Frommer's®

POSTCARDS

FROM

EUROPE

Summer visitors can gaze on fields of sunflowers as they drive through southern France—
as if through a Van Gogh painting. See chapter 6. © Bob Krist Photography.

The Acropolis in Athens stands as an ancient symbol of "the glory that was Greece."
See chapter 8. © Kindra Clineff Photography.

The Louvre and I. M. Pei's controversial glass pyramid reflect the convergence of old and new in Paris. See chapter 6. © Bob Krist Photography.

Magnificent Chambord is the largest château in the Loire Valley. See chapter 6. © Kevin Galvin Photography.

Marie Antoinette played shepherdess at this quaint hamlet near the Petit Trianon in Versailles. See chapter 6. © Kindra Clineff Photography.

The Arc de Triomphe has witnessed some of France's proudest moments and some of its more humiliating defeats. See chapter 6. © Kevin Galvin Photography.

Rising above the steets of Montmartre is the central dome of the gleaming white Sacré-Coeur. See chapter 6. © Bob Krist Photography.

Walking the cobblestone streets of Stockholm's Gamla Stan (Old Town) at night is a trip back in time. See chapter 17. © Bob Krist Photography.

Restaurant-lined rue des Bouchers is in Brussels's historic heart. See chapter 2. © Kevin Galvin Photography.

"Checkmate." Men playing chess relax in one of Budapest's thermal baths. See chapter 9. © *Catherine Karnow Photography.*

Medieval castles, Gothic cathedrals, cobblestone streets, and tranquil canals hauntingly evoke Bruges's past. See chapter 2. © *Kevin Galvin Photography.*

The Vltava River winds through historic Prague, one of Europe's most vibrant and beautiful cities. See chapter 3. © Anthony Cassidy/Tony Stone Images.

Baroque Salzburg's alpine setting is on the banks of the Salzach River. See chapter 1. © Kevin Galvin Photography.

Amsterdam's graceful cityscape is lined with canals, bridges, and 17th-century town houses. See chapter 12. © Kevin Galvin Photography.

In the Netherlands, watery expanses are punctuated by scenic windmills. See chapter 12. © Michael Defreitas Photography.

*Capped by Brunelleschi's dome—
an amazing architectural feat—
the Duomo dominates Florence's
skyline. See chapter 11.
© Kevin Galvin Photography.*

*Olive trees and grapevines dot Tuscany's rolling hills in the heart of Italy. See chapter 11.
© Jean Miele/The Stock Market Photography.*

Visitors are no longer allowed to climb the fragile Leaning Tower of Pisa, one of the most recognizable buildings in the Western world. See chapter 11.
© Massimo Mastrorillo/The Stock Market.

The maritime province of the Algarve is dotted with hundreds of Portugal's finest beaches. See chapter 14. © Foto World/The Image Bank.

Hiking is the best way to see the Dingle Peninsula on the lush Emerald Isle. See chapter 10.
© M. Timothy O'Keefe Photography.

St. Paul's Cathedral in London is a monument to beauty and tranquillity. See chapter 5.
© Kelly/Mooney Photography.

Rich in history, Edinburgh Castle is one of the highpoints of a visit to Scotland. See chapter 15. © Kindra Clineff Photography.

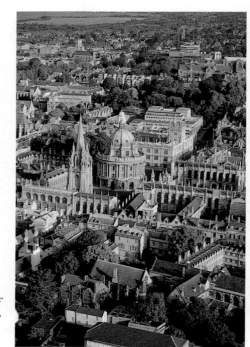

In Oxford, the towers and spires of one of the world's great universities rise majestically skyward. See chapter 5. © Chris Donaghue Photography.

Segovia's glorious 12th-century El Alcázar has been the residence of Spanish monarchs since the days of Ferdinand and Isabella. See chapter 16. © *Ric Ergenbright Photography.*

Neuschwanstein Castle's gothic turrets rise from the rugged Bavarian Alps. See chapter 7.
© *Jeff Hunter/The Image Bank.*

When should I travel to get the best airfare?
Where do I go for answers to my travel questions?
What's the best and easiest way to plan and book my trip?

www.frommers.travelocity.com

Frommer's, the travel guide leader, has teamed up with **Travelocity.com**, the leader in online travel, to bring you an in-depth, easy-to-use resource designed to help you plan and book your trip online.

At **www.frommers.travelocity.com**, you'll find free online updates about your destination from the experts at Frommer's plus the outstanding travel planning and purchasing features of Travelocity.com. Travelocity.com provides reservations capabilities for 95 percent of all airline seats sold, more than 47,000 hotels, and over 50 car rental companies. In addition, Travelocity.com offers more than 2,000 exciting vacation and cruise packages. Travelocity.com puts you in complete control of your travel planning with these and other great features:

> **Expert travel guidance from Frommer's** - over 150 writers reporting from around the world!
>
> **Best Fare Finder** - an interactive calendar tells you when to travel to get the best airfare
>
> **Fare Watcher** - we'll track airfare changes to your favorite destinations
>
> **Dream Maps** - a mapping feature that suggests travel opportunities based on your budget
>
> **Shop Safe Guarantee** - 24 hours a day / 7 days a week live customer service, and more!

Whether you're traveling on a tight budget, looking for a quick weekend getaway, or planning the trip of a lifetime, Frommer's guides and Travelocity.com will make your travel dreams a reality. You've bought the book, now book the trip!

Other Great Guides for Your Trip:

Frommer's Europe from $70 a Day

Frommer's Gay & Lesbian Europe

Hanging Out in Europe

Frommer's Road Atlas Europe

Here's what the critics say about Frommer's:

"Amazingly easy to use. Very portable, very complete."

—*Booklist*

♦

"The only mainstream guide to list specific prices. The Walter Cronkite of guidebooks—with all that implies."

—*Travel & Leisure*

♦

"Complete, concise, and filled with useful information."

—*New York Daily News*

♦

"Hotel Information is close to encyclopedic."

—*Des Moines Sunday Register*

♦

"Detailed, accurate and easy-to-read information for all price ranges."

—*Glamour Magazine*

Frommer's® 2001

Europe

IDG Books Worldwide, Inc.
An International Data Group Company
Foster City, CA • Chicago, IL • Indianapolis, IN • New York, NY

IDG BOOKS WORLDWIDE, INC.

An International Data Group Company
919 E. Hillsdale Blvd.
Suite 400
Foster City, CA 94404

Find us online at **www.frommers.com**

ISBN 0-02-863863-8
ISSN 1091-9511

Editors: Ron Boudreau and Matthew Kiernan
Production Editor: Donna Wright
Photo Editor: Richard Fox
Design by Michele Laseau
Staff Cartographers: John Decamillis, Roberta Stockwell, Elizabeth Puhl
Page creation by IDG Books Indianapolis Production Department

Front cover photo: Ramsau in Bavaria, Germany

SPECIAL SALES

For general information on IDG Books Worldwide's books in the U.S., please call our Consumer Customer Service Department at 1-800-762-2974. For reseller information, including discounts, bulk sales, customized editions, and premium sales, please call our Reseller Consumer Service Department at 1-800-434-3422.

Manufactured in the United States of America.

5   4   3   2

Contents

12   The Netherlands   778

by George McDonald

13   Norway   808

by Darwin Porter & Danforth Prince

14   Portugal   834

by Darwin Porter & Danforth Prince

15   Scotland   879

by Darwin Porter & Danforth Prince

16   Spain   929

by Darwin Porter & Danforth Prince

17   Sweden   1015

by Darwin Porter & Danforth Prince

18   Switzerland   1040

by Darwin Porter & Danforth Prince

Appendix   1083

Index   1087

List of Maps

ABOUT THE AUTHORS

Darwin Porter, a native of North Carolina, was assigned to write the very first edition of a Frommer's guide devoted solely to one European country. Since then, he has written many best-selling Frommer's guides to all the major European destinations. In 1982, he was joined in his research efforts by **Danforth Prince,** formerly of the Paris bureau of the *New York Times,* who has traveled and written extensively about Europe.

All four of **Joseph S. Lieber**'s grandparents emigrated from Eastern Europe at the turn of the 20th century, settling in New York City, where he was born and raised. Mr. Lieber lived in Hungary for several years in the early 1990s. He presently practices law in Boston and is the coauthor of *Frommer's Budapest & the Best of Hungary* and *Frommer's Europe from $70 a Day.* **Christina Shea** served as a Peace Corps volunteer in Hungary and subsequently directed Peace Corps language-training programs in Lithuania and Kyrghyzstan. She's the author of the novel *Moira's Crossing* (St. Martin's) and a coauthor of *Frommer's Budapast & the Best of Hungary* and *Frommer's Europe from $70 a Day.*

Robert Emmet Meagher, a dual citizen of Ireland and the United States, is professor of humanities at Hampshire College in Amherst, Massachusetts. The author of more than a dozen books, plays, and translations, he has lived and worked in Ireland, twice holding visiting professorships at Trinity College Dublin.

George McDonald has lived in Amsterdam and Brussels as a former editor of the Sabena Belgian World Airlines and deputy editor of the KLM Royal Dutch Airlines in-flight magazines. He is now a freelance journalist and travel writer, and has written extensively about the Netherlands and Belgium for international magazines and guidebooks, such as *Frommer's Amsterdam* and *Frommer's Belgium, Holland & Luxembourg.*

Sherry Marker's love of Greece began when she majored in classical Greek at Harvard. She has studied at the American School of Classical Studies in Athens and studied ancient history at the University of California at Berkeley. Author or coauthor of a number of guides to Greece (such as *Frommer's Greece* and *Frommer's Greek Islands*), she has published articles in the *New York Times, Travel & Leisure,* and *Hampshire Life.* She's also the coauthor of *Frommer's Europe from $70 a Day* and has written books on a variety of subjects, including a history of London for young adults.

John Mastrini is a former television news anchor from the United States. He has lived in Prague since 1989, where he works as a journalist and media consultant. He's coauthor of *Frommer's Prague & the Best of the Czech Republic.* **Hana Mastrini** is a native of the western Czech spa town of Karlovy Vary who became a veteran of "Velvet Revolution" as a student in Prague in 1989. She began contributing to Frommer's guides while helping her husband, John, better understand his new home in the Czech Republic.

AN INVITATION TO THE READER

In researching this book, we discovered many wonderful places—hotels, restaurants, shops, and more. We're sure you'll find others. Please tell us about them, so we can share the information with your fellow travelers in upcoming editions. If you were disappointed with a recommendation, we'd love to know that, too. Please write to:

Frommer's Europe 2001
IDG Books Worldwide, Inc.
909 Third Avenue
New York, NY 10022

AN ADDITIONAL NOTE

Please be advised that travel information is subject to change at any time—and this is especially true of prices. We therefore suggest that you write or call ahead for confirmation when making your travel plans. The authors, editors, and publisher cannot be held responsible for the experiences of readers while traveling. Your safety is important to us, however, so we encourage you to stay alert and be aware of your surroundings. Keep a close eye on cameras, purses, and wallets, all favorite targets of thieves and pickpockets.

WHAT THE SYMBOLS MEAN

✪ Frommer's Favorites

Our favorite places and experiences—outstanding for quality, value, or both.

The following abbreviations are used for credit cards:

AE	American Express	EURO	EuroCard
CB	Carte Blanche	JCB	Japan Credit Bank
DC	Diners Club	MC	MasterCard
DISC	Discover	V	Visa
ER	EnRoute		

FIND FROMMER'S ONLINE

www.frommers.com offers up-to-the-minute listings on almost 200 cities around the globe—including the latest bargains and candid, personal articles updated daily by Arthur Frommer himself. No other Web site offers such comprehensive and timely coverage of the world of travel.

Introduction: Planning a Trip to Europe

by Darwin Porter & Danforth Prince

Irresistible and intriguing, the ever-changing Europe at the beginning of the new millennium offers you more excitement, experiences, and memories than ever. In compiling this book, we've tried to open the door to Europe's famous cities (their art and architecture, restaurants and theater, hotels and history) and guide you to all the experiences no one would want to miss on even a cursory visit. So though this guide has to skim the highlights, we've also tossed in offbeat destinations and adventurous suggestions leading to surprises and delights around every corner.

As it moves into the 21st century, Europe, or at least the 11-nation "euro zone" (Austria, Belgium, Finland, France, Germany, Ireland, Italy, Luxembourg, the Netherlands, Portugal, Spain) has a dream to steer the continent toward the type of robust growth known in the States during the Clinton years. During the 1990s, each member nation was burdened with high unemployment, recession, and slow growth, preventing fast economic recovery. Economic reforms, especially in the big three (Germany, Italy, France), are on the horizon but face stiff opposition from the public. By becoming part of the euro zone, these nations have pledged themselves to cut budget deficits and squeeze chronic inflation. And by adopting the euro and yielding to fiercely competitive global pressures, these 11 nations have been sent kicking and screaming into the 2000s whether major political groups in any country wanted it or not.

Of course, you don't visit Europe to fret over economies. The rich culture and histories in each of its myriad countries and regions have always been the lure, and they remain so today. From the splendor of a walled hill town rising above the verdant Tuscan landscape to the majestic snowcapped peaks of the Alps, from the sound of flamenco in a Madrid tablaos to the blasting of a brass band in Munich's Hofbräuhaus—one Europe it may be on the map (and now on the bankbooks), but on the ground it's still a Europe of countless facets and proud, distinct, diverse heritages. There's no other place where you can experience such enormous cultural changes by driving from one mountain valley to the next, where in only a few miles you're likely to encounter not only a different language but also different food, architecture, and culture.

Europe has seen some of the greatest intellectual and artistic developments the world has ever known, and the landscape is dense with museums, cathedrals, palaces, and monuments serving as repositories

Europe

Number, Please: Calling Europe

To make a phone call **from the United States to Europe,** dial the international access code, **011,** then the **country code** for the country you're calling, then the **city code** for the city you're calling, and then the regular phone number. For an operator-assisted call, dial **01,** then the country code, then the city code, and then the regular phone number; an operator then comes on the line.

The following are the codes for the countries and major cities in this guide. These are the codes you use to call from overseas or from another European country; if you're calling from within the country or within the city, see the "Telephone" entry in the "Fast Facts" section for each city.

European phone systems are undergoing a prolonged change. **Italy, France, Spain, Monaco, Copenhagen, and now Portugal no longer use separate city codes.** The code is now built into all phone numbers, and you must always dial the initial zero or nine (which was previously—and still is in most other countries—added before a city code only when dialing from another city within the country). Also, be aware of these two recent changes: The city codes for London (171 and 181) have been replaced by a new single code, 20, which is then followed by an eight-digit number beginning with either 7 or 8; and the city code for Lisbon has changed from 1 to 21.

Austria	43	**Denmark**	45
Innsbruck	512	**England**	44
Salzburg	662	Bath	1225
Vienna	1	London	20
Belgium	32	Oxford	1865
Bruges	50	Stratford-upon-Avon	1789
Brussels	2	**France**	33
Ghent	9	**Germany**	49
Czech Republic	420	Berlin	30
Prague	2	Munich	89

for much of this past glory. But the good news is that the continent is still in a dynamic creative mode; artistic and cultural ferment are still very much part of the present, and Europe still helps set the trends in fashion, industrial design, cinema, technology, music, literature, and science. The dynamic environment is all about life, innovation, entertainment, and food, which exist side by side with the artistic and cultural grandeur of the past.

Europe is also about people. Europeans have seen the best and the worst of times, and a better-educated, more sophisticated younger generation is waiting to welcome you. They're as diverse and fascinating as the lands they come from, and throughout this book we've noted places not only where you'll meet other visitors, but also where you'll have a chance to meet and chat with the locals, enriching your experience immeasurably.

We've tried to prepare this edition to help you discover where you want to go and what you want to see. This introductory chapter is designed to equip you with what you need to know before you go—the advance-planning tools for an enjoyable and successful trip.

Greece	**30**	Norway	**47**
Athens	1	Oslo	22
Delphi	265	**Portugal**	**351**
Hungary	**36**	**Scotland**	**44**
Budapest	1	Edinburgh	131
Ireland	**353**	**Spain**	**34**
Dublin	1	**Sweden**	**46**
Italy	**39**	Stockholm	8
Monaco	**377**	**Switzerland**	**41**
Netherlands	**31**	Bern	31
Amsterdam	200	Geneva	22

The easiest and cheapest way to call home from abroad is with a calling card. On the road, you just dial a local access code (almost always free) and then punch in the number you're calling as well as the calling-card number. If you're in a non–Touch-Tone country, just wait for an English-speaking operator to put your call through. The "Telephone" entry in the "Fast Facts" for each city gives the AT&T, MCI, and Sprint access codes for that country (your calling card will probably come with a wallet-sized list of local access numbers). You can also call any one of those companies' numbers to make a collect call as well; just dial it and wait for the operator.

When it comes to dialing direct, calling from the United States to Europe is much cheaper than the other way around, so whenever possible, have friends and family call you at your hotel rather than you calling them. To dial direct back to the United States and Canada from Europe, the international access code is often, but not always, 00; the country code is 1, and then you punch in the area code and number. For Australia and New Zealand, the access code is also 00; the country codes are 61 and 64, respectively.

1 Visitor Information

TOURIST OFFICES

Start with the **European tourist offices** in your own country; for a complete list, see below. If you aren't sure which countries you want to visit, send for an information-packed free booklet called *Planning Your Trip to Europe,* revised annually by the 28-nation **European Travel Planner,** P.O. Box 1754, New York, NY 10185 (☎ 800/816-7530; www.visiteurope.com). Or check out *Europe for Dummies,* available at most bookstores.

AUSTRIAN NATIONAL TOURIST OFFICE

IN THE U.S.   P.O. Box 1142, Times Square Station, New York, NY 10108-1142 (☎ 212/944-6880; fax 212/730-4568).

IN CANADA   1010 Sherbrooke St. W., Suite 1410, Montréal, PQ H3A 2R7 (☎ 514/849-3709; fax 514/849-9577); 2 Bloor St. E., Suite 3330, Toronto, ON

M4W 1A8 (☎ **416/967-3381;** fax 416/967-4101); 200 Granville St., Suite 1380, Vancouver, BC V6C 1S4 (☎ **604/683-5808;** 604/662-8528).

IN THE U.K.   14 Cork St., London W1X 1PF (☎ **020/7629-0461;** fax 020/7499-6038).

IN AUSTRALIA   36 Carrington St., 1st Floor, Sydney, NSW 2000 (☎ **02/9299-3621;** fax 02/9299-3808).

E-MAIL   oewlon@easynet.co.uk or oesyd@world.net.

WEB SITE   www.anto.com.

BELGIAN TOURIST OFFICE

IN THE U.S.   780 Third Ave., New York, NY 10017 (☎ **212/758-8130;** fax 212/355-7675).

IN CANADA   P.O. Box 760 NDG, Montréal, PQ H4A 3S2 (☎ **514/489-3594;** fax 514/489-8965).

IN THE U.K.   31 Pepper St., London E14 9RW (☎ **0891/887-799;** fax 020/7458-2999).

E-MAIL   info@belgium-tourism.org.

WEB SITE   www.visitbelgium.com.

BRITISH TOURIST AUTHORITY

IN THE U.S.   551 Fifth Ave., Suite 701, New York, NY 10176-0799 (☎ **800/462-2748** or 212/986-2200; fax 212/986-1188).

IN CANADA   111 Avenue Rd., Suite 450, Toronto, ON M5R 3J8 (☎ **888/847-4885** in Canada, or 905/405-1840 in Toronto; fax 416/961-2175).

IN AUSTRALIA   Level 16, Gateway, 1 Macquarie Place, Sydney, NSW 2000 (☎ **02/9377-4400;** fax 02/9377-4499).

IN NEW ZEALAND   Dilworth Bldg., Suite 305, Customs and Queen streets, Auckland 1 (☎ **09/303-1446;** fax 09/377-6965).

E-MAIL   travelinfo@bta.org.uk.

WEB SITE   www.visitbritain.com.

CZECH TOURIST AUTHORITY

IN THE U.S.   1109 Madison Ave., New York, NY 10028 (☎ **212/288-0830**).

IN CANADA   P.O. Box 198, Exchange Tower, 130 King St. W., Suite 715, Toronto, ON M5X 1A6 (☎ **416/367-3432**).

IN THE U.K.   95 Great Portland St., London W1N 5RA (☎ **020/7291-9920;** fax 020/7436-1300).

E-MAIL   nycenter@ny.czech.cz.

WEB SITE   wwwczech.cz/newyork.

FRENCH GOVERNMENT TOURIST OFFICE

IN THE U.S.   444 Madison Ave., 16th Floor, New York, NY 10022 (☎ **212/838-7800**); 676 N. Michigan Ave., Suite 3360, Chicago, IL 60611 (☎ **312/751-7800**); 9454 Wilshire Blvd., Suite 715, Beverly Hills, CA 90212 (☎ **310/271-6665;** fax 310/276-2835). To request information at any of these offices, call the **France on Call hot line** at ☎ **410/286-8310** (50¢ per minute).

IN CANADA   Maison de la France/French Government Tourist Office, 1981 av. McGill College, Suite 490, Montréal, PQ H3A 2W9 (☎ **514/288-4264;** fax 514/845-4868); 30 St. Patrick St., Suite 700, Toronto, ON M5T 3A3 (☎ **416/491-7622;** fax 416/979-7587).

IN THE U.K.   Maison de la France/French Government Tourist Office, 178 Piccadilly, London, W1V 0AL (☎ **0891/244-123;** fax 020/7943-6594).

IN AUSTRALIA   French Tourist Bureau, 25 Bligh St., Sydney, NSW 2000 (☎ **02/9231-5244**).

E-MAIL   info@francetourism.com.

WEB SITE   www.fgtousa.org or www.francetourism.com.

GERMAN NATIONAL TOURIST OFFICE

IN THE U.S.   122 E. 42nd St., 52nd Floor, New York, NY 10168-0072 (☎ **212/661-7200;** fax 212/661-7174).

IN CANADA   175 Bloor St. E., Suite 604, Toronto, ON M4W 3R8 (☎ **416/968-1570;** fax 416/968-1986).

IN THE U.K.   P.O. Box 2695, London W1A 3PM (☎ **020/7317-0908** or 0891/600-100).

IN AUSTRALIA   P.O. Box A980, Sydney, NSW 2000 (☎ **02/9267-8148;** fax 02/9267-9035).

E-MAIL   gntony@aol.com or germanto@idirect.com.

WEB SITE   www.germany-tourism.de.

GREEK NATIONAL TOURIST ORGANIZATION

IN THE U.S.   645 Fifth Ave., 5th Floor, New York, NY 10022 (☎ **212/421-5777;** fax 212/826-6490); 168 N. Michigan Ave., Suite 600, Chicago, IL 60601 (☎ **312/782-1084;** fax 312/782-1091); 611 W. 6th St., Suite 2198, Los Angeles, CA 92668 (☎ **213/626-6696;** fax 213/489-9744).

IN CANADA   1300 Bay St., Toronto, ON M5R 3K8 (☎ **416/968-2220;** fax 416/968-6533); 1233 rue de la Montagne, Suite 101, Montréal, PQ H3G 1Z2 (☎ **514/871-1535;** fax 514/871-1498).

IN THE U.K.   4 Conduit St., London W1R 0DJ (☎ **020/7734-5997;** fax 020/7287-1369).

IN AUSTRALIA   51–57 Pitt St., Sydney, NWS 2000 (☎ **02/9241-1663;** fax 02/9235-2174).

E-MAIL   None.

WEB SITE   www.hellas.de or www.greektourism.com.

HUNGARIAN NATIONAL TOURIST OFFICE

IN THE U.S. & CANADA   150 E. 58th St., 33rd Floor, New York, NY 10155 (☎ **212/355-0240;** fax 212/207-4103).

IN THE U.K.   ᶜ/ₒ Embassy of the Republic of Hungary, Trade Commission, 46 Eaton Place, London, SW1X 8AL (☎ **020/7823-1032;** fax 020/7823-1459).

E-MAIL   htnewyork@hungarytourism.hu or htlondon@hungarytourism.hu.

WEB SITE   www.hungarytourism.hu.

IRISH TOURIST BOARD

IN THE U.S.   345 Park Ave., New York, NY 10154 (☎ **800/223-6470** or 212/418-0800; fax 212/371-9052).

IN CANADA   160 Bloor St. E., Suite 1150, Toronto, ON M4W 1B9 (☎ **416/487-3335;** fax 416/929-6783).

IN THE U.K.   150 New Bond St., London W1Y OAQ (☎ **020/7493-3201;** fax 020/7493-9065).

IN AUSTRALIA   36 Carrington St., 5th Floor, Sydney, NSW 2000 (☎ **02/9299-6177;** fax 02/9299-6323).

E-MAIL   info@irishtouristboard.com.

WEB SITE   www.ireland.travel.ie.

ITALIAN GOVERNMENT TOURIST BOARD

IN THE U.S.   630 Fifth Ave., Suite 1565, New York, NY 10111 (☎ **212/245-4822;** fax 212/586-9249); 500 N. Michigan Ave., Suite 2240, Chicago, IL 60611 (☎ **312/644-0996;** fax 312/644-3019); 12400 Wilshire Blvd., Suite 550, Beverly Hills, CA 90025 (☎ **310/820-1898;** fax 310/820-6357).

IN CANADA   1 place Ville-Marie, Suite 1914, Montréal, PQ H3B 3M9 (☎ **514/866-7667;** fax 514/392-1429).

IN THE U.K.   1 Princes St., London W1R 8AY (☎ **020/7408-1254;** fax 020/7493-6695).

E-MAIL   enitny@bway.net, 739145@icam.net, or enitlond@globalnet.co.uk.

WEB SITE   None.

MONACO GOVERNMENT TOURIST OFFICE

IN THE U.S. & CANADA   565 Fifth Ave., New York, NY 10017 (☎ **800/753-9696** or 212/286-3330; fax 212/286-9890).

IN THE U.K.   3–8 Chelsea Garden Market, Chelsea Harbour, London, SW10 0XE (☎ **020/7352-9962;** fax 020/7352-9103).

E-MAIL   mgto@monaco1.org.

WEB SITE   www.monaco.mc/usa.

NETHERLANDS BOARD OF TOURISM

IN THE U.S.   355 Lexington Ave., 21st Floor, New York, NY 10017 (☎ **212/370-7360**); 225 N. Michigan Ave., Suite 1854, Chicago, IL 60601 (☎ **888/464-6552** or 312/819-0300; fax 312/819-1740).

IN CANADA   Box 1078, Toronto, ON M5C 2K5 (☎ **888/464-6552** or 416/363-1577; fax 416/363-1470).

IN THE U.K.   18 Buckingham Gate, London, SW1E 6LD (☎ **0891/717-777** or 020/7828-7900; fax 020/7828-7941).

E-MAIL   go2holland@aol.com.

WEB SITE   www.goholland.com.

PORTUGUESE NATIONAL TOURIST OFFICE

IN THE U.S.   590 Fifth Ave., 4th Floor, New York, NY 10036 (☎ **212/354-4403;** fax 764-6137).

IN CANADA   60 Bloor St. W., Suite 1005, Toronto, ON M4W 3B8 (☎ **416/ 921-7376;** fax 416/921-1353).

IN THE U.K.   22–25A Sackville St., 2nd Floor, London W1X 2LY (☎ **0891/ 600-370** or 020/7494-1441; fax 020/7494-1868).

E-MAIL   aavila@portugal.org or iceptor@direct.com.

WEB SITE   www.portugal.org.

SCANDINAVIAN TOURIST BOARDS (DENMARK, NORWAY & SWEDEN)

IN THE U.S. & CANADA   P.O. Box 4649, Grand Central Station, New York, NY 10163-4649 (☎ **212/885-9700;** fax 212/885-9710).

IN THE U.K.   Danish Tourist Board, 55 Sloane St., London SW1X 95Y (☎ **0891/600-109** or 020/7259-5959; fax 020/7259-5955); Norwegian Tourist Board, Charles House, 5 Regent St., London, SW1Y 4LR (☎ **020/7839-2650;** fax 020/7839-6014); Swedish Travel and Tourism Council, 11 Montagu Pl., London W1H 2AL (☎ **020/7870-5600;** fax 020/7724-5872).

E-MAIL   usa@nortra.no, info@gosweden.org, dtb.london@dt.dk, or greatbritain@ nortra.no.

WEB SITES   www.visitdenmark.com or www.gosweden.org.

SWITZERLAND TOURISM

IN THE U.S.   608 Fifth Ave., New York, NY 10020 (☎ **212/757-5944;** fax 212/262-6116); 150 N. Michigan Ave., Suite 2930, Chicago, IL 60601 (☎ **312/630-5840;** fax 312/630-5848); 222 N. Sepulveda Blvd., Suite 1570, El Segundo, CA 90245 (☎ **310/335-5980;** fax 310/335-5982).

IN CANADA   926 The East Mall, Etobicoke, ON M9B 6KI (☎ **416/695-2090;** fax 416/695-2774).

IN THE U.K.   Swiss Centre, 1 New Coventry St., London, W1V 8EE (☎ **020/ 7734-1921;** fax 020/7437-4577).

E-MAIL   stnewyork@switzerlandtourism.com or london@switzerlandvacation.ch.

WEB SITE   www.switzerlandtourism.com.

TOURIST OFFICE OF SPAIN

IN THE U.S.   666 Fifth Ave., 35th Floor, New York, NY 10103 (☎ **212/ 265-8822;** fax 212/265-8864); 845 N. Michigan Ave., Suite 915E, Chicago, IL 60611 (☎ **312/642-1992;** fax 312/642-9817); 8383 Wilshire Blvd., Suite 960, Beverly Hills, CA 90211 (☎ **213/658-7188;** fax 213/658-1061); 1221 Brickell Ave., Suite 1850, Miami, FL 33131 (☎ **305/358-1992;** fax 305/358-8223).

IN CANADA   2 Bloor St. W., 34th Floor, Toronto, ON M5S 1M9 (☎ **416/ 961-3131;** fax 416/961-1992).

IN THE U.K.   22–23 Manchester Sq., London W1M 5AP (☎ **0891/669-920** or 020/7486-8077; fax 020/7486-8034).

IN AUSTRALIA   203 Castlereagh St., Suite 21A (P.O. Box 675), Sydney, NSW 2000 (☎ **02/9264-7966**).

E-MAIL   oetny@here-i.com.

WEB SITE   www.okspain.org.

Europe Online

For country- and city-specific Web sites, see the **"Planning Your Trip: An Online Directory"** following this chapter.

THE INTERNET

The Internet can provide lots of travel information. **Yahoo!** (www.yahoo.com), **Excite** (www.excite.com), **Lycos** (www.lycos.com), **Infoseek** (www.infoseek.com), and the other major Internet indexing sites all have subcategories for travel, country/regional information, and culture—click on all three for links to travel-related Web sites. One of the best hot lists for travel and destination information is Excite's **City.Net** (www.city.net).

Other good clearinghouse sites for information are **Microsoft's Expedia** (www.expedia.com), **Travelocity** (www.travelocity.com), the **Internet Travel Network** (www.itn.com), **TravelWeb** (www.travelweb.com), and the **European Travel Commission** (www.visiteurope.com). Of the many, many online travel magazines, two of the best are **Arthur Frommer's Budget Travel Online** (www.frommers.com), written and updated by the guru of budget travel himself, and **Condé Nast's Epicurious** (www.epicurious.com), based on articles from the company's glossy magazines.

The site **www.guidebookwriters.com** will put you in direct contact with professional guidebook writers who specialize in different countries, regions, and cities around the world. These expert consultants can give you personalized advice, pass along the latest travel tips and news, and even help you plan your trip, from exploring the back roads of Bavaria to planning a Europe-wide jaunt.

That covers some of the top general Web sites. As often as possible throughout this chapter, we've included specific Web sites along with phone numbers and addresses.

TRAVEL AGENTS

Travel agents can save you plenty of time and money by hunting down the best airfare for your route and arranging for rail passes and rental cars. For now, most travel agents still charge you nothing for their services—they're paid through commissions from the airlines and other agencies they book for you. However, a number of airlines have begun cutting commissions, and increasingly, agents are finding they have to charge you a fee to hold the bottom line (or else unscrupulous agents will offer you only the travel options that bag them the juiciest commissions). Shop around and ask hard questions.

If you decide to use a travel agent, make sure the agent is a member of the **American Society of Travel Agents (ASTA),** 1101 King St., Alexandria, VA 22314 (☎ **703/739-8739;** www.astanet.com). If you send them a self-addressed stamped envelope, ASTA will mail you the booklet *Avoiding Travel Problems* for free.

TRAVEL BOOKSTORES

If you live outside a large urban area, you can order maps or travel guides from bookstores specializing in mail- or phone-order service. Some of these are **Book Passage,** 51 Tamal Vista Blvd., Corte Madera, CA 94925 (☎ **800/321-9785** or 415/927-0960; www.bookpassage.com); and **Forsyth Travel Library,** 1780 E. 131st St., P.O. Box 480800, Kansas City, MO 64148-0800 (☎ **800/FORSYTH;** www.forsyth.com). And of course there are huge online bookstores at **Amazon** (www.amazon.com) and **Barnes & Noble** (www.barnesandnoble.com).

Canadians can contact **Ulysses Travel Bookshop,** 4176 rue St-Denis, Montréal, PQ H2W 2M5 (☎ **514/843-9447;** www.ulysses.ca), or 101 Yorkville Ave., Toronto,

ON M5R 1C1 (☎ **416/323-3609**). In London, try **Daunt Books,** 83 Marylebone High St. (☎ **020/7224-2295**), or any branch of the **Travel Bookshop,** at 13–15 Blenheim Crescent (☎ **020/7229-5260**), in the Campus Travel office at 52 Grosvenor Gardens (☎ **020/7730-1314**), or in the British Airways office at 156 Regent St. (☎ **020/7434-4744**).

2 Entry Requirements & Customs

PASSPORTS

If you don't already have one, you can download a passport application from the Web sites listed below. Countries covered in this guide do *not* require visas for U.S. or Canadian citizens for stays less than 90 days. Though a valid U.S. state driver's license usually suffices, it's wise to carry an **International Driving Permit** ($12), which you can obtain from any AAA branch if you bring two passport-size photos.

U.S. CITIZENS   If applying for a first passport, you need to do it in person at one of 13 passport offices throughout the States; a federal, state, or probate court; or a major post office (though not all post offices accept applications; call the number below to find ones that do). You need to present a certified birth certificate as proof of citizenship, and it's wise to bring along your driver's license, state or military ID, and social security card as well. You also need two identical passport-sized photos (2 in. by 2 in.), taken at any corner photo shop (not one of the strip photos, however, from a photo-vending machine).

For people over 15, a passport is valid for 10 years and costs $60 ($45 plus a $15 handling fee); for those 15 and under, it's valid for 5 years and costs $40. If you're over 15 and have a valid passport that was issued within the past 12 years, you can renew it by mail and bypass the $15 handling fee. Allow plenty of time before your trip to apply; processing normally takes 3 weeks but can take longer during busy periods (especially spring). For general information, call the **National Passport Agency** at ☎ **202/647-0518.** To find your regional passport office, call the **National Passport Information Center** at ☎ **900/225-5674** (www.travel.state.gov).

CANADIAN CITIZENS   You can pick up a passport application at one of 28 regional passport offices or most travel agencies. The passport is valid for 5 years and costs $60. Children under 16 may be included on a parent's passport but need their own to travel unaccompanied by the parent. Applications, which must be accompanied by two identical passport-sized photographs and proof of Canadian citizenship, are available at travel agencies throughout Canada or from the central **Passport Office, Department of Foreign Affairs and International Trade,** Ottawa, ON K1A 0G3 (☎ **800/567-6868;** www.dfait-maeci.gc.ca/passport). Processing takes 5 to 10 days if you apply in person or about 3 weeks by mail.

U.K. CITIZENS   As a member of the European Union (EU), you supposedly need only an identity card, not a passport, to travel to other EU countries. However, you

Traveler's Tip

Safeguard your passport in an inconspicuous, inaccessible place like a money belt. If you lose it, visit the nearest consulate of your native country as soon as possible for a replacement. Before leaving home, make two photocopy collages of your important documents: the first page of your passport (the page with the photo and identifying info), driver's license, and other ID. Leave one copy at home with a family member or friend and carry the other with you (separate from the originals!).

should bring a passport anyway. To pick up an application for a 10-year passport, visit your nearest passport office, major post office, or travel agency. You can also contact the **London Passport Office** at ☎ 020/7271-3000 (www.open.gov.uk/ukpass/ukpass. htm). Passports are £21 for adults and £11 for children under 16.

IRISH CITIZENS   You can apply for a 10-year passport, costing IR£45, at the **Passport Office,** Setanta Centre, Molesworth Street, Dublin 2 (☎ 01/671-1633; www.irlgov.ie/iveagh/foreignaffairs/services). Those under age 18 and over 65 must apply for a IR£10 3-year passport. You can also apply at 1A South Mall, Cork (☎ 021/272-525) or over the counter at most main post offices.

AUSTRALIAN CITIZENS   Apply at your local post office or passport office or search the government Web site at **www.dfat.gov.au/passports/**. Passports for adults are A$126 and for those under 18 A$63. Note that Australians now need visas to enter Portugal.

NEW ZEALAND CITIZENS   You can pick up a passport application at any travel agency or Link Centre. For more info, contact the **Passport Office,** P.O. Box 805, Wellington (☎ 0800/225-050). Passports for adults are NZ$80 and for those under 16 NZ$40.

CUSTOMS

U.S. CITIZENS   If you've been away 48 hours or more, you're allowed to bring back, once every 30 days, $400 worth of merchandise duty-free. You'll be charged a flat rate of 10% duty on the next $1,000 worth of purchases. Be sure to have your receipts handy. On gifts, the duty-free limit is $100. You can't bring fresh foodstuffs into the United States; tinned foods, however, are allowed. For more information, contact the **U.S. Customs Service,** 1301 Constitution Ave. (P.O. Box 7407), Washington, DC 20044 (☎ 202/927-6724; www.customs.ustreas.gov), and request the free pamphlet *Know Before You Go.*

U.K. CITIZENS   If you're **returning from a European Union (EU) country,** you'll go through a separate Customs Exit ("Blue Exit") especially for EU travelers. In essence, there's no limit on what you can bring back from an EU country, as long as the items are for personal use (this includes gifts) and you've already paid the necessary duty and tax. However, customs law sets out guidance levels. If you bring in more than these levels, you might be asked to prove the goods are for your own use. Guidance levels on goods bought in the EU for your own use are 800 cigarettes, 200 cigars, 1 kilogram smoking tobacco, 10 liters of spirits, 90 liters of wine (of this, not more than 60 liters can be sparkling wine), and 110 liters of beer. For more information, contact **HM Customs & Excise,** Passenger Enquiry Point, 2nd Floor Wayfarer House, Great South West Road, Feltham, Middlesex, TW14 8NP (☎ 020/ 8910-3744; www.open.gov.uk).

If you're **returning from a non-EU country,** you have a customs allowance of 200 cigarettes; 50 cigars; 250 grams of smoking tobacco; 2 liters of still table wine; 1 liter of spirits or strong liqueurs (over 22% volume); 2 liters of fortified wine, sparkling wine, or other liqueurs; 60 cubic centimeters (ml) perfume; 250 cubic centimeters (ml) of toilet water; and £145 worth of all other goods, including gifts and souvenirs. People under 17 can't have the tobacco or alcohol allowance. For more information, contact **HM Customs & Excise,** Passenger Enquiry Point, Wayfarer House, 2nd Floor, Great South West Road, Feltham, Middlesex, TW14 8NP (☎ 020/8910-3744, or 44/181-910-3744 outside the U.K.; www.open.gov.uk).

CANADIAN CITIZENS   For a clear summary of rules, write for the booklet *I Declare,* issued by **Revenue Canada,** 2265 St. Laurent Blvd., Ottawa, ON K1G 4KE

(☎ 613/993-0534). Canada allows you a $750 exemption, and you're allowed to bring back duty-free 200 cigarettes, 2.2 pounds of tobacco, 40 imperial ounces of liquor, and 50 cigars. In addition, you're allowed to mail gifts to Canada from abroad at the rate of Can$60 a day, provided they're unsolicited and don't contain alcohol or tobacco (write on the package "Unsolicited Gift, Under $60 Value"). All valuables should be declared on the Y-38 form before departure from Canada, including serial numbers of valuables you already own, such as expensive foreign cameras. *Note:* The $500 exemption can be used only once a year and only after an absence of 7 days.

AUSTRALIAN CITIZENS   The duty-free allowance is A$400 or, for those under 18, A$200. Personal property mailed back should be marked "Australian Goods Returned" to avoid payment of duty. Upon returning to Australia, you can bring in 250 cigarettes or 250 grams of loose tobacco and 1,125 milliliters of alcohol. If you're returning with valuable goods you already own, such as foreign-made cameras, you should file form B263. A helpful brochure, available from Australian consulates or Customs offices, is *Know Before You Go.* For more information, contact **Australian Customs Services,** GPO Box 8, Sydney NSW 2001 (☎ 02/9213-2000).

NEW ZEALAND CITIZENS   The duty-free allowance is NZ$700. Citizens over 17 can bring in 200 cigarettes, 50 cigars, or 250 grams of tobacco (or a mix of all three if their combined weight doesn't exceed 250 grams); plus 4.5 liters of wine and beer or 1.125 liters of liquor. New Zealand currency doesn't carry import or export restrictions. Fill out a certificate of export, listing the valuables you're taking out of the country; that way, you can bring them back without paying duty. Most questions are answered in a free pamphlet available at New Zealand consulates and Customs offices: *New Zealand Customs Guide for Travelers,* Notice no. 4. For more information, contact **New Zealand Customs,** 50 Anzac Ave., P.O. Box 29, Auckland (☎ 09/359-6655).

3 Money

Traveler's checks, while still the safest way to carry money, are going the way of the dinosaur. The aggressive evolution of international computerized banking and ATM networks has led to the triumph of plastic in Europe—even if cold cash is still the most trusted currency. Odds are you can saunter up to an ATM in the dinkiest Bavarian village with your bankcard or PIN-enabled Visa and get some local cash out of it. Never rely on credit cards and ATMs alone, however. Though most hotels and many restaurants around Europe accept plastic, smaller towns and cheaper places are still wary, and occasionally the phone lines and computer networks used to verify your card can go down and render your plastic useless. Always carry some local currency and some traveler's checks for insurance.

Although currency conversions in this guide were accurate at press time, European exchange rates fluctuate. For up-to-date rates, look in the business pages or travel section of any major U.S. newspaper, check online at the **Universal Currency Converter** (www.xe.net/currency), or call **Thomas Cook** (see "Traveler's Checks," below).

It's more expensive to purchase foreign currency in your own country than once you've reached your destination. But it's a good idea to arrive in Europe with a bit of the local currency—at least enough to get you from the airport to your hotel, so you can avoid the bad rates you get at airport exchanges. Bring along about $30 to $50 in the local currencies of every European city you'll be visiting (call around to the major branches of local banks in your hometown to find the best rate).

While traveling, either withdraw local currency from an ATM (see below) or convert your cash or traveler's checks at a bank whenever possible—banks invariably give better rates than tourist offices, hotels, travel agencies, or exchange booths. You lose money every time you make a transaction, so it's often better to convert large sums at once (especially in flat-fee transactions). The rates for converting traveler's checks are usually better than those for cash, but you get the best rates by withdrawing money from an ATM with your bank or credit card.

ATMS

Plus, Cirrus, and other networks work on many ATMs in Europe, giving you local currency and drawing it directly from your checking account. This is the fastest, easiest, and least expensive way to change money. You take advantage of the bank's bulk exchange rate (better than anything you'll get on your own exchanging cash or traveler's checks) and, unless your home bank charges you for using a nonproprietary ATM, you won't have to pay a commission. Make sure the PINs on your bank and credit cards will work in Europe; you usually need a four-digit code (six digits often won't work). Keep in mind you're usually able to access only your checking account, not savings, from ATMs abroad.

Both the **Cirrus** (☎ 800/424-7787; www.mastercard.com/atm) and the **Plus** (☎ 800/843-7587; www.visa.com/atms) networks have ATM locators listing the banks in each country that accept your card; alternately, you can just search out any machine with your network's symbol on it. Europe is getting to be like America—a bank on virtually every corner—and most are globally networked. You can also get a cash advance through Visa or MasterCard (contact the issuing bank to enable this feature and get a PIN), but note the credit-card company will begin charging you interest immediately, and many have begun assessing a fee every time. American Express card cash advances are usually available only from AMEX offices, which you'll find in every European city.

CREDIT CARDS

Most middle-bracket and virtually all first-class and deluxe hotels, restaurants, and shops in Europe accept major credit cards—American Express, Diners Club, MasterCard, and Visa (not Discover). Some budget establishments accept plastic; others don't. The most widely accepted cards these days are Visa and MasterCard, but it pays to carry American Express too. Note that you can now often choose to charge credit-card purchases at the price in euros or in the local currency; since most European currencies are now locked together, the dollar amount always comes out the same, but it could help you comparison-shop.

TRAVELER'S CHECKS

Most large banks sell traveler's checks, charging fees of 1% to 2% of the value of the checks. AAA members can buy American Express checks commission-free. Traveler's checks are great travel insurance because if you lose them—and have kept a list of their numbers (and a record of which ones were cashed) in a safe place separate from the checks themselves—you can get them replaced at no charge. Hotels and shops usually accept them, but you get a lousy exchange rate. Use traveler's checks to exchange for local currency at banks or American Express offices. Personal checks are next to useless in Europe.

American Express (☎ 800/221-7282; www.americanexpress.com) is one of the largest issuers of traveler's checks, and theirs are the most commonly accepted. They also sell checks to holders of certain types of American Express cards at no commission. **Thomas Cook** (☎ 800/223-7373 in the U.S. and Canada, 020/7480-7226 in London, or 609/987-7300 collect from other parts of the world;

What's Up with the Euro?

In 1999, the new single European currency called the **euro** (€ or EUR) was launched in Austria, Belgium, Finland, France, Germany, Ireland, Italy, Luxembourg, the Netherlands, Portugal, and Spain. The other countries covered in this guide, including the Czech Republic, Denmark, England, Greece, Scotland, and Sweden, among others, aren't under the euro umbrella. However, for the life of this edition, you'll continue to trade in the old currency of all the countries covered.

Though the actual paper notes and coins won't be introduced until January 1, 2002—and the national currencies won't be fully phased out until July 1, 2002—banks and stock exchanges are obligated in the meantime to carry out all non-cash transactions in euros, and you can make your credit-card purchases in euros. This allows you to more easily compare the cost of something in Paris to its cost in Rome, without having to juggle conversion rates. This is good news for travelers and even better news for Europe's economic strength as its markets can now compete on an even footing. As 2002 approaches, you'll note that more and more European shops and restaurants and so forth will list prices in euros beside the prices in francs, pesetas, or whatever.

At press time, the euro had fallen 12% since its introduction and had almost reached a 1:1 conversion rate with the American dollar.

www.thomascook.com) issues MasterCard traveler's checks. **Citicorp** (☎ **800/645-6556** in the U.S. and Canada, or 813/623-1709 collect from anywhere else in the world; www.citicorp.com) and many other banks issue checks under their own name or under MasterCard or Visa. Get checks issued in dollar amounts (as opposed to, say, French francs) as they're more widely accepted abroad.

WIRE SERVICES

American Express MoneyGram, Wadsworth St., Englewood, CO 80155 (☎ **800/926-9400**), allows friends back home to wire you money in an emergency in less than 10 minutes. Senders should call AMEX to learn the address of the closest outlet that handles MoneyGrams. Cash, credit card, or the occasional personal check (with ID) are acceptable forms of payment. AMEX's fee is $40 for the first $500 with a sliding scale for larger sums. The service includes a short telex message and a 3-minute phone call from sender to recipient. The beneficiary must present a photo ID at the outlet where the money is received.

VALUE-ADDED TAX (VAT)

All European countries charge a **value-added tax (VAT)** of 15% to 33% on goods and services—it's like a sales tax that's already included in the price. Rates vary from country to country (as does the name—it's called the IVA in Italy and Spain, the TVA in France, and so on), though the goal in EU countries is to arrive at a uniform rate of about 15%. Citizens of non-EU countries can, as they leave the country, get back most of the tax on purchases (not services) if they spend above a designated amount (usually $80 to $200) in a single store.

Regulations vary from country to country, so inquire at the tourist office when you arrive to find out the procedure; ask what percentage of the tax is refunded, and if the refund is given to you at the airport or mailed to you later. Look for a **TAX FREE SHOPPING FOR TOURISTS** sign posted in participating stores. Ask the storekeeper for the necessary forms, save all your receipts, and, if possible, keep the purchases in their original packages. Save all your receipts and VAT forms from each EU country to process all of them at the **"Tax Refund"** desk in the airport of the last country you visit before flying home (allow an extra 30 minutes or so at the airport to process forms).

4 When to Go

Europe is a continent for all seasons, offering everything from a bikini beach party on the Riviera in summer to the finest skiing in the world in the Alps in winter.

Europe has a continental climate with distinct seasons, but there are great variations in temperature from one part to another. Northern Norway is plunged into Arctic darkness in winter, but in sunny Sicily the climate is usually temperate—though snow can fall even on the Greek Islands in winter, and winter nights are cold anywhere. Europe is north of most of the United States, but along the Mediterranean they see weather patterns more along the lines of the U.S. southern states. In general, however, seasonal changes are less extreme than in most of the United States.

The **high season** lasts mid-May to mid-September, with the most tourists hitting the continent mid-June to August. In general, this is the most expensive time to travel, except in Austria and Switzerland, where prices are actually higher in winter during the ski season. And since Scandinavian hotels depend on business clients instead of tourists, lower prices can often be found in the fleeting summer, when business clients vacation and a smaller number of tourists take over.

You'll find smaller crowds, relatively fair weather, and often lower prices at hotels in the **shoulder seasons,** Easter to mid-May and mid-September to mid-October. **Off-season** (except at ski resorts) is November to Easter, with the exception of December 25 to January 6. Much of Europe, Italy especially, takes August off, and August 15 to August 30 is vacation time for many locals, so expect the cities to be devoid of natives but the beaches packed.

WEATHER

BRITAIN & IRELAND   Everyone knows it rains a lot in Britain and Ireland. Winters are rainier than summers; August and September to mid-October are the sunniest months. Summer daytime temperatures average in the low to mid-60s (° Fahrenheit), dropping to the 40s on winter nights. Ireland, whose shores are bathed by the Gulf Stream, has a milder climate and the most changeable weather—a dark rainy morning can quickly turn into a sunny afternoon, and vice versa. The Scottish Lowlands have a climate similar to England's, but the Highlands are much colder, with storms and snow in winter.

CENTRAL EUROPE   In Vienna and along the Danube Valley the climate is moderate. Summer daytime temperatures average in the 70s, falling at night to the 50s. Winter temperatures are in the 30s and 40s during the day. In Budapest, temperatures can reach 80°F in August and 30°F in January. Winter is damp and chilly, spring is mild, and May and June are usually wet. The best weather is in the late summer through October. In Prague and Bohemia, summer months have an average temperature of 65°F but are the rainiest, while January and February are usually sunny and clear, with temperatures around freezing.

FRANCE & GERMANY   The weather in Paris is approximately the same as in the U.S. mid-Atlantic states, but like most of Europe, there's less extreme variation. In summer, the temperature rarely goes beyond the mid-70s. Summers are fair and can be hot along the Riviera. Winters tend to be mild, averaging in the 40s, though it's

---

What Time Is It, Anyway?

Based on U.S. Eastern Standard Time, Britain, Ireland, and Portugal are 5 hours ahead of New York City; Greece is 7 hours ahead of New York. The rest of the countries in this book are 6 hours ahead of New York. For instance, when it's noon in New York, it's 5pm in London and Lisbon; 6pm in Paris, Copenhagen, and Amsterdam; and 7pm in Athens. The European countries now observe daylight saving time. The time change doesn't usually occur on the same day or in the same month as in the United States.

If you plan to travel to Ireland or continental Europe from Britain, keep in mind that the time will be the same in Ireland and Portugal, 2 hours later in Greece, and 1 hour later in the other countries in this guide.

---

warmer along the Riviera. Germany's climate ranges from the moderate summers and chilly, damp winters in the north to the mild summers and very cold, sunny winters of the alpine south.

NORTHERN EUROPE   In the Netherlands, the weather is never extreme at any time of year. Summer temperatures average around 67°F and the winter average is about 40°F. The climate is rainy, with the driest months February to May. Mid-April to mid-May, the tulip fields burst into color. The climate of northern Germany is very similar. Belgium's climate is moderate, varying from 73°F in July and August to 40°F in December and January. It does rain a lot, but the weather is at its finest in July and August.

SCANDINAVIA   Summer temperatures above the Arctic Circle average in the mid-50s, dropping to the midteens during the dark winters. In the south, summer temperatures average around 70°F, dropping to the 20s in winter. Fjords and even the ocean are often warm enough for summer swimming, but rain is frequent. The sun shines 24 hours in midsummer above the Arctic Circle, where winter brings semipermanent twilight. Denmark's climate is relatively mild by comparison, with moderate summer temperatures and winters that can be damp and foggy, with temperatures in the mid-30s.

SOUTHERN EUROPE   Summers are hot in Italy, Spain, and Greece, with temperatures in the high 80s or even higher in some parts of Spain. Along the Italian Riviera, summer and winter temperatures are mild, and except in the alpine regions, Italian winter temperatures rarely drop below freezing. The area around Madrid is dry and arid, and summers in Spain are coolest along the Atlantic coast, with mild temperatures year-round on the Costa del Sol. Seaside Portugal is very rainy but has a temperature range between 50°F and 75°F year-round. In Greece there's sunshine all year, and winters are usually mild, with temperatures around 50°F to 55°F. Hot summer temperatures are often helped by cool breezes. The best seasons to visit Greece are mid-April to June and mid-September to late October, when the wildflowers bloom and the tourists go home.

SWITZERLAND & THE ALPS   The alpine climate is shared by Bavaria in southern Germany and the Austrian Tyrol and Italian Dolomites—winters are cold and bright and spring comes late, with snow flurries well into April. Summers are mild and sunny, though the alpine regions can experience dramatic changes in weather any time of year.

5 Active & Other Special-Interest Vacations

CYCLING

Cycling tours are a great way to see Europe at your own pace. Some of the best are conducted by the **Cyclists' Tourist Club,** 69 Meadrow, Godalming, Surrey, England GU7 3HS (☎ **01483/417-217;** www.ctc.org.uk). **Holland Bicycling Tours, Inc.,** P.O. Box 6485, Thousand Oaks, CA 91359 (☎ **800/852-3258;** fax 805/495-8601), leads 8-day bicycle tours throughout Europe, and **Experience Plus** (☎ **800/685-4565;** www.experienceplus.com) runs bike tours across Europe. **Cicilsmo Classico,** 13 Marathon St., Arlington, MA 02174 (☎ **800/866-7314;** fax 781/641-1512; www.ciclismoclassico.com), is an excellent outfit running tours of Italy, and Florence-based ✪ **I Bike Italy** (☎ **055-234-2371;** www.ibikeitaly.com: e-mail: i_bike_italy@compuserve.com), offers guided single-day rides in the Tuscan countryside.

HIKING

Wilderness Travel, 1102 9th St., Berkeley, CA 94710 (☎ **800/368-2794;** www.wildernesstravel.com), specializes in walking tours, treks, and inn-to-inn hiking tours of Europe, as well as less strenuous walking tours. **Sherpa Expeditions,** 131A Heston Rd., Hounslow, Middlesex, England TW5 ORD (☎ **020/8577-2717;** www.sherpa-walking-holidays.co.uk), offers both self-guided and group treks through off-the-beaten-track regions; it's represented in the United States by **Himalayan Travel,** 110 Prospect St., Stamford, CT 06901 (☎ **800/225-2380;** www.gorp.com/ hmtravel.htm). Two somewhat upscale walking tour companies are **Butterfield & Robinson,** 70 Bond St., Suite 300, Toronto, ON M5B 1X3 (☎ **800/678-1147;** fax 416/864-0541; www.butterfield.com), and **Country Walkers,** P.O. Box 180, Waterbury, VT 05676-0180 (☎ **800/464-9255;** fax 802/244-5661; www.countrywalkers.com).

Most European countries have associations geared toward aiding hikers and walkers. In England it's the **Ramblers' Association,** 1–5 Wandsworth Rd., London SW8 2XX (☎ **020/7339-8500;** www.ramblers.org.uk); in Italy, contact the **Club Alpino Italiano,** 7 Via E. Fonseca Pimental, Milan 20127 (☎ **02-205-7231;** www.cai.it); for Austria, try the **Österreichischer Alpenverein (Austrian Alpine Club),** Wilhelm-Greil-Strasse 15, Innsbruck, A-6020 (☎ **0512/595470;** www.alpenrerein.at); in Norway, it's the **Norwegian Mountain Touring Association,** Storgata 3, Box 7, Sentrum 0101 Oslo (☎ **22-82-28-22;** fax 22-82-28-55; www.turistforeningen.no).

HORSEBACK RIDING

One of the best companies is **Equitour,** P.O. Box 1262, Dubois, WY 82513 (☎ **800/545-0019** or 307/455-3363; fax 307/455-2354; www.ridingtours.com), with 5- to 7-day rides through many of Europe's most popular areas, such as Tuscany and the Loire Valley.

HOME EXCHANGES

Intervac U.S., P.O. Box 590504, San Francisco, CA 94159 (☎ **800/756-HOME** or 415/435-3497; www.intervac.com), is part of the largest worldwide home-exchange network, with a special emphasis on Europe. It publishes four catalogs a year, listing homes in more than 36 countries. Members contact each other directly. Listing fees vary from country to country; contact them for complete details and costs.

EDUCATIONAL TRAVEL

The best (and one of the most expensive) of the escorted tour operators is **IST Cultural Tours** (☎ 800/833-2111; www.ist-tours.com), whose tours are first class all the way and accompanied by a certified expert in whatever field the trip focuses on. If you missed out on study abroad in college, the brainy **Smithsonian Study Tours** (☎ 202/357-4700; www.si.edu/tsa) may be just the ticket, albeit a pricey one. The cheaper alternative is **Smithsonian Odyssey Tours** (☎ 800/258-5885; www2. smithsonianmag.51.edu), run by Saga International Holidays (these trips cost less because you stay in three- or four-star hotels rather than deluxe). Also contact your alma mater or local university to see if it offers summer tours open to the public and guided by a professor specialist.

The **National Registration Center for Studies Abroad (NRCSA),** P.O. Box 1393, Milwaukee, WI 53203 (☎ 414/278-7410; www.NRCSA.com), and the **American Institute for Foreign Study (AIFS),** 102 Greenwich Ave., Greenwich, CT 06830 (☎ 800/727-2437 or 203/869-9090; www.AIFS.com), can both help you arrange study programs and summer programs abroad.

The biggest organization dealing with higher education in Europe is the **Institute of International Education,** with headquarters at 809 United Nations Plaza, New York, NY 10017-3580 (☎ 212/984-5400; www.iie.org). A few of its booklets are free, but for $42.95, plus $5 postage, you can buy the more definitive *Vacation Study Abroad.* To order publications, check out the IIE's online bookstore at www.iie.org; call ☎ 800/445-0443 or 301/617-7804; fax 301/206-9789; or write to the Institute of International Education, P.O. Box 371, Annapolis Junction, MD 20701-0371.

A clearinghouse for information on European-based language schools is **Lingua Service Worldwide,** 211 E. 43rd St., Suite 1303, New York, NY 10017 (☎ 800/ 394-LEARN or 212/867-1225; fax 212/983-2590; www.linguaserviceworld.de.com).

CULINARY SCHOOLS

Cuisine International, P.O. Box 25228, Dallas, TX 75225 (☎ 214/373-1161; fax 214/373-1162; www.cuisineinternational.com), brings together some of the top independent cooking schools and teachers based in various European countries so you can book your weeklong culinary dream vacation.

Italian Cuisine in Florence, Via Trieste 1, 50139 Firenze (☎ 055-480041; e-mail: mirel@boxl.tin.it), provides several gourmet classes in regional as well as *nouva cucina.* Most courses are 5 days, but short workshops for larger groups are also available. May to October, the **International Cooking School of Italian Food and Wine,** 201 E. 28th St., New York, NY 10016-8538 (☎ 212/779-1921; fax 212/779-3248; www.intl-kitchen.com), offers courses in Bologna, the "gastronomic capital of Italy." **Le Cordon Bleu,** rue Léon-Delhomme 8, 75015 Paris (☎ 800/457-2433 in the U.S., or 01-53-68-22-50; www.cordonbleu.net), was established in 1895 as a means of spreading the tenets of French cuisine to the world at large. It offers many programs outside its flagship Paris school.

6 Health & Insurance

HEALTH

You'll encounter few health problems traveling in Europe. The tap water is generally safe to drink (except on trains and elsewhere it's marked as nondrinking water), the milk pasteurized, and health services good to superb. You will, however, be eating foods and spices your body isn't used to, so you might want to bring along Pepto-Bismol tablets in case indigestion or diarrhea strikes.

A Packing Tip

Pack prescription medications in your carry-on luggage. Carry written prescriptions in generic (not brand-name) form, and dispense all prescription medications from their original labeled vials. This helps foreign pharmacists fill them and customs officials approve them. If you wear contact lenses, pack an extra pair in case you lose one.

If you worry about getting sick away from home, you may want to consider **medical travel insurance** (see below). In most cases, however, your existing health plan will provide all the coverage you need. Be sure to carry your ID card in your wallet.

If you suffer from a chronic illness, consult your doctor before your departure. For conditions like epilepsy, diabetes, or heart problems, wear a **Medic Alert Identification Tag** (☎ **800/825-3785;** www.commedicalert.org), which immediately alerts doctors to your condition and gives them access to your records through Medic Alert's 24-hour hotline. Membership is $35, plus a $15 annual fee.

Contact the **International Association for Medical Assistance to Travelers (IAMAT)** (☎ **716/754-4883** or 416/652-0137; www.sentex.net/~iamat), for tips on travel and health concerns in the countries you'll be visiting and a list of local English-speaking doctors. When you're abroad, any local consulate can provide a list of area doctors who speak English. If you do get sick, you might want to ask the concierge at your hotel to recommend a local doctor.

Many European hospitals are partially socialized, and you'll usually be taken care of speedily, often at no charge for simple ailments. If you have to be admitted, most health insurance plans and HMOs will cover, at least to some extent, out-of-country hospital visits and procedures. However, most make you pay the bills up front at the time of care and reimburse you after you've returned and filed all the paperwork. Members of Blue Cross/Blue Shield can now use their cards at select hospitals in most major cities worldwide (call ☎ **800/810-BLUE** or www.bluecares.com for a list of participating hospitals).

INSURANCE

Comprehensive insurance programs, covering basically everything from trip cancellation and lost luggage to medical coverage abroad and accidental death, are offered by the following companies: **Access America,** 6600 W. Broad St., Richmond, VA 23286-4991 (☎ **800/284-8300**); **Travelex Insurance Services,** P.O. Box 9408, Garden City, NY 11530-9408 (☎ **800/228-9792**); **Travel Guard International,** 1145 Clark St., Stevens Point, WI 54481 (☎ **800/826-1300;** www.travel-guard.com); and **Travel Insured International,** P.O. Box 280568, East Hartford, CT 06128-0568 (☎ **800/243-3174;** www.travelinsured.com). British travelers can try **Columbus Travel Insurance,** 17 Devonshire Square, London EC2M 4SQ (☎ **020/7375-0011** in London; www.columbusdirect.co.uk).

Medicare covers only U.S. citizens traveling in Mexico and Canada. Two companies specializing in accident and medical care are **MEDEX International,** P.O. Box 5375, Timonium, MD 21094-5375 (☎ **888/MEDEX-00,** or 410/453-6300 outside the U.S. and Canada; fax 410/453-6301; www.medexassist.com); and **Travel Assistance International (Worldwide Assistance Services),** 1133 15th St. NW, Suite 400, Washington, DC 20005 (☎ **800/821-2828** or 202/828-5894; fax 202/828-5896).

For information on **car renter's insurance,** see "Getting Around," below.

7 Tips for Travelers with Special Needs

FOR TRAVELERS WITH DISABILITIES

Europe won't win any medals for handicapped-accessibility, but in the past few years its big cities have made an effort to accommodate travelers with disabilities. *A World of Options,* a 658-page book of resources for travelers with disabilities, covers everything from biking trips to scuba outfitters. It costs $35 ($30 for members) and is available from **Mobility International USA,** P.O. Box 10767, Eugene, OR 97440 (☎ **541/343-1284,** voice and TDD; www.miusa.org); annual membership is $35. In addition, **Twin Peaks Press,** P.O. Box 129, Vancouver, WA 98666 (☎ **360/ 694-2462**), publishes travel-related books for people with disabilities. The **Moss Rehab Hospital** (☎ **215/456-9600**) has been providing friendly and helpful phone advice and referrals to travelers with disabilities for years through its **Travel Information Service** at ☎ **215/456-9603** (www.mossresourcenet.org).

You can join the **Society for the Advancement of Travel for the Handicapped (SATH),** 347 Fifth Ave. Suite 610, New York, NY 10016 (☎ **212/447-7284;** fax 212-725-8253; www.sath.org), for $45 annually or $30 for seniors/students. It provides info sheets on travel destinations and referrals to tour operators who specialize in traveling with disabilities. Its quarterly magazine, *Open World for Disability and Mature Travel,* is full of good information and resources and costs $13 ($21 outside the U.S.) per year.

You might also want to consider joining a tour catering specifically to travelers with disabilities. One of the best operators is **Flying Wheels Travel,** 143 West Bridge (P.O. Box 382), Owatonna, MN 55060 (☎ **800/535-6790**), offering escorted tours and cruises, with an emphasis on sports, as well as private tours in minivans with lifts. Other reputable specialized tour operators are **Access Adventures** (☎ **716/ 889-9096**), which offers sports-related vacations; **Accessible Journeys** (☎ **800/ TINGLES** or 610/521-0339), for slow walkers and wheelchair travelers; **The Guided Tour** (☎ **215/782-1370**); **Wilderness Inquiry** (☎ **800/728-0719** or 612/ 379-3858); and **Directions Unlimited** (☎ **800/533-5343**).

You can get a copy of *Air Transportation of Handicapped Persons* by writing to Free Advisory Circular No. AC12032, Distribution Unit, U.S. Department of Transportation, Publications Division, M-4332, Washington, DC 20590. Vision-impaired travelers should contact the **American Foundation for the Blind,** 11 Penn Plaza, Suite 300, New York, NY 10001 (☎ **800/232-5463**), for information on traveling with Seeing Eye dogs.

The **Royal Association for Disability and Rehabilitation (RADAR),** Unit 12, City Forum, 250 City Rd., London EC1V 8AF (☎ **020/7250-3222**), publishes three holiday "fact packs." The first provides general info, including planning and booking a holiday, insurance, finances, and useful organizations and holiday providers; the second outlines transportation and rental equipment options; and the third deals with specialized accommodations. Another good service is the **Holiday Care Service,** Imperial Building, 2nd Floor, Victoria Road, Horley, Surrey RH6 7PZ (☎ **01293/774-535;** fax 01293/784-647), a national charity that advises on accessible accommodations for seniors and persons with disabilities. Annual membership is £30.

FOR FAMILIES

Europeans expect to see families traveling together. It's a multigenerational continent, and you sometimes see the whole clan traveling around. And Europeans tend to love kids. You'll often find a child guarantees you an even warmer reception at hotels and restaurants.

At **restaurants,** ask waiters for a half portion to fit junior's appetite. If you're traveling with small children, three- and four-star hotels may be your best bet—**baby-sitters** are on call so you can take the occasional romantic dinner, and such hotels have a better general ability to help you access the city and its services. But even cheaper hotels can usually find you a sitter. Traveling with a pint-sized person usually means pint-sized rates. An **extra cot** in the room won't cost more than 30% extra (if anything), and most museums and sights offer **reduced or free admission** for children under a certain age (which can range from 6 to 18). Kids almost always get discounts on plane and train tickets too.

Several books offer tips to help you travel with kids. *Family Travel* (Lanier Publishing International) and *How to Take Great Trips with Your Kids* (Harvard Common Press) are full of good general advice that can apply to travel anywhere. Another reliable tome, with a worldwide focus, is *Adventuring with Children* (Foghorn Press). *Family Travel Times* is published six times a year by TWYCH (Travel with Your Children; ☎ **888/822-4388** or 212/477-5524) and offers a weekly call-in service for subscribers. Subscriptions are $40 per year for quarterly editions. A free publication list and sample issue are available by calling the above number.

The University of New Hampshire runs **Familyhostel** (☎ **800/733-9753**), an intergenerational alternative to standard guided tours. You live on a European college campus for the 2- or 3-week program, attend lectures, seminars, go on lots of field trips, and sightsee—all of it guided by a team of experts and academics. It's designed for children 8 to 15, parents, and grandparents.

FOR GAYS & LESBIANS

Much of Europe has grown to accept same-sex couples over the past few decades, and in most countries homosexual sex acts are legal. To be on the safe side, do a bit of research and test the waters for acceptability in any one city or area. As you might expect, smaller towns tend to be less accepting than cities. Gay centers include London, Paris, Amsterdam, Berlin, Milan, and the Greek Islands (Mykonos). For fabulous coverage of the gay scene in Europe's top destinations, get a copy of *Frommer's Gay & Lesbian Europe.*

The **International Gay & Lesbian Travel Association** (IGLTA) (☎ **800/448-8550** or 954/776-2626; fax 954/776-3303; www.iglta.org), links travelers up with the gay-friendly service organizations or tour specialists. With around 1,200 members, it offers quarterly newsletters, marketing mailings, and a membership directory updated quarterly. Membership is usually gay/lesbian businesses but is open to individuals for $150 yearly, plus a $100 administration fee for new members. Members are kept informed of gay and gay-friendly hoteliers, tour operators, and airline and cruise-line representatives. Contact the IGLTA for a list of its member agencies, who'll be tied into IGLTA's resources.

General gay and lesbian travel agencies include **Family Abroad** (☎ **800/999-5500** or 212/459-1800; www.familyabroad.com; gay/lesbian); and **Above and Beyond Tours** (☎ **800/397-2681;** www.abovebeyondtours.com; mainly gay).

Besides *Frommer's Gay & Lesbian Europe,* two good biannual English-language guidebooks focus on gays but include information for lesbians as well. You can get the Spartacus or Odysseus guides (and Frommer's guide) from most gay and lesbian bookstores or order them from **Giovanni's Room** (☎ **215/923-2960**) or **A Different Light Bookstore** (☎ **800/343-4002** or 212/989-4850; www.adlbooks.com). Both lesbians and gays might want to pick up a copy of *Gay Travel A to Z* ($16). The Ferrari Guides (www.q-net.com) is another good series of guidebooks.

Out and About, 8 W. 19th St. #401, New York, NY 10011 (☎ **800/929-2268** or 212/645-6922; www.outandabout.com), offers guides and a monthly newsletter packed with details on the global gay and lesbian scene. A year's subscription to the newsletter is $49. **Our World,** 1104 North Nova Rd., Suite 251, Daytona Beach, FL 32117 (☎ **904/441-5367;** www.ourworldmag.com), is a slicker monthly magazine promoting and highlighting travel bargains and opportunities. Annual subscription rates are $35 inside the United States and $45 outside.

FOR SENIORS

Don't be shy about asking for discounts but always carry some kind of ID, such as a driver's license, showing your date of birth. Also mention that you're a senior when you first make your travel reservations. Many hotels offer seniors discounts, and in most cities, people over age 60 qualify for reduced admission to theaters, museums, and other attractions as well as discounted fares on public transportation.

Members of the **American Association of Retired Persons (AARP),** 601 E St. NW, Washington, DC 20049 (☎ **800/424-3410** or 202/434-2277; www.aarp.org), get discounts not only on hotels but also on airfares and car rentals. AARP offers members a wide range of special benefits, including *Modern Maturity* magazine and a monthly newsletter.

Grand Circle Travel, 347 Congress St., Suite 3A, Boston, MA 02210 (☎ **800/221-2610** or 617/350-7500; www.gct.com), is also one of the hundreds of travel agencies specializing in vacations for seniors. Many of these packages, however, are of the tour-bus variety, with free trips thrown in for those who organize groups of 10 or more. Seniors seeking more independent travel should consult a regular travel agent. **SAGA International Holidays,** 222 Berkeley St., Boston, MA 02116 (☎ **800/343-0273;** www.sagaholidays.com), offers inclusive tours and cruises for those 50 and older. It also sponsors the more substantial "Road Scholar Tours" (☎ **800/621-2151**), which are fun-loving but have an educational bent.

If you want something more than the average vacation or guided tour, try **Elderhostel,** 75 Federal St., Boston, MA 02110-1941 (☎ **877/426-8056;** www.elderhostel.org), or the University of New Hampshire's **Interhostel** (☎ **800/733-9753**), both variations on the same theme: educational travel for seniors. These escorted tours are packed with seminars, lectures, field trips, and sightseeing, led by academic experts. Elderhostel arranges study programs for those 55 and over (and a spouse or companion of any age) in the United States and 77 countries around the world. Most courses last about 3 weeks and many include airfare, accommodations in student dorms or modest inns, meals, and tuition. Write or call for a free catalog. Interhostel takes travelers 50 and over (with companions over 40) and offers 2- and 3-week trips, mostly international. The courses in both programs are ungraded, involve no homework, and often focus on the liberal arts. They're not luxury vacations but are fun and fulfilling.

Though these specialty books are U.S.-focused, they do provide general advice and contacts for savvy travelers: *The 50+ Traveler's Guidebook* (St. Martin's Press), *The Seasoned Traveler* (Country Roads Press), and *Unbelievably Good Deals and Great Adventures That You Absolutely Can't Get Unless You're Over 50* (Contemporary Books). Also check out your newsstand for the quarterly magazine *Travel 50 & Beyond.*

FOR STUDENTS

The best resource is the **Council on International Educational Exchange (CIEE).** It can set you up with an ID card (see below), and its travel branch, **Council Travel Service** (☎ **800/226-8624;** www.counciltravel.com), is the world's biggest student travel agency. It can get you discounts on plane tickets, rail passes, and the like. Ask for a list of CTS offices in major cities so you can keep the discounts flowing (and aid lines open) as you travel.

From CIEE you can get the student traveler's best friend, the $18 **International Student Identity Card (ISIC).** It's the only officially acceptable form of student ID, good for cut rates on rail passes, plane tickets, and other discounts. It also provides you with basic health and life insurance and a 24-hour help line. If you're no longer a student but are still under 26, you can buy a **GO 25** card from the same people, getting you the insurance and some of the discounts (but not student admission prices in museums).

In Canada, **Travel CUTS,** 200 Ronson St., Suite 320, Toronto, ONT M9W 5Z9 (☎ **800/667-2887** or 416/614-2887; www.travelcuts.com), offers similar services. **Campus USIT,** 52 Grosvenor Gardens, London SW1W 0AG (☎ **020/7730-3402;** www.usitcampus.co.uk), opposite Victoria Station, is Britain's leading specialist in student and youth travel.

8 Getting There

FLYING FROM NORTH AMERICA

Most major airlines charge competitive fares to European cities, but price wars break out regularly and fares can change overnight. Tickets tend to be cheaper if you fly mid-week or off-season. **High season** on most routes is usually June to mid-September—the most expensive and most crowded time to travel. **Shoulder season** is April to May, mid-September to October, and December 15 to 24. **Low season**—with the cheapest fares—is November to December 14 and December 25 to March.

MAJOR NORTH AMERICAN AIRLINES   North American carriers with frequent service and flights to Europe are **Air Canada** (☎ 800/776-3000 in the U.S., or 800/555-1212 in Canada; www.aircanada.ca), **American Airlines** (☎ 800/433-7300; www.americanair.com), **Canadian Airlines** (☎ 800/426-7000 in the U.S., or 800/665-1177 in Canada; www.cdnair.ca), **Continental Airlines** (☎ 800/231-0856; www.flycontinental.com), **Delta Airlines** (☎ 800/241-4141; www.delta-air.com), **Northwest Airlines** (☎ 800/447-4747; www.nwa.com), **Tower Air** (☎ 800/221-2500; www.towerair.com), **TWA** (☎ 800/892-4141; www.twa.com), and **US Airways** (☎ 800/622-1015; www.usairways.com).

For the latest on airline Web sites, check **www.itn.com**.

EUROPEAN NATIONAL AIRLINES   Not only will the national carriers of European countries offer the greatest number of direct flights from the States (and can easily book you through to cities beyond the major hubs), but since their entire U.S. market is to fly you to their home country, they often run more competitive deals than most North American carriers. Major national and country-affiliated European airlines include the following:

- **Austria:** Austrian Airlines. *In the U.S. and Canada:* 800/843-0002. *In the U.K.:* 020/7434-7300. *In Australia:* 02/9241-4277. www.aua.com.
- **Belgium:** Sabena. *In the U.S. and Canada:* 800/955-2000. *In the U.K.:* 020/7494-2629. www.sabena-usa.com.
- **Czech Republic:** CSA Czech Airlines. *In the U.S. and Canada:* 800/223-2365. *In the U.K.:* 0171/255-1898. *In Australia:* 02/9247-6196. www.csa.cz.
- **France:** Air France. *In the U.S.:* 800/237-2747. *In Canada:* 514/847-1106. *In the U.K.:* 020/8742-6600. *In Australia:* 02/9321-1000. *In New Zealand:* 068/725-8800. www.airfrance.com.

- **Germany:** Lufthansa. *In the U.S.:* 800/645-3880. *In Canada:* 800/563-5954. *In the U.K.:* 0345/737-747. *In Australia:* 02/9367-3888. *In New Zealand:* 09/303-1529. www.lufthansa.com.
- **Greece:** Olympic Airways. *In the U.S.:* 800/223-1226, or 212/735-0200 in New York State. *In Canada:* 514/878-3891 (Montréal) or 416/920-2452 (Toronto). *In the U.K.:* 020/7409-2400. *In Australia:* 02/9251-2044. agn.hol.gr/info/olympic1.htm.
- **Hungary:** Malev Hungarian Airlines. *In the U.S.:* 800/262-5380. *In Canada:* 416/9440-093. *In the U.K.:* 020/7439-0577. *In Australia:* 02/9321-9111. *In New Zealand:* 09/379-4455. www.malev-airlines.com.
- **Ireland:** Aer Lingus. *In the U.S.:* 800/474-7424. *In the U.K.:* 020/8899-4747 (London) or 0645/737-747 (all other areas). *In Australia:* 02/9321-9123. *In New Zealand:* 09/379-4455. www.aerlingus.ie.
- **Italy:** Alitalia. *In the U.S.:* 800/223-5730. *In Canada:* 514/842-8241 (Montréal) or 416/363-1348 (Toronto). *In the U.K.:* 020/8745-8200. *In Australia:* 02/9247-1307. *In New Zealand:* 09/379-4457. www.alitalia.com.
- **The Netherlands:** KLM Royal Dutch Airlines. *In the U.S.:* 800/374-7747. *In Canada:* 514/939-4040 (Montréal) or 416/204-5100 (Toronto). *In the U.K.:* 0990/750-9900. *In Australia:* 02/9231-6333. *In New Zealand:* 09/309-1782. www.klm.nl.
- **Portugal:** TAP Air Portugal. *In the U.S.:* 800/221-7370. *In the U.K.:* 020/7828-0262. www.tap-airportugal.pt.
- **Scandinavia (Denmark, Norway, Sweden):** SAS Scandinavian Airlines. *In the U.S.:* 800/221-2350. *In the U.K.:* 020/7734-6777. *In Australia:* 02/9299-6688. www.flysas.com.
- **Spain:** Iberia. *In the U.S.:* 800/772-4642. *In Canada:* 800/363-4534. *In the U.K.:* 020/7830-0011. *In Australia:* 02/9283-3660. *In New Zealand:* 09/379-3076. www.iberia.com.
- **Switzerland:** Swissair. *In the U.S. and Canada:* 800/221-4750. *In the U.K.:* 020/7434-7300. *In Australia:* 02/9232-1744. www.swissair.com.
- **United Kingdom:** (1) British Airways. *In the U.S. and Canada:* 800/247-9297. *In the U.K.:* 020/8897-4000 or 034/522-2111. *In Australia:* 02/9258-3300. www.british-airways.com. (2) Virgin Atlantic Airways. *In the U.S. and Canada:* 800/862-8621. *In the U.K.:* 01293/616-161 or 01293/747-747. *In Australia:* 02/9352-6199. www.fly.virgin.com.

PACKAGE TOURS Package tours aren't the same thing as escorted tours. They're simply a way of buying your airfare and accommodations at the same time and getting an excellent rate on both. Your trip is your own. In many cases, a package including airfare, hotel, and transportation to and from the airport costs less than the hotel alone if you booked it yourself. The downside is that many stick you in large international-style hotels (which in Europe are often outside the historic city center). You do get a good rate for that sort of hotel, but with a little more work (and the hotel reviews in this book), you can easily find on your own a midrange pension or friendly B&B for the same price or less and right in the heart of the action.

All major airlines flying to Europe sell vacation packages (see phone numbers and Web sites above). The best place to start looking for independent packagers is the travel section of your local Sunday newspaper and national travel magazines. **Central Holidays** (☎ 800/935-5000; www.book.centralh.) is one of the best and most reputable package-tour operators. **Liberty Travel** (☎ 888/271-1584); www.libertytravel. com) is one of the biggest packagers in the Northeast and usually boasts a full-page

Flying for Less: Tips for Getting the Best Airfares

- **Take advantage of APEX fares.** Advance-purchase booking (APEX) fares are often the key to getting the lowest fare. You generally must be willing to make your plans and buy your tickets as far ahead as possible: The **21-day APEX** is seconded only by the **14-day APEX,** with a stay of 7 to 30 days. Since the number of seats allocated to APEX fares is sometimes less than 25% of plane capacity, the early bird gets the low-cost seat. There's often a surcharge for flying on a weekend, and cancellation and refund policies can be strict. A more flexible, but more expensive, option is the regular **economy fare,** allowing for a stay shorter than the 7-day APEX minimum. You're also usually free to make last-minute changes in flight dates and have unrestricted stopovers.

- **Watch for sales.** You'll almost never see them during July and August or the Thanksgiving or Christmas seasons, but at other times you can get great deals. If you already hold a ticket when a sale breaks, it may even pay to exchange it, which usually incurs a $50 to $75 charge.

- **Check out budget travel agencies.** An agency like **Council Travel** (☎ 800/ 2-COUNCIL;** www.counciltravel.com), a student travel specialist, always has the scoop on the latest cheap fares, and you don't have to be a student, under 26, or a teacher to use it (though you'll save more if you are). In addition, all specialize in finding the lowest fares. You can often get discounted fares on short notice without all the advance-purchase requirements.

- **Ask if you can secure a cheaper fare by staying an extra day or flying mid-week.** If your schedule is flexible, you can definitely save money this way. Many airlines won't volunteer this information.

- **Be aware that consolidators (aka bucket shops) are good places to find low fares.** They buy seats in bulk from airlines and sell them to you at prices below even the airlines' discounted rates. Their small boxed ads usually run in the Sunday travel section. One of the biggest U.S. consolidators is **Travac,** 989 Sixth Ave., New York, NY 10018 (☎ 800/TRAV-800** or 212/563-3303; www.travac.com). **Council Travel** (☎ 800/226-8624;** www.counciltravel. com) and **STA Travel** (☎ 800/781-4040;** www.sta.travel.com) cater to young

ad in Sunday papers. **American Express Vacations** (☎ 800/241-1700;** www. americanexpress.com/travel) and **Kemwel** (☎ 800/678-0678;** www.kemwel.com) are both reputable options too.

FLY/DRIVE TOURS   Fly/drive vacations, which combine airfare and car rental, are increasing in popularity and are a lot cheaper than booking both airfare and car rental independently. They're available mainly through major European airlines (see above).

ESCORTED GROUP TOURS   With a good escorted group tour, you'll know ahead of time what your trip will cost and won't have to worry about transportation, luggage, hotel reservations, communicating in foreign languages, and other basics— an experienced guide will take care of all that and lead you through all the sightseeing. The downside of a guided tour is you trade much of the freedom and personal free time independent travel grants you and often see only the canned postcard-ready side of Europe through the tinted windows of a giant bus. You get to *see* Europe, but rarely travelers, but their bargains are available to all ages. **Travel Bargains** (☎ **800/AIR-FARE;** www.1800airfare.com) was once owned by TWA but now offers the deepest discounts on many other airlines, with a 4-day advance purchase. Other consolidators are **1-800-FLY-CHEAP** (www.1800flycheap. com); **Cheap Tickets** (☎ **800/377-1000;** www.cheaptickets.com); **1-800/FLY-4-LESS** (www.lowairfare.com); and "rebators" like **Travel Avenue** (☎ **800/333-3335** or 312/876-1116; www.travelavenue.com) and **Smart Traveller** (☎ **800/448-3338** or 305/448-3338; www.smarttraveller@ juno.com). In the United Kingdom, **Trailfinders** (☎ **020/7937-5400;** www.trailfinders.com), is a consolidator offering access to tickets on major European carriers.

- **Book a seat on a charter flight.** Most charter operators advertise and sell their seats through travel agents. Before deciding to take a charter, however, check the ticket restrictions: You may be asked to buy a tour package, pay in advance, be amenable if the departure day is changed, pay a service charge, fly on an airline you're not familiar with (unusual), and pay harsh penalties if you cancel (but be understanding if the charter doesn't fill up and is canceled up to 10 days before departure). Summer charters fill up more quickly than others and are almost sure to fly, but if you decide on a charter, consider cancellation and baggage insurance. **Council Travel,** 205 E. 42nd St., New York, NY 10017 (☎ **800/226-8624;** www.counciltravel.com), arranges charter seats on regularly scheduled aircraft. One of the biggest charter operators is **Travac** (see above). For Canadians, good charter deals are offered by **Martinair** (☎ **800/627-8462;** www.martinair.com) and **Travel CUTS** (☎ **800-667-2887;** www.travelcuts.com), which also has an office at 295A Regent St. in London (☎ **020/7528-6113**).

- **Search for deals on the Web.** It's possible to get some great deals on airfare, hotels, and car rentals via the Internet. See **"Planning Your Trip: An Online Directory"** following this chapter for details on getting the most from the Web.

do you get the chance to really *know* it. Consult a good travel agent for the latest offerings and advice.

Two of the top escorted tour operators are **American Express Vacations,** with the most comprehensive tours to Europe, and **Kemwel** (for both, see "Package Tours," above). If you want a tour that balances independent-style travel and plenty of free time with all the pluses of a guided tour, try the very popular itineraries offered by **Europe Through the Back Door,** 120 Fourth Ave. North, P.O. Box 2009, Edmonds, WA 98020-2009 (☎ **425/771-8303;** www.ricksteves.com), run by Rick Steves, of public TV's *Travels in Europe* fame.

GETTING TO THE CONTINENT FROM THE UNITED KINGDOM

BY TRAIN   Many rail passes and discounts are available in the United Kingdom for travel in continental Europe. One of the most complete overviews is available from **Rail Europe Special Services Department,** 10 Leake St., London SE1 7NN (☎ **0990/848-848**), or **Wasteels,** Platform 2, Victoria Station, London SW1V 1JT

(☎ **020/7834-7066**). Wasteels, and also the London Branch of **Campus USIT,** 52 Grosvenor Gardens, London SW1W OAG (☎ **020/7730-3402;** www. usitcampus.co.uk), are particularly well-versed in information about discount travel as it applies to persons under 26, full-time or part-time students, and seniors.

The most prevalent option for younger travelers, the **EuroYouth passes,** are available only to travelers under 26 and entitle the pass holder to unlimited second-class rail travel in 26 European countries.

BY CHUNNEL   The Eurostar train shuttles between London and both Paris and Brussels; the trip time is less than 3 hours (compared to 10 hours on the traditional train-ferry-train route). **Rail Europe** (☎ **800/94-CHUNNEL;** www.raileurope.com) sells tickets on the Eurostar between London and Paris or Brussels (both $149 one-way).

For Eurostar reservations, call ☎ **0990/300-003** in London, 01-44-51-06-02 in Paris, or 800/EUROSTAR in the U.S. (www.eurostar.com). Eurostar trains arrive at/depart from Waterloo Station in London, Gare du Nord in Paris, and Central Station in Brussels.

BY FERRY & HOVERCRAFT   Brittany Ferries (☎ **01705/892-200;** www. brittany-ferries.com) is the largest British ferry/drive outfit, sailing from the southern coast of England to five destinations in Spain and France. From Portsmouth, sailings reach St-Malo and Caen; from Poole, Cherbourg. From Plymouth, sailings go to Santander in Spain. **P&O Stena Lines** (☎ **087/6000-0611;** www.posl.com) operates car and passenger ferries between Portsmouth and Cherbourg (three departures a day; 5 to 7 hours); between Portsmouth and Le Havre, France (three a day; 5¹/₂ hours); and between Dover and Calais, France (25 sailings a day; 1¹/₄ hours).

Unless you're interested in a leisurely sea voyage, passengers without cars might be better off using the quicker, and slightly cheaper, **Hoverspeed** (☎ **08705/240-241;** www.hoverspeed.co.uk). Hoverspeeds make the 35-minute crossing between Calais and Dover 7 to 15 times per day, with the more curtailed schedule in winter. Prices are £25 ($43) adults on foot or £14 ($24) children; vehicle fares are £78 to £139 ($133 to $236). Prices are one way or 5-day return.

BY CAR   Many car-rental companies won't let you rent a car in Britain and take it to the Continent, so always check ahead. There are many "drive-on/drive-off" car-ferry services across the Channel; see "By Ferry & Hovercraft," above. There are also Chunnel trains that run a drive-on/drive-off service every 15 minutes (once an hour at night) for the 35-minute ride between Ashford and Calais.

BY COACH   Though travel by coach is considerably slower and less comfortable than travel by train, if you're on a budget you might opt for one of Eurolines's regular departures from London's Victoria Coach Station to destinations throughout Europe. Contact **Eurolines** at 52 Grosvenor Gardens, Victoria, London SW1W OAU (☎ **0990/143219** or 01582/404511; www.eurolines.co.uk).

9 Getting Around

BY TRAIN

In Europe, the shortest—and cheapest—distance between two points is lined with rail tracks. European trains are less expensive than those in the United States, far more advanced in many ways, and certainly more extensive. Modern high-speed trains (130 m.p.h.) make the rails faster than the plane for short journeys, and overnight trains get you where you're going without wasting valuable daylight hours—and you save money on lodging to boot.

SOME TRAIN NOTES   Many European high-speed trains, including the popular EC (EuroCity), IC (InterCity), and EN (EuroNight), require you to pay a **supplement** in addition to the regular ticket fare. It's included when you buy tickets but not in any rail pass, so check at the ticket window before boarding; otherwise, the conductor will sell you the supplement on the train—along with a fine. **Seat reservations** ($15 to $50 or more, when a meal's included) are required on some high-speed runs— any marked with an *R* on a printed train schedule. You can usually reserve a seat within a few hours of departure, but be on the safe side and book your seat a few days in advance. You need to reserve any sleeping couchette or sleeping berth, too.

With two exceptions, there's no need to buy individual train tickets or make seat reservations **before you leave the States.** However, on the high-speed Artesia run (Paris-Turin and Milan) you must buy a supplement, on which you can get a substantial discount if you have a rail pass, but only if you buy the supplement in the States along with the pass. It's also wise to reserve a seat on the Eurostar, as England's frequent "bank holidays" (long weekends) book the train solid with Londoners taking a short vacation to Paris.

The difference between **first class** and **second class** on European trains is minor— a matter of 1 or 2 inches of extra padding and maybe a bit more elbow room. European **train stations** are usually as clean and efficient as the trains, if a bit chaotic at times. In stations you'll find posters showing the track number and timetables for regularly scheduled runs (departures are often on the yellow poster). Many stations also have tourist offices and hotel reservations desks, banks with ATMs, and newsstands where you can buy phone cards, bus and metro tickets, maps, and local English-language event magazines.

You can get many more details about train travel in Europe and automated schedule information by fax by contacting **Rail Europe** (☎ **800/438-7245;** fax 800/432-1329; www.raileurope.com). If you plan on doing a lot of train travel, consider buying the *Thomas Cook European Timetable* ($27.95 from travel specialty stores or order it at ☎ **800/FORSYTH**). Each country's national railway Web site, which includes schedules and fare information, occasionally in English, is hot-listed at **Mercurio** (mercurio.iet.unipi.it).

RAIL PASSES   The greatest value in European travel has always been the **rail pass,** a single ticket allowing you unlimited travel (or travel on a certain number of days) within a set time period. If you plan on going all over Europe by train, buying a rail pass will end up being much less expensive than buying individual tickets. Plus, a rail pass gives you the freedom to hop on a train whenever you feel like it, and there's no waiting in ticket lines. For more focused trips, you might want to look into national or regional passes or just buy individual tickets as you go.

Passes Available in the United States   The granddaddy of passes is the **Eurailpass,** covering 17 countries (most of western Europe except Britain). It has been joined by the **Europass,** covering 5 to 12 countries (depending on which version you buy); this pass is mainly for travelers who are going to stay in the heart of western Europe.

Rail passes are available in either **consecutive-day** or **flexipass** versions (in which you have, say, 2 months in which to use 10 days of train travel). Consecutive-day passes are best for those taking the train frequently (every few days), covering a lot of ground, and making many short train hops. Flexipasses are for folks who want to range far and wide, but plan on taking their time over a long trip and intend to stay in each city for a while. If you're under 26, you can opt to buy a regular first-class pass or a second-class youth pass; if you're 26 or over, you're stuck buying a first-class pass. Passes for kids 4 to 11 are half-price, and kids under 4 travel free.

It's best to buy these passes in the States (they're available from some major European train stations but are up to 10% more expensive). You can get them from most travel agents, but the biggest supplier is **Rail Europe** (☎ 800/438-7245; www.raileurope.com), which also sells most national passes, except for a few minor British ones. You can also contact Rick Steve's **Europe Through the Back Door** (☎ 425/771-8303; www.ricksteves.com), which sells all Europe-wide and national rail passes and sends a free video and guide on how to use rail passes; he doesn't tack on the $10 handling fee all other agencies do.

The rates below are for 2000; they rise each year, usually after press time, so we can't include rates for 2001 here.

- **Eurailpass:** Consecutive-day Eurailpass at $554 for 15 days, $718 for 21 days, $890 for 1 month, $1,260 for 2 months, or $1,558 for 3 months.
- **Eurail Flexipass:** Good for 2 months of travel at $654 for 10 days (consecutive or not) or $862 for 15 days.
- **Eurail Saverpass:** Good for two to five people traveling together at $470 per person for 15 days, $610 for 21 days, $756 for 1 month, $1,072 for 2 months, or $1,324 for 3 months.
- **Eurail Saver Flexipass:** Good for two to five people traveling together at $556 per person for 10 days within 2 months or $732 per person for 15 days within 2 months.
- **Eurail Youthpass:** Second-class pass for travelers under 26 at $388 for 15 days, $499 for 21 days, $623 for 1 month, $882 for 2 months, or $1,089 for 3 months.
- **Eurail Youth Flexipass:** Only for travelers under 26 at $458 for 10 days of travel within 2 months or $599 for 15 days within 2 months.
- **Europass:** For trips focusing on the core of western Europe (France, Germany, Switzerland, Italy, Spain), giving 5, 6, 8, 10, or 15 days of train travel for 2 months. Expand the scope of the pass by buying add-on "zones" (Austria/Hungary; Belgium/Netherlands/Luxembourg; Greece, including the ferry from Brindisi: Portugal). Base pass at $348 for 5 days to $728 for 15 days.
- **Europass Youth:** Second-class pass for travelers under 26 granting 5, 6, 8, 10, or 15 days of unlimited train travel in France, Germany, Italy, Spain, and Switzerland within 2 months. Cost is $233 for 5 days, $253 for 6 days, $313 for 8 days, $363 for 10 days, or $513 for 15 days.
- **EurailDrive Pass:** Mixes train travel and rental cars (through Hertz or Avis) for less money than it would cost to do them separately (and one of the only ways to get around the high daily car-rental rates in Europe when you rent for less than a week). You get 4 rail days and 2 car days within a 2-month period. Prices (per person for one adult/two adults) vary with the class of the car: $399/$339 economy class, $439/$359 compact, and $459/$369 midsized. You can add up to

Countries Honoring Train Passes

Eurail Countries: Austria, Belgium, Denmark, Finland, France, Germany, Greece, Hungary, Ireland, Italy, Luxembourg, the Netherlands, Norway, Portugal, Spain, Sweden, Switzerland.
Europass Core Countries: France, Germany, Switzerland, Italy, Spain.
Europass Add-on "Zones": Austria/Hungary, Belgium/Netherlands/Luxembourg, Greece (including the ferry from Brindisi, Italy), Portugal.
Note: Great Britain isn't included in any pass.

Train Trip Tips

To make your train travels as pleasant as possible, remember a few general rules:

- Hold on to your train ticket after it's been marked or punched by the conductor. Some European railroad systems require that you present your ticket when you leave the station platform at your destination.

- While you sleep—or even nap—be sure your valuables are in a safe place; you might temporarily attach a small bell to each bag to warn you if someone attempts to take it. If you've left bags on a rack in the front or back of the car, consider securing them with a small bicycle chain and lock to deter thieves, who consider trains happy hunting grounds.

- Few European trains have drinking fountains and the dining car may be closed just when you're at your thirstiest, so take along a bottle of mineral water. As you'll soon discover, the experienced European traveler comes loaded with hampers of food and drink and munches away throughout the trip.

- If you want to leave bags in a train station locker, don't let anyone help you store them in it. A favorite trick among thieves is feigned helpfulness, then pocketing the key to your locker while passing you the key to an empty one.

---

5 extra rail and/or car days. Extra rail days are $59 each; car days are $61 each for economy class, $80 compact, and $90 midsized. You have to reserve the first car day a week before leaving the States but can make other reservations as you go (always subject to availability). If there are more than two adults, the extra passengers get the car portion free but must buy the 4-day rail pass for $280.

- **Eurodrive Pass:** A similar deal but good for Europass countries only (and no add-on zones) and for shorter trips. It's good for 3 rail days and 2 car days within a 2-month period. Prices (per person for one adult/two adults) are $345/$284 economy class, $379/$304 compact, and $399/$314 midsized. You can add up to 7 extra rail days at $45 each, and unlimited extra car days for $59 to $89 each, depending on the class of car.

There are also **national rail passes** of various kinds and **regional passes** like ScanRail (Scandinavia), BritRail (Great Britain), and the European East Pass (Austria, Czech Republic, Slovakia, Hungary, Poland). Some national passes you have to buy in the States, some you can get on either side of the Atlantic, and still others you must buy in Europe. Remember: Seniors, students, and youths can usually get discounts on European trains—in some countries just by asking, in others by buying a discount card good for a year (or whatever). Rail Europe or your travel agent can fill you in on all the details.

BritRail (☎ **888/BRITRAIL;** www.britrail.com) specializes in rail passes in Great Britain, and **DER Tours** (☎ **800/782-2424;** www.dertravel.com) is a Germany specialist that also sells other national passes (except French and British ones).

Passes Available in the United Kingdom   Many rail passes are available in the United Kingdom for travel in Britain and Europe.

The **InterRail Card** is the most popular rail ticket for anyone who has lived in Europe at least 6 months and is 26 or under (an over-26 version exists but offers discounts in fewer countries). It costs around £279, is valid for 1 month, and entitles you to unlimited second-class travel in 28 European countries. It also gives you a 34%

discount on rail travel in Britain and Northern Ireland, plus an up-to-50% discount on the rail portion of travel from London to various continental ports, plus special rates on Eurostar trains. You'll also get a reduction (30% to 50%) on most sailings to Europe and a variety of other shipping services around the Mediterranean and Scandinavia. If you're not planning to travel in 28 countries, you can buy a lower-price card for more limited travel.

Another good option for travelers 26 and under, **Eurotrain** tickets are valid for 2 months and allow you to choose your own route to a final destination and stop off as many times as you like along the way. **Eurotrain "Explorer"** tickets are slightly more expensive but allow you to travel to your final destination along one route and back on another. The price includes round-trip ferry crossing as well as round-trip rail travel from London to the port.

For help in determining the best option for your trip and to buy tickets, stop in London at the **International Rail Centre,** in Victoria Station (☎ **0990/848-848**); **Wasteels,** also in Victoria Station (☎ **020/7834-7066**), adjacent to Platform 2; or **Campus Travel,** 52 Grosvenor Gardens (☎ **020/7730-3402**).

BY CAR

Many rental companies grant discounts if you **reserve in advance** (usually 48 hours) from your home country. Weekly rentals are almost always less expensive than day rentals. Three or more people traveling together can usually get around cheaper by car than by train (even with rail passes).

When you reserve a car, be sure to ask if the price includes the EU **value-added tax (VAT), personal accident insurance (PAI), collision-damage waiver (CDW),** and any other **insurance options.** If not, ask what these extras cost, because at the end of your rental, they can make a big difference in your bottom line. The CDW and other insurance might be covered by your credit card if you use the card to pay for the rental; check with the card issuer to be sure.

If your credit card doesn't cover CDW, **Travel Guard International,** 1145 Clark St., Stevens Point, WI 54481-9970 (☎ **800/826-1300;** www.travel-guard.com), offers it for $5 per day. Avis and Hertz, among other companies, require that you purchase a theft-protection policy in Italy.

The main car-rental companies are **Avis** (☎ **800/331-1212;** www.avis.com), **Budget** (☎ **800/527-0700;** www.budgetrentacar.com/), **Europcar** (known as Dollar in the U.S.; ☎ **800/800-6000;** www.europcar.com), **Hertz** (☎ **800/654-3131;** www.hertz.com), and **National** (☎ **800/227-7368;** www.nationalcar.com). U.S.-based companies specializing in European rentals are **Auto Europe** (☎ **800/223-5555;** www.autoeurope.com), **Europe by Car** (☎ **800/223-1516,** or 212/581-3040 in New York; www.europebycar.com), and **Kemwel Holiday Auto** (☎ **800/678-0678;** www.kemwel.com). Europe by Car and Kemwel also offer a low-cost alternative to renting for longer than 15 days: **short-term leases** in which you technically buy a fresh-from-the-factory car and then sell it back when you return it. All insurance is included, from liability and theft to personal injury and CDW, with no deductible.

The AAA supplies good maps to its members. **Michelin maps** (☎ **800/423-0485;** www.michelin.com) are made for the tourist. The maps rate cities as "uninteresting" (as a tourist destination); "interesting"; "worth a detour"; or "worth an entire journey." They also highlight particularly scenic stretches of road in green, and have symbols pointing out scenic overlooks, ruins, and other sights along the way.

The Rules of the Road: Driving in Europe

- First off, know that European drivers tend to be more aggressive than their American counterparts.
- Drive on the right except in England, Scotland, and Ireland, where you drive on the left. And *do not ride* in the left lane on a four-lane highway; it is truly only for passing.
- If someone comes up from behind and flashes his lights at you, it's a signal for you to slow down and drive more on the shoulder so he can pass you more easily (two-lane roads here routinely become three cars wide).
- Except for the German autobahn, most highways do indeed have speed limits of around 60 to 80 miles per hour (100 to 135 kmph).
- Remember that everything's measured in kilometers here (mileage and speed limits). For a rough conversion, 1 kilometer = 0.6 miles.
- Be aware that although gas may look reasonably priced, the price is per liter, and 3.8 liters = 1 gallon—so multiply by four to estimate the equivalent per-gallon price.
- Never leave anything of value in the car overnight and nothing visible any time you leave the car (this goes double in Italy, triple in Naples).

BY PLANE

Though trains remain the cheapest and easiest way to get around in Europe, air transport options have improved drastically in the past few years. Intense competition with rail and ferry companies has slowly forced airfares into the bargain basement. **British Airways** (☎ **800/AIRWAYS** in the U.S., or 0345/222111 in the U.K.; www.britishairways.com) and other scheduled airlines now fly regularly from London to Paris for only £98 to £105 ($167 to $179) round-trip, depending on the season. Lower fares usually apply to midweek flights and carry advance-purchase requirements of 2 weeks or so.

The biggest airline news in Europe is the rise of the **no-frills airline** modeled on American upstarts like Southwest. By keeping their overheads down through electronic ticketing, forgoing meal service, and flying from less popular airports, these airlines are able to offer low fares. Most round-trip tickets are $60 to $160. This means now you can save lots of time, and even money, over long train hauls, especially from, say, London to Venice or from central Europe out to peripheral countries like Greece and Spain. Budget airlines include **EasyJet** (☎ **870/6-000-000;** www.easyjet.com), and British Airway's subsidiary **Go** (☎ **1279/666-388**) in England; **Ryanair** (☎ **353/1609-7889** in Ireland; 541/569-569 in England; www.ryanair.com) in Ireland; and **Virgin Express** (☎ **2/752-0505;** www.virgin-express.com), an offshoot of Virgin Air, in Belgium. Be aware, though, that the names might change because these small airlines are often economically vulnerable and can fail or merge with a big airline. Still, as quickly as one disappears, another will take off.

Lower airfares are also available throughout Europe on **charter flights** rather than regularly scheduled ones. Look in local newspapers to find out about them. Consolidators cluster in cities like London and Athens.

Flying across Europe on regularly scheduled airlines can destroy a budget and be super expensive. Whenever possible, book your total flight on one ticket before leaving. For example, if you're flying from New York to Rome, but also plan to visit Palermo, Florence, and Turin, have the total trip written up on one ticket. Don't arrive in Rome and book separate legs of the journey, which costs far more when it's done piecemeal.

Sometimes national carriers offer remarkable deals to non-European residents, which cuts down costs of flying within Europe. For example, **Lufthansa** offers a "Discover Europe" package of three flight coupons, which vary in price, depending on the nation of origin. Another bargain is **Alitalia**'s "Europlus." First, you have to book a transatlantic flight, perhaps from New York to Rome. After that, and for only $299, you can buy a package of three flight coupons entitling you to fly on any three flights anywhere in Europe served by Alitalia (not just Italy). You can also purchase unlimited additional tickets, one way, for another $100 per ticket.

Another fine deal is offered in London by **Go Fly Limited** (☎ **84-56-05-43-21** in London; www.go-fly.com), a subsidiary of British Airways. Go Fly offers 40% off standard round-trip airfares. There is a 2-night minimum stay. Sample round-trip air fares from London are as follows: Edinburgh £100 ($170), Copenhagen £150 ($255), Rome £160 ($272), and Lisbon £160 ($272).

American citizens can call **Europe by Air** (☎ **888/387-2479** or 512/404-1291; www.eurair.com) for their Europe flight pass serving 20 countries, 13 airlines, and 62 European cities. It costs only $90 each to travel one way between these cities.

Because discount passes are always changing on air routes within Europe, it's best to check in with **Air Travel Advisory Bureau** in London (☎ **020/7636-5000;** www.atab.co.uk). This bureau offers a free service directory to the public for suppliers of discount airfares from all major U.K. airports.

BY BUS

Bus transportation is readily available throughout Europe; it sometimes is less expensive than train travel and covers a more extensive area but can be slower and much less comfortable. European buses, like the trains, outshine their American counterparts, but they're perhaps best used only to pick up where the extensive train network leaves off. One major bus company serves all the countries of western Europe (no service to Greece): **Eurolines** in London at ☎ **0990/143219,** whose staff can check schedules, make reservations, and quote prices.

10 Tips on Accommodations

Traditional European hotels tend to be simpler than American ones and emphasize cleanliness and friendliness over amenities. For example, even in the cheapest American chain motel, free cable is as standard as indoor plumbing. In Europe, however, few hotels below the moderate level even have in-room TVs.

Unless otherwise noted, all hotel rooms in this book have **private en-suite bathrooms.** However, the standard European hotel bathroom might not look like what you're used to. For example, the European concept of a shower is to stick a nozzle in the bathroom wall and a drain in the floor. Shower curtains are optional. In some cramped private bathrooms, you'll have to relocate the toilet paper outside the bathroom before turning on the shower and drenching the whole room. Another interesting fixture is the "half tub," in which there's only room to sit, rather than lie down. The half tub usually sports a shower nozzle that has nowhere to hang—so your knees get very clean and the floor gets very wet. Hot water may be available only once a day and not on demand—this is especially true with shared bathrooms. Heating water is costly, and many smaller hotels do it only once daily, in the morning.

GETTING THE BEST ROOM AT THE BEST RATE

The *rack rate* is the maximum rate a hotel charges for a room—the rate you'd get if you walked in off the street and asked for a room for the night. In our hotel entries, we list these rack rates. But hardly anybody pays these prices, however, and there are many ways around them. Below are some suggestions for getting the most for your money:

- **Don't be afraid to bargain.** Most rack rates include commissions of 10% to 25% or more for travel agents, which many hotels cut if you make your own reservations and haggle a bit. Always ask politely about the availability of a room less expensive than the first one mentioned or whether any special rates apply to you. You may qualify for corporate, student, military, senior, or other discounts. Be sure to mention membership in AAA, AARP, frequent-flyer programs, or trade unions, which could entitle you to special deals too.

- **You don't have to take the first room they show you.** Unless you really love the first room you're shown, ask to see several. Open and close windows to see how well they shut out noise. Check the firmness of the mattress and the cleanliness of the bathroom. Always ask for a corner room—they're usually larger, quieter, and closer to the elevator and often have more windows and light than standard rooms. When making your reservation, ask if the hotel is renovating; if it is, request a room away from the renovation work and one that has already been redone. Many hotels now offer no-smoking rooms; if smoke bothers you, by all means ask for one. Inquire too about the location of the restaurants, bars, and discos in the hotel—they could all be a source of irritating noise.

- **Rely on a qualified professional.** Certain hotels give travel agents discounts in exchange for steering business their way, so if you're shy about bargaining, an agent may be better equipped to negotiate discounts for you.

- **Dial direct.** When booking a room in a chain hotel, call the hotel's local line and then its toll-free number to see where you get the best deal. A hotel makes nothing on a room that stays empty. The clerk who runs the place is more likely to know about vacancies and often grants deep discounts to fill up.

- **Remember the law of supply and demand.** Resort hotels are most crowded and therefore most expensive on weekends, so discounts are usually available for mid-week stays. To the contrary, business hotels in downtown locations are busiest during the week; expect discounts over the weekend. Avoid high-season stays whenever you can: Planning your vacation just a week before or after official peak season can mean big savings.

- **Look into group or long-stay discounts.** If you come as part of a large group, you should be able to negotiate a bargain, since the hotel can then guarantee occupancy in a number of rooms. Likewise, when you're planning a long stay

A Traveler's Tip

If you call a hotel from home to reserve a room, *always follow up with a confirmation fax.* Not only is it what most hotels prefer, but it is printed proof you've booked a room. Keep the language simple—state your name, number of people, what kind of room (like "double with bathroom and one bed" or "double with bathroom and two beds"), how many nights you'd like to stay, and the starting date for the first night. Remember that Europeans abbreviate dates day/month/year, not month/day/year.

(usually 5 days to a week) you'll qualify for a discount. As a general rule, you get 1 night free after a 7-night stay.

- **Avoid excess charges.** When you book a room, ask whether the hotel charges for parking. Most hotels have free available space, but many urban or beachfront hotels don't. Also find out before you dial whether your hotel imposes a surcharge on local or long-distance calls. A pay phone, however inconvenient, may save you money. And don't open that minibar!

- **Consider a suite.** If you're traveling with your family or another couple, you can pack more people into a suite (which usually comes with a sofa bed), and thereby reduce your per-person rate. Remember that some places charge for extra guests and some don't.

- **Book an efficiency.** A room with a kitchenette allows you to grocery shop and eat some meals in. Especially during long stays with families, you're bound to save money on food this way. And you get the added thrill of shopping in a European food store or (even better) a European street market.

- **Investigate reservation services.** These outfits usually buy up or reserve rooms in bulk and deal them out to you at a profit, garnering special deals at 10% to 50% off; but these discounts apply to rack rates, inflated prices people rarely pay. You're probably better off dealing directly with a hotel, but if you don't like bargaining, this is a viable option. Most offer online reservation services as well. Some of the more reputable providers are **Accommodations Express** (☎ **800/950-4685;** www.accommodationsxpress.com); **Hotel Reservations Network** (☎ **800/96HOTEL;** www.180096HOTEL.com); **Quikbook** (☎ **800/789-9887,** includes fax on demand service; www.quikbook. com); and **Room Exchange** (☎ **800/846-7000** in the U.S., or 800/486-7000 in Canada). Online, try booking your hotel through **Arthur Frommer's Budget Travel** (www.frommers.com) and save up to 50%. **Microsoft Expedia** (www.expedia. com) features a "Travel Agent" that directs you to affordable lodgings.

HOTEL BOOKING SERVICES

When you arrive in town, you'll find that a desk in the train station or at the tourist office (or both) acts as a central hotel reservations service for the city. Tell them your price range, where you'd like to be in the city, and sometimes even the style of hotel, and they'll use a computer database to find you a room in town.

The advantages of booking services are that they do all the room-finding work for you—for a nominal fee—and always speak English, while individual hoteliers may not. When every hotel in town seems to be booked up (during a convention or festival or just in high season), they can often find space for you at inns not listed in guidebooks or other main sources. On the downside, hotels in many countries often charge higher rates to people booking through such a service.

Planning Your Trip: An Online Directory

by Lynne Bairstow

Lynne Bairstow is the coauthor of *Frommer's Mexico* and the editorial director of *e-com* magazine.

Day by day, the Internet becomes more integrated into our lives—including the way we plan and book our travel. By early 2000, 1 in every 10 trips was being booked online, a trend that's sure to accelerate.

The Internet not only provides a wealth of destination information but also gives you the chance to compare experiences with fellow travelers, ask experts for pretrip advice, seek out discounted fares once accessible only to travel industry insiders, and stay in touch via e-mail while you're away. The instant communication and storehouse of information has revolutionized the way travel is researched, reserved, and realized.

This Online Directory will help you take better advantage of the travel planning information available online, and it's best used in conjunction with this book. Part 1 lists general Internet resources that can make any trip easier, such as sites for obtaining the best possible prices on airline tickets. In Part 2 you'll find some top online guides for Europe, organized first by Europe in general and then by country.

Keep in mind this isn't a comprehensive list but a discriminating selection to get you started. Recognition is given to sites based on their content value and ease of use and aren't paid for—unlike some Web-site rankings, which are based on payment. Finally, remember this is a press-time snapshot of leading Web sites—some undoubtedly will have evolved, changed, or moved by the time you read this.

1 Top Travel Planning Web Sites

While the Internet was once a conglomerate of sites for researching places to visit, several key companies have emerged that offer comprehensive travel planning and booking. In addition to the Frommer's Online (see box, below), we list the other top online travel agencies below, along with some more specialized services.

WHY BOOK ONLINE?

Online agencies have come a long way over the past few years, now providing tips for finding the best fare and giving suggested dates or times to travel that yield the lowest price if your plans are flexible. Other sites even allow you to establish the price you're willing to pay, and they check the airlines' willingness to accept it. However, in some

What You'll Find at the Frommer's Site

We highly recommend **Arthur Frommer's Budget Travel Online** (**www.frommers.com**) as an excellent travel planning resource. Of course, we're a little biased, but you'll find indispensable travel tips, reviews, monthly vacation giveaways, and online booking. Among the site's most popular features is the regular "Ask the Expert" bulletin boards, which feature one of the Frommer's authors answering your questions via online postings.

Subscribe to Arthur Frommer's Daily Newsletter (**www.frommers.com/newsletters**) to receive the latest travel bargains and inside travel secrets in your e-mailbox every day. You'll read daily headlines and articles from the dean of travel himself, highlighting last-minute deals on airfares, accommodations, cruises, and package vacations. You'll also find great travel advice by checking our Tip of the Day or Hot Spot of the Month.

Search our Destinations archive (**www.frommers.com/destinations**) of more than 200 domestic and international destinations for great places to stay, tips for traveling there, and what to do while you're there. Once you've researched your trip, the online reservation system (**www.frommers.com/booktravelnow**) takes you to Frommer's favorite sites for booking your vacation at affordable prices.

cases, these sites may not always yield the best price. Unlike a travel agent, for example, they may not have access to charter flights offered by wholesalers.

Online booking sites aren't the only places to reserve airline tickets—all major airlines have their own Web sites and often offer incentives—bonus frequent-flyer miles or net-only discounts, for example—when you buy online or buy an e-ticket.

The new trend is toward conglomerated booking sites. By mid-2000, a consortium of U.S. and European airlines are planning to launch an as-yet unnamed Web site that will offer fares lower than those available through travel agents. United, Delta, Northwest, and Continental have initiated this effort, based on their success at selling airline seats at their own online sites.

The best of the travel planning sites are now highly personalized; they store your seating preferences, meal preferences, tentative itineraries, and credit-card information, allowing you to quickly plan trips or check agendas.

In many cases, booking your trip online can be better than working with a travel agent. It gives you the widest variety of choices, control, and the 24-hour convenience of planning your trip when you choose. All you need is some time—and often a little patience—and you're likely to find the fun of online travel research will greatly enhance your trip.

WHO SHOULD BOOK ONLINE?

Online booking is best for travelers who want to know as much as possible about their options, those who have flexibility in their travel dates and are looking for the best price, and bargain hunters driven by a good value who are open-minded about where they travel.

One of the biggest successes in online travel for both passengers and airlines is the offer of last-minute specials, such as American Airlines' weekend deals or other Internet-only fares you must purchase online. Another advantage is that

More people still look online than book online, partly due to fear of putting their credit card numbers out on the Net. Secure encryption and increasing experience buying online have removed this fear for most travelers. In some cases, however, it's simply easier to buy from a local travel agent who can deliver your tickets to your door (especially if your travel is last minute or you have special requests). You can find a flight online and then book it by calling a toll-free number or contacting your travel agent, though this is somewhat less efficient. To be sure you're in secure mode when you book online, look for a little icon of a key (in Netscape) or a padlock (in Internet Explorer) at the bottom of your Web browser.

you can cash in on incentives for booking online, such as rebates or bonus frequent-flyer miles.

Business and other frequent travelers also have found numerous benefits in online booking, as the advances in mobile technology provide them with the ability to check flight status, change plans, or get specific directions from handheld computing devices, mobile phones, and pagers. Some sites will even e-mail or page passengers if their flights are delayed.

Online booking is increasingly able to accommodate complex itineraries, even for international travel. The pace of evolution on the Net is rapid, so you'll probably find additional features and advancements by the time you visit these sites. What the future holds for online travelers is ever-increasing personalization, customization, and reaching out to you.

TRAVEL PLANNING & BOOKING SITES

Below are listings for the top sites for planning and booking travel. The following sites offer domestic and international flight, hotel, and rental car bookings, plus news, destination information, and deals on cruises and vacation packages. Free (one-time) registration is required for booking.

✪ **Expedia. expedia.com**

Expedia is known as the fastest and most flexible online travel planner for booking flights, hotels, and rental cars. It offers several ways of obtaining the best possible fares: The **Flight Price Matcher** service allows your preferred airline to match an available fare with a competitor; the comprehensive **Fare Compare** area shows the differences in fare categories and airlines; and the **Fare Calendar** helps you plan your trip around the best possible fares. Its main limitation is that like many online databases, Expedia focuses on the major airlines and hotel chains so don't expect to find too many budget airlines or one-of-a-kind B&Bs here.

Personalized features allow you to store your itineraries, and receive weekly fare reports on favorite cities. You can also check on the status of flight arrivals and departures and, through MileageMiner, track all your frequent-flyer accounts.

Expedia also offers vacation packages, cruises, information on specialized travel (like family vacations, casino destinations, and adventure, ski, and golf travel). There are also special features for travelers accessing information on mobile devices.

(*Note:* In early 2000, Expedia bought travelscape.com and vacationspot.com and incorporated these sites into expedia.com.)

Airline Web Sites

Below are the Web sites for the major airlines. These sites offer schedules and flight booking, and most have pages where you can sign up for e-mail alerts for weekend deals and other late-breaking bargains:

Aer Lingus. www.aerlingus.com
Air France. www.airfrance.com
Alitalia. www.alitalia.it
American Airlines. www.aa.com
Austrian Airlines. www.aua.com
British Airways. www.british-airways.com
Continental Airlines. www.continental.com
CSA Czech Airlines. www.csa.cz
Delta. www.delta-air.com
Iberia. www.iberia.com
KLM Royal Dutch Airlines. www.klm.nl
Lufthansa. www.lufthansa.com
Malev Hungarian Airlines. www.malev-airlines.com
Northwest Airlines. www.nwa.com
Olympic Airways. http://agn.hol.gr/info/olypimic1.htm
Sabena. www.sabena-usa.com
SAS. www.sas.se
Swissair. www.swissair.com
TAP Air Portugal. www.tap-airportugal.pt
TWA. www.twa.com
United Airlines. www.ual.com
US Airways. www.usairways.com
Virgin Atlantic. www.fly.virgin.com

Travelocity (incorporates Preview Travel). www.travelocity.com; www.previewtravel.com

Travelocity uses the SABRE system to offer reservations and tickets for more than 400 airlines, plus reservations and purchase capabilities for more than 45,000 hotels and 50 car rental companies. An exclusive feature of the SABRE system is its **Low Fare Search Engine,** which automatically searches for the three lowest-priced itineraries based on a traveler's criteria. Last-minute deals and consolidator fares (provided by Travel Information Software Systems, or TISS) are included in the search. If you book with Travelocity, you can select specific seats for your flights with online seat maps and also view diagrams of the most popular commercial aircraft. Its hotel finder provides street-level location maps and photos of selected hotels.

Travelocity features an inviting interface for booking trips, though the wealth of graphics involved can make the site somewhat slow to load, and any adjustment in desired trip planning means you'll need to completely start over.

This site also has some very cool tools. With the **Fare Watcher** feature, you can select up to five routes and will receive e-mail notices when the fare changes by $25 or more. If you own an alphanumeric pager with national access that can receive e-mail, Travelocity's **Flight Paging** can alert you if your flight is delayed. You can also access real-time departure and arrival information on any flight within the SABRE system.

Note to AOL Users: You can book flights, hotels, rental cars, and cruises on AOL at keyword: Travel. The booking software is provided by Travelocity/Preview Travel and is similar to the Internet site. Use the AOL "Travelers Advantage" program to earn a 5% rebate on flights, hotel rooms, and car rentals.

TRIP.com. www.trip.com

TRIP.com began as a site geared for business travelers, but its innovative features and highly personalized approach have broadened its appeal to leisure travelers as well. It's the leading travel site for those using mobile devices to access Internet travel information.

TRIP.com includes a trip-planning function that provides the average and lowest fare for the route requested, in addition to the current available fare. An on-site "newsstand" features breaking news on airfare sales and other travel specials. Among its most popular features are Flight TRACKER and intelli-TRIP. **Flight TRACKER** allows users to track any commercial flight en route to its destination anywhere in the U.S., while accessing real-time FAA-based flight monitoring data. **intelliTRIP** is a travel search tool that allows users to identify the best airline, hotel, and rental car fares in less than 90 seconds.

In addition, it offers e-mail notification of flight delays, plus, city resource guides, currency converters, and a weekly e-mail newsletter of fare updates, travel tips, and traveler forums.

Yahoo Travel. www.travel.yahoo.com

Yahoo is currently the most popular of the Internet information portals, and its travel site is a comprehensive mix of online booking, daily travel news, and destination information. The **Best Fares** area offers what it promises and provides feedback on refining your search if you have flexibility in travel dates or times. There's also an active section of Message Boards for discussions on travel in general and for specific destinations.

SPECIALTY TRAVEL SITES

Although the sites listed above provide the most comprehensive services, some travelers have specialized needs that are best met by a site catering specifically to them.

For adventure travelers, **iExplore** (**www.iexplore.com**) is a great source for information and booking adventure and experiential travel, as well as related services and products. The site combines the secure Internet booking functions with hands-on expertise and 24-hour live customer support by seasoned adventure travelers, for those interested in trips off the beaten path. The company is a supporting member of the Ecotourism Society and is committed to environmentally responsible travel worldwide.

Another excellent site for adventure travelers is **Away.com** (**www.away.com**), which features unique vacations for challenging the body, mind, and spirit. Trips may include cycling in the Loire Valley, taking an African safari, or assisting in the excavation of a Mayan ruin. For those without the time for such an extended exotic trip, offbeat weekend getaways are also available. Services include a customer service center staffed with experts to answer calls and e-mails, plus a network of over 1,000 prescreened tour operators. Trips are categorized by cultural, adventure, and green travel. Away.com also offers a Daily Escape e-mail newsletter.

GORP (Great Outdoor Recreation Pages; **www.gorp.com**) has been a standard for adventure travelers since its founding in 1995 by outdoor enthusiasts Diane and Bill Greer. Tapping their own experiences, they created this Web site that offers the unique travel destinations and encourages active participation by fellow GORP visitors through the sophisticated menu of online forums, contests, and discussions.

For travelers who prefer more unique accommodations, **InnSite** (**www.innsite.com**) offers listings for inns and B&Bs in all U.S. states and dozens of countries around the globe. Find an inn at your destination, have a look at images of the rooms, check prices and availability, and then send e-mail to the innkeeper if you have further questions. This is an extensive directory of bed-and-breakfast inns but includes listings only if the proprietors submitted one (*Note:* It's free to get an inn listed). The descriptions are written by the innkeepers, and many listings link to the inn's own Web sites, where you can find more information and images.

Another good resource for mostly one-of-a-kind places in the U.S. and abroad is **Places to Stay** (**www.placestostay.com**), which focuses on resort accommodations.

"Have Kids, Still Travel!" is the motto of the **Family Travel Forum** (FTF; **www.familytravelforum.com**), a site dedicated to the ideals, promotion, and support of travel with children. FTF is supported by memberships, which are available in flexible prices from a $2.95 monthly fee to a heftier annual fee for more comprehensive services. Since no advertising is accepted, FTF provides its members with honest, unbiased information, informed advice, and practical tips designed to make traveling with children a healthier, safer, hassle-free experience, not to mention a better value.

TOP VACATION PACKAGE SITES

Both **Expedia** and **Travelocity** (see above) offer excellent selections and searches for complete vacation packages. Travelers can search by destination and desired dates coupled with how much they're willing to spend. Travelocity has a valuable "Cruise Critic" function, to help would-be cruisers obtain first-hand accounts of the quality and details of a cruise from recent passengers.

Travel wholesalers, like **Apple Vacations** (**www.applevacations.com**) and **Funjet** (**www.funjet.com**) are also good starting points, but they still require that the final booking be handled through a travel agent.

As travel agents tend to be more expert at sorting through the values in vacation packages, you might find **Vacation.com** (**www.vacation.com**) helpful in previewing packages and finding an appropriate agent to help you book the deal. This site represents a nationwide network of 9,800 local travel agencies that specialize in finding the best values in cruises, vacation packages, tours, and other leisure travel services. To find a Vacation.com member agency, enter your Zip code and the Vacation.com Agency Finder will locate a nearby office.

LAST-MINUTE DEALS & OTHER ONLINE BARGAINS

There's nothing airlines hate more than flying with lots of empty seats. The Net has enabled airlines to offer last-minute bargains to entice travelers to fill those seats. Most of these are announced on Tuesday or Wednesday and are valid for travel the following weekend, but some can be booked weeks or months in advance. You can sign up for weekly e-mail alerts at airlines' sites (for their Web sites, see "Airline Web Sites," above) or check sites that compile lists of these bargains, such as **Smarter Living** or **WebFlyer** (see below). To make it easier, visit a site that'll round up all the deals and send them in one convenient weekly e-mail. But last-minute deals aren't the only online bargains; other sites can help you find value even if you haven't waited until the eleventh hour. Increasingly popular are services that let you name the price you're willing to pay for an air seat or vacation package at travel auction sites.

Cheap Tickets. www.cheaptickets.com
Cheap Tickets has exclusive deals that aren't available through more mainstream channels. One caveat about the Cheap Tickets site is that it'll offer fare quotes for a route and later show this fare isn't valid for your dates of travel—most other Web sites, such as Expedia, consider your dates of travel before showing what fares are available. Despite its problems, Cheap Tickets can be worth the effort because its fares can be lower than those offered by its competitors.

✪ **1travel.com. www.1travel.com**
Here you'll find deals on domestic and international flights, cruises, hotels, and all-inclusive resorts like Club Med. 1travel.com's **Saving Alert** compiles last-minute air deals so you don't have to scroll through multiple e-mail alerts. A feature called "Drive a little using low-fare airlines" helps map out strategies for using alternate airports to find lower fares. And **Farebeater** searches a database that includes published fares, consolidator bargains, and special deals exclusive to 1travel.com. *Note:* The travel agencies listed by 1travel.com have paid for placement.

Bid for Travel. www.bidfortravel.com
Bid for Travel is another of the travel auction sites, similar to Priceline (see below), which are growing in popularity. In addition to airfares, Internet users can place a bid for vacation packages and hotels.

Go4less.com. www.go4less.com
Specializing in last-minute cruise and package deals, Go4less has some excellent offers. The **Hot Deals** section gives an alphabetical listing by destination of super discounted packages.

LastMinuteTravel.com. www.lastminutetravel.com
Suppliers with excess inventory come to this online agency to distribute unsold airline seats, hotel rooms, cruises, and vacation packages. It's got great deals, but you have to put up with an excess of advertisements and slow-loading graphics.

Moment's Notice. www.moments-notice.com
As the name suggests, Moment's Notice specializes in last-minute vacation and cruise deals. You can browse for free, but if you want to purchase a trip you have to join Moment's Notice, which costs $25. Go to **World Wide Hot Deals** for a complete list of special deals in international destinations.

✪ **Priceline.com. travel.priceline.com**
Even people who aren't familiar with many Web sites have heard about Priceline.com. Launched in 1998 with a $10-million ad campaign featuring William Shatner, Priceline lets you "name your price" for domestic and international airline tickets and hotel rooms. In other words, you select a route and dates, guarantee with a credit card, and make a bid for what you're willing to

Know When the Sales Start

While most people learn about last-minute weekend deals from e-mail dispatches, it can be best to find out precisely when these deals become available. Because the deals are limited, they can vanish within hours—sometimes even minutes—so it pays to log on as soon as they're available. Check the pages devoted to these deals on airlines' Web pages to get the info. An example: Southwest's specials are posted at 12:01am Tuesdays (Central time). So if you're looking for a cheap flight, stay up late and check Southwest's site to grab the best new deals.

pay. If one of the airlines in Priceline's database has a fare lower than your bid, your credit card will automatically be charged fo a ticket.

But you can't say when you want to fly—you have to accept any flight leaving between 6am and 10pm on the dates you selected, and you may have to make a stopover. No frequent-flyer miles are awarded, and tickets are nonrefundable and can't be exchanged for another flight. So if your plans change, you're out of luck. Priceline can be good for travelers who have to take off on short notice (and thus unable to qualify for advance-purchase discounts). But be sure to shop around first, because if you overbid, you'll be required to purchase the ticket—and Priceline will pocket the difference between what it paid for the ticket and what you bid.

Priceline says that over 35% of all reasonable offers for domestic flights are being filled on the first try, with much higher fill rates on popular routes (New York to San Francisco, for example). They define "reasonable" as not more than 30% below the lowest generally available advance-purchase fare for the same route.

Smarter Living. www.smarterliving.com
Best known for its e-mail dispatch of weekend deals on 20 airlines, Smarter Living also keeps you posted about last-minute bargains on everything from Windjammer Cruises to flights to Iceland.

SkyAuction.com. www.skyauction.com
This auction site has categories for airfare, travel deals, hotels, and much more.

Travelzoo.com. www.travelzoo.com
At this Internet portal, over 150 travel companies post special deals. It features a Top 20 list of the best deals on the site, selected by its editorial staff each Wednesday night. This list is also available via an e-mailing list, free to those who sign up.

WebFlyer. www.webflyer.com
WebFlyer is a comprehensive online resource for frequent flyers and also has an excellent listing of last-minute air deals. Click on **Deal Watch** for a roundup of weekend deals on flights, hotels and rental cars from domestic and international suppliers.

ONLINE TRAVELER'S TOOLBOX

Veteran travelers usually carry some essential items to make their trips easier. The following is a selection of online tools to smooth your journey.

ATM Locator: Visa. www.visa.com/pd/atm/
ATM Locator: MasterCard. www.mastercard.com/atm
Use these sites to find ATMs in hundreds of cities in the U.S. and around the world. Both include maps for some locations and both list airport ATM locations, some with maps. *Tip:* You'll usually get a better exchange rate using ATMs than exchanging traveler's checks at banks, but check in advance to see what kind of fees your bank will assess for using an overseas ATM.

CDC Travel Information. www.cdc.gov/travel/index.htm
Health advisories and recommendations for inoculations from the U.S. Centers for Disease Control. The CDC site is good for an overview, but it's best to consult your personal physician to get the latest information on required vaccinations or other health precautions.

✪ **Foreign Languages for Travelers. www.travlang.com**
Here you can learn basic terms in more than 70 languages and click on any underlined phrase to hear what it sounds like. (*Note:* Free audio software and

One of the best sources of travel information is word-of-mouth from someone who has just been there. Internet discussion groups are offering an unprecedented way for travelers around the globe to connect and share experiences. The **Frommer's Online** site (**www.frommers.com**) offers these message boards and also areas where you can pose questions to the guidebook writers themselves in the section "Ask the Expert." **Yahoo Travel, Expedia,** and **Travelocity** are other good sources of online travel discussion groups. The granddaddy of specialized discussions on particular topics, is **Usenet,** a collection of over 50,000 newsgroups. You'll find a comprehensive listing at **Deja News** (**www.dejanews.com/usenet/**) or at **www.liszt.com**.

speakers are required.) It also offers hotel and airline finders with excellent prices and a simple system to get the listings you're looking for.

Intellicast. www.intellicast.com
Here you'll find weather forecasts for all 50 states and cities around the world. Note that temperatures are in Celsius for many international destinations, so don't think you'll need that winter coat for your next trip to Athens.

✪ Mapquest. www.mapquest.com
The best of the mapping sites lets you choose a specific address or destination, and in seconds it'll return back a map and detailed directions. It really is easier than calling, asking, and writing down directions. The site also links to special travel deals and helpful sites.

Net Cafe Guide. www.netcafeguide.com/mapindex.htm
Stop here to locate Internet cafes at hundreds of locations around the globe. Catch up on your e-mail, log onto the Web, and stay in touch with the home front, usually for just a few dollars per hour.

Tourism Offices Worldwide Directory. www.towd.com
This is an extensive listing of tourism offices, some with links to these offices' Web sites.

Travelers' Tales. www.travelerstales.com
Considered the best in compilations of travel literature, Travelers' Tales are an award-winning series of books grouped by destination (Mexico, Italy, France, China.) or by theme (Love & Romance, The Ultimate Journey, Women in the Wild, The Adventure of Food). It's a new kind of travel book that offers a description of a place or type of journey through the experiences of many travelers. It makes for a perfect traveling companion.

The Travelite FAQ. www.travelite.org
Here you'll find tips on packing light, choosing luggage, and selecting appropriate travel wear—helpful if you always tend to pack too much or are a compulsive list maker.

Universal Currency Converter. www.xe.net/currency
Come here to see what your dollar or pound is worth in more than a hundred other countries.

U.S. Customs Service Traveler Information.
  www.customs.ustreas.gov/travel/index.htm
Wondering what you're allowed to bring in to the U.S.? Check at this thorough site, which includes maximum allowance and duty fees.

U.S. State Department Travel Warnings. travel.state.gov/travel_warnings.html

You'll find reports on places where health concerns or unrest might threaten U.S. travelers. Keep in mind that these warnings can be somewhat dated and conservative. You can also sign up to receive State Department briefings via e-mail.

Web Travel Secrets. www.web-travel-secrets.com

If this list leaves you yearning for more travel-oriented sites, Web Travel Secrets offers one of the best compilations around. One section offers advice and tips on how to find the lowest prices for airlines, hotels, and cruises. The other section provides a comprehensive listing of Web travel links for airfare deals, airlines, booking engines, cars, cruise lines, discount travel and best deals, general travel resources, hotels and hotel discounters, search engines, and travel magazines and newsletters.

2 Top Web Sites for Europe

Information updated by Herbert Bailey Livesey

Herbert Bailey Livesey is coauthor of *Frommer's Europe from $70 a Day* and *Frommer's New England* as well as author of *Frommer's Montréal & Québec City.*

Bear in mind that some of the best sites are listed in the first category covering Europe in general. So if you're looking for information on Italy, don't just check the Italy section—also see sites like Europe and TimeOut.com.

GENERAL SITES FOR EUROPE

About.com: Europe. about.com/travel/index.htm

Formerly known as Miningco.com, this still rounds up some of the best Web sites and separates them by country, city, and specific subjects. The selections are culled by "human guides" hired for each subject; some are uneven, so About.com is worth a look primarily for its wealth of links.

Europe. www.visiteurope.com

This encompassing site is maintained by the European Travel Commission, comprised of the government tourism offices of 29 nations. It has mountains of advice by country, with updated planning info that includes passports, visas, weather conditions, international phone codes, and much more.

Europe Online. www.europeonline.com

Similar to About.com, this site has individual human guides for each country who select the best links related to travel categories. The site looks more comprehensive than it is, and some sections are very strong while others need work, but it still contains useful information about individual cities.

✪ RailEurope. www.raileurope.com

This is a one-stop shopping site for European train travel, whether you're looking for fares and schedules, a Eurail pass, or a ride through the Chunnel. And you can book tickets online.

Rail Pass Express. www.eurail.com

Here's a good source for Eurail pass information, purchasing, and deals. Also, see Rick Steves' Europe Through the Back Door (below) for insider tips on Eurail passes.

Checking E-mail at Internet Cafes

Until a few years ago, most travelers who checked their e-mail while traveling carried a laptop—an expensive and often technologically problematic option. Thankfully, Web-based free e-mail programs have made it much easier to check your mail.

Just open an account at any one of the numerous "freemail" providers—the original leaders continue to be **Hotmail** (hotmail.com), **Excite** (www.excite.com), and **Yahoo! Mail** (mail.yahoo.com), though many are available. AOL users should check out **AOL Netmail,** and USA.NET (**www.usa.net**) comes highly recommended for functionality and security. You can find hints, tips, and a mile-long list of freemail providers at **www.emailaddresses.com**. Then all you'll need to check your mail is a Web connection, easily available at Net cafes and copy shops around the world. After logging on, just point the browser to your freemail's Internet address, enter your username and password, and you'll have access to your mail. From these sites, you can download all your e-mail—even from office accounts—or your local or national Internet Service Provider address. There'll be a section generally called "check other mail" that allows you to add the names of other e-mail servers.

The downside is that most Web-based e-mail sites allow a maximum of only 3MB capacity per mail account, which can fill up quickly. Also, message sending and receiving isn't immediate; some messages may be delayed by several hours or even days.

Internet cafes have become ubiquitous, so for a few dollars an hour you'll be able to check your mail and send messages from virtually anywhere in the world (see the "Fast Facts" section in each chapter for one or two places to get on the Net).

Rick Steves' Europe Through the Back Door. www.ricksteves.com
The man who made himself an industry writing about Europe offers a great deal of information here, from Eurail pass comparisons to nude beaches and jet lag cures. He shares tips and discoveries he's made from 25 years of travel and provides message boards with hints from fans.

Subway Navigator. subwaynavigator.com/bin/cities/english
This site is one of those technological wonders that instantly produces detailed subway maps for dozens of European cities. Select a city and enter your departure and arrival points. Subway Navigator outlines your route, shows it on a map, and tells you how long the trip should take.

✪ TimeOut.com. www.timeout.com
An outstanding guide from the Britishpublisher of travel books and magazines, this site covers 16 European cities, with a particular focus on entertainment and what's on this month. Its hip and savvy advice is applied as well to hotels, restaurants, shops, galleries, museums, and music venues.

UK Golf. www.uk-golf.com
Over 3,000 European courses are listed here, complete with greens fees and directions to get there. Though the name implies it's just for the United Kingdom, courses in France, Spain, and Portugal are included.

COUNTRY SITES
AUSTRIA

Austria National Tourist Office. www.anto.com
This official site is geared for English speakers and has current information on culture and events. The tour finder includes advice for all sorts of vacations, from brewery tours to trips for the physically challenged. You'll also find magazine-style features and city guides for nine Austrian cities.

LiveCam Vienna. rhwcam.markant.at/snap.cgi
Suggested mainly for its curiosity value, this site offers round-the-clock live views of Vienna. It's in German, but the purpose is visual, and no special software is required.

Mozart Concerts. www.mozart.co.at/concerts
Here you can learn about where and when to see performances, such as recitals by the Vienna Mozart Orchestra. Click the Union Jack for the site in English.

Vienna Tourist Board. www.info.wien.at.
This is an up-to-date guide with listings for cultural events, museums exhibits, and more. The 72-hour guide is a fine whirlwind tour for those who have only 3 days in the city. You'll also find advice on getting around Vienna. Click on "Vienna Scene" for the English version.

Tourist.net: Austria. www.tourist-net.co.at/main1e.htm
This modest region-by-region guide to Austria includes a number of photos, updated events listings, and advice on dining and attractions, such as the basket-weaving community of Piringsdorf.

BELGIUM

Belgium: Official Travel Guide. www.visitbelgium.com/bxhome.htm
The site is boosterish, hardly surprising given its sponsorship by the tourism office. But it's still a good place to research tours, see images of attractions, and find out what's new.

Belgium Tourism. www.belgique-tourisme.net
Covering both Brussels and the rural Ardennes region, this site describes native gastronomy, accommodation, châteaux, and participant sports (golf, biking, and sailing). With the companion site about Flanders, **www.toervl.be**, all of this small nation is covered.

Brussels. www.trabel.com/brussels.htm
This solid roundup of attractions, cultural events, and museums comes complete with insider advice. Some of the categories are whimsical, such as "City of Beer" and "Brussels Lace."

Hotels Belgium. www.hotels-belgium.com
Here's a good place to research hotels, where you can compare prices, see pictures of the rooms, and use e-mail to get in touch with proprietors.

✪ **Welcome to Belgium. www.trabel.com/index.htm**
This extensive overview of the country includes tourism advice, airport info, and a search feature. If you like, you can sign up for a free e-mail newsletter.

CZECH REPUBLIC

CzechSite. www.czechsite.com
This well-designed site offers tips on getting around, attractions, museums, galleries, and restaurants. You can book your lodging and a rental car and also find an online message board.

Czech Tourism Pages. czech-tourism.com
This extensive roundup of links to other Web sites was pulled together by a Net veteran who awards a Czech flag icon to sites he considers especially worthy.

✪ **HotelsCzech. www.HotelsCzech.com**
This well-organized site shows hotels by the number of stars bestowed by the government. Click on a hotel to find prices by date and photos of the buildings and rooms. Reservations aren't instant—after you fill out the form, an agent is supposed to get back to you within 48 hours.

DENMARK

Welcome to Denmark. www.visitdenmark.com
This wide-ranging site is from the Danish Tourist Board. The accommodation section, for example, ranges from "Castles and Manor Houses" to "Farm Holidays." You'll also find late news and transportation tips.

Wonderful Copenhagen. www.woco.dk
A product of Copenhagen's official visitors bureau, this comprehensive site takes a while to load but is worth the wait. Click on "Index" for all the basics on dining, lodging, and attractions.

ENGLAND

✪ **Automobile Association UK. www.theaa.co.uk**
This outstanding site provides a routing service similar to its U.S. counterpart. It also lays out lodging listings, ranked by price and quality; many accept online bookings.

British Museum. www.british-museum.ac.uk
At press time, the site was under construction, but information was still available about current exhibits, the permanent collections, opening times, and entrance fees.

Buckingham Palace. www.royal.gov.uk/palaces/bp.htm
The official site from the British monarchy offers history, images, and descriptions of the "working palace" and "visitors' palace."

Houses of Parliament. www.parliament.uk
This straightforward visitors' guide to the House of Commons and the House of Lords includes tour times and schedules. Go to "visits" in the Index for details on opening times and whether the Commons and the Lords are in session.

London Airports. www.heathrow.co.uk
Come here for a guide and terminal maps for Heathrow, Gatwick, Stansted, and other lesser airports, including flight arrival times, duty-free shops, airport restaurants, and info on getting from the airports to downtown London. Also see the animated **www.heathrowexpress.co.uk** for information about the train that takes just 15 minutes to get from Heathrow to downtown London.

London Theatre Guide. www.officiallondontheatre.co.uk
This extensive guide carries not only information on half-price tickets and what's on but also, casting news, impending openings, and "last chances."

London Transport. www.londontransport.co.uk
London Transport is the agency that operates the subway ("Underground") and city bus systems. This extensive site includes maps, fare information, and advice to help you get around London easily and cheaply.

The National Trust: Travel. www.nationaltrust.org.uk/travel.htm

The National Trust, an architectural preservation organization, maintains more than 200 cottages and other unusual lodgings throughout the United Kingdom, many of which you can rent for short periods. Some sample pictures and prices are given, and bookings can be made on line.

Original London Walks. www.walks.com

London's most established walking tour company posts its schedule here. Click on a day and get a list of more than a dozen tours, often with themes like "In the Footsteps of Sherlock Holmes" and "Jack the Ripper Haunts."

⭐ **Tower of London Tour.** www.toweroflondontour.com

Here you'll find an illuminating photographic virtual tour—with music—of one of London's oldest and most intriguing attractions.

⭐ **Visit Britain.** www.usagateway.visitbritain.com

Designed by the British Tourist Authority expressly for U.S. travelers, this site lets you order brochures online, provides trip-planning hints, and even allows e-mail questions for prompt answers. All of Great Britain is covered.

⭐ **Westminister Abbey.** www.westminster-abbey.org

This superb historical tour of one of the world's most magnificent churches has lots of photos. Included are basic visitor info (tours of the nave, sanctuary, Henry VII Chapel), news of upcoming events, and a section on the coronations that have occurred at the abbey.

FRANCE

All Things French. www.allthingsfrench.com

Much of this site is concerned with shopping—glassware, toys, beauty products—but check out the vacation packages for ballooning holidays over Burgundy and Bordeaux, river barging, and alpine adventures.

Beyond the French Riviera. www.beyond.com

The Travel section of this guide deals with the regions of southeast France, explaining train, bus, air, and sea travel in detail. A directory of towns brings you to photos, history, and excursions.

Channels Paris. www.paris.cx

Centering on an elaborate virtual tour, this site has hundreds of photos, maps, links, and a search page for available hotels. Drop in on the chatbox and check out the Q&A on its Paris Forum.

Eiffel Tower. www.tour-eiffel.fr

Read the history of the tower and practical information about its hours, tours, restaurants, and boutiques.

⭐ **Château Versailles.** www.chateauversailles.com

Before visiting the country residence of Louis XIV, print out pages from this inventive reference, full of pictures of its works of art, of its history, and of its grounds. It has appropriate music and moving 360-degree films of a few of the most important rooms.

⭐ **FranceWay.** www.franceway.com

Wit lots of suggestions for your trip to France—especially Paris—this guide covers dining, lodging, and transportation. The detailed listings of restaurants in Paris don't appear to be paid ads.

⭐ **Giverny and Vernon.** www.giverny.org

Visitors to the region forever associated with Claude Monet will find loads of useful travel and transportation information. Run down details on the area's castles, museums, places of archaeological interest, as well as the artist's famous gardens.

The Louvre. www.louvre.fr
After checking out the descriptions of the guided tours, permanent collections, and temporary exhibits, download the free QuickTime VR software to take a virtual stroll through the museum. *Venus de Milo* and *Mona Lisa* are merely tastes of what lies ahead.

Nice, French Riviera. www.nice-cotazur.org
While this official tourism site is a little thin, it's helpful for its calendar of events and hotel search.

✪ Paris Pages. www.paris.org
Descriptions of lodgings are the strength of this site. Hotels are organized by arrondissements and price ranges, supplemented with guest reviews. The city guide includes an event calendar, shops, a map of attractions with details about each, and a photo tour.

✪ Provence Touristic Guide. www.provence.guideweb.com
Dig into the "Leisure and Culture" section for pictures, exhibit descriptions, and contact information for museums. There's also a directory of hotels and guest houses that includes photos and the possibility of online reservations.

Travel France. www.bonjour.com
Here, you can pick one of the country's regions and peruse a directory of links to attractions, tour operators, and city visitor bureaus. Check out the hints for getting around Paris.

GERMANY

Bavaria Alpine Net Guide. www.bavaria.com
Here all things Bavarian are touched on, such as Mad King Luwig's castle and an Oktoberfest beer and music raft ride down the river Isar. There's advice on shopping, getting around, and enjoying the Alps, among many other nuggets.

Berlin Info. www.berlin-info.de/index_e.html
Come here for a virtual tour of Berlin's sights, but be aware that some of the links go to German-only pages.

Eat Germany. www.eat-germany.net
This definitive dining guide lets you search the site or view its Top 10 for each city. The restaurants are selected by users who rate them, giving an aura of objectivity. With lots of detail about type of food, hours, locations, and kinds of patrons, searches can be narrowed by nation, state, or city.

German Castles. www.germancastles.com
This guide to 48 castles and manors comes complete with lots of photos and suggestions about lodging, river cruises, and vacation packages. There's a form to request further information.

German National Tourist Board. www.us.germany-tourism.de
This informative site includes basics on lodging, getting around, links, and upcoming events, such as the celebrations commemorating the 250th anniversary of the death of Bach.

Hotels and Travel in Germany. www.hotelstravel.com/germany.html
This site not only provides detailed listings for hotels in Germany but also has links to related sites, like Ritz-Carlton and Relais & Châteaux, that offer lodging and general travel info.

Oktoberfest. www.munich-tourist.de
Updated for each year's festival, this site from the Munich Tourist Office includes a program of events, a guide to various beer tents, and images from past festivals. Descriptions of hotel packages and discount voucher packages are added.

GREECE

✪ **Aegean. aegean.ch/main.htm**
This easy-to-use travel guide to Greece includes detailed hotel information, travel agencies, special offers (such as Net-only discounts) and more. Use the "Map of Greece" link for in-depth guides to various islands.

Athens Guide. www.athensguide.com
This wide-ranging yet personal guide includes getting around, walking tours, dining, and nightlife. There are discussions of such varied topics as Athens's outdoor markets, public gardens, and Internet cafes.

GoGreece.com. www.gogreece.com
This search site for Greece includes destination advice, maps, and current news, as well as fun extras likes games, chat rooms, and live Greek radio stations.

Greek National Tourism Office. www.vacation.net.gr
Taxi fares, museum hours, ferry schedules—whatever you're looking for, there's a good chance you'll find it here.

Greek National Tourism. www.greektourism.gr
This site is updated by the tourism organization. A music loop and spiffy graphics now enliven galleries of photos and rare posters and comprehensive guides to archaeological sites, monasteries, islands, flora and fauna, and a good hotel search page.

HUNGARY

Budapest.com. www.budapest.com
Come here to view a virtual slideshow, consult the shopping guide, or see what the city looked like a century ago. Use the forum link for online discussions.

Hungarian Cultural and Information Center. hungary.org
Use the extensive collection of links as a jumping-off point for learning more about Hungary's history, culture, cuisine, and more. Of course, there's also a travel section.

✪ **Hungarian National Tourist Office. gotohungary.com**
This U.S.-based site loads far more quickly than sites based in Europe and has a wealth of information. Especially useful is the up-to-date events calendar and special-interest guide, with links, for example, to spas and thermal baths.

IRELAND

Event Guide. www.eventguide.com
Log on before you leave to see what's happening this month—theater, film, clubbing and pubbing, and jazz, folk, pop, and classical concerts.

✪ **Go Ireland. www.goireland.com**
The breadth of this guide is almost overwhelming: more than 11,000 lodging listings (many with pictures) and thousands of restaurants (some with menus), though in some cases the info is pretty thin.

✪ **Heritage of Ireland. www.heritageireland.ie**
Use this site to get visitor information and view images of historic sites, parks, gardens, and cultural attractions, such as the Irish Museum of Modern Art.

Ireland Tourism. www.shamrock.org
Come here to learn about package vacations and find some special deals, such as off-peak fares on Aer Lingus.

Irish Tourist Board. www.ireland.travel.ie
Use this well-designed site for tips on getting around, places to stay, and things to do. You'll also find a listing of major events, such as the Dublin Film Festival and Galway Art Festival.

Virtual Tour of Ireland. www.iol.ie/tip
With this site, it's not such a long way to Tipperary. See images of various towns, peruse the destination information, and find tips for getting around, lodging, and dining.

ITALY

Carnival of Venice. www.carnivalofvenice.com/uk
Find out what's afoot for the Carnavale celebration in the city of gondolas. There's also information about transportation, city services, and other basics. Also see **www.doge.it**, with a modest amount of information about hotels and happenings.

Christus Rex. www.christusrex.org
This unrelentingly religious site provides a photo tour of the Vatican and its art treasures. Also see **www.vatican.va**, the Vatican's official Web site.

Dolce Vita. www.dolcevita.com
The self-proclaimed "insider's guide to Italy" is all about style—as it pertains to fashion, cuisine, design, and travel. Dolce Vita is a good place to stay up to date on trends in modern Italian culture.

Enjoy Rome. wwwenjoyrome.com
Maintained by a private company, this site promotes its walking tours in Rome, Florence, and Venice as well as guided trips to Pompeii.

Firenze By Net. www.mega.it/florence
Updated weekly for news and notices about concerts and dance recitals, this site also lets you explore the art scene by clicking on the museum map, then switch to the monument version for both the city and surrounding regions, including Chianti.

✪ In Italy Online. www.initaly.com
This extensive site helps you find all sorts of accommodations (country villas, historic residences, convents, and farmhouses) and includes tips on shopping, dining, driving, and viewing works of art.

ItalyTour.com. www.italytour.com
Check out this vast directory for coverage of the arts, culture, business, tours, entertainment, restaurants, lodging, media, shopping, sports, and major Italian cities. See photo collections and videos in the "Panorama" section.

Know It All: Know Tuscany. www.knowital.com
As the name suggests, this travel guide does seem to know it all about lodging, dining, and wine in the Italian region of Tuscany.

Meeting Venice. www.meetingvenice.it
Intended for both leisure and business travelers, this guide to the magical city provides a calendar of events, weather forecasts, a hotel search, and brief descriptions of *hundreds* of eating places.

The Rome Page. www.comune.roma.it

It takes a while to load, but this official site has a fair amount of info on most aspects of the Rome experience. It appears to be only in Italian, but click on the "Roma Review" box on the welcome page and then on the English phrases of interest—what's on, what to hear, what to see.

Traveling with Ed and Julie. www.twenj.com/romevisit.htm

These two seasoned travelers give novice visitors their subjective but realistic take ancient Rome. The amiably opinionated pair guides tourists to hotels, restaurants, excursions, kids' activities, and major attractions.

Venezia. www.provincia.venezia.it/aptve

In addition to listings of events, sights, and suggested itineraries, this official tourist-board site piles on scores of pages of hotel descriptions.

THE NETHERLANDS

Amsterdam Hotspots. www.amsterdamhotspots.nl

And they mean "hot." Here are *the* places to fill your nights, from eating and drinking to where to toke, what the top gay bars are, and where to see those famous working girls on display behind picture windows.

✪ Channels Amsterdam. www.channels.nl

This is one of the best virtual tours on the Net—the images are clear, you can direct your own tour, and you can chat with others about Amsterdam. Visitors offer their impressions of restaurants, hotels, museums, and hash houses.

Go Amsterdam. www.go-amsterdam.org

This cleanly designed site includes an extensive "A–Z Index" with listings for museums, hotels, transportation, and other categories.

Hollandlinks. www.regiolicht.nl/homepages/fkleuve1/holland.htm

This ungainly Web address is worth typing for this well-organized extensive list of links, including sites for Webcams, newspapers, dining, Amsterdam, and many others.

Visit Amsterdam. www.visitamsterdam.nl

This site lays out the details on sightseing, walking routes, wining and dining, shopping for antiques, and current events. There's even a page warning you about streets that can be dangerous at night.

Welcome to Holland. www.visitholland.com

The official site from the Netherlands Board of Tourism is awkwardly designed (expanding your browser to its full size helps). But it does have useful advice for upcoming events, cycling, and culture—and it even lets you know when the tulips bloom.

NORWAY

Welcome to My Norway. www.mynorway.org

This personal site has photos of fjords, stave churches, and ski jumps, as well as brief essays on government, history, and even prehistoric rock carvings. Check out the Official Guide to Oslo, which has a hotel booking service.

Norway Info. www.cyberclip.com/Katrine/NorwayInfo/index.html

Thousands of interesting tidbits appear on this one-woman site (though they need updating), along with a virtual bookstore and links. There are explanations of native foods and a Norwegian vocabulary, and click on "A Year in Norway" to learn more about festivals, holidays, traditions, and folklore.

✪ **Visiting Norway. www.norway.org/travel**
This well-designed site offers an expansive introduction to the country's cities and regions, with information on lodging, attractions, cruises, shopping, and much more.

PORTUGAL

Lisbon Pages. www.kpnqwest.pt.lisboa
After a general description of the city, this site gets down to abundant specifics about restaurants, bars, discos, hotels, and fado clubs.

Nancy's Portugal Site. home.sol.no/~nancys/portugal/index.html
Nancy's Norwegian, not Portuguese, but she's put together a refreshingly personal love letter to her second home. Her attention is directed primarily on Lisbon and Madeira.

Virtual Portugal. www.portugalvirtual.pt
A extensive collection of Web links is provided for exploring Portugal in depth. Main categories include "Tourism," "Shopping," "Accommodation," and "Restaurants."

SCOTLAND

Discover Scotland. www.discover-scotland.com
This site from the *Daily Record* and *Sunday Mail* combines news headlines with travel advice ranging from fine dining to golf.

Edinburgh and Lothians Tourist Board. www.edinburgh.org
An official site, this discusses what's new, travel tips, and events and festivals for city, coast, and country. They also include something other webmasters might keep in mind—a page about what to do with kids, written *by* kids.

Golf Courses of Scotland. www.uk-golf.com/courses/scotland/index.shtml
Some say you haven't played golf until you've teed up in Scotland. This site, which lists locations and greens fees, will help you find a course wherever you plan to be.

Holidays in Scotland. www.holiday.scotland.net
An official site of the Scottish Tourist Board, this is an excellent source for events, lodging, getting around, and outdoor activities. However, the "Special Offers" section requires a lot of clicks for little payoff.

Scotland Holiday Net. www.aboutscotland.co.uk
This site combines an effective collection of information on dining, lodging, and sightseeing with some personal accounts, such as a letter from an author who lives in the West Coast Highlands.

✪ **Travel Scotland. www.travelscotland.co.uk**
Curious about Scotland's top 20 free attractions? Interested in restaurant reviews from other diners? Try this site.

SPAIN

All About Spain. www.red2000.com
This deep and well-organized travel guide encompasses all sorts of attractions, from museums to fiestas. A section called "Yellow Pages" provides easy access to topics.

✪ **CyberSpain. www.cyberspain.com**
Guilty of almost too much information, this site has the basics on lodging and dining but much more, like background on Spanish traditions like La Tuna and an extensive section on artists like Goya.

Go Spain. www.clark.net/pub/jumpsam
This extensive site ranges from Jewels of Spain (Picasso, the Alhambra) to Spanish cooking. You'll also find a photo archive, links to news outlets, and a search engine for other resources covering Spain.

MadridMan's Yankee Home Page. www.madridman.com
On the Web for years, this guy from Ohio hides a surprising amount of info behind a home page that may sound frivolous but isn't. The museum descriptions, for example, are both long and insightful, with nuts-and-bolts details that surpass most other sources.

The Prado Museum. www.museoprado.mcu.es
Just click on the English words at the bottom of the homepage for Spain's most important museum to get news about gallery closings and openings, current exhibits, floor plans, and hours and fees.

✪ Softguide Madrid. www.softguides.com/index.Madrid
Come here for reams of material about Madrid, including substantial essays on food and culture, suggested day trips, concerts (with price ranges), and where to find movies in English, with only a few bare spots.

Tourist Office of Spain. www.okspain.org
This can help plan your trip with listings of lodging options, attractions, and tour operators and packages. You'll also find handy tips on getting around.

SWEDEN

CityGuide Sweden. www.cityguide.se
Upcoming events, entertainments, and places of tourist interest are outlined for the cities of Stockholm, Göteborg, and Malmö. A hotel reservation page is included.

Stockholm Information Service. www.stockholmtown.com
Check this site just before you go for updated events listings. You'll also find advice for dining, lodging, and museums, as well as links to media outlets.

Swedish Information Smorgasbord. www.sverigeturism.se/smorgasbord
Interested in a steamship ride to the islands in Storsjön? This site will help you learn about this and thousands of other intriguing ways to spend your time in the Land of the Midnight Sun.

Travelets Sweden. www.travelets.com/sweden
The real utility here is the roster of available rental properties, with photos. To encourage you to hang around, there's a free Lotto game with real cash prizes.

SWITZERLAND

GoSki: Switzerland. www.goski.com/switz.htm
Get the lowdown on skiing the high country. This site will help you find a resort, tell you the best time to go, and keep you posted about conditions.

Switzerland.com. www.switzerland.com/travel.html
Not so much a destination in itself as a launching pad to other Web sites, Switzerland.com can point the way to museums, hotels, restaurants, and other attractions.

Switzerland Tourism. www.myswitzerland.com
Although awkwardly designed, this site does have useful travel advice on hotels and travel packages and throws in current snow reports.

Austria 1

by Darwin Porter & Danforth Prince

Austria now stands at the crossroads of Europe, as it did in the heyday of the Austro-Hungarian Empire. Its capital, Vienna, stranded during the postwar years on the edge of Western Europe, is taking its place again as an important international city.

The country offers a lot to do, from exploring historic castles and palaces to skiing on some of the world's finest alpine slopes or hiking in the Danube Valley.

1 Vienna & the Danube Valley

Vienna still retains much of the glory and grandeur of the empire's heady days. Museum treasures from all over Europe, baroque palaces through which Maria Theresa and her brood wandered, Johann Strauss's lively music, Gustav Klimt's paintings, the concert halls, the unparalleled opera—it's all still here, as if the empire were still flourishing.

Tourism is growing as thousands arrive every year to view Vienna's great art and architecture, to feast on lavish Viennese pastries, to explore the Vienna Woods, to sail down the Danube, to attend Vienna's balls, operas, and festivals, and to listen to the "music that never stops."

Visitors today face a newer and brighter Vienna, a city with more joie de vivre and punch than it's had since before the war. There's also a downside: Prices are on the rise—they haven't reached the height of the Ferris wheel at the Prater, but they're climbing there.

ORIENTATION

ARRIVING **By Plane** Vienna's international airport, **Wien Schwechat** (☎ **01/700-70**), is about 19km (12 miles) southeast of the city center. There's regular **bus service** between the airport and the City Air Terminal (Wien Mitte) at the Hotel Hilton. Buses run 24 hours a day every 20 to 60 minutes. The one-way fare is 70AS ($5). There's also service between the airport and two rail stations, the Westbahnhof and the Südbahnhof, with buses leaving the airport every 30 minutes throughout the day. For the return trip to the airport, buses depart the Westbahnhof every 30 minutes 5:30am to midnight (reaching the Südbahnhof 15 minutes later). The trip takes 20 to 25 minutes from the airport to the Inner City. Fares between the airport and the train station are 120AS ($9) per person.

Vienna

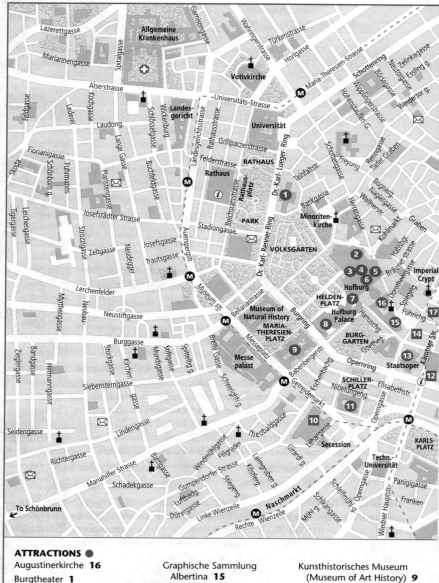

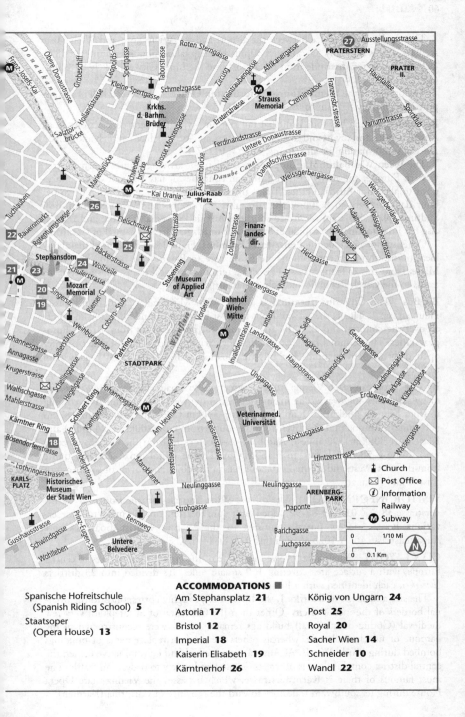

Spanische Hofreitschule
(Spanish Riding School) **5**

Staatsoper
(Opera House) **13**

ACCOMMODATIONS ■

Am Stephansplatz **21**

Astoria **17**

Bristol **12**

Imperial **18**

Kaiserin Elisabeth **19**

Kärntnerhof **26**

König von Ungarn **24**

Post **25**

Royal **20**

Sacher Wien **14**

Schneider **10**

Wandl **22**

There's also **train** service between the airport and the Wien Nord and Wien Mitte stations. Trains run daily 5:07am to 9:30pm. The trip takes about 45 minutes at 38AS ($2.95). A one-way **taxi** ride from the airport into the Inner City will likely be 410AS ($32).

The branch of the **Vienna Tourist Information Office** in the arrival hall of the airport is open daily 8:30am to 9pm.

By Train Vienna has four principal rail stations, with frequent connections to all Austrian cities and towns and to all major European cities, such as Munich and Milan. For train information for all stations, call ☎ **01/17-17.**

The **Wien Westbahnhof,** Europaplatz, is for trains arriving from western Austria, western Europe, and many eastern European countries. It has frequent train connections to all major Austrian cities. Trains from Salzburg pull in at the rate of two per hour daily 5:40am to 8:40pm; the trip takes $3^1/4$ hours. The **Wien Südbahnhof,** Südtirolerplatz, has train service to southern Austria, Slovenia, Croatia, and Italy. It also has links to Graz, the capital of Styria, and to Klagenfurt, the capital of Carinthia.

Other stations include the **Franz-Josef Bahnhof,** Franz-Josef-Platz, used mainly by local trains, although connections are made here to Prague and Berlin. The **Wien Mitte,** Landstrasser Hauptstrasse 1, is also a terminus of local trains, plus a depot for trains to the Czech Republic and Schwechat Airport.

By Bus The **City Bus Terminal** is at the Wien Mitte rail station, Landstrasser Hauptstrasse 1. This is the arrival depot for Post buses and Bundesbuses from points all over the country, and also, the arrival point for private buses from various European cities. The terminal has lockers, currency-exchange kiosks, and a ticket counter open daily 6:15am to 6pm. For bus information, call ☎ **01/711-01** daily 6am to 9pm.

By Car You can reach Vienna from all directions via major highways (*autobahnen*) or by secondary highways. The main artery from the west is Autobahn **A-1,** coming in from Munich 468km (291 miles), Salzburg 336km (209 miles), and Linz 187km (116 miles). Autobahn **A-2** arrives from the south, from Graz 200km (124 miles) and Klagenfurt 309km (192 miles). Autobahn **A-4** comes in from the east, connecting with Route **E-58,** which runs to Bratislava and Prague. Autobahn **A-22** takes traffic from the northwest, and Route **E-10** connects to the cities and towns of southeastern Austria and Hungary.

VISITOR INFORMATION The official **Wien Tourist-Information** is at Kärntnerstrasse 38 (☎ **01/513-88-92**), open daily 9am to 7pm. You can make room reservations here. Address postal inquiries to the Vienna Tourist Board, Obere Augartenstrasse 40, A-1025 Vienna (fax 01/211-14-57).

CITY LAYOUT Vienna has evolved into one of the largest metropolises of central Europe, with a surface area covering 160 square miles. It's divided into 23 districts (*bezirke*), each identified with a Roman numeral.

The size and shape of **Bezirke I,** the **Inner City,** roughly corresponds to the original borders of the medieval city. Other than the Cathedral of St. Stephan, very few medieval (Gothic or medieval) buildings remain—many were reconstructed in the baroque or neoclassical style, whereas others are modern replacements of buildings bombed during World War II. As Austria's commercial and cultural nerve center, the central district contains dozens of streets devoted exclusively to pedestrian traffic. The most famous of these is **Kärntnerstrasse,** which bypasses the Vienna State Opera House during its southward trajectory toward the province of Carinthia (Kärnten).

The **Ringstrasse,** a circular boulevard about 4km (2¹/₂ miles) long whose construction between 1859 and 1888 was one of the most ambitious (and controversial) examples of urban restoration in the history of central Europe, surrounds the Inner City. Confusingly, the name of this boulevard changes many times during its encirclement of the Inner City. Names that apply to it carry the suffix *-ring:* for example, Opernring, Schottenring, Burgring, Dr.-Karl-Lueger-Ring, Stubenring, Parkring, Schubertring, and Kärntner Ring.

Surrounding the Ringstrasse are the **inner suburban districts** (Bezirkes II through IX). These contain most of the villas and palaces of Vienna's 18th-century nobility, as well as complexes of modern apartment houses and the 19th-century homes of middle-class entrepreneurs. The **outer suburban districts** embrace a wide range of residential, industrial, and rural settings.

Northeast of the center, beyond the Danube Canal, is the **Second District,** with the famous amusement park, the Prater. East of the center, in the **Third District,** you'll find the art treasures and baroque setting of the Belvedere Palace. West of the center is Schönbrunn Palace.

GETTING AROUND   By Public Transportation   Vienna Transport (*Wiener Verkehrsbetriebe*), with its network of facilities covering hundreds of miles, can take you where you want to go—by U-Bahn (subway), tram (streetcar), or bus. Vienna Public Transport has **Information Centers** at Karlsplatz, open Monday to Friday 7am to 6pm and Saturday, Sunday, and holidays 8:30am to 4pm; on Stephansplatz, open Monday to Friday 6:30am to 6:30pm and Saturday to Sunday 8:30am to 4pm; and on Praterstern, open Monday to Friday 7am to 6:30pm. Centers are also at each of the larger Metro stations. For information, call ☎ **01/79-09-105.**

Vienna has a **uniform fare,** allowing the same tickets to be used on all means of transportation as well as on the **Schnelbahn (Rapid Transit)** of the Austrian Federal Railways in the Vienna area and on some connecting private bus lines. A single (one-ride) ticket costs 20AS ($1.55); that's also the price for two rides by a child. Children under 6 ride free.

It's wise to buy your tickets in advance at a *tabak-trafik* (tobacconist shop) or at an advance-sales office in one of the three public transport information centers (see above for locations). All advance-sales offices are open Monday 6am to noon, Tuesday and Wednesday 6:30am to 12:30pm, and Thursday and Friday 12:30 to 6:30pm. Most buses and streetcars don't have conductors, which means you must have the correct change, 20AS ($1.55), when you buy your ticket aboard or from a vending machine at the station. A ticket bought from a machine will be stamped with the date and time of purchase. Tickets purchased in advance must be stamped before you start your ride by the machine on conductorless streetcars or at the platform barriers of the

---

Traveler's Tip

The **Vienna Card** gives you access to all public modes of transportation (subway, bus, and tram) within Vienna—as well as discounts in city museums, shops, and restaurants—for a single **discounted price.** A 24-hour network pass costs 60AS ($4.60) and is good for a full day of public transport. A 72-hour network pass sells for 140AS ($11). For 220AS ($17), you can purchase a versatile **3-day strip ticket,** which can be used for 3 separate days of travel; a rail attendant punches the ticket each day it's used. Vienna Cards are easy to find throughout the capital, or you can buy one outside Vienna by calling ☎ **01/798-44-00-28** with a credit card.

Vienna Metro

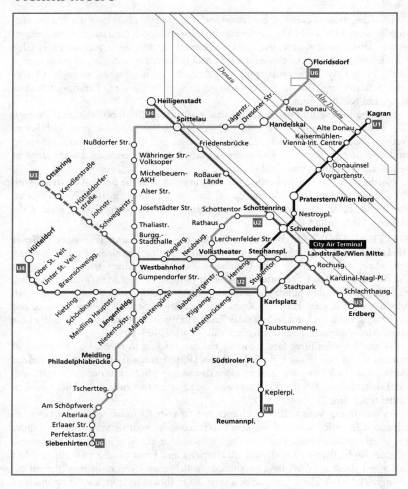

underground or Stadtbahn. Once a ticket is stamped, it may be used for one trip in one direction, including transfers.

By Bus & U-Bahn (Subway)   You can ride directly into the Inner City on the U-Bahn U1 or on city bus no. 1A, 2A, or 3A. The U-Bahn runs daily 6am to midnight; buses operate Monday to Saturday 6am to 10pm and Sunday 6am to 8pm.

By Tram   More and more tram routes are being phased out in favor of buses or the U-Bahn, but trams are still in heavy use within the center, especially lines 1 and 2. Trams are also in use between the Westbahnhof and Burgring (take line 58), and between the Westbahnhof and the Südbahnhof (take line 18). Finally line D runs between the Südbahnhof and the Ring.

By Taxi   Taxi stands are marked by signs, or you can call for a radio cab by phoning ☎ **31-300,** 60-160, 81-400, 91-011, or 40-100. Fares are indicated on an officially calibrated taximeter. The basic fare is 27AS ($2.10), plus 15AS ($1.15) per kilometer.

There's an extra charge of 13AS ($1) for luggage carried in the trunk. For rides after 11pm, and for trips on Sunday and holidays, there's a surcharge of 4AS (30¢). If you call for a radio cab, additional charges apply.

By Car   Major car-rental companies operating in Vienna include **Avis,** Opernring 3–5 (☎ **800/654-3001** in the U.S., or 01/587-62-41 in Vienna; U-Bahn: Karlsplatz); **Budget Rent-a-Car,** City/Hilton Air Terminal (☎ **800/472-3325** in the U.S., or 01/714-6565 in Vienna; U-Bahn: Landstrasse/Wien Mitte); and **Hertz,** Kärntnerring 17 (☎ **1/512-86-77**; U-Bahn: Stephansplatz).

By Bicycle   Vienna has more than 155 miles of marked bicycle paths within the city limits. In fact, city officials encourage bicycle riding. In July and August, many Viennese leave their cars in the garage and ride bikes. Specially marked cars of the U-Bahn will transport bicycles free in July and August, Monday to Friday 9am to 3pm and after 6:30pm until the trains stop running, and on weekends from 9am until the trains stop running. All other times, you pay half the regular U-Bahn fare to take a bike on the U-Bahn.

Rental stores abound at such places as the Prater amusement park and along the banks of the Danube Canal, which is the favorite venue for most Viennese to go bicycling. One of the best of the many sites specializing in bike rentals is **Copacagrana,** Reichsbrücke, on the Donauinsel (☎ **064/34-58-515**; U-Bahn: Handelskai), open May to October daily 9am to 9pm. Alternatively, you can rent from a kiosk within the **Westbahnhof** (☎ **01/58-00-329**), between May and October every day 8am to 10pm. The Vienna Tourist Board can also supply a list of rental shops and more information about bike paths throughout the city. Bike rentals begin at around 200AS ($15) a day.

Fast Facts: Vienna

American Express   The most convenient office is at Kärntnerstrasse 21–23 (☎ **01/515-40**; U-Bahn: Stephansplatz), open Monday to Friday 9am to 6pm and Saturday 9am to noon.

Business Hours   Most shops are open Monday to Friday 9am to 6pm and Saturday 9am to noon, 12:30pm, or 1pm. On the first Saturday of every month, the custom is for shops to remain open until 4:30 or 5pm. The tradition is called *langer Samstag.*

Currency   The Austrian currency is the **schilling,** written ASch, AS, Ös, or simply S. A schilling is made up of 100 groschen (which are seldom used). Coins are minted as 5, 10, and 50 groschen, and 1, 5, 10, 20, and 50 schilling. Banknotes appear as 20, 50, 100, 500, 1,000, and 5,000 schilling. At this writing $1 = 12.93 schillings, or 1 schilling = 8¢ (the rate used in this chapter). The ratio of the British pounds to the schillings fluctuates constantly. At press time, £1 = approximately 21.34AS (or 1AS = 0.046p). The euro rate was currently fixed at 13.76AS (or 1AS = 0.07€—or 7 "eurocents").

Dentists/Doctors   For dental problems during the night or on Saturday and Sunday, call ☎ **01/512-20-78.** If you have a medical emergency during the night, call ☎ **141** daily 7pm to 7am. See also "Emergencies" and "Hospitals," below.

Drugstores   Called *apotheke,* they're open Monday to Friday 8am to noon and 2 to 6pm and Saturday 8am to noon. Each apotheke posts in its window a list of shops that take turns staying open at night and on Sunday.

Embassies/Consulates   The Embassy of the **United States** is at Boltzmann-gasse 16, A-1090 Vienna (☎ **01/313-39;** U-Bahn: Stadtpark). The consular section is at Gartenbaupromenade 2–4, A-1010 Vienna (☎ **01/313-39**). Lost passports, tourist emergencies, and other matters are handled by the consular section. The embassy and consulate are open Monday to Friday 8:30am to noon and 1 to 3:30pm.

The Embassy of **Canada,** Laurenzerberg 2 (☎ **01/531-38-30-00;** U-Bahn: Schwedenplatz), is open Monday to Friday 8:30am to 12:30pm and 1:30 to 3:30pm; the **United Kingdom,** Jauresgasse 12 (☎ **01/716-13-0;** tram: 71), open Monday to Friday 9:15am to noon and 2 to 4pm; **Australia,** Mattiellis-trasse 2–4 (☎ **01/512-85-80;** U-Bahn: Karlsplatz), open Monday to Friday 8:30am to 1pm and 2 to 5:30pm; and **New Zealand,** Springsiedelgasse 28 (☎ **01/318-85-05;** bus: 26A, 391, 392, or 590), open Monday to Friday 8:30am to 5pm; **Ireland,** Hilton Center, Landstrasser Hauptstrasse 2 (☎ **01/715-42-47;** Tram: 1), open Monday to Friday 9 to 11:30am and 1:30 to 4pm.

Emergencies   Call ☎ **122** to report a fire, ☎ **133** for the police, or ☎ **144** for an ambulance.

Hospitals   The major hospital is **Allgemeines Krankenhaus,** Währinger Gürtel 18–20 (☎ **01/404-00;** U-Bahn: Michel Beuern).

Internet Access   Try the **National Library,** 1 Neue Burg 1 (☎ **01/53-41-00;** U-Bahn: Maria Hilfer), in Heldenplatz at the Hofburg, which offers free access at numerous terminals Monday to Saturday 10am to 4pm and Sunday 10am to 1pm.

Police   The emergency number is ☎ **133.**

Post Office   Addresses for these can be found in the telephone directory under "Post." Post offices are generally open for mail services Monday to Friday 8am to noon and 2 to 6pm. The central post office, the **Hauptpostamt,** at Fleischmarkt 19 (☎ **01/515-09-0;** U-Bahn: Schwedenplatz), and most general post offices are open daily 24 hours.

Telephone   The **country code** for Austria is **43.** The **city code** for Vienna is **1;** use this code when you're calling from outside Austria. If you're within Austria, use **01.**

A **local call** costs 2AS (15¢) for 1 minute. Hotels add huge surcharges to **long-distance calls;** go to the post office instead where it costs 31.50AS ($2.45) to call the United States for 3 minutes during peak hours Monday to Friday 8am to 6pm. Otherwise, it is only 28AS ($2.15) for 3 minutes. Consider purchaising a **phone card** at any post office for 50AS ($3.85), 100AS ($8), or 200AS ($15). **International direct dial** numbers include **AT&T** (☎ **022-90-30-11**); **MCI** (☎ **022-90-30-12**), and **Sprint** (☎ **0800-20-02-36**).

Taxes   Vienna imposes no special city taxes, other than the national value-added tax that's tacked on to all goods and services. The tax depends on the item, but can range up to 34% on luxury goods, 21% on car rentals.

WHERE TO STAY
ON OR NEAR KÄRNTNERSTRASSE
Very Expensive

✪ **Bristol.** Kärntner Ring 1, A-1015 Vienna. ☎ **800/325-3535** in the U.S., or 01/515-160. Fax 01/515-16-550. www.luxurycollection.com/bristol. E-mail: hotel-bristol@sheraton.com.

140 units. A/C MINIBAR TV TEL. 4,100–17,200AS ($316–$1,324) double; from 15,000AS ($1,155) suite. AE, DC, MC, V. Parking 350AS ($27). U-Bahn: Karlsplatz. Tram: 1 or 2.

This six-story landmark is a superb choice. When it was constructed in 1894 next to the State Opera it was the ultimate in luxury style, but it's been updated to give guests the benefit of black-tile bathrooms and modern conveniences. Bedrooms are sumptuously appointed. The club floor offers luxurious comfort, enhanced by period furnishings. Every year a different floor of the hotel is completely renovated. The Bristol's restaurant, the Korso, is one of the best in Vienna, and the modern Rôtisserie Sirk and the elegant Café Sirk are also meeting places for gourmets.

Imperial. Kärntner Ring 16, A-1015 Vienna. ☎ **800/325-3535** in the U.S., or 01/501-10-0. Fax 01/501-10-410. www.luxurycollection.com/imperial. 128 units. A/C MINIBAR TV TEL. 5,500–8,600AS ($424–$662) double; from 14,000AS ($1,078) suite. AE, DC, MC, V. Parking 450AS ($35). U-Bahn: Karlsplatz.

This hotel is Vienna's grandest and the most "imperial" looking in Austria, 2 blocks from the State Opera and 1 block from the Musikverein. The hotel was built in 1869 as the private residence and was converted into a private hotel in 1873. Everything is outlined against a background of polished marble, crystal chandeliers, Gobelin tapestries, and fine rugs. Some of the royal suites are palatial, but all rooms are soundproof and generally spacious. Courtyard rooms are more tranquil but lack views. The elegant restaurant, Zur Majestät, has a late-19th-century atmosphere and offers traditional Austrian dishes done with a light touch.

Sacher Wien. Philharmonikerstrasse 4, A-1010 Vienna. ☎ **01/514-56.** Fax 01/51-45-68-10. www.sacher.com. E-mail: hotel@sacher.com. 108 units. A/C MINIBAR TV TEL. 3,950–9,000AS ($304–$693) double; from 14,000AS ($1,078) suite. AE, DC, MC, V. Parking 390AS ($30). U-Bahn: Karlsplatz. Bus: 4A. Tram: 1, 2, 62, 65, D, or J.

Much of the glory of the Hapsburgs is still evoked by the public rooms here. The red velvet, crystal chandeliers, traditional wallpaper, and brocaded curtains are reminiscent of Old Vienna. The hotel is popular with groups, however, and the heavy traffic is taking a toll. Although it has its die-hard admirers, if you're going truly grand, the Imperial and Bristol are superior. Demisuites and chambers with drawing rooms are more expensive. The reception desk is fairly flexible about making arrangements for salons, apartments, or joining two rooms together.

Expensive

Am Stephansplatz. Stephansplatz 9, A-1010 Vienna. ☎ **01/534-05-0.** Fax 01/534-05-711. E-mail: hotel@stephansplatz.co.at. 60 units. MINIBAR TV TEL. 2,160–2,360AS ($166–$182) double. Rates include breakfast. AE, DC, MC, V. Parking 350AS ($27). U-Bahn: Stephansplatz.

You'll walk out your door and face the front entrance to Vienna's cathedral if you stay in this hotel, with its unadorned circa-1956 facade. The location is unbeatable, although many other Viennese hotels have more charm and a more helpful staff. Nevertheless, the place has many winning qualities and isn't overrun with groups on package tours. Some bedrooms contain painted reproduction rococo furniture and references to imperial Austria. Most accommodations, however, are rather sterile and functional, and 10 are equipped with showers only instead of tubs. The most interesting units overlook the facade of the cathedral, whereas the more tranquil ones open onto an inner courtyard. Lack of air-conditioning could be a problem here in midsummer, as guests must open their windows onto Stephansplatz, which is noisy until late at night. The hotel's dining choice, Domcafé, serves everything from drinks and snacks to full-fledged meals.

Astoria. Kärntnerstrasse 32–34, A-1015 Vienna. ☎ **01/515-77-0.** Fax 01/515-77-82. www.austria-friend.at. E-mail: astoria@austria-friend.at. 108 units. MINIBAR TV TEL. 2,600AS ($200) double; 4,000AS ($308) suite. Rates include breakfast. AE, DC, MC, V. Parking 300AS ($23). U-Bahn: Stephansplatz.

Hotel Astoria is for nostalgia buffs who want to recall the grand life of the closing days of the Austro-Hungarian Empire. A first-class hotel, the Astoria has a desirable location on the shopping mall close to St. Stephan's Cathedral and the State Opera. Decorated in a slightly frayed late-19th-century style, the hotel offers well-appointed and traditionally decorated bedrooms. The interior rooms tend to be too dark, and singles are just too cramped. Of course, it has been renovated over the years, most recently in 1996, but the old style has been respected. The management offers a good standard at a decent but not cheap price.

✪ **Kaiserin Elisabeth.** Weihburggasse 3, A-1010 Vienna. ☎ **01/515-260.** Fax 01/515-267. 63 units. MINIBAR TV TEL. 2,550AS ($196) double; 2,850AS ($219) suite. Rates include buffet breakfast. AE, DC, MC, V. Parking 350AS ($27). U-Bahn: Stephansplatz.

This hotel of yellow stone is only 1 block from St. Stephan's. The interior offers Oriental rugs on well-maintained marble or wood floors. The soundproof rooms have been considerably updated since Richard Wagner, Franz Liszt, and Edvard Grieg each spent a night here. Modern composers are still attracted to the place. Although some parts of the building date from the 14th century, you're likely to see an up-to-date decor of polished wood, clean linen, and perhaps, an Oriental rug in your room.

Moderate

König von Ungarn. Schulerstrasse 10, A-1010 Vienna. ☎ **01/515-840.** Fax 01/515-848. 32 units. A/C MINIBAR TV TEL. 2,350AS ($181) double; 2,750AS ($212) suite. Rates include breakfast. AE, DC, MC, V. Parking 200AS ($15). U-Bahn: Stephansplatz.

In a choice site on a narrow street near the cathedral, this hotel has been in the business for more than 4 centuries and is Vienna's oldest continuously operated accommodation. It's an evocative, intimate, and cozy retreat in an early 17th-century building, once a pied-à-terre for Hungarian noble families visiting the Austrian capital. Mozart reportedly lived here in 1791. The interior is filled with interesting architectural details, and the King of Hungary restaurant—under separate management—is one of the city's finest (see "Where to Dine"). Bedrooms have low-key luxury, old tradition, and modern convenience, along with some Biedermeier decorative touches. In spite of frequent renovations, the hotel is committed to preserving its sense of nostalgia.

Royal. Singerstrasse 3, A-1010 Vienna. ☎ **01/515-68-0.** Fax 01/513-96-98. www.kremslehner.hotels.or.at/royal. E-mail: royal@kremslehner.hotels.or.at. 82 units. MINIBAR TV TEL. 1,650–2,000AS ($127–$154) double; 2,800AS ($216) suite. Rates include breakfast. AE, DC, MC, V. U-Bahn: Stephansplatz.

The lobby of this nine-story hotel less than a block from St. Stephan's contains the piano where Wagner composed *Die Meistersinger von Nürnberg.* Each room is furnished differently, in a style influenced by 19th-century Italy, with some good reproductions of antiques and an occasional original. The entire facility was built in 1960 and reconstructed in 1982. Try for a room with a balcony and a view of the cathedral. Corner rooms with spacious foyers are also desirable, although those facing the street tend to be noisy. The on-site restaurant, Firenze, serves Tuscan food, of course.

Schneider. Getreidemarkt 5, A-1060 Vienna. ☎ **01/588-380.** Fax 01/588-38-212. E-mail: schneider@hotels.or.at. 70 units. MINIBAR TV TEL. 1,720–2,200AS ($132–$169) double. Rates include buffet breakfast. AE, DC, MC, V. Parking 250AS ($19). U-Bahn: Karlsplatz.

This hotel stands in the center of Vienna between the State Opera and the famous Nasch Market. It's a modern five-story building with panoramic windows on the ground floor and a red-tile roof. The interior is warmly decorated in part with 19th-century antiques and comfortably upholstered chairs. Musicians, singers, actors, and other artists form part of the loyal clientele. This is one of Vienna's better small hotels, and families are especially fond of the place because each suite contains a kitchenette. Some units are air-conditioned.

Inexpensive

Kärntnerhof. Grashofgasse 4, A-1010 Vienna. ☎ **01/512-19-23.** Fax 01/513-22-28-33. www.karntnerhof.com. E-mail: kaerntnerhof@netway.at. 44 units. TEL. 1,240–1,850AS ($96–$142) double; 2,400–3,000 AS ($185–$231) suite. Rates include breakfast. AE, DC, MC, V. Parking 200AS ($15). U-Bahn: Stephansplatz.

Only a 4-minute walk from the cathedral, Kärntnerhof advertises itself as a *gutbürgerlich* family oriented hotel. The public rooms are tastefully decorated; the bedrooms are up-to-date. The bathrooms glisten with tile walls and floors.

✪ **Post.** Fleischmarkt 24, A-1010 Vienna. ☎ **01/51-58-30.** Fax 01/515-83-808. 107 units, 80 with bathroom. TV TEL. 860AS ($66) double without bathroom, 1,420AS ($109) double with bathroom; 1,100AS ($85) triple without bathroom, 1,740AS ($134) triple with bathroom. Rates include buffet breakfast. AE, DC, MC, V. Parking 220AS ($17). Tram: 1 or 2.

Hotel Post lies in the medieval slaughterhouse district, today an interesting section full of hotels and restaurants. The manager is quick to tell you that both Mozart and Haydn frequently stayed in a former inn at this address, although the structure as it stands today is only about a century old. In 1996 and 1997, all the furnishings in the rooms were replaced and upgraded. The well-maintained bedrooms are streamlined and functional.

Wandl. Petersplatz 9, A-1010 Vienna. ☎ **01/53-45-50.** Fax 01/53-455-77. E-mail: reservation@hotelwandl.com. 138 units (137 with bathroom). TV TEL. 1,200AS ($92) double without bathroom, 1,650–1,950AS ($127–$150) double with bathroom. Rates include breakfast. AE, DC, MC, V. Parking 250AS ($19). U-Bahn: Stephansplatz.

Despite a discreet 1997 renovation, this hotel still exudes a sense of history—it has been under the same ownership for generations. Built around 1700, the establishment has views of the steeple of St. Stephan's from many of its windows, which often open onto small balconies. The bedrooms are quite spacious, with the bathrooms small but adequate. Room service is available 24 hours a day.

WHERE TO DINE

ON OR NEAR KÄRNTNERSTRASSE

Very Expensive

✪ **Drei Husaren.** Weihburggasse 4. ☎ **01/512-10-92.** Reservations required. Main courses 220–395AS ($17–$30); tasting menu (6 courses) 920AS ($71). AE, DC, MC, V. Daily noon–3pm and 6pm–1am. U-Bahn: Stephansplatz. VIENNESE/INTERNATIONAL.

Just off Kärntnerstrasse, this enduring favorite—a Viennese landmark since it opened in 1935—serves an inventive and classic Viennese cuisine. To the background music of Gypsy melodies, you'll dine on freshwater salmon with pike soufflé, mussel soup, breast of guinea fowl, an array of sole dishes, and such old-timey favorites as *tafelspitz* (boiled beef). The chef specializes in veal, including his deliciously flavored *kalbsbrücken metternich*. The place is celebrated for its repertoire of more than 35 hors d'oeuvres, which are rolled around the dining room on four separate carts. Every diner pays a supplemental music charge of 50AS ($3.85).

König von Ungarn (King of Hungary). In the Hotel König von Ungarn, Schulerstrasse 10. ☎ **01/512-53-19.** Reservations required. Main courses 220–350AS ($17–$27); fixed-price menu 340–450AS ($26–$35) at lunch, 490–700AS ($38–$54) at dinner. AE, DC, MC, V. Sun–Fri noon–2:30pm and 6–10:30pm. U-Bahn: Stephansplatz. Bus: 1A. VIENNESE/INTERNATIONAL.

This beautifully decorated restaurant is inside the famous hotel of the same name (see "Where to Stay"). The restaurant has operated since the 1600s, the present management dating from 1979. Food is well prepared but traditional—not at all experimental. You dine under a vaulted ceiling in an atmosphere of crystal, chandeliers, antiques, and marble columns. If you're in doubt about what to order, try the *tafelspitz,* a savory boiled-beef specialty elegantly dispensed from a cart. Other menu choices, which change seasonally, include venison in a Chinese mushroom sauce, a ragout of fish with fresh mushrooms, grilled sea bass with crabmeat sauce and a spinach-flavored strudel, or tournedos with a mustard-and-horseradish sauce. The service is superb.

Sacher Hotel Restaurant. Philharmonikerstrasse 4. ☎ **01/514-560.** Reservations required. Main courses 260–380AS ($20–$29). AE, DC, MC, V. Daily noon–2:30pm and 6–11pm. U-Bahn: Karlsplatz. AUSTRIAN/VIENNESE/INTERNATIONAL.

This has long been an enduring favorite, for either pre- or post-opera dining. It seems like all celebrities who come to Vienna eventually are seen either in the Red Bar with its adjacent dining room, where live piano music is presented every evening from 7 to midnight, or in the brown-and-white Anna Sacher Room, the site of many a high-powered meal. There's no better place in Vienna to sample the restaurant's most famous dish, *tafelspitz,* the Viennese boiled-beef platter that is fit for an emperor. The chef serves it here with a savory, herb-flavored sauce. Other excellent dishes include fish terrine, Styrian-style lamb chops with cream cabbage, veal steak with morels, and rib steak with onions. There's also Viennese fried chicken with potato salad. For dessert, enjoy the world-renowned Sacher torte, said to have been created in 1832 by Franz Sacher while he served as Prince Metternich's apprentice.

Moderate

Dö & Co. Akademiestrasse 3. ☎ **01/512-64-74.** Reservations recommended for one of the tables. Main courses 100–225AS ($8–$17). AE, DC, MC, V. Mon–Fri 10:30am–7:30pm, Sat 10am–6pm. U-Bahn: Karlsplatz. DELI.

This sophisticated delicatessen is next to the State Opera. Depending on the season, the asparagus might have been flown in from Paris or Argentina, whereas the shellfish may have come from either the North Sea or the Bosphorus. Sprawling glass cases are laden with rich displays of pâtés, seafood salads, and Viennese pastries. You can get your purchases to go or sit at one of a tiny, somewhat-cramped table near the entrance.

✪ **Plachutta.** Wollzeile 10. ☎ **01/512-1577.** Reservations recommended. Main courses 195–290AS ($15–$22). DC, MC, V. Daily 11:30am–11:15pm. U-Bahn: Stubentor. VIENNESE.

Few restaurants have built such a culinary shrine around one dish. The platter is produced in 10 variations. Its *tafelspitz,* the boiled beef dish that was the favorite of Emperor Franz Josef throughout his prolonged reign. Whichever of the versions you order, it will invariably come with sauces and garnishes that perk up what sounds like a dull dish into a delectable culinary traipse through the tastes of yesteryear. The differences between the versions are a function of the cut of beef you request as part of your meal. Two of the ones most often associated with the dish include *schulterscherzel* (shoulder of beef or *beinfleisch* (shank of beef). Regardless of the cut you specify, your meal will be accompanied with hash brown potatoes, chives, and a very appealing version of horseradish and chopped apples.

Coffeehouses & Cafes

The windows of the much-venerated ✪ **Café Demel,** Kohlmarkt 14 (☎ **01/533-55-16;** U-Bahn: Stephansplatz; bus: 1A or 2A), are filled with fanciful spun-sugar creations of characters from folk legends. Perhaps Lady Godiva's 5-foot tresses will shelter a miniature village of Viennese dancers or the Empress Sisi in her royal finery will grace the window. You can definitely expect to see St. Nicholas at Christmastime. Inside is a splendidly baroque Viennese landmark with black marble tables, cream-colored embellished plaster walls, elaborate half paneling, and crystal chandeliers covered with white milk-glass globes. Dozens of pastries are offered every day, including cream-filled horns (*gugelhupfs*). Coffee costs 52AS ($4), and those tempting cakes begin at 50AS ($3.85). It's open daily 10am to 7pm.

One of the city's most atmospheric cafes, not far from Schönbrunn Palace, **Café Dommayer,** Dommayergasse 1 (☎ **01/877-54-65;** tram: U4 [green line] to Schönbrunn), is where both Johann Strausses (father and son) played waltzes for members of Vienna's *grande bourgeoisie.* Opened in 1787 by a local writer, the cafe still has an old-world atmosphere, with Biedermeier accessories set amid silver samovars, formally dressed waiters (many of whom are short-tempered), and a stylish and very Viennese clientele. A special Viennese coffee costs 45AS ($3.45). It's open daily 7am to midnight.

One of the Ring's great cafes, **Café Landtmann,** Dr.-Karl-Lueger-Ring 4 (☎ **01/532-06-21;** tram: 1, 2, or D), dates from the 1880s. Overlooking the Burgtheater, it has traditionally drawn a mix of politicians, journalists, and actors and was also Freud's favorite. The original chandeliers and the prewar chairs have been refurbished. We highly suggest spending an hour or so here, whether perusing the newspapers, sipping on coffee, or planning the day's itinerary. A large coffee costs 44AS ($3.40), and full meals are available. A fixed-price lunch costs 105AS ($8). Meals are served daily 11:30am to 3pm and 5 to 11:30pm, but the cafe is open daily 8am to midnight.

Inexpensive

Augustinerkeller. Augustinerstrasse 1. ☎ **01/533-10-26.** Main courses 94–180AS ($7–$14); lunch menu buffet 248AS ($19); glass of wine 34–37AS ($2.60–$2.85). AE, MC, V. Daily 11am–midnight. U-Bahn: Stephansplatz or Karlsplatz. AUSTRIAN.

Augustinerkeller, in the basement of the part of the Hofburg complex that shelters the Albertina Collection, has served wine, beer, and food since 1857, although the vaulted ceilings and sense of timelessness evoke an establishment even older than that. It attracts a lively group of patrons from all walks of life, and sometimes they get boisterous, especially when the *schrammel* music goes late into the night. It's one of the best values for wine tasting in Vienna. Aside from the wine and beer, the establishment serves simple food, including roast chicken on a spit, roast pork shank, schnitzel, and *tafelspitz.*

✪ **Buffet Trzesniewski.** Dorotheergasse 1. ☎ **01/512-32-91.** Reservations not accepted. Sandwiches 10AS (75¢); pastries 20AS ($1.55). No credit cards. Mon–Fri 8:30am–9:30pm, Sat 9am–5pm. U-Bahn: Stephansplatz. SANDWICHES.

Everyone in Vienna knows about this place, from the most hurried office worker to the city's elite hostesses. Franz Kafka lived next door and used to come in for sandwiches and beer. Its current incarnation is unlike any buffet you may have seen, with six or seven cramped tables and a rapidly moving queue of clients who jostle for space next to the glass countertops. You'll indicate to the waitress the kind of sandwich you want, and if you can't read German signs, you just point. Most people come here for the delicious finger sandwiches, which include 18 combinations of cream cheese, egg and onion, salami, mushroom, herring, green and red peppers, tomatoes, lobster, and many more.

✪ **Gulaschmuseum.** Schulerstrasse 20. ☎ **01/512-1017.** Reservations recommended. Main courses 95–160AS ($7–$12). MC, V. Mon–Fri 9am–midnight. Sat–Sun 10am–midnight. U-Bahn: Wollzeile or Stephansplatz. AUSTRIAN/HUNGARIAN.

If you thought that *gulasch* (goulash) was available in only one form, think again. This restaurant celebrates at least 15 varieties of it, each of them an authentic survivor of the culinary traditions of Hungary, and each redolent with the taste of that country's most distinctive spice, paprika. You can order versions of goulash based on roast beef, veal, pork, fried chicken livers, and even all-vegetarian versions made with either potatoes, beans, or mushrooms. Boiled potatoes and rough-textured brown or black bread will usually accompany your choice. An excellent beginning is a dish so firmly associated with Hungary that it's been referred to as the national crepe of the Magyars, *hortobágyi palatschinken,* stuffed with minced beef and paprika-flavored cream sauce.

Wiener Rathauskeller. Rathausplatz 1. ☎ **01/405-12-190.** Reservations required. Main courses 146–240AS ($11–$19); Vienna music evening with dinner (Tues–Sat at 8pm) 450AS ($35). AE, DC, MC, V. Mon–Sat 11:30am–3pm and 6–11pm. U-Bahn: Rathaus. VIENNESE/INTERNATIONAL.

City halls throughout the Teutonic world have traditionally maintained restaurants in their basements, and Vienna is no exception. Although its famous Rathaus was built between 1871 and 1883, its cellar-level restaurant wasn't added until 1899. Today, in half a dozen richly atmospheric dining rooms, you'll enjoy the high vaulted ceilings and stained-glass windows of their neo-Gothic heyday, as well as good and reasonably priced food. The chef's specialty is a Rathauskellerplatte for two, consisting of various cuts of meat, including a veal schnitzel, lamb cutlets, and pork medallions. One section of the cellar is devoted every evening to a Viennese musical soiree beginning at 8pm. Live musicians ramble through the world of operetta, waltz, and *schrammel* music—suitable dining entertainment.

Zwölf-Apostelkeller. Sonnenfelsgasse 3. ☎ **01/512-67-77.** Main courses 85–155AS ($7–$12). AE, DC, MC, V. Daily 4:30pm–midnight. Closed 3 weeks in July. Bus: 1A. Tram: 1, 2, 21, D, or N. VIENNESE.

Sections of this old wine tavern's walls predate 1561. Rows of wooden tables stand under vaulted ceilings, with lighting provided partially by streetlights set into the masonry floor. It's so deep that you feel you're entering a dungeon. This place is popular with students, partly because of its low prices and because of its proximity to St. Stephan's. In addition to beer and wine, the establishment serves hearty Austrian fare. Specialties include roast pork with dumplings, Hungarian goulash soup, a limited number of vegetarian dishes, and a *schlachtplatte* (hot black pudding, liverwurst, pork, and pork sausage with a hot bacon-and-cabbage salad).

NEAR FLEISCHMARKT
Moderate
Griechenbeisl. Fleischmarkt 11. ☎ **01/533-19-77.** Reservations required. Main courses 168–275AS ($13–$21); fixed-price menu 270–445AS ($21–$34). AE, DC, MC, V. Daily 11am–midnight (last orders at 11:30pm). Tram: N. U-Bahn: Schwedenplatz. AUSTRIAN.

Griechenbeisl opened in 1450 and is still one of Vienna's leading restaurants. It has a labyrinthine collection of dining areas on three floors, all with low vaulted ceilings, smoky paneling, wrought-iron chandeliers, and Styrian-vested waiters who scurry around with large trays of food. As you go in, be sure to see the so-called inner sanctum, with signatures of such former patrons as Mozart, Beethoven, and Mark Twain. The food is *gutbürgerlich*—hearty, ample, and solidly bourgeois. Menu items include deer stew, both Hungarian and Viennese goulash, sauerkraut garni, Wiener schnitzel, and venison steak—in other words, all those favorite recipes from Grandmother's kitchen. A 25AS ($1.95) cover charge is assessed for candles, bread, wine, flowers, and a napkin on the table.

✪ **Steirereck.** Rasumofskygasse 2. ☎ **01/713-31-68.** Reservations required. Main courses 265–410AS ($20–$32); 3-course fixed-price lunch 465AS ($36); 5-course fixed-price dinner 980AS ($75). AE, V. Mon–Fri 10:30am–3pm and 7pm–midnight. Closed holidays and weekends. Bus: 4. Tram: N. VIENNESE/AUSTRIAN.

Steirereck means "corner of Styria," which is exactly what Heinz and Margarethe Reitbauer have created in the rustic decor of this intimate restaurant. On the Danube Canal, between Central Station and the Prater, it has been acclaimed by some Viennese as the best in the city. The Reitbauers offer both traditional Viennese dishes and "new Austrian" selections. You might begin with a caviar-semolina dumpling, roasted turbot with fennel (served as an appetizer), or the most elegant and expensive item of all, goose-liver *steirereck.* Enticing main courses are asparagus with pigeon and saddle of lamb for two diners. The menu is wisely limited and well prepared, changing daily depending on the fresh produce available at the market.

Wein-Comptoir. Bäckerstrasse 6. ☎ **01/51-21-760.** Reservations recommended. Main courses 125–290AS ($10–$22). AE, DC, MC, V. Mon–Sat 11am–3pm and 5pm–2am (last orders at 1am). U-Bahn: Stephansplatz. AUSTRIAN/INTERNATIONAL.

This is one of the most charming wine-tavern restaurants in the Old Town. You can visit just to sample a wide selection of wines, mostly Austrian, on the street level, or descend into the brick-vaulted cellar, where tables are arranged for meals. Here, waiters run up and down the steep steps, serving not only wine but also standard platters of Austrian and international food. Since most dishes are cooked to order, prepare yourself for a long wait. Full meals might include breast of venison in a goose-liver sauce, *tafelspitz,* or breast of pheasant with bacon, and such vegetarian dishes as spinach dumplings with fresh Parmesan and hot butter sauce.

Moderate

Kardos. Dominikaner Bastei 8. ☎ **01/512-69-49.** Reservations recommended. Main courses 100–220AS ($8–$17). AE, DC, MC, V. Mon–Sat 11:30am–2:30pm and 6–11pm. Closed Aug. U-Bahn: Schwedenplatz. HUNGARIAN/SLOVENIAN/BALKAN.

This restaurant specializes in the strong flavors and mixed grills of the Great Hungarian Plain, turning out such traditional specialties as *hortobágyi palatschinken,* fish soup in the style of Lake Balaton, piquant little rolls known as *grammel* seasoned with minced pork and spices, and a choice of grilled meats. In an atmospheric cellar, the restaurant is filled with bold colors and Hungarian accessories, with a sense of Gypsy schmaltz. There's sometimes a strolling violinist during the winter months.

AT SCHOTTENRING

Inexpensive

Zum Schwarzen Kameel. Bognergasse 5. ☎ **01/533-81-25.** Main courses 160–290AS ($12–$22). MC, V. Mon–Fri 9am–8pm, Sat 8:30am–4pm. U-Bahn: Schottentor. Bus: 2A or 3A. INTERNATIONAL.

This restaurant has been in the same family since 1618. A delicatessen against one of the walls sells wine, liquor, and specialty meat items, although most of the action takes place in the cafe, which on Saturday mornings is packed with Viennese recovering from a late night with massive doses of caffeine. The restaurant beyond the cafe, with only 11 tables, is a perfectly preserved art nouveau room. Specialties include herring fillet Oslo, potato soup, tournedos, Roman saltimbocca (veal with ham), and daily fish specials, along with those old favorites like boiled ham on the bone, veal goulash, and *tafelspitz.*

SEEING THE SIGHTS OF VIENNA

The Inner City (*Innere Stadt*) is the tangle of streets from which Vienna grew in the Middle Ages. Much of your exploration will be confined to this area, encircled by the boulevards of "The Ring" and the Danube Canal. The main street of the Inner City is **Kärntnerstrasse,** most of which is a pedestrian mall. The heart of Vienna is **Stephansplatz,** the square on which St. Stephan's Cathedral sits.

SIGHTSEEING SUGGESTIONS FOR FIRST-TIME VISITORS

If You Have 1 Day   Begin at **St. Stephan's Cathedral** and from there branch out for a tour of the enveloping Inner City. But first climb the tower of the cathedral for a panoramic view of the city (you can also take an elevator to the top). Stroll down **Kärntnerstrasse,** the main shopping artery, and enjoy the 11am ritual of coffee in a grand cafe, such as the **Café Imperial.** In the afternoon, visit **Schönbrunn,** seat of the Hapsburg dynasty. Have dinner in a typical Viennese wine tavern.

If You Have 2 Days   On the second day, explore other major attractions of Vienna, including the **Hofburg,** the **Imperial Crypts,** and the **Kunsthistorisches Museum.** In the evening, attend an opera performance or some other musical event.

If You Have 3 Days   On your third day, try to attend a performance of either the **Spanish Riding School** (Tuesday through Saturday) or the **Vienna Boys' Choir** (singing at masses on Sunday). Explore the **Belvedere Palace** and its art galleries; stroll through the **Naschmarkt,** the city's major open-air market; and cap the day by a visit to one or more of Vienna's cabarets, wine bars, or beer cellars.

If You Have 4 or 5 Days   On day 4, take a tour of the **Vienna Woods** and then visit **Klosterneuburg Abbey,** the major abbey of Austria. Return to Vienna for an evening of fun.

On day 5, "mop up" all the attractions you missed on your first 4 days. These might include a visit to the **Graphische Sammlungen Albertina,** the most important graphic-arts collection in the world; and a walk through the **Stadtpark** at Parkring.

EXPLORING THE HOFBURG PALACE COMPLEX

The winter palace of the Hapsburgs, known for its vast, impressive courtyards, the **Hofburg** sits in the heart of Vienna. To reach it (you can hardly miss it), head up Kohlmarkt to Michaelerplatz 1, Burgring (☎ **01/587-55-54**). You can also take the U-Bahn to Herrengasse or tram no. 1, 2, D, or J to Burgring.

This complex of imperial edifices, the first of which was constructed in 1279, grew and grew as the empire did, so that today the Hofburg Palace is virtually a city within a city. The palace, which has withstood three major sieges and a great fire, is called simply *die Burg,* or "the palace," by Viennese. Of its more than 2,600 rooms, fewer than two dozen are open to the public.

✪ **Schatzkammer (Imperial Treasury).** Hofburg, Schweizerhof. ☎ **01/533-79-31.** Admission 100AS ($8) adults; 70AS ($5) children, seniors, and students. Wed–Mon 10am–6pm.

The Schatzkammer is the greatest treasury in the world. It's divided into two sections: the Imperial Profane and the Sacerdotal Treasuries. One part displays the crown jewels and an assortment of imperial riches and the other, of course, ecclesiastical treasures. The most outstanding exhibit in the Schatzkammer is the imperial crown, dating from 962. It's so big that, even though padded, it was likely to slip down over the ears of a Hapsburg at a coronation. Studded with emeralds, sapphires, diamonds, and rubies, this 1,000-year-old symbol of sovereignty is a priceless treasure. Also on display is the imperial crown worn by the Hapsburg rulers from 1804 to the end of the empire. You'll see the saber of Charlemagne and the holy lance from the 9th century. Among great Schatzkammer prizes is the Burgundian Treasure seized in the 15th century, rich in vestments, oil paintings, gems, and robes.

✪ **Kaiserappartements (Imperial Apartments).** Michaelerplatz 1. ☎ **01/533-75-70.** Admission 95AS ($7) adults, 75AS ($6) students under 25, 50AS ($3.85) children 6–15; children 5 and under free. Daily 9am–5pm.

The Hofburg complex also includes the Kaiserappartements, where the emperors and their wives and children lived, on the first floor. To reach these apartments, you enter via the rotunda of Michaelerplatz. The apartments are richly decorated with tapestries, many from Aubusson. The Imperial Silver and Porcelain Collection provides an insight to Hapsburg court etiquette. Most of these pieces are from the 18th and 19th centuries. Leopoldinischer Trakt (Leopold's apartments) date from the 17th century. These Imperial Apartments are more closely associated with Franz Josef than with any other emperor.

✪ **Hofmusikkapelle Wien (Vienna Boys' Choir).** Die Burgkapelle (Palace Chapel), Hofburg (entrance on Schweizerhof). ☎ **01/533-99-27.** Tickets, 60–350AS ($4.60–$27). Masses (performances) held only Jan–June and mid-Sept until the end of Dec, Sun and holidays at 9:15am.

Construction of this Gothic chapel began in 1447 during the reign of Emperor Frederick III, but it was subsequently massively renovated. From 1449, it was the private chapel of the royal family. Today the Burgkapelle is the home of the Hofmusikkapelle Wein, an ensemble consisting of the Vienna Boys' Choir and members of the Vienna State Opera chorus and orchestra. Written applications for reserved seats should be sent at least 8 weeks in advance of the time you wish to attend, but send no checks or money. For reservations, write to Verwaltung der Hofmusikkapelle, Hofburg, A-1010 Vienna. If you failed to reserve in advance, you may be lucky enough to secure tickets from a block sold at the Burgkapelle box office every Friday 3 to 5pm, but the queue starts lining up at least half an hour before that. Or you might settle for standing room (it's free).

Neue Burg. Heldenplatz. ☎ **01/521-770.** Admission to Hofjagd and Rüstkammer, Musikinstrumentensammlung, and Ephesos-Museum, 30AS ($2.30) adults, 15AS ($1.15) children. Hofjagd and Rüstkammer and Musikinstrumentensammlung and Ephesos-Museum, Wed–Mon 10am–6pm.

The last addition to the Hofburg complex was the Neue Burg (New Château). Construction was started in 1881 and continued until work was halted in 1913. The palace was the residence of Archduke Franz Ferdinand, the nephew and heir apparent of Franz Josef, whose assassination at Sarajevo set off the chain of events that led to World War I. The arms and armor collection is second only to that of the Metropolitan Museum of Art in New York. It's in the **Hofjagd and Rüstkammer,** on the second floor of the New Château. On display are crossbows, swords, helmets, pistols, and armor. Another section, the **Musikinstrumentensammlung** (☎ **01/521-77-470**), is devoted to musical instruments, mainly 17th- and 18th-century. In the

Ephesos-Museum (Museum of Ephesian Sculpture), Neue Burg 1, Heldenplatz, with an entrance behind the Prince Eugene monument (☎ **01/521-77-0**), you'll see the Parthian monument, the most important relief frieze from Roman times ever found in Asia Minor.

Graphische Sammlung Albertina. Augustinerstrasse 1. ☎ **01/53-483.** Admission 70AS ($5) adults, 35AS ($2.70) students; children under 11 free. Tues–Sun 10am–5pm.

The development of graphic arts since the 14th century is explored at this Hofburg museum, named for a son-in-law of Maria Theresa. It houses one of the world's greatest graphics collections, and the most outstanding treasure in the Albertina is the Dürer collection, though what you'll usually see are copies—the originals are shown only on special occasions. Here, you can see Dürer's *Praying Hands*, which has been reproduced throughout the world.

Augustinerkirche. Augustinerstrasse 3. ☎ **01/533-70-99.** Guided tour, 10AS (75¢) contribution. To arrange a visit, contact the church office, Pfarre St. Augustin, Augustinerstrasse 3, or the music office (☎ 01/533-69-63). The most convenient, and dramatic, time to visit is Sunday at 11am, when a high mass is celebrated, with choir, soloists, and orchestra.

This church was constructed in the 14th century as part of the Hofburg complex to serve as the parish church of the imperial court. In the latter part of the 18th century it was stripped of its baroque embellishments and returned to the original Gothic features. The Chapel of St. George, dating from 1337, is entered from the right aisle. The royal weddings of Maria Theresa and François of Lorraine (1736), Marie Antoinette and Louis XVI of France (1770), Marie-Louise of Austria to Napoléon (1810, but by proxy—he didn't show up), and Franz Josef and Elizabeth of Bavaria (1854) were all held here.

✪ **Spanische Hofreitschule (Spanish Riding School).** Michaelerplatz 1, Hofburg. ☎ **01/533-90-32.** Regular performances, 250–290AS ($19–$22) seats, 200AS ($15) standing room. Training performances with music, 100AS ($8). (Children under 3 not admitted, but children 3–6 attend free with adults.) Training session, 100AS ($8) adults, 30AS ($2.30) children. Regular performances, Apr–June and Sept, Sun 10:45am, most Weds 7pm. Training performances with music, Mar and Oct–Dec Sun at 10:45am. Apr–June and Sept–Oct Sat at 10am.

The Spanish Riding School is in the crystal-chandeliered white ballroom in an 18th-century building of the Hofburg complex. We always marvel at the skill and beauty of the sleek Lippizaner stallions as their adept trainers put them through their paces in a show that hasn't changed in 4 centuries. Reservations for performances must be made in advance, as early as possible. Order your tickets for the Sunday and Wednesday shows in writing to Spanische Reitschule, Hofburg, A-1010 Vienna (fax 43/1/535-01-86), or through a travel agency in Vienna. (Tickets for Saturday shows can be ordered only through a travel agency.) Tickets for training sessions with no advance reservations can be purchased at the entrance Innerer Burghof-In der Burg.

Lippizaner Museum. Reitschulgasse 2, Stallburg. ☎ **01/533-78-11.** Admission 70AS ($5) adults, 50AS ($3.85) children. Daily 9am–6pm. U-Bahn: Stephansplatz.

The latest attraction at the Hofburg is this museum near the stables of the famous white stallions. The exhibition begins with the historic inception of the Spanish Riding School in the 16th century and extends to the stallions' near destruction in the closing weeks of World War II. Exhibits such as paintings, historic engravings, drawings, photographs, uniforms and bridles, plus video and film presentations, bring to life the history of the Spanish Riding School, offering an insight into the breeding and training of these champion horses. Visitors to the museum are able to see through a window into the stallions' stables while they are being fed and saddled.

OTHER TOP ATTRACTIONS IN THE INNER CITY

✪ **Domkirche St. Stephan (St. Stephan's Cathedral).** Stephansplatz 1. ☎ **01/ 515-52-37-67.** Cathedral, free. Tour of catacombs 40AS ($3.10) adults, 15AS ($1.15) children under 15. North Tower 40AS ($3.10) adults, 15AS ($1.15) children under 15. South Tower 30AS ($2.30) adults, 10AS (75¢) children under 15. Two-hour evening tours, conducted only in German and including a visit to the roof, 130AS ($10) adults, 50AS ($3.85) children under 15. Cathedral open daily for prayer and contemplation 6–10pm, touristic visits Mon–Sat 9am–11:30pm and 1–4pm, Sun 1–4pm. English-language tour offered cathedral Mon–Sat (Mar–Oct only) at 3:45pm. Tour of catacombs Mon–Sun at half-hour intervals between 10am and 4:30pm. North Tower Oct–Mar daily 8:30am–5pm, Apr–Sept daily 9am–6pm. South Tower daily 9am–5:30pm. Between June and Sept, a special 2-hour evening tour is offered, in German only, at 7pm. Bus: 1A, 2A, or 3A. U-Bahn: Stephansplatz.

A basilica built on the site of a Romanesque sanctuary, the cathedral was founded in the 12th century in what even in the Middle Ages was the town's center. Stephansdom was virtually destroyed in a 1258 fire that swept through Vienna, and toward the dawn of the 14th century the ruins of the Romanesque basilica gave way to a Gothic building. The cathedral suffered terribly in the Turkish siege of 1683, but then was allowed a rest from destruction until the Russian bombardments of 1945. Reopened in 1948 after restoration, the cathedral is today one of the greatest Gothic structures in Europe, rich in wood carvings, altars, sculptures, and paintings. The steeple, rising some 450 feet, has come to symbolize the very spirit of Vienna. You can climb the 343-step south tower, which dominates the Viennese skyline and offers a view of the Vienna Woods. Called Alter Steffl (Old Steve), the tower with its needlelike spire was built between 1350 and 1433. The North Tower (Nordturm), reached by elevator, was never finished to match the South Tower, but was crowned in the Renaissance style in 1579. You view a panoramic sweep of the city and the Danube.

Gemäldegalerie Akademie der Bildenden Künste (Academy of Fine Arts). Schiller-platz 3. ☎ **01/58-816.** Admission 50AS ($3.85) adults and children. Tues–Sun 10am–4pm. U-Bahn: Karlsplatz.

When in Vienna, visit this painting gallery to see the *Last Judgment* by the incomparable Hieronymus Bosch. In this work, the artist conjured up all the demons of the nether regions for a terrifying view of the suffering and sins of humankind. There are many 15th-century Dutch and Flemish paintings and several works by Lucas Cranach, the Elder. The academy is noted for its 17th-century art by van Dyck, Rembrandt, Botticelli, and a host of others.

✪ **Kunsthistorisches Museum (Museum of Art History).** Maria-Theresien-Platz, Bur-gring 5. ☎ **01/525-24-0.** Admission 100AS ($8) adults, 70AS ($5) students and senior citizens, free for children under 11. Tues–Sun 10am–6pm. U-Bahn: Mariahilferstrasse. Tram: 52, 58, D, or J.

Across from the Hofburg Palace, this huge building houses many of the fabulous art collections gathered by the Hapsburgs when they added new territories to their empire. A highlight is the fine collection of ancient Egyptian and Greek art. The museum also has works by many of the greatest European masters, such as Velázquez and Titian.

ATTRACTIONS OUTSIDE THE INNER CITY

✪ **Schönbrunn Palace.** Schönbrunner Schlossstrasse. ☎ **01/811-13.** Admission 120AS ($9) adults, 105AS ($8) students under 25, 60AS ($4.60) children 6–15; children under 6 free. Apartments, Apr–Oct daily 8:30am–5pm; Nov–Mar daily 9am–4:30pm. U-Bahn: U4 (green line) to Schönbrunn.

A Hapsburg palace of 1,441 rooms, Schönbrunn was designed and built between 1696 and 1712 in a grand baroque style meant to surpass that of Versailles. When

Maria Theresa became empress in 1740, she changed the original plans, and the Schönbrunn we see today, with its delicate rococo touches, is her conception. It was the imperial summer palace during Maria Theresa's 40-year reign, the scene of great ceremonial balls and lavish banquets, and the fabulous receptions held here during the Congress of Vienna in 1815. The State Apartments are the most stunning. Much of the interior ornamentation is in $23^1/_2$-karat gold, and many porcelain tile stoves are in evidence. Of the 40 rooms that you can visit, particularly fascinating is the "Room of Millions," decorated with Indian and Persian miniatures, the grandest rococo salon in the world.

Österreichische Galerie Belvedere. Prinz-Eugen-Strasse 27. ☎ **01/795-57.** Admission 60AS ($4.60) adults, 30AS ($2.30) children. Tues–Sun 10am–5pm. Tram: D to Schloss Belvedere.

The Belvedere Palace was built as a summer home for Prince Eugene of Savoy and consists of two palatial buildings. The pond reflects the sky and palace buildings, which are made up of a series of interlocking cubes, and the interior is dominated by two great, flowing staircases. The Unteres Belvedere (Lower Belvedere), with its entrance at Rennweg 6A, was constructed from 1714 to 1716 and contains the Gold Salon, one of the palace's most beautiful rooms. It also houses the Barockmuseum (Museum of Baroque Art). The Oberes Belvedere (Upper Belvedere) was started in 1721 and completed in 1723. It contains the Gallery of 19th- and 20th-Century Art, with an outstanding collection of the works of Gustav Klimt (1862–1918); be sure to see his extraordinary *Judith*. The Museum of Medieval Austrian Art is in the Orangery.

ORGANIZED TOURS

Wiener Rundfahrten (Vienna Sightseeing Tours), Stelzhamergasse 4–11 (☎ **01/712-468-30;** U-Bahn: Landstrasse Wien Mitte), offers some of the best organized tours of Vienna and its surroundings. Tours depart from a signposted area in front of the State Opera and include running commentary in both German and English.

CITY TOURS   The historical city tour costs 400AS ($31) for adults and is free for children 12 and under. It's ideal for visitors who are pressed for time and yet want to be shown the major (and most frequently photographed) monuments of Vienna. It takes you past the historic buildings of Ringstrasse—the State Opera, Hofburg Palace, museums, Parliament, City Hall, Burgtheater, the University, and the Votive Church—into the heart of Vienna. Tours leave from the State Opera daily at 9:30 and 10:30am and at 2:30 and 4:30pm.

The company's **"Grand City Tour,"** a bus tour with commentary that includes an exterior view of the Belvedere Palace and a walk through Schönbrunn Palace, departs daily from the State Opera at 9:15am and 2:15am. From April to November, an additional tour is offered at 10:15am. The tour costs 400AS ($31) for adults and 200AS ($15) for children under 12.

TOURS OUTSIDE THE CITY   Looking to travel farther afield? Vienna Sightseeing's bus tour to the **"Vienna Woods and Mayerling"** includes a tour of Baden, a spa once favored by the Hapsburg aristocracy, and a stop at Mayerling, site of the still-unexplained sudden death of Crown Prince Rudolf (the only son of Austria's last emperor, Franz Josef) and his mistress, Baroness Maria Vetsera. The tour is long on schmaltz and nostalgia and costs 500AS ($39) for adults and 200AS ($15) for children.

If you're interested in visiting **Budapest,** once the co-capital of the Austro-Hungarian Empire, the company offers a full-day bus tour daily between April and October. The tour departs at 8am, returns at 8:30pm, and includes lunch and a

3-hour bus tour of Budapest's most evocative monuments. The cost is 1,300AS ($100) for adults and 1,000AS ($77) for children. Between November and March, the day trip to Budapest is offered only on Tuesday, Thursday, and Saturday.

THE SHOPPING SCENE

Vienna is known for the excellent quality of its works, including petit point and hand-painted porcelain. Also popular is loden, a boiled and rolled wool fabric made into overcoats, suits, and hats, as well as knitted sweaters. The most famous shopping streets are in the city center (First District), including **Kärntnerstrasse, Graben, Kohlmarkt,** and **Rotensturmstrasse.** Other shopping streets include Mariahilfer-strasse, Favoritenstrasse, and Landstrasser Hauptstrasse.

Albin Denk, Graben 13 (☎ 01/512-44-39; U-Bahn: Stephanplatz), is the oldest continuously operating porcelain store in Vienna, in business since 1702. You'll see thousands of objects from Meissen, Dresden, and other regions. The state-owned **Dorotheum,** Dorotheergasse 17 (☎ 01/515-60-0; U-Bahn: Stephanplatz), is the oldest auction house in Europe, dating from 1707, when it was founded by Emperor Josef I as an auction house where impoverished aristocrats could fairly (and anony-mously) get good value for their heirlooms. Today the Dorotheum is also the scene of many art auctions. If you're interested in what's being auctioned off, you give a small fee to a *sensal,* one of the licensed bidders, and he or she will bid in your name. Auc-tions are usually conducted every Monday to Saturday at 2pm, though in particularly busy periods, additional auctions might be held at 11am and at 3pm. Viewing of the pieces about to go on the block is possible every Monday to Friday 10am to 6pm and every Saturday 9am to 5pm.

Opened in 1830 by the Plankl family, **Loden Plankl,** Michaelerplatz 6 (☎ 01/533-80-32; U-Bahn: Stephanplatz), is the oldest and most reputable outlet in Vienna for traditional Austrian clothing. You'll find Austrian loden coats, shoes, trousers, dirndls, jackets, lederhosen, and suits for men, women, and children. The building, opposite the Hofburg, dates from the 17th century. The three-floor ✪ **Ö. W. (Österreichische Werkstatten),** Kärntnerstrasse 6 (☎ 01/512-24-18; U-Bahn: Stephanplatz), sells hundreds of handmade art objects from Austria. Some 200 leading artists and craftspeople throughout the country organized this cooperative to showcase their wares. It's easy to find, only half a minute's walk from St. Stephan's Cathedral.

VIENNA AFTER DARK

The best source of information about what's happening on the cultural scene is *Wien Monatsprogramm,* distributed free at tourist information offices and at many hotel reception desks. *Die Presse,* the Viennese daily, publishes a special magazine in its Thursday edition outlining the major cultural events for the coming week. It's in German but might still be helpful.

THE PERFORMING ARTS

OPERA & CLASSICAL MUSIC   Music is at the heart of the cultural life in Vienna. This has been true for a couple of centuries or so, and the city continues to lure com-posers, musicians, and music lovers. Vienna's opera is still the world's quintessential opera house, one of the three most important in the world.

When the **Staatsoper (State Opera),** Opernring 2 (☎ 01/514-44-29-60; U-Bahn: Karlsplatz), was bombed into a shell in World War II, the Viennese made its restoration their top priority, finishing it in time for the country's celebration of inde-pendence from occupying forces in 1955. A repertoire of some 40 works is given every season, with the Vienna Philharmonic in the pit and leading stars of the world on the stage. In their day, Gustav Mahler and Richard Strauss worked here as directors. The New Year usually starts off with a gala performance of *Die Fledermaus*. Tickets are 130 to 2,450AS ($10 to $189). Tours are offered two to five times daily, 40AS ($3.10) per person; tour times are posted on a board outside the entrance.

When the prestigious **Wiener Philharmoniker (Vienna Philharmonic)** is not traveling throughout the world, its home is the **Musikverein,** Bösendorferstrasse 12 (☎ **01/ 505-65-25;** U-Bahn: Karlsplatz). Opened in 1870, the concert hall is suitably ornate, and is the site of the famous New Year's Day concert, broadcast internationally. Tours are offered Wednesday to Monday at 1:30pm, 70AS ($6) adults, 50AS ($4) children 12 to 16, children under 12 free.

Besides the world-renowned Vienna Philharmonic, Vienna is home to three other major orchestras: the Vienna Symphony, the ÖRF Symphony Orchestra, and the Niederösterreichische Tonkünstler. The Wiener Sympohniker (Vienna Symphony) performs in the **Konzerthaus,** Lothringerstrasse 20 (☎ **01/712-12-11;** U-Bahn: Stadt-Park), a major concert hall with three auditoriums, also the venue for chamber music and a diversity of programs.

In summer when the state theaters are closed, the Vienna Opera Festival presents performances and movie screenings of highlights from past opera seasons. The venue is the plaza in front of City Hall, and everything is free.

THEATER   For performances in English, head to **Vienna's English Theatre,** Josefsgasse 12 (☎ **01/402-12-60;** U-Bahn: Rathaus). The **Burgtheater (National Theater),** Dr.-Karl-Lueger-Ring 2 (☎ **01/514-44-2959;** tram: J; bus: 13A), produces classical and modern plays, and even if you don't understand German, you might want to attend a performance here, especially if a familiar Shakespeare play is being staged. This is one of Europe's premier repertory theaters; it is the dream of every German-speaking actor to appear here. Tickets are 180AS to 480AS ($14 to $37).

NIGHTCLUBS, CABARETS, BARS & CASINOS

The noteworthy architect Adolf Loos designed the very dark, sometimes mysterious ✪ **Loos American Bar,** Kärntnerdurchgang 10 (☎ **01/512-3283;** U-Bahn: Stephansplatz), in 1908. Today it welcomes singles, couples who tend to be bilingual and very hip, and all manner of clients from the arts and media scene of Vienna. The mixologist's specialties include 15 kinds of martinis, plus 11 kinds of Manhattans. It's open Monday to Friday noon to 4am and Saturday to Sunday noon to 5am.; There's no cover.

Nestled into the vaulted early 20th-century niches created by the trusses of the U-Bahn, the hip, multicultural, and electronically sophisticated **Rhiz Bar Modern,** Llerchenfeldergürtel, 37–38 Stadtbahnbögen (☎ **01/409-2505;** U-Bahn: Josefstädterstrasse), is about 4km (2¹/₂ miles) west of St. Stephan's, a few blocks west of the Ring. Here, within the once-grimy architecture of the Industrial Revolution, a team of entrepreneurs installed stainless steel ventilation ducts, a green plastic bar, a sophisticated stereo system, and a TV camera that constantly broadcasts images of the hipster clientele over the Internet (www.rhiz.org) every night between 10pm and 3am. There's no cover.

Named after the patron saint of wine making, **St. Urbani-Keller,** Am Hof 12 (☎ **01/533-91-02;** U-Bahn: Stephansplatz or Herrengasse), this cellar is one of the most historic in Vienna, having opened in 1906. The artifacts inside include paneling in the German romantic style and fanciful wrought-iron lighting fixtures. The cellar has brick vaulting dating from the 13th century and sections of solid Roman walls you can admire while listening to the folk music at night. Open Monday to Friday 11am

Wine Tasting in the *Heurigen*

Heurigen are Viennese wine taverns, celebrated in operettas, films, and song. They are found on the outskirts of Vienna, principally in Grinzing (the most popular district) and in Sievering, Neustift, Nussdorf, or Heiligenstadt. **Grinzing** lies at the edge of the Vienna Woods, a 15-minute drive northwest of the center. Take tram no. 38 to Grinzing.

Only 20 minutes from Vienna, ✪ **Weingut Wolff,** Rathstrasse 50, Neustift (☎ **01/440-37-27**), is one of the most endurable and beloved of heurigen. Although aficionados claim the best are "deep in the countryside" of Lower Austria, this one comes closest on the borderline of Vienna to offering an authentic experience. In summer, you're welcomed to a flower-decked garden set against a backdrop of ancient vineyards. You can really fill up your platter here, with some of the best wursts (sausages), and roast meats (especially the delectable pork), as well as fresh salads. Find a table under a cluster of grapes and sample the fruity young wines, especially the Chardonnay, Sylvaner, and Gruner Veltliner. The tavern is open from Monday to Saturday 2pm to 1am and Sunday 11am to 1am, with main courses from 130 to 220AS ($10 to $17).

Altes Presshaus, Cobenzigasse 15 (☎ **01/320-02-03**), was established in 1527, the oldest continuously operating Heurige in Grinzing, with an authentic cellar you might ask to visit. The place has an authentic, smoked-stained character with wood paneling and antique furniture. The garden terrace blossoms throughout the summer. Meals cost 150 to 350AS ($12 to $27), with glasses of wine beginning at 30AS ($2.30). Try such heurigen-inspired fare as smoked pork shoulder, roast pork shank, sauerkraut, potatoes, and dumplings. Open March to December daily 4pm to midnight.

to 11pm and Saturday and Sunday 4 to 10pm; with no cover. Watch your step on the way up or down.

Volksgarten, entrances from the Heldenplatz and from Burgring 1 (☎ **01/533-05-180;** U-Bahn: Volkstheatre), is the largest and most diverse entertainment complex within Vienna's Ring. Established in 1946, it intersperses a series of dining and drinking emporiums within a labyrinth of rooms and outdoor spaces that interconnect into a happy-go-lucky maze. Many visitors prefer the area with the evergreen music, where Tyrolean and Bavarian oom-pah-pah music alternates with classic rock 'n' roll. A restaurant on the premises is open continuously 11am to midnight. Cover is 70AS ($5) for the evergreen music (8pm to 2am nightly), 80 to 150AS ($6 to $12) for the disco music (nightly 11pm to 4am).

Set on the city's main shopping thoroughfare, a 5-minute walk from the Bristol Hotel, **Casino Wien,** Esterházy Palace, Kärntnerstrasse 41 (☎ **01/512-48-36;** tram: 1, 2, or D), is the only casino in Vienna. You'll find gaming tables for French and American roulette, blackjack, poker, a dice game known as 7–11, and chemin de fer, as well as the ever-present slot machines and a bar. Men are encouraged to wear jackets and ties. It's open Monday to Thursday 9pm to 3am and Friday to Sunday 3pm to 4am; with no cover. You'll need to show your passport to enter.

GAY BARS

Alfi's Goldener Spiegel, Linke Wienzeile 46 (entrance on Stiegengasse; ☎ **01/58-66-608;** U-Bahn: Ketten Brückeng), is one of the most popular gay havens in

Vienna, attracting a lot of foreigners. It's a combination restaurant and bar. Food items, which include well-seasoned and well-prepared versions of Wiener schnitzel, are served Wednesday to Monday 7pm to 2am.

Alte Lampe, Heumühlgasse 13 (☎ **01/587-34-54;** U-Bahn: Ketten Brückeng), is the oldest gay bar in Vienna, established in the 1960s. Today's patrons listen to the same schmaltzy piano music that has been played here for years. Open Sunday, Wednesday, and Thursday 6pm to 1am, Friday and Saturday 8pm to 3am.

Frauencafé, Langegasse 11 (☎ **01/406-37-54;** U-Bahn: Rathaus), is exactly what a translation of its name would imply: A politically conscious cafe for lesbian and (to a lesser degree) heterosexual women who appreciate the company of other women. Established in 1977, it has an interior filled with magazines, newspapers, modern paintings, and an international female clientele. Open Tuesday to Saturday; in summer 8pm to 1am, in winter 7pm to 1am.

DAY TRIPS ALONG THE DANUBE

KLOSTERNEUBURG   On the northwestern outskirts of Vienna, this old market town is the site of **Klosterneuburg Abbey (Stift Klosterneuburg),** Stiftsplatz 1 (☎ **02243/411-0),** the most historically significant abbey in Austria. Its art treasures include the world-famous 12th-century enamel altar of Nikolaus of Verdun. The monastery also boasts the largest private library in Austria, with more than 1,250 handwritten books and many antique paintings. You can visit the monastery only as part of 1-hour guided tours daily 9am to noon and 2:30 to 5:30pm, costing 65AS ($5). Most tours are conducted in German with occasional brief English translations.

Getting There   By **car,** follow Route 14 northwest of Vienna along the south bank of the Danube. Otherwise, take the U-Bahn from the Westbahnhof heading for Heiligenstadt, where you can then board a bus marked Klosterneuburg.

HERZOGENBURG MONASTERY   Founded in the 12th century by a German bishop from Passau, this Augustinian monastery, A-3130 Herzogenburg (☎ **02782/83112),** lies 6km (7 miles) south of Traismauer and 16km (10 miles) south of the Danube. The present complex of buildings comprising the church and the abbey was reconstructed in the baroque style. Outstanding is the high altar and the series of 16th-century paintings on wood. The monastery is known for its library containing more than 80,000 works. Entrance costs 55AS ($4.25) for adults, 12AS (90¢) for students, 45AS ($3.45) for those over 65. You can wander around alone or participate in a guided tour, departing daily at 9am, 10am, 11am, and at 1pm, 2pm, 3pm, 4pm, and 5pm. The attraction is open only April to October daily 9am to 6pm. There's a wine tavern in the complex where you can eat platters of Austrian specialties and drink the product of local grapes.

Getting There   By **car,** head west from Vienna via Autobahn A-1, following the signs to Salzburg and Linz, exiting at the signposted turnoff for Heiligenkreuz.

KREMS   In the eastern part of the Wachau on the left bank of the Danube lies 1,000-year-old Krems. The city today encompasses Stein and Mautern, once separate towns. Krems is a mellow town of courtyards, old churches, and ancient houses in the heart of vineyard country, with some partially preserved town walls. Just as the Viennese flock to Grinzing and other suburbs to sample new wine in heurigen, so the people of the Wachau come here to taste the vintners' products, which appear in Krems earlier in the year.

The most interesting part of Krems today is what was once the little village of Stein. Narrow streets are terraced above the river, and the single main street, **Steinlanderstrasse,** is flanked with houses, many from the 16th century. The **Grosser Passauerhof,**

Steinlanderstrasse 76, is a Gothic structure decorated with an oriel. Another house, at Steinlanderstrasse 84, once the imperial tollhouse, combines Byzantine and Venetian elements.

The **Pfarrkirche St. Veith (parish church)** stands in the center of town at the Rathaus, reached by going along either Untere Landstrasse or Obere Landstrasse. Rich with gilt and statuary, it's the town's most visible church and the ecclesiastical centerpiece of the local parish.

The **Wein Stadt Museum Krems (Historical Museum of Krems),** Körnermarkt 14 (☎ **02732/801-567**), is in a restored Gothic-style Dominican monastery. It has a gallery displaying the paintings of Martin Johann Schmidt, a noted 18th-century artist better known as Kremser Schmidt. The museum is open March to November Tuesday to Sunday 1 to 6pm. Admission is 40AS ($3.10) for access to both areas of the museum.

Getting There　Krems is 80km (50 miles) west of Vienna and 29km (18 miles) north of St. Pölten. By **car,** drive north from Vienna along Autobahn A-22 until it splits into three roads near the town of Stockerau. Once here, drive due west along Route 3, following the signs into Krems.

Trains depart from both the Wien Nord Station and the Wien Franz-Josefs Bahnhof for Krems every 2 hours daily 8am until around 2pm. Many are direct, although some will require a transfer in the railway junctions of Absdorf-Hippersdorf or St. Pölten. The trip takes 1 to 1¹/₂ hours. Call ☎ **01/17-17** for schedules.

Between mid-May and late September, **river cruisers** depart westward from Vienna every Sunday at 8:30am en route to Passau, in Germany. They arrive upstream in Tulln around 11:15am, then continue westward to Krems, arriving there around 1:40pm. For more information, call the DDSG-Donaureisen Shipping Line in Vienna (☎ **01/588-800**) or the tourist office in either Tulln (Albrechtsgasse 32, ☎ **02272/658-36**) or Krems (Undstrasse 6, ☎ **02732/82676**).

DÜRNSTEIN   Less than 8km (5 miles) west of Krems is the loveliest town along the Danube, Dürnstein, which draws throngs of tour groups in summer. Terraced vineyards mark this as a Danube wine town, and the town's fortified walls are partially preserved.

The **ruins of a castle fortress,** 520 feet above the town, are a link with the Crusades. Here Richard the Lion-Hearted of England was held prisoner in 1193. You can visit the ruins if you don't mind a vigorous climb (allow an hour). The castle isn't much, but the view of Dürnstein and the Wachau is more than worth the effort.

The 15th-century **Pfarrkirche (parish church)** also merits a visit. The building was originally an Augustinian monastery, reconstructed in the baroque style; the church tower is the finest baroque example in the whole country.

Getting There   By **car,** take Route 3 west from Krems. **Train** travel to Dürnstein from Vienna requires a transfer in Krems (see above). In Krems, trains depart approximately every 2 hours on routes that parallel the northern bank of the Danube on their way to Linz. These departures connect with trains from Vienna. Call ☎ **01/17-17** in Vienna for information.

About eight **buses** a day travel between Krems and Dürnstein, some of which coordinate with the arrival time of one of the many daily trains from Vienna. The bus trip between Krems and Dürnstein takes 20 minutes.

MELK   One of the chief sightseeing goals of every visitor to Austria is Melk. In the words of Empress Maria Theresa, "If I had never come here, I would have regretted it." Melk's major attractions are the **Melk Abbey,** Dietmayerstrasse 1 (☎ **02752/523-12**), one of the finest baroque buildings in the world, and the **Stiftskirche** (abbey church).

The rock-strewn bluff where the abbey now stands overlooking the river was the seat of the Babenbergs, who ruled Austria from 976 until the Hapsburgs took over in 1278. The abbey's influence as a center of learning and culture spread all over Austria, a fact familiar to readers of the Umberto Eco's *The Name of the Rose.* Most of the design of the present abbey was by the baroque architect Jakob Prandtauer. The Marmorsaal (marble hall) contains pilasters coated in red marble. Despite all this adornment, the abbey takes second place in lavish glory to the **Stiftskirche,** the golden abbey church, damaged by fire in 1947 but now almost completely restored.

The abbey is open daily, with tours leaving at 15- to 20-minute intervals 9am to 5pm (to 4pm October to March). Guides make efforts to translate into English a running commentary that is otherwise German. Adults pay 85AS ($7) for guided tours and 65AS ($5) for unguided tours; children 50AS ($3.85) and 30AS ($2.30), and family tickets are available for 170AS ($13) with two children under 15.

Getting There   By **car,** drive about 88km (55 miles) west of Vienna, along Autobahn A-1, on the right bank of the Danube. Melk marks the western terminus of the Wachau, lying upstream from Krems. Trains leave frequently from Vienna's Westbahnhof to Melk, with two brief stops; the trip takes about 1 hour.

2 Salzburg & Environs

A baroque city on the banks of the Salzach River, set against a mountain backdrop, Salzburg is the beautiful capital of the state of Salzburg. The city and the river were named after its early residents earned their living in the salt mines. In this "heart of the heart of Europe," Mozart was born in 1756, and the composer's association with the city beefs up tourism.

The **Old Town** lies on the left bank of the river, where a monastery and bishopric were founded in 700. From that start, Salzburg grew in power and prestige, becoming an archbishopric in 798. In the heyday of the prince-archbishops, the city became known as the "German Rome." Responsible for much of its architectural grandeur are those masters of the baroque, Fischer von Erlach and Lukas von Hildebrandt.

The city of Mozart, "Silent Night," and *The Sound of Music*—Salzburg lives essentially off its rich past. Site of the world's snobbiest summer musical festival, it is a front-ranking cultural Mecca for classical music year-round. Its natural setting among alpine peaks on both banks of the Salzach River gives it the backdrop needed to perpetuate its romantic image.

One of Europe's greatest tourist capitals, most of Salzburg's day-to-day life spins around promoting its music and its other connections. Although *The Sound of Music* was filmed way back in 1964, this Julie Andrews blockbuster has become a cult attraction and is definitely alive and well in Salzburg. Ironically, Austria was the only country in the world where the musical failed when it first opened. It played for only a single week in Vienna, closing after audiences dwindled.

Salzburg is only a short distance from the Austrian-German frontier, so it's convenient for exploring many of the nearby attractions of Bavaria (see chapter 7). On the northern slopes of the Alps, the city is at the intersection of traditional European trade routes and is well served today by air, autobahn, and rail.

ORIENTATION

ARRIVING **By Plane** The **Salzburg Airport,** Innsbrucker Bundesstrasse 95 (☎ 0662/8580), lies 3km (2 miles) southwest of the city center. It has regularly scheduled service to all Austrian airports, as well as to Frankfurt, Amsterdam, Brussels, Berlin, Dresden, Düsseldorf, Hamburg, Paris, and Zurich. Major airlines serving the Salzburg Airport are **Austrian Airlines** (☎ 0662/85-45-11), **Lauda Air** (☎ 0662/85-63-64), **Air France** (☎ 0662/17-89), **Lufthansa** (☎ 0662/88580), and **Tyrolean** (☎ 0662/85-45-33).

Bus no. 77 runs between the airport and the main rail station of Salzburg. The bus departs every 30 minutes during the day, and the trip takes 20 minutes and costs 20AS ($1.55) one way. A taxi takes about 15 minutes, and you're likely to pay at least 150AS ($12).

By Train Salzburg's main rail station, the **Salzburg Hauptbahnhof,** Südtirolerplatz (☎ 0662/8887-3163), is on the major rail lines of Europe, with frequent arrivals from all the main cities of Austria and European cities such as Munich. Between 5:05am and 8:05pm, trains arrive every 30 minutes from Vienna (trip time: $3^1/_2$ hours). There are eight daily trains from Innsbruck (trip time: 2 hours). For central rail information, call ☎ 0662/17-17. Trains also arrive every 30 minutes from Munich (trip time: $2^1/_2$ hours).

From the train station, buses depart to various parts of the city, including the Altstadt. Or you can walk from the rail station to the Altstadt in about 20 minutes. Taxis are also available, and the rail station has a currency exchange and storage lockers.

By Car   Salzburg is 334km (209 miles) southwest of Vienna and 152km (95 miles) east of Munich. It's reached from all directions by good roads, including Autobahn **A-8** from the west (Munich), **A-1** from the east (Vienna), and **A-10** from the south. **Route 20** comes into Salzburg from points north and west, and **Route 159** serves towns and cities from the southeast.

VISITOR INFORMATION   The **Salzburg Information Office,** Mozartplatz 5 (☎ **0662/88987-330**), is open in July to September daily 9am to 8pm and off-season Monday to Saturday 9am to 6pm. The office makes hotel reservations for a 7.2% deposit plus a 30AS ($2.30) booking fee for two people. To reach it, take bus no. 5, 6, or 51 into the center. There's also a tourist information office on Platform 2A of the Hauptbahnhof, Südtirolerplatz (☎ **0662/88987-340**).

CITY LAYOUT   Most of what visitors come to see lies on the left bank of the Salzach River in the **Altstadt** (Old Town). If you're driving, you must leave your car in the modern part of town—the right bank of the Salzach—and descend on foot to the Altstadt pedestrian zone.

The heart of the inner city is **Residenzplatz,** with the largest and finest baroque fountain this side of the Alps. On the western side of the square stands the **Residenz,** palace of the prince-archbishops, and on the southern side of the square is the **Salzburg Cathedral (Dom).** To the west of the Dom lies **Domplatz,** linked by archways dating from 1658. The squares to the north and south appear totally enclosed.

On the southern side of Max-Reinhardt-Platz and Hofstallgasse, toward **Mönchsberg**—a mountain ridge slightly less than 3km (2 miles) long—stands the **Festspielhaus** (Festival Theater).

GETTING AROUND   **By Bus/Tram**   A quick, comfortable service is provided by city buses through the center of the city from the Nonntal parking lot to Sigsmundsplatz, the city-center car park. Fares for one ride are 20AS ($1.55) adult, 11AS (85¢) children 6 to 15; those 5 and under travel free. *Be warned:* Buses stop running at 11pm.

By Taxi   You'll find taxi stands scattered at key points all over the city center and in the suburbs. To order a taxi in advance, call **Salzburg Funktaxi-Vereinigung** (radio taxis), Rainerstrasse 27 (☎ **0662/8111**). Taxi fares start at 30AS ($2.30).

By Car   Driving a car in Salzburg isn't recommended. However, you'll probably want a car for touring around Salzburg, as using public transportation can be time consuming. Arrangements for car rentals are always best if made in advance. Try **Avis**

Traveler's Tip

The **Salzburg Card** not only entitles you to use **public transportation** but also acts as an **admission ticket** to the city's most important cultural sights and institutions. With it, you can visit Mozart's birthplace, the Hohensalzburg fortress, the Residenz gallery, the water fountain gardens at Hellbrunn, the Baroque Museum in the Mirabell Garden, and the gala rooms in the Archbishop's Residence. The card can also be used to take in sights outside town, such as Hellbrunn Zoo, the open-air museum in Grossingmain, the salt mines of the Dürnberg, and a gondola trip at Untersberg. You'll also receive a brochure with maps and sightseeing hints. Cards are valid for 24, 48, and 72 hours and cost 200AS ($15), 290AS ($22), and 380AS ($29), respectively. Children up to 15 receive a 50% discount. You can buy the pass from Salzburg travel agencies, hotels, tobacconists, and municipal offices.

Salzburg

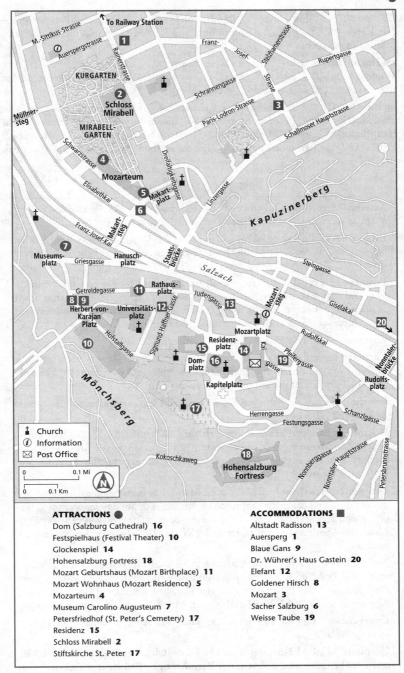

Church ✝
Information ⓘ
Post Office ✉

0   0.1 Mi
0   0.1 Km

ATTRACTIONS ●

Dom (Salzburg Cathedral) **16**
Festspielhaus (Festival Theater) **10**
Glockenspiel **14**
Hohensalzburg Fortress **18**
Mozart Geburtshaus (Mozart Birthplace) **11**
Mozart Wohnhaus (Mozart Residence) **5**
Mozarteum **4**
Museum Carolino Augusteum **7**
Petersfriedhof (St. Peter's Cemetery) **17**
Residenz **15**
Schloss Mirabell **2**
Stiftskirche St. Peter **17**

ACCOMMODATIONS ■

Altstadt Radisson **13**
Auersperg **1**
Blaue Gans **9**
Dr. Wührer's Haus Gastein **20**
Elefant **12**
Goldener Hirsch **8**
Mozart **3**
Sacher Salzburg **6**
Weisse Taube **19**

(☎ **0662/877278**) or **Hertz** (☎ **0662/876674**), both at Ferdinand-Porsche-Strasse 7 and open Monday to Friday 8am to 6pm and Saturday 8am to 1pm. A 21.2% tax is added to car rentals.

By Horse-Drawn Cab   There are horse-drawn cabs (*fiakers*) at Residenzplatz. Four people usually pay 350AS ($27) for 20 minutes or 680AS ($52) for 50 minutes. But all fares are subject to negotiation, of course.

By Bicycle   City officials have developed a network of bicycle paths, which are indicated on city maps. Between April and November, bicycles can be rented at the **Hauptbahnhof,** Desk 3 (☎ **0662/8887-3163**), on Südtirolerplatz. The cost is about 150AS ($12) per day, unless you have a rail ticket; then you pay 100AS ($8) per day.

Fast Facts: Salzburg

American Express   The office is at Mozartplatz 5–7 (☎ **0662/8080**), open Monday to Friday 9am to 5:30pm and Saturday 9am to noon.

Baby-Sitters   English-speaking students at the University of Salzburg often baby-sit; call ☎ **0662/8044-6001.** Make arrangements as far in advance as possible.

Business Hours   Most shops and stores are open Monday to Friday 9am to 6pm and Saturday, usually 9am to noon. Some of the smaller shops shut down at noon for a lunch break. Salzburg observes *langer Samstag,* which means that most stores stay open until 5pm on selected Saturdays.

Currency   See "Fast Facts: Vienna" in section 1.

Currency Exchange   Banks are open Monday to Friday 8am to noon and 2 to 4:30pm. You can exchange money at the Hauptbahnhof on Südtirolerplatz daily 7am to 10pm and at the airport daily 9am to 4pm.

Dentists   For an English-speaking dentist, call **Dentistenkammer,** Faberstrasse 2 (☎ **0662/87-34-66**).

Doctors   Call **Ärztekammer für Salzburg** (☎ **0662/87-13-27**). For emergencies, the **Medical Emergency Center,** Paris-London-Strasse 8A (☎ **141**), is on duty 7pm Friday to 7am Monday; it's also open on public holidays. See also "Hospitals" below.

Drugstores (Apotheke)   They're open Monday to Friday 8am to 12:30pm and 2:30 to 6pm and Saturday 8am to noon. For night or Sunday service, shops display a sign giving the address of the nearest open pharmacy. You can also go to **Elisabeth-Apotheke,** Elisabethstrasse 1 (☎ **0662/87-14-84**), near the railway station.

Embassies/Consulates   The Consular Agency of the **United States** at Altermarkt (☎ **0662/84-87-76**) is open Monday, Wednesday, and Thursday 9am to noon to assist U.S. citizens with emergencies. The Consulate of **Great Britain** at Altermarkt 4 (☎ **0662/84-81-33**) is open Monday to Friday 9am to noon.

Emergencies   Call ☎ **133** for police, ☎ **122** to report a fire, and ☎ **144** for an ambulance.

Hospitals   **Unfahl Hospital** is on Dr.-Franz-Rehrl-Platz (☎ **0662/65-80-0**), and **Krankenhaus und Konvent der Barmherzigen Brüder** is at Kajetanerplatz 1 (☎ **0662/80-88-0**).

Internet Access   Visit the **Cybercafe,** Gstätteng 29 (☎ **0662/84-26-16-22**), open Monday to Thursday 2 to 11pm and Friday to Sunday 2pm to 1am.

Post Office   The main post office is at Residenzplatz 9 (☎ **0662/844-1210**), open Monday to Friday 7am to 7pm and Saturday 8 to 10am. The post office at the main rail station is open 24 hours.

Telephone   The **country code** for Austria is **43.** The **city code** for Salzburg is **662;** use this code when you're calling from outside Austria. If you're within Austria, use **0662.** Phone numbers in Salzburg are undergoing a change. If you can't reach a number we've listed, dial 11181 for information if you're within Austria. If calling from outside Austria, dial 11813 for information.

WHERE TO STAY
ON THE LEFT BANK (ALTSTADT)
Very Expensive
Altstadt Radisson. Rudfolkskai 28 & Judengasse 15, A-5020 Salzburg. ☎ **800/333-3333** in the U.S., or 0662/848-571. Fax 0662/848-571-6. 60 units. MINIBAR TV TEL. Low season: 2,800–3,400AS ($216–$262) double; 4,950–7,800AS ($381–$601) suite. High season: 5,000–6,600AS ($385–$508) double; 7,400–9,800AS ($570–$755) suite. Rates include buffet breakfast. AE, DC, MC, V. Parking 300AS ($23).

This is not your typical Radisson property—in fact, it's a radical departure for the chain in style and charm. Dating from 1377, it's a luxuriously and elegantly converted Altstadt hostelry, with a second entrance on Judengasse. Its closest rival in town is the old-world Golener Hirsch, to which it comes in second. The old and new are blended in perfect harmony here, and the historic facade conceals top-rate comforts and amenities. The cozy antique-filled lobby sets the tone. In a structure of this size, bedrooms naturally vary greatly in size, but all have a certain charm and sparkle, and are exceedingly comfortable with some of the city's best beds. Overlooking the river, the Restaurant Symphonie is one of the best hotel dining rooms in the city.

✪ **Goldener Hirsch.** Getreidegasse 37, A-5020 Salzburg. ☎ **800/325-3535** in the U.S., or 0662/8084. Fax 0662/8485-178-45. www.goldenerhirsh.com. E-mail: welcome@ goldenerhirsch.com. 69 units. A/C MINIBAR TV TEL. 4,500–4,900AS ($347–$377) double; from 7,550AS ($581) suite. Higher rates reflect prices at festival time (1st week of Apr and mid-July to Aug). AE, DC, MC, V. Valet parking 350AS ($27). Bus: 55.

The award for the finest hotel in Salzburg goes to this place, steeped in legend and with a history dating from 1407, though it was last renovated in 1997. Near Mozart's birthplace, the hotel is composed of four medieval town houses, three of which are joined together in a labyrinth of rustic hallways and staircases. The fourth, called "The Coppersmith's House," is across the street and contains 17 charming spacious rooms. All rooms are beautifully furnished and maintained. The hotel is home to two of the most important restaurants of Salzburg. Its charm and personal service are outstanding.

Moderate
Blaue Gans. Getreidegasse 41–43, A-5020 Salzburg. ☎ **0662/84-13-17.** Fax 0662/84-13-179. www.blauegans.at. E-mail: office@blauegans.at. 45 units. TV TEL. 1,250–1,950AS ($96–$150) double. Rates include breakfast. AE, DC, MC, V. Parking 168AS ($13). Bus: 1 or 2.

Only a short walk from the much more expensive Goldener Hirsch, the much-renovated "Blue Goose" has been functioning as an inn for more than 400 years within a 500-year-old building. Bedrooms were renovated between 1995 and 1998. Each is cozy, comfortable, and in many cases, contains a TV. All have good beds with firm mattresses. On the premises is the Stadtgasthof Blaue Gans, which functions of as a cafe, a beer hall, and a cozy and conservatively traditional bistro.

Elefant. Sigmund-Haffner-Gasse 4, A-5020 Salzburg. ☎ **0662/84-33-97.** Fax 0662/84-01-0928. E-mail: reception@elefant.at. 35 units. MINIBAR TV TEL. 1,555–2,275AS ($120–$175) double. Rates include buffet breakfast. AE, DC, MC, V. Parking 100AS ($8). Bus: 1, 5, 6, or 51.

Near the Rathaus in the Old Town, in a quiet alley off Getreidegasse, is this well-established family run hotel. It's one of the most ancient buildings of Salzburg—more than 700 years old—but was last renovated in 1992. One of our favorite rooms is the vaulted Bürgerstüberl, where high wooden banquettes separate the tables. The well-furnished and high-ceilinged bedrooms have radios, safes, and hair dryers.

Inexpensive

Weisse Taube. Kaigasse 9, A-5020 Salzburg. ☎ **0662/84-24-04.** Fax 0662/84-17-83. www.weissetaube.at. E-mail: hotel@weissetaube.at. 31 units. MINIBAR TV TEL. 1,220–1,820AS ($94–$140) double. Rates include breakfast. AE, DC, MC, V. Parking garage 120AS ($9). Bus: 5, 51, or 55.

"The White Dove" is a few steps from Mozartplatz in the pedestrian zone of the Old Town, but you can drive up to it to unload baggage. Constructed in 1365, the Weisse Taube has been owned by the Haubner family since 1904. Some of the public rooms contain the original massive ceiling beams, but the bedrooms were renovated in the 1990s and are comfortably streamlined, with traditional furnishings, including frequently renewed beds. The hotel has a TV room and a bar.

ON THE RIGHT BANK
Expensive

Sacher Salzburg. Schwarzstrasse 5–7, A-5020 Salzburg. ☎ **800/223-6800** in the U.S. and Canada, or 0662/889-77. Fax 0662/889-77-551. www.sacher.com. E-mail: oehof@sacher.com. 120 units. A/C MINIBAR TV TEL. 2,700–4,200AS ($208–$323) double; from 14,000AS ($1,078) suite. Rates include buffet breakfast. AE, DC, MC, V. Parking 320AS ($25). Bus: 1, 5, 29, or 51.

Built as the Hotel d'Autriche in 1866, this hotel has survived the toils of war and has been renovated countless times. A new era began when the Gürtler family, owners of the Hotel Sacher in Vienna, took over in 1988. A year-long renovation has turned the hotel into a jewel amid the villas on the riverbank. The cheerful rooms are well furnished, quite spacious, and individually decorated. Try to reserve one overlooking the river. A host of drinking and dining facilities is available, including the Roter Salon, an elegant dining room facing the river, and the Zirbelzimmer, an award-winning wood-paneled restaurant.

Moderate

✪ **Auersperg.** Auerspergstrasse 61, A-5027 Salzburg. ☎ **0662/889-44-0.** Fax 0662/889-44-55. www.auesperg.at. E-mail: hotel.auersperg@magnet.at. 63 units. MINIBAR TV TEL. 1,260–2,280AS ($97–$176) double; 1,660–2,480AS ($128–$191) suite. Rates include breakfast. AE, DC, MC, V. Free parking. Bus: 15 from the train station.

With its own sunny gardens, this traditional family- run hotel consists of two buildings, a main structure and a less expensive annex. There's an old-fashioned look of charm wherever you go, from the reception hall with its molded ceilings to the antique-filled drawing room. The warm, cozy, and large rooms are especially inviting, with excellent beds and well-equipped bathrooms with hair dryers. The hotel also has a good restaurant, bar, sauna, and steam bath. Its fitness center is on the top floor with a roof terrace offering panoramic views of Salzburg.

Dr. Wührer's Haus Gastein. Ignaz-Rieder-Kai 25, A-5020 Salzburg. ☎ **0662/62-25-65.** Fax 0662/62-25-659. E-mail: gastein@salzburginfoor.at. 13 units. MINIBAR TV TEL.

1,400–2,100AS ($108–$162) double; from 3,000AS ($231) suite. Rates include breakfast. MC, V. Parking 300AS ($23). Bus: 49.

This prosperous-looking Teutonic villa, amid calm scenery on the bank of the Salzach River, was built as a private home in 1953. Guests appreciate the spacious flowering garden, a setting for breakfast or afternoon tea. The interior is sparsely but pleasantly furnished. Bedrooms—often quite large—contain cozy Salzburg furniture crafted by regional artisans. Many accommodations have private balconies.

Mozart. Franz-Josef-Strasse 27, A-5020, Salzburg. ☎ **0662/87-22-74.** Fax 0662/87-00-79. www.hotel-mozart.at. E-mail: hotel-mozart.sbg@magnet.at. 33 units. MINIBAR TV TEL. 1,560–2,060AS ($120–$159) double. Rates include breakfast. AE, DC, MC, V. Closed Jan–Mar. Free parking. Bus: 15, 27, or 29.

The Mozart is a comfortable family- run hotel, a 10-minute walk from the train station and 5 minutes from the Linzergasse and the famous Mirabell Garden. Bedrooms are often sunny and have all the standard amenities, including duvet-covered twin beds with firm mattresses and tiled bathrooms equipped with hair dryers. The hotel prides itself in its careful service and courteously attentive staff.

WHERE TO DINE

Two special desserts you'll want to sample while here are the famous *Salzburger nockerln,* a light mixture of stiff egg whites, as well as the elaborate confection known as the *Mozart-Kugeln,* with bittersweet chocolate, hazelnut nougat, and marzipan. You'll also want to taste the beer in one of the numerous Salzburg breweries.

ON THE LEFT BANK (ALTSTADT)
Very Expensive
Goldener Hirsch. Getreidegasse 37. ☎ **0662/8084-861.** Reservations required. Main courses 290–420AS ($22–$32); 5-course fixed-price menu 690AS ($53). AE, DC, MC, V. Daily noon–2:30pm and 6:30–9:30pm. Bus: 55. AUSTRIAN/VIENNESE.

The best restaurant in Salzburg's best hotel attracts the brightest luminaries of the international music and business community. It's staffed with a superb team of chefs and waiters who preside over an atmosphere of elegant simplicity. Specialties include parfait of smoked trout in a mustard-dill sauce, saddle of venison in a cranberry cream sauce, veal in saffron sauce, roast fillet of char with dill mustard and asparagus, *tafelspitz* (boiled beef), and roast duck in its own gravy. Dishes are impeccably prepared and beautifully served.

Expensive
✪ **Alt-Salzburg.** Bürgerspitalgasse 2. ☎ **0662/84-14-76.** Reservations required. Main courses 120–250AS ($9–$19); fixed-price menu 480–560AS ($37–$43). AE, DC, MC, V. Mon 6–11:30pm, Tues–Sat 11:30am–2pm and 6–11:30pm (to midnight in Aug). Closed Feb 3–16. Bus: 1, 15, or 49. AUSTRIAN/INTERNATIONAL.

This restaurant, a bastion of formal service and refined cuisine, offers a retreat into old-world elegance. The building, right in the town center, dates from 1648 and has a wood-ceilinged room, crafted to reveal part of the chiseled rock of the Mönchsberg. Main dishes include lamb chops in red-wine sauce; fillet of river char sautéed with tomatoes, mushrooms, capers, spinach, and potatoes; and saddle of venison with morel-flavored cream sauce with red cabbage and dumplings.

Purzelbaum. Zugallistrasse 7. ☎ **0662/84-88-43.** Reservations required. Main courses 270–290AS ($21–$22); 4-course fixed-price menu 540AS ($42). AE, DC, MC, V. Mon 6–11pm; Tues–Sat noon–2pm and 6–11pm. Bus: 55. AUSTRIAN/VIENNESE.

In a residential neighborhood, this restaurant is near a duck pond at the bottom of a steep incline leading up to Salzburg Castle. Guests reserve tables in one of the three

Cafe Society

The ✪ **Café-Restaurant Glockenspiel,** Mozartplatz 2 (☎ **0662/84-14-03-0;** bus: 55), is the city's most popular cafe, with about 100 tables with armchairs out front. You might want to spend an afternoon here, particularly when there's live chamber music. Upon entering, you can't miss a glass case filled with every caloric delight west of Vienna. Coffee starts at 35AS ($2.70) and comes in many varieties, including Maria Theresa, which contains orange liqueur. Summer hours are daily 9am to midnight (food served to 11pm); the rest of the year hours are daily 9am to 7pm (food served to 6pm). It's closed the second and third weeks of November and January.

Opened in 1705, ✪ **Café Tomaselli,** Altermarkt 9 (☎ **0662/84-44-88;** bus: 2, 5, 6, 51, or 55), opens onto one of the Altstadt's most charming cobblestone squares. Aside from the outdoor summer chairs, you'll find inside a room with many tables and lots of elegant conversation among the haute bourgeoisie. A waiter brings a pastry tray filled with 40 kinds of cakes. Other menu items include omelets, wursts, ice cream, and a wide range of drinks. Pastries begin at 27AS ($2.10), and the most elaborate cakes cost 39AS ($3). Coffee costs 38AS ($2.95) for a mélange. It's open Monday to Saturday 7am to 9pm and Sunday and holidays 8am to 9pm (closed 5 days in January).

rooms containing marble buffets from a French buttery and art nouveau ceilings. Menu items change according to the inspiration of the chef. Look for venison in red-wine sauce, sole meunière, beefsteak cooked in a savory casserole or grilled and served with pepper sauce, and the house specialty, scampi Grüstl, composed of fresh shrimp with sliced potatoes and baked with herbs in a casserole.

Moderate

Café Winkler. Mönchsberg Terrace, Mönchsberg. ☎ **0662/847-738.** Reservations recommended for meals, not for cafe items. Main courses 120–320AS ($9–$25). AE, DC, MC, V. Tues–Sun noon–2pm and 6–11pm. Limited food items available Tues–Sun 2–6pm. Also open Mon (same hours) during Salzburg Festival. Access via the Mönchsberg elevator. INTERNATIONAL.

On the rocky Mönchsberg Terrace in an isolated position high above the city, the Winkler was built during the 1950s and has been drawing tourists like a magnet ever since. Ringed with large expanses of glass, it offers the best panoramas in Salzburg. The menu is broad enough to satisfy someone who wants a full Austrian meal or merely a caffeine fix. If you wish to dine, an employee will whip out a tablecloth and silverware, take your order, and provide a menu listing dishes that include a gratin of scampi; fillet steaks with peppercorns or with mushroom sauce; or saddle of venison with a sauce made from seasonal berries. The food is surprisingly good for such a touristy place.

Inexpensive

Festungsrestaurant. Hohensalzburg Schloss, Mönchsberg 34. ☎ **0662/84-17-80.** Reservations required July–Aug. Main courses 125–250AS ($10–$19). MC, V. Apr–May and Oct daily 10am–8pm, June–Sept daily 10am–10pm, Nov–Mar Wed–Sun 10am–5pm. Funicular from the Old Town. SALZBURG/AUSTRIAN.

Since the Middle Ages, this pair of solid dining rooms has been dispensing food and drink to archbishops, priests, servants, travelers, and (during wartime) soldiers and their commanders. The compound is poised 400 feet above the Altstadt and the Salzach River, with a panoramic view over the spires and cupolas of the city and its nearby alpine peaks. In warm weather, tables are set up within nearby gardens. The menu presents well-flavored and time-tested cuisine that includes *Salzburger bierfleische* (goulashlike stew) and a succulent version of *Salzburger schnitzel* (pork scallop stuffed with mushrooms, bacon, and tomatoes).

✪ **Humboldtstube.** Gstättengasse 6. ☎ **0662/843-171.** Reservations recommended. Main courses 95–145AS ($7–$11); set menus 90–120AS ($7–$9). AE, DC, MC, V. Daily 11am–1am. Bus: 1 or 2. AUSTRIAN.

This restaurant, in a building from 1492, is a charming evocation of old-fashioned Austria. A staff of hardworking, and sometimes harassed, women carry heaping platters that most older Austrians remember from their childhood. Examples include goulash soup; Wiener schnitzels or pork schnitzels; roasted beef with onions; noodles flavored with ham, cheese, mushrooms, herbs, and onions; and the dessert most closely associated with Salzburg, Salzburger nockerln. Be alert to the appeal of the well-supplied salad bar.

Krimpelstätter. Müllner Hauptstrasse 31. ☎ **0662/43-22-74.** Reservations recommended. Main courses 79–265AS ($6–$20). No credit cards. Tues–Sat 11:45am–2pm and 6pm–midnight (and on Mon, May–Sept). Closed 3 weeks in Jan. Bus: 49 or 95. SALZBURGER/AUSTRIAN.

An enduring Salzburg favorite dating from 1548, it was constructed as an inn. In summer, the beer garden, full of roses and trellises, attracts up to 300 visitors at a time. If you want a snack, a beer, or a glass of wine, head for the paneled door marked *Gastezimmer* in the entry corridor. If you're looking for a more formal, less visited area, three cozy antique dining rooms sit atop a flight of narrow stone steps. The menu offers the same dishes in each of the different areas, a hearty Salzburg regional cuisine featuring homemade sausages, spinach noodles, and wild game dishes.

Sternbräu Gastronomie Welt. Griesgasse 23. ☎ **0662/84-21-40.** Main courses 90–155AS ($7–$12); fixed-price 145–210AS ($11–$16). AE, DC, MC. Daily 9am–midnight. Bus: 2, 5, 12, 49, or 51. AUSTRIAN.

This place seems big enough to have fed half the Austro-Hungarian army, with a series of rooms that follow one after the other in varying degrees of formality. The Hofbräustübl is a rustic fantasy. You can also eat in the chestnut tree–shaded beer garden, usually packed on a summer's night, or under the weathered arcades of an inner courtyard. Daily specials include typical Austrian dishes such as Wiener and chicken schnitzels, some trout recipes, cold marinated herring, Hungarian goulash, hearty regional soups, and lots of other *gutbürgerlich* selections. You come here for hearty portions—not for refined cuisine.

✪ **Stiftskeller St. Peter (Peterskeller).** St.-Peter-Bezirk 1–4. ☎ **0662/84-12-680.** Reservations recommended. Main courses 115–265AS ($9–$20). AE, MC, V. Daily 11am–midnight. Bus: 29. AUSTRIAN/VIENNESE.

Legend has it that Mephistopheles met with Faust in this tavern, which isn't that far-fetched, considering it was established by Benedictine monks in A.D. 803. In fact, it's the oldest restaurant in Europe and is housed in the abbey of the church that supposedly brought Christianity to Austria. Aside from a collection of baroque banquet rooms, there's an inner courtyard with rock-cut vaults, a handful of dignified wood-paneled rooms, and a brick-vaulted cellar. In addition to the wine fermented from the abbey's vineyards (*Prelaten,* a young fruity white wine, is the most popular), the tavern serves good home-style Austrian cooking, including braised oxtail with mushrooms and fried polenta, and braised veal knuckle with anchovy sauce. Other menu items include *tafelspitz* and *bauernpfandl,* a succulent version of pork fillet stuffed with mushrooms and served with spaetzle.

ON THE RIGHT BANK
Moderate
Hotel Stadtkrug Restaurant. Linzer Gasse 20. ☎ **0662/87-35-45.** Reservations recommended. Main courses 98–265AS ($8–$20); fixed-price menu 130–400AS ($10–$31). AE, DC, MC, V. Wed–Mon noon–2pm and 6–11pm. Bus: 27 or 29. AUSTRIAN/INTERNATIONAL.

Across the river from the Altstadt, on the site of a 14th-century farm, this restaurant occupies a structure rebuilt from an older core in 1458. In the 1960s, a modern hotel was added in back. The old-fashioned dining rooms serve as one of the neighborhood's most popular restaurants. In an antique and artfully rustic setting, you can enjoy hearty, traditional Austrian cuisine, such as cream of potato soup "Old Vienna" style, braised beef with burgundy sauce, roast duckling with bacon dumplings and red cabbage/apple dressing, and glazed cutlet of pork with caraway seeds and deep-fried potatoes.

Zum Fidelen Affen. Priesterhausgasse 8. ☎ **0662/877-361.** Main courses 110–125AS ($8–$10). No credit cards. Mon–Sat 5pm–midnight. Bus: 1 or 2. AUSTRIAN.

On the eastern edge of the river near the Staatsbrücke, this is the closest thing in Salzburg to a loud, animated, and jovial pub with food service. It's in one of the city's oldest buildings, from 1407. Management's policy is to allow only three reserved tables on any particular evening; the remainder are given to whomever happens to show up. Menu items are simple, inexpensive, and based on regional culinary traditions. A house specialty is a gratin of green (spinach-flavored) noodles in cream sauce with strips of ham. Also popular are casseroles of seasonal meats and mushrooms, and at least three different kinds of main-course dumplings flavored with meats, cheeses, herbs, and various sauces. Everyone' favorite drink is Trumer pils beer.

SEEING THE SIGHTS IN THE CITY OF MOZART
The Old Town lies between the left bank of the Salzach River and the ridge known as the **Mönchsberg,** which rises to a height of 1,650 feet and is the site of Salzburg's gambling casino. The main street of the Altstadt is **Getreidegasse,** a narrow little thoroughfare lined with five- and six-story burghers' buildings. Most of the houses along the street are from the 17th and 18th centuries. Mozart was born at no. 9 (see below). Many lacy-looking wrought-iron signs are displayed, and a lot of the houses have carved windows.

You might begin your tour at **Mozartplatz,** with its outdoor cafes. From here you can walk to the even more expansive **Residenzplatz,** where torchlight dancing is staged every year, along with outdoor performances.

SIGHTSEEING SUGGESTIONS FOR FIRST-TIME VISITORS
If You Have 1 Day   Start slowly with a cup of coffee at the **Café-Restaurant Glockenspiel** on Mozartplatz. Then from the Altstadt, take the funicular to the **Hohensalzburg Fortress** for a tour. After lunch in an old tavern, visit **Mozart's birthplace** on Getreidegasse, and stroll along the narrow street, most typical in the city. Later, visit the **Residenz.**

If You Have 2 Days   In the morning of your second day, explore the **Dom** and the **cemetery of St. Peter's.** Take a walking tour through the **Altstadt.** In the afternoon, explore **Hellbrunn Palace,** 5km (3 miles) south of the city.

If You Have 3 Days   On day 3, visit the many attractions of Salzburg you've missed so far: the **Mönchsberg,** the **Mozart Wohnhaus,** and the **Museum Carolino Augusteum** in the morning. In the afternoon, see the **Mirabell Gardens** and **Mirabell Palace** and at least look at the famous **Festspielhaus** (Festival Hall); tours are sometimes possible.

If You Have 4 or 5 Days On day 4, head for some of the sights in the environs of Salzburg. Go to **Gaisberg** in the morning, which at 4,250 feet offers a panoramic view of the Salzburg Alps. After lunch, head for **Hallein,** the second-largest town in Land Salzburg, for a look at its salt mines. On day 5, take the *"Sound of Music* **Tour"** (see "Organized Tours," below) and visit the places where this world-famous musical was filmed. Return to Salzburg in time to hear a Mozart concert, if one is featured (as it often is).

THE TOP ATTRACTIONS

✪ **Residenz.** Residenzplatz 1. ☎ **0662/80-42-26-90.** Admission to Residenz state rooms, 70AS ($5) adults, 40AS ($3.10) students 16–18 and seniors, 25AS ($1.95) children 6–15; children 5 and under free. Residenz Gallery, 70AS ($5) adults, 25AS ($1.95) students 16–18 and seniors; children 15 and under free. Combined ticket to state rooms and gallery, 100AS ($8). Jan–Apr and Nov Mon–Fri 10am–5pm, May–Oct and Dec daily 10am–5pm. Bus: 5 or 6.

This opulent palace, just north of Domplatz in the pedestrian zone, was the seat of the Salzburg prince-archbishops after they no longer needed the protection of the gloomy Hohensalzburg Fortress of Mönchsberg. The Residenz dates from 1120, but work on its series of palaces, which comprised the ecclesiastical complex of the ruling church princes, began in the late 1500s and continued until about 1796. The 17th-century Residenz fountain is one of the largest and most impressive baroque fountains north of the Alps. The child prodigy Mozart often played in the Conference Room for guests. More than a dozen state rooms, each richly decorated, are open to the public via guided tour. On the second floor you can visit the **Residenzgalerie Salzburg** (☎ 0662/84-04-51), an art gallery containing European paintings from the 16th to the 19th century.

Glockenspiel (Carillon). Mozartplatz 1. ☎ **0662/80-42-27-84.**

The celebrated glockenspiel with its 35 bells stands across from the Residenz. You can hear this 18th-century carillon at 7am, 11am, and 6pm. Visits are no longer allowed within the Glockenspiel.

✪ **Dom (Salzburg Cathedral).** Domplatz. ☎ **0662/84-41-89.** Cathedral free; excavations 30AS ($2.30) adults, 20AS ($1.55) students and children 6–15, children 5 and under free; museum, 60AS ($4.60) adults, 20AS ($1.55) students and children 6–15, children 5 and under free. Cathedral daily 8am–8pm (until 6pm in winter); excavations Easter–mid-Oct daily 9am–5pm; museum May 16–Oct 26 daily 10am–5pm. Bus: 1.

Located where Residenzplatz flows into Domplatz, this cathedral is world renowned for its 4,000-pipe organ. The original foundation dates from A.D. 774, superseded in the 12th century by a late-Romanesque structure that was destroyed by fire in 1598. Italian architect Santino Solari built the present cathedral, which was consecrated in 1628 by Archbishop Paris Count Lodron. Hailed by some critics as the "most perfect" northern Renaissance building, the cathedral has a marble facade and twin symmetrical towers. The mighty bronze doors were created in 1959. The interior has a rich baroque style with elaborate frescoes, the most important of which, along with the altarpieces, were designed by Mascagni of Florence. In the crypt, traces of the old Romanesque cathedral have been unearthed.

The treasure of the cathedral and the "arts and wonders" the archbishops collected in the 17th century are displayed in the **Dom Museum** (☎ 0662/84-41-89), entered through the cathedral. The **cathedral excavations** (☎ 0662/84-52-95), entered around the corner (left of the Dom entrance), show the ruins of the original foundation.

Stiftskirche St. Peter. St.-Peter-Bezirk. ☎ **0662/844-578.** Admission 12AS (90¢). Daily 9:30am–5pm.

Founded in A.D. 696 by St. Rupert, whose tomb is here, this is the church of St. Peter's Abbey and Benedictine Monastery. Once a Romanesque basilica with three aisles, it was completely overhauled in the 17th and 18th centuries in elegant baroque style. The west door dates from 1240. The church is richly adorned with art treasures including some altar paintings by Kremser Schmidt.

Petersfriedhof (St. Peter's Cemetery). St.-Peter-Bezirk. ☎ **0662/84-45-78-0.** Tours 12AS (90¢). Catacombs May–Sept daily 10am–5pm every 60 minutes; Oct–Apr daily 9am–5pm. Bus: 1.

This cemetery lies at the stone wall that merges into the Mönchsberg. Many of the aristocratic families of Salzburg lie buried here as well as many other noted persons, including Nannerl Mozart, sister of Wolfgang Amadeus. You can also see the Romanesque Chapel of the Holy Cross and St. Margaret's Chapel, dating from the 15th century. *Warning:* Tours of the catacombs in theory follow the hours outlined above; however, they may not be offered for almost any reason.

Hohensalzburg Fortress. Mönchsberg 34. ☎ **0662/84-24-30-11.** Admission (including audio tour and museum) 42AS ($3.25) adults, 21AS ($1.60) children 6–19; children 5 and under free. Fortress and museum Nov–Mar daily 9am–5pm; Apr–June and Oct daily 9am–6pm; July–Sept daily 8am–7pm. The funicular from Festungsgasse (☎ **0662/ 84-26-82**) runs every 10 min. during daylight hours and the round-trip costs 69AS ($5) for adults and 37AS ($2.85) for children 6–16; children 5 and under free. If you're athletic you can reach the fortress on foot from Kapitelplatz by way of Festungsgasse or from the Mönchsberg via the Schartentor.

The stronghold of the ruling prince-archbishops before they moved "downtown" to the Residenz, this fortress towers 400 feet above the Salzach River on a rocky Dolomite ledge. The massive fortress crowns the Festungsberg and literally dominates Salzburg. Work on Hohensalzburg began in 1077 and wasn't finished until 1681. This is the largest completely preserved castle left in central Europe. The elegant state apartments, once the courts of the prince-archbishops, are on display. The **Burgmuseum** contains a collection of medieval art. Plans and prints tracing the growth of Salzburg are on exhibit, as well as instruments of torture and many Gothic artifacts. The **Rainermuseum** has displays of arms and armor. The beautiful late-Gothic **St. George's Chapel** (1501) is adorned with marble reliefs of the apostles.

MORE ATTRACTIONS

✪ **Mozart Gerburtshaus (Mozart's Birthplace).** Getreidegasse 9. ☎ **0662/84-43-13.** Admission 70AS ($5) adults, 55AS ($4.25) students, 20AS ($1.55) children. Daily 9am–6pm (last entrance at 5:30pm).

The house where Wolfgang Amadeus Mozart was born on January 27, 1756, contains exhibition rooms and the apartment of the Mozart family. The main treasures are the valuable paintings (such as the well-known unfinished oil painting, *Mozart and the Piano,* by Joseph Lange) and the original instruments: the violin Mozart used as a child, his concert violin, his viola, fortepiano, and the clavichord.

Mozart Wohnhaus (Mozart Residence). Makartplatz 8. ☎ **0662/88-34-54-40.** Admission 70AS ($5) adults, 55AS ($4.25) students, 20AS ($1.55) children 15 and under. June–Sept daily 10am–5pm, Oct–May daily 10am–4pm. Bus: 1 or 5.

In 1773, the Mozart family vacated the cramped quarters of Mozart's birthplace, and the young Mozart lived here with his family until 1780. In the rooms of the former Mozart family apartments, a museum documents the history of the house and the life and work of Wolfgang Amadeus. This isn't the original house. Destroyed by bombing in 1944, it was rebuilt according to the specifics of an 1838 engraving and reopened on January 26, 1996—the eve of Mozart's birthday. A mechanized audio tour in six languages with relevant musical samples accompanies the visitor through the rooms of the museum.

Schloss Mirabell (Mirabell Palace). Off Makartplatz. ☎ **0662/8072-0.** Free admission. Staircase: daily 8am–6pm. Marmorsaal: Mon, Wed–Thurs 8am–4pm; Tues and Fri 1–4pm. Bus: 1, 5, 6, or 51.

This palace and its gardens were built as a luxurious private residence called Altenau. Prince-Archbishop Wolf Dietrich had it constructed in 1606 for his mistress and the mother of his children, Salome Alt. Not much remains of the original grand structure. Lukas von Hildebrandt rebuilt the *schloss* in the first quarter of the 18th century, and it was modified after a great fire in 1818. The official residence of the mayor of Salzburg is now in the palace, which is like a smaller edition of the Tuileries in Paris. The ceremonial marble *Barockstiege-Englesstiege,* "angel staircase," with sculptured cherubs, carved by Raphael Donner in 1726, leads to the Marmorsaal, a marble and gold hall used for concerts and weddings. Chamber music concerts are staged here.

Museum Carolino Augusteum. Museumsplatz 1. ☎ **0662/841-134-0.** Admission 40AS ($3.10) adults, 30AS ($2.30) seniors over 60; 15AS ($1.15) students and children 6–19; children 5 and under free. Thurs 9am–8pm, Fri–Sun and Tues–Wed 9am–5pm. Bus: 1, 49, or 95.

Several collections are brought together under one roof in this museum reflecting Salzburg's cultural history. The archaeological collection contains the well-known Dürnberg beaked pitcher, as well as Roman mosaics. Some 15th-century Salzburg art is on view, and there are many paintings from the Romantic period, as well as works by Hans Makart, born in Salzburg in 1840.

Mönchsberg. West of the Hohensalzburg Fortress. ☎ **0662/6205-51-180.** Express elevators leave from Gstättengasse 13, daily 9am–11pm; round-trip fare 27AS ($2.10) adults, 14AS ($1.10) children 6–15, free for children 5 and under.

This heavily forested ridge extends for some 2km (1¹/₂ miles) above the Altstadt and has fortifications dating from the 15th century. A panoramic view of Salzburg is possible from Mönchsberg Terrace just in front of the Grand Café Winkler.

THE MIRABELL GARDENS

The **Mirabell-Garten (Mirabell Gardens)** are on the right bank of the river off Makartplatz. Laid out by Fischer von Erlach, these baroque gardens are studded with statuary and reflecting pools, making the gardens a virtual open-air museum. Be sure to visit the bastion with fantastic marble baroque dwarfs and other figures, by the Pegasus Fountains in the lavish garden west of Schloss Mirabell. From the garden you have an excellent view of the Hohensalzburg Fortress. Admission is free, and the gardens are open June to September daily 7am to 8pm. The rest of the year, hours are daily 7am to dusk. Take bus 1, 5, 6, or 51.

ORGANIZED TOURS

Bookings may be made at the bus terminal at Mirabellplatz/St. Andrä Kirche (☎ **0662/87-40-29**). Tour prices are the same for all ages. The best tours are offered by **Salzburg Panorama Tours,** Mirabellplatz (☎ **0662/88-32-11-0**). The original *"Sound of Music* **Tour"** combines the city tour with an excursion to the lake district and the places where the film was shot. The English-speaking guide also shows you the historical and architectural landmarks of Salzburg, as well as a part of the Salzkammergut countryside. The 4¹/₂-hour tour departs daily at 9:30am and 2pm and costs 350AS ($27).

You must take your passport along for any of three trips into **Bavaria** in Germany. One of these, called the **"Eagle's Nest Tour,"** takes visitors to Berchtesgaden and on to Obersalzberg, where Hitler and his followers had a vacation retreat. The 4¹/₂-hour tour departs daily at 9am, May 15 to October 31, and costs 550AS ($42). Among other tours offered, **"The City & Country Highlights"** takes in historic castles and the surrounding landscape. The 5-hour tour departs daily at 1pm and costs 550AS ($42).

THE SHOPPING SCENE

Salzburg obviously doesn't have Vienna's wide range of merchandise. However, if you're not going on to the Austrian capital, you may want to patronize some of the establishments recommended below. Good buys in Salzburg include souvenirs of Salzburg state, dirndls, lederhosen, petit point, and all types of sports gear. **Getreidegasse** is a main shopping thoroughfare, but you'll also find some intriguing little shops on **Residenzplatz.**

Opened in 1871, **Drechslerei Lackner,** Badergasse 2 (☎ **0662/84-23-85**), offers both antique and modern country wood furniture. Among the new items are chests, chessboards, angels, cupboards, crèches, candlesticks, and most definitely, chairs. **Musikhaus Pühringer,** Getreildegasse 13 (☎ **0662/84-32-67**), established in 1910, sells all kinds of classical musical instruments, especially those popular in central Europe, as well as a large selection of electronic instruments (including synthesizers and amplifiers). You'll find classical and folk -music CDs and tapes, plus many classical recordings, especially those by Mozart. The store is only a few buildings away from the composer's birthplace.

Salzburger Heimatwerk, Am Residenzplatz 9 (☎ **0662/84-41-10**), is one of the best places in town to buy local Austrian handcrafts and original regional clothing. Items for sale include Austrian silver and garnet jewelry, painted boxes, candles, wood carvings, copper and brass ceramics, tablecloths, and patterns for cross-stitched samplers in alpine designs. Another section sells dirndls and the rest of the regalia native to the land and still donned during commemorative ceremonies and festivals.

Wiener Porzellanmanufaktur Augarten Gesellschaft, Alter Markt 11 (☎ **0662/84-07-14**), might very well tempt you to begin a porcelain collection. The origins of this world-class manufacturer go back 275 years, when it originated as one of several branches of the Meissen porcelain manufacturers in Germany. Today, its product is legendary and its patterns, such as *Wiener Rose, Maria Theresia,* and the highly distinctive *Biedermeier,* are well known. The company also produces such historical pieces as the black-and-white demitasse set created by architect/designer Josef Hoffman.

SALZBURG AFTER DARK
The Performing Arts

It's said there's a musical event—often a Mozart concert—staged virtually every night in Salzburg. To find the venue, visit the Salzburg tourist office, Mozartplatz 5 (☎ **0662/88987-330**). Here you'll be given a free copy of *Veranstaltungen,* a frequently updated pamphlet listing all major, and many minor, local cultural events.

The major ticket agency affiliated with the city of Salzburg is located adjacent to Salzburg's main tourist office, at Mozartplatz 5. The **Salzburger Ticket Office** (☎ **0662/84-03-10**) is open Monday to Friday 10am to 6pm (to 7pm in midsummer) and Saturday 9am to noon.

If you don't want to pay a ticket agent's commission, you can go directly to the box office of a theater or concert hall. However, many of the best seats may have already been sold, especially those at the Salzburg Festival.

Getting Tickets to the Salzburg Festival

One of the premier music attractions of Europe, the **Salzburg Festival** reached its 79th season in 1999. Composer Richard Strauss founded the festival, aided by director Max Reinhardt and writer Hugo von Hofmannsthal. Details on the festival are available by writing to Salzburg Festival, Hofstallgasse 1, A-5020 Salzburg, Austria (☎ **0662/8045-579**). You can buy tickets Monday to Friday 8am to 12:30pm and 1 to 4:30pm and Saturday 8am to 2pm.

Festival tickets are in great demand, and there are never enough of them. Don't arrive expecting to get into any of the major events unless you've booked your tickets far ahead. Travel agents can often get tickets for you, and you can also go to branches of the Austrian National Tourist Office at home or abroad.

An annual event is Hofmannsthal's adaptation of the morality play *Everyman,* which is staged (in German) outside the cathedral in Domplatz.

Subject to many exceptions and variations, and excluding ticket agent commissions, drama tickets generally run 200 to 2,500AS ($15 to $193). Opera tickets can begin as low as 600AS ($46), ranging upward to 4,200AS ($323).

CONCERTS & OTHER ENTERTAINMENT

The rich collection of concerts that combine every summer to form the Salzburg Festival's program are presented in several different concert halls scattered throughout Salzburg. The largest is the **Festspielhaus**, Hofstallgasse 1 (☎ **0662/8045;** bus: 1, 5, or 6), which contains at least two different theaters, with easy accessibility to other areas nearby. Within the Festspielhaus complex you'll find the **Grosses Haus** (Big House), seating 2,170, and the **Kleines Haus** (Small House), which with a seating capacity of 1,323 isn't really that small. There's also the **Felsenreitschule**, an outdoor auditorium with a makeshift roof. Originally built in 1800 as a riding rink, it's famous as the site where scenes from *The Sound of Music* were filmed. Tickets are 100 to 4,000AS ($8 to $308); average but good seats run 550 to 1,050AS ($42 to $81). Information and tickets are also available through the **Kulturvereiningung** ticket office at Waagplatz 1A, near the tourist office (☎ **0662/84-26-65**); their services are available Monday to Friday 9:30am to 5pm.

On the right back of the Salzach River, near the Mirabell Gardens, is the **Mozarteum,** Schwarzstrasse 26 and Mirabellplatz 1 (☎ **0662/87-31-54;** bus 1, 5, 6, or 51), the major music and concert hall of Salzburg. All the big orchestra concerts, as well as organ recitals and chamber-music evenings, are offered by the Mozarteum. In the old building at Schwarzstrasse there are two concert halls, the Grosser Saal and the Wiener Saal. However, in the newer building on Mirabellplatz, concert halls include the Grosses Studio, the Leopold-Mozart Saal, and the Paumgartner Studio. The box office is open Monday to Thursday 9am to 2pm and Friday 9am to 4pm. Performances are at 11am or 7:30pm. Tickets are 250 to 800AS ($19 to $62); the best seats run 1,200 to 2,500AS ($92 to $193).

Besides the venues above, you can attend a concert in dramatic surroundings in the Fürstenzimmer (Prince's Chamber) of the **Hohensalzburg Fortress.** Guest musicians of international renown perform on occasion. The box office, at Adlgasser-Weg 22 (☎ **0662/82-58-58**), is open daily 9am to 10pm. Performances are daily mid-May to mid-October, at either 8 or 8:30pm, and tickets are 360 to 450AS ($28 to $35).

BEER GARDENS & THE CASINO

Regardless of the season, you'll have one of your most enjoyable and authentic evenings in Salzburg at ✪ **Augustiner Bräustübl,** Augustinergasse 4 (☎ **0662/ 43-12-46;** bus: 27). This bierstube and biergarten has been dispensing oceans of beer since it was established in 1622. Depending on the weather, the city's beer-drinking fraternity gathers either within the cavernous interior, where three separate rooms each hold up to 400 people, or in the leafy, chestnut-shaded garden. Brewed on the premises, the beer is excellent and is served Monday to Friday 3 to 11pm and Saturday and Sunday 2:30 to 11pm. Throughout the year, the staple here is Märzen beer, which sells for 34AS ($2.60) for a brimming half-liter mugful.

Immediately below the Hohensalzburg Fortress and established in the early 1800s, part of the **Stiegelbräu Keller,** Festungsgasse 10 (☎ **0662/84-26-81**), is carved into the rocks of Mönchsberg. To get here, you'll have to negotiate a steep cobblestone street that drops off on one side to reveal a panoramic view of Salzburg. Most of the staff here is preoccupied with supplying large volumes of the local brew (Steigelbräu) and food to enthusiastic locals. If the weather permits, you can head to the leafy garden, or else you'll have to sip your suds in the cavernous interior. Mugs of beer, costing 39AS ($3) each, are supplemented with small to enormous platters of such traditional bierkeller food as sausages and schnitzels. It's open May to September daily 10am to midnight.

Within a separate room, you can participate in folkloric **"Sound of Music" dinner shows.** These are presented May to September daily 7:30 to 10pm. A three-course meal plus the show costs 520AS ($40). If you prefer to skip the dinner, you can show up at 8:15pm and pay 380AS ($29), which includes the show, dessert, and coffee.

The **Casino Salzburg Schloss Klessheim,** A-5071 Walzsezenheim (☎ **0662/ 854-4550**), is the only year-round casino in Salzburg state, occupying the Schloss Klessheim, a baroque palace. On the premises is a stylish restaurant, plus bars. Monday night is poker night. You must show some form of identification—a driver's license or a passport—and except during the hottest months of summer, men are encouraged to wear jackets and ties. The complex is open daily 3pm to 3am. The cover of 260AS ($20) includes 300AS ($23) worth of casino chips. To get here, drive west along Autobahn A-1, exiting at the "Schloss Klessheim" exit, about a mile west of the center of Salzburg. Also, the casino maintains a flotilla of red-sided free shuttle buses that depart from the rocky base of the Mönchsberg every hour on the half-hour, daily 3pm to 3am.

DAY TRIPS FROM SALZBURG

SCHLOSS HELLBRUNN   This early 17th-century palace was built as a hunting lodge and summer residence for Prince-Archbishop Markus Sittikus. The **Hellbrunn Zoo,** also here, was formerly the palace's deer park. The palace **gardens,** some of the oldest baroque formal gardens in Europe, are known for their trick fountains. As you walk through, take care—you may be showered when you least expect it. Some 265 figures in a mechanical theater are set in motion by a hydraulic movement to the music of an organ, also powered by water. The rooms of the schloss are furnished and decorated in 18th-century style. See, in particular, the **banquet hall** with its trompe l'oeil painting. The gardens are at Fürstenweg 37, Hellbrunn (☎ **0662/820-372-16**). Admission is 70AS ($5) for adults for both the gardens and 90AS ($7) for adults for the banquet hall. All children's tickets are half price. Open April and October daily 9am to 4:30pm; May, June, and September daily 9am to 3:30pm; July and August daily 9am to 10pm.

Getting There   Bus 55 from Salzburg runs here in 18 minutes.

✪ **DÜRNBERG SALT MINES (SALZBERGWERK HALLEIN)**   These salt mines (☎ **06245/83511-0**) are the big lure at Hallein, south of Salzburg. On guided tours, you'll walk downhill from the ticket office to the mine entrance, then board an electric mine train that takes you deep into the caverns. From here, you go on foot through galleries, changing levels by sliding down polished wooden slides, then exit on the train that brought you in. An underground museum traces the history of salt mining back to remote times.

Tours lasting 1¹/₂ hours are conducted April to October daily 9am to 5pm and November to March daily 11am to 3pm. Admission is 195AS ($15) for adults and 95AS ($7) for children between 6 and 15, and 65AS ($5) for children between 4 and 6. Free for children under 3.

Getting There   Hallein is connected to Salzburg, 10 miles away, by both train and bus. From Hallein there's a cable railway to Dürnberg. There's also a modern road from Hallein directly to a large parking lot near the ticket office to the mines.

✪ **EISRIESENWELT**   One of the region's most unusual geological oddities, Eisriesenwelt lies in the Pongau basin, on the western cliffs of the Hochkogel, towering over the Salzach valley. This is the "World of Ice Giants," the largest known **ice caves** in the world. The caves stretch for about 42km (26 miles), although only a portion of that length is open to the public. You'll see fantastic ice formations at the entrance, extending for half a mile. The climax of this chilly underworld tour is the spectacular "Ice Palace."

The ice caves are open between May and October and must be visited as part of an organized tour. Two-hour supervised tours begin at hourly intervals every day between 9:30am and 3:30pm, with more frequent departures offered during July and August when the caves are open until 4:30pm. For more information, call ☎ **06468/5248.** Tours begin at a mountain outpost set 5,141 feet above sea level. From here, you walk to the nearby entrance to the caves. Tour, with the cable car (see below) included, costs 200AS ($15) for adults and 95AS ($7) for children 4 to 14.

Getting There   To reach the Eisriesenwelt, head for Werfen, a village that's the center for exploring the ice caves. If go by train to Werfen, 48km (30 miles) south of Salzburg, you can take a taxi bus that's marked "Eisriesenwelt," which departs for the ice caves at 15-minute intervals from Werfen's Hauptplatz (main square). The round-trip fare is 70AS ($5) per person. Some hardy travelers opt to hike the steep road, a strenuous 3¹/₂-mile, uphill trek that rises abruptly from 1,600 to 3,000 feet. The bus will deposit you at the same point you'll reach if you're traveling in your own car. From the parking lot, a cable car hauls you uphill to the entrance of the caves. Once again, some hardy travelers opt to hike uphill to the entrance of the caves, though this is recommended only if you have lots of time and lots of energy.

BERCHTESGADEN   Although it lies in Germany, Berchtesgaden is one of the most popular day trips from Salzburg, about 22km (14 miles) south. Berchtesgaden is situated below the many summits of Watzmann Mountain (8,900 feet at the highest point)—according to legend, these mountain peaks were once a king and his family who were so evil God punished them by turning them into rocks.

Many visitors expect to see one of Hitler's favorite haunts, since the name Berchtesgaden is often linked with the Führer and the Nazi hierarchy. This impression is erroneous. Hitler's playground was actually at Obersalzberg (see below), on a wooded plateau about half a mile up the mountain. Berchtesgaden itself is an old alpine village with ancient winding streets and a medieval marketplace and castle square.

The **Schlossplatz** is partially enclosed by the castle and the **Stiftskirche** (Abbey Church), dating from 1122, a Romanesque foundation with Gothic additions. The church interior contains many fine works of art; the high altar has a painting by Zott dating from 1669. The **Königliches Schloss Berchtesgaden** (☎ **08652/20-85**) is now a museum, and the exhibition is mainly devoted to the royal collection of sacred art, including wood sculptures by the famed artists Veit Stoss and Tilman Riemenschneider. You can also explore a gallery of 19th-century art. Admission is 6DM ($3.25) for adults and 3DM ($1.60) for children 6 to 16 (free for children 5 and under). Easter to September, hours are Sunday to Friday 10am to 1pm. Off-season, hours are Monday to Friday 10am to 1pm and 2 to 5pm. Tours are conducted at 11am and 2pm.

On the opposite side of the square from the church is a 16th-century arcade that leads to **Marktplatz,** with typical alpine houses and a wooden fountain from 1677 (restored in 1860). Some of Berchtesgaden's oldest inns and houses border this square.

Salzbergwerk Berchtesgaden, Bergwerkstrasse 83 (☎ **08652/6-00-20**), lies at the eastern edge of town. These salt mines have been worked since 1517; the deposits are more than 990 feet thick and are still processed today. Older children will especially enjoy the guided tours that begin with a ride into the mine on a small wagonlike train after donning protective miner's clothing. After nearly a half-mile ride, visitors explore the rest of the mine on foot, sliding down a miner's slide and riding on the salt lake in a ferry. The highlight of the tour is the "chapel," a grotto containing unusually shaped salt formations illuminated for an eerie effect. The 1^1/$_2$-hour tour can be taken any time of the year, in any weather. Admission is 21DM ($11) for adults and 11DM ($6) for children 4 to 14. The mines are open May to October 15 daily 9am to 5pm. In the off-season, hours are Monday to Saturday 11am to 3:30pm.

Getting There　**Trains** run every hour during the day from Salzburg to Berchtesgaden; you'll have to change trains at Freilassing. Frequent **buses** also travel from Salzburg to Berchtesgaden. Motorists take Route 20 south of Salzburg (the route is signposted all the way).

✪ OBERSALZBERG　The drive from Berchtesgaden to Obersalzberg at 3,300 feet is along one of Bavaria's most scenic routes. Here Hitler settled down in a rented cottage while he completed *Mein Kampf.* After he came to power in 1933, he bought Haus Wachenfeld near the hamlet of Hintereck and had it remodeled into his residence, the Berghof. Obersalzberg became the center for holiday living for Nazis leaders who included Martin Bormann and Hermann Göring.

A major point of interest to visitors is the **Kehlstein,** or Eagle's Nest, which can be reached only by a thrilling bus ride up a 7km-long (4^1/$_2$-mile) mountain road that was blasted out of solid rock, an outstanding feat of construction and engineering when begun in 1937. To reach the spot, you must enter a tunnel and take a 400-foot elevator ride through a shaft to the summit of the Kehlstein Mountain. Here you can enjoy the panoramic view and explore the rooms of the Nazi hierarchy's original teahouse, which includes Eva Braun's living room. Of the many buildings that once comprised the lavish vacation compound favored by Hitler, this is the only one that wasn't bombed into oblivion by Allied troops near the end of the war.

Getting There　For information about trips to Kehlstein, call ☎ **08652/54-73.** RVO **buses** (local buses based in Berchtesgaden) run from the Berchtesgaden Post Office 4km (2^1/$_2$ miles) uphill to Obersalzberg-Hintereck; the round-trip journey costs 6.80DM ($3.65). From Hintereck, a special mountain bus will carry you another 6km (4 miles) uphill to the Kehlstein parking lot. The bus departs Hintereck every half-hour. The ticket price of 20DM ($11) includes the elevator ride from the Kehlstein parking lot up to the teahouse itself.

3 Innsbruck & the Tyrol

Land of ice and mountains, dark forests and alpine meadows full of spring wildflowers, summer holidays and winter sports—that's Tyrol. Those intrepid tourists, the British, discovered its vacation delights and made it a fashionable destination in the last century. Munich is only a few hours away, and even the Bavarians head for Tyrol when they want a change of scenery. Tyrol is the most frequented winter playground in Austria, and in summer, the extensive network of mountain paths lures visitors.

Skiers flock here in winter for a ski season that runs from mid-December to the end of March. Many prefer its ski slopes to those of Switzerland. It's been a long time since the eyes of the world focused on Innsbruck at the Winter Olympics in 1964 and 1976, but the legacy lives on in the ski conditions and facilities on some of the world's choicest slopes.

INNSBRUCK

Innsbruck is a city with a long imperial past, and even though it is littered with cultural artifacts of a bygone era, most visitors don't come for the history, but for the mountains. Alpine peaks surround Innsbruck, protecting it from the cold winds of the north (we've seen vegetable gardens growing in January).

Innsbruck has a particularly lovely medieval town center, and town planners have protected this historic Altstadt. New structures in the inner city are in harmony with the Gothic, Renaissance, and baroque buildings already standing, and modern urban development spreads along the Inn River east and west, away from the center. Visitors can take countless excursions in the environs; at the doorstep of Innsbruck lie some of the most beautiful drives in Europe. Just take your pick: Head in any direction, up any valley, and you'll be treated to mountains and alpine beauty almost unmatched anywhere else, including Switzerland.

Innsbruck is easily reached from Salzburg (189km/118 miles) to the northeast and from Munich (105km/99 miles to the north). But it's a long, 486km (304-mile) haul west of Vienna.

ORIENTATION

ARRIVING   By Plane   Innsbruck's airport, **Flughafen Innsbruck-Kranebitten,** Fürstenweg 180 (☎ 0512/22525), is 3km (2 miles) west of the city. It offers regularly scheduled air service from the major airports of Austria and Europe's major cities. The region's local carrier, **Tyrolean Airways** (☎ 0512/2222) is by far the most visible and aggressively marketed carrier at this airport, so much so that the only other regularly scheduled airline is a handful of flights that Tyrolean comanages with **Austrian Airlines** (☎ 0512/582-9850). The airport also receives a handful of charter flights from throughout Europe.

From the airport, **bus F** leads to the center of the city. Tickets cost 21AS ($1.60). A taxi ride takes about 10 minutes and costs from 120AS ($9).

By Train   Innsbruck is connected with all parts of Europe by international railway links. Arrivals are at the **Hauptbahnhof,** Südtirolerplatz (☎ 0512/17-17 for all rail information). Frequent trains pull in here from all major European and Austrian cities. There are at least 10 daily trains from Munich (trip time: 2 hours) and about a dozen from Salzburg (trip time: 2 to $3^1/_2$ hours, depending on the route).

By Bus   Bus service to all Austrian cities is provided by both **Postal Buses** and **Federal Railway Buses.** You can take a bus from Salzburg, although the train is more

efficient. For central information about various bus routings through Tyrol, call
☎ **0512/53-07-102.**

By Car   If you're driving down from Salzburg in the northeast, take Autobahn **A-8**
west, which joins Autobahn **A-93** (later it becomes the A-12), heading southwest to
Innsbruck. This latter autobahn (A-93/A-12) is the main artery in from Munich.
From the south you can take the Brenner toll motorway.

VISITOR INFORMATION   The **tourist office,** Burggraben 3 (☎ **0512/59850**),
is open Monday to Friday 8am to 6pm and Saturday 8am to noon. It will supply you
with a wealth of information, as well as a list of inexpensive private rooms for rent in
Innsbruck. On the first floor of the same building is **Innsbruck-Information**
(☎ **0512/5356**), which arranges tours, sells concert tickets, and makes hotel reservations. It's open Monday to Saturday 8am to 6pm and Sunday 9am to 6pm.

CITY LAYOUT   This historic city is divided by the Inn River into left- and right-
bank districts. Two major bridges cross the Inn, the **Universitätssbrücke** and the **Alte
Innsbrücke (Old Inn Bridge).** Many of the attractions, including the Hofkirche and
the Goldenes Dachl, are on the right bank. If you arrive at the Hauptbahnhof, take
Salurner Strasse and Brixener Strasse to Maria-Theresien-Strasse, which will put you
into the very heart of Innsbruck.

The **Altstadt** is bounded on the north by the Inn River and on the south by
Burggraben and Marktgrabben. The main street of this historic district is **Herzog-
Friedrich-Strasse,** which becomes **Maria-Theresien-Strasse,** the axis of the
postmedieval new part of town. The Altstadt becomes a pedestrian zone after 10:30am
(wear good shoes on the cobblestone streets).

GETTING AROUND   A network of three **tram** and 25 **bus** lines covers all of Innsbruck and its environs. Single tickets in the central area cost 21AS ($1.60), and a
booklet of four tickets goes for 54AS ($4.30). For information about various routes,
call the **Innsbrucker Verkehrsbetriebe** (☎ **0512/53-07-102**). You can buy tickets at
the Innsbruck tourist office (above), tobacco shops, and vending machines.

Postal buses leave from the Central Bus Station, adjacent to the Hauptbahnhof on
Sterzinger Strasse, for all parts of Tyrol. The station is open Monday to Friday 7am to
5:30pm and Saturday 7am to 1pm. For information about bus schedules, call
☎ **0512/58-51-55.**

Taxi stands are in all parts of town, or you can call a radio car (☎ **0512/5311**). You
can take a ride in a horse-drawn cab, starting in front of Tiroler Landestheater,
Rennweg. The cost for a 30-minute ride is 320AS ($25).

April to early November, you can rent bikes at the Hauptbahnhof, the main rail station. The cost is 150 to 200AS ($12 to $15) per day, although if you carry a Eurail or
Interrail pass, the charge is only 90 to 160AS ($7 to $12) per day. You can return bikes
to any rail station in Austria if you don't plan to come back to Innsbruck.

For exploring Tyrol by car, try either **Avis,** Salurner Strasse 15 (☎ **0512/
57-17-54**), open Monday to Friday 8am to 6pm and Saturday and Sunday 9am to
noon; or **Hertz,** Südtirolerplatz 1 (☎ **0512/58-09-01**), across from the Hauptbahnhof, open Monday to Friday 7:30am to 6pm and Saturday 8am to 1pm. Prices at both
agencies fluctuate throughout the year, based partly on special promotions and
supply and demand. Remember that you'll always get a cheaper rental rate if you
reserve your car from North America through either company's toll-free reservations
networks.

Innsbruck

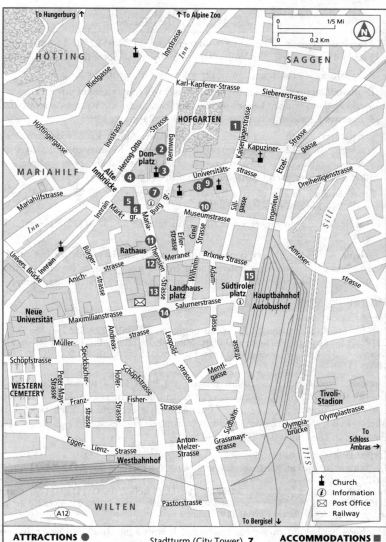

ATTRACTIONS ●

Annasäule
  (St. Anna's Column) **11**
Dom zu St. Jakob
  (Cathedral of St. James) **2**
Goldenes Dachl (Golden Roof)
  & Maximilianeum **4**
Herzog-Friedrich-Strasse **5**
Hofburg **3**
Hofkirche **8**

Stadtturm (City Tower) **7**
Tiroler Landsmuseum
  Ferdinandeum
  (Ferdinandeum Tyrol
  Museum) **10**
Tiroler Volkskunst-Museum
  (Tyrol Museum
  of Popular Art) **9**
Triumphpforte
  (Triumphal Arch) **14**

ACCOMMODATIONS ■

Europa Tyrol **15**
Goldene Krone **13**
Goldener Adler **6**
Maria Theresia **12**
Schwarzer-Adler **1**
Weisses Kreuz **5**

Fast Facts: Innsbruck

American Express   The office at Brixnerstrasse 3 (☎ **0512/58-24-910**; tram: 1 or 3) is open Monday to Friday 9am to 5:30pm and Saturday 9am to noon.

Baby-Sitters   Most hotel concierges will make arrangements for you.

Dentists/Doctors   The tourist office (above) will supply a list of private English-speaking dentists and doctors in the Innsbruck area. Or you can contact the **University Clinic,** Anichstrasse 35 (☎ **0512/504**; tram: 1 or 3).

Drugstores   In the heart of Innsbruck, **St.-Anna Apotheke,** Maria-Theresien-Strasse 4 (☎ **0512/58-58-47**; tram: 1 or 3), is open Monday to Friday 8am to 12:30pm and 2:30 to 6pm and Saturday 8am to noon; it also posts addresses of other pharmacies open nights and weekends.

Emergencies   In case of trouble, call ☎ **133** for the police, ☎ **122** for a fire, or ☎ **144** for an ambulance.

Hospitals   Try the **University Clinic,** Anichstrasse 35 (☎ **0512/504**; tram: 1 or 3).

Telephone   The **country code** for Austria is **43.** The **city code** for Innsbruck is **512;** use this code when you're calling from outside Austria. If you're within Austria, use **0512.** For additional information, see "Fast Facts: Vienna," above.

WHERE TO STAY

Very Expensive

Europa Tyrol. Südtirolerplatz 2, A-6020 Innsbruck. ☎ **800/223-5652** in the U.S., or 0512/5931. Fax 0512/58-78-00. 140 units. MINIBAR TV TEL. 1,900–4,800AS ($146–$370) double; 4,200–4,800AS ($323–$370) suite. Rates include breakfast. AE, DC, MC, V. Parking 160AS ($12).

Opposite Innsbruck's rail station, this elegant hotel has a formal lobby with an English-style bar. The rooms and suites are handsomely furnished, with all the modern conveniences and Tyrolean or Biedermeier-style decorations. Each tasteful unit offers a radio, a marble bathroom, and a hair dryer. The restaurant Europa Stüberl is the finest in Innsbruck (see "Where to Dine").

Expensive

✪ **Schwarzer Adler.** Kaiserjägerstrasse 2, A-6020 Innsbruck. ☎ **0512/58-71-09.** Fax 0512/56-16-97. www.tiscover.com/romantikhotel-schwarzer-adler. E-mail: romantikhotel-innsbruck@netway.at. 28 units. MINIBAR TV TEL. 1,800–2,300AS ($139–$177) double; 3,400–4,600AS ($262–$354) suite. Rates include breakfast. Half board 330AS ($25) per person. AE, DC, MC, V. Parking 120AS ($9). Tram: 1 or 3.

The hotel lies behind an antique stucco facade with a big-windowed tower. Its owners, the Ultsch family, have furnished the charming interior with hand-painted regional furniture, antiques, and lots of homey clutter, making for a cozy and inviting ambience. The rooms are virtually one of a kind, each with its special character. Beds are exceedingly comfortable, with some of the thickest mattresses in town and well-stuffed duvets. Bathrooms have dual basins with powerful showerheads and hair dryers. The original Tiroler Stube has a history going back 4 centuries, and the K. u K. (Kaiser und König) Restaurant has won awards for its modern Austrian cuisine.

Moderate

✪ **Goldener Adler.** Herzog-Friedrich-Strasse 6, A-6020 Innsbruck. ☎ **0512/57-11-11.** Fax 0512/58-44-09. 33 units. MINIBAR TV TEL. 1,760–2,300AS ($136–$177) double; from 2,750AS ($212) suite. Rates include breakfast. AE, DC, MC, V. Parking 196AS ($15). Tram: 1 or 3.

Famous guests of this 600-year-old hotel have included Goethe, Mozart, and the violinist Paganini, who cut his name into the windowpane of his room. The handsomely styled rooms in this family- run hotel sport leaded windows with stained-glass inserts, travertine floors, and ornate carved Tyrolean furniture. All the rooms have private safes, firm mattresses, and well-maintained bathrooms.

Maria Theresia. Maria-Theresien-Strasse 31, A-6020 Innsbruck. ☎ **800/528-1234** in the U.S., or 0512/5933. Fax 0512/57-56-19. 107 units. MINIBAR TV TEL. 1,600–2,200AS ($123–$169) double; 2,300AS ($177) suite. Rates include American breakfast. AE, DC, MC, V. Parking 140AS ($11). Tram: 1 or 3.

This Best Western is on Innsbruck's famous shopping street a few blocks away from the winding alleys of the oldest parts of the city. The helpful staff will do everything possible to make you feel comfortable. All rooms have been recently redecorated. Most are medium-sized and each is well appointed with firm mattresses. Bathrooms are tiny but equipped with a hair dryer. Restaurant Tyrol serves a local and international cuisine.

Inexpensive

Goldene Krone. Maria-Theresien-Strasse 46, A-6020. Innsbruck. ☎ **0512/58-61-60.** Fax 0512/580-18-96. www.touringhotels.at. E-mail: r.pischl@tirol.com. 37 units. TV. 920–1,350AS ($71–$104) double; from 1,440–1,680AS ($111–$129) suite. Rates include breakfast. AE, MC, V. Parking 100AS ($8). Bus: A, H, K, or N. Tram: 1.

Near the Triumphal Arch on Innsbruck's main street, this baroque house offers three-star comfort: modern well-maintained rooms with soundproof windows. A Viennese-inspired coffeehouse/restaurant, the Café, is open Monday to Saturday 7am to 11pm and serves a salad buffet daily 11:30am to 2pm.

Weisses Kreuz. Herzog-Friedrich-Strasse 31, A-6020 Innsbruck. ☎ **0512/59479.** Fax 0512/59-47-990. E-mail: hotel.weisses.kreuz@eunet.at. 39 units, 30 with bathroom. TEL. 820–860AS ($63–$66) double without bathroom, 1,060–1,220AS ($82–$94) double with bathroom. Rates include breakfast. AE, MC, V. Parking 100AS ($8). Tram: 1 or 3.

This atmospheric and historic inn located in the center of Innsbruck has been changed and altered over the years to keep abreast of shifting tastes and requirements. Bedrooms have been modernized and updated frequently, with stylish but simple furnishings, including good beds. In 1769, 13-year-old Wolfgang Mozart and his father, Leopold, stayed here. The hotel's facade is graced by an extended bay window, stretching from the second to the fourth floor.

WHERE TO DINE
Expensive

Europastüberl. In the Hotel Europa Tyrol, Brixner Strasse 6. ☎ **0512/5931.** Reservations required. Main courses 95–320AS ($7–$25); fixed-price menus 350–460AS ($27–$35). AE, DC, MC, V. Daily 11am–2pm and 6:30–10pm. AUSTRIAN/INTERNATIONAL.

Traditional regional and creative cookery is the chef's motto at this distinguished restaurant filled with delightful Tyrolean ambience. Fresh Tyrolean trout almost always appears on the menu, and meat dishes range from red deer ragout to saddle of venison to such exotica as fried jelly of calf's head Vienna style with a lamb's tongue salad. Many dishes are served for two people, including roast pike-perch with vegetables and buttery potatoes, and Bresse guinea hen roasted and served with an herb sauce. There's also a heaping platter known as a Europastuberl Rindl that contains portions of sirloin steak, veal cutlet, calves' liver, and venison sausage garnished with fresh vegetables and sauerkraut, and a succulent version of gratin of veal "Old Innsbruck" with mushroom-cheese sauce and gratin of potatoes. Smaller appetites appreciate such main course regulars as Tyrolean dumplings stuffed with bacon, spinach, and cheese, and served with sauerkraut. Although many of the staples of this restaurant are offered throughout the year, some seasonal specialties change every 2 weeks.

✪ Restaurant Goldener Adler. Herzog-Friedrich-Strasse 6. ☎ **0512/57-11-11.** Reservations recommended. Main courses 150–275AS ($12–$21); set-price menus 160–500AS ($12–$39). AE, DC, MC, V. Daily 11:30am–10:30pm, with a limited menu 2–6pm. Tram: 1 or 3. AUSTRIAN/TYROLEAN/INTERNATIONAL.

Richly Teutonic and steeped in the decorative traditions of the Tyrolean Alps, this beautifully decorated restaurant with four separate dining rooms has a loyal following among locals. The menu includes good, hearty fare based on cold-weather outdoor life—the chefs aren't into delicate subtleties. Examples include Tyrolean bacon served with horseradish and farmer's bread; carpaccio of fillet of beef with Parmesan and olive oil; cream of cheese soup with croutons; and *Tyroler Zopfebraten,* a flavorful age-old specialty consisting of strips of veal steak served with herb-enriched cream sauce and spinach dumplings. A well-regarded specialty is a platter known as *Adler Tres.* It contains spinach dumplings, stuffed noodles, and cheese dumplings, unified with a brown butter sauce and a gratin of mountain cheese.

Moderate

Altstadtstüberl. Riesengasse 13. ☎ **0512/58-23-47.** Reservations recommended. Main courses 80–200AS ($6–$15). AE, DC, MC, V. Mon–Sat 11am–3pm and 6pm–midnight. Tram: 1 or 3. AUSTRIAN/ITALIAN.

This is one of the best moderately priced restaurants in Innsbruck. There's a salad buffet and a satisfying roster of dishes that include both international choices (steaks, salads, roast lamb, and pastas) as well as Austrian favorites, including *tafelspitz* (boiled beef) with horseradish sauce, Wiener schnitzel, rack of lamb, and a frequently changing selection of homemade pastries. Foremost among these are *Kaiserschmarrn,* a doughy crepe filled with a slow-cooked mixture of plum and apricot marmalade enhanced with raisins, cut into bite-sized portions, and served with a compote of apples.

Hirschen-Stuben. Kiebachgasse 5. ☎ **0512/58-29-79.** Reservations recommended. Main courses 165–255AS ($13–$20); fixed-price lunch 110–270AS ($8–$21). DC, MC, V. Tues–Sat 11am–2pm; Mon–Sat 6–10pm. Tram: 1 or 3. AUSTRIAN/ITALIAN.

Beneath a vaulted ceiling in a house built in 1631, Hirshchen-Stuben is charming and well recommended. Down a short flight of stairs from the street, you'll find brocaded chairs and a warm ambience that is especially attractive in spring, autumn, and winter. The food is well prepared and the staff is helpful, polite, and efficient. Menu items include steaming platters of pasta, fish soup, monkfish in a tomato-basil sauce, and sliced veal in cream sauce Zurich style.

Inexpensive

Restaurant Ottoburg. Herzog-Friedrich-Strasse 1. ☎ **0512/57-46-52.** Reservations recommended. Main courses 250–460AS ($19–$35); 2-course fixed-price lunch 98–230AS ($8–$18). AE, DC, MC, V. Daily 11am–3pm and 5–11pm. Closed Tues Oct–June. Tram: 1 or 3. AUSTRIAN/INTERNATIONAL.

This historic restaurant opened around 1745 and occupies two floors of a 13th-century building some historians say is the oldest in Innsbruck. Inside are four intimate and atmospheric dining rooms with a 19th-century neo-Gothic decor. Dishes include venison stew, mixed grill, fried trout, and three varieties of roasts.

Stiegl-Bräu Innsbruck. Wilhelm-Greil-Strasse 25. ☎ **0512/58-43-38.** Main courses 350–480AS ($27–$37); fixed-price menu 130–145AS ($10–$11). AE, DC, MC, V. Daily 10am–midnight (last orders at 11pm). Tram: 1 or 3. AUSTRIAN/INTERNATIONAL.

A Salzburg-based brewery (Stiegl-Bräu) whose product has been brewed nearby since 1492 owns this animated beer hall/restaurant, one of the most atmospheric of the city's cost-conscious restaurants. Its interior contains two crowded and well-used dining rooms and an outdoor beer garden that's open only in summer. Menu items are described by the hardworking staff as "the people's food," and include rib-sticking versions of braised beef, braised veal, hearty stews, Irish mutton, lamb and pork chops, sausages, and schnitzels that are often accompanied with braised cabbage or sauerkraut and dumplings.

EXPLORING THE TOWN

The Altstadt and the surrounding alpine countryside are Innsbruck's main attractions. Often it's fascinating just to watch the passersby, who are occasionally attired in Tyrolean regional dress.

✪ **Maria-Theresien-Strasse,** which cuts through the heart of the city from north to south, is the main street and a good place to begin to explore the city. Many 17th- and 18th-century houses line this wide street. On the south end of the street, there's a **Triumphpforte** (Triumphal Arch), modeled after those in Rome. Maria Theresa ordered it built in 1765 with a twofold purpose: to honor her son's marriage and to commemorate the death of her beloved husband, Emperor Franz I. From this arch southward the street is called Leopoldstrasse.

Going north from the arch along Maria-Theresien-Strasse, you'll see **Annasäule (St. Anna's Column)** in front of the 19th-century Rathaus (town hall). The column was erected in 1706 to celebrate the withdrawal in 1703 of invading Bavarian armies during the War of the Spanish Succession. Not far north of the Annasäule, the wide street narrows and becomes Herzog-Friedrich-Strasse, running through the heart of the medieval quarter. This street is arcaded and flanked by a number of well-maintained burghers' houses with their jumble of turrets and gables; look for the multitude of dormer windows and oriels.

Hofburg. Rennweg 1. ☎ **0512/58-71-86.** Admission 70AS ($5) adults, 45 AS ($3.45) students, 10AS (75¢) children under 10. Daily 9am–5pm. Last admission at 4:30pm. Tram: 1 or 3.

The 15th-century imperial palace of Emperor Maximilian I, flanked by a set of domed towers, was rebuilt in rococo style in the 18th century on orders of Maria Theresa. It's a fine example of baroque secular architecture, with four wings and a two-story Riesensaal (Giant's Hall), painted in white and gold and filled with portraits of the Hapsburgs. You can visit the state rooms, the house chapel, the private apartment, and the Riesensaal on a guided tour, lasting about half an hour.

✪ **Goldenes Dachl (Golden Roof) & Maximilianeum.** Herzog-Friedrich-Strasse 15. ☎ **0512/581-111.** Admission to the Maximilianeum 60AS ($4.60) adults, 50AS ($3.85) seniors, 20AS ($1.55) children, 30AS ($2.30) students. No charge for views of the Goldenes Dachl, and no restrictions as to when it can be viewed. Museum Tues–Sun 10am–5pm. Tram: 1 or 3.

"The Golden Roof," Innsbruck's greatest tourist attraction and its most characteristic landmark, is a three-story balcony on a house in the Altstadt; the late-Gothic oriels are capped with 2,657 gold-plated tiles. It was constructed for Emperor Maximilian I in the beginning of the 16th century to serve as a royal box where he could sit in luxury and enjoy tournaments in the square below.

In 1996, the city of Innsbruck added a small museum, the **Maximilianeum,** to the second floor of the municipal building attached to the Goldenes Dachl. Inside are exhibits celebrating the life and accomplishments of the Innsbruck-based Hapsburg emperor, Maximilian I, who bridged the gap between the Middle Ages and the German-speaking Renaissance. Look for costumes, silver chalices and coins, portraits, and a video depicting his era and personality.

With the same ticket, you can also visit the **Stadtturm (City Tower),** Herzog-Friedrich-Strasse 21 (☎ **0512/52-23-56-269**). Formerly a prison cell, the tower dates from the mid-1400s and stands adjacent to the Rathaus. Its top affords a panoramic view of the city rooftops and the mountains beyond.

Museums & Churches

Hofkirche. Universitätsstrasse 2. ☎ **0512/58-43-02.** Church admission 30AS ($2.30) adults, 20AS ($1.55) students, 15AS ($1.15) children under 15. Museum admission 60AS ($4.60) adults, 35AS ($2.70) students, 20AS ($1.55) children under 15. Combined admission 75AS ($6) adults, 55AS ($4.25) students, 35AS ($2.70) children under 15. Mon–Sat 9am–5:30pm. Tram: 1 or 3.

The most important treasure in the Hofkirche is the cenotaph of Maximilian I, a great feat of German Renaissance style. It has 28 bronze 16th-century statues of Maximilian's real and legendary ancestors surrounding the kneeling emperor, with 24 marble reliefs on the sides depicting scenes from his life.

Dom zu St. Jakob (Cathedral of St. James). Domplatz 6. ☎ **0512/58-39-02.** Free admission. Winter daily 7:30am–6:30pm; summer daily 7:30am–7:30pm. Closed Fri noon–3pm. Tram: 1 or 2.

Designed and rebuilt from 1717 to 1724 by Johann Jakob Herkommer, the Dom has a lavishly embellished baroque interior. A chief treasure is Lucas Cranach the Elder's *Maria Hilf (St. Mary of Succor)* on the main altar.

Tiroler Landesmuseum Ferdinandeum (Ferdinandeum Tyrol Museum). Museumstrasse 15. ☎ **0512/59-489.** Admission 60AS ($4.60) adults, 20AS ($1.55) children. May–Sept daily 10am–5pm, Thurs 10am–5pm and 7–9pm. Oct–Apr Tues–Sat 10am–noon and 2–5pm, Sun 10am–1pm. Tram: 1 or 3.

This museum has a gallery of Flemish and Dutch masters and also traces the development of popular art in the Tyrolean country. You'll also see the original bas-reliefs used in designing the Goldenes Dachl.

Tiroler Volkskunst-Museum (Tyrol Museum of Popular Art). Universitätsstrasse 2. ☎ **0512/58-43-02.** Admission 60AS ($4.60) adults, 35AS ($2.70) students, 20AS ($1.55) children. Mon–Sat 9am–5pm, Sun 9am–noon. Tram: 1 or 3.

This popular art museum is in the Neues Stift (New Abbey) adjoining the Hofkirche on its eastern side. It contains one of the largest and most impressive collections extant of Tyrolean artifacts, ranging from handcrafts, furniture, Christmas cribs, and national costumes to religious and secular popular art.

Zoos & Views

Alpenzoo. Weiherburggasse 37. ☎ **0512/29-23-23.** Admission 70AS ($5) adults, 50AS ($3.85) students, 35AS ($2.70) children 6–15, 20AS ($1.55) children 4–5. Daily 9am–6pm (to 5pm in winter). Bus: 2 (May 15–Sept only). Tram: 1 to the Hungerburgbahn (cog railway).

From this zoo on the southern slope of the Hungerburg plateau, you'll get a panoramic view of Innsbruck and the surrounding mountains. The zoo contains only those animals indigenous to the Alps, plus alpine birds, reptiles, and fish. More than 800 animals belong to more than 140 different and rare species, including otters, eagles, elk, rabbits, vultures, wildcats, bison, and wolves.

The Most Beautiful Spot in the Tyrol

The ✪ **Hungerburg mountain plateau** (2,860 feet) is the most beautiful spot in the Tyrol, affording the best view of Innsbruck, especially on summer nights, when much of the city, including fountains and historic buildings, is floodlit. You can drive to the plateau or take a cog railway, the **Hungerburgbahn,** which departs from a point about a half-mile east of the center of Innsbruck, at the corner of Rennweg and Kettenbrücke. (To reach the cog railway's departure point from Innsbruck's center, take tram 1 or bus C.) In summer, the cog railway departs at 15-minute intervals daily 9am to 8pm, then runs at 30-minute intervals until 10:30pm. The rest of the year, it operates at 30-minute intervals daily 8:30am to between 5 and 6pm, depending on the hour of dusk. Round-trip fares on the cog railway cost 45AS ($3.45) for adults and 33AS ($2.55) for children. For schedules and information, call ☎ **0512/58-61-58.**

Once you arrive at the Hungerburg plateau, you can progress even farther into the alpine wilds via the Nordkette cable car. Designed as a skier-friendly gondola suspended high above the rocky terrain, it will carry you up to the Seegrube and the Hafelekar (7,655 feet), for a sweeping view over the Tyrol region's alpine peaks and glaciers. Hill climbers and rock climbers appreciate this route as the debut of a labyrinth of mountain trails; skiers consider it the departure point for dozens of downhill runs. Throughout the year, the Nordkette cable car runs daily, at 20-minute intervals, from 8:30am to 5:30pm. A round-trip between Innsbruck and Hafelekar costs 225AS ($18) for adults and 110AS ($8) for students and children under 16.

ENJOYING THE GREAT OUTDOORS

Five sunny snow-covered, avalanche-free **ski areas** around the Tyrol are served by 5 cableways, 44 chairlifts, and ski hoists. The area is also known for bobsled and toboggan runs and ice-skating rinks.

In summer you can play tennis at a number of courts, golf on either a 9- or an 18-hole course, or go horseback riding, mountaineering, gliding, swimming, hiking, and shooting.

The **Hofgarten,** a public park containing lakes and many shade trees, lies north of Rennweg.

ORGANIZED TOURS

The best way to get a quick and convenient overview of Innsbruck is to take a 2-hour **bus tour** of the city's major monuments. Tours depart from a clearly marked point in front of the city's main railway station on the Südtirolerplatz and cost 160AS ($12) per adult or 70AS ($5) for those under 16. The experience includes multilingual running commentary on the city's history and architectural highlights and a 20-minute walk through the heart of the old city. April to September, tours depart at 10am, noon, and 2pm; October to March, one tour a day departs at noon.

If you're really crunched for time, there's a 1-hour bus tour of the city, with no walking, that provides a very basic introduction to the city. Hours vary, according to demand, but since the 1-hour tour costs 130AS ($10), almost as much as the 2-hour tour, most visitors opt for the latter. For information on either tour, contact the **Innsbruck Tourist Information Office,** Burggraben 3 (☎ **0512/5356**).

THE SHOPPING SCENE

You'll find a large selection of Tyrolean specialties and all sorts of skiing and mountain-climbing equipment. Stroll around **Maria-Theresien-Strasse, Herzog-Friedrich-Strasse,** and **Museumstrasse,** ducking in and making discoveries of your own. Here are some suggestions.

Lodenbaur, Brixner Strasse 4 (☎ **0512/58-09-11**), is devoted to regional Tyrolean dress, most of which is made in Austria. There's a full array for men, women, and children. **Tiroler Heimatwerk,** Meraner Strasse 2 (☎ **0512/58-23-20**), is one of the best stores in Innsbruck for handcrafted sculpture and pewter, carved chests, and furniture. The store carries textiles, lace, bolts of silk, and dress patterns for those who want to whip up their own dirndl. The elegant decor includes ancient stone columns and vaulted ceilings.

Using old molds discovered in abandoned Tyrolean factories, **Zinnreproduktionen Rudolf Boschi,** Kiebachgasse 8 (☎ **0512/58-92-24**), produces fine reproductions of century-old regional pewter at reasonable prices. Mr. Boschi also reproduces rare pewter objects acquired from auctions throughout Europe. Look for a copy of the 18th-century pewter barometer emblazoned with representations of the sun and the four winds. The work is done in a nearby foundry south of Innsbruck.

INNSBRUCK AFTER DARK

THE PERFORMING ARTS   The major venue for the performing arts is the 150-year-old **Landestheater,** Rennweg 2 (☎ **0512/52074**), with a variety of programs. The box office is open Monday to Saturday 8:30am to 8:30pm and Sunday 5:30 to 8:30pm, and performances usually begin at 7:30 or 8pm. Tickets cost 85 to 460AS ($7 to $35) for operettas and opera and 70 to 390AS ($5 to $30) for theater. Concerts are often presented at the Kunstpavillon in the Hofgarten in summer.

BARS, CLUBS & FOLK MUSIC   In summer, the outdoor bar at **Club Filou,** Stiftsgasse 12 (☎ **0512/58-02-56**), blossoms with ivy-covered trellises and parasols. Inside you'll find an intimate hangout filled with Victorian settees and pop art. In a separate, very old room is the disco, with a ceiling supported by medieval stone columns and ringed with a high-tech steel balcony. Long drinks in both the cafe and the disco begin at around 68AS ($5); a beer costs 38AS ($2.95). The cafe is open daily 6pm to 4am; the disco is open daily 9pm to 4am. Food is available until 3am. Admission to both the cafe and disco is free.

If you want to try an award-winning martini, go to **Sparkling Cocktails,** Innstrasse 45 (☎ **0512/28-78-80**), where virtually any kind of mixed drink or cocktail, including an almost lethal zombie, can be crafted by the highly experienced staff. Drinks range from 68 to 125AS ($5 to $10) and are served Monday to Saturday 7pm to 2am.

Young people hang out at **Treibhaus,** Angerzellgasse 8 (☎ **0512/58-68-74**), a combination cafe, bar, and social club. Within its battered walls, you can attend a changing roster of art exhibitions, cabaret shows, and protest rallies, daily 10am to 1am, with live music presented at erratic intervals. Cover for live performances is 180 to 220AS ($14 to $17).

Goethe Stube, Restaurant Goldener Adler, Herzog-Friedrich-Strasse 6 (☎ **0512/57-11-11**), offers authentic folk music programs throughout the Christmas-New Year's season, Easter, and the winter season. There's no cover, but a one-drink minimum; a large beer costs 40AS ($3.10); meals start at 200AS ($15). Open daily 7pm to midnight.

ST. ANTON AM ARLBERG

A modern resort has grown out of this old village on the Arlberg Pass that was the scene of ski history in the making. The Ski Club Arlberg was born here in 1901, and in 1911, the first Arlberg-Kandahar Cup competition was held. At St. Anton (elev. 4,225 feet), Hannes Schneider developed modern skiing techniques and began teaching tourists how to ski in 1907. Before his death in 1955, Schneider saw his ski school rated as the world's finest. Today the school is still one of the world's largest and best, with about 300 instructors (most of whom speak English). St. Anton am Arlberg in winter is quite fashionable, popular with the wealthy and occasional royalty—a more conservative segment of the rich and famous than you'll see at other posh ski resorts.

There's so much emphasis on skiing here that few seem to talk of the summertime attractions. In warm weather, St. Anton is tranquil and bucolic, surrounded by meadowland. A riot of wildflowers blooming in the fields announces the beginning of spring.

St. Anton is 595km (372 miles) west of Vienna and 99km (62 miles) west of Innsbruck.

ESSENTIALS

ARRIVING   By Train   Because of St. Anton's good rail connections to eastern and western Austria, most visitors arrive by train. St. Anton is an express stop on the main rail lines crossing over the Arlberg Pass between Innsbruck and Bregenz. Just to the west of St. Anton, trains disappear into the Arlberg tunnel, emerging almost 7 miles later on the opposite side of the mountain range. About one train per hour arrives in St. Anton from both directions. Trip time from Innsbruck is 75 to 85 minutes, depending on the train; from Bregenz, around 85 minutes. For local rail information, call ☎ **05446/24020.**

By Bus   The town is the point of origin for many bus travelers who travel from St. Anton on to such other resorts as Zürs and Lech. There is no local number to call for bus information.

By Car   Motorists should take Route 171 west from Innsbruck.

VISITOR INFORMATION   The **tourist office** is in the Arlberghaus in the center of town (☎ **05446/22690**) and is open July to mid-September Monday to Friday 8am to noon and 2 to 6pm, Saturday to Sunday 10am to noon; May to June and mid-September to December Monday to Friday 8am to noon and 2 to 6pm; January to April Monday to Friday 8am to 6pm, Saturday 9am to noon and 1 to 7pm, Sunday 10am to noon and 2 to 6pm.

WHERE TO STAY

✪ **Schwarzer Adler.** A-6580 St. Anton am Arlberg. ☎ **800/528-1234** in the U.S., or 05446/22440. Fax 05446/224462. E-mail: schwarzer.adler@st-anton.at. 50 units. TV TEL. Winter 2,200–4,800AS ($169–$370) double. Summer 1,400–2,400AS ($108–$185) double. Rates include half board. AE, DC, MC, V. Closed May–June and Oct–Nov. Free parking.

This hotel has been owned/operated by the Tschol family since 1885. The beautiful building in the center of St. Anton was constructed as an inn in 1570 and became known for its hospitality to pilgrims crossing the treacherous Arlberg Pass. The 400-year-old frescoes on the exterior were discovered during a restoration and have been faithfully restored to their original grandeur. The interior is rustic yet elegant, with blazing fireplaces, painted Tyrolean baroque armoires, and Oriental rugs. There are handsomely furnished and well-equipped rooms in the main hotel, plus 13 slightly less well-furnished (but less expensive) rooms in the annex, which is across the street above the Café Aquila. There's a sauna and a fitness center, and the hotel's restaurant is known for its excellent cuisine.

WHERE TO DINE

Raffl-Stube. In the Hotel St. Antoner Hof, St. Anton am Arlberg. ☎ **05446/2910.** Reservations required. Main courses 150–300AS ($12–$23); fixed-price menu 1,500–2,000AS ($116–$154). AE, DC, MC, V. Daily 11am–2pm and 7–10:30pm. Closed mid-Oct to mid-Dec and mid-Apr to mid-June. AUSTRIAN.

This isn't the most visible or flamboyant restaurant in St. Anton, but it's one of the most cozy. Containing only a half-dozen tables, it occupies an enclosed corner off the lobby of one of the resort's most prominent hotels, and because of its small scale and emphasis on well-prepared food, it can get very exclusive. Reservations are essential, especially if you're a nonresident. Overflow diners are offered a seat in a spacious but less special dining room across the hall. The hotel has long enjoyed a reputation for its cuisine, but somehow the food in the stube tastes even better. Quality ingredients are always used, and the kitchen prepares such tempting specialties as roast goose liver with salad, cream of parsley soup with sautéed quail eggs, fillet of salmon with wild rice and trout "prepared as you like it," along with the ever-popular fondue bourguignonne.

MORE DINING   If you're not able to secure a reservation at Raffl-Stube, don't despair. St. Anton has plenty of other less expensive options, usually hotel dining rooms open to nonguests. You can get classic Austrian dishes at the historic **Hotel Alte Post Restaurant** (☎ **05446/25530**) and the first-rate **Hotel Kertess Restaurant** (☎ **05446/2005**), located high on a slope in the suburb of Oberdorf. For superb international cuisine, head to the medieval **Hotel Schwarzer Adler Restaurant** (☎ **05446/22440**). Although none of these hotels have a street address, they're all signposted at various places in town, so you should have no trouble finding them.

HITTING THE SLOPES IN ST. ANTON

The snow in this area is perfect for skiers, and the total lack of trees on the slopes makes the situation ideal. The ski fields of St. Anton stretch over a distance of some 6 square miles. Beginners stick to the slopes down below, whereas more experienced skiers head to the runs from the Galzig and Valluga peaks. A cableway will take you to **Galzig** (6,860 feet), where there's a self-service restaurant. You go from here to **Vallugagrat** (8,685 feet), the highest station reached. The peak of the **Valluga,** at 9,220 feet, commands a panoramic view. St. Christoph is the mountain annex of St. Anton.

Other major ski areas include the **Gampen/Kapall,** an advanced-intermediate network of slopes, whose lifts start just behind St. Anton's railway station; and the **Rendl,** a relatively new labyrinth of runs to the south of St. Anton that offers many novice and intermediate slopes.

OTHER ACTIVITIES & ATTRACTIONS

There are many other cold-weather pursuits than just skiing, including ski jumping, mountain tours, curling, skating, tobogganing, and sleigh rides, plus après-ski on the quiet side.

Ski und Heimat Museum (Skiing and Local Museum), in the Arlberg-Kandahar House (☎ **05446/2475**), traces the development of skiing in the Arlberg, as well as the history of the region from the days of tribal migrations in Roman times. The museum, in the imposing structure at the center of the Holiday Park in St. Anton, is open from December through April on Monday through Saturday 2:30pm to midnight. Mid-June to late September, it's open Thursday to Tuesday 10am to 6pm. Admission is 20AS ($1.55) for adults and 10AS (75¢) for children.

Side Trips to Bavaria

While you're based in Seefeld, it's relatively easy to explore part of Bavaria in Germany. You may or may not get to see little **Wildmoos Lake.** It can, and sometimes does, vanish in a day or so, and then you may find cows grazing on what has become meadowland. However, the lake will suddenly come back again, and if conditions are right, it will become deep enough for swimmers. Wildmoos Lake comes and goes more frequently than Brigadoon.

Wildmoos Lake is a 5-minute drive west from Seefeld (it's signposted from the center of town). Cars are not permitted on the drive until after 5pm. Buses run from the center of Seefeld several times a day. Or it's a 10- to 15-minute walk from the center of town.

The little German town of **Mittenwald,** one of the highlights of Bavaria, can also be easily explored on a day trip from Seefeld. It's best to take the train, which departs from Seefeld hourly until 9pm (trip time: 1 hour). Two buses per day also make the trip, although the traffic is so congested the bus trip often takes twice as long as the train. Contact the tourist office for the bus schedule.

SEEFELD

Seefeld, 24km (15 miles) northwest of Innsbruck, is a member of Austria's "big three" international rendezvous points for winter-sports crowds (St. Anton and Kitzbühel are the other two). Seefeld hosted the 1964 and 1976 Nordic events for the Olympic Winter Games and the 1985 Nordic Ski World Championships. The fashionable resort lies some 3,450 feet above sea level on a sunny plateau.

ESSENTIALS

ARRIVING   By Train   More than a dozen trains per day arrive from Innsbruck (trip time: around 40 minutes). There's also train service from Munich and Garmisch-Partenkirchen, Germany. For rail information, call ☎ **05212/2438.**

By Bus   Buses depart daily from Innsbruck's Hauptbahnhof; trip time is around 45 minutes. For bus information, call ☎ **0512/58-51-55** in Innsbruck.

By Car   From Innsbruck, head west along Route 171 until you reach the junction with Route 313, at which point turn north.

VISITOR INFORMATION   The **Seefeld tourist office** is at Klosterstrasse 43 (☎ **05212/2313**) and is open mid-June to mid-September and mid-December to February Monday to Saturday 8:30am to 6:30pm; mid-September to mid-December and March to mid-June Monday to Saturday 8:30am to 12:15pm and 3 to 6pm.

WHERE TO STAY

✪ **Klosterbräu.** Klosterstrasse 30, A-6100 Seefeld. ☎ **05212/26210.** Fax 05212/3885. www.klosterbraeu.com. E-mail: info@klosterbraeu.com. 136 units. MINIBAR TV TEL. Winter 3,700–3,900AS ($285–$300) double; from 4,700AS ($362) suite. Summer 1,400–1,600AS ($108–$123) double; 1,900–2,370AS ($146–$183) suite. Rates include Half board. AE, DC, MC, V. Closed Apr–May and Oct–Nov. Parking 160AS ($12).

The town's most unusual and elegant hostelry is constructed around a 16th-century cloister. The dramatic entrance is under a thick stucco arch. The interior contains soaring vaults supported by massive columns of the same kind of porous stone that built Salzburg (you can still see prehistoric crustaceans embedded in the stone). The well-furnished and elegant rooms are encased in a towering chalet behind the front entrance. Restaurants on the premises include a country-style Bräukeller, a rustic Tyrolean room, and a more formal dining room where guests sit below ancient ceiling vaults. Dishes include international and Austrian specialties. The person at the next table might be a vacationing celebrity traveling incognito. À la carte dinners go for 350 to 600AS ($28 to $48), and reservations are necessary. In the evening, Die Kanne is a nightclub, and a daily afternoon tea dance in winter allows the hotel guests to meet one another. There are indoor and outdoor swimming pools, a sauna, health club, solarium, golf, tennis, mountain climbing, and skiing within walking distance.

WHERE TO DINE

Sir Richard. Innsbruckerstrasse 162. ☎ **05212/2093.** Reservations required. Main courses 200–320AS ($15–$25). DC, MC, V. Daily 11:30am–2pm and 6:30–10pm. Closed 2 weeks in Nov and Tues in winter. AUSTRIAN/ITALIAN.

On the southern outskirts of town, this restaurant creates an elegant aura of year-round Christmastime because of its masses of flowers, dozens of burning candles, and immaculately pressed linen. The menu is short and well composed, and everything on it is mouth-watering, made with the freshest of ingredients. You might begin with watercress soup, followed by one of the lamb, veal, or fish dishes, often accompanied by masterful sauces. Even the fresh leafy salads have just the right degree of tartness. For a taste of Italy, try one of the pastas or risottos or even one of the many Italian reds.

HITTING THE SLOPES & OTHER ACTIVITIES

SKIING   Skiers are served with one funicular railway, two cable cars, three chairlifts, and 14 drag lifts. The beginner slopes lie directly in the village center. The base stations of the lifts for the main skiing areas (known as **Gschwandtkopt** and **Rosshutte/Seefelder Joch**) are at most half a mile away from the center, and are serviced by free daily nonstop bus service. There are 198km (124 miles) of prepared **cross-country tracks.**

OTHER WINTER ACTIVITIES   Other winter activities offered here include curling, horse-drawn sleigh rides, outdoor skating (ice-skating school, with artificial and natural ice rink), horseback riding, indoor tennis (Swedish tennis school), tube sliding (you slide on rubber inner tubes), indoor golf facilities, parasailing, bowling, squash, hiking (60 miles of cleared paths), fitness studio, swimming, and saunas.

SUMMER ACTIVITIES   Summer visitors can enjoy swimming in three lakes, in a heated open-air swimming pool on Seefeld Lake, or at the Olympia indoor and outdoor pools. Other summer sports include tennis on 18 open-air and 8 indoor courts (Swedish tennis school), horseback riding (two stables with indoor schools), and golf on the 18-hole course, which has been rated by golf insiders as one of the 100 most beautiful courses in the world. Hiking on 198km (124 miles) of walks and mountain paths, cycling, minigolf, parasailing, and rafting can also be enjoyed.

THE KITZBÜHEL ALPS

Hard-core skiers and the rich and famous are attracted to this ski region. The Kitzbühel Alps are covered with such a dense network of lifts that they now form the largest skiing complex in the country, with a series of superlative runs. The action centers on the town of Kitzbühel, but there are many satellite resorts that are much less expensive, including St. Johann in Tyrol.

Kitzbühel is, in a sense, a neighbor of Munich, 130km (81 miles) to the northeast, whose municipal airport is the entry point for most wintertime visitors.

Edward, prince of Wales (you may remember him better as the duke of Windsor), may have put Kitzbühel on the international map with his 1928 "discovery" of what was then a town of modest guest houses. Certainly his return a few years later with Mrs. Simpson caused the eyes of the world to focus on this town, and the "upper crust" of England and other countries began flocking here. At the time of this 20th-century renaissance, however, Kitzbühel itself was already some 8 centuries old, and a settlement has been here much, much longer than that.

ESSENTIALS

ARRIVING   By Train   Kitzbühel sits astride the main train lines between Innsbruck and Salzburg, receiving between one express train and about two local trains per hour from both of these cities. Trip time from Innsbruck is about 1 hour; from Salzburg, around 2¹/₂ hours. For rail information, call ☎ **05356/64055.**

By Bus   Two buses travel daily from Salzburg's main railway station to Kitzbühel (trip time: around 2¹/₄ hours). Nine local bus lines run into and up the surrounding valleys. A bus runs every 30 to 60 minutes between Kitzbühel and St. Johann in Tyrol (trip time: 25 minutes). For information, call ☎ **05356/627-15.**

By Car   Kitzbühel is 99km (62 miles) east of Innsbruck. From Innsbruck, take Autobahn A-12 east to the junction with Route 312 heading to Ellmau. After bypassing Ellmau, continue east to the junction with Route 342, which you take south to Kitzbühel.

VISITOR INFORMATION   The **tourist office** is at Hinterstadt 18 (☎ **0 5356/ 621-55**). In the winter ski season and in July and August it's open Monday to Friday 8:30am to 6:30pm, Saturday 8:30am to noon and 4 to 6pm, and Sunday 10am to noon and 4 to 6pm. In off-season, hours are Monday to Friday 8:30am to 12:30pm and 2:30 to 6pm and Saturday 8:30am to noon. In winter, call ☎ 182 for snow reports.

WHERE TO STAY

Bruggerhof. Reitherstrasse 24, A-6370 Kitzbühel. ☎ **05356/62806.** Fax 05356/644-7930. 25 units. TV TEL. Winter 1,500–1,840AS ($116–$142) double; summer 1,160–1,300AS ($89–$100) double. Rates includes half board. AE, DC, V. Free parking. Closed Apr to mid-May and mid-Oct to Dec 15.

About a mile west of the town center, near the Schwarzsee, is this countryside chalet with a sun terrace. Originally a 1920s farmhouse, the interior has massive ceiling beams and a corner fireplace. In 1960 it was expanded and enlarged into a three-star hotel that's family oriented and well maintained. Rooms are comfortable and cozy, decorated in an alpine style. The dining room is graced with wooden ceilings and wrought-iron chandeliers. A whirlpool, steam bath, and solarium are just a few of the amenities guests enjoy year-round; tennis and miniature golf facilities are available in summer.

✪ **Zur Tenne.** Vorderstadt 8–10, A-6370 Kitzbühel. ☎ **05356/644440.** Fax 05356/64803-56. 50 units. MINIBAR TV TEL. Winter 2,530–3,500AS ($195–$270) double; 3,250–5,500AS ($250–$424) suite for three. Rates include breakfast. Half board 560AS ($43) per person in winter, 350AS ($27) in summer. AE, DC, MC, V. Free parking outdoors; 100AS ($8) in covered garage nearby.

This hotel combines Tyrolean *gemütlichkeit* with urban style and panache. The staff shows genuine concern for their clientele. The hotel was created in the 1950s when three 700-year-old houses were joined into one unit. Accommodations come in a wide range of sizes—each elegantly furnished, with firm mattresses, and often French doors leading to private patios or balconies. Suites have fireplaces. The hotel sports the most luxurious health complex in town, complete with a tropical fountain, two hot tubs, a sauna, and a hot and cold foot bath. The elegant Zur Tenne Restaurant serves an international cuisine.

WHERE TO DINE

Florianistube. In the Gasthof Eggerwirt, Gaensbachgasse 12. ☎ **05356/62437.** Reservations recommended. Main courses 110–150AS ($8–$12). AE, MC, V. Daily 11am–2pm and 6–10pm. Closed Nov 1–Dec 6 and Easter to end of May. INTERNATIONAL.

Named after St. Florian, patron saint of the hearth, this restaurant is in one of the resort's less ostentatious guest houses, and it welcomes outsiders. The menu is comprehensive for such a stube-type place—it might include typical Austrian or Tyrolean dishes, or tournedos with mushroom sauce, spaghetti with clam sauce, or fondue bourguignonne. For something really local, order *bauernschmaus,* a heaping hot platter of smoked pork, roast pork, pork sausages, sauerkraut, potatoes, and dumplings. In summer, a lunch or dinner buffet is served outside under the trees of the rear garden.

Wirtshaus Unterberger-Stuben. Wehgasse 2. ☎ **05356/66127.** Reservations recommended. Main courses 190–340AS ($15–$26); fixed-price menus 460–920AS ($35–$71). AE, MC, V. Daily noon–1:30pm and 6:30–10:30pm. Closed June and Nov and Tues in summer. INTERNATIONAL.

Throughout the 1980s, this was the preferred hangout for the rich and famous. Although the stars of yesteryear might have faded a bit, the place still has a lot of prestige, and you're likely to be served one of your finest meals in Tyrol. If it's on the menu, try the poppy seed soufflé, or specialties such as terrine of roast chicken liver with a salad of wild mushrooms or fillet of pike-perch with mountain herbs and baby vegetables. The establishment is open for snacks, coffee, and drinks 9am to midnight, but meals are only served during lunch and dinner hours.

SEEING THE SIGHTS IN TOWN

The town has two main streets, both pedestrian walkways, **Vorderstadt** and **Hinterstadt.** Kitzbühel has preserved its traditional style of structure, at least along these streets. You'll see three-story stone houses with oriels and scrollwork around the doors and windows, heavy overhanging eaves, and Gothic gables.

The **Pfarrkirche (parish church)** was built from 1435 to 1506 and renovated in the baroque style in the 18th century. The lower part of the **Liebfrauenkirche (Church of Our Lady)** dates from the 13th century, the upper part from 1570. Between these two churches stands the **Ölbergkapelle (Ölberg Chapel)** with a 1450 "lantern of the dead" and frescoes from the latter part of the 16th century.

In the **Heimatmuseum,** Hinterstadt 34 (☎ **05356/645-88**), you'll see artifacts from prehistoric European mining eras and the north alpine Bronze Age, a wintersports section with trophies of Kitzbüheler skiing greats, and exhibits detailing the town's history. The museum is open Monday to Saturday 9am to 12:30pm; admission is 40AS ($3.10) for adults and 15AS ($1.15) for children and students.

HITTING THE SLOPES & OTHER OUTDOOR ACTIVITIES

SKIING In winter the emphasis in Kitzbühel, 2,300 feet above sea level, is on skiing, and facilities are offered for everyone from novices to experts. The ski season starts just before Christmas and goes until late March. With more than 62 lifts, gondolas (cable cars), and mountain railroads on five different mountains, Kitzbühel has two main ski areas, the **Hahnenkamm** (renovated in 1995) and the **Kitzbüheler Horn.** Cable cars are within easy walking distance, even for those in ski boots.

The linking of the lift systems on the Hahnenkamm has created the celebrated ✪ **Kitzbühel Ski Circus,** which makes it possible to ski downhill for more than 80km (50 miles), with runs that suit every stage of proficiency. Numerous championship ski events are held here; the World Cup event each January pits the skills of top-flight skiers against the toughest, fastest downhill course in the world, a stretch of the Hahnenkamm especially designed for maximum speed. Its name, *Die Streif,* is both feared and respected among skiers. A ski pass costing 2,000AS ($154) entitles the holder to use of all the lifts that form the Ski Circus.

Skiing became a fact of life in Kitzbühel as long ago as 1892, when the first pair of skis was imported from Norway and intrepid daredevils began to slide down the snowy slopes at breakneck speeds. Many great names in skiing have since been associated with Kitzbühel, the most renowned being Toni Sailer, a native, who was the triple Olympic champion in the 1956 Winter Games in Cortina.

OTHER WINTER ACTIVITIES   There are many other winter activities: ski-bobbing, ski jumping, ice-skating, tobogganing, hiking on cleared trails, curling, and hang gliding, as well as such indoor activities as tennis, bowling, and swimming. The children's ski school provides training for the very young. And don't forget the lively après-ski scene, with bars, nightclubs, and dance clubs rocking from tea time until the wee hours.

SUMMER ACTIVITIES   Kitzbühel has plenty of summer pastimes too, including walking tours, visits to the **Wild Life Park** at Aurach (about 2 miles from Kitzbühel), tennis, horseback riding, golf, squash, brass band concerts in the town center, cycling, and swimming. There's an indoor swimming pool, but we recommend going to the **Schwarzsee** (Black Lake), a peat lake about a 15-minute walk from the center of town. Here you'll find bathing establishments, boats to rent, fishing, windsurfing, a water-ski school, and restaurants.

One of the region's most exotic collections of alpine flora is clustered into the jagged and rocky confines of the **Alpine Flower Garden Kitzbühel,** where various species of edelweiss, gorse, heather, and lichens are found on the sunny slopes of the Kitzbüheler Horn. Set at a height of around 6,000 feet above sea level, the garden—which the municipality of Kitzbühel owns and maintains as an incentive to midsummer tourism—is open late May to early September daily 8:30am to 5:30pm. It's at its most impressive June to August. Admission to the garden is free, and many visitors opt to view it by taking the Kitzbüheler Horn gondola (cable car) to its uppermost station and then descending on foot via the garden's labyrinth of footpaths to the gondola's middle station. The **Kitzbüheler Horn gondola** (☎ **05356/6951**) departs from the Kitzbühel at 20-minute intervals daily throughout the summer and winter months from 8:30am to 5:30pm; a round-trip ticket is 180AS ($14).

2 Belgium

by George McDonald

Modest little Belgium has never been known to boast of its charms, yet its variety of language, culture, history, and cuisine would do credit to a country many times its size. Belgium's diversity stems from its location at the cultural crossroads of Europe. The boundary between the continent's Germanic north and Latin south cuts clear across the country's middle, leaving Belgium divided into two major ethnic regions: Dutch-speaking Flanders and French-speaking Wallonia.

Although international attention is focused on Brussels as the "capital of Europe," the stage on which the unfolding drama of uniting Europe is playing, there's another Belgium of Gothic cathedrals, medieval castles, cobblestone streets, and tranquil canals waiting in the wings. In a country about the size of Maryland, the timeless beauty of Bruges and Ghent are accessible, even to the most hurried visitor.

1 Brussels

A city with a notable history, Brussels seems headed for a bright future, too. The "capital of Europe" has already begun to act like Europe's Washington, D.C., a focus of political and economic power, where decisions that affect the lives of people around the world are made. After centuries of occupation by Spain, Austria, and France, whose power struggles tore Europe apart, the city now hosts the bureaucratic empire trying to bring it all together. As headquarters of the European Union (EU), Brussels is a bastion of officialdom, a breeding ground for the regulations that govern and often exasperate the rest of Europe.

Bruxellois are more than a little ambivalent about their city's transformation into a power center. At first, the waves of Eurocrats seemed to bring a new cosmopolitan air to a slightly provincial city, but as old neighborhoods were leveled to make way for office towers, people wondered whether Brussels was losing its soul. After all, Brussels doesn't only mean politics and business. This city inspired surrealism and worships comic strips, prides itself on handmade lace and chocolate, and serves each one of its artisanal beers in its own unique glass.

Fortunately, not all of Brussels's individuality has been lost in this transition, and although the urban landscape has suffered from wanton destruction, the city's spirit survives in traditional cafes, bars, bistros, and restaurants—its French- and Dutch-speaking residents may have their differences, but they both love a good meal. Whether elegantly art nouveau or eccentrically festooned with posters, curios, and knickknacks, such centuries-old establishments provide a warm, convivial ambience that is peculiarly Belgian.

ORIENTATION

ARRIVING   By Plane   In addition to the national carrier Sabena, Brussels National-al Airport, at Zaventem, 14km (9 miles) northeast of the city center, is served by most major European airlines and many other international carriers. Trains to Brussels's three main stations (Gare du Nord, Gare Centrale, Gare du Midi) run every 20 minutes from the airport's underground railway station between 5:43am and 11:14pm (trip time to Gare Centrale: 25 minutes). One-way fare is 140BF ($3.70) first-class and 90BF ($2.35) second. Most trains have wide corridors and extra space for baggage.

Taxi fare is around 1,200BF ($32) to the city center. Use only official taxis from the rank outside Arrivals.

By Train   Brussels is served by Eurostar trains from London, and high-speed Thalys from Paris, Amsterdam, and Cologne, in addition to slower Eurocity (EC) and Intercity (IC) international services from many continental cities. For all international schedule and fare information, call ☎ **0900/10-366;** for service in Belgium call ☎ **02/555-25-25.** Tickets are sold at all stations. There are timetables at all stations; main stations have information and reservation counters.

If you are arriving from another European country, you will get out at **Gare Centrale,** Carrefour de l'Europe, downtown; **Gare du Midi,** rue de France (the Eurostar and Thalys terminal), south of the city center; or **Gare du Nord,** rue du Progrès, north of the city center.

By Bus   **Eurolines** has daily return services from London, Paris, Amsterdam, and many other cities to Brussels. For schedule and fare information on this and services from other European cities, contact Eurolines (☎ **0990/808080** in the U.K., or ☎ **02/203-07-07** in Belgium). International buses arrive at **Gare du Nord** railway station's bus terminal.

By Car   Major expressways to Brussels are the E19 from Amsterdam and Paris, and E40 from Ostend and Cologne.

By Boat   **P&O North Sea Ferries** (☎ **0148/237-7177** in the U.K.) has a daily overnight car ferry service from Hull in northern England to Zeebrugge (trip time: 14 hours). **Hoverspeed** (☎ **0870/524-0241** in the U.K.) offers fast catamaran car ferry service five to seven times daily from Dover, England, to Ostend (trip time: under 2 hours).

VISITOR INFORMATION   **Tourist Information Brussels (T.I.B.)** on the ground floor of the Hôtel de Ville (Town Hall), Grand-Place, 1000 Brussels (☎ **02/513-89-40;** fax 02/514-45-38; e-mail: tourism.brussels@tib.be; Métro: Centrale) sells a comprehensive visitors' booklet, *Brussels Guide & Map,* for 70BF ($1.85); makes same-day hotel reservations; organizes guided walking tours in summer; and has multilingual guides who can be engaged by the hour or day. It is open April to December, daily 9am to 6pm; January to March, Monday to Saturday 9am to 6pm. **Tourist Information Belgium,** rue du Marché-aux-Herbes 63, 1000 Brussels (☎ **02/504-03-90;** fax 02/504-02-70; www.toervl.be; e-mail: info@toervl.be; Métro: Centrale), is open June to September, Monday to Saturday 9am to 7pm, Sunday 9am to 6pm; October to March, Monday to Saturday 9am to 6pm, Sunday (April, May, October) 9am to 6pm or (November to March) 1 to 5pm.

Brussels

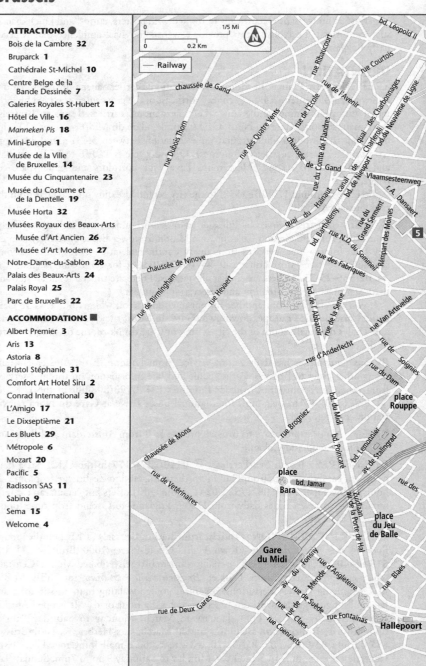

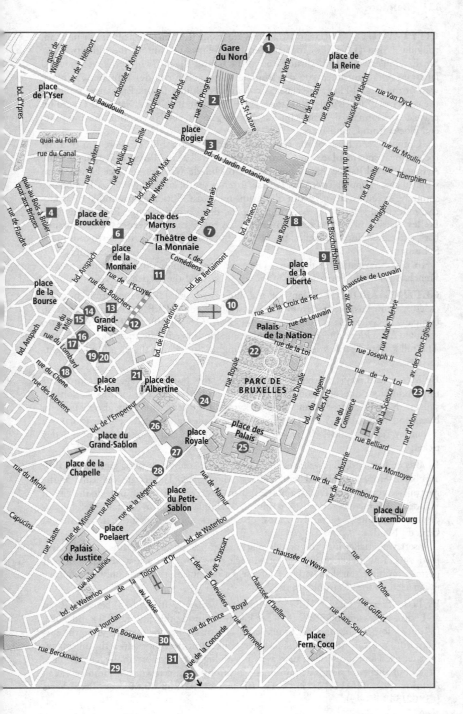

Gare
du Nord

place de
la Reine

quai de
Willebroek

av. de l'Héliport

chaussée d'Anvers

rue du Marché

rue du Progrès

bd. St-Lazare

rue Verte

rue de la Poste

rue Royale

chaussée de Haecht

rue Van Dyck

1

place
de l'Yser

bd. d'Ypres

bd. Baudouin

Jacqmain

Émile

2

place
Rogier

3

bd. du Jardin Botanique

rue du Moulin

rue du Méridien

rue de la Limite

rue Tiberghien

quai au Foin

rue du Canal

rue de Laeken

rue du Pélican

bd.

bd. Adolphe Max

rue Neuve

rue du Marais

rue Pacheco

rue Royale

8

bd. Bisschoffsheim

rue Potagère

quai au Bois à Brûler

quai aux Briques

rue de Flandre

4

place de
Brouckère

6

place des
Martyrs

Théâtre de
la Monnaie

7

9

place
de la
Liberté

chaussée de Louvain

place
de la
Monnaie

r. des
Comédiens

11

bd. Anspach

rue de l'Ecuyer

bd. de Berlaimont

av. des Arts

rue Marie-Thérèse

rue des Bouchers

place
de la
Bourse

14

13

15

Grand-
Place

12

rue de l'Impératrice

10

rue de la Croix de Fer

Palais
de la Nation

rue de Louvain

rue Joseph II

av. des Deux-Églises

rue du Midi

17

16

rue du Lombard

19 **20**

rue Royale

22

rue de la Loi

rue de la Loi

23 →

bd. Anspach

rue du Chêne

18

place
St-Jean

21

place de
l'Albertine

24

PARC DE
BRUXELLES

bd. du Régent

av. des Arts

rue Ducale

rue du Commerce

rue de la Science

rue d'Arlon

rue des Alexiens

bd. de l'Empereur

26

place des
Palais

rue Belliard

place du
Grand-Sablon

place
Royale

25

27

rue Montoyer

place de la
Chapelle

28

rue du Miroir

rue de la Régence

place
du Petit-
Sablon

rue de Namur

rue de l'Industrie

rue du Luxembourg

place du
Luxembourg

rue Haute

rue de Minimes

rue Allard

place
Poelaert

bd. de Waterloo

Capucins

Palais
de Justice

rue aux Laines

bd. de Waterloo

av. de la Toison d'Or

av. Louise

r. des Chevaliers

rue de Strassart

chaussée du Wavre

rue du Trône

rue Goffart

rue Sans-Souci

chaussée d'Ixelles

rue du Prince Royal

rue de la Concorde

rue Keyenveld

place
Fern. Cocq

rue Jourdan

rue Bosquet

30

31

rue Berckmans

29

32 ↓

CITY LAYOUT   Most main attractions are inside the heart-shaped inner ring-road, roughly 2.5km (1.5 miles) in diameter, that follows the line of the old city walls. Small, cobblestone streets cluster around the **Grand-Place.** Two nearby well-traveled lanes are restaurant-lined **rue des Bouchers** and **petite rue des Bouchers.** A block west of the Grand-Place, the classical colonnaded Bourse (Stock Exchange) stands at the center of Brussels's nightlife zone. A few blocks north is the **National Opera** on place de la Monnaie. The city's busiest shopping street, **rue Neuve,** runs north for several blocks from Grand-Place.

"Uptown," southeast of the center and literally atop a hill, is where you find the second great square, **place du Grand-Sablon,** as well as the **Royal Museums of Fine Arts** and **Royal Palace.** Head southwest across bd. de Waterloo to place Louise, from which a chic shopping street, **av. Louise,** extends south, and a slightly less fashionable shopping street, **av. de la Toison d'Or,** runs northeast. Both are surrounded by attractive residential side streets, containing typical Belgian architecture. East of this zone **Ixelles** district, near the **Free University,** has many casual, inexpensive restaurants, bars, and cafes. North of Ixelles, the modern European Union district surrounds **place Schuman.**

To make navigating challenging, maps list street names within the city limits in French and Dutch. For consistency and ease, I've used the French names.

GETTING AROUND   Maps of the integrated public transportation network (Métro, tram, bus) are free from the tourist office, the **S.T.I.B.** public transportation company at Galerie de la Toison d'Or 20 (☎ **02/515-20-00**), and from main Métro stations. All stations and many bus and tram stops have public transportation maps. The full system operates from 6am to midnight, after which there's a limited night-bus system.

By Métro (Subway)   Although not extensive, this fast and efficient system covers important city center locations and reaches the suburbs. You can identify stations by signs with a white letter M on a blue background. Tickets, which can also be used on buses and trams, cost 50BF ($1) for a single (called a "direct"); 240BF ($6) for a 5-journey ticket; 340BF ($9) for a 10-journey ticket; and 130BF ($3) for a 1-day ticket.

By Bus & Tram   Urban vehicles are yellow; stop them by extending your arm as they approach. Stops are marked with red-and-white signs. Tickets are the same as the Métro (see above). The **De Lijn** bus company has service to points outside the city in Flanders; **T.E.C.** has service to points in Wallonia. Belgium has few useful long-distance bus routes, as trains do most of the work; those there are generally stop at Gare du Nord.

Insert your ticket into the orange machines inside buses and trams and at Métro platforms. Your ticket must be inserted each time you enter a new vehicle, but as it permits multiple transfers within a 1-hour period, during that time only one journey is canceled by the electronic scanner.

By Taxi   Starting rate is 95BF ($2.50) during the day, 170BF ($4.45) between 10pm and 6am, increasing by 38BF ($1) per kilometer inside the city (tariff 1) and 76BF ($2) per kilometer beyond city limits (tariff 2)—make sure the meter is set to the correct tariff. You can round up the fare if you like, but need not add a tip unless you have received an extra service, such as help with luggage. Taxis cannot be hailed on the street, but there are stands at prominent locations around town. For radio cabs, call **Autolux** (☎ **02/411-12-21**), **Taxis Bleus** (☎ **02/268-00-00**), or **Taxis Verts** (☎ **02/349-49-49**).

By Car   At rush hour (8 to 10am and 4 to 6pm), it's almost impossible to move on main roads inside the city and on the R0 outer ring-road. Do yourself a favor: Leave the car at a parking garage. Brussels's proximity to the rest of the country, as well as to France, Germany, and Holland, makes a car an attractive option for continuing on. All the top U.S. firms rent here—including **Hertz,** bd. Maurice-Lemmonier 8 (☎ 02/726-49-50; Métro: Anneesens); **Avis,** rue Américaine 145 (☎ 02/720-09-44; tram: 91 or 92); and **Budget,** av. Louise 327 (☎ 02/646-51-30; Métro: Place Louise). Note that car rentals are taxed 21% in Belgium.

Fast Facts: Brussels

American Express   The AMEX office is at bd. du Souverain 100, 1000 Brussels (☎ 02/676-21-11; Métro: Horrmann-Debroux). It's open Monday to Friday 9am to 1pm and 2 to 5pm; however, call ahead before visiting, as the office is out in the suburbs.

Business Hours   Banks are open Monday to Friday 9am to 1pm and 2 to 4:30 or 5pm. Shopping hours are Monday to Saturday 9 or 10am to 6 or 7pm. Some stores, such as bakers and news vendors, open earlier, and some open the same hours on Sunday. Many stores stay open on Friday until 8 or 9pm.

Currency   The exchange rate used in this chapter is $1 = 38 Belgian francs (BF) or 1BF = 2.5¢. At press time, £1 = 62BF. The euro rate was currently fixed at €1 = 40.34BF.

Currency Exchange   Banks offer the best rates, and exchange offices in railway stations come close. If you carry American Express traveler's checks, change them at **American Express** (see above), where there's no commission charge. Hotels and street bureaux de change offer poorer rates and may charge high commissions, but are open in the evenings and on weekends. **Thomas Cook,** Grand-Place 4 (☎ 02/513-28-45; Métro: Centrale), has reasonable rates. There are many ATMs around town, connected to Cirrus and Plus, and identified by "Bancontact" and "Mister Cash" logos. You must have a four-digit PIN to access the ATMs.

Dentists/Doctors   For emergency medical service around the clock, call ☎ 02/479-18-18; ask for an English-speaking doctor. For emergency dental care, call ☎ 02/426-10-26.

Embassies   The **U.S. Embassy** is at bd. du Regent 27, 1000 Brussels (☎ 02/508-21-11; Métro: Arts-Loi); **Canadian Embassy,** av. de Tervuren 2, 1040 Brussels (☎ 02/741-06-11); **U.K. Embassy,** rue Arlon 85, 1040 Brussels (☎ 02/287-62-11; Métro: Maalbeek); **Irish Embassy,** rue Froissart 89, 1040 Brussels (☎ 02/230-53-37; Métro: Schuman); **Australian Embassy,** rue Guimard 6–8, 1040 Brussels (☎ 02/286-05-00; Métro: Merode); **New Zealand Embassy,** bd. du Regent 47, 1000 Brussels (☎ 02/512-10-40; Métro: Trone).

Emergencies   For an ambulance, call ☎ 100; for police assistance, ☎ 101; for fire, ☎ 100.

Internet Access   Try **@Internem,** bd. Général Jacques 68, 1050 Ixelles (☎ and fax 02/649-45-09; www.internem.be; tram: 23 or 90), a Vietnamese restaurant and cybercafe; open daily noon to midnight.

Post Office   The office at **Gare du Midi,** av. Fonsny 1E/F (☎ **02/538-33-98;** Métro: Midi), is open 24 hours a day. Others are open Monday to Friday 9am to 5pm; closed weekends and public holidays; the **Centre Monnaie** office, place de la Monnaie (☎ **02/226-21-11;** Métro: De Brouckère), is also open Saturday 9:30am to 3pm).

Safety   Brussels is generally safe, but there's a rise in crime, in particular pickpocketing, theft from cars and of cars, and muggings in Métro station foot tunnels. Tourists are targets of pickpockets on the Métro and in tourist areas such as the Grand-Place.

Telephone   Belgium's country code is **32.** Brussels's city code is **2;** use this code when calling from outside Belgium. In Belgium, use **02.**

A local call costs 15BF (40¢) for 3 minutes. To make international calls, use a Belgacom telecard, available at Belgacom offices and many news vendors for 200BF ($5), 500BF ($13), or 1,000BF ($26). It costs 120BF ($3.15) for a 3-minute call to the United States with a telecard. To make a collect or calling card call from a pay phone, deposit 10BF (25¢) and dial one of the following access numbers to reach an American operator or an English-language voice prompt: **AT&T** (☎ **0800/10-010**); **MCI** (☎ **0800/10-012**); **Sprint** (☎ **0800/11-605**).

WHERE TO STAY

The business of Brussels is business, a fact reflected in the cost and nature of available accommodations. Hotels in the upper price range have a wealth of facilities for business travelers—conference rooms, fax machines, and efficient, though impersonal, service. At every level, hotels fill up during the week and empty out on weekends and during July and August. In off-peak periods, rates can drop as much as 50% from those quoted below; be sure to ask for lower rates and that you're quoted the correct rates, which include 21% value added tax (TVA) and service.

The **T.I.B.** office in the Grand-Place and the **Belgian Tourist Office** at rue du Marché-aux-Herbes 63 (see "Visitor Information," above) make reservations for the same day, if you go in person, for a small fee (deducted by the hotel from its room rate). T.I.B. publishes an annual *Hotel Guide* with listings by price range, and can provide complete information, including space availability, on hostels. **Belgian Tourist Reservations,** bd. Anspach 111, 1000 Brussels (☎ **02/513-74-84;** fax 02/513-92-77), reserves hotel rooms throughout Belgium and often gets substantial discounts.

An alternative to hotels is a bed-and-breakfast. Brussels has several good B&B organizations: **Bed & Brussels,** rue Kindermans 9, 1050 Brussels (☎ **02/644-07-37;** fax 02/644-01-14); and **New Windrose,** av. Brugman 11, 1060 Brussels (☎ **02/ 534-71-91;** fax 02/534-71-92). All will send you a list of host families (the Windrose includes a profile of the families) and rates. Booking fee is 500BF ($13) per reservation; rates vary from 1,500BF to 2,200BF ($39 to $58) for a double.

The **Sheraton Brussels Airport,** Luchthaven Brussel Nationaal (facing Departures), 1930 Zaventem (☎ **800/325-3535** in the U.S. and Canada, or 02/725-10-00; fax 02/710-80-80; www.sheraton.com), couldn't be more convenient to the airport without being on the runway. You have all the comfort you would expect of a top-flight Sheraton. Doubles cost 14,500BF to 15,500BF ($382 to $408) per night. For a cheaper airport option, try the **Holiday Inn Express Brussels Airport,** Berkenlaan 5 (access road opposite NATO HQ), 1831 Diegem (☎ **02/725-33-80;** fax 02/725-38-10). Doubles cost 4,950BF to 7,000BF ($130 to $184), and are frequently discounted. You can dine at its big brother Holiday Inn next door. There's free parking and an airport shuttle.

VERY EXPENSIVE

Conrad International. Av. Louise 71, 1050 Brussels (at place Stéphanie). ☎ **02/542-42-42.** Fax 02/542-42-00. www.brussels.conradinternational.com. E-mail: bruhc—rm@hilton.com. 269 units. A/C MINIBAR TV TEL. 15,000BF ($395) double; 35,000BF ($921) suite. AE, CB, DC, DISC, MC, V. Parking 490BF ($13). Métro: Louise.

Big, bright, and fancy, this hotel offers luxuriously furnished spacious rooms that include trouser presses, hair dryers, icemakers, and huge tubs. French restaurant La Maison du Maître provides all the refinements of haute cuisine; Café Wiltshire maintains a less formal tone. Service and amenities are all you would expect from a hotel in its price category—24-hour room service, sports and fitness center, wheelchair access, parking garage.

Métropole. Place de Brouckère 31 (close to Centre Monnaie), 1000 Brussels. ☎ **02/217-23-00.** Fax 02/218-02-20. www.metropolehotel.be. E-mail: info@metropolehotel.be. 410 units. MINIBAR TV TEL. 12,500–16,500BF ($329–$434) double; from 18,000BF ($474) suite. Rates include buffet breakfast. AE, CB, DC, JCB, MC, V. Parking 500BF ($13). Métro: De Brouckère.

An ornate marble-and-gilt interior distinguishes this 19th-century hotel several blocks from the Grand-Place. Spacious rooms have classic furnishings and some modern luxuries, including heated towel racks, hair dryers, and trouser presses. French restaurant L'Alban Chambon caters to the sophisticated diner; belle epoque Café Métropole to the sophisticated cafe hound. There's a heated sidewalk terrace, though it has an uninspiring view of a busy street. Amenities include a relaxation center with sauna, Turkish bath, Jacuzzi, solarium, and flotation tank.

✪ **Radisson SAS.** Rue du Fossé-aux-Loups 47 (close to Galeries Royales Saint-Hubert). ☎ **800/333-3333** in the U.S. and Canada, or 02/219-28-28. Fax 02/219-62-62. www.radisson.com/brussels.be. E-mail: sales@bruzh.rdsas.com. 281 units. A/C MINIBAR TV TEL. 13,000–17,000BF ($342–$447) double; from 19,000BF ($500) suite. Rates in some doubles include buffet breakfast. AE, CB, DC, MC, V. Parking 770BF ($20). Métro: Centrale.

Modern, yet in harmony with its neighborhood a few blocks from the Grand-Place, this highly regarded hotel incorporates part of the medieval city wall. Large rooms are decorated in a variety of styles, including Scandinavian, Asian, and Italian. All rooms have personal answering machines and hair dryers. The Sea Grill restaurant wins plaudits for its seafood; the Atrium serves Belgian and Scandinavian specialties; and the Bar Dessinée has a Belgian comic strip theme. Amenities include a health club and sauna.

EXPENSIVE

✪ **Astoria.** Rue Royale 103 (close to Colonne du Congrès), 1000 Brussels. ☎ **800/SOFI-TEL** in the U.S. and Canada, or 02/227-05-05. Fax 02/217-11-50. www.sofitel.com. E-mail: h1154@accor-hotels.com. 118 units. A/C MINIBAR TV TEL. Mon–Fri 13,000BF ($342), Sat–Sun 5,500BF ($145) double; from 18,000BF ($474) suite. Weekend double rates include buffet breakfast. AE, CB, DC, MC, V. Valet parking 600BF ($16). Métro: Botanique.

You are transported to a more elegant age the moment you walk into the belle epoque foyer. The Astoria dates from 1909, and its plush interior recalls the panache of that vanished heyday. Rooms are attractively furnished, though not extravagantly so, and include the latest fixtures and fittings, such as wall-mounted hair dryers.

Bristol Stephanie. Av. Louise 91–93, 1050 Brussels. ☎ **02/543-33-11.** Fax 02/538-03-07. www.bristol.be. E-mail: hotel_bristol@bristol.be. 142 units. A/C MINIBAR TV TEL. 11,200BF ($295) double; from 20,500BF ($539) suite. AE, CB, DC, MC, V. Parking 350BF ($9). Métro: Louise.

Every feature of this sleek Norwegian-owned hotel, from its lobby fittings to furnishings in the 16 kitchenette suites, is streamlined, functional, and representative of the best in Nordic design. It's in a pretty section of one of the city's toniest shopping streets, and has an indoor pool. Restaurant Le Chalet d'Odin's international menu is strong on Norwegian specialties.

L'Amigo. Rue de l'Amigo 1–3 (off the Grand-Place), 1000 Brussels. ☎ **02/547-47-47.** Fax 02/513-52-77. www.hotelamigo.com. E-mail: hotelamigo@hotelamigo.com. 185 units. MINIBAR TV TEL. 8,900–11,500BF ($234–$303) double; from 15,500BF ($408) suite. Rates include continental breakfast. AE, DC, JCB, MC, V. Parking 490BF ($13). Métro: Bourse.

In Brussels slang, an "amigo" is a prison, and indeed, a prison once stood here, but any resemblance to the former accommodations is nominal. Understated old European refinement permeates the stately corridors. Rooms are lushly outfitted, about two-thirds have air-conditioning, all have hair dryers. Although the restaurant is unremarkable and fitness buffs have to go elsewhere to exercise, the hotel provides world-class comforts.

MODERATE

○ **Albert Premier.** Place Rogier 20 (beside Gare du Nord), 1210 Brussels. ☎ **02/203-31-25.** Fax 02/203-43-31. 287 units. TV TEL. 3,000–5,500BF ($79–$145) double. Rates include buffet breakfast. DC, MC, V. Limited parking available on street. Métro: Rogier.

With a fully renovated art deco interior behind a 19th-century facade, the Albert, named after Belgium's dashing World War I "Soldier King," has retained a certain cachet despite paralleling the mixed fortunes of the square on which it stands. Once-elegant, then seedy, this neighborhood on the edge of the city center has been turned around and is now a thriving business district. Rooms are minimalist in terms of facilities, yet modern, comfortable, attractively decorated, and have hair dryers.

Aris. Rue du Marché-aux-Herbes 78–80, 1000 Brussels (off Grand-Place). ☎ **02/514-43-00.** Fax 02/514-01-19. 55 units. A/C TV TEL. 6,500BF ($171.05) double. Rates include buffet breakfast. DC, JCB, MC, V. Limited parking available on street. Métro: Centrale.

What this shiny hotel lacks in personality it makes up for in amenities and position. Rooms are impersonal but well outfitted with double-glazed windows, firm beds, a private safe, and hair dryers. Charming it isn't, but you'll have most of the comforts of home.

Comfort Art Hotel Siru. Place Rogier 1 (opposite Gare du Nord), 1210 Brussels. ☎ **800/228-3323** in the U.S. and Canada, or 02/203-35-80. Fax 02/203-33-03. E-mail: art.hotel.siru@skynet.be. 101 units. MINIBAR TV TEL. 3,200–6,200BF ($84–$163) double. Rates include buffet breakfast. AE, CB, DC, MC, V. Parking 425BF ($11). Métro: Rogier.

The owner of this art-gallery-cum-hotel in the middle of a redeveloped business district persuaded 130 Belgian artists, including some of the country's biggest names, to "decorate" each of the coolly modern, well-equipped rooms (all have hair dryers) and the corridors with a work on travel. Given the unpredictable nature of reactions to modern art, some clients apparently reserve the same room time after time; others ask for a room change in the middle of the night. It is not easily forgotten.

Le Dixseptième. Rue de la Madeleine 25, 1000 Brussels (off place de l'Albertine). ☎ **02/502-57-44.** Fax 02/502-64-24. 24 units. MINIBAR TV TEL. 6,600BF ($174) studio; 9,800–13,600BF ($258–$358) suite. AE, DC, MC, V. Limited parking available on street. Métro: Centrale.

This graceful, 17th-century house stands close to the Grand-Place in a neighborhood of restored dwellings. Rooms are as big as suites in many hotels, and some have balconies. All are in 18th-century style and are named after Belgian painters from Brueghel to Magritte. Two beautiful lounges are decorated with carved wooden medallions and 18th-century paintings.

Mozart. Rue du Marché-aux-Fromages 15a, 1000 Bruxelles (close to Grand-Place). ☎ **02/502-66-61.** Fax 02/502-77-58. www.hotel-mozart.be. E-mail: hotel.mozart@ skynet.be. 47 units. TV TEL. 3,500BF ($92) double. Rates include continental breakfast. AE, DC, MC, V. Limited parking available on street. Métro: Centrale.

Go a flight up from the busy, cheap-eats street level, and guess which famous composer's music wafts through the lobby? Salmon-colored walls, plants, and old paintings create a warm, intimate ambience that's carried into the rooms. Although furnishings are blandly modern, colorful fabrics and exposed beams lend each room a rustic originality. Several are duplexes with a sitting room underneath the loft bedroom. Top rooms have a great view. All have hair dryers.

Sema. Rue des Harengs 6–8, 1000 Brussels (close to Grand-Place). ☎ **02/514-07-60.** Fax 02/548-90-39. 11 units. TV TEL. 4,500BF ($118) double. Rates include buffet breakfast. AE, DC, MC, V. Limited parking available on street. Métro: Centrale.

This small, modern hotel is warmly inviting. Its cozy lobby is up a flight of stairs, and from there an elevator takes you to your room. Gleaming wood floors, white walls, and bright bedcovers create a cheerful setting in quite large rooms. Windows are double-glazed and rooms have hair dryers.

INEXPENSIVE

Les Bluets. Rue Berckmans 124, 1060 Brussels (off av. Louise). ☎ **02/534-39-83.** Fax 02/543-09-70. E-mail: bluets@eudoramail.com. 10 units. TV TEL. 2,650BF ($70) double. Rates include continental breakfast. MC, V. Limited parking available on street. Métro: Hôtel des Monnaies.

In a house dating from 1864, you step into a fine old family hotel with a proprietress, Mme Myriam Heller, who considers her guests almost as members of the family. Each room is different, but all have high ceilings and unusual antiques—statuettes, stained glass, paintings—and knickknacks. The effect is more that of a comfortable country house than a hotel. All rooms have hair dryers. Smoking is not allowed anywhere in the hotel.

Pacific. Rue Antoine Dansaert 57 (2 blocks from the Bourse), 1000 Brussels. ☎ and fax **02/511-84-59.** 15 units (2 with shower only; none with toilet). 1,800–2,300BF ($47–$61) double. Showers 100BF ($3) extra for rooms without bathrooms. Rates include full breakfast. No credit cards. Parking 200BF ($5). Métro: Bourse.

In a bohemian neighborhood, this hotel is a 5-minute walk from Grand-Place. Most rooms are large, though with plumbing from 80 years ago; front rooms have small balconies. Breakfast is served in a room eclectically decorated with a zebra skin, a Canadian World War II steel helmet, railway signal lamps, copper pots, and a Buddhist prayer wheel. Monks from the Dalai Lama's entourage once stayed here and left mystical symbols in some rooms. Just the place if you prefer atmosphere over comfort.

Sabina. Rue du Nord 78 (close to Colonne du Congrès), 1000 Brussels. ☎ **02/218-26-37.** Fax 02/219-32-39. 24 units. TV TEL. 2,500BF ($66) double. Rates include buffet breakfast. AE, DC, MC, V. Limited parking available on street. Métro: Madou.

This small hostelry is like a private residence, presided over by hospitable owners. A grandfather clock in the reception area and polished wood along the restaurant walls give it a warm, homey atmosphere. Rooms vary in size, but all are comfortable and simply, yet tastefully done in modern style with twin beds. Three rooms have kitchenettes for 100BF ($2.65) extra; all have hair dryers.

✪ **Welcome.** Quai au Bois-à-Brûler 23, 1000 Brussels (at the Marché-aux-Poissons). ☎ **02/ 219-95-46.** Fax 02/217-18-87. www.hotelwelcome.com. E-mail: info@hotelwelcome.com. 10 units. A/C MINIBAR TV TEL. 2,600–4,100BF ($68–$108) double; 4,600BF ($121) suite. DC, MC, V. Free parking. Métro: Ste-Catherine.

You'll be hard put to imagine a hotel that leaves you with fonder memories, though the Welcome, up now from six rooms to 10, is no longer the city's smallest. It has such fiercely loyal regulars that it is often fully booked—admittedly not a difficult feat—so you should reserve far ahead. The enthusiastic couple who own it, Michel and Sophie Smeesters, has generated a loyal following with their bright, cheerful rooms and superb attached seafood restaurant, La Truite d'Argent (see "Where to Dine," below).

WHERE TO DINE

Imaginatively decorated restaurant interiors reflect the importance Bruxellois attach to culinary pleasure. In this, they have been joined by the Euro and international crowd. From crisp "French" fries and waffles on the street corner to succulent Flemish and Walloon specialties, it's almost impossible to eat badly in Brussels, and with 2,000 restaurants to choose from you'll have no problem eating well at a reasonable price.

Most of the city's favorite dishes are based on local products, with the notable exception of its beloved fresh *moules* (mussels), served in multitudinous variations from July through the winter, which come from Zeeland in the Netherlands. A steaming bowl of mussels, or a user-friendly *steak-frites* (steak and french fries), always goes down well with Belgian diners.

Belgium is renowned for 400 brands of beer produced by hundreds of small breweries; Belgian chefs use beer in their sauces the way French chefs use wine. Beef, chicken, and fish are often bathed in a savory sauce based on the local *gueuze, faro,* and *kriek* brews. Beer is the perfect accompaniment to the sturdy regional dishes you find on menus around town: *waterzooï,* fish or chicken stew with a parsley-and-cream sauce; *stoemp,* a puree of vegetables and potatoes with sausage, steak, or chop; *paling in 't groen,* eel in a grass-green sauce; *ballekes,* spicy meatballs; *hochepot,* stew; *lapin à la gueuze,* rabbit with a Brussels beer sauce; and *carbonnades à la flamande,* beef stew with a beer sauce. A selection of the country's 300 artisanal cheeses, or waffles and whipped fresh cream, is a good way to finish off.

There are good restaurants all around town, with the main dining-out areas centering around the Grand-Place and the Marché-aux-Poissons (Fish Market) in the Center; and in trendy Ixelles and St-Gilles south of the Center. Vegetarian restaurants are thin on the ground, though many places have a vegetarian listing on their menu offering at least a few items. If you are a nonsmoker you're mostly out of luck—get ready to consume a garnish of secondhand smoke with your meal.

Don't fret if service is slow: People take their time dining out here, and just sitting in a good restaurant is part of the pleasure. Service is included in most, but not all, checks, so you usually don't have to do much more than round the total up to the nearest handy amount, unless you're especially pleased with the service, in which case a 10% tip is adequate—even generous by Belgian standards.

VERY EXPENSIVE

✪ **Comme Chez Soi.** Place Rouppe 23. ☎ **02/512-29-21.** Reservations required for lunch and dinner. Main courses 1,250–3,550BF ($33–$93); set-price menus 2,150–4,950BF ($57–$130). AE, DC, MC, V. Tues–Sat noon–1:30pm and 7–9:30pm (closed July and Christmas/ New Year holidays). Métro: Anneessens. CLASSIC FRENCH.

Looking for unforgettable French cuisine in an art nouveau setting? An expedition inside the hallowed portals of "Just Like Home," sporting the maximum three Michelin stars, will surely be the culinary highlight of your trip to Brussels. Although the food is a long way from what most people eat at home, the welcome from master chef Pierre Wynants is warm, and his standards are high enough for the most rigorous taste buds. Ask for a table in the kitchen, where you can watch the master at work. The sautéed lobster with truffles and chanterelles and the roast saddle of lamb are memorable main courses; for dessert, try the soufflé of preserved oranges in Mandarine Napoléon liqueur.

La Maison du Cygne. Grand-Place 9 (entrance at rue Charles Buls 2). ☎ **02/511-82-44.** Reservations recommended on weekends. Main courses 950–1,600BF ($25–$42); set-price menu 2,200BF ($58). AE, DC, MC, V. Mon–Fri noon–2:15pm and Mon–Sat 7pm–midnight (closed 3 weeks in Aug). Métro: Centrale. CLASSIC FRENCH.

This grande dame of Brussels restaurants has one Michelin star and overlooks the Grand-Place from the former Butchers' Guildhouse. "The House of the Swan's" service, though a tad stuffy, is as elegant as the polished walnut walls, bronze wall sconces, and green velvet. Among the classics offered, try the souplike lobster stew, tournedos with green peppercorns, oysters in champagne, or sole mousse. Because of its location, Cygne is usually crowded at lunch, but dinner reservations are likely to be available.

Villa Lorraine. Av. du Vivier d'Oie 75. ☎ **02/374-31-63.** Main courses 1,200–1,800BF ($32–$47); menu gastronomique 3,000BF ($79). AE, DC, MC, V. Mon–Sat noon–2:30pm and 7–9:30pm. Closed 3 weeks in July. Going by car or taxi is the most practical way to get there. CLASSIC FRENCH.

You'll find one of the city's top kitchens in this renovated château on the fringes of the Bois de la Cambre park. The dining rooms are spacious, with wicker furnishings, flower arrangements everywhere, and a skylight. In good weather you may elect to have drinks outside under the trees. Among the classic French offerings are saddle of lamb in a delicate red-wine-and-herb sauce, cold salmon in an herb sauce, partridge cooked with apples, and baked lobster with butter rose.

EXPENSIVE

De l'Ogenblik. Galerie des Princes 1. ☎ **02/511-61-51.** Main courses 800–1,000BF ($21–$26); plat du jour 440BF ($12). AE, DC, MC, V. Mon–Sat noon–2:30pm and 7pm–midnight (Fri–Sat to 12:30am). Métro: Centrale. FRENCH/BELGIAN BISTRO.

In the elegant surroundings of the Galeries Royales St-Hubert, this restaurant supplies good taste in a Parisian bistro setting, popular with off-duty actors from the Gallery theater. It often gets busy, but the ambience in the two-level, wood-and-brass dining room, with a sand-strewn floor, is convivial, if a little too tightly packed. Look for garlicky seafood and meat menu dishes, and expect to pay a smidgen more for atmosphere than might be strictly justified by results on the plate.

✪ **La Quincaillerie.** Rue du Page 45 (at rue Américaine). ☎ **02/538-25-53.** Main courses 640–960BF ($17–$25); menu du jour 1,750BF ($46). AE, CB, DC, MC, V. Mon–Fri noon–2:30pm and 7pm–midnight; Sat–Sun 7pm–midnight. Tram: 81, 82, 91, or 92 to chaussée de Charleroi. MODERN FRENCH/OYSTER BAR.

In Ixelles, a part of the city where fine restaurants are as common as streetlights, this spot stands out, even though it may be a little too aware of its own modish good looks and a shade pricey. The setting is a traditional former hardware store, with wood paneling and masses of wooden drawers, designed by students of art nouveau master Victor Horta. It's busy enough to get the wait staff harassed and absent-minded, yet they are always friendly. Specialties include salmon in roasted rock salt and baby duck with a crust of honey and lime.

La Truite d'Argent. Quai aux Bois-à-Brûler 23 (at the Marché-aux-Poissons). ☎ **02/219-95-46.** Main courses 720–1,080BF ($19–$28); set-price menu 1,250BF ($33).

DC, MC, V. Mon–Fri noon–2:30pm and 7–11:30pm. Métro: Ste-Catherine. CLASSIC FRENCH/SEAFOOD.

Enthusiastic owners of an 1896 restaurant that once boasted Jacques Brel among its regular customers, Michel and Sophie Smeesters positively insist on delivering savory seafood specialties. *Superb* is the best word to describe the dishes, which include meat choices. All are prepared from fine ingredients, and the presentation is exquisite, so pleasing to the eye you might hesitate to destroy the image by eating it. You can dine on a sidewalk terrace on the Fish Market in good weather.

MODERATE

L'Amadeus. Rue Veydt 13. ☎ **02/538-34-27.** Main courses 545–875BF ($14–$23); plat du jour (Mon–Fri) 355BF ($9); Sun brunch 670BF ($18). AE, DC, MC, V. Tues–Fri and Sun noon–2:30pm and 7pm–1am; Mon, Sat 7pm–1am. Métro: Louise. MODERN BELGIAN.

The postmodern chic of this restaurant/wine bar/oyster bar in a former sculptor's studio with a garden-courtyard terrace makes a refreshing change from traditional Belgian style. Its candlelit interior is so dim you would think they're hiding something, but the cooking is nothing to be ashamed of. The menu includes such vegetarian treats as vegetarian lasagna and ricotta and spinach tortellini, and for meat eaters, caramelized spare ribs and several salmon dishes, all accompanied by delicious homemade nut bread. The Sunday brunch is an all-you-can-eat affair, that includes smoked fish, cheese, eggs, bread, cereal, juice, and coffee.

✪ La Roue d'Or. Rue des Chapeliers 26 (off Grand-Place). ☎ **02/514-25-54.** Main courses 495–875BF ($13–$23); menu du jour 1,650–2,000BF ($43–$53). AE, DC, MC, V. Daily noon–12:30am; closed mid-July to mid-Aug. Métro: Centrale. TRADITIONAL BELGIAN.

This welcoming, art nouveau brasserie with lots of dark wood, mirrors, a frescoed ceiling, Magritte images on the walls, and marble-topped tables, has a loyal local following. An extensive menu, ranging from grilled meats to a good selection of cooked salmon and other seafood, as well as old Belgian favorites like *stoemp*, caters to just about any appetite, and the beer, wine, and spirits list is equally long. Jeff De Gelas, the colorful owner (he also owns 't Kelderke, see below), is known locally as the "King of Stoemp."

Le Falstaff Gourmand. Rue des Pierres 38 (near the Bourse). ☎ **02/512-17-61.** Main courses 480–720BF ($13–$19); menu gourmand 1,000BF ($26). AE, DC, MC, V. Tues–Sun 11:30am–3pm and 7–11pm (except Sun evening). Métro: Bourse. CLASSIC BELGIAN/FRENCH.

Le Falstaff cafe across from the Bourse (see "Brussels After Dark," below) is widely renowned as a classic art nouveau bar and eatery. Around the corner, its sister establishment has a different but equally notable style. Service is attentive, prompt, and friendly. First-class Belgian and French menu dishes include one of the best deals in Brussels: a three-course *menu gourmand*, which includes an aperitif, glass of wine with the starter, and a small pitcher of wine with the main course.

Le Joueur de Flûte. Rue de l'Epée 26 (beside the Palais de Justice). ☎ **02/513-43-11.** Reservations required. Set-price menu 1,200BF ($32). MC, V. Mon–Fri 8–10pm. Métro: Louise. MODERN FRENCH/BELGIAN.

Dining in this tiny Marolles restaurant is nothing if not straightforward. There is only one menu, with a couple of variations for the main course. Don't let that, or the fact that it serves only 16 diners each evening, put you off. Owner/chef Philippe Van Cappelen, who has had more than a passing acquaintance with Michelin stars in his time, now likes to keep things simple. He changes the decor to suit the changing seasons and cooks whatever he feels like cooking—and it's guaranteed to be delicious.

Le Marmiton. Rue des Bouchers 43 (off Grand-Place). ☎ **02/511-79-10.** Main courses 480–720BF ($13–$19); menu du jour 395–725BF ($10–$19). AE, DC, MC, V. Daily noon–3pm and 6–11:30pm (12:30am on weekends). Métro: Centrale. BELGIAN/FRENCH.

A welcoming environment, hearty servings, and commitment to satisfying customers are hallmarks at this cozy restaurant, now on two floors. On a menu that emphasizes fish, the seafood cocktail starter is a heap of shellfish and crustaceans substantial enough to be a main course, and the sole is excellent. Meat dishes are available, too. The menu is complemented by an excellent wine list selected by Portuguese/Belgian owner and chef, Antonio Beja da Silva, whose love of his own cooking shows in his waistline and in the attention he devotes to his customers.

Shanti. Av. Adolphe Buyl 68. ☎ **02/649-40-96.** Main courses 300–450BF($8–$12); set-price menus 450–1,000BF ($12–$26). AE, DC, MC, V. Tues–Sat noon–2pm and 6:30–10pm. Bus: 71. VEGETARIAN.

An exotic look keeps faith with its multicultural menus: lots of greenery and flowers create a gardenlike feel, and crystal lamps, mirrors and old paintings adorn the walls. Try "Neptune's pleasure," crab with avocado and seaweed, as a starter. For a main course, shrimp Marsala with mixed vegetables and coriander is excellent, as is eggplant with ricotta in a tomato-and-basil sauce. There is also a big choice in set-price menus.

INEXPENSIVE

In 't Spinnekopke. Place du Jardin-aux-Fleurs 1 (off rue Van Artevelde). ☎ **02/511-86-95.** Main courses 400–780BF ($11–$21); plat du jour 295BF ($8). AE, DC, MC, V. Mon–Fri noon–3pm and 6–11pm; Sat 6pm–midnight. Métro: Bourse. TRADITIONAL BELGIAN.

A coaching inn from 1762, just far enough off the beaten track downtown to be frequented mainly by "those in the know." Hardy standbys of Belgian cuisine, such as stoemp and waterzooï, are given all the care and attention they deserve, from kitchen staff and diners alike, generally accompanied by an artisanal beer from a list of 500. You dine in a tilting, tiled-floor building, at plain tables, and more likely than not squeezed into a tight space—but getting caught "In the Spider's Web" is well worth it.

L'Auberge des Chapeliers. Rue des Chapeliers 1–3 (off Grand-Place). ☎ **02/513-73-38.** Main courses 300BF–635BF ($8–$17); menus 605BF–820BF ($16–$22). AE, DC, MC, V. Mon–Thurs noon–2pm and 6–11pm; Fri noon–2pm and 6pm–midnight; Sat noon–3pm and 6pm–midnight; Sun noon–3pm and 6–11pm. Métro: Centrale. TRADITIONAL BELGIAN.

Bistro food has been served up in this 17th-century former Hatmakers' Guildhouse for more than a quarter of a century. Popular with locals who live and work in the area, as well as with tourists fortunate enough to find it, it can be crowded at the height of lunch hour, so it's a good idea to come just before noon or just after 2pm. There are traditional Belgian dishes, many cooked in beer, and mussels on the menu, and servings are more than ample.

La Manufacture. Rue Notre-Dame du Sommeil 12–22 (off place du Jardin-aux-Fleurs). ☎ **02/502-25-25.** Main courses 450–705BF ($–$); menu du jour (lunch only) 500BF ($13). AE, DC, MC, V. Mon–Fri noon–2pm and 6–11pm; Sat 6pm–midnight. Métro: Centrale. FRENCH/INTERNATIONAL.

Even in its former industrial incarnation, this place was concerned with style—it was the factory of chic leather goods maker Delvaux. Fully refurbished, with parquet floors, polished wood, and stone tables set amid iron pillars and exposed air ducts, it produces trendy world cuisine from a French foundation for a mostly youthful public. It might at first seem disconcerting to find dim sum, sushi, Moroccan couscous, Lyon sausage, and Belgian waterzooi on the same menu, but don't worry—everything is tasty. There's piano music some evenings.

✪ **'t Kelderke.** Grand-Place 15. ☎ **02/513-7344.** Main courses 360–450BF ($9–$12); plat du jour 390BF ($10). AE, DC, MC, V. Daily noon–2am. Métro: Centrale. TRADITIONAL BELGIAN.

Despite being on the Grand-Place, this is far from being a tourist trap. As many Bruxellois as tourists throng the long wooden tables in a 17th-century, brick-arched cellar, and all are welcomed with zeal. Memorable traditional Belgian fare, with little in the way of frills, is served up from the open kitchen. It's a great place to try local specialties such as sausage, Flemish beef stew, rabbit in Brussels beer, and big steaming pans piled high with Zeeland mussels.

SEEING THE SIGHTS
SIGHTSEEING SUGGESTIONS FOR FIRST-TIME VISITORS

If You Have 1 Day   Spend the day exploring the historic Center. Beginning in the magnificent **Grand-Place,** visit the 15th-century **Town Hall, Brussels City Museum,** and elegant **guild houses,** before moving on to *Manneken-Pis,* **St-Michel Cathedral,** and the 19th-century **Galeries Royales St-Hubert** for some serious shopping (or window shopping). Buy a bag of chocolates at Wittamer on **place du Grand-Sablon** and browse the antiques shops around the square before heading over to tranquil **place du Petit-Sablon** for a rest. After a dinner that should include mussels, in season, spend the evening checking out one or more of the city's famed cafes.

If You Have 2 Days   On the second day, explore Belgian art and architecture in their many permutations. Begin with Brueghel and Rubens at the **Musée d'Art Ancien,** then move into the 20th century with Magritte and Delvaux at the **Musée d'Art Moderne** next door. While you're in the neighborhood, take a look at the neoclassical harmony of **place Royale** and the elegant **Royal Palace.** At the **Belgian Center for Comic-Strip Art,** follow the adventures of comic-book heroes and admire the art nouveau architecture of this restored department store. Continue your art nouveau explorations by strolling the side streets off **av. Louise** and around **square Ambiorix.**

If You Have 3 Days   On the third day get up early and stop by the **flea market** in place du Jeu de Balle. Then, head out to **Bruparck,** an attractions park on the city's northern edge that includes **Mini-Europe** and the **Océade** water leisure center. Nearby are the giant spheres of the **Atomium** and a panoramic view of the city from its viewing deck. For your last night in Brussels, have dinner or drinks in one of the **guild hall restaurants,** such as La Maison du Cygne, that overlook the Grand-Place. The illuminated square is even more beautiful at night than during the day.

BRUSSELS'S HISTORIC SQUARES & STREETS

GRAND-PLACE   Ornamental gables, medieval banners, gilded facades, sunlight flashing off gold-filigreed rooftop sculptures, a general impression of harmony and timelessness—there's a lot to take in all at once when you first enter the Grand-Place. Once the pride of the Hapsburg Empire, the Grand-Place has always been the very heart of Brussels. Characterized by Jean Cocteau as "a splendid stage," it's the city's theater of life.

Your tour should include a visit to the Gothic Hôtel de Ville (Town Hall); the neo-Gothic Maison du Roi (King's House), which houses the Musée de la Ville de Bruxelles (Brussels City Museum); and the Musée de la Brasserie (Brewers Museum), in the beautiful old brewers' guild house at Grand-Place 10.

PLACE DU GRAND-SABLON   Considered classier than the Grand-Place by the locals, though busy traffic diminishes your enjoyment of its cafe-terraces, the Grand-Sablon is lined with gabled mansions. This is antiques territory, and many of those mansions house antiques shops or private art galleries, with pricey merchandise on display. The dealerships have spread into neighboring side streets, and on Saturday and Sunday an excellent antiques market sets up its stalls in front of **Notre-Dame au Sablon Church,** a flamboyantly Gothic edifice with five naves, built by the city's Guild of Crossbowmen in the 15th century. The statue of Minerva in the square dates from 1751. Take tram 92, 93, or 94.

PLACE DU PETIT-SABLON   Across rue de la Régence, the Grand-Sablon's little cousin is an ornamental garden with a fountain and pool, a magical little retreat from the city bustle. The 48 bronze statuettes adorning the surrounding wrought-iron fence symbolize Brussels's medieval guilds, and a sculpture group by the fountain commemorates Counts Egmont and Hornes, beheaded in 1568 for protesting the extravagant cruelties of the Council of Blood, the Spanish Inquisition's enforcement arm in the Low Countries. Take tram 92, 93, or 94.

PLACE ROYALE   Meeting point of rue de la Régence and rue Royale, streets on which stand many of the city's premier attractions, the square is graced by an **equestrian statue** of Duke Godefroi de Bouillon, leader of the First Crusade. Its inscription describes him as the "First King of Jerusalem," a title Godefroi himself refused, accepting instead that of "Protector of the Holy Places." Also in place Royale is the neoclassical **St-Jacques-sur-Coudenberg Church.** Take tram 92, 93, or 94.

MUSEUMS, CHURCHES & MONUMENTS

Manneken Pis. Corner of rue du Chêne and rue de l'Etuve (2 blocks east of the Grand-Place). Métro: Bourse.

Brussels's favorite little boy gleefully does what a little boy's gotta do, generally ogled by a throng of admirers snapping pictures. Children especially seem to enjoy his bravura performance. This isn't the original statue, which was prone to theft and anatomical "maltreatment" and was removed for safekeeping. Louis XV of France began the tradition of presenting colorful costumes to "Little Julian" to make amends for Frenchmen having kidnapped the statue in 1747; the outfits are housed in the Musée de la Ville de Bruxelles in the Grand-Place. Incidentally, the *Manneken-Pis* has a female counterpart called the *Jeanneke-Pis,* located on the dead-end impasse de la Fidélité off rue des Bouchers. It was the 1987 brainstorm of a local restaurateur who wanted to attract business; its lack of grace is an embarrassment to many Bruxellois.

✪ **Hôtel de Ville (Town Hall).** Grand-Place. ☎ **02/279-43-55.** Admission 80BF ($2.10) for guided tours only. Apr–Sept Tues 11:30am and 3:15pm, Wed 3:15pm, Sun 12:15pm; Oct–Mar Tues 11:30am and 3:15pm, Wed 3:15pm. Métro: Centrale.

The spectacular Gothic Hall chamber is open for visits when Brussels's council of aldermen is not in session. You should begin with the exterior, however, in particular with the sculptures on the facade, many of which are 15th- and 16th-century jokes. Inside are superb 16th- to 18th-century tapestries; one depicts the duke of Alba, whose cruel features reflect the brutal oppression he and his Council of Blood imposed on Belgium; others are scenes from the life of Clovis, first king of the Franks. The aldermen meet in a plush, mahogany-paneled room surrounded by mirrors—presumably so that each party can see what underhanded maneuvers the others are up to.

Palais Royal (Royal Palace). Place des Palais. ☎ **02/551-20-20.** Free admission. July 22 to late Sept Tues–Sun 10:30am–4:30pm. Métro: Parc.

Work on the palace began in 1820, and it was given a grandiose Louis XVI–style facelift in 1904. King Albert II has his offices here and it is used for state receptions, but he and Queen Paola live at the Royal Palace in suburban Laeken. You can visit the ornate throne room, which has magnificent chandeliers, and other public rooms.

Cathédrale St-Michel. Parvis Ste-Gudule (2 blocks west of Gare Centrale). ☎ **02/217-83-45.** Free admission to church; crypt 40BF ($1.05). Daily 7am–6pm. Métro: Centrale.

Victor Hugo considered this magnificent church to be the "purest flowering of the Gothic style." Begun in 1226, it was officially dedicated as a cathedral only in 1961. The 16th-century Hapsburg Emperor Charles V took a personal interest in its decoration, donating the superb stained-glass windows. In recent years its stonework has undergone cleaning and restoration, and the dazzlingly bright exterior makes a superb sight. Inside, spare decoration focuses attention on its soaring columns and arches.

✪ **Musées Royaux des Beaux-Arts (Royal Museums of Fine Arts).** Rue de la Régence 3 (at place Royale)). ☎ **02/508-32-11.** Admission 150BF ($3.95) adults, 50BF ($1.30) children. Ancient Art Museum Tues–Sun 10am–noon and 1–5pm; Modern Art Museum Tues–Sun 10am–1pm and 2–5pm. Métro: Parc; tram: 92, 93, or 94 to place Royale.

Beyond the main entrance, the Musée d'Art Ancien (Museum of Ancient Art) has Brueghel and Rubens as the stars of the show, but the greater history of Belgian painting is well represented. The collection includes international masters, with works by Van Gogh and the French impressionists. Next-door, the Musée d'Art Moderne (Museum of Modern Art) has an emphasis on underground works—if only because the museum's eight floors are all below ground level. Magritte is well represented; so are Delvaux, De Braekeleer, Dalí, Permeke, and many others.

Musée de la Ville de Bruxelles (Brussels City Museum). Grand-Place. ☎ **02/279-43-50.** Admission 100BF ($2.65) adults, 80BF ($2.10) children 5–15; children under 5 free. Mon–Thurs 10am–12:30pm and 1:30–5pm (Oct–Mar to 4pm), Sat–Sun 10am–1pm. Métro: Centrale.

In the neo-Gothic Maison du Roi (King's House), the displays cover Brussels through the ages, including its traditional arts and crafts of tapestry and lace making. Among its most fascinating exhibits are old paintings and scale reconstructions of the historic city center, particularly those showing the riverside ambience along the now-vanished River Senne. Pride of place goes to more than 500 costumes—including an Elvis costume—belonging to Manneken Pis.

Musée Horta (Horta Museum). Rue Américaine 25. ☎ **02/543-04-90.** Admission 150BF ($3.95) on weekdays; 200BF ($5) on weekends. Tues–Sun 2–5:30pm. Tram: 81, 82, 91 or 92.

Brussels owes much of its rich art nouveau heritage to Victor Horta (1861–1947), a resident architect who led the development of the style. His home and adjoining studio in St-Gilles are now a museum. Restored to their original condition, they showcase his use of flowing, sinuous shapes and colors, in both interior decoration and architecture.

Musée du Cinquantenaire (Cinquantenaire Museum). Parc du Cinquantenaire 10. ☎ **02/741-72-11.** Admission 150BF ($3.95). Tues–Fri 9:30am–5pm; Sat–Sun 10am–5pm. Métro: Mérode.

In the monumental Cinquantenaire Park, the museum traces the story of civilization, especially but not exclusively European civilization. Collections include antiquities (including a giant model of Imperial Rome), Islam, Byzantine art, India, Southeast Asia, and European decorative arts.

Musée du Costume et de la Dentelle (Museum of Costume and Lace). Rue de la Violette 6. ☎ **02/512-77-09.** Admission 100BF ($2.65) adults, 80BF ($2.10) children 5–16, free for children under 5. Mon–Sat 10am–12:30pm and 1:30–5pm (Oct–Mar until 4pm); Sat–Sun 2–4:30pm. Métro: Centrale.

In a city famous for its lace, the marvelous antique creations in this museum near the Grand-Place. Besides examples of historic Belgian lace, the museum displays costumes, including dress from the 16th to the 19th centuries.

✪ **Centre Belge de la Bande Dessinée (Belgian Center for Comic-Strip Art).** Rue des Sables 20. ☎ **02/219-19-80.** Admission 250BF ($7) adults, 100BF ($2.65) ages 11 and under. Tues–Sun 10am–6pm. Métro: Centrale.

Called the "CéBéBéDé" for short, the center displays such popular cartoon characters as Lucky Luke, Thorgal, and, of course, Belgium's own Tintin, complete with red-and-white-checkered moon rocket, yet does not neglect the likes of Superman, Batman, and the Green Lantern. As icing on the cake, it's in a Victor Horta building, the Magasins Waucquez, which was slated for demolition when the center took it over.

PARKS & GARDENS

The **Parc de Bruxelles** borders rue Royale, between Parliament and the Royal Palace (Métro: Parc). Once a hunting preserve of the dukes of Brabant, it is now a landscaped garden. In 1830, Belgian patriots confronted Dutch troops here during the War of Independence. Although not very big, the park manages to contain everything from carefully trimmed borders to rough patches of trees and bushes, and has fine views along its main axes.

The city's big public park, the **Bois de la Cambre,** begins at the top of av. Louise in the city's southern section. This is the lung of Brussels, and it gets pretty busy on sunny weekends. Its centerpiece is a small lake with an island in the center reached by an electrically powered pontoon. Some busy roads run through the park and traffic moves fast on them, so be careful with children. Take tram 23, 90, or 93.

Kids especially enjoy the sights at **Bruparck,** on the city's northern edge, at bd. du Centenaire, Laeken. There's nothing else quite like the **Atomium** (☎ 02/474-89-77), a cluster of giant spheres that represent the atomic model of an iron molecule enlarged 165 billion times, built for the 1958 World's Fair. You can wander around inside the spheres; the sight from the viewing deck is marvelous. The Atomium is open from April to August 9am to 8pm; September to March 10am to 6pm. Admission is 200BF ($5) for adults, 150BF ($4) for children 3 to 12, and free for children under 1m 20cm (47 inches); look out for reduced-rate combined tickets if you also plan to visit Mini-Europe and the Océade.

Adults and kids alike get a kick out of strolling around the landmarks of **Mini-Europe** (☎ 02/478-05-50; Métro: Heysel), which include Big Ben, the Leaning Tower of Pisa, the Seville bullring, and more modern emblems of continental achievement like the Channel Tunnel. As the scale is 1:25, everyone feels like a giant. July and August, it's open daily 9:30am to 7pm; before and after this, it opens progressively later and closes progressively earlier as the season moves from high to low; it's closed in January and February. Admission is 360BF ($9) adults, 250BF ($7) children 16 and under, and free for children under 1m 20cm (47 inches). Mini-Europe is next to the **Océade** water leisure center.

ORGANIZED TOURS

Three-hour coach tours are available from **De Boeck,** rue de la Colline 8 (☎ 02/513-77-44). Each tour costs 790BF ($21) for adults and 395BF ($10) for children. You can book at most hotels, and arrangements can be made for hotel pick-up. Regular tours operate throughout the year; private tours can also be arranged.

Chatterbus, rue des Thuyas 12 (☎ 02/673-18-35), operates a daily 3-hour tour, June 15 to September 15, starting at 10am from the Galeries Royales St-Hubert, next to rue du Marché-aux-Herbes 90, a few steps from the Grand-Place. The walking tour covers the historic center, followed by a bus ride through areas most tourists never see. You hear about life in Brussels and get a better feel for the city. The price is 300BF ($8).

ARAU, the Workshop for Urban Research and Action, bd. Adolphe Max 55 (☎ 02/219-33-45), is a committee of concerned Brussels residents who give 3-hour themed coach tours, including "Surprising Parks and Squares," "Brussels 1900 Art Nouveau," "Grand-Place and Its Surroundings," and "Alternative Brussels." You are advised to book ahead. Tours cost 600BF ($16) and operate on a rotating basis on Saturdays from March to November; private group tours can be arranged throughout the year.

THE SHOPPING SCENE

Don't look for many bargains in Brussels. As a general rule, the upper city around av. Louise and Porte de Namur is more expensive than the lower city around rue Neuve and the shopping malls on place de la Monnaie and place Brouckère. (For shopping hours, see "Business Hours" under "Fast Facts: Brussels," above.) A useful source of information is the weekly English-language magazine *The Bulletin,* which keeps tabs on shopping trends, reviews stores, and carries advertising.

Galeries Royales St-Hubert, which claims to be Europe's oldest shopping mall, is a light and airy arcade hosting boutiques, cafe-terraces, and street musicians playing classical music. Opened in 1847, architect Pierre Cluysenaer's Italian neo-Renaissance gallery has a touch of class and is well worth a stroll through, even if you have no intention of shopping. The elegant triple gallery—Galerie du Roi, Galerie de la Reine, and Galerie des Princes—is near the Grand-Place, between rue du Marché-aux-Herbes and rue de l'Ecuyer, and split by rue des Bouchers. There are accesses on each of these streets (Métro: Centrale).

At the **Vieux Marché (Old Market)** flea market on place du Jeu-de-Balle (Métro: Porte de Hal), a large square in the Marolles district, you can find some exceptional decorative items, many recycled from the homes of the "recently deceased," as well as unusual postcards, clothing, and household goods. Everything from antiques to junk, from North African clothes to Soviet chic, is sold here. The market is held daily 7am to 2pm. Every weekend, place du Grand Sablon hosts a fine **Antiques Market** (Métro: Centrale). Salesmanship is low-key, interest pure, prices not unreasonable, and quality of merchandise—including silverware, pottery, paintings, and jewelry—high. The market is open Saturday 9am to 6pm and Sunday 9am to 2pm.

Manufacture Belge de Dentelle, Galerie de la Reine 6–8 (☎ 02/511-44-77; Métro: Centrale), specializes in top-quality handmade Belgian lace. Another good lace store is **Maison Antoine,** Grand-Place 26 (☎ 02/512-48-59; Métro: Centrale), in a former guild house where Victor Hugo lived in 1852. The quality is superb, service friendly, and prices reasonable. The Grand-Place has a **Flower Market,** daily 7am to 2pm, and a weekly **Bird Market,** with many varieties of birds for sale. Nearby, at the top end of rue du Marché-aux-Herbes, in the Agora, the weekend **Crafts Market** has lots of fine little specialized jewelry and other items, most of which are inexpensive.

Forget computer games and Disney stores—if you need to buy a gift for the kids, take home some Tintin mementos from **Boutique de Tintin,** rue de la Colline 13 (☎ 02/514-45-50; Métro: Centrale). Visit **De Boe,** rue de Flandre 36 (☎ 02/511-13-73; Métro: Ste-Catherine), a small shop near the Fish Market, for the heavenly aromas of roasted and blended coffee, a superb selection of wines in all price categories, and an array of specialty crackers, nuts, spices, teas, and gourmet snacks, many of which come in tins that make them easy to pack.

Buying Belgian Chocolates & Pastries

Belgian chocolates are rightly famous around the world. You find some of the best handmade pralines at: **Chocolatier Mary,** rue Royale 73 (☎ **02/217-45-00;** Métro: Parc), a supplier to the royal court; **Neuhaus,** Galerie de la Reine 25 (☎ **02/502-59-14;** Métro: Centrale); **Wittamer,** place du Grand-Sablon 12 (☎ **02/512-37-42;** tram 92, 93, or 94), whose rolls, breads, pastries, and cakes have also been winning fans since 1910. **Dandoy,** rue au Beurre 31 (☎ **02/511-81-76;** Métro: Bourse), is for cookies-and-cakes fans. Try traditional Belgian specialties such as spicy *speculoos* cookies and *pain à grecque.*

Among shops selling fashionable clothing and accessories, try **Delvaux,** Galerie de la Reine 31 (☎ **02/512-71-98;** Métro: Gare Centrale), a local company making and selling some of the best, and priciest, handbags and leather goods in Belgium. **Olivier Strelli,** av. Louise 72 (☎ **02/511-21-34;** Métro: Louise), is owned by the top-rated Belgian fashion designer, whose line is strong on elegant, ready-to-wear items. For the most books and magazines in English, visit **Waterstone's,** bd. Adolphe Max 71 (☎ **02/219-27-08;** Métro: Rogier).

BRUSSELS AFTER DARK

The city offers a full range of evening activities, including dance, opera, classical music, jazz, film, theater, and discos. For an exhaustive listing of events, consult the "What's On" section of the English-language weekly *The Bulletin.*

THE PERFORMING ARTS

The main performing-arts season is September to May, with performances in summer as well. The superb **Théâtre Royal de la Monnaie,** place de la Monnaie (☎ **02/229-12-11;** Métro: De Brouckère), founded in the 17th century, is home to the **Opéra National** and the **Orchestre Symphonique de la Monnaie.** The resident ballet company is Belgian choreographer Anna Theresa de Keersmaeker's **Group Rosas.** The box office is open Tuesday to Saturday 11am to 6pm; tickets are 300BF to 3,500BF ($8 to $92), but 5 minutes before a show, students 25 and under pay only 200BF ($5).

The **Palais des Beaux-Arts,** rue Royale 10 (☎ **02/507-84-66;** Métro: Parc), is home to the Belgian National Orchestra. The box office is open Monday to Saturday 11am to 6pm, with tickets running 400BF to 3,000BF ($11 to $79). The **Cirque Royal,** rue de l'Enseignement 81 (☎ **02/218-20-15;** Métro: Parc), formerly a real circus, is used for music, opera, and ballet. The box office is open Tuesday to Saturday 11am to 6pm, with tickets at 300BF to 2,500BF ($8 to $66).

Theaters concentrate on French- and Dutch-language plays, many adapted from English, with occasional English-language performances. The **Théâtre Royal du Parc,** rue de la Loi 3 (☎ **02/512-23-39;** Métro: Parc), a magnificent edifice, occupies a corner of the Parc de Bruxelles opposite Parliament. Most performances of classic and contemporary drama and comedies here are in French. (At press time, the theater is being rebuilt after having been heavily damaged by fire.)

Traditional Bruxellois marionette theater is maintained in an old cafe, the **Théâtre Toone VII,** Impasse Schuddeveld, Petite rue des Bouchers 6 (☎ **02/217-27-53;** Métro: Centrale). Often treating sophisticated subjects, puppet master José Géal

---
Getting Tickets

You can order tickets for all performing-arts venues from the **Central Booking Office** (☎ **0800/21-221;** open Monday to Friday 9am to 7pm and Saturday 10am to 7pm) and from individual box offices, or you can reserve them against a credit card for pick-up the night of the performance.

---

presents adaptations of classic tales in the local dialect, Brusseleir, as well as in English, French, Dutch, and German.

THE CLUB & MUSIC SCENE

Brussels isn't as noted for nightlife as some neighboring capitals—dining out being the most popular activity. However, nightlife is alive and well, and if its range is smaller than that of bigger cities like London and Paris, the quality is not.

CABARETS & DANCE CLUBS   Brussels isn't Paris when it comes to putting on Moulin Rouge–type shows, but **Le Show Point,** place Stéphanie 14 (☎ **02/511-53-64;** Métro: Louise), adopts a similar approach. From 10pm until dawn, showgirls, scantily clad or wearing fanciful costumes, strut their stuff in a variety of fetching choreographies. Drinks cost 1,000BF ($26). No cover. Open Monday to Saturday 10pm dawn (show begins at 12:30am). A bit of a hoot, **Chez Flo,** rue au Beurre 25 (☎ **02/513-31-52;** Métro: Bourse), is a popular transvestite cabaret and dinner show that is outrageous and comfortable at the same time. Dinner and floor show are 1,475 to 2,950BF ($39 to $78); the highest price includes a half-bottle of champagne per person. Show begins at 8pm.

The disco **Le Sparrow,** rue Duquesnoy 16 (☎ **02/512-66-22;** Métro: Centrale), always seems on the verge of going out of style, yet never quite gets there, even if it has lost the wildness of its younger days. A location off the Grand-Place helps. So does an up-to-date approach to music—techno, house, trip-hop, garage, whatever. It's open Thursday to Saturday 10pm to dawn, and cover is 320BF ($8), including a drink. Open Tuesday to Saturday 10pm to 4 or 5am, **Griffin's Night Club,** in the Royal Windsor Hotel, rue Duquesnoy 5 (☎ **02/505-55-55;** Métro: Centrale), is a fashionable kind of disco with a varied taste in musical styles and periods. There's no cover.

Le Fuse, rue Blaes 208 (☎ **02/511-97-89;** bus: 20 or 48), is the place if only techno will do. On the first Friday of every month, it reinvents itself as the women-only Pussy Lounge and every Sunday as the men-only La Démence. Cover varies: Saturday techno evenings, Pussy Lounge and La Démence are free 10 to 11pm, thereafter 300BF ($8). It's open Tuesday to Sunday 10pm to 5am.

JAZZ & BLUES   Jazz has taken a hit in recent years, with some of the city's best-loved spots closing down, but enough remain, and new ones have opened, to feel the city's collective foot tapping.

Very chichi and not the friendliest of scenes, the art deco bar **L'Archiduc,** rue Antoine Dansaert 6 (☎ **02/512-06-52;** Métro: Bourse), serves up a sophisticated program of jazz on weekends, usually beginning at 5pm. A stylish crowd lounges about in the blue light and nods appreciatively at the mellow sounds. Sunday jazz cover is 400 to 500BF ($11 to $13). Open daily 4pm to 4am. **Marcus Mingus Jazz Spot,** Impasse de la Fidelité 10, off rue des Bouchers (☎ **02/502-02-97;** Métro: Centrale), is a popular jazz cafe that attracts top local performers and an occasional international name. Concerts begin a couple of hours after opening time. There's a jam session on Thursday. Open Monday to Saturday 7:30pm to 2am. Cover is 200BF ($5) Wednesday, 300BF ($8) Friday and Saturday.

Belgian Brews

Be warned: Belgian beers are stronger than their American counterparts—alcohol content can be as high as 12%. Try a rich, dark Trappist ale brewed by monks from Chimay, Orval, Rochefort, Sint-Benedictus, Westmalle, and West-vleteren monasteries. Brussels is well known for its lambic beers, which use naturally occurring yeast for fermentation, are often flavored with fruit, and come in bottles with champagne-type corks. Unlike any other beer, they're more akin to a sweet sparkling wine. Gueuze, a blend of young and aged lambic beers is one of the least sweet. If you prefer something sweeter, try raspberry-flavored framboise or cherry-flavored kriek. Faro is a low-alcohol beer, sometimes sweetened or lightly spiced.

THE BAR SCENE

Now you're talking. Bars are where Brussels really dwells. The city's cafes and bars run the gamut from art nouveau palaces to convivial local watering holes. Don't leave without lingering a few hours in one, savoring Belgium's incredible variety of beers.

Although its name means "Sudden Death," don't worry. You'll probably survive ✪ **A la Morte Subite,** rue Montagne-aux-Herbes-Potagères 7 (☎ **02/513-13-18;** Métro: Centrale), a fine old cafe, which appeals to an eclectic cross-section of society, from little old ladies to bank managers, dancers and musicians from top cultural venues, and students. Decor consists of stained glass, old photographs, paintings, prints, and plain wooden chairs and tables. Specialties are traditional Brussels beers: gueuze, faro, and kriek, as well as abbey brews such as Chimay, Maredsous, and Grimbergen. The staff's attitude takes a little getting used to, especially if you need more than 3 seconds to decide what you want. If you can be decisive, you have a friend for life—or at any rate, for the evening.

The decor at **Halloween,** rue des Grands-Carmes 10 (☎ **02/514-12-56;** Métro: Bourse), is enough to give you the creeps: Gargoyles, devils, and other assorted creatures from the darker recesses of the human mind create a disturbing ambience in what is an unforgettable bar inhabited mostly by the young and the trendy. By contrast, **Le Cirio,** rue de la Bourse 18 (☎ **02/512-13-95;** Métro: Bourse), is a quiet, refined place to sip your drink in surroundings that make the exercise seem worthwhile. Many customers look like they've made their pile across the road at the Stock Exchange and retired here to a state of genteel splendor.

Shock and horror reverberated through the city in 1999 when the legendary 1904 art nouveau tavern enlivened with a dash of art deco, **Le Falstaff,** rue Henri Maus 17–25 (☎ **02/511-98-77;** Métro: Bourse), went bankrupt and closed. Reopened under new management, it has shed its famously vain wait staff and slipped a few notches on the hip scale as a result. If such considerations don't worry you, there's still the same stunning decor, and reasonably priced brasserie food.

Le Fleur en Papier Doré, rue des Alexiens 53 (☎ **02/511-16-59;** Métro: Bourse), calls itself a "temple of surrealism," but old prints, plates, horns, porcelain, and knick-knacks on the walls are more evocative of a cozy hunting lodge than a room Magritte might have painted—although he and other surrealists used to hang out here. Now painters, poets, and an after-theater crowd sip beer, munch on snacks, and enjoy the relaxed atmosphere. On weekend nights, there's an accordion player; poetry readings are held upstairs several times a month.

THE GAY & LESBIAN SCENE

Brussels's gay scene is developing and can claim a substantial clutch of clubs and bars as its own. Lesbians have a harder time of it, with venues thin on the ground.

Rue des Riches-Claires and **rue du Marché-au-Charbon,** south of the Bourse, host some gay and lesbian bars. **Macho 2,** rue du Marché-au-Charbon 108 (☎ 02/513-56-67; Métro: Bourse), houses a gay men's sauna, pool, steam room, and cafe. It's open Monday to Thursday noon to 2am, Friday and Saturday noon to 4am, and Sunday noon to midnight, and admission is 450BF ($12) or 300BF ($8) for men under 25 (on Thursday it's 300BF/$8 for everyone); students enter for 200BF ($5). **Le Fuse** and **Le Sparrow** (above) have gay nights. **Le Sapho,** rue St-Géry 1 (☎ 02/512-45-52; Metro: Bourse), is the place for lesbians, though it's more relaxed about men entering than most gay places are about letting in women. It's open Friday and Saturday 10pm to 5am, with no cover.

For more information, contact **Infor Homo,** av. de Roodebeek 57 (☎ 02/733-10-24; Métro: Diamant), open Tuesday to Friday 8am to 6pm. Or stop by the gay and lesbian community center, **Telsquels,** rue du Marché-au-Charbon 81 (☎ 02/512-45-87; Métro: Bourse), open Saturday to Thursday 5pm to 2am and Friday 8am to 4am.

A DAY TRIP TO WATERLOO

Europe's Gettysburg, the battle that ended Napoléon's empire was fought 10km (6 miles) south of Brussels, on a stretch of rolling farmland near Waterloo that remains much as it was on June 18, 1815. Before touring it, you should study a 360° **Panorama** mural and see a short audiovisual presentation of the battle, including scenes from Sergei Bondarchuk's epic movie *Waterloo,* at the **Centre du Visiteur,** route du Lion 252–254, Braine l'Alleud (☎ 02/385-19-12). To survey the battlefield, climb the nearby **Butte du Lion** (Lion Mound) monument, a pyramid-like hill behind the center.

These three sites are open daily: April to September 9:30am to 6:30pm; October 9:30am to 5:30pm; November to February 10:30am to 4pm; March 10am to 5pm. The combined ticket costs 300BF ($8) adults, 200BF ($5) students/seniors, and 150BF ($3.95) children 6 to 12; children under 6 are free. A **Waxworks Museum,** and the **Hougoumont** and **La Haie-Sainte** farms that played a crucial role in the battle are only a short stroll from the visitor center.

You can fill in details of the battle at the **Wellington Museum,** chaussée de Bruxelles 147, Waterloo (☎ 02/354-78-06), a former inn that was Wellington's headquarters, and where wrote his victory dispatch. The museum is open from April to September daily 9:30am to 6:30pm; October to March daily 10:30am to 5pm. Admission is 100BF ($2.65) for adults, 80BF ($2.10) for seniors and students, 40BF ($1.05) for children ages 6–12, and free for children under 6.

GETTING THERE   T.E.C. bus "W" leaves on the half hour and the hour from a bus terminal on av. de Stalingrad, a block south of place Rouppe, in Brussels. It stops at both the museum in Waterloo and the visitor center at Braine l'Alleud. By car, take the N5 south through the Bois de la Cambre and Forêt de Soignes.

2 Bruges & Ghent

Both Flemish cities are showcases of medieval art and architecture, yet each has a distinctive character that makes visiting them complementary. Walking around Bruges is like taking a step back in time. This almost perfectly preserved medieval city, with graceful squares, such as the Markt and Burg, is a sight in itself. Ghent is austere but more authentic, with a forbidding castle and three-towered cathedral. Some of the northern Renaissance's most outstanding paintings hang in the cities' museums and churches, most notably in Bruges's Church of Our Lady and Groeninge Museum, and Ghent's St. Bavo's Cathedral.

BRUGES (BRUGGE)

From its 13th-century origins as a cloth-manufacturing town to its current incarnation as a tourism magnet, Bruges seems to have changed little. As in a fairy tale, swans glide down the winding canals and the stone houses look like they're made of gingerbread. Even though modern glass-fronted stores have taken over the ground floors of ancient buildings, and the swans scatter before tour boats chugging along the canals, Bruges has managed the transition from medieval to modern with remarkable grace. The town seems revitalized rather than crushed by the tremendous influx of tourists. Even more amazing is the warm welcome that the populace extends to its visitors. Tourism is an economic necessity, of course, but the people of Bruges love their beautiful town and take great pride in showing it off.

ESSENTIALS

ARRIVING   By Train   Frequent trains arrive, via Ghent, from Brussels and Antwerp and from the ferry ports of Ostend (Oostende) and Zeebrugge. The trip is about an hour. A train from Lille in northern France connects Bruges with Eurostar trains from London through the Channel Tunnel to Paris and Brussels. Look for "Brugge," the town's Flemish name, on destination boards at the station, which is on Stationsplein, 1.5km (1 mile) south of the city center. For train information, call ☎ **050/38-23-82** between 6:30am and 10:30pm. From the train station you can take any bus labeled "Centrum" (center) and get out at Markt.

By Bus   Eurolines' twice-daily service between London and Brussels stops at Bruges. For reservations in Brussels, contact Eurolines (☎ **02/203-03-07**). There are Eurolines connections from many European cities via Brussels. Bruges's main bus station adjoins the train station. From the station you can take any bus labeled "Centrum" (center) and get out at Markt.

By Car   The main expressways to Bruges are the E40 from Brussels and Ghent, the E17 and then E40 from Antwerp, and the E40 from Ostend.

VISITOR INFORMATION   The tourist office, **Toerisme Brugge,** Burg 11, 8000 Brugge (☎   050/44-86-86; fax 050/44-86-00; www.brugge.be; e-mail: toerisme@brugge.be), is open April to September Monday to Friday 9:30am to 6:30pm, Saturday and Sunday 10am to noon and 2 to 6:30pm; October to March Monday to Friday 9:30am to 5pm, Saturday and Sunday 9:30am to 1pm and 2 to 5:30pm. Friendly and efficient, the office dispenses brochures that outline walking, coach, canal, and horse-drawn cab tours, as well as detailed information on many sightseeing attractions and cultural events.

CITY LAYOUT   Bruges has two hearts, in side-by-side monumental squares the **Markt** and the **Burg.** Narrow streets fan out from these squares, and a network of *reien* (canals) threads its way through every section of this small city. The center is almost encircled by a canal that opens at its southern end into the Minnewater (Lake of Love), filled with swans and bordered by the Begijnhof and a park.

GETTING AROUND   Although street signs and transportation information are in Dutch, English is widely spoken, so you should have no problem getting directions.

By Bus   Most city buses depart the bus station beside the train station, or from a second bus station at the big square called 't Zand, west of the Markt. Several bus routes pass through the Markt. For city and regional bus information, call ☎ **059/56-53-53.**

By Car   It's all but impossible to use a car in the confusing and narrow streets of the city center. Leave your car at your hotel parking garage, at one of the big, prominently signposted underground lots in the center (they get expensive for long stays), or at a free parking zone by the train station. It's a short walk into the heart of the city from any of the parking lots.

By Taxi   There are taxi stands at the Markt (☎ **050/33-44-44**) and outside the train station (☎ **050/38-46-60**).

By Bike   You can rent a bike at the train station's Baggage Department (☎ **050/38-58-71**) for 325BF ($9) per day or 250BF ($7) with a train ticket, plus a deposit. Some hotels and shops rent bikes. Biking is a terrific way to get around town, and to the nearby village of Damme by way of beautiful canal-side roads.

WHERE TO STAY

Bruges's hotels fill up fast. Don't arrive without a reservation, especially in summer. If you do, the tourist office has a reservation service; you can book in advance here and in tourist offices throughout the country. Accommodations are less heavily booked during the week than on weekends.

Expensive

De Snippe. Nieuwe Gentweg 53, 8000 Brugge. ☎ **050/33-70-70.** Fax 050/33-76-62. E-mail: de.snippe@flanderscoast.be. 9 units. MINIBAR TV TEL. 5,750–6,000BF ($151–$158) double; 7,750–8,000BF ($204–$211) double junior suite. Rates include full breakfast. AE, CB, DC, MC, V. Free parking.

In an early 18th-century building in the town center, De Snippe has luxurious and spacious rooms. Many have fireplaces, and all are furnished with restrained elegance. De Snippe is also one of Bruges's leading restaurants (see "Where to Dine," below).

Die Swaene. Steenhouwersdijk 1, 8000 Brugge. ☎ **050/34-27-98.** Fax 050/33-66-74. www.dieswaene-hotel.com. E-mail: info@dieswaene-hotel.com. 22 units. MINIBAR TV TEL. 6,250–9,250BF ($165–$243) double; 11,600BF ($305) suite. Rates include buffet breakfast. AE, DC, JCB, MC, V. Parking 350BF ($9).

This small hotel on the beautiful city-center Groenerei canal has been called one of the most romantic in Europe, thanks in part to the care lavished on it by the Hessels family. All of the comfortable rooms are elegantly and individually furnished; some are air-conditioned and all have hair dryers. The lounge, from 1779, was formerly the Tailors' Guild Hall, and there's a sauna and indoor swimming pool. There's an annex across the canal. The restaurant, whose specialty is seafood, has won favorable reviews from guests and critics alike.

✪ **Romantik Pandhotel.** Pandreitje 16, 8000 Brugge. ☎ **050/34-06-66.** Fax 050/34-05-56. E-mail: info@pandhotel.com. 24 units. MINIBAR TV TEL. 5,290–6,290BF ($139–$166) double; 7,290–10,990BF ($192–$289) family rooms and suites. Rates include buffet breakfast. AE, CB, DC, JCB, MC, V. Parking in nearby garage 350BF ($9).

Close to the Markt, this lovely 18th-century mansion surrounded by plane trees is an oasis of tranquillity. Although it provides modern conveniences, such as hair dryers, its exquisite, old-fashioned furnishings lend special grace to comfortable rooms. Guests praise Mrs. Chris Vanhaecke-Dewaele for her hospitality and attention to detail. There's an Internet-connected computer in the lobby which guests can use to send and receive e-mail.

Bruges

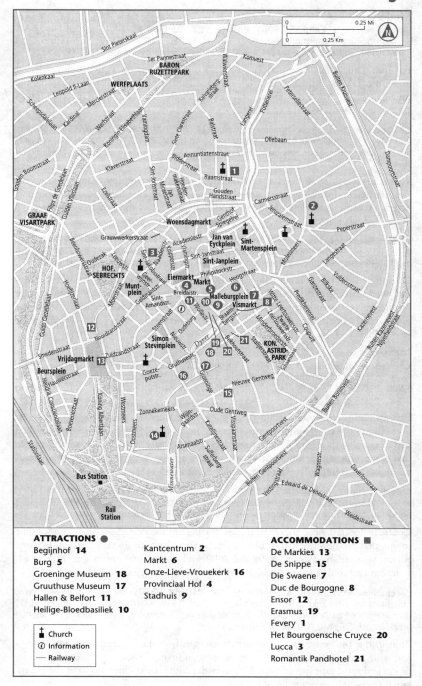

ATTRACTIONS ●

Begijnhof **14**
Burg **5**
Groeninge Museum **18**
Gruuthuse Museum **17**
Hallen & Belfort **11**
Heilige-Bloedbasiliek **10**

Kantcentrum **2**
Markt **6**
Onze-Lieve-Vrouekerk **16**
Provinciaal Hof **4**
Stadhuis **9**

‡ Church
ⓘ Information
— Railway

ACCOMMODATIONS ■

De Markies **13**
De Snippe **15**
Die Swaene **7**
Duc de Bourgogne **8**
Ensor **12**
Erasmus **19**
Fevery **1**
Het Bourgoensche Cruyce **20**
Lucca **3**
Romantik Pandhotel **21**

Moderate

De Markies. 't Zand 5, 8000 Brugge. ☎ **050/34-83-34.** Fax 050/34-87-87. www.brugge.internetgids.be/demarkies. 18 units. TV TEL. 3,000–3,400BF ($79–$89) double. Rates include buffet breakfast. AE, CB, MC, V. Parking in nearby garage 350BF ($9).

For those who want to experience Bruges's old-world charm without surrendering modern comforts or their wallet, this is a good bet. Its position on a corner of the big square, 't Zand, makes it convenient for exploring the old center. The spacious rooms are decorated with modern furnishings.

✪ **Duc de Bourgogne.** Huidenvettersplein 12, 8000 Brugge. ☎ **050/33-20-38.** Fax 050/34-40-37. E-mail: duc.Bourgogne@ssi.be. 10 units. TV TEL. 4,000–5,400BF ($105 –$142) double. Rates include continental breakfast. AE, CB, DC, MC, V. Limited parking available on street.

This is an elegant small hotel in a 17th-century canal-side building. Fairly large rooms are luxuriously furnished, with antiques scattered throughout. All rooms have hair dryers. A good restaurant on the ground floor overlooks the canal (see "Where to Dine," below).

✪ **Het Bourgoensche Cruyce.** Wollestraat 41–43, 8000 Brugge. ☎ **050/33-79-26.** Fax 050/34-19-68. E-mail: bour.cruyce@ssi.be. 8 units. TV TEL. 3,500–4,900BF ($92–$129) double. Rates include continental breakfast. AE, DC, MC, V. Parking in nearby garage 350BF ($9).

Opening onto a lovely inner courtyard, right in the middle of town, this tiny family-run hotel epitomizes the Bruges experience. Rooms are quite large with contemporary furnishings; modern bathrooms have hair dryers. Best of all is the hospitality of the proprietors, who also oversee one of the best restaurants in town on the ground floor (see "Where to Dine," below).

Inexpensive

✪ **Ensor.** Speelmansrei 10, 8000 Brugge. ☎ **050/34-25-89.** Fax 050/34-20-18. www.Brugesonline.com/hotelensor.htm. E-mail: hotel_ensor@unicall.be. 12 units. TEL. 1,960–2,300BF ($52–$61) double. Rates include continental breakfast. AE, MC, V. Parking (book ahead) BF250 ($61).

If you want to open your window and know right away you're in Bruges, get a room overlooking the canal. Though most rooms are relatively large and neatly furnished and all come with bright modern bathrooms, it's the leafy canal view at a budget price that makes this family hotel a standout. There's a radio in every room, plus an elevator and a TV lounge. The hotel rents bicycles at BF250 ($7).

Fevery. Collaert Mansionstraat 3, 8000 Brugge. ☎ **050/33-12-69.** Fax 050/33-17-91. www.hotelfevery.be. E-mail: paul@hotelfevery.be. 11 units. TV TEL. 2,000–2,600BF ($53–$68) double. Rates include full breakfast. AE, CB, JCB, MC, V. Free parking.

Centrally located near the Markt, this small family-owned hotel has comfortable rooms that are beautifully furnished in modern style, with a small table and chairs. Rooms were enlarged during 1999 and 2000, and all have hair dryers. There's a downstairs bar and dining room, and baby-sitting can be arranged.

Lucca. Naaldenstraat 30, 8000 Brugge. ☎ **050/34-20-67.** Fax 050/33-34-64. www.hotellucca.be. E-mail: lucca@hotellucca.be. 17 units, 13 with bathroom. TEL. 1,950BF ($51) double without bathroom; 2,500BF ($66) double with bathroom. Rates include continental breakfast. AE, DC, MC, V. Parking 350BF ($9).

Built in the 14th century by a wealthy merchant from Lucca, Italy, the high ceilings and wide halls of this mansion convey a sense of luxury. Rooms are in excellent condition and sport pine furnishings. Rooms with private bathrooms also have TV. Breakfast is served in a cozy medieval cellar.

TIMBUKTU   KALAMAZOO

AT&T Direct® Service

The easy way to call home from anywhere.

Global connection with the AT&T Network | **AT&T** direct service

For the easy way to call home, take the attached wallet guide.

Make Learning Fun & Easy

With IDG Books Worldwide

Frommer's

WEBSTER'S NEW WORLD™

the Unofficial Guide®

ARCO®

HOWELL BOOK HOUSE™

W E I G H T (W) W A T C H E R S®

Available at your local bookstores

WHERE TO DINE

Bruges isn't short of restaurants. You'll be tripping over the places all the time in the city center. Most are okay, even if some have gotten too complacent about the tourists that are their main market. The restaurants featured below aim to make dining a memory of Bruges that you'll still savor back home.

Very Expensive

✪ **De Karmeliet.** Langestraat 19. ☎ **050/33-82-59.** Reservations required. Main courses 750–1,250BF ($20–$33); set-price menus 2,600–3,200BF ($68–$84). AE, DC, V. Tues–Sat noon–2pm and 7–9:30pm; Sun 7–9:30pm except June–Sept. Closed Jan, last week of Aug, first week of Sept. BELGIAN/FRENCH

In 1996 chef Geert Van Hecke became the first Flemish chef to be awarded three Michelin stars. He has described his award-winning menu as "international cuisine made with local products" that aims to combine French quality with Flemish quantity. The result is outstanding, and the decor is as elegant as the fine cuisine deserves.

De Snippe. Nieuwe Gentweg 53. ☎ **050/33-70-70.** Reservations required. Main courses 850–1,350BF ($22–$36). AE, DC, MC, V. Tues–Sat noon–2:30pm; daily 7–10pm. FLEMISH/FRENCH.

In the 18th-century mansion hotel of the same name, this restaurant enjoys a well-earned reputation as one of Bruges's finest regional choices. Try the crayfish creations, scampi, or sliced wild duck.

Expensive

Duc de Bourgogne. Huidenvettersplein 12. ☎ **050/33-20-38.** Reservations required. Main courses 950–2,000BF ($25–$53); set-price menus 1,275–2,150BF ($34–$57). AE, CB, DC, MC, V. Tues 7–9pm; Wed–Sun noon–2pm and 7–9pm. Closed for 3 weeks during Jan and July. FRENCH.

This splendidly aristocratic dining room, overlooking a canal illuminated at night, is a Bruges classic. The menu is lengthy; the set-price lunch menu changes daily, and the set-price dinner every 2 weeks. Specialties include veal filets in a port sauce.

't Bourgoensche Cruyce. Wollestraat 41–43. ☎ **050/33-79-26.** Reservations required. Main courses 550–850BF ($14–$22); 3-course set-price meal 1,400BF ($37) lunch, 2,200BF ($58) dinner. AE, DC, MC, V. Thurs–Mon noon–2:30pm and 7–9:30pm. Closed Nov. CONTI-NENTAL.

You'd be hard put to find a better location, finer food, or a friendlier welcome. The rustic charm of this small dining room overlooking a canal in the town center is only one intimation of the culinary delights in store. Its regional specialties are perfection, and the menu, reflecting the best ingredients available, includes superb seafood dishes.

Moderate

Graaf van Vlaanderen. 't Zand 19. ☎ **050/33-31-50.** Main courses 375–450BF ($10–$12). AE, DC, MC, V. Fri–Wed 8am–10pm. STEAK/SALADS.

This reasonably priced restaurant in a small hotel near the railway station has an extensive menu and a decor that relies heavily on mirrors and plants. The food is equally simple, featuring minute steak (steak so thin it cooks in a minute) and french fries, spaghetti, and salads.

Kasteel Minnewater. Minnewater 4. ☎ **050/33-42-54.** Main courses 520–980BF ($14–$26); menu gastronomique 1,200BF ($32). V. Daily 11:30am–2:30pm and 6:30–10pm. FRENCH/SEAFOOD.

Old paintings on the walls, chandeliers, and fine table linen complement this château/restaurant's location close to the Begijnhof, with a garden terrace on the Min-newater (Lake of Love). It exudes an unstuffy charm, and though its prices are edging up, still provides a good deal considering the setting. Its Belgian specialties include sole Ostendaise, North Sea shrimp, and lamb cutlet with potatoes gratinée.

Inexpensive

Brasserie Erasmus. Wollestraat 35. ☎ **050/33-57-81.** Main courses 300–750BF ($8–$20). AE, CB, MC, V. Tues–Sun 11am–midnight. FLEMISH.

This small, popular restaurant is a great stop after viewing the cathedral and nearby museums. It serves a large variety of dishes, including a very good waterzooï with fish and rabbit in a beer sauce. About 150 different brands of beer are also offered here.

't Koffieboontje. Hallestraat 4. ☎ **050/33-80-27.** Main courses 350–650BF ($9–$17). AE, DC, JCB, MC, V. Daily noon–11pm. SEAFOOD/FLEMISH.

The bright, modern interior here strikes a noticeably stylish contrast to the often-dark ambience of many Bruges restaurants. An extensive menu is equally cheery, featuring good, but not fancy, seafood specialties like lobster and salmon, and such Belgian staples as mussels, steak, and sole.

EXPLORING HISTORIC BRUGES

Walking is by far the best way to see Bruges, whose town center is traffic-free. Wear good walking shoes, as those charming cobblestones can be hard going. Begin at the **Markt,** where a **sculpture group** depicts two Flemish heroes, butcher Jan Breydel and weaver Pieter de Coninck, who led an uprising in 1302 against the wealthy merchants and nobles who dominated the guilds, and went on to an against-all-odds victory over French knights in the Battle of the Golden Spurs later that same year. The 19th-century neo-Gothic **Provinciaal Hof** houses the West Flanders provincial government.

An array of beautiful buildings, which form a trip through the history of Bruges architecture, stand in the **Burg,** a square just steps away from the Markt. Here the Count of Flanders, Baldwin "Iron Arm," built a fortified castle (burg), around which grew the village that developed into Bruges.

Belfort (Belfry) and Hallen (Halls). Markt 7. ☎ **050/44-87-11.** Admission 100BF ($2.65) adults, 50BF ($1.30) children. Apr–Sept daily 9:30am–5pm; Oct–Mar daily 9:30am–12:30pm and 1:30–5pm.

The 13th- to 16th-century Belfry's octagonal tower soars 84 meters (272 feet) and holds a magnificent 47-bell carillon. Climb the 366 steps to the Belfry's summit for a panoramic view all the way to the sea. Much of the city's commerce was conducted in the Hallen in past centuries. Today local art dealers use them for exhibitions. The Belfry and Halls are open daily.

Stadhuis (Town Hall). Burg 11. ☎ **050/44-87-11.** Admission 60BF ($1.60) adults, 20BF (55¢) children. Daily Apr–Sep 9:30am–5pm; Oct–Mar 9:30am–12:30pm and 2–5pm.

Belgium's oldest town hall is an intricate Gothic structure from the late 1300s. Don't miss the upstairs ✪ **Gotische Zaal (Gothic Room),** with its ornate decor and wall murals depicting highlights of the city's history. Admission includes entry to the neighboring Renaissance **Zaal van de Brugse Vrije (Hall of the Liberty of Bruges),** which has been restored to its 16th-century condition. It has a superb black marble fireplace decorated with an alabaster frieze and topped by a carved oak chimney-piece with statues of Emperor Charles V and his illustrious grandparents: Emperor Maximilian of Austria, Duchess Mary of Burgundy, King Ferdinand II of Aragon, and Queen Isabella I of Castile.

Heilige-Bloedbasiliek (Holy Blood Basilica). Burg 10. ☎ **050/33-67-92.** Admission: basilica free; museum, 40BF ($1.05) adults, 20BF (55¢) children. Apr–Sep daily 9:30am–noon and 2–6pm; Oct–Mar daily 10am–noon and 2–4pm; closed Wed afternoon.

Since 1149, this richly decorated Romanesque church has been the repository of a cloth fragment holding what is said to be the blood of Christ, brought to Bruges after the Second Crusade by the count of Flanders. Every Ascension Day (May 24 in 2001), in the Procession of the Holy Blood, the bishop carries the relic through the streets, accompanied by costumed residents acting out Biblical scenes. The relic is kept in the basilica museum inside a rock-crystal vial, which is in a magnificent gold-and-silver reliquary.

Begijnhof. Wijngaardstraat. ☎ **050/33-00-11.** Courtyard permanently open and free. Admission to Begijn's House 60BF ($1.60) adults, 30BF (80¢) children; the. Mar–Nov daily 10am–noon and 1:45–5pm (Apr–Sep weekends to 5:30pm); Dec–Feb Mon, Tues, Fri 11am–noon, Wed–Thurs 2–4pm.

Through the centuries, one of the city's most tranquil spots has been the Begijnhof. *Begijns* were religious women, comparable to nuns, who accepted vows of chastity and obedience but drew the line at poverty. Today, the begijns are no more and the Begijnhof is occupied by Benedictine nuns who keep the begijns' traditions alive. Their tree-sprinkled lawn, surrounded by little whitewashed houses, makes a marvelous place to escape from the hurly-burly of the outside world.

Onze-Lieve-Vrouwekerk (Church of Our Lady). Mariastraat. ☎ **050/34-53-14.** Admission to church and Madonna and Child altar free; chapel of Charles and Mary, 60BF ($1.60) adults, 30BF (80¢) children. Apr–Sept Mon–Sat 10–11:30am and 2:30–5pm (Sat to 4pm), Sun 2:30–5pm; Oct–Mar Mon–Sat 10–11:30am and 2:30–4:30pm (Sat to 4pm), Sun 2:30–4:30pm.

It took 2 centuries (from the 13th until the 15th) to build this church. Its soaring 122m (396-foot) spire can be seen from a wide area around the city. Among its many art treasures are a beautiful marble *Madonna and Child* by Michelangelo (one of his few works to be seen outside Italy); a *Crucifixion* by Anthony Van Dyck; and impressive side-by-side bronze tomb sculptures of Charles the Bold, who died in 1477, and Mary of Burgundy, who died in 1482.

✪ **Groeninge Museum.** Dijver 12. ☎ **050/44-87-11.** Admission 200BF ($5) adults, 100BF ($2.65) children. Apr–Sept daily 9:30am–5pm; Oct–Mar Wed–Mon 9:30am–12:30pm and 2–5pm.

One of Belgium's leading fine arts museums, this collection covers painting in the Low Countries from the 15th to the 20th century. Its Flemish Primitives Gallery holds 30 works by such painters as Jan van Eyck (portrait of his wife, Margerita van Eyck), Rogier van der Weyden, Hieronymus Bosch *(The Last Judgment),* and Hans Memling. Works by Magritte and Delvaux are also on display.

Gruuthuse Museum. Dijver 17. ☎ **050/44-87-11.** Admission 130BF ($3.40) adults, 70BF ($1.85) children, 250BF ($7) families with children under 18. Apr–Sept daily 9:30am–5pm; Oct–Mar Wed–Mon 9:30am–12:30pm and 2–5pm.

In a courtyard next to the Groeninge is an ornate mansion where Flemish nobleman and herb merchant Louis de Gruuthuse lived in the 1400s. It contains thousands of antiques and antiquities, including paintings, sculptures, tapestries, lace, weapons, glassware, and richly carved furniture.

Kantcentrum (Lace Center). Peperstraat 3a. ☎ **050/33-00-72.** Admission 60BF ($1.60) adults, 40BF ($1.05) children. Mon–Sat 10am–noon and 2–6pm (Sat to 5pm).

A popular attraction, needless to say, is the Lace Center. Bruges lace is famous the world over, and there's no lack of shops offering you the opportunity to take some home. At the center, the ancient art of lace making is passed on to a new generation, while you get a firsthand look at artisans making many of the items sold in the city's lace shops. Lace-making demonstrations are in the afternoon.

BOAT TRIPS & OTHER ORGANIZED TOURS

If you'd like a trained, knowledgeable **guide** to accompany you, the tourist office can provide one for 1,500BF ($39) for the first 2 hours, 750BF ($20) for each additional hour. In July and August, join a daily guided walking tour at 3pm from the tourist office for 150BF ($3.95); free for children under 14.

Make sure you take an ✪ **open-top canal boat tour;** it's a fine way to view the city. Departure points are marked with an anchor icon on tourist office maps. Boats operate from March to November daily 10am to 6pm; December to February on weekends, school holidays, and public holidays 10am to 6pm (unless the canals are frozen). A half-hour cruise costs 170BF ($4.45) for adults, 85BF ($2.25) for children over 4. Wear something warm for cold or windy weather.

Another lovely way to tour Bruges is by **horse-drawn carriage.** From March to November, they are stationed in the Burg (Wednesday in the Markt); a 30-minute ride costs 900BF ($24) per cab, and 450BF ($12) for each additional 15 minutes. **Horse-drawn trams** are a cheaper, but no less romantic option: **Den Oekden Peerdentram** (☎ 050/79-04-37) does 30-minute tours from 't Zand, costing 200BF ($5) for adults, 100BF ($2.65) for children ages 4 to 11. **Firmin's Paardentram** (☎ 050/33-61-36) has 45-minute tours from the Markt, costing BF300 ($8) for adults, BF150 ($3.95) for children ages 4 to 11.

Sightseeing Lines coach tours (50 minutes) depart hourly every day from the Markt; first bus at 10am, last bus at 7pm in July and August, and at 4, 5, or 6pm in other months. Fares are 380BF ($10) for adults, 250BF ($7) for children; call ☎ 050/31-13-55.

Get out of town and into the West Flanders countryside on a **Back Road Bike Co.** bicycle tour (☎ 050/34-30-45). Call ahead to book; meeting and departure point is the Burg.

BRUGES AFTER DARK

For what's on information, pick up the tourist office's free monthly brochure *Exit* and free monthly newsletter *Agenda Brugge.*

THE PERFORMING ARTS   The **Koninklijke Stadsschouwburg,** Vlamingstraat 29 (☎ 050/44-86-86), from 1869, is the city's main opera, classical music, theater, and dance venue. Another important venue is the **Joseph Ryelandtzaal,** Achiel Van Ackerplein (☎ 050/44-86-86). Smaller-scale events, such as recitals, are held at the **Prinsenhof,** Prinsenhof 8 (☎ 050/34-50-93), the former palace of the dukes of Burgundy, and at **Sint-Salvators Kathedraal, Sint-Jacobskerk,** and other churches.

Theater—mostly in Dutch—is performed at **De Korre Theater,** Sint-Jacobsstraat 36 (☎ 050/34-47-60), which also has a puppet theater, **Marionettentheater Brugge,** for this sophisticated, centuries-old local art.

A different kind of theater is on the menu at **Brugge Anno 1468,** Celebration Entertainment, Vlamingstraat 86 (☎ 050/34-75-72). In a former Jesuit church, actors re-enact the wedding of Duke Charles the Bold of Burgundy to Margaret of York while customers pile into a medieval banquet. Performances take place from April to October, Thursday to Saturday 7:30 to 10pm; November to March, Saturday 7.30 to 10pm.

CLUBS & DANCING   The **Cactus Club,** Sint-Jacobsstraat 33 (☎ 050/33-20-14), presents an eclectic concert schedule Friday and Saturday nights. Try **De Vuurmolen,** Kraanplein 5 (☎ 050/33-00-79), for a raucous dancing-on-the-tables kind of night; it's open nightly from 10pm until the wee small hours.

✪ **Ma Rica Rokk,** 't Zand 7–8 (☎ 050/33-83-58), a bar with dancing, attracts a young, techno-oriented crowd nightly from 7pm to 4am (9pm to 6am on weekends).

Gays should visit bar/disco **Ravel,** Karel de Stoutelaan 172 (☎ **050/31-52-74**), open Wednesday and Friday to Monday from 10pm.

Vino Vino, Grauwwerkersstraat 15 (☎ **050/34-51-15**), somehow successfully combines Spanish tapas and the blues. For jazz, from bebop to modern, you won't do better than ✪ **De Versteende Nacht,** Langestraat 11 (☎ **050/34-32-93**).

BARS & TAVERNS ✪ Traditional cafe **'t Brugs Beertje,** Kemelstraat 5 (☎ **050/ 33-96-16**), serves more than 300 kinds of beer. **'t Dreupelhuisje,** Kemelstraat 9 (☎ **050/34-24-21**), does something similar with *jenever,* serving up dozens of artisanal examples of the deadly art. **Gran Kaffee De Passage,** Dweersstraat 26 (☎ **050/34-02-32**), is a quiet and elegant cafe that does inexpensive meals.

GHENT (GENT)

At the confluence of the Rivers Leie and Scheldt, Ghent was the seat of the powerful counts of Flanders, whose great castle, built in 1180, still stands as a gloomy reminder of their dominance.

For years the city was considered by tourists to be a poor relation of Bruges, only to be visited if there was time at the end of a trip. That's no longer true. The old town has been spruced up to attract more visitors, and Ghent has never looked so good. Although it's larger and more citified than Bruges, its center has enough cobblestone streets, meandering canals, and antique Flemish architecture to make it nearly as magical as its more famous sister.

ESSENTIALS

ARRIVING   By Train   Ghent is 32 minutes by rail from Brussels. There are trains about every half an hour for the 30-minute trip. The main train station, **Sint-Pieters** (☎ **09/222-44-44**), on Maria Hendrikaplein, is 1.5km (1 mile) south of the city center. Take tram 1, 10, 11, or 12 into town.

By Bus   The bus station (☎ **09/210-94-91**) adjoins Sint-Pieters train station.

By Car   You get to Ghent on the E40 from Brussels, E17 from Antwerp, and E40 from Bruges and Ostend.

VISITOR INFORMATION   The **Tourist Office,** Predikherenlei 2, 9000 Gent (☎ **09/225-36-41;** fax 09/225-62-88; www.gent.be; e-mail: toerisme@gent.be), is open Monday to Friday 8:30am to noon and 1 to 4:30pm. More convenient for personal visits, the **Infokantoor (Inquiry Desk)** is in the cellar of the Belfry, Botermarkt 17a, 9000 Gent (☎ **09/266-52-32;** fax 09/224-15-55), open April to October daily 9:30am to 6:30pm; November to March 9:30am to 4:30pm.

CITY LAYOUT   **Korenmarkt** is the city's heart. The most important sights, including the **Town Hall, St. Bavo's Cathedral,** and **Belfry,** lie within a short walking distance. The **River Leie** winds through the center and connects with the River Scheldt and canals that lead to a busy port area. Citadel Park, home to the **Fine Arts Museum,** is close to Sint-Pieters train station.

GETTING AROUND   Ghent has an excellent tram and bus system, with many lines converging at Korenmarkt. Walking is the best way to see the city center and experience at a human pace its effortless combination of history and modernity. Beyond the center, use public transportation.

SPECIAL EVENTS   The last week of July witnesses the **Gentse Feesten (Ghent Festivities),** a time of music, dancing, and generally riotous fun and games throughout the city.

WHERE TO STAY

The tourist office provides a free "Hotels and Restaurants" booklet and makes hotel reservations for a returnable deposit. Considering its popularity, Ghent has fewer hotels than you might expect, and city-center lodgings are often full at peak times, so try to book ahead.

Very Expensive

Novotel Gent Centrum. Gouden Leeuwplein 5, 9000 Gent. ☎ **800/221-4542** or 09/224-22-30. Fax 09/224-32-95. www.hotelweb.fr. E-mail: h0840@accor-hotels.com. 117 units. A/C MINIBAR TV TEL. 5,150–5,850BF ($136–$154) double; 6,950BF ($183) suite. AE, DC, MC, V. Parking 300BF ($8).

This modern hotel near the Town Hall is within easy walking distance of all the city's major sights. A modern edifice has been designed to fit, more or less, into its ancient surroundings. Rooms are nicely furnished and have individual heating controls. The facilities are all you'd expect from a top hotel, and include light, airy public rooms and a garden terrace.

Expensive

Sofitel Gent Belfort. Hoogpoort 63, 9000 Gent. ☎ **09/233-33-31.** Fax 09/233-11-02. E-mail: h1673hr@accor_hotels.com. 128 units. A/C MINIBAR TV TEL. 8,500–10,150BF ($224–$267) double; 15,150BF ($399) suite. AE, DC, MC, V. Parking 300BF ($8).

Ghent's top hotel has an enviable position across from the Town Hall, within easy reach of the main tourist attractions. Its big rooms are furnished in a modern, efficient style, and come with hair dryers. The hotel is bright and modern and has been designed to at least partly fit in with its venerable surroundings.

Moderate

✪ **Erasmus.** Poel 25, 9000 Gent. ☎ **09/224-21-95.** Fax 09/233-42-41. 12 units. TV TEL. 3,500–4,200BF ($92–$111) double; 5,000BF ($132) suite. Rates include buffet breakfast. AE, MC, V. Parking nearby 200BF ($5).

Each room is different in this converted 16th-century house, and all are plush, furnished with antiques and knickknacks. Rooms have high oak-beam ceilings, and baths are luxuriously modern. Some rooms have leaded-glass windows, some overlook a carefully manicured inner garden, and some have elaborate marble fireplaces; all have hair dryers and coffeemakers. Breakfast is served in an impressive room that would have pleased the counts of Flanders.

Ibis Gent Centrum Opera. Nederkouter 24–26, 9000 Gent. ☎ **800/221-4542** in the U.S. and Canada, or 09/225-07-07. Fax 09/223-59-07. E-mail: h1455@accor_hotels.com. 134 units. TV TEL. 3,350BF ($88) double. Rates include buffet breakfast. AE, CB, DC, MC, V. Parking 300BF ($8).

Rooms in this modern hotel between the city center and the train station are bright and comfortably furnished. There's a nice bar, and although there's no restaurant, several good ones are nearby. The hotel offers good accommodations at moderate rates. A program of room renovations, begun in 1997, continues.

✪ **Sint-Jorishof (aka Cour St-Georges).** Botermarkt 2, 9000 Gent. ☎ **09/224-24-24.** Fax 09/224-26-40. www.hotelbel.com/cour-st-georges.htm. E-mail: courstgeorges@ skynet.be. 28 units. TV TEL. 3,900–4,600BF ($103–$121) double. Rates include full breakfast. AE, DC, MC, V. Parking 200BF ($5).

In the city center opposite the town hall, this historical treasure has been a quality inn since 1228. If you stay here you're be in good company, historically speaking: Mary of Burgundy, Charles V, and Napoléon have all spent the night. Try to get a room in the old building rather than in the modern annex across the street. Decor in the pleasant

Ghent

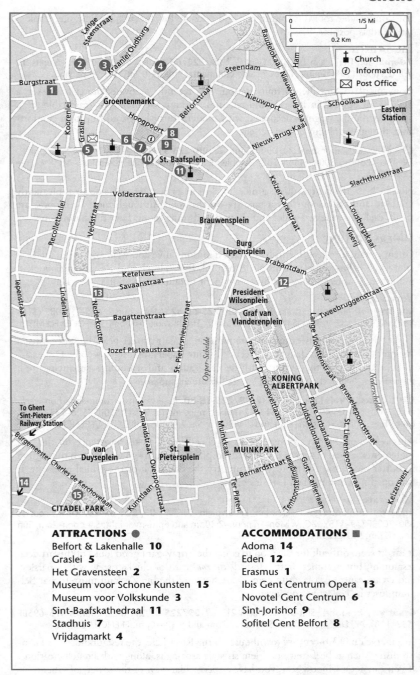

0   1/5 Mi
0   0.2 Km

✝ Church
ⓘ Information
✉ Post Office

Lange Steenstraat
Kraanlei Oudburg
Steendam
Burgstraat
1
Groentenmarkt
Hoogpoort
Belfortstraat
Nieuwport
Baudelokaai Nieuw-Brug-Kaai
Ham
Schoolkaai
Eastern Station
Koorenlei
Graslei
5
6
7
8
9
10
St. Baafsplein
11
Nieuw-Brug-Kaai
Keizer-Karelstraat
Slachthuisstraat
Volderstraat
Recollettenlei
Veldstraat
Brauwensplein
Burg Lippensplein
Brabantdam
Lousbergskaai
Viserij
Ketelvest
Savaanstraat
 Nederkouter
Bagattenstraat
Jozef Plateaustraat
13
Iependenstraat
Lindenlei
St. Pietersnieuwstraat
Opper-Schelde
President Wilsonplein
Graf van Vlanderenplein
12
Pres. Fr.-D.-Rooseveltlaan
Lange Violettenstraat
Tweebruggenstraat
Frère Orbanlaan
Brusselsepoortstraat
St. Lievenspoortstraat
Nederschelde
To Ghent Sint-Pieters Railway Station
Burgemeester Charles de Kerchovelaan
Leie
KONING ALBERTPARK
Hofstraat
Zuidstationlaan
van Duyseplein
St. Amandstraat
Overpoortstraat
St. Pietersplein
Muinkkaai
MUINKPARK
Bernardstraat
Ter Platen
Tentoonstellingslaan
Gust. Callierlaan
Keizersvest
14
15
CITADEL PARK
Kunstlaan

ATTRACTIONS ●
Belfort & Lakenhalle **10**
Graslei **5**
Het Gravensteen **2**
Museum voor Schone Kunsten **15**
Museum voor Volkskunde **3**
Sint-Baafskathedraal **11**
Stadhuis **7**
Vrijdagmarkt **4**

ACCOMMODATIONS ■
Adoma **14**
Eden **12**
Erasmus **1**
Ibis Gent Centrum Opera **13**
Novotel Gent Centrum **6**
Sint-Jorishof **9**
Sofitel Gent Belfort **8**

and comfortable rooms is traditional, and rates are low for such a prime site. Book as far ahead as possible.

Inexpensive

Adoma. Sint-Denijslaan 19, 9000 Gent. ☎ **09/222/65-50.** Fax 09/245-09-37. 15 units. TV TEL. 2,100BF ($55) double. Rates include continental breakfast. MC, V. Free parking.

Convenient to Sint-Pieters train station, this recently renovated hotel has taken a major leap upward in its style and facilities, without sacrificing its reasonable rates. Spacious rooms, brightly decorated with modern furnishings, add up to a comfortable, though not luxurious, experience.

✪ **Eden.** Zuidstationstraat 24, 9000 Gent. ☎ **09/223-51-51.** Fax 09/233-34-57. 28 units. TV TEL. 2,500–3,300BF ($66–$87) double. Rates include buffet breakfast. MC, V. Free parking.

Not far from the center, this is a nice hotel in its price range. The decor is pleasantly modern, and each room has a tapestry on the wall. Although most bathrooms are small, each has at least a toilet and shower, and some rooms have full bathrooms.

WHERE TO DINE

Ghent restaurants keep Flemish culinary traditions alive and well, and prices are generally well below those in Brussels. A helpful, free "Hotels and Restaurants" booklet published by the tourist office lists prominent restaurants in all price brackets.

Very Expensive

Jan Breydel. Jan Breydelstraat 10. ☎ **09/225-62-87.** Main courses 675–1,150BF ($18–$30). AE, DC, MC, V. Tues–Sat noon–2pm and 7–10pm; Mon 7–10pm. SEAFOOD/FLEMISH.

High honors go to this exquisite restaurant on a quaint street near the Gravensteen. Its interior is a garden delight of greenery, white napery, and light woods. Dishes are as light and airy as the setting, with delicate sauces and seasonings enhancing fresh ingredients. Seafood and regional specialties are all superb.

✪ **'t Buikske Vol.** Kraanlei 17. ☎ **09/225-18-80.** Reservations recommended on weekends. Main courses 495–895BF ($13–$24); fixed-price menus 975–1,650BF ($26–$43). AE, V. Mon, Tues, Thurs, Fri noon–2pm and 7–9:30pm; Sat 7–9:30pm. BELGIAN/FRENCH.

This is one of the city's gems, thanks to chef Peter Vyncke's insistence on the best ingredients, served in a cozy, intimate atmosphere. You can't go wrong with the salmon in butter sauce, but for more adventure, try the doe steak or the grilled pheasant. It isn't open much, but when it is, it's busy.

Moderate

Auberge de Fonteyne. Gouden Leeuwplein 7. ☎ **09/221-69-26.** Main courses 350–700BF ($9–$18). MC, V. Mon–Fri noon–2:30pm and 6pm–midnight; Sat noon–2am; Sun noon–2pm. MUSSELS/FLEMISH.

It might seem difficult for the food to equal the extravagant good looks of this art deco restaurant, but it comes pretty close. *Waterzooï* (fish or chicken stew with a parsley-and-cream sauce) is a favorite here, as are heaps of the big Zeeland mussels that Belgium loses its collective cool over.

Graaf van Egmond. Sint-Michielsplein 21. ☎ **09/225-07-27.** Main courses 475–695BF ($13–$18). AE, DC, MC, V. Tues–Sun noon–2pm and 6:30–10pm. FRENCH/FLEMISH.

In a marvelous 13th-century townhouse on the River Leie, the restaurant serves Flemish dishes such as beef stew and Flemish-style asparagus, along with French creations. If you can get a window seat, you have a spectacular view of the towers of Ghent.

Guido Meerschaut. Kleine Vismarkt 3. ☎ **09/223-53-49.** Main courses 320–495BF ($8–$13); fixed-price menu 880BF ($23). AE, DC, MC, V. Tues–Sat noon–2:30pm and 6–10:30pm. SEAFOOD/FLEMISH.

Guido owns a fish shop in the Fish Market, so it's no surprise that his restaurant specializes in seafood. Well-prepared fish fresh from the North Sea is served in a simple yet elegant room painted with scenes from Fish Market history. Dover sole, sole Ostendaise, a variety of cod, herring, and other fish dishes predominate, along with North Sea shrimp, oysters, and mussels prepared in a variety of ways.

Inexpensive

Amadeus. Plotersgracht 8. ☎ **09/225-13-85.** Reservations required. Spareribs dinner 450BF ($12). No credit cards. Mon–Thurs 7pm–midnight; Fri–Sat 6pm–midnight; Sun noon–3pm and 6pm–midnight. RIBS/CONTINENTAL.

Sure, there are vegetarian and fish plates, but all Ghent comes here for the all-you-can-eat spareribs dinner: a slab of perfectly cooked ribs served on a tray with a choice of delicious sauces and a baked potato. If you're up to it, you can order another and another and another. A bottle of wine is on the table, and you pay for what you drink from it. The decor is sumptuously art nouveau with burnished wood, mirrors, and colored glass, and the ambience is fun and relaxed.

EXPLORING HISTORIC GHENT

The city's historic monuments have a solemnity that gives them a somewhat forbidding look. In the case of the Castle of the Counts of Flanders, it was meant to look this way because Ghent's citizens were so often in revolt against their overlord. The "Three Towers of Ghent"—St. Bavo's, the Belfry, and St. Nicholas—form an almost straight line pointing toward St. Michael's Bridge.

A row of gabled ✪ **guild houses** built along Graslei between the 1200s and 1600s, when the waterway was Ghent's harbor, forms a perfect ensemble of colored facades reflected in the River Leie. To view them as a whole, cross the bridge over the Leie to Korenlei, and walk along the bank past each one. These buildings once housed the craftsmen, tradespeople, and merchants who formed the city's commercial core and this is an ideal spot to snap a picture that captures the essence of Ghent.

The **Vrijdagmarkt (Friday Market Square),** a popular meeting spot today, was a rallying point in times past. A statue of Jacob Van Arteveld pays tribute to this rebel leader of the 1300s, and its base is adorned by the insignia of some 52 guilds. The square is now a major shopping area and hosts a lively street market every Friday. A short distance away, smaller **Kanonplein** is guarded by a gigantic cannon known as Mad Meg (Dulle Griet), which thundered away in the 1400s in the service of Burgundian armies.

Sint-Baafskathedraal (St. Bavo's Cathedral). Sint-Baafsplein. ☎ **09/223-10-46.** Cathedral, free; **Mystic Lamb** chapel and Crypt, 60BF ($1.60) adults, 50BF ($1.30) children. Cathedral, daily 8:30am to 6pm, except during religious services; **Mystic Lamb** chapel and Crypt Apr–Oct Mon–Sat 9:30am–noon and 2–6pm, Sun 1–6pm; Nov–Mar Mon–Sat 10:30am–noon and 2:30–4pm, Sun 2–5pm.

Within this 14th-century cathedral's plain Gothic exterior lies a splendid baroque interior and some priceless art. A 24-panel altarpiece, *The Adoration of the Mystic Lamb,* completed by Jan van Eyck in 1432, is St. Bavo's showpiece. Other treasures include Rubens's *The Conversion of St. Bavo* (1624), in the Rubens Chapel off the semicircular ambulatory behind the high altar.

⭕ **Belfort (Belfry) and Lakenhalle (Cloth Hall).** Sint-Baafsplein. ☎ **09/223-99-22.** Tickets 100BF ($2.65) adults, 30BF (80¢) children ages 7–16 (under 7 free). Tours Tues–Sun hourly 2:10–5:10pm.

Across the square from St. Bavo's, the Belfry and Cloth Hall form a glorious medieval ensemble. From the 14th-century Belfry, great bells have rung out Ghent's civic pride down through the centuries, and a 54-bell carillon does so today. You can get high in the Belfry with a guide and the aid of an elevator. The 1425 Cloth Hall was the gathering place of medieval wool and cloth merchants.

Het Gravensteen (Castle of the Counts). Sint-Veereplein. ☎ **09/225-93-06.** Admission, 200BF ($5), children under 12 free. Daily Apr–Sept 9am–6pm; Oct–Mar 9am–5pm.

Crouching like a gray stone lion over the city, grim-looking Gravensteen was clearly designed by the counts of Flanders to send a message to rebellion-inclined Gentenaars: Keep your thoughts to yourself; better still, don't have any at all. Surrounded by the waters of the River Leie, the castle was begun by Count Philip of Alsace, fresh from the Crusades in 1180. If its 2m- (6-foot-) thick walls, battlements, and turrets failed to intimidate attackers, the counts could turn to the accoutrements of a well-equipped torture chamber, some of which can be seen in a small museum. The view from the ramparts of the central keep, or donjon, is worth the climb. Call ahead if you want a guided tour.

⭕ **Stadhuis (Town Hall).** Botermarkt and Hoogpoort. ☎ **09/223-99-22.** Admission, 100BF ($2.65) adults, 30BF (80¢) children. Guided tours, May–Oct Mon–Thurs 2pm from tourist office in Belfry "Raadskelder."

The Town Hall has what you might call a split personality. A plain Renaissance facade fronts Botermarkt, and a garishly ornamented Gothic side faces Hoogpoort. Work began in 1518 and continued until the 18th century, and the building's many styles reflect the changing tastes of those centuries, as well as availability or lack of money. In its **Pacificatiezaal (Pacification Room),** the Pacification of Ghent, signed in 1567, declared the Low Countries' repudiation of Spanish rule and their intention to permit religious freedom.

Museum voor Schone Kunsten (Fine Arts Museum). Citadel Park, Nicolaas de Liemaeckereplein 3. ☎ **09/222-17-03.** Admission 100BF ($2.65), children under 12 free. Tues–Sun 9:30am–5pm.

This large museum is home to ancient and modern masterpieces, including works by Van der Weyden, Brueghel, Rubens, Van Dyck, and Bosch, along with moderns such as James Ensor and Constant Permeke.

Museum voor Volkskunde (Folklore Museum). Kraanlei 65. ☎ **09/223-13-36.** Admission 100BF ($2.65) adults, 50BF ($1.30) children ages 12–18, children under 12 free. Apr–Oct daily 9am–12:30pm and 1:30–5:30pm; Nov–Mar Tues–Sun 10am–12:30pm and 1:30–5pm.

In a group of former almshouses from the 1300s, this museum displays authentic replicas of rooms where craft skills were practiced around 1900. There is an attached marionette theater (check with the museum for the performance schedule). The museum is open.

BOAT RIDES & OTHER ORGANIZED TOURS

A **boat ride** on the canals (☎ 09/282-92-48) is an ideal way to see the city's highlights. From April to October, open and covered boats leave every 30 minutes, daily from 10am to 7pm from the Graslei and Korenlei. The narrated trip lasts 35 minutes; the fare is 160BF ($4.20) for adults, 80BF ($2.10) for children under 12.

Qualified guides (☎ **09/233-07-72**) lead private **walking tours** from the **Tourist Office Infokantoor** Monday to Friday at a charge of 1,500BF ($39) for the first 2 hours, 600BF ($16) for each additional hour.

Horse-drawn carriages leave from Sint-Baafsplein and Korenlei daily from 10am to 7pm, from Easter to October. A half-hour ride costs 800BF ($21).

GHENT AFTER DARK

THE PERFORMING ARTS   Opera is performed in the 19th-century **Vlaamse Opera,** Schouwburgstraat 3 (☎ **09/225-24-25**), October to mid-June. For non-premier performances, tickets cost 250 to 2,500BF ($7–$66). Most performances begin at 8pm, with occasional 3pm matinees. It's best to book ahead.

Ghent venues for puppet shows are the **Museum voor Volkenkunde,** Kraanlei 65 (☎ **09/223-13-36**); **Taptoe Teater,** Forelstraat 91c (☎ **09/223-67-58**); and **Magie,** Haspelstraat 39 (☎ **09/226-42-18**). Check with the tourist office for performance schedules during your visit.

BARS & TAVERNS   In typical Flemish fashion, Ghent's favorite after-dark entertainment is frequenting atmospheric cafes and taverns. You should have a memorable evening in any one you choose. **De Witte Leeuw,** Graslei 6 (☎ **09/233-37-33**), has a 17th-century setting and more than 300 varieties of beer. At **Dulle Griet,** Vrijdagmarkt 50 (☎ **09/224-24-55**), you'll be asked to deposit one of your shoes before being given a potent Kwak beer in the too-collectible glass with a wood frame that allows the glass to stand up—you too may need artificial support if you drink too many. The smallest building on Graslei, the former Toll House, is now a nice little tavern called **Het Tolhuisje,** Graslei 10 (☎ **09/224-30-90**).

Groentenmarkt, near the Gravensteen, makes for a pretty good pub-crawl in an easily navigable area. Try **Het Waterhuis aan de Bierkant,** Groentenmarkt 9 (☎ **09/225-06-80**), which has more than 100 different Belgian beers, including locally made Stopken. A couple of doors along is **'t Dreupelkot,** Groentenmarkt 12 (☎ **09/224-21-20**), a specialist in deadly little glasses of jenever (a stiff spirit similar to gin). Ask owner Paul to recommend one of his 100 or so varieties, or walk straight in and boldly ask for a 64-proof Jonge Hertekamp or a 72-proof Pekèt de Houyeu; if they don't knock you down, you may be up for an 8-year-old 100-proof Filliers Oude Graanjenever or a 104-proof Hoogspanning. Across the tramlines is **Het Galgenhuisje,** Groentenmarkt 5 (☎ **09/233-42-51**), a tiny and, perforce, intimate place popular with students.

3 The Czech Republic

by John Mastrini & Hana Mastrini

If you have time to visit only one Eastern European city, the place to go is Prague. The quirky Czech capital, often called a "baroque Disneyland" because of its fairy-tale architecture, is a perfect new cusp-of-the-millennium destination. Here you'll encounter the triumphs and tragedies of the past 10 centuries spiked with the peculiarity of the post-Communist reconstruction.

But Prague isn't the Czech Republic's only draw. Visitors are again flocking to west Bohemia after some of the world's best-known spas were restored to their Victorian-era splendor.

1 Prague & Environs

Almost 75 years after native-son Franz Kafka's death, Prague's mix of the melancholy and the magnificent, the shadows and the fog of everyday life, set against some of Europe's most spectacular architecture, still confounds all who live or visit here. Its tightly wound brick paths have felt the hooves of kings' horses, the jackboots of Hitler's armies, the heaving tracks of Soviet tanks, and the shuffle of students in passive revolt. The 6-centuries-old Charles Bridge is today jammed with visitors and venture capitalists looking for memories or profits from a once-captive city now enjoying yet another renaissance.

A turbulent past and promising future gives Prague its eclectic energy, while its baroque and Renaissance atmosphere provides its gravity.

ORIENTATION

ARRIVING By Plane Newly rebuilt **Ruzyně Airport** (☎ **02/2011 1111**) is 19km (12 miles) west of the city center. You'll find a bank for changing money (usually open daily 7am to 11pm), telephones, and several car-rental offices.

Plenty of **taxis** line up in front of the airport. The fancy cars parked in front of the terminal cost about twice the price of the rickety Škoda and Lada taxis off to the right. **ČSA,** the Czech national airline main office is at V Celnici 5 (☎ **02/2010 4111**). CEDAZ operates an **airport shuttle bus** to nám. Republiky in central Prague. It leaves the airport daily every 30 minutes from 6am to 9pm and stops near the Náměstí Republiky metro station (trip time: 30 minutes). Returning, the bus leaves every 30 minutes 5:30am till 9:30pm. The shuttle costs 90Kč ($2.65). You can also take **city bus 119** to the Dejvická metro station (Line A) for 12Kč (35¢).

Traveler's Tip

Most of Prague's taxi drivers will take advantage of you; getting an honestly metered ride from the airport is close to impossible. The fare from the airport to Wenceslas Square should be no more than about 500Kč ($15). If you pay only twice this, consider yourself lucky.

By Train   Of the two central rail stations, **Hlavní nádraží,** Wilsonova třída 80, Praha 1 (☎ 02/2461 1111), is the grander and more popular; however, it's also seedier. The basement holds a 24-hour luggage-storage counter charging 15Kč (44¢) per bag up to 15kg (33 lbs.) per day (counted from midnight). The nearby lockers aren't secure and should be avoided. Beneath the main hall are surprisingly clean public showers that are a good place to refresh yourself for just 40Kč ($1.17); they're open Monday to Friday 6am to 8pm, Saturday 7am to 7pm, and Sunday 8am to 4pm. On the second floor is the train information office (marked by a lowercase "i"), open daily 6am to 10pm. From the main train station it's a 5-minute stroll to the "top" end of Wenceslas Square or a 15-minute walk to Old Town Square. Metro Line C connects the station to the rest of the city. Metro trains depart from the lower level, and city-center no-transfer tickets, costing 8Kč (23¢), are available at the newsstand near the metro entrance. Taxis line up outside the station day and night.

   Nádraží Holešovice, Partyzánská at Vrbenského, Praha 7 (☎ 02/2422 4200), usually serves trains from Berlin and other points north. Although it isn't as centrally located as the main station, its more manageable size and position at the end of metro Line C make it almost as convenient.

VISITOR INFORMATION   Those arriving by train at either of the two primary stations can get information from **AVE Ltd.** (☎ 02/2422 3226 or 02/2422 3521; fax 02/5731 2984; www.avetravel.cz; e-mail: ave@avetravel.cz), an accommodations agency that also distributes printed information. The two train station offices are open daily 6am to 10pm. **Tom's Travel** has developed a fantastic set of Web sites, including www.travel.cz for general Czech tourist information and accommodation (see below).

   The city's **Cultural and Information Center,** on the ground floor of the remodeled Municipal House (Obecní dům), Náměstí Republiky 5, Praha 1, ☎ 02/2200 2100; fax 02/2200 2636; e-mail: od@monet.cz; metro: Náměstí Republiky), is a new attempt at visitor-friendly relations, offering advice, tickets, souvenirs, refreshments, and rest rooms. It's open daily 9am to 5pm.

CITY LAYOUT   The **River Vltava** bisects Prague. **Staré Město (Old Town)** and **Nové Město** (New Town) are on the east (right) side of the river, while the **Hradčany** (Castle District) and **Malá Strana** (Lesser Town) are on the west (left) bank.

   Bridges and squares are the most prominent landmarks. **Charles Bridge,** the oldest and most famous of those spanning the Vltava, is at the epicenter and connects Old Town with Lesser Town and the Castle District. Several important streets radiate from Old Town Square, including fashionable **Pařížská** to the northwest, historic **Celetná** to the east, and **Melantrichova,** connecting to **Wenceslas Square (Václavské náměstí)** to the southeast.

   On the west side of Charles Bridge is **Mostecká,** a 3-block-long connection to **Malostranské náměstí,** Malá Strana's main square. Hradčany, the Castle District, is just northwest of the square, while a second hill, **Petřín,** is just southwest.

   When reading maps or searching for addresses, keep in mind that *ulice* (abbreviated ul.) means "street," *třída* means "avenue," *náměstí* (abbreviated nám.) is a "square" or

Prague

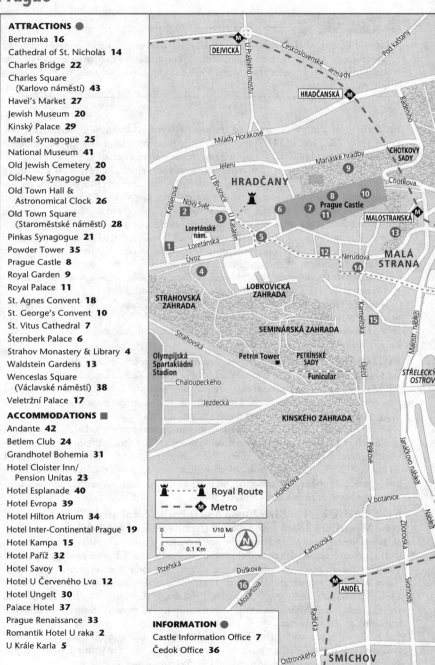

🏰 ---- 🏰 **Royal Route**
--- Ⓜ **Metro**

0 _____ 1/10 Mi
0 _____ 0.1 Km

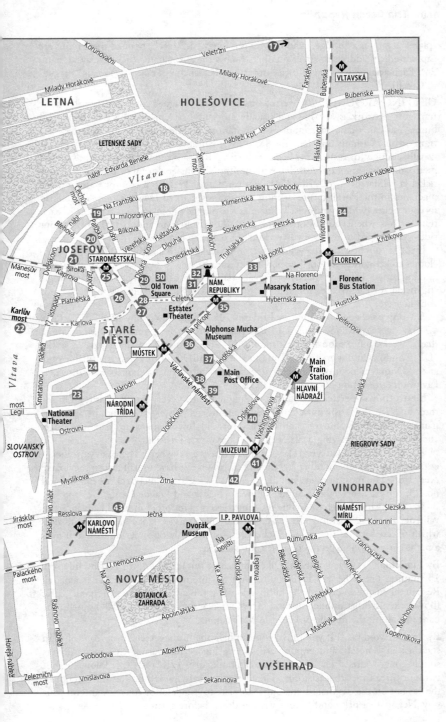

"plaza," a *most* is a "bridge," and *nábřeží* is a "quay." In Czech, none of these terms are capitalized. In addresses, street numbers follow the street name (like Václavské nám. 25). Each address is followed by a district number, such as Praha 1 (*Praha* is "Prague" in Czech).

GETTING AROUND   By Metro, Bus & Tram   Prague's communist-built public transport network is a vast—and usually efficient—system of subways, trams, and buses. You can ride a maximum of four stations on the metro or 15 minutes on a tram or bus, without transfers, for 8Kč (23¢); children 5 and under are free. This is usually enough for trips in the historic districts. Rides of more than four stops on the metro, or longer tram or bus rides, with unlimited transfers for up to 1 hour after your ticket is validated, cost 12Kč (35¢). You can buy tickets from coin-operated orange machines in metro stations or at most newsstands marked *tabák* or *trafika*. Hold on to your ticket (which you must validate at the orange or yellow stamp clocks in each tram or bus when you get on board or at the entrance to the metro) during your ride—you'll need it to prove you've paid if a ticket collector asks.

If you're caught without a valid ticket, you have to pay a 200Kč ($6) fine to a plain-clothes ticket controller on the spot. Make sure he or she shows you a very official-looking badge. *Warning:* Oversized luggage (larger than carry-on size) requires a single trip ticket for each piece. You may be fined 400Kč ($12) for not having tickets for your luggage.

A **1-day pass** good for unlimited rides is 70Kč ($2.05); a **3-day pass** 200Kč ($6); a **7-day pass** 250Kč ($7); and a **15-day pass** 280Kč ($8). If you're staying for more than 2 weeks, buy a **monthly pass** for 420Kč ($12). You can buy the day passes at the "DP" windows at any metro station, but the photo ID monthly pass is available only at the Dopravní podnik (transport department) office on Na bojišti, near the I. P. Pavlova metro station (☎ **02/9619 1111**).

Metro trains operate daily 5am to midnight and run every 3 to 8 minutes. On the three lines (A, B, C), the most convenient stations are Můstek, at the foot of Václavské náměstí (Wenceslas Square); Staroměstská, for Old Town Square and Charles Bridge; and Malostranská, serving Malá Strana and the Castle District.

The **electric tram** (streetcar) lines run practically everywhere. There's always another tram with the same number traveling back. You never have to hail trams; they make every stop. The most popular, no. 22 (the "tourist tram" or "pickpocket express") and no. 23, run past top sights like the National Theater and Prague Castle.

To ride the **bus,** you have to buy the same tickets as for other modes in advance and validate them on boarding. Regular bus and tram service stops at midnight, after which selected routes run reduced schedules, usually only once per hour. If you miss a night connection, expect a long wait for the next.

By Funicular   The cog railway makes the scenic run up and down Petřín Hill every 15 minutes or so 9:15am to 8:45pm, with an intermediate stop at the Nebozízek Restaurant in the middle of the hill overlooking the city. It requires the same 12Kč (35¢) ticket as other public transport. The funicular departs from a small house in the park just above the middle of Újezd in Malá Strana.

By Taxi   Avoid taxis! If you must, you can hail one in the streets or in front of train stations, large hotels, and popular attractions, but be forewarned that many drivers simply gouge tourists. The best fare you can hope for is 17Kč (50¢) per kilometer, but twice or three times that isn't rare. The rates are usually posted not on the exterior of the car but on the dashboard, making it too late to haggle once you're in and on your way. Negotiate a price and have it written down before getting in. Better yet, go on

Prague Metro

foot or by public transport. Somewhat reputable companies with English-speaking dispatchers are **AAA Taxi** (☎ **02/2432 2432** or local phone 1080); **SEDOP** (local phone ☎ **1087**) and the unfortunately named **ProfiTaxi** (local phone ☎ **1035**). Get a receipt (and send it to the mayor).

By Car   Driving in Prague is not worth the money or effort. The roads are frustrating and slow, and parking is minimal and expensive. If you want to rent a car to explore the environs, try **Europcar/InterRent,** Pařížská 28, Praha 1 (☎ **02/2481 0039**), open daily 8am to 8pm. Also there's **Hertz,** Karlovo nám. 28, Praha 2 (☎ **02/ 291 851** or 02/290 122), and **Budget,** at Ruzyně Airport (☎ **02/316 5214**) and in the Hotel Inter-Continental, náměstí Curieových, Praha 1 (☎ **02/2488 9995**).

Local Czech car-rental companies sometimes offer lower rates than the big international firms. Try **SeccoCar,** Přístavní 39, Praha 7 (☎ **02/6671 0602**).

Fast Facts: Prague

American Express   For travel arrangements, traveler's checks, currency exchange, and other member services, visit the city's sole office at Václavské nám. 56 (Wenceslas Square), Praha 1 (☎ **02/2280 0251;** fax 02/2221 1131; metro: Můstek). It's open daily from 9am to 7pm. To report lost or stolen cards, call ☎ **02/2280 0800.**

Prague Online

The city's own information service, PIS, has regularly updated cultural information in English and acts as a gateway to other tourism Web sites at **www.prague-info.cz**. For visa and other consular information, the Foreign Ministry site is **www.czech.cz**. For the latest local news updates and tourism info, try the Globe Bookstore's eclectic English-language Web site **www.globopolis.com**, the Internet Café supremo Terminal Bar site at **www.terminal.cz** or the *Prague Post* at **www.praguepost.cz**.

Business Hours Most **banks** are open Monday to Friday 8am to 6pm. Business **offices** are generally open Monday to Friday 8am to 6pm. **Pubs** are usually open daily 11am to midnight. Most **restaurants** open for lunch noon to 3pm and for dinner 6 to 11pm; only a few stay open later.

Currency The basic unit of currency is the **koruna** (plural, **koruny**) or crown, abbreviated **Kč**. Each koruna is divided into 100 haléřů or hellers. Notes, each of which bears a forgery-resistant metal strip and a prominent watermark, are issued in 20, 50, 100, 200, 500, 1,000, 2,000, and 5,000 koruny denominations. Coins are 10, 20, and 50 hellers and 1, 2, 5, 10, 20, and 50 koruny. At this writing, $1 = approximately 34Kč and £1 = 55Kč, or 1Kč = 3¢. Also, €1 = 36.5Kč.

Currency Exchange Banks generally offer the best exchange rates. Don't hesitate to use a credit or debit card to draw cash for the best rates. **Komerční banka** has three convenient Praha 1 locations with ATMs accepting Visa, MasterCard, and American Express: Na Příkopě 33, Národní 32, and Václavské nám. 42 (☎ **02/2442 1111** central switchboard for all branches; metro: Můstek). The exchange offices are open Monday to Friday 8am to 5pm, but the ATMs are accessible 24 hours.

Doctors/Dentists If you need a doctor or dentist and your condition isn't life-threatening, you can visit the **Polyclinic at Národní,** Národní 9, Praha 1 (☎ **02/2207 5120;** for emergencies, ☎ 02/0600 111; operator 02/140 533; metro: Můstek), during walk-in hours, 8am to 5pm. Dr. Stránský is an Ivy League–trained straight-talking physician. For **emergency medical aid,** call the **Foreigners' Medical Clinic,** Na Homolce Hospital, Roentgenova 2, Praha 5 (☎ **02/5292 2146** or 02/5292 2191 after hours; metro: Anděl).

Embassies The **U.S. Embassy** is at Tržiště 15, Praha 1 (☎ **02/5732 0663**). The **Canadian Embassy** is at Mickiewiczova 6, Praha 6 (☎ **02/7210 1800**). The **U.K. Embassy** is at Thunovská 14, Praha 1 (☎ **02/5732 0355**). The **Australian Honorary Consul** is at Na Ořechovce 38, Praha 6 (☎ **02/2431 0743**). The **Embassy of Ireland** is at Tržiště 13, Praha 1 (☎ **02/5753 0061**).

Emergencies You can reach Prague's **police** and **fire** services by dialing ☎ **158** from any phone. To call an **ambulance,** dial ☎ **155.**

Hospitals Particularly welcoming to foreigners is **Nemocnice Na Homolce,** Roentgenova 2 , Praha 5 (☎ **02/5292 2146** or 02/5292 2191 after hours; metro: Anděl). The English-speaking doctors can also make house calls.

Internet Access The best of the cybercafes is **Terminal Bar** at Soukenická 6, three blocks from nám. Republiky on the yellow line (☎ **02/2187 1999;** metro: Náměstí Republiky), where about a dozen twin-seater work stations are available for 100Kč ($2.95) an hour for non-members (charged by the quarter hour with a 15-minute minimum).

Pharmacies   The most central pharmacy (*lékárna*) is at Václavské nám. 8, Praha 1 (☎ **02/2422 7532;** metro: Můstek), open Monday to Friday 8am to 6pm. The nearest emergency (24-hour) pharmacy is at Palackého 5, Praha 1 (☎ **02/2494 6982**). If you're in Praha 2, there's an emergency pharmacy on Belgická 37 (☎ **02/2423 7207**).

Taxes   A 22% **value-added tax (VAT)** is built into the price of most goods and services rather than being tacked on at the register. (A plan to lower the VAT on hotels and restaurants to 5% began in mid-2000 to make the country even more attractive for tourists). Most restaurants include VAT in the prices stated on their menus. If they don't, that fact should be stated somewhere on the menu.

Telephone   The **country code** for the Czech Republic is **420.** The **city code** for Prague is **2;** use it if you're calling from outside the country. If you're within the Czech Republic but not in Prague, use **02.** If you're calling within Prague, simply leave off the code and dial the regular phone number.

For **directory assistance** in English, dial (without charge) **0149.** For **information on services** and rates, dial **0139.** Dial tones are continual high-pitched beeps that sound something like busy signals in America. After dialing a number from a pay phone, you might hear a series of very quick beeps that tell you the line is being connected. Busy signals sound similar to dial tones only quicker.

There are two kinds of **pay phones.** One accepts coins and the other operates only with a phone card, available from post offices and news agents in denominations ranging from 50Kč to 500Kč ($1.45 to $15). The minimum cost of a **local call** is 3Kč (10¢). Coin-op phones, if they work, have displays telling you the minimum price for your call. They don't make change, so don't load more than you have to. You can add more coins as the display gets near zero. The more efficient phone card telephones deduct the price of your call from the card. If you're calling home, get a phone card with plenty of points, as calls run about 42Kč ($1.25) per minute to the United States and 25Kč (45p) to the United Kingdom. Hotels usually add their own surcharge, sometimes as hefty as 100% to 200%, which may surprise you when you're presented with the bill. Ask before placing any call from a hotel. Charging to your phone credit card from a public telephone is often the most economical way to call home.

A fast, convenient way to call home from Europe is via services that bypass the foreign operator and automatically link you to an operator with your long-distance carrier in your home country. The access number in the Czech Republic for **AT&T USA Direct** is ☎ **0042 000 101,** for **MCI World Phone** ☎ **0042 000 112,** and for **Sprint Global One** ☎ **00 420 87187.** Canadians can connect with **Canada Direct** at ☎ **00 420 00151** and Brits with **BT Direct** at ☎ **00 420 04401** or **Mercury Call UK** at ☎ **00 420 04450.** From a pay phone in the Czech Republic, your local phone card will be debited only for a local call.

Tipping   At most restaurants and pubs, locals just round the bill up to the nearest few koruny. When you're given good service at tablecloth places, a 10% tip is proper. Washroom and cloakroom attendants usually demand a couple of koruny, and porters in airports and rail stations usually receive 20Kč (60¢) per bag. Taxi drivers should get about 10%, unless they've already ripped you off.

WHERE TO STAY

Prague's full-service hotels have had to tighten efficiency in the face of heavier international competition, but due to low supply, room rates still top those of many similar or better quality hotels in Western Europe. Pensions with limited services are cheaper than hotels, but compared with similar Western B&Bs, they're pricey. The best budget accommodations are rooms in private homes or apartments.

Expect to pay between 750Kč and 1,500Kč ($22 and $44) for a single and between 1,500Kč and 6,000Kč ($44 and $176) for an apartment for two. All kinds of private housing are offered by several local agencies. The leader now is Prague-based **Tom's Travel** at **www.travel.cz**, which offers all types of accommodation at their main site, or you can tap their large pictured database of apartments at **www.apartments.cz**. Tom's office is near the National Theater at Ostrovní 7 (☎ **02/2499 0983;** fax 02/2499 0999; metro: Národní třída). Another agency, especially for those arriving late by train or air, is **AVE Travel Ltd.** (☎ **02/2422 3226;** fax 02/5155 6005; www.avetravel.cz; e-mail: ave@avetravel.cz). It has outlets at the airport (7am to 10pm), at the main train station, Hlavní nádraží (6am to 11pm), and at the north train station, nádraží Holešovice (7am to 9pm).

STARÉ MĚSTO (OLD TOWN) & JOSEFOV
Very Expensive
Grandhotel Bohemia. Královdorská 4, Praha 1. ☎ **02/2480 4111.** Fax 02/232 9545. www.austria-hotels.co.at. E-mail: grand-hotel-bohemia@austria-hotels.icom.cz. 78 units. A/C MINIBAR TV TEL. 14,824Kč ($436) double; from 20,740Kč ($610) suite. Rates include breakfast. AE, DC, MC, V. Metro: Náměstí Republiky.

Opened in 1994, the Bohemia is sophisticated and comfortable, and if you don't care about being overcharged, it's certainly the place to stay. In this wonderfully restored art nouveau–style hotel, the extravagant, gilded public areas are impressive and quite different from the contemporary guest rooms. The bright and cheerful accommodations aren't large but are fitted with extras. Use the unspectacular restaurant only as a matter of convenience. There's also a small cafe.

Hotel Intercontinental Prague. Nám. Curieových 43/5, Praha 1. ☎ **02/2488 1111.** Fax 02/2481 0071. www.interconti.com. E-mail: prague@interconti-com. 364 units. A/C MINIBAR TV TEL. From 8,840Kč ($260) double; from 13,600Kč ($400) suite. Rates include buffet breakfast. Children under 10 free in parents' room. AE, DC, MC, V. Metro: Staroměstská.

The upper suites have hosted luminaries such as Michael Jackson, Madeleine Albright, and, so legend has it, terrorist Carlos the Jackal. The 1970s design has been updated with a glittering modern fitness center and an atrium restaurant. The standard rooms aren't very large but are comfortable, with decent but not exceptional furniture and computer ports. A riverside window might give you a glimpse of the castle or the metronome at the top of Letná park across the river.

Expensive
✪ **Hotel Paříž.** U Obecního domu 1, Praha 1. ☎ **02/2219 5195.** Fax 02/2422 5475. www.hotel-pariz.cz. E-mail: booking@hotel-pariz.cz. 93 units. TV TEL. 9,180Kč ($270) double; from 12,920Kč ($380) suite. Rates include breakfast. AE, CB, DC, MC, V. Metro: Náměstí Republiky.

At the edge of náměstí Republiky and across from the Municipal House, the Paříž provides a rare glimpse back into the gilded First Republic. Each light fixture, etching, and curve at this art nouveau landmark recalls the days when Prague was one of the world's richest cities. For a glimpse of the hotel's atmosphere, rent the film *Mission Impossible;* you can see Tom Cruise plotting his revenge from within one of the fine suites. The rooms are some of the most comfortable in Prague, with modern updates of art deco accents.

Hotel Ungelt. Štupartská 1, Praha 1. ☎ **02/2482 8686.** Fax 02/2482 8181. www. interacta.cz/accol.htm. 9 units. MINIBAR TV TEL. 6,330Kč ($186) 1-bedroom suite for 2;

8,640Kč ($254) two-bedroom suite for 3 or 4. Rates include breakfast. AE, MC, V. Metro: Staroměstská or Náměstí Republiky.

The three-story Ungelt offers airy, spacious suites. Each contains a living room, a full kitchen, and a bathroom. Bedrooms have standard-issue beds, but do boast luxurious accents like huge chandeliers; some have magnificent hand-painted ceilings. One of our editors and his family raved about the location and spaciousness, especially with two small boys in tow.

Moderate

✪ **Betlem Club.** Betlémské nám. 9, Praha 1. ☎ **02/2222 1575.** Fax 02/2222 0580. 22 units. MINIBAR TV TEL. 3,300Kč ($97) double. Rates include breakfast. No credit cards. Metro: Národní třída.

This small hotel offers a great location on a cobblestoned square across from where Protestant firebrand Jan Hus once preached. Rooms are bland but comfortable and fairly priced. One great advantage is that if you come by car, the Betlem lets you park in front of the hotel, a rarity for this parking-deficient city.

Inexpensive

✪ **Hotel Cloister Inn/Pension Unitas.** Bartolomějská 9, Praha 1. ☎ **02/232 7700.** Fax 02/232 7709. www.cloister-inn.cz. E-mail: cloister@cloister-inn.cz. Pension: 32 units, none with bathroom; 1,200Kč ($35) double. Hotel: 25 units with en suite showers; 3,800Kč ($111) double. Both rates include breakfast (a more extensive buffet on the hotel side). AE, MC, V (hotel only). Metro: Národní třída.

Between Old Town Square and the National Theater, the Cloister Inn/Unitas is half a pension and half a hotel, occupying a building that was a convent before the secret police converted it into holding cells. It sounds ominous, but the Unitas offers sparse, clean accommodations at an unbeatable price for the location. Proprietor Jiří Tlaskal has taken over management from the secret police and the Sisters of Mercy (the nuns, not the rock group). George (in English, as he prefers) has refurbished the hotel side with comfortable Scandinavian furniture. For a bizarre treat in the pension, you might like to stay down in Cell P6, once occupied by dissident playwright Václav Havel, a frequent "guest" of the secret police and now president of the country.

NOVÉ MĚSTO (NEW TOWN)

Very Expensive

Hotel Hilton Atrium. Pobřežní 1, Praha 8. ☎ **02/2484 1111.** Fax 02/2484 2378. www.hilton.com. E-mail: sales_prague@hilton.com. 788 units. A/C MINIBAR TV TEL. 7,885Kč ($232) double; from 12,350Kč ($363) suite. AE, CB, DISC, MC, V. Metro: Florenc.

The Atrium was built in a galleria style seemingly out of place in Prague, and its rooms are relatively cushy and functional, somewhat like those in a better-than-average U.S. motel. The building is packed with amenities, including a tennis club, pool, fitness center, and casino. The location of this modern mammoth just outside the central city isn't ideal, but the overpriced hotel Mercedes are ready to take you where you want, and the service is pure Hilton.

Palace Hotel. Panská 12, Praha 1. ☎ **02/2409 3111.** Fax 02/2422 1240. www.hotel-palace.cz. E-mail: palhoprg@mbox.vol.cz. 124 units. A/C MINIBAR TV TEL. From 9,826Kč ($289) double; from 11,900Kč ($350) suite. Rates include breakfast. AE, DC, MC, V. Metro: Můstek.

Now surpassed in overall comfort by only the Savoy in Hradčany, the Palace is a top, upscale, central-city offering, a block from Wenceslas Square, although if given the choice, the Paříž has far more character. Rooms are some of the largest and most modern luxury accommodations in Prague. Two rooms for travelers with disabilities are available.

Expensive

Hotel Esplanade. Washingtonova 19, Praha 1. ☎ **800/444-7462** in the U.S.; 800/181-535 in the U.K.; or 02/2421 3696. Fax 02/2422 9306. 74 units. TV TEL. 8,400Kč ($247) double; from 8,950Kč ($263) suite. Rates include breakfast. AE, MC, V. Metro: Muzeum.

Located on a side street at the top of the square, the Esplanade began life as a bank and the offices of an Italian insurance company. Rooms are bright and airy, some with standard beds, others with French provincial headboards, and others with extravagant canopies. Number 101 is over-the-top with antique wooden chairs, intricate inlaid tables, and a fascinating embossed wall covering. You might be put off by having the main train station across the street, but an honest-looking doorman says the hotel is safe. Just the same, be advised not to stroll alone in the neighborhood at night.

Prague Renaissance. V Celnici 7, Praha 1. ☎ **02/2182 1111.** Fax 02/2182 2200. www.renaissancehotel.com. E-mail: RenPrgBusiness@compuserve.com. 315 units. A/C MINI-BAR TV TEL. 6,800Kč ($200) double; from 11,600Kč ($341) suite. AE, CB, DC, MC, V. Metro: Náměstí Republiky.

The Renaissance, opened in 1993, has the standard comforts of most top-level business hotels. It's around the corner from the central bank and caters to conferences and entrepreneurs. Suites on the top floor are spacious and have walk-in closets and sizable bathrooms. A few standard rooms are wheelchair accessible.

Moderate

✪ **Andante.** Ve Smečkách 4, Prague 1. ☎ **02/2221 1616.** Fax 02/2221 0584. www.andante.cz. E-mail: andante@netforce.cz. 32 units. MINIBAR TV TEL. 224DM ($124) double; 296DM ($164) suite. Rates, which fluctuate based on the latest crown rate against the German mark because of the crown's volatility, include breakfast. AE, MC, V. Metro: Muzeum.

A new addition as the best value choice near Wenceslas Square, the understated Andante is tucked away on a dark side street, about 2 blocks off the top of the square. Despite its less than appealing neighborhood, this is the most comfortable property in the $100 to $125 range. It lacks the character of the old Hotel Evropa, but also the neglect. With en suite bathrooms for every room and higher-grade Scandinavian furniture, you will gain in comfort what you lose in adventure. A close friend of ours, a young businesswoman, said she enjoyed the stay at the Andante, but she felt safer having her boyfriend with her.

Inexpensive

Hotel Evropa. Václavské nám. 25, Praha 1. ☎ **02/2422 8117.** Fax 02/2422 4544. 90 units (23 with bathroom). 1,490Kč ($43) single without bathroom, 2,700Kč ($79) single with bathroom, 2,490Kč ($73) double without bathroom, 3,740Kč ($110) double with bathroom; from 4,700Kč ($138) suite. Rates include continental breakfast. AE, MC, V. Metro: Můstek.

The statue-studded exterior is still one of the most striking landmarks on Wenceslas Square, but unlike other early 20th-century gems, it hasn't been polished and continues to get duller. Rooms are aging and most don't have baths; some are just plain shabby. The best choice is a room facing the square with a balcony, but all are falling into various levels of disrepair. Still, this is an affordable chance to stay in one of Wenceslas Square's once-grand addresses.

MALÁ STRANA (LESSER TOWN)

We used to recommend the **Hotel U Červeného lva,** Nerudova 41 (☎ **02/5753 3832**), as the top pick near the castle, but with ever more tourists walking up Nerudova, the noise has become prohibitive in summer, according to a few Frommer's regulars. Try this place during the colder months when your windows will remain closed.

Expensive

⊙ U Krále Karla. Nerudova-úvoz 4, Praha 1. ☎ **02/5753 2869.** Fax 02/5753 3591. www.romantichotels.cz. E-mail: Ukrale@tnet.cz. 19 units. MINIBAR TV TEL. 6,100 Kč ($179) double; 6,700 Kč ($197) suite. Rates include breakfast. AE, MC, V. Tram: 22 or 23 to Malostranské náměstí.

This Castle Hill property does so much to drive home its Renaissance roots, King Charles's heirs should be getting royalties. Replete with period-print open-beamed ceilings and stained-glass windows, the atmosphere is almost Disneyesque in its pretense, but somehow appropriate for this location at the foot of Prague Castle. This is a fun, comfortable choice, with heavy period furniture and colorful angelic accents everywhere. Two ornate vaulted dining rooms serve breakfast, lunch, and dinner until 11pm.

Moderate

Hotel Kampa. Všehrdova 16, Praha 1. ☎ **02/5732 0404.** Fax 02/5732 0262. www. euroagentur.cz. E-mail: hotel.kampa@mbox.vol.cz. 84 units. TEL. 3,550Kč ($104) double. Rates include breakfast. AE, MC, V. Metro: Malostranská, then tram 12, 22, or 23 to Hellichova.

The Kampa has a choice location on a quiet winding alley off the park, giving you quick access to Malá Strana and Charles Bridge. The rooms smack of Communist chintz, but they're comfortable if you don't expect first-class surroundings. The best rooms boast a park view, so request one when booking or checking in.

HRADČANY

Very Expensive

Hotel Savoy. Keplerova 6, Praha 1. ☎ **02/2430 2430.** Fax 02/2430 2128. www. hotel-savoy.cz. E-mail: savhoprg@mbox.vol.cz. 61 units. A/C MINIBAR TV TEL. From 9,044Kč ($266) double; from 12,444Kč ($366) suite. Rates include breakfast. AE, DC, MC, V. Tram: 22 or 23.

Prague's finest new hotel, opened in 1994, belongs to the company that manages the more venerable Palace on Wenceslas Square. Behind the massive Foreign Ministry, Černín Palace, and a few blocks from the castle, it welcomes you with a tastefully modern lobby. Rooms are richly decorated and boast every amenity, including VCRs, faxes, and computer data ports. Beds are consistently huge, a rejection of the central-European twin-beds-shoved-together look. The pleasant staff provides attention to detail a cut above most hotels here. The Savoy's Hradčany Restaurant is also one of the finest dining rooms in town (see "Where to Dine," below).

Expensive

⊙ Romantik Hotel U raka. Černínská 10, Praha 1. ☎ **02/2051 1100.** Fax 02/2051 0511. www.romantikhotels.com/uraka. E-mail: uraka@login.cz. 6 units. A/C MINIBAR TV TEL. 6,200Kč ($182) double; 7,200Kč ($212) suite. Rates include breakfast. AE, MC, V. Tram: 22 or 23.

Hidden among the stucco houses and cobblestoned streets of a pristine medieval neighborhood on the far side of Prague Castle is this most pleasant surprise. In a ravine below the Foreign Ministry gardens, the old-world farmhouse has been lovingly reconstructed. This is the quietest getaway you could imagine in tightly packed Prague. The rustic rooms have heavy wooden furniture, open-beam ceilings, and exposed brick. The much-sought-after suite has a fireplace and adjoins a private garden, making it a favorite for honeymooners.

WHERE TO DINE

The true Czech dining experience can be summed up in three native words: *vepřo, knedlo, zelo*—pork, dumplings, cabbage. If that's what you want, try most any *hostinec*

Traveler's Tip

Beware: Some restaurants gouge customers by charging exorbitant amounts for nuts or other seemingly free premeal snacks left on your table. Ask before you eat.

(Czech pub). Most offer a hearty *guláš* or pork dish with dumplings and cabbage for about 80Kč to 150Kč ($2.35 to $4.40). After you wash it down with Czech beer, you won't care about the taste—or your arteries.

At most restaurants, menu prices include VAT. Tipping has become more commonplace in restaurants where the staff is obviously trying harder; rounding up the bill to about 10% or more is usually adequate.

STARÉ MĚSTO (OLD TOWN) & JOSEFOV
Expensive

✪ **Bellevue.** Smetanovo nábřeží 18, Praha 1. ☎ **02/2222 1449.** Reservations recommended. Main courses 650–990Kč ($19–$29); fixed-price menu 1,190Kč ($35). AE, DC, MC, V. Daily noon–3pm and 5:30–11pm; Sun brunch 11am–4pm. Metro: Staroměstská. INTERNATIONAL/WILD GAME.

In short, when in Prague, go to the Bellevue, just a few dozen steps from Charles Bridge on the Old Town side of the river. The intelligent menu boasts choice beef, nouvelle sauces, well-dressed fish and game, delicate pastas, and gorgeous desserts. Poached Norwegian salmon glistens in a light herb sauce and prawns dance on a piquant garlic glaze. Several wild game options stand out, like Fallow deer with oysters and mushrooms. The consistent food and presentation and the pleasant and perfectly timed service make the Bellevue an evening to remember.

V zátiší. Liliová 1, Praha 1. ☎ **02/2222 0627.** Reservations recommended. Main courses 400–600Kč ($12–$18); fixed-price menu 775–1,075Kč ($23–$32). AE, DC, MC, V. Mon–Sun noon–3pm and 5:30–11pm; brunch Sun 11am–2pm. Metro: Národní třída. INTERNATIONAL.

V zátiší (still life) has a casual elegance, like the living room of a beachfront Mediterranean villa with cushy, upholstered, wrought-iron chairs and plenty of artfully arranged flora. Here, you'll find several fish and game choices, and a scampi that never disappoints. The dessert selections often echo those at the Bellevue, which is run by the same restaurant group, but a flaming vodka-doused Siberian palačinka one snowy Christmas Eve here stands out in our memories. Maybe one of the helpful waiters will convince the chef to do it again.

Moderate
La Provence. Štupartská 9, Praha 1. ☎ **02/232 4801.** Reservations recommended. Main courses 170–650Kč ($4.40–$19). AE, MC, V. Daily noon–midnight. Metro: Náměstí Republiky. FRENCH.

A French country wine cellar meets urban kitsch. The din of the crowd allows you to discuss private matters without too much eavesdropping. La Provence offers a wide array of French provincial dishes, as well as tangy Italian pastas and the spiciest scampi in Prague. Salads, from Caesar to Niçoise, are large and fresh; they come with fresh French bread and garlic butter. Weekends often attract drag queens from the Banana Cafe upstairs for a funky lip-synch floor show.

Inexpensive
Klub architektů. Betlémské nám. 5a, Praha 1. ☎ **02/2440 1214.** Reservations recommended. Main courses 70–130Kč ($2.10–$3.95). AE, MC, V. Daily 11:30am–midnight. Metro: Národní třída. CZECH/INTERNATIONAL.

Across the courtyard from Jan Hus's Bethlehem Chapel, this eclectic clubhouse for the city's progressive architects is the best nonpub value in Old Town. Sitting in the stone cellar, among industrial swag lights, you can choose from baked chicken, pork steaks, pasta, stir-fry chicken, and even vegetarian burritos. Wicker seats and torches set up in the courtyard make for an enjoyable summer night, although the alfresco menu is limited.

✪ **Pivnice Radegast.** Templová 2, Praha 1. ☎ **02/232 8237.** Main courses 60–140Kč ($1.75–$4). AE, MC, V. Daily 10am–midnight. Metro: Můstek or Náměstí Republiky. CZECH.

The raucous Radegast dishes up Prague's best pub *guláš* in a single narrow vaulted hall, where the namesake Moravian brew seems to never stop flowing from its taps. Around the corner from a bunch of popular bars, the Radegast attracts a good mix of visitors and locals and a young upwardly mobile crowd.

Pizzeria Rugantino. Dušní 4, Praha 1. ☎ **02/231 8172.** Individual pizzas 100–300Kč ($2.95–$9). No credit cards. Mon–Sat 11am–11pm; Sun 6–11pm. Metro: Staroměstská. PIZZA.

The wood-fired stoves and handmade dough result in a crisp, delicate crust, a perfect platform for a multitude of cheeses, vegetables, and meats. The Diabolo with fresh garlic bits and very hot chiles goes nicely with a cool iceberg salad and a pull of Krušovice beer. The constant buzz, no-smoking area, and heavy childproof wooden tables make this place a family favorite.

✪ **U medvídků.** Na Perštýně 7, Praha 1. ☎ **02/2421 1916.** Main courses 90–250Kč ($2.65–$7). AE, MC, V. Daily 11am–11pm. Metro: Národní třída. CZECH.

Bright and noisy, the House at the Little Bears serves a better-than-average *vepřo, knedlo, zelo* with two-color cabbage. The pub, on the right after entering, is much cheaper and more lively than the bar to the left. It's a hangout for locals, German tour groups, and foreign journalists in search of the original Czech Budweiser beer, *Budvar*. In high season, an oompah band plays in the beer wagon.

NOVÉ MĚSTO (NEW TOWN)
Moderate
✪ **Restaurant U Čížků.** Karlovo nám. 34, Praha 2. ☎ **02/2223 2257.** Reservations recommended. Main courses 170–320Kč ($5–$9). AE, MC, V. Daily noon–10pm. Metro: Karlovo náměstí. CZECH.

One of the city's first private restaurants, this cozy cellar-cum-hunting lodge on Charles Square can be recognized by the long line of German tour buses outside. The fare is purely Czech, and the massive portions of game, smoked pork, and other meats will stay with you for a while. The traditional *Starý český talíř* (local meat, dumplings, and cabbage) is about as authentic Czech as it gets. The still excellent value earns this pioneer a star.

Inexpensive
Café-Restaurant Louvre. Národní třída 20, Praha 1. ☎ **02/297 223.** Reservations not accepted. Main courses 60–300Kč ($1.75–$9). AE, DC, MC, V. Daily 8am–11pm. Metro: Můstek. CZECH/INTERNATIONAL.

This big breezy upstairs hall, the artsy restaurant formerly known as Gany's, is great for a coffee, an inexpensive pretheater meal, or an upscale game of pool. A fabulous art nouveau interior, with huge original chandeliers, buzzes with local coffee talk, the shopping crowd, business lunches, and students. Starters include smoked salmon, battered and fried asparagus, and ham au gratin with vegetables. Main dishes range from trout with horseradish to beans with garlic sauce. Avoid the always-overcooked pastas

Kavárna Society

Cafe life is back in a big way in Prague, now that the Slavia and the Municiple House Kavárna have returned. From dissident blues to high society, these are the places where nonpub Praguers spend their afternoons and evenings, sipping coffee and smoking cigarettes while reading, writing, or talking with friends.

The ✪ **Kavárna (Cafe) Slavia,** Národní at Smetanovo nábřeží 2, Praha 1 (☎ **02/2422 0957;** metro: Národní třída), reopened in 1997, after a half-decade sleep, prolonged by a Boston real estate speculator who was sitting on the property. President Havel (a Slavia regular when it was the dissident hangout) intervened, and after a long legal battle, the Slavia returned on the Velvet Revolution's eighth anniversary. "A small victory for reason over stupidity," Havel called it. The restored crisp art deco room recalls the Slavia's 100 years as the meeting place for the city's cultural and intellectual crowd. You'll still find a relatively affordable menu of light fare served with the riverfront views of Prague Castle and the National Theater. Open daily 8am to midnight.

The quaint **Café Milena,** Staroměstské nám. 22, Praha 1 (☎ **02/2163 2609;** metro: Staroměstská), is managed by the Franz Kafka Society and named for Milena Jesenská, one of the writer's lovers. The draw is a great view of the Orloj, the astronomical clock with the hourly parade of saints on the side of Old Town Square's city hall. It's open daily 10am to 10pm, and no credit cards are accepted.

Of all the beautifully restored spaces in the Municipal House, the **Kavárna Obecní dům,** náměstí Republiky 5, Praha 1 (☎ **02/2200 2763;** metro: Náměstí Republiky), might be its most spectacular room. Lofty ceilings, marble accents and tables, an altarlike mantle, huge windows, and period chandeliers provide the awesome setting for coffees, teas, and other drinks, along with pastries and light sandwiches. A true turn-of-the-century afternoon. It's open daily 7:30am to 11pm, and no credit cards are accepted.

The newer Bohemians have made **Velryba,** at Opatovická 24 on a small side street near Národní třída (metro: Národní třída), the late 20th-century version of the Slavia. Here, cheap pasta salads mix with clove cigarette smoke and pop art. It's very difficult to get a table more than a few minutes after noon as the students and young intellectuals homestead. It's open 11am to 2am, and no credit cards are accepted.

and stick to the basic meats and fish. In the snazzy billiards parlor in back, you can have drinks and light meals served.

MALÁ STRANA
Expensive
✪ **Ostroff.** Střelecký ostrov 336, Praha 1. ☎ **02/2491 9235.** Reservations recommended. Main courses 400–600Kč ($12–$18). AE, MC, V. Open for lunch Mon–Fri noon–2pm, for dinner Mon–Sat 7–11:30pm, closed Sun. Tram 22, 23, 9, 6 to Národní divadlo, then walk midway across the bridge (most Legií), down the stairs to the island below (Střelecký ostrov). ITALIAN.

Nowhere else in Prague is Italian as intricately prepared as at Ostroff, on a river island across from the National Theater. Here immigrant cooks bring new twists to northern Italian fare, which is served attentively in a classical vaulted wine cellar with modern Milano chic. Begin with a flaky vegetable flan laden with goat cheese, a wafer-thin sea bass carpaccio, or oysters on the half shell, then a second plate of tagliatelle in a white bean sauce or a fine minestrone soup. Meat and fresh seafood top the entrees including a tender grilled rack of lamb or entrecôte on rosemary. The daily three-course lunch special, for under 450Kč ($13) without wine, is a great value. Before or after, you can have a cocktail at the riverside bar with a stunning view of the gold-domed National Theater, casting a romantic nighttime glow on the Ostroff and your partner.

✪ **U Malířů.** Maltézské nám. 11, Praha 1. ☎ **02/5732 0317.** Reservations recommended. Main courses 520–1,490Kč ($15–$44); set-price menu 1,190Kč ($35) and 1,490Kč ($44). AE, DC, MC, V. Daily 7–2am. Metro: Malostranská. FRENCH.

The owners of U Malířů have given in to the pressure of competition and are now offering a more affordable chance to sample the finer attributes of a Parisian kitchen. Surrounded by Romantic-age murals and gorgeously appointed tables in three intimate dining rooms, you're faced with some tough choices. Creamy scallops ragout swim in light vanilla sauce, pike perch comes with truffles, rack of lamb is glazed in tarragon, and an exotic set of quail chicks bathe in Armagnac. If you want a truly Old-World evening of elegant romance and French specialties, U Malířů is finally getting to be worth it.

Moderate
U modré kachničky. Nebovidská 6, Praha 1. ☎ **02/5732 0308.** Reservations recommended. Main courses 300–500Kč ($9–$15). AE, MC, V. Daily noon–4pm and 6:30–11:30pm. Metro: Malostranská. CZECH/WILD GAME.

The "Blue Duckling," on a narrow Malá Strana street, tries (and often succeeds) at turning traditional Czech food into Bohemian cuisine, but sometimes its results fall short. A series of small dining rooms with vaulted ceilings and playfully frescoed walls is packed with antique furniture and pastel-flowered linen upholstery. The menu is loaded with wild game and quirky spins on Czech village favorites. Try the Malá Strana Templar's Sword, a skewer sampling of several domesticated and wild meats.

Inexpensive
Bohemia Bagel. Újezd 16, Praha 1. ☎ **02/531 002.** E-mail: bagel@terminal.cz. Bagels and sandwiches 20–135Kč (60¢–$4). No credit cards. Mon–Thurs 7am–midnight, Fri 7am–2am, Sat 8am–2am, Sun 8am–midnight. Tram: 6, 9, 12, 22, or 23 to újezd. BAGELS/SANDWICHES.

Bohemia Bagel emerged in 1997 at the base of Petřín Hill as the answer to the lazy-morning bagel-less blues. The roster of golden-brown, hand-rolled, stone-baked bagels is stellar. Plain, cinnamon raisin, garlic, or onion provide a sturdy but tender frame for Scandinavian lox and cream cheese or jalapeño-cheddar cheese (on which you can lop Tex-Mex chili for the Sloppy Bagel). The cushioned wooden booths in an earthy contemporary setting are comfortable.

HRADČANY
Expensive
Hradčany Restaurant. In the Hotel Savoy, Keplerova 8, Praha 1. ☎ **02/2430 2150.** Reservations recommended. Main courses 510–930Kč ($15–$27). AE, MC, V. Daily noon–3pm, 6:30–11pm. Tram: 22 or 23, 2 stops past Prague Castle. INTERNATIONAL.

Matching the crisp English setting of the Savoy Hotel in which it resides, the Hradčany is the most elegant choice this side of the castle. The menu lists a variety of beef, pork, and seafood, including succulent poached salmon and lean sliced veal in herb cream sauce. There are also surprises, such as herb-stuffed tortellini and prawns in avocado mousse. The service sets the standard for Prague, and the new lunch sitting is sure to attract a solid crowd to this jewel beyond the castle gates.

Inexpensive

Saté Indonesian Restaurant. Pohořelec 3, Praha 1. ☎ **02/2051 4552.** Main courses 80–200Kč ($2.35–$6). No credit cards. Daily 11am–10pm. Tram: 22 or 23. INDONESIAN.

A lunchtime savior near the castle, the Saté has made quite a business out of its simple Indonesian dishes at simple prices. The unassuming Saté storefront on the same side as the Swedish embassy doesn't scream out to you, so look closely. The pork saté comes in a peanut sauce along with a hearty noodle Migoreng. The casual atmosphere eagerly welcomes foot-dragging visitors in search of a bite and a rest.

IN VINOHRADY

Moderate

Ponte. Anglická 15, Praha 2. ☎ **02/2422 1665.** Reservation recommended. Main courses 350–500Kč ($10–$15).AE, MC, V. Daily 11:30am–11pm. Metro: I. P. Pavlova or Náměstí Míru. INTERNATIONAL.

Our favorite choice above Wenceslas Square in Vinohrady, Ponte is especially great for shunning the cold of an autumn or winter evening near the roaring fire in the brick cellar dining room. As its name suggests, this place is a bridge between Italian cuisine and other continental foods. Beyond the penne and pesto, you can start with black bean soup with bacon and fresh tomato or tangy spinach salad chunks of niva cheese. There are several vegetarian and low-calorie, chicken-based selections. Jazz combos play on most nights from a small stage in the corner. Ponte is one of the best values in a full-service restaurant in Prague.

Inexpensive

Radost FX. Bělehradská 120, Praha 2. ☎ **02/2425 4776.** Main courses 60–150Kč ($1.80–$4.55). MC, V. Daily 11am–5am. Metro: I.P. Pavlova. VEGETARIAN.

En vogue and vegetarian, Radost is a clubhouse for hip New Bohemians. The veggie burger is well seasoned and substantial on a grain bun, and the soups, like lentil and onion, are light and full of flavor. The dining area is a dark rec room of upholstered armchairs, chaise lounges, couches from the 1960s, and coffee tables from which you eat.

SEEING THE SIGHTS

In Prague, you'll get the most enjoyment from a slow, aimless wander through the city's heart. Except for the busy main streets, where you may have to dodge traffic, Prague is ideal for walking. Actually, walking is really the only way to explore Prague. Most of the town's oldest areas are walking zones, with motor traffic restricted. If you have the time and energy, absorb the grand architecture of Prague Castle and the Old Town skyline (best from Charles Bridge) at sunrise and then at sunset. You'll see two completely different cities.

SIGHTSEEING SUGGESTIONS FOR FIRST-TIME VISITORS

If You Have 1 Day   If you have only 1 day, do what visiting kings and potentates do on a short visit: Walk the **Royal Route** from the top of the Hradčany hill (tram 22 or 23 or a taxi is suggested for the ride up unless you're very fit). Tour **Prague Castle,** and then stroll across **Charles Bridge** on the way to the winding alleys of **Old Town (Staré Město).**

If You Have 2 Days   On day 2, explore the varied sights of **Old Town, Lesser Town (Malá Strana),** and the **Jewish Quarter (Josefov).** Wander and browse through numerous **shops** and **galleries** offering the finest Bohemian crystal, porcelain, and modern artwork, as well as top **boutiques, cafes,** and **restaurants.**

If You Have 3 Days   On day 3, visit the **National Art Gallery** at Šternberk Palace and the **Strahov Monastery** with its ornate libraries, and the **Loreto Palace** with its peculiar artwork.

If You Have 4 or 5 Days   Beyond day 3, tour one of the many other museums of galleries. For a great respite from the crowded city, visit the old southern citadel over the Vltava, Vyšehrad, where you get a completely different view of the city you've just explored.

PRAGUE CASTLE & CHARLES BRIDGE

Dating from the 14th century, ✪ **Charles Bridge (Karlův most),** Prague's most celebrated structure, links Prague Castle to Staré Město. For most of its 600 years, the 518m (1,700-foot) span has been a pedestrian promenade, although for centuries walkers had to share the concourse with horse-drawn vehicles and trolleys. Today, the bridge is filled with hordes walking among folksy artists and street musicians.

The best times to stroll across the bridge are in early morning or around sunset, when the crowds have thinned and the shadows are more mysterious, but you'll be crisscrossing the bridge throughout your stay.

✪ **Prague Castle (Pražský Hrad).** Hradčanské nám., Hradčany, Praha 1. ☎ **02/2437 3368.** Fax 02/2431 0896. www.hrad.cz. E-mail:pdo@hrad.cz. Grounds, free. Combination ticket to 4 main attractions (St. Vitus Cathedral, Royal Palace, St. George's Basilica, Powder Tower), 120Kč ($3.50) adults, 60Kč ($1.75) students without guide; 180Kč ($5) with English-speaking guide. V. Ticket valid 3 days. Castle, daily 9am–5pm (to 4pm Nov–Mar). Metro: Malostranská, then tram 22 or 23, up the hill two stops.

The huge hilltop complex known collectively as **Pražský Hrad** encompasses dozens of towers, churches, courtyards, and monuments. A visit could easily take an entire day or more. Still, you can see the top sights—St. Vitus Cathedral, the Royal Palace, St. George's Basilica, the Powder Tower, plus Golden Lane—in the space of a morning or an afternoon.

St. Vitus Cathedral (Chrám sv. Víta), constructed in A.D. 926 as the court church of the Premyslid princes, was named for a wealthy 4th-century Sicilian martyr and has long been the center of Prague's religious and political life. The key part of its Gothic construction took place in the 14th century. In the 18th and 19th centuries, subsequent baroque and neo-Gothic additions were made. In 1997, Pope John Paul II visited Prague to honor the 1,000th anniversary of the death of 10th-century Slavic evangelist St. Vojtěch. He conferred the saint's name on the cathedral along with St. Vitus's, but officially the Czech state calls it just St. Vitus.

The ✪ **Royal Palace (Královský palác),** in the third courtyard of the castle grounds, served as the residence of kings between the 10th and the 17th centuries. Vaulted Vladislav Hall, the interior's centerpiece, was used for coronations and special occasions. Here Václav Havel was inaugurated president. The adjacent Diet was where the king met with advisers and where the supreme court was held. You'll find a good selection of guidebooks, maps, and other related information at the entrance.

St. George's Basilica (Kostel sv. Jiří), adjacent to the Royal Palace, is Prague's oldest Romanesque structure, dating from the 10th century. It was also Bohemia's first convent, which now houses a museum of historic Czech art.

Golden Lane (Zlatá ulička) is a picturesque, fairy-tale street of tiny 16th-century servants' houses built into the castle fortifications. The houses now contain shops, galleries, and refreshment bars. In 1917, Franz Kafka lived briefly at no. 22.

The **Powder Tower (Prašná věž aka Mihulka)** forms part of the northern bastion of the castle complex just off the Golden Lane. Originally a gunpowder storehouse and a cannon tower, it was turned into a laboratory for the 17th-century alchemists serving the court of Emperor Rudolf II.

GETTING TICKETS   Tickets are sold at the **Prague Castle Information Center** (☎ 02/2437 3368), in the second courtyard after passing through the main gate from Hradčanské náměstí. The center also arranges tours in various languages and sells tickets for individual concerts and exhibits.

THE JEWISH MUSEUM

The Jewish Museum manages all the Jewish landmarks in Josefov, which forms the northwest quarter of Old Town. The museum offers guided package tours as part of a comprehensive admission price, with an English-speaking guide. The package includes the **Ceremonial Hall, Old Jewish Cemetery, Old-New Synagogue, Pinkas Synagogue, Klaus Synagogue, Maisel Synagogue,** and the newly refurbished **Spanish Synagogue.**

• **Maisel Synagogue.** Maiselova 10 (between Široká and Jáchymova 3), Praha 1. ☎ **02/2481 0099.** Fax 02/231 0681. www.jewishmuseum.cz. E-mail: zmp@ecn.cz. Admission to all museum sites 480Kč ($14) adults, 340Kč ($10) students. May–Oct tours for groups of 10 or more on the hour starting 9am (last tour 4pm). Nov–Apr tours leave whenever enough people gather in same language. Metro: Staroměstská.

Maisel Synagogue is used as the exhibition space for the Jewish Museum. Most of Prague's ancient Judaica was destroyed by the Nazis during World War II. Ironically, those same Germans constructed an "exotic museum of an extinct race," thus salvaging thousands of objects, such as the valued Torah covers, books, and silver now displayed at the Maisel Synagogue.

✪ **Old-New Synagogue (Staronová synagoga).** Červená 3. ☎ **02/2481 0099.** Admission 200Kč ($6) adults, 1400Kč ($4) students. Sun–Thurs 9am–6pm, Fri 9am–5pm. Metro: Staroměstská.

First called the New Synagogue to distinguish it from an even older one that no longer exists, the Old-New Synagogue, built around 1270, is Europe's oldest Jewish house of worship. Jews have prayed here continuously for more than 700 years, carrying on even after a massive 1389 pogrom in Josefov that killed more than 3,000 Jews. It was interrupted only between 1941 and 1945 during the Nazi occupation. The synagogue is also one of Prague's largest Gothic buildings, with vaulted ceilings and Renaissance-era columns.

✪ **Old Jewish Cemetery (Starý židovský hřbitov).** U Starého hřbitova 3A. ☎ **02/2481 0099.** Fax 02/231 0681. www.jewishmuseum.cz. E-mail: zmp@ecn.cz. Admission to all Jewish Museum sites 480Kč ($14) adults, 340Kč ($10) students. Sun–Fri 9am–6pm. Metro: Staroměstská.

Dating from the mid-15th century, this is one of Europe's oldest Jewish burial grounds, 1 block from the Old-New Synagogue. Because the local government of the time didn't allow Jews to bury their dead elsewhere, graves were dug deep enough to hold 12 bodies vertically, with each tombstone placed in front of the last. The result is one of the world's most crowded cemeteries: a 1-block area filled with more than 20,000 graves. Among the most famous persons buried here are the celebrated Rabbi Loew (died 1609), who created the legendary Golem (a clay "monster" to protect Prague's Jews), and banker Markus Mordechai Maisel (died 1601), then the richest man in Prague and protector of the city's Jewish community during the reign of Rudolf II. The adjoining **Ceremonial Hall** at the end of the path is worth a look for the heart-wrenching drawings by children held at the Terezín concentration camp during World War II (see "Day Trips from Prague," below, for more on Terezín).

THE NATIONAL GALLERY

The national collection of fine art is grouped for display in the series of venues known collectively as the National Gallery (**Národní Galerie**). Remember, this term refers to several locations, not just one gallery.

The most extensive collection of classic European works spanning the 14th to 18th centuries is found at the Archbishop's Palace complex in the **Šternberský palác** across from the main gate to Prague Castle. **Veletržní Palace** houses most of the 20th-century art collection, and now also shows the important national revival works from Czech artists of the 19th century. Much of the rest of the national collection is divided between Kinský Palace on Old Town Square, with Gothic pieces at **St. George's Convent** at Prague Castle, and 19th-century Czech painters and sculptors to be shown from September 2000 at **St. Agnes Convent** near the river in Old Town.

Hradčany

✪ **Šternberk Palace (Šternberský palác).** Hradčanské nám. 15, Praha 1. ☎ **02/2051 4599.** Admission 90Kč ($2.65) adults, 50Kč ($1.45) students and children. Tues–Sun 10am–6pm. Metro: Malostranská or Hradčanská.

The jewel in the National Gallery crown (also known casually as the European Art Museum), the gallery at Šternberk Palace, adjacent to the main gate of Prague Castle, displays a wide menu of European art throughout the ages. It features 5 centuries of everything from Orthodox icons to Renaissance oils from Dutch masters. Pieces by Rembrandt, El Greco, Goya, and van Dyck are mixed among numerous pieces from Austrian imperial-court painters.

St. Agnes Convent (Klášter sv. Anežky české). U milosrdných 17, Praha 1. ☎ **02/2481 0628.** Admission 90Kč ($2.65) adults, 50Kč ($1.50) children. Tues–Sun 10am–6pm. Metro: Staroměstská.

This complex of early Gothic buildings and churches dates from the 13th century. The convent, tucked in a corner of Staré Město, is scheduled to feature 19th-century Czech painters and sculptors after September 2000.

St. George's Convent at Prague Castle (Klášter sv. Jiří na Pražském hradě). Jiřské nám. 33. ☎ **02/5732 0536.** Admission 90Kč ($2.65), 50Kč ($1.45) students. Tues–Sun 10am–6pm. Metro: Malostranská or Hradčanská.

Dedicated to displaying traditional Czech art, the castle convent is especially packed with Gothic and baroque Bohemian iconography as well as portraits of patron saints. The most famous among the unique collection of Czech Gothic panel paintings are those by the Master of the Hohenfurth Altarpiece and the Master Theodoricus.

Staré Město (Old Town)

✪ **Kinský Palace (Palác Kinských).** Staroměstské náměstí, Praha 1. ☎ **02/2481 0758.** Admission and hours not set at press time. Metro: Staroměstská.

The rococo palace houses graphic works from the National Gallery collection, including pieces by Georges Braque, André Derain, and other modern masters. Pablo Picasso's 1907 *Self-Portrait* is here and has virtually been adopted as the National Gallery's logo. At this writing, the Kinsky is undergoing a massive renovation but should be reopened by the time you get there.

Veletržní Palace (National Gallery). Veletržní at Dukelských hrdinů 47, Praha 7. ☎ **02/2430 1111.** Admission 120Kč ($3.55), 60Kč ($1.75) students; Thurs 6–9pm 40Kč ($1.20). Tues–Sun 10am–6pm (Thurs to 9pm). Metro: Vltavská; tram 17.

This 1925 constructivist palace, built for trade fairs, holds the bulk of the National Gallery's collection of 20th-century works by Czech and other European artists. Three atrium-lit concourses provide a comfortable setting for some catchy and kitschy Czech sculpture and multimedia works. Alas, the best cubist works from Braque and Picasso, Rodin bronzes, and many other primarily French pieces have been relegated to the second floor. Other displays are devoted to peculiar works from Czech artists that demonstrate how creativity flowed even under the weight of the Iron Curtain.

FAMOUS SQUARES

The most celebrated square, **Old Town Square (Staroměstské náměstí),** is surrounded by baroque buildings and packed with colorful craftspeople, cafes, and entertainers. In ancient days, the site was a major crossroad on central European merchant routes. In its center stands a memorial to Jan Hus, the 15th-century martyr who crusaded against Prague's German-dominated religious and political establishment. Unveiled in 1915, on the 500th anniversary of Hus's execution, the monument's most compelling features are the asymmetry of the composition and the fluidity of the figures.

The **Astronomical Clock (orloj)** at **Old Town Hall (Staroměstská radnice)** performs a glockenspiel spectacle daily on the hour from 8am to 8pm. Originally constructed in 1410, the clock has long been an important symbol of Prague. **Wenceslas Square (Václavské náměstí),** a former horse market, has thrice been the focal point of riots and revolutions—in 1918, 1968, and 1989.

MORE ATTRACTIONS

Bertramka (Museum W. A. Mozart). Mozartova 169, Praha 5. ☎ **02/543 893.** Admission 90Kč ($2.65) adults, 50Kč ($1.45) students. Daily 9:30am–6pm. Metro: Anděl, then tram 2, 6, 7, 9, 14.

Mozart loved Prague, and when he visited he often stayed with the family that owned this villa, the Dušeks. Now a museum, the villa contains displays that include his written work and harpsichord. There's also a lock of Mozart's hair, encased in a cube of glass. Much of the Bertramka villa was destroyed by fire in the 1870s, but Mozart's rooms, where he finished composing *Don Giovanni,* miraculously remained untouched.

Estates' Theater (Stavovské divadlo). Ovocný trh 1, Praha 1. ☎ **02/2490 1487.** Metro: Můstek.

The theater was completed in 1783 by the wealthy Count F. A. Nostitz, and Mozart staged the premier of *Don Giovanni* here in 1787 because he felt the conservative patrons in Vienna didn't appreciate him or his passionate and often shocking work. "Praguers understand me," Mozart was quoted as saying. Czech director Miloš Forman returned to his native country to film his Oscar-winning *Amadeus,* shooting the scenes of Mozart in Prague with perfect authenticity at the Estates'. The theater doesn't give daily tours, but tickets for performances—and the chance to sit in one of the elegant private boxes—are usually available. Tour events are occasionally scheduled, and you can arrange individual tours by calling the city heritage group **Pražská vlastivěda** at ☎ **02/2171 4152.**

✪ **Strahov Monastery and Library (Strahovský klášter a knihovna).** Strahovské nádvoří 1, Praha 1. ☎ **02/2051 6654.** Admission 40Kč ($1.15) adults, 20Kč (60¢) students. Tues–Sun 9am–noon and 1–5pm. Metro: Malostranská, then tram 22 or 23.

The second oldest monastery in Prague, Strahov was founded high above Malá Strana in 1143 by Vladislav II. It's still home to Premonstratensian monks, a scholarly order closely related to the Jesuits, and their dormitories and refectory are off-limits. What draws visitors are the monastery's ornate libraries, holding more than 125,000 volumes.

Cathedral of St. Nicholas (Chrám sv. Mikuláše). Malostranské nám., Praha 1. Free admission. Daily 9am–5pm. Metro: Malostranská, then tram 22, 23, or 12 one stop to Malostranské nám.

This church is critically regarded as one of the best examples of the high baroque north of the Alps. K. I. Dienzenhofer's 1711 design was augmented by his son Kryštof's 80m (260-foot) dome, which has dominated the Malá Strana skyline since its completion in 1752. Prague's smog has played havoc with the building's exterior, but its gilded interior is stunning. Gold-capped marble-veneered columns frame altars packed with statuary and frescoes.

PARKS & GARDENS

From **Vyšehrad,** Soběslavova 1 (☎ **02/296 651**), legend has it that Princess Libuše looked out over the Vltava valley toward the present-day Prague Castle and predicted the founding of a great state and capital city. Vyšehrad was the seat of the first Czech kings of the Premyslid dynasty before the dawn of this millennium.

Today within the confines of the citadel, lush lawns and gardens are crisscrossed by dozens of paths, leading to historic buildings and cemeteries. From here you'll see one of the city's most panoramic views. Take tram 3 from Karlovo náměstí to Výtoň south of New Town.

The **Royal Garden (Královská zahrada)** at Prague Castle, once the site of the sovereigns' vineyards, was founded in 1534. Dotted with lemon trees and surrounded by 16th-, 17th-, and 18th-century buildings, the park is laid out with abundant shrubbery and fountains. Enter from U Prašného mostu street north of the castle complex.

In Hradčany, the castle's **Garden on the Ramparts (Zahrada na Valech),** below the castle with a gorgeous city panorama, was reopened in spring 1995 after being thoroughly refurbished. The park is open Tuesday to Sunday 9am to 5pm. Part of the excitement of **Waldstein (Wallenstein) Gardens (Valdštejnská zahrada)** is its location, behind a 9m (30-foot) wall on the back streets of Malá Strana. Inside, elegant, leafy gravel paths, dotted by classical bronze statues and gurgling fountains, fan out in every direction.

A SPECIAL GROUP TOUR

If you're traveling in a large group and really want a unique sightseeing experience, why not rent your own classic trolley? With enough people, it really can be affordable, thanks to the **Historic Tram Tour (Elektrické dráhy DP),** Patočkova 4, Praha 6 (☎ and fax **02/312 3349**).

If you send a fax with details 1 day ahead, the city transport department can arrange a private tour using one of the turn-of-the-century wooden trams that once traveled on regular lines through Prague. Up to 24 people can fit in one car, which sports wooden-planked floors, cast-iron conductor's levers, and the "ching-ching" of a proper tram bell.

It costs 2,940Kč ($87) per hour. Up to 60 people can fit into a double car for 3,780Kč ($111) per hour. You can also order a cold smorgasbord with coffee, beer, champagne, a waiter to serve, and an accordion player. You can choose the route the tram takes—the no. 22 route is best.

THE SHOPPING SCENE

Czech porcelain, glass, and cheap but well-constructed clothing draw hoards of day-trippers from Germany. Private retailers have been allowed to operate here only since late 1989, but many top international retailers have already arrived. Shops lining the main route from Old Town Square to Charles Bridge are also great for browsing. For clothing, porcelain, jewelry, garnets, and glass, stroll around **Wenceslas Square** and **Na Příkopě,** connecting Wenceslas Square with náměstí Republiky.

For glass and crystal, try ✪ **Moser,** at Na Příkopě 12, Praha 1 (☎ **02/2421 1293;** metro: Můstek), or at Malé nám, 11, Praha 1 (☎ **02/2161 1520;** metro: Můstek). The Moser family began selling Bohemia's finest crystal in central Prague in 1857, drawing customers from around the world. The dark-wood showroom upstairs at Na Příkopě is worth a look if only to get the feeling of Prague at its most elegant. Open Monday to Friday 9am to 8pm, Saturday and Sunday 10am to 6pm at Na Příkopě; Monday to Friday 10am to 7pm, Saturday and Sunday 10am–6pm at Malé nám.

At **Cristallino,** Celetná 12 (metro: Nám. Republiky) (☎ **02/2422 5173**), you'll find a good selection of stemware and vases in traditional designs. The shop's central location belies its excellent prices. At **Pavilon,** Vinohradská 50 (metro: Jiřího z Poděbrad) (☎ **02/2209 7111**), a new four-tiered galleria, fashion junkies can browse in stores from Lacoste to Diesel, have their hair done, buy some Timberlands, and bring home a hunk of bacon from the Belgian Butcher.

Havelský trh (Havel's Market), Havelská ulice, Praha 1 (metro: Můstek), is on a short street running perpendicular to Melantrichova, the main route connecting Staroměstské náměstí with Václavské náměstí. This open-air market (named well before a Havel became president) features dozens of private vendors selling seasonal home-grown fruits and vegetables. Other goods, including flowers and cheese, are also for sale. Since this place is designed primarily for locals, the prices are exceedingly low by Western European standards. The market is open Monday to Friday 7am to 6pm.

PRAGUE AFTER DARK

Prague's nightlife has changed completely since the Velvet Revolution—for the better if you plan to go clubbing, for the worse if you hope to sample the city's classical offerings. Still, seeing *Don Giovanni* in the Estates' Theater, where Mozart first premiered it, is worth the admission. Ticket prices, while low by Western standards, have become prohibitively high for the average Czech. However, you'll find the exact reverse in the rock and jazz scene. Dozens of clubs have opened, and world-class bands are finally adding Prague to their European tours.

Turn to the Prague Post for listings of cultural events and nightlife around the city; it's available at most newsstands in Old Town and Malá Strana.

Once in Prague, you can buy tickets at theater box offices or from any one of dozens of agencies throughout the city center. Large centrally located agencies (take the metro to Můstek for all) are **Prague Tourist Center,** Rytířská 12, Praha 1 (☎ **02/ 2421 2209**), open daily 9am to 8pm; **Bohemia Ticket International,** Na Příkopě 16, Praha 1 (☎ **02/2421 5031**); and **Čedok,** Na Příkopě 18, Praha 1 (☎ **02/2481 1870**).

THE PERFORMING ARTS

Although there's plenty of music year-round, the symphonies and orchestras all come to life during the ✪ **Prague Spring Music Festival,** a 3-week series of concerts featuring the country's top performers, as well as noted guest conductors, soloists, and visiting symphony orchestras. The festival runs May 12 to June 2. Tickets for concerts are 250Kč to 2,000Kč ($7 to $59).

The Czech Philharmonic and Prague Symphony orchestras usually perform at the **Rudolfinum,** náměstí Jana Palacha, Praha 1 (☎ **02/2489 3352;** metro: Staroměstská). The Czech Philharmonic is the traditional voice of the country's national pride, often playing works by Dvořák and Smetana; the Prague Symphony ventures into more eclectic territory. Tickets are 100Kč to 600Kč ($2.95 to $18). Ticket orders and purchases can be made in advance (and you are advised to book well in advance) through the agency **TICKETPRO**, Salvátorská 10, 110 00 Praha 1, Czech Republic, by phone, mail, fax or E-mail: ☎ **02/2481 4020**, fax: 02/2481 4021, E-mail: orders@ticketpro.cz, mail:orders@ticketpro.cz>. All major credit cards accepted.

Any remaining tickets are sold at the venues of the performances, which have various opening hours, but usually few seats remain within a month of the festival.

In a city full of spectacularly beautiful theaters, the massive pale-green **Estates' Theater (Stavovské divadlo),** Ovocný trh 1, Praha 1 (☎ **02/2421 5001**; metro: Můstek), is one of the most awesome. Built in 1783 and site of the premiere of Mozart's *Don Giovanni* (conducted by the composer), the theater now hosts many of the classic productions of European opera and drama. Simultaneous English translation, transmitted via headphone, is available for most plays. Tickets cost 200Kč to 1,000Kč ($6 to $29). The theater doesn't have daily tours, but tour events are occasionally scheduled, and individual tours can be arranged by calling the city heritage group **Pražská vlastivěda** at ☎ **02/2171 4152.**

Lavishly constructed in the late-Renaissance style of northern Italy, the gold-crowned **Národní divadlo (National Theater),** Národní třída 2, Praha 1 (☎ **02/2490 1448**; metro: Národní třída), overlooking the Vltava River, is one of Prague's most recognizable landmarks. Completed in 1881, the theater was built to nurture the Czech National Revival—a grassroots movement to replace the dominant German culture with that of native Czechs. Today, classic productions are staged here in a larger setting than at the Estates' Theater, but with about the same ticket prices.

The National Theater Ballet performs at the National Theater. The troupe has seen most of its top talent go west since 1989, but it still puts on a good show. Some critics have complained that Prague's top company has been performing virtually the same dances for many years and they're in serious need of refocusing. Choreographer Libor Vaculík has responded with humorous and quirky stagings of off-the-wall ballets such as *Some Like It Hot* and *Psycho.* Tickets cost 200Kč to 600Kč ($6 to $18).

Laterna Magika, Národní třída 4, Praha 1 (☎ **02/2491 4129**; metro: Národní třída), is a performance-art show in the new wing of the National Theater. The multimedia show, which combines live theater with film and dance, was once considered on the radical edge. The shows are not for those easily offended by nudity. Tickets are 400Kč ($12).

THE CLUB & MUSIC SCENE

Prague's club and music scene is limited but lively. Local acts still have a garage-band sound, but are adding more sophisticated numbers to their gigs. Many venerable jazz groups who toiled in the underground caverns are finding a new audience in visitors who stumble on their clubs. It is no longer a huge shock to see well-known Western bands playing a couple of sets in Prague.

ROCK & DANCE CLUBS   At **Club Lávka,** Novotného lávka 1, Praha 1 (☎ **02/2421 4797**; www.lavka.cz; metro: Staroměstská), straightforward dance hits attract one of Prague's best-looking young crowds. Because of its location next to the Staré Město foot of Charles Bridge, it also attracts a lot of less well-dressed visitors. Open 24 hours, the club is one of the nicest in town, offering a large bar, a good dance floor, and fantastic outdoor seating in warm months. Cover is 50Kč to 100Kč ($1.45 to $2.95): ticket prices for performing art 120Kč to 150Kč ($3.50 to $4.40).

Popular with a mixed gay and model crowd, **Radost FX,** Bělehradská 120, Praha 2 (☎ **02/2251 3144**; metro: I. P. Pavlova), is built in the American mold. In a subterranean labyrinth of nooks and crannies there's a pulsating techno-heavy dance floor with good sight lines for wallflowers. Radost, extremely stylish and self-consciously urban, is open daily 9pm to 5am. Cover is usually 50Kč ($1.45). No credit cards.

One of the city's most unusual venues, **Roxy Experimental Space,** Dlouhá 33, Praha 1 (☎ **02/2481 0951;** metro: Náměstí Republiky), is a subterranean theater with a wraparound balcony overlooking a concrete dance floor. The club is ultra-downscale and extremely popular on Friday and Saturday. Persian rugs and lanterns soften the atmosphere but don't improve the lousy acoustics. Acid jazz, funk, techno, ambient, and other danceable tunes attract an artsy crowd after midnight. Several live acts are also featured here each month, with music ranging from Czech acid jazz to Allanah Miles. Cafe open noon to midnight; club 10pm to 6am. Cover is 100Kč to 150Kč ($2.95 to $4.40). No credit cards.

JAZZ CLUBS   Upscale by Czech standards, **AghaRTA Jazz Centrum,** Krakovská 5, Praha 1 (☎ **02/2221 1275;** metro: Muzeum), regularly features some of the best music in town, from standard acoustic trios to Dixieland, funk, and fusion. Hot Line, the house band led by AghaRTA part-owner and drummer extraordinaire Michael Hejuna, regularly takes the stage with its keyboard-and-sax Crusaders-like sound. Bands usually begin at 9pm. The club is open Monday to Friday 5pm to 1am and Saturday and Sunday 7pm to 1am. Cover is 60Kč to 100Kč ($1.75 to $2.95). **Reduta Jazz Club,** Národní třída 20, Praha 1 (☎ **02/2491 2246;** metro: Národní třída), is a smoky subterranean room that looks exactly like a jazz cellar should. An adventurous booking policy, which even included a saxophone gig with a U.S. president in 1994, means that different bands play almost every night. Music usually starts around 9pm. It's open 9pm to midnight. Cover is usually 100Kč ($2.95).

Pubs & Bars

You'll experience true Czech entertainment in only one kind of place—a smoky local pub serving some of the world's best beer. Remember to put a cardboard coaster in front of you to show you want a mug, and never wave for service, as the typically surly waiter will just ignore you.

Hidden on a small Old Town back street, **Chapeau Rouge/Banana Café,** Jakubská 2, Praha 1 (no phone; metro: Staroměstská), is loud and lively, if slightly seedy. The place has twin bars, plank floors, and a good sound system playing contemporary rock. They have four types of beer on tap and feature regular drink specials. Open daily noon to 5am, it's busy and fun—if you avoid the headache-inducing concoctions from the frozen drink machine.

Originally a brewery dating from 1459, **U Fleků,** Křemencova 11, Praha 2 (☎ **02/2491 5118;** metro: Národní třída), is Prague's most famous beer hall, and one of the only pubs that still brews its own beer. This huge place has a myriad of timber-lined rooms and a large, loud courtyard where an oompah band performs. Tourists come here by the busload, so U Fleků is avoided by disparaging locals who don't like its German atmosphere anyway. The pub's special dark beer is excellent, however, and not available anywhere else. Open daily 9am to 11pm.

One of the most famous Czech pubs, **U Zlatého tygra,** Husova 17, Praha 1 (☎ **02/2222 1111;** metro: Staroměstská or Můstek), was a favorite watering hole of President Havel and the late writer Bohumil Hrabal. Particularly smoky, and not especially tourist friendly, At the Golden Tiger is a one-stop education in Czech culture. Havel and President Bill Clinton joined Hrabal for a traditional Czech pub evening here during Clinton's 1994 visit to Prague. It's open daily 3pm to 10:30pm.

Gay & Lesbian Bars

For details on the gay and lesbian community, call the **SOHO Infocentrum** at ☎ **02/2422 0327.** For a stylish place to dance, try **Radost FX** (see "The Club & Music Scene," above). Lesbians should look for the sharply decorated **"A" Klub Milíčova 32,**

Praha 3 (no phone; metro: Flora, then tram 9), covered with the works of female artists and sporting cushy chairs and couches. Friday's are women only. Men are allowed on other nights, but only in the company of a woman. There's dancing and relaxed chat here daily 6pm to 6am. Cover is 25Kč (75¢).

Just across the tracks from the main train station is **Fire Club,** Seifertova 3, Praha 3 (no phone; metro: Hlavní nádraží), which used to be the rock palace Alterna Komotovka. It has been transformed into a wild pink-and-neon cavern serving an almost exclusively gay crowd, offering original Budweiser on tap. It's open Friday and Saturday 9pm until whenever they feel like closing. There's no cover.

CASINOS

Prague has many casinos, most offering blackjack, roulette, and slot machines. House rules are usually similar to those in Las Vegas. **Casino Palais Savarin,** Na Příkopě 10 (☎ 02/2422 1636; metro: Můstek), occupying a former rococo palace, is the city's most beautiful game room, open daily 1pm to 4am. Other recommended casinos are **Casino de France,** in the Hotel Hilton Atrium, Pobřežní 1 (☎ 02/2484 1111), open daily 2pm to 6am; and **Casino U Nováků,** Vodičkova 30 (☎ 02/2422 2098), open daily 1pm to 5am. For both, a picture ID or passport is necessary!

DAY TRIPS FROM PRAGUE

KARLŠTEJN CASTLE   By far the most popular day trip from Prague, this medieval castle, 30km (18 miles) southwest of Prague, which has been restored to its original state, was built by Charles IV in the 14th century to safeguard the crown jewels of the Holy Roman Empire. As you approach, little can prepare you for your first view: a spectacular Disney-like castle perched high on a hill, surrounded by lush forests and vineyards. The **Holy Rood Chapel** is famous for the more than 2,000 precious and semiprecious inlaid gems that adorn its walls, and the **Chapel of St. Catherine** was King Karel IV's private oratory. (*Warning:* Both chapels were closed for a short time recently; check ahead to make sure that they will be open during your visit.) Both the **Audience Hall** and the **Imperial Bedroom** are impressive, despite being stripped of their original furnishings.

Admission is 150Kč ($4.40) adults and 100Kč ($2.95) students, children from 6 without guide; 200Kč ($6)/100Kč ($2.95) with an English-speaking guide. It's open Tuesday to Sunday, January to March 9am to noon, 1pm to 4pm; April to June, September, and October 9am to noon and 12:30 to 6pm; July and August 9am to noon and 12:30 to 7pm; November, and December 25 to 31, 9am to noon and 1 to 4pm.

Getting There   The best way to get to Karlštejn is by **train** (there's no bus service). Most trains leave from Prague's Smíchov Station (metro: Smíchovské nádraží) hourly throughout the day (trip time: 45 minutes). One-way second-class fare is 22Kč (65¢). You can also **drive:** Leave Prague on Highway 4 southwest in the direction of Strakonice and take the Karlštejn cutoff, following the signs (and traffic!).

KUTNÁ HORA   A medieval town that grew fantastically rich from the silver deposits beneath it, Kutná Hora, 72km (45 miles) east of Prague, is probably the second most popular day trip. The town's ancient heart is quite decayed, making it hard to believe that this was once the second most important city in Bohemia.

Getting There   The **bus** departs from the terminal at Prague's Želivského metro station (trip time: 1 hour). To **drive,** take Vinohradská ulice, due east from behind the National Museum at the top of Wenceslas Square, straight to Kutná Hora (trip time: 50 minutes). Once out of the city, the road turns into Highway 333.

Exploring Kutná Hora　The main attraction is the enormous **St. Barbara's Cathedral (Chrám sv. Barbory)** at the southwestern edge of town. Soaring arches, dozens of spires, and intricate designs raise expectations that the interior will be just as impressive—and you won't be disappointed. On entering (from the side, not the front), you see several richly decorated frescoes full of symbols denoting the town's two main industries of mining and minting. Admission is 40Kč ($1.15) for adults and 20Kč (60¢) for children. It's open Tuesday to Sunday 9am to noon and 1 to 5pm.

When you leave the cathedral, head down the statue-lined **Barborská street,** where you'll pass the early **Baroque Jesuit College** built in the late 17th century.

A visit to Kutná Hora isn't complete without a trip to ✪ **Kostnice,** the "bone church." It's located just down the road in Sedlec; those who don't want to walk can board a local bus on Masarykova street; the fare is 6Kč (15¢). From the outside, Kostnice looks like most other Gothic churches. But once you go inside, you know this is no ordinary church. All the decorations, designed by František Rint, are made from human bones. The bones came from victims of the 14th-century plague and the 15th-century Hussite wars; both events left thousands of dead, who were buried in mass graves. As the area developed, the bones were uncovered, and the local monks came up with this idea. Admission is a bargain at 25Kč (75¢) for adults and 10Kč (30¢) for children. It's open July and August, daily 9am to noon and 1 to 5pm; the rest of the year, Tuesday to Sunday 9am to noon and 1 to 4pm.

TEREZÍN (THERESIENSTADT)　The name Terezín (*Theresienstadt* in German) occupies a unique place in the atrocious history of Nazism. This former Austro-Hungarian imperial fortress, turned into a concentration camp, 50km (30 miles) northwest of Prague, witnessed no gas chambers, mass machine-gun executions, or medical testing; it was used instead as a transit camp. About 140,000 people passed though Terezín's gates; many died here, and more than half ended up at the death camps of Auschwitz and Treblinka.

Terezín will live in infamy for the cruel trick played by SS chief Heinrich Himmler. On June 23, 1944, three foreign observers came to Terezín to find out if the rumors of Nazi atrocities were true. They left under the impression that all was well, duped by a carefully planned "beautification" of the camp. So the observers wouldn't think the camp was overcrowded, the Nazis transported some 7,500 of the sick and elderly to Auschwitz. The trick worked so well that the Nazis made a film of the camp while it was still "self-governing," called *A Town Presented to the Jews from the Füehrer.* Terezín was liberated by Russian forces on May 10, 1945, eight days after Berlin had fallen to the Allies.

Today, Terezín stands as a memorial to the dead and a monument to human depravity. Once inside the **Major Fortress,** you'll immediately be struck by its drab, plain streets. Just off the main square lies the **Museum of the Ghetto,** chronicling the rise of Nazism and life in the camp. English pamphlets describing the exhibits are provided. Admission is 50Kč ($1.45) for adults and 25Kč (75¢) for children. A ticket to enter both the Major and Minor Fortresses is 100Kč ($2.95) for adults and 50Kč ($1.45) for children. The Major Fortress is open daily 9am to 6pm. The **Minor Fortress** is about a 10-minute walk from the Major Fortress over the Ohře River. Just in front of the fortress's main entrance is the **National Cemetery (Národní hřbitov),** where the bodies exhumed from the mass graves were buried. As you enter the main gate, the sign above it, ARBEIT MACHT FREI (WORK SETS ONE FREE), sets a gloomy tone. You can walk through the prison barracks, execution grounds, workshops, and isolation cells.

Getting There　Terezín is a 45-minute **drive** from Prague, on the main highway north towards Berlin via Dresden. Six **buses** leave daily from Florenc Bus Station (trip time: 1 hour). The Prague-based **Wittman Tours** (☎ **02/2481 2325**) offers a bus tour to Terezín that costs 1,150Kč ($34), 850Kč ($25) for students. Call for times.

2 West Bohemia & the Spas

The Czech Republic is composed of two regions: Bohemia and Moravia. The larger of the two, Bohemia, occupying the central and western areas of the country, has for centuries been caught between a rock (Germany) and a hard place (Austria). Bohemia was almost always in the center of regional conflicts, both secular and religious. But the area also flourished, as witnessed by the wealth of castles that dot the countryside and the spa towns that were once the playgrounds of the rich and famous.

Although Bohemia is historically undivided, there are clear-cut distinctions in the region's geography that make going from town to town easier if you "cut" Bohemia into sections. This section focuses on west Bohemia, home to the country's spa towns. It's also one of the few regions in the Czech Republic where a full-blown tourist infrastructure is already in place. Its main towns—Karlovy Vary (Carlsbad), Mariánské Lázně (Marienbad), and to a lesser extent Plzeň and Cheb, offer a wide array of accommodations, restaurants, and services. All are constantly being reconstructed, renovated, and restored.

A relatively inexpensive network of trains and buses covers the region. West Bohemia is generally rougher terrain, so only serious cyclists should consider touring the area on two wheels. For those with a car, the highways can range from top-notch, such as the newly built Prague-Plzen motorway, to an asphalt horror ride such as the Prague–Karlovy Vary route. Roads generally are much slower than in Western Europe, so leave yourself plenty of time. Gas stations are constantly springing up, so stops for food and fuel are rarely hard to come by. *Note:* If you drive the D-5 (Prague-Plzeň) and D-1 (Prague-Brno) highways, your car must display the country's highway sticker; these stickers, which you can buy at most gas stations and border crossings, cost 800Kč ($24) and save you from being hassled by the police.

Most towns are distant enough that you should drive from one to another. However, if you'd rather stay in one place and make day trips, we'd recommend staying in Karlovy Vary. The **Kur-Info Vřídelní kolonáda,** 360 01 Karlovy Vary (☎ **017/322 9312** or 017/322 4097; fax 017/246 67) can provide information on bus trips to Mariánské Lázně and other regional sights.

KARLOVY VARY (CARLSBAD)

The discovery of Karlovy Vary (Carlsbad), 120km (75 miles) west of Prague, by Charles IV reads something like a 14th-century episode of *The Beverly Hillbillies.* According to local lore, the king was out huntin' for some food when up from the ground came a-bubblin' water (though discovered by his dogs, not an errant gunshot). Knowing a good thing when he saw it, Charles immediately set to work building a small castle, naming the town that evolved around it Karlovy Vary (Charles's Boiling Place). The first spa buildings were built in 1522, and before long, notables like Albrecht of Wallenstein, Russian Czar Peter the Great, and later Bach, Beethoven, Freud, and Marx all came to take the waters.

Warning to Drivers

Be warned that highway E-48 from Prague to Karlovy Vary is a popular route for reckless drivers heading to and from the capital. Please take extra care when driving.

After World War II, East Bloc travelers (following in the footsteps of Marx, no doubt) discovered the town, and Karlovy Vary became a destination for the proletariat. On doctor's orders, most workers enjoyed regular stays of 2 or 3 weeks, letting the mineral waters ranging from 43.5°C to 72°C (110.3°F to 161.6°F) from the town's 12 spas heal their tired and broken bodies. Even now, most spa guests are there by doctor's prescription.

Most of the 40-plus years of communist neglect have been erased by a barrage of renovators who are restoring almost all the spa's former glory. Gone is the statue of Yuri Gagarin, the Russian cosmonaut. Gone are almost all the crumbling building facades that used to line both sides of the river. In their place now stand restored buildings, cherubs, caryatids, and more.

Nearly 100,000 people travel annually to the spa resort to sip, bathe, and frolic. Most enjoy the 13th spring, a hearty herb-and-mineral liqueur called Becherovka, more than the 12 nonalcoholic versions. Czechs will tell you that all have medicinal benefits.

ESSENTIALS

GETTING THERE   By Train   *At all costs, avoid the train from Prague* (trip time: over 4 hours). If you're arriving from another direction, Karlovy Vary's main train station is connected to the town center by bus 11.

By Bus   Frequent express buses make the trip from Prague's Florenc station, platform 21 or 22, to Karlovy Vary (trip time: 2¹/₂ hours). Take a 10-minute walk or local bus 4 into Karlovy Vary's center. Note that you must have a ticket to board local transport. You can buy tickets for 8Kč (25¢) at the main station stop, or, if you have no change, the kiosk across the street sells tickets during regular business hours.

By Car   The drive from Prague isn't difficult but can be at times a little hair-raising (trip time: 2 hours). Take highway E-48 from the western end of the city and follow it straight through to Karlovy Vary. This two-lane highway widens in a few spots to let cars pass slow-moving vehicles on hills.

VISITOR INFORMATION   Kuri-Info, inside the Vřídelní kolonáda (☎ 017/ 322 9312 or 017/322 4097; fax 017/246 67), is open Monday to Friday 7am to 5pm, Saturday and Sunday 9am to 3pm. It provides accommodation services, arranges guided tours and spa treatments, and sells tickets for some events. Be sure to pick up the *Cultural Calendar,* a comprehensive collection of events with a small map of the town center.

There are also two privately run **Info-Centrum** booths: one in the train station and the other in a parking lot at the base of Jana Palacha ulice. Both give away free maps and a brochure of current cultural listings and events called *Promenáda*. Info-Centrum also books accommodations in private rooms and sells tours.

SPECIAL EVENTS   The **Karlovy Vary International Film Festival** is one of the few places to see and be seen. Each summer (usually at the beginning of July), film stars and celebrities take part in one of Europe's biggest film festivals. Six venues screen more than 200 films during the 8- to 10-day festival.

Karlovy Vary plays host to several other events, including a **jazz festival** and **beer Olympiad** in May, the **Dvořák singing contest** in June, the **Summer Music Festival** in August, and the **Dvořák Autumn Music Festival** in September and October.

For more information on any of the festivals, contact **Kuri-Info,** Vřídelní kolonáda, 360–01 Karlovy Vary (☎ **017/322 9312** or 017/322 4097; fax 017/246 67).

WHERE TO STAY

Private rooms used to be the best places to stay in Karlovy Vary for both quality and price, but this is changing as more and more hotels renovate and raise standards—as

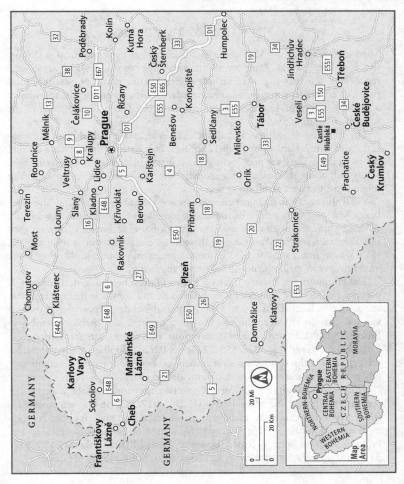

well as prices. Private accommodation can still provide better value, but it takes a little extra work. If you want to arrange a room, try the **Info-Centrum** (see "Visitor Information," above). Expect to pay about 500Kč to 1,000Kč ($15 to $29) for a single and 750Kč to 1,200Kč ($22 to $35) for a double.

Some of the town's major spa hotels accommodate only those who are paying for complete treatment, unless their occupancy rates are particularly low. The hotels I've listed below accept guests for stays of any length.

Grandhotel Pupp. Mírové nám. 2, 360 91, Karlovy Vary. ☎ **017/310 9111.** Fax 017/322 4032. www.pupp.cz. 110 units. MINIBAR TV TEL. 5,610Kč ($165) double deluxe; 7,310Kč ($215) studio deluxe; 10,710Kč ($315) apt; 13,600Kč ($400) Imperial apt; 28,390Kč ($835) Presidential apt. Breakfast not included (extra $11). The crown rate for the room fluctuates, based on the latest crown rate against the dollar on the day the payment is made because of the crown's volatility. The dollar rate remains constant for those paying in dollars or by credit card. A daily exchange rate is used for those who want to pay in crowns by cash. AE, DC, MC, V.

Spa Cures & Treatments

Most visitors to Karlovy Vary come specifically to get a spa treatment, a therapy that lasts 1 to 3 weeks. After consulting with a spa physician, guests are given a regimen of activities that may include mineral baths, massages, waxings, mud packs, electrotherapy, and pure oxygen inhalation. After spending the morning at a spa or sanatorium, guests are then usually directed to walk the paths of the town's surrounding forest.

The common denominator of all the cures is an ample daily dose of hot mineral water, which bubbles up from 12 springs. This water definitely has a distinct odor and taste. You'll see people chugging it down, but it doesn't necessarily taste very good. Some thermal springs actually taste and smell like rotten eggs. You might want to take a small sip at first.

You'll also notice that almost everyone in town seems to be carrying "the cup," basically a mug with a built-in straw that runs through the handle. Young and old alike parade through town with their mugs, filling and refilling them at each new thermal water tap. You can buy these mugs everywhere for as little as 50Kč ($1.45) or as much as 500Kč ($15); they make a quirky souvenir. *Warning:* None of the mugs can make the hot springs taste any better!

The minimum spa treatment lasts 1 week and must be arranged in advance. A package traditionally includes room, full board, and complete therapy regimen; the cost varies from about $40 to $100 per person per day, depending on the season and facilities. Rates are highest May to September and lowest November to February. For information and reservations in Prague, contact **Čedok,** Na Příkopě 18, Praha 1 (☎ **02/2419 7111;** fax 02/2421 0502). Many hotels also offer spa and health treatments, so ask when you book your room. Most will happily arrange a treatment if they don't provide it directly.

Visitors to Karlovy Vary for just a day or two can experience the waters on an "outpatient" basis. The **State Baths III** (☎ **017/322 5641**) welcomes daytrippers with mineral baths, massages, saunas, and a cold pool. It's open for men on Tuesday, Thursday, and Saturday and for women on Monday, Wednesday, and Friday 7:45am to 3pm. **Vojenský lázeňský ústav,** Mlýnské nábřeží 7 (☎ **017/ 311 9111**), offers similar services and costs about 500Kč ($15) per day.

Well known as one of Karlovy Vary's best hotels, the Pupp, built in 1701, is also one of Europe's oldest. While the hotel's public areas ooze with splendor and charm, rooms aren't as consistently enchanting. The best tend to be on the upper floors facing the town center. The Grand Restaurant serves up as grand a dining room as you'll find, with the food to match (see "Where to Dine," below).

Hotel Dvořák. Nová Louka 11, 360 21, Karlovy Vary. ☎ **017/322 4145.** Fax 017/322 2814. www.hotel-dvorak.cz. 79 units. MINIBAR TV TEL. 140–203DM ($74–107) double; 240DM ($126) suite. A daily exchange rate is used for those who want to pay in crowns by cash. AE, DC, MC, V.

Now part of the Vienna International hotel/resort chain, the Dvořák has improved immensely over the past year or two, especially in terms of service. If the Pupp has the history and elegance, the Dvořák has the facilities, including a well-equipped fitness center, a sauna, and an indoor pool. However, the rooms, for all their creature comforts, lack the Old World charm found at the Pupp.

Hotel Embassy. Nová Louka 21, 360 01, Karlovy Vary. ☎ **017/322 1161-5.** Fax 017/322 3146. 20 units. TV TEL. 2,788–3,468Kč ($82–$102) double; 3,060–3,740Kč ($90–$110) double deluxe; 3,570–4,420Kč ($105–$130) suite. Rates include breakfast. AE, V. Free parking.

This family-run hotel manages to evoke the turn of the last century with elegantly decorated rooms. Although smaller than those at the Pupp, they're impeccably furnished and overlook the river. The restaurant downstairs is where a lot of movers and shakers at the Karlovy Vary film festival get away from the glitz and get down to business.

Parkhotel Pupp. Mírové nám. 2, 360 91, Karlovy Vary. ☎ **017/310 9111.** Fax 017/322 4032. 255 units. MINIBAR TV TEL. 3,400Kč ($100) double; 4,420Kč ($130) apt. Breakfast $8 extra. AE, DC, MC, V.

This is how the other half live at the Pupp. At four stars, this wing of the Grandhotel Pupp is housed within the same complex as its five-star cousin, but a world apart in terms of frills—and price. Still, rooms are large and all the same facilities are available; the views are just less spectacular.

WHERE TO DINE

Embassy. Nová Louka 21. ☎ **017/322 1161.** Reservations recommended. Main courses 145–895Kč ($4.25–$26). AE, V. Daily noon–11pm. CZECH/CONTINENTAL.

On the ground floor of the hotel of the same name, the Embassy restaurant has a pub on one side and an intimate dining room on the other. On a cold day the pub works wonders with a hearty goulash soup. But the dining is the Embassy's hidden treasure. What the meals lack in flair, they more than make up for with sophistication. Salmon with a delicate dill sauce or beef with a surprisingly light mushroom sauce are two of the choices that set this restaurant apart.

Grand Restaurant. In the Grandhotel Pupp, Mírové nám. 2. ☎ **017/310 9111.** Reservations recommended. Main courses 240–1,100Kč ($7–$32). AE, V. Daily noon–3pm and 6–11pm. CONTINENTAL.

It's no surprise that the Grandhotel Pupp has the nicest dining room in town, an elegant affair with tall ceilings, huge mirrors, and glistening chandeliers. A large menu gives way to larger portions of salmon, chicken, veal, pork, turkey, and beef in a variety of heavy and heavier sauces. Even the trout with mushrooms is smothered in butter sauce.

Hospoda U Švejka. Stará Louka 10. ☎ **017/ 323 2276.** Main courses 99–214Kč ($2.90–$6); beer 20Kč (60¢). MC, V. Daily 11am–11pm. CZECH.

A new addition to the pub scene, U Švejka plays on the tried and true Good Soldier Švejk tourist theme. Luckily the tourist trap goes no further, and once inside, you find a refreshingly unsmoky although thoroughly Czech atmosphere. Locals and tourists, alike, rub elbows while throwing back some fine lager and standard pub favorites, such as goulash and beef tenderloin in cream sauce.

✪ **Promenáda.** Tržiště 31. ☎ **017/322 5648.** Reservations highly recommended. Main courses 139–498Kč ($4.10–$15). AE, V. Daily noon–11pm. CZECH/CONTINENTAL.

This intimate spot may not be as elegant as the Grand, but for Karlovy Vary residents, it has become one of *the* places to dine. Across from the Vřídelní kolonáda, the Promenáda serves the best food around, offering a wide selection of generous portions. The daily menu usually includes well-prepared wild game, but the mixed grill for two or the chateaubriand, both flambéed at the table, are the chef's best dishes.

EXPLORING KARLOVY VARY

The town's slow pace and pedestrian promenades, lined with art nouveau buildings, turn strolling into an art form. Nighttime walks take on an even more mystical feel as the sewers, river, and many major cracks in the roads emit steam from the hot springs underneath.

If you're traveling here by train or bus, a good place to start is the **Hotel Thermal** at the north end of the old town's center. The 1970s glass, steel, and concrete Thermal, between the town's eastern hills and the Ohře River, sticks out like a sore communist thumb amid the 19th-century architecture. Nonetheless, you'll find three important places here: its outdoor pool with mineral water, the only centrally located outdoor public pool; its upper terrace, boasting a spectacular view; and its theater, Karlovy Vary's largest, which holds many of the film festival's premier events. Look at it, and then turn and walk away. Try not to picture it again.

As you enter the heart of the town on the river's west side, you'll see the ornate white wrought-iron **Sadová kolonáda** adorning the beautifully manicured park **Dvořákovy sady.** Continue following the river, and about 100m (110 yards) later you'll encounter the **Mlýnská kolonáda,** a long, covered walkway housing several Karlovy Vary springs, which you can sample 24 hours a day. Each spring has a plaque beside it telling which mineral elements are present and the temperature of the water. Bring your own cup or buy one just about anywhere to sip the waters since most are too hot to drink from your hands. Remember, some springs are rather hot.

When you hit the river bend, the majestic **Church of St. Mary Magdalene** sits perched atop a hill, overlooking the **Vřídlo,** the hottest spring in town. Built in 1736, the church is the work of Kilian Ignac Dientzenhofer, who also created two of Prague's more notable churches—both named St. Nicholas. Housing Vřídlo, which blasts water some 15m (50 feet) into the air, is the glass building where the statue of Soviet astronaut Gagarin once stood. (Gagarin's statue has since made a safe landing at the Karlovy Vary airport.) Now called the **Vřídelní kolonáda,** the structure, built in 1974, houses several hot springs you can sample for free. The building also holds the Kuri-Info information center and several kiosks selling postcards, stone roses, and drinking cups.

Heading away from the Vřídelní kolonáda are Stará and Nová Louka streets, which line either side of the river. Along **Stará (Old) Louka** you'll find several fine cafes and glass and crystal shops. **Nová (New) Louka** is lined with hotels and the historic town's main theater, currently under reconstruction.

Both streets lead to the **Grandhotel Pupp.** After a massive reconstruction, the Pupp is once again the crown jewel of the town. Gone are the effects of nearly 50 years of communism (it was temporarily called the Grand Hotel Moskva); once again, splendor radiates from its restored facade. Regardless of capitalism or communism, the Pupp remains what it always was: the grand dame of hotels in the area. Once catering to nobility from all over central Europe, the Pupp still houses one of the town's finest restaurants, the Grand, and its grounds are a favorite with the hiking crowd. The reconstruction has also brought with it a plethora of designer shops catering to those who just don't know what to wear.

If you still have the energy, atop the hill behind the Pupp stands the **Diana Lookout Tower.** Footpaths leading through the forests eventually spit you out at the base of the tower, as if to say, "Ha, the trip is only half over." The five-story climb tests your stamina, but the view of the town is more than worth it. For those who aren't up to the climb just to get to the tower, a cable car runs to the tower every 15 minutes or so.

THE SHOPPING SCENE

Crystal and porcelain are Karlovy Vary's other claims to fame. Dozens of shops throughout town sell everything from plates to chandeliers.

Traveler's Tip

Consider yourself warned: Word has spread about Český Krumlov. Summer season can be unbearable, as thousands of visitors blanket its medieval streets. If possible, try to visit in the off-season—we suggest autumn to take advantage of the colorful surrounding hills—when the crowds recede, the prices decrease, and the town's charm can really shine. Who knows? You might even hear some Czech!

Ludvík Moser founded his first glassware shop in 1857 and soon became one of the country's foremost names in glass. Now his name can be found in almost every store along the river. Many of the stores will pack and ship your purchases, either back to Prague or all the way home. We recommend comparison shopping as prices can sometimes vary greatly for similar items.

ČESKÝ KRUMLOV

If you have time for only one day trip, consider making it Český Krumlov, 155km (96 miles) south of Prague. One of Bohemia's prettiest towns, Krumlov is a living gallery of elegant Renaissance-era buildings housing charming cafes, pubs, restaurants, shops, and galleries. In 1992, UNESCO named Český Krumlov a World Heritage Site for its historic importance and physical beauty.

Bustling since medieval times, the town, after centuries of embellishment, is exquisitely beautiful. In 1302, the Rožmberk family inherited the castle and used it as their main residence for nearly 300 years. Looking out from the Lazebnický bridge, with the waters of the Vltava below snaking past the castle's gray stone, you'll feel that time has stopped. At night, with the castle alight, the view becomes even more dramatic.

Few deigned to change the appearance of Český Krumlov over the years, not even the Schwarzenbergs, who usually had an unrestrained flair for opulence. At the turn of the 19th century, several house facades in the town's outer section were built, as were inner courtyards. Thankfully, economic stagnation in the area during communism meant little money for "development," so no glass-and-steel edifices, like the Hotel Thermal in Karlovy Vary, jut out to spoil the architectural beauty. Instead, a medieval impression reigns supreme, now augmented by the many festivals and renovations that keep the town's spirit alive.

ESSENTIALS

GETTING THERE   By Train   The only way to reach Český Krumlov by train from Prague is via České Budějovice, a slow ride that deposits you at a station relatively far from the town center (trip time: 3¹/₂ hours); the fare is 180Kč ($5)first class or 120Kč ($3.55) second class.

By Bus   The nearly 3-hour bus ride from Prague usually involves a transfer in České Budějovice and costs 149Kč ($4.40). The bus station in Český Krumlov is a 15-minute walk from the town's main square.

By Car   From Prague, it's a 2-hour drive along E-55.

VISITOR INFORMATION   On the main square, the **Information Centrum,** náměstí Svornosti 1, 381 00 Český Krumlov (☎ and fax **0337/711 183**), offers a complete array of services from booking accommodations to ticket reservations for events, as well as a phone and fax service. It's open daily 9am to 6pm.

SPECIAL EVENTS   After being banned during communism, the **Slavnost pětilisté růže (Festival of the Five-Petaled Rose)** has made a triumphant comeback. It's held each year on the summer solstice. Residents of Český Krumlov dress up in Renaissance costume and parade through the streets. Afterward, the streets become a stage with plays, chess games with people dressed as pieces, music, and even duels "to the death."

Český Krumlov also plays host to a 2-week **International Music Festival** every August, attracting performers from all over the world. Performances are held in nine spectacular venues. For information or ticket reservations, contact the information center's ticket hotline at ☎ **0337/711 650.**

WHERE TO STAY

Hotels are sprouting up, or are getting a "new" old look; PENSION and ZIMMER FREI signs line Horní and Rooseveltova streets and offer some of the best values in town. For a comprehensive list of area hotels and help with bookings, call or write to the Infocentrum listed above.

Moderate

Hotel Růže (Rose Hotel). Horní 153, 381 01 Český Krumlov. ☎ **0337/711 141.** Fax 0337/711 128. 53 units. MINIBAR TV TEL. 1,530–3,420Kč ($45–$11) double; 1,800–4,230Kč ($53–$124) small suite; 2,700–4,950Kč ($79–$146) large suite. Rates include breakfast. AE, MC, V.

Once a Jesuit seminary, this stunning Italian Renaissance building has been turned into a well-appointed hotel. Comfortable in a big-city kind of way, it's packed with amenities and is one of the top places to stay in Český Krumlov. But for all of the splendor of the building, you may find the Růže a bit of a disappointment. Rooms, although clean and spacious, look as though they were furnished from a Sears warehouse in the U.S. Midwest. The promise of a Renaissance stay dissipates quickly.

Inexpensive

Hotel Konvice. Horní ul. 144, 381 01 Český Krumlov. ☎ **0337/711 611.** Fax 0337/711 327. 10 units. 1,300Kč ($38) double; 1,600–2,500Kč ($47–$74) suite. Rates include breakfast. No credit cards.

If you can get a room with a view out the back, take it immediately. Rooms themselves are small but clean and comfortable, with nice parquet floors and well-appointed baths. As you overlook the river and the castle on the opposite bank, you'll wonder why anyone would stay at the Růže just a few doors up.

✪ **Pension Anna.** Rooseveltova 41, 381 01 Český Krumlov. ☎ **0337/711 692.** 8 units. 800–1,000Kč ($24–$29) double; 1,100–1,300Kč ($32–38) suite. Rates include breakfast. No credit cards.

Along "pension alley," this is a comfortable and rustic choice. What makes this a favorite is the friendly management and the homey feeling you get as you walk up to your room. Forget hotels—this is the kind of place where you can relax. The owners even let you buy drinks and snacks at the bar downstairs and take them to your room. Suites, with four beds and a living room, are great for families and groups.

Pension Na louži. Kájovská 66, 381 01 Český Krumlov. ☎ and fax **0337/712 880.** 5 units. 1,000Kč ($29) double; 1,200Kč triple ($35). Rates include breakfast. No credit cards.

Smack-dab in the heart of the Inner Town, the small Na louzi, built in 1459 and decorated with early 20th-century wooden furniture, is full of charm. The only drawback is beds with footboards that can be a little short for tall people. Don't worry about the noise—the pub downstairs is not open late!

✪ **Pension Ve Věži (In the Tower).** Latrán 28, 381 01 Český Krumlov. ☎ **0337/711 742.** 4 units (none with bathroom). May–Sept 1,400Kč ($41) double; 1,800Kč ($53) quad. Oct–Apr 750Kč ($22) double; 1,200Kč ($35) quad. Rates include breakfast. No credit cards.

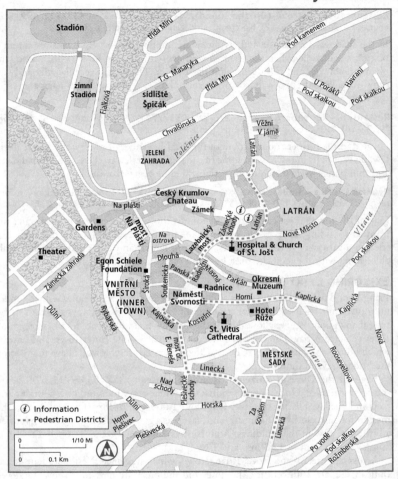

A private pension in a renovated medieval tower just a 5-minute walk from the castle, Ve Věži is one of the most magnificent places to stay in town. It's not the rooms themselves that are so grand—none have a bathroom and all are sparsely decorated—it's the wonderful ancient ambience. Advance reservations are always recommended.

WHERE TO DINE

Hospoda Na louži. Kájovská 66. ☎ **0337/711 280.** Main courses 49–129Kč ($1.45–$3.80). No credit cards. Daily 10am–10pm. CZECH.

The large wooden tables encourage you to get to know your neighbors in this Inner Town pub, located in a 15th-century house. The atmosphere is fun and the food above average. If no table is available, stand and have a drink; the seating turnover is pretty fast, and the staff is accommodating. In summer, the terrace seats only six, so dash over if a seat becomes empty.

Restaurant Na Ostrově (On the island). Na Ostrově 171. ☎ **0337/711 699.** Main courses 60–245Kč ($1.75–$7). No credit cards. Daily 11am–11pm. CZECH.

In the shadow of the castle and, as the name implies, on an island, this restaurant is best on a sunny day when the terrace overflows with flowers, hearty Czech food with plenty of chicken and fish dishes, and lots of beer. The staff is very friendly and very slow—usually only two waiters work a shift. This is a great place to relax and enjoy the view.

Restaurant Eggenberg. Latrán 27. ☎ **0337/711 761.** Main courses 80–195Kč ($2.35–$6). MC, V. Daily 10am–11pm. CZECH.

Located in the former cooling room of the local Eggenberg Brewery, this is one of the few big beer halls in town, with some of the freshest draft anywhere. Traditional meat-and-dumplings–style Czech food is augmented by vegetarian dishes.

Rybářská bašta Jakuba Krčína. Kájovská 54. ☎ **0337/712 692.** Reservations recommended. Main courses 110–340Kč ($3.25–$10). AE, MC, V. Daily 7am–11pm. CZECH.

One of the town's most celebrated restaurants, this place specializes in freshwater fish from surrounding lakes. Trout, perch, pike, and eel are sautéed, grilled, baked, and fried in a variety of herbs and spices. Venison, rabbit, and other game are also available, along with the requisite roast beef and pork cutlet.

Exploring Český Krumlov

Bring a good pair of walking shoes and be prepared to wear them out. Český Krumlov not only lends itself to hours of strolling, but its hills and alleyways demand it. No cars, thank goodness, are allowed in the historic town, and the cobblestones keep most other vehicles at bay. The town is split into two parts—the **Inner town** and **Latrán,** which houses the castle. They're best tackled separately, so you won't have to crisscross the bridges several times.

Begin at the **Okresní Muzeum (Regional Museum)** (☎ 0337/711 674) at the top of Horní ulice. Once a Jesuit seminary, the three-story museum now contains artifacts and displays relating to Český Krumlov's 1,000-year history. The highlight of this mass of folk art, clothing, furniture, and statues is a giant model of the town that offers a bird's-eye view of the buildings. Admission is 20Kč (60¢), and it's open Tuesday to Sunday from 10am to 12:30pm and 1 to 6pm.

Across the street is the **Hotel Růže (Rose),** which was once a Jesuit student house. Built in the late 16th century, the hotel and the prelature next to it show the development of architecture; Gothic, Renaissance, and rococo influences are all present. If you're not staying at the hotel, don't be afraid to walk around and even ask questions at the reception desk.

Continue down the street to the impressive late Gothic **St. Vitus Cathedral.** Be sure to climb the church tower, which offers one of the most spectacular views of both the Inner Town and the castle across the river.

As you continue down the street, you'll come to **náměstí Svornosti.** For such an impressive town, the main square is a little disappointing, with few buildings of any character. The **Radnice (Town Hall),** at náměstí Svornosti 1, is one of the few exceptions. Its Gothic arcades and Renaissance vault inside are exceptionally beautiful in this otherwise rundown area. From the square, streets fan out in all directions. Take some time just to wander through them. You might want to grab a light snack before crossing the bridge.

As you cross the bridge and head toward the castle, you'll see immediately to your right the former **hospital and church of St. Jost.** Founded at the beginning of the

14th century, it has since been turned into apartments. Feel free to snoop around, but don't enter the building.

One of Český Krumlov's most famous residents was Austrian-born 20th-century artist Egon Schiele. He was a bit of an eccentric who, on more than one occasion, raised the ire of the town's residents (many were distraught with his use of their young women as his nude models); his stay was cut short when residents' patience ran out. But the town readopted the artist in 1993, setting up the **Egon Schiele Foundation** and the **Egon Schiele Centrum** in Inner Town, Široká 70–72, 381 01, Český Krumlov (☎ **0337/711 224;** fax 0337/711 191). Back across the river from the castle, it documents his life and work, housing a permanent selection of his paintings as well as exhibitions of other 20th-century artists. Admission depends on the exhibitions being displayed. It's open daily 10am to 6pm.

For a different perspective on what the town looks like, take the stairs from the **Městské divadlo (Town Theater)** on Horní ulice down to the riverfront and rent a boat from **Maláček boat rentals** at 40Kč ($1.20) per hour. Always willing to lend his advice, the affable Pepa Maláček will tell you what to watch out for and where the best fishing is (no matter how many times you say that you don't want to fish!).

SEEING THE ČESKÝ KRUMLOV CHÂTEAU

Reputedly the second-largest castle in Bohemia (after Prague Castle), the **Český Krumlov Château** was constructed in the 13th century as part of a private estate. Throughout the ages, it has passed to a variety of private owners, including the Rožmberk family, Bohemia's largest landholders, and the Schwarzenbergs, the Bohemian equivalent of *Dynasty*'s Carrington family.

From the entrance, by the bear moat, you'll begin the long climb up to the **castle.** Greeting you is a round 12th-century tower—painstakingly renovated—with its Renaissance balcony. You'll pass over the moat, now occupied by two brown bears. Beyond it is the **Dolní Hrad (Lower Castle)** and then the **Horní Hrad (Upper Castle).**

Perched high atop a rocky hill, the château is open from April to October only, exclusively by guided tour. Visits begin in the rococo **Chapel of St. George,** continue through the portrait-packed **Renaissance Hall,** and end with the **Royal Family Apartments,** outfitted with ornate furnishings that include Flemish wall tapestries and European paintings. Tours last 1 hour and depart frequently. Most are in Czech or German, however. If you want an English-language tour, arrange it ahead of time by calling ☎ **0337/711 465** (fax 0337/711 687).

The tour costs 100Kč ($2.95) for adults and 50Kč ($1.45) for students. The castle hours are Tuesday to Sunday: May to August 7:45am to noon and 12:45 to 4pm, September 8:45am to noon and 12:45 to 4pm, and April and October 8:45am to noon and 12:45 to 3pm. The last entrance is 1 hour before closing.

Once past the main castle building, you can see one of the more stunning views of Český Krumlov from **Most Na Plášti,** a walkway that doubles as a belvedere over the Inner Town. Even farther up the hill lies the castle's riding school and gardens.

Most visitors don't realize that beyond this part of the castle they can have one of the Czech Republic's finest dining experiences at ✪ **Krčma Markéta,** Latrán 67 (☎ **0337/711 453**). To get there, walk all the way up the hill through the castle, past the Upper Castle and past the Castle Theater. Walk through the raised walkway and into the Zámecká zahrada (Castle Garden), where you'll eventually find this Renaissance pub. Going inside is like leaving this century. There's no need for plates here, as meals are served on wooden blocks. Drinks come in pewter mugs.

Although owners have come and gone, the atmosphere and good times are still the same. There's no menu—just go up to the spit and see what's roasting; usually there's a wide variety of meat, including succulent pork cutlets, rabbit, chickens, and pork knees, a Czech delicacy. The waiter/cook will bring bread and a slab of spiced pork fat (considered a good base for drinking), but don't worry—refusing to eat it won't raise anyone's ire. Instead, wait until the entree comes. Yes, that obligatory smattering of cabbage is all the vegetables you're going to get. Vegetarians need not apply. Krčma Markéta is open daily 6 to 11pm. Reservations are recommended. Main courses are 75Kč to 155Kč ($2.20 to $4.55). No credit cards are accepted.

MARIÁNSKÉ LÁZNĚ (MARIENBAD)

When Thomas Alva Edison visited Mariánské Lázně in the late 1800s, he proclaimed, "There is no more beautiful spa in all the world." The town is 47km (29 miles) southwest of Karlovy Vary and 160km (100 miles) west of Prague.

While the spa town stands in the shadow of the Czech Republic's most famous spa town, Karlovy Vary, it wasn't always that way. First mentioned in 1528, the town's mineral waters gained prominence at the end of the 18th century and the beginning of the 19th. Nestled among forested hills and packed with romantic and elegant pastel hotels and spa houses, the town, commonly known by its German name, Marienbad, has played host to such luminaries as Goethe (where his love for Ulrika von Levetzow took root), Mark Twain, composers Chopin, Strauss, and Wagner, as well as Freud and Kafka. England's Edward VII found the spa resort so enchanting he visited nine times and even commissioned the building of the country's first golf club.

ESSENTIALS

GETTING THERE   By Train   The express train from Prague costs 165Kč ($4.85) for first class; 110Kč ($3.25) for second class (trip time: 3 hours). Mariánské Lázně train station, Nádražní nám. 292 (☎ **0165/625 321**), is south of the town center; take bus 5 into town.

By Bus   The 3-hour bus trip from Prague costs 120Kč ($3.65). The Mariánské Lázně bus station is adjacent to the train station on Nádražní náměstí; take bus 5 into town. Thre buses run daily between Prague and Marianske Lazne. Eight trains run to Marianske Lazne from Prague every 2 to 3 hours beginning at 6am with the last train leaving Prague just after 10pm.

By Car   Driving from Prague, take E-50 through Plzeň to Stříbro—about 22km (14 miles) past Plzeň—and head northwest on highway 21. The clearly marked route can take up to 2 hours. From Karlovy Vary, the trip is about 80km (50 miles). Take highway 20 south and then turn right onto highway 24 in the town of Bečov.

VISITOR INFORMATION   Along the main strip lies **Infocentrum KaSS,** Dům Chopin, Hlavní 47, 353 01, Mariánské Lázně (☎ and fax **0165/622 474**). In addition to dispensing advice, the staff sells maps and concert tickets and can arrange accommodations in hotels and private homes. It's open Monday to Friday 7am to 7pm, Saturday and Sunday 9am to 6pm.

SPECIAL EVENTS   Mariánské Lázně honors one of its frequent visitors, Chopin, with a yearly festival devoted to the Polish composer and his works. The **Chopin Festival** usually runs for 8 to 10 days near the end of August. Tickets range from 70Kč to 1,500Kč ($2.05 to $44).

Each June, the town also plays host to a **classical music festival** featuring many of the Czech Republic's finest musicians, as well as those from around the world. For more information or ticket reservations for either event, contact **Infocentrum KaSS** (see "Visitor Information," above).

Patriotic Americans can show up on **July 4** for a little down-home fun, including a parade and other flag-waving special events commemorating the town's liberation by U.S. soldiers in World War II.

WHERE TO STAY

The main strip along **Hlavní třída** is lined with hotels, many with rooms facing the colonnade. If you feel comfortable about doing this, I suggest walking the street and shopping around for a room; most hotels charge from 2,000Kč to 3,500Kč ($58 to $102) for a double May to September. Off-season prices can fall by as much as half.

For private accommodations, try **Palackého ulice,** running south of the main spa area.

Hotel Golf. Zádub 55, 353 01 Mariánské Lázně. ☎ **0165/622 651.** Fax 0165/622 655. 28 units. MINIBAR TV TEL. 2,278–3,604Kč ($67–$106) double; 4,318–5,576Kč ($127–$164) suite. Rates include breakfast. AE, DC, MC, V.

One of the more luxurious hotels, the Golf isn't actually in town but across from the golf course about 3km (2 miles) down the road leading to Karlovy Vary. This hotel is busy, so reservations are recommended. The English-speaking staff delivers on its pledge to cater to every wish. Rooms are bright and spacious—but sparsely decorated and far from luxurious—a hangover from the Communist era when golf was considered taboo in the worker's paradise. There's an excellent restaurant and terrace on the first floor. Not surprisingly, the staff can help arrange a quick 18 holes across the street. The hotel has also recently opened its own spa center. In the winter, the golf course is used freely by cross-country skiers.

✪ **Hotel Koliba.** Dusíkova 592, 353 01 Mariánské Lázně. ☎ **0165/625 169.** Fax 0165/763 10. 10 units. MINIBAR TV TEL. 1,200–1,470Kč ($35–$43) double. AE, MC, V.

Away from the main strip but still only a 7-minute walk from the colonnade, the Koliba is a rustic hunting lodge set in the hills on Dusíkova, the road leading to the golf course and Karlovy Vary. The rooms are very comfortable. The hotel offers a wide array of spa and health treatments, which cost extra. A small hill directly outside the hotel, serviced by two ski lifts, is perfect for teaching the children how to ski or for a romantic cross-country skiing weekend. The restaurant is a good choice for lunch or dinner (see "Where to Dine," below).

Hotel Palace. Hlavní třída 67, 353 01 Mariánské Lázně. ☎ **0165/622 222.** Fax 0165/624 262. 45 units. MINIBAR TV TEL. 2,150–3,570 Kč ($63–$105) double; 2,810–5,100 ($82–$150) suite. AE, DC, MC, V.

The 1920s Palace is a beautiful art nouveau hotel just 90m (300 feet) from the colonnade. Rooms are not tremendously spacious, but they're comfortable and tastefully, almost regally, decorated with early 20th-century furniture and lavish curtains and chandeliers. In addition to a good Bohemian restaurant with one of the nicest terraces in town, there's a cafe, wine room, and snack bar.

Hotel Villa Butterfly. Hlavní třída 72, 353 01 Mariánské Lázně. ☎ **0165/626 201.** Fax 0165/626 210. 94 units. MINIBAR TV TEL. 2,100–3,300Kč ($61–$97) double; 3,250–5,400Kč ($95–$158) suite; 4,500–7,200Kč ($132–$211) apt. Rates include breakfast. AE, DC, MC, V.

The Butterfly has upgraded its rather ordinary rooms into 94 first-rate spacious living quarters. In fact, from the front hall to the fitness room and down to its underground parking, the Butterfly has really taken off. Oddly enough, the renovations have had a reverse effect on the hotel's prices, now a good 15% lower. An English-speaking staff and a good selection of foreign-language newspapers at the reception are added bonuses, as is one of the better cups of coffee in town at the ground floor cafe.

Hotel Zvon. Hlavní třída 68, 353 01 Mariánské Lázně. ☎ **0165/622 015.** Fax 0165/623 245. 79 units. MINIBAR TV TEL. 1,720–4,720Kč ($50–$139) double; 2,370–8,460Kč ($69–$248) suite. AE, DC, MC, V.

Next to the Palace, in a prime spot directly across from the colonnade, the Zvon lacks a bit of the panache that its smaller neighbor has, but it still ranks as one of the town's nicer hotels. Ask for a room facing the Kolonada. Not only is the view spectacular, rooms on this side tend to be larger and brighter.

WHERE TO DINE

Churchill Club Restaurant. Hlavní třída 121. ☎ **0165/622 705.** Main courses 150–400Kč ($4.40–$12). AE, MC, V. Daily 11am–11pm. CZECH.

A lively bar atmosphere makes the Churchill one of the few fun places to be after dark. Don't let the name fool you—the food is traditional Czech with few surprises, which is both good and bad. A large selection of beers also sets the Churchill apart from other places along the main strip.

✪ **Hotel Koliba Restaurant.** Dusíkova 592. ☎ **0165/625 169.** Reservations recommended. Main courses 85–385Kč ($2.50–$11). No credit cards. Daily 11am–11pm. CZECH.

Like the hotel it occupies, the Koliba restaurant is a shrine to the outdoors. The rustic dining room, centered on an open fire grill, boasts a hearty rustic atmosphere that goes perfectly with the restaurant's strength: wild game. Check the daily menu to see what's new or choose from the wide assortment of specialties *na roštu* (from the grill), including wild boar and venison. The second room off the dining area makes for a great lunch stop, especially on a cold winter day when the fireplace is roaring.

Restaurant Fontaine. In the Villa Butterfly, Hlavní třída 72. ☎ **0165/626 201.** Main courses 90–300Kč ($2.65–$9). AE, DC, MC, V. Daily 6–11pm. CZECH/INTERNATIONAL.

The restaurant has undergone a major transformation for the better. The dining room is large but remains quiet, although a little too well lit. Bow-tied waiters serve traditional Bohemian specialties, like succulent roast duck, boiled trout, and chateaubriand, as well as some inventive variations such as shark.

TAKING THE WATERS AT MARIÁNSKÉ LÁZNĚ

When walking through the town, it's almost impossible to miss the **Lázeňská kolonáda,** just off Skalníkovy sady. From Hlavní třída, walk east on Vrchlického ulice. Recently restored to its former glory, the eye-catching cast-iron and glass colonnade is adorned with ceiling frescoes and Corinthian columns. Built in 1889, it connects a half-dozen major springs in the town center; this is the focal point of those partaking in the ritual. Bring a cup to fill or, if you want to fit in with the thousands of guests who are serious about their spa water, buy one of the porcelain mugs with a built-in straw that are offered just about everywhere. Do keep in mind that the waters are used to treat internal disorders, so the minerals may act to cleanse the body thoroughly. You can wander the colonnade any time; water is distributed daily 6am to noon and 4 to 6pm.

For a relaxing mineral bubble bath or massage, make reservations through the **Spa Information Service,** Mírové nám. 104, 353 29, Mariánské Lázně (☎ **0165/655 555** or 0165/655 550; fax 0165/655 500). Also ask your hotel about spa treatments and massages they offer or can arrange. Treatments cost from 300Kč ($9) and up.

More to See & Do

There's not much town history, since Mariánské Lázně officially came into existence only in 1808, but engaging brevity is what makes the two-story **Muzeum hlavního města (City Museum),** Goetheovo nám. 11 (☎ **0165/622 740**), recommendable. Chronologically arranged displays include photos and documents of famous visitors. Goethe slept in the upstairs rooms in 1823, when he was 74 years old. If you ask nicely, the museum guards will play an English-language tape that describes the contents of each of the rooms. You can also request to see the museum's English-language film about the town. Admission is 20Kč (60¢), and it's open Tuesday to Sunday 9am to 4pm.

You can also take a walk in the woods. The surrounding **Slavkovský les (Slavkov Forest)** has about 70km (45 miles) of marked footpaths and trails through the area's gentle hills.

The **Mariánské Lázně Golf Club** (☎ **0165/624 300**), a 6,195m (6,775-yard), par-72 championship course, lies on the edge of town. The club takes pay-as-you-play golfers, and a fully equipped pro shop rents clubs. Greens fees are 1,200Kč ($35) and club rental is 500Kč ($15).

ČESKÉ BUDĚJOVICE

This fortress town was born in 1265, when Otakar II decided that the intersection point of the Vltava and Malše rivers would be the perfect site to protect the approaches to southern Bohemia. Although Otakar was killed at the battle of the Moravian Field in 1278, and the town subsequently ravaged by the rival Vítkovic family, the construction of České Budějovice continued, eventually taking the shape originally envisaged.

Today, České Budějovice, hometown of the original Budweiser brand beer, is more a bastion for the beer drinker than a protector of Bohemia. But its slow pace, relaxed atmosphere, and interesting architecture make it a worthy stop, especially as a base for exploring southern Bohemia or for those heading on to Austria.

Essentials

GETTING THERE   By Train   Daily express trains from Prague make the trip to České Budějovice in about 2¹/₂ hours. The fare is 165Kč ($4.85) first class or 110Kč ($3.25) second class.

By Bus   Several express buses run from Prague's Florenc station each day, taking 2 hours and costing 109Kč ($3.20).

By Car   Leave Prague to the south via the main D-1 expressway and take the cutoff for Highway E-55, which runs straight to České Budějovice (trip time: 1¹/₂ hours).

VISITOR INFORMATION   Tourist Infocentrum, náměstí Přemysla Otakara II 2 (☎ and fax **038/635 9480**), provides maps and guidebooks and finds lodging.

SPECIAL EVENTS   Each August, České Budějovice hosts the largest **International Agricultural Show,** the country's massive "state fair."

Where to Stay

Several agencies can locate reasonably priced private rooms. Expect to pay about 500 Kč ($15) per person, in cash. **Tourist Infocentrum** (see "Visitor Information," above) can point you toward a wide selection of conveniently located rooms and pensions.

Hotel Malý Pivovar (Small Brewery). Ulice Karla IV 8–10, 370 01 České Budějovice. ☎ **038/636 0471.** Fax 038/636 0474. E-mail: budvar.hotel@cbu.pvtnet.cz. 28 units. MINIBAR TV TEL. 1,890–2,450Kč ($56–$72) double; 1,690–2,750Kč ($50–$81) suite. Rates include breakfast. AE, MC, V.

Around the corner from the Zvon (see below), a renovated 16th-century microbrewery combines the charms of a B&B with the amenities of a modern hotel. Rooms are bright and cheery, with antique-style wooden furniture. Exposed wooden ceiling beams lend a farmhouse feel in the center of town. It's definitely worth consideration if being only 30m (100 feet) from the square isn't a problem.

Hotel Zvon. Náměstí Přemysla Otakara II 28, 370 42 České Budějovice. ☎ **038/731 1384.** Fax 038/731 1385. www.hotel-zvon.cz. 75 units. MINIBAR TV TEL. 1,450–2,900Kč ($43–$85) double; 1,800–3,800Kč ($53–$112) suite. AE, DC, MC, V.

Location is everything for the city's most elegant hotel, which occupies several historic buildings on the main square. Upper-floor rooms have been renovated and tend to be more expensive, especially those with a view of the square, which aren't only brighter, they're larger and nicer, too. Others are relatively plain and functional. Try to avoid the smaller rooms, usually reserved for tour groups. There's no elevator, but if you don't mind the climb, stay on the fourth floor. One of the biggest changes here in recent years has been the staff, which seems to be learning that guests like respect and quality treatment.

WHERE TO DINE

Masné Krámy (Meat Shops). Krajinská 29. ☎ **038/633 7957.** Main courses 85–180Kč ($2.50–$5). No credit cards. Daily 10am–11pm. CZECH.

If you've pledged not to go to any "tourist traps," you might make an exception for this one housed in a historic building. Just northwest of náměstí Přemysla Otakara II, labyrinthine Masné Krámy occupies a series of drinking rooms on either side of a long hall, and is a must for any serious pub-goer. The inexpensive and filling food is pure Bohemia, including several pork, duck, and trout dishes. Come for the boisterous atmosphere, or for what's possibly the best goulash in the Czech Republic.

U paní Emy. Široká 25. No phone. Main courses 69–200Kč ($2.05–$6). No credit cards. Daily 10am–3am. CZECH/INTERNATIONAL.

Usually crowded, U paní Emy has a good selection on the menu, with reasonable prices for both food and beverages. The chicken and fish dishes are the most popular. The panfried trout tastes very light, not oily as most Czech restaurants tend to make it. A wine bar here stays open to the wee hours.

EXPLORING THE TOWN

You can comfortably see České Budějovice in a day. At its center is one of central Europe's largest squares, the cobblestoned **náměstí Přemysla Otakara II.** The square contains the ornate **Fountain of Sampson,** an 18th-century water well that was once the town's principal water supply, plus a mishmash of baroque and Renaissance buildings. On the southwest corner is the **town hall,** an elegant baroque structure built by Martinelli between 1727 and 1730. On top of the town hall, the larger-than-life statues by Dietrich represent the civic virtues: justice, bravery, wisdom, and diligence.

One block northwest of the square is the **Černá věž (Black Tower),** visible from almost every point in the city. Its 360 steps are worth the climb to get a bird's-eye view in all directions. The most famous symbol of České Budějovice, the 70m (232-foot) 16th-century tower was built as a belfry for the adjacent **St. Nicholas Church.** This 13th-century church, one of the town's most important sights, was a bastion of Roman Catholicism during the 15th-century Hussite rebellion. You shouldn't miss the flamboyant white-and-cream 17th-century baroque interior.

Keeping Up with the Schwarzenbergs: Visiting a 141-Room English Castle

Only 8km (5 miles) north from České Budějovice lies **Hluboká nad Vltavou.** The distance is short enough to make a pleasant bike trip from the city or a quick stop on the way to, or coming from, Prague, Třeboň, or Tábor. The castle is open from April to October Tuesday to Sunday from 10am to 5:30pm. Tours in English run at 11am and 2 and 4pm and cost 75Kč ($2.20).

Built in the 13th century, Hluboká has undergone many face-lifts over the years, but none that left as lasting an impression as those ordered by the Schwarzenberg family. As a sign of the region's growing wealth and importance in the mid–19th century, the Schwarzenbergs remodeled the 141-room castle in the neo-Gothic style of England's Windsor Castle. Robin Leach would be proud; no expense was spared. The Schwartzenbergs removed the impressive wooden ceiling from their residence at Český Krumlov and reinstalled it in the large dining room. Other rooms are equally garish in their appointments, making a guided tour worth the time, even though only about a third of the rooms are open to the public.

To complete the experience, the **Alšova Jihočeská Galerie (Art Gallery of South Bohemia),** in the riding school at Hluboká, houses the second-largest art collection in Bohemia, including many interesting Gothic sculptures from the area.

If you're driving to Hluboká from České Budějovice, take Highway E-49 north and then Highway 105 just after leaving the outskirts of České Budějovice. For cyclists or drivers who prefer a slower, more scenic route, take the road that runs behind the brewery; it passes through the village of Obora.

TOURING A BEER SHRINE

On the town's northern edge sits a shrine for those who pray to the gods of the amber nectar. This is where it all began, where **Budějovický Budvar,** the original brewer of Budweiser brand beer, has its one and only factory. Established in 1895, Budvar draws on more than 700 years of Bohemian brewing tradition to produce one of the world's best beers. Contact Budvar n.p., Karolíny Světlé 4, České Budějovice (☎ **038/770 5340**).

Trolley buses 2, 4, 6, and 8 stop by the brewery; this is how it ensures that its workers and visitors reach the plant safely each day. The trolley costs 8Kč (25¢) to the brewery. You can also hop a cab from the town square for about 100Kč to 150Kč ($2.95 to $4.40).

Tours can be arranged by phoning ahead, but only for groups. If you're traveling alone or with only one or two other people, ask a hotel concierge at one of the bigger hotels (we suggest the Zvon) if he or she can put you in with an already scheduled group. Failing that, you might want to take a chance and head up to the brewery, where, if a group has arrived, another person or two won't be noticed.

PLZEŇ (PILSEN)

Some 400 years ago, a group of men formed Plzeň's first beer-drinking guild, and today, beer is probably the only reason you'll want to stop at this industrial town 90km (55 miles) southwest of Prague. Alas, the town's prosperity and architecture were ravaged during World War II, leaving few buildings untouched. The main square, náměstí Republiky, is worth a look, but after that, there's not much to see.

ESSENTIALS

GETTING THERE   By Train   It's more comfortable taking the train to Plzeň than the bus, although a lot slower now that the motorway connects the city to Prague (trip time: 2 hours). Trains between the two cities are plentiful and fit most every schedule. Fare costs 111Kč ($3.25) first class or 74Kč ($2.20) second. To get from the train station to town, walk out the main entrance and take Americká street across the river, and then turn right onto Jungmannova, which leads to the main square.

By Bus   The bus from Prague costs 69Kč ($2) but tends to be cramped (trip time: 1 hour). If you do take the bus, head back into town along Husova to get to the square.

By Car   A newly finished highway makes the drive between Prague and Plzeň, one of the few worry-free trips a motorist can make in the country. Go west from Prague on D-5 (trip time: 40 minutes).

VISITOR INFORMATION   The **City Information Center Plzeň,** náměstí Republiky 41, 301 16 Plzeň (☎ **019/723 6535;** fax 019/722 4473), is packed with literature to answer travelers' questions. A helpful, multilingual staff will also point you in the right direction. Open Monday to Friday 10am to 5pm, Saturday and Sunday 10am to 3:30pm.

SPECIAL EVENTS   If you're an American, or speak English, being in Plzeň in May is quite an experience. On May 8, Gen. George S. Patton was forced to halt his advance after liberating the area, in accordance with an Allied agreement. The Russians were then allowed to liberate Prague. Forty years of communist oppression, however, means that the town now celebrates May 8 or **Liberation Day** with a vengeance. Although the celebrations have cooled some from the heady days just after the Velvet Revolution of 1989, you'll still be feted and praised into the wee hours, as the city's people give thanks to the forces that ended Nazi occupation.

Anxious to capitalize on its beer heritage and always happy to celebrate, Plzeň has started its own Oktoberfest, called **Pivní slavnosti.**

WHERE TO STAY

For private rooms that are usually outside the town center but a little cheaper, try **Čedok** at Sedláčkova 12 (☎ **019/723 7419;** fax 019/722 3703), open Monday to Friday 9am to noon and 1 to 5pm (to 6pm in summer) and Saturday 9am to noon. Expect to pay about 500Kč to 1,000Kč ($15 to $29) for a double.

Hotel Central. Náměstí Republiky 33, 305 28 Plzeň. ☎ **019/722 6059.** Fax 019/722 6064. 50 units. TV. 1,250Kč ($37) double. AE, MC, V.

This rather sterile building is across from St. Bartholomew's Church and has generously given itself a four-star rating. The surly staff notwithstanding, it is clean and quiet for such a central location. Rooms are very plain, but beds are surprisingly comfortable. With few choices around, you could do worse than the Central.

Interhotel Continental. Zbrojnická 8, 305 34 Plzeň. ☎ **019/723 6479.** Fax 019/722 1746. 55 units (10 with shared shower/bathroom, 20 with private shower only, 25 with private bathroom). TV TEL. 850Kč ($25) double without bathroom; 1,590Kč ($47) double with shower only; 2,150Kč ($63) double with bathroom; 3,700Kč ($109) deluxe double. AE, MC, V.

About a block from the old town square, the modern Continental is considered by locals to be one of the best in town, but keep in mind that there's not much to choose from. Rooms are spacious and comfortable.

WHERE TO DINE

Městařská Beseda. Smetanovy sady 13. ☎ **019/723 6667.** Main courses 39–149Kč ($1.15–$4.40). MC, V. Sun–Thurs 10am–11pm; Fri–Sat 10am–midnight. CZECH/ CONTINENTAL.

The high ceilings and wall murals add a touch of elegance to this large restaurant frequented by the theater crowd. The prices are reasonable for the center, but the meals are unimaginative. It's a great place to stop for a late-evening coffee and some strudel or a nightcap.

Pilsner Urquell Restaurant. U Prazdroje 1 (just outside the brewery gates). No phone. Main courses 65–220Kč ($1.95–$7). AE, MC, V. Mon–Sat 10am–10pm. CZECH.

This isn't a visitor-oriented pub; in the same building that houses the brewery's management, the pub has remained true to its beer suppliers by cooking hearty basic Czech meals, although it has become a little pricey.

Restaurace Na Spilce (At the fermenting cellar). U Prazdroje (just inside the brewery gates). ☎ **019/706 2754.** Main courses 32–195Kč (95¢–$6). AE, MC, V. Mon–Thurs 11am–10pm; Fri–Sat 11am–11pm; Sun 11am–9pm. CZECH.

The Na Spilce looks like a 600-seat tourist trap, but the food is quite good and reasonably priced. The standard *řízky* (schnitzels), goulash, and *svíčková na smetaně* (pork tenderloin in cream sauce) are hearty and complement the beer that flows from the brewery. If you've got a big appetite or just can't decide, try the Plzeňská bašta, with ample servings of roasted pork, smoked pork, sausage, sauerkraut, and two kinds of dumplings.

EXPLORING PLZEŇ

Founded in 1295 by Přemysl King Václav II, Plzeň was, and remains, western Bohemia's administrative center. Václav's real gift to the town, however, was granting it brewing rights. As a result, more than 200 microbreweries popped up in almost every street-corner basement. Realizing the brews they were drinking had become mostly inferior by the late 1830s, rebellious beer drinkers started demanding quality from their brewers. "Give us what we want in Plzeň, good and cheap beer!" became the battle cry. By 1842, the brewers had combined their expertise to produce a superior brew through what became known as the Pilsner brewing method.

Plzeňský Prazdroj (Pilsner Breweries), at U Prazdroje 7, will interest anyone who wants to learn more about the brewing process. It's actually made up of several breweries, pumping out brands like Pilsner Urquell and Gambrinus, the most widely consumed beer in the Czech Republic. The 1-hour tour of the factory (which has barely changed since its creation) includes a 15-minute film and visits to the fermentation cellars and brewing rooms. The tour is at 12:30pm Monday to Saturday. It costs 30Kč (90¢) Monday to Friday and 50Kč ($1.45) Saturday; the price includes a dozen beer-oriented postcards and a tasting of some freshly brewed beer (for details on other tours available, call ☎ **019/706 2017**).

If you didn't get your fill of beer facts at the brewery, the **Pivovarské muzeum (Beer Museum)** (☎ **019/722 4955;** fax 019/723 5574), is 1 block away on Veleslavínova. Inside this former 15th-century house, you'll learn everything there is to know about beer but were afraid to ask. In the first room, once a 19th-century pub, the guard winds up an old German polyphone music box from 1887 that plays the sweet though scratchy strains of Strauss's *Blue Danube.* Subsequent rooms display a wide collection of pub artifacts, brewing equipment, and mugs. Most displays have English captions, but ask for a more detailed museum description in English when you enter. Admission is 30Kč (90¢), and it's open Tuesday to Sunday 10am to 6pm.

Now full of more brewing knowledge than you might have wanted, proceed to the main square to see what's hopping (sorry, we couldn't resist). Dominating the center is the Gothic **Cathedral of St. Bartholomew,** boasting the tallest steeple in the Czech Republic at 100m (333 feet). Inside the church, a beautiful marble Madonna graces the main altar.

You'll see an Italian flair to the first four floors of the 16th-century **Town Hall** and in the *sgrafitto* adorning its facade. Later on, more floors were added, as well as a tower, gables, and brass flags, creating the illusion that another building had just fallen on top of the original. In front of the town hall, a 1681 **memorial** commemorates victims of the plague.

Just west of the square on Sady pětatřicátníků lies the shattered dreams of the 2,000 or so Jews who once called Plzeň home. The **Great Synagogue,** the world's third largest, was built in the late 19th century. Sadly, its doors remain locked, although funds are being raised to support urgent repairs.

CHEB (EGER) & FRANTIŠKOVY LÁZNĚ (FRANZENSBAD)

As with Plzeň, few people who travel through Cheb, 170km (105 miles) west of Prague and 40km (25 miles) southwest of Karlovy Vary, actually stop and look around. From the outside, that's understandable, but it's too bad. The center of Cheb is one of the more architecturally interesting places in west Bohemia, and its history is fascinating as well.

A former stronghold for the Holy Roman Empire on its eastern flank, Eger, as it was then known, became part of Bohemia in 1322. Cheb stayed under Bohemian rule until it was handed to Germany as part of the 1938 Munich Pact. After World War II, it returned to Czech hands, when most of the area's native Germans, known as Sudeten Germans, were expelled for their open encouragement of the invading Nazis. This bilingual, bicultural heritage can be seen in the town's main square, which could easily sit on either side of the border if it weren't for the Czech writing on the windows. These days, the Germans have returned, but only for a few hours at a time, many for the town's thriving sex trade and cheap alcohol. Don't be surprised to see women around almost every corner looking to ply their trade. Still, Cheb is worth exploring for its melange of architectural styles, the eerie Jewish quarter Špalíček, and the enormous Romanesque Chebský Hrad (Cheb Castle).

Only about 20 minutes up the road from Cheb is the smallest of the three major west Bohemian spa towns, **Františkovy Lázně (Franzensbad).** Although it pales in comparison to Karlovy Vary and Mariánské Lázně, Františkovy Lázně has taken great strides in the past few years to try to erase the decline it experienced under communism. There's not much to see save for the **Spa Museum,** which holds an interesting display of bathing artifacts, but it's a much quieter and cleaner place to spend the night than Cheb.

To get to Františkovy Lázně from Cheb by car, take E-49 (trip time: 20 minutes). You can also take a taxi; just agree with the driver before you get in that the fare won't be more than 250Kč ($7).

ESSENTIALS

GETTING THERE   By Train   Express trains from Prague usually stop in Cheb, as do several trains daily from Karlovy Vary. Cheb is on a main train route, so it's easy to catch many international connections here. The train costs 195Kč ($6) first class and 130Kč ($3.80) second class (trip time: 3½ hours).

By Bus   Cheb is a long bus ride from Prague, and I suggest avoiding it if possible. It's more manageable to take the bus from Karlovy Vary to Cheb.

By Car   Cheb is located on E-48, one of the main highways leading to Germany. If you're driving from Prague, take the same route as you would to Karlovy Vary, which eventually brings you to Cheb (trip time: $2^1/_2$ hours).

VISITOR INFORMATION   You'll find maps, guidebooks, lodging, and even a currency exchange (at a fairly steep price, so use it only if desperate) at the **Informační Centrum Goetz & Hanzlík,** náměstí Přemysla Otakara II 2 (☎ **0166/459 480;** fax 0166/459 291).

WHERE TO STAY

Hotel Hvězda. Náměstí Krále Jiřího z Poděbrad 4, 350 01 Cheb. ☎ **0166/422 549.** Fax 0166/422 546. 44 units. TV TEL. 1,150Kč ($34) double. AE, MC, V.

Overlooking the rather noisy main square, the Hvězda is a lone star in the Cheb hotel universe. Small but clean rooms make it bearable, and the staff tries to make your stay comfortable. If you can't stay in Františkovy Lázně and don't want to drive farther, this is really the only hotel we'd recommend in town.

Hotel Tři lilie. Jiráskova 17, 351 01 Františkovy Lázně. ☎ **0166/942 350.** Fax 0166/942 970. 32 units. TV TEL. 3,250Kč ($96) double; 4,700Kč ($138) suite. AE, MC, V.

In 1808, Goethe stayed here, and he knew what he was doing. The Three Lilies is worth the extra money since it's only luxury hotel in the area. Cheb needs a nice hotel like this. You can relax here; the spotless, spacious, well-appointed rooms block out any noise. The staff is very attentive and can arrange spa treatments, massages, and other health services. On the main floor is a nice, but a bit pricey, bar and restaurant.

WHERE TO DINE

Restaurace Fortuna. Náměstí Krále Jiřího z Poděbrad 29. ☎ **0166/422 110.** Main courses 79–185Kč ($2.30–$5). No credit cards. Daily 10am–2am. CZECH.

If you need to have one last schnitzel before leaving, this is as good a place as any. The food is uniformly good but not great, with most Czech specialties accounted for. It's one of the only restaurants open late, and a terrace right on the main square lends to its appeal.

Staročeská Restaurace. Kamenná 1. No phone. Main courses 69–190Kč ($2.05–$6). No credit cards. Daily 10am–10pm. CZECH/CHINESE.

This restaurant serves much the same fare as all the other restaurants on or around the square, but what caught my eye were the few Chinese meals offered. The *kuře kung-pao* (kung pao chicken) was a good spicy alternative to the sausages, meat, and dumplings most of the other diners were having.

EXPLORING CHEB

The main square, **náměstí Krále Jiřího z Poděbrad,** attracts most of the attention, and is a good place to begin a tour of the old town. Although it has been overrun with touristy shops and cafes that serve mediocre German fare, the square still shines with Gothic burgher houses and the baroque **old town hall (stará radnice).** At its south end, the **statue of Kašna Roland,** erected in 1591, is a former symbol of capital punishment, reminding people of the strength justice can wield. At the other end of the square stands the **Kašna Herkules,** a monument to the town's former strength and power. Next to it is a cluster of 11 timber houses, called **Špalíček.** These houses used to be owned by Jews in the early 14th century, but a fervently anti-Semitic clergy in the area incited such hatred against them that they were forced into an alley now called ulička Zavražděných (Murder Victim's Lane), where they were unceremoniously slaughtered in 1350.

Across from Špalíček is the **Cheb Museum** (☎ **0166/422 246**), where another murder took place almost 300 years later in 1634—that of Albrecht von Wallenstein, a major player in the Thirty Years' War and hero of a dramatic trilogy by Schiller. On the upper level a display vividly depicts the assassination. The museum's first floor displays many 20th-century paintings from which you can trace the town's slow demise. Admission is 25Kč (75¢), and it's open Tuesday to Sunday 9am to noon and 1 to 5pm.

The old town of Cheb is also packed with several churches. The most interesting is **St. Nicholas,** around the corner from the museum. It's a hodgepodge of architectural styles: Romanesque tower windows, a Gothic portal, and a baroque interior.

TOURING CHEB CASTLE

An excellent example of Romanesque architecture is **Cheb Castle,** in the northeast part of the old town. Overlooking the Elbe River, the late 12th-century castle is one of central Europe's largest Romanesque structures.

The castle's main draws are its **chapel of Sts. Erhard and Ursala** and the **Černá věž (Black Tower).** The two-tiered early Gothic chapel has a somber first floor where the proletariat would congregate, while the emperor and his family enjoyed the much cheerier and brighter second floor with its Gothic windows. Alas, there are no tours of the castle, and the English text provided at the entrance does little to inform you. Admission is 50Kč ($1.45). It's open Tuesday to Sunday: June to August 9am to noon and 1 to 6pm, May and September 9am to noon and 1 to 5pm, and April and October 9am to noon and 1 to 4pm.

Across the courtyard from the chapel stands the **Černá věž (Black Tower).** From its 18m (60-foot) lookout, you can see the best views of the town. The tower seems dusty and smeared with pollution, but its color isn't from the emissions of the Trabants and Škodas that drive through the streets. Rather, the tower is black because it's actually made from lava rocks taken from the nearby Komorní Hůrka volcano (now dormant).

Denmark 4

by Darwin Porter & Danforth Prince

In this chapter, we've concentrated on Copenhagen, Denmark's capital, and added a few important side trips you can take in a day or two. The name for Copenhagen came from the word *københavn,* meaning "merchants' harbor." This city grew in size and importance due to its position on the Øresund (the Sound) between Denmark and Sweden, guarding the entrance to the Baltic. From its humble beginnings, Copenhagen has become the largest city in Scandinavia, home to 1.5 million people.

In summer 2000, Denmark was linked to Sweden by the 16km (10-mile) Øresund Bridge. The two cities of Copenhagen and Malmö (in Sweden) are the hubs of the Øresund Region, northern Europe's largest domestic market, larger than Stockholm and equal in size to Berlin, Hamburg, and Amsterdam. At a cost of $3 billion, the bridge is the longest combined rail-and-road bridge in the world.

Copenhagen

Copenhagen is a city with much charm, as reflected in its canals, narrow streets, and old houses. Its most famous resident was Hans Christian Andersen, whose memory still lives on. Another of Copenhagen's world-renowned inhabitants was Søren Kierkegaard, who used to take long morning strolls in the city, planning his next essay; his completed writings eventually earned him the title "father of existentialism."

But few modern Copenhageners are reading Kierkegaard today, and neither are they as melancholy as Hamlet. Most of them are out having too much fun. Copenhagen epitomizes a Nordic joie de vivre, and the city is filled with a lively atmosphere, good times (none better than at the Tivoli Gardens), sex shows, countless outdoor cafes, and all-night dance clubs. Of course, if you come in winter, the fierce realities of living above the 55th parallel set in. That's when Copenhageners retreat inside their smoky jazz clubs and beer taverns.

Modern Copenhagen still retains some of the characteristics of a village. If you forget the suburbs, you can cover most of the central belt on foot, which makes it a great tourist spot. It's almost as if the city were designed for pedestrians, as reflected by its Strøget (strolling street), Europe's longest and oldest walking street.

Copenhagen

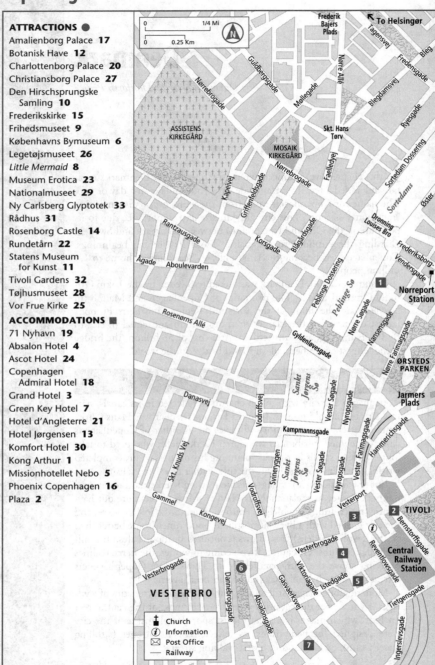

✝ Church
ⓘ Information
✉ Post Office
— Railway

VESTERBRO

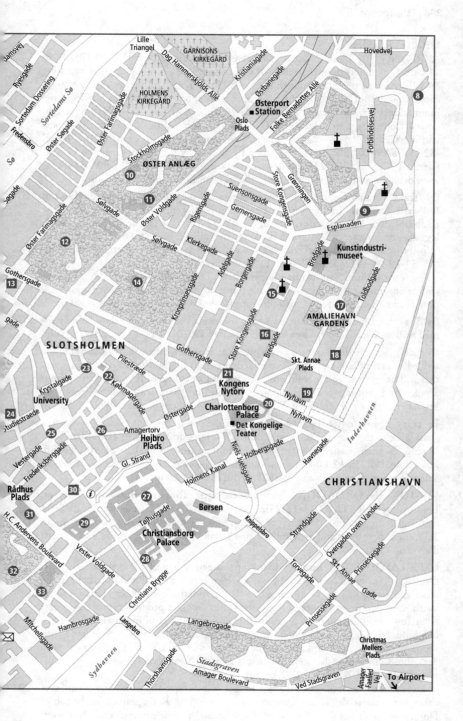

ORIENTATION

ARRIVING   By Plane   When you arrive at **Kastrup Airport** (☎ 70-10-20-00) 11.5km (7¹/₄ miles) from the center of Copenhagen, you can reduce costs by taking an SAS coach to the city terminal; the fare is 35DKK ($5). A taxi to the city center costs around 130DKK ($19). Even cheaper is local bus no. 250S, leaving from the international arrivals terminal every 15 to 20 minutes for the Town Hall Square in central Copenhagen and costing 15DKK ($2.15). Air/rail links connect the airport with the Central Railway Station. The ride takes only 11 minutes, costing 16.40DKK ($2.35). **SAS** (☎ 800/221/2350; www.flysas.com) is the major carrier to Copenhagen. **TWA** (☎ 800/221-2000; www.twa.com) and **Delta** (☎ 800/241-4141; www.delta-air.com) have daily nonstop flights from New York's JFK airport.

By Train   Trains from the continent arrive at the **Hoved Banegård (Central Railroad Station),** in the very center of Copenhagen, near the Tivoli and the Rådhuspladsen. For **rail information,** call ☎ 33-14- 17-01. The station operates a luggage-checking service but room bookings are available only at the tourist office (see "Visitor Information" below). You can also exchange money at the **Den Danske Bank** (☎ 33-12-04-11), open daily 8am to 8pm.

From the Central Railroad Station, you can connect with **S-tog,** the local subway, with trains leaving from platforms in the terminus itself. Ask at the information desk near Tracks 5 and 6 about which train you should board to reach your destination.

By Bus   Buses from Zealand or elsewhere in Denmark also pull into the Central Railroad Station (see above). For **bus information,** call ☎ 70-13-14-15 daily 8am to 7pm.

By Car   If you're driving from Germany, a car-ferry will take you from Travemünde to Gedser in southern Denmark. From Gedser, get on E-55 north, an express highway that will deliver you to the southern outskirts of Copenhagen. If you're coming from Sweden and crossing at Helsingborg, you'll land on the Danish side at Helsingør. From here, take express highway E-55 south to the northern outskirts of Copenhagen.

By Ferry   Most ferries land at Havnegade at the end of the south side of Nyhavn, a short walk to the center. Taxis also wait here for ferry arrivals. Most arrivals are from Malmö, Sweden; ferries from continental Europe usually land in South Zealand. Hydrofoils (☎ 33-12-80-88) arrive hourly during the day from Malmö, Sweden. The trip takes 40 minutes and costs 20 to 50DKK ($2.85 to $7).

VISITOR INFORMATION   The **Copenhagen Tourist Information Center,** Bernstorffsgade 1 (☎ 33-11-13-25), is across from Tivoli's main entrance. It's open September 16 to April, Monday to Friday 9am to 4:30pm and Saturday 9am to 1:30pm; May to June and September 1 to 15, daily 9am to 9pm; and July to August, daily 8am to 11pm.

CITY LAYOUT   The heart of Old Copenhagen is a maze of pedestrian streets, formed by Nørreport Station to the north, Town Hall Square (Rådhuspladsen) to the west, and Kongens Nytorv to the east, and the Inderhavnen (Inner Harbor) to the south. One continuous route, Strøget, the world's longest pedestrian street, goes east from Town Hall Square to Kongens Nytorv and is made up of five streets: Frederiksberggade, Nygade, Vimmelskaftet, Amagertorv, and Østergade. Strøget is lined with shops, bars, restaurants, and sidewalk cafes in summer. Pistolstraede, a narrow street a 3-minute walk west of Kongens Nytorv, is a maze of galleries, restaurants, and boutiques, all housed in restored 18th-century buildings.

Fiolstraede (Violet Street), a dignified street with antique shops and bookshops, cuts through the university (Latin Quarter). If you turn into Rosengaarden at the top of Fiolstraede, you'll come to **Kultorvet** (Coal Square) just before you reach Nørreport

Station. Here you join the third main pedestrian street, **Købmagergade** (Butcher Street), which winds around and finally meets Strøget on Amagertorv.

At the end of Strøget you approach **Kongens Nytorv** (King's Square), the site of the Royal Theater and Magasin, the largest department store. This will put you at the beginning of **Nyhavn,** the former seamen's quarter that has been gentrified into an upmarket area of expensive restaurants, apartments, cafes, and boutiques. The government of Denmark is centered on the small island of **Slotsholmen,** connected to the center by eight bridges. Several museums, notably Christiansborg Castle, are found here.

The center of Copenhagen is **Rådhuspladsen** (Town Hall Square). From here it's a short walk to the Tivoli Gardens, the major attraction, and the Central Railroad Station, the main railroad and subway terminus. The wide boulevard, **Vesterbrogade,** passes by Tivoli until it reaches the Central Railroad Station. Another major street is named after Denmark's most famous writer; **H. C. Andersens Boulevard,** runs along Rådhuspladsen and the Tivoli Gardens.

GETTING AROUND   A joint zone fare system includes Copenhagen Transport buses and State Railway and S-tog trains in Copenhagen and North Zealand, plus some private rail routes in a 40km (25-mile) radius of the capital, enabling you to transfer from train to bus and vice versa with the same ticket.

A *grundbillet* (basic ticket) for both buses and trains costs 11DKK ($1.55). You can buy 10 tickets for 75DKK ($11). Children under 12, half fare; those under 5 free on local trains, and those under 7 free on buses. You can purchase a ticket allowing 24-hour bus and train travel through nearly half of Zealand for 70DKK ($10); children 7 to 11 half price; children under 7 free.

Students who have an **International Student Identity Card (ISIC)** are entitled to a number of travel breaks. You can buy a card in the United States at any Council Travel office; for the office nearest you, call ☎ **800/GET-AN-ID.**

For information about low-cost train and plane trips, go to Waastels, Skoubogade 6 (☎ **33-14-46-33**). Hours are Monday to Friday 9am to 6pm and Saturday 11am to 3pm. Wasteels specializes in inexpensive travel by plane within Europe, and they also are the experts on special youth fares.

Eurailpasses and Nordturist Pass tickets are accepted on local trains.

By Bus   Copenhagen's well-maintained buses are the least expensive method of getting around. Most buses leave from Rådhuspladsen. A basic ticket allows 1 hour of travel and unlimited transfers within the zone where you started your trip. For information, call ☎ **36-13-14-45.**

By S-tog (Subway)   The S-tog connects heartland Copenhagen with its suburbs. Use of the tickets is the same as on buses (above). You can transfer from a bus line to an S-train on the same ticket. Eurailpass holders generally ride free. For more information, call ☎ **33-14-17-01** between 6:30am and 11pm.

By Car   It's best to park your car in any of the dozens of city parking lots, then retrieve it when you're ready to explore the capital's environs. Many parking lots are open 24 hours a day; a few others tend to close between 1am and 7am. Some close on Saturday afternoon and on Sunday during nonpeak business hours when traffic is presumably lighter. Costs tend to range from 22DKK ($3.15) per hour or 220DKK ($31) per 24 hours. Two of the most central parking lots are Industriens Hus, H. C. Andersens Blvd. 18 (☎ **33-91-21-75**), which is open Monday to Friday 7am to 12:45am and Saturday and Sunday 9am to 12:45am; and the more reasonable Statoil, Israels Plads (☎ **33-14-37-76**), open 24 hours.

A Traveler's Tip

The **Copenhagen Card** entitles you to free and unlimited travel by bus and rail throughout the metropolitan area (including North Zealand), 25% to 50% discounts on crossings to and from Sweden, and free admission to many sights and museums. The card is available for 1, 2, or 3 days and costs 155DKK ($22), 255DKK ($36), and 320DKK ($46), respectively. Children 11 and under are given a 50% discount. For more information, contact the Copenhagen Tourist Information Center (see above).

By Taxi   Watch for the *fri* (free) sign or green light to hail a taxi. Be sure the taxis are metered. Københavns Taxa (☎ **35-35-35-35**) operates the largest fleet of cabs. Tips are included in the meter price: 25DKK ($3.55) at the drop of the flag and 13DKK ($1.85) per kilometer thereafter, Monday to Friday 6am to 6pm. From 6pm to 6am and all day and night on Saturday and Sunday, the cost is 14DKK ($2) per kilometer. Basic drop-of-the-flag costs remain the same, however. Many drivers speak English.

By Bicycle   To reduce pollution from cars, Copenhageners ride bicycles. You can rent a bike at Københavns Cyklebors, Gothersgade 157, next to the botanical gardens (☎ **33-14-07-17**) for 40DKK ($6) per day or 185DKK ($26) per week. Shop hours are Monday to Friday 8:30am to 5:30pm and Saturday 10am to 1:30pm.

Fast Facts: Copenhagen

American Express   Its office, more limited than in other European capitals, offers only foreign exchange and customer service for Amex cardholders who lose their cards or need travel checks. Their office is care of **Nyman and Schultz,** Nørregade 7A, 3rd floor (☎ **33-12-23-01;** S-Tog: Nørreport). It's open Monday to Friday 9am to 5pm, Saturday 9am to noon.

Business Hours   Most **banks** are open Monday to Friday 9:30am to 4pm (Thursday to 6pm). **Stores** are generally open Monday to Thursday 9am to 5:30pm, Friday 9am to 7 or 8pm, and Saturday 9am to 2pm; most are closed Sunday.

Currency   The Danish currency is the **krone** (crown), or **DKK** in its plural form, made up of 100 **øre.** Banknotes are issued in 50, 100, 500, and 1,000DKK. Coins come in 25 and 50 øre, and 1, 2, 5, 10, and 20DKK; the 1-, 2-, and 5-krone coins have a hole in the center. The rate of exchange used in this chapter was $1 = 6.98DKK, or 1DKK = 15¢. The ratio of the British pound to the krone fluctuates constantly. At press time, £1 = approximately 11.54DKK (or 1DKK = 0.14 = 0.009p). The euro rate was currently fixed at 7.43DKK (or 1DKK = €0.14).

Currency Exchange   Banks are generally your best bet to exchange currency. When banks are closed, you can exchange money at **Forex** (☎ **33-11-29-05;** S-tog: Central Station) in the Central Railroad Station, open daily 8am to 9pm, or **The Change Group** (☎ **33-93-04-55;** bus 1, 6, or 9), Østergade 61, open Monday to Saturday 9am to 10pm and Sunday 9am to 8pm.

Dentists/Doctors   For emergency dental treatment, go to **Tandlaegevagten,** Oslo Plads 14 (☎ **35-38-02-51;** S-tog: Østerport), near Østerport Station and the U.S. Embassy. It's open Monday to Friday 8am to 9:30pm and Saturday,

Sunday, and holidays 10am to noon. Be prepared to pay in cash. To reach a doctor, dial ☎ **33-93-63-00** Monday to Friday 9am to 5pm or ☎ **38-88-60-41** after hours. The doctor's fee is payable in cash. Virtually every doctor speaks English.

Embassies   The embassy of the **United States** is at Dag Hammarsjölds Allé 24, DK-2100 København (☎ **35-55-31-44;** bus 1 or 6); the embassy of the **United Kingdom,** Kastelsvej 36–40, DK-2100 København (☎ **35-44-52-00;** bus 1 or 6); the embassy of **Canada,** Kristen Berniskowsgadei, DK-1105 København K (☎ **33-48-32-00;** bus 28); the embassy of **Ireland,** Østbanegade 21, DK-2100 København (☎ **35-42-32-33;** S-tog: Østerport); and the embassy of **Australia,** Strandboulevarden, DK-2100 København (☎ **39-29-20-77;** bus 40). There's no **New Zealand** embassy.

Emergencies   Dial ☎ **112** for the fire department, the police, an ambulance, or to report a sea or air accident. Emergency calls from public phone kiosks are free (no coins needed).

Internet Access   You can send e-mails or check on your messages at **Cyberia Café,** Whitfield Street, W1 (☎ **020/7813-9659;** e-mail: cyberia@easynet.co. uk; Tube: Goodge St.), open Monday to Friday 10am to 8pm, Saturday 11am to 7pm, and Sunday 11am to 6pm.

Post Office   For information about the Copenhagen post office, call ☎ **33-33-89-00.** The main post office, where you can pick up your general delivery letters, is Tietgensgade 35–39, DK-1704 København (☎ **33-33-89-00;** S-tog: Central Station), open Monday to Friday 11am to 6pm, Saturday 10am to 1pm. The post office at the Central Railroad Station is open Monday to Friday 8am to 10pm, Saturday 9am to 4pm, and Sunday 10am to 4pm.

Telephone   The **country code** for Denmark is **45,** and this two-digit number will precede any call that's intended for Denmark dialed from another country. Danish phones are fully automatic. Dial just the eight-digit number, for there are no city area codes.

At public phone booths, use two 50-øre coins or a 1-krone or 5-krone coin only. Don't insert coins until your party answers. You can make more than one call on the same payment if your time hasn't run out. Available at post offices, phone cards cost 30DKK ($4.30), 50DKK ($7), and 100DKK ($14). Remember it can be expensive to phone from your hotel room. Emergency calls are free. To make phone calls or send faxes or telexes, go to the **Telecom Denmark** at the Central Railroad Station open Monday to Friday 8am to 10pm and Saturday and Sunday 9am to 9pm. You can reach a U.S. operator with an **AT&T** calling card, by dialing ☎ **800-10022.** For **Sprint,** dial ☎ **80-01-08-77;** for **MCI** dial ☎ **80-01-00-22.**

WHERE TO STAY
NEAR KONGENS NYTROV & NYHAVN
Very Expensive
Hotel d'Angleterre. Kongens Nytorv 34, DK-1050 København. ☎ **800/44-UTELL** in the U.S., or 33-12-00-95. Fax 33-12-11-18. E-mail: anglehot@remmen.dk. 130 units. A/C MINI-BAR TV TEL. 2,180–3,500DKK ($312–$501) double; from 3,450DKK ($493) suite. AE, DC, MC, V. Parking 150DKK ($21). Bus: 1, 6, or 9.

At the top of Nyhavn, this seven-story hotel, built in 1755 and extensively renovated in the 1980s, is the premier choice for Denmark (though a bit staid and stodgy). The rooms are beautifully furnished with art objects and the occasional antique. They vary in size, but each has a good bed with a firm mattress; the bathrooms come with robes, hair dryers, phones, thick towels, and scales. The hotel features the main dining room, Wiinblad, along with the upscale gourmet eatery, Restaurant d'Angleterre. Both serve a Danish/French cuisine. Facilities include a health club, sauna, pool, Turkish bath, and solarium.

✪ Phoenix Copenhagen. Bredgade 37, DK-1260 København. **☎ 33-95-95-00.** Fax 33-33-98-33. E-mail: phoenix@vip.cypercity.dk. 213 units. MINIBAR TV TEL. 1,590–2,390DKK ($227–$342) double; from 2,800DKK ($400) suite. AE, DC, MC, V. Parking 90DKK ($13). Bus: 1, 5, 9, or 10.

More than any other hotel, this top-of-the-line newcomer poses a challenge to the nearby d'Angleterre. Opened in 1991, the Phoenix rose from the ruins of an 18th-century royal house. The rooms are tastefully elegant and discreet interpretations of Louis XVI. Beds are large with firm mattresses. The bathrooms have hair dryers and robes. The very best rooms also have faxes, trouser presses, and phones in the bathrooms. On the premises are a Danish/French restaurant, the Von Plessen, and an English-inspired pub, Murdoch's.

Moderate

Copenhagen Admiral Hotel. Toldbodgade 24–28, DK-1253 København. **☎ 33-74-14-14.** Fax 33-74-14-16. www.admiral-hotel.dk. E-mail: admiral@admiral-hotel.dk. 366 units. TV TEL. 1,040–1,315DKK ($149–$188) double; from 1,885DKK ($270) suite. AE, DC, MC, V. Free parking. Bus: 1, 9, 10, 28, or 41.

Two blocks from Nyhavn Canal, this hotel was built as a granary in 1787 and last renovated in 1997. The building still features thick timbers and stone arches, though modern partitions have created a series of well-furnished first-class bedrooms. The rooms may lack charm, but they're well maintained. Some have harbor views or open onto French balconies. Bathrooms are small but have bidets and hair dryers. The hotel restaurant, the Pinafore, specializes in seafood. A lunch plate offers a sampling of the menu's various fish dishes.

✪ 71 Nyhavn. Nyhavn 71, DK-1051 København. E-mail: arp@isa.dknet.dk **☎ 33-11-85-85.** Fax 33-93-15-85. 82 units. MINIBAR TV TEL. Mon–Thurs 1,450–1,725DKK ($207–$247) double. Fri–Sun 1,195DKK ($171) double. Suite 2,895DKK ($414) all week. AE, DC, MC, V. Free parking. Bus: 650.

On the corner between Copenhagen harbor and Nyhavn Canal, this hotel is a restored old warehouse from 1804, and it was thoroughly renovated in 1997. Most of the rooms have a harbor and canal view. Mattresses are firm but the beds are narrow; bathrooms are rather small and contain hair dryers; most have a stall shower. The best units are also equipped with ironing boards, faxes, and bathrobes, and computer plugs are available at the reception desk. No-smoking accommodations are available. In the cellar, the Restaurant Pakhuskælderen offers rustic charm and good food.

NEAR RÅDHUSPLADSEN & TIVOLI

Expensive

Plaza. Bernstorffsgade 4, DK-1577 København. **☎ 800/223-5652** or 33-14-92-62. Fax 33-93-93-62. www.phg.dk. E-mail:booking@phg.dk 93 units. MINIBAR TV TEL. 1,850DKK ($265) double; from 3,250DKK ($465) suite. AE, DC, MC, V. Parking 120DKK ($17). Bus: 1 or 6.

This successful overhaul of an older hotel near the rail station combines first-class comfort and antique furnishings. Opposite the Tivoli Gardens, the hotel was commissioned by King Frederik VIII in 1913 and has entertained its share of celebrities and royalty. Rooms vary greatly in size and resemble what you might find in an English country house, but with all the modern amenities. Double-glazed windows with views make this a good choice. There're some smoke-free accommodations. Rooms on the top floor have dormer windows. Bathrooms are generous in size and contain hair dryers and make-up mirrors. The Library Bar is one of Copenhagen's most charming oases. Off the lobby, the Flora Danica Restaurant serves a sumptuous Scandinavian break-fast buffet and a good lunch with such dishes as roast beef sandwiches, cognac-flavored blini, and American rib-eye steak with stuffed potato. There's access to a 24-hour health club and 24-hour room service, along with dry cleaning/laundry and secretarial services.

Moderate

Ascot Hotel. Studiestraede 61, DK-1554 København. ☎ **33-12-60-00.** Fax 33-14-60-40. www.ascothotel.dk. E-mail: hotel@ascothotel.dk. 155 units. TV TEL. 1,060–1,370DKK ($152–$196) double; 1,090–2,090DKK ($156–$299) suite. Rates include buffet breakfast. AE, DC, V. Free parking. Bus: 14 or 16.

On a side street, about a 2-minute walk from Town Hall Square, sits one of Copenhagen's best small hotels. The Ascot was built in 1902 and enlarged and modernized in 1994. The furniture is standard; the firm mattresses are renewed as frequently as needed. The finest units open onto the street, though the rooms in the rear get better air circulation and more light. Bathrooms are large. Facilities include a small gymnasium.

Grand Hotel. Vesterbrogade 9A, DK-1620 København. ☎ **33-27-69-00.** Fax 33-27-69-01. 151 units. www.grandhotelcopenhagen.dk. E-mail: grandhotel@arp-hansen.dk. 151 units. MINIBAR TV TEL. 1,495–1,960DKK ($214–$280) double; 2,195–2,795DKK ($314–$400) suite. Rates include buffet breakfast. AE, DC, MC, V. Bus: 1, 6, 16, 27, 28, or 29.

Built in 1880, this surprisingly elegant landmark hotel near the Central Railroad Station was most recently renovated in 1997. Rooms are tastefully furnished and well maintained with excellent, sleep-inducing beds. The superior bathrooms are large and furnished with a goodly assortment of towels and a hair dryer. The Grand Bar over-flows onto a sidewalk cafe in summer and Oliver's Restaurant serves freshly prepared Danish specialties.

Komfort Hotel. Løngangstræde 27, DK-1468 København. ☎ **33-12-65-70.** Fax 33-15-28-99. E-mail: booking@principal.dk. 201 units. TV TEL. 1,250DKK ($179) double. Extra bed 225DKK ($32). Rates include buffet breakfast. AE, DC, MC, V. Parking 90DKK ($13). Bus: 1, 5, or 6.

In the heart of Copenhagen, close to the Town Hall, the Komfort offers good value. In just 2 minutes you can walk to the Tivoli Gardens. All its medium-sized bedrooms are furnished in a modern Danish design and contain firm mattresses. The overall look, however, including the small but well-maintained bathrooms, is somewhat motel-like. Towels are a bit skimpy, so ask for extras. The hotel's restaurant, Hatte-hylden, serves traditional Danish food; or try the John Bull Pub, the oldest English pub in the city. There's even a pool room.

Kong Arthur. Nørre Søgade 11, DK-1370 København. ☎ **33-11-12-12.** Fax 33-32-61-30. www.kongarthur.dk. E-mail: hotel@kongarthur.dk. 107 units. MINIBAR TV TEL. 1,280–1,480DKK ($183–$212) double; 2,900DKK ($415) suite. Rates include buffet breakfast. AE, DC, MC, V. Free parking. Bus: 5, 7, or 16.

An orphanage when it was built in 1882, this good-value hotel sits behind a private courtyard next to the tree-lined Peblinge Lake. A wing with more spacious rooms, including 20 for nonsmokers, was added in 1993. Each of the comfortably furnished rooms has an in-house video and safe. Bathrooms are medium-sized and contain hair dryers. The hotel's Restaurant Brøchner is recommended for its reasonably priced Danish and French cuisine, and a Japanese restaurant serves full meals from a sushi bar.

Inexpensive

Absalon Hotel. Helgolandsgade 15, Dk-1653 København. ☎ **33-24-22-11.** Fax 33-24-34-11. www.absalon/hotel.dk. E-mail: info@absalon/hotel.dk. 265 units, 165 with bathroom. MINIBAR TV TEL. 790DKK ($113) double without bath; 1,100DKK ($157) double with bathroom. 1,300–1,500DKK ($186–$215) suite. Rates include breakfast. AE, DC, MC, V. Parking 75DKK ($11). Bus: 16.

This family-run lodging, one of the best-managed hotels in the neighborhood, consists of four townhouses that were joined into one building and became a hotel in 1938. It has a spacious blue-and-white breakfast room, and an attentive staff. The rooms are simple and modern, but cramped. Those with private bathrooms also have TVs, trouser presses, and hair dryers. There are laundry facilities.

Green Key Hotel. Sønder Blvd. 53, DK-1720 København. ☎ **33-25-25-19.** Fax 33-25-25-83. www.greenk.dk. E-mail:hotelinfo@greenkey.dk. 20 units, none with bathroom. TV TEL. 400DKK ($57) double. No credit cards. Free parking. Bus: 10.

Simple and plain but well kept, this five-story hotel is about a 10-minute walk from the main rail station. Renovated in the late 1980s, it's unpretentious and unassuming, with bright, acceptably decorated rooms. Beds are reasonably comfortable if a bit narrow. Each room has a sink with hot and cold running water; toilets and showers are off the central corridors. Breakfast is the only meal served.

Missionshotellet Nebo. Istedgade 6, DK-1650 København. ☎ **33-21-12-17.** Fax 33-23-47-74. www.nebo.dk. E-mail: nebo@email.dk. 150 units, 37 with bathroom. TV TEL. 610DKK ($87) double without bathroom, 830DKK ($119) double with bathroom. Extra bed 200DKK ($29). AE, DC, MC, V. Parking 25DKK ($3.55). Bus: 1, 6, 16, 28, or 41.

This hotel near the rail station is a quiet retreat, with a tiny lobby and a lounge that opens onto a side courtyard. The small rooms are clean and up-to-date, though Spartan. Some beds are comfortable, others sag in the middle. There are bathrooms on all floors.

A GAY HOTEL

Hotel Jørgensen. Rømersgade 11, DK-1362 København. ☎ **33-13-81-86.** Fax 33-15-51-05. 24 units; 13 dorm rms (72 beds). TV TEL. 600DKK ($86) double; 115DKK ($16) per person in dorm. Rates include breakfast. MC, V. Free parking. Bus: 14 or 16.

In 1984 the Jørgensen was transformed into Denmark's first gay hotel. A white stucco establishment, it's on a busy boulevard in the central city, with a patronage mainly of gays and lesbians, though all are welcome. The rooms are conventional and have dormitory-style beds. Family rooms house four to five people, whereas the 12 rooms accommodate 6 to 14 each. Rental of either requires guests to provide their own sheets or sleeping bag. Breakfast is the only meal served.

WHERE TO DINE

That national institution, the *smørrebrød* (open-face sandwiches), is introduced at lunch. Literally, this means "bread and butter," but the Danes stack this sandwich as if it were the Leaning Tower of Pisa—then they throw in a slice of curled cucumber and bits of parsley or perhaps sliced peaches or a mushroom for added color.

NEAR KONGENS NYTORV & NYHAVN

Very Expensive

✪ **Kong Hans Kaelder.** Vingårdsstraede 6. ☎ **33-11-68-68.** Reservations required. Main courses 265–335DKK ($38–$48); fixed-price menu 645–725DKK ($92–$104). AE, DC, MC, V. Mon–Sat 6pm–midnight. Closed Dec 23–30, Jan 1–2. Bus: 1, 6, or 9. INTERNATIONAL.

This vaulted Gothic cellar, once owned by King Hans, may be the best restaurant in Denmark. Its most serious competition comes from Kommandanten, which many discriminating palates hail as the best. On "the oldest corner of Copenhagen," it has been carefully restored and is now a Relais Gourmand. A typical three-course lunch would be smoked salmon from the restaurant's own smokery with aquavit and grain mustard, salmis of mallard duckling with spätzle, then caramelized vanilla crème with pears. At dinner, you might choose lobster consommé with basil and ravioli, young pigeon with jasmine rice galette, a selection of Danish and French cheeses, finished with Valrhona chocolate in variations with citrus fruit marmalade.

Expensive

✪ **Kommandanten.** Ny Adelgade 7. ☎ **33-12-09-90.** Reservations required. Main courses 280–330DKK ($40–$47); fixed-price menu 350–690DKK ($50–$99). AE, DC, MC, V. Mon–Fri noon–2pm; Mon–Sat 6–10pm. Bus: 1 or 6. INTERNATIONAL.

Built in 1698 and the former residence of the military commander of Copenhagen, Kommandanten is the epitome of Danish chic and charm, famously decorated in shades of blue and silver. The menu offers a mouthwatering array of classical dishes mixed with innovative selections, a medley of strong yet subtle flavors. The finest seasonal ingredients are used, and the menu changes every 2 weeks. You might be offered the grilled catch of the day, breast of duck with port-wine sauce, grilled turbot with spinach sauce, or gratinée of shellfish; or oxtails removed from the bone and served with fried lobster, puree of potatoes and parsley, and a lobster cream sauce.

Moderate

Café Lumskebugten. Esplanaden 21. ☎ **33-15-60-29.** Reservations recommended. Main courses 168–250DKK ($24–$36); 3-course fixed-price lunch 275DKK ($39); 4-course fixed-price dinner 465DKK ($67). AE, DC, MC, V. Mon–Fri 11am–midnight; Sat 4pm–midnight. Bus: 1, 6, or 9. DANISH/FRENCH.

This restaurant is a well-managed bastion of Danish charm, with an unpretentious elegance. Now-legendary matriarch Karen Marguerita Krog established it in 1854 as a rowdy tavern for sailors. A tastefully gentrified version of the original beef hash is still served. Two glistening-white dining rooms are decorated with antique ships' models, oil paintings, and pinewood floors. The food and service are excellent. Menu specialties include Danish fish cakes with mustard sauce and minced beets, fried platters of herring, sugar-marinated salmon with mustard-cream sauce, and a symphony of fish with saffron sauce and new potatoes.

Inexpensive

Ida Davidsen. Store Kongensgade 70. ☎ **33-91-36-55.** Reservations recommended. Sandwiches 45–150DKK ($6–$21). AE, DC, MC, V. Mon–Fri 10am–4am. Bus: 1 or 9. DANISH.

This restaurant has flourished within the Danish psyche since 1888, when the forebears of its present owner, Ida Davidsen, established a sandwich shop. Today, five generations later, the family matriarch and namesake is known as the "smørrebrød queen of Copenhagen" selling a greater variety of open-faced sandwiches (177) than anyone else in Denmark. If you opt for a sandwich here, you'll be in good company: Her fare has even been featured at royal buffets at Amalienborg Palace. You'll select your choice by pointing to it within a glass-fronted display case, after which a staff member will carry it to your table. The vast selection includes sandwiches made with salmon, lobster, shrimp, smoked duck with braised cabbage and horseradish, liver pâté, ham, herring, and boiled egg.

NEAR RÅDHUSPLADSEN & TIVOLI
Moderate

Restaurant Flyvefisken. Lars Bjørnstr. 18. ☎ **33-14-95-15.** Reservations recommended. Main courses 55–150DKK ($8–$21). Set-price dinners 148–210DKK ($21–$30). DC, MC, V. Mon–Sat 5:30–10:30pm. Bus: 5. THAI.

The decor of this restaurant is authentically Danish, complete with colors of the national flag, thick wooden tables, and paneling. Beginning at 5:30pm, the culinary venue of the fiery cuisine of Thailand becomes the norm. Expect strong curries and lemongrass, the hot fish soups of Bangkok, grilled lamb, shark in basil sauce, chicken with cashews and fiery peppers; steaming cupfuls of green and black tea, and bottles of Singha beer. It's a marvelous change of pace from typically Danish fare.

Inexpensive

✪ **Riz Raz.** Kompagnistræde 20 (at Knabrostræde). ☎ **33-15-05-75.** Reservations not necessary. Vegetarian buffet 59DKK ($8.45) per person; main courses 79–169DKK ($11.30–$24.15). DC, MC, V. Daily 11:30am–midnight. Bus: 5 or 6. MEDITERRANEAN.

Bustling and unpretentious, this decidedly un-Danish hideaway offers the best all-vegetarian buffet. Help yourself from a sprawling network of buffet tables laden with each of the vegetarian specialties of the Mediterranean world, including Morocco, Egypt, Lebanon, Greece, and Italy, all for a price that by Scandinavian standards is highly reasonable. Carry your selections to a warren of small dining rooms. There's additional seating outdoors during nice weather, or upstairs. Expect a medley of virtually every vegetable known to humankind, prepared either au naturel, or as part of a marinated fantasy that might include antipasti of Italy, hummus of Lebanon, or an array of long-simmered casseroles inspired by the cuisines of the Moroccan highlands.

NEAR ROSENBORG SLOT
Very Expensive

St. Gertruds Kloster. Hauser Plads 32. ☎ **33-14-66-30.** Reservations required. Fixed-price menus 370–825DKK ($53–$118); children's menu 99DKK ($14); main courses 248–295DKK ($35–$42). AE, DC, MC, V. Daily 4pm–2am. Closed Dec 24–26. Bus: 4E, 5, 7E, 14, or 16. INTERNATIONAL.

Near Nørreport Station and south of Rosenborg Castle, this is the most romantic restaurant. There's no electricity in the labyrinth of 14th-century underground vaults, and the 1,500 flickering candles, open grill, iron sconces, and rough-hewn furniture create an elegant medieval ambience. At dinner, you might start with a pâté of fresh foie gras with a Madeira glacé and duck bacon or king prawn sautéed in parsley butter and served in red curry cream with honey-preserved apples and shallots, then move on to a combination of three kinds of fish with crayfish tails, mild curry jus, and a ratatouille of vegetables and rice. Every flavor is fully focused, each dish balanced to perfection.

AT GRÅBRØDRETORV
Moderate

Bøf & Ost. Gråbrødretorv 13. ☎ **33-11-99-11.** Reservations required. Main courses 135–179DKK ($19–$26); fixed-price meals 75–100DKK ($11–$14) at lunch, 345DKK ($49) at dinner. DC, MC, V. Mon–Sat 11:30am–11pm. Closed Jan 1 and Dec 24–25. Bus: 5. DANISH/FRENCH.

"Beef & Cheese" is housed in a 1728 building, and its cellars come from a medieval monastery. In summer a pleasant outdoor terrace overlooks Gray Friars Square. Specialties include lobster soup, fresh Danish bay strips, a cheese plate with six selections, and entrecôte with various sauces and butters and a baked potato. Seasonal dishes rotate in and out of the menu, making good use of regional mushrooms, fish, and game.

Inexpensive

Pasta Basta. Valkendorfsgade 22. ☎ **33-11-21-31.** Reservations recommended. Main courses 69–159DKK ($10–$23). No credit cards. Sun–Thurs 11:30am–3am, Fri–Sat 11:30am–5am. Bus: 5. ITALIAN/INTERNATIONAL.

Its main attraction is a loaded table of cold antipasti and salads, which many diners believe is one of the best values in town. The restaurant is divided into half a dozen cozy dining rooms, each with a decor inspired by ancient Pompeii. Menu choices include at least 15 kinds of pasta (all made fresh on the premises), raw marinated fillet of beef (carpaccio) served with olive oil and basil, a platter with three kinds of Danish caviar (whitefish, speckled trout, and vendace, all served with chopped onions, lemon, toast, and butter), and fresh mussels cooked in a dry white wine with pasta and creamy saffron sauce. Late nights are often lively, so if you can't sleep and you're hungry, this can be an entertaining option.

Peder Oxe's Restaurant/Vinkaelder Wine Bar. Gråbrødretorv 11. ☎ **33-11-00-77.** Reservations recommended. Main courses 75–189DKK ($11–$27); fixed-price lunch 98DKK ($14). DC, MC, V. Daily 11:30am–11pm. Bus: 5. DANISH.

In the Middle Ages this was the site of a monastery, but the present building dates from the 1700s. The restaurant/wine bar was established in the 1970s and is popular among young people. A salad bar is included in the price of the main course, but it's so tempting that many prefer to enjoy it alone for 69DKK ($10) per person. Dishes include lobster soup, Danish bay shrimp, open-face sandwiches, hamburgers, and fresh fish. The bill of fare, though standard, is well prepared.

AT CHRISTIANSBORG

Very Expensive

Krogs Fiskerestaurant. Gammel Strand 38. ☎ **33-15-89-15.** Reservations required. Main courses 248–395DKK ($35–$57); fixed-price menu 395DKK ($57) for 3 courses, 485DKK ($69) for 5 courses. AE, DC, MC, V. Mon–Sat 11:30am–4pm and 5:30–10:30pm. Bus: 2, 10, or 29. SEAFOOD.

Classically elegant and opposite the old fish market, this restaurant's premises were built in 1789 as a fish shop. The canal-side plaza where fishers moored their boats is now the site of the outdoor dining terrace. Converted into a restaurant in 1910, the establishment serves very fresh seafood in a single large room. The well-chosen menu includes lobster soup, bouillabaisse, natural oysters, mussels steamed in white wine, and sautéed turbot with corn cassoulet. Each dish is impeccably prepared and filled with flavor. A limited selection of meat dishes is also available.

Expensive

Nouvelle. 34 Gammel Strand. ☎ **33-13-50-18.** Reservations recommended. Main courses 195–225DKK ($28–$32); 3-course fixed-price lunch menu 275DKK ($39); 5-course fixed-price dinner 495DKK ($71). AE, DC, MC, V. Mon–Fri 11:30am–3pm and 5:30–10pm, Sat 5:30–10pm. Closed Dec 22–Jan 6. Bus: 29 or 41. DANISH.

Within one of the oldest surviving houses, a prosperous-looking villa built around 1700, this restaurant lies upstairs from the also-recommended and less expensive Thorvaldsen (below). Dine in one of three elegantly rustic rooms overlooking a nearby canal and whose ambience emulates an upscale Danish *kro* (country inn). Chefs here are known for their finesse in creating modern adaptations of traditional Danish favorites. Menu items change with the season but might include herring in puff pastry with caviar; turbot in a fruity gewürtztraminer sauce; fillet of veal with truffle sauce; and an unusual starter known as "egg nouvelle," a simple boiled egg with a significant difference (it's stuffed with a mousseline of lobster and accompanied with a dollop of caviar). A thrilling dessert specialty is an assortment of three sherbets: white chocolate, blackberries, and pear.

Moderate

Den Gyldne Fortun. Ved Stranden 18. ☎ **33-12-20-11.** Reservations recommended. Main courses 145–265DKK ($21–$38); 3-course fixed-price menu 325DKK ($46). AE, DC, V. Mon–Sat noon–3pm and 5:30–10:30pm, Sun 5:30–10:30pm. Bus: 1, 6, or 10. SEAFOOD.

Though the building dates from 1750, Den Gyldne Fortun was opened in 1975 and is today the best seafood restaurant. The restaurant prides itself on fresh fish from the Mediterranean and the North Atlantic. Warmly nautical in decor, it has a bubbling lobster tank and an ice table displaying the fish of the day. Try the lobster bisque with fish and lobster roe, Danish fish soup, stuffed sole poached in white wine and glazed with hollandaise sauce, fried plaice with potatoes, or fricassee of three types of fish in saffron-flavored bouillon with noodles. Some beef dishes, such as Charolais sirloin, are also served.

Inexpensive

Thorvaldsen. 34 Gammel Strand. ☎ **33-32-04-00.** Reservations recommended. Main courses 60–135DKK ($9–$19). AE, DC, MC, V. Mon–Sat 11:30am–4pm. Bus: 27, 28, 29 or 61. DANISH.

Part of the success of this artfully simple Danish bistro derives from its association with Nouvelle, one of Copenhagen's most talked-about modern restaurants (above). Open only for lunch, it lies on the street level of the 1700 mansion it occupies, adjacent to a canal. Named after the 18th-century merchant, who occupied the site originally, it features a single blue-and-white dining room and menu specialties that taste best when accompanied by beer, aquavit, or any selection from the copious wine list. Menu items include a tasty version of traditional herring in cream-and-onion sauce; fillet of eel simmered with white beans and onions; and an all-Danish platter whose four components change with the seasons.

IN TIVOLI

Food prices inside Tivoli are about 30% higher than elsewhere. Try skipping dessert at a restaurant and picking up a less expensive treat at one of the many stands. Take bus no. 1, 6, 8, 16, 29, 30, 32, or 33 to reach the park and either of the following restaurants. *Note:* These restaurants are open only from May to mid-September.

Very Expensive

Divan II. Vesterbrogade 3. ☎ **33-12-51-51.** Reservations recommended. Main courses 265–345DKK ($38–$49); fixed-price meal 325DKK ($46) at lunch, 385–585DKK ($55–$84) at dinner. AE, DC, MC, V. Daily 11am–midnight. DANISH/FRENCH.

This is one of the finest restaurants in Tivoli, established in 1843, the same year as Tivoli itself. Despite its designation as Divan II, it's nonetheless older than its nearby competitor, the less formal Divan I. Service is almost unrelentingly impeccable in a garden setting where the cuisine is among the most urbane in the Danish capital. Examples include fried fillet of salmon served with a turbot bisque and tomato-and-basil concassé, a paupiette of fillet of sole with lobster mousseline with fried oyster mushrooms and turbot bisque, and monkfish medallions sautéed with veal bacon and served with fricassee of morels. Dinners here are elaborate, memorable, and highly ritualized.

Expensive

Restaurant P.H. Vesterbrogade 3, Tivoli. ☎ **33-75-07-75.** Reservations recommended. Main courses 195DKK ($28); set-price lunch 98–185DKK ($14–$26); set-price dinner 295–395DKK ($42–$57). AE, DC, MC, V. Daily noon–10:30pm (last order). DANISH/FRENCH.

One of the most upscale and elegant restaurants in Tivoli bears the initials of Paul Hemmingsen (1894–1967), an architect, interior designer, and writer, whose works are known to virtually every Dane. A relative newcomer to the Tivoli restaurant scene, where owners and venues rarely change, the restaurant has gained a flash of fame since it opened in the late 1990s, thanks to intelligent cuisine and a freshness of image that older, more jaded restaurants here might've lost. You'll dine in a modern-looking building that Hemmingsen designed, with a sun-flooded, cheerfully modern decor. Menu items are based on French and Danish traditions, with touches of Asian pepper and spice to heat things up a bit. The menu intelligently draws on fine Danish culinary traditions without the heaviness. Opt for the North Sea turbot, with white asparagus and spring cabbage or the Danish veal cutlet with a panade of ham and shallots served with potato baked in a calf's tail confit and a creamy morel sauce.

EXPLORING COPENHAGEN
SIGHTSEEING SUGGESTIONS FOR FIRST-TIME VISITORS

If You Have 1 Day   Take a walking tour through the heart of the old city, which will give you time to recover from jet lag. Spend the late afternoon at Christiansborg Palace on Slotsholmen Island where the queen of Denmark receives guests. Early in the evening, head to the Tivoli.

If You Have 2 Days   On day 2, visit Amalienborg Palace, the queen's residence. Try to time your visit to witness the changing of the guard. Continue beyond the palace to *The Little Mermaid* statue. In the afternoon, see the art treasures of Ny Carlsberg Glyptotek. At night, seek out a local tavern.

If You Have 3 Days   In the morning of the third day, journey to Rosenborg Castle, summer palace of King Christian IV, then wander through the park and gardens. Have lunch at one of the restaurants lining the canal at Nyhavn, the traditional seamen's quarter of Copenhagen. In the afternoon, go to Rundetårn (Round Tower) for a panoramic view of the city, and if time remains, stop in at the National Museum and Denmark's Fight for Freedom Museum.

If You Have 4 Days   Head north to Louisiana, the modern-art museum, and continue on to Helsingør to visit Kronborg Castle, famously associated with Shakespeare's *Hamlet.* Return by train to Copenhagen in time for a stroll along the Strøget, Europe's longest walking street. For dinner, visit the village of Dragør.

If You Have 5 Days   On the fifth day, visit Frilandsmuseet, at Lyngby, a half-hour train ride from Copenhagen. Have lunch at the park. Return to Copenhagen and take a walking tour along its canals. If time remains, tour the Carlsberg brewery. Pay a final visit to the Tivoli to cap your adventure in the Danish capital.

THE TIVOLI GARDENS

✪ **Tivoli Gardens.** Vesterbrogade 3. ☎ **33-15-10-01.** Admission 11am–1pm, 35DKK ($5) adults, 20DKK ($2.85) children under 12; 1–9:30pm, 45DKK ($6) adults, 20DKK ($2.85) children; 9:30pm–midnight, 39DKK ($6) adult, 20DKK ($2.85) children. Rides 20DKK ($2.85) each. Daily 11am–midnight. Closed mid-Sept–Apr. Bus: 1, 16, or 29.

Since it opened in 1843, this 20-acre garden and amusement park in the center of Copenhagen has been a resounding success, with its thousands of flowers, merry-go-round of tiny Viking ships, games of chance and skill, and Ferris wheel of hot-air balloons and cabin seats. There's even a playground for children. The newest attraction is "The Golden Tower," toped by a shining golden cupola. The ride takes passengers 190 feet above ground to enjoy a panoramic view of the city before being dropped to the ground at a blazing speed, even faster than a natural free fall. An Arabian-style fantasy

Copenhagen's *Little Mermaid*

The one statue *everybody* wants to see is the life-size bronze of **Den Lille Havfrue,** inspired by Hans Christian Andersen's "The Little Mermaid," one of the world's most famous fairy tales. The statue, unveiled in 1913, was sculpted by Edvard Eriksen and rests on rocks right off the shore. The mermaid has been attacked more than once, losing an arm in one misadventure, decapitated as recently as January 6, 1998.

All year, there's a 2¹/₂-hour Grand Tour of Copenhagen that makes a significant stop at the *Little Mermaid* and costs 160DKK ($23). In summer, a special "Mermaid Bus" leaves from Rådhuspladsen (Vester Voldgade) at 10:30am and then at half-hour intervals until 5:30pm. On the "Langelinie" bus there's a 20-minute stop at *The Little Mermaid.* If you want more time, take bus no. 1, 6, or 9.

palace, with towers and arches, houses more than two dozen restaurants in all price ranges, from a lakeside inn to a beer garden. Take a walk around the edge of the tiny lake with its ducks, swans, and boats.

A parade of the red-uniformed Tivoli Boys Guard takes place on weekends at 5:20 and 7:20pm, and their regimental band gives concerts Friday at 10pm on the open-air stage. The oldest building at Tivoli, the Chinese-style Pantomime Theater, with its peacock curtain, stages pantomimes in the evening.

THE TOP MUSEUMS

Don't worry about not understanding the explanations in the museums; virtually all have write-ups in English.

✪ **Ny Carlsberg Glyptotek.** Dantes Plads 7. ☎ **33-41-81-41.** Admission 30DKK ($4.30) adults, children under 16 free. Free admission Wed and Sun. Tues–Sun 10am–4pm. Bus: 1, 5, 10, 550S, or 650S.

The Glyptotek, behind the Tivoli, is one of Scandinavia's most important art museums. Founded by 19th-century art collector Carl Jacobsen, the museum comprises two distinct departments: modern works and antiquities. The modern section has both French and Danish art, mainly from the 19th century; sculpture, including works by Rodin; and works of the Impressionists and related artists, including van Gogh's *Landscape from St-Rémy.* Antiquities include Egyptian, Greek, Roman, and Etruscan art. The Egyptian collection is outstanding; the prize is a prehistoric rendering of a hippopotamus. A favorite of ours is the Etruscan art display. In 1996, the Ny Glyptotek added a French Masters' wing, where you'll find an extensive collection of masterpieces.

Statens Museum for Kunst (Royal Museum of Fine Arts). Sølvgade 48–50. ☎ **33-74-84-94.** Admission 40DKK ($6) adults, children under 16 free. Tues and Thurs–Sun 10am–5pm, Wed 10am–8pm. Bus: 10 or 14.

After its major 1998 restoration, this well-stocked museum houses painting and sculpture from the 13th century to the present. There're Dutch golden-age landscapes and marine paintings by Rubens and his school, plus portraits by Frans Hals and Rembrandt. Eckersberg, Købke, and Hansen represent the Danish golden age. French 20th-century art includes 20 works by Matisse. In the Royal Print Room are 300,000 drawings, prints, lithographs, and other works by such artists as Dürer, Rembrandt, Matisse, and Picasso.

Den Hirschsprungske Samling (The Hirschsprung Collection). Stockholmsgade 20. ☎ **35-42-03-36.** Admission 25DKK ($3.55) adults; children under 16 free; 40DKK ($6) for special exhibits. Free admission on Wed. Wed 11am–9pm, Thurs–Mon 11am–4pm. Bus: 14, 42, or 43.

This collection of Danish art from the 19th and early 20th centuries is in Ostre Anlaeg, a park in the city center. Tobacco merchant Heinrich Hirschsprung (1836–1908) created the collection, and it has been growing ever since. The emphasis is on the Danish golden age, with such artists as Eckersberg, Købke, and Lundbye, and on the Skagen painters, P. S. Krøyer, and Anna and Michael Ancher. Some furnishings from the artists' homes are exhibited.

Nationalmuseet (National Museum). Ny Vestergade 10. ☎ **33-13-44-11.** Admission 35DKK ($5) adults, children under 16 free. Tues–Sun 10am–5pm. Closed Dec 24–25 and 31. Bus: 1, 2, 5, 6, 8, 10, 28, 29, 30, 32, 33, 34, or 35.

A gigantic repository of anthropological artifacts, this museum is divided primarily into five departments. The first section focuses on prehistory, the Middle Ages, and the Renaissance in Denmark. These collections date from the Stone Age and include Viking stones, helmets, and fragments of battle gear. Especially interesting are the "lur" horn, a Bronze Age musical instrument among the oldest in Europe, and the world-famous Sun Chariot, an elegant Bronze Age piece of pagan art. The Royal Collection of Coins and Medals contains various coins from antiquity. There're also an outstanding collections of Egyptian and Classical antiquities.

Frihedsmuseet (Museum of Danish Resistance, 1940–45). Churchillparken. ☎ **33-13-77-14.** Free admission. May–Sept 15 Tues–Sat 10am–4pm, Sun 10am–5pm; Sept 16–Apr Tues–Sat 11am–3pm, Sun 11am–4pm. Bus: 1, 6, or 9.

On display here are relics of torture and concentration camps, the equipment used for the wireless and illegal films, British propaganda leaflets, satirical caricatures of Hitler, information about both Danish Jews and Danish Nazis, and the paralyzing nationwide strikes. Also look for an armed car used for drive-by shootings of Danish Nazi informers and collaborators.

Frilandsmuseet (Open-Air Museum). Kongevejen 100. ☎ **33-13-44-11.** Admission 40DKK ($6) adults; children free. Free admission on Wed. Easter–Sept Tues–Sun 10am–5pm; Oct 1–21 Tues–Sun 10am–4pm. Closed Oct 22–Easter. S-tog: From Copenhagen Central Station to Sorgenfri (leaving every 20 minutes). Bus: 184 or 194.

This reconstructed village in Lyngby, on the fringe of Copenhagen, captures Denmark's one-time rural character. The "museum" is nearly 90 acres, a 3.2km (2-mile) walk around the compound reveals a dozen authentic buildings—farmsteads, windmills, fishers' cottages. Exhibits include a half-timbered 18th-century farmstead from one of the tiny windswept Danish islands, a primitive longhouse from the remote Faroe Islands, thatched fishers' huts from Jutland, tower windmills, and a mid–19th-century potter's workshop.

Museum Erotica. Købmagergade 24. ☎ **33-12-03-11.** Admission 65DKK ($9). May–Sept daily 10am–11pm; Oct–Apr Mon–Fri 11am–8pm, Sat 10am–9pm, Sun 10am–8pm. Bus: 1, 2, 6, 10, or 29.

The only museum in the world where you learn about the sex lives of such famous people as Freud, Marilyn Monroe, Hugh Heffner, Nietzsche, and Duke Ellington, this museum of erotica opened in summer 1992. Founded by Ole Ege, a well-known Danish photographer of nudes, it's within walking distance of the Tivoli and the Central Railroad Station. In addition to revealing a glimpse into the sex lives of the famous, it presents a survey of erotica around the world and through the ages. The exhibits range from "the tame to the tempestuous"—from Etruscan drawings and Chinese paintings to Greek vases depicting sexual activity.

Tøjhusmuseet (Royal Arsenal Museum). Tøjhusgade 3. ☎ **33-11-60-37.** Admission 20DKK ($2.85) adults, 5DKK (70¢) children 6–12, children under 6 free. Tues–Sun noon–4pm. Closed Jan 1 and Dec 24–25 and 31.

This museum features a fantastic display of weapons used for hunting and warfare. On the ground floor is the Canon Hall, the longest vaulted Renaissance hall in Europe, stocked with artillery equipment from 1500 up to the present day. Above the Canon Hall is the impressive Armory Hall with one of the world's finest collections of small arms, colors, and armor.

THE ROYAL PALACES

✪ **Amalienborg Palace.** Amalienborg Slotsplads. ☎ **33-12-21-86.** Admission 40DKK ($6) adults, 5DKK (70¢) children 5–12 , children under 5 free. Jan–Apr and Nov–Dec Tues–Sun 11am–4pm, May–Oct 10am–4pm. Closed Dec 18–26. Bus: 1, 6, 9, 10, 19, or 29.

These four 18th-century French-style rococo mansions have been the home of the Danish royal family since 1794, when Christiansborg burned. Visitors flock to witness the changing of the guard at noon when the royal family is in residence. A swallowtail flag at mast signifies that the queen is in Copenhagen and not at her North Zealand summer home, Fredensborg Palace.

The Royal Life Guard in black bearskin busbies like the hussars leaves Rosenborg Castle at 11:30am and marches along Gothersgade, Nørrevold, Frederiksborggade, Købmagergade, Østergade, Kongens Nytorv, Bredgade, Sankt Annae Plads, and Amaliegade to Amalienborg. After the event, the guard, still accompanied by the band, returns to Rosenborg Castle via Frederiksgade, Store Kongensgade, and Gothersgade.

In 1994 some of the official and private rooms in Amalienborg were opened to the public for the first time. The rooms, reconstructed to reflect the period 1863 to 1947, belonged to members of the reigning royal family, the Glücksborgs, who ascended the throne in 1863. The highlight is the period devoted to the long reign (1863–1906) of King Christian IX and Queen Louise.

✪ **Christiansborg Palace.** Christiansborg Slotsplads, Prins Jørgens Gård 1. ☎ **33-92-64-92.** Admission to Royal Reception Rooms, 40DKK ($6) adults, 10DKK ($1.45) children; parliament, free; castle ruins, 20DKK ($2.85) adults, 5DKK (70¢) children. Reception Rooms, May and Sept, guided tours Tues–Sun at 11am and 3pm; June–Aug, guided tours daily at 11am, 1pm, and 3pm; Oct–Apr, guided tours Tues, Thurs, Sat–Sun at 11am and 3pm. English-language tours given only mid-June to late Sept Tues, Thurs, Sat–Sun 10am–4pm. Ruins, May–Sept Tues–Fri and Sun 9:30am–3:30pm. Bus: 1, 2, 6, 8, or 10.

This granite-and-copper palace on the Slotsholmen—a small island that has been the center of political power in Denmark for more than 800 years—houses the Danish parliament, the Supreme Court, the prime minister's offices, and the Royal Reception Rooms. A guide will lead you through richly decorated rooms, including the Throne Room, banqueting hall, and Queen's Library. Before entering, you'll be asked to put on soft overshoes to protect the floors. Under the palace, visit the well-preserved ruins of the 1167 castle of Bishop Absalon, founder of Copenhagen.

Rosenborg Castle. Øster Voldgade 4A. ☎ **33-15-32-86.** Admission 50DKK ($7) adults, 10DKK ($1.45) children 5–12, under 5 free. Palace and treasury (royal jewels), Jan–Apr Tues–Sun 11am–2pm; May–Sept daily 10am–4pm; Oct daily 11am–3pm; Nov–Dec 18 daily 11am–2pm; Dec 27–30 daily 11am–3pm. Closed Dec 19–26. S-tog: Nørreport. Bus: 5, 10, 14, 16, 31, 42, 43, 184, or 185.

This redbrick Renaissance-style castle houses everything from narwhal-tusk and ivory coronation chairs to Frederik VII's baby shoes—all from the Danish royal family. Its biggest draws are the dazzling crown jewels and regalia in the basement Treasury, where a lavishly decorated coronation saddle from 1596 is also shown. Try to see the Knights Hall (Room 21), with its coronation seat, three silver lions, and relics from the 1700s. Room 3 was used by founding father Christian IV, who died in this bedroom decorated with Asian lacquer art and a stucco ceiling.

CHURCHES & OTHER ATTRACTIONS

Frederikskirke. Frederiksgade 4. ☎ **33-15-01-44.** Free admission to church; 20DKK ($2.85) adults, 10DKK ($1.45) children to dome. Church: Mon–Tues and Thurs-Sat 10am–5pm; Wed 10am–6pm; Sun noon–5pm. Dome: Oct–May Sat–Sun 1–3pm; June–Aug daily 1–3pm. Bus: 1, 6, or 9.

This 2-centuries-old church, with its green copper dome—one of the largest in the world—is a short walk from Amalienborg Palace. After an unsuccessful start during the neoclassical revival of the 1750s in Denmark, the church was finally completed in Roman baroque style in 1894. In many ways, it's more impressive than Copenhagen's cathedral.

Vor Frue Kirke (Copenhagen Cathedral). Nørregade. ☎ **33-14-41-28.** Free admission. Mon–Fri 9am–5pm. Bus: 5.

This Greek Revival–style church, built in the early 19th century near Copenhagen University, features Bertel Thorvaldsen's white marble neoclassical works, including *Christ and the Apostles.* The funeral of H. C. Andersen took place here in 1875, and that of Søren Kierkegaard in 1855.

Rådhus (Town Hall). Rådhuspladsen. ☎ **33-66-25-82.** Admission to Rådhus, 30DKK ($4.30); clock, 10DKK ($1.45) adults, 5DKK (70¢) children. Guided tour: Rådhus, Mon–Fri 3pm, Sat 10am and 11am; tower, Oct–May Mon–Sat at noon; June–Sept Mon–Fri 10am, noon, 2pm; Sat noon. Bus: 1, 6, or 8.

Built in 1905, the Town Hall has impressive statues of H. C. Andersen and Niels Bohr, the Nobel Prize–winning physicist. Jens Olsen's famous **World Clock** is open for viewing Monday to Friday 10am to 4pm and Saturday at noon. The clockwork is so exact that the variation over 300 years is 0.4 seconds. Climb the tower for an impressive view.

Rundetårn (Round Tower). Købmagergade 52A. ☎ **33-73-03-73.** Admission 15DKK ($2.15) adults (14 and older), 5DKK (70¢) children 5–13, under 5 free. Tower, Sept–May Mon–Sat 10am–5pm, Sun noon–5pm; June–Aug Mon–Sat 10am–8pm, Sun noon–8pm. Observatory, Oct 15–Mar 20 Tues–Wed 7–10pm. S-tog: Nørreport. Bus: 5, 7E, 14, 16, or 42.

This 17th-century public observatory, attached to a church, is visited by thousands who climb the spiral ramp (no steps) for a panoramic view of Copenhagen. The tower is one of the crowning architectural achievements of the Christian IV era. Peter the Great, in Denmark for a state visit, galloped up the ramp on horseback.

Botanisk Have (Botanical Gardens). Öesterfarimadsdade 2 B ☎ **35-32-22-22.** Free admission. May–Sept daily 8:30am–6pm; Oct–Apr daily 8:30am–4pm. S-tog: Nørreport. Bus: 5, 7, 14, 16, 24, 40, or 43.

Planted from 1871 to 1874, the Botanical Gardens, across from Rosenborg Castle, are on a lake that was once part of the city's defensive moat. Special features include a cactus house and a palm house, all of which appear even more exotic in the far northern country of Denmark. An alpine garden contains mountain plants from all over the world.

ORGANIZED TOURS

BUS & BOAT TOURS For orientation, try the 1¹/₂-hour **City Tour** (2¹/₂ hours with a visit to a brewery) that covers major scenic highlights like *The Little Mermaid,* Rosenborg Castle, and Amalienborg Palace. On workdays, tours also visit the Carlsberg brewery. Tours depart May 30 to September 13 daily at 1pm and cost 125DKK ($18) adults and 20DKK ($2.85) children.

The **City and Harbor Tour,** a 2¹/₂-hour trip by launch and bus, departs from Town Hall Square. The boat tours the city's main canals, passing *The Little Mermaid* and the Old Fish Market. It operates May 30 to September 13 daily at 1pm. Tours cost 165DKK ($24) adults and 30DKK ($4.30) children under 12.

Shakespeare buffs will be interested in an afternoon excursion to the castles of North Zealand. The 7-hour English-language tour explores the area north of Copenhagen, including visits to Kronborg (Hamlet's Castle), a brief trip to Fredensborg, the queen's residence, and a stopover at Frederiksborg Castle and the National Historical Museum. Tours depart from the Town Hall Square, May 2 to October 16 Wednesday, Saturday, and Sunday at 10:15am. The cost is 335DKK ($48) adults and 40DKK ($6) children.

One of the most appealing of the guided tours is the **Hans Christian Andersen Tour,** which involves a 10-hour bus trip to the verdant island of Funen. It departs every Wednesday and Sunday between June and September at 8:30am from Rådhusplads. The cost of 500DKK ($72) includes transit from Copenhagen through Zealand, over the recently completed High Bridge spanning the Great Belt, to Odense, birthplace of Hans Christian Andersen. The price of lunch and admission to the various museums and castles visited is extra. Stops along the way include Egeskov Castle, built in 1554, and the house and museum of the fabled storyteller himself. Advance reservations are necessary. For more information about these English-language tours, contact **Copenhagen Excursions** at ☎ **32-54-06-06** or **Vikingbus** at ☎ **32-55-44-22.**

GUIDED WALKS English-language guided walking tours of Copenhagen are offered May 1 to September 30 at 50DKK ($7) adults and 25DKK ($3.55) children. Tours begin outside the tourist office. Contact the Copenhagen Tourist Information Center, Bernstorffsgade 1 (☎ **33-11-13-25**).

THE SHOPPING SCENE

✪ **Royal Copenhagen** and **Bing & Grøndahl Porcelain,** Amagertorv 6 (☎ **33-13-71-81;** bus: 1, 2, 6, 8, 28, 29, or 41 for the retail outlet or 1 or 14 for the factory), was founded in 1775. Royal Copenhagen's trademark, three wavy blue lines, has come to symbolize quality in porcelain throughout the world. The factory was a royal possession for a century before passing into private hands in 1868 and has turned out a new plate each year since 1908; most of the motifs depict the Danish countryside in winter.

In the Royal Copenhagen retail center, legendary ✪ **Georg Jensen,** Amagertorv 6 (☎ **33-11-40-80;** bus: 1, 6, 8, 9, or 10), is known for its fine silver. For the connoisseur, there's no better address—this is the largest and best collection of Jensen hollowware in Europe. Jewelry in traditional and modern design is also featured. One department specializes in seconds produced by various porcelain and glassware manufacturers. In the Royal Copenhagen retail center, **Holmegaards Glasvaerker,** Amagertorv 6 (☎ **33-12-44-77;** bus: 1, 6, 8, 9, or 10), is the only major producer of glasswork in Denmark. Look for the solidly crafted 1859 Wellington pattern, Holmegaard glasses, and Regiment Bar set.

Customers refer to the two owners of **The Amber Specialist,** Frederiksberggade 28 (☎ **33-11-88-03;** bus: 28, or 29, or 41), as "The Amber Twins." These blonde-haired ladies specialize in "the gold of the north." This stone—really petrified resin—originated in the large coniferous forests that covered Denmark some 35 million years ago.

A center for modern Scandinavian and Danish design, **Illums Bolighus,** Amagertorv 10, on Strøget (☎ **33-14-19-41;** bus: 28, 29, or 41), is one of Europe's finest showcases for household furnishings and accessories of every kind. The store also sells fashions and accessories for women and men. There's even a gift shop. At **Sweater Market,** Frederiksberggade 15 (☎ **33-15-27-73;** bus: 2, 8, or 30), take your pick from Scandinavian and Icelandic top-grade sweaters, hats, and scarves, hand knit in 100% wool. There's also a large selection of Icelandic wool jackets and coats.

One of Denmark's top department stores, **Illum's,** Østergade 52 (☎ **33-14-40-02;** bus: 1, 6, 9, or 10), is on the Strøget. Take time to browse through its vast world of Scandinavian design. There's a restaurant and a special export cash desk at street level. The elegant **Magasin,** Kongens Nytorv 13 (☎ **33-11-44-33;** bus: 1, 6, 9, or 10), is the biggest department store in Scandinavia. It offers an assortment of Danish designer fashion, glass and porcelain, and souvenirs. Goods are shipped abroad tax-free.

Established in 1926, **Kunsthallens Kunstauktioner,** Gothersgade 9 (☎ **33-32-52-00;** bus: 1, 6, 9, or 10), is Europe's leading dealer in the pan-European school of painting known as COBRA (Copenhagen, Brussels, and Amsterdam). These works, produced from 1948 to 1951, were an important precursor of abstract expressionism. The gallery holds 12 auctions yearly, 8 with modern art, others with 19th-century art. **Boghallen,** Rådhuspladsen 37 (☎ **33-11-85-11;** bus: 2, 8, or 30), is a big store carrying many books in English (including translations of Danish works) as well as a wide selection of travel-related literature, including maps. The shop is at Town Hall Square.

COPENHAGEN AFTER DARK

In Copenhagen, a good night means a late night. On warm weekends hundreds of rowdy revelers crowd Strøget until sunrise, and jazz clubs, traditional beer houses, and wine cellars are routinely packed. The city has a more serious cultural side as well, exemplified by excellent theaters, operas, and ballets. **Half-price tickets** for some concerts and theater productions are available the day of the performance from the ticket kiosk opposite the Nørreport rail station, at Nørrevoldgade and Fiolstræde; it's open Monday to Friday noon to 7pm and Saturday noon to 3pm. On summer evenings there're outdoor concerts in Fælled Park near the entrance, near Frederik V's Vej; inquire about dates and times at the Copenhagen Tourist Office.

THE PERFORMING ARTS

Det Kongelige Teater (Royal Theater), Kongens Nytorv (☎ **33-69-69-69;** bus: 1, 6, 9, or 10), which dates from 1748, is home to the world-renowned **Royal Danish Ballet** and the **Royal Danish Opera.** Because the arts are state subsidized in Denmark, ticket prices are comparatively low, and some seats may be available at the box office the day before a performance. We recommend making reservations in advance. The season runs from August to May. Tickets are 60 to 600DKK ($9 to $86), half price for seniors 67 and over and those under 26 (1 week before a show begins). Box office open Monday to Saturday 1 to 8pm; telephone hours Monday to Saturday 1 to 7pm.

NIGHTCLUBS

Across the boulevard from the Tivoili, **Rosie McGee's,** Vesterbrogade 2A (☎ **33-32-19-23;** bus: 250E or 350E), is a funky, American-style nightclub that caters to high-energy Generation X-ers (aged 21 to 40), whom you may or may not find enchanting.

Lots of young people come here to mingle, compare notes, and dance, dance, dance. The simple restaurant serves mostly Mexican food and frothy, foamy drinks. The bars and restaurant open nightly 5pm, with disco featured every Thursday to Saturday 11:30pm till dawn. Cover is 40DKK ($6) on disco nights only. Discos come and go with alarming frequency in the Danish capital, but **Slide/The Fever/Vasa,** Gothersgade 8F, Bolthensgaard (☎ **33-93-74-15;** Bus: 1, 6, or 9), remains one of the hotter, more popular venues for a late-night crowd of 25- to 35-year-olds, some of whom are avid fans of whatever musical innovation has just emerged in London or Los Angeles. The decorative themes derive from the 1960s cult classic *A Clockwork Orange.* Looking for insights into the heady world of the Danish arts? Head for the club's lower level, where luminaries from ballet, high fashion, and other fields are likely to be gossiping. The club is open Thursday to Saturday 11pm to 5am. Cover 50 to 100DKK ($7 to $14) after midnight.

LIVE-MUSIC CLUBS

In the very heart of the city, **Den Røde Pimpernel** (the Scarlet Pimpernel), Kattasundit 4 (☎ **33-12-20-32;** S-tog: Vesterport.), with its lively atmosphere, is a good place for people watching and dancing to an odd mix of contemporary pop and old-time evergreen ensembles. There's a bit of an attitude; the clientele is admitted only after being inspected through a peephole. The club is open Tuesday to Saturday 9pm to 5am. There's no cover Tuesday to Thursday, but there's a 50DKK ($7) cover Friday and Saturday.

    Copenhagen JazzHouse, Niels Hammingsensgade 10 (☎ **33-15-26-00;** S-tog: Nørreport), rocks and rolls, offering an all-purpose venue that plays—depending on the night of the week—everything from live jazz concerts to late-night disco. There's dancing to electronically amplified music Wednesday to Sunday 11pm to at least 3am. The quality and breed of jazz depends entirely on whoever is scheduled to appear on any particular evening. Live music tends to begin around 8:30pm. There's a cafe on the premises and tableside seating for up to 300 jazz fans at a time. Cover 40 to 70DKK ($5.70 to $10). **Mojo Blues Bar,** Løngangsstraede 21C (☎ **33-11-64-53;** bus: 2, 8, or 30), is one of the leading blues clubs in Scandinavia. Softly lit by candle and globe lamps, Mojo seats about 90 people at wooden tables and chairs and on a long bench along one wall. On weekends, which are often standing room only, up to 125 people cram through the door. Most come for the live blues performed mainly by Danish groups, although German, American, and British bands sometimes take the stage. It's open daily 8pm to 5am. No cover Sunday to Thursday, 50DKK ($7) Friday and Saturday.

A DANCE CLUB

Set a short walk from Tivoli, **Baron & Baroness,** Vesterbrøgade 2E (☎ **33-16-01-01;** bus: 250E or 350E), is a relatively upscale nightclub whose decor incorporates faux-medieval crenellations, attracting a crowd that's a bit more prosperous, and a bit more mature, than nearby competitors catering only to teenagers. Full meals cost 150 to 250DKK ($21to $36), and on nights when there's no disco, you'll find a solo musician playing a fiddle, piano, harmonica, or whatever. The bars are open nightly 5pm until at least 4:30am; the restaurant 5pm to 11:30pm. Disco, which is featured one floor above the street restaurant, is presented only Thursday to Saturday, 10pm till dawn. Cover 50DKK ($7) for disco only.

BARS

Det Lille Apotek, Stor Kannikestraede 15 (☎ **33-12-56-06;** bus: 2, 5, 8, or 30), is a good spot for English-speaking foreign students to meet their Danish contemporaries.

Though the menu varies, keep an eye out for the prawn cocktail and tenderloin. The main courses run about 88 to 128DKK ($13 to $18) at dinner. The kitchen is open daily 11:30am to 5pm, The bar is open daily 11am to midnight (closed December 24 to 26). Frequented by celebrities and royalty, the ✪ **Library Bar,** in the Hotel Plaza, Bernstorffsgade 4 (☎ **33-14-92-62;** bus: 6), was rated by the late Malcolm Forbes as one of the top five bars in the world. In a setting of antique books and works of art, you can order everything from a cappuccino to a cocktail. The setting is the lobby level of the landmark Plaza, commissioned in 1913 by King Frederik VIII. The bar was designed and built as the hotel's ballroom and Oregon pine was used for the paneling. The mural of George Washington and his men dates from 1910. It's open Monday to Saturday 11:30am to 1am and Sunday 11:30am to midnight.

Nyhavn 17, Nyhavn 17 (☎ **33-12-54-19;** bus: 1, 6, 27, or 29), is the last of the honky-tonks that used to make up the former sailors' quarter. This cafe is a short walk from the Kongens Nytorv and d'Angleterre hotels. In summer you can sit outside. On Tuesday to Saturday evenings there's free entertainment from a solo guitarist or guitar duet. It's open Sunday to Thursday 9:30am to 2am and Friday and Saturday until 4am. Built in 1670, **Hvids Vinstue,** Kongens Nytorv 19 (☎ **33-15-10-64;** bus: 1, 6, 9, or 10), is a wine cellar that's a dimly lit safe haven for an eclectic crowd, many patrons—both theater-goers and actors and dancers—drawn from the Royal Theater across the way. In December only, a combination of red wine and cognac is served. It's open Monday to Saturday from 10am to 2am; closed Sunday in July and August.

GAY & LESBIAN CLUBS

Café Babooshka, Turensensgade 6 (☎ **33-15-05-36;** bus: 5, 7, or 16), is Copenhagen's premier lesbian bar, owned and managed by women. Near the Ørsteds Parken and Gyldenløvesgade, it welcomes men, gay and straight, but primarily identifies itself as a spot where lesbians can be themselves. After 8pm, the cafe-style format is transformed into a disco. Friday and Saturday nights are reserved for women only. The place is open Sunday to Thursday 4pm to 1am, and Friday and Saturday 4pm to 2am. There's no cover. **Pan Society,** Knabrostræde 3 (☎ **33-13-19-48** or 33-11-37-84); bus: 28, 29, or 41), is a nationwide organization established in 1948 for the protection and advancement of gay and lesbian rights. Its headquarters is a 19th-century yellow building off the Strøget. A dance club occupies three of its floors, and a modern cafe is situated on the ground floor. Every night is gay night, although a lot of straights come here because the music is good. The cafe is open daily 8pm to 5am. The dance club, however, is open Wednesday 11pm to 3am, Thursday 10pm to 4am, Friday and Saturday 10pm to 5am, and Sunday 11pm to 3am. Admission to the dance club is 55DKK ($8).

A CASINO

At the **Casino Copenhagen,** in the SAS Scandinavia Hotel, Amager Blvd. 70 (☎ **33-96-59-65;** bus: 5, 11, 30, or 34), gamblers play such popular games as roulette, baccarat, punto banco, blackjack, and slots. The operation is overseen by Casinos of Austria, Europe's largest casino operator. It's open daily 2pm to 4am. Cover is 80DKK ($11). Jackets are required for men and a valid picture ID for all.

DAY TRIPS FROM COPENHAGEN

DRAGØR   Visit the past in this old seafaring town on the island of Amager, 4.8km (3 miles) south of Copenhagen's Kastrup Airport. It's filled with well-preserved half-timbered, ocher-and-pink 18th-century cottages with steep red-tile or thatch roofs, many of which are under the protection of the National Trust.

Dragør (pronounced *Drah-wer*) was a busy port on the herring-rich Baltic Sea in the early Middle Ages, but when fishing fell off, it became just another sleepy waterfront village. After 1520, Amager Island and its villages—Dragør and Store Magleby—were inhabited by the Dutch, who brought their own customs, Low-German language, and agricultural expertise, especially their love of bulb flowers. In Copenhagen, you still see wooden-shoed Amager selling their hyacinths, tulips, daffodils, and lilies in the streets.

A rich trove of historic treasures is in the **Amager Museum,** Hovedgaden 4–12, Store Magleby (☎ **32-53-93-07;** bus: 30, 33, or 350S), outside Dragør. The exhibits reveal the affluence achieved by the Amager Dutch, with rich textiles, fine embroidery, and amenities like carved silver buckles and buttons. The interiors of a Dutch house are especially interesting. Admission is 20DKK ($2.85) adults, 10DKK ($1.45) children. It's open April to September Tuesday to Sunday noon to 4pm; October to March Wednesday and Sunday noon to 4pm.

The exhibits at the harbor-front **Dragør Museum,** Havnepladsen 2–4 (☎ **32-53-41-06;** bus: 30, 33, or 350S), show how the Amager Dutch lived from prehistoric times to the 20th century. Farming, goose breeding, seafaring, fishing, ship piloting, and ship salvage are delineated through pictures and artifacts. Admission is 20DKK ($2.85) adults, 10DKK ($1.45) children. It's open May to September Tuesday to Sunday noon to 4pm; closed October to April.

Getting There   Dragør is a 35-minute trip on bus no. 30, 33, or 73E from Rådhuspladsen (Town Hall Square) in Copenhagen.

LOUISIANA   Established in 1958, the ✪ **Louisiana Museum of Modern Art,** Gl. Strandvej 13 (☎ **49-19-07-19**), is idyllically situated in a 19th-century mansion on the Danish Riviera surrounded by a sculpture park, opening directly onto the Øresund. Paintings and sculptures by modern masters, such as Giacometti and Henry Moore, as well as the best and most controversial works of modern art are displayed. The museum name came from the estate's first owner, Alexander Brun, who had three wives, each named Louise. Admission is 55DKK ($8) adults, 15DKK ($2.15) children 4 to 16, and children under 4 free. It's open daily 10am to 5pm; closed December 24, 25, and 31.

Getting There   **Humlebaek,** the nearest town to Louisiana, may be reached by train from Copenhagen (København-Helsingør). Two trains an hour leave from the main station in Copenhagen (trip time: 40 minutes). Once you're at Humlebaek, follow signs to the museum, a 15-minute walk.

HELSINGØR (ELSINORE)   Helsingør is visited chiefly for "Hamlet's Castle." Aside from its literary associations, the town has a certain charm: a quiet market square, medieval lanes, and old half-timbered and brick buildings, remains of its once-prosperous shipping industry. The **Tourist Office,** Havnepladsen 3 (☎ **49-21-13-33**), is open Monday to Friday 9:30am to 6pm and Saturday 9am to 4pm.

There's no evidence Shakespeare ever saw this sandstone-and-copper Dutch Renaissance–style castle, full of intriguing secret passages and casemates, but he made **Kronborg Slot,** Kronborg (☎ **49-21-30-78**), famous in *Hamlet.* According to 12th-century historian Saxo Grammaticus, though, if Hamlet had really existed, he would've lived centuries before Kronborg was erected (1574–85). Over the years, some famous productions of *Hamlet* have been staged here, the castle's bleak atmosphere providing a good foil to the drama.

During its history, the castle has been looted, bombarded, gutted by fire, and used as a barracks (1785–1922). The starkly furnished Great Hall is the largest in northern Europe. The church with its original oak furnishings and the royal chambers is also worth exploring. Admission to the castle is 30DKK ($4.30) adults, 10DKK ($1.45) children 6 to 14. May to September, it's open daily 10:30am to 5pm; October and April, hours are Tuesday to Sunday 11am to 4pm; November to March, it's open Tuesday to Sunday 11am to 3pm (closed Christmas). Guided tours are given every half hour October to April. In summer you can walk around on your own. The castle is .8km ($^1/_2$ mile) from the rail station.

Getting There   Once you reach Helsingør, 40.2km (25 miles) north of Copenhagen, you'll be deposited in the center of town and can cover all the major attractions on foot. There are frequent trains from Copenhagen, taking 50 minutes. Some 30 buses daily leave Copenhagen for the 1-hour trip to Helsingør.

5

England

by Darwin Porter & Danforth Prince

London is the most happening city in Europe—lively, fast-paced, and teeming with action. London now touts its fascinating contradictions: It's both an overwhelming jumble of antiquity and a world leader in the latest music, fashion, and food (the cuisine is better than ever). As stimulating as the city is, however, you'll want to tear yourself away from it to visit legendary Stonehenge on the Salisbury Plain, Oxford University, and the unspoiled stone-built villages of the Cotswolds. The classic city of Bath isn't just a museum of the past, with echoes ranging from the Romans to 18th-century Jane Austen, but a vibrant fashionable city of today, renowned for its shopping and architectural monuments.

1 London

Samuel Johnson said, "When a man is tired of London, he is tired of life; for there's in London all that life can afford." In this section, we'll survey a segment of that life: ancient monuments, literary shrines, museums, walking tours, Parliament debates, royal castles, waxworks, palaces, cathedrals, and parks.

ORIENTATION
ARRIVING   By Plane   Heathrow Airport (☎ 020/8759-4321) is divided into four terminals, each relatively self-contained. Terminal 4 handles many of the long-haul and transatlantic operations of British Airways; most U.S. airline flights arrive at Terminal 3. Terminals 1 and 2 receive intra-European flights. There's an Underground (subway) connection to central London; the 50-minute trip costs £3.40 ($6). Airbuses take about an hour; they cost £7 ($12) adults; up to four children ride free if accompanied by an adult. A taxi usually costs from £35 to £40 ($60 to $68), but may be higher. For more information about train or bus connections, call ☎ 020/7222-1234.

The **London-Heathrow Express** (☎ 0845/600-1515) is a 160kph (100 m.p.h.) train running every 15 minutes daily 5:10am to 11:40pm to Paddington Station. Trips cost £12 ($20) in economy class or £20 ($34) in first class; children up to 15 ride free (trip time: 15 to 20 minutes). There are special areas for wheelchairs. From Paddington, passengers can connect to other trains or hail a taxi. You can buy tickets on the train or at self-service machines at Heathrow (also available from travel agents).

Gatwick (☎ **01293/535353** for flight information) is 40km (25 miles) south of London. Trains leave for London every 15 minutes during the day and every hour at night; they cost £10.20 ($17) adults, children aged 5 to 15 half price, and under 5 free. There's also an express Flightline bus (no. 777) from Gatwick to Victoria Station that departs every half hour from 6:30am to 8pm and every hour from 8 to 11pm; it costs £8 ($14). A taxi from Gatwick to central London usually costs £55 to £65 ($94 to $111); however, you must negotiate a fare with the driver before you get into the cab. The London meter doesn't apply since Gatwick lies outside the Metropolitan Police District.

By Train   Most trains from Paris traveling through the "Chunnel" pull in at **Waterloo Station.** Visitors from Amsterdam arrive at the **Liverpool Street Station,** and those journeying south by rail from Edinburgh disembark at **King's Cross Station.** All are connected to the vast bus and Underground network, and have phones, restaurants, pubs, luggage-storage areas, and London Regional Transport Information Centres.

By Car   If you're taking a car across the channel, you can quickly connect by motorway (superhighway) into London. London is encircled by a ring road. Determine which part of the city you wish to enter and follow the signs. You should confine your driving in London to the *bare minimum;* before you arrive, call your hotel for advice on where to park. Be warned—parking is scarce and expensive. Most important driving tip in England: *Remember to drive on the left.*

VISITOR INFORMATION   The **British Visitors Centre,** 1 Regent St., London SW1 4XT (tube: Piccadilly Circus), caters to walk-in visitors (phone information has been suspended). It's often a long wait. On the premises you'll find a British Rail ticket office, a travel agency, theater-ticket agency, hotel-booking service, bookshop, and souvenir shop, all in one well-equipped and very modern facility. It's open Monday to Friday 9am to 6:30pm and Saturday and Sunday 10am to 4pm, with extended Saturday hours June to September.

For a full information pack on London, write to the London Tourist Board, 26 Grosvenor Gardens, SW1 WODU.

CITY LAYOUT   For our purposes, London begins at **Chelsea,** on the north bank of the river, and stretches for roughly 8km (5 miles) north to **Hampstead.** Its western boundary runs through Kensington, whereas the eastern boundary lies 8km (5 miles) away, at Tower Bridge. Inside this 8-by-8km (5-by-5-mile) square, you'll find all the hotels and restaurants and nearly all the sights that are usually of interest to visitors.

The logical, though not geographical, center of this area is **Trafalgar Square,** which we'll take as our orientation point. Stand here facing the steps of the imposing National Gallery; you're looking northwest. That's the direction of **Piccadilly Circus**—the real core of tourist London—and the maze of streets that makes up **Soho.** Farther north runs **Oxford Street,** London's gift to moderately priced shopping, and still farther northwest lies Regent's Park and the zoo.

At your back (south) runs **Whitehall,** which houses or skirts nearly every British government building, including the official residence of the prime minister at **10 Downing Street.** In the same direction, a bit farther south, stand the Houses of Parliament and Westminster Abbey. Flowing southwest from Trafalgar Square is the table-smooth **Mall,** flanked by parks and mansions and leading to Buckingham Palace, the queen's residence. Farther along in the same direction lie **Belgravia** and **Knightsbridge,** the city's plushest residential areas, and south of them is chic **Chelsea** and **King's Road,** an upscale boulevard for shopping.

Due west stretches the superb and high-priced shopping area bordered by **Regent Street** and **Piccadilly.** Farther west lie the equally elegant shops and even more elegant homes of **Mayfair.** Then comes **Park Lane,** with its deluxe hotels. Beyond is **Hyde Park,** the biggest park in central London and one of the largest in the world. **Charing Cross Road** runs north from Trafalgar Square, past **Leicester Square,** and intersects with **Shaftesbury Avenue.** This is London's Theaterland. A bit farther along, Charing Cross Road turns into a browser's paradise, lined with shops selling new and secondhand books. At last, it funnels into **St. Giles Circus.** Beyond is **Bloomsbury,** site of the University of London, the British Museum, and erstwhile stamping ground of the famed "Bloomsbury group," led by Virginia Woolf. Northeast lies **Covent Garden,** known for its Royal Opera House; today it's a major shopping, restaurant, and cafe district.

Follow **The Strand** eastward from Trafalgar Square and you'll come to **Fleet Street.** From the 19th century through most of the 20th century, this area was the most concentrated newspaper district in the world. **Temple Bar** stands where The Strand becomes Fleet Street, and only here do you enter the actual City of London, or "the City." Its focal point and shrine is the Bank of England on **Threadneedle Street,** with the Stock Exchange next door and the Royal Exchange across the street. In the midst of all the hustle and bustle rises **St. Paul's Cathedral,** Sir Christopher Wren's monument to beauty and tranquillity. At the far eastern fringe of the City looms the **Tower of London,** shrouded in legend, blood, and history and permanently besieged by battalions of visitors.

GETTING AROUND   By Public Transportation   Both the Underground (subway) and bus systems are operated by **London Transport.** Travel Information Centres are in the Underground stations at King's Cross, Hammersmith, Oxford Circus, St. James's Park, Liverpool Street Station, and Piccadilly Circus, as well as in the British Rail stations at Euston and Victoria and in each of the terminals at Heathrow Airport. They take reservations for London Transport's guided tours and have free Underground and bus maps and other information. A **24-hour telephone information** service is available by calling ☎ **020/7222-1234.**

Travelcards for use on most buses, the Underground, and British Rail inside Greater London can be purchased at Underground ticket offices, Travel Information Centres, and some newsstands. For short stays, a **1-Day Off-Peak Travelcard** can be used Monday to Friday after 9:30am and any time on weekends and bank holidays. A two-zone card costs £4.50 ($8) adults and £2.80 ($4.75) children 5 to 15;, children 4 and under are free. Travelcards are also available for periods of 7 days to 1 year. A 7-day Travelcard allowing travel in two zones costs £17.60 ($30) adults and £6.50 ($11) children.

By Underground (Subway)   The Underground is known locally as "the tube"; all stations are clearly marked with a red circle and blue crossbar. Fares are based on zones. The flat fare for one trip within the zone 1 is £1.40 ($2.40). Trips from the zone 1 to destinations in the suburbs generally range from £1.40 to £4.40 ($2.40 to $8). Be sure to keep your ticket, as it must be presented when you exit at your destination.

By Bus   The bus system is almost as good as the Underground, and you'll have a better view of the city. To find out about current routes, pick up a free bus map at one of the Travel Information Centres listed above.

A Map Note

See the inside front cover of this guide for a map of the London Underground.

Fares vary according to the distance traveled. Generally, the cost is 50p to £1.20 (85¢ to $2.05). If you travel for two or three stops, the cost is 60p ($1); longer runs within zone 1 are charged 90p ($1.55). If you want to be warned when to get off, simply ask the driver or conductor. For schedules and fares, call the 24-hour hot line at ☎ **020/7222-1200.**

By Taxi   For a radio cab, phone ☎ **020/7272-0272** or 020/7253-5000. The minimum fare is £2.70 ($4.60) for the first half kilometer (third of a mile) or 1 minute and 51 seconds, with increments of 20p (35¢) thereafter, based on distance or time. Each additional passenger is charged 40p (70¢). Passengers pay 10p (15¢) for each piece of luggage in the driver's compartment and any other item more than 2 feet long. Surcharges are imposed after 8pm and on weekends and public holidays. All these tariffs include VAT, and fares usually increase annually. It's recommended that you tip 10% to 15% of the fare.

By Car   Rent a car only if you plan to take excursions into the environs. Because of traffic and parking difficulties, it's virtually impossible to see London by car.

By Bicycle   One of the most popular bike rental shops is **On Your Bike,** 52–54 Tooley St., London Bridge, SE1 (☎ **020/7378-6669;** tube: London Bridge), open Monday to Friday 9am to 6pm, Saturday 9:30am to 5:30pm, and Sunday 11am to 4pm. The first-class mountain bikes, with high seats and low-slung handlebars, cost £15 ($26) per day or £30 ($51) per weekend, or £60 ($102) per week and require a £200 ($340) deposit on a credit card.

Fast Facts: London

American Express   The main office is at 6 Haymarket, SW1 (☎ **020/ 7930-4411;** tube: Piccadilly Circus). Full services are available Monday to Saturday 9am to 5:30pm; foreign-exchange only is open Sunday 10am to 1pm.

Baby-Sitters   The best is **Childminders,** 6 Nottingham St., London W1M 3RB (☎ **020/7935-3000;** tube: Baker St.). You pay £5.80 ($10) per hour in the daytime and £4.30 to £5.50 ($7 to $9) per hour at night. There's a 4-hour minimum, and hotel guests are charged a £10 ($17) booking fee each time they use a sitter.

Business Hours   **Banks** are usually open Monday to Friday 9:30am to 3:30pm. **Pubs and bars** are open Monday to Saturday 11am to 11pm and Sunday noon to 10:30pm; some pubs close Sunday 3 to 7pm. **Stores** are generally open daily 9am to 5:30pm, to 7pm Wednesday or Thursday. Most central shops close Saturday around 1pm.

Currency   The basic unit of currency is the **pound sterling** (£), which is divided into 100 pence (p). There are 1p, 2p, 10p, 20p, 50p, and £1 and £2 coins; banknotes are issued in £1, £5, £10, £20, and £50 denominations. The rate of exchange used in this chapter was £1 = $1.70.

Dentists/Doctors   For dental emergencies, call **Eastman Dental Hospital** (☎ **020/7915-1000;** tube: King's Cross). Some hotels have doctors on call. In an emergency, contact **Doctor's Call** (☎ **020/8037-2255). Medical Express,** 117A Harley St., W1 (☎ **020/7499-1991;** tube: Regent's Park), is a private British clinic that's not part of the free British medical establishment. It's open Monday to Friday 9am to 6pm and Saturday 9:30am to 2:30pm.

Drugstores　In Britain they're called "chemists." **Bliss The Chemist,** 5 Marble Arch, W1 (☎ **020/7723-6116;** tube: Marble Arch), is open daily 9am to midnight. Every London neighborhood has a branch of **Boots.**

Embassies　The **U.S. Embassy** is at 24 Grosvenor St., W1 (☎ **020/ 7499-9000;** tube: Bond St.). For passport and visa information, go to the U.S. Passport and Citizenship Unit, 55–56 Upper Brook St., London, W1 (☎ **020/7499-9000,** ext. 2563 or 2564; tube: Marble Arch). Hours are Monday to Friday 8:30am to 11:30am and 2 to 4pm (Tuesday the office closes at noon). The **Canadian High Commission,** MacDonald House, 38 Grosvenor St., W1 (☎ **020/7258-6600;** tube: Bond St.), handles visas for Canada. It's open Monday to Friday 8 to 11am. The **Australian High Commission,** at Australia House, Strand, WC2 (☎ **020/7379-4334;** tube: Charing Cross or Aldwych), is open Monday to Friday 9:30am to 3:30pm. The **New Zealand High Commission,** at New Zealand House, 80 Haymarket at Pall Mall, SW1 (☎ **020/7930-8422;** tube: Charing Cross or Piccadilly Circus), is open Monday to Friday 10am to noon and 2 to 4pm. The **Irish Embassy,** at 17 Grosvenor Place, SW1 (☎ **020/7235-2171;** tube: Hyde Park Corner), is open Monday to Friday 9:30am to 1pm and 2:15 to 5pm. The **South African High Commission**, South Africa House, Trafalgar Square, WC2 (☎ **020/7451-7299;** tube: Charing Cross), is open Monday to Friday 10am to noon and 2 to 4pm.

Emergencies　In London, for police, fire, or an ambulance, dial ☎ **999.**

Hospitals　Emergency care 24 hours a day, with the first treatment free under the National Health Service, is offered by Royal Free Hospital, Pond Street, NW10 (☎ **020/7794-0500;** tube: Belsize Park), and University College Hospital, Gower Street, WC1 (☎ **020/7387-9300;** tube: Warren St.).

Internet Access　You can send e-mails or check on your messages at **Cyberia Café,** Whitfield Street, W1 (☎ **020/7813-9659;** e-mail: cyberia@easynet. co.uk; tube: Goodge St.), open Monday to Friday 10am to 8pm, Saturday 11am to 7pm, and Sunday 11am to 6pm.

Post Office　The **Main Post Office,** 24 William IV St., WC2N 4DL (☎ **020/ 7484-9307;** tube: Charing Cross), operates as three separate businesses: inland and international postal service and banking; philatelic postage stamp sales; and the post shop, selling greeting cards and stationery. All are open Monday to Saturday 8am to 8pm.

Taxes　The British government levies a 25% tax on gasoline ("petrol"). In 1994, Britain imposed a departure tax: either £10 ($17) for flights within Britain and the EU or £20 ($34) for passengers flying elsewhere. This tax is generally written into the price of your ticket.

Telephone　To call London from the United States, dial the international code **44** (Britain's country code) and **20** and then the 8-digit local telephone number. To call outside London, dial the international code 44, and then the exchange code and the local telephone number.

　　To place a local call for 2 minutes costs 10p (15¢), and you can buy phone cards at newsstands for £1 ($1.70), £2 ($3.40), £4 ($7), £10 ($17), and £20 ($34). To make an international call, dial 155 to reach the international operator. To dial direct, dial 00. For the United States, you reach AT&T at 0800-89-0077, MCI at 0800-89-0222, and Sprint at 0800-89-0877.

WHERE TO STAY

In most of the places listed, a service charge ranging from 10% to 15% will be added to your bill. The British government also imposes a VAT of 17.5% to your bill. Those looking to splurge on very special accommodations may like to stay at Henry XIII's **Hampton Court Palace** for 4 to 7 days (see "Side Trips from London").

MAYFAIR

Very Expensive

✪ **Brown's Hotel.** 29–34 Albemarle St., London W1A 4SW. ☎ **020/7493-6020.** Fax 020/7493-9381. www.brownshotel.com. 118 units. A/C MINIBAR TV TEL. £280 ($476) double; from £360 ($612) suite. VAT extra. AE, DC, MC, V. Tube: Green Park.

Brown's, the quintessential London hotel, was created by a former manservant of Lord Byron and opened in 1837, the year Queen Victoria ascended the throne. Today, Brown's occupies some 14 historic houses on two streets just off Berkeley Square. Bedrooms, many quite small, are furnished traditionally with old-fashioned comfort. In the formal restaurant the table d'hôte changes frequently, and dishes have a lighter, more contemporary touch than before, though the "trolley roast" is still here for long-time devotees.

Park Lane Hotel. Piccadilly, London W1Y 8BX. ☎ **800/325-3535** in the U.S., or 020/7499-6321. Fax 020/7499-1965. 305 units. MINIBAR TV TEL. £260 ($442) double; from £360 ($612) suite. AE, DC, MC, V. Parking £26 ($44). Tube: Hyde Park Corner or Green Park.

The most traditional of the Park Lane mansions, its silver entrance is an art deco marvel and has been used in many films. Some 150 rooms were recently redecorated. The accommodations are luxurious and spacious and many rooms have marble fireplaces. Bracewell's, the hotel's award-winning restaurant, competes favorably with other grand hotel dining rooms. There're also fitness facilities and a business center on the premises.

Expensive

Hotel Chesterfield. 35 Charles St., London W18 LX. ☎ **020/7491-2622.** Fax 020/7491-4793. E-mail: reservations@chesterfield.viewinn.co.uk. 110 units. A/C MINIBAR TV TEL. £190 ($323) double; from £325–£350 ($552–$595) suite. AE, DC, MC, V. Tube: Green Park.

An air of Victorian respectability and the easy access to Berkeley Square form part of the allure of this Mayfair hotel, once partly the home of the Earl of Chesterfield. The owners take great pride and care in their decorative techniques: Each room contains rich-looking accessories, an antique or two, or some artifact that might remind you of a stately English home. There's a restaurant on the premises, open daily for lunch and dinner, and a bar in a glass-roofed conservatory that fills what was an outdoor courtyard.

Inexpensive

Ivanhoe Suite Hotel. 1 St. Christopher's Place, Barrett St. Piazza, London W1M 5HB. ☎ **020/7935-1047.** Fax 020/7224-0563. www.scoot.co.uk/ivanhoe-suite-hotel. 8 units. TV. £79 ($134) double; £89 ($151) triple. Rates include continental breakfast. AE, DC, MC, V. Tube: Bond St.

Shopping buffs flock to this little jewel tucked away off Oxford Street, close to the shop-flanked New and Old Bond streets. Above a restaurant, it's on a pedestrian street of boutiques and restaurants. The recently redecorated singles and doubles are attractively furnished, each with a sitting area, entry security video, beverage-making facilities, fridge/bar, plus a wide selection of videotapes.

London Accommodations

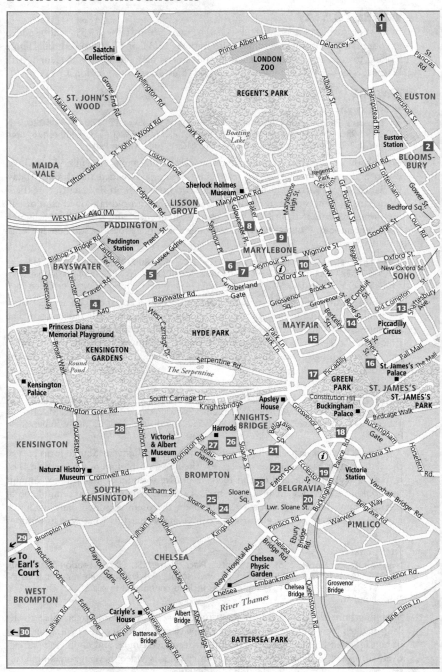

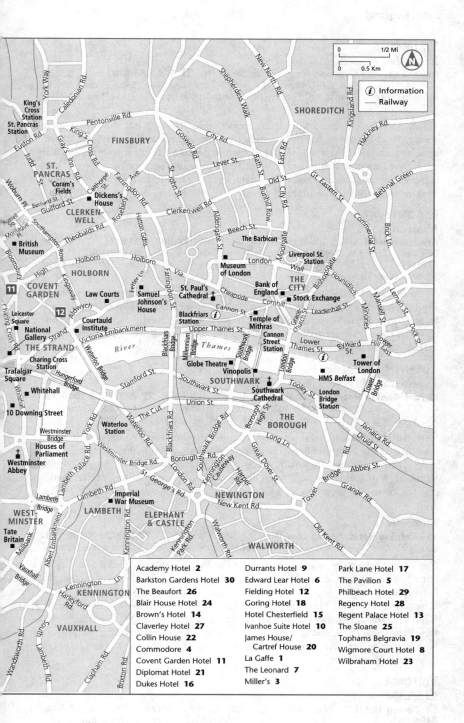

Academy Hotel **2**
Barkston Gardens Hotel **30**
The Beaufort **26**
Blair House Hotel **24**
Brown's Hotel **14**
Claverley Hotel **27**
Collin House **22**
Commodore **4**
Covent Garden Hotel **11**
Diplomat Hotel **21**
Dukes Hotel **16**

Durrants Hotel **9**
Edward Lear Hotel **6**
Fielding Hotel **12**
Goring Hotel **18**
Hotel Chesterfield **15**
Ivanhoe Suite Hotel **10**
James House/
    Cartref House **20**
La Gaffe **1**
The Leonard **7**
Miller's **3**

Park Lane Hotel **17**
The Pavilion **5**
Philbeach Hotel **29**
Regency Hotel **28**
Regent Palace Hotel **13**
The Sloane **25**
Tophams Belgravia **19**
Wigmore Court Hotel **8**
Wilbraham Hotel **23**

ST. JAMES'S
Expensive

Dukes Hotel. 35 St. James's Place, London SW1A 1NY. ☎ **800/381-4702** in the U.S., or 020/7491-4840. Fax 020/7493-1264. www.dukes.hotel.co.uk. E-mail: dukeshotel@ compuserve.com. 81 units. A/C TV TEL. £200 ($340) double; from £310 ($527) suite. AE, DC, MC, V. Parking £32 ($54). Tube: Green Park.

Dukes provides elegance without ostentation. Since 1908, it has stood in a quiet courtyard off St. James's Street. It attracts the urbane guest who's looking for charm, style, and tradition. Each well-furnished room is decorated in the style of a particular period, ranging from Regency to Edwardian. All rooms are equipped with private bars and luxurious mattresses. Dukes Restaurant is small, tasteful, and elegant, combining both classic British and continental cuisine.

BLOOMSBURY
Moderate

Academy Hotel. 17–25 Gower St., London WC1E 6HG. ☎ **800/678-3096** in the U.S., or 020/7631-4115. Fax 020/7636-3442. www.etontownhouse.com. 48 units. A/C TV TEL. £125–£145 ($213–$247) double; £185 ($315) suite. AE, DC, MC, V. Tube: Tottenham Court Rd. or Goodge St.

In the heart of London's publishing district, the hotel was substantially upgraded in the 1990s, with a bathroom added to every room—whether there was space or not. Rooms are decorated in a neutral style, but they are well cared for. Facilities include an elegant bar, a library room, a secluded patio garden, and two restaurants serving French and continental food.

COVENT GARDEN
Expensive

Covent Garden Hotel. 10 Monmouth St., London WC2H 9HB. ☎ **020/7806-1000.** Fax 020/7806-1100. 50 units. A/C MINIBAR TV TEL. £200 ($340) double; £295 ($502) suite. AE, MC, V. Parking: £30 ($51). Tube: Leicester Sq. or Covent Garden.

Originally built as a hospital around 1850, the premises were reconfigured in 1996 into a charming boutique hotel. Soundproof rooms are lushly outfitted in English style. Their decorative trademark? Each contains a clothier's mannequin—a lithe female form draped in the same fabric that went into the composition of that particular bedroom. The hotel also has two charming restaurants and bar with full English fare.

Moderate

The Fielding Hotel. 4 Broad Court, Bow St., London WC2B 5QZ. ☎ **020/7836-8305.** Fax 020/7497-0064. 26 units. £95–£120 ($162–$204) double. AE, DC, MC, V. Tube: Covent Garden.

One of London's more eccentric hotels, the Fielding is cramped, quirky, and quaint, but an enduring favorite nonetheless. Almost opposite the Royal Opera House, the hotel is just outside Covent Garden with its pubs, shops, markets, and restaurants. It is named after novelist Henry Fielding of *Tom Jones* fame who lived in Broad Court. Rooms are small, but they are so old-fashioned and traditional they have their devotees. Bathrooms are minuscule. Floors dip and sway, and the furnishings and fabrics have known better times, so be duly warned. There's a small bar where guests can enjoy a traditional pint.

VICTORIA
Expensive

✪ **Goring Hotel.** 15 Beeston Place, Grosvenor Gardens, London SW1W 0JW. ☎ **020/ 7396-9000.** Fax 020/7834-4393. www.goringhotel.co.uk. E-mail: reception@goringhotel.

co.uk. 75 units. TV TEL. £195–£235 ($332–$400) double; from £260 ($442) suite. AE, DC, MC, V. Parking £21 ($36). Tube: Victoria Station.

Built in 1910, this was the first hotel in the world to have central heating and a private bathroom in every bedroom. Just behind Buckingham Palace, it's our premier choice for the Victoria area. The charm of a traditional English country home is reflected in the paneled drawing room, where fires burn in ornate fireplaces. All the well-furnished rooms (called apartments) have been refurbished; some are air-conditioned. The Goring is one of the best places in London for afternoon tea, and its restaurant and bar offer the area's finest traditional English dishes and drinks. Guests have free use of a nearby health club.

Moderate
Tophams Belgravia. 28 Ebury St., London SW1W 0LU. ☎ **020/7730-8147.** Fax 020/7823-5966. www.tophams.com. E-mail: Tophams_Belgravia.compuserve.com. 39 units, 38 with bathroom. TV TEL. £110 ($187) double without bathroom, £130–£140 ($221–$238) double with bathroom; £260 ($442) suite. AE, DC, MC, V. Tube: Victoria Station.

Tophams, opened in 1937 and completely renovated in 1997, retains its country-house flavor, complete with flower-filled window boxes. All rooms have hair dryers, satellite TV, and beverage-making facilities; the finest have en suite bathrooms and four-poster beds. The best feature of this hotel, however, is that it's only a 3-minute walk from Victoria Station.

Inexpensive
Collin House. 104 Ebury St., London SW1W 9QD. ☎ **020/7730-8031.** Fax 020/7730-8031. 13 units, 8 with bathroom. £62 ($105) double without bathroom, £73 ($124) double with bathroom. Rates include English breakfast. No credit cards. Tube: Victoria Station.

This is a good, clean, no-smoking B&B where everything is well maintained. The rooms come in various shapes and sizes, the largest on the lower floors, and there are a number of family rooms. The units at the back are quiet, while those in the front face a lot of traffic noise (no soundproofing). The main bus, rail, and tube stations are all about a 5-minute walk from the hotel.

✪ **James House/Cartref House.** 108 Ebury St. and 129 Ebury St., London, SW1W 9QD. ☎ **020/7730-7338** for James House, **020/7730-6176** for Cartref House. Fax 020/7730-7338. 20 units, 11 with bathroom. £62 ($105) double without bathroom, £73 ($124) double with bathroom; £104 ($177) quad with bathroom. AE, MC, V. Tube: Victoria Station.

Hailed by many publications as one of the top 10 B&Bs in London, James House and Cartref House (across the street) deserve the accolades. Derek and Sharon James run both properties and are the finest hosts in the area. They're constantly refurbishing, so everything looks state-of-the-art. Each room is individually designed, and some of the large rooms have bunk beds suitable for families. The generous English breakfast means you might skip lunch. Don't worry about which house you're assigned. Each is equally good.

KNIGHTSBRIDGE
Expensive
The Beaufort. 33 Beaufort Gardens, London SW3 1PP. ☎ **800/888-1199** in the U.S and Canada, or 020/7584-5252. Fax 020/7589-2834. www.thebeaufort.co.uk/index.htm. 28 units. TV TEL. £200 ($340) double; £325 ($553) junior suite for 2. Rates include continental breakfast and afternoon tea. AE, DC, MC, V. Tube: Knightsbridge.

One of London's finest boutique hotels has an elegant town-house atmosphere, with personal service and the ultimate in tranquillity. A short walk from Harrods, it sits behind two Victorian porticoes and an iron fence. Each room features a painting by a London artist, plush carpeting, and a kind of grace throughout. Light meals are available from room service, and the hotel has a health club.

Moderate

Claverley Hotel. 13–14 Beaufort Gardens, London SW3 1PS. ☎ **800/747-0398** in the U.S., or 020/7589-8541. Fax 020/7584-3410. www.camelotintl.com. 29 units, 27 with bathroom. TV TEL. £120–£190 ($204–$323) double; £160 ($272) junior suite. Rates include English breakfast. AE, DC, MC, V. Tube: Knightsbridge.

On a quiet cul-de-sac, this tasteful hotel, one of the neighborhood's very best, is just a few blocks from Harrods. It's a small, cozy place accented with Georgian-era accessories. The lounge evokes a country house. Most rooms have wall-to-wall carpeting and comfortably upholstered armchairs.

BELGRAVIA
Moderate

Diplomat Hotel. 2 Chesham St., London SW1X 8DT. ☎ **020/7235-1544.** Fax 020/7259-6153. www.btinternet.com/~diplomat.hotel. E-mail: Diplomat.Hotel@btinternet. co.uk. 26 units. TV TEL. £125–£155 ($213–$264) double. Rates include English breakfast buffet. AE, DC, MC, V. Tube: Sloane Sq. or Knightsbridge.

This is a small, reasonably priced hotel in an otherwise expensive neighborhood. It was built in 1882 by one of the neighborhood's most famous architects, Thomas Cubitt. Rooms are comfortable and many were renovated in 1996. Modern bathrooms are equipped with hair dryers. The staff is very helpful and light meals and snacks are available in the hotel bar area.

CHELSEA
Moderate

Blair House Hotel. 34 Draycott Place, London SW3 2SA. ☎ **020/7581-2323.** Fax 020/7823-7752. 11 units. TV TEL. £110–£118 ($187–$201) double. Rates include continental breakfast. AE, DC, MC, V. Tube: Sloane Sq.

This comfortable hotel is a good reasonably priced choice in the heart of Chelsea. In terms of price, it comes as a relief when compared to the rates of some of Chelsea's luxurious hotels. The old-fashioned building has been modified and completely refurbished. The comfortable rooms sport radios, hair dryers, and beverage-making facilities. The quieter rooms are in the back.

The Sloane. 29 Draycott Place, London SW3 2SH. ☎ **020/7581-5757.** Fax 020/7584-1348. 12 units. A/C TV TEL. £140 ($238) double; £225 ($383) suite. AE, DC, MC, V. Tube: Sloane Sq.

Set in a redbrick Victorian-era townhouse, this hotel combines worthy 19th-century antiques with modern comforts and a desirable Chelsea location near Sloane Square. The rooms come in varying sizes but are opulently furnished, many with four-poster or canopied beds. There's 24-hour room service as well as a top-floor bar with a limited menu and a panoramic view. The staff is accommodating, pan-European, and tactful.

Inexpensive

Wilbraham Hotel. 1–5 Wilbraham Place (off Sloane St.), London SW1X 9AE. ☎ 020/7730-8296. Fax 020/7730-6815. 46 units. TV TEL. £100–£106 ($170–$180) double. No credit cards. Nearby parking £12 ($20). Tube: Sloane Sq.

This is a dyed-in-the-wool British hotel set on a quiet residential street near Sloane Square. The well-maintained rooms are furnished in a traditional style. On the premises is an attractive and old-fashioned lounge, The Bar and Buttery.

SOUTH KENSINGTON
Moderate
Regency Hotel. 100 Queen's Gate, London SW7 5AG. ☎ **800/223-5652** in the U.S., or 020/7370-4595. Fax 020/7370-5555. 209 units. A/C MINIBAR TV TEL. £149 ($253) double; from £215 ($366) luxury suite. AE, DC, MC, V. Parking: £30 ($51). Tube: South Kensington.

The Regency is convenient to museums and Knightsbridge. Its rooms are a bit small, furnished in a standard modern style, with trouser presses and hair dryers. The suites also have Jacuzzi tubs and iron/ironing boards. The hotel's restaurant, the Pavillion, serves moderately priced international dishes. At your disposal are the Regency Health Club (with steam rooms, minigym, saunas, and a sensory-deprivation tank), a business center, plus a bar and restaurant.

PADDINGTON
Inexpensive
The Pavilion. 34–36 Sussex Gardens, London W2 1UL. ☎ **020/7262-0905.** Fax 020/7262-1324. www.msi.com.mt/pavilion. 27 units. TV TEL. £90 ($153) double. Rates include breakfast. AE, DC, MC, V. Parking £5 ($9). Tube: Edgware Rd.

In the early 1990s, a team of entrepreneurs with inroads to the fashion industry radically redecorated the rooms in a theatrical and often outrageous decor that's much appreciated by the fashion models and music-industry buffs who make this their temporary home in London. Examples include a "kitsch '70s" room ("Honky-Tonk Afro"); an oriental bordello theme ("Enter the Dragon") and even some with 19th-century ancestral themes. One Edwardian-style room, a gem of emerald brocade and velvet, is called "Green with Envy." Rooms contain tea-making facilities, and, regrettably, are rather small. Breakfast is the only meal served.

MARYLEBONE
Expensive
The Leonard. 15 Seymour St., London W1H 5AA. ☎ **020/7935-2010.** Fax 020/7935-6700. www.theleonard.com. E-mail: the.leonard@dial.pipex.com. 31 units. A/C TV TEL. £190 ($323) double; £240–£480 ($408–$816) suite. AE, DC, MC, V. Tube: Marble Arch.

Near Marble Arch in 1996, a quartet of 17th-century town houses was combined into a tasteful hotel. Rooms have double-glazed windows to keep out noises; some have fireplaces. Each unit also has a VCR and a hi-fi stereo system. There's no restaurant on the premises, but a 24-hour cafe near the reception area serves sandwiches and simple platters. There's a small-scale exercise room as well.

Moderate
Durrants Hotel. 26–32 George St., London W1H 6BJ. ☎ **020/7935-8131.** Fax 020/7487-3510. 92 units. TV TEL. £135 ($230) double; £175 ($298) family room; £260 ($442) suite. AE, MC, V. Tube: Bond St.

Established in 1789 off Manchester Square, this historic hotel is a snug, cozy, and traditional retreat—almost a poor man's Browns. All rooms are very comfortably furnished. Many contain air-conditioning and minibars. There's also 24-hour room service. The hotel restaurant and bar offer full English fare.

Inexpensive
Edward Lear Hotel. 28–30 Seymour St., London W1H 5WD. ☎ **020/7402-5401.** Fax 020/7706-3766. www.edlear.com. E-mail: edwardlear@aol.com. 36 units, 5 with bathroom. TV TEL. £60 ($102) double without bathroom; £89.50 ($152) double with bathroom; £105 ($179) suite. Rates include English breakfast. MC, V. Tube: Marble Arch.

Edward Lear is a popular budget hotel, 1 block from Marble Arch in a pair of brick town houses dating from 1780. The cozy rooms are fairly small. The only major drawback is that this is an extremely noisy part of London.

Wigmore Court Hotel. 23 Gloucester Place, London, W1N 3PB. ☎ **020/7935-0928.** Fax 020/7487-4294. www.wigmore-court-hotel.co.uk. E-mail: info@wigmore-court-hotel.co.uk. 19 units. TV TEL. £89 ($151) double. Rates include English breakfast. MC, V. Tube: Marble Arch.

This small family friendly hotel enjoys an enviable location close to Hyde Park, Marble Arch, Oxford Street, and Madame Tussaud's. Personal service and a welcoming atmosphere distinguish it from many others. The owners frequently upgrade, and their well-furnished rooms are comfortable with good, firm beds. Amenities are few, though there are laundry facilities. The hotel serves only breakfast, although many restaurants are easily within reach.

BAYSWATER
Moderate

Commodore. 50 Lancaster Gate, London W2 3NA. ☎ **020/7402-5291.** Fax 020/7262-1088. www.commodore/hotel.com. 88 units. A/C MINIBAR TV TEL. £110–£125 ($187–$213) double; £115 ($196) suite. Rates include breakfast. AE, DC, MC, V. Tube: Lancaster Gate.

This 25-year-old hotel is newly fashionable since the traveling public has rediscovered the charm of its eclectic and somewhat eccentric rooms. About a quarter of the rooms are split-level, with a sleeping gallery set at the top of a short flight of stairs. Others have stained glass, a larger-than-expected closet, or an unexpected layout. Overall, the decor is comfortable and cozy. The bar and a restaurant serve lunches and dinners daily except Sunday night.

✪ Miller's. 111A Westbourne Grove, London W2 4UW. ☎ **020/7243-1024.** Fax 020/7243-1064. E-mail: enquiries@millersuk.com. 8 units. TV TEL. £140 ($238) double; £160 ($272) suite. Rates include continental breakfast. AE, DISC, MC, V. Tube: Bayswater or Notting Hill Gate.

It's been said that staying here is like spending a night in the Old Curiosity Shop. Others claim the little hotel looks like a set of *La Traviata*. Miller's calls itself an 18th-century rooming house. Regardless of which images come to mind, there's nothing quite like this in London. A roaring log fire blazes in the large book-lined drawing room in winter. The individually designed rooms are named after romantic poets. They vary in shape and size, but all are luxuriously furnished with cushy mattresses. A fine breakfast is served, and there's also limited room service, along with laundry and baby-sitting.

EARL'S COURT
Inexpensive

Barkston Gardens Hotel. 34–44 Barkston Gardens, London SW5 0EW. ☎ **020/7373-7851.** Fax 020/7370-6570. 93 units. A/C MINIBAR TV TEL. £99 ($168) double. AE, DISC, MC, V. Tube: Earl's Court.

Although refurbished and altered over the years, it still retains much of its original early 20th-century elegance. Most of the rooms are small, though the high ceilings give the aura of more space. They're comfortably furnished with excellent beds. The hotel offers a little bistro-style restaurant for continental dining, and amenities include room service, laundry, and baby-sitting.

HAMPSTEAD HEATH
Inexpensive

✪ La Gaffe. 107–111 Heath St., Hampstead, London NW3 6SS. ☎ **020/7435-8965.** Fax 020/7794-7592. E-mail: La-Gaffe@msn.com. 18 units. TV TEL. £85 ($145) double; £115 ($196) honeymoon room or triple. Rates include continental breakfast. AE, DISC, MC, V. Tube: Hampstead Heath.

A 15-minute tube ride from central London, this little nugget is nestled in exclusive Hampstead Heath. It dates from 1734 and was a shepherd's cottage before being turned into a residential inn. Although relatively small, it offers many of the amenities its large competitors do. The well-furnished rooms are small but cozy, with firm beds, hair dryers, and beverage makers. Special rooms include a honeymoon room with a four-poster and a Jacuzzi, plus a triple room with a queen-size four-poster. There's an excellent little Italian restaurant and a bar.

AT HEATHROW AIRPORT
Inexpensive
Ibis Hotel. 112–114 Bath Rd., Hayes UB3 5AL. ☎ **020/8759-4888.** Fax 020/8564-7894. 345 units. TV TEL. £58 ($99) double. Rates include buffet breakfast. AE, MC, V.

The best budget hotel in the Heathrow area, the Ibis evokes a Howard Johnson's Motor Lodge. The rooms are cramped and blandly furnished, but the comfort is reasonably good—even great for the price—as the beds are firm. Don't expect frills. There's a beverage maker, but the towels are sparse and gone are the free toiletries of most airport hotels. There are smoking and no-smoking rooms. A breakfast buffet is served daily 6 to 10am. A full bar comes alive at night.

A GAY HOTEL
Philbeach Hotel. 30–31 Philbeach Gardens, London SW5. ☎ **020/7373-1244.** Fax 020/7244-0149. 40 units, 16 with bathroom. TV TEL. £48 ($78) single without bathroom, £60 ($97) single with bathroom; £63 ($102) double without bathroom, £85 ($138) double with bathroom. Rates include continental breakfast. AE, DC, MC, V. Tube: Earl's Court.

One of Europe's largest gay hotels, the Philbeach is a Victorian row house on a wide crescent behind the Earl's Court Exhibition Centre, open to both men and women. It offers standard budget-hotel rooms; the showers are tiny, but the shared baths are clean. Room no. 8A, a double with bathroom, has a balcony overlooking the small back garden. There's a basement bar, and the glass-walled dining room is used for breakfast and at night becomes a good French restaurant called Wilde About Oscar.

Next door is the more upscale but equally gay **New York Hotel,** 32 Philbeach Gardens, London SW5 (☎ **020/7244-6884;** fax 020/7370-4961), offering 14 units, 12 with bathroom. Rates are £70 to £90 ($114 to $147) double with bathroom, including continental breakfast.

WHERE TO DINE
All restaurants and cafes in Britain are required to display the prices of their food and drink in a place that the customer can see before entering the eating area. Charges for service and any minimum charge or cover must also be made clear. The prices shown must include 17.5% VAT. Most restaurants add a 10% to 15% service charge to your bill, but if nothing has been added, leave a 12% to 15% tip.

MAYFAIR
Very Expensive
✪ **Chez Nico at Ninety Park Lane.** 90 Park Lane, W1. ☎ **020/7409-1290.** Reservations required (2 days in advance for lunch, 10 days for dinner). Fixed-price 3-course lunch £35 ($60); à la carte dinner £53 ($90) for 2 courses, £66 ($112) for 3 courses. AE, DC, MC, V. Mon–Fri noon–2pm; Mon–Sat 7–11pm. Closed 10 days around Christmas/New Year's. Tube: Marble Arch. FRENCH.

Nico Ladenis is one of the most talked-about chefs in Britain—and certainly the only one who's a former oil company executive, economist, and self-taught cook. As befits any three-star Michelin restaurant, dinners are memorable in the very best gastronomic tradition of postnouvelle cuisine, in which the tenets of classical cuisine are creatively adapted to local fresh ingredients. The menu changes frequently, according to Nico's inspiration. Specialties include a warm salad of foie gras on toasted brioche with caramelized orange or a Bresse pigeon rivaled only by La Gavroche. Desserts are sumptuous.

Le Gavroche. 43 Upper Brook St., W1. ☎ **020/7408-0881.** Reservations required, as far in advance as possible. Main courses £27–£36 ($46–$61); fixed-price lunch £37 ($63); *menu exceptionnel* £78 ($133). AE, MC, V. Mon–Fri noon–2pm and 7–11pm. Tube: Marble Arch. FRENCH.

Le Gavroche has long stood for quality French cuisine, perhaps the finest in Britain, though Michelin gives it only two stars. It's the creation of two Burgundy-born brothers, Albert and Michel Roux. Service is faultless, the ambience chic and formal without being stuffy. The menu changes constantly, depending on the chefs' inclinations and what fresh produce is available. Their wine cellar is among London's most interesting, with many quality Burgundies and Bordeaux. Try, if featured, the soufflé Suissesse, *papillote* of smoked salmon, or *tournedos gratinés aux poivres* (pears).

Moderate

L'Oranger. 5 St. James's St. SW1A. ☎ **020/7839-3774.** Reservations recommended. Set-price lunch £23.50 ($39.95); set-price dinner £33.50 ($56.95). AE, DC, MC, V. Mon–Fri noon–3pm; Mon–Sat 6-11:15pm. Tube: Green Park. CONTINENTAL.

This bistro-cum-brasserie manages to elevate a Gallic brasserie into an artfully upscale dining experience for a clientele that has been described as "people who have made it." The set-price menus are likely, depending on the inspiration of the chef, to include foie gras poached in a red Pessac wine sauce and panfried fillet of sea bass with zucchini, tomatoes, basil, and a black-olive vinaigrette. Other staples might be crispy cod fillets with bouillabaisse sauce and new potatoes and braised leg of rabbit in Madeira sauce with whole cloves of yellow garlic *en confit* and braised cabbage. Particularly artful starters include a terrine of ham and tongue served with gherkins and parsley, bound together with a layer of spinach and served on a bed of choron sauce.

PICCADILLY & LEICESTER SQUARE

Very Expensive

✪ **Oak Room/Marco Pierre White.** In Le Méridien Piccadilly, 21 Piccadilly, W1. ☎ **020/7437-0202.** Reservations required as far in advance as possible. Fixed-price lunch £37.50 ($64); fixed-price menu gourmand £90 ($153). Mon–Fri noon–2:30pm; Mon–Sat 7-11:15pm. Closed 2 weeks for Christmas and New Year's. Tube: Piccadilly Circus. MODERN BRITISH.

Put simply, "MPW" is the best chef in London. He serves London's finest cuisine in the city's most beautiful dining room, which has been restored to its original oak-and-gilt splendor and filled with art. Unlike major competitors making names for themselves by reinterpreting English cuisine, White remains a French classicist who refuses to Anglicize or even diversify his cooking. Sail into his menu with its caramelized wing of skate with winkles, fillet of sea bass with fennel, and braised pig's trotters (which sounds pedestrian but is elegantly refined fare). One diner claimed that White makes the world's greatest mashed potatoes, described as "sieved, pureed, and squeezed through silk stockings." White vies with Nico Ladenis as the most temperamental chef in London, but he's clearly a magician. If you can afford it, catch his show.

Expensive

Coast. 26B Albemarle St., W1X 3FA. ☎ **020/7495-5999.** Reservations required. Main courses £7–£19 ($12–$32); fixed-price 2-courses £19.50 ($33), 3-courses £25 ($43). AE, DC,

MC, V. Mon–Sat noon–3pm and 6pm–midnight, Sun noon–3:30pm and 6–11pm. Tube: Green Park or Piccadilly Circus. MODERN INTERNATIONAL.

This place, in a former automobile showroom, is so cutting edge, so 21st century, that you might feel it strains a bit to maintain its avant-garde image as one of the hippest restaurants in London. Food is eclectic and international. Textures are well handled, and flavor is paramount, especially in the lightness of the cuisine and the fish dishes. Coast tempts with their pressed terrine of grilled quail, panfried foie gras, celeriac with toasted brioche, and the baked halibut with shrimp and chervil mousseline. Then it's on to steamed salmon with a watercress and scallop mousse wrapped in prosciutto, or roast rack of new season lamb with grilled polenta and pequillo peppers.

J. Sheekey. 28–32 St. Martin's Lane, WC2. ☎ **020/7240-2565.** Reservations recommended. Main courses £9.50–£26.75 ($16–$46). AE, DC, DISC, MC, V. Daily noon–3pm and 7:30pm–midnight. Tube: Charing Cross. SEAFOOD.

British culinary tradition lives on in this restored fish joint, long a favorite of West End actors. The same jellied eels that delighted Laurence Olivier and Vivien Leigh are still here, along with an array of fresh oysters from the coasts of Ireland and Brittany, plus that Victorian favorite, fried whitebait. Sheekey's fish pie is still on the menu, as is a delightful Dover sole, even a Cornish fish stew that's quite savory. The old "mushy" vegetables still appear but the chefs also get experimental and occasionally more daring and offer the likes of steamed organic sea beet. The double chocolate pudding soufflé is a delight, and many old-fashioned favorite puddings remain. But look for something daring every now and then—perhaps fried plum ravioli with yogurt ice cream.

Moderate

Atlantic Bar & Grill. 20 Glasshouse St., W1. ☎ **020/7734-4888.** Reservations required. Main courses £13–£18 ($22–$31); fixed-price lunch £14.90 ($25), including 2 glasses of wine. AE, MC, V. Mon–Fri noon–2:45pm, Mon–Sat 6pm–3am, Sun 6–10:30pm. Tube: Piccadilly Circus. MODERN BRITISH.

In a former art deco ballroom off Piccadilly Circus, this titanic 160-seat restaurant draws trendsetters to an untrendy part of London. Classically trained executive chef Richard Sawyer is at the helm, still serving the world's most sublime potato and chive hash, which seems incidental to the accompanying smoked salmon. Try, for example, the delectable Helbridean salmon in a creamy champagne sauce with summer sorrel, the Thai spiced lamb fillet with pressed lime and roasted peanuts, or the hickory-smoked Aberdeen Angus beef fillet with a green Szechuan peppercorn sauce. The menu changes every 2 months but is always strong on seafood.

The Criterion Brasserie—Marco Pierre White. 224 Piccadilly, W1. ☎ **020/7930-0488.** Main courses £11–£15 ($19–$26); fixed-price 2-course lunch £14.99 ($26), fixed-price 3-course lunch £17.99 ($31). AE, MC, V. Daily noon–2:30pm and 6pm–midnight. Tube: Piccadilly Circus. FRENCH/MEDITERRANEAN.

Called the "bad boy" of British cookery, Marco Pierre White runs what he calls his "junior" restaurant here. The Criterion knew its greatest fame in World War II when it was the site of tea dances. This palatial neo-Byzantine mirrored marble hall is now a glamorous backdrop for the master chef's cuisine, served under a golden ceiling, with peacock-blue theater-size draperies. The menu is wide ranging, from Paris brasserie food to "nouvelle-classical." The food is excellent but falls just short of sublime. Start with squid ink risotto with roast calamari. The roast skate wing with deep-fried snails is especially delectable, as is the roast saddle of lamb stuffed with mushrooms and spinach.

Soho
Expensive
Quo Vadis. 26–29 Dean St., W1. ☎ **020/7437-9585.** Reservations required. Main courses £10.50–£19.50 ($18–$33); set lunches £14.75–£19.75 ($25–$34). AE, MC, V. Sun–Fri noon–2:30pm, Mon–Sat 5:30–11:30pm, Sun 5:30–10:30pm. Tube: Leicester Sq. or Tottenham Court Rd. EUROPEAN.

This hyper-trendy restaurant occupies the former apartment house where Karl Marx once lived. He'd never recognize it today. Its interior was ripped apart and reconfigured into the stylish, postmodern ode to cutting-edge art you'll see today. Although the restaurant is associated with culinary superstar Marco Pierre White, the actual nectar and ambrosia you get will be prepared and compiled by his designated underling, Philip Cooper. This is one of the flashiest restaurants in London. And the food? Although competent and highly appealing, cuisine is only secondary to the social blitz of hipdom generated by the clientele, the setting, and the vagaries of fashion.

Moderate
The Ivy. 1–5 West St., WC2. ☎ **020/7836-4751.** Reservations required. Main courses £11–£24 ($19–$41); Sat–Sun lunch £49 ($83). AE, DC, MC, V. Daily noon–3pm and 5:30pm–midnight (last order). Tube: Leicester Sq. ENGLISH/FRENCH.

Effervescent and sophisticated, the Ivy has been intimately associated with the West End since it opened in 1911. Meals are served until very late, ideal for after theater. With its ersatz 1930s look, the Ivy is fun and humming. The menu choices appear deceptively simple, but the fresh ingredients are skillfully prepared. Dishes include white asparagus with sea kale and truffle butter; seared scallops with spinach, sorrel, and bacon; and salmon fish cakes.

Mezzo. 100 Wardour St., W1. ☎ **020/7314-4000.** Reservations required for Mezzo. Mezzonine main courses £15–£20 ($26–$34); Mezzo 3-course dinner £35 ($60). £5 ($9) cover at Mezzo Thurs–Fri after 10:30pm. AE, DC, MC, V. Mezzo: daily noon–2:30pm; Mon–Thurs 6pm–midnight, Fri–Sat 6pm–3am, Sun 6–11:30pm. Mezzonine: daily noon–2:30pm, Mon–Thurs 5:30pm–1am, Fri–Sat 5:30pm–3am, Sun 5:30–11:30pm. Tube: Tottenham Court Rd. EUROPEAN.

This all-out blockbuster, the latest creation of entrepreneur Sir Terence Conran, is a 750-seat eatery, dubbed the biggest restaurant in Europe. The mammoth space has been split into several separate restaurants, including the Mezzonine upstairs, serving a Thai/Asian cuisine with European flair. Downstairs is the swankier Mezzo, which can seat 400 at a time in an atmosphere evoking Hollywood in the 1930s. There's even a Mezzo Café, stocked with sandwiches and drinks. Mezzonine serves dishes such as marinated salmon with ginger, star anise, and shallots; and roast marinated lamb with yogurt and cumin on flat bread. In the basement, the cuisine is more ambitious, with a view of 100 chefs working behind glass. Here a modern British menu includes shoulder of lamb slow-roasted and enlivened with lemon zest and anchovies.

✪ **Rasa Samundra.** 5 Charlotte St., W1. ☎ **020/7637-0222.** Reservations required. Main courses £8.50–£30 ($14–$51); fixed-price menus £4.25–£7.50 ($7–$13). AE, DC, MC, V. Daily noon–11pm. Tube: Tottenham Court Rd. INDIAN.

This outpost offers the best Indian cuisine in London. All house chefs have been trained personally by the owner Das Sreedharan's mother and the results are delectable. The specialties are Keralan seafood dishes. Try *malslam pattichathu* (king fish cooked in fresh spices, with green chile and coconut paste), *para konju nirachathu* (lobster cooked with black pepper, garlic and Indian shallots and served with whole lemon and beet root curry), *masala dosa* (paper-thin rice and black gram pancake filled with potato and ginger Masala) and *moru kachlathu* (green bananas and mangoes cooked in a yogurt sauce with turmeric and onions). Rasa also offers a full range of Keralan appetizers, side orders, breads, rices, and desserts.

Soho Spice. 124–126 Wardour St., W1. ☎ **020/7434-0808.** Reservations recommended. Main courses £10.50–£14 ($18–$24); set menus £16.95–£23.95 ($29–$40). AE, MC, V. Sun–Wed noon–midnight, Thurs noon–midnight, Fri–Sat noon–3pm. Tube: Tottenham Court Rd. SOUTH INDIAN.

One of Central London's most stylish Indian restaurants combines a sense of media and fashion hip with the flavors and scents of southern India. You might opt for a drink at the cellar-level bar before heading to the large street-level dining room. A staff member will propose choices from a wide array of dishes, including a range of slow-cooked Indian *tikkas* that feature combinations of spices with lamb, chicken, fish, or all-vegetarian. The cuisine will satisfy traditionalists but has a nouveau-Soho flair. The presentation takes it a step above typical Indian restaurants.

Inexpensive
Chuen Cheng Ku. 17 Wardour St., W1. ☎ **020/7437-1398.** Reservations recommended on weekend afternoons. Main courses £11.50–£30 ($205–$51). AE, DC, MC, V. Daily 11am–11:45pm. Closed Dec 24–25. Tube: Piccadilly Circus or Leicester Sq. CHINESE.

One of the finest eateries in Soho's "New China," this large restaurant on several floors seats 400 diners and is noted for its Cantonese food and its long and interesting menu. Specialties are paper-wrapped prawns, rice in lotus leaves, steamed spareribs in black-bean sauce, and shredded pork with cashew nuts, all served in generous portions.

BLOOMSBURY
Moderate
Townhouse Brasserie. 24 Coptic St., WC1. ☎ **020/7636-2731.** Reservations recommended. Main courses £6.95–£10.35 ($12–$18). AE, DC, MC, V. Mon–Fri 11am–11pm, Sat 4–11pm, Sun 10am–6pm. Tube: Tottenham Court Rd. or Holborn. INTERNATIONAL.

Near the British Museum, this old Georgian townhouse is one of the newest and most up-and-coming restaurants in Bloomsbury. The ground floor is enhanced with contemporary art, and upstairs is a traditional old English dining room, except for an infusion of Peruvian art. The frequently changing menu is a culinary tour de force, drawing inspiration from around the world. Ingredients are very fresh and deftly handled by a skilled kitchen staff. Launch your repast with the cream of leek soup or sweet potato soup with basil. Then it's on to a delectable charcoal-grilled duck breast with an Asian-style salad. Especially pleasing is a fresh seafood pasta flavored with chives, thick cream, and white wine. It's worth it to save up room for one of the tempting desserts, made fresh daily.

Villandry. 170 Great Portland St., W1. ☎ **020/7631-3131.** Reservations recommended. Main courses £12–£15 ($20–$26). AE, MC, V. Mon–Sat 8am–10pm, Sun 11am–4pm. Tube: Great Portland St. INTERNATIONAL/CONTINENTAL.

Food lovers and gourmands flock to this combination food store, florist, delicatessen, and restaurant. The setting is an oversized Edwardian-style storefront north of Oxford Circus. Inside, the venue is artfully minimalist and immaculate. Ingredients change here so frequently the menu is revamped and rewritten twice a day—during a recent visit, the menu offered such perfectly crafted dishes as breast of duck with fresh spinach and a gratin of baby onions; boiled haunch of pork with blood sausages, mashed potatoes, kale, and mustard sauce; fillets of black codfish with prosciutto, radicchio, and creamed lentils; and panfried turbot with deep-fried celery, artichoke hearts, and hollandaise sauce.

Inexpensive

Wagamama. 4 Streatham St., WC1. ☎ **020/7323-9223.** Reservations not accepted. Main courses £10–£12 ($17–$20). AE, MC, V. Mon–Sat noon–11pm, Sun 12:30–10pm. Tube: Tottenham Court Rd. JAPANESE.

This noodle joint, in a basement just off New Oxford Street, is noisy, overly crowded, and you'll have to wait in line for a table. This fast-serve, fast-out concept calls itself a "non-destination food station" and caters to some 1,200 customers a day. All dishes are built around ramen noodles with your choice of chicken, beef, or salmon served with gyoza, a light pancake filled with vegetables. Vegetarian dishes are available, but skip the so-called Korean-style dishes.

COVENT GARDEN & THE STRAND
Moderate

Belgo Centraal. 50 Earlham St., WC2. ☎ **020/7813-2233.** Reservations required for the restaurant. Main courses £9.95–£18.95 ($17–$32); set menus £7–£13 ($12–$22). AE, DC, MC, V. Mon–Sat noon–11:30pm, Sun noon–10:30pm. Closed Christmas. Tube: Covent Garden. BELGIAN.

Chaos reigns supreme in this audacious and cavernous basement where mussels marinière with fries and 100 Belgian beers are the raison d'être. Take a freight elevator down past the busy kitchen and into a converted cellar that has been divided into two large eating areas. One is a beer hall seating about 250. The menu here is the same as in the restaurant, but reservations aren't needed. Reservations are required for the restaurant side, which has three nightly seatings: 5:30, 7:30, and 10pm. Although mussels are the big attraction, you can also opt for fresh Scottish salmon, roast chicken, a perfectly done steak, or one of the vegetarian specialties. Gargantuan plates of wild boar sausages arrive with *stoemp,* a Belgian version of mashed spuds and cabbage.

Porter's English Restaurant. 17 Henrietta St., WC2. ☎ **020/7836-6466.** Reservations recommended. Main courses £7–£10 ($11.90–$17); fixed-price menu £16.50 ($28). AE, DC, MC, V. Mon–Sat noon–11:30pm, Sun noon–10:30pm. Tube: Covent Garden or Charing Cross. ENGLISH.

Porter's specializes in classic English meat pies. Main courses are so generous that the menu eliminates appetizers. The traditional bangers-and-mash plate is featured daily. With whipped cream or custard, the "puddings" come hot or cold, including bread-and-butter pudding or steamed syrup sponge. Although the English call all desserts puddings, at Porter's they're in fact puddings in the American sense.

Rules. 35 Maiden Lane, WC2. ☎ **020/7836-5314.** Reservations recommended. Main courses £14.95–£18 ($25–$31). AE, DC, MC, V. Daily noon–11:15pm. Tube: Covent Garden. ENGLISH.

London's most quintessentially British restaurant opened in 1798 as an oyster bar and is lined with the framed memorabilia of the British Empire at its height. Around the turn of the century, Edward VII, portly future king of England, used to arrive here with his famous mistress, Lillie Langtry. Their signed portraits still embellish the yellowing walls, along with that of Charles Dickens, who crafted several of his novels here. You can order such classic dishes as jugged hare, Greshingham duckling in a bramley apple and five-spice chutney sauce, and game dishes.

FLEET STREET
Inexpensive

Ye Olde Cheshire Cheese. Wine Office Court, 145 Fleet St., EC4. ☎ **020/7353-6170.** Main courses £8.95–£13.25 ($15–$23). AE, DC, MC, V. Daily noon–9:30pm. Drinks and bar snacks available daily 11:30am–11pm. Tube: St. Paul's or Blackfriars. ENGLISH.

Taking Afternoon Tea in London:
Where to Have a Cuppa

The lounge at **Brown's Hotel,** 29–34 Albemarle St., W1 (☎ **020/7493-6020;** tube: Green Park), is decorated with English antiques, oil paintings, and floral chintz, much like an English country estate. Give your name to the concierge upon arrival (reservations aren't accepted); arrangements will be made for you to be seated on clusters of sofas and settees or at low tables. Served daily 3 to 5:45pm, the regular afternoon tea (£18.95/$32) includes a choice of 10 teas, plus sandwiches, scones, and pastries. The teatime rituals at **Claridge's,** Brook Street, W1 (☎ **020/7629-8860;** tube: Bond St.), have managed to persevere through the years with as much pomp and circumstance as the empire itself. A portrait of Lady Claridge gazes beneficently from the paneled walls as a choice of 17 teas is served ever-so-politely. Reservations are recommended, and jackets are required for men. Served daily 3 to 5pm, high tea runs £19 to £27 ($32 to $46).

A flood of visitors is somehow gracefully herded into the high-volume but nevertheless elegant **Georgian Restaurant,** on the fourth floor of Harrods, 87–135 Brompton Rd., SW1 (☎ **020/7255-6800;** tube: Knightsbridge), in a room so long its staff refers to its shape and size as the "Mississippi River." The list of teas available—at least 50—is sometimes so esoteric the experience might remind you of the choosing among vintages in a sophisticated wine cellar. Served Monday to Saturday 3:45 to 5:15pm (last order), high tea runs £17 ($29) per person; reservations are recommended. **The Orangery,** in the gardens just north of Kensington Palace, W8 (☎ **020/7376-0239;** tube: Kensington High St. or Queensway), occupies a long and narrow garden pavilion built in 1704 by Queen Anne as a site for her tea parties. Tea is still served amid rows of potted orange trees basking in sunlight from soaring windows. Tea is served daily: April to September 10am to 6pm and October to March 10am to 4pm. Reservations aren't accepted. A pot of tea is £2.60 ($4.40), and summer cakes and puddings run £2 to £5 ($3.40 to $9).

Dating from the 13th century, this is the most famous of the old City chophouses (restaurants) and pubs. It claims to be the spot where Samuel Johnson entertained admirers. Later, many of the ink-stained journalists and scandalmongers of Fleet Street made its four-story premises their "local." Within, you'll find six bars and two dining rooms. The house specialties include "ye famous pudding"—steak, kidney, mushrooms, and game—and Scottish roast beef, with Yorkshire pudding and horseradish sauce.

WESTMINSTER
Moderate

Tate Gallery Restaurant. Millbank, SW1. ☎ **020/7887-8877.** Reservations required 2 days in advance. Main courses £10–£16 ($17–$27); 2-course fixed-price lunch £16.75 ($28); 3-course fixed-price lunch £19.50 ($33). AE, MC, V. Mon–Sat noon–3pm and Sun noon–4pm, Mon–Sat 3–5pm for afternoon tea. Tube: Pimlico. Bus: 77 or 88. ENGLISH.

The restaurant at Tate Britain is particularly attractive to wine fanciers, offering what may be the best bargains for superior wines to be found anywhere in the country. It's especially strong on Bordeaux and Burgundies. Wine connoisseurs frequently come for lunch, regardless of the current exhibitions on view at the museum. The restaurant specializes in French cuisine. The menu changes every month and may include duck prepared in a variety of ways or lamb or veal dishes.

KNIGHTSBRIDGE
Expensive
Zafferano. 15 Lowndes St., SW1. ☎ **020/7235-5800.** Reservations required. Set menus £18.50 ($31) or £39.50 ($67). AE, MC, V. Mon–Sat noon–2:30pm and 7–11pm. Tube: Knightsbridge. ITALIAN.

There's something honest and satisfying about this restaurant, where Margaret Thatcher, Michael Hesseltine, Richard Gere, Princess Margaret, and Eric Clapton have dined. Some of the allure derives from an elegantly modernized interpretation of Italian cuisine, which incorporates such dishes as ravioli of pheasant with black truffles, rabbit with Parma ham and polenta, sea bream with spinach and balsamic vinegar, and monkfish with almonds. The owners pride themselves on one of the most esoteric and well-rounded collections of Italian wine in London: You'll find as many as 20 different vintages each of Brunello and Barolos, and about a dozen vintages of Sassecaia.

Moderate
English Garden. 10 Lincoln St., SW3. ☎ **020/7584-7272.** Reservations required. Main courses £11.50–£19.25 ($20–$33); fixed-price lunch £16.75 ($28). AE, DC, MC, V. Daily 12:30–11:30pm. Closed Dec 25–26. Tube: Sloane Sq. ENGLISH.

In this historic Chelsea town house, the Garden Room, with its domed conservatory and banks of plants, is a metropolitan restaurant par excellence. Every component is well prepared and proportioned. Well-crafted old-fashioned dishes include Arbroath smokie fish cake, saddle of venison and "potted" cabbage, and roast rump of lamb with butter beans and bacon. Save room for the mango fool with macaroons or the white chocolate cheesecake, each delectable.

KENSINGTON
Moderate
Joe's. 126 Draycott Ave., SW3. ☎ **020/7225-2217.** Reservations recommended. Main courses £9–£13 ($15–$22). AE, DC, MC, V. Mon–Sun 9am–6pm. Tube: South Kensington. MODERN BRITISH.

One of three London restaurants established by fashion designer Joseph Ettedgui, Joe's is often filled with well-known names from the fashion, music, and entertainment industries. The atmosphere is laid-back but stuffy, and the food is safe but a bit unexciting. You can enjoy such dishes as crab-crusted halibut, breast of duck with roasted root vegetables, charcoal-grilled swordfish with cracked wheat and salsa verde (green sauce), or tiger prawns and monkfish kebabs with sesame balsamic dressing. No one will mind if your meal consists exclusively of appetizers. There's a bar near the entrance, tables for quick meals near the door, and more leisurely (and gossipy) dining a few steps up from the bar. Brunch is served on Sunday, which is the cheapest way to enjoy this place.

Pasha. 1 Gloucester Rd., SW7. ☎ **020/7589-7969.** Reservations recommended. Main courses £11–£18 ($19–$31). AE, DC, MC, V. Daily noon–3pm and 7–11:30pm. Tube: Gloucester Rd. MOROCCAN/MEDITERRANEAN.

Few ethnic restaurants equal the zest and stylishness of this re-created Marrakech palace. Within a duet of dining rooms outfitted with rich upholsteries, flickering candles, belly dancing music, and artifacts from the sub-Sahara, you'll enjoy regional and time-honored specialties. Examples include a crispy lamb salad with pomegranate and mint, grilled sea bass with warm hummus and parsley salad, chicken merguez (spicy sausage) with a coriander tagine; and charcoal-grilled skewered chicken with green chile salsa. And if you like couscous, you'll have at least three kinds to choose from.

SOUTH KENSINGTON
Expensive
Bibendum/Oyster Bar. 81 Fulham Rd., SW3. ☎ **020/7581-5817.** Reservations required in Bibendum; not accepted in Oyster Bar. Main courses £19–£27 ($32–$46); 3-course fixed-price lunch £23–£27 ($39–$46); cold seafood platter in Oyster Bar £22 ($37) per person. AE, DC, MC, V. Bibendum, daily noon–2:30pm and 7–11:15pm. Tube: South Kensington. MODERN FRENCH/MEDITERRANEAN.

This fashionable eatery occupies two floors of the former British headquarters of the Michelin tire company. Bibendum, the more visible eatery, is one floor above street level in a white-tiled room whose stained-glass windows, streaming sunlight, and chic clientele make meals extremely pleasant. Menu choices are carefully planned interpretations of seasonal ingredients, known for their freshness and simplicity, including roast quail flavored with Marsala and thyme, braised oxtail with prunes and almonds, and *ris de veau* (sweetbreads) with black butter and capers. Simpler meals and cocktails are available on the building's street level, in the Oyster Bar.

The Collection. 264 Brompton Rd., SW3. ☎ **020/7225-1212.** Reservations recommended. Main courses £12–£18 ($20–$31); set-price menu £35 ($60). AE, MC, V. Daily noon–3pm and 6:30–11pm. Tube: South Kensington. INTERNATIONAL.

This temple to voyeurism and the vanities occupies an echoing warehouse, where a 30-foot underlit catwalk (the only access to the place) emulates what you'd expect at one of next season's couture shows. Don't worry about a snobbish chill: Manager Julian Shaw is adept, humorous, and something of a celebrity in his own right because of his skill at dealing with big-ego fashion moguls. Yummy menu items include crispy duck with yaki soba noodles; sesame-crusted tuna steak with sweet potatoes and bok choy; sea bream with cilantro; and panfried calves' liver with sage and onions. Don't overlook this site as a venue for your after-dark bar-hopping.

Hilaire. 68 Old Brompton Rd., SW7. ☎ **020/7584-8993.** Reservations recommended. 2-course fixed-price lunch £18.50 ($31); 3-course fixed-price lunch £23.50 ($40); 3-course fixed-price dinner £36 ($61); 4-course fixed-price dinner £42 ($71); dinner main courses £23 ($39). AE, DC, MC, V. Mon–Fri 12:15–2:30pm; Mon–Sat 6:30–11pm. Closed Sun and bank holidays. Tube: South Kensington. MODERN BRITISH.

Hilaire is a jovially cramped restaurant, housed in a Victorian storefront. Chef Bryan Webb prepares a mixture of classical French and cuisine moderne; thus, this has become one of London's most stylish restaurants. The menu always reflects the best of the season's offerings, and main courses at dinner might include rack of lamb with tapenade and wild garlic, saddle of rabbit, or grilled tuna with Provençal vegetables.

CHELSEA
Inexpensive
Admiral Codrington. 17 Mossop St., SW3. ☎ **020/7581-0005.** Reservations recommended. Main courses £3.75–£12.25 ($6–$21). MC, V. Daily noon–11:30pm. Tube: South Kensington. INTERNATIONAL.

Once a lowly pub, this stylish bar and restaurant is all the rage. The exterior has been maintained, but the old "Cod," as it is affectionately known, has emerged to offer plush dining with a revitalized decor by Nina Campbell and a glass roof that rolls back on sunny days. The bartenders still offer a traditional pint, but the sophisticated menu features such delectable fare as linguine with zucchini, crab, and chile peppers, or rib-eye steak with slow-roasted tomatoes. Opt for the grilled breast of chicken salad with bean sprouts, apple, or cashews, or the perfectly grilled tuna with a couscous salad and eggplant "caviar."

MARYLEBONE
Moderate

Caldesi. 15–17 Marylebone Lane, W1. ☎ **020/7935-9226.** Reservations required. Main courses £5.50–£15 ($9–$26). AE, MC, V. Mon–Fri noon–2:30pm and 6–11pm, Sat 6–11pm. Tube: Bond St. TUSCAN.

Good food, reasonable prices, fresh ingredients, and authentic Tuscan family recipes have attracted a never-ending stream to this eatery founded by owner and head chef, Giancarlo Caldesi. The extensive menu includes a wide array of pasta, antipasti, fish, and meat dishes. Start with an excellent insalata Caldesi, made with tomatoes slow roasted in garlic and rosemary oil and served with mozzarella flown in from Tuscany. Pasta dishes include an especially flavor-filled homemade tortelloni stuffed with salmon and ricotta and served with a creamy spinach sauce. Monkfish and prawns are flavored with wild fennel and fresh basil, or you might sample the tender duck breast with fresh peaches, steeped in white wine, honey, thyme, and rosemary.

NOTTING HILL GATE
Moderate

Pharmacy. 150 Notting Hill Gate, W11. ☎ **020/7221-2442.** Reservations required Fri–Sat; otherwise strongly recommended. Main courses £15–£21 ($26–$36). MC, V. Daily noon–2:30pm and 6:45pm–midnight. Tube: Notting Hill Gate. MODERN EUROPEAN/ MEDITERRANEAN.

This place can be a lot of fun. The "medical chic" restaurant created by Damien Hirst will remind you of a harmless small-town pharmacy or a drug lord's secret stash of mind-altering pills, an ambiguity richly appreciated by the arts-conscious crowd that flocks here. In the street-level bar, a drink menu lists lots of highly palatable martinis as well as a somewhat icky concoction known as a Cough Syrup (cherry liqueur, honey, and vodka). Bottles of pills, aspirin-shaped bar stools, and painted representa-tions of Fire, Water, Air, and Earth decorate a scene favored by minor celebs and party people. Upstairs in the restaurant the hospital theme is less pronounced. Menu items include such trendy but comforting food items as a carpaccio of sea bass; lamb cooked with celery, spinach, and herb juices; fisherman's pie; home-salted cod and eggplant pie; and roasted duck with white peaches and French fries.

SEEING THE SIGHTS

London isn't a city to visit hurriedly. It is so vast, so stocked with treasures, that it would take a lifetime to explore it thoroughly. But even a quick visit will give you a chance to see what's creating the hottest buzz in shopping and nightlife as well as the city's time-tested treasures.

SIGHTSEEING SUGGESTIONS FOR FIRST-TIME VISITORS

If You Have 1 Day   No first-time visitor should leave London without visiting West-minster Abbey. See Big Ben and the Houses of Parliament, then walk over to see the Changing of the Guard at Buckingham Palace if it's being held. Have dinner in Covent Garden, perhaps at Porter's English Restaurant. For your nightcap, head over to the Red Lion, 2 Duke of York St. (☎ **020/7930-2030**), in Mayfair, quite a Victo-rian pub.

If You Have 2 Days   Devote a good part of your second day to exploring the British Museum, one of the world's largest and best museums. Spend the afternoon visiting the Tower of London and seeing the crown jewels (but expect slow-moving lines). Cap your day by boarding one of the London Launches to experience the city from the river. Go to one of London's landmark restaurants such as Rules, 35 Maiden Lane.

If You Have 3 Days   In the morning of your third day, go to the National Gallery on Trafalgar Square. Then enjoy an afternoon at Madame Tussaud's Waxworks. Take some time to stroll through St. James's and try to catch a cultural performance at the South Bank Centre, site of the Royal Festival Hall, or a play or musical in the West End.

If You Have 4 Days   In the morning of your fourth day, head for the City, the financial district. Tour St. Paul's Cathedral. Spend a few hours strolling the City and visit a few of its many attractions. In the late afternoon, head down King's Road in Chelsea to shop the many and varied boutiques.

If You Have 5 Days   On your fifth day, explore the Victoria and Albert Museum in the morning, then head to the Tate Gallery for lunch. Finally, see where history was made during the dark days of World War II in the Cabinet War Rooms at Clive Steps, where Churchill directed the British operations against the Nazis. In the evening, attend the theater.

THE TOP ATTRACTIONS

✪ **Tower of London.** Tower Hill, on the north bank of the Thames, EC3. ☎ **020/7709-0765.** Admission £10.50 ($18) adults, £7.90 ($13) students and senior citizens, £6.90 ($11.75) children, children under 5 free. Family ticket for 5 members (but no more than 2 adults), £31 ($53). Mar–Oct Mon–Sat 9am–5pm, Sun 10am–5pm; Nov–Feb Sun–Mon 10am–4pm; Tues–Sat 9am–4pm. Closed Dec 24–26 and Jan 1. Tube: Tower Hill. Boats: From Westminster Pier.

This ancient fortress continues to pack in visitors because of its macabre associations with all the legendary figures who were imprisoned and/or executed here (Sir Walter Raleigh, Anne Boleyn and her daughter Elizabeth, Lady Jane Grey). The finest structure is the White Tower, begun by William the Conqueror. Here you can view the Royal Armouries collection of armor and weapons. Instruments of torture and execution are on view in Bowyer Tower. In summer, go early in the day to see the **Crown Jewels** because long lines often form. Uniformed Beefeater guides give 1-hour tours at frequent intervals, starting at 9:30am from the Middle Tower near the main entrance. The tour includes the Chapel Royal of St. Peter ad Vincula (St. Peter in Chains). The last guided walk starts about 3:30pm in summer or 2:30pm in winter.

✪ **Westminster Abbey.** Broad Sanctuary, SW1. ☎ **020/7222-7110.** Free admission to cloisters. Abbey, £5 ($9) adults, £3 ($5) students, £2 ($3.40) children 11–18 (free 10 and under). Family ticket (2 adults, 2 children) £10 ($17). Mon–Fri 9:30am–3:45pm, Sat 9:15am–1:45pm and 4–4:45pm. Tube: Westminster or St. James's Park.

In 1065, the Saxon king, Edward the Confessor, founded a Benedictine abbey on this spot overlooking Parliament Square. The first king crowned in the abbey was Harold in 1066. The coronation tradition has continued to the present day, broken only twice (Edward V and Edward VIII). The abbey is the site of state occasions, including the September 1997 funeral of Diana, Princess of Wales, which led to a 25% increase in attendance at the abbey. The Gothic structure existing today owes more to Henry III's plans than to those of any other sovereign, although many architects, including Wren, have contributed to the abbey. Henry VII Chapel is one of the loveliest in Europe, with its fan vaulting, Knights of Bath banners, and Torrigiani-designed tomb of the king. You can also visit the most hallowed spot in the abbey, the shrine of Edward the Confessor (canonized in the 12th century). In the saint's chapel is the Coronation Chair, made at the command of Edward I in 1300 to display the Stone of Scone.

London Attractions

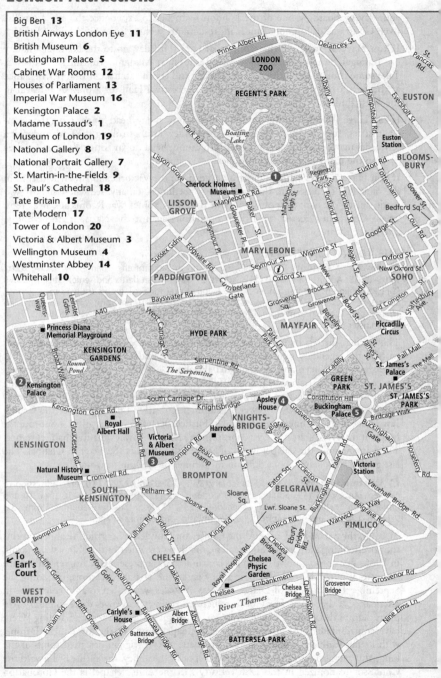

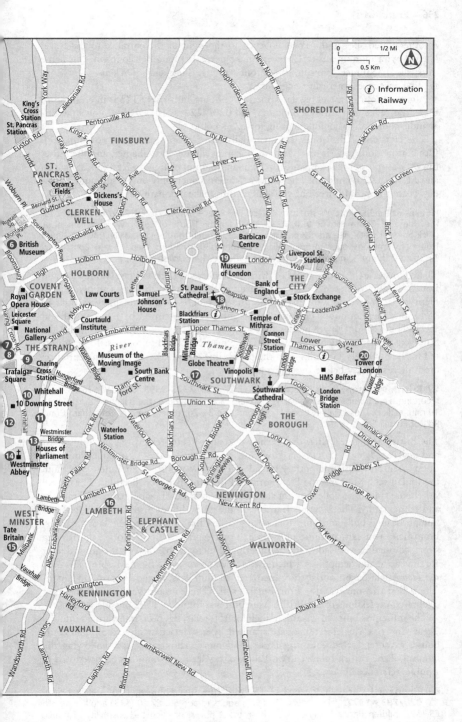

Another noted spot is the Poets' Corner, to the right of the entrance to the Royal Chapel, with monuments to Chaucer, Shakespeare, "O Rare Ben Johnson" (his name misspelled), Samuel Johnson, the Brontë sisters, Thackeray, Dickens, Tennyson, Kipling, even the American Longfellow.

A guided tour of the abbey lasts about 1¹/₂ hours and costs £3 ($5) in addition to the entrance fee. For advance bookings, call **020/7222-7110.** Or else enjoy a personal audio tour, an Audioguide renting for £2 ($3.40).

The cloisters of the abbey are open daily 9am to 6pm, charging no admission. Other attractions to visit on site are the Chapter House, Pyx Chapter, and the museum of Westminster relics, open daily 10:30am to 4pm, charging £2.50 ($4.25) adults and £1.30 ($2.20) children. The College Garden is open only on Tuesday and Thursday 10am to 6pm. It's free but you're invited to make a donation.

Houses of Parliament. Westminster Palace, Old Palace Yard, SW1. ☎ **020/7219-4272** for the House of Commons, or **020/7219-3107** for the House of Lords. www.parliament.uk (click on V for visit). Free admission. House of Lords, open to the public daily 2:30–10:30pm. House of Commons, open to the public Mon–Tues 2:30–10:30pm, Wed 9:30am–2pm, Thurs 11:30am–7:30pm. Join line at St. Stephen's entrance. Tube: Westminster.

These Houses are the stronghold of Britain's democracy. Both Houses (Commons and Lords) are situated in the former royal Palace of Westminster, the king's residence until Henry VIII moved to Whitehall. The present Houses of Parliament were built in 1840, but the Commons chamber was bombed and destroyed by the Luftwaffe in 1941. The 320-foot tower houses Big Ben, the "symbol of London." Except for the Strangers' Galleries, the two Houses of Parliament are closed to tourists. To be admitted to the Strangers' Galleries, join the public line outside the St. Stephen's entrance; often there's a delay before the line is admitted.

☉ British Museum. Great Russell St., WC1. ☎ **020/7323-8599,** or 020/7636-1555 for recording. Free admission. Mon–Sat 10am–5pm, Sun noon–6pm (the galleries start to close 10 min. earlier). Closed Jan 1, Good Friday, and Dec 24–26. Tube: Holborn, Tottenham Court Rd., or Russell Sq.

The British Museum shelters one of the world's most comprehensive collections of art and artifacts. Even on a cursory first visit, be sure to see the Asian collections (the finest assembly of Islamic pottery outside the Islamic world), the Chinese porcelain, the Indian sculpture, and the Prehistoric and Romano-British collections. The overall storehouse splits into collections of antiquities; prints and drawings; coins and medals; and ethnography. The Assyrian Transept on the ground floor displays the winged and human-headed bulls and lions that once guarded the gateways to the king's palaces. From here, you can continue into the hall of Egyptian sculpture to see the Rosetta stone, whose discovery led to the deciphering of hieroglyphs. Also on the ground floor are the Parthenon Sculptures, which used to be known as the Elgin Marbles. The *Sutton Hoo* Anglo-Saxon burial ship discovered in Suffolk is, in the words of an expert, "the richest treasure ever dug from English soil." The Portland Vase, one of the most celebrated possessions of the British Museum, was found in 1582 outside Rome.

The museum's inner courtyard, hidden for 150 years, has been transformed into the Great Court, a 1ha (2-acre) square spanned by a spectacular glass roof. The court houses a center for education, galleries, and more exhibition space. Following the removal of the British Library to St. Pancras, the Reading Room has been restored as a public reference library.

Buckingham Palace. At the end of The Mall (the street running from Trafalgar Sq.). ☎ **020/7839-1377.** Palace tours £10 ($17) adults to age 60, £7.50 ($13) adults over 60, £5 ($9) children under 17. (*Warning:* These ticket prices, or even the possibility of public

The Plundering Empire

For decades, Greece has demanded the return of the Parthenon Sculptures, calling them "war loot." Greece claims these sculptures as part of its heritage, although so far Britain has refused its demands.

admission to Buckingham Palace, are subject to change.) Aug–Sept daily 9:30am–4:15pm. Tube: St. James's Park, Green Park, or Victoria.

This massively graceful building is the official residence of the queen. You can tell when Her Majesty is at home by the Royal Standard flying over the palace. The state rooms and picture gallery are usually open to the public for 8 weeks in August and September, when the royal family is away on vacation. The tours include the Throne Room and the grand staircase. The queen's picture gallery has some world-class masterpieces rarely on public view.

Buckingham Palace's most famous spectacle is the **Changing of the Guard.** The new guard, marching behind a band, comes from either the Wellington or Chelsea Barracks and takes over from the old guard in the forecourt of the palace. When this martial ceremony occurs is the subject of mass confusion—*when* it happens, it begins at 11:30am. In theory, that is supposed to be from mid-April to July and on alternate days the rest of the year. It can be canceled in bad weather and during major state events. Call ☎ **020/7414-2497** to see if this world-famous military ritual is likely to be staged during your visit.

Madame Tussaud's. Marylebone Rd., NW1. ☎ **020/7935-0207.** Admission £10.50 ($18) adults, £8 ($14) senior citizens, £7 ($12) children under 16. Combination tickets, including the new planetarium, £12.75 ($22) adults, £9.80 ($17) seniors, £8.50 ($14) children 5–16, and children under 5 are free. Mon–Sat 10am–5:30pm. Tube: Baker St.

In 1770, an exhibition of life-size wax figures was opened in Paris by Dr. Curtius. He was soon joined by his niece, Strasbourg-born Marie Tussaud, who learned the secret of making lifelike replicas of the famous and the infamous. During the French Revolution, the head of almost every distinguished victim of the guillotine was molded by Madame Tussaud or her uncle. An enlarged Grand Hall continues to house years of old favorites, as well as many of today's heads of state and political leaders. In the Chamber of Horrors, you can have the vicarious thrill of walking through a Victorian London street where special effects include the shadowy terror of Jack the Ripper. Planetarium shows begin at 10:20am daily and are presented every 40 minutes.

Tate Britain. Millbank, SW1. ☎ **020/7887-8000.** www.tate.org.uk. Free admission; special exhibits sometimes £3–£6 ($5–$10). Daily 10am–5:50pm. Tube: Pimlico. Bus: 77am, 88, or C10.

What's now known as Tate Britain was originally known as the Tate Gallery before the modern works in its collection were moved to a new building (see below). Fronting the Thames near Vauxhall bridge in Pimlico, the most prestigious gallery in Britain houses the national collections covering British art from the 16th century to the present. Since only a portion of the collections can be displayed at any one time, the works on view change from time to time. We suggest you try to schedule two visits—the first to see the classic British works, the second to concentrate on whichever other section interests you most.

The older works include some of the best of Gainsborough, Reynolds, Stubbs, Blake, Constable, and Hogarth (particularly his satirical *O the Roast beef of Old England*, known as *The Gate of Calais*). The illustrations of William Blake, the incomparable mystical poet of such works as *The Book of Job, The Divine Comedy,* and

Paradise Lost are here. The collection of works by J. M. W. Turner is its largest collection by a single artist; Turner himself willed most of the paintings and watercolors here to the nation. Also on display are the works of many major 19th- and 20th-century painters, including Paul Nash. In the modern collections are works by Matisse, Dalí, Modigliani, Munch, Bonnard, and Picasso. Truly remarkable are the several enormous abstract canvases by Mark Rothko, the group of paintings and sculptures by Giacometti, and the paintings of one of England's best-known modern artists, the late Francis Bacon. Sculptures by Barbara Hepworth are also occasionally displayed.

Tate Modern. 25 Sumner St., SE1. ☎ **020/7887-8000.** www.tate.org.uk. Free admission. Sun–Thurs 10am–6pm, Fri–Sat 10am–8pm. Tube: Southwark.

In the spring of 2000, the Tate opened a new gallery to display its collection of 20th- and 21st-century art. You can cross the Millennium Bridge, a pedestrian-only walk from the steps of St. Paul's, over the Thames to the new gallery. The Tate Modern was converted from the former Bankside Power Station, and extensive use of glass for both the exterior and the interior characterize the stunning new gallery, offering panoramic views. Galleries showing art are arranged over three levels and provide different kinds of space for display. Instead of exhibiting art chronologically and by school, the Tate Modern, in a radical break from tradition, takes a thematic approach. This allows displays to cut across movements. Photographs will be displayed for the art form they are, including rare photographs on loan.

National Gallery. Trafalgar Sq., WC2. ☎ **020/7839-3321.** Free admission. Daily 10am–6pm (9pm Wed). Closed Jan 1, Good Friday, and Dec 24–26. Tube: Charing Cross, Embankment, or Leicester Sq.

The National Gallery houses a comprehensive collection of Western paintings, representing all the major schools from the 13th to the early 20th century. Of the early Gothic works, the *Wilton Diptych* is the rarest treasure; it depicts Richard II being introduced to the Madonna and child by John the Baptist and the Saxon king, Edward the Confessor. The 16th-century Venetian masters and the northern European painters are well represented.

✪ St. Paul's Cathedral. St. Paul's Churchyard, EC4. ☎ **020/7236-4128.** Cathedral, £4 ($7) adults, £2 ($3.40) children 6–16. Galleries, £3.50 ($6) adults, £1.50 ($2.55) children. Guided tours, £3.50 ($6), recorded tours £3 ($5), children 5 and under free. Sightseeing, Mon–Sat 8:30am–4pm; galleries, Mon–Sat 10am–4:15pm. No sightseeing Sun (services only). Tube: St. Paul's.

It was during the Great Fire of 1666 that the old St. Paul's was destroyed, making way for a baroque structure designed by Sir Christopher Wren and built between 1675 and 1710. The dome of St. Paul's dominates the City's square mile. The cathedral houses few art treasures but has many monuments, including a memorial chapel to American service personnel who lost their lives in World War II. Encircling the dome is the Whispering Gallery, where vocal discretion is advised. Wren lies in the crypt, along with the duke of Wellington and Lord Nelson. Of course, this was where Prince Charles married Lady Diana Spencer in 1981. From the steps of St. Paul's, you can cross the Millennium Bridge, a pedestrian-only walk, over the Thames to the new Tate Modern gallery (see above).

✪ Victoria & Albert Museum. Cromwell Rd., SW7. ☎ **020/7938-8500.** £5 ($9) adults, £3 ($5) students/seniors; children under 18 free. Daily 10am–5:45pm. Tube: South Kensington.

On display here are fine and decorative arts. Medieval holdings include many treasures, such as the Eltenberg Reliquary; the Early English Gloucester Candlestick; the

For Diana Fans

Princess Diana is buried on an island on the Oval Lake at Althorp, the Spencer family estate at Great Brington in Northamptonshire. You won't have access to the gravesite or the island, but you can view the island from across the lake. Admission is £9.50 ($16) adults, £7.50 ($13) seniors, and £5 ($9) children.

You must book tickets long in advance by calling **01604/592-020** or writing **Althorp Admissions,** c/o Wayhead, The Hollows, St. James's Street, Nottingham, NG1 6FJ. A special train is operated by Virgin Trains which runs coaches to Althorp daily, costing £12.50 ($21) for a one-day round-trip ticket. For schedules and more information, call **National Rail** at ☎ **0345/484-950.**

At Althorp, Earl Spencer, Diana's brother, opened a $5 million shrine to the late princess, including a museum, a gift shop, and a cafe. The museum contains, among other exhibits, letters she wrote as a schoolgirl, the silk dress she wore as a bride at Westminster Abbey, and the high-fashion outfits she later appeared in. Some exhibits are almost embarrassingly personal, such as a toy rabbit with an ear missing. You can also see poignant films of her as a carefree child dancing in the gardens and later on a ride with her sons, William and Harry. Other relics include the christening robe worn at her baptism in 1961; two bridesmaids dresses worn at her wedding; Sir Elton John's and Sir George Martin's autographed musical score and parts and Bernie Taupin's hand-written annotated manuscript of *Candle in the Wind '97*. The men in her life—Prince Charles, James Hewitt, and even Dodi al Fayed—are notable only by their absence from the museum.

Byzantine Veroli Casket, with its ivory panels based on Greek plays; and the Syon Cope, an English embroidery from the early 14th century. Islamic art includes the 16th-century Persian Ardabil carpet. The V&A has the largest collection of Renaissance sculpture outside Italy, including a Donatello marble relief. Raphael's cartoons for tapestries for the Sistine Chapel, owned by the queen, can also be seen here.

Kensington Palace. The Broad Walk, Kensington Gardens, W8. ☎ **020/7937-9561.** Admission £8.50 ($14) adults, £6.70 ($11) seniors and students, £6.10 ($10) children, £26.10 ($44) family ticket. June–Sept daily 10am–5pm; off-season, daily 10am–4pm. Tube: Queensway or Bayswater on north side of gardens; High St. Kensington on south side.

Kensington Palace dates from about 1605 but was redesigned by Sir Christopher Wren in 1689. Since the end of the 18th century, it has been home to various members of the royal family, and the State Apartments are open for tours. The palace is now the London home of Princess Margaret as well as the duke and duchess of Kent. It was once the home of Diana, princess of Wales, and her two sons. Newly restored, the State Apartments and Ceremonial Dress Collection display trompe l'oeil murals by William Kent and ceremonial robes belonging to Queen Mary and George V. Visitors are guided through a series of theme rooms, including a tailor shop stocked with materials used in court dress. One section includes state-occasion dresses, hats, and shoes worn by queens in the 20th century. The State Apartments were first opened to the public a century ago by Queen Victoria, who was born here. Of the 30 rooms, 15, including the restored King's Gallery and the Cupola Room, where Queen Victoria was baptized, are permanently opened to the public. In the northwestern corner of Kensington Gardens (see below), you'll find the new **Princess Diana Memorial Playground.**

MORE SIGHTS
Official London
Whitehall and Cabinet War Rooms. Clive Steps at the end of King Charles St., SW1, off Whitehall near Big Ben. ☎ **020/7930-6961.** Admission £4.80 ($8); children under 15 free. Apr–Sept daily 9:30am–6pm (last admission 5:15pm); Oct–Mar daily 10am–5:30pm. Closed Christmas and holidays. Tube: Westminster or St. James's.

Whitehall extends south from Trafalgar Square to Parliament Square. Along it you'll find the Home Office, the Old Admiralty Building, and the Ministry of Defence. Visitors today can see the **Cabinet War Rooms,** a bombproof bunker suite of rooms, just as they were left by Winston Churchill at the end of World War II. You can see the Map Room with its huge wall maps; the Atlantic map is a mass of pinholes (each hole represents at least one convoy). Next door is Churchill's bedroom-cum-office, which has two BBC microphones on the desk for his broadcasts of those famous speeches that stirred the nation.

Museums
Imperial War Museum. Lambeth Rd., SE1. ☎ **020/7416-5000.** Admission £5.20 ($9) adults, £4.20 ($7) senior citizens and students, children under 16 free; free daily 4:30–6pm. Daily 10am–6pm. Closed Dec 24–26. Tube: Lambeth North or Elephant & Castle.

Constructed around 1815 as the Bethlehem Royal Hospital for the Insane (or Bedlam), this large domed building houses collections relating to the two world wars and other military operations. There are four floors of exhibitions, including a vast area showing historical displays, two floors of art galleries, and a dramatic re-creation of London at war during the blitz.

Wellington Museum. Apsley House, Hyde Park Corner, SW1. ☎ **020/7499-5676.** Admission £4.50 ($8) adults, £3 ($5) seniors, children under 18 free. Tues–Sun 11am–5pm. Closed Jan 1, May Day, and Dec 24–26. Tube: Hyde Park Corner.

This former town house of the Iron Duke, the British general (1769–1852) who defeated Napoléon at the Battle of Waterloo and later became prime minister, was opened as a public museum in 1952. The building was designed by Robert Adam and constructed in 1771–78.

Museum of London. 150 London Wall, EC2. ☎ **020/7600-3699.** Admission £5 ($9) adults, £3 ($5) students/seniors, £12 ($20) family ticket; free 16 and under. Tues–Sat 10am–5:50pm, Sun noon–5:50pm. Tube: St. Paul's, Barbican, or Moorgate.

In the Barbican near St. Paul's, the museum traces London's history from prehistoric times through relics, costumes, household effects, maps, and models. Anglo-Saxons, Vikings, Normans—they're all here, displayed on two floors around a central courtyard.

National Portrait Gallery. St. Martin's Place, WC2. ☎ **020/7306-0055.** Free admission. Mon–Sat 10am–6pm, Sun noon–6pm. Tube: Charing Cross or Leicester Sq.

The National Portrait Gallery was founded in 1856 to collect the likenesses of famous British men and women. Today the collection is the most comprehensive of its kind in the world and constitutes a unique record of those who created the history and culture of the nation. A few paintings will catch your eye, including Sir Joshua Reynold's portrait of Samuel Johnson ("a man of most dreadful appearance"). You'll also see a portrait of William Shakespeare, which is claimed to be the most "authentic contemporary likeness" of its subject, and the portrait of the Brontë sisters, painted by their brother Branwell. The most recent addition to the gallery includes portraits of British sports figures, a tribute to athletic icons from the *Chariots of Fire* athletes of the 1920s to the superstars of today.

A Millennium Marker

Note that the long-ballyhooed **Millennium Dome** in Greenwich was open for just 2000 (and was pretty much a financial fiasco). There's talk of turning it into an Olympic or sports arena. Stay tuned.

British Airways London Eye. Jubilee Gardens, SE1. ☎ **020/7487-0294.** Admission £7.45 ($13) adults, £5.95 ($10) seniors, £4.95 ($8) children. Tube: Embankment or Waterloo.

Opened in early 2000 (it was scheduled to have opened in December 1999), this extraordinary Ferris wheel is the world's highest observation wheel. Protected from the elements inside 32 high-tech capsules, passengers rise slowly to a height of 450 feet and receive a 30-minute slow-moving "flight" over the heart of the capital, complete with commentary and bird's-eye views that are "usually only accessible by helicopter or aircraft."

LONDON'S PARKS

London's parklands easily rate as the greatest "green lung" system of any large city. One of the largest is **Hyde Park.** With the adjoining Kensington Gardens, it covers 257ha (636 acres) of central London with velvety lawn interspersed with ponds, flowerbeds, and trees. **Kensington Gardens** are home to the celebrated statue of Peter Pan with the bronze rabbits that toddlers are always trying to kidnap. In the northwestern corner of the gardens is the new **Princess Diana Memorial Playground.** East of Hyde Park, across Piccadilly, stretch **Green Park** and **St. James's Park,** forming an almost-unbroken chain of landscaped beauty. This is an ideal area for picnics. You'll find it hard to believe this was once a festering piece of swamp near the leper hospital. **Regent's Park,** north of Baker Street and Marylebone Road, was designed by the 18th-century genius John Nash to surround a palace that never materialized. The **open-air theater** and the **London Zoo** are in this most classically beautiful of London's parks.

In July 2000, a 7-mile **walk commemorating the life of Princess Diana** opened. The walk passes through four of London's royal parks—St. James's Park, Green Park, Hyde Park, and Kensington Gardens. Along the way there are 70 plaques pointing out sites associated with Diana, including Kensington Palace (her home for 15 years), Buckingham Palace, St. James's Palace (where she once shared an office with Prince Charles), and Spencer House (once her family's mansion and now a museum).

ORGANIZED TOURS

One of the most popular bus tours is called **"The Original London Sightseeing Tour,"** where London unfolds from a traditional double-decker bus, with live commentary by a guide. The 1½-hour tour costs £12.50 ($21) adults and £6.50 ($11) children under 16. The tour plus Madame Tussaud's costs £21 ($36) adults and £12 ($20) children. You can buy tickets on the bus or from any London Transport or London Tourist Board Information Centre, where you can receive a discount. Departures are from convenient points within the city. For information or ticket purchases on the phone, call ☎ **020/8877-1722.**

To Vent or Not to Vent

Speakers' Corner in the northeast corner of Hyde Park is one of the most bizarre sights in London. Political activists, evangelists, and every crackpot in Britain who wishes to be heard can hop on a soapbox and speak their minds every Sunday from 11am to dusk. Democracy in action has never been so colorful!

Touring boats operate on the Thames all year and can take you to various places within Greater London and beyond. Main embarkation points are Westminster Pier, Charing Cross Pier, and Tower Pier, a system that enables you, for instance, to take a "water taxi" from the Tower of London to Westminster Abbey, or a more leisurely cruise from Westminster to Hampton Court Palace or Kew Gardens. Several companies operate motor launches offering panoramic views en route. For information and reservations, call the **Westminster/Greenwich** service at ☎ **020/7930-2062, Hampton Court** service at ☎ **020/7930-2062,** and **Tower** service at ☎ **020/7237-5134.** Westminster Pier is on Victoria Embankment, SW1 (tube: Embankment).

The best regularly scheduled walking tours of London are offered by **The Original London Walks** (☎ **020/7624-3978**). The tours range from ghost walks to one that features sites important in the history of the Beatles. The guides are superb and include prominent actors and actresses and the man many consider to be the foremost authority on Jack the Ripper. Walks cost £4.50 ($8) adults or £3.50 ($6) students/seniors; children under 15 are free. No reservations are needed; call the number above for walk times and starting locations.

THE SHOPPING SCENE
THE TOP SHOPPING STREETS & NEIGHBORHOODS

There are several key streets that offer some of London's best retail stores—or simply one of everything—in a niche or neighborhood, so you can just stroll and shop.

THE WEST END   As a neighborhood, the West End includes Mayfair and is home to the core of London's big-name shopping. Most of the department stores, designer shops, and chain stores have their flagships in this area.

The key streets are **Oxford Street** for affordable shopping (tube: Marble Arch if you're ambitious, Bond St. if you just want to see some of it), and **Regent Street,** which intersects Oxford Street at Oxford Circus tube: Oxford Circus). **Marks & Spencer**'s Marble Arch store (on Oxford Street) is their flagship and worth shopping for their high-quality goods. There's a grocery store in the basement and a home furnishings department upstairs. Regent Street has fancier shops—more upscale department stores (including the famed **Liberty of London**), chain stores **(Laura Ashley),** and specialty dealers—and leads all the way to Piccadilly.

In between the two, parallel to Regent Street, is **Bond Street.** Divided into New and Old, Bond Street (tube: Bond St.) also connects Piccadilly with Oxford Street and is synonymous with the luxury trade. Bond Street has had a recent revival and is the hot address for international designers. **Burlington Arcade** tube: Piccadilly Circus), the famous glass-roofed, Regency-style passage leading off Piccadilly, is lined with intriguing shops and boutiques specializing in fashion, jewelry, Irish linen, cashmere, and more.

Just off Regent Street, **Carnaby Street** (tube: Oxford Circus) might sound like a tired name from the '60s, but it's still alive and flourishing. The area includes surrounding streets as well: Newburg, Ganton, Marlborough Court, Lowndes Court, Marshall, Beak, Kingly, and Foubert's Place. Each of these streets has new and exciting shops along with trendy cafes and bars. New retailers are moving in all the time, including a concept by Levi's to sell its vintage clothing under the label "Red." You can expect the unexpected here, and innovative boutiques come and go virtually every week. The entire district is also a place to hang out at such bars as JUS Cafe, on Foubert's Place, the most fashionable juice bar in London.

For a total contrast, check out **Jermyn Street,** on the far side of Piccadilly, a tiny 2-block-long street devoted to high-end men's haberdashers and toiletries shops; many have been doing business for centuries. Several hold royal warrants, including **Turn-ball & Asser,** where HRH Prince Charles has his pj's made.

The West End also includes the theater district, so there's two more shopping areas: the still-not-ready-for-prime-time **Soho,** where sex shops are slowly being turned into cutting-edge designer shops; and **Covent Garden,** which is a masterpiece unto itself. The original marketplace has taken over the surrounding neighborhood so that even though the streets run a little higgledy-piggledy and you can easily get lost, it's fun to just wander and shop. Covent Garden is especially mobbed on Sundays (tube: Covent Garden).

KNIGHTSBRIDGE & CHELSEA   This is the second-most famous retail district because it's the home of **Harrods,** 87–135 Brompton Rd., Knightsbridge (☎ 020/7730-1234; tube: Knightsbridge). Harrods is London's—indeed Europe's—top department store. The sheer range, variety, and quality of merchandise are dazzling; be sure not to miss the delicatessen and food halls. A small street nearby, Sloane Street, is chockablock with designer shops; and another street in the opposite direction, **Cheval Place,** is also lined with designer resale shops.

Walk toward Museum Row and you'll soon find **Beauchamp Place** (pronounced *Bee*-cham). The street is only 1 block long, but it features the kinds of shops where young British aristos buy their clothing. Head out at the **Harvey Nichols (Harvey Nicks)** end of Knightsbridge, away from Harrods, and shop your way through the designer stores on Sloane Street (**Hermès, Armani, Prada,** and the like), then walk past Sloane Square and you're in an altogether different neighborhood: King's Road.

King's Road (tube: Sloane Sq.), the main street of Chelsea, which starts at Sloane Square, will forever remain a symbol of London in the swinging sixties. More and more in the 1990s, King's Road is a lineup of markets and "multistores," large or small conglomerations of indoor stands, stalls, and booths within one building or enclosure. Chelsea doesn't begin and end with King's Road. If you choose to walk the other direction from Harrods, you connect to a part of Chelsea called **Brompton Cross,** another hip and hot area for designer shops made popular when Michelin House was rehabbed by Sir Terence Conran for **The Conran Shop,** 81 Fulham Rd., SW 3 (☎ 020/7589-7401).

Also, seek out **Walton Street,** a tiny little snake of a street running off Brompton Cross. About 2 blocks are devoted to fairy-tale shops where a *lady* buys aromatherapy, needlepoint, costume jewelry, or meets with her interior designer. Finally, don't forget all those museums right there in the corner of the shopping streets. They all have great gift shops.

KENSINGTON & NOTTING HILL   **Kensington High Street** (tube: High St. Kensington) is the most recent hangout of the classier breed of teen, who has graduated from Carnaby Street and is ready for street chic. While there're a few staples of basic British fashion on this strip, most of the stores feature items that stretch, are very, very short, or very, very tight.

From Kensington High Street, you can walk up **Kensington Church Street,** which, like Portobello Road, is one of the city's main shopping avenues for antiques. Kensington Church Street dead-ends into the Notting Hill Gate tube station, which is where you would arrive for shopping in **Portobello Road.** The weekend market is 2 blocks beyond.

THE TOP MARKETS

THE WEST END   The most famous market in all of England, **Covent Garden Market** (☎ 020/7836-9136; tube: Covent Garden), offers several different markets daily 9am to 5pm (we think it's most fun to come on Sunday). **Apple Market** is the fun, bustling market in the courtyard, where traders sell, well, everything. Many of the items are what the English call collectible nostalgia; they include a wide array of glassware and ceramics, leather goods, toys, clothes, hats, and jewelry. Some of the merchandise is truly unusual. This becomes an antique market on Mondays. Meanwhile, out back is **Jubilee Market** (☎ 020/7836-2139), which is also an antique market on Mondays. Every other day of the week, it's sort of a fancy hippie-ish market with cheap clothes and books. Out front there're a few tents of cheap stuff, except again on Monday, when antique dealers take over here, too.

   St. Martin-in-the-Fields Market (tube: Charing Cross) is good for teens and hipsters who don't want to trek all the way to Camden Market (see below) and can be satisfied with imports from India and South America, crafts, and some local football souvenirs. It's near Trafalgar Square and Covent Garden; hours are Monday to Saturday 11am to 5pm, and Sundays noon to 5pm.

NOTTING HILL   The area has become synonymous with the Julia Roberts and Hugh Grant movie, but Londoners already know, whatever you collect, you'll find it at the **Portobello Market** (tube: Notting Hill Gate). It's mainly a Saturday happening, from 6am to 5pm. You needn't be here at the crack of dawn; 9am is fine. You just want to beat the motor-coach crowd. Once known mainly for fruit and vegetables (still sold here throughout the week), Portobello in the past 4 decades has become synonymous with antiques. But don't take the stallholder's word for it that the fiddle he's holding is a genuine Stradivarius left to him in the will of his Italian great-uncle; it might just as well have been nicked from an East End pawnshop.

   The market is divided into three major sections. The most crowded is the antique section, running between Colville Road and Chepstow Villas to the south. (*Warning:* There's a great concentration of pickpockets in this area.) The second section (and the oldest part) is the "fruit and veg" market, lying between Westway and Colville Road. In the third and final section, there's a flea market, where Londoners sell bric-a-brac and lots of secondhand goods they didn't really want in the first place. But, looking around still makes for interesting fun.

NORTH LONDON   If it's Wednesday, it's time for **Camden Passage** (☎ 020/7351-5353; tube: Angel) in Islington, where each Wednesday and Saturday there's a very upscale antique market. It starts in Camden Passage and then sprawls into the streets behind. It's on Wednesdays 7am to 5:30pm and Saturdays 9am to 5:30pm.

   Don't confuse Camden Passage with **Camden Market** (very, very downtown). Camden Market (tube: Camden Town) is for teens and others into body piercing, blue hair (yes, still), and vintage clothing. Serious collectors of vintage may want to explore during the week, when the teen scene isn't quite so overwhelming. Market hours are 9:30am to 5:30pm daily, with some parts opening at 10am.

LONDON AFTER DARK

Weekly publications such as *Time Out* and *Where,* available at newsstands, give full entertainment listings and contain information on restaurants, nightclubs, and theaters. You'll also find listings in daily newspapers, notably *The Times* and *The Telegraph.*

THE PERFORMING ARTS

If you want to see specific theatrical performances—especially hit ones—purchase your tickets in advance. The best way to do this is to buy your ticket from the theater's box office. Often you can call in advance; many theaters will accept bookings by telephone if you give your name and credit-card number when you call. You can also make theater reservations through ticket agents, such as **Keith Prowse/First Call,**

Fringe Benefits

Some of the best theater in London is performed on the "fringe"—at the dozens of so-called fringe theaters that usually attempt more adventurous productions than the established West End theaters; they're also dramatically lower in price and staged in more intimate surroundings. Check the weekly listings in *Time Out* for schedules and show times.

234 W. 44th St., Suite 1000, New York, NY 10036 (☎ **800/669-8687** or 212/398-1430 in the U.S., or 020/7911-3403 in London). The fee for booking a ticket in the United States is 35%; in London, it's 25%.

THEATER   Occupying a prime site on the South Bank of the River Thames is the flagship of British theater, the **Royal National Theatre,** South Bank, SE1 (☎ **020/7452-3000;** tube: Waterloo, Embankment, or Charing Cross). The National houses three theaters. The largest is the Olivier, with 1,200 seats. Tickets are £12 to £30 ($20 to $51).

The **Royal Shakespeare Company (RSC),** Barbican Centre, Silk St., Barbican, EC2 (☎ **020/7638-8891;** tube: Barbican, Moorgate, or Liverpool St.), is one of the world's finest theater companies. The core of the company's work remains the plays of William Shakespeare, but it also presents a wide-ranging program. There are three different productions each week in the Barbican Theatre, a 1,200-seat main auditorium with excellent sight lines throughout; and the Pit, the small studio space where much of the company's new writing is presented. Barbican Theatre tickets are £8 to £33 ($14 to $56); The Pit, £14 to £18.50 ($24 to $31).

A recent addition to London's theater scene is the replica of Shakespeare's **Globe Theatre,** New Globe Walk, Bankside, SE1 (☎ **020/7401-9919;** tube: Mansion House). Performances are staged, on the theater's original site, as they were in Elizabethan times: without lighting, scenery, or such luxuries as cushioned seats or a roof over the audience. Tours are £7 ($12) adults, £5 ($9) students and seniors, and £4 ($7) children. Performance tickets and schedules vary; call for details. Tours daily 9:15am to 12:15pm.

Sadler's Wells Theatre, Rosbery Ave., EC1 (☎ **020/7314-8800;** tube: Angel), is London's premier venue for dance. This new theater has a huge stage double its previous size, a 1,500-seat capacity, improved sight lines, and added foyers featuring cafes, bars, and space for art. The new theater can change its interior shape, size, mood, and even color for almost any performance. The program for Sadler's for each year will be approximately 25 weeks of dance and 10 to 12 weeks of opera. The remaining time will be a medley of visual theater. Box office Monday to Saturday 10am to 8pm. Tickets are £7.50 to £35 ($13 to $60).

CLASSICAL MUSIC & OPERA   The **Royal Opera** and **Royal Ballet** are back at the newly restored **Royal Opera House,** Bow St., Covent Garden, WC2 (☎ **020/7212-9123;** tube: Covent Garden). New additions include two annexes with shops and restaurants, and rehearsal rooms. The Studio Theater and the backstage area of the opera house have been enlarged. Opera performances are usually sung in the original language with English subtitles. The Royal Ballet performs a repertory with a tilt toward the classics, including works by its earlier choreographer-director, Sir Frederick Ashton, and Sir Kenneth MacMillan. Opera tickets are £8 to £100 ($13.60 to $170), ballet £6 to £60 ($10 to $102).

The **London Coliseum,** St. Martin's Lane, WC2 (☎ **020/7632-8300;** tube: Leicester Sq.), is London's largest and most splendid theater. The **English National**

Opera performs a wide range of works in English, from great classics to Gilbert and Sullivan to new and experimental works, staged with flair and imagination. Tickets are £6 to £55 ($10 to $94). About 100 discount balcony tickets are sold on the day of performance.

The **Royal Albert Hall,** Kensington Gore, SW7 (☎ **020/7589-8212;** tube: South Kensington), is the annual setting for the BBC Henry Wood Promenade Concerts ("The Proms") from mid-July to mid-September. A British tradition since 1895, the programs are outstanding, often presenting newly commissioned works for the first time. Tickets are £3 to £90 ($5 to $153).

Across Waterloo Bridge rises **South Bank Centre,** South Bank, SE1 (☎ **020/7960-4242;** tube: Waterloo or Embankment). Here are three of the most comfortable and acoustically perfect concert halls in the world: Royal Festival Hall, Queen Elizabeth Hall, and the Purcell Room. Within their precincts, more than 1,200 performances a year are presented. Tickets are £5 to £80 ($9 to $136).

THE CLUB & MUSIC SCENE

NIGHTCLUBS & CABARETS   The premises of **Bagley's Studios,** King's Cross Freight Depot, off York Way, N1 (☎ **020/7278-2777;** tube: King's Cross), are vast, echoing, a bit grimy, and very evocative of a munitions warehouse during the dark days of World War II. Set in the bleak industrial landscapes behind King's Cross Station, its interior is radically transformed three nights a week into one of London's most animated Rave events. It's scattered over two floors, each the size of an American football field, and each divided into a trio of individual rooms, with its own ambience and sound system. You'll be happiest here if you wander from room to room, searching out the site that best corresponds to your energy level at the moment. Guaranteed openings Friday to Sunday 10pm to 7am; otherwise, openings depend on whatever promoter wants to book the space. Cover is £10 to £20 ($17 to $34).

Set in a dingy residential neighborhood in north London, **Barfly Club,** at the Falcon Pub, 234 Royal College St., NW1 (☎ **020/7482-4884;** tube: Camden Town), is a traditional-looking pub that's distinguished every night by the roster of rock-and-roll bands that come in from throughout the United Kingdom for bouts of beer and high-energy music. A recorded announcement tells fans what to expect on any given night, along with explicit instructions on how to reach it through a warren of narrow streets. You're likely to get virtually anything here—which adds considerably to the sense of fun and adventure. Open nightly 7:30 to 2 or 3am, with most musical acts beginning at 8:15pm. Cover is £7 to £11 ($12 to $19).

Camden Palace, 1A Camden High St., NW1 (☎ **020/7387-0428;** tube: Camden Town or Mornington Crescent), is housed inside what was originally a theater built around 1910. It draws an over-18 crowd that flocks there in various costumes and energy levels according to the night of the week. Since it offers a rotating style of music, it's best to phone in advance to see if that evening's musical genre appeals to your taste. Open Tuesday 10am to 2am, Friday 10am to 6am, and Saturday 10am to 7am. Cover is £5 to £20 ($9 to $34).

ROCK   A long-established venue for rock-and-roll, blues, and indie bands, **The Rock Garden,** 6–7 The Piazza, Covent Garden (☎ **020/7836-4052;** tube: Covent Garden), maintains a bar and a stage in the cellar and a restaurant on the street level. The cellar area, known as The Venue, has hosted such bands as Dire Straits, The Police, and U2 before they became famous. Open daily 5pm to 2am Sunday to Thursday, 3am Friday and Saturday). Cover is £5 to £10 ($9 to $17); diners enter free. No cover before 8pm, 10pm Friday and Saturday.

Wag Club, 35 Wardour St., W1 (☎ 020/7437-5534; tube: Piccadilly Circus or Leicester Sq.), hides behind an innocuous brick facade. The popular dance club covers two floors, one decorated with Celtic designs in gold with colorful renditions of medieval tarot cards, the other in bright primary colors, with huge black-and-white canvasses. White fur fabric sculptures adorn the walls; high-tech lighting illuminates the dance floor. The music policy alternates between live bands and recorded music. Call to see what's happening any given night. Open Tuesday to Thursday 10pm to 3am, Friday 10pm to 4am, and Sunday 10pm to 5am. Cover is £5 to £10 ($9 to $17).

JAZZ & BLUES   The reasonably priced **100 Club,** 100 Oxford St., W1 (☎ 020/7636-0933; tube: Tottenham Court Rd.), is a serious rival to the city's upscale jazz clubs. Its cavalcade of bands includes the best British jazz musicians, as well as many touring Americans. Rock, R&B, and blues are also presented. It's open Monday to Friday 8:30pm to 3am, Saturday 7:30pm to 1am, and Sunday 7:30 to 11:30pm. Cover is £8 ($14) members, £9 ($15) nonmembers; Sun £6 ($10).

Mention the word *jazz* in London and people immediately think of **Ronnie Scott's,** 47 Frith St., W1 (☎ 020/7439-0747; tube: Leicester Sq.), long the citadel of modern jazz in Europe, where the best English and American groups are booked. Featured on almost every bill is an American band, often with a top-notch singer. In the Main Room, you can either stand at the bar to watch the show or sit at a table, where you can order dinner. The Downstairs Bar is more intimate. On weekends, the separate Upstairs Room has a disco called Club Latino. Open Monday to Saturday 8:30pm to 3am. Cover is £15 ($26) Monday to Thursday, £20 ($34) Friday and Saturday.

DANCE CLUBS

The Annexe, 1 Dean St., W1 (☎ 020/7287-9608; tube: Tottenham Court Rd.), is in the heart of the Soho area and is a combination of a New York–style lounge and a funky hip music scene for young Londoners. The decor is posh but relaxed. The establishment can accommodate 250 people with its two bars and large dance floor. The DJ's program varies from top 10 dance music, soul, and funk to pop and rock played on a powerful stereo system. The club also features fashion shows, band showcases, photographic exhibitions, and short film and video screenings. It's open Tuesday to Thursday 5pm to 11pm, Friday and Saturday 5pm to 5am. Cover is £5 to £10 ($9 to $17).

Equinox, Leicester Sq., WC2 (☎ 020/7437-1446; tube: Leicester Sq.), has nine bars, the largest dance floor in London, and a restaurant modeled along the lines of an American diner from the 1950s. Virtually every kind of dance music, save "rave," is featured here. It's open Monday to Thursday 9pm to 3am and Friday and Saturday 9pm to 4am. Cover is £5 to £12 ($9 to $20); £3 ($5) students. **Hippodrome,** Leicester Sq., WC2 (☎ 020/7437-4311. Tube: Leicester Sq.), is one of London's greatest discos, an enormous place where light and sound envelop you from all directions. Revolving speakers even descend from the roof to deafen you in patches, and you can watch yourself on closed-circuit video. It's open Monday to Saturday 9pm to 3am. Cover is £3 to £12 ($5 to $20).

Because it's removed from the city center, **Ministry of Sound,** 103 Gaunt St., SE1 (☎ 020/7378-6528; tube: Elephant & Castle), is popular with the local set and relatively devoid of tourists. It has a big bar and an even bigger sound system that blasts garage and house music to enthusiastic crowds, who fill the two dance floors or relax in the cinema room. Be warned that entrance to this place isn't particularly cheap and the door policy is selective. Open Friday 10:30pm to 6am, Saturday midnight to 9am. Cover is £10 to £15 ($17 to $26).

Wednesday is one of the most popular nights at **The Office,** 3–5 Rathbone Place, W1 (☎ 020/7636-1598; tube: Tottenham Court Rd.), when the "Double Six Club"

The World's Greatest Pub Crawl

Dropping into the local pub for a pint of real ale or bitter is the best way to soak up the character of the different villages that make up London. You'll hear the accents and slang and see first-hand how far removed upper-crust Kensington is from blue-collar Wapping. Catch the local gossip or football talk—and, of course, enjoy some of the finest ales, stouts, ciders, and malt whiskies in the world.

Central London is awash with wonderful historic pubs as rich and varied as the city itself. The **Cittie of Yorke,** 22 High Holborn, WC1 (☎ **0171/242-7670;** tube: Holborn or Chancery Lane), boasts the longest bar in all Britain, rafters ascending to the heavens, and a long row of immense wine vats, all of which give it the air of a great medieval hall—appropriate since a pub has existed at this location since 1430. Samuel Smiths is on tap, and the bar offers novelties like chocolate-orange-flavored vodka. Dickens once hung out in the **Lamb & Flag,** 33 Rose St., off Garrick Street, WC2 (☎ **0171/497-9504;** tube: Leicester Sq.), and the room itself is little changed from the days when he prowled this neighborhood. The pub has an amazing and somewhat scandalous history. Dryden was almost killed by a band of thugs outside its doors in December 1679; the pub gained the nickname the "Bucket of Blood" during the Regency era (1811–20) because of the routine bare-knuckled prizefights that broke out. Tap beers include Courage Best and Directors, Old Speckled Hen, John Smiths, and Wadworths 6X.

The **Olde Mitre,** Ely Place, EC1 (☎ **0171/405-4751;** tube: Chancery Lane), is the namesake of a working-class inn built here in 1547, when the Bishops of Ely controlled the district. It's a small pub with an odd assortment of customers. Friary Meux, Ind Coope Burton, and Tetleys are on tap. **Seven Stars,** 53 Carey St., WC2 (☎ **0171/242-8521;** tube: Holborn), is tiny and modest except for its collection of toby mugs and law-related art, the latter a tribute to the pub's location at the back of the Law Courts and the large clientele of barristers who drink here. It's a great place to pick up some British legal jargon. Courage Best and Directors are on tap, as well as a selection of single malts.

Black Friar, 174 Queen Victoria St., EC4 (☎ **0171/236-5650;** tube: Blackfriars), will transport you to the Edwardian era. The wedge-shaped pub reeks of marble and bronze art nouveau, featuring bas-reliefs of mad monks, a low-vaulted mosaic ceiling, and seating carved out of gold marble recesses. It's especially popular with the city's after-work crowd, and it features Adams, Wadsworth 6X, Tetleys, and Brakspears on tap.

features easy-listening music and board games from 6pm to 2am. Other nights are devoted to recorded pop, rock, soul, and disco. Come for the fun not the decor. Open Monday to Friday 11am to 3am, Saturday 9:30pm to 3:30am. Cover is £6 to £8 ($10 to $14).

THE GAY & LESBIAN SCENE

The most reliable source of information on gay clubs and activities is the (always busy) 24-hour **Gay Switchboard** at ☎ **020/7837-7324.** Offering similar help for women is the **Lesbian Line** at ☎ **020/7251-6911,** staffed Tuesday to Thursday 7 to 10pm and Monday and Friday 2 to 10pm.

Adjacent to one of Covent Garden's best-known traffic junctions, **The Box,** at Seven Dials, 32–34 Monmouth St., WC2 (☎ **020/7240-5828;** tube: Covent Garden or Leicester Sq.), is a Mediterranean-style bar. Gay men outnumber lesbians, though the venue is sophisticated and blasé about sexual definitions. Year-round, the place defines itself as a "summer bar," throwing open its doors and windows to a cluster of outdoor tables that attracts a crowd at the slightest hint of warmth. It's open Monday to Saturday 11:30am to 11pm and Sunday noon to 6pm.

Candy Bar, 4 Carlisle St., London, W1 (☎ **020/7494-4041;** tube: Tottenham Court Rd.), is a trilevel dance club that's a hot spot for London's lesbian crowd, whether young or of a certain age. The top floor is a lounge with pool tables and comfortable couches. The second floor is a dimly lit bar area. The lower floor is a large dance floor with live DJs playing everything from rock and pop to top 10 R&B, soul, and reggae. The decor is rather plain with more subdued lighting for a more cruisy atmosphere. Providing they appear on the arm of a woman, men are allowed to visit as well. Hours are Monday to Thursday 5pm to midnight, Friday 5pm to 2am, Saturday 2pm to 2am, and Sunday 5 to 11pm. Cover is £3 ($5) Friday and Saturday.

Few bars in London exemplify tolerance, humor, and sexual sophistication as well as **The Edge,** 11 Soho Sq., W1 (☎ **020/7439-1313;** tube: Tottenham Court Rd.). You'll get the idea the moment you enter; the first two floors are painted in intertwined shades of red and blue, with accessories that change, like the fixtures of an English garden, with the season. The clientele ranges from the ostentatiously gay to "Randy Andy" types slumming on a pub crawl away from the Royal Palace. It's open Monday to Saturday 11am to 1am and Sunday noon to 10:30pm. **First Out,** 52 St. Giles High St., WC2 (☎ **020/7240-8042;** tube: Tottenham Court Rd.), prides itself on being the first (est. 1986) all-gay coffee shop in London. Set in a 19th-century building whose venerable wood panels have been painted all colors of the Rainbow, it maintains two intimate floors (read: not particularly cruisy) where menu items are exclusively vegetarian and invariably priced at £3.80 ($6). Cappuccino and whisky are the preferred drinks, while curry dishes, pot pies in phyllo pastries, and salads are the foods of choice. Don't expect raucousness; some clients have even brought their grandmothers here. Look for the bulletin board, where the leaflets and business cards of gay and gay-friendly entrepreneurs add an aura of resource center to this cozy venue. Open Monday to Saturday 10am to 11pm and Sunday 11am to 10:30pm.

✪ **Heaven,** The Arches, Craven St., WC2 (☎ **020/7930-2020;** tube: Charing Cross or Embankment), is a London landmark club within the vaulted cellars of Charing Cross Railway Station. Black inside and reminiscent of a very large air-raid shelter, Heaven is one of England's biggest and best-established gay venues. It's four different areas are connected by a labyrinth of stairs, catwalks, and hallways. The club features different theme nights, where, depending on the night, gay men, gay women, or mostly heterosexuals predominate. Call before you go to learn the latest format. It's open Monday and Wednesday 10:30pm to 3am, Friday and Saturday 10:30pm to 6am. Cover is £6 to £10 ($10 to $17).

THE BAR SCENE

At the **American Bar,** in The Savoy, The Strand, WC2 (☎ **020/7836-4343;** tube: Embankment or Covent Garden), still one of the most sophisticated gathering places in London, the bartender is known for such special concoctions as the "Savoy Affair" and the "Prince of Wales," as well as for pouring the best martini in town. The bar is open Monday to Saturday 11am to 11pm with jazz piano music beginning at 7pm. On Sunday, it's open noon to 3pm and 7 to 10:30pm.

Rumours, 33 Wellington St., WC2 (☎ **020/7836-0038;** tube: Covent Garden), is the kind of place where you might expect Tom Cruise to turn up as bartender. Set within what functioned a century ago as a wholesale flower market, Rumours combines 1990s sophistication with a flamboyant marine theme. Open Monday to Saturday 11:30am to 11pm, Sunday 2 to 10:30pm.

DAY TRIPS FROM LONDON

❂ **HAMPTON COURT PALACE**   On the north side of the Thames, 21km (13 miles) west of London in East Molesey, Surrey, this 16th-century palace of Cardinal Wolsey can teach us a lesson: Don't try to outdo your boss, particularly if he happens to be Henry VIII. The rich cardinal did just that. He eventually lost his fortune, power, and prestige—and he ended up giving his lavish palace to the Tudor monarch. Although the palace enjoyed prestige and pomp in Elizabethan days, it owes much of its present look to William and Mary—or rather to Sir Christopher Wren, who designed and built the Northern or Lion Gates. You can parade through the apartments today, filled as they are with porcelain, furniture, paintings, and tapestries. The Renaissance Gallery is graced with some of the best art, mainly paintings by old masters on loan from Queen Elizabeth II.

The cloisters, courtyards, state apartments, great kitchen, cellars, and Hampton Court exhibition are open April to October Monday 10:15am to 6pm and Tuesday to Sunday 9:30am to 6pm. November to March, hours are Monday 10:15am to 4:30pm and Tuesday to Sunday 9:30am to 4:30pm. The Tudor tennis court and banqueting house are open the same hours as above, but only mid-March to mid-October. Admission to all these attractions is £10 ($17) adults, £7.60 ($13) students/seniors, and £6.60 ($11) children 5 to 15, and £29.90 ($51) families (2 adults and up to 3 children); children under 5 are free. The gardens—including the Great Vine, King's Privy Garden, Great Fountain Gardens, Sunken Gardens, Board Walk, Tiltyard, and Wilderness—are open daily 7am to dusk (but not later than 9pm) and can be visited free except for the Privy Garden, for which admission is £2 ($3.40), unless you pay for a palace ticket.

The **Landmark Trust,** Shootesbrooke, Maidenhead, Berkshire SL6 3SW (☎ **0168/825-925;** www.landmarktrust.co.uk; e-mail: bookings@landmarktrust. co.uk), oversees two palace buildings offering modest self-catering facilities. The Fish Court, sleeping six, was originally the quarters of the pastry chefs; 4-day bookings are £531 ($903) and 7-day bookings £1,515 ($2,576). Sleeping eight, the Georgian House is a former kitchen for the palace with a private garden; 4-night bookings for £578 ($983) and 7-day bookings £1,857 ($3,157).

You can get to Hampton Court (☎ **020/8781-9500**) by bus, train, boat, or car. Frequent trains from Waterloo Station (Network Southeast) go to Hampton Court Station. London Transport buses 111, 131, 216, 267, and 461 make the trip, as do Green Line Coaches (ask at the nearest London Country Bus office for routes 715, 716, 718, and 726). If you have the time (about 4 hours), boat service is offered to and from Kingston, Richmond, and Westminster.

❂ **WINDSOR CASTLE**   When William the Conqueror ordered a castle built on this spot, he began a legend and a link with English sovereignty that has known many vicissitudes, the most recent being a 1992 fire. The state apartments display many works of art, porcelain, armor, furniture, three Verrio ceilings, and several 17th-century Gibbons carvings. Several works by Rubens adorn the King's Drawing Rooms. Of the apartments, the grand reception room, with its Gobelin tapestries, is the most spectacular.

Queen Mary's Doll's House is a palace in perfect miniature. It was given to Queen Mary in 1923 as a symbol of national goodwill. The house, designed by Sir Edwin Lutyens, was created on a scale of 1 to 12. It took 3 years to complete and involved the work of 1,500 tradesmen and artists.

St. George's Chapel is a gem of the Perpendicular style, sharing the distinction with Westminster Abbey as a pantheon of English monarchs (Victoria is a notable exception). The present St. George's was founded in the late 15th century by Edward IV on the site of the original Chapel of the Order of the Garter (Edward III, 1348).

Admission is £10 ($17) adults, £7.50 ($13) students/seniors, £5 ($9) children 16 and under, £22.50 ($38) families (2 adults and 2 children). The castle at Castle Hill is open March to October daily 10am to 5pm and November to February daily 10am to 4pm. Lying 34km (21 miles) west of London, Windsor Castle (☎ **01753/831118**) can be reached in 50 minutes by train from Paddington Station.

2 Oxford, the Cotswolds & Stratford-upon-Avon

One of England's most picturesque areas is the Cotswolds, with its sleepy old wool towns, and the country around Shakespeare's birthplace, Stratford-upon-Avon. After visiting London, many move on to visit the ancient university city of Oxford and the still untouched Cotswold villages that, despite attracting healthy amounts of tourism, retain their authentic character. Both time and tradition beckon you on to these places.

TOWN & GOWN: OXFORD

Oxford is a city of business and commerce, home to several industries; it's much more of a real city than Cambridge. Oxford isn't entirely dominated by its university, although the college spires are the reason the hordes, including tour buses, flock here. The fast-flowing pedestrian traffic may cause you to think you've been transported back to London instead of delivered to not-so-sleepy Oxford.

At any time of the year, you can tour the colleges, many of which represent a peak in England's architectural kingdom, as well as a valley of Victorian contributions. The Oxford Information Centre (see below) offers guided walking tours daily throughout the year. Just don't mention the other place (Cambridge), and you shouldn't have any trouble. Comparisons between the two universities are inevitable of course, Oxford being better known for the arts and Cambridge more for the sciences.

The city predates the university—in fact, it was a Saxon town in the early part of the 10th century. By the 12th century, Oxford was already growing in reputation as a seat of learning, at the expense of Paris. The first colleges were founded in the 13th century. The story of Oxford is filled with local conflicts: The relationship between town and gown wasn't as peaceful as it is today, and riots often flared over the rights of the university versus the town. Nowadays, the young people of Oxford take out their aggressions in sporting competitions.

Ultimately, the test of a great university lies in the caliber of the people it turns out. Oxford can name-drop a mouthful: Roger Bacon, Sir Walter Raleigh, John Donne, Sir Christopher Wren, Samuel Johnson, William Penn, Lewis Carroll, Harold Macmillan, Graham Greene, T. E. Lawrence, just to name a select few.

ESSENTIALS

GETTING THERE   Oxford is 87km (54 miles) northwest from London.

By Train   Trains from Paddington Station reach Oxford in 1¹/₄ hours. Service is hourly. A cheap, same-day round-trip ticket costs £28.80 ($49); call **British Rail** at ☎ **0345/484-950** for more detailed information.

By Bus   Oxford Citylink provides coach service from London's Victoria Station (☎ 020/7824-0056) to the Oxford bus station. Coaches usually depart about every 20 minutes during the day from gate 10 (trip time: about 1³/₄ hours). A same-day round-trip ticket costs £7.50 ($13).

By Car   Take M-40 west from London and follow the signs. Traffic and parking are a disaster in Oxford; you may want to use one of the four "Park and Ride" lots just outside of the city.

VISITOR INFORMATION   The **Oxford Tourist Information Centre,** at The Old School, Gloucester Green (☎ 01865/726871), sells maps, brochures, souvenir items, as well as the famous Oxford University T-shirt. It also provides hotel booking services for £2.50 ($4.25). Guided walking tours leave from the center daily (see below). It's open Monday to Saturday 9:30am to 5pm and Sunday and bank holidays in summer 10am to 3:30pm.

GETTING AROUND   Since Oxford is relatively flat, a good way to see the colleges is by bicycle. **Bike Zone,** 6 Lincoln House Market St. (☎ 01865/728877), rents 15-speed hybrid bicycles for £15 ($26) a day or £20 ($34) for the week with a £50 ($85) refundable deposit. The staff is very friendly and helpful. It's open Monday to Saturday 9am to 5:30pm.

WHERE TO STAY

The **Oxford Tourist Information Centre,** Gloucester Green, opposite the bus station (☎ 01865/726871), operates a year-round room-booking service for a fee of £2.50 ($4.25), plus a refundable deposit. The center has a list of accommodations, maps, and guidebooks.

Expensive

Old Bank Hotel. 92–94 High St., Oxford OX1 4BN. ☎ **0186/579-9599.** Fax 0186/579-9598. www.oxford-hotels-restaurants.co.uk. 44 units. A/C TV TEL. £160–£170 ($272–$289) double; from £195 ($332) suite. Rates include English breakfast. AE, DC, DISC, MC, V. Bus: 7.

The first hotel created in the center of Oxford in 135 years, it opened late in 1999. The good-sized rooms are comfortably and elegantly appointed, often with views. The hotel has a dynamic restaurant, Alto Bar & Grill, serving an Italian-influenced cuisine in a contemporary setting.

Old Parsonage Hotel. 1 Banbury Rd., Oxford OX2 6NN. ☎ **01865/310210.** Fax 01865/311262. E-mail: info@oldparsonage-hotel.co.uk. 30 units. MINIBAR TV TEL. £150–£175 ($255–$298); from £200 ($340) suite. Rates include English breakfast and afternoon tea. AE, DC, MC, V. Bus: 7.

This hotel near St. Giles Church and Keble College is so old (1660) it looks like an extension of one of the ancient colleges. Oscar Wilde once lived here. In 1991 it was completely renovated and transformed into a first-rate hotel. The rooms are individually designed but not large, with such amenities as a remote-control radio and hair dryer. The bathrooms have their own phone extensions and are the only place in the hotel with air-conditioning. All suites and some rooms have sofa beds. There's 24-hour room service available.

The Randolph. Beaumont St., Oxford, Oxfordshire OX1 2LN. ☎ **800/225-5843** in the U.S. and Canada, or 01865/247481. Fax 01865/791678. 119 units. TV TEL. £155–£375 ($263.50–$637.50) double; from £225–£375 ($382.50–$637.50) suite. AE, DC, MC, V. Parking £10 ($17). Bus: 7.

Since 1864, the Randolph, with its striking arched stone entrance, has overlooked St. Giles, the Ashmolean Museum, and the Cornmarket. The hotel illustrates how

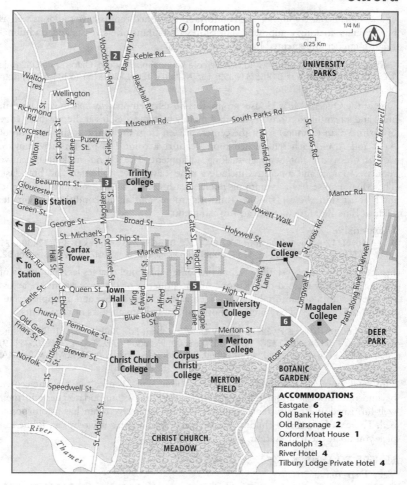

ACCOMMODATIONS
Eastgate **6**
Old Bank Hotel **5**
Old Parsonage **2**
Oxford Moat House **1**
Randolph **3**
River Hotel **4**
Tilbury Lodge Private Hotel **4**

historic surroundings can be combined with modern conveniences to make for elegant accommodations. The furnishings are traditional, and all rooms have a hair dryer and hot beverage-making facilities. Some rooms are quite large, although others are a bit cramped. The double glazing on the windows seems inadequate to keep out the mid-town traffic noise. In this price range, we'd opt first for the Old Parsonage. The hotel's Spires Restaurant presents both time-tested English and modern cuisine in a high-ceilinged Victorian dining room.

Moderate

Eastgate Hotel. 23 Merton St., Oxford, Oxfordshire, OX1 4BE. ☎ **01865/248244.** Fax 01865/791681. 64 units. TV TEL. £130–£155 ($221–$264) double; from £155 ($264) suite. AE, DC, MC, V. Bus: 7.

The Eastgate stands opposite the ancient Examination Halls, next to Magdalen Bridge, within walking distance of Oxford colleges and the city center. Recently refurbished, it offers modern facilities while retaining in the public rooms, the atmosphere of an English country house. The comfortably furnished rooms have radios as well as hot beverage-making equipment. The Shires Restaurant offers roasts and traditional English fare, complemented by a choice of wines.

Oxford Moat House. Godstow Rd., Wolvercote Roundabout, Oxford, Oxfordshire OX2 8AL. ☎ **01865/489988.** Fax 01865/310259. 155 units. TV TEL. £120–£151 ($204–$257) double. AE, MC, V. Bus: 60.

One of the Queens Moat Houses group, this hostelry, emphasizes spacious, glassed-in areas and streamlined rooms. Patronized mainly by motorists, it's at the northern edge of Oxford 3km (2 miles) from the center, hidden from the traffic at the junction of A-40 and A-34. Each refurbished room features a color TV, pay-for-view movies, trouser press, and hot beverage-making equipment. The 10 no-smoking executive rooms are larger and amenities include a robe, newspaper, toiletries, and breakfast. The Moat House has a swimming pool, squash courts, sauna, solarium, punt and pitch court (nine holes), snooker (billiards) room, and an air-conditioned gym. Its Oxford Blue Restaurant serves an English menu.

Inexpensive
River Hotel. 17 Botley Rd., Oxford OX2 OAA. ☎ **01865/243475.** Fax 01865/724306. 21 units. TV TEL. £67.50–£90 ($115–$153) double. Rates include breakfast. MC, V. Bus: 4C or 52.

Just beyond the railway station west of the center, this hotel charges less than many of its more centrally located competitors. About a quarter of the cozy rooms are across the street, within a comfortable stone-sided annex. There's a bar and a simple restaurant on the premises. The hotel is a short walk away from all sorts of restaurants.

Tilbury Lodge Private Hotel. 5 Tilbury Lane, Eynsham Rd., Botley, Oxford, Oxfordshire OX2 9NB. ☎ **01865/862138.** Fax 01865/863700. 9 units. TV TEL. £62–£70 ($105–$119) double, £75 ($128) double with 4-poster bed. Rates include English breakfast. MC, V. Bus: 4A, 4B, or 100.

This small hotel is on a quiet country lane about 3km (2 miles) west of the center, beyond the railway station. Eddie and Eileen Trafford accommodate guests in their well-furnished and comfortable rooms. The most expensive room has a four-poster bed. There's a Jacuzzi and children are welcome. If you don't arrive by car, Eddie can pick you up at the train station.

WHERE TO DINE
Very Expensive
Le Manoir aux Quat' Saisons. Great Milton, Oxfordshire OX44 7PD. ☎ **01844/278881.** Fax 01844/278847. Reservations required. Main courses £32–£37 ($54–$63); lunch menu du jour £32 ($54); lunch or dinner menu gourmand £72 ($122). AE, DC, MC, V. Daily noon–2:15pm and 7:15–10:15pm. Take Exit 7 off M-40 and head along A-329 toward Wallingford; look for signs for Great American Milton Manor about 2km (1 mi.) later. FRENCH.

Some 19km (12 miles) southeast of Oxford, Le Manoir aux Quat' Saisons offers the finest cuisine in the Midlands. The stone manor house was originally built by a Norman nobleman in the 1300s. The connection with France has been masterfully revived by the Gallic owner and chef, Raymond Blanc. You can enjoy such highly creative specialties as quail eggs, spinach, Parmesan, and black truffle ravioli in a rosemary *jus;* light crab bisque with ginger and lemongrass; or braised boned oxtail filled with shallots and wild mushrooms in a Hermitage red-wine sauce with puree of parsnips. Each dish is an exercise in studied perfection.

The gabled house was built in the 1500s, improved and enlarged in 1908. Inside, there are 32 luxurious rooms, each decorated boudoir style with radio, color TV, phone, and private bathroom; the cost is £230 to £340 ($391 to $578) for a double, £550 ($935) for a suite.

Expensive

Elizabeth. 82 St. Aldate's St. ☎ **01865/242230.** Reservations recommended. Main courses £13.25–£18.75 ($23–$32); lunch £16 ($27) 3 courses. AE, DC, MC, V. Tues–Sat 12:30–2:30pm and 6:30–11pm; Sun 7–10:30pm. Closed Good Friday and Christmas week. Bus: 7. FRENCH/CONTINENTAL.

Despite the portraits of Elizabeth II that hang near the entrance, this restaurant is named after its original owner, a matriarch who founded the place in the 1930s opposite Christ Church College. Today, the well-trained staff serves beautifully presented dishes in the French style. The larger of the two dining rooms displays reproductions of paintings by Goya and Velázquez and exudes a restrained kind of dignity; the smaller room is devoted to *Alice in Wonderland* designs inspired by Lewis Carroll. The dishes that show the kitchen at its best include chicken royale; Scottish steaks; several different fish served in white-wine or lemon-butter sauce; and Basque pipérade.

Moderate

Cherwell Boathouse Restaurant. Bardwell Rd. ☎ **01865/552746.** Reservations recommended. Fixed-price 3-course dinner £20.50 ($35); Sun lunch £19.50 ($33). AE, DC, MC, V. Tues 6–11:30pm, Wed–Sat noon–2pm and 6–11:30pm, Sun noon–2pm. Closed Dec 24–30. Bus: Banbury Rd. FRENCH.

This Oxford landmark on the River Cherwell is owned by Anthony Verdin, who is assisted by a young crew. The cooks change the menu every 2 weeks to take advantage of the availability of fresh vegetables, fish, and meat. There's a very reasonable, even exciting, wine list. In summer, the restaurant also serves on the terrace. The chefs turn out the best roast pheasant in Oxford, and other dishes are delicately handled as well, including a loin of free-range pork in a creamy tarragon and green peppercorn sauce.

Inexpensive

✪ **Entrees and Exits.** 6 Park End St. ☎ **01865/245710.** Reservations recommended. Main courses £4.95–£7.50 ($8–$13). AE, MC, V. Tues–Sun noon–3pm, Wed–Thurs and Sun 5:30–10:30pm, Fri–Sat 5:30–11:30pm. Bus: 52. AUSTRALIAN/INTERNATIONAL.

Near the train station, this restaurant, newly opened in 1999, has been hailed by Oxford students as one of the best food values in town. Allegedly the owner opened it because you couldn't get a decent cappuccino or dessert in Oxford late at night. The kitchen staff does both of those admirably, and a lot more, offering fresh, imaginatively prepared dishes. Begin with Outback nachos or the crumbled Brie with cranberry sauce. You'll also delight in the catch of the day in Aussie beer batter or the Thai green curry with bok choy and mangoes. The fresh pasta of the day is posted on the blackboard. The desserts are among the town's finest, especially the raspberry cheesecake or the almond, ginger, and pear tart. The wines are the finest from New Zealand and Australia.

PUBS WITH PEDIGREE

Bear Inn. Alfred St. ☎ **01865/721783.** Snacks and bar meals £2–£6 ($3.40–$10). DC, MC, V. Daily noon–11pm. Bus: 2A or 2B. ENGLISH.

A short block from The High, overlooking the north side of Christ Church College, this is the village pub, an Oxford tradition since the 13th century. Its swinging inn sign depicts the bear and ragged staff, old insignia of the earls of Warwick, who were among the early patrons. Some former owners developed an astonishing habit: clipping neckties. Around the lounge bar you'll see the remains of thousands of ties, which have been labeled with their owners' names.

Turf Tavern. 4 Bath Place (off Holywell St.). ☎ **01865/243235.** Main dishes £3–£5.50 ($5–$9). MC, V. Mon–Sat 11am–11pm, Sun noon–3pm and 7–10:30pm. Bus: 52. ENGLISH.

This 13th-century tavern lies on a very narrow passageway near the Bodleian Library. Thomas Hardy used the place in *Jude the Obscure.* During his student days at Oxford, Bill Clinton was a frequent visitor. At night, the nearby old tower of New College and part of the old city wall are floodlit, and during warm weather you can sit in any of the three gardens that radiate outward from the pub's central core. For wintertime warmth, braziers are lighted in the courtyard and in the gardens. A separate food counter, set behind a glass case, displays the day's fare.

WALKING AROUND THE COLLEGES

The best way to get a running commentary on the important sightseeing attractions is to go to the Oxford Information Centre. **Two-hour walking tours** through the city and the major colleges leave daily at 11am and 2pm, and cost £4.50 ($8) adults and £2.50 ($4.25) children. The tours don't include New College or Christ Church.

OVERVIEW   For a bird's-eye view of the city and colleges, climb **Carfax Tower** (☎ **01865/792653**), in the city center. This structure is distinguished by the clock and figures that strike the quarter hours. Carfax Tower is all that remains from St. Martin's Church, where William Shakespeare once stood as godfather for William Davenant, who also became a successful playwright. A church stood on this site from 1032 until 1896. The tower used to be higher, but after 1340 it was lowered, following complaints from the university to Edward III that townspeople threw stones and fired arrows at students during town-and-gown disputes. Admission is £1.20 ($2.05) adults, 60p ($1) children. The tower is open April to October daily 10am to 5:30pm; November to March it's open Monday to Saturday 10am to 3:30pm.

CHRIST CHURCH   Begun by Cardinal Wolsey as Cardinal College in 1525, Christ Church (☎ **01865/276492**), known as the House, was founded by Henry VIII in 1546. Facing St. Aldate's Street, Christ Church has the largest quadrangle of any college in Oxford. Tom Tower houses Great Tom, the 18,000-pound bell referred to earlier. It rings at 9:05pm nightly, signaling the closing of the college gates. The 101 times it peals originally signified the number of students in residence at the time of the founding of the college.

The college chapel was constructed over a period of centuries, beginning in the 12th century. The cathedral's most distinguishing features are its Norman pillars and the vaulting of the choir, dating from the 15th century. In the center of the great quadrangle is a statue of Mercury mounted in the center of a fishpond. The college and cathedral can be visited daily 9am to 5:30pm. The entrance fee is £3 ($5) adults and £2 ($3.40) children.

MAGDALEN COLLEGE   Magdalen (pronounced *Maud*-lin) College, High Street (☎ **01865/276000**), was founded in 1458 by William of Waynflete, bishop of Winchester and later chancellor of England. Its alumni range from Wolsey to Wilde. Opposite the botanic garden, the oldest in England, is the bell tower, where the choristers sing in Latin at dawn on May Day. The reflection of the 15th-century tower is cast in the waters of the Cherwell below. On a not-so-happy day, Charles I—with his days numbered—watched the oncoming Roundheads from this tower. Visit the 15th-century chapel, in spite of many of its latter-day trappings. Ask when the hall and other places of special interest are open. The grounds of Magdalen are the most extensive of any Oxford college; there's even a deer park. You can visit Easter to September daily noon to 6pm; off-season, daily 2 to 6pm. Admission is £2.50 ($4.25), but it's charged only from Easter to September.

MERTON COLLEGE   Founded in 1264, Merton College, Merton Street (☎ **01865/276310**), is among the three oldest colleges at the university. It stands near Corpus Christi College on Merton Street, the sole survivor of Oxford's medieval cobbled streets. Its library, built between 1371 and 1379, is said to be the oldest college library in England. There was once a tradition of keeping some of its most valuable books chained. Now only one book is so secured, to illustrate that historical custom. One treasure of the library is an astrolabe (an astronomical instrument used for measuring the altitude of the sun and stars) thought to have belonged to Chaucer. You pay £1 ($1.70) to visit the ancient library, as well as the Max Beerbohm Room (the satirical English caricaturist who died in 1956). The library and college are open Monday to Friday 2 to 4pm and Saturday 10am to 4pm (closed for 1 week at Easter and Christmas).

A favorite pastime is to take **Addison's Walk** through the water meadows. The stroll is so named after a former alumnus, Joseph Addison, the 18th-century essayist and playwright noted for his contributions to *The Spectator* and *The Tatler*.

UNIVERSITY COLLEGE   University College, High Street (☎ **01865/276602**), is the oldest one at Oxford and dates back to 1249, when money was donated by an ecclesiastic, William of Durham (the old claim that the real founder was Alfred the Great is more fanciful). The original structures have all disappeared, and what remains today represents essentially 17th-century architecture, with subsequent additions in Victoria's day, as well as in more recent times. The Goodhart Quadrangle was added as late as 1962. The college's most famous alumnus, Shelley, was "sent down" for his part in collaborating on a pamphlet on atheism. However, all is forgiven today, as the romantic poet is honored by a memorial erected in 1894. The hall and chapel of University College can be visited daily during vacations, with special permission from the bursar office, from 2 to 4pm for £1.50 ($2.55) adults, 60p ($1) children. No paid tours are available. Chapel services are held daily at 4 and 6pm.

NEW COLLEGE   New College, New College Lane, off Queen's Lane (☎ **01865/ 279555**), was founded in 1379 by William of Wykeham, bishop of Winchester and later lord chancellor of England. His college at Winchester supplied a constant stream of students. The first quadrangle, dating from before the end of the 14th century, was the initial quadrangle to be built in Oxford and formed the architectural design for the other colleges. In the antechapel is Sir Jacob Epstein's remarkable modern sculpture of *Lazarus* and a fine El Greco painting of St. James. One of the treasures of the college is a crosier (bishop's staff) belonging to the founding father. In the garden, you can stroll among the remains of the old city wall and the mound. The college (entered at New College Lane) can be visited Easter to September daily 11am to 5pm; off-season, daily 2 to 4pm. Admission is £1.50 ($2.55), after October admission is free.

Punting: A Sport & a Pastime

At **Punt Station,** Cherwell Boathouse, Bardwell Road (☎ **01865/515978**), you can rent a punt (flat-bottom boat maneuvered by a long pole and a small oar) for £8 to £10 ($14 to $17) per hour, plus a £40 to £50 ($68 to $85) deposit. Similar charges are made for punt rentals at Magdalen Bridge Boathouse. Punts are rented from March to mid-June and late August to October, daily 10am to dusk; from mid-June to late August, when a larger inventory of punts is available, it's open daily 10am to 10pm.

Calling on Churchill at Blenheim Palace

Just 13km (8 miles) northwest of Oxford stands the extravagantly baroque ✪ **Blenheim Palace** (☎ **01993/811325**), England's answer to Versailles. Blenheim is the home of the 11th duke of Marlborough, a descendant of John Churchill, the first duke, who was an on-again, off-again favorite of Queen Anne's. In his day (1650–1722), the first duke became the supreme military figure in Europe. Fighting on the Danube near a village named Blenheim, Churchill defeated the forces of Louis XIV, and the lavish palace of Blenheim was built for the duke as a gift from the queen. It was designed by Sir John Vanbrugh; the landscaping was created by the famous 18th-century landscape gardener, Capability Brown. You may recognize Blenheim because it was used as the setting for Kenneth Branagh's *Hamlet*.

The palace is loaded with riches: antiques, porcelain, oil paintings, tapestries, and chinoiserie. North Americans know Blenheim as the birthplace of Sir Winston Churchill. His birth room is included in the palace tour, as is the Churchill exhibition, four rooms of letters, books, photographs, and other relics. Today the former prime minister lies buried in Bladon Churchyard, near the palace.

Blenheim Palace is open mid-March to October daily 10:30am to 5:30pm. Admission is £8.50 ($14) adults, £6.50 ($11) seniors/children 16 to 17, and £4.50 ($8) children 5 to 15; children 4 and under are free. If you're driving, take the A-44 from Oxford; otherwise, the no. 20 Gloucester Green bus (☎ **01865/772250**) leaves Oxford about every 30 minutes during the day for the half-hour trip.

THE SHOPPING SCENE

In its way, **Alice's Shop,** 83 St. Aldate's (☎ **01865/723793**), might have played a more important role in English literature than any other shop in Britain. Set in a 15th-century building that has housed some kind of shop since 1820, it functioned as a general store (brooms, hardware, and so on) during the period that Lewis Carroll, at the time a professor of mathematics at Christ Church College, was composing *Alice in Wonderland*. As such, it is believed to have been the model for important settings in the book. Today, the place is a favorite stop of Lewis Carroll fans, who gobble up commemorative pencils, chess sets, party favors, bookmarks, and in rare cases, original editions of some of Carroll's works.

The **Bodleian Library Shop,** Old School's Quadrangle, Radcliffe Sq., Broad St. (☎ **01865/277216**), specializes in Oxford-derived souvenirs. There're more than 2,000 objects inventoried here, including books describing the history of the university and its various colleges, paperweights made of pewter and crystal, and Oxford banners and coffee mugs. **Castell & Son (The Varsity Shop),** 13 Broad St. (☎ **01865/244000**), is the best outlet for clothing emblazoned with the Oxford logo or heraldic symbol. Objects include both whimsical and dead-on-serious neckties, hats, T-shirts, sweatshirts, pens, bookmarks, beer and coffee mugs, and cuff links. At **The Oxford Collection,** 106 High St. (☎ **01865/247414**), you'll find Oxford souvenirs such as glass beer steins etched with the university's logo and a wool cardigan-like sweater with brass buttons bearing the university crest.

Magna Gallery, 41 High St. (☎ **01865/245805**), is one of the best-respected antiquarian galleries in Oxford, with engravings, maps, and prints made between 1550 and 1896. The shop also stocks general topography, botanical prints, caricatures, and maps of Oxford and Oxfordshire. Few other shops in England glorify trees and wood products as artfully as **Once a Tree,** 99 Gloucester Green (☎ **01865/793558**). A member of a rapidly blossoming chain, it stocks wood-carved objects that range from the functional and utilitarian (kitchen spoons and breadboards) to the whimsical and exotic (carved wooden flowers, chunky jewelry, boxes, bowls, mirror frames, furniture, mantelpieces).

BURFORD: GATEWAY TO THE COTSWOLDS

This unspoiled medieval town, built of Cotswold stone, is 32km (20 miles) west of Oxford. The town is largely famous for its **Norman church** (ca. 1116) and **High Street** lined with coaching inns. Oliver Cromwell passed this way, as (in a happier day) did Charles II and his mistress, Nell Gwynn. Burford was one of the last of the great wool centers. You'll likely want to photograph the bridge across the Windrush River where Queen Elizabeth I once stood. Burford today is definitely equipped for tourists, as the antique shops along the High will testify.

ESSENTIALS

GETTING THERE   By Train   The nearest station is at Oxford, so take a train from London (a 1¼-hour trip), and at Oxford, walk a very short distance to the entrance of the Taylor Institute, from which about three or four buses per day make the 30-minute run to Burford. Round-trip tickets cost £7.50 ($13). Call **Thames Transit** at **01865/772250** for details.

By Bus   A National Express coach runs from London's Victoria Coach Station to Burford several times a day; the trip, with many stops, takes 2 hours. For more information, call ☎ **08705/808080.**

By Car   From Oxford, take the A-40 west for 32km (20 miles).

VISITOR INFORMATION   The **Tourist Information Centre,** The Brewery, Sheep Street (☎ **01993/823558**), is open Monday to Saturday 10am to 5:30pm and Sunday 1 to 5pm.

WHERE TO STAY & DINE

Bay Tree Hotel. 12–14 Sheep St., Burford, Oxfordshire OX18 6LW. ☎ **01993/822791.** Fax 01993/823008. 30 units. TV TEL. £135 ($229.50) double; from £175–£210 ($298–$357) suite. Rates include English breakfast. AE, DC, MC, V.

The house was built for Sir Lawrence Tanfield, the unpopular lord chief baron of the Exchequer to Elizabeth I. He was definitely not noted for his hospitality. But time has erased his unfortunate memory, and the splendor of this Cotswold manor house remains, even more so after a major overhaul. The house has tastefully decorated oak-paneled rooms with stone fireplaces. Twentieth-century comforts have been discreetly installed throughout the house. Try to get a room overlooking the terraced gardens at the rear of the house. The oak-beamed restaurant, which overlooks the gardens, retains all of its original charm. The chef is well known for his tempting menus, with dishes based on local and seasonal produce.

Golden Pheasant Hotel. 91 High St., Burford, Oxfordshire OX18 4QA. ☎ **01993/823223.** Fax 01993/822621. 12 units. TV TEL. £75–£103 ($128–$175) double. Rates include English breakfast. AE, MC, V.

On the main street, the Golden Pheasant has the oldest set of property deeds surviving in Burford. It's the second best place to stay in town. In the 1400s, it was the home of a prosperous wool merchant, but it began serving food and drink in the 1730s. The rooms are comfortable and cozy; three have four-poster beds. Within view of dozens

A Side Trip to Bibury

Most visitors in a rush head north from Burford to Stow-on-the-Wold and Broadway (see below). But if you have the time you can dip south and in less than an hour you'll be in Bibury. From Burford, go southwest along the A-433 to reach one of the loveliest spots in the Cotswolds.

The utopian romancer of Victoria's day, the poet William Morris, called it England's most beautiful village. On the banks of the tiny Coln River, Bibury is noted for **Arlington Row,** a group of 15th-century gabled cottages, its most-photographed attraction. You can admire the cottages from the outside; however, you're not supposed to peer into the windows, as they're still private homes.

The main thing to do here is enjoy the village scene. Attractions in the area include the **Cotswold Heritage Center** (☎ **01451/860715**), in a former mill, with an impressive collection of old carts and industrial machines. Rooms show how locals lived and worked in the 19th century. Admission is £2.50 ($4.25) adults, £2 ($3.40) senior citizens, and 80p ($1.35) children. Open mid-March to mid-November, Monday to Saturday 10am to 4pm, Sunday 1 to 4pm; off-season Saturday and Sunday 10am to dusk.

If you'd like to stay in Bibury, the finest hotel and restaurant in the village is **The Swan,** Bibury, Gloucestershire GL7 5NW (☎ **01285/740695;** fax 01285/740473). The owners outfitted parts of the interior in a cozily overstuffed mode, and the charming and tasteful rooms have antique furniture along with TV and telephones. On the premises is an informal brasserie, with outdoor seating in the courtyard. A more formal restaurant, with crystal chandeliers and heavy damask curtains, specializes in modern British food. Three-course meals start at £28 ($48) and 2 courses, £21.50 ($37). Rates are £165 to £235 ($281 to $400) for a double and include English breakfast. American Express, Master-Card, and Visa are accepted.

of old beams and a blazing fireplace, a candlelit restaurant serves both French and English specialties; the new bar serves food and merits a visit.

BOURTON-ON-THE-WATER

Its fans define it as the quintessential Cotswold village, with a history going back to the Celts. Residents fiercely protect the heritage of 15th- and 16th-century architecture, even though their town is singled out for practically every bus tour that rolls through the Cotswolds. Populated in Anglo-Saxon times, Bourton-on-the-Water developed into a strategic outpost along the ancient Roman road, Fosse Way, that traversed Britain from the North Sea to the St. George's Channel. During the Middle Ages, its prosperity came from wool, which was shipped all over Europe. During the Industrial Revolution when the greatest profits lay in finished textiles, it became a backwater as a producer of raw wool—albeit with the happy result for us that it was never "modernized," and its traditional appearance was preserved.

ESSENTIALS

GETTING THERE   By Train   Trains make the 2-hour trip from Paddington Station in London to nearby Moreton-in-Marsh; call **0345/484950** for schedules. From Moreton-in-Marsh, Pulhams Bus Company (☎ **08705/808080**) runs buses for the 15-minute journey to Bourton-on-the-Water. Trains also run from London to

Cheltenham or Kingham; while somewhat more distant than Moreton-in-Marsh, both towns also have bus connections into Bourton-on-the-Water.

By Bus   National Express coaches, from Victoria Coach Station in London, travel to both Cheltenham and Stow-in-the-Wold. From either of those towns, Pulhams Bus Company (see above) operates about four buses per day into Bourton-on-the-Water.

WHERE TO STAY & DINE

Old Manse Hotel. Victoria St., Bourton-on-the-Water, Cheltenham, Gloucestershire GL54 2BX. ☎ **01451/820082.** Fax 01451/810381. 15 units. TV TEL. Sun–Thurs £65–£85 ($111–$145) double. Fri–Sat £72–£96 ($122–$163) double; £120 ($204) suite. Rates include English breakfast. AE, MC, V.

An architectural gem reminiscent of the setting of Nathaniel Hawthorne's *Mosses from an Old Manse,* this hotel sits by the slow-moving river that wanders through the village green. The rooms have recently been refurbished to a high standard. Dining is a treat in the Le Jardin du Vin, which serves dinner daily 7 to 9:15pm. Typical dishes include blackened chicken, raspberry duck, rack of lamb, salmon, monkfish, and tiger prawns. Sometimes roast pheasant is featured.

Old New Inn. High St., Bourton-on-the-Water, Cheltenham, Gloucestershire GL54 2AF. ☎ **01451/820467.** Fax 01451/810236. 11 units (10 with bathroom). TV. £76 ($129) double with bathroom. Rates include English breakfast. MC, V.

Old New Inn puts aside the contradiction inherent in its moniker. On the main street, overlooking the river, it's a good example of Queen Anne design (the miniature model

---

Back Roads to Bourton-on-the-Water

If you have a car, the best way to get a feel for the scenic beauty of the Cotswolds is to ditch the main routes in favor of the back roads. From Oxford, follow A-40 northwest to Buford, gateway to the Cotswolds, and then follow the signs to Great Barrington, about 6.4km (4 miles) away, by turning left onto an unclassified road just north of the bridge over the Windrush River. After passing through Great Barrington's double row of Cotswold cottages, continue west toward Windrush. From here, take an unnumbered road northwest to Sherborne, and, once here, go another 9.6km (6 miles) north to Bourton-on-the-Water.

---

village in its garden is referred to below). Hungry or tired travelers are drawn to the old-fashioned comforts and cuisine of this most English inn. The comfortable rooms have homelike furnishings and soft beds. Nonresidents are also welcome here for meals, with lunches priced at £10 to £15 ($17 to $26), dinner costing from £15 ($26), and Sunday brunch (three courses) costing £11.95 ($20). You may want to spend an evening in the redecorated pub lounge either playing darts or chatting with the villagers.

EXPLORING THE TOWN

A handful of minor museums can be visited within the town, each of which grew up from idiosyncratic collections amassed over the years by local residents. They include the **Cotswold Motor Museum** (☎ 01451/821255), open daily 11am to 5pm. Admission is £1.50 ($2.55) adults and £1.20 ($2.05) children. The **Bourton Model Railway Exhibition and Toy Shop** (☎ 01451/820686), open daily 10am to 6pm. Admission is £2 ($3.40) adults and £1 ($1.70) children, and **Birdland** (described below). But these museums don't compare with the evocative history of Bourton-on-the-Water itself.

The **Model Village at the Old New Inn,** High St. (☎ 01451/820467), was constructed by a local hotelier during the Great Depression. His scale model (1:9) is big enough to allow viewers to walk through a re-creation of the town. If you opt to visit, you won't be alone: the Queen has marveled at the site's workmanship and detailing, and Ford Motor Company used it as the centerpiece of an ad campaign for its compact Fiesta. Admission is £2 ($3.40) adults, £1.80 ($3.05) senior citizens, and £1.50 ($2.55) children. It's open daily 9am to 6pm or until dusk in summer; daily 10am to 4pm in winter.

About 2km (1 mile) east of Bourton-on-the-Water, on the banks of Windrush River, is **Birdland,** Rissington Road. (☎ 01451/820480). Established in 1958 on 3.5ha (8^1/$_2$ acres) of field and forests, this handsomely designed homage to ornithological splendors houses about 1,200 birds representing 361 species. Included is the largest and most varied collection of penguins in any zoo, with glass-walled tanks that allow observers to appreciate their agile underwater movements. Birdland provides a picnic area and a children's playground in a wooded copse. Admission is £6 ($10) adults, £3 ($5) senior citizens, and £2.50 ($4.25) children ages 4 to 14. Birdland is open April to October, daily 10am to 6pm; November to March, daily 10am to 4pm.

STOW-ON-THE-WOLD

This Cotswold market town remains unspoiled, despite the busloads of tourists who stop off en route to Broadway and Chipping Campden. Stow-on-the-Wold lies 14km (9 miles) southeast of Broadway, 16km (10 miles) south of Chipping Campden, 6.5km (4 miles) south of Moreton-in-Marsh, and 34km (21 miles) south of

Stratford-upon-Avon. The town is the loftiest in the Cotswolds, built on a wold or rolling hill about 240m (800 feet) above sea level. In its open market square, you can still see the stocks where offenders in the past were jeered at and punished by the townspeople, who threw rotten eggs at them. The final battle between the Roundheads and the Royalists took place in Stow-on-the-Wold. This is a good base for exploring the Cotswold wool towns, as well as Stratford-upon-Avon.

ESSENTIALS

GETTING THERE   By Train   From London, take a train to Moreton-in-Marsh (see below) from London's Paddington Station, a service that runs several times a day. From Moreton-in-Marsh, continue by a Pulhams bus for the 10-minute ride to Stow-on-the-Wold.

By Bus   National Express (☎ **08705/808080**) coaches also run daily from London's Victoria Coach Station to Moreton-in-Marsh, where a Pulhams Bus Company coach goes the rest of the way to Stow-on-the-Wold. Several Pulhams coaches also run daily to Stow-on-the-Wold from Cheltenham.

VISITOR INFORMATION   The **Tourist Information Centre,** at Hollis House, The Square (☎ **01451/831082**), is open April to October, Monday to Saturday 9:30am to 5:30pm and Sunday 10:30am to 4pm; November to March, Monday to Saturday 9:30am to 4:30pm.

WHERE TO STAY & DINE

Fosse Manor Hotel. Fosse Way, Stow-on-the-Wold, Cheltenham, Gloucestershire GL54 1JX. ☎ **01451/830354.** Fax 01451/832486. 22 units. TV TEL. £118 ($201) double; £160 ($272) suite. Rates include English breakfast. "Bargain Breaks" (2-night minimum required): £65–£78 ($111–$133) per person, including half board. AE, CB, DC, MC, V. Take A-429 2km (1¼ miles) south of Stow-on-the-Wold.

Although lacking the charm of the Grapevine (see below), Fosse Manor is at least "second best" in town. Its stone walls and neo-Gothic gables almost concealed by strands of ivy, the hotel lies near the site of an ancient Roman road. From some of the high stone-sided windows, you can enjoy a view of a landscaped garden with a sunken lily pond, flagstone walks, and an old-fashioned sundial. The bedrooms are homelike. There's a padded and upholstered bar and a dining room where dinners cost £25 ($43).

Grapevine Hotel. Sheep St., Stow-on-the-Wold, Cheltenham, Gloucestershire GL54 1AU. ☎ **800/528-1234** in the U.S. and Canada, or 01451/830344. Fax 01451/832278. www.vines.co.uk. 22 units. TV TEL. £105–£125 ($179–$213) double. Rates include breakfast. "Bargain Breaks" (2-night minimum): £72–£92 ($122–$156) per person, including half board. AE, DC, MC, V.

The Grapevine, facing the village green, mixes urban sophistication with reasonable prices, rural charm, and intimacy. Although it's the best inn within the town, it doesn't have the charm and grace of Wyck Hill House. The Grapevine was named after the ancient vine that shades the beautiful conservatory restaurant. Each room has tasteful furnishings, radio, hair dryer, and a tea and coffeemaker. Six rooms offer a minibar. Full meals feature English, French, and Italian cuisine.

✪ **Wyck Hill House.** Burford Rd., Stow-on-the-Wold, Cheltenham, Gloucestershire GL54 1HY. ☎ **01451/831936.** Fax 01451/832243. 32 units. TV TEL. £195–£245 ($332–$417) double; £220 ($374) suite. Rates include English breakfast. AE, DC, MC, V. Drive 4km (2½ miles) south of Stow-on-the-Wold on A-424.

Parts of this otherwise Victorian country house, which sits on 40ha (100 acres) of grounds and gardens, date from 1720. Now the area's showcase country inn, Wyck

A Cotswold Ramble: Walking Between the Slaughters

Midway between Bourton-on-the-Water and Stow-on-the-Wold are the twin villages of Upper and Lower Slaughter, two of the prettiest villages in the Cotswolds. (The name "Slaughter" is a corruption of *de Scoltre,* the name of the original Norman landowner.) The houses are constructed of honey-colored Cotswold stone, and a stream meanders right through, providing a home for the ducks that wander freely about, begging scraps from kindly visitors.

Of course, you can drive to these delightful villages, lying on back roads, but it's more fun to walk. The walk between the two, with an optional extension to Bourton-on-the-Water, is 1.5km (1 mile) each way between the Slaughters, or 4km (2¹/₂ miles) from Upper Slaughter to Bourton-on-the-Water. Your walk could take between 2 and 4 hours. A well-worn footpath, Warden's Way, meanders beside the edge of the swift-moving River Eye. Originating in Upper Slaughter (where its start is marked at the central parking lot), the path beckons all kinds of nature enthusiasts. En route, you will pass sheep grazing in meadows, antique stone houses, stately trees arching over ancient millponds, and footbridges that have endured centuries of traffic and rain.

Don't think for a moment that the rivers of this region (including the Eye, Colne, Diklar, and Windrush) are sluggish, slow-moving streams: Between Upper and Lower Slaughter, the water literally rushes down the incline, powering a historic mill that you'll find on the northwestern edge of Lower Slaughter. In quiet eddies, you'll see ample numbers of waterfowl and birds, including wild ducks, gray wagtails, mute swans, coots, and Canadian geese. You could follow this route in reverse, although since parking is more plentiful in Upper Slaughter than in Lower Slaughter, it's more convenient to begin in the former town.

Most visitors prefer to end their outdoor ramble here, retracing their steps upstream to the car park at Upper Slaughter. But you could continue your walk for another 2.5km (1¹/₂ miles) to Bourton-on-the-Water. To extend your trip, follow Warden's Way across the A-429 highway, which is identified by locals as Fosse Way. Your path will leave the river's edge and strike out across cattle pastures in a southerly direction. Most of the distance from Lower Slaughter to Bourton-on-the-Water is paved; it's closed to motor traffic, but ideal for trekkers or cyclists. Watch for bird life, and remember that you're legally required to close each of the several gates that stretch across the footpath.

Warden's Way will introduce you to Bourton-on-the-Water through the hamlet's northern edges. The first landmark you'll see will be the tower of St. Lawrence's Anglican Church. From the base of the church, walk south along The Avenue (one of the hamlet's main streets) and end your Cotswold ramble on the Village Green, directly in front of the War Memorial.

Hill House offers well-furnished rooms in the main hotel, the coach-house annex, or the orangery. Excellent food is served, with a two-course lunch costing £13.95 ($24) and a three-course lunch going for £19.95 ($34). Dinners are à la carte, averaging £32.50 to £48 ($55 to $82) per meal.

ANTIQUES HEAVEN

Don't be fooled by the hamlet's sleepy, bucolic setting: Stow-on-the-Wold has developed over the past two decades into the antique buyer's centerpiece of Britain, and as such has at least 60 merchandisers scattered throughout the village and its environs.

Some visitors thrill to the chance to rummage at random through the town's various venues, dusty and otherwise. Here's a selection of the town's most interesting and unusual emporiums.

In four showrooms inside an 18th-century building on the town's main square, **Anthony Preston Antiques, Ltd.,** The Square (☎ **01451/831586**), specializes in English and French furniture, including some very large pieces such as bookcases, and decorative objects that include paperweights, lamps, paintings on silk, and more.

Baggott Church Street, Ltd., Church Street (☎ **01451/830370**), is the smaller, and perhaps more intricately decorated, of two shops founded and maintained by a well-regarded local antiques merchant, Duncan ("Jack") Baggott. The shop contains four showrooms loaded with furniture and paintings from the 17th to the 19th century. More eclectic and wide-ranging in its inventory is **Woolcomber House,** Sheep Street (☎ **01451/830662**), the second of Baggott's two shops. This contains about 17 rooms that today are decorated according to a particular era of English history.

Covering about half a block of terrain in the town center, **Huntington's Antiques, Ltd.,** Church Street (☎ **01451/830842**), contains one of the largest stocks of quality antiques dating from the Middle Ages through the 17th century, and for informal (country "vernacular") pieces, includes the Middle Ages to the end of the 18th century. Wander at will through 10 ground-floor rooms, then climb to the second floor, where a long gallery and a quartet of additional showrooms bulge with refectory tables, unusual cupboards, and much more.

MORETON-IN-MARSH

Moreton-in-Marsh, near many villages of interest, is an important center for rail passengers headed for the Cotswolds. The town is 6.5km (4 miles) north of Stow-on-the-Wold, 11km (7 miles) south of Chipping Campden, and 27km (17 miles) south of Stratford-upon-Avon. Don't take the name "Moreton-in-Marsh" too literally; "marsh" derives from an old word meaning "border," so you won't be wading through wetlands on your visit.

The town, which once lay on the ancient Fosse Way, is itself the central attraction, rather than specific sights or museums. Look for the 17th-century market hall and the old curfew tower, and then walk down the shop-flanked High Street, where Roman legions trudged centuries ago. Look for the Market Hall on High Street, a Victorian Tudor structure from 1887. The Curfew Tower on Oxford Street dates from the 1600s. However, far more alluring are the antique shops along the wide Fosse Way. Moreton-in-Marsh doesn't rival Stow-on-the-Wold in shopping, but everybody seems to be a shopkeeper here.

ESSENTIALS

GETTING THERE   By Train   You can take a train from London's Paddington Station, arriving in about 2 hours. For schedules and information, call ☎ **0345/484950.**

By Bus   National Express coaches run from London's Victoria Coach Station to Moreton-in-Marsh daily. Call ☎ **08705/808080** for details.

VISITOR INFORMATION   The nearest tourist office is at Stow-on-the-Wold (see above).

WHERE TO STAY

Manor House Hotel. High St., Moreton-in-Marsh, Gloucestershire GL56 0LJ. ☎ **800/876-9480** in the U.S., or 01608/650501. Fax 01608/651481. 40 units. TV TEL. £90–£135 ($153–$230) double; £135 ($230) suite. Rates include English breakfast. AE, DC, MC, V.

The town's best address, the Manor House comes complete with a host of idiosyncratic amenities: its own ghost, a priest's hiding hole, a secret passage, and a moot room used centuries ago by local merchants to settle arguments over wool exchanges. The rooms are tastefully furnished, many with fine old desks set in front of windows with a view of the garden and ornamental pond. The hotel has a heated indoor pool, a spa bath, and a sauna.

White Hart Royal Hotel. High St., Moreton-in-Marsh, Gloucestershire GL56 0BA. ☎ **01608/650731.** Fax 01608/650880. 19 units. TV TEL. £68–£96 ($116–$163) double. Rates include English breakfast. MC, V.

A mellow old Cotswold inn once graced by Charles I (in 1644), the White Hart provides modern amenities without compromising the personality of yesteryear. It long ago ceased to be the premier inn of town, but it's still a good, comfortable place to spend the night. The well-furnished rooms have a few antiques intermixed with basic 20th-century pieces.

WHERE TO DINE

Marsh Goose. High St. ☎ **01608/652111.** Reservations recommended. Lunch main courses £11–£15 ($19–$26); 4-course fixed-price dinner £29.50 ($50). AE, DC, MC, V. Tues–Sun 12:30–2:30pm; Tues–Sat 7:30–9:45pm. MODERN BRITISH.

In a highly competitive area of England, the food here, a creative seasonal cuisine that showcases the talents of chef Matthew Laughton, ranks at the top. Despite its unique allure and country-house elegance, this is very much an outpost of young and sophisticated Londoners. The unusual cuisine is modern British, with good doses of Caribbean style thrown in. Examples include panfried salmon served with artichoke hearts, lime dressing, and strips of smoked goose breast; grilled veal and pigeon served with fresh jam; and grilled goat cheese in a warm basil vinaigrette. A favorite dessert is the hot dark chocolate soufflé with white chocolate sauce.

CHIPPING CAMPDEN

Regardless of how often they visit the Cotswolds, the English are attracted in great numbers to this town, once an important wool center. Off the main road, it's easily accessible to major points of interest, and double-decker buses frequently run through here on their way to Oxford or Stratford-upon-Avon. It lies 58km (36 miles) northwest of Oxford, 19km (12 miles) south of Stratford-upon-Avon, and 150km (93 miles) northwest of London.

On the northern edge of the Cotswolds above the Vale of Evesham, Campden, a Saxon settlement, was recorded in the *Domesday Book.* In medieval times, rich merchants built homes of Cotswold stone along its model High Street—described by the historian G. M. Trevelyan as "the most beautiful village street now left in the island." Today, the houses have been so well preserved that Chipping Campden remains a gem of the Middle Ages. Its church dates from the 15th century, and its old market hall is the loveliest in the Cotswolds. Look also for its almshouses, which, along with the market hall, were built by a great wool merchant, Sir Baptist Hicks, whose tomb is in the church.

The Bard Alfresco

In summer, you'll likely find Shakespeare performed free outdoors (donations welcome though) in towns like Moreton-in-Marsh and Chipping Campden—there's nothing as memorable as watching *A Midsummer's Night Dream* on a balmy July evening in the middle of the Cotswolds.

ESSENTIALS

GETTING THERE   By Train   Trains depart from London's Paddington Station for Moreton-in-Marsh (trip time: about 2 hours). Call ☎ **0345/484950** for schedules. At Moreton-in-Marsh, a bus operated by Castleway's travels the 11km (7 miles) to Chipping Campden five times a day. Many visitors opt for a taxi at Moreton-in-Marsh.

By Bus   The largest and most important nearby bus depot is Cheltenham, which receives service several times a day from London's Victoria Coach Station. From Cheltenham, however, bus service (by Barry's Coaches) is infrequent and uncertain, departing at the most only three times per week.

VISITOR INFORMATION   The summer-only **Tourist Information Centre** is at Noel Court, High Street (☎ **01386/841206**), open daily 10am to 5:30pm.

WHERE TO STAY & DINE

✪ **Cotswold House Hotel.** The Square, Chipping Campden, Gloucestershire GL55 6AN. ☎ **01386/840330.** Fax 01386/840310. www.cotswold-house.demon.co.uk. E-mail: reception@cotswold-house.demon.co.uk. 15 units. TV TEL. £140–£200 ($238–$340) double; £190 ($323) 4-poster room. Rates include English breakfast. AE, MC, V.

A stately, formal Regency house dating from 1800, right in the heart of the village opposite the old wool market, Cotswold House sits amid a tended, walled garden with shaded seating. It's the best place to stay in town. Note the fine winding Regency staircase in the reception hall. The rooms are furnished with themes ranging from Gothic to French to military, with many others included along the way. You can dine in the restaurant, which serves first-class English and French food in a formal, elegant dining room, or in Forbes Brasserie.

Noel Arms Hotel. High St., Chipping Campden, Gloucestershire GL55 6AT. ☎ **800/528-1234** in the U.S. and Canada, or 01386/840317. Fax 01386/841136. 26 units. TV TEL. £105 ($179) double; half board £140 ($238) per person. Children up to 10 stay free in parents' room. Rates include English breakfast. AE, DC, MC, V.

This old coaching inn has been famous since the 14th century, although it long ago lost its supremacy to the Cotswold House. In 1651, Charles II rested here after his defeat at the Battle of Worcester. Tradition is kept alive in the decor, with fine antiques, muskets, swords, and shields. There's a private sitting room for residents, but you may prefer the lounge with its 12-foot-wide fireplace. Twelve rooms date from the 14th century; others, comfortably furnished and well appointed, are in a more sterile modern wing built of Cotswold stone. The oak-paneled Gainsborough Restaurant offers an extensive menu, with an international wine list. Typical English dishes such as venison and mushroom pie or roast prime sirloin of beef with Yorkshire pudding are featured.

BROADWAY

The most overrun and tourist-trodden town of the Cotswolds is also one of the most beautiful. Hence, its enduring popularity. Many of the Cotswolds' prime attractions, as well as Shakespeare country, lie within easy reach of Broadway, which is near Evesham at the southern tip of Hereford and Worcester. Broadway lies 24km (15 miles) southwest of Stratford-upon-Avon, 8km (5 miles) west of Chipping Campden, and 150km (93 miles) northwest of London.

The best-known of the Cotswold villages, Broadway has a wide and beautiful High Street flanked with honey-colored stone buildings, remarkable for their harmonious style and design. Overlooking the Vale of Evesham, it's a major stop for bus tours and is mobbed in summer. However, it still manages to retain its charm in spite of the tourist invasion.

ESSENTIALS

GETTING THERE   By Train   Connections are possible from London's Paddington Station via Oxford. The nearest railway stations are 11km (7 miles) away at Moreton-in-Marsh or 8km (5 miles) away at Evesham. Call ☎ **0345/484950** for schedules. Frequent buses arrive from Evesham, but you'll have to take a taxi from Moreton.

By Bus   From London's Victoria Coach Station, one coach daily runs to Broadway, taking 2½ hours. Call ☎ **08705/808080** for details.

By Car   From Chipping Campden take the B-4081 southwest to the junction with A-44, at which point you cut northwest to Broadway. The town is entered via B-4632.

VISITOR INFORMATION   The **Tourist Information Centre,** 1 Cotswold Court (☎ **01386/852937**), is open March to December, Monday to Saturday 10am to 1pm and 2 to 5pm.

WHERE TO STAY

Broadway Hotel. The Green, Broadway, Hereford and Worcestershire WR12 7AA. ☎ **01386/852401.** Fax 01386/853879. www.cotswold-inns-hotel.co.uk. E-mail: bookings@ cotswold-inns-hotel.co.uk. 20 units. TV TEL. £110–£125 (187–$213) double. Rates include English breakfast. AE, DC, MC, V.

Right on the village green, one of the most colorful places in Broadway is this converted 15th-century house, formerly used by the abbots of Pershore, combining the half-timbered look of the Vale of Evesham with the stone of the Cotswolds. While keeping its old-world charm, the hotel has been modernized and converted to provide comforts. All the pleasantly furnished rooms have hot-beverage facilities and central heating. One room has a four-poster bed. The cooking is fine, the service personal, and the dining room attractive.

Dormy House. Willersey Hill, Broadway, Worcestershire WR12 7LF. ☎ **01386/852711.** Fax 01386/858636. E-mail: reservations@dormyhouse.co.uk. 48 units. TV TEL. £146 ($248) double; £174 ($296) 4-poster room; from £186 ($316) suite. Rates include English breakfast. AE, DC, MC, V. Closed Dec 24–29. Free parking. Take A-44 3km (2 miles) southeast of Broadway.

This manor house high on a hill above the village boasts panoramic views in all directions. Its position has made it a favorite place for a meal, afternoon tea, or lodgings. The owners transformed it from a sheep farm, furnishing the 17th-century house with a few antiques, good soft beds, and full central heating. They also extended these amenities to an old adjoining timbered barn, which they converted into studio rooms, with open-beamed ceilings. The establishment serves an excellent cuisine, and the cellar houses a superb selection of wines.

✪ Lygon Arms. High St., Broadway, Worcestershire WR12 7DU. ☎ **01386/852255.** Fax 01386/858611. www.savoy-group.co.uk. E-mail: info@the-lygon-arms.co.uk. 65 units. TV TEL. £178–£198 ($303–$337) double; £255 ($434) 4-poster room; from £285 ($485) suite. VAT extra. Rates include continental breakfast. AE, DC, MC, V. Free parking.

This many-gabled structure basks in its reputation as one of the greatest Old English inns. In the rear the inn opens onto a private garden, with 1.2ha (3 acres) of lawns, trees, and borders of flowers, stone walls with roses, and nooks for tea or sherry. Each room is furnished with a radio, hair dryer, and trouser press. You may dine in the oak-paneled Great Hall, with a Tudor fireplace, a vaulted ceiling, and a minstrels' gallery.

WHERE TO DINE

Tapestry Restaurant. In Dormy House, off the A-44, Willersey Hill, Broadway. ☎ **01386/852711.** Reservations recommended. Lunch main courses (Mon–Sat) £9–£11

($15–$19), set-price Sun lunch £20 ($34); dinner main courses £16–£24 ($27–$41). Table d'hôte menus (dinner only) £30.50–£38 ($52–$65). AE, DC, MC, V. Sun–Fri noon–2pm; Mon–Sat 7–9:30pm; Sun 7–9pm. MODERN BRITISH.

On the highway leading to Moreton-in-Marsh and Oxford, 3km (2 miles) from the center of Broadway, is this charming and well-managed restaurant. The setting is as pastoral as a painting by Constable. You'll dine in a room ringed with Cotswold stone or in an adjacent glass-sided (and no-smoking) conservatory. Chef Alan Cutler creates imaginative dishes and presents them with a stylish flair. For an appetizer, you might choose the seared escallop of Scottish smoked salmon on caper and horseradish butter sauce. Main courses include pheasant, grouse, and partridge with a bread sauce parfait and rich game sauce; and saffron-laced tagliatelle with deep-fried vegetables in tempura batter and Provençale sauce. The cellar houses a superb collection of wines.

STRATFORD-UPON-AVON

Stratford is virtually overrun by visitors in the summer months; the crowds dwindle in winter, allowing you at least to walk on the streets and seek out the places of genuine historic interest. Stratford is 146km (91 miles) northwest of London and 64km (40 miles) northwest of Oxford.

William Shakespeare, of course, was born here. Little is known about his early life, and many of the stories connected with Shakespeare's days in Stratford are largely fanciful, invented to amuse the vast number of literary fans who make the pilgrimage. David Garrick, the actor, really launched the shrine in 1769 when he organized the first of the Bard's commemorative birthday celebrations.

Tourist magnets include the Royal Shakespeare Theatre, where the Royal Shakespeare Company performs for 11 months each year. Visitors often rush back to London after a performance. Despite the crowds, Stratford's literary pilgrimage sights merit your interest. The town today aggressively hustles the Shakespeare connection, a bit suffocatingly so; everybody seems in business to make a buck off the Bard.

ESSENTIALS

GETTING THERE By Train Amazingly, considering the demand, there're no direct trains from London to Stratford-upon-Avon. However, from London's Paddington Station you can take the train to Leamington Spa, then change trains for Stratford-upon-Avon. The journey takes about 3 hours and costs £22 ($37) round-trip. For schedules and information, call ☎ **0345/484950.**

By Bus Eight **National Express** (☎ **08705/808080**) coaches a day leave from Victoria Station (trip time: 3¹/₄ hours). A single-day round-trip ticket costs £14.50 ($25) except Friday when the price is £17.50 ($30).

By Car From Broadway, continue northeast along A-46 directly into Stratford-upon-Avon to call on the Bard.

VISITOR INFORMATION The **Tourist Information Centre,** Bridgefoot (☎ **01789/293127**), will provide any details you might wish about the Shakespeare houses, theater, and other attractions, and will assist you in booking rooms. It's open March to October Monday to Saturday 9am to 6pm, and Sunday 11am to 5pm. In the off-season, hours are Monday to Saturday 9am to 5pm.

WHERE TO STAY

Very Expensive

✪ **Welcombe Hotel.** Warwick Rd., Stratford-upon-Avon, Warwickshire CV37 ONR. ☎ **01789/295252.** Fax 01789/414666. 65 units. TV TEL. £175 ($298) double; £250 ($425) suite. Rates include English breakfast. AE, DC, MC, V. Take A-439 2.5km (1¹/₂ miles) northeast of the town center.

For a formal, historic hotel, there's none better in Stratford. One of England's great Jacobean country houses, this hotel is a 10-minute ride from the heart of Stratford. The home once belonged to Sir Archibald Flower, the philanthropic brewer who helped create the Shakespeare Memorial Theatre. Converted into a hotel, it is surrounded by 64ha (157 acres) of grounds. Its keynote feature is an 18-hole golf course. The public rooms are heroic in size, with high windows providing views of the park. Rooms—some big enough for tennis matches—are luxuriously furnished; those in the garden wing, although comfortable, are small.

Expensive

Alveston Manor Hotel. Clopton Bridge, Stratford-upon-Avon, Warwickshire CV37 7HP. ☎ **800/225-5843** in the U.S. and Canada, or 08704/008181. Fax 01789/414095. 114 units. TV TEL. £125 ($213) double; from £240 ($408) suite. AE, DC, MC, V.

This black-and-white timbered manor is perfect for theatergoers. It's just a 2-minute walk from the Avon off B-4066. Whereas the Welcombe is on the outskirts and has cornered the deluxe trade, the Alveston—along with the Shakespeare (see below)—are tied for the most atmospheric choices within the town itself. The hotel has everything from an Elizabethan gazebo to Queen Anne windows. Mentioned in the *Domesday Book*, the building predates the arrival of William the Conqueror. The rooms in the manor house will appeal to those who appreciate old slanted floors, overhead beams, and antique furnishings. Some triples or quads are available in the modern section, which is connected by a covered walk through the rear garden. The rooms here have built-in pieces; 20 are set aside for nonsmokers.

Moderate

Arden Thistle Hotel. 44 Waterside, Stratford-upon-Avon, Warwickshire CV37 6BA. ☎ **01789/294949.** Fax 01789/415874. E-mail: stradford.uponavon@thistle.co.uk. 63 units. TV TEL. £135 ($230) double. AE, DC, MC, V.

Across the street from the main entrance of the Royal Shakespeare Theatre, the hotel was completely refurbished in 1993. Theatergoers flock here. Its redbrick main section dates from the Regency period. Today, the interior has a lounge and bar, a dining room (Bards), a covered garden terrace, and comfortable but narrow rooms with trouser presses, hair dryers, and hot-beverage facilities.

Falcon. Chapel St., Stratford-upon-Avon, Warwickshire CV37 6HA. ☎ **01789/279953.** Fax 01789/414260. 84 units. TV TEL. £105 ($179) double; from £130 ($221) suite. AE, DC, MC, V.

The Falcon blends the very old and the very new. At the rear of a half-timbered inn, licensed 25 years after Shakespeare's death, is a modern extension, joined by a glass-covered passageway. In the heart of Stratford, the inn faces the Guild Chapel and the New Place Gardens. The recently upgraded bedrooms in the mellowed part have oak beams and diamond-shaped windows. Each room includes a radio, electric trouser press, and hot-beverage facilities, but not enough soundproofing to prevent you from hearing the BBC show your neighbor is watching.

Shakespeare. Chapel St., Stratford-upon-Avon, Warwickshire CV37 6ER. ☎ **800/225-5843** in the U.S. and Canada, or 01789/294771. Fax 01789/415411. 74 units. TV TEL. £150 ($255) double; $180 ($306) suite. Children up to 12 stay free in parents' room. AE, DC, MC, V.

This hotel snatched up the premium name in town. Filled with historical associations, the original parts of this hotel date from the 1400s. In the 1880s, the hotel was restored to its original Tudor look. It is rivaled within central Stratford only by Alveston Manor. Residents relax in the post-and-timber-studded public rooms with

Stratford-upon-Avon

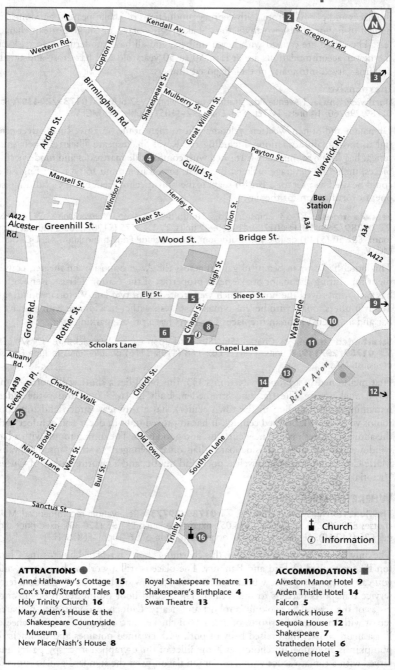

ATTRACTIONS ●
Anne Hathaway's Cottage **15**
Cox's Yard/Stratford Tales **10**
Holy Trinity Church **16**
Mary Arden's House & the
  Shakespeare Countryside
  Museum **1**
New Place/Nash's House **8**

Royal Shakespeare Theatre **11**
Shakespeare's Birthplace **4**
Swan Theatre **13**

ACCOMMODATIONS ■
Alveston Manor Hotel **9**
Arden Thistle Hotel **14**
Falcon **5**
Hardwick House **2**
Sequoia House **12**
Shakespeare **7**
Stratheden Hotel **6**
Welcome Hotel **3**

✝ Church
ⓘ Information

fireplaces and playbills from 19th-century productions of Shakespeare. The rooms are named in honor of noteworthy actors, Shakespeare's plays, or Shakespearean characters. The oldest are capped with hewn timbers, and all have modern comforts. Even the newer accommodations are at least 40 to 50 years old and have rose-and-thistle patterns carved into many of their exposed timbers.

Inexpensive

Hardwick House. 1 Avenue Rd., Stratford-upon-Avon, CV37 6UY. ☎ **01789/204307.** Fax 01789/296760. 14 units. TV TEL. £54–£62 ($92–$105) double. AE, MC, V.

Drenaugh and Simen Weetten welcome you to their home on a tree-lined street central to most main attractions, including the Royal Shakespeare Theatre. Their snug retreat has ample rooms, each furnished with comfortable mattresses and modern, tidy pieces, including beverage makers. Breakfast, served in a room so typically English it could be used as a set for a British soap, is the only meal offered, but it's a full English one, fit fortification for the day.

Sequoia House. 51–53 Shipston Rd., Stratford-upon-Avon, Warwickshire CV37 7LN. ☎ **01789/268852.** Fax 01789/414559. 22 units. TV TEL. £75 ($128) double without bathroom, £82.50 ($140) double with bathroom. Rates include English breakfast. AE, DC, DISC, MC, V.

This hotel has its own beautiful garden across the Avon opposite the theater, convenient for visiting the major Shakespeare properties of the National Trust. Renovation has vastly improved the house, which was created from two late Victorian buildings. Today it offers rooms with beverage-makers. Guests gather in a lounge with a licensed bar and an open Victorian fireplace. The hotel has a private parking area.

Stratheden Hotel. 5 Chapel St., Stratford-upon-Avon, Warwickshire CV37 6EP. ☎ **01789/297119.** 9 units. TV TEL. £62–£68 ($105–$116) double. Rates include English breakfast. MC, V.

First mentioned in a property deed in 1333, this hotel lies a short walk north of the Royal Shakespeare Theatre. The Stratheden, built in 1673 (and today the oldest remaining brick building in the town center), has a tiny rear garden and top-floor rooms with slanted, beamed ceilings. It has improved in both decor and comfort with the addition of fresh paint, new curtains, and good beds. The dining room, with a bay window, has an overscale sideboard that once belonged to the "insanely vain" Marie Corelli, an eccentric novelist, poet, and mystic, and a favorite author of Queen Victoria.

WHERE TO DINE

The Boat House. Swan's Nest Lane. ☎ **01789/297733.** Reservations recommended. Main courses £10.50–£16.50 ($17.85–$28.05); fixed-price lunch £11.95 ($20.30); fixed-price dinner £25 ($42.50). AE, MC, V. Tues–Fri noon–2pm; Mon–Sat 6–10pm. ENGLISH.

The only restaurant set on the Avon, this charming choice is reached by crossing Clopton Bridge toward Oxford and Banbury. The place is still a working boathouse, and you can rent punts and row boats for an intimate view of the Avon. A gondola ferry service transports patrons to the theater. The second-floor dining room opens onto vistas of the river. The cooking is robust and hearty. Launch into your well-prepared repast with the likes of a risotto of green Thai chicken or a tagliatelle of goat's cheese. For a main course, the braised belly of pork with creamed potatoes and caramelized pumpkin is an exuberant choice, as is the fillet of tuna wrapped in crispy pastry and served with a tomato sauce with a cardamon flavor. Even the standard grilled rump of lamb is given added zest and flavor with a rosemary and red pepper broth.

Box Tree Restaurant. In the Royal Shakespeare Theatre, Waterside. ☎ **01789/403415.** Reservations required. Matinee lunch £16 ($27); dinner £26.50 ($45). AE, MC, V. Thurs–Sat noon–2:30pm; Mon–Sat 5:45pm–midnight. FRENCH/ITALIAN/ENGLISH.

This restaurant is right in the theater itself, with glass walls providing an unobstructed view of the Avon and its swans. During intermission, there's a snack feast of smoked salmon and champagne. You dine by flickering candlelight. There's a special phone for reservations in the theater lobby. Many dishes are definitely Old English (apple and parsnip soup); others reflect a continental touch. For your main course, you might select Dover sole, salmi of wild boar, pheasant suprême, or roast loin of pork. Homemade desserts are likely to include crème brûlée, an old-time favorite at the Box Tree. Better food can be had at other places, such as Hussain's, but none are as convenient for theatergoers.

Greek Connection. 1 Shakespeare St. ☎ **01789/292214.** Reservations recommended. Main courses £9–£14 ($15–$24). DC, MC, V. Daily noon–2:30pm in summer; daily 5:30pm–12:30am year-round. GREEK.

This restaurant occupies a high-ceilinged building from 1854 that originally served as a Methodist chapel. Today, authentic Greek food is accompanied by live music and dancing nightly. Chefs George and Spiros serve up such favorites as moussaka (freshly minced meat embedded in layers of eggplant, zucchini, and potatoes with a dome of creamy béchamel) and stuffed grape leaves. Many patrons say that ordering the Mezedakia is the best option; you'll get a wide sampling of Greek hors d'oeuvres and won't have to choose only one from the enticing menu.

Hussain's. 6A Chapel St. ☎ **01789/267506.** Reservations recommended. Main courses £5.95–£7.25 ($10–$12). AE, MC, V. Daily 12:30–2:30pm and 5pm–midnight. INDIAN.

Dining here has been compared to a visit to a private Indian home. Some consider the restaurant one of the brighter spots on the bleak culinary landscape. The well-trained, alert staff welcomes guests. You can select from an array of northern Indian dishes. Herbs and spices are blended imaginatively in the kitchen to impart a distinctive flavor. Many tandoori dishes are offered, along with various curries with lamb or prawn. Hussain's is across from the Shakespeare Hotel and historic New Place.

PUBS

Dirty Duck. Waterside. ☎ **01789/297312.** Reservations required for dining. Main courses £7–£12.50 ($12–$21); bar snacks £8 ($14). AE, MC, V (restaurant only). Pub, Mon–Sat 11am–11pm, Sun noon–3pm and 7–10:30pm. Restaurant, Tues–Sun noon–2pm; Mon–Sat 5:30–11:30pm. ENGLISH.

This has been a popular hangout for Stratford players since the 18th century. The wall is lined with autographed photos of past patrons, such as Lord Laurence Olivier. The front lounge and bar crackles with intense conversation. In the spring and fall, an open fire blazes. In the Dirty Duck Grill Room, typical English grills, among other dishes, are featured, although no one ever accused the Dirty Duck of serving the best food in Stratford. Main dishes include braised kidneys or oxtails, roast chicken, or honey-roasted duck.

Garrick Inn. 25 High St. ☎ **01789/292186.** Main courses £5–£11 ($9–$19). MC, V. Meals daily noon–10pm. Pub, Mon–Sat 11am–11pm, Sun noon–10:30pm. ENGLISH.

This half-timbered Elizabethan pub from 1595 near Harvard House has an unpretentious charm. It's named for the great actor, David Garrick. The front bar is decorated with tapestry-covered settles, an old oak refectory table, and an open fireplace that attracts the locals. The back bar has a circular fireplace with a copper hood and mementos of the triumphs of the English stage. The specialty is homemade pies such as steak and ale, steak and kidney, or chicken and mushroom.

THEATER

✪ **Royal Shakespeare Company** has a major showcase at the Royal Shakespeare Theatre, Waterside, Stratford-upon-Avon CV37 6BB (☎ **01789/403403**), on the banks of the Avon. Plays, including on average five by Shakespeare each season, are staged at the 1,500-seat Royal Shakespeare and 450-seat Swan theaters as well as 170-seat The Other Place, a smaller more experimental venue.

It's important to reserve tickets in advance, which you can book by phone or from a travel agent. In New York try Edwards and Edwards (☎ **800/223-6108**) or Keith Prowse (☎ **800/669-8687**); a service charge will be added. You can also call the theater box office (payment by major credit card) at the number listed above; it's open Monday to Saturday 9am to 8pm, closing at 6pm on days with no performances. Seat prices are £75 to £93 ($128 to $158). A small number of tickets are always held for sale on the day of a performance. You can pick up your ticket on the day it is to be used, but you can't cancel once your reservation is made unless 2 full weeks advance notice is given.

SHAKESPEARE PILGRIMAGE SIGHTS

Besides the attractions on the periphery of Stratford, there are many Elizabethan and Jacobean buildings in town, many of them administered by the Shakespeare Birthplace Trust. The combination ticket costing £10 ($17) adults, £9 ($15) seniors and students, and £5 ($9) children lets you visit the five most important sights. You can buy tickets at any of the Trust properties.

Hall's Croft. Old Town (near Holy Trinity Church). ☎ **01789/292107.** Admission £3.50 ($5.95) adults, £1.90 ($3.25) children; £29 ($49.30) families (2 adults, 3 children) for all 5 Shakespeare-related houses. Mar 20–Oct 19 Mon–Sat 10:30am-5pm, Sun 10am–5pm; off-season Mon–Sat 10am–4pm, Sun 10:30am–4pm. Closed Dec 23–26. To reach Hall's Croft, walk west from High St., which becomes Chapel St. and Church St. At the intersection with Old Town, go left.

It was here Shakespeare's daughter Susanna probably lived with her husband, Dr. John Hall. Furnished in the style of a middle-class home of the time, Hall's Croft is an outstanding Tudor house with a beautiful walled garden. Dr. Hall was widely respected and built up a large medical practice in the area, and exhibits illustrating the theory and practice of medicine in Dr. Hall's time are on view. You're welcome to use the adjoining Hall's Croft Club, which serves morning cofeee, lunch, and afternoon tea.

✪ **Shakespeare's Birthplace.** Henley St. ☎ **01789/204016.** Admission £4.90 ($8) adults, £2.20 ($3.75) children. Mar 20–Oct 19 Mon–Sat 9am–5pm, Sun 9:30am–5pm; off-season Mon–Sat 9:30am–4pm, Sun 10am–4pm. Closed Dec 23–26.

The son of a glover and whittawer (leather worker), the Bard was born on St. George's day (April 23) in 1564 and died 52 years later on the exact same date. Filled with Shakespeare memorabilia, including a portrait and furnishings of the writer's time, the Trust property is a half-timbered structure, dating from the first part of the 16th century. The house, bought by public donors in 1847, is preserved as a national shrine. You can visit the oak-beamed living room, the bedroom where Shakespeare was probably born, a fully equipped kitchen of the period (look for the "baby-minder"), and a Shakespeare Museum, illustrating his life and times.

✪ **Anne Hathaway's Cottage.** Cottage Lane, Shottery. ☎ **01789/204016.** Admission £3.90 ($7) adults, £1.60 ($2.70) children. Mar 20–Oct 19 Mon–Sat 9:30am–5pm, Sun 10am–5pm; off-season Mon–Sat 9:30am–4pm, Sun 10am–4pm. Closed Dec 23–26. You can walk across the meadow to Shottery from Evesham Place in Stratford (pathway marked), or take a bus from Bridge St.

In the hamlet of Shottery, 1.5km (1 mile) from Stratford, is the thatched, wattle-and-daub cottage where Anne Hathaway lived before her marriage to Shakespeare. It's the most interesting of the Trust properties, and the most unchanged. The Hathaways were yeoman farmers, and the cottage provides a rare insight into the life of a family of Shakespeare's day. Many original furnishings, including the courting settle and utensils, are preserved inside the house, which was occupied by descendants of Shakespeare's wife's family until 1892.

New Place/Nash's House. Chapel St. ☎ **01789/204016.** Admission £3.30 ($6) adults, £1.60 ($2.70) children. Mar 20–Oct 19 Mon–Sat 9:30am–5pm, Sun 10am–5pm; Oct 20–Mar 19 Mon–Sat 10am–4pm, Sun 10:30am–4pm. Closed Dec 23–26. Walk west down High St.; Chapel St. is a continuation of High St.

This is the site where Shakespeare retired in 1610, a prosperous man. He died 6 years later, at the age of 52. Regrettably, his former home was torn down, and only the site remains. You enter the gardens through Nash's House (Thomas Nash married a granddaughter of the poet). The house has 16th-century period rooms and an exhibition illustrating the history of Stratford. The delightful Knott Garden adjoins the site and represents the style of a fashionable Elizabethan garden. New Place has its own great garden, which once belonged to Shakespeare.

Mary Arden's House and the Shakespeare Countryside Museum. Wilmcote. ☎ **01789/293455.** Admission £4.40 ($8) adults, £2.20 ($3.75) children. Mar 20–Oct 19 Mon–Sat 9:30am–5pm, Sun 10am–5pm; off-season Mon–Sat 10am–4pm, Sun 10:30am–4pm. Closed Dec 23–26. Take the A-3400 (Birmingham) road for 5.5km (3^1/$_2$ miles).

This Tudor farmstead, with its old stone dovecote and various outbuildings, may have been the girlhood home of Shakespeare's mother. There's no definite evidence that this was the actual home where Mary Arden dwelled. Nonetheless, it's situated at Wilmcote, outside Stratford. The house contains country furniture and domestic utensils. In the barns, stable, cowshed, and farmyard you'll find an extensive collection of farming implements illustrating life and work in the local countryside from Shakespeare's time to the present.

Cox's Yard/Stratford Tales. Cox's Yard. ☎ **01789/404600.** Admission £3.95 ($7) adults, £3.25 ($6) seniors and students, £2.50 ($4.25) children. Cox's Yard daily 9am–11pm, Stratford Tales daily 10am–5pm.

The Bedford-based brewery, Charles Wells, leased a former timber yard adjacent to Bancroft Garden in the town center in 1996 and turned it into an array of attractions. Chief among these is the Stratford Tales, which uses elaborate visual and audiovisual displays as well as historic objects to illustrate town stories from the 16th century to the present day. On site is a microbrewery that brews a variety of cask ales sold in a traditional English pub where you can enjoy a pint. Other attractions include a restaurant, a gift shop, a tearoom, and even wildlife habitats. Throughout the year, a program of special events also takes place in the yard, including traditional crafts exhibitions.

ORGANIZED TOURS

Guided tours leave daily from the Guide Friday Tourism Center, Civic Hall, Rother Street (☎ **01789/294466**). In summer, open-top double-decker buses depart every 15 minutes 9:30am to 5:30pm. You can take a 1-hour ride without stops, or you can get off at any or all of the town's five Shakespeare's Properties. Anne Hathaway's

Stopping at Warwick Castle

Perched on a rocky cliff above the Avon in the town center, **Warwick Castle** is a stately late 17th-century–style mansion surrounded by a magnificent 14th-century fortress. The first significant fortifications were built by Ethelfleda, daughter of Alfred the Great, in 914. Two years after the Norman Conquest in 1068, William the Conqueror ordered the construction of a motte and bailey castle. The mound is all that remains today of the Norman castle.

The Beauchamp family, earls of Warwick, are responsible for the appearance of the castle today, and much of the external structure remains unchanged from the mid-14th century. The staterooms and Great Hall house fine collections of paintings, furniture, arms, and armor. The armory, dungeon, torture chamber, ghost tower, clock tower, and Guy's tower create a vivid picture of the castle's turbulent past and its important role in the history of England.

Sir Walter Scott described Warwick Castle in 1828 as "that fairest monument of ancient and chivalrous splendor which yet remains uninjured by time." Visitors can also see the Victorian rose garden, a re-creation of an original design from 1868 by Robert Marnock. On Castle Hill, Warwick Castle (☎ **01926/406600**) is open daily 10am to 5pm. Admission is £10.50 ($18) adults, £6.25 ($11) children 4 to 16, £7.50 ($13) seniors and students, children 3 and under free, £28 ($48) family of 4.

Trains run frequently between Stratford and Warwick, and a Midland Red Bus leaves every hour (no. 18 or X16) during the day (trip time: 15 to 20 minutes). Motorists should take A-46 north from Stratford.

Cottage and Mary Arden's House are the two likely stops to make outside the town center. Although the bus stops are clearly marked along the historic route, the most logical starting point is on the sidewalk in front of the Pen & Parchment Pub, at Bridgefoot, at the bottom of Bridge Street. Tour tickets are valid all day, so you can hop on and off the buses wherever you want. The tour price is £8 ($14) adults, £6.50 ($11) senior citizens or students, and £2.50 ($4.25) children under 12.

THE SHOPPING SCENE

At the **National Trust Shop,** 45 Wood St. (☎ **01789/262197**), you'll find textbooks and guidebooks describing esoteric places in the environs of Stratford, descriptions of National Trust properties throughout England, stationery, books, china, pewter, and toiletries, each inscribed, embossed, or painted with logos that evoke some aspect of English tastes and traditions. Set in an antique house that lies across from the Birthplace, the **Shakespeare Bookshop**, 39 Henley St. (☎ **01789/292176**), is the region's premier source for textbooks and academic treatises on the Bard and his works. It specializes in books conceived for every level of expertise, from picture books for junior high school students to weighty tomes geared toward anyone pursuing a Ph.D. in literature.

Arbour Antiques, Ltd., Poet's Arbour, Sheep St. (☎ **01789/293453**), sells antique weapons, used for both warfare and sport, from Britain, Europe, and in some cases, India and Turkey. If you've always hankered after a full suit of English armor, this place will be able to sell you one. Everything at the **Pickwick Gallery,** 32 Henley St. (☎ **01789/294861**), is a well-crafted work of art produced by copper or steel engraving plates, or printed by means of a carved wooden block. Look for the engravings by

William Hogarth showing satirical scenes that lampooned Parliamentary corruption during the late 18th century. More than any other pottery studio in Stratford, **Dianthus,** 1 Centre Craft Yard, off Henley St. (☎ **01789/292252**), benefits from an intimate knowledge of Pacific Rim ceramics, with emphasis on unique creative statements in stoneware. In spacious quarters, three potters display their technique on their potter's wheels.

Scattered over three floors of an Elizabethan house said to have been occupied by one of Shakespeare's daughters as an adult, **Trading Post,** 1 High St. (☎ **01789/267228**), offers a jammed and slightly claustrophobic assortment of gift items that might appeal to your taste for the kitschy and nostalgic. Included in the roster of items are doll's houses and furnishings, a scattering of small, easy-to-transport antiques, and memorabilia of your visit to the Midlands.

3 Stonehenge & Bath

Many visitors with very limited time head for the West Country, where they explore its two major attractions: Stonehenge—the most important prehistoric monument in Britain—and Bath, England's most elegant city, famed for its architecture and its hot springs. If you have the time, you might also visit Salisbury Cathedral and the other prehistoric sites in the area, at Avebury and Old Sarum.

STONEHENGE

At the junction of A-303 and A-344/A-360, 3km (2 miles) west of Amesbury and about 15km (9 miles) north of Salisbury, stands the renowned monument of Stonehenge, a stone circle believed to be anywhere from 3,500 to 5,000 years old. This circle of lintels and megalithic pillars is the most important prehistoric monument in Britain.

ESSENTIALS

GETTING THERE   By Car   To reach Stonehenge from London, head in the direction of Salisbury, 145km (90 miles) to the southwest. Take the M-3 to the end of the run, continuing the rest of the way on A-30. Once at Salisbury, after stopping to view its cathedral (see below), head north on Castle Road. At the first roundabout (traffic circle), take the exit toward Amesbury (A-345) and Old Sarum. Continue along this route for 13km (8 miles) and then turn left onto A-303 in the direction of Exeter. Stonehenge is signposted, leading you up the A-344 to the right. In all, it's about 19km (12 miles) from Salisbury.

By Train or Bus   You can also reach Stonehenge by train and bus from London. A Network Express train departs hourly from Waterloo Station bound for Salisbury (trip time: 2 hours). Buses also depart four or five times per day from Victoria Station heading for Salisbury (trip time: 2¹/₂ hours). Once at Salisbury, take a Wilts & Dorset bus (☎ **01722/336855** for schedules), which runs several vehicles daily, depending on demand, from Salisbury to Stonehenge. This company's buses depart from the train station at Salisbury, heading directly to Stonehenge (trip time: 30 minutes).

A Stonehenge Tip

We like to visit Stonehenge at twilight, when the last of the photo-snapping bus hordes have departed. Amid relative calm, you can ponder the monument's occult origins. The setting rays of sunshine reflect off the ancient stones and seem to heighten their mystery.

Round-trip fare is £4.80 ($8) adults, £2.40 ($4.10) children under 14. Use Salisbury (see below) as a refueling stop.

EXPLORING STONEHENGE

Despite its familiarity, visitors cannot help but be impressed when they first see Stonehenge, an astonishing engineering feat. The boulders, the bluestones in particular, were moved many miles, possibly from as far away as southern Wales, to this site.

The widely held view of the 18th- and 19-century romantics that Stonehenge was the work of the Druids is without foundation. The boulders, many weighing several tons, are believed to have predated the arrival in Britain of the Celtic Druidic cult. Recent excavations continue to bring new evidence to bear on the origin and purpose of the prehistoric circle; controversy has surrounded the site, especially since the publication of *Stonehenge Decoded* by Gerald S. Hawkins and John B. White, which maintains that Stonehenge was an astronomical observatory—that is, a Neolithic calendar capable of predicting eclipses.

The site is now surrounded by a fence to protect it from vandals and souvenir hunters. Your ticket permits you to go inside the fence, all the way up to a short rope barrier about 15m (50 feet) from the stones. Spring 1996 saw the start of the full circular tour around Stonehenge; a modular walkway has been introduced to cross the archaeologically important area that runs between the Heel Stone and the main circle of stones. This lets you complete a full circuit of the stones, an excellent addition to the well-received audio tour.

Admission to Stonehenge (☎ **01980/623108**) is £4 ($7) adults, £3 ($5) students and seniors, and £2 ($3.40) children. It's open March 16 to May and September to October 15 daily 9:30am to 6pm; June to August daily 9am to 7pm; and October 16 to March 15 daily 9:30am to 4pm.

After visiting Stonehenge, you might wish to move on to Bath. But if you have an extra day or so, you shouldn't miss the other attractions nearby, Avebury and Salisbury.

AVEBURY

Avebury, one of Europe's largest prehistoric sites, lies 32km (20 miles) north of Stonehenge on the Kennet River, 11km (7 miles) west of Marlborough. The small village actually lies within the vast stone circle. Unlike Stonehenge, you can walk around the 11ha (28-acre) site, winding in and out of the circle of more than 100 stones, some of which weigh up to 50 tons. The stones are made of sarsen, a sandstone found in Wiltshire. Inside this large circle are two smaller ones, each with about 30 stones standing upright. Native Neolithic tribes are believed to have built these circles.

Avebury is on A-361 between Swindon and Devizes and 1.5km (1 mile) from the A-4 London-Bath road. The closest rail station is at Swindon, some 19km (12 miles) away, which is served by the main rail line from London to Bath. A limited bus service (no. 49) runs from Swindon to Devizes through Avebury.

You can also reach Avebury by bus from Salisbury by taking one of two buses (no. 5 and 6) run by Wilts & Dorset (☎ **01722/336855**). The buses leave three times a day Monday to Saturday and twice on Sunday (trip time: 1^1/$_2$ hours).

AN ARCHAEOLOGICAL MUSEUM

Founded by Alexander Keiller, the **Avebury Museum** (☎ **01672/539250**) houses one of Britain's most important archaeological collections. It began with material from excavations at Windmill Hill and Avebury, and now includes artifacts from other prehistoric digs at West Kennet, Long Barrow, Silbury Hill, West Kennet Avenue, and the Sanctuary. Admission is £1.70 ($2.90) adults, 80p ($1.35) children. Open April to October daily 10am to 6pm; November to March daily 10am to 4pm.

SALISBURY

Long before you enter Salisbury, the spire of the cathedral comes into view, just as John Constable painted it many times. Salisbury lies in the Avon River Valley, and is a fine place to stop for lunch and a look at the cathedral on your way to Stonehenge.

For driving directions, see above. Salisbury can be reached by bus from the Victoria Coach Station in London. There's also direct rail service from London from Waterloo Station. Call ☎ **0345/484950** for schedules and information.

WHERE TO DINE

Harper's Restaurant. 6–7 Ox Row, Market Sq. ☎ **01722/333118.** Reservations recommended. Main courses £5.50–£12.50 ($9–$21); fixed-price 2-course menu £8.50 ($14). AE, DC, MC, V. Mon–Sat noon–2pm and 6–10pm and Sun 6–9pm (June–Sept only). ENGLISH.

The chef-owner of this place prides himself on specializing in homemade and wholesome "real food." The pleasantly decorated restaurant is on the second floor of a red-brick building at the back side of Salisbury's largest parking lot, in the town center. You can order from two different menus, one featuring cost-conscious bistro-style platters, including beefsteak casserole with "herbey dumplings." A longer menu includes all-vegetarian pasta diavolo or spareribs with french fries and rice.

Salisbury Haunch of Venison. 1 Minster St. ☎ **01722/322024.** Main courses £8.50–£13.95 ($14–$24); bar platters for lunches, light suppers, and snacks £3.95–£5.75 ($7–$10); set menus £9.95–£11.95 ($17–$20). AE, MC, V. Daily noon–3pm; Mon–Sat 6:30–9:30pm. Pub, Mon–Sat 11am–11pm, Sun noon–3pm and 7–11pm. Closed Christmas. ENGLISH.

Right in the heart of Salisbury, this creaky-timbered 1320 restaurant serves excellent dishes, especially English roasts and grills. Stick to what it's known for, and you'll rarely go wrong. Begin perhaps with tasty grilled venison sausages in a Dijon mustard sauce, then follow with the time-honored house specialty: roast haunch of venison with gin and juniper berries. Many other classic English dishes are served, such as a medley of fish and shellfish or else grilled Barnsley lamb chops with "bubble and squeak" (cabbage and potatoes).

Silver Plough. White Hill, Pitton, near Salisbury. ☎ **01722/712266.** Reservations recommended. Main courses £8–£15 ($14–$26); bar platters £4.50–£7.50 ($8–$13). AE, DC, MC, V. Restaurant, daily noon–2:30pm; Mon–Sat 7–10pm, Sun 7–9pm. Pub, Mon–Sat 11am–3pm and 6–11pm, Sun noon–3pm and 7–10:30pm. Closed Dec 25–26 and Jan 1. Take A-30 for 8km (5 miles) east of Salisbury; it's at the southern end of the hamlet of Pitton. ENGLISH.

Built as a stone-sided farmhouse 150 years ago, the Silver Plough is now a charming country pub with an attached restaurant. Snacks available in the bar include ratatouille au gratin and grilled sardines with garlic butter and freshly baked bread. In the somewhat more formal dining room, the chef prepares such dishes as fresh Dorset mussels in a white wine, garlic, and cream sauce; sliced breast of duck in cracked pepper or orange sauce; and roast guinea fowl in a sharp strawberry sauce. The Silver Plough has known many famous visitors, but the management prefers to stick to its quiet, country atmosphere and concentrate on making its guests feel at home.

IN & AROUND SALISBURY

✪ **Salisbury Cathedral.** The Close. ☎ **01722/555120.** Admission £3 ($5) adults, £2 ($3.40) students and seniors, £1 ($1.70) children, or £6 ($10) family of 4. Daily Sept–May 7am–6:15pm, June–Aug 7am–8:15pm.

You can search all of England, but you'll find no better example of early English or pointed style than Salisbury Cathedral. Construction began as early as 1220 and took 38 years to complete; this was rather fast since it was customary in those days for a cathedral building to require at least 3 centuries. The soaring spire was completed at the end of the 13th century. Despite an ill-conceived attempt at renovation in the 18th century, the architectural integrity of the cathedral has been retained.

The 13th-century octagonal chapter house (note the fine sculpture), which is especially attractive, possesses one of the four surviving original texts of the Magna Carta, along with treasures from the diocese of Salisbury and manuscripts and artifacts belonging to the cathedral. The cloisters enhance the beauty of the cathedral, and the exceptionally large close, with at least 75 buildings in its compound (some from the early 18th century, others earlier), sets off the cathedral most effectively.

Old Sarum. Castle Rd. ☎ **01722/335398.** Admission £2 ($3.40) adults, £1.50 ($2.55) senior citizens, £1 ($1.70) children. Daily Apr–Sept, 10am–6pm, off-season 10am–4pm. 3km (2 miles) north of Salisbury off A-345. Bus: 3, 5, 6, 7, 8, and 9 from Salisbury run every 20 minutes.

Old Sarum is believed to have been an Iron Age fortification. The earthworks were known to the Romans as *Sorbiodunum.* Much later, Saxons also used the fortification. The Normans built a cathedral and a castle here in what was then a Middle Ages walled town. Parts of the old cathedral were taken down to build the city of New Sarum (Salisbury).

✪ **Wilton House.** Wilton. ☎ **01722/746729.** Admission £6.55 ($11) adults, £4 ($7) children 5–15 (under 5 free); grounds only £3.75 ($6) adults, £2.50 ($4.25) children. Daily Apr–Oct 10am–5:30pm (last admission at 4:30pm). About 4km (2¹/₂ miles) west of Salisbury on A-30. Bus: 60 and 61 from Salisbury run every 10 minutes.

Wilton House, one of England's great country estates, is the home of the earls of Pembroke. The house dates from the 16th century, but has undergone numerous alterations. It is believed that Shakespeare's troupe may have entertained here. Celebrated 17th-century architect Inigo Jones designed the staterooms. Preparations for the D-day landings at Normandy were laid out here by Eisenhower and his advisors, with only the silent Van Dyck paintings in the Double Cube room as witnesses.

The house displays paintings by Van Dyck, Rubens, Brueghel, and Reynolds. A dynamic film introduced and narrated by Anna Massey brings to life the history of the family since 1544, the year it was granted the land by Henry VIII. You then visit a reconstructed Tudor kitchen and Victorian laundry plus "The Wareham Bears," a unique collection of some 200 miniature dressed teddy bears.

Giant Cedars of Lebanon grow on the 8.5ha (21-acre) estate, the oldest of which were planted in 1630. The Palladian Bridge was built in 1737 by the ninth earl of Pembroke and Roger Morris. There're rose and water gardens, riverside and woodland walks, and a huge adventure playground for children.

BATH

The city of Bath has had two lives. Originally, it was a Roman spa known as Aquae Sulis. The foreign legions founded their baths here (which may be visited today) to ease their rheumatism in the curative mineral springs. In 1702 Queen Anne made the trek from London, 185km (115 miles) west to the mineral springs of Bath, thereby launching a fad that was to make the city England's most celebrated spa.

The most famous personage connected with Bath's growing popularity was the 18th-century dandy Beau Nash. The master of ceremonies of Bath, Nash cut a striking figure. In all the plumage of a bird of paradise, he was carted around in a sedan chair, dispensing (at a price) trinkets to courtiers and aspirant gentlemen. This polished arbiter of taste and manners succeeded in making dueling déclassé.

The 18th-century architects John Wood the Elder and his son envisioned a proper backdrop for Nash's activities. They designed a city of honey-colored stone from the nearby hills, a feat so substantial and lasting that Bath today is the most harmoniously laid-out city in England. The city attracted leading political and literary figures, such as Dickens, Thackeray, Nelson, and Pitt, and most important, of course, Jane Austen. Canadians may already know that General Wolfe lived on Trim Street, and Australians may want to visit the house at 19 Bennett St. where their founding father, Admiral Phillip, lived.

Remarkable restoration and careful planning have ensured that Bath retains its handsome look today. It has somewhat of a museum appearance, with the attendant gift shops. Prices, stimulated by massive tourist invasion, tend to be high. But Bath remains one of the high points of the West Country.

ESSENTIALS

GETTING THERE   By Train   At least one train an hour leaves London's Paddington Station bound for Bath during the day (trip time: 70 to 90 minutes). For rail schedules and information, call ☎ **0345/484950.**

By Bus   One National Express coach leaves London's Victoria Coach Station every 2 hours during the day (trip time: 2¹/₂ hours). For schedules and information, call ☎ **08705/808080.**

By Car   From London, drive west on M-4 to the junction with A-4, on which you continue west to Bath. From Salisbury take A-36 west to Bath. You'll enter at the southern tier of the city.

VISITOR INFORMATION The **Bath Tourist Information Centre,** at Abbey Chambers, Abbey Church Yard (☎ **01225/477101**), opposite the Roman Baths, is open Monday, Tuesday, Friday, and Saturday 9am to 5:30pm, Wednesday and Thursday 9:45am to 5:30pm, and Sunday 10am to 4pm.

SPECIAL EVENTS For 17 days in late May and early June the city is filled with more than 1,000 performers—orchestras, soloists, and artists from all over the world. The **Bath International Music Festival** focuses on classical music, jazz, new music, and opening night celebrations with fireworks. There's also all the best in walks, tours, and talks, plus free street entertainment. For more information, contact the **Bath Festivals Box Office,** 2 Church St., Abbey Green, Bath BA1 1NL (☎ **01225/463362**).

GETTING AROUND One of the best ways to explore Bath is by bike. You can rent one from **Somerset Valley Bike Hire** (☎ **01225/442442**), behind the train station. It's open daily 9am to 5:30pm, charging £14 to £25 ($24 to $43) per day, £9 ($15) per half day, £50 ($85) per week, depending on the type of bike. Deposits range from £20 to £75 ($34 to $128).

WHERE TO STAY
Very Expensive
✪ **Bath Spa Hotel.** Sydney Rd., Bath, Somerset BA2 6JF. ☎ **01225/444424.** Fax 01225/444006. www.bathspahotel.com. E-mail: fivestar@bathspa.u-net.com. 98 units. MINIBAR TV TEL. Sun–Thurs £174 ($296) double; Fri–Sat £219 ($372) double. Weeklong £254–£354 ($432–$602) suite for 2. AE, DC, MC, V. Free parking. East of the city off A-36.

This restored 19th-century mansion, which lies at the end of a tree-lined drive on landscaped grounds, is a 10-minute walk from the center of Bath. It is an even more stunning addition to the Bath hotel scene than the Royal Crescent. The drawing room of what was once an English general's house has been restored, and fireplaces, elaborate moldings, oak paneling, and staircases create a warm country-house charm. The rooms, most quite spacious, are handsomely furnished with the best English furniture. The hotel features an indoor swimming pool, gymnasium, tennis court, health and leisure spa, beauty treatment rooms, and a very English croquet lawn.

The premier hotel restaurant, Vellore House, serves continental cuisine. You'll find immaculate service and superb food and wine; a fixed-price dinner is served from 7 to 10pm daily. A second restaurant, the Alfresco, offers a Mediterranean-style menu. In summer, guests can dine outside in an informal garden with a fountain.

Priory Hotel. Weston Rd., Bath, Somerset BA1 2XT. ☎ **01225/331922.** Fax 01225/448276. 28 units. TV TEL. £180 ($306) standard double; £240 ($408) deluxe room for 2. Rates include English breakfast. AE, DC, MC, V. Free parking.

Converted from one of Bath's Georgian houses in 1969, the Priory is set amidst formal and award-winning gardens with manicured lawns and flower beds, a swimming pool, and a croquet lawn. The hotel was recently refurbished and improved; if anything, it is more inviting than ever. It's not as overly commercial as the Francis, but is less expensive than the Bath Spa or Royal Crescent, while offering somewhat the same town-house aura. The rooms are individually decorated; our personal favorite is Clivia (all rooms are named after flowers or shrubs), a nicely appointed duplex in a circular turret.

The restaurant consists of three separate dining rooms, one in a small salon in the original building; the others have views over the garden. The menu is varied and reflects seasonal availability. Grouse, partridge, hare, and venison are served in season, as is the succulent best end of lamb roasted with herb-flavored breadcrumbs. A three-course dinner is offered, and on Sunday, traditional roasted meats are featured.

Bath

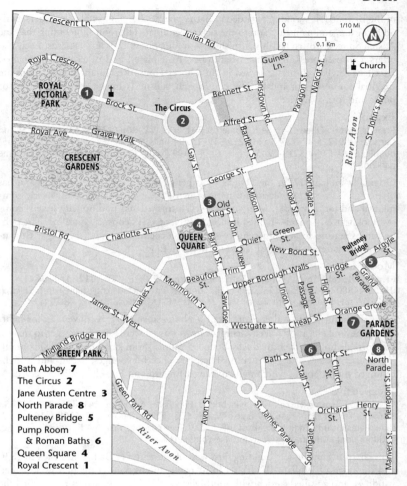

Church

ROYAL VICTORIA PARK

Brock St.

The Circus ②

CRESCENT GARDENS

ROYAL CRESCENT ①

Royal Ave.

Gravel Walk

Julian Rd.

Guinea Ln.

Bennett St.

Alfred St.

Bartlett St.

Lansdown Rd.

Paragon St.

Walcot St.

River Avon

St. John's Rd.

Gay St.

George St.

Milsom St.

Broad St.

Northgate St.

③ Old King St.

④ QUEEN SQUARE

Barton St.

John St.

Quiet

Green St.

New Bond St.

Pulteney Bridge ⑤

Argyle St.

Bristol Rd.

Charlotte St.

Queen St.

Trim

Upper Borough Walls

Bridge St.

Grand Parade

Beaufort St.

Monmouth St.

Sawclose

Charles St.

James St. West

Union Passage

Union St.

High St.

Orange Grove

Westgate St.

Cheap St.

⑦ PARADE GARDENS

Midland Bridge Rd.

GREEN PARK

Green Park Rd.

River Avon

Bath St.

⑥

York St.

Stall St.

Church St.

North Parade ⑧

Avon St.

St. James Parade

Southgate St.

Orchard St.

Henry St.

Pierrepont St.

Manvers St.

Bath Abbey **7**
The Circus **2**
Jane Austen Centre **3**
North Parade **8**
Pulteney Bridge **5**
Pump Room
   & Roman Baths **6**
Queen Square **4**
Royal Crescent **1**

Queensberry Hotel. Russel St., Bath, Somerset BA1 2QF. ☎ **800/323-5463** in the U.S., or 01225/447928. Fax 01225/446065. 29 units. TV TEL. £120–£210 ($204–$357) double. Rates include continental breakfast. MC, V. Parking £1 ($1.70) per hour.

Although hardly as grand as the addresses previously considered, this place derives much of its beauty from the many original fireplaces, ornate ceilings, and antiques. The Marquis of Queensberry commissioned John Wood to build this house in 1772. Each room has antique furniture, in keeping with the character of the house. Open since 1988, the Queensberry has become one of Bath's most important hotels. You can dine at the exceptional Olive Tree, offering a contemporary English cuisine (see below).

✪ **Royal Crescent Hotel.** 16 Royal Crescent, Bath, Somerset BA1 2LS. ☎ **800/457-6000** in the U.S., or 01225/823333. Fax 01225/339401. 45 units. TV TEL. £190–£290 ($323–$493) double; from £380 ($646) suite. AE, DC, MC, V. Free parking.

Standing proudly in the center of the famed Royal Crescent, this Georgian colonnade of town houses was designed by John Wood the Younger in 1767. Before the arrival of the Bath Spa, it was long regarded as Bath's premier hotel. Crystal chandeliers, period furniture, and paintings add to the rich adornment. The rooms, including the Jane Austen Suite, are often lavishly furnished with four-poster beds and Jacuzzis. Each also offers a trouser press, hair dryer, bathrobes, fruit plates, and other special touches. Excellent English cuisine is served in the Dower House Restaurant. Reservations are essential for rooms or meals. The continental cuisine is imaginative, with ever-so-polite and formal service.

Expensive

Francis Hotel. Queen Sq., Bath, Somerset BA1 2HH. ☎ **800/225-5843** in the U.S. and Canada, or 01225/424257. Fax 01225/319715. 94 units. TV TEL. £124–£144 ($211–$245) double; £129–£144 ($219–$245) triple; £179–£199 ($304–$338) suite. AE, DC, MC, V. Free parking.

Originally built in 1729, the Francis was opened as a private hotel in 1884 and has offered guests first-class service for more than 100 years, though it seems overly commercial and touristy today. Many of the well-furnished and traditionally styled rooms overlook Queen Square—named in honor of George II's consort, Caroline. The public rooms feature some 18th-century antiques, a cocktail bar, and the Edgar Restaurant, which offers both British and international food.

Moderate

Pratt's Hotel. South Parade, Bath, Somerset BA2 4AB. ☎ **01225/460441.** Fax 01225/448807. 46 units. TV TEL. £95 ($162) double. Rates include English breakfast. Children under 15 stay free in a room shared with 2 adults. AE, DC, MC, V. Parking £8.50 ($14).

Once the home of Sir Walter Scott, Pratt's, a hotel since 1791, is convenient for sightseeing. Several elegant terraced Georgian town houses were joined together to make a comfortable hotel with individually designed rooms (from small to spacious) containing trouser presses and hair dryers. There are cheerful lounges, a bar, and a high-ceilinged dining room, where well-conceived English and French cuisine is served.

Inexpensive

✪ **Apsley House Hotel.** 141 Newbridge Hill, Bath, Somerset BA1 3PT. ☎ **01225/336966.** Fax 01225/425462. 9 units. TV TEL. £75 ($128) double; £95–£105 ($162–$179) suite. Rates include English breakfast. AE, MC, V. Free parking. Take A-4 to Upper Bristol Rd. and fork right at the traffic signals into Newbridge Hill.

This charming and stately building, just west of the center of Bath, dates back to 1830 and the reign of William IV. It's set in its own gardens, with a square tower, arched windows, and a walled garden with south views. In 1994, new owners refurbished the hotel, filling it with country-house chintzes and antiques. The rooms are comfortably furnished and filled with attractive accessories.

Dukes' Hotel. 53–54 Great Pulteney St., Bath, Somerset BA2 4DN. ☎ **01225/463512.** Fax 01225/483733. 23 units. TV TEL. £70–£100 ($119–$170) double; £120 ($204) family room. Rates include English breakfast. AE, MC, V. Bus: 18.

A short walk from the heart of Bath, this building dates from 1780. It has been completely restored and rather elegantly furnished and modernized. Many of the original Georgian features have been retained. Amenities include electric trouser presses and hair dryers. Guests can relax in a refined drawing room or patronize the cozy bar. A traditional English menu is also offered.

Laura Place Hotel. 3 Laura Place, Great Pulteney St., Bath, Somerset BA2 4BH. ☎ **01225/463815.** Fax 01225/310222. 8 units. TV TEL. £68–£88 ($116–$150) double; £110 ($187) family suite. Rates include English breakfast. AE, MC, V. Free parking. Bus: 18 or 19.

Built in 1789, this hotel won a civic award for the restoration of its stone facade. On the corner of a residential street overlooking a public fountain, it's a 2-minute walk from the Roman Baths and Bath Abbey. The hotel has been skillfully decorated with antique furniture and fabrics evocative of the 18th century, and its medium-sized rooms are very cozy in the best tradition of an English B&B.

Number Ninety Three. 93 Wells Rd., Bath, Somerset BA2 3AN. ☎ **01225/317977.** 4 units. TV. £38–£58 ($65–$99) double; £60–£75 ($102–$128) triple. Rates include English breakfast. Bus: 3, 13, 14, 17, 23, or 33.

This elegant Victorian guest house is a traditional British B&B: small but immaculate and well maintained, within easy walking distance from the center and rail and National Bus stations. Its owner is a mine of local information, who serves a traditional English breakfast. The rooms, small to medium, are very nice, with cozy beds. Parking can be difficult in Bath, but the hotel will advise.

Paradise House Hotel. 86–88 Holloway, Bath, Somerset BA2 4PX. ☎ **0122/5317723.** Fax 01225/482005. www.gratton.co.uk/paradise. E-mail: paradise@apsleyhouse.easynet.co.uk. 10 units. TV TEL. Standard double £75–£85 ($128–$145), deluxe double £85–£90 ($145–$153). Rates include breakfast. AE, MC, V.

Dating from 1735, this Georgian House is set among manicured gardens on the southern slopes of the city, about a 7-minute walk from the center. Join in a game of croquet on the lawns and step back in time. David and Annie Lanz have restored the house to its original charm, and they offer individually decorated rooms, most often with a romantic decor, as evoked by a garden room with a four-poster. Beds are sumptuous, and amenities range from excellent mattresses to hair dryers and beverage makers. Guests relax and meet each other in the drawing room with its arched windows plus an open fire in winter. The hotel also has a small bar. The place is a real find.

Sydney Gardens Hotel. Sydney Rd., Bath, Somerset BA2 6NT. ☎ **01225/464818.** Fax 01225/484347. www.sydneygardens.co.uk. 6 units. TV TEL. Sun–Thurs £69 ($117) double; Fri–Sat £75 ($128) double. Rates include English breakfast. AE, MC, V. Free parking.

This spot recalls the letters of Jane Austen, who wrote to friends about the long walks she enjoyed in Sydney Gardens, a public park just outside the city center. In 1852, an Italianate Victorian villa was constructed here on a lot immediately adjacent to the gardens. Three rooms have twin beds and the other three have 5-foot-wide double beds. Each room is decorated with an English country-house charm. Amenities include hair dryers and beverage-making facilities. Only breakfast is served. There's also a footpath running beside a canal. No smoking.

Nearby Places to Stay

Homewood Park. Hinton Charterhouse, Bath, Somerset BA3 6BB. ☎ **01225/723731.** Fax 01225/723820. 19 units. £139–£249 ($236–$423) double; £249 ($423) suite. Rates include English breakfast. AE, DC, MC, V. Free parking. Take A-36 (Bath-Warminster rd.) 10km (6 miles) south of Bath.

Overlooking the Limpley Stoke Valley, this small, family-run hotel is a large Victorian house with grounds adjoining the 13th-century ruin of Hinton Priory. You can play tennis and croquet in the garden. Riding and golf are available nearby, and beautiful walks in the Limpley Stoke Valley lure guests. Each room is luxuriously decorated and furnished with taste and charm. Most overlook the gardens and grounds or offer views of the valley. Most visitors, however, come here for the French and English cuisine, which is prepared with skill and flair. The dining room faces south, overlooking the gardens.

Hunstrete House. Hunstrete, Pensford, near Bristol, Somerset BS39 4NS. ☎ **01761/490490.** Fax 01761/490732. 23 units. TV TEL. £130–£180 ($221–$306) double; £250–£320 ($425–$544) suite. Half board £200–£250 ($340–$425) double; £250 ($425) suite for 2.

Rates include English breakfast. AE, DC, MC, V. Free parking. Take A-4 about 6.5km (4 miles) west of Bath, then A-368 another 7km (4¹/₂ miles) toward Weston-super-Mare.

This fine Georgian house, which has earned Relais & Châteaux distinction, is situated on 37ha (92 acres) of private parkland. Six units are in the Courtyard House, attached to the main structure and overlooking a paved courtyard with its Italian fountain and flower-filled tubs. Swallow Cottage, which adjoins the main house, has its own private sitting room, double bedroom, and bathroom. Units in the main house are individually decorated. There's a heated swimming pool in a sheltered corner of the walled garden. Part of the pleasure of staying at Hunstrete is the contemporary and classic cuisine served in the dining room.

✪ **Ston Easton Park.** Ston Easton, Somerset BA3 4DF. ☎ **01761/241631.** Fax 01761/241377. 21 units. TV TEL. £190–£255 ($323–$434) double; £320–£405 ($544–$689) suite. Children under 7 not accepted. AE, DC, MC, V. Free parking. Follow A39 south from Bath until you see the signposted turnoff to Ston Easton.

From the moment you pass a group of stone outbuildings and the century-old beeches of the 12ha (30-acre) park, you know you've come to a very special place. The mansion was created in the mid-1700s from the shell of an Elizabethan house. In 1977, Peter and Christine Smedley acquired the property and poured money, love, and labor into its restoration. Now it's one of the great country hotels of England. A pair of carved mahogany staircases is ringed with ornate plaster detailing, and the place is replete with antiques. Tasteful rooms are filled with flowers. A gardener's cottage comprises two separate suites, and the stateroom is regal with a four-poster bed and a private seating area. A sunflower-colored formal dining room displays museum-quality oil portraits, grandeur, and exquisite attention to detail. The chef prepares superb food from an imaginative menu.

WHERE TO DINE
Expensive
✪ **Lettonie Restaurant.** 35 Kelston Rd. ☎ **0122/5446676.** Reservations required. Fixed-price dinner £44.50 ($76); fixed-price lunch £20–£25 ($34–$43). AE, DC, MC, V. Tues–Sat noon–2pm and 7–9:30pm. FRENCH.

Moving here from Bristol, this restaurant quickly became the talk of Bath and the city's best dining choice. In a Georgian house with a lounge bar, it has a terraced garden sloping toward the Avon Valley. Sian and Martin Blunos have won an entire coterie of new admirers with their French-inspired cuisine. Each dish is the result of time-consuming preparation in the kitchen, and the results are always worthy, as evoked by such appetizers as scrambled duck egg topped with Sevruga caviar and served with blini pancakes or kipper tortellini with scallops and tomato in a sauternes cream sauce. Main dishes are represented by a delectable medley of deep-fried frog's legs with a lemon and crumb crust, served with a nettle risotto. If not that, then try the beet-root mousse with seared chicken livers and oak-smoked bacon. Desserts are worth the calories, especially the hot gingerbread tart with poached glazed pear and the to-die-for banana and caramel soufflé with banana ice cream and caramel sauce.

Moderate
Moon and Sixpence. 6A Broad St. ☎ **01225/460962.** Reservations recommended. Main courses £11–£15 ($19–$26); fixed-price lunch £8.95–£12.95 ($15–$22); 2-course lunch buffet in the wine bar £7.95 ($14); fixed-price dinner £24.95 ($42). AE, MC, V. Daily noon–2:30pm and 5:30–10:30pm (until 11pm Fri–Sat). INTERNATIONAL.

One of Bath's finest restaurants and wine bars, the Moon and Sixpence occupies a stone structure just off Broad Street east of Queen Square, with an extended conservatory and sheltered patio. The food may not be outstanding, but the value is unbeatable.

At lunch, a large cold buffet with a selection of hot dishes is featured in the wine bar section. In the upstairs restaurant overlooking the bar, full service is offered. Main courses might include such dishes as fillet of lamb with caramelized garlic or medallions of beef fillet with a bacon, red wine, and shallot sauce. Look for the daily specials on the continental menu.

Olive Tree. In the Queensberry Hotel, Russel St. ☎ **01225/447928.** Reservations recommended. Main courses £11.50–£19 ($20–$32); fixed-price 3-course lunch £14.50 ($25); fixed-price 3-course dinner £24 ($41). MC, V. Mon–Sat noon–2pm and 7–10pm; Sun 7–9:30pm. MODERN ENGLISH/MEDITERRANEAN.

In the basement of this hotel (see above), Stephen and Penny Ross operate one of the most sophisticated little restaurants in Bath. Stephen uses the best of local produce, with an emphasis on freshness. The menu is changed to reflect the season, with game and fish being the specialties. You might begin with a Provençal fish soup with *rouille* and croutons, or eggplant and mozzarella fritters with a sweet red pepper sauce— unless the grilled scallops with noodles and pine nuts tempt you instead. Then you could move on to Gressingham duck breast lightly grilled with shallots and kumquats, or loin of venison with wild rice and morels delicately flavored with a tarragon sauce. Stephen is also known for his desserts; they might include a hot chocolate soufflé or an apricot and almond tart.

Popjoy's Restaurant. Sawclose. ☎ **01225/460494.** Reservations recommended. Main courses £14–£20 ($24–$34); fixed-price 3-course lunch £11 ($19). AE, DC, MC, V. Mon–Sat noon–2pm and 6–11pm. BRITISH/INTERNATIONAL.

In this Georgian home, where Beau Nash and his mistress, Julianna Popjoy, entertained their friends, two dining rooms are on separate floors. Dishes display inventiveness and solid technique. Menu choices include terrine of duck and chicken liver wrapped in bacon with a tomato coulis; watercress and potato soup; sautéed lamb kidneys with crispy smoked bacon; braised lamb shoulder with a sage and garlic stuffing; and tagliatelle with leeks and cream sauce.

Inexpensive

Beaujolais. 5 Chapel Row, Queen Sq. ☎ **01225/423417.** Reservations recommended. Fixed-price 2-course lunch £8.50 ($14); fixed-price, 2-course dinner £13.50 ($23); dinner main courses £11–£14.50 ($19–$25). AE, MC, V. Daily noon–2:30pm and 7–11pm. FRENCH.

This is the best-known bistro in Bath, attracting new admirers every year. Established in 1973, it is the oldest restaurant in Bath under its original ownership. Diners are drawn to the good, honest cooking and good value. Begin perhaps with a salad of warm scallops, or rabbit terrine served with chutney. You might follow that with an excellent grilled loin of lamb topped with a crispy julienne of ginger and leeks. House wines are modestly priced. One area of the restaurant is reserved for nonsmokers, and people with disabilities (wheelchair access), children (special helpings), and vegetarians will all find comfort here.

Woods. 9–13 Alfred St. ☎ **01225/314812.** Reservations recommended. Main courses £11–£17 ($19–$29); fixed-price lunches £7 ($12); fixed-price dinners £12.25 ($21). AE, MC, V. Mon–Sat noon–2:30pm and 6–10:30pm; Sun noon–4pm. Closed Dec 25–26. ENGLISH/FRENCH/ASIAN.

Named after John Wood the Younger, this restaurant in a Georgian building is run by horse-racing enthusiast David Price and his French-born wife, Claude. A printed fixed-price menu and a seasonally changing array of à la carte items noted on a chalkboard detail the choices. Good bets include pear and parsnip soup; smoked chicken salad with Stilton and avocado; panfried cod roe; and a perfectly prepared breast of chicken with tomatoes, mushrooms, red wine, and tarragon.

EXPLORING BATH

In addition to the attractions listed below, you'll want to visit some of the buildings, crescents, and squares in town. John Wood the Elder's **North Parade** (where Oliver Goldsmith lived) and **South Parade** (where English novelist and diarist Frances Burney once resided) are the architectural idealization of harmony. The younger Wood designed the **Royal Crescent,** an elegant half-moon row of town houses. One of the most beautiful squares is **Queen Square,** which displays the work of Wood the Elder. Both Jane Austen and Wordsworth once lived here. Also of interest is **The Circus,** built in 1754, as well as the shop-lined **Pulteney Bridge,** designed by Robert Adam and often compared to the Ponte Vecchio of Florence.

Bath's newest attraction, the **Jane Austen Centre**, 40 Gay St. (☎ **01225/443-000**), is located in a Georgian town house on an elegant street where Miss Austen once lived. Exhibits and a video convey a sense of what life was like in Bath during the Regency period. The center is open Monday to Saturday 10am to 5pm and Sunday 10:30am to 5:30pm. Admission is £4 ($7).

Bath Abbey. Orange Grove. ☎ **01225/422462.** Free admission; donation requested £1.50 ($2.55). Heritage Vaults £2 ($3.40) adults, £1 ($1.70) students, children, and senior citizens. Abbey, Apr–Oct Mon–Sat 9am–6pm; Nov–Mar Mon–Sat 9am–4:30pm; year-round, Sun 1–2:30pm and 4:30–5:30pm. Heritage Vaults, Mon–Sat 10am–4pm.

Built on the site of a much larger Norman cathedral, the present-day abbey is a fine example of the late Perpendicular style. When Queen Elizabeth I came to Bath in 1574, she ordered a national fund set up to restore the abbey. The interior and its many windows plainly illustrate why the abbey is called the "Lantern of the West." Note the superb fan vaulting, with its scalloped effect. Beau Nash was buried in the nave and is honored by a simple monument totally out of keeping with his flamboyant character. In 1994 the Bath Abbey Heritage Vaults opened on the south side of the abbey. This subterranean exhibition traces the history of Christianity at the abbey site since Saxon times.

Pump Room and Roman Baths. Abbey Church Yard. ☎ **01225/477785.** Admission £7.10 ($12.05) adults, £4 ($7) children. Oct–Mar Mon–Sat 9:30am–5pm, Sun 10:30am–5pm; Apr–June and Sept daily 9am–6pm; Aug daily 9am–10pm. Last admission 1 hour before closing.

Founded in A.D. 75 by the Romans, the baths were dedicated to the goddess Sulis Minerva; in their day they were an engineering feat. Even today, still fed by Britain's most famous hot-spring water, they're among the finest Roman remains in the country. After centuries of decay, the original baths were rediscovered during Queen Victoria's reign. The site of the Temple of Sulis Minerva has been excavated and is now open to view. The museum displays many interesting objects from Victorian and recent digs (look for the head of Minerva). Coffee, lunch, and tea, usually with music from the Pump Room Trio, can be enjoyed in the 18th-century pump room, overlooking the hot springs. There's also a drinking fountain with hot mineral water that tastes horrible, but is supposedly beneficial.

No. 1 Royal Crescent. 1 Royal Crescent. ☎ **01225/428126.** Admission £4 ($7) adults, £3 ($5) children; £8 ($14) family ticket. Mar–Oct Tues–Sun 10:30am–5pm; Nov–Dec 1 Tues–Sun 10:30am–4pm (last admission 30 minutes before closing). Closed Good Friday.

The interior of this Bath town house has been redecorated and furnished by the Bath Preservation Trust to look as it might have toward the end of the 18th century. The house is at one end of Bath's most magnificent crescent, west of the Circus.

American Museum. Claverton Manor, Bathwick Hill. ☎ **01225/460503.** Admission £5 ($9) adults, £4.50 ($8) students and senior citizens, £2.50 ($4.25) children. Late Mar to late Oct daily 2–5pm. Bus: 18.

Two More Magnificent Houses:
Longleat House & Stourhead

Between Bath and Salisbury, 6.5km (4 miles) southwest of Warminster and 7km (4¹/₂ miles) southeast of Frome on A-362, is **Longleat House,** Warminster, Wiltshire (☎ **01985/844400**), owned by the seventh marquess of Bath. The first view of this Elizabethan house, built in the early Renaissance style, is romantic enough, but the wealth of paintings and furnishings in its lofty rooms is dazzling. From the Elizabethan Great Hall to the library, staterooms, and grand staircase, the house is filled with fine tapestries and paintings. The library contains the finest private collection in the country. The Victorian kitchens are open, and various exhibitions are mounted in the stable yard.

Events are staged frequently on the grounds. The Safari Park has a vast array of animals in open parklands, including Britain's only white tiger. The Maze, the longest in the world, was added to the attractions by the current marquess. It has more than 2.5km (1¹/₂ miles) of paths; the first part is comparatively easy, but the second is rather more complicated.

Admission is £5 ($9) adults, £4 ($7) children; admission to Safari Park is £6 ($10) adults, £4.50 ($8) children. Special exhibitions and rides require separate admission. Passport tickets for all Longleat's attractions cost £13 ($22) adults and £10 ($17) children, including admission to the Butterfly Garden, Simulator Dr. Who Exhibition, Postman Pat's Village, Adventure Castle, and more. It's open daily mid-March to September 10am to 5pm, October to Easter 10am to 4pm. The park itself is open daily mid-March to October 31, 10am to 6pm (last cars are admitted at 5:30pm or sunset).

After a visit to Longleat, you can drive 10km (6 miles) down B-3092 to Stourton, a village just off the highway 5km (3 miles) northwest of Mere (A-303). A Palladian house, **Stourhead** (☎ **01747/841152**), was built in the 18th century by the banking family of Hoare. The fabulous gardens, blending art and nature, became known as *le jardin anglais.* Set around an artificial lake, the grounds are decorated with temples, bridges, islands, and grottoes, as well as statuary. The gardens are open daily 9am to 7pm (or until dusk), and cost £4.60 ($8) adults and £2.60 ($4.40) children from March to October. Off-season tickets cost £3.50 ($6) adults and £1.50 ($2.55) children. The house is open April 30 to October 30 Saturday to Wednesday noon to 5:30pm. Admission is £4.50 ($8) adults and £2.50 ($4.25) children. A combination ticket to both attractions goes for £8 ($14) adults or £3.80 ($7) children.

Some 4km (2¹/₂ miles) from Bath is the first American museum established outside the United States. In a Greek Revival house (Claverton Manor), the museum sits on extensive grounds high above the Avon valley. Authentic exhibits of pioneer days have been shipped over from the States. On the grounds is a copy of Washington's flower garden at Mount Vernon and an American arboretum. A permanent exhibition in the New Gallery displays the Dallas Pratt Collection of Historical Maps.

ORGANIZED TOURS

The **Heart of England Tourist Board** (☎ **01905/763436**) and the **West Country Tourist Board** (☎ **01392/276351**) have details of numerous guided tours within their regions, and the staff can book you with registered guides for outings ranging from short walks to luxury tours that include accommodations in stately homes.

Free, 1³/₄-hour walking tours are conducted throughout the year by the Mayor's Honorary Society (☎ **01225/477786**). Tours depart from outside the Roman Baths Monday to Friday 10:30am and 2pm, Sunday 2:30pm, and Tuesday, Friday, and Saturday 7pm. A slightly different tour by Bath Parade Tours, costing £3.50 ($6) per person, leaves Saturday 2:30pm from outside the Roman Baths. Reservations aren't needed for either tour.

Jane Austen Tours take you in the footsteps of the author and her characters. These tours leave Saturday from the Abbey Lace Shop, York Street (☎ **01225/463030**), and cost £3 ($5) per person. You'll be told the time to meet when you make a reservation.

To tour Bath by bus, you can choose among several tour companies; some have open-top buses leaving from the Tourist Information Centre, which supplies details of changing schedules and prices. Among the best bus tours is **Patrick Driscoll/Beau Nash Guides,** Elmsleigh, Bathampton, BA2 6SW (☎ **01225/46210**); these tours are more personalized than most. Another good outfitter is **Sulis Guides,** 2 Lansdown Terrace, Weston, Bath BA1 4BR (☎ **01225/429681**).

THE SHOPPING SCENE

Bath has the finest shopping possibilities outside of London. We'll give you a sampling to get you started. The four floors of merchandise at **Rossiter's,** 38–41 Broad St. (☎ **01225/462227**), might remind you of a very English version of a department store. They'll ship any of the Royal Doulton, Wedgwood, or Spode to anywhere in the world. Look especially for the displays of ginger jars, vases, and clocks manufactured by Moorcroft, and perfumes by London-based Floris.

The most charming and unusual emporium in Bath, **Whittard of Chelsea,** 14 Union Passage (☎ **01225/447787**), supplies everything you'll need to duplicate the dearly held tea-drinking ritual. If you want a quite exotic tea to wow your friends back home, ask for Monkey-Picked Oolong, a Chinese tea from plants so difficult to reach that leaves can be gathered only by trained monkeys.

Walcot Reclamation, 108 Walcot St. (☎ **01225/444404**), is a sprawling and dusty storeroom selling 19th-century architectural remnants. The 20,000-square-foot warehouse is just northeast of Bath. Anything can be shipped or altered on-site.

The most important gallery of contemporary art in Bath, **Beaux Arts Gallery,** 13 York St. (☎ **01225/464850**), specializes in well-known British artists. The gallery occupies a pair of interconnected, stone-fronted Georgian houses, set close to Bath Abbey. The **Bath Stamp & Coin Shop,** 12–13 Pulteney Bridge (☎ **01225/463073**), is the largest purveyor of antique coins and stamps in Bath, with hundreds of odd or unusual numismatics from throughout England and its former empire. Look also for antique Venetian glass and a scattering of English antiques.

BATH AFTER DARK

Theatre Royal, next to the new Seven Dials development at Sawclose (☎ **01225/448844;** for credit-card bookings, call 01225/448861), was restored in 1982 and refurbished with plush seats, red carpets, and a painted proscenium and ceiling. Now the most beautiful theater in Britain, it has 940 seats, a small pit and grand tiers rising to the upper circle. A **studio theater** at the rear of the main building opened in 1996. The theater publishes a list of forthcoming events; its repertoire includes, among other offerings, West End shows. It operates only 6 to 8 weeks a year. Prices vary, but tickets generally begin at £9 ($15).

Beneath the theater, reached from the back of the stalls or by a side door, are the theater vaults, where you will find a bar and a restaurant, serving an array of dishes from soup to light à la carte meals.

France 6

by Darwin Porter & Danforth Prince

France presents visitors with an embarrassment of riches—no other country concentrates such a diversity of sights and scenery into so compact an area. This chapter explores that diversity: Paris and the Ile de France; the Loire Valley in the northwest with its châteaus and vineyards; Provence, in the southwest, with its ancient culture; and the lush semitropical coast of the Mediterranean, the French Riviera, and the Côte d'Azur.

1 Paris

Today, Paris is in many ways less French and more international. Those Parisians who were born and bred in the city and who have French ancestry have accepted the fact that they may one day become a minority in their own hometown, as waves of immigrants from the far stretches of the former empire, including Vietnam and North Africa, flood their gates. And with the millions of visitors pouring in annually from all over the world, you can no longer separate Paris from its visitors—they have virtually become one and the same.

Legendary Paris style and chic are changing, too. Unless you frequent upscale watering holes, you'll see very few Parisians dressed quite as alluringly and formally as they did a few years ago. Many young Parisians have adopted the casual attire of their American counterparts. And while the old haute couture houses have experienced rough times, pret-a-porter designers are flourishing.

The late president François Mitterrand wanted to leave an architectural legacy to rival or surpass that of the autocratic "Sun King," Louis XIV. Mitterrand's dream was to make Paris the undisputed capital of the European Union. To do that, he virtually painted Paris in gold (well, gilt at least), cleaned the Louvre's facade, spruced up the Champs-Elysées, and ran up a $6 billion tab as he built, restored, and recast. The most famous and controversial of these projects was I. M. Pei's metal-and-glass pyramid entrance for the Louvre, a design selected by Mitterrand himself.

Thanks to Mitterrand, a more glamorous Paris is the stage on which lovers walk arm in arm along the Seine, children scamper about in the Tuileries, cafes fill with animated conversation, and women dance the cancan at the Moulin Rouge.

ORIENTATION

GETTING THERE   By Plane   Paris has two major international airports: Aéroport d'Orly, 13km (8¹/₂ miles) south, and Aéroport Roissy—Charles de Gaulle, 23km (14 miles) northeast of the city. The Air France bus that travels between Orly and Roissy airports departs at 20-minute intervals daily between 6am and 11pm. The trip takes an hour and costs 75F ($12).

At **Charles de Gaulle (Roissy) Airport** (☎ **01-48-62-22-80**), foreign carriers use Aérogare (terminal) 1, and Air France flies into Aérogare 2. The two terminals are linked by a shuttle bus (navette). The **free shuttle bus** connecting Aérogare 1 with Aérogare 2 also transports passengers to the Roissy rail station, from which fast RER trains leave every 15 minutes heading to such Métro stations as Gare du Nord, Châtelet, Luxembourg, Port-Royal, and Denfert-Rochereau. A typical train fare from Roissy to any point in central Paris is 49F ($8). Passengers arriving on chartered flights from virtually anywhere tend to arrive at Terminal T-9, a relatively simple facility without the architectural drama of either of the other two aérogares. It lies immediately adjacent to the RER station, a short walk from Aérogare 1, and as such, is accessible via the above-mentioned shuttle bus network described above.

You can also take an Air France shuttle bus, which departs about every 12 minutes, 5:40am and 11pm, and costs 60 to 70F ($10 to $11), to Palais des Congrès (Port e Maillot), then continue on to place de l'Etoile, Gare de Montparnesse, and Gare de Lyon, where metro lines can carry you to any other point in Paris (trip time: 45 to 55 minutes). Another option is Roissybus, which departs daily 5:45am to 11pm and costs 45F ($7). The bus takes you near the corner of rue Scribe and place de l'Opéra (trip time: 45 to 50 minutes). A more recent service, **Airport Shuttle,** 2 av. Général-Leclerc, 14e (☎ **04-01-43-21-06-78;** Métro: Denfert-Rochereau), will transport you to and from Orly or Charles de Gaulle in a minivan. The cost is 120F ($19) per person or else 89F ($14) if the van is shared.

A **taxi** from Roissy into the city will cost about 300F ($48). From 8pm to 7am, fares are 40% higher. Long queues of both taxis and passengers form outside each of the airport's terminals but are surprisingly orderly.

Orly Airport (☎ **01-49-75-15-15**) also has two terminals—Orly Sud (south) for international flights and Orly Ouest (west) for domestic flights. They're linked by a free shuttle bus. **Air France buses** leave from Exit H of Orly Sud and from Exit D of Orly Ouest every 12 minutes, 5:45am and 11pm, heading for Gare de Montparnasse and Gare des Invalides. The fare for the trip is 45F ($7). At Exit J arrival level in Orly Ouest and Exit H, Platform 4, in Orly Sud, you can board an **Orly bus** to Denfert-Rochereau in central Paris. Expect to pay 30F ($4.80).

An alternative method for reaching central Paris involves taking a combination of conveyances that includes a monorail (**Orly Val**) to the nearby RER station of Anthony, then the RER train into downtown Paris. The Orly Val makes stops at both the north and the south terminals, then continues at 8-minute intervals for the 10-minute ride to the Anthony RER station. The fare, 57F ($9) each way, seems relatively expensive but offsets the horrendous construction costs of a monorail that sails above the congested roadways encircling the airport. At Anthony, RER trains (line B) make the 30-minute ride into the city for 8F ($1.30) extra per person.

A taxi from Orly to the center of Paris costs about 225F ($36), more at night. Don't take a meterless taxi from Orly Sud or Orly Ouest—it's much safer and usually cheaper to hire a metered cab from the lines, which are under the scrutiny of a police officer.

Returning to the airport, buses leave the Invalides terminal heading either to Orly Sud or Orly Ouest every 15 minutes (trip time: 30 minutes).

By Train   There are six major train stations in Paris: **Gare d'Austerlitz,** 55 quai d'Austerlitz, 13e (servicing the southwest with trains to the Loire Valley, the Bordeaux country, and the Pyrénées); **Gare de l'Est,** place du 11-Novembre-1918, 10e (servicing the east, with trains to Strasbourg, Nancy, Reims, and beyond to Zurich, Basel, Luxembourg, and Austria); **Gare de Lyon,** 20 bd. Diderot, 12e (servicing the southeast with trains to the Côte d'Azur, Provence, and beyond to Geneva, Lausanne, and Italy); **Gare de Montparnasse,** 17 bd. Vaugirard, 15e (servicing the west with trains to Brittany); **Gare du Nord,** 18 rue de Dunkerque, 15e (servicing the north with trains to Holland, Denmark, Belgium, and the north of Germany); and **Gare St-Lazare,** 13 rue d'Amsterdam, 8e (servicing the northwest with trains to Normandy and London).

For **general train information,** or to make reservations, call ☎ **08-36-35-35-35** if your destination takes you from Paris to anywhere else in France or Europe. If your ride will be limited to Paris and its suburbs, call ☎ **01-53-90-20-20** instead.

Buses operate between the stations, and each of these stations has a Métro stop. Taxis are also available at every station at designated stands. *Note:* The stations and surrounding areas are usually seedy and are frequented by pickpockets, hustlers, hookers, and drug addicts. Be alert, especially at night.

By Bus   Most buses arrive at **Gare Routière Internationale du Paris-Gallieni,** 28 av. du Général-de-Gaulle, Bagnolet (☎ **08-36-69-52-52;** Métro: Gallieni). Bagnolet is a 35-minute Métro ride from central Paris.

By Car   Driving a car in Paris is definitely *not* recommended. Parking is difficult and traffic dense. If you do drive, remember that Paris is encircled by a ring road called the *périphérique.* The major highways into Paris are the **A-1** from the north (Great Britain and Benelux); the **A-13** from Rouen, Normandy, and other points of northwest France; the **A-109** from Spain, the Pyrénées, and the southwest; the **A-7** from the French Alps, the Riviera, and Italy; and the **A-4** from eastern France.

VISITOR INFORMATION   The city's main **tourist information office** is at 127 av. des Champs-Elysées, 8e (☎ **08-36-68-31-12**), where you can secure information about both Paris and its provinces. The office is open daily April to October, 9am to 8pm (closed May 1); November to March, 11am to 6pm (closed December 25). Although the above-mentioned address is the largest tourist information post in the city, it's supplemented with an additional branch in the base of the Eiffel Tower (open only May to October, Monday to Saturday, 8am to 8pm), and within the arrivals hall of the Gare de Lyon (Monday to Saturday, 8am to 8pm). Any of the above-mentioned tourist offices will give you free copies of 50-page English-language leaflets *Time Out* and *Paris Users' Guide.*

CITY LAYOUT

Paris is surprisingly compact. Occupying slightly more land space than San Francisco, it's home to more than 10 million people. The River Seine divides Paris into the **Right Bank (Rive Droite)** to the north and the **Left Bank (Rive Gauche)** to the south. These designations make sense when you stand on a bridge and face downstream, watching the waters flow out toward the sea—to your right is the north bank; to your left the south. Thirty-two bridges link the Right Bank and the Left Bank, some providing access to the two small islands at the heart of the city, **Ile de la Cité**—the city's birthplace and site of Notre-Dame—and **Ile St-Louis,** a moat-guarded oasis of sober 17th-century mansions.

Between 1860 and 1870, Baron Georges-Eugène Haussmann, at the orders of Napoléon III, forever changed the look of Paris by creating the legendary *grands*

A Map Note

See the inside back cover of this guide for a map of the Paris Métro.

---

boulevards: St-Michel, St-Germain, Haussmann, Sébastopol, Magenta, Voltaire, and Strasbourg.

The "main street" on the Right Bank is the **avenue des Champs-Elysées,** beginning at the Arc de Triomphe and running to **place de la Concorde.** Haussmann also created avenue de l'Opéra and the 12 avenues that radiate starlike from the Arc de Triomphe, giving it its original name, place de l'Etoile (*étoile* means "star"). It was renamed place Charles-de-Gaulle following the general's death; today it's often referred to as **place Charles-de-Gaulle-Etoile.**

ARRONDISSEMENTS IN BRIEF   The heart of medieval Paris was the **Ile de la Cité** and the areas immediately surrounding it. As Paris grew it absorbed many of the once-distant villages, and even today each of these *arrondissements* (districts) retains a distinct character. They're numbered from 1 to 20 starting at the center around the Louvre and progressing in a clockwise spiral. The key to finding any address in Paris is looking for the arrondissement number, rendered either as a number followed by "e" or "er" (1er, 2e, and so on). If the address is written out more formally, you can tell what arrondissement it's in by looking at the postal code. For example, the address may be written with the street name then "75014 Paris." The last two digits, 14, indicate that the address is in the 14th arrondissement, Montparnasse.

On the Right Bank, the **1er** is home to the Musée du Louvre, place Vendôme, rues de Rivoli and St-Honoré, Palais Royal, and Comédie-Française—an area filled with grand institutions and grand stores; at the center of the **2e** is the Bourse (stock exchange), making it the city's financial center; most of the **3e** and the **4e** is referred to as the Marais, the old Jewish quarter that in the 17th century was home to the aristocracy—today it's a trendy area of boutiques and restored mansions as well as the center of Paris's gay and lesbian community. On the Left Bank, the **5e** is known as the Latin Quarter, home to the Sorbonne and associated with the intellectual life that thrived in the 1920s and 1930s; the **6e,** known as St-Germain-des-Prés, stretches from the Seine to boulevard du Montparnasse, and is associated with the 1920s and 1930s—as well as being a center for art and antiques, it boasts the Palais and Jardin du Luxembourg within its boundaries. The **7e,** containing both the Tour Eiffel and Hôtel des Invalides, is a residential district for the well heeled.

Back on the Right Bank, the **8e** epitomizes monumental Paris: with the triumphal avenue des Champs-Elysées, the Elysées Palace, and the fashion houses along avenue Montaigne and the Faubourg St-Honoré. The **18e** is home to Sacré-Coeur and Montmartre and all that the name conjures of the bohemian life painted most notably by Toulouse-Lautrec. The **14e** incorporates most of Montparnasse, including its cemetery, whereas the **20e** is where the city's famous lie buried in Père-Lachaise and where today the recent immigrants from North Africa live. Beyond the arrondissements stretch the vast *banlieue,* or suburbs, of Greater Paris, where the majority of Parisians live.

GETTING AROUND

Paris is a city for strollers whose greatest joy is rambling through unexpected alleys and squares. Given a choice of conveyance, try to make it on your own two feet whenever possible.

You can purchase a Paris-Visite, a tourist pass valid for 1, 2, 3, or 5 days on the public transportation system, including the Métro, buses, and RER (Réseau Express Régional) trains. (The RER has both first- and second-class compartments, and the pass lets you travel in first class.) As a bonus, the funicular ride to the top of Montmartre is included. A 1-day pass costs 55F ($9), a 2-day pass 90F ($14), a 3-day pass 120F ($19), and a 5-day pass 175F ($28). The card is available at RATP (Régie Autonome des Transports Parisiens), tourist offices, or the main Métro stations (☎ **01-44-68-20-20** or 08-36-68-77-14).

There are other discount passes as well, though most are available only to French residents with government ID cards and proof of taxpayer status. One available to temporary visitors is **Carte Mobilis,** which allows unlimited travel on all bus, subway, and RER lines during a 1-day period. A 1-day pass costs 32F ($5). Ask for it at any Métro station. The pass is valid only within the 20 arrondissements—not within the suburbs of Paris.

BY MÉTRO   The Paris Métro (subway) runs daily 5:30am to around 1:15am, at which time all underground trains reach their final terminus. (Be alert that their arrivals within the central Paris stations might be as much as an hour before the end of their run.) The Métro is reasonably safe at any hour, but beware of pickpockets. Transfer stations are known as *correspondances.* Note that some transfers require long walks (Châtelet is the most notorious), but most trips will require only one transfer. On the urban lines, it costs the same to any point. One ticket costs 8F ($1.30).

BY BUS   Buses are much slower than the Métro. Most run 7am to 8:30pm (a few operate to 12:30am, and 10 operate during the early morning hours). Service is limited on Sundays and holidays. Bus and Métro fares are the same and you can use carnet tickets on both. Most bus rides (including all of those that begin and end within the 20 arrondissements of Paris), require one ticket, but there are some destinations in the city's suburbs that require up to, but never more than, two.

If you intend to use the buses a lot during your stay in Paris, pick up an **RATP bus map** at their office on Place de la Madeleine, 8e, at any tourist information office, or at RATP headquarters, 52–54 quai de la Rapée, 12e (☎ **01-44-68-20-20**). For detailed information on bus and Métro routes, call ☎ **08-36-68-41-14.**

BY TAXI   The flag drops at 14F ($2.25), and you pay 3.36F (55¢) per kilometer. At night, expect to pay 5.45F (85¢) per kilometer. On airport trips you're not required to pay for the driver's empty return ride. Should you get tied up in a traffic jam and have a long wait, a basic charge of 120F ($19) per hour will be assessed, or 60F ($10) per 30 minutes of waiting time. Tip 12% to 15%—the latter usually elicits a *merci.* For radio cabs, call ☎ **01-49-36-10-10** or 01-42-70-00-42—note that you'll be charged from the point where the taxi begins the drive to pick you up.

BY CAR   Don't even consider driving in Paris, unless you're a battle-hardened veteran of urban guerilla tactics. The streets are narrow and parking is next to impossible.

BY BICYCLE   **Paris-Vélos,** 2 rue du Fer-à-Moulin, 5e (☎ **01-43-37-59-22;** Métro: Censier-Daubenton), rents by the day, weekend, or week, charging 90 to 160F ($14 to $26) per weekday, 160 to 220F ($26 to $35) Saturday and Sunday, and 450 to 600F ($72 to $96) for a week. Deposits of 2,000F ($320) are required. Bikes are rented Monday to Saturday 10am to 12:30pm and 2 to 7pm.

Traveler's Tip

When purchasing Métro tickets, a *carnet* is the best buy—10 tickets for 52F ($8).

BY BOAT The **Batobus** (☎ **01-44-11-33-44**), a series of 150-passenger ferryboats with big windows suitable for viewing the passing riverfronts, operates every day between April and mid-October along the Seine, stopping at five points of tourist interest. You can board at the Eiffel Tower, Musée d'Orsay, Louvre, Notre-Dame, or the Hôtel de Ville docks. Transit between each stop costs 20F ($3.20), and departures are about every 30 minutes from 10am to 7pm.

Fast Facts: Paris

American Express   American Express operates a 24-hour-a-day hot line from its administrative headquarters in the Paris suburb of Reuil-Malmaison (☎ **01-47-77-70-00**). Don't expect to walk in for help, as it's geared only for telephone-related handling of emergencies like lost cards. The day-to-day services, like tours and money changing, are available at affiliates in central Paris. They include an Amex branch at 11 rue Scribe, 9e (☎ **01-47-77-77-07;** Métro: Opéra), and a smaller affiliate at 38 av. Wagram, 8e (☎ **01-42-27-58-80;** Métro: Ternes). Both of the branches are open Monday to Friday 9am to 6:30pm, with money-changing services ending at 4:45pm.

Baby-Sitters   **Institut Catholique,** 21 rue d'Assas, 6e (☎ **01-45-48-31-70**), runs a service staffed by students. The price is 35F ($6) per hour, plus 10F ($1.60) for insurance. The main office is open Monday to Friday 9am to noon and 2 to 5:30pm, and Saturday 9 to 11:30am.

Business Hours   Most **banks** in Paris are open Monday to Friday 9am to 4:30pm; only a few are open on Saturday. The *grands magasins* (**department stores**) are generally open Monday to Saturday 9:30am to 6:30pm; **smaller shops** close for lunch and reopen around 2pm, but this has become rarer. Many stores stay open to 7pm in summer; others are closed Monday, especially in the morning. Large **offices** remain open all day, but some also close for lunch.

Currency   American Express (see above) can fill most banking needs. For the best exchange rate, cash your traveler's checks at banks or foreign-exchange offices, not at shops and hotels. The French franc (F) is divided into 100 centimes. There are coins of 5, 10, 20, and 50 centimes (the latter is usually referred to as a half-franc coin); and 1, 2, 5, 10, and 20 francs. Bills come in 20, 50, 100, 200, and 500 franc denominations. At this writing $1 = approximately 6.16F (or 1F = 15¢), and this is the rate of exchange used to calculate the dollar values in this chapter. The ratio of the British pound to the franc fluctuates constantly. At press time, £1 = approximately 10.18F (or 1F = £0.10p). The euro rate was currently fixed at 6.56F (or 1F = € 0.15).

Dentists/Doctors   For emergency dental service, call **S.O.S. Dentaire** at ☎ **01-43-37-51-00** Monday to Friday 8pm to midnight and Saturday and Sunday 8am to midnight. **American Hospital of Paris,** 63 bd. Victor-Hugo, Neuilly (☎ **01-46-41-25-43;** Métro: Pont de Levallois or Pont de Neuilly; bus: 82), operates a 24-hour medical and dental service.

Drugstores   After regular hours, have your concierge contact the Commissariat de Police for the nearest 24-hour *pharmacie.* You'll find the address posted on the doors or windows of all other drugstores. One of the most central all-nighters is **Pharmacie "les Champs,"** in La Galerie Les Champs, 84 av. des Champs-Elysées, 8e (☎ **01-45-62-02-41;** Métro: George V).

Embassies & Consulates   Call before you go, as they often keep strange hours and observe both French and home-country holidays. The Embassy of the **United States,** at 2 av. Gabriel, 8e (☎ **01-43-12-22-22;** Métro: Concorde), is open Monday to Friday 9am to 6pm. Passports are issued (for $55) at its consulate at 2 rue St-Florentin (☎ **01-43-12-22-22;** Métro: Concorde). The Embassy of **Canada** is at 35 av. Montaigne, 8e (☎ **01-44-43-29-00;** Métro: Franklin D. Roosevelt or Alma-Marceau), open Monday to Friday 9am to noon and 2 to 4pm. The Embassy of the **United Kingdom** is at 35 rue du Faubourg St-Honoré, 8e (☎ **01-44-51-31-00;** Métro: Concorde or Madeleine), open Monday to Friday 9:30am to 12:30pm and 2:30 to 5pm. The consulate is at 16 rue d'Anjou, 8e (☎ **01-44-66-29-79;** Métro: Madeleine), and is open Monday to Friday 9:30am to 12:30pm and 2:30 to 5pm. The Embassy of **Australia** is at 4 rue Jean-Rey, 15e (☎ **01-40-59-33-00;** Métro: Bir Hakeim), open Monday to Friday 9:15am to noon and 2 to 4:30pm. The embassy of **New Zealand** is at 7 ter rue Léonard-de-Vinci, 16e (☎ **01-45-00-24-11;** Métro: Victor Hugo), open Monday to Friday 9am to 1pm and 2:30 to 6pm. The Embassy of **Ireland** is at 12 av. Foch, 16e (☎ **01-44-17-67-00;** Métro: Charles de Gaulle-Etoile). The **Embassy of South Africa** is at 59 quai d'Orsay, 7e (☎ **01-53-59-23-23;** Métro: Invalides). Hours are Monday to Friday 9am to noon.

Emergencies   For the police, call ☎ **17;** to report a fire, call ☎ **18.** For an ambulance, phone the fire department at ☎ **01-45-78-74-52;** a fire vehicle rushes cases to the nearest emergency room. **S.A.M.U** is an independently operated, privately owned ambulance company; call ☎ **15.** For nonemergencies, the police can be reached at 9 bd. du Palais, 4e (☎ **01-53-71-53-71** or 01-53-73-53-73; Métro: Cité).

Holidays   On national holidays, shops, businesses, government offices, and most restaurants close. They include New Year's Day (January 1); Easter Monday (late March or early April, April 16, 2001); Labor Day (May 1); Ascension Thursday (40 days after Easter, May 24, 2001); Whit Monday, also called Pentecost Monday (51st day after Easter, June 12, 2001); Bastille Day (July 14); Assumption Day (August 15); All Saints Day (November 1); Armistice Day (November 11); and Christmas Day (December 25). In addition, schedules may be disrupted on Shrove Tuesday (the Tuesday before Ash Wednesday, in January or February) and Good Friday (late March or early April).

Hospitals   See "Dentists/Doctors" above.

Internet Access   In the Latin Quarter is **Cybercafé Latino,** 13 rue de l'Ecole Polytechnique, 5e (☎ **01-40-51-86-94;** www.cybercafelatino.com; Métro: Maubert-Mutualité), open Monday to Saturday 10am to midnight.

Police   In an emergency call ☎ **17.** The principal Prefecture is at 9 bd. du Palais, 4e (☎ **01-53-71-53-71;** Métro: Cité).

Post Office   Each of the arrondissements of Paris maintains its own postal headquarters, but the one that remains open longer, and which is more centrally located than any other in the French capital is the one in the 1st arrondissement. The **Bureau de Poste,** 52 rue du Louvre, 75001 Paris (☎ **01-40-28-20-00;** Métro: Louvre-Rivoli), is open 24 hours a day for the sale of stamps and expedition of faxes and telegrams, with limited hours—8am to 5pm Monday to Friday and 8am to noon on Saturday—for other financial services such as the sale of money orders. Your mail can be sent to this post office *poste restante* (general delivery) for a small fee. Take an ID such as a passport.

Airmail letters to North America cost 4.50F (70¢); to other European countries 3F (50¢); to Australia and New Zealand 5.10F (80¢).

Safety   Especially beware of child pickpockets. They roam Paris, preying on tourists around such sites as the Louvre, Eiffel Tower, Notre-Dame, and Montmartre, and they especially like to pick pockets in the Métro, often blocking the entrance and exit to the escalator.

Telephones   The country code for France is **33.** All phone numbers in France have 10 digits, and this includes the **area code** (or regional prefix). For example, the phone number for the Hôtel Regina—01-42-60-38-09—contains the area code (01) for Paris and the Ile de France. To make a **long-distance call within France,** you would just dial this 10-digit number. **When calling from outside France,** dial the international prefix for your country (**011** for the United States and Canada), the country code for France, and then the last 9 digits of the number, dropping the 0 (zero) from the regional prefix.

   Public phone booths are in cafes, restaurants, Métro stations, post offices, airports, train stations, and sometimes on the streets. Finding a coin-operated phone in France may be an arduous task; a simpler option is to use the *télécarte,* a prepaid calling card available for purchase at most post offices and Métro stations.

   From a *télélcabine,* using a *télélcarte,* a 3-minute local call will cost around 2F (30¢); a call to the United States will cost around 3F (30¢) per minute. Note that these rates apply to public phone booths; hotels will add surcharges. Télécartes are sold in denominations of 50F to 200F ($8 to $32). Access codes for the major U.S.-based carriers are as follows: To access **ATT,** dial **0800-99-00-11;** to access **MCI,** dial **0800-99-00-19;** to access **Sprint,** dial **0800-99-00-87.**

Transit Information   For information on public transport, stop in at the office of the **Services Touristiques de la RATP,** 53 quai des Grands-Augustins, 6e (Métro: St-Michel), or call ☎ **01-43-46-14-14** for recorded information, in French, about stoppages, subway or bus breakdowns, or exceptionally heavy traffic on any particular bus or Métro line.

WHERE TO STAY

Many travelers with an early morning flight at Charles de Gaulle (or those who arrive very late at night) check into the **Hotel Sofitel Paris Aéroport CDG,** Aéroport Charles de Gaulle, Zone Central at Roissy (☎ **800/221-4542** in the U.S. and Canada, or 01-49-19-29-29; fax 01-49-29-00), doubles from 980 to 1,500F ($157 to $240). International food with French overtones is served at a comfortable first-class restaurant and bar on the hotel's ground floor, and other amenities include 24-hour room service and a swimming pool and sauna.

RIGHT BANK: 1ST ARRONDISSEMENT
Very Expensive
Hôtel Costes. 239 rue St-Honoré, 75001 Paris. ☎ **01-42-44-50-50.** Fax 01-42-44-50-01. 83 units. A/C MINIBAR TV TEL. 2,250–3,500F ($360–$560) double; 5,250–5,500F ($840–$880) suite. AE, DC, MC, V. Métro: Tuileries or Concorde.

Grand style and a location close to some of the most upscale shops in Paris attract high-style fashion types. The five-story town house–style premises functioned as a maison bourgeoise for many generations. Today, everything about it evokes the rich days of France's Gilded Age. Although small, rooms are cozy and ornate, with one or two large beds, sumptuous mattresses, CD player, and fax machine. Bathrooms are fairly spacious, with deluxe toiletries and tub/shower combinations. Each of four dining rooms offers a different decorative theme and overlooks the Italianate inner courtyard.

Hôtel de Vendôme. 1 Place Vendôme, 75001 Paris. ☎ **01-42-60-32-84.** Fax 01-49-27-97-89. E-mail: reservations@hoteldevendome.com. 23 units. A/C MINIBAR TV TEL. 2,800–3,200F ($448–$512) double; 4,500–5,500F ($720–$880) suite. AE, DC, MC, V. Métro: Concorde or Opéra.

Once the home of the Embassy of Texas when the state was a nation, this 18th-century jewel box opened in summer 1998 at one of the world's most prestigious addresses. Although the sumptuous rooms are only moderate in size, you live in opulent comfort here. Most rooms are decorated in a classic Second Empire style with luxurious beds and mattresses. Bathrooms are equally sumptuous, with tub/shower combinations. Security is fantastic, with TV intercoms. The hotel restaurant, Café de Vendôme, features an imaginative cuisine in an austere but elegant setting.

✪ Hôtel Ritz. 15 place Vendôme, 75001 Paris. ☎ **800/448-8355** in the U.S. and Canada, or 01-43-16-30-30. Fax 01-43-16-31-78. E-mail: resa@ritzparis.com. 175 units. A/C MINIBAR TV TEL. 3,600–4,500F ($576–$720) double; from 6,500F ($1,040) suite. AE, DC, MC, V. Parking 230F ($37). Métro: Opéra.

Site of Princess Diana's tragic last dinner, the Ritz is an enduring symbol of elegance on one of Paris's most beautiful and historic squares. Rooms are individually decorated with thick rugs, tapestries, large mirrors, marble fireplaces, double-glazed windows, and brass beds. The spacious bathrooms are among the city's most luxurious, filled with deluxe toiletries, hair dryers, scales, private phones, cords to summon mail and valets, robes, dual basins, deep and big tubs. The Espadon grill room is one of the finest in Paris, and the Ritz Club includes a bar, a salon with a fireplace, a restaurant, and a dance floor. You can order drinks in either the Bar Vendôme or the Bar Hemingway. At ground level is a luxury health club with a pool and massage parlor.

Expensive

Hôtel du Louvre. Place André-Malraux, 75001 Paris. ☎ **800/888-4747** in the U.S. and Canada, or 01-44-58-38-38. Fax 01-44-58-38-01. 222 units. A/C MINIBAR TV TEL. 1,850–2,500F ($296–$400) double; from 3,000F ($480) suite. AE, DC, MC, V. Ask about midwinter discounts. Parking 125F ($20). Métro: Louvre-Rivoli.

Situated between the Musée du Louvre and the Palais Royal, this hotel is quintessentially Parisian. Rooms have double-glazed windows, hair dryers, robes, and trouser presses. Newer rooms have shower stalls but older rooms are fitted with large tubs. Le Bar "Defender" is a cozy hideaway, and Bistro-style food is served in the French Empire Brasserie du Louvre, with outside terrace tables. Services include 24-hour room service, baby-sitting, laundry, and valet; there's also a business center.

Hôtel Regina. 2 place des Pyramides, 75001 Paris. ☎ **800/448-8355** in the U.S. and Canada, or 01-42-60-31-10. Fax 01-40-15-95-16. www.regina/hotel.com. E-mail: reservation@ regina/hotel.com. 120 units. A/C MINIBAR TV TEL. 1,550–2,250F ($248–$360) double; from 2,250F ($360) suite. AE, DC, MC, V. Free parking. Métro: Pyramides or Tuileries.

Until a radical renovation upgraded its old-fashioned grandeur in 1995, this hotel slumbered peacefully in a prime location. Rooms are richly decorated in such French styles as Directoire, Louis XVI, or Art Nouveau. Bathrooms have hair dryers and combination tubs and showers. Pluvinel serves a conservative French cuisine in an art deco ambience of deliberate nostalgia.

Paris Accommodations

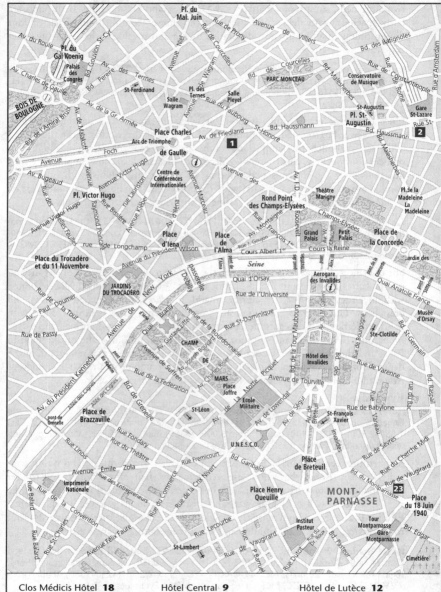

Clos Médicis Hôtel **18**

Grand Hôtel St-Michel **17**

Hôtel Abbatial St-Germain **14**

Hôtel Aviatic **23**

Hôtel Britannique **8**

Hôtel Central **9**

Hôtel Concorde St-Lazare **2**

Hôtel Costes **5**

Hôtel de Fleurie **19**

Hôtel de l'Académie **22**

Hôtel de Lutèce **12**

Hôtel des Deux-Iles **13**

Hôtel des Grands Ecoles **15**

Hôtel de Vendôme **4**

Hôtel du Louvre **7**

Hôtel du Quai-Voltaire **21**
Hôtel Regina **6**
Hôtel Ritz **3**
Hôtel St-Louis **11**
L'Hôtel **20**

Libertel Quartier Latin **16**
Pavillon de la Reine **10**
Résidence Lord Byron **1**

ⓘ Information
✉ Post Office
--- Railway

0   1/4 Mi
0   0.25 Km

Inexpensive

✪ **Hôtel Britannique.** 20 av. Victoria, 75001 Paris. ☎ **01-42-33-74-59.** Fax 01-42-33-82-65. 40 units. MINIBAR TV TEL. 895–1,025F ($143–$164) double. AE, DC, MC, V. Parking 120F ($19). Métro: Châtelet.

Though the 1st arrondissement has far better hotels, the Britannique is a superior value. Rooms may be small, but they're clean, comfortable, and adequately equipped. Centrally located near Les Halles, the Centre Pompidou, and Notre-Dame, the Britannique was completely renovated in 1998. Bathrooms are small but efficiently organized and have hair dryers.

RIGHT BANK: 3RD & 4TH ARRONDISSEMENTS

Expensive

✪ **Pavillon de la Reine.** 28 place des Vosges, 75003 Paris. ☎ **01-40-29-19-19.** Fax 01-40-29-19-20. E-mail: pavillon@club.internet.fr. 55 units. A/C MINIBAR TV TEL. 1,900–2,150F ($304–$344) double; 2,350–3,900F ($376–$624) suite or duplex. AE, DC, MC, V. Free parking. Métro: Bastille.

Opened in 1986, this neoclassical villa blends into an area that was once home to Victor Hugo. Wing chairs with flame-stitched upholstery combined with iron-banded Spanish antiques create a rustic feel. Each well-furnished and traditional room is different; some are duplexes with sleeping lofts set above cozy salons, but all have a warm decor of weathered beams, reproductions of famous oil paintings, and double-glazed windows. Bathrooms are generally roomy, with robes and a hair dryer. In the more deluxe rooms, private safes are also provided. There's 24-hour room service.

Moderate

Hôtel de Lutèce. 65 rue St-Louis-en-l'Ile, 75004 Paris. ☎ **01-43-26-23-52.** Fax 01-43-29-60-25. 23 units. A/C TV TEL. 870F ($139) double; 990F ($158) triple. AE, MC, V. Parking nearby 110F ($18). Métro: Pont Marie.

Going into this hotel is much like walking into a country house in Brittany. Each of the individualized rooms is furnished with antiques. The hotel is comparable in style and amenities with Deux-Iles (same ownership). Many of the rooms were renovated in 1998 and plush French mattresses were added. Bathrooms are small but have hair dryers.

Hôtel des Deux-Iles. 59 rue St-Louis-en-l'Ile, 75004 Paris. ☎ **01-43-26-13-35.** Fax 01-43-29-60-25. 17 units. A/C TV TEL. 870F ($139) double. AE, MC, V. Parking nearby 130F ($21). Métro: Pont Marie.

This 17th-century hotel is the most appealing on Ile St-Louis. The rather small rooms have exposed beams, which lend a sense of old-fashioned charm. The small bathrooms have hair dryers. In the cellar is a rustic-looking breakfast room whose decor was inspired by a medieval tavern, complete with an open fireplace. Visible from the reception area is a glassed-in courtyard whose landscaping can be admired through glass windows, but not entered. Although the Deux-Iles has nowhere near the style, charm, comfort, and grace of the Pavillon de la Reine, it's a lot cheaper.

✪ **Hôtel St-Louis.** 75 rue St-Louis-en-l'Ile, 75004 Paris. ☎ **01-46-34-04-80.** Fax 01-46-34-02-13. www.paris-hotel.tm.fr. 21 units. TEL. 775–875F ($124–$140) double. MC, V. Parking nearby 100F ($16). Métro: Pont Marie.

This small hotel occupies a 17th-century town house romantically positioned on Ile St-Louis. Guy Record and his wife Andrée maintain a charming family atmosphere that's increasingly hard to find in Paris. Hôtel St-Louis may not be in the same league as its major rivals, Lutéce and Deux-Iles, but it's an even better value. We prefer the rooms on the fifth floor (no elevator), which have the most atmosphere and views over rooftops. A full renovation in 1998 updated the plumbing.

RIGHT BANK: 8TH ARRONDISSEMENT

Expensive

Hôtel Concorde St-Lazare. 108 rue St-Lazare, 75008 Paris. ☎ **800/888-4747** in the U.S. and Canada, 0171/630-1704 in London, or 01-40-08-44-44. Fax 01-42-93-01-20. 280 units. A/C MINIBAR TV TEL. 1,450–2,400F ($232–$384) double; from 4,500F ($720) suite. AE, DC, MC, V. Parking 115F ($18). Métro: St-Lazare.

This, the best hotel in the Gare St-Lazare area, sits across from the rail station. In the 1990s the main lobby, a historic monument, was restored. Rooms and bathrooms were recently renovated, redecorated, and soundproofed. Bathrooms have hair dryers. An American bar, Le Golden Black, bears fashion designer Sonia Rykiel's signature decor of black lacquer with touches of gold and amber. Bistrot 108 offers provincial dishes with vintages you can order by the glass.

Moderate

Résidence Lord Byron. 5 rue de Chateaubriand, 75008 Paris. ☎ **01-43-59-89-98.** Fax 01-42-89-46-04. www.escapade.paris.com. E-mail: lord.byron@escapade.paris.com. 31 units. MINIBAR TV TEL. 870–990F ($139–$158) double; 1,390F ($222) suite. AE, MC, V. Métro: George V. RER: Etoile.

Lord Byron, just off the Champs-Elysées on a curving street, may not be as monumentally grand as other hotels of the 8th, but it's a good price performer. No style setter, it's solid and reliable (and maybe a little stuffy). Owner Françoise Benoit has added many personal touches such as framed prints of butterflies and historic French scenes. Rooms are very *hôtel de charme*, with flowery wallpaper, bedspreads, and curtains. Bathrooms are small with tub/shower combinations (or else only a shower) and hair dryers.

LEFT BANK: 5TH ARRONDISSEMENT

Moderate

Grand Hôtel St-Michel. 19 rue Cujas, 75005 Paris. ☎ **01-46-33-33-02.** Fax 01-40-46-96-33. www.123.france.com. E-mail: grand.hotel.st.michel@wanadoo.frweb. 46 units. MINIBAR TV TEL. 890F ($142) double. AE, DC, MC, V. Métro: Cluny–La Sorbonne. RER: Luxembourg.

This hotel is larger and more business-like than many of the smaller town house–style inns that lie within the same neighborhood. In 1997, the hotel was renovated and some rooms enlarged. Rooms have quality French mattresses, private safes, and minibars. Fifth floor rooms (no elevators) have wrought-iron balconies overlooking the surrounding neighborhood, and sixth floor rooms have interesting views over the surrounding rooftops. Bathrooms are small, but have hair dryers.

Inexpensive

Hôtel Abbatial St-Germain. 46 bd. St.-Germain, 75005 Paris. ☎ **01-46-34-02-12.** Fax 01-43-25-47-73. E-mail: abbatial@hotellerie.net. 43 units. A/C MINIBAR TV TEL. 740–850F ($118–$136) double. AE, DC, MC, V. Parking nearby 100F ($16). Métro: Maubert-Mutualité.

Renovations of this hotel have revealed such 17th-century touches as dovecotes and massive oaken beams. Rooms are very much French boudoir in style, with many well-crafted decorative touches. Towels in the small bathrooms are rather thin, but there's a hair dryer. All rooms are double-glazed, and many on the fifth and sixth floors enjoy views over the cathedral of Notre-Dame. Fifth floor rooms have small balconies.

✪ **Hotel des Grandes Écoles.** 75 rue de Cardinal Lemoine, 75005 Paris. ☎ **01-43-26-79-23.** Fax 01-43-25-28-15. www.hotel-grandes-ecoles.com. E-mail: hotel.grandes.ecoles@wanadoo.fr. 51 units. TEL. 530–630F ($85–$101) double. MC, V. Parking 100F ($16). Métro: Cardinal Lemoine or Place Monge.

Few hotels in the neighborhood offer so much low-key charm at such reasonable prices. This trio of high-ceilinged buildings connected by a sheltered courtyard owes its present look to renovations completed in the 1990s. Rooms are artfully old-fashioned with comfortable mattresses and hair dryers. Many offer views of a bucolic garden whose trellises and flowerbeds evoke the countryside. There are dozens of restaurants in the surrounding rue Mouffetard neighborhood, and weather permitting, breakfast is served in the garden.

LEFT BANK: 6TH ARRONDISSEMENT

Expensive

L'Hôtel. 13 rue des Beaux-Arts, 75006 Paris. ☎ **01-44-41-99-00.** Fax 01-43-25-64-81. www.l-hotel.com. E-mail: reservation@L-hotel.com. 27 units. A/C MINIBAR TV TEL. 600–3,000F ($96–$480) double; 1,700–4,000F ($272–$640) suite. AE, DC, MC, V. Métro: St-Germain des Prés.

L'Hôtel was once a 19th-century fleabag whose major distinction was that Oscar Wilde died here. Throughout the building is an eclectic collection of antiques. Rooms vary widely in size, style, and price; some are quite small, others are deluxe chambers fit for the occasional celebrity guest. Regardless of size, rooms have decorative fireplaces and private safes. The relatively small bathrooms are well equipped with deluxe toiletries and hair dryers; however, about half of them are tiny tubless nooks.

Moderate

Clos Médicis Hôtel. 56 rue Monsieur-le-Prince, 75006 Paris. ☎ **01-43-29-10-80.** Fax 01-43-54-26-90. E-mail: clos_medicis@compuserve.com. 38 units. A/C MINIBAR TV TEL. 780–990F ($125–$158) double; 1,200F ($192) duplex suite. AE, DC, MC, V. Métro: Odéon. RER: Luxembourg.

One of this hotel's major advantages is its location adjacent to the Luxembourg Gardens in the heart of the Latin Quarter. You'll find a verdant garden, a lobby with modern spotlights and simple furniture, and a multilingual staff. The warmly colored rooms are uncomplicated and comfortable. Bathrooms are small but have hair dryers. Breakfast is the only meal served.

Hôtel de Fleurie. 32-34 rue Grégoire-de-Tours, 75006 Paris. ☎ **01-53-73-70-00.** Fax 01-53-73-70-20. www.hotel-de-fleurie.com.fr. E-mail: bonjour@hotel-de-fleurie.tm.fr. 29 units. A/C MINIBAR TV TEL. 950–1,300F ($152–$208) double. AE, DC, MC, V. Métro: Odéon.

Just off boulevard St-Germain on a colorful little street, the Fleurie is one of the best of the "new" old hotels. A 1997 renovation upgraded all beds and restored the lobby. Rooms, though generally small, have an 18th-century aura with a mixture of antiques and reproductions, trouser presses, and private safes. Bathrooms are surprisingly luxurious for a hotel of this rating, and have both hair dryers and deluxe toiletries; most have a tub/shower combination, but seven come only with a shower. A spiral staircase leads down to the breakfast room.

Libertel Quartier Latin. 9 rue des Ecoles, 75006 Paris. ☎ **800/949-7562** or 01-44-27-06-45. Fax 01-43-25-36-70. 29 units. MINIBAR TV TEL. 1,050F ($168) double; 1,200F ($192) suite. Nearby parking 100F ($16) per night. AE, DC, MC, V. Métro: Jussieu.

This century-old building in a neighborhood crowded with Quartier Latin color received a radical upgrade in 1997 that transformed the rooms into testimonials to French literature. Proust and Gide used to live here, and the place remains gay friendly. Expect a hardworking and articulate staff and small, cozy rooms. Bathrooms are small but efficiently organized and have hair dryers. Breakfast is the only meal served, but many restaurants lie within the area.

Inexpensive

Hôtel Aviatic. 105 rue de Vaugirard, 75006 Paris. ☎ **01-53-63-25-50.** Fax 01-53-63-25-55. www.aviatic.fr. E-mail: welcome@aviatic.fr. 43 units. A/C MINIBAR TV TEL.

680–980F ($109–$157) double. AE, DC, MC, V. Parking 120F ($19). Métro: Montparnasse-Bienvenue.

The Aviatic is a bit of old Paris—it's been a family-run hotel of character and elegance for a century. The reception lounge, with its marble columns, brass chandeliers, antiques, and petit salon, provides an attractive traditional setting. There's also a modest inner courtyard. Although it doesn't have the decorative style and flair of some hotels in the 6th, it offers good comfort and a warm ambience. The rather small rooms were renovated in various stages throughout the 1990s; each has a safe and bathrooms have hair dryers.

LEFT BANK: 7TH ARRONDISSEMENT
Moderate
Hôtel de l'Académie. 32 rue des Sts-Peres, 75007 Paris. ☎ **01-45-49-80-00.** Fax 01-45-49-80-10. E-mail: aaacademie@aol.com. 34 units. A/C MINIBAR TV TEL. 990–,290F ($158–$206) double, 1,590F ($254) junior suite. AE, DC, MC, V. Parking 150F ($24). Métro: St-Germain des Prés.

In 1998 rooms were renovated with strict allegiance to the 17th-century building's original ceiling beams and exposed stone walls, but with a Second Empire style. Bathrooms are attractive but functional, and have hair dryers. Views from the upper floors sweep out over the historic buildings of the surrounding neighborhood.

Inexpensive
✪ **Hôtel du Quai-Voltaire.** 19 quai Voltaire, 75007 Paris. ☎ **01-42-61-50-91.** Fax 01-42-61-62-26. www.hotelduquaivoltaire.com. E-mail: hotelduquaivoltaire@dial.oleane.com. 33 units. TV TEL. 670–720F ($107–$115) double; 870F ($139) triple. AE, DC, MC, V. Parking 110F ($18) nearby. Métro: Palais Royal–Musée du Louvre.

Built in the 1600s as an abbey, then transformed into a hotel in 1856, Quai-Voltaire is best known for its illustrious guests, who have included Wilde, Baudelaire, and Wagner. Twenty-eight rooms have views over the Seine. In 1998, double-glazed windows were added to block out traffic noise. Rooms tend to be small, and bathrooms are a bit cramped. You can have drinks in the bar or the small salon, and simple meals can be prepared for those who prefer to eat in.

A GAY HOTEL
Hôtel Central. 33 rue Vieille-du-Temple, 75004 Paris. ☎ **01-48-87-99-33.** Fax 01-42-77-06-27. 7 units, 1 with bathroom. TEL. 535F ($86) double with or without bathroom. MC, V. Métro: Hôtel de Ville.

This is the most visible gay hotel in Paris. Rooms are on the upper floors of this 18th-century building, which contains the Marais's major gay bar, Le Central (see below). If you arrive between 8am and 5pm, you'll find a registration staff one floor above street level; if you arrive at any other time, you'll have to retrieve your key and register at the street-level bar. Accessible via an antique wooden staircase that's as old as the building itself, rooms are simple and serviceable.

WHERE TO DINE
RIGHT BANK: 1ST ARRONDISSEMENT
Very Expensive
✪ **Le Grand Véfour.** 17 rue de Beaujolais, 1er. ☎ **01-42-96-56-27.** Reservations required. Main courses 290–550F ($46–$88); set price lunch 345–750F ($55–$120); set price dinner 780F ($125). AE, DC, MC, V. Mon–Fri 12:30–2:15pm and 7:30–10pm. Métro: Louvre-Rivoli. FRENCH.

Dining here is a great gastronomic experience. Specialties, served on Limoges china, include noisettes of lamb with star anise, and lobster. An exciting dish on a menu of delightful surprises is homemade ravioli stuffed with foie gras and served with an emulsion of truffle-flavored créme fraîche. Desserts are often grand, like the gourmandises au chocolat, a richness of chocolate served with chocolate sorbet.

Moderate

Chez Vong. 10 rue de la Grande-Truanderie, 1er. ☎ **01-40-26-09-36.** Reservations recommended. Main courses 100–145F ($16–$23). Fixed-price lunch 150F ($24). AE, DC, MC, V. Mon–Sat noon–2:30pm and 7pm–midnight. Métro: Etienne Marcel. CANTONESE.

This trendsetter, full of folk from the worlds of entertainment and the arts, is the kind of place you head when you're sick of grand French cuisine and grander culinary pretentions. The decor is a soothing mixture of green and browns, steeped in a Chinese colonial ambience. Menu items include shrimps and scallops served with any degree of spiciness you specify, including a superheated version with garlic and red peppers; "joyous beef" that mingles sliced fillet with pepper sauce; chicken in puff pastry with ginger; and a tempting array of fresh fish dishes.

Le Fumoir. 6 rue de l'Amiral Coligny, 1er. ☎ **01-42-92-00-24.** Reservations recommended. Main courses 110–125F ($18–$20). AE, DC, MC, V. Daily for salads, pastries, and snacks 11am–1am; complete menu daily noon–3pm and 7pm–12:30am. AE, DC, MC, V. Métro: Louvre-Rivoli. INTERNATIONAL.

Stylish and breezy, a few steps from the Louvre, this upscale brasserie is the most fashionable place to be seen eating or drinking in Paris today. Within a high-ceilinged ambience of warm but somber browns and indirect lighting, you can order salads, pastries, and drinks during the off-hours noted above, and platters of more substantial food during conventional meal times. Examples include fillets of codfish with onions and herbs; sliced rack of veal simmered in its own juices with tarragon; calves liver with onions; a combination platter of lamb chops with grilled tuna steak; and herring in a mustard-flavored cream sauce.

Inexpensive

✪ **Lescure.** 7 rue de Mondovi, 1er. ☎ **01-42-60-18-91.** Reservations not accepted. Main courses 50–85F ($8–$14); set price 4-course menu 170F ($27). MC, V. Mon–Fri noon–2:15pm and 7–10:15pm. Closed 2 weeks in Aug. Métro: Concorde. FRENCH.

This minibistro is a major discovery because reasonably priced restaurants near place de la Concorde are difficult to find. The tables on the sidewalk are tiny and there isn't much room inside, but what this place does have is rustic charm. The kitchen is wide open, and the aroma of drying bay leaves, salami, and garlic hanging from the ceiling fills the room. Don't expect anything overly thrilling, just hearty fare. House specialties include *confit de canard* (duckling) and salmon in green sauce. A favorite dessert is one of the chef's fruit tarts.

RIGHT BANK: 3RD ARRONDISSEMENT

Moderate

L'Ambassade d'Auvergne. 22 rue de Grenier St-Lazare, 3e. ☎ **01-42-72-31-22.** Reservations recommended. Main courses 88–110F ($14–$18); set price menu 170F ($27). MC, V. Daily noon–2pm and 7:30–11pm. Métro: Rambuteau. FRENCH.

In an obscure district, this rustic tavern serves food derivative of the rib-sticking, hearty, savory cuisine associated with Auvergne. You enter through a busy bar, with heavy oak beams and hanging hams; rough wheat bread is stacked in baskets, and rush-seated ladder-back chairs are placed at tables covered with bright cloths, mills to grind your own salt and pepper, and a jug of mustard. Tried-and-true favorites include a parmentier of blood sausage with fried apples; pork sausages served with *aligot* (mashed potatoes with garlic and Cantal cheese); a *potée d'Auvergne* (stewed pork with cabbage, carrots, and white beans); and fillet of salmon *à l'Auvergnate* that's prepared with lard, bacon, garlic, and potatoes.

RIGHT BANK: 4TH ARRONDISSEMENT
Very Expensive
☺ **L'Ambroisie.** 9 place des Vosges, 4e. ☎ **01-42-78-51-45.** Reservations required. Main courses 320–530F ($51–$85). AE, V. Tues–Sat noon–1:30pm and 8–9:30pm. Métro: St-Paul. FRENCH.

Bernard Pacaud is one of the most talented chefs in Paris, and his restaurant occupies an early 17th-century town house built for the duc de Luynes. In summer there's outdoor seating. The dishes change seasonally but may include crayfish tails with sesame seeds and curry sauce; fillet of turbot braised with celery and celeriac, served with a julienne of black truffles; fricassee of lobster; and one of our favorites, Bresse chicken roasted with black truffles and truffled vegetables.

Moderate
Blue Elephant. 43 rue de la Roquette, 11e. ☎ **01-47-00-42-00.** Reservations recommended. Main courses 85–160F ($14–$26). Set price dinners 275F ($44). AE, DC, MC, V. Sun–Fri noon–2:30pm; Mon–Sat 7pm–midnight; Sun 7–11pm. Métro: Bastille. THAI.

This is the Paris branch of an international chain that prides itself on having the most glamorous, stylish and best Thai restaurant in whatever city they happen to be in. In this version, the decor is an artful version of the jungles of Southeast Asia, with a labyrinth of waterfalls, replicas of garden paths, potted plants, and bridges. Menu items, infused with the lemongrass, coconut milk, coriander, chile, and basil that distinguish Thai cooking, are savory, spicy and full of deep, intense flavors. Try the salad made with a Thai fruit that's larger and more tart than a grapefruit, a *pomelo*, studded with shrimp and herbs; the salmon soufflé served in banana leaves; or the chicken in green curry sauce.

Inexpensive
Brasserie de l'Ile St-Louis. 55 quai de Bourbon, 4e. ☎ **01-43-54-02-59.** Reservations recommended. Main courses 70–120F ($11–$19). MC, V. Thurs–Tues 11:30am–1am. Métro: Pont Marie. FRENCH/ALSATIAN.

This retro-chic brasserie is the perfect place for an impromptu rendezvous. Little about the establishment's patina and paneled decor has changed since it was founded in the 1880s, a fact that adds an allure not equaled in many more modern nearby competitors. Menu items are conservative, flavorful, and well prepared; don't expect cutting-edge culinary fads and trends. Examples include an always-popular version of Alsatian sauerkraut, cassoulet in the old-fashioned style of Toulouse; stingray with a nut and butter sauce; calf's liver; and a succulent version of loin of pork with warm apple marmalade.

RIGHT BANK: 8TH ARRONDISSEMENT
Expensive
Buddha Bar. 8 rue Boissy d'Anglas, 8e. ☎ **01-53-05-90-00.** Reservations recommended. main courses 115–260F ($18–$42). AE MC, V. Mon–Fri noon–3pm; daily 6pm–2am. Métro: Concorde. FRENCH/PACIFIC RIM.

This place is hot, hot, hot—truly the restaurant of the moment in Paris. A location on a chic street near the Champs-Elysées, and allegiance to a fashionable fusion of French, Asian, and California cuisine, almost guarantees a clientele devoted to the whims of fashion. A cutting-edge culinary theme combines Japanese sashimi, Vietnamese spring rolls, lacquered duck, sautéed shrimp with black bean sauce, grilled chicken skewers with orange sauce, sweet-and-sour spareribs, and crackling squab à l'orange. Many come here just for a drink in the carefully lacquered, hip-looking bar, upstairs from the street-level dining room.

⭕ **L'Astor.** In the Hôtel Astor. 11 rue d'Astorg, 8e. ☎ **01-53-05-05-20.** Reservations recommended. Main courses 110–240F ($18–$38); set-price menus 298–580F ($48–$93). AE, DC, MC, V. Mon–Fri noon–2pm and 7:30–10pm. Métro: St-Augustin. FRENCH.

When culinary guru Joël Robuchon retired from his citadel on avenue Raymond Poincaré (see Alain Ducasse, below) he started dropping in here as a "culinary consultant." L'Astor's current chef is the well-respected Eric Lecerf, who has created his own specialties, such as roasted and braised rack of lamb and a galette of scallops with sea urchins; but those dishes invented by and forever associated with Robuchon are still on the menu. These include truffle tart, Bresse chicken with truffles and macaroni, and a gelée of caviar with cauliflower cream sauce.

Spoon Food & Wine. In the Marignan-Elysée Hotel, 14 rue Marignan, 8e. ☎ **01-40-76-34-44.** Reservations required. Appetizers, main courses, vegetable side dishes each 70–180F ($11–$29). Mon–Fri noon–2:30pm and 7–11:30pm. AE, DC, MC, V. Metro: Franklin-D-Roosevelt. INTERNATIONAL.

Alain Ducasse's newest restaurant has been both praised and condemned by Parisian food critics. Surreal, a bit absurd, the hypermodern, claustrophobic dining room evokes Paris and California. The cuisine roams the world, there are American classics such as macaroni and cheese (rather bland), and barbecued ribs, as well as dishes from Italy, Latin America, and Asia. Some dishes are more successful than others (try the steamed lobster with mango chutney, a real winner). You have great leeway in creating your own meal; for a "vegetable garden," you can mix and match 15 ingredients, including iceberg lettuce, and for the one basic pasta you have a selection of five sauces.

Moderate

Androuët. 6 rue Arsene Houssaye, 8e. ☎ **01-42-89-95-00.** Reservations required. Main courses 95–280F ($15–$45); set-price menus 140–230F ($22–$37) at lunch, 250–300F ($40–$48) at dinner; *dégustation des fromages* 300F ($48). DC, MC, V. Mon–Fri noon–2:30pm and Mon–Sat 7:30–11pm. Métro: Charles de Gaulle–Etoile. FRENCH.

Androuët isn't merely chic—it's an institution whose trademark involves combining top-notch, traditional French ingredients with cheeses and cheese sauces from throughout the country. Choices include noisettes of lamb with a Saint-Marcellin sauce (a goat cheese from France's southwest); lobster with Roquefort sauce; sea bass with a soft and sweet *gratte paille* from the Ile de France, and fillet steak with Roquefort sauce, flambéed with Calvados. Dishes, if you prefer, can be prepared without cheese as well.

RIGHT BANK: 9TH & 10TH ARRONDISSEMENTS
Moderate

⭕ **Au Petit Riche.** 25 rue Le Peletier, 9e. ☎ **01-47-70-68-68.** Reservations recommended. Main courses 92–135F ($15–$22); set price lunches 165F ($26); set price dinner 140–180F ($22–$29). AE, MC, V. Mon–Sat noon–2:15pm and 7pm–midnight. Métro: Le Peletier or Richelieu-Drouot. LOIRE VALLEY (ANJOU).

This bistro serves up simple well-prepared food and a sense of nostalgia. You'll be ushered to one of five different "compartments," each of which was crafted for maximum intimacy, with red velour banquettes, ceilings painted with allegorical themes, and accents of brass and frosted glass. The wine list favors Loire Valley vintages that go well with such dishes as *rillettes* and *rillons* (potted fish or meat, especially pork) in an aspic of Vouvray wine; a platter of poached fish with a buttery white wine sauce; seasonal game dishes; and duck breast with green peppercorns.

Brasserie Flo. 7 cour des Petites-Ecuries, 10e. ☎ **01-47-70-13-59.** Reservations recommended. Main courses 90–168F ($14–$27); set price lunch 138F ($22); set price dinner 189F ($30); set price late-night supper (after 10pm) 142F ($23). AE, DC, MC, V. Daily noon–3pm and 7pm–1:30am. Métro: Château d'Eau or Strasbourg–St-Denis. ALSATIAN.

This restaurant is remote and a bit hard to find, but once you arrive (after walking through passageway after passageway), you'll see that fin-de-siècle Paris lives on. The restaurant was established in 1860 and has changed its decor very little since. The house specialty is *la formidable choucroute* (a heaping mound of sauerkraut surrounded by boiled ham, bacon, and sausage) for two. It's bountiful in the best tradition of Alsace. The onion soup and sole meunière are always good, as is the warm foie gras and guinea hen with lentils. Look for the *plats du jour* (plates of the day), ranging from roast pigeon to fricassee of veal with sorrel.

16TH ARRONDISSEMENT
Very Expensive

✪ **Alain Ducasse.** 59 av. Raymond Poincaré, 16e. ☎ **01-47-27-12-27.** Reservations 2 months in advance. Main courses 350–500F ($56–$80); set lunch 480F ($77); set dinner 950–1,490F ($152–$238). AE, DC, MC, V. Mon–Fri 12:15–2pm and 7:45–10pm. Métro: Trocadéro. FRENCH/MEDITERRANEAN.

In the jaded culinary landscape of Paris, the celebrated Ducasse spends hours trying to inject new culinary ideas into the restaurant scene. Food has been rarefied to the point where it's so experimental it appears almost hallucinogenic. Examples from the menus include half-dried pasta, creamed and studded with truffles, enriched with sweetbreads and the crest and kidneys of a rooster, slices of crispy lard served with caramelized potatoes, pig's head salad, bitter herbs, and truffles (believe it or not, this is all one dish); monkfish with endive and essence of truffles; and chilled crayfish served in a reduction of its own juices and caviar. The food remains sober in presentation, true, precise, and authentic in its flavor. On the ground floor of the restored four-story mansion is a bar stocked with rare brandies and fine cigars.

LEFT BANK: 5TH ARRONDISSEMENT
Very Expensive

La Tour d'Argent. 15–17 quai de la Tournelle, 5e. ☎ **01-43-54-23-31.** Reservations required 2 months in advance. Main courses 250–600F ($40–$96); set price lunch 350F ($56). AE, DC, MC, V. Tues–Sun noon–2:30pm and 7:30–9:30pm. Métro: Maubert-Mutualité or Pont Marie. FRENCH.

From La Tour d'Argent, a national institution, the view over the Seine and the apse of Notre-Dame is panoramic. Although this penthouse restaurant's long-established reputation as "the best" in Paris has long since faded, dining at this temple of gastronomy remains an unsurpassed theatrical event. The restaurant became famous when it was owned by Frédéric Delair, who began issuing certificates to diners who ordered the house specialty, pressed duck (*caneton*)—it's sensational. A new, lighter dish that is divinely refined is asparagus and lobster in puff pastry. You might also try fillet of sole cardinal with a mousse of pike-perch and a crayfish sauce or fillet Tour d'Argent with a chive sauce and a slice of warm foie gras resting atop the perfect piece of fillet of beef.

Inexpensive

Al Dar. 8 rue Frédéric Sauton, 5e. ☎ **01-43-25-17-15.** Reservations recommended. Main courses 85–92F ($14–$15). AE, DC, MC, V. Daily noon–midnight. Métro: Maubert-Mutualité. LEBANESE.

This well-respected restaurant works hard to promote Lebanon's savory cuisine. In a room lined with photographs of Lebanese architecture and scenery, you can enjoy such dishes as *taboulé*, a refreshing combination of finely chopped parsley, mint, bulgur, tomatoes, onions, lemon juice, olive oil, and salt; baba ghanoush (pulverized and seasoned eggplant); and hummus. Any of these can be followed with roasted chicken; minced lamb prepared with mint, cumin, and Mediterranean herbs; and any of several kinds of tagines and couscous.

Brasserie Balzar. 49 rue des Ecoles, 5e. ☎ **01-43-54-13-67.** Reservations required. Main courses 78–125F ($13–$20). AE, MC, V. Daily noon–12:30am. Métro: Cluny–La Sorbonne. FRENCH.

Opened in 1898, this brasserie is a bit battered yet cheerful, with some of the friendliest waiters in Paris. It enjoys an increasing reputation as a hip and desirable brasserie with a scene of retro charm. The menu makes almost no concessions to nouvelle cuisine and includes steak au poivre (pepper steak), sauerkraut garnished with ham and sausage, pigs' feet, and calves' liver. The food is decently prepared, and who wants to come up with anything new when what has been served for more than 40 years is just fine?

✪ **La Petite Hostellerie.** 35 rue de la Harpe (just east of bd. St-Michel), 5e. ✪ **01-43-54-47-12.** All main courses 59F ($9), set price menus 59–89F ($9–$14). AE, DC, MC, V. Mon–Sat noon–2pm and 6:30–10:45pm. Métro: St-Michel or Cluny–La Sorbonne. FRENCH.

This place has a usually crowded ground-floor dining room and a larger one (seating 100) upstairs with attractive 18th-century woodwork. People come for the cozy ambience and decor, decent French country cooking, polite service, and excellent prices. The set price menu might feature favorites like *coq au vin* (chicken cooked in wine), *canard* (duckling) *à l'orange*, or *entrecôte à la moutarde* (steak with mustard sauce). Start with onion soup or stuffed mussels and finish with cheese or salad and peach Melba or apple tart. The menu and everything else remains virtually unchanged year after year.

LEFT BANK: 6TH ARRONDISSEMENT
Expensive
Jacques Cagna. 14 rue des Grands-Augustins, 6e. ☎ **01-43-26-49-39.** Reservations required. Main courses 180–350F ($29–$56); set price menu 270F ($43) at lunch, 490F ($78) at dinner. AE, DC, MC, V. Tues–Fri noon–2pm and Mon–Sat 7:30–10:30pm. Closed 3 weeks in Aug. Métro: St-Michel. FRENCH.

Both the food and the clientele in this 17th-century town house are among the grandest in Paris. Menu items are flavorful and creative. Examples include prawns roasted in a lobster sauce with lemon; and snails "surprise-style à la Jacques Cagna" whereby they're removed from their shells and served with butter within a small roasted potato. A particular favorite of ours involves a chicken from Houdan (an Ile de France town known for its poultry) that's served as a main course in two separate servings: The first part involves the roasted breast *demi-deuil*, in which truffles have stained the white meat dark. The second combines the roasted thigh with garden vegetables.

Moderate
Alcazar Bar & Restaurant. 62 rue Mazarine, 6e. ☎ **01-53-10-19-99.** Reservations recommended. Set price lunches 140–160F ($22–$26); Main courses 95–160F ($15–$26). AE, DC, MC, V. Daily noon–5:30pm and 7pm–1am. Métro: Odéon. FRENCH.

One of Paris' newest high-profile, high-style brasseries deluxe is this artfully hi-tech establishment. It features an all-white, futuristic decor within a large, street-level dining room and a busy and hyper-stylish bar one floor above. Especially good dishes include grilled entrecôte with béarnaise sauce and fried potatoes; Charolais duckling with honey and spices; sashimi and sushi with lime; fillet of monkfish with saffron in puff pastry; and a comprehensive collection of shellfish and oysters from the waters of Brittany. Wines are stylish and diverse; and the clientele includes lots of trendsetters wearing lots of black.

Inexpensive

Crémerie-Restaurant Polidor. 41 rue Monsieur-le-Prince, 6e. ☎ **01-43-26-95-34.** Reservations not accepted. Main courses 40–75F ($6–$12); set price lunch (Mon–Fri) 55–110F ($9–$18); set price dinner 110F ($18). No credit cards. Mon–Sat noon–2:30pm and 7pm–12:30am, Sun noon–2:30pm and 7–11pm. Métro: Odéon. FRENCH.

Frequented by students and artists, this is one of the Left Bank's most established literary bistros, and has changed little since opening in 1930. Lace curtains and brass hat racks, drawers in the back where repeat customers lock up their cloth napkins, and clay water pitchers add to the old-fashioned atmosphere. Food is traditional: pumpkin soup, snails from Burgundy, veal in white sauce, confit of duckling, and a supremely old-fashioned holdover from the France of yesterday—roasted guinea fowl with cabbage and ham. The *"crémerie"* of its name refers to its specialty, frosted crème desserts.

LEFT BANK: 7TH ARRONDISSEMENT

Expensive

✪ **Le Violon d'Ingres.** 135 rue St-Dominique, 7e. ☎ **01-45-55-15-05.** Fax 01-45-55-48-42. Reservations required. Main courses 130–190F ($21–$30); fixed-price menu 240–400F ($38–$64) lunch, 490F ($78) at dinner. AE, MC, V. Tues–Sat noon–2:30pm and 7–10:30pm. Métro: Ecole Militaire. FRENCH.

For a chance to experience chef/owner Christian Constant's gastronomic masterpieces, you have to reserve a table a minimum of 3 to 4 days in advance. Those who are fortunate enough to dine in the Violin's warm atmosphere of rose-colored wood, soft cream walls, and elegant chintz fabrics patterned with old English tea roses always rave about the cleverly artistic dishes. They range from a starter of panfried foie gras with gingerbread and spinach salad to more elegant main courses such as lobster ravioli with crushed vine-ripened tomatoes, roasted veal in a light and creamy milk sauce served with tender spring vegetables, or even a selection from the popular rôtisserie, like spit-roasted leg of lamb rubbed with fresh garlic and thyme. Even his familiar dishes seem new at each tasting. Chef Constant keeps a copious and well-chosen selection of wine to accompany his overwhelmingly satisfying meals. The service is charming and discreet.

Moderate

La Petite Chaise. 36–38 rue de Grenelle, 7e. ☎ **01-42-22-13-35.** Reservations required. Set price menus 160–195F ($26–$31). AE, MC, V. Daily noon–2pm and 7–11pm. Métro: Sèvres-Babylone. FRENCH.

This is Paris's oldest restaurant, established by the baron de la Chaise in 1680. The baron, according to the restaurant's lore, maintained a series of upstairs rooms for afternoon dalliances. The "Little Chair" invites you into a very Parisian world of cramped but attractive tables, old wood paneling, and ornate wall sconces. The only option is a cost-conscious four-course set menu with a large choice of dishes. Choices might include marinated salmon with anise and a creamy mustard sauce; a selection of fresh fish and scallops in saffron sauce with pink potatoes; a salad of leeks and country ham with red-beet vinaigrette; a mignon of pork with figs and honey; and a special dessert of roasted figs with pistachios and vanilla ice cream.

Inexpensive

Chez L'Ami Jean. 27, rue Malar, 7e. ☎ **01-47-05-86-89.** Reservations recommended. Main courses 80–100F ($13–$16). Set menu 99F ($16). MC, V. Mon–Sat noon–3pm and 7–10:30pm. Métro: Invalides. BASQUE/SOUTHWESTERN FRENCH.

Cafe Society

In Paris, cafes are catch-all institutions for social rendezvous, business meetings, letter writing, coffee or wine drinking, snacking, flirting, people watching, fashion gazing, and so on. Here's our pick of some of the city's most appealing and interesting.

Brasserie Lipp, 151 bd. St-Germain, 6e (☎ **01-45-48-53-91;** Métro: St-Germain-des-Prés), is known as the "rendezvous for le tout Paris." There's an upstairs dining room, but it's more fashionable to sit in the back room. It's open daily 9am to 1am, though restaurant service is available only noon to 1am. Across from the Centre Pompidou, the avant-garde **Café Beaubourg,** 100 rue St-Martin, 4e (☎ **01-48-87-63-96;** Métro: Rambuteau or Hôtel de Ville), boasts a minimalist decor by architect Christian de Portzamparc. In summer, tables are set on the terrace, providing a panoramic view of the neighborhood. It's open Sunday to Thursday 8am to 1am and Friday and Saturday 8am to 2am.

Fouquet's, 99 av. des Champs-Elysées, 8e (☎ **01-47-23-70-60;** Métro: George V), is the premier cafe on the Champs-Elysées. The outside tables are separated from the sidewalk by a barricade of potted flowers. Throughout, you'll find a decor of leather banquettes, rattan furniture, and a sense of Champs-Elysées bustle. Fouquet's street level is open as a cafe that serves platters of food, salads, tea, omelets, ice cream, and light platters of food every day 8am till 2am. One floor above street level is a comfortable and relatively formal restaurant open daily noon to 3pm and 7pm to 12:30am.

The legendary **Deux Magots,** 6 place St-Germain-des-Prés, 6e (☎ **01-45-48-55-25;** Métro: St-Germain-des-Prés), is still the hangout for sophisticated neighborhood residents and a tourist favorite in summer. Inside are two large Asian statues that give the cafe its name. It's open daily 7:30am to 1:30am. At **La Coupole,** 102 bd. Montparnasse, 14e (☎ **01-43-20-14-20;** Métro: Vavin), the clientele ranges from artists' models to young men dressed like Rasputin. The dining room looks like a rail station but serves surprisingly good food daily 7:30am to 2am.

The **Café de la Musique,** 212 av. Jean-Jaurès, 19e (☎ **01-48-03-15-91;** Métro: Porte de Pantin), lies within the Cité de la Musique—one of the grandest of Mitterrand's *grands travaux.* The site guarantees the presence of a crowd passionately devoted to music. Consequently, the recorded sounds playing in the background are diverse and eclectic. Its red-and-green velour setting has a theatricality evocative of a modern opera house (it was designed by decorating superstars Elizabeth and Christian). The windows overlook the lions of the modern fountains within nearby place de la Fontaine. It's open daily 7am to 2am, and there's live jazz every Wednesday 10pm to 1am.

Ardent fans claim that this is the most authentic Basque restaurant on the Left Bank. You'll dine amid a decor that's as close to an authentic Basque *auberge* (inn) as any other in Paris, with wood panels, sports memorabilia, and red and white woven tablecloths like the ones sold in Bayonne. Menu items include cured Bayonne ham; earthy and herb-laden vegetable soups in the style of Béarn; marinated anchovies and fresh duck liver; confit de canard (duckling), a succulent omelette (*piperade basque*) laden with peppers, tomatoes, and onions.

SEEING THE SIGHTS IN THE CITY OF LIGHT

The best way to discover Paris is on foot. Walk along the grand avenue des Champs-Elysées, tour the quays of the Seine, wander around Ile de la Cité and Ile St-Louis, browse through the countless shops and stalls, wander through the famous squares and parks. Each turn will open a new vista.

SIGHTSEEING SUGGESTIONS FOR FIRST-TIME VISITORS

If you really want to see a lot of sights in a short time, consider taking a 2-hour City-rama bus tour (see "Organized Tours," below).

If You Have 1 Day   Get up early and find a little cafe for a typical Parisian breakfast of coffee and croissants. If you're a museum and monument junkie, you'll already know that two most popular museums are the **Louvre** and the **Musée d'Orsay,** and the three most enduring monuments are the **Eiffel Tower,** the **Arc de Triomphe,** and **Notre-Dame** (which you can save for later in the day). If it's a toss-up between the Louvre and the d'Orsay, we'd make it the Louvre if you're a first-timer; if it's a toss-up between monuments, we'd make it the Eiffel Tower, for the panoramic view of the city. If you feel your day is too short to visit museums, then spend your time strolling—the streets of Paris are live theater. The most elegant place for a walk in Paris is Ile St-Louis, filled with 17th-century mansions. On the **Left Bank,** wander St-Germain-des-Prés or the area around place St-Michel, the heart of the student quarter. As the sun sets over Paris, head for **Notre-Dame,** which stands majestically along the banks of the Seine, and watch the shadows fall over Paris and the lights come on for the night.

If You Have 2 Days   If you explored the Left Bank on your first day, spend your second day taking in the glories of the Right Bank. Begin at the **Arc de Triomphe** and stroll down the grand **Champs-Elysées,** the main boulevard of Paris, until you reach the Egyptian obelisk at the **place de la Concorde.** The place de la Concorde—where some of France's most notable figures met the guillotine—affords terrific views of the **Madeleine,** the **Palais Bourbon,** the Arc de Triomphe, and the Louvre. After all this walking, we'd suggest a rest stop in the **Jardin de Tuileries,** or a long lunch in a Right Bank bistro. After exploring the heart of elegant, monumental Paris, why not go for a walk on the seedy side? Our favorite is a stroll along rue des Rosiers in the **Marais,** a narrow street that's the heart of the Jewish community. After a rest back at your hotel, follow Hemingway's footsteps and head down to **Montparnasse** for a lively dinner.

If You Have 3 Days   This is the day to follow your special interests. Most visitors will want to select the newly opened **Centre Pompidou,** which will eat up most of your day. You might save time to explore the **Musée Picasso** as well, along with some of the trendy art galleries of the Marais. At midday, head for lunch to Paris's oldest and most charming square, **place des Vosges.** Reserve the afternoon for the **Ile-de-la-Cité,** where you can revisit Notre-Dame and see the **Conciergerie,** where Marie Antoinette and others were held prisoner before beheading, and the **Sainte-Chapelle** in the Palais de Justice with its stunning stained glass. For dinner, we suggest a bistro in Le Marais.

If You Have 4 or 5 Days   On your fourth day, go on your own or take and orga-nized tour to **Versailles.** Then head back to the city for dinner and an evening stroll in the **Latin Quarter.** Some of the livelier streets for wandering include the rue de la Huchette and rue Monsieur-le-Prince.

On your fifth day, devote at least a morning to **Montmarte,** the former artists' com-munity perched on top of the highest of Paris' seven hills. Visit the **Basilica du Sacré-Coeur,** for the view if nothing else.

Paris Attractions

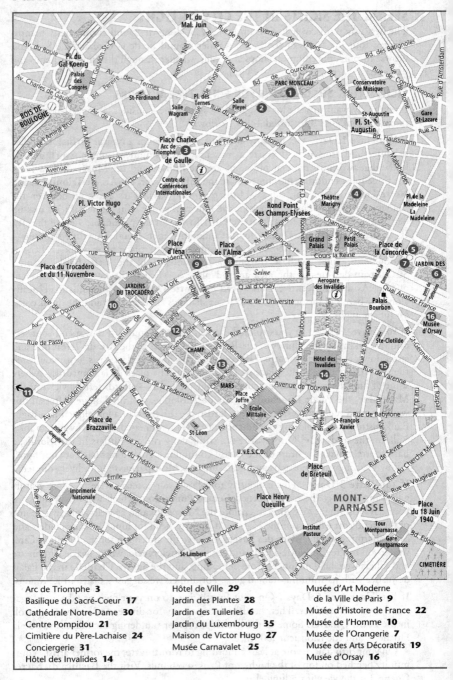

Arc de Triomphe **3**
Basilique du Sacré-Coeur **17**
Cathédrale Notre-Dame **30**
Centre Pompidou **21**
Cimitière du Père-Lachaise **24**
Conciergerie **31**
Hôtel des Invalides **14**

Hôtel de Ville **29**
Jardin des Plantes **28**
Jardin des Tuileries **6**
Jardin du Luxembourg **35**
Maison de Victor Hugo **27**
Musée Carnavalet **25**

Musée d'Art Moderne
  de la Ville de Paris **9**
Musée d'Histoire de France **22**
Musée de l'Homme **10**
Musée de l'Orangerie **7**
Musée des Arts Décoratifs **19**
Musée d'Orsay **16**

Musée du Louvre **20**
Musée National du Moyen Age/
   Thermes de Cluny **36**
Musée Jacquemart-André **2**
Musée Marmottan **11**
Musée Picasso **23**
Musée Rodin **15**

Palais de l'Elysée **4**
Palais du Luxembourg **34**
Panthéon **37**
Parc du Champ-de-Mars **13**
Parc Monceau **1**
Place de la Concorde **5**
Place de l'Alma **8**

Place des Vosges **26**
Place Vendôme **18**
Sainte-Chapelle **32**
St-Germain-des-Prés **33**
Tour Eiffel **12**

Attention Museums Mavens

Le Pass-Musée (Museum and Monuments Pass) is available at any of the museums that honor it or at any branch of the Paris Tourist Office (above). It offers
entrance to the permanent collections of 65 monuments and museums in Paris and
the Ile de France. A 1-day pass is 80F ($13), a 3-day pass 160F ($26), and a 5-day
pass 240F ($38).

THE TOP MUSEUMS

✪ **Musée du Louvre.** Pyramid, 1er. ☎ **01-40-20-53-17**, or 01-40-20-51-51 for recorded
information; advance credit card sales 01-49-87-54-54. Admission 45F ($7) before 3pm, 26F
($4.15) after 3pm and all day Sun; free for children 17 and under. Free first Sun of every
month. Mon and Wed 9am–9:45pm (Mon, short tour only), Thurs–Sun 9am–6pm. 90-minute
English-language tours leave Mon and Wed–Sat at various times for 17F ($2.70) adults and
children alike. Métro: Palais Royal-Musée du Louvre.

The Louvre is the world's largest palace and largest museum. You'll have no choice but
to miss certain masterpieces since you won't have the time or stamina to see everything—the Louvre's collection is truly staggering. People on one of those "Paris-in-a-
day" tours try to break track records to stand with the crowds and see the two most
famous ladies here: the *Mona Lisa* and the *Venus de Milo*. Those with an extra 5 minutes go in pursuit of *Winged Victory*, the headless statue discovered at Samothrace and
dating from about 200 B.C.

To enter the Louvre, you pass through the 22m (71-foot) I. M. Pei glass pyramid
in the courtyard. The collections are divided into departments; those with little time
should go on one of the guided tours (in English), lasting about 1¹/₂ hours.

Our favorite works include *Ship of Fools* by Hieronymous Bosch (tucked in the
Flemish galleries)—no one can depict folly and greed more vividly; *Four Seasons* by
Nicolas Poussin, the canonical work of French classicism; Eugène Delacroix's *Liberty
Leading the People*, the ultimate endorsement of revolution (Louis-Philippe purchased
the painting and hid it during his reign); and Veronese's gigantic *Wedding Feast at
Cana*, showing how stunning colors can be when used by a master. The Richelieu
Wing, inaugurated in 1993, houses the museum's collection of northern European
and French paintings, along with decorative arts, French sculpture, Asian antiquities
(a rich collection of Islamic art), and the grand salons of Napoléon III. In 1998, the
museum inaugurated a site for its splendid collection of Egyptian artifacts, portrait
busts, and sarcophagi, on the ground floor and first floor of the Sully Wing. Also in
the Sully Wing, inaugurated at the same time, is one of the world's largest collections
of ancient Greek ceramics.

✪ **Musée d'Orsay.** 1 rue de Bellechasse or 62 rue de Lille, 7e. ☎ **01-40-49-48-14**. Admission 40F ($6) adults, 30F ($4.80) ages 18–24 and seniors, free for children 17 and under.
Tues–Wed and Fri–Sat 10am–6pm, Thurs 10am–9:45pm, Sun 9am–6pm. June 20-Sept 20,
museum opens 9am. Métro: Solférino. RER: Musée-d'Orsay.

The handsome neoclassical Gare d'Orsay rail station has been transformed into a
repository of 19th-century art and civilization. The museum houses sculptures and
paintings spread across 80 galleries, plus belle epoque furniture, photographs, objets
d'art, architectural models, and even a cinema. One of Renoir's most joyous paintings
is here—*Moulin de la Galette* (1876). Another celebrated work is by American James
McNeill Whistler—*Arrangement in Grey and Black: Portrait of the Painter's Mother*.
The most famous piece in the museum is Manet's 1863 *Déjeuner sur l'herbe (Picnic on
the Grass)*, which created a scandal when it was first exhibited.

⊙ **Musée Picasso.** 5 rue de Thorigny, 3e. ☎ **01-42-71-25-21.** Admission 30F ($4.80) adults, 20F ($3.20) ages 19–24 and over 60, free for ages 18 and under. Apr–Sept Wed–Mon 9:30am–6pm; Oct–Mar Wed–Mon 9:30am–5:30pm. Métro: St-Paul, Filles du Calvaire, or Chemin Vert.

When it opened in the beautifully restored Hôtel Salé (salt mansion, built in 1656 for Aubert de Fontenay, collector of the dreaded salt tax), a state-owned property in the Marais, the press hailed it as a "museum for Picasso's Picassos," meaning those he chose not to sell. The greatest Picasso collection in the world, acquired by the state in lieu of $50 million in inheritance taxes, consists of 203 paintings, 158 sculptures, 16 collages, 19 bas-reliefs, 88 ceramics, and more than 1,500 sketches and 1,600 engravings, along with 30 notebooks. These works span 75 years of Picasso's life and changing styles. The range of paintings includes a remarkable 1901 self-portrait and embraces such masterpieces as *Le Baiser (The Kiss)*, painted at Mougins in 1969, and *Reclining Nude* and *The Man with a Guitar. Note:* Higher admission prices (see above) are charged only during special exhibitions.

⊙ **Centre Pompidou.** Place Georges-Pompidou, 4e. ☎ **01-44-78-12-33.** Admission 30F ($4.80) adults, 20F ($3.20) students, free under 13. Special exhibitions 40F ($6) adults, 30F ($4.80) students, free under 13. Wed–Mon 11am–9pm. Métro: Rambuteau, Hôtel de Ville, or Châtelet-Les-Halles.

Relaunched in January 2000, in what in the 1970s was called "the most avant-garde building in the world," the restored Pompidou Center is packing in the art-loving crowds again. The dream of former president Georges Pompidou, this center for 20th-century art (designed by Renzo Piano) opened in 1977 and immediately became the focus of loud controversy: Its bold exoskeletal architecture and the brightly painted pipes and ducts crisscrossing its transparent facade were jarring in the old Beaubourg neighborhood. Perhaps the detractors were right all along—within 20 years the building began to deteriorate so badly that a major restoration was called for.

The Centre Pompidou encompasses four separate attractions. The **Musée National d'Art Moderne** (National Museum of Modern Art) offers a large collection of 20th-century art. If you want to view some real charmers, see Alexander Calder's 1926 *Josephine Baker*, one of his earliest versions of the mobile. Marcel Duchamps's *Valise* is a collection of miniature reproductions of his fabled Dada sculptures and drawings; they're displayed in a carrying case. And every time we visit Paris we have to see Salvador Dali's *Portrait of Lenin Dancing on Piano Keys.* In the **Public Information Library** the public has free access to a million French and foreign books, periodicals, films, records, slides, and microfilms in nearly every area of knowledge. The **Center for Industrial Design** emphasizes the contributions made in the fields of architecture, visual communications, publishing, and community planning; and the **Institute for Research and Coordination of Acoustics/Music** brings together musicians and composers interested in furthering the cause of music, both contemporary and traditional. Finally, you can also visit a recreation of the jazz-age studio of Romanian sculptor Brancusi **(l'Atelier Brancusi),** which is configured as a mini-museum that's slightly separate from the rest of the action.

More Museum Tips

Museums require that you check shopping bags and book bags, and sometimes lines for these can be longer than ticket and admission lines. Visitors who value their time should leave these bags behind or do shopping afterward. Ask if a museum has more than one coat line; if so, avoid the main one and go to the less frequented ones.

ON THE CHAMPS-ELYSÉES

In late 1995, Paris's most prominent triumphal promenade was augmented with several important improvements. The *contre-allées* (side lanes that had always been clogged with parked cars) have been removed, new lighting and underground parking garages added, sidewalks widened, and new trees planted. Now the Grand Promenade truly is grand again.

Arc de Triomphe. Place Charles-de-Gaulle-Etoile, 16e. ☎ **01-55-37-73-77.** Admission 40F ($6) adults, 25F ($4) ages 13–25 and over 60, free for children 12 and under. Apr–Sept daily 9:30am–11pm; Oct–Mar daily 10am–10:30pm. Métro: Charles de Gaulle-Etoile.

At the western end of the Champs-Elysées, the Arc de Triomphe is the world's largest triumphal arch, about 50m (163 feet) high and 45m (147 feet) wide. This arch has witnessed some of France's proudest moments and some of its more humiliating defeats, notably those of 1871 and 1940. Commissioned by Napoléon in 1806 to commemorate his Grande Armée's victories, it wasn't completed until 1836, under Louis-Philippe. Four years later, Napoléon's remains—brought from his grave on St. Helena—passed under the arch on their journey to his tomb at the Invalides. Since then it has become the focal point for state funerals. It's also the site of the tomb of the unknown soldier, where an eternal flame is kept burning.

ILE DE LA CITÉ: WHERE PARIS WAS BORN

Medieval Paris, that architectural blending of grotesquerie and gothic beauty, began on this island in the Seine. Explore as much of it as you can, but if you're in a hurry, try to visit at least Notre-Dame, the Sainte-Chapelle, and the Conciergerie.

Cathédrale Notre-Dame. 6 place du Parvis Notre-Dame, 4e. ☎ **01-42-34-56-10.** Cathedral, free. Towers 35F ($6) adults, 23F ($3.70) ages 12–25 and over 60. Free under 12. Museum and treasury 15F ($2.40) adults, 10F ($1.60) ages 12–25 and over 60, free under 12. Crypt 33F ($5) ages 27–60, free otherwise. Cathedral daily 8am–6:45pm year-round. Towers, Apr–Sept daily 9:30am–6pm, Oct–Mar daily 10am–5:15pm; museum Wed and Sat–Sun 2:30–5pm; treasury Mon–Sat 9am–noon and 1–5:30pm. Tues–Sun 10am–5:30pm. Métro: Cité or St-Michel. RER: St-Michel-Notre-Dame.

This is the world's most famous Gothic cathedral. From square Parvis, you can view the trio of 13th-century sculptured portals: On the left, the Portal of the Virgin depicts the signs of the Zodiac and the Virgin's coronation. The restored central Portal of the Last Judgment is divided into three levels: The first shows Vices and Virtues; the second, Christ and his Apostles; the third, Christ in triumph after the Resurrection. On the right is the Portal of St. Anne, depicting such scenes as the Virgin enthroned with Child, the most perfect piece of sculpture in Notre-Dame. Equally interesting (though often missed) is the Portal of the Cloisters around on the left.

The interior is typical Gothic, with slender, graceful columns. Over the central portal is the remarkable rose window, 9m (31 feet) in diameter. The carved-stone choir screen from the early 14th century depicts such biblical scenes as the Last Supper. Near the altar stands the highly venerated 14th-century Virgin and Child. To visit those grimy gargoyles (immortalized by Victor Hugo as Quasimodo's hangout), you have to scale steps leading to the twin square towers, rising to a height of 69m (225 feet).

The **crypt** (La crypte archéologique du parvis Notre-Dame), lying under the square in the front of the cathedral has been turned into an archaeological museum, containing artifacts from previous churches that have stood on this site. There are even artifacts from the Parisii who lived here some 20 centuries ago. Excavations carried out in the 1960s unearthed many of these relics. You can also view the foundations of a Gallo-Roman rampart from the 3rd century and the foundations of the Merovingian church from the 6th century. The history of Ile de la Cité is revealed in slides and models.

Sainte-Chapelle. Palais de Justice, 4 bd. du Palais, 1er. ☎ **01-53-73-78-50.** Admission 35F ($6) adults, 23F ($3.70), students and ages 12–25, free for children under 12. Apr–Sept daily 9:30am–6:30pm; Oct–Mar daily 10am–5pm. Métro: Cité, St-Michel, or Châtelet.

Sainte-Chapelle is Paris's second most important medieval monument after Notre-Dame. It was erected in the flamboyant Gothic style to enshrine relics no longer there, including the Crown of Thorns and two pieces from the True Cross. The walls of the upper chapel consist almost entirely of 15 superb stained-glass windows, and viewed on a bright day with the sun streaming in, they glow with marvelous ruby reds and Chartres blues. The lower level of the chapel is supported by flying buttresses and ornamented with fleurs-de-lis—it was used by the palace servants, the upper chapel by the king and his courtiers.

Conciergerie. 1 quai de l'Horloge, 1er. ☎ **01-53-73-78-50.** Admission 35F ($6) adults, 23F ($3.70) ages 12–25 and over 60, free children under 12. Apr–Sept daily 9:30am–6:30pm; Oct–Mar daily 10am–5pm. Métro: Cité or Châtelet.

The Conciergerie has been called the most sinister building in France. Though it had a long regal history before the revolution, it's visited today chiefly by those wishing to bask in the Reign of Terror's horrors. You approach the Conciergerie through its landmark twin towers, the Tour d'Argent and Tour de César, but the 14th-century vaulted Guard Room is the actual entrance. Also from the 14th century—and even more interesting—is the vast, dark, foreboding Salle des Gens d'Armes (People at Arms), chillingly changed from the days when the king used it as a banqueting hall.

ANOTHER ISLAND IN THE STREAM: ILE ST-LOUIS

As you walk across the iron footbridge from the rear of Notre-Dame, you enter into a world of tree-shaded quays, aristocratic town houses and courtyards, restaurants, and antique shops.

The sibling island of Ile de la Cité, Ile St-Louis is primarily residential; its denizens fiercely guard their heritage, privileges, and special position. It was originally two "islets," one named Island of the Heifers. Plaques on the facades make it easier to identify former residents. Madame Curie, for example, lived at 36 quai de Bethune, near ponte de la Tournelle, from 1912 until her death in 1934.

The most exciting mansion is the **Hôtel de Lauzun,** built in 1657, at 17 quai d'Anjou; it's named after a 17th-century rogue, the duc de Lauzun, famous lover and on-again/off-again favorite of Louis XIV. French poet Charles Baudelaire lived here in the 19th century with his "Black Venus," Jeanne Duval. Voltaire resided in the **Hôtel Lambert,** 2 quai d'Anjou, with his mistress, Emilie de Breteuil, the marquise du Châteley, (who had an understanding husband).

THE EIFFEL TOWER & ENVIRONS

From place du Trocadéro, you can step between the two curved wings of the Palais de Chaillot and gaze out on a panoramic view. At your feet lie the Jardins du Trocadéro, centered by fountains. Directly in front of you, the pont d'Iéna spans the Seine, leading to the iron immensity of the Tour Eiffel. And beyond, stretching as far as your eye can see, is the Champ-de-Mars, once a military parade ground but now a garden with arches, grottoes, lakes, and cascades.

Tour Eiffel. Champ-de-Mars, 7e. ☎ **01-44-11-23-23.** First landing, 21F ($3.35); second landing, 43F ($7); third landing, 60F ($10); stairs to second landing, 15F ($2.40). Sept–May daily 9:30am–11pm; June–Aug daily 9am–midnight (in fall and winter the stairs close at 6:30pm). Métro: Bir Hakeim, Trocadéro, or Ecole Militaire. RER: Champ de Mars-Tour Eiffel.

Except for the Leaning Tower of Pisa, this is the single most recognizable structure in the world—the symbol of Paris. Weighing 7,000 tons but exerting about the same pressure on the ground as an average-size person sitting in a chair, the tower was never meant to be permanent. It was built for the Universal Exhibition of 1889 by Gustave-Alexandre Eiffel, the engineer whose fame rested mainly on his iron bridges. The tower, including its 17m (55-foot) TV antenna, is 322m (1,056 feet) tall. On a clear day, you can see it from some 65km (40 miles) away. An open-framework construction, the tower ushered in the almost-unlimited possibilities of steel construction, paving the way for the 20th century's skyscrapers. You can visit the tower in three stages: Taking the elevator to the first landing, you have a view over the rooftops of Paris; the second landing provides a panoramic look at the city; the third gives the most spectacular view, allowing you to identify monuments and buildings.

Hôtel des Invalides (Napoléon's Tomb). Place des Invalides, 7e. ☎ **01-44-42-37-72.** Admission to Musée de l'Armée, Napoléon's Tomb, and Musée des Plans-Reliefs (☎ 01-45-51-95-05) 38F ($6) adults, 28F ($4.50) children 12–18, free for children 11 and under. Oct–Mar daily 10am–5pm, Apr–May and Sept daily 10am–6pm, June–Aug daily 10am–7pm. Closed Jan 1, May 1, Nov 1, and Dec 25. Métro: Invalides, Varenne, or Latour-Maubourg.

The glory of the French military lives on here in the Musée de l'Armée, the world's greatest army museum. It was the Sun King who decided to build the "hotel" to house soldiers who'd been disabled. Among the collections are Viking swords, Burgundian bacinets, 14th-century blunderbusses, Balkan khandjars, salamander-engraved Renaissance serpentines, and American Browning machine guns. As a sardonic touch, there's even General Daumesnil's wooden leg. To accommodate the Tomb of Napoléon—red porphyry on a green granite base—the architect Visconti had to redesign the high altar in 1842. Surrounding the tomb are a dozen amazon-like figures representing Napoléon's victories. Almost lampooning the smallness of the man, everything is made awesome: You'd think a real giant was buried here, not a symbolic one.

At the **Musée des Plans-Reliefs,** you'll find detailed sketches and scale models of the many fortresses of France, beginning with the Middle Ages. It's a subcomponent of the Musée de l'Armée.

IN MONTMARTRE

From the 1880s to just before World War I, Montmartre enjoyed its golden age as the world's best-known art colony. *La Vie de bohème* reigned supreme. Following World War I the pseudoartists flocked here in droves, with camera-snapping tourists hot on their heels. The real artists had long gone to such places as Montparnasse.

Before its discovery and subsequent chic, Montmartre was a sleepy farming community, with windmills dotting the landscape. Since it's at the highest point in the city, if you find it too much of a climb you may want to take the miniature train along the steep streets: **Le Petit Train de Montmartre,** which passes all the major landmarks and seats 55 passengers who can listen to the recorded English-language commentary. Board the train at the bottom of the hill, at Place Blanche (Métro: Blanche), near the Moulin Rouge, and ride it uphill to place du Tertre, within a very short walk of the crest of the hill and its monumental basilica. June to August, trains run daily 10am to midnight (at other times to 6pm). The price of 30F ($4.80) for adults and 15F ($2.40) for ages 2 to 12 allows you to ascend and descend *la butte* within any of the trains, getting on or off wherever you please en route. Ascents and descents of the hill take about 20 minutes each. For information, contact **Promotrain,** 131 rue de Clignancourt, 18e (☎ **01-42-62-24-00**).

The simplest way to reach Montmartre is to take the Métro to Anvers, then walk up rue du Steinkerque to the funicular, which runs to the precincts of Sacré-Coeur daily 6am to 11pm.

Sacré-Cake?

One Parisian called Sacré-Coeur "a lunatic's confectionery dream." Zola declared it "the basilica of the ridiculous." But Utrillo never tired of drawing and painting it, and he and Max Jacob came here regularly to pray.

Basilique du Sacré-Coeur. Place St-Pierre, 18e. ☎ **01-53-41-89-00.** Basilica, free; joint ticket to dome and crypt 30F ($4.80) adults, 16F ($2.55) students and children. Apr–Sept daily 9am–6:45pm, Oct–Mar daily 9am–5:45pm. Métro: Abbesses; then take the elevator to the surface and follow the signs to the funiculaire, which goes up to the church for the price of one Métro ticket.

Montmartre's crowning achievement is Sacré-Coeur, though the view of Paris from its precincts takes precedence over the basilica itself. In gleaming white, it towers over Paris—its five bulbous domes suggesting some 12th-century Byzantine church and its campanile inspired by Roman-Byzantine art. After France's defeat by the Prussians in 1870, the basilica was planned as an offering to cure the country's misfortunes. Both rich and poor contributed money to build it. Construction began in 1873, but the church was not consecrated until 1919. On a clear day the vista from the dome can extend for 56km (35 miles).

IN THE LATIN QUARTER

This is the Left Bank precinct of the **University of Paris** (the **Sorbonne**). Rabelais called it the Quartier Latin, because of the students and professors who spoke Latin in the classrooms and on the streets. The sector teems with belly dancers, exotic restaurants from Vietnamese to Balkan, sidewalk cafes, bookstalls, and caveaux.

A good starting point is **place St-Michel** (Métro: St-Michel), where Balzac used to get water from the fountain when he was a youth. This center was the scene of much Resistance fighting in summer 1944. The quarter centers around **boulevard St-Michel,** to the south (the students call it "Boul Mich").

Musée National du Moyen Age/Thermes de Cluny (Musée de Cluny). 6 place Paul-Painlevé, 5e. ☎ **01-53-73-78-00.** Admission 30F ($4.80) adults, 20F ($3.20) ages 18–25, free for age 17 and under. Wed–Mon 9:15am–5:45pm. Métro: Cluny-La Sorbonne.

There are two reasons to go here: The museum houses the world's finest collection of art from the Middle Ages, including jewelry and tapestries, and it's all displayed in a well-preserved manor house built on top of Roman bathrooms. In the cobblestone Court of Honor, you can admire the flamboyant Gothic building with its clinging vines, turreted walls, gargoyles, and dormers with seashell motifs. Along with the Hôtel de Sens in the Marais, this is all that remains in Paris of domestic medieval architecture. Most people come primarily to see the Unicorn Tapestries—all the romance of the age of chivalry lives on in these remarkable yet mysterious tapestries, showing a beautiful princess and her handmaiden, beasts of prey, and just plain pets. They were discovered only a century ago in the Château de Boussac in the Auvergne. Downstairs are the ruins of Roman bathrooms, dating from around A.D. 200. You wander through a display of Gallic and Roman sculptures and an interesting marble bathtub engraved with lions.

HISTORIC GARDENS & SQUARES

GARDENS   Bordering place de la Concorde, the statue-studded **Jardin des Tuileries** (☎ 01-40-20-90-43; Métro: Tuileries) are as much a part of Paris as the Seine. They were designed by Le Nôtre, Louis XIV's gardener and planner of the Versailles

Gone with the Wind

The most violent windstorm in France's history thundered through Paris on Christmas Day 1999, causing extensive damage to parks and gardens in the Ile de France. At Versailles, the wind toppled 10,000 trees and blew out some windows at the magnificent château. In Paris, Parc Monceau and the Tuileries were the hardest hit, with hundreds of trees uprooted or damaged. At the Père-Lachaise cemetery, the dense foliage protecting the gravesites was destroyed. Minor damage also occurred to Notre-Dame and Sainte-Chapelle. All these places have now reopened for visits and most of the visible structural damage has been fixed, but the difficult task of replanting the thousands of trees will take some time and it'll be years before they return to their lush grandeur.

grounds. About 100 years before that, Catherine de Médici ordered a palace built here, connected to the Louvre. Twice attacked by enraged Parisians, it was finally burned to the ground in 1871 and never rebuilt.

Hemingway told a friend that the **Jardin du Luxembourg** (☎ 01-53-35-89-35), 6e (Métro: Odéon; RER: Luxembourg), "kept us from starvation." He related that in his poverty-stricken days in Paris, he wheeled a baby carriage through the gardens because it was known "for the classiness of its pigeons." When the gendarme left to get a glass of wine, the writer would eye his victim, then lure it with corn and snatch it. "We got a little tired of pigeon that year," he confessed, "but they filled many a void." Before it became a feeding ground for struggling artists in the 1920s, the Luxembourg Gardens knew greater days. But they've always been associated with artists, though students from the Sorbonne and children predominate nowadays. The gardens are the best on the Left Bank (if not in all of Paris). Marie de Médici, the much-neglected wife and later widow of the roving Henri IV, ordered the Palais du Luxembourg built on this site in 1612.

SQUARES   In **place de la Bastille** on July 14, 1789, a mob of Parisians attacked the Bastille and thus sparked the French Revolution. Nothing remains of the historic Bastille, built in 1369. Many prisoners—some sentenced by Louis XIV for "witchcraft"—were kept within its walls, the best known was the "Man in the Iron Mask." When the fortress was stormed, only seven prisoners were discovered (the marquis de Sade had been transferred to the madhouse 10 days earlier). Bastille Day is celebrated with great festivity on July 14. In the center of the square is the Colonne de Juillet (July Column), but it doesn't commemorate the revolution. It honors the victims of the 1830 July revolution, which put Louis-Philippe on the throne.

✪ **Place des Vosges,** 4e (Métro: St-Paul or Chemin Vert), is Paris's oldest square and was once the most fashionable. In the heart of the Marais, it was called the Palais Royal in the days of Henri IV, who planned to live here—but his assassin, Ravaillac, had other ideas. Henry II was killed while jousting on the square in 1559. Place des Vosges was one of the first planned squares in Europe. Its grand siècle redbrick houses are ornamented with white stone. Its covered arcades allowed people to shop at all times, even in the rain—quite an innovation at the time.

The Champs-Elysées begins at **place de la Concorde,** an octagonal traffic hub ordered built in 1757 to honor Louis XV and one of the world's grandest squares. The statue of the king was torn down in 1792 and the name of the square changed to place de la Révolution. Floodlit at night, it's dominated now by an Egyptian obelisk from Luxor, the oldest man-made object in Paris; it was carved circa 1200 B.C. and presented to France in 1829 by the viceroy of Egypt. During the Reign of Terror,

Dr. Guillotin's little invention was erected on this spot and claimed thousands of lives—everybody from Louis XVI, who died bravely, to Mme du Barry, who went kicking and screaming all the way.

For a spectacular sight, look down the Champs-Elysées—the view is framed by Coustou's Marly horses, which once graced the gardens at Louis XIV's Château de Marly (these are copies—the originals are in the Louvre).

HISTORIC PARKS & A CEMETERY

PARKS   One of the most spectacular parks in Europe is the **Bois de Boulogne,** Porte Dauphine, 16e (☎ **01-53-92-82-82;** Métro: Les-Sablons, Porte-Maillot, or Porte-Dauphine). Horse-drawn carriages traverse it, but you can also drive through. Many of its hidden pathways, however, must be discovered by walking. West of Paris, the park was once a forest kept for royal hunts. When Napoléon III gave the grounds to the city in 1852, they were developed by Baron Haussmann. Separating Lac Inférieur from Lac Supérieur is the Carrefour des Cascades (you can stroll under its waterfall). The Lower Lake contains two islands connected by a footbridge.

Parc Monceau, 8e (☎ **01-43-18-70-70;** Métro: Monceau or Villiers), is ringed with 18th- and 19th-century mansions, some of them evoking Proust's *Remembrance of Things Past.* It was built in 1778 by the duc d'Orléans, (or Philippe Egalité, as he became known). Parc Monceau was laid out with an Egyptian-style obelisk, a medieval dungeon, a thatched alpine farmhouse, a Chinese pagoda, a Roman temple, an enchanted grotto, various chinoiseries, and a waterfall. The park was opened to the public during Napoléon III's Second Empire.

A CEMETERY   The **Cemetière du Père-Lachaise,** 16 rue de Repos, 20e (☎ **01-43-70-70-33;** Métro: Père-Lachaise), is Paris's largest and contains more illustrious dead than any other. When it comes to name-dropping, this cemetery knows no peer—it's been called the "grandest address in Paris." Everybody from Sarah Bernhardt to Oscar Wilde is buried here. So are Balzac, Delacroix, and Bizet. Colette's body was taken here in 1954, and her pink and black granite slab always sports flowers (legend has it that cats replenish the red roses). In time, the "little sparrow," Edith Piaf, followed. Marcel Proust's black tombstone rarely lacks a tiny bunch of violets. Some tombs are sentimental favorites—Jim Morrison's reportedly draws the most visitors. Another stone is marked Gertrude Stein on one side and Alice B. Toklas on the other. Open Monday to Friday 8am to 6pm, Saturday 8:30am to 6pm, and Sunday 9am to 6pm (closes at 5:30pm November to early March).

ORGANIZED TOURS

BY BUS   A highly visible option for seeing Paris are the get-acquainted tours offered by **Cityrama,** 147–149 rue Saint-Honoré, 1er (☎ **01-44-55-61-00;** Métro: Palais Royal-Musée du Louvre). The company operates a flotilla of double-decker red-and-yellow buses, each with oversize windows and a series of multilingual recorded commentaries that recite an overview of Paris's history and monuments. The most popular tour is a 2-hour affair that departs from the Place des Pyramides, adjacent to the rue de Rivoli and the Tuileries Gardens, every day at 9:30am, 10:30am, 1:30pm, and 2:30pm. Throughout the year, there are additional tours every Saturday and Sunday at 11:30am, and between March and October, there are additional tours every day at 3:30 and 4:30pm. The price is 150F ($24) per person. Other, more detailed tours are also available. They include a 3¹/2-hour morning tour (Monday, Wednesday, Friday, and Saturday) to the interiors of Notre-Dame and the Louvre, priced at 295F ($47) per person. There are 3¹/2-hour morning tours to Versailles at 320F ($51) per person. and 3¹/2-hour afternoon tours to Chartres at 275F ($44) per person. If you buy tickets for the tours of Versailles and Chartres simultaneously, you'll pay only 500F ($80) for both. And if you're interested in a night tour of Paris as a means of under-standing how the City of Light got its name, tours depart every evening at 10pm in summer and at 7pm in Winter at a cost of 150F ($24) per person.

BY BOAT   A boat tour on the Seine provides sweeping vistas of the riverbanks and some of the best views of Notre-Dame. Many of the boats have open sundecks, bars, and restaurants. **Bateaux-Mouche** cruises (☎ **01-42-25-96-10** for reservations, or 01-40-76-99-99 for schedules; Métro: Alma Marceau) depart from the Right Bank of the Seine, adjacent to pont de l'Alma, and last about 75 minutes each. Tours leave every day at 20- to 30-minute intervals May to October, beginning at 10am and end-ing at 11:30pm. November to April, there're at least nine departures every day between 11am and 9pm, with a schedule that changes frequently according to demand and the weather. Fares cost 40F ($6) for adults and 20F ($3.20) for children aged 5 to 15. Dinner cruises depart every evening at 8:30pm, last 2 hours and 15 min-utes, and cost between 500 and 800F ($80 and $128), depending on which of the set price menus you order. Aboard dinner cruises, jackets and ties are required for men.

THE SHOPPING SCENE

You don't have to buy anything to appreciate shopping in Paris; just soaking up mass consumerism as the true art form the French have made it is enough. Gawking at the vitrines (display windows) will give you a whole new education in style.

THE BEST BUYS   **Perfumes** and **cosmetics,** including such famous brands as Guerlain, Chanel, Schiaparelli, and Jean Patou, are almost always cheaper in Paris than in the United States. Paris is also a good place to buy Lalique and Baccarat **crystal.** They're expensive but still priced below international market value.

Of course, many people come to Paris just to shop for **fashions.** From Chanel to Yves Saint Laurent, Nina Ricci to Sonia Rykiel, the city overflows with fashion bou-tiques, ranging from haute couture to the truly outlandish. Fashion accessories, such as Louis Vuitton and Céline, are among the finest in the world. Smart Parisians know how to dress in style without mortgaging their condos: they head for discount and resale shops. One of the most visible of these is **Anna Lowe,** 104 rue du Faubourge St-Honoré, 8e (☎ **01-42-66-11-32;** Métro: Miromesnil), one of the busiest fashion discounters for women's clothing in Paris, and located within a few steps of the ultra-exclusive Bristol Hotel. Her inventory includes garments by Thierry Mugler, Chanel, Valentino, Givency, Ungaro, and Lacroix from the present or previous season, usually sold at wholesale prices. There's also an inventory of fashion accessories such as belts, shawls, and scarves.

Michel Swiss, 16 rue de la Paix, 2e (☎ **01-42-61-61-11;** Métro: Opéra), looks like the other chic boutiques near place Vendôme. But once you're inside (there's no storefront window), you'll see major brands of luxury perfumes, makeup, leather bags, pens, neckties, accessories, and giftware—all discounted.

Lingerie is another great French export. All the top lingerie designers are repre-sented in boutiques as well as in the major department stores, Galeries Lafayette and Le Printemps.

Chocolate lovers will find much to tempt them in Paris. **Christian Constant,** 37 rue d'Assas, 6e (☎ **01-53-63-15-15;** Métro: Rennes), produces some of Paris's most sinfully delicious chocolates. Racks and racks of chocolates are priced individually or by the kilo at **Maison du Chocolat,** 225 rue du Faubourg St-Honoré, 8e (☎ **01-42-27-39-44;** Métro: Ternes), though it'll cost you nearly or over 500F ($80) for a kilo. There are five other branches around Paris.

Paris Shopper's Secret

For bargain cosmetics, try out French dime store (such as **Monoprix** and **Prisunic**) brands. Brands to look for include **Bourjois** (made in the same factories as Chanel cosmetics), **Lierac,** and **Galenic. Vichy,** famous for its water, has a complete skin care and makeup line.

BUSINESS HOURS Shops are usually open Monday to Saturday 9:30am , 10am to 7pm or 8pm, but the hours vary greatly and Monday mornings aren't full throttle. Small shops sometimes take a 2-hour lunch break and may not open until after lunch on Monday. Thursday is traditionally devoted to late-night shopping, with stores open until 9 or 10pm.

Sunday shopping is currently limited to tourist areas and flea markets, though there's growing demand for full-scale Sunday hours. The big department stores now open for the five Sundays before Christmas; otherwise they're dead on Sundays, too.

The **Carrousel du Louvre,** an underground mall adjacent to the Louvre, is open and hopping on Sunday but closed on Monday. The tourist shops lining rue de Rivoli across from the Louvre are all open on Sunday, as are the antique villages, assorted flea markets and specialty events, and several good food markets in the streets.

GREAT SHOPPING AREAS

1er & 8e Because these two adjoin each other and form the heart of what is Paris's best Right Bank shopping, they really function as one shopping neighborhood. This area includes the famed **rue du Faubourg St-Honoré,** where the big designer houses are, and **avenue des Champs-Elysées,** where the mass-market and teen scenes are hot.

At one end of the 1st is the **Palais Royal,** where an arcade of boutiques flanks the garden of the former palace. At the other side of town, at the end of the 8th, lies **avenue Montaigne** (Métro: Franklin D. Roosevelt or Alma Marceau), 2 blocks of the fanciest shops in the world, where you simply float from big name to big name and in a few hours can see everything from **Louis Vuitton** at no. 54 (☎ **01-45-62-47-00**) to **Inès de la Fressange** (Chanel model turned retailer) at no. 14 (☎ **01-47-23-08-94**). **Ferragamo** (☎ **01-47-23-36-37**) is at no. 45 in one of the most beautiful apartment buildings in Paris. In addition, you'll find fabulous perfumes at **Parfums Caron** (☎ **01-47-23-40-82**). The shop, which was founded in 1904, can be visited at no. 34.

2e Right behind the Palais Royal lies the **Garment District (Sentier),** as well as very upscale shopping secrets like **place des Victoires.** This area hosts a few old-fashioned passages, alleys filled with tiny stores, such as **Galerie Vivienne** on rue Vivienne.

3e & 4e The difference between these two arrondissements gets fuzzy, especially around **place des Vosges**—center stage of Le Marais. Even so, they offer several dramatically different shopping experiences.

On the surface, the shopping includes the real-people stretch of **rue de Rivoli** (which becomes **rue St-Antoine**). Two department stores are in this area: **La Samaritaine,** 19 rue de la Monnaie (☎ **01-40-41-20-20;** Métro: Pont Neuf), occupies four architecturally noteworthy buildings erected between 1870 and 1927. Of special interest are the annual sales that go on here during October and November, when much, but not all, of the merchandise is reduced by between 20% and 40%. **BHV (Bazar de l'Hôtel de Ville),** which was first opened in 1856, has seven floors loaded with merchandise. It lies adjacent to Paris's City Hall at 52–64 rue de Rivoli (☎ **01-42-74-90-00;** Métro: Hôtel de Ville).

Paris's Most Famous Flea Market

The **Marché aux Puces de Clignancourt** (flea market), avenue de la Porte de Clignancourt (Métro: Vanves), has an enormous mixture of vintage bargains and old junk. It's estimated that the complex has 2,500 to 3,000 open stalls. Monday is traditionally the day for bargain hunters, and negotiating is a must (you'll usually be able to find someone who speaks English). Once you arrive at Porte de Clignancourt, turn left and cross boulevard Ney, then walk north on avenue de la Porte de Clignancourt. You'll pass stalls offering cheap clothing, but continue walking until you see the entrances to the first maze of flea-market stalls on the left.

Meanwhile, hidden away in the Marais is a medieval warren of tiny twisting streets chockablock with cutting-edge designers and up-to-the-minute fashions and trends. Start by walking around place des Vosges for art galleries, designer shops, and fabulous little finds, then dive in and get lost in the area leading to the Musée Picasso.

Place de la Bastille—an up-and-coming area for artists and galleries—is in the 4th arrondissement (leading to the 12th), as is the Ile St-Louis. One of the newest entries to the retail scene, the **Viaduc des Arts,** begins at Bastille but technically stretches to the 12th arrondissement.

6e & 7e   Whereas the 6th arrondissement is one of the most famous shopping districts—it's the soul of the Left Bank—a lot of the really good stuff is hidden in the zone that becomes the wealthy residential 7th. **Rue du Bac,** stretching from the 6th to the 7th in a few blocks, stands for all that wealth and glamour can buy. The street is jammed with art galleries, home-decorating stores, and gourmet-food shops.

9e   To add to the fun of shopping the Right Bank, the 9th arrondissement sneaks in behind the 1st, so if you don't choose to walk toward the Champs-Elysées and the 8th, you can head to the city's big department stores, built in a row along **boulevard Haussmann** in the 9th. These department stores include not only the two mammoth French icons, **Au Printemps,** 64 bd. Haussmann, 9e (☎ **01-42-82-50-00;** Métro: Havre-Caumartin; RER: Auber), and **Galeries Lafayette,** 40 bd. Haussmann, 9e (☎ **01-42-82-34-56;** Métro: Chausée d'Antin-La Fayette; RER: Auber), but also a large branch of Britain's **Marks & Spencer** at 35 bd. Haussman, 9e (☎ **01-47-42-42-91;** Métro: Chausée-d-Antin-La Fayette; RER: Auber).

PARIS AFTER DARK

Parisians tend to do everything later than their Anglo-American counterparts. Once the workday is over, people head straight to the cafe to meet up with friends, and from there they go to a restaurant or bar, and finally to a nightclub.

THE PERFORMING ARTS

Listings of what's playing can be found in *Pariscope,* a weekly entertainment guide, or the English-language *Boulevard.* Performances start later in Paris than in London or New York City—anywhere from 8 to 9pm—and Parisians tend to dine after the theater. There are many ticket agencies in Paris, but most are found near the Right Bank hotels. *Avoid them if possible*—usually, the cheapest tickets can be purchased at the box office.

We do recommend checking a few agencies that sell tickets for cultural events and plays at discounts of up to 50%. One outlet for discount tickets is the **Kiosque Théâtre,** 15 place de la Madeleine, 8e (no phone; Métro: Madeleine), offering leftover tickets for about half price for tickets sold only on the day of a performance. Tickets for evening performances are sold Tuesday to Friday 12:30 to 8pm and Saturday 2 to 8pm. If you'd like to attend a matinee, buy your ticket Saturday 12:30 to 2pm or Sunday 12:30 to 4pm.

For discounts of 20% to 40% on tickets for festivals, concerts, and theater performances, try one of two locations of the **FNAC** department store chain: 136 rue de Rennes, 6e (☎ **01-49-54-30-00;** Métro: Montparnasse-Bienvenue), or in the **Forum des Halles,** 1–7 rue Pierre-Lescot, 1er (☎ **01-40-41-40-00;** Métro: Châtelet-Les Halles). To obtain discounts on tickets, you must purchase a carte FNAC, which is valid for 3 years and costs 160F ($26) for adults or 100F ($16) for students.

Those with a modest understanding of French can still delight in a sparkling production of Molière at the **Comédie-Française,** 2 rue de Richelieu, 1er (☎ **01-44-58-15-15;** Métro: Palais Royal-Musée du Louvre), established to keep the classics alive and promote the most important contemporary authors. Nowhere else will you see the works of Molière and Racine so beautifully staged. In 1993, a much-neglected wing of the building was renovated and launched as the Théâtre du Vieux Colombier, specializing in avant-garde productions, with all tickets costing 160F ($26). The box office is open daily 11am to 6pm (closed July 21 to September 5). Tickets cost 70 to 190F ($11 to $30).

Opéra Bastille, Place de la Bastille, 120 rue de Lyon, 12e (☎ **01-43-43-96-96;** Métro: Bastille), is the home of the **Opera National de Paris.** The controversial building was designed by Canadian architect Carlos Ott, with curtains created by Japanese fashion designer Issey Miyake. The showplace was inaugurated in July 1989 for the Revolution's bicentennial. The main hall is the largest of any French opera house, with 2,700 seats. The building contains two additional concert halls, including an intimate room, usually used for chamber music, with only 250 seats. Both traditional operas and symphony concerts are presented. Several concerts are presented free, in honor of certain French holidays. Write ahead to the above address for tickets, which cost 60 to 680F ($10 to $109).

Opéra Garnier (Palais Garnier), Place de l'Opéra, 9e (☎ **01-40-01-17-89;** Métro: Opéra), is the home of the **Ballet National de Paris,** one of the world's great companies, always a leading innovator in the world of dance. This rococo wonder was designed as a contest entry by architect Charles Garnier in the heyday of the empire. Months of painstaking restorations returned the Garnier to its former glory. In mid-1995 the Garnier reopened grandly. Tickets cost 60 to 670F ($10–$107). The box office is open Monday to Saturday 11am to 6:30pm. Additionally, on evenings when there's a performance, it reopens between 6:45 and 7:30pm.

A particularly charming venue for opera on a smaller scale than those that are the norm within either of Paris's major opera houses is the **Opéra-Comique,** 5 rue Favart, 2e (☎ **01-42-44-45-45;** Métro: Richelieu-Drouot). Built in the late 1890s in an ornate style reminiscent of the Palais Garnier, it's the site of such operas as Carmen, Don Giovanni, Tosca, and Palleas & Melisande. There are no performances between mid-July and late August. The box office, however, is open year-round, Monday to Saturday 11am to 7pm. Tickets cost 50 to 610F ($8 to $98).

Another worthy musical venue in Paris is **Salle Pleyel,** 232 rue du Faubourg St-Honoré, 8e (☎ **01-45-61-53-00;** Métro: Ternes). Built in 1927 in a conservative Art Deco style, it's the site of appearances by such organizations as the Orchestre de Paris, the Orchestre Philharmonique de Radio-France, and L'Ensemble Orchestrale de Paris. The box office is open Monday to Saturday 11am to 6pm. Tickets cost 60 to 320F ($10 to $51).

For access to some of the most modern and avant-garde music in France, try the **Radio France Salle Oliver Messian,** 116 av. Président-Kennedy, 16e (☎ **01-42-30-15-16;** Métro: Passy or Ranelagh), site of many of the performances of the Orchestre Philharmonique de Radio-France. A different organization that performs within the same concert hall is the somewhat more conservative Orchestre National de France. The box office is open Monday to Saturday 11am to 6pm. Tickets cost 50 to 100F ($8 to $16).

Of the half-dozen grands travaux conceived by the Mitterrand administration, the **Cité de la Musique,** 221 av. Jean Jaurès, 19e (☎ **01-44-84-45-00** or 01-44-84-44-84; Métro: Porte de Pantin), has been the most widely applauded, the least criticized, and the most innovative. It incorporates a network of concert halls, a library and research center for the study of all kinds of music from around the world, and a museum. Concerts, presented within any of several of the compound's auditoriums, are presented at 4:30pm and 8pm every day except Monday. Tickets cost 80 to 200F ($13 to $32).

NIGHTCLUBS & CABARETS

Since it was established in 1951, ❂ **Crazy Horse Saloon,** 12 av. Georges-V, 8e (☎ **01-47-23-32-32;** Métro: Georges V or Alma Marceau), a sophisticated strip joint, has thrived as a staple on the Paris theatrical circuit thanks to good choreography and a sly, often coquettish philosophy that celebrates and exalts the female form. The theme that binds each of the 5-minute dance numbers together is *La Femme* in her various emotional textures: temperamental, sad, dancing/bouncy, or joyful. Each of the numbers features gorgeous girls, girls, girls, each outfitted in the kind of costumes that support Paris's image as one of the erotic capitals of Europe. If you opt for dinner as part of the show, it will be a tasteful, well-prepared event served with flair at Chez Francis, a restaurant under separate management a few steps from the cabaret itself. Shows last for 1³/₄ hours each, and are attended by men, and to a lesser extent, women. Reservations are recommended. Cover is 450 to 560F ($72 to $90), including two drinks, at a table; or 290F ($46) including two drinks, for standing room at the bar; dinner spectacle (floor show) is 660F ($106). Shows are Sunday to Friday 8:30pm and 11pm; Saturday 7:30pm, 9:45pm and 11:50pm.

The **Folies-Bergère,** 32 rue Richer, 9e (☎ **01-44-79-98-98;** Métro: Rue Montmartre or Cadet), is a Paris institution. Since 1886, foreigners have been flocking here for performances, excitement, and scantily clad dancers. Josephine Baker, the African American singer who used to throw bananas into the audience, became "the toast of Paris" at the Folies-Bergère. The Folies has radically changed its context into a less titillating, more conventional format. It often presents bemused, lighthearted French-language comedies and musicals. Cover is 150 to 350F ($24 to $56); dinner and show 370 to 550F ($59 to $88). Performances are Tuesday to Saturday 9pm, Sunday 3pm. Restaurant opens at 7pm. Box office is open Tuesday to Saturday 10am to 6pm, Sunday noon to 6pm.

Moulin Rouge, Place Blanche, 18e (☎ **01-53-09-82-82;** Métro: Blanche), the establishment that Toulouse-Lautrec immortalized in his paintings, is still here. But the artist would probably have a hard time recognizing it today. Try to get a table, as the view is much better on the main floor than from the bar. What's the underlying theme that drives spectators back to the Moulin Rouge generation after generation? It's an ongoing emphasis on the strip routines and saucy sexiness of *La Belle Époque,* and of permissive, promiscuous Paris between the World Wars. Handsome men and girls, girls, girls, virtually all of them topless, contribute to the enduring appeal that survives despite an increasing jadedness on the part of both audiences and staff. Dance finales usually include two dozen of the belles ripping loose with a topless cancan in a style that might have been appreciated by Gigi herself. Cover including champagne is 560F ($90); dinner and show 890 to 990F ($142 to $158). Dinner is nightly at 7pm, revues at 9 and 11pm.

JAZZ & ROCK CLUBS

Within a cellar lined with jazz-related paintings, with a large central bar and an ongoing roster of videos showing great jazz moments (Charlie Parker, Miles Davis) of the past, **Baiser Salé,** 58 rue des Lombards, 1er (☎ **01-42-33-37-71;** Metro: Châtelet), is an appealing and musically varied club. Everything is very mellow and laid-back, with an emphasis on grooving to whatever form of jazz happens to be featured that evening. Genres include Afro-Caribbean, Afro-Latino, salsa, merengue, rhythm and blues, and less frequently, fusion. It's open daily 6pm to 6am, with music nightly 10pm to 3am. Entrance is free Monday and Tuesday. Cover is 50 to 100F ($8 to $16) Wednesday to Sunday.

Jazz maniacs come to drink, talk, and dance at **New Morning,** 7–9 rue des Petites-Ecuries, 10e (☎ **01-45-23-51-41;** Métro: Château d'Eau), which is now in the same league as the Village Vanguard in New York's Greenwich Village. The high-ceilinged former newspaper office was turned into a nightclub in 1981. The club remains on the see-and-be-seen circuit. Many styles of music are played and performed. Jazz groups from Central and South Africa are especially popular. Sometimes they're open on Sunday. Cover is 100F ($16). Hours are generally Monday to Saturday 8pm to 1:30am. No food is served.

Don't expect any techno, punk, jazz, or blues at **Bus Palladium,** 6 rue Fontaine, 9e (☎ **01-53-21-07-33;** Métro: Blanche or Pigalle). This temple to 1960s-style rock and roll has varnished hardwoods and fabric-covered walls that absorb only some of the reverberations of the nonstop recorded music. Straight singles age 25 to 35 come here. An alcoholic drink will set you back a hefty 80F ($13), except on Tuesdays, when women drink free. Cover is 100F ($16) for men Tuesday, Friday, and Saturday; 100F ($16) for women Friday to Saturday. Open Tuesday to Saturday 11pm to 6am.

DANCE CLUBS

The chic **Les Bains,** 7 rue du Bourg-l'Abbé, 3e (☎ **01-48-87-01-80;** Métro: Réaumur), has been pronounced "in" and "out" of fashion, but lately it's very "in." The place was formerly a Turkish bath attracting gay clients, none more notable than Marcel Proust. Today, it's predominantly straight, with an emphasis on the young, the trendy, and the fashionable, who usually range in age from 20 to around 45. It can be hard to get in if those at the door don't deem you acceptable. Cover is 120F ($19), including the first drink. It's open nightly 11:30pm to 6am.

A popular nightspot in a former bakery with a vaulted masonry ceiling, **Club Zed,** 2 rue des Anglais, 5e (☎ **01-43-54-93-78;** Métro: Maubert-Mutualité), may surprise you with its mix of musical offerings, including samba, rock, 1960s pop, and jazz. Cover is 50F to 100 F ($8 to $16), including the first drink, and it's open Wednesday and Thursday 10:30pm to 3am and Friday and Saturday 11pm to 5:30am.

WINE BARS

The tiny **Au Sauvignon,** 80 rue des Sts-Pères, 7e (☎ **01-45-48-49-02;** Métro: Sèvres-Babylone), has tables overflowing onto a covered terrace. Wines served range from the cheapest Beaujolais to expensive white Bordeaux. To go with your wine, choose an Auvergne specialty, such as goat cheese and terrines. Open Monday to Saturday 8:30am to 10:30pm. Closed August and major religious holidays.

A wide assortment of chic Parisians patronize the increasingly popular ✪ **Willi's Wine Bar,** 13 rue des Petits-Champs, 1er (☎ **01-42-61-05-09;** Métro: Louvre-Rivoli, Bourse, or Palais Royal-Musée du Louvre), in the center of the financial district. About 250 kinds of wine are offered, including a dozen "wine specials" you can taste by the glass for 17 to 80F ($2.70 to $13). Lunch is the busiest time—on quiet evenings, you can better enjoy the warm ambience. Open for meals Monday to Saturday noon to 2:30pm and 7 to 11pm; the bar is open Monday to Saturday 11am to midnight.

GAY & LESBIAN CLUBS

Banana Café, 13 rue de la Ferronnerie, 1er (☎ **01-42-33-35-31;** Métro: Châtelet or Les Halles), is the most popular gay bar in the Marais, a ritualized stopover for European homosexuals (mostly male and to a much lesser extent, female) visiting or doing business in Paris. Occupying two floors of a 19th-century building, it has dim lighting and a well-publicized policy of raising the price of drinks after 10pm, after the joint starts to become really interesting. There's a street-level bar and a dance floor in the cellar featuring a live pianist and recorded music. On many nights, go-go dancers perform from spotlit platforms. It's open daily 4pm to around 5:30am. **Le Bar Central,** 33 rue Vielle-du-Temple, 4e (☎ **01-48-87-99-33;** Métro: Hôtel de Ville), is one of the leading bars for men in the Marais. Open Monday to Thursday 4pm to 2am, Friday and Saturday 2pm to 2am. The club has opened a small hotel upstairs. The hotel caters mostly to gay men, less frequently to lesbians. No cover.

Le Pulp, 25 bd. Poissonnière, 2e (☎ **01-40-26-01-93;** Métro: Rue Montmartre), is one of the most visible and popular lesbian discos in Paris. Outfitted like a burgundy-colored 19th-century French music hall, a new management has made its seedy past a distant memory. Today it's fun, trendy, and chic. It's best to show up before midnight. The venue, as the French like to say, is very cool, with all types of cutting-edge music played in a setting that just happens to discourage the presence of men. Le Pulp is open Tuesday to Saturday midnight to at least 5am. Entrance to Le Pulp is free Wednesday and Thursday, and costs 50F ($8) Friday and Saturday.

DAY TRIPS FROM PARIS: THE ILE DE FRANCE

VERSAILLES   Within 50 years the ✪ **Château de Versailles** (☎ **01-39-24-88-88**) was transformed from Louis XIII's simple hunting lodge into an extravagant palace, a monument to the age of absolutism. What you see today is the greatest living museum of a vanished way of life. Begun in 1661, the construction of the château involved 32,000 to 45,000 workmen, some of whom had to drain marshes—often at the cost of their lives—and move forests. Louis XIV set out to create a palace that would awe all Europe, and the result was a symbol of pomp and opulence that was to be copied, yet never quite duplicated, all over Europe and even in America.

The six magnificent **Grands Appartements** are in the Louis XIV style; each takes its name from the allegorical painting on its ceiling. The most famous room is the 72m (236-foot) **Hall of Mirrors.** Begun by Mansart in 1678 in the Louis XIV style, it was decorated by Le Brun with 17 large arched windows matched by corresponding beveled mirrors in simulated arcades.

Spread across 100ha (250 acres), the **Gardens of Versailles** were laid out by the great landscape artist André Le Nôtre. A long walk across the park will take you to the **Grand Trianon,** in pink-and-white marble, designed by Hardouin-Mansart for Louis XIV in 1687. Traditionally it's been a place where France has lodged important guests. Gabriel, the designer of place de la Concorde in Paris, built the **Petit Trianon** in 1768 for Louis XV; its construction was inspired by Mme de Pompadour, who died before it was completed. In time, Marie Antoinette adopted it as her favorite residence.

May 2 to September 30, the palace is open Tuesday to Sunday 9am to 6pm (to 5pm the rest of the year). The grounds are open daily dawn to dusk. Admission to the palace is 45F ($7) for adults, 35F ($6) for those 18 to 25, and free for those under 18 and over 60. Admission to the Grand Trianon is 25F ($4) for adults, 15F ($2.40) for those 18 to 25, and free for those under 18. Admission to the Petit Trianon is 15F ($2.40) for adults, 10F ($1.60) for those 18 to 25, and under 18 free. Admission to both Trianons is 30F ($4.80) for adults, 20F ($3.20) for those 18 to 25, and free for those under 18. Adults pay the reduced rates for all attractions after 3:30pm.

Getting There   To get to Versailles, 21km (13 miles) southwest of Paris, catch the RER line C at the Gare d'Austerlitz, St-Michel, Musée d'Orsay, Invalides, Pont-de-l'Alma, Champ-de-Mars, or Javel station and take it to the Versailles Rive Gauche station(trip time: 35 to 40 minutes). From there you can take a shuttle bus or walk to the château. The fare is 35F ($6); Eurailpass holders travel free on the train, but pay 20F ($3.20) for a ride on the shuttle bus. Regular SNCF trains also make the run from Paris to Versailles: One train departs from the Gare St-Lazare for the Versailles Rive Droite RER station; another departs from the Gare Montparnasse for Versailles Chantiers station. From there it's a 15-minute walk from the château or you can take bus B to the Château for 8F ($1.30).

As a final resort you can always go via a combination of Métro and city bus. Travel to the Pont de Sèvres stop by Métro, then transfer to bus 171 (trip time: 20 to 45 minutes, depending on traffic). The bus costs you 3 Métro tickets, and will deposit you near the gates of the palace.

If you're driving, take route N-10 and park on the Place d'Armes in front of the Château.

FONTAINEBLEAU   Napoléon joined the grand parade of French rulers who used the **Palais de Fontainebleau** (☎ **01-60-71-50-70**) as a resort, hunting in its magnificent forest. Under François I the hunting lodge was enlarged into a royal palace in the Italian Renaissance style that he admired. Artists from the School of Fontainebleau adorned the 64m (210-foot) **Gallery of François I.**

Fontainebleau found renewed glory under Napoléon. You can wander around much of the palace on your own, but the **Musée Napoléon and the Petits Appartements** are accessible by guided tour only. Most impressive are his throne room and his bedroom (look for his symbol, a bee). The furnishings in the grand apartments of Napoléon and Joséphine evoke the imperial heyday.

The interior is open Wednesday to Monday 9:30am to 12:30pm and 2 to 5pm. In July and August, it's open 9:30am to 6pm. A ticket allowing visits to the Grands Appartements costs 35F ($6) for adults and 23F ($3.70) for students 18 to 25; under 18 free. A ticket allowing access to the Petits Appartements and the Musée Napoléon goes for 16F ($2.55) for adults and 12F ($1.90) for students 18 to 25; under 18 free.

Getting There   Trains to Fontainebleau, 60km (37 miles) south of Paris, depart from the Gare de Lyon in Paris (trip time: 45 to 60 minutes), and cost 94F ($15.05) round-trip. Fontainebleau's railway station lies 5km (3 miles) from the château, within the suburb of Avon. A local bus marked CHÂTEAU leaves at 15-minute intervals every Monday to Saturday, and at 30-minute intervals every Sunday, for 10F ($1.60) each way.

CHARTRES   The architectural aspirations of the Middle Ages reached their highest expression in the ✪ **Cathédrale Notre-Dame de Chartres,** 16 Cloître Notre-Dame

(☎ **02-37-21-56-33**). A mystical light seems to stream through this stained glass, which gave the world a new color—Chartres blue. One of the greatest of the world's high Gothic cathedrals, Chartres contains some of the oldest (some of it created as early as the 12th century) and most beautiful medieval stained glass anywhere. It was spared in both world wars; the glass removed painstakingly piece by piece for storage and safekeeping.

The cathedral you see today dates principally from the 13th century. It was the first to use flying buttresses, giving it a higher and lighter construction. French sculpture in the 12th century broke into full bloom when the Royal Portal was added; the sculptured bodies are elongated and formalized in their long flowing robes, but the faces are amazingly lifelike. Admission free, the cathedral is open Monday to Saturday 7:30am to 7pm and Sunday 8:30am to 7pm. The crypt can only be visited on a guided tour, costing 11F ($1.75) for adults or 8F ($1.30) for students and children. From April to October, there are five tours daily, curtailed to two per day off-season. Inquire locally about times of tours, as they change frequently.

Getting There   Chartres is 97km (60 miles) southwest of Paris. Direct trains leave from Gare Montparnasse (trip time: 55 minutes) and pass through the sea of wheat fields that characterize Beauce, the granary of France.

2 The Loire Valley Châteaux

Bordered by vineyards, the winding Loire Valley cuts through the land of castles deep in France's heart. When royalty and nobility built châteaux throughout this valley during the French Renaissance, sumptuousness was uppermost in their minds. An era of excessive pomp reigned until Henri IV moved his court to Paris, marking the Loire's decline.

The Loire is blessed with abundant attractions—there's even the castle that inspired the fairy tale Sleeping Beauty. Tours is the traditional gateway; once here you can explore either east or west, depending on your interests. From Paris, you can reach Tours by autoroute (take A-10 southwest).

In general, Loire Valley **tourist Offices** are open October to March, Monday to Saturday 9am to 6:30pm and Sunday 10am to noon; the rest of the year, hours are Monday to Saturday 9am to 7pm and Sunday 9:30am to 12:30pm.

TOURS

Tours, 232km (144 miles) southwest of Paris and 113km (70 miles) southwest of Orléans, is at the junction of the Loire and Cher Rivers. The devout en route to Santiago de Compostela in northwest Spain once stopped off here to pay homage at the tomb of St. Martin, the Apostle of Gaul, bishop of Tours in the 4th century. Tours is the traditional place to begin your exploration of the Loire Valley.

ESSENTIALS

GETTING THERE   About 10 **trains** make the run from Paris to Tours every day. At least eight of them are TGVs (*trains à grande vitesse*) that roar their way from Gare Montparnasse (trip time: 55 minutes). TGVs arrive at the railway station in St-Pierre-de-Corps, a hamlet about 3km (2 miles) southeast of Tours, and which is connected to the city's main rail station (La Gare SNCF de Tours, at Place Maréchal Leclerc) by a free shuttle train. If you're coming into Tours on any of the trains that fan out into the Loire Valley, chances are you'll arrive via conventional train at Place Maréchal

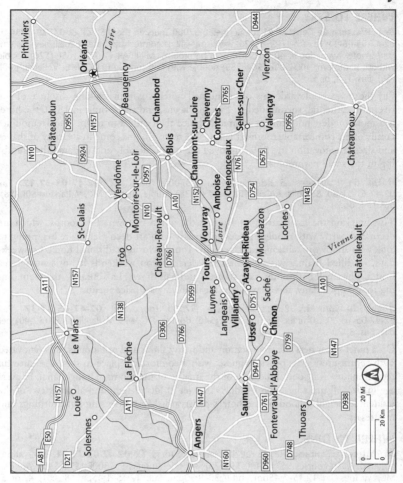

Leclerc, and thereby avoid the need to make the transfer from the TGV station at St-Pierre-de-Corps. For rail information and schedules in Tours, the Loire Valley, and the rest of France, call ☎ **08-36-35-35-35.**

Once you're in Tours, you can rely on public transport to see much of the Loire; you can also rent a **bike** and tour—the region is relatively flat. Try **Amster'Cycle,** 8 rue Édouard Vaillant (☎ **02-47-61-22-23**), which rents both mountain bikes and all-purpose road bikes for 80F ($13) per day. A deposit is required in the form of a passport, 1,500F ($240), or a valid credit card. The shop is only 45m (50 yards) from the rail station.

VISITOR INFORMATION   The **Office de Tourisme** is at 78 rue Bernard-Palissy (☎ **02-47-70-37-37**).

DEPARTING BY CAR   To reach your first major château in the Loire, follow D-7 for 18km (11 miles) west to Villandry.

WHERE TO STAY

Best Western Le Central. 21 rue Berthelot, 37000 Tours. In the U.S. ☎ **800/528-1234** or 02-47-05-46-44. Fax 02-47-66-10-26. www.tour-online.com/central-hotel. E-mail: bestwestern. centralhotel@wanadoo.fr. 40 units (38 with bathroom). MINIBAR TV TEL. 165F ($26) double without bathroom; 400–500F ($64–$80) double with bathroom. AE, DC, MC, V. Parking 40F ($6). Bus: 1, 4, or 5.

Off the main boulevard, this old-fashioned hotel is within walking distance of the river and cathedral, surrounded by gardens, lawns, and trees. Built in 1850, the hotel is a more modest but more economical choice than others in town. The Tremouilles family offers comfortable rooms at reasonable rates. Rooms come in a variety of shapes and sizes; a renovation in 1999 improved them considerably and updated the plumbing in the small bathrooms.

Hôtel de l'Univers. 5 bd. Heurteloup, 37000 Tours. ☎ **02-47-05-37-12.** Fax 02-47-61-51-80. 85 units. A/C TV TEL. 860F ($138) double. AE, DC, MC, V. Parking 50F ($8). Bus 1, 4, or 5.

This hotel on the main artery of Tours is the oldest in town. The rooms, which are decorated partly with modern pieces and partly with art deco pieces, are beginning to look a bit shopworn, although this remains Tours' favorite traditional hotel. On weekdays, it's filled mainly with business travelers and on weekends it hosts many area brides. The small bathrooms have showers and hair dryers. La Touraine, the main dining room, open daily, serves excellent meals from a set price menu.

Hôtel du Manoir. 2 rue Traversière, 37000 Tours. ☎ **02-47-05-37-37.** Fax 02-47-05-16-00. 20 units. TV TEL. 290F ($46) double. DC, MC, V. Parking 15F ($2.40) per day. Bus: 3, 70.

On a quiet street near the train station and many shops and restaurants, this renovated 19th-century residence provides guests with a comfortable place to stay. The cheerful reception area is a good indication of the quality of the rooms. Though small to average in size, all units have big windows that let in lots of light and afford views of the residential neighborhood or the hotel's courtyard. Most have simple furnishings and mattresses.

WHERE TO DINE

La Rôtisserie Tourangelle. 23 rue du Commerce Tours. ☎ **02-47-05-71-21.** Reservations required. Main courses 95–125F ($15–$20); set price menus 95–300F ($15–$48). AE, DC, MC, V. Tues–Sat 12:15–1:45pm and 7:30–9:30pm, Sun 12:15–1:45pm. Bus: 1, 4, or 5. FRENCH.

This is a local favorite, where you can dine on a terrace in summer (though there's not much to see). It's better to concentrate on the ever-changing menu, which may include homemade foie gras and white fish caught in the Loire served with *beurre blanc* (white butter sauce). Regional ingredients mix well with the local wines, as exemplified by pike-perch with sabayon and *magret de fillet de canard* (duckling) served with a "jam" of red Chinon wine. In summer, strawberry parfait with raspberry coulis is a perfect end to the meal. If only the service were a little better.

Le Relais Buré. 1 place de la Résistance. ☎ **02-47-05-67-74.** Main courses 68–115F ($11–$18); set price menu (Mon–Fri only) 120F ($19). AE, DC, MC, V. Daily noon–2pm and 7pm–midnight. Bus: 1 or 5. FRENCH.

A 5-minute walk east of the center of Tours, this brasserie specializes in shellfish and regional recipes, though it's somewhat unimaginative. It has a busy bar and a front terrace, with tables scattered inside on the street level and mezzanine. Menu items include six well-flavored versions of sauerkraut, a wide choice of grilled meats, including steak au poivre, foie gras and smoked salmon, and a tempting array of desserts.

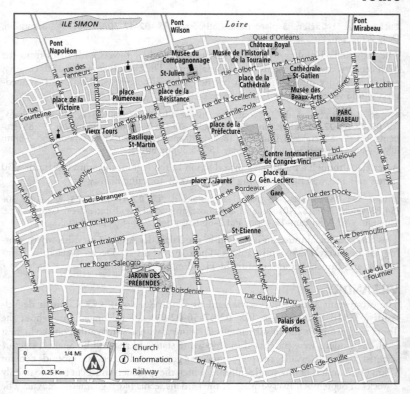

The map shows the following labels:

ILE SIMON · Pont Napoléon · Pont Wilson · Loire · Pont Mirabeau · Quai d'Orléans · Château Royal · Musée de l'Historial de la Touraine · Musée du Compagnonnage · rue A.-Thomas · rue Mirabeau · rue des Tanneurs · St-Julien · rue Colbert · Cathédrale St-Gatien · rue Lobin · rue de la Victoire · rue Bretonneau · rue du Commerce · place de la Cathédrale · Musée des Beaux-Arts · rue des Ursulines · place Plumereau · place de la Résistance · rue de la Scellerie · rue des Petit-Pré · PARC MIRABEAU · place de la Victoire · rue Courteline · rue des Halles · rue de la Scellerie · rue Emile-Zola · rue du Petit-Pré · Vieux Tours · Basilique St-Martin · rue Marceau · place de la Préfecture · rue Jules-Simon · rue G. Delpérier · rue Nationale · rue Briçon · Centre International de Congrès Vinci · bd. Heurteloup · rue de la Fuye · rue Charpentier · place J.-Jaurès · place du Gén.-Leclerc · bd. Béranger · rue de Bordeaux · Gare · rue des Docks · rue Léon-Boyer · rue de la Grandière · rue Fouquet · rue Charles-Gille · rue Victor-Hugo · rue Desmoulins · rue d'Entraigues · av. de Grammont · rue E. Vaillant · rue du Gén.-Chanzy · rue George-Sand · St-Etienne · rue Michelet · rue du Dr Fournier · rue Roger-Salengro · JARDIN DES PRÉBENDES · rue de Boisdenier · bd. de Lattre de Tassigny · rue Giraudeau · rue Lakanal · rue Galpin-Thiou · rue Chevallier · Palais des Sports · bd. Thiers · av. Gén.-de-Gaulle

0   1/4 Mi
0   0.25 Km

† Church
ⓘ Information
— Railway

✪ **Parc de Belmont (Jean Bardet).** 57 rue Groison, 37100 Tours. ☎ **02-47-41-41-11.**
Fax 02-47-51-68-72. Reservations recommended. Main courses 210–380F ($34–$61); set
price menu 250–750F ($40–$120). AE, DC, MC, V. Nov–Mar, Tues–Sat noon–2pm and
7:30–9:30pm, Sun noon–2:30pm; Apr–Oct, Tues–Sun noon–2pm and daily 7:30–9:30pm.
Bus: 9. FRENCH.

Set in three rooms of a 19th-century château and opened in 1987, this fine restaurant
is the creation of the famous, Michelin two-star chef Jean Bardet, who considers all
meals here to be "an orchestration of wines, alcohol, food, and cigars." However, that's
not to say that you must partake of all four elements to have one of the best meals in
the region. Specialties of spectacular flavor include a lobster ragout, sliced sea bass with
a confit of tomatoes and artichoke hearts, and scallops with a puree of shallots and
truffle cream. The duck giblets and lobster accompanied by a red wine and orange
sauce is reason enough to visit.

The rest of the château has been transformed into a luxury hotel and is the domain
of chef Bardet's wife, Sophie. The spacious rooms are individually decorated and have
high ceilings, cozy fireplaces, and antique furnishings. Some have private balconies
that open onto the gardens. A double room ranges from 750 to 1,050F ($120 to
$168), and suites cost from 1,500 to 1,900F ($240 to $304).

EXPLORING TOURS

The heart of town is **place Jean-Jaurès. Rue Nationale** is the principal street (the valley's Champs-Elysées), running north to the Loire River. Head along rue du Commerce and rue du Grand-Marché to reach la vieille ville, the old town.

Cathédrale St-Gatien. 5 place de la Cathédrale. ☎ **02-47-70-21-00.** Free admission. Daily 9am–7pm. Bus: 3.

The cathedral's Flamboyant Gothic facade is flanked by towers with bases from the 12th century, though the lanterns are Renaissance. The choir is from the 13th century, and each century through the 16th saw new additions. Some of the glorious stained-glass windows are from the 13th century.

Musée de l'Historial de la Touraine. In the Château Royal, 25 av. André Malraux. ☎ **02-47-61-02-95.** Admission 35F ($6) adults, 30F ($4.80) senior citizens, 24F ($3.85) students, 16F ($2.55) children. Daily May 16–June 30 and Sept 1–Oct 31 9am–noon and 2–6pm; July 1–Aug 31 9am–6:30pm; Nov 1–May 15 2–5:30pm. Bus: 3.

A perfect, although a bit kitschy, introduction to the region, this museum features 30 scenes and 165 wax figures tracing 1,000 years of Touraine history.

Musée des Beaux-Arts. 18 place François-Sicard. ☎ **02-47-05-68-73.** Museum: 30F ($4.80) adults, 15F ($2.40) students and those over 65; 12 and under free. Gardens free. Museum: Wed–Mon 9am–12:45pm and 2–6pm. Gardens 7am–8:30pm. Bus: 3.

This fine provincial museum is housed in the Palais des Archevêques. It's worth visiting for its lovely rooms and gardens. There are works by Degas, Delacroix, Rembrandt, and Boucher, and sculpture by Houdon and Bourdelle.

VILLANDRY

The extravagant 16th-century–style gardens of the Renaissance ✪ **Château de Villandry,** 37510 Joué-les-Tours (☎ **02-47-50-02-09**), are celebrated throughout the Touraine. Forming a trio of superimposed cloisters, with a water garden on the highest level, the gardens were purchased in a decaying state and restored by Spanish doctor/scientist Joachim Carvallo, the present owner's great-grandfather. The grounds contain 17km (10½ miles) of boxwood sculpture, which the gardeners must cut to style in only 2 weeks in September. Every square of the gardens seems like a geometric mosaic. The borders represent the many faces of love: for example, tender, tragic (with daggers), or crazy, the last evoked by a labyrinth that doesn't get you anywhere.

Originally a feudal castle stood at Villandry, but in 1536 Jean Lebreton, the chancellor of François I, built the present château; the buildings form a U and are surrounded by a two-sided moat.

Admission to the gardens with a tour of the château is 45F ($7) for adults, 38F ($6) for children. Visiting the gardens separately without a guide costs 33F ($5) for adults, 26F ($4.15) for children. The château is open mid-February to mid-November, and guided tours are conducted daily 9am to 6:30pm. The gardens are open year-round 9am to 5:30pm. Tours are given in French with leaflets in English.

ESSENTIALS

GETTING THERE   Unfortunately, Villandry doesn't have train or bus service from Tours, 18km (11½ miles) away. Rent a **bike** in Tours (see above) and ride along the Cher or go by car (see above); the ride will take 60 to 90 minutes.

DEPARTING BY CAR   From Villandry, continue west along D-7, then take D-39 south for 11km (7 miles) to Azay-le-Rideau.

WHERE TO STAY & DINE

Le Cheval Rouge. Villandry, 37510 Joué-les-Tours. ☎ **02-47-50-02-07.** Fax 02-47-50-08-77. Reservations recommended. Main courses 80–120F ($13–$19). Set price menus 95–180F ($15–$29). MC, V. Tues–Sun noon–2pm and 7:30–9pm. Closed Feb to mid-Mar. Open Sun night and Mon if it's a holiday. FRENCH.

This is a well-known lunch stopover near the château, in spite of a stiff, sometimes unpleasant welcome and difficult staff. Set within a conservatively decorated dining room, about 90m (100 yards) from the banks of the Cher, it won't be your most memorable meal in the Loire Valley; the food is competent, but not brilliant. Specialties include lobster Thermidor, medallions of veal with morels, and turbot with hollandaise sauce. The inn also rents 20 rooms, all with bathroom and telephone. A double is 230 to 280F ($37 to $45). Parking is free.

AZAY-LE-RIDEAU

This château's machicolated towers and blue-slate roof pierced with dormers shimmer in the moat, creating a reflection like a Monet painting. But the defensive medieval look is all for show; the ✪ **Château d'Azay-le-Rideau,** 37190 Azay-le-Rideau (☎ 02-47-45-42-04), was created as a private residence during the Renaissance at an idyllic spot on the Indre River. Gilles Berthelot, François I's finance minister, commissioned the castle, and his spendthrift wife, Philippa, supervised its construction. So elegant was the creation that the chevalier king grew immensely jealous. In time, Berthelot was forced to flee and the château reverted to the king.

Before entering, circle the château, enjoying the perfect proportions of this crowning achievement of the Renaissance in Touraine. Its most fanciful feature is a bay enclosing a grand stairway with a straight flight of steps. The Renaissance interior is a virtual museum. From the second-floor Royal Chamber, look out at the gardens. This bedroom, also known as the Green Room, is believed to have sheltered Louis XIII.

The château is open daily: July to August 9am to 7pm, April to June and October 9:30am to 6pm, and November to March 9:30am to 12:30pm and 2 to 5:30pm. Admission is 35F ($6) for adults and 23F ($3.70) for children. May to July, *son et lumière* (sound-and-light) performances are staged at 10:30pm; August at 10pm, and September at 9:30pm. Tickets cost 60F ($10) for adults and 35F ($6) for children.

ESSENTIALS

GETTING THERE   Azay-le-Rideau lies astride the railway lines that interconnect Tours with Chinon. The SNCF maintains about seven **trains** or **buses** a day that make the transit from both (trip time: 25 and 30 minutes). Trains arrive at the railway station west of Azay's center; buses arrive in the town center. For information about either buses or trains, call ☎ **02-47-93-11-04** (Chinon railway station) or ☎ **08-36-35-35-35** (SNCF information throughout France).

VISITOR INFORMATION   The **Syndicat d'Initiative** (tourist office) is at place de l'Europe (☎ **02-47-45-44-40**).

DEPARTING BY CAR   After seeing Villandry and Azay-le-Rideau, return to Tours. From Tours, head east for 35km (22 miles) to Amboise. To reach Amboise, take either D-751 on the south bank of the Loire or N-152 on the north bank (both good roads). If you take the northern route, you can follow the signs to Vouvray, which turns out the most famous white wine of the Touraine. Vintners post signs if they allow visits and tastings.

WHERE TO DINE

L'Aigle d'Or. 10 av. Adélaïde-Riché. ☎ **02-47-45-24-58.** Reservations recommended. Main courses 80–115F ($13–$18); set price lunch 105F ($17); set price dinner 155–250F ($25–$40). V. Daily 12:30–2pm and 7:30–9:30pm. Closed Wed and Sun and Tues night in Winter also all of Feb and Nov 20–30. FRENCH.

The service is professional, the welcome often charming, and the food the best in Azay. The selection of appetizers ranges from a mousseline of scallops with a crayfish coulis, to foie gras. Main dishes often feature fresh fish from the Loire with sauces made from regional wines. Desserts are made fresh daily and vary with the chef's moods.

AMBOISE

On the banks of the Loire, Amboise is in the center of vineyards known as Touraine-Amboise. Leonardo da Vinci spent his last years in this city. Dominating the town is the ✪ **Château d'Amboise** (☎ **02-47-57-00-98**), the first in France to reflect the Italian Renaissance. A combination of both Gothic and Renaissance, this 15th-century château is mainly associated with Charles VIII, who built it on a rocky spur separating the valleys of the Loire and the Amasse.

You enter via a ramp, opening onto a panoramic terrace fronting the river. At one time, this terrace was surrounded by buildings, and fetes were staged in the enclosed courtyard. At the time of the revolution, the castle declined and only a quarter or even less remains of this once-sprawling edifice. First you come to the flamboyant Gothic Chapelle St-Hubert, distinguished by its lacelike tracery. It allegedly contains Leonardo's remains; actually the great artist was buried in the castle's Collegiate Church, which was destroyed between 1806 and 1810. During the Second Empire, excavations here revealed bones "identified" as Leonardo's.

Today the walls of the château are hung with tapestries and the rooms furnished grandly. The Logis du Roi (king's apartment) escaped destruction and can be visited. The château is open daily July and August 9am to 7:30pm, April to June 9am to 6:30pm, September and October 9am to 6pm, and November to March 9am to noon and 1:30 to 5:30pm. Admission is 60F ($10) for adults, 33F ($5) for students, and 21F ($3.35) for children.

You might also wish to visit **Clos-Lucé**, 2 rue de Clos-Lucé (☎ **02-47-57-62-88**), a 15th-century brick-and-stone manor. In what had been an oratory for Anne de Bretagne, François I installed "the great master in all forms of art and science," Leonardo da Vinci. Venerated by the chevalier king, Leonardo lived here for 3 years, dying at the manor in 1519. (Those paintings of Leonardo dying in François's arms are symbolic; the king was supposedly away at the time.) The manor's rooms are well furnished, some with reproductions from Leonardo's time. Clos-Lucé is open March through September daily from 9am to 7pm; Off-season daily from 9am to 6pm. Admission is 39F ($6) for adults and 32F ($5) for students, 20F ($3.20) ages 6 to 15 (free 5 and under).

ESSENTIALS

GETTING THERE   Amboise lies on the main Paris-Blois-Tours rail line, with 14 trains per day arriving from both Tours (trip time: 20 minutes) and Blois (trip time: 15 minutes). Five trains arrive daily from Paris (trip time: 2¹/₂ hours). For train information and schedules, call ☎ **08-36-35-35-35. Tourisme Verney** (☎ **02-47-57-00-44**), runs five **buses** a day connecting Tours and Amboise (trip time: about 30 minutes). The train station is along Boulevard Gambetta and buses leave from the parking lot adjacent to the tourist office.

VISITOR INFORMATION   The **Office de Tourisme** is on quai du Général-de-Gaulle (☎ **02-47-57-09-28**).

DEPARTING BY CAR   To reach Blois from Amboise, continue along either the south bank (D-751) or the north bank (N-152). Blois is 60km (37 miles) northeast of Tours.

WHERE TO STAY

Belle-Vue. 12 quai Charles-Guinot, 37400 Amboise. ☎ **02-47-57-02-26.** Fax 02-47-30-51-23. 32 units. TV TEL. 420F ($67) double. Rates include breakfast. MC, V. Closed Nov 15–Mar 15.

This modest inn lies at the bridge crossing the Loire at the foot of the château. Rooms are furnished in an old-fashioned French style, with low beds and rather thin mattresses. Try to stay in the main building, which has more charm and character than the less convenient annex across the river. Bathrooms are small and have showers. Breakfast is the only meal served.

Hostellerie du Château-de-Pray. Route de Chargé (D-751), 37400 Amboise. ☎ **02-47-57-23-67.** Fax 02-47-57-32-50. www.chateauxethotels.com. E-mail: chateaudepray@wanadoo.fr. 19 units. TV TEL. 490–850F ($78–$136) double; 750–990F ($120–$158) suite. Half board 225F ($36) per person extra. AE, DC, V. Closed Jan 2–Feb 10. Free parking.

East of the town center, this château from 1224 resembles a tower-flanked castle on the Rhine. Inside, you'll find antlers, hunting trophies, antiques, and a paneled drawing room with a fireplace and a collection of antique oils. Rooms in the main building were renovated in 1998 and are stylishly conservative and comfortable. The more spacious chambers are near the ground floor. Small but efficiently organized bathrooms contain hair dryers. Try to avoid the four rooms in the 1990s annex; they're rather impersonally furnished and lack character. The hotel restaurant, open to nonguests, offers set price menus of excellent quality.

✪ Le Choiseul. 36 quai Charles-Guinot, 37400 Amboise. ☎ **02-47-30-45-45.** Fax 02-47-30-46-10. www.choiseul.com. E-mail: choiseul@wanadoo.fr. 32 units. MINIBAR TV TEL. 470–1,450F ($75–$232) double; 1,130–1,950F ($181–$312) suite. AE, DC, MC, V. Closed Dec 8–Jan 24.

There's no better address in Amboise or any better place for cuisine than this 18th-century hotel. This hotel is set in the valley between a hillside and the Loire River, close to the château, and there's a garden with flowering terraces on the grounds. Rooms, 16 of which are air-conditioned, are luxurious; though recently modernized, they've retained their old-world charm. The small bathrooms contain tub/shower combinations and hair dryers. The food is better than that found in Tours or the surrounding area. The formal dining room has a view of the Loire and welcomes nonguests who phone ahead. It's open daily noon to 2pm and 7 to 9:30pm, with set price menus ranging from 290 to 500F ($46 to $80). The wine list is the best in the area. Facilities include an outdoor pool, a tennis court, and a Ping-Pong table.

WHERE TO DINE

Le Manoir St-Thomas. Place Richelieu. ☎ **02-47-57-22-52.** Reservations required. Main courses 130–150F ($21–$24). Set price menu 175–295F ($28–$47). AE, DC, MC, V. Tues 7:15–9:30pm, Wed–Sat 12:15–2:30pm and 7:15–9:30pm, Sun 12:15–2:30pm. Closed Jan 15–Mar 15. FRENCH.

The best food in town outside of Le Choiseul is served at this Renaissance house in the shadow of the château. The restaurant is in a pleasant garden, and the elegant dining room is richly decorated with a polychrome ceiling and a massive stone fireplace. Owner/chef François Le Coz's specialties include truffles with foie gras, lamb fillet with port, and red mullet fillet with cream of sweet pepper sauce. The tender saddle of hare is perfectly flavored. Some special culinary delights are the goose liver pâté wrapped in a combination of truffles and wild black mushrooms, and duck flavored with honey, cinnamon, and ginger.

BLOIS

Blois is the most attractive of the major Loire towns. It rises on the right bank of the Loire, its skyline dominated by its château, where the duc de Guise was assassinated on December 23, 1588, on orders of his archrival, Henri III; it's one of the most famous murders in French history. Several French kings lived here, and the town has a rich architectural history.

The murder of the duc de Guise is only one of the memories evoked by the ✪ **Château de Blois** (☎ 02-54-90-33-33), begun in the 13th century by the comtes de Blois. Charles d'Orléans (son of Louis d'Orléans, assassinated by the Burgundians in 1407) lived at Blois after his release from 25 years of English captivity. He'd married Mary of Cleves and brought a "court of letters" to Blois. In his 70s, Charles became the father of the future Louis XII, who was to marry Anne de Bretagne. Blois was then launched in its new role as a royal château. In time it was to be called the second capital of France, with Blois, the city of kings.

However, Blois soon became a palace of banishment. Louis XIII got rid of his interfering mother, Marie de Médici, by sending her here; but this plump matron escaped by sliding into the moat down a mound of dirt left by the builders. Then in 1626 the king sent his conspiring brother, Gaston d'Orléans, here; he stayed.

If you stand in the courtyard, you'll find the château is like an illustrated storybook of French architecture. The Hall of the Estates-General is a beautiful 13th-century work; the Charles d'Orléans gallery was actually built by Louis XII from 1498 to 1501, as was the Louis XII wing. The Gaston d'Orléans wing was constructed by Mansart between 1635 and 1638. The most remarkable is the François I wing, a masterpiece of the French Renaissance, containing a spiral staircase with elaborately ornamented balustrades and the king's symbol, the salamander.

The château is open daily mid-October to mid-March from 9am to 12:30pm and 2 to 5pm; mid-March through June and September from 9am to 6:30pm; July and August from 9am to 7:30pm. Admission 35F ($6) for adults, 25F ($4) for students under 25, and 20F ($3.20) for children under 7. A *son et lumière* presentation in French is sponsored nightly between May and September, beginning in most cases at 10:30pm, but in rare instances, including throughout the month of May, at 9:30 or 10:15, depending on the school calendar. As a taped lecture is played, colored lights and dramatic readings, in French, evoke the age in which the château was built. Participation in the sound-and-light show costs 60F ($10) for adults and 30F ($4.80) for children 7 to 15. Free for children 6 and under.

ESSENTIALS

GETTING THERE   The Paris-Austerlitz line via Orléans delivers 8 **trains** per day from Paris (trip time: 2 hours). From Tours, 10 trains arrive per day (trip time: 45 minutes), and from Amboise, 10 trains per day arrive (trip time: 20 minutes). For train information and schedules, call ☎ 08-36-35-35-35. The train station is at place de la Gare. If you'd like to explore the area by **bike,** go to **Cycles Le Blond,** 44 levée des Tuileries (☎ 02-54-74-30-13), where rentals range from 30 to 120F ($4.80 to $19) per day, depending on the model. You have to leave your passport, a credit card, a driver's license, or a deposit of between 500 and 1,500F ($80 and $240), depending on the value of the bike.

VISITOR INFORMATION   The **Office de Tourisme** is at Pavillon Anne-de-Bretagne, 3 av. Jean-Laigret (☎ 02-54-90-41-41).

DEPARTING BY CAR   To reach Chaumont sur-Loire, take D-751 for 19km (12 miles) south of Blois.

WHERE TO STAY

Hôtel le Savoie. 6–8 rue du Docteur-Ducoux, 41000 Blois. ☎ **02-54-74-32-21.** Fax 02-54-74-29-58. www.citote.com. 26 units. TV TEL. 230–280F ($37–$45) double. MC, V.

This modern hotel is both inviting and livable, from its courteous staff to the rooms, which though small, are nonetheless quiet and cozy. They were last renovated in 1998. Bathrooms are small but have sufficient shelf space. In the morning, a breakfast buffet is set up in the bright dining room.

Mercure Centre. 28 quai St-Jean, 41000 Blois. ☎ **02-54-56-66-66.** Fax 02-54-56-67-00. www.mercure.blois.fr. E-mail: mercure-blois@wanadoo.fr. 96 units. A/C MINIBAR TV TEL. 580F ($93) double; 650–680F ($104–$109) suite. AE, DC, MC, V. Parking 40F ($6). Bus: Quayside marked PISCINE.

This is the newest and best-located hotel in Blois—three stories of reinforced concrete and big windows beside the quays of the Loire, a 5-minute walk from the château. Rooms never rise above their chain format and are very roadside motel in look, but they're roomy and soundproof and equipped with satellite TV. Bathrooms are excellent, with a shower-and-tub combination and a hair dryer. French and international meals are served daily in the pleasant restaurant.

WHERE TO DINE

Le Médicis. 2 allée François-1er, 41000 Blois. ☎ **02-54-43-94-04.** Fax 02-54-42-04-05. www.le-medicis.com. E-mail: christiangaranger@wanadoo.fr. Reservations required. Main courses 80–165F ($13–$26); set price menus 110F ($18), 165F ($26), 275F ($44), and 420F ($67). AE, MC, V. Daily noon–2pm and 7–10pm. Closed Jan. Bus: 2. FRENCH.

Christian and Annick Garanger maintain one of the most sophisticated inns in Blois—ideal for a gourmet meal or an overnight stop. Fresh fish is the chef's specialty. Typical main courses are asparagus in mousseline sauce, scampi ravioli with saffron sauce, and suprême of perch with morels. Chocolate in many manifestations is the dessert specialty. In addition, the Garangers rent 12 elegant rooms, each with bathroom, air-conditioning, minibar, TV, phone, and hair dryer. The rates are 450 to 550F ($72 to $88) double; there is one suite that goes for 700F ($112).

✪ Rendezvous des Pêcheurs. 27 rue du Foix. ☎ **02-54-74-67-48.** Reservations recommended. Main courses 96–130F ($15–$21); set price menu 150F ($24). MC, V. Mon 7:30–10pm, Tues–Sat noon–2pm and 7:30–10pm. Closed 3 weeks in Aug and 1 week in Feb. FRENCH.

This restaurant occupies a small, 16th-century house a 5-minute walk from the château. The chefs here, the finest in this part of France, continue to maintain their reputation for quality ingredients, generous portions, and creativity. The chef prepares only two or three meat dishes, including roasted chicken with a medley of potatoes and mushrooms and a confit of garlic; and a fricassee of sweetbreads. These appear alongside a much longer roster of fish and seafood dishes, such as a poached fillet of zander served with fresh oysters; and fillet of sea bass served with a champagne sauce on a bed of sea urchins.

CHAUMONT-SUR-LOIRE

On the morning when Diane de Poitiers crossed the drawbridge, the ✪ **Château de Chaumont** (☎ 02-54-51-26-26) looked fiercely grim, with its battlements and pepper-pot turrets crowning the towers. Henri II, her lover, had recently died. The king had given her Chenonceau, but his widow, Catherine de Médici, banished her from her favorite château and sent her into exile at Chaumont. Inside, portraits reveal that Diane truly deserved her reputation as forever beautiful. A portrait of Catherine looking like a devout nun invites unfavorable comparisons.

Chaumont (Burning Mount) was built during the reign of Louis XII by Charles d'Amboise, and spans the period between the Middle Ages and the Renaissance. It was privately owned and inhabited until it was acquired by the state in 1938. Its prize exhibit is a rare collection of medallions by the Italian artist, Nini. A guest of the château, he made medallion portraits of kings, queens, and nobles—even Benjamin Franklin, who once visited. In the bedroom once occupied by Catherine de Médici is a rare portrait, painted when she was young.

The château is open daily January to mid-March and October to December 10am to 4:30pm; mid-March to September, it's open daily 9:30am to 6pm. Admission is 32F ($5) for adults and 21F ($3.35) for children 12 to 17. Free for children 11 and under.

ESSENTIALS

GETTING THERE   Seventeen trains per day travel from both Blois (trip time: 15 minutes) and Tours (trip time: about 45 minutes). The train station is in Onzain, 2.5km (1½ miles) north of the château, a pleasant walk. For transportation information, call ☎ **08-36-35-35-35.** From June 15 to September 15, you can take a bus in Blois operated by Point Bus, 2 place Victor Hugo (☎ 02-54-78-15-66). The bus leaves Blois at 9:10am, returning at 6pm daily.

VISITOR INFORMATION   The **Office de Tourisme** is on rue du Maréchal-Leclerc (☎ **02-54-20-91-73**).

DEPARTING BY CAR   Blois (above) also makes a perfect launching pad for visiting another important château in the area, that of Chambord, which lies 18km (11 miles) east of Blois along D-33 near Bracieux.

WHERE TO STAY & DINE NEARBY

Domaine des Hauts de Loire. Route d'Herbault, 41150 Onzain. ☎ **02-54-20-72-57.** Fax 02-54-20-77-32. www.relaischateau.fr/hauts-loire. E-mail: hauts-loire@relaischateaux.fr. 35 units. MINIBAR TV TEL. 700–1,500F ($112–$240) double; from 1,850F ($296) suite. AE, DC, MC, V.

Less than 3km (2 miles) from the Château of Chaumont, on the opposite side of the Loire, this Relais & Châteaux property is a stately manor house built by the prosperous owner of a Paris-based newspaper in 1840 and called, rather coyly at the time, a "hunting lodge." It's the most appealing stopover in the neighborhood, with a roster of intensely decorated rooms each in Louis Philippe or Empire style. About half the rooms lie within a half-timbered annex that was originally the stables.

The site also offers a restaurant that's open to nonguests who phone in advance. Its well-prepared food served in a stately dining room is a local favorite. Set price menus ranging from 320 to 700F ($51 to $112) include a salad of marinated eel with shallot-flavored vinaigrette; oysters on a layered sheet of sardines; fillet of sole with black pepper and watercress; roasted fillet of Loire Valley whitefish (sandre) served with parsley-flavored cream sauce and cabbage stuffed with a compote of snails; and the ultimate Loire valley main course, a fillet of smoked eel prepared with Vouvray wine.

CHAMBORD

When François I used to say, "Come on up to my place," he meant the ✪ **Château de Chambord,** 41250 Bracieux (☎ **02-54-50-40-00**), not Fontainebleau or Blois. Some 2,000 workers began to piece together "the pile" in 1519. What emerged after 20 years was the pinnacle of the French Renaissance, the largest château in the Loire Valley. It was ready for the visit of Charles V of Germany, who was welcomed by nymphets in transparent veils gently tossing wildflowers in his path. French monarchs like Henri II and Catherine de Médici, Louis XIV, and Henri III came and went from Chambord, but none developed an affection for it to match François I's. The state acquired Chambord in 1932.

The château is in a park of more than 5,200ha (13,000 acres), enclosed within a wall stretching some 32km (20 miles). Looking out a window in one of the 440 rooms, François is said to have carved these words on a pane with a diamond ring: "A woman is a creature of change; to trust her is to play the fool." Chambord's facade is dominated by four monumental towers. The keep has a spectacular terrace the ladies of the court used to stand on to watch the return of their men from the hunt.

The three-story keep also encloses a corkscrew staircase, superimposed so one person may descend at one end and a second ascend at the other without ever meeting. The apartments of Louis XIV, including his redecorated bedchamber, are also in the keep.

The château is open daily: January through March and October through December from 9am to 5:15pm; April through June, it closes at 6:15pm and July and August it closes at 7:15pm. Admission is 40F ($6) for adults and 25F ($4) for ages 12 to 25. it's free for children 11 and under. At the tourist office you can pick up tickets for the *son et lumière* presentation in summer, called *Jours et Siècles* (Days and Centuries), but check the times. A ticket costs 50F ($8).

ESSENTIALS

GETTING THERE   It's best to travel to Chambord by car so you can explore the beautiful countryside on the way there and back. You could rent a **bicycle** in Blois (see above) and cycle to Chambord (a trip of 30km/18¹/₂ miles lasting 90 to 120 minutes). June 15 to September 15 **Point Bus,** 2 place Victor Hugo (☎ **02-54-78-15-66**), operates a bus service to Chambord, leaving Blois at 9:10am and again at 1:20pm with a return at 1 and 6:10pm.

VISITOR INFORMATION   The **Office de Tourisme** is on place St-Michel (☎ **02-54-20-34-86**).

DEPARTING BY CAR   Back at the launching pad of Blois, you can strike out in another direction for yet another major château. Cheverny lies 19km (12 miles) south of Blois, reached by taking D-765.

WHERE TO STAY & DINE

Hôtel du Grand-St-Michel. 103 place St-Michel, 41250 Chambord, near Bracieux. ☎ **02-54-20-31-31.** Fax 02-54-20-36-40. 39 units. TV TEL. 300–450F ($48–$72) double. MC, V. Closed Nov 14–Dec 20. Free parking.

Across from the château, this inn is really the only one of any substance in town. Try for a front room overlooking the château, which is dramatic when floodlit at night. Rooms are plain but comfortable, with provincial decor. Most visitors arrive for lunch, which in summer is served on an awning-shaded terrace. The regional dishes are complemented by a marvelous collection of Loire wines so good they almost overshadow the cooking itself.

CHEVERNY

The *haut monde* still come to the Sologne area for the hunt as if the 17th century had never ended. However, 20th-century realities, like taxes, are *formidable* here—hence the **Château de Cheverny** (☎ **02-54-79-96-29**) must open some of its rooms for inspection by paying guests. At least that keeps the tax collector at bay and the hounds fed in winter.

Unlike most of the Loire châteaux, Cheverny is actually lived in by the descendants of the original owner, the vicomte de Sigalas. The family's lineage can be traced back to Henri Hurault, the son of the chancellor of Henri III and Henri IV, who built the château here in 1634. Designed in classic Louis XIII style, it boasts square pavilions flanking the central pile.

Inside, the antique furnishings, tapestries, decorations, and objets d'art are quite impressive. A 17th-century French artist, Jean Mosnier, decorated the fireplace with motifs from the legend of Adonis. In the Guards' Room is a collection of medieval armor.

The château is open daily: November through February from 9:30am to noon and 2:15 to 5pm; in March, the last part of September, and October it closes at 5:30pm, in April and May at 6:30pm, and from June to mid-September at 6:45pm. Admission is 34F ($5) adults and 17F ($2.70) children 7 to 14. It's free for children 6 and under.

ESSENTIALS

GETTING THERE   Cheverny is 19km (12 miles) south of Blois, along D-765. It's best reached by car or on an organized **bus tour** from Blois. From the railway station at Blois, there's a bus that departs for Cheverney once a day, at noon, returning to Blois four hours later, according to an oft-changing schedule that's dependent on the season and the day of the week. Frankly, most visitors find it a lot easier to take their own car or a taxi from the railway station at Blois.

DEPARTING BY CAR   If after exploring Cheverny you have enthusiasm for one more château, strike out for Valençay. From Cheverny head south on D-102 for 10km (6 miles), crossing the border of the forest of Cheverny. At the town of Contres, connect with the junction of D-956, which traverses the Cher River 19km (12 miles) farther south at Selles-sur-Cher. From here, continue the final signposted 14km (9 miles) to Valençay.

WHERE TO STAY & DINE

Les Trois Marchands. Place de l'Eglise, 41700 Cour-Cheverny. ☎ **02-54-79-96-44.** Fax 02-54-79-25-60. Main courses 70–185F ($11–$30). Set price menus 125–255F ($20–$41). AE, DC, MC, V. Tues–Sun noon–2:15pm and 7:30–9:15pm. Closed Feb 1–Mar 15. FRENCH.

This much-renovated coaching inn, more comfortable than Saint-Hubert, has been handed down for many generations. Today Jean-Jacques Bricault owns the three-story building that sports awnings, a mansard roof, a glassed-in courtyard, and sidewalk tables with bright umbrellas. In the large tavern-style dining room, the menu might include foie gras, lobster salad, frogs' legs, fresh asparagus in mousseline sauce, or fish cooked in a salt crust. The inn also rents 38 well-furnished and comfortable rooms, costing 260 to 350F ($42 to $56) for a double with bathroom; 180F ($29) without bathroom.

Saint-Hubert. Rue Nationale. 41700 Cour-Cheverny. ☎ **02-54-79-96-60.** Fax 02-54-79-21-17. Main courses 85–160F ($14–$26); set price menus 80–280F ($13–$45). MC, V. Thurs–Tues 12:15–2pm and 7:30–9:30pm. Closed Jan 10–Feb 17 and Sun night in low season. FRENCH.

About 730m (800 yards) from the château, this roadside inn was built in the old provincial style. Chef Jean-Claude Pillaut is the secret of the Saint-Hubert's success. The least expensive menu might include terrine of quail, pike-perch with beurre blanc, a selection of cheeses, and a homemade fruit tart. The most expensive menu may offer lobster, an aiguillette of duckling prepared with grapes, or wild boar with a creamy sauce. Game is featured here in season. The Saint-Hubert offers 19 rooms with bathroom, charging 200 to 320F ($32 to $51) double.

VALENÇAY

One of the Loire's handsomest Renaissance châteaux, 56km (35 miles) south of Blois, the **Château de Valençay** (☎ **02-54-00-10-66**) was acquired in 1803 by Talleyrand on the orders of Napoléon, who wanted his minister of foreign affairs to receive dignitaries in great style. In 1838 Talleyrand was buried at Valençay, the château passing to his nephew, Louis de Talleyrand-Périgord. Before the Talleyrand ownership, Valençay was built in 1550 by the d'Estampes family. The dungeon and great west tower are of this period, as is the building's main body; other wings were added in the 17th and 18th centuries. The effect is grandiose, almost too much so, with domes, chimneys, and turrets. The private apartments are open to the public; they're sumptuously furnished, mostly in Empire style but with Louis XV and Louis XVI trappings as well.

Admission to the castle, an antique car museum, and the park is 49F ($8) for adults, 37F ($6) for seniors, students, and those 17 and under. It's open daily April through June and September through October from 10am to 6pm; daily July and August from 9:30am to 6:30pm; and on Saturday, Sunday, and school holidays November through March 2 to 5pm.

ESSENTIALS

GETTING THERE   There are frequent SNCF rail connections from Blois. Call ☎ **08-36-35-35-35** for **train** information and schedules. The station is near the village center.

VISITOR INFORMATION   The **Office de Tourisme** is on route de Blois (☎ **02-54-00-04-42**).

DEPARTING BY CAR   To continue château-hopping, drive north from Valençay until you come to Selles-sur-Cher at the river. This time head west in the direction of Amboise, taking N-76 along the south bank. Chenonceaux lies 16km (10 miles) south of Amboise.

WHERE TO STAY & DINE

✪ **Hôtel d'Espagne.** 9 rue du Château, 36600 Valençay. ☎ **02-54-00-00-02.** Fax 02-54-00-12-63. 16 units. TV TEL. 450–650F ($72–$104) double; 900F ($144) suite. AE, DC, MC, V. Parking 25F ($4). Closed Feb.

This former coaching inn is maintained by the Fourré family, which provides an old-world ambience. The unique rooms are named after different ancestral manor houses in the region. Bathrooms are exceedingly well maintained with a tub/shower combination and a hair dryer. Lunch is served in the dining room or gardens Tuesday to Sunday. Specialties include noisettes of lamb with tarragon and sweetbreads with morels. Within the hotel's dining room, set price menus range from 180 to 260F ($29 to $42).

CHENONCEAUX

A Renaissance masterpiece, the **Château de Chenonceau** (☎ **02-47-23-90-07**) is best known for the *dames de Chenonceau* who have occupied it. (Note that the town is spelled with a final x, but the château is not.) Originally it was owned by the Marqués family, whose members were far too extravagant. Deviously, Thomas Bohier, the comptroller-general of finances in Normandy, began buying up land around the château. The Marqués family was forced to sell to Bohier, who tore down Chenonceau, preserving only the keep and building the rest in the emerging Renaissance style.

Many of the château's walls are covered with Gobelin tapestries, including one depicting a woman pouring water over the back of an angry dragon, another of a three-headed dog and a seven-headed monster. The chapel contains a delicate marble

Virgin and Child, plus portraits of Catherine de Médici in her traditional black and white. There's even a portrait of the stern Catherine in the former bedroom of her rival, Diane de Poitiers. In François I's Renaissance bedchamber, the most interesting portrait is that of Diane de Poitiers as the huntress Diana.

The history of Chenonceau is related in 15 tableaux in the wax museum, which charges 10F ($1.60). Diane de Poitiers, who, among other accomplishments, introduced the artichoke to France, is depicted in three tableaux. One portrays Catherine de Médici tossing out her husband's mistress.

The château is open daily mid-March through mid-September 9am to 7pm; the rest of the year it closes between 4:30 and 6pm. Admission is 50F ($8) for adults and 40F ($6) for children 7 to 15; children 6 and under free. A *son et lumière* spectacle, *In the Old Days of the Dames of Chenonceau,* is staged daily in summer at 10:15pm; admission is 50F ($8) for adults and 35F ($6) for children.

ESSENTIALS

GETTING THERE   There are 3 daily **trains** from Tours to Chenonceaux (trip time: 45 minutes). The train deposits you near the base of the château. Call ☎ **08-36-35-35-35** for train information and schedules.

VISITOR INFORMATION   The **Syndicat d'Initiative** (tourist office) is at rue Bretonneau (☎ **02-47-23-94-45**), open Easter to September.

DEPARTING BY CAR   Continue back to Tours on the N-76, branching out this time for the best of the châteaux in the west. The first stop is Ussé, of *Sleeping Beauty* fame. Follow the directions to the previously visited Azay-le-Rideau. From Tours, it's a short ride down the Indre Valley on D-17 and then D-7 to Ussé.

WHERE TO STAY

Hôtel du Bon-Laboureur et du Château. 6 rue du Dr. Bretonneau, Chenonceaux, 37150 Bléré. ☎ 02-47-23-90-02. Fax 02-47-23-82-01. E-mail: bon-laboureur.fr@lemel.fr. 29 units. TV TEL. 350–700F ($56–$112) double; 850–1,000F ($136–$160) suite. AE, DC, MC, V.

This country inn is within walking distance of the château and is your best bet for a comfortable night's sleep and good food. The rear garden has a little guest house, plus formally planted roses. Founded in 1880, the hotel maintains the flavor of that era, thanks to thick walls, solid masonry, and a scattering of antiques. Most rooms are small, especially those on the upper floors. The place is noted for its restaurant, which receives notably fewer bus groups than many of its competitors within the region. In fair weather, tables are set up within the courtyard, amid trees and flowering shrubs. Set-price menus in the restaurant cost 155 to 315F ($25 to $50) each. On the premises is a heated outdoor swimming pool.

✪ **La Roseraie.** 7 rue du Dr. Bretonneau, Chenonceaux, 37150 Bléré. ☎ **02-47-23-90-09.** Fax 02-47-23-91-59. 16 units. TV TEL. 280–800F ($45–$128) double. AE, DC, MC, V. Closed Dec–Jan.

Thanks to hotelier Laurent Fiorito, who radically upgraded this hotel in 1993, La Roseraie is the most charming and appealing hotel in Chenonceaux. The inviting rooms are individually decorated. Well-kept gardens dominate the property, and there's a heated swimming pool. Some of the finest meals in town are served at lunch and dinner in the hotel's restaurant. Set menus range in price from 98 to 170F ($16 to $27); our favorite dishes include house-style foie gras; magret of duckling with pears and cherries; and an unusual and very delicious invention—*emincée* (a dish made with braised meat) of rump steak with wine-marinated pears.

WHERE TO DINE

Au Gateau Breton. 16 rue du Dr. Bretonneau. ☎ **02-47-23-90-14.** Reservations required July–Aug. Set price menus 60–115F ($10–$18). MC, V. May–Sept, Tues 7–9:30pm, Wed 11:30am–2pm, Thurs–Mon 11:30am–2pm and 7–9:30pm; Oct–Apr, Thurs–Tues 11:30am–2:30pm and 7–9:30pm. FRENCH.

The sun terrace in back of this Breton-type inn, a short walk from the château, is a refreshing place for dinner or tea. Gravel paths run among beds of pink geraniums and lilacs, and the red tables have bright canopies and umbrellas. The chef provides home cooking and cherry liqueur—a specialty of the region. In cool months meals are served in rustic dining rooms. Specialties are small chitterling sausages of Tours, chicken with Armagnac sauce, and coq au vin (chicken cooked in wine). The medallions of veal with mushroom-cream sauce are excellent. Tasty pastries are sold in the front room.

USSÈ

At the edge of the hauntingly dark forest of Chinon, the **Château d'Ussè** (☎ **02-47-95-54-05**) was the inspiration behind Perrault's legend of *Sleeping Beauty (La Belle au bois dormant)*. On a hill overlooking the Indre River, it's a complex of steeples, turrets, towers, chimneys, and dormers. Conceived as a medieval fortress, Ussè was erected at the dawn of the Renaissance. Two powerful families, the Bueil and d'Espinay, lived here in the 15th and 16th centuries. The terraces, laden with orange trees, were laid out in the 18th century.

The guided tour begins in the Renaissance chapel, with its sculptured portal and handsome stalls. Then you proceed to the royal apartments, furnished with tapestries and antiques. One gallery displays an extensive collection of swords and rifles. A spiral stairway leads to a tower with a waxwork Sleeping Beauty, and a panoramic view of the river.

The château is open daily February to October 9am to 6:30pm; it's closed from November to January. Admission is 59F ($9) for adults and 19F ($3.05) for children 8 to 16 (free 7 and under).

ESSENTIALS

GETTING THERE From Tours, motorists can follow D7 into Ussè, 28km (17 miles) away. The nearest rail station, Langrais, is 12km (7¹/₂ miles) away; from Langeais you have to take a taxi.

DEPARTING BY CAR Chinon is easily reached from Ussè via D-7 and D-17. You approach this ancient town with its rock-of-ages castle looming on the horizon.

CHINON

In the film *Joan of Arc,* Ingrid Bergman sought out the dauphin as he tried to conceal himself among his courtiers—an action whose real-life equivalent took place at the **Château de Chinon,** one of the oldest fortress-châteaux in France. Charles VII, mockingly known as the King of Bourges, centered his government at Chinon from 1429 to 1450. In 1429, with the English besieging Orléans, the Maid of Orléans, that "messenger from God," prevailed on the weak dauphin to give her an army. The rest is history. The seat of French power stayed at Chinon until the Hundred Years' War ended.

Chinon retains a medieval atmosphere. It consists of winding streets and turreted houses, many built in the 15th and 16th centuries in the heyday of the court. For the best view, drive across the river, turning right onto quai Danton. From that vantage point, you'll have the best perspective, seeing the castle in relation to the village and the river. The gables and towers make Chinon look like a toy village. The most typical street is **rue Voltaire,** lined with 15th- and 16th-century town houses. At no. 44,

Richard the Lion-Hearted died on April 6, 1199, after being mortally wounded while besieging Chalus in Limousin. In the heart of Chinon, the **Grand Carroi** was the crossroads of the Middle Ages.

The most famous son of Chinon, François Rabelais, the earthy and often bawdy Renaissance writer, lived on the Rue de la Lamproie where today a plaque marks the spot where his father practiced law and maintained a prestigious and prosperous home and office. The isolated cottage 6km (3½ miles) west of Chinon where he was born is the site of the **Musée François Rabelais,** La Devinière, 37500 Seuilly (☎ **02-47-95-91-18**). Entrance costs 24F ($3.85) for adults, and 17F ($2.70) for students and those under 24, and it's open as follows: January 1 to March 13 and October 1 to December 31, daily 9:30am to 12:30pm and 2 to 5pm; March 14 to April 30 daily 9:30am to 12:30pm and 2 to 6pm; May 1 to September 14, daily 10am to 7pm. To reach it from Chinon, follow the road signs pointing to Saumur and the D-17.

Château de Chinon (☎ **02-47-93-13-45**) is three separate strongholds, once badly ruined, but today at least two of the buildings, the Château du Milieu and Château du Coudray, have been entirely restored, with the exception of their still nonexistent roofs. Some of the grim walls from other dilapidated edifices remain, though many of the buildings—including the Great Hall where Joan of Arc sought out the dauphin—have been torn down. Some of the most destructive owners were the heirs of Cardinal Richelieu. Now gone, the Château de St Georges was built by Henry II of England, who died here in 1189. The Château du Milieu dates from the 11th to the 15th century, containing the keep and the clock tower, where the Musée Jeanne d'Arc has been installed. Separated from the latter by a moat, the Château du Coudray contains the Tour du Coudray, where Joan of Arc stayed during her time at Chinon. In the 14th century the Knights Templar were imprisoned here before meeting their violent deaths.

The château is open daily January 11 through March 14 from 9am to noon and 2 to 5pm, March 15 through June 30 and all of September from 9am to 6pm, July through August from 9am to 7pm, and October from 9am to 5pm. Admission is 28F ($4.50) for adults and 19F ($3.05) for children.

ESSENTIALS

GETTING THERE　　There are three **trains** daily from Tours (trip time: 1 hour). Call ☎ **08-36-35-35-35** for information and schedules. The train station lies at the edge of this very small town. Once leaving it, you walk along quai Jeanne d'Arc, taking a right at the Café de la Paix to get to place de l'Hôtel de Ville, the town hall, and the tourist office. There are three **buses** a day from Tours (trip time: 1½ hours).

VISITOR INFORMATION　　The **Office de Tourisme** is at 12 rue Voltaire (☎ **02-47-93-17-85**).

DEPARTING BY CAR　　Angers is generally considered the western end of the Loire Valley, though the Loire River continues for another 130km (80 miles) before reaching Nantes. To reach Angers, continue north from Chinon toward the river. The D-7 connects to the N-152 heading west all the way to Saumur. Once at Saumur, the D-952 continues west into Angers, a distance of 51km (32 miles).

WHERE TO STAY

Chris' Hôtel. 12 place Jeanne-d'Arc, 37500 Chinon. ☎ **02-47-93-36-92.** Fax 02-47-98-48-92. E-mail: infos@chris-hotel.fr. 33 units. TV TEL. 220–380F ($35–$61) double. AE, DC, MC, V. Free parking.

This well-run hotel is housed in a 19th-century building near the town's historic district. Many of the rooms are small but offer views of the castle and river. Most are furnished in a Louis XV style and all have modern amenities. Bathrooms are quite cramped. Breakfast is the only meal served.

WHERE TO DINE

✪ **Au Plaisir Gourmand.** 2 rue Parmentier. ☎ **02-47-93-20-48.** Reservations required. Main courses 80–150F ($13–$24); set price menus 175–340F ($28–$54). AE, V. Tues–Sat noon–2pm and 7:30–9:30pm, Sun noon–2pm. Closed Feb. FRENCH.

This is the premier restaurant in the area, owned by Jean-Claude Rigollet, who used to direct the chefs at the fabled Les Templiers in Les Bézards. His restaurant offers an intimate dining room with a limited number of tables in a charming 18th-century building. Menu items are likely to include roast rabbit in aspic with foie-gras sauce, oxtail in a Chinon red wine sauce, zander in beurre blanc, and sautéed crayfish with a spicy salad. For dessert, try the prunes stuffed in puff pastry.

ANGERS

Once the capital of Anjou, Angers straddles the Maine River. Although it suffered extensive damage in World War II, it has been considerably restored, somehow blending provincial charm with the suggestion of sophistication. The town is often used as a base for exploring the château district to the west.

The moated **Château d'Angers** (☎ **02-41-87-43-47**) from the 9th century, was once the home of the comtes d'Anjou. After the castle was destroyed, it was reconstructed by St. Louis. From 1230 to 1238 the outer walls and 17 massive towers were built, creating a formidable fortress well prepared to withstand invaders. The château was favored by Good King René; until he was forced to surrender Anjou to Louis XI, a brilliant court life flourished here. Louis XIV turned the château into a prison, dispatching his finance minister, Fouquet, to one of its cells. In the 19th century, the castle was also used as a prison, and during World War II, it was used by the Nazis as a munitions depot. Allied planes bombed it in 1944.

The castle displays the ✪ **Apocalypse Tapestries,** masterpieces of medieval art. (This series of tapestries wasn't always so highly regarded, they once served as a canopy for orange trees to protect the fruit from unfavorable weather and at another time to cover the damaged walls of a church.) The tapestries were created by Nicolas Bataille, master weaver, perhaps in the Parisian workshop of Robert Poinçon based on cartoons by Hennequin of Bruges. The series illustrates the book of St. John in 77 pieces that stretch 102m (335 feet). One scene is called *La Grande Prostituée,* and another shows Babylon invaded by demons; yet another is a peace scene with two multiheaded monsters holding up a fleur-de-lis.

You can tour the fortress, including the courtyard of the nobles, prison cells, ramparts, windmill tower, 15th-century chapel, and royal apartments. The château is open daily June to September 15 9:30am to 7pm and September 16 to May 10am to 5pm. Admission is 35F ($6) for adults, 23F ($3.70) for ages 13 to 25, and children 12 and under are free.

Cathédrale St-Maurice, place Monsigneur Shappoulie (☎ **02-41-87-58-45**), is mostly from the 12th and 13th centuries; the main tower, however, dates from the 16th century. The statues on the portal represent everybody from the Queen of Sheba to David at the harp. On the tympanum is depicted Christ Enthroned; the symbols, such as the lion for St. Mark, represent the Evangelists. The stained-glass windows from the 12th through the 16th century have made the cathedral famous. The oldest one illustrates the martyrdom of St. Vincent (the most unusual is of former St. Christopher with the head of a dog). Once all the Apocalypse Tapestries were shown here; now only a few remain, and they are mainly exhibited in summer. The 12th-century nave is a landmark in cathedral architecture, a clear, coherent plan that's a work of harmonious beauty, the start of the Plantagenet architecture. It's open daily 9am to 7pm.

ESSENTIALS

GETTING THERE   Trains arrive from Saumur (trip time: 30 minutes), Tours (trip time: 1 hour), and Paris-Montparnasse (trip time: 1½ hours). The station at place de la Gare in Angers is a convenient walk from the château. For information and schedules, call ☎ **08-36-35-35-35**. There are three bus connections a day from Saumur, Monday to Saturday (trip time: 1½ hours). Buses depart and arrive at Place de la République. Call ☎ **02-41-88-59-25** for schedules and information.

VISITOR INFORMATION   The **Office de Tourisme** is on place Kennedy (☎ **02-41-23-51-11**).

WHERE TO STAY

Hôtel d'Anjou. 1 bd. Foch, 49100 Angers. ☎ **800/528-1234** in the U.S., or 02-41-88-24-82. Fax 02-41-87-22-21. 51 units. MINIBAR TV TEL. 480–680F ($77–$109) double. AE, DC, MC, V. Parking 45F ($7).

Situated next to a large park, this hotel is the best choice for overnighting in the area. Although comparable in price to the Hôtel de France, it has more upscale appointments and amenities, and a better restaurant. The high-ceilinged and more spacious rooms are closer to the ground. All rooms and the small bathrooms were overhauled in 1998. Dining here is also satisfying. Set price menus from 130 to 210F ($21 to $34) are served in a setting that includes carefully maintained paneling, an antique tapestry, and a wood-burning fireplace.

Quality Hôtel de France. 8 place de la Gare, 49100 Angers. ☎ **02-41-88-49-42.** Fax 02-41-86-76-70. E-mail: hotel.de.france.anjou@wanadoo.fr. 57 units. MINIBAR TV TEL. 400–600F ($64–$96) double. AE, DC, MC, V. Parking 40F ($6).

This 19th-century hotel, one of the most respected in town, has been run by the Bouyers since 1893. It's the best choice near the rail station. Rooms are soundproof, but only four are air-conditioned (it can get hot on a summer night). Many of the rooms were renovated in the late 1990s. Bathrooms are very small with a shower stall and a hair dryer. The restaurant, Les Plantagenets, serves reliable set price meals.

WHERE TO DINE

Hôtel d'Anjou (see above) boasts the town's best restaurant.

Provence Caffè. 9 place du Ralliement. ☎ **02-41-87-44-15.** Reservations recommended. All main courses 85F ($14); set price menus 98–149F ($16–$24). AE, MC, V. Tues–Sat noon–2pm and 7–10pm. PROVENÇAL.

This restaurant celebrates the herbs, spices, and seafood of Provence. The decor includes bundles of herbs, bright colors, and souvenirs of the Mediterranean; the ambience is casual and sunny. Recommended dishes include a risotto served with asparagus and basil or with snails, grilled salmon with Provençal herbs, and a ballotine of chicken with ratatouille. The chef here continues to delight, perhaps with carpaccio of foie gras or sea wolf grilled with mushrooms and sprinkled with virgin olive oil.

3 Provence & the Côte d'Azur

Provence has been called a bridge between the past and present, where yesterday blends with today in a quiet, often melancholy way. Peter Mayle's best-selling *A Year in Provence* and *Toujours Provence* (as well as his other books about the area) has played no small part in the burgeoning popularity that this sunny corner of southern France has enjoyed during recent years.

The Greeks and Romans filled the landscape with cities boasting theaters, bathrooms, amphitheaters, and triumphal arches. Romanesque fortresses and Gothic cathedrals followed in the Middle Ages. In the 19th century, Provence's light and landscapes attracted illustrious painters like Cézanne and van Gogh to Aix and Arles and other towns.

Provence has its own language and customs. The region is bounded on the north by the Dauphine, the west by the Rhône, the east by the Alps, and the south by the Mediterranean. We cover the northern area of this region, what's traditionally thought of as Provence, and then head down to the southern part, what's known as the glittering Côte d'Azur, or French Riviera.

The Riviera has been called the world's most exciting stretch of beach and "a sunny place for shady people." Each resort on the Riviera—be it Beaulieu by the sea or eagle's-nest Eze—has a unique flavor and special merits. Glitterati and eccentrics have always been drawn to this narrow strip of fabled real estate. A trail of modern artists, attracted to the brilliant light, have left a rich heritage: Matisse in his chapel at Vence, Cocteau at Menton and Villefranche, Picasso at Antibes and seemingly everywhere else, Léger at Biot, Renoir at Cagnes, and Bonnard at Le Cannet. The best art collection of all is at the Maeght Foundation in St-Paul-de-Vence.

The Riviera's high season used to be winter and spring only. However, with changing tastes, July and August have become the most crowded months, and reservations are imperative. The average summer temperature is 24°C (75°F); the average winter temperature, 10°C (49°F).

The Corniches of the Riviera, depicted in countless films, stretch from Nice to Menton. The Alps drop into the Mediterranean and roads were carved along the way. The lower road, about 32km (20 miles) long, is the **Corniche Inférieure.** Along this road are the ports of Villefranche, Cap-Ferrat, Beaulieu, and Cap-Martin. Built between World War I and the beginning of World War II, the **Moyenne Corniche** (Middle Road), 30km (19 miles) long, also runs from Nice to Menton, winding spectacularly in and out of tunnels and through mountains. The highlight is at mountaintop Eze. The **Grande Corniche**—the most panoramic—was ordered built by Napoléon in 1806. La Turbie and Le Vistaero are the principal towns along the 32km (20-mile) stretch, which reaches more than 488m (1,600 feet) high at Col d'Eze.

In general, **tourist offices** in Provence are open April to September Monday to Friday 9am to 1pm and 2 to 6pm and Saturday and Sunday 9am to 1pm and 2 to 5pm (closed Sunday the rest of the year).

Our tour begins in Avignon, 684km (425 miles) south of Paris, 80km (50 miles) northwest of Aix-en-Provence, and 106km (66 miles) northwest of Marseille. Most motorists approach the city from Lyon in the north, taking the autoroute (A-7) south. If you haven't arranged for a rental before leaving home, you can head to the following offices in Avignon: **Budget** at the airport (☎ **04-90-27-94-95**) and at 2 av. de Montclair-Gare (☎ 04-90-27-94-95); **Hertz** at the airport (☎ **04-90-84-19-50**) and at 2 av. Montclair (☎ 04-90-82-37-67); and **Avis** at the airport (☎ **04-90-87-17-75**) and at 160 bis av. Pierre-Senmard (☎ 04-90-87-17-75).

Provence

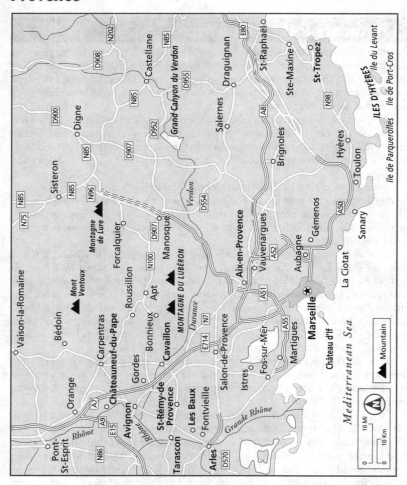

AVIGNON

In the 14th century, Avignon was the capital of Christendom; the popes lived here during what was called "the Babylonian Captivity." The legacy left by that "court of splendor and magnificence" makes Avignon one of the most interesting and beautiful of Europe's medieval cities.

ESSENTIALS

GETTING THERE   Avignon is a junction for bus routes throughout the region. For information about bus routes in the area, call ☎ **04-90-82-07-35;** you'll find the depot on boulevard St-Roch. Train service from other towns is also frequent. The TGV **trains** from Paris arrive 13 times per day (trip time: 4 hours), and 17 trains per day arrive from Marseille (trip time: 1¹/₂ hours). For train information and schedules, call ☎ **08-36-35-35-35;** the station at porte de la République. If you'd like to explore the area by **bike,** go to **Cycles Peugeot,** 80 rue Guillaume-Puy

(☎ 04-90-86-32-49), which rents all sorts of bikes for 60F ($10) per day, including 10-speed road bikes and mountain bikes. A deposit of 1,000F ($16) is required, either in the form of cash or a credit-card imprint.

VISITOR INFORMATION   The **Office de Tourisme** is at 41 cours Jean-Jaurès (☎ 04-32-74-32-74).

DEPARTING BY CAR   From Avignon, D-571 continues south to St-Rémy-de-Provence.

WHERE TO STAY

Hôtel d'Angleterre. 29 bd. Raspail, 84000 Avignon. ☎ 04-90-86-34-31. Fax 04-90-86-86-74. www.hotelangleterre.fr. 40 units (39 with bathroom). TV TEL. 190F ($30) double without bathroom; 300–360F ($48–$58) double with bathroom. MC, V. Free parking. Closed Dec 20–Jan 20.

In the heart of Avignon, this classical structure is the city's best budget hotel. Small rooms are comfortably but basically furnished; bathrooms are also small and shower-only. Breakfast is the only meal served.

✪ La Mirande. 4 place Amirande, 84000 Avignon. ☎ 04-90-85-93-93. Fax 04-90-86-26-85. E-mail: mirande@la-mirande.fr. 20 units. A/C MINIBAR TV TEL. 1,700–2,600F ($272–$416) double; 3,700F ($592) suite. AE, DC, V. Parking 80F ($13).

This restored 700-year-old town house in the heart of Avignon is one of France's grand little luxuries, far better than anything else in town. The individually designed rooms, most of which are quite spacious, have bedside controls, antiques, and art. Bathrooms are sumptuous, with hair dryers and make-up mirrors. The restaurant earns its one star in Michelin and is among the finest in Avignon. Set price menus run 240 to 480F ($38 to $77).

Mercure Palais-des-Papes. Quartier de la Balance, rue Ferruce, 84000 Avignon. ☎ 04-90-85-91-23. Fax 04-90-85-32-40. E-mail: ho549@accor-hotels.com. 87 units. A/C MINIBAR TV TEL. 550–595F ($88–$95) double. AE, DC, MC, V. Parking 47F ($8). Bus: 11.

This chain hotel is one of the best in Avignon, and is a good value for what it offers. It lies within the city walls, at the foot of the Palace of the Popes. Rooms are well furnished yet functional; what they lack in style they make up for in comfort. Bathrooms are small, but often contain a tub/shower combination. There's a small bar but breakfast is the only meal served.

WHERE TO DINE

✪ Christian Etienne. 10 rue Mons. ☎ 04-90-86-16-50. Reservations recommended. Main courses 170–210F ($27–$34); set price lunch (Mon–Fri) 170F ($27); set price dinners 320F ($51), 430F ($69), 500F ($80). AE, DC, MC, V. July, daily 12:30–1:30pm and 7:30–9:30pm; the rest of the year, Tues–Fri noon–2:30pm and 8–10:30pm, Sat and Sun 8–10:30pm. FRENCH.

This restaurant serves the best food in Avignon. The dining room contains very old ceiling and wall frescoes honoring the marriage of Anne de Bretagne to the French king in 1491. Several of the set price menus present specific themes, from vegetarian to lobster. À la carte specialties include a fillet of red snapper with a coulis of black olives; roasted pigeon with a truffle-enhanced sauce, and a dessert specialty of fennel-flavored sorbet with saffron-flavored English cream sauce.

La Fourchette. 7 rue Racine. ☎ 04-90-85-20-93. Set price lunch 100–150F ($16–$24); set price dinner 150F ($24). MC, V. Mon–Fri 12:30–2pm and 7:30–9:30pm. Closed Aug 5–29. Bus: 11. FRENCH.

This bistro offers creative cooking at a moderate price. There are two dining rooms, one like a summerhouse with walls of glass, the other more like a tavern with oak beams. You might begin with fresh sardines flavored with coriander, ravioli filled with haddock, or parfait of chicken liver with a spinach flan and confiture of onions. Grilled lambs' liver with raisins is a main course specialty.

EXPLORING THE TOWN

Even more famous than the papal residency is the ditty "*Sur le pont d'Avignon, l'on y danse, l'on y danse,*" echoing through every French nursery and around the world. Ironically, **pont St-Bénézet** was far too narrow for the danse of the rhyme, inspired, according to legend, by a vision a shepherd named Bénézet had while tending his flock. Spanning the Rhône and connecting Avignon with Villeneuve-lèz-Avignon, the bridge is now only a fragmented ruin. Built between 1177 and 1185, it suffered various disasters from then on; in 1669 half of it toppled into the river. On one of the piers is the two-story Chapelle St-Nicolas—one story in Romanesque style, the other Gothic. The bridge is open daily 9am to 6pm. Admission is 15F ($2.40) for adults and 7F ($1.10) for students, children, and seniors.

Dominating Avignon from a hill is the **Palais des Papes,** place du Palais-des-Papes (☎ **04-90-27-50-74**). You're shown through on a guided tour, usually lasting 50 minutes. Most of the rooms have been stripped of their finery; the exception is the Chapelle St-Jean, known for its beautiful frescoes of scenes from the life of John the Baptist and John the Evangelist, attributed to the school of Matteo Giovanetti and painted between 1345 and 1348. The Grand Tinel, or banquet hall, is about 41m (135 feet) long and 9m (30 feet) wide, and the pope's table stood on the southern side. The pope's bedroom is on the first floor of the Tour des Anges.

It's open daily November to March, 9:30am to 6:45pm; April to June and August to October, 9am to 7pm; July, 9am to 9pm. Admission is 45F ($7) for adults and 36F ($6) for students, children, and seniors. A guided tour, via either a trained staff member or a prerecorded cassette, is included in the price.

Near the palace is the 12th-century **Cathédrale Notre-Dame,** place du Palais-des-Papes (☎ **04-90-86-81-01**), containing the flamboyant Gothic tomb of Pope John XXII, who died at age 90. Benedict XII is also buried here. The cathedral's hours vary, but generally it's open daily 9am to 6pm and admission is free. From the cathedral, enter the promenade du Rocher-des-Doms to stroll through its garden and enjoy the view across the Rhône to Villeneuve-lèz-Avignon.

THE SHOPPING SCENE

Véronique Pichon, place Crillon (☎ **04-90-85-89-00**), is the newest branch of a porcelain manufacturer whose colorful products have been a regional fixture since the 1700s. Manufactured in the nearby town of Uzès, the tableware, decorative urns, statues, and lamps are cost-effective enough to be shipped virtually anywhere.

ST-RÉMY-DE-PROVENCE

Nostradamus, the French physician/astrologer and author of more than 600 obscure verses, was born here in 1503. In 1922 Gertrude Stein and Alice B. Toklas found St-Rémy after "wandering around everywhere a bit," as Stein once wrote to Cocteau. But mainly St-Rémy is associated with van Gogh, who committed himself to an asylum here in 1889 after cutting off his left ear. Between moods of despair, he painted such works as *Olive Trees* and *Cypresses* here. The town lies 26km (16 miles) northeast of Arles and 13km (8 miles) north of Les Baux.

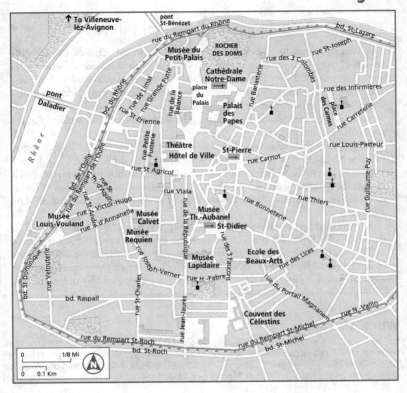

ESSENTIALS

GETTING THERE   There are local buses (no trains) from Avignon, which will let you off in the center of town (trip time: 45 minutes); between four to nine buses run per day. Call ☎ **04-90-82-07-35** in Avignon for information and schedules.

VISITOR INFORMATION   The **Office de Tourisme** is at place Jean-Jaurès (☎ **04-90-92-05-22**).

DEPARTING BY CAR   From St-Rémy-de-Provence, head south for 13km (8 miles) along the winding D-5 until you reach Les Baux.

WHERE TO STAY

Les Antiques. 15 av. Pasteur, 13210 St-Rémy-de-Provence. ☎ **04-90-92-03-02.** Fax 04-90-92-50-40. 27 units. MINIBAR TEL. 370–750F ($59–$120) double. AE, DC, MC, V. Closed Oct 20–Apr 7.

This stylish 19th-century villa is in a 3ha (7-acre) park with a pool. It contains an elegant reception lounge, which opens onto several salons, and Napoléon III furnishings. Handsomely furnished rooms come in a variety of styles and shapes. Those in the modern pavilion are more comfortable, larger, and have direct access to the garden, but they don't have much character as those in the main building. Bathrooms are small. In summer you're served breakfast (the only meal) in the former Orangerie.

Shopping for Provençal Fabric

The Avignon branch of **Les Olivades,** 28 rue des Marchands (☎ **04-90-86-13-42**), is one of the most visible of a chain of outlets associated in the States with Pierre Deux. Look for fabrics by the yard, bedcovers, slipcovers, draperies, and tablecloths. Fabrics, printed often by hand in a factory only 10km (6 miles) from Avignon, tend to feature intricate designs in colors inspired by 19th-century models or, to a somewhat lesser extent, Creole designs with butterflies, pineapples, bananas, and flowers.

The vision that launched **Les Indiens de Nîmes,** 4 rue Joseph-vernet (☎ **04-90-86-32-05**), in the early 1980s involved the duplication of 18th- and 19th-century Provençal fabric patterns. They're sold as fabric by the meter as well as clothing for men, women, and children. Kitchenware and a selection of furniture inspired by originals from Provence and the steamy wetlands west of Marseille are also sold.

All the clothing at **Souleiado,** 5 rue Joseph-Vernet (☎ **04-90-86-47-67**), derives from a Provençal model, and even the Provençal name (which translates as "first ray of sunshine after a storm") evokes a spirit on which the owners want to capitalize. Most, but not all, of the clothing is designed for women; there are some garments—shirts mostly—for men. Fabrics are also sold by the meter.

WHERE TO DINE

La Maison Jaune. 15 rue Carnot. ☎ **04-90-92-56-14.** Reservations recommended. www.franceweb.org/lamaisonjaune. E-mail: lamaisonjaune@wanadoo.fr. Set price lunches 120–295F ($19–$47); set price dinners 175–295F ($28–$47). MC, V. June–Sept Wed–Sun noon–2pm and Tues–Sun 7:30–9:30pm. Oct–May Tues–Sat noon–2pm and Mon–Sat 7:30–9:30pm. FRENCH/PROVENÇAL

One of the most enduringly popular restaurants in St-Remy lies within what was built during the 1700s as the home of a wealthy merchant. Today, in a pair of dining rooms scattered over two floors of the yellow-fronted building, you'll appreciate meals prepared and served with flair. An additional 34 seats are available in nice weather on an outdoor terrace. Good choices include pigeon roasted in wine from Les Baux; grilled sardines with candied lemon and raw fennel; artichoke hearts marinated in white wine; and a succulent roasted rack of lamb served with a black olive and anchovy tapenade.

EXPLORING ST-RÉMY & ENVIRONS

One interesting activity is visiting the cloisters of the asylum van Gogh made famous in his paintings at the 12th-century **Monastère de St-Paul-de-Mausolée.** Now a psychiatric hospital, the former monastery is east of D-5, a short drive north of Glanum (see below). You can't visit the cell in which van Gogh was confined, but it's still worth coming to explore the Romanesque chapel and cloisters with their circular arches and columns, which have beautifully carved capitals. The cloisters are open Tuesday to Sunday 9:30am to 6:30pm between June and September and Tuesday to Friday 11am to 5pm October to May. On your way to the church, you'll see a bust of Van Gogh. Admission costs 15F ($2.40) for adults, 10F ($1.60) ages 12 to 16, free 11 and under. There's no number that's available to the public within the monastery, but you can call the nearby clinic (☎ **04-90-92-77-00**) for information.

In the center of St-Rémy, **Musée Archéologique,** in the Hôtel de Sade, rue du Parage (☎ **04-90-92-64-04**), displays both sculptures and bronzes excavated at Glanum. It's open daily April to September, 10am to noon and 2 to 7pm; October to March, 10am to noon and 2 to 5pm. Admission is 15F ($2.40) for adults and 15F ($2.40) for students. Free for children 11 and under.

Just south of St-Rémy on D-5 is **Ruines de Glanum,** avenue Vincent-van-Gogh (☎ **04-90-92-23-79**), a Gallo-Roman city (follow the signs to Les Antiques). Its historical monuments include an Arc Municipal, a triumphal arch dating from the time of Julius Caesar, and a cenotaph called the Mausolée des Jules. Garlanded with sculptured fruits and flowers, the arch dates from 20 B.C. and is the oldest in Provence. The mausoleum was raised to honor the grandsons of Augustus and is the only extant monument of its type. In the area are entire streets and foundations of private residences from the 1st-century town. Some remains are from an even earlier Gallo-Greek town dating from the 2nd century B.C. Admission is 32F ($5) for adults, 21F ($3.35) ages 12 to 25, free 11 and under. The excavations are open daily April to September, 9am to 7pm; October to March, 9am to noon and 2 to 5pm.

LES BAUX

What Cardinal Richelieu called "a nesting place for eagles" lies 19km (12 miles) north of Arles and 80km (50 miles) north of Marseille and the Mediterranean. Once it was the citadel of the powerful seigneurs of Les Baux, today, in its lonely position high on a windswept plateau overlooking the southern Alpilles, Les Baux is a ghost of its former self. Still, there is no more dramatically situated town in Provence than this one nestled in a valley surrounded by mysterious, shadowy rock formations.

ESSENTIALS

GETTING THERE   There's no railway station in Les Baux, so consequently most rail passengers get off at Arles. From Arles, there're four **buses** daily that stop at Les Baux (trip time: 25 minutes), and an additional four or five that stop in the nearby hamlet of Maussane-les-Alpilles, 4km (2¹/₂ miles) to the south. The frequency of the bus service is reduced by about half between November and March. For information about buses, call ☎ **04-90-49-38-01** in Arles for information and schedules.

VISITOR INFORMATION   The **Office de Tourisme** is on Ilôt Post Tenebras Lux (☎ **04-90-54-34-39**).

DEPARTING BY CAR   From Les Baux continue southwest on D-17 for 19km (12 miles) to Arles.

WHERE TO STAY & DINE

✪ **La Riboto de Taven.** Le Val d'Enfer, 13520 Les Baux. ☎ **04-90-54-34-23.** Fax 04-90-54-38-88. Reservations required. Main courses 150–190F ($24–$30); set price lunch 220F ($35); set price dinners 300–450F ($48–$72). AE, DC, MC, V. Thurs–Mon noon–1:30pm and 7:30–9pm. Closed Jan 15–Mar 1. FRENCH.

This 1835 farmhouse outside the medieval section of town serves food filled with brawny flavors and the heady perfumes of Provençal herbs. In summer, you can sit out at the beautifully laid tables (one of which is a millstone). Menu items may include sea bass in olive oil, fricassee of mussels flavored with basil, and lamb en croute with olives—plus homemade desserts.

It's also possible to rent three double rooms so large they're like suites, each at 1,100F ($176), breakfast included.

Exploring Les Baux

Some one million visitors a year flock here to wander the feudal ruins, inspect the foundation of a demolished castle, and explore the facades of gracefully restored Renaissance homes. The **Château des Baux** (☎ **04-90-54-55-56**) is carved out of the rocky mountain peak; the site of this former castle covers an area at least five times that of Les Baux itself below. As you stand here, you can look out over the **Valley of Hell** (Val d'Enfer). (Later, you might be tempted to drive through its bleak and rugged scenery—access is from the D27 and D78G). At the castle you can enjoy panoramas from Tour Paravel and Tour Sarascenes. The site is open daily July and August, 9am to 8:30pm; September to February, 9am to 5pm; March to June, 9am to 6pm. Admission is 37F ($6) for adults, 28F ($4.50) for students, and 20F ($3.20) for ages 7 to 17 (free 6 and under).

ARLES

Arles, 35km (22 miles) southwest of Avignon and 88km (55 miles) northwest of Marseille, has been called "the soul of Provence," and art lovers, archaeologists, and historians alike are attracted to this town on the Rhône. Van Gogh left Paris for Arles in 1888 and painted some of his most celebrated works here—*Starry Night, The Bridge at Arles, Sunflowers,* and *L'Arlésienne* among others. Many of these luminous scenes remain to delight visitors today.

Arles isn't quite as charming as Aix-en-Provence, but it has first-rate museums, excellent restaurants, and summer festivals, such as an international photography festival in early June. Though not as lovely as it was when Picasso came here, Arles has enough antique Provençal flavor to keep the appeal alive.

Essentials

GETTING THERE   Arles lies on the Paris-Marseille and Bordeaux-St-Raphaël rail lines, so has frequent connections from most French cities. Ten **trains** arrive daily from Avignon (trip time: 20 minutes) and 10 per day from Marseille (trip time: 1 hour). From Aix-en-Provence, 10 trains arrive per day (trip time: $1^3/_4$ hours). Call ☎ **08-36-35-35-35** for details. There are about five **buses** per day from Aix-en-Provence (trip time: $1^3/_4$ hours). Call ☎ **04-90-49-38-01** for information and schedules. The bus station is adjacent to the railway station, a 10-minute walk from the center.

VISITOR INFORMATION   The **Office de Tourisme,** where you can buy a *Billet Global* (see below) is on the esplanade des Lices (☎ **04-90-18-41-20**). If you'd like to get around by bicycle, head for the newspaper kiosk immediately adjacent to the town's tourist information office, a site that doubles as the town's only bike rental outfit: **Europbike,** Kiosk à Journaux Le Provençal, Esplanade Charles de Gaulle (☎ **04-90-96-44-20**). A six-speed road bike—all that this emporium stocks—rents for 70F ($11) per day, and requires a deposit of 1,000F ($160). **Cycles peugeot,** 15 rue du Pont (☎ **04-90-96-03-77**), rents bikes at comparable rates.

DEPARTING BY CAR   From Arles, head east toward Aix-en-Provence on N-113. Once at Salon-de-Provence, take the autoroute southeast for 37km (23 miles) to Aix-en-Provence, the conclusion of your driving tour of Provence. After that, it's south to the French Riviera.

Where to Stay

Hôtel d'Arlatan. 26 rue du Sauvage, 13631 Arles. ☎ **04-90-93-56-66.** Fax 04-90-49-68-45. E-mail: hotel-arlatan@provenet.fr. 48 units. A/C MINIBAR TV TEL. 500–850F ($80–$136) double; 1,050–1,450F ($168–$232) suite. AE, DC, MC, V. Parking 70F ($11).

In the former residence of the comtes d'Arlatan de Beaumont, near place du Forum, this hotel has been managed by the same family since 1920. It was built in the 15th century on the ruins of an old palace—in fact, there's still a 4th-century wall. Rooms are furnished with authentic Provençal antiques and walls covered by tapestries. Try to get a room overlooking the garden. Those on the ground floor are largest. The bathrooms have hair dryers and often a tub/shower combination.

✪ **Hôtel Jules César et Restaurant Lou Marquês.** 7 bd. des Lices, 13200 Arles. ☎ **04-90-93-43-20.** Fax 04-90-93-33-47. www.julescesar.fr. E-mail: julescesar@calvanet.fr. 58 units. MINIBAR TV TEL. 850–1,250F ($136–$200) double; from 1,500F ($240) suite. AE, DC, MC, V. Parking 65F ($10). Closed Nov 12–Dec 23.

In the town center, this 17th-century former Carmelite convent is now a stately hotel with the best restaurant in Arles. Though this is a noisy neighborhood, most rooms face the quiet, unspoiled cloister. You wake to the scent of roses and the sounds of birds singing. The decoration is luxurious, with antique Provençal furnishings. Interior rooms are the most tranquil, but also the darkest. Most downstairs rooms are spacious; those upstairs have certain old-world charm that offsets their smaller size. Rooms in the modern extensions, though large and comfortable, lack character. In all cases, the bathrooms are supplied with deluxe toiletries, a hair dryer, and most have a tub/shower combination.

The restaurant, Lou Marquês, has tables outside on the front terrace. The food is extremely fresh. From the à la carte menu, we recommend bourride à la Provençale or Arles lamb. À la carte dinners average 210 to 380F ($34 to $61).

WHERE TO DINE

El Quinto Toro. 12 rue de la Liberté. ☎ **04-90-49-62-29.** Reservations recommended in summer. Main courses 50–80F ($8–$13). AE, V. Thurs–Tues noon–2:30pm and 7–10:30pm. PROVENÇAL/SPANISH.

Set within a few steps of the Place du Forum, and outfitted with a decor that's inspired by the *corrida* (bullfights) that are held in and around Arles, this is a well-managed restaurant with no more than 30 seats and a following of local fans. Some of the best food here is grilled over live coals that waft aromas from the busy kitchens into the dining rooms. You might begin with a platter of Spanish tapas, many of which derive from fresh seafood or vegetables; then follow with generous slabs of duck breast or fresh fish, both grilled, both succulent. A noteworthy specialty, not widely available, is a slab of wood-grilled bull steak from the Camargue. The owners pride themselves on the earthy simplicity of their cuisine, and don't provide fancy sauces, preferring instead to emphasize the natural juices and flavors of the meat or fish. A wide selection of French and Spanish wines and beers can accompany your meal.

EXPLORING ARLES

At the tourist office you can purchase a Billet Global, the all-inclusive pass that admits you to the town's museums, Roman monuments, and major attractions; it costs 60F ($10) for adults and 40F ($6) for children.

The town is full of Roman monuments. The general vicinity of the old Roman forum is occupied by **place du Forum,** shaded by plane trees. Once the Café de Nuit, immortalized by van Gogh, stood on this square. Two Corinthian columns and pediment fragments from a temple can be seen at the corner of the Hôtel Nord-Pinus. South of here is **place de la République** (also known as the place de l'Hôtel de Ville), the principal plaza, dominated by a 15m (50-foot) blue porphyry obelisk. On the north is the impressive Hôtel-de-Ville (town hall) from 1673, built to Mansart's plans and surmounted by a Renaissance belfry.

On the east side of the square is the **Eglise St-Trophime** (☎ 04-90-96-07-38), noted for its 12th-century portal, one of the finest achievements of southern Romanesque style. In the pediment Christ is surrounded by the symbols of the Evangelists. The cloister, in both the Gothic and Romanesque styles, is noted for its medieval carvings. Admission is free. The church is open Monday to Saturday 8:30am to 6:30pm, Sunday 8:30am to 6pm. The cloister's hours are Monday to Saturday 9am to noon and 2:30 to 6pm. Admission is 15F ($2.40) for adults and 9F ($1.45) for students and children under 12.

Museon Arlaten (☎ 04-90-96-08-23) is entered at 29 rue de la République (its name is written in old Provençal style.) It was founded by Frédéric Mistral, the Provençal poet and leader of a movement to establish Modern Provençal as a literary language, using the money from his Nobel Prize for literature in 1904. This is really a folklore museum, with regional costumes, portraits, furniture, dolls, a music salon, and one room devoted to mementos of Mistral. The museum is open April to October daily 9am to noon and 2 to 6pm (until 6:30pm in July and August); November to March Tuesday to Sunday 9:30am to 12:30pm and 2 to 5pm. Admission is 25F ($4) for adults and 20F ($3.20) for ages 12 to 18, free 11 and under.

The city's two great classical monuments are the **Théâtre Antique,** rue du Cloître (☎ 04-90-96-93-30), and the Amphitheater. The Roman theater begun by Augustus in the 1st century, was mostly destroyed and only two Corinthian columns remain. Now rebuilt, the theater is the setting for an annual drama festival in July. The theater was where the Venus of Arles was discovered in 1651. Take rue de la Calade from the town hall. The theater is open daily March to November 10am to noon and 2 to 4:30pm; off-season 10 to 11:30am and 2 to 4pm. Admission is 15F ($2.40) for adults, 9F ($1.45) for children.

Nearby, the **Amphitheater,** Rond-Pont des Arènes (☎ 04-90-49-36-36), also built in the 1st century, seats almost 25,000 and still hosts bullfights in summer. The government warns you to visit the old monument at your own risk because of the worn and uneven masonry. For a good view, you can climb the three towers that remain from medieval times, when the amphitheater was turned into a fortress. Admission is 15F ($2.40) for adults and 9F ($1.45) 16 and under. Hours are daily March to November 10am to noon and 2 to 4:30pm; off-season 10 to 11:30am and 2 to 4pm.

The most memorable sight in Arles is **Les Alyscamps,** rue Pierre-Renaudel (☎ 04-90-49-36-36), once a necropolis established by the Romans, converted into a Christian burial ground in the 4th century. As the latter, it became a setting for legends in epic medieval poetry and was even mentioned in Dante's Inferno. Today, it's lined with poplars and the remaining sarcophagi; a cool oasis in hot weather. Open daily June to September 8:30am to 7pm, October and March to May 9am to noon and 2 to 4:30pm, and November to February 10 to 11:30am and 2 to 4pm. Admission is 15F ($2.40) for adults and 9F ($1.45) for children. Another ancient monument is the **Thermes de Constantin,** rue Dominique-Maisto, near the banks of the Rhône. Today, only the bathrooms (*thermae*) remain of a once-grand imperial palace. Visiting hours and admission prices are the same as at Les Alyscamps.

AIX-EN-PROVENCE

Founded in 122 B.C. by Roman general Caius Sextius Calvinus, who named it Aquae Sextiae after himself, Aix evolved from a Roman military outpost to a provincial administrative capital, the seat of an archbishop, and the official residence of the medieval comtes de Provence.

The celebrated son of this old capital city of Provence is Paul Cézanne, who immortalized the countryside nearby. Montagne Ste-Victoire looms over the town today just as it did in Cézanne's time, though a string of high rises has cropped up. This faded university town, Provence's most charming center, was once a seat of aristocracy, its streets walked by counts and kings. It's 80km (50 miles) southeast of Avignon and 32km (20 miles) north of Marseille.

ESSENTIALS

GETTING THERE   As a rail and highway junction, the city is easily accessible, with **trains** arriving hourly from Marseille (trip time: 40 minutes) at the station off rue Gustave Desplace at the end of avenue Victor Hugo. For details, call ☎ **08-36-35-35-35.** There's frequent **bus** service in and out of Aix's **Gare Routière** (☎ **04-42-91-26-80** for information), including four a day to and from Avignon (trip time: 1¹/₂ hours). Buses arrive at the station on rue Lapierre at intervals of between 15 and 30 minutes throughout the day from Marseille. If you'd like to explore the region by bike, contact **Cycles Naddeo,** 54 av. de Lattre-de-Tassigny (☎ **04-42-21-06-93**), which rents 10-speeds for 80F ($13) per day or mountain bikes for 100F ($16) per day. Either a passport or some form of currency representing between 1,000F ($160) and 2,500F ($400), depending on the value of the bike, is required at the time of rental. The shop lies in the heart of town, midway between town hall and the town's main police station.

VISITOR INFORMATION   The **Office de Tourisme** is at 2 place du Général-de-Gaulle (☎ **04-42-16-11-61**).

DEPARTING BY CAR   From Aix-en-Provence, the best way to reach St-Tropez is to take the autoroute (A-8) southeast to the junction with Route 25, then cut south to Ste-Maxime. Once at Ste-Maxime, follow N-98 west to Port Grimaud, at which point you connect with D-98A going east for the final lap to St-Tropez.

WHERE TO STAY

Hôtel Cardinal. 22-24 rue Cardinale, 13100 Aix-en-Provence. ☎ **04-42-38-32-30.** Fax 04-42-26-39-05. 29 units. TV TEL. 280–400F ($45–$64) double. MC, V.

Not everything is state of the art, but to many, the Cardinal is still the best value in Aix. Lying on the other side of the Cours in the Mazarin quarter, it is distinguished by a lingering air of fragility and nostalgia. Guests stay in simply furnished old rooms either in the main building or in the annex up the street. Some of the annex rooms have serviceable kitchens. Bathrooms tend to be small but each has a good shower.

✪ **Villa Gallici.** Av. de la Violette (impasse des Grands Pins), 13100 Aix-en-Provence. ☎ **04-42-23-29-23.** Fax 04-42-96-30-45. E-mail: villagallici@relaischateaux.fr. 22 units. A/C MINIBAR TV TEL. 1,000–2,500F ($160–$400) double; 2,500–3,050F ($400–$488) suite. AE, DC, MC, V.

This elegant inn is the most stylishly decorated in Aix. Each large room has a safe and a king-sized bed, often canopied. Some rooms boast a private terrace or garden. Bathrooms are large with hair dryers and makeup mirrors. The villa sits in a large enclosed garden in the heart of town, close to one of the best restaurants, Le Clos de la Violette. Simple meals can be ordered from this restaurant and eaten beside the pool. The hotel also has its own restaurant, serving an à la carte menu. On the premises are limited spa facilities.

WHERE TO DINE

Le Bistro Latin. 18 rue de la Couronne. ☎ **04-42-38-22-88.** Reservations recommended. Set price lunch 75–95F ($12–$15); set price dinner 125–145F ($20–$23) and 185F ($30). MC, V. Mon 7–10:30pm and Tues–Sat noon–2pm and 7–10:30pm. Bus: 27, 42, or 51. FRENCH.

This is the best little bistro in Aix for the price. Provençal music plays in two intimate, antique-decorated dining rooms, and the staff is young and enthusiastic. Try the chartreuse of mussels, one of the meat dishes with spinach-and-saffron cream sauce, or crepe of hare with basil sauce. We've enjoyed the classic cuisine, particularly the scampi risotto, on all our visits.

✪ **Le Clos de la Violette.** 10 av. de la Violette. ☎ **04-42-23-30-71.** Reservations required. Main courses 185–210F ($30–$34); set price lunch 300–600F ($48–$96); set price dinner 600F ($96). AE, V. Mon 7:30–9:30pm, Tues–Sat noon–1:30pm and 7:30–9:30pm. Closed 2 weeks in Nov and 1 week in Feb. Bus: 27, 42, or 51. FRENCH.

In an elegant residential neighborhood, which most visitors reach by taxi, this is the most innovative restaurant in town. The food produced by Jean-Marc and Brigitte Banzo has been called a "song of Provence." Typical dishes—though they change every 2 months—are an upside-down tart of snails with parsley juice, slow-cooked lamb with brown sauce, scallops with artichoke hearts, and a sumptuous array of desserts.

EXPLORING THE CITY

✪ **Cours Mirabeau,** the main street, is one of the most beautiful in Europe. Plane trees act like umbrellas, shading the street from the hot Provençal sun and filtering the light into shadows that play on the rococo fountains. On one side are shops and sidewalk cafes, on the other richly embellished sandstone *hôtels particuliers* (mansions) from the 17th and 18th centuries. The street, which honors Mirabeau, the revolutionary and statesman, begins at the 1860 landmark fountain on place de la Libération.

Cathédrale St-Sauveur, place des Martyrs de la Résistance (☎ **04-42-23-45-65**), is dedicated to Christ under the title St-Sauveur (Holy Savior). Its baptistery dates from the 4th and 5th centuries, but the architectural complex as a whole has seen many additions. It contains a brilliant Nicolas Froment triptych, *The Burning Bush,* from the 15th century. One side depicts the Virgin and Child, the other Good King René and his second wife, Jeanne de Laval. It's open daily 7:30am to noon and 2 to 6pm; masses are Sunday at 9am, 10:30am, and 7pm.

Nearby in a former archbishop's palace is the **Musée des Tapisseries,** 28 place de l'Ancien Archeveche (☎ **04-42-23-09-91**). Lining its gilded walls are three series of tapestries from the 17th and 18th centuries collected by the archbishops to decorate the palace: *The History of Don Quixote* by Natoire, *The Russian Games* by Leprince, and *The Grotesques* by Monnoyer. In addition, the museum exhibits rare furnishings from the 17th and 18th centuries. It's open Wednesday to Monday 10am to noon and 2 to 5:45pm; admission is 10F ($1.60).

Up rue Cardinale is the **Musée Granet,** place St-Jean-de-Malte (☎ **04-42-38-14-70**), which owns a not-very-typical collection Cézannes. Matisse donated a nude in 1941. Housed in the former center of the Knights of Malta, the fine-arts gallery contains work by Van Dyck, Van Loo, and Rigaud; portraits by Pierre and François Puget; and (the most interesting) a Jupiter and Thetis by Ingres. Ingres also did an 1807 portrait of the museum's namesake, François Marius Granet. Granet's own works abound. The museum is open Wednesday to Monday 10am to noon and 2 to 6pm; closed January. Admission is 10F ($1.60).

Outside town, at 9 av. Paul-Cézanne, is the **Atelier de Cézanne** (☎ **04-42-21-06-53**), the studio of the painter who was the major forerunner of cubism.

Surrounded by a wall, the house was restored by American admirers. Repaired again in 1970, it remains much as Cézanne left it in 1906. It's open daily 10am to noon and from 2 to 6pm (till 5pm between October and May). Admission costs 25F ($4) for adults and 10F ($1.60) for students and seniors, free 15 and under.

THE SHOPPING SCENE

Founded in 1934 and set on a busy boulevard just outside the center of Aix, the show-room and factory of **Santons Fouque,** 65 cours Gambetta (Route de Nice, RN7) (☎ **04-42-26-33-38**), stocks the largest assortment of santons in Aix. More than 1,800 figurines are cast in terra cotta, finished by hand, then painted according to 18th-century models. Each of the trades practiced in medieval Provence is represented, including grizzled but awestruck shoemakers, barrel makers, copper- and ironsmiths, and rope makers, each poised to welcome the newborn Jesus. Depending on their size and complexity, figurines range from 22 to 5,600F ($3.50 to $896). At **Girault,** 35 rue Bedarrides (☎ **04-42-27-17-35**), another outlet for santons, a faithful allegiance to the models of long ago is extremely important. Prices are competitive with those charged by Santons Foque, above.

Few boutiques carry so many *santons* (carved Nativity figurines), locally woven tex-tiles and carvings, and an assortment of *calissons* (sugared confections made with almonds and a *confit* of melon) as **La Boutique du Pays d'Aix,** 2 place du Général-de-Gaulle, in the Aix-en-Provence Tourist Information Office (☎ **04-42-16-11-61**). Established a century ago and a standard stop for anyone planning a dinner party in and around Aix, **Bechard,** 12 cours Mirabeau (☎ **04-42-26-06-78**), is the most famous bakery in town. It takes its work so seriously that it refers to its underground kitchens as a *laboratoire* (laboratory). The pastries are truly gorgeous, in most cases made fresh every day.

ST-TROPEZ

Sun-kissed lasciviousness is rampant in this carnival town, 76km (47 miles) southwest of Cannes, but the true Tropezian resents the fact that the port has such a bad repu-tation. "We can be classy, too," one native insisted. Creative people in the arts and ordinary folk create a compelling mixture.

Colette lived here for many years. Diarist Anaïs Nin, confidante of Henry Miller, posed on the beach in 1939 in a Dorothy Lamour bathing suit. Earlier, St-Tropez was known to Guy de Maupassant, Matisse, and Bonnard. Today, artists, composers, nov-elists, and the film colony come to St-Tropez in summer. Trailing them is a line of humanity unmatched anywhere else on the Riviera for sheer flamboyance.

ESSENTIALS

GETTING THERE   The nearest rail station is in St-Raphaël, a neighboring resort; at the Vieux Port, four or five boats per day leave the **Gare Maritime de St-Raphaël,** rue Pierre Auble (☎ **04-94-95-17-46**), for St-Tropez (trip time: 50 minutes). Some 15 **Sodetrav buses** per day leave from the **Gare Routière** in St-Raphaël (☎ **04-94-95-24-82**), for St-Tropez (trip time: 1¹/₂ to 2¹/₄ hours). Buses also run directly to St-Tropez from its nearest airport at Toulon-Hyères, 56km (35 miles) away. If you drive, be aware that parking in St-Tropez is extremely difficult, especially in summer, when the carnival atmosphere virtually guarantees a shortage of parking spots. In 1998, some of the situation was relieved with the construction of a multi-storied parking lot beneath the Place des Lices, **Parc des Lices** (☎ **04-94-97-34-46**), whose entrance is on the Avenue Paul Roussel. Designed for 471 cars, it charges between 8 to 13F ($1.30 to $2.10) for the first hour, and between 8 to 12F ($1.30 to $1.90) for each subsequent hour, depending on the season. Many visitors with expensive cars prefer this site, as it's more carefully supervised and guarded than other parking lots in St-Tropez.

VISITOR INFORMATION   The **Office de Tourisme** is on quai Jean-Jaurès (☎ 04-94-97-45-21).

DEPARTING BY CAR   After leaving St-Tropez, take the D-98A northwest again (the same route you traveled to get here), and link up with D-559 at the junction, heading east to Ste-Maxime. This route, which becomes N-98, will take you all the way to Cannes.

WHERE TO STAY

✪ **Hôtel Byblos.** Av. Paul-Signac, 83990 St-Tropez. ☎ **800/223-6800** in the U.S., or 04-94-56-68-00. Fax 04-94-56-68-01. www.byblos.com. E-mail: saint-tropez@byblos.com. 98 units. A/C MINIBAR TV TEL. 1,750–3,350F ($280–$536) double; from 6,200F ($992) suite. AE, DC, MC, V. Parking 150F ($24). Closed Oct 15–Apr 17.

This deluxe complex on a hill over the harbor resembles a palace in Beirut with salons decorated with Phoenician gold statues from 3000 B.C. Rooms are imaginative—for example, with a fireplace on a raised hearth with beds recessed on a dais. Le Hameau contains 10 duplex apartments built around a small courtyard with an outdoor spa. Some rooms have balconies overlooking an inner courtyard; others open onto a terrace of flowers. About 10 rooms are completely rejuvenated every season. Bathrooms are well equipped with robes, step-down tubs, and deluxe toiletries. You can dine by the pool at Les Arcades, enjoying Provençal food, or try the Italian restaurant.

Hôtel Ermitage. Av. Paul-Signac, 83990 St-Tropez. ☎ **04-94-97-52-33.** Fax 04-94-97-10-43. 26 units. TV TEL. 630–990F ($101–$158) double. AE, DC, MC, V.

Attractively isolated amid the rocky heights of St-Tropez, this hotel was built in the 19th century as a private villa. A walled garden is illuminated at night, and a cozy corner bar near a wood-burning fireplace takes the chill off blustery evenings. Rooms, although a bit small, offer good value for St-Tropez, and have an efficiently organized and well-maintained bathroom with a shower. The staff can be charming. Breakfast is the only meal served.

Hôtel la Tartane. Route des Salins, 83990 St-Tropez. ☎ **04-94-97-21-23.** Fax 04-94-97-09-16. 14 units. A/C MINIBAR TV TEL. 650–1,000F ($104–$160) double. AE, DC, V. Closed Oct 15–Easter.

This cozy, small-scale hotel was built in the 1980s midway between the center of St-Tropez and the Plage des Salins, about a 3-minute drive from each. There's a stone-rimmed pool set into the garden, attractively furnished public rooms with terra-cotta floors, and an attentive management that works hard to keep everything pulled together. Rooms are well-furnished bungalows centered around the pool, but the bathrooms are on the small side. Breakfasts are elaborate and attractive; bouillabaisse and fresh fish from the Mediterranean are the specialties in the hotel restaurant.

WHERE TO DINE

L'Echalotte. 35 rue Allard. ☎ **04-94-54-83-26.** Reservations recommended in summer. Main courses 80–140F ($13–$22); set price menus 105–160F ($17–$26). AE, MC, V. Thurs 8–11:30pm, Fri–Wed 12:30–2pm and 8–11:30pm. Closed Nov 15–Dec 15. FRENCH.

This charming restaurant, with a tiny garden, serves consistently good food for moderate prices. You can enjoy lunch on the veranda or dinner indoors. The food is solidly bourgeois, including grilled veal kidneys, crayfish with drawn-butter sauce, and fillet of turbot with truffles. The major specialty is several kinds of fish, like sea bass and daurade royale cooked in a salt crust.

The French Riviera

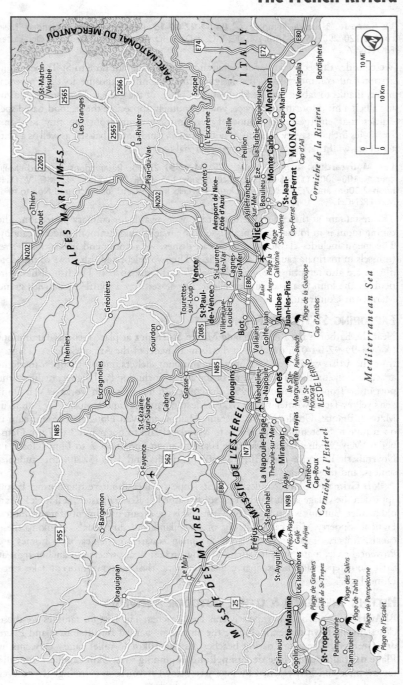

La Ramade. 3 rue du Temple. ☎ **04-94-97-00-15.** Reservations recommended. Main courses 120–290F ($19 –$46). AE, DC, MC, V. Daily 8pm–midnight. Closed: mid-Oct–Easter. PROVENÇAL.

We consider this courtyard-style restaurant an appealing antidote to St-Tropez's congestion and commercialism. It's designed for maximum exposure to the Provençal night, thanks to tables arranged beneath the tables of the garden. Despite the charming albeit a bit disorganized service, you'll genuinely appreciate the seafood-based specialties that emerge amid clouds of herb-infused steam from the tiny kitchens. Examples include savory versions of both *bourrides* and bouillabaisses; as well as a platter of sea wolf that's slow-roasted over charcoal flames.

Les Mouscardins. 1 rue Portalet. ☎ **04-94-97-29-00.** Reservations required. Main courses 100–300F ($16–$48); set price menus 135–210F ($22–$34). AE, MC, V. Daily noon–2:30pm and 7:30–11:30pm. Closed 2 weeks in Nov, and for lunch mid-Nov to mid-Mar. FRENCH.

This restaurant at the end of the harbor has won awards for culinary perfection. The dining room is in formal Provençal style with an adjoining sunroom under a canopy. The menu includes classic Mediterranean dishes; we recommend *moules marinières* (mussels in marinara sauce) as an appetizer. The two celebrated fish stews of the Côte d'Azur are also tempting: *bourride Provençale* and bouillabaisse. The fish dishes, particularly the loup (sea bass), are excellent. For dessert, try a soufflé made with grand Marnier or Cointreau.

EXPLORING ST-TROPEZ & ENVIRONS

Near the harbor is the **l'Annonciade Musée St-Tropez** at place Georges-Grammont (☎ **04-94-97-04-01**), installed in the former chapel of the Annonciade. As a legacy from the artists who loved St-Tropez, the museum shelters one of the finest modern-art collections on the Riviera. Many of the artists, including Paul Signac, depicted the port of St-Tropez. Opened in 1955, the collection includes such works as Van Dongen's yellow-faced Women of the Balustrade and paintings and sculpture by Bonnard, Matisse, Braque, Utrillo, Seurat, Derain, Maillol, and Van Dongen. The museum is open June to September Wednesday to Monday 10am to noon and 3 to 7pm; October to May Wednesday to Monday 10am to noon and from 2 to 6pm (closed in November). Entrance costs 30F ($4.80) for adults and 15F ($2.40) for students, seniors, and those under 16.

Port Grimaud, 3km (2 miles) from St-Tropez, makes an interesting outing. If you approach the village at dusk, when it's softly bathed in Riviera pastels, it'll look like an old hamlet. But this is a mirage. Port Grimaud is the dream fulfillment of its promoter, François Spoerry, who carved it out of marshland and dug canals. Flanking these canals, fingers of land extend from the main square to the sea. The homes are Provençal style, many with Italianate window arches. Boat owners can anchor right at their doorsteps. One newspaper called the port "the most magnificent fake since Disneyland."

HITTING THE BEACH & OTHER OUTDOOR ACTIVITIES

BEACHES   St-Tropez has the Riviera's best beaches. The best for families are those closest to the town center, including the amusingly named **Bouillabaisse** and **Plage des Greniers.** The more daring beaches are the 10km (6-mile) sandy crescents at **Plage des Salins** and **Plage de Pampellone,** beginning some 3km (2 miles) from the town center and best reached by bike (see below) if you're not driving. If you ever wanted to go topless, bottomless, or wear a truly daring bikini, this is the place!

BICYCLING   The largest outfitter for bikes and motor scooters is Louis Mas, 5 rue Josef-Quaranta (☎ **04-94-97-00-60**). Bikes rent for plus 48F ($8) per hour; motor scooters go for 190 to 275F ($30 to $44) per hour, depending on the size. A deposit of 1,000F ($160), payable with American Express, MasterCard, or Visa, is also required.

BOATING   We recommend **Suncap Company,** 15 Quai de Suffren (☎ **04-94-97-11-23**), which rents boats that range from 5.5m (18 feet) to 12m (40 feet). The smallest can be rented to qualified sailors without a captain, whereas the larger ones come with a captain at the helm. Daily rates start at 3,000F ($480).

GOLF   The nearest golf course, at the edge of Ste-Maxime, across the bay from St-Tropez, is the **Golf Club de Beauvallon,** bd. des Collines, Grimaud, 83120 Ste-Maxime (☎ **04-94-96-16-98**), a popular course that brought its complement of holes up to 18 after a massive improvement and enlargement in 1996. No golf carts are available. Greens fees range from 250 to 300F ($40 to $48) for 18 holes, and a set of golf clubs rents for 100F ($16) per set.

Sprawling over a rocky, vertiginous landscape that requires a golf cart and a lot of physical labor is the Don Harradine-designed **Golf de Ste-Maxime-Plaza,** Route de Débarquement, B.P. 1, 83120 Ste-Maxime (☎ **04-94-55-02-02**). Built in 1991 and associated with the four-star Plaza de Ste-Maxime, it also welcomes nonguests; phone to reserve tee times. Greens fees for 18 holes are 250 to 280F ($40 to $45) per person; renting a cart for two golfers and their equipment costs 125F ($20) per 18 holes.

SCUBA DIVING   A team of dive enthusiasts who are ready, willing, and able to show you the azure depths off the coast of St-Tropez operate from the *Octopussy I and II,* based year-round in St-Tropez's Nouveau Port. Experienced divers pay 230F ($37) for a one-tank exploration dive, and novices are charged 250F ($40) for a *baptème,* which includes one-on-one supervision from a monitor and a descent to a depth of around 5m (15 feet). For reservations and information, call or write Les Octopussys, Quartier de Berteau, Gassin, 83990 St-Tropez (☎ **04-94-56-53-10**).

TENNIS   Anyone who phones in advance can use the eight courts (both artificial grass and "Quick," a form of concrete) at the **Tennis-Club de St-Tropez,** Route des Plages, in St-Tropez's industrial neighborhood of St-Claude (☎ **04-94-97-15-52**), about ¹/₂ mile from the resort's center. The courts are open year-round and rent for 100F ($16) per hour until 5pm and 130F ($21) per hour after 5pm.

The Shopping Scene

In a resort that's increasingly loaded with purveyors of suntan lotion, touristy souvenirs, and T-shirts, **Jacqueline Thienot,** 12 rue Georges-Clemenceau (☎ **04-94-97-05-70**), maintains an inventory of Provençal antiques, prized by dealers from as far away as Paris. The one-room shop is housed in a late 18th-century building that shows the 18th- and 19th-century antiques to their best advantage.

Although better stocked than the norm, **Choses,** Quai Jean-Jaurès (☎ **04-94-97-03-44**), is a women's clothing store typical of the hundreds of middle-bracket, whimsically nonchalant emporiums that thrive throughout the Riviera. Its specialty includes clingy and often provocative T-shirt dresses. **Galeries Tropéziennes,** 56 rue Gambetta (☎ **04-94-97-02-21**), crowds hundreds of unusual gift items, some worthwhile, some rather silly, and textiles into its rambling showrooms near place des Lices. The inspiration is Mediterranean, breezy and sophisticated.

St-Tropez After Dark

Located on the lobby level of the hyperexpensive, hyperelegant Hôtel Byblos, **Les Caves du Roy,** av. Paul-Signac (☎ **04-94-97-16-02**), is the most prestigious and most self-consciously chic nightclub in St-Tropez. Entrance is free, but drinks cost a whooping 120F ($19) each. It's open nightly from 11:30pm till dawn, but only from Easter to late September.

Le Papagayo, in the Residence du Nouveau Port, rue Gambetta (☎ **04-94-97-07-56**), is one of the largest nightclubs in St-Tropez, with two floors, three bars, and lots of attractive women and men from throughout the Mediterranean eager to pursue their bait. The decor is neopsychedelic, and the clientele is youthful and high-energy. Between Easter and late September, it's open nightly 11:30pm till dawn. The rest of the year, it's open only on preselected weekends, usually as part of the celebrations of local charities and sports clubs, events to which the public is welcome. Cover is 110F ($18) and includes one drink.

Most of the socializing at the largely gay **Le Pigeonnier,** 13 rue de la Ponche (☎ **04-94-97-84-26**), revolves around the long and narrow bar, where drinks cost around 75F ($12). The crowd is composed of some lesbians, but mostly gay men in their 20s or early 30s from all over Europe. There's also a dance floor. Cover is 90F ($14) and includes one drink.

CANNES

When Coco Chanel came here and got a suntan, returning to Paris bronzed, she startled the milk-white ladies of society. But they quickly began copying her. Today the bronzed bodies—in nearly nonexistent swimsuits—still line the sandy beaches of this chic resort.

Popular with celebrities, Cannes is at its most frenzied during the **International Film Festival** at the Palais des Festivals on promenade de la Croisette, held in either April or May. On the seafront boulevards, flashbulbs pop as the stars emerge. International regattas, galas, concours d'élégance, even a Mimosa Festival in February—something is always happening at Cannes, except in November, traditionally a dead month.

Cannes, sheltered by hills, lies 26km (16 miles) southwest of Nice. For many it consists of only one street, **promenade de la Croisette** (or just La Croisette), curving along the coast and split by islands of palms and flowers. A port of call for cruise liners, the seafront is lined with hotels, apartment houses, and chic boutiques. Many of the bigger hotels, some dating from the 19th century, claim part of the beaches for the private use of their guests. But there are also public areas.

ESSENTIALS

GETTING THERE   Cannes lies on the major coastal rail line along the Riviera, with trains arriving at the station at 1 rue Jean-Laurès from Antibes (trip time: 15 minutes) and Nice (trip time: 35 minutes). The TGV from Paris going via Marseille (trip time: $4^1/_2$ hours) also services Cannes. For information and schedules, call ☎ **08-36-35-35-35. Bus** service is available from the Nice airport to Cannes every hour during the day (trip time: 35 minutes). For bus information about Cannes routes, call ☎ **04-93-45-20-08;** the station is at place de l'Hôtel de Ville. There's also one bus every half-hour from Antibes. The international airport at Nice is only 20 minutes northeast of Cannes.

VISITOR INFORMATION   The **Office de Tourisme** is in the Palais des Festivals, Esplanade Georges Pompidou (☎ **04-93-39-24-53**).

DEPARTING BY CAR   From Cannes, N-7 heads directly east to the resort of Juan-les-Pins, a distance of 10km (6 miles).

WHERE TO STAY

Although hotels in Cannes might elect to have their own e-mail address, there is a shared and collective e-mail number for al hotels in the city: infos@cannes.hotel.com.

Very Expensive

Hôtel Carlton Inter-Continental. 58 bd. de la Croisette, 06400 Cannes. ☎ **800/327-0200** in the U.S., or 04-93-06-40-06. Fax 04-93-06-40-25. www.interconti. com. E-mail: canne@interconti.com. 338 units. A/C MINIBAR TV TEL. 2,040–4,090F ($326–$654) double; from 6,490F ($1,038) suite. AE, DC, MC, V. Parking 180F ($31). Bus: 11.

Today, except for the Cannes Film Festival, you are more likely to see conventions and groups than the stars and royalty of past years. Rooms feature double-glazed windows and big combination bathrooms with hair dryers. The most spacious rooms are in the west wing, and many on the upper floors open onto balconies fronting the sea. The Carlton Casino Club opened in 1989, and La Côte restaurant, open only June to September, is one of the most distinguished along the Riviera. Otherwise, la Belle Otéro is open for lunch and dinner most of the year. The cuisine here, some of the finest along the entire Riviera, wins two stars from Michelin, and is the only restaurant in Cannes to rival Palme d'Or. There's a private beach, health club with spa facilities, and a glass-roofed indoor pool.

Expensive

Hôtel Gray-d'Albion. 38 rue des Serbes, 06400 Cannes. ☎ **04-92-99-79-79.** Fax 04-93-99-26-10. www.graydalbion@lucienbarriere.com. E-mail: graydalbion@lucienbaniere. com. 189 units. A/C MINIBAR TV TEL. 920–2,020F ($147–$323) double; from 2,920F ($467) suite. AE, DC, MC, V. Bus: 1.

Because it offers a luxurious setting on a scale smaller than the Carlton and the Majestic, we count the Gray d'Albion among the Riviera's more desirable hotels. Rooms are fairly standard, with private safes and bedside controls. Each has a balcony; those on the 8th and 9th floors have views of the Mediterranean, otherwise the views aren't notable. Bathrooms are well equipped and clad in marble and granite, each with deluxe toiletries, hair dryers, and make-up mirrors. Dining selections include Le Royal Gray (one of Cannes's best), a beach-club restaurant, and a brasserie featuring special dishes from Lebanon.

Moderate

Hôtel le Fouquet's. 2 rond-point Duboys-d'Angers, 06400 Cannes. ☎ **04-92-59-25-00.** Fax 04-92-98-03-39. 10 units. A/C MINIBAR TV TEL. 590–990F ($94–$158) double. AE, DC, MC, V. Closed Oct–late Mar. Parking 80F ($13). Bus 1.

This is an intimate hotel drawing a discreet clientele, often from Paris, who'd never think of patronizing the grand palace hotels. Very "Riviera French" in design and decor, it's several blocks from the beach. Each attractive, airy room contains a loggia and a dressing room. Bathrooms, although small, are efficiently organized, with shower and hair dryer.

Inexpensive

Hôtel de Provence. 9 rue Molière, 06400 Cannes. ☎ **04-93-38-44-35.** Fax 04-93-39-63-14. 30 units. A/C MINIBAR TV TEL. 420–530F ($67 –$85) double. AE, DC, MC, V. Parking 60F ($10). Bus: 1.

Hôtel de Provence stands in its own walled garden of palms and flowering shrubs on a quiet inner street. Most rooms have private balconies and many overlook the garden. Small bathrooms have showers. In warm weather, breakfast is served under the vines and flowers of an arbor.

Hôtel Le Florian. 8 rue Commandant-André, 06400 Cannes. ☎ **04-93-39-24-82.** Fax 04-92-99-18-30. 20 units. A/C TV TEL. 200–350F ($32–$56) double. AE, MC, V. Parking 45F ($7) per night in a nearby public facility. Bus 1.

This hotel is set on a busy but narrow, densely commercial street that leads directly into La Croisette, near both the beach and the city's largest convention hall, Palais des Festivals. Built about a century ago, it has been maintained by three different generations of the Giordano family since the 1950s. Basic, but comfortable, most rooms are rather small but have fine mattresses. Bathrooms are compact with a shower. No meals are served other than breakfast.

WHERE TO DINE
Expensive
Gaston-Gastounette. 7 quai St-Pierre. ☎ **04-93-39-49-44.** Reservations required. Main courses 160–300F ($26–$48); set price lunch 125–170F ($20–$27); set price dinner 200F ($32). AE, DC, MC, V. Daily noon–2pm and 7–11pm. Closed Nov 30–Dec 19. Bus: 1. FRENCH.

This is the best restaurant to offer views of the marina. Located in the old port, it has a stucco exterior with oak moldings and big windows and a sidewalk terrace surrounded by flowers. Inside you'll be served a delectable bouillabaisse, breast of duckling in garlic-cream sauce, *pot-au-feu de la mer* (seafood stew), and perfectly prepared fish platters such as turbot and sole.

✪ **La Palme d'Or.** In the Hôtel Martinez, 73 bd. de la Croisette. ☎ **04-92-98-74-14.** Reservations required. Main courses 250–480F ($40–$77); set price lunch 295F ($47); set price dinner 390–850F ($62–$136). AE, DC, MC, V. Wed–Sun 12:30–2pm and 7:30–10:30pm. Also Tues 7:30–10:30pm mid-June to mid-Sept. Closed Nov 15–Dec 24. Bus: 1. FRENCH.

When this hotel was renovated by the Taittinger family of Champagne fame, one of their primary concerns was to establish a restaurant that could rival the tough competition in Cannes. Well, they've succeeded. The result is a light wood-paneled, art deco marvel overlooking the pool and La Croisette. Chef Christian Willer has worked at some of France's greatest restaurants. Here his sublime specialties include warm foie gras with fondue of rhubarb, fillets of fried red mullet with a beignet of potatoes, zucchini, and an olive cream sauce, or a medley of crayfish, clams, and squid marinated in peppered citrus sauce.

Moderate
✪ **La Mère Besson.** 13 rue des Frères-Pradignac. ☎ **04-93-39-59-24.** Reservations required. Main courses 75–120F ($12–$19); set price dinners 140–170F ($22–$27). AE, DC, MC, V. Apr–Oct Tues–Fri 12:15–2pm and 7:30–10:30pm, Mon and Sat 7:30–10:30pm (open Sun in summer). Nov–Mar Mon–Sat 7:30–10:30pm. Bus: 1. FRENCH.

The references here are Provençal, set within a venue that's as authentic and nostalgic as you're likely to find anywhere in Cannes. The most appealing of the menu items are the Provençal dishes like a savory *bourride* made from monkfish and court bouillon that's featured on Wednesday; and a savory kettle of fish made from a medley of steamed vegetables, mussels, and assorted fish that's offered every Friday with a creamy garlic sauce. There's also an *estouffade Provençal* made with braised beef, red wine, and a rich stock flavored with garlic, onions, herbs, and mushrooms, that's the featured dish every Monday. Come with an appetite and a sense of conviviality.

EXPLORING CANNES
Above the harbor, the old town of Cannes sits on Suquet Hill, where you'll see a 14th-century tower, which the English dubbed the **Lord's Tower.**

Nearby is the **Musée de la Castre,** in the Château de la Castre, Le Suquet (☎ **04-93-38-55-26**), containing fine arts, with a section on ethnography. The latter includes relics and objects from everywhere from the Pacific islands to Southeast Asia, including both Peruvian and Mayan pottery. There's also a gallery with relics of ancient Mediterranean civilizations. Five rooms are devoted to 19th-century paintings. The museum is open April to June Wednesday to Monday 10am to noon and 2 to 6pm; July to September 10am to noon and 3 to 7pm; October to March 10am to noon and 2 to 5pm (closed in January). Admission is 10F ($1.60) for adults and free for those under 16.

Another museum of note, the **Musée de la Mer,** Fort Royal (☎ **04-93-38-55-26**), displays artifacts from Ligurian, Roman, and Arab civilizations, including paintings, mosaics, and ceramics. You can also see the jail where the "Man in the Iron Mask" was incarcerated. Temporary exhibitions of photography are also shown. It's open July to September 10:30am to 12:15pm and 2:15 to 6:30pm; October to June it closes at sundown (4:30 to 5:30pm). Admission is 10F ($1.60) for adults and free for students and children 12 and under.

HITTING THE BEACH & OTHER OUTDOOR PURSUITS

BEACHES   The best beach is **Plage du Midi,** west of the old harbor front, with the best sun in the afternoon. **Plage Gazagnaire,** another good beach, is east of the new port, ideal in the morning. Between these two public beaches are many private ones where you can gain entrance by paying a fee that includes a mattress and sun umbrella. Waiters at these private beach clubs come by to take your lunch order.

BICYCLING & MOTOR SCOOTERING   Despite the roaring traffic, the flat landscapes between Cannes and such satellite resorts as La Napoule are well suited for riding a bike or motor scooter. **Cannes Location Deux Roues,** 11 rue Hélène-Vagliano (☎ **04-93-39-46-15**), across from the Gray d'Albion, rents pedal bikes for 62F ($10) per day and requires a 1,000F ($160) deposit (payable with American Express, MasterCard, or Visa). Motor scooters cost 160 to 200F ($26 to $32) per day and require a deposit of 4,000 to 10,000F ($640 to $1,600), depending on their value. A worthwhile competitor for the rentals of bikes and motor scooters is **Cycles Daniel,** 2 rue du Pont Romain (☎ **04-93-99-90-30**), where *vélos tout terrain* (mountain bikes) cost 70F ($11) a day. At both of the establishments recommended above, renters of motorized bikes and scooters must be at least 14 years old. For the larger of the scooters, potential renters must present à valid driver's license.

BOATING   Several companies can rent you a boat of any size, with or without a crew, for a day, a week, or a month, depending on your priorities, your bankroll, and your schedule. An outfit known for its short-term rentals of small craft, including motorboats and sailboats, is **Elco Marine**, 106 Bd. Du Midi (☎ **04-93-47-12-62**). Two others that provide access to larger boats, including motor-driven and sailing yachts and craft suitable for deep-sea fishing, include **MS Yachts,** 57 La Croisette (☎ **04-93-99-03-51**); and **Mediterranée Courtage** (Agence Y.P.), 22 quai St-Pierre (☎ **04-93-38-30-40**).

GOLF   The dry and rolling landscapes of Provence contribute to memorable golfing. One of the region's most challenging and interesting courses, **Country-Club de Cannes-Mougins,** 175 rte. d'Antibes, Mougins (☎ **04-93-75-79-13**), 6km (4 miles) north of Cannes, was a 1976 reconfiguration by Dye & Ellis of an outmoded, underaccessorized course laid out in the 1920s. Noted for olive trees and cypresses that adorn a relatively flat terrain, the par-72 course has many water traps and a deceptively tricky layout loaded with technical challenges. It's the host of the Royal Mougins Open, an important stop on the PGA European Tour. The course is open to anyone with proof of his or her handicap—24 for men, 28 for women—willing to pay greens fees of 400 to 450F ($64 to $72), depending on the day of the week. An electric golf cart rents for 280F ($45), and golf clubs can be rented for 150F ($24) per set. Reservations are recommended.

SWIMMING   Most of the larger hotels in Cannes have their own pools. In addition to the tennis courts described below, the **Complexe Sportif Montfleury,** 23 av. Beauséjour (☎ **04-93-38-75-78**), boasts a large modern pool. Entrance fee is 25F ($4) for adults, 20F ($3.20) for those under 16.

TENNIS   **Complexe Sportif Montfleury,** 23 av. Beauséjour (☎ **04-93-38-75-78**) has eight hard-surfaced courts that rent for 80F ($13) per hour, and two clay-surfaced courts that rent for 100F ($16) per hour.

THE SHOPPING SCENE

You're likely to find branch outlets of virtually every stylish Paris retailer in Cannes. Most of the big names in designer fashion line **La Croisette.** The best names are closest to the high-rise **Gray-d'Albion,** 17 La Croisette, which is both a mall and a hotel.

At the edge of the Quartier Suquet, **Marché Forville** is the town's primary fruit, flower, and vegetable market. On Monday it's a flea market. There's a somewhat disorganized and invariably busy outdoor flea market every Saturday along the edges of the allée de la Liberté, across from the Palais des Festivals.

The distinctive and charmingly old-fashioned **Cannolive,** 16–20 rue Vénizelos (☎ **04-93-39-08-19**), owned by the Raynaud family, who founded the place in 1880, sells Provençal olives and all of their by-products—purées (tapenades) that connoisseurs refer to as "Provençal caviar," black "olives de Nice," and green "olives de Provence," as well as three grades of olive oil from several regional producers. Oils and food products are dispensed from no. 16, but gift items (fabrics, porcelain, and Provençal souvenirs) are sold next door.

Maiffret, 31 rue d'Antibes (☎ **04-93-39-08-29**), specializes in chocolates and candied fruit, made by culinary processes that must be seen to be fully appreciated. Pâtés and confits of fruit, some of which decorate cakes and tarts, are also sold as desirable confections in their own right. Look for the Provençal national confection, *calissons,* crafted from almonds, a confit of melon, and sugar. Richly stocked with books and periodicals from virtually every English-speaking country in the world, **Cannes English Bookshop,** 11 rue Bivouac Napoléon (☎ **04-93-99-40-08**), near the main post office, has attracted readers since 1984.

CANNES AFTER DARK

CASINOS   The largest and most legendary casino in Cannes is the Casino Croisette, in the Palais des Festivals, 1 jetée Albert-Edouard, near promenade de la Croisette (☎ **04-92-98-78-00**). Within its glittering confines you'll find all the gaming tables you'd expect. A small subdivision of the casino opens daily at 10am for access to slot machines. The main areas, including the ones with the roulette and baccarat tables, open every day at 7:30pm and close down at 5am. The Palais des Festivals also contains one of the best nightclubs in town, **Jimmy's de Regine** (☎ **04-93-68-00-07**), outfitted in shades of red. Jimmy's is open Thursday to Sunday 11pm to dawn. You must present your passport to enter the gambling room. Admission is 100F ($16) and includes a drink.

Considerably smaller than its major competitor, **Le Carlton Casino Club,** in the Carlton Inter-Continental, 50 bd. de la Croisette (☎ **04-92-99-51-00**), nonetheless draws its share of devotees. Jackets are required for men, and a passport or government-issued identity card is necessary for admission. It's open daily 8pm to 4am. Admission is 70F ($11).

CLUBS   Jane's, in the cellar of the Gray d'Albion, 38 rue des Serbes (☎ **04-92-99-79-79**), is a stylish and appealing nightclub with an undercurrent of coy permissiveness. The well-dressed crowd (many of the men in jacket and tie) is made up of all ages. The cover ranges from 50 to 100F ($8 to $16), depending on business; on some slow nights women enter for free. Open Thursday to Sunday 11pm to 5am.

JUAN-LES-PINS

This suburb of Antibes is a resort that was developed in the 1920s by Frank Jay Gould. At that time, people flocked to "John of the Pines" to escape the "crassness" of nearby Cannes. In the 1930s, Juan-les-Pins drew a chic crowd during winter. Today, Juan-les-Pins is often called a honky-tonk town or the "Coney Island of the Riviera," (but anyone who calls it that hasn't seen Coney Island in a long time). One newspaper writer labeled it "a pop-art Monte Carlo, with burlesque shows and nude beaches"— a description much too provocative for such a middle-class resort.

The town has some of the best nightlife on the Riviera, and the action reaches its frenzied height during the **Festival International de Jazz** in July. Many revelers stay up all night in the smoky jazz joints, then sleep the next day on the beach. For more information on the festival, contact the tourist office. The **casino,** in the town center, offers cabaret entertainment, often until daybreak. During the day, skin-diving and waterskiing predominate. The pines sweep down to a good beach, crowded with summer sunbathers, most often in skimpy swimwear.

ESSENTIALS

GETTING THERE   Juan-les-Pins is connected by rail and bus to most other coastal resorts. Frequent **trains** arrive from Nice throughout the day (trip time: 30 minutes). For more information and schedules, call ☎ **08-36-35-35-35.** The station is on avenue l'Esterel. A bus leaves from Antibes at place Guynemer (☎ **04-93-34-37-60**), daily every 20 minutes and costs 7.50F ($1.20) one way (trip time: 10 minutes).

VISITOR INFORMATION   The **Office de Tourisme** is at 51 bd. Charles-Guillaumont (☎ **04-92-90-53-05**).

DEPARTING BY CAR   After Juan-les-Pins, ignore the "Direct to Antibes" signs and follow D-2559 around the cape. You'll come first to Cap d'Antibes before approaching the old city of Antibes itself.

WHERE TO STAY

Belles-Rives. Bd. Baudoin, 06160 Juan-les-Pins. ☎ **04-93-61-02-79.** Fax 04-93-67-43-51. E-mail: belles.rives@atsat.com. 45 units. A/C MINIBAR TV TEL. 1,150–2,900F ($184–$464) double; from 3,200F ($512) suite. AE, MC, V. Closed mid-Oct to Mar.

This is one of the fabled addresses on the Riviera. Over, the years it has hosted such illustrious guests as Zelda and F. Scott Fitzgerald, the duke and duchess of Windsor, and Edith Piaf. A certain 1930s aura still lingers, and the sea views are as enchanting as ever. Rooms range from small to spacious, all with luxurious mattresses. Bathrooms have a tub/shower combination and a hair dryer. The lower terraces are devoted to garden dining rooms and a waterside aquatic club with a snack bar/lounge and a jetty extending into the water. Also on the premises are a private beach and a landing dock.

✪ **Hôtel Juana.** La Pinède, av. Gallice, 06160 Juan-les-Pins. ☎ **04-93-61-08-70.** Fax 04-93-61-76-60. www.hotel-juana.com. E-mail: info@hotel-juana.com. 50 units. A/C TV TEL. 950–2,550F ($152–$408) double; from 2,800F ($448) suite. AE, MC, V. Parking 50F ($8). Closed Nov–Mar.

This balconied art deco building is separated from the sea by a park of pines. The hotel has a private swimming club where guests can rent a "parasol and pad" on the sandy beach. The hotel is constantly being refurbished, and the very attractive rooms come complete with mahogany pieces, safes, and large bathrooms with hair dryers. Some have balconies. There's a bar in the pool house. Also on the premises are a private beach and a heated outdoor pool.

WHERE TO DINE

✪ **La Terrasse.** In the Hôtel Juana, La Pinède, av. Gallice. ☎ **04-93-61-20-37.** Reservations required. Main courses 240–390F ($38–$62); set price lunch 290F ($46); set price dinners 490–660F ($78–$106). AE, MC, V. July–Aug daily 12:30–2pm and 7:30–10:30pm; Apr–June and Sept–Oct Tues and Thurs–Sun 12:30–2pm; Thurs–Mon 7:30–10:30pm. Closed Nov–Mar. FRENCH/MEDITERRANEAN.

The cuisine here is the best in Juan-les-Pins. Bill Cosby is such a fan he's been known to fly chef Christian Morisset to the States to prepare dinner for him. Morisset cooks with a light, precise, and creative hand, both interpreting traditional dishes and creating his own. The ideal place to dine in summer is the terrace, among a lively, sophisticated crowd. His saddle of lamb is cooked to your taste and served with a rosemary jus, stuffed zucchini flowers, and fresh white beans. Or try the limousine fillet of beef—tender and juicy and straight from the charcoal grill. The seafood, including red mullet and sea bass, is caught fresh daily.

ANTIBES & CAP D'ANTIBES

On the other side of the Bay of Angels, 21km (13 miles) southwest of Nice, is the port of Antibes. This old Mediterranean town has a quiet charm, unusual for the Côte d'Azur. Its little harbor is filled with fishing boats, the marketplaces with flowers, mostly roses and carnations. If you're in Antibes in the evening, you can watch fishers playing the popular Riviera game of *boule.*

Spiritually, Antibes is totally divorced from Cap d'Antibes, a peninsula studded with the villas and pools of the *haut monde.* In *Tender Is the Night,* F. Scott Fitzgerald described it as a place where "old villas rotted like water lilies among the massed pines."

ESSENTIALS

GETTING THERE   **Trains** from Cannes arrive every 30 minutes (trip time: 16 minutes); trains from Nice also pull in every 30 minutes (trip time: 18 minutes). For rail information, call ☎ **08-36-35-35-35.** The station is on avenue Robert Soleau.

VISITOR INFORMATION   The **Office de Tourisme** is at 11 place du Général-de-Gaulle (☎ **04-92-90-53-00**).

DEPARTING BY CAR   After leaving Antibes, you can take an excursion to the most famous hill towns on the French Riviera: St-Paul-de-Vence and Vence. Follow N7 to Cagnes-sur-Mer, where you can connect with D36 heading first to St-Paul-de-Vence, then continuing north to Vence.

WHERE TO STAY

Auberge de la Gardiole. Chemin de la Garoupe, 06600 Cap d'Antibes. ☎ **04-93-61-35-03.** Fax 04-93-67-61-87. 20 units. A/C MINIBAR TV TEL. 490–590F ($78–$94) double; from 790F ($126) suite. AE, MC, V. Free parking. Closed Nov–Mar. Bus: A2.

M. and Mme Courtot run this country inn with a delightful personal touch. The large villa, surrounded by gardens and pergola, is in an area of private estates. The charming rooms, on the upper floors of the inn and in the little buildings in the garden, contain personal safes. The cheerful dining room has a fireplace and hanging pots and pans, and in good weather, you can dine under a wisteria-covered trellis near the swimming pool.

Hôtel du Cap–Eden Roc. Bd. J-F-Kennedy, 06601 Cap d'Antibes. ☎ **04-93-61-39-01.** Fax 04-93-67-76-04. E-mail: edenroc-hotel@wanadoo.fr. 140 units. A/C TEL. 2,050–4,400F ($328–$704) double; from 4,800F ($768) suite. No credit cards. Free parking. Closed mid-Oct–mid-Apr. Bus: A2.

This Second Empire hotel, opened in 1870, is surrounded by 9ha (22 acres) of splendid gardens. It's like a great country estate, with spacious public rooms, marble fireplaces, scenic paneling, and richly upholstered armchairs. Rooms are among the most sumptuous on the Riviera. Bathrooms are roomy with posh toiletries, a hair dryer, and a tub/shower combination. The staff is famed for its snobbery. The world-famous Pavillon Eden Roc, near a rock garden apart from the hotel, has a panoramic Mediterranean view.

Hotel Imperial Garoupe. 770 Chemin de la Garoupe, 06600 Antibes. ☎ **800/525-4800** in the U.S., or 04-92-93-31-61. Fax 04-92-93-31-62. www.imperial-garoupe.com. E-mail: hotel-imp@webstore.fr. 34 units. A/C MINIBAR TV TEL. 1,250–2,900F ($200–$464) double; 2,300–5,100F ($368–$816) suite. AE, DC, MC, V. Free parking. Bus A2.

One of the Riviera's newest upscale hotels is a charming pocket of posh that's a bit less intimidating than the more monumental Hotel du Cap. The one-story building is designed around a landscaped patio with architectural elements that evoke both Tudor England and the deserts of Morocco, with a view over a swimming pool. The large, luxurious rooms are filled with oversized furniture. Bathrooms have plenty of shelf space, a hair dryer, and deluxe toiletries. Set within 45m (50 yards) of the beach, the hotel is the centerpiece of a 1.5ha (3½-acre) park whose rows of pines block some of the views of the sea.

WHERE TO DINE

La Bonne Auberge. Quartier de Brague, route N-7. ☎ **04-93-33-36-65.** Reservations required. Set price menu 210F ($34). MC, V. Tues–Sun noon–2pm and 7–10pm. Closed mid-Nov to mid-Dec. Take the coastal highway (N-7) 2½ miles from Antibes. FRENCH.

For many years after its 1975 opening, this was one of the most famous restaurants on the French Riviera. In 1992, following the death of its famous founder, Jo Rostang, his culinary heir Philippe Rostang wisely limited its scope and transformed it into a worthwhile but less ambitious restaurant. The set price menu offers a wide selection. Choices vary but may include Basque-inspired pipérade with poached eggs, savory swordfish tart, chicken with vinegar and garlic, and perch-pike dumplings Jo Rostang. Dessert might be an enchanting peach soufflé.

Restaurant de Bacon. Bd. de Bacon. ☎ **04-93-61-50-02.** Reservations required. Set price menus 280–450F ($45–$72). AE, DC, MC, V. Tues–Sun noon–2pm and 8–10pm (open Mon dinner in July–Aug). Closed Nov–Jan. SEAFOOD.

Bouillabaisse aficionados claim, and we agree, that Bacon's offers France's best version. In its deluxe version, saltwater crayfish float atop the savory brew; we prefer the simple version—a waiter adds the finishing touches at your table. You can also try a fish soup with the traditional garlic-laden rouille sauce; fish terrine, sea bass, John Dory, or one of the exotic fish, such as sar, pageot, or denti, unknown in North America. The venue evokes the chic 1950s, within a low, sprawling, big-windowed building set within a rocky landscape across the coastal highway from the sea.

TWO MUSEUMS WORTH VISITING

On the ramparts above the port is the Château Grimaldi, place du Château, which contains the **Musée Picasso** (☎ **04-92-90-54-26,** or 04-92-90-54-20 for a recorded message). Once the home of the princes of Antibes of the Grimaldi family, who ruled the city from 1385 to 1608, today it houses one of the greatest Picasso collections in the world. Picasso came to the small town after his bitter war years in Paris and stayed in a hotel at Golfe-Juan until the museum director at Antibes invited him to work and live at the museum. Picasso then spent 1946 painting at the museum. When he departed he gave the museum all the work he'd done that year—two dozen paintings, nearly 80 pieces of ceramics, 44 drawings, 32 lithographs, 11 oils on paper, 2 sculptures, and 5 tapestries. In addition, a gallery of contemporary art exhibits Léger, Miró, Ernst, and Calder, among others. The museum is open Tuesday to Sunday 10am to noon and 2 to 6pm, except June to September, 10am to 6pm. Admission costs 30F ($4.80) for adults, 18F ($2.90) for students 15 to 24 and people over 60, and free for children 14 and under.

Cap d'Antibes has the **Musée Naval et Napoléonien,** Batterie du Grillon, boulevard J-F-Kennedy (☎ **04-93-61-45-32**). This ancient military tower contains an interesting collection of Napoleonic memorabilia, naval models, paintings, and mementos. It's open Monday to Friday 9:30am to noon and 2:15 to 6pm and Saturday 9:30am to noon. Admission is 20F ($3.20).

ST-PAUL-DE-VENCE & VENCE

Of all the perched villages of the Riviera, St-Paul-de-Vence, 27km (17 miles) east of Cannes and 30km (19 miles) north of Nice, is the best known. It was popularized in the 1920s when many noted artists occupied the 16th-century houses flanking the narrow cobblestone streets. The feudal hamlet grew up on a bastion of rock, almost blending into it. Its ramparts—allow about 30 minutes to encircle them—overlook a peaceful setting of flowers and olive and orange trees. As you make your way through the warren of streets, you'll pass endless souvenir shops, a charming old fountain carved in the form of an urn, and a 13th-century Gothic church. St-Paul-de-Vence and Vence itself are most often visited as a day trip from either Cannes or Nice; allow at least an afternoon for this jaunt.

ESSENTIALS

GETTING THERE   Some 20 **buses** per day leave from Nice's gare routière to drop you in the town center (trip time: 55 minutes).

VISITOR INFORMATION   The **Office de Tourisme** is at Maison Tours, rue Grande (☎ **04-93-32-86-95**).

DEPARTING BY CAR   To reach Nice, take the N-202 south to the junction with the N-7; follow the N-7 east to Nice.

EXPLORING ST-PAUL-DE-VENCE & VENCE

The ✪ **Fondation Maeght** (☎ **04-93-32-81-63**) is one of the most modern art museums in Europe. On a hill in pine-studded woods, the Maeght Foundation is like a Shangri-la. Not only is the architecture avant-garde, but the building houses one of the finest collections of contemporary art on the Riviera. Natural and human creations blend harmoniously in this unique achievement of architect José Luís Sert. Its white concrete arcs give the impression of a giant pagoda.

A stark Calder rises like some futuristic monster on the grassy lawns. In a courtyard, the elongated bronze works of Giacometti form a surrealistic garden, creating a hallucinatory mood. Sculpture is also displayed inside, but it's at its best in a natural setting of surrounding terraces and gardens.

A library, cinema, and cafeteria (open July to September only) are also here. In one showroom, original lithographs by artists like Chagall and Giacometti and limited-edition prints are for sale. Admission is 50F ($8) for adults and 40F ($7) for students and children 12 to 18; free 11 and under. It's open daily July to September 10am to 7pm and October to June 10am to 12:30pm and 2:30 to 6pm.

North of St-Paul, you can visit the sleepy old town of Vence, with its **Vieille Ville** (Old Town). If you're wearing solid, comfortable shoes, the narrow, steep streets are worth exploring. The **cathedral** on place Godeau is unremarkable except for some 15th-century choir stalls. If it's a Tuesday or Thursday, however, most visitors pass quickly through the narrow gates of this once-fortified walled town on their way to the **Chapelle du Rosaire,** 466 av. Henri-Matisse (☎ **04-93-58-03-26**), created by Henri Matisse.

Matisse was 77 when, after a turbulent time of introspection, he set out to create this masterpiece, in his own words, "the culmination of a whole life dedicated to the search for truth." From the front you might find the chapel of the Dominican nuns of Monteils unremarkable—until you spot a 40-foot crescent-adorned cross rising from a blue-tile roof.

The light inside picks up the subtle coloring in the simply rendered leaf forms and abstract patterns: sapphire blue, aquamarine, and lemon yellow. In black-and-white ceramics, St. Dominic is depicted in a few lines. The Stations of the Cross are also black-and-white tile, with Matisse's self-styled "tormented and passionate" figures. The bishop of Nice himself came to bless the chapel in the late spring of 1951, when the artist's work was completed. Matisse died 3 years later. Admission is 13F ($2.10), 5F (80¢) 12 and under; donations are welcomed. October and December to June, it's open Tuesday and Thursday 10am to 11:30am and 2:30 to 5:30pm; July to September it's also open on Wednesday, Friday, and Saturday 2:30 to 5:30pm. Closed in November.

NICE

The Victorian upper class and czarist aristocrats loved Nice in the 19th century, but it's solidly middle class today. Of all the major resorts, from Deauville to Biarritz to Cannes, Nice is the least expensive. It's also the best excursion center on the Riviera, especially if you're dependent on public transportation. For example, you can go to San Remo, "the queen of the Italian Riviera," returning to Nice by nightfall. From the Nice airport, the second largest in France, you can travel by bus along the entire coast to resorts like Juan-les-Pins and Cannes, the latter only 32km (20 miles) to the west.

Nice is the capital of the Riviera, the largest city between Genoa and Marseille (also one of the most ancient, having been founded by the Greeks, who called it Nike, or Victory). Because of its brilliant sunshine and relaxed living, Nice has attracted artists and writers, among them Matisse, Dumas, Nietzsche, Apollinaire, Flaubert, Hugo, Stendhal, and Mistral.

ESSENTIALS

GETTING THERE   You can take an airport bus (no. 23) that travels at 20-minute intervals throughout the day and evening between the **Aéroport Nice-Côte d'Azur** (☎ **04-93-21-30-30**) and the city's **Gare Routière,** promenade du Paillon (☎ **04-93-85-61-81**), in the city center. Buses run daily 6am to 10:30pm, and cost 9F ($1.45) per person. A somewhat more luxurious mode of transport involves a specially conceived navette de l'aéroport (airport shuttle bus) that charges 21F ($3.35) for a ride from the airport to Nice's main railway station. A taxi ride into the city center will cost at least 150 to 200F ($24 to $32) for a carload of up to four passengers. **Trains** arrive at **Gare Nice-Ville,** avenue Thiers (☎ **08-36-35-35-35**). From here you can take frequent trains to Cannes, Monaco, and Antibes, among other destinations.

VISITOR INFORMATION   Thanks to its status as the tourist centerpiece of the Côte d'Azur. Nice maintains three tourist information offices, the largest and most central of which is at 5 promenade des Anglais (☎ **04-92-14-48-00**), near the Place Massena. Additional tourist offices are in the arrivals hall of the **Aèroport Nice-Côte d'Azur** (☎ **04-93-21-44-11**); and at the railway station (☎ **04-93-87-07-07**). Any of the three can make you a hotel reservation (but only for the night of the day you happen to show up); charging a modest fee that varies according to the classification of the hotel you book.

You can rent bicycles and mopeds from **Nicea Rent,** 9 av. Thiers (☎ **04-93-82-42-71**), or from a competitor, **Arnaud,** 4 place Grimaldi (☎ **04-93-87-88-55**). Both are open daily from 9am to noon, and 2 to 7pm, with a Sunday closing between October and April. Rentals begin at around 100F ($16) per day, plus a deposit of at least 2,000F ($320) or more, depending on the value of the machine you rent. If you want to rent a car here, try the following: **Budget** at the airport (☎ **04-93-21-36-50**) and at 23 rue de Belgique, opposite the rail station (☎ 04-93-16-24); **Hertz** at the airport (☎ **04-93-21-36-72**) and at 12 av. de Suède (☎ 04-93-87-11-87); and **Avis** at the airport (☎ **04-93-21-36-33**) and at 2 av. des Phocéens (☎ 04-93-80-63-52).

DEPARTING BY CAR   Leaving Nice, drive east along the Corniche Inférieure until reaching Villefranche; turn right onto D-25, which takes you in a very short distance to the wooded peninsula of St-Jean-Cap-Ferrat, 10km (6 miles) east of Nice.

WHERE TO STAY
Very Expensive
Hôtel Négresco. 37 promenade des Anglais, 06007 Nice CEDEX. ☎ **04-93-16-64-00.** Fax 04-93-88-35-68. E-mail: negresco@nicematin.fr. 141 units. A/C MINIBAR TV TEL. 1,350–2,750F ($216–$440) double; from 3,400F ($544) suite. AE, DC, MC, V. Parking 160F ($26). Bus: 8, 9, 10, or 11.

This Victorian wedding-cake hotel is one of the many superglamorous hotels along the French Riviera. It was built on the seafront, in the French château style, with a mansard roof and domed tower, and its interior design was inspired by the country's châteaux. Rooms contain antiques, tapestries, paintings, and art and come in the widest range of styles and shapes of any hotel in town. Least desirable are the street-side units on the ground floors, where, in spite of double glazed windows, you can still hear traffic. The most expensive rooms contain balconies and face the Mediterranean. Bathrooms are spacious and each has a hair dryer, deluxe toiletries, and dual basins. Reasonably priced meals are served in La Rotonde, though the featured restaurant— one of the greatest on the Riviera—is Chantecler (see "Where to Dine," below).

Expensive
✪ **Château des Ollières.** 39 av. des Baumettes, 06000 Nice. ☎ **04-92-15-77-99.** Fax 04-92-15-77-98. www.chateaudesollieres. E-mail: chateaudesollieres.com. 6 units. A/C MINI-BAR TV TEL. 800–2,000F ($128–$320) double; 1,100–3,300F ($176–$528) suite. AE, MC, V. Bus: 38.

The most appealing and unusual hotel to open in Nice in many years lies within a 5-minute walk from the Négresco and the promenade des Anglais, within a 8ha (20-acre) park loaded with exotic trees and shrubs. Its centerpiece is a beaux-arts villa built in the 1870s. Inside, you'll find a noteworthy collection of oil paintings and "neo-Napoléonienne" and Empire-inspired antiques. Rooms are outfitted in the same high-ceilinged, richly ornate style as the public areas, and have supremely comfortable mattresses and the kind of decorative porcelain and accessories you'd expect in an impeccably upscale private home. Bathrooms are quite luxurious, with generous shelf space, a tub/shower combination, and a hair dryer.

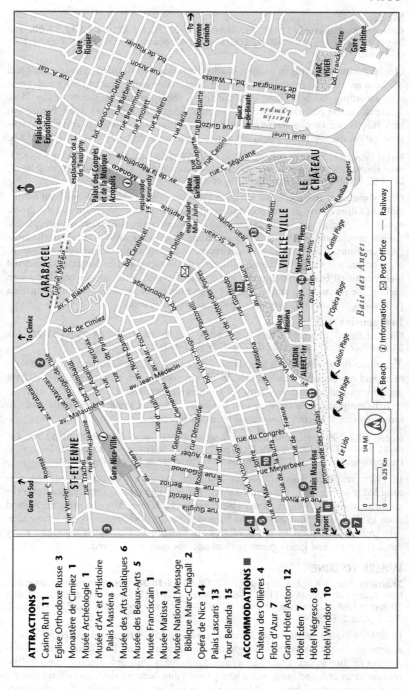

ATTRACTIONS ●
Casino Ruhl **11**
Eglise Orthodoxe Russe **3**
Monastère de Cimiez **1**
Musée Archéologie **1**
Musée d'Art et d'Histoire
 Palais Masséna **9**
Musée des Arts Asiatiques **6**
Musée des Beaux-Arts **5**
Musée Franciscain **1**
Musée Matisse **1**
Musée National Message
 Biblique Marc-Chagall **2**
Opéra de Nice **14**
Palais Lascaris **13**
Tour Bellanda **15**

ACCOMMODATIONS ■
Château des Ollières **4**
Flots d'Azur **7**
Grand Hôtel Aston **12**
Hôtel Eden **7**
Hôtel Négresco **8**
Hôtel Windsor **10**

Key elements on map:
CARABACEL
ST-ETIENNE
VIEILLE VILLE
LE CHÂTEAU
Baie des Anges

Beach · (i) Information · ⊠ Post Office · — Railway

1/4 Mi
0.25 Km

Moderate

Grand Hôtel Aston. 12 av. Félix-Faure, 06000 Nice. ☎ **04-92-17-53-00.** Fax 04-93-80-53-11. 156 units. 900–1,500F ($144–$240) double. AE, DC, MC, V. Parking 100F ($16). Bus: 12.

One of the most alluring in its price bracket, this elegantly detailed 19th-century hotel has been radically renovated. Rooms have comfortable mattresses and price scales that vary according to their views over the street, the splashing fountains of the Place Massena, or the panorama over the coastline from the uppermost floor. Bathrooms have tub/shower combinations and hair dryers. On summer evenings visit the garden-style bar on the top floor. The hotel is associated with Holland's Golden Tulip chain.

Hotel Windsor. 11 rue Dalpozzo, 06000 Nice. ☎ **04-93-88-59-35.** Fax 04-93-88-94-57. www.windsor@webstore.fr. E-mail: windsor@webstore.fr. 420–750F ($67–$120) double. AE, DC, MC, V. Parking 60F ($10). Bus: 9, 10, or 22.

One of the most arts-conscious hotels in Provence is set within what was built by disciples of Gustav Eiffel as a maison bourgeoise, near the Hotel Negresco and the Promenade des Anglais, in 1895. Inside, you'll find an artsy, somewhat claustrophobic environment that nonetheless is very appealing to artists or those with ties to the artistic community. Rooms have good mattresses, and small, tidily maintained bathrooms. High points include a fifth-floor health club, steam room, and sauna, that's considered highly unusual by local architects; and a one-of-a-kind series of frescoes that adorn each of the rooms. The dining room is open only to residents of the hotel. There's a pool and a garden with scores of tropical and exotic plants.

Inexpensive

Flots d'Azur. 101 promenade des Anglais, 06000 Nice. ☎ **04-93-86-51-25.** Fax 04-93-97-22-07. 21 units. A/C TEL. 270–420F ($43–$67) double. MC, V. Bus: 8.

This three-story villa-hotel is located next to the sea, a short walk from the more elaborate and costlier promenade hotels. While the rooms vary in size and decor, all have good views and sea breezes, with 12 containing minibars. Double-glazed windows were recently added to cut down on the noise. There's a small sitting room and sun terrace in front, where a continental breakfast is served.

Hôtel Eden. 99 bis promenade des Anglais, 06000 Nice. ☎ **04-93-86-53-70.** Fax 04-93-97-67-97. 10 units. A/C TV TEL. 320–390F ($51–$62) single or double. AE, DC, MC, V. Free parking. Bus: 3, 9, 10, 22, 23, or 24 from the center or 12 from the train station.

In 1925, an exiled Russian countess built this art deco villa on the seafront, surrounded it with a wall, and planted a tiny garden. The villa still remains, despite the construction of much taller modern buildings on both sides. You can enjoy the ivy and roses in the garden and stay in old-fashioned partly modernized rooms whose sizes vary greatly. Bathrooms are old-fashioned but functional. The owner maintains a wry sense of humor and greets guests at breakfast, the only meal served.

WHERE TO DINE

Brasserie Flo. 2–4 rue Sacha-Guitry. ☎ **04-93-13-38-38.** Reservations recommended. Main courses 80–120F ($13–$19). Set price menus 119F ($19) served only at lunch and after 10:30pm; 169F ($27) served anytime. AE, DC, MC, V. Daily noon–3pm and 7pm–midnight. Bus: 1, 2, or 5. FRENCH.

In 1991, a France-based restaurant chain (Jean-Paul Bucher group), noted for its skill at restoring historic brasseries, bought the premises of a faded but historic turn-of-the-century restaurant near Place Masséna and injected it with new life. It's now a stylish, reasonably priced, and fun place, where patrons dine beneath the high ceilings that are covered with original frescoes. Menu items include an array of grilled fish, *choucroute* (sauerkraut) in the Alsatian style, steaks with brandied pepper sauce, and fresh oysters and shellfish.

✪ **Chantecler.** In the Hôtel Négresco, 37 promenade des Anglais. ☎ **04-93-16-64-00.** Reservations required. Main courses 210–350F ($34–$56); set price lunch 245F ($39); set price dinner 415–590F ($66–$94). AE, DC, MC, V. Daily 12:30–2:30pm and 7:30–10:30pm. Closed mid-Nov to mid-Dec. Bus: 8, 9, 10, or 11. FRENCH.

This restaurant, with its beautifully restored setting—the wall panels are from a château in Puilly-Fusse—is the most prestigious in Nice, and chef Alain Llorca offers the most sophisticated and creative dishes. Menu items change almost weekly, but may include fillet of turbot served with a puree of broad beans, sun-dried tomatoes, and fresh asparagus; roasted suckling lamb served with beignets of fresh vegetables and ricotta-stuffed ravioli; and a melt-in-your-mouth fantasy of marbled hot chocolate drenched in an almond-flavored cream sauce.

Chez Michel (Le Grand Pavois). 11 rue Meyerbeer. ☎ **04-93-88-77-42.** Reservations required. Main courses 135–160F ($22–$26); bouillabaisse from 300F ($48); set price menus 195–255F ($31–$41); menu gastronomique 300F ($48); set lunch 130F ($21). AE, DC, MC, V. Daily noon–2:30pm and 7–11pm. Bus: 8. SEAFOOD.

Chez Michel is nestled under an art deco apartment building near the water. One of the partners, Jacques Marquise, is from Golfe-Juan, where for 25 years he managed the famous fish restaurant Chez Tétou. His bouillabaisse has been widely celebrated. Other recommended specialties are baked sea bass in white wine, herbs, and lemon sauce and grilled flambé lobster.

✪ **Le Safari.** 1 Cours Saleya. ☎ **04-93-80-18-44.** Reservations recommended. Main courses 65–150F ($10–$24); set menu 150F ($24). AE, DC, MC, V. Daily noon–2:30pm and 7–11:30pm. Bus: 1, 2, or 5. PROVENÇAL/NIÇOISE.

The decor couldn't be simpler, outfitted as it is with a black ceiling, white walls, and an old-fashioned terra-cotta floor, and the youthful staff is mellow. Expect mobs of clients here, many of whom prefer the outdoor terrace overlooking the nearby *Marché aux Fleurs,* and all of whom appreciate the earthy, unpretentious, reasonably-priced, and generously-proportioned meals. Examples include a pungent *bagna cauda,* where vegetables are immersed in a sizzling brew of hot oil and anchovy paste; grilled peppers bathed in olive oil; *daube* (stew) of beef; fresh pasta with basil; an omelette with *blettes* (tough but flavorful greens); and the unfortunately named *merda de can* (dog shit), which is gnocchi stuffed with spinach—it's a lot more appetizing than it sounds.

IN & AROUND NICE

The wide **boulevard des Anglais** fronts the bay. Split by "islands" of palms and flowers, it stretches for about 6km (4 miles). Fronting the beach are rows of grand cafes, the Musée Masséna, villas, and hotels—some good, others decaying.

In the east, the promenade becomes **quai des Etats-Unis,** the original boulevard, lined with some of the best restaurants in Nice, each specializing in bouillabaisse. Rising sharply on a rock is the site known as **Le Château,** the spot where the ducs de Savoie built their castle, which was torn down in 1706. The steep hill has been turned into a garden of pines and exotic flowers. To reach the site, many prefer to take an elevator; actually, many prefer to take the elevator up, then walk down. The park is open daily 8am to 7:30pm.

The center of Nice is **place Masséna,** with pink buildings in the 17th-century Genoese style and the **Fontaine du Soleil** (Fountain of the Sun) by Janoit. Stretching from the main square to the promenade is the **Jardin Albert-Ier,** with an open-air

Nice Beach?

Some of the world's most attractive (and skimpily dressed) people cross the boulevard des Anglais heading for the beach, or "on the rocks," as it's called here. Tough on tender feet, the beach is shingled with rocks, one of the least attractive (and least publicized) aspects of this cosmopolitan resort. Many bathhouses provide mattresses for a charge.

terrace and a Triton Fountain. Palms and exotic flowers make this the most relaxing oasis at the resort.

A Trio of Museums Worth a Look

Musée d'Art et d'Histoire Palais Masséna. 65 rue de France. ☎ **04-93-88-11-34.** Admission 25F ($4) adults, 15F ($2.40) children. Free first Sun every month; Tues–Sun 10am–noon and 2–6pm. Bus: 3, 7, 8, 9, 10, 12, 14, or 22.

The fabulous villa housing this museum was built in 1900 in the style of the First Empire as a residence for Victor Masséna, the prince of Essling and grandson of Napoléon's marshal. The city of Nice has converted the villa, next door to the Négresco, into a museum of local history and decorative art. A remarkably opulent drawing room, with mahogany-veneer pieces and ormolu mounts, is on the ground floor. At press time the museum was closed for extensive renovations; check its status at the time of your visit.

✪ **Musée des Beaux-Arts.** 33 av. des Baumettes. ☎ **04-92-15-28-28.** Admission 25F ($4) adults, 15F ($2.40) students. Free under 18. Tues–Sun 10am–noon and 2–6pm. Bus: 9, 12, 22, 23, or 38.

Housed in the former residence of Ukrainian Princess Kotchubey, this museum has an important gallery devoted to the masters of the Second Empire and belle époque. The gallery of sculptures includes works by J. B. Carpeaux, Rude, and Rodin. Note the important collection by a dynasty of painters, the Dutch Van Loo family. A fine collection of 19th- and 20th-century art is displayed, including works by Ziem, Raffaelli, Boudin, Renoir, Monet, Guillaumin, and Sisley.

Musée des Arts Asiatiques. 405 promenade des Anglais. ☎ **04-92-29-37-00.** Mid-Apr to mid-Oct, Wed–Mon 10am–6pm. Mid-Oct to mid-Apr Wed–Mon 10am–5pm. Admission 35F ($6) adults, 25F ($4) children and students. Free 6 and under.

Set very close to Nice's airport, this museum opened in 1998 as a tribute to the sculpture and paintings of Cambodia, China, India, Tibet, and Japan. Inside are some of the best ceramics and devotional carvings ever found, many of them hauled back to France by colonials during the 19th and early 20th centuries. Of special interest are the accoutrements associated with Japan's tea-drinking ceremony, and several monumental representations of Buddha.

Exploring Nearby Cimiez

Founded by the Romans, who called it Cemenelum, Cimiez, a hilltop suburb, was the capital of the Maritime Alps province. Recent excavations have uncovered the ruins of a Roman town, and you can wander around the digs. To reach this suburb, take bus 15 or 17 from place Masséna.

Monastère de Cimiez (Cimiez Convent), place du Monastère (☎ **04-93-81-00-04**), embraces a church that owns three of the most important works from the primitive painting school of Nice by the Bréa brothers. The most stunning is a 1475 Pietà to the right of the entrance as you come in. A Crucifixion on the left in the choir is a later work dating from 1512. Finally, in the third chapel, is a Deposition. In addition, note the huge altarpiece, half in the Renaissance style, half in the Baroque, carved in wood and decorated with gold leaf screens. In a restored part of the convent where some Franciscan friars still live, **Musée Franciscain** is decorated with 17th-century frescoes. Some 350 documents and works of art from the 15th to the 18th century are displayed, and a monk's cell has been re-created.

In the gardens, you can get a panoramic view of Nice and the Bay of Angels. Matisse and Dufy are buried in the cemetery. The museum is open Monday to Saturday 10am to noon and 3 to 6pm; the church is open daily 8am to 12:30pm and 2 to 7pm. There is no admission charge.

Musée Matisse, in the Villa des Arènes-de-Cimiez, 164 av. des Arènes-de-Cimiez (☎ **04-93-81-08-08**), honors the great artist who spent the last years of his life in Nice; he died here in 1954. The museum has several permanent collections, many donated by Matisse and his heirs. These include *Nude in an Armchair with a Green Plant* (1937), *Nymph in the Forest* (1935/1942), and a chronologically arranged series of paintings from 1890 to 1919. The most famous of these is *Portrait of Madame Matisse* (1905), usually displayed near another portrait of the artist's wife, by Marquet, painted in 1900. The museum is open Wednesday to Monday 10am to 6pm (closes at 5pm off-season). Admission is 25F ($4) for adults, 15F ($2.40) for students, and free for children 17 and under; it's free for everyone the first Sunday of every month.

THE SHOPPING SCENE

You might want to begin with a stroll through the streets and alleys of Nice's historic core. The densest concentrations of boutiques are along **rue Masséna, place Magenta,** and **rue Paradis,** as well as on the streets funneling into and around them. Nice is also known for its colorful street markets. The **flower market,** Marché aux Fleurs, cours Saleya, is open 6am to 5:30pm except Monday and Sunday afternoon. The main Nice **flea market,** Marché à la Brocante, also at cours Saleya, takes place every Monday. There's another flea market on the port, Les Puces de Nice, place Robilante, open Tuesday to Saturday 10am to 6pm.

If you're thinking of indulging in a Provençal picnic, you'll find everything you need at **Nicola Alziari,** 14 rue St-François de Paule (☎ **04-93-85-76-92**), from olives, anchovies, and pistous to aïolis and tapenades. It's one of the oldest stores of its kind in Nice. The house brand of olive oil comes in two strengths, a light version that aficionados claim is vaguely perfumed with Provence and a stronger version well suited to the earthy flavors and robust ingredients of a Provençal winter. Also, look for a range of objects crafted from olive wood.

One of the oldest chocolatiers in Nice, **Confiserie/Salon de Thé Auer,** 7 rue St-François-de-Paule (☎ **04-93-85-77-98**), was established five generations ago, in 1820, in a position near the opera house. Since then, few of the original decorative accessories have been changed, allowing tea drinkers to wax nostalgic for an era when taking tea was an integral part of the Niçois afternoon ritual. Today, tea is served Tuesday to Sunday 8am to 12:30pm and 2:30 to 6pm. Hot chocolate is made the old-fashioned way, by melting bars of chocolate directly into hot milk; and the array of *confits de fruits* is almost comprehensive.

Established in 1949 by the grandfather, Georges Fuchs, of the present English-speaking owners, **Confiserie Florian du Vieux-Nice,** 14 quai Papacino (☎ **04-93-55-43-50**), near the historic center's Old Port specializes in glazed fruits crystallized in sugar or artfully arranged into chocolates. Look for exotic jams (rose-petal preserves or mandarin marmalade) as well as candied violets, verbena leaves, and rosebuds.

Façonnable, 7–9 rue Paradis (☎ 04-93-87-88-80), is the site that sparked the creation of what is today several hundred Façonnable menswear stores around the world. Here you'll find one of the largest Façonnable stores, with a wide range of men's suits, raincoats, overcoats, sportswear, and jeans. The look is youthful and conservatively stylish.

HITTING THE LINKS & OTHER OUTDOOR PURSUITS

GOLF The oldest golf course on the Riviera is about 16km (10 miles) from Nice: **Golf Bastide du Roi** (also known as the Golf de Biot), avenue Jules-Grec, Biot (☎ 04-93-65-08-48). This is a flat, not particularly challenging, and much-used seafronting course. Regrettably, you have to cross over a highway midway through the course to complete the full 18 holes. Open daily throughout the year, tee-off times begin at 8am and continue until 6pm, with the understanding that players then continue their rounds as long as the daylight allows. Reservations aren't necessary, though on weekends you should expect a delay. Greens fees are 240F ($38) for 18 holes, and clubs can be rented for 80F ($13). No carts are available.

SCUBA DIVING The best-respected underwater outfitter is the **Centre International de Plongée de Nice,** 2 Ruelle des Moulins (☎ 04-93-55-59-50). Adjacent to the city's old port, it lies midway between quai des Docks and boulevard Stalingrad. A Baptême (initiatory dive for first-timers) costs 200F ($32), and a one-tank dive for experienced divers, with all equipment included, is 190F ($30). This outfitter is open only from mid-March to mid-November.

TENNIS The oldest tennis club in Nice is the **Nice Lawn Tennis Club,** Parc Impérial, 5 av. Suzanne-Lenglen (☎ 04-92-15-58-00), located near the rail station. It's open daily 9am to 9pm (8pm mid-October to mid-April), and charges 120F ($19) per person for two noncontiguous hours of court time, or a reduced rate of 300F ($48) per person for unlimited access to the courts for a 1-week period. The club has a cooperative staff, 13 clay courts, and 6 hard-surfaced courts. Reservations should be made the evening before.

NICE AFTER DARK

Nice has some of the most active nightlife along the Riviera; pick up a copy of *La Semaine de Spectacles,* which outlines the week's nighttime diversions, for clues on what's hot. The major cultural center along the Riviera is the **Opéra de Nice,** 4 rue St-François-de-Paule (☎ 04-92-17-40-40; bus: 15), with a busy season in winter. A full repertoire is presented, including both operas and the popular French Opéra Comique. In one season you might see *La Bohème, Tristan und Isolde,* and *Carmen,* as well as a *saison symphonique,* dominated by the Orchestre Philharmonique de Nice. The opera hall is also the major venue for concerts and recitals. The box office is open Tuesday to Saturday 10am to 5:30pm, with tickets ranging from 40F ($6) to 800F ($128), depending on the event.

Le Cabaret du Casino Ruhl, in the Casino Ruhl, 1 promenade des Anglais (☎ 04-93-87-95-87; airport bus), is Nice's answer to the cabaret glitter that appears in more ostentatious forms in Monte Carlo and Las Vegas. It includes just enough flesh to titillate; lots of spangles, feathers, and sequins; a medley of cross-cultural jokes and nostalgia for the good old days of French *chanson;* and an acrobat or juggler. The cover of 100F ($16) includes the first drink; dinner and the show, complete with a bottle of wine per person, costs 300F ($48). Shows are presented every Friday and Saturday at 10pm.

The casino contains an area devoted exclusively to slot machines, open daily noon to 4 or 5am, entrance is free. A more formal gaming room, replete with blackjack, baccarat, chemin de fer, and 21 tables, is open nightly, at a fee of 75F ($12) per person, every Monday to Friday 8pm to 4am, and every Saturday and Sunday 5pm to 5am. Bring your passport.

Near the Négresco and the promenade des Anglais, **Le Blue Boy,** 9 rue Spinetta (☎ **04-93-44-68-24;** bus: 15), is the oldest gay disco on the Riviera. With two bars and two floors, it's a vital nocturnal stopover for passengers aboard the dozens of all-gay cruises that make regular stops at Nice. Cover is 60F ($10) on Saturday or 30F ($4.80) otherwise. Ask the tourist office for a free copy of two of their periodicals, *L'X* and *L'Exces* that list the entertainment and nightlife options for gay travelers in Nice.

ST-JEAN-CAP-FERRAT

This has been called Paradise Found. Of all the oases along the Côte d'Azur, no place has the snob appeal of Cap-Ferrat. It's a 14km (9-mile) promontory sprinkled with luxurious villas, outlined by sheltered bays, beaches, and coves. The vegetation is lush. In the port of St-Jean, the harbor accommodates yachts and fishing boats.

The Italianate **Musée Ile-de-France,** avenue Denis-Séméria (☎ **04-93-01-33-09**), allows you to visit one of the most legendary villas along the Côte d'Azur, built by the Baronne Ephrussi de Rothschild. She died in 1934, leaving the building and its magnificent gardens to the Institut de France on behalf of the Académie des Beaux-Arts. The wealth of her collection is preserved: 18th-century furniture; Tiepolo ceilings; Savonnerie carpets; screens and panels from the Far East; tapestries from Gobelins, Aubusson, and Beauvais; original drawings by Fragonard; canvases by Renoir, Sisley, and Boucher; rare Sèvres porcelain; and more. Covering 5ha (12 acres), the gardens contain fragments of statuary from churches, monasteries, and torn-down palaces.

Between mid-February and October, the museum and its gardens are open daily 10am to 6pm. From November to mid-February, they're open Monday to Friday 2pm to 6pm and Saturday and Sunday 10am to 6pm. The entrance fee is 49F ($8) for adults and 37F ($6) for children and students 18 to 24. A 14F ($2.25) supplement is charged for anyone who wants to participate in a guided tour. These are conducted in English every day at 11:30am, 2:30pm, 3:30pm, and 4:30pm.

ESSENTIALS

GETTING THERE   Most visitors drive or take the hourly bus (trip time: 25 minutes) or a taxi from the rail station at nearby Beaulieu. There's also **bus service** from Nice (no. 111). For bus information and schedules, call ☎ **04-93-85-61-81.** Buses pull into the center of town, but there's no station.

VISITOR INFORMATION   The **Office de Tourisme** is at 54 av. Denis-Séméria (☎ **04-93-76-08-90**).

DEPARTING BY CAR   From St-Jean-Cap-Ferrat, you can head east toward Monaco by taking D-25 along the coast to the resort of Beaulieu, which is almost as chic as Cap-Ferrat. Continue along N-98 for about 11km (7 miles) into Monaco.

WHERE TO STAY

✪ **Grand Hôtel du Cap-Ferrat.** Bd. du Général-de-Gaulle, 06230 St-Jean-Cap-Ferrat. ☎ **04-93-76-50-50.** Fax 04-93-76-04-52. www.grand-hotel-cap-ferrat.com. E-mail: reserve@grand-hotel-cap-ferrat.com. 53 units. A/C MINIBAR TV TEL. 950–3,200F ($152–$512) double; from 3,600F ($576) suite. AE, DC, MC, V. Parking from 300F ($48).

This turn-of-the-century palace is at the tip of the peninsula in the midst of a 6ha (14-acre) garden of semitropical trees and manicured lawns. Parts of the exterior have open loggias and big arched windows, and guests enjoy the views from the elaborate flowering terrace over the sea. Rates include admission to the pool, Club Dauphin. Most rooms are quite spacious, and elegantly appointed. Each comes with a sumptuously fitted bed containing the town's most comfortable mattresses. Bathrooms feature power showerheads, robes, a hair dryer, and dual basins. The indoor/outdoor restaurant's cuisine is based on market-fresh ingredients.

Hôtel Clair Logis. 12 av. Centrale, 06230 St-Jean-Cap-Ferrat. ☎ **04-93-76-04-57.** Fax 04-93-76-11-85. www.hoteclairlogis.fr. 18 units. TEL. 440–740F ($70–$118) double. AE, DC, MC, V. Free parking. Closed Jan 10–Feb and Nov–Dec 15.

In an otherwise pricey resort strip of deluxe hotels and homes, this 19th-century former villa surrounded by semitropical gardens is a rare find. The pleasant rooms are scattered over three buildings in the confines of the garden. The most romantic and spacious ones are in the main building; units in the annex are the most modern but have the least character.

WHERE TO DINE

Le Provençal. 2 av. Denis-Séméria. ☎ **04-93-76-03-97.** Reservations required. Main courses 230–360F ($37–$58). Set price menus 280–350F ($45–$56). MC, V. Apr–Oct 14, daily noon–2:30pm and 7:30–11pm. Oct 15–Mar Fri–Sun noon–2:30pm and 7:30–11pm. FRENCH.

This restaurant, one of the finest in the area, occupies what was a 2-century-old stone-sided farmhouse above the center of St-Jean-Cap Ferrat. The venue is very much in the old Provençal style. You can enjoy marinated artichoke hearts with half a lobster, a tart fine of potatoes served with deliberately undercooked foie gras; rack of lamb with local herbs and tarragon sauce; and crayfish served with asparagus and black olive tapenade. A dessert sampler, "les cinq desserts du Provençal," includes five luscious sweets, such as macaroons with chocolate or crème brûlée. The food is solemnly served, as if part of a grand ritual.

MONACO

Monaco—or rather its capital, Monte Carlo—has for a century been a symbol of glamour. Its legend was further enhanced by the 1956 marriage of the man who was at that time the world's most eligible bachelor, Prince Rainier III, to American actress Grace Kelly. Although not always happy in her role, Princess Grace soon won the respect and adoration of her people. The Monégasques still mourn her death in a 1982 car accident.

Monaco became a property of the Grimaldi clan, a Genoese family, as early as 1297. With shifting loyalties, it has maintained something resembling independence ever since. In a fit of impatience, the French annexed it in 1793, but the ruling family recovered it in 1814, though the prince at the time couldn't bear to tear himself away from the pleasures of Paris for "dreary old Monaco."

ESSENTIALS

GETTING THERE   Monaco has rail, bus, and highway connections from other coastal cities, especially Nice. There are no border formalities for anyone entering Monaco from mainland France. **Trains** arrive at the station on avenue Prince Pierre every 30 minutes from Cannes, Nice, Menton, and Antibes. For rail information and schedules, call ☎ **08-36-35-35-35.** For **bus** information call ☎ **377/93-50-62-41.** Most buses leave from place du Casino (no station).

VISITOR INFORMATION   The **Direction du Tourisme** is at 2A bd. des Moulins (☎ **377/92-16-61-16**).

Phone Tips

On June 21, 1996, Monaco's phone system underwent drastic changes. It's now a separate entity from France, which means that calls to and from such nearby places as Nice are long-distance. If you're calling Monaco from France, dial 00 followed by Monaco's new country prefix, 377, then the 8-digit local phone number. To call from the United States, use the international access code, 011, then 377 plus the 8-digit local number.

WHERE TO STAY

Hôtel Alexandra. 33 bd. Princesse-Charlotte, 98000 Monaco. ☎ **377/93-50-63-13.** Fax 377/92-16-06-48. 56 units. A/C TV TEL. 650–880F ($104–$141) double. AE, DC, MC, V. Parking 45F ($7.20).

This hotel is in the center of the business district, on a busy and often noisy street corner. Its comfortably furnished rooms aren't that exciting, but they're reliable and respectable. The Alexandra knows it can't compete with the giants of Monaco and doesn't even try, but if you want to visit the principality without spending a fortune, it's a good deal.

Hôtel Cosmopolite. 4 rue de la Turbie, 98000 Monaco. ☎ **377/93-30-16-95.** Fax 377/93-30-23-05. 24 units, none with bathroom. 250–320F ($40–$51) double. No credit cards.

This century-old three-story hotel is down a set of steps from the train station. Madame Gay Angèle, the English-speaking owner, is proud of her "Old Monaco" establishment. Her more expensive rooms have showers, but the cheapest way to stay here is to request a room without shower—there are adequate facilities in the hall.

Hôtel de Paris. Place du Casino, 98000 Monaco. ☎ **377/92-16-30-00.** Fax 377/92-16-38-50. www.montecarloresort.com. E-mail: hp@sdm.mc 197 units. A/C MINIBAR TV TEL. 2,240–3,710F ($358–$594) double; from 4,730F ($757) suite. AE, DC, MC, V. Parking 130F ($21).

On the main plaza, this is one of the most famous hotels in the world and the choicest address in Monaco. The hotel is furnished with a dazzling decor of marble pillars, statues, crystal chandeliers, sumptuous carpets, Louis XVI chairs, and a wall-size fin-de-siècle mural. Rooms are, in many cases, sumptuous, each with an elaborate period decor or a stylish contemporary one. Bathrooms are large, and come with hair dryers, dual basins, robes, and deluxe toiletries. On top of the Hôtel de Paris, the Louis XIV royal galley-style Le Grill has an impressive sliding roof. The elegant Le Louis XV is recommended under "Where to Dine." Thermes Marins spa, connected to the hotel, offers complete cures of thalassotherapy under medical supervision.

Hôtel Mirabeau. 1 av. Princesse-Grace, MC 98000 Monaco. ☎ **377/92-16-65-65.** Fax 377/93-50-84-85. www.montecarloresort.com. E-mail: a.arena@sbm.mc 103 units. A/C MINI-BAR TV TEL. 1,400–2,450F ($224–$392) double; from 3,250F ($520) suite. AE, DC, MC, V. Parking 125F ($20).

In the heart of Monte Carlo, next to the casino, the contemporary Mirabeau combines modern design with refined atmosphere. Large mirrors, spacious lighted closets, safes, and sumptuous beds with luxurious mattresses make living here idyllic; many rooms also have terraces with romantic views over the pool and Mediterranean. Although the newest rooms are as fine as those in the main building, many prefer older ones for their old-fashioned French decor and street-front exposures. Bathrooms are roomy and well appointed with robes, deluxe toiletries, dual basins, and a hair dryer. La Coupole restaurant is highly praised among restaurants of the Riviera for its inventive yet classical cooking (closed in August).

WHERE TO DINE

Café de Paris. Place du Casino. ☎ **377/92-16-20-20.** Reservations recommended. Main courses 98–210F ($16–$34). AE, DC, MC, V. Daily 8am–4am. INTERNATIONAL.

This is the best positioned cafe and restaurant in Monaco, very close to both the casino and the Hôtel de Paris, and so close to the tourist center of things that you might get more of a dose of Las Vegas than you might care for. But why not revel in the crowds and the hurly-burly? This site provides a front-row seat to the never-ending spectacle of Monte Carlo. Food is professional and well-prepared: About a half-dozen *plats du jour* are available, including fried trout with almonds, pepper steak, osso bucco, and turbot with hollandaise.

✪ **Le Louis XV.** In the Hôtel de Paris, place du Casino. ☎ **377/92-16-30-01.** Reservations recommended. Jacket/tie for men. Main courses 310–590F ($50–$94); set price dinner 860–980F ($138–$157). Set lunch 500F ($80). AE, DC, MC, V. July–Aug Wed 8–10pm, Thurs–Mon noon–2pm and 8–10pm; Sept–June Thurs–Mon noon–2pm and 8–10pm. Closed Feb 2–17 and first 3 weeks Dec. FRENCH/ITALIAN.

On the lobby level of the five-star Hôtel de Paris, Le Louis XV offers what one critic called "down-home Riviera cooking within a Fabergé egg." In these regal trappings, the chef, the great six-star Alain Ducasse, creates a cuisine that is light and attuned to the seasons, with an intelligent modern interpretation of both Provençal and northern Italian courses. Always count on Ducasse for delightful surprises. He stopped being a very good chef a long time ago and became a great one. He commands the finest ingredients in Europe, and his menu is ever changing to take advantage of what is best in any season. The service is superb.

EXPLORING MONACO

The second-smallest state in Europe (Vatican City is the tiniest), Monaco consists of four parts: The old town, **Monaco-Ville,** on a promontory, The Rock, 60m (200 feet) high, is the seat of the royal palace and the government building, as well as the home of the Oceanographic Museum. To the west of the bay, **La Condamine,** the 19th-century home of the Monégasques, is at the foot of the old town, forming its harbor and port sector. Up from the port (walking is steep in Monaco) is **Monte Carlo,** once the playground of European royalty and still the center for wintering wealthy, the setting for the casino and its gardens and the deluxe hotels. The fourth part, **Fontvieille,** is a neat industrial suburb.

Ironically, **Monte-Carlo Beach,** at the far frontier, is on French soil. It attracts a chic crowd, including movie stars. The resort has a freshwater pool, an artificial beach, and a sea-bathing establishment.

The Italianate home of Monaco's royal family, the **Palais du Prince,** dominates the principality from "The Rock." When touring Les Grands Appartements du Palais, place du Palais (☎ **377/93-25-18-31**), you're shown the Throne Room and allowed to see some of the art collection, including works by Brueghel and Holbein, as well as Princess Grace's stunning state portrait. The palace was built in the 13th century and part of it is from the Renaissance. The ideal time to arrive is 11:55am to watch the 10-minute changing of the guard. The palace is open daily June to September 9:30am to 6:30pm and October from 10am to 5pm. Admission is 30F ($4.80) for adults, 15F ($2.40) for children ages 8 to 14, and free for children 7 and under.

Monaco

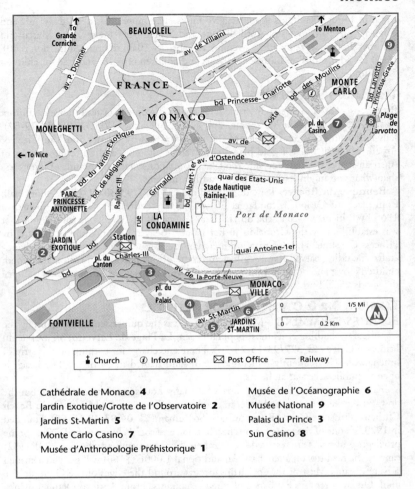

Church ✝ **Information** ⓘ **Post Office** ✉ **Railway** —

Cathédrale de Monaco **4**

Jardin Exotique/Grotte de l'Observatoire **2**

Jardins St-Martin **5**

Monte Carlo Casino **7**

Musée d'Anthropologie Préhistorique **1**

Musée de l'Océanographie **6**

Musée National **9**

Palais du Prince **3**

Sun Casino **8**

Jardin Exotique, boulevard du Jardin-Exotique (☎ 377/93-15-29-80), was built on the side of a rock and is known for its cactus collection. The gardens were begun by Prince Albert I, who was both a naturalist and a scientist. He spotted some succulents growing in the palace gardens, and knowing that these plants were normally found only in Central America or Africa, he created the garden from them. You can also explore the grottoes here, as well as the **Musée d'Anthropologie Préhistorique** (☎ 377/93-15-80-06). The view of the principality is splendid. The site is open daily June to September 9am to 7pm and October to May 9am to 6pm. Admission is 39F ($6) for adults and 18F ($2.90) for children 6 to 18; admissions is free for children 5 and under.

Musée de l'Océanographie, avenue St-Martin (☎ 377/93-15-36-00), was founded by Albert I, great-grandfather of the present prince. In the main rotunda is a statue of Albert dressed as a sea captain. Displayed are specimens he collected during 30 years of expeditions aboard his oceanographic boats. The aquarium, one of the finest in Europe, contains more than 90 tanks. The museum is open daily July and August from 9am to 8pm; April to June and September 9am to 7pm; March and October 9:30am to 7pm; and November to February 10am to 6pm. Admission is 60F ($10) for adults, 30F ($4.80) for students and children 6 to 18, and free for children 5 and under.

TWO SHOPS WORTH A LOOK

Rising costs and an increase in crime have changed women's tastes in jewelry. **Bijoux Cascio,** Les Galeries du Metropole, 207 av. des Spélugues (☎ 377/93-50-17-57), sells imitation gemstones, copies of the real ones sold by Cartier and Van Cleef & Arpels. Made in Italy of gold-plated silver, cubic zirconia, and glittering chunks of Austrian-made Swarovski crystal, the fake jewelry costs many thousands of francs less than what you might have paid for the authentic gems.

Boutique du Rocher, 1 av. de la Madone (☎ 377/93-30-91-17), a short walk from place du Casion, is the larger of two roughly equivalent boutiques opened in 1966 by Princess Grace as the official retail outlets of the charitable foundation that was established by the Grimaldis in her name. Today the foundation is directed by Princess Caroline. The organization merchandises Monégasque and Provençal hand-crafts, including carved frames; gift items crafted from porcelain, textiles, and wood; children's toys; and dolls. On the premises are workshops where local artisans produce the goods you'll find for sale.

TAKING A DIP & OTHER OUTDOOR ACTIVITIES

BEACHES/SWIMMING   Monaco, in its role as the quintessential kingdom by the sea, offers sea bathing at its most popular beach, **La Plage de Larvetto,** off avenue du Princesse-Grace (☎ 377/93-15-28-76). There's no charge for bathing on this strip of beach, which is frequently replenished with sand hauled in by barge. The beach is open to public access at all hours.

If a pool is more to your tastes, most of the large hotels in town boast pools, but the dowager empress, across the border in neighboring France, is **Le Monte Carlo Beach Club,** av. Princesse-Grace, Roquebrune—St-Roman (☎ 04-93-28-66-66). Founded in 1929, it's one of the most famous beach, pool, and social clubs on the Riviera. Some privileges and perks are reserved for members, but nonmembers who pay 200F ($32) can use the facilities on a day pass. An additional 1,000F ($160) will get you a striped private cabana. Most of the socializing occurs around the edges of the Olympic-size pool. On the premises are bars and three restaurants. From April to October, wind-surfing and waterskiing are popular diversions that are conducted from the stony beach of this club.

GOLF   The **Monte Carlo Golf Club,** Route N-7, La Turbie (☎ 04-93-41-09-11), lying within France, is a par-72 golf course with equal parts prestige, scenic panoramas, and local history. Certain perks, including use of electric golf buggies, are reserved exclusively for members. Before they're allowed to play, nonmembers will be asked to show proof of membership in another golf club and provide evidence of their handicap ratings. Greens fees for 18 holes are 400F ($64) Monday to Friday and 500F ($80) Saturday and Sunday. Clubs can be rented for 80F ($13). The course is open daily 8am to sunset.

TENNIS & SQUASH   In addition to 23 tennis courts (21 clay and 2 concrete), the **Monte Carlo Country Club,** av. Princesse-Grace, Roquebrune—St-Roman (☎ 04-93-41-30-15), has enough other warm-weather distractions to keep you amused for a week. An entrance fee of 220F ($35) gets you access to a restaurant, a health club with Jacuzzi and sauna, a putting green, a beach, squash courts, and the above-mentioned roster of well-maintained tennis courts. Residents of the hotels administered by the Societé des Bains de Mer (the Hotel de Paris, the Hermitage, the Mirabeau, and the Monte Carlo Beach Club) pay half-price. It's open daily 8am to 8 or 9pm, depending on the season.

GAMBLING & OTHER AFTER-DARK DIVERSIONS

The **Sun Casino,** in the Monte Carlo Grand Hotel, 12 av. des Spélugues (☎ 377/93-50-65-00), is a huge room filled with the one-armed bandits. It also features blackjack, craps, and American roulette. Additional slot machines are available on the roof starting at 11am—for those who want to gamble with a wider view of the sea. It's open daily 5pm to 4am (until 5am for slot machines). Admission is free. Bring your passport.

A speculator, François Blanc, made the **Monte Carlo Casino,** place du Casino (☎ 377/92-16-21-21), the most famous in the world, attracting Sarah Bernhardt, Mata Hari, King Farouk, and Aly Khan (Onassis used to own a part-interest). The architect of Paris's Opéra Garnier, Charles Garnier, built the oldest part of the casino, and it remains an extravagant example of period architecture.

The **Salle Américaine,** containing only Vegas-style slot machines, opens at noon, as do doors for roulette and trente-quarente. A section for roulette and chemin-de-fer opens at 3pm. Everything heats up at 4pm when the full casino swings into action with more roulette, craps, and blackjack. Gambling continues until very late, and closing time depends on the crowd. To enter the casino, you must be at least 21 and have a passport, driver's license, or identity card. Admission to private rooms is 50 to 100F ($8 to $16).

The foremost winter establishment, under the same ownership, is the **Cabaret** in the Casino Gardens, where you can dance to the music of a smooth orchestra. A good cabaret with feathers, glitter, and Riviera-style seminudity is presented at 10pm Wednesday to Monday mid-September to June. From 9pm you can enjoy dinner for 450F ($72). Drinks ordered separately begin at 150F ($24). For reservations, call ☎ 377/92-16-36-36.

In the **Salle Garnier** of the casino, concerts are held periodically; for information, contact the tourist office (above). The music is usually classical, featuring the Orchestre Philharmonique de Monte Carlo.

The casino also contains the **Opéra de Monte-Carlo,** whose patron is Prince Rainier. This world-famous house, opened in 1879 by Sarah Bernhardt, presents a winter and spring repertoire that traditionally includes Puccini, Mozart, and Verdi. The famed Ballets Russes de Monte-Carlo, starring Nijinsky and Karsavina, was created in 1918 by Sergei Diaghilev. The national orchestra and ballet company of Monaco appear here. Tickets may be hard to come by; your best bet is to ask your hotel concierge. You can make inquiries about tickets on your own at the **Atrium du Casino** (☎ 377/92-16-22-99), open Tuesday to Sunday 10am to 12:15pm and 2 to 5pm. Standard tickets generally cost 150 to 800F ($24 to $128).

7

Germany

by Darwin Porter & Danforth Prince

At the millennium, Berlin is the capital of unified Germany, and the rebuilding of the city for the 21st century continues at a rapid pace. What was once the city's biggest tourist attraction, the Berlin Wall, is now a bicycle path where Berliners push baby strollers. Restored baroque Munich, in the south, known as Germany's "secret capital," is the gateway to the Bavarian Alps and the colorful alpine villages. For a taste of medieval Germany, explore the untouched towns of the Romantic Road and Ludwig II's fairy-tale castle of Neuschwanstein.

1 Berlin

When Heinrich Heine arrived in Berlin in 1819, he exclaimed, "Isn't the present splendid!" Were he to arrive today, he might make the same remark. Visitors who come by plane to Berlin see a splendid panorama. Few metropolitan areas are blessed with as many lakes, woodlands, and parks—these cover one-third of the city's area, and small farms with fields and meadows still exist within the city limits.

Berlin today is an almost completely modern city. Regrettably, Berlin is hardly the architectural gem that old-time visitors remember from the pre-Nazi era; it wasn't rebuilt with the same kind of care lavished on Munich and Cologne. But in spite of its decades-long "quadripartite status," it's a vibrant city, always receptive to new ideas, a major economic and cultural center, and a leader in development and research. Because of its excellent facilities, it is a favored site for trade fairs, congresses, and conventions, attracting six million visitors a year.

Since the Berlin Wall came down, change within the city has been so rapid that the government has resorted to painting a red line through its central district so that baffled visitors can tell where it stood. The city still seems to have two of everything—two zoos, two opera companies, two major international airports, to name a few. However, there're also new problems for the reunited Berlin. Economic devastation has affected the eastern sector and panhandling and crime on the streets have become major problems in some areas of the city.

ORIENTATION

ARRIVING By Plane Tegel Airport is the city's busiest, serving most flights from the west. Historic **Tempelhof Airport,** made famous as the city's lifeline during the Berlin Airlift, has declined in importance. **Schönefeld,** the airport in the eastern sector, is used primarily by Russian and Eastern European airlines. Private bus shuttles among the three airports operate constantly so you can make connecting flights at a different airport. Buses from each airport will also take you into the center. For information on every airport, call ☎ **0180/500-00-186.**

Lufthansa (☎ **800/645-3880** in the U.S., or 0181/750-3300 in London) is the premier airline flying into Berlin, followed closely by **Delta** (☎ **800/221-1212**). **British Airways** (☎ **800/247-9297** in the U.S. and Canada, or 0345/222-111 in the U.K.) offers direct flights into Berlin from London's Heathrow and Gatwick airports and from Birmingham.

By Train   Frankfurt and Hamburg, among other cities, have good rail connections to Berlin. From Frankfurt to Berlin takes about 7 hours. Eurailpass and GermanRail passes are valid. Most arrivals from western European and western German cities are at the **Bahnhof Zoologischer Garten** (☎ **030/194-19**), the main train station, called "Bahnhof Zoo," in western Berlin. In the center of the city, close to the Kurfürstendamm, it's well connected for public transportation. Facilities include a tourist information counter dispensing free maps and tourist brochures open daily 5am to 11pm. The staff will also make same-day hotel reservations for 5DM ($2.70).

Berlin has two other train stations, the **Berlin Hauptbahnhof** and **Berlin Lichtenberg.** Call the main station at (☎ **030/1-94-19**) for information.

By Bus   The operations center for several independent bus operators are headquartered within a central arrivals and departures point, the **ZOB Omnibusbahnhof am Funkturm,** Messedamm 8 (☎ **030/301-80-28**). Call for departure times and fare information for routes to and from other parts of Europe.

By Car   From Frankfurt, take A-66 to Bad Herzfeld, and either go east on A-4 to pick up A-9 to Berlin, or continue on A-7 to Braunschweig and east on A-2 toward Berlin. North of Nürnberg, A-9 leads to Berlin. From Leipzig take A-14 in the direction of Halle; at the intersection of A-9, head northeast into Berlin. From Dresden, head northeast on A-13 into Berlin. Expect heavy traffic delays on autobahnen, especially on weekends and sunny days when everybody is out touring.

VISITOR INFORMATION   For tourist information and hotel bookings, head for the **Berlin Tourist Information Center,** in the Europa-Center near the Memorial Church, entrance on the Budapesterstrasse side (☎ **030/25-00-25;** information@btm.de or reservations@btm.de), open Monday to Saturday 8am to 10pm and Sunday 9am to 9pm. You can learn about Berlin on the Internet at **www.berlin.de.**

CITY LAYOUT   The center of activity in the western part of Berlin is the 3km (2-mile)-long **Kurfürstendamm,** called the Ku'damm by Berliners. Along this wide boulevard you'll find the best hotels, restaurants, theaters, cafes, nightclubs, shops, and department stores. The huge **Tiergarten,** the city's largest park, is crossed by Strasse des 17 Juni, which leads to the famed **Brandenburger Tor (Gate);** just north is the Reichstag. On the southwestern fringe of the Tiergarten is the **Berlin Zoo (Zoologischer Garten).** From the Ku'damm you can take Hardenbergstrasse, crossing Bismarckstrasse and traversing Otto-Suhr-Allee, which leads to **Schloss Charlottenburg** and museums, one of your major sightseeing goals. The Dahlem Museums are on the southwestern fringe, often reached by going along Hohenzollerndamm.

The **Brandenburger Tor** is the start of Berlin's most celebrated street, **Unter den Linden,** the cultural heart of Berlin before World War II. The famous street runs from

Western Berlin

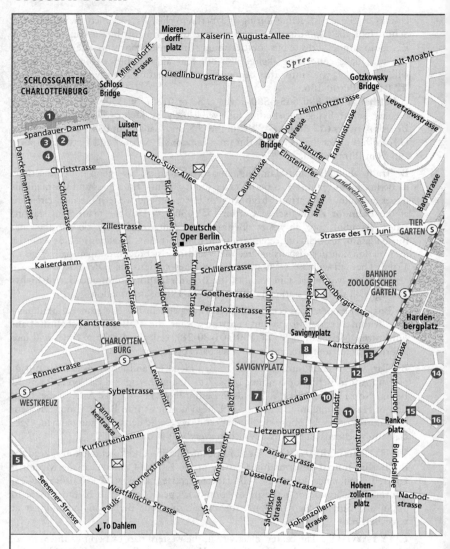

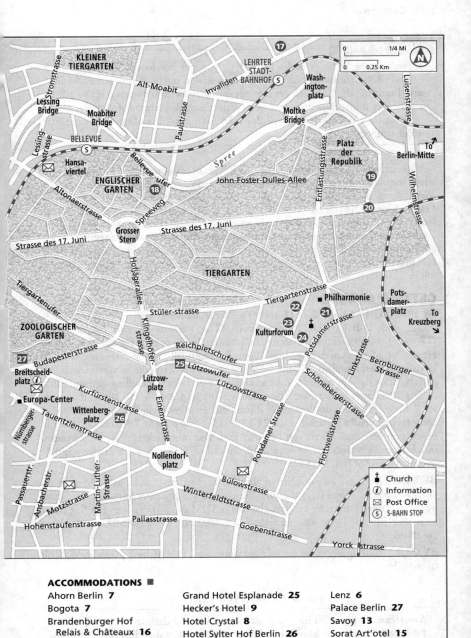

ACCOMMODATIONS ■

Ahorn Berlin **7**

Bogota **7**

Brandenburger Hof
  Relais & Châteaux **16**

Golden Tulip Hotel
  Kronprinz Berlin **5**

Grand Hotel Esplanade **25**

Hecker's Hotel **9**

Hotel Crystal **8**

Hotel Sylter Hof Berlin **26**

Kempinski Hotel
  Bristol Berlin **12**

Lenz **6**

Palace Berlin **27**

Savoy **13**

Sorat Art'otel **15**

Traveler's Tip

If you're going to be in Berlin for 3 days, you can purchase a **WelcomeCard** for 29DM ($16), entitling holders to 72 free hours on public transportation in Berlin and Brandenburg. You also get free admission or price reductions up to 50% on sightseeing tours, museums, and other attractions. Reductions of 25% are granted at 10 of the city's theaters as well. It's valid for one adult and up to three children 13 or younger.

---

west to east, cutting a path through the city. It leads to **Museumsinsel** (Museum Island), where the most outstanding museums of eastern Berlin, including the Pergamon, are situated. As it courses along, Unter den Linden crosses another major Berlin artery, **Friedrichstrasse.** If you continue south along Friedrichstrasse, you'll reach the former location of **Checkpoint Charlie,** the famous border-crossing site of the cold war days.

Unter den Linden continues east until it reaches **Alexanderplatz,** the center of eastern Berlin, with its TV tower (Fernsehturm). A short walk away is the restored **Nikolai Quarter** (Nikolaiviertel), a neighborhood of bars, restaurants, and shops that evoke life in the prewar days.

GETTING AROUND

BY PUBLIC TRANSPORTATION   The Berlin transport system consists of buses, trams, and U-Bahn and S-Bahn trains. The network is run by the **BVG** (☎ 030/1-94-49), which operates an information booth outside the Bahnhof Zoo on Hardenbergplatz, open daily 8am to 10pm. The staff will provide details about which U-Bahn (underground) or S-Bahn (elevated railway) line to take to various locations and the ticket options possible. You can also purchase tickets, including discount cards.

The **BVG standard ticket** (Einzelfahrschein) is 3.90DM ($2.10) and is valid for 2 hours of transportation in all directions, transfers included. Also available at counters and vending machines is a 24-hour ticket; the price is 7.80DM ($4.20). On buses, only standard tickets can be purchased, and tram tickets must be purchased in advance. Tickets should be kept until the end of the journey; otherwise you'll be liable for a fine of 60DM ($32).

BY TAXI   Taxis are available throughout Berlin. The meter starts at 4DM to 6DM ($2.15 to $3.25). The longer the ride, the cheaper the price per kilometer. For short distances, either 5 minutes or 2km, the fare is 5DM ($2.70). Visitors can flag down taxis that have a T-sign illuminated. For a taxi, call ☎ **21-02-02,** 6-90-22, or 26-10-26.

BY CAR   Touring Berlin by car isn't recommended. Free parking places are difficult to come by.

Fast Facts: Berlin

American Express   The main office at Uhlandsdtrasse 173 (☎ **030/ 88-45-88-21**) is open Monday to Friday 9am to 5:30pm and Saturday 9am to noon. Branch offices are at Bayreuthstrasse 23 (☎ **030/21-49-83-63**) and Friedrichstrasse 172 (☎ **030/20-17-40-12**).

Business Hours   Most **banks** are open Monday through Friday 9am to 1 or 3pm. Most other **businesses** and **stores** are open Monday to Friday 9 or 10am to 6 or 6:30pm and Saturday 9am to 2pm. On *langer Samstag,* the first Saturday of the month, shops stay open until 4 or 6pm. Some stores observe late closing on Thursday, usually at 8:30pm.

Currency   The German monetary unit is the **deutsche mark (DM),** which is divided into 100 pfennig. Bills exist in denominations of 5, 10, 20, 50, 100, 200, 500, and 1,000 marks; coins come in denominations of 1, 2, and 5 marks and in 1, 2, 5, 10, and 50 pfennig. The rate of exchange for the deutsche mark used throughout this chapter was $1 = 1.85DM, or 1DM = 55¢. The ratio of the British pound to the mark fluctuates constantly. At press time, £1 = approximately 3.04DM. The euro rate is currently fixed at 1.9DM (or 1DM = € 0.53).

Currency Exchange   You can exchange money at all airports, major department stores, any bank, and the American Express office (above).

Dentists/Doctors   The Berlin tourist office in the Europa-Center (see "Visitor Information" above) keeps a list of English-speaking dentists and doctors in Berlin. In case of a medical emergency, call ☎ **030/31-00-31.**

Drugstores   If you need a pharmacy (*Apotheke*) at night, go to one on any corner. There you'll find a sign in the window giving the address of the nearest drugstore open at night; such posting is required by law. A central pharmacy is **Europa-Apotheke,** Tauentzienstrasse 9–12 (☎ **030/2-61-41-42**), by the Europa-Center. It's open Monday to Friday 9am to 8pm and Saturday to 4pm.

Embassies & Consulates   The embassy of the **United States** is at Neustaedtische Kirchstrasse 4–5 (☎ **030/2-38-51-74;** U-Bahn: Friedrichstrasse) and a consulate at Clayallee 170 (☎ **030/8-32-92-33;** U-Bahn: Hüttenweg). The **British Embassy's** Berlin office is at Unter den Linden 32–34 (☎ **030/ 20-18-40;** U-Bahn: Friedrichstrasse). The embassy of **Australia** is on Kempinski Plaza, at Uhlandstrasse 181–183 (☎ **030/8-80-08-80;** U-Bahn: Uhlandstrasse). The embassy of **Canada** maintains a consulate at Friedrichstrasse 95 (☎ **030/20-31-20;** U-Bahn: Friedrichstrasse). The embassy of **New Zealand** is at Friedrichstrasse 60 (☎ **030/20-62-10;** U-Bahn: Fredrichstrasse). The consulate of **Ireland** is at Ernst-Reuter-Platz 10 (☎ **030/34-80-08-22;** U-Bahn: Tiergarten) in Berlin.

Emergencies   Call the police at ☎ **110;** dial ☎ **112** to report a fire or to call an ambulance.

Internet Access   If you're feeling out of touch, visit the **Virtuality Café,** Lewishamstrasse 1 (☎ **030/32-75-143;** www.vrcafe.de; S-Bahn: Charlottenburg).

Post Office   The post office at the Bahnhof Zoo is open Monday through Saturday 6am to midnight and Sunday 8am to midnight. If you have mail sent here, have it marked Hauptpostlagernd, Postamt 120, Bahnhof Zoo, D-10612, Berlin. There's also a post office at Hauptbahnhof, open Monday to Friday 7am to 8pm and Saturday 8am to 1pm. For postal information, call ☎ **030/311-00-20.** You can make long-distance calls at post offices at far cheaper rates than at hotels.

Taxes   A 16% value-added tax (VAT) is included in the price of restaurants, hotels, and material goods. On many objects, however, temporary visitors to Germany can obtain a VAT refund if you purchase 60DM ($32) worth of goods from one outlet.

Telephone   The **country code** for Germany is **49;** the **city code** for Berlin is **30** for calls from outside Germany or 030 if you're calling within the country.

If you're going to make a lot of phone calls or wish to make an international call from a phone booth, you'll probably want to purchase a **telephone card.**

Berlin U-Bahn & S-Bahn

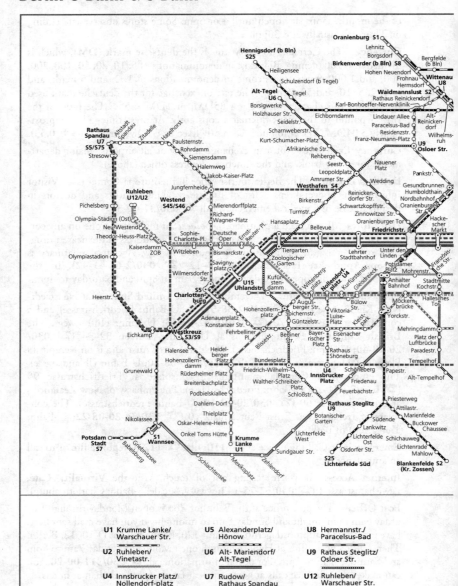

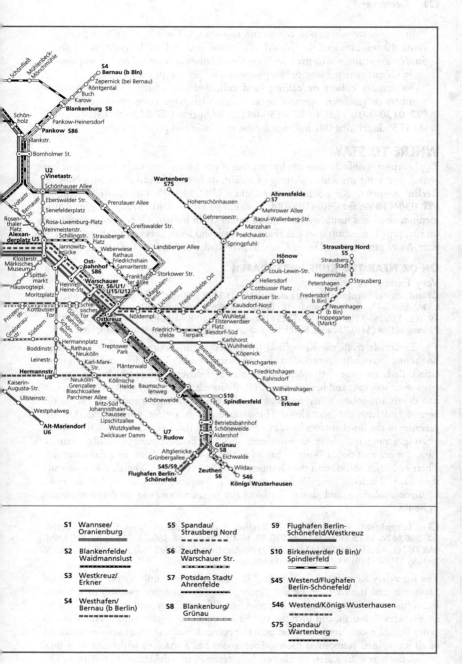

Schönfließ
Mühlenbeck-Mönchmühle

S4
Bernau (b Bln)
Zepernick (bei Bernau)
Röntgental
Buch
Karow

Blankenburg S8

Schön-
holz
Pankow-Heinersdorf

Pankow S86

Wollankstr.

Bornholmer St.

U2
Vinetastr.

Schönhauser Allee

Eberswalder Str.   Prenzlauer Allee

Voltastr.
Bernauer Str.
Senefelderplatz

Rosen-
thaler
Platz
Rosa-Luxemburg-Platz

Alexander-
platz U5
Weinmeisterstr.
Schillingstr.   Strausberger
Platz

Jannowitz-
brücke
Weberwiese
Rathaus
Friedrichshain
Samariterstr.

Klosterstr.
Märkisches
Museum
Ost-
bahnhof
S86
Heinrich-
Heine-Str.
Warschauer
Str. S6/U1/
U15/U12
Frankfurter Allee
Magdalenenstr.   Lichtenberg

Spittel-
markt
Hausvogteipl.
Moritzplatz

Schlesisches
Tor
Köpenicker
Tor
Schön-
leinstr.
Ostkreuz
Nöldnerpl.

Prinzen-
str.
Gneisenau-
str.
Kottbusser
Tor
Südstern

Boddinstr.
Hermannplatz
Rathaus
Neukölln
Treptower
Park

Leinestr.
Karl-Marx-
Str.
Plänterwald

Hermannstr.
U8
Neukölln
Grenzallee
Blaschkoallee
Parchimer Allee
Köllnische
Heide
Baumschul-
enweg

Kaiserin-
Augusta-Str.
Britz-Süd
Johannisthaler
Chaussee
Schöneweide

Ullsteinstr.
Lipschitzallee
Wutzkyallee
Zwickauer Damm

Westphalweg

Alt-Mariendorf
U6
U7
Rudow

Altglienicke
Grünberggallee

S45/S9
Flughafen Berlin-
Schönefeld

S75
Wartenberg

Hohenschönhausen

Gehrenseestr.

Ahrensfelde
S7
Mehrower Allee
Raoul-Wallenberg-Str.
Marzahn
Poelchaustr.
Springpfuhl

Landsberger Allee

Storkower Str.

Friedrichsfelde Ost

Biesdorf

Hönow
U5
Louis-Lewin-Str.
Hellersdorf
Cottbusser Platz
Grottkauer Str.
Kaulsdorf-Nord

Wuhletal
Elsterwerdaer
Platz
Biesdorf-Süd
Kaulsdorf
Mahlsdorf

Strausberg Nord
S5
Strausberg
Stadt
Hegermühle   Strausberg
Petershagen
Nord
Fredersdorf
(b Bln)
Neuenhagen
(b Bin)
Hoppegarten
(Markt)
Birkenstein

Friedrich-
sfelde
Tierpark

Karlshorst
Wuhlheide
Köpenick
Hirschgarten
Friedrichshagen
Rahnsdorf
Wilhelmshagen

Betriebsbahnhof
Rummelsburg

S10
Spindlersfeld

S3
Erkner

Oberspree
Betriebsbahnhof
Schöneweide
Adlershof

Grünau
S8
Eichwalde
Wildau

Zeuthen
S6

S46
Königs Wusterhausen

Phone cards are sold at post offices and newsstands. The 12DM ($7) card offers about 40 minutes and the 50DM ($27) card is useful for long-distance calls. Simply insert them into the telephone slot. Phone cards are becoming so popular in Germany that many public phones no longer accept coins.

To make a **collect or calling card call,** dial one of the following access numbers to reach an operator or an English-language voice prompt: **AT&T** (☎ **0130-0010**), **MCI** (☎ **0130-0012**), or **Sprint** (☎ **0130-0013**). To call the U.S. direct, dial 001 followed by the area code and phone number.

WHERE TO STAY

Tegel Airport is only 20 minutes by taxi, but if you have a very early departure or late arrival, and want the added security of an airport hotel, you can check into **Novotel Berlin Airport,** Kurt-Schumacher-Damm 202, 13405 Orsteil-Reinickendorf (☎ **030/41060;** fax 030/4106700). Doubles go for 225DM ($122) a night; they're medium-sized and furnished in standard motel-chain format. There's also a restaurant on site, plus a free shuttle service that runs back and forth between the hotel and airport. American Express, Diners Club, MasterCard, and Visa are accepted.

ON OR NEAR THE KURFÜRSTENDAMM
Very Expensive

Grand Hotel Esplanade. Lützowufer 15, D-10785 Berlin. ☎ **030/25-47-80.** Fax 030/2-65-11-71. www.esplanade.de. E-mail: info@esplanade.de. 400 units. A/C MINIBAR TV TEL. 550DM–610DM ($297–$329) double; from 800DM ($432) suite. AE, DC, MC, V. Parking 30DM ($16). U-Bahn: Kurfürstenstrasse, Nollendorfplatz, or Wittenbergplatz.

The Esplanade rivals the Kempinski for supremacy in Berlin. Rooms are spacious, bright and cheerfully decorated, with such extras as cable TV, video, and sound insulation. Beds are large with quality mattresses and duvets. Bathrooms are among the city's most spacious and luxurious, with fluffy towels (and plenty of them) along with hair dryers and robes. When reserving, ask for one of the corner rooms, as they're the biggest and have the best views. Thirty-three rooms are for nonsmokers. On the premises of the hotel are two bars, Harry's New York Bar, open daily noon to 2:30am, offering a modern, young environment; and The EckKneipe, open daily 11am to 1am, a more traditional German bar with a wide variety of beers in a rustic setting. There's a buffet breakfast in the Orangerie from 6:30 to 11am. There's also a gourmet restaurant, Harlekin (see "Where to Dine"). Facilities include an indoor pool, whirlpool, solarium, and sauna. The hotel also organizes visits to the major museums in Berlin.

✪ **Kempinski Hotel Bristol Berlin.** Kurfürstendamm 27, D-10719 Berlin. ☎ **800/426-3135** in the U.S., or 030/88-43-40. Fax 030/88-360-75. 315 units. A/C MINIBAR TV TEL. 425DM–560DM ($230–$302) double; from 660DM ($356) suite. AE, DC, MC, V. Parking 35DM ($19). U-Bahn: Kurfürstendamm.

The legendary Kempinski, or "Kempi," is matched in style only by the Grand Hotel Esplanade and the Maritim Grand. Rooms range in size from medium to spacious. Furnishings are elegant and the mattresses firm. The cheapest (and smallest) rooms are on the second, fourth, and fifth floors, and are called the Berlin rooms. The high category Bristol rooms are larger and better appointed, and the finest accommodations of all are refined Kempinski rooms. Each room has a spacious bathroom with dual basins, fluffy towels, scales, shoehorns, hair dryers, and a deluxe set of toiletries. The hotel contains three dining areas. Facilities include a recreation center with an indoor pool, a sauna, massage facilities, a solarium, and a fitness center.

Expensive

✪ **Brandenburger Hof Relais & Châteaux.** Eislebener Strasse 14, D-10789 Berlin. ☎ **030/21-40-50.** Fax 030/21-40-51-00. www.brandenburger-hof.com. E-mail: info@ brandenburger-hof.com. 82 units. A/C MINIBAR TV TEL. 345DM–465DM ($186–$251) double; from 745DM ($402) suite. Rates include breakfast buffet. AE, DC, MC, V. Parking 25DM ($14). U-Bahn: Kurfürstendamm or Augsburger Strasse. S-Bahn: Zoologischer Garten.

Rooms at this white-fronted classic, though perhaps too severe and minimalist for some tastes, are among the most stylish in the city. This is authentic Bauhaus— torchere lamps, black leather upholstery, and platform beds with deluxe mattresses. French doors open to small balconies, but not on the top floors. Baths are spacious, with large combination tub and showers, scales, and hair dryers. Housekeeping is among the finest in Berlin. There's state-of-the-art security. Besides the Die Quadriga restaurant, open Monday to Friday 7 to 10:30pm, there's also the Wintergarten, open daily noon to 11pm, a colorful combination of an Italian monastery and a Japanese garden. There's also a piano bar with live music daily 7pm to closing.

Golden Tulip Hotel Kronprinz Berlin. Kronprinzendamm 1, D-10711 Berlin. ☎ **030/ 89-60-30.** Fax 030/8-93-12-15. www.kronprinz-hotel.de. E-mail: reception@kronprinz-hotel.de. 68 units. MINIBAR TV TEL. 260DM ($140) double; from 380DM ($205) suite. Children 12 and under stay free in parents' room. Rates include buffet breakfast. AE, DC, MC, V. Free parking. Bus: 104, 110, 119, 129, or 219.

Kronprinz is at the far western edge of the Ku'damm, about half-an-hour walk from the Gedächtniskirche. Established in a town house that dates from 1894, the hotel has in recent years been renovated and redecorated in the art-deco style. Rooms range from medium to large and include a balcony. Mattresses are firm, high quality, and renewed every other year. Bathrooms have tub and shower combinations and deluxe toiletries. Many guests congregate in the cozy bar, or in summer gather in the garden under the chestnut trees for draft beer and wine.

✪ **Savoy.** Fasanenstrasse 9–10, D-10623 Berlin. ☎ **800/223-5652** in the U.S. and Canada, or 030/3-11-0-30. Fax 030/3-11-03-333. www.hotel-savoy.com. E-mail: info@ hotel-savoy.com. 130 units. MINIBAR TV TEL. 289DM–389DM ($156–$210) double; 520DM–900DM ($281–$486) suite. Children under 12 stay free in parents' room. AE, DC, MC, V. Parking 18DM ($10). U-Bahn: Kurfürstendamm.

If you don't demand the full-service facilities of the grander choices, this might be the hotel for you. In general, rooms are a bit small but they are comfortable nonetheless, with such amenities as private safes, double-glazed windows, trouser presses, and quality mattresses. Bathrooms are decently sized, maintained spotlessly, and contain a shower and tub combination. Try the restaurant, Belle Époque, and its cozy Times Bar. There's also a sauna and a fitness club.

Moderate

Ahorn Berlin. Schlüterstrasse 40, D-10707 Berlin. ☎ **030/8-71-98-00.** Fax 030/8-87-19-871. www.hotel-ahorn.com. E-mail: info@hotel-ahorn.com. 28 units. MINIBAR TV TEL. 160DM–210DM ($86–$113) double; 180DM–240DM ($97–$130) triple; 30DM ($16) supplement for kitchenette. Discounts sometimes granted in Dec and Aug. Rates include continental breakfast. AE, DC, MC, V. Parking 10DM ($5). U-Bahn: Adenauerplatz. S-Bahn: Savignyplatz. Bus: 109, 119, or 219.

This simple, clean, cost-conscious hotel is near a corner of the Ku'damm. Stay here more for price than any grand comfort, but rooms are inviting nonetheless, with excellent mattresses and tidy maintenance. Bathrooms are routine. Families often book here, not only for the kitchenettes, but because so many rooms are suitable for three or four guests.

Lenz. Xantenerstrasse 8, D-10707 Berlin. ☎ **030/8-81-51-58.** Fax 030/8-81-55-17. 28 units. TV TEL. 160DM–255DM ($86–$138) double; 180DM–315DM ($97–$170) family room. Rates include buffet breakfast. AE, DC, MC, V. U-Bahn: Adenauerplatz.

Although it may be a bit creaky, many appreciate the old-fashioned, homelike atmosphere of the Lenz. Rooms vary in size and decor; the most spacious are on the ground floor. Try to book 103, the largest and best furnished. Those on the top floor have better views, but are small. All rooms have firm mattresses and rather small bathrooms. There's also a small but convivial bar and breakfast room.

Inexpensive
Bogatà. Schlüterstrasse 45, D-10707 Berlin. ☎ **030/881-50-01.** Fax 030/88-35-887. www.bogota.de. E-mail:hotel.bogota@t-online.de. 130 units (12 with shower only, 65 with bathroom). TV TEL. 125DM–150DM ($68–$81) double without bathroom; 145DM–165DM ($78–$89) double with shower only; 170DM–210DM ($92–$113) double with bathroom. Rates include continental breakfast. AE, DC, MC, V. Parking 20DM ($11). U-Bahn: Adenauerplatz or Uhlandstrasse. S-Bahn: Savignyplatz. Bus: 109, 119, or 129.

Although it's one of the town's most popular budget hotels, the Bogatà's facilities are less than state-of-the-art. Rooms are small but tidy with aging but still comfortable mattresses. Some have computer connections. Housekeeping is tidy. Bathrooms, though small, are efficiently organized with a tiled shower, and a rack of medium-sized towels.

Hotel Crystal. Kantstrasse 144, D-10623 Berlin. ☎ **030/312-90-47.** Fax 030/312-64-65. 33 units (5 with shower only, 16 with bathroom). TEL. 110DM ($59) double without bathroom; 130DM ($70) double with shower only; 180DM ($97) double with bathroom. Rates include continental breakfast. AE, MC, V. Free parking. S-Bahn: Savignyplatz.

This hotel is owned and operated by American John Schwarzrock and his German wife, Dorothée, who are always glad to welcome visitors from the States. The rooms are comfortable and well kept, although very basic. There's a small bar just off the lobby.

NEAR THE MEMORIAL CHURCH & ZOO
Expensive
✪ **Sorat Art'otel.** Joachimstalerstrasse 29, D-10719 Berlin. ☎ **030/88-44-70.** Fax 030/88-44-77-00. 133 units. A/C MINIBAR TV TEL. 220DM–415DM ($119–$224) double. Rates include buffet breakfast. AE, DC, MC, V. U-Bahn: Kurfürstendamm.

Those partial to the more famous and highly regarded Brandenburger Hof (above) also like this tasteful, discreet hotel. Chic and avant-garde, the Sorat is unlike any other hotel in Berlin. Rooms, all medium size, are minimalist, with a touch of industrial design. Although they will not please clients seeking a traditional Berlin hotel, modernists will be at home with the pedestal tables evoking cable spools and chrome-legged furnishings, and everyone will appreciate the deluxe mattresses on the large beds and private safes. Bathrooms are generously proportioned and contain deluxe toiletries, hair dryers, and a set of fluffy towels. The hotel restaurant Anteo features Greek and international cuisine.

Palace Berlin. In the Europa-Center, Budapesterstrasse 41, D-10789 Berlin. ☎ **800/ 457-4000** in the U.S., or 030/2-50-20. Fax 030/2502-1161. www.palace.de. E-mail: hotel@palace.de. 282 units. A/C MINIBAR TV TEL. 410DM–590DM ($221–$319) double; from 650DM ($351) suite. AE, DC, MC, V. Parking 30DM ($16). U-Bahn: Zoologischer Garten.

The stylish and comfortable Palace is much improved over recent years. However, in some rooms, the double-glazing on the windows is unable to deafen the noise from the adjacent Europa-Center. The entire seventh floor and some of the sixth is no-smoking. The best rooms are in the more recent Casino Wing. Rooms range from medium to spacious, each with deluxe bed, quality mattress, and trouser press. The bathrooms are medium size, most often with combination tub and shower (sometimes with shower only), but always with fluffy towels and a hair dryer. Along with the First Floor (see "Where to Dine"), there're several other restaurants and bars on site or within close proximity to the hotel. Sam's Bar is a classic with a warm and welcoming atmosphere, open Monday to Saturday 8pm to 2am. In the Europa-Center, there's Alt Nurnberg (see "Where to Dine") and Tifany's, open Sunday to Thursday 11:30am to 11pm and Friday and Saturday 11am to midnight, ideal for a fast snack or late brunch during the day or an elegant meal in the evening. The Thermen am Europa-Center, a large health club, offers indoor and outdoor pools, exercise equipment, and a sauna.

Moderate

Hecker's Hotel. Grolmanstrasse 35, D-10623 Berlin. ☎ **030/8-89-00.** Fax 030/8-89-02-60. www.heckers-hotel.com. E-mail: info@heckers-hotel.com. 72 units. A/C MINIBAR TV TEL. 380DM ($205) double; 400DM ($216) suite. AE, DC, MC, V. Parking 20DM ($11). U-Bahn: Uhlandstrasse. Bus: 109 from Tegel Airport to Uhlandstrasse or 119.

This hotel is near the Ku'damm and the many bars, cafes, and restaurants around the Savignyplatz. Rooms range from small to medium, but are fairly routine despite good beds and frequently renewed mattresses. There's a sterility here but also up-to-date comfort and top-notch maintenance. Bathrooms are small. Some rooms are no-smoking. The hotel restaurant Cassambalis serves excellent Mediterranean cuisine. There's also a bar and a little cafe in the lobby. In summer, guests sit on the rooftop terrace, enjoying the lights of Berlin at night.

Hotel Sylter Hof Berlin. Kurfürstenstrasse 116, D-10787 Berlin. ☎ **030/2-12-00.** Fax 030/214-28-26. 161 units. MINIBAR TV TEL. 282DM ($152) double; from 293DM ($158) suite. Rates include buffet breakfast. AE, DC, MC, V. Parking 16DM ($9). U-Bahn: Wittenbergplatz. Bus: 119, 129, 146, or 185.

Sylter Hof offers rich trappings at good prices. The main lounges are warmly decorated in old-world style. The well-maintained rooms, most of which are singles, may be too small for most tastes, but the staff pay special attention to your comfort. Baths are small but efficiently arranged. The Friesenstube is a conservative dining room serving Prussian and continental cuisine. There's also a coffee bar and nightclub, **Kleine Nachtreuve.**

IN BERLIN-MITTE
Very Expensive

✪ **Hotel Adlon.** Unter den Linden 77, D-10117 Berlin. ☎ **800/426-3135** or 030/22-61-0. Fax 030/22-61-11-16. www.hotel-adlon.de. E-mail: adlon@kempinski.com. 337 units. A/C MINIBAR TV TEL. 490DM–660DM ($265–$356) double; from 800DM ($432) suite. AE, DC, MC, V. Parking 40DM ($22). S-Bahn: Unter den Linden.

Only steps from the Brandenburg Gate, this hotel is considered one of Berlin's premier addresses and is famous among celebrities. The large, beautifully appointed rooms contain CD players, fax machines, and king-size or twin beds with luxury mattresses. Bathrooms are spacious with deluxe toiletries, hair dryer, a phone, and tiled shower stalls. There are two restaurants, two bars, and a coffee shop. The Adlon Spa features a swimming pool, fitness room (personal trainers are available), saunas, tanning beds, and massage room. A health club features indoor and outdoor swimming pools, jogging path that begins across the street, and access to bicycling, golf, and horseback riding in the city limits of Berlin.

⊕ **The Westin Grand.** Friedrichstrasse 158–164, D-10117 Berlin. ☎ **800/843-3311** in the U.S., or 030/2-02-70. Fax 030/20-27-33-62. www.westin-grand.com. E-mail: info@westin-grand.com. 358 units. A/C MINIBAR TV TEL. 430DM–530DM ($232–$286) double; from 750DM ($405) junior suite; from 1,400DM ($756) apt suite. AE, DC, MC, V. Parking 40DM ($22). U-Bahn: Französische Strasse. S-Bahn: Friedrichstrasse.

Many hotels call themselves grand—this one truly is, rivaled only by the Kempinski. Since taking over, Westin has spent a fortune in making the rooms among the finest in the city. All are tastefully decorated, with deluxe mattresses. Bathrooms are spacious, with large tubs, hair dryers, and deluxe toiletries. Your dining choices are the posh Peacock Bar or the more traditional Goldene Gans (see "Where to Dine"). Facilities include a fitness club, whirlpool, marble pool, saunas, and solarium.

Expensive

Radisson SAS Hotel Berlin. Karl-Liebknecht-Strasse 5, D-10178 Berlin. ☎ **800/333-3333** in the U.S. or 030/23828. Fax 030/2382-7590. www.radisson.com/berlinde. E-mail: guest@radissonsas.com. 540 units. A/C MINIBAR TV TEL. 360DM–520DM ($194–$281) double; from 650DM ($351) suite. AE, DC, DISC, MC, V. Parking 30DM ($16). S-Bahn: Alexanderplatz.

This hotel ranks near the top of the four-star choices. Most rooms open onto a view and are medium to large. They've been carefully planned with private safes and either queen size or twin beds with comfortable mattresses. The bathrooms feature private phones, deluxe toiletries and hair dryers. The Orangerie is an intimate restaurant serving international cuisine; the Bistretto offers moderate Italian cuisine of pastas and salads; and the Garden Lounge Bar features live music every night. The hotel has a gymnasium with the biggest hotel pool in Berlin.

Moderate

Art Nouveau. Leibnizstrasse 59, D-10629 Berlin. ☎ **030/3-27-74-40.** Fax 030/327-744-40. www.hotelartnouveau.de. E-mail: hotelartnouveau@snafu.de. 15 units. TV TEL. 210DM ($113) double; 350DM ($189) suite. U-Bahn: Adenauerplatz.

On the fourth floor of an art nouveau apartment house, this little-known hotel is an atmospheric choice. Even the elevator is considered a historic gem of the upmarket and desirable neighborhood. Art Nouveau was fully renovated in 1998. The comfortable rooms are pleasantly decorated and high ceilinged, with excellent beds and white tiled bathrooms. Rooms in the rear are more tranquil except when the schoolyard is full of children. There's an honesty bar in the lobby where guests keep track of their own drinks. A generous breakfast is the only meal served.

⊕ **Hotel Luisenhof.** Köpenicker Strasse 92, 10179 Berlin. ☎ **030/2-41-59-06.** Fax 030/2-79-29-83. 27 units. MINIBAR TV TEL. 250DM ($135) double; 450DM ($243) suite. Rates include breakfast. AE, DC, MC, V. U-Bahn: Märkisches Museum.

One of the most desirable small hotels in Berlin's eastern district, the Luisenhof occupies a dignified 1822 house. Five floors of high-ceilinged rooms will appeal to those desiring to escape modern Berlin's sterility. Rooms range greatly in size, but each is equipped with good queen or twin beds and firm mattresses. Bathrooms, though small, are beautifully appointed, with a rack of plentiful fluffy towels, toilet articles, and shower stalls (often with a large tub). Beneath vaulted ceilings in the cellar, you'll find a very appealing restaurant, the Alexanderkeller.

IN GRÜNEWALD
Very Expensive

⊕ **Schlosshotel Vier Jahreszeiten Berlin.** Brahmsstrasse 10, D-14193 Berlin-Grünewald. ☎ **030/89-58-40.** Fax 030/89-58-48-00. 52 units. MINIBAR TV TEL. 595DM–780DM ($321–$421) double; from 995DM ($537) suite. AE, DC, MC, V. Parking 35DM ($19). Bus: 219.

This Italian Renaissance–style palace was built in 1912 and is a good choice for those who gravitate to German castle hotels. In 1994, it reopened after a 3-year renovation by German-born fashion superstar Karl Lagerfeld, who added grand touches such as rich brass and beautiful mahogany woodwork throughout. Rooms are larger and more elegant than average and come with VCRs, CD players, fax machines, data ports—even "Do Not Disturb" switches on the doors. Bathrooms are roomy, with makeup mirrors, robes, phones, radiantly heated floors, lots of fluffy towels, and bedroom slippers. The hotel has two restaurants; the more unusual and better of which is Vivaldi's.

WHERE TO DINE

For food on the run, try one of the dozens of kabob stalls (Imbisse) that dot the streets. Some 200,000 Turks live in Berlin and the food that they've introduced—meat- or *Scharfskäse-* (sheep's cheese, virtually identical to feta) stuffed pitas—make a filling, cheap meal—but watch out for the cascades of cabbage. Good sit-down Turkish restaurants are harder to find, but one of the best is **Hitit,** Knobelsdorffstrasse 35 (☎ **030/322-45-57**), near Charlottenburg Schloss, with a full array of Turkish specialties, some 150 dishes in all. It's open daily noon to 1am.

ON OR NEAR THE KURFÜRSTENDAMM

Very Expensive

✪ **Bamberger Reiter.** Regensburgerstrasse 7. ☎ **030/218-42-82.** Reservations required. Main courses 52DM–60DM ($28 –$32); 6- or 7-course fixed-price menu 165DM–195DM ($89–$105). AE, DC, MC, V. Tues–Sat 6pm–1am (last order). U-Bahn: Spichernstrasse. CONTINENTAL.

Bamberger Reiter is the city's best restaurant, serving French, German, and Austrian dishes. Only Rockendorf's or Alt Luxemburg can pretend to have better fare. Don't judge it by its location in an undistinguished 19th-century apartment house. Excellent in its forthright approach to fresh ingredients and meticulous in its preparation and service, the restaurant enjoys a loyal following among Berlin's business elite. The decor evokes old Germany, with lots of mirrors and fresh flowers. The menu changes daily according to the availability of fresh ingredients and the chef's inspiration, but might include a roulade of quail, bass with Riesling sauce, lamb with beans and potato croutons, and a date strudel with almond ice cream.

Expensive

✪ **Harlekin.** In the Grand Hotel Esplanade, Lützowufer. ☎ **030/254-78-858.** Reservations recommended. Main courses 45DM–50DM ($24–$27); 4- to 6-course fixed-price menu 130DM–165DM ($70–$89). AE, DC, MC, V. Tues–Sat 6–11pm. Closed $3^{1}/_{2}$ weeks in July (dates vary). U-Bahn: Nollendorfplatz or Wittenbergplatz. FRENCH/INTERNATIONAL.

Chefs at traditional favorites like the Kempinski were chagrined at this restaurant's success. The menu is perfectly balanced between tradition and innovation. Appetizers are likely to include such dishes as calves' consommé with crayfish or osso buco consommé with lobster spätzle. For your main course, you might be won over by the saddle of lamb baked in a spring roll or turbot roasted with mixed root vegetables.

✪ **Mensa.** Am Lützowplatz. ☎ **030/579-93-33.** Reservations required. Main courses 47DM–49DM ($25–$26); 4-course menu 99DM ($53), 6-course menu 145DM ($78). Mon–Fri 11:15am–2:30pm and Mon–Sat 6–10:30pm. AE, MC, V. U-Bahn: Nollendorfplatz.

Mensa ("table" in Latin) has quickly moved to the cutting edge in Berlin, attracting chic models, rising politicians, visiting stars, and new money. Established in 1999, the bright, airy restaurant has a Mediterranean decor and a helpful, hip staff. The cuisine is perfectly seasoned and cooked, and you can sample such delights as lobster salad with wild herbs in a dressing of sauterne and shallots, roasted goose liver with vanilla stalk and salsify (oyster plant), and fillet of sea bass with a braised eel ragout and a parsnip cream sauce.

Paris Bar. Kantstrasse 152. ☎ **030/313-80-52.** Reservations recommended. Main courses 36DM–45DM ($19–$24). AE. Daily noon–1am. U-Bahn: Uhlandstrasse. FRENCH.

This French bistro has been a local favorite since the postwar years, when two Frenchmen established the restaurant to bring a little Parisian cheer to the dismal gray of bombed-out Berlin. The place is just as crowded with elbow-to-elbow tables as a Montmartre tourist trap, but you'll find it a genuinely pleasing little eatery. It's a true restaurant on the see-and-be-seen circuit between Savignyplatz and Gedächtniskiche. The food is invariably fresh and well prepared but not particularly innovative.

Moderate

Hardtke's. Meinekestrasse 27A. ☎ **030/881-98-27.** Reservations required. Main courses 20DM–32DM ($11–$17); fixed-price menu 16.50DM–18.90DM ($9–$10) available Mon–Fri until 8pm. No credit cards. Daily 8am–midnight. U-Bahn: Kurfürstendamm. BERLINER.

These Teutonic recipes haven't changed during the 40 years of Hardtke's operation. German retirees like dining here; they're fond of the cuisine they enjoyed in the 1940s and 1950s before the "new German cookery" became all the rage. You can overdose on all the potatoes and sauerkraut, the blood-and-liver sausage (from the in-house butcher shop), and the monstrous bockwurst. The true Berliner asks for the *grosse Schlachteplatte*—fresh black pudding and liver sausage, small pickled knuckle of pork, liver dumpling, shredded pickled white cabbage, mashed peas, and boiled potatoes.

Istanbul. Knesebeckstrasse 77. ☎ **030/883-27-77.** Main courses 20DM–35DM ($11–$19). Daily noon–midnight. AE, DC, MC, V. S-Bahn: Savignyplatz. TURKISH

Vegetarians patronize Berlin's oldest Turkish restaurant for its selection of hot and cold appetizers. The dark and lavishly decorated interior evokes old Constantinople (as do the belly dancers performing in a back room). Try the stuffed grape leaves or the hummus (chickpeas with garlic), or the meat-topped Turkish pizza. Shish kebab is the most popular item, and there's a wide array of succulent lamb dishes. A chef's specialty is veal grilled on a roasting spit.

La Table. Damaschkestrasse 26. ☎ **030/3-23-14-04.** Reservations required. Main courses 12.50DM–36DM ($7–$19). MC. Mon–Sat 5pm–midnight. U-Bahn: Adenauerplatz. GERMAN.

La Table has gained a reputation as a select dining spot and social center. Your host, Mr. Seidler, has a devoted local following among theater and media personalities. The ambience is that of a Berlin bistro, charmingly cluttered with kitsch from all over the world. Savor the *Kohlroulade,* a stuffed cabbage roll—few chefs would want to compete with it. Other highlights are *tafelspitz* (boiled beef with vegetables) and rack of lamb with honey onions and rosemary potatoes. Look for market-fresh daily specials. The chef believes in strong flavors and good hearty cookery.

✪ **Marjellchen.** Mommsenstrasse 9. ☎ **030/883-26-76.** Reservations required. Main courses 20DM–40DM ($11–$22). AE, DC, MC, V. Mon–Sat 5pm–midnight. Closed Dec 23, 24, and 31. U-Bahn: Adenauerplatz or Uhlandstrasse. Bus: 109, 119, or 129. EAST PRUSSIAN.

This is the only restaurant in Berlin specializing in the cuisine of Germany's long-lost province of East Prussia, along with the cuisines of Pomerania and Silesia. Deriving its unusual name from an East Prussian word meaning "young girl," the establishment divides its space among three rooms, the first dominated by a German-style bar. Amid a Bismarckian ambience of still lifes, vested waiters, and oil lamps, you can enjoy a savory version of red-beet soup with strips of beef, East Prussian potato soup with crabmeat and bacon, *falscher Gänsebraten* (pork spareribs stuffed with prunes and bread crumbs), and *mecklenburger Kümmelfleisch* (lamb with chives and onions).

Restaurant Mario. Carmerstrasse 2. ☎ **030/312-31-15.** Reservations recommended. Main courses 19.50DM–31DM ($11–$17); fixed-price menus 25DM–65DM ($14–$35). AE, MC, V. Mon–Fri noon–midnight; Sat 4pm–1am. S-Bahn: Savignyplatz. NORTHERN ITALIAN.

Named for its owner, this restaurant serves some of the most imaginative northern Italian food in Berlin. It was created by an East Berliner who'd never been to Italy but wanted to "cook Italian," nevertheless. Today the chefs are fully grounded in the repertoire of Italy, and use the best market-fresh ingredients in creating their culinary offerings. The innovative and refreshing dishes might include platters of the most delectable antipasti in town or else carpaccio. At least two different kinds of pastas are offered nightly, including a favorite made with a green pepper pesto. Savory ravioli and rigatoni appear several different ways.

Zlata Praha. Meinekestrasse 4. ☎ **030/881-97-50.** Reservations recommended. Main courses 20DM–40DM ($11–$22). AE, MC, V. Daily noon–midnight. U-Bahn: Joachimstaler Strasse. BOHEMIAN/HUNGARIAN.

Zlata Praha serves the best Bohemian cuisine in Berlin. German, French, and Austrian wines are featured. However, the pièce de résistance is the special tap beer, Pilsner Urquell das Echte. Many of the food items spark an instant recognition (paprika lovers take note) and evoke childhood memories from the restaurant's many regular clients. The *Szegendiner goulash* is as fine as any we've had during our tours of Hungary.

Inexpensive
Karavan. Kurfürstendamm 11. ☎ **303/881-50-05.** Reservations not necessary. Most plates 10DM ($5). No credit cards. Daily 11am–midnight. U-Bahn to Kürfurstendamm. TURKISH.

The chefs claim (with some justification) to make the best Turkish pizza in Berlin. Sandwiches, salads, spinach-filled pastries, and even Turkish-style burgers fill out the bill of fare. There are a few barstools inside for dining, or you can go sit on one of the benches on the square outside.

La Table. Damaschkestrasse 26. ☎ **030/323-14-04.** Reservations recommended. Main courses 18.50DM–36DM ($10–$19). MC, V. Mon–Sat 5pm–midnight. U-Bahn: Adenauerplatz. GERMAN.

West of the center, La Table has gained a reputation as a select dining spot and social center. Savor the recipes that much of Berlin craves, including the *Kohlroulade,* a stuffed cabbage roll, which is the best in town, but served only in winter. The *tafelspitz,* boiled beef with vegetables, would have pleased Emperor Josef of Austria (it was his favorite dish). Look also for the market-fresh daily specials, especially if fresh fish is featured. Diners enjoy these dishes in a charmingly cluttered Berlin bistro ambience, with kitsch from all over the world.

NEAR THE MEMORIAL CHURCH & ZOO
Very Expensive
✪ **First Floor.** In the Palace Berlin Hotel, Budapesterstrasse 42. ☎ **030/25-02-10-20.** Reservations recommended. Main courses 46DM–75DM ($25–$41). Set menus 78DM ($42) at lunch only; and 130DM–158DM ($70–$85) at lunch and dinner. AE, DC, MC, V. Sun–Fri noon–2:30pm and 6–11pm, Sat 6–11pm. U-Bahn: Zoologischer Garten. REGIONAL GERMAN/FRENCH.

This is the showcase restaurant within one of the most spectacular hotels ever built near the Tiergarten. Set one floor above street level, it features a perfectly orchestrated service and setting that revolves around the cuisine of master chef Rolf Schmidt. Carefully rehearsed staff members smooth over the logistics and details of an upscale meal. Menu items include a terrine of veal with arugala-flavored butter; sophisticated variations of Bresse chicken; guinea fowl stuffed with foie gras and served with a truffled

Cafe Society

At the turn of the 20th century, the **Café Adlon,** Kurfürstendamm 69 (☎ **030/883-76-82;** U-Bahn: Adenauerplatz), was one of the most prestigious cafes in its neighborhood. It still offers charming summer vistas from its sidewalk tables and a view of Berlin kitsch from its interior. You'll find a huge selection of cakes. Open daily 8am to midnight.

The family-owned **Café/Bistro Leysieffer,** Kurfürstendamm 218 (☎ **030/885-74-80;** U-Bahn: Kurfürstendamm), opened in the early 1980s within what had been the Chinese embassy. The street level contains a pastry and candy shop, but most clients climb the flight of stairs to a marble- and wood-sheathed cafe with a balcony overlooking the busy Ku'damm. The breakfast menu is one of the most elegant in town: Parma ham, smoked salmon, a fresh baguette, French butter, and—to round it off—champagne. Open Sunday to Thursday 10am to 8pm, Friday and Saturday 10am to 10pm, and Sunday 10am to 8pm.

✪ **Café Kranzler,** Kurfürstendamm 18–19 (☎ **030/882-69-11;** U-Bahn: Kurfürstendamm), one of Berlin's most famous and visible cafes, opened in 1825 on the Unter den Linden. After the war, it moved to the then-less-imposing district around the Ku'damm. Today owned by Swiss investors, the cafe/restaurant offers a variety of Swiss specialties, among them shredded veal Zurich style. Also available are ice creams, pastries, coffee, and drinks. Open daily 8am to midnight.

vinaigrette sauce; a cassolette of lobster and broad beans in a style vaguely influenced by the culinary precepts of southwestern France; fillet of sole with champagne sauce; and a mascarpone mousse with lavender-scented honey.

Inexpensive

Alt Nürnberg. Europa-Center. ☎ **030/2-502-1117.** Reservations recommended weekends. Main courses 12DM–30DM ($7–$16). AE, DC, MC, V. Sun–Thurs 11:30am–11pm, Fri–Sat 11:30am–midnight. U-Bahn: Kurfürstendamm or Zoologischer Garten. GERMAN/BAVARIAN.

This ground-level restaurant handsomely captures the ambience of an old Bavarian tavern. The food is solid German fare, standard and reliable, though hardly exciting. The house specialty is *Nürnberger Rostbratwürstl* (little finger sausages). You might begin with a typical Berlin pea soup with croutons or Hungarian *Goulashsouppe.* The Wiener schnitzel is always reliable, as are the herring salad and the pork fillet in pepper sauce with broccoli or the Baden-Baden saddle of venison. Inexpensive platters are usually a meal in themselves.

IN & AROUND CHARLOTTENBURG

Expensive

✪ **Alt-Luxemburg.** Windscheidstrasse 31. ☎ **030/323-87-30.** Reservations required. Fixed-price 3-course menu 95DM ($51); fixed-price 4-course menu 120DM ($65); fixed-price 5-course menu 135DM ($73). AE, DC, MC, V. Mon–Sun 7–11pm. U-Bahn: Sophie-Charlotteplatz. CONTINENTAL.

The Bamberger Reiter may be the leader among Berlin restaurants, but the Alt-Luxemburg is nipping at its heels. Chef Karl Wannemacher is one of the most outstanding in eastern Germany. Known for his quality and market-fresh ingredients, he prepares a seductively sensual plate. Everything shows his flawless technique, especially the stuffed and stewed oxtail or the saddle of venison with elderberry sauce. Taste his excellent lacquered duck breast with honey sauce or saddle of lamb with stewed peppers. Alt-Luxemburg offers a finely balanced wine list. The service is both unpretentious and gracious.

Moderate

Bierhaus Luisen-Bräu. Luisenplatz 1, Charlottenburg (close to Charlottenburg Castle). ☎ **030/3-41-93-88.** Reservations recommended on weekends. Main courses 9.80DM–20DM ($5–$11). AE, MC, V. Sun–Thurs 9am–1am, Fri–Sat 9am–2am. U-Bahn: Richard-Wagner-Platz. GERMAN.

Luisen-Bräu brewery established this restaurant in 1987. The decor includes enormous stainless-steel vats of the fermenting brew, from which the waiters refill your mug. There's no subtlety of cuisine here; it's robust and hearty fare. You serve yourself from a long buffet table. The seating is indoor or outdoor, depending on the season, at long picnic tables that encourage a sense of beer-hall *Bruderschaft* (camaraderie).

Ponte Vecchio. Spielhagenstrasse 3. ☎ **030/342-19-99.** Reservations required. Main courses 30DM–46DM ($16–$25). DC. Wed–Mon 6:30–11pm. Closed 4 weeks in summer. U-Bahn: Bismarckstrasse. TUSCAN.

This is one of Berlin's finest Italian restaurants. It's not the most elaborately decorated, but it caters to patrons primarily concerned with what's on the plate. Market-fresh ingredients result in winning dishes with a Tuscan focus. If you don't opt for the fresh fish of the day, you'll find any number of other dishes to tempt the palate, especially several variations of veal. Assorted shellfish is always deftly handled according to Tuscan style, with fresh basil and olive oil.

IN BERLIN-MITTE

Expensive

✪ **Restaurant Vau.** Jägerstrasse 54 (near the Four Seasons Hotel and the Gendamenmarkt). ☎ **030/202-9730.** Reservations recommended. Main courses 48DM–65DM ($26–$35). Set-price lunches 60DM ($32); set-price dinners 90DM–120DM ($49–$65). AE, DC, MC, V. Mon–Sat noon–3pm and 7–10:30pm. S-Bahn: Hausvoigteiplatz. GERMAN.

This restaurant is the culinary showcase of up-and-coming chef Kolja Kleeberg. Choices, which are based on fresh and seasonal ingredients include terrine of salmon and morels with rocket salad; aspic of suckling pig with sauerkraut; salad with marinated red mullet, mint, and almonds; crisp-fried duck with marjoram; ribs of suckling lamb with thyme-flavored polenta; and desserts such as woodruff soup with champagne-flavored ice cream. The wine list is international and well chosen.

Moderate

Französischer Hof. Jagerstrasse 56. ☎ **030/204-35-70.** Reservations recommended. Main courses 28DM–45DM ($15–$24). AE, DC, MC, V. Daily noon–11pm. Closed Dec 24. U-Bahn: Hausvogteiplatz. GERMAN/INTERNATIONAL.

Französischer Hof, which opened in 1989, evokes a turn-of-the-century Paris bistro. The cookery is hardly the finest in eastern Berlin, but the ingredients are fresh and deftly handled. One recent memorable dinner included roast duck breast with Calvados along with zucchini and potato pancakes. Many guests begin with the terrific selection of fish canapés, then proceed to the main courses. Saddle of lamb is always admirably done, as is the saddle of venison with juniper-berry sauce (served with red cabbage). The white fish, zander, is grilled and appears with an herb sauce. The soups are also a delight here, especially on a winter day and especially the potato and leek served with croutons.

Restaurant Borchardt. Französische Strasse 47. ☎ **030/2038-7110.** Reservations recommended. Daily specials 20DM ($11); main courses 30DM–50DM ($16–$27). AE, V. Daily 11:30am–2am (kitchen closes at midnight). U-Bahn: Französische Strasse. FRENCH/INTERNATIONAL.

This restaurant is elegant, lighthearted, and fashionable among the city's artistic movers and shakers. It occupies a monumental dining area, complete with marble accents and partially gilded columns. You can order anything from a simple salad (as supermodel Claudia Schiffer often does) to the more substantial cream of potato soup with bacon and croutons; fillet of carp prepared with Riesling and herbs, and finished with champagne; foie gras served with caramelized apples; chicken stuffed with morels and served with cream-and-herb sauce; and a pistachio mousse garnished with essence of fresh fruit.

Inexpensive

Keller Restaurant im Brecht-Haus. Chausseestrasse 125. ☎ **030/28-23-843.** Reservations recommended. Main courses 20DM–32DM ($11–$17). AE, DC, MC. Sun–Fri noon–midnight, Sat 6pm–midnight. U-Bahn: Oranienburger Tor. SOUTH GERMAN/AUSTRIAN.

This unusual restaurant occupies the cellar of a building where Bertolt Brecht once lived. The restaurant is trimmed with white plaster and exposed stone, and has scores of photographs of the playwright's theatrical productions. It serves copious portions of traditional south German and Austrian food, including *Fleisch Laberln*—tasty meatballs made with minced pork, beef, green beans, and bacon, served with dumplings. No one will mind if you just stop in for a glass of one of the restaurant's many wines.

Zur Letzten Instanz. Waisenstrasse 14–16. ☎ **030/242-55-28.** Main courses 19DM–36DM ($10–$19); fixed-price menu 25DM–35DM ($14–$19). AE, DC, V. Mon–Sat noon–1am; Sun noon–11pm. S-Bahn: Kloster Strasse. GERMAN.

Reputedly Berlin's oldest restaurant, dating from 1525, Zur Letzten Instanz in its day was frequented by everybody from Napoléon to Beethoven. Prisoners used to stop off here for one last beer before going to jail. It occupies two floors of a baroque building whose facade is ornamented with a row of stone bas-reliefs of medieval faces. Double doors open on a series of small woodsy rooms, one with a bar and ceramic stove. At the back a circular staircase leads to another series of rooms, where every evening at 6pm, only food and wine (no beer) are served. On both floors you can select from a limited and old-fashioned menu of Berlin staples.

IN WAIDMANNSLUST

Very Expensive

✪ **Rockendorf's Restaurant.** Düsterhauptstrasse 1. ☎ **030/402-30-99.** Reservations required. Fixed-price lunch 110DM–175DM ($59–$95); fixed-price dinner 175DM–198DM ($95–$107). AE, DC, MC, V. Tues–Sat noon–2pm and 7–9:30pm. Closed Dec 22–Jan 6 and July. S-Bahn: Waidmannslust. CONTINENTAL.

Rockendorf's occupies a 19th-century art nouveau villa near the Englischer Garten in north Berlin, a 20-minute taxi ride from the center. Chef Siegfried Rockendorf achieves a happy marriage between modern cuisine and classic specialties. The restaurant is the only one in Berlin to mount a serious challenge to the Bamberger Reiter and the Alt-Luxemburg. Try such dishes as fillet of turbot in Ricard sauce, which succeeds despite being neither new nor exciting. The same could be said of the goose meat pâté in sauterne with cranberries. The service is exquisitely refined—attentive without being cloying.

SEEING THE SIGHTS
SIGHTSEEING SUGGESTIONS FOR FIRST-TIME VISITORS

If You Have 1 Day   Get up early and visit the **Brandenburg Gate,** symbol of Berlin, then walk down **Unter den Linden** and have coffee and pastry at the Operncafé. Visit the **Gemäldegalerie,** to see some of the world's greatest masterpieces. Afterward, go to **Charlottenburg Palace** and its museums to view the celebrated bust of Queen Nefertiti in the **Egyptian Museum.** In the evening, walk along the Kurfürstendamm, visit the **Kaiser Wilhelm Memorial Church,** and dine in a local restaurant.

If You Have 2 Days   On Day 2, visit the **Pergamon Museum** on Museum Island, seeing the Pergamon Altar. Explore the **National Gallery** and the **Bode Museum,** then head for Alexanderplatz. Take the elevator up for a view from its TV tower, before exploring the **Nikolai Quarter** on foot.

If You Have 3 Days   On Day 3, go to **Potsdam** (see "Day Trips from Berlin").

If You Have 4 or 5 Days   On Day 4, visit the museums of **Dahlem,** especially the **Sculpture Gallery** and **Ethnographical Museum.** In the afternoon return to Charlottenburg Palace and explore the **Historical Apartments,** and in the evening visit the **Europa-Center** for drinks and dinner. On Day 5, see some of the sights you might have missed. Take some walks through Berlin and stop at the Cold War's **Checkpoint Charlie,** with its museum. If time remains, visit the **Berlin Zoo,** stroll through the **Tiergarten,** and attend a cabaret in the evening.

THE TOP MUSEUMS
In the Tiergarten

✪ **Gemäldegalerie (Picture Gallery).** Mattäiskirchplatz 4. ☎ **030/20-90-5555.** Admission 8DM ($4.30) adults, 4DM ($2.15) children. Tues–Fri 10am–5pm, Sat–Sun 10am–6pm. U-Bahn: Kurfürstenstrasse, then bus 148. Bus 129 from Ku'damm (plus a 4-minute walk).

Opening in its new home in 1998, this is one of Germany's greatest galleries. Of the nearly 3,000 paintings it owns, some 600 or more are on display. Several rooms are devoted to early German masters, with panels from altarpieces dating from the 13th, 14th, and 15th centuries. Note the panel of *The Virgin Enthroned with Child* (1350), surrounded by angels that resemble the demons so popular in the later works of Hieronymus Bosch. Eight paintings make up the Dürer collection in adjacent rooms.

Another gallery is given over to Italian painting. Here are five Raphael Madonnas, works by Titian (*The Girl with a Bowl of Fruit*), Fra Filippo Lippi, Botticelli, and Correggio (*Leda with the Swan*). There're also early Netherlandish paintings from the 15th and 16th centuries (Van Eyck, Van der Weyden, Bosch, and Bruegel). Several galleries are devoted to Flemish and Dutch masters of the 17th century, with no fewer than 20 works by Rembrandt, including the *Head of Christ*. One painting, famous for years as a priceless Rembrandt, *The Man with the Golden Helmet,* was proven by radioactive testing in 1986 to have been painted in Rembrandt's era by an imitator of his style. This remarkable painting is now accepted as an independent original.

Neue Nationalgalerie (New National Galerie). Potsdamerstrasse 50 (just south of the Tiergarten). ☎**030/2-66-26-62.** Permanent collection, 10DM ($5) adults, 4DM ($2.15) children; temporary exhibitions, 12DM ($7). Tues–Fri 10am–6pm; Sat–Sun 11am–6pm. Closed Jan 1–Dec 24–25 and 31, and the Tues after Easter and Whitsunday. U-Bahn: Kurfürstenstrasse. S-Bahn: Potsdamer Platz.

In its modern glass-and-steel home designed by Ludwig Mies van der Rohe (1886–1969), the Neue Nationalgalerie is a sequel of sorts to the art at Dahlem. It contains a continually growing collection of modern European and American art.

New Meets Old

On the Kurfürstendamm in the western part of the city, Berliners often glance at a sobering reminder of less happy days. At the end of the street stands the **Kaiser-Wilhelm-Gedächtniskirche (Kaiser Wilhelm Memorial Church)** Breitscheidplatz (☎ **030/218-5023**), with only the shell of its neo-Romanesque bell tower (1895) remaining. (You can wander through the ruins Monday to Saturday 10am to 4:30pm. Admission is free.) In striking contrast is the new church, constructed west of the old tower in 1961, and nicknamed "lipstick and powder box" by Berliners. Its octagonal hall is lit solely by thousands of colored-glass windows set into the honeycomb framework. Ten-minute services are held in the church daily at 5:30 and 6pm for those going home from work. There's a Saturday concert at 6pm, and an English-language service is held daily at 9am June to August. The church is open daily 9am to 7pm. This remarkable combination of old and new is what Berlin, which was almost flattened in World War II, is all about.

Here you'll find works of 19th-century artists, with a concentration on French impressionists. German art starts with Adolph von Menzel's paintings from about 1850. The 20th-century collection includes works by Max Beckmann, Edvard Munch, and E. L. Kirchner (*Brandenburger Tor*), as well as a few paintings by Bacon, Picasso, Ernst, Klee, and American artists such as Barnett Newman. There's food service in the cafe on the ground floor. Hot meals are served from 10:30am to 6pm.

Museumsinsel (Museum Island)

✪ **Pergamon Museum.** Kupfergraben, Museumsinsel. ☎ **030/2090-50.** Admission 8DM ($4.30) adults, 4DM ($2.15) children; free the first Sun of the month. Tues–Sun 10am–6pm. U-Bahn/S-Bahn: Friedrichstrasse. Tram: 1, 2, 3, 4, 5, 13, 15, or 53.

The Pergamon Museum houses several departments, but if you have time for only one exhibit, go to the central hall of the U-shaped building to see the **Pergamon Altar,** still under restoration. This Greek altar (180–160 B.C.) has a huge room all to itself. Some 27 steps lead up to the colonnade. Most fascinating is the frieze around the base, tediously pieced together over a 20-year period. Depicting the struggle of the Olympian gods against the Titans as told in Hesiod's *Theogony,* the relief is strikingly alive, with figures projecting as much as a foot from the background. This, however, is only part of the attraction of the **Department of Greek and Roman Antiquities,** housed in the north and east wings. You'll also find a Roman market gate discovered in Miletus and sculptures from many Greek and Roman cities, including a statue of a goddess holding a pomegranate (575 B.C.), found in southern Attica. The **Near East Museum,** in the south wing, contains one of the largest collections anywhere of antiquities discovered in the lands of ancient Babylonia, Persia, and Assyria. Among the exhibits is the Processional Way of Babylon with the Ishtar Gate (580 B.C.).

Altes Museum. Bodestrasse 13. Museumsinsel. ☎ **030/20-90-5801.** Admission 8DM ($4.30), 4DM ($2.15) children. Tues–Sun 9am–5pm. U-Bahn/S-Bahn: Friedrichstrasse. Bus: 100 to Lustgarten.

Karl Friedrich Schinkel, the city's greatest architect, designed this structure, which resembles a Greek Corinthian temple, in 1822. On its main floor is the **Antikensammlung** or Museum of Greek and Roman Antiquities. This great collection of world-famous works of antique decorative art was inaugurated in 1960. It's rich in pottery; Greek, Etruscan, and Roman bronze statuettes and implements; ivory carvings, glassware, objects in precious stone, and jewelry of the Mediterranean region, as well as gold and silver treasures; mummy portraits from Roman Egypt; wood and stone sarcophagi; and a few marble sculptures. The collection includes some of the finest Greek vases of the black- and red-figures style dating from the 6th to the 4th century B.C. The best known is a large Athenian wine jar (amphora) found in Vulci, Etruria, dating from 490 B.C., which shows a satyr with a lyre and the god Hermes.

The **Alte Nationalgalerie** above may still be closed for renovation, but about 150 of its major art works are on display. The gallery displays paintings and sculpture from the end of the 18th to the beginning of the 20th, including works by van Gogh, Manet, Monet, Renoir, and Cézanne. The gallery is especially proud to own the world's largest collection of Adolph von Menzel, a famous Berlin artist. The full gallery is scheduled to reopen sometime in 2001.

In Charlottenburg

Charlottenburg is the quarter of Berlin just west of the Tiergarten. In addition to viewing the exhaustive collections in Charlottenburg Palace, you can enjoy a relaxing ramble through Schlossgarten Charlottenburg. The gardens have been restored and landscaped much as they were in the days of Friedrich Wilhelm II.

Schloss Charlottenburg (Charlottenburg Palace). Luisenplatz. ☎ **030/320-91-275.** Combined ticket for all buildings and historical rooms 15DM ($8) adults, 10DM ($5) children under 14 and students. Palace, Tues–Fri 9am–5pm, Sat 10am–5pm; Museum, Tues–Fri 10am–6pm (free admission) daily 6:30am–8pm. Gardens (free admission) daily 6:30am–8pm. U-Bahn: Sophie-Charlotte-Platz or Richard-Wagner-Platz. Bus: 109, 121, 245, or 204.

Napoléon exaggerated a bit in comparing Schloss Charlottenburg to Versailles when he invaded Berlin in 1806, but in its heyday this palace was the most elegant residence for Prussian rulers outside the castle in Potsdam. Begun in 1695 as a summer palace for the Electress Sophie Charlotte, patron of philosophy and the arts and wife of King Frederick I (Elector Frederick III), the little residence got out of hand until it grew into the massive structure you see today. Parts of the palace were badly damaged during the war, but most of it has now been completely restored. Many furnishings were saved, especially the works of art, and are again on display. The main wing contains the apartments of Frederick I and his "philosopher queen." The **new wing,** known as the Knobelsdorff-Flügel and built from 1740 to 1746, shelters the apartments of Frederick the Great, which have in essence been converted into a museum of paintings, many of which were either collected or commissioned by the king.

✪ Ägyptisches Museum (Egyptian Museum). Schloss-strasse 70. ☎ **030/32-09-11.** Admission 8DM ($4.30) adults, 4DM ($2.15) children. Tues–Fri 10am–6pm, Sat–Sun 11am–6pm. U-Bahn: Sophie-Charlotte-Platz or Richard-Wagner-Platz. Bus: 109, 110, or 145.

The western Berlin branch of the Egyptian Museum is housed in the east guardhouse built for the king's bodyguard. It's worth the trip just to see the famous colored bust of Queen Nefertiti, dating from the Egyptian Amarna period (about 1340 B.C.) and discovered in 1912. The bust, stunning in every way, is all by itself in a dark first-floor

A Museum Update

Though there could be delays, several museum reopenings are scheduled for 2001 following years of renovation. These include the **Alte Nationalgalerie** on Museum Island, the **Berlin Museum** and its **Jüdisches Museum (Jewish Museum)** in Kreuzberg, and the **Deutsches Historisches Museum** in Berlin-Mitte. Ask at the tourist office for exact opening dates, hours, and admissions.

room, illuminated by a spotlight. It is believed that the bust never left the studio in which it was created but served as a model for other portraits of the queen. The left eye of Nefertiti was never drawn in. In addition, look for the head of Queen Tiy and the world-famous head of a priest in green stone.

✪ **Die Sammlung Berggruen: Picasso und Seine Zeit (The Berggruen Collection: Picasso and his Era).** Schlosstrasse 1. ☎ **030/830-1466.** Admission 8DM ($4.30) adults, 4DM ($2.15) students and children. Tues–Fri 10am–6pm, Sat–Sun 11am–6pm. U-Bahn: Richard-Wagner-Platz, followed by a 10-minute walk. Bus: 21, 109, 110, 145.

One of the most unusual private museums in Berlin has accumulated the awesome private collection of respected art and antiques dealer Heinz Berggruen. A native of Berlin who fled the Nazis in 1936, he later established a mini-empire of antique dealerships in Paris and California before returning, with his collection, to his native home in 1996. There's a distinct likelihood that octogenarian Mr. Berggruen himself, who maintains an apartment adjacent to his museum, might be conducting a lecture on his favorite painter, or strolling among his paintings, sometime during your visit. The setting, which was provided after extensive negotiations by the city of Berlin, is a renovated former army barracks designed by noted architect August Stüler, in 1859. Although most of the collection is devoted to Picasso, there're also works by Cézanne, Braque, Klee, and van Gogh. Some 60 or more works in all, the Picasso collection alone is worth the trip, ranging from his teenage efforts to all of his major periods.

Bröhan Museum. Schlossstrasse 1a. ☎ **030/3269-0600.** Admission 6DM ($3.10) adults, 3DM ($1.55) students/children. Tues–Sun 10am–6pm. U-Bahn: Sophie-Charlotte-Platz. Bus: 109 or 145 to Luisenplatz/Schloss Charlottenburg.

This wonderful museum specializes in decorative objects of the art nouveau (Jugendstil in German) and art deco periods (1889–1939), with exquisite vases, glass, furniture, silver, paintings of artists belonging to the Berlin Secession, and other works of art arranged in drawing-room fashion, including an outstanding porcelain collection.

Other Museums

Deutsche Guggenheim Berlin. Unter den Linden 13–15. ☎ **030/2020-930.** Admission 8DM ($4.30) adults, 5DM ($2.70) children. Free on Mon. Daily 11am–8pm. S-Bahn: Unter den Linden.

Opened in autumn 1997, this state-of-the-art museum, a joint venture of Deutsche Bank and the Solomon R. Guggenheim Foundation, is devoted to organizing and presenting exhibitions of modern and contemporary art. At the intersection of Unter den Linden and Charlottenstrasse, the exhibition space on the ground floor of the newly restored Berlin branch of Deutsche Bank was designed by Richard Gluckman. The Guggenheim Foundation conceives, organizes, and installs several exhibitions annually, and also presents exhibitions of newly commissioned works created specifically for this space by world-renowned artists. The bank is also a major player, supporting young artists from the German-speaking world by purchasing their works and displaying them throughout the company's offices and public spaces. In addition to contemporary artists, exhibitions in the past have ranged from everybody Picasso and Cézanne to Andy Warhol.

Käthe-Kollwitz Museum. Fasanenstrasse 24. ☎ **030/882-52-10.** Admission 8DM ($4.30) adults, 4DM ($2.15) children and students. Wed–Mon 11am–6pm. U-Bahn: Uhlandstrasse or Kurfürstendamm. Bus: 109, 119, 129, 219, or 249.

More than any other museum in Germany, this one reflects the individual sorrow of the artist whose work it contains. Some visitors call it a personalized revolt against the agonies of war, as well as a welcome change from the commercialism of the nearby

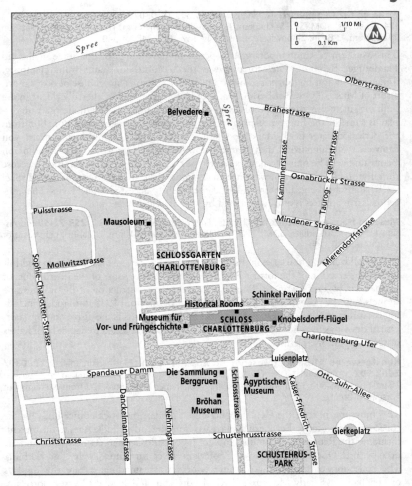

Ku'damm. Established in 1986, it was inspired by Berlin-born Käthe Kollwitz, an ardent socialist, feminist, and pacifist whose stormy social commentary led to the eventual banning of her works by the Nazis. Many Kollwitz works show the agonies of wartime separation of mother and child, inspired in part by her loss of a son in Flanders during World War I and a grandson during World War II.

Märkisches Museum. Am Köllnischen Park 5. ☎ **030/30-86-60.** Admission 3DM ($1.60) adults, 1DM (55¢) children. Tues–Sun 10am–6pm. U-Bahn: Märkisches Museum. Bus: 147, 240, or 265.

The full cultural history of Berlin is displayed in one of the most prominent buildings on the banks of the Spree; 42 rooms contain collections of artifacts from excavations, plus such art treasures as Slav silver items and Bronze Age finds. You can learn about Berlin's theaters and literature, the arts in Berlin and Brandenburg, and the life and work of Berlin artists. Most visitors like the array of mechanical musical instruments that can be played Wednesday 3 to 4pm and Sunday 11am to noon, for an extra 2DM ($1.10).

Museum für Gegenwart. Invalidenstrasse 50–51. ☎ **030/20-90-55-55.** Admission 8DM ($4.30) adults, 4DM ($2.15) children. Tues–Wed, Fri 10am–6pm, Thurs 10am–8pm, Sat–Sun 11am–6pm. U-Bahn: Zinnowitzer Strasse. Bus: 157, 245, 248, or 340.

This Museum of Contemporary Art opened in 1996 north of the Spree in the old Hamburger Bahnhof. The structure was the terminus for trains from Hamburg. Today, the station no longer receives trains but is a premier storehouse of postwar art, a sort of Musée d'Orsay of Berlin. Traces of its former function are still evident in the building, including the high roof designed for steam engines. The modern art on display is some of the finest in Germany, the nucleus of the collection a donation from the Berlin collector Erich Marx (no relation to Karl Marx). A multimedia event, you can view everything from Andy Warhol's now legendary *Mao* to an audiovisual Joseph Beuys archive. The museum houses one of the best collections of Cy Twombly because the curator, Heiner Bastian, was once an assistant to the artist. Other works on display are by Rauschenberg, Lichtenstein, and the recently deceased Dan Flavin. The conceptual artist, Beuys is also represented by 450 drawings.

Museum Haus am Checkpoint Charlie. Friedrichstrasse 44. ☎ **030/253-72-50.** Admission 8DM ($4.30) adults, 5DM ($2.70) children. Daily 9am–10pm. U-Bahn: Kochstrasse or Stadtmitte. Bus: 129.

This small building houses exhibits depicting the tragic events leading up to and following the erection of the former Berlin Wall. You can see some of the instruments of escape used by East Germans. Photos document the construction of the wall, escape tunnels, and the postwar history of both parts of Berlin from 1945 until today, including the airlift of 1948–49. One of the most moving exhibits is the display on the staircase of drawings by schoolchildren who, in 1961–62, were asked to depict both halves of Germany in one picture.

Kunstgewerbe Museum (Museum of Applied Arts). Matthäiskirchplatz. ☎ **030/2662-902.** Admission 4DM ($2.05) adults, 2DM ($1.05) students/children. Tues–Fri 10am–6pm, Sat–Sun 11am–6pm. U-/S-Bahn: Potsdamer Platz. Bus: 129 from Ku'damm to Potsdamer Brücke.

This museum, next to the Gemäldegalerie in a modern redbrick edifice built for the collection, is devoted to European applied arts from the early Middle Ages to the present, including the Renaissance, baroque, rococo, Jugendstil (German art nouveau), and art deco periods. Displayed are glassware, porcelain, silver, furniture, jewelry, and clothing. The collection of medieval goldsmiths' works is outstanding, as are the displays of Venetian glass, early Meissen and KPM porcelain, and Jugendstil vases, porcelain, furniture, and objects.

The Story of Berlin. Ku'damm-Karree, Kurfürstendamm 207–208 (at the corner of Uhlandstrasse). ☎ **030/1805-992010.** Admission 18DM ($9) adults, 14DM ($7) students/children, 40DM ($21) families. Daily 10am–8pm (you must enter by 6pm). S-Bahn: Ulandstrasse.

This multimedia extravaganza attempts to portray 8 centuries of the city's history through photos, films, sounds, and colorful displays. Beginning with the founding of Berlin in 1237, it chronicles the plague, the Thirty Years' War, Frederick the Great's reign, military life, the Industrial Revolution and the working poor, the Golden 1920s, World War II, divided Berlin during the Cold War, and the fall of the Wall. Lights flash in a media blitz as you enter the display on the fall of the Wall, making you feel like one of the first East Berliners to wonderingly cross to the West. Conclude your tour on the 14th floor with a panoramic view over today's Berlin. Allow at least

Berlin-Mitte

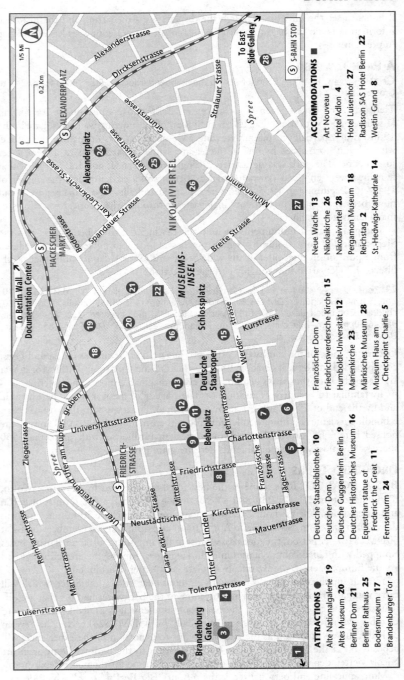

ATTRACTIONS ●
Alte Nationalgalerie **19**
Altes Museum **20**
Berliner Dom **21**
Berliner Rathaus **25**
Bodesmuseum **17**
Brandenburger Tor **3**

Deutsche Staatsbibliothek **10**
Deutscher Dom **6**
Deutsche Guggenheim Berlin **9**
Deutsches Historisiches Museum **16**
Equestrian statue of
  Frederick the Great **11**
Fernsehturm **24**

Französicher Dom **7**
Friedrichswerdersche Kirche **15**
Humboldt-Universität **12**
Marienkirche **23**
Märkisches Museum **28**
Museum Haus am
  Checkpoint Charlie **5**

Neue Wache **13**
Nikolaikirche **26**
Nikolaiviertel **28**
Pergamon Museum **18**
Reichstag **2**
St.-Hedwigs-Kathedrale **14**

ACCOMMODATIONS ■
Art Nouveau **1**
Hotel Adlon **4**
Hotel Luisenhof **27**
Radisson SAS Hotel Berlin **22**
Westin Grand **8**

437

2 hours to see the museum. Though the displays are a bit jarring and the historical information is too jumbled to be truly educational, the museum does leaves a lasting impression.

A PARK & A ZOO

✪ **Tiergarten.** From the Bahnhof Zoo to the Brandenburger Tor. Bus: 100, 141, or 341 to Grosser Stern.

Tiergarten, the largest green space in central Berlin, covers just under 2.5 sq. km (1 square mile), with more than 23km (14 miles) of meandering walkways. Late in the 19th century, partially to placate growing civic unrest, it was opened to the public, with a layout formalized by one of the leading landscape architects of the era, Peter Josef Lenné. The park was devastated during World War II, and the few trees that remained were chopped down for fuel as Berlin shuddered through the winter of 1945–46. Beginning in 1955, trees were replanted and alleyways, canals, ponds, and flowerbeds rearranged in their original patterns through the cooperative efforts of many landscape architects.

The park's largest monuments include the Berlin Zoo, described below, and the **Siegessäule** (Victory Column), which perches atop a soaring red-granite pedestal from a position in the center of the wide boulevard (Strasse des 17 Juni) that neatly bisects the Tiergarten into roughly equivalent sections.

✪ **Zoologischer Garten Berlin (Berlin Zoo).** Hardenbergplatz 8. ☎ **030/25-40-10.** Zoo, 13DM ($7) adults, 7DM ($3.80) children. Aquarium, 13DM ($7) adults, 7DM ($3.80) children. Combined ticket 19DM ($10) adults, 9.50DM ($5) children. Zoo, Apr–Oct daily 9am–6:30pm; Nov–Mar daily 9am–5pm. Aquarium, year-round, daily 9am–6pm. S-Bahn/ U-Bahn: Zoologischer Garten.

Occupying most of the southwest corner of Tiergarten is Germany's oldest and finest zoo. Founded in 1844, it's a short walk north from the Ku'damm. Until World War II, the zoo boasted thousands of animals of every imaginable species and description— many familiar to Berliners by nicknames. The tragedy of the war struck here as well, and by the end of 1945, only 91 animals remained. Since the war, the city has been rebuilding its large and unique collection; today there're more than 13,000 animals are housed here. The zoo has Europe's most modern birdhouse, with more than 550 species. The most valuable inhabitants here are giant pandas.

ORGANIZED TOURS

BUS & BOAT TOURS   Some of the best tours are operated by **Severin + Kühn,** Kurfürstendamm 216 (☎ **030/880-41-90**), which offers half a dozen tours of Berlin and its environs. Their 2-hour **"12 Stops City Tour"** departs at 30-minute intervals daily 10am and 3pm November to April, 10am and 4pm May to October. Priced at 30DM ($16) per person, the tour passes most of the important attractions using buses equipped with taped commentaries in eight languages. Among the attractions visited are the Europa-Center, the Brandenburg Gate, and Unter den Linden.

You can supplement this bus tour with a 3-hour boat ride on the Spree, which will carry you past the riverbanks and among some of the backwater harbors that are difficult to access except by water. The boat-tour supplement is available only May to October, with departures 10:30am to 1pm daily for 45DM ($24) each. The Severin & Kühn drivers and staff, at the end of the bus tour portion of the experience, will deposit you at the appropriate quays (either adjacent to the Berliner Dom or in the Nicolaiviertel, depending on the day of your visit) in time for the boat's departure.

More appealing and personalized is the 3-hour **"Big Berlin Tour,"** which departs 10am and 2pm daily, costs around 39DM ($21) per person, and—depending on the itinerary—usually incorporates sights not included on the shorter tour. Among the attractions is a section of the Grünewald Forest.

One interesting tour lasts 4 hours and visits Potsdam and Sans Souci Palace, former residence of Frederick the Great. The price is 59DM ($32) per person. Departures are Tuesday through Sunday 10am; May and October, there are additional departures Friday, Saturday, and Sunday 2:15pm.

THE SHOPPING SCENE

The central shopping destinations are **Kurfürstendamm, Tauentzienstrasse, Am Zoo,** and **Kantstrasse.** You might also want to walk up streets that intersect with Tauentzienstrasse: Marburger, Ranke, and Nürnberger. Most stores are open Monday to Friday 9 or 10am to 6 or 6:30pm. Many stores stay open late on Thursday evening, usually until about 8:30pm. Saturday hours for most stores are 9 or 10am to 2pm.

Berlin's largest indoor shopping center, topped by the Mercedes-Benz logo, is the **Europa-Center,** Breitscheidplatz Tauentzienstrasse (☎ **030/348-0088;** U-Bahn: Kurfürstendamm), in the heart of the western city. You'll find the Berlin casino and a number of restaurants and cafes, in addition to an array of shops offering wide-ranging merchandise.

THREE STORES WORTH A LOOK

Known popularly as KaDeWe (pronounced kah-*day*-vay), **Kaufhaus des Westens,** Wittenbergplatz (☎ **030/21-21-0;** U-Bahn: Kurfürstendamm), is about 2 blocks from the Kurfürstendamm. The huge luxury store, whose name means "department store of the west," was established some 75 years ago. Displaying extravagant items, it's known mainly for its sixth-floor food department. It's been called the greatest food emporium in the world. More than 1,000 varieties of German sausages are displayed, and delicacies from all over the world are shipped in.

Despite its abbreviated name, ✪ **KPM,** Kurfürstendamm 26A (☎ **030/88-67-21-10;** U-Bahn: Kurfürstendamm), is one of Europe's most prestigious emporiums of luxury dinnerware. Königliche Porzellan Manufaktur was founded in 1763 when Frederick the Great invested his personal funds in a lackluster porcelain factory and elevated it to royal status. Each item is hand painted, hand decorated, and hand packed in almost unbreakable formats that can be shipped virtually anywhere.

In the heart of the city near the Europa-Center, **Wertheim,** Kurfürstendamm 231 (☎ **030/8800-3206;** U-Bahn: Kurfürstendamm, is a good all-around store for travel aids and general basics. It sells a number of perfumes, clothing for the entire family, jewelry, electrical devices, household goods, photography supplies, and souvenirs. It also has a shoe-repair section. Shoppers can fuel up at a large restaurant with a grand view over half the city.

BERLIN'S MARKETS

Berliner Antik & Flohmarkt, in the Friedrichstrasse S-Bahn station (☎ **030/208-2645**), is one of Berlin's latest flea markets. Some 100 vendors try to tempt buyers with porcelain, brassware, and assorted bric-a-brac. Some have new or used clothing and others may even be selling World War II mementos. The market is open Monday and Wednesday to Sunday 11am to 6pm. The **Turkish Bazaar** (U-Bahn: Kottbusser Tor, then a 5-minute walk) is held on the bank of the Maybachufer in Kreuzberg. This area adjacent to the Maybachufer Canal has been converted by Germany's "guest workers." Although much of the merchandise involves food, especially grilled kebabs, there's also a good selection of jewelry, glassware, onyx, and copper items. The market is open Tuesday and Friday noon to 6:30pm. The Friday market is busier and is the best time to attend if you have a choice.

BERLIN AFTER DARK

The German *Zitty* and *Tip* include some listings in English, and keep you informed about various nightlife and cultural venues. Both *Berlin Programm* and *Kultur!news* also contain theater listings and other diversions. Performance arts are also covered in *Berlin,* a quarterly published in both English and German. These pamphlets and magazines are available at news kiosks.

THE PERFORMING ARTS

The ✪ **Berliner Philharmonisches Orchester** (Berlin Philharmonic) is one of the world's premier orchestras. Its home, **the Philharmonie,** Matthäikirchstrasse 1, (☎ 030/254-88-0; bus: 129 or 148), is a significant piece of modern architecture; you may want to visit even if you do not attend a performance. None of the 2,218 seats are more than 100 feet from the rostrum. The box office is open Monday to Friday 3:30 to 6pm and Saturday and Sunday 11am to 2pm. You can't place orders by phone. If you're staying in a first-class or deluxe hotel, you can usually get the concierge to obtain seats for you. Tickets are 26 to 80DM ($14to $43); special concerts 40 to 250DM ($22 to $135).

Because of the east-west split, Berlin has two famous opera companies. The famed ✪ **Deutsche Oper Berlin** (Berlin Opera), Bismarckstrasse 35 (☎ **030/34-384-01;** U-Bahn: Deutsche Oper; S-Bahn: Charlottenburg; bus: 101 or 109), performs in one of the world's great opera houses, built on the site of the prewar opera house in Charlottenburg. The structure is a notable example of modern theater architecture that seats 1,885. A ballet company performs once a week. Concerts, including Lieder evenings, are also presented on the opera stage. Tickets are 26 to 150DM ($14 to $81).

The **Deutsche Staatsoper** (German State Opera), Unter den Linden 7 ☎ **030/ 20-35-45-55;** U-Bahn: Französische Strasse), presents some of the finest opera in the world, along with a regular repertoire of ballet and concerts. Its home was rebuilt within the walls of the original 1740s Staatsoper, destroyed in World War II. The box office generally sells tickets Monday to Friday 10am to 6pm and Saturday and Sunday noon to 6pm. Tickets for concerts are 12 to 80DM ($7 to $43), opera are 12 to 200DM ($7 to $108). The opera closes from late June to the end of August.

Komische Oper Berlin, Behrensstrasse 55–57 (☎ **030/20-26-00;** U-Bahn: Französische Strasse; S-Bahn: Friedrichstrasse or Unter den Linden), lies in the middle of the city near Brandenburger Tor. Over the years, it has become one of the most innovative theater ensembles in Europe, presenting many avant-garde productions. The box office is open Monday to Saturday 11am to 7pm and Sunday 1pm until 1¹/₂ hours before the performance. Tickets are 16 to 115DM ($9 to $62).

LIVE-MUSIC CLUBS

A-Trane, Pestalozzistrasse 105 (☎ **030/313-25-50;** S-Bahn: Savignyplatz), is small and smoky jazz house where virtually everyone seems to have a working familiarity with great names from the jazz world's past and present. The name is a hybrid of the old Big Band standard, "Take the A-Train," with the 'e' derived from the name of the legendary John Coltrane. It's open Wednesday to Saturday 9pm, music begins around 10pm. Closing hours vary. Cover is 15 to 25DM ($8 to $14), depending on who's playing. Popular, well managed, and noted for its revolving array of international jazz acts, **Ewige Lampe,** Niebuhrstrasse 11A (☎ **030/324-39-18;** S-Bahn: Savignyplatz), was originally established in 1964 as a working-class restaurant near Savignyplatz. In 1988, the owners abandoned food and transformed the place into a hard-drinking enclave of jazz—blues, boogie-woogie, New Orleans, and traditional. The club is open

Come to the Cabaret!

If you know how to sing "Life is a cabaret, old chum," in German no less, you may enjoy an evening in this postwar "Porcupine." Like its namesake, **Die Stachelschweine,** Tauentzienstrasse and Budapester Strasse (in the basement of the Europa-Center) (☎ **030/261-47-95;** U-Bahn: Kurfürstendamm), pokes prickly fun at both German and often American politicians. Get a ticket early, because the Berliners love this one. The box office is open Tuesday to Friday 10am to 2pm and 3 to 7:30pm and Saturday 10am to 2pm and 3 to 8:45pm. Shows are presented Tuesday to Friday at 7:30pm and Saturday at 6 and 8:45pm. Cover is 20 to 40DM ($11 to $22). The cabaret is closed during July.

Opened in 1893 as one of the most popular purveyors of vaudeville in Europe, the **Wintergarten,** Potsdamer Strasse 96 (☎ **030/230-88-230;** U-Bahn: Kurfürstenstrasse), operated in fits and starts throughout the war years, until it was demolished in 1944 by Allied bombers. In 1992, a modernized design reopened. Today, it's the largest and most nostalgic Berlin cabaret, laden with schmaltzy reminders of yesteryear and staffed with chorus girls; magicians from America, Britain, and countries of the former Soviet bloc; circus acrobats; political satirists; and musician/dancer combos. Shows begin Monday to Saturday at 8pm and Sunday at 3:30 and 8:30pm. Shows last around $2^1/4$ hours. The box office is open daily 7pm to midnight. Cover Friday and Saturday is 59 to 98DM ($32 to $53), Sunday to Thursday 35 to 80DM ($19 to $43), depending on the seat. Price includes first drink.

Wednesday to Sunday 8pm to 2am, with live music from 9pm. Cover is 10 to 20DM ($5 to $11).

Large and artfully drab, **Far Out,** Kurfürstendamm 156 (☎ **030/320-00-717;** U-Bahn: Adenauerplatz), plays danceable rock from the '70s to the '90s that manages to get hundreds of high-energy dancers up and out on the floors. Clientele includes lots of students and artists, who dress up in artfully bizarre clothing that has lots of punk-rock overtones. It occasionally imports celebrity DJs from other disco-crazed cities of Europe. The place only really comes alive after midnight. Open Tuesday to Sunday 10am to between 4 and 6am, depending on the crowd. Cover is 6DM ($3.25). **Knaack-Klub,** Greifswalderstrasse 224 (☎ **030/442-7060;** S-Bahn: Alexanderplatz; tram: No. 2, 3, or 4), features a live music venue, two floors of dancing, and a floor dedicated to games. There're usually four live rock shows a week, with a fairly even split between German and international touring bands. The music ranges from techno to hip-hop to '80s. Disco music is played on Wednesday, Friday, and Saturday nights. Open nightly 10pm. Cover is 5 to 10DM ($2.70 to $5).

The premises that contains **Opernschänke,** in the Opernpalais, Unter den Linden 5 (☎ **030/20-26-83;** U-Bahn: Friedrichstrasse; bus: 100), were built in 1762, a fact that seems to add a certain importance to a setting that's undeniably historic, and to the artists who perform their music live. For the most part, this is a restaurant serving Continental food every day noon to midnight, with the last order accepted at 11:30pm. Main courses cost 20 to 30DM ($11 to $16). The food is augmented with live music, usually jazz, Thursday, Friday, and Saturday nights between 6pm and 1am, as well as Sunday afternoons between 11am and 2pm as part of set-price "Jazz Brunch" costing 39DM ($21). After the end of the jazz brunch, the restaurant remains open till 7pm, for food and drink.

DANCE CLUBS

Local clubbies define **E-Werk,** Wilhelmstrasse 43 (☎ **030/617-93-70;** U-Bahn: Mohrenstrasse), as "the apotheosis of techno," complete with industrial machines and colored strobe lights. Several bars and nonstop beats keep this former power station lively—that is, if you show up after 1am. The largest dance floor is in the cavernous main hall. Old machinery is still scattered about, which adds to the offbeat ambience but doesn't make room for any chill-out area. To wind down, you have to escape to the outside courtyard. A lot of gays show up on Saturday. The club is open Friday and Saturday 11pm to 5 and often 8am. Cover on Friday and Saturday is 15 to 20DM ($8 to $11).

Gays, straights, and everybody in between show up at **SO 36,** Oranienstrasse 190 (☎ **030/61-40-13-06;** U-Bahn: Görlitzer Bahnhof), for wild action and frantic dancing into the wee hours. A young, vibrant Kreuzberg crowd is attracted to this joint where the scene changes nightly. On Wednesday it's strictly gay and lesbian disco. On Friday and Saturday the parties "get really wild, man," as the bartender accurately promised. Some nights are devoted to themes such as James Bond where you can show up looking like a Cold War spy. Wednesdays and Sundays are generally all gay. Open Wednesday to Saturday 11pm until "we feel like closing," and Sunday 5 to 11pm. Cover is 8 to 12DM ($4.30 to $7).

Metropole, Nollendorfplatz 5, Schöneberg (☎ **030/217-36-80;** U-Bahn: Nollendorfplatz), one of the leading dance clubs in Berlin, opens only on weekends and attracts patrons ages 18 to 38. Built as a theater around the turn of the century, Metropole hosts live concerts and offers special events (by special arrangement only) for gay people. It is open Wednesday and Saturday 9pm to 6am. Cover is 10 to 20DM ($5 to $11).

One of Berlin's most rocking techno venues, **Tresor Globus,** Leipzigerstrasse 126A (☎ **030/229-06-11;** U-Bahn: Mohrenstrasse), has been packing 'em in since 1991. The building was once part of Globus Bank. Downstairs there's a bunkerlike atmosphere with prison-type metal bars and harsh acoustics. The spacious dance floor upstairs has lighter house sounds. There's also a bar in the back when you want to chill out. In summer, tables are placed outside, with lights strung among the shrubbery. The club is open Wednesday from 10pm and Friday to Sunday from 11pm; it often closes at 6am. Cover on Wednesday is 5DM ($2.70), Friday 10DM ($5), Saturday and Sunday 15 to 20DM ($8 to $11).

POPULAR BARS

In the heart of old East Berlin, a complex of about 30 bars, shops, and restaurants, called **Die Hackeschen Höfe** (S-Bahn: Hackescher Markt) is one of the best places to drink in the evening. The stylish and hip minimall attracts counterculture denizens. You can wander through the galleries, boutiques, and cafes; the most happening spot is **Oxymoron,** in the courtyard at Rosenthaler Strasse 40–41 (☎ **030/283-91-88-5**), whose red-velvet decor evokes Jazz Age decadence. The site is primarily a restaurant and bar rather than a nightclub, although some form of live music begins most evenings at 8pm. Menu items are international, and themes range from "gangster nights" to just dancing and jazz. The club is open daily 11am to 2am (dining), although the bar doesn't shut down until 3am. On weekends, the music is played by popular DJs whose musical programs keep patrons dancing until after 4am.

GAY & LESBIAN BERLIN

Andreas Kneipe, Ansbacher Strasse 29 (☎ **030/218-32-57;** U-Bahn: Wittenbergplatz), is as warm, cozy, and convivial as many of the other traditional bars scattered throughout Berlin, with a distinct appeal for the many gay men and women who consider it their neighborhood hangout. It's been in business since 1938, making it the oldest gay bar in Berlin. Few of the clients dance, and there's no food served, so this is a place just to talk and drink in a convivial setting. Open daily 11am to 4am. The **Begine Café-und-Kulturzentrum für Frauen,** Potsdamerstrasse 139 (☎ 030/215-43-25; U-Bahn: Bülowstrasse; bus: 119 or 48), established in 1986, is one of Berlin's most visible headquarters for feminists and the most obvious place for women seeking to meet other women. Within its inner sanctums is a changing array of art exhibitions, poetry readings, music venues, German-language discussions, comedy showcases, lectures, and social events. You can phone in advance for the schedule. The premises are occasionally transformed into a disco. Open daily 5pm to 1am.

Both gays and straights are welcomed at **Kumpelnest 3000,** Lützowstrasse 23 (☎030/2616-918; U-Bahn: Kurfürstenstrasse). All that's asked is that you enjoy a kinky nightclubbing good time in what used to be a Berlin brothel. It's really a bar but there's dancing to disco classics. Berliners often show up here for early morning fun after they've exhausted the action at the other hot spots. It's crowded and chaotic. Open daily 5pm to 5am, but if the house crowd merits it, they'll stay open even later on weekends. **Tom's Bar,** Motzstrasse 19 (☎ 030/2-13-45-70; U-Bahn: Nollendorfplatz), becomes crowded after 11pm with young gay men. Upstairs, the porno action is merely on the screen; downstairs it's real. The back room is hot, hot, and hotter. Monday nights feature two-for-one drinks. There's a cover charge for special occasions only. Open daily 10pm to 6am.

DAY TRIPS FROM BERLIN

POTSDAM   Of all the tours possible from Berlin, the three-star attraction is the baroque town of Potsdam, 24km (15 miles) southwest of Berlin on the Havel River, often called Germany's Versailles. From the beginning of the 18th century it was the residence and garrison town of the Prussian kings. World attention focused on Potsdam from July 17 to August 2, 1945, when the Potsdam Conference shaped postwar Europe.

West of the historic core lies **Sans Souci Park,** with its palaces and gardens. Northwest of Sans Souci is the New Garden and the Cecilienhof Palace, on the Heiliger See.

Getting There   There're 29 daily connections by rail from Bahnhof Zoo (trip time: 23 minutes) and Berliner Hauptbahnhof (trip time: 54 minutes). For rail information in Potsdam, call ☎ 018/05-99-66-33. Potsdam can also be reached by S-Bahn S3 and S7 (trip time: 30 minutes). Car access is via the E-30 autobahn east and west or the E-53 north and south.

Visitor Information   For tourist information, contact **Potsdam-Information,** Friedrich-Ebert-Strasse 5 (☎ 0331/275580). Its hours are April to October Monday to Friday 9am to 8pm, Saturday 10am to 6pm, and Sunday 10am to 4pm; November to March Monday to Friday 10am to 6pm and Saturday to Sunday 10am to 2pm.

Exploring Potsdam   With its palaces and gardens, ✪ **Sans Souci Park,** Zur historischen Mühle (☎ 0331/96-94-202; Tram 94 or 95; Bus 612, 614, 631, 632, 692, or 695), was the work of many architects and sculptors. The park covers an area of about a square mile. Once at Potsdam, you might consider an organized tour of the park and various palaces: unguided tours 10DM ($5) adults, 5DM ($2.70) children. Two-hour guided tours, 15DM ($8) adults, 8DM ($4.30) children. For information on English-speaking tours, call ☎ 0331/96-94-200.

Frederick II ("the Great") chose Potsdam rather than Berlin as his permanent residence. The style of the buildings he ordered erected is called Potsdam rococo, an

A Fabulous Place to Dine in Potsdam

In 1878, a courtier in the service of the Prussian monarch built an elegant villa on the shore of the Heiliger See. During the 1920s, author Bernhardt Kellerman wrote some of his best work here. After a cold war stint as a base for Russian officers, it now functions as the most talked-about restaurant in Potsdam: **Villa Kellerman,** Mangerstrasse 33–36 (☎ **0331/29-15-72;** bus: 695). The classical Italian cuisine might include marinated carpaccio of whitefish; a mixed platter of antipasti; spaghetti with scampi, herbs, and garlic; or John Dory in butter-and-caper sauce. Reservations are recommended. American Express and Visa accepted. It's open Tuesday and Wednesday 2pm to midnight and Thursday to Sunday noon to midnight.

achievement primarily of Georg Wenzeslaus von Knobelsdorff. Knobelsdorff built **Sans Souci Palace,** with its terraces and gardens, as a summer residence for Frederick II. The palace, inaugurated in 1747, is a long one-story building crowned by a dome and flanked by round pavilions. The music salon is the supreme example of the rococo style, and the elliptical Marble Hall is the largest in the palace. As a guest of the king, Voltaire visited in 1750. Sans Souci is open April to October 9am to 5pm; November to March 9am to 4pm; closed Mondays. Admission is 10DM ($5) for adults and 5DM ($2.70) for children.

Schloss Charlottenhof, south of Okonomieweg (☎ **0331/969-42-00;** tram: 1 or 4), was designed by Karl Friedrich Schinkel, the great neoclassical master, and built between 1826 and 1829. He erected the palace in the style of a villa and designed most of the furniture inside. Open daily May through October 10am to 5pm. Admission is 6DM ($3.25) adults and 3DM ($1.60) children.

North of the 200-acre park, the ✪ **Cecilienhof Palace,** Im Neuer Garten (☎ **0331/969-42-44;** bus: 694), was ordered built by Kaiser Wilhelm II between 1913 and 1917 and was completed in the style of an English country house. The 176-room mansion became the new residence of Crown Prince Wilhelm of Hohenzollern. It was occupied as a royal residence until March 1945, when the crown prince and his family fled to the West, taking many of their possessions. Cecilienhof was the headquarters of the 1945 Potsdam Conference. It is open April to October daily 9am to 5pm, November to March daily 9am to 4pm. Admission is 6DM ($3.25) for adults and 4DM ($2.15) for children, without tour guide. Admission with tour guide 8DM ($4.30) adults and 6DM ($3.25) children (visits must be guided November to March).

THE SPREEWALD This landmass southeast of Berlin is flat and water-soaked—but celebrated for its eerie beauty. For at least 1,000 years, residents of the region have channeled the marshlands here into a network of canals, streams, lakes, and irrigation channels and built unusual clusters of houses, barns, and chapels on the high points of otherwise marshy ground. Ethnologists consider it one of central Europe's most distinctive adaptations of humans to an unlikely landscape, and botanists appreciate the wide diversity of bird and animal life that flourishes, according to the seasons, on its lush and fertile terrain. And legends of the spirits that inhabit the thick forests of the Spreewald abound.

Many of the people you'll meet here belong to a linguistic subdivision of the German-speaking people, the Sorbs, descendants of Slavic tribes who settled in the region around 600 B.C. Most modern-day Sorbs remain fiercely proud of their dialect and traditions and continue to till the soil of the Spreewald using labor-intensive methods, producing crops of mostly cucumbers and radishes.

The Spreewald is at its most appealing in early spring and autumn, when the crowds of sightseers depart and a spooky chill descends with the fog over these primeval forests and shallow medieval canals.

Getting There   The Spreewald lies 97km (60 miles) southeast of Berlin, and the best gateway is Lübben, 60 minutes by train from Berlin-Lichtenberg station. At the Lübben station, head straight out the front exit and walk in the same direction on a tree-lined street leading into the center of town. Once here, follow the signs directing you to *Kahfahrten* (boat rides) or *Paddlebooten* (paddleboats) and you're off to discover Spreewald.

Visitor Information   The tourist office in Lübben, Ernst von Huwald Damm 16 (☎ **03546/3090**), is the main point of departure for most Spreewald cruises. a secondary point of departure for Spreewald tours, 10km (6 miles) away, is the tourist office in the hamlet of Lübbenau, Ehm-Welk-Strasse 15 (☎ **03542/3668**).

Exploring the Spreewald   The shallow, nutrient-rich waters of the Spreewald seem ideally suited to boat tours along its timeless surface. If you're interested, several companies offer tours from the piers in the hamlet of Lübben. Each charges equivalent rates of 9.50DM ($5) for a 3-hour tour. Your best bet involves wandering down to the piers near the hamlet's center and hopping aboard the next departure, as virtually no one will speak English. Each of the companies operates only April to October, with departures scheduled every day between 9am and 4pm. If you're interested in renting a canoe or rowboat and paddling around the Spreewald on your own, head for **Bootsverleih Gebauer,** Lindenstrasse (☎03546/7194), where canoes can be rented for 8DM ($4.30) per person hourly, 5DM ($2.70) each additional hour, and 32DM ($17) per week.

2 Munich & the Bavarian Alps

Sprawling Munich, home of some 1.3 million people and such industrial giants as Siemens and BMW, is the pulsating capital and cultural center of Bavaria. One of Germany's most festive cities, Munich exudes a hearty Bavarian *Gemütlichkeit.*

Longtime resident Thomas Mann wrote: "Munich sparkles." Although the city he described was swept away by some of the most severe bombing of World War II, Munich continues to sparkle, as it introduces itself to thousands of new visitors annually.

The Munich cliché as a beer-drinking town of folkloric charm is marketed by the city itself. Despite a roaring gross national product, Munich likes to present itself as a large, agrarian village peopled by jolly beer drinkers who cling to rustic origins despite the presence on all sides of symbols of the computer age, high-tech industries, a sophisticated business scene, a good deal of Hollywood-style glamour, and fairly hip night action. Bavarians themselves are in danger of becoming a minority in Munich—more than two-thirds of the population comes from other parts of the country or from outside Germany—but everybody buys into the folkloric charm and schmaltz.

ORIENTATION

GETTING THERE   By Plane The **Franz Josef Strauss Airport** (☎ **089/ 97-52-13-13**), inaugurated in 1992, is among the most modern in the world. It lies 27km (17 miles) northeast of central Munich at Erdinger Moos.

S-Bahn (☎ **089/41-42-43-44**) trains connect the airport with the Hauptbahnhof (main railroad station) in downtown Munich, with departures every 20 minutes for the 40-minute trip. The fare is 14DM ($8); Eurailpass holders ride free. A taxi into

Munich

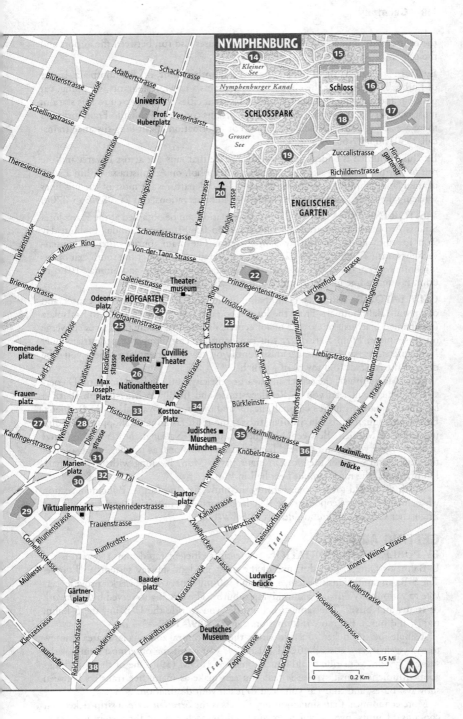

NYMPHENBURG

14 Kleiner See

15

Nymphenburger Kanal

Schloss 16

SCHLOSSPARK

17

Grosser See

18

19

Zuccalistrasse

Richildenstrasse

Hirsch-gartenstr.

Blütenstrasse

Adalbertstrasse

Schackstrasse

Schellingstrasse

Türkenstrasse

University

Prof.-Huberplatz

Prof.- Veterinärstr.

Theresienstrasse

Amalienstrasse

Ludwigstrasse

Kaulbachstrasse

Königin strasse

20

ENGLISCHER GARTEN

Türkenstrasse

Oskar- von- Miller- Ring

Schoenfeldstrasse

Von-der-Tann Strasse

Prinzregentenstrasse

22

Lerchenfeld strasse

21

Oettingenstrasse

Brienerstrasse

Galeriestrasse

Theater-museum

Unsöldstrasse

Wagmüllerstr.

Odeons-platz

HOFGARTEN

24

K. Scharnagl -Ring

23

Christophstrasse

St.-Anna-Pfarrstr.

Thierschstrasse

Liebigstrasse

Reitmorstrasse

Promenade-platz

Hofgartenstrasse

25

Residenz-strasse

Residenz

26

Cuvilliés Theater

Karl-Fauhaber-Strasse

Theatinerstrasse

Max Joseph-Platz

Nationaltheater

Marstallstrasse

Am Kosttor-Platz

34

Bürkleinstr.

St.-Anna-Platz

Sternstrasse

Widenmayer strasse

I s a r

Frauen-platz

27

28

Weinstrasse

Pfisterstrasse

33

Judisches Museum München

35

Maximilianstrasse

36

Maximilians-brücke

Kaufingerstrasse

Diener strasse

31

Marien-platz

30

32

Im Tal

Th. Wimmer-Ring

Knöbelstrasse

29

Viktualienmarkt

Westenriederstrasse

Isartor-platz

Cornelliusstrasse

Blumenstrasse

Frauenstrasse

Kanalstrasse

Thierschstrasse

Steinsdorfstrasse

I s a r

Müllerstr.

Rumfordstr.

Zweibrücken strasse

Innere Weiner Strasse

Gärtner-platz

Baader-platz

Morassistrasse

Ludwigs-brücke

Rosenheimerstrasse

Kellerstrasse

Klenzestrasse

Fraunhofer

Reichenbachstrasse

Baaderstrasse

Erhardtstrasse

Deutsches Museum

I s a r

38

37

Zeppelinstrasse

Lillenstrasse

Hochstrasse

0   1/5 Mi

0   0.2 Km

the center costs about 100DM ($54). Airport buses also run between the airport and the center.

By Train   Munich's main rail station, the **Hauptbahnhof,** on Bahnhofplatz, is one of Europe's largest. Near the city center, it contains a hotel, restaurants, shopping, car parking, and banking facilities. All major German cities are connected to this station, most with service every hour. Some 20 daily trains connect Munich to Frankfurt, and there are about 23 trains daily to Berlin. For information about long-distance trains, call ☎ **01805/99-66-33.**

By Bus   Munich is a focal point for bus service that fans out across Bavaria and the rest of Germany. The West-wing-Starnberger Bahnhof, on Arnulfstrasse within a wing of the Hauptbahnhof, is the point of arrivals and departures for most of the bus lines servicing the city. For schedules, information, and reservations, call ☎ **089/545-8700.**

VISITOR INFORMATION   Tourist information can be obtained at the Franz Josef Strauss Airport in the central area (☎ **089/233-03-00**), open Monday to Thursday 9am to 4pm, Friday to Sunday 9am to 3pm. The main tourist office, **Fremden-verkehrsamt** (☎ **089/23-33-02-72**), is at the Hauptbahnhof at the south exit opening onto Bayerstrasse. Open Monday to Saturday 9am to 8pm and Sunday 10am to 6pm, it offers a free map of Munich and will also reserve hotel rooms.

CITY LAYOUT   Munich's Hauptbahnhof lies just west of the town center and opens onto Bahnhofplatz. From the square, you can take Schützenstrasse to Karlsplatz (nicknamed Stachus), one of the major centers of Munich. Many tram lines converge on this square. From Karlsplatz, you can continue east along the pedestrians-only Neuhauserstrasse and Kaufingerstrasse until you reach Marienplatz, where you'll be deep in the Altstadt (old town) of Munich.

From **Marienplatz,** the center and heart of the city, you can head north on Diener-strasse, which will lead you to Residenzstrasse and finally to **Max-Joseph-Platz,** a landmark square, with the National Theater and the former royal palace, the Residenz. East of this square runs **Maximilianstrasse,** the most fashionable shopping and dining street of Munich. Between Marienplatz and the National theater is the **Platzl** quarter, where you'll want to head for nighttime diversions, as it's the seat of some of the finest (and some of the worst) restaurants in Munich, along with the landmark Hofbräuhaus, the most famous beer hall in Europe.

North of the old town is **Schwabing,** the university and former Bohemian section whose main street is Leopoldstrasse. The large, sprawling municipal park grounds, the Englischer Garten, are found due east of Schwabing.

GETTING AROUND

BY PUBLIC TRANSPORTATION   The city's efficient rapid-transit system is the **U-Bahn,** or Untergrundbahn, one of the most modern subway systems in Europe. The **S-Bahn** rapid-transit system, a 420km (260-mile) network of tracks, provides service to various city districts and outlying suburbs. The city is also served by a network of **trams** and **buses.** The same ticket entitles you to ride the U-Bahn, the S-Bahn, trams, and buses. For more information, call ☎ **089/41-42-43-44.**

A single-journey ticket for a ride within the city's central zone—a large area that few tourists ever leave—costs 3.40DM ($1.85). If you go to the outermost zones of the subway system, your ride could cost as much as 16DM ($9). One of the best things about Munich's transit system is that you can make as many free transfers between subways, buses, and trams as you need to reach your destination.

More economical than single-journey tickets is the ***Streifencarte,*** a strip-ticket that contains 11 units, two of which are annulled for each zone of the system you travel

Munich U-Bahn & S-Bahn

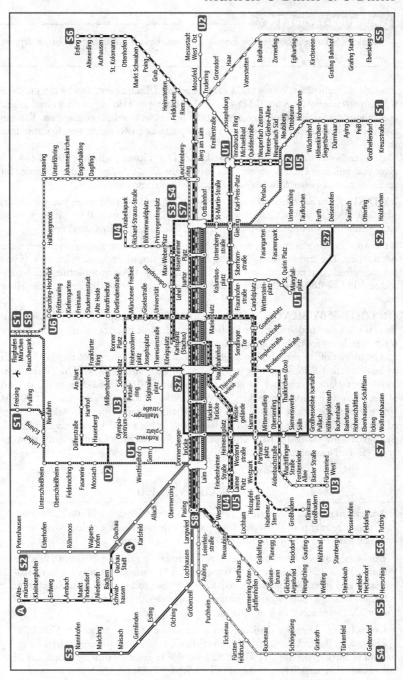

A Money-Saving Tip

Munich's S-Bahn is covered by Eurail, so if you have a railpass, don't buy a separate ticket.

---

through. A Streifencarte costs 15DM ($8) for adults. Children ages 4 to 14 can purchase a *Kinderstreifencarte* for 8.50DM ($4.60). With this type of ticket, you can travel in one continuous direction during any 2-hour time period with unlimited transfers. You can also use it for multiple passengers (for two people to ride two zones, simply stamp four strips).

An even better deal may be the **Tageskarte (Day Ticket),** which for 9DM ($4.85) gives you unlimited access within the central zone for a full day. Double the price for access to all of Greater Munich—an 80km (50-mile) radius.

BY TAXI   Cabs are relatively expensive—you'll pay 5DM ($3) when you get inside, plus 2.20DM ($1.20) per kilometer, add 2DM ($1.10) if you call for pick-up. In an emergency, call ☎ **089/2161-0** or 089/194-10 for a radio-dispatched taxi.

BY CAR   Driving in the city, which has an excellent public transportation system, is not advised. The streets around Marienplatz in the Altstadt are pedestrian only. If you are interested in renting a car locally, try **Sixt/Budget Autovermietung,** Einstein-strasse 106 (☎ **089/550-24-47**), or look under *Autovermietung* in the Munich yellow pages.

ON FOOT & BY BICYCLE   Of course, the best way to explore Munich is on foot, since it has a vast pedestrian zone in the center. Many of its attractions can, in fact, be reached only on foot. Pick up a good map and set out.

The tourist office also sells a pamphlet that outlines itineraries for touring Munich by bicycle called *Radl-Touren für unsere Gäste,* costing .50DM (25¢). One of the most convenient places to rent a bike is **Radius Bikes** (☎ **089/59-61-13**), at the far end of the Hauptbahnhof, near lockers opposite tracks 30 and 31. The charge is 10DM ($5) per 2 hours, or else 25DM ($14) from 10am to 6pm. Mountain bikes are rented for about 25% more. A deposit of 100DM ($54) is assessed; students and Eurail-pass holders are granted a 10% discount. Open April to early October daily 10am to 6pm, closed November to March.

Fast Facts: Munich

American Express   American Express, Promenadeplatz 6 (☎ **089/290-900;** U-Bahn: Marienplatz), is open for mail pickup and check cashing Monday to Friday 9am to 5:30pm and Saturday 9:30am to 12:30pm.

Business Hours   Most **banks** are open Monday to Friday 8:30am to 12:30pm and 1:30 to 3:30pm (many stay open until 5:30pm on Thursday). Most **businesses** and **stores** are open Monday to Friday 9am to 6pm and Saturday 9am to 2pm. On *langer Samstag* (first Saturday of the month) stores remain open until 6pm. Many observe an 8 or 9pm closing on Thursday.

Consulates   There's a **United States** consulate at Königstrasse 5 (☎ **089/288-80;** U-Bahn: Universität); a Consulate General Office for the **United Kingdom** at Bürkleinstrasse 10 (☎ **089/21-10-90;** U-Bahn: Isartor); a Consulate of **Ireland** at Mauerkircherstrasse 1a (☎ **089/98-57-23;** bus: 87), and a consulate of **Canada** at Tal Strasse 29 (☎ **089/219-95-70;** U-Bahn: Marienplatz). The governments and Australia and New Zealand do not maintain offices in Munich.

Currency   See "Fast Facts: Berlin."

Currency Exchange   You can get a better rate at a bank than at your hotel. American Express traveler's checks are best cashed at the local American Express office (see above). On weekends or at night, you can exchange money at the Hauptbahnhof exchange, open daily 6am to 11:30pm.

Dentists/Doctors   For an English-speaking dentist, go to **Klinik und Poliklinik für Kieferchirurgie der Universität München,** Lindwurmstrasse 2A (☎ **089/51-60-0;** U-Bahn: Goetheplatz); it deals with emergency cases and is always open. The American, British, and Canadian consulates keep a list of recommended English-speaking physicians. For dental or medical emergencies at night or on Saturday and Sunday, call **Notfallpraxis,** Elisenstrasse (☎ **089/55-17-17;** bus: 69). It's open Monday, Tuesday, and Thursday 7pm to midnight; Wednesday and Friday 2pm to midnight, and Saturday, Sunday, and holidays, 7pm to midnight.

Drugstores   For an international drugstore where English is spoken, go to **Bahnhof Apotheke,** Bahnhofplatz (☎ **089/59-41-19;** U-Bahn/S-Bahn: Hauptbahnhof), open Monday to Friday 8am to 6:30pm and Saturday 8am to 2pm. If you need a prescription filled in off-hours, call ☎ **089/59-44-75** for information about what's open. The information is recorded and in German only, so you may need to get someone from your hotel staff to assist you.

Emergencies   For emergency medical aid, phone ☎ **089/55-17-71.** Call the police at ☎ **110.**

Internet Access   You can send e-mails or check your messages at the **Internet-Café,** Bayer-Strasse 10A (☎ **089/55-08-800;** www.icafe.space.de; bus: 2, 19, 20, or 29). This is also the site of a cafe, bar, disco, bistro, pastry shop, and pizzeria.

Post Office   A central post office is at Arnulfstrasse 32 (☎ **089/16-39-80;** U-Bahn: Briennerstrasse), north of the Hauptbahnhof, open Monday to Friday 8am to 8pm. You can have your mail sent here Poste Restante (general delivery), but include the zip code D-80335. You'll need a passport to reclaim mail. Packages can also be mailed from the above address.

Telephone   The **country code** for Germany is **49.** The **city code** for Munich is **89.** Use this code when you're calling from outside Germany; if you're within Germany, use **089.** For more information on making calls from Germany, see "Fast Facts: Berlin."

WHERE TO STAY

All the hotels listed here are in the very center of Munich.

VERY EXPENSIVE

✪ **Bayerischer Hof & Palais Montgelas.** Promenadeplatz 2–6, D-80333 München. ☎ **800/223-6800** in the U.S., or 089/2-12-00. Fax 089/21-20-906. www.bayerischerhof. de. E-mail: hbh@compuserve.com. 495 units. MINIBAR TV TEL. 499DM–599DM ($269–$323) double; from 819DM ($442) suite. AE, DC, MC, V. Parking 35DM ($19). Tram: 19.

A Bavarian version of New York's Waldorf-Astoria, this hotel is in a swank location, opening onto a little tree-filled square. Rooms range from medium to extremely spacious, each with plush duvets topping firm mattresses; many of the beds are four-posters. Decor ranges from Bavarian provincial to British country house chintz. The large bathrooms have private phones. The major dining room, the Garden-Restaurant, evokes the grandeur of a small palace. A clubby bar serves generous drinks and charcoal specialties, and there's Trader Vic's for Polynesian nights. Facilities include a rooftop pool and garden with bricked sun terrace, gym, sauna, and massage rooms.

○ **Hotel Vier Jahreszeiten München.** Maximilianstrasse 17, D-80539 München. ☎ **800/426-3135** in the U.S., or 089/2125-0. Fax 089/2125-2777. www. kepindki-vierjahreszeilen.de. E-mail: reservations.hyj@kempinski.com. 366 units. A/C MINIBAR TV TEL. 520DM–820DM ($281–$443) double; from 920DM–1,950DM ($497–$1,053) suite. AE, DC, MC, V. Parking 30DM ($16). Tram: 19.

This grand hotel, with a tradition dating from 1858, is the most elegant place to stay in Munich. Rooms range from medium to very spacious. Bedside controls, luxury mattresses and Oriental rugs, plus spacious bathrooms with soft towels, hair dryers, robes, and deluxe toiletries will keep any guest comfortable. Vier Jahreszeiten Restaurant, the hotel's finest dining spot, is open daily; or try the completely refurnished Bistro Eck. There's an indoor pool and sauna, solarium, and sun terrace.

EXPENSIVE

Eden-Hotel-Wolff. Arnulfstrasse 4–8, D-80335 München. ☎ **089/55-11-50.** Fax 089/551-15-555. www.ehw.de. E-mail: sales@ehw.de. 210 units. MINIBAR TV TEL. 290DM–480DM ($157–$259) double; 400DM–600DM ($216–$324) suite. One child up to age 6 stays free in parents' room. Rates include buffet breakfast. AE, DC, MC, V. Parking 20DM ($11). U-Bahn/S-Bahn: Hauptbahnhof.

If you must stay near the train station, this is your best bet. With some exceptions, most rooms are spacious, their styles ranging from modern to rustic Bavarian. Rooms have luxurious mattresses, safes, and double-glazed windows; and the large bathrooms have hair dryers. Some units are hypoallergenic with special beds and a private ventilation system. The main dining room, with its natural-pine ceiling, gleaming brass lantern sconces, and thick stone arches, serves excellent Bavarian dishes.

MODERATE

Advocat Hotel. Baaderstrasse 1, 80469 München. ☎ **089/21-63-10.** Fax 089/21-63-190. E-mail: advokathot@aol.com. 50 units. MINIBAR TV TEL. 260DM ($140). AE, DC, MC, V. S-Bahn: Isartor.

This hotel occupies a six-story 1930s apartment house. Its streamlined interior borrows in discreet ways from Bauhaus and minimalist models. One Munich critic said the rooms look as if Philippe Starck had gone on a shopping binge at Ikea. The result is an aggressively simple, clean-lined, and artfully Spartan hotel with very few amenities and facilities. The German government gave it three stars. There's no restaurant on the premises, though there is a cozy bar. But the prices are reasonable, and the staff is helpful.

An der Oper. Falkenturmstrasse 11, D-80331 München. ☎ **089/290-02-70.** Fax 089/290-02-729. 68 units. TV TEL. 260DM–320DM ($140–$173) double. Rates include buffet breakfast. AE, MC, V. Tram: 19.

Just off Maximilianstrasse, near Marienplatz, this is a superb choice for sightseeing or shopping in the traffic-free malls, just steps from the Bavarian National Theater. Built in the 1970s, it's one of the best-run hotels in this price category. Recently renovated rooms, which range from small to medium, have such amenities as double-glazed windows, firm beds, a small sitting area, and a table for those who want breakfast in their rooms. Bathrooms are medium in size and beautifully maintained.

○ **Gästehaus Englischer Garten.** Liebergesellstrasse 8, D-80802 München-Schwabing. ☎ **089/38-39-41-0.** Fax 089/38-39-41-33. 25 units, 19 with bathroom. MINIBAR TV TEL. 130DM ($70) double without bathroom; 158DM–206DM ($85–$111) double with bathroom; from 220DM ($119) apt. AE, DC, MC, V. Parking 10DM ($5). U-Bahn: Münchner Freiheit.

This oasis of charm and tranquillity, close to the Englischer Garten, is one of our preferred stopovers. The decor of the rooms might be termed "Bavarian grandmother." Antiques, and old-fashioned but comfortable beds (with duvets and fine linen covering firm mattresses), evoke coziness, while Oriental carpets add extra warmth. Bathrooms are small and not one of the hotel's stronger features. In an annex across the street are 15 small apartments, each with bathroom and a tiny kitchenette. Try for room 16, 23, 26, or especially 20; all are more spacious, better furnished, and have better views. In fair weather, breakfast is served in a rear garden for 15DM ($8).

Hotel Mark. Senefelderstrasse 12, D-80336 München. ☎ **089/55-98-20.** Fax 089/559-82-333. 90 units. MINIBAR TV TEL. 190DM–220DM ($103–$119) double. Rates include buffet breakfast. AE, DC, MC, V. Parking 15DM ($8). U-Bahn/S-Bahn: Hauptbahnhof.

This hotel near the Hauptbahnhof's south exit should be considered for its comfort and moderate prices. The rooms are functionally furnished, although a bit cramped, and mattresses were recently renewed, so you should sleep in peace. Bathrooms are small but tidily maintained. Breakfast is the only meal served.

Splendid. Maximilianstrasse 54, D-80538 München. ☎ **089/29-66-06.** Fax 089/29-131-76. 36 units, 30 with bathroom. TV TEL. 205DM–315DM ($111–$170) double without bathroom; 140DM–340DM ($76–$184) double with bathroom; 265DM–520DM ($143–$281) suite. AE, DC, MC, V. U-Bahn: 4 or 5. Tram: 17 or 19.

Splendid is one of the most attractive old-world hotels in Munich, with antiques, Oriental rugs, and chandeliers decorating the public rooms. Room size ranges from small (usually singles) to quite spacious. You'll be comfortable on the firm beds. Bathrooms are medium-sized. You can order breakfast, the only meal served, in your room if you wish, or sit on a trellised patio.

INEXPENSIVE

Am Markt. Heiliggeistrasse 6, D-80331 München. ☎ **089/22-50-14.** Fax 089/22-40-17. 32 units (12 with bathroom). TV TEL. 110DM–116DM ($59–$63) double without bathroom; 150DM–160DM ($81–$86) double with bathroom. Rates include continental breakfast. No credit cards. Parking 12DM ($7). U-Bahn/S-Bahn: Marienplatz.

This popular but basic Bavarian hotel stands in the heart of the older section. You're likely to find yourself surrounded by opera and concert artists who stay here to be close to where they perform. The rooms are trim, neat, and small—space to store your stuff is at a minimum. Mattresses are well worn, but with enough life for comfort. Private bathrooms are also small, and corridor bathrooms are kept quite fresh.

Hotel Jedermann. Bayerstrasse 95, D-80335 München. ☎ **089/54-32-40.** Fax 089/54-32-41-11. www.hotel-jedermann.de. E-mail: hotel-jedermann@cube.net. 55 units (34 with bathroom). TV TEL. 95DM–110DM ($51–$59) double without bathroom; 150DM–240DM ($81–$130) double with bathroom; 130DM–185DM ($70–$100) triple without bathroom; 190 DM–290DM ($103–$157) triple with bathroom. Rates include buffet breakfast. MC, V. Parking 10DM ($5). U-Bahn/S-Bahn: Hauptbahnhof.

This pleasant spot's central location and value make it a good choice. It's especially good for families as both cribs and cots are available. Rooms are generally small and old fashioned, but are cozy and comfortable, with firm mattresses. Private bathrooms are also small but contain adequate towels and a hair dryer. Corridor bathrooms are numerous enough so you don't usually have to wait in line. Most rooms also have a safe. A generous breakfast buffet is served in a charming room.

Pension Westfalia. Mozartstrasse 23, D-80336 München. ☎ **089/53-03-77.** Fax 089/54-39-120. E-mail: pension-westfalia@t-online.de. 19 units (11 with bathroom). TV ☎ 85DM–95DM ($46–$51) double without bathroom; 115DM–130DM ($62–$70) double with bathroom. Rates include buffet breakfast. Credit cards only for reservations. Parking, when available, is free on the street. U-Bahn: Goetheplatz. Bus: 58.

Facing the meadow where the annual Oktoberfest takes place, this four-story town house near Goetheplatz is another of Munich's top pensions. Rooms range from small to medium, but the owner takes great pride in seeing that they are well maintained and comfortable, renewing mattresses as needed. There are few extras, though some rooms have TV. Private bathrooms are small with shower stalls. Corridor bathrooms are well maintained and do the job just as well.

Uhland Garni. Uhlandstrasse 1, 80336 München. ☎ **089/54-33-50.** Fax 089/54-33-52-50. www.hotel-uhland.de. E-mail: hotel-uhland@compuserve.com. 30 units. MINIBAR TV TEL. 150DM–199DM ($81–$107) double. Rates include buffet breakfast. AE, DC, MC, V. Free parking. Bus: 58.

In a residential area, just a 10-minute walk from the Hauptbahnhof, the Uhland could easily become your home in Munich. It offers friendly, personal service. The stately town mansion, built in art-nouveau style, stands in its own small garden. Its rooms are soundproof, snug, traditional, and cozy. The bathrooms contain hair dryers. Only breakfast is served.

WHERE TO DINE

As with the hotels, most of the restaurants listed are in the heart of the city. For beer halls serving plenty of low-priced food, see the box "What's Brewing at the Beer Halls?" later in this chapter.

VERY EXPENSIVE

Gasthaus Glockenbach. Kapuzinerstrasse 29, corner of Maistrasse. ☎ **089/53-40-43.** Reservations recommended. Main courses 40DM–55DM ($22–$30); fixed-price menus 60DM–170DM ($32–$92). AE, MC, V. Tues–Fri noon–2pm (last order); Tues–Sat 7–10pm (last order). Closed for 2 weeks in Aug, 1 week at Christmas. U-Bahn: Goetheplatz. MODERN CONTINENTAL.

The setting is a 200-year-old building, close to a tributary (the Glockenbach) of the Isar. The dignified country-baroque interior is accented with vivid modern paintings and the most elegant table settings in town, including a lavish array of porcelain by a company not well known in the New World, Hutchenreuther. Cuisine changes with the season and according to the inspiration of the chef. Examples include imaginative preparations of venison and pheasant in autumn, lamb and veal dishes in springtime, preparations of whatever shellfish is seasonal at the time, and a medley of ultrafresh vegetables and exotica imported from local farms and from sophisticated purveyors throughout Europe and the world.

✪ **Boettner's.** Pfisterstrasse 9. ☎ **089/22-12-10.** Reservations required. Main courses 48DM–68DM ($26–$37). AE, DC, MC, V. Summer Mon–Sat 11:30am–3pm and 6–10pm. Sept–May Mon–Sat 11:30am–10pm. Sept–May Mon–Sat 11:30am–10pm. U-Bahn/S-Bahn: Marienplatz. INTERNATIONAL.

Long featured in this guide, Boettner's— first opened in 1901 as a tea and oyster shop—has moved to a new location where it has kept its old devotees but gained new and younger fans. The restaurant today is housed in Orlandohaus, a Renaissance structure in the very heart of Munich. Culinary fans from yesterday will recognize its wood-paneled interior, which was dismantled and moved to the site. The cookery is lighter and more refined and seems better than ever. Try the lobster stew in a cream sauce and almost any dish with white truffles. Pike balls appear delectably in a Chablis herb sauce, and succulent lamb or venison also appears enticingly in a woodsy morel sauce. Desserts are as sumptuous as ever. The French influence is very evident, as are many traditional Bavarian recipes.

Restaurant Königshof. In the Hotel Königshof, Karlsplatz 25 (Am Stachus). ☎ **089/55-13-60.** Reservations required. Main courses 48DM–68DM ($2690–$37); fixed-price menus 144DM–174DM ($78–$94). AE, DC, MC, V. Daily noon–2:30pm and 6:45pm–midnight. S-Bahn: Karlsplatz. Tram: 19, 20, or 21. INTERNATIONAL.

The Königshof is no longer the finest hotel dining room in Munich, but it's still near the top. The Geisel family has made major renovations to the dining room, with its oyster-white oak panels and polished bronze chandeliers. The chefs here are both inventive and creative. Culinary masterpieces depend on their whims and what's available in season. Extremely fresh ingredients are used in all the dishes. Perhaps you'll get to try the foie gras with sauternes, loin of lamb with *fines herbes*, lobster with vanilla butter, or sea bass suprême.

✪ **Tantris.** Johann-Fichte-Strasse 7, Schwabing. ☎ **089/3-61-95-90.** Reservations required. Fixed-price 5-course lunch 198DM ($107); fixed-price dinner 198DM ($107) for 5 courses, 225DM ($122) for 8 courses. AE, DC, MC, V. Tues–Sat noon–3pm and 6:30pm–1am (last order 11:30pm). Closed public holidays; annual holidays in Jan and May. U-Bahn: Dietlin-denstrasse. FRENCH/INTERNATIONAL.

Tantris serves Munich's finest cuisine. Chef Hans Haas was voted the top in Germany in 1994, and, if anything, he has refined and sharpened his culinary technique since winning that honor. Once inside, you're transported into an ultramodern atmosphere with fine service. The food is a treat to the eye as well as to the palate. You might begin with a terrine of smoked fish served with green cucumber sauce, then follow with classic roast duck on mustard-seed sauce, or perhaps a delightful concoction of lobster medallions on black noodles. These dishes show a refinement and attention to detail, plus a quest for technical perfection, that you find nowhere else in Munich.

EXPENSIVE

✪ **Alois Dallmayr.** Dienerstrasse 14–15. ☎ **089/213-51-00.** Reservations required. Main courses 25.50DM–43DM ($14–$23). AE, DC, MC, V. Mon–Wed 9:30am–7pm, Thurs–Fri 9:30am–8pm, Sat 9am–4pm. Tram: 19. CONTINENTAL.

Alois Dallmayr's history can be traced back to 1700. Near the Rathaus, it is Germany's most famous delicatessen. After looking at its tempting array of delicacies from around the globe, you'll think you're lost in a millionaire's supermarket. The upstairs dining room serves a subtle German version of continental cuisine, owing a heavy debt to France. The food array is dazzling, ranging from the best herring and sausages we've ever tasted to such rare treats as perfectly vine-ripened tomatoes flown in from Morocco, and papayas from Brazil. Also shipped in is the famous French *poulet de Bresse,* believed by many gourmets to be the world's finest.

Austernkeller. Stollbergstrasse 11. ☎ **089/29-87-87.** Reservations required. Main courses 33DM–49DM ($18–$26). AE, DC, MC, V. Daily 5pm–1am. Closed Dec 23–26. S-Bahn: Isar-torplatz; U-Bahn/S-Bahn: Marienplatz. SEAFOOD.

Here you can feast on the largest selection of the finest oysters in town. Many gourmets make an entire meal of raw oysters; others prefer them elaborately prepared. A delectable dish to start is the shellfish platter with fresh oysters, mussels, clams, scampi, and sea snails, or you might begin with a richly stocked fish soup and go on to lobster thermidor or shrimp grilled in the shell. French meat specialties are also offered. The decor, under a vaulted ceiling, relies on everything from plastic lobsters to old porcelain.

Spatenhaus. Residenzstrasse 12. ☎ **089/290-70-60.** Reservations recommended. Main courses 24.50DM–42.50DM ($13–$23). AE, MC, V. Daily 9:30am–12:30pm and 2–11pm. U-Bahn: Odeonsplatz or Marienplatz. BAVARIAN/INTERNATIONAL.

One of Munich's best-known beer restaurants has wide windows overlooking the opera house on Max-Joseph-Platz. Of course, to be loyal, you should accompany your meal with the restaurant's own beer, Spaten-Franziskaner-Bier. You can sit in an intimate, semiprivate dining nook or at a big table. The Spatenhaus has old traditions, offers typical Bavarian food, and is known for generous portions and reasonable prices. If you want to know what all this fabled Bavarian gluttony is all about, order the "Bavarian plate," which is loaded down with various meats, including lots of pork and sausages.

MODERATE

Buon Gusto (Talamonti). Hochbruckenstrasse 3. ☎ **089/296-383.** Reservations recommended. Main courses 22DM–50DM ($12–$27). AE, MC, V. Mon–Sat noon–11pm. Closed Dec 24–Jan 15. U-Bahn/S-Bahn: Marienplatz. ITALIAN.

Two dining areas include a simple, rustic-looking bistro which looks over an open kitchen, and a more formal and more upscale-looking dining room. Menu items and prices are identical in both areas. Owned and managed by an extended family, the Talamontis, whose members are likely not to speak anything except Italian and German, the restaurant emphasizes fresh ingredients, strong and savory flavors, and food items inspired by the Italian Marches and Tuscany. Examples include ravioli stuffed with mushrooms and herbs, roasted lamb with potatoes, lots of scaloppinis, and fresh fish that seems to taste best when served simply, with oil or butter and lemon. Especially flavorful are the array of risottos whose ingredients change with the seasons. During Oktoberfest and trade fairs, the place is mobbed.

✪ **Hunsiger's Pacific.** Maximiliansplatz 5 (entrance is on the Max-Joseph-Strasse). ☎ **089/5502-9741.** Main courses 26DM–45DM ($14–$24). AE, DC, MC, V. Mon–Fri noon–3pm, daily 6–10:30pm. Closed Sun May–Sept. U-Bahn: Stachus/Odeonsplatz. INTERNATIONAL.

This restaurant is the creative statement of one of the city's most innovative young chefs, Werner Hunsiger. Despite the name, don't expect the menu to be devoted exclusively to Pacific Rim cuisine. Fish is the premier item here. Preparation is based on classic French-inspired methods, but the innovative flavors come from Malaysia (coconut milk), Japan (wasabi), Thailand (lemongrass), and India (curry). You could begin with a tuna carpaccio with sliced plum, fresh ginger, and lime. Main courses include a succulent version of bouillabaisse with aïoli, which you might follow with cold melon soup garnished with a dollop of tarragon-flavored granita. Fried monkfish in the Malaysian style and turbot in chile and ginger sauce are evocative of Hawaii. Prices here are relatively low compared to its competitors.

✪ **Ratskeller München.** Im Rathaus, Marienplatz 8. ☎**089/219-98-90.** Reservations required. Main courses 12DM–28DM ($7–$15). AE, MC, V. Daily 10am–midnight. U-Bahn/ S-Bahn: Marienplatz. BAVARIAN.

Munich is proud to possess one of the best rathskellers in Germany. The decor is typical: lots of dark wood and carved chairs. The most interesting tables, the ones staked out by in-the-know locals, are the semiprivate dining nooks in the rear, under the vaulted painted ceilings. Bavarian music adds to the ambience. The menu, a showcase of regional fare, includes many vegetarian choices, which is unusual for a rathskeller. Some of the dishes are a little heavy and too porky, but you can find lighter fare if you search the menu.

INEXPENSIVE

Andechser am Dom. Weinstrasse 7A. ☎ **089/29-84-81.** Reservations recommended. Main courses 17.50DM–29DM ($9–$16). AE, DC, MC, V. Daily 10am–1am. U-Bahn/S-Bahn: Marienplatz. GERMAN.

Set on two floors of a postwar building erected adjacent to the back side of the Frauenkirche, this restaurant and beer hall serves copious amounts of a beer brewed in a monastery near Munich (Andechser) as well as generous portions of German food. Order a snack, a full meal, or just a beer, and enjoy the frothy fun of it all. Menu items are often accompanied with German-style potato salad and green salad, and include such dishes as veal schnitzels, steaks, turkey croquettes, roasted lamb, fish, and several kinds of sausages that taste best with tangy mustard. During clement weather, tables are set up on the building's roof and on the sidewalk in front, both of which overlook the back of one of the city's most evocative churches.

✪ **Donisl.** Weinstrasse 1. ☎ **089/22-01-84.** Reservations recommended. Main courses 10.50DM–11.95DM ($5–$6). AE, DC, MC, V. Daily 9am–midnight. U-Bahn/S-Bahn: Marienplatz. BAVARIAN/INTERNATIONAL.

Donisl is one of Munich's oldest beer halls, dating from 1715. The seating capacity of this relaxed and comfortable restaurant is about 550, and in summer you can enjoy the hum and bustle of Marienplatz while dining in the garden area out front. The standard menu offers traditional Bavarian food, as well as a weekly changing specials menu. The little white sausages, Weisswürst, are a decades-long tradition here.

Hundskugel. Hotterstrasse 18. ☎ **089/26-42-72.** Reservations required. Main courses 15DM–38DM ($8–$21). No credit cards. Daily 10am–midnight. U-Bahn/S-Bahn: Marienplatz. BAVARIAN.

The city's oldest tavern, Hundskugel dates back to 1440, and apparently serves the same food as it did back then. If it was good a long time ago, why mess with the menu? Built in an alpine style, it's within easy walking distance of Marienplatz. Perhaps half the residents of Munich have at one time or another made their way here to enjoy the honest Bavarian cookery that has no pretensions. Although the chef specializes in *Spanferkel* (roast suckling pig with potato noodles), you might prefer *tafelspitz* (boiled beef) in dill sauce, or roast veal stuffed with goose liver.

Nürnberger Bratwurst Glöckl Am Dom. Frauenplatz 9. ☎ **089/29-52-64.** Reservations recommended. Main courses 20DM–30DM ($11–$16). No credit cards. Daily 9am–1am. U-Bahn/S-Bahn: Marienplatz. BAVARIAN.

In the coziest and warmest of Munich's local restaurants, the chairs look as if they were made by some Black Forest woodcarver, and the place is full of memorabilia—pictures, prints, pewter, and beer steins. Upstairs through a hidden stairway is a dining room decorated with reproductions of Dürer prints. The restaurant has a strict policy of shared tables, and service is on tin plates. The homesick Nürnberger comes here just for one dish: *Nürnberger Schweinwurstl mit Kraut* (little sausages with kraut). Last food orders go in at midnight.

SEEING THE SIGHTS
SIGHTSEEING SUGGESTIONS FOR FIRST-TIME VISITORS

If You Have 1 Day Local tourist tradition calls for a morning breakfast of Weisswürst; head for Donisl (see "Where to Dine"). A true Münchener downs them with a mug of beer. Then walk to **Marienplatz,** with its glockenspiel and **Altes Rathaus** (old town hall). Later, stroll along **Maximilianstrasse,** one of Europe's great shopping streets. In the afternoon, visit the **Neue Pinakothek** and see at least some exhibits at the **Deutsches Museum.** Cap the evening with a night of Bavarian food, beer, and music at the **Hofbräuhaus am Platzl.**

If You Have 2 Days   In the morning of Day 2, visit the **Bayerisches Nationalmuseum (Bavarian National Museum),** with three vast floors devoted to Bavaria's artistic and historical riches. If the weather's right, plan a lunch in one of the beer gardens of the **Englischer Garten.** In the afternoon, visit the **Nymphenburg Palace,** summer residence of the Wittelsbach dynasty, longtime rulers of Bavaria.

If You Have 3 Days   Pass your third day exploring the sights you've missed so far: the **Residenz,** the **Antikensammlungen (Museum of Antiquities),** and the **Glyptothek.** If you have any more time, return to the Deutsches Museum. Enjoy dinner or at least a drink at **Olympiapark,** enjoying a panoramic view of the Alps.

If You Have 4 or More Days   As fascinating as Munich is, tear yourself away on Day 4 for a excursion to the **Royal Castles** once occupied by the "mad king" Ludwig II (see "Organized Tours" and "The Romantic Road"). On Day 5, take an excursion to **Dachau,** the notorious World War II concentration camp, and in the afternoon visit **Mittenwald** for a taste of the Bavarian Alps.

EXPLORING THE ALTSTADT (OLD TOWN)

Marienplatz, dedicated to the patron of the city whose statue stands on a huge column in the center of the square, is the heart of the Altstadt. On its north side is the **Neues Rathaus** (New City Hall) built in 19th-century Gothic style. Each day at 11am, and also at noon and 5pm in the summer, the **Glockenspiel** on the facade performs a miniature tournament, with enameled copper figures moving in and out of the archways. Since you're already at the Rathaus, you may wish to climb the 55 steps to the top of its tower (an elevator is available if you're conserving energy) for a good overall view of the city center. The **Altes Rathaus** (Old City Hall), with its plain Gothic tower, is to the right. It was reconstructed in the 15th century, after being destroyed by fire.

MUSEUMS & PALACES

By summer 2001, a new museum, the **Pinakothek der Moderne,** will open beside the Alte Pinakothek, with international art of the 20th century, including works by Braque, Matisse, Marc, Kandinsky, Ernst, Kirchner, Dix, Rauschenberg, Picasso, and Jasper Johns. Check with the tourist office for details.

✪ **Alte Pinakothek.** Barer Strasse 27. ☎ **089/238-050.** Admission 7DM ($3.80) adults, 4DM ($2.15) students, free for children 14 and under. Combination ticket to Neue Pinakothek, Alte Pinakothek, and State Gallery of Modern Art, 12DM ($7) adults, 6DM ($3.25) students and seniors, 4DM ($2.15) children. Tues–Wed and Fri–Sun 10am–5pm, Tues and Thurs 10am–8pm. U-Bahn: Theresienstrasse. Tram: 27. Bus: 53.

This is one of the most significant art museums in Europe. The nearly 900 paintings on display in this huge neoclassical building represent the greatest European artists of the 14th through the 18th century. Begun as a small court collection by the royal Wittelsbach family in the early 1500s, the collection has grown and grown. There are two floors with exhibits, but the museum is immense.

Albrecht Altdorfer, landscape painter *par excellence* of the Danube school, is represented by no fewer than six monumental works. Albrecht Dürer's works include his greatest—and final—*Self-Portrait* (1500). Here the artist has portrayed himself with almost Christ-like solemnity. Also displayed is the last great painting by the artist, his two-paneled work called *The Four Apostles* (1526).

Antikensammlungen (Museum of Antiquities). Königsplatz 1. ☎ **089/59-83-59.** Admission 6DM ($3.25) adults, 3.50DM ($1.90) students and children. Combination ticket to the Museum of Antiquities and the Glyptothek, 10DM ($5) adults, 5DM ($2.70) students and children. Tues and Thurs–Sun 10am–5pm, Wed 10am–8pm. U-Bahn: Königsplatz.

On the south side of Königsplatz, five main-floor halls house more than 650 Greek vases. The oldest piece is "the goddess from Aegina" from 3000 B.C. This pre-Mycenaean figure, carved from a mussel shell, is on display with the Mycenaean pottery exhibits in Room I. Take the stairs down to the lower level to see the collection of Greek, Roman, and Etruscan jewelry.

✪ Bayerisches Nationalmuseum (Bavarian National Museum). Prinzregentenstrasse 3. ☎ **089/21-124-1.** Admission 4DM ($2.15) adults, 3DM ($1.60) students and seniors, free for children under 15. No admission on Sun. Tues–Sun 9:30am–5pm. U-Bahn: Lehel. Tram: 17. Bus: 53.

Three vast floors of sculpture, painting, folk art, ceramics, furniture, textiles, and scientific instruments demonstrate Bavaria's artistic and historical riches. Entering the museum, turn to the right and go into the first large gallery called the **Wessobrunn Room.** Devoted to early church art from the 5th to the 13th century, this room holds some of the oldest and most valuable works. The desk case contains ancient and medieval ivories, including the so-called Munich ivory, from about A.D. 400.

The **Riemenschneider Room** is devoted to the works of the great sculptor Tilman Riemenschneider (ca. 1460–1531) and his contemporaries. The second floor contains a fine collection of stained and painted glass—an art in which medieval Germany excelled—baroque ivory carvings, Meissen porcelain, and ceramics.

✪ Deutsches Museum (German Museum of Masterpieces of Science and Technology). Museuminsel 1. ☎ **089/2-17-91.** Admission 12DM ($7) adults, 7DM ($3.80) seniors, 5DM ($2.70) students; children 6 and under free. Daily 9am–5pm (closes at 2pm the second Wed in Dec). Closed major holidays. S-Bahn: Isartor. Tram: 18.

On an island in the Isar River is the largest technological museum of its kind in the world. Its huge collection of priceless artifacts and historic originals includes the first electric dynamo (Siemens, 1866), the first automobile (Benz, 1886), the first diesel engine (1897), and the laboratory bench at which the atom was first split (Hahn, Strassmann, 1938). There are hundreds of buttons to push, levers to crank, and gears to turn, as well as a knowledgeable staff to answer questions and demonstrate how steam engines, pumps, or historical musical instruments work. Among the most popular displays are those on mining, with a series of model coal, salt, and iron mines, as well as the electrical power hall, with high-voltage displays that actually produce lightning. There are many other exhibits, covering the whole range of science and technology.

Glyptothek. Königsplatz 3. ☎ **089/28-61-00.** Admission 6DM ($3.25) adults, 3DM ($1.60) students and seniors, 1DM (55¢) children. Combination ticket to the Museum of Antiquities and the Glyptothek, 10DM ($5), 5DM ($2.70) for students and children, free for children under 14. Tues–Sun 10am–5pm. U-Bahn: Königsplatz.

The Glyptothek supplements the pottery and smaller pieces of the main museum with an excellent collection of ancient Greek and Roman sculpture. Included are the famous pediments from the temple of Aegina, two marvelous statues of *kouroi* (youths) from the 6th century B.C., the colossal figure of a *Sleeping Satyr* from the Hellenistic period, and a splendid collection of Roman portraits.

Neue Pinakothek. Barer Strasse 29. ☎ **089/23-80-51-95.** Admission 7DM ($3.80) adults, 4DM ($2.15) students and seniors, free for children 15 and under. Combination ticket to Neue

Pinakothek, Alte Pinakothek, and State Gallery of Modern Art, 12DM ($7) adults, 6DM ($3.25) students and seniors, 4DM ($2.15) children. Tues 10am–8pm; Wed–Sun 10am–5pm. U-Bahn: Theresienstrasse. Tram: 27. Bus: 53.

Neue Pinakothek offers a survey of 18th- and 19th-century art. Across Theresienstrasse from the Alte Pinakothek, the museum has paintings by Gainsborough, Goya, David, Manet, van Gogh, and Monet. Among the more popular German artists represented are Wilhelm Leibl and Gustav Klimt. Note particularly the genre paintings by Carl Spitzweg.

✪ **Residenz.** Max-Joseph-Platz 3. ☎ **089/29-06-71.** Combination ticket for Residenzmuseum and Schatzkammer 12DM ($7) adults, 8DM ($4.30) students/seniors, free for ages 15 and under. Ticket for either Schatzkammer or Residenzmuseum 7DM ($3.80) adults, 5DM ($2.70) seniors/students, free for age 15 and under. Museum and Treasury, Tues–Sun 10am–4:30pm (last tickets sold at 4pm); Theater, Mon–Sat 2–5pm, Sun 10am–5pm. U-Bahn: Odeonsplatz.

The official residence of Bavaria's rulers from 1385 to 1918, the complex is a conglomerate of various styles of art and architecture. Depending on how you approach the Residenz, you might first see a German Renaissance hall (the western facade), a Palladian palace (on the north), or a Florentine Renaissance palace (on the south facing Max-Joseph-Platz). The Residenz has been completely restored since its almost total destruction in World War II and now houses the Residenz Museum, a concert hall, the Cuvilliés Theater, and the Residenz Treasure House.

Residenzmuseum, Max-Joseph-Platz 3 (☎089/29-06-71), comprises the southwestern section of the palace, some 120 rooms of art and furnishings collected by centuries of Wittelsbachs. To see the entire collection, you'll have to take two tours, one in the morning and the other in the afternoon. You may also visit the rooms on your own.

If you have time to view only one item in the **Schatzkammer** (Treasure House), make it the 16th-century Renaissance statue of *St. George Slaying the Dragon.* The equestrian statue is made of gold, but you can barely see the precious metal for the thousands of diamonds, rubies, emeralds, sapphires, and semiprecious stones embedded in it.

From the Brunnenhof, you can visit the **Cuvilliés Theater,** whose rococo tiers of boxes are supported by seven bacchants. The huge box, where the family sat, is in the center. In summer, this theater is the scene of frequent concert and opera performances. Mozart's *Idomeneo* was first performed here in 1781.

✪ **Schloss Nymphenburg.** Schloss Nymphenburg 1. ☎ **089/17-908-668.** Admission to all attractions 8DM ($4.30), free for children 14 and under. Nymphenburg Palace, Amalienburg, Marstallmuseum, and museum of porcelain 5DM ($2.70), free for children 14 and under. Apr–Sept Tues–Sun 10am–noon and 1:30–5pm. Oct–Mar Tues–Sun 10am–noon and 1:30–4pm. Parking beside the Marstallmuseum. U-Bahn: Rotkreuzplatz, then tram no. 17 toward Amalienburgstrasse. Bus: 41.

In summer, the Wittelsbachs would pack up their bags and head for their country house, Schloss Nymphenburg. A more complete, more sophisticated palace than the Residenz, it was begun in 1664 in Italian villa style and went through several architectural changes before completion.

The main building's great hall, decorated in rococo colors and stuccos with frescoes by Zimmermann (1756), was used for both banquets and concerts in the 18th century. Concerts are still presented here in summer. From the main building, turn left and head for the arcaded gallery connecting the northern pavilions. The first room in the arcade is the Great Gallery of Beauties. More provocative, however, is Ludwig I's

Gallery of Beauties in the south pavilion (the apartments of Queen Caroline). Ludwig commissioned no fewer than 36 portraits of the most beautiful women of his day. The paintings by J. Stieler include the *Schöne Münchnerin (Lovely Munich Girl)* and a portrait of Lola Montez, the dancer whose "friendship" with Ludwig I caused a scandal that factored into the Revolution of 1848.

CHURCHES

When the smoke cleared from the 1945 bombings, only a fragile shell remained of Munich's largest church, the ✪ **Frauenkirche** (Cathedral of Our Lady), Frauenplatz 1 (U-Bahn/S-Bahn: Marienplatz). Workmen and architects who restored the 15th-century Gothic cathedral used whatever remains they could find in the rubble, along with modern innovations. The overall effect of the rebuilt Frauenkirche is strikingly simple yet dignified. The twin towers, which remained intact, have been a city landmark since 1525. Instead of the typical flying buttresses, huge props on the inside that separate the side chapels support the edifice. The gothic vaulting over the nave and chancel is borne by 22 simple octagonal pillars. Except for the tall chancel window, when you enter the main doors at the west end, you don't notice windows; they're hidden by the enormous pillars. According to legend, the devil laughed at the notion of hidden windows and stamped in glee at the stupidity of the architect—you can still see the strange footlike mark called "the devil's step" in the entrance hall.

Peterskirche (St. Peter's Church), Rindermarkt 1 (☎ **089/260-48-28;** U-Bahn/S-Bahn: Marienplatz), is Munich's oldest church (1180). Its tall steeple is worth the climb in clear weather for a view as far as the Alps. In its gilded baroque interior are murals by Johann Baptist Zimmermann. The **Asamkirche,** Sendlinger Strasse (U-Bahn/S-Bahn: Sendlingertor), is a remarkable example of rococo, designed by the Asam brothers, Cosmas Damian and Edgar Quirin, in 1733 to 1746. The **Michaelskirche,** Neuhauser Strasse 52 (U-Bahn/S-Bahn: Karlsplatz), has the distinction of being the largest Renaissance church north of the Alps. The lovely **Theatinerkirche,** Theatinerstrasse 22 (U-Bahn/S-Bahn: Odeonsplatz), with its graceful fluted columns and arched ceilings, is the work of the court architect, François Cuvilliés and his son.

ORGANIZED TOURS

The easiest, and fastest, ways to gain an overview of Munich is on a guided tour. One of the largest organizers of these tours is **Panorama Tours** (an affiliate of Gray Line), Arnulfstrasse 8 (☎ **089/550-28995;** U-Bahn/S-Bahn: Hauptbahnof), just north of the Hauptbahnof. At least a half-dozen touring options are available, ranging from a quickie 1-hour overview of the city to full-day excursions to such outlying sites as Berchtesgaden, Oberammergau, and Hohenschwangau, site of three of Bavaria's most stunning palaces.

City tours encompass aspects of both modern and medieval Munich, and depart from the main railway station aboard blue-sided buses. Departures, depending on the season and the tour, occur between two and eight times a day, and tours are conducted in both German and English. Most tours don't last more than 2^1/2 hours, with the exception of a scientific odyssey that focuses on the technological triumphs of Munich as witnessed by various museums that include the Deutsches Museum. That experience usually lasts for a minimum of 4 hours, plus whatever time you spend wandering through museums at the end of your tour.

Depending on the tour, adults pay 17DM to 49DM ($9 to $26); children under 12 pay between 9DM to 29DM ($4.85 to $16). Advance reservations for most city tours aren't required, and you can buy your ticket from the bus driver at the time you board.

If you want to participate in any tour that covers attractions outside the city limits, advance reservations are required, especially if you want the bus to pick you up at any of Munich's hotels. Travel agents in Munich, as well as the concierge or reception staff at your hotel, can book any of these tours, but if you want to contact Panorama Tours directly, they're open May and October, daily 7:30am to 6pm; November to April, Tuesday, Thursday, and Saturday 7:30am to 6pm, and Monday, Wednesday, and Friday 9am to 6pm.

Pedal pushers will want to try Mike Lasher's **Mike's Bike Tour** (☎ 089/651-4275). His bike rentals for 33DM ($18) include maps and locks, child and infant seats, and helmets at no extra charge. English and bilingual tours of central Munich run March through November, leaving daily at 12:30pm (call to confirm). The cost of the tour is included in rental fee.

THE SHOPPING SCENE

The most interesting shops are concentrated on Munich's pedestrians-only streets between **Karlsplatz** and **Marienplatz.**

Handmade crafts can be found on the fourth floor of Munich's major department store, **Ludwig Beck am Rathauseck,** Am Marienplatz 11 (☎ 089/236-91-00; U-Bahn/S-Bahn: Marienplatz), and ✪ **Wallach,** Residenzstrasse 3 (☎ 089/22-08-71; U-Bahn/S-Bahn: Odeonplatz), is a fine place to obtain handcrafts and folk art, both new and antique. Shop here for a memorable object to remind you of your trip. You'll find antique churns, old hand-painted wooden boxes and trays, painted porcelain clocks, and many other items.

✪ **Dirndl-Ecke,** Am Platzl 1/Sparkassenstrasse 10 (☎ 089/22-01-63; U-Bahn/S-Bahn: Marienplatz), 1 block up from the famed Hofbräuhaus, gets our unreserved recommendation as a stylish place specializing in dirndls, feathered alpine hats, and all the clothing associated with the alpine regions. Everything is of the best quality—there's no tourist junk. Bavarian clothing for children is also available.

The founders of **Hemmerle,** Maximilianstrasse 14 (☎ 089/24-22-600), made their fortune designing bejeweled fantasies for the Royal Bavarian Court of the fairy-tale king, Ludwig II. Today, all pieces are limited editions, designed and made in-house by Bavarian craftspeople.

On the grounds of Schloss Nymphenburg at Nördliches Schlossrondell 8, you'll find **Nymphenburger Porzellan-manufaktur** (☎ 089/17-91-970; U-Bahn: Rotkreuzplatz, then tram no. 17 toward Amalienburgstrasse; Bus: 41), one of Germany's most famous porcelain makers. You can visit the exhibition and sales rooms; shipments can be arranged if you make purchases. There's also a branch in Munich's center, at Odeonsplatz 1 (☎ 089/28-24-28; U-Bahn/S-Bahn: Odeonplatz).

MUNICH AFTER DARK

To find out what's happening in the Bavarian capital, go to the tourist office and buy a copy of *Monats-programm.* This pamphlet contains complete information about what's going on in Munich and how to purchase tickets.

THE PERFORMING ARTS

Nowhere else in Europe, other than London and Paris, will you find so many musical and theatrical performances. And the good news is the low cost of the seats—you'll get good tickets if you're willing to pay anywhere from 15DM to 75DM ($8 to $41).

A part of the Residenz (see "Museums & Palaces"), ✪ **Altes Residenztheater** (Cuvilliés Theater), Residenzstrasse 1 (☎ 089/2185-19-40; U-Bahn: Odeonsplatz), is a sightseeing attraction in its own right, and Germany's most outstanding example of a rococo tier-boxed theater. During World War II, the interior was dismantled and stored. You can tour it Monday to Friday 2 to 5pm and Sunday 10am to 5pm. The **Bavarian State Opera** and the **Bayerisches Staatsschauspiel (State Theater Company)** perform smaller works here in keeping with the tiny theater's intimate character. Box-office hours are Monday to Friday 10am to 6pm, plus 1 hour before performances; Saturday 10am to 1pm only. Opera tickets are 30 to 255DM ($16 to $138); theater tickets, 20 to 71DM ($11 to $38); building tours 3DM ($1.60).

The regular season of the **Deutsches Theater,** Schwanthalerstrasse 13 (☎ 089/552-34-444; U-Bahn: Karlsplatz/Stachus), lasts throughout the year. Musicals, operettas, ballets, and international shows are performed here. During carnival season (January to February) the theater becomes a ballroom for more than 2,000 guests. Tickets are 40 to 115DM ($22 to $62), higher for special events.

The ✪ **Gasteig München GmbH,** Rosenheimer Strasse 5 ☎ 089/48-09-80; S-Bahn: Rosenheimerplatz; tram: 18; bus: 51), is the home of the **Münchner Philharmoniker** (Munich Philharmonic), founded in 1893. Its present home opened in 1985 and shelters the Richard Strauss Conservatory and the Munich Municipal Library. The orchestra performs in Philharmonic Hall, which has the largest seating capacity of the center's five halls. Purchase tickets Monday to Friday 9am to 6pm, Saturday 9am to 2pm. The Philharmonic season runs mid-September to July. Tickets are 17 to 95DM ($9 to $51).

Practically any night of the year, except August to mid-September, you'll find a performance at the ✪ **Nationaltheater,** Max-Joseph-Platz 2 (☎ 089/2185-1920; U-Bahn/S-Bahn; Marienplatz or Odeonsplatz), home of the **Bavarian State Opera,** one of the world's great opera companies. The productions are beautifully mounted and presented, and sung by famous singers. Hard-to-get tickets may be purchased Monday to Friday 10am to 6pm, plus 1 hour before performance; Saturday 10am to 1pm. The Nationaltheater is also home to the Bavarian State Ballet. Opera tickets are 12 to 375DM ($7 to $203); ballet tickets, 8 to 130DM ($4.30 to $70).

THE CLUB & MUSIC SCENE

You'll find some of Munich's most sophisticated entertainment at **Bayerischer Hof Night Club,** in the Hotel Bayerischer Hof, Promenadeplatz 2–6 (☎ 089/212-09-94; tram: 19). Within one very large room is a piano bar where a musician plays melodies every night except Monday 7 to 10pm. Behind a partition that disappears at 10pm, there's a bandstand for live orchestras, which play to a crowd of dancing patrons until 3 or 4am. The piano bar is free, but there's a nightclub cover charge of 45DM ($24). Daily happy hour is 7 to 8:30pm in the piano bar with drinks starting at 9DM ($4.85).

Jazzclub Unterfahrt, Einstienstrasse 42 (☎ 089/448-27-94; U-Bahn/S-Bahn: Ostbahnhof), is Munich's leading jazz club, lying near the Ostbahnhof in the Haidhausen district. The club presents live music Tuesday to Sunday 8:30pm to 1am (it opens at 8pm). Wine, small snacks, beer, and drinks are sold as well. Sunday night there's a special jam session for improvisation. Cover Tuesday to Saturday is 18 to 28DM ($10 to $15), Sun jam session 30DM ($16). Club members pay half of regular cover. Small, dark, and popular with blues and jazz aficionados, **Mister B's,** Herzog-Heinrichstrasse 38 (☎ 089/534901; U-Bahn: Goetheplatz), hosts a slightly older, mellower crowd than the rock and dance clubs. Open Tuesday to Sunday 8pm to 3am. Blues, jazz, and rhythm-and-blues combos take the stage Thursday to Saturday. Cover is 8 to 10DM ($4.30 to $5).

Set in a huge factory warehouse, **Nachtwerk,** Landesbergerstrasse 185 (☎ 089/578-3800; S-Bahn: Donnersbergerbrücke), is a mostly straight dance club

What's Brewing at the Beer Halls?

The world's most famous beer hall, ✪ **Hofbraühaus am Platzl,** Am Platzl 9 (☎ **089/22-16-76;** U-Bahn/S-Bahn: Marienplatz), is a legend. Visitors with only 1 night in Munich usually target the Hofbräuhaus as their top nighttime destination. Owned by the state, the present Hofbräuhaus was built at the end of the 19th century, but the tradition of a beer house on this spot dates from 1589. In the 19th century it attracted artists, students, and civil servants and was known as the Blue Hall because of its dim lights and smoky atmosphere. When it grew too small to contain everybody, architects designed another in 1897. This one was the 1920 setting for the notorious meeting of Hitler's newly launched German Workers Party. Today, 4,500 beer drinkers can crowd in on a given night. Several rooms are spread over three floors, including a top-floor room for dancing. The ground floor, with its brass band (which starts playing at 11am), is exactly what you expect of a beer hall—here it's eternal Oktoberfest. It's open daily 9:30am to midnight.

In a century-old house northwest of Schwabing at the edge of Luitpold Park, **Bamberger Haus,** Brunnerstrasse 2 (☎ **089/308-89-66;** U-Bahn: Scheidplatz), is named after the city most noted for the quantity of beer its residents drink. Bavarian and international specialties served in the street-level restaurant include well-seasoned soups, grilled steak, veal, pork, and sausages. If you only want to drink, visit the rowdier and less expensive beer hall in the cellar, where a large beer is 5.50DM ($2.95). The restaurant is open daily noon to midnight and the beer hall daily 5pm to 1am; in summer, weather permitting, a beer garden is open daily 11am to 11pm.

Englischer Garten, the park between the Isar River and Schwabing, is the biggest city-owned park in Europe. It has a main restaurant and several beer gardens, of which the ✪ **Biergärten Chinesischer Turm,** Englischer Garten 3 (☎ **089/38-38-730;** U-Bahn: Giselastrasse; bus: 54 or 154), is our favorite. It takes its name from its location at the foot of a pagoda-like tower. Plenty of beer and cheap Bavarian food are what you get here. A large glass or mug of beer (ask for *ein mass Bier*), enough to bathe in, costs 9.50DM ($5). Homemade dumplings are a specialty, as are all kinds of tasty sausage. Oompah bands often play. It's open daily 10am to 11pm (closed January 11 to February 5).

On the principal pedestrian-only street of Munich, **Augustinerbrau,** Neuhäuserstrasse 27 (☎ **089/231-83-257;** U-Bahn/S-Bahn: Stachus; tram: 19), offers generous helpings of food, good beer, and a mellow atmosphere. It's been around for a little less than a century, but beer was first brewed on this spot in 1328. The cuisine is not for dieters: It's hearty, heavy, and starchy, but it sure soaks up that beer. Hours are daily 9am to midnight. **Waldwirtschaft Grosshesslohe,** George-Kalb-Strasse 3 (☎ **089/74-99-4030;** tram: 7), is a popular summertime rendezvous seating some 2,000 drinkers. The gardens are open daily 11am to 11pm (they have to close early because neighborhood residents complain). Music ranges from Dixieland to English jazz to Polish bands. Entrance is free and you bring your own food. It's above the Isar River in the vicinity of the zoo.

that also books bands. It's a festive place that's not nearly as pretentious as other more "exclusive" discos (the doorman won't send you away for wearing the wrong shoes or pants). Open Thursday 10pm to 4am; Friday and Saturday 10:30pm. Cover is 10DM ($6). **Parkcafé,** Sophienstrasse 7 (☎ **089/59-83-13;** U-Bahn: Lebachplatz), contains five lively bars, two of them outfitted like the inside of a ship plus a strident color scheme using oranges and reds, among other colors. Who'd ever guess this home to chic freaks was a Nazi hangout in the 1930s? Many nights are themed, ranging from "Black Beat" music on Wednesday to "gay Sundays." It's open Wednesday to Sunday 10pm to 4am. It's also open the first Tuesday of every month from 11pm to 4am. Cover 10DM ($5).

THE BAR & CAFE SCENE

Once a literary cafe, **Alter Simpl,** Türkenstrasse 57 (☎ **089/272-30-83;** U-Bahn: University; tram: 18; bus: 53), attracts a diverse crowd of locals, including young people. The real fun begins after 11pm, when the iconoclastic artistic ferment becomes more reminiscent of Berlin than Bavaria. Open Sunday to Thursday 11am to 3am, Friday and Saturday 11am to 4am.

Nachtcafé, Maximilianplatz 5 (☎ **089/59-59-00;** tram: 19), hums, thrives, and captures the nocturnal imagination of everyone—no other nightspot in Munich attracts such an array of soccer stars, film celebrities, literary figures, and, as one employee put it, "ordinary people, but only the most sympathetically crazy ones." Waves of patrons appear at different times of the evening: at 11pm, when live concerts begin; at 2am, when the restaurants close; and at 4am, when die-hard revelers seek a final drink in the predawn hours. The music is jazz, blues, funk, and soul and the decor is updated 1950s. There's no cover. Open daily 9pm to 6am.

Schumann's, Maximilianstrasse 36 (☎ **089/22-90-60;** tram: 19), doesn't waste any money on decor—it depends on the local *beau monde* to keep it looking chic. In warm weather the terrace spills out onto the street. Schumann's is known as a "thinking man's bar." Charles Schumann, author of three bar books, wanted a bar that would be an artistic, literary, and communicative social focus of the metropolis. Popular with the film, advertising, and publishing worlds, his place is said to have contributed to a remarkable renaissance of bar culture in the city. Open Sunday 6pm to 3am, Monday to Friday 5pm to 3am, closed Saturday.

GAY & LESBIAN CLUBS

Much of Munich's gay and lesbian scene takes place in the blocks between the Viktualienmarkt and Gärtnerplatz, particularly on Hans-Sachs-Strasse.

The strident rhythms and electronic sounds of **New York,** Sonnenstrasse 25 (☎ **089/59-10-56;** U-Bahn: Sendlingertorplatz), might just have been imported from New York, Los Angeles, or Paris. The sound system is accompanied by laser-light shows. This is Munich's premier gay male disco. Most clients, ranging in age from 20 to 35, wear jeans. There's no cover Monday to Thursday; Friday to Sunday cover is 10DM ($5) including the first drink. It's open daily 11pm. **Soul City,** Maximilianplatz 5 (☎ **089/595272;** U-Bahn: Karlsplatz), is *the* gay dance club in Munich. Scattered nooks allow conversation sheltered from one of the best sound systems in the city, as well as offering a brief respite from the throng on the dance floor and at the bar. The 10DM ($5) cover charge on Thursday and Friday includes free drinks, and on Saturday you get discounted drink coupons. Open Sunday to Thursday 10pm to 4am, and Friday and Saturday 10pm to 6am.

Teddy Bar, Hans-Sachsstrasse 1 (☎ **089/260-33-59;** U-Bahn: Sendlingertor; tram: 17, 18 or 27), is a small, cozy gay bar decorated with teddy bears. It draws a congenial crowd, both foreign and domestic. There's no cover. From October to April, there's a Sunday brunch 11am to 3pm. Open daily 6pm to 3am. Other hot spots include **Mylord,** Ickstattstrasse 2A (☎ **089/260-44-98;** U-Bahn: Sendlingertorplatz; tram: 17), for 3 decades a lesbian hangout, although drawing a mixed crowd these days, often actors, writers, and musicians, even transvestites and transsexuals. It has a cozy living room atmosphere. Open Sunday to Thursday 6pm to 1am, Friday and Saturday 6pm to 3am.

It is said that if Rick (that is, Bogie of *Casblanca*) were alive today, he'd be operating **Club Morizz,** Klenzestrasse 43 (☎ **089/2-01-67-76;** U-Bahn: Fraunhofer-strasse), a stylish gay bar ringed with mirrors. Relax with drinks or food in red leather armchairs clustered around marble-topped tables. The electric menu includes well-prepared Thai dishes, as well as European specialties. Open Sunday to Thursday 7pm to 2am, Friday and Saturday 7pm to 3am.

DAY TRIPS FROM MUNICH

DACHAU In 1933, what had once been a quiet little artists' community just 16km (10 miles) from Munich became a tragic symbol of the Nazi era. In March, shortly after Hitler became chancellor, Himmler and the SS set up the first German concentration camp on the grounds of a former ammunition factory. Countless prisoners arrived at Dachau between 1933 and 1945. Although the files show a registry of more than 206,000, the exact number of people imprisoned here is unknown.

Entering the camp, **KZ-Gedenkstätte Dachau,** Alte-Römar-Strasse 75 (☎ **08131/1741**), you are faced by three memorial chapels—Catholic, Protestant, and Jewish. Immediately behind the Catholic chapel is the Lagerstrasse, the main camp road lined with poplar trees, once flanked by 32 barracks, each housing 208 prisoners. Two barracks have been rebuilt to give visitors insight into the conditions endured by the prisoners.

The **museum** is housed in the large building that once contained the kitchen, laundry, and shower bathrooms where the SS often brought prisoners for torture. Photographs, documents, and exhibits depict the rise of the Nazi regime and the history of the camp.

Getting There Take the frequent S-Bahn S2 train (direction: Petershausen) from the Hauptbahnhof to the Dachau station, and then bus 724 or 726 from the station to the camp. Admission is free, the camp is open Tuesday to Sunday 9am to 5pm. The English version of a documentary film, *KZ-Dachau,* is shown at 11:30am, 2:30 and 3:30pm.

HERRENCHIEMSEE & THE NEUES SCHLOSS Known as the "Bavarian Sea," Chiemsee is one of the Bavarian Alps' most beautiful lakes in a serene landscape. Its main attraction lies on the island of Herrenchiemsee where "Mad" King Ludwig II built one of his fantastic castles.

✪ **Neues Schloss,** begun in 1878, was never completed because of the king's death in 1886. The castle was to have been a replica of the grand palace of Versailles that Ludwig so admired. One of the architects was Julius Hofmann, whom the king had also employed for the construction of his alpine castle, Neuschwanstein. When work was halted in 1886, only the center of the enormous palace had been completed. The palace and its formal gardens remain one of the most fascinating of Ludwig's adventures, in spite of their unfinished state.

The splendid Great Hall of Mirrors most authentically replicates Versailles. The 17 door panels contain enormous mirrors reflecting the 33 crystal chandeliers and the 44 gilded candelabra. The vaulted ceiling is covered with 25 paintings depicting the life of Louis XIV. The dining room is a popular attraction because of "the little table that lays itself." A mechanism in the floor permitted the table to go down to the room below to be cleared and relaid between courses.

You can visit Herrenchiemsee at any time of the year. From April to September 30, tours are given daily 9am to 5pm; off-season, 10am to 4pm. Admission (in addition

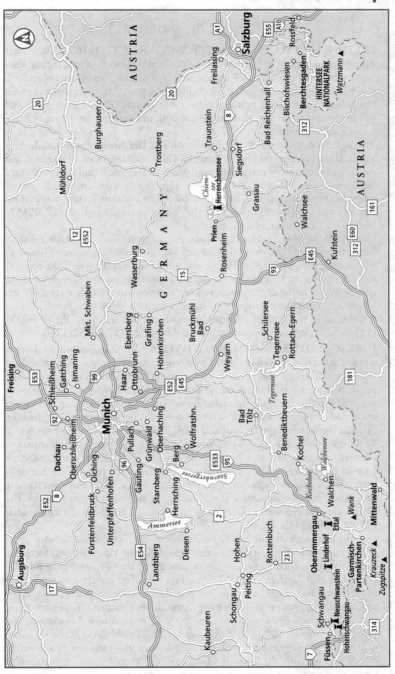

Outdoors in the Bavarian Alps

HITTING THE SLOPES & OTHER WINTER ACTIVITIES   The winter **skiing** here is the best in Germany. A regular winter snowfall in January and February measures from 12 to 20 inches, which in practical terms means about 6 feet of snow in the areas served by ski lifts. The great **Zugspitzplatt** snowfield can be reached in spring or autumn by a rack railway. The Zugspitze at 9,720 feet above sea level is the tallest mountain peak in Germany. Ski slopes begin at a height of 8,700 feet.

The second great ski district in the Alps is **Berchtesgadener Land,** with alpine skiing centered on Jenner, Rossfeld, Götschen, and Hochschwarzeck, and consistently good snow conditions until March. Here you'll find a cross-country skiing center and many miles of tracks kept in first-class condition, natural toboggan runs, one artificial ice run for toboggan and skibob runs, artificial ice skating, and ice-curling rinks. Call the local "Snow-Telefon" at ☎ **08652/967-297** for current snow conditions.

Between October and February, you can use the world-class **ice-skating** rink in Berchtesgaden (the Eisstadion). Less reliable, but more evocative of Bavaria's wild open spaces, involves skating on the surface of the Hintersee Lake once it's sufficiently frozen. Rarer is an ice-skating experience on the Königsee, whose surface freezes to the degree where you can skate on average only once every ten winters. A particularly cozy way to spend a winter's night is to huddle with a companion in the back of a **horse-drawn sled.** For a fee of 40DM to 50DM ($22 to $27) per hour, this can be arranged by calling ☎ **08652/1760.**

HIKING & OTHER SUMMER ACTIVITIES   In summer, **alpine hiking** is a major attraction—climbing mountains, enjoying nature, watching animals in the forest. Hikers are able at times to observe endangered species firsthand. One of the best areas for hiking is the 4,060-foot **Eckbauer,** lying on the southern fringe of Partenkirchen (the tourist office at Garmisch-Partenkirchen will supply maps and details). Many visitors come to the Alps in summer just to hike through the **Berchtesgaden National Park,** bordering the Austrian province of Salzburg. The 8,091-foot Watzmann Mountain, the Königssee (Germany's cleanest, clearest lake), and parts of the Jenner—the pride of Berchtesgaden's four ski areas—are within the boundaries of the national park, which has well-mapped trails cut through protected areas, leading the hiker along spectacular flora and fauna. Information about hiking in the park is provided by the **Nationale Parkverwaltung,** Franciscanalplatz 7, D-83471 Berchtesgaden (☎ **08652/64343).**

From Garmisch-Partenkirchen, serious hikers can embark on full-day or, if they're more ambitious, overnight alpine treks, following clearly marked footpaths and staying in isolated mountain huts maintained by the German Alpine Association (Deutscher Alpenverein/DAV). Some huts are staffed and serve meals. For the truly remote unsupervised huts, you'll be provided with information on how to gain access, and your responsibility in leaving them tidy after your visit. For information, inquire at the local tourist office or write to the **German Alpine Association,** Am Franciscanalplatz 7, D-83471, Berchtesgaden (☎ **08652/64343**). At the same address and phone number, you'll also be routed to staff members of a privately owned tour operator, the **Summit Club,** an outfit devoted to the organization of high-altitude expeditions throughout Europe and the world.

If you're a true outdoors person, you'll briefly savor the somewhat touristy facilities of Garmisch-Partenkirchen, and then use it as a base for exploring the rugged **Berchtesgaden National Park,** which is within an easy commute of Garmisch. You can also stay at one of the inns in Mittenwald or Oberammergau and take advantage of a wide roster of sporting diversions within the wild open spaces. Any of the outfitters below will provide directions and link-ups with their sports programs from wherever you decide to stay. Street maps of Berchtesgaden and its environs are usually available for free from the **Kurdirektion** (the local tourist office) at Berchtesgaden (☎ **08652/967-0**), and more intricately detailed maps of the surrounding alpine topography are available for a fee.

In addition to hill climbing and rock climbing, summertime activities include **ballooning,** which, weather permitting, can be arranged through **Outdoor Club Berchtesgaden,** Am Gmundberg (☎ **08652/50-01**). Local enthusiasts warn that ballooning is not a sport for the timid or anyone who suffers unduly in the cold: Warm thermal currents that prevail around Berchtesgaden in summer limit the sport to the cold-weather months. Consequently, the seasonal heyday for ballooning is between December and February. A local variation of **curling** (*Eisstock*) that makes use of wooden, rather than stone, instruments can usually be arranged even when ice and snows have melted on the surrounding slopes at the town's biggest ice rink, Berchtesgaden Eisstadion, An der Schiessstätte (☎ **08652/61405**). If you opted not to carry your ice skates within your luggage during your transatlantic flight, don't worry: A kiosk (☎ **08652/3384**) within the ice stadium rents a wide spectrum of ice skates in all sizes for around 6DM ($3.25) adults, 5DM ($2.70) children per hour.

Cycling and **mountain biking,** available through the rental facilities of **Full Stall,** Maximilianstrasse 16 (☎ **08652/948450**), give outdoor enthusiasts an opportunity to enjoy the outdoors and exercise their leg muscles simultaneously. Open Monday to Friday 9am to noon and 2 to 6pm, Saturday 9am to 1pm.

Anglers will find plenty of **fishing** opportunities (especially salmon, pike-perch, and trout) at Lake Hintersee and the rivers Ramsauer Ache and Königseer Ache, although in most cases it's best to obtain a fishing permit. To acquire one, contact either the Kurdirektion (tourist office) at Berchtesgaden, which will direct you to any of four different authorities.

Despite its obvious dangers, **hang gliding** or **para gliding** from the vertiginous slopes of Mount Jenner can be thrilling. To arrange it, contact the previously recommended Full Stall (see above), or Full Stall's competitor, **Para-Taxi**, Maximilianstrasse 15 (☎ **08652/948450**), at the same address. The headquarters for a loosely allied group of parasailing enthusiasts, the **Berchtesgaden Gleitschirmflieger** (☎ **08652/23-63**), whose members sometimes arrange communal paragliding excursions on which qualified newcomers are invited. Practice your **kayaking** or **white-water rafting** techniques on one of the many rivers in the area, such as the Ramsauer, Königisser, Bischofswiesener, and the Berchtesgadener Aches. For information and options, contact the above-mentioned **Outdoor Club Berchtesgaden.**

If you'd like to go **swimming** in an alpine lake—not to everyone's body temperature—there're many "lidos" found in the Bavarian Forest.

to the 10DM ($5) for the round-trip boat fare) is 8DM ($4.30) for adults, 5DM ($2.70) for students, and free for children under 15.

Getting There　Take the train to Prien am Chiemsee (trip time: about 1 hour). For information, call ☎ **08051/99-66-33.** There's also regional bus service offered by **RVO Regionalver-kehr Oberbayern** (☎ **08021/948274**). Access by car is via A-8 Autobahn.

From Prien, lake steamers make the trip to Herrenchiemsee. They are operated by **Chiemsee-Schiffahrt Ludwig Fessler** (☎ **08051/60-90**). The round-trip fare is 10DM ($5). For visitor information, contact the **Kur und Verkehrsamt,** Alte Rathausstrasse 11, in Prien am Chiemsee (☎ **08501/6-90-50**), open Monday to Friday 8:30am to 6pm, Saturday 9am to noon.

GARMISCH-PARTENKIRCHEN

In spite of its urban flair, Garmisch-Partenkirchen, Germany's top alpine resort, has maintained the charm of an ancient village. Even today, you occasionally see country folk in traditional costumes, and you may be held up in traffic while the cattle are led from their mountain grazing grounds down through the streets of town. Garmisch is about 88km (55 miles) southwest of Munich.

ESSENTIALS

GETTING THERE　By Train　The **Garmisch-Partenkirchen Bahnhof** lies on the major Munich-Weilheim-Garmisch-Mittenwald-Innsbruck rail line with frequent connections in all directions. Twenty trains per day arrive from Munich (trip time: 1 hour 22 minutes). For rail information and schedules, call ☎ **01805/99-66-33.**

By Bus　Both long-distance and regional buses through the Bavarian Alps are provided by **RVO Regionalverkehr Oberbayern** in Garmisch-Partenkirchen (☎ **08821/948-274** for information).

By Car　Access is via A-95 Autobahn from Munich; exit at Eschenlohe.

VISITOR INFORMATION　For tourist information, contact the **Kurverwaltung und Verkehrsamt,** Richard-Strauss-Platz (☎ **08821/18-06**), open Monday to Saturday 8am to 6pm, Sunday 10am to noon.

GETTING AROUND　An unnumbered municipal bus services the town, depositing passengers at Marienplatz or the Bahnhof, from where you can walk to all central hotels. This free bus runs every 15 minutes.

WHERE TO STAY

Gästehaus Trenkler. Kreuzstrasse 20, D-82467 Garmisch-Partenkirchen. ☎ **08821/ 34-39.** Fax 08821/15-67. 10 units, 5 with shower. 90DM–95DM ($49–$51) double without shower, 99DM–105DM ($53–$57) double with shower. Rates include continental breakfast. No credit cards. Free parking. Bus: Eibsee no. 1.

For a number of years, Frau Trenkler has made travelers feel well cared for in her quiet, centrally located guest house. She rents five doubles with showers and toilets and five doubles with hot and cold running water. Each duvet-covered bed is equipped with a good mattress. Rooms range from small to medium. Corridor bathrooms are adequate and tidily maintained.

✪　**Post-Hotel Partenkirchen.** Ludwigstrasse 49, D-82467 Garmisch-Partenkirchen. ☎ **08821/9363-0.** Fax 08821/9363-2222. www.post-hotel.de. 59 units. MINIBAR TV TEL. 250DM–280DM ($135–$151) double. Rates include buffet breakfast. AE, DC, MC, V.

This is one of the town's most prestigious hotels, especially with the added asset of its unusually fine restaurant (see "Where to Dine"). The U-shaped rooms are generally medium size. Duvets rest on comfortable beds with firm mattresses, mostly doubles or twins. Bathrooms are handsomely maintained with a hair dryer. The balconies overlook a garden and offer a view of the Alps. Golf, tennis, swimming, hiking, mountain climbing, skiing, cycling, hiking, horseback riding, and para gliding can be arranged.

✪ **Reindl's Partenkirchner Hof.** Bahnhofstrasse 15, D-82467 Garmisch-Partenkirchen. ☎ **08821/5-80-25.** Fax 08821/73-401. www.garmisch-partenkirchen.com/reindl. E-mail: riendl@oberland.net. 65 units. MINIBAR TV TEL. 170DM–282DM ($92–$152) double; 278DM–470DM ($150–$254) suite. AE, DC, MC, V. Parking 14DM ($8). Closed Nov 10–Dec 15.

This special Bavarian retreat maintains a high level of luxury and hospitality. The annexes have balconies and the main four-story building has wraparound verandas, giving each room an unobstructed view of the mountains and town. Rooms have a cozy charm. The best are suites opening onto panoramic views of mountains or the garden. Rustic pine furniture and excellent mattresses add to the allure of this place. Bathrooms have hair dryers and plenty of fluffy towels. Facilities include the much-honored Reindl's restaurant (see "Where to Dine"), a covered pool, sauna, sunroom, health club, open terrace for snacks, and two attractive gardens.

✪ **Romantik-Hotel Clausing's Posthotel.** Marienplatz 12, D-82467 Garmisch-Partenkirchen. ☎ **08821/7090.** Fax 08821/70-92-05. www.clausingsposthotel.de. E-mail: info@clausings-posthotel.de. 43 units. TV TEL. 160DM–300DM ($86–$162) double; 400DM ($216) suite. DC, MC, V. Free parking.

This hotel in the heart of town was originally built in 1512 as a tavern and has retained its *gemütlich* antique charm. In the early 1990s, it was radically upgraded. Rooms range from rather small and cozy Bavarian nests to spacious. The owners have installed state-of-the-art German mattresses. Bathrooms are beautifully kept and have hair dryers and an ample supply of soft towels. The Stüberl is an enclave of warmth and carefully presented cuisine.

WHERE TO DINE

Flösserstuben. Schmiedstrasse 2. ☎ **08821/28-88.** Reservations recommended. Main courses 10DM–32DM ($5–$17). AE, MC, V. Daily 11am–2:30pm and 5:30–10pm. Town bus. INTERNATIONAL.

Regardless of the season, a bit of the Bavarian Alps always seems to flower amid the wood-trimmed nostalgia of this intimate restaurant close to the town center. You can select a seat at a colorful wooden table or on an ox yoke–inspired stool in front of the spliced saplings that decorate the bar. Moussaka and souvlaki, as well as sauerbraten and all kinds of Bavarian dishes, are abundantly available. You can also order Mexican tacos and tortillas or even *tafelspitz* from the Austrian kitchen.

Post-Hotel Partenkirchen. Ludwigstrasse 49, Partenkirchen. ☎ **08821/5-10-67.** Reservations required. Main courses 25DM–50DM ($14–$27); fixed-price menus 35DM–55DM ($19–$30). AE, DC, MC, V. Daily noon–2pm and 6–9:30pm. CONTINENTAL.

Post-Hotel Partenkirchen is renowned for its distinguished cuisine. The interior dining rooms are rustic, with lots of mellow, old-fashioned atmosphere. You could imagine meeting Dürer here. Everything seems comfortably subdued, including the guests. The best way to dine is to order one of the fixed-price menus, which change daily, depending on the availability of seasonal produce. The à la carte menu is extensive, featuring game in the autumn. The Wiener schnitzel served with a large salad is the best we've had in the resort.

✪ **Reindl's Restaurant.** In the Partenkirchner Hof, Bahnhofstrasse 15. ☎ **08821/ 5-80-25.** Reservations required. Main courses 27DM–41DM ($15–$22); fixed-price lunch 50DM ($27); fixed-price gourmet dinner 120DM ($65). AE, DC, MC, V. Daily noon–2:30pm and 6:30–11pm. Closed Nov 10–Dec 15. CONTINENTAL.

Reindl's is first class all the way. The seasonal menu comprises *cuisine moderne* as well as regional Bavarian dishes. The chef de cuisine is Marianne Holzinger, daughter of founding father Karl Reindl. Among main dishes, we recommend *coq au Riesling* (chicken with wine) with noodles, or veal roasted with *Steinpilzen*, a special mushroom from the Bavarian mountains. For dessert, try Grand Marnier sabayon with strawberry and vanilla ice cream or a *Salzburger nockerln* (a feathery light soufflé made of eggs, flour, butter, and sugar) for two.

SEEING THE SIGHTS IN TOWN

The symbol of the city's growth and modernity is the **Olympic Ice Stadium,** built for the 1936 Winter Olympics and capable of holding nearly 12,000 people. On the slopes at the edge of town is the much larger **Ski Stadium,** with two ski jumps and a slalom course. In 1936 more than 100,000 people watched the events in this stadium. Today it's still an integral part of winter life in Garmisch—the World Cup Ski Jump is held here every New Year.

Garmisch-Partenkirchen is a center for winter sports, summer hiking, and mountain climbing. In addition, the town environs offer some of the most panoramic views and colorful buildings in Bavaria. The **Philosopher's Walk** in the park surrounding the pink and silver 18th-century pilgrimage **Chapel of St. Anton** is a delightful spot to enjoy the views of the mountains around the low-lying town.

EXPLORING THE ENVIRONS

One of the most beautiful of the alpine regions around Garmisch is the ✪ **Alpspitz region,** which hikers and hill climbers consider uplifting and healing for both body and soul. Here, you'll find alpine meadows, masses of seasonal wildflowers, and a rocky and primordial geology whose savage panoramas might strike you as Wagnererian. Ranging in altitude from 1,200m to 1,800m (4,000 to 6,000 feet) above sea level, the Alps around Garmisch-Partenkirchen are accessible via more than 30 ski lifts and funiculars, many of which run throughout the year.

The most appealing and panoramic of the lot includes the Alpspitz (Osterfelderkopf) cable car that runs uphill from the center of Garmisch to the top of the Osterfelderkopf peak, at a height of 1,980m (6,500 feet). It makes its 9-minute ascent at least every hour, year-round, 8am to 5pm. The round-trip cost is 37DM ($20) for adults, 22DM ($12) for children ages 4 to 15, and 26DM ($14) for persons aged 16 to 18. After admiring the view at the top, you can either return directly to Garmisch, or continue your journey into the mountains via other cable cars. If you opt to continue, take the Hochalm cable car across the high-altitude plateaus above Garmisch. At its terminus, you'll have two options, both across clearly marked alpine trails. The 20-minute trek will take you to the uppermost station of the Kreuzbergbahn, which will carry you back to Garmisch. The 75-minute trek will carry you to the upper terminus of the Hausbergbahn, which will also carry you back to Garmisch.

Another of the many cable car options within Garmisch involves an eastward ascent from the center of Partenkirchen to the top of the 1,780m (5,850-foot) Wank via the Wankbahn, for a round-trip price of 28DM ($15) for adults and 20DM ($11) for persons aged 16 to 18, and 17DM ($9) for children. From here, you'll get a sweeping view of the plateau upon which the twin villages of Garmisch and Partenkirchen sit. In winter, the top of the Wank is a favorite departure point for many downhill ski runs. It's also, however, a favorite with the patrons of Garmisch's spa facilities because the plentiful sunshine makes it ideal for the *Liegekur* (deck-chair cure).

If you plan on pursuing any of these options, it's to your advantage to invest in a day pass, the Classic Garmisch Pass, with which you'll be able to ride most of the cable cars in the region (including those to the above-recommended Alpspitz, Kreuzeck, and Wank, as well as several others that fan out over the Eckbauer and the Ausberg) as many times as you like within the same day. Priced 48DM ($26) to 53DM ($29) per person, depending on the season, the pass is available from any of the town's cable car stations. For information on all the cable car schedules and itineraries within the region, call ☎ 08821/7970.

Another option for exploring the environs of Garmisch involves an ascent to the top of the ❂ **Zugspitze,** at 2,960m (9,720 feet) the tallest mountain in Germany, with a base set astride the Austrian frontier. Ski slopes begin at 2,650m (8,700 feet). For a panoramic view over both the Bavarian and Tyrolean Alps, go to the summit. The first stage begins in the center of Garmisch by taking the cog railway to an intermediary alpine plateau (Zugspitzplatz). Trains depart hourly throughout the year 7:39am to 2:39pm, although we recommend that you begin by 1:39pm (and preferably earlier) and not wait until the cog railway's final ascent from Garmisch. At Zugspitzplatz, you can continue uphill on the same cog railway to the debut of a high-speed, four-minute ride aboard the Gletscherbahn cable car, the high-altitude conveyance you'll ride to the top of the Zugspitz peak. (The distance between Zugspitzplatz and debut of the Gletscherbahn can also be transited aboard a secondary cable car—the Eibsee-Seil-bahn, but this will require that you walk uphill for part of the route). Regardless of the exact route you follow, round-trip transit between the center of Garmisch and the top of the Zugspitz costs 62 to 76DM ($34 to $41) for adults, 44 to 53DM ($24 to $29) for persons 16 to 17, and 37 to 45DM ($20 to $24) for children 5 to 15. Children under 4 ride free. Note that the price of the ascent to the Zugspitz is not included in the above-mentioned Classic Garmisch Pass, as it forms part of an independent net-work of cable cars that's not associated with the other cable cars within the region. For more information, call the tourist office or ☎ 08821/1806.

MITTENWALD

Seeming straight out of *The Sound of Music,* the year-round resort of Mittenwald lies in a pass in the Karwendel Range, 18km (11 miles) southeast of Garmisch-Partenkirchen. Especially noteworthy and photogenic are the painted Bavarian hous-es with overhanging eaves. Even the baroque church tower is covered with frescoes. On the square stands a monument to Mathias Klotz, who introduced violin making to Mittenwald in 1684. The town is a major international center for this highly spe-cialized craft.

ESSENTIALS

GETTING THERE   By Train   Mittenwald lies on the express rail line between Munich and Innsbruck and can be reached by almost hourly train service from Munich (trip time: 1¹/₂ to 2 hours). Call ☎ 01805/99-66-33 for information.

By Bus   Regional bus service from Garmisch-Partenkirchen and nearby towns is fre-quent; call **RVO Regionalverkehr Oberbayern** at Garmisch (☎ 08821/94-82-74 for information).

By Car   Access by car is via A-95 Autobahn from Munich.

VISITOR INFORMATION   Contact the **Kurverwaltung und Verkehrsamt,** Dammkarstrasse 3 (☎ 08823/3-39-81), open Monday to Friday 8am to noon and 1 to 6pm, Saturday 10am to 2pm.

WHERE TO STAY

Alpenrose. Obermarkt 1, D-82481 Mittenwald. ☎ **08823/92-700.** Fax 08823/37-20. 18 units. MINIBAR TV TEL. 142DM–166DM ($77–$90) double; 192DM ($104) suite. Rates include buffet breakfast. AE, DC, DISC, MC, V. Free parking.

In the village center at the foot of a rugged mountain, this inn is covered with decorative designs and window boxes holding flowering vines. The main building, a former 14th-century monastery, is much more desirable than more functionally furnished annex, the Bichlerhof. Rooms in the main building are very charming with their old-fashioned farmhouse cupboards and dark wood paneling. The private bathrooms are well kept but a bit small.

Gästehaus Franziska. Innsbrucker-Strasse 24, D-82481 Mittenwald. ☎ **08823/92030.** Fax 08823/3893. www.franziskatourism.de. E-mail: franziskahmiltenwald.de. 19 units. MINIBAR TV TEL. 126DM ($68) double; from 168DM ($91) suite. Rates include buffet breakfast. AE, V. Free parking. Closed Nov 10–Dec 12.

The Kufler family labors to make this the most personalized guest house in town. Each room is comfortably furnished and beautifully maintained—first-rate beds feature crisp linen duvets and fine mattresses. All have balconies with mountain views; suites have safes and tea or coffee facilities. Bathrooms are a bit small but inviting and tidy. Breakfast is the only meal served. It's extremely difficult to obtain bookings June 20 to October 2.

Hotel Post. Obermarkt 9, D-82481 Mittenwald. ☎ **08823/10-94.** Fax 08823/10-96. 81 units. TV TEL. 140DM–240DM ($76–$130) double; 220DM–300DM ($119–$162) suite. Rates include buffet breakfast. No credit cards. Parking 8DM ($4.30).

The Post, dating from 1632, remains Mittenwald's finest address. A delightful breakfast is served on the sun terrace, with a view of the Alps; in cool weather you can enjoy a beer in the snug lounge-bar with its open fireplace. For a night of hearty Bavarian specialties, head for the wine tavern or the Poststüberl. Rooms are comfortable but standard. Beds (twin or double) and mattresses are among the most comfortable in town. Bathrooms are small. The maids are especially helpful if you need something extra. An indoor pool, massage facilities, and sauna are available

WHERE TO DINE

Restaurant Arnspitze. Innsbruckerstrasse 68. ☎ **08823/24-25.** Reservations required. Main courses 29DM–43DM ($16–$23); fixed-price lunch 43DM ($23); fixed-price dinner 83DM ($45). AE. Thurs noon–2pm; daily 6–9pm; closed Tues all day and Wed for lunch. Closed Oct 25–Dec 19. Bus: RVO. BAVARIAN.

Housed in a modern chalet hotel on the outskirts, this is the finest dining room in town. The restaurant is decorated in the old style; the cuisine is solid, satisfying, and wholesome. You might order sole with homemade noodles or veal steak in creamy smooth sauce, then finish with one of the freshly made desserts. There's an excellent fixed-price lunch.

SEEING THE SIGHTS

The town's museum, with a workshop, has exhibits devoted to the evolution of violins and other string instruments. The **Geigenbau-und Heimatmuseum,** Ballenhausgasse 3 (☎ **08823/25-11**), is open Monday to Friday 10 to noon and 2 to 5pm, Saturday and Sunday 10 to noon. Admission is 3DM ($1.60) for adults and 1DM (55¢) for children. The museum is closed November 1 to December 20.

In the countryside, you are constantly exposed to the changing scenery of the Wetterstein and Karwendel ranges. Horse and carriage trips are available as well as coach tours from Mittenwald to nearby villages. In the evening there's typical Bavarian entertainment, often consisting of folk dancing and singing, zither playing, and yodeling, but you also have your choice of concerts, dance bands, discos, and bars. Mittenwald has good spa facilities, in large gardens landscaped with tree-lined streams and trout pools. Concerts during the summer are held in the music pavilion.

Outdoor Activities

In winter, the town is a skiing center, but it remains equally active throughout the summer. Some 130km (80 miles) of paths wind up and down the mountains around the village, with chairlifts making the hiking trails readily accessible. Of course, where there are trails, there's mountain biking. A biking map is available from the tourist office (see above), and mountain climbing expeditions are also available. You can always go swimming to cool off on a hot summer's day—the Lautersee and Ferchensee are brisk waters that, even in summer, might be forfeited by the fainthearted for the heated adventure pool in Mittenwald.

OBERAMMERGAU

A visit to Oberammergau, 19km (12 miles) north of Garmisch-Partenkirchen, is ideal in summer or winter. It stands in a wide valley surrounded by forests and mountains, with sunny slopes and meadows. The world-famous **passion play** is presented here, usually every 10 years; the next one is scheduled for 2010. It has also long been known for the skill of its woodcarvers. Here in this village right under the Kofel, farms are still intact, and tradition prevails.

Essentials

GETTING THERE   By Train   The Oberammergau Bahnhof is on the Murnau-Bad Kohlgrum-Oberammergau rail line, with frequent connections in all directions. Murnau has connections to all major German cities. Daily trains from Munich take 2 hours. For information, call ☎ **01805/99-66-33.**

By Bus   Regional bus service to nearby towns is offered by **RVO Regionalverkehr Oberbayern** in Garmisch-Partenkirchen (☎ **08821/948-274**). An unnumbered bus travels between Oberammergau and Garmisch-Partenkirchen.

By Car   Take A-95 Munich-Garmisch-Partenkirchen Autobahn and exit at Eschenlohe (trip time: 1¹/₂ hours).

VISITOR INFORMATION   Contact the **Oberammergau Tourist Information Office,** Eugen-Papst-Strasse 9A (☎ **08822/92310**), open Monday to Friday 8am to 6pm, Saturday 8am to noon.

Seeing the Sights

Oberammergau's most respected citizens include an unusual group, the woodcarvers, many of whom have been trained in the village's woodcarver's school. In the **Pila-tushaus,** Ludwigthomstrasse (☎ **08822/1682**), you can watch local artists at work, including woodcarvers, painters, sculptors, and potters. Hours are Monday to Friday 1 to 6pm May to October. You'll see many examples of these art forms throughout the town, on the painted cottages and inns and in the churchyard. Also worth seeing when strolling through the village are the houses with 18th-century frescoes by Franz Zwink that are named after fairy-tale characters, such as "Hansel and Gretel House" and the "Little Red Riding Hood House."

   Heimatmuseum, Dorfstrasse 8 (☎ **08822/94136**), has a notable collection of Christmas crêches, all hand carved and painted, and dating from the 18th through the

20th century. It's open mid-April to mid-October, Tuesday through Saturday 2 to 6pm; off-season, only on Saturday 2 to 6pm. Admission is 4DM ($2.15) for adults and 1.50DM (80¢) for children.

NEARBY ATTRACTIONS   The Ammer Valley, with Oberammergau in the (almost) center, offers easy access to many nearby attractions. **Schloss Linderhof** (☎ **08822/92030**), designed as a French rococo palace, the smallest and the most successful of Ludwig II's constructions, is open throughout the year. This is in many ways the most successful of his palaces. The gardens and smaller buildings here are even more elaborate than the two-story main structure. Especially outstanding is a Hall of Mirrors, set in white and gold panels, decorated with gilded wood carvings. The king's bedchamber overlooks a Fountain of Neptune and the cascades of the garden. The palace is open daily April to September 9am to 12:15pm and 1pm to 5:30pm, October to March 9:30am to noon and 1pm to 4pm. Admission is 7DM ($3.80), children under 15 free. Buses arrive from Garmisch-Partenkirchen throughout the day. Motorists can leave Oberammergau following the road signs to Ettal, 5km (3 miles) away. From Ettal, follow the signs for another 5km (3 miles) to Draswang, at which point the road into Schloss Linderhof is signposted.

OUTDOOR ACTIVITIES

Numerous **hiking trails** lead through the mountains around Oberammergau to hikers' inns such as the **Kolbenalm** and the **Romanshohe.** You can, however, simply go up to the mountaintops on the Laber cable railway or the Kolben chairlift. Oberammergau also offers opportunities to tennis buffs, minigolf players, cyclists, swimmers, hang-gliding enthusiasts, and canoeists. The recreation center **Wellenberg,** with its large alpine swimming complex with open-air pools, hot water and fountains, sauna, solarium, and restaurant, is one of the Alps' most beautiful recreation centers.

WHERE TO STAY & DINE

Alte Post. Dorfstrasse 19, D-82487 Oberammergau. ☎ **08822/91-00.** Fax 08822/910-100. E-mail: altepost@ogan.de 32 units. TV TEL. 120DM–140DM ($65–$76) double. Rates include buffet breakfast. AE, DC, MC, V. Parking 6DM ($3.25). Closed Oct 25–Dec 19. Bus: 30.

This provincial inn in the village center with a wide overhanging roof, green-shuttered windows, and tables set on a sidewalk under a long awning, is the village social hub. The interior has storybook charm, with a ceiling-high green ceramic stove, alpine chairs, and shelves of pewter plates. Most of the rustic rooms have views. Wide comfortable beds with giant posts range in size from cozy to spacious. Bathrooms are medium size with a good set of fluffy towels. The restaurant serves excellent Bavarian dishes, and there's an intimate drinking bar.

Hotel Café-Restaurant Friedenshöhe. König-Ludwig-Strasse 31, D-82487 Oberammergau. ☎ **08822/35-98.** Fax 08822/43-45. 17 units. TEL. 110DM–170DM ($59–$92) double. Rates include buffet breakfast. AE, DC, MC, V. Closed Nov–Dec 14.

This 1906 villa enjoys a beautiful location and is among the town's best bargains. Well-maintained rooms range from rather small singles to spacious doubles. Corner rooms are bigger. Bathrooms tend to be small. TVs are available on request. There are four dining rooms, including both indoor and outdoor terraces with panoramic views. The Bavarian and international cuisine is known for its quality.

Hotel Restaurant Böld. König-Ludwig-Strasse 10, D-82487 Oberammergau. ☎ **08822/91-20.** Fax 08822/71-02. 57 units. TV TEL. 180DM–238DM ($97–$129) double. Rates include continental breakfast. AE, MC, V. Free outside parking; 10DM ($5) in the garage.

A stone's throw from the river, this well-designed chalet hotel is one of the town's premier choices. Rooms in both the main building and the annex have equally good beds, usually doubles or twins, each with a firm German mattress. Most rooms open onto balconies. The spotless bathrooms are medium size with fluffy towels. Facilities include a sauna, solarium, and whirlpool. The restaurant features both international and regional cuisine. In the bar (where food is served), you'll find a tranquil atmosphere and attentive service.

3 The Romantic Road

No area of Germany is more aptly named than the Romantische Strasse. Stretching 290km (180 miles) from Würzburg to Füssen in the foothills of the Bavarian Alps, it passes through untouched medieval villages and 2,000-year-old towns.

The best way to see the Romantic Road is by car, stopping whenever the mood strikes you and then driving on through vineyards and over streams until you arrive at the alpine passes in the south. Frankfurt and Munich are convenient gateways. Access is by A-7 Autobahn from north and south, or A-3 Autobahn from east and west; A-81 Autobahn has links from the southwest. You can also explore the Romantic Road by train or bus, or by organized tour.

ROTHENBURG OB DER TAUBER

This city was first mentioned in written records in 804 as Rotinbure, a settlement above (*ob*) the Tauber River that grew to be a free imperial city, reaching its apex of prosperity under a famous Burgermeister, Heinrich Toppler, in the 14th century.

The place is such a gem and so well known that its popularity is its chief disadvantage—tourist hordes march through here, especially in summer, and the concomitant souvenir peddlers hawk kitsch. Even so, if your time is limited and you can visit only one town on the Romantic Road, make it Rothenburg.

Contemporary life and industry have made an impact, and if you arrive at the railroad station, the first things you'll see are factories and office buildings. But don't be discouraged. Inside those undamaged 13th-century city walls is a completely preserved medieval town, relatively untouched by the passage of time.

ESSENTIALS

GETTING THERE   By Train   Rothenburg lies on the Steinach-Rothenburg rail line, with frequent connections to all major German cities, including Nürnberg and Stuttgart. Daily trains arrive from Frankfurt (trip time: 3 hours), Hamburg (trip time: 5½ hours), or Berlin (trip time: 7 hours). For information, call ☎ 01805/99-66-33.

By Bus   The bus that traverses the length of the Romantic Road is EB189 or EB189E, operated by Deutsche Touring Frankfurt (☎ 069/790-3281 for information and reservations). Two buses operate along this route every day, but only April to October. Know in advance that although you'll see a lot of romantic color en route, travel time to Rothenburg from Frankfurt via these buses is 6½ hours because of frequent stops en route. Any travel agent in Germany or abroad can book you a seat on any of these buses, each of which stops at sites along the Romantic Road that include Würzburg, Augsburg, Füssen, and Munich.

Regional bus service that's limited to towns and hamlets within the vicinity of Rothenburg and the rest of the Romantic Road is provided by **OVF Omnibusverkehr Franken GmbH,** Kopernikusplatz 5, 90159 Nürnberg (☎ 0911/43-90-60) for information.

VISITOR INFORMATION   Contact **Stadt Verkehrsamt,** Marktplatz (☎ **09861/ 40-492**), open Monday to Friday 9am to 12:30pm and 2 to 6pm, Saturday and Sunday 10am to 3pm (November to March closes at 6pm on weekdays).

WHERE TO STAY
Expensive

✪ **Burg Hotel.** Klostergasse 1–3, D-91541 Rothenburg o.d.T. ☎ **09861/94-89-0.** Fax 09861/94-89-40. www.burghotel.rothenburg.de. E-mail: burghotel.rothenburg@t-online.de. 15 units. MINIBAR TV TEL. 180DM–300DM ($97–$162) double; from 320DM ($173) suite. Rates include buffet breakfast. V. Parking 10DM ($5).

This old-fashioned timbered house at the end of a cul-de-sac is out of the Brothers Grimm. Its Tauber Valley view, picket fences, and window boxes exude of German charm. Rooms spread across three floors (no elevator). Mattresses are deluxe; extras include safes and spacious bathrooms with combination shower and tub, hair dryer, and large mirrors. Any room is likely to please, but if you want a view, ask for numbers 7, 12, or 25.

✪ **Eisenhut.** Herrngasse 3–5, D-91541 Rothenburg o.d.T. ☎ **09861/70-50.** Fax 09861/70-545. www.eisenhut.com. E-mail: hotel@eisenhut.com. 70 units. MINIBAR TV TEL. 300DM–395DM ($162–$213) double; 540DM–660DM ($292–$356) suite. AE, DC, MC, V. Parking 15DM ($8).

The most celebrated inn on the Romantic Road, Eisenhut is also the finest small hotel in Germany. Four medieval patrician houses, dating from the 12th century, were joined to make this distinctive inn. Demand for rooms is great, and the staff appears forever overworked. No two rooms are alike—yours may contain hand-carved, monumental pieces or have a 1940s Hollywood touch with a tufted satin headboard. All are enhanced by comforters and pillows piled high on state-of-the-art German mattresses. Extras include bedside controls, safes, spacious bathrooms outfitted with hair dryers, fluffy towels, and often twin basins. There's an impressive three-story galleried dining hall, with ornate classic wood paneling and balconies. Other places to dine are richly decorated and furnished, although in sunny weather they're all deserted in favor of the multitiered flagstone terrace on the Tauber.

Goldener Hirsch. Untere Schmiedgasse 16–25, D-91541 Rothenburg o.d.T. ☎ **09861/ 70-80.** Fax 09861/70-81-00. 72 units. MINIBAR TEL. 180DM–320DM ($97–$173) double. Rates include breakfast. AE, DC, MC, V. Parking 4DM ($2.15).

This first-class hotel 3 blocks from the main square is a remake of a 17th-century inn. It looks more austere and institutional and lacks the coziness of some of the other leading inns. Rooms are very modern with built-in furniture more Scandinavian than Bavarian. Bathrooms are tiny; only the most superior rooms have hair dryers. Room service and laundry are available. The Blue Terrace for dining offers a panoramic view of the Tauber Valley, or you may prefer to take your dinner in the wood-paneled, cozy Ratsherrenstube.

Hotel Tilman Riemenschneider. Georgengasse 11–13, D-91541, Rothenburg o.d.T. ☎ **09861/9790.** Fax 09861/29-79. www.tilman-riemenschneider.de. E-mail: hotel@tilman. rothenburg.de. 65 units. TV TEL. 200DM–420DM ($108–$227) double. Rates include buffet breakfast. AE, DC, MC, V. Parking 10DM ($5).

This hotel's half-timbered facade rises directly above one of Rothenburg's busy historic streets. Its rear courtyard, adorned with geraniums, offers a cool and calm oasis from the heavy pedestrian traffic in front. Most rooms are medium size though a few are small. All have exceedingly comfortable mattresses. Room service, laundry, and dry

The Romantic Road

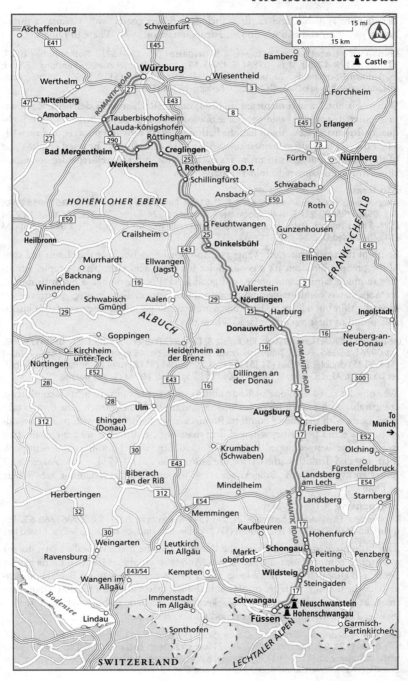

cleaning are available, and facilities include a fitness center with a sauna, a turbo-skylab solarium, and two whirlpools. For its restaurant, see "Where to Dine."

Romantik Hotel Markusturm. Rödergasse 1, D-91541 Rothenburg o.d.T. ☎ **09861/9-42-80.** Fax 09861/9-42-81-13. romantikhotel.com/rothenburg. E-mail: markusturm@t-online.de. 25 units. TV TEL. 220DM–350DM ($119–$189) double. Rates include buffet breakfast. AE, DC, MC, V. Parking 12DM ($7).

When this hotel was constructed in 1264, one of Rothenburg's defensive walls was incorporated into the building. Some rooms have four-poster beds; all have high-quality firm mattresses. About half the bathrooms have tubs and showers, and each has a hair dryer. Many guests request room 30, a cozy attic retreat. The hotel employs one of the most helpful staffs in town. It's open all year, but the well-regarded restaurant closes from mid-January to mid-February.

Moderate

Hotel Gasthof Glocke. Am Plönlein 1, D-91541 Rothenburg o.d.T. ☎ **09861/95899-0.** Fax 09861/95899-22. E-mail: glocke@ringshotels.de. 24 units. TV TEL. 168DM–188DM ($91–$102) double. Rates include continental breakfast. AE, DC, MC, V. Parking 8.50DM ($4.60). Closed Dec 24–Jan 6.

South of the town center off Wenggasse, this hotel does not have the charm and style of the premier inns, but it's a good choice for those who want plain, simple, affordable rooms, a family atmosphere, and good food. Rooms, though a bit institutional, are nonetheless comfortable and a good value for pricey Rothenburg. Mattresses are generally thin but adequate. Bathrooms are exceedingly small. The owners are justifiably proud of their restaurant (see "Where to Dine").

Hotel Reichs-Küchenmeister. Kirchplatz 8, D-91541 Rothenburg o.d.T. ☎ **09861/9700.** Fax 09861/86-965. E-mail: hotel@reichskuechenmeister.de. 48 units. TV TEL. 150DM–250DM ($81–$135) double; 250DM ($135) suite for 2; 330DM ($178) suite for 5. Rates include buffet breakfast. AE, DC, MC, V. Parking 6DM ($3.25) in lot, 10DM ($5) in garage.

We consider this hotel, one of Rothenburg's oldest structures, near St. Jakobskirche, comparable with Tilman Riemenschneider and the Goldener Hirsch. The owners take special care with the guests' comfort. Rooms are nicely furnished with painted wooden furniture and frequently renewed firm mattresses. Bathrooms are a bit small. This is one of the best equipped hotels in Rothenburg, with Finnish sauna, whirlpool, solarium, and Turkish bath. Use of the sauna costs 20DM ($11) extra. An extra 17 rooms are available in the duller annex across the street. For its restaurant, see "Where to Dine."

Inexpensive

Bayerischer Hof. Ansbacherstrasse 21, D-91541 Rothenburg o.d.T. ☎ **09861/60-63.** Fax 09861/86-56-1. 9 units. TV TEL. 130DM ($70) double. Rates include breakfast. MC, V. Closed Jan.

This little place, midway between the Bahnhof and the medieval walled city, doesn't even try to compete with the grand inns. And why should it? It's found a niche as a B&B, and although the outside looks rather sterile, many cozy warm Bavarian touches grace the interior. Beds are comfortable though mattresses are a bit thin. Rooms are small, as are the bathrooms, but housekeeping is excellent and the staff is most hospitable. The international/Bavarian food is also very good.

Gasthof Goldener Greifen. Obere Schmiedgasse 5, D-91541 Rothenburg o.d.T. ☎ **09861/22-81.** Fax 09861/86-374. 21 units (20 with bathroom). 74DM ($40) double without bathroom; 138DM ($75) double with shower or bathroom. Rates include buffet breakfast. AE, MC, V. Closed Aug 22–Sept 2 and Dec 22–Feb.

This is one of the very best B&Bs in town if you want Bavarian home-style warmth. Fine mattresses, tidy housekeeping, and a willing staff make this patrician 1374 house off Marktplatz extremely comfortable. Corridor bathrooms are adequate, and generally spruced up after use. Those in units with private bathroom will find them small but well maintained. You can order your morning coffee in the garden amid roses and geraniums.

WHERE TO DINE
Expensive
✪ **Restaurant Bärenwirt.** In the Hotel Bären, Hofbronnengasse 9. ☎ **09861/951-880.** Reservations recommended. Main courses 42DM–80DM ($23–$43). AE, MC, V. Daily 10am–11pm. FRANCONIAN/INTERNATIONAL.

Many food critics, including *VIF Gourmet Journal,* cite the "Bear," owned by Fritz and Elisabeth Müller, as one of the finest restaurants in all Germany. The decor is elegantly subdued and the service impeccable. On occasion, the chef is known to serve a historical menu from the Middle Ages. Menu changes are based on the chef's inspiration and use the best seasonal produce.

Moderate
Baumeisterhaus. Obere Schmiedgasse 3. ☎ **09861/94-700.** Reservations required for courtyard tables. Main courses 13.50DM–35DM ($7–$19). AE, DC, MC, V. Daily 10am–9pm. FRANCONIAN.

Right off Marktplatz, the Baumeisterhaus is housed in an ancient patrician residence, built in 1596. It has Rothenburg's most beautiful courtyard (which only guests can visit), with colorful murals, serenely draped by vines. Frankly, although the menu is good, the romantic setting is better. The food, for the most part, is rib-sticking fare beloved of Bavarians, including roast suckling pig with potato dumplings, and one of the chef's best dishes, sauerbraten (braised beef marinated in vinegar), served with spätzle (small flour dumplings).

Ratsstube. Marktplatz 6. ☎ **09861/55-11.** Reservations recommended. Main courses 18DM–32DM ($10–$17). MC, V. Mon–Sat 9am–11pm, Sun noon–6pm. Closed Jan 7–Feb. FRANCONIAN.

Ratsstube enjoys a position right on the market square, one of the most photographed spots in Germany. It's a bustling center of activity throughout the day—a day that begins when practically every Rothenburger stops by for a cup of coffee. Inside, a true tavern atmosphere prevails with hardwood chairs and tables, vaulted ceilings, and pierced copper lanterns. The à la carte menu of Franconian wines and dishes includes sauerbraten and venison, both served with fresh vegetables and potatoes. For dessert, you can order homemade Italian ice cream and espresso. This is a longtime favorite of those who prefer typical Franconian cookery without a lot of fuss and bother. If you arrive at 9am, the staff will serve you an American breakfast.

Reichs-Küchenmeister. Kirchplatz 8. ☎ **09861/9700.** Reservations required. Main courses 19.50DM–45DM ($11–$24). AE, DC, MC, V. Daily 11am–2pm and 6–10pm. FRANCONIAN.

The main dishes served here are the type Bavarians have loved for years, including sauerbraten, or pork tenderloin; white herring and broiled salmon are also available. The *Lebensknodel* (liver dumpling) or goulash soup is perfect for cold days. The chef makes one of the best Wiener schnitzels in town. The restaurant is near St. Jakobskirche and has a typical weinstube decor, along with a garden terrace and a *Konditorei* (cake shop). Service is warm and efficient.

Inexpensive

Hotel Gasthof Glocke. Am Plönlein 1. ☎ **09861/958-990.** Reservations recommended. Main courses 16DM–66DM ($9–$36). AE, DC, MC, V. Daily 11am–2pm; Mon–Sat 6–9pm. Closed Dec 24–Jan 6. FRANCONIAN.

This traditional hotel and guest house (previously recommended) serves regional specialties along with a vast selection of local wine. Meals emphasize seasonal dishes and range from a simple vegetarian plate to lobster. Service is polite and attentive.

Tilman Riemenschneider. Georgengasse 11. ☎ **09861/9790.** Main courses 18.50DM–34DM ($10–$18); fixed-price menu 30DM–36DM ($16–$19). AE, DC, MC, V. Daily 11:30am–2pm and 6–9pm. FRANCONIAN.

This traditional old weinstube is housed in one of Rothenburg's finest hotels. The old-fashioned cookery is served in generous portions. You might begin with air-dried beef or smoked fillet of trout, then follow with poached eel, halibut steak, or loin of pork.

EXPLORING THE MEDIEVAL TOWN

The ✪ **Rathaus (Town Hall)** on the Marktplatz (☎ 09861/404-92) and the Jakobskirche are the outstanding attractions, along with the medieval walls. The town hall consists of two sections: The older, Gothic section dates from 1240. From the 50m (165-foot) tower of the Gothic hall, you get an overview of the town. The belfry has quite a history—in 1501, fire destroyed part of the building, and after that the belfry became a fire watchtower. Guards had to ring the bell every quarter hour to prove they were awake and on the job. The newer Renaissance section, built in 1572, is decorated with intricate friezes, an oriel extending the building's full height, and a large stone portico opening onto the square. The octagonal tower at the center of the side facing the square contains a grand staircase leading to the upper hall. On the main floor is the large courtroom.

Admission to the tower is 1DM (55¢) for adults, .50DM (25¢) children. The Rathaus is open Monday to Friday 8am to 6pm; the tower is open April to October, daily 9:30am to 12:30pm and 1 to 5pm; November to March, Saturday, Sunday, and holidays only noon to 3pm.

✪ **St. Jakobskirche (Church of St. James),** Klostergasse 15 (☎ 09861/70-06-20), contains the famous *Altar of the Holy Blood* (west gallery), a masterpiece of the Würzburg sculptor and woodcarver Tilman Riemenschneider (1460–1531). The Rothenburg Council commissioned the work in 1499 to provide a worthy setting for the *Reliquary of the Holy Blood*. The relic is contained in a rock-crystal capsule set in the reliquary cross (about 1270) in the center of the shrine, and beneath it the scene of the *Last Supper* makes an immediate impact on the viewer—Jesus is giving Judas the morsel of bread, marking him as the traitor. The altar wings show (left) the *Entry of Christ into Jerusalem* and (right) *Christ Praying in the Garden of Gethsemane.*

The vertical Gothic church has three naves. The choir, dating from 1336, is the oldest section and has fine late Gothic painted-glass windows. To the left is the tabernacle (1390–1400), which was recognized as a "free place," a sanctuary for condemned criminals where they could not be touched. Open April to October Monday to Saturday 9am to 5:30pm, Sunday 11am to 5:30pm. In December, it's open daily 10am to 3pm. And during November and from January to March, it's open daily 10am to noon and from 2 to 4pm. Admission costs 2.50DM ($1.35) for adults, and 1DM (55¢) for children under 6 and for students of any age.

Also of interest is the **Reichsstadtmuseum,** Klosterhof 5 (☎ 09861/939-043). This is Rothenburg's historical collection, housed in a 13th-century Dominican nunnery with well-preserved cloisters. You'll find on display here an enormous tankard that holds 3.5 liters (3¹/₂ quarts) whose story has echoes all over the city. In 1631, during the Thirty Years' War, the Protestant city of Rothenburg was captured by General Tilly, commander of the armies of the Catholic League. He promised to spare the town from destruction if one of the town burghers would drink the huge tankard full of wine in one draught. Burgermeister Nusch accepted the challenge and succeeded, and so saved Rothenburg. There's a festival every spring at Whitsuntide to celebrate this event. Among the exhibits is the 1494 *Rothenburg Passion* series, 12 pictures by Martinus Schwartz, and works by English painter Arthur Wasse (1854–1930), whose pictures managed to capture in a romantic way the many moods of the city. Admission to the museum is 5DM ($2.70) for adults, 3DM ($1.60) for children; a family card costs 10DM ($5). It's open daily April to October, 10am to 5pm; November to March, 1 to 4pm.

The **Kriminal Museum,** Burggasse 3 (☎ **09861/53-59**), is the only one of its kind in Europe. The museum's four floors display 10 centuries of legal history and provides insight into the life, laws, and punishments of medieval days. You'll see chastity belts, shame masks, a shame flute for bad musicians, and a cage for bakers who baked bread too small or too light. It's open daily April to October, 9:30am to 6pm; November and January to March, 2 to 4pm; and December, 10am to 4pm. Admission is 5DM ($2.70) for adults and 3DM ($1.60) for children under 13.

DINKELSBÜHL

Still surrounded by medieval walls and towers, Dinkelsbühl is straight out of a Brothers Grimm story, even down to the gingerbread, which is one of its main products. Behind the ancient 10th-century walls is a town that retains its quiet, provincial ambience in spite of the many tourists who come here. The cobblestone streets are lined with fine 16th-century houses, many with carvings and paintings depicting biblical and mythological themes. In the center of town, on Marktplatz, is the late Gothic **Georgenkirche** (1448–99). It contains a carved Holy Cross Altar and pillar sculptures.

ESSENTIALS

GETTING THERE   By Train   The nearest train station is in Ansbach, which has several trains arriving daily from Munich and Frankfurt (trip time: 2¹/₂ to 3 hours), Nürnberg, and Stuttgart. From Ansbach, Dinkelsbhl can be reached by bus. For information, call ☎ **01805/99-66-33.**

By Bus   For long-distance bus service along the Romantic Road, see "Rothenburg," above. Regional buses link Dinkelsbühl with local towns. There're three to five buses a day to Rothenburg and five or six to Nördlingen.

By Car   Take B-25 south from Rothenburg.

VISITOR INFORMATION   Contact   **Stadt Verkehrsamt,**   Marktplatz (☎ **09851/9-02-40**). April to October, hours are Monday to Friday 9am to noon and 2 to 6pm, Saturday 10am to 1pm and 2 to 4pm, and Sunday 10am to 1pm. November to March, open only on Saturday 10am to 1pm.

SPECIAL EVENTS   The **Kinderzeche (Children's Festival),** held for 10 days in July, commemorates the saving of the village by its children in 1632. According to the story, the children pleaded with conquering Swedish troops to leave their town without pillaging and destroying it—and got their wish. The pageant includes concerts given by the local boys' band dressed in historic military costumes.

WHERE TO STAY & DINE

Blauer Hecht. Schweinemarkt 1, D-91150 Dinkelsbühl. ☎ **09851/5810.** Fax 09851/581170. E-mail: hotel@t-online.de. 44 units. TV TEL. 150DM–174DM ($81–$94) double. Rates include continental breakfast. AE, DC, MC, V. Free parking. Closed Jan.

The inn is the best in town. The elegant ocher 17th-century building was once a brewery tavern, and the owners still brew in the backyard. Although it's central, rooms are tranquil and sunny. The mattresses are the newest and finest in town, and most rooms have bedside controls. Bathrooms are routine but well maintained. Good regional food is served in the hotel restaurant.

Deutsches Haus. Weinmarkt 3, D-91550 Dinkelsbühl. ☎ **09851/60-58.** Fax 09851/79-11. E-mail: deutscheshaus@t-online.de. 15 units. TV TEL. 150DM–210DM ($81–$113) double; 240DM ($130) suite. Rates include continental breakfast. AE, DC, MC, V. Parking 15DM ($8). Closed Dec 23–Jan 6.

The facade of Deutsches Haus, which dates from 1440, is rich in painted designs and festive wood carvings. Rooms are unique; you may find yourself in one with a ceramic stove or in another with a Biedermeier desk. For the tradition-minded, there're no finer rooms in town. Bathrooms are spotless, often with a shower and tub combination.

The **Altdeutsches Restaurant** is one of the finest in Dinkelsbühl. It's an attractive rendezvous, intimate and convivial. Franconian and regional specialties are served daily 11:30am to 2pm and 6 to 11pm. In the afternoon many visitors drop in for coffee and freshly baked pastries.

✪ **Eisenkrug.** Dr.-Martin-Luther-Strasse 1, D-91550 Dinkelsbühl. ☎ **09851/57700.** Fax 09851/577070. www.hotel-eisenkrug.de. E-mail: eisenkrug@t-online.de. 23 units. MINIBAR TV TEL. 135DM–160DM ($73–$86) double. Rates include continental breakfast. MC, V. Parking 10DM ($5).

The sienna walls of this central hotel were originally built in 1620. The stylish rooms are filled with engaging old furniture. A newer wing contains the most contemporary rooms, all rather standard and modern, each medium in size. The older rooms offer more charm, although some tend to be smaller. Some beds are canopied, and all have first-class German mattresses. Housekeeping and maintenance are topnotch. Bathrooms vary small to spacious; all but one have a shower instead of a tub.

Mediterrano serves a gourmet international cuisine—the finest dining along the entire road. The chef invents his own recipes and carefully selects ingredients that go into his market-fresh cuisine. His is an indigenous Franconian-Swabian approach, with many innovative touches. The superior wine cellar has some really unusual vintages. À la carte meals cost 25DM to 45DM ($14 to $24). It's open noon to 2pm and 7 to 10pm; closed Monday and Tuesday evenings.

Goldene Rose. Marktplatz 4, D-91550, Dinkelsbühl. ☎ **09851/57-750.** Fax 09851/57-75-75. E-mail: hotel-goldene-rose@t-online.de. 34 units. MINIBAR TV TEL. 140DM–220DM ($76–$119) double. Rates include continental breakfast. AE, DC, MC, V. Parking 6DM ($3.25) in lot, 15DM ($8) in garage.

A landmark in the heart of this village since 1450, the intricately timbered Goldene Rose rises three stories, with a steeply pitched roof and overflowing window boxes. Although it doesn't match the impressive standards of the Eisenkrug, it is one of Dinkelsbühl's best values. The small to medium-size rooms have been modernized in a style more institutional and functional than traditional Bavarian. The more expensive units offer more charm. Bathrooms are rather small, but 10 have full tub and shower.

The dining rooms are country-inn style, with an international cuisine (menu in English). The à la carte menu offers such tempting items as tenderloin of wild hare flavored with hazelnuts, and rump steak. Meals cost 16DM to 30DM ($9 to $16), and service is daily 11:30am to midnight.

NÖRDLINGEN

One of the most irresistible and perfectly preserved medieval towns along the Romantic Road, Nördlingen is still completely encircled by its well-preserved 14th- to 15th-century **city fortifications.** You can walk around the town on the covered parapet, which passes 11 towers and 5 fortified gates set into the walls.

Things are rather peaceful around Nördlingen today, and the city still employs sentries to sound the message, *"So G'sell so"* ("All is well"), as they did in the Middle Ages. However, events around here weren't always so peaceful. The valley sits in a gigantic crater, the Ries. Once thought to be the crater of an extinct volcano, it is now known that a large meteorite was responsible. It hit the ground at more than 100,000 miles per hour, the impact having the destructive force of 250,000 atomic bombs. Debris was hurled as far as Slovakia, and all plant and animal life within a radius of 160km (100 miles) was destroyed. This momentous event took place some 15 million years ago. Today it is the best preserved and most scientifically researched meteorite crater on earth. The American Apollo 14 and 17 astronauts had their field training in the Ries in 1970.

ESSENTIALS

GETTING THERE   By Train Nördlingen lies on the main Nördlingen-Aalen-Stuttgart line, with frequent connections in all directions (trip time: 2 hours from Stuttgart and Nürnberg, 1 hour from Augsburg). Call ☎ **01805/99-66-33** for information.

By Bus   The long-distance bus that operates along the Romantic Road includes Nördlingen; see "Rothenburg" above.

By Car   Take B-25 south from Dinkelsbühl.

VISITOR INFORMATION   Contact the **Verkehrsamt,** Marktplatz 2 (☎ **09081/ 43-80**). The office is open Easter to October, Monday to Thursday 9am to 5pm, and Friday 9am to 3:30pm. The rest of the year, hours are Monday to Thursday 9am to 6am, and Friday 9am to 4:30pm.

WHERE TO STAY

Flamberg Hotel Klösterle. Am Klösterle 1, D-86720 Nördlingen. ☎ **09081/88-054.** Fax 09081/22-740. E-mail: nordlingen@astronhotels.de. 90 units. MINIBAR TV TEL. 202DM ($109) double; from 256DM ($138) suite. Rates include breakfast. AE, DC, MC, V. Parking 15DM ($8).

This is the best place to stay in town. In 1991, this 13th-century former monastery was renovated, a new wing added, and the entire complex transformed into the town's most luxurious hotel. Rated four stars, it offers elevator access, a cozy bar, and a hard-working, polite staff. Rooms have excellent mattresses, lots of electronic extras, and large bathrooms with hair dryers. Under the sloping eaves of the top floor, are a sauna, a fitness center, and a series of conference rooms. The restaurant serves meals every day noon to 2pm and 6 to 10pm.

Kaiser Hotel Sonne. Marktplatz 3, D-86720 Nördlingen. ☎ **09081/50-67.** Fax 09081/23-999. E-mail: kaiserhofhotelsonnet-online.de. 43 units (35 with bathroom). MINIBAR TV TEL. 150DM ($81) double without bathroom; 185DM ($100) double with bathroom; 230DM ($124) suite. Rates include breakfast and parking. AE, DC, MC, V.

Next to the cathedral and the Rathaus, is the Sonne, an inn since 1405. Among its guests have been Frederick III, Maximilian I, Charles V, and, in more recent times, the American Apollo astronauts. Many of the rooms contain hand-painted four-posters to bring out the romantic in you. Others are regular doubles or twins, but each has a firm mattress. Goethe may have complained of the lack of comfort he found here, but you'll fare well. Bathrooms are fresh and immaculate. In the dining rooms, you can order the soup of the day, main courses such as rump steak Mirabeau, and fattening German desserts. It's all quite casual; the waitresses even urge you to finish the food on your plate.

WHERE TO DINE

Meyer's Keller. Marienhöhe 8. ☎ **09081/44-93.** Reservations required. Main courses 26DM–36DM ($14–$19); fixed-price meals 49DM–129DM ($26–$70). AE, MC, V. Wed–Sun noon–2pm; Tues–Sun 6–10pm. Local bus to Marktplatz. CONTINENTAL.

The conservative, modern decor here seems a suitable setting for the restrained *neue Küche* of talented chef and owner, Joachim Kaiser, adroit with both rustic and refined cuisine. The menu changes according to availability of ingredients and the chef's inspiration; typical selections are likely to include roulade of sea wolf and salmon with baby spinach and wild rice, or John Dory with champagne-flavored tomato sauce. The wine list is impressive, with many bottles quite reasonably priced.

SEEING THE SIGHTS

At the center of the circular Altstadt within the walls is **Rübenmarkt.** If you stand in this square on market day, you'll be swept into a world of the past—the country people have preserved many traditional customs and costumes here, which, along with the ancient houses, create a living medieval city. Around the square stand a number of buildings, including the Gothic **Rathaus.** An antiquities collection is displayed in the **Stadtmuseum,** Vordere Gerbergasse 1 (☎ **09081/84-120**), open Tuesday to Sunday 1:30 to 4:30pm; closed November to February. Admission is 7DM ($3.80) for adults and 3.50DM ($1.90) for children.

The 15th-century Hallenkirche, the **Church of St. George,** on the square's northern side, is the town's most interesting sight and one of its oldest buildings. Plaques and epitaphs commemorating the town's more illustrious 16th- and 17th-century residents decorate the fan-vaulted interior. Although the original Gothic altarpiece by Friedrich Herlin (1470) is now in the Reichsstadt Museum, a portion of it, depicting the crucifixion, remains in the church. Above the high altar today stands a more elaborate baroque altarpiece. The church's most prominent feature, however, is the 90m (295-foot) French Gothic tower, called the "Daniel." At night, the town watchman calls out from the steeple, his voice ringing through the streets. The tower is open daily April to October 9am to 8pm. Admission is 3DM ($1.60) for adults and 2DM ($1.10) for children.

Rieskrater-Museum, Hintere Gerbergasse (☎ **09081/273-8220**), documents the impact of the stone meteorite that created the Ries. Examine fossils from Ries Lake deposits and learn about the fascinating evolution of this geological wonder. Hours are Tuesday to Sunday 10am to noon and 1:30 to 4:30pm. Admission is 5DM ($2.70) for adults and 2.50DM ($1.35) for students, seniors, and large groups. Tours of the crater are possible through the museum.

EN ROUTE TO AUGSBURG

After Nördlingen, B-25 heads south to Augsburg. After a 19km (12-mile) ride you can stop to visit **Schloss Harburg** (it's signposted), one of the best-preserved medieval castles in Germany. It once belonged to the Hohenstaufen emperors and contains treasures collected by the family over the centuries. It is open mid-March to September, Tuesday to Sunday 10am to 5pm; October, Tuesday to Sunday 10am to 4pm. Admission is 6DM ($3.25) for adults and 4DM ($2.15) for children, including a guided tour. There's no number to call for information.

After exploring the castle, continue 11km (7 miles) south to the walled town of **Donauwörth,** where you can stop to walk through the oldest part of the town, on an island in the river, connected by a wooden bridge. Here the Danube is only a narrow, placid stream. The town's original walls overlook its second river, the Woernitz.

After a brief stopover, continue your southward trek for 48km (30 miles) to Augsburg, the largest city on the Romantic Road.

AUGSBURG

Augsburg is near the center of the Romantic Road and the gateway to the Alps and the south. Founded 2,000 years ago by the Roman emperor Augustus, for whom it was named, it once was the richest city in Europe. Little remains from the early Roman period. However, the wealth of Renaissance art and architecture is staggering. Over the years, Augsburg has boasted an array of famous native sons, including painters Hans Holbein the Elder and Hans Holbein the Younger, and playwright Bertolt Brecht. It was here in 1518 that Martin Luther was summoned to recant his 95 theses before a papal emissary. Only 15% of the city was left standing after World War II, but there's still much here to intrigue. Today, Augsburg is an important industrial center on the Frankfurt-Salzburg autobahn, and Bavaria's third largest city after Munich and Nürnberg.

ESSENTIALS

GETTING THERE   By Train   About 90 Euro and InterCity trains arrive here daily all major German cities. For information, call ☎ **01805/99-66-33.** There are 60 trains a day from Munich (trip time: 30 to 50 minutes), and 35 from Frankfurt (trip time: 3 to 4^1/₂ hours).

By Bus   Long-distance buses (lines EB190 and 190A, plus line 189) service the Romantic Road. The buses are operated by **Deutsche Touring GmbH** at Am Römerhof in Frankfurt (☎ **069/790-32-56** for reservations and information).

VISITOR INFORMATION   Contact **Tourist-Information,** Bahnhofstrasse (☎ **0821/50-20-70**), Monday to Friday 9am to 6pm, Saturday at Rathausplatz 10am to 4pm, closed Sunday.

GETTING AROUND   The public transportation system in Augsburg consists of four tram and 31 bus lines covering the inner city and reaching into the suburbs. Public transportation operates daily 5am to midnight, and service is provided by **Augsburger Verkehrsverband AVV** (☎ **0821/15-70-07**).

WHERE TO STAY
Very Expensive

✪   **Steigenberger Drei Mohren.** Maximilianstrasse 40, D-86150 Augsburg. ☎ **800/223-5652** in the U.S. and Canada, or 0821/5-03-60. Fax 0821/15-78-64. 107 units. MINIBAR TV TEL. 329DM–379DM ($178–$205) double; 290DM–550DM ($157–$297) suite. Rates include buffet breakfast. AE, DC, MC, V. Parking 22DM ($12). Tram: 1.

The original hotel, dating from 1723, was renowned in Germany before its destruction in an air raid. In 1956, it was rebuilt in a modern style, and it remains the premier hotel in town. Decorators worked hard to create a decor that was both comfortable and inviting, with thick carpets, subdued lighting, double glazing at the windows, and such extra amenities as safes and trouser presses. Rooms vary in size and appointments, however, ranging from some economy specials that are a bit small with narrow twin beds and showers (no tubs) to spacious, luxurious units with full shower and tub. Each has a good mattress, however. Many rooms are smoke free, and most bathrooms are fairly spacious. The formal dining room offers an international cuisine. The staff can arrange golf nearby.

Moderate

Dom Hotel. Frauentorstrasse 8, D-86152 Augsburg. ☎ **0821/34-39-30.** Fax 0821/34-39-32-00. E-mail:domhotel.augsburg@t-online.de 43 units. TV TEL. 137DM–198DM ($74–$107) double. Rates include buffet breakfast. AE, DC, MC, V. Free parking or 10DM ($5) garage. Tram: 2.

Although it may not have the decorative flair of the more expensive hotels, the low rates and an indoor pool make this one of the most appealing choices in town. The hotel is a half-timbered structure, next to Augsburg's famous cathedral, and was built in the 15th century. Rooms on most floors are medium size and nicely appointed, although we prefer the smaller attic accommodations where you can rest under a beamed ceiling and enjoy a panoramic sweep of the rooftops of the city. All rooms have good beds with firm mattresses. Bathrooms are small. In warm weather, breakfast—the only meal served—can be enjoyed in a garden beside the town's medieval fortifications.

Hotel Am Rathaus. Am Hinteren Perlachberg 1, D-86150 Augsburg. ☎ **0821/34-64-90.** Fax 0821/346-49-99. www.pyramide.de. 32 units. MINIBAR TV TEL. 205DM ($111) double. AE, DC, MC, V. Parking 15DM ($8). Tram: 1.

Many repeat guests consider this hotel's location just behind the town hall to be its best asset. Built in a three-story contemporary format in 1986, it offers comfortable rooms and a well-stocked breakfast buffet. It may be short on style but it's long on value. There's no restaurant or bar.

Romantik Hotel Augsburger Hof. Auf dem Kreuz 2, D-86152 Augsburg. ☎ **0821/ 34-30-50.** Fax 0821/343-0555. www.romantikhotel.de. E-mail: info@romantik.de. 36 units. MINIBAR TV TEL. 130DM–280DM ($70–$151) double. Rates include buffet breakfast. AE, DC, MC, V. Parking 10DM ($5). Tram: 1.

Originally built in 1767 in a solid, thick-walled design with exposed beams and timbers, this hotel was carefully restored in 1988. In the town center, it's a favorite for its traditional atmosphere and its excellent food. In spite of the Renaissance interior, the rooms are completely up to date and not as romantic as the name of the hotel suggests. They range from cozy to spacious, each with a fine bed and quality mattress. Those overlooking the calm inner courtyard are more expensive than ones facing the street. Some bathrooms seemed crowded in as an afterthought, but each is beautifully maintained. On the premises a restaurant serves German and international food.

Inexpensive

Hotel Garni Weinberger. Bismarckstrasse 55, D-86391 Stadtbergen. ☎ **0821/24-39-10.** Fax 0821/43-88-31. 31 units (26 with bathroom). 130DM ($70) double without bathroom; 150DM ($81) double with bathroom. Rates include buffet breakfast. No credit cards. Closed Aug 15–30. Tram: 3.

One of the best budget accommodations in the area lies about 3km (2 miles) from the center along Augsburgerstrasse in the western sector. Rooms are small but well kept with good beds and firm mattresses. The private bathrooms are rather cramped, the towels a bit thin, but housekeeping is excellent. Corridor bathrooms are adequate and kept tidy. The place is well patronized by bargain-hunting Germans, and its cafe is one of the most popular in the area for snacks.

WHERE TO DINE

Die Ecke. Elias-Holl-Platz 2. ☎ **0821/51-06-00.** Reservations required. Main courses 26DM–45DM ($14–$24); fixed-price dinner 65DM ($35) for 4 courses, 98DM ($53) for 6 courses. AE, DC, MC, V. Daily 11:30am–2:30pm and 5:30pm–1am. Tram: 2. FRENCH/SWABIAN.

Since Die Ecke was founded in the year Columbus sighted the New World, its guests have included Hans Holbein the Elder, Wolfgang Amadeus Mozart, and, in more contemporary times, Bertolt Brecht, whose sharp-tongued irreverence tended to irritate diners of more conservative political leanings. The weinstube ambience belies the skilled cuisine of the chef, which wins us over year after year. Breast of duckling might be preceded by pâté, and the fillet of sole in Riesling is deservedly a classic. Venison dishes in season are a specialty—the best in town.

Fuggerei Stube. Jakoberstrasse 26. ☎ **0821/3-08-70.** Reservations recommended. Main courses 19.50DM–28DM ($11–$15), set price menu 36DM ($19). AE, MC, V. Tues–Sun 11:30am–2pm; Tues–Sat 6:30pm–1:30am. GERMAN/SWABIAN.

The building that contains this carefully maintained restaurant was constructed in 1546 as the home of a local politician and merchant. The large dining room, suitable for 60 persons, has welcomed diners since 1946, with very little change in the menu, the decor, or the ambience. Expect generous portions of well-prepared food such as sauerbraten, roasted pork, pork schnitzel; game dishes such as venison, pheasant, and rabbit; and fish such as fillet of sole served with boiled potatoes and parsley. The beer foaming out of the taps here is Storchenbräu, and most visitors find that it goes wonderfully with the conservative German specialties.

✪ **Oblinger.** Pfäarrle 14. ☎ **0821/345-83-92.** Reservations required. Main courses 22DM–42DM ($12–$23). AE, DC, MC, V. Tues–Sun 11am–2pm; Tues–Sat 6–11pm. Closed Aug 1–19. Tram: 12. CONTINENTAL.

Near the cathedral, in the heart of the historic section, Oblinger is the best restaurant within the city. It's a charming, intimate 20-seat choice offering a changing array of seasonal specialties. The surroundings are unpretentious, the waiters attentive, and there's a superb collection of wine. You can savor the goose-liver terrine with mushrooms and cabbage, going on to an equally well-prepared sole roulade with crepes. The turbot with chanterelles and the stuffed Bresse pigeon are also successes—quite simply, the cuisine has personality.

SEEING THE SIGHTS IN TOWN

Rathaus. Am Rathausplatz 2. ☎ **0821/3241.** Admission 3DM ($1.60) adults, 1DM (55¢) children 7–14. Daily 10am–6pm. Tram: 1.

In 1805 and 1809, Napoléon visited the Rathaus, built by Elias Holl in 1620. Regrettably, it was also visited by an air raid in 1944, leaving a mere shell of the building that had once been a palatial eight-story monument to the glory of the Renaissance. Its celebrated "golden chamber" was left in shambles. Now, after costly restoration, the Rathaus is open to the public.

Dom St. Maria. Hoher Weg. ☎ **0821/31-66-353.** Free admission. Mon–Sat 7am–6pm, Sun noon–6pm. Tram: 1.

The cathedral of Augsburg has the distinction of containing the oldest stained-glass windows in the world. Those in the south transept, dating from the 12th century, depict Old Testament prophets in a severe but colorful style. They are younger than the cathedral itself, which was begun in 944. You'll find the ruins of the original basilica in the crypt beneath the west chancel. Partially Gothicized in the 14th century, the

Exploring the Fuggerei

Throughout its history, Augsburg has been an important city, but during the 15th and 16th centuries it was one of Europe's wealthiest communities, mainly because of its textile industry and the political and financial clout of its two banking families, the Welsers and the Fuggers. The Welsers, who once owned nearly all of Venezuela, have long since faded from the minds of Augsburgers. But the founders of the powerful Fugger family have established themselves forever in the hearts of townsfolk by an unusual legacy, the ✪ **Fuggerei,** created in 1519 to house poorer Augsburgers. A master mason fallen on hard times, Franz Mozart (great-grandfather of Wolfgang Amadeus Mozart), once lived at Mittlere Gasse 14. The quarter consists of several streets lined with well-maintained Renaissance houses, as well as a church and administrative offices, all enclosed within walls. The Fugger Foundation still owns the Fuggerei.

The house at Mittlere Gasse 13, next to the one once occupied by Mozart's ancestor, is now the Fuggerei's **museum** (☎ **0821/30-868**). The rough 16th- and 17th-century furniture, wood-paneled ceilings and walls, and cast-iron stove, as well as other objects of everyday life, show what it was like to live there in earlier times. Admission is 1DM (55¢). It's open March to October, daily 9am to 6pm. Take tram no. 1.

church stands on the edge of the park, which also fronts the **Episcopal Palace,** where the basic Lutheran creed was presented at the Diet of Augsburg in 1530. The 11th-century bronze doors, leading into the three-aisle nave, are adorned with bas-reliefs of biblical and mythological characters. The cathedral's interior, restored in 1934, contains side altars with altarpieces by Hans Holbein the Elder and Christoph Amberger.

Church of St. Ulrich and St. Afra. Ulrichplatz 19. ☎ **0821/34-55-60.** Free admission. Daily 9am–6pm. Tram: 1.

This is the most attractive church in Augsburg. It was constructed between 1476 and 1500 on the site of a Roman temple. The church and the dom, one Protestant, one Catholic, stand side by side, a tribute to the 1555 Peace of Augsburg, which recognized the two denominations, Roman Catholic and Lutheran. Many of the church's furnishings, including the three altars representing the birth and resurrection of Christ and the baptism of the church by the Holy Spirit, are baroque. In the crypt are the tombs of the Swabian saints, Ulrich and Afra.

Schaezlerpalais. Maximilianstrasse 46. ☎ **0821/324-21-71.** Admission 4DM ($2.15) adults, 2DM ($1.10) children. Wed–Sun 10am–4pm. Tram: 1.

Facing the Hercules Fountain is the Schaezlerpalais, home to the city's art galleries. Constructed as a 60-room mansion between 1765 and 1770, it was willed to Augsburg after World War II. Most of the paintings are Renaissance and baroque. One of the most famous is Dürer's portrait of Jakob Fugger the Rich, founder of the dynasty that was once powerful enough to influence the elections of the Holy Roman emperors. Other works are by local artists Hans Burgkmair and Hans Holbein the Elder; Rubens, Veronese, and Tiepolo are also represented.

NEUSCHWANSTEIN & HOHENSCHWANGAU: THE ROYAL CASTLES

The 19th century saw a great classical revival in Germany, especially in Bavaria, mainly because of the enthusiasm of Bavarian kings for ancient art forms. Beginning with

Ludwig I (1786–1868), who was responsible for many Greek Revival buildings in Munich, this royal house ran the gamut of ancient architecture in just 3 short decades. It culminated in the remarkable flights of fancy of "Mad" King Ludwig II, who died under mysterious circumstances in 1886. In spite of his rather lonely life and controversial alliances, both personal and political, he was a great patron of the arts.

Although the name "Royal Castles" is limited to Hohenschwangau (built by Ludwig's father, Maximilian II) and Neuschwanstein, the extravagant king was responsible for the creation of two other magnificent castles, Linderhof (near Oberammergau) and Herrenchiemsee (on an island in Chiemsee).

In 1868, after a visit to the great castle of Wartburg, Ludwig wrote to his good friend, composer Richard Wagner: "I have the intention to rebuild the ancient castle ruins of Hohenschwangau in the true style of the ancient German knight's castle." The following year, construction began on the first of a series of fantastic edifices, a series that stopped only with Ludwig's death in 1886, only 5 days after he was deposed because of alleged insanity.

The nearest towns to the castles are **Füssen,** 3km (2 miles) away at the very end of the Romantic Road, and **Schwangau,** where accommodations can be found.

ESSENTIALS

GETTING THERE   By Train   There're frequent trains from Munich (trip time: 2¹⁄₂ hours) and Augsburg (trip time: 3 hours) to Füssen. For information, call ☎ **01805/99-66-33.** Frequent buses travel to the castles.

By Bus   Long-distance bus service into Füssen from other parts of the Romantic Road including Würzburg, Augsburg, and Munich, is provided by the **Deutsche Touring GmbH** bus EB189 or EB189E. For information and reservations, call ☎ **069/790-3281** in Frankfurt. Regional service to villages around Füssen is provided by **RVA Regionalverkehr Allgau GmbH** in Füssen (☎ **08362/37771**). It's most important routing, at least for visitors to Füssen, includes about 14 orange, yellow, or white-sided buses that depart every day Füssen's railway station for the village of Hohenschwangau, site of both Hohenschwangau Palace and Neuschwanstein Palace, a 10-minute ride. The cost of a one-way ticket to the village or to either of the two palaces is 3.50DM ($1.90). For more information, contact the Füssen Tourist office.

By Car   Take B-17 south to Füssen, then head east from Füssen on B-17.

VISITOR INFORMATION   For information about the castles and the region in general, contact the **Kurverwaltung,** Kaiser-Maximilian-Platz 1, Füssen (☎ **08362/ 938-50**), open Monday to Friday 8am to noon and 2 to 5pm, Saturday 10am to noon. Information is also available at the **Kurverwaltung,** Rathaus, Münchenerstrasse 2, Schwangau (☎ **08362/8-19-80**). It's open Monday to Friday 8am to 5pm.

WHERE TO STAY
In Hohenschwangau

Hotel Lisl and Jägerhaus. Neuschwansteinstrasse 1–3, D-87645 Hohenschwangau. ☎ **08362/88-70.** Fax 08362/81-107. www.lisl.de. E-mail: info@lisl.de. 47 units. TV TEL. 190DM–368DM ($103–$199) double. AE, DC, MC, V. Closed Christmas and New Year's. Free parking.

This graciously styled villa and its annex across the street sit in a narrow valley, surrounded by their own gardens. Most rooms have a view of at least one of the two royal castles and some units open onto views of both. We prefer the rooms in the main building to the more sterile annex, but all are comfortable, and have good, firm mattresses. Bathrooms, though small, are adequate. Two well-styled dining rooms serve decent meals; the restaurant features both international and local dishes.

Hotel Müller Hohenschwangau. Alpseestrasse 16, D-87645 Hohenschwangau. ☎ **08362/8-19-90.** Fax 08362/81-99-13. www.hotel-mueller.de. E-mail: info@hotel-mueller.de. 43 units. TV TEL. 220DM–300DM ($119–$162) double; 350DM–600DM ($189–$324) suite. Rates include buffet breakfast. DC, MC, V. Free parking. Closed Jan–Feb.

As if the yellow walls, green shutters, and gabled alpine detailing of this hospitable inn weren't incentive enough, its location near the foundation of Neuschwanstein Castle makes it even more alluring. Rooms are inviting and have a bit of Bavarian charm, each with a good bed. The shower-only bathrooms are spotless. On the premises are two pleasant restaurants. Nature lovers usually enjoy hiking the short distance to nearby Hohenschwangau Castle.

In or Near Füssen

AlstadHotel Zum Hechten. Ritterstrasse 6, D-87629 Füssen. ☎ **08362/91-600.** Fax 08362/91-6099. www.hotel-hechten.com. E-mail: hotel.hechten@t-online.de. 35 units, 29 with bathroom. 100DM ($54) double without bathroom; 120DM–145DM ($65–$78) double with bathroom. Rates include buffet breakfast. No credit cards. Free outside parking, 5DM ($2.70) garage.

Family owners have maintained this impeccable guest house for generations—it's one of the oldest (and most comfortable) in town. In spring, you'll open your window to a flower box of geraniums, and feel like Gretel (or Hansel) getting ready to milk the cows. Rooms are small to medium size; the bathrooms spotless but a bit cramped. Corridor bathrooms are adequate and well maintained. The guest house offers two restaurants. A typical Swabian and Bavarian cuisine is served, with plenty of dishes to please the vegetarian as well.

Hotel Christine. Weidachstrasse 31, D-87629 Füssen. ☎ **08362/72-29.** Fax 08362/940554. 13 units. TV TEL. 160DM–260DM ($86–$140) double. Rates include breakfast. No credit cards. Closed Jan 15–Feb 15.

The Christine, 5 minutes by taxi from the train station in Füssen, is one of the best local choices for accommodation. The staff spends the winter months refurbishing the rooms so they'll be fresh and sparkling for spring visitors. A Bavarian charm pervades the hotel, and rooms are cozy, though hardly fit for King Ludwig. Each is well maintained and supplied with firm German mattresses. The shower-only bathrooms are a bit cramped. Breakfast, the only meal offered, is served on beautiful regional china as classical music plays in the background.

Seegasthof Weissensee. An der B-310, D-87629 Füssen-Weissensee. ☎ **08362/91780.** Fax 08362/917888. 19 units. MINIBAR TEL. 136DM ($73) double. Rates include breakfast. No credit cards. Free parking.

The paneled rooms at this hotel have sliding glass doors opening onto a balcony overlooking the lake, 6.5km (4 miles) from central Füssen on B-310. Each room has a minibar stocked with beer, wine, and champagne. Owners are extra careful about the comfort of their guests, maintaining quality mattresses in the small but very well-maintained rooms. Bathrooms, also small, are well kept with shower stalls. Breakfast is an appetizing and generous meal of cheese, cold cuts, bread, pastry, eggs, and beverages. The fish that your obliging hosts serve you for dinner might have been caught in the ice-blue waters of the nearby lake, whose far shore you can see from the dining room.

Steig Mühle. Alte Steige 3, D-87629 Weissensee-Oberkirch. ☎ **08362/91-76-0.** Fax 08362/31-48. 13 units. TV TEL. 98DM–111DM ($53–$60) double. Rates include buffet breakfast. No credit cards. Free outside parking, 4.50DM ($2.45) in garage. From Füssen, take Route B310 north toward Kempten, a 5-minute drive.

Owners and hosts Gunter and Nedwig Buhmann like things to be cozy, and their chaletlike guest house is almost a cliché of Bavarian charm. The rooms open onto a view of the lake or mountains, and many have their own balconies. Each room has been outfitted with double or twin beds and firm mattresses. Private bathrooms (shower only) are well kept. There aren't a lot of frills, but the place offers one of the most exceptional hotel values in the area.

WHERE TO DINE

Fischerhütte. Uferstrasse 16, Hopfen am See. ☎ **08362/91-97-0.** Reservations recommended. Main courses 30DM–42DM ($16–$23). AE, DC, MC, V. Daily 11am–2pm and 6–10pm. Closed Tues in Jan–Mar. SEAFOOD.

In the hamlet of Hopfen am See, at the edge of the lake within sight of dramatic mountain scenery 5km (3 miles) northwest of Füssen, lie four old-fashioned dining rooms, plus a terrace in summer. As the name "Fisherman's Cottage" suggests, the establishment specializes in an array of international fish dishes: half an Alaskan salmon (for two); a garlicky version of French bouillabaisse; fresh alpine trout, pan-fried or with aromatic herbs in the style of Provence; North Atlantic lobster; and grilled halibut. A few meat dishes are also offered, as well as tempting desserts.

Zum Schwanen. Brotmarkt 4, Füssen. ☎ **08362/61-74.** Reservations required. Main courses 15DM–28DM ($8–$15). AE, DC, V. Tues–Sun 11:30am–2pm; Tues–Sat 5:30–9pm. Closed Nov. SWABIAN/BAVARIAN.

This small, old-fashioned restaurant serves a conservative yet flavorful blend of Swabian and Bavarian specialties. Good-tasting and hearty specialties include homemade sausage, roast pork, lamb, and venison.

VISITING THE ROYAL CASTLES

There are often very long lines in summer, especially August. With 25,000 people a day visiting , the wait in peak summer months can be as long as 4 or 5 hours for a 20-minute tour. The telephone number for Neuschwanstein is ☎ **08362/8-10-35;** for Hohenschwangau, ☎ **08362/8-11-27.**

✪ Neuschwanstein

This is the fairy-tale castle of Ludwig II. Construction went on for 17 years, until the king's death, when all work stopped, leaving a part of the interior uncompleted. Ludwig lived here on and off for about 6 months from 1884 to 1886.

The doorway off the left side of the vestibule leads to the king's apartments. The study, like most of the rooms, is decorated with wall paintings showing scenes from the Nordic legends (which inspired Wagner's operas). The theme of the study is the Tannhäuser saga, painted by J. Aigner. The curtains and chair coverings are in hand-embroidered silk, designed with the Bavarian coat of arms.

From the vestibule, you enter the throne room through the doorway at the opposite end. This hall, designed in Byzantine style by J. Hofmann, was never completed. The floor, a mosaic design, depicts the animals of the world. The columns in the main hall are the deep copper red of porphyry.

The king's bedroom is the most richly carved and decorated in the entire castle—it took 4¹/₂ years to complete. Aside from the mural showing the legend of Tristan and Isolde, the walls are decorated with panels carved to look like Gothic windows. In the center is a large wooden pillar completely encircled with gilded brass sconces. The ornate bed is on a raised platform with an elaborately carved canopy.

The fourth floor of the castle is almost entirely given over to the **Singer's Hall,** the pride of Ludwig II and all of Bavaria. Modeled after the hall at Wartburg, where the legendary song contest of Tannhäuser supposedly took place, this hall is decorated with marble columns and elaborately painted designs interspersed with frescoes depicting the life of Parsifal.

The castle is open year-round, and in September, visitors have the additional treat of hearing Wagnerian concerts and other music in the Singer's Hall. For information and reservations, contact the tourist office in Schwangau, **Verkehrsamt,** at the Rathaus (☎ **08362/8-19-80**). The castle, which is seen by guided tour, is open daily April to September 9am to 5:30pm, October to March 10am to 4pm. Admission is 12DM ($7) for adults, 9DM ($4.85) for students and seniors over 65; children 5 and under enter free.

Reaching Neuschwanstein involves a steep .8km (half-mile) climb from the parking lot of Hohenschwangau Castle, about a 25-minute walk for the energetic, an eternity for anybody else. To cut down on the climb, you can take a bus to Marienbrücke, a bridge that crosses over the Pollat Gorge at a height of 93m (305 feet). From that vantage you, like Ludwig, can stand and meditate on the glories of the castle and its panoramic surroundings. If you want to photograph the castle, don't wait until you reach the top, where you'll be too close. It costs 3.50DM ($1.90) for the bus ride up to the bridge or 2DM ($1.10) if you'd like to take the bus back down the hill. From the Marienbrücke bridge it's a 10-minute walk to Neuschwanstein over a very steep footpath that is not easy to negotiate for anyone who has trouble walking up or down precipitous hills.

The most colorful way to reach Neuschwanstein is by horse-drawn carriage, costing 8DM ($4.30) for the ascent, 4DM ($2.15) for the descent. However, some readers have objected to the rides, complaining that too many people are crowded in.

✪ Hohenschwangau

Not as glamorous or spectacular as Neuschwanstein, the neo-Gothic Hohenschwangau Castle nevertheless has a much richer history. The original structure dates back to the 12th-century knights of Schwangau. When the knights faded away, the castle began to do so too, helped along by the Napoleonic Wars. When Ludwig II's father, Crown Prince Maximilian (later Maximilian II), saw the castle in 1832, he purchased it and 4 years later had completely restored it. Ludwig II spent the first 17 years of his life here and later received Richard Wagner in its chambers, although Wagner never visited Neuschwanstein on the hill above.

The rooms of Hohenschwangau are styled and furnished in a much heavier Gothic mode than those in Ludwig's castle and are typical of the halls of medieval knights' castles. Also unlike Neuschwanstein, this castle has a comfortable look about it, as if it actually were a home, not just a museum. The small chapel, once a reception hall, still hosts Sunday Mass. The suits of armor and the Gothic arches set the stage. Among the most attractive chambers is the **Hall of the Swan Knight,** named for the wall paintings that tell the saga of Lohengrin.

Hohenschwangau is open daily March 15 to mid-October 8:30am to 5:30pm, off-season 9:30am to 4pm. Admission is 12DM ($7) for adults and 9DM ($4.85) for children 6 to 15 and seniors over 65; children 5 and under free. Several parking lots nearby enable you to leave your car while visiting both castles.

OUTDOOR ACTIVITIES IN THE AREA

Most visitors come to Füssen for views of its magnificent Bavarian castles, testimonials to the megalomania of a demented king. But if you want to get away the grandeur of his dreams, nearby Forggensee and Hopfensee provide lots of opportunities for windsurfing, swimming, and sailing. The focal points for all of these include the

Forggensee's **Yachtschule Forggensee,** Seestrasse 10, 87669 Rieden (☎ **08367/ 471**), and the Hopfensee's **Selbach Bootsvermietung,** Höhenstrasse 51, 87629 Hopfen (☎ **08362/1487**). At both of these sites, instruction for, and rentals of wind-surfers and sailboats is available.

There's also a limited amount of midwinter skiing available in the area, at lower altitudes and with less reliable snowfall, than that which prevails at more visible resorts such as Garmisch. About 6.5km (4 miles) from Füssen, the **Schigebiet Tegelberg,** near the hamlet of Schwangau (☎ **08362/98-36-0**), provides a half-dozen lifts and a cable car that ascend the slopes of the Tegelberg.

Frankly, your best bet for recreation, diversion, and distraction will probably involve hiking and hill climbing in the foothills around Füssen and Schwangau. Maps, guide services, and hiking-related information of all kinds are available from the local tourist offices.

A SIDE TRIP TO WIESKIRCHE

A fascinating excursion is to the ✪ **Wieskirche** (☎ **08861/8173**), one of the most extravagant and flamboyant rococo buildings in the world, a masterpiece of Dominikus Zimmermann. On the slopes of the Ammergau Alps, between Ammer and Lech, the Wieskirche is a noted pilgrimage church, drawing visitors from all over the globe. It's in an alpine meadow just off the Romantic Road near Steingaden. Ask at the tourist office for a map and the exact location before setting out. The church, which in German means "in the meadows," was built to honor the memory of Jesus Scourged. With the help of his brother, Johann Baptist, Zimmermann worked on the building from 1746 to 1754. Around the choir, the church has "upside-down" arches, and its ceiling is richly frescoed. Hours are daily 8am to 7pm. A bus heading for the church leaves Füssen Monday to Saturday at 11:15am and on Sunday at 1:05pm. You can return on the 3:50pm bus from the church. The trip takes an hour and costs 16.50DM ($9) round-trip.

8 Greece

by Sherry Marker

The "glory that was Greece" continues to lure visitors to see the Acropolis in Athens; Olympia, where the games began; Delphi, with the magnificent temple of Apollo; Mycenae, where Agamemnon met his bloody death when he returned home from Troy; and Epidauros, with its astonishingly well-preserved ancient theater. There's also a profusion of less well-known ancient sites—such as Nemea, home to a newly restored stadium—as well as a wealth of Byzantine monuments, including the churches of Daphni and Osios Loukas. Greece is the quintessential land of mountains and seashore, where you can laze the day away on a perfect beach before dancing the night away on Mykonos or Santorini or one of the other breathtakingly beautiful "isles of Greece."

1 Athens

Athens is the city that Greeks love to hate, complaining that it's too expensive, too crowded, and too polluted. Some 40% of Greece's population lives here, and with five million inhabitants, a rumored 17,000 taxis, and streets so congested you'll suspect that each of those five million Athenians has a car, the city is bursting at the seams. The new Metro (subway) station in Syntagma Square opened on January 28, 2000, although work on the Metro elsewhere in Athens proceeds at a snail's pace, with the tunneling disrupting traffic in much of central Athens. So, why are you here? Because you, too, will probably soon develop a love-hate relationship with Athens, snarling at the traffic and gasping in wonder at the Acropolis, fuming at the taxi driver who tries to overcharge you, and marveling at the stranger who realizes that you're lost and walks several blocks out of his way to take you where you're going.

Allow yourself some time to make haste slowly in Athens. Your best moments may come at a small cafe, sipping a tiny cup of the sweet sludge that Greeks call coffee, or getting hopelessly lost in the Plaka—only to find yourself in the shady courtyard of an old church. With only a little planning, you should find a good hotel, eat well in convivial restaurants, and leave Athens expecting to return, as the Greeks say, *Tou Chronou:* next year.

ORIENTATION
GETTING THERE   By Plane   Athens's **Ellinikon International Airport** is only 11km (7 miles) south of Syntagma (Constitution)

Square, but traffic to and from the airport is often so heavy you should allow an hour for the trip. Most visitors arrive at the **East (Anatoliko) Air Terminal,** on the eastern side of the runways. You can change money at one of the major Greek bank branches here (usually open 24 hours) or at the ATM and get a free luggage cart while waiting for your luggage to arrive in the baggage area or after you clear Customs in the main airport. The **Greek National Tourist Organization** (GNTO or EOT) information desk, slightly to the left as you come out of Customs, usually has pamphlets on Athens, and for a small fee its staff will book you into a hotel in your price range. Outside the terminal, a taxi rank is to the right and buses are to the left.

All domestic and international flights of the national airline, **Olympic Airways,** arrive at the newer **West (Dytiko) Air Terminal.** For information about incoming Olympic flights, call ☎ **01/926-9111** or 01/966-6666. Bank offices are in the arrivals area and are officially open 7am to 11pm, but often closed by 7pm; ATMs usually operate 24 hours. Olympic has an information booth, and the Tourist Police have a corner office in the building across from the terminal entrance.

Many charter flights now use the **Charter Terminal,** south of the East Air Terminal. The information numbers for the Charter Terminal are ☎ **01/997-2581** or 01/997-2686.

If you arrive at one of these three terminals and have to make connections at another, you can take either the shuttle bus service for 200Dr (65¢) or a taxi. The shuttle bus service officially runs once an hour from 8:30am to 8:30pm, but actually runs on an erratic schedule.

If you're heading into Athens, a **taxi** into the center (kentro) from any of the three terminals should cost about 2,000Dr to 3,000Dr ($7 to $10), double that between midnight and 5am. *Note:* If you decide to take a taxi, ask an airline official or a policeman what the fare should be, and let the taxi driver know that you have been told the official rate before you begin your journey.

All **bus schedules** are erratic, and those posted at the airports are frequently months out of date. **Buses** 91 and 101 run from the East and West Terminals into central Athens for 200Dr (65¢). Schedules are *very* erratic, with both buses officially running 7am to 10pm, and no. 91 continuing service until midnight. In addition, bus 101 runs from the West Terminal to Athens and continues to Piraeus; the official schedule for service is hourly 8am to midnight for 100Dr (35¢). There's sometimes hourly express bus service to Athens, continuing on to Piraeus. In short, all bus schedules are erratic, and schedules posted at the airport are often months—sometimes years—out of date. Due to ongoing roadwork between Athens and Piraeus, journey times and routes are constantly subject to change.

Athens's new airport, **Eleftherios Venizelos International,** is currently under construction and scheduled to open at Spata, 23km (14 miles) outside Athens, in March 2001. If you are traveling around this time, be sure to check with your travel agent to see whether the new airport has, in fact, opened.

By Train   Trains from the west, including Eurail connections via Patra, arrive at the **Peloponnese Station (Stathmos Peloponnissou),** about 1.5km (1 mile) northwest of Omonia Square. Trains from the north arrive 3 blocks north at the **Larissa Station (Stathmos Larissis),** on the opposite side of the tracks from the Peloponnese Station. If you are making connections from one station to the other, allow 10 to 15 minutes for the walk. Both stations have currency-exchange offices that are usually open daily 8am to 9pm and a luggage-storage office usually open 6am to 9pm that charges 500Dr ($1.65) per bag per day. A taxi into the center of town from either station should cost about 1,000Dr ($3.35).

Athens

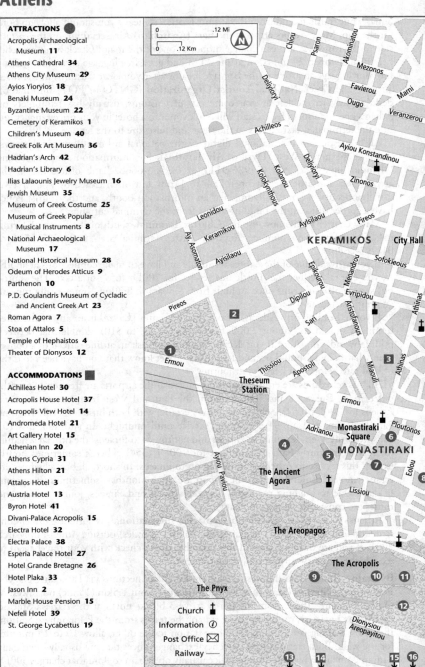

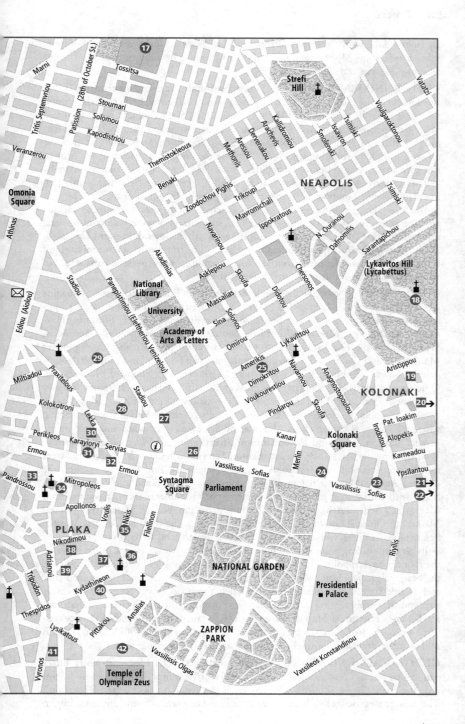

By Boat   Athens's main seaport, **Piraeus,** 11km (7 miles) southwest, is a 15-minute subway ride from Monastiraki and Omonia squares. The subway runs from about 5am to midnight and costs 250Dr (85¢).

VISITOR INFORMATION   **The Greek National Tourist Organization** (EOT, also known as the Hellenic Tourism Organization) has its central office on the ground floor at 2 Amerikis St. (☎ **01/331-0437** or 01/331-0561), 2 blocks west of Syntagma Square between Stadiou and Venizelou. It's open weekdays 9am to 7pm and Saturday 9:30am to 2pm (closed holidays). No sign identifies the building as an EOT office, but there's a round sign with an "i" above the door. Information about Athens, free city maps, transportation schedules, hotel lists, and other booklets on many regions of Greece are available in Greek, English, French, and German—although many publications on popular sites seem to be perpetually out of print.

You can also get information on the Internet. Web sites for Greece include **www.phantis.com** (search engine for Hellenic Resources); **www.ellada.com** (general information); **city.net** (Athens Information); **www.athensnews.dolnet.gr** (*The Athens News)*; **www.compulink.gr/tourism** (general information); **www.areianet.gr/ infoxenios** (Greek National Tourism Organization); **www.perseus.tufts.edu** (an excellent source for information on ancient Greece).

CITY LAYOUT   If you, like the Greek mathematician Euclid, find it easy to imagine geometric forms, it will help you to think of Central Athens as an almost perfect equilateral triangle, with its points at **Syntagma (Constitution) Square, Omonia (Harmony) Square,** and **Monastiraki (Little Monastery) Square,** near the **Acropolis.** With luck, by the time you arrive in Athens, the construction cranes towering over Monastiraki and Omonia, like those in Syntagma, will be gone, and more of the new Athens subway will be open. In government jargon, the area bounded by Syntagma, Omonia, and Monastiraki Squares is defined as the commercial center, from which cars are banned (in theory, if not in practice) except for several cross streets. Most Greeks consider Omonia the city center, but visitors usually get their bearings from Syntagma, where the House of Parliament is. Omonia and Syntagma squares are connected by the parallel **Stadiou Street** and **Panepistimiou Street,** also called Eleftheriou Venizelou. West from Syntagma Square, ancient **Ermou Street** and broader **Mitropoleos Street** lead slightly downhill to Monastiraki Square. Here you'll find the **flea market,** the **Ancient Agora (Market)** below the Acropolis, and the **Plaka,** the oldest neighborhood, with many street names and a scattering of monuments from antiquity. From Monastiraki Square, **Athinas Street** leads north past the modern Market (the Central Market) to Omonia Square. Bustling with shoppers in the daytime, Athinas Street is best avoided at night, when prostitutes and drug dealers tend to hang out here.

In general, finding your way around Athens is relatively easy, except in the Plaka, at the foot of the Acropolis. This labyrinth of narrow, winding streets can challenge even the best navigators. Don't panic: The area is small enough that you can't go far astray, and its side streets, with small houses and neighborhood churches, are so charming that you won't mind being lost. One excellent map may help: the Greek Archaeological Service's **Historical Map of Athens,** which has maps of Plaka and of the city center showing the major archaeological sites. The map costs about 500Dr ($1.65) and is sold at many bookstores, museums, ancient sites, and newspaper kiosks.

GETTING AROUND   By Public Transportation   The **blue-and-white buses** run regular routes in Athens and its suburbs every 15 minutes from 5am to midnight. (For the more distant suburbs, you may need to change buses at a transfer station.) The **orange electric trolley buses** serve areas in the city center from 5am to midnight.

A Metro Museum

The Metro station at Syntagma Square displays finds from the subway excavations in what amounts to Athens's newest small museum.

The **green buses** run between the city center and Piraeus every 20 minutes from 6am to midnight, then hourly until 6am. Tickets cost 120Dr (40¢) and must be purchased in advance, usually in groups of 10, from any news kiosk or special bus ticket kiosks at the main stations.

When you board, validate your ticket in the automatic machine. Hold on to your ticket: Uniformed and plainclothes inspectors periodically check tickets and can levy fines of 1,500Dr ($5) on the spot.

The **Athens map** distributed by the Greek National Tourist Organization indicates major public transportation stops and routes. Keep in mind that the buses are usually very crowded and their schedules are erratic. Furthermore, construction on the Metro, as well as the opening of new Metro stops, is affecting bus routes and schedules. In January 2000, buses running on Panepistimiou Street were given their own lane, going against the traffic—keep this in mind when you cross this busy street.

The original **Metro** line linked Piraeus, Athens's seaport; central Athens; and Kifissia, an upscale northern suburb. A second line, with its main station in Syntagma Square, opened on January 28, 2000, to link the Defense Ministry on Mesogheion Avenue with central Athens and the northwest suburb of Sepolia. (Press releases trumpeted that pollution was cut by 70 tonnes on the first day the new Metro ran, when 100,000 fewer vehicles entered central Athens; as this reduction in pollution continues day by day, Athens's infamous *nefos* (smog) should diminish considerably and city buses should have a fighting chance of running on schedule.) Plans are for the entire 21-station Metro carrying 400,000 passengers a day to be running by 2002—certainly by 2004 for the Olympics.

In the city center, the trains run underground, and the main stops are **Syntagma, Monastiraki, Omonia,** and **Viktorias (Victoria).** Trains run about every 5 to 15 minutes daily 5am to midnight, with tickets at 250Dr (85¢). Validate your ticket in the machine as you enter the waiting platform or risk a fine. Metro and bus tickets aren't interchangeable.

By Taxi Supposedly there're 17,000 taxis in Athens, but finding one empty is almost never easy. Especially if you have travel connections to make, it's a good idea to reserve a radio taxi.

When you get into a taxi, check to see that the meter is turned on and set on "1" rather than "2"; it should be set on "2" (double fare) only between midnight and 5am or if you take a taxi outside the city limits. (If you plan to do this, try to negotiate a flat rate in advance.) Unless your cab is caught in very heavy traffic, a trip to the center of town from the airport between 5am and midnight should not cost more than 4,000Dr ($13). Don't be surprised if your driver picks up other passengers en route; he will work out everyone's share, and probably the worst that will happen is that you'll get less of a break than you would if you spoke Greek.

At press time, the minimum fare was 200Dr (65¢), and the "1" meter rate was 62Dr (20¢) per kilometer, with a surcharge of 150Dr (50¢) for service from a port or rail or bus station, 300Dr ($1) for service from the airport, and a luggage fee of 50Dr (20¢) for every bag over 10kg (22 lb.). These prices may well be higher by the time you visit Greece, as changes were due to go into effect at press time.

There're about 15 radio taxi companies, including **Athina** (☎ **01/921-7942**), **Express** (☎ **01/993-4812**), **Parthenon** (☎ **01/581-4711**), and **Piraeus** (☎ **01/418-2333-5**). If you're trying to make travel connections or traveling during rush hours, the service will be well worth the 300Dr ($1) surcharge.

Keep in mind that your driver may have difficulty understanding your pronunciation of your destination. If you are taking a taxi from your hotel, a staff member can tell the driver your destination or write down the address for you to show to the driver. If you carry a business card from your hotel, you can show it to the driver when you return. If you suspect you have been overcharged, ask for help at your hotel or other destination before you pay the fare. Most restaurants will also call for a taxi at no charge.

The Hellenic Tourism Organization's pamphlet **"Helpful Hints for Taxi Users"** has information on fares as well as a complaint form, which you can send to the Ministry of Transport and Communication, 13 Xenophondos, 101 91 Athens. Replies to complaints should be forwarded to the *Guinness Book of Records.*

On Foot   Most of what you probably want to see and do in Athens is in the city center, allowing you to sightsee mostly on foot. Wheelchair users will find Athens a challenge, although curbs on many streets are being redesigned to accommodate wheelchairs. All visitors should keep in mind that a red traffic light or stop sign is no guarantee that cars will stop for pedestrians. The pedestrian zones in sections of the Plaka, the commercial center, and Kolonaki make strolling, window-shopping, and sightseeing infinitely more pleasant than on other, traffic-clogged streets. Don't relax completely even on pedestrianized streets, though: Athens's multitude of kamikaze motorcycles seldom respects the rules.

By Car   Parking is so difficult and traffic so heavy in Athens that you should use a car only for trips outside the city. Keep in mind that on any day-trip (to Sounion or Daphni, for example) you'll spend at least several hours leaving and reentering central Athens.

Car-rental agencies in the Syntagma Square area include **Avis,** 48 Amalias Ave. (☎ **800/331-1084** in the U.S., or 01/322-4951); **AutoEurope,** 29 Hatzihristou St., right off Syngrou (☎ **01/924-2206;1-800/223-5555** in the U.S.); **Budget,** 8 Syngrou Ave. (☎ **01/921-4711; 800/527-0700** in the U.S.). Prices for one-day rentals range from 15,000Dr to 30,000Dr ($50 to $100) and usually include unlimited mileage but not full insurance, which I strongly recommend. You can usually reduce the price considerably by booking from outside Greece; sometimes, especially in the off-season, on-the-spot bargaining is effective.

Warning: Most companies add, and do not always mention, the hefty surcharge for picking up or dropping off your car at the airport. And be sure to take full insurance; if you are renting with a credit card, check with your company to see exactly what, if any, insurance it provides.

A Taxi Warning

There're increasing numbers of unlicensed cab drivers in Athens and Piraeus. Usually, these pirate cabbies (many from Eastern Europe) drive not the standard gray Athens taxi, but a gray car you might mistake for an Athens cab. It's always a good idea to make sure your cab driver has a meter and a photo ID.

Fast Facts: Athens

American Express   The office at 2 Ermou St., near the southwest corner of Syntagma Square (☎ **01/324-4975;** fax 01/322-7893), offers currency exchange and other services weekdays 8:30am to 4pm and Saturday 8:30am to 1:30pm.

Area Code   The country code for Greece is **30.** The city code for Athens is **1;** use this code when you're calling from outside Greece. If you're within Greece, use **01.**

ATMs   ATM cash dispensers are increasingly common in Athens, and the National Bank of Greece operates a 24-hour ATM next to the tourist information office on Syntagma Square. It's *not* a good idea to rely on using ATMs exclusively in Athens because the machines are often out of service when you need them most: on holidays or during bank strikes.

Banks   Banks are generally open Monday to Thursday 8am to 2pm and Friday 8am to 1:30pm. Most have currency-exchange counters that use the rates set daily by the government, which are usually more favorable than those offered at unofficial exchange bureaus. It's worth doing a little comparison shopping for the best rate of exchange; for example, many hotels offer rates (usually only for cash) that are better than the official bank rates.

Business Hours   In **winter,** shops are generally open Monday and Wednesday 9am to 5pm; Tuesday, Thursday, and Friday 10am to 7pm; and Saturday 8:30am to 3:30pm. In **summer,** shops are generally open Monday, Wednesday, and Saturday 8am to 3pm; and Tuesday, Thursday, and Friday 8am to 1:30pm and 5:30 to 10pm. Note that many shops geared to visitors keep especially long hours, and some close from about 2 to 5pm. Most **food stores** and the **Central Market** are open Monday and Wednesday 9am to 4:30pm, Tuesday 9am to 6pm, Thursday 9:30am to 6:30pm, Friday 9:30am to 7pm, and Saturday 8:30am to 4:30pm.

Currency   The **drachma** (Dr) is the Greek national currency. Coins are issued in 5, 10, 20, 50, and 100Dr; bills are denominated in 50, 100, 500, 1,000, 5,000, and 10,000Dr. At press time, $1 = 300Dr, €1 = 324Dr, or £1 = 492Dr, or 100Dr = 33¢, €.30, or £.20.

Dentists & Doctors   If you need an English-speaking doctor or dentist, call your embassy for advice or try **SOS Doctor** (☎ 01/331-0310 or 01/331-0311). The English-language *Athens News* lists some American- and British-trained doctors and hospitals offering emergency services. Most of the larger hotels have doctors whom they can call for you in an emergency.

Drugstores   *Pharmakia,* identified by green crosses, are scattered throughout Athens. Hours are usually 8am to 2pm weekdays. In the evening and on weekends most are closed, but they usually post a notice listing the names and addresses of pharmacies that are open or will open in an emergency. Newspapers, including the *Athens News,* list the pharmacies open outside regular hours.

Embassies/Consulates   United States, 91 Vasilissis Sofias Ave. (☎ **01/721-2951**); **Canada,** 4 Ioannou Yenadiou St. (☎ **01/723-9511** or 727-3400); **United Kingdom,** 1 Ploutarchou St. (☎ **01/723-6211**); **Ireland,** Odos Stratigou Kalari 16, Psychiko (☎ **01/723-27710**); **Australia,** 37 Dimitriou Soutsou Ave. (☎ **01/645-0405**); **New Zealand** (consulate), 24 Xenias, Ambelokipi (☎ **01/771-0112**). Embassies are usually closed on their own important national holidays and sometimes on Greek holidays as well.

Emergencies In an emergency, dial ☎ **100** for fast **police** assistance and ☎ **171** for the **Tourist Police** (see "Police," below). Dial ☎ **199** to report a **fire** and ☎ **166** for an **ambulance** and **hospital.**

Holidays Major public holidays in Athens include New Year's Day (January 1), Epiphany (January 6), Ash Wednesday, Independence Day (March 25), Good Friday, Easter Sunday and Monday (Orthodox Easter can coincide with or vary by 2 weeks from Catholic and Protestant Easter), Labor Day (May 1), Assumption Day (August 15), National Day (October 28), and Christmas (December 25 and 26). Some shops and offices close for at least a week at Christmas and Easter.

Internet Access You can check your e-mail or send messages at the **Astor Internet Café,** 17 Patission St., a block off Omonia Square (☎ **01/523-8546**), open Monday to Saturday 10am to 10pm and Sunday 10am to 4pm; it charges 1,500Dr ($5) per hour. **Sofokleous.com Internet c@fe**, 5 Stadiou, a block off Syntagma Square (☎ **01/324-8105** also charges 1,500Dr ($5) an hour and is open daily 10am to 10pm. Across from the National Archaeological Museum is the **Central Music Coffee Shop,** 28 Octobriou St., also called Patission St. (☎ **01/883-3418**), open daily 9am to 11pm; it also charges 1,500Dr ($5) per hour.

Laundry The self-service **launderette** at 10 Angelou Yeronda St., off Kidathineon, Plaka, is open daily 8:30am to 7pm; it charges 2,000Dr ($7) for wash, dry, and soap. The **National Dry Cleaners and Laundry Service,** 17 Apollonos St. (☎ **01/323-2226**), next to the Hermes Hotel, is open Monday and Wednesday 7am to 4pm and Tuesday, Thursday, and Friday 7am to 8pm; laundry costs 1,500Dr ($5) per kilo. Hotel chambermaids will often do laundry for you at a reasonable price.

Police In an emergency, dial ☎ **100.** For help dealing with a troublesome taxi driver, hotel, restaurant, or shop owner, stand your ground and call the **Tourist Police** at ☎ **171.**

Post Office The main **post offices** in central Athens are at 100 Eolou St., just south of Omonia Square, and in Syntagma Square on the corner of Mitropoleos Street. They're open Monday to Friday 7:30am to 8pm, Saturday 7:30am to 2pm, and Sunday 9am to 1pm. The two post offices at the East and West Air Terminals keep the same hours. Oddly, mail posted at the air terminals almost always takes longer to arrive than mail posted in Athens itself.

All the post offices can accept small parcels. The **parcel post office,** 4 Stadiou St., inside the arcade (☎ **01/322-8940**), is open Monday to Friday 7:30am to 8pm. Parcels must be open for inspection before you seal them at the post office.

Tax Value-added tax (VAT) is included in the price of all goods and services in Athens, ranging from 4% on books to 36% on certain luxury items. Some shops attempt to mislead you by quoting you one price and then, when you hand over your credit card, adding on a hefty VAT charge. Be wary. In theory, if you are not a citizen of a European Union country, you can get a refund on major purchases at Hellenikon airport when you leave Greece. In practice, you would virtually have to arrive at the airport a day before your flight to get to the head of the line, do the paper work, get a refund, and catch your flight.

Telephone/Telegrams/Telefaxes Many of the city's public phones now accept only **phone cards,** available at newsstands and OTE offices in several denominations starting at 1,700Dr ($6). The card works for 100 short local calls (or briefer long distance or international calls). Some kiosks still have **metered phones;** you pay what the meter records. Local phone calls cost 20Dr (5¢). North Americans can phone home directly by contacting **AT&T** at ☎ **00-800-1311, MCI** at ☎ **00-800-1211,** or **Sprint** at ☎ **00-800-1411;** calls can be collect or billed to your phone charge card. You can send a telegram or fax from offices of the **Telecommunications Organization of Greece (OTE).** At press time, the OTE office at 15 Stadiou, near Syntagma, was temporarily closed, leaving the Omonia Square OTE office and the Victoria Square Office at 85 Patission St. as Athens's most central OTE offices.

Tipping   Restaurants include a service charge in the bill, but many visitors add a 10% tip. Most Greeks do not give a percentage tip to taxi drivers, but often round the fare to the nearest 1,000Dr, for example, on a fare of 950Dr.

WHERE TO STAY

Warning: Hotel prices were accurate at press time, but price increases of 10% to 15% are rumored. Virtually all Greek hotels are clean and comfortable; few are charming or elegant. If shower and tub facilities are important to you, be sure to have a look at the bathroom: Many Greek tubs are tiny, and the showers handheld. Don't assume that just because a hotel says it has air-conditioning, the air-conditioning is working—and check to see if there's functioning central heating in the winter. And keep in mind that very few Greek hotel rooms have hair dryers or coffee- and tea-making facilities.

The area south and west of Syntagma Square and the neighborhoods of Plaka, Kolonaki, Koukaki, **Makriyanni,** and **Monastiraki** offer the most convenient and comfortable choices. For pure convenience, the **Syntagma** hotels and those in the lively **Plaka** area can't be beat. **Kolonaki** is an upscale neighborhood on the slopes of Mount Likavitos—but keep in mind that you'll have an uphill walk to your hotel. The **Koukaki** district, near Philopappos Hill and off the non-Acropolis side of Dionysiou Areopayitou Avenue, offers quiet residential back streets and the feeling of a real Greek neighborhood. Keep in mind that from Koukaki, almost everything you want to do, including buying an English-language newspaper, involves extra walking.

Finally, staying in a hotel near the airport is not recommended. Should you have an early morning/late evening, it's easy to get back and forth into Athens at these times.

IN PLAKA
Expensive
Electra Palace. 18 Nikodimou St., Plaka, 105 57 Athens. ☎ **01/324-1401** or 01/324-1407. Fax 01/324-1875. 106 units. A/C MINIBAR TV TEL. 39,800–49,400Dr ($133–$165) double. Rates include breakfast. AE, DC, MC, V.

The Electra, just a few blocks southwest of Syntagma Square, is the most modern and stylish Plaka hotel; it even has a decent restaurant. There's a rooftop pool, rooms are decent sized and have balconies. Top-floor rooms are smallish, but they're where you want to be, both for the Acropolis view and to escape traffic noise. And that's the problem: if you sit on your balcony on one of the lower floors, you'll inhale lots of fumes and hear lots of traffic noise.

Moderate
Acropolis House Hotel. 6–8 Kodrou St., 105 58 Athens. ☎ **01/322-2344.** Fax 01/324-4143. 25 units, 15 with bathroom. A/C TEL. 16,104 Dr ($54) double without bathroom, 18,920Dr ($63) double with bathroom. 4,000Dr ($13) surcharge for A/C. Rates include continental breakfast. V. Walk 2 blocks out of Syntagma Sq. on Mitropoleos St. and turn left on Voulis, which becomes pedestrianized Kodrou.

Planning Ahead

If you're visiting Athens in the summer, **write or fax ahead of time for reservations** because the best-value hotels tend to be full then. If you arrive without a reservation, you can try to book a room at the tourist information booth at the West Air Terminal, run by a private tourist agency and open 7am to 1am; the agency charges a small fee. If you visit Athens in the off-season, especially in the winter, you may be pleasantly surprised at the not-always-publicized low rates available in even the most expensive hotels.

This small hotel in a renovated 150-year-old villa with many of its original classical architectural details offers the convenience of a central location, and the charm of a quiet pedestrian side street. Rooms 401 and 402 have Acropolis views and can be requested, but not guaranteed, when making a reservation. The newer wing (only 60 years old) isn't architecturally special and each room's spartan bathroom is across the hall. There's a book-swap spot and a washing machine, free after a 4-day stay.

Byron Hotel. 19 Vyronos St., 105 58 Athens. ☎ **01/325-3554.** Fax 01/323-0327. 20 units. TEL. 25,000Dr ($83) double. Rates include breakfast. No credit cards. From Syntagma Sq., walk south on Amalias Ave. past Hadrian's Arch, stay right, and turn right on Dionysiou Areopayitou St.; Vyronos (Byron in Greek) is 2nd street on right, and hotel (with a portrait of Lord Byron by the door) is on right.

When we visited The Byron, it was in the throes of remodeling. Whether the promised air-conditioning and all new bathrooms and furniture materialize, only time will tell. What won't change is this small hotel's convenient Plaka location just off recently pedestrianized Dionysiou Areopayitou St. What one hopes will change is the Byron's frequently haphazard management.

✪ **Hotel Nefeli.** 16 Iperidou St., 105 58 Athens. ☎ **01/322-8044.** Fax 01/322-5800. 18 units. TEL. 21,200 Dr ($71) double. Rates include continental breakfast. AE, V. Walk 2 blocks west from Syntagma Sq. on Mitropoleos St., turn left on Voulis, cross Nikodimou St., and turn right on Iperidou.

The charming little Nefeli was completely redecorated in 1998, with new beds and furniture. Rooms (some with old-fashioned ceiling fans, others with air-conditioning) are small but comfortable, the quietest overlooking pedestrianized Angelikis Hatzimihali Street, though the entire hotel is very quiet, considering its central location. I found the staff, including manager Tasos Kanellopoulos, courteous and helpful, and friends who've stayed here say the same.

✪ **Hotel Plaka.** Mitropoleos and 7 Kapnikareas St., 105 56 Athens. ☎ **01/322-2096.** Fax 01/322-2412. E-mail: rofos@ath.forthnet.gr. 67 units. A/C TV TEL. 30,000Dr ($100) double. Rates include breakfast. AE, EURO, MC, V. Follow Mitropoleos St. out of Syntagma Sq. past cathedral and turn left onto Kapnikareas.

This 10-year-old hotel—popular with Greeks, who prefer its modern conveniences to the old-fashioned charms of most other hotels in the Plaka area, as well as with gays—has a terrific location and fair prices. Many rooms have balconies. Rooms on the fifth and sixth floors in the rear (where it's usually quieter) have views of the Plaka and the Acropolis, also splendidly visible from the roof garden (which has a snack bar). Friends who stayed here recently were not charmed by the service, but found it adequate.

NEAR MONASTIRAKI SQUARE
Moderate
Attalos Hotel. 29 Athinas St., 105 54 Athens. ☎ **01/321-2801.** Fax 01/324-3124. E-mail: atthot@hol.gr. www.attalos.gr. 80 units. A/C TV TEL. 18,000Dr ($60) double; 24,000Dr ($80) triple. Rates include buffet breakfast. AE, V. From Monastiraki Sq. walk about 1¹/₂ blocks north on Athinas St.

One of the pleasures of staying at the six-story (with elevator) Attalos is taking in the frenzied street life of the nearby Central Market. The nighttime scene here is less attractive, with streetwalkers and drug dealers in evidence. Rooms are plain, but most have TV and hair dryers and 44 have balconies. The roof garden has fine city and Acropolis views. The Attalos provides free luggage storage and often offers a discount for Frommer's readers.

✪ **Jason Inn Hotel.** 12 Ayion Assomaton St., 105 53 Athens. ☎ **01/325-1106.** Fax 01/324-3123 & 01/523-4786. Email: Douros@hotelnet.gr. 57 units. A/C TV TEL MINIBAR. 18,000Dr ($60) double. Rates include American buffet breakfast. From Monastiraki Sq., head west on Ermou, turn right at Thisio Metro station, pass small belowground-level church and bear left (hotel sign visible).

If you don't mind walking a few extra blocks to Syntagma, this is one of the best values in Athens, with an eager-to-help staff. The recently renovated Jason Inn (admittedly on a dull street) has attractive rooms with modern amenities and double-paned windows. If the Jason is full, the staff may be able to find you a room in one of its other hotels: the similarly priced Adrian, in the Plaka, or the slightly less expensive King Jason or Jason, both a few blocks from Omonia Square.

ON & AROUND SYNTAGMA SQUARE
Very Expensive
Hotel Grande Bretagne. Syntagma Sq., 105 63 Athens. ☎ **800/325-3535** reservations through Sheraton Hotels in the U.S., or 01/321-5555 in Greece. Fax 01/322-0211. 365 units, 33 suites. A/C MINIBAR TV TEL. 52,500–121,500Dr ($175–$405) double; from 195,000Dr ($650) suite. AE, CB, DC, MC, V. Across from the Parliament Building in Syntagma Square.

This venerable 1864 hotel with elegant beaux arts decor is an Athens landmark. Political and social movers and shakers pass through the lobby, with its ornately carved wood paneling, soaring ceilings, and polished marble floors, for power lunches at the popular GB Corner. (So, increasingly, do the tour groups staying here, which doesn't help the ambience.) Many of the courtyard rooms look the worse for wear and utterly lack the elegance of the front rooms, which have marvelous views over Syntagma Square and toward the National Gardens and Acropolis.

Expensive
Electra Hotel. 5 Ermou St., 105 63 Athens. ☎ **01/322-3223.** Fax 01/322-0310. E-mail: electrahotels@ath.Forthnet.gr. 110 units. A/C TV TEL. 48,400Dr ($161) double. Rates include buffet breakfast. AE, DC, MC, V.

If Ermou Street remains pedestrianized, and the Electra sticks to its present rates, this hotel is excellent value, with a location that is both central (steps from Syntagma Square) and quiet (despite the presence of lots of tour groups). Most rooms, though not large, have comfortable armchairs, large windows, and modern bathrooms with hair dryers; about half have balconies. The front desk is sometimes understaffed, but the service is generally acceptable. Prices off season are usually considerably lower.

Esperia Palace Hotel. 22 Stadiou St., 105 61 Athens. ☎ **800/528-1234** reservations through Best Western in the U.S., or 01/323-8001 in Greece. 185 units. A/C MINIBAR TV TEL. 58,000–73,500Dr ($193–$245) double. Rates include breakfast. AE, DC, MC, V. Take Stadiou out of Syntagma Square toward Omonia Square. The Esperia Palace is on the right-hand side of the street.

This is a reasonably good-value hotel with a very convenient location near Syntagma Square. Rooms are large and perfectly acceptable, although rather plain; some carpets are in need of cleaning. The buffet breakfast is a plus. Many tour groups stay here, which you might find a drawback if you are on your own.

Moderate
Athens Cypria. 5 Diomias St., 105 62 Athens. ☎ **01/323-8034.** Fax 01/324-8792. 71 units. A/C MINIBAR TV TEL. 28,000Dr ($94) double. Rates include breakfast. AE, MC, V. Take Karagiorgi Servias out of Syntagma Sq.; Diomias St. is on the left, after Lekka St.

After extensive renovations, the former Diomia Hotel has been reborn as the Athens Cypria. Gone are the Diomia's gloomy lobby and rooms, but the convenient central location on a street with (usually) no traffic and the splendid Acropolis views from no. 603 to 607 remain. Halls and rooms have been painted bright white, the units have cheerful floral bedspreads and curtains, and the bathrooms (with hair dryers) are freshly tiled with all new fixtures. The breakfast buffet offers hot and cold dishes 7 to 10am in a mirrored dining room. The Cypria promises to be an excellent addition to Athens's moderately priced hotels.

Hotel Achilleas. 21 Lekka St., 105 62 Athens. ☎ **01/323-3197.** Fax 01/324-1092. E-mail: rofos@ath.forthnet.gr. 34 units. A/C TV TEL. 24,000Dr ($80) double. Rates include breakfast. AE, DC, EU, MC, V. With Hotel Grande Bretagne on your right, walk 2 blocks out of Syntagma Sq. on Karayioryi Servias and turn right into Lekka.

The Achilleas (Achilles), on a relatively quiet side street steps from Syntagma Square, is showing signs of wear since its renovation in 1995, although rooms are good-sized and light; some rear rooms have small balconies. The Achilleas's very central location and fair prices make it a good choice, but don't expect to be charmed by your room or the service.

IN KOLONAKI
Very Expensive
Saint George Lycabettus Hotel. 2 Kleomenous St., 106 75 Athens. ☎ **01/729-0711.** Fax 01/721-0439. www.sglycabettus.gr. E-mail: info@sglycabettus.gr. 167 units. A/C TEL TV. 58,500–83,300Dr ($195–$278) double. Breakfast 5,400Dr ($18). AE, DC, MC, V. From Kolonaki Square, take Patriarchou Ioachim to Loukianou; follow Loukianou uphill to Kleomenous; turn left on Kleomenous; the hotel overlooks Dexamini Park.

As yet, the Saint George Lycabettus does not get many tour groups, which contributes to the tranquil tone here. The nicely appointed rooms look toward Mt. Likavitos or a small park (some corner rooms have spectacular views of both Likavitos and the Acropolis), although the surrounding street traffic keeps this from being a real oasis of calm. The rooftop pool is a real plus, and the hotel is steps from the chic Kolonaki restaurants and shops—but keep in mind that when you head back to the hotel, those steps are steeply uphill!

Moderate
✪ **Athenian Inn.** Athenian Inn. 22 Haritos St., Kolonaki, 106 75 Athens. ☎ **01/723-8097.** Fax 01/724-2268. 28 units. A/C TEL. 31,350Dr ($104) double; 39,120Dr ($130) triple. Rates include breakfast. AE, DC, V. From Syntagma Sq., go east on Vasilissis Sofias Ave. to Loukianou; turn left on Loukianou and take it 6 blocks uphill to Haritos; hotel is a block up on the right.

The quiet location 3 blocks from Kolonaki Square is a blessing, as are the clean accommodations and friendly staff. (A quote from British author and Hellenophile Lawrence Durrell in the guest book states: "At last the ideal Athens hotel, good and modest in scale but perfect in service and goodwill.") Breakfast is served in a small lounge with a fireplace and piano (and, of late, a TV). Between stays, I tend to forget how small the rooms are here, which suggests to me that the staff is doing a good job of making guests feel comfortable.

IN THE EMBASSY DISTRICT
Very Expensive

✪ **Andromeda Hotel.** 22 Timoleontos Vassou St. (off Plateia Mavili), 115 21 Athens. ☎ **01/643-7302.** Fax 01/646-6361. 42 units. A/C MINIBAR TV TEL. 90,000–105,000Dr ($300–$350) double. Special rates sometimes available. AE, DC, EURO, MC, V. From Syntagma Sq. take Vas. Sophias Ave. to Plateia Mavili; follow D. Soustou out of Plateia Mavili to T. Vassou St; turn left into T. Vassou; the Andromeda is on the right.

The city's only boutique hotel is easily the most charming in Athens, with a staff that makes you feel that this is your home away from home. Rooms are large and elegantly decorated, with hair dryers. This very quiet hotel overlooks the garden of the American ambassador's home, and has marvelous breakfasts and snacks (at present there's no restaurant). The only drawbacks: It's a serious hike (20 to 30 minutes) or 10-minute taxi ride to Syntagma, and there're few restaurants in this residential neighborhood, although the superb Vlassis is just around the corner. If you're planning a long stay in Athens, check out the Andromeda's new (and very lovely) service apartments just across the street.

Athens Hilton. 46 Vasilissis Sofias Ave., 115 28 Athens. ☎ **800/445-8667** or 01/722-0301. Fax 01/721-3110. 446 units. A/C MINIBAR TV TEL. 85,500–126,000Dr ($285–$420) double. AE, DC, EURO, MC, V. From Syntagma Square, take Vas. Sofias Ave. about half a mile to the Hilton (on the right-hand side of Vas. Sofias Ave.)

The Athens Hilton, near the U.S. Embassy, is a brisk 10-minute walk from Syntagma Square. It's something of an Athenian institution, where businesspeople and diplomats meet for a drink or a meal. A number of small shops, a beauty parlor, and cafes and restaurants surround the seriously glitzy marble and crystal lobby. Rooms (looking toward either the hills outside Athens or the Acropolis) have large marble bathrooms with hair dryers and are decorated in the generic but comfortable international Hilton style, with some Greek touches. The Plaza Executive floor of rooms and suites offers a separate business center and higher level of service. Sports options include a pool and a health club. The Hilton often runs promotions, so check about special rates before booking.

NEAR THE ACROPOLIS (MAKRIYANNI & KOUKAKI DISTRICTS)
Very Expensive

Divani-Palace Acropolis. 19–25 Parthenonos St., Makriyanni, 117 42 Athens. ☎ **01/92-22-2945.** Fax 01/92-14-993. www.otenet.gr. E-mail: acropol@otenet.gr. 253 units. A/C MINIBAR TV TEL. 60,000–75,000Dr ($200–$250) double. AE, DC, MC, V. From Syntagma Square take Amalias Ave. to pedestrianized Dionysiou Areopagitou; turn left into Parthenonos; the hotel is on your left after about 3 blocks.

Just 3 blocks south of the Acropolis, in a quiet residential neighborhood (there's a handy Veropoulos SPAR supermarket a block away at 4 Parthenos St., and a shop at 7 Parthenos that sells American and English newspapers), the Divani Palace Acropolis does a brisk tour business, but is welcoming to independent travelers. The blandly decorated rooms are large and comfortable and the large bathrooms have hair dryers (some have two wash basins). There's a small, handsome pool, a bar, restaurant, and a lovely roof garden with the view you'd expect. A section of Athens's 5th-century B.C. defense wall is preserved behind glass in the basement, by the gift shop. The same hotel group operates the **Divani Caravel Hotel,** near the National Art Gallery and Hilton Hotel at 2 Vas. Alexandrou Ave. (☎ **01/725-3725;** fax 01-725-3770).

Moderate

✪ **Acropolis View Hotel.** Rovertou Galli & 10 Webster St., 117 42 Athens. ☎ **01/ 921-7303.** Fax 01/923-0705. 32 units. A/C TV TEL. 33,000Dr ($110) double. Rates include generous breakfast. Substantial reductions Nov–Apr 1. AE, EURO, MC, V. From Syntagma Sq. take Amalias Ave. to Dion. Areopagitou; head west past Herodes Atticus theater to Rovertou Galli St. Webster (Gouemster on some maps) is the little street intersecting Rovertou Galli St. between Propilion and Garabaldi.

This nicely maintained hotel with helpful staff is on a residential side street off Rovertou Galli, not far from the Herodes Atticus theater. The usually quiet neighborhood, at the base of Philopappos Hill, is a 10- to 15-minute walk from the heart of the Plaka. Rooms (most freshly painted each year) are small but clean and pleasant, with good bathrooms; 16 rooms have balconies. Some, like no. 405, overlook Philopappos Hill, and others, like no. 407, face the Acropolis. There's a congenial breakfast room and bar in the lobby.

Art Gallery Hotel. 5 Erechthiou St., Koukaki, 117 42 Athens. ☎ **01/923-8376.** Fax 01/923-3025. www.greekhotels.com/ht328.htm. E-mail: ecotec@atenet.gr. 22 units. TEL. 16,500Dr ($55) double. No credit cards. Follow Dionysiou Areopayitou St. around south side of Acropolis to Odeum of Herodes Atticus and turn left on Erechthiou.

As you might expect, this small hotel—in a half-century-old house that has been home to several artists—has an artistic flair (and a nice old-fashioned cage elevator). Rooms are plain but comfortable, with polished hardwood floors and ceiling fans. On the fourth floor is a nice Victorian-style breakfast room with heavy marble-topped tables and velvet-covered chairs. In January 2000, the manager mentioned plans to "modernize"; not too much, I hope.

Austria Hotel. 7 Mousson St., Filopappou, 117 42 Athens. ☎ **01/923-5151.** Fax 01/924-7350. www.austriahotel.com. E-mail: austria@topservice.com or austria@hol.gr. 37 units, 9 with shower only. A/C TEL. 26,200Dr ($87) double with or without bathroom. Rates include breakfast. AE, MC, V. Follow Dionysiou Areopagitou St. around the south side of the Acropolis to where it meets Roverto Galli St.; take Garivaldi around the base of Filopappou Hill until you reach Mouson St.

This well-maintained little hotel at the base of wooded Filopappos Hill is operated by a Greek-Austrian family. They offer use of the hotel safe-deposit box and a fax service, will exchange your foreign money into drachmas (which not all small hotels are prepared to do), and can point you to the convenient neighborhood laundry. Rooms and bathrooms are rather spartan (the linoleum floors aren't enchanting) but tidy. There's a great view over Athens and out to sea (I could see the island of Aegina) from the rooftop, where you can sun or sit under an awning.

Inexpensive

✪ **Marble House Pension.** 35 A. Zinni St., Koukaki, 117 41 Athens. ☎ **01/923-4058.** Fax 01/922-6461. 17 units, 12 with bathroom. A/C MINIBAR TEL. 13,500Dr ($45) double with bathroom; 12,000Dr($40) double without bathroom. Oct–May double rooms can be rented for the month for 100,000Dr ($333). No credit cards. From Syntagma Square take Amalias Ave. into Syngrou Ave; turn right into Zinni; the hotel is in the cul de sac beside the small church (allow at least 20 minutes for this walk).

Named for its marble facade, usually covered by bougainvillea, this small hotel whose front rooms have balconies overlooking quiet Zinni Street, is famous among budget travelers (including many teachers) for its friendly helpful staff. The hotel was recently remodeled, and all new bathrooms, furniture, and minibars should be ready for your visit. If you're spending more than a few days in Athens and don't mind being out of the center, this is a homey base. Luggage storage is free and there's a satellite TV in the library/lounge.

WHERE TO DINE

Athens has an astonishing number of restaurants and tavernas (and a growing number of fast-food joints) offering everything from good, cheap Greek food in plain surroundings to fine Greek, French, Asian, and other international cuisines served in luxurious surroundings. **Warning: Many Athenian restaurants do not accept credit cards.** If you want to pay with a credit card, double-check to make sure the restaurant will accept your card before going there.

Most restaurants have menus in Greek and English, but many don't keep their printed (or handwritten) menus up to date. If a menu is not in English, there's almost always someone working at the restaurant who will either translate or rattle off suggestions for you in English. That may mean you'll be offered some fairly repetitive suggestions because restaurant staff members tend to suggest what most tourists request. In Athens, that means *moussaka* (baked eggplant casserole, usually with ground meat), *souvlakia* (chunks of beef, chicken, pork, or lamb grilled on a skewer), *pastitsio* (baked pasta, usually with ground meat and béchamel sauce), or *dolmadakia* (grape leaves, stuffed usually with rice and ground meat). Although all these dishes can be delicious, all too often restaurants catering to tourists serve profoundly dull moussaka and unpleasantly chewy souvlakia.

Mezedes (appetizers served with bread) are one of the great delights of Greek cuisine, and often can be enjoyed in lieu of a main course. Some perennial favorites include *tzatziki* (garlic, cucumber, dill, and yogurt dip), *melitzanosalata* (eggplant dip), *skordalia* (garlic sauce), *taramosalata* (fish roe dip), *keftedes* (crispy meatballs), *kalamaria* (squid), *gigantes* (large white beans in tomato sauce), *loukanika* (little sausages), and *oktopodi* (octopus).

If you're wondering what to use to wash all this down, the most popular Greek table wine is *retsina*. It's usually white, although sometime rosé or red, and flavored with pine resin. In theory, the European Union now controls the amount of resin added, so you're less likely to come across the harsh retsina that some compare to turpentine. If you don't like the taste of retsina, try *aretsinato* (wine without resin).

If you want to find out more about Greek wine, pick up a copy of Dimitri Hadjinicolaou's *The A to Z Guide of Greek Wines* (Oenos O Agapitos Publisher). This handy pocket-sized Greek/English guide has illustrations of labels, information on vintages, and sells for about 2,400Dr ($8).

<hr>

Eating Well

To avoid the ubiquitous favorites-for-foreigners, you might prefer to tell your waiter you'd like to have a look at the food display case, often positioned just outside the kitchen, and then point out what you'd like to order. Many restaurants are perfectly happy to have you take a look in the kitchen itself, but it's not a good idea to do this without checking first. Not surprisingly, you'll get the best value and the tastiest food at establishments serving a predominantly Greek, rather than a transient tourist, clientele.

When it comes time for dessert or a midafternoon infusion of sugar, Greeks usually head to a *zaharoplastion* (sweet shop). Consequently, most restaurants don't offer a wide variety of desserts. Almost all do serve fruit (stewed in winter, fresh in season), and increasingly, many serve sweets such as *baklava* (pastry and ground nuts with honey), *halva* (sesame, chopped nuts, and honey), and *kataifi* (shredded wheat with chopped nuts and lots of honey). All these sweets are seriously sweet. If you want **coffee** with your dessert, keep in mind that for Greeks, regular coffee usually includes a mere teaspoon of sugar. Sweet coffee seems to be about a fifty-fifty mixture of coffee and sugar. Watch out for the grounds in the bottom of the cup.

Greek **brandy** is a popular after-dinner drink (although—you guessed it—a bit sweet for non-Greek tastes), but the most popular Greek hard drink is *ouzo.* The anise-flavored liqueur is taken either straight or with water, which turns it cloudy white. You may see Greek men drinking quarter- and even half-bottles of ouzo with their lunch; if you do the same, you'll find out why the after-lunch siesta is so popular. There're many cafes (*ouzeri*) where ouzo, wine, and a selection of mezedes are served from breakfast to bedtime.

IN PLAKA

Some of the most charming old restaurants in Athens are in Plaka—as are some of the worst tourist traps. Here are a few things to keep in mind when you head off for a meal.

Some Plaka restaurants station waiters outside who don't just urge you to come in and sit down, but virtually pursue you down the street with an unrelenting sales pitch. The hard sell is almost always a giveaway that the place caters to tourists.

In general, it's a good idea to avoid places with floor shows; many charge outrageous amounts (and levy surcharges not always openly stated on menus) for drinks and food. If you get burned, stand your ground, phone the **Tourist Police** (☎ **171**), and pay nothing before they arrive. Often the mere threat of calling the Tourist Police has the miraculous effect of causing a bill to be lowered.

Expensive

⭕ **Daphne's.** 4 Lysikratous St. ☎ and fax **01-322-7971.** Main courses 4,500–8,500Dr ($15–$28), with some fish priced by the kilo. Daily 1:30pm–6pm and 8pm–2am. AE DC MC V. ELEGANT GREEK/NOUVELLE.

There're frescoes on the walls of this neoclassical 1830s former home, a shady garden with bits of ancient marble found when the restaurant was built, and sophisticated Athenians at many tables. The cuisine here (recommended in *The New York Times* and *Travel and Leisure*) gives you all the old favorites (try the zesty eggplant salad) with new distinction, and combines familiar ingredients in innovative ways (delicious hot pepper and feta cheese dip). I could cheerfully just eat the hors d'oeuvres all night, but have also enjoyed the *stifado* (stew) of rabbit in *mavrodaphne* (sweet wine) sauce and the tasty prawns with toasted almonds. Most nights, there's a pair of strolling musicians, whose repertoire ranges from Greek favorites to "My Darling Clementine."

Moderate

⭕ **Platanos Taverna.** 4 Dioyenous St. ☎ **01/322-0666.** Main courses 2,500Dr–3,500Dr ($8–$12). No credit cards. Mon–Sat noon–4:30pm and 8pm–midnight. From Syntagma Sq., head south on Filellinon or Nikis St. to Kidathineon; turn right on Adrianou St., and take Mnissikleos up 1 block toward Acropolis and turn right on Dioyenous. GREEK.

This traditional taverna on a quiet pedestrian square has tables outdoors in good weather beneath a spreading plane tree (*Platanos* means "plane tree"). Inside, where locals usually congregate to escape the summer sun at midday and the tourists in the evening, you can enjoy looking at the old paintings and photos on the walls. The Platanos has been serving good *spitiko fageto* (home cooking) since 1932 and has managed to keep steady customers happy while enchanting visitors. If artichokes or spinach with lamb are on the menu, you're in luck: They're delicious. The house wine is tasty, and there's a wide choice of bottled wines from many regions of Greece.

Taverna Xinos. 4 Agelou Geronta St. ☎ **01/322-1065.** Main courses 1,500Dr–4,000Dr ($5–$13). No credit cards. Daily 8pm–anywhere from 11pm–1am; sometimes closed Sun, usually closed part of July–Aug. From Syntagma Sq., head south on Filellinon or Nikis St. to Kidathineon; turn right on Angelou Geronta and look for the sign for Xinos in the cul de sac. GREEK.

Despite the forgivable lapse in spelling, Xinos's business card says it best: "In the heart of old Athens there's still a flace [*sic*] where the traditional Greek way of cooking is upheld." In summer, there're tables outside in the courtyard; in winter, you can warm yourself by the coal-burning stove. Year-round you can enjoy the hearty, generous portions; lamb lovers should try the lamb with artichokes (usually available in the spring), or the lamb with egg, lemon, and dill sauce. The strolling musicians sing wonderful Greek golden oldies, accompanying themselves on the guitar and bouzouki. (If you are serenaded, you might want to give the musicians a small tip. If you want to hear the theme from *Never on Sunday*, ask to hear "Ena Zorbas.") Most evenings, tourists predominate until around 10pm, when locals begin to arrive, as they have since Xinos opened in 1935.

Inexpensive

✪ **Damigos (The Bakaliarakia).** 41 Kidathineon St. ☎ **01/322-5084.** Main courses 1,000Dr–2,500Dr ($3.35–$8). No credit cards. Daily 7pm to anywhere from 11pm–1am. Usually closed June–Sept. From Syntagma Sq., head south on Filellinon or Nikis St. to Kidathineon; Damigos is downstairs on the left just before Adrianou St. GREEK/CODFISH.

Damigos has been serving delicious deep-fried codfish and eggplant, as well as chops and stews, since 1865 in this basement taverna. Don't miss the enormous wine barrels in the back room and an ancient column supporting the roof in the front room. The wine comes from the family vineyards, and there're few pleasures greater than sipping retsina while you watch the cook—who manages to look genial while never smiling—turn out unending meals in his absurdly small kitchen. Try the delicious *skordalia* (garlic sauce), equally good with cod, eggplant, bread—well, you get the idea.

Kouklis Ouzeri (To Yerani). 14 Tripodon St. ☎ **01/324-7605.** Appetizers 600Dr–1,500Dr ($2–$5). No credit cards. Daily 11am–2am. From Syntagma Sq., head south on Filellinon or Nikis St. to Kidathineon; take Kidathineon across Adrianou to Thespidos and climb toward Acropolis; Tripodon is first street on right after Adrianou. GREEK.

Besides Kouklis Ouzeri and To Yerani, Greeks call this popular old favorite with its winding staircase to the second floor the "Skolario" because of the nearby school. Sit down at one of the small tables and a waiter will present a large tray with about a dozen plates of *mezedes*—appetizer portions of fried fish, beans, grilled eggplant, taramosalata, cucumber-and-tomato salad, olives, fried cheese, sausages, and other seasonal specialties. Accept the ones that appeal. If you don't order all 12, you can enjoy a tasty and inexpensive meal, washed down with the house *krasi* (wine). (No prices are posted, but the waiter will tell you what everything costs if you ask.) Now, if only the staff here could be just a bit more patient when foreigners are trying to decide what to order.

NEAR MONASTIRAKI SQUARE
Moderate
✪ **Abyssinia Cafe.** Plateia Abyssinia, Monastiraki. ☎ **01/321-7047.** Appetizers and main courses 1,000–2,000Dr ($3.35–$7). No credit cards. Tues–Sun 10:30am–2pm; often open evenings as well. Closed Mon. Usually closed for a week at Christmas and Easter, sometimes closed part of Jan and Feb. Abyssinia Sq. is just off Ifaistou (Hephaistos) St. across from the entrance to the Ancient Agora on Adrianou. GREEK.

This small cafe in a ramshackle building has a nicely restored interior featuring lots of gleaming dark wood and polished copper. It faces a lopsided square where furniture restorers ply their trade. You can sit indoors or outside and have just a coffee, but it's tempting to snack on Cheese Abyssinia (feta cheese scrambled with spices and garlic), mussels and rice pilaf, or *keftedes* (meatballs).

Taverna Sigalas. 2 Monastiraki Sq. ☎ **01/321-3036.** Main courses 1,500–2,700Dr ($5–$9). No credit cards. Daily 7am–2am. Sigalas is across Monastiraki Square from the Metro station. GREEK.

This worthy taverna in an 1879 commercial building with a newer outdoor pavilion boasts it's open 365 days a year. Inside, there're huge old retsina kegs and dozens of black-and-white photos of Greek movie stars. After 8pm nightly, there's recorded Greek music. At all hours, Greeks and tourists wolf down large portions of stews, moussaka, grilled meatballs, baked tomatoes, gyros, and other tasty dishes.

Inexpensive
Diporto. Athens Central Market. No phone. Main courses 900–2,500Dr ($3–$8). No credit cards. Mon–Sat 6am–6pm. The Central Market is on Athinas Street, which runs between Omonia and Monastiraki Squares. GREEK.

Sandwiched between shops selling olives, this little place serves up salads, stews, and delicious *revithia* (chickpeas, a popular Greek winter dish) to market stall owners, shoppers, and Athenians who make their way here for the cheap and delicious food. If you like Diporto, try Papandreou, in the meat section of the Central Market; the tripe soup here is reputed to cure all ills.

✪ **Thanasis.** 69 Mitropoleos St. ☎ **01/324-4705.** Main courses 500–2,500Dr ($1.65–$8). No credit cards. Daily 9am–2am. Thanasis is on the northeast corner of Monastiraki Sq. Hermou St. leads directly from Syntagma Sq. to Monastiraki Sq. GREEK.

Thanasis serves very good souvlakia and pita and exceptionally good french fries, both "to go" and at its outdoor and indoor tables; as always, prices are higher if you sit down to eat. On weekends, it often takes the strength and determination of an Olympic athlete to get through the door and place an order here. Yes, it's worth the effort: This is both a great budget choice and a great place to take in the local scene.

NEAR SYNTAGMA SQUARE
Moderate
Gerofinikas. 10 Pindar St. ☎ **01/363-6710.** Reservations strongly recommended. Main courses 3,000–6,200Dr ($10–$21); set-price menu 6,000Dr ($20), not including beverage. AE, DC, MC, V. From Syntagma Square take Vas. Sofias Ave. to Akadamias Ave; turn left into Pindarou. GREEK/INTERNATIONAL.

For years, this was *the* place to go for a special lunch or dinner, and the food is still very good—which is why tour groups have, alas, discovered it. Still, it's always pleasant to walk down the passageway into Gerofinikas (the name means "the old palm tree"), look at the long display cases of tempting dishes, and try to decide between shrimp with feta cheese, rabbit stew with onions, the tasty eggplant dishes—all the while keeping room for one of the rich desserts.

Quick Bites

In general, the Syntagma Square area is not known for its food, but it has a number of places to get a snack. The **Apollonion Bakery,** 10 Nikis St., and the **Elleniki Gonia,** 10 Karayioryis Servias St., make sandwiches to order and sell croissants, both stuffed and plain. **Ariston** is a small chain of *zaharoplastia* (confectioners), with a branch at the corner of Karayioryis tis Servias and Voulis streets (just off the square) that sells snacks as well as pastries. **Floca** is another excellent chain of pastry shops, with 14 branches; there's one in the arcade on Panepistimiou Street near Syntagma Square and another just south of the Center for Acropolis Studies, at Makriyanni and Hatzihristou streets. As always, you pay extra to be served at a table.

For the quintessential Greek sweet *loukoumades*—round doughnut-centerlike pastries deep-fried and then drenched with honey and topped with powdered sugar and cinnamon—nothing beats **Doris,** 30 Praxiteles St. (a continuation of Lekka Street), a few blocks from Syntagma Square. If you're still hungry, Doris serves hearty stews and pasta dishes for absurdly low prices Monday to Saturday until 3:30pm. **Aigaion,** 46 Panepistimiou St. is a good place to stop on the way to or from the National Archaeological Museum for some *loukoumades* or creamy rice pudding. **Everest** is another chain worth trying; there's a branch 1 block north of Kolonaki Square at Tsakalof and Iraklitou streets. Also in Kolonaki Square, **To Kotopolo** ("the Chicken Place") serves succulent grilled chicken to take out or eat in. In Plaka, you'll find excellent coffee and sweets at the **K. Kotsolis Pastry Shop,** 112 Adrianou St., an oasis of old-fashioned charm in the midst of the souvenir shops. The **Orea Ellada** (Beautiful Greece) cafe is at the Center of Hellenic Tradition, opening onto 36 Pandrossou St. and 59 Mitropoleos St. near the flea market. You can revive yourself with a cappuccino and snack on pastries while you enjoy a spectacular view of the Acropolis.

Inexpensive

Neon. 3 Mitropoleos St. (on the southwest corner of Syntagma Sq.). ☎ **01/322-8155.** Snacks 200–650Dr (70¢–$2.15); sandwiches 450–1,200Dr ($1.50–$4); main courses 1,000–3,200Dr ($3.35–$11). No credit cards. Daily 9am—midnight. GREEK/INTERNATIONAL.

This new addition to the Neon chain is convenient, although not as charming as the original on Omonia Square. You're sure to find something to your taste—maybe a Mexican omelette, spaghetti Bolognese, the salad bar, or sweets ranging from Black Forest cake to tiramisu. If you're tired of practicing your restaurant Greek, this is a good place to eat, since most things are self-service.

IN KOLONAKI

Expensive

✪ **To Kafeneio.** 26 Loukianou St. ☎ **01/722-9056.** Main courses 1,800–6,000Dr ($6–$20). No credit cards. Mon–Sat 11am–midnight or later. From Kolonaki Sq., follow Patriarkou Ioakim St. several blocks uphill to Loukianou and turn right to Kafeneio. GREEK/INTERNATIONAL.

This is hardly a typical rough-and-ready Kafeneio (coffee shop/cafe): There're pictures on the walls, pink tablecloths on the tables, and a clientele of ladies who lunch, as well as staff from the many embassies located in Kolonaki. In short, it's a great people-watching place, where you can easily run up a substantial tab, but where you will also eat elegantly. Try the artichokes à la polita (tender artichokes flanked by carrots and potatoes in an egg-lemon sauce) or leeks in crème fraîche, washed down with draft beer or the house wine—and save room for the delectable profiteroles. I've always found this an especially congenial spot when I'm eating alone (perhaps because I love people-watching and profiteroles).

Moderate

Dimokritos. 23 Dimokritou St. ☎ **01/361-3588.** Main courses 4,200–4,800Dr ($14–$16). No credit cards. Mon–Sat 1–5pm and 8pm–1am. From Syntagma Square take Vas. Sofias Ave. to Akadamias Ave; take Akadamias Ave. to Dimokritou; turn right into Dimokritou and climb until you see the Church of Ayios Dionysios. The restaurant is marked only by the word *taverna* on the doors. GREEK.

Overlooking the Church of Ayios Dionysios, this cozy taverna serves good food to lots of steady customers. The large menu features grilled veal, rabbit, fish, and lamb, and usually has excellent swordfish souvlaki. A variety of Greek salads and hors d'oeuvres are usually on display in a case by the entrance, and you can usually point out what you want for starters on your way to your table.

Rhodia. 44 Aristipou St. ☎ **01/722-9883.** Main courses 2,000–3,500Dr ($7–$12). No credit cards. Mon–Sat 8pm–2am. From Kolonaki Sq. take Patriarkou Ioakim uphill to Loukianou; turn left on Loukianou and climb steeply uphill to Aristipou; turn right on Aristipou. GREEK.

This long-time taverna in a handsome old Kolonaki house has tables in its small garden in good weather—although the interior, with its tile floor and old prints is so charming that you might be tempted to eat indoors. The Rodia is a favorite of visiting archaeologists from the nearby British and American Schools of Classical Studies, as well as of Kolonaki residents. It may not sound like just what you'd always hoped to have for dinner, but the octopus in mustard sauce is terrific, as are the veal and *dolmades* (stuffed grape leaves) in egg-lemon sauce. The house wine is excellent, as is the halva, which manages to be both creamy and crunchy.

To Ouzadiko. 25–29 Karneadou (in the Lemos International Shopping Center), Kolonaki. ☎ **01/729/5484.** Mezedes and main courses 2,000–4,000Dr ($7–$14). No credit cards. Mon–Sat 9pm–12:30am. From Kolonaki Square take Kapsali St. across Irodotou St. into Karneadou St. The Lemos Center is the miniskyscraper on your left. GREEK.

This cozy ouzo bar has at least 40 kinds of ouzo and as many mezedes, including fluffy *keftedes* (meatballs) that make all others taste leaden. If you can find a seat at this popular hangout, it's a great place for a snack or a full meal. A serious foody friend of mine goes here especially for the wide variety of *horta* (greens), which she says are the best she's ever tasted.

To Prytaneion. 7 Milioni, Kolonaki. ☎ **01-364-3353-4.** Mezedes and snacks 1,700–6,000Dr ($6–$20). No credit cards. Mon–Sat 10am–3am. From Kolonaki Square take Kanari to Milioni, a pedestrianized street on your right. GREEK/INTERNATIONAL.

The trendy bare stone walls here are decorated with movie posters and illuminated by baby spotlights. Waiters dressed mostly in black serve customers glued to cellular phones plates of some of Athens's most expensive and eclectic mezedes, including beef carpaccio, smoked salmon, bruschetta, and shrimps in fresh cream, as well as Greek olives and that international favorite, the hamburger.

Around Omonia Square & the National Archaeological Museum

Expensive

Restaurant Kostoyannis. Restaurant Kostoyannis. 37 Zaimi St. (2 blocks behind the National Archaeological Museum). ☎ **01/822-0624.** Main courses 2,500–6,800Dr ($8–$23). No credit cards. Mon–Sat 8pm–2am. From Omonia Sq. take Patission (28 Oktovriou) toward the National Museum to Tositsa; turn right on Tositsa and then left on Zaimi. GREEK/SEAFOOD.

It's not easy to simply walk into Kostoyannis and sit down: Just inside the entrance is a show-stopping display of shrimp, mussels, fresh fish, seemingly endless appetizers, tempting stews (*stifada*) in ceramic pots, and yards of chops that could almost make a dedicated vegetarian fall off the wagon. You can choose the items you'd like to sample, or you could make an entire meal just from the *mezedes* (appetizers), which I think are even better than the entrees. Don't be put off by this restaurant's slightly out-of-the-way location on a rather uninteresting street: It's well worth the trip.

Moderate

✪ **Athinaikon.** 2 Themistokleous St. ☎ **01/383-8485.** Main courses 1,000–4,000Dr ($3.35–$13). No credit cards. Mon–Sat 11am–midnight. Closed Aug. From Omonia Sq. take Panepistimou St. a block to Themistokleous St.; the Athinaikon is almost immediately on your right. GREEK.

This is a favorite haunt of lawyers and businesspeople working in the Omonia Square area. You can have just some appetizers (technically, this is an *ouzeri)* or a full meal. Obviously, the way to have a reasonably priced snack is to stick to the appetizers, including delicious *loukanika* (sausages) and *keftedes* (meatballs) and pass on the more pricey grilled shrimp or seafood casserole. Whatever you have, you'll enjoy taking in the old photos on the walls, the handsome tiled floor, and the marble-topped tables and bentwood chairs.

Inexpensive

Taygetos. 4 Satovriandou St. ☎ **01/523-5352.** Main courses 1,000–2,300Dr ($3.35–$8). No credit cards. Mon–Sat 9am–1am. From Omonia Sq. take Patision (28 Oktovriou) toward the National Museum; Satovriandou is the third major street on your left. GREEK/SOUVLAKIA.

This is a great place to stop in on your way to or from the museum. Service is swift, and the souvlakia and fried potatoes are excellent, as are the grilled lamb and chicken (priced by the kilo). The menu sometimes includes delicious *kokoretsia* (grilled entrails). The Ellinikon Restaurant next door is also a good value.

NEAR THE OLYMPIC STADIUM

Very Expensive

✪ **Bajazzo.** 1 Tyrteou & 14 Anapafseos sts. (corner), Mets. ☎ and fax **01/921-3013.** Reservations required Fri–Sat and recommended otherwise. Dinner for two from 45,000Dr ($150). Prices vary according to the daily menu. AE, DC, MC, V. Mon–Sat 8pm–1am. Take a taxi to this hard-to-find restaurant, off Ardittou St., south of the Temple of Olympian Zeus. INTERNATIONAL.

Bajazzo put Greek cuisine on the map when it won its Michelin star in 1998. Chef Klaus Feuerbach rightly says that two can eat here for $150, but I have friends who have eaten at Bajazzo and cheerfully spent almost twice that on the fine food and wine. Specialties include the feta tart, langostino souvlaki, kid with Peloponnesian herbs, and sea bass with mustard sauce—perhaps not to be eaten all at one sitting. The menu changes from night to night, so part of the fun is finding out what's being prepared on any given night.

NEAR THE ACROPOLIS

Moderate

Socrates' Prison. 20 Mitseon St. ☎ **01/922-3434.** Main courses 3,000–4,5000Dr ($9–$15). AE DC M/C V. Mon–Sat 11am–4pm; 7pm–1am. Closed Aug. From Syntagma Sq. take Amalias Ave. to pedestrianized Dionysiou Areopayitou St., walk away from Temple of Zeus on side of Dionysiou Areopagitou across from the Acropolis and turn left onto Mitseon (across from Theater of Dionysios). GREEK/CONTINENTAL.

This is a favorite with both Greeks and American and European expatriates living in Athens, who lounge at tables outdoors in good weather and in the pleasant indoor rooms year-round. Some long tables are communal, and there're also tables for four. The food here is noticeably more imaginative than average Greek fare (try the veggie croquettes), and includes continental dishes such as salade Niçoise and pork roll stuffed with vegetables. The retsina is excellent, and there's a wide choice of bottled wines and beers. This is a good place to head if you don't want to eat in the Plaka but enjoy strolling through on your way to or from dinner.

WORTH A (SHORT) TRIP
Expensive

✪ **Varoulko.** 14 Deligeorgi, Piraeus. ☎ **01/411-2043.** Fax 01/422-1283. Reservations required (make them several days before you plan to eat here). Fish priced by the kilo; prices vary according to what's available. Dinner for two easily 30,000Dr ($100). No credit cards. Open for dinner only daily except Sun. We recommend taking a taxi to this restaurant, which is hard to find and not in central Piraeus. FISH/SEAFOOD.

In an unlikely location on a side street in Piraeus, chef-owner Lefteris Lazarou has created what many consider not just the finest seafood restaurant, but the finest *restaurant* in the greater Athens area. I had one of the best meals in my life here—smoked eel, artichokes with fish roe, crayfish with sun-dried tomatoes, monkfish livers with soy sauce, honey, and balsamic vinegar—and the best sea bass and monkfish I have ever eaten. Everything is beautifully presented, and everything is delicious.

Vitrina. 7 Navarchou Apostoli St., Psiri. ☎ **01/321-1200.** Reservations required. Main courses 4,500–9,000Dr ($15–$30). No credit cards. Daily 8pm–late. NOUVELLE GREEK/INTERNATIONAL.

This drop-dead-fashionable restaurant is one of several new hot spots in the old warehouse district of Psirri off Ermou Street. The walls are pale gold, the tablecloths and chairs are pale gray, and many of the young waiters and waitresses are aspiring actors and writers. The kitchen seems to try too hard with some dishes (shrimp in Muscatel and lavender sauce, for example), but the food is usually both delicious and beautifully presented, and there's a serious wine list. The fashion accessory of choice is a cellular phone—so useful for calling people at the next table—and almost no one arrives before 10pm.

Moderate

✪ **Vlassis.** 8 Paster St. (off Plateia Mavili). ☎ **01/722-9056.** Main courses 1,800–3,600Dr ($6–$12). No credit cards. Mon–Sat noon–5pm and 9pm–1am. Closed much of June–Sept. From Syntagma Sq. take Vas. Sophias Ave. to Plateia Mavili; follow D. Soustou out of Plateia Mavili to Chatzikosta; Paster is the cul-de-sac on the left after you turn right into Chatzikosta. GREEK.

Greeks call this kind of food *paradisiako*—traditional, but paradisiacal is just as good a description. This is traditional food fit for the gods: delicious fluffy vegetable croquettes, eggplant salad that tastes like no other eggplant salad you've had, hauntingly tender lamb in egg-lemon sauce. It's a sign of Vlassis's popularity with Athenians—the last time I ate there, I was the only obvious foreigner in the place—that there's not even a discreet sign announcing its presence in a small apartment building on hard-to-find Paster Street. Take a taxi; you may feel so giddy with delight after eating that you won't mind the half-hour walk back to Syntagma Square.

Zeidoron. 10 Taki and Ayios Anaryiron. ☎ **01/321-5368.** www.psirri.gr.Zeidoron. Appetizers 1,500–3,500Dr ($5–$12). No credit cards. Mon–Sat 7pm–at least midnight. Closed Aug. From Syntagma Sq. take Ermou to Navarchou Apostoli, which runs into Taki, which intersects

Ayios Anayiron. Zeidoron is by the Ayios Anayiron church (this is at least a 20-min. walk from Syntagma). GREEK/MEZEDES.

This *mezedopolio* (hors d'oeuvres place) is one of a number of restaurants springing up in the old warehouse district of Psirri, now on the verge of being reclaimed and guppified, as the Greeks term their version of yuppification. There're lots of delicious *mezedes* to choose from, including vegetable croquettes, several eggplant dishes, and some heartier meat dishes, like pork in mustard.

SEEING THE SIGHTS
SIGHTSEEING SUGGESTIONS FOR FIRST-TIME VISITORS

If You Have 1 Day   Try to be at the **Acropolis** as soon as it opens so that you can take in the site and enjoy seeing the **Parthenon** and the Acropolis Museum before the crowds arrive. Afterward, walk downhill to visit the **Ancient Agora** and then head into **Monastiraki** and **Plaka,** where you can window-shop and relax over lunch or dinner.

Keep an eye out for the **Plaka tram.** The half-hour ride begins in Palia Agora Square, loops through the Plaka, and then heads past the Acropolis on Dionissiou Areopayitou Boulevard before heading back into Plaka (10am to 10pm in summer; 1,000Dr/$3.35). This is a great (and relaxing) way to get a sense of what you may want to explore on foot in the Plaka.

If You Have 2 Days   On Day 1, follow the suggestions above. It's worth spending several hours of Day 2 at the **National Archaeological Museum** (again, try to arrive the minute it opens to beat the crowds). Then, visit some of Athens's smaller museums—or, if you need a change of pace, head up **Mount Likavitos** on the funicular that leaves from the top of Ploutarchou Street (500Dr/$1.70, 10am to midnight, about every 20 minutes in summer). If the *nefos* (smog) isn't too bad, you'll have a wonderful view of Athens, Piraeus, and the Saronic Gulf. If you have an extra hour, take one of the paths from the summit and stroll down Likavitos, enjoying the scent of the pine trees and the changing views of the city.

If You Have 3 Days or More   For Days 1 and 2, follow the suggestions above. For the rest of your stay, visit more of the museums listed below, or consider a day trip to one of the great sights of antiquity, such as **Delphi** or **Sounion;** a day excursion to **Corinth, Mycenae,** and **Epidaurus** (best done on a bus tour); or a visit to the Byzantine monasteries of **Daphni** or **Kaisariani** (see "Day Trips from Athens," below). If you don't want to go home without seeing one of the "isles of Greece," take a day trip by boat from Piraeus to one of the islands of the Saronic Gulf. **Aegina (Egina), Poros,** and **Hydra (Idra)** are all feasible day trips—but best not done the day before you leave Athens, lest bad weather strands you on an island.

Whatever else you do, be sure to give yourself time to sit in cafes and watch the world go by.

Strike!

Strikes that close museums and archaeological sites can occur without warning. Decide what you most want to see, and go there as soon as possible after your arrival. The fact that something is open today says nothing about tomorrow. If you're visiting in the off-season, check with the **Greek National Tourist Organization** (☎ 01/331-0437) for the abbreviated winter hours of sites and museums.

THE TREASURES OF ANTIQUITY

✪ **The Acropolis. ☎ 01/321-0219.** Admission 4,000Dr ($14) adults (includes same-day admission to the National Archaeological Museum). Free Sun. Admission includes entrance to Acropolis Museum, which sometimes closes earlier, other times later, than the site. Summer daily 8am–7pm; winter daily 8:30am–2:30pm. From Syntagma Sq., take Amalias Ave. into pedestrianized Dionysiou Areopayitou St. and follow the marble path up to the Acropolis. The ticket booth, along with a small post office and a snack bar, are slightly below the entrance to the Acropolis.

When you climb up the Acropolis—the heights above the city—you'll realize why people seem to have lived here as long ago as 5000 B.C. The sheer sides of the Acropolis make it a superb natural defense, just the place to avoid enemies and to be able to see invaders coming across the sea or the plains of Attica. And, of course, it helped that in antiquity there was a spring here, ensuring a steady supply of water.

In classical times, when Athens's population had grown to around 250,000, people lived on the slopes below the Acropolis, which had become the city's most important religious center. Athens's civic and business center, the Agora, and its cultural center, with several theaters and concert halls, bracketed the Acropolis; when you peer over the sides of the Acropolis at the houses in Plaka and the remains of the ancient Agora and the Theater of Dionysos, you'll see the layout of the ancient city. Syntagma and Omonia squares, the heart of today's Athens, were well out of the ancient city center.

Even the Acropolis's height couldn't protect it from the Persian invasion of 480 B.C., when most of its monuments were burned and destroyed. You may notice some immense column drums built into the Acropolis's walls. When the great Athenian statesman Pericles ordered the monuments rebuilt, he had the drums from the destroyed Parthenon built into the walls lest Athenians forget what had happened—and so they would remember that they had rebuilt what they had lost. Pericles's rebuilding program began about 448 B.C.; the new Parthenon was dedicated 10 years later, but work on other monuments continued for a century.

The **Parthenon**—dedicated to Athena Parthenos (the Virgin), patron goddess of Athens—was the most important religious monument, but there were shrines to many other gods and goddesses on the Acropolis's broad summit. As you climb up, you pass through first the **Beule Gate,** built by the Romans, and now known by the name of the French archaeologist who discovered it in 1852. Next comes the **Propylaia,** the monumental 5th-century B.C. entranceway. You'll notice the little **Temple of Athena Nike** (Athena of Victory) perched above the Propylaia; the beautifully proportioned Ionic temple was built in 424 B.C. and restored in the 1930s. Off to the left of the Parthenon is the **Erechtheion,** which the Athenians honored as the tomb of Erechtheus, a legendary king of Athens. A hole in the ceiling and floor of the northern porch indicates the spot where Poseidon's trident struck to make a spring (symbolizing control of the sea) gush forth during his contest with Athena to be the city's chief deity. Athena countered with an olive tree (symbolizing control of the rich Attic plain); the olive tree planted beside the Erechtheion reminds visitors of her victory. Give yourself a little time to enjoy the delicate carving on the Erechtheion, and be sure to see the original Caryatids (the monumental female figures who served as columns on the Erechteion's porch) in the Acropolis Museum.

However charmed you are by these elegant little temples, you're probably still heading resolutely toward the **Parthenon,** and you may be disappointed to realize that visitors are not allowed inside, both to protect the monument and to allow ongoing restoration work to proceed safely (eight of the Parthenon's columns are being taken apart and painstakingly reassembled). If you find this frustrating, keep in mind that in antiquity only priests and honored visitors were allowed in to see

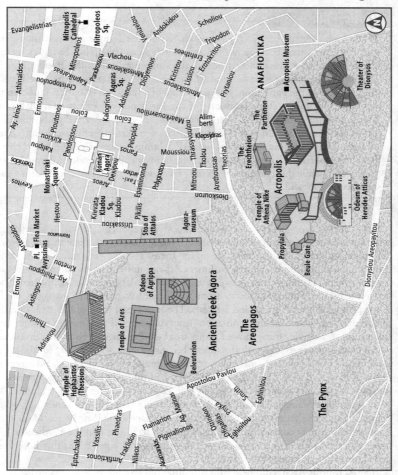

the monumental—some 11m (36 feet) tall—statue of Athena designed by the great Phidias, who supervised Pericles's building program. Nothing of the huge gold-and-ivory statue remains, but there's a small Roman copy in the National Archaeological Museum—and horrific renditions on souvenirs ranging from T-shirts to ouzo bottles. The floor of the room in which the statue stood was covered in olive oil, so that the gold and ivory reflected through the dimly lit room.

The Parthenon's entire roof and much of the interior were blown to smithereens in 1687, when a party of Venetians attempted to take the Acropolis from the Turks. A shell fired from nearby Mouseion Hill struck the Parthenon—where the Turks were storing gunpowder and munitions—and caused appalling damage to the building and its sculptures. Most of the remaining sculptures were carted off to London by Lord Elgin in the first decade of the 19th century. Those surviving sculptures—the **Elgin Marbles**—are on display in the British Museum, causing ongoing pain to generations of Greeks, who continue to press for their return.

Optical Illusions

If you look over the edge of the Acropolis toward the Temple of Hephaistos in the Ancient Agora, then back up at the Parthenon, you can't help but be struck by how much lighter, how much more graceful, the Parthenon is than the Theseion (as the Temple of Hephaistos is known today). Scholars tell us that this is because Iktinos, the architect of the Parthenon, was something of a magician of optical illusions: the columns and stairs—even the floor—of the Parthenon all appear straight because they're minutely curved. The exterior columns, for example, are slightly thicker in the middle (a device known as *entasis*), which makes the entire column appear straight. That's why the Parthenon, with 17 columns on each side and 8 at each end (creating a **peristyle,** or exterior colonnade, of 46 relatively slender columns), looks so graceful, while the Theseion, with only 6 columns at each end and 13 along each side, seems so stolid.

The Parthenon originally had sculpture in both its pediments, as well as a frieze running around the entire temple. Alternating *triglyphs* (panels with three incised grooves) and *metopes* (sculptured panels) made up the frieze. The east pediment showed scenes from the birth of Athena, the west pediment Athena and Poseidon's contest for possession of Athens. The long frieze showed the battle of the Athenians (led by the hero Theseus) against the Amazons, scenes from the Trojan War, and the struggles of the Olympian gods against giants and centaurs. The message of most of this sculpture was the triumph of knowledge and civilization (read: Athens) over the forces of darkness and barbarians. An interior frieze showed scenes from the Panathenaic Festival each August, when citizens processed through the streets, bringing a new *peplos* (tunic) for the statue of Athena. Only a few fragments of any of the sculptures remain in place, and every visitor will have to decide whether it's a good or a bad thing that Lord Elgin removed so much before the smog spread over Athens and ate away at the remaining sculpture.

If you're lucky enough to visit the Acropolis on a smog-free and sunny day, you'll see the golden and cream tones of the Parthenon's handsome Pentelic marble at their most subtle. It may come as something of a shock to realize that the Parthenon, like most other monuments here, was painted in antiquity, with gay colors that have since faded, revealing the tones of the marble.

The **Acropolis Archaeological Museum** hugs the ground to detract as little as possible from the ancient monuments. Inside, you'll see the four original **Caryatids** from the Erechtheion that are still in Athens (one disappeared during the Ottoman occupation, and one is in the British Museum). Other delights here include sculpture from the Parthenon burnt by the Persians, statues of *korai* (maidens) dedicated to Athena, figures of *kouroi* (young men), and a wide range of finds from the Acropolis.

Those interested in learning more about the Acropolis should check to see if the **Center for Acropolis Studies,** on Makriyanni Street just southeast of the Acropolis (☎ **01/923-9381**), temporarily closed in early 2000, has reopened. If so, it should be open daily 9am to 2:30pm; admission is free. On display are artifacts, reconstructions, photographs, drawings, and plaster casts of the Elgin Marbles. A museum is being built here to house the marbles themselves when (if) they're returned to Athens. Construction has been slowed by the discovery of important Byzantine remains here.

Ancient Agora. Below the Acropolis on the edge of Monastiraki (entrance on Adrianou St., near Ayiou Philippou Sq., east of Monastiraki Sq.). ☎ **01/321-0185.** Admission (includes museum) 1,200Dr ($4) adults, 900Dr ($3) seniors, 600Dr ($2) students. Tues–Sun 8:30am–3pm.

The Agora was Athens's commercial and civic center, with buildings used for a wide range of political, educational, philosophical, theatrical, and athletic purposes—which may be why what remains seems such a jumble. This is a nice place to wander and enjoy the views up toward the Acropolis; take in the herb garden and flowers planted around the 5th century B.C. **Temple of Hephaistos (the Theseion);** peek into the heavily restored 11th-century church of Ayii Apostoli (Holy Apostles); and admire the 2nd-century B.C. **Stoa of Attalos,** totally reconstructed by American archaeologists in the 1950s.

The **museum** in the Stoa's ground floor has finds from 5,000 years of Athenian history, including sculpture and pottery, as well as a voting machine and a child's potty seat, all with labels in English. The museum (which has excellent toilet facilities) closes 15 minutes before the site.

Cemetery of Keramikos. 148 Ermou St. ☎ **01/346-3552.** Admission 500Dr ($1.70) adults, 400Dr ($1.35) seniors, 300Dr ($1) students. Tues–Sun 8:30am–3pm. Walk west from Monastiraki Sq. on Ermou St. past Thisio Metro station; cemetery is on the right.

This ancient cemetery, where Pericles gave his famous funeral oration, is a short walk from the Ancient Agora and not far from the presumed site of Plato's Academy. There're a number of well-preserved funerary monuments and the remains of the colossal **Dipylon Gate,** the main entrance to the ancient city of Athens. You can also see substantial remains of the 5th-century B.C. fortifications known as the "Long Walls" that ran from Athens to Piraeus. The Keramikos can be a pleasant spot to sit and read because it's seldom crowded. If you like cemeteries, be sure to take in Athens's enormous **First Cemetery,** near the Athens Stadium, where notables such as former Prime Minister George Panandreou are buried beneath elaborate monuments.

THE TOP MUSEUMS

✪ **National Archaeological Museum.** 44 Patission St. ☎ **01/821-7717.** Fax 01/821-3573. E-mail: protocol@eam.culture.gr. Admission 4,000Dr ($14) adults (includes same-day admission to the Acropolis). Summer daily 8am–7pm; winter 8am–3pm. (Be sure to double-check that these hours are in effect when you visit. Budget considerations may force the museum to revert to its former closing time of 5pm in winter, 3pm on Sun and holidays, and its midday opening on Mon). Walk 10 minutes—about $1/2$km ($1/3$ mile)—north of Omonia Sq. on the road officially named 28 Oktobriou Ave. but usually called Patission.

This is an enormous and enormously popular museum; try to arrive as soon as it opens so you can see the exhibits and not just the other visitors' backs. Early arrival should give you at least an hour before most tour groups turn up. Don't miss the stunning gold masks, cups, dishes, and jewelry unearthed from the site of Mycenae by Heinrich

A National Archaeological Museum Update

The second floor of the National Archaeological Museum has been closed since an earthquake shook Athens in 1999. At press time, this floor hadn't reopened, and there were plans to move the restored 3500 B.C. Thira frescoes (on that floor) back to the island of Thira (Santorini). In addition, a number of splendid marble statues on the ground floor are still under protective wraps.

Many guards are strictly enforcing long-ignored rules regulating the size of bags, briefcases, and knapsacks allowed into the museum. Don't be surprised if you're told to check your bag at the cloakroom—be sure to remove any valuables. The GNTO recently announced plans to keep the museum open to 7pm in summer. You may wish to check to see if this has taken place by the time you visit.

Schliemann in 1876, on display in the first room, and the elegant marble Cycladic figurines (ca. 2000 B.C.) in the adjacent room. The museum's extensive collection of black and the red figure vases are on the museum's second floor, which may not have reopened when you visit. Frustratingly, the museum shop displays a wide range of excellent reproductions—almost none of which are in stock.

N.P. Goulandris Foundation Museum of Cycladic Art. 4 Neophytou Douka St. ☎ 01/
722-8321. Admission 800Dr ($2.70) adults, 250Dr (85¢) students. Mon, Wed–Fri
10am–4pm; Sat 10am–3pm. From Syntagma Sq., walk 7 blocks east along Vasilissis Sofias,
then ¹/₂ block north on Neophytou Douka; museum is on right.

This handsome new museum houses the largest collection of Cycladic art outside the National Archaeological Museum, with some 230 stone and pottery vessels and figurines from the 3rd millennium B.C. on display. See if you agree with those who have compared the faces of the Cycladic figurines to the work of the Italian painter, Modigliani. Be sure to go through the courtyard into the museum's newest acquisition: an elegant 19th-century house with some of its original furnishings and visiting exhibits. The museum shop has a wide variety of books and reproductions—and wildly unhelpful staff.

Benaki Museum. 1 Koumbari St. (at Vasilissis Sofias Ave., Kolonaki). From Syntagma Sq.,
walk a long 5 blocks east on Vas. Sophias Ave to the museum, which is on your left).
☎ 01/361-1617.

The Benaki Museum, closed for several years for major alterations, was scheduled to reopen in 2000. If it has reopened by the time you're here, you're in luck. The costume collection is superb, and the relics of Greece's 1821 War of Independence, including Lord Byron's writing desk and pen, are fascinating. If the museum has not reopened, it's still worth a visit for its special exhibitions in a reopened gallery and its excellent museum store. If the rooftop cafe has reopened, be sure to enjoy the superb view of the National Gardens and Acropolis.

Byzantine Museum. 22 Vasilissis Sofias Ave. (at Vassileos Konstandinou Ave.). ☎ 01/
723-1570 or 01/721-1027. Admission 500Dr ($1.70) adults, 250Dr (85¢) students. Tues–Sun
8:30am–3pm. From Syntagma Sq., walk along Vasilissis Sofias Ave. (also known as Venizelou
Ave.) for about 15 minutes. The museum is on the right, on the same side of the street as the
National Garden.

As its name makes clear, this museum, in a 19th-century Florentine-style former villa, is devoted to the art and history of the Byzantine era. Greece's most important collection of icons and religious art—along with sculptures, altars, mosaics, religious vestments, bibles, and a small-scale reconstruction of an early Christian basilica—are exhibited on several floors around a courtyard.

✪ **Greek Folk Art Museum.** 17 Kidathineon St., Plaka. ☎ **01/322-9031.** Admission
500Dr ($1.65) adults, 400Dr ($1.35) seniors, 300Dr ($1) students. Tues–Sun 10am–2pm.
From Syntagma, take Filellinon St. to Kidathineon.

This endearing small museum has dazzling embroideries and costumes from all over the country, plus a small room with zany frescoes of gods and heroes done by the eccentric artist Theofilos Hadjimichael, who painted in the early part of the 20th century.

✪ **Museum of Greek Popular Musical Instruments.** 1–3 Diogenous St. ☎ **01/
325-0198.** Free admission. Tues, Thurs–Sun 10am–2pm; Wed noon–8pm.

Photos show the musicians, and recordings let you listen to the tambourines, Cretan lyres, lutes, pottery drums, and clarinets on display here. The shop has a wide selection of CDs and cassettes.

Ilias Lalaounis Jewelry Museum. 12 Kalisperi (at Karyatidon). ☎ **01/922-1044.** Fax 01/
923-7358. Karyatidon). ☎ **01/922-1044.** Fax 01/923-7358. www.lalounis-jewelrymuseum.
gr. E-mail: jewelrymuseum@ath.forthnet.gr. Admission 1,000Dr ($3.35) adults, 500Dr ($1.65)
students/seniors/children. Mon and Thurs–Sat 9am–4pm, Wed 9am–9pm (entrance free after
3pm), Sun 10am–4pm. Walk 1 block south of the Acropolis between the Theater of Dionysos
and the Odeum of Herodes Atticus.

The 3,000 pieces on display here are so spectacular that even nonjewelry lovers will
enjoy this glitzy small museum, founded by one of Greece's most successful jewelry
designers. The first floor has a boutique stocking 2,000 items and a small workshop.
The second and third floors display pieces inspired by ancient, Byzantine, and
Cycladic designs, as well as by plants and animals. The museum has frequent special
exhibitions.

SOME SMALL MUSEUMS ALSO WORTH A LOOK

Athens has a number of excellent small museums. Some of the nicest include the **Center of Folk Art and Tradition** (also known as the Cultural Center of the Municipality of Athens), 6 Angelikis Hatzimihali St. (☎ **01/324-3987**); the **Children's Museum,** 14 Kidathineon St. (☎ **01/331-2995**); the **Jewish Museum,** 39 Nikis St. (☎ **01/323-1577**); the **Museum of Greek Costume,** 7 Dimokritou St. (☎ **01/362-9513**); and the **Athens City Museum,** 7 Paparigopoulou St. (☎ **01/324-6164**).

THE NATIONAL GARDEN & MOUNT LIKAVITOS

The National Garden, between Amalias Avenue and Irodou Attikou, south of Vasilissis Sofias Avenue, was once the royal family's palace garden. Today it encompasses a
park, garden, and small, rather sad, zoo. It has shade trees, benches, and small lakes
and ponds with ducks, swans, and a few peacocks. There're several cafes tucked away,
and you can also picnic here. The large neoclassical exhibition and reception hall was
built by the brothers Zappas and is known as the Zappion. Keep an eye out for the
bust of Melina Mercouri, the Greek actress and political figure, across from the gardens on Vas. Amalias Ave. The garden is officially open daily 7am to 10pm. This is
not a good place to wander alone at night, unless you enjoy encounters with strangers.

Mount Likavitos (Lycabettus), which dominates the northeast part of the city, is
a favorite retreat for Athenians and a great place to get a bird's-eye view of Athens and
its environs—if the *nefos* (smog) isn't too bad. Even when the *nefos* is bad, sunsets can
be spectacular here. On top, there's a small **chapel of Ayios Yioryios (St. George),**
whose name day is April 23. There're performances at the **Likavitos Theater** each
summer, and the expensive cafes on the summit are usually open all year. You can take
the **funicular** from the top of Ploutarchou Street for 500Dr ($1.70), 10am to midnight, about every 20 minutes in summer, or walk up from Dexameni Square, the
route preferred by young lovers and the energetic.

ORGANIZED TOURS

Tours of Athens are often no more expensive, and considerably less stressful, than renting a car for the day and driving yourself. You can book through most hotels or any
travel agency. A half-day tour of city highlights should cost about 15,000Dr ($50).
Night tours can include a sound-and-light show, Greek folk dancing at the Dora Stratou Folk Dance Theater, or dinner and Greek dancing. They range from 15,000Dr to
30,000Dr ($50 to $100).

Educational Tours & Cruises, 9 Irving St., Medford, MA 02111 (☎ **800/
275-4109;** e-mail: edtours@ars.nep.gr), and 1 Artemídos St., Glyfáda 16674, Athens
(☎ **01/898-1741**), can arrange tours in Athens and throughout Greece, including
individual tours with an emphasis on Greek culture. **CHAT Tours,** 4 Stadiou St.

(☎ 01/322-3137); **GO Tours,** 31–33 Voulis St. (☎ 01/322-5951); and **Key Tours,** 4 Kaliroïs St. (☎ 01/923-3166), are all reliable, established companies that offer tours of Athens and various day trips. Destinations include the temple of Apollo at Sounion, Delphi, and the Peloponnese (usually taking in Corinth, Mycenae, and Epidauros).

THE SHOPPING SCENE

If you want to pick up retro clothes or old copper, try the **flea market,** a daily spectacle between Plaka and Monastiraki Square. It's most lively on Sunday, but you can find the usual touristy trinkets, copies of ancient artifacts, jewelry, sandals, and various handmade goods, including embroideries, any day. Keep in mind that not everything sold as an antique is genuine, and that it's illegal to take antiquities and icons more than 100 years old out of the country without a hard-to-obtain export license.

In the Plaka-Monastiraki area, several shops with nicer-than-usual arts and crafts and fair prices include **Stavros Melissinos,** the Poet-Sandalmaker of Athens, 89 Pandrossou St. (☎ 01/321-9247); **Iphanta,** the weaving workshop, 6 Selleu St. (☎ 01/322-3628); **Emanuel Masmanidis' Gold Rose Jewelry** shop, 85 Pandrossou St. (☎ 01/321-5662); and the **Center of Hellenic Tradition,** 59 Mitropoleos and 36 Pandrossou sts. (☎ 01/321-3023), which sells arts and crafts. At the **Hellenic Folk-Art Gallery,** 6 Ipatias and Apollonos sts., Plaka (☎ 01/324-0017), a portion of the proceeds from everything sold (including handsome woven and embroidered carpets), goes to the National Welfare Organization, which encourages traditional crafts. Finally, don't forget that most museums have excellent shops.

The biggest **foreign-language bookstore** in Athens is **Eleftheroudakis,** which has a branch at 4 Nikis St. (☎ 01/322-2255) and a new headquarters at 17 Panepistimiou St. (☎ 01/331-4480). The new store has eight stories filled with a full range of subjects, plus a cafe and a music shop, and stages a series of small concerts and readings by local authors.

Compendium, 28 Nikis St. (☎ 01/322-1248), on the edge of Plaka near Syntagma Square, is a good English-language bookstore, selling new and used fiction and nonfiction, plus magazines and maps. **Reymondos,** 18 Voukourestiou St., a pedestrianized street just off Syntagma Square (☎ 01/364-8189), has a good selection in English, including some dazzling photo books on Greece, and is often open after usual shop hours.

On your way there, you can ogle the window displays at **Zolotas,** 10 Panepistimiou St. (☎ 01/361-3782), and **Lalounis,** 6 Panepistimiou St. (☎ 01/362-1371), Greece's two finest jewelers, which have branches at the foot of Voukourestiou Street.

ATHENS AFTER DARK

Greeks enjoy their nightlife so much that they take an afternoon nap to rest up for it. The evening often begins with a leisurely *volta* (stroll); you'll see it in most neighborhoods, including Plaka and Kolonaki Square. Most Greeks don't think of dinner until at least 9pm—when there's still no hurry. Around midnight the party may move on to a club for music and dancing.

Check the daily *Kathimerini* insert in the *International Herald-Tribune* or the *Athens News,* both sold at most major newsstands, for current cultural and entertainment events, including films, lectures, theater, music, and dance. The weekly *Hellenic Times* and *Athenscope* and the monthly *Now in Athens* list nightspots, restaurants, movies, theater, and much else. The weekly Greek publication *Athinorama* has comprehensive listings of events.

THE PERFORMING ARTS

The **Athens Festival** at the Odeon of Herodes Atticus has famous Greek and foreign artists performing music, plays, opera, and ballet from the beginning of June to the beginning of October in a beautiful open-air setting. Find out what's being presented through the English-language press or at the **Athens Festival Office,** 4 Stadiou St. (☎ **01/322-1459,** 01/322-3111, or 01/322-3110, ext. 137). The office is open Monday to Saturday 8:30am to 2pm and 5 to 7pm, and Sunday 10am to 1pm. If available—and that's a big "if"—tickets, which range from about $10 to $30, can also be purchased at the **Odeon** (☎ **01/323-2771**) several hours before a performance.

The acoustically marvelous new **Megaron Mousikis Concert Hall,** 89 Vasilissis Sofias Ave. (☎ **01/729-0391** or 01/728-2333), hosts a wide range of classical music programs that include chamber music, operas in concert, symphonic concerts, and recitals. The box office is open weekdays 10am to 6pm, Saturday 10am to 2pm, and Sunday 6 to 10:30pm on performance nights only. Tickets, costing about 1,000Dr to 20,000Dr ($3.35 to $67), depending on the performance, are also sold weekdays 10am to 5pm in the Megaron's convenient downtown kiosk in the Spiromillios Arcade, 4 Stadiou St. The Megaron has a limited summer season but is in full swing the rest of the year.

Most major jazz and rock concerts, as well as some classical performances, take place at the **Pallas Theater,** 1 Voukourestiou St. (☎ **01/322-8275**).

English-language theater and American-style music are performed at the **Hellenic American Union Auditorium,** 22 Massalias St., between Kolonaki and Omonia squares (☎ **01/362-9886**); you can usually get a ticket for around 3,000Dr ($10). Arrive early and check out the art show or photo exhibition at the adjacent gallery. The **Greek National Opera** performs at the Olympia Theater, 59 Akadimias St., at Mavromihali (☎ **01/361-2461**).

The **Dora Stratou Folk Dance Theater,** which performs on Philopappos Hill, is the best known of the traditional dance troupes. Regional dances are performed in costume with appropriate musical accompaniment nightly at 10:15pm, with additional shows at 8:15pm on Wednesday and Sunday. You can buy tickets 8am to 2pm at the box office, 8 Scholio St., Plaka (☎ **01/924-4395,** or 01/921-4650 after 5:30pm); prices are 3,000Dr to 4,200Dr ($10 to $14), or higher.

Sound-and-light shows, seen from the Pnyx, the hill across Dionysiou Areopayitou Street from the Acropolis, illuminate (sorry) Athens's history by focusing on the history of the Acropolis. Try to sit away from the (very) loud speakers, so you won't be deafened by the booming historical narrative and all-too-stirring music and can concentrate instead on the play of lights on the monuments of the Acropolis. Shows are held April to October. Performances in English begin at 9pm and last 45 minutes. Tickets can be purchased at the **Athens Festival Office,** 4 Stadiou St. (☎ **01/322-7944**), or at the entrance to the Sound and Light (☎ **01/922-6210**), which is signposted on the Pnyx. Tickets are 1,800Dr ($6) for adults and 600Dr ($2) students.

THE CLUB, MUSIC & BAR SCENE

Walk the streets of Plaka any night and you'll find plenty of tavernas offering pseudo-traditional live music. Many are clip joints playing the equivalent of Muzak, but some do better. **Taverna Mostrou,** 22 Mnissikleos St. (☎ **01/324-2441**), is one of the largest, oldest, and best known for traditional Greek music and dancing. Shows begin at about 11pm and usually last until 2am. Cover is 6,000Dr ($20) and includes a set-menu supper. À la carte fare is available but expensive. Nearby, **Palia Taverna Kritikou,** 24 Mnissikleos St. (☎ **01/322-2809**), is another lively open-air taverna with music and dancing. Other reliable tavernas with live traditional music include **Nefeli,** 24 Panos St. (☎ **01/321-2475**); **Dioyenis,** 3 Sellei St. (☎ **01/324-7933**); **Stamatopoulou,** 26 Lissiou St. (☎ **01/322-8722**); and **Xinos,** 4 Agelou Geronta St. (☎ **01/322-1065**).

For Greek pop music, try **Zoom,** 37 Kidathineon St., in the heart of Plaka (☎ **01/322-5920**). Performers, who are likely to have current hit albums, are showered with carnations by adoring fans. The minimum order is 6,000Dr ($20). If you want to check out the local rock and blues scene along with small doses of metal, Athenian popsters play at **Memphis,** 5 Ventiri St., near the Hilton Hotel east of Syntagma Square (☎ **01/722-4104**); it's open Tuesday to Friday 10:30pm to 2:30am.

Those interested in authentic *rebetika* (music of the urban poor and dispossessed) should consult their hotel receptionist or the current issue of *Athenscope* or *Athinorama* (in Greek) to see which clubs are featuring the best performers. Shows usually don't start until nearly midnight, and though there's usually no cover, a 5,000Dr ($17) charge per drink is not uncommon. Most clubs are closed during summer, and many are far from the town center, so budget another 2,500Dr to 5,000Dr ($8 to $17) for round-trip taxi fare.

One of the more central clubs is the **Stoa Athanaton,** 19 Sofokleous, in the Central Meat Market (☎ **01/321-4362**), which has live rebetika Monday to Saturday 3 to 6pm and after midnight and serves good food; minimum is 3,000Dr ($10). **Taximi,** 29 Odos Isavron, Exarchia (☎ **01/363-9919**), is consistently popular. Drinks cost 3,500Dr ($12). It's closed Sunday and July and August. **Frangosyriani,** 57 Odos Arachovis, Exarchia (☎ **01/360-0693**), specializes in the music of rebetika legend Markos Vamvakaris. It's closed Tuesday and Wednesday. The downscale, smoke-filled **Rebetiki Istoria,** in a neoclassical building at 181 Ippokratous St. (☎ **01/642-4937**), features old-style rebetika music, played to a mixed crowd of older regulars and younger students and intellectuals. The music usually starts at 11pm, but arrive earlier to get a seat. The legendary Maryo I Thessaloniki (Maryo from Thessaloniki), sometimes described as the Bessie Smith of Greece, sometimes sings rebetika at **Perivoli t'Ouranou,** 19 Lysikratous St. (☎ **01/323-5517** or 01/322-2048) in Plaka; cover is around 10,000Dr ($34).

A number of clubs and cafes specialize in jazz, but also offer everything from Indian sitar music to rock and punk. The **Café Asante,** 78 Damareos (☎ **01/756-0102**) in Pangrati has music most nights from 11pm; cover varies, but count on spending around 10,000Dr ($34) if you go and have a couple of drinks. The very popular **Half Note Jazz Club,** 17 Trivonianou St., Mets (☎ **01/921-3310**), has everything from medieval music to jazz nightly; performance times vary from 8 to 11pm and later; cover is usually between 4,000 and 6,000Dr ($13 and $20). At **The House of Art,** 4 Sahtouri and Sari, Psirri (☎ **01/321-7678**) and **Pinakothiki,** 5 Agias Theklas

Open in August

Many popular after-dark spots close in August, when Athenians flee the summer heat to the country. You'll find that a number of bars, cafes, ouzeries, and tavernas on the pedestrianized **Irakleidon** walkway off Apostolos Pauvlos Street across from the Theseion stay open in August: **Stavlos,** the restaurant/bar/disco popular with all ages, remains open on August weekends. A few doors away, the **Berlin Club,** which caters to a young crowd and specializes in rock, is open most nights, and **Ambibagio** has quite genuine Greek music. The sweet shop **Aistisis** offers great views of the Acropolis and stays open as late as the nearby bars.

(☎ 01/324-7741), both in newly fashionable Psyrri, you can often hear jazz from 11pm; cover is around 7,000Dr ($23), first drink included. **The Rodon Club,** 24 Marni St. (☎ 01/523-6293), west of Omonia Square, also has jazz and pop concerts many nights from 10pm; cover is from 7,000Dr ($23).

GAY & LESBIAN BARS

The gay scene is fairly low key; get-togethers are sometimes advertised in the English-language press. Information is also available from the Greek national gay and lesbian organization **AKOE-AMPHI,** P.O. Box 26002, 10022 Athens; office at 6 Zalongou (☎ 01/771-9221). The friendliest bar is **Aleko's Island,** 42 Tsakalof St., Kolonaki (no phone), a fun place where you can actually have a conversation. **Granazi,** 20 Lebesi St. (☎ 01/325-3979), attracts a loud and lively young crowd. The disco **Lambda,** 15 Lembessi St. and Syngrou Av. 9 (☎ 01/922-4202), is hip and trendy with the young locals. In Kolonaki, **Alexander's,** 44 Anagnostopoulou, Kolonaki (☎ 01/364-6660), is more sedate, with more variety. And **Porta,** 10 Phalirou St. (☎ 01/924-3858), is the only true lesbian bar in town.

DANCE CLUBS

Hidden on the outskirts of the Plaka, **Booze,** 57 Kolokotroni St., second floor (☎ 01/324-0944), blasts danceable rock to a hip student crowd. There's art on every wall, jelled stage lights, and two bars. Admission is 1,500Dr ($5), plus 1,000Dr ($3.35) per drink. If it's disco you're craving, head east to **Absolut,** 23 Filellinon St. (no phone), **Q Base** 49 Evripidou, Omonia (☎ 01/321-8256), or **R-Load,** 161 Ermou (☎ 01/345-6187). If you feel a bit too old there, head north to Panepistimiou Street, where the **Wild Rose,** in the arcade at 10 Panepistimiou St. (☎ 01/364-2160), and **Mercedes Rex,** at 48 Panepistimiou St. (☎ 01/361-4591), usually have varied programs.

DAY TRIPS FROM ATHENS
PIRAEUS

You probably won't fall in love with Piraeus, but if you have some time to kill—or want to escape Athens's summer heat—you can find lots to enjoy.

Piraeus has been the port of Athens since antiquity and is still where you catch most island boats and cruise ships. Keep in mind that there are three harbors: the **main harbor** (*Megas Limani*), where you'll see everything from tankers to island boats and cruise ships; **Zea Marina** (also called *Zea Limani*), the port for most of the swift hydrofoils; and **Little Harbor** (*Microlimani,* also called *Turkolimani,* or Turkish Harbor), the location of many fish restaurants. As in antiquity, today's Piraeus has the seamier side of a sailors' port of call and the color and bustle of an active harbor—both aspects, somewhat sanitized, were portrayed in the film *Never on Sunday.* Piraeus also has a sprawling market where you can buy produce shipped in each day, including bread baked that morning on distant islands. There're a number of fish restaurants, but many are overpriced and serve fish that is not as fresh as the bread.

GETTING THERE   By Metro   The fastest and easiest way to Piraeus is to take the Metro from Omonia Square or Monastiraki to the last stop. It costs 250Dr (85¢) and leaves you 1 block from the principal domestic port.

By Bus   From Syntagma Square, take bus 40 from the corner of Filellinon Street; it leaves you 1 block from the international port, about a 10-minute walk along the water from the domestic port. From the airport, bus 91 goes to Piraeus. The fare is 300Dr ($1).

By Taxi   A taxi from Syntagma Square or the airport costs about 2,400Dr ($8). When tourists headed back to Athens disembark, taxi drivers usually offer flat fees that are wildly out of line. Either insist on the metered rate, or walk away from the harbor and try again.

VISITOR INFORMATION   For boat schedules, transit information, and other tourist information 24 hours a day, dial ☎ **171.**

If you need a travel agency to make reservations or to recommend a particular service, try **Explorations Unlimited,** 2 Kapodistriou St. (☎ **01/411-6395** or 01/411-1243), just off Akti Posidonos near the Metro station. It's open weekdays 8am to 7pm and Saturday 9am to 2pm.

FERRIES TO THE ISLANDS   The boats to the islands are opposite the Metro station. Boats to the **Saronic Gulf** and hydrofoils (Flying Dolphins) to **Aegina** are opposite and to the left of the station; the hydrofoils leave from the foot of Gounari Street. Boats to the other islands are around to the right and away from the station. Boats to **Italy** and **Turkey** are a mile or so to the left. Hydrofoils to other destinations leave from Zea Marina, a separate harbor some distance from the Metro station. Very few signs point the way, so try to arrive early.

Ferry **tickets** can be purchased at a ticket office up to 1 hour before departure; after that they can be bought on the boat. To book **first-class cabins** or purchase **advance tickets,** see one of the harborside travel agents around Karaiskaki Square by the domestic ferries and along Akti Miaouli, opposite the Crete ferries. Most open at 6am, and some will hold your baggage for the day (but there's no security). The Greek National Tourist Organization (EOT) publishes a list of weekly sailings, and the **Tourist Police** (☎ 171) or the **Port Authority** (☎ 01/451-1311) can provide schedule information. Keep in mind that all such schedules are tentative.

SEEING THE SIGHTS ON LAND   The **Maritime Museum** at Akti Themistokleous (☎ **01/451-6264**), near the departure pier for the Flying Dolphin hydrofoils, has handsome models of ancient, medieval, and modern ships. The museum is open Tuesday to Saturday 9am to 2pm; admission is 500Dr ($1.70). The nearby **Archaeological Museum,** 32 Harilaou Trikoupi St. (☎ **01/452-1598**), is open Tuesday to Sunday 8:30am to 3pm, and also costs 500Dr ($1.70). The stars of the museum are the three superb monumental bronzes of a youth, the goddess Artemis, and the goddess Athena. If you have time for only one museum, you'll probably find the Maritime Museum a pleasant departure from what you've seen in other archaeological museums.

WHERE TO DINE   Piraeus has some good restaurants, but the places to eat along the harbor are generally mediocre. If you decide to try one of the seafood restaurants in central Piraeus or Microlimani, make sure you know the price before ordering; if the final tab seems out of line, insist on a receipt, and phone the Tourist Police. In addition to our suggestions here, don't forget ✪ **Varoulko** at 14 Deligeorgi, Piraeus, which serves the best fish in Greece (See "Where to Dine—Worth a (Short) Trip," above).

Traveler's Tip

Whatever your destination from Piraeus, don't be too surprised if your boat leaves late. Schedules depend on the weather, and sailings are often delayed or canceled. It's not a good idea to plan to arrive back in Athens less than 24 hours before your flight home, lest bad weather strands you on an island.

Dourambeis. 29A Dilaveri St., Piraeus. ☎ **01/412-2092.** Reservations recommended. Fish around 9,000–15,000Dr ($30–$50) per kilo; priced daily. No credit cards. Mon–Sat 8:30pm–1am. Take a cab from the Metro station. SEAFOOD.

This taverna near the Delphinario theater in Piraeus is where locals go when they want to splurge on a good fish dinner. The decor is simple, the food excellent. The crayfish soup alone is excellent, as is the grilled fish.

✪ **Vassilenas.** 72 Etolikou, Ayia Sofia. ☎ **01/461-2457.** Reservations recommended Fri–Sat. Meals 6,000Dr ($20). No credit cards. Mon–Sat 8pm–midnight. From Akti Kondili, which runs between the Northern and Peloponnesian train stations, take Etolikou (approximaely halfway between the two stations) to Vassilenas (a vigorous 20-minute walk). SEAFOOD/GREEK.

There's no menu at this restaurant in an old grocery store in a suburb just north of Piraeus; for a flat fee of 6,000Dr ($20) per person, you're presented with a steady flow of more than 15 dishes. Even if you come here hungry, you probably won't be able to eat everything set before you. There's plenty of seafood, plus good Greek dishes.

THE MONASTERY OF DAPHNI & ANCIENT ELEUSIS

THE MONASTERY OF DAPHNI Laden with dazzling mosaics, the **Monastery of Daphni** (☎ 01/581-1558) is one of the masterpieces of Byzantine art—but since the 1999 earthquake, Daphni has been closed as often as has been open, so check with the GNTO to see if Daphni is open. Sir David Talbot-Rice, the great art historian of Byzantine Greece, has called Daphni "the most perfect monument" of the 11th century. There were shrines on this spot even in antiquity, when Apollo was honored here, as the name "Daphni"—laurel, Apollo's favorite plant—suggests. The present monastery was begun in the late 11th century; in the centuries that followed, it was repeatedly damaged by invaders and earthquakes, and repeatedly rebuilt. After the crusaders captured Constantinople in 1204, Daphni was used as a Catholic monastery by Cistercian monks who installed the twin Gothic arches in front of the west entrance to the church. After the Greek War of Independence in the 1820s, the Greek Orthodox Church reclaimed Daphni and restored it to its former glory.

A severe earthquake in the 1980s prompted another round of restoration. The church has been strengthened and its dazzling mosaic cycle restored. The central dome has the commanding mosaic of **Christ Pantocrator (the Almighty).** The image is of an awesome judge rather than the Western conception of a suffering mortal. As is traditional, the **Annunciation, Nativity, Baptism,** and **Transfiguration** are in the squinches (quarter-circles) supporting the dome, and the 16 Major **Prophets** are displayed between the dome's windows. **The Adoration of the Magi** and the **Resurrection** are in the barrel vault inside the main (southern) entrance of the church, and the **Entry into Jerusalem** and the **Crucifixion** are in the northern barrel vault. Mosaics showing scenes from the **life of the Virgin** are in the south bay of the narthex (passage between the entrance and nave).

The monastery is open daily, except major holidays, 8:30am to 3pm. Admission is 800DDr ($2.70).

Getting There Daphni is 9km (5¹/₂ miles) west of Athens on the highway to Corinth. Take bus 860 from Panepistimiou Street, north of Sina (behind the university); bus 853, 862, 873, or 880 from Eleftheria Square off Pireos Avenue (northwest of Monastiraki); or bus A 15 ("Elefsina") from Sachtouri Street, southeast of Eleftheria Square. The trip should take about half an hour, and the bus stop at Daphni is about 140m (450 feet) from the monastery. From Daphni, you can continue by bus to Ancient Eleusis.

ANCIENT ELEUSIS   Eleusis was the site of the most famous and revered of all the ancient Mysteries. The unknown and the famous were initiated into the sacred rites here, yet we know almost nothing about the Eleusinian Mysteries. What we do know is that the Mysteries commemorated the abduction of Demeter's daughter Persephone by the god of the underworld, Hades (Pluto). Demeter was able to strike a bargain with the god, who allowed Persephone to leave the underworld and rejoin her mother for 6 months each year. The mysteries celebrated this—and the cycle of growth, death, and rebirth of each year's crops.

The **Sanctuary of Eleusis** (☎ **01/554-6019**), in the modern industrial city of Elefsina, is 23km (14 miles) west of central Athens on the highway to Corinth. Despite its substantial remains and glorious past—Eleusis was already a religious site in Mycenaean times—the sanctuary's present surroundings are so grim that it's not easy to warm to the spot. You'll see remains of a **Temple of Artemis**, a 2nd-century A.D. **Roman propylaia** (monumental entrance), and **triumphal arches** dedicated to the Great Goddesses and to the emperor Hadrian. (Hadrian's arch inspired the Arc de Triomphe in Paris.) Nearby is the **Kallichoron Well**, where Demeter wept over the loss of Persephone. The cave here, the **Ploutonion**, was believed to be the entrance to the underworld through which Persephone vanished. Nearby is the **Telesterion**, the Temple of Demeter; only initiates of the cult knew what really happened there.

The small **museum**, with finds from the site, including the greater part of a famous Demeter by Agoracritis, may still be closed due to damage from the 1999 earthquake. The Sanctuary and museum are open Tuesday to Sunday and holidays 8:30am to 3pm; admission is 500Dr ($1.70), free on Sunday. There's also a small **museum**, with finds from the site, including the greater part of a famous statue of Demeter. The sanctuary and museum are open Tuesday to Sunday and holidays 8:30am to 3pm; admission is 500Dr ($1.70), free on Sunday.

Getting There   Take bus 853 or 862 from Eleftheria, a square off Pireos Avenue (northwest of Monastiraki), or bus A15 ("Elefsina") from Sachtouri Street, southeast of Eleftheria Square. When you get into Eleusis, tell the bus driver that you want to see *"ta archaia"* (the antiquities). If you come by car, count on getting lost: Signs for the site are totally inadequate.

PICNICKING AT THE TEMPLE OF POSEIDON

One of the most popular, and easiest, day trips from Athens is to the 5th-century B.C. **Temple of Poseidon** at **Cape Sounion** (☎ **0292/39-363**), about 2 hours by bus outside Athens. The temple, which was built at about the same time as the Parthenon, occupies a dramatic position on a cliff high above the sea. In antiquity, as today, sailors knew they were nearing Athens when they caught sight of the temple's slender Doric columns. Fifteen of them remain; try to find the spot on one where Lord Byron carved his name. Then you can swim in the sea below and grab a snack at one of the over-priced restaurants. (Better yet, bring a picnic.) This is a good place *not* to go on the weekend, when it's very crowded and the traffic to and from beaches outside Athens is very heavy.

The archaeological site is open daily from 10am to sunset. Admission is 800Dr ($2.70) for adults, 600Dr ($2) for seniors, and 400Dr ($1.35) for students.

GETTING THERE   Buses to Sounion leave hourly on the half-hour 6:30am to 6:30pm from the **station** at 14 Mavromateon St. (☎ **01/821-3203**), at the southwest corner of Areos Park, well north of Omonia Square—best reached by taxi.

2 Delphi & the Northern Peloponnese

With the exception of the Acropolis in Athens, the most famous and beautiful ancient sites in Greece bracket the Gulf of Corinth. Apollo's sanctuary at Delphi is on the mainland north of the gulf, and Agamemnon's palace at Mycenae, the Mycenaean fortress of Tiryns, the spectacular 4th century B.C. theater of Epidauros and the birthplace of the Olympic Games at Olympia, are south of the gulf in the northern Peloponnese.

EXPLORING THE REGION BY CAR   Thanks to the excellent road linking Athens and the Peloponnese at Corinth, and the frequent ferry service across the Gulf of Corinth between Rio and Anti-Rio, it's easy to combine a visit to Delphi with a tour of the most important ancient sites in the Peloponnese. Try to allow at least 4 days (spending 2 nights at Nafplion and 1 night each at Olympia and Delphi).

If traffic is light (and it almost never is), you can drive the 88km (55 miles) from Athens to Corinth on the National Road in an hour. After you take a look at the Corinth Canal and the sprawling site of ancient Corinth, an hour's drive (less if you take the new National Road to Argos and double back) through the farmland of Corinthia and Argolis will take you to Mycenae, 114km (71 miles) southwest of Athens. From Mycenae, it's less than an hour to Nafplion, 145km (90 miles) southwest of Athens. Generally considered the prettiest town in the Peloponnese, Nafplion is the perfect spot to spend the night before visiting Epidauros.

Although it's only 32km (20 miles) from Nafplion to Epidauros, the road is usually clogged with tour buses, especially when there are performances at the ancient theater; allow at least an hour for the drive. From Nafplion and Epicauros, two routes lead across the Peloponnese to Olympia. You can return to Corinth and join the National Road, which runs as far as Patras, where you take the good coast road on to Olympia. (Although there're signs in Patras pointing you toward Olympia, the heavy traffic in Patras means that you can easily spend an hour getting across town).

If you want to avoid Patras, you can join the new National Road at Argos and drive through the Arcadian mountains via Tripolis to Olympia, 320km (199 miles) west of Athens. Either way, expect to spend at least 4 hours en route—and try to spend more, so that you can enjoy the coastal scenery or the mountain villages of Arcadia. Then, to reach Delphi from Olympia, simply head to Rio, just north of Patras, and catch one of the frequent ferries across the gulf to Anti-Rio, where a new road runs all the way to Delphi, 177km (110 miles) west of Athens. Allow at least 5 hours for the trip from Olympia to Delphi, and 3 hours to get from Delphi to Athens.

THE NORTHERN PELOPONNESE & THE CLASSICAL SITES

One of the delights of visiting the northern Peloponnese is that it's relatively uncrowded when many of the Aegean islands are sagging under the weight of tourists each summer.

Driving Tip

Keep in mind that although most Greek roads are quite good, much of your journey to and around the Peloponnese will be on beautiful, but sometimes vertiginous, winding mountain and coastal roads that make distances deceptive. Therefore, I've indicated how long you should expect each part of the trip to take, rather than giving you a false sense of how quickly you can travel by just telling you how much distance you'll cover. Also keep in mind that only Portugal has more traffic fatalities each year than Greece: buckle up and be careful out there!

That doesn't mean you'll have famous spots like Mycenae, Epidauros, and Olympia to yourself if you arrive at high noon in August. It does mean that if you arrive just as they open or just before they close, you may have an hour under the pine trees at Olympia or Epidauros virtually alone, and be able to stand in Mycenae's Treasury of Atreus with swallows as your only companions.

Because even the most avid tourists do not live by culture alone, it's good to know that one of the great delights of spending time in the northern Peloponnese comes from quiet hours in shady *plateias* (squares), watching fishers mend their nets while local families settle down for a leisurely meal. An hour in a seaside cafe watching the locals watching you watch them is the ideal way to unwind after a day's sightseeing. By the way, if you visit here in the winter, make sure your hotel has functioning heating.

CORINTH

Corinth exported its pottery around the Mediterranean and dominated trade in Greece for much of the 8th and 7th centuries B.C. It experienced a second golden age under the Romans in the 2nd century A.D. Today, as in antiquity, Corinth and Patras are the two major gateways to the Peloponnese. As you pause here, you'll want to leave the main highway (look for the turn-off for the Canal Tourist Area) saying to take a look at the Corinth Canal and visit ancient Corinth before heading deeper into the northern Peloponnese.

Essentials

GETTING THERE   By Train   Several trains a day run from Athens's Stathmos Peloponnisou to the Corinth station off Odos Demokratias (☎ **0741/22-522**). The trains are almost invariably late, often taking 3 hours or more. Refreshments sometimes are available on board. For information on schedules and fares, call ☎ **01/512-4913** in Athens.

By Bus   At least 15 buses a day run to Corinth from the Stathmos Leoforia Peloponnisou, 100 Odos Kifissou in Athens. For schedule and fare information, call ☎ **01/512-8233** in Athens. Buses to and from Athens come and go from the bus station at Ermou and Koliatsou streets (☎ **0741/25-645**). Buses for ancient Corinth sometimes leave from this station and sometimes leave from another bus stop on Odos Koliatsou. Inquire upon arrival and allow 20 minutes for bus ride to Archaia Korinthos (Ancient Corinth); buses usually run once an hour from about 8am to 8pm. Buses from Corinth for the Peloponnese leave from the station at the corner of Konstantinou and Aratou streets (☎ **0741/24-403**).

By Car   Corinth is 88km (55 miles) west of Athens on the National Highway; the toll is 500Dr ($1.70). Work to widen the highway to seven lanes is almost finished, but there're still a few particularly dangerous three-lane stretches. The highway now continues past the Corinth Canal; just after the canal, you'll see signs for Ancient Corinth (the archaeological site) and Corinth (the uninteresting modern town).

FAST FACTS   The telephone **area code** for Corinth is **0741**. The **police station** is on Ermou Street (☎ **0741/22-143**).

The Corinth Canal

When the main road ran directly past the restaurants and cafes on either side of the canal, almost everyone used to stop here for a coffee, a souvlaki, and a look at the canal that separates the Peloponnese from the mainland. Now buses, trucks, and most cars stay on the new highway, but you can still take the exit for the Canal and Tourist Area to see the canal and have a snack. There's a small post office at the canal and a kiosk with postcards and English-language newspapers. Most of the large souvlaki places

Central Greece & the Northern Peloponnese

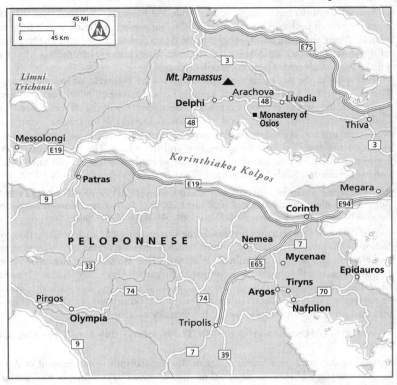

have surprisingly clean toilet facilities (and very tough souvlaki). One word of warning that's necessary here and almost nowhere else in Greece: Be sure to lock your car door. This is a popular spot for thieves to prey on unwary tourists.

The French engineers who built the Corinth Canal between 1881 and 1893 used lots of dynamite, blasting through 87m (285 feet) of sheer rock to make this 6km-long (4-mile), 27m-wide (30-yard) passageway. The canal utterly revolutionized shipping in the Mediterranean; vessels that previously had spent days making their way around Cape Matapan, at the southern tip of the Peloponnese, could dart through the canal in hours.

Exploring Ancient Corinth

To reach Ancient Corinth, follow the signs after the Corinth Canal for Ancient and Old Corinth. It's a 20-minute bus ride from the train station or 10 minutes by taxi.

Ancient Corinth. Old Corinth. ☎ **0741/31-207.** Admission to archaeological site and museum 1,200Dr ($4). Summer, Mon–Fri 8am–7pm, Sat–Sun 8am–3pm; winter, Mon–Fri 8:45am–3pm, Sat–Sun 8:30am–3pm.

The most conspicuous—and the most handsome—surviving building at Ancient Corinth is clearly the 6th-century B.C. **Temple of Apollo,** which stands on a low hill overlooking the extensive remains of the **Roman Agora** (marketplace). Only seven of the temple's 38 monolithic Doric columns are standing, the others having long since been toppled by earthquakes.

Ancient Corinth's main drag, the 12m-wide (40-foot) marble-paved road that ran from the port of Lechaion into the heart of the marketplace, is clearly visible from the temple. Along the road, and throughout the Agora, are the foundations of hundreds of the stores that once stocked everything from spices imported from Asia Minor to jugs of wine made from Corinth's excellent grapes.

Two spots in the Agora are especially famous—the **Fountain of Peirene** and the **Bema.** In the 2nd century A.D., the famous Roman traveler, Philhellene, and bene-factor Herodes Atticus encased the modest Greek fountain in the elaborate two-story building with arches, arcades, and the 5-square-meter (50-square-foot) courtyard whose remains you see today. Peirene was a woman who wept so hard when her son died that she dissolved into the spring that still flows here. The Bema (public plat-form) was where St. Paul had to plead his case when the Corinthians, irritated by his constant criticisms, hauled him in front of the Roman governor Gallo in A.D. 52.

Archaeological Museum. Ancient Corinth, in the town of Old Corinth. ☎ **0741/31-207.** Admission to museum and archaeological site 1,200Dr ($4). Summer, Mon–Fri 8am–7pm, Sat–Sun 8am–3pm; winter, Mon–Fri 8:45am–3pm, Sat–Sun 8:30am–3pm.

As you'd expect, this museum just inside the site entrance has a particularly fine col-lection of the famous Corinthian pottery, which is often decorated with charming red and black figures of birds and animals. Alas, many fine pieces were stolen in 1991; it's hoped that they will someday be recovered and returned here. There're also a number of statues of Roman worthies and several mosaics, including one in which Pan is shown piping away to a clutch of cows. The museum courtyard is a shady spot to sit and read up on the ancient site, which has virtually no shade.

Acrocorinth. Old Corinth. Admission 500Dr ($1.70). Summer, daily 8am–7pm; winter, daily 8am–5pm.

A winding dirt road runs from the site of Ancient Corinth to the summit of Acro-corinth, the rugged limestone sugarloaf mountain topped by centuries of fortifications that dominates the plain of Corinth. A superb natural acropolis, Acrocorinth was for-tified first by the Greeks and later by the Byzantines, Franks, Venetians, and Turks. Extensive remains of the centuries of walls, turrets, and towers built here still remain. After you roam around enjoying the seemingly endless view over the rich plain below, you can relax at the small cafe just outside the site entrance.

✪ NAFPLION

With two hilltop Venetian fortresses, shady parks, an interesting assortment of small museums, and better-than-average hotels, restaurants, and shops—and even a minia-ture castle (the Bourtzi) in the harbor—this port town on the northeast coast of the Gulf of Argos is almost everyone's first choice as the most charming town in the Pelo-ponnese. A good deal of Nafplion's appeal comes from the fact that for several years after the Greek War of Independence (1821–28), this was the country's first capital. Although the palace of Greece's young King Otto—a mail-order monarch from Bavaria—burnt down in the 19th century, an impressive number of handsome neo-classical civic buildings and private houses have survived, as have a scattering of Turk-ish fountains and several mosques.

Essentials
GETTING THERE   By Bus   At least a dozen buses a day run to Nafplion from the **Stathmos Leoforia Peloponnisou,** 100 Odos Kifissou (☎ **01/513-4110** or 01/513-4588), Athens. The trip takes about 4 hours because the bus goes into Corinth and Argos before reaching Nafplion.

By Boat   Minoan Flying Dolphin hydrofoil service runs from Marina Zea, Piraeus, to Nafplion, Monday to Saturday, weather permitting. The hydrofoil makes a number of stops and takes almost as long as the bus to reach Nafplion. For fare and schedule information, call ☎ **01/419-9200** or 01/453-6107 in Athens.

By Car   From Athens, head south to the Corinth Canal. Take the new Corinth-Tripolis road to the Argos exit and follow signs into Argos and Nafplion. You'll almost certainly get lost at least once in Argos, which has an abysmal system of directional signs. Allow at least 3 hours for the drive from Athens to Nafplion. When you reach Nafplion, park in the large, free municipal lot by the harbor. If you want to stop at Mycenae or Nemea, take the winding old road to Nafplion. If you want to stop at Epidauros, take the sign-posted turn for Epidauros just after the canal.

VISITOR INFORMATION   The **Greek National Tourist Organization (EOT)** office is at 16 Photomara St. (☎ **0752/28-131**), catercorner from the bus station in Plateia Nikitara. It's usually open weekdays 9am to 2pm, but seems to have frequent unscheduled closings. The helpful brochure *Nafplion Day and Night* is sometimes available here, sometimes in shops and hotels.

FAST FACTS   The telephone **area code** for Nafplion is **0752.** The **post office** is open weekdays 8am to 2pm, and the **OTE telephone and telegraph** office is open weekdays 8am to 7pm. Both are signposted from the bus station. The **National Bank of Greece** has a branch on the main square, Syntagma Square. There're a number of **travel agencies** in Nafplion, including Staikos Travel, by the harbor (☎ **0752/ 27-950**). The best place to swim is at the **beach** beneath the Palamidi, a 15-minute walk (with the sea on your right) from the harborside cafes.

Where to Stay

✪ **Byron Hotel.** Plateia Agiou Spiridona, Nafplion 21100. ☎ **0752/22-351.** Fax 0752-26338. E-mail: byronhotel@otenet.gr. 13 units. A/C MINIBAR TV TEL. 21,000Dr ($70) double. AE, EURO, MC, V.

This pleasant small hotel, painted a distinctive pink with blue shutters, is in a quiet, breezy location overlooking the Church of Agiou Spiridona, a short, steep hike up from the main plateia. There're a number of nice bits of Victoriana in the sitting rooms and bedrooms (some of which are quite small for two), as well as modern conveniences such as air conditioning, hair dryers, and in-room television with CNN. Word has gotten out about the Byron's charm, and it's almost impossible to stay here in July or August without a reservation.

Epidauros Hotel. 2 Kokkinou St., Nafplion 21100 (beside the Commercial Bank). ☎ and fax **0752/27-541.** 15 units. 12,600Dr ($42) double. No credit cards.

The Epidauros has an annex across the street, as well as nearby pension quarters at 7,500Dr ($25) for a double. Rooms are small but pleasant, with good, firm beds. The location, on a quiet street just off the main square, is excellent; the staff is neither wildly welcoming nor noticeably efficient.

Hotel Nafsimedon. 9 Sideras Merarhias St., Nafplion 21100 (On Kolokotronis Park). ☎ **0752/25-060.** Fax 0752/26-913. 13 units. A/C TV TEL. 18,000Dr–21,000Dr ($60–$70) double. No credit cards.

This new "boutique" hotel in a handsome mid–19th-century neoclassical house is a welcome addition to Nafplion's hotels. The hotel, with two ornamental palms in its front garden, is set back from the street and overlooks relatively quiet Kolokotronis Park. The exterior is a warm peach color and the interior walls are peach and apricot (sponge painted, of course). The rooms are attractively furnished, some with four-poster beds; most are larger than those in most Greek hotels. We're eager to hear readers' reports on this new hotel, which was still experiencing some growing pains when we visited.

✪ Omorphi Poli Pension. 5 Sofroni St., Nafplion 21100. ☎ **0752/21-565.** 10 units. TV TEL. 15,000Dr ($50) double. Rates include breakfast. MC, V. Sometimes closed off-season.

What a lovely place! This new (1998) small pension/hotel above the charming cafe by the same name (Beautiful City) has gone all-out to restore a building to give guests the sense that they're staying in a Nafplion home—but with privacy. There's nothing to fault here: good beds, nice tile floors, and air-conditioning promised for 2000. In short, this is a pleasant place to use as a base for touring the area. Families will like the rooms with sleeping lofts for children at 18,000Dr ($60) for three.

Xenia Palace Hotel. Acronafplia, 210 00 Nafplion. ☎ **0752/28-981.** Fax 0752/28-987. 51 units, 50 bungalows. A/C MINIBAR TV TEL. 60,000–78,000Dr ($200–$260) double. Rates include breakfast and lunch or dinner. Off-season discounts sometimes available. AE, DC, EURO, MC, V.

The Xenia Palace boasts the best view in town; whether you think it's in the best location depends on whether you want to be in town or up here on the slopes of Acronafplia, looking across the harbor to the Bourtzi and the mountains of the Peloponnese. Unfortunately, the rugs and chairs in many of the rooms are showing signs of wear, and the dining room has indifferent "international" and Greek cuisine. One big plus is the swimming pool, the perfect place to cool off after a day's sightseeing. You can sometimes make arrangements to use the pool if you're staying at the nearby **Xenia Hotel** (same phone and fax), the Xenia Palace's less expensive sibling, where rooms are usually at least $25 cheaper.

Where to Dine

Oddly enough, the restaurants in and just off Syntagma Square are not the tourist traps you'd expect. Furthermore, you'll see a good number of Greeks at the big harborside cafes on Akti Miaoulis. In short, Nafplion has lots of good restaurants, as well as one superb pastry shop and any number of ice cream parlors selling elaborate gooey confections.

Benetsianiko. Akti Miaoulis (by the playground). ☎ **0752/23-598.** Ouzo and standard mezedes from 900Dr ($3); ouzo and meal of mezedes from 2,700Dr ($9); fish by the kilo. No credit cards. Daily 10am–midnight. SNACKS.

The Benetsianiko (Venetian) has taken over the old Pharos restaurant, which specialized in *mezedes* (hors d'oeuvres) and added charcoal grills and an expanded menu of fresh fish to its original offerings. We haven't eaten here yet, but a friend has sent us a favorable report.

Hellas Restaurant. Syntagma Sq. ☎ **0752/27-278.** Main courses 1,800–3,600Dr ($6–$12). AE, MC, V. Daily 9am–midnight. GREEK.

Kostas, the omnipresent host of the Hellas, says that there's been a restaurant here for more than 100 years. Shady trees and awnings make this a cool spot to eat outdoors; there's also an inside dining room, where locals tend to congregate year-round. Excellent dolmades with egg-lemon sauce are usually on the menu, as well as stuffed tomatoes and peppers in season. Just about everyone in town passes through Syntagma Square, so this is a great spot to people-watch.

Karamanlis. 1 Leoforos Bouboulinas. ☎ **0752/27-668.** Main courses 1,500–2,700Dr ($6–$9); fish priced daily by the kilo. AE, EURO, MC, V. Daily 11am–midnight. GREEK.

This simple harbor-front taverna several blocks east of the cluster of harbor-front cafes tends to get fewer tourists than most of the places in town. It serves good grills and several kinds of meatballs (*keftedes, sousoutakia,* and *yiouvarlakia*). If you like the food here, you'll probably also enjoy the **Kanares Taverna** and the **Hundalos Taverna,** both also on Bouboulinas.

✪ **Noufara.** Plateia Syntagma, Nafplion. ☎ **0752/23-648.** Fax 0752/23-945. Main courses 1,500–4,000Dr ($5–$13). EURO, MC, V. Daily about 8am–1am. ITALIAN/GREEK.

If you're not sure you can face another stuffed tomato, head for the Noufara, which has a wide range of Italian dishes as well as the usual Greek favorites. You can sit under the umbrellas and have a cool drink or a full meal—or you can retreat inside to the air-conditioned dining room. The Noufara also has a branch with the same menu (but a wider offering of fish) just outside Nafplion on the shore in Nea Chios (☎ 0752/52-314).

Savouras Psarotaverna. 79 Leoforos Bouboulinas. ☎ **0752/27-704.** Fish priced daily by the kilo. AE, EURO, MC, V. Daily noon–11pm. SEAFOOD.

This restaurant has been here more than 20 years, and its fresh fish attracts Greek day-trippers from Tripolis and even Athens. What you eat depends on what was caught that day—and it's always a good idea to check the price before ordering. Expect to pay $50 (and easily more) for two fish dinners, a salad, and some house wine. On summer weekends this restaurant can be terribly crowded.

Sokaki. Corner of Eth. Antistaseos and Nafpleo sts. ☎ **0752/26-032.** Daily 9am–2pm and 6 till at least 10pm. CREPES/SWEETS/BREAKFASTS/COFFEES.

In the morning, tourists tuck into the full American breakfast here, while locals toy with a tiny cup of Greek coffee. In the evening, young men lounge here, some eyeing the women who pass by, others eyeing the men. A nice place to take a break and watch people watching people.

Exploring the Town

Nafplion is a stroller's delight, and one of the great pleasures here is simply walking through the parks, up and down the stepped side streets, and along the harbor. Don't make the mistake of stopping your harborside stroll when you come to the last of the large seaside cafes by the Hotel Agamemnon. If you continue, you can watch fishing boats putting in at the pier and explore several cliff-side chapels. Nafplion is so small that you can't get seriously lost, so have fun exploring. Here are some suggestions on how to take in the official sights after you've had your initial stroll.

ACRONAFPLIA & THE PALAMIDI Nafplion's two massive fortresses, Acronafplia and the Palamidi, dominate the skyline. There's no charge to visit the cliffs known as **Acronafplia,** where there are considerable remains of Greek, Frankish, and Venetian fortresses, as well as two modern hotels, the Xenia and Xenia Palace. The easiest way to get up Acronafplia is to drive or hitch a ride on the elevator (signposted) that conveys guests from the lower town to the **Xenia Palace Hotel.** If you want to walk up, follow signs in the lower town to the **Church of Saint Spyridon,** one of whose walls has the mark left by one of the bullets that killed Ianni Kapodistria, the first governor of modern Greece. From Saint Spyridon, follow the signs farther uphill to the **Catholic Church of the Metamorphosis.**

This church is as good a symbol as any for Nafplion's vexed history. Built by the Venetians, it was converted into a mosque by the Turks, and then reconsecrated as a church after the War of Independence. Inside, an ornamental doorway has an inscription listing Philhellenes who died for Greece, including nephews of Lord Byron and George Washington. As you continue to climb to Acronafplia, keep an eye out for several carvings of the winged lion that was the symbol of Saint Mark, the patron saint of Venice.

If you're not in the mood to climb the 800-plus steps to the summit of the **Palamidi,** you can take a taxi up and then walk down. The Venetians spent 3 years building the Palamidi, only to have it conquered the next year (1715) by the Turks. You'll enter the fortress the way the Turkish attackers did, through the main gate to the east. Once inside, you can trace the course of the massive wall that encircled the entire summit and wander through the considerable remains of the five fortresses that failed to stop the Turkish attack. In June, there're sometimes concerts here in the evening. The Palamidi is open weekdays 8am to 7pm in summer, 8:30am to 5pm in winter. Admission is 800Dr ($2.70).

NAFPLION'S MUSEUMS   All four of Nafplion's museums are within easy walking distance of one another. Almost as soon as it opened in 1981, the **Folk Art Museum** (1 Odos V. Alexandros; ☎ **0752/28-947;** fax 0752/27-960; e-mail: pff@otenet.gr), with its superb collection of Greek costumes, won the European Museum of the Year Award. In September 1999, it reopened after extensive renovations and reinstallations. The display highlights "The Best of the Peloponnesian Folk Foundation," with exhibits from its more than 25,000-object collection, which includes coins, ceramics, furniture, and farm implements as well as all those costumes. The museum occupies three floors in an elegant 18th-century house with a shady courtyard and a welcome snack bar. Throughout, labels are in English as well as Greek and a number of dioramas (my favorite shows nine elegant matrons in a 19th-century parlor) help visitors to imagine life in Greece, especially during the 19th century when the western world impinged on the Greek world. The small gift shop is excellent, with fine ceramic and copper reproductions.

The **Museum of Childhood,** Stathmos, Kolokotronis Park, an offshoot of the Folk Art Museum, has an eclectic collection of dolls, baby clothes, and toys. It's open year-round, weekdays 4 to 8pm and Saturday 9am to 1pm, with frequent unscheduled closings. Admission is 400Dr ($1.35).

The **Archaeological Museum,** Syntagma Square (☎ **0752/27-502**), is housed in the handsome 18th-century Venetian arsenal that dominates Syntagma Square. The thick walls make it a deliciously cool place to visit on even the hottest day. Displays are from sites in the area and include pottery, jewelry, and some horrific Mycenaean terra-cotta idols, as well as a handsome bronze Mycenaean suit of armor. Open Tuesday to Sunday 8:30am to 1pm; admission is 500Dr ($1.70).

If you like old prints and old photographs, not to mention muskets, you'll enjoy strolling through the exhibits at the **Military Museum,** on Leoforos Amalias (☎ **0752/25-591**). It covers Greek wars from the War of Independence to World War II. Open Tuesday to Sunday 9am to 2pm; admission is free.

The Shopping Scene

Nafplion has not escaped the invasion of T-shirt and mass-produced-souvenir shops that threatens to overwhelm Greece, but there're some genuinely fine shops. Many are on or just off Odos Spiliadou, the street immediately above Plateia Syntagma. As in most Greek towns heavily dependent on tourism, many of the shops are closed in the winter.

There're lots of jewelry shops in Nafplion, but one that stands out is **Preludio,** 2 Vas. Constantinou (just off Syntagma Square), Nafplion (☎ **0752/25-277**). Preludio has a surprisingly wide range of handsome earrings, necklaces, bracelets, and rings. Some designs are modern, some traditional, others are replicas of ancient and Byzantine styles (including some nice rings and necklaces with good reproductions of ancient coins). The staff speaks excellent English and is very helpful.

In her shop near the waterfront, **Helene Papadopoulou,** 5 Odos Spiliadou (☎ **0752/25-842**), sells traditional weavings and dolls made from brightly painted gourds. Prices start at 10,000Dr ($33). Next door, her husband has a wide collection of excellent-quality Greek costume dolls (from 12,000Dr/$40), as well as some nice ceramic jewelry of Greek ships and flowers from 1,500Dr ($5).

Konstantine Beselmes, 6 Athan Siokou St. (☎ **0752/27-274**), sells his own magical paintings of village scenes, sailing ships, idyllic landscapes, and family groups. Although new, the paintings are done on weathered boards, which gives them a pleasantly aged look. Prices begin at around 15,000Dr ($50). The **Komboloi Museum,** 25 Staikopoulou St., Nafplion (☎ and fax **0752/21-618**), is a fascinating shop with its own museum of komboloi, usually referred to as "worry beads." Both the shop and museum have examples of Muslim prayer beads, Catholic rosaries, and the secular Greek worry bead. Prices range from a few dollars to several hundred. Admission is 500Dr ($1.70).

The Corner, Staikopoulou and Koletti, just off Syntagma Square (☎ **0752/ 21-359**), often has old photographs, prints, wood and copper, and, sometimes, handsome old embroidered aprons and vests from traditional costumes. **The Wine Shop,** 5 Amalias, Nafplion (☎ and fax **0752/24-446**), is one of the best wine shops in the Peloponnese and an excellent place to head if you want to browse and learn about Greek wines. Owner Dimitris Karonis is usually happy to talk to browsers about his wide selection of Greek wines, and he also stocks wines and spirits from Europe and North America. The **Odyssey** (no phone) book shop, Syntagma Square, has a wide selection of newspapers, magazines, and books in English, as well as a collection of startling pornographic drink coasters.

Day Trips from Nafplion

TIRYNS The **archaeological site** of Tiryns is 5km (3 miles) outside Nafplion on the Argos road (before you visit here, check with the GNTO to make sure that the site is open. It has had several unscheduled closings recently due to damage from several recent earthquakes). From the moment you see it, you'll understand why Homer called this **citadel,** which may have been Mycenae's port, "well walled." Tiryns stands on a rocky outcropping 27m (87 feet) high and about 302m (990 feet) long, girdled by the massive walls that so impressed Homer—but that didn't keep Tiryns from being destroyed around 1200 B.C. Later Greeks thought that only the giants known as Cyclopes could have hefted the 14-ton red limestone blocks into place for the walls that archaeologists still call "cyclopean." Even today, Tiryns's walls stand more than 9m (30 feet) high; originally, they were twice as tall—and as much as 17m (57 feet) thick. The citadel is crowned by the palace, whose *megaron* (**great hall**) has a well-preserved circular hearth and the base of a throne. This room would have been gaily decorated with frescoes (the surviving frescoes are now in the National Archaeological Museum in Athens).

The site is officially open daily, 8am to 7pm in the summer, 8am to 5pm in the winter. Admission is 500Dr ($1.70). Visitors without cars can reach Tiryns from Nafplion by taxi (expect to pay about $20 for a 1-hour round-trip) or the frequent (about every half-hour) Nafplion-Argos-Nafplion bus (about $2; tell the driver you want to get off at Tiryns).

NEMEA Nemea is signposted on the both the old and new highways from Corinth into the Peloponnese. Throughout antiquity, panhellenic games were held every 4 years at Olympia and Delphi and every 2 years at Isthmia (near Corinth) and Nemea, in a gentle valley in the eastern foothills of the Arcadian mountains. Thanks to the Society for the Revival of the Nemean Games, games were held again at Nemea in 1996 and 2000. The stadium you visit here is not only the place where athletes once contended, but the site of the new Nemean Games.

The **Nemea Museum,** set on an uncharacteristically green Greek lawn, is one of the most charming small museums in Greece, with helpful labels in English. Two excellent site guides are on sale here: *Nemea* and *The Ancient Stadium of Nemea,* 500Dr ($1.70) each. When you're in the museum, be sure to peer out one of the large picture windows that overlook the shaded ancient site where the coins, vases, athletic gear, and architectural fragments on display were found. A raised stone path tactfully suggests the route from the museum to the site. It passes a carefully preserved early Christian **tomb** and skirts a large Christian **basilica** and Hellenistic bath before arriving at the **Temple of Zeus,** where 3 of the 32 original Doric columns still stand.

The stadium is signposted across the road from the site. Athletes would have stripped down in the locker room, whose foundations are visible just outside the stadium, and then oiled their bodies with olive oil before sprinting into the stadium through the vaulted tunnel. In the stadium, spectators sprawled on earthen benches carved out of the hillside and watched the athletes take their places at the well-preserved stone starting line.

The site is open year-round, Tuesday to Sunday 8:30am to 3pm. Admission to the museum and the ancient site is 500Dr ($1.70), plus another 500Dr ($1.70) for the stadium.

MYCENAE

Greek legend and the poet Homer tell us that King Agamemnon of Mycenae was the most powerful leader in Greece at the time of the Trojan War. In about 1250 B.C., Homer says, Agamemnon led the Greeks from Mycenae to Troy, where they fought for 10 years to reclaim fair Helen, the wife of Agamemnon's brother Menelaus, from the Trojan prince Paris. The German archaeologist Heinrich Schliemann, who found and excavated Troy, began to excavate at Mycenae in 1874. Did Schliemann's excavations here prove that what Homer wrote was based on an actual event, not myth and legend? Scholars are suspicious, although most admit that Mycenae could have been built to order from Homer's descriptions of its palaces.

Essentials

GETTING THERE   By Bus   Buses run frequently from Athens's **Stathmos Leoforia Peloponnisou,** 100 Odos Kifissou (☎ **01/513-4100**), to Corinth, Argos, and Nafplion. Allow 3 to 4 hours. From any of those places, allow an hour for the trip to Mycenae.

By Car   Mycenae is 114km (71 miles) southwest of Athens and 50km (31 miles) south of Corinth. From Corinth, take the old Corinth–Argos highway south for about 48km (30 miles), and then take the left turn to Mycenae, which is about 8km (5 miles) down the road. From Nafplion, take the road out of town toward Argos. When you reach the Corinth-Argos highway, turn right and then, after about 16km (10 miles), right again at the sign for Mycenae. If you're going to Nafplion when you leave Mycenae, try the pleasant back road that runs through villages and rich farmland. You'll see the sign for Nafplion on your left shortly after you leave Mycenae.

Traveler's Tip

There's almost no shade at Mycenae, where the terrain is alternately rough and slippery. Be sure to wear a hat, sunscreen, and good shoes.

FAST FACTS   The telephone **area code** for the modern village of Mycenae is **0751.** You can buy stamps and change money at the mobile **post office** at the ancient site weekdays 8am to 2pm. This office is sometimes open on weekends and after 2pm, but don't count on it.

Where to Stay

La Belle Helene. Mycenae, 212 00 Argolis.   ☎ **0751/76-225.** Fax 0751/76-179. 8 units, none with bathroom. 18,000–22,500Dr ($60–$75) double. Rates include breakfast. Off-season discounts sometimes available. DC, V. On the main road to Mycenae, on the left as you approach the site.

The real reason to stay here is to add your name to those of Schliemann and other luminaries in the guest book. Tradition aside, this small hotel is usually quiet, and the simple rooms are clean and comfortable. If you stay here, be sure to drive or walk up to the ancient site at night, especially if it's a full moon.

La Petite Planete. Mycenae, 212 00 Argolis.   ☎ **0751/76-240.** Fax 0751/76-610. 30 units. TEL. 22,500Dr ($75) double. Rates include breakfast. Off-season discounts sometimes available. AE, V. On the main road to Mycenae, on the left as you approach the site.

The bright, good-sized rooms would make this a nice place to stay even without its swimming pool, which is irresistible after a hot day's trek around Mycenae. We've usually found it quieter here than at La Belle Helene, and friends who stayed here recently praised the restaurant (in the evening, not lunch, which is aimed at tour groups) and enjoyed the view over the hills from their window.

Where to Dine

Most of the restaurants specialize in serving set-price meals to groups. If you eat at one of the big, impersonal roadside restaurants, you're likely to be served a bland, luke-warm "European-style" meal of overcooked roast veal, underripe tomatoes, and, even in summer, canned vegetables. You'll have better luck at the smaller restaurants at the hotels listed above.

Exploring Ancient Mycenae

The Citadel & the Treasury of Atreus. No phone. Admission 1,500Dr ($5). Summer, Mon–Fri 8am–7:30pm, Sat–Sun 8am–3pm; winter, Mon–Fri 8am–5pm, Sat–Sun 8:30am–3pm.

Just as when you visit the Acropolis in Athens, when you walk uphill to Mycenae, you begin to get an idea of why people settled here as long ago as 5000 B.C. Mycenae strad-dles a low bluff between two protecting mountains and is a superb natural citadel overlooking one of the richest plains in Greece. By the time of the classical era, almost all memory of the Mycenaeans had been lost, and Greeks speculated that places like Mycenae and Tiryns had been built by the Cyclopes. Only such enormous giants, peo-ple reasoned, could have moved the huge rocks used to build the ancient citadels' defense walls.

You enter Mycenae through just such a wall, passing under the massive **Lion Gate,** whose two lions probably symbolized Mycenae's strength. The door itself (missing, like the lions' heads) probably was made of wood, covered with bronze for additional protection; cuttings for the doorjambs and pivots are clearly visible in the lintel. Sol-diers stationed in the round **tower** on your right would have shot arrows down at any attackers who tried to storm the citadel.

One of the most famous spots at Mycenae is immediately ahead of the Lion Gate—the so-called **Grave Circle A,** where Schliemann found the gold jewelry now on dis-play at the National Archaeological Museum in Athens. When Schliemann opened the tombs and found some 14kg (30 pounds) of gold here, including several solid-gold face masks, he concluded he had found the grave of Agamemnon himself. However, recent scholars have concluded that Schliemann was wrong, and that the kings buried here died long before Agamemnon was born.

From the grave circle, head uphill past the low remains of a number of houses. Mycenae was not merely a palace, but a small village, with administrative buildings and homes on the slopes below the palace. The **palace** had reception rooms, bedrooms, a throne room, and a large *megaron* (ceremonial hall). You can see the imprint of the four columns that held up the roof in the megaron, as well as the outline of a circular altar on the floor.

If you're not claustrophobic, head to the northeast corner of the citadel and climb down the flight of stairs to have a look at Mycenae's enormous **cistern.** (You may find someone here selling candles, but it's a good idea to bring your own flashlight.) Along with Mycenae's great walls, this cistern, which held a water supply channeled from a spring 450m (500 yards) away, helped to make the citadel impregnable for several centuries.

There's one more thing to see before you leave Mycenae. The massive tomb known as the **Treasury of Atreus,** is the largest of the *tholos* tombs found here. You'll see signs for the Treasury of Atreus on your right as you head down the modern road away from Mycenae. The Treasury of Atreus may have been built around 1300 B.C., at about the same time as the Lion Gate, in the last century of Mycenae's real greatness. The enormous tomb, with its 118-ton lintel, is 13m (43 feet) high and 14m (47 feet) wide. To build the tomb, workers first cut the 35m (115-foot) passageway into the hill and faced it with stone blocks. Then the *tholos* chamber itself was built, by placing slightly overlapping courses of stone one on top of the other until a capstone could close the final course. As you look up toward the ceiling of the tomb, you'll see why these are called "beehive tombs." Once your eyes get accustomed to the poor light, you can make out the bronze nails that once held hundreds of bronze rosettes in place in the ceiling. This tomb was robbed even in antiquity, so we'll never know what it contained, although the contents of Grave Circle A give an idea of what riches must have been here. If this was the family vault of Atreus, it's entirely possible that Agamemnon himself was buried here.

EPIDAUROS

Epidauros, dedicated to the healing god Asclepios, was one of the most famous shrines in ancient Greece. Greeks came to the shrine of Asclepios in antiquity as they go to the shrine of the Virgin on the island of Tinos today, to give thanks for good health and in hopes of finding cures for their ailments. While at Epidauros, patients and their families could "take the waters" at any one of a number of healing springs and in the superb baths. Visitors could also take in a performance in the theater, just as you can today.

Essentials

GETTING THERE   By Bus   Two buses a day run from the **Stathmos Leoforia Peloponnisou,** 100 Odos Kifissou, Athens (☎ **01/513-4100**). The trip takes about 3 hours. There're three buses a day to Epidauros from the Nafplion bus station, off Plateia Kapodistrias (☎ **0752/27-323**), with extra buses when there are performances at the Theater of Epidauros. The trip takes about an hour.

By Car   Epidauros is 63km (39 miles) south of Corinth and 32km (20 miles) east of Nafplion. If you're coming from Athens or Corinth, turn left at the sign for Epidauros immediately after the Corinth Canal and take the coast road to the Theatro (ancient theater), *not* to Nea Epidauvos or Palaia Epidauros. From Nafplion, follow the signs for Epidauros. If you drive to Epidauros from Nafplion for a performance, be alert; the road will be clogged with tour buses and other tourists who are driving the road for the first time.

THEATER PERFORMANCES   There are usually performances at the ancient theater on Saturday and Sunday June to September. Many are given by the National Theater of Greece, some by foreign companies. For information and ticket prices, contact the **Athens Festival Office,** 4 Odos Stadiou (☎ 01/322-1459). Most of the travel agencies in Nafplion sell tickets, as does the theater itself, from 5pm on the day of a performance. The performance starts around 9pm. The ancient tragedies are usually performed in classical or modern Greek; programs cost 1,000Dr ($3.35) and usually have a full translation or a full synopsis of the play. The excellent Odyssey bookstore on Syntagma Square in Nafplion often has English translations of the plays being performed at Epidauros.

A SPECIAL EVENT   Beginning in 1995, the Society of the Friends of Music have sponsored the **Little Epidauros Music Festival** during the last two weekends of July at the recently restored 4th-century theater at Palea Epidaurus, 7km (4 miles) from Epidaurus. Check with the Greek National Tourist Office or the **Municipality of Palea Epidauros** (☎ 0753/41-250) for the schedule of performances. The **Athens Concert Hall,** the Megaron Musikis (☎ 01/728-2333), also sometimes has information. Poetry readings are scheduled in July at the Little Epidauros theater, which seats 4,000.

Where to Stay & Dine

Epidauros Xenia Hotel. Ligourio, Nafplias, Peloponnese. ☎ **0753/22-003-5.** 26 units, 12 with bathroom. TEL. 22,250Dr ($75) double. Rates include breakfast. Off-season discounts sometimes available. No credit cards.

The best place to stay overnight at Epidauros is here, at the site itself. Once everyone leaves, this is a lovely, quiet spot, in a pine grove beside the ancient site. The bungalow-like units (which could use some serious sprucing up and redecoration) go quickly, so reserve well in advance if you plan to be here the night of a performance. The restaurant serves bland but acceptable food, so you may want to try the **Leonides Restaurant** (☎ **0752/22-115**) in the village of Epidauros; this restaurant is usually packed after performances at the ancient theater.

Exploring the Ancient Site

The **excavation museum** at the entrance to the site helps put some flesh on the bones of the confusing remains of the Sanctuary of Asclepios. The museum has an extensive collection of architectural fragments from the sanctuary, including lovely acanthus flowers from the mysterious *tholos,* which you'll see when you visit the site. Also on view are an impressive number of votive offerings that pilgrims dedicated: The terracotta body parts show precisely what part of the anatomy was cured. The display of surgical implements will send you away grateful that you didn't have to go under the knife here, although hundreds of inscriptions record the gratitude of satisfied patients.

It's pleasant to wander through the shady **Sanctuary of Asclepios,** but it's not at all easy to decipher the scant remains. The Asklepion had accommodations for visitors, several large bathhouses, civic buildings, a stadium and gymnasium, and several temples and shrines. The remains are so meager that you might have to take this on faith. Try to find the round *tholos,* which you'll pass about halfway into the sanctuary. The famous 4th-century B.C. architect Polykleitos, who built similar round buildings at Olympia and Delphi, was the designer here. If you wonder why the inner foundations of the *tholos* are so convoluted and labyrinthine, you're in good company—scholars still aren't sure what went on here, although some suspect that Asclepios's healing serpents lived in the labyrinth.

The museum and archaeological site are open in summer, weekdays 8am to 7pm and Saturday and Sunday 8:30am to 3:15pm; in winter, weekdays 8am to 5pm and Saturday and Sunday 8:30am to 3:15pm. Admission (also covering the theater; see below) is 1,500Dr ($5). There're several kiosks selling snacks and cold drinks near the ticket booth.

The Theater

If you found the remains of the ancient sanctuary a bit of a letdown, don't worry—the **Theater of Epidauros** is one of the most impressive sights in Greece. Probably built in the 4th century B.C., possibly by Polykleitos, the architect of the *tholos,* the theater seats some 14,000 spectators. Unlike so many ancient buildings, and almost everything at the Sanctuary of Asclepios, the theater was not pillaged for building blocks in antiquity. As a result, it's astonishingly well preserved; restorations have been minimal and tactful.

If you climb to the top, you can look down over the seats, divided into a lower section of 34 rows and an upper section with 21 rows. The upper seats were added when the original theater was enlarged in the 2nd century B.C. The theater's acoustics are famous; you'll almost certainly see someone demonstrating that a whisper can be heard all the way from the orchestra to the topmost row of seats. Just as the stadium at Olympia brings out the sprinter in many visitors, the theater at Epidauros tempts many to step center stage and recite poetry, declaim the opening of the Gettysburg Address, or burst into song. It's always a magical moment when a performance begins, as the sun sinks behind the orchestra and the first actor steps onto the stage.

Admission to the museum and archaeological site (see above) includes the theater; they keep the same hours.

OLYMPIA

With its shady groves of pine, olive, and oak trees, the considerable remains of two temples, and the stadium where the first Olympic races were run in 776 B.C., Olympia is the most beautiful major site in the Peloponnese. When you realize that the archaeological museum is one of the finest in Greece, you'll see why you can easily spend a full day or more here. The straggling modern village of Olympia (confusingly known as Ancient Olympia) is bisected by its one main street, Leoforos Kondili. The town has the usual assortment of tourist shops as well as more than a dozen hotels and restaurants.

The ancient site of Olympia lies a 15-minute walk south of the modern village, but if you have a car, you might as well drive; the road teems with tour buses, and the walk is less than relaxing.

Essentials

GETTING THERE   By Train   Several trains a day run from Athens to Pirgos, where you change to the train for Olympia. Information on schedules and fares is available from the **Stathmos Peloponnisou (Railroad Station for the Peloponnese)** in Athens (☎ **01/513-1601**).

By Bus   Three buses a day run to Olympia from the Stathmos Leoforia Peloponnisou, 100 Odos Kifissou, Athens (☎ **01/513-4110**). There're also frequent buses from Patras to Pirgos, with connecting service to Olympia. In Patras, **KTEL** buses leave from the intersection of Zaimi and Othonos streets (☎ **061/273-694**).

By Car   Olympia, 320km (199 miles) from Athens, is at least a 6-hour drive whether you take the coast road that links Athens to Corinth, Patras, and Olympia or head inland to Tripolis and Olympia on the new Corinth-Tripolis road. Heavy traffic in

Patras, 159km (99 miles) south, means that the drive from Patras to Olympia can easily take 2 hours.

VISITOR INFORMATION   The office of the Greek National Tourist Organization (EOT) is on the way to the ancient site near the south end of Leoforos Kondili, the main street (☎ **0624/23-100** or 0624/23-125). It's usually open daily, 9am to 10pm in the summer and 11am to 6pm in the winter.

FAST FACTS   The telephone **area code** for Olympia is **0624.** The **OTE telephone and telegraph** office on Odos Praxitelous is open weekdays 7:30am to 10pm. The **train station** is at the north end of town, one street off Leoforos Kondili. You can call ☎ **0624/22-580** for a taxi.

Where to Stay

Olympia has more than 20 hotels, which means you can almost always find a room, although if you arrive without a reservation in July or August, you might not get your first choice. In the winter, many hotels are closed.

Hotel Europa. 270 65 Ancient Olympia, Peloponnese. ☎ **800/528-1234,** 0624/22-650, or 0624/22-700. Fax 0624/23-166. 118 units. A/C TV TEL. 32,000Dr ($106) double. Considerable reductions off-season. Rates include breakfast. AE, DC, MC, V.

The Europa is clearly the best hotel in town—and one of the best in the entire Peloponnese. Part of the Best Western chain, it's a few minutes' drive out of town on a hill overlooking both the modern village and the ancient site. Most rooms overlook a large pool and garden, and several have views of the ancient site. The Europa recently added another 38 units in a separate building on its grounds. Rooms are large, with colorful rugs, extra-firm mattresses, hair dryers, and sliding glass doors opening onto generous balconies.

Hotel Neda. Odos Praxiteles, 270 65 Ancient Olympia, Peloponnese. ☎ **0624/22-563.** Fax 0624/22-206. 43 units. TEL. 25,500Dr ($75) double. AE, V.

With a pleasant rooftop cafe, a comfortable lobby, a serviceable restaurant, and a distinctive red-and-white facade, the Neda (off the noisy main drag) offers good value. Rooms are large, with colorful shaggy flokakia rugs on the floor and good bedside reading lamps. Some of the doubles have double beds, but most have twins, so specify which you want. Each room has a good-sized balcony, and the bathrooms are better than those usually found in hotels in this price category (thanks to the presence of shower curtains, which help you to avoid spraying the entire room). Rooms here are usually quieter than those at hotels on the main street.

Hotel Praxiteles. 7 Odos Spiliopoulou, 270 65 Ancient Olympia, Peloponnese. ☎ **0624/ 22-592.** 10 units. 9,000Dr ($30) double. AE, EURO, V.

Just one street back from Olympia's main street, Odos Spiliopoulou has a nice neighborhood feel and is the best bargain in town—if you don't mind a no-frills approach.

Shopping Suggestion

For a break from Olympia's tourist-oriented commerce, seek out Antonios Kosmopoulos' **Galerie Orphee** bookstore on Leoforos Kondili (☎ **0624/23-555**). With its extensive range of cassettes and CDs of Greek music and frequent displays of contemporary art, it makes a pleasant contrast to Olympia's other shops, which have all too many T-shirts, museum reproductions, and machine-made rugs and embroideries sold as "genuine handmade crafts."

(Someone may, or may not, be on duty at the front desk and there's neither air-conditioning nor central heating.) Rooms are small and spare, with narrow beds; those in front have balconies. If you want to avoid the sounds of conversation from the hotel's excellent restaurant on the sidewalk below the balconies, ask for a room at the back (and hope that the neighborhood dogs don't bark too much).

Where to Dine

There're almost as many restaurants as hotels in Olympia. The ones on and just off the main street with large signs in English and German tend to have indifferent food and service, although it's possible to get good snacks of yogurt or *tiropites* (cheese pies) in most of the cafes.

Taverna Ambrosia. Behind the train station. ☎ **0624/23-414.** Main courses 1,500–3,600Dr ($5–$12). AE, MC, V. Daily 7–11pm and some weekends noon–4pm. GREEK.

This large restaurant with a pleasant outside veranda continues to attract locals, although it does a brisk business with tour groups. You'll find the usual grilled chops and souvlakia here, and the vegetable dishes are unusually good, as is the lamb stew with lots of garlic and oregano.

Taverna Kladeos. Behind the train station. ☎ **0624/23-322.** Main courses about 3,000Dr ($10). No credit cards. Daily 7–11pm. Closed in winter. GREEK.

The charming Kladeos, with the best food in town, is at the end of the little paved road that runs steeply downhill past the Ambrosia restaurant. You may not be the only foreigner, but you'll probably find lots of locals here. In good weather, tables are set up under canvas awnings and roofs made of rushes. The menu changes according to what's in season. The lightly grilled green peppers, zucchini, and eggplant are especially delicious. The house wine, a light rosé, is heavenly. If you want to buy a bottle to take with you, give your empty water bottle to your waiter and ask him to fill it with *krasi* (wine).

Taverna Praxiteles. In the Hotel Praxiteles, 7 Odos Spiliopoulou. ☎ **0624/23-570** or 0624/22-592. Main courses 900–3,000Dr ($3–$10). No credit cards. Daily usually noon–2pm and 7pm–midnight. GREEK.

The reputation of the Hotel Praxiteles's excellent and reasonably priced restaurant has spread rapidly. It's packed almost every evening, first with foreigners eating unfashionably early, then with locals, who start showing up around 10pm. Although the entrées are very good—especially the rabbit stew with onions (*stifado*)—it's easy to make a meal of the delicious and varied appetizers. A sampling of mezedes costs about 1,500Dr ($5) and may include octopus, eggplant salad, taramosalata and Russian salad, meatballs stuffed with zucchini, fried cheese, and a handful of olives. In good weather, tables are outside on the sidewalk; the rest of the year, meals are in the pine-paneled dining room.

The Museums & the Ancient Site

Archaeological Museum. ☎ and fax **0624/22-529.** www.culture.gr. E-mail: pzepka@culture.gr. Admission 1,200Dr ($4). Summer, Mon noon–7pm, Tues–Sun 8am–7pm; winter, Mon noon–5pm, Tues–Sat 8am–5pm; Sat–Sun 8:30am–5pm. The museum is directly across the road from the Ancient Site (see below).

Even though you'll be eager to see the ancient site, it's a good idea to begin your visit with the museum, whose collection makes clear Olympia's astonishing wealth and importance in antiquity. Every victorious city and almost every victorious athlete dedicated a bronze or marble statue here. Nothing but the best was good enough for Olympia, and many of the superb works of art found since excavations began here more than 150 years ago are on view in the museum. Most of the exhibits are in galleries on either side of the main entrance and follow a chronological sequence, from severe Neolithic vases to baroque Roman imperial statues. The museum's superstars are in the central galleries directly ahead of the entrance.

The monumental images from the **Temple of Zeus** are probably the finest surviving examples of archaic Greek sculpture. The sculpture from the west pediment shows the battle of the Lapiths and Centaurs raging around the magisterial figure of Apollo. On the east pediment, Zeus oversees the chariot race between Oinomaos, king of Pisa, and Pelops, the legendary figure who wooed and won Oinomaos' daughter by the unsporting expedient of loosening his opponent's chariot pins. On either end of the room, sculptured metopes show scenes from the labors of Hercules, including the one he performed at Olympia: cleaning the Augean stables.

Just beyond the sculpture from the Temple of Zeus are the 5th-century B.C. **winged victory** done by the artist Paionios and the 4th-century B.C. figure of Hermes and the infant Dionysios known as the *Hermes of Praxiteles.* The Hermes has a room to itself—or would, if tourists didn't make a beeline to admire Hermes smiling with amused tolerance at his chubby half-brother Dionysios. If you want to impress your companions, mention casually that many scholars think it's not an original work by Praxiteles, but a Roman copy. In addition to several cases of glorious bronze heads of snarling griffins and the lovely terra-cotta of a resolute Zeus carrying off the youthful Ganymede, the museum has a good deal of **athletic paraphernalia** from the ancient games. You'll see stone and bronze weights used for balance by long jumpers, bronze and stone discuses, and even an enormous stone with an inscription boasting that a weight lifter raised it over his head with only one hand.

Before you leave the museum, have a look at the two excellent **site models** just inside the main entrance. As the models make clear, a low wall divided ancient Olympia into two distinct parts: the *Altis,* or religious sanctuary, containing temples and shrines, and the civic area, with athletic and municipal buildings. Between festivals, Olympia was crowded only with its thousands of statues. Every 4 years, during the games, so many people thronged here that it was said by the time the games began, not even one more spectator could have wedged himself into the stadium. So if the site is crowded when you visit, just remember it would have been much worse in antiquity.

The Ancient Site. Admission 1,200Dr ($4). Summer, Mon–Fri 7:30am–7pm, Sat–Sun 8:30am–3pm; winter, Mon–Fri 8am–5pm, Sat–Sun 8:30am–3pm.

Olympia's setting is magical—pine trees shade the little valley, dominated by the conical Hill of Kronos that lies between the Alphios and Kladeos rivers. The handsome temples and the famous stadium are not at once apparent as you enter the site. Immediately to the left are the unimpressive low walls that are all that remain of the **Roman baths** where athletes and spectators could enjoy hot and cold plunge baths. The considerably more impressive remains with the slender columns on your right mark the **gymnasium** and **palestra,** where athletes practiced their footracing and boxing skills. The enormous gymnasium had one roofed track, precisely twice the length of the stadium, where athletes could practice in bad weather. Also on the right are the fairly meager remains of a number of structures, including a swimming pool and the large square **Leonidaion,** which served as a hotel for visiting dignitaries until a Roman governor decided it would do nicely as his villa. If you want, you can continue around the outskirts of the site, identifying other civic buildings, but you'll probably want to enter the sanctuary itself.

The **religious sanctuary** is dominated by two shrines: the good-sized Temple of Hera and the massive Temple of Zeus. The **Temple of Hera,** with its three standing columns, is the older of the two, built around 600 B.C. If you look closely, you'll see that the temple's column capitals and drums are not uniform. That's because this temple was originally built with wooden columns, and as each column decayed, it was replaced; inevitably, the new columns had variations. The *Hermes of Praxiteles* was found here, buried under the mud that covered Olympia for so long, caused by the repeated flooding of the rivers. The **Temple of Zeus,** which once had a veritable thicket of 34 stocky Doric columns, was built around 456 B.C. The entire temple— so austere and gray today—was anything but plain in antiquity. Gold, red, and blue paint was everywhere, and inside the temple stood an enormous gold-and-ivory statue of Zeus seated on an ivory-and-ebony throne. The statue was so ornate that it was considered one of the Seven Wonders of the Ancient World—and so large that people joked that if Zeus stood up, his head would go through the temple's roof. In fact, the antiquarian Philo of Byzantium suggested that Zeus had created elephants simply so that the sculptor Phidias would have the ivory to make his statue.

Not only do we know that Phidias made the 13m (42-foot) statue, we know where he made it: The **Workshop of Phidias** was on the site of the well-preserved brick building clearly visible west of the temple just outside the sanctuary. How do we know that this was Phidias' workshop? Because a cup with "I belong to Phidias" on it and artists' tools were found here. Between the Temples of Zeus and Hera you can make out the low foundations of a round building: This is all that remains of the shrine that Philip of Macedon, never modest, built here to pat himself on the back after conquering Greece in 338 B.C. Beyond the two temples, built up against the Hill of Kronos itself, are the curved remains of a once-elegant **Roman fountain** and the foundations of 11 **treasuries** where Greek cities stored votive offerings and money. In front of the treasuries are the low bases of a series of bronze statues of Zeus dedicated not by victorious athletes but by those caught cheating in the stadium. The statues would have been the last thing competitors saw before they ran through the vaulted tunnel into the stadium.

Museum of the Olympic Games. Admission 500Dr ($1.70). Mon–Sat 8am–3:30pm; Sun and holidays 9am–2:30pm.

When you head back to town, try to set aside half an hour or so to visit the Museum of the Olympic Games. Not many tourists come here, and the guards are often glad to show visitors around. Displays include victors' medals, commemorative stamps, and photos of winning athletes, such as former King Constantine of Greece and the great American athlete Jesse Owens. There's also a photo of the bust of the founder of the modern Olympics, Baron de Coubertin. (The bust itself stands just off the main road east of the ancient site and marks the spot where de Coubertin's heart is buried.)

Olympic Traditions

Ancient tradition makes it clear that the Olympic games began here in 776 B.C. and ended in A.D. 395, but is less clear on why they were held every 4 years. According to one legend, Herakles (Hercules) initiated the games to celebrate completing his 12 labors, one of which took place nearby when the hero diverted the Alphios River to clean the fetid stables that King Augeas had neglected for more than a decade. The stables clean, Herakles paced off the stadium and then ran its entire length—600 Olympic feet (192.27m)—without having to take a single breath.

DELPHI

Delphi, which the ancient Greeks believed was the center of the world, is the big enchilada of Greek sites. Even more than Olympia, it has everything: a long and glorious history as the scene of Apollo's famous oracle and the Pythian games; spectacular ancient remains, including the Temple of Apollo and the well-preserved stadium where the ancient games took place; a superb museum; and a heartachingly beautiful location on the slopes of Mount Parnassus. Look up and you see the cliffs and crags of Parnassus; look down at Greece's most beautiful plain of olive trees stretching as far as the eye can see toward the town of Itea on the Gulf of Corinth.

Many tour groups offer day trips to ✪ **Delphi,** stopping at the Byzantine Monastery of Osios Loukas (see "Organized Tours," above). In the summer, tour groups clog Delphi's few streets by day, but many head elsewhere for the night, which means that hotel rooms are usually available—although often all the cheap rooms are gone by midmorning. In the winter, thousands of Greeks head here each weekend, not for the archaeological site, but for the excellent skiing on Mount Parnassus. Getting a room in the once-sleepy nearby hamlet of Arachova is virtually impossible without a reservation on winter weekends, and Delphi itself is often full.

ESSENTIALS

GETTING THERE   By Bus   Depending on the season, as many as five daily buses make the 3-hour trip to Delphi from the Athens station, 260 Liossion St. (☎ 01/831-7096), north of Omnia Square.

By Car   Take the Athens-Corinth National Highway 74km (46 miles) west of Athens to the Thebes turnoff and continue 40km (25 miles) west to Levadia. If you want to stop at the monastery of Osios Loukas, take the Distomo turnoff for 9km (5¹/₂ miles). Return to Distomo and continue via Arachova for 26km (16 miles) to Delphi or via the seaside town of Itea for 64km (40 miles) to Delphi. The approach from Itea is well worth the time if you aren't in a hurry.

VISITOR INFORMATION   The **GNTO** Office (☎ **0265/82-900**) in the town hall on the main street (Odos Frederikis) is usually open 8am to 3pm (sometimes later in summer).

FAST FACTS   The telephone **area code** for Delphi is **0265.** Most services are available on Odos Frederikis Street. The **post office** is usually open 8am to 4pm, and sometimes also open Sunday 9am to 1pm. The **OTE telephone and telegraph office** is open Monday to Saturday 7:30am to 3pm and Sunday 9am to 1pm. Both banks on Frederikis Street have ATMS (not always in service).

GETTING AROUND   The village of Delphi, with its handful of long, parallel streets connected by stepped side streets, is small enough that most visitors find it easiest to abandon their cars and explore on foot. If you have to drive to the site rather than making the 5- to 10-minute walk from town, be sure to set off early to get one of the few parking places. Whether you walk or drive, keep an eye out for the enormous tour buses that barrel down the center of the road—and for the not-terribly-well-marked one-way streets in the village.

WHERE TO STAY

There's no shortage of hotels in Delphi, and you can usually get a room even in July and August. Still, if you want a room in a specific price category, or with a view, it's best to make a reservation. Finally, in summer (but not in winter when the skiers take over this hamlet) consider staying in nearby **Arachova,** where the hotels are usually less crowded (see "Day Trips from Delphi," below). Be sure to check whether your hotel has functioning heating if you visit here in the winter.

Castalia Hotel. 13 Frederikis St. (at Vasileos Pavlou), 33054 Delphi. ☎ **0265/82-205.** 26 units. TEL. 26,000Dr ($87) double. Rates include breakfast. AE, DC, V. Closed weekdays Jan–Feb.

The Castalia, a white stucco building with projecting balconies on Delphi's main street, has been here since 1938 and was completely remodeled in 1986. Most of the good-sized rooms have hand-loomed rugs, and the rear ones have fine views over the olive plain.

✪ **Hotel Varonos.** 25 Frederikis St. (at Vasileos Pavlou), 33054 Delphi. ☎ and fax **0265/82-345.** 9 units. TV TEL. 15,000Dr ($50) double. Breakfast supplement 2,000Dr ($7). AE, MC, V.

This small, family owned hotel has very clean, spare rooms; many overlook the olive plain. This is a very welcoming hotel—we once arrived with an ailing gardenia plant, and the entire family pitched in to make sure it was well taken care of.

✪ **Hotel Vouzas.** 1 Frederikis St. (at Vasileos Pavlou), 33054 Delphi. ☎ **0265/82-232.** Fax 0265/82-033. 59 units. TV TEL. 45,000Dr ($150) double. AE, DC, MC, V.

If you don't mind not having a swimming pool, this is the place to stay. It has a cozy fireplace in the lobby and spectacular views, and is a short walk from everything you've come to see. The rooms and bathrooms are very comfortable, and the balconies have not only a table and chairs, but also, when we stayed there, a welcoming pot of basil.

WHERE TO DINE

You won't starve in Delphi, but there's no really outstanding restaurant, so you may prefer to head to the village of Arachova, 10km (6 miles) to the north (see "Day Trips from Delphi," below).

That said, in Delphi you might try **Topiki Gefsi,** Odos Pavlou and Frederikis 19 (☎ **0265/82-480**), the **Taverna Vakchos,** 31 Apollonos St. (☎ **0265/82-448**), or the family run **Taverna Lekaria,** 33 Apollonos St. (☎ **0265/82-864**). Its main street location, periodic live music, and usual fine views probably makes **Topiki Gefsi** the most expensive of the three (about $15 per person). I've often enjoyed the simple food (and tasty toasted bread, sometimes topped with garlic and cheese) at the Lekaria, but this is not a good place to come if you are in a hurry.

EXPLORING THE SITE

If possible, begin your visit when the site and museum open in the morning (both are sometimes relatively uncrowded in the hour before closing, too). If you begin your visit at the museum, you'll arrive at the site already familiar with many of the works of art that once decorated the sanctuary.

Delphi Archaeology Museum. ☎ **0265/82-313.** Admission (which includes the site) 2,0000Dr ($7) adults, 900Dr ($3) seniors, and 600Dr ($2) students. Summer, Mon noon–5:30pm, Tues–Fri 7:30am–6:30pm, Sat–Sun 8:30am–3pm; winter, usually 8:30am–3pm.

Each of the museum's 13 rooms has a specific focus: sculpture from the elegant Sifnian treasury in one room, finds from the Temple of Apollo in two rooms, discoveries from the Roman period (including the Parian marble statue of the epicene youth Antinous, the beloved of the emperor Hadrian) in another. If you're lucky, the museum extension will have opened by the time you visit here and there'll be lots more to see. Just outside the first display room stands a 4th-century B.C. marble egg, a symbol of Delphi's position as the center of the world. According to legend, when Zeus wanted to determine the earth's center, he released two eagles from Mount Olympus. When the eagles met over Delphi, Zeus had his answer. (You can still see eagles in the sky above Delphi, but as often as not, the large birds circling overhead are the less distinguished Egyptian vultures.)

The star of the museum, with a room to himself, is the famous 5th-century B.C. *Charioteer of Delphi,* a larger-than-life bronze figure that was part of a group that originally included a four-horse chariot. It's an irresistible statue—don't miss the handsome youth's delicate eyelashes shading wide enamel and stone eyes or the realistic veins that stand out in his hands and feet.

Although the charioteer is the star of the collection, he's in good company. Delphi was chockablock with superb works of art given by wealthy patrons, such as King Croesus of Lydia, who contributed the massive silver bull that's on display. Many of the finest exhibits are quite small, such as the elegant bronzes in the museum's last room, including one that shows Odysseus clinging to the belly of a ram. According to Homer, this is how the wily hero escaped from the cave of the ferocious (but nearsighted) monster Cyclops.

Sanctuary of Apollo, Castalian Spring & Sanctuary of Athena Pronaia. ☎ **0265/ 82-313.** Admission (which includes the museum) 2,000Dr ($7) adults, 900Dr ($3) seniors, and 600Dr ($2) students. Summer, Mon–Fri 7:30am–6:30pm and Sat, Sun, holidays 8:30am–3pm; winter, usually 8:30am–3pm.

As you enter the **Sanctuary of Apollo,** just past the museum, you'll be on the marble **Sacred Way,** following the route that visitors to Delphi have taken for thousands of years. The Sacred Way twists uphill past the remains of Roman **stoas** and a number of Greek **treasuries** (including the Siphnian and Athenian treasuries, whose sculpture is in the museum). Just as modern cities compete to see who can construct the tallest skyscraper, ancient cities tried to build the most elegant of these elaborate small temples, storehouses for works of art dedicated to Apollo. Take a close look at the treasury walls: You'll see not only beautiful dry-wall masonry, but countless inscriptions. The ancient Greeks were never shy about using the walls of their buildings as bulletin boards. Alas, so many contemporary visitors have added their own names to the ancient inscriptions that the Greek archaeological service no longer allows visitors inside the massive 4th-century B.C. **Temple of Apollo,** which was built here after several earlier temples were destroyed.

From the temple, it's a fairly steep uphill climb to the remarkably well-preserved 4th-century B.C. theater and the stadium, which was extensively remodeled by the Romans. In antiquity, contests in the Pythian festivals took place in both venues. Today the theater and stadium are used most summers for the Festival of Delphi— which, on occasion, has featured exceptionally unclassical pop music.

Keep your ticket as you leave the Sanctuary of Apollo and begin the 10-minute walk along the Arachova-Delphi road to the Sanctuary of Athena (also called the Marmaria, which refers to all the marble found here). En route, you'll pass the famous Castalian

The Delphic Oracle

In antiquity, one of the three priestesses on duty gave voice to Apollo's oracles from a room deep within the **Temple of Apollo.** That much is known, although the details of precisely what happened here are obscure. Did the priestess sit on a tripod balanced over a chasm, breathing in hallucinatory fumes? Did she chew various herbs, including the laurel leaf sacred to Apollo, until she spoke in tongues, while priests interpreted her sayings? Perhaps wisely, the oracle has kept its secrets.

Spring, where Apollo planted a laurel. Above are the rose-colored cliffs known as the **Phaedriades (the Bright Ones),** famous for the way they reflect the sun's rays. Drinking from the Castalian Spring has inspired legions of poets; however, poets now have to find their inspiration elsewhere because the spring is off-limits to allow repairs to the Roman fountain facade. Poets, be warned: Once an antiquity is closed in Greece, it often stays closed for quite a while.

A path descends from the main road to the **Sanctuary of Athena,** goddess of wisdom, who shared the honors at Delphi with Apollo. The remains here are quite fragmentary, except for the large 4th-century B.C. gymnasium, and you might choose simply to wander about and enjoy the site without trying too hard to figure out what's what. The round 4th-century B.C. *tholos* with its three graceful standing Doric columns is easy to spot—but no one knows why the building was constructed, why it was so lavishly decorated, or what went on inside. Again, the oracle is silent.

DAY TRIPS FROM DELPHI

ARACHOVA   The mountain village of Arachova, 10km (6 miles) north of Delphi, clings to Mount Parnassus some 945m (3,100 feet) above sea level. Arachova is famous for its hand-loomed *tagari* shoulder bags, heavy blankets, and fluffy *flokakia* rugs. When several tour buses stop here during the daytime, the tiny village can be seriously crowded. Don't despair—come in the evening, when the shops are still open and the cafes and restaurants allow you to escape from the tourist world of Delphi to the village world of Greece—except, of course, in winter, when Athenian skiers in full après-ski outfits roam the village. Year-round, in decent weather, there's usually an energetic evening *volta* (stroll) on the main street, and if you climb the steep stairs to the upper town, you'll find yourself on quiet neighborhood streets where children play and families sit in front of their homes.

On main street, have a look at the weavings in Georgia Charitou's shop, **Anemi** (☎ 0267/31-701), which also offers some nice reproductions of antiques. **Katina Panagakou's shop,** on the main street (☎ 0267/31-743), has examples of local crafts, too.

For lunch or dinner, try one of the restaurants strung out along the main street with its lovely fresh water springs and cafes: the **Taverna Karathanassi** (☎ 0267/31-360), the **Taverna Dasargyri** (also known as Barba Iannis) (☎ 0267/31-391), or the **Taverna Kaplanis** (☎ 0267/31-891). The Dasargyri has tasty *loukanika* (sausages) and delicious *kokoretsi*, the stuffed entrails that are not perhaps to every traveler's taste. No credit cards are accepted; all are open daily approximately noon to midnight, but sometimes close from about 4pm to 7pm. Dinner for two costs about 6,000 to 7,500Dr ($20 to $25) at all these restaurants.

If you want to stay in Arachova, the **Xenia Hotel** (☎ 0267/31-230; fax 0267/32-175) in town, with 42 rooms, each with a balcony, has doubles at 21,000Dr ($70). The very pleasant **Best Western Anemolia** (☎ 800/528-1234 in the U.S., or 0267/31-640), with 52 rooms, on a hill just outside Arachova above the Delphi road, charges 25,000Dr ($83) for a double (prices sometimes are much as $20 higher on the weekend). **The Arachova Inn** (☎ 0267/31-353; fax 0267/31-134; www.arachova.com/arachova-inn), with 42 rooms, charges 25,000Dr ($83) all summer and on winter weekdays and 29,000Dr ($97) on winter weekends.

MOUNT PARNASSUS   Parnassus is an odd mountain: Its peaks are difficult to see from Delphi or Arachova, but if you approach from the north, you'll have fine views of its twin summits. You can drive up to the ski resort at Fterolaki in about an hour from either Delphi or Arachova. It's a lively place in winter during the ski season, but usually nothing is open during the summer.

If you want to go **hiking** on Mount Parnassus, there're two possibilities. From Delphi, head uphill on the paved road that runs above the cemetery and stadium, and keep going. Four hours will bring you to the upland meadows known as the **Plateau of Livadi,** where shepherds traditionally pasture their flocks. As always in the mountains, it's not a good idea to make such an excursion alone. If you plan to continue past the meadows to the **Corcyrian Cave** (known locally as *Sarantavli,* or "Forty Rooms"), where Pan and the nymphs once were thought to live, or to the summits, you should check on conditions locally or with the **Hellenic Mountaineering Club** in Athens (☎ **01/323-4555**).

THE MONASTERY OF OSIOS LOUKAS   You can visit Osios Loukas en route to or from Delphi, or make the 97km (60-mile) round-trip from Delphi in a day. If you go to Osios Loukas via Levadia, pause at **Schiste (Triodos),** where three roads cross. This is the spot where the ancients believed that Oedipus unknowingly slew his father.

The 10th-century **Monastery of Osios Loukas (Saint Luke)** is a lavishly decorated complex. A wide variety of jewel-like polychrome marbles were used in the monastery's construction. The two churches have superb **mosaics;** along with the mosaics at Daphni, outside Athens (see "Day Trips from Athens," above), and those in the splendid churches of Thessaloniki, these are the finest mosaics in Greece.

Bear in mind that Osios Loukas is not a tourist destination, but a holy spot for Greek Orthodox visitors. This is not the place for sleeveless shirts, shorts, or a casual attitude toward the icons or the tomb of Saint Luke. The monastery is usually open daily 8am to 2pm and 4 to 7pm May 3 to September 15 and 8am to 5pm the rest of the year; admission is 800Dr ($2.70).

3 The Cyclades

When most people think of the "Isles of Greece," they're thinking of the Cyclades, the rugged (even barren) chain of Aegean islands whose villages of dazzling white houses look from a distance like so many sugar cubes. The Cyclades got their name from the ancient Greek word meaning "to circle," or surround, because the island chain encircles the sacred island of Delos. Today, especially in the summer, it's the visitors who circle these islands, taking advantage of the swift island boats and hydrofoils that link them.

If you were to describe the best-known Cycladic islands (roughly from north to south), **Tinos** would probably be called the "Lourdes of Greece." Its famous church of the Panagia Evangelistria is Greece's most important pilgrimage destination, especially on the Feast of the Assumption (August 15). **Mykonos's** superior amenities (you can get a margarita as easily as an ouzo) first made it popular in the '60s, and although the Beautiful People might have moved on, Mykonos remains a favorite, although expensive, island—especially in the summer, when reservations are imperative. The crescent of **Santorini (Thira),** with its black sand beaches and blood-red cliffs, is all that remains of the island that was blown apart in antiquity by a volcano that still steams and hisses today. Santorini's exceptional physical beauty, dazzling relics, and elegant restaurants and boutiques cause people to call it "sophisticated." Unfortunately, Santorini's charms draw so many day-trippers from cruise ships that the island almost sinks under the weight of tourists each summer. **Sifnos,** long popular with Athenians, increasingly draws summer visitors to its handsome whitewashed villages, which many consider to have the finest architecture in all the Cyclades. In the spring it's one of the greenest and most fertile of the islands. Finally, some think of **Paros** as the poor man's Mykonos, with excellent windsurfing and a profusion of restaurants and nightspots less pricey than those on its better-known neighbor.

The islands are crowded and expensive in the high season, roughly mid-June to mid-September—and the season seems to get longer every year. If this doesn't appeal to you, visit the Cyclades in the off-season; the best times are in the autumn (mid-September to October) or in the spring (May to early June—April can still be very cold in these islands). Note that while the restaurant you'd hoped to eat in may be closed, and some of the chic shops shuttered, you'll be able to enjoy the islands without feeling that you're surrounded by other visitors. Should you visit in winter, keep in mind that many island hotels have minimal heating; make sure that your hotel has genuine heat before you check in.

On most of these islands, the capital town has the name of the island itself. It's also sometimes called "Hora," or "Chora," a term meaning "the place" that's commonly used for the most important regional town. The capital of Paros, Parikia, is also called Hora, as is Apollonia, the capital of Sifnos.

One note of explanation: We've dropped our coverage of the island of Ios. Alas, in recent years some visitors have transformed Ios from a lively "party island" into an Aegean Animal House, complete with food fights in the tavernas. Let's hope that things calm down on the once-lovely island so that we can again recommend visiting.

GETTING TO THE CYCLADES

BY AIR   Olympic Airways (☎ **01/926-7593** or 01/966-6666 in Athens) has frequent daily service from Athens to Mykonos, Paros, and Santorini; there's service several times a week from Mykonos or Santorini to Thessaloniki, Iraklio, Crete, and Rhodes. In addition, an increasing number of charter flights from all over Europe fly into the various islands. Several small, private Greek airlines serving the islands have gone in (and out) of business in recent years.

BY SEA   Ferries leave daily from Athens's main port of Piraeus and from Rafina, the port east of Athens; contact the Piraeus Port Authority (☎ **01/451-1310** or 01/451-1311) or the Rafina Port Police (☎ **0294/22-300**) for schedules. The speedy Seajet (☎ **01/414-1250**) catamaran service also departs from Rafina and zips between Andros, Syros, Tinos, Mykonos, Paros, Naxos, and Santorini (Thira).

Ilio Lines (☎ **01/422-4772** in Athens or 0294/22-888 in Rafina) offers regular hydrofoil service from Rafina to a number of destinations.

It can take an hour for the 27km (17-mile) bus ride from Athens to Rafina (the most convenient port for Tinos, Mykonos, and sometimes Paros), but you save about an hour of sailing time and usually about 20% on the fare. Buses leave every 30 minutes 6am to 10pm from 29 Mavromateon St. (☎ **01/821-0872**), near Areos Park north of the National Archaeological Museum (indicated on most city maps).

In the summer there's regular ferry service to Iraklio, Crete, from Piraeus, the port of Athens. There're also ferry and hydrofoil connections three to four times a week in the summer between Paros and Samos, Ikaria, Karpathos, and Rhodes; several times a week between Mykonos and Kos and Rhodes; twice a week between Mykonos and Skyros, Skiathos, and Thessaloniki; and two or three times a week between Syros and the Dodecanese.

GETTING AROUND THE CYCLADES

There's frequent ferry service between most of the islands. Schedules can be erratic, and service diminishes suddenly at the end of the season. Smaller excursion vessels are easily affected by high winds. To further complicate matters, a line will sometimes authorize only one agent to sell tickets or limit the number of tickets available to an agency, giving other agents little incentive to tout its service. You may want to visit

several agents or inquire at the port authority. (For specifics, see "Getting There" under "Essentials" for each island.)

The easiest, most comfortable, and most expensive way to island-hop is on a **chartered yacht cruise;** you don't have to worry about ferry connections, hotel reservations, and most meals. **Viking Star Cruises,** 1 Artemidos St., Glyfada, 166 74 Athens (☎ **01/898-0729;** fax 01/894-0952; e-mail: vikings@forum.ars.net.gr or bjgh44a@prodigy.com) offers 7-day cruises beginning every Friday, April to early November. They stop on Tinos, Ios, Santorini, Paros, Naxos, Mykonos, and Delos. Last-minute discount fares are occasionally available.

If you want to cruise around the Cyclades (or elsewhere in Greece) for a week or two, and don't want to travel with strangers, put together your own group and contact **Ari Drivas Yachting** (☎ **01/411-3194;** fax 01/411-4459, e-mail: drivasy@ath.forthnet.gr). Choose among a stunning array of motor yachts and sailing

---

The winds frequently complicate sea travel on the Aegean. For this reason, plan to arrive back in Athens from the islands at least 24 hours before you have to make any air or sea connections. In July the strong winds known as the *meltemi* usually kick up, often playing havoc with hydrofoil schedules. The larger ferries still run—although if you're prone to seasickness, take precautions. In the winter the strong north winds (*vorias*) frequently make sea travel impossible for days at a time.

---

vessels with from 2 to 24 cabins. Drivas prides itself on its superbly trained crews, which include excellent cooks.

For more information on cruises, contact the **Greek National Tourist Organization** (☎ **212/421-5777** in New York; 020/7734-5997 in London; or 01/331-0437 or 01/331-0561 in Athens) or the **Greek Island Cruise Center** (☎ **800/342-3030** in the U.S.). **Sea Cloud Cruises** (☎ **888/732-2568** or 201/884-0407), uses a four-masted private yacht that take up to 60 passengers on Aegean cruises.

TINOS

An island of green hills and austere mountains, Tinos (pop. 9,500; 160km or 87 nautical miles southeast of Piraeus) is home to the famous icon of the Panagia Evangelistria (Virgin of the Annunciation), housed in the handsome church of the same name. Tinos has some good beaches, and there's good walking through the countryside. The area is dotted with small villages and the distinctive dovecotes (some dating from the Venetian occupation) for which this island, like neighboring Andros, is known.

Keep in mind that almost every Greek visiting here is on a pilgrimage, especially on and around March 25 (Feast of the Annunciation) and August 15 (Feast of the Assumption), the most significant pilgrimage days. Be sure to act and dress respectfully (no halters, shorts, or slacks for women; no shorts or sleeveless shirts for men) when you visit Panagia Evangelistria—or any other church. On Tinos alone there're said to be at least 1,000 chapels to visit—although because of vandalism and theft, many remain locked except on feast days.

Note: Unless you have firm hotel reservations, don't plan an overnight visit to Tinos on summer weekends or during important religious holidays, especially March 25 (Feast of the Annunciation) and August 15 (Feast of the Assumption)—unless you're willing to rough it and sleep outside.

ESSENTIALS

GETTING THERE   By Boat   There're several ferries daily from Piraeus and three daily from Rafina; you should confirm schedules with **Tourist Information** in Athens (☎ **143**), the **Piraeus Port Authority** (☎ **01/422-6000** or 01/451-1311), or the **Rafina Port Police** (☎ **0294/22-300** or 0294/25-200). **Ilio Lines** (☎ **01/422-4772** in Athens, or 0294/22-888 in Rafina) runs hydrofoil service from Rafina. From Tinos, there are connections several times daily with nearby Andros, Mykonos, and Syros, and several daily excursions to Mykonos and Delos from about 12,000Dr ($40).

There are three piers in Tinos harbor; be sure to find out from which your ship will depart. The **port authority** can be reached at ☎ **0283/22-348.**

VISITOR INFORMATION   The small tourist information office (☎ **0283/22-255**) is near the waterfront at the corner of Kionion and Vlachaki. There are also several helpful travel agents along the waterfront, including the consistently reliable

Windmills Travel (☎ **0283/23-398;** e-mail: tinos@windmills-travel.com), as well as **Tinos Mariner** (☎ **0283/23-193**), and **Nicholas Information Center,** 24 Evangelistria St. (☎ **0283/24-142;** fax 0283/24-049). Nicholas usually also has information on renting rooms on the island. (Evangelistria is the main market street to the left and perpendicular to the port.)

FAST FACTS   The telephone **area code** for Tinos is **0283.** The **banks** are on the waterfront. The **police station** (☎ **0283/22-255**) is signposted on the harbor. The **OTE telephone office** (☎ **0283/22-399**) is on Megaloharis Avenue, the main street leading up to the Church of Panagia Evangelistria. It's open Monday to Friday 8am to midnight. The **post office** is at the southeast end of the waterfront.

GETTING AROUND   The **bus station** is at the harbor; check at the KTEL office there for the schedule (which is erratic) and rates. The **taxi stand** is also nearby on the harbor. Several shops on the harbor front rent **mopeds;** rates start at about 5,500Dr ($18) a day. **Vidalis** (☎ **0283/23-400**), **Nicholas** (☎ **0283/24-142**), and **Moto Mike** (☎ **0283/23-304**) are usually reliable. Cars can be rented from several harborfront agencies; rates in summer are steep, at about 22,500Dr ($75) a day. Make sure the rate includes full insurance.

WHERE TO STAY

If you avoid the religious holidays and summer weekends, you'll have no trouble finding a room. People will offer to rent you rooms in their homes at the landing.

✪ **Avra Hotel.** Tinos town, 842 00 Tinos. ☎ **0283/22-242.** Fax 0283/22-176. 17 units. 15,000Dr ($50) double. Continental breakfast 1,000Dr ($3.35) extra. No credit cards. On the harborfront.

This charming century-old neoclassical hotel has simple, spacious, high-ceilinged rooms. Its plant-filled, tiled courtyard is a pleasant place to relax after sightseeing. This is the place to stay in Tinos town if you do not need all the modern conveniences to be happy in a hotel, and don't mind the sometimes noisy bustle of the harbor.

Hotel Eleana. Ierarchon Sq., Tinos town, 842 00 Tinos. ☎ **0283/22-561.** 17 units. 13,500Dr ($45) double. V. Just off the harbor and about 365m (400 yards) past the conspicuous Hotel Poseidon.

This hotel is an excellent value. It doesn't have harbor views, but the rooms are large, comfortable, and usually quiet.

Tinion. Constantinou Alavanou 1, Tinos town, 842 00 Tinos. ☎ **0283/22-261.** Fax 0283/24-754. E-mail: kchatzi@ath.forthnet.gr. 21 units. A/C TEL. 15,000Dr ($50) double. Continental breakfast 2,000Dr ($7). MC, V. Just off the harbor.

If you don't mind not having an elevator and think you'd enjoy sitting on a balcony overlooking the bustling harbor, this is the place to stay. The Tinion has been here since 1925, and has the high-ceilinged rooms, nicely tiled floors, and many of the original solid old furnishings to prove it. The Tinion added air-conditioning in 2000.

Tinos Beach Hotel. Kionia, 84200 Tinos (4km/2.5 mi. west of Tinos town on the coast road). ☎ **0283/22-626.** Fax 0283/23-153. 180 units. TEL. 30,000Dr ($100) double. Rates include breakfast. AE, DC, MC, V. Usually closed Nov–Mar.

This sprawling 1960s beachfront resort hotel with pools, tennis courts, and a restaurant, is a good choice for families (there's a separate children's pool). Rooms, all with balconies, are perfectly utilitarian and comfortable, but could use sprucing up (carpets, furniture, and grounds here have all been neglected).

WHERE TO DINE

Tinos has a number of good restaurants (probably because most of its customers are Greeks). As in most Greek ports, you should (with one exception) avoid harbor-front joints; the food is often inferior and expensive, and the service can be rushed.

Lefteris. Harbor front, Tinos town. ☎ **0283/24-213.** Main courses 1,000–3,700Dr ($3.35–$12); fish priced daily by the kilo. V. Daily 11am–midnight. GREEK.

This place is an exception to the rule that waterfront restaurants and/or those that cater to tourists are best avoided. Look for a blue sign on the harbor over an arched entrance that leads to a large courtyard decorated with fish plaques. The menu is large and varied; the grilled sea bass, veal *stifado* (stew), and *dolmades* (stuffed grape leaves) in lemon sauce are tasty. Waiters here perform Greek dances and urge diners to join in.

O Kipos. Tinos town. ☎ **0283/22-838.** Main courses 900–3,000Dr ($3–$10). No credit cards. Daily noon–midnight. Just off the harbor near the conspicuous Hotel Poseidon. GREEK.

At this small taverna, the cooking is typical down-home Greek, with the usual dishes, including moussaka and souvlakia. You can have a complete meal with good retsina for around 6,000Dr ($20).

Peristerionas. 12 Paksimadi Fraiskou St., Tinos town. ☎ **0283/23-425.** E-mail: tonyk@mail.otenet.gr. Main courses 2,500–4,000Dr ($8–$13). No credit cards. Daily noon–3pm and 7–11:30pm. Closed in winter. GREEK.

On a small lane uphill behind the Lido Hotel, this restaurant, decorated like one of the island's famous dovecotes, has outdoor tables. You can get good grilled meats and fish here, but also try the delicious fennel pancakes, a house specialty.

Xinari. Plateia Evangelistria, Tinos town. ☎ **0283/23-337.** Reservations recommended. Main courses 2,400–6,000Dr ($8–$20). MC, V. Daily noon–4pm and 8pm–12am. Closed Oct–Apr. GREEK.

This chic spot serves a combination of traditional dishes with a difference (roast pork—but with plums), nouvelle Greek food (familiar dishes with a less heavy hand pouring out the olive oil), and some Lebanese dishes. Meals aren't cheap, but the food is usually very good and the surroundings charming.

EXPLORING THE ISLAND

Each year, the ✪ **Church of Panagia Evangelistria (Our Lady of Good Tidings)** draws thousands of pilgrims seeking the aid of the church's miraculous icon. According to local lore, one night in 1822, a nun named Pelagia dreamed that a miraculous icon was buried nearby. Pelagia led her neighbors to the place she had seen in her dream, and when they began to dig, they discovered the remains of a Byzantine church with the icon. As is the case with many of the most holy icons, the Panagia Evangelistria is believed to be the work of Saint Luke. The massive church—made of marble from the islands of Paros and Tinos, with a distinctive bell tower—was built in 1824 to house the icon.

A broad flight of marble stairs flanked by lovely pebble mosaics leads to the church; inside, hundreds of gold and silver hanging lamps illuminate the holy icon of the Virgin and the gifts—many in gold, silver, and precious jewels—dedicated by the faithful. Even those who do not make a lavish gift customarily light one of the many candles burning inside the church. The pilgrims' devotion is manifest in these gifts—and in the piety of the visitors who crawl on their knees to the church from the dock.

The church is open daily, 8am to 8pm in the summer and noon to 6pm in the winter; the small **museum** is usually open Tuesday to Sunday 8:30am to 3pm; admission is 500Dr ($1.70). To enter the church, men must wear long pants and shirts with sleeves, and women must wear dresses or skirts and blouses with sleeves. If there's a church service while you are here, you will hear the beautiful, resonant chanting that typifies a Greek Orthodox service—but remember that it's not appropriate to explore the church during a service.

On the other hand, the **town** of Tinos, sprawled within eyesight of the inland Venetian fortress of **Exobourgo**, is always a pleasant place to explore. There's a lively **flea market** and a great many shops selling religious souvenirs, delicate embroidery, and the special sweet of the island, nougat.

The **Weaving School** on Evangelistrias Street sells handsome hand-loomed fabrics made by its students. Several **ceramics shops** on the waterfront, including **Margarita, Bernardo, and Manina,** have interesting pottery, jewelry, and copperware at moderate prices. Those interested in contemporary hand-painted icons might ask to be directed to **Maria Vryoni,** off Leoforos Megaloharis, the street from the port to the Panagia Evangelistria. The shop accepts credit cards.

Once you're away from the shops near the harbor, you'll find yourself on quiet residential streets where many of the houses have small gardens—or, at a minimum, some bright geraniums planted in whitewashed metal containers that once held olive oil. The small **Archaeological Museum** (☎ **0283/22-670**) near the Panagia Evangelistria has finds from the Sanctuary of Poseidon at Kionia. It's usually open Tuesday to Sunday 8:30am to 3pm; admission is 500Dr ($1.70). There's also a **Gallery of Modern Greek Painters** and a **Gallery of Tiniot Artists** near the Panagia Evangelistria.

The famous **Venetian dovecotes** (*peristerionas*), many dating from the 17th century, are scattered throughout the island. You can see several, as well as the scattered remains of the **Temple of Poseidon,** by taking the coastal road 2km (1¼ miles) west of Tinos to the town of Kionia ("Columns"), a pleasant 30-minute hike past the Hotel Aigli. Another hike, from the village of Xinara, leads 565m (1,850 feet) steeply uphill to the ruins of the **Venetian Fortress of Exoburgo** (Xombourgo, on some maps). The less energetic may prefer to enjoy some of the island's small villages, such as **Steni** and **Pirgos.**

Tinos has several good **beaches:** The sand beach at Kionia, about 3km (2 miles) west of Tinos town, and at Kolimbithra, on the north coast, are especially good. About 2.5km (1½ miles) east of Tinos town, the beach at Ayios Fokas has a small hotel; more hotels are rumored to be in the works for Kionia and Kolimbithria.

There's **bus service** (usually four times a day) from Tinos town to Ayios Fokas and farther east to the resort of Porto, which has two beaches and several new hotel complexes.

TINOS AFTER DARK

Tinos is not known for its nightlife, but there's a small enclave of music bars off the harbor, including **Argonautis, Fevgatos, Koutsaros,** the **Sibylla Bar,** and **George's Place,** which features Greek dancing. Things usually get going around 10pm.

MYKONOS

If you haven't been to Mykonos (pop. 15,000; 178km or 96 nautical miles southeast of Rafina) for a number of years, you'll probably wander around muttering "ruined" when you arrive. Then you'll realize that once you're away from the shops, bars, and restaurants along the harbor, you're pleasantly surprised at how familiar many of the twisting back streets seem. You might even admit that it's not half bad to have such a wide choice of restaurants. If this is your first visit, you'll find lots to enjoy—especially if you avoid July and August, when it seems that every one of the island's 800,000 annual visitors is here.

What makes this small, arid island so popular? At least initially, it was the exceptionally handsome Cycladic architecture—and the fact that many on the poor island were more than eager to rent their houses to visitors. First came the jet-setters, artists, and expatriates (including many sophisticated gay visitors), as well as the mainland Greeks who opened many of the chic shops and restaurants—all followed by a curious mixture of jet-set wannabes and backpackers. Now, with cruise ships lined up in the harbor all summer and as many as 10 flights each day from Athens, it's easier to say who doesn't come to Mykonos than to define who does. That's why it's *very* important not to arrive here without reservations in the high season, unless you enjoy sleeping outdoors—and don't mind being moved from your sleeping spot by the police, who are not always charmed to find foreigners alfresco.

ESSENTIALS

GETTING THERE　By Air　Olympic Airways has as many as 10 flights daily between Athens and Mykonos. In addition, there's usually one flight daily between Mykonos and Iraklio (Crete), Rhodes, and Santorini, and three flights a week between Mykonos and Ios, Lesvos, and Samos. It's difficult to get a seat on any of these flights, so make reservations early and reconfirm them at the office in Athens (☎ **01/961-6161** or 01/966-6666) or Mykonos (☎ **0289/22-490** or 0289/22-237).

By Sea　From Piraeus, **Ventouris Lines** (☎ **01/482-5815**) has departures at least once daily, usually at 8am, with a second on summer afternoons; check schedules in Athens by calling the **Tourist Police** (☎ **171**). From Rafina, **Strintzis Lines** has daily ferry service; schedules can be checked with the **Port Police** (☎ **0294/22-300**). There're daily ferry connections between Mykonos and Andros, Paros, Syros, and Tinos; five to seven trips a week to Ios; four a week to Iraklio, Crete; several a week to Kos and Rhodes; and two a week to Ikaria, Samos, Skiathos, Skyros, and Thessaloniki. **Ilio Lines** (☎ **01/422-4772** in Athens, or 0294/22-888 in Rafina) offers daily hydrofoil service to Mykonos from Rafina.

On Myconos, your best bet for getting boat information is to check at individual agents, or to see if either the **tourist police** (☎ **0289/22-482**) at the north end of the harbor, or the **tourist office** (☎ **0289/23-990;** fax 0289/22-229), also on the harbor, has an up-to-date list of sailings.

Check each travel agent's current schedule because most ferry tickets are not interchangeable. **Sea & Sky Travel,** Taxi Square, Mykonos town (Hora) (☎ **0289/22-853;** fax 0289/24-753), represents the Strintzis, Ilio, and Agapitos lines, changes money, and offers excursions to Delos. The **Veronis Agency** (☎ **0289/22-687;** fax 0289/23-763), also on the main square, offers information, luggage facilities, and other services.

Hydrofoil service to Crete, Ios, Paros, and Santorini is often irregular. For information, check at the **Port Authority** in Piraeus (☎ **01/451-1311**), Rafina (☎ **0294/23-300**), or Mykonos (☎ **0289/22-218**).

VISITOR INFORMATION　The **Mykonos Tourist Office** (☎ **0289/23-990;** fax 0289/22-229) is on the west side of the port near the excursion boats to Delos. Look for a copy of the free *Mykonos Summertime* magazine. The **Mykonos Accommodations Center,** at the corner of Enoplon Dhinameon and Malamatenias (☎ **0289/23-160;** e-mail: mac@mac.myk.forthnet.gr), as its name implies, helps visitors find accommodations.

TOWN LAYOUT　Legend has it that the streets of Mykonos town—which locals call Hora—were designed to confuse pirates, so your own confusion will be understandable. As you get off the ferry, you can see the main square south across the harbor beyond the small town beach and a cluster of buildings; we refer to it as **Taxi Square,** although it's officially called Plateia Manto Mavroyennis, after a local heroine. Here you'll find several travel agents, kiosks, snack bars, and of course, the town's taxi stand. The map published by **Stamatis Bozinakis** is sold at most kiosks for 400Dr ($1.35) and is quite decent; the excellent **Mykonos Sky Map** is free at some hotels and shops.

The main street, **Matoyanni,** leads south off Taxi Square behind the church; it's narrow, but you can hardly miss the bars, boutiques, and restaurants. Several "blocks" along it you'll find a "major" cross street, **Kaloyera,** and by turning right, you'll find several of the hotels and restaurants we recommend. If you get lost—and you will—remember that in Mykonos that's part of the fun.

GETTING AROUND   On Foot   One of Hora's greatest assets is the government decree that made the town an architectural landmark and prohibited motorized traffic on its streets. If you don't arrive with your donkey or bicycle, you can walk around town. Much of the rest of the island is served by local buses.

By Bus   Mykonos has one of the best bus systems in the Greek islands; the buses run frequently and on schedule. They cost 200 to 800Dr (70¢ to $2.70) one way. There're two bus stations in Hora: the **north station,** near the middle of the harbor below the Leto Hotel; and the **south station,** about a 10-minute walk from the harbor, near the Olympic Airways office (follow the helpful blue signs). Schedules are posted, although subject to change. Bus information in English is sometimes available from the **KTEL** office (☎ **0289/23-360**).

By Boat   Weather permitting, excursion boats to **Delos** depart every day at 9am from the west side of the harbor near the tourist office. For more information, see "An Excursion to the Island of Delos," below, or consult a travel agent; guided tours are available. Caïques to the beaches of **Super Paradise, Agrari,** and **Elia** depart from the town harbor every morning, weather permitting. Caïques to **Paradise, Super Paradise, Agrari,** and **Elia** also leave from Plati Yialos every morning, weather permitting. (Caïque service is almost continuous during the high season, when boats also depart from Ornos Bay.)

By Car & Moped   Rental cars and Jeeps are available from travel agents for about 15,000Dr ($50) per day, including full insurance, during the high season, and substantially less at other times if you bargain. Mopeds can be a fun way to get around if you know how to handle one and can negotiate the sometimes treacherous roads. Mopeds (around 6,000 to 12,000Dr/$20 to $40 a day) are available from shops near both bus stations.

Note: If you park in town or in a no-parking area, the police will remove your license plates, and you—not the rental office—will have to find the police station and pay a steep fine to get them back.

By Taxi   Getting a taxi in Hora is easy; walk to Taxi Square, near the statue, and get in line; a notice board gives rates for each destination for both high and low seasons. You can also phone (☎ **0289/22-400,** or 0289/23-700 for late-hours and out-of-town service). You'll be charged the fare from Hora to your pickup point plus the fare to your destination, so before calling, try to find an empty taxi returning to Hora or flag one down along the road. You can also take a moped taxi in Mykonos town—but only if you like to live dangerously.

FAST FACTS   Area Code   The telephone area code for Mykonos is **0289.**

Banks   The Commercial Bank and the National Bank of Greece are on the harbor a couple of blocks west of Taxi Square. Both are open weekdays 8am to 2pm. The ATMs usually (but not always) function after hours. Traveler's checks can be cashed at the post office and at many travel agents and hotels, usually at a less favorable rate than at banks.

Hospital   The **Mykonos Health Center** (☎ **0289/23-994** or 0289/23-996) handles routine medical complaints; serious cases are usually airlifted to the mainland.

Internet Access   The **Mykonos Cyber Café**, 26 M. Axioti, on the road between the south bus station and the windmills (☎ **0289/27-684;** www.mykonos-cyber-café.com) is usually open daily 9am to 10pm and charges 6,000Dr ($20) per hour or 1,500Dr ($5) for 15 minutes).

Laundry   The **Ace Laundry** is on Ayios Efthimiou (☎ **0289/28-389**) near the bus station. A self-service **launderette** is on Ayion Anaryiron Street at Scarpa, behind the Church of Paraportiani. Hotel chambermaids often do laundry for a reasonable fee.

Police   The **Tourist Police** office (☎ **0289/22-482**) is on the west side of the port near the ferries to Delos. The **Port Police** office (☎ **0289/22-218**) is on the east side of the harbor front near the post office. The **local police** office (☎ **0289/22-235**) is behind the grammar school.

Post Office   The post office (☎ **0289/22-238**), on the east side of the harbor near the Port Police, is open weekdays 7:30am to 2pm.

Telephones   The **OTE telephone office** (☎ **0289/22-499**) on the east side of the harbor beyond the Hotel Leto, is usually open daily 7:30am to 10pm.

WHERE TO STAY

If you arrive by ferry, you're met by a throng of people hawking rooms, some in small hotels, others in private homes. If you don't have a hotel reservation, one of these rooms may be very welcome. If you're pretty sure that won't suit your needs, be sure you have reserved a room 1 to 3 months in advance of your visit. Many hotels are fully booked all summer by tour groups or regular patrons. The **Mykonos Accommodations Center (MAC),** 46 Odos Matoyianni (☎ **0289/23-160** or 0289/23-408; fax 0289/24-137) or the **Mykonos tourist office** (☎ **0289/22-201**) should be able to advise you. Keep in mind that Mykonos is an easier, more pleasant place to visit in the spring or fall—and off-season hotel rates are sometimes half the quoted high-season rate. The water temperature is cool to cold in spring; warm to cool in fall.

In & Around Hora

✪ **Belvedere Hotel**. Hora, 846 00 Mykonos (Rohari District). ☎ **800/345-8236** or 0289/25-112. Fax 0289/25-126. www.belvederehotel.com. E-mail: belvedere@myk.forthnet.gr. 47 units. A/C MINIBAR TV TEL. 52,000–65,000Dr ($173–$217) double. Rates include breakfast. Considerable off-season reductions usually available. AE, MC, V.

The spiffy new (1998) Belvedere, on the main road into town, has a sauna, Jacuzzi, large pool, and stunning views over the town and harbor, a few minutes' walk away. Rooms are nicely furnished, with some local decorative touches—and 10 rooms are wired for direct Internet connection. This is the place to stay if you want the amenities of Mykonos's beach resorts (pool, hair dryers, minibars), but prefer to be within walking distance of Hora. The in-house Remvi restaurant, in a handsomely restored 1850s house that is part of the hotel, is excellent (and pricey). In 1999, the Belvedere added the Campani Lounge, with full conference facilities, including state of the art digital video display and constant Greek stock market reports.

Cavo Tagoo. Hora, 846 00 Mykonos. ☎ **0289/23-692**, 0289/23-693, or 0289/23-694. Fax 0289/24-923. 72 units. A/C TV TEL. 52,500–60,000Dr ($175–$200) double. Rates include buffet breakfast. AE, MC, V. Closed Nov–Mar.

This elegant hotel is hard to resist—its island-style architecture has won awards, and its wooden furniture and local-style weavings are a genuine pleasure. It's only a 10-minute walk to Hora's harbor, although you may find it hard to budge: A pool and a good restaurant are right here. Rooms have hair dryers.

Matina Hotel. 3 Fournakion St., Hora, 846 00 Mykonos. ☎ **0289/22-387.** Fax 0289/24-501. 14 units. 29,300Dr ($98) double. Continental breakfast 2,200Dr ($7). AE, MC, V.

This small hotel is inside a large garden that makes it especially quiet for its central location. Rooms are small, modern, and comfortable, and the owner has been described by several readers as "very helpful."

✪ **Pension Stelios.** 9 Apollonos St., Hora, 846 00 Mykonos. ☎ **0289/24-641.** 21 units (all with shower only). 22,500Dr ($75) double. Rates include breakfast. No credit cards.

This small inn on the hill above the OTE office (take the broad stone steps above the road) has a convenient, central location, and most rooms have terrific views of the harbor. The Pension expanded in 1998, and the new rooms have balconies or terraces, and are airy and comfortable, if not cozy (the usual pine bedroom furniture predominates).

Philippi Hotel. 25 Kaloyera St., Hora, 846 00 Mykonos. ☎ **0289/22-294.** Fax 0289/24-680. 13 units. 15,000Dr ($50) double. No credit cards.

Each room in this homey little hotel in the heart of Mykonos town is different, so you might want to have a look at several before choosing yours. The owner tends a lush garden that often provides flowers for her son's restaurant, the elegant Philippi (see "Where to Dine," below), which can be reached through the garden.

Around the Island
Although most visitors prefer to stay in Hora and commute to the beaches, there are hotels near many of the more popular island beaches.

There are private studios and simple pensions at Paradise and Super Paradise beaches, but rooms are almost impossible to get, and prices more than double in July and August. Contact the **Mykonos Accommodations Center** (☎ 0289/23-160)—or, for Super Paradise, **GATS Travel** (☎ 0289/22-404)—for information on the properties they represent. The tavernas at each beach may also have suggestions.

AT KALAFATI   The **Paradise Aphrodite Hotel** (☎ 0289/71-367) has a large pool, two restaurants, and 150 rooms. It's a good value in May, June, and October, when a double costs about 30,000Dr ($100).

AT ORNOS BAY   Try elegant new **Kivotos Clubhouse,** Ornos Bay, 846 00 Mykonos (☎ **800/345-8236** or 0289/25-795; fax 0289/22-844), where most of the 21 units overlook the sea. If you don't like saltwater, head for the freshwater pool, or the Jacuzzi and sauna. Kivotos Clubhouse is small enough to be intimate and tranquil. Small wonder that this is a popular honeymoon destination. If you ever want to leave (there are several restaurants), the hotel minibus will whisk you into town. Doubles run 45,000 to 120,000Dr ($150 to $400).

AT PLATI YIALOS   The 82 units at the **Hotel Petassos Bay,** Plati Yialos, 846 00 Mykonos (☎ **0289/23-737;** fax 0289/24-101; www.vacation.forthnet.gr/petabeac. htm; e-mail: petasos@myk.forthnet.gr) all have air-conditioning, minibars, and telephones, and are large and comfortable. Doubles rent for 45,000Dr ($150). Each has a balcony overlooking the (relatively secluded) beach, which is less than 36m (40 yards) away. The hotel has a good-sized pool and sundeck, Jacuzzi, gym, and sauna, and offers free round-trip transportation from the harbor or airport, safety boxes, and laundry service. The new seaside restaurant has a great view and serves a big buffet breakfast (not included in room rate).

AT AYIOS STEPHANOS   This popular resort, about 4km (2¹/₂ miles) north of Hora, has a number of hotels; the 38-unit **Princess of Mykonos,** Ayios Stephanos beach, 846 00 Mykonos (☎ **0289/23-806;** fax 0289/23031) is the most elegant. The Princess has bungalows, a gym, a pool, and an excellent beach; doubles from 52,500Dr ($175). The **Hotel Artemis,** Ayios Stephanos, 846 00 Mykonos (☎ **0289/ 22-345**), near the beach and bus stop, offers 23 units with bathroom for 30,000Dr ($100), breakfast included. The small **Hotel Mina,** Ayios Stephanos, 846 00 Mykonos (☎ **0289/23-024**), uphill behind the Artemis, has 15 doubles with bathroom that go for 18,000Dr ($60). All these hotels are usually closed from November to March.

WHERE TO DINE

Unfortunately, most restaurants here know that you're probably just passing through—hardly an incentive to offer the best in food or service. Restaurants also come and go here, so if possible, check with other travelers or locals as to what's new and good.

As usual on the islands, most of the harborside tavernas are expensive and mediocre, although **Kounelas** on the harbor (no phone; no credit cards) is still a good value.

Antonini's. Plateia Manto, Hora. ☎ **0289/22-319.** Main courses 3,000–5,000Dr ($10–$17). No credit cards. Daily noon–3pm and 7pm–1am in summer. Usually closed Nov–Mar. GREEK.

Antonini's is one of the oldest of Mykonos's restaurants, and it serves consistently decent stews, chops, and *mezedes.* Locals still eat here, although in summer, they tend to leave the place to tourists.

✪ Edem. Signposted off Matoyanni St. (near the church). ☎ **0289/22-855.** Reservations recommended July–Aug. Main courses 3,700–6,100Dr ($12–$20). AE, DC, MC, V. Daily noon–3pm and 7pm–midnight in summer (hours are flexible; sometimes open in winter). GREEK/CONTINENTAL.

This restaurant beside a pool in a garden has a quiet location—unless you have the bad luck to arrive here, as I once did, just before a raucous tour group occupied all the other tables. If that happens, console yourself with the food: excellent appetizers, lots of tasty (and very pricey) seafood, and lamb stews with delicate seasonings.

Philippi. 32 Kalogera, off Matoyanni St. ☎ **0289/22-294.** Reservations recommended July–Aug. Main courses 3,000–6,500Dr ($10–$22). AE, MC, V. Daily 7pm–1am. Walk up the main street, past Kaloyera, and you'll find it on the right. GREEK/CONTINENTAL.

This restaurant in the garden of the Hotel Philippi is a nice place to go to escape the hurly-burly of the harbor. Old Greek favorites share space on the menu with French dishes and a more than usually impressive wine list.

Sesame Kitchen. Odos Dinameon, Tria Pigadia Sq. ☎ **0289/24-710.** Main courses 2,000–5,000Dr ($7–$17). V. Daily 7pm–12:30am. Walk up the main street, turn right on Enoplon Dinameon, and it's on the right next to the Nautical Museum. GREEK/INTERNATIONAL/ VEGETARIAN.

This small, health-conscious taverna offers spinach, vegetable, cheese, and chicken pies baked fresh daily. There's a large variety of salads, brown rice, and soy dishes, including a vegetable moussaka, and lightly grilled and seasoned meat dishes.

EXPLORING THE ISLAND

Even if you're here for the beaches or to visit the island of Delos, you'll probably want to spend some time exploring Hora and enjoying the twists and turns of the narrow streets—and admiring the harbor-front's resident pelican.

The **Archaeological Museum** (☎ **0289/22-325**), near the harbor, has finds from Delos; it's open Monday and Wednesday to Saturday 9am to 3:30pm, Sunday and holidays 10am to 3pm. Admission is 600Dr ($2); free on Sunday. The **Nautical Museum of the Aegean** (☎ **0289/22-700**) across from the park on Enoplon Dinameon St., has just what you'd expect, including some handsome ship models. It's open daily 10:30am to 1pm and 7 to 9pm; admission is 300Dr ($1). The **Museum of Folklore** (☎ **0289/25-591**), in a 19th-century sea captain's mansion near the quay, has examples of local crafts and furnishings and a re-created 19th-century island kitchen. It's usually open Monday to Saturday 4 to 8pm; admission is free.

Hora also has the remains of a small **Venetian Kastro** (fortress) and the island's most famous church, the **Panagia Paraportiani (Our Lady of the Postern Gate),** a thickly whitewashed asymmetrical edifice made up of four small chapels. Beyond the Panagia Paraportiani is the Alefkanda quarter, better known as **Little Venice,** for its cluster of homes built overhanging the sea. Many buildings here have been converted into fashionable bars prized for their sunset views; you can sip a margarita and listen to Mozart most nights at the Montparnasse or Kastro bar (see "Mykonos After Dark," below).

Another nearby watering spot is at the famous **Tria Pigadia (Three Wells).** Local legend says that if a virgin drinks from all three she is sure to find a husband, but it's probably not a good idea to test this hypothesis by drinking the brackish well water. After you visit the Tria Pigadia, you may want to take in the famous **windmills** of Kato Myli and enjoy the views back toward Little Venice.

Mykonos has a lot of shops, mostly selling overpriced souvenirs, clothing, and jewelry. The finest jewelry shop is **Lalaounis,** 14 Polykandrioti St. (☎ **0289/22-444**), associated with the famous Lalaounis museum and shops in Athens. It has superb reproductions of ancient and Byzantine jewelry as well as original designs. If you can't afford Lalaounis, you might have a look at **Delos Dolphins,** Matoyanni at Enoplon Dimameon (☎ **0289/22-765**), which specializes in copies of museum pieces, or **Vildiridis,** 12 Matoyanni St. (☎ **0289/23-245**), which also has designs based on ancient jewelry. If you want to see some serious works of art, try the **Scala Gallery,** 48 Matoyianni (☎ **0289/23-407;** fax 0289/26-993), which represents a wide range of contemporary Greek artists and frequently has exhibitions.

THE BEACHES   If you've come to Mykonos to find a secluded beach, you have made a serious mistake. People come to Mykonos to see and be seen, whether in their best togs at cafes or naked on nudist beaches. If you want to hit the "in" beaches, take a little time to ask around, because beaches go in and out of favor quickly. Then catch the bus or a caïque to the beach of your choice. If you want a quick swim, the closest beach to Hora is **Megali Ammos (Big Sand),** about a 10-minute walk south of town, and usually very crowded. A better but still-crowded beach is 4km (2¹/₂ miles) farther north of Megali Ammos at **Ayios Stephanos,** a major resort center with water sports.

Plati Yialos is another favorite. It's served by a bus that runs every 15 minutes from 8am to 8pm, then every 30 minutes until midnight during the summer. If Plati Yialos is too crowded, you can catch a caïque there for the more distant beaches of Paradise, Super Paradise, Agrari, and Elia. **Paradise,** the island's most famous nude beach, remains beautiful, despite the crowds and activity, with especially clear water. Paradise is also easily reached by local bus or taxi.

Super Paradise (Plindri) is accessible only by a very poor road, footpath, or caïque, so it's less crowded. It's predominantly gay and nude, but clothed sunbathing by heterosexuals is tolerated. Farther east across the little peninsula is **Agrari,** a lovely cove sheltered by lush foliage, with a good little taverna.

Elia, a 45-minute caïque ride from Plati Yialos, is one of the island's best and largest beaches, attracting many nudists. It's usually one of the least crowded, although bus service from the north station will probably soon put an end to that. If it gets too crowded, head back west to Agrari.

The next major beach, **Kalo Livadi (Good Pasture),** a beautiful spot in an idyllic farming valley, is accessible by a scramble over the peninsula east from Elia and by bus from the north station in the summer. There's even a nice restaurant.

The last resort area on the southern coast accessible by bus from the north station is at **Kalafati,** a fishing village that was once the port for the ancient citadel of Mykonos. It's now dominated by the large Aphrodite Beach Hotel complex. Several miles farther east, accessible by a fairly good road from Kalafati, is **Lia,** which has fine sand, clear water, bamboo windbreaks, and a small taverna.

MYKONOS AFTER DARK

Mykonos has the liveliest, most abundant (and expensive), and most chameleon-like nightlife—especially gay nightlife—in the Aegean. Don't be surprised if the places we suggest have closed, moved, or changed their name or image.

Watching the sunset is a popular sport at the sophisticated bars in Little Venice. The **Kastro** (☎ **0289/23-070**), near the Paraportiani Church, is famous for classical music and frozen daiquiris. This is a great spot to watch handsome young men flirting with each other. If you find it too crowded or tame, sashay along to **Le Caprice,** which also has a seaside perch. The **Montparnasse** (☎ **0289/23-719**), on the same lane, is cozier, with classical music and Toulouse-Lautrec posters. The **Veranda** (☎ **0289/23-290**), in an old mansion overlooking the water with a good view of the windmills, is as relaxing as its name implies.

The decibel level is considerably higher along the harbor, where **Pierro's** (☎ **0289/22-177,** popular with gay visitors, rocks all night long to American and European music. The **Anchor** plays blues, jazz, and classic rock for its 30-something clients, as does **Argo. Stavros Irish Bar** (☎ **0298/23-359**) behind the town hall, is among the wildest places on the island. The **Windmill Disco** draws a younger crowd interested in chatting before anything significant happens. And if you'd like to sample some Greek music and dancing, try **Thalami,** a small club underneath the town hall.

The **City Club Disco** has a nightly drag show, and the **Factory,** near the windmills, is the place for gay striptease.

AN EXCURSION TO THE ✪ ISLAND OF DELOS

According to legend, Delos is the spot where Leto gave birth to the twins Artemis and Apollo. Why did Leto pick this tiny—less than 5 square kilometers (2 square miles)—barren island as her nursery? Because she hoped to escape her lover Zeus's jealous spouse Hera by hiding on the smallest of the Cycladic islands. Although remote and tiny, Delos had an excellent harbor (long since silted up) that made it a vital way station for ancient ships plying the Aegean. The island was also a significant religious shrine in the cult of Apollo, with an oracle second in importance only to Delphi. In addition, the Delian Festival was an important ancient athletic festival. Less endearingly, in Roman times Delos was the most important slave market in the Aegean; there're reports of as many as 10,000 slaves being sold here in a single day. Today, the extensive ruins on Delos make the island rival Delphi and Olympia as one of the most impressive ancient sites in all Greece—although you'll long for the shady pine trees of Delphi and Olympia when you visit virtually shadeless Delos.

GETTING THERE   Delos can be visited only by sea—and many days the sea is too rough for boats to put in here. The site is usually open 8:30am to 3pm and is always closed on Monday. Most people visit on excursion boats from nearby Mykonos, although there are excursions from other neighboring islands, and Delos is a prominent stop for cruise ships and yachts. Spending the night is not allowed. From Mykonos, organized guided and unguided excursions leave Tuesday to Sunday from the west end of the harbor; the trip takes about 40 minutes and costs about 3,000Dr ($10) round-trip for transportation alone (departure from Mykonos around 8:30am; return to Mykonos around 3pm). **Yiannakis Tours** (☎ **0289/22-089**) offers guided tours for 12,000Dr ($40) that depart at 9 or 10am and return at 12:30 or 2pm.

Note: Try to leave as early as possible in the morning for Delos, especially in the summer, when both the afternoon heat and the crowds are intense. Be sure to wear sturdy shoes and a hat and bring water and a snack. (There's a cafe near the museum, but the prices are high and the quality is poor.)

EXPLORING THE ISLAND

Delos flourished from the earliest days of Greek history through the Roman era, and the remains here attest to its life as the most important religious, maritime, and commercial center in the Aegean. Still, the 3 hours allotted by most excursion boats should be enough for all except the most avid archaeology enthusiasts to explore the site and museum.

Entrance to the site costs 1,500Dr ($5) unless it was included in your tour; site plans and picture guides are sold at the ticket facility. If you intend to explore the sprawling remains, be sure to get a site plan. If you're energetic enough, climb up **Mount Kythnos,** at 113m (371 feet), the highest point on the island, for an overview of the site (and a fine view of the neighboring Cyclades).

French archaeologists have been excavating Delos since 1872, and there's a lot to see on and off the **Sacred Way,** the route that runs to the Sanctuary of Apollo. Note that most visitors are more interested in the marble phalluses in the **Sanctuary of Dionysos** than in the remains of houses, stoas, and religious shrines here—although the marble lions along the **Avenue of the Lions** have their admirers. (Some lions may not be in place when you visit, having been taken off-island for restoration work.) If you've never seen ancient mosaics, be sure to take in the handsome pebble mosaics in the **House of the Dolphins,** the **House of the Masks,** and the **House of the Tridents.**

✪ SANTORINA (THIRA)

Especially if you arrive by sea, you won't confuse Santorini with any of the other Cyclades—although you might be confused to learn that it's also known as Thira. Ships arrive at Santorini (pop. 8,000; 240km or 130 nautical miles southeast of Piraeus) in a spectacular harbor that's part of the enormous *caldera* (crater) formed when a volcano blew out the island's center around 1450 B.C. To this day, some scholars speculate that the destruction gave birth to the myth of the lost continent of Atlantis.

Your first choice upon disembarking will be to decide whether you want to ride the funicular or a donkey 335m (1,100 feet) up the sheer sides of the caldera to the island's capital, Fira. Once there, you may decide to reward yourself with a glass of the island's rosé wine before you explore the shops and restaurants of Fira, swim at the black volcanic beach of Kamari, or visit the dazzling site of Akrotiri, an Aegean Pompeii destroyed when the volcano erupted. In case you were wondering, the volcano is now officially dormant, so you don't have to fret about the plumes of steam you might see around the islands of Kamenes in the harbor.

ESSENTIALS

GETTING THERE   By Air   Olympic Airways has several (six in the high season) daily flights between Athens and the airport at Monolithos (☎ **0286/31525**), which also receives European charters. There're also daily connections with Mykonos, three or four a week with Rhodes, two or three a week with Iraklion, Crete, and three a week during the high season with Thessaloniki. For schedule information and reservations, check with the Olympic Airways office on Ayiou Athanassiou Street (☎ **0286/ 22-493**, or 01/961-6161 or 01/966-6666 in Athens).

By Sea   Several companies operate **ferry service** at least twice daily from Piraeus; the trip takes 10 to 12 hours, and costs about 6,000Dr ($20) one way. If you can book a day sailing, you'll pass many of the Cyclades. In summer, there are often daily ferry connections from Santorini to Ios, Mykonos, and Paros. **Excursion boats** go to and from Iraklion, Crete, almost daily. The fare is about 4,000Dr ($13) one way. Because this is an open-sea route, the trip can be an ordeal in bad weather. Check the schedules with the **Tourist Police** in Athens (☎ **171**) or the **Port Authority** in Piraeus (☎ **01/451-1310**) or Santorini (☎ **0286/22-239**).

The high-speed **hydrofoil** *Nearchos* connects Santorini with Ios, Paros, Mykonos, and Iraklio, Crete, almost daily in the high season and three times weekly in the low season, if the winds aren't too strong.

VISITOR INFORMATION   There's no official government tourist office, but there're a number of travel agencies. Several travelers have written of good experiences dealing with **Kamari Tours,** 2 blocks south of the main square on the right (☎ **0286/ 22-666;** fax 0286/22-971; e-mail: kamaritours@santonet.gr). Other agencies include **Joint Travel Service** (☎ **0286/2 4900;** fax 0286/24992), next to the Olympic Airways Office in Fira; **Nomikos Travel** (☎ **0286/23-660**), with offices in Fira, Karterados, and Perissa; also, **Damigos Tours,** on the main Fira square (☎ **0286/22-504;** fax 0286/22-266), the first agency established in Fira, often offers excellent guided tours at slightly lower prices than the others. Any of these agencies should be able to help you find accomodations, rent a car, get boat tickets, or book a tour. Expect to pay about 6,000Dr ($20) to join a bus tour to Akrotiri or Ancient Thira.

GETTING AROUND   By Bus   Santorini has very good bus service. The island's central bus station is just south of the main square in Fira. Schedules are posted on the wall of the office above it; most routes are serviced every half hour 7am to 11pm in the summer, less frequently in the off-season.

By Car   Most travel agents can help you rent a car. You might find that a local company such as **Zeus** (☎ **0286/24-013**) offers better prices than the big names, although the quality might be a bit lower. Of the better-known agencies, try **Budget Rent-A-Car,** a block below the bus stop square in Fira (☎ **0286/22-900;** fax 0286/22-887), where a four-seat Fiat Panda should cost about 21,000Dr ($70) a day, with unlimited mileage. If you reserve in advance through Budget in the United States (☎ **800/527-0700**), you should be able to beat that price.

By Moped   The roads on the island are notoriously treacherous, narrow, and winding; add local drivers who take the roads at high speed and visiting drivers who aren't sure where they're going, and you'll understand the island's high accident rate. If you're determined to use two-wheeled transportation, expect to pay about 3,000 to 9,000Dr ($10 to $30) per day, depending on size and season.

By Taxi   The taxi station is just south of the main square. In high season, you should book ahead by phone (☎ **0286/22-555** or 0286/23-700) if you want a taxi for an excursion; prices are standard from point to point. If you call for a taxi outside Fira, you're required to pay the fare from there to your pickup point, although you can sometimes find one that has dropped off a passenger. Taxis are not cheap and not always easy to find, so it's a good idea to book one well in advance if you want to plan a trip around the island by taxi. On the other hand, after the bus service shuts down at midnight, taxis (or walking) are your best options for getting around.

FAST FACTS   American Express   The **X-Ray Kilo Travel Service,** near the Tropical Bar at the head of the steps up to Fira from the harbor (☎ **0286/22-624;** fax 0286/23-600), is the American Express representative on Santorini.

Area Code   The telephone area code for Santorini is **0286.**

Banks   The **National Bank** (open weekdays 8am to 2pm; ATM machine) is a block south from the main square on the right near the taxi station. Many travel agents also change money; most are open daily 8am to 9:30pm.

Hospital   The small **Health Clinic** is on the southeast edge of town on Ayiou Athanassiou Street (☎ **0286/22-238**), to the left after the playground, near the Santorini Hotel.

Internet Access   The **PC Club** (☎ **0286/24-600**) is in Fira. It's usually open Monday to Saturday 9am to 2pm and 5pm to 8pm; 1,500Dr ($5) per hour for use.

Police   The police station is on Dekigala Street (☎ **0286/22-649**), several blocks south of the main square, on the left. The **port authority** can be reached at ☎ **0286/ 22-239.**

Post Office   The **post office** (☎ **0286/22-238;** fax 0286/22-698) is off to the right of the bus station. It's open weekdays 8am to 1pm.

Telephone   The **OTE telephone** office is just off Ypapantis Street, up from the post office. It's usually open Monday through Friday 8am to 4pm.

WHERE TO STAY

Santorini is packed in July and August, so if you plan a summer visit, make a reservation with a deposit at least 2 months in advance or be prepared to accept potluck. Don't accept rooms offered at the port unless you're exhausted and don't care how remote the village is that you wake up in. If you come between April and mid-June or in September or October, when the island is less crowded and far more pleasant, the rates can be nearly half the high-season rates we quote. Most of the hotels recommended below don't have air-conditioning, but with cool breezes blowing through, you won't need it. Many don't have televisions either—but with the superb views here, you shouldn't miss TV too much.

✪ **Astra Apartments.** Imerovigli, 847 00 Santorini. ☎ **0286/23-641.** Fax 0286/24-765. E-mail: astra-ae@oenet.gr. 18 units. A/C TV TEL. 36,000–99,000Dr ($120–$330) double. AE, MC, V.

Perched on a cliff side with spectacular views, looking like a miniature village set within the tiny hamlet of Imerovigli, the Astra Apartments are quietly elegant, with a drop-dead pool. Each unit has a kitchenette, but breakfast is served on your private terrace or balcony, and there's also a poolside bar that serves delicious snacks. This is an ideal place to escape the hustle and bustle of Fira or Oia and enjoy life. Every detail here is right, the views are spectacular, and the service is outstanding. Not surprisingly, reservations are often hard to come by; this is also a popular place for weddings and honeymoons.

✪ **Katikies.** Oia, 847 02 Santorini. ☎ **800/345-8236** or 0286/71-401. Fax 0286/71-129. E-mail: katikies@otenet.gr. 22 units. A/C MINIBAR TV TEL. 45,000–84,000Dr ($150–$280) double. MC, V.

If you find a more spectacular pool anywhere on the island, let us know: This one runs virtually to the side of the caldera, so that you can paddle about and enjoy an endless view. (There's also a smaller pool intended for the use of guests who have suites.) The hotel's island-style architecture incorporates twists and turns, secluded patios, and antiques. If the people in the next room like to sing in the shower, you might hear them—but most people who stay here treasure the tranquility. The top-of-the-line honeymoon suite has its own Jacuzzi, just in case you can't be bothered going to either outdoor pool.

Loucas Hotel. Fira, 847 00 Santorini. ☎ **0286/22-480** or 0286/22-680. Fax 0286/24-882. 22 units. A/C TV TEL. 34,500Dr ($115) double. Rates include breakfast. MC, V.

This is one of the oldest and best hotels on the caldera, with barrel-ceilinged "caves" built to prevent collapse during an earthquake. Rooms are newly renovated; some were enlarged and furnished with handsome lively blue furniture, and have shared patios overlooking the caldera. It's an excellent value for the location, amenities, and view, although it's sufficiently in the heart of things in Fira that it can be noisy here at night.

WHERE TO DINE

Camille Stephani. Kamari Beach. ☎ **0286/31-716.** Reservations recommended July–Sept. Main courses 3,600–7,500Dr ($12–$25). AE, DC, MC, V. Daily 1–4pm and 6:30pm–midnight (but often open all day; often closed off-season). GREEK/INTERNATIONAL.

Even if you're not staying at Kamari, this restaurant on the north end of the beach, 460m (500 yards) from the bus stop, will make the trip worthwhile. The house specialty is a tender beef fillet with green pepper in Madeira sauce. You can take a moonlight stroll along the beach after dinner.

Katina Fish–Taverna. Port of Oia (Ammoudi). ☎ **0286/71-280.** Fish priced daily by the kilo. No credit cards. Daily 11am–1am. SEAFOOD.

One of the best places to eat in Oia isn't in town but down in the port of Ammoudi, which is best reached by donkey (ask in the village about hiring a donkey), or you can walk, or take a taxi. Katina Pagoni is considered one of the very best local cooks, and the setting beside the glittering Aegean is romantic.

Kukumavolos. Port of Oia (Ammoudi). ☎ **0286/71-413.** Fish priced daily by the kilo. No credit cards. Daily 8pm–midnight. NOUVELLE GREEK.

This elegant restaurant has delicious fresh fish and an adventurous menu of "nouvelle Greek" cuisine (dishes are lighter and less oil-saturated than is customary in Greece). There's a wide selection of island and off-island wines and wonderful views over the sea.

✪ **Selene.** Fira (in the passageway between the Atlantis and Aressana Hotels). ☎ **0286/ 22-249.** Fax 0286/24-395. Reservations recommended. Main courses 3,000–6,000Dr ($10–$20). AE, MC, V. Mid-Apr to early Oct, Mon–Sat noon–3pm; daily 7pm–midnight. Closed late Oct to early Apr. ELEGANT GREEK.

The best restaurant on Santorini—and one of the best in all Greece—Selene uses local produce to highlight what owners Evelyn and George Hatziyiannakis call the "creative nature of Greek cuisine." The appetizers, including a delicious eggplant salad with octopus and tomato, mushrooms with crabmeat and cheese, and fluffy fava balls with caper sauce, are deservedly famous. Entrees include sea bass grilled with pink peppers, rabbit, quail, and saddle of lamb with yogurt and mint sauce. If you eat only one meal on Santorini, eat it here, in a truly distinguished restaurant with distinctive local archi-tecture—and be sure to try the enormous local capers.

EXPLORING THE ISLAND

FIRA If you're staying overnight on Santorini, take advantage of the fact that almost all the day-trippers from cruise ships leave in the late afternoon, and explore the cap-ital in the evening. As you stroll, you may be surprised to discover that Fira has a Roman Catholic cathedral and convent in addition to the predictable Greek Ortho-dox cathedral, a legacy from the days when the Venetians controlled much of the Aegean. The name *Santorini,* in fact, is a Latinate corruption of the Greek for "Saint Irene." The small **Archaeological Museum** (☎ **0286/22-217**), with both Minoan and classical finds, is near the cable car station in Fira. It's open Tuesday to Sunday 8:30am to 3pm; admission is 800Dr ($2.65). You might find it almost deserted, as most visitors head directly for Thira's shops. (The new archaeological museum should open sometime in 2000.) In addition to the inevitable mass-produced souvenir and T-shirt shops, Fira has a number of nice, small galleries selling watercolors, posters, ceramics, and handcrafted glass—and a great many shops selling jewelry.

It's a good idea to remember the maxim that all that glitters is not necessarily gold as you scout out Fira's seemingly nonstop jewelry shops. The best-known jeweler here is probably **Kostas Antoniou,** on Ayiou Ioannou Street (☎ **0286/22-633;** ☎ and fax 0296/23-557), north of the cable-car station. **Porphyra,** in the Fabrica Shopping Center near the cathedral (☎ **0286/22-981**), also has some impressive work. Most jewelers will first weigh, then price, what you're interested in—and some will bargain.

VILLAGES Two island villages well worth visiting are **Pirgos (Tower),** the oldest and highest settlement on the island, and **Oia** (also spelled Ia), on a cliff above the caldera. Badly damaged in a massive earthquake in 1956, Oia was virtually a ghost town until it was rebuilt in the 1960s and '70s and resettled. Now its chic shops and gorgeous sunsets make it an increasingly popular place to stay or to visit—especially with those who find Fira too frenetic. If you travel to either village (local buses run there from Fira, or you can take a taxi), keep a lookout for some of the island's cave dwellings (homes hollowed out of Santorini's soft volcanic stone).

BEACHES Santorini does not have the soft sand beaches of Mykonos, but the black volcanic sand and pebble beach make **Kamari** a very nice place to swim, especially in the morning, before the all-day sunbathers arrive (and before the black sand gets seri-ously hot). On the way to or from Kamari from Fira by local bus or taxi, you can stop at the **Antoniou, Roussos,** or **Boutari** vintners to see how wine is made, have a free sample, and perhaps buy a bottle or two to sample later. Be warned: Vino Santo, San-torini's sweet wine, is *very* sweet. **Boutari,** Megalohori (☎ **0286/81-011**), is the island's largest vintner. For 1,500Dr ($5) you can see the wine press, sample the wines, and snack on *mezedes* (hors d'oeuvre). The **Antoniou winery** (run by the same fami-ly who has the Antoniou jewelry in Fira) is especially charming, with the old wine press and barrels on display

ANCIENT THIRA & AKROTIRI Above Kamari beach on a rocky promontory are the ruins of **Ancient Thira** (☎ **0286-22-217** or 0286-22-366), settled in the 9th century B.C., although most of the scattered remains date from the Hellenistic era. At press time, it was open Tuesday to Friday 8am to 2:30pm, Sunday and holidays 8am to 2:30pm; it was also sometimes open on Saturday 8am to 2:30pm; admission is 1,200Dr ($4). A good, but alarmingly narrow, road now runs almost to the summit, which can also be reached on foot or by donkey (for hire from some travel agents) by a path. The hilltop site is very fine, but if you have to choose between Ancient Thira and Akrotiri, head for Akrotiri.

The excavations at **Akrotiri,** the Minoan settlement destroyed when the volcano erupted around 1450 B.C., have unearthed buildings three stories tall that were lavishly decorated with frescoes (which are now on view in the National Archaeological Museum in Athens). It's still breathtaking to walk down the streets and peek in the windows of houses in a town whose life was extinguished in a torrent of lava and ash so long ago. The site (☎ **0286/81-366**) is open Tuesday to Sunday 8:30am to 3pm; admission is 1,500Dr ($5). Akrotiri can be reached by public bus or private bus tour; **Damigos Tours,** on the main square (☎ **0286/22-504**), has knowledgeable and entertaining guides.

SANTORINI AFTER DARK

Most people will want to start the evening with a drink on the caldera watching the sunset. **Franco's** (☎ **0286/22-881**) is the most famous place for this magic hour, but drinks are expensive; the nearby **Tropical** (no phone) has almost as good a view and charges less. **Archipelago** (☎ **0286/23-673**) and the **Canava Cafe** (☎ **0286/22-565**) also have good views. For more reasonable prices and the same fantastic view, continue past the Loucas Hotel to the **Renaissance Bar** (☎ **0286/22-880**).

Most of the action is north and west of the main square. Underneath the square, the **Kirathira Bar** plays jazz at a level that permits conversation. The **Town Club** appeals to clean-cut rockers, while the **Two Brothers** pulls in the biggest, chummiest crowd on the island. For Greek music, find the **Apocalypse Club,** or **Bar 33** for bouzouki. Discos come and go; follow your ears to find them. The **Koo Club** is the biggest, and **Enigma** is popular with those interested in good music. In Oia, **Melissa's Piano Bar** and **Zorba's** are good spots for a drink at sunset.

None of the places recommended above have specific street addresses; it's best just to ask someone for directions.

SIFNOS

Sifnos (pop. 2,500; 172km or 93 nautical miles southeast of Piraeus) is the most beautiful of the western Cyclades, with unusually green hills and valleys, particularly lovely villages, and a reputation for especially good olive oil and distinguished cooking. All this has made the island a favorite summer retreat for Athenians, and now that foreign visitors have discovered Sifnos's charms, the island can be terribly crowded in July (especially around the feast day of the Prophet Elias, the patron saint of the island's most important monastery) and in August. If possible, don't visit then, unless you like your restaurants and beaches very busy.

ESSENTIALS

GETTING THERE   There's at least one boat daily from Piraeus, in addition to daily (twice daily in summer) connections to the other western Cyclades, Serifos and Milos, and less frequently to Kimolos and Kythnos. There are ferry connections four times a week with Santorini; three times a week with Folegandros, Ios, and Sikinos; and once a week with Andros, Crete, Mykonos, Paros, Rafina, Syros, and Tinos. There's a weekly connection with the Dodecanese islands of Karpathos, Kassos, Rhodes, and Symi. Contact the **Port Authority** in Piraeus (☎ **01/171,** 01/451-1130, or 01/322-2545) or in Sifnos (☎ **0284/31-617**) for information.

VISITOR INFORMATION   You can book a room, buy ferry tickets, rent a car or motorbike, arrange excursions, and usually leave your luggage at the **Aegean Thesaurus Travel and Tourism office** on the port (☎ **0284/32-190;** e-mail: thesaurus@travelling.gr), at **Siphanto Travel** (☎ **0284/32-034;** fax 0284/31-024), or at **Katzoulakis Tourist Agency** (☎ **0284/32-362**) on the port. Check to see if Aegean

Thesaurus, which also has an office on the main square in Apollonia (☎ 028431-151; fax 0284/332-190), still has its excellent information packet on Sifnos for 400Dr ($1.35). At press time, **Ventouris Ferries** (☎ 0284/31-700) in Kamares had the concession for tickets for most ferry lines, while Aegean Thesaurus handled hydrofoil (flying dolphin) tickets.

FAST FACTS   The telephone **area code** for Sifnos is **0284.** Tourist services are centered around the main square, Plateia Iroon ("Heroes' Square"), in Apollonia, the capital. The **post office** (☎ 0284/31-329) is open weekdays 8am to 3pm, and in the summer, Saturday and Sunday 9am to 1:30pm. The **National Bank** (☎ 0284/31-317) is open Monday to Thursday 8am to 2pm and Friday 8am to 1:30pm. The **OTE telephone office,** is open daily 8am to 3pm, and in summer 5 to 10pm. The **news kiosk** on the square has a metered phone for after-hours calls. The **police station** (☎ 0284/31-210), which also functions as an informal information center, is just east of the square, and a first-aid station is nearby; for **medical emergencies,** phone ☎ 0284/31-315.

GETTING AROUND   Many visitors come to Sifnos just for the wonderful hiking and mountain trails. A car or moped isn't really necessary, but cars can be rented at **FS** (☎ 0284/31-795) and **Aegean Thesaurus** (☎ 0284/32-190) in Apollonia, or in Kamares at **Sifnos Car** (☎ 0284/31-793). Apollonia has a few moped dealers; try **Yanni's** (☎ 0284/31-155), on the main square, or **Easy Rider** (☎ 0284/31-001), on the road circling the village. As always, exercise caution if you do decide to rent a car or moped; many drivers, like you, will be unfamiliar with the island roads.

By Bus   Apollonia's Heroes' Square is the central bus stop for the island. The system is fairly efficient; buses run regularly to and from the port at Kamares, north to Artemonas, east to Kastro, and south to Faros and Plati Yialos. A bus schedule is usually posted by the stop in Heroes' Square.

By Taxi   Apollonia's Heroes' Square is also the main taxi stand, although there aren't many of them on the island. Some mobile phone numbers for taxis are ☎ 094/642-680, 094/444-904, 094/761-210, or 094/936-111.

WHERE TO STAY

Many young Athenians vacation on Sifnos, particularly on summer weekends, when it can be very difficult to find a room. If you plan to be in Kamares during the high season, be sure to make reservations by May. If you're here off-season, many of these hotels are closed, but several remain open all year. The efficient **Aegean Thesaurus Travel Agency** (see "Visitor Information," above) can place you in a room in a private house with your own bathroom, in a studio with a kitchenette, or in other, more stylish accommodations.

Hotel Anthoussa. Apollonia, 840 03 Sifnos. ☎ **0284/31-431.** 15 units. A/C TV TEL. 19,500Dr ($65) double. Continental breakfast 1,500Dr ($5). MC, V.

This hotel is above the excellent and popular Yerontopoulos cafe and patisserie, on the right past Heroes Square. Although street-side rooms offer wonderful views over the hills, they overlook the late-night sweet-tooth crowd and can be recommended only to night owls. Back rooms are quieter and overlook a beautiful bower of bougainvillea.

✪ **Hotel Petali.** Ano Petali, Apollonia, 840 03 Sifnos. ☎ and fax **0284/33-024.** 11 units. A/C MINIBAR TV. 18,000–24,000Dr ($60–$80) double. No credit cards. Hotel not always open in winter.

This would be a nice place to stay a week. There are lovely views over Ano Petali (a suburb of Apollonia) to the sea, a large terrace with handsome, comfortable chairs, rooms furnished in Cycladic style, good beds, modern bathrooms, and a small restaurant that serves delicious Sifnian specialties. The hotel offers an American breakfast for 2,000Dr ($6.65). Although the Hotel Petali does not accept credit cards, its managing office, **Aegean Thesaurus Travel Agency** (☎ **0284/33-151;** fax 0284/32-190) accepts MasterCard and Visa.

✪ **Hotel Plati Yialos.** Plati Yialos, 840 03 Sifnos. ☎ **0284/31-324,** or 0831/22-626 in winter. Fax 0284/31-325, or 0831/55-049 in winter. 34 units. A/C TV TEL. 45,000Dr ($150) double. Rates include breakfast. No credit cards. Hotel usually open in winter.

Thanks to a recent renovation, the island's first beach hotel is still the best. It overlooks the beach on the west side of the cove. Ground-floor rooms have private patios, and all rooms have modern bathrooms and are nicely decorated with ceramics and painted tiles. There are also a number of suites, which are ideal for families. The Plati Yialos's flagstone sundeck extends from the beach to a dive platform at the end of the cove, with a bar and restaurant sharing the same Aegean views.

✪ **Hotel Sifnos.** Apollonia, 840 03 Sifnos. ☎ **0284/31-624.** 9 units. 16,500Dr ($55) double. AE, EURO, MC, V. Usually open in winter.

Many consider this hotel on a quiet pedestrianized street the best in Apollonia. The owners have tried hard to make it reflect island taste, using local pottery and weavings in the good-sized, bright rooms. It's usually open year-round and has an excellent restaurant.

WHERE TO DINE

Apostoli's Koutouki Taverna. Apollonia. ☎ **0284/31-186.** Main courses 1,500–4,500Dr ($5–$15). No credit cards. Daily noon–midnight. GREEK.

There are several tavernas in Apollonia, and this one on the main pedestrian street is generally the best for Greek food. The service is usually leisurely at best. All the vegetable dishes, most made from locally grown produce, are tasty, but portions are on the skimpy side.

Captain Andreas. Kamares. (☎ **0284/32-356.** Main courses 1,500– 2,500Dr ($5–$8). Fish priced by the kilo. No credit cards. Daily 1pm–midnight. GREEK/SEAFOOD.

This is a typical fish taverna, on the beach, with the catch of the day on the menu, as well as the usual chops and salads. Captain Andreas has many fans, although some find him a bit dour.

Sifnos Cafe–Restaurant. Apollonia. ☎ **0284/31-624.** Main courses 1,500–4,600Dr ($5–$15). AE, EURO, MC, V. Daily 8am–midnight. GREEK.

You can start the day here with breakfast, including fresh fruit juice and your choice of a dozen coffees. Stop by later in the day for a snack, light meal, ouzo and mezedes, or dessert. This place often has *rivithia* (chickpeas), a Sifnian specialty, on Sunday.

To Liotrivi (Manganas). Artemona. ☎ **0284/31-246.** Main courses 1,300–4,500Dr ($4.35–$15). No credit cards. Daily noon–midnight. GREEK.

One of the island's favorite tavernas is in the pretty village of Artemona, just over a mile's walk from Apollonia. Taste for yourself why the Sifnians consider Yannis Yiorgoulis one of their best cooks. Try his delectable *kaparosalata* (minced caper leaves and onion salad), *povithokeftedes* (croquettes of ground chickpeas), or *ambelofasoula* (crisp local black-eyed peas in the pod). In short, there're lots of vegetarian delights here, but there's also a very tasty beef fillet with potatoes baked in foil. This place usually has the excellent Siphnian specialty of chickpeas *rivithia* on Sundays.

EXPLORING THE ISLAND

Kamares, on the west coast, is the island's port and will be most visitors' introduction to Sifnos—a pity, because it has none of the charm of the capital, Apollonia, or the inland villages. Still, there's a good **sand beach** at Kamares, and the usual assortment of restaurants and shops, some of which sell the distinctive local pottery, made from island clay.

From Kamares, you can catch a bus for the 5km (3-mile) trip to **Apollonia** (also called Hora), with almost 700 year-round inhabitants, the largest of the island's seven villages. En route up the hill to Apollonia, you'll begin to get a sense of the island's handsome architecture, especially its stone paths and small, cubical, whitewashed houses, almost all with whitewashed containers of geraniums.

Apollonia's **Heroes Square (Plateia Iroon)** is the site of a monument to Sifnos's World War II veterans. Home to a number of small cafes, restaurants, and shops, it's the transportation hub of the island, where its vehicular roads converge. There's also a **Museum of Folk Art** on the square. It's usually open July to mid-September 10am to 1pm and 6pm to 10pm; admission is 400Dr ($1.35).

More and more asphalt roads are appearing on Sifnos, but you'll still be able to do most of your walking on the island's distinctive flagstone and marble paths. You'll probably see village women whitewashing the edges of the paving stones, transforming the monochrome paths into elaborate abstract patterns. Apollonia gleams with whitewash, as does the handsome village of Kastro, the former capital, where you can see remains of the walls of the **medieval fortress (kastro).** Throughout the island, you'll see dovecotes, windmills, and small white chapels in amazingly remote spots.

Most connoisseurs rank **Plati Yialos** on the island's south coast as Sifnos's best beach. Don't expect to be alone: A hotel and a campground are on the popular, long crescent beach. There's also good swimming at **Heronissos, Vroulidia,** and **Faros,** a small resort on the east coast with some good budget accommodations and tavernas. **Apokofto** has a good sand beach, and you can often reach the lovely beach at **Vathy** by one of the caïques that leave from Kamares, or by bus on the new road. **Aegean Thesaurus Travel** (see "Visitor Information," above) has caïque excursions to a number of isolated beaches.

SIFNOS AFTER DARK

In Apollonia, the **Argo Bar, Botzi,** and **Volto,** on the main pedestrian street, are good for the latest European and American pop. In summertime the large **Dolphin Pub** becomes a lively nightspot (it closes in mid-September). At Kamares, the **Old Captain's Bar, Collage Bar, Mobilize Dance Club** and the more elegant **Follie-Follie,** all on the beach, compete most nights to see who can crank up the volume for disco music the loudest.

PAROS

You can catch a boat from Paros (pop. 12,000; 176km or 95 nautical miles southeast of Piraeus) to most of the Aegean islands, which means that a lot of people pass through here, especially in summer. Some decide to stay: Paros's good beaches, lovely villages, and increasingly sophisticated nightlife, especially in the village of Naoussa and the capital town Parikia (also known as Hora), have earned it a reputation for being a less expensive Mykonos. In addition, Paros has attractions its better-known neighbor lacks, including extensive vineyards, the substantial remains of a Venetian castle, and the finest Byzantine cathedral in the Cyclades. The celebrations here of the Feast of the Assumption (August 15) make Paros *very* crowded in August.

ESSENTIALS

GETTING THERE   **By Air**   **Olympic Airlines** has five flights daily (10 in summer) between Athens and Paros. For schedule information and reservations, call ☎ **01/966-6666** in Athens, or 0284/21-900 in Parikia, or call the **Paros airport** (☎ **0284/91-257**).

By Sea   The main port, Parikia, has ferry service from Piraeus at least once daily and four times daily in the summer. The trip takes 6 hours. Confirm schedules with the **Tourist Police** in Athens (☎ **171** or 01/322-2545) or the **Port Authority** in Piraeus (☎ **01/451-1310**). **Strintzis Lines** (☎ **01/422-5000** in Athens) and **Ventouris Ferries** (☎ **01/482-8901** in Athens) operate from Piraeus via Syros three or four times a week. **Ilio Lines** (☎ **01/422-4772** in Athens) has hydrofoil service almost daily from Rafina.

Daily ferry service from Parikia links Paros with Ios, Mykonos, Santorini (Thira), and Tinos. Daily excursion tours link Parikia and Naoussa (the north coast port) with Mykonos. Call the **port authority** (☎ **0284/21-240**) or check each travel agent's current schedule. Most ferry tickets are not interchangeable.

VISITOR INFORMATION   The **Paros Information Bureau** is inside the windmill on the harbor (☎ **0284/22-078** or 0284/21-673). In theory, it's open June to September, daily 9am to 11pm; the staff speaks English, provides local schedules, and changes traveler's checks. **Paros Travel** (☎ **0284/21-582**; fax 0284/22-582) is a good, helpful travel agent near the pier.

GETTING AROUND   The capital, Parikia, is best enjoyed by simply strolling about and getting pleasantly lost. Naoussa can also be enjoyed on foot. If you plan to explore the island, however, you may want to rent a car, or take one of the guided tours of the island offered by **Paros Travel** (☎ **0284/21-582**).

By Bicycle   With its rolling, fertile hills, Paros is well suited to exploration by bike, although some of the pebble-and-dirt roads will require strong tires. **Mountain Bike Club Paros,** just off the waterfront (☎ **0284/23-778**), supplies bikes for their organized tours as well as such essentials as a helmet, insurance, repair kits, and water bottles.

By Bus   The **bus station** in Parikia is on the waterfront (☎ **0284/21-395,** left from the windmill. There's hourly public bus service between Parikia and Naoussa. The other public buses from Parikia run hourly. Schedules are posted at the stations.

By Car   There're several agencies along the waterfront, and except in July and August you should be able to bargain. **Rent-A-Car Acropolis,** left from the windmill on the waterfront (☎ **0284/21-830**), has wildly painted dune buggies or Suzuki jeeps. **Budget Rent-a-Car** (☎ **0284/22-320**) and **Paros Europcar S.A.** (☎ **0284/ 24-408;** fax 0284/22-544 in Parikia) usually have a good selection. Purchasing full insurance is recommended. You'll probably get the best rate if you reserve in advance through **Budget** in the United States (☎ **800/527-0700**). Expect to pay at least $50 per day in the summer.

By Moped   There're several moped dealers along the waterfront. Make sure the cycle is in proper condition before you accept it, and be careful on pebble-and-dirt surfaces. Expect to pay about $15 per day in the summer.

By Taxi   Taxis can be booked (☎ **0284/21-500**) or hailed at the windmill taxi stand. If you're coming off the ferry with lots of luggage and a hotel reservation in Naoussa, it's worth the fee of around 2,000Dr ($7) to take a taxi directly there.

FAST FACTS   Area Code   The telephone area code for Paros is **0284.**

Banks   The three banks on Mavroyenous Square (to the right behind the windmill) are open Monday to Friday 8am to 2pm and Friday 8am to 1:30pm.

Hospital   The private **Medical Center of Paros** (☎ **0284/24-410**) is left (west) of Parikia's central square, across from the post office, a block off the port. The public **Parikia Health Clinic** (☎ **0284/22-500**) is down the road from the Ekantopyliani Church.

Internet Access   Try **Sindemeno Café** (☎ **0284/22-003**) on Market Street in Parikia; the user's fee is 2,500Dr ($8) per hour. The **Wired Café** (stnicolas@ bigfood.com), on the market street by the kastro has Internet service for 2,400Dr ($8) per hour.

Police   The **police station** is on the central square (☎ **100** or 0284/23-333). The **Tourist Police** are behind the windmill on the port (☎ **0284/21-673**). In Marpissa, call ☎ **0284/41-202;** in Naoussa, ☎ **0284/51-202.**

Post Office   The **post office** (☎ **0284/21-236**) is on the waterfront road; it's open Monday to Friday 7:30am to 2pm, with extended hours in July and August. It offers fax service at 0284/22-449.

Telephone   The **OTE telephone office** (☎ **0284/22-135**) is to the right of the windmill; it's open Monday through Friday 7:30am to midnight. (If the front door is closed, go around to the back—wind direction determines which door is open.)

WHERE TO STAY

Most hotels require reservations for July and August; it's advisable to book at least a month in advance. If you arrive without a room, you can often get one in a private house from one of the hawkers who meet ships. If you don't like what you're offered, the **Hotelliers Association of Paros** (☎ **0284/24-555** or 0284/24-556) in Mavroyenous Square may be able to help. Keep in mind that all hotels in Parikia are likely to be noisy in season.

✪ **Astir of Paros.** Kolimbithres Beach, Naoussa, 844 01 Paros. ☎ **0284/51-976.** Fax 0284/51-985. E-mail: astir@mail.otenet.gr; agn.hol.gr/hotels/astir/astir/htm. 57 units. A/C MINIBAR TV TEL. 61,000Dr ($203) double; 69,000–165,000Dr ($230–$550) suite. AE, DC, MC, V.

The Hotel Astir of Paros, on Kolymbithres Beach across from the village of Naoussa, is one of the glamour spots of the Cyclades. There's just about everything you'd expect here: large, quiet suites and rooms, a freshwater pool, miniature golf for the kiddies— in other words, this is as close to a full resort hotel (built to suggest an island village) as you'll find in the Aegean. That said, rooms are comfortable, but not luxurious (although bathrooms are large and modern).

Hotel Fotilia. Naoussa, 844 01 Paros. ☎ **0284/51-480.** Fax 0284/51-189. 14 units. TEL. 30,000Dr ($100) double. Rates include breakfast. No credit cards. Climb to the top of the steps at the end of town and to the left of the church you'll see a restored windmill behind a stone archway.

The Fotilia's large rooms are furnished in tasteful country style and have doors opening to balconies overlooking the old harbor and bay. There're also some studio apartments with simple kitchenettes.

✪ **Lefkes Village Hotel.** P.O. Box 71, Lefkes Village 844 00 Paros. ☎ **0284/41-827** or 01/251-6497. Fax 0284/41-827 or 01/675-5019. 25 units. A/C MINIBAR TV TEL. In season 44,000Dr ($147) double; off-season 26,000–35,000Dr ($87–$117) double. Rates include buffet breakfast. No credit cards.

This handsome new hotel 10km (6 miles) from Parikia is designed to look like a small island village, and is situated in Lefkes, one of Paros's most charming inland villages, with views over the countryside to the sea. Rooms are light and bright, with good bathrooms; some have balconies. There's a restaurant, a handsome swimming pool, a Jacuzzi, and even a small Museum of Popular Aegean Culture and a winery.

✪ **Papadakis Hotel.** Naoussa, 84410 Paros. ☎ **0284/51-643.** Fax 0284/51-269. 19 units. 21,600Dr ($72) double. Breakfast 1,800Dr ($6) extra. No credit cards.

This new hotel is comfortable and charming, with lovely views over the village and sea. In 1999, the hotel was remodeled from top to bottom, and an outdoor pool and Jacuzzi were added to the Papadakis's allures. Ten rooms have satellite TV and mini-bars, five are air-conditioned, and several have kitchenettes.

WHERE TO DINE

Aligaria Restaurant. Plateia Aligari, Parikia. ☎ **0284/22-026.** Main courses 1,500–3,700Dr ($5–$12). EURO, MC, V. Daily noon–3:30pm and 6:30pm–midnight. Turn left off Mavroyenous Sq. behind the Hotel Kontes. GREEK.

Owner Elizabeth Nikolousou is an excellent cook; her zucchini pie and generous portions of stuffed tomatoes disappear early. There's a good selection of local wines.

Barbarossa Ouzeri. On the waterfront, Naoussa. ☎ **0284/51-391.** Mezedes 600–1,800Dr ($2–$6). No credit cards. Daily 7:30–11:30pm. SNACKS.

This authentic ouzeri is right on the port. Wind-burned fishermen sit for hours nursing their milky ouzo in water and their miniportions of grilled octopus and olives. This is a good spot to sit and watch the world go by.

✪ **Lalula.** Naoussa. ☎ **0284/51-547.** Reservations recommended July–Aug. Main courses 2,000–5,500Dr ($7–$18). No credit cards. Daily 7–11:45pm. Take a left at the post office; it's across from the Minoa Hotel. GREEK/MEDITERRANEAN/VEGETARIAN.

A gifted German restaurateur is responsible for the delicious and distinctive food, subdued decor, and interesting but unobtrusive music at Lalula. There's a lovely little garden in the back. The cooking is lighter than typical Greek cuisine; the menu depends on what's fresh at the market. Regular items include vegetable quiche, sweet-and-sour chicken with rice and ginger chutney, and fish steamed in herbs. Check to see if there's a set-price menu; it's usually an excellent value.

Levantis Restaurant. Market St., Parikia on island or Paros: ☎ **0284/23-613.** Fax 0284/21-453. E-mail: levantis@parosweb.com. Reservations recommended July–Aug. Main courses 2,500–4,600Dr ($8–$15). AE, DC, EURO, MC, V. Daily 6pm–1am. GREEK/EASTERN MEDITERRANEAN.

This restaurant serves dinner under a splendid grape arbor that some of the older diners remember from when they were young. The Levantis added an Internet cafe in 1999, and is adding Asian and Western cuisine to its popular Mediterranean and Near Eastern specialties, which include spiced Moroccan lamb and a variety of seafood.

Traveler's Warning

Several places in Paros offer very cheap drinks or "buy one, get one free" deals—usually the locally brewed alcohol that the natives call **bomba.** If you drink it, you'll know why: intoxication and nausea are virtually simultaneous.

EXPLORING THE ISLAND

Parikia, site of the ancient capital, is the main port and largest town on the island, with a busy harbor front whose best-known landmark is the squat, whitewashed windmill just off the main pier. Most of what you'll need—banks, travel agents, several hotels, restaurants, and shops—is clustered nearby in Mavroyenous Square. Things get more interesting when you head inland to Parikia's picturesque **Agora (market)** section, a mixture of food markets and handicraft shops. The nicest part of town is around the 13th-century **Venetian Kastro (fortress).** Like a number of houses and churches here, the Kastro was built of the famous Parian marble originally used to build the temples of Apollo and Demeter.

Today, the churches of Ayios Konstantinos and Ayia Eleni form part of the Kastro, but Parikia's most famous church is the 6th-century **Panayia Ekatondapyliani (Our Lady of a Hundred Doors).** This hyperbolic name simply suggests that the church has more than the usual number of doors. The church is usually open daily 8am to 1pm and 5 to 8pm; admission is free. There's a 500Dr ($1.70) fee for the small **Cathedral Museum.** As on Tinos, many pilgrims come here on the feast of the Virgin on August 15, when finding accommodations on Paros is virtually impossible.

Parikia's **Archaeological Museum** (☎ 0284/21-231) is open Tuesday to Sunday 8:30am to 2:30pm; admission is 500Dr ($1.70). Enter just behind the Panayia Ekatondapyliani. The museum has a lovely statue of a **winged victory** and part of the famous **Parian Chronicle,** a 3rd-century B.C. inscription recording important happenings in the history of ancient Greece.

Paros's best-known and most picturesque fishing village, **Naoussa,** with the remains of a Venetian castle, is in the throes of overdevelopment. Much of the construction is concentrated along the shore, and you can still find pleasant old streets in the village itself, as well as a number of new bars, restaurants, boutiques, and hotels. If you want a quieter spot and like butterflies, head for ✪ **Petaloudes,** the **Valley of the Butterflies,** about 6km (4 miles) out of Parikia. You can visit the colorful butterflies—actually moths—daily in season (usually May to July) from 9am to 8pm for 800Dr ($2.70). (Take the main coast road south out of Parikia; turn left at the sign for the Convent of Christou Dassos, and follow the signs.) The small **Museum of Popular Aegean Culture** (free) in the Lefkes Village Hotel in the village of Lefkes has examples of island pottery, furniture, and farm implements.

If you find Paros too crowded for your tastes, you can take a caïque over to **Antiparos,** a small island with some nice beaches, small tavernas (and rapidly increasing touristic development) half a mile offshore. Spelunkers will want to visit the **Cave of Antiparos,** open daily 10am to 4pm; admission is 500Dr ($1.65).

OUTDOOR ACTIVITIES   The free booklet *Paros Windsurfing Guide* has a good small map of the island, maps of several beaches, and useful information. It's especially good for those interested in water sports. The free publication *Summer Paros/Antiparos* also has a map of the island, a fairly good map of Parikia, and information.

There're **beaches** north along Parikia Bay, but beach seekers will probably want to head east to Naoussa Bay. One of the island's best and most famous beaches, picturesque **Kolymbithres,** where smooth giant rocks divide the golden sand beach into little coves, is an hour's walk or a 10-minute moped ride west from Naoussa. There're several tavernas and hotels nearby.

North of Kolymbithres, by Ayios Ioannis Church, is **Monastery Beach,** where there's some nudism, and the **Monasteri Club,** a bar and restaurant with music and beach service. Most of the other beaches west of Naoussa are overcrowded because of all the new hotels. Sandy **Santa Maria Beach,** on the northeast coast, is particularly popular with windsurfers; the Santa Maria Surf Club rents gear and sometimes gives lessons. There is also a fine beach and windsurfing facilities at **Chrissi Akti (Golden Beach),** half a mile of fine golden sand, which some consider the island's best beach. The frequent stiff winds make it a better spot for windsurfers than for sunbathers. South of the village of Drios, **Lolantonis Beach** is often surprisingly uncrowded. There're small tavernas on all these beaches.

PAROS AFTER DARK

Just behind the windmill is a local landmark, the **Port Cafe,** a basic *kafenio* lit by bare incandescent bulbs and filled day and night with tourists waiting for a ferry, bus, taxi, or fellow traveler. The **Saloon d'Or,** south of the port, is another spot for cheap drinks. If you're not in a mood to party, try the **Pebbles Bar,** where you can usually hear tapes of classical music at sunset, or the **Pirate Bar** (☎ 0284/21-114), in the Agora, where classical music alternates with jazz and blues. For partiers, there's the **Rendezvous,** where you'll hear rock music, and **Black Bart's** (☎ 0284/21-802), with loud music and a boisterous, boozy crowd.

In Naoussa, try **Leonardo's, Agosta,** or the **Sofrano Bar,** all on the harbor, or **Banana Moon,** just off the harbor.

Two movie theaters, the **Cine Rex** (☎ 0284/21-676) in Parika, and the **Makis** (☎ 0284/22-221) in Naoussa, are open all summer, and often have English language films.

Hungary 9

by Joseph S. Lieber & Christina Shea

The dramatic political changes of 1989 have irreversibly altered life in Hungary. Awakened after its long slumber behind the Iron Curtain, Hungary is now one of Europe's hottest destinations. Poised between East and West, both geographically and culturally, it's at the center of the region's rebirth. To best understand and appreciate Hungary, you ought to go beyond its stately capital. Get to know the great river that runs through the country's heart. take a slow boat (or a fast hydrofoil) up the Danube to the "Bend" towns of Szentendre, Esztergom, or Visegrád. For pure relaxation, you can sample the resorts at Europe's largest inland pond, Lake Balaton.

1 Budapest

Budapest came of age in the 19th century, at the start of which the two towns of Buda and Pest were little more than provincial outposts on the Danube. The dawning of a modern Hungarian identity spawned the city's neoclassical development. The rise of the eclectic style coincided with the great post-1867 boom, creating most of the historic inner city. Indeed, Budapest, notwithstanding its long and tattered history of Roman, Mongol, and Turkish conquest, is very much a late-19th-century city, with its characteristic coffeehouse and music hall culture. The decades after World War I and the fall of the Hapsburg monarchy weren't kind to Hungary's charming capital, and until recently Budapest's glory seemed irretrievably lost. How fitting it is, then, that Budapest's post–Cold War renaissance comes when it does: The city is once again attracting visitors from far and wide as the new century dawns.

Budapest retains an exotic feeling seldom experienced in the better-known capitals of Europe. Take a turn off any of the city's main boulevards and you'll quickly find yourself in a quiet residential neighborhood, where the scent of a hearty *gulyás* wafts from a kitchen window and cigarette smoke fogs the cavelike entry of the corner pub.

ORIENTATION

ARRIVING   By Plane   All flights arrive at **Ferihegy II,** located in the XVIII district in southeastern Pest. There are several main numbers: for arrivals, call ☎ **061/296-5052;** for departures, ☎ **061/ 296-5883;** and for general info, ☎ 061/**296-7155.**

Budapest

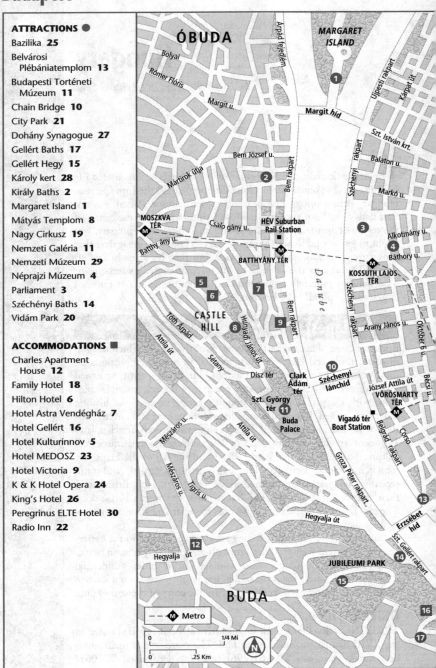

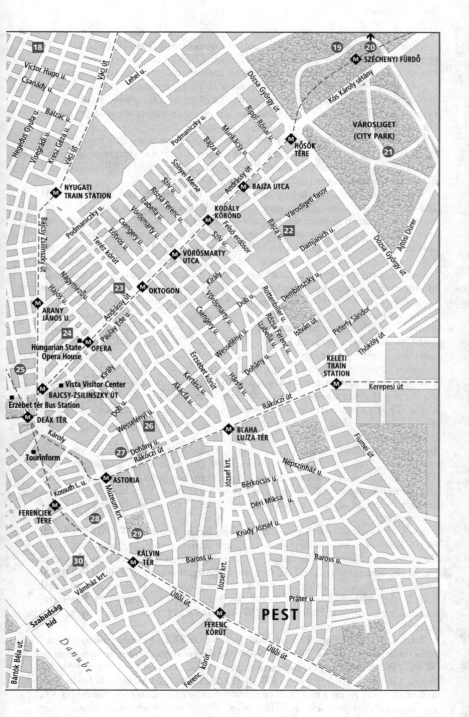

- 18
- Víctor Hugo u.
- Csanády u.
- Hegedűs Gyula u.
- Balzac u.
- Viségrádi u.
- Kresz Géza u.
- Váci út
- Lehel u.
- Váci út
- 19
- 20
- SZÉCHENYI FÜRDŐ
- Dózsa György út
- Kós Károly sétány
- VÁROSLIGET (CITY PARK)
- 21
- Podmaniczky u.
- Munkácsy u.
- Bajza u.
- Rippl-Rónai u.
- HŐSÖK TERE
- NYUGATI TRAIN STATION
- Szinyei Merse
- Szív u.
- Rózsa Ferenc u.
- Izabella u.
- Vörösmarty u.
- Podmaniczky u.
- Csengery u.
- Eötvös u.
- Teréz körút
- Andrássy út
- BAJZA UTCA
- KODÁLY KÖRÖND
- Felső erdősor
- Szív u.
- Városligeti fasor
- Bajza u.
- Damjanich u.
- Ajtósi Dürer
- Dózsa György út
- 22
- VÖRÖSMARTY UTCA
- Bajcsy Zsilinszky út
- Nagymező u.
- Hajós u.
- 23
- OKTOGON
- Király
- Vörösmarty u.
- Csengery u.
- Dob u.
- Rottenbiller u.
- Rózsa Ferenc u.
- Izabella u.
- István út
- Dembinszky u.
- Péterfy Sándor
- Thököly út
- ARANY JÁNOS U.
- Andrássy út
- Paulay Ede u.
- 24
- OPERA
- Hungarian State Opera House
- 25
- Vista Visitor Center
- BAJCSY-ZSILINSZKY ÚT
- Erzsébet tér Bus Station
- DEÁK TÉR
- Károly
- Tourinform
- Király
- Dob u.
- Wesselényi u.
- 26
- Erzsébet körút
- Kertész u.
- Akácfa u.
- Wesselényi u.
- Dohány u.
- Hársfa u.
- Rákóczi út
- KELETI TRAIN STATION
- Kerepesi út
- BLAHA LUJZA TÉR
- 27
- Dohány u.
- Rákóczi út
- ASTORIA
- Kossuth L. u.
- Múzeum krt.
- FERENCIEK TERE
- 28
- 29
- KÁLVIN TÉR
- 30
- Vámház krt.
- Szabadság híd
- Bartók Béla út.
- Danube
- József krt.
- Népszínház u.
- Bérkocsis u.
- Déri Miksa u.
- Krúdy József u.
- Baross u.
- Baross u.
- József krt.
- Üllői út
- Práter u.
- PEST
- FERENC KÖRÚT
- Ferenc körút
- Üllői út
- Filunei út

The easiest way into the city is probably the **Airport Minibus** (☎ 061/296-8555 or 061/296-8993), a service of the LRI (Budapest Airport Authority). The minibus, leaving every 10 or 15 minutes throughout the day, takes you directly to any city address and costs 1,200Ft ($5). The trip takes 30 minutes to an hour, depending on how many stops are made before your own. The Airport Minibus desk is easily found in the main hall. Minibuses also provide the same efficient service returning to the airports; arrange for your pickup *a full day in advance.*

LRI also runs an **Airport-Centrum** shuttle bus, leaving every half hour (5am to 9pm). Passengers are dropped off at Erzsébet tér, across from the Kempinski Hotel and just off Deák tér, where all three metro lines converge. The price is 600Ft ($2.50), and tickets are sold aboard the bus (trip time: 30 to 40 minutes).

We strongly *discourage* the use of cabs from the **Airport Taxi** fleet (☎ 061/ 282-2222), which is notoriously overpriced. A ride downtown from one of these cabs might cost as much as twice the fare in a cheaper fleet. Alas, for reasons no one has been able to explain to us with a straight face, cabs from the Airport Taxi fleet are the only cabs permitted to wait for fares on the airport grounds. However, dozens of cabs from the cheaper fleets we recommend are at all times stationed at roadside pullouts just off the airport property, a stone's throw from the terminal, waiting for radio calls from their dispatchers. You can phone from the terminal to any of these fleets and a cab will be there for you in a few minutes. (See "Getting Around" by taxi, below, for phone numbers.) For three or more people traveling together (and maybe even two people), a taxi from a recommended fleet to the city will be cheaper than the combined minibus fares, at about 2,900Ft ($12). A taxi from the airport to downtown takes about 20 to 30 minutes (see "Getting Around," below).

It's also possible (and very cheap) to get to the city by public transportation; the bus-to-metro-to-town trip takes about 1 hour total. Take the red-lettered **bus 93** to the last stop, Kóbánya-Kispest. From there, the Blue metro line runs to the Inner City of Pest. The cost is two transit tickets, which is 180Ft (75¢); you can buy tickets from the automated vending machine at the bus stop (coins only) or from any newsstand in the airport.

By Train   Budapest has three major train stations: Keleti pályaudvar (Eastern Station), Nyugati pályaudvar (Western Station), and Déli pályaudvar (Southern Station). The stations' names, curiously, correspond neither to their geographical location in the city nor to the origins or destinations of trains serving them. Each has a metro station beneath it and an array of accommodation offices, currency-exchange booths, and other services.

Most international trains pull into bustling **Keleti Station** (☎ 061/314-5010; metro: Keleti pu.), a classic steel-girdered European train station located in Pest's seedy Baross tér. In addition to the metro, numerous bus, tram, and trolleybus lines serve Baross tér. Some international trains arrive at **Nyugati Station** (☎ 061/349-0115; metro: Nyugati pu.), another classic of a station designed by the Eiffel company and built in the 1870s. Numerous tram and bus lines serve busy Nyugati tér. Few international trains arrive at **Déli Station** (☎ 061/375-6293; metro: Déli pu.), an ugly modern building in central Buda.

Train station phone numbers are good 8pm to 6am. During the day, obtain **in-land train information** at ☎ 061/461-5400 and **international train information** at ☎ 061/461-5500. Purchase **tickets** at train station ticket windows or from the MÁV Service Office, VI. Andrássy út 35 (☎ 061/322-8042), open Monday to Friday 9am to 6pm. You can access a timetable on the Web at www.elvira.mavinformatika.hu. (As you must conduct your search in Hungarian, it's helpful to know that *honnan* means "from where," *hova* "to where," *ma* "today," *holnap* "tomorrow," and *keres* "ask" or, in this context, "search.")

MÁV operates a **minibus** that'll take you from any of the three stations to any point in the city for 900Ft ($3.80) per person or between stations for 600Ft ($2.50) per person. To order the minibus, call ☎ **061/353-2722** or 061/357-2617. Often, however, a taxi fare will be cheaper, especially for groups of two or more travelers.

By Bus   Buses use three terminals, though plans are afoot to close the Erzsébet tér station and expand the Népstadion station. At the moment, however, buses to and from Western Europe and points in Hungary west of the Danube call at the **Erzsébet tér bus station** (☎ **061/317-2966** in-land info and 061/317-2562 international info; metro: Deák tér), in central Pest. Buses to and from Eastern and Central Europe, as well as points in Hungary east of the Danube, call at the **Népstadion bus station** (☎ **061/252-2995** in-land info and 061/252-1896 international info; metro: Népstadion). Buses to/from the Danube bend and other points north of Budapest call at the **Árpád híd bus station** (☎ **061/320-9229** or 317-9886; metro: Árpád híd).

By Car   Vienna, 275km (170 miles) from Budapest, connects to the Hungarian capital by the Austrian A4 superhighway, which becomes the M1 and feeds into the city via southern Buda. The border crossings from Austria and Slovakia are generally hassle-free. You may be requested to present your driver's license, vehicle registration, and proof of insurance (the number plate and symbol indicating country of origin are acceptable proof). Hungary doesn't require an international driver's license. Cars entering Hungary are required to have a decal indicating country of registration, a first-aid kit, and an emergency triangle.

By Hydrofoil   The Hungarian state shipping company **MAHART** operates hydrofoils on the Danube between Vienna and Budapest in spring and summer. It's an extremely popular route, so book your tickets well in advance; contact your local Austrian National Tourist Board. In Vienna, contact MAHART, Handelskai 265 (☎ **061/729-2161;** fax 061/729-2163). The Budapest office of **MAHART** is at V. Belgrád rakpart (☎ **061/318-1704** or 061/318-1586). Boats and hydrofoils from Vienna arrive at the international boat station next door to the MAHART office on the **Belgrád rakpart,** which is on the Pest side of the Danube, between the Szabadság and Erzsébet bridges.

VISITOR INFORMATION   The city's best info source is **Tourinform,** V. Sütó u. 2, just off Deák tér in Pest (☎ **061/317-9800** or 061/317-8992; www.hungarytourism. hu; metro: Deák tér). It's open daily 8am to 8pm. Another useful source is the **Vista Visitor Center,** V. Paulay Ede u. 7 (☎ **061/267-8603;** www.vista.hu; metro: Deák tér). It's open Monday to Friday 8am to 10pm and Saturday and Sunday 10am to 10pm.

CITY LAYOUT   The city of Budapest was founded in 1873 by joining three cities: Buda, Pest, and Óbuda. Budapest, like Hungary itself, is defined by the River Danube (Duna), along which many historic sites are found. Eight bridges join the two banks; five of them are in the city center.

On the right bank lies **Pest,** the commercial and administrative center. Central Pest is that part of the city between the river and the semicircular **Outer Ring boulevard (Nagykörút),** stretches of which take the names of former monarchs: Ferenc, József, Erzsébet, Teréz, and Szent István. The Outer Ring begins at the Pest side of the Petófi Bridge in the south and wraps itself around the center, ending at the Margit Bridge in the north. Several of Pest's busiest squares are along the Outer Ring, and Pest's major east–west avenues bisect it at these squares.

A Note on Addresses

Budapest is divided into 22 districts called **kerülets** (abbreviated ker.). A Roman numeral followed by a period precedes every written address in Budapest, signifying the kerület; for example, XII. Csörsz utca 9 is in the 12th kerület. Because many street names are repeated in different parts of the city, it's very important to know which kerület a certain address is in.

Central Pest proper is defined by the **Inner Ring (Kiskörút).** It starts at Szabadság híd (Freedom Bridge) in the south and is alternately named Vámház körút, Múzeum körút, Károly körút, Bajcsy-Zsilinszky út, and József Attila utca before ending at the Chain Bridge (Széchenyi lánchíd). Inside this ring is the **Belváros,** the historic Inner City of Pest.

Váci utca is a popular pedestrian shopping street between the Inner Ring and the Danube. It spills into **Vörösmarty tér,** one of the best-known squares. The **Dunakorzó (Danube Promenade),** a popular evening stroll, runs along the river in Pest, between the Chain Bridge and the Erzsébet Bridge. The **historic Jewish district** of Pest is in the Erzsébetváros, between the two ring boulevards. **Margaret Island (Margit-sziget)** is in the middle of the Danube. Accessible by the Margaret Bridge or Árpád Bridge, it's a popular park without vehicular traffic.

On the left bank is **Buda;** to its north, beyond the city center, lies Óbuda. Buda is as hilly as Pest is flat. **Castle Hill** is widely considered the most beautiful part of Budapest. A number of steep paths, staircases, and small streets go up to Castle Hill, but no major roads. The easiest access is from **Clark Ádám tér** (at the head of the Chain Bridge) by funicular, or from **Várfok utca** (near Moszkva tér) by foot or bus. Castle Hill consists of the royal palace itself, home to numerous museums, and the so-called **Castle District,** a lovely neighborhood of small, winding streets, centered on the Gothic Matthias Church. Below Castle Hill, along the Danube, is a long, narrow neighborhood, historically populated by fishermen and other river workers, known as the **Víziváros (Watertown). Central Buda** is a collection of low-lying neighborhoods below Castle Hill. The main square is **Moszkva tér,** just north of Castle Hill. Beyond Central Buda, mainly to the east, are the Buda Hills.

Óbuda is on the left bank of the Danube, north of Buda. Although the greater part of Óbuda is modern and drab, it features a beautiful old city center and impressive Roman ruins.

GETTING AROUND

Budapest has an extensive and inexpensive public transportation system. Its biggest disadvantage is that, except for 17 well-traveled bus and tram routes, all forms of transport shut down nightly at around 11:30pm; certain areas of the city, most notably the Buda Hills, are beyond the reach of the limited night service, so you have to take a taxi. Be on the alert for pickpockets when on crowded public transportation. Keep your money and valuables inside your clothing in a money belt.

All forms of public transportation require the self-validation of prepurchased **tickets (vonaljegy),** costing 90Ft (40¢) apiece (children under 6 travel free). Single tickets can be bought at metro ticket windows, newspaper kiosks, and the occasional tobacco shop. There are also automated machines in most metro stations and at major transportation hubs, but the older ones among these are not too reliable. On weekends and at night it can be rather difficult to find an open ticket window, so buy enough to avoid the trouble of constantly having to replenish your stock. For 810Ft

($3.40) you can get a **10-pack (*tizes csomag*),** and for 1,500Ft ($6), you can get a **20-pack (*huszos csomag*).**

Your best bet is to buy a day pass or multiday pass. Passes are inexpensive and need be validated only once. A pass will probably save you some money too, as you're likely to be getting on and off public transportation all day long. **Day passes (*napijegy*)** cost 700Ft ($3.15) and are valid until midnight of the day of purchase. Buy them from metro ticket windows; the clerk validates the pass at the time of purchase. A **3-day pass (*turistajegy*)** costs 1,400Ft ($6) and a **7-day pass (*hétibérlet*)** 1,750Ft ($7); these have the same validation procedure as the day pass. Anyone under 25 qualifies for a **10-day youth pass (*tiz napos ifjusági jegy*),** costing 1,500Ft ($6).

Plainclothes inspectors (who flip out a hidden red armband for ID) frequently come around checking for valid tickets, particularly at the top or bottom of the escalators to metro platforms. On-the-spot fines (1,200Ft/$5) are assessed to fare dodgers. All public transport operates on rough schedules, posted at bus and tram shelters and in metro stations. The Budapest Transport Authority (BKV térkép) produces a more detailed transportation map, available at most metro ticket windows for 200FT (85¢).

By Metro   The metro is clean and efficient, with trains running every 3 to 5 minutes from about 4:30am until about 11:30pm. The three lines are universally known by color—Yellow, Red, and Blue. Officially they have numbers as well (1, 2, and 3 respectively), but all signs are color-coded. All three lines converge at **Deák tér,** the only point where any meet.

The **Yellow (1) line** is the oldest metro on the European continent, but was fully renovated in 1996. This easily accessible line, just a few steps underground, runs from Vörösmarty tér in the heart of central Pest, out the length of Andrássy út, past the Városliget (City Park), ending at Mexikói út. Tickets for the Yellow line are validated on the train itself. The **Red (2) and Blue (3) lines** are modern metros, deep underground and accessible by escalator. The Red line runs from eastern Pest, through the center, across the Danube to Déli Station. The Blue line runs from southeastern Pest, through the center, to northern Pest. Tickets should be validated at the automated timestamp boxes before you descend the escalator. When changing lines at Deák tér, you must validate a new ticket at the orange machines in the hallway between lines.

By Bus   Many parts of the city, most notably the Buda Hills, are best accessed by bus **(*busz*).** Most lines are in service from about 4:30am to about 11:30pm, with less frequent weekend service on some. You must validate your bus ticket on board at the mechanical red box found by each door. Tickets cannot be purchased from the driver. You can board the bus by any door.

Black-numbered local buses constitute the majority of bus lines. Red-numbered are express. If the red number on the bus is followed by an *E,* the bus runs nonstop between terminals (whereas an *É*—with an accent—signifies *észak,* meaning night). A few buses are labeled by something other than a number; one you'll probably use is the **Várbusz (Palace Bus),** a minibus that runs between Várfok utca, off Buda's Moszkva tér, and the Castle District.

By Tram   You'll find Budapest's bright-yellow trams (known as *villamos* in Hungarian) very useful, particularly the **4 and 6,** which travel along the Outer Ring (Nagykörút). You must validate your ticket on board. As with buses, tickets are valid for one ride, not for the line itself. Trams stop at every station, and all doors open, regardless of whether anyone is waiting to get on. The buttons near the tram doors are for emergency stops, not stop requests.

By Trolleybus Red trolleybuses are electric buses that get power from a cable above the street. There are only 14 trolleybus lines in Budapest, all in Pest. Of particular interest to train travelers is no. 73, the fastest route between Keleti Station and Nyugati Station. All the information in the "By Bus" section above on boarding and ticket validation applies to trolleybuses as well.

By HÉV The HÉV is a suburban railway network that connects Budapest to various points along the city's outskirts. There are four HÉV lines; only one, the **Szentendre line,** is of serious interest to tourists. The terminus for the Szentendre HÉV line is Buda's Batthyány tér, also a station of the Red metro line. To reach Óbuda's Fó tér (Main Square), get off at the Árpád híd (Árpád Bridge) stop. The HÉV runs regularly between 4am and 11:30pm. For trips within the city limits, you need one transit ticket, available at HÉV ticket windows at the Batthyány tér station or from the conductor on board. These tickets are different from the standard transportation tickets and are punched by conductors on board. If you have a valid day pass, you do not need to buy a ticket for trips within the city limits.

By Taxi Budapest taxis are unregulated, so fares vary tremendously. Perhaps because there are more taxi drivers than the level of business can support, many drivers are experts at fleecing foreigners. However, if you watch out, taxis are still a bit cheaper than in the West. Several fleet companies have good reputations, honest drivers, and competitive rates. We particularly recommend **Fó Taxi** (☎ **061/222-2222**). Other reliable fleets are **Volántaxi** (☎ **061/466-6666**), **City Taxi** (☎ **061/211-1111**), **Tele5** (☎ **061/355-5555**), and **6x6** (☎ **061/266-6666**).

By Car We don't recommend using a car for sightseeing in Budapest. You may, however, want to rent one for trips outside the capital. We recommend **Denzel Europcar InterRent,** VIII. Üllői út 60–62 (☎ **061/313-1492** or 061/313-0207; fax 061/313-1492), where you can rent a Suzuki Swift for 5,500Ft ($23) per day (insurance included), plus 33Ft (14¢) per kilometer. They also have a rental counter at the airport (☎ **061/296-6610**), but there you pay an 11% airport tax. You might also try **LRI Airport Rent-A-Car,** with a counter at the airport (☎ or fax **061/296-7170**); they offer a Volkswagen Polo for $35 per day (insurance included) and 23¢ per kilometer.

Fast Facts: Budapest

American Express Budapest's only Amex office is between Vörösmarty tér and Deák tér in central Pest, at V. Deák Ferenc u. 10, 1052 Budapest (☎ **061/ 235-4330** or 061/235-4300; fax 061/267-2028; metro: Deák tér). Summer hours are Monday to Saturday 8:30am to 6:30pm and Sunday 8:30am to 2pm; winter hours are Monday to Friday 8:30am to 5:30pm and Saturday 9:30am to 2pm. There's an ATM on the street in front. Depending on whether your account allows it, it dispenses either cash (Forints only) or traveler's checks (U.S. dollars only). Check with American Express beforehand if you wish to use these ATMs abroad.

For lost traveler's checks, come to the office as soon as you can and they'll assist you. If you don't want to wait that long, use a 20Ft coin to initiate a call to England; the call is otherwise toll-free. Dial ☎ **00-800-11128.** For a lost credit card, make a local call to ☎ **061/235-4310** during business hours or 061/460-5233 after hours. If this is unsuccessful, try calling England at ☎ **00-44-181-551-1111** (or dial 00/800-04411 for the U.K. direct operator and ask to call collect).

Budapest Metro

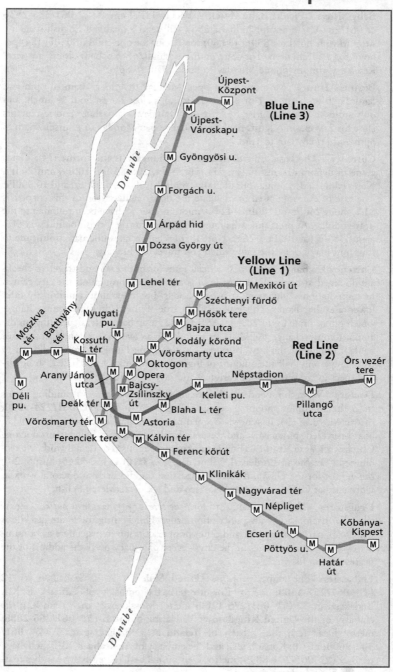

Újpest-
Központ

**Blue Line
(Line 3)**

Újpest-
Városkapu

Gyöngyösi u.

Forgách u.

Árpád hid

Dózsa György út

**Yellow Line
(Line 1)**

Lehel tér

Mexikói út

Széchenyi fürdő

Hősök tere

Nyugati
pu.

Bajza utca

Kodály körönd

Vörösmarty utca

Moszkva
tér

Batthyány
tér

Kossuth
L. tér

Oktogon

**Red Line
(Line 2)**

Örs vezér
tere

Arany János
utca

Opera

Bajcsy-
Zsilinszky
út

Népstadion

Deák tér

Keleti pu.

Blaha L. tér

Pillangő
utca

Déli
pu.

Vörösmarty tér

Astoria

Ferenciek tere

Kálvin tér

Ferenc körút

Klinikák

Nagyvárad tér

Népliget

Kőbánya-
Kispest

Ecseri út

Pöttyös u.

Határ
út

Danube

Baby-Sitters   **Ficuka Baby Hotel,** V. Váci u. 11b, I em. 9 (☎ **061/338-2836** or 061/267-0330; ask for Judit Zámbo), will send a qualified English-speaking sitter to your hotel for 850Ft ($3.60) for 1 hour for one child or 950Ft ($4) per hour for two children. For four or more children, two baby-sitters are sent. Reserve a sitter by phone Monday to Friday 8am to 8pm.

Business Hours   Most stores are open Monday to Friday 10am to 6pm and Saturday 9 or 10am to 1 or 2pm. Many shops close for an hour at lunch, and only stores in central tourist areas are open Sunday. Many shops and restaurants close for 2 weeks in August. Banks are usually open Monday to Thursday 8am to 3pm and Friday 8am to 1pm.

Currency   The basic unit of currency in Hungary is the **forint (Ft)**. Coins come in denominations of 1Ft, 2Ft, 5Ft, 10Ft, 20Ft, 50Ft, 100Ft, and 200Ft. Notes come in denominations of 200Ft, 500Ft, 1,000Ft, 5,000Ft, and 10,000Ft. The rate of exchange used to calculate the dollar values given in this chapter is $1 = about 240Ft (or 100Ft = 42¢). Amounts over $5 have been rounded to the nearest dollar. At press time, the rate of exchange for the British pound was £1 = about 385Ft (or 100Ft = 26p). Note that exchange rates fluctuate from time to time and may not be the same when you travel to Hungary.

Currency Exchange   The best official rates for both cash and traveler's checks are obtained at banks. Exchange booths are located throughout the city center, in train stations, and in most luxury hotels, but they almost uniformly offer lower rates than banks. This is particularly true of one chain called Inter Change, which offers a rate up to 20% lower than the going bank rate, depending on the amount you exchange. ATMs (Cirrus and Plus networks) are found in front of banks throughout the city. *Warning:* On departing Hungary, you're allowed to reexchange only half the amount of forints you originally purchased, so be circumspect in converting your currency and save all exchange receipts.

Doctors   We recommend the **American Clinic,** in a modern building across from the Mammut shopping center at I. Hattyu u. 14 (☎ **061/224-9090;** metro: Moszkva tér); its a newly opened private outpatient clinic with two U.S. board-certified physicians and several English-speaking Hungarian doctors. Check with Vista Visitor Center for discount coupons. For dental work, we recommend **Dr. Susan Linder,** II. Vihorlat u. 23 (☎ **061/335-5245;** bus: 5, 29), the dentist for the U.S. and British embassies; she did her postdoctoral work at University of California at San Francisco and speaks flawless English.

Drugstores   The Hungarian word for *drugstore* is *gyógyszertár* or *patika*. Generally, pharmacies carry only prescription drugs. Hotel "drugstores" are just shops with soap, perfume, aspirin, and other nonprescription items. There are a number of 24-hour pharmacies in the city—every pharmacy posts the address of the nearest one in its window.

Embassies   The embassy of the **United States** is at V. Szabadság tér 12 (☎ **061/267-4400;** metro: Kossuth tér); the embassy of **Canada** at XII. Budakeszi út 32 (☎ **061/275-1200;** metro: Moszkva tér, then tram 22); the embassy of the **United Kingdom** at V. Harmincad u. 6 (☎ **061/266-2888;** metro: Deák tér); the embassy of **Ireland** at V. Szabadság tér 7 (☎ **061/ 302-9600;** metro: Kossuth tér); and the embassy of **Australia** at XII. Királyhágo tér 8–9 (☎ **061/201-8899;** metro: Déli pu.). The U.K. embassy handles matters for **New Zealand** citizens.

Emergencies   Dial ☎ **104** for an ambulance, ☎ **105** for the fire department, or ☎ **107** for the police.

Internet Access   We generally use **Vista Visitor Center,** V. Paulay Ede u. 7 (☎ **061/267-8603;** metro: Deák tér), with about 10 terminals costing 11Ft (4¢) per minute; the wait is sometimes pretty long. It's open Monday to Friday 8am to 10pm and Saturday and Sunday 10am to 10pm. Another option, with less risk of a wait, is the **Internet Café,** V. Kecskeméti u. 5 (☎ **061/328-0292;** metro: Kálvin tér), with about 20 terminals costing 700Ft ($2.95) per hour, with pricing by 30-minute intervals (except 10 minutes or less, which costs 150Ft [65¢]).

Laundry & Dry Cleaning   Self-service launderettes (*patyolat*) are scarce in Budapest. The city's only centrally located Laundromat is at V. Varmegye u. 1, on the corner of Varosház utca, open Monday to Friday 7am to 7pm and Saturday 8am to 1pm (metro: Ferenciek tere). The chain *A Házimosoda* ("The Home Laundry"), with locations throughout Buda but none in Pest (☎ **061/275-6008**), is a new full-service laundry/dry-cleaning business that also offers a convenient pick-up and delivery service. Open Monday to Friday 7am to 7pm and Saturday 8am to 3pm. For 1-hour dry cleaning, try **Ruhatisztító Top Clean,** VI. Nyugati Skala, across from the train station (metro: Nyugati pu.); it's open Monday to Friday 7am to 7pm and Saturday 9am to 2pm.

Post Office   The main branch of the Hungarian Postal Service (Magyar Posta) is at V. Petófi Sándor u. 17–19, 1052 Budapest, Hungary (metro: Deák tér). This rather confusing office is open Monday to Friday 8am to 8pm and Saturday 8am to 2pm. The post office at VIII. Baross tér 11/c (metro: Keleti pu.) is open Monday to Saturday 7am to 9pm. The post office at VI. Teréz krt. 51 (metro: Nyugati pu.) is open Monday to Saturday 7am to 9pm and Sunday 8am to 8pm. At press time, an airmail postcard costs 95Ft (40¢); an airmail letter 140Ft (59¢) and up. The rate for letters mailed in Budapest to a Budapest address is 27Ft (11¢), and postcards to a Budapest address cost 24Ft (10¢). For letters mailed to other parts of Hungary, the rate is 32Ft (13¢); for postcards, 27Ft (11¢). At press time, an airmail postcard costs 95Ft (40¢); an airmail letter, 140Ft (59¢) and up.

Safety   By U.S. standards, Budapest is a relatively safe city—muggings and violent attacks are rare. Nevertheless, foreigners are always prime targets. Though they're clearly less of a threat now than a few years ago, teams of professional pickpockets still plague Budapest, operating on crowded trams, metros, and buses. Be particularly careful on bus 26 (Margaret Island) and trams 4 and 6 or in any other crowded setting. The pickpockets' basic trick is to create a distraction to take your attention away from yourself and your own security. Avoid being victimized by wearing a money belt under your clothes instead of wearing a fanny pack or carrying a wallet or purse. No valuables should be kept in the outer pockets of a knapsack.

Taxes   Taxes are included in all restaurant prices, hotel rates, and shop purchases. Refunds on the 25% **value-added tax (VAT),** which is built into all prices, is available for most consumer goods purchases of more than 50,000Ft ($210)—look for stores with the "Tax-Free" logo in the window. The refund process, however, is elaborate and confusing. In most shops, the salesperson can provide you with the necessary documents: the store receipt, a separate receipt indicating the VAT amount on your purchase, the VAT reclaim form, and the mailing envelope. The salesperson should also be able to help you fill out the paperwork. You'll need to include your currency exchange receipt if it was a cash purchase (or credit-card receipt for credit card purchase). You must hold on to the full packet until you leave Hungary, at which point you can get your forms certified by Customs. Then mail in your envelope and wait for your refund. Two wrinkles: You must get your forms certified by Customs within 90 days of the purchase and must mail in your forms within 183 days of the date of export certification to the refund claim form. Use a separate claim form for each applicable purchase. For more details, contact **Global Refund,** II. Bég u. 3–5, 1022 Budapest (☎ **061/212-4734,** ext. 118; fax 061/212-4906; taxfree@hu. globalrefund.com; www.globalrefund.com).

Telephone   The **country code** for Hungary is **36.** The **city code** for Budapest is **1;** use this code when you're calling from outside Hungary. If you're within Hungary but not in Budapest, first dial **06;** when you hear a tone, dial the city code and phone number. If you're calling within Budapest, simply leave off the code and dial only the regular seven-digit phone number.

Be aware that Budapest phone numbers are constantly changing as MATÁV continues to upgrade its system. Note, for instance, that any number beginning with a "1" has been changed; try replacing the 1 with a 3 or 4. Usually, if the number you're dialing has changed, you'll get a recording first in Hungarian and than in English, indicating the new number. If further information is needed, dial ☎ **198** for directory assistance.

The Hungarian phone company MATÁV provides much better service than in the past, but it still falls significantly short of Western standards. For best results, dial slowly and don't be too quick to trust a busy signal—try again.

Numbers beginning with 06-20 or 06-30, followed by a seven-digit number, are **mobile phone numbers.** If the mobile number you've been given has only six digits, it's incorrect; add a 9 before the other six digits. Be aware that you pay for a long-distance call when you call a mobile phone. A GTE Hungarian yellow pages phone number search is available in English on the Web at www. gte-yellow-pages.com/2Eng.htm.

Public **pay phones** charge varying amounts for local calls depending on the time of day you place your call. It's apparently cheapest to call late in the evenings and on weekends. Public phones operate with 20Ft coins or with phone cards (in 50 or 120 units) you can buy from post offices, tobacco shops, supermarkets, travel agencies, and any MATÁV customer service office (MATÁV Pont).

For **international calls,** there are several options. Our preferred method is to make all international calls from abroad through a U.S.-based "callback" service. Calls made in this manner are billed at competitive U.S. calling rates, which are significantly cheaper than Hungarian international rates. These services generally charge an activation fee and a monthly maintenance fee, as well as other fees, so you ought to make a judgment as to whether you're likely to be making enough calls for it to be worthwhile. A company called **Kallback** seems to offer the best package (☎ **800/959-5255** or 800/516-9992; www.kallback.com). Other "callback" companies worth looking into are **Justice Technology** (☎ **310/526-2000;** www.justicecorp.com), **New World Telecommunications** (☎ **201/287-8400;** www.newworldtele.com), and **Frontier Communications** (☎ **800/584-3384;** www.frontiercorp.com).

Alternatively, you can use a phone card and access the international operator through a public phone, though older phones are less reliable; again, a 20Ft coin is required to start the call. You can also place an international call at the post office at VI. Teréz krt. 51 (metro: Nyugati pu.), as well as from these MATÁV offices: MATÁV Pont Mammut at I. Széna tér and MATÁV Pont Budai Skála at XI. Október 23 u. The main telecommunications office, at Petőfi Sándor u. 17 (metro: Deák tér), also provides telephone service but at press time was closed indefinitely for reconstruction. The above-mentioned phone card will allow you to call the United States and Canada for 138Ft (58¢) per minute, 24 hours a day. There's a 9Ft connecting fee. Purchase either 50-unit (800Ft/$3.35) or 120-unit (1,800Ft/$8) cards.

You can reach the **AT&T** operator at ☎ **00/800-01111,** the **MCI** operator at ☎ **00/800-01411,** and the **Sprint** operator at ☎ **00/800-01877.**

Tipping   Tipping is generally 10%. Among those who welcome tips are waiters, taxi drivers, hotel employees, barbers, cloakroom attendants, toilet attendants, masseuses, and tour guides.

WHERE TO STAY

One of the happy developments of the post-1989 boom in Budapest has been the proliferation of new pensions and small hotels. The better choices among these—and the less expensive—are usually outside the city center, but all the places we list can easily be reached by public transportation. Notwithstanding the arrival of these new places, Budapest retains its reputation as a city without enough guest beds. Indeed, in high season it can be difficult to secure a hotel or pension room or hostel bed, so make reservations and get written confirmation well ahead if possible.

An alternative is a room in a **private apartment.** Typically, you share the bath with the hosts or with other guests. Breakfast isn't officially included, but the host will often offer continental breakfast for 400Ft to 600Ft ($1.70 to $2.50). You may have limited kitchen privileges (ask in advance). Some hosts will greet you when you arrive, give you a key, and seemingly disappear; others will want to befriend you, show you around, and cook for you. Most rooms are adequate, some even memorable, but any number of reasons may cause you to dislike yours: Noisy neighborhoods, tiny baths, and bad coffee are among the complaints we've heard. The great majority of visitors, though, appear to be satisfied; at the very least, staying in a private room provides a window into everyday Hungarian life you'd otherwise miss.

The most established agencies are the former state-owned travel agents **Ibusz, Cooptourist,** and **Budapest Tourist.** Although newer, private agencies have proliferated, the older ones tend to have the greatest number of rooms listed. There are agencies at the airport, all three major train stations, throughout central Pest, and along the main roads into Budapest for travelers arriving by car. The main **Ibusz reservations office** is at Ferenciek tere 10 (☎ **061/318-6866;** fax 061/318-2805; metro: Ferenciek tere), open summer Monday to Friday 8:15am to 5:30pm and Saturday 9am to 1pm; off-season, Monday to Friday to 4:30. All major credit cards are accepted.

IN THE INNER CITY & CENTRAL PEST
Very Expensive

✪ **K & K Hotel Opera.** VI. Révay u. 24, 1065 Budapest. ☎ **061/269-0222.** Fax 061/269-0230. www.kkhotels.com. 205 units. A/C MINIBAR TV TEL. 270DM ($146) double. Rates 5% lower in low season. Rates include breakfast. AE, DC, EURO, MC, V. Parking 13DM ($7). Metro: Opera.

Operated by the Austrian K & K hotel chain, this tasteful, elegant establishment opened in 1994 and expanded in 1997. Directly across the street from the Opera House in central Pest, the hotel blends nicely with its surroundings. The interior is equally pleasing. The staff is uniformly friendly and helpful. Rooms have safes. No-smoking rooms are available. Pets are welcome. The hotel has a sauna and fitness room and a business center.

Moderate

King's Hotel. VII. Nagydiófa u. 25–27 Budapest. ☎ and fax **061/352-7675.** 79 units. A/C TV TEL. $70–$80 double; $140 suite. Rates include breakfast. AE, DC, MC, V. Parking available on street for $5 per day. Metro: Astoria.

King's Hotel opened for business in 1995 in a beautifully renovated and restored fin de siècle building in the heart of Pest's Jewish district. The reception is uniformly friendly and helpful. Despite the somewhat drab modern furnishings, rooms retain a 19th-century atmosphere, many with small balconies overlooking the quiet residential street. Most, but not all have a private bathroom. The hotel restaurant is strictly kosher and is open for breakfast, lunch, and dinner; food is prepared under the observation of Rabbi Hoffman. Conference rooms are available.

Inexpensive

Hotel MEDOSZ. VI. Jókai tér 9, 1061 Budapest. ☎ **061/374-3000.** Fax 061/332-4316. 68 units. TV TEL. 80DM ($43) double. Rates include breakfast. Rates 15% lower in low season. No credit cards. Parking difficult in neighborhood. Metro: Oktogon.

The MEDOSZ's location on sleepy Jókai tér, in the heart of Pest's theater district and not far from the Opera House, is as good as it gets off the river in central Pest. Though the hotel hasn't been renovated since privatization (it once was a trade-union hotel), it remains a great value given its location, with simple but clean rooms. Next door is one of Budapest's special treats for children: a puppet theater (*bábszínház*). Note that there's talk of changing the hotel name to Cédrus (Cedar).

☉ **Peregrinus ELTE Hotel.** V. Szerb u. 3, 1056 Budapest. ☎ **061/266-4911.** Fax 061/266-4913. 26 units. MINIBAR TV TEL. 13,200Ft ($71) double. Rates include breakfast. No credit cards. No parking. Metro: Kálvin tér.

This is the guest house of Pest's ELTE University, and its location couldn't be better—in the heart of the Inner City, on a small side street just half a block from the quiet southern end of the popular pedestrians-only Váci utca. Reserve at least a week ahead. The building dates from the early 1900s and was renovated in 1994, when the guest house was opened. Rooms are simple but comfortable.

JUST BEYOND CENTRAL PEST

Expensive

Family Hotel. XIII. Ipoly u. 8/b, 1133 Budapest. ☎ **061/320-1284.** Fax 061/329-1620. E-mail: family.hotel@mail.matav.hu. 13 units. A/C MINIBAR TV TEL. 160DM–180DM ($86–97) double; 240DM ($130) suite. Rates include breakfast. Rates 20% lower in low season. AE, DC, JCB, MC, V. Parking available on the street. Metro: Keleti pu., then trolleybus 79 to Ipoly utca.

Traveler's Tip

Most hotels and pensions in Budapest divide the year into three seasons. **High season** is roughly from March or April to September or October and the week between Christmas and New Year's. **Midseason** is usually considered March and October and/or November. **Low season** is roughly November to February, except Christmas week. Some hotels discount as much as 50% in low season, while others offer no winter discount; be sure to inquire.

A charming, elegant little place opened in 1991, the Family Hotel stands 2 blocks from the Danube in a quiet, mostly residential neighborhood in the Újlipótváros (New Leopold Town), just north of the Inner City of Pest. Perhaps the nicest thing about this hotel is the low-key atmosphere; it has only one bar (in the Hungarian/international restaurant) and there's very little for sale elsewhere. The suites, all duplexes, are among the nicest in the city, with skylights over the upstairs bedrooms and enormous floor-to-ceiling windows. All rooms are spacious, with simple wood furniture and large bathrooms.

Inexpensive

✪ Radio Inn. VI. Benczúr u. 19, 1068 Budapest. ☎ **061/342-8347** or 061/322-8284. Fax 061/322-8284. 32 units. TV TEL. 9,500–19,500Ft ($40–$82) apt for 1 to 3. Breakfast 1,050Ft ($4.40). MC, V. Parking available on street. Metro: Bajza utca.

As the official guest house of Hungarian National Radio, the Radio Inn houses many visiting dignitaries, and also offers apartments to individual tourists. Reserve well ahead. The inn is in an exclusive embassy neighborhood (next door to the embassy of China), a stone's throw from City Park, and a block from Pest's grand Andrássy út. The Yellow line takes you into the center of Pest in 5 minutes; alternatively, it's a 30-minute walk. Behind the building, there's an enormous private courtyard full of flowers. The huge apartments (all with fully equipped, spacious kitchens) are comfortably furnished and painstakingly clean. Note that the toilets and bathrooms are separate, European style. The management is somewhat old-system (read: begrudging with information, slightly suspicious of foreigners), yet cordial enough. Laundry service is available.

IN CENTRAL BUDA & THE CASTLE DISTRICT

Very Expensive

Hilton Hotel. I. Hess András tér 1–3, 1014 Budapest. ☎ **061/488-6600.** Fax 061/488-6644. www.hilton.com. 322 units. A/C MINIBAR TV TEL. 390DM–580DM ($211–$313) double; 650DM–900DM ($351–$486) suite. Children stay free in parents' room. Breakfast 29DM ($16). AE, DC, MC, V. Parking for a fee in garage. Metro Moszkva tér, then bus "Várbusz"; or Deák tér, then bus 16.

One of only two hotels in Buda's elegant Castle District (the other is Hotel Kulturinnov), the Hilton, built in 1977, is widely considered the city's classiest hotel. Its location, on Hess András tér, next door to Matthias Church and the Fisherman's Bastion, is no less than spectacular. The award-winning design incorporates the ruins of a 13th-century Dominican church and the baroque facade of a 17th-century Jesuit college (the main entrance). Although the building is clearly modern, its tasteful exterior blends in fairly well with the surrounding Castle District architecture. More expensive rooms have views over the Danube, with a full Pest skyline; rooms on the other side of the hotel overlook the delightful streets of the Castle District. Bathrooms have hair dryers.

Hotel Gellért. XI. Gellért tér 1, 1111 Budapest. ☎ **061/385-2200.** Fax 061/466-6631. www.danubiusgroup.com/danubius/gellert.html. 233 units. MINIBAR TV TEL. 350DM–376DM ($189–$203) double; 466DM–500DM ($252–$270) suite. Rates include breakfast. Spa packages available. AE, DC, MC, V. Free parking. Metro: Deák tér, then tram 47 or 49.

First opened in 1918, this splendid, sprawling art nouveau hotel, located in Buda at the base of Gellért Hill on the bank of the Danube, has not seen renovation since 1970. It's pretty run-down now, but still one of the most charming hotels in Budapest. The quality and size of the rooms vary greatly—it seems to be hit or miss. Only 20 rooms have air-conditioning. Some rooms with balconies offer great views over the

Danube, but these can be noisy since the hotel fronts loud and busy Gellért Square. The Gellért is one of several thermal hotels managed or owned by Danubius Hotels. While the majority of guests don't come for the official spa treatment, there are a number of spa-related facilities available free of charge: indoor swimming pool and outdoor pool with waves (in summer), steam room, and the Gellért Baths, perhaps the most popular of Budapest's thermal baths.

Expensive

✪ **Hotel Astra Vendégház.** I. Vám u. 6, 1011 Budapest. ☎ **061/214-1906.** Fax 061/214-1907. 12 units. A/C MINIBAR TV TEL. 190DM ($102) double. Rates include breakfast. Rates 10% lower in low season. No credit cards. Parking available on street. Metro: Batthyány tér.

This little gem was opened in 1996 in a renovated 300-year-old building on a quiet side street in Buda's lovely Watertown. Rooms are large, and far more homey and pleasant than most hotel rooms. Indeed, the hotel is tasteful throughout and the staff friendly. Some rooms overlook the inner courtyard, while others face onto the street.

Hotel Victoria. I. Bem rakpart 11, 1011 Budapest. ☎ **061/457-8080.** Fax 061/457-8088. www.victoria.hu. 27 units. A/C MINIBAR TV TEL. 199DM ($107) double; 350DM ($189) suite for two. Rates include breakfast. Rates 25% lower in low season. AE, DC, EURO, MC, V. Parking in garage 17DM ($9). Metro: Batthyány tér, then tram 19 to first stop.

The Hotel Victoria, located in Buda's lovely Watertown district, is separated from the Danube bank by the busy road that runs alongside the river. The narrow building has only three rooms on each of its nine floors. Two-thirds are corner rooms with large double windows providing great views over the river to Pest. Rooms are quite large, with spacious bathrooms. Middle rooms, though smaller than corner ones, also have windows facing the river. Unfortunately, noise from the busy road beneath your window may disturb your rest. The hotel is just minutes by foot from both Batthyány tér and Clark Ádám tér, with dozens of metro, tram, and bus connections.

Moderate

✪ **Hotel Kulturinnov.** I. Szentháromság tér 6, 1014 Budapest. ☎ **061/355-0122** or 061/375-1651. Fax 061/375-1886. 16 units. TEL. $75 double. Rates include breakfast. AE, DC, MC, V. Parking 2,000Ft ($8). Metro: Moszkva tér, then bus "Várbusz"; or Deák tér, then bus 16.

This little guest house of the Hungarian Culture Foundation, in the very heart of Buda's Castle District, is dedicated to forging ties with ethnic Hungarians in neighboring countries. It's open to the public, but few travelers know about it. Rooms are small and simple; nothing is modern, but everything works and the bathrooms are clean. Though located in the large building directly across from Matthias Church and the Plague Column, it can be a bit hard to find; the entrance is unassuming and practically unmarked. Go through the iron grille door and pass through an exhibition hall, continuing up the grand red-carpeted staircase to the right.

Inexpensive

✪ **Charles Apartment House.** I. Hegyalja út 23, 1016 Budapest. ☎ **061/201-1796.** Fax 061/202-2984. E-mail: charles@mail.matav.hu. 26 units. TV TEL. $44–$55 apt for 1 or 2, $70 apt for 3. Rates include breakfast. Rates 10%–15% lower in low season. AE, DC, MC, V. Parking 1,000Ft ($4.20) per day or for free on nearby side street. Metro: Keleti pu., then bus 78 to Mészáros utca.

Owner Károly Szombati has amassed 22 apartments in a building in a dull but convenient Buda neighborhood (near the large luxury Novotel), as well a handful of apartments in nearby buildings. All are average Budapest apartments with full kitchens.

The furnishings are comfortable and clean. Hegyalja út is a very busy street, but only two apartments face onto it; the rest are in the interior or on the side of the building.

IN THE BUDA HILLS
Moderate
Gizella Panzió. XII. Arató u. 42/b, 1121 Budapest. ☎ and fax **061/249-2281.** E-mail: gazella@mail.matav.hu. 14 units. MINIBAR TV TEL. 125DM ($68) double; 140DM ($76) suite. Rates include breakfast. Rates lower in low season. EURO, MC, V. Free parking. Metro: Moszkva tér, then tram 59 to the last stop.

This fine pension in the Buda Hills is a 10-minute walk from the tram station. Built on the side of a hill, it has a lovely view and a series of terraced gardens leading down to the swimming pool. The pension also features a sauna, solarium, fitness room, and bar. Rooms are unique but uniformly quaint, sunny, and tasteful. Owner Gizella Varga also rents fully furnished apartments in the center of town for 110DM to 180DM ($59 to $97), depending on the number of people.

WHERE TO DINE
You can get more for your money dining in Budapest than anywhere in Western Europe. The selection of international eateries is wide, and the Hungarian cuisine itself adventurous with spices. In most restaurants, you have to initiate the paying and tipping ritual by summoning the waiter. The bill is then written out on the spot. If you think the bill is incorrect, don't be embarrassed to call it into question; waiters readily correct the bill when challenged. In all but the fanciest restaurants, the waiter stands there waiting patiently for payment after handing over the bill. The tip (generally about 10%) should be included in the amount you give him. State the full amount you are paying (bill plus tip) and the waiter will make change. Hungarians never leave tips on the table.

Étterem is the most common Hungarian word for restaurant and is used for everything from cafeteria-style eateries to first-class restaurants. A *vendéglő*, or guest house, is a smaller, more intimate restaurant, often with a Hungarian folk motif; a *csárda* is a countryside vendéglő. An *étkezde* is an informal lunchroom open only in the daytime. *Önkiszolgáló* means self-service cafeteria, typically open only for lunch. Stand-up *bufes* are often found in bus stations and near busy transport hubs. A *cukrászda* or *kávéház* is a classic Central European coffeehouse, where lingering has developed into an art form. A *borozó* is a wine bar, a *söröző* is a beer bar; sandwiches are usually available at both. Finally, a *kocsma* is a sort of roadside tavern; the Buda Hills are filled with them. Most kocsmas serve full (if greasy) dinners, but the kitchens close very early.

IN THE INNER CITY & CENTRAL PEST
Expensive
Légrádi & Társa. V. Magyar u. 23. ☎ **061/318-6804.** Reservations highly recommended. Soup 600–700Ft ($2.50–$2.95); main courses 2,000–3,000Ft ($8–$13). AE, CB, MC, V. Mon–Sat 6pm–midnight. Metro: Kálvin tér. HUNGARIAN.

Very small (nine tables) and inconspicuously marked, on a sleepy side street in the southern part of the Inner City, this is one of the city's most elegant and formal restaurants. The food is served on Herend china, the cutlery is sterling, and an excellent string trio livens the atmosphere. We suggest you pass on the initial premenu offer of hors d'oeuvres costing 1,500Ft ($6). If you'd like to try a soup, the cream of asparagus is a fine interpretation of a Hungarian favorite. The chicken paprika served with cheese dumplings seasoned with fresh dill will surpass any you've tried elsewhere, and the veal, smothered in cauliflower-cheese sauce, is delightful.

Lou Lou. V. Vigyázó F. u. 4. ☎ **061/312-4505.** Reservations recommended. Appetizers 400–1,500Ft ($1.70–$6); main courses 1,000–2,700Ft ($4.20–$11). DC, DISC, MC, V. Mon–Fri noon–3pm and 7pm–midnight; Sat 7pm–midnight. Closed Sun. Metro: Deák tér or Kossuth tér. FRENCH.

Located on a quiet side street not far from Parliament in the financial district, this is a handsome new addition to the Budapest dining scene. The decor is rustic and taste-ful, with Roman yellow walls and a vaulted ceiling. For starters, you might try the cold peach soup, excellent and refreshing, followed by the vegetarian strudel, a good deal at 1,000Ft ($4.20). Lou Lou features an extensive wine list, ranging to 4,500Ft ($19) a bottle. House wine is also available.

Moderate

✪ **Marquis de Salade.** VI. Hajós u. 43. ☎ **061/302-4086.** Appetizers 750–2,500Ft ($3.15–11); main courses 1,200–2,800Ft ($5—$12). V. Daily 11am–midnight. Metro: Arany János u. ASIAN/MIDDLE EASTERN/AFRICAN.

Vegetarians will feel right at home here. On the edge of Pest's theater district, this recently renovated restaurant employs eight cooks from various countries (Russia, Bangladesh, East Africa, Hungary, China, Italy, and the Caucasus Mountains) and turns out an amazing assortment of exceptional dishes from a number of cuisines. The offerings are sophisticated yet earthy. Try the lamb with rice (Caucasian) or the borscht (Russian). A no-smoking area is available, and tablecloths and tapestries are for sale.

Inexpensive

Kádár Étkezde. VII. Klauzál tér 9. ☎ **061/321-3622.** Soup 140Ft (60¢); main courses 360–570Ft ($1.50–$2.40). No credit cards. Tues–Sat 11:30am–3:30pm. Metro: Astoria or Deák tér. HUNGARIAN.

By 11:45am, Uncle Kádár's, in the heart of the Jewish district, is filled with regulars—from paint-spattered workers to elderly Jewish couples. Uncle Kádár, a neighborhood legend, personally greets them as they file in. From the outside the only sign of the place is a very small red sign saying "Kádár Étkezde." The place is no more than a lunchroom, but it has a great atmosphere: high ceilings, wood-paneled walls with pho-tos (many autographed) of actors and athletes, and old-fashioned seltzer bottles on every table. The food is simple but hearty and the service friendly. Table sharing is the norm.

Mérleg Vendéglő. V. Mérleg u. 6. ☎ **061/317-6911.** Soup 180–260Ft (75¢–$1.10); main courses 500–1,180Ft ($2.10–$4.95). MC, V. Mon–Sat 8am–11pm. Metro: Deák tér. HUNGARIAN.

This inexpensive little restaurant, a few minutes' walk from the central tourist area of the Inner City, serves traditional Hungarian cuisine in an authentic atmosphere with shared tables. It's the perfect alternative to the expensive tourist traps on Váci utca. The specials are written on chalkboard in Hungarian only, but are worth asking about. Start with the cold cucumber soup in summer, then try stuffed cabbage (*töltött kaposz-ta*) or chicken paprika (*paprikás csirke*) for your main dish.

JUST BEYOND CENTRAL PEST
Very Expensive

Gundel. XIV. Állatkerti út 2. ☎ **061/322-1002** or 061/321-3550. Reservations highly rec-ommended. Soup 800Ft ($3.35); main courses 2,500–4,980Ft ($11–$21). AE, DC, EURO, MC, V. Daily noon–4pm and 7pm–midnight. Metro: Hősök tere. HUNGARIAN/INTERNATIONAL.

Budapest's fanciest and most famous historic restaurant, Gundel was reopened in 1992 by the well-known restaurateur George Lang, owner of New York's Café des Artistes. Located in City Park, Gundel has an opulent dining room and a large, carefully

Coffeehouse Culture

Imperial Budapest, like Vienna, was famous for its coffeehouse culture. Literary movements and political circles alike were identified in large part by which coffeehouse they met in. You can still go to several classic coffeehouses, all of which offer delicious pastries, coffee, and more in an atmosphere of splendor. Table sharing is common.

The best are **Gerbeaud's,** in the Inner City at V. Vörösmarty tér 7 (☎ 1/ 318-1311); ✪ **Művész Kávéház,** across the street from the Opera House at VI. Andrássy út 29 (☎ 1/352-1337) (Yellow line, Opera); the **New York Kávéház,** on the Outer Ring at VII. Erzsébet krt. 9–11 (☎ 1/322-3849) (but avoid the overpriced and mediocre dinners here) (Red line, Blaha Lujza tér); **Ruszwurm Cukrászda,** in the Castle District at I. Szentháromság u. 7 (☎ 1/375-5284) (Várbusz [Castle Bus] from Moszva tér); and ✪ **Angelika Cukrászda,** also in Buda, at I. Batthyány tér 7. (☎ 1/201-4847) (Red line, Batthyány tér).

groomed garden. The kitchen prides itself on preparing traditional dishes in an innovative fashion. Lamb and wild-game entrees are house specialties. The menu highlights fruits and vegetables in season. In late spring, don't miss out on the asparagus served in hollandaise with grilled salmon. Gundel has an extensive wine list, and the waiters are well versed in its offerings. Homemade fruit ice cream served in the shape of the fruit makes for a delectable dessert, as does the famous Gundel torta, a decadently rich chocolate layer cake.

IN CENTRAL BUDA

Expensive

Kacsa Vendéglő. I. Fő u. 75. ☎ **061/201-9992.** Reservations recommended. Soup 400–500Ft ($1.70–$2.10); main courses 1,900–3,000Ft ($8–$13). MC, V. Daily 6pm–1am. Metro: Batthyány tér. HUNGARIAN.

Kacsa (meaning "duck") is located on the main street of Watertown, the Buda neighborhood that lies between Castle Hill and the Danube. Here you'll find an intimate, elegant, and understated dining atmosphere, though the service seems overly attentive and ceremonious. Enticing main courses include roast duck with Morello cherries, haunch of venison with grapes, and pike-perch Russian style. The vegetarian plate is the best we've had anywhere.

Moderate

Le Jardin de Paris. I. Fő u. 20. ☎ **061/201-0047.** Reservations recommended. Soup 550–850Ft ($2.30–$3.55); appetizers 750–2,000Ft ($3.15–$8); main courses 950–2,000Ft ($4–$8). AE, DC, MC, V. Daily noon–12am. Metro: Batthyány tér. FRENCH.

This wonderful little French bistro is in the heart of Buda's Watertown, across from the hideous Institut Français. A cozy cellar space, it's decorated with an eclectic collection of graphic arts, with a jazz trio entertaining diners. The menu contains nouvelle French specialties, and the wine list features French as well as Hungarian vintages. The presentation is impeccable and the waiters aren't overbearing. In summer there's outdoor seating in a new garden area.

Taverna Ressaikos. I. Apor Péter u. 1. ☎ **061/212-1612.** Reservations recommended. Soup and appetizers 300–800Ft ($1.25–$3.35); main courses 750–1,300Ft ($3.15–$5). AE, EU, MC. Daily noon–midnight. Metro: Deák tér, then bus 16 to Clark Ádám tér. GREEK.

In the heart of Buda's Watertown, next to the Hotel Carlton Budapest, the Ressaikos features generous portions of carefully prepared food at reasonable prices. Try the calamari or the lamb in wine sauce. The menu also features a number of interesting goat dishes. Vegetarians can easily make a meal of the appetizers: stuffed tomatoes, spanakopita, tsatsiki, and the like. The live guitar music (weekends only) can get a bit loud, and the service, while attentive, is definitely slow.

IN THE BUDA HILLS
Moderate

✪ **Náncsi Néni Vendéglője.** II. Órdögárok út 80. ☎ **061/397-2742.** Reservations recommended for dinner. Main courses 500–950Ft ($2.10–$4). AE, CB, DC, DISC, EURO, JCB, MC, V. Daily noon–11pm. Metro: Moszkva tér, then tram 56 to last stop, then bus 63 to Széchenyi utca. HUNGARIAN.

Decorated with photographs of early 1900s Budapest, this popular but remote restaurant is located high in the Buda Hills. There's outdoor garden dining in the summer, with live accordion music at night. The menu features typical Hungarian dishes, prepared with great care.

Szép Ilona. II. Budakeszi út 1–3. ☎ **061/275-1392.** Soup 290–610Ft ($1.20–$2.55); main courses 780–1,800Ft ($3.30–$8). No credit cards. Daily 11:30am–10pm. Metro: Moszkva tér, then bus 158 (departs from Csaba utca, at the top of the stairs, near the stop from which the Várbusz departs for the Castle District). HUNGARIAN.

This cheerful, unassuming restaurant serves a mostly local crowd. There's a good selection of specialties: Try the *borjúpaprikás galuskával* (veal paprika) served with *galuska* (a typical Central European style of dumpling). There's a small sidewalk garden for summer dining. The Szép Ilona is in a pleasant Buda neighborhood; after your meal, have a stroll through the tree-lined streets.

IN NORTHERN BUDA & ÓBUDA
Expensive

✪ **Kis Buda Gyöngye.** III. Kenyeres u. 34. ☎ **061/368-6402** or 061/368-9246. Reservations highly recommended. Soup 450–600Ft ($1.90–$2.50); main courses 980–3,500Ft ($4.10–$15). AE, DC, MC, V. Mon–Sat noon–midnight. Tram: 17 from Margit híd (Buda side). HUNGARIAN.

On a quiet side street in a residential Óbuda neighborhood, Kis Buda Gyöngye ("Little Pearl of Buda") is a favorite of Hungarians and visitors, serving standard Hungarian fare. This cheerful place features an interior garden, which sits in the shade of a wonderful old gnarly tree. Inside, an eccentric violinist entertains diners. Consider the goose plate, a rich combination platter including a roast goose leg, goose cracklings, and goose liver.

SEEING THE SIGHTS
SIGHTSEEING SUGGESTIONS FOR FIRST-TIME VISITORS

If You Have 1 Day Spend a few hours in the morning exploring the **Inner City** and **central Pest.** Stroll along the Danube as far as the neo-Gothic **Parliament,** noting along the way the **Chain Bridge.** In the afternoon, visit the major sites of **Castle Hill** and meander the cobblestone streets of the **Castle District.**

If You Have 2 Days On Day 1, head for Buda's **Gellért Hotel** and take a dip in its spa waters. Then hike up the stairs of **Gellért Hill** for an unparalleled panorama. Devote most of Day 2 to the **Castle District** and the sites of **Castle Hill** and visit some of the smaller museums. Head back to Pest to see **Heroes' Square** and **City Park,** and in the evening stroll the length of grand **Andrássy út** back to the center of Pest.

If You Have 3 Days Or More   On Day 3, take a boat up the Danube to visit **Szentendre,** a charming riverside town. On Days 4 and 5, visit some of the central sites you may have missed, and after lunch cross the Chain Bridge to **Watertown** to explore Buda's historic riverside neighborhood. See **St. Anne's Church,** the **Capuchin Church,** and the **Király Baths.** Check out Pest's indoor **market halls** and visit **Margaret Island.**

THE TOP ATTRACTIONS
In Pest
Néprajzi Múzeum (Ethnographical Museum). V. Kossuth tér 12. ☎ **061/312-4878.** Admission 300Ft ($1.25). Tues–Sun 10am–6pm (to 5pm in winter). Metro: Kossuth tér.

Directly across from Parliament, the vast Ethnographical Museum features an ornate interior equal to that of the Opera House. A ceiling fresco of Justitia, the goddess of justice, by artist Károly Lotz, dominates the lobby. Although a third of the museum's holdings are from outside Hungary, most concentrate on the items from Hungarian ethnography. The fascinating permanent exhibition, "From Ancient Times to Civilization," features everything from drinking jugs to razor cases to chairs to clothing.

✪ **Nemzeti Múzeum (Hungarian National Museum).** VIII. Múzeum krt. 14. ☎ **061/338-2122.** Admission 400Ft ($1.70). Tues–Sun 10am–6pm. Metro: Kálvin tér.

This enormous neoclassical structure, built in 1837–47, played a major role in the beginning of the Hungarian Revolution of 1848–49; on its wide steps on March 15, 1848, poet Sándor Petófi and other young radicals are said to have exhorted the people of Pest to revolt against the Hapsburgs. The two main museum exhibits on view are "The History of the Peoples of Hungary from the Paleolithic Age to the Magyar Conquest" and "The History of the Hungarian People from the Magyar Conquest to 1989." "The Hungarian Royal Insignia" is another permanent exhibit.

In Buda
Budapesti Történeti Múzeum (Budapest History Museum). I. In Buda Palace, Wing E, on Castle Hill. ☎ **061/375-7533** or 061/355-8849. Admission 300Ft ($1.25). Guided tours in English for serious history buffs, 5,000Ft ($21) available on advance request. May 15–Sept 15 Wed–Mon 10am–6pm; Sept 16–May 14 Wed–Mon 10am–5pm. Metro: Moszkva tér, then bus "Várbusz"; or Deák tér, then bus 16. Funicular: From Clark Ádám tér to Castle Hill.

This museum, also known as the Castle Museum, is the best place to get a sense of the once-great medieval Buda. It's probably worth splurging for a guided tour; even though the museum's descriptions are written in English, the history of the palace's repeated construction and destruction is so arcane it's difficult to understand what you're really seeing.

Nemzeti Galéria (Hungarian National Gallery). I. In Buda Palace, Wings B, C, and D, on Castle Hill. ☎ **061/375-5567.** Admission 300Ft ($1.25). Guided tours in English for 2,000ft–3,000Ft ($8–$13). Mar 16–Nov 14 Tues–Sun 10am–6pm; Nov 15–Mar 15 Tues–Sun 10am–4pm. Metro: Moszkva tér, then bus "Várbusz"; or Deák tér, then bus 16. Funicular: From Clark Ádám tér to Castle Hill.

Hungary has produced some fine artists, particularly in the late 19th century, and this is the place to view their work. The giants of the time are the brilliant but moody Mihály Munkácsy; László Paál, a painter of village scenes; Károly Ferenczy, a master of light; and Pál Szinyei Merse, the plein-air artist and contemporary of the early French impressionists.

Where Have All the Statues Gone?

Ever wonder where all the vanished Communist statues went after the fall? Just a decade ago Budapest and the rest of Hungary was filled with memorials to Lenin, Marx, Engels, the Red Army, and the many lesser-known figures of Hungarian and international Communist history. Torn from their pedestals in the aftermath of 1989, they sat for a few years in warehouses until a controversial plan for a **Szoborpark Múzeum (Socialist Statue Park)** was realized. The park's inconvenient location and the relatively small number of statues displayed (reflecting nothing of their former ubiquitousness) make it less than it could be. Moreover, the best examples of the genre, from the Stalinist period of the late 1940s and 1950s, were removed from public view long before 1989 and have presumably been destroyed.

In extreme southern Buda on Balatoni út (☎ **061/227-7446**), the museum park costs 200Ft (85¢). March 16 to November 13, it's open daily 10am to dusk; November 14 to March 15, hours are weekends only. To get there, take the black-lettered bus no. 7 from Ferenciek tere to Kosztolányi Dezső tér. Board a yellow Volán bus (to Érd) at Platform 6 for a 20-minute ride to the park.

MORE ATTRACTIONS

✪ **Vidám Park (Amusement Park).** XIV. Állatkerti krt. 14–16. ☎ **061/343-0996.** Admission 100Ft (42¢) adults, 50Ft (20¢) children; rides 150–300Ft (65¢–$1.25). Apr–Sept daily 10am–8pm; Oct–Mar 10am–7pm. Metro: Széchenyi fürdő.

This is a must if you're traveling with kids, but two rides in particular aren't to be missed. The 100-year-old **Merry-Go-Round** *(Körhinta)*, constructed almost entirely of wood, was recently restored to its original grandeur. The riders must actively pump to keep the horses rocking and authentic Würlitzer music plays. As the carousel spins round and round, it creaks mightily. The **Ferris wheel** *(Óriáskerék)* is also wonderful, though it has little in common with rambunctious modern Ferris wheels. A gangly bright-yellow structure, it rotates at a liltingly slow pace, gently lifting you high for a remarkable view. The Vidám Park also features Europe's longest wooden roller-coaster.

Historic Buildings

✪ **Magyar Állami Operaház (Hungarian State Opera House).** VI. Andrássy út 22. ☎ **061/353-0170.** Admission (by guided tour only) 600FT ($2.50). Tours daily at 3 and 4pm. Metro: Opera.

Completed in 1884, Budapest's Opera House boasts a fantastically ornate interior featuring frescoes by two of the best-known Hungarian artists of the day, Bertalan Székely and Károly Lotz. Home to both the State Opera and the State Ballet, the Opera House has a rich and evocative history.

Parliament. V. Kossuth tér. ☎ **061/268-4904.** Admission (by guided tour only): 30-min tour in English, 900Ft ($3.80). Tickets available at gate X, enter at gate XII. Summer, tours Mon–Fri at 10am and 2pm and Sat–Sun at 10am; winter, tours daily 10am. Closed when Parliament is in session. Metro: Kossuth tér.

Budapest's great Parliament, an eclectic design mixing the predominant neo-Gothic style with a neo-Renaissance dome, was completed in 1902. Standing proudly on the Danube bank, visible from almost any riverside point, it has from the outset been one of Budapest's symbols, though until 1989 a democratically elected government had convened here only once (just after World War II, before the Communist takeover).

The main cupola is decorated with statutes of Hungarian kings. On either side of the cupola are waiting rooms leading into the respective houses of Parliament. Here the MPs gather during session breaks in the session to smoke and chat. The waiting room on the Senate side (blue carpet) is adorned with statues of farmers, peasants, tradesmen, and workers. The statues that decorate the waiting room on the representatives' side (red carpet) are of sailors, soldiers, postal officials, etc. The interior decor is predominantly neo-Gothic. The ceiling frescoes are by Károly Lotz, Hungary's best-known artist of that genre. Note the purportedly largest handmade carpet in Europe, from the small Hungarian village of Békésszentandrás.

Churches & Synagogues

✪ Dohány Synagogue. VII. Dohány u. 2–8. ☎ **061/342-8949.** Admission by donation. Officially Tues–Thurs 10am–5pm, Fri 10am–3pm, Sat 10am–1pm. Metro: Astoria or Deák tér.

Built in 1859 and just recently restored, this is said to be the largest synagogue in Europe and the second largest in the world. The architecture has striking Moorish elements; the interior is vast and ornate, with two balconies, and the unusual presence of an organ. The synagogue has a rich but tragic history. There's a Jewish museum next door that traces the origins of Hungarian Judaism and features exhibits of ceremonial Judaica throughout the centuries, including Torah covers, scholarly writings, and documents.

Bazilika (St. Stephen's Church). V. Szent István tér 33. ☎ **061/117-2859.** Church, free; treasury, 130Ft (55¢); tower, 400Ft ($1.70). Church, daily 7am–7pm, except during services; treasury, daily 9am–5pm (10am–4pm in winter); Szent Jobb Chapel, Mon–Sat 9am–5pm (10am–4pm in winter) and Sun 1–5pm; tower, daily Apr–May 10am–4:30pm, June–Aug 9:30am–6pm, Sept–Oct 10am–5:30pm. Metro: Arany János utca or Bajcsy-Zsilinszky út.

The country's largest church, this basilica took more than 50 years to build (the 1868 collapse of the dome caused significant delay) and was finally completed in 1906. However, during this time Pest underwent radical growth—while the front of the church dominates sleepy Szent István tér, the rear faces out onto the far busier Inner Ring boulevard. In the Chapel of the Holy Right (Szent Jobb Kápolna), you can see Hungarian Catholicism's most cherished—and bizarre—holy relic: the preserved right hand of Hungary's first Christian king, Stephen.

✪ Mátyás Templom (Matthias Church). I. Szentháromság tér 2. ☎ **061/315-5657.** Church free; exhibit rooms beneath altar 150Ft (65¢). Daily 9am–6pm. Metro: Moszkva tér, then bus "Várbusz"; or Deák tér, then bus 16. Funicular: From Clark Ádám tér to Castle Hill.

Officially named the Church of Our Lady, this symbol of Buda's Castle District is popularly known as Matthias Church after the 15th-century king who was twice married here. Though it dates from the mid–13th century, like other old churches in Budapest it has an interesting history of destruction and reconstruction, always being refashioned in the architectural style of the time.

PARKS & PANORAMAS

Gellért Hegy (Gellért Hill), towering 230m (750 feet) above the Danube, offers the city's single best panorama. It's named after the Italian Bishop Gellért, who assisted Hungary's first Christian king, Stephen I, in converting the Magyars. Gellért became a martyr when vengeful pagans, outraged at the forced and violent nature of Stephen's proselytization, rolled him in a barrel to his death from the side of the hill on which his enormous statue now stands. On top of Gellért Hill you'll find the Liberation Monument, built in 1947 to commemorate the Red Army's liberation of Budapest from Nazi occupation. Also atop the hill is the Citadella, built by the Austrians shortly after they crushed the Hungarian War of Independence of 1848–49. Take bus 27 from Móricz Zsigmond körtér.

Budapest's Most Popular Thermal Baths

Budapest's baths have a proud history stretching back to Roman times. Under Turkish occupation the bath culture flourished, and several still-functioning bathhouses—Király, Rudas, and Rac—are among the period's architectural relics. In the late 19th and early 20th centuries, Budapest's "golden age," several fabulous bathhouses were built: the extravagant eclectic Széchenyi Baths in City Park, the splendid art nouveau Gellért Baths, and the solid neoclassical Lukács Baths. All are still in use.

Thermal bathing is an activity steeped in ritual. For this reason, and because bathhouse employees tend to be unfriendly relics, many foreigners find a trip to the baths stressful or confusing at first. As with any ritualistic activity, it helps to spend some time observing before joining in. Even then, you're likely not to know what to do or where to go. The most confusing step may well be the first: the ticket window with its endless list of prices for facilities and services, often without English translations. Chances are you're coming to use one of these facilities or services: *uszoda,* pool; *termál,* thermal pool; *fürdő,* bath; *gőzfürdő,* steam bath; massage; and sauna. There's no particular order in which people move from one modality to the next; do whatever feels most comfortable. Towel rental is *törülköző* or *lepedő.* An entry ticket generally entitles you to a free locker in the locker room (*öltöző*); at some bathhouses you can opt to pay an additional fee for a private cabin (*kabin*). At the Kiraly everyone gets a private dressing room and there's an employee to lock and unlock the rooms.

Remember to pack a bathing suit—and a bathing cap, if you wish to swim in the pools—so you won't have to rent 1970 models. In the single-sex baths, nude bathing is the custom. Towels are provided, but usually as you reenter the locker area *after* bathing. For this reason, you may want to bring your own towel into the bathing areas. Flip-flops are also a good idea. Soap and shampoo are only allowed in the showers, but should be brought out to the bath area to avoid having to return to the comparatively cold locker room prematurely. You will, most likely, want to wash your hair after soaking in the sulfury waters. Long hair must be tied back when bathing. Leave your eyeglasses in the locker as they'll be fogged up in the baths.

Margaret Island (Margit-sziget) has been a public park since 1908. The long, narrow island, connected to both Buda and Pest by the Margaret and Árpád bridges, is barred to most vehicular traffic. Facilities on the island include the Palatinus Strand open-air baths (see the box "Budapest's Most Popular Thermal Baths,"), which draw upon the famous thermal waters under Margaret Island; the Alfréd Hajós Sport Pool; and the Open Air Theater. Sunbathers line the steep embankments along the river and bicycles are available for rent. Despite all this, Margaret Island is a quiet, tranquil place. It's best reached by bus 26 from Nyugati tér, which runs the length of the island, or tram 4 or 6, which stop at the entrance to the island midway across the Margaret Bridge. (*Warning:* These are popular lines for pickpockets.)

City Park (Városliget) is an equally popular place to spend a summer day. Heroes' Square, at the end of Andrássy út, is the most logical starting point for a walk in City Park. The lake behind the square is used for boating in summer and ice-skating in winter. The park's Zoo Boulevard (Állatkerti körút), the favorite street of generations of

Generally, extra services (massage, pedicure) are received after a bath. Tipping is tricky; locker room attendants do not expect (except perhaps at the Gellért) but would welcome a tip of 50Ft to 100Ft (21¢ to 42¢), while masseurs and manicurists expect a tip of 150Ft to 200Ft (65¢ to 85¢).

Although there are drinking fountains in the bath areas, it's a good idea to drink plenty of water *before* a bath and don't bathe on an empty stomach; the hot water and steam take a toll on the unfortified body. Most bathhouses have snack bars in the lobbies where you can pick up a cold juice or sandwich on your way out. After the baths, you'll be thirsty and hungry. Be sure to replenish yourself.

The most spectacular bathhouse, the **Gellért Baths** are located in Buda's Hotel Gellért, at XI. Kelenhegyi út 4 (☎ 1/466-6166; metro: Deák tér, then tram 47 or 49). Go in through the side entrance. The unisex indoor pool is exquisite, with marble columns, majolica tiles, and stone lion heads spouting water. The segregated Turkish-style thermal baths, one off to each side of the pool through badly marked doors, are also glorious, though in need of restoration. The outdoor roof pool attracts great attention for 10 minutes every hour on the hour when the artificial wave machine is turned on. Admission to the thermal bath is 800Ft ($3.35); 15-minute massage is 750Ft ($3.15) plus tip. Lockers are free; a cabin is 300Ft ($1.25). Admission to all pools and the baths is 1,500Ft ($6) adults and 750Ft ($3.15) children. Prices and the lengthy list of services are posted in English. The thermal baths are open in summer daily 6am to 7pm (in winter closing on the weekend at 2pm), with the last entrance 1 hour before closing.

The **Király Baths,** at I. Fó u. 84 (☎ 1/202-3688; metro: Batthyány tér), are one of Budapest's most important monuments to Turkish rule. Built in the late 16th century, is housed under an octagonal domed roof with stained-glass windows. There are also sauna and steam bath facilities. After your treatment, wrap yourself in a cotton sheet and lounge with a cup of tea in the relaxation room. The Király baths are open on different days for men and women. Men can use the baths on Monday, Wednesday, and Friday 9am to 6pm. Women are welcome Tuesday and Thursday 6:30am to 6pm and Saturday 6:30am to noon. It costs 500Ft ($2.10) to bathe.

Hungarian children, is where the **zoo,** the **circus,** and the **amusement park** are all found. **Gundel,** Budapest's most famous restaurant, is also here, as are the **Széchenyi Baths.** The Yellow line makes stops at Hósök tere (Heroes' Square), at the edge of the park, and Széchenyi Fürdó, in the middle of it.

Károly kert (Charles Garden), a little enclosed park in the southern half of the Inner City (Red line, Astoria), is the location of what we consider to be Budapest's most charming playground. To enter the park, you must pass through a gigantic wrought-iron gate. The equipment here might not be as modern or as varied as at some of the city's other playgrounds, but the place has a distinct old-world charm and its location in the Inner City makes it a convenient destination.

ORGANIZED TOURS
BUS & BOAT TOURS   **Ibusz** (☎ 061/318-1139 or 061/318-1043), with decades of experience, sets the standard with organized tours in terms of quality and quantity. It offers 11 boat and bus tours, from basic city tours to special folklore-oriented tours.

Ibusz tours operate all year, with an abbreviated schedule off-season. Bus tours leave from the Erzsébet tér bus station (metro: Deák tér) and boat tours from the Vigadó tér landing on the Pest waterfront, between the Erzsébet Bridge and the Chain Bridge (metro: Vörösmarty tér). There's also a free hotel pickup service 30 minutes before departure.

A boat tour is a great way to get your measure of the scope and scale of the Hungarian capital, and you can see a majority of the city's grand sights from the river. The Hungarian state company **MAHART,** V. Belgrád rakpart (☎ **061/318-1704** or 061/318-1586), operates daily sightseeing cruises on the Danube. Boats depart frequently from Vigadó tér on weekends and holidays in spring and every day in summer.

WALKING TOURS   We recommend "Walking Tours in Budapest" offered by a company called **Image Advantage** (☎ **06-30/211-8861** [cell phone]; www.iatours.com). The tours, conducted by knowledgeable and personable guides, start on the front steps of the Műcsarnok (metro: Hősök tere). Mid-May to September, tours are daily at 10am and 2pm; October to mid-December and February to early May, tours are daily at 10am. Tickets are 2,500Ft ($11); children under 12 are free. Show this book (or the company's flyer, found at many tourist haunts) and you'll get a 500Ft ($2.10) discount. Buy your ticket from the guide at the start of the tour. Tours last anywhere from 3¹/₂ to 5 hours, depending on the mood of the group, and take you throughout central Pest and central Buda. You get quite a comprehensive introduction to the city, but be aware that it's practically an entire day on your feet.

THE SHOPPING SCENE

All year long, shoppers fill the pedestrians-only **Váci utca,** from the stately Vörösmarty tér, the center of Pest, across the roaring Kossuth Lajos utca, all the way to Vámház krt (Yellow line). The **Castle District** in Buda, with many folk-art boutiques and galleries, is another popular area for souvenir hunters. Locals (and budget travelers) might window-shop in these two neighborhoods, but they do their serious shopping elsewhere. One popular street is Pest's **Outer Ring (Nagykörút);** another bustling shopping street is Pest's **Kossuth Lajos utca,** off the Erzsébet Bridge, and its continuation **Rákóczi út,** extending all the way out to Keleti Station.

BEST BUYS   Folkloric Objects   Hungary's famous folkloric objects are the most popular souvenirs among foreign visitors. The state-owned Folkart shops (Népművészeti Háziipar) have a great selection of handmade goods. Popular items include pillowcases, pottery, porcelain, dolls, dresses, skirts, and sheepskin vests. The main store, **Folkart Centrum,** is at V. Váci u. 14 (☎ **061/318-5840**), and is open daily 9:30am to 7pm (to 9pm July and August). One outstanding private shop on Váci utca is ✪ **Vali Folklór,** in the courtyard of Váci u. 23 (☎ **061/337-6301**). This cluttered shop is run by a soft-spoken man named Bálint Ács who travels the villages of Hungary and neighboring countries in search of authentic folk items.

✪ **Holló Folkart Gallery,** at V. Vitkovics Mihály u. 12 (☎ **061/317-8103**), is an unusual gallery selling handcrafted reproductions of folk-art pieces from various regions of the country.

Porcelain & Pottery   Another popular Hungarian item is porcelain, particularly from the country's two best-known producers, Herend and Zsolnay. Although both brands are available in the West, here you'll find a better selection and prices about 50% lower.

You'll find world-renowned hand-painted Herend porcelain (www.herend.com), first produced in 1826 in the town of Herend near Veszprém in western Hungary, at the **Herend Shop,** V. József nádor tér 11 (☎ **061/317-2622**). This shop has the widest Herend selection in the capital, but unfortunately, it can't arrange shipping. There are also two new Herend shops at the following locations: V. Kígyó u. 5 (☎ 061/318-3439)—this shop offers shipping—and I. Szentháromság u. 5 (☎ 061/375-5857) in the Castle District. If Herend porcelain isn't within your price range, you'll find lovely pottery at ✪ **Herend Village Pottery,** V. Váci u. 23 (☎ 061/318-2094). This shop sells Herend porcelain as well as a lovely casual "village-style" pottery. There is a second shop at II. Bem rakpart 37 (☎ 061/ 356-7899) in Buda's Watertown. Delightfully gaudy Zsolnay porcelain from the southern city of Pécs is Hungary's second-most celebrated brand of porcelain; you'll find it at **Zsolnay Márkabolt,** V. Kígyó u. 4 (☎ 061/318-3712).

Hungarian Foods   Connoisseurs generally agree that **Pick Salami** from the southeastern city of Szeged is the best of world-renowned Hungarian salami, and it's easy to carry home without giving your clothes an unforgettable aroma. Chestnut paste (*gesztenye püré*), found in a tin or block wrapped in foil, is rare abroad and used primarily as a pastry filling, but can also top desserts and ice cream. Paprika paste (*pirosarany*) is also hard to find outside Hungary; it comes in a bright-red tube in hot (*csípós*), deli-style (*csemege*), and sweet (*édes*) varieties. All these can be found in grocery stores (*élelmiszer*) and delicatessens (*csemege*).

Hungarian Wines   Fine, affordable Hungarian wines from the Szekszárd, Villány, Tokaj, and Eger regions are abundant. The most renowned red wines come from the region around Villány, a town to the south of Pécs by the Croatian border. As a result of the aggressive marketing strategy of the former Communist regime, many foreigners are familiar with the red wines from Eger, especially *Egri Bikavér* (Eger Bull's Blood). Eger wines, though rich and fruity, are markedly inferior to Villányi reds. The country's best white wines are generally believed to be those from the Lake Balaton region, though some Hungarians insist that white wines from the Sopron region (by the Austrian border) are better. *Tokaj* wines—*száraz* (dry) or *édes* (sweet)—are popular as aperitifs and dessert wines.

MARKETS   Budapest has a handful of **vintage market halls (vásárcsarnok),** wonders of steel and glass, built in the 1890s in the ambitious grandiose style of the time. Three are still in use and provide a measure of local color you won't find in the grocery store. The **Központi Vásárcsarnok (Central Market Hall),** on IX. Vámház körút, is the largest and most spectacular market hall. In the Inner Ring (Kiskörút), on the Pest side of the Szabadság Bridge, this trilevel hall was impeccably reconstructed in 1995. Other vintage market halls include the **Belvárosi Vásárcsarnok (Inner City Market Hall),** on V. Hold utca, behind Szabadság tér in central Pest, the **Józsefváros Vásárcsarnok,** on VIII. Rákóczi tér. Other active and lively markets are found in unspectacular buildings, such as the **Fehérvári úti Vásárcsarnok,** on XI. Fehérvári út, in front of the Buda Skála department store, just a block from the Móricz Zsigmond körtér transportation hub; and the **Fény utca Piac,** on II. Fény utca, just off Moszkva tér in Buda.

MALLS   Several new American-style malls have sprung up in Budapest over the past few years, and have proven immensely popular to Budapesters. **Duna Plaza,** XII. Váci út 178 (☎ 061/465-1220), is probably the most popular shopping center/entertainment complex, comprised of 120 different shops (including a Virgin Records Megastore), a nine-screen "Hollywood Cineplex," snackbars and pubs, the best bowling alley in the city, and even a small ice-skating rink. Duna Plaza also features an Internet Club (☎ 061/465-1126; www.plazaclub.com), providing 15 PCs and a Mac for use at 600Ft ($2.50) per hour, 12Ft (5¢) per minute. Duna Plaza is open daily 9am to 9pm; the entertainment complex closes later.

Polus Center, at XV. Szentmihályi út 131 (☎ 061/419-4028), is now the largest shopping mall in the region. It is home to TESCO, the British supermarket chain, as well as to countless other shops. Wings in the mall have flashy American street names: Rodeo Drive, Sunset Boulevard, Wall Street. Open weekdays 10am to 8pm, weekends 10am to 6pm. A mall shuttle bus or else bus 73 (red-lettered) departs for Polus Center from Keleti station.

Mammut, the most recently built mall (1998), is located at II. Lövőház u. 2–6, next to Fény utca market (☎ 061/345-8024; metro: Moszkva tér, or tram: 4 or 6). **West End,** a behemoth mall under construction right behind Nyugati railway station and scheduled to open in 2000, has generated lots of concern about the future of downtown shops and boutiques.

BUDAPEST AFTER DARK

The most complete schedule of mainstream performing arts is found in the free bimonthly Koncert Kalendárium at the Central Philharmonic Ticket Office in Vörösmarty tér. The *Budapest Sun* is a good source, as is the new magazine *Scene,* and the *Budapest Week* Web site (www.budapestweek.hu).

The **Central Theater Ticket Office (Színházak Központi Jegyiroda),** VI. Andrássy út 18 (☎ 061/312-0000; metro: Opera), sells tickets to just about everything, from theater and operetta to sports events and rock concerts; it's open Monday to Thursday 9am to 1pm and 1:45 to 6pm (Friday to 5pm). A second branch is at II. Moszkva tér 3 (☎ 061/335-9136; metro: Moszkva tér), with similar hours except that it opens at 10am. For **classical performances,** go to the National Philharmonic Ticket Office (Filharmónia Nemzeti Jegyiroda), V. Vörösmarty tér 1 (☎ 061/ 318-0281; metro: Vörösmarty tér). For **opera and ballet,** go to the Hungarian State Opera Ticket Office (Magyar Állami Opera Jegyiroda), VI. Andrássy út 20 (entrance inside the courtyard) (☎ 061/332-7914; metro: Opera). For events in the **Spring Festival,** go to the Festival Ticket Service, V. 1081 Rákóczi út 65 (☎ 061/333-2337) (Red line, Blaha Lujza Tér). For **rock and jazz concert** tickets, try Ticket Express, VI. Jókai u. 40 (☎ 061/353-0692) (Yellow line, Opera).

THE PERFORMING ARTS

Completed in 1884, the **Magyar Állami Operaház (Hungarian State Opera House),** VI. Andrássy út 22 (☎ 061/331-2550; metro: Opera), is Budapest's most famous performance hall and a tourist attraction in its own right. Hungarians adore opera, and a large percentage of seats are sold on a subscription basis; buy your tickets a few days ahead if possible. The box office is open Monday to Friday 11am to 6pm. Ticket prices range from 2,200 to 5,600Ft ($9 to $24).

The Great Hall (Nagyterem) of the ✪ **Zeneakadémia (Ferenc Liszt Academy of Music),** VI. Liszt Ferenc tér 8 (☎ 061/341-4788; metro: Oktogon), is the premier music hall. The Academy was built in the art nouveau style of the early 20th century with the best acoustics in the city. Box office hours are 2pm to show time on the day of performance. Tickets range from 400 to 3,000Ft ($1.70 to $13).

LIVE-MUSIC CLUBS

The club scene has found fertile ground since 1989's political changes—so much so, in fact, that clubs come in and out of fashion overnight. Check the *Budapest Sun* for up-to-the-minute club listings.

The popular **Made Inn Mine,** VI. Andrássy út 112 (☎ 061/311-3437; metro: Bajza utca), has a subterranean cavelike atmosphere. Wednesday features a funk dance party, with all drinks half price. For some reason, Thursday is *the* night to be here; you

---

Music for a Summer Evening

During the warm lazy days, you'll find several special venues for classical music. Tickets for them are available at the **National Philharmonic Ticket** Office, V. Vörösmarty tér 1 (☎ **061/318-0281;** metro: Vörösmarty tér).

The historic outdoor Dominican Courtyard, inside the Castle District's Hilton Hotel, I. Hess András tér 1–3 (☎ **061/488-6600;** metro: Moszkva tér, then bus "Várbusz"; or Deák tér, then bus 16), is the site for a series of classical recitals during the summer. The District's beautiful **Matthias Church (Mátyás Templom),** next door at I. Szentháromság tér 2, holds a regular Tuesday and Friday-night series of organ concerts June through September. Concerts start at 7:30pm. Tickets can be purchased before the performance at the church entry.

Organ concerts are also held Monday evenings at 7pm during July and August and **St. Stephen's Church (Basilica),** Hungary's largest church, V. Szent István tér 33 (☎ **061/317-2859;** metro: Arany János utca or Bajcsy-Zsilinszky út). You can buy tickets at the church entry before the performance.

The **Dohány Synagogue,** VII. Dohány u. 2–8. (☎ **061/342-8949;** metro: Astoria or Deák tér), is the venue for occasional concerts from May to September. Concerts begin at 7pm, but days are not regular. For information and tickets, call the **Central Theater Ticket Office** (☎ **061/312-0000;** metro: Opera).

---

may have to wait in line to enter. It's open daily 8pm to 5am, with the kitchen open to 3am. Cover is 300Ft ($1.25), but 500Ft ($2.10) on Thursday. ✪ **TRAFO,** XI. Liliom u. 41 (☎ **061/454-2049;** tram: 4 or 6 to Üllöi út), is an old electric power station renovated and transformed into a cultural center for young alternative artists. It also hosts the hippest disco in town. *The* night is Tuesday with DJ Palotai, with the party starting at 9pm.

The **Fél 10 Jazz Klub,** VIII. Baross u. 30 (no phone; metro: Kálvin tér), is a classy multilevel club. The place features live jazz performances nightly, while techno-free dance parties get going in the wee hours Thursday to Saturday. It's open Monday to Friday noon to 4am and Saturday and Sunday 7pm to 4am. ✪ **Old Man's,** VIII. Akácfa u. 13 (☎ **061/322-7645;** metro: Blaha Luzja tér), is the place to take in the best jazz and blues in Hungary. The Pege Quartet plays here, as does Hobo and his blues band. This very hip spot is open daily 3pm to 3am.

BARS

The ✪ **Irish Cat Pub,** V. Múzeum krt. 41 (☎ **061/266-4085;** metro: Kálvin tér), is an Irish-style pub with Guinness on tap and a whiskey bar. It's a popular meeting place for expatriates and travelers, serving a full menu, and is open Monday to Thursday and Sunday 11am to 3am and Friday and Saturday 11am to 5am. **Morrison's Music Pub,** VI. Révay u. 25 (☎ **061/269-4060;** metro: Opera [Yellow line]), is a casual place packed by an almost-20-something crowd. There's a small dance floor, an eclectic variety of loud live music, and a number of beers on tap. It's open Monday to Saturday 8:30pm to 4am.

An American-style microbrewery on one of Pest's busiest squares, **Chicago Sörgyár,** VII. Erzsébet krt. 2. ☎ **061/269-6753;** metro: Blaha Lujza tér), has a diehard expatriate crowd that comes not just for the fairly good home-brewed beer but for the hamburgers, nachos, and fries. Happy hour is weekdays 4 to 6pm, with half-price drinks. It's open Monday to Thursday noon to midnight, Friday and Saturday noon to 1am, and Sunday noon to 11pm.

HUNGARIAN DANCE HOUSES

Recent years have seen the growth of an urban-centered folk revival movement known as the táncház **(dance house).** This interactive evening of **folk music** and **folk dancing,** held in community centers around town, is one of the best cultural experiences you can have in Hungary. The format usually consists of about an hour of dance-step instruction, followed by several hours of dancing accompanied by a live band, which might include some of Hungary's best folk musicians, in an authentic, casual atmosphere.

The leading Hungarian folk band Muzsikás, whose lead singer is the incomparable Márta Sebestyén, hosts a táncház every Thursday (September to June only) at 8pm for 300Ft ($1.25) at the ✪ **Marczibányi Square Cultural House (Marczibányi tér Művelődésiház),** II. Marczibányi tér 5/a (☎ **061/212-0803;** metro: Moszkva tér). If you're in town and have an evening to catch a Muzsikás performance, don't miss it. The **FMH Cultural House (Szakszervezetek Fővárosi Művelődési Háza),** XI. Fehérvári út 47 (☎ **061/203-3868;** metro: Deák tér, then tram 47), hosts a táncház for kids every Tuesday (except in July and August), from 5pm to 6pm, for 150Ft (50¢). Téka, a well-known folk band that performs on traditional instruments, plays every Friday evening, September to May for 300Ft ($1.25). The evening kicks off with a táncház hour for kids, at 5pm. A csángó táncház, the oldest and most authentic type of traditional Hungarian folk dance, is held on Saturdays, from 6pm to 11pm, for 200Ft (85¢).

GAY & LESBIAN BARS

As with the fickle club scene, "in" bars become "out," or even close down, at a moment's notice. See the *Budapest Sun* for additional, and always current, listings.

Angel Bar & Dance Club, VII. Szövetség u. 33 (☎ **061/351-6490;** metro: Blaha Lujza tér [Red line]), is a basement place with a bar, restaurant, and huge dance floor. It has been around for a while now and is presumably here to stay. The club isn't exclusively gay; many straights attend, especially on Friday. Friday and Sunday, Angel hosts a now-famous transvestite show at 11pm. Cover is 500Ft ($2.10), but there are no shows and no cover on Thursday. It's open Thursday to Sunday 10pm to dawn. **Mystery Bar,** V. Nagysándor József u. 3 (☎ **061/312-1436;** metro: Arany János utca [Blue line]), is a smaller place, with a larger foreign crowd. There are occasional drag shows and live lounge music. Hours vary. **Eklektika Café**, V. Semmelweis u. 21 (☎ **061/266-3054;** metro: Deák tér [all lines]), is a wonderfully appointed place with 1950s socialist realist furnishings; it features live jazz on Wednesday, Friday, and Sunday. An intimate place, Eklektika hosts a women-only night every second Saturday. It's open Monday to Saturday 10am to midnight and Sunday 5pm to midnight.

DAY TRIPS ALONG THE DANUBE BEND

The delightful towns along the Bend—Szentendre, Esztergom, and Visegrád—are easy day trips from Budapest. The great natural beauty of the area, where forested hills loom over the river, makes it a welcome departure for the city weary.

GETTING THERE   By Boat & Hydrofoil   From April to September, **boats** run between Budapest and the towns of the Danube Bend. All boats leave Budapest's Vigadó tér boat landing, stopping to pick up passengers 5 minutes later at Buda's Batthyány tér landing, before continuing up the river.

Schedules and towns served are complicated, so contact **MAHART,** the state shipping company, at the Vigadó tér landing (☎ **061/318-1223**) for information. Round-trip prices are 900Ft ($3.80) to Szentendre, 975Ft ($4.10) to Visegrád, and 1,035Ft ($4.35) to Esztergom. Children aged 4 to 14 receive a 50% discount. Travel time is 1½ hours to Szentendre, 3½ hours to Visegrád, and 5 hours to Esztergom.

By Train   To Szentendre: The HÉV suburban railroad connects Budapest's Batthyány tér with Szentendre. Trains leave daily, year-round, every 20 minutes or so from 4am to 11:30pm (trip time: 45 minutes). The one-way fare is 240Ft ($1); subtract 90Ft (35¢) if you have a valid Budapest public transportation pass.

To Visegrád: There's no direct train service to Visegrád. Instead, take one of 20 daily trains departing from Nyugati Station for Nagymaros (trip time: 1 hour). From Nagymaros, take a ferry across the river to Visegrád. The ferry dock (RÉV) is a 5-minute walk from the train station. A ferry leaves every hour throughout the day. The train ticket to Nagymaros costs 348Ft ($1.45); the ferry boat ticket to Visegrád costs 100Ft (42¢).

To Esztergom: Ten trains daily make the run between Budapest's Nyugati Station and Esztergom (trip time: 1¼ hours). Train tickets cost 266Ft ($1.10).

SZENTENDRE   Peopled in medieval times by Serbian settlers, Szentendre (pronounced *Sen*-ten-dreh), 21km (13 miles) north of Budapest, counts half a dozen Serbian churches among its rich collection of historical buildings. Since the turn of the century, Szentendre has been home to an artist's colony and has a wealth of museums and galleries. The town is an extremely popular tourist destination.

Visitor Information   The information office **Tourinform** is at Dumtsa Jenő u. 22 (☎ **26/317-965**), with maps of Szentendre (and the Danube Bend region), as well as concert and exhibition schedules. The office can also provide accommodations information and is open Monday to Friday 9:30am to 5pm and weekends in summer 10am to 2pm. If you arrive by train, you'll come upon this office as you follow the flow of pedestrian traffic into town on Kossuth Lajos utca. If you arrive by boat, you may find the **Ibusz** office sooner, corner of Bogdányi út and Gőzhajó utca (☎ **26/313-597**). It's open April to October, Monday to Friday 9am to 6pm and weekends 10am to 2pm; November to March, weekdays only, 9am to 4pm.

Exploring the Museums & Churches   The ✪ **Margit Kovács Museum,** Vastagh György u. 1 (☎ **26/310-244**), is a must-see, displaying the exceptional and highly original work of Hungary's best-known ceramic artist. Her sculptures of elderly women and friezes of village life are particularly moving. The museum is open April to October Tuesday to Sunday 10am to 6pm (November to March to 4pm). Admission is 250Ft ($1.05). The **Blagovestenska church** at Fó tér 4 dates from 1752. A rococo iconostasis features paintings of Mihailo Zivkovic—notice that the eyes of all the icons are on you; the effect is extraordinary. Next door at Fó tér 6 (☎ **26/310-244**) is the ✪ **Ferenczy Museum,** dedicated to the art of the prodigious Ferenczy family. The paintings of Károly Ferenczy, one of Hungary's leading impressionists, are featured. It's open April to October Tuesday to Sunday 10am to 4pm; November to March Friday to Sunday 10am to 4pm. Admission is 150Ft (65¢).

The **Ámos and Anna Muzeum,** Bogdány u. 10 (☎ **26/310-790**), was the former home of artist couple Imre Ámos and Margit Anna, whose work represents the beginning of expressionist painting in Hungary. Opened after Anna's death in 1991, the collection is Szentendre's best-kept secret. It's open Tuesday to Sunday 10am to 6pm, and admission is 150Ft (65¢).

Where to Dine   If you get hungry, **Aranysárkány Vendégló (Golden Dragon Inn),** Alkotmány u. 1/a (☎ **26/301-479**), just east of Fó tér on Hunyadi utca, is always crowded, often with locals (a definite good sign in a tourist town like Szentendre). Choose from such enticing offerings as alpine lamb, roast leg of goose, quail, and venison ragout. A very tasty vegetarian plate is also offered. Various beers are on draft.

If you walk directly south from Fó tér, you'll find **Régimodi,** Fútó u. 3 (☎ **26/ 311-105**). This elegant restaurant in a former private home serves Hungarian specialties, with an emphasis on game dishes. The wild-boar stew in red wine is particularly sumptuous. Be sure to stop in at the ✪ **Dobos Museum & Cafe,** Dumtsa Jenó u. 7, for a slice of authentic *dobos torta,* a sumptuously rich layer cake named after pastry chef József Dobos, who experimented with butter frostings in the 19th century. The success of his recipe was immediate, and he was quickly appointed official baker to the Hapsburg emperor.

ESZTERGOM   Formerly a Roman settlement, Esztergom (pronounced *Ess*-tair-gome), 46km (29 miles) northwest of Budapest, was the seat of the Hungarian kingdom for 300 years. Hungary's first king, István I (Stephen I), crowned by the pope in A.D. 1000, converted Hungary to Catholicism, and Esztergom became the country's center of the early church. Although its glory days are long gone, the quiet town remains the seat of the archbishop-primate—the "Hungarian Rome."

Visitor Information   **Gran Tours,** Széchenyi tér 25 (☎ **33/413-756**), is the best source of information. Summer hours are Monday to Friday 8am to 6pm and Saturday 9am to noon; winter hours are Monday to Friday 8am to 4pm and Saturday 9am to noon.

Exploring the Town   The massive, neoclassical **Esztergom Cathedral** in Szent István tér on Castle Hill, is Esztergom's most popular attraction and one of Hungary's most impressive buildings. It was built in the last century to replace the cathedral ruined during the Turkish occupation. The cathedral ✪ **Treasury** (*Kincstár*) contains a stunning array of ecclesiastical jewels and gold works. Since Cardinal Mindszenty's body was moved to the crypt in 1991 (he died in exile in 1975), it has been a place of pilgrimage for Hungarians. If you brave the ascent of the cupola, you're rewarded at the top with unparalleled views of Esztergom and the surrounding Hungarian and Slovak countryside. The cathedral is open daily, summer 8am to 8pm, winter 9am to 3pm. The treasury, crypt, and cupola are open daily, summer 9am to 5pm, winter 10am to 3pm. Admission to the cathedral and the crypt are free, but it costs 200Ft (85¢) to see the treasury and 100Ft (40¢) to see the cupola.

It's definitely worth taking a break from the crowds at the cathedral and strolling through the quiet cobblestone streets of **Víziváros (Watertown).** There you'll find the **Keresztény Múzeum (Christian Museum),** Mindszenty tér 2 (☎ **33/313-880**), in the neoclassical former primate's palace. It houses Hungary's largest collection of religious art and the largest collection of medieval art outside the National Gallery. Hours are Tuesday to Sunday 10am to 6pm, and admission is 100Ft (40¢).

Where to Dine   The food at ✪ **Szalma Csárda,** Nagy-Duna sétány 2 (☎ **33/ 315-336**), is absolutely first-rate, with everything made to order and served piping hot. The excellent house soups—fish soup (*halászlé*), goulash (*gulyásleves*), and bean soup (*babgulyás*)—constitute meals in themselves. It's open daily 10am to 10pm and doesn't accept credit cards.

VISEGRÁD   Halfway between Szentendre and Esztergom, Visegrád (pronounced *Vee*-sheh-grod) is a sparsely populated, sleepy riverside village, which makes its history all the more fascinating and hard to believe. The Romans built a fort here, which

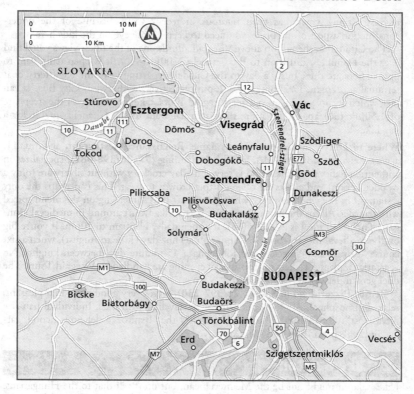

was still extant when Slovak settlers gave the town its present name (meaning "High Castle") in the 9th or 10th century. After the Mongol invasion (1241–42), construction began on both the present ruined hilltop citadel and the former riverside palace. Eventually, Visegrád could boast one of the finest royal palaces ever built in Hungary. Only one king, Charles Robert (1307–42), actually used it as his primary residence, but monarchs from Béla IV, in the 13th century, through Matthias Corvinus, in the late 15th century, spent time in Visegrád and contributed to its development, the latter expanding the palace into a great Renaissance center known throughout Europe.

Visitor Information **Visegrád Tours,** RÉV u. 15 (☎ **26/398-160**) is located across the road from the RÉV ferry boat landing (not to be confused with the MAHART boat landing, just down the road). It is open daily April to October, 9am to 6pm; November to March weekdays, 10am to 4pm.

Each summer on the second weekend in July, Visegrád hosts the **International Palace Tournament,** an authentic medieval festival replete with dueling knights on horseback, early music, and dance. For more information, contact Visegrád Tours.

Exploring the Palace & the Citadel The **Royal Palace** covered much of the area where the MAHART boat landing and Fő utca (Main Street) are now found. Indeed, the entrance to its open-air ruins, called the ✪ **King Matthias Museum,** is at Fő u. 27 (☎ **26/398-023**). Admission is 120Ft (50¢). The museum is open daily 9am to 5pm. The buried ruins of the palace, having achieved a near-mythical status, were not discovered until this century. Almost all of what you see is the result of ongoing reconstruction, which has been rigorous in recent years. Because of the under-construction aspect of the place, you need to keep a close eye on the kids here.

The **Citadel** on the hilltop above Visegrád affords one of the finest views you'll find over the Danube. Admission to the Citadel is 200Ft (85¢). It is open daily 9am to 6pm. There are three buses a day to the Citadel, departing from the RÉV ferry boat terminal at 9:26am, 12:26pm, and 3:26pm respectively. Otherwise "City Bus," a van taxi, which awaits passengers outside Visegrad Tours, takes people up for the steep fare of 1,500Ft ($6) apiece. It's more than a casual walk to the Citadel, suitable for a day hike.

Where to Dine   In keeping with its name, **Renaissance Restaurant,** at Fő u. 11, across the street from the MAHART boat landing (☎ **26/398-081**), specializes in authentic medieval cuisine. Food is served in clay crockery without silverware (only a wooden spoon) and guests are offered paper crowns to wear. This is perhaps the only restaurant in the whole country where you won't find something on the menu spiced with paprika. All for the sake of authenticity; paprika wasn't around in medieval Hungary. The menu meal is 2,000Ft ($8). It's open daily, 11:30am to 10pm. If you're big on the medieval theme, come for dinner on a Thursday (June to August), when a six-course "Royal Feast" is celebrated following a 45-minute duel between knights. No vegetarians, please! Tickets for this special evening are handled by Visegrád Tours. The duel gets underway at 5:15pm sharp.

Benito Pizzeria, Fő u. 83 (☎ **26/397-230**), serves very good pizza in a pleasant, relaxed atmosphere. A good option if you're traveling with kids. Individual pan-size pizzas cost 400 to 700Ft ($1.70 to $2.95). Try the "Benito," a delicious ricotta, garlic, and herb pizza. Beer and wine are served.

2 Lake Balaton

Lake Balaton might not be the Mediterranean, but don't tell that to the Hungarians. Somehow, over the years, they have managed to create their own Central European hybrid variety of a Mediterranean culture along the shores of their long, shallow, milky-white lake, Europe's largest at 80km (50 miles) long and 15km (10 miles) wide at its broadest stretch.

Throughout the long summer, swimmers, windsurfers, sailboats, kayaks, and cruisers enjoy the warm and silky-smooth waters; people cast their reels for pike, play tennis, ride horses, and hike in the hills.

The **south shore** towns are as flat as Pest; walk 10 minutes from the lake and you're in farm country. The air here is still and quiet; in summer, the sun hangs heavily in the sky. Teenagers, students, and young travelers tend to congregate in the hedonistic towns of the south shore. Here, huge 1970s-style beachside hotels are filled to capacity all summer long, and disco music pulsates into the early morning hours.

On the more graceful **north shore,** little villages are neatly tucked away in the rolling countryside, where the grapes of the popular Balaton wines ripen in the strong southern sun. Traveling from Budapest, the northern shore of the lake at first appears every bit as built up and crowded as the southern shore. Beyond Balatonfüred, this impression begins to fade. You'll discover the **Tihany Peninsula,** a protected area whose 12 square kilometers (4³/₄ square miles) jut out into the lake like a knob. Stop for a swim—or the night—in a small town like **Szigliget.** Moving westward along the coast, you can make forays inland into the rolling hills of the Balaton wine country. The city of **Keszthely,** sitting at the lake's western edge, marks the end of its northern shore.

Passenger boat travel on Lake Balaton lets you travel across the lake as well as between towns on the same shore. It's both extensive and cheap, but considerably slower than surface transportation. All major towns have a dock with departures and arrivals. Children 3 and under travel free, and those 13 and under get half-price tickets. A single ferry (*komp*) running between Tihany and Szántód lets you transport a car across the width of the lake. Boat and ferry information is available from the **MAHART** office in Siófok (☎ **84/310-050**). Local tourist offices along the lake also have schedules and information.

Because hotel prices are unusually high in the Balaton region, and because just about every local family rents out a room or two in summer, we especially recommend private rooms. You can reserve a room through a local tourist office, or you can just look for the ubiquitous **SZOBA KIADÓ** (or **ZIMMER FREI**) signs along the roads. When you take a room without using a tourist agency as the intermediary, prices are generally negotiable. In the height of the season, you shouldn't have to pay more than 9,600Ft ($40) for a double room within reasonable proximity of the lake.

ESSENTIALS

ARRIVING   By Train   From Budapest, trains to the various towns along the lake depart from Déli Station. The local (sebes) trains are interminably slow, stopping at each village along the lake. Unless you're going to one of these little villages (sometimes a good idea), try to get on an express (gyors). To Keszthely, the trip takes about 4 hours and costs 1,310Ft ($6). To reach Tihany, take a train to Balatonfüred for 920Ft ($4) (travel time 2 hours), and then a local bus to Tihany.

By Car   If you're driving from Budapest, take the M-7 motorway south through Székesfehérvár until you hit the lake. Route 71 circles the lake.

VESZPRÉM

On your way to Lake Balaton, you might want to make a stop in this charming town. Just 16km (10 miles) from Lake Balaton, Veszprém (pronounced *Vess*-praym), 116km (72 miles) southwest of Budapest, surely ranks as one of Hungary's most vibrant small cities, and is often used as a starting point for trips to that popular resort area. In Veszprém you'll find a harmonious mix of old and new: A delightfully self-contained and well-preserved 18th-century baroque Castle District spills effortlessly into a typically modern city center, itself distinguished by lively wide-open, pedestrian-only plazas.

ESSENTIALS

GETTING THERE   Six daily trains depart Budapest's Déli Station for Veszprém (trip time: 1³/₄ hours). Tickets cost 786Ft ($3.30).

VISITOR INFORMATION   Tourinform, Rákóczi u. 3 (☎ **88/404-548**), is open Monday to Friday 9am to 6pm, Saturday 9am to 1pm (open only weekdays in winter); and **Ibusz,** Kossuth u. 10, in the odd modern structure marked KINIZSI ÜZLETHÁZ (☎ **88/426-492** or 88/427-604), is open Monday to Friday 9am to 5pm and Saturday 9am to noon. Both offices provide information, sell city maps, and help with hotel or private-room bookings.

WHERE TO DINE

For fast food, try **Mackó Cukrászda,** at Kossuth u. 6, ☎ **88/426-686.** Open daily 7:30am to 7:30pm (opening at 9amd closing at 5:30pm on Sunday). This stand-up eatery, which is somewhat grungy yet always bustling, is popular with young locals. Pizza, hot dogs, french fries, fried chicken, and various sweets are served. ✪ **Cserhát**

Lake Balaton

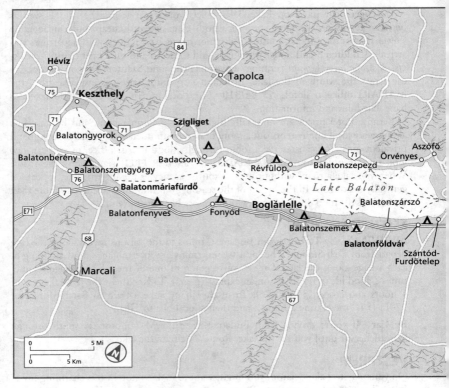

Étterem ☎ 88/425-441), housed in the same structure, is an authentic *önkiszólgáló* (self-service cafeteria). You'll find the restaurant behind the Nike store; go up the winding staircase inside the building. A menu is posted.

For something more upscale, try ✪ **Villa Medici Étterem,** next to the zoo at Kittenberger u. 11 (☎ 88/321-273). Reputedly one of Hungary's best restaurants, it's also relatively expensive. Villa Medici serves Hungarian and continental cuisine. Open daily from 11am to 11pm.

SEEING THE SIGHTS

Most of Veszprém's main sights are clustered along Vár utca, the street that runs the length of the city's small but lovely **Castle District.**

Housed inside the 18th-century canon's house, the **Exhibition of Religious Art,** Vár u. 35, has a fine collection of Roman Catholic art. Admission is 20Ft (8¢). Open daily from 9am to 5pm; closed October to April. At Vár u. 16, the vaulted **Gizella Chapel,** named for King Stephen's wife, was unearthed during the construction of the adjoining Bishop's Palace in the 18th century. Today it houses a modest collection of ecclesiastical art, but is best known for the 13th-century **frescoes** that, in various states of restoration, decorate its walls. Admission is 20Ft (10¢). Open daily from 9am to 5pm; closed October to April.

For a wonderful view of the surrounding Bakony region, climb up the steps to the narrow observation deck at the top of the ✪ **Fire Tower,** at Áváros tér. Although the

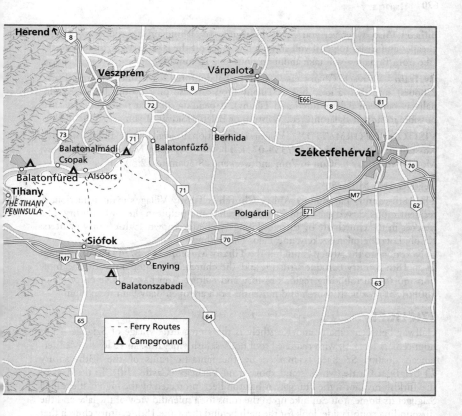

tower's foundations are medieval, the structure itself was built in the early 19th century. Enter through the courtyard of Vár u. 17, behind Áváros tér. Admission is 100Ft (40¢). Open daily from 9:30am to 6pm.

THE TIHANY PENINSULA

The Tihany (pronounced *Tee*-hine) Peninsula is a protected area, and building is heavily restricted. Consequently, it maintains a rustic charm that's unusual in the Balaton region. The peninsula also features a lush, protected interior, accessible by a trail from Tihany Village, with several little inland lakes as well as a lookout tower offering views over the Balaton.

ESSENTIALS

GETTING THERE   The rail line that circles Lake Balaton does not serve the Tihany Peninsula. The nearest station is in Aszófó, about 5km (3 miles) from Tihany Village. A local bus comes to Tihany from the nearby town of Balatonfüred. You can also go by ferry from Szántód or Balatonföldvár, or by boat from Balatonfüred.

By Car   From Budapest, take M7 south through Székesfehérvár until you hit the lake. Route 71 circles the lake. If you're planning a trip to Lake Balaton for more than a day or two, you should consider renting a car, which will give you much greater mobility. The various towns differ enough from one another that you may want to keep driving until you find the place that's right for you. Without a car, this is obviously more difficult. Also, wherever you go in the region, you'll find private rooms to be both cheaper and easier to get if you travel a few miles off the lake. Driving directly to the lake from Budapest will take about an hour and 15 minutes.

By Train   To reach Tihany, take a train to Balatonfüred for 920Ft ($4) (travel time 2 hours), and then a local bus to Tihany (You can also pick up this bus at Aszófó, halfway between Balatonfüred and Tihany). depending on what train you take, it is possible to stop at Balatonfüred, Szántód, or Balatonföldvár, if you are so inclined.

VISITOR INFORMATION   Visitor information is available at **Balatontourist,** Kossuth u. 20 (☎ and fax **87/538-071**). The office is open May to October only, Monday to Friday 8:30am to 7pm and weekends 8:30am to 12:30pm.

SEEING THE SIGHTS

The 18th-century baroque ✪ **Abbey Church** is Tihany Village's main attraction. A resident monk carved the exquisite wooden altar and pulpit in the 18th century. The frescoes in the church are by three of Hungary's better-known 19th-century painters: Károly Lotz, Bertalan Székely, and Lajos Deák-Ébner.

Next door to the Abbey Church is the **Tihany Museum** (☎ **87/448-650**), housed in an 18th-century baroque structure like the church. The museum features exhibitions on the surrounding region's history and culture. You pay a single entry fee of 180Ft (75¢) for both church and museum. Both are open daily 9am to 5:30pm.

SZIGLIGET

Halfway between Tihany and Keszthely is the scenic little village of Szigliget (pronounced *Sig*-lee-get), with thatched roof houses, lush vineyards, and a lovely Mediterranean quality. Szigliget is marked by the fantastic ruins of the 13th-century ✪ **Szigliget Castle,** which stand above it on **Várhegy (Castle Hill).** In the days of the Turkish invasions, the Hungarian Balaton fleet, protected by the high castle, called Szigliget its home. You can hike up to the ruins for a splendid view of the lake and the surrounding countryside; look for the path behind the white 18th-century church that stands on the highest spot in the village. A good place to fortify yourself for the hike is the **Vár Vendéglő** (on the road up to the castle), a casual restaurant with plenty of outdoor seating, serving traditional Hungarian fare.

The lively **beach** at Szigliget provides a striking contrast to the quiet village. In summer, buses from neighboring towns drop off hordes of beach-goers. The beach area is crowded with fried food and beer stands, ice cream vendors, a swing set, and a volleyball net. Admission to the beach is 200Ft (85¢). Szigliget is also home to the **Eszterházy Wine Cellar,** the largest wine cellar in the region. After a hike in the hills or a day in the sun, a little wine tasting just might be in order.

Natur Tourist (☎ **87/461-399**), in the village center, is your best (and only) source of information in Szigliget. Open daily 9am to 7pm (closing earlier in winter).

KESZTHELY

At the western edge of Lake Balaton, Keszthely (pronounced *Kest*-hay), 188km (117 miles) southwest of Budapest, is one the largest towns on the lake. Although Keszthely was largely destroyed during the Turkish wars, the town was rebuilt in the 18th century by the Festetics family, an aristocratic family who made Keszthely their home through World War II.

The center of Keszthely's summer scene, just like that of every other settlement on Lake Balaton, is down by the water on the "strand." Keszthely's beachfront is dominated by several large hotels. Regardless of whether you're a guest, you can rent Windsurfers, boats, and other water-related equipment from these hotels.

Heating Things Up at the Thermal Lake in Hévíz

If you find the water of Lake Balaton warm, just wait until you jump into the lake at Hévíz (pronounced *Hay*-veez), a town about 8km (5 miles) northwest of Keszthely.

This is Europe's largest ✪ **thermal lake** (and the second largest in the world). The lake's water temperature seldom dips below 30 to 32°C (85 to 90°F), even in the bitterest storm of winter. Consequently, people swim in the lake year-round. Hévíz has been one of Hungary's leading spa resorts for more than 100 years, and it retains some of the 19th-century character that's more typical of the spas in the Czech Republic than of those in the Hungary.

You can easily reach Hévíz by bus from Keszthely. Buses depart every half hour or so from the bus station (conveniently stopping to pick up passengers in front of the church on Fó tér). The entrance to the lake is just opposite the bus station. You'll see a whimsical wooden facade and the words TÓ FÜRDÓ (Bathing Lake) (☎ **83/340-587**). Tickets cost 480Ft ($2) for up to 3 hours or 920Ft ($3.85) for a day pass. Your ticket entitles you to a locker. Keep the ticket until exiting, as the attendant needs to see it to determine whether you've stayed a half-day or a full day.

ESSENTIALS

VISITOR INFORMATION   For visitor information, stop at **Tourinform,** Kossuth u. 28 (☎ and fax **83/314-144**), open Monday to Friday 9am to 4pm and Saturday (and Sundays in high season) 9am to 1pm. For private-room bookings, try **Zalatours,** Kossuth u. 1 (☎ **83/312-560**), or **Ibusz,** Kossuth u. 27 (☎ **83/314-320**).

A BAROQUE MANSION

✪ **Festetics Mansion.** Szabadsag u. 1. ☎ **83/312-190.** Admission 1,000Ft ($4.20) for foreigners. Summer: daily 9am–6pm; winter: Tues–Sun 9am–5pm.

The highlight of a visit to Keszthely is the splendid baroque 18th-century home (with its 19th-century additions) of the Festetics family. Part of the mansion is now open as a museum, the main attraction of which is the ornate library. The museum also features hunting gear and trophies of a bygone era.

The mansion's lovely concert hall is the site of **classical music concerts** almost every night throughout the summer (just two or three times a month from September through May). Concerts usually start at 8pm; tickets, at 750Ft ($3.15) apiece, are available at the door or earlier in the day at the museum cashier. Another part of the mansion has in the past—and, we are informed, may again—serve as a hotel.

10

Ireland

by Robert Meagher

If you haven't been to Ireland lately, then you haven't been to Ireland. The scale and pace of change here is dizzying. Once the donkey-cart of the European Union, Ireland is now the pacesetter—a young, turbulent, venturesome nation that's slow to look back and quick to outreach itself. If you look for it, the old Ireland lingers here and there, and, to be sure, Ireland remains a land of breathtaking beauty, whose people possess more than their share of wit and charm. What's new is that Ireland at the millennium is where "it's" happening—a boom, a renaissance, a revolution. No one knows what to call it, because no one knows where it's going. All the same, six million annual visitors come a long way to see it for themselves.

1 Dublin

"Seedy elegance" may have aptly described much, if not most, of Dublin until quite recently, but no longer. Named by *Fortune* magazine as the number one European city in which to do business, and edging out Rome, Venice, and Prague as the fifth most visited city in Europe, Dublin is no backwater. In fact, at the turn of the millennium Dublin was named by the annual Mercer survey as one of the world's top 10 places to live.

Needless to say Dublin is a great place to visit. The Liffey may never be potable, but otherwise the sky seems to be the limit here. More than 40 new hotels have sprouted up in the past several years alone in what seems a nearly hopeless race to keep up with tourist demand. Dublin is "ground zero" for the new Ireland, the lair of the "Celtic Tiger," and without any contest the hottest spot on the island.

ORIENTATION

ARRIVING By Plane The **Dublin International Airport** (☎ **01/704-4222**) is located 11km (7 miles) north of the city center. **Dublin Bus** (☎ **01/873-4222**) provides express coach service from the airport into the city's central bus station, **Busaras,** on Store Street. Service runs daily, 7:30am to 7:45pm (8:30pm Sundays), with departures every 20 to 30 minutes. One-way fare is £3.50 ($4.90) for adults and £1.25 ($1.75) for children under age 12. These services are expanded during high season, and a local city bus (no. 41) is also available to the city center for £1.10 ($1.55). There is also a new private licensed coach service called "AirCoach" operating 60 services a day at

15-min intervals between 5:30am and 11pm. AirCoach runs direct from the airport to Dublin's south side, servicing St. Stephen's Green, Fitzwilliam Square, Merrion Square, Ballsbridge and Donnybrook—the key hotel and business districts. The one-way fare is £4 ($6).

For speed and ease, a **taxi** is the best way to get directly to your hotel or guest house. Depending on your destination, fares average between £15 ($21) and £20 ($28). A 10% tip is standard. Taxis are lined up at a first-come, first-served taxi stand outside the arrivals terminal.

By Ferry   Passenger/car ferries from Britain arrive at the **Dublin Ferryport** (☎ 01/ 855-2222), on the eastern end of the North Docks, and at the **Dun Laoghaire Ferryport** (☎ 01/661-0511), about 16km (10 miles) south of the city center. There is bus and taxi service from both ports.

By Train   Irish Rail (☎ 01/836-6222) operates daily train service into Dublin from Belfast in Northern Ireland and all major cities in the Irish Republic, including Cork, Galway, Limerick, Killarney, Sligo, Wexford, and Waterford. Trains from the south, west, and southwest arrive at **Heuston Station,** Kingsbridge, off St. John's Road; from the north and northwest at **Connolly Station,** Amiens Street; and from the southeast at **Pearse Station,** Westland Row, Tara Street.

By Bus   Bus Eireann (☎ 01/836-6111) operates daily express coach and local bus services from all major cities and towns in Ireland into Dublin's central bus station, Busaras, on Store Street.

By Car   If you are arriving by car from other parts of Ireland or via car ferry from Britain, all main roads lead into the heart of Dublin and are well signposted to An Lar (City Centre). To bypass the city center, the East Link (toll bridge 60p/85¢) and West Link are signposted, and the M50 circuits the city on three sides.

VISITOR INFORMATION   Dublin Tourism operates five year-round walk-in visitor centers in greater Dublin. The principal center is at **St. Andrew's Church,** Suffolk Street, Dublin 2, open June to August Monday to Saturday 9am to 8:30pm, Sunday and Bank Holidays 10:30am to 2:30pm, and the rest of the year Monday to Saturday 9am to 5:30pm. Services include a currency exchange counter, a car-rental counter, accommodation reservations, bus and rail information desks, a gift shop, and a cafe. The other four centers are at the Arrivals Hall of **Dublin Airport;** the new ferry terminal, **Dun Laoghaire;** the **Baggot Street Bridge,** Dublin 2; and **The Square,** Tallaght, Dublin 24 (all phone inquiries should be directed to the numbers below). All centers are open year-round with at least the following hours: Monday to Friday 9am to 5:30pm and Saturday 9am to 1pm.

For accommodation reservations throughout Ireland by credit card, contact **Dublin Tourism** at ☎ **011 800/668-668-66** (within Ireland, omit the 011), reservations@ dublintourism.ie, or www.visitdublin.com. For other information contact **Bord Failte** at ☎ **1850/230330** within Ireland (a local call from anywhere in the country) or ☎ **066/979-2083;** or information@dublintourism.ie.

In addition, an independent center offers details on concerts, exhibits, and other arts events in the **Temple Bar** section at 18 Eustace St., Temple Bar, Dublin 2 (☎ 01/ 671-5717), open year-round Monday to Friday 9:30am to 5:30pm and Saturday 10am to 5:30pm.

At any of these centers you can pick up the free *Tourism News;* or the free *Event Guide,* a biweekly entertainment guide, online at www.eventguide.ie. *In Dublin,* a biweekly arts-and-entertainment magazine selling for £2.90 ($4.05), is available at most newsstands. Dublin Tourism is also online at www.visitdublin.com.

Dublin

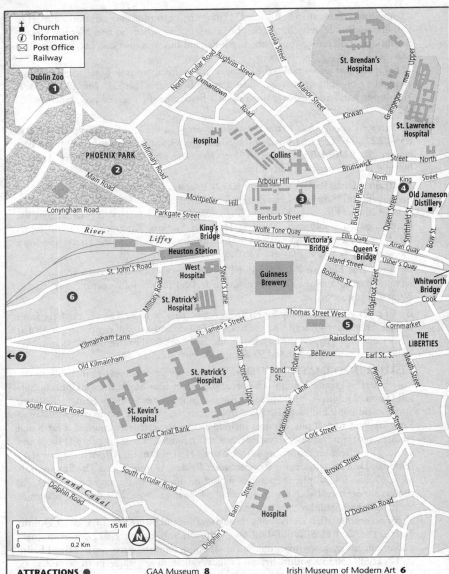

Legend:
- ✝ Church
- ⓘ Information
- ✉ Post Office
- — Railway

Dublin Zoo ①

PHOENIX PARK ②

Hospital

PRUSSIA STREET

North Circular Road Aughrim Street
Oxmantown
Manor Street

St. Brendan's Hospital

Kirwan

St. Lawrence Hospital

Collins

Brunswick Street North

North King Street ④

Old Jameson Distillery ■

Arbour Hill ③

Benburb Street

Infirmary Road
Main Road
Montpelier Hill
Conyngham Road
Parkgate Street

Blackhall Place
Queen Street
Smithfield Street
Bow St.

River Liffey
King's Bridge
Heuston Station
West Hospital
St. Patrick's Hospital

Wolfe Tone Quay
Victoria Quay
Victoria's Bridge
Ellis Quay
Arran Quay

Queen's Bridge
Island Street
Usher's Quay

Whitworth Bridge
Cook

Guinness Brewery

Bonham St.
Bridgefoot Street

Military Road
Steven's Lane

Irish Museum of Modern Art ⑥

⑦ ←

Kilmainham Lane
Old Kilmainham

St. James's Street

Thomas Street West ⑤
Rainsford St.
THE LIBERTIES
Cornmarket

Basin Street Upper
Robert St.
Bellevue
Earl St. S.
Maath Street

St. Patrick's Hospital

Bond St.
Pimlico
Ardee Street

Marrowbone Lane

South Circular Road
St. Kevin's Hospital
Grand Canal Bank

Cork Street

Brown Street

Grand Canal
Dolphin Road
South Circular Road
Barn Street
Dolphin's

Hospital

O'Donovan Road

0   1/5 Mi
0   0.2 Km
N

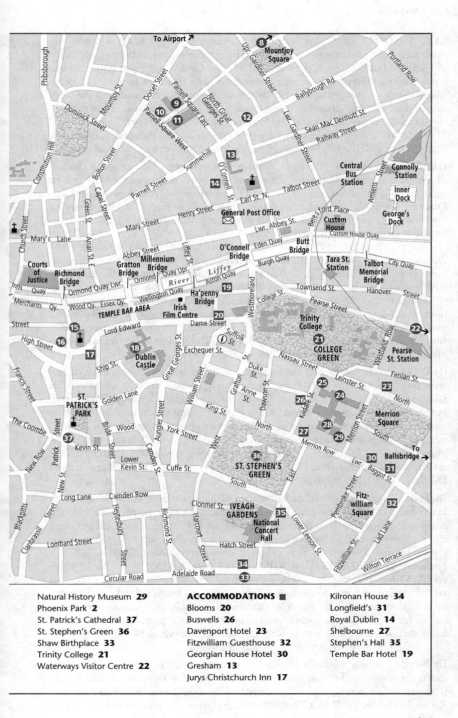

CITY LAYOUT   Compared with other European capitals, Dublin is a relatively small metropolis and easy to get to know. The downtown core of the city, identified in Gaelic on bus destination signs as **AN LAR** (the Center), is shaped somewhat like a pie, with the **River Liffey** cutting across the middle from east to west. The north side of the city is rimmed in a semicircular sweep by the **Royal Canal,** and the south side is edged in a half-circle shape by the waters of the **Grand Canal.** To the north of the Royal Canal are the suburbs of Drumcondra, Glasnevin, Howth, Clontarf, and Malahide; to the south of the Grand Canal are the suburbs of Ballsbridge, Blackrock, Dun Laoghaire, Dalkey, Killiney, Rathgar, Rathmines, and other residential areas.

GETTING AROUND   By Bus   Dublin Bus operates a fleet of green double-decker buses, frequent single-deck buses, and minibuses throughout the city and its suburbs. Most buses originate on or near **O'Connell Street, Abbey Street,** or **Eden Quay** on the north side, and from **Aston Quay, College Street,** or **Fleet Street** on the south side. Destinations and bus numbers are posted above the front windows; buses destined for the city center are marked **AN LAR.**

Bus service runs daily throughout the city, 6am (10am on Sunday) to 11:30pm; Friday and Saturday there's a Nitelink service from the city center to the suburbs midnight to 3am. Schedules are posted on revolving notice boards at each bus stop. City bus fares are calculated on the distances traveled and run from a base fare of 80p ($1.10) to £1.25 ($1.75). The NiteLink fare is a flat £2.50 ($3.50). Buy your tickets from the driver as you enter the bus; exact change is not required. One-day, 4-day, and weekly passes are available at reduced rates. For more information, contact **Dublin Bus,** 59 Upper O'Connell St. (☎ **01/873-4222**). Dublin Bus also operates an information desk at the central Tourist Office on Suffolk Street.

By DART   Although Dublin has no subway in the strict sense, there is an electrified train system, known as **DART** (Dublin Area Rapid Transit). It travels mostly at ground level or on elevated tracks, linking the city-center stations at **Tara Street, Pearse Street,** and **Amiens Street** with suburbs and seaside communities as far as Howth to the north and Bray to the south. Service operates roughly every 10 to 20 minutes Monday to Saturday 7am to midnight and Sunday 9:30am to 11pm. Minimum fare is 80p ($1.10). One-day, 4-day, and weekly passes, as well as family tickets, are available at reduced rates. For further information, contact **DART,** Pearse Station, Dublin 2 (☎ **01/7-3-3054**).

By Taxi   Dublin taxis do not cruise the streets looking for fares; instead, they line up at stands (called ranks). Stands are located outside all the leading hotels, at bus and train stations, and on prime thoroughfares, such as Upper O'Connell Street, College Green, and the north side of St. Stephen's Green. You can also phone for a taxi. Some of the companies that operate a 24-hour radio-call service are **Co-Op** (☎ **01/677-7777**), **National** (☎ **01/677-2222**), and **VIP Taxis** (☎ **01/478-3333**). If you need a wake-up call, **VIP** offers that service, along with especially courteous dependability. Taxi rates are fixed by law and posted in each taxi. At peak times in Dublin's often backed-up traffic, it's the minutes and not the miles that are going to add up. The most costly add-ons are for dispatched pick-up and for service from Dublin airport. Some hotel or guest house staff, when asked to arrange for a taxi, tack on as much as £4 ($6) for their services, although this practice violates city taxi regulations.

By Bicycle   Riding a bike in Dublin isn't recommended. Traffic is very heavy, the streets are narrow, and pedestrians crowd every corner. For those determined to take to the streets on wheels, a good option is **Dublin Bike Tours,** 3 Morningside Rd., Ranelagh, Dublin 6 (☎ **01/679-0899**), offering 3-hour tours of the city. The cost is

£15 ($21) per person; tours depart three times daily (10am, 2pm, and 6pm). Dublin Bike Tours also offer a variety of other cycle tours in the Dublin area.

Parking   The bottom line here is that you're better off without a car in Dublin, as the city is aggressively discouraging the car as the vehicle of choice for commuters, much less for tourists. During normal business hours, **free parking** on Dublin streets is an endangered option soon to be extinct. Never park in bus lanes or along a curb with double yellow lines. Fines for parking illegally start at £21 ($23); if a car is towed away, it costs at least £100 ($140) to retrieve it. What's more the infamous "Denver boot," or wheel clamp, has come to Ireland, and the cost of removing it starts at £65 ($91).

Individual **parking meters** in the city center are currently being phased out in favor of multibay meters and "pay-and-display" **disk parking.** In Dublin, five disks can be purchased for £4 ($6), and each ticket is good for either 1 or 2 hours, depending on the location of the parking site. By 2001, Dublin plans to introduce "smart cards" for city parking, though the details of the plan have not yet been released at press time. The most reliable and safest places to park are at surface parking lots or in multistory parking lots (called car parks) in central locations, such as Kildare Street, Lower Abbey Street, Marlborough Street, and St. Stephen's Green West. Parking lots charge on average £1.50 ($2.10) per hour and £14 ($20) for 24 hours. Night rates vary from £4 ($6) to £6 ($8).

On Foot   Small and compact, Dublin is ideal for walking, but be careful to look left and right for oncoming traffic and to obey traffic signals. Each traffic light has timed "walk/don't walk" signals for pedestrians. Pedestrians have the right of way at specially marked zebra-striped crossings; as a warning, there are usually two flashing lights at these intersections. For some walking-tour suggestions, see "Organized Tours" under "Exploring Dublin," below).

Fast Facts: Dublin

American Express   The Dublin office of American Express International is a full-service travel agency also offering currency exchange, traveler's checks, and (for members) mail-holding. It is located opposite Trinity College, just off College Green, at 41 Nassau St., Dublin 2 (☎ **01/679-9000**), and is open Monday to Saturday 9am to 5pm. American Express also has a desk at the Dublin Tourism Office on Suffolk Street (☎ **01/605-7709**). In an emergency, traveler's checks can be reported lost or stolen by dialing collect ☎ **1-44-1-273-571-600.**

Baby-Sitters   With advance notice, most hotels and guest houses will arrange for baby-sitting.

Banks   Two convenient banks are the **National Irish Bank,** 66 Upper O'Connell St., open Monday to Friday 10am to 4pm (to 5pm Thursday), and the **Allied Irish Bank,** 100 Grafton St., open Monday to Friday 10am to 4pm (to 5pm Thursday). Both have ATMs that accept Cirrus network cards as well as MasterCard and Visa.

Business Hours   **Banks** are open Monday to Wednesday and on Friday 10am to 12:30pm and 1:30 to 3pm, on Thursday 10am to 12:30pm and 1:30 to 5pm. Some banks stay open through the lunch hour. Most **business offices** are open Monday to Friday 9am to 5pm. **Stores and shops** are open Monday to Wednesday and Friday to Saturday 9am to 5:30pm, and Thursday 9am to 8pm. Some bookshops and tourist-oriented stores also open on Sunday 11am or noon to 4 or 5pm. During the peak season (May through September), many gift and souvenir shops post Sunday hours.

Currency   Ireland, as of January 1999, has adopted the single European currency known as the euro. Although the euro will not appear as hard currency until 2002, it is already the actual medium of exchange in the Republic. The punt or Irish pound no longer trades as an independent currency, its value permanently fixed at €1.27. Already in shops and elsewhere, prices are cited in both punts and euros; in this guide prices in the Republic are still given in punts. The punt is divided into 100 **pence (p).** There are lp, 2p, 5p, 10p, 20p, 50p, and £1 coins, and punt notes of 5, 10, 20, 50, and 100 punts. It is, of course, difficult to predict the future course of the punt, which has had a disappointing debut. The rate of exchange used in this chapter is: $1 = 71p or Irish £1 = $1.40.

Currency Exchange   Currency-exchange services, signposted as BUREAU DE CHANGE, are in all banks and at many post offices (An Post). A bureau de change operates daily during flight arrival and departure times at Dublin airport; a foreign currency note-exchanger machine is also available on a 24-hour basis in the main arrivals hall. Many hotels and travel agencies offer bureau de change services, although the best rate of exchange is usually given at banks or, better yet, when you use your credit card for purchases or expenses.

Dentist   For dental emergencies, contact the Eastern Health Board Headquarters, Dr. Steevens Hospital, Dublin 8 (☎ **01/679-0700**). See also "Dental Surgeons" in the Golden Pages (yellow pages) of the telephone book.

Doctor   In an emergency, most hotels and guest houses will contact a house doctor for you. You can also call the Eastern Health Board Headquarters, Dr. Steevens Hospital, Dublin 8 (☎ **01/679-0700**); or the Irish Medical Organization, 10 Fitzwilliam Place, Dublin 2 (☎ **01/676-7273**), 9:15am to 5:15pm. See also "Doctors—Medical" in the Golden Pages of the phone book.

Drugstores   Centrally located drugstores, known locally as pharmacies or chemists, include **Hamilton Long and Co.,** 5 Lower O'Connell St. (☎ **01/874-8456**); and **Dame Street Pharmacy,** 16 Dame St., Dublin 2 (☎ **01/670-4523**). A late-night chemist shop is **Byrnes Late Night Pharmacy,** 4 Merrion Rd., Dublin 4 (☎ **01/668-3287**).

Embassies/Consulates   The **United States** Embassy is located at 42 Elgin Rd., Ballsbridge, Dublin 4 (☎ **01/668-8777**); **Canadian** Embassy, 65/68 St. Stephen's Green, Dublin 2 (☎ **01/478/1988**); **British** Embassy, 29 Merrion Rd., Dublin 4 (☎ **01/205-3700**); **Australian** Embassy, Fitzwilton House, Wilton Terrace, Dublin 2 (☎ **01/676-1517**).

Emergencies   For the **Garda** (police), fire, or other emergencies, dial ☎ **999.**

Holidays   Dublin holidays are January 1 (New Year's Day), March 17 (St. Patrick's Day), Good Friday and Easter Monday, May Day (the first Monday in May), the first Monday in June and August (Summer Bank Holidays), the last Monday in October (Autumn Bank Holiday), December 25 (Christmas Day), and December 26 (St. Stephen's Day). Most stores remain closed between Christmas and the first Monday after New Year's Day.

Hospitals   For emergency care, two of the most modern health-care facilities are **St. Vincent's Hospital,** Elm Park (☎ **01/269-4533**), on the south side of the city, and **Beaumont Hospital,** Beaumont Road, Dublin 9 (☎ **01/837-7755**), on the north side.

Internet Access   In Internet-savvy Dublin, public access terminals are no longer hard to find, appearing in shopping malls, hotels, and hostels throughout the city center. One of the most convenient and comfortable of the many cyber-cafes in town is **Betacafe,** Curve St., Temple Bar, Dublin 2 (☎ **01/605-6800;** www.betacafe.com), located above the Arthouse. Fifteen minutes on-line will set you back £1.50 ($2.10). It's open Monday to Saturday 10am to 10:30pm and Sunday noon to 6pm. At the **Planet Cybercafe** (☎ **01/679-0583**), 23 South Great Georges St., Dublin 2, 30 minutes on-line costs £2.75 ($3.85). Fast transmission rates are assured at **Cyberia Cafe,** Eustace Street, Temple Bar, Dublin 2 (☎ **01/679-7607;** www.cyberiacafe.net), where 15 minutes on-line is £1.50 ($2.10), or £1.25 ($1.75) for students. It's open Monday to Saturday 10am to 11pm and Sunday noon to 8pm.

Laundry   In the city center, try **Suds,** 60 Upper Grand Canal St., Dublin 2 (☎ **01/668-1786**). Take your dry cleaning to **Craft Cleaners,** 12 Upper Baggot St., Dublin 4 (☎ **01/668-8198**).

Post Office   The **General Post Office** (GPO) is located on O'Connell Street, Dublin 1 (☎ **01/705-7000**). Hours are Monday to Saturday 8am to 8pm, Sunday and holidays 10:30am to 6:30pm. Branch offices, identified by the sign OIFIG AN POST/POST OFFICE, are open Monday to Saturday 9am to 6pm.

Telephone   The **country code** for the Republic of Ireland is **353.** The **city code** for Dublin is **01.** If you're calling from outside Ireland, drop the initial 0 from the city code. Thus, to call the Georgian House from the United States, you would dial ☎ **011-353-1/661-8832.** For direct-dial calls to the United States, dial the international access code (**00** from Ireland), and then the country code (**1**), followed by area code and number. To place a collect call to the United States from Ireland, dial ☎ **1-800/550-000** for USA Direct service. The toll-free international access codes are: **AT&T** ☎ 1-**800/550-000,** **Sprint** ☎ **1-800/ 552-001,** and **MCI** ☎ **1-800/55-1001.**

Ireland has one of Europe's most sophisticated phone systems, and the quality of international connections is exceptional. Throughout the city you can find pay phones that accept coins, both on the street and in pubs; a **local call** costs 20p (30¢). If you want to use one of the many yellow Callcard phones, almost as common as coin phones, you have to buy a **Callcard** (available at post offices, newsstands, and many convenience stores). The Callcard is available in denominations of 10, 20, 50, and 100 units, priced at £2 ($2.80), £3.50 ($4.90), £8 ($11), and £16 ($22), respectively. There's a local and international phone center at the General Post Office on O'Connell Street. Pay phones accept a variety of coins or a phone card (available at post offices). For information on finding a telephone number, dial ☎ **1190.**

Tipping & Service Charges   Many hotels and guest houses add a service charge to the bill, usually 12.5% to 15%, although some places add only 10% or nothing at all. For restaurants, the policy is usually printed on the menu—either a gratuity of 10% to 15% is added to your bill, or in some cases, no service charge is added, in which case it is up to you to decide how much tip you want to leave. As a rule, bar staff do not expect a tip, except when table service is provided. Taxi drivers don't expect a tip, but if you want to give one, 10% is appropriate.

VAT   All goods and services in Ireland are subject to a 17.36% tax, known as the **VAT (value-added tax).** For non-European visitors to Ireland, it's relatively easy to arrange a **refund** of all VAT tax paid on goods (the tax paid on services is nonrefundable). See "Money" in the "Introduction: Planning a Trip to Europe" for more information, or contact the tourist office.

WHERE TO STAY
HISTORIC OLD CITY & TEMPLE BAR/TRINITY COLLEGE AREA
Expensive
Temple Bar Hotel. Fleet St., Temple Bar, Dublin 2. ☎ **800/44-UTELL** in the U.S., or 01/677-3333. Fax 01/677-3088. www.towerhotelgroup.ie. 129 units, 13 with shower only. TV TEL. £109–£189 ($153–$265) double. Rates include full breakfast. No service charge. AE, DC, MC, V. DART to Tara St. Station. Bus: 78A or 78B.

If you want to be in the heart of the action in the Temple Bar district, then this is a prime place to stay. Opened in summer 1993, this five-story hotel was developed from a row of townhouses. Rooms are modern with traditional furnishings, including amenities such as a garment press, towel warmer, hair dryer, and tea/coffeemaker. Two rooms are wheelchair accessible. Facilities include the Terrace Café, a skylit garden-style restaurant, and Buskers, an Old Dublin–theme pub, as well as access to a nearby health club.

Moderate
Blooms. Anglesea St., Dublin 2. ☎ **800/44-UTELL** from the U.S., or 01/671-5622. Fax 01/671-5997. www.blooms.ie. 86 units. TV TEL. £110 ($154) double. Service charge 12.5%. DC, MC, V. No parking provided. DART: Tara St. Bus: 21A, 46A, 46B, 51B, 51C, 68, 69, or 86.

Lovers of Irish literature will feel at home at Blooms. Named after Leopold Bloom, a character in James Joyce's *Ulysses*, this hotel is near Trinity College and on the edge of the artsy Temple Bar district. Rooms are modern and functional, with garment presses and hair dryers. The hotel has concierge service, 24-hour room service, and valet/laundry service. Bia is the formal restaurant, but for more casual fare, try the Anglesea Bar. Late-night entertainment is available in the basement-level nightclub, known simply as M.

Inexpensive
Jurys Christchurch Inn. Christchurch Place, Dublin 8. ☎ **800/44-UTELL** in the U.S., or 01/454-0000. Fax 01/454-0012. www.jurys.com. 182 units. A/C TV TEL. £65–£68 ($91–$95) double. No service charge. AE, DC, MC, V. Bus: 21A, 50, 50A, 78, 78A, or 78B.

Across from Christchurch Cathedral, this relatively new four-story hotel was designed in keeping with the area's Georgian/Victorian architecture. Geared to the cost-conscious traveler, it's the first of its kind in the city's historic district, offering quality hotel lodgings at guest-house prices. Rooms, decorated with contemporary furnishings, can accommodate up to three adults or two adults and two children—all for the same price. All have coffeemakers and hair dryers. Facilities include a moderately

---

Traveler's Tip

In general, rates for Dublin hotels don't vary as greatly with the seasons as they do in the Irish countryside. Hotels often charge higher prices, however, during special events, such as the Dublin Horse Show. For the best deals, try to reserve a room in Dublin over a weekend, and ask if there's a reduction or a weekend package in effect. Some Dublin hotels cut their rates by as much as 50% on Friday and Saturday nights, when business traffic is low. Also, significant reductions are sometimes available when rooms are booked from the States using the 800 numbers listed in this book.

priced restaurant, a pub lounge, and an adjacent multistory parking area. There are 38 no-smoking rooms available, and two rooms specially adapted for guests with disabilities.

ST. STEPHEN'S GREEN/GRAFTON STREET AREA
Very Expensive
✪ **Shelbourne.** 27 St. Stephen's Green, Dublin 2. ☎ **800/225-5843** in the U.S., or 01/676-6471. Fax 01/661-6006. www.shelbourne.ie. 190 units. MINIBAR TV TEL. £240–£322($336–$450) double. Rates include full breakfast. Service charge 15%. AE, DC, MC, V. DART: Pearse. Bus: 10, 11A, 11B, 13, or 20B.

This grand six-story redbrick and white-trimmed hostelry stands out on the north side of St. Stephen's Green. Built in 1824, it has played a significant role in Irish history (the new nation's constitution was signed in room 112 in 1921) and is often host to international leaders, stars of stage and screen, and literary giants. The public areas, replete with glowing fireplaces, Waterford chandeliers, and original art, are popular rendezvous spots for Dubliners. Rooms vary in size, but all offer up-to-date comforts and are furnished with antique and period pieces. Front units overlook St. Stephen's Green. Needless to say, you don't stay here just for the beds, which represent the Irish preference for a mattress somewhere beyond soft and short of firm.

Stephen's Hall. Earlsfort Centre, 14–17 Lower Leeson St., Dublin 2. ☎ **01/638-1111.** Fax 01/638-1122. www.premgroup.ie. 37 units. MINIBAR TV TEL. £175–£260 ($245–$364) double. No service charge. AE, DC, MC, V. DART: Pearse. Bus: 14A, 11A, 11B, 13, 46A, 46B, or 86.

On the southeast corner of St. Stephen's Green, with a gracious Georgian exterior, this is Dublin's first all-suite hotel. It's ideal for visitors who plan an extended stay or want to entertain. Newly renovated and furnished in a contemporary motif, each suite contains a hallway, sitting room, dining area, kitchen, bathroom, and one or two bedrooms, with orthopedic beds. Luxury suites on the upper floors offer city views, while ground-level townhouse suites have private entrances. Twelve have computers. All have CD/radio, hair dryers, and coffeemakers.

Expensive
Buswells. 25 Molesworth St., Dublin 2. ☎ **800/473-9527** in the U.S., or 01/614-6500. Fax 01/676-2090. www.quinn-group.com. 69 units. TV TEL. £165 ($231) double. Rates include full breakfast. No service charge. AE, DC, MC, V. Free overnight parking (5:30pm–9:30am). DART: Pearse. Bus: 10, 11A, 11B, 13, or 20B.

Situated on a quiet street 2 blocks from Trinity College and opposite the National Museum, this vintage four-story hotel has long been a meeting point for artists, poets, scholars, and politicians. Originally two 1736 Georgian townhouses, it was launched as a hotel in 1928 and has been managed by three generations of the Duff family. The public rooms have period furniture and intricate plasterwork. Rooms have been updated in a contemporary decor with Victorian touches and come with such amenities as tea/coffeemakers and hair dryers. No-smoking rooms are available; one room is specially designed for travelers with disabilities. Facilities include a restaurant, two bars, concierge, and room service.

Moderate
Georgian House Hotel. 18–22 Lower Baggot St., Dublin 2. ☎ **01/661-8832.** Fax 01/661-8834. E-mail: hotel@georgianhouse.ie. 47 units. TV TEL. £110–£150 ($154–$210) double. Rates include full breakfast. No service charge. AE, CB, DC, MC, V. Free parking. DART to Pearse Station. Bus: 10.

Located less than 2 blocks from St. Stephen's Green, this four-story, 200-year-old brick townhouse sits in the heart of Georgian Dublin, within walking distance of most major attractions. During the past year, nearly 20 new spacious rooms have been added and the smallish older ones have been fully renovated to a high standard of comfort. All have hair dryers. The hotel's restaurant, the Celts Banquet, specializes in seafood and Celtic fare such as suckling pig and pheasant pie, accompanied by open logs fires and traditional music. There's also a lively in-house pub, Maguire's, in the basement. Current plans call for new executive rooms, a leisure center and indoor pool, an underground garage, and a new dining room perhaps by spring 2001.

FITZWILLIAM/MERRION SQUARE AREA

Very Expensive

Davenport Hotel. Merrion Sq., Dublin 2. ☎ **800/327-0200** in the U.S., or 01/661-6800. Fax 01/661-5663. www.davenporthotel.ie. 116 units. A/C TV TEL. £210–£300 ($294–$420) double. Rates include full breakfast. Service charge 12.5%. AE, DC, MC, V. DART: Pearse. Bus: 5, 7A, 8, or 62.

The hotel building incorporates the neoclassical facade of Merrion Hall, an 1863 church. Inside is an impressive domed entranceway, with a six-story atrium lobby. Rooms, in a new section, have traditional furnishings, orthopedic beds, three telephone lines plus a computer data port, work desk, safe, trouser press, tea/coffee welcome tray, and hair dryer. It's a sister hotel to the Mont Clare across the street and shares valet car-parking arrangements.

Expensive

✪ **Longfield's.** 10 Lower Fitzwilliam St., Dublin 2. ☎ **01/676-1367.** Fax 01/676-1542. E-mail: lfields@indigo.ie. 26 units. TV TEL. £110–£160 ($154–$224) double. Rates include full breakfast. No service charge. AE, DC, MC, V. DART to Pearse Station. Bus: 10.

Created from two 18th-century Georgian townhouses, this small, classy hotel combines Georgian decor and reproduction period furnishings of dark woods and brass trim. Rooms offer hair dryers and coffeemakers. Although situated in a busy area, Longfield's is remarkably quiet, an elegant yet unpretentious getaway 5 minutes' walk from St. Stephen's Green. Facilities include a restaurant with bar, room service, and foreign currency exchange.

Moderate

✪ **Fitzwilliam Guesthouse.** 41 Upper Fitzwilliam St., Dublin 2. ☎ **01/662-5155.** Fax 01/676-7488. 12 units, all with bathroom. TV TEL. £60–£84 ($84–$118) double. Rates include full breakfast. AE, DC, MC, V. DART: Pearse (then a 10-minute walk southeast). Bus: 10.

This guest house occupies a meticulously restored 18th-century townhouse on Fitzwilliam Street, the best-preserved Georgian thoroughfare in Dublin and a convenient location for exploring the city. The entrance parlor has a homey atmosphere, with a carved marble fireplace and antique furnishings. The bright rooms have hair dryers; bathrooms are somewhat small, but impeccably clean. Tea/coffeemakers are available just outside every room. A full Irish breakfast is served in the vaulted basement restaurant.

Kilronan House. 70 Adelaide Rd., Dublin 2. ☎ **01/475-5266.** Fax: 01/478-2841. www.dublinn.com. 15 units, all with shower only. TV TEL. £70–£90 ($98–$126) double. Children under 7 free. Rates include full breakfast. AE, MC, V. Free parking. Bus: 14, 15, 19, 20, or 46A.

Noel Comer is the outgoing proprietor at this comfortable guest house, located within 5 minutes' walk of St. Stephen's Green, just north of the Royal Canal. The sitting room on the ground floor is small and intimate, with a fire glowing through the cold months of the year. Rooms are well kept, and those facing the front have commodious bay windows; each offers tea and coffee facilities and hair dryers. If you don't like stairs, request a room on the second floor, as there's no elevator. The front rooms, facing Adelaide Street, are also preferable to those in back, which face onto office buildings and a parking lot. When you book, ask about a reduction for Frommer's readers.

O'CONNELL STREET AREA

Very Expensive

Gresham. 23 Upper O'Connell St., Dublin 1. ☎ **01/874-6881.** Fax 01/878-7175. 288 units. A/C TV TEL. £180–£280 ($252–$392) double; from £280 ($392) suite. Service charge 12.5%. AE, CB, DC, MC, V. Parking £5 ($7) daily. DART: Connolly. Bus: 40A, 40B, 40C, or 51A.

Centrally located on the city's main business thoroughfare, this Regency-style hotel is one of Ireland's oldest (1817) and best-known lodgings. Although much of the tourist trade in Dublin has shifted south of the Liffey in recent years, the Gresham is still synonymous with stylish Irish hospitality and provides easy access to the Abbey and Gate Theatres and other north-side attractions. The newly renovated rooms vary in size and style. One-of-a-kind luxury terrace suites grace the upper-front floors.

Moderate

Royal Dublin. 40 Upper O'Connell St., Dublin 1. ☎ **800/528-1234** in the U.S., or 01/873-3666. Fax 01/873-3120. E-mail: enq@royaldublin.com. 117 units. TV TEL. £105–£154 ($147–$216) double. Rates include full Irish breakfast and service charge. AE, DC, MC, V. Free parking nearby. DART: Connolly. Bus: 36A, 40A, 40B, 40C, or 51A.

Romantically floodlit at night, this modern five-story hotel is positioned near Parnell Square at the north end of Dublin's main thoroughfare, within walking distance of all the main theaters and north-side attractions. It combines a contemporary skylit lobby full of art deco overtones with adjacent lounge areas that were part of an original building, dating from 1752. Rooms are strictly modern, with full-length windows that extend over the busy street below.

BALLSBRIDGE/EMBASSY ROW AREA

Situated south of the Grand Canal, this is Dublin's most prestigious suburb, yet it is within walking distance of downtown. Although primarily a residential area, it is also the home of some of the city's leading hotels, restaurants, and embassies.

Very Expensive

✪ **Berkeley Court.** Lansdowne Rd., Ballsbridge, Dublin 4. ☎ **800/42-DOYLE** in the U.S., or 01/660-1711. Fax 01/661-7238. www.doylehotels.com. 186 units. TV TEL. £172–£278 ($240–$389) double; from £250 ($388) suite. Rates include full breakfast. Service charge 15%. AE, DC, MC, V. Free valet parking. DART: Lansdowne Rd. Bus: 7, 8, or 45.

The flagship of the Irish-owned Doyle Hotel group, and the first Irish member of Leading Hotels of the World, the Berkeley Court is nestled in a residential area near the American Embassy on well-tended grounds that were once part of the Botanic Gardens of University College. A favorite haunt of diplomats and international business leaders, the hotel is known for its posh lobby decorated with fine antiques, original paintings, and Irish-made carpets and furnishings. The newly redecorated rooms with semicanopy beds convey an air of elegance. No-smoking rooms are available. Facilities include a restaurant, conservatory, bar and lounge, minigym, hair salon, boutiques, and gift shop.

Jurys Hotel and Towers. Pembroke Rd., Ballsbridge, Dublin 4. ☎ **800/843-3311** in the U.S., or 01/660-5000. Fax 01/667-5471. www.jurys.com. 390 units. A/C MINIBAR TV TEL. Main hotel £195 ($273) double; Towers wing (with continental breakfast) £220 ($308) double. Service charge 12.5%. AE, DC, MC, V. Limited free parking. DART: Lansdowne Rd. Bus: 5, 7, 7A, or 8.

Setting a progressive tone in a city steeped in tradition, this massive hotel, which enjoyed a major refurbishment in 1999, welcomes guests to a skylit, three-story atrium lobby. Situated opposite the American Embassy, this sprawling property is actually two interconnected hotels in one: a modern, eight-story high-rise and a new 100-unit tower with its own check-in desk, separate elevators, and private entrance, as well as full access to all the main hotel's amenities. Rooms have computer key-card access, stocked minibar, three telephone lines, well-lit work area with desk, reclining chair, and either a king- or queen-size bed. The Towers section features oversized concierge-style rooms with bay windows. Towers guests also enjoy exclusive use of a private hospitality lounge with library, boardroom, and access to complimentary continental breakfast, daily newspapers, and coffee/tea service throughout the day.

Expensive

Butlers Town House. 44 Lansdowne Rd., Ballsbridge, Dublin 4. ☎ **800-44-UTELL** in the U.S., or 01/667-4022. Fax 01/667-3960. E-mail: info@butlers-hotel.com. 20 units, 1 with shower only. A/C TV TEL. £80–£160 ($112–$224) double. Rates include full breakfast. AE, DC, MC, V. DART: Lansdowne Rd. Bus: 7, 7A, 8, 45.

This beautifully restored and expanded Victorian townhouse has a formal yet welcoming elegance—class without the starched collar. Rooms are richly furnished with either four-poster or half-tester beds, equipped with climate control, computer modems, hair dryers, and coffeemakers. It's hard to elude comfort here, and the staff is especially solicitous. The gem, in our opinion, is the Glendalough Room, which can be requested if you book early. In addition to laundry and dry cleaning, secretarial services are available. Amenities include free tea or coffee anytime; breakfast, afternoon tea, and high tea served in the atrium dining room; room service, baby-sitting, and one handicapped-equipped room. You'll find that there isn't much Helen Finnegan, the manager, has overlooked here.

Moderate

✪ **Ariel House.** 50/52 Lansdowne Rd., Ballsbridge, Dublin 4. ☎ **01/668-5512.** Fax 01/668-5845. 40 units. TV TEL. £100 –£158 ($140–$221) double (rates vary seasonally). Full Irish breakfast £8.50 ($12). MC, V. Free parking available. DART: Lansdowne Rd. Bus: 7, 7A, 8, or 45.

In the age of the generic, Ariel House remains a bastion of distinction and quality. For Dublin guest houses, this one sets the standard. Michael and Maurice O'Brien are warm and consummate hosts. Guests are welcome to relax in the Victorian-style drawing room with its Waterford glass chandeliers and open fireplace. Rooms are individually decorated, with period furniture. Facilities include a conservatory-style dining room where breakfast, morning coffee, and afternoon tea are served; there's also a wine bar.

Mount Herbert. 7 Herbert Rd., Ballsbridge, Dublin 4. ☎ **01/668-4321.** Fax 01/660-7077. www.mountherberthotel.ie. 200 units. TV TEL. £70–£99 ($98–$139) double. Rates include full breakfast. No service charge. AE, DC, MC, V. Limited free parking. DART: Lansdowne Rd. Bus: 3, 5, 7, 7A, 8, 18, or 45.

More than 40 years ago, the Loughran family welcomed their first guests to what had once been the family home of Lord Robinson. This gracious residence, with its own mature floodlit gardens, forms the core of a now somewhat sprawling complex. In 4 decades, the Mount Herbert has expanded from 4 rooms to 200. The result is a curious mix of family hospitality and large-scale uniformity. Rooms are bright, comfortable, and convenient to the city center, although without remarkable charm. Tea/coffee-making facilities, hair dryers, garment presses, and orthopedic beds are standard. Guest facilities include a restaurant, wine bar, sauna, indoor solarium, gift shop.

Inexpensive

Bewley's Hotel. Merrion Rd., Ballsbridge, Dublin 4. ☎ **01/668-1111.** Fax 01/668-1999. www.bewleyshotels.com. TV TEL. 220 units. £69 ($97) per room (sleeps up to 3 adults), £138 ($193) suite. AE, DC, MC, V. DART: Sandymount (5-minute walk). Bus: 7, 7A, 7X, 8, 45.

The new Bewley's Hotel, located in a fashionable suburb 3km (2 miles) south of the city center, occupies an elegant 19th-century brick Masonic school building next to the British Embassy. Public lounges and reception areas are spacious and thoughtfully restored. Rooms are spacious. All have a writing desk, armchair, trouser press, tea/coffee facilities, and either a king bed or a double and a twin bed. Bathrooms are moderate. The suites include an additional room with foldout couch, table (seats six), a tiny kitchen/bar cleverly hidden in a cabinet, and an additional bathroom (shower only). A basement restaurant (O'Connell's) is run by the Allen family of Ballymaloe fame, and offers very good food at reasonable prices; there's also an informal Bewley's tearoom. The *per room* rate makes this hotel excellent value for families and groups; the only downside is it's location, a small obstacle given the frequent bus and DART service.

Self-Catering

Lansdowne Village. Newbridge Ave. off Lansdowne Rd., Ballsbridge, Dublin 4. ☎ **01/668-3534.** Fax 01/660-6465. 19 units (2 or 3 bedrooms). TV TEL. £400–£595 ($560– $833) per week, depending on size of apt and season. Shorter periods available at reduced rates Oct–Mar. MC, V. DART: Lansdowne Rd. Bus: 2, 3, 5, 7, 7A, 8, 18, 45.

Lansdowne Village is a modest and appealing residential development on the banks of the River Dodder and directly across from Lansdowne Stadium. Within this community, Trident Holiday Homes offers fully equipped two- and three-bedroom rental units, each with an additional pullout double-bed sofa in the living room. They are bright and comfortable, trim, and well maintained. The location is ideal. Not only are you a 5-minute walk from the DART and less than a half-hour's walk from St. Stephen's Green, but the Sandymount Strand, a favorite walking spot for Dubliners, is only 10 minutes away on foot. Shops and supermarkets are nearby, so you can manage here quite well without a car, feeling apart from the city's frenzy and yet not at all cut off. The smaller units are perfect for couples, perhaps with one child; the considerably more spacious three-bedroom units are recommended for larger families or for more than one couple.

WHERE TO DINE

HISTORIC OLD CITY & TEMPLE BAR/TRINITY COLLEGE AREA

Expensive

Les Frères Jacques. 74 Dame St., Dublin 2. ☎ **01/679-4555.** Reservations recommended. Set-price lunch £13.50 ($19); set-price dinner £21 ($29). À la carte also available. AE, DC, MC, V. Mon–Fri 12:30–2:30pm and 7:30–11pm; Sat 7–11pm. Bus: 50, 50A, 54, 56, or 77. FRENCH.

Well situated between Crampton Court and Sycamore Street opposite Dublin Castle, this restaurant brings a touch of haute cuisine to the lower edge of the trendy Temple Bar district. The menu offers such creative main courses as fillet of beef in red wine and bone marrow sauce; duck suprême on a sweet corn pancake in tangy ginger sauce; rosette of spring lamb in meat juice sabayon and tomato coulis with crispy potato straws; and grilled lobster from the tank flamed in whiskey.

Lord Edward. 23 Christchurch Place, Dublin 8. ☎ **01/454-2420.** Reservations required. Main courses £9.95–£15.95 ($14–$22); set-price dinner £20 ($28). AE, DC, MC, V. Mon–Fri noon–10:45pm; Sat 6–10:45pm. Bus: 50, 54A, 56A, 65, 65A, 77, 77A, 123, or 150. SEAFOOD.

Established in 1890, this cozy upstairs dining room claims to be Dublin's oldest seafood restaurant. A dozen different preparations of sole (including au gratin and Véronique) are served, as are seven variations of prawns (from Thermidor to Provençal), and fresh lobster is prepared au naturel or in sauces. There's also fresh fish from salmon and sea trout to plaice and turbot—grilled, fried, or poached. Vegetarian dishes are also available. At lunchtime, light snacks and simpler fare are served in the bar.

Moderate

bruno's. 30 E. Essex St., Dublin 2. ☎ **01/670-6767.** Reservations recommended. Dinner main courses £10.95–£13.95 ($15–$20). Service charge 10% on tables over 4. AE, CB, DC, MC, V. Mon–Fri 12:30–10:30pm; Mon–Sat 5–10:30pm. DART: Tara St. Bus: 21A, 46A, 46B, 51B, 51C, 68, 69, 86. FRENCH/MEDITERRANEAN.

This is a surefire spot for a flawlessly prepared, interesting lunch or dinner without serious damage to the budget. The atmosphere is light and modern, with the focus on food that is consistently excellent without flourish or pretense. The spinach and goat cheese tart, salad of prawns with honey, lime, sesame seeds, and jalapeño peppers, and the bruschetta of chicken are all worthy of mention. The new Millennium Bridge makes bruno's all the more convenient as it crosses the Liffey at Eustace Street directly opposite the restaurant. You can now also find a bruno's at 21 Kildare St., Dublin 2 (☎ **01/662-4724**).

Café Auriga. Temple Bar Square, Dublin 2. ☎ **01/671-8228.** Main courses £8.95–£14.95 ($13–$21); early bird menu (5:30–7:30pm) 3 courses for the price of the main course £8.95–£10.50 ($13–$15). AE, MC, V. Tues–Sat 5:30–11:00pm. Bus: Any city-center bus. CONTEMPORARY IRISH

Café Auriga is a stylish, second-floor cafe whose main dining room overlooks Temple Bar Square. Dinner is served under a ceiling of twinkling stars and is accompanied not by the sweet serenade of a lone violinist, but by the louder melodies of Dublin's top 40. The decor is stylish and simple and the crowd young, sleek, and professional. The food demonstrates the chef's facility in combining simple ingredients to create a piquant surprise for the palate. Subtly spiced, imaginative sauces accompany well-prepared fish and meat dishes, such as salmon in ginger soy sauce or breast of chicken stuffed with basil mousse. Vegetarian offerings include a succulent tagliatelle of goat cheese, cherry tomatoes, spinach, fresh herbs, and cream.

Chameleon. No. 1 Fownes St. Lower, Temple Bar, Dublin 2. ☎ **01/671-0362.** Set menus £13.50–£21.50 ($19–$30); early bird main courses £6.50–£7 ($9 –$10). MC, V. Tues–Sat 6–11:30pm; Sun 6–10pm. Bus: Any city-center bus. INDONESIAN.

Only a dim candlelit window and an orange sign signal Chameleon, well camouflaged on a small side street off Temple Bar Square. The air is tinged with incense, and rich Indonesian batiks are sumptuous backdrops for the traditional puppets and dark wood carvings that lurk in the corners. The Chameleon offers a variety of menus featuring samplings of seven different dishes and an assortment of condiments. The staff is quick in explaining how to best complement chicken saté with roasted peanuts. Sambal-badjak, a red curry paste, gives the rice a robust, pleasantly spicy flavor. Finally, a small morsel of pickled vegetable is suggested as a "palate cleanser"—good advice to swallow if you want to take advantage of the abundance of delicately flavored dishes that Chameleon has to offer.

Dish. 2 Crow St., Dublin 2. ☎ **01/671-1248.** Reservations recommended. Main courses £10.50–£13.95 ($15–$20). Service charge 10% on tables over 5. AE, DC, MC, V. Daily noon–11:30pm. DART: Tara St. Bus: 21A, 46A, 46B, 51B, 51C, 68, 69, or 86. NOUVEAU INTERNATIONAL.

With expansive floor-to-ceiling windows, wide-beamed pine floors, light walls, and dark blue linens, Dish offers a relaxed, tasteful atmosphere. The menu is eclectic and enticing, with an emphasis on fresh grilled seafood and Mediterranean flavors that are complex without being confusing. The grilled salmon with avocado, papaya, and tequila-lime dressing, the baked hake, and the charcoal-grilled tiger prawns are particularly outstanding. The desserts I tried—caramelized lemon tart with cassis sauce and the amaretti chocolate cheesecake—were superior. Dish promises to be one of Temple Bar's finest venues, and at a modest price.

Juice. Castle House, 73 S. Great George's St., Dublin 2. ☎ **01/475-7856.** Reservations recommended Fri–Sat. Main courses £4.95–£7.25 ($7–$10); early bird set-price dinner (Mon–Fri 5:30–7pm) £8.95 ($14). MC, V. Sun–Wed 9am–10:30pm; Thurs–Sat 5:30pm–4am. Bus: 50, 50A, 54, 56, or 77. VEGETARIAN.

Juice tempts carnivorous, vegan, macrobiotic, celiac, and yeast-free diners alike, using organic produce to create delicious dressings and entrees among its largely conventional but well-prepared offerings. The avocado fillet of blue cheese and broccoli wrapped in phyllo was superb, and I also highly recommend the spinach-and-ricotta cannelloni. The latter is included in the early-bird dinner—a great deal. Coffees, fresh-squeezed juices, organic wines, and late weekend hours add to the lure of this casual modern place frequented by mature diners who know their food.

Inexpensive
Govinda's. 4 Aungier St., Dublin 2. ☎ **01/475-0309.** Main courses £4.95 ($7); soup and freshly baked bread £1.75 ($2.45). MC, V. Mon–Sat 11am–9pm. Bus: 16, 16A, 19, or 22. VEGETARIAN.

Govinda's serves healthy square meals on square plates for very good prices. The meals are generous, belly warming concoctions of vegetables, cheese, rice, and pasta. Two main courses are offered cafeteria-style: one East Indian and the other a simple, plainly flavored staple like lasagna or macaroni and cheese. Veggie burgers are also prepared to order. All are accompanied with a choice of two salads (and are unaccompanied by smoke as the restaurant is no smoking throughout). Desserts are healthful and huge, like the rich wedge of carob cake with a dollop of cream or homemade ice cream—each £1.40 ($1.95).

Leo Burdock's. 2 Werburgh St., Dublin 8. ☎ **01/454-0306.** Main courses £2.50–£4.50 ($3.50–$6). No credit cards. Mon–Sat noon–midnight; Sun 4pm–midnight. Bus: 21A, 50, 50A, 78, 78A, or 78B. FISH-AND-CHIPS.

For three generations, Brian Burdock's family has been serving up the country's best fish-and-chips. Cabinet ministers, university students, poets, Americans who have had the word passed by locals, and almost every other type can be found in the queue, waiting for fish bought fresh that morning and those good Irish potatoes, both cooked in "drippings" (none of that modern cooking oil!). Service is take-out only, but you can sit on a nearby bench or stroll down to the park at St. Patrick's Cathedral. It's located across from Christchurch, around the corner from Jury's Inn.

ST. STEPHEN'S GREEN/GRAFTON STREET AREA
Very Expensive
The Commons. 85–86 St. Stephen's Green, Dublin 2. ☎ **01/479-0530.** Reservations required. Set-price lunch £22 ($31); set-price dinner £45 ($63). AE, DC, MC, V. Mon–Fri 12:30–2:15pm and 7–10pm; Sat 7–10pm. DART: Pearse. Bus: 10, 11, 13, or 46A. MODERN EUROPEAN.

Nestled on the south side of St. Stephen's Green, this Michelin-starred restaurant occupies the basement level of Newman House, the historic seat of Ireland's major university. The interior is a blend of Georgian architecture, cloister-style arches, and original contemporary artworks with Joycean influences. For an aperitif in fine weather, there is a lovely stone courtyard terrace surrounded by a "secret garden" of lush plants and trees. The inventive menu changes daily, but you'll often see dishes such as confit of duck leg on a beet boxty, grilled shark with peppered carrot, and loin of rabbit with a stuffing of marinated prune.

Moderate

✪ **Fitzers Cafe.** 51 Dawson St., Dublin 2. ☎ **01/677-1155.** Reservations recommended. Lunch main courses£6.95–£11.50 ($10–$16); dinner main courses £7.50–£14.50 ($11–$20). AE, DC, MC, V. Daily 9am–4:30pm and 5–11pm. DART: Pearse. Bus: 10, 11A, 11B, 13, or 20B. INTERNATIONAL.

In the middle of a busy shopping street, this airy Irish-style bistro has a multiwindowed shop-front facade and a modern Irish decor of light woods. The food is excellent and reasonably priced, contemporary and quickly served, with choices ranging from penne with chorizo, tomato, basil and feta cheese or roasted salmon or cod to charcoal-grilled venison with grain mustard mash.

Fitzers has three other locations, each with a different menu and character: in the National Gallery, Merrion Square, Dublin 2 (☎ **01/661-4496**); in the Royal Dublin Society (RDS), Ballsbridge, Dublin 4 (☎ **01/667-1302**); and in Temple Bar Square, Dublin 2 (☎ **01/679-0440**). *Consistency* is the operative word here. You can count on Fitzers not to disappoint.

✪ **Il Primo.** 16 Montague St., Dublin 2 (off Harcourt St., 50 yards down from St. Stephen's Green). ☎ **01/478-3373.** Reservations required on weekends. Dinner main courses £7.50–£11.80 ($11–$17). No service charge. AE, DC, MC, V. Mon–Sat 12–3pm and 6–11pm; Sun 6–11pm. MODERN ITALIAN.

Word of mouth is what brought me to Il Primo—little else would have, so obscurely is it tucked away off Harcourt Street. From the street all you see are several tables, a bar, an assembly of wooden stools, and a staircase, which happens to lead to some of the most distinguished, innovative Italian cuisine you'll ever meet up with outside Rome or Tuscany. Awaken your palate with a glass of sparkling Venetian prosecco; open with a plate of Parma ham, avocado, and balsamic vinaigrette; and then go for broke with the ravioli Il Primo, an open handkerchief of pasta over chicken, Parma ham, and mushrooms in a light tarragon cream sauce. The proprietor, Dieter Bergman, will assist gladly in selecting appropriate wines, all of which he personally chooses and imports from Tuscany. Wines are by the milliliter, not the bottle. Open any bottle and you pay for only what you drink. Il Primo is full of surprises.

Inexpensive

Bewley's Cafe. 78 Grafton St. (between Nassau St. and St. Stephen's Green). ☎ **01/677-6761.** Homemade soup £2.25 ($3.15); main courses £3–£6.50 ($4.20–$9); lunch specials from £5 ($7). Dinner main courses £12–£20 ($17–$28). AE, DC, MC, V. Daily 7:30am–11pm (continuous service for breakfast, hot food, and snacks). Bus: Any city-center bus. TRADITIONAL/PASTRIES.

This is Dublin's old reliable, a chain with a 150-year history. The interior is a subdued, mellow mix of dark wood, amber glass, and deep red velvet. Bewley's bustles with the clink of teapots and the satisfied hum of customers sated on scones, almond buns, and baked goods. Less appealing but equally filling are warm suppers of lasagna, sausages and chips, or a variety of casseroles. Most Bewley's are self-service cafeterias, but Grafton Street also has several full-service tearooms. Other locations include 11 Westmoreland St., Dublin 2; 13 S. Great George's St., Dublin 2; 40 Mary St., Dublin 1 (near the ILAC shopping center north of the Liffey); and Dublin Airport.

Café Bell. St. Teresa's Courtyard, Clarendon St., Dublin 2. ☎ **01/677-7645.** All items £2–£5 ($2.80–$7). No credit cards. Mon–Sat 9am–5:30pm. Bus: 16, 16A, 19, 19A, 22A, 55, or 83. IRISH/SELF-SERVICE.

In the cobbled courtyard of early 19th-century St. Teresa's Church, this serene little place is one of a handful of dining options springing up in historic or ecclesiastical surroundings. With high ceilings and an old-world decor, Café Bell is a welcome contrast to the bustle of Grafton Street a block away and Powerscourt Town House Centre across the street. The menu changes daily but usually includes homemade soups, sandwiches, salads, quiches, lasagna, sausage rolls, hot scones, and other baked goods.

FITZWILLIAM/MERRION SQUARE AREA

Very Expensive

✪ **Restaurant Patrick Guilbaud.** 21 Upper Merrion St., Dublin 2. ☎ **01/676-4192.** Reservations required. Set-price lunch £22 ($31); main courses around £26 ($36). AE, DC, MC, V. Jan–Nov Tues–Sat 12:30–2pm and 7:30–10:15pm; Dec 1–Dec 24 Mon–Sat 12:30–2pm and 7:30–10:15pm. DART: Westland Row. Bus: 5, 7A, or 8. FRENCH NOUVELLE.

After being tucked away for many years on James Place, this distinguished restaurant has transferred to new quarters but kept its glowing Michelin reputation (Ireland's only two-star restaurant) for fine food and artful service. The menu features such dishes as casserole of black sole and prawns, steamed salmon with orange and grapefruit sauce, fillet of spring lamb with parsley sauce and herb salad, roast duck with honey, and breast of guinea fowl with Madeira sauce and potato crust.

Expensive

✪ **L'Ecrivain.** 109 Lower Baggot St., Dublin 2. ☎ **01/661-1919.** Reservations recommended. Fixed-price 3-course lunch: £16.50 ($23). Early bird fixed-price dinner £17.50 ($25) inclusive of VAT and service, Mon–Thurs (6:30–7:30pm). Fixed-price 3-course dinner: £31.50 ($44). Main courses £19.50 ($27). 10% service charge on food only. AE, DC, MC, V. Mon–Fri 12:30–2pm and 7–11pm; Sat 7–11pm. Bus: 10. FRENCH/IRISH.

This is one of Dublin's truly fine restaurants, from start to finish. The atmosphere is relaxed and welcoming, without the bother of pretense. You can choose to dine on the garden terrace, weather permitting. Each course seems to receive the same devoted attention, and most consist of traditional "best of Irish" ingredients, allowed to make their own best case without having to argue through dense sauces. The seared sea trout with sweet potato puree and the entrecôte steak with caramelized onion were perfectly prepared for me. Desserts are not an afterthought, but the creations of a talented pastry chef. The crème brûlée here is the best we've tasted north of the Chunnel.

Moderate

Lloyds Brasserie. 20 Upper Merrion St., Dublin 2. ☎ **01/662-7240.** Reservations recommended. Set-price 2-course lunch £10.50 ($15); 3-course £13.50 ($19); main courses £8.95–£15.95 ($13–$22). No service charge. AE, DC, MC, V. Daily 10am for coffee; lunch Mon–Fri noon–2:30pm; brunch Sat–Sun 1–4pm; dinner daily 6pm–2am. DART: Westland Row. Bus: 10, 11A, 11B, 13, or 20B. FRENCH NOUVELLE.

This is famed chef Conrad Gallagher's latest venture. The decor is minimalist, contemporary, with hints of art deco—clear, bright, and simple. The food is another matter—bold, often intense, and in presentation nothing less than architectural. The menu, on the page and on the plate, certainly commands attention, although the essential ingredients are often in danger of being taken for granted, even overlooked. A meal here is an adventure, well worth the relatively moderate price, and where else will you find "bubble and squeak" (corned beef, ground lamb, and cabbage), a surprisingly subtle dish?

Inexpensive

✪ **The Steps of Rome.** Chatham Court, off Chatham St., Dublin 2. ☎ **01/670-5630.**
Main courses £4.50–£9 ($6 –$13); pizza slices £1.60–£2 ($2.24–$2.80). No credit cards. Daily
10am–2pm and 7–11pm. Bus: 10, 11A, 11B, 13, 20B. ITALIAN/PIZZA.

Word is out that this restaurant just off Grafton Street offers some of the best simple
Italian fare in Dublin. Large, succulent pizza slices available for take-out are one way
to enjoy the wonders of this authentic Italian kitchen when the dining room is full—
the seven tables huddled within this tiny restaurant seem to be perennially occupied.
The potato, mozzarella and rosemary pizza, with a thick crust resembling focaccia, is
unusual and exceptionally delicious. Although the pasta dishes are also quite good, it's
that pizza that remains unforgettable.

O'CONNELL STREET AREA
Moderate

✪ **101 Talbot.** 100 Talbot St., Dublin 1. ☎ **01/874-5011.** Reservations recommended.
Dinner main courses £8.25–£11.50 ($12–$16). AE, MC, V. Mon 5–10pm, Tues–Sat 5–11pm.
DART: Connolly. Bus: 27A, 31A, 311B, 32A, 32B, 42B, 42C, 43, or 44A. INTERNATIONAL/
VEGETARIAN.

This second-floor shop-front restaurant features light and healthful foods, with a
strong emphasis on vegetarian dishes, including choices for vegans. The setting is
bright and casual, with contemporary Irish art on display, big windows, yellow rag-
rolled walls, ash-topped tables, and newspapers for browsing. Main courses include
jambalaya of lamb, smoked sausage, and black-eyed peas; vegetable saté with rice; and
tandoori chicken with mango. The lunch menu changes daily, and the dinner menu
weekly. Espresso and cappuccino are always available for sipping, and there's a full
bar. It's located at Talbot Lane near Marlborough Street, convenient to the Abbey
Theatre.

Inexpensive

Winding Stair. 40 Lower Ormond Quay, Dublin 1. ☎ **01/873-3292.** All items £1.50–£4
($2.10–$6). MC, V. Mon–Sat 10am–6pm; Sun 1–6pm. Bus: 70 or 80. IRISH.

Those who resist reading the texts that paper the walls of this cafe's three-storied 18th-
century winding stair will soon find themselves in a comforting enclave overlooking
the Ha'penny bridge and the River Liffey. Solicitous staff are quick to serve bookish
clientele who are as satisfied with the tea, espresso, and healthful sandwiches and cakes
as they are with the surrounding shelves filled with new and used books. Thick sandwiches heaped with fresh vegetables and a choice of cheeses and salamis are made to
order. Salads include the exotic and the local with both a hearty tabouli and an Irish
Brie and Cranberry gracing the chalkboard menu. A banana and honey sandwich as
well as carrot cake and lemon–poppy-seed loaf make up the "sweet" menu. Soup is
also offered—but go early if it's your lunchtime goal as it tends to disappear quickly
on rainy Dublin days. Evening events include poetry readings and recitals.

BALLSBRIDGE/EMBASSY ROW AREA
Expensive

Le Coq Hardi. 35 Pembroke Rd., Ballsbridge, Dublin 4. ☎ **01/668-9070.** Reservations
required. Set-price lunch £24.50 ($34) for full menu; set-price dinner £35 ($49). AE, CB, MC,
V. Mon–Fri 12:30–2:30pm and 7–10.30pm; Sat 7–10:30pm. DART: Lansdowne Rd. Bus: 18,
46, 63, or 84. FRENCH.

Newly redecorated in radiant autumn colors and offering a new cocktail bar, this plush
50-seat restaurant draws a well-heeled local and international business clientele. Chef
John Howard has garnered many an award by offering such specialties as Dover sole

stuffed with prawns, Irish wild salmon on fresh spinach leaves, fillet of hake roasted on green cabbage and bacon with Pernod butter sauce, and fillet of prime beef flamed in Irish whiskey. The 700-bin wine cellar boasts a complete collection of Château Mouton Rothschild, dating from 1945 to the present. Le Coq Hardi's latest trophy was the Year 2000 "Restaurant of the Year" award from Bord Bia.

Moderate

✪ **Rolys Bistro.** 7 Ballsbridge Terrace, Dublin 4. ☎ **01/668-2611.** Reservations required. Main courses £9.50–£14.95 ($13 –$21); set-price lunch £12.50 ($18). AE, DC, MC, V. Daily noon–3pm and 6–10pm. DART: Lansdowne Rd. Bus: 5, 6, 7, 8, 18, or 45. IRISH/INTERNATIONAL.

Opened in 1992, this two-story shop-front restaurant quickly skyrocketed to success, thanks to its genial and astute host Roly Saul and its master chef Colin O'Daly. What you get is excellent and imaginatively prepared food at mostly moderate prices. The main dining rooms, with a bright and airy decor and lots of windows, can be noisy when the house is full, but the nonsmoking section has a quiet enclave of booths for those who prefer a quiet tête-à-tête. Main courses include roasted venison, panfried Dublin Bay prawns, game pie with chestnuts, and wild mushroom risotto. An excellent array of international wines is offered, starting at £10.95 ($15) a bottle.

Inexpensive

✪ **Da Vincenzo.** 133 Upper Leeson St., Dublin 4. ☎ **01/660-9906.** Reservations recommended. Main courses £6.50–£10 ($9 –$14). AE, DC, MC, V. Mon–Sat 12:30–11:45pm; Sun 1–10pm. Bus: 10, 11A, 11B, 46A, or 46B. ITALIAN.

Occupying a shop-front location within a block of the Hotel Burlington, this informal and friendly owner-run bistro offers ground level and upstairs seating. The casual decor consists of glowing brick fireplaces, pine walls, vases and wreaths of dried flowers, modern art posters, blue and white pottery, and a busy open kitchen. Pizza with a light, pita-style dough, cooked in a wood-burning oven, is a specialty here. Other main courses range from pastas to veal and beef dishes, including an organically produced filet steak.

SEEING THE SIGHTS
SIGHTSEEING SUGGESTIONS FOR FIRST-TIME VISITORS

If You Have 1 Day   Start at the beginning—Dublin's medieval quarter, the area around **Christchurch** and **St. Patrick's cathedrals.** Tour these great churches and then walk the cobblestoned streets and inspect the nearby old city walls at **High Street.** From Old Dublin, take a turn eastward and see **Dublin Castle** and then **Trinity College** with the famous *Book of Kells.* Cross over the River Liffey to **O'Connell Street,** Dublin's main thoroughfare. Walk up this wide street, passing the landmark General Post Office (GPO), to Parnell Square and the picturesque Garden of Remembrance. If time permits, visit the **Dublin Writers Museum,** and then hop on a double-decker bus heading to the south bank of the Liffey for a visit to **St. Stephen's Green** for a relaxing stroll amid the greenery. Cap the day with a show at the **Abbey Theatre** and maybe a drink or two at a nearby pub.

If You Have 2 Days   On your second day, take a **Dublin Bus city sightseeing tour** to give you an overview of the city. You'll see all the local downtown landmarks, plus some of the leading sites on the edge of the city, such as the **Guinness Brewery,** the **Royal Hospital,** and **Phoenix Park.** In the afternoon, head for **Grafton Street** for some shopping. If time allows, stroll around **Merrion** or **Fitzwilliam squares** to give you a sampling of the best of Dublin's Georgian architecture.

If You Have 3 Days   Make Day 3 a day for Dublin's artistic and cultural attractions—visit the **National Museum** and **National Gallery,** the **Guinness Hop Store,** or a special-interest museum, such as the **Writers Museum.** Save time for a walk around **Temple Bar,** the city's Left Bank district, lined with art galleries and film studios, interesting secondhand shops, and casual eateries.

If You Have 4 Days   On Day 4, take a ride aboard DART, Dublin's rapid-transit system, to the suburbs, either southward to **Dun Laoghaire** or **Dalkey,** or northward to **Howth.** The DART routes follow the rim of Dublin Bay in both directions, so you'll enjoy a scenic ride and get to spend some time in an Irish coastal village. Or take a trip to the **Boyne Valley** and the north coast to visit the burial mounds at Newgrange, the site of the Battle of the Boyne, King William's Glen, and other sites. This trip is also worthwhile for the glimpses of Irish countryside it affords.

DUBLIN'S TOP ATTRACTIONS

✪ **Trinity College and the *Book of Kells*.** College Green, Dublin 2. ☎ **01/608-2320.** www.tcd.ie/library. Free admission to college grounds. Old Library/*Book of Kells*, £4.50 ($6) adults, £4 ($6) seniors/students, £9 ($13) families, free for children under 12; Dublin Experience, £3 ($4.20) adults, £2.50 ($3.50) seniors/students, £1.50 ($2.10) children, £6 ($8) family. Combination tickets also available. Library, Mon–Sat 9:30am–5pm, Sun noon–4:30pm (opens at 9:30am June–Sept); Dublin Experience, May–Sept daily 10am–5pm, closed Oct–Apr. Bus: All city-center buses.

The oldest university in Ireland, Trinity was founded in 1592 by Queen Elizabeth I. It sits in the heart of the city on a beautiful 16ha (40-acre) site just south of the Liffey, with cobbled squares, gardens, a picturesque quadrangle, and buildings dating from the 17th to the 20th centuries. The college is home to the *Book of Kells*, an 8th-century version of the four Gospels with elaborate scripting and illumination. This famous treasure and other early Christian manuscripts are on permanent public view in the Colonnades, an exhibition area on the ground floor of the Old Library. Also housed in the Old Library is the Dublin Experience (☎ **01/608-1177**), an excellent multimedia introduction to the history and people of Dublin.

Archaeology and History Museum. Kildare St., Dublin 2. ☎ **01/677-7444.** Free admission. Tues–Sat 10am–5pm; Sun 2–5pm. DART: Pearse. Bus: 7, 7A, 8, 10, 11, or 13.

This important museum reflects Ireland's heritage from 2000 B.C. to the present. It's the home of many of the country's greatest historical finds, including the Ardagh Chalice, Tara Brooch, and Cross of Cong. Other highlights range from the artifacts from the Wood Quay excavations of the Old Dublin Settlements to an extensive exhibition of Irish gold ornaments from the Bronze Age.

Collins Barracks. Benburb St., Dublin 7. ☎ **01/677-7444.** Free admission. Tours at varying hours, depending on groups, £1 ($1.55). Tues–Sat 10am–5pm; Sun 2–5pm. Bus: 25, 66, 67, or 90.

This is the latest venue of the National Museum, which has already occupied 2 of the 4 blocks available here. Even if it were empty, Collins Barracks—the oldest military

National Museum

✪ **The National Museum of Ireland** currently comprises three separate venues—Archaeology and History Museum, Collins Barracks, and Natural History Museum—and plans to add a fourth. A special MuseumLink shuttle bus (Route 172) runs daily between these museums, and the cost of a day-ticket is £2 ($2.80) adults, £1 ($1.40) children, seniors free.

barracks in Europe—would be well worth a visit; the structure is a splendidly restored early 18th-century masterwork by Col. Thomas Burgh, Ireland's Chief Engineer and Surveyor General under Queen Anne.

So far, the collection housed here focuses on the decorative arts and weaponry. Most notable is the extraordinary display of Irish silver and furniture. Collins Barracks also houses a cafe and gift shop.

Natural History Museum. Merrion St., Dublin 2. ☎ **01/677-7444.** Free admission. Tues–Sat 10am–5pm, Sun 2–5pm. Bus: 7, 7A, 8.

The recently renovated Natural History Museum is considered one of the finest traditional museums in the world. In addition to presenting the zoological history of Ireland, there are examples of major animal groups from around the world, including many rare or extinct groups. The Blaschka glass models of marine animals are quite famous.

✪ **Dublin Castle.** Palace St. (off Dame St.), Dublin 2. ☎ **01/677-7129.** www.historic-centres.com. Admission £3 ($4.20) adults, £2 ($2.80) seniors and students, £1.25 ($1.75) children under 12, £7.50 ($11) family. Mon–Fri 10am–5pm; Sat–Sun and holidays 2–5pm. Guided tours are conducted every 20–25 minutes. Bus: 50, 50A, 54, 56A, 77, 77A, or 77B.

Built between 1208 and 1220, this complex represents some of the oldest surviving architecture in the city and was the center of British power in Ireland for more than 7 centuries until it was taken over by the new Irish government in 1922. Highlights include the 13th-century Record Tower; the State Apartments, once the residence of English viceroys; and the Chapel Royal. The newest developments are the Undercroft, an excavated site on the grounds where an early Viking fortress stood, and the Treasury, built between 1712 and 1715 and believed to be the oldest surviving office building in Ireland. At hand, as well, are a craft shop, heritage center, and restaurant.

Dublin Writers Museum. 18–19 Parnell Sq. N., Dublin 1. ☎ **01/872-2077.** Fax 01/872-2231. Admission £3.15 ($4.40) adults, £2.65 ($3.70) seniors/students, £1.50 ($2.10) ages 3–11, £8.50 ($12) families (2 adults and up to 4 children). AE, DC, MC, V. Mon–Sat 10am–5pm (6pm June–Aug); Sun and holidays 11am–5pm. DART: Connolly. Bus: 11, 13, 16, 16A, 22, or 22A.

Housed in a stunning 18th-century Georgian mansion with splendid plasterwork and stained glass, the museum is itself an impressive reminder of the grandeur of the Irish literary tradition. Yeats, Joyce, Beckett, Shaw, Wilde, Swift, and Sheridan are among those whose lives and works are celebrated here. One of the museum's rooms is devoted to children's literature.

Christchurch Cathedral. Christchurch Place. ☎ **01/677-8099.** Admission: suggested donation £2 ($2.80) adults, £1 ($1.40) students and children under 15, £5 ($7) family. Daily 10am–5:30pm. Closed Dec 26. Bus: 21A, 50, 50A, 78, 78A, or 78B.

Standing on a ridge above the site of the original Norse town, the cathedral was founded in 1038, although the present building dates from around 1172, with substantial renovations from 1871 to 1878. Inside you'll find a monument to Strongbow, the ruler who had the cathedral built. Make sure to look back from the altar and note the leaning wall of Dublin, which has been on a lean (by some 45cm 18 inches) since 1562. The newly restored crypt, intact since the 13th century, is one of the largest medieval crypts in either Britain or Ireland.

St. Patrick's Cathedral. 21–50 Patrick's Close, Patrick St., Dublin 8. ☎ **01/475-4817.** www.stpatrickscathedral.ie. Admission £2.30 ($3.22) adults, £1.60 ($2.25) students and seniors, £5.50 ($8) family. MC, V. Mon–Fri 9am–6pm year-round; Mar–Oct Sat 9am–6pm and Sun 9–11am, 12:45–3pm, 4:15–6pm; Nov–Feb Sat 9am–5pm and Sun 10–11am, 12:45–3pm. Closed except for services Dec 24–26 and Jan 1. Bus: 65, 65B, 50, 50A, 54, 54A, 56A, 77.

It is said that St. Patrick baptized converts on this site and consequently a church has stood here since A.D. 450, making it the oldest Christian site in Dublin. The present cathedral dates from 1190, but because of a fire and subsequent rebuilding in the 14th century, not much remains from the cathedral's foundation days. It's mainly early English in style, with a square medieval tower that houses the largest ringing peal bells in Ireland, an 18th-century spire, and a 90m (300-foot) interior, making it the longest church in the country. St. Patrick's is closely associated with Jonathan Swift, who was dean here from 1713 to 1745 and whose tomb lies in the south aisle. St. Patrick's is the national cathedral of the Church of Ireland.

MORE ATTRACTIONS

Dublinia. St. Michael's Hill, Christchurch, Dublin 8. ☎ **01/679-4611.** Admission £3.95 ($6) adults, £3 ($4.20) seniors, students, and children, £10 ($14) family. AE, MC, V. Apr–Sept daily 10am–5pm; Oct–Mar Mon–Sat 11am–4pm, Sun 10am–4:30pm. Bus: 50, 78A, or 123.

What was Dublin like in medieval times? Here is a historically accurate presentation of the Old City from 1170 to 1540, re-created through a series of theme exhibits, spectacles, and experiences. Highlights include an illuminated Medieval Maze complete with visual effects, background sounds, and aromas that lead you on a journey through time from the first arrival of the Anglo-Normans in 1170 to the closure of the monasteries in the 1530s. The next segment depicts everyday life in medieval Dublin with a diorama, as well as a prototype of a 13th-century quay along the banks of the Liffey. The finale takes you to The Great Hall for a 360-degree wrap-up portrait of medieval Dublin via a 12-minute cyclorama-style audiovisual.

GAA Museum. Croke Park, Dublin 3. ☎ **01/855-8176.** Admission £3 ($4.20) adults, £2 ($2.80) students, £1.50 ($2.10) children, £6 ($8) families. May–Sept daily 9:30am–4:30pm; Oct–Apr Tues–Sat 10am–4:30pm, Sun 12–4:30pm. Bus: 3, 11, 11A, 16, 16A, 51A, 123.

On the grounds of Croke Park, principal stadium of the Gaelic Athletic Association, this museum dramatically presents the athletic heritage of Ireland. The Gaelic Games (Gaelic football, hurling, handball, and camogie) have long been contested on an annual basis between teams representing the various regions of Ireland. Test your skills with interactive exhibits, and peruse the extensive video archive of football finals dating from 1931. The 12-minute film *A Sunday in September* captures admirably the hysteria of final match. Note that on match days the museum is open only to new stand ticket holders.

Guinness Brewery Hop Store/Visitor Centre. James's Gate, Dublin 8. ☎ **01/408-4800.** www.guinness.ie. Admission £5 ($7) adults, £4 ($6) seniors and students, £1 ($1.40) children under 12. AE, MC, V. Apr–Sept Mon–Sat 9:30am–5pm, Sun 10:30am–4:30pm; Oct–Mar Mon–Sat 9:30am–4pm, Sun noon–4pm. Guided tours every half hour. Bus: 51B, 78A, or 123.

Founded in 1759, Guinness is one of the world's largest breweries, producing the distinctive dark beer called stout, famous for its thick, creamy head. Although tours of the brewery itself are no longer allowed, visitors are welcome to explore the adjacent Guinness Hopstore. It houses the World of Guinness Exhibition and an audiovisual presentation showing how the stout is made. You'll also find the Cooperage Gallery, displaying one of the finest collections of tools in Europe, and the Gilroy Gallery, dedicated to the graphic design work of John Gilroy. Last but not least is a bar where visitors can sample a glass of the famous brew.

Irish Traditional Music Centre (Ceol). Smithfield Village, off Arran Quay, Dublin 1. ☎ **01/817-3820.** www.ceol.ie. Admission £3.95 ($6) adults, £3.50 ($4.90) students, £3 ($4.20) children, £12 ($17) families. Mon–Sat 9:30am–6pm, Sun noon–7pm (last film 45 minutes before closing). Bus: 67, 67A, 68, 69, 79, 90.

A Ramble from Bray to Greystones

The walk from Bray to Greystones along the rocky promontory of Bray Head is a great excursion, with beautiful views back toward Killiney Bay, Dalkey Island, and Howth. Bray, the southern terminus of the DART line, is readily accessible from Dublin. In Bray, follow the beachside promenade south through town; at the outskirts of town the promenade turns left and up, beginning the ascent of Bray Head. Shortly after the beginning of this ascent, a trail branches to the left—this is the cliff-side walk, which continues another 6km (3½ miles) along the coast to Greystones. From the center of Greystones, there's a train that takes you back to Bray. This is an easy walk, about 2 hours one way.

This new attraction (opened in 1999) offers a good introduction to Irish traditional music for the uninitiated, and a few items that may be of interest to experienced listeners and performers. The centre consists of several interactive audiovisual displays that present the basic components of Irish traditional music—song, dance, and instruments. An impressive diversity of material is packed into the small space, the most interesting of which is an archive of songs, categorized by region and topic. Videos demonstrating set dancing are projected onto 2m (6-foot) screens, and audio recordings of early Irish radio broadcasts are continuously played in small circular chamber at the center of the museum. A 30-minute film intersperses brief interviews with performers, clips from live sessions, and spectacular views of the Irish countryside. Adjacent to the centre is the "Jameson Chimney," a recently restored industrial tower with a separate charge for this new view of Dublin.

James Joyce Centre. 35 N. Great George's St., Dublin 1. ☎ **01/878 8547.** Fax 01/878-8488. www.jamesjoyce.ie. Admission £3 ($4.20) adults, £2 ($2.80) student/senior, 75p ($1.05) child, £6 ($8) family; walking tours £6.50 ($9) adults, £5 ($7) student/senior, £12 ($17) family; tour of house with Ken Monaghan £4.50 ($6) adults, £4 ($6) student/senior. AE, MC, V. Mon–Sat 9:30am–5pm; Sun 12:30–5pm. Closed Dec 24–26. DART: Connolly. Bus: 1, 40A, 40B, 40C.

Located near Parnell Square and the Dublin Writers Museum, this newly restored Georgian townhouse, built in 1784 gives literary enthusiasts one more reason to visit Dublin's north side. The house itself was once the home of Denis J. Maginni, a dancing instructor who appears briefly in *Ulysses*. The Ulysses Portrait Gallery on the second floor has a fascinating collection of photographs and drawings of characters from *Ulysses* who had a life outside the novel. A recently opened exhibition room holds the table and writing table used by Joyce in Paris when he was working on *Finnegans Wake*. In addition, there are talks and audiovisual presentations daily. The latest addition to the centre is a new coffee shop. Guided walking tours are offered through the neighboring streets of "Joyce Country" in Dublin's northern inner city.

✪ **Joyce Tower Museum.** Sandycove, County Dublin. ☎ **01/280-9265.** Admission £2.60 ($3.65) adults, £2.10 ($2.95) seniors and students, £1.30 ($1.80) children, and £7.75 ($11) family. Apr–Oct Mon–Sat 10am–1pm and 2–5pm; Sun 2–6pm; open Nov–Mar by appointment only (call ☎ 01/872-2077). DART: Sandycove. Bus: 8.

No James Joyce fan should miss this small museum housed in the Sandycove Martello Tower where Joyce lived for a while in 1904—it's described in the first chapter of *Ulysses*. The museum contains exhibits on Joyce and Dublin at the time *Ulysses* was written. If you pick up a copy of the "Ulysses Map of Dublin," you can make this the starting point of a Joyce tour of the city. Robert Nicholson, the museum's curator, is a great source of information on all topics relating to Joyce, and has published the best guide to Ulysses sites in Dublin, titled simply *The Ulysses Guide.*

Kilmainham Gaol Historical Museum. Kilmainham. ☎ **01/453-5984.** Admission £3.50 ($4.90) adults, £2.50 ($3.50) seniors, £1.50 ($2.10) children and students, £8 ($11) family. MC, V. Tours Apr–Sept daily 9:30am–4:45pm; Oct–Mar Mon–Fri 9:30am–4pm, Sun 10am–5pm. Bus: 51, 51B, 78, 78A, 78B, or 79 at O'Connell Bridge.

Within these walls, political prisoners were incarcerated, tortured, and killed from 1796 until 1924, when the late president Eamon de Valera left as its final prisoner. To walk along these corridors, through the exercise yard, or into the Main Compound is a moving experience that lingers hauntingly in the memory.

The **War Memorial Gardens** (☎ **01/677-0236**), located along the banks of the Liffey, are a 5-minute walk from nearby Kilmainham Gaol. The gardens were designed by the famous British architect Sir Edwin Lutyens (1869–1944), who completed a number of commissions for houses and gardens in Ireland. Thankfully, the gardens are fairly well maintained and continue to present a moving testimony to Ireland's war dead. This is one of the finest small gardens in Ireland. The opening times are Monday to Friday 8am to dark and Saturday 10am to dark.

Hugh Lane Municipal Gallery of Modern Art. Parnell Sq. N., Dublin 1. ☎ **01/874-1903.** Free admission but donations accepted. Tues–Thurs 9:30am–6pm; Fri–Sat 9:30am–5pm; Sun 11am–5pm. DART: Connolly or Tara. Bus: 10, 11, 11A, 11B, 13, 16, 16A, 19, 19A, 22, 22A, and 36.

Housed in a finely restored 18th-century building known as Charlemont House, this gallery is situated next to the Dublin Writers Museum. It is named after Hugh Lane, an Irish art connoisseur who died when the *Lusitania* sank in 1915 and who willed his collection (including works by Courbet, Manet, Monet, and Corot) to be shared between the government of Ireland and the National Gallery of London. With the Lane collection as its nucleus, this gallery also contains paintings from the Impressionist and post-Impressionist traditions, sculptures by Rodin, stained glass, and works by modern Irish artists. In 1998 the museum received its most important donation since its establishment in 1908: the studio of Irish painter Francis Bacon, which will open in 2001. The bookshop is open during museum hours.

✪ **National Gallery.** Merrion Sq. West, Dublin 2. ☎ **01/661-5133.** www.nationalgallery.ie. Free admission. Mon–Wed and Fri–Sat 10am–5:30pm; Thurs 10am–8:30pm; Sun 2–5pm. Free public tours: Sat 3pm; Sun 2:15, 3, and 4pm. DART: Pearse. Bus: 5, 6, 7, 7A, 8, 10, 44, 47, 47B, 48A, or 62.

Established by an act of Parliament in 1854, this gallery first opened its doors in 1864, with just over 100 paintings. Today the collection of paintings, drawings, watercolors, miniatures, prints, sculpture, and objets d'art is considered one of Europe's finest. Every major European school of painting is represented, including an extensive assemblage of Irish work. Of special note is the new Yeats Museum, dedicated to Jack B. Yeats (1871–1957). The museum features a fine gallery shop and an excellent self-service restaurant. All public areas are wheelchair-accessible.

Irish Museum of Modern Art. Royal Hospital, Military Road, Kilmainham, Dublin 8. ☎ **01/612-9900.** Fax 01/612-9999. E-mail: info@modernart.ie. Free admission. Tues–Sat 10am–5:30pm; Sun noon–5:30pm. Bus: 68A, 69, 78A, 90, and 123. DART: Feeder bus from Connolly and Tara to Heuston.

One of the city's newest museums is located in its oldest classical building, the stately Kilmainham Hospital. Modeled on Les Invalides in Paris, the old hospital is a quadrangle with chapel and majestic dining hall in the north wing and a row of stables to the south, now converted to artists' studios. Situated in an expansive parkland setting, the building has an elaborate formal garden on its north side and a long, tree-lined ceremonial entrance to the west, extending all the way to the Kilmainham Gaol. The museum occupies the east, west, and south wings of the hospital; the high entrance hall on the south side is adjoined by a fine bookshop and tea house, serving light meals under £5 ($7). The galleries contain the work of Irish and international artists from the small but impressive permanent collection, with numerous temporary exhibitions at any given time. There's even a drawing room, where kids and parents can record their impressions of the museum with the crayons provided.

Waterways Visitor Centre. Grand Canal Quay, Ringsend Road, Dublin 2. ☎ **01/ 677-7510.** Admission £2 ($2.80) adults, £1.50 ($2.10) seniors, £1 ($1.40) children or students, £5 ($7) families. June–Sept daily 9:30am–6:30pm; Oct–May Wed–Sun 12:30–5pm. DART: Pearse (5-minute walk). Bus: 1, 3.

Heading south from Dublin on the DART you may have noticed the tiny Waterways Visitor Centre, a brilliant white cube floating on the Grand Canal Basin amidst massive derelict brick warehouses. This intriguing modern building is home to a fascinating exhibit describing the history of Ireland's inland waterways, a network of canals connecting Dublin westward and northward to the Shannon watershed. The centre's shiny white exterior gives way inside to the subdued tones of Irish oak wall panels and a hardwood ship's floor—a series of exhibits describe aspects of canal design, and several interactive models attempt to demonstrate dynamically the daily operations of the canals. No longer used for transporting goods, the canals of Ireland are now popular with boaters and hikers, and there's some information here for those interested in these activities.

PARKS & ZOOS

✪ **St. Stephen's Green,** in the heart of Dublin 2, has been preserved as an open space for Dubliners since 1690. A short walk from most city center locations, this large park is popular for picnics, reading, a quiet stroll, and summertime concerts. The hours are Monday to Saturday 8am to dark and Sunday 10am to dark. **Iveagh Gardens,** a small garden hidden behind the National Concert Hall, is largely neglected by visitors. The main entrance is from Clonmel Street, off Harcourt Street, less than 5 minutes from Stephen's Green. The hours are the same as those for St. Stephen's Green.

✪ **Phoenix Park.** Parkgate St., Dublin 7. ☎ **01/677-0095.** Free admission. Daily 24 hours. Visitor Centre: Admission £2 ($2.80) adults, £1.50 ($2.10) seniors, £1 ($1.40) students and children, £5 ($7) families. Jan–mid-Mar Sat–Sun 9:30am–4:30pm; mid-Mar to end of Mar daily 9:30am–4:30pm; Apr–May daily 9:30am–5:30pm; June–Sept daily 10am–6pm; Oct daily 9:30am–5pm; Nov–Dec Sat–Sun 9:30am–4:30pm. Bus: 37, 38, 39.

Dublin's 712ha (1,760-acre) playground—Europe's largest enclosed urban park—opened in 1747. Situated 3km (2 miles) west of the city center, it is traversed by a network of roads and quiet pedestrian walkways, and informally landscaped with ornamental gardens, nature trails, and broad expanses of grassland separated by avenues of trees, including oak, beech, pine, chestnut, and lime. The homes of the Irish president (see below) and the U.S. ambassador are on its grounds. Livestock graze peacefully on pasturelands, deer roam the forested areas, and horses romp on polo fields. The new Phoenix Park Visitor Centre, adjacent to Ashtown Castle, has exhibitions and an audiovisual presentation on the history of the Phoenix Park, and houses its own restaurant.

For tours of **Áras an Uachtaráin (The Irish White House),** tickets are issued at the Phoenix Park Visitor Center every Saturday 9:40am to 4:20pm except December 24 to 26. Admission is free. No advance booking is possible. The entire tour lasts one hour. As only 525 tickets are given out, first come first served, every Saturday, it is advisable, especially in the summer months, to arrive before 1:30pm. The **Dublin Zoo** (☎ 01/677-1425), also located here in the Phoenix Park, was established in 1830 and is the third-oldest zoo in the world (after London and Paris).

National Botanic Gardens. Botanic Rd., Glasnevin, Dublin 9. ☎ **01/837-4388.** Free admission. Gardens: Summer Mon–Sat and Fri 9am–6pm, Sun 11am–6pm; winter Mon–Sat 10am–4:30pm, Sun 11am–4:30pm. Glass houses: Summer Mon–Wed and Fri 9am–3:15pm, Thurs 9am–3:15pm, Sat 9am–5:45pm and Sun 2–5:45pm; winter Mon–Wed and Fri–Sat 10am–4:15pm, Thurs 10am–3:15pm, and Sun 2–4:15pm. Bus: 13, 19, or 134.

Established by the Royal Dublin Society in 1795 on a rolling 20ha (50-acre) expanse of land north of the city center, this is Dublin's horticultural showcase. The attractions include more than 20,000 different plants and cultivars, a Great Yew Walk, a bog garden, a water garden, a rose garden, and an herb garden. There are also a variety of Victorian-style glass houses filled with tropical plants and exotic species.

ORGANIZED TOURS

BUS TOURS   For the standard see-it-all-in-under-3-hours tour, climb aboard the **Dublin Bus** open-deck sightseeing coach. Tours leave from the Dublin Bus office at 59 Upper O'Connell St. (☎ 01/873-4222), departing at 10:15am and 2:15pm. You can purchase your ticket at the office or on the bus: £9 ($13) adults, £4 ($6) children under age 14, and £20 ($28) for a family of four. This tour takes in most of the important sights but doesn't stop at any.

For more flexible touring, there's the **Dublin City Tour,** a continuous guided bus service connecting 10 major points, like museums, art galleries, churches and cathedrals, libraries, and historic sites. For £6 ($8) adults, £3 ($4.20) under age 14, £12 ($17) for a family of four, you can ride the bus for a full day, getting off and on as often as you wish. It operates daily 9:30am to 4:30pm.

WALKING TOURS   You can set out on your own with a map, but the best way to avoid any hassles or missed sights is following one of the four signposted and themed "tourist trails": Old City Trail for historic sights; Georgian Trail for the landmark buildings, streets, squares, terraces, and parks; Cultural Trail for a circuit of the top literary sites, museums, galleries, theaters, and churches; and the Rock 'n' Stroll Trail for a tour of contemporary music enclaves, pubs, breweries, nightspots, and more. Each trail is mapped out in a handy booklet, available for £2.50 ($3.50) from the Dublin Tourism Office, Suffolk Street, Dublin 2 (☎ 01/605-7700).

A number of firms offer tours led by knowledgeable local guides. Tour times and charges vary, but most last about 2 hours and cost between £4 and £7 ($6 and $10). Discover Dublin Tours (☎ 01/478-0193) offers a **Traditional Music Pub Crawl** led by two professional musicians. The **Jameson Dublin Literary Pub Crawl** (☎ 01/454-0228) departs evenings from the Duke Pub, Duke Street; your guides will recount the stories connecting these pubs with Dublin's literary greats. Information/booking for these and other theme tours may be had at the Dublin Tourism Office, Suffolk Street, Dublin 2 (☎ 01/605-7700). **Historical Walking Tours of Dublin** (☎ 01/878-0227) depart from the front gate of Trinity College. Many guides are history graduates of Trinity College, and participants are encouraged to ask questions. Between May and October, **Trinity College Walking Tours** depart every 40 minutes (approximately) from Trinity's front gate.

HORSE-DRAWN CARRIAGE TOURS   If you don't mind being conspicuous, you can tour Dublin in style in a handsomely outfitted horse-drawn carriage while your driver points out the sights. To arrange a ride, consult with one of the drivers stationed with carriages on the Grafton Street side of St. Stephen's Green. Rides range from a short swing around the Green to an extensive half-hour Georgian tour or an hour-long Old City tour. Rides are available on a first-come basis and cost anywhere from £9 to £35 ($13 to $49) for two to five passengers, depending on the duration of the ride. They run from April to October, daily and nightly, depending on the weather.

THE SHOPPING SCENE

In general, Dublin shops are open Monday to Saturday 9 or 9:30am to 5:30 or 6pm, with late hours Thursday to 8pm. In tourist season, many shops also post Sunday hours. **Grafton Street,** a pedestrians-only zone near Trinity College, is a chic shopping district where trendy boutiques, department stores, and specialty shops proliferate. **Powerscourt Townhouse Centre** and **St. Stephen's Green Centre** are two of this area's focal points and prime examples of Dublin's ongoing renovation and gentrification. In the **Temple Bar area** are unusual shops selling Asian and Latin American imports, secondhand clothes, and hard-to-find records. North of the Liffey, shopping is best on and just off of **O'Connell Street** and on **Henry Street.**

BOOKS   This city of literary legends has quite a few fine bookstores. For new books, try **Fred Hanna,** 27–29 Nassau St., Dublin 2 (☎ 01/677-1255; e-mail: fred@hannas.ie); or **Waterstones Bookshop,** 7 Dawson St., Dublin 2 (☎ 01/679-1415). For fine used books, including first editions of works by famous Irish authors, try **Cathach Books,** 10 Duke St., Dublin 2 (☎ 01/671-8676; fax 01/671-5120; e-mail: cathach@rarebooks.ie; www.rarebooks.ie.); more prosaic (and affordable) used books can be found at **Greene's Bookshop,** 16 Clare St., Dublin 2 (☎ 01/676-2554; fax 01/678-9091; e-mail: greenes@iol.ie); or **The Winding Stair,** 40 Lower Ormond Quay, Dublin 1 (☎ 01/873-3292).

CHINA & CRYSTAL   **China Showrooms,** 32–33 Abbey St. (☎ 01/878-6211), is a one-stop source of fine china such as Belleek, Aynsley, Royal Doulton, and hand-cut crystal from Waterford, Tipperary, and Tyrone. The **Dublin Crystal Glass Company,** Brookfield Terrace, Carysfort Avenue, Blackrock (☎ 01/288-7932), is Dublin's own distinctive hand-cut crystal business, founded in 1764 and revived in 1968. Visitors are welcome to browse in the factory shop and to see the glass being made and engraved.

CRAFTS & GIFTS   The ✪ **Powerscourt Townhouse Centre,** 59 S. William St. (☎ 01/679-4144), is a four-story complex with more than 60 boutiques, craft shops, art galleries, snackeries, wine bars, and restaurants. The wares include all kinds of crafts, antiques, paintings, prints, and hand-dipped chocolates and farmhouse cheeses.

If you're searching for contemporary Irish design, head to **The Kilkenny Shop,** 6–10 Nassau St. (☎ 01/677-7066), a modern multilevel showplace for original Irish designs and quality products including pottery, glass, candles, woolens, pipes, knitwear, jewelry, books, and prints; and **DESIGNyard,** 12 E. Essex St. (☎ 01/677-8453), a nonprofit gallery for the finest contemporary Irish and European jewelry, furniture, ceramics, glass, lighting, and textiles. Also, the **House of Ireland,** 37–38 Nassau St. (☎ 01/677-7473), is a happy blend of European and Irish products, from Waterford and Belleek to Wedgwood and Lladró, as well as tweeds, linens, knitwear, Celtic jewelry, mohair capes, shawls, kilts, blankets, and dolls. For quality ceramics, the creations of **Louis Mulcahey,** a noted Kerry potter, now have a Dublin home at 17 Kildare St. (☎ 01/662-8787).

FASHIONS   **Cleo,** 18 Kildare St. (☎ 01/676-1421), is the shop for the Joyce family's designer ready-to-wear clothing in a rainbow of vibrant tweed colors. **Pat Crowley,**

3 Molesworth Place (☎ 01/661-5580), is known for her exclusive line of tweeds and couture evening wear. Men shouldn't miss **Kevin and Howlin,** 31 Nassau St. (☎ 01/677-0257), a shop that has specialized in men's tweed garments for more than 50 years. There's also a selection of sweaters, scarves, vests, and hats. **Louis Copeland,** 39–41 Capel St. (☎ 01/872-1600), is known for high-quality work in made-to-measure and ready-to-wear men's suits, coats, and shirts. There are also branches at 30 Pembroke St. and 18 Wicklow St.

HERALDRY **Heraldic Artists,** 3 Nassau St. (☎ 01/679-7020), has been known for helping visitors celebrate their family roots for more than 20 years. In addition to tracing surnames, it also sells all the usual heraldic items, from parchments and mahogany wall plaques to crests, scrolls, and books on researching ancestry.

KNITWEAR The **Blarney Woolen Mills,** 21–23 Nassau St. (☎ 01/671-0068), known for its competitive prices, stocks a wide range of woolen knitwear made at its home base in Blarney, as well as crystal, china, pottery, and souvenirs. The **Dublin Woolen Mills,** 41 Lower Ormond Quay (☎ 01/677-0301), is on the north side of the River Liffey next to the Ha'penny Bridge, a leading source of Aran hand-knit sweaters as well as vests, hats, jackets, and tweeds. If you want a cashmere sweater, go to ✪ **Monaghan's,** 15–17 Grafton Arcade, Grafton Street (☎ 01/677-0823), which has the best selection of colors, sizes, and styles for both men and women anywhere in Ireland. It's also located at 4–5 Royal Hibernian Way, off Dawson Street (☎ 01/679-4451).

MARKETS For a walk into the past, don't miss the **Moore Street Market,** Moore Street, full of street-side barrow vendors plus plenty of local color and chatter. It's the principal open-air fruit, flower, fish, and vegetable market of the city. Up and running Monday to Saturday 9am to 6pm—or until supplies run out.

At the **Blackrock Market,** 19a Main St., Blackrock (☎ 01/283-3522) (DART to Blackrock), more than 60 vendors sell a wide variety of old and new goods at great prices in this indoor/outdoor setting; it's open Saturday 11am to 5:30pm and Sunday noon to 5:30pm.

The ✪ **Mother Red Caps Market,** Back Lane, off High Street (☎ 01/454-4655) (Bus: 21A, 50, 50A, 78, 78A, 78B), is one of Dublin's best, an enclosed market in the heart of Old Dublin. The stalls offer everything from antiques and used books and coins to silver, handcrafts, music tapes, furniture, and even a fortune teller! It's worth a trip here just to sample the farm-made cheeses, baked goods, and jams at the Rye-field Foods stall. Open Friday to Sunday, 10am to 5:30pm.

DUBLIN AFTER DARK

The best way to find out what's going on is to consult *In Dublin,* the leading maga-zine for upcoming events and happenings. The *Event Guide* also contains a useful and up-to-date listing of events throughout Ireland, with a focus on Dublin.

THE PERFORMING ARTS

For more than 90 years, **Abbey Theatre,** Lower Abbey St., Dublin 1 (☎ 01/878-7222; www.abbeytheatre.ie; bus: 29A, 31, 31A, 32, 32A, 32B, 38, 42A, 42B), has been the national theater of Ireland. The original theater, destroyed by fire in 1951, was replaced in 1966 by this functional-though-uninspired 600-seat house. The Abbey's artistic reputation within Ireland has risen and fallen many times and is at pre-sent reasonably strong. The box office is open Monday to Saturday 10am to 6pm; per-formances begin at 8 or 8:15pm. Tickets are £8 to £16 ($11 to $22); reduced tickets for students Monday to Thursday.

Just north of O'Connell Street off Parnell Square, the recently restored 370-seat ✪ **The Gate,** 1 Cavendish Row, Dublin 1 (☎ **01/874-4368;** fax 01/874-5373; DART: Connolly; bus: 40A, 40B, 40C, 51A), was founded in 1928 by Hilton Edwards and Michael MacLiammoir to provide a showing for a broad range of plays. This policy prevails today, with a program that includes a blend of modern works and the classics. Although less well known by visitors, the Gate is easily as distinguished as the Abbey. The box office is open Monday to Saturday 10am to 7pm. Tickets are £13 to £15 ($18 to $21) or £10 ($14) for previews. The relatively new **Andrews Lane Theatre,** 12–16 Andrews Lane, Dublin 2 (☎ **01/679-5720;** Pearse St. bus: 10, 11, 13B, 15A, 15B), has an ascending reputation for fine theater. It consists of a 220-seat main theater where contemporary works from home and abroad are presented, and a 76-seat studio geared for experimental productions. The box office is open Monday to Saturday 10:30am to 7pm. Tickets are £8 to £12 ($11 to $17).

Dublin's main venue for classical music is the **National Concert Hall,** Earlsfort Terrace, Dublin 2 (☎ **01/475-1572;** www.nch.ie; DART: Pearse St. bus: 14, 14A, 15A, 15B, 15C, 44, 48A). Originally part of University College, the hall stays busy with performances several nights a week for much of the year and is home to the National Symphony Orchestra. The box office is open Monday to Friday 10am to 3pm and 6pm to close of concert, weekends one hour before concerts. Tickets are £8 to £25 ($11 to $35); lunchtime concerts are £4 ($6).

With its Victorian jewel-box facade and garish red lobby, the **Olympia Theatre,** 72 Dame St., Dublin 2 (☎ **01/677-7744;** bus 50, 50A, 54, 56, 77), looks as though it should be home to high-stepping cancan girls. However, it's one of Dublin's busier old theaters, hosting everything from contemporary Irish plays to rock concerts. The box office is open 10:30am to midnight on show nights. Tickets are £7.50 to £15 ($12 to $23). With a seating capacity of 3,000, **The Point,** East Link Bridge, North Wall Quay (☎ **01/836-3633;** DART: Tara St. bus: 53A), is Ireland's newest large theater/concert venue, attracting top Broadway-caliber shows and international stars. The box office is open Monday to Saturday 10am to 6pm. Tickets are £10 to £50 ($14 to $70).

The City Arts Centre, 23–25 Moss St., at City Quay ☎ **01/677-0643;** DART: Tara St.), is an affiliate of Trans Europe Halles, the European network of independent arts centers. It presents a varied program, from dramatic productions, theatrical discussions, and readings by local writers to shows by touring companies from abroad. In May 2000, it was home to the World Stories Festival. Average ticket prices are £5 to £7 ($7 to $10).

THE PUB SCENE

The center of Irish social life, the pub is the place where Dubliners gather for conversation, music, and foaming pints of local brews. Day and night, the pub is for Dubliners, an extension of the household, both dining room and parlor. Though pub meals are rarely exciting, they're always filling and offer budgeters an inexpensive alternative to the city's restaurants.

FOR CONVERSATION & ATMOSPHERE The brass-filled and lantern-lit ✪ **Brazen Head,** 20 Lower Bridge St. (☎ **01/679-5186**), claims to be the city's oldest pub—and with good reason, considering that it was licensed in 1661 and occupies the site of an earlier tavern dating from 1198. On the south bank of the River Liffey, it's at the end of a cobblestoned courtyard and was once the meeting place of Irish freedom fighters, such as Robert Emmet and Wolfe Tone. Situated between Dublin Castle and Christchurch Cathedral, the recently rejuvenated bilevel **The Castle Inn,** Christchurch Place, Dublin 8 (☎ **01/475-1122**), exudes an "old city" atmosphere,

Traditional Irish Entertainment

The Irish cultural organization Comhaltas Ceoltoiri Eireann has been the prime mover in encouraging the renewal of Irish traditional music. An authentic fully costumed show featuring traditional music, song, and dance is staged mid-June through early September, Monday to Thursday at 9pm at ✪ **Culturlann Nah Eireann,** 32 Belgrave Sq., Monkstown (☎ **01/280-0295;** www.comhaltas. com). No reservations are necessary. Year-round, ceili dances are performed Friday 9pm to midnight; informal music sessions are held Friday and Saturday at 9:30pm. Tickets for ceilis are £5 ($7); informal music sessions £2 ($3.10); stage shows £7 ($10).

A mix of traditional Irish music and Broadway classics, set dancing, humorous monologues, and audience participation is offered at **Jury's Irish Cabaret,** Pembroke Road, Ballsbridge (☎ **01/660-5000**), Ireland's longest-running show (over 30 years). Shows take place May through October, Tuesday to Sunday with dinner at 7:15pm and the show at 8pm. Dinner and show are £36.50 ($51); show with two drinks £23 ($32).

There are several venues in Dublin where you can have dinner and listen to traditional music. At the **Abbey Tavern,** Abbey Road, Howth, County Dublin. (☎ **01/839 0307**), a complete four-course meal is accompanied by authentic Irish ballad music, with its blend of fiddles, pipes, tin whistles, and spoons. Tickets for dinner and entertainment are from £30 ($42). The box office is open Monday to Saturday 9am to 5pm; dinner and shows are daily March to October. From November to February it's best to call ahead to find out on which nights shows will be offered.

with stone walls, flagstone steps, knightly suits of armor, big stone fireplaces, beamed ceilings, and lots of early Dublin memorabilia. It is also the setting for an Irish Ceili and Banquet (May to September) featuring Irish traditional musicians and set dancers.

Referred to as a "moral pub" by James Joyce in *Ulysses,* **Davy Byrnes,** 21 Duke St. (just off Grafton St.) (☎ **01/677-5217**), is an imbibers' landmark that has drawn poets, writers, and lovers of literature ever since. Davy Byrnes first opened the doors in 1873; he presided here for more than 50 years and visitors today can still see his likeness on one of the turn-of-the-century murals hanging over the bar. In the heart of the trendy Temple Bar district on the corner of Temple Lane, the small three-room **Flannery's Temple Bar,** 47–48 Temple Bar (☎ **01/497-4766**), was established in 1840. The decor is an interesting mix of crackling fireplaces, globe ceiling lights, old pictures on the walls, and shelves filled with local memorabilia.

Tucked into a busy commercial street, **The Long Hall,** 51 S. Great George's St. (☎ **01/475-1590**), is one of the city's most photographed pubs, with a beautiful Victorian decor of filigree-edged mirrors, polished dark woods, and traditional snugs. The hand-carved bar is said to be the longest counter in the city.

Adjacent to the back door of the Gaiety Theatre, the celebrated **Neary's,** 1 Chatham St., Dublin 2 (☎ **01/677-7371**), is a favorite with stage folk and theatergoers. Trademarks here are the pink-and-gray marble bar and the brass hands that support the globe lanterns adorning the entrance. Three generations of the Ryan family have contributed to the success of ✪ **W. Ryan,** 28 Parkgate St. (☎ **01/677-6097**), located on the north side of the Liffey near Phoenix Park. The pub has such fine features as a metal ceiling and domed skylight, beveled mirrors, etched glass, brass lamp holders, a mahogany bar, and four old-style snugs.

FOR TRADITIONAL & FOLK MUSIC   South of the Grand Canal, ✪ **Kitty O'Shea's,** 23–25 Upper Grand Canal St. (☎ **01/660-9965**), is named after the sweetheart of 19th-century Irish statesman Charles Stewart Parnell. The decor reflects the Parnell era, with ornate oak paneling, stained-glass windows, old political posters, cozy alcoves, and brass railings. Traditional Irish music is on tap every night. For fans of traditional Irish music, **O'Donoghue's,** 15 Merrion Row, Dublin 2 (☎ **01/660-7194**), is a must. The Dubliners, one of Ireland's favorite traditional bands, got their start here, and impromptu music sessions are held almost every night.

Situated in the heart of Temple Bar and named for one of Ireland's literary greats, **Oliver St. John Gogarty,** 57–58 Fleet St. (☎ **01/671-1822.**), has an inviting old-world atmosphere, with shelves of empty bottles, stacks of dusty books, a horseshoe-shaped bar, and old barrels for seats. There are traditional music sessions every night from 9 to 11pm. A Saturday session is at 4:30pm, and Sunday from noon to 2pm.

Located on the north side of the Liffey, **Slattery's,** 129–130 Capel St. (☎ **01/873-1979**), has a classic facade and an interior of brass trim, dark wood, gas lamps, and church pew benches. On Sunday at 12:30 and 2pm, it's a focal point for traditional Irish music and ballads, with as many as 20 musicians playing in an informal session in the main bar. Rock and blues music are featured in the upstairs lounge Wednesday to Sunday 9 to 11:30pm. No cover for Irish-music sessions; £4 to £5 ($6 to $8) for rock or blues.

THE CLUB & MUSIC SCENE

The club and music scene in Dublin is confoundingly complex and changeable. Jazz, blues, folk, country, traditional, rock, and comedy move from venue to venue, night by night. The same club could be a gay fetish scene one night and a traditional music hotspot the next, so you have to stay on your toes to find what you want. The first rule is to get the very latest listings and see what's on and where.

Dozens of clubs and pubs all over town feature rock, folk, jazz, and traditional Irish music. This includes the so-called "late-night pubs"—pubs with an exemption allowing them to remain open past the usual closing time, mandated by law (11pm in winter, 11:30pm in summer). Check *In Dublin* magazine or the *Event Guide* for club schedules.

One of the most popular rock clubs is **Whelan's,** 25 Wexford St., Dublin 2 (☎ 01/478-0766); you should also visit the new **Hot Press Irish Music Hall of Fame,** 57 Middle Abbey St., Dublin 1 (☎ 01/878-3345), with music from Celtic to Rock most nights, and the second-oldest pub in Dublin, **Bleeding Horse,** 24–25 Camden St., Dublin 2 (☎ 01/475-2705). Other venues, especially popular with the over-30 late crowd, include: **Break for the Border,** Lower Steven's Street, Dublin 2 (☎ 01/478-0300); **Bad Bob's Backstage Bar,** East Essex Street, Dublin 2 (☎ 01/677-5482); **Major Tom's,** South King Street, Dublin 2 (☎ 01/478-3266); **the Baggot Inn,** Baggot Street, Dublin 4 (☎ 01/676-1430); and **Sinnotts,** South King Street, Dublin 2 (☎ 01/478-4698). All are open daily, with live music most nights. Where there is a cover charge, it's usually £2 to £6 ($2.80 to $8).

GAY & LESBIAN BARS

A great pub to check out is **The George,** 89 S. Great George's St., Dublin 2 (☎ 01/478-2983). Upstairs at The George is a club called **The Block** (☎ 01/478-2983), open Wednesday to Saturday 11pm to 2am, with a cover charge of £3 ($4.20); it's a comfortable mixed-age venue with something for everyone. **Stonewallz,** The Barracks,

Griffith College, South Circular Road, Dublin 8 (☎ 01/872-7770), is a women-only club currently open only on Saturday 9pm to 2am; the cover is £3 ($4.20). **Out on the Liffey,** 27 Upper Ormond Quay, Dublin 1 (☎ 01/872-2480), is a relaxed, friendly pub catering to a balance of men and women that serves up pub food with good conversation. In 1998, "Out" expanded to include a new and happening late-night venue called Oscar's, where you can dance (or drink) until you drop.

DANCE CLUBS

Here are the most established cutting-edge clubs (with correspondingly strict door policies): **The Kitchen,** in the Clarence Hotel, 6–8 Wellington Quay, Dublin 2 (☎ 01/677-6178), open Wednesday to Sunday 11pm to 2am; **POD** ("Place of Dance"), Harcourt Street, Dublin 2 (☎ 01/478-0166), open Wednesday to Saturday 11pm to 2am or later; and **Lillie's Bordello,** 45 Nassau St., Dublin 2 (☎ 01/679-9204), open daily 10pm to 1am or later.

There are also a few clubs with less strict door policies and a mixed-age crowd: **Club M,** in Blooms Hotel, Anglesea Street, Dublin 2 (☎ 01/671-5622), open Tuesday to Sunday 11pm to 2am; **Ri-Ra,** 1 Exchequer St., Dublin 2 (☎ 01/677-4835), open daily 11:30pm until 4am or later; and **Annabel's,** in the Burlington Hotel, Leeson Street Upper, Dublin 4 (☎ 01/660-5222), open Tuesday to Saturday 10pm to 2am.

Admission charges for these clubs range from £4 to £8 ($6 to $11).

SIDE TRIPS FROM DUBLIN

✪ **Malahide Castle.** Malahide, County Dublin. ☎ 01/846-2184. Admission to castle £3.10 ($4.80) adults, £2.60 ($4.05) students and seniors, £1.70 ($2.65) children under 12, £8.50 ($13) family. AE, DC, MC, V. Combination tickets available with Fry Model Railway and Newbridge House. Apr–Oct Mon–Fri 10am–5pm, Sat 11am–6pm, Sun 11:30am–6pm; Nov–Mar Mon–Fri 10am–5pm, Sat–Sun 2–5pm; gardens May–Sept daily 2–5pm. Closed for tours 12:45–2pm (restaurant remains open). Bus: 42.

About 13km (8 miles) north of Dublin, Malahide is one of Ireland's most historic castles, founded in the 12th century by Richard Talbot and occupied by his descendants until 1973. The fully restored interior of the building is the setting for a comprehensive collection of Irish furniture, dating from the 17th through the 19th centuries, and the walls are lined with one-of-a-kind Irish historical portraits and tableaux on loan from the National Gallery. The furnishings and art reflect life in and near the house over the past 8 centuries.

After touring the house, you can explore the 100ha (250-acre) estate, which includes 8ha (20 acres) of prized gardens with more than 5,000 species of plants and flowers. The Malahide grounds also contain the Fry Model Railway Museum, an exhibit of rare handmade models of more than 300 Irish trains, from the introduction of rail to the present.

✪ **Newgrange.** Off N51, Slane, County Meath. ☎ 041/988-0300. Admission to Newgrange and Brugh na Boinne Centre £4 ($6) adults, £3 ($4.20) seniors, £2 ($2.80) students and children over 6, £10 ($14) family. No credit cards accepted. Open daily Nov–Feb 9:30am–5pm; Mar–Apr 9:30am–5:30pm; May 9am–6:30pm; June to mid-Sept 9am–7pm; mid- to end Sept 9am–6:30pm; Oct 9:30am–5:30pm.

Newgrange is Ireland's best-known prehistoric monument and one of the archaeological wonders of Western Europe. Built as a burial mound more than 5,000 years ago—long before the Great Pyramids and Stonehenge—it sits atop a hill near the Boyne, massive and impressive. The huge mound—11m (36 feet) tall and approximately 80m (260 feet) in diameter—consists of 200,000 tons of stone, a 6-ton capstone, and other stones weighing up to 16 tons each, many of which were hauled from as far away as County Wicklow and the Mountains of Mourne. Each stone fits perfectly in the overall pattern and the result is a watertight structure, an amazing feat of engineering. Carved into the stones are myriad spirals, diamonds, and concentric circles. Inside, a passage 18m (60 feet) long leads to a central burial chamber with a 6m (19 foot) ceiling.

Fascination with Newgrange reaches a peak each winter solstice, when at 8:58am, as the sun rises to the southeast, sunlight pierces the inner chamber with an orange-toned glow for about 17 minutes. This occurrence is so remarkable that, as of this writing, the waiting list for viewing extends through the year 2004. Admission to Newgrange is by guided tour only. It's located 3km (2 miles) east of Slane, off N51.

All tickets are issued at the new visitor center. Combined tickets with Knowth, another nearby megalithic passage tomb, are available at the center. Because of the great numbers of visitors to Newgrange, especially in the summer, delays are to be expected and access is not guaranteed.

✪ Knowth. Off N51, Slane, County Meath. ☎ **041/988-0300.** Admission to Knowth and Brugh na Boinne Centre £3 ($4.20) adults, £2 ($2.80) seniors, £1.25 ($1.75) students and children over 6, £7.50 ($11) family. No credit cards accepted. Open daily May 9am–6:30pm; June to mid-Sept 9am–7pm; mid- to end Sept 9am–6:30pm; Oct 9:30am–5:30pm.

Dating from the Stone Age and under seemingly perpetual excavation, this great mound is believed to have been a burial site for the high kings of Ireland. Archaeological evidence points to occupation from 3000 B.C. to A.D. 1200. Located 1.5km (1 mile) northwest of Newgrange (see listing above), between Drogheda and Slane, Knowth is more complex than Newgrange, with two passage tombs surrounded by another 17 smaller satellite tombs. The site has the greatest collection of passage tomb art ever uncovered in Western Europe. All tickets, including combined tickets with Newgrange, are issued at the new visitor center.

2 Kerry & the Dingle Peninsula

Kerry is a place of disorienting contrasts, where the tackiest tourist attractions coexist with some of Ireland's most spectacular scenic wonders. It's a rugged place for the most part, some of it so rugged that it's seldom visited and remains quite pristine; Ireland's two highest mountains, Carrantuohill and Mount Brandon, are two examples. You could be driving along—say, on the famous and popular Ring of Kerry, which traces the shores of the Iveragh Peninsula—make one little detour from the main road, and be in wild and unfrequented territory. The transition can be startling.

Thanks to its remoteness, County Kerry has always been an outpost of Gaelic culture. Poetry and music are intrinsic to Kerry lifestyle, as is a love of the outdoors and sports. Gaelic football is an obsession in this county, and Kerry wins most of the national championships. You'll also find some of Ireland's best golf courses here, and the fishing for salmon and trout is equally hard to resist.

GETTING TO COUNTY KERRY   By Plane   Aer Lingus offers daily direct flights from Dublin into **Kerry County Airport,** Farranfore, County Kerry (☎ **066/ 64644**), about 16km (10 miles) north of Killarney and 24km (15 miles) south of Tralee.

By Car   Roads leading into Kerry include N21 and N23 from Limerick, N22 from Cork, N72 from Mallow, and N70 from West Cork.

KILLARNEY TOWN

Killarney is a relatively small town with a population of around 7,000 people. The town is very walkable, although the streets are usually crowded with tourists, especially in summer. The busiest section of town is at the southern tip of Main Street, where it meets East Avenue Road. Here the road curves and heads southward out to Muckross Road and the entrance to Killarney National Park.

It's important to remember that the reason why Killarney draws millions of visitors a year has nothing to do with Killarney town. Rather, it's all about the lakes and mountains of quite enchanting beauty just beyond the town's reach; and it's ever so easy to enter these wonders. Just walk from the town car park towards the cathedral and turn left into the National Park. In a matter of minutes you'll see for yourself why there's all the fuss. During the summer, the evenings are long, the light is often inde-scribable, and you needn't share the lanes with jaunting cars. Apart from deer and locals, the park is all yours till dark.

ESSENTIALS

GETTING THERE   By Train   Irish Rail offers daily service from most major Irish cities, arriving at **Killarney Railway Station,** Railway Road, off East Avenue Road (☎ **064/31067**).

By Bus   Bus Eireann operates regularly scheduled bus service from all parts of Ire-land. The **bus station** is adjacent to the train station at Railway Road, off East Avenue Road, Killarney (☎ **064/34777**).

VISITOR INFORMATION   The Killarney Tourist Office, Aras Fáilte, is located at the Town Centre Car Park, Beech Road, Killarney (☎ **064/31633**). It's open Jan-uary to April, Monday to Saturday 9:15am to 1pm and 2:15 to 5:30pm; May, Mon-day to Saturday 9:15am to 5:30pm; June, Monday to Saturday 9am to 6pm, Sunday 10am to 1pm and 2 to 6pm; July to August, Monday to Saturday 9am to 8pm, Sun-day 10am to 1pm and 2 to 6pm; September, Monday to Saturday 9am to 6pm, Sun-day 10am to 1pm and 2:15 to 6pm; October to December, Monday to Saturday 9:15am to 1pm and 2:15 to 5:30pm. It offers many helpful booklets, including the Tourist Trail walking-tour guide and the Killarney Area Guide with maps.

Useful local publications include *Where: Killarney,* a quarterly magazine distributed free at hotels and guest houses. It's packed with all types of current information on tours, activities, events, and entertainment.

GETTING AROUND   The town is so small and compact that it's best traversed on foot. Taxis line up at the stand on College Square (☎ **064/31331**). You can also phone for a taxi from **John Burke** (☎ **064/32448**), **Dero's Taxi Service** (☎ **064/31251**), or **O'Connell Taxi** (☎ **064/31654**).

You can drive to Killarney National Park, or go by **jaunting car.** The horse-drawn jaunting cars line up at Kenmare Place, offering rides to Killarney National Park sites and other scenic areas.

WHERE TO STAY

Expensive

✪ **Killarney Park Hotel.** Kenmare Place, Killarney, County Kerry. ☎ **064/35555.** Fax 064/35266. www.killarneyparkhotel.ie. 78 units. A/C TV TEL. £150–£190 ($210–$266) dou-ble; £220–£450 ($308–$630) suite. No service charge. Rates include full breakfast. AE, DC, MC, V.

With a striking yellow neo-Georgian facade, this new four-story property is located on the eastern edge of town. Public rooms are posh and spacious, with open fireplaces and a sunlit conservatory-style lounge overlooking the gardens. Rooms have wood fur-nishings and hair dryers. Public areas include a restaurant, piano bar, patio, billiard room, indoor heated swimming pool, outdoor hot tub, Jacuzzi, sauna, gym, and steam room. Among the hotel's recent plaudits are the 1997/98 AA "Irish Hotel of the Year" award as well as several RAC dining awards for 1999/2000.

Blennerville Windmill **3**	Gap of Dunloe **13**	Kerry the Kingdom **1**
Crag Cave **14**	Ionad An Bhlascaoid	Skellig Experience **8**
Derrynane House	(The Blasket Centre) **5**	Skellig Islands **9**
National Historic Park **11**	Kenmare Heritage Town	Staigue Fort **10**
Dingle Oceanworld **6**	Exhibition Centre **12**	Tralee Steam Railway **2**
Gallarus Oratory **4**	Kerry Bog Village Museum **7**	

Moderate

Castlerosse. Killorglin Rd., Killarney, County Kerry. ☎ **800/528-1234** in the U.S., or 064/31114. Fax 064/31031. E-mail: castler@iol.ie. 121 units. TV TEL. £70–£104 ($98–$146) double. Rates include full Irish breakfast and service charge. AE, DC, MC, V. Closed Dec–Feb.

Set on its own parkland between Lower Lake and surrounding mountains, this modern, rambling, ranch-style inn is 3km (2 miles) from the heart of town and next to Killarney's two golf courses. The recently refurbished rooms offer contemporary furnishings and views of the lake. No-smoking rooms and ones specially fitted for guests with disabilities are available on request. Facilities include a nine-hole golf course, a new leisure and fitness center, two tennis courts, putting green, walking paths, and jogging trails. New self-catering minisuites, sleeping up to five persons, are also available.

Earls Court Guesthouse. Woodlawn Junction, Muckross Rd., Killarney, County Kerry. ☎ **064/34009.** Fax 064/34366. www.killarney-earlscourt.ie. 11 units (1 single with shower only). TV TEL. £57–£90 ($80–$126) double. Rates include full Irish breakfast and service charge. MC, V. Closed Nov 6–Feb. Follow the sign off N71; it's a 5-minute walk from Killarney center.

Earls Court is among Killarney's newest and most attractive quality guest houses. The spacious and immaculately clean rooms are furnished with exceptional style and taste. Some have sitting areas, and nearly all have balconies. The second-floor rooms, in particular, have clear views of the mountains. All rooms have firm beds and hair dryers, and all are no-smoking. Room service and laundry services available by request. In 1998 Earls Court won the "RAC Small Hotel of the Year" award for Ireland.

⭕ Kathleen's Country House. Madam's Height, Tralee road (N22), Killarney, County Kerry. ☎ **064/32810.** Fax 064/32340. www.kathleens.net 16 units. TV TEL. £63–£85 ($88–$119) double. No service charge. Rates include full breakfast. AE, MC, V. Closed mid-Nov to early Mar.

Of the many guest houses in this area, this one stands out. Located just north of town next to a dairy farm, it is a two-story contemporary house with a modern mansard-style roof and many picture windows. Enthusiastic and efficient hostess Kathleen O'Regan-Sheppard has also outfitted all the rooms with orthopedic beds, hair dryers, trouser presses, and tea/coffeemakers. Quite recently, all rooms have been totally refurbished in antique pine furniture. A cozy new library/drawing room has been added. Smoking is permitted only in the enclosed front foyer of the house.

Inexpensive

⭕ Gleann Fia Country House. Deerpark, Killarney, County Kerry. ☎ **064/35035.** Fax 064/35000. E-mail: gleanfia@iol.ie. 17 units. TV TEL. £46–£60 ($64–$84) double. No service charge. Rates include full breakfast. AE, MC, V. Closed Dec–Feb.

Although just out of town, this modern guest house feels pleasantly secluded, tucked away as it is in 10ha (26 acres) of lawns and woodlands. Rooms in the most recent addition are slightly larger and more elegantly furnished than those in the main house, and are correspondingly pricier. All are nonsmoking. There's also a spacious family room on the ground floor of the main house with a double bed, single bed, and couch. Amenities include an airy conservatory with tea-making facilities, a guest lounge, and an unusually extensive breakfast menu. There is a nature walk along the stream that runs by one side of the house. Bicycles may be rented on the premises.

WHERE TO DINE

Expensive

⭕ Gaby's Seafood Restaurant. 27 High St., Killarney. ☎ **064/32519.** Reservations recommended. Main courses £12.90–£28 ($18–$39). AE, DC, MC, V. Mon–Sat 6–10pm. Closed mid-Feb to mid-Mar. SEAFOOD.

One of Killarney's longest established restaurants, this nautically themed place is a mecca for lovers of fresh seafood. It's known for its succulent lobster, served grilled or in a house sauce of cognac, wine, cream, and spices. Other choices include turbot, haddock in wine, local salmon, and a giant Kerry shellfish platter, a veritable feast of prawns, scallops, mussels, lobster, and oysters.

Moderate

⭕ Bricín. 26 High St., Killarney. ☎ **064/34902.** Reservations recommended for dinner. Main courses £8.50–£13.50 ($12–$19); snacks £1.60–£5 ($2.25–$7). AE, CB, DC, MC, V. Year-round Tues–Sat 10am–4:30pm; Easter–Oct Mon–Sat 6–9:30pm. IRISH.

Traditional Kerry boxty dishes (potato pancakes with various fillings, such as chicken, seafood, curried lamb, or vegetables) are the trademark of this upstairs restaurant. The menu also offers a variety of fresh seafood, pastas, Irish stew, and specials. Housed in one of Killarney's oldest buildings, Bricín sports original stone walls, turf fireplaces, and, something very rare in Ireland—a completely smoke-free room seating 40.

⭕ Coopers Café and Restaurant. Old Market Lane, off High St. (where New St. intersects High), Killarney. ☎ **064/37716.** Reservations recommended. Dinner main courses £8.95–£14.25 ($13–$20). MC, V. Mon–Thurs 12:30–3pm and 6:30–9:30pm, Fri–Sat 12:30–3pm and 6:30–10pm, Sun 4–9:30pm. IRISH/CONTINENTAL.

This recent (1999) creation of "Martin and Mo"—two of Ireland's most touted restaurateurs—is already creating quite a buzz among both locals and tourists. Coopers has clearly broken the mold here in Killarney, with its chic, urban, nightclub decor. Overhead, the many-tendriled wire-sculpture chandeliers with flower-cup lights cast a magical fairylike illumination. The total effect is as captivating as the menu, which while inventive and varied focuses on local Irish seafood and wild game. The skillfully rendered options comprise such specialties as wild pheasant cooked in Irish cream liqueur, escallope of venison, fillet of wild pigeon, grilled swordfish and salmon, wild fillet of sea trout, and baked cod Provençale. For vegetarians, the warm goat's cheese salad with two pestos is but one fully satisfying selection. Finally, the luring array of desserts include crumbles, tarts, homemade ice creams, meringues, and crème brûlées, although it requires rare strength of character to get past the duo of dark chocolate and pistachio mousse.

Greenes. 4 Bridewell Lane, off New St. across from Dunnes Stores, Killarney. ☎ **064/ 33083.** Reservations recommended. Dinner main courses £8.95–£11.95 ($13–$17). MC, V. Apr–June Tues–Sat 12:30–3pm and 6:30–9:30pm, Sun 6:30–9:30pm; July–Oct Mon–Sat 12:30–3pm and 6:30–9:30pm, Sun 6:30–9:30pm; Nov–Dec Tues–Sat 12:30–3pm. Closed Jan–Mar. VEGETARIAN.

Good things often come in small parcels, and it's no exception with this uncommonly good, fanciful nook of a restaurant tucked away in one of Killarney's many off-street lanes. A little persistent looking will turn it up, and the reward is a tranquil, fresh, delicious meal seemingly far from the madding crowd. The menu changes with the season and with what is at its best in the markets; but you can expect the likes of carrot and coriander loaf with crème fraîche, whole-wheat spinach crepe filled with organic avocado and brazil nuts and three cheeses, or baked eggplant gâteau. The modest selection of house wines, by bottle or glass, suits well the cuisine. An assortment of puddings, tarts, and other sweet whims await you at the finish line. This new contender in the Killarney cuisine scene is well worth one of your afternoons or nights out.

✪ KILLARNEY NATIONAL PARK

This is Killarney's centerpiece: a 10,000ha (25,000-acre) area of natural beauty. You'll find three-storied lakes—Lower Lake (or Lough Leane), Middle Lake (or Muckross Lake), and Upper Lake—myriad waterfalls, rivers, islands, valleys, mountains, bogs, and woodlands, and lush foliage and trees, including oak, arbutus, holly, and mountain ash. There's also a large variety of wildlife, including a rare herd of red deer. No automobiles are allowed within the park, so touring is best done on foot, bicycle, or horse-drawn jaunting car. The park offers four signposted walking and nature trails along the lakeshore.

Access is available from several points along the Kenmare road (N71), with the main entrance being at Muckross House, where there is a new visitor center featuring background exhibits on the park and a 20-minute film titled *Mountain, Wood, Water.* Admission is free, and the park is open year-round during daylight hours.

VIEWS & VISTAS   The journey through the ✪ **Gap of Dunloe** is a must. The winding and rocky Gap of Dunloe is situated amid mountains and lakelands about 10km (6 miles) west of Killarney. The route through the gap passes a kaleidoscope of craggy rocks, massive cliffs, meandering streams, and deep valleys. The road through the gap ends at Upper Lake. One of the best ways to explore the gap is by bicycle. Horse fanciers may want to take one of the horseback excursions offered by **Castlelough Tours,** 7 High St. (☎ **064/31115**); **Corcoran's Tours,** Kilcummin (☎ **064/36666**); and **Dero's Tours,** 22 Main St. (☎ **064/31251**).

Aghadoe Heights, on Tralee Road (off N22) is a spectacular viewing point over the lakes and town. To your left is the ruin of the 13th-century Castle of Parkvonear, erected by Norman invaders and well worth a visit. In the nearby churchyard are the remains of a stone church and round tower dating from 1027.

MORE ATTRACTIONS

✪ **Muckross House and Gardens.** Kenmare Rd. (N71), Killarney. ☎ **064/31440.** Admission to house £4 ($6) adults, £3 ($4.20) seniors, £1.60 ($2.25) students and children, £10 ($14) family. Daily mid-Mar to June and Sept–Oct 9am–6pm; July–Aug 9am–7pm; Nov to mid-Mar 9am–5:30pm. Gardens open year-round without admission fee.

The Muckross Estate is the focal point of Middle Lake. The gracious ivy-covered, Elizabethan-style residence with its colorful and well-tended gardens was built by Henry Arthur Herbert in 1843 and visited by Queen Victoria in 1861. The house is now a folk museum, and the cellars have been converted into craft shops where local artisans demonstrate the traditional trades of bookbinding, weaving, and pottery making. The adjacent gardens are known for their fine collection of rhododendrons and azaleas.

Just across from Muckross House is an attraction you might overlook but which is really quite fascinating, especially for families with children. **Muckross Traditional Farms,** a 28ha (70-acre) park, is home to displays of traditional farm life and artisans' shops. The farmhouses and buildings are so authentically detailed that visitors feel they are dropping in on working farms and lived-in houses. The animals and household environments are equally fascinating for children and adults. Combined tickets are available with Muckross House.

Ross Castle. Ross Rd., off Kenmare Rd. (N71), Killarney. ☎ **064/35851.** Admission £3 ($4.20) adults, £2 ($2.80) seniors, £1.25 ($1.75) students and children, and £7.50 ($10) family. Apr daily 10am–5pm; May and Sept daily 10am–6pm; June–Aug daily 9am–6:30pm; Oct Tues–Sun 10am–5pm.

Newly restored, this 15th-century fortress sits on the edge of the Lower Lake, 3km (2 miles) outside Killarney Town. Built by the O'Donoghue chieftains, this castle distinguished itself in 1652 as the last stronghold in Munster to surrender to Cromwell's forces. All that remains today is a tower house, surrounded by a fortified bawn with rounded turrets. The tower has been furnished in the style of the late 16th and early 17th centuries and offers a magnificent view of the lakes and islands from its top. Access is by guided tour only. A lovely lakeshore walk stretches for 3km (2 miles) between Killarney and the castle.

SIGHTSEEING TOURS

Bus Tours   To get your bearings in Killarney, consider one of two sightseeing tours. **Killarney Highlights** is offered by **Dero's Tours,** 7 Main St., Killarney (☎ 064/ 31251 or 064/31567; www.derostours.com). Besides showing off Killarney's lakes from the best vantage points, this 3-hour tour takes you to Aghadoe, the Gap of Dunloe, Ross Castle, Muckross House and Gardens, and Torc Waterfall. Frommer's readers who book directly with the Deros office may receive a 5% discount. Tours cost £8 ($11) and are given May to September daily at 10:30am, but schedules vary, so check in advance. **Castlelough Tours,** 7 High St., Killarney (☎ 064/31115), takes you through the spectacularly scenic **Gap of Dunloe** and includes a boat tour of the Killarney lakes. Tours cost £13 ($18) and are given May to September. Call for current hours and bookings.

In addition to Killarney's main sights, some bus tours also venture into the two prime scenic areas nearby: the Ring of Kerry and Dingle Peninsula. In the May-to-September period, tours are offered daily; prices average £14 ($20) per person. Check the following companies if that's the kind of tour for you: **Bus Eireann,** Bus Depot, Railway Road, off East Avenue Road (☎ **064/34777**); **Castlelough Tours,** 7 High St. (☎ **064/31115**); **Corcoran's Tours,** 10 College St. (☎ **064/36666**); and **Dero's Tours,** 22 Main St. (☎ **064/31251** or 064/31567).

Jaunting Car Tours   These quaint horse-driven buggies are one of the main features of the landscape here, and if you decide to give them a try, keep in mind that rates are set and carefully monitored by the Killarney Urban District Council. Current rates, all based on four persons to a jaunting car, run roughly £4 to £12 ($6 to $17)) per person round-trip, depending on destinations, which include Ross Castle, Muckross House and Gardens, Torc Waterfall, Muckross Abbey, Dinis Island, and Kate Kearney's Cottage, gateway to the Gap of Dunloe. To arrange a tour in advance, contact **Tangney Tours,** Kinvara House, Muckross Road, Killarney (☎ **064/33358**).

Boat Tours   There is nothing quite like seeing the sights from a boat on the lakes of Killarney. Two companies operate regular boating excursions, with full commentary. **M.V. Pride of the Lakes Tours,** Scotts Gardens, Killarney (☎ **064/32638**), offers daily sailings on an enclosed boat from the pier at Ross Castle. The trip lasts just over an hour, and reservations are suggested. Tours are given April to October at 11am, 12:30pm, 2:30pm, 4pm, and 5:15pm, and cost £5 ($7) adults, £2.50 ($3.50) children, £12.50 ($18) family. **M.V. Lily of Killarney Tours,** 3 High St., Killarney (☎ **064/31068**), offers similar tours April to October at 10:30am, noon, 1:45pm, 3:15pm, and 4:30pm for £5 ($7) adults, £2.50 ($3.50) children, £12 ($17) family.

Enjoying the Great Outdoors

BICYCLING   The **Killarney National Park** is a paradise for bikers. Various types of bikes, from 21-speed touring bikes and mountain bikes to tandems, are available. Rental charges average £6 ($8) per day or £25 ($35) per week. Try one of the following shops: **Killarney Rent-a-Bike,** High Street (☎ **064/32578**); **O'Neills Cycle Shop,** 6 Plunkett St., Killarney (☎ **064/31970**); and D. O'Sullivan's **The Bike Shop,** High Street, Killarney (☎ **064/31282**). Most shops are open year-round 9am to 6pm daily, with extended hours until 8 or 9pm in the summer months.

One great ride beginning in Killarney takes you through the Gap of Dunloe along a dirt forest road, where you'll see some of the best mountain scenery in the area; it can be made into a 56km (35-mile) loop if you return on N71.

FISHING   Fishing for salmon and brown trout in Killarney's unpolluted lakes and rivers is a big attraction. Brown trout fishing is free on the lakes, but a permit is necessary for the Rivers Flesk and Laune. A trout permit costs £3 to £10 ($4.20 to $14) per day.

Salmon fishing anywhere in Ireland requires a license; the cost is £3 ($4.20) per day or £10 ($14) for 21 days. In addition, some rivers also require a salmon permit, which costs £8 to £10 ($11 to $14) per day. Permits and licenses can be obtained at the Fishery Office at the **Knockreer Estate Office,** New Street, Killarney (☎ **064/31246**).

For fishing tackle, bait, rod rental, and other fishing gear, as well as permits and licenses, try **O'Neill's,** 6 Plunkett St., Killarney (☎ **064/31970**). This shop also arranges the hire of boats and ghillies (fishing guides), for £60 ($93) per day on the Killarney Lakes, leaving from Ross Castle. Gear and tackle can also be purchased from Michael O'Brien at **Angler's Paradise,** Loreto Road, Killarney (☎ **064/33818**).

GOLF   Visitors are always welcome at the twin 18-hole championship courses of the **Killarney Golf & Fishing Club,** Killorglin Road, Fossa, Killarney (☎ **064/31034**), located 5km (3 miles) west of the town center. Widely praised as one of the most scenic golf settings in the world, these courses, known as "Killeen" and "Mahony's

Point," are surrounded by lake and mountain vistas. Greens fees are £40 ($56) on either course.

HORSEBACK RIDING   Many trails in the Killarney area are suitable for horseback riding. Hiring a horse ranges from £10 to £15 ($14 to $21) per hour at the following establishments: **Killarney Riding Stables,** R562, Ballydowney, Killarney (☎ **064/ 31686**); **O'Donovan's Farm,** Mangerton Road, Muckross, Killarney (☎ **064/32238**); and **Rocklands Stables,** Rockfield, Tralee Road, Killarney (☎ **064/32592**). Lessons and week-long trail rides can also be arranged.

WALKING   Killarney is ideal for walking enthusiasts. On the outskirts of town, the **Killarney National Park** offers four sign-posted nature trails. Leaflets with maps of these four trails are available at the park's visitor center. For long-distance walkers, there is the 200km (125-mile) "Kerry Way," a sign-posted walking route that extends from Killarney around the Ring of Kerry.

THE SHOPPING SCENE: KERRY GLASS & WOOLENS

The ✪ **Kerry Glass Studio and Visitor Centre,** Killorglin Road, Fossa (☎ **064/ 44666**), produces Killarney's distinctive colored glass. Visitors are welcome to watch and photograph the craftspeople firing, blowing, and adding color to the glass. The center includes a factory shop and snack bar.

The **Blarney Woolen Mills,** 10 Main St. (☎ **064/33222**), has everything from hand-knit or hand-loomed Irish-made sweaters to tweeds, crystal, china, pottery, and souvenirs. **Quill's Woolen Market,** 1 High St. (☎ **064/32277**), is one of the best shops in town for hand-knit sweaters of all kinds, as well as tweeds, mohair, and sheepskins.

THE RING OF KERRY

Undoubtedly Ireland's most popular scenic drive, the Ring of Kerry is a 177km (110-mile) panorama of seacoast, mountain, and lakeland vistas. Bicyclists usually avoid this route, since the scores of tour buses that thunder through here every day in the summer aren't always generous about sharing the road.

ESSENTIALS

MAKING THE DRIVE   By Bus   Bus Eireann (☎ 064/34777) provides limited daily service from Killarney to Caherciveen, Waterville, Kenmare, and other towns on the Ring of Kerry.

By Car   This is by far the best way to get around the Ring. For the most part, the route follows N70.

VISITOR INFORMATION   For year-round information, stop in at the **Killarney Tourist Office,** Town Centre Car Park, Beech Road, Killarney (☎ 064/31633), before you begin your drive. June to September, **The Barracks Tourist Office,** Caherciveen (☎ **066/72589**), is open; Easter to September, the **Kenmare Tourist Office,** Market Square, Kenmare (☎ **064/41233**), is open. Most telephone numbers on the Ring of Kerry use the 064 or 066 code.

WHERE TO STAY AROUND THE RING

✪ **Park Hotel Kenmare.** Kenmare, County Kerry. ☎ **800/525-4800** in the U.S., or 064/41200. Fax 064/41402. www.parkkenmare.com. 48 units. TV TEL. £244–£484 ($342–$678) double. No service charge. Rates include full breakfast. AE, DC, MC, V. Closed Nov–Dec 23 and Jan 2 to mid-Apr.

Ensconced amid palm tree–lined gardens beside Kenmare Bay, this 1897 Victorian-style château is a haven of impeccable service and luxurious living. The interior is rich with high-ceilinged sitting rooms, fireplaces, plush furnishings, and museum-worthy antiques. Rooms are decked out in a mix of Georgian and Victorian styles, many with four-poster or canopy beds. Most have views of the river and mountains. No-smoking rooms are available; all are wheelchair accessible. The dining room is one of the most highly acclaimed hotel restaurants in Ireland, meriting a Michelin star. Facilities include an 18-hole golf course, joggers' trail, tennis court, croquet lawn, and salmon fishing. In 1998, the Park Hotel was named the Condé Nast "Best Hotel in Ireland."

Parknasilla Great Southern Hotel. Ring of Kerry Rd. (N70), Parknasilla, County Kerry. ☎ **064/45122.** Fax 064/45323. E-mail: www.gsh.ie. 84 units. TV TEL. £160–£212 ($224–$297) double. Service charge 12.5%. AE, DC, MC, V. Closed Jan to mid-Mar.

Facing one of the loveliest seascape settings in Ireland, this château-style hotel is set amid 120ha (300 acres) of lush, subtropical palm trees and flowering shrubs. George Bernard Shaw stayed here and was inspired to write much of his play *Saint Joan.* The hotel has a private nine-hole golf course, a heated indoor saltwater swimming pool, saunas, and tennis courts, and offers riding, fishing, and boating. Rooms are individually furnished, and most look out onto broad vistas of the Kenmare River and the Atlantic.

Towers. Ring of Kerry Rd. (N70), Glenbeigh, County Kerry. ☎ **066/976-8212.** Fax 066/976-8260. E-mail: towers@tinet.ie. 28 units. TV TEL. £76–£94 ($106–$132) double. Service charge 12.5%. Rates include full breakfast. AE, MC, V. Closed Nov–Mar.

If you'd like to be right in the heart of one of the Ring's most delightful towns, then this vintage brick-faced country inn is for you. Shaded by ancient palms, it sits in the middle of a small fishing village, yet is near the sandy Rossbeigh Strand. Recently refurbished and updated, most of the rooms are in a contemporary-style new wing with lovely views of the nearby waters. Facilities include a lively old-fashioned pub and a good seafood restaurant.

WHERE TO DINE AROUND THE RING

The Huntsman. The Strand, Waterville. ☎ **066/947-4560.** Reservations recommended. Main courses £9.95–£18.95 ($14–$27); four-course fixed-price dinner £25 ($35). AE, DC, MC, V. Mar–Oct daily 10am–10pm; Nov–Feb Sat–Sun noon–9pm. INTERNATIONAL.

It's worth a trip to Waterville just to dine at this contemporary beachfront restaurant on the shore of Ballinskelligs Bay. Owner/chef Raymond Hunt takes the time to offer suggestions from the extensive menu, specializing in seafood and featuring only the freshest local catch and produce. Skellig lobster fresh from the tank, swordfish, and Kenmare Bay scampi are among the seafood dishes; meat dishes include rack of lamb, venison, seasonal pheasant, rabbit, duck, and Irish stew. All this is assisted by an extensive award-winning wine list. In addition, there's a complimentary feast comprised of spectacular views of ocean headlands and mountains.

✪ **Lime Tree.** Shelbourne Rd., Kenmare. ☎ **064/41225.** Reservations recommended. Main courses £9.95–£13.50 ($14–$19). MC, V. Apr–Oct daily 6:30–10pm. IRISH.

Innovative cuisine is the focus at this restaurant in an 1821 landmark renovated schoolhouse next to the grounds of the Park Hotel. The decor includes a skylit gallery and stone walls lined with paintings by local artists, and the menu offers such dishes as goat's cheese potato cake with balsamic glaze, oak-planked wild salmon, fillet of Irish beef with colcannon (mashed potatoes and cabbage), and oven-roasted Kerry lamb.

Packie's. Henry St., Kenmare, County Kerry. ☎ **064/41508.** Reservations recommended. Main courses £8.90–£18.90 ($12–$26). MC, V. Easter to mid-Nov Tues–Sat 5:30–10pm. IRISH.

With window boxes full of colorful seasonal plantings, this informal, bistro-style restaurant in the middle of town exudes a welcoming atmosphere. The interior has a slate floor, stone walls, and dark oak tables and chairs. On the walls is a collection of wonderful contemporary Irish art, and on the menu are tried-and-true favorites: Irish stew and rack of lamb. Also offered are creative combinations, such as gratin of crab and prawns, beef braised in Guinness with mushrooms, and blackboard fish specials. Chef-owner Maura Foley uses herbs from her own garden to enhance each dish.

EXPLORING THE RING

The drive can be undertaken in either direction, but I strongly recommend a counterclockwise route for the most spectacular views. It's worth noting that the farther you get along the road, the more the signs tend to be in Gaelic only. Since the maps are all in English, this can be somewhat confusing. Careful study of the maps is suggested when exploring away from N20. You can buy an Ordnance Survey map (sheet 83) from the tourist office, which gives names in both English and Gaelic.

Leave Killarney on R562 and follow the signs for **Killorglin.** Be sure to make the detour to visit **Ballymalis Castle.** Probably built by the Ferris family at the end of the 16th century, this ruin is typical of the tower houses built by wealthy landlords to protect their households from unwelcome intruders. Climbing the narrow, winding staircase, you're rewarded with splendid views over mountains, rivers, and fields. Backtrack to the main road and continue.

When you arrive in **Killorglin,** you might want to stop and walk around this spot, known far and wide for its annual mid-August horse, sheep, and cattle fair. Its official name is Puck Fair. The locals capture a wild goat from the mountains and enthrone it in the center of town as a sign to begin unrestricted merrymaking—although not necessarily for the goat.

Continuing on N70, follow the signs for **Glenbeigh,** with views to your left of 1,040m (3,414-foot) **Carrantuohill,** Ireland's tallest mountain. Open bog land is a constant companion on this stretch, and locals dig peat, or turf, to burn in their fireplaces. On your right just before you reach Glenbeigh is the **Kerry Bog Village Museum** (☎ 066/ 69184), where a cluster of thatched cottages illustrates Kerry life in the early 1800s. As you explore the blacksmith's forge, the turf cutter's house, and the laborer's cottage, the smell of burning peat hangs heavy in the air. The village is also home to the Kerry Bog pony, a breed that has been saved from extinction and is now unique to this museum.

The next town on the Ring is **Glenbeigh,** a palm tree–lined fishing resort with a lovely duney beach called Rossbeigh Strand. You may want to stop here, or continue on the Ring, with the first sightings of the Atlantic appearing away to your right. The views on the next section of the Ring are breathtaking, although the drive can be a bit hair-raising since the road twists and winds around the cliffs. There's a gorgeous view down over **Kells Bay,** best viewed from the road, instead of making the drive down to it. The route then moves inland with mountains to your right and a patchwork of fields in many shades of green to your left.

When you reach **Cahersiveen,** follow the signs right for the two forts, reached along a scenic though narrow road. You need to park a little way past the first fort, **Cahergeal,** and walk back along a rough track. The fort is made from gray stones and boulders piled one on top of the other. Staircases and walkways snake their way up and around ramparts, and the view across the bay is magical. The second fort can be reached along a narrow road to the right a little farther along. This is **Leacanabuaile Fort,** one of the few stone forts to have been excavated. The objects found suggest that the fort was in use until the 9th or 10th century. The castle that can be seen from both forts is Ballycarbery, but isn't really worth a visit, being best viewed from the distance.

Return to Cahersiveen and rejoin N70, and then follow the signs right marked VALENTIA VIA FERRY. **Valentia** (also spelled Valencia) can also be reached by road (R565), following the signs for Portmagee farther along N70, but the ferry crossing saves a good deal of time and costs just £3 ($4.20) for the car. Valentia Island, 11km (7 miles) long, is one of the most westerly points in Europe. It has the distinction of being the place from which the first telegraph cable was laid across the Atlantic in 1866.

Once ashore at Knightstown, follow the signs for **Glanleam Gardens,** Glanleam House (☎ **066/76176**). Created over 150 years ago by the Knights of Kerry, the gardens are justly famous for a unique collection of Southern Hemisphere plants. Broad walks weave through junglelike plantings of South American palms, Australian tree ferns, bananas, giant groves of bamboo, and rust-colored myrtles from Chile.

Leaving the gardens, follow the signs for **Portmagee,** stopping on the outskirts to visit **The Skellig Experience,** Skellig Heritage Centre (☎ **066/76306**). This attraction blends right in with the terrain, with a stark, stone facade, framed by grassy mounds. The center gives you a detailed look at the bird and plant life of the Valentia area. In particular, it tells the story of the **Skellig rocks**—Skellig Michael and Little Skellig—two rocky islands sitting off the coast in the Atlantic. In the 6th century, Skellig Michael, the larger of the two, became home to a group of monks who founded a monastery that survived for more than 600 years. Today, the other Skellig is one of the largest breeding grounds for the gannet in Western Europe. Admission to the Skellig Experience, for the exhibition and audiovisual, is £3 ($4.20) for adults, £2.70 ($3.80) for seniors and students, £1.50 ($2.10) for children under 12, and £7 ($10) for a family of two adults and up to four children; for the exhibition, audiovisual, and sea cruise circuiting the Skelligs, the fee is £15 ($21) for adults, £13.50 ($19) for seniors and students, £7.50 ($11) for children under 12, £40 ($56) for a family. It's open April to September, 10am to 7pm.

It's well worth making the 13km (8-mile) sea journey to the Skelligs, if only to climb the "stairway to Heaven," leading to the remains of the monastic settlement where you can marvel at the lifestyle of the monks who once lived here. Thanks to the degree to which the place has been preserved, little imagination is needed to picture those early years of Irish Christianity. Ferries leave daily from Ballyferriter, usually between 9am and noon; call **Joe Roddy** (☎ 066/74268) or **Sean Feehan** (☎ 066/79182). Ferries departing from Portmagee are run by **Murphy's** (☎ 066/ 77156). The cost is £20 ($28) per person.

In the 18th century Valentia harbor was famous as a refuge for smugglers and privateers; tradition has it that John Paul Jones, the Scottish-born American naval officer in the War of Independence, anchored here frequently.

The route now continues into **Portmagee** and on through the **Coomanaspig Pass,** with dramatic views across St. Finan's Bay. This remote Irish-speaking area is an outpost of Gaelic culture and has an Irish college to which children come in the summer months to learn their native language. Continue through the glen, passing miles of golden, sandy beaches. When you reach Ballinskelligs, follow the road (R566 and N70) around the bay to **Waterville.** An overnight at this idyllic spot is highly recommended. There are many excellent restaurants, and from 9pm on, almost every bar on the seafront comes alive with the singing of traditional Irish songs.

Leaving Waterville, continue along N70. If time allows (you'll need a good 50 minutes), take the first left turn, sign-posted CLUB MED (yes, you'll pass their only branch in Ireland) and enjoy a spectacular drive along the shores of **Lough Currane.** This is a very narrow and little-used road, but the dramatic views are well worth the effort.

To your left, the dark waters of the lough and the towering ruggedness of the purple mountains suddenly give way to a patchwork of green fields. Take your time and take it all in. The road ends at a cottage, where you'll need to turn around and backtrack to N70.

Continuing on N70 through the Coomakista Pass, you arrive at another viewpoint at the crest of the road, where there's a statue of the Virgin Mary looking down onto the mouth of the Kenmare River and back along the pass to Waterville.

The next village is **Caherdaniel,** where a right turn leads to **Derrynane House** (☎ **066/75113**), the home, for most of his life, of Daniel O'Connell, the liberator. The house is now a museum dedicated to his struggle, with documents, maps, and memorabilia. Nature trails twist and turn through the 130ha (320-acre) grounds and an explanatory booklet is available.

Return to N70 and continue on until you reach signs to the left for the **Staigue Fort,** which possibly dates from around 1000 B.C. Forts such as this, with massive stone walls, were built as centers for communal refuge. The fort is nestled between the hills and mountains, and the views down over the treetops across the bay and estuary are magnificent.

Back on N70, you'll arrive at the pretty, colorful village of **Sneem,** its houses painted in vibrant shades of blue, pink, yellow, and purple. There's a memorial commemorating General de Gaulle's visit in 1969, and don't miss, to the right of the Catholic church, The Way the Fairies Went, a creation by James Scanlon, with four pyramid-shaped natural-stone structures with stained-glass panels.

Once through Sneem, you have a choice. You can continue on the Ring to Kenmare, a route that's pretty but at times tedious and uneventful. Or for a truly awe-inspiring scenic drive, follow the signs left to **Killarney,** on a route (R568) that takes you through the mountains. At every twist and turn of the road, a spectacular new vista opens out before you—myriad shades of green, surrounded on all sides by the moody, purple mountains, and babbling brooks that trickle into dark roadside lakes. When you reach Molls Gap, turn right (N71) for a visit to **Kenmare,** an enchanting place originally called Neidin, meaning "Little Nest." Well laid out and immaculately maintained by its proud residents (pop. 1,200), Kenmare more than rivals Killarney as a base for County Kerry sightseeing.

However, our last section of the Ring and the grand finale beckons. Backtrack to Molls Gap and then follow the signs for **Killarney** (N71). Soon you're crossing the boundary of the national park, and every viewpoint is well worth the time it takes to stop and gaze across the lakes of Killarney. Most popular is **Ladies View,** so called because of the pleasure expressed by Queen Victoria's ladies in waiting when they visited this picturesque spot in 1861. Farther on, don't miss the **Torc Waterfall,** signposted from the road and located in a peaceful woodland setting. From here it's a short distance to Muckross House and then back to Killarney.

TRALEE

Tralee, with its population of 22,000, is County Kerry's chief town and the gateway to the Dingle Peninsula. A busy, bustling, and not particularly attractive place, its greatest claim to fame is that it was the inspiration for the song "The Rose of Tralee," composed by local resident William Mulninock more than 100 years ago. Consequently, Tralee is now the setting for the Rose of Tralee festival, the country's largest annual festival, held in August. It's also the permanent home of the National Folk Theatre of Ireland, Siamsa Tire.

ESSENTIALS

GETTING THERE   By Air   Aer Lingus operates daily nonstop flights from Dublin into **Kerry County Airport,** Farranfore, County Kerry (☎ **066/976-4644**), about 24km (15 miles) south of Tralee.

By Train   Trains from major cities arrive at the **Tralee Railway Station** on John Jo Sheehy Road (☎ **066/712-3522**).

By Bus   Buses from all parts of Ireland arrive daily at the **Bus Eierann Depot** on John Jo Sheehy Road, near the train station (☎ **066/712-3566**).

VISITOR INFORMATION   The **Tralee Tourist Office,** in Ashe Memorial Hall, Denny Street, Tralee (☎ **066/712-1288**), is open year-round Tuesday through Saturday 9am to 1pm and 2 to 5pm, with extended hours in the summer season. There is also a first-rate cafe on the premises.

WHERE TO STAY

Abbey Gate Hotel. Maine St., Tralee, County Kerry. ☎ **066/712-9888.** Fax 066/712-9821. 100 units. TV TEL. £50–£98 ($70–$137) double. No service charge. AE, DC, MC, V.

This modern three-story hotel is located in the center of Tralee. Rooms are spacious, tastefully decorated, and have coffeemakers. Public areas are modern and functional. No-smoking rooms are available, and all beds are orthopedic. The hotel's pub, the Old Market Place, is a lively nightspot; and for dinner you have two in-house options, the Bistro Marché for casual dining and the Vineyard Restaurant for something a little more formal.

Ballyseede Castle Hotel. Tralee-Killarney rd., Tralee, County Kerry. ☎ **066/712-5799.** Fax 066/712-5287. 12 units. TV TEL. £140–£200 ($196–$280) double. Full breakfast £8.50 ($12). Service charge 12.5%. DC, MC, V.

This turreted four-story castle was once the chief garrison of the legendary Fitzgeralds, the earls of Desmond. The lobby has Doric columns and a hand-carved oak staircase. The two drawing rooms are warmed by marble fireplaces. Residents can feel like royalty in the elegant rooms (no-smoking available), a feeling that's reiterated in the newly refurbished Regency restaurant. It goes without saying that the castle is haunted.

The Shores. Cappatigue, Castlegregory, County Kerry. ☎ **066/713-9196.** 5 units (4 with bathroom). £44 ($62) double. Rates include full breakfast. AE, DC, MC, V. Closed Dec–Jan. 1km (¹/₂ mile) west of Stradbally on the Conor Pass Rd.

The Shores, a modern house on the south side of Brandon Bay, commands good views of Tralee Bay and Mount Brandon. Annette O'Mahoney is an avid interior decorator, and she has done a great job of giving each room a unique ambience. Furnishings are lavish, with a canopy bed in one of the upstairs rooms. All rooms are nonsmoking and have hair dryers, trouser presses, and coffeemakers. The downstairs room has a private entrance and a fireplace. Breakfast options are particularly extensive, with smoked salmon and waffles given as alternatives to the standard fry.

WHERE TO DINE

In addition to the recommendation below, you can get excellent pub grub, especially steaks, at **Kirby's Olde Brogue Inn,** Rock Street, Tralee (☎ **066/712-3357**). This pub has a barnlike layout, with an interior that incorporates agricultural instruments, farming memorabilia, and rush-work tables and chairs. Sometimes traditional music and folk ballads are served up too.

✪ **Larkins.** Princes St., Tralee. ☎ **066/712-1300.** Main courses £7.90–£16 ($11–$22); set-price menu £13.90 ($19) May–Sept. DC, MC, V. Mon–Fri 12:30–2pm and 6:30–9:30pm; Sat 6:30–9:30pm (Sun hours June–Sept). IRISH/SEAFOOD/VEGETARIAN.

This bright, welcoming Irish-country restaurant is widely acclaimed for its catch of the day and its roast rack of Irish lamb. Modestly priced and immodestly tasty, Larkins's offerings are well worth a stop.

The Tankard. Kilfenora, Fenit. ☎ **066/713-6164.** Reservations recommended. Main courses £10–£18 ($14–$25). AE, DC, MC, V. Daily 12:30–2pm and 6–10pm. SEAFOOD/IRISH.

Ten kilometers (6 miles) northwest of Tralee, this is one of the few restaurants in the area that capitalizes on sweeping views of Tralee Bay. Situated right on the water's edge, it is outfitted with wide picture windows and a sleek contemporary decor. The straightforward and extensive menu primarily features local shellfish and seafood such as lobster, scallops, prawns, and black sole, but also includes rack of lamb, duck, quail, and a variety of steaks, as well as a range of vegetarian options. Bar food is available all day, but this restaurant is at its best in the early evening, especially at sunset.

SEEING THE SIGHTS

One of Ireland's largest indoor heritage centers, **Kerry the Kingdom,** Ashe Memorial Hall, Denny Street, Tralee (☎ **066/712-7777**), offers three separate attractions that give an in-depth look at 7,000 years of life in County Kerry. A 10-minute video, "Kerry in Colour," presents the seascapes and landscapes of Kerry; the Kerry County Museum chronologically examines the county's music, history, legends, and archaeology through interactive and hands-on exhibits; and the exhibit on Gaelic football is unique. Many items of local origin that were previously on view at the National Museum in Dublin are now here. Complete with lighting effects and aromas, a theme park–style ride called "Geraldine Tralee" takes you through a re-creation of Tralee's streets, houses, and abbeys during the Middle Ages. Admission is £5.50 adults ($8), £4.75 ($7) students, £3 ($4.20) children, £17 ($24) family. Open March to October, daily 10am to 6pm, and November to December, daily 2 to 5pm; closed January to February.

The restored ✪ **Tralee Steam Railway** (☎ **066/712-8888**) offers 3km (2-mile) narrated scenic trips from Tralee's Ballyard Station to Blennerville. It uses equipment that was once part of the Tralee & Dingle Light Railway, one of the world's most famous narrow-gauge railways. Trains run on the hour from Tralee and on the half hour from Blennerville, and the trip costs £2.75 adults ($3.85), £2.25 ($3.15) seniors and students, £1.50 ($2.10) children, £7 ($10) family. It operates daily April to September; closed on the second Monday of each month for maintenance.

TRALEE AFTER DARK

Siamsa Tire, the National Folk Theatre of Ireland, is located at Town Park, Tralee (☎ **066/712-3055;** fax 066/27246). Founded in 1974, Siamsa (pronounced *Sheemsha*) offers a mixture of music, dance, and mime, and its programs focus on three different themes: Fado Fado/The Long Ago; Sean Agus Nua/Myth and Motion; and Ding Dong Dedero/Forging the Dance. The scenes depict old folk tales and farmyard activities such as thatching a cottage roof, flailing sheaves of corn, and twisting a sugan (straw) rope.

In addition to these folk theater entertainments, Siamsa presents a full program of drama and musical concerts (from traditional to classical) performed by visiting amateur and professional companies. Admission is £12 ($17) for adults, £10 ($14) for seniors, students, and children. The schedule is Monday, Tuesday, Thursday, and

Saturday in May; Monday, Tuesday, Wednesday, Thursday, and Saturday in June; Monday through Saturday in July and August; Monday, Tuesday, Thursday, and Saturday from September to mid-October. Curtain time is 8:30pm.

PUBS Tralee pubs can be a little crowded and impersonal. **Olde Macs,** The Mall (☎ **066/712-1572**), is an exception. From the delightful flowers in the hanging baskets outside to the dark-wood interior, the pub exudes atmosphere. Conversation is lighthearted, and the regulars are extremely friendly.

THE DINGLE PENINSULA

While the Dingle Peninsula is an ideal drive, it also makes a fine bicycling tour. Dingle village is a delightful place to stay (see below) while exploring the peninsula.

The best route to the Dingle Peninsula is to follow the camp road (N86) from Tralee. You'll pass the **Blennerville Windmill** (☎ **066/712-1064**) 5km (3 miles) to the west. This is the largest working windmill in Ireland and was built in 1850. After years of neglect, it was recently restored and now produces 5 tons of whole-meal flour per week. The visitors complex has an emigration exhibition center, craft workshops, and a cafe. Admission is £2.75 ($3.85) for adults, £2.25 ($3.15) for seniors and students, and £1.50 ($2.10) for children over 5; it's open March to October, Monday to Saturday 10am to 6pm, and Sunday 11am to 6pm.

The route continues with delightful vistas over Tralee Bay, passing through the town of **Camp.** From here on, the road hugs the shore with vistas of **Brandon Mountain,** Ireland's second highest. Follow the signs for the **Conor Pass,** a spectacular drive through the mountains that reaches a height of 455m (1,500 feet). Rising steeply, the often very narrow road passes through a landscape of rocky mountain slopes, dark lakes, and cliffs. On a clear day, the views of Tralee and Brandon Bays are superb. Be sure to stop at the viewpoint when you reach the top of the pass. The final descent offers views over Dingle Bay and an enticing glimpse of Dingle itself (see below).

From **Dingle,** follow the signs for **Slea Head Drive,** a route that takes you on a spectacular, often rugged trip, returning eventually to Dingle. The **Beehive Huts** that stand to the right of the road past **Ventry** are worth a stop. These unmortared, prehistoric cells or huts owe their shape to the ancient method of construction known as drystone corbelling, in which the circular walls are constructed of overlapping stones and curve gradually inward until they can be covered with a capstone at the top.

Also worth a visit is the **Dunbeg Fort,** situated on an ocean-side site with beautiful sea views. A viewpoint at **Slea Head** overlooks a mountainous curve at the end of the peninsula; it's been the setting for many a picture postcard and sea-splashed landscape painting. You also have a view of the seven **Blasket Islands,** sitting out in the Atlantic. Until 1953 the largest of these, Great Blasket, was still inhabited. Great Blasket was once an outpost of Irish civilization and nurtured a small band of Irish-language writers. The quite splendid **Blasket Centre,** on the westerly tip of the Dingle Peninsula near Dunquin (☎ **066/915-6371**), has a series of displays, exhibits, and a video presentation that celebrate the cultural and literary traditions of the Blaskets. Admission is £2.50 ($3.50) for adults, £1.75 ($2.45) for seniors, £1 ($1.40) for children and students, and £6 ($8) for families; it's open Easter through June and September through October daily 10am to 6pm; July through August daily 10am to 7pm.

The route now continues to **Ballyferriter,** a largely Gaelic-speaking village. From here you head east and follow the signs to the **Gallarus Oratory,** one of the best-preserved early Christian church buildings in Ireland. Constructed of unmortared stone and shaped like an upturned boat, it's still watertight even after a thousand years.

Continue following the signs marked SLEA HEAD DRIVE until you arrive at the **Kilmalkedar Church,** dating from the 12th century. Inside the ruined church is an abecedarian stone, with the Latin alphabet crudely carved, a relic of a 7th-century school and probably the oldest-surviving Irish relic of Roman script. Don't miss the 15th-century ruins of **St. Brendan's House,** hidden among the bushes a little way past the church, once a substantial priests' dwelling.

Continue on the road and turn right, following the signs to **Brandon Creek.** It was from here, in the 6th century, that St. Brendan reputedly set out for the Islands of Paradise in the Western Ocean, a 7-year voyage that led him, it has been claimed, to discover America. The life of the saint and the story of his voyage, *Navigation Sancti Brendai Abbatis,* was written in the 9th century. The Latin narrative was popular reading in medieval Europe and the inspiration for many voyagers and explorers, including Christopher Columbus.

Backtrack to Slea Head Drive and follow it on a picturesque route back to Dingle. From here take R561 eastward along Dingle Bay, through the villages of Lispole and Annascaul to **Inch,** one of Dingle's most beautiful seascapes, a 6km (4-mile) stretch of sandy beach, with distant views of the Ring of Kerry and Killarney. From here you can return to Camp or Tralee or continue to Castlemaine (where the Wild Colonial Boy was born) and onward to Limerick or other parts of Kerry and Cork.

DINGLE TOWN

With a charter dating back many centuries, Dingle was Kerry's principal harbor in medieval times. Even though it's just a small town (pop. 1,500), Dingle has more fine restaurants than many of Ireland's major cities, and is known for the traditional Irish music in its pubs.

WHERE TO STAY

✪ **Doyle's Townhouse.** 5 John St., Dingle, County Kerry. ☎ **800/223-6510** in the U.S., or 066/915-1174. Fax 066/915-1816. www.doylesofdingle.com. 16 units. TV TEL. £72–£80 ($101–$112) double. Service charge 10%. Rates include full breakfast. MC, V. Closed mid-Nov to mid-Mar.

This old-world guest house is just a few minutes' walk away from Dingle's main street. It has a lovely Victorian fireplace in the main sitting room area and many of the antique furnishings are more than 250 years old. Period pieces and country pine predominate in the rooms, although the fixtures and fittings are modern and include semiorthopedic beds. Some back rooms face a garden with mountain vistas in the background.

✪ **Greenmount House.** John St., Dingle, County Kerry. ☎ **066/915-1414.** Fax 066/915-1974. www.greenmounthouse.com. 12 units. TV TEL. £40–£80 ($56–$112) double. No service charge. Rates include full breakfast. MC, V. Closed Dec 20–26.

Perched on a hill overlooking Dingle Bay and town, this modern bungalow-style bed-and-breakfast is a standout in its category. It has all the comforts of a hotel at bargain prices, including rooms decorated with contemporary furnishings and orthopedic beds, a public sitting room with an open fireplace, and a sunlit conservatory filled with plants. Rooms have coffeemakers, unstocked refrigerators, and hair dryers. No smoking is allowed in the rooms or dining room.

✪ **Milltown House.** Dingle, County Kerry. ☎ **066/915-1372.** Fax 066/915-1095. E-mail: milltown@indigo.ie. 10 units. TV TEL. £45–£75 ($63–$105) double. Rates include full breakfast. AE, MC, V.

You couldn't wish for a more picturesque Dingle setting than this bayside haven. A narrow road leads to it and, once inside, you'll see why much of their business is repeat. Rooms are tastefully and individually furnished, several offering bay windows that gaze out onto a bay and harbor panorama. All have coffeemakers and hair dryers. The public areas include a peaceful lounge with an open fire and a bright, airy conservatory. The owners, John and Angela Gill, go out of their way to leave you wanting for nothing. A four-course evening meal is offered with a full wine list. There are also on-site stables for riding and trekking.

WHERE TO DINE

✪ **Doyle's Seafood Bar.** 4 John St., Dingle. ☎ **066/915-1174.** Reservations required. Main courses £12–£20 ($17–$28). DC, MC, V. Mon–Sat 5:30–10pm. Closed mid-Nov to mid-Dec. SEAFOOD.

Owned by John and Steela Doyle, this excellent establishment has won international acclaim and is the benchmark of all Dingle's restaurants. The atmosphere is homey with stone walls and floors, sugan (a kind of straw) chairs, and old Dingle sketches. All the ingredients come from the sea, the Doyles' garden, or nearby farms. Specialties include the Doyles' own smoked salmon, baked fillet of lemon sole with prawn sauce, hot poached lobster, and a signature platter of seafood (sole, salmon, lobster, oysters, and crab claws).

✪ **Waterside Cafe.** Strand St., Dingle. ☎ **066/9151458.** Strand St., Dingle. ☎ **066/ 915-1458.** Reservations recommended for dinner. Cafe items £2–£10 ($2.80 –$14); restaurant main courses £9–£13 ($13–$18). MC, V. Easter–Sept cafe daily 10am–6pm; restaurant Mar–Oct 7–10pm; dinner 7–10pm Nov–Easter. INTERNATIONAL.

For a daytime snack with a Dingle ambience, this restaurant offers a setting opposite the busy town marina. It's a bright and airy place with a decor of blue and white, enhanced by seasonal flowers and plants. There is seating in a sunlit conservatory-style room as well as on an outdoor patio. It operates as a cafe by day and as a full-service restaurant on summer nights. The choices include oysters on the half-shell, cockles and mussels sandwiches, prawn and crab seafood salads, and soups, as well as quiches, omelettes, crepes, and pastries. The evening menu concentrates on local seafood and steaks.

EXPLORING THE TOWN

The new gem in Dingle town is ✪ **Dingle Oceanworld,** Dingle Harbour, Dingle (☎ **066/915-2111;** fax 066/52155; e-mail: marabeo@iol.ie). Admission is £5 ($7) adults, £4 ($6) seniors and students, £3 ($4.20) children, and £12 ($17) family. It's open September, May, and June daily 9:30am to 7pm, July to Aug daily 9:30am to 8:30pm, and October to May daily 9:30am to 6pm. This new harborside aquarium, which is dedicated to the exploration and understanding of the nearby ocean's depths and its critters, is already a main family attraction. All but the sharks are indigenous to local waters. In addition, there are exhibits on Brendan the Navigator and the Spanish Armada, as well as a cafe and gift shop.

Just west of the Dingle Marina is **Ceardlann Na Coille** (☎ **066/915-1797**), a cluster of traditional cottages in a circular craft village. Each craft worker produces and sells his or her own wares, which include knitwear, leather goods, hand weaving, and wood turning. It's open daily 10am to 6pm.

In 1984 Fungie, an adult male bottlenose dolphin, swam solo into the waters of Dingle harbor. Since then a whole industry has grown up around him. **Fungie the Dolphin Tours** (☎ **066/915-1967**) will ferry you out to find him (if there's no sighting, you don't pay). Fungie happily swims alongside the boats, although his enthusiasm has abated slightly in recent years. Fares for the 1-hour boat trip are £6 ($8) for adults and £3 ($4.20) for children 11 and under. More adventurous visitors can swim with him on a dolphin encounter, arranged by Bridgit Flannery at ☎ **066/915-1967** or 066/915-1163, most any day from 8am to 8pm. The procedure is to book a swim the day before, when you rent your gear (semidry suit, mask, snorkel, boots, and fins—all in one duffel). The full overnight outfitting cost is £24 ($34) per person. Then you show up in your gear early the next morning to be brought out by boat to your aquatic rendezvous. The 2-hour escorted swim period costs an additional £10 ($14). If you prefer, you can use your rented outfit and swim out on your own. Fungie also welcomes drop-ins. This outing is for teenagers on up, although smaller children will certainly enjoy watching.

ENJOYING THE GREAT OUTDOORS

BICYCLING   Rentals begin at £5 ($8) per day or £25 ($39) per week. Contact **Foxy John's Hardware Store,** Main Street (☎ **066/915-1316**). Mountain bikes can be rented at **The Mountain Man,** Strand Street, Dingle (☎ **066/915-2400**), for £6 ($8) per day or £30 ($42) per week.

HORSEBACK RIDING   At **Dingle Horse Riding,** Ballinaboula House, Dingle (☎ **066/915-2199**), rides are available along nearby beaches or through the mountains; the cost is £15 ($21) for a 1-hour ride. Half-day, full-day, and 3- to 5-day packages including accommodation, meals, and riding can be arranged.

SAILING   The **Dingle Sailing Club,** c/o The Wood, Dingle (☎ **066/915-1984;** e-mail: lfarrell@tinet.ie), offers an array of sailing courses taught by experienced, certified instructors. Summer courses run £70 to £90 ($98 to $126). To charter a yacht, **contact Dingle Sea Ventures,** Dingle (☎ **066/915-2244;** www.charterireland.com). Yachts, sleeping from 6 to 10 persons, are available, ranging in price from £865 to £2,085 ($1,211 to $2,919) per week, depending on boat and season. Skipper's fees are £50 ($70) per day.

SEA ANGLING   For sea angling packages and day trips, contact Nicholas O'Connor at **Angler's Rest,** Ventry (☎ **066/915-9947**); or Seán O'Conchúir (☎ **066/915-5429**), representing the **Kerry Angling Association**.

WALKING   The **Dingle Way** begins in Tralee and circles the peninsula, covering 150km (95 miles) of gorgeous mountain and coastal landscape. The most rugged section is along Brandon Head, where the trail passes between Mount Brandon and the ocean; the views are tremendous, but the walk is about 24km (15 miles), 9 hours, and strenuous, and should be attempted only when the sky is clear. The 24km (15-mile) section between Dunquin and Ballyferriter follows an especially lovely stretch of coast. For more information see The Dingle Way Map Guide, available in local tourist offices and shops.

THE SHOPPING SCENE

Brian De Staic, The Wood (☎ **066/915-1298**), is Ireland's leading goldsmith. His workshop is just west of the Dingle Pier. He specializes in unusual Irish jewelry, hand-crafted and engraved with the letters of the Ogham alphabet, an ancient Irish form of writing dating from the 3rd century.

At **The Weavers Shop,** Green Street (☎ **066/915-1688**), Lisbeth Mulcahy, one of Ireland's leading weavers, creates fabrics and tapestries inspired by seasonal changes in the Irish land- and seascapes. Pure Irish wool, linen/cotton, and alpaca are used in weaving wall hangings and tapestries, as well as scarves, shawls, and knee rugs. At **Holden Dingle,** Main Street (☎ **066/915-1896**), Jackie and Conor Holden offer beautiful handcrafted leather handbags lined with suede and silk pockets as well as duffel and travel bags and briefcases.

DINGLE AFTER DARK

At night, virtually every pub in Dingle offers live music from 9pm on. One of Dingle's most atmospheric pubs, **An Droichead Beag/The Small Bridge,** Lower Main St. (☎ **066/915-1723**), has a dark, cavernous interior that's filled with banter and laughter. Traditional Irish music takes place every night at 9pm. But be warned: It's popular, so get there early if you want a seat.

Although Richard "Dick" Mack died a few years ago, his family keeps up the traditions of the unique **Dick Mack's "Haberdashery,"** Green St. (☎ **066/915-1070**), where Dick handcrafted leather boots, belts, and other items in between pub chores. Corridors lined with old pictures and mugs lead into tiny snug bars where locals and visitors stand around sipping stout and exchanging jokes and gossip. It's been a favorite pub with celebrities such as Robert Mitchum, Timothy Dalton, and Paul Simon, whose names are now commemorated with stars on the sidewalk just outside.

Deep in the outer reaches of the Dingle Peninsula, **Kruger's Guest House and Bar,** Ballinaraha, Dunquin (☎ **066/915-6127**), is a social center of the Irish-speaking district, and an entertainment hub, with nightly performances of the "sean-nos" Irish singing (an old unaccompanied style), plus traditional music and step dancing on weekends. Guest house is open March to October

11 Italy

by Darwin Porter & Danforth Prince

A feast for the senses and the intellect, Italy and especially Rome are the virtual nerve center for the celebration of the millennium, which will continue throughout 2001. All roads won't lead just to Rome, but to Florence, Venice, and countless other destinations. With or without a millennium, Italy calls up visions of Pompeii, the Renaissance, and Italy's rich treasury of art and architecture. But some of the country's best experiences can involve the simple act of living in the Italian style, eating regional cuisines, and enjoying the countryside.

1 Rome

The city of Rome, the city of the millennium, is simultaneously strident, romantic, and sensual. And although the romantic poets would probably be horrified at today's traffic, pollution, overcrowding, crime, political discontent, and the barely controlled chaos of modern Rome, the city endures and thrives in a way that is called "eternal."

It would take a lifetime to know a city filled with 27 centuries of artistic achievement. A cradle of Western civilization, Rome is timeless with it ancient history, art, and architecture, containing more treasures per square foot than any other city in the world. Caesar was assassinated here, Charlemagne crowned, and the list of the major events goes on and on.

In between all that absorption of culture and history, take time to relax and meet the Romans. Savor their succulent pastas while enjoying a fine glass of wine on one of the city's splendid squares where one of the reigning Caesars might have gone before you, or perhaps Michelangelo or Raphael.

ORIENTATION

ARRIVING By Plane Chances are that you'll arrive in Italy at Rome's **Leonardo da Vinci International Airport** (☎ **06-65951** or 06-65953640 for information), popularly known as Fiumicino, 30km (18¹/₂ miles) from the city center. Domestic flights arrive at one terminal, international ones at the other. If you're flying by charter, you might arrive at Ciampino Airport.

To get into the city, there's a **shuttle service** directly from Fiumicino to Stazione Termini, the main train station. Upon leaving Customs, follow the signs marked TRENI. Trains go back and forth between the airport and the rail station daily 7:30am to 10pm. A one-way ticket costs 16,000L ($8).

Taxis from Fiumicino to city center are expensive—75,000L ($38) and up.

Should you arrive on a charter flight at **Ciampino Airport** (☎ **06-794941**), take a COTRAL bus, departing every 30 minutes or so, which will deliver you to the Anagnina stop of Metropolitana (subway) line A. At Anagnina you can take line A to Stazione Termini, where your final connections can be made. The trip takes about 45 minutes and costs 1,500L (75¢).

By Train Trains arrive in the center of old Rome at **Stazione Termini,** Piazza dei Cinquecento (☎ **1478-88088**), the train and subway transportation hub for the city. Many hotels lie near the station, and you can walk to your hotel if you don't have too much luggage. Otherwise, an array of taxi, bus, and subway lines awaits you.

If you're taking the **Metropolitana** (subway), follow the illuminated M sign in red that points the way. To catch a bus, go straight through the outer hall of the Termini and enter the sprawling bus lot of Piazza dei Cinquecento. Taxis are also found here.

By Bus Arrivals are at the **Stazione Termini** (see "By Train," above).

By Car From the north the main access route is **A-1 (Autostrada del Sole),** cutting through Milan and Florence, or you can take the coastal route, SSI Aurelia, from Genoa. If you're driving north from Naples, you take the southern lap of the **Autostrada del Sole (A-2).** All these autostrade join with the **Grande Raccordo Anulare,** a ring road that encircles Rome, channeling traffic into the congested city.

VISITOR INFORMATION Information is available at three locations maintained by the Azienda Provinciale di Turismo (APT). They include kiosks at **Leonardo da Vinci Airport** (☎ **06-6595-6074**) and **Stazione Termini** (☎ **06-487-1270**), and their headquarters at Via Parigi 5 (☎ **06-4889-9253**). Via Parigi 5 is open Monday to Friday 8:15am to 7:15pm, Saturday to 2pm. The airport and Stazione Termini kiosks are open daily 8:15am to 7:15pm. However, don't expect much from these offices.

More helpful, stocking maps and brochures, are the offices maintained by the **Comune di Roma** at half a dozen sights around the city. You can identify them by their red-and-orange or yellow-and-black signs saying COMUNE DI ROMA—PUNTI DI INFORMAZIONE TURISTICA. They're staffed daily 9am to 6pm, and can be found in Piazza Pia, near the Castel Sant'Angelo (☎ **06-6880-9707**); in Piazza San Giovanni in Laterano (☎ **06-7720-3598**); along Largo Carlo Goldoni, near the intersection of Via del Corso and Via Condotti (☎ **06-6813-6061**); on Via Nazionale, near the Palazzo delle Esposizioni (☎ **06-4782-4525**); on Largo Corrado Ricci, near the Colosseum (☎ **06-6992-4307**); and in Trastevere on Piazza Sonnino (☎ **06-5833-3457**). The Stazione Termini office (☎ **06-4890-6300**) is open daily 8am to 9pm. Other offices have also opened, including Piazza 5 Lune, near piazza Navona (☎ **06-6880-9240**); piazza Santa Maria Maggiore (☎ **06-4788-0294**); and piazza dei 500, outside Stazione Termini (☎ **06-4782-5194**).

CITY LAYOUT The drive into the city from the airport is rather uneventful until you pass through the still remarkably intact **Great Aurelian Wall,** begun in A.D. 271 to calm Rome's barbarian jitters. Suddenly, ruins of imperial baths loom on one side and great monuments can be seen in the middle of blocks.

Stazione Termini, the modern railroad station, faces the huge **Piazza dei Cinquecento,** named after 500 Italians who died heroically in a 19th-century battle in Africa.

The bulk of ancient, Renaissance, and baroque Rome lies on the east side of the **Fiume Tevere (Tiber River),** which meanders between 19th-century stone embankments. However, several important monuments are on the other side: **St. Peter's Basilica** and the **Vatican,** the **Castel Sant' Angelo** (formerly the tomb of the emperor Hadrian), and the colorful section known as **Trastevere.** The city's various quarters are linked by boulevards that have mostly been laid out since the late 19th century.

Major streets fan out from **Piazza Venezia** in front of the **Vittorio Emmanuele monument,** a highly controversial pile of snow-white Brescian marble. Running north to **Piazza del Popolo** and the city wall is **Via del Corso,** one of Rome's main streets. Called simply "Il Corso," it's noisy, congested, and always crowded with buses and shoppers. Going west across the Tiber toward St. Peter's is **Corso Vittorio Emanuele.** Running toward the Colosseum is **Via dei Fori Imperiali,** named for the excavated ruins of the imperial forums that flank this avenue. **Via Quattro Novembre** runs east and becomes **Via Nazionale** before terminating at **Piazza della Repubblica.**

GETTING AROUND

Much of the inner core of Rome is traffic-free—so you'll need to walk whether you like it or not. However, walking in many parts of the city is hazardous and uncomfortable because of overcrowding, heavy traffic, and very narrow and uneven sidewalks.

By Subway   The **Metropolitana,** or **Metro** for short, is the fastest means of transportation in Rome. It has two underground lines: **Line A** and **Line B.** A big red letter M indicates the subway entrance. The fare is 1,500L (75¢). Tickets are available from vending machines at all stations. These machines accept 50L, 100L, and 200L coins. Ticket booklets are available at *tabacchi* (tobacco) shops and in some terminals. Some machines change 1,000L (50¢) notes into coins. *Tip:* Avoid riding the trains when the Romans are going to or from work or you'll be mashed flatter than fettuccine.

By Bus/Tram   Roman buses are operated by **ATAC (Azienda Tramvie e Autobus del Comune di Roma),** Via Volturno 65 (☎ **06-46951** for information). The service is quite good and you can ride to most parts of Rome for only 1,500L (75¢). The ticket is valid for 1¹/₄ hours, and you can get on as many buses during that time period as you want, using the same ticket; you can also transfer free between the metro and the bus within the 75 minutes of validity.

By Taxi   Don't count on hailing a taxi on the street or even getting one at a stand. If you're going out, have your hotel call one. At a restaurant, ask the waiter or cashier to dial for you. If you want to call yourself, try one of these numbers: ☎ **06-6645,** 06-3570, or 06-4994. The meter begins at 4,500L ($2.25) for the first 3km, then 1,300L (65¢) per kilometer. On Sunday, a 2,000L ($1) supplement is assessed, plus another 5,000L ($2.50) supplement from 10pm to 7am. There's yet another 2,000L ($1) supplement for every suitcase. The driver will expect a 10% tip.

By Car   You can rent a car from **Hertz,** near the parking lot of the Villa Borghese, Via Veneto 156 (☎ **06-3216831); Italy by Car**, via Ludovisi 60 (☎ **06-4820966);** or the local Italian company **Maggiore,** Via di Tor Cervara 225 (☎ **06-229351); Avis** at Stazione Termini (☎ **06-428-24-728**).

Traveler's Tip

At the Stazione Termini, you can purchase a special **tourist bus and subway pass,** which costs 6,000L ($3) for 1 day or 24,000L ($12) for a week. The tourist pass is also valid on the subway.

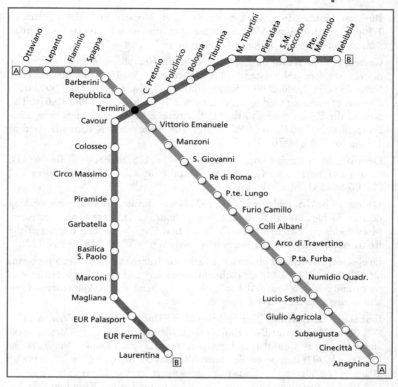

Rome Metropolitana

By Bicycle   You can rent bicycles at many places throughout Rome. Ask at your hotel for the nearest rental location, or else go to **I Bike Rome**, Via Veneto 156 (☎ **06-322-5240**), which rents bicycles from the underground parking garage at the Villa Borghese. Most bikes cost 4,000L ($2) per hour or 10,000L ($5) per day. It's open daily 9am to 7pm. Bring an ID card with you.

Fast Facts: Rome

American Express   The offices are at Piazza di Spagna 38 (☎ **06-67641**; Metro: Spagna). The travel service and tour desk are open Monday to Friday 9am to 5:30pm and Saturday 9am to 12:30pm. Hours for financial and mail services are Monday to Friday 9am to 5pm and Saturday 9am to noon.

Baby-Sitters   Most hotel desks in Rome will help you secure a baby-sitter. Inquire as far in advance as possible. Request an English-speaking sitter. You won't always get one but it pays to ask. **Angels Baby Sitting Services,** Via delle quattro Fontane (☎ **06-420-13-0803**; Metro: Repubblica), offers British, American, or Australian babysitters, available for a few hours or even one or more days. Rates range from 12,000 to 25,000L ($6 to $13) per hour.

Business Hours In general, banks are open Monday to Friday 8:30am to 1:30pm and 3 to 4pm. Most stores are open year-round Monday to Saturday 9am to 1pm and 3:30 or 4pm to 7:30 or 8pm.

Currency The Italian unit of currency is the **lira,** almost always used in the plural form, **lire** (abbreviated "L"). Coins come in 50, 100, 200, 500, 1,000L. Notes come in 1,000, 2,000, 5,000, 10,000, 50,000, 100,000, and 500,000L. The rate of exchange used in this chapter was $1 = 1,818L, or 100L = 0.05¢. The ratio of the British pound to the lira fluctuates constantly. At press time, £1 = approximately 3,007L (or 100L = 3p). The Euro rate was currently fixed at 1,936L (or 100 L = €0.05).

Dentist For an English-speaking dentist, call the U.S. Embassy (☎ **06-46741**). There's also the 24-hour **G. Eastman Dental Hospital,** Viale Regina Elena 287 (☎ **06-844831;** Metro: Policlinico).

Doctor The U.S. Embassy (☎ **06-46741**) will provide a list of English-speaking doctors. All big hospitals in Rome have a 24-hour first-aid service (go to the emergency room or "pronto soccorso"). You'll find English-speaking doctors at the **Rome American Hospital,** Via Emilio Longoni 69 (☎ **06-22551;** bus: 112).

Drugstores A reliable pharmacy is **Farmacia Internazionale,** Piazza Barberini 49 (☎ **06-4871195;** Metro: Barberini), open day and night. Most pharmacies are open 8:30am to 1pm and 4 to 7:30pm. In general, they follow a rotation system so that several are always open on Sunday.

Embassies/Consulates The Embassy of the **United States**, Via Veneto 119A (☎ **06-46741;** Metro: Barberini), is open Monday to Friday 8:30am to noon and 2 to 4pm. Consular and passport services for **Canada,** Via Zara 30 (☎ **06-445981;** bus: 36 or 60; Metro: Policlinico), are open Monday to Friday 10am to 12:30pm; the Canadian Embassy is at Via G. B. De Rossi 27 (☎ **06-445-981;** bus: 36 or 60). The office of the **United Kingdom,** Via XX Settembre 80A (☎ **06-4825441;** Metro: Barberini), is open Monday to Friday 9:15am to 1:30pm. The Embassy of **Australia,** Via Alessandria 215 (☎ **06-852721;** bus: 36 or 60; Metro: Policlinico), is open Monday to Thursday 8:30am to 12:30pm and 1:30 to 5:30pm and Friday 8:30am to 1:15pm; the Australian Consulate is at Corso Trieste 25 (☎ **06-852-721;** bus: 36 or 60). The **New Zealand** office, Via Zara 28 (☎ **06-441-71-71;** bus: 36 or 60; Metro: Policlinico), is open Monday to Friday 8:30am to 12:45pm and 1:45 to 5pm. The Embassy of **Ireland** is at Piazza di Campitelli 3 (☎ **06-697-912;** bus: 46; Metro: Circo Massimo); for consular queries call ☎ **06-697-91211.** In case of emergency, embassies have a 24-hour referral service.

Emergencies Dial ☎ **113** for an ambulance, police, or fire. In case of a breakdown on an Italian road, dial ☎ **116** at the nearest telephone box; the nearest Automobile Club of Italy (ACI) will be notified to come to your aid.

Internet Access You can log onto the Web in central Rome at **Thenetgate,** Piazza Firenze 25 (☎ **06-689-3445;** bus: 116). Summer hours are Monday to Saturday 10:30am to 12:30pm and 3:30 to 10:30pm and winter hours daily 10:40am to 8:30pm. A 20-minute visit costs 5,000L ($2.50), with 1 hour (including mailbox) at 10,000L ($5.00). Access is free Saturdays 10:30 to 11am and 2 to 2:30pm. You can kill two birds with one stone just north of Stazione Termini at **Splash,** Via Varese 33 (☎ **06-4938-2073;** Metro: Termini), a do-it-yourself Laundromat (13,000L/$7 per load, including soap) with a satellite TV and four computers hooked up to the Net (5,000L/$2.50 per half hour).

Post Office   The **central post office,** Piazza San Silvestro 19, behind the Rinascente department store on Piazza Colonna (☎ **06-6771;** bus: 52, 53, 58, 61, or 160), is open Monday to Friday 9am to 6pm and Saturday 9am to 2pm.

Safety   Purse snatching is commonplace in Rome. Young men on Vespas ride through the city looking for victims. To avoid trouble, stay away from the curb and hold on tightly to your purse. Don't lay anything valuable on tables or chairs where it can be grabbed up easily. Gypsy children are a particular menace. You'll often virtually have to flee, if they completely surround you. They'll often approach you with pieces of cardboard hiding their hands.

Taxes   A value-added tax (called IVA in Italy) is added to all consumer products and most services, including restaurants and hotels. The tax is not the same for all goods and services. The average tax on most items is 19% but it could rise as much as 35% on certain luxury goods.

Non-EU (European Union) citizens are entitled to a **refund of the IVA** if they spend more than 300,000L ($180) at any one store, before tax. To claim your refund, request an invoice from the cashier at the store and take it to the Customs office (*dogana*) at the airport to have it stamped before you leave. If you're going to another EU country before flying home, have it stamped at the airport Customs office of the last EU country you'll be in (for example, if you're flying home via Britain, have your Italian invoices stamped in London). Once back home, mail the stamped invoice (keep a photocopy for your records) back to the original vendor within 90 days of the purchase. The vendor will, sooner or later, send you a refund of the tax you paid at the time of your original purchase. Reputable stores view this as a matter of ordinary paperwork and are businesslike about it. Less honorable stores might lose your dossier. It pays to deal with established vendors on large purchases. You can also request that the refund be credited to the credit card with which you made the purchase; this is usually a faster procedure.

Many shops are now part of the **"Tax Free for Tourists"** network (look for the sticker in the window). Stores participating in this network issue a check along with your invoice at the time of purchase. After you have the invoice stamped at Customs, you can redeem the check for cash directly at the Tax Free booth in the airport—in Rome, it's past Customs; in Milan's airports the booth is inside the Duty Free shop—or mail it back in the envelope provided within 60 days.

Telephone   The **country code** for Italy is **39.** The **city code** for Rome is **06,** which is the code you'll use every time you dial a party located within Rome, regardless of whether you're within the city limits or not.

To call **from one city code to another** within Italy, dial the city code, complete with the initial zero, then the local number. To **dial direct internationally,** dial 00, then the country code for the country you are calling, then the area or city code and then the local number. Direct-dial calls from the United States to Italy are usually cheaper than calls placed from an Italian hotel to most phones in North America, so if possible, try to arrange for friends and acquaintances to call you at your hotel at prearranged times.

To ring national **telephone information** (in Italian) in Italy dial **12.** International information is available at **176,** but costs 1,200L (60¢) per request.

To make a **collect or calling-card call** from a public phone, drop in 200L or insert a prepaid phone card (available from most *tabacchi*) and dial one of the following access numbers to reach an American operator or an English-language voice prompt: **AT&T** ☎ **172-10-11** (if calling a country other than the United

States, after access code dial 01, the country code of country you are calling, city code, and local number); **MCI** ☎ **172-1022;** and **Sprint** ☎ **172-1877.**

WHERE TO STAY
NEAR STAZIONE TERMINI
Expensive
Hotel Artemide. Via Nazionale 22, 00184 Roma. ☎ **06-489911.** Fax 06-48991700. www.spacehotels.it or www.travel.it. E-mail: artemide@spacehotels.it. 79 units. A/C MINIBAR TV TEL. 490,000–540,000L ($245–$270) double; 630,000L ($315) suite. Rates include breakfast. AE, MC, DC, V. Parking 30,000L ($15). Metro: Repubblica.

A refined four-star hotel, this establishment was transformed from a 19th-century palazzetto into an elegant hotel named for Artemis, the Greek goddess. Close to the Opera, it combines stylish simplicity with modern comforts against an Art Nouveau backdrop. The original stained-glass skylight dome was retained in the lobby. Rooms have good furnishings and such extras as safes. The spacious bathrooms have hair dryers and generous towels. No-smoking units are available. The Caffè Caffeteria Nazionale restaurant serves Mediterranean cuisine along with international dishes and also offers light buffet dinner and lunch, afternoon tea, and cold and hot snacks. It is open daily from 7am to 10pm. There's also an American bar.

Hotel Diana. Via Principe Amedeo 4, 00185 Roma. ☎ **06-4827541.** Fax 06-486998. www.hoteldianaroma.com. E-mail: diana@venere.it. 186 units. A/C MINIBAR TV TEL. 330,000L ($165) double; 450,000L ($225) junior suite. Rates include breakfast. AE, DC, MC, V. Parking 35,000L ($18). Metro: Termini.

The Diana has recaptured the flavor of its heyday at the turn of the century when both the aristocracy and the bourgeoisie dropped in for a drink after the Opera. In the heart of 19th-century Rome, Diana offers an elegant yet comfortable atmosphere. Rooms are tastefully furnished. Bathrooms offer hair dryers, heated towel racks, and a choice of tub or shower. No-smoking units are available. The restaurant offers a menu selection of classic Italian dishes and daily seasonal specialties. The American Bar in summer moves to the panoramic rooftop terrace where lunch and dinner can also be served. Here shaded by tents and surrounded by plants, you'll have sweeping views over the ancient roofs.

Moderate
Aberdeen Hotel. Via Firenze 48, 00184 Roma. ☎ **06-4823920.** Fax 06-4821092. www.travel.it/roma/aberdeen. E-mail: hotelaberdeen@travel.it. 26 units. A/C MINIBAR TV TEL. 300,000L ($150) double. Rates include buffet breakfast. AE, DC, MC, V. Parking 38,000L ($19). Metro: Repubblica. Bus: 64 or 170.

This completely renovated 26-room hotel near the Opera is centrally located for most landmarks and for rail and bus connections. It's located in front of the Ministry of Defense, a rather quiet and fairly safe area of Rome. The recently renovated rooms, furnished with an uninspired modern styling, have hair dryers and firm, frequently renewed mattresses. The breakfast buffet is the only meal served, but it is easy to find a good restaurant nearby.

Hotel Ranieri. Via XX Settembre 43, 00187 Roma. ☎ **06-481-4467.** Fax 06-481-8834. www.hotelranieri.com. E-mail: hotelranieri@italyhotel.com. 47 units. A/C MINIBAR TV TEL. 230,000–350,000L ($115–$175) double. Rates include breakfast. AE, MC, V. Parking 30,000–45,000L ($15–$23). Metro: Repubblica.

Ranieri is a winning three-star hotel in a very old, freshly restored building. From the hotel you can stroll to the Opera, Piazza Della Repubblica, and Via Veneto.

Rooms feature double-panel windows and rejuvenated bathrooms. You can arrange for a home-cooked meal—both regional or national—in the dining room, with a choice of five fixed-price menus ranging from 30,000 to 50,000L ($15 to $25) per person.

Medici. Via Flavia 96, 00187 Roma. ☎ **06-482-7319.** Fax 06-474-0767. www.hotelmedici. com. 69 units. MINIBAR TV TEL. 260,000–330,000L ($130–$165) double. Rates include breakfast. AE, DC, MC, V. Parking 35,000–40,000L ($18–$20). Metro: Repubblica.

The Medici, built in 1906, is a substantial hotel that has easy access to the shops along Via XX Settembre. Many of its better rooms overlook an inner patio garden. Rooms are a generous size and were renovated in 1997 in a classic Roman style. The cheapest rooms are called standard; superior units offer air conditioning, more antiques, and superior furnishings. Breakfast is the only meal served.

Inexpensive
Hotel Pavia. Via Gaeta 83, 00185 Roma. ☎ **06-483-801.** Fax 06-481-9090. www.travel.it/roma/hotelpavia. E-mail: hotpavia@hotmail.com. 25 units. A/C MINIBAR TV TEL. 250,000L ($125) double. Rates include breakfast. AE, DC, MC, V. Parking 25,000L ($13). Metro: Termini.

Hotel Pavia is a popular choice on this quiet street near the gardens of the Baths of Diocletian. Established in the 1980s, it occupies a much-renovated century-old building. The front rooms tend to be noisy, but that's the curse of all Termini hotels. Nevertheless, the rooms are comfortable and fairly attractive, and were last renovated in 1998.

NEAR VIA VENETO & PIAZZA BARBERINI
Very Expensive
✪ **Hotel Eden.** Via Ludovisi 49, 00187 Roma. ☎ **800/225-5843** in the U.S., or 06-478121. Fax 06-4821584. www.hotel-eden.it. E-mail: reservations@hotel-eden.it. 119 units. A/C MINIBAR TV TEL. 1,034,000–1,210,000L ($517–$605) double; from 2,640,000L ($1,320) suite. AE, DC, MC, V. Parking 45,000L ($23). Metro: Barberini.

During the heyday of this ornate hotel, all the big names—Hemingway, Maria Callas, Ingrid Bergman, Fellini—checked in here. In 1994, it reopened after a 2-year (and $20 million) radical renovation that enhanced its original fin de siècle grandeur and added the modern amenities its five-star status calls for. Its hilltop position guarantees a panoramic city view from most rooms. Understated elegance is the rule. On the premises are a gym and health club, a piano bar, and a glamorous restaurant, La Terrazza.

✪ **Hotel Majestic.** Via Veneto 50, 00187 Roma. ☎ **06-486841.** Fax 06-4880984. www.primahotels.it. E-mail: hotelmajestic@flashnet.it. 96 units. A/C MINIBAR TV TEL. 790,000–850,000L ($395–$425) double; from 1,600,000L ($800) suite. Rates include breakfast. AE, DC, MC, V. Parking 40,000L ($20). Metro: Barberini.

An architectural triumph of the Gilded Age and one of the grandest buildings along the Via Veneto, the Majestic has welcomed Eleonora Duse, most of the politicians of Italy and trade representatives from the rest of Europe, Bruce Springsteen, Bill Gates, and both George Bush and George W. Bush. Each room is uniquely decorated, always with a rich and sophisticated mixture of upscale furnishings and accessories. That includes supremely comfortable mattresses and a decor by noted designer Luigi Sturchio. The hotel's two restaurants include the brasserie-style La Ninfa and the more formal La Veranda.

Rome Accommodations

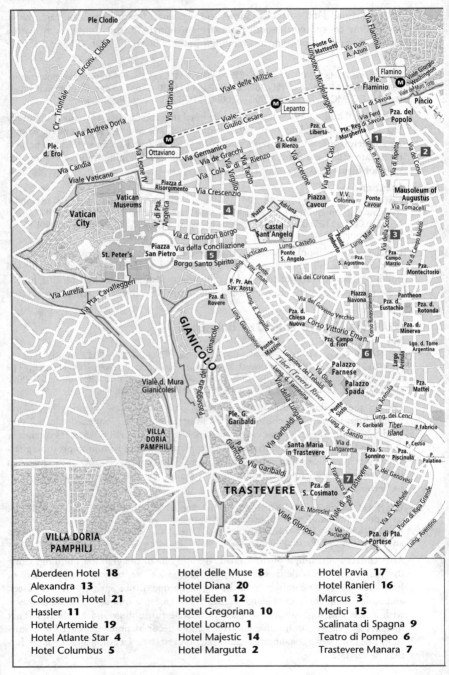

Aberdeen Hotel **18**
Alexandra **13**
Colosseum Hotel **21**
Hassler **11**
Hotel Artemide **19**
Hotel Atlante Star **4**
Hotel Columbus **5**

Hotel delle Muse **8**
Hotel Diana **20**
Hotel Eden **12**
Hotel Gregoriana **10**
Hotel Locarno **1**
Hotel Majestic **14**
Hotel Margutta **2**

Hotel Pavia **17**
Hotel Ranieri **16**
Marcus **3**
Medici **15**
Scalinata di Spagna **9**
Teatro di Pompeo **6**
Trastevere Manara **7**

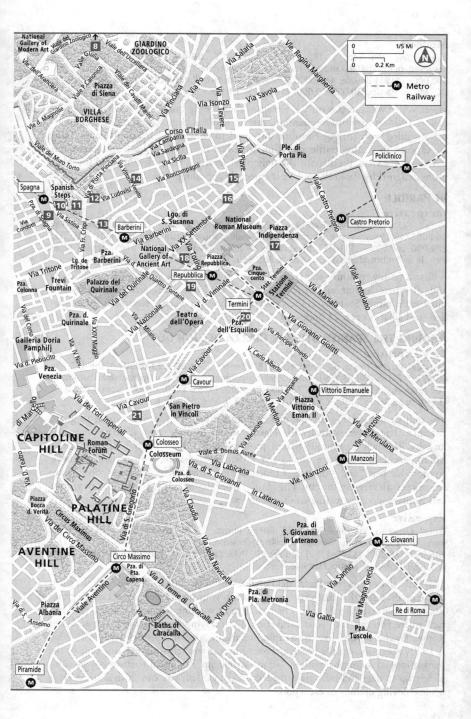

Moderate

Alexandra. Via Veneto 18, 00187 Roma. ☎ **06-4881943.** Fax 06-4871804. www.venere.it/roma/alexandra. E-mail: alexandra@venere.it. 46 units. A/C MINIBAR TV TEL. 390,000L ($195) double; 450,000L ($225) suite for two. Rates include buffet breakfast. AE, DC, MC, V. Parking 30,000–50,000L ($15–$25). Metro: Barberini.

Here's where you can stay on Via Veneto without going broke. Set in what was originally a 19th-century private mansion, this hotel offers clean, comfortable accommodations filled with antique furniture and modern conveniences. Rooms facing front are exposed to roaring traffic and animated street life; those in back are quieter but have less of a view. Breakfast is the only meal served. The garden-inspired breakfast room designed by Paolo Portoghesi is especially appealing.

IN PARIOLI
Inexpensive

Hotel delle Muse. Via Tommaso Salvini 18, 00197 Roma. ☎ **06-8088333.** Fax 06-8085749. www.venere.it/roma/muse. E-mail: hmuse@flashnet.it. 61 units. TV TEL. 220,000–260,000L ($110–$130) double; 240,000–290,000L ($120–$145) triple. Rates include buffet breakfast. AE, DC, MC, V. Bus: 360. Tram: 19.

A classic, family run three-star establishment, this hotel is 1km ($^1/_2$ mile) north of the Villa Borghese, a winning but unheralded choice. Most rooms have been renovated but remain rather Spartan. In the summer the hotel operates a restaurant in the garden, and a bar is open 24 hours a day.

AROUND THE SPANISH STEPS & PIAZZA DEL POPOLO
Very Expensive

Hassler. Piazza Trinità d. Monti 6, 00187 Roma. ☎ **800/223-6800** in the U.S., or 06-699-340. Fax 06-678-9991. www.hotelhasslerroma.com. E-mail: info@hotelhasslerroma.it. 100 units. A/C MINIBAR TV TEL. 730,000–860,000L ($365–$430) double; from 1,080,000L ($540) suite. AE, DC, MC, V. Parking 45,000L ($23). Metro: Spagna.

The only deluxe hotel in this old part of Rome, it uses the Spanish Steps as its grand entrance. The crown worn by the Hassler is still in place after all these years; the hostelry has such a mystique that it prospers and endures in spite of high-prices. Rooms, some of which are small, have a personalized look, with French windows, comfortable beds, and—the nicest touch of all—bowls of fresh flowers. Some have balconies with views of the city. The Hassler Roof Restaurant is a favorite with visitors and Romans alike for its fine cuisine and view.

Expensive

Hotel Locarno. Via della Penna 22, 00186 Roma. ☎ **06-3610841.** Fax 06-3215249. www.hotellocarno.com. E-mail: info@hotellocarno.com. 52 units. MINIBAR TV TEL. 346,000–378,000L ($173–$189) double; 410,000L ($205) suite. Rates include buffet breakfast. AE, DC, MC, V. Metro: Flaminio.

This little charmer is near Piazza del Popolo, said to be haunted by the imperial ghost of Nero, although that isn't expected to disturb your night's sleep. You can count on Rome's heavy traffic to do that. The hotel's most winning feature is its large roof terrace where you can take your breakfast while enjoying some of the major sights of Rome's skyline. If you'd like to go exploring, the Locarno will provide you with a bike. A 1920s aura pervades the hotel, as evoked by the wrought-iron elevator cage or the marble-topped walnut bar with its Tiffany-style lamp. Rooms and bathrooms are completely up to date and safes are provided. In the garden, you can sit in a rattan chair while enjoying orchids in cachepots.

○ **Scalinata di Spagna.** Piazze. Trinità dei Monti 17, 00187 Roma. ☎ **06-6793006.** Fax 06-69940598. www.italyhotel.com/home/roma/scalinata/scalinata.html. 16 units. A/C MINI-BAR TV TEL. 400,000–500,000L ($200–$250) double; from 600,000L ($300) suite. Rates include breakfast. AE, MC, V. Parking 45,000L ($23). Metro: Spagna.

This upscale B&B near the Spanish Steps has always been one of the most sought-after in Rome. It's right at the top of the steps, directly across the small piazza from the deluxe Hassler. Decor varies radically from one room to the next; some have low, beamed ceilings and ancient-looking wood furniture, others offer loftier ceilings and more average appointments. All rooms were renovated and upgraded in 1998, the bathrooms receiving special attention. In season, breakfast is served on the rooftop garden terrace with its sweeping view of the dome of St. Peter's across the Tiber.

Moderate

Hotel Gregoriana. Via Gregoriana 18, 00187 Roma. ☎ **06-6794269.** Fax 06-6784258. 20 units. A/C TV TEL. 380,000L ($190) double. Rates include breakfast. AE, DC, V. Parking 30,000–40,000L ($15–$20). Metro: Spagna.

Although surrounded by much more expensive neighbors like the pricey Hassler, the small Gregoriana in a former 17th-century convent has its own fans—mainly members of the Italian fashion industry. Rooms are small but comfortable. The elevator cage is a black-and-gold art deco fantasy, and the door to each room has a reproduction of an Erté print whose fanciful characters indicate the letter designating that room. You'll pay the bill in the tiny, bamboo-covered lobby.

Inexpensive

Hotel Margutta. Via Laurina 34, 00187 Roma. ☎ **06-3223674.** Fax 06-3200395. 24 units. TEL. 190,000–260,000L ($95–$130) double; 250,000L ($125) triple. Rates include breakfast. AE, DC, MC, V. Metro: Flaminio.

Located on a cobblestone street near Piazza del Popolo, this hotel offers attractively decorated but exceedingly small rooms and cramped private bathrooms. Its helpful staff makes it an enduring favorite, nonetheless. The best rooms are on the top floor; two of these share a terrace, and another larger room has a private terrace. The hotel is not air-conditioned, nor does it have room TVs. Off the lobby is a simple breakfast room.

Marcus. Via del Clementino 94 (corner of Via Ripetta and Via della Scrofa), 00186 Roma. ☎ **06-6830-0320.** Fax 06-6830-0312. www.venere.it/roma/marcus. E-mail: solemarco@hotmail.com. 18 units, 17 with bathroom. MINIBAR TV TEL. 160,000–230,000L ($80–$115) double. Rates include breakfast. AE, MC, V. Metro: Spagna.

This family-run hotel is near the Spanish Steps, right in the historical and shopping center of Rome. It is housed in a 16th-century palace that offers all modern comforts with reasonable prices. Rooms, in a variety of sizes, are tastefully furnished and the windows are double-glazed. About 50% are air-conditioned, which costs an extra 20,000L ($10) in summer. Baths are simple, with shower stalls and hair dryers. Breakfast is the only meal served. The helpful Salvatore de Caro and his family will be glad to make you feel at home in this charming two-star hotel.

NEAR CAMPO DE' FIORI

Moderate

Teatro di Pompeo. Largo del Pallaro 8, 00186 Roma. ☎ **06-68300170.** Fax 06-68805531. 13 units. A/C TV TEL. 350,000L ($175) double. Rates include breakfast. AE, DC, MC, V. Bus: 46, 62, or 64.

Built on the top of the ruins of the Theater of Pompey, which dates from about 55 B.C., this small charmer lies near the spot where Julius Caesar met his fate. Intimate and refined, it's on a quiet piazzetta near the Palazzo Farnese and Campo de' Fiori. Rooms, all doubles, are decorated in an old-fashioned Italian style with handpainted tiles, and the beamed ceilings date from the days of Michelangelo. There's no restaurant, but breakfast is served.

NEAR VATICAN CITY

Very Expensive

Hotel Atlante Star. Via Vitelleschi 34, 00193 Roma. ☎ **06-6873233.** Fax 06-6872300. www.atlantehotels.com. E-mail: atlante.star@atlantehotels.com. 90 units. A/C MINIBAR TV TEL. 500,000L ($250) double; from 700,000L ($350) suite. Rates include buffet breakfast. AE, MC, V. Parking 40,000L ($20). Metro: Ottaviano. Tram: 19 or 30.

Atlante Star is a first-class hotel a short distance from St. Peter's. The upper floors give the impression of being inside a luxuriously appointed ocean liner. Rooms are small but posh, outfitted with all the modern comforts. A royal suite features a Jacuzzi. The views of St. Peter's are the most striking of any hotel in Rome. The restaurant, Les Etoiles (see "Where to Dine," below), is an elegant roof-garden choice at night, offering a 360° panoramic view of Rome. There's also a less formal year-round rooftop cafe and restaurant called Terrazza Paradiso, where you can enjoy good Italian food and a panoramic view on Ancient Rome, surrounded by a cascade of Mediterranean plants and flowers.

Expensive

Hotel Columbus. Via della Conciliazione 33, 00193 Roma. ☎ **06-6865435.** Fax 06-6864874. 92 units. A/C MINIBAR TV TEL. 570,000L ($285) double; 660,000L ($330) suite. Rates include buffet breakfast. AE, DC, MC, V. Hotel has a few free parking spaces. Bus: 62 or 64.

In an impressive 15th-century palace, Hotel Columbus is a few minutes' walk from St. Peter's. It was once the private home of a wealthy cardinal who later became Pope Julius II and had Michelangelo paint the Sistine Chapel. The building looks much as it must have those long centuries ago. Rooms are considerably simpler than the tiled and tapestried salons. All are spacious; a few are enormous and still have such original details as decorated wood ceilings and frescoed walls. La Veranda restaurant, with frescoes from the school of Pittoricchio, serves a good Roman and international cuisine. In summer, meals are served in a garden.

NEAR ANCIENT ROME

Inexpensive

Colosseum Hotel. Via Sforza 10, 00184 Roma. ☎ **06-4827228.** Fax 06-4827285. www.venere.it/home/roma/colosseum/colosseum.html. E-mail: colosseum@venere.it. 47 units. TV TEL. 239,000–245,000L ($120–$123) double. Rates include breakfast. AE, DC, MC, V. Parking 35,000L ($18). Metro: Cavour.

Not far from the Santa Maria Maggiore, the Colosseum offers baronial living on a miniature scale. The tasteful hotel reflects the best of Italy's design heritage. Rooms are furnished with well-conceived antique reproductions. Most are air-conditioned. The drawing room, with its long refectory table, white walls, red tiles, and provincial armchairs, invites lingering.

IN TRASVETERE

Trastevere Manara. Via L. Manara 24–25, 00153 Roma. ☎ **06-581-4713.** Fax 06-588-1016. 9 units. TV TEL. 130,000L ($65) double. Continental breakfast 10,000L ($5) per person. AE, MC, V. Free parking on street. Bus: H. Tram: 8.

Deep in the heart of Trastevere, which tourists used to avoid in the '50s and '60s, there's today a demand for suitable lodgings. Manara fits the bill. Time was, you'd stay here only if you were writing a book called *Down and Out in Roma*. But those cobweb memories have been chased away, and this little gem has emerged with freshly decorated rooms and a price that's hard to beat for those who want to stay in one of the most atmospheric sections of Rome. Most rooms open onto Piazza San Cisimato, and all have comfortable albeit functional furnishings. Bathrooms are quite small. Breakfast is the only meal served, but many good restaurants lie just minutes outside the door.

WHERE TO DINE
NEAR STAZIONE TERMINI
Expensive

Agata e Romeo. Via Carlo Alberto 45. ☎ **06-4466115.** Reservations recommended. Main courses 40,000–50,000L ($20–$25). AE, DC, MC, V. Mon–Sat 1–3pm and 8–10:30pm. Metro: Vittorio Emanuele. ROMAN.

Named after the husband-wife team Romeo and Agata Caraccio), this is a small-scale and charming enclave of culinary creativity in the shadow of Santa Maria Maggiore. Menus are changed with the seasons to reflect the bounty of the Italian harvest, as well as the whims and inspiration of both kitchen and wine cellar. Examples include a puree of eggplant capped with slices of rabbit fillet; or a deceptively simple version of white beans capped with fried cuttlefish. Spaghetti is often prepared with shellfish, especially clams. Breast of duck with porcini and herb sauce, or rack of lamb with rosemary sauce are perennial favorites. One of their most enduring dessert specialties is their own version of *millefiori*—chantilly cream laced with liqueur and served in puff pastry.

Moderate

Scoglio di Frisio. Via Merulana 256. ☎ **06-4872765.** Reservations recommended. Main courses 12,000–32,000L ($6–$16). AE, DC, MC, V. Mon–Fri 12:30–3pm and 7:30–11pm, Sat–Sun 7:30–11pm. Bus: 714 from Stazione Termini. NEAPOLITAN/PIZZA.

South of the Stazione Termini, Scoglio di Frisio is the choice *suprême* to introduce yourself to the Neapolitan kitchen. While here, you should get reacquainted with pizza—this is the genuine article. At night, you can begin with a plate-size Neapolitan pizza (crunchy, oozy, and excellent) with clams and mussels. After a medley of stuffed vegetables and antipasti, you may settle for chicken cacciatore or veal scaloppini. Scoglio di Frisio also presents Neapolitan songs, so it makes for an inexpensive night on the town.

Inexpensive

Il Dito e La Luna. Via dei Sabelli 49–51, San Lorenzo. ☎ **06-4940726.** Reservations recommended. Main courses 19,000–24,000L ($10–$12). No credit cards. Mon–Sat 8pm–midnight. Metro: Vittorio Emanuele. SICILIAN/ITALIAN.

At this charming, small restaurant the menu is equally divided between traditional Sicilian recipes and more creative up-to-date recipes prepared with gusto and flair. The setting emulates an unpretentious bistro. Menu items include fresh orange-infused anchovies served on orange segments; a creamy flan of mild onions and mountain cheese; seafood couscous loaded with shellfish; and such succulent pastas as square-cut spaghetti (tonnarelli) prepared with mussels, bacon, and tomatoes, and exotic mushrooms.

NEAR VIA VENETO & PIAZZA BARBERINI
Very Expensive

✪ **Sans Souci.** Via Sicilia 20. ☎ **06-4821814.** Reservations recommended. Main courses 35,000–68,000L ($18–$34). AE, DC, MC, V. Tues–Sun 8pm–1am. Closed Aug 10–30. Metro: Barberini. FRENCH/ITALIAN.

The Cafe Scene

Caffè de Paris, Via Vittorio Veneto 90 (☎ 06-4885284; Metro: Barberini), rises and falls in popularity depending on the decade. In the 1950s, it was a haven for the fashionable and now it's a popular restaurant in summer where the tables spill out onto the sidewalk filled with patrons. Open Wednesday to Monday 8am to 1:30am, Tuesday 8am to midnight. **Canova Café,** Piazza del Popolo 16 (☎ 06-3612231; Metro: Flaminio), has a sidewalk terrace for people-watching, plus a snack bar, a restaurant, and a wine shop inside. In summer you'll have access to a courtyard with ivy-covered walls. Meals cost 25,000L ($13) and up. Open daily 8am to midnight or later depending on the crowd.

Since 1760, **Antico Caffè Greco,** Via Condotti 84 (☎ 06-6791700; Metro: Spagna), has been Rome's most posh and fashionable coffee bar. It has for years enjoyed a reputation as the gathering place of the literati. In the front is a wooden bar, and beyond that a series of small salons, decorated in a 19th-century style. Open Monday to Saturday 8am to 9pm. **Caffè Sant'Eustachio,** Piazza Sant'Eustachio 82 (☎ 06-6861309; bus: 116), is one of the city's most celebrated espresso shops, on a small square near the Pantheon. The water supply comes from a source outside Rome, which the emperor Augustus funneled into the city with an aqueduct in 19 B.C. Rome's most experienced espresso judges claim that the water plays an important part in the coffee's flavor, although steam forced through ground Brazilian coffee roasted on the premises has an important effect as well. Open Tuesday to Friday and Sunday 8:30am to 1am, Saturday 8:30am to 1:30am.

Sans Souci, which was getting a little tired, has now bounced back, and Michelin has restored its coveted star. It is now the market leader for glitz, glamour, and nostalgia for *la dolce vita*. This is a major stop on the see-and-be-seen circuit, and might be your best bet for spotting a movie star, albeit a faded one. The menu is ever changing, as "new creations" are devised. You might begin with a terrine of goose liver with truffles, a special creation of the chef. The fish soup, according to one Rome restaurant critic, is "a legend to experience." The soufflés are also deservedly popular; artichoke, asparagus, and spinach are our favorites.

Expensive

Colline Emiliane. Via Avignonesi 22. ☎ 06-4817538. Reservations required. Main courses 45,000–60,000L ($23–$30). MC, V. Sat–Thurs 12:45–2:45pm and 7:45–10:45pm. Closed Aug. Metro: Barberini. EMILIANA-ROMAGNOLA.

This small restaurant right off Piazza Barberini serves *classica cucina bolognese*. It's a family-run place where everybody helps out. The owner is the cook and his wife makes the pasta, which, incidentally, is about the best you'll encounter in Rome. The house specialty is an inspired *tortellini alla panna* (cream sauce) with truffles. To start your meal, we suggest *culatello di Zibello,* a delicacy from a small town near Parma that's known for having the finest prosciutto in the world. An excellent main course is *braciola di maiale*—boneless rolled pork cutlets that have been stuffed with ham and cheese, breaded, and sautéed. *Bollito misto* (mixed boiled meats) is another specialty.

Moderate

Césarina. Via Piemonte 109. ☎ 06-4880828. Reservations recommended. Main courses 18,000–26,000L ($9–$13). AE, DC, MC, V. Mon–Sat 12:30–3pm and 7:30–11pm. Bus: 52, 53, 56, or 910 from Stazione Termini. EMILIANA-ROMAGNOLA/ROMAN.

This restaurant perpetuates the culinary traditions of the late Cesarina Masi in a newer manifestation of the original hole-in-the-wall. Today, with three dining rooms and more than 200 seats, the restaurant serves excellent versions of *bollito misto* (an array of well-seasoned boiled meats), rolled from table to table on a cart; and *misto Cesarina*—three kinds of pasta, each handmade and served with a different sauce. Equally appealing is *saltimbocca* (veal with ham) and *cotoletta alla bolognese* (veal cutlet baked with ham and cheese).

✪ **Girarrosto Toscano.** Via Campania 29. ☎ **06-4823835.** Reservations required. Main courses 25,000–40,000L ($13–$20). AE, CB, DC, MC, V. Thurs–Tues 12:30–2:30pm and 7:30–11pm. Bus: 90B, 95, 490, or 495. Metro: Barberini, then a long stroll. TUSCAN.

You may have to wait for a table at this popular place facing the walls of the Borghese Gardens. Under vaulted ceilings in a cellar setting, fine Tuscan specialties are served. Begin with an enormous selection of antipasti: succulent little meatballs, vine-ripened melon with prosciutto, mozzarella, and especially savory Tuscan salami. You're then given a choice of pasta. *Bistecca alla fiorentina* (grilled steak seasoned with oil, salt, and pepper) is the best item to order, although it's expensive. Oysters and fresh fish from the Adriatic are also served every day. Meat and fish dishes are priced according to weight and costs can run considerably higher than the prices quoted above.

IN PARIOLI
Very Expensive
Relais Le Jardin. In the Hotel Lord Byron, Via G. de Notaris 5. ☎ **06-3613041.** Reservations required. Main courses 45,000–55,000L ($23–$28). AE, DC, MC, V. Mon–Sat 1–3pm and 8–10:30pm. Bus: 26 or 52. ITALIAN/INTERNATIONAL.

For both a traditional and creative cuisine in an elegantly romantic and classic setting, Relais Le Jardin is the place to go. A chichi crowd with demanding palates patronizes it nightly, even in August when the menu is curtailed. A member of Relais Gourmands, the establishment serves a frequently changing array of seasonal dishes. The pasta and soups are among the best in town—the tonnarelli pasta with asparagus and smoked ham served with concassé tomatoes is delectable, as is the pasta with ricotta sauce, black olives, corn, and oregano. For your main course you face such selections as roast loin of lamb with artichoke romana, pork fillet stuffed with crab, or grilled beef sirloin with hot chicory and sautéed potatoes.

Moderate
Al Ceppo. Via Panama 2. ☎ **06-8419696.** Reservations recommended. Main courses 19,000–35,000L ($10–$18). AE, DC, MC, V. Tues–Sun 12:30–3pm and 8–11pm. Closed the last 3 weeks of Aug. Bus: 4, 52, or 53. ROMAN.

This restaurant's somewhat hidden location (although it's only 2 blocks from the Villa Borghese, near Piazza Ungheria) means that the clientele is likely to be Roman rather than foreign. At this longtime and enduring favorite, the cuisine is as good as it ever was in its heyday. "The Log" features an open fireplace where the chef prepares lamb chops, liver, and bacon to charcoal perfection. The beefsteak, which hails from Tuscany, is also succulent. Other dishes include *linguine monteconero* (made with clams and fresh tomatoes), and a savory version of spaghetti with pepperoni, fresh basil, and pecorino cheese.

NEAR THE SPANISH STEPS & PIAZZA DEL POPOLO
Expensive
El Toulà. Via della Lupa 29B. ☎ **06-6873498.** Reservations required for dinner. Main courses 40,000–46,000L ($20–$23); five-course menu *degustazione* 120,000L ($60); four-course menu veneto 100,000L ($50). AE, DC, MC, V. Tues–Fri noon–3pm and Mon–Sat 7:30–11pm. Closed Aug. Bus: 81, 90, 90b, 628, or 913. ROMAN/VENETIAN.

El Toulà offers quintessential Roman haute cuisine with a creative flair in an elegant setting of vaulted ceilings and large archways. Guests stop in the charming bar to order a drink while deciding on their food selections from the impressive menu, which changes every month. One section is devoted exclusively to culinary specialties of Venice, including Venice's classic dish, *fegato* (liver) *alla Veneziana;* calamari stuffed with vegetables; *baccalà* mousse (codfish) with polenta, and another Venetian classic, *broetto* (fish soup made with monkfish and clams). El Toulà usually isn't crowded at lunchtime.

Moderate

Dal Bolognese. Piazza del Popolo 1–2. ☎ **06-3611426.** Reservations required. Main courses 18,000–30,000L ($9–$15). AE, DC, MC, V. Tues–Sun 12:30–3pm and 8:15pm–1am. Closed 20 days in Aug. Metro: Flaminio. BOLOGNESE.

If *La Dolce Vita* were being filmed now, this restaurant would be used as a backdrop, its patrons photographed in their latest Fendi drag. It's one of those rare dining spots that's not only chic, but noted for its food as well. Young actors, shapely models, artists from nearby Via Margutta, even industrialists on an off-the-record evening on the town show up here, occupying the sidewalk tables on the terrace when the weather is fair. To begin your meal, we suggest *misto di pasta*—four pastas, each flavored with a different sauce, arranged on the same plate. For your main course, specialties include *lasagne verdi, tagliatelle alla bolognese,* and a most recommendable *cotoletta alla bolognese* (veal cutlet topped with cheese). Although almond cake is the house specialty, it's hard to resist the fresh strawberry tart.

Otello alla Concordia. Via della Croce 81. ☎ **06-6791178.** Reservation recommended. Main courses 14,000–30,000L ($7–$15); fixed-price menu 40,000L ($20). AE, DC, MC, V. Mon–Sat 12:30–3pm and 7:30–11pm. Closed 2 weeks in Feb. Metro: Spagna. ROMAN.

On a side street amid the glamorous boutiques near the northern edge of the Spanish Steps, this is a popular and consistently reliable restaurant. Diners enter from a stone corridor that leads from the street into a dignified building and then choose a table (space permitting) in either an arbor-covered courtyard or in a cramped but convivial series of inner dining rooms. The *spaghetti alle vongole veraci* (spaghetti with clams) and the pasta with chickpeas are excellent, as are Roman-style *abbacchio arrosto* (roasted baby lamb), a selection of grilled or sautéed fish dishes, and classic eggplant parmigiana.

Ristorante Nino dal 1934. Via Borgognona 11. ☎ **06-6795676.** Reservations recommended. Main courses 20,000–50,000L ($10–$25). AE, DC, MC, V. Mon–Sat 12:30–3pm and 7:30–11pm. Closed Aug. Metro: Spagna. TUSCAN.

Ristorante Nino, off Via Condotti a short walk from the Spanish Steps, is a tavern mecca for writers, artists, and international models from one of the nearby high-fashion houses. The Guarnacci brothers, the owners, deserve acclaim for their Tuscan dishes, such as pappardelle with hare sauce or bean soup from the Tuscan hills. The hearty cooking is completely unpretentious. The restaurant is particularly known for its steaks, shipped in from Florence and charcoal broiled (priced according to weight). Cannelloni Nino is one of the chef's specialties, as are ravioli di tartufo (dumplings stuffed with truffles) or baccalà (dried cod fish, usually on Friday).

NEAR CAMPO DE' FIORI & THE JEWISH GHETTO
Moderate

Da Giggetto. Via del Portico d'Ottavia 21–22. ☎ **06-6861105.** Reservations recommended. Main courses 20,000–28,000L ($10–$14). AE, DC, MC, V. Tues–Sun 12:30–3pm and 7:30–11pm. Closed Aug 1–15. Bus: 62, 64, 75, 90, or 170. ROMAN.

Da Giggetto, in the old ghetto, is a short walk from the Theater of Marcellus. Romans flock to this bustling trattoria for their special traditional dishes. None are more typical than *carciofi alla giudea,* baby-tender fried artichokes. This is a true delicacy! The cheese concoction, mozzarella in carrozza, is another good choice, as are the zucchini flowers stuffed with mozzarella and anchovies, even the dried salted cod fillet. Also sample *fettuccine al 'Amatriciana,* with shrimp sautéed in garlic and olive oil.

Il Drappo. Vicolo del Malpasso 9. ☎ **06-6877365.** Reservations required. Main courses 20,000–45,000L ($10–$23); fixed-price menus (including Sardinian wine) 65,000–70,000L ($33–$35). AE, MC, V. Mon–Sat 7pm–midnight. Closed Aug 15–31. Bus: 46, 62, or 64. SARDINIAN.

Il Drappo, on a hard-to-find, narrow street off a square near the Tiber, is operated by a woman known to her habitués only as "Valentina." The facade is graced with a modernized trompe-l'oeil painting above the stone entrance, flanked with potted plants. Fixed-price dinners may include a wafer-thin appetizer called *carte di musica* (sheet-music paper), topped with tomatoes, green peppers, parsley, and olive oil, followed by fresh spring lamb in season, or a changing selection of strongly flavored regional specialties that are otherwise difficult to find in Rome. Among these is roast suckling Sardinian pig with an herb sauce, casserole of rabbit with black olives and capers. For dessert, try a Sardinian sweet known as *sebadas,* like a little crepe stuffed with cheese and honey and served very hot. Only Sardinian wines are served; one of the best being a red wine known as Cannolau di Erzo.

Vecchia Roma. Via della Tribuna di Campitelli 18. ☎ **06-6864604.** Reservations recommended. Main courses 24,000–40,000L ($12–$20). AE, DC. Thurs–Tues 1–3:30pm and 8–11pm. Closed 10 days in Aug. Bus: 64, 90, 90b, 97, or 774. ITALIAN/ROMAN.

Vecchia Roma is a charming, moderately priced trattoria in the heart of the Jewish ghetto (a short walk from the Campidoglio). The owners are known for their selection of fresh seafood, and the minestrone of the day is made with fresh vegetables. An interesting selection of antipasti is always presented, including salmon and a vegetable antipasto. The pastas and risottos are also excellent; the "green" risotto with porcini mushrooms is invariably good. Lamb is a specialty of the chef.

NEAR PIAZZA NAVONA & THE PANTHEON
Very Expensive
✪ **Quinzi & Gabrieli.** Via delle Coppelle 5/6, 00185 Roma. ☎ **06-6879389.** Reservation required as far in advance as possible. Main courses 40,000–60,000L ($20–$30). AE, DC, MC, V. Mon–Sat 7:30–11:30pm. Closed Aug. Bus: 44, 46, 55, 60, 61, 62, 64, or 65. SEAFOOD.

We've never found better, or fresher, seafood than that served here in a 15th-century building attracting the most discriminating of Rome's fish fanciers. Don't be put off by the rough and ready service, but come here for the great taste instead. Be prepared to pay for the privilege, as fresh seafood is extremely expensive in Rome. Partners Alberto Quinzi and Enrico Gabrieli have earned their reputation on their simply cooked and presented fish. Everything tastes natural and fresh, and heavy sauces aren't used to disguise old fish as they are in many restaurants. In fact, the restaurant is known for its raw seafood such as a delicate carpaccio of swordfish, sea bass, and deep-sea shrimp. The house specialty is spaghetti with lobster, but all sorts of fish are served, including sea urchins, octopus, sole, and red mullet. Check out what's available in a special display on ice at the entrance. Sometimes the headwaiters will prepare wriggling crab or scampi right on the grill before you—that way you know it's fresh. In summer French doors lead to a small dining terrace.

Expensive

Troiani. Via dei Soldati 28. ☎ **06-688805950.** Reservations recommended. Main courses 43,000L ($22). AE, DC, MC, V. Tues–Sat 1–2:30pm and Tues–Sun 8–10:30pm. Bus: 70, 87, or 90. ITALIAN.

In a new location that's a great improvement over the former cramped setting, Chef Angelo Troiana still is on the A-list of Roman chefs, even though he now has a lot more diners to feed. Since 1989, Angelo and his two brothers have excited discriminating palates with seasonal Italian cooking and creative culinary innovation. Launch yourself into the excitement with a warm seafood salad made with clams, mussels, white fish, and a giant prawn with al dente vegetables and a "mayonnaise of the sea," a fragrant lemony sauce. Even the ravioli is stuffed creatively, with ingredients and inspiration that changes with the seasons. Worthy main courses include saddle of rabbit that might be stuffed with porcini mushrooms and served with an onion marmalade, or boned rack of lamb cooked in an herb and vegetable crust. For dessert, consider a slice of almond and bitter chocolate cake accented with fresh currants.

Moderate

Bramante. Via della Pace 25. ☎ **06-68803916.** Reservations recommended. Main courses 20,000–30,000L ($10–$15). AE, DC, MC, V. Mon–Sat 5pm–1am, Sun noon–1am. Closed Dec 24. Bus: 44, 46, 55, 60, 61, 62, 64, 65. ROMAN.

On a cobblestone street in back of the Piazza Navona, this cafe-restaurant opens onto a delightful small square of vine-draped taverns. The establishment is named for the 16th-century church on the square, which was designed by the Bramante. Behind the ivy-covered facade the interior is completely hand painted, as white candles illuminate the marble bar, making for a cozy, inviting atmosphere. The owner, Mr. Giuseppe, tries to make visitors appreciate Italian food and traditions, and succeeds admirably. Almost all his dishes are handmade, and the cooks use only the freshest ingredients. Recipes are simple but rich in Mediterranean flavor. You can taste wonderful pastas made just with fresh tomato sauce, garlic, and pasta, or else something heavier such as braised beef or tender grilled steak flavored with herbs and served with potatoes. They don't serve fish, however.

La Carbonara. Piazza Campo de' Fiori 23. ☎ **06-6864783.** Reservations recommended. Main courses 16,000–24,000L ($8–$12). AE, MC, V. Wed–Mon noon–2:30pm and 6:30–10:30pm. Closed 3 weeks in Aug. Bus: 64. ROMAN.

In a palazzetto at the edge of the market square, this amicable trattoria claims to be the home of the original spaghetti carbonara. The much-disputed legend claims that the dish was invented when American GIs donated their K-rations of powdered eggs and salted bacon to the chef—the result was that tempting concoction of egg, cheese, and bacon-enriched pasta that has become well-loved throughout the world. Actually the name comes from the Carbonari, men who delivered coal for heating, who were served meals here. The owner's father was a carbonaro, so he dedicated the restaurant to his memory. The current chef still prepares the dish as his predecessor did, as well as succulent antipasti, grilled meats, and fresh seasonal vegetables. A dish that is truly *divino* is the sautéed artichokes with pumpkin flowers. In addition to typically Roman dishes, the chef also specializes in a wide selection of risottos, flavored with asparagus, porcini mushrooms, zucchini, or fresh artichokes—whatever is in season. In summer, some sidewalk tables are available for people-watchers.

L'Eau Vive. Via Monterone 85. ☎ **06-68801095.** Reservations recommended. Main courses 25,000–70,000L ($13–$35); fixed-price menus 22,000L ($11), 30,000L ($15), and 50,000L ($25). AE, MC, V. Mon–Sat 12:30–2:30pm and 8–10:30pm. Closed Aug 1–20. Bus: 46, 62, 64, 70, or 115. FRENCH/INTERNATIONAL.

L'Eau Vive is run by lay missionaries who wear the dress or costumes of their native countries. The restaurant occupies the cellar and the ground floor of a 17th-century palace, and is filled with monumental paintings. In this formal atmosphere, at 10pm nightly, the waitresses sing religious hymns and "Ave Marias." Your gratuity for service will be turned over for religious purposes. Pope John Paul II used to dine here when he was still archbishop of Kraków. Specialties include hors d'oeuvres and frogs' legs. Main dishes range from guinea hen with onions and grapes in a wine sauce to couscous. Other selections include salad niçoise, several kinds of homemade pâté, and beefsteak in wine sauce. A smooth finish is the chocolate mousse.

Osteria dell'Antiquario. Piazzetta di S. Simeone 26/27, Via dei Coronari. ☎ **06-6879694.** Reservations recommended. Main courses 28,000–40,000L ($14–$20). AE, DC, MC, V. Tues–Sat 12:30–2:30pm and 8–11pm, Mon 8–11pm. Closed 15 days in mid-Aug, Christmas, Jan 1–15. Bus: 70, 87, or 90. INTERNATIONAL/ROMAN.

Virtually undiscovered, this little Roman osteria lies a few blocks down the Via dei Coronari as you leave the Piazza Navona and head toward St. Peter's. In a stone-built stable from the 1500s, it has three dining rooms and a terrace for fair-weather dining. We prefer to begin with a delectable appetizer of sautéed shellfish (usually mussels and clams), although you might opt for the risotto with porcini mushrooms. For a main course, you can go experimental with the fillet or ostrich covered by a slice of ham and grated Parmesan, or else opt for shellfish flavored with saffron. The fish soup with fried bread is excellent, as is an array of freshly made soups and pastas. Veal rolls Roman style and turbot flavored with fresh tomatoes and basil are other excellent choices. This is dining in the classic Roman style.

Inexpensive

Pizzeria Baffetto. Via del Governo Vecchio 114. ☎ **06-686-1617.** Reservations not accepted. Pizza 6,000–10,000L ($3–$5). No credit cards. Daily 6:30pm–1am. Closed Aug. Bus: 46, 62, 64. PIZZA.

Our Roman friends always take out-of-towners here when they request the best pizza in Rome. Arguably, Pizzaria Baffetto fills the bill and has done so admirably for the past 80 years. Pizzas are sold as *piccolo* (small), *media* (medium), or *grande* (large). Most pizza aficionados order the margherita, the simplest version with mozzarella and a delectable tomato sauce, but a wide range of toppings is served. The chef is preening proud of his pizza Baffetto, the house specialty. It comes with a topping of tomato sauce, mozzarella, mushrooms, onions, sausages, roasted peppers, and eggs. The pizza crusts are delightfully thin, and the pies are served piping hot from the intense heat of the ancient ovens.

Tre Scalini. Piazza Navona 30. ☎ **06-6879148.** Reservations recommended. Main courses 24,000–32,000L ($12–$16). AE, DC, MC, V. Thurs–Tues noon–3pm and 7–11pm. Closed Dec–Feb. Bus: 70, 87, or 90. ROMAN/ITALIAN.

Established in 1882, this is the most famous and respected restaurant on Piazza Navona—a landmark for ice cream as well as more substantial meals. Yes, it's literally crawling with tourists, but its waiters are friendly and helpful. Although there's a cozy bar on the upper floor with a view over the piazza, most visitors opt for a seat either in the ground-floor cafe or at tables on the piazza. House specialties include risotto with porcini mushrooms, spaghetti with clams, roast duck with prosciutto, a carpaccio of sea bass, and roast lamb in the Roman style. No one will object if you order just a pasta and salad, unlike at other restaurants nearby. Their famous *tartufi* (ice cream disguised with a coating of bittersweet chocolate, cherries, and whipped cream) and other ice creams cost 12,000L ($6) each.

NEAR VATICAN CITY
Very Expensive

✪ **Les Etoiles.** In the Hotel Atlante Star, Via dei Bastioni 1. ☎ **06-689-9494.** Reservations required. Main courses 45,000–80,000L ($23–$40). AE, DC, MC, V. Daily 12:30–2:30pm and 7:30–11pm. Metro: Ottaviano. MEDITERRANEAN.

Les Etoiles deserves all the stars it receives—both for its cuisine and for its panoramic view of Rome. At this garden in the sky you'll have an open window over the rooftops of Rome. In summer everyone wants a table outside, but in winter almost the same view can be seen through the picture windows. Refined Mediterranean cuisine, with perfectly balanced flavors, is served here. Dishes include quail cooked either with radicchio or in a casserole with mushrooms and herbs, artichokes stuffed with ricotta and pecorino cheese, Venetian-style risotto with squid ink, and roast suckling lamb with mint.

Moderate

Ristorante Il Matriciano. Via dei Gracchi 55. ☎ **06-3212327.** Reservations required. Main courses 14,000–28,000L ($7–$14). AE, DC, MC, V. Daily 12:30–3pm and 8pm–midnight. Closed Aug 5–25. Metro: Ottaviano. ROMAN.

Il Matriciano is a family restaurant with a devoted following among many actors from the Italian stage. The food is good country fare—nothing fancy. In summer, try to sit at a sidewalk table behind a green hedge under a shady canopy. For openers, we suggest *tagliolini con tartufi* (truffles). For a main course, we recommend *abbacchio al forno* (oven-roasted lamb) and *trippa alla romana* (tripe). The house specialty is based on that Roman favorite, Amatriciana sauce. Here, it's prepared with bucatini pasta and richly flavored with bacon, tomatoes, and basil. In honor of its namesake, another specialty is bucatini alla matriciana, served with a tomato sauce enriched with fried bacon, onion, and hot pepper powder, covered with a topping of pecorino cheese.

Inexpensive

Ristorante Giardinaccio. Via Aurelia 53. ☎ **06-631367.** Reservations recommended, especially on weekends. Main courses 15,000–40,000L ($8–$20); fixed-price menus 15,000–60,000L ($8–$30). AE, DC, MC, V. Daily 12:15–3:15pm and 7:15–11:15pm. Bus: 46, 62, or 98. ITALIAN/MOLISIAN/ROMAN.

This popular restaurant is only 200 yards from St. Peter's. Unusual for Rome, it offers specialties from the provincial Molise region in southeast Italy, and is appropriately decorated in rustic country-tavern style. Flaming grills provide succulent versions of perfectly done quail, goat, and other dishes, but you might want to be adventurous and try the mutton goulash. Many pastas are featured, including *taconelle,* a homemade pasta with lamb sauce. Vegetarians and others will like the large self-service selection of antipasti.

IN ANCIENT ROME
Inexpensive

Abruzzi. Via del Vaccaro 1. ☎ **06-6793897.** Reservations recommended. Main courses 15,000–20,000L ($8–$10). AE, DC, MC, V. Sun–Fri 12:30–3pm and 7–10:30pm. Closed 2 weeks in Aug (dates vary). Bus: 57, 64, 70, or 17. ABRUZZESE.

Abruzzi takes its name from a little-explored region east of Rome known for its haunting beauty and curious superstitions. The restaurant is located at one side of piazza SS. Apostoli, just a short walk from piazza Venezia. Good food at reasonable prices makes it enduringly popular among students. The chef is justly praised for his satisfying assortment of cold antipasti. For a starter, you'll find good *stracciatella* (an egg-and-Parmesan cheese soup). A typical main dish is *vitello tonnato con capperi* (veal in tuna fish sauce with capers).

Alvaro al Circo Massimo. Via dei Cerchi 53. ☎ **06-6786112.** Reservations required. Main courses 18,000–35,000L ($9–$18). AE, MC, V. Tues–Sat 12:30–3:30pm and 7:30–11pm, Sun 12:30–3:30pm. Closed Aug. Metro: Circo Massimo. ITALIAN.

Alvaro al Circo Massimo, at the edge of the Circus Maximus, is the closest thing in Rome to a genuine provincial inn. Here is all the decor associated with Italian taverns, including corncobs hanging from the ceiling and rolls of fat sausages. The antipasti and pasta dishes are fine, the meat courses well prepared, and there's an array of fresh fish—never overcooked. Other specialties include tagliolini with mushrooms and truffles, and roasted turbot with potatoes. They're especially well stocked with exotic seasonal mushrooms, including black truffles so good you'd have to go directly to Spoleto to find better.

IN TRASTEVERE
Expensive
Alberto Ciarla. Piazza San Cosimato 40. ☎ **06-5818668.** Reservations required. Main courses 20,000–48,000L ($10–$24); fixed-price menus 80,000–120,000L ($40–$60). AE, DC, MC, V. Mon–Sat 8:30pm–12:30am. Closed 1 week in Jan and 1 week in Aug. Bus: 44, 75, 170, 280, or 718. SEAFOOD.

Alberto Ciarla is the best and most expensive restaurant in Trastevere, although it's not as chic as it was in the 1980s. It serves some of the most elegant fish dishes in the city. Specialties include a handful of ancient recipes subtly improved by Signor Ciarla, such as soup of pasta and beans with seafood. Original dishes include a delectable salmon Marcel Trompier with lobster sauce, as well as well-flavored sushi, a full array of shellfish, and fillet of sea bass prepared in at least three different ways, including an award-winning version with almonds.

Moderate
La Cisterna. Via della Cisterna 13. ☎ **06-5812543.** Reservations recommended. Main courses 20,000–32,000L ($10–$16). AE, DC, MC, V. Mon–Sat 7pm–1:30am. Bus: 44, 75, 170, 280, or 710. ROMAN.

La Cisterna lies deep in the heart of Trastevere. For more than half a century it has been run by the Simmi family, who are genuinely interested in serving only the best as well as providing a good time for all guests. The cistern in the name comes from an ancient Roman well discovered in the cellar. If you like traditional cookery based on the best of regional produce, come here. In summer you can inspect the antipasti—a mixed selection of hors d'oeuvres—right out on the street before going in. House specialties include Roman-style suckling lamb (*abbacchio*), *rigatoni a l'Amatriciana* (with diced bacon, olive oil, garlic, tomatoes, red peppers, and onions), and fresh fish—especially sea bass baked with herbs.

EXPLORING THE ETERNAL CITY
Rome is studded with ancient monuments that silently evoke its history as one of the greatest centers of Western civilization—once all roads led to Rome, with good reason. It was the first cosmopolitan city in Europe, importing everything from slaves and gladiators to great art from the far corners of the empire. With all its carnage and mismanagement, it left a legacy of law and order and an uncanny lesson in how to conquer enemies by absorbing their cultures. But ancient Rome is only part of the spectacle. The Vatican also made the city a center of the world in art as well as religion. And although Vatican architects rifled much of the glory of the past for their projects, they also created the great Renaissance treasures we come to see today.

Rome Attractions

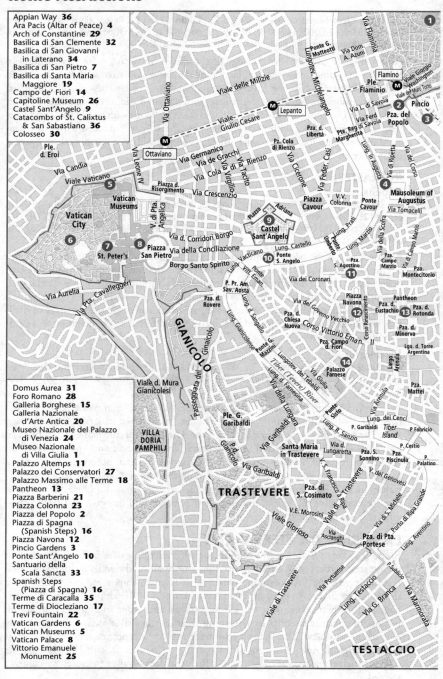

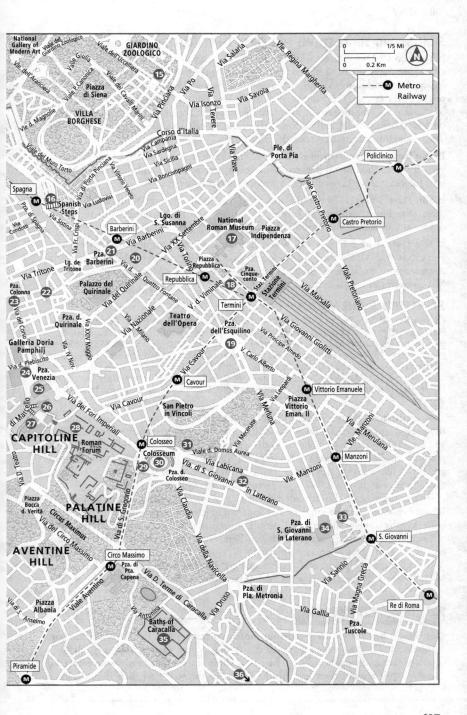

SIGHTSEEING SUGGESTIONS FOR FIRST-TIME VISITORS

If You Have 1 Day Rome wasn't built in a day and you aren't likely to see it in a day either, but make the most of your limited time. You'll basically have to decide on the legacy of imperial Rome—the Roman Forum, the Imperial Forum, and the Colosseum— or else St. Peter's and the Vatican. Walk along the Spanish Steps at sunset. At night go to Piazza del Campidoglio for a fantastic view of the Forum below. Have a nightcap on Via Veneto, which, although past its prime, is still appealing. Toss a coin in the Trevi fountain and promise yourself you'll return.

If You Have 2 Days If you elected to see the Roman Forum and the Colosseum on your first day, then spend the second day exploring St. Peter's and the Vatican Museums (or vice versa). Have dinner in a restaurant in Trastevere.

If You Have 3 Days In the morning go to the Pantheon in the heart of Old Rome, then, after lunch, explore the Castel Sant'Angelo and the Etruscan Museum. Have dinner at a restaurant in or around Piazza Navona.

If You Have 4 or 5 Days On Day 4 head for the environs, notably Tivoli, where you can see the Villa d'Este and Hadrian's Villa. On Day 5 explore the ruins of Ostia Antica, return to Rome for lunch, and visit the Capitoline Museum and Basilica di San Giovanni in Laterano in the afternoon.

ST. PETER'S & THE VATICAN

✪ **Basilica di San Pietro (St. Peter's Basilica).** Piazza San Pietro. ☎ **06-6988-4466.** Piazza San Pietro. ☎ **06-688-4466** (for information on celebrations). Basilica (including grottoes), free; guided tour of excavations around St. Peter's tomb, 15,000L ($8) (children younger than 15 are not admitted); stairs to the dome 7,000L ($3.50); elevator to the dome 8,000L ($4); Sacristy (with Historical Museum) 9,000L ($4.50). Basilica (including the sacristy and treasury), Oct–Mar daily 7am–6pm; Apr–Sept daily 7am–7pm. Grottoes daily 8am–5pm. Dome, Oct–Mar daily 8am–5pm; Apr–Sept 8am–6pm. Bus: 46. Metro: Ottaviano then a long stroll.

To tour the area around St. Peter's tomb, you must apply several days in advance to the excavations office (☎ 06-69885318), open Monday to Saturday 9am to noon and 2 to 5pm. Pass under the arch to the left of the facade of St. Peter's to find it. As you stand in Bernini's **Piazza San Pietro** (St. Peter's Square), you'll be in the arms of an ellipse; like a loving parent, the Doric-pillared colonnade reaches out to embrace the faithful. Holding 300,000 is no problem for this square.

Inside, the size of this famous church is awe-inspiring—though its dimensions (about two football fields long) are not apparent at first. St. Peter's is said to have been built over the tomb of the crucified saint. The original church was erected on the order of Constantine, but the present structure is Renaissance and baroque; it showcases the talents of some of Italy's greatest artists.

In such a grand church, don't expect subtlety. But the basilica is rich in art. Under Michelangelo's dome is the celebrated **baldacchino** by Bernini. In the nave on the

A St. Peter's Warning

St. Peter's has a strict dress code: no shorts, no skirts above the knee, and no bare shoulders. They will not let you in if you don't come dressed appropriately. In a pinch, men and women alike can buy a big cheap scarf from a nearby souvenir stand and wrap it around their legs as a long skirt or throw it over their shoulders as a shawl.

A Vatican Tip

On the left side of Piazza San Pietro is the **Vatican Tourist Office** (☎ **06-6988-4466** or 06-6988-4866), open Monday to Saturday 8:30am to 7pm with maps and guides and reservations for Vatican Gardens tours.

right (the first chapel) is the best-known piece of sculpture, the *Pietà* that Michelangelo sculpted while still in his early twenties. You can visit the **treasury,** filled with jewel-studded chalices, reliquaries, and copes. One robe worn by Pius XII strikes a simple note in these halls of elegance. The sacristy now contains a **Historical Museum (Museo Storico)** displaying Vatican treasures, including the large 1400s bronze tomb of Pope Sixtus V by Antonio Pollaiuolo and several antique chalices. In addition you can visit the **Vatican grottoes,** with their tombs, both ancient and modern (Pope John XXII gets the most adulation).

The grandest sight is yet to come: the climb to **Michelangelo's dome,** which towers about 115m (375 feet) high. Although you can walk up the steps, we recommend the elevator as far as it'll carry you. You can walk along the roof, for which you'll be rewarded with a panoramic view of Rome and the Vatican.

○ **Vatican Museums and the Sistine Chapel.** Viale Vaticano, Vatican City. ☎ **06-69883333.** Admission 18,000L ($9), free for everyone the last Sun of each month (be ready for a crowd). Mar 16–Oct 30 Mon–Fri 8:45am–3:45pm, Sat and the final Sun of the month 8:45am–12:45pm. Off-season, Mon–Sat and the final Sun of the month 8:45am–12:45pm. Last admission 1 hour before closing. Closed religious holidays (except Easter week), and Aug 15–16. Metro: Ottaviano. The museum entrance is a long walk around the Vatican walls north from St. Peter's Square.

The Vatican Museums contain a gigantic repository of treasures. You can follow one of four itineraries—A, B, C, or D—according to the time you have (from $1\frac{1}{2}$ to 5 hours) and your special interests. You can choose from the picture gallery, which houses paintings from the 11th to the 19th century, the Egyptian collection, the Etruscan museum, Greek and Roman sculpture, and, of course, the **Sistine Chapel.** Consult the large panels at the entrance, then follow the letter and color of the itinerary chosen. Facilities for persons with disabilities are available.

Michelangelo labored for 4 years (1508–12) over the epic Sistine Chapel, now restored, although not without controversy, to its original glory. The work was so physically taxing that it permanently damaged his eyesight. Glorifying the human body as only a sculptor could, Michelangelo painted nine panels taken from the pages of Genesis, and surrounded them with prophets and sibyls. Also, visit the Stanze di Raphael, rooms decorated by Raphael when still a young man.

THE FORUM, THE COLOSSEUM & THE HIGHLIGHTS OF ANCIENT ROME

○ **Foro Romano (Roman Forum).** Via dei Fori Imperiali. ☎ **06-6990110.** Foro Romano free; Palatine Hill 12,000L ($7). Apr–Sept daily 9am–8pm; Oct–Mar daily 9am–3:30pm; last admission 1 hour before closing. Closed Dec 25, Jan 1, and May 1. Metro: Colosseo.

The Roman Forum was built in the marshy land between the Palatine and the Capitoline Hills. It flourished as the center of Roman life in the days of the Republic,

A Sistine Chapel Tip

To get the best view of the Sistine Chapel's frescoes, bring binoculars.

before it gradually lost prestige to the Imperial Forum. By day the columns of now-vanished temples and the stones from which long-forgotten orators spoke are mere shells. But at night, when the Forum is silent in the moonlight, it isn't difficult to imagine that Vestal Virgins still guard the sacred temple fire.

If you want the stones to have some meaning, you'll have to purchase a detailed plan, as the temples can be hard to locate. The best of the lot is the handsomely adorned **Temple of Castor and Pollux,** erected in the 5th century B.C. in honor of a battle triumph. The **Temple of Faustina,** with its lovely columns and frieze (griffins and candelabra), was converted into the San Lorenzo in Miranda Church. The **Temple of the Vestal Virgins** is a popular attraction; some of the statuary, mostly headless, remains.

A long walk up from the Roman Forum leads to the **Palatine Hill,** one of the seven hills of Rome; your ticket from the Forum will admit you to this attraction (it's open the same hours). The Palatine, tradition tells us, was the spot on which the first settlers built their huts, under the direction of Romulus. In later years, the hill became a patrician residential district that attracted citizens like Cicero. It's worth the climb for the panoramic, sweeping view of both the Roman and Imperial Forums, as well as the Capitoline Hill and the Colosseum. Of the ruins that remain, none is finer than the so-called **House of Livia** (the "abominable grandmother" of Robert Graves's *I, Claudius*).

When the glory that was Rome has completely overwhelmed you, you can enjoy a respite in the cooling **Farnese Gardens,** laid out in the 16th century, which incorporate some of Michelangelo's designs.

✪ **Colosseo (Colosseum).** Piazzale del Colosseo, Via dei Fori Imperiali. ☎ **06-7004261.** Admission 10,000L ($5) all levels. Oct–Jan 15 daily 9am–3pm; Jan 16–Feb 15 daily 9am–4pm, Feb 16–Mar 17 daily 9am–4:30pm, Mar 18–Apr 16 daily 9am–5pm, Apr 17–Sept daily 9am–6pm. Metro: Colosseo.

In spite of the fact that it's a mere shell, the Colosseum remains the greatest architectural inheritance from ancient Rome. It was inaugurated by Titus in A.D. 80 with a weeks-long bloody combat between gladiators and wild beasts. At its peak, the Colosseum could seat 50,000 spectators, and exotic animals—humans also—were shipped in from the far corners of the empire to satisfy jaded tastes. Many historians now believe that one of the most enduring legends linked to the Colosseum—that Christians were fed to the lions here—is unfounded.

Next to the Colosseum is the **Arch of Constantine,** erected in honor of Constantine's defeat of the pagan Maxentius (A.D. 306).

Domus Aurea (Golden House of Nero). Via della Domus Aurea, on the Esquiline Hill. ☎ **06-3974-9907.** Admission 10,000L ($5), plus 2,000L ($1.10) for advance reservation (highly recommended). Audio tour 3,000L ($1.60); guided tour 6,000L ($3.25), plus additional 1,000L (55¢) reservation. Daily 9am–7pm. Metro: Colosseo.

Nero's fabulous Golden House reopened in 1999 after a 15-year restoration. In A.D. 64, Rome was swept by a disastrous fire—contrary to gossip it has never been proven that Nero set the fire. The emperor did, however, seize more than 200 acres of the burned-out historic core to create one of the most sumptuous palaces in history. Subsequent emperors, seeking to distance themselves from their unpopular predecessor, destroyed much of the place by using its vast network of rooms and walls as a foundation for new construction. Out of its original 250 rooms, 30 are now open to the public, decorated with some of the sculptures, mosaics, and frescoes that have survived the past 2,000 years. When Nero moved in, he shouted, "At last I can start living like a human being!"

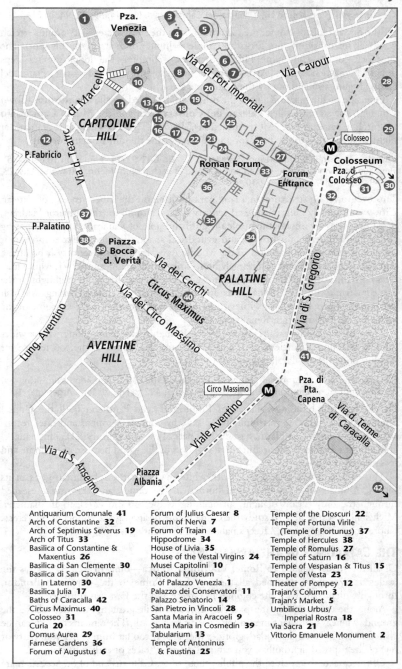

Ancient Rome & Attractions Nearby

Pza. Venezia

Via dei Fori Imperiali

Via Cavour

di Marcello

CAPITOLINE HILL

P.Fabricio

Via d. Teatro

Roman Forum

Forum Entrance

Colosseo

M Colosseum
Pza. d. Colosseo

P.Palatino

Piazza Bocca d. Verità

Via dei Cerchi

PALATINE HILL

Circus Maximus

Via dei Circo Massimo

Via di S. Gregorio

AVENTINE HILL

Lung. Aventino

Circo Massimo **M**

Pza. di Pta. Capena

Via d. Terme di Caracalla

Viale Aventino

Via di S. Anselmo

Piazza Albania

Campidoglio (Capitoline Hill). Piazza del Campidoglio. Bus: 44, 89, 92, 94, or 716.

Of the Seven Hills of Rome, the Campidoglio is the most sacred—its origins stretch way back into antiquity (an Etruscan temple to Jupiter once stood on this spot). The approach to the Capitoline Hill is dramatic—climbing the long, sloping steps designed by Michelangelo. At the top is a perfectly proportioned square, Piazza del Campidoglio, also laid out by the Florentine artist.

One side of the piazza is open; the others are bounded by the **Senatorium** (Town Council), the statuary-filled **Palazzo dei Conservatori,** and the **Museo Capitolinio** (Capitoline Museum; see "More Attractions," below). The Campidoglio is dramatic at night (walk around to the back for a regal view of the floodlit Roman Forum).

Castel Sant'Angelo. Lungotevere Castello 50. ☎ **06-681-91-11.** Admission 10,000L ($5). Tues–Sun 9am–8pm. Closed second and last Wed of each month. Metro: Ottaviano. Bus: 23, 46, 49, 62, 64, 87, 98, 280, or 910.

This overpowering structure, in a landmark position on the Tiber just east of Vatican City, was originally built in the 2nd century A.D. as a tomb for the emperor Hadrian; it continued as an imperial mausoleum until the time of Caracalla. It's an imposing and grim castle with thick walls and cylindrical shape. If it looks like a fortress, it should, as that was its function in the Middle Ages. In the 14th century it became a papal residence. Its legend rests largely on its link with Pope Alexander VI, whose mistress bore him two children—Cesare and Lucrezia Borgia. Today the highlight of the castle is a trip through the Renaissance apartments with their coffered ceilings and lush decoration. Their walls have witnessed plots and intrigues that make up some of the arch-treachery of the High Renaissance.

The castle halls display the history of the Roman mausoleum, along with a wide-ranging selection of ancient arms and armor. You can climb to the top terrace for another one of those dazzling views of the Eternal City.

✪ **Pantheon.** Piazza della Rotonda. ☎ **06-68300230.** Free admission. Mon–Sat 9am–6:30pm, Sun 9am–1pm. Bus: 46, 62, 64, 170, or 492 to Lgo. di Torre Argentina.

Of all the great buildings of ancient Rome, only the Pantheon ("All the Gods") remains intact today. It was built in 27 B.C. by Marcus Agrippa, and later reconstructed by the emperor Hadrian in the first part of the 2nd century A.D. This remarkable building is among the architectural wonders of the world because of its dome and its concept of space.

The Pantheon was once ringed with white marble statues of Roman gods in its niches. Animals were sacrificed and burned in the center, and the smoke escaped through the only means of light, an opening at the top 8m (27 feet) in diameter. Michelangelo came here to study the dome before designing the cupola of St. Peter's, whose dome is only .5m (2 feet) smaller than the Pantheon's.

THE CATACOMBS OF THE APPIAN WAY

Of all the roads that led to Rome, **Via Appia Antica**—built in 312 B.C.—was the leader. It eventually stretched all the way from Rome to the seaport of Brindisi, through which trade with the colonies in Greece and the East was funneled.

Along the Appian Way the patrician Romans built great monuments above the ground, whereas Christians met in the catacombs beneath. The remains of both can be visited today. In some dank, dark grottoes (never stray too far from either your party or one of the exposed lightbulbs), you can still discover traces of early Christian art.

Of the catacombs open to the public, those of St. Callixtus and of St. Sebastian are the most important. Both can be reached by bus 118, which leaves from near the Colosseo metro station.

Catacombe di San Sebastiano are at Via Appia Antica 136 (☎ **06-7887035;** bus: 118). Today the tomb of the martyr is in the basilica, but was originally in the catacomb under the building. From the reign of Valerian to that of Constantine, the bodies of Sts. Peter and Paul were hidden in these catacombs. The tunnels, if stretched out, would reach a length of 11km (7 miles). Admission is 8,000L ($4) adults, 4,000L ($2) children 6 to 15, free for children 5 and under. Open April to October Monday to Saturday 9am to noon and 2:30 to 5:30pm; November to March Monday to Saturday 8:30am to noon and 2:30 to 5pm.

The **Catacombe di San Callisto,** Via Appia Antica 110 (☎ **06-51301580;** bus: 118), are the first cemetery of the Christian community of Rome, burial place of 16 popes in the 3rd century. They bear the name of St. Callixtus, the deacon whom the pope St. Zephyrinus put in charge of them. Callixtus himself was later elected pope (217–22). The cemeterial complex is made up of a network of galleries stretching for nearly 19km (12 miles), structured in five different levels, reaching a depth of about 20m (65 feet). Admission is 8,000L ($4) adults, 4,000L ($2) children 6 to 15, free for children 5 and under. Hours are April to October Thursday to Tuesday 8:30am to noon and 2:30 to 5:30pm; November to February Thursday to Tuesday 8:30am to noon and 2:30 to 5pm.

MORE ATTRACTIONS

⊙ **Spanish Steps (Scalinata di Spagna).** Piazza di Spagna. Metro: Spagna.

The steps—filled in spring with azaleas and other flowers, flower vendors, jewelry dealers, and photographers snapping pictures of visitors—and the square take their names from the Spanish Embassy, which used to be headquartered here. Designed by Italian architect Francesco de Sanctis and built from 1723 to 1725, they were funded almost entirely by the French as a preface to Trinità dei Monti at the top. At the foot of the steps is a boat-shaped fountain designed by Pietro Bernini (not to be confused with his son, Giovanni Lorenzo Bernini, a far greater sculptor). The steps and the piazza below are always packed with a crowd: strolling, reading in the sun, browsing the vendors' carts, and people-watching.

Terme di Caracalla (Baths of Caracalla). Via delle Terme di Caracalla 52. ☎ **06-5758626.** Admission 8,000L ($4). Oct–Jan 15 daily 9am–4pm; Jan 16–Feb 15 daily 9am–4:30pm; Feb 16–Mar 15 daily 9am–5pm; Mar 16–Mar 31 daily 9am–5:30; Apr–Sept daily 9am–7pm. Last admission 1 hour before closing. Closed holidays. Bus: 628.

Named for the emperor Caracalla, the baths were completed in the early part of the 3rd century. The richness of decoration has faded and the lushness can only be judged from the shell of brick ruins that remain.

Basilica di San Clemente. Via San Giovanni in Laterano at Piazza San Clemente, Via Labicana 95. ☎ **06-7045-1018.** Church, free; excavations, 4,000L ($2). Mon–Sat 9am–12:30pm and 3–6pm, Sun 10am–12:30pm and 3–6pm. Metro: Colosseo.

From the Colosseum, head up Via di San Giovanni in Laterano, which leads to the Basilica of Saint Clement. In this church-upon-a-church, centuries of history peel away: A 4th-century church was built over a secular house from the 1st century A.D., beside which stood a pagan temple dedicated to Mithras; Normans destroyed the lower church, and a new one was built in the 12th century. Down in the eerie grottoes (which you can explore on your own—unlike the catacombs on the Appian Way), you'll discover well-preserved frescoes from the 1st to the 3rd centuries.

Basilica di San Giovanni in Laterano. Piazza San Giovanni in Laterano 4. ☎ **06-69886433.** Basilica, free; cloisters, 4,000L ($2). Summer, daily 7am–6:45pm (off-season to 6pm). Metro: San Giovanni.

This church—not St. Peter's—is the cathedral of the diocese of Rome. Catholics all over the world refer to it as their "mother church." Originally built in A.D. 314 by Constantine, the cathedral has suffered many vicissitudes and was forced to rebuild many times. The present structure is characterized by its 18th-century facade by Alessandro Galilei (statues of Christ and the Apostles ring the top). Borromini gets the credit—some say blame—for the interior, built for Innocent X. It's said that in the misguided attempt to redecorate, frescoes by Giotto were destroyed.

The most unusual sight is across the street at the "Palace of the Holy Steps," called the **Santuario della Scala Sancta,** Piazza San Giovanni in Laterano (☎ **06-70494619**). It's alleged that these were the actual steps that Christ climbed when he was brought before Pilate. These steps are supposed to be climbed only on your knees, which you're likely to see the faithful doing throughout the day. Visiting hours are daily 6:15am to noon and 3:30 to 6:30pm. Admission is free.

Basilica di Santa Maria Maggiore (Saint Mary the Great). Piazza Santa Maria Maggiore. ☎ **06-4881094.** Free admission. Daily 7am–7pm. Metro: Termini.

This great church was originally founded by Pope Liberius in A.D. 358 but was rebuilt by Pope Sixtus III in 432–40. Its campanile, erected in the 14th century, is the loftiest in the city. Much doctored in the 18th century, the facade is not an accurate reflection of the treasures inside. The basilica is especially noted for the 5th-century Roman mosaics in its nave, as well as for its coffered ceiling, said to have been gilded with gold brought from the New World. In the 16th century Domenico Fontana built a now-restored "Sistine Chapel." The church contains the tomb of Bernini, Italy's most important architect during the flowering of the baroque in the 17th century.

✪ **Museo Capitolino and Palazzo dei Conservatori.** Piazza del Campidoglio. ☎ **06-67102071.** Admission to both museum and palace 10,000L ($5) adults, 5,000L ($2.50) children 18 and under and seniors 60 and over. Tues–Sun 9am–7pm. Bus: 44, 81, 95, 160, 170, 715, or 780.

The Capitoline Museum was built in the 17th century, based on an architectural sketch by Michelangelo. In the first room is *The Dying Gaul,* a work of majestic skill; in a special gallery all her own is *The Capitoline Venus,* who demurely covers herself—this statue (a Roman copy of the Greek original) has been a symbol of feminine beauty and charm down through the centuries.

The famous statue of *Marcus Aurelius* is the only bronze equestrian statue to have survived from ancient Rome. It was retrieved from the Tiber where it had been tossed by marauding barbarians. For centuries it was thought to be a statue of Constantine the Great; this mistake protected it further, since papal Rome respected the memory of the first Christian emperor.

The **Palazzo dei Conservatori,** across the way, is rich in classical sculpture and paintings. In the courtyard are fragments of a colossal statue of Constantine. One of the most notable bronzes is the *Spinario* (little boy picking a thorn from his foot), a Greek classic from the 1st century B.C. In addition, you'll find *Lupa Capitolina* (Capitoline She-Wolf), a rare Etruscan bronze possibly from the 5th century B.C. (Romulus and Remus, the legendary twins that the she-wolf suckled, were added at a later date.)

✪ **Galleria Borghese.** Piazza Scipione Borghese, off Via Pinciano. ☎ **06-32010** for reservations, or 06-8417645 for information. Admission 12,000L ($6). Nov–Apr Tues–Sun 9am–7pm; May–Oct Tues–Sun 9am–9pm. Bus: 56 or 910. *Note:* No more than 300 visitors at a time are allowed on the ground floor, no more than 90 on the upper floor. Reservations are essential (call Mon–Fri 9am–6pm).

Closed for 14 years, this jewel box collection of masterworks is finally back. The masterpieces are displayed in what was once Borghese's summer residence. However, in spring 1997, after a complete restoration, it was back in all its fabulous glory. The bad news is that it may be hard to get in because of limited access (see above). This treasure trove of art includes such masterpieces as Bernini's *David, The Rape of Persephone,* and his *Apollo and Daphne;* Titian's *Sacred and Profane Love;* Raphael's *Deposition;* even Caravaggio's *Jerome.* One of the most viewed pieces of sculpture in today's gallery is Canova's life-size sculpture of Napoléon's sister, Pauline, in the pose of "Venus Victorious." When Pauline was asked if she felt uncomfortable about posing in the nude, she replied, "Why should I? The studio was heated."

Galleria Nazionale d'Arte Antica. Via delle Quattro Fontane 13. ☎ **06-4814430.** Admission 10,000L ($5). Tues–Sun 9am–10pm. Metro: Barberini.

Palazzo Barberini, right off piazza Barberini, is one of Rome's most magnificent baroque palaces. It was begun by Carlo Maderno in 1627 and completed in 1633 by Bernini, whose lavishly decorated rococo apartments are on view. The palace houses the Galleria Nazionale. On the first floor, a splendid array of paintings includes works that date from the 13th and 14th centuries, notably the *Mother and Child* by Simone Martini. Art from the 15th and 16th centuries include works by Filippo Lippi, Andrea Solario, Francesco Francia, Il Sodoma, and Raphael. Since 1998, you can visit a newly restored 18th-century apartment decorated with frescoes from the school of Barberini. Admission is 2,000L ($1), and hours are Tuesday to Sunday 9am to 10pm.

✪ **Museo Nazionale di Villa Giulia (Etruscan).** Piazzale di Villa Giulia 9. ☎ **06-3201951.** Admission 8,000L ($4). Tues–Sat 9am–7pm, Sun 9am–2pm. Metro: Flaminio. Tram: 225.

A 16th-century papal palace in the Villa Borghese shelters this priceless collection of art and artifacts of the mysterious Etruscans, who predated the Romans, and of whom little is known except for their sophisticated art and design. If you have time only for the masterpieces, head for Sala 7, which has a remarkable *Apollo* from Veio from the end of the 6th century B.C. (clothed, for a change). Two other widely acclaimed pieces of statuary in this gallery are *Dea con Bambino* (goddess with a baby) and a greatly mutilated, but still powerful, *Hercules* with a stag. In the adjoining Sala 8, you'll see the lions' sarcophagus from the mid–6th century B.C., which was excavated at Cerveteri, north of Rome. Finally, in Sala 9, is one of the world's most important Etruscan art treasures, the bride and bridegroom coffin from the 6th century B.C., also from Cerveteri.

Museo Nazionale Romano

Originally the museum occupied only the Diocletian Baths; today it's divided into four sections: Palazzo Massimo alle Terme; Terme di Diocleziano (Diocletian Baths) with the annex Octagonal Hall; and Palazzo Altemps.

Palazzo Massimo alle Terme. Largo di Villa Peretti 67. ☎ **06-489-035-00.** Admission 12,000L ($6) (ticket includes Diocletian Baths). Tues–Sun 9am–8pm. Last admission 1 hour before closing. Metro: Termini.

If you'd like to go wandering in a virtual garden of classical statues, head for this 19th-century palazzo built to resemble the patrician palaces from the baroque period. If you ever wanted to know what emperors looked like, this museum will make them live again, togas and all. In the central hall are works representing the political and social life of Rome at the time of Augustus. Other works include an altar from Ostia Antica, the ancient port of Rome, plus a statue of a wounded Niobid from 440 B.C. that is a masterwork of expression and character. Upstairs stand in awe at frescoes, stuccoes, and mosaics from the 1st century B.C. to the Imperial Age. The most celebrated mosaic is of the Four Charioteers. In the basement are a rare numismatic collection and an extensive collection of Roman jewelry.

Palazzo Altemps. Piazza San Apollinare 44. ☎ **06-489-035-00.** Admission 12,000L ($6). Tues–Fri 9am–9pm, Sat 9am–midnight, Sun 9am–8pm. Last admission 1 hour before closing. Metro: Termini.

This other branch of the National Roman Museum is housed in a 15th-century palace only a few steps from the Piazza Navona. It is home to the fabled Ludovisi Collection of Greek and Roman sculpture. Among the masterpieces of the Roman Renaissance, you'll find the *Ares Ludovisi,* a Roman copy of the original dated 330 B.C. and restored by Bernini. In the *Sala delle Storie di Mosè* is the *Ludovisi's Throne* representing the birth of Venus. The *Sala delle Feste* (The Celebrations' Hall) is dominated by *Grande Ludovisi,* a sarcophagus depicting the Romans fighting against the Ostrogoth Barbarians from the 2nd century A.D. Other outstanding art includes a 1st-century B.C. copy of Phidias's celebrated Athena that once stood in the Parthenon.

Terme di Diocleziano (Diocletian Bath) and the Aula Ottagona (Octagonal Hall). Viale E. di Nicola 79. ☎ **06-489-035-00.** Admission to the Baths 12,000L ($6) (ticket includes Palazzo Massimo alle Terme), Octagonal Hall, free. Tues–Fri 9am–2pm. Sat–Sun 9am–1pm. Last admission 1 hour before closing. Metro: Termini.

This museum occupies part of the 3rd-century A.D. baths of Diocletian and part of a convent that may have been designed by Michelangelo. The Diocletian baths were the biggest thermal baths in the world. Nowadays they host a marvelous collection of funereal art and decorations from the Aurelian period. The Octagonal Hall occupies the southwest corner of the central building. Here you can see the *Lyceum Apollo.* This statue was found in the area surrounding the Trajan Baths. Worthy of a note is the *Aphrodite of Cyrene,* discovered in Cyrene, Libya.

ORGANIZED TOURS

One of the leading tour operators (among the zillions of possibilities) is **American Express,** Piazza di Spagna 38 (☎ **06-67641;** Metro: Spagna), open Monday to Friday 9am to 5:30pm and Saturday 9am to 12:30pm. One popular tour is a 4-hour orientation tour of Rome and the Vatican, which departs most mornings at 9:30am and costs 70,000L ($35) per person. Another 4-hour tour, which focuses on ancient Rome (including visits to the Colosseum, the Roman Forum, the Imperial Palace, and the Church of San Pietro in Vincoli), costs 60,000L ($30). Outside Rome, a popular excursion April to October is a 5-hour bus tour to Tivoli, where visits are conducted of the Villa d'Este and its spectacular gardens and the ruins of the Villa Adriana, all for the price of 70,000L ($35) per person.

If your time in Italy is rigidly limited, you might opt for 1-day excursions to points farther afield on tours that are marketed (but not conducted) by American Express. A series of 1-day tours is offered to Pompeii, Naples, and Sorrento for 160,000L ($80) per person; to Florence for 190,000L ($95); and to Capri and Sorrento for 210,000L ($105). These trips, which include lunch, depart from Rome around 7am and return to your hotel sometime after 9 or 10pm.

THE SHOPPING SCENE

Shopping hours are generally Monday 3:30 to 7:30pm and Tuesday to Saturday 9:30 or 10am to 1pm and from 3:30 to 7 or 7:30pm. Some shops are open on Monday mornings, however, and some shops don't close for the afternoon break.

To Market, To Market

At the sprawling **Porta Portese** open-air flea market, held every Sunday morning, every peddler from Trastevere and the surrounding Castelli Romani sets up a temporary shop. Vendors sell merchandise ranging from secondhand paintings of Madonnas to pseudo-Etruscan hairpins. The flea market is near the end of Viale Trastevere (bus 75 to Porta Portese), then a short walk to Via Portuense. By 10:30am, the market is full of people. As you would at any street market, beware of pickpockets. Open Sunday 7am to 1pm.

THE BEST SHOPPING STREETS

The posh shopping streets **Via Borgognona** and **Via Condotti** begin near piazza di Spagna. For the most part, the merchandise on both is chic and very, very expensive. **Via Frattina** runs parallel to Via Condotti, its more famous sibling. Part of its length is closed to traffic; here, the concentration of shops is densest. **Via del Corso** doesn't have the image or the high prices of Via Condotti or Via Borgognona; the styles here are aimed at younger consumers. There're, however, some gems scattered amid the shops selling jeans and sporting equipment. The most interesting shops are on the section of the street nearest the fashionable cafes of piazza del Popolo.

Beginning at the top of the Spanish Steps, **Via Sistina** runs to piazza Barberini. The shops are small, stylish, and based on the personalities of their owners. The pedestrian traffic is less dense than on other major streets. Most shoppers reach **Via Francesco Crispi** by following Via Sistina 1 long block from the top of the Spanish Steps. Near the intersection of these streets are several shops full of unusual and less expensive gifts. Evocative of *La Dolce Vita* fame, **Via Veneto** is filled these days with expensive hotels and cafes and an array of relatively expensive stores selling shoes, gloves, and leather goods.

Traffic-clogged **Via Nazionale**—just crossing the street is no small feat—begins at piazza della Repubblica and runs down almost to piazza Venezia. Here you'll find an abundance of leather stores—more reasonable in price than those in many other parts of Rome—and a welcome handful of stylish boutiques.

Via dei Coronari, a good street for antiques, is buried in a colorful section of the Campus Martius, and is an antiquer's dream, literally lined with magnificent vases, urns, chandeliers, breakfronts, chaises, refectory tables, and candelabra. To find the entrance to the street, turn left out of the north end of piazza Navona, pass the excavated ruins of Domitian's Stadium, and the street will be just ahead of you. There are more than 40 antique stores in the next 4 blocks.

SOME SHOPS WORTH SEEKING OUT

Anatriello del Regalo, Via Frattina 123 (☎ **06-6789601;** Metro: Spagna), stocks new and antique silver, some of it quite unusual. New items are made by Italian silversmiths in designs ranging from the whimsical to the severely formal. **E. Fiore**, Via Ludovisi 31 (☎ **06-4819296;** Metro: Spagna), sells a wide assortment of charms, bracelets, necklaces, rings, brooches, and cameos. The store also carries elegant watches, silverware, and gold ware.

La Rinascente, Via del Corso 189 (☎ **06-6797691** at the Piazza Colonna; Metro: Barberini or Spagna), is Rome's most famous department store. Rather upscale, it has a little bit of everything: clothing, hosiery, perfume, cosmetics, housewares, and even furniture, plus its own line of clothing (Ellerre) for men, women, and children. At **Farnese,** Piazza Farnese 52 (☎ 06-6896109; bus: 64), you'll find Rome's most evocative collection of patterned tiles, which can be used on walls or floors. Motifs depict everything from the scenes of ancient Roman mosaics to the glazed tiles of Capodimonte in Naples.

Head to **Salvatore Ferragamo,** Via Condotti 73 (☎ 06-6798402; Metro: Spagna), for elegant footwear, women's clothing and accessories, and ties, in an atmosphere full of Italian style. Figure on a 30-minute wait outside. Ferragamo's male collection is a few steps away at Via Condotti 66 (☎ 06-678-1130). At **Emporio Armani,** Via del Babuino 140 (☎ 06-3600-2197; Metro: Spagna), you'll find moderately priced men's wear crafted by the couturier who has dressed more stage and screen stars than any other designer in Italy. The designer's more expensive line—sold at prices that are sometimes 30% less than what you'd pay in the United States—lies a short walk away, at **Giorgio Armani,** Via Condotti 77 (☎ 06-6991460; Metro: Spagna). **Saddlers Union,** Via Condotti 26 (☎ 06-6798050; Metro: Spagna), is a great place to look for well-crafted leather accessories—handbags, belts, wallets, shoes, briefcases, and other high-quality items.

ROME AFTER DARK

There're few evening diversions quite as pleasurable as a stroll past the solemn pillars of old temples or the cascading torrents of Renaissance fountains glowing under the blue-black sky. Of the **fountains,** the Naiads (piazza della Repubblica), the Tortoises (piazza Mattei), and, of course, the Trevi are particularly beautiful at night. The **Capitoline Hill** is magnificently lit after dark, with its Renaissance facades glowing like jewel boxes. Behind the Senatorial Palace is a fine view of the **Roman Forum.** If you're staying across the Tiber, **piazza San Pietro,** in front of St. Peter's Basilica, is impressive at night without tour buses and crowds. And a combination of illuminated architecture, Renaissance fountains, and, frequently, sidewalk shows and art expositions is at **piazza Navona.** If you're ambitious and have a good sense of direction, try exploring the streets to the west of piazza Navona, which look like a stage set when lit at night.

The minimagazines *Metropolitan* and *Wanted in Rome* have listings of jazz, rock, and such and give an interesting look at expatriate Rome. The daily *Il Messaggero* lists current cultural news, especially in its Thursday magazine supplement, *Metro.* And *Un Ospite a Roma,* available free from the concierge desks of top hotels, is full of details on what's happening. Even if you don't speak Italian, you can generally follow the listings featured in *TrovaRoma,* a special weekly entertainment supplement published in the newspaper *La Repubblica* on Thursday.

THE PERFORMING ARTS

If you're in the capital for the opera season, usually from December to June, you can attend a performance at the historic **Teatro dell'Opera (Rome Opera House),** located off Via Nazionale, at Piazza Beniamino Gigli 1 (☎ 06-481601; Metro: Repubblica). In the summer the venue switches to Piazza di Siena. The **Rome Opera Ballet** also performs at the Teatro dell'Opera. Look for announcements of classical concerts that take place in churches and other venues.

THE CLUB & MUSIC SCENE

Clubs are generally open Monday to Saturday from 9 or 10pm to 2 to 4am.

NIGHTCLUBS Arciliuto, Piazza Monte Vecchio 5 (☎ 06-6879419; bus: 70, 81, or 87), reputedly the former studio of Raphael, is one of the most romantic candlelit spots in Rome. From 10pm to 2am, Monday to Saturday guests enjoy a musical salon

A Meal & a Song

Roman rusticity is combined with theatrical flair at **Fantasie di Trastevere,** Via di Santa Dorotea 6 (☎ **06-5881671;** tram: 8, 20, 170, or 280), the "people's theater" where the famous actor Petrolini made his debut. Waiters dressed in regional garb serve with drama. The cuisine isn't subtle but is bountiful, and expect to pay 80,000L to 120,000L ($40 to $60) for a full meal; your first drink will cost 35,000L ($18). Some two dozen folk singers and musicians in regional costumes perform, making it a festive affair. Meals are served daily beginning at 8pm, and piano bar music is offered from 8:30 to 9:30pm, followed by the show, lasting until 10:30pm.

ambience, listening to a guitarist, a pianist, and a violinist. The evening's presentation also includes live Neapolitan songs, and new Italian madrigals, even current hits from Broadway or London's West End. Cover (including one drink) is 35,000L ($18). Closed July 20 to September 6.

JAZZ, SOUL & FUNK   Every night but Sunday **Alexanderplatz,** Via Ostia 9 (☎ **06-39742171;** tram: 907 or 991), features live jazz. There's also a good restaurant here that serves everything from gnocchi alla romana to Japanese cuisine. A 2-month membership costs 12,000L ($6). **Big Mama,** Vicolo San Francesco a Ripa 18 (☎ **06-5812551;** bus: 44, 75, or 170), is a hangout for jazz and blues musicians; you're likely to meet the up-and-coming jazz stars of tomorrow. Sometimes the big names appear as well. Closed June to September. No cover for minor shows, 20,000 to 30,000L ($10 to $15) for big acts, plus 20,000L ($10) for a seasonal membership.

Gilda, Via Mario dei Fiori 97 (☎ 06-6784838; Metro: Spagna), is an adventurous combination of nightclub, disco, and restaurant known for the glamorous acts it books. The artistic direction assures first-class shows, a well-run restaurant, and disco music played between the live musical acts. The restaurant and pizzeria open at 9:30pm and occasionally present shows. International cuisine is featured as well, meals begin at 45,000L ($23). The nightclub, opening at midnight, presents music of the 1960s as well as modern recordings. Cover (including 1 drink) is 40,000L ($20).

GAY & LESBIAN CLUBS

The Hangar, Via in Selci 69 (☎ **06-4881397;** Metro: Cavour), is the premier gay bar in Rome, on one of the city's oldest streets, adjacent to the Roman Forum. Women are welcome any night except Monday, when videos and entertainment for gay men are featured. The busiest nights are Saturday, Sunday, and Monday, when as many as 500 patrons cram inside. The Hangar is closed for 3 weeks in August. Open Wednesday to Monday 10:30pm to 2:30am. No cover, but there's a card membership of 3,000L ($1.50). **L'Alibi,** Via Monte Testaccio 44 (☎ **06-574-3448;** bus: 95), is a year-round venue on many a gay man's agenda, and is one of the hottest clubs in Rome. The crowd, however, tends to be mixed, both Roman and international, straight and gay, male and female. Music ranges from garage to '70s disco. One room is devoted to dancing. Open Thursday to Sunday 11pm to 4am. Cover is 25,000L ($13).

Angelo Azzuro, Via Cardinal Merry del Val 13 (☎ 06-5800472; bus: 44, 75, or 170), a gay "hot spot" deep in the heart of Trastevere, is open Friday to Sunday 11pm to 4am. No food is served, nor is there live music. Friday is for women only. Cover (including one drink) is 10,000L ($5) Friday and Sunday, 20,000L ($10) Saturday. **New Joli Coeur,** Via Sirte 5 (☎ **06-8621-6240;** bus: 38 or 58), in a seedy neighborhood, caters mainly to lesbians and is open on Saturday and Sunday 11pm to 5am only. Saturday night is reserved for women only, although Sunday the crowd can be mixed. Cover (including 1 drink) is 20,000L ($10).

SIDE TRIPS FROM ROME

TIVOLI   Tivoli, known as Tibur to the ancient Romans, was the playground of emperors. Today its reputation continues unabated: It's the most popular half-day jaunt from Rome.

While the ✪ **Villa d'Este,** Piazza Trento, Viale delle Cento Fontane (☎ **0774/ 312070),** is just a dank Renaissance palace with second-rate paintings that's hardly worth the trek from Rome, its gardens—designed by Pirro Ligorio—dim the luster of Versailles. Visitors descend a cypress-studded slope, and on their way are rewarded with everything from lilies to gargoyles spouting water, torrential streams, and waterfalls. The loveliest fountain—on this there's some agreement—is the **Fontana dell' Ovato,** designed by Ligorio. But nearby is the most spectacular achievement, the **hydraulic organ fountain,** dazzling visitors with its water jets in front of a baroque chapel, with four maidens who look tipsy. The best walk is along the promenade, which has 100 spraying fountains. Admission is 10,000L ($5). The villa opens Tuesday to Sunday at 9am; closing times vary according to the season (one hour before the sunset). From November to January it closes at 4pm; closing times may be as late as 6:45pm in high season.

Whereas the Villa d'Este dazzles with artificial glamour, **Villa Gregoriana,** Largo Sant'Angelo (☎ **0774/334522),** relies more on nature. The gardens were built by Pope Gregory XVI in the 19th century. At one point on the circuitous walk carved along a slope, visitors stand and look out onto Tivoli's most panoramic waterfall (Aniene). The trek to the bottom on the banks of the Anio is studded with grottoes and balconies that open onto the chasm. From one belvedere, there's a panoramic view of the Temple of Vesta on the hill. Admission is 3,500L ($1.75). It's open May to August daily 10am to 7:30pm; September daily 9:30am to 6:30pm; October to March daily 9:30am to 4:30pm; April daily 9:30am to 6pm.

Of all the Roman emperors dedicated to *la dolce vita,* the globetrotting Hadrian spent the last 3 years of his life in the grandest style. Less than 6.5km (4 miles) from Tivoli he built his great estate—the ✪ **Villa Adriana (Hadrian's Villa),** Via di Villa Adriana (☎ **0774/530203)**—and filled acre after acre with some of the architectural wonders he'd seen on his many trips. Hadrian directed the construction of much more than a villa—it's a self-contained world for a vast royal entourage, the guards required to protect them, and the hundreds of servants needed to bathe them, feed them, and satisfy their libidos. On the estate were theaters, baths, temples, fountains, gardens, and canals bordered with statuary. For a glimpse of what the villa once was, see the plastic reconstruction at the entrance. Admission is 8,000L ($4). Open daily 9am to sunset (about 7:30pm in summer, 4pm November to March).

Getting There   The town of Tivoli is 32km (20 miles) east of Rome on Via Tiburtina—about an hour's drive with traffic. You can also take public transportation: An autobus marked Tivoli leaves every 15 to 20 minutes during the day from Via Gaeta (west of via Volturno), near the Stazione Termini.

OSTIA ANTICA   This major attraction is particularly interesting to those who can't make it to Pompeii. At the mouth of the Tiber, it was the port of ancient Rome.

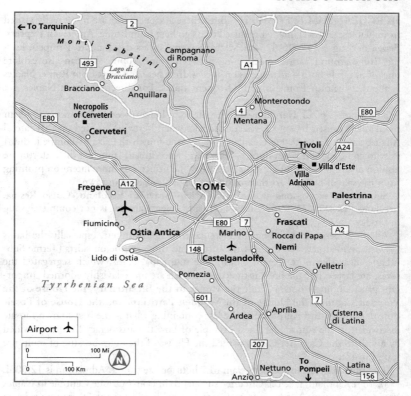

Through it were funneled riches from the far corners of the empire. It was founded in the 4th century B.C., and became a major port and naval base primarily under the emperors Claudius and Trajan. A thriving, prosperous city developed, full of temples, bathrooms, theaters, and patrician homes. Ostia Antica flourished for about 8 centuries before it began eventually to wither and the wholesale business of carting off its art treasures began.

Although a papal-sponsored commission launched a series of digs in the 19th century, the major work of unearthing was carried out under Mussolini's orders from 1938 to 1942. The city is only partially dug out today, but it's believed that all the chief monuments have been uncovered.

All the principal monuments are clearly labeled. The most important spot in all the ruins is **Piazzale delle Corporazioni,** an early version of Wall Street. Near the theater, this square contained nearly 75 corporations; the nature of their businesses was identified by the patterns of preserved mosaics.

Ostia Antica is entered on Viale dei Romagnoli 717 (☎ **06-56358099**). Admission is 8,000L ($4). Open Tuesday to Sunday 9am to 6pm.

Getting There   Take the Metro to the Magliana stop, then change for the Lido train to Ostia Antica, about 26km (16 miles) from Rome. Departures are about every half hour, and the trip takes only 20 minutes. The train lets you off across the highway that connects Rome with the coast. It's just a short walk to the excavations.

HERCULANEUM & POMPEII   Both these ancient sights are more easily visited from Naples; however, many organized tours go here from Rome. **American Express,** Piazza di Spagna (☎ **06-67641;** Metro: Spagna) offers day tours to Pompeii, leaving Rome around 7am and returning between 9 and 10pm. You can also explore one—but rarely both—attractions on a day's drive here and back from Rome. Naples is about 2¹/₂ hours from Rome by frequent trains. For directions from Naples, see below.

The builders of ✪ **Herculaneum** (Ercolano in Italian) were still working to repair the damage caused by an A.D. 62 earthquake when Vesuvius erupted on that fateful August day in A.D. 79. Herculaneum, about one-fourth the size of Pompeii, didn't start to come to light again until 1709, when Prince Elbeuf launched the unfortunate fashion of tunneling through it for treasures. The prince was more intent on profiting from the sale of objets d'art than in uncovering a dead Roman town.

Subsequent excavations at the site, **Ufficio Scavi di Ercolano,** Corso Resina, Ercolano (☎ **081/7390963**), have been slow. Herculaneum is not completely dug out today.

All the streets and buildings of Herculaneum hold interest, especially the baths (*terme*), divided between those at the forum and those on the outskirts (Terme Suburbane, near the more elegant villas). The municipal baths, which segregated the sexes, are larger, but the ones at the edge of town are more lavishly adorned. Important private homes to see include the **House of the Bicentenary,** the **House of the Wooden Cabinet,** the **House of the Wooden Partition,** and the **House of Poseidon (Neptune) and Amphitrite,** the last containing what is the best-known mosaic discovered in the ruins. The finest example of how the aristocracy lived is provided by a visit to the **Casa dei Cervi,** named the House of the Stags because of sculpture found inside.

The ruins may be visited daily 9am to 1 hour before sunset. Admission is 12,000L ($6). To reach them, take the Circumvesuviana train from Stazione Centrale in Naples leaving about every half hour from Corso Garibaldi 387 for the 20-minute ride; or take bus 255 from Piazza Municipio. The excavations are a short walk from the train station. Otherwise, it's a 7km (4¹/₂-mile) drive on the autostrada to Salerno (turn off at Ercolano).

When Vesuvius erupted in A.D. 79, Pliny the Younger, who later recorded the event, thought the end of the world had come. Lying 24km (15 miles) south of Naples, the ruined Roman city of ✪ **Pompeii** (Pompei in Italian) has been dug out from the inundation of volcanic ash and pumice stone. At the excavations, the life of 19 centuries ago is vividly experienced.

The **Ufficio Scavi di Pompei** is entered at Piazza Esedra (☎ **081/8610744**). The most elegant of the patrician villas, the **House of Vettii** has a courtyard, statuary (such as a two-faced Janus), paintings, and a black-and-red Pompeiian dining room frescoed with cupids. The second important villa, the **House of Mysteries** (Villa dei Misteri) near the Herculaneum Gate (Porto Ercolano), lies outside the walls. What makes the villa exceptional are its remarkable frescoes. The **House of the Faun** (Casa del Fauno), so called because of a bronze statue of a dancing faun found there, takes up a city block and has four different dining rooms and two spacious peristyle gardens. In the center of town is the **Forum**—although rather small, it was the heart of Pompeiian life.

Pompeii's ruins may be visited daily 9am to 1 hour before sunset. Admission is 12,000L ($6). From Stazione Centrale in Naples, take the Sorrento-bound Circumvesuviana train leaving about every half hour and get off at the Pompei Scavi station; the excavations are across from the station.

2 Florence

No other city in Europe, with the exception of Venice, lives off its past in the way Florence does. The Renaissance began here. Florence is a bit foreboding and architecturally severe; many of its palazzi (palaces), as was the Medici style, look like fortresses. But you must remember that when these structures were built the aim was to keep foreign enemies at bay. And these facades guard treasures within, as the thousands of visitors who overrun the narrow streets know and appreciate.

Since the 19th century, Florence has been visited by seemingly half the world—the city has impressed some hard-to-impress people, including Mark Twain, who found it overwhelmed with "tides of color that make all the sharp lines dim and faint and turn the old city to a city of dreams."

It may appear that Florence is caught in a time warp—a Medici returning to the city from the past would have no trouble finding his way around. But Florence virtually pulsates with modern life. Students racing to and from the university quarter add vibrancy to the city, and it's amusing to watch the way many local businesspeople avoid the city's impossible traffic today, whizzing by on Vespas past cars stalled in traffic.

Florentines like to present *una bella figura* (a good appearance) to the rest of the world and are incredibly upset when that appearance is attacked, as in the case of the May 1993 bombing of the Uffizi. The entire city rallied to reopen this treasure trove of Renaissance art.

Try to visit this city, even on the most rushed of European itineraries. There's nothing like it anywhere else. Venice and Rome are too different from Florence to invite meaningful comparisons. Florence is also an ideal base from which to explore Tuscany. Though increasingly built up, Tuscany has enough old hill towns and rolling hills studded with olives and grapevines to attract the romantic. Florence and Siena are the chief drawing cards, but Fiesole and Pisa also have their allure.

ORIENTATION

ARRIVING By Plane If you're flying from New York, a much flown route is Rome, where you can board a domestic flight to the **Galileo Galilei Airport** at Pisa (☎ **050-500707**), 93km (58 miles) west of Florence. **Air Europe** (☎ **888/ 999-9090;** www.aireurope.it) also offers six flights a week from New York to Pisa. You can then take an express train for the hour-long trip to Florence. There's also a small domestic airport, **Amerigo Vespucci,** on Via del Termine, near A-11 (☎ **055-30615**), 6km (3½ miles) northwest of Florence, a 15-minute drive. This airport can be reached by ATAF bus 62, departing from the main Santa Maria Novella rail terminal. Domestic air service is provided by **Alitalia,** with offices at Lungarno degli Acciaiuoli 10–12 in Florence (☎ **055-27881**).

By Train If you're coming north from Rome, count on a 2- to 3-hour trip, depending on your connection. **Santa Maria Novella rail station,** in Piazza della Stazione, adjoins Piazza di Santa Maria Novella. For railway information, call ☎ **055-2351.** Some trains into Florence stop at the **Stazione Campo di Marte,** on the eastern side of Florence. A 24-hour bus service (91) runs between the two rail terminals.

By Bus Long-distance buses service Florence, run by **SITA,** Viale Cadorna 105 (☎ **055-483651**), and **Lazzi Eurolines,** via Mercadante 2 (☎ **055-363041**). Both SITA and Lazzi Eurolines offer transfers from Florence to Arezzo, Pisa, and San Gimignano. A one-way ticket from Florence to Arezzo, for example, costs 11,000L ($6). If you're traveling on SITA, and you want to go to Pisa, the one-way fare is 20,000L ($10), but you'll have to call SITA 3 days in advance to reserve a seat.

Florence

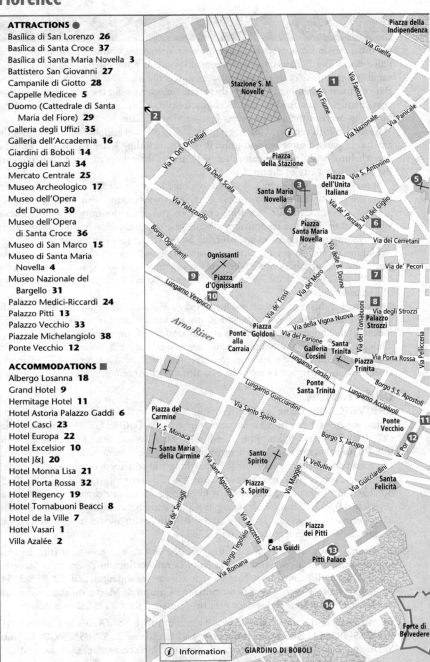

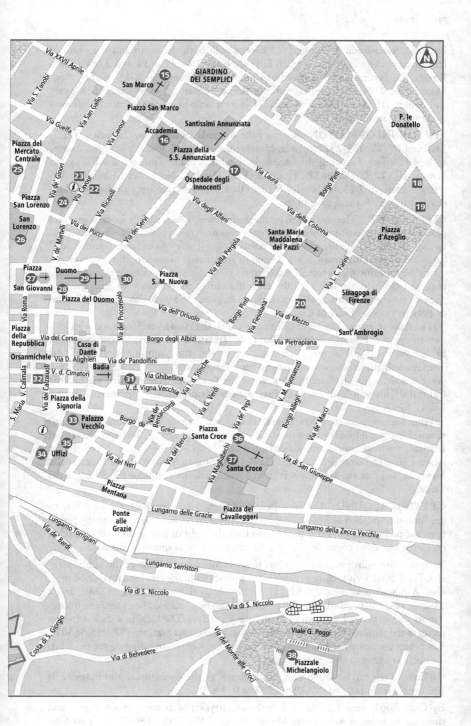

N

Via XXVII Aprile

Via S. Zanobi

Via San Gallo

Via Guelfa

Via Cavour

15 San Marco ✝

GIARDINO DEI SEMPLICI

Piazza San Marco

Accademia **16**

Santissimi Annunziata

Piazza della S.S. Annunziata

P. le Donatello

Piazza del Mercato Centrale **25**

Via de' Ginori

23

ⓘ Via Cavour **22**

17 Via Laura

Ospedale degli Innocenti

Borgo Pinti

18

Piazza San Lorenzo **24**

San Lorenzo **26**

V. de' Martelli

Via Ricasoli

Via dei Pucci

Via de' Servi

Via degli Alfani

Via della Colonna

Via L. C. Farini

19

Piazza d'Azeglio

Santa Maria Maddalena dei Pazzi ✝

Piazza San Giovanni **27**

Duomo **29** ✝

28

Piazza del Duomo

30

Via del Proconsolo

Piazza S. M. Nuova

Via della Pergola

21

20

Sinagoga di Firenze

Via Roma

Via dell'Oriuolo

Borgo Pinti

Via Fiesolana

Via di Mezzo

Sant'Ambrogio

Piazza della Repubblica

Via del Corso

Orsanmichele

Casa di Dante

Via D. Alighieri

Badia ✝

V. d. Cimatori

32

Via dei Calzaiuoli

S. Maria V. Calimala

Borgo degli Albizi

Via Pietrapiana

Via de' Pandolfini

Via Ghibellina

31

V. d. Vigna Vecchia

Via I. d. Stinche

Via G. Verdi

Via de' Pepi

V. M. Buonarroti

Borgo Allegri

Via de' Macci

Piazza della Signoria

33 Palazzo Vecchio

35

34 Uffizi

Borgo de' Greci

Via de' Bentaccordi

Via dei Benci

Piazza Santa Croce **36**

37

Via Magliabechi

Santa Croce

Via di San Giuseppe

Piazza Mentana

ⓘ

Lungarno delle Grazie

Piazza dei Cavalleggeri

Ponte alle Grazie

Lungarno Torrigiani

Via de' Bardi

Lungarno della Zecca Vecchia

Lungarno Serristori

Via di S. Niccolo

Via di S. Niccolo

Costa di S. Giorgio

Via del Monte alle Croci

Via di Belvedere

Viale G. Poggi

38 Piazzale Michelangiolo

By Car **Autostrada A-1** connects Florence with both the north and the south of Italy. It takes about an hour to reach Florence from Bologna and about 3 hours from Rome. The Tyrrhenian coast is only an hour from Florence on **A-11** heading west. Florence lies 277km (172 miles) north of Rome, 105km (65 miles) west of Bologna, and 298km (185 miles) south of Milan. Use a car only to get to Florence. Don't even contemplate its use once here.

VISITOR INFORMATION Contact the **Azienda Promozione Turistica,** Via A. Manzoni 16 (☎ 055-23220), open Monday to Saturday 8:30am to 1:30pm. Another helpful office, handling data about both Florence and Tuscany, is **APT** at Via Cavour 1R (☎ **055-290832**). Hours here are March to November Monday to Saturday 8:15am to 7:15pm, Sunday 8:15am to 1:45pm; November to February Monday to Saturday 8:15am to 1:45pm.

CITY LAYOUT The city is split by the **Arno River,** which usually looks serene and peaceful but can turn ferocious with floodwaters on rare occasions. The major monumental and historical core lies on the north ("right") side of the river. But the "left" side—called the **Oltrarno**—is not devoid of attractions. Many long-time visitors frequent the Oltrarno for its tantalizing trattoria meals; they also maintain that the shopping here is less expensive. Even the most hurried visitor will want to cross over the Arno to see the Pitti Palace with its many art treasures and walk through the Giardini di Boboli, a series of formal gardens.

The Arno is spanned by eight bridges, of which the **Ponte Vecchio,** lined with jewelry stores, is the most celebrated. **Ponte S. Trinità** is the second-most important bridge spanning the Arno. After crossing it you can continue along **Via dei Tornabuoni,** the most important right-bank shopping street. At the Ponte Vecchio you can walk, again on the right bank, along **Via Por Santa Maria,** which will become Calimala. This will lead you into **Piazza della Repubblica,** a commercial district known for its cafes.

From here, you can take **Via Roma,** which leads directly into **Piazza di San Giovanni.** Here you'll find the baptistery and its neighboring sibling, the larger **Piazza del Duomo,** with the world-famous cathedral and bell tower by Giotto. From the far western edge of Piazza del Duomo, **Via del Proconsolo** heads south to **Piazza della Signoria,** sight of the landmark Palazzo Vecchio and its sculpture-filled Loggia dei Lanzi.

GETTING AROUND **On Foot** Because Florence is so compact, the ideal way to get around town is on foot—at times it's the only way, because there're so many pedestrian zones. In theory at least, pedestrians have the right of way at uncontrolled zebra crossings, but don't count on that should you encounter a speeding Vespa.

By Bus You must purchase your bus ticket before boarding one of the public vehicles. For 1,500L (75¢), you can ride on any public bus in the city for a total of 60 minutes. A 3-hour pass costs 2,500L ($1.25), a 4-hour ticket is 5,800L ($2.90), and a 24-hour pass costs 7,500L ($3.75). Bus tickets can be purchased from *tabacchi* (tobacconists shops, marked by a white T) and news vendors. The local bus station (which serves as the terminal for ATAF city buses) is at Piazza della Stazione (☎ **055-56501**). Bus routes are posted at bus stops, but inquire the day you're riding to get exact bus numbers as they can change overnight.

By Taxi Taxis can be found at stands at nearly all the major squares in Florence. If you need a radio taxi, call ☎ **055-4390** or 055-4798.

By Car You'll need a car to explore the countryside of Tuscany in any depth, and these are available at **Avis,** Borgo Ognissanti 128R (☎ **055-213629**); **Italy by Car,**

Borgo Ognissanti 134R (☎ **055-287161**); and **Hertz,** Via del Termine 1 (☎ **055-307370**).

By Bicycle or Motorscooter   **Alinari** is near the rail station at Via Guelfa 85R (☎ **055-280500**). Depending on the model of bike you rent, it will cost 4,000 to 5,000L ($2 to $2.50) per hour or 20,000 to 30,000L ($10 to $15) per day. If you want to rent a scooter, it costs 15,000L ($8) per hour, 50,000L ($25) for 5 hours, or 80,000L ($40) per day.

Fast Facts: Florence

American Express   Amex is at Via Dante Alighieri 22R (☎ **055-50981**), open Monday to Friday 9am to 5:30pm and Saturday 9am to 12:30pm.

Business Hours   From mid-June to mid-September most shops and businesses are open Monday to Friday 9am to 1pm and 4 to 8pm. Off-season hours, in general, are Monday 3:30 to 7:30pm and Tuesday to Saturday 9am to 1pm and 3:30 to 7:30pm.

Consulates   The Consulate of the **United States** is at Lungarno Amerigo Vespucci 38 (☎ **055-2398276**), open Monday to Friday 9am to 12:30pm and 2 to 3:30pm. The Consulate of the **United Kingdom** is at Lungarno Corsini 2 (☎ **055-284133**), near Piazza Santa Trinità, open Monday to Friday 9:30am to 12:30pm and 2:30 to 4:30pm. Citizens of Australia, Canada, and New Zealand should consult their missions in Rome (see above).

Currency Exchange   Local banks in Florence grant the best rates. Most banks are open Monday to Friday 8:30am to 1:30pm and 2:45 to 3:45pm. The tourist office (see "Orientation," above) exchanges money at official rates when banks are closed and on holidays, but a commission is often charged. You can also go to the Ufficio Informazione booth at the rail station, open daily 7:30am to 7:40pm. See "Fast Facts: Rome" for the exchange rate used in this chapter.

Dentists/Doctors   For a list of English-speaking dentists, consult your consulate if possible or contact **Tourist Medical Service,** Via Lorenzo il Magnifico 59 (☎ **055-475411**). Visits without an appointment are possible Monday to Friday 11am to noon and 5 to 6pm. After hours, an answering service gives names and phone numbers of dentists and doctors on duty.

Emergencies   For fire, call ☎ **115;** for an ambulance, call ☎ **118;** for the police, ☎ **113;** and for road service, ☎ **116.**

Hospitals   Call the **General Hospital of Santa Maria Nuova,** Piazza Santa Maria Nuova 1 (☎ **055-27581**).

Internet Access   You can check your messages or send e-mail at **Internet Train,** Via dell'Orvio 25R (☎ **055-234-5322;** e-mail: info@fionline.it; www.fionline.it).

Police   Dial ☎ **113** in an emergency. Foreigners who want to see and talk to the police should go to the Ufficio Stranieri station at Via Zara 2 (☎ **055-49771**), where English-speaking personnel are available daily 9am to 2pm.

Post Office   The Central Post Office is at Via Pellicceria 3, off Piazza della Repubblica (☎ **055-2774539;** 055-2774322 for English-speaking operators). It's open Monday to Saturday 8:15am to 7pm. Stamps are purchased in the main post office at windows 21–22. If you want your mail sent to Italy general delivery (*fermo posta*), have it sent in care of this post office (use the 50100 Firenze postal code). Mail can be picked up at windows 23–24.

Safety Violent crimes are rare in Florence; crime consists mainly of pickpockets who frequent crowded tourist centers, such as the corridors of the Uffizi Galleries. Members of group tours who cluster together are often singled out as victims. Car thefts are relatively common: Don't leave your luggage in an unguarded car, even if it's locked in the trunk. Women should be especially careful in avoiding purse snatchers, some of whom grab a purse while whizzing by on a Vespa, often knocking the woman down. Documents such as passports and extra money are better stored in the safe at your hotel.

Telephones The **country code** for Italy is **39.** The **city code** for Florence is **055,** which is the code you'll use every time you dial a party located within Florence, regardless of whether you're within the city limits or not. We emphasize that newly imposed technologies will require the use of the "0" and then "55" for calls to parties in Florence, regardless of whether you're within the city limits or not. For additional information, see "Fast Facts: Rome," above.

WHERE TO STAY
NEAR THE DUOMO
Expensive

✪ **Hotel J and J.** Via di Mezzo 20, 50121 Firenze. ☎ **055-2345005.** Fax 055-240282. www.jandjhotel.com. E-mail: jandj@dada.it. 20 units. A/C MINIBAR TV TEL. 450,000L ($225) double; 550,000L ($275) junior suite; 630,000–680,000L ($315–$340) suite. Rates include buffet breakfast. AE, DC, MC, V. Parking 50,000L ($25). Bus: A.

This charming hotel was built in the 16th century as a monastery. It's 5-minute walk from the church of Santa Croce. You'll find many a flagstone-covered courtyard and a salon with vaulted ceilings and several preserved ceiling frescoes. Rooms combine an unusual mixture of modern furniture with the monastery's original beamed ceilings. Suites usually contain sleeping lofts and, in some cases, rooftop balconies overlooking the historic core.

Hotel Monna Lisa. Borgo Pinti 27, 50121 Firenze. ☎ **055-2479751.** Fax 055-2479755. www.monnalisa.it. E-mail: monnalis@ats.it. 30 units. A/C MINIBAR TV TEL. 350,000–500,000L ($175–$250) double; 430,000–620,000L ($215–$310) triple. Rates include breakfast. AE, DC, MC, V. Parking 20,000L ($10). Bus: A, 6, 31, or 32.

Hotel Monna Lisa (yes, that's the right spelling) is a privately owned Renaissance palazzo, 4 blocks east of the Duomo. Most of the great old rooms overlook either an inner patio or a modest rear garden. Each of the salons is handsomely furnished. Rooms vary greatly—some are quite large, though no two are alike.

Hotel Porta Rossa. Via Porta Rossa 19. 50123 Firenze. ☎ **055-287551.** Fax 055-282179. 79 units. A/C MINIBAR TV TEL. 285,000L ($143) double; 355,000–410,000L ($178–$205) suite for 3 or 4. Rates include breakfast. AE, DC, MC, V. Parking 40,000–55,000L ($20–$28). Bus: A.

The hotel occupies the top three floors of a six-story building. Reportedly, this is the second oldest hotel in Italy, dating from 1386. The place is a bit dark, but on a hot Tuscan summer day you welcome that in lieu of air conditioning. Since it isn't as well known or publicized as some of its competitors such as the Hermitage or Tornabuoni, you stand a better chance for getting a reservation. In spite of its antiquity, the hotel has kept abreast of the times, installing modern conveniences, good beds, and ample bathrooms. The managers have resisted making two new rooms out of one of the old spacious ones from centuries ago. Breakfast is the only meal served, and a little terrace offers a panoramic view.

NEAR THE PONTE VECCHIO
Moderate

Hermitage Hotel. Vicolo Marzio 1, Piazza del Pesce I, 50122 Firenze. ☎ **055-287216.** Fax 055-212208. www.venere.it/firenze/hermitage/hermitage_it.html. E-mail: florence@ hermitagehotel.com. 29 units. A/C TV TEL. 300,000–350,000L ($150–$175) double; 350,000–400,000L ($175–$200) triple; 500,000L ($250) family room. Rates include breakfast. MC, V. Parking 30,000–40,000L ($15–$20). Bus: B.

The offbeat, intimate Hermitage is a charming place, with a sun terrace on the roof providing a view. You can take your breakfast under a leafy arbor surrounded by potted roses and geraniums. The extremely small rooms are pleasantly furnished. Bathrooms are superb and contain lots of gadgets. Some recently restored ones have hydro massage tubs. Those rooms overlooking the Arno offer the most scenic view, and they've been fitted with double-glazed windows, which reduces the traffic noise by 40%.

NEAR PIAZZA SANTA TRINITÀ
Moderate

Hotel Tornabuoni Beacci. Via Tornabuoni 3, 50123 Firenze. ☎ **055-212645.** Fax 055-283594. www.italyhotel.com. E-mail: beacci.tornabuoni@italyhotel.com. 30 units. A/C MINIBAR TV TEL. 340,000–370,000L ($170–$185) double. Rates include buffet breakfast. AE, DC, MC, V. Parking 40,000L ($20). Bus: B, 6, 11, or 36.

Near the Arno and Piazza S. Trinità, on the principal shopping street, this pensione occupies the top three floors of a 14th-century palazzo. The public rooms have been furnished in a tatty provincial style. The hotel was completely renovated recently, but it still bears an air of old-fashioned gentility. The rooms are moderately well furnished. The roof terrace, surrounded by potted plants and flowers, is for breakfast or late-afternoon drinks. Dinner, typically Florentine and Italian dishes, is served here in summer, except in August when the restaurant is closed. The view of the nearby churches, towers, and rooftops is worth experiencing.

NEAR PIAZZA SAN LORENZO & THE MERCATO CENTRALE
Inexpensive

Hotel Casci. Via Cavour 13, 50129 Firenze. ☎ **055-211686.** Fax 055-2396461. www.emmeti.it/casci.html. E-mail: casci@italyhotel.com. 25 units. A/C TV TEL. 190,000L ($95) double; 255,000L ($128) triple; 320,000L ($160) quad. Rates include buffet breakfast. AE, DC, MC, V. Parking 35,000–40,000L ($18–$20). Bus: 1, 7, 25, or 33.

Casci is a well-run little hotel, 100m (110 yards) from Piazza del Duomo and 200m (220 yards) from the main rail station. The building dates from the 14th century, and some of the public rooms feature frescoes. The hotel is both traditional and modern, and the English-speaking reception staff is attentive. Rooms are comfortably furnished. Each year four or five are upgraded and renovated.

Hotel Europa. Via Cavour 14, 50129 Firenze. ☎ **055-210361.** Fax 055-210361. 13 units. A/C TV TEL. 180,000L ($90) double; 240,000L ($120) triple. Rates include buffet breakfast. AE, MC, V. Parking 30,000–40,000L ($15–$20) in nearby garage. Bus: 1, 7, 25, or 33.

Two long blocks north of the Duomo, this 16th-century building has functioned as a family-run hotel since 1925. Homey touches remind newcomers of its ongoing administration by members of the Gassim family. All but four rooms overlook the back and usually open onto a view of the campanile and dome of the Duomo. Those that face the street are noisier but benefit from double-glazing that keeps out at least some of the traffic noises.

NEAR PIAZZA SANTA MARIA NOVELLA & THE TRAIN STATION
Expensive
Hotel Astoria Palazzo Gaddi. Via del Giglio 9, 50123 Firenze. ☎ **055-2398095.** Fax 055-214632. 106 units. A/C MINIBAR TV TEL. 490,000–540,000L ($245–$270) double; from 700,000L ($350) suite. Rates include buffet breakfast. AE, DC, MC, V. Parking 40,000L ($20) nearby. Bus: 4.

In spite of its location in a setting of cheap railroad station hotels, this is an impressive Renaissance palace still containing 16th-century frescoes by Luca Giordano. In the 17th century, John Milton wrote parts of *Paradise Lost* in one of the rooms. The Astoria has been renovated and turned into a serviceable and enduring choice, with a helpful staff. From the rooms on the upper floors, you'll have a view over the rooftops. Rooms have stylish traditional furnishings for the most part; some are decorated in more modern style. Inside the hotel is a well-known restaurant, Palazzo Gaddi, offering excellent Tuscan and Italian dishes. In summer on the roof garden, you can order drinks and a wide choice of cold dishes, salads, and sandwiches while taking in a panoramic view.

Hotel de la Ville. Piazza Antinori 1, 50123 Firenze. ☎ **055-2381805.** Fax 055-2381809. www.hoteld.aville.it. E-mail: info@hoteld.aville.it. 79 units. A/C MINIBAR TV TEL. 450,000–560,000L ($225–$280) double; 650,000–850,000L ($325–$425) suite. Rates include buffet breakfast. AE, DC, MC, V. Parking 45,000–50,000L ($23–$25). Bus: 6, 11, 36, 37, or 68.

On the most elegant street of the historic center, close to the Arno and the rail station, this recently refurbished hotel has a loyal following among Italian business travelers. It has a conservatively contemporary appearance. Rooms are soundproof and have safes. There's an American bar, a breakfast room, and a parking area reserved for guests. Laundry and baby-sitting are available. Guests have access to a nearby pool in the private club, Parco delle Cascine.

Moderate
Villa Azalée. Viale Fratelli Rosselli 44, 50123 Firenze. ☎ **055-214242.** Fax 055-268264. E-mail: villaazalee@fi.flashnet.it. 25 units. A/C MINIBAR TV TEL. 268,000L ($134) double; 360,000L ($180) triple. Rates include buffet breakfast. AE, DC, MC, V. Parking from 35,000L ($18) nearby. Bus: 80.

Villa Azalée, set on a street corner with a big garden, is a private home built in the 1860s and transformed into a hotel in 1964 with an annex added. The decorating is tasteful. Rooms have distinction (one boasts a flouncy canopy bed). The hotel is a 5-minute walk from the rail station. You can rent bicycles at the hotel for 5,000L ($2.50) per day.

Inexpensive
Hotel Vasari. Via B. Cennini 9–11, 50123 Firenze. ☎ **055-212753.** Fax 055-294246. 27 units. A/C MINIBAR TV TEL. 230,000L ($115) double. Rates include breakfast. AE, DC, MC, V. Parking 20,000L ($10). Bus: 4, 7, 10, 13, 14, 23, or 71.

Built in the 1840s as a private home, this was a rundown two-star hotel until 1993, when its owners upgraded it to one of the most fairly priced three-star hotels in town. Its three stories are somewhat Spartan.

ON PIAZZA OGNISSANTI
Piazza Ognissanti is a fashionable but car-clogged Renaissance square opening onto the Arno. It's home to two of the most legendary hotels in the city (see below).

Very Expensive

Grand Hotel. Piazza Ognissanti 1, 50123 Firenze. ☎ **800/325-3589** in the U.S. and Canada, or 055-288781. Fax 055-217400. www.firenzealbergo.it/home/grandhotel. E-mail: info@theluxurycollection.firenze.net. 107 units. A/C MINIBAR TV TEL. 750,000–950,000L ($375–$475) double; from 1,520,000L ($760) suite. AE, DC, MC, V. Parking from 60,000L ($30). Bus: 6 or 17.

The Grand is a bastion of luxury, although neither it nor the Excelsior (see below) are as exclusive as the Regency (see below). A hotel of history and tradition, the Grand is known for its halls and salons. Rooms and suites have a refined elegance, and the most desirable overlook the Arno. A highlight of the hotel is the Winter Garden, an enclosed court lined with arches where regional and international dishes are served.

Hotel Excelsior. Piazza Ognissanti 3, 50123 Firenze. ☎ **800/325-3535** in the U.S. and Canada, or 055-264201. Fax 055-210278. www.firenzealbergo.it/home/excelsior. E-mail: info@theluxurycollection.firenze.net. 191 units. A/C MINIBAR TV TEL. 680,000–770,000L ($340–$385) double; from 1,100,000L ($550) junior suite. AE, DC, MC, V. Parking 60,000L ($30). Bus: 6 or 17.

The Excelsior, a former patrician mansion, is the ultimate in luxury. Cosmopolitan and sophisticated, it has the best-trained staff in town. If you like glamour and glitz, stay here. The opulent rooms have 19th-century Florentine antiques and sumptuous fabrics. Some of the more desirable rooms open onto views of the Arno. In these old palaces, expect the accommodations to come in a variety of configurations. Il Cestello, the hotel's deluxe restaurant, attracts an upper-crust clientele.

ON OR NEAR PIAZZA MASSIMO D'AZEGLIO

Piazza Massimo d'Azeglio is a 12-minute walk northeast of the historic core of Florence.

Very Expensive

○ **Hotel Regency.** Piazza Massimo d'Azeglio 3, 50121 Firenze. ☎ **055-245247.** Fax 055-2346735. www.regency-hotel.com. E-mail: info@regency-hotel.com. 34 units. A/C MINIBAR TV TEL. 620,000–720,000L ($310–$360) double; from 970,000L ($485) suite. Rates include buffet breakfast. AE, DC, MC, V. Parking 50,000L ($25). Bus: 6, 31, or 32.

The Regency is an intimate villa of taste and exclusivity. This well-built old-style villa, a member of Relais & Châteaux, has its own garden across from a park in a residential area. It's a luxurious hideaway, filled with stained glass, paneled walls, and reproduction antiques, and offers exquisitely furnished rooms. The dining room, Relais le Jardin, is renowned for its *alta cucina.*

Inexpensive

Albergo Losanna. Via Vittorio Alfieri 9, 50121 Firenze. ☎ and fax **055-245840.** 8 units (3 with bathroom). TEL. 95,000L ($48) double without bathroom; 130,000L ($65) double with bathroom. Rates include breakfast. AE, MC, V. Parking 30,000–35,000L ($15–$18). Bus: 6.

A good choice, Albergo Losanna is a tiny family run place off Viale Antonio Gramsci, between Piazzale Donatello and Piazza Massimo d'Azeglio. It offers utter simplicity and cleanliness. Rooms are homey and well kept, but the furnishings are simple and a bit tired.

WHERE TO DINE
NEAR THE DUOMO
Inexpensive

Il Cavallino. Piazza della Signoria, Via della Farine 6R. ☎ **055-215818.** Reservations recommended. Main courses 15,000–28,000L ($8–$14); fixed-price menu 32,000L ($16). AE, DC, MC, V. Mar–Oct daily noon–3pm and 7–10:30pm; off-season Thurs–Tues noon–3pm and Thurs–Mon 7–10:30pm. Bus: A or B. TUSCAN/ITALIAN.

A local favorite since the 1930s, Il Cavallino is the kind of discreetly famous restaurant where Florentines invariably go to be with one another. It's on a tiny street (which probably won't even be on your map) that leads off piazza della Signoria at its northern end, not far from the equestrian statue. There's usually a gracious reception at the door, especially if you've called ahead for a reservation. Two of the three dining rooms have vaulted ceilings and peach-colored marble floors. The main room looks out over the piazza. Menu items are typical hearty Tuscan fare, including an assortment of boiled meats in green herb sauce, grilled fillet of steak, breast of chicken Medici style, and the inevitable Florentine spinach.

Paoli. Via dei Tavolini 12R. ☎ **055-216215.** Reservations required. Main courses 16,000–40,000L ($8–$20). AE, DC, MC, V. Wed–Mon noon–2:30pm and 7–10:30pm. Closed 3 weeks in Aug. Bus: A. TUSCAN/ITALIAN.

Paoli, housed in a building from 1824 between the Duomo and piazza della Signoria, is one of Florence's finest restaurants. It turns out a host of specialties, but could be recommended almost solely for its medieval-tavern atmosphere, with arches and ceramics stuck into the walls like medallions. All pastas are homemade, and the fettuccine alla Paoli is served piping hot and full of flavor. The chef also does a superb *rognoncino trifolato* (thinly sliced kidney cooked with oil, garlic, and parsley) and sole meunière. A recommendable side dish is *piselli* (garden peas) in the Florentine style.

NEAR THE PONTE VECCHIO
Inexpensive
Buca dell'Orafo. Via Volta dei Girolami 28R. ☎ **055-213619.** Reservations recommended. Main courses 15,000–35,000L ($8–$18). No credit cards. Tues–Sat 12:30–2:30pm and 7:30–10:30pm. Closed Aug and 2 weeks in Dec. Bus: A. FLORENTINE.

This little dive is one of many cellars or *buca*-type establishments beloved by Florentines. The trattoria is usually stuffed with regulars, so if you want a seat, go early. Over the years the chef has made little concession to the foreign palate, turning out genuine Florentine specialties, like tripe and mixed boiled meats with a green sauce and *stracotto e fagioli* (beef braised in a sauce of chopped vegetables and red wine), served with beans in a tomato sauce.

NEAR PIAZZA SAN LORENZO & THE MERCATO CENTRALE
Inexpensive
Le Fonticine. Via Nazionale 79R. ☎ **055-282106.** Reservations recommended for dinner. Main courses 17,000–30,000L ($9–$15). AE, DC, MC, V. Tues–Sat noon–2:30pm and 7–10pm. Closed Jan 1–15 and Aug. Bus: 7, 10, 11, 12, 25, 31, 33, or 70. TUSCAN/BOLOGNESE.

Owner Silvano Bruci converted both this former convent and its adjoining garden into one of the most hospitable restaurants in Florence. The richly decorated interior contains the second passion of Signor Bruci's life, his collection of modern paintings. The first passion, as a meal here reveals, is the cuisine he and his wife produce from recipes she collected from her childhood in Bologna. The food, served in copious portions, is both traditional and delectable. Begin with a platter of fresh antipasti, then enjoy samplings of three of the most excellent pasta dishes of the day. This might be followed by veal scaloppini, or stewed wild boar.

Trattoria Antellesi. Via Faenza 9R. ☎ **055-216990.** Reservations recommended. Main courses 18,000–30,000L ($9–$15). AE, DC, MC, V. Nov–Aug Mon–Sat noon–3pm and 7–10:30pm; Sept–Oct daily noon–3pm and 7–10:30pm. Bus: 7, 10, 11, 12, 25, 31, 33, or 70. TUSCAN.

The Cafe Scene

Café Rivoire, Piazza della Signoria 4R (☎ **055-214412;** bus: B), offers a classy and amusing old-world ambience with a direct view of the statues of one of our favorite squares. Try the hot chocolate. Behind three Tuscan arches on a fashionable shopping street in the center of the old city, **Giacosa,** Via. Tornabuoni 83R (☎ **055-2396226;** bus: B, 6, 11, 36, 37, or 68), has a warmly paneled interior, a lavish display of pastries and sandwiches, and a reputation as the birthplace of the Negroni, a drink that's a combination of gin, Campari, and red vermouth.

A few minutes' walk from the Duomo, **Gilli,** Piazza della Repubblica 39R (☎ **055-213896;** bus: A), is the oldest and most beautiful café in Florence, founded in 1733. The interior is all wood and brass, and tables are placed outside in summer. **Giubbe Rosse,** Piazza della Repubblica 13R (☎ **055-212-280;** bus: A), has always been known as a literary cafe, where intellectuals and writers met each other to discuss the Italian politics and literature. It survived the Mussolini era and continues to function as a rendezvous for cultural debates. You can enjoy coffee, drinks, and also salads and sandwiches surrounded by early 1900s chandeliers and polished granite floors.

On the ground floor of a 15th-century historic monument, a few steps from the Medici Chapel, this restaurant is devoted almost exclusively to Tuscan recipes that have stood the test of time. Owned by the Italian American team of Enrico Verrecchia and his Arizona-born wife, Janice, the restaurant prepares at least seven *piatti del giorno* that change according to the availability of the ingredients. Menu items may include tagliatelle with porcini mushrooms or with braised arugula, *crespelle alla fiorentina* (a Tuscan Renaissance cheesy spinach crepe introduced to France by Catherine de Medici's kitchen staff), market-fresh fish (generally on Friday), and delicious Valdostana chicken.

NEAR PIAZZA SANTA MARIA NOVELLA & THE TRAIN STATION
Expensive
I Quattro Amici. Via degli Orti Oricellari 29. ☎ **055-215413.** Reservations recommended. Main courses 30,000–50,000L ($15–$25). AE, DC, MC, V. Daily noon–2:30pm and 7–10:30pm. Bus: D, 26, 27, or 35. SEAFOOD.

Opened in 1990 by four Tuscan entrepreneurs, this restaurant occupies the street level of a modern building near the rail station. Amid a vaguely neoclassical decor, the place serves endless quantities of fish. Specialties include such dishes as pasta with fish sauce and sausage; fish soup; fried shrimp and squid in the style of Livorno; and grilled, stewed, or baked versions of all the bounty of the Mediterranean. The roast sea bass and roast snapper, flavored with Mediterranean herbs, are among the finest dishes, as is the fresh lobster with mixed vegetables.

Moderate
Buca Lapi. Via del Trebbio 1R. ☎ **055-213768.** Reservations required for dinner. Main courses 25,000–45,000L ($13–$23). AE, DC, MC, V. Tues–Sat 12:30–2:30pm, and Mon–Sat 7:30–10:30pm. Closed 2 weeks in Aug. Bus: 6, 11, 36, or 37. TUSCAN.

Buca Lapi, a cellar restaurant under the Palazzo Antinori, is big on glamour, good food, and the enthusiasm of fellow diners. Its decor alone makes it fun: Vaulted ceilings are covered with travel posters from all over the world. There's a long table of interesting fruits, desserts, and vegetables. The cooks know how to turn out the most classic dishes of the Tuscan kitchen with superb finesse. Specialties include pâté, cannelloni, *scampi giganti alla griglia* (a supersize shrimp), and *bistecca alla fiorentina* (local beefsteak), still cooked over coals in the old-fashioned way. In season, the *fagioli toscani all'olio* (Tuscan beans in the native olive oil) are a delicacy. Owner and the chef Luciano Ghinasi puts all his passion for good and genuine food in his recipes. His cookbook, available in English, reveals some of his secrets in preparing succulent Tuscan dishes.

✪ **Don Chisciotte.** Via Ridolfi 4R. ☎ **055-475430.** Reservations recommended. Main courses 28,000–40,000L ($14–$20); *menu degustazione* 90,000L ($45). AE, DC, MC, V. Mon 8–10:30pm, Tues–Sat 1–2:30pm and 8–10:30pm. Bus: 20. ITALIAN/SEAFOOD.

One floor above the street level in a Florentine palazzo, this restaurant is known for its creative cuisine and changing array of very fresh fish. Creative menu items are produced with a flourish from the kitchens. Examples include red taglierini with clams, pesto, and cheese; risotto of broccoli and baby squid; and black ravioli colored with squid ink and stuffed with a puree of shrimp and crayfish. Chefs also prepare one of the city's most flavor-filled Florentine steaks along with a succulent medley of boiled meats with fresh herb seasonings.

Sabatini. Via de'Panzani 9A. ☎ **055-211559.** Reservations recommended. Main courses 25,000–48,000L ($13–$24). AE, DC, MC, V. Tues–Sun 12:30–2:30pm and 7:30–10:30pm. Bus: 1, 6, 14, 17, or 22. FLORENTINE.

Despite its location near the rail station, Sabatini has long been extolled by Florentines and visitors alike as the finest of the restaurants characteristic of the city. To celebrate our return visit every year, we order the same main course—boiled Valdarno chicken with savory green sauce. Other main courses are also delicious, especially the veal scaloppini with artichokes. Of course, you can always order a good sole meunière and the classic beefsteak Florentine.

Inexpensive

Ristorante Otello. Via degli Orti Oricellari 36R. ☎ **055-216517.** Reservations recommended. Main courses 20,000–35,000L ($10–$18). AE, DC, MC, V. Daily noon–3pm and 7:30–11pm. Bus: D, 26, 27, or 35. FLORENTINE.

Beside the train station, Ristorante Otello is a long-established comfortable Florentine dining room. Its antipasto Toscano is one of the best in town, an array of appetizing hors d'oeuvres that practically becomes a meal in itself. The waiter urges you to *"Mangi, mangi, mangi!"* ("Eat, eat, eat!"). Order one of the succulent pasta dishes, such as spaghetti with baby clams or pappardelle with garlic sauce. The meat and poultry dishes are equally delectable, including sole meunière and veal pizzaiola with lots of garlic.

✪ **Trattoria Sostanza.** Via del Porcellana 25R. ☎ **055-212691.** Reservations recommended. Main courses 15,000–29,000L ($8–$15). No credit cards. Mon–Fri noon–2:10pm and 7:30–9:30pm. Closed Aug and 2 weeks at Christmas. Bus: 12. FLORENTINE.

Sostanza is a tucked-away little trattoria where working people have gone since 1869 to get excellent, reasonably priced food. It's the city's oldest and most revered trattoria with a real Tuscan atmosphere. The small dining room has crowded family tables. The rear kitchen is open, its secrets exposed to diners. Specialties include breaded chicken breast and a succulent T-bone steak. You might also want to try tripe the Florentine way—cut into strips and baked in a casserole with tomatoes, onions, and Parmesan.

NEAR PIAZZA GOLDONI
Moderate

Harry's Bar. Lungarno Vespucci 22R. ☎ **055-2396700.** Reservations required. Main cours-es 20,000–36,000L ($10–$18). AE, MC, V. Mon–Sat noon–3pm and 7–11pm. Closed 1 week in Aug and Dec 18–Jan 8. Bus: B. INTERNATIONAL/ITALIAN.

Harry's Bar, in a prime position on the Arno, is an enclave of expatriate and well-heeled visiting Yankees that deserves its reputation. Patrons can order from an inter-national menu—small but select and beautifully prepared, featuring fresh fish on its menu every day. A specialty is risotto or tagliatelle with ham, onions, and cheese. Harry has created his own tortellini (stuffed pasta), but Harry's hamburger and his club sandwich are the most popular items. The chef also prepares about a dozen spe-cialties every day, like breast of chicken "our way," grilled giant-size scampi, and lean broiled sirloin.

Trattoria Coco Lezzone. Via del Parioncino 26R. ☎ **055-287178.** Reservations accepted only for groups of 10 or more. Main courses 16,000–45,000L ($8–$23). No credit cards. Mon–Sat noon–2:30pm and 7–10pm. Closed last week of July–Aug and Dec 25–Jan 6. Bus: 27 or 31. FLORENTINE.

In Florentine dialect, the establishment's name refers to the sauce-stained apron of the extroverted chef who established this place more than a century ago. Today, this remains a good place to sample the nearby food of the Tuscan countryside. Go before the rush begins if you want a seat in this bustling trattoria. The rib-sticking fare includes gener-ous portions of boiled meats with a green sauce, pasta fagiole (beans), osso buco (beef or veal knuckle braised in wine, butter, garlic, and lemon), tripe, and beefsteak Florentine, which is superexpensive, although most dishes are very moderate in price.

NEAR PIAZZA SANTA CROCE
Expensive

Alle Murate. Via Ghibellina, 52R. ☎ **055-240618.** Reservations recommended. Main courses 45,000–70,000L ($23–$35). AE, DC, MC, V. Tues–Sun 7:30–11:30pm. Closed 15 days at Christmas. Bus: 14. TUSCAN/SOUTHERN ITALIAN.

Owned by young Umberto Montano, this sophisticated eatery with a softly lit unclut-tered dining room prepares some of the most creative and classic Tuscan dishes in town. Yet at the same time, it allows you to take a night off from Tuscan fare by offer-ing some of the classics of the south, including the famous pasta, orecchiette sauced with broccoli, fish poached acqua pazza (tomatoes, garlic, and parsley), or five bean puree topped with cooked chicory. The chefs make the best lasagna in town with moz-zarella and fresh tomatoes. Several soufflés are prepared with seasonal vegetables such as leeks or artichokes. Handmade tortelli (a kind of ravioli) is stuffed with small egg-plants and served with a butter and thyme sauce. Brasato di chianina is veal braised with Brunello di Montalcino red wine. There's nothing finer here than the baked sea bream with crunchy potatoes. In an adjacent smaller room, Vineria, the menu is dif-ferent, the service not as good, but the food is slightly cheaper.

You may also want to check out Montano's **Osteria del Caffè Italiano,** Via Isola delle Stinche 11–13R, 2 blocks west of piazza Santa Croce (☎ **055-28-93-68;** bus: A or 14) and **Caffè Italiano,** V. Condotta 56R, off Via dei Calzaiuoli (☎ **055-29-1082;** bus: 14, 23, or 71).

Moderate

Cibreo. Via dei Macci 118R. ☎ **055-2341100.** Reservations recommended in the restau-rant, not accepted in the trattoria. Main courses 30,000–45,000L ($15–$23) in the restaurant, 20,000–30,000L ($10–$15) in the trattoria. AE, DC, MC, V (restaurant only). Tues–Sat 12:30–3pm and 7:30–11pm. Closed late July to early Sept. Bus: A. MEDITERRANEAN.

Cibreo is one of the largest eateries in the neighborhood. From a small and impossibly old-fashioned kitchen, it prepares food for a restaurant, a less formal tavern-style trattoria, and a cafe-bar across the street. *The New York Times* called the chef and owner, Fabio Picchi, a poet for how he talks and a magician for how he cooks. The kitchens are noteworthy for not containing a grill and not serving pastas. They specialize in foodstuffs cooked in a wood-burning oven and cold marinated dishes, especially vegetables. Menu items include *sformato* (soufflé made from potatoes and ricotta, served with Parmesan and tomato sauce) and flan of Parmesan, veal tongue, and artichokes. A favorite dish of the chef is roast pigeon flavored with a fruity mustard. Among his classic recipes are *zuppa di cavolo* (cabbage soup), *polenta alle erbe* (polenta flavored with seasonal herbs), and *insalata di fave* (fava bean salad with parmigiano flakes).

ACROSS THE ARNO
Moderate
Mamma Gina. Borgo Sant'Jacopo 37R. ☎ **055-2396009.** Reservations required for dinner. Main courses 20,000–32,000L ($10–$16). AE, DC, MC, V. Mon–Sat noon–2:30pm and 7–10:30pm. Closed Aug 9–23. Bus: B or D. TUSCAN.

Named after its founding matriarch, Mamma Gina is a rustic left-bank restaurant in a 15th-century building that's a winner for fine foods prepared in the traditional bustling manner. This exceptional trattoria, well worth the trek across the Ponte Vecchio, is a center for hearty Tuscan fare. The menu items are rich, savory, and tied to the seasons and include such dishes as cannelloni Mamma Gina (stuffed with a puree of minced meats, spices, and vegetables); tagliolini with artichoke hearts or mushrooms and whatever else is in season at the time; and chicken breast Mamma Gina, baked in the northern Italian style with prosciutto and Emmenthaler cheese. Trust Mamma Gina's recipes and try the panzerotti, savory turnovers made with pizza dough and stuffed with several different types of cheese, including mozzarella, plus prosciutto.

EXPLORING THE RENAISSANCE CITY
Florence was the fountainhead of the Renaissance, the city of Dante and Boccaccio. Florentines are noted for their cunning, as represented by Machiavelli; however, they're not noted for their religious zeal, as evoked by Savonarola, who might've found a better reception in Geneva. For 3 centuries, Florence was dominated by the Medici family, patrons of the arts and masters of assassination. But it's chiefly through its artists that we know of the apogee of the Renaissance: Ghiberti, Fra Angelico, Donatello, Brunelleschi, Botticelli, and the incomparable Leonardo da Vinci and Michelangelo.

○ **Piazza della Signoria,** though never completed, is one of the most beautiful in Italy. On the square is the Fountain of Neptune. Nearby is the spot where Savonarola walked his last mile. This zealous monk was a fire-and-brimstone reformer who rivaled Dante in conjuring up the punishment hell would inflict on sinners. For centuries Michelangelo's *David* stood in this piazza, but it was moved to the Accademia in the 19th century. The work you see here today is a copy.

On the piazza, the 14th-century **Loggia dei Lanzi** (sometimes called the Loggia della Signoria) is a gallery of sculpture that often depicts fierce, violent scenes. The best piece is a rare work by Benvenuto Cellini, the goldsmith and tell-all autobiographer. Critics have said that his exquisite *Perseus,* who holds the severed head of Medusa, is the most significant Florentine sculpture since Michelangelo's *Night* and *Day.*

For a view of the wonders of Florence below and Fiesole above, climb aboard bus 13 from the central station and head for **Piazzale Michelangiolo,** a 19th-century belvedere with a view seen in many a Renaissance painting. It's best at dusk, when the purple-fringed Tuscan hills form a frame for Giotto's bell tower, Brunelleschi's dome, and the towering stones sticking up from the Palazzo Vecchio. Another copy of Michelangelo's *David* dominates the square.

SIGHTSEEING SUGGESTIONS FOR FIRST-TIME VISITORS

If You Have 1 Day   You'll have to accept the inevitable—you can only visit a small fraction of Florence's stellar attractions. Go to the **Uffizi Galleries** as soon as they open and concentrate only on some of the masterpieces or your favorite artists. Have lunch on **Piazza della Signoria,** dominated by the Palazzo Vecchio, and admire the statues in the Loggia dei Lanzi. After lunch, visit the **Duomo** and **Baptistry,** before continuing north to see Michelangelo's *David* at the **Accademia.** Next, head back south toward the Arno and the Ponte Vecchio. On the way do a little shopping at the fabled **Straw Market** (Mercato Nuovo). Sunset should find you at the landmark **Ponte Vecchio.** Finish your very busy day with a hearty Tuscan dinner in one of Florence's many *bucas* (cellar restaurants).

If You Have 2 Days   Spend your first day as suggested above. On Day 2, you can spend a fascinating morning visiting the **Bargello** to see some of the Renaissance, including another version of Michelangelo's *David.* A short walk will take you to the **Palazzo Vecchio,** where you can explore the Hall of the 500 to see the Vasari Renaissance frescoes. Then in the afternoon visit the **Pitti Palace,** on the other side of the Arno, and wander through the Galleria Palatina, with its 16th- and 17th-century masterpieces, including 11 works by Raphael alone. After a visit, stroll through the adjoining **Boboli Gardens.** At sunset, go again to the Duomo and the Baptistry for a much better look.

If You Have 3 Days   Spend your first 2 days as suggested above. In the morning of Day 3, head for the **Medici Chapels** adjacent to the Basilica of San Lorenzo. Here you can stand by Michelangelo. Look especially for the figures of *Dawn* and *Dusk.* Later in the morning you can go to the **Museo di San Marco,** a small museum that's a monument to the work of Fra Angelico. After lunch, visit the **Museo dell'Opera del Duomo,** with its sculptural masterpieces from the Duomo, including Donatello's *Mary Magdalene.*

If You Have 4 Days or More   Spend days 1 to 3 as suggested above. On Day 4, begin with a morning visit to the Palazzo Medici-Riccardi, near the Duomo. Here you can view the mid–15th-century frescoes by Benozzo Gozzoli in the Medici Chapel. Later that morning pop into Santa Maria Novella, one of Florence's most distinguished churches with its Gondi Chapel containing Brunelleschi's wooden Christ on the Cross. Before it closes at 6:30pm, call at the Basilica di Santa Croce, with its two restored chapels by Giotto.

On Day 5, leave Florence, as fascinating as it is, and head south to yet another fascinating art city, **Siena,** the most important of the Tuscan hill towns.

THE TOP MUSEUMS

✪ **Galleria degli Uffizi.** Piazzale degli Uffizi 6. ☎ **055-23885.** www.uffizi.firenze.it. Admission 12,000L ($6). Mon–Fri 8:30am–9pm, Sat 8:30am–midnight, Sun 8:30am–8pm (last entrance 45 minutes before closing).

This is one of the world's outstanding museums and Italy's finest collection of art. The Uffizi is nicely grouped into periods or schools to show the progress of Italian and

---

Reserving Tickets for the Uffizi & Other Museums

Finally, you can bypass the hours-long ticket line at the **Uffizi Galleries** by reserving a ticket and an entry time in advance by calling ☎ **055-294883** or checking on the Web at **www.arca.net/uffizi/reservation.htm**. By March, entry times can already be booked up over a week in advance. You can also reserve for the **Accademia Gallery** (another interminable line, to see *David*), as well as the **Galleria Palatina** in the Pitti Palace and the **Bargello** (you don't really need it for those last two) and several others. There's a nominal fee (worth every penny), and you can pay by credit card.

European art. The first room begins with classical sculpture. A special treasure is a work by Masaccio, who died at an early age but is credited as the father of modern painting. In his madonnas and bambini you can see the beginnings of the use of perspective. The Botticelli rooms contain his finest works, including *The Birth of Venus*. In another room you'll see Leonardo da Vinci's unfinished but brilliant *Adoration of the Magi* and Verrocchio's *Baptism of Christ*, not a very important painting but noted because Leonardo painted one of the angels when he was 14. Also in this salon hangs Leonardo's *Annunciation*.

In the rooms that follow are works by Perugino, Dürer, Mantegna, Bellini, Giorgione, and Correggio. Finally, you can view Michelangelo's Holy Family, as well as Raphael's Madonna of the Goldfinch, plus his portraits of Julius II and Leo X. There's also what might be dubbed the Titian salon, which has two of his interpretations of Venus (one depicted with Cupid).

After much renovation, following a terrorist bomb in 1993, the Uffizzi has a new look. The refurbishment of the building, designed by Giorgio Vasari, is now complete. The galleries at the upper two floors are three times their previous size, and the trompe-l'oeil painting in the Loggiato sull'Arno has been restored to its original beauty. Walking down this hall, looking through its high windows, you'll have enchanting views of Florence.

Remember to call ahead to reserve tickets (see above)!

✪ **Galleria dell'Accademia.** Via Ricasoli 60. ☎ **055-2388609.** Admission 12,000L ($6). Tues–Fri 8:30am–9pm, Sat 8:30am–midnight, Sun 8:30am–8pm. Bus: 1, 6, 11, or 17.

This museum boasts many paintings and sculptures, but they're completely overshadowed by one work: Michelangelo's colossal *David*, unveiled in 1504 and now the world's most fabled sculpture. It first stood in Piazza della Signoria but was moved to the Accademia in 1873 and placed beneath the rotunda of a room build exclusively for its display. When he began work, Michelangelo was just 29 and only recently recognized for his talents following his creation of the *Pietà*, now in St. Peter's Basilica in Rome. In the connecting picture gallery is a collection of Tuscan masters, such as Botticelli, and Umbrian works by Perugino (teacher of Raphael).

✪ **Palazzo Pitti and the Giardini di Boboli (Boboli Gardens).** Piazza de'Pitti. ☎ **055-23885.** Palatina, 12,000L ($6); Modern Art Gallery, 8,000L ($4); Argenti, 4,000L ($2); Boboli Gardens, 4,000L ($2). Galleria Palatina and Appartamenti Reali, Tues–Fri 8am–9pm, Sat 8am–midnight, and Sun 8am–8pm. Museo degli Argenti and Modern Art Gallery daily 8:30am–1:30pm, closed the first, third, and fifth Mon and the second and fourth Sun of each month. Boboli Gardens, June–Sept daily 8:30am–7:45pm; Apr–May and Oct daily 8:30am–6:45pm; Nov–Mar daily 9am–5:45pm, closed the first and the last Mon of each month. Ticket office closes 1 hour before the gardens. Bus: D.

The Pitti Palace, on the left bank (a 5-minute walk from the Ponte Vecchio), actually contains several museums, the most important of which is the **Galleria Palatina,** a repository of old masters. This gallery houses one of Europe's great art collections, with masterpieces hung one on top of the other, as in the days of the Enlightenment. If for no other reason, come here for the Raphaels. In the **Sala di Saturno,** look to the left of the entrance wall to see Raphael's *Madonna of the Canopy.* On the third wall near the door is the greatest Pitti prize, Raphael's *Madonna of the Chair,* his best-known interpretation of the Virgin. The Pitti, built in the mid-15th century (Brunelleschi was the original architect), was once the residence of the powerful Medici family.

Other museums are the **Appartamenti Reali,** which the Medici family once called home; the **Museo degli Argenti,** 16 rooms devoted to displays of the "loot" acquired by the Medici dukes; the **Coach and Carriage Museum;** the **Galleria d'Arte Moderna;** the **Museo delle Porcellane** (porcelain); and the **Galleria del Costume.** The **Museo degli Argenti** has a separate number to call for information (☎ 055-2388-709), as does the **Modern Art Gallery** (☎ 055-2388-616).

Behind the Pitti Palace are the **Boboli Gardens,** Piazza de'Pitti 1 (☎ 055-265171), through which the Medici romped. The gardens were laid out in the 16th century by the great landscape artist, Triboli. The Boboli is ever popular for a promenade or an idyllic interlude in a pleasant setting. The gardens are filled with fountains and statuary, such as a Giambologna *Venus* in the "Grotto" of Buontalenti. You can climb to the top of the Fortezza di Belvedere for a dazzling city view.

Cappelle Medicee (Medici Chapels). Piazza Madonna degli Aldobrandini 6. ☎ 055-23885. Admission 13,000L ($7). Tues–Sat 8:30am–4:15pm, Sun 8:30am–1:50pm. Closed 2nd and 4th Sun, and 1st, 3rd, 5th Mon of each month.

The Medici tombs are adjacent to the Basilica of San Lorenzo (see "Other Churches," below). You enter the tombs, housing the "blue-blooded" Medici, behind the church by going around to Piazza di Madonna degli Aldobrandini. The "New Sacristy" was designed by Michelangelo. Working from 1521 to 1534, he created the Medici tomb in a style that foreshadowed the baroque. Lorenzo the Magnificent was buried near Michelangelo's uncompleted *Madonna and Child* group. Ironically, the finest groups of sculpture were reserved for two Medici "clan" members, who (in the words of Mary McCarthy) "would better have been forgotten." They're represented as armored, idealized princes. The other two figures on Lorenzo's tomb are most often called *Dawn* (represented as woman) and *Dusk* (as man). The best-known figures are *Night* (chiseled as a woman in troubled sleep) and *Day* (a man of strength awakening to a foreboding world) at the feet of Giuliano, the duke of Nemours.

Museo Nazionale del Bargello. Via del Proconsolo 4. ☎ 055-2388606. Admission 8,000L ($4). Tues–Sat 8:30am–1:50pm. Closed 1st, 3rd, 5th Sun and 2nd and 4th Mon of each month.

The National Museum, a short walk from piazza della Signoria, is a 13th-century fortress palace whose dark underground chambers once resounded with the cries of the tortured. Today it's a vast repository of some of the most important Renaissance sculpture, including works by Michelangelo and Donatello.

Here you'll see another Michelangelo *David* (formerly referred to as *Apollo*), chiseled perhaps 25 to 30 years after the figure in the Accademia. The Bargello *David* is totally different—even effete when compared to its stronger brother. Among the more significant sculptures is Giambologna's *Winged Mercury.* The Bargello displays two versions of Donatello's *John the Baptist*—one emaciated, the other younger and much kinder. Look for two more *Davids*—Donatello's and Verrocchio's. The Bargello contains a large number of terra-cottas by the della Robbia clan.

Museo di San Marco. Piazza San Marco 1. ☎ **055-2388608.** Admission 8,000L ($4). Daily 8:30am–1:50pm. Closed 1st, 3rd, and 5th Sun of the month, and 2nd and 4th Mon of the month. Bus: 1, 7, 25, or 33.

This state museum is a handsome Renaissance palace whose cell walls are decorated with 15th-century frescoes by the mystical Fra Angelico. In the days of Cosimo dei Medici, San Marco was built by as a Dominican convent. It originally contained bleak, bare cells, which Angelico and his students then brightened considerably. One of his better-known paintings here is *The Last Judgment,* which depicts people with angels on the left dancing in a circle and lordly saints towering overhead. On the second floor—at the top of the hall—is Angelico's masterpiece, *The Annunciation.*

THE DUOMO, CAMPANILE & BAPTISTRY

✪ **Cattedrale di Santa Maria del Fiore (Duomo).** Piazza del Duomo. ☎ **055-2302885.** Cathedral, free; excavations, 5,000L ($2.50); cupola, 10,000L ($5). Mar–Oct Mon–Sat 8:30am–6:30pm, off-season Mon–Sat 8:30am–5:30pm.

The Duomo, graced by Brunelleschi's dome, is the crowning glory of Florence. But don't rush inside too quickly, as the view of the exterior, with its geometrically patterned bands of white, pink, and green marble, is, along with the dome, the best feature. One of the world's largest churches, the Duomo represents the flowering of the "Florentine Gothic" style. Begun in 1296, it was finally consecrated in 1436, yet finishing touches on the facade were applied as late as the 19th century.

Inside, the overall effect is bleak, except when you stand under the cupola, frescoed in part by Vasari. Some of the stained-glass windows in the dome were based on designs by Donatello (Brunelleschi's friend) and Ghiberti (Brunelleschi's rival). If you resist scaling Giotto's bell tower (below), you may want to climb Brunelleschi's ribbed dome. The view is well worth the trek.

Campanile (Giotto's Bell Tower). Piazza del Duomo. ☎ **055-2302885.** Admission 10,000L ($5). Daily 8am–7pm.

Giotto left to posterity the most beautiful campanile (bell tower) in Europe, rhythmic in line and form. He designed it in the last 2 or 3 years of his life and died before its completion. The final work was admirably carried out by Andrea Pisano, one of the greatest Gothic sculptors in Italy (see his bronze doors on the nearby Baptistery). The 84m (274-foot) tower, a "Tuscanized" Gothic, with bands of colored marble, can be scaled for a panorama of the sienna-colored city. The view will surely rank among your most memorable—it encompasses the enveloping hills and Medici villas.

Battistero San Giovanni (Baptistry). Piazza S. Giovanni. ☎ **055-2302885.** Admission 5,000L ($2.50). Mon–Sat noon–6:30pm, Sun 9am–1pm.

Named after the city's patron saint, Giovanni (John the Baptist), the present octagonal Battistero dates from the 11th and 12th centuries. The oldest structure in Florence, the baptistery is a highly original interpretation of the Romanesque style, with its bands of pink, white, and green marble. Visitors from all over the world come to gape at its three sets of bronze doors. The east door is a copy; the other two are originals. In his work on two sets of doors, Lorenzo Ghiberti reached the pinnacle of his artistry in *quattrocento* Florence. The gilt panels—representing scenes from the New Testament, including the *Annunciation,* the *Adoration,* and Christ debating the elders in the temple—make up a flowing, rhythmic narration in bronze.

OTHER CHURCHES

Basilica di San Lorenzo. Piazza San Lorenzo. ☎ **055-214443.** Free admission or 5,000–15,000L ($2.50–$8) for special exhibitions. Library, Mon–Sat 7:30–11:45am and 3:30–5:30pm. Bus: 1, 6, 14, or 23.

This is Brunelleschi's 15th-century Renaissance church, where the Medici used to attend services from their nearby palace on Via Larga, now Via Camillo Cavour. Most visitors flock to see Michelangelo's Medici Chapels (see "The Top Museums," above), but Brunelleschi's handiwork deserves some time, too. Built in the style of a Latin cross, the church is distinguished by harmonious grays and rows of Corinthian columns.

Biblioteca Medicea Laurenziana (☎ 055-210760) is entered separately at Piazza San Lorenzo 9 and was designed by Michelangelo to shelter the expanding library of the Medici. Beautiful in design and concept, and approached by exquisite stairs, the library is filled with some of Italy's greatest manuscripts—many of which are handsomely illustrated. Hours are Monday to Saturday 9am to 1pm. Admission is free; the only time you'll be charged is if there's some special exhibition mounted.

Basilica di Santa Croce. Piazza Santa Croce 16. ☎ **055-244619.** Church, free; cloisters and church museum, 8,000L ($4). Church, Mon–Sat 8am–6:30pm, Sun 3–6:30pm. Museum and cloisters, Thurs–Tues 10am–7pm. Bus: 23 or 71.

The Pantheon of Florence, this church shelters tombs or monuments of everyone from Michelangelo to Machiavelli, from Dante to Galileo. Santa Croce was the church of the Franciscans. In the right nave (first tomb) is the Vasari-executed monument to Michelangelo, whose body was smuggled back to his native Florence from its original burial place in Rome. The Trecento frescoes are reason enough for visiting Santa Croce—especially those by Giotto to the right of the main chapel.

Basilica di Santa Maria Novella. Piazza Santa Maria Novella. ☎ **055-282187.** Church, free; Spanish Chapel and cloisters, 5,000L ($2.50). Church, Mon–Fri 7am–noon and 3–6pm, Sat–Sun 3–5pm, Spanish Chapel and cloisters, Sat–Thurs 8am–2pm. Bus: A, 6, 11, 12, 36, 37, or 68.

Near the railway station is one of Florence's most distinguished churches, begun in 1278 for the Dominicans. Its geometric facade, with bands of white and green marble, was designed in the late 15th century by Leon Battista Alberti, an aristocrat and true Renaissance man. The church borrows from and harmonizes the Romanesque, Gothic, and Renaissance styles. In the left nave as you enter, (the third large painting) is Masaccio's *Trinity,* a curious work that has the architectural form of a Renaissance stage setting, but whose figures—in perfect perspective—are like actors in a Greek tragedy. Head straight up the left nave to the Gondi Chapel for a look at Brunelleschi's wooden *Christ on the Cross,* said to have been carved to compete with Donatello's same subject in Santa Croce.

PALACES

Palazzo Vecchio. Piazza della Signoria. ☎ **055-2768325.** Admission 10,000L ($5). Mon–Wed and Fri–Sat 9am–7pm, Thurs and Sun 9am–2pm; July 15–Sept 15 Mon and Fri 9am–11pm. Ticket office closes 1 hour before palace.

The secular "Old Palace" is without doubt the most famous and imposing palace in Florence. It dates from the closing years of the 13th century. Its remarkable architectural feature is its 308-foot tower, an engineering feat that required supreme skill. Once home to the Medici, the Palazzo Vecchio (also called the Palazzo della Signoria) is occupied today by city employees, but much of it is open to the public. The 16th-century

"Hall of the 500" (Dei Cinquecento), the most outstanding part of the palace, is filled with Vasari & Co. frescoes as well as sculpture. As you enter the hall, look for Michelangelo's *Victory*. Later you can stroll through the apartments and main halls. You can also visit the private apartments of Eleanor of Toledo, wife of Cosimo I, and a chapel that was begun in 1540 and frescoed by Bronzino.

Palazzo Medici-Riccardi. Via Camillo Cavour 1. ☎ **055-2760340.** Admission 6,000L ($3). Mon–Tues and Thurs–Sat 9am–12:30pm and 3–5pm, Sun 9am–noon.

A short walk from the Duomo, this 15th-century palace was the home of Cosimo dei Medici before he took his household to the Palazzo Vecchio. The brown stone building was also the scene, at times, of the court of Lorenzo the Magnificent. Art lovers visit today chiefly to see the Medici Chapel with its mid–15th-century frescoes by Benozzo Gozzoli, which depict the *Journey of the Magi*.

OTHER MUSEUMS

Museo Archeologico. Via della Colonna 38. ☎ **055-23575.** Admission 8,000L ($4). Nov–Aug Tues–Sat 9am–2pm, Sept also Sat 9–midnight, Oct also Sun 9am–8pm. Bus: 6, 31, or 32.

The Archaeological Museum, a short walk from piazza della Santissima Annunziata, houses one of Europe's most outstanding Egyptian and Etruscan collections. Egyptian mummies and sarcophagi are on the first floor, along with Etruscan works. Pause to look at the lid of the coffin of a fat Etruscan. Look for the bronze Chimera, a lion with a goat sticking out of its back, a masterpiece of Etruscan art.

Museo dell'Opera del Duomo. Piazza del Duomo 9. ☎ **055-2302885.** Admission 10,000L ($5). Apr–Oct, Mon–Sat 9am–6:50pm; Nov–Mar, Mon–Sat 9am–5:20pm.

Museo dell'Opera del Duomo, behind the cathedral, is beloved by connoisseurs of Renaissance sculptural works. It shelters the sculpture removed from the campanile and the Duomo. A major attraction of this museum is Michelangelo's unfinished *Pietà*, carved between 1548 and 1555 when the artist was in his seventies. Also look for the marble choirs (*cantorie*) of Donatello and Luca della Robbia. The Luca della Robbia choir is more restrained, but it still "praises the Lord" in marble—with clashing cymbals and sounding brass that constitute a reaffirmation of life.

THE SHOPPING SCENE

Skilled craftsmanship and traditional design unchanged since the days of the Medici have made Florence a destination for serious shoppers. Florence is noted for its hand-tooled **leather goods** and its **straw merchandise,** as well as superbly crafted **gold jewelry.** Its reputation for fashionable custom-made clothes is no longer what it was, having lost its position of supremacy to Milan.

Florence is not a city for bargain shopping. Most visitors interested in gold or silver jewelry head for the **Ponte Vecchio** and its tiny shops. It's difficult to tell one from the other, but you really don't need to since the merchandise is similar. If you're looking for a charm or souvenir, these shops are fine. But the heyday of finding gold jewelry bargains on the Ponte Vecchio is long gone.

The street for antiques in Florence is **Via Maggio;** some of the furnishings and objets d'art here are from the 16th century. Another major area for antiques shopping is **Borgo Ognissanti.**

Florence's Fifth Avenue is **Via dei Tornabuoni.** This is the place to head for the best-quality leather goods, the best clothing boutiques, and stylish but costly shoes. Here you'll find everyone from Armani to Ferragamo. You'll find better shops on **Via Vigna Nuova, Via Porta Rossa,** and **Via degli Strozzi,** too. You might also stroll on

Florence's Famous Markets

After checking into their hotels, the most intrepid shoppers head for **Piazza del Mercato Nuovo (Straw Market),** called "Il Porcellino" by the Italians because of the bronze statue of a reclining wild boar here. (It's a copy of the one in the Uffizi.) Tourists pet its snout (which is well worn) for good luck. The market stands in the monumental heart of Florence, an easy stroll from the Palazzo Vecchio. It sells not only straw items but leather goods as well, along with an array of typically Florentine merchandise—frames, trays, hand embroidery, table linens, and hand-sprayed and painted boxes in traditional designs. Open Monday to Saturday 9am to 7pm.

However, even better bargains await those who make their way through push-carts to the stalls of the open-air **Mercato Centrale** (also called the Mercato San Lorenzo), in and around Borgo San Lorenzo, near the train station. If you don't mind bargaining, which is imperative here, you'll find an array of merchandise, including raffia bags, Florentine leather purses, salt-and-pepper shakers, straw handbags, and art reproductions.

the Lungarno along the Arno. For some of the best buys in leather, check out **Via del Parione,** a short narrow street of Tornabuoni.

Shopping hours are generally Monday 4 to 7:30pm and Tuesday to Saturday 9 or 10am to 1pm and 3:30 or 4 to 7:30pm. During the summer some shops are open Monday mornings. However, don't be surprised if shops close for several weeks in August, if not for the entire month.

SOME SHOPS WORTH A LOOK

In front of the palazzo Vecchio, **Befani E Tai,** Via Vacchereccia 13R (☎ **055-287825**), is one of the most unusual jewelry stores in Florence—some of its pieces date back to the 19th century. The store was established right after World War II by expert goldsmiths who were childhood friends. Some of their clients design their own jewelry and have the store's artisans handcraft their creations.

Beltrami, Via del Tornabuoni 48 (☎ **055-287779**), sells well-known leather goods as well as expensive evening clothes, heavyweight silk scarves, and fashions of the best quality. This is one of several Beltrami shops in the area. High fashion, high prices, and high quality are what you'll find here, but prices are significantly lower than what you'll pay for Beltrami in the States. The **Beltrami Spa,** Via del Panzani 1 (☎ **055-212661**), offers last season's fashions at discounts of 20% to 50%. There are further discounts for multiple purchases, and since the original prices are still on the items, you can tell how much you're saving.

Sergio Bojola, a leading name in leather, has distinguished himself in Florence by the variety of his selections, in both synthetic materials and beautiful leathers. At **Bojola**, Via dei Rondinelli 25R (☎ **055-211155**), you'll find first-class quality and craftsmanship. You might be especially interested in their beautiful leather suitcases.

Galleria Masini, Piazza Goldoni 6R (☎ **055-294000**), is the oldest art gallery in Florence. The selection of modern and contemporary paintings by top artists is extensive, representing the work of more than 700 Italian painters. Even if you're not a collector, this is a good place to select a picture that will be a lasting reminder of your visit to Italy—you can take it home duty-free.

The wide inventory at **Menegatti,** Piazza del Pesce, Ponte Vecchio 2R (☎ 055-215202), includes pottery from Florence, Faenza, and Deruta. There're also della Robbia reproductions made in red clay like the originals. Items can be sent home if you arrange it at the time of your purchase.

Officina Profumo Farmaceutica di Santa Maria Novella, Via della Scala 16N (☎ 055-216276), is the most fascinating pharmacy in Italy. Located northwest of the Church of Santa Maria Novella, it opened its doors to the public in 1612, offering a selection of herbal remedies that were created by friars of the Dominican order. Those closely guarded secrets have been retained, and many of the same elixirs are still sold today. A wide selection of perfumes, scented soaps, shampoos, and of course potpourris, along with creams and lotions, is also sold. The shop is closed on Saturday afternoon in July and August.

FLORENCE AFTER DARK

For theatrical and concert listings, pick up a free copy of *Welcome to Florence,* available at the tourist office. This helpful publication contains information on recitals, concerts, theatrical productions, and other cultural presentations.

Many cultural presentations are performed in churches. These might include openair concerts in the cloisters of the Badia Fiesolana in Fiesole (the hill town above Florence) or at the Ospedale degli Innocenti, the foundling "hospital of the innocents" (on summer evenings only).

THE PERFORMING ARTS

Teatro Comunale di Firenze, Corso Italia 16 (☎ 055-211158; bus: B), is the main theater in Florence, with an opera and ballet season presented from September to December, and a concert season from January until April. This is also the venue for the **Maggio Musicale Fiorentino** (www.maggiofiorentino.com), Italy's oldest and most prestigious festival. It takes place from May until July and offers opera, ballet, concerts, recitals, and cinema productions. The box office is open Tuesday to Friday 10am to 4:30pm, Saturday 9am to 1pm, and 1 hour before curtain. Tickets are 35,000 to 150,000L ($18 to $75). During the Maggio Musicale, tickets usually range from 40,000 to 200,000L ($20 to $100).

You'll have to understand Italian to appreciate most of the plays presented at **Teatro della Pergola,** Via della Pergola 18 (☎ 055-2479651 bus: 6, 14, or 23). Plays are performed year-round except during the Maggio Musicale, when the theater becomes the setting for the many musical presentations of the festival. Performances are Tuesday to Saturday at 8:45pm and Sunday at 3:45pm. The box office is open Tuesday to Saturday 9:30am to 1pm and 3:30 to 6:45pm and on Sunday 10am to noon. Tickets are 22,000 to 44,000L ($11 to $22); 14,500 to 28,500L ($7 to $14) ages 24 and under.

MUSIC & DANCE CLUBS

Contained in the cellar of an antique building in the historic heart of town, the wellknown **Full-Up,** Via della Vigna Vecchia 23–25R (☎ 055-293006; bus: A or 14.), attracts college students from the city's many universities, although older clients usually feel at ease, too. One section contains a smallish dance floor and recorded dance music; another is devoted to the somewhat more restrained ambience of a piano bar. Open Wednesday to Monday 9pm to 3am. Cover (including 1 drink) is 15,000 to 25,000L ($8 to $13).

Set within a 20-minute bus ride from Piazza Duomo, near the Parco della Cascine, **Meccanò,** Viale degli Olmi 1 (☎ 055-331371; bus: P), is one of the few discos in

Italy to offer an indoor-outdoor setting that includes century-old trees, a terrace, and three dance floors on two different levels. Gays mix with mostly straight people with ease, and the average age of patrons is 18 to around 32. Dancing reigns supreme every night except Sunday, Monday, and Wednesday, from 11:30pm till 4am. There's also a restaurant offering modern Italian cuisine. It's open same days of the disco from 9 to 11:30pm. Cover (including 1 drink) is 25,000L ($13). The popular dance club **Yab,** Via Sassetti 5R (☎ **055-215161;** bus: A), is located in the heart of Florence's historic core. Owned and operated by the same entrepreneurs who maintain the larger, more fun, and less inhibited Meccanò, it offers much the same kind of scene, albeit in a smaller and more cramped setting. It's open Wednesday to Saturday 9pm to 3am and is closed between May and October. Cover (including 1 drink) is 20,000 to 30,000L ($10 to $15).

IRISH PUBS

If you ask whether **Dublin Pub,** Via Faenza 27R (☎ **055-293049;** bus: 7, 10, 11, 12, 25, 31, or 70), is an Italian pub, the all-Italian staff will respond rather grandly that such a concept doesn't exist, and that pubs are by definition Irish. And once you get beyond the fact that virtually no one on the staff here has ever been outside of Tuscany, and that there's very little to do here except drink and perhaps practice your Italian, you might settle down and have a rollicking old (very Latin) time. Beers, at least, are appropriately Celtic, and include Harp, Guinness, Kilkenny, and Strong's on tap. It's near the Santa Maria Novella train station and is open daily from 5pm to 2am. After an initial success in Rome, **Fiddler's Elbow,** Piazza Santa Maria Novella 7R (☎ **055-215056;** bus: A), also located near the train station, has now invaded the city of Donatello and Michelangelo. It has quickly become one of the most popular bars in Florence. It's open Monday to Friday 5pm to 1am, Saturday and Sunday 5pm to 2am.

GAY & LESBIAN BARS

ArciGay/Lesbica (aka Azione Gay e Lesbica), Italy's largest and oldest gay organization, has a center in Florence at Via San Zanobi 54r (☎ and fax **055-476-557;** www.agora.stm.it/gaylesbica.fi). It's open for visits Monday to Saturday 4 to 8pm.

Tabasco, Piazza Santa Cecilia 3 (☎ **055-213-000**), is Florence's (and Italy's) oldest gay dance club, open Thursday to Tuesday 10pm to 3am, with a 15,000L to 30,000L ($8 to $16) cover. The crowd is mostly men in their 20s and 30s. Florence's leading gay bar, **Crisco,** Via San Egidio 43r (☎ **055-248-0580**), is for men only, open Sunday, Monday, Wednesday, and Thursday 10:30pm to 3:30am and Friday and Saturday 10:30pm to 5 or 6am. The cover is 12,000L to 16,000L ($6 to $9). In summer at **Flamingo Bar,** Via del Pandolfini 26 (☎ **055-243-356**), the crowd is international. Thursday to Saturday it's a mixed gay/lesbian party; the rest of the week, men only. It's open Sunday to Thursday 10pm to 4am and Friday and Saturday 10pm to 6am. The bar is open year-round; the disco only September to June. Cover, including the first drink, is 12,000L ($6) Sunday to Thursday and 15,000L to 20,000L ($8 to $11) Friday and Saturday.

A SIDE TRIP TO FIESOLE

This town, once an Etruscan settlement, is the most popular outing from Florence. Bus 7, which leaves from piazza San Marco, brings you here in 25 minutes and gives you a panoramic view along the way. You'll pass fountains, statuary, and gardens strung out over the hills like a scrambled jigsaw puzzle.

You won't find anything as dazzling here as the Renaissance treasures of Florence— the charms of Fiesole are more subtle. Fortunately, all major sights branch out within walking distance of the main piazza, beginning with the **Cattedrale di San Romolo.** Dating from 1000, it was much altered during the Renaissance. In the Salutati Chapel, are important sculptural works by Mino da Fiesole. It's open daily 7:30am to noon and 4 to 7pm.

The ecclesiastical **Bandini Museum,** Via Dupre 1 (☎ **055-59477**), around to the side of the Duomo, belongs to the Fiesole Cathedral Chapter. On the ground floor are della Robbia terra-cotta works, as well as art by Michelangelo and Nino Pisano. March to September hours are daily 9:30am to 6:30pm; October daily 9:30am to 5:30pm; November to February daily 9:30am to 4:30pm. It's always closed the first Tuesday of every month. Admission is 10,000L ($5). The ticket is valid 24 hours and also includes admission to the Teatro Romano e Museo Civico (see below).

The hardest task you'll have in Fiesole is to take the steep goat-climb up to the **Museo Missionario Francescano Fiesole,** Via San Francesco 13 (☎ **055-59175**). You can visit the Franciscan church, built in the Gothic style in the first years of the 1400s. The church was consecrated in 1516. Inside are many paintings by well-known Florentine artists. In the basement of the church is the ethnological museum. Begun in 1906, the collection has a large section of Chinese artifacts, including ancient bronzes, as well as Etruscan, Roman and Egyptian objects. Admission is free (donation expected). It's open Monday to Saturday 9:30am to 12:30pm and 3 to 7pm in summer (closes at 6pm off-season).

On the site of the **Teatro Romano e Museo Civico,** Via Portigiani 1 (☎ **055-59477**), is the major surviving evidence that Fiesole was an Etruscan city 6 centuries before Christ, then later a Roman town. In the 1st century B.C., a theater was built, the restored remains of which you can see today. Near the theater are the skeleton-like ruins of the baths, which may have been built at the same time. The Etruscan-Roman museum contains many interesting finds that date from the days when Fiesole, not Florence, was supreme (a guide is on hand to show you through). For admission and hours, see the Bandini Museum above.

3 Highlights of the Tuscan & Umbrian Countryside

Rome may rule Italy, but **Tuscany** presides over its heart. The Tuscan landscapes, little changed since the days of the Medicis, look just like Renaissance paintings, with cypress trees, olive groves, evocative hill towns, and those fabled Chianti vineyards.

Tuscany was the place where the Etruscans first appeared in Italy. The Romans followed, absorbing and conquering them, and by the 11th century, the region had evolved into a collection of independent city-states, such as Florence and Siena, each trying to dominate the other. Although the Renaissance was immensely popular in Florence, it was slow to spread into the surrounding region.

When the Renaissance did arrive, however, with its titans of art, like Giotto, Michelangelo, and Leonardo, critics claim that Western civilization was "rediscovered" in Tuscany. According to D. H. Lawrence, Tuscany became "the perfect center of man's universe." Art flourished under the patronage of the powerful Medicis, and the legacy remains of Masaccio, della Francesca, Signorelli, Raphael, Donatello, Botticelli, and countless others. Tuscany also became known for its men of letters, like Dante, Petrarch, and Boccaccio (who wrote in the vernacular rather than in Latin).

Umbria, a small region at the heart of the Italian peninsula, is associated mainly with saints, like St. Francis of Assisi, founder of the Franciscan order, but Umbrian painters (such as Il Perugino) also contributed to the glory of the Renaissance. The landscape is as alluring as that of Tuscany, with fertile plains of olive groves and vineyards.

Tuscan Tours

If you love to walk or bike, **I Bike Italy** (☎ 055-2342371 Monday to Friday, or 0368/459123 weekends) books guided bike rides through the countryside March to November. **Country Walks in Italy** can be booked with the same outfit year-round. If you want to see Italy as did the Romans and the Renaissance *condottieri,* you can book a horseback trek through **Equitour** (☎ 800/545-0019 in the U.S.).

SIENA

In Rome you see classicism and the baroque; in Florence, the Renaissance; but in the walled city of Siena you stand solidly planted in the Middle Ages. On three sienna-colored hills in the center of Tuscany, Sena Vetus lies in Chianti country, 34km (21 miles) south of Florence. Preserving its original character more markedly than any other Italian city, it's even today a showplace of the Italian Gothic.

Had Siena continued to expand and change after reaching the zenith of its power in the 14th century, chances are it would be markedly different today, influenced by the rising tides of the Renaissance and the baroque (represented here only to a small degree). But Siena retained its uniqueness.

Trains arrive hourly from both Florence and Pisa, and **TRA-IN,** Piazza San Domenico 1 (☎ 0577-204245), in Siena, offers bus service to all of Tuscany, with air-conditioned coaches. The one-way fare between Florence and Siena is 11,000L ($7). Motorists can head south from Florence along the Firenze-Siena autostrada, a superhighway linking the cities, going through Poggibonsi.

The **tourist information office** is at Piazza del Campo 56 (☎ 0577-280551), open Monday to Saturday 8:30am to 7:30pm, Sunday 8:30am to noon. From November to February hours are Monday to Saturday 8:30am to 1pm and 3 to 7pm.

WHERE TO DINE

Al Marsili (Ristorante Enoteca Gallo Nero). Via del Castoro 3. ☎ 0577-47154. Reservations recommended. Main courses 18,000–28,000L ($9–$14). AE, DC, MC, V. Tues–Sun 12:30–2:30pm and 7:30–10:30pm. SIENESE/ITALIAN.

The beautiful Al Marsili is the best in Siena, standing between the Duomo and Via della Città in a neighborhood packed with medieval and Renaissance buildings. You dine beneath crisscrossed ceiling vaults whose russet-colored brickwork was designed centuries ago. Specialties include roast boar with tomatoes and herbs, *ribollita* (savory vegetable soup in the Sienese style), spaghetti with a sauce of seasonal mushrooms, and veal scaloppini with tarragon and tomato sauce.

EXPLORING SIENA

Start in the heart of Siena, the shell-shaped **Piazza del Campo (Il Campo),** described by Montaigne as "the finest of any city in the world." Pause to enjoy the Fonte Gaia, with embellishments by Jacopo della Quercia (the present sculptured works are reproductions; the badly beaten original ones are found in the town hall).

Museo Civico and Torre del Mangia. In the Palazzo Pubblico, Piazza del Campo. ☎ 0577-292263. Admission 10,000L ($5). July–Sept 16 daily 10am–11pm; Sept 17 to end of the month daily 10am–7pm; Oct daily 10am–6pm; Nov–Dec daily 10am–4pm; Jan–June daily 10am–5pm. Bus: A, B, or N.

The Palazzo Pubblico dates from 1288 to 1309 and is filled with important art works by some of the leaders in the Sienese school of painting and sculpture. This collection is the Museo Civico. Upstairs in the museum is the **Sala della Pace,** painted from

Tuscany & Umbria

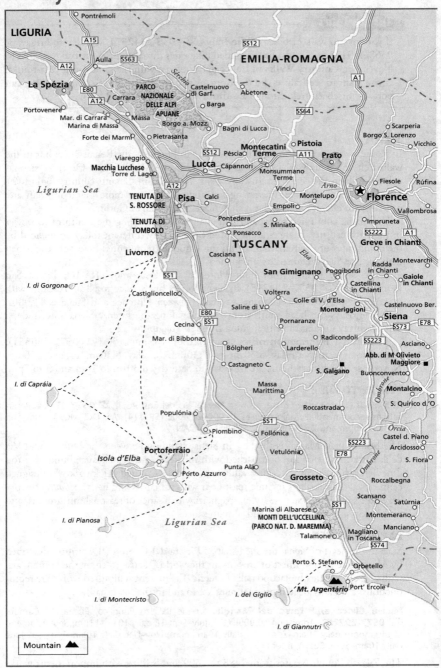

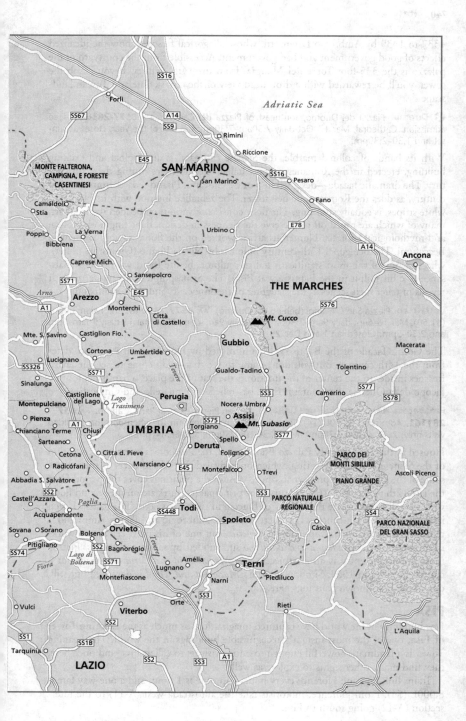

Adriatic Sea

SS16

Forlì

SS67

A14

SS9

Rimini

Riccione

SAN MARINO

SS16

MONTE FALTERONA,
CAMPIGNA, E FORESTE
CASENTINESI

San Marino

Pesaro

E45

Fano

Camáldoli

Stia

E78

A14

Poppi

La Verna

Urbino

Bibbiena

Ancona

Caprese Mich.

SS71

Sansepolcro

THE MARCHES

Arno

Arezzo

E45

SS76

Monterchi

A1

Città
di Castello

Mt. Cucco

Mte. S. Savino

Castiglion Fio.

Gubbio

Macerata

Cortona

Umbértide

Lucignano

Gualdo-Tadino

Tolentino

SS326

SS71

SS3

Camerino

SS77

Sinalunga

SS78

Lago
Trasimeno

Perugia

Nocera Umbra

Castiglione
del Lago

SS75

Assisi

Mt. Subasio

Montepulciano

Torgiano

Pienza

A1

Chiusi

Spello

SS77

Chianciano Terme

UMBRIA

Deruta

Sarteano

Foligno

Cetona

Città d. Pieve

Montefalco

Trevi

PARCO DEI
MONTI SIBILLINI

Radicófani

Marsciano

E45

Abbadia S. Salvatore

Ascoli Piceno

PIANO GRANDE

SS2

Paglia

SS3

Castell'Azzara

PARCO NATURALE
REGIONALE

Acquapendente

Todi

SS448

SS4

Sovana

Sorano

Orvieto

Spoleto

Cáscia

PARCO NAZIONALE
DEL GRAN SASSO

Bolsena

Pitigliano

SS2

Bagnorégio

Tevere

SS74

Fiora

SS71

Amélia

Lago di
Bolsena

Montefiascone

Lugnano

Terni

Piediluco

Narni

Vulci

Orte

SS3

Rieti

Viterbo

SS2

L'Aquila

SS1

SS1B

Tarquinia

SS2

SS3

A1

LAZIO

1337 to 1339 by Ambrogio Lorenzetti, whose allegorical frescoes show the idealized effects of good government and bad government. Accessible from the courtyard of the palazzo is the 335-foot **Torre del Mangia,** from the 14th century. If you climb the tower, you'll be rewarded with a drop-dead view of the city skyline and Tuscan landscape.

✪ **Duomo.** Piazza del Duomo, southeast of Piazza del Campo. ☎ **0577-283048.** Free admission. Cathedral, Mar 17–Oct daily 7:30am–7:30pm; the rest of the year, closes at sunset and 1:30–2:30pm.

With its bands of colored marble, the Sienese cathedral is an original and exciting building, erected in the Romanesque and Italian Gothic styles during the 12th century. The dramatic facade—designed in part by Giovanni Pisano—dates from the 13th century, as does the Romanesque bell tower. The zebralike interior, with its black and white stripes, is equally stunning. The floor consists of various embedded works of art, many of which are roped off to preserve the richness in design, depicting both biblical and mythological subjects. Numerous artists worked on the floor, notably Domenico Beccafumi. The octagonal 13th-century pulpit is by Nicola Pisano (Giovanni's father), who was one of the most significant Italian sculptors before the dawn of the Renaissance (see his pulpit in the Baptistery at Pisa). The Siena pulpit is his masterpiece; it reveals in relief such scenes as the slaughter of the innocents and the Crucifixion.

Battistero. Piazza San Giovanni (behind the Duomo). ☎ **0577-283048.** Admission 3,000L ($1.50). Mar 16–Sept daily 9am–7:30pm; Oct daily 9am–6pm; Nov–Mar 15 daily 10am–1pm and 2:30–5pm. Closed Jan 1 and Dec 25.

The Gothic facade of the Baptistry, left unfinished by Domenico di Agostino, dates from the 14th century. But you don't come to see that—you come to see the lavish frescoes inside. In the center of the interior is the star of the place, a baptismal font by Jacopo della Quercia that contains some bas-reliefs by Donatello and Ghiberti.

Pinacoteca Nazionale (Picture Gallery). Via San Pietro 29, near Pz. d. Campo. ☎ **0577-281161.** Admission 8,000L ($4). Tues–Sat 8:30am–1:30pm (in the afternoon three guided visits only: 2:30, 4, and 5:30pm), Mon 8:30am–1:30pm, Sun 8am–1pm.

Housed in the 14th-century Palazzo Buonsignori, the Pinacoteca contains a collection of the Sienese school of painting, which once rivaled that of Florence. Displayed are some of the giants of the pre-Renaissance. Most of the paintings cover the period from the late 12th to the mid-16th century. The principal treasures are on the second floor, where you'll contemplate the artistry of Duccio in the early salons. The gallery is rich in the art of the 14th-century Lorenzetti brothers, Ambrogio and Pietro. Ambrogio is represented by an *Annunciation* and a *Crucifix,* but one of his most celebrated works is an almond-eyed *Madonna and Bambino* surrounded by saints and angels. Pietro's most important entry is an altarpiece—*The Madonna of the Carmine*—made for a church in Siena in 1329. Simone Martini's *Madonna and Child* is damaged but still, one of the best-known paintings here.

PISA

Few buildings in the world have captured imaginations as much as the **Leaning Tower of Pisa,** one of the most instantly recognizable buildings in the world. The Leaning Tower is a landmark powerful enough to entice visitors to call at Pisa, and once here, they find many other sights to explore as well.

Trains link Pisa and Florence every hour. Trip time is 1 hour, and a one-way fare is 8,000L ($4). From Florence, motorists take the autostrada west (A-11) to the intersection (A-12) going south to Pisa.

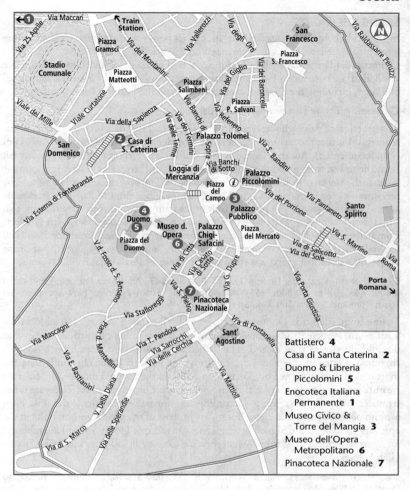

The **tourist information office** is at Via Carlo Cammeo 2 (☎ **050-560464**), open March to October Monday to Saturday 8:30am to 7:30pm; off-season, Monday to Saturday 9:30am to 1pm and 2:30 to 5:30pm. There's also another office at piazza della Stazione.

WHERE TO DINE

✪ **Al Ristoro dei Vecchi Macelli.** Via Volturno 49. ☎ **050-20424.** Reservations required. Main courses 18,000–36,000L ($9–$18). Mon–Tues and Thurs–Sat 1–3pm and 8–10:30pm, Sun 8–10:30pm. AE, DC. Closed 2 weeks in Aug. INTERNATIONAL/PISAN.

Near Piazzetta di Vecchi Macelli, is the best restaurant in Pisa. After selecting from a choice of two dozen varieties of seafood antipasti, you can enjoy a homemade pasta with scallops and zucchini or fish-stuffed ravioli in shrimp sauce. Other dishes are gnocchi with pesto and shrimp and roast veal with a velvety truffle-flavored cream sauce.

Seeing the Sights

In the Middle Ages, Pisa reached the apex of its power as a maritime republic before it eventually fell to its rivals, Florence and Genoa. Its greatest legacy remains at ✪ **Piazza del Duomo,** which D'Annunzio labeled piazza dei Miracoli (miracles). Here you'll find an ensemble of the top three attractions—original "Pisan-Romanesque" buildings, including the Duomo, the Baptistery, and the Leaning Tower itself.

✪ **Leaning Tower (Campanile).** Piazza del Duomo. Bus: 1.

Construction of this eight-story campanile began in 1174 by Bonanno, and a persistent legend is that the architect deliberately intended the bell tower to lean (that claim is undocumented). Another legend is that Galileo let objects of different weights fall from the tower, then timed their descent to prove his theories on bodies in motion.

Alas, the tower is in serious danger of collapse. The government is taking various measures to keep it from falling, including clamping five rings of half-inch steel cable around its lower stones and pouring tons of lead around its base to keep it stabilized. The tower floats on a sandy base of water-soaked clay; it leans at least 4m (14 feet) from perpendicular. If it stood up straight, the tower would measure about 55m (180 feet) tall. In 1990, the government suspended visits inside. In years gone by one of the major attractions in Europe was to climb the Tower of Pisa—taking all 294 steps.

✪ **Il Duomo.** Piazza del Duomo 17. ☎ **050-560547.** Admission (including Battistero) 3,000L ($1.50) or 10,000L ($5). May–Oct daily 10am–7:30pm; Nov–Apr Mon–Sat 10am–1pm and 3–5pm, Sun 3–4:45pm.

Dating from 1063, the Duomo was designed by Buschetto, though Rainaldo in the 13th century erected the unusual facade with its four layers of open-air arches that diminish in size as they ascend. The cathedral is marked by three bronze doors—rhythmic in line—that replaced those destroyed in a fire in 1596. The south door, the most notable, was designed by Bonanno in 1180. In the restored interior, the chief art treasure is the pulpit by Giovanni Pisano, which was finished in 1310. There are other treasures, too: Galileo's lamp (according to unreliable tradition, the Pisa-born astronomer used the chandelier to formulate his laws of the pendulum); mosaics in the apse said to have been designed by Cimabue; the tomb of Henry VII of Luxembourg; *St. Agnes* by Andrea del Sarto; *Descent from the Cross* by Il Sodoma; and a Crucifix by Giambologna.

Battistero (Baptistry). Piazza del Duomo. ☎ **050-560547.** Admission (including Duomo) 10,000L ($5). June–Aug daily 8am–7:30pm, closes 1 to 2 hours earlier rest of the year. Closed Dec 31 and Jan 1.

Begun in 1153, the Baptistry is like a Romanesque crown. Although it's most beautiful on the exterior, with its arches and columns, venture inside to see the hexagonal pulpit made by Nicola Pisano in 1260. Supported by pillars resting on the backs of three marble lions, the pulpit contains bas-reliefs of the Crucifixion, the Adoration of the Magi, the presentation of the Christ child at the temple, and the Last Judgment (many angels have lost their heads over the years).

Museo Nazionale di San Matteo. Piazzetta San Matteo 1. ☎ **050-541865.** Admission 8,000L ($4). Tues–Sat 9am–7pm and Sun 9am–1:30pm.

Near Piazza Mazzini, the National Museum contains a good assortment of paintings and sculpture, many dating from the 13th to the 16th century. In the museum are statues by Giovanni Pisano; Simone Martini's *Madonna and Child with Saints,* a polyptych; Nino Pisano's *Madonna de Latte,* a marble sculpture; Masaccio's *St. Paul,* painted in 1426; Domenico Ghirlandaio's two *Madonna and Saints* depictions; works by Strozzi and Alessandro Magnasco; and old copies of works by Jan and Pieter Bruegel. You enter from Piazza San Matteo.

SAN GIMIGNANO

The golden lily of the Middle Ages is called the Manhattan of Tuscany since it preserves 13 of its noble towers, giving it a skyscraper skyline. It lies 42km (26 miles) northwest of Siena and 55km (34 miles) southwest of Florence.

Poggibonsi, serviced by regular trains from Florence and Siena, is the **rail** station nearest to San Gimignano. At Poggibono, buses depart from in front of the station at frequent intervals to the center of San Gimignano. For information, call **0577-204-111. Buses** operated by **TRA-IN** (☎ **0577-204-111**) service San Gimignano from Florence with a change at Poggibonsi (trip time: 75 minutes). The same company also operates service from Siena, with a change at Poggibonsi (trip time: 50 minutes). In San Gimignano, buses stop at Piazzale Montemaggio, outside Porta San Giovanni, the southern gate. You'll have to walk into the center, as vehicles aren't allowed in most of the town's core.

If you've got a **car,** leave Florence (trip time: 1½ hours) or Siena (1¼ hours) by the Firenze-Siena autostrada and drive to Poggibonsi, where you'll need to cut west along a secondary route (S324) to San Gimignano.

For tourist information, go to **Associazione Pro Loco,** Piazza del Duomo 1 (☎ **0577-940-008**), open November to February daily 9am to 1pm and 2 to 6pm (March to October to 7pm).

WHERE TO STAY

Since you'll want to spend as much time here as possible, an overnight stay is recommended.

Hotel La Cisterna. Piazza della Cisterna 24, 53037 San Gimignano. ☎ **0577-940-328.** Fax 0577-942-080. E-mail: lacisterna@i0l.it. 49 units. TV TEL. 155,000–195,000L ($78–$98) double, 220,000L ($110) suite. Rates include breakfast. AE, DC, MC, V. Closed Jan–Feb. Parking 25,000L ($13).

Opened in 1919, the ivy-covered La Cisterna is modernized but still retains its medieval lines (it was built at the base of some 14th-century patrician towers). For years, it was the only hotel in town, and it's still one of the leading inns. Many people visit it just to patronize Ristorante Le Terrazze (See "Where to Dine," below). Rooms are generally large; some of the best ones open onto terraces with views of the Val d'Elsa.

✪ **Relais Santa Chiara.** Via Matteotti 15, 53037 San Gimignano. ☎ **0577-940-701.** Fax 0577-942-096. www.rscit. E-mail: rsci@rsc.it. 41 units. A/C MINIBAR TV TEL. 250,000–390,000L ($125–$195) double, 460,000L ($230) suite. Rates include buffet breakfast. AE, DC, MC, V. Closed Dec-Mar.

This solid comfortable hotel lies in a residential neighborhood about a 10-minute walk south of the medieval ramparts. It's the prestigious place to stay, far superior to La Cisterna. It's surrounded with elegant gardens and a pool, and its spacious public rooms contain Florentine terra-cotta floors and mosaics. Rooms are comfortable and include a Jacuzzi, radio, and hair dryer. Though the hotel is relatively new, the furnishings and ambience blend in harmoniously with the Tuscan countryside. There's no restaurant, but the hotel serves a buffet breakfast and snacks at lunch in summer.

WHERE TO DINE

Ristorante Bel Soggiorno. In the Hotel Bel Soggiorno, Via San Giovanni 91. ☎ **0577-940-375.** Reservations recommended. Main courses 20,000–32,000L ($10–$16); fixed-price menu 45,000L ($23). AE, DC, MC, V. Thurs–Tues 12:30–2:30pm and 7:30–10pm. Closed Jan 7–Feb. TUSCAN.

Thanks to windows overlooking the countryside and a devoted use of fresh ingredients from nearby farms, you'll get a strong sense of Tuscany's agrarian bounty here. Two of the most appealing specialties (available only late summer to late winter) are roasted wild boar with red wine and mixed vegetables and pappardelle pasta garnished with a savory ragout of pheasant. Other pastas are pappardelle with roasted hare and risotto with herbs and seasonal vegetables.

Ristorante Le Terrazze. In La Cisterna, Piazza della Cisterna 24. ☎ **0577-940-328.** Reservations required. Main courses 25,000–35,000L ($13–$18). AE, DC, MC, V. Wed 7:30–10pm, Thurs–Mon 12:30–2:30pm and 7:30–10pm. Closed Nov–Feb. TUSCAN.

The newer of this restaurant's two dining rooms has large windows overlooking the old town and the Val d'Elsa. The setting is one of a country inn, and the food features an assortment of produce from the surrounding farms. Soups and pastas make fine beginnings, and specialties of the house include delectable items like sliced fillet of wild boar with polenta and Chianti, breast of goose with walnut sauce, vitello (veal) alla Cisterna with buttered beans, and Florence-style steaks.

EXPLORING THE TOWN

In the town center is the palazzo-flanked **Piazza della Cisterna,** so named because of the 13th-century cistern in its heart. Connected with the irregularly shaped square is its satellite, **Piazza del Duomo,** whose medieval architecture—towers and palaces— is almost unchanged. It's the most beautiful spot in town. On the square, the **Palazzo del Popolo**'s **Torre Grossa,** at 54m (178 feet), is believed to have been the tallest "skyscraper" in town.

Note: One ticket, available at any of the sites below, allows admission to all of them for 18,000L ($9).

Duomo Collegiata o Basilica di Santa Maria Assunta. Piazza del Duomo. ☎ **0577-940-316.** Church, free; chapel, 3,000L ($1.50). Daily 9:30am–12:30pm and 3–5:30pm.

Residents of San Gimignano still call this a Duomo (cathedral), even though it was demoted to a "Collegiata" once the town lost its bishop. Plain and austere on the outside, it's richly decorated inside. Retreat inside to a world of tiger-striped arches and a galaxy of gold stars. Head for the north aisle, where in the 1360s Bartolo di Fredi depicted scenes from the Old Testament. Two memorable ones are *The Trials of Job* and *Noah with the Animals.* In the right aisle, panels trace scenes from the life of Christ—the kiss of Judas, the Last Supper, the Flagellation, and the Crucifixion. The chief attraction is the **Chapel of Santa Fina,** designed by Giuliano and Benedetto da Maiano. Michelangelo's fresco teacher, Domenico Ghirlandaio, frescoed it with scenes from the life of a local girl, Fina, who became the town's patron saint.

Civic Museum (Museo Civico). In the Palazzo del Popolo, Piazza del Duomo 1. ☎ **0577-940-340.** Admission 7,000L ($3.50). Apr–Oct daily 9:30am–7pm; Nov–Mar Tues–Sun 9:30am–1pm and 2:30–4:30pm.

This museum is installed upstairs in the Palazzo del Popolo (town hall). Most notable is the **Sala di Dante,** where the White Guelph-supporting poet spoke out for his cause in 1300. Look for one of the masterpieces of San Gimignano—the *Maestà* (Madonna enthroned) by Lippo Memmi (later touched up by Gozzoli). The first large room upstairs contains other masterpiece: a *Madonna in Glory,* with Sts. Gregory and Benedict, painted by Pinturicchio. On the other side of it are two depictions of the *Annunciation* by Filippino Lippi.

Passing through the Museo Civico, you can scale the **Torre Grossa** and be rewarded with a bird's-eye view of this most remarkable town. The tower, the only one in town you can climb, is open March to October daily 9:30am to 7:30pm; off-season, Tuesday to Saturday 9:30am to 1:30pm and 2:30 to 4:30pm. Admission is 8,000L ($4).

LUCCA

In 56 B.C., Caesar, Crassus, and Pompey met in **Lucca** and agreed to rule Rome as a triumvirate. By the time of the Roman Empire's collapse, it was virtually the capital of Tuscany. Periodically in its valiant, ever-bloody history, Lucca was an independent principality, similar to Genoa. This autonomy attests to the fame and prestige it enjoyed. Now, however, Lucca is largely bypassed by time and travelers, rewarding the discriminating few.

By the late 1600s, Lucca had gained its third and final set of city walls. This girdle of ramparts is largely intact and is one of the major reasons to visit the town, with its medley of architecture ranging from Roman to Liberty (the Italian term for art nouveau).

Today, Lucca is best known for its *olio d'oliva lucchese,* quality olive oil produced in the region outside the town's walls. Lucca is a sort of Switzerland of the south: the banks have latticed Gothic windows, the shops look like well-stocked linen cupboards, children play in landscaped gardens, and geraniums bloom from the roofs of medieval tower houses.

At least 20 **trains** travel daily between Florence and Lucca (trip time: 1¼ hours). The rail station lies about .5km (¼-mile) south of Lucca's historic core, a short walk from the city's ramparts. For rail information in Lucca, call **0583-467-013.** The **Lazzi bus** company (☎ **0583-584-877**) operates buses traveling between Florence and Lucca (trip time: 1 hour). If you've got a **car,** leave Florence and take A11 through Prato, Pistoia, and Montecatini before reaching the outskirts of Lucca. If you're in Pisa, take SS12.

The Lucca **tourist office** is on Piazzale Verdi (☎ **0583-419-689**), open daily 9:30am to 6:30pm April to October (off-season to 3:30pm). They also have a 24-hour answering machine service (in both English and Italian), giving information on events and monuments.

WHERE TO STAY

Since Lucca will absorb so much of your time, consider it as an overnight stopover from Florence.

✪ **Locanda l'Elisa.** Strada Statale del Brennaro 1952, 55050 Mass Pisana (Lucca). ☎ **0583-379-737.** Fax 0583-379-019. www.lunet.it/aziende/locandaelisa. E-mail: locanda. elisa@lunet.it. 10 units. A/C MINIBAR TV TEL. 450,000L ($225) double, 550,000L ($275) junior suite for two. AE, DC, MC, V. Free parking. Bus: 2 from center of Lucca.

This Relais & Châteaux hotel is the region's most elegant, 3km (2 miles) south of the city walls. During the mid–19th century, it was the home of an army officer who was the preferred escort and intimate companion of Napoléon's sister Elisa. Behind a dignified neoclassical facade, this locanda (inn) has verdant gardens, discreet and charming service, and large and plushly decorated rooms. All but two are skillfully decorated junior suites with views of either gardens or a park. The restaurant, Il Gazebo, serving an Italian and Tuscan cuisine, is one of the area's finest choices for dining. Il Gazebo is a Victorian-style conservatory inserted in a charming garden where you'll also find the pool.

Piccolo Hotel Puccini. Via di Poggio 9, 55100 Lucca. ☎ **0583-55-421.** Fax 0583-53-487. www.onenet.it/lu/hotel_puccini. E-mail: hotelpuccinilu@onenet.it. 14 units. TV TEL. 130,000L ($65) double. Rates include breakfast. AE, MC, V. Free parking nearby.

Your best bet in the center is this 15th-century palace across from the Puccini birth-place. The classical music played in the lobby area (often Puccini) commemorates the long-ago association. Right off Piazza San Michele, one of the most enchanting in Lucca, this little hotel is better than ever now that an energetic couple, Raffaella and Paolo, has taken it over, breathing new life into the property. Intimate and comfort-able rooms are beautifully maintained with good beds. Some windows open onto the small square in front with a bronze statue of Puccini.

WHERE TO DINE

Even if you don't stay over, consider lunch at one of the following for the best food in Lucca.

✪ **Buca di Sant'Antonio.** Via della Cervia 1. ☎ **0583-55-881.** Reservations recom-mended. Main courses 22,000–30,000L ($11–$15). AE, DC, MC, V. Tues–Sun noon–3pm, Tues–Sat 7:30–10:30pm. Closed 2 weeks in July. TUSCAN.

On a difficult-to-find alleyway near Piazza san Michele, this is Lucca's finest restau-rant. The 1782 building was constructed on the site of a chapel that was believed to be favorable for invoking the protective powers of St. Anthony. The cuisine is refined and inspired, respecting the traditional ways but also daring to be innovative. Menu items include homemade ravioli stuffed with ricotta and pulverized zucchini, grilled meat and fish dishes, and roast Tuscan goat with roast potatoes and braised greens.

Giglio. Piazza del Giglio 2. ☎ **0583-494-058.** Reservations recommended. Main courses 15,000–25,000L ($8–$13). AE, DC, MC, V. Thurs–Tues noon–3pm, Thurs–Mon 7–10pm. Closed Feb. REGIONAL/TUSCAN.

In regional appeal and popularity, this place is rivaled only by the Buca di Sant'Anto-nio. The secret to its appeal might be its rustic decor, its attentive staff, and its fine interpretations of time-honored Tuscan and regional recipes. Menu items usually include steaming bowls of *minestre di farro,* homemade tortellini with meat sauce, roasted codfish with virgin olive oil, a savory stewed rabbit with olives, and *tortes* made from vegetables like carrots or with a base of cream and chocolate.

EXPLORING THE TOWN

✪ **Le Mura** enclose the old town. The Lucchesi are fiercely proud of these city walls, the best-preserved Renaissance defense ramparts in Europe. The present walls, mea-suring 35m (115 feet) at the base and soaring 12m (40 feet) high, replaced crumbling ramparts built during the Middle Ages. If you'd like to join in one of the grand prom-enades of Tuscany, you can gain access to the ramparts from one of 10 bastions, the most frequently used of which is in back of the tourist office at **Piazzale Verdi.** For orientation, you may want to walk completely around the city on the tree-shaded ram-parts, a distance of 4km (2¹/₂ miles).

Cattedrale di San Martino (Duomo). Piazza San Martino. ☎ **0583-494-726.** Admis-sion: Cathedral, free; sacristy and inner sanctum, 4,000L ($2). Church and sacristy, Apr–Oct daily 10am–6pm; Nov–Mar Mon–Fri 10am–2pm, Sat–Sun 10am–5pm.

On Piazza San Martino, the Duomo is the town's most visible monument, dating back to 1060, though the present structure was mainly rebuilt during the following cen-turies. The facade is exceptional, evoking the Pisan-Romanesque style but with enough originality and idiosyncrasies to distinguish it from the Duomo at Pisa. Designed mostly by Guidetto da Como in the early 13th century, the west front con-tains three wide ground-level arches, surmounted by three scalloped galleries with taffy-like twisting columns tapering in size. The main relic inside—in some ways the religious symbol of Lucca itself—is the *Volto Santo,* a crucifix carved by Nicodemus (so tradition has it) from a cedar of Lebanon. The face of Christ was supposedly chiseled onto the statuary.

Chiesa San Frediano. Piazza San Frediano. ☎ **0583-493-627.** Free admission. Mon–Sat 7:30am–noon and 3–6pm, Sun 9am–1pm and 3–6pm.

Romanesque in style, this is one of Lucca's most important and famous churches, built in the 12th and 13th centuries when the town enjoyed its greatest glory. A mosaic of the Ascension relieves the severe white facade, and the campanile or bell tower rises majestically. Inside the bas-reliefs on the Romanesque font add a note of comic relief: Supposedly depicting the story of Moses, among other themes, they show Egyptians in medieval armor chasing after the Israelites.

National Picture Gallery and Palazzo Mansi Museum (Pinacoteca Nazionale e Museo di Palazzo Mansi). Via Galli Tassi 43. ☎ **0593-55-570.** Admission 8,000L ($4). Tues–Sat 9am–7pm, Sun 9am–2pm.

The Lucchesi horde their art treasures in this palace built for the powerful Mansi family, whose descendants are still movers and shakers in town. Though Tuscany has far greater preserves of art, there're some treasures here, notably a portrait of Princess Elisa by Marie Benoist, Elisa Bonaparte (1777–1820), who married into a local wealthy family, the Bacceocchis, and was "given" the town by her brother Napoléon in 1805 when he made her princess of Lucca and Piombino. The collection is enriched by works from Lanfranco, Luca Giordano, and Tintoretto, among others, though not their greatest works.

AREZZO

The most landlocked of all towns or cities of Tuscany, Arezzo, 80km (50 miles) southeast of Florence, was originally an Etruscan settlement and later, a Roman center. The city flourished in the Middle Ages before its capitulation to Florence.

The walled town grew up on a hill, but large parts of the ancient city, including native son Petrarch's house, were bombed during World War II. Another famous son is Vasari, the painter/architect remembered chiefly for his history of the Renaissance artists.

Today, Arezzo looks a little rustic, but it really isn't. The city has one of the biggest jewelry industries in western Europe. Little firms on the outskirts turn out an array of rings and chains, and bank vaults are overflowing with gold ingots. Because of the lack of any really good hotels, you may want to return to Florence for the night.

A **train** comes from Florence at intervals of 20 to 60 minutes throughout the day (trip time: 40 to 60 minutes). In Arezzo, trains depart and arrive at the **Stazione Centrale,** Piazza della Repubblica (☎ **1478-88-088**). Because of complicated transfers required en route and travel time of as much as 2¹/₂ hours each way, a trip by **bus** from Florence to Arezzo isn't a good idea. If you have a **car** and are in Rome, head north on A1; from Florence, head south on A1. In both directions, the turnoff for Arezzo is clearly marked.

The **tourist office** at Piazza della Repubblica 28 (☎ **0575-377-678**), is open April to September every Monday to Saturday 9am to 1pm and 3 to 7pm and Sunday 9am to 1pm; October to March, it's open Monday to Saturday 9am to 1pm and 3 to 6:30pm, first Sunday of every month 9am to 1pm.

WHERE TO DINE

✪ **Buca di San Francesco.** Via San Francesco 1. ☎ **0575-23-271.** Reservations recommended. Main courses 25,000–40,000L ($13–$20). AE, DC, MC, V. Wed–Sun 12:30–3pm and 7–11pm, Mon 12:30–3pm. ITALIAN.

This is the city's finest dining choice, housed in the historic core of Arezzo in the cellar of a building from the 1300s; it's decorated with medieval references and strong Tuscan colors of sienna and blue. Menu items include pollo del Valdarno arrosto (roast chicken from the valley of the Arno) flavored with anise, homemade tagliolini with tomatoes and ricotta, and calves' liver with onions. All ingredients are fresh, many of the stapes are produced in-house, and even the olive oil is from private sources not shared by other restaurants.

EXPLORING AREZZO

The biggest event on the Arezzo calendar is the **Giostra del Saraceno,** staged the third Sunday of June and the first Sunday of September on Piazza Grande. Horsemen in medieval costumes reenact the lance-charging joust ritual—with balled whips cracking in the air—as they have since the 13th century. But you should visit **Piazza Grande** at any time of the year for the medieval and Renaissance palaces and towers that flank it, including the 16th-century loggia by Vasari.

✪ **Basilica di San Francesco.** Piazza San Francesco. ☎ **0575-20-630.** Free admission. Daily 8:30am–noon and 2–6:30pm.

If you have only an hour for Arezzo, race to this Gothic church finished in the 14th century for the Franciscans. Inside is Piero della Francesca's fresco cycle, *Legend of the True Cross.* They're remarkable for their grace, clearness, dramatic light effects, well-chosen colors, and ascetic severity. The frescoes depict the burial of Adam; Solomon receiving the queen of Sheba at the court (the most memorable scene); the dream of Constantine with the descent of an angel; and the triumph of the Holy Cross with Heraclius, among other subjects.

Santa Maria della Pieve. Corso Italia. ☎ **0575-22-629.** Free admission. Mon–Sat 8am–1pm and 3–7pm, Sun 8am–1pm and 3–6:30pm.

This Romanesque church is fronted by three open-air loggias (each pillar designed uniquely). The 14th-century bell tower is known as "the hundred holes," as it's riddled with windows. Inside, the church is bleak and austere, but there's a notable polyptych, *The Virgin with Saints,* by Pietro Lorenzetti.

Petrarch's House. Via dell'Orto 28A. ☎ **0575-24-700.** Free admission. Mon–Fri 10am–noon and 3–5pm; Sat 10am–noon. Closed Aug 1–25.

A short walk from Santa Maria della Pieve is the house of Francesco Petrarch (1304–74), rebuilt after war damage. Born at Arezzo, he was a great lyrical poet and humanist who immortalized his love, Laura, in his sonnets. His house is filled with memorabilia. Ring the bell to enter.

GUBBIO

Lying 92km (57 miles) southeast of Arezzo, Gubbio is one of the best-preserved medieval towns in Italy. Once you press through the modern apartments and stores on the outskirts, you're firmly back in the Middle Ages. The best-known streets of its medieval core are **Via XX Settembre, Via dei Consoli, Via Galeotti,** and **Via Baldassini.** All these are in the old town (Città Vecchia), set against the steep slopes of Monte Ingino.

Since Gubbio is off-the-beaten track, it remains a fairly sleepy backwater except for intrepid shoppers who drive here for the ceramics. Today, the central **Piazza dei Quaranta Martiri** is named for and honors victims of Nazi atrocities in 1944.

Gubbio doesn't have a rail station of its own, so **train** passengers headed for Gubbio from other parts of Italy get off at the nearby railway station of Fossato di Vico,

19km (12 miles) away, then transfer to one of the frequent buses that make the short trip on to Gubbio. Fosato di Vico lies astride the rail lines stretching between Rome and Ancona. Motorists from Florence can take the A1 south to Orte, then take SS3 north 142km (88 miles) to its intersection with SS298 at Schéggia. Go southwest on SS298 for 13km (8 miles) to Gubbio.

The **tourist office** is at Piazza Oderisi 6 (☎ **075-922-0693**), open October to February Monday to Friday 8am to 2pm and 3 to 6pm, Saturday 9am to 1pm and 3 to 6pm. March to September Monday to Friday 8am to 2pm and 3:30 to 6:30pm, Saturday 9am to 1pm and 3:30 to 6:30pm. Sunday year-round 9:30am to 12:30pm.

WHERE TO STAY

Gubbio is one of the best centers in Tuscany for overnighting.

✪ **Hotel Relais Ducale.** Via Ducale 2, 06024 Gubbio. ☎ **075-922-0157.** Fax 075-922-0159. www.mencarelligroup.com. E-mail: mencarelli@mencarelligroup.com. 32 units. MINIBAR TV TEL. 280,000–320,000L ($140–$160) double; 350,000L ($175) suite. Rates include breakfast. AE, DC, V.

Once this palazzo was the guesthouse for the dukes of Urbino, built in a palace between Piazza Grande and Palazzo Ducale in the very heart of town. Nowadays the former guest quarters have been converted into a charming hotel with exotic hanging gardens and terraces overlooking the main piazza of town. Rooms come in a variety of sizes, many quite large. All have been modernized with amenities such as Jacuzzis. The restaurant, Taverna del Lupo, is worth a detour even if you're not staying here. It offers a well-balanced menu of Italian specialties. In addition, the Caffè Ducale is the best place in central Gubbio for meeting people and sipping a cappuccino or one of their drinks.

Palace Hotel Bosone. Via XX Settembre 22, 06024 Gubbio. ☎ **075-922-0698.** Fax 075-922-0552. 30 units. MINIBAR TV TEL. 180,000–200,000L ($90–$100) double, 350,000L ($175) suite. AE, DC, MC, V. Closed Jan 10–Mar 15. Free self-parking nearby.

This hotel is in the town's most scenic location, and it's also one of the most historic, having once housed Dante. Set at the meeting point of an almost endless flight of stone steps and a narrow street in the upper regions of town, it was built in the 1300s and enlarged during the Renaissance. The three-story stone building was converted from a private home into a hotel in 1974, welcoming guests ever since into cozy rooms. Breakfast is the only meal served.

WHERE TO DINE

Taverna del Lupo. Via Giovanni Ansid. 21. ☎ **075-927-4368.** Reservations recommended. Main courses 16,000–32,000L ($8–$16). AE, DC, MC, V. Tues–Sun 12:15–3pm and 7pm–midnight. ITALIAN/UMBRIAN.

Gubbio has many taverns that will feed you well. The most authentically medieval is Taverna del Lupo. Built in the 1200s, with unusual rows of tiles, it contains ceilings supported by barrel vaults and ribbing of solid stone, from which hang iron chandeliers. For such a relatively modest place, the menu is sophisticated and filled with the rich bounty from this part of Italy, each dish deftly prepared by a talented kitchen staff. Menu items include a terrine of duck studded with truffles, suprême of pheasant, rich minestrone, and many of the pork, veal, and beef dishes that are distinctly Tuscan.

EXPLORING THE OLD TOWN

If the weather is right, you can take a cable car up to **Monte Ingino,** at a height of 820m (2,690 feet), for a panoramic view. Service is daily: June to August 8:30am to

8pm (to 7:30pm April, May, and September to March). A round-trip ticket is 6,500L ($3.25).

Back in Gubbio, you can set about exploring a town that knew its golden age in the 1300s. Begin at **Piazza Grande,** the most important square.

Palazzo dei Consoli. Piazza Grande. ☎ **075-927-4298.** Admission 7,000L ($3.50). Apr–Sept daily 10am–1pm and 3–6pm; Oct–Mar daily 10am–1pm and 2–5pm.

The Gothic Consuls' Palace houses the famed bronze *tavole eugubine,* a series of tablets as old as Christianity, discovered in the 15th century. The tablets contain writing in the mysterious Umbrian language.

Ducal Palace (Palazzo Ducale). Via Ducale. ☎ **075-927-5872.** Admission 4,000L ($2). Mon–Sat 9am–6:30pm and Sun 9am–1:30pm. Closed first Mon of the month.

Associated with the memories (not always good ones) of the ruling dukes of Urbino, the Ducal Palace was built for Federico of Montefeltro. Most of the elegant decor and artworks have long been stripped away, but you can still see a collection of baroque paintings and some of the original palace frescoes. In summer, you can also explore the hanging gardens.

Il Duomo. Via Ducale. ☎ **075-927-3980.** Free admission. Daily 9am–12:30pm and 3:30–8:30pm.

The cathedral is across the way from the Ducal Palace. It's a relatively unadorned pink Gothic building with some 12th-century stained-glass windows. Inside, several arches support the ceiling. Of particular interest are the wood cross above the altar, an exquisite example of the 13th-century Umbrian school, and a painting of Mary Magdelene, a Piero della Francesca masterpiece, in the Bishop's chapel.

SHOPPING

This is the major reason many visitors flock here. Gubbio's fame as a ceramics center had is beginnings in the 14th century. Two of the best ceramics outlets are in the town center. Head for **Ceramica Rampini,** Via Leonardo da Vinci 94 (☎ **075-927-2963**), where you can visit the workshop; the Rampini store is at Via dei Consoli 52 (same phone). Its largest competitor, **Mastro Giorgio,** is at Piazza Grande 3 (☎ **075-927-1574**). La Mastro Giorgio opens its factory, at Via Tifernate 10 (☎ **075-927-3616**), about .8km (¹/₂ mile) from the center, to well-intentioned visitors who phone in advance for a convenient hour.

ASSISI

Ideally placed on the rise to Mt. Subasio, watched over by the medieval **Rocca Maggiore,** this purple-fringed Umbrian hill town retains a mystical air. The site of many a pilgrimage, Assisi is forever linked in legend with is native son, St. Francis. The gentle saint founded the Franciscan order and shares honors with St. Catherine of Siena as the patron saint of Italy. But he's remembered by many, even non-Christians, as a lover of nature (his preaching to an audience of birds is one of the legends of his life). Dante compared him to John the Baptist. St. Francis put Assisi on the map, and making a pilgrimage here is one of the highlights of a visit to Umbria. Assisi is still recovering from twin earthquakes that struck in the autumn of 1997.

Although there's no rail station in Assisi, the town, which lies 177km (110 miles) north of Rome and 24km (15 miles) southeast of Perugia, is but a 30-minute bus or taxi ride from the nearby Santa Maria degli Angeli rail station. Buses depart at 30-minute intervals for Piazza Matteotti, in the heart of Assisi. **Trains** between Florence and Assisi usually require a transfer at Terontola. Frequent **buses** connect Perugia with

Assisi

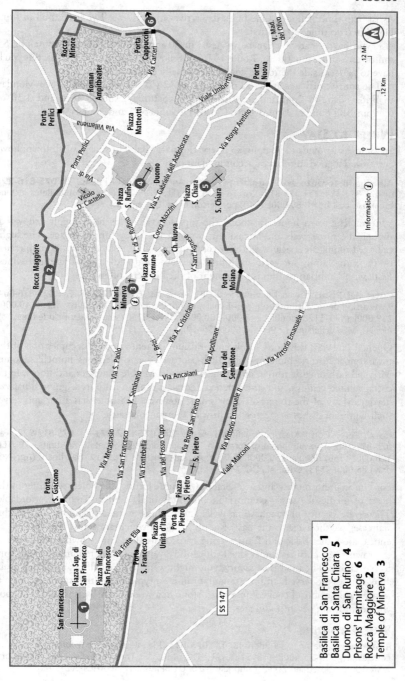

Basilica di San Francesco **1**
Basilica di Santa Chiara **5**
Duomo di San Rufino **4**
Prisons' Hermitage **6**
Rocca Maggiore **2**
Temple of Minerva **3**

Information ⓘ

.12 Mi
.12 Km

SS 147

Assisi (trip time: 1 hour). One bus a day arrives from Rome. Two buses pull in from Florence (trip time: 2¹/₂ hours).

If you have a **car**, you can be in Assisi in 30 minutes from Perugia by taking S3 southwest. At the junction of Route 147, just follow the signs toward Assisi. But you'll have to park outside the town's core, as it's usually closed to traffic.

The **tourist office** is at Piazza del Comune 12 (☎ **075-812-534**), open Monday to Friday 8am to 2pm and 3:30 to 6:30pm, Saturday 9am to 1pm and 3:30 to 6:30pm, and Sunday 9am to 1pm. Closed December 25 and January 1.

WHERE TO STAY

Space in Assisi tends to be tight, so reservations are vital. For such a small town, how-ever, it has a good number of accommodations.

Albergo Ristorante del Viaggiatore. Via San Antonio 14, 06081 Assisi. ☎ **075-816-297** or 075-812-424. Fax 075-813-051. 16 units. TV TEL. 115,000L ($58) double. Rates include breakfast. Half board 80,000L ($40) per person extra. DC, MC, V.

This ancient town house is among the tops for value. It's been totally renovated, though the stone walls and arched entryways of the lobby hint at its age. The high-ceilinged rooms are spacious and very contemporary. The restaurant has been operated by the same family for years and offers excellent local and regional fare and wines. Pasta with Umbrian truffles is a highlight of the kitchen's offerings.

Hotel del Priori. Corso Mazzini 15, 06081 Assisi. ☎ **075-812-237.** Fax 075-816-804. www.assind.perugia.it/hotel/dpriori. E-mail: hpriori@edisons.it. 34 units. TEL. 140,000–239,000L ($70–$120) double; 248,000–300,000L ($124–$150) suite. Rates include breakfast. AE, DC, MC, V. Parking 12,000–18,000L ($6–$9).

Opened in 1923, this hotel has been continuously renovated. It occupies one of the town's most historic buildings, the 17th-century Palazzo Nepis. A homelike, some-what old-fashioned Umbrian atmosphere prevails. Marble staircases and floors, terra-cotta, vaulted ceilings, and stone-arched doorways remain from its seigniorial palazzo heyday. Many of the rooms are a bit small, however. The hotel has a bar and serves such Umbrian dishes as green gnocchi with Gorgonzola sauce.

Hotel Sole. Corso Mazzini 35, 06081 Assisi. ☎ **075-812-373** or 075-812-922. Fax 075-813-706. www.umbria.org/Hotel/sole. E-mail: sole@technonet.it. 36 units. TV TEL. 120,000L ($60) double, 150,000L ($75) triple. Rates include breakfast. Half board (Apr–Nov only) 85,000L ($43) extra. AE, DC, MC, V.

For Umbrian hospitality and a general down-home feeling, the Sole is a winner in the heart of medieval Assisi—comfortable but traditional, a bit tattered but affordable. The severe beauty of rough stone walls and ceilings, terra-cotta floors, and marble staircases pay homage to the past. Rooms, some of which are across the street in an annex, are rather basic and feature aging bathrooms. The family owners offer one of the town's best cuisines under the 15th-century vaults of their restaurant open April to November. The food is so savory; you might want to take half board. When avail-able, truffles are served, and the restaurant offers a typical Umbrian specialty: torta al testo, a kind of bread cooked on a black stone in a wood oven. This would be a good choice for dining even if you aren't a guest.

WHERE TO DINE

Il Medioevo. Via Arco dei Priori 4B. ☎ **075-813-068.** Reservations recommended. Main courses 15,000–25,000L ($8–$13). AE, DC, MC, V. Thurs–Tues noon–2:30pm and 7:30–10pm. Closed Jan 7–Feb 7 and July 1–20. UMBRIAN/INTERNATIONAL.

Assisi's best restaurant is one of the architectural oddities of the town's historic center, with foundations at least 1,000 years old. The structure was enlarged and modified until today it's an authentic medieval gem, conserving and exhibiting archaeological finds from the area. Alberto Falsinotti and his family prepare superb versions of Umbrian recipes whose origins are as old as Assisi itself. Specialties are tortelloni stuffed with minced turkey, veal, and beef and served with butter and Parmigiano Reggiano; gnocchi stuffed with ricotta and spinach and sprinkled with Parmigiano Reggiano; roasted rabbit with red-wine sauce and truffles; roast lamb with rosemary, potatoes, and herbs; homemade pasta stuffed with black truffles; and grilled fillet of veal with herb sauce.

Ristorante Buca di San Francesco. Via Brizi 1. ☎ **075-812-204.** Reservations recommended. Main courses 28,000–40,000L ($14–$20). AE, DC, MC, V. Tues–Sun noon–2:30pm and 7:30–9:30pm. Closed July 1–15. UMBRIAN/ITALIAN.

Hospitable and evocative of the Middle Ages, this restaurant occupies a cave near the foundation of a 12th-century palace. There're about 100 seats in the dining room and another 60 in the garden, overlooking the buildings in Assisi's historic center. Menu items change frequently, based on the availability of ingredients, but what you're likely to find are *spaghetti alla buca,* with exotic mushrooms and meat sauce; *umbricelli* (big noodles) with asparagus sauce; *cannelloni* (stuffed pasta tubes baked in the oven) with ricotta, spinach, and tomatoes; *carlacca* (baked crepes stuffed with cheese, prosciutto, and roasted veal); and *piccione alla sisana* (roasted pigeon with olive oil, capers, and aromatic herbs).

EXPLORING THE TOWN

In the heart of Assisi, **Piazza del Comune** is a dream for a lover of architecture from the 12th to the 14th century. On the square is a pagan structure, with six Corinthian columns, called the **Temple of Minerva (Tempio di Minerva),** from the 1st century B.C. With Minerva-like wisdom, the people of Assisi turned it into a baroque church inside so as not to offend the devout. Adjoining the temple is the 13th-century **Tower (Torre),** built by Ghibelline supporters. The site is open daily 7am to noon and 2:30pm to dusk. In the wake of the earthquakes, the tower can no longer be visited.

✪ **Basilica di San Francesco.** Piazza. San Francesco. ☎ **075-819-001.** Free admission. Daily 7am–5:30pm.

This great basilica, with both an upper and a lower church, houses some of the most important cycles of frescoes in Italy, including works by such pre-Renaissance giants as Cimabue and Giotto. The basilica and its paintings form the most significant monument to St. Francis. Disaster struck in 1997 when a series of devastating earthquakes hit Umbria, causing much damage. After a major restoration effort, involving some of Europe's greatest restorers, the basilica reopened to the public late in 1999.

Giotto's most celebrated frescoes, St. Francis preaching to the birds, can be seen on the entrance wall. In the nave are the cycle of 27 frescoes, some by Giotto, though the authorship of the entire cycle is a subject of controversy. Many frescoes are almost surrealistic, like stage sets that allow you to see the actors inside. In the cycle, you can see pictorial evidence of the rise of humanism that led to Giotto's and Italy's split from the rigidity of Byzantium.

The upper church also contains the damaged masterpiece by Cimabue, his *Crucifixion.* Time and quakes have robbed the fresco of its former radiance, but its power and ghostlike drama remain at least on video. The cycle of badly damaged frescoes in the transept and apse are other works by Cimabue and his helpers. Rather tragically, art experts spend hours daily sorting through boxes of rubble, trying to piece together the jigsaw puzzle caused by the quakes. There's a debate about whether the Cimbaue and Giotto frescoes will ever be in good-enough condition to be restored to their historic place.

From the transept of the upper church, proceed down the stairs through the two-tiered cloisters to the lower church. In the south transept, look for Cimabue's faded but masterly *Virgin and Child* with four angels and St. Francis looking on from the far right; it's often reproduced in detail as one of Cimabue's greatest works. You'll also find works here by Giotto, Pietro Lorenzetti, and Simone Martini.

Prisons' Hermitage (Eremo delle Carceri). Via Eremo delle Carceri. ☎ **075-812-301.** Free admission (donations accepted). Apr–Oct daily 7am–7pm; Nov–Mar daily 7am–5pm. About 4km (2¹/₂ miles) east of Assisi (out V. Eremo d. Carceri).

Eremo delle Carceri dates from the 14th and 15th centuries. The "prison" isn't a penal institution but rather a spiritual retreat. It's believed that St. Francis retired to this spot for meditation and prayer. Out back is a moss-covered gnarled ilex (live oak) more than 1,000 years old, where St. Francis is believed to have blessed the birds, after which they flew in the four major compass directions to symbolize that Franciscans, in coming centuries, would spread from Assisi all over the world. The friary contains some faded frescoes. One of the handful of friars who still inhabit the retreat will show you through.

Basilica di Santa Chiara (Clare). Piazza di Santa Chiara. ☎ **075-812-282.** Basilica, free; however, the custodian turns away visitors in shorts, miniskirts, plunging necklines, and backless or shoulderless attire. Nov–Mar daily 8:30am–noon and 3–5pm; Apr–Oct daily 8:30am–12:05pm and 2–6:55pm.

The basilica is dedicated to "the little plant of Blessed Francis," as St. Clare liked to describe herself. Born in 1193 into one of the noblest families of Assisi, Clare gave all her wealth to the poor and founded, together with St. Francis, the Order of the Poor Clares. She was canonized by Pope Alexander IV in 1255. Pope Pius XII declared her Patroness of Television in 1958. It was decided to entrust to her this new means of social communication based on a vision she had on Christmas Eve 1252 while bedridden in the Monastery of San Damiano: She saw the manger and heard the friars sing in the Basilica of St. Francis. Though many of the frescoes that once adorned the basilica have been completely or partially destroyed, much remains that's worthy of note. The basilica also houses the remains of St. Clare as well as the crucifix under which St. Francis received his command from above.

4 Venice

Venice is a preposterous monument to both the folly and the obstinacy of humankind. It shouldn't exist, but it does, much to the delight of thousands of tourists, gondoliers, lace makers, hoteliers, restaurateurs, and glassblowers.

Fleeing the barbarians centuries ago, Venetians left dry-dock and drifted out to a flotilla of "uninhabitable" islands in the lagoon. Survival was difficult enough, but no Venetian has ever settled for mere survival. The remote ancestors of today's inhabitants created the world's most beautiful and unusual city.

However, it's sinking at a rate of about 6cm (2¹/₂ inches) per decade, and it's estimated that one-third of the city's art will have deteriorated hopelessly within the next few decades if action isn't taken to save it. Clearly, Venice is in peril, under assault by uncontrolled tides, pollution, atmospheric acid, and old age.

This is one of the most enchantingly evocative cities on earth, but you must pay a price for all this beauty. In the sultry heat of the Adriatic in summer, the canals become a smelly stew. Steamy, overcrowded July and August are the worst times to visit; May and June or September and October are much more ideal.

ORIENTATION

GETTING THERE   All roads lead not necessarily to Rome but, in this case, to the docks of mainland Venice. The arrival scene at the unattractive Piazzale Roma is filled with nervous expectation, and even the most veteran traveler can become confused. Whether you arrive by train, bus, car, or airport limousine, there's one common denominator—everyone walks to the nearby docks to select a method of transport to his or her hotel. The cheapest way is by vaporetto, the more expensive by gondola or motor launch.

By Plane   You'll land at Mestre, with its **Marco Polo Aeroporto** (☎ 041-2606111). **Boats** depart every 30 minutes directly from the airport, taking you to a terminal near Piazza San Marco. The fare is 17,000L ($9).

It's less expensive to take a **bus** from the airport to Piazzale Roma (☎ 041-5287-886), a trip of less than 8km (5 miles); a one-way fare is 1,400L (70¢). Departures are usually every 30 minutes (trip time: 30 minutes). Once at Piazzale Roma, you can make transportation connections to most parts of Venice, including the Lido.

By Train   Trains pull into the **Stazione di Santa Lucia,** at Piazzale Roma. Travel time by train from Rome is about $5^1/_4$ hours; from Milan, $3^1/_2$ hours; from Florence, 4 hours; and from Bologna, 2 hours. For information about rail connections, call ☎ 01478-88088. The best and least expensive way to get from the station to the rest of town is to take a vaporetto, which departs near the main entrance to the station.

By Bus   Buses arrive from points on the mainland of Italy at **Piazzale Roma.** For information about schedules, call the office of **ACTV** at Piazzale Roma (☎ 041-5287886). If you're coming from a distant city in Italy, it's better to take the train.

By Car   Venice has autostrada links with the rest of Italy, with direct routes from such cities as Trieste (driving time: $1^1/_2$ hours), Milan (driving time: 3 hours), and Bologna (driving time: 2 hours). Bologna is 151km (94 miles) southwest of Venice; Milan, 265km (165 miles) west of Venice; and Trieste, 156km (97 miles) east. Rome is 526km (327 miles) to the southwest.

If you arrive by car, there're several multitiered parking areas at the terminus where the roads end and the canals begin. One of the most visible is the **Garage San Marco,** Piazzale Roma (☎ 041-5235101), near the vaporetto, gondola, and motor-launch docks. You'll be charged 35,000 to 46,000L ($18 to $23) per day, maybe more, depending on the size of your car.

VISITOR INFORMATION   You can get information at the **Azienda di Pro-mozione Turistica,** Calle Ascensione, San Marco 71F (☎ 041-5208964). Another office is at Santa Lucia railway station. Both are open daily from 9am to 1pm and from 1:30 to 5pm.

CITY LAYOUT   Venice, 4km ($2^1/_2$ miles) from the Italian mainland and 2km ($1^1/_4$ miles) from the Adriatic, is an archipelago of some 117 islands. Most visitors, however, concern themselves only with Piazza San Marco and its vicinity. In fact, the entire city has only one piazza: San Marco. Venice is divided into six quarters that locals call *sestieri.* These include the most frequented, San Marco, but also Santa Croce, San

Venice

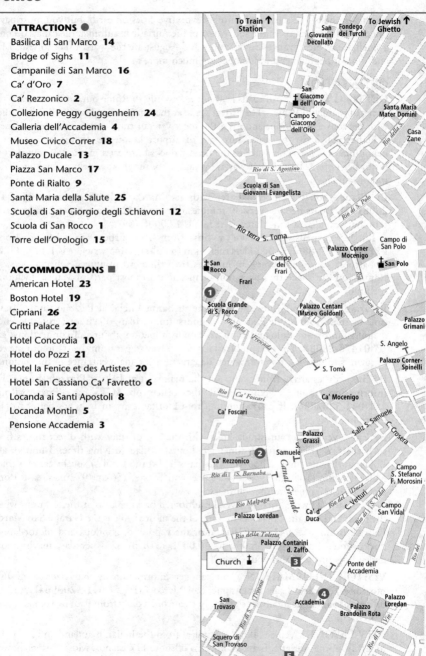

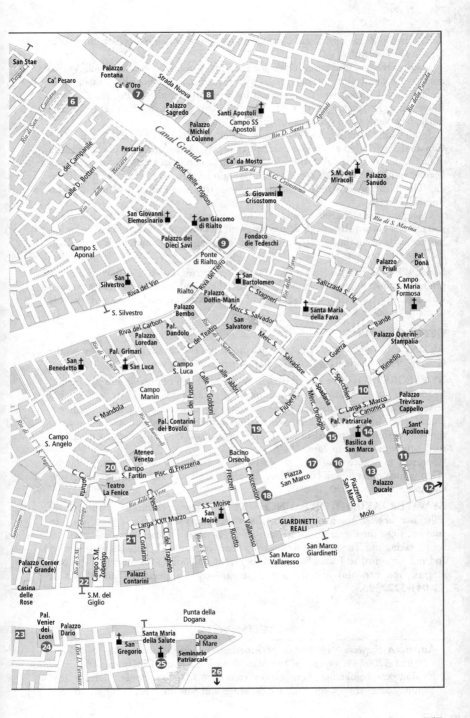

Polo, Castello, Cannaregio, and Dorsoduro, the last of which has been compared to New York's Greenwich Village.

Many of the so-called streets of Venice are actually **canals,** some 150 in all. A canal is called a *rio,* and a total of 400 bridges span these canals. If Venice has a main street, it's the **Grand Canal,** which is spanned by three bridges: the Rialto, the Academy Bridge, and the stone Railway Bridge (the last dating from the 20th century). The canal splits Venice into two unequal parts.

South of the section called Dorsoduro, which is south of the Grand Canal, is the **Canale della Giudecca,** a major channel separating Dorsoduro from the large island of La Giudecca. At the point where the Canale della Giudecca meets the Canale di San Marco, you'll spot the little **Isola di San Giorgio Maggiore,** with a church by Palladio. The most visited islands in the lagoon, aside from the **Lido,** are **Murano, Burano,** and **Torcello.**

Once you land and explore Piazza San Marco and its satellite, Piazzetta San Marco, you can head down **Riva degli Schiavoni,** with its deluxe and first-class hotels, or follow the signs along the **Mercerie,** the major shopping artery, which leads to the Rialto, site of the market area.

Maps & Finding an Address   The system of addresses in Venice is so confusing it's probably known only to the postman, if that. The best thing to do is to arm yourself with a good map, such as the **Falk** map of Venice, which is pocket size and available in many kiosks and bookstores.

GETTING AROUND

Walking is the only way to explore Venice unless you plan to see it from a boat on the Grand Canal. Everybody walks in Venice—there's no other way.

BY VAPORETTO   The motorboats, or *vaporetti,* of Venice provide inexpensive and frequent, if not always fast, transportation in this canal-riddled city. An *accelerato* is a vessel that makes every stop and a *diretto* makes only express stops. The average fare is 6,000L ($3). In summer, the vaporetti are often fiercely crowded. Pick up a map of the system from the tourist office. There's frequent service daily 7am to midnight, then hourly midnight to 7am.

Visitors to Venice may avail themselves of a 10-tickets carnet costing 50,000L ($25), which must be validated before use and shown together with the matrix (the last ticket of the booklet).

BY WATER TAXI/MOTOR LAUNCH   The city's many private motor launches are called *taxi acquei.* You may or may not have the cabin of one of these sleek vessels to yourself, since the captains fill their boats with as many passengers as the law allows before taking off. The price of a transit by water taxi from Piazzale Roma (the road and rail terminus) to Piazza San Marco begins at 80,000L ($40) for one to six passengers. You can also call for a taxi acquei—try **Cooperativa San Marco** at ☎ **041-5222303.**

Fast Facts: Venice

American Express   The office of American Express is at San Moisè 1471 (☎ **041-5200844;** vaporetto: San Marco), in San Marco. City tours and mail handling can be obtained here. The office is open May to October, Monday to Saturday 8am to 8pm for currency exchange and 9am to 5:30pm for all other

Getting Around by Gondola

When riding in a gondola, two major agreements have to be reached: the price of the ride and the length of the trip. The official rate is 100,000L ($60), but virtually no one pays that amount; prices really start at about 150,000L ($90) for up to 50 minutes. Two major stations at which you can hire gondolas are Piazza San Marco (☎ 041-5200685) and the Ponte Rialto (☎ 041-5224904). Both organize gondola tours, lasting about 50 minutes and costing from 120,000 to 150,000L ($60 to $75) per person.

transactions. From November to April, Saturday hours are 9am to 12:30pm; weekday hours are 9am to 5:30pm.

Consulates   There's no U.S. consulate in Venice; the closest is in Milan, at Via Principe Amedeo 2 (☎ 02-290351). The British consulate is at Dorsoduro 1051 (☎ 041-5227207), open Monday to Friday 10am to noon and 2 to 3pm.

Currency   See "Fast Facts: Rome," above.

Currency Exchange   There're many banks in Venice where you can exchange money. Try the **Deutsch Bank SPA,** San Marco 2216 (☎ 041-5207024; vaporetto: San Marco). Hours are Monday to Friday 8:30am to 1:30pm and 2:45 to 4pm. Many travelers find that **Guetta Viaggi,** San Marco 1261 (☎ 041-5285101; vaporetto: San Marco), offers the best rates in Venice. Hours are Monday to Friday 9am to 12:30pm and 3 to 6:30pm. From April to October also Saturday 9am to noon.

Dentist/Doctor   Your best bet is to have your hotel call and set up an appointment with an English-speaking dentist or doctor. The American Express office and the British Consulate also have a list.

Drugstores   If you need a drugstore in the middle of the night, call ☎ 192 for information about which one is open. Pharmacies take turns staying open late. A well-recommended, centrally located one is the **International Pharmacy,** Via XXII Marzo 2067 (☎ 041-5222311; vaporetto: San Marco).

Emergencies   Emergency phone numbers are ☎ 113 for the police, ☎ 118 for an ambulance, and ☎ 115 to report a fire.

Hospitals   Get in touch with the **Ospedale Civile Santi Giovanni e Paolo,** Campo Santi Giovanni e Paolo in Castello (☎ 041-52394517).

Post Office   The main post office is at Fondaco dei Tedeschi (☎ 041-2717111; vaporetto: Rialto), near the Rialto Bridge. It's open Monday to Saturday 8:15am to 5pm. For information call ☎ 160.

Safety   The curse of Venice is the pickpocket. Violent crime is rare, but because of the overcrowding on vaporetti and even on the small, narrow streets, it's easy to pick pockets. Purse snatchings are commonplace as well. A purse-snatcher seemingly darts out of nowhere, grabs a purse, and in seconds seems to have disappeared down some narrow, dark alley. Secure your valuables, and if your hotel has safes, keep them locked there when not needed.

Telephones   The **country code** for Italy is **39.** The **city code** for Venice is **041,** which is the code you'll use every time you dial a party located within Venice, regardless of whether you're within the city limits or not. We emphasize that newly imposed technologies will require the use of the "0" and then "41" for calls to parties in Venice, regardless of whether you're within the city limits of Venice or not. For additional information, see "Fast Facts: Rome," above.

WHERE TO STAY
NEAR PIAZZA SAN MARCO
Very Expensive

✪ **Gritti Palace.** Campo Santa Maria del Giglio, San Marco 2467, 30124 Venezia. ☎ **800/325-3535** in the U.S., 416/947-4864 in Canada, or 041-794611. Fax 041/5200942. www.sheraton.com. E-mail: reso73grittipalace@ittsheraton.com. 93 units. A/C MINIBAR TV TEL. 1,100,000–1,400,000L ($550–$700) double; from 2,400,000L ($1,200) suite. Rates include buffet breakfast. AE, DC, MC, V. Vaporetto: Santa Maria del Giglio.

In a stately setting on the Grand Canal, Gritti Palace is the renovated four-story palazzo of the 15th-century doge Andrea Gritti. It's a bit starchy but is topped only by the Cipriani in terms of prestige. "Our home in Venice" to Ernest Hemingway, it has for years drawn a clientele of theatrical, literary, political, and royal figures. The range and variety of the rooms seem almost limitless, from elaborate suites to relatively small singles. But in every case the stamp of glamour is evident. For a splurge, ask for Hemingway's old suite or the Doge Suite, once occupied by Somerset Maugham. The hotel restaurant, Club del Doge, offers international food along with modern version of Venetian dishes, and a very romantic view of the city. The Bar Longhi is an ideal rendezvous to have a drink and a talk with Venetians as well as with international visitors.

Expensive

Hotel Concordia. Calle Larga, San Marco 367, 30124 Venezia. ☎ **041-5206866.** Fax 041-5206775. www.venere.it/home/venezia/concordia/concordia.html. E-mail: veniceitaly@hotelconcordia.com. 57 units. A/C MINIBAR TV TEL. 320,000–620,000L ($160–$310) double; 450,000–720,000L ($225–$360) suite. Rates include buffet breakfast. AE, DC, MC, V. Vaporetto: San Marco.

The Concordia is the only hotel in Venice that has rooms overlooking St. Mark's Square. A series of gold-plated marble steps takes you to the lobby, where you'll find a comfortable bar area. All rooms are decorated in a Venetian antique style and contain a safe, hair dryer, and other amenities. Light meals and Italian snacks are available in the bar from noon to midnight.

Hotel la Fenice et des Artistes. Campiello de la Fenice, San Marco 1936, 30124 Venezia. ☎ **041-5232333.** Fax 041-5203721. E-mail: fenice@fenicehotels.it. 69 units. TV TEL. 240,000–360,000L ($120–$180) double; 420,000–480,000L ($210–$240) suite. Rates include breakfast. AE, DC, MC, V. Vaporetto: San Marco.

This hotel offers widely varying accommodations in two connected buildings, each at least 100 years old. One building is rather romantic yet time worn, with overly decorated rooms. Your satin-lined room may have an inlaid desk and a wardrobe painted in the Venetian manner to match a baroque bed frame. The carpets might be thin, however, and the fabrics aging. Bathrooms, still a little cramped, were renewed in 1999. Chambers in the other building are far less glamorous. The older of the two has no elevator, and the newer building's modern rooms have conservative, rather sterile furniture.

Moderate

Boston Hotel. Ponte dei. Dai, San Marco 848, 30124 Venezia. ☎ **041-5287665.** Fax 041-5226628. 42 units. A/C TEL. 260,000–320,000L ($130–$160) double. Rates include breakfast. AE, DC, MC, V. Closed Nov–Feb. Vaporetto: San Marco.

Boston Hotel, run by Mario and Adriana Bernardi, is a whisper away from St. Mark's. The hotel was named after an uncle who left to seek his fortune in Boston and never returned. The little living rooms contain many antiques and Venetian ceilings. For the skinny guest, there's a tiny self-operated elevator and a postage-stamp–size street entrance. Most of the rooms have built-in features, snugly designed beds, chests, and wardrobes. Several have tiny balconies opening onto canals.

Hotel Do Pozzi. Corte do Pozzi, San Marco 2373, 30124 Venezia. ☎ **041-5207855.** Fax 041-5229413. 35 units. MINIBAR TV TEL. 330,000L ($165) double. Rates include breakfast. AE, DC, MC, V. Vaporetto: Santa Maria del Giglio.

Small, modernized, and centrally located just a short stroll from the Grand Canal and Piazza San Marco, this place is more like a country tavern than a hotel. Its original structure is 200 years old, and it opens onto a paved front courtyard with potted greenery. The sitting and dining rooms are furnished with antiques (and near antiques) mixed with utilitarian modern decor. A major refurbishing has given everything a fresh touch. Laundry and baby-sitting are available.

IN THE DORSODURO
Moderate
American Hotel. Campo San Vio, Dorsoduro 628, 30123 Venezia. ☎ **041-5204733.** Fax 041-5204048. www.hotelamerican.com. E-mail: hotelameri@tin.it. 29 units. A/C MINIBAR TV TEL. 340,000–370,000L ($170–$185) double; 425,000–455,000L ($213–$228) triple. Rates include breakfast. AE, MC, V. Vaporetto: Accademia.

Set on a small waterway, the American Hotel (there's nothing American about it) occupies an ochre building across the Grand Canal from the most heavily touristed areas. It's one of your best budget bets. The modest lobby is filled with murals, warm colors, and antiques, and the location is perfect for anyone wanting to avoid the crowds that descend in summer. The rooms are comfortably furnished in a Venetian style, but vary in size; some of the smaller ones are a bit cramped. Many rooms with a private terrace face the canal. On the second floor is a beautiful terrace where guests relax over drinks.

○ **Pensione Accademia.** Fondamenta Bollani, Dorsoduro 1058, 30123 Venezia. ☎ **041-5237846.** Fax 041-5239152. E-mail: pensione.accademia@flashnet.it. 27 units. A/C TV TEL. 270,000–360,000L ($135–$180) double. Rates include breakfast. AE, DC, MC, V. Vaporetto: Accademia.

This is the most patrician of the pensioni, in a villa whose garden extends into the angle created by the junction of two canals. Iron fences, twisting vines, and neo-classical sculpture are a part of the setting. There's an upstairs sitting room and a formal rose garden that's visible from the breakfast room. The rooms are spacious and decorated with 19th-century furniture, and some are air-conditioned and recently renovated.

Inexpensive
○ **Locanda Montin.** Fondamenta di Borgo, Dorsoduro 1147, 31000 Venezia. ☎ **041-5227151.** Fax 041-5200255. 10 units (5 with bathroom). 155,000L ($78) double without bathroom; 200,000L ($100) double with bathroom. AE, DC, MC, V. Vaporetto: Accademia.

The well-recommended Locanda Montin is an old-fashioned Venetian inn whose adjoining restaurant is one of the most loved in the area. The hotel is across the Grand Canal from the most popular tourist zones. It's officially listed as a fourth-class hotel, but the accommodations are considerably larger and better than that rating suggests. Reservations are virtually mandatory, because of the reputation of this locanda. Marked only by a small carriage lamp etched with the name of the establishment, the inn is a little difficult to locate but worth the search.

IN SANTA CROCE
Moderate

Hotel San Cassiano Ca'Favretto. Calle della Rosa, Santa Croce 2232, 30135 Venezia. ☎ **041-5241768.** Fax 041-721033. www.sancassiano.it. E-mail: info@sancassiano.it. 35 units. A/C MINIBAR TV TEL. 200,000–450,000L ($100–$225) double. Rates include breakfast. AE, DC, MC, V. Vaporetto: San Stae.

San Cassiano Ca'Favretto was once the studio of 19th-century painter Giacomo Favretto. The views from the hotel's gondola pier and from the dining room's porch encompass the lacy facade of the Ca' d'Oro, considered the most beautiful building in Venice. The hotel was constructed in the 14th century as a palace. The present owner has worked closely with Venetian authorities to preserve the original details. Fifteen of the conservatively decorated rooms overlook one of two canals. There's an American bar with a spacious terrace on the canal.

IN CANNAREGIO
Expensive

Locanda ai Santi Apostoli. Strada Nuova, Canaregio 4391, 30123 Venezia. ☎ **041-5212612.** Fax 041-5212611. 11 units. TV TEL. 380,000L ($190) double, 480,000L ($240) double with view on the Canal Grande; 680,000L ($340) suite. Rates include breakfast. AE, DC, MC, V. Vaporetto: Ca d'Oro.

If you can't afford the Gritti Palace (and few can), but still fantasize about living in a palazzo overlooking the Grande Canal, near the Rialto, here is a possibility. The Locanda knows the advantage of its location, however, and doesn't come cheap. But it's a lot less expensive than the grand palaces nearby. It's situated on the top floor of a 15th-century building, and the rooms, although simple, are rather inviting. Naturally, the two rooms actually opening onto the Grand Canal are the most requested. Even if you don't have an accommodation overlooking the Grand Canal, there's a view from the main salon. Breakfast is the only meal served.

ON ISOLA DELLA GIUDECCA
Very Expensive

✪ **Cipriani.** Isola della Giudecca 10, 30133 Venezia. ☎ **800/992-5055** in the U.S., or 041-5207744. Fax 041-5207745. www.orient-expresshotels.com. E-mail: info@ hotelcipriani.it. 110 units. A/C MINIBAR TV TEL. 1,450,000–2,500,000L ($725–$1,250) double; from 2,850,000L ($1,425) suite. Rates include buffet breakfast. AE, DC, MC, V. Closed Nov–Mar. Vaporetto: Zitelle.

Isolated, security-conscious, and elegant, the Cipriani occupies a 16th-century cloister on the residential island of Giudecca. This refined, tranquil, and sybaritic resort hotel was established in 1958 by the late Giuseppe Cipriani, the founder of Harry's Bar and the one real-life character in Hemingway's Venetian novel. Rooms have different decors—ranging from tasteful contemporary to antique—but all have splendid views. Lunch is served at Il Gabbiano, either indoors or on terraces overlooking the water; more formal meals are served at night in the restaurant The Terrace. There's an Olympic-size pool with filtered saltwater, tennis courts, a sauna, and a fitness center. The hotel runs a 24-hour motor boat shuttle to and from San Marco.

WHERE TO DINE
NEAR PIAZZA SAN MARCO
Very Expensive

Harry's Bar. Calle Vallaresso, San Marco 1323. ☎ **041-5285777.** Reservations required. Main courses 80,000–95,000L ($40–$48). AE, DC, MC, V. Apr–Oct daily 10:30am–1am; Nov–Mar daily 10:30am–11pm. Vaporetto: San Marco. VENETIAN.

Harry's Bar serves the best food in Venice, though Quadri and the Antico Martini (see below) have more elegant atmospheres. Its fame was spread by Ernest Hemingway. A. E. Hotchner, in *Papa Hemingway,* quoted the writer as saying, "We can't eat straight hamburger in a Renaissance palazzo on the Grand Canal." So he ordered a 5-pound "tin of beluga caviar" to, as he said, "take the curse off it." Hemingway would skip the place today, fleeing from the foreign visitors, and the prices would come as a shock even to him. You can have your choice of dining in the bar downstairs or the room with a view upstairs. We recommend the Venetian fish soup, followed by scampi Thermidor with rice pilaf or seafood ravioli.

Expensive

✪ Antico Martini. Campo San Fantin, San Marco 1983. ☎ **041-5224121.** Reservations required. Main courses 36,000–52,000L ($18–$26); 4-course, fixed-price menus 78,000–98,000L ($39–$49); 6-course *menu degustazione* 136,000L ($68). AE, DC, MC, V. Wed 7–11:30pm, Thurs–Mon noon–2:30pm and 7–11:30pm. Vaporetto: San Marco or Santa Maria del Giglio. VENETIAN/INTERNATIONAL.

As the city's leading traditional restaurant, Antico Martini, located near La Fenice, elevates Venetian cuisine to its highest level. The walls are paneled, elaborate chandeliers glitter overhead, and gilt-framed oil paintings adorn the walls. The courtyard is favored in summer. An excellent beginning to your meal is the *risotto di frutti di mare,* creamy Venetian style with plenty of fresh seafood. For a main dish, try the *fegato alla veneziana,* which is tender liver fried with onions and served with polenta, a yellow cornmeal mush. The chefs are better at regional dishes than they are with those of the international kitchen.

Da Ivo. Calle dei Fuseri, San Marco 1809. ☎ **041-5285004.** Reservations required. Main courses 44,000–55,000L ($22–$28). AE, DC, MC, V. Mon–Sat noon–2:30pm and 7pm–midnight. Closed Jan 6–31. Vaporetto: San Marco. TUSCAN/VENETIAN.

Da Ivo has such a faithful clientele that you'll think at first you're in a semiprivate club. The rustic atmosphere is both cozy and relaxing, with candles on the well-set tables. Homesick Florentines go here for fine Tuscan cookery; regional Venetian dishes are also served. In season, game, according to an ancient tradition, is cooked over an open charcoal grill. On one cold day, our hearts and plates were warmed when we ordered homemade tagliatelle. It came topped with slivers of tartufi bianchi, the pungent white truffle from the Piedmont district that's unforgettable to the palate. Dishes change according to the season and the availability of ingredients. You'll also find such a delicacy as giant scampi with cherry tomatoes and black pepper, or a beef carpaccio covered by arugula and parmigiana flakes.

Quadri. Piazza San Marco, San Marco 120–124. ☎ **041-5289299.** Reservations required. Main courses 45,000–79,000L ($23–$40). AE, DC, MC, V. Tues–Sun noon–2:30pm and 7–10:30pm; July–Aug Tues–Sun 7–210:30pm. Vaporetto: San Marco. VENETIAN/INTERNATIONAL.

One of Europe's famous restaurants, the deluxe Quadri is on the second floor, overlooking the "living room" of Venice. The setting is one of gilt and rosy velvet, evoking the world of its former patrons, Marcel Proust and Stendhal. Many diners come here just for the setting and are often surprised when they're treated to high-quality cuisine and impeccable service. You pay for all this nostalgia, however. The Venetian cuisine has been acclaimed—at least by one food critic—as "befitting a doge," though we doubt if those old doges ate as well. The chef is likely to tempt you with such dishes as octopus in fresh tomato sauce, salt codfish with polenta, or sea bass with crab sauce. Try the "baked" ice cream for dessert.

The Cafe Scene

Venice's most famous cafe is the ❂ **Florian,** Piazza San Marco, San Marco 56–59 (☎ **041-5285338;** vaporetto: San Marco). It was built in 1720 and remains romantically and elegantly decorated—pure Venetian salons with red plush banquettes, elaborate murals under glass, and art-nouveau lighting and lamps. It's open Thursday to Tuesday 9:30am to midnight. Closed the first week in December and the first week in January.

❂ **Quadri,** Piazza San Marco, San Marco 120–124 (☎ **041-5222105;** vaporetto: San Marco), stands opposite the Florian. Founded in 1638, it's elegantly decorated in an antique style. Wagner used to drop in for a drink when he was working on *Tristan und Isolde.* The restaurant on the second floor offers refined Venetian cuisine. Both are open April to October daily 9am to midnight; off-season, Tuesday to Sunday 9am to midnight.

Moderate

Ristorante da Raffaele. Calle Larga XXII Marzo (Fond. d. Ostriche), San Marco 2347. ☎ **041-5232317.** Reservations recommended Sat–Sun. Main courses 25,000–45,000L ($13–$23). AE, DC, MC, V. Fri–Wed noon–3pm and 7–10:30pm. Closed Dec 10–mid-Feb. Vaporetto: San Marco or Santa Maria del Giglio. ITALIAN/VENETIAN.

This place, a 5-minute walk from Piazza San Marco and a minute from the Grand Canal, has long been a favorite canal-side stop. It's often overrun with tourists, but the veteran kitchen staff holds up well. The huge inner sanctum has a high-beamed ceiling, 17th- to 19th-century pistols and sabers, exposed brick, wrought-iron chandeliers, a massive fireplace, and hundreds of copper pots. The food is excellent, beginning with a choice of tasty antipasti or well-prepared pastas. Seafood specialties include scampi, squid, or a platter of deep-fried fish from the Adriatic. The grilled meats are also succulent and can be followed by rich, tempting desserts.

Taverna la Fenice. Campiello de la Fenice, San Marco 1938. ☎ **041-5223856.** Reservations required. Main courses 22,000–38,000L ($11–$19). AE, DC, MC, V. Mon–Sat noon–3pm, and 7–11pm. Vaporetto: San Marco. ITALIAN/VENETIAN.

Opened in 1907, when Venetians were flocking in record numbers to hear the *bel canto* performances in the opera house nearby, this restaurant is one of Venice's most romantic dining spots. Gabriele D'Annunzio himself provided the name for this historic place. The interior is suitably elegant, but the preferred spot in clement weather is out beneath a canopy, a few steps from the burned Teatro La Fenice, where Stravinsky introduced works that included *The Rake's Progress.* The service is smooth and efficient. You might enjoy risotto with scampi and arugula, freshly made tagliatelle with cream and exotic mushrooms, or John Dory fillets with artichokes. Among the wide selection of fresh fish, you may be tempted by the exquisite simplicity of the sea bream garnished with seasonal herbs. For pasta lovers the choice ranges from traditional black tagliolini with squid ink and crabmeat, to the more creative tagliatelle with a combination of scampi and artichokes.

Trattoria La Colomba. Piscina Frezzeria, San Marco 1665. ☎ **041-5221175.** Reservations recommended. Main courses 35,000–65,000L ($18–$33). AE, DC, MC, V. Daily noon–3pm and 7–11pm. Closed Wed Nov–Apr. Vaporetto: San Marco or Rialto. VENETIAN/INTERNATIONAL.

This is one of the most distinctive and popular trattorie in town, with a history going back at least a century and a by now legendary association with some of Venice's leading painters. Menu items are likely to include at least five daily specials based exclusively on the time-honored cuisine of Venice. Otherwise, you can order *risotto di funghi del Montello* (risotto with mushrooms from the local hills of Montello) or *baccalà alla vicentina* (milk-simmered dry cod seasoned with onions, anchovies, and cinnamon, then served with polenta). The chef uses only the freshest ingredients on the market. Every day two boxes of giant scampi arrive directly from Sicily to your table. If you're a meat fan, try the chateaubriand accompanied by steamed vegetables and almost a dozen different sauces.

Vini da Arturo. Calle degli Assassini, San Marco 3656. ☎ **041-5286974.** Reservations recommended. Main courses 30,000–45,000L ($15–$23). No credit cards. Mon–Sat noon–2:30pm and 7–10:30pm. Closed Aug. Vaporetto: San Marco or Rialto. VENETIAN.

Vini da Arturo attracts many devoted regulars, including artists and writers. Here you get some of the most delectable local cooking—and not just the standard cliché Venetian dishes and not seafood, which may be unique for a Venetian restaurant. Instead of ordering plain pasta, try a tantalizing dish called *spaghetti alla gorgonzola*. The beef is also good, especially when prepared with a cream sauce flavored with mustard and freshly ground pepper. The salads are made with crisp, fresh ingredients, often in unusual combinations. The place is small and contains only seven tables; it's between the Fenice Opera House and St. Mark's Square.

Inexpensive

Da Bruno. Calle del Paradiso, Castello 5731. ☎ **041-5221480.** Main courses 20,000–40,000L ($10–$20); fixed-price menu 25,000L ($13). AE, DC, MC, V. Daily noon–3pm and 7–11pm. Vaporetto: San Marco or Rialto. VENETIAN.

Da Bruno is like a country tavern in the center of Venice. On a narrow street about halfway between the Rialto Bridge and Piazza San Marco, this restaurant attracts its crowds by grilling meats on an open-hearth fire. Get your antipasti at the counter and watch your prosciutto being prepared—paper-thin slices of spicy flavored ham wrapped around breadsticks (*grissini*). In the right season, da Bruno does some of the finest game specialty dishes in Venice. If it's featured, try *capriolo* (roebuck) or *fagiano* (pheasant). Another great dish is veal scaloppini with wild mushrooms. If you feel more in a pasta mood, try the "black spaghetti" with tomato sauce.

Sempione. Ponte dei Beretteri, San Marco 578. ☎ **041-5226022.** Reservations recommended. Main courses 20,000–35,000L ($10–$18). AE, DC, MC, V. Daily 11:30am–3pm and 6:30–10pm. Closed Thurs Nov–Dec. Vaporetto: Rialto. VENETIAN.

This restaurant has done an admirable job of feeding local residents and visitors for 90 years. Set adjacent to a canal, within a 15th-century building near St. Marks Square, it contains three dining rooms outfitted in a soothingly traditional style, a well-trained staff, and a kitchen that focuses on preparations of traditional Venetian cuisine. Examples include grilled fish, spaghetti with crabmeat, risotto with fish, fish soup, and a timeless and delectable version of Venetian calf's liver. If you like surprises, try spaghetti with crabmeat flavored with a mysterious sauce whose ingredients the chef doesn't want to reveal. Try for a table by the window so you can watch the gondolas slide by.

Trattoria alla Madonna. Calle de la Madonna, San Pollo 594. ☎ **041-5223824.** Reservations recommended but not always accepted. Main courses 20,000–40,000L ($10–$20). AE, MC, V. Thurs–Tues noon–3pm and 7:15–10pm. Closed Dec 24–Jan and Aug 4–17. Vaporetto: Rialto. VENETIAN.

This restaurant was opened in 1954 in a 300-year-old building of historic distinction. Named after *another* famous Madonna, it's one of the most popular and characteristic trattorie of Venice, specializing in traditional recipes and an array of grilled fresh fish. A suitable beginning may be the antipasto *frutti di mare.* Pastas, polentas, risottos, meats (including *fegato alla veneziana,* liver with onions), and many kinds of irreproachably fresh fish are widely available.

EAST OF PIAZZA SAN MARCO
Moderate
Ristorante Corte Sconta. Calle del Pestrin, Castello 3886. ☎ **041-5227024.** Reservations required. Main courses 25,000–40,000L ($13–$20); fixed-price menu 70,000–90,000L ($35–$45). AE, DC, MC, V. Tues–Sat 12:30–2:30pm and 7:30–9:30pm. Closed Jan 7–Feb 7 and July 15–Aug 15. Vaporetto: Arsenale. SEAFOOD.

On a narrow alley, whose name is shared by at least three other streets in Venice (this particular one is near Campo Bandiere Moro and San Giovanni in Bragora), the modest restaurant whose name in Italian means "hidden courtyard" has a multicolored marble floor, plain wooden tables, and no serious attempt at decoration. It has become well known, however, as a sophisticated gathering place for artists, writers, and filmmakers. This restaurant serves a variety of flawlessly grilled fish (much of the "catch" is largely unknown in North America). It's also flawlessly fresh—the gamberi, for example, is placed live on the grill. Begin with marinated salmon with arugula and pomegranate seeds in rich olive oil. If you don't like fish, a tender fillet of beef is available.

Inexpensive
Nuova Rivetta. Campo San Filippo, Castello 4625. ☎ **041/5287302.** Reservations required. Main courses 18,000–32,000L ($9–$16). AE, MC, V. Tues–Sun 10am–10pm. Closed July 23–Aug 20. Vaporetto: San Zaccaria. SEAFOOD.

Nuova Rivetta is an old-fashioned Venetian trattoria where you eat well without having to pay a lot. The restaurant stands in the monumental heart of the old city. Many find it best for lunch during a stroll around Venice. The most representative dish to order is *frittura di pesce,* a mixed fish fry from the Adriatic, which includes squid or various other "sea creatures" that turned up at the market that day. Other specialties are gnocchi stuffed with Adriatic spider crab, pasticcio of fish (a main course), and spaghetti flavored with squid ink.

NEAR THE PONTE DI RIALTO
Moderate
"Al Graspo de Ua." Calle dei Bombaseri, San Marco 5094. ☎ **041-5200150.** Reservations required. Main courses 26,000–40,000L ($13–$20). AE, DC, MC, V. Tues–Sun noon–3pm and 8–11pm. Closed Aug 5–20. Vaporetto: Rialto. SEAFOOD/VENETIAN.

"Al graspo de ua" is one bunch of grapes you'll want to pluck. For that special meal, it's a winner. Decorated in the old tavern style, it offers several air-conditioned dining rooms. Among the best fish restaurants in Venice, this place has been patronized by such celebs as Elizabeth Taylor, Jeanne Moreau, and even Giorgio de Chirico. You can help yourself to all the hors d'oeuvres you want—known on the menu as "self-service mammoth." The wonderful *gran fritto dell'Adriatico* is a mixed treat of deep-fried fish from the Adriatic.

✪ **Poste Vechie.** Pescheria Rialto, San Polo 1608. ☎ **041-721822.** Reservations recommended. Main courses 21,000–45,000L ($11–$23). AE, DC, MC, V. Wed–Mon noon–3:30pm and 7–10:30pm. Vaporetto: Rialto. SEAFOOD.

This is one of Venice's most charming restaurants, near the Rialto fish market and connected to the rest of the city by a small, privately owned bridge. It was established in the early 1500s as the local post office—food was served to the mail carriers to fortify them for their deliveries. Today, it's one of the oldest restaurants in town, with two intimate dining rooms and a verdant courtyard. Menu items include a super fresh array of fish from the nearby markets; a salad of shellfish and exotic mushrooms; a spicy soup of Adriatic fish; tagliolini flavored with squid ink, crabmeat, and fish sauce; and the restaurant's pièce de résistance, *seppie* (cuttlefish) *alla veneziana* with polenta. If you don't like fish, calf's liver or veal shank with ham and cheese are also well prepared. The desserts come rolling to your table on a trolley and are usually sumptuous.

Ristorante à la Vecia Cavana. Rio Terà SS. Apostoli, Cannaregio 4624. ☎ **041-5287106.** Reservations recommended. Main courses 40,000–60,000L ($20–$30); fixed-price menu 50,000L ($25). AE, DC, MC, V. Tues–Sun noon–3pm and 6:30–10:30pm. Vaporetto: Ca' d'Oro. SEAFOOD.

This restaurant is off the tourist circuit and well worth the trek through winding streets to find it. When you enter, you'll be greeted with brick arches, stone columns, terra-cotta floors, framed modern paintings, and a photograph of 19th-century fishermen relaxing after a day's work. It's an appropriate introduction to a menu that specializes in seafood, including a mixed grill from the Adriatic, fresh sole, three types of risotto (each prepared with seafood), and spicy *zuppa di pesce* (fish soup). Another specialty is *antipasti di pesce Cavana,* which includes just about every sea creature. It's worth the trek across Venice if you wish to sample the chef's special linguine with lobster and a velvety cream sauce enriched with freshly ground black pepper.

IN SAN POLO
Moderate
Osteria da Fiore. Calle del Scaletèr, San Polo 2202. ☎ **041-72-13-08.** Reservations required. Main courses 36,000–48,000L ($18–$24). AE, DC, MC, V. Tues–Sat 12:30–2:30pm and 8–10:30pm. Closed 3 weeks in Aug and Dec 25–Jan 14. Vaporetto: San Tomà. SEAFOOD.

The breath of the Adriatic seems to blow through this place, although how the wind finds this little restaurant tucked away in a labyrinth is a mystery. The restaurant serves only fish, and has done so since 1910. An imaginative and changing fare is offered, depending on the availability of fresh fish and produce. You'll find everything from scampi (a sweet Adriatic prawn, cooked in as many different ways as there are chefs) to granzeola, a type of spider crab. Try such dishes as *capelunghe alla griglio* (razor clams opened on the grill), *masenette* (tiny green crabs that you eat shell and all), and *canoce* (mantis shrimp). For your wine, we suggest Prosecco, which has a distinctive golden-yellow color and a bouquet that's refreshing and fruity.

IN THE DORSODURO
Moderate
La Furatola. Calle Lunga San Barnaba, Dorsoduro 2870A. ☎ **041-5208594.** Reservations required. Main courses 26,000–45,000L ($13–$23). AE, DC, MC, V. Mon 7:30–10:30pm; Fri–Sun and Tues 12:30–2:30pm and 7:30–10:30pm. Closed Jan Aug. Vaporetto: Ca' Rezzonico. SEAFOOD.

La Furatola (an old Venetian word meaning "restaurant") is very much a Dorsoduro neighborhood hangout, but it has captured the imagination of local foodies. It's in a 300-year-old building, along a narrow flagstone-paved street that you'll need a good map and a lot of patience to find. The specialty is fish brought to your table in a wicker basket so you can judge its size and freshness by its bright eyes and red gills. A display of seafood antipasti is set out near the entrance. A standout is the baby octopus boiled and eaten with a drop of red-wine vinegar.

Inexpensive

✪ **Locanda Montin.** Fondamenta di Borgo, Dorsoduro 1147. ☎ **041-5227151.** Reservations recommended. Main courses 20,000–36,000L ($10–$18). AE, DC, MC, V. Tues 12:30–2:30pm, Thurs–Mon 12:30–2:30pm and 7:30–9:30pm. Closed 10 days in mid-Aug and 20 days in Jan. Vaporetto: Accademia. INTERNATIONAL/ITALIAN.

Since this restaurant opened just after World War II, its famous patrons have included Ezra Pound, Jackson Pollock, Mark Rothko, and Peggy Guggenheim's artist friends. The inn is owned and run by the Carretins, who have covered the walls with paintings donated by or purchased from their many friends and diners. Today the arbor-covered garden courtyard of this 17th-century building is filled with regulars, many of whom allow their favorite waiter to select most of their dishes. The frequently changing menu includes a variety of salads, grilled meats, and fish caught in the Adriatic. Specialties include fresh crab with virgin olive oil and lemon, tortelloni (a kind of dumpling) stuffed with artichokes and covered in a scampi cream sauce, and seasonal fish often served in a Barolo red wine sauce.

SEEING THE SIGHTS IN VENICE

Ahead, we'll explore the city's great art and architecture. But, unlike Florence, Venice would reward you with treasures even if you never ducked inside a museum or church. In the city on the islands, the frame eternally competes with the picture inside.

SIGHTSEEING SUGGESTIONS FOR FIRST-TIME VISITORS

If You Have 1 Day   Get up early and watch the sun rise over **Piazza San Marco,** as the city wakes up. The pigeons will already be here to greet you. Have an early morning cappuccino on the square, then visit the **Basilica of San Marco** and the **Palazzo Ducale.** We recommend a lunch stop at **Poste Vecchie,** at Pescheria Rialto, San Polo 1608 (tel. **041-721-822;** vaporetto: Rialto). This restaurant, near the fish market is the oldest in Venice, open Wednesday to Monday noon to 3pm and 7:30 to 10:30pm. Ride the **Grand Canal** in a gondola 2 hours before sunset and spend the rest of the evening wandering the narrow streets of this strangely unreal and most fascinating city. Apologize to yourself for such a short visit and promise to return.

If You Have 2 Days   Spend your first day as above. On Day 2 it's time for more concentrated sightseeing. Begin at Piazza San Marco (viewing it should be a daily ritual, regardless of how many days you have in Venice), then head for the major museum, the **Accademia,** in the morning. In the afternoon, visit the **Collezione Peggy Guggenheim** (modern art) and perhaps the **Ca' d'Oro** and **Ca' Rezzonico.**

If You Have 3 Days   Spend your first 2 days as above. Begin Day 3 by having a cappuccino on Piazza San Marco, then inspect the Campanile di San Marco. Later in the morning visit the Museo Correr. In the afternoon, go to the Scuola Grande di San Rocco to see the works of Tintoretto. Spend the rest of the day strolling the streets of Venice and ducking into shops that capture your imagination. Even if you get lost, you'll eventually return to a familiar landmark, and you can't help but see the signs pointing you back to Piazza San Marco. Have dinner in one of the most typical of Venetian trattorias, such as Locanda Montin.

If You Have 4 or 5 Days   Spend Days 1 to 3 as above. On Day 4 plan to visit the islands of the lagoon, including Murano, Burano, and Torcello. All three can be covered, at least briefly, on 1 busy day. On Day 5, relax, wander around the streets, and take in some of the many attractions you may have missed.

THE GRAND CANAL

Peoria may have its Main Street, Paris its Champs-Elysées—but Venice, for uniqueness, tops them all with its ✪ **Canal Grande (Grand Canal).** Lined with *palazzi* (palaces)—many in elegant Venetian-Gothic style—this great road of water is today filled with vaporetti, motorboats, and gondolas. Along the canal, the boat moorings are like peppermint sticks. It begins at Piazzetta San Marco on one side and Longhena's Salute Church on the opposite bank. At midpoint it's spanned by the Rialto Bridge. Eventually the canal winds its serpentine course to the railway station. We can guarantee that there's not a dull sight en route.

THE BASILICA, DOGES' PALACE & CAMPANILE

✪ **Piazza San Marco (St. Mark's Square)** was the heartbeat of La Serenissima (the Serene Republic) in the heyday of its glory as a seafaring state, the crystallization of its dreams and aspirations. If you have only 1 day for Venice, you need not leave the square, as the city's major attractions, such as the Basilica of St. Mark and the Doges' Palace, are centered here or nearby. Thanks to Napoléon, the square was unified architecturally. The emperor added the Fabbrica Nuova, thus bridging the Old and New Procuratie. Flanked with medieval-looking palaces, Sansovino's Library, elegant shops and colonnades, the square is now finished—unlike Piazza della Signoria in Florence.

If Piazza San Marco is the drawing room of Europe, then its satellite, **Piazzetta San Marco,** is the antechamber. Hedged in by the Doges' Palace, Sansovino's Library, and a side of St. Mark's Basilica, the tiny square faces the Grand Canal. One of the two tall granite columns in the piazzetta is surmounted by a winged lion, which represents St. Mark. The other is topped by a statue of a man taming a dragon, supposedly the dethroned patron saint Theodore. Both columns came from the East in the 12th century.

✪ **Basilica di San Marco.** Piazza San Marco. ☎ **041-5225205.** Basilica, free; treasury, 4,000L ($2); presbytery, 3,000L ($1.50); Marciano Museum, 3,000L ($1.50). Basilica and presbytery, Apr–Sept Mon–Sat 9:30am–5:30pm, Sun 2–5:30pm; Oct–Mar Mon–Sat 10am–4:30pm, Sun 2–4:30pm. Treasury, Mon–Sat 9:30am–5pm, Sun 2–5pm. Marciano Museum, Apr–Sept Mon–Sat 10am–5:30pm, Sun 2–4:30pm; Oct–Mar Mon–Sat 10am–4:45pm, Sun 2–4:30pm. Vaporetto: San Marco.

This so-called "Church of Gold" dominates Piazza San Marco, and is one of the world's greatest and most richly embellished churches—in fact, it looks as if it had been moved intact from Istanbul. The basilica is a conglomeration of styles, yet it's particularly indebted to Byzantium. It incorporates other schools of design, such as Romanesque and Gothic, with freewheeling abandon. Like Venice itself, it's adorned with booty from every corner of the city's once far-flung mercantile empire—capitals from Sicily, columns from Alexandria, porphyry from Syria, sculpture from Constantinople. The basilica is capped by a dome that, like a spider plant, sends off shoots, in this case, a quartet of smaller-scale cupolas. Spanning the facade is a loggia, surmounted by replicas of the four famous St. Mark's horses—the *Triumphal Quadriga.*

A St. Mark's Warning

St. Mark's has a strict **dress code:** no shorts, no skirts above the knee, and no bare shoulders. *They will not let you in if you don't come dressed appropriately.* You also must remain silent and cannot take photographs.

If you look back at the aperture over the entryway, you can see a mosaic, the dance of Salome in front of Herod and his court. Wearing a star-studded russet-red dress and three white fox tails, Salome dances under a platter holding John's head. Her glassy face is that of a Madonna, not an enchantress. Proceed up the right nave to the doorway to the **treasury** (*tesoro*). The entrance to the **presbytery** is nearby. On the high altar, the alleged sarcophagus of St. Mark rests under a green marble blanket and is held up by four sculptured alabaster Corinthian columns. The Byzantine-style **Pala d'Oro,** from Constantinople, is the rarest treasure at St. Mark's—made of gold and studded with precious stones.

On leaving the basilica, head up the stairs in the atrium for the **Marciano Museum** and the Loggia dei Cavalli. The star attraction of the museum is the world-famous *Quadriga,* four horses looted from Constantinople by Venetian crusaders in the sack of that city in 1204. This is the only quadriga (a quartet of horses yoked together) to have survived from the classical era.

✪ **Palazzo Ducale.** Piazzetta San Marco. ☎ **041-5224951.** Admission 18,000L ($9) adults; 10,000L ($5) students 15–29 years old; 6,000L ($3) ages 7–14 (free 6 and under). Mar–Oct daily 9am–5:30pm; off-season daily 9am–3:30pm. Vaporetto: San Marco.

You enter the Palace of the Doges through the magnificent 15th-century Porta della Carta on the piazzetta. It's somewhat like a frosty birthday cake in pinkish red marble and white Istrian stone. The Venetian-Gothic palazzo—with all the architectural intricacies of a doily—gleams in the tremulous Venetian light. The grandest civic structure in Italy, it dates back to 1309, though a fire in 1577 destroyed much of the original.

After climbing the Sansovino stairway of gold, proceed to the Anti-Collegio salon, which houses the palace's greatest artworks—notably Veronese's *Rape of Europa,* to the far left on the right wall. Tintoretto is well represented with his *Three Graces* and *Bacchus and Ariadne.* Some critics consider the latter his supreme achievement.

Now trek downstairs through the once-private apartments of the doges to the grand Maggior Consiglio, with its allegorical *Triumph of Venice* on the ceiling, painted by Veronese. What makes the room outstanding, however, is Tintoretto's *Paradise,* over the Grand Council chamber—said to be the largest oil painting in the world.

Reenter the Maggior Consiglio and follow the arrows on their trail across the **Bridge of Sighs,** linking the Doges' Palace with the Palazzo delle Prigioni, where the cell blocks are found, the ones that lodged the prisoners who felt the quick justice of the Terrible Ten. The "sighs" in the bridge's name stemmed from the sad laments of the numerous victims led across it to certain torture and possible death.

Campanile di San Marco. Piazza San Marco. ☎ **041-5224064.** Admission 8,000L ($4). Oct–Feb daily 9:30am–4pm, Mar–June daily 9am–7pm, July–Sept daily 9am–9pm. Closed Jan 7–31. Vaporetto: San Marco.

One summer night back in 1902, the bell tower of the Basilica of St. Mark on Piazza San Marco, which was suffering from years of rheumatism in the damp Venetian climate, gave out a warning sound that sent the fashionable crowd scurrying from the Florian Caffè in a dash for their lives. But the campanile gracefully waited until the next morning, July 14, before it tumbled into the piazza. The Venetians rebuilt their belfry, and it's now safe to ascend. A modern elevator takes you up for a pigeon's view of the city. It's a particularly good vantage point for viewing the cupolas of St. Mark's Basilica.

MUSEUMS & GALLERIES

✪ **Galleria dell'Accademia.** Campo della Carità, Dorsoduro. ☎ **041-5222247.** Admission 12,000L ($6). Mar–Oct Tues–Fri 9am–9pm, Sat 9am–11pm, Sun 9am–8pm; Nov–Feb Tues–Sat 9am–6:30pm, Sun 9am–1:30pm. Vaporetto: Accademia.

The pomp and circumstance, the glory that was Venice, lives on in this remarkable collection of paintings spanning the 14th to the 18th century. The hallmark of the Venetian school is color and more color. From Giorgione to Veronese, from Titian to Tintoretto, with a Carpaccio cycle thrown in, the Accademia has samples—often their best—of its most famous sons.

You'll first see works by such 14th-century artists as Paolo and Lorenzo Veneziano, who bridged the gap from Byzantine art to Gothic (see the latter's *Annunciation*). Next, you'll view Giovanni Bellini's *Madonna and Saint* (poor Sebastian, not another arrow), and Carpaccio's fascinating yet gruesome work of mass crucifixion. Two of the most important works with secular themes are Mantegna's armored *St. George*, with the dragon slain at his feet, and Hans Memling's 15th-century portrait of a young man. Giorgione's *Tempest* is the most famous painting at the Accademia.

Collezione Peggy Guggenheim. Ca' Venier dei Leoni, Dorsoduro 701. ☎ **041-5206288.** Admission 12,000L ($6) adults, 8,000L ($4) students, free children 9 and under. Wed–Mon 11am–6pm. Vaporetto: Accademia.

This is one of the most comprehensive and brilliant modern-art collections in the Western world, and it reveals the foresight and critical judgment of its founder. The collection is housed in an unfinished palazzo, the former home of Peggy Guggenheim, who died in 1979. In the tradition of her family, Guggenheim was a lifelong patron of contemporary painters and sculptors. As her private collection increased, she decided to find a larger showcase and selected Venice. Displayed here are works not only by Pollock and Ernst but also by Picasso (see his cubist *The Poet* of 1911), Duchamp, Chagall, Mondrian, Brancusi, Delvaux, and Dalí, plus a garden of modern sculpture that includes works by Giacometti.

Ca' d'Oro. Cannaregio 3931–3932. ☎ **041-5238790.** Admission 6,000L ($3). Daily 9am–1:30pm. Closed Jan 1, May 1, and Dec 25. Vaporetto: Ca' d'Oro.

This is one of the most handsomely embellished palaces along the Grand Canal. Although it contains the important **Galleria Giorgio Franchetti,** the House of Gold (so named because its facade was once gilded) competes with its own paintings. Built in the first part of the 15th century in the ogival style, it has a lacy look. Baron Franchetti, who restored the palace and filled it with his collection of paintings, sculpture, and furniture, presented it to Italy during World War I. In a special niche reserved for the masterpiece of the Franchetti collection is Andrea Mantegna's icy-cold *St. Sebastian,* the central figure of which is riddled with what must be a record number of arrows.

Museo Civico Correr. In the Procuratie Nuove, Piazza San Marco. ☎ **041-5225625.** Admission 18,000L ($9) adults, 10,000L ($5) ages 14–29, 6,000L ($3) children 6–14, free for children 6 and under. Mar–Oct daily 9am–7pm, Nov–Mar daily 9am–5pm. Vaporetto: San Marco. (The admission ticket includes entrance to Palazzo Ducale.)

This museum traces the development of Venetian painting from the 14th to the 16th century. On the second floor, are the red and maroon robes once worn by the doges, plus some fabulous street lanterns. There's also an illustrated copy of *Marco Polo in Tartaria*. You can see Cosmé Tura's *La Pietà,* a miniature of renown from the genius in the Ferrara School. This is one of his more gruesome works, depicting a bony, gnarled Christ sprawled on the lap of the Madonna. Farther on, search out a Schiavone *Madonna and Child* (no. 545), our candidate for ugliest bambino ever depicted on canvas (no wonder the mother looks askance). One of the most important rooms at the Correr is filled with three masterpieces: Antonello da Messina's *Pietà,* Hugo van der Goes's *Crucifixion,* and Dieric Bouts's *Madonna and Child.* The star attraction of the Correr is the Bellini salon, which includes works by founding padre Jacopo and his son, Gentile. But the real master of the household was the other son, Giovanni.

Ca' Rezzonico. Fondamenta Rezzonico, Dorsoduro 3136. ☎ **041-2410100.** Admission 14,000L ($7) adults. Oct–Apr Sat–Thurs 10am–4pm, May–Sept daily 10am–5pm. Vaporetto: Ca' Rezzonico.

This 17th- and 18th-century palace along the Grand Canal is where Robert Browning set up his bachelor headquarters. Pope Clement XIII also stayed here. It's a virtual treasure house, known for its baroque paintings and furniture. You first enter the Grand Ballroom with its allegorical ceiling, then proceed through lavishly embellished rooms with Venetian chandeliers, brocaded walls, portraits of patricians, tapestries, gilded furnishings, and touches of chinoiserie. At the end of the first walk is the Throne Room, with its allegorical ceilings by Giovanni Battista Tiepolo.

Upstairs you'll find a survey of 18th-century Venetian art. Head for the first salon on your right (facing the canal) that contains paintings from the brush of Pietro Longhi. His most famous work, *The Lady and the Hairdresser,* is the first canvas to the right on the entrance wall.

THE SCUOLE

Scuola di San Rocco. Campo San Rocco, San Polo. ☎ **041-5234864.** Admission 9,000L ($4.50) adults, 6,000L ($3) students. Mar 28–Nov 2 daily 9am–5:30pm; Nov 3–30 and Mar 1–27 daily 10am–4pm; Dec–Feb Mon–Fri 10am–1pm; Sat–Sun 10am–4pm. Ticket office closes 30 minutes before last entrance. Closed Easter and Dec 25–Jan 1. Vaporetto: San Tomà; from the station, walk straight onto Ramo Mondoler, which becomes Larga Prima; then take Salizzada San Rocco, which opens into Campo San Rocco.

Of Venice's *scuole* (in the Renaissance, scuole were centers used by social and religious organizations affiliated with the local parish), none are as richly embellished as the Scuola di San Rocco, filled with epic canvases by Tintoretto. By clever trick, he won the competition to decorate the darkly illuminated early 16th-century building. He began painting in 1564 and the work stretched on till his powers as an artist waned. The paintings sweep across the upper and lower halls, mesmerizing the viewer with a kind of passion play. In the grand hallway, they depict New Testament scenes, devoted largely to episodes in the life of Mary (*Flight into Egypt* is among the best). In the top gallery are works illustrating Old and New Testament, the most renowned devoted to the life of Christ. In a separate room is Tintoretto's masterpiece—a mammoth *Crucifixion,* one of the world's most celebrated paintings.

Scuola di San Giorgio degli Schiavoni. C.alle dei Furiani, Castello. ☎ **041-5228828.** Admission 5,000L ($2.50). Nov–Mar Tues–Sat 10am–12:30pm and 3–6pm, Sun 10am–12:30pm. Apr–Oct Tues–Sat 9:30am–12:30pm and 3:30–6:30pm, Sun 9:30am–12:30pm. Last entrance 20 minutes before closing. Vaporetto: San Zaccaria.

At the St. Antonino Bridge (Fondamenta dei Furlani) is the second important scuola to visit in Venice. Between 1502 and 1509, Vittore Carpaccio painted a pictorial cycle here of exceptional merit and interest. Of enduring fame are his works of St. George and the dragon—these are our favorite pieces of art in all of Venice and certainly the most delightful. In one frame, St. George charges the dragon on a field littered with half-eaten bodies and skulls. Gruesome? Not at all. Any moment you expect the director to call "Cut!"

ORGANIZED TOURS

Daily at 9:10am, **American Express,** San Marco 1471 (☎ **041-5200844;** vaporetto: San Marco), offers a 2-hour guided tour of the city, costing 40,000L ($20). Sights include St. Mark's Square, the basilica, the Doges' Palace, the prison, the bell tower, and in some cases a demonstration of the art of Venetian glassblowing. Monday to Saturday at 3pm, a 2-hour guided tour incorporates visits to the exteriors of several palaces along Campo San Benetto and other sights of the city. The tour eventually crosses the Grand Canal to visit the Church of Santa Maria dei Frari, which contains an *Assumption* by Titian. The tour continues by gondola down the canal to visit the Ca' d'Oro and ends at the Rialto Bridge. The cost of the afternoon tour is 45,000L ($23).

The **Evening Serenade Tour,** at 55,000L ($28) per person, allows a nocturnal view of Venice accompanied by the sound of singing musicians in gondolas. From April to October there're two daily departures, at 7:30 and 9:30pm, leaving from Campo Santa Maria del Giglio but from November to March there's just one departure at 3:30pm. Five to six occupants fit in each gondola as a singer and a handful of musicians perform throughout the Venetian evening. The experience lasts 50 minutes.

The **Islands Tour** is a 3-hour tour of Murano, Burano, and Torcello available for 30,000L ($15) per person. Departures are at 2:30pm year-round and also at 9:30am from March 15 to October.

THE SHOPPING SCENE

Venetian **glass** and **lace** are known throughout the world. However, selecting quality products in either craft requires a shrewd eye, as there's much that is tawdry and shoddily crafted. Some of the glassware hawked isn't worth the cost of shipping it home. Yet other pieces represent some of the world's finest artistic and ornamental glass. Murano is famous for its handmade glass. However, you can find little glass animal souvenirs in shops all over Venice.

For lace, head out to Burano where the last of a long line of women put in painstaking hours to produce some of the finest lace in the world.

SHOPPING STROLLS   All the main shopping streets of Venice, even the side streets, are touristy and overrun. The greatest concentration of shops is around Piazza San Marco and around the Rialto Bridge. Prices are much higher at San Marco, but the quality of merchandise is better. There're two major shopping strolls in Venice. First, from Piazza San Marco you can stroll through Venice toward the spacious square of **Campo Morosini.** You just follow one shop-lined street all the way to its end (although the name will change several times along the way). You begin at Salizzada San Moisè, which becomes Via 22 Marzo, and then Calle delle Ostreghe, before it opens onto Campo Santa Maria Zobenigo. The street then narrows again and changes its name to Calle Zaguri before widening once more into Campo San Maurizio, finally becoming Calle Piovan before it reaches Campo Morosini. The only deviation from this tour is a detour down Calle Vallaressa, between San Moisè and the Grand Canal, which is one of the major shopping arteries with some of the biggest designer names in the business.

The other great shopping stroll in Venice wanders from Piazza San Marco to the Rialto in a succession of streets collectively known as **The Mercerie.** It's virtually impossible to get lost because each street name is preceded by the word *merceria,* such as Merceria dell'Orologio, which begins near the clock tower in Piazza San Marco. Many commercial establishments, mainly shops, line the Mercerie before it reaches the Rialto, which then explodes into one vast shopping emporium.

SOME SHOPS WORTH A LOOK

At **Pauly & Co.,** Ponte Consorzi, San Marco (☎ **041-5209899;** vaporetto: San Zaccaria), you can wander through 21 salons, enjoy an exhibition of artistic glassware, and later see a furnace in full action. Pauly's production, which is mainly made-to-order, consists of continually renewed patterns, subject to change and alteration based on

Tips on Shopping for Venetian Glass & Lace

Venice is literally crammed with **glass** shops. It's estimated that there're at least 1,000 of them in the sestiere of San Marco alone. Unless you go to an absolutely top-quality and reliable dealer, such as those we recommend, most stores sell both shoddy and high-quality glassware. Sometimes, only the most trained eye can tell the difference. The big secret (which is becoming less a secret all the time) is that a lot of so-called Venetian glass isn't Venetian at all, but comes from former Eastern Bloc countries, including the Czech Republic. Of course, the Czech Republic has some of the finest glassmakers in Europe, so that may not be bad either. If you're looking for an heirloom, stick to such award-winning houses as **Pauly & Co.** or **Venini** (see below).

Most of the **lace** vendors are centered around Piazza San Marco. Although high, prices of Venetian lace are still reasonable considering the painstaking work that goes into it. Much of the lace is shoddy, and some of it—a lot of it, really—isn't Venetian lace but machine made in who knows what country. *The* name in Venetian lace is **Jesurum** (see below), which has stood for quality since the last century.

customer desire. The Venetian glass of **Venini,** Piazzetta Leoncini, San Marco 314 (☎ **041-5224045;** vaporetto: San Zaccaria), has won collector fans all over the globe. The store sells lamps, bottles, and vases, but not ordinary ones. Many are works of art, representing the best of Venetian craftsmanship in design and manufacture. Their best-known glass has a distinctive swirl pattern in several colors, which is called a *venature.*

The elegant **Jesurum,** Mercerie del Capitello, San Marco 4857 (☎ **041-5206177;** vaporetto: San Zaccaria or Rialto), the best place in Venice for serious lace purchases, has been in a 12th-century church since 1868. You'll find Venetian hand- or machine-made lace and embroidery on table, bed, and bath linens; and hand-printed bathing suits. **Laboratorio Artigiano Maschere,** Barbaria delle Tole, Castello 6657 (☎ **041-5223110;** vaporetto: Rialto), is one of the best places to purchase carnival masks handcrafted in papier-mâché or leather. The masks carry names and symbols, the best known being the birdlike luck bringer, called *Buonaventura* in Italian.

Il Papiro, Calle del Piovan, San Marco 2764 (☎ **041-5223055;** vaporetto: Accademia), is mainly noted for its stationery supplies, but it also carries and sells many textures and colors of writing paper and cards. In addition to hand-printed paper, the store stocks any number of easy-to-pack gift items.

VENICE AFTER DARK

The tourist office distributes a free pamphlet (part in English, part in Italian), called *Un Ospite di Venezia.* A section of this useful publication lists events, including any music and opera or theatrical presentations, along with art exhibitions and local special events.

In addition, classical concerts are often at various churches, such as the Chiesa di Vivaldi. To see if any **church concerts** are being presented at the time of your visit, call **Kele and Teo Travel Agency** (☎ **041/5208722**) for information.

THE PERFORMING ARTS

In January 1996, a dramatic fire left the fabled **La Fenice** at Campo San Fantin, the city's main venue for performing arts, a blackened shell and a smoldering ruin. The Italian government has pledged $12.5 million for the reconstruction of the theater, one of the most beautiful in Italy. However, you can still see performances of the Orchestra and Caro della Fenice in a temporary venue, **PalaFenice** in the Tronchetto parking facilities near Piazzale Roma (☎ **041-786500** for information; vaporetto: Tronchetto). Tickets for most events range from 30,000 to 150,000L ($15 to $75), but this could vary. The **box office** is open Monday to Friday 8:30am to 1:30pm and 1 hour before performance (☎ **041-521-0161**).

   Teatro Goldoni, Calle Goldoni, near Campo San Luca (☎ **041-5205422;** vaporetto Rialto), close to the Ponte Rialto in the San Marco district, honors Carlo Goldoni (1707–93), the most prolific—critics say the best—Italian playwright. The theater presents a changing repertoire of productions, often plays in Italian, but musical presentations as well. The box office is open Monday to Saturday 10am to 1pm and 4:30 to 7pm. Tickets are 20,000 to 45,000L ($10 to $23).

PIANO BARS & DANCE CLUBS

The pub **Il Piccolo Mondo,** Calle Contarini Corfu 1056A (☎ **041-520-0371;** vaporetto: Accademia), near the Accademia, is open during the day, and at night features disco dancing and organized parties. The crowd is often young, and dance music prevails. It's open from Thursday to Tuesday 10pm to 4am, but the action actually doesn't begin until after midnight. Cover (including the first drink) is 15,000L ($8) Thursday and Friday, 20,000L ($10) Saturday, otherwise free.

   Martini Scala Club, Campo San Fantin, San Marco 1980 (☎ **041-5224121;** vaporetto: San Marco or Santa Maria del Giglio), is an elegant restaurant with a piano bar that has functioned as some kind of an inn since 1724. You can enjoy its food and wine until 2am—it's the only kitchen in Venice that stays open late. After 10pm, you can come here to enjoy the piano bar. The restaurant is open March to November, Wednesday to Monday 7pm to 11:30pm; December to February, Wednesday to Monday noon to 2:30pm and from 7 to 11:30pm. The bar, which offers a piano bar and food, is open every day but Tuesday 10pm to 3am, and closed in July and August.

CASINOS

If you want to risk your luck and your lire, you can take a vaporetto ride on the Casino Express, which leaves from the stops at the rail station, Piazzale Roma, and Piazzetta San Marco and delivers you to the landing dock of the **Casino Municipale,** Lungomare G. Marconi 4, Lido (☎ **041-5297111**). Admission is 10,000L ($5), and bring your passport to get in. The building itself is foreboding, almost as if it could've been inspired by Mussolini-era architects. However, the action gets hotter once you step inside. At the casino, you can play blackjack, roulette, baccarat, or whatever. You can also dine, drink at the bar, or enjoy a floor show. It's open July to September daily from 3pm to 2:30am.

   October to June, the casino action moves to the **Vendramin-Calergi Palace,** Strada Nuova, Cannaregio 2040 (☎ **041-5297111;** vaporetto: San Marcuola). Incidentally, in 1883 Wagner died in this house, which opens onto the Grand Canal. The casino is open daily 3pm to 2:30am. Admission is 10,000L ($5), and bring your passport.

DAY TRIPS FROM VENICE

MURANO   On this island, **glassblowers** have for centuries performed oral gymnastics to turn out those fantastic chandeliers that Victorian ladies used to prize so highly. They also produce heavily ornamented glasses so ruby red or so indigo blue you can't tell if you're drinking blackberry juice or pure wood grain. Happily, the glassblowers are still plying their trade, though increasing competition, notably from Sweden, has

---

Sipping a Bellini at Harry's Bar

The single most famous of all the watering holes of Ernest Hemingway, **Harry's Bar,** Calle Vallaresso, San Marco 1323 (☎ **041-5285777;** vaporetto: San Marco), is known for inventing its own drinks and exporting them around the world. It's also said that *carpaccio,* the delicate raw-beef dish, was invented here. Devotees say that Harry's makes the best Bellini of any bar in the world. In Venice, this bar is a tradition and landmark, not quite as famous as the Basilica di San Marco, but almost.

---

compelled a greater degree of sophistication in design. You can combine a tour of Murano with a trip along the lagoon. To reach it, take vaporetto 5 at Riva degli Schiavoni, a short walk from Piazzetta San Marco. The boat docks at the landing platform at Murano where the first furnace conveniently awaits. It's best to go Monday to Friday 10am to noon if you want to see glassblowing action.

BURANO   Burano became world famous as a center of **lace making,** a craft that reached its pinnacle in the 18th century. If you can spare a morning to visit this island you'll be rewarded with a charming little fishing village far removed in spirit from the grandeur of Venice, but lying only half an hour away by ferry. Boats leave from Fondamente Nuove, overlooking the Venetian graveyard (which is well worth the trip all on its own). Take vaporetto 12 or 52 from Riva degli Schiavoni, get off at Fondamente Nuove, and catch boat 12, marked Burano.

Once at Burano, you'll discover that the houses of the islanders come in varied colors—sienna, robin's-egg or cobalt blue, barn-red, butterscotch, grass green. **Scuola Merietti** stands in the center of the fishing village on Piazza Baldassare Galuppi. The Burano School of Lace was founded in 1872 as part of a resurgence movement aimed at restoring the age-old craft that had earlier declined, giving way to such other lace-making centers as Chantilly and Bruges. By going up to the second floor you can see the lace makers, mostly young women, at painstaking work and can purchase hand-embroidered or handmade lace items.

After visiting the lace school, you can walk across the square to the **Duomo** and its leaning campanile (inside, look for a *Crucifixion* by Tiepolo). However, walk quickly; the bell tower is leaning so precariously it looks as if it may topple at any moment.

TORCELLO   Of all the islands of the lagoon, Torcello—the so-called Mother of Venice—offers the most charm. If Burano is behind the times, Torcello is positively antediluvian. You can follow in the footsteps of Hemingway and stroll across a grassy meadow, traverse an ancient stone bridge, and step back into that time when the Venetians first fled from invading barbarians to create a city of Neptune in the lagoon. To reach Torcello, take vaporetto 12 from Fondamenta Nuova on Murano. The trip takes about 45 minutes.

Cattedrale di Torcello, also called the Church of Santa Maria Assunta Isola di Torcello (☎ **041-730084**), was founded in A.D. 639 and was subsequently rebuilt. It stands in a lonely, grassy meadow beside a campanile dating from the 11th century. It's visited chiefly because of its Byzantine mosaics. Clutching her child, the weeping Madonna in the apse is a magnificent sight, whereas on the opposite wall is a powerful *Last Judgment.* It's open daily April to October 10am to 12:30pm and 2:30 to 6:30pm; November to March 10am to 12:30pm and 2:30 to 5pm. Admission is 2,000L ($1).

While on the island, you can dine in Venice's most idyllic luncheon stopover, ✪ **Locanda Cipriani,** Piazza San Fosca 29 (☎ **041-730150**), operated by Bonifacio Brass, nephew of Harry Cipriani of Hotel Cipriani and Harry's Bar fame. This low-key, deliberately rustic locanda serves an authentic Venetian cuisine, everything from a succulent risotto made from fresh vegetables and herbs from the family garden to fil-let of John Dory in the style of Carla, a late and much-revered matriarch here (the fish is flavored with tomatoes and capers). Main courses run from 30,000 to 45,000L ($15 to $23) and hours are Wednesday to Monday noon to 3pm and Friday and Saturday 7 to 10pm. Closed January 15 to February 15. American Express, Diners Club, MasterCard, and Visa are accepted.

THE LIDO   Near the turn of the century the Lido began to blossom into a fash-ionable beachfront resort, complete with deluxe hotels and its Casino Municipale.

The Lido today is past its heyday. The fashionable and chic of the world still patron-ize the **Excelsior Palace** and the **Hotel des Bains,** but the beach strip is overtourist-ed and opens onto polluted waters. It's not just the beaches around Venice that are polluted—the entire Adriatic is reputedly polluted. For swimming, guests use the pools of their hotels. They can, however, still enjoy the sands along the Lido. Try the **Lungomare G. d'Annunzio Public Bathing Beach** at the end of the Gran Viale (Piazzale Ettore Sorger), a long stroll from the vaporetto stop. You can book cabins—called *cabine*—and enjoy the sand. Rates change seasonally.

To reach the Lido, take vaporetto 6 from Riva Schiavoni, a landing stage near the Doges' Palace (the ride takes about 15 minutes).

Accommodations   The ✪ **Excelsior Palace,** Lungomare Marconi 41, 30126 Venezia Lido (☎ **800/325-3535** in the U.S. and Canada, or 041-5260201; fax 041-5267276; www.starwood.com, e-mail: res_excelsior@sheraton.com; vaporetto: Lido, then bus A, B, or C), is a monument to *la dolce vita* and did much to make the Lido fashionable. Today it is the Lido's most luxurious hotel. Rooms range in style and amenities from cozy singles to suites. Most of the social life takes place around the angular pool or on the flowered terraces leading up to the cabanas on the sandy beach. All 197 guest rooms—some big enough for tennis games—have been modernized, often with vivid colors. On the premises is one of the most elegant dining rooms of the Adriatic, the Tropicana. Rates, including breakfast, are 837,000 to 1,073,000L ($419 to $537) for a double and from 2,300,000L ($1,150) for a suite. American Express, Diners Club, MasterCard, and Visa are accepted. The hotel is closed Novem-ber to March 15.

✪ **Hotel des Bains,** Lungomare Marconi 17, 30126 Venezia Lido (☎ **800/325-3535** in the U.S. and Canada, or 041-5265921; fax 041-5260113; www.starwood.com; e-mail: res_desbains@sheraton.com; vaporetto: Lido, then bus A, B, or C), was built in the grand era of European resort hotels. It has its own wooded park and private beach with individual cabanas along with a kind of confectionery facade from the turn of the century. Thomas Mann stayed here several times before making it the setting for *Death in Venice,* and later it was used as a set for the film of the same name. The hotel has fairly large, well-furnished rooms, 191 in all. Many resort-type amenities are offered, including tennis courts, a large pool, a private pier, and a park. Rates are 695,000 to 975,000L ($348 to $488) for a double; suites begin at 1,450,000L ($725). American Express, Diners Club, MasterCard, and Visa are accepted. It's closed November to March.

12

The Netherlands

by George McDonald

This chapter mainly covers easygoing, prosperous Amsterdam, full of canals, bridges, and world-class museums. It includes day trips to historic Haarlem; the seaside resort Zandvoort; Delft, famous for its blue-and-white earthenware; the flower centers; and two IJsselmeer lakeside villages, Volendam and Marken.

Amsterdam

Amsterdam has never entirely shed its reputation as a hippie haven of peace, love, pot, and tulips, even with an economy that has become the envy of Europe. Fueled more by business than the combustion of semi-legal exotic plants, prosperity has sifted like a North Sea fog through the graceful cityscape of canals and 17th-century townhouses, bringing disruptive side effects in its wake. The historic city center recalls Amsterdam's golden age as the command post of a vast trading network and colonial empire, when wealthy merchants constructed gabled residences along neatly laid-out canals. Now a new generation of entrepreneurs is revitalizing old neighborhoods such as the Jordaan, turning some of the distinctive houses into bustling shops, cafes, hotels, and restaurants.

A delicious irony is that the placid 17th-century structures also host brothels, smoke shops, and some of Europe's wildest nightlife. The Dutch are proud of their live-and-let-live attitude, which is based on pragmatism as much as the country's long history of tolerance. Deciding to control what they cannot effectively outlaw, they permit prostitution in the red light district and the sale of marijuana and hashish in designated "coffee shops."

But don't think Amsterdammers drift around in a drug-induced haze. They are too busy whizzing around the city on bicycles, jogging through Vondelpark, feasting on arrays of ethnic dishes, or simply watching the parade of street life from the terrace of an outdoor cafe. Their zest for living is infectious. Between dips into Amsterdam's trove of artistic and historical treasures, take time out to absorb the freewheeling spirit of Europe's most vibrant city.

ORIENTATION

ARRIVING By Plane Amsterdam's **Schiphol Airport** (☎ **0900/0141** for flight information), is served by Dutch national carrier KLM in association with Northwest Airlines, in addition to

American Airlines, United Airlines, and many other international carriers. You emerge from baggage retrieval into Schiphol Plaza, a combined arrivals hall, railway station, and shopping mall.

The **KLM hotel shuttle bus** operates between the airport and city center on a circular route directly connecting 16 top hotels, with stops close to many others. The one-way fare is 17.50Dfl ($9); no reservations are needed, and buses leave from in front of Schiphol Plaza every 20 minutes from 7am to 6pm and every 30 minutes from 6 to 9:30pm.

Trains leave from Schiphol Station, downstairs from Schiphol Plaza, for Amsterdam's Centraal Station. Departures range from one per hour at night to six per hour at peak times. The fare is 6.25Dfl ($3) one way, and the trip takes about 20 minutes. Other stations—Amsterdam Zuid (South) and RAI among them—are also served, so be sure to check which one is best (including any tram or bus connection) for your hotel.

From the airport to the city center, **taxis** charge about 60Dfl ($29).

By Train   International trains arrive at Amsterdam's Centraal Station from Brussels, Paris (including the Thalys high-speed train), and several German cities, as well as from more distant locations in eastern Europe, Switzerland, and Italy, and from towns and cities all over Holland. For schedule and fare information on travel in Holland, call ☎ **0900/9292;** for international trains, call ☎ **0900/9296.**

To get to your hotel, trams or taxis can be found in front of the station.

By Bus   International coaches arrive at the main bus terminal opposite Centraal Station, and at Amstel bus station, beside Amstel railway station, which has metro and tram service to the center.

By Ship   **Scandinavian Seaways** has a daily overnight car ferry service from Newcastle in northeast England to IJmuiden on the North Sea coast west of Amsterdam; for reservations, call ☎ **01255/240240** in the United Kingdom, or 0255/534-546 in the Netherlands. **P&O North Sea Ferries** has a daily overnight car ferry service from Hull in northeast England to Rotterdam (Europoort); for reservations, call ☎ **0148/237-7177** in the United Kingdom, or 0181/255-555 in the Netherlands. **Stena Line** sails four times a day from Harwich in southeast England to Hoek van Holland (Hook of Holland) near Rotterdam; for reservations, call ☎ **01233/647047** in the United Kingdom, or 0174/389-333 in the Netherlands.

By Car   European expressways E19, E35, E231, and E22 reach Amsterdam from Belgium and Germany.

VISITOR INFORMATION   Holland Tourist Information (HTI) has an office in Schiphol Plaza at Schiphol Airport. Amsterdam's tourist information organization, **VVV Amsterdam** (☎ **0900/400-4040**), has offices inside Centraal Station beside platform 1, outside the station on Stationsplein, at Leidseplein 1, and on Stadionplein. VVV Amsterdam can help you with almost any question about the city, and can supply brochures, maps, and more. There are separate desks for reserving hotel rooms.

CITY LAYOUT   Amsterdam center is small enough that its residents think of it as a village. However, as villages go, it can be confusing until you get the hang of it. The concentric rings of major canals are its defining characteristic, along with several important squares that act as focal points. It's easy to think you're headed in one direction along the canal ring, only to find out you're going in exactly the opposite direction. A map is essential. VVV offices have maps and guides, including the small but detailed VVV Amsterdam map, which sells for 4Dfl ($1.90).

Amsterdam

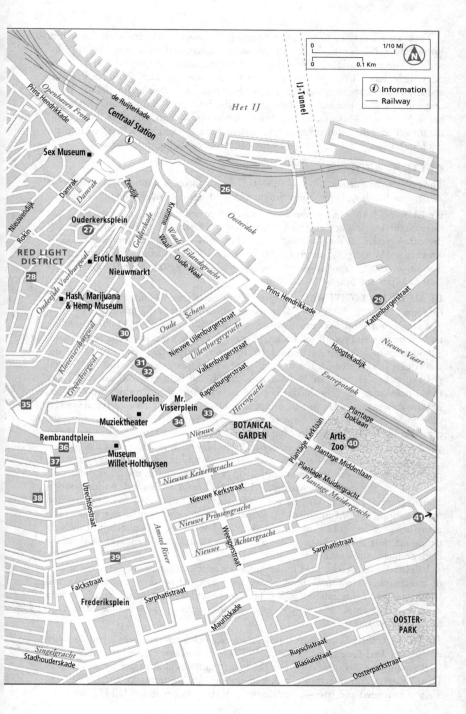

There are six major squares. Dam Square is the heart of the city, encircled by the Royal Palace, Nieuwe Kerk, department stores, hotels, and restaurants. Leidseplein, and the streets around it, is Amsterdam's Times Square, glittering with restaurants, cafes, nightclubs, discos, performance centers, and movie theaters. Rembrandtplein is another entertainment center, bustling with restaurants, cafes, and a casino. Museumplein and Waterlooplein are the cultural hubs, with the Rijksmuseum, Concertgebouw, Van Gogh Museum, and Stedelijk Museum of Modern Art all in and around the former, and the Muziektheater (plus a superb flea market) at the latter. Muntplein is a transportation hub, identified by the Munt Tower, dating from 1620.

GETTING AROUND

The public-transportation system runs daily 6am to around midnight (trams start at 7:30am on Sunday). Night buses run on a limited service, usually one per hour.

BY BUS & TRAM　An extensive bus network complements 17 tram routes; 11 of them begin and end at Centraal Station. Most bus/tram shelters have maps showing the entire system. A detailed map is available from VVV tourist offices and GVB/Amsterdam Municipal Transport ticket booths on Stationsplein in front of Centraal Station, or call transportation information (☎ **0900/9292**), Monday to Saturday 7am to 10pm and Sunday 8am to 10pm.

BY METRO & LIGHT RAIL　Amsterdam has two subway lines and four light rail (*sneltram*) lines (50, 51, 53, or 54) to get people to and from the suburbs.

A single-journey **ticket** (an *enkeltje*) costs 3 to 7.50Dfl ($1.45 to $3.60) depending on how many zones you travel through. There are 11 fare zones in greater Amsterdam, although tourists rarely travel beyond the city center zone 5700 (Centrum). Make sure your ticket is validated for the number of zones you plan to travel through. Several types of tickets are valid on buses, trams, metro, and light rail. You can buy a **day ticket** (*dagkaart*), valid for the day of purchase and the night following, from any bus or tram driver, conductor, or ticket dispenser for 12Dfl ($6). Also available are tickets valid for 2 to 9 days, priced from 16 to 42.25Dfl ($8 to $20); they have to be purchased at the GVB/Amsterdam Municipal Transport ticket booths. Bear in mind that you need to take a lot of trams for day and multiday cards to be worthwhile.

If you plan to do a lot of walking and take trams only around the city center, you're probably better off with a *strippenkaart* (strip card) that you can use throughout your stay. You can buy an eight-strip card for 12Dfl ($6) from drivers and conductors, or a 15-strip card (11.50Dfl/$6) and a 45-strip card (33.75Dfl/$16) from railway and metro stations, GVB/Amsterdam Municipal Transport ticket booths, post offices, and many news vendors. The card is easy to use: Fold at the line and punch it in the validating machine aboard the tram. On some trams a conductor at the rear validates the card; on buses, the driver does it.

Validated cards can be used for any number of transfers between lines and modes of transportation, within 1 hour of the time stamped on them at validation and within the paid-for number of zones. The fare system is based on canceling one strip more than the number of zones you travel within—two strips for one zone, three strips for two zones, and so on.

BY TAXI　Officially, you can't simply hail a cab, but often they stop if you do. Otherwise, call **Taxi Centrale** (☎ **020/677-7777**) or find one of the taxi stands sprinkled around the city, generally near the luxury hotels and at major squares such as Dam Square, Centraal Station, Spui, Rembrandtplein, Westermarkt, and Leidseplein. Taxis are metered and fares—which include the tip—begin at 5.80Dfl ($2.80) when you get in and run up at the rate of 2.85Dfl ($1.35) per kilometer. For a **water taxi,** call ☎ **020/622-2181.**

BY CAR   Don't rent a car to get around Amsterdam—you'll regret the expense and hassle. The city is a jumble of one-way streets, narrow bridges, and no-parking zones. In addition, car break-ins are not uncommon, especially at night.

Outside the city, driving is another story; you may want to rent a car for a trip into the countryside. Call **Avis,** Hogehilweg 7 (☎ **020/430-9611**); **Budget,** Overtoom 121 (☎ **020/612-6066**); or **Hertz,** Overtoom 333 (☎ **020/612-2441**).

BY BICYCLE   Follow the Dutch example and cycle. Sunday, when the city is quiet, is a good day to pedal through the parks and to practice riding on cobblestones and dealing with trams before venturing into the rush-hour fray. Bike-rental rates average 12.50Dfl ($6) per day or 60Dfl ($29) per week, with a deposit required. You can rent bikes from **MacBike,** Mr. Visserplein 2 (☎ **020/620-0985**); **MacBike Too,** Marnixstraat 220 (☎ **020/626-6964**); and **Bike City,** Bloemgracht 70 (☎ **020/626-3721**).

BY WATER BUS   The **Canal Bus** (☎ **020/623-9886**) runs daily 10am to 5pm and has three routes—Green, Red, and Blue—that connect important museums, and shopping and entertainment districts. There are two buses an hour at peak times. A day pass, valid until noon next day and including a discount on museum admissions, costs 29.50Dfl ($14) adults and 17.50Dfl ($8) age 13 and under.

BY PEDAL BOAT   Rent one from **Canal Bike** (☎ **020/626-5574**) and pedal yourself along the canals. They seat two or four; the hourly rate is 12.50Dfl ($6) per person for one or two people, 10Dfl ($4.80) per person for three or four. Moorings are at Leidseplein; Westerkerk, near the Anne Frankhuis; Stadhouderskade, between the Rijksmuseum and Heineken Reception Center; and Toronto Bridge on the Keizersgracht, near Leidsestraat. You can rent a water bike at one mooring and leave it at another.

Fast Facts: Amsterdam

American Express   Offices are at Damrak 66 (☎ **020/504-8777;** tram: Any tram to Centraal Station) and Van Baerlestraat 39 (☎ **020/673-8550;** tram: 2, 3, 5, 12, or 20). Both are open Monday to Friday 9am to 5pm and Saturday 9am to noon. The Damrak office books tours and excursions and offers a full range of services, including currency exchange. The Van Baerlestraat office only books tours and excursions.

Business Hours   Banks are open Monday to Friday 9am to 4 or 5pm (some until 7pm on Thursday). Regular shopping hours are Monday 11am to 6pm, Tuesday, Wednesday, and Friday 9am to 6pm, Thursday 9am to 9pm, Saturday 9am to 5pm, and Sunday (some stores only) noon to 5pm.

Currency   Holland's monetary unit is the **guilder,** yet you see it written as **Dutch florins** (abbreviated *f*, fl, Hfl, or **Dfl**); since this is a holdover from the past, ignore the written symbol and read all prices as guilders. There are 100 Dutch cents to a guilder. The exchange rate used in this chapter is $1 = 2.08Dfl or 1Dfl = 48¢. Also, €1 = 2.2Dfl or £1 = 3.45Dfl.

Currency Exchange   Change your money at **VVV tourist offices,** or if you carry American Express traveler's checks, at **American Express,** Damrak 66 (see above), where there's no commission charge. Other fair-dealing options are the **GWK exchanges** at Schiphol Airport and Centraal Station, which also handle money transfers via Western Union.

Doctors & Dentists   Contact the Central Medical Service at ☎ **020/ 592-3434.**

Drugstores   In Holland a pharmacy is called an *apotheek*. Try **Dam Apotheek,** Damstraat 2 (☎ **020/624-4331;** tram: 4, 9, 14, 16, 20, 24, or 25). All pharmacies have the name of an all-night pharmacy posted on the door.

Embassies & Consulates   The **U.S. Consulate** is at Museumplein 19 (☎ **020/575-5309;** tram: 3, 5, 12, 16, or 20); the U.S. Embassy is at Lange Voorhout 102, The Hague (☎ **070/310-9209**). The **U.K. Consulate-General** is at Koningslaan 44 (☎ **020/676-4343;** tram: 2); the British Embassy is at Lange Voorhout 10, The Hague (☎ **070/364-5800**).

Emergencies   In an emergency, dial ☎ **112** to call the police, report a fire, or summon an ambulance.

Internet Access   In de Waag, Nieuwmarkt 4 (☎ **020/422-7772;** metro: Nieuwmarkt), in the castle in the middle of Nieuwmarkt, is a popular cybercafe and restaurant, with free terminals. **Cyber C@fé,** Nieuwendijk 19 (☎ **020/ 623-5146;** tram: 1, 2, 5, 13, 17, or 20), is an Internet cafe.

Post Office   The main post office is at Singel 250–256 (☎ **020/556-3311;** tram: 13, 14, 17, or 20), at the corner of Radhuisstraat. It's open Monday to Friday 9am to 6pm and Saturday 9am to 3pm.

Taxes   Citizens from outside the European Union can shop tax free. If you spend more than 300Dfl ($144) in one store, you can ask for a Tax Free Shopping Cheque, which is stamped by Customs when you leave the European Union. A refund of 13.5% can be paid to your credit card account.

Telephone   The country code for the Netherlands is **31.** The city code for Amsterdam is **20** from outside the Netherlands, **020** inside the country (no code at all if you're in the city).

A local call in Amsterdam costs .50Dfl (25¢) for 3 minutes. Most pay phones in the Netherlands accept only phone cards, which are sold at newsstands, post offices, tobacconists, and railway stations for 10Dfl ($4.80), 25Dfl ($12), and 50Dfl ($24). Coin phones take 0.25, 1, 2.50, or 5Dfl. On both coin and card phones, watch the digital reading, which tracks your decreasing deposit so you'll know when to add more coins or another card. For directory assistance within the country, call ☎ **0900/8008;** for international assistance, dial ☎ **0900/8418.**

To charge a call to your calling card, dial AT&T (☎ 0800/022-9111); MCI (☎ 0800/022-9122); Sprint (☎ 0800/022-9119); Canada Direct (☎ 0800/022-9116); British Telecom (☎ 0800/022-9944).

WHERE TO STAY

Most Amsterdam hotels, whatever their cost, are clean and tidily furnished, and in many cases they've been recently renovated or redecorated. Booking ahead is always advised. The Dutch hotel industry runs a free hotel-booking service: the **NRC/Netherlands Reservations Center,** P.O. Box 404, 2260 AK Leidschendam (☎ **070/419-5500;** fax 070/419-5519).

If you arrive in Amsterdam without a reservation, the **VVV tourist offices** inside and outside Centraal Station will help you for the moderate charge of 5Dfl ($2.40) per person.

If you need to stay near the airport, try the **Sheraton Amsterdam Airport,** Schiphol Boulevard 101, 1118 BG Schiphol Airport (☎ **800/325-3535** in the U.S.

and Canada, or 020/316-4300; fax 020/316-4399; www.sheraton.com/amsterdam). You have all the comfort you would expect of a top-flight Sheraton. Doubles cost 870Dfl ($418). For a cheaper option, try the **Dorint Schiphol Amsterdam,** Sloterweg 299, 1171 VB Badhoevedorp (☎ **020/658-8111;** fax 020/658-8100; www.dorint.de; e-mail: reservations@dha.dorint.nl). Doubles cost 380 to 440Dfl ($183 to $212).

VERY EXPENSIVE

✪ **American Hotel.** Leidsekade 97 (facing Leidseplein), 1017 PN Amsterdam. ☎ **020/624-5322.** Fax 020/625-3236. www.interconti.com. E-mail: american@ interconti.com. 188 units. A/C MINIBAR TV TEL. 550–650Dfl ($264 –$313) double; 750Dfl ($361) suite; add 5% city tax. AE, CB, DC, JCB, MC, V. Parking at nearby lot 60Dfl ($29). KLM Hotel Shuttle from Schiphol Airport stops nearby. Tram: 1, 2, 5, 6, 7, or 10 to Leidseplein.

Art nouveau, neo-Gothic, and castlelike, the American has been a city landmark and meeting place since the early 1900s. Its location is one of the best in town if you want to be where the action is—some rooms overlook kaleidoscopic Leidseplein and others the tranquil Singelgracht canal. Rooms are decorated in art deco style, with clean lines and subtle lighting. All have hair dryers. Dine in the magnificent Café Américain (see "Where to Dine"), and watch the street life from the Nightwatch Bar's glassed-in sidewalk terrace. Amenities include a concierge, 24-hour room service, dry cleaning/laundry, and a health center with a sauna and solarium.

Grand Hotel Krasnapolsky. Dam 9 (facing the Royal Palace), 1012 JS Amsterdam. ☎ **020/554-9111.** Fax 020/622-8607. www.krasnapolsky.nl. E-mail: book@krasnapolsky.nl. 469 units. A/C MINIBAR TV TEL. 725Dfl ($348) double; 955–1,495Dfl ($460–$719) suite; add 5% city tax. Children under 2 stay free in parents' room; children 2–12 charged half price. AE, CB, DC, MC, V. Valet and self-parking 45Dfl ($22). KLM Hotel Shuttle from Schiphol Airport. Tram: 4, 9, 14, 16, 20, 24, or 25 to Dam Square.

One of the city's landmarks, the "Kras," as it's known locally, began life in 1866 as the Wintertuin (Winter Garden) restaurant, which still dominates the hotel's ground floor. The size and shape of the rooms vary, with 36 converted into miniapartments. All have hair dryers and coffeemakers. Recent enhancements include a new wing with a Japanese garden and Dutch roof garden. The Winter Garden is complemented by the French Brasserie Reflet, Japanese Edo and Kyo restaurants, and the Bedouin Shibli. Amenities include concierge, 24-hour room service, dry cleaning and laundry, health club, beauty salon, and boutiques.

Hôtel de l'Europe. Nieuwe Doelenstraat 2–8 (facing Muntplein), 1012 CP Amsterdam. ☎ **800/223-6800** in the U.S. and Canada, or 020/531-1777. Fax 020/531-1778. www. leurope.nl. E-mail: hotel@leurope.nl. 100 units. A/C MINIBAR TV TEL. 630Dfl ($303) double; suites from 870Dfl ($418); add 5% city tax. AE, DC, MC, V. Valet parking 6Dfl ($2.90) per hour. Tram: 4, 9, 14, 16, 20, 24, or 25 to De Munt.

Built in 1896, the Europe has a grand style and sense of ease. Its pastel-red-and-white facade overlooks the Amstel where it runs into the city's canal network. Rooms and bathrooms are spacious and bright, furnished with classic good taste. Some have

A Canal-House Warning

Be prepared to climb hard-to-navigate stairways if you want to save money on lodging in Amsterdam. Narrow and steep as ladders, these stairways were designed to conserve space in the narrow houses along the canals. Today they're an anomaly that'll make your stay even more memorable. If you have difficulty climbing stairs, ask for a room on a lower floor.

mini-balconies on the river, and all have hair dryers. About 20 units are updated each year. Dine in the elegant Excelsior restaurant or in the less formal Le Relais. Le Bar and La Terrasse (summer only) serve drinks and hors d'oeuvres daily. There's a waterside cafe terrace in summer. Amenities include concierge, 24-hour room service, heated indoor pool, and health club with sauna and massage.

Pulitzer Sheraton. Prinsengracht 315–331 (near Westermarkt), 1016 GZ Amsterdam. ☎ **800/325-3535** or 020/523-5235. Fax 020/627-6753. www.sheraton.com. 226 units. A/C MINIBAR TV TEL. 495–585Dfl ($238–$281) double; 1,570Dfl ($755) suite; add 5% city tax. AE, CB, DC, JCB, MC, V. Valet and self-parking 49.50Dfl ($24). KLM Hotel Shuttle from Schiphol Airport. Tram: 13, 14, 17, or 20 to Westermarkt.

This real prizewinner was constructed within the walls of 25 adjoining canal houses, most of which are between 200 and 400 years old. You walk between two houses to enter the lobby and climb the steps of a former merchant's house to enter the cheerful bar. Rooms are spacious and modern with views on one of two historic canals, Prinsengracht and Keizersgracht, or on the hotel garden. All have hair dryers. Dine in the tony De Goudsbloem restaurant or snack in the chic Pulitzer's cafe. A restored saloon cruiser from 1909 awaits your pleasure at the hotel's jetty. Amenities include a concierge, 24-hour room service, and laundry/dry cleaning.

EXPENSIVE

Dikker & Thijs Fenice. Prinsengracht 444 (at Leidsestraat), 1017 KE Amsterdam. ☎ **020/626-7721.** Fax 020/625-8986. www.dikkerenthijsfenice.nl. E-mail: info@ dikkerenthijsfenice.nl. 26 units. MINIBAR TV TEL. 450–495Dfl ($216–$238) double. Rates include continental breakfast. Children 12 and under stay free in parents' room. AE, DC, JCB, MC, V. Parking at nearby lot 50Dfl ($24). Tram: 1, 2, or 5 to Prinsengracht.

Small and homey, this hotel reveals a cozy character behind its stylish facade. Spacious rooms, tastefully styled in a modern version of art deco, are clustered in groups of two or four around small lobbies, which makes the hotel feel more like an apartment building. Double-glazed windows eliminate the noise from Leidsestraat. All rooms were renovated during 1997 and 1998 and have hair dryers and in-room movies. Those at the front have a great view of Prinsengracht. The Prinsenkelder restaurant serves fine French and Italian cuisine. Amenities include a concierge, room service, and dry cleaning and laundry.

Estheréa. Singel 303–309 (near Spui), 1012 WJ Amsterdam. ☎ **020/624-5146.** Fax 020/623-9001. www.estherea.nl. E-mail: estherea@xs4all.nl. 70 units. MINIBAR TV TEL. 380–450Dfl ($183–$216) double; add 5% city tax. One child 12 and under may stay free in parents' room. AE, DC, JCB, MC, V. Limited parking available on street. Tram: 1, 2, or 5 to Spui.

This large family-owned hotel occupying neighboring 17th-century canal houses has the intimacy and personality of a much smaller establishment. Most rooms and bathrooms are good size. All have hair dryers, and several have extra beds, making them ideal for families. There's a comfortable lounge and bar. As an added touch, the hotel offers guests free coffee and tea. The Greek Traîterie Grekas restaurant next door delivers room-service meals. Amenities include a concierge, limited-hours room service, and dry cleaning and laundry.

Jan Luyken. Jan Luykenstraat 54–58 (near Van Gogh Museum), 1071 CS Amsterdam. ☎ **020/573-0730.** Fax 020/676-3841. www.janluyken.nl. E-mail: info@janluyken.nl. 62 units. A/C TV TEL. 370–540Dfl ($178–$260) double. Children under 4 stay free in parents' room; extra person 85Dfl ($41). Rates include Dutch buffet breakfast. AE, DC, MC, V. Limited parking available on street. Tram: 2, 5, or 20 to Paulus Potterstraat; 3 or 12 to Eerste Constantijn Huygensstraat.

In a residential neighborhood 1 block from the P.C. Hooftstraat shopping street, this is best described as a small hotel with many of the amenities and facilities of a big one. Rooms are classically furnished; modern bathrooms have hair dryers. The owners are proud of the setting they've created and are constantly improving the hotel's facilities. Amenities include a health center with Jacuzzi, steam bath, and solarium.

○ **Schiller.** Rembrandtplein 26–36, 1017 CV Amsterdam. ☎ **020/554-0777.** Fax 020/626-6831. www.goldentulip.com. E-mail: sales@gtschiller.goldentulip.nl. 92 units. TV TEL. 420–530Dfl ($202–$255) double; 750Dfl ($361) suite. AE, DC, JCB, MC, V. Limited parking available on street. Tram: 4, 9, 14, or 20 to Rembrandtplein.

A blend of Jugendstil (art nouveau) and art deco, whose sculpted facade, wrought-iron balconies and stained-glass windows stand out on brash Rembrandtplein, the Schiller was constructed by painter/hotelier Frits Schiller during the 1890s, and no fewer than 600 of his works are on view inside. The tastefully decorated rooms have trouser presses, coffeemakers, and hair dryers. One in three has a minibar. Dine in the oak-paneled Brasserie Schiller (see "Where to Dine," below), and join the in crowd for a drink in the art deco Café Schiller. Amenities include 24-hour room service, laundry, and dry cleaning.

MODERATE

Amsterdam Wiechmann. Prinsengracht 328–330 (at Looiersgracht), 1016 HX Amsterdam. ☎ **020/626-3321.** Fax 020/626-8962. 40 units. TV TEL. 200–250Dfl ($96–$120) double. Rates include continental breakfast. No credit cards. Limited parking available on street. Tram: 1, 2, or 5 to Prinsengracht.

It takes only a moment to feel at home in the antique-adorned lobby. Owned for years by American T. Boddy and his Dutch wife, Nicky, the Wiechmann is comfortable and casual. Like a good wine, it gets better with age, and the location is one of the best you'll find in this or any price range. Most rooms are standard, with twin or double beds, some have big bay windows. Higher-priced doubles have antique furnishings, and many have a view of the canal. There's a breakfast room with white linen cloths on the tables, a lounge, and a bar.

Apollofirst. Apollolaan 123 (off Minervalaan), 1077 AP Amsterdam. ☎ **020/673-0333.** Fax 020/675-0348. E-mail: apolfi@xs4all.nl. 38 units. TEL. 325Dfl ($156) double; 495Dfl ($238) suite. Rates include buffet breakfast. AE, DC, MC, V. Limited parking available on street. Tram: 5 or 24 to Beethovenstraat.

This intimate and elegant family owned hotel, set amid the Amsterdam School architecture of Apollolaan, advertises itself as the "best quarters in town in the town's best quarter." That boast may be debatable, but all rooms are quiet, spacious, and grandly furnished. Those at the back overlook well-kept gardens as well as the summer terrace where guests can have a snack or a cocktail. There's an elegant French restaurant, the Chambertin. Amenities include room service and laundry and dry cleaning service.

○ **Canal House.** Keizersgracht 148 (near Leliegracht), 1015 CX Amsterdam. ☎ **020/622-5182.** Fax 020/624-1317. www.canalhouse.nl. E-mail: info&canalhouse.nl. 26 units. TEL. 265–365Dfl ($127–$176) double. Rates include continental breakfast. DC, JCB, MC, V. Limited parking available on street. Tram: 13, 14, 17, or 20 to Westermarkt.

A contemporary approach to reestablishing the elegant canal-house atmosphere has been taken by the owner of this small hotel in an effort to create a home away from home. Three adjoining houses dating from 1630 were rebuilt to provide private bathrooms, and then filled with antiques, quilts, and Chinese rugs. Room 26 has a panoramic view of the canal. The elegant breakfast room, seemingly unchanged since the 17th century, overlooks the back garden, and there's a cozy Victorian-style saloon.

De Filosoof. Anna van den Vondelstraat 6, 1054 GZ Amsterdam. ☎ **020/683-3013.** Fax 020/685-3750. www.xs4all.nl/~filosoof. E-mail: filosoof@xs4all.nl. 28 units. TV TEL. 215Dfl–245Dfl ($103–$118) double. Rates include buffet breakfast. AE, MC, V. Limited parking available on street. Tram: 1 or 6 to Overtoom.

On a quiet street near Vondelpark, one of the owners, a philosophy professor, has chosen posters, painted ceilings, framed quotes, and unusual objects to represent philosophical and cultural themes. Rooms are dedicated to Goethe, Wittgenstein, Nietzsche, Marx, and Einstein or based on motifs like Eros, the Renaissance, astrology, and women. Rooms in an annex across the street are larger; some open onto a private terrace. All-round improvements in services and facilities raised the hotel's local rating from two to three stars in 2000.

○ **Die Port van Cleve.** Nieuwezijds Voorburgwal 176–180 (behind the Royal Palace), 1012 SJ Amsterdam. ☎ **020/624-4860.** Fax 020/622-0240. E-mail: dieportvancleve. amsterdam@wxs.nl. 120 units. TV TEL. 340–415Dfl ($163–$200) double; 650–780Dfl ($313–$375) suite; extra person 95Dfl ($46). Rates include buffet breakfast. AE, CB, DC, MC, V. Nearby parking lot 40Dfl ($19). KLM Hotel Shuttle from Schiphol Airport. Tram: 1, 2, 5, 13, 17, or 20 to Dam Square.

Oozing history and class, this is one of the city's oldest hotels; it began its life in 1864 as the first Heineken brewery. Behind the ornamental facade, complete with turrets and alcoves, rooms, though on the small side, are comfortably furnished in modern yet cozy style. All have hair dryers and in-room movie channels, and some have minibars. You won't eat better Dutch food than in the Brasserie de Poort, and you can drink in the Bodega de Blauwe Parade watched over by Delft Blue tiles.

Seven Bridges. Reguliersgracht 31, 1017 LK Amsterdam. ☎ **020/623-1329.** 10 units. 220–360Dfl ($106–$173) double. Rates include full breakfast. AE, MC, V. Limited parking available on street. Tram: 16, 24, or 25 to Keizersgracht.

Owners Pierre Keulers and Gunter Glaner have made this one of the city's gems, and it has recently been virtually rebuilt inside, to provide every room with a bathroom. Some attic rooms have sloped ceilings and exposed wood beams. Big, bright basement rooms are done almost entirely in white. Decor includes handmade Italian drapes, hand-painted tiles, and wood-tiled floors.

INEXPENSIVE

○ **Acacia.** Lindengracht 251 (off Prinsengracht and Brouwersgracht), 1015 KH, Amsterdam. ☎ **020/622-1460.** Fax 020/638-0748. www.hotelnel.nl. E-mail: acacia.nl@wxs.nl. 18 units. TV TEL. 155Dfl ($75) double; 235Dfl ($113) houseboat double. Rates include full breakfast. MC, V. Parking 25Dfl ($12). Tram: 3 to Nieuwe Willemstraat; bus: 18 to Willemstraat.

Fronting a canal in the Jordaan, this well-kept hotel is run by Hans and Marlene van Vliet, who've worked hard to make it welcoming. Rooms, recently furnished with new beds, tables, and chairs, are simple but comfortable, and all have writing tables. Breakfast is served in a triangular breakfast room, with windows on both sides giving a nice view of the canal. Two houseboats for guests on nearby Lijnbaansgracht add an authentic local touch.

Amstel Botel. Oosterdokskade 2–4 (beside Centraal Station), 1011 AE Amsterdam. ☎ **020/626-4247.** Fax 020/639-1952. 176 units. TV TEL. 159Dfl ($76) double. AE, DC, JCB, MC, V. Limited parking available on quayside. Turn left out of Centraal Station, pass the bike rental, and you'll see it floating in front of you. Tram: Any tram to Centraal Station.

Where better to experience a city built on water than on a boat-hotel? Launched in 1993 to serve as a hotel, the boat has become very popular because of its location, adventurous quality, and comfort at reasonable rates. Four decks accommodate 176 cabins. Be sure to ask for a room with a view on the waterside, not on the uninspiring quayside. There's a concierge, in-room movie channel, and dry cleaning.

Casa Cara. Emmastraat 24 (at Koninginneweg), 1075 HV Amsterdam. ☎ **020/662-3135.** Fax 020/676-8119. www.com-all.nl/hotels/casa-cara. 9 units, 6 with bathroom. TEL. 85–100Dfl ($41–$48) double without bathroom; 130–155Dfl ($63–$75) double with bathroom. Summer rates include continental breakfast. AE, DC, MC, V. DC, MC, V. Limited parking available on street. Tram: 2 or 16 to Koninginneweg.

Gradually and faithfully trying to meet the demands of the 21st century traveler, the Casa Cara, near Vondelpark, is a simple but well-crafted conversion of a residential house in a neighborhood with deep front lawns. The hotel has two large rooms with a private shower and toilet on each floor (they also have a TV), and a trio of rooms without bathrooms that, as a result, have the hall facilities almost to themselves.

✪ **De Admiraal.** Herengracht 563 (at Thorbeckeplein), 1071 CD Amsterdam. ☎ **020/626-2150.** Fax 020/623-4625. 9 units. TV. 105–165Dfl ($51–$79) double; 200–320Dfl ($96–$154) family room. MC, V (5% surcharge). Limited parking available on street. Tram: 4, 9, 14, or 20 to Rembrandtplein.

Occupying a building from 1666, part of which was a spice warehouse for the East Indies trade, this hotel still has a nautical feel, with a bar and breakfast room that looks like an old sailing-ship officer's quarters. The simply furnished but clean and comfortable rooms—three of which are family rooms—are reached by a narrow staircase and have a fine view of the canal or adjacent Thorbeckeplein. Room 6 is the best, with two double beds, a panoramic view, and a balcony.

Piet Hein. Vossiusstraat 52–53 (facing Vondelpark), 1071 AK Amsterdam. ☎ **020/662-7205.** Fax 020/662-1526. www.hotelpiethein.com. E-mail: info@ hotelpiethein.nl. 36 units. TV TEL. 155–225Dfl ($75–$108) double. Rates include continental breakfast. AE, DC, JCB, MC, V. Parking at nearby garage 30Dfl ($14). Tram: 2 or 5 to Paulus Potterstraat.

The Piet Hein, occupying a villa near the city's most important museums, is named after a Dutch folk hero, a 17th-century admiral who captured a Spanish silver shipment. Rooms are spacious and well furnished, and the staff friendly and professional. Half the rooms overlook the park; two second-floor doubles have semicircular balconies; and there is a honeymoon suite with waterbed. Lower-priced rooms are in the annex. Hair dryers are available on request, and the hotel provides concierge, room service for drinks, dry cleaning and laundry, baby-sitting, and in-room movies.

Prinsenhof. Prinsengracht 810 (at Utrechtsestraat), 1017 JL Amsterdam. ☎ **020/623-1772.** Fax 020/638-3368. www.hotelprinsenhof.com. E-mail: info@ hotelprinsenhof.com. 10 units, 2 with bathroom. TEL. 125Dfl ($60) double without bathroom; 165Dfl ($79) double with bathroom. Rates include continental breakfast. AE, MC, V. Limited parking available on street. Tram: 4 to Prinsengracht.

Owner Ives Molin takes pride in his hotel, a modernized canal house near the River Amstel, and will make you feel welcome. Most rooms are large, with basic yet reasonably comfortable beds. The hotel has recently been redecorated, and new showers and carpets installed. Front rooms look out onto the Prinsengracht, where colorful houseboats are moored. Breakfast is served in an attractive dining room. There's no elevator, but a pulley hauls your luggage up and down the stairs.

WHERE TO DINE

As a trading city, a gateway city, and one that positively revels in its status as a melting pot, Amsterdam has absorbed culinary influences from far and wide. Just about any international cuisine can be found on the city's restaurant roster.

A True Amsterdam Dining Experience

You haven't eaten in Amsterdam until you've had an **Indonesian *rijsttafel* dinner,** a traditional "rice table" banquet of as many as 20 succulent and spicy foods served in tiny bowls. Pick and choose from among the bowls and add your choice to the pile of rice on your plate. It's almost impossible to eat all the food set on your table, but give it a shot—it's delicious. For an abbreviated version served on one plate, try ***nasi rames.*** At lunch, the standard Indonesian fare is ***nasi goreng*** (fried rice with meat and vegetables) or ***bamo goreng*** (fried noodles prepared in the same way).

Our suggestion of where to have your first *rijsttafel* is **Kantjil en de Tijger** (see below).

In general, with the exception of late-night restaurants, kitchens in Amsterdam take their last dinner orders at 10 or 11pm. Restaurants with outside terraces are always in big demand on pleasant summer evenings, and few take reservations.

One way to combat escalating dinner tabs is to take advantage of the low-cost tourist menu offered by some restaurants and the *dagschotel* (dish of the day) offered by many.

VERY EXPENSIVE

✪ **La Rive.** In the Amstel Intercontinental Hotel, Professor Tulpplein 1 (off Weesperstraat). ☎ **020/520-3273.** Main courses 45–130Dfl ($22–$63); set-price menus 135–195Dfl ($65–$94). AE, DC, MC, V. Mon–Fri noon–2pm; Mon–Sat 6:30–10:30pm. Tram: 6, 7, 10, or 20 to Sarphatistraat. FRENCH.

Earning the restaurant in his charge two Michelin stars, chef Robert Kranenborg has created a menu combining the finesse of classical French cuisine with the modern trend toward lighter, healthier eating. Luxury isn't forgotten either. The freshest seasonal fish and game is enhanced by sauces of truffles, cèpes, and foie gras. The setting is intimate but formal (a jacket is required for men), and several tables are next to the tall French windows that overlook the water.

EXPENSIVE

De Silveren Spiegel. Kattengat 4–6 (off Singel). ☎ **020/624-6589.** Main courses 47.50–55Dfl ($23–$26); set-price menus 75–85Dfl ($36–$41). AE, MC, V. Daily 6–11pm (open for lunch on reservation). Tram: 1, 2, 5, 13, 17, or 20 to Martelaarsgracht. DUTCH/FRENCH.

The two houses forming the premises were constructed in 1614 for wealthy soap-maker Laurens Jansz Spieghel. It's typically Old Dutch inside, with the bar downstairs and more dining rooms where the bedrooms used to be. There's a garden in back, and the whole place emanates a traditionally Dutch tidiness that's very welcoming. The updated menu features finely prepared seafood and meat dishes, such as baked sole fillets with wild spinach, Texel lamb with ratatouille, and traditional Zaanse mustard is always available.

✪ **D'Vijff Vlieghen.** Spuistraat 294–302 (entrances on Singel and Spuistraat). ☎ **020/624-8369.** Main courses 47–58Dfl ($23–$28); set-price menus 75–97.50Dfl ($36–$47). AE, DC, MC, V. Daily 5:30pm–10:30. Tram 1, 2, or 5 to Spui. DUTCH.

Occupying five canal houses, the restaurant is a kind of Dutch theme park with seven separate dining rooms decorated with artifacts from Holland's golden age. Don't miss the four original Rembrandt etchings and the collection of handmade glass. Yes, it's touristy, but at the "Five Flies," the food is authentic stick-to-the-ribs Dutch fare. The chef is passionate about an updated form of Dutch cuisine he calls "the new Dutch kitchen." The menu offers a selection of seasonal fish and game often marinated with fresh herbs and served with unusual vegetables such as chard, wild spinach, and brussels sprouts. If you're feeling adventurous, try the wild boar with sweet chestnuts and gin sauce.

Mangerie de Kersentuin. In the Bilderberg Garden Hotel, Dijsselhofplantsoen 7 (off Apollolaan). ☎ **020/664-2121.** Reservations recommended on weekends. Main courses 42.50–49Dfl ($20–$24); set-price menus 57.50–67.50Dfl ($28–$32). AE, DC, JCB, MC, V. Mon–Fri noon–2pm; Mon–Sat 6–11pm. Tram: 5 or 24 to Apollolaan; 16 to De Lairessestraat. INTERNATIONAL.

All cherry red and gleaming brass, the "Cherry Orchard" has floor-to-ceiling windows overlooking a residential street and semi-screened interior windows looking into the glimmering kitchen. It follows its own unique culinary concept, based on regional recipes from around the world, using fresh ingredients from Dutch waters and farmlands. The menu changes every two months, but you might find such dishes as lamb fillet prepared in goose fat with creamy salsifies and coriander-scented vanilla sauce; or sea bass sautéed with peppers, garlic, sea salt, and sesame seeds, served on stir-fried bok-choy and tofu, with lemongrass butter.

't Swarte Schaep. Korte Leidsedwarsstraat 24 (at Leidseplein). ☎ **020/622-3021.** Main courses 45–52.50Dfl ($22–$25); set-price menu 77.50Dfl ($37). AE, DC, JCB, MC, V. Daily noon–11pm. Tram: 1, 2, 5, 6, 7, or 10 to Leidseplein. DUTCH.

In a house from 1687, the "Black Sheep" still seems like an Old Dutch home. You climb a steep flight of tiled steps to reach the second-floor dining room, where the beams and ceiling panels are dark with age. It's a cozy, almost crowded place made both fragrant and inviting by the fresh flowers on every table and those that spill from the polished brass buckets hanging from the ceiling beams. The "Black Sheep" is well known for its wine list and its crepes Suzette. Other menu items might include sole meunière with asparagus or grilled salmon with fresh thyme.

MODERATE

✪ Amsterdam. Watertorenplein 6 (off Haarlemmerweg). ☎ **020/682-2666.** Reservations recommended on weekends. Main courses 16.50–40Dfl ($8–$19). AE, DC, MC, V. Daily 11:30am–1am. Tram: 10 to Van Halstraat. CONTINENTAL.

This restaurant in a century-old water-pumping station was an instant hit when it opened in the redeveloping Westerpark district. It's a little bit out of the way, but easily worth the tram ride. You dine amid a buzz of conviviality in the big, brightly lit former pumping hall. Service is breezy, the food is good, and the menu long. The emphasis is on seafood, but lots of meat and vegetarian dishes are offered too. If you're feeling flush, you could spring for a double starter of a half lobster with six Zeeland oysters.

Bodega Keyser. Van Baerlestraat 96 (beside the Concertgebouw). ☎ **020/671-1441.** Main courses 39.50–68.50Dfl ($19–$33); set-price menu 63Dfl ($30). AE, DC, MC, V. Mon–Sat 9am–midnight; Sun 11am–midnight. Tram: 2 to Willemsparkweg; 3, 5, 12, or 20 to Van Baerlestraat; 16 to De Lairessestraat. DUTCH.

Whether or not you attend a concert at the Concertgebouw, you may want to plan a visit to its next-door neighbor. An Amsterdam landmark since 1903, the Keyser has enjoyed a colorful joint heritage with the world-famous concert hall. There's an elegance here that combines traditional dark-and-dusky decor and highly starched pink linens. The menu leans heavily toward local fish and, in season, game specialties, such as hare and venison.

Brasserie Schiller. In the Hotel Schiller, Rembrandtplein 26–36. ☎ **020/554-0700.** Main courses 29.50–35Dfl ($14–$17); set-price menu 49.50Dfl ($24). AE, DC, MC, V. Daily 7am–11pm. Tram: 4, 9, 14, or 20 to Rembrandtplein. DUTCH.

Beamed and paneled in well-aged oak and graced with etched-glass panels and stained-glass skylights, this century-old Jugendstil landmark is a splendid sight. Paintings by Frits Schiller, the artist who constructed the hotel, adorn the walls, and the menu harks back to the early 1900s. (Elderly former chefs were even consulted on old recipes and cooking styles.) Among the classic dishes are stewed eel and potato-and-cabbage casserole, T-bone steak, roast leg of lamb with mint sauce, and spaghetti bolognese.

Café Américain. In the American Hotel, Leidsekade 97 (at Leidseplein). ☎ **020/556-3232.** Main courses 35–52Dfl ($17–$25). AE, CB, DC, MC, V. Daily 7am–12:30am. Tram: 1, 2, 5, 6, 7, or 10 to Leidseplein. INTERNATIONAL.

Café Américain is a national monument of Dutch Jugendstil and art deco. Mata Hari held her wedding reception here in her pre-espionage days, and since its 1900 opening, the place has been a haven for Dutch and international artists, writers, dancers, and actors. Leaded windows, newspaper-littered reading tables, bargello-patterned velvet upholstery, frosted-glass chandeliers from the 1920s, and tall, carved columns are all part of the dusky sit-and-chat setting. Menu dishes include monkfish, perch, rack of Irish lamb, and rosé breast of duck with creamed potatoes. Jazz lovers can stock up on good music at a Sunday jazz brunch.

De Belhamel. Brouwersgracht 60 (at Herengracht). ☎ **020/622-1095.** Reservations recommended. Main courses 28.50–44.50Dfl ($14–$21); set-price menu 49.50Dfl ($24). AE, MC, V. Daily 6pm–midnight. Tram: 1, 2, 5, 13, 17, or 20 to Martelaarsgracht. CONTINENTAL.

Classical music compliments art nouveau in a graceful setting overlooking the Herengracht and Brouwersgracht canals. The menu changes seasonally and game is a specialty. You can expect such menu dishes as puffed pastries layered with salmon, shellfish, crayfish tails, and chervil beurre-blanc to start; and beef tenderloin in Madeira sauce with zucchini rösti and puffed garlic for a main course. They serve vegetarian dishes, too.

De Oesterbar. Leidseplein 10. ☎ **020/623-2988.** Main courses 38.50–85Dfl ($19–$41). AE, DC, MC, V. Daily noon–1am. Tram: 1, 2, 5, 6, 7, or 10 to Leidseplein. SEAFOOD/DUTCH.

The decor at this 50-year-old restaurant is a delight: white tiles with fish tanks bubbling at your elbows on street level, and Victorian brocades and etched glass in the more formal dining room upstairs. The menu is a regular compendium of the variety of fish available in Holland and the variety of ways they can be prepared but also includes a few meat selections. Choices include sole Danoise with tiny North Sea shrimp, sole Véronique with muscadet grapes, stewed eel in wine sauce, and the assorted fish plate of turbot, halibut, and fresh salmon.

Haesje Claes. Spuistraat 275 (beside Spui). ☎ **020/624-9998.** Main courses 24.75–35.50Dfl ($12–$17). AE, DC, MC, V. Daily noon–midnight. Tram: 1, 2, or 5 to Spui. DUTCH.

If you're yearning for a cozy Old Dutch environment and hearty Dutch food at moderate prices, go to Haesje Claes. It's an inviting, intimate place with lots of nooks and crannies and with brocaded benches and traditional Dutch hanging lamps. The menu covers a lot of ground, ranging from canapés to caviar, but you'll be happiest with such Dutch stalwarts as omelets, tournedos, *hutspot* (stew), *stampot* (mashed potatoes and cabbage), or various fish stews, including those with IJsselmeer *paling* (eel).

Kantjil en de Tijger. Spuistraat 291–293 (beside Spui). ☎ **020/620-0994.** Main courses 21.50–29.50Dfl ($10–$14); *rijsttafel* 77.50–97.50Dfl ($37–$47). AE, DC, MC, V. Daily 4:30–11pm. Tram: 1, 2, or 5 to Spui. INDONESIAN.

Unlike Indonesian restaurants that wear their ethnic origins on their sleeve, the "Antelope and the Tiger" is modern and cool. Two best-sellers are *nasi goreng Kantjil* (fried rice with pork kebabs, stewed beef, pickled cucumbers, and mixed vegetables) and the 20-item *rijsttafel* (rice with meat, seafood, and vegetables) for two. Other choices are stewed chicken in soja sauce, tofu omelet, shrimp with coconut dressing, Indonesian pumpkin, and mixed steamed vegetables with peanut-butter sauce. Finish with the multilayered cinnamon cake or the coffee with ginger liqueur and whipped cream.

✪ Kort. Amstelveld 12 (at Prinsengracht). ☎ **020/626-1199.** Reservations required for sidewalk terrace. Main courses 32.50–39.50Dfl ($16–$19); menus 50–70Dfl ($24–$34). AE, CB, DC, MC, V. Summer daily 11:30am–midnight; winter Wed–Mon 11:30am–midnight. Tram: 4 to Prinsengracht. CONTINENTAL.

This is one of the few restaurants that takes reservations for evening dining outdoors in good weather. On the edge of a canal and a wide, open square, the tree-shaded terrace is far enough away from traffic to be unaffected by noise. Service is friendly, and menu dishes include excellent vegetarian choices, such as grilled goat's cheese with spinach and salad. Look also for the Eastern spiced fish, a house specialty. Dining indoors in the restored 17th-century Amstelkerk is recommended too, with fancier table sets than outside.

INEXPENSIVE

✪ Café Luxembourg. Spuistraat 22–24 (beside Spui). ☎ **020/620-6264.** Snacks 9.50–19.50Dfl ($4.55–$10). MC, V. Sun–Fri 9am–1am; Fri–Sat 9am–2am. Tram: 1, 2, or 5 to Spui. GRAND CAFE.

The New York Times called Café Luxembourg "one of the world's great cafes." The large portions of food at reasonable prices in a stylish and relaxing setting attract all kinds of people. Soup, club sandwiches, and such menu dishes as meat loaf join with specialties taken from other well-known restaurants in the city. Between 5 and 7pm, the bar is packed with tired nine-to-fivers and in summer, there's sidewalk dining. International newspapers are provided to encourage lingering.

Café-Restaurant Blincker. Sint-Barberenstraat 7 (off Rokin and Nes, near Theater Frascati). ☎ **020/627-1938.** Main courses 10–30Dfl ($4.80–$14). AE, DC, MC, V. Mon–Sat 4pm–1am. Tram: 4, 9, 16, 20, 24, or 25 to Rokin. CONTINENTAL.

This intimate restaurant in the Frascati Theater building, on a small side street off Rokin, attracts actors, journalists, artists, and other assorted bohemians. At night the place is jammed with people who cluster around the bar. The food is simple but tasty, including lamb chops with garlic, pancakes with cheese and mushrooms, homemade pasta, and cheese fondue.

De Jaren. Nieuwe Doelenstraat 20–22 (near Muntplein). ☎ **020/625-5771.** Main courses 18–30Dfl ($9–$14); set-price menus 38–45Dfl ($18–$22). No credit cards. Daily 10am–1am; Fri–Sat until 2am. Tram: 4, 9, 16, 20, 24, or 25 to the Munt. GRAND CAFE.

This big cafe has 300 seats inside and 150 more on a terrace beside the River Amstel. Students from the nearby campus often lunch here, contributing to its informality. Originally a bank, the renovated building has unusually high ceilings and a tiled mosaic floor. You can enjoy everything from a cup of coffee or a glass of *jenever* (potent Dutch gin) to spaghetti bolognese and rib-eye steak.

De Prins. Prinsengracht 124 (at Leliegracht). ☎ **020/624-9382.** Reservations not accepted. Main courses 12–25Dfl ($6–$12); dish of the day 20.50Dfl ($10); specials 23.50–28.50Dfl ($11–$14). AE, CB, DC, MC, V. Daily 10am–1 or 2am. Tram: 13, 14, 17, or 20 to Westermarkt. DUTCH/FRENCH.

This companionable, brown cafe (bar) and restaurant opposite the Anne Frankhuis serves the kind of food you'd expect from a much more expensive place. The clientele is loyal, so the relatively few tables fill up quickly. It's a quiet neighborhood restaurant—nothing fancy or trendy, but quite appealing, housed in a 17th-century canal house, with the bar on a slightly lower level than the restaurant, and a sidewalk terrace for drinks in summer.

Keuken van 1870. Spuistraat 4 (at Martelaarsgracht). ☎ **020/624-8965.** Reservations not accepted. Main courses 9–18.50Dfl ($4.35–$9). AE, DC, MC, V. Mon–Fri 12:30pm–8pm; Sat–Sun 4–9pm. Tram: 1, 2, 5, 13, 17, or 20 to Martelaarsgracht. DUTCH.

This is one of the cheapest and plainest places to eat in Amsterdam. Opened in 1870 as a public soup kitchen, it serves meals cafeteria-style. Tables are bare, and menu dishes are basic, but the food is good. Pork chops, fish, and chicken—all accompanied by vegetables and potatoes—are some of the main courses on the menu. It's a good place to go if you're on a tight budget.

La Place. Rokin 160 (near Muntplein). ☎ **020/622-0171.** Main courses 7.50–17.50Dfl ($3.60–$8). MC, V. Mon–Sat 9:30am–8pm; Sun 11am–8pm. Tram: 4, 9, 14, 16, 20, 24, or 25 to Muntplein. DUTCH.

This vast, multilevel food depot has something for everyone. The ground floor offers thick slabs of quiche, an assortment of pizzas, and deliciously flavored fresh breads—the cheese-onion loaf is a meal in itself. An airy, glass-topped cafeteria covers the three upstairs floors. Menu dishes include a meat or fish of the day, often with an Indonesian touch, along with vegetables and potatoes. Vegetarians love the soup and salad selection, and there's an assortment of freshly squeezed fruit juices.

SEEING THE SIGHTS
SUGGESTIONS FOR FIRST-TIME VISITORS

If You Have 1 Day   For the perfect introduction to the city, take a cruise on its canals and admire the many gabled merchants' houses and almost 1,200 bridges. (The canals are even more special after dark, when the glow of street and house lights shimmers on the water). In the afternoon, visit the Rijksmuseum to see Rembrandts and works by other golden age masters. In the evening, dine at a traditional restaurant or opt for an Indonesian *rijsttafel,* and end your day by dropping into a brown cafe (a traditional Amsterdam bar, see "Brown Cafes").

If You Have 2 Days   Day 1 as above. On Day 2, visit the Anne Frank house in the morning. In the afternoon, explore the historic center on foot, visiting Dam Square and the Royal Palace and other major squares. In the evening attend a concert at the Concertgebouw, or opera or dance at the Muziektheater (book ahead).

Passport to Amsterdam
_____

The **Amsterdam Culture & Leisure Pass** is a sound investment if you plan to do a lot of sightseeing. Some 30 coupons allow free entry into top museums, a free canal cruise and diamond factory tour, and discounts on many other attractions and purchases. The pass costs 39.50Dfl ($19) and is available from any of the city's VVV tourist offices or from Holland Tourist Information at Schiphol Plaza.

If You Have 3 Days   Days 1 and 2 as above. On Day 3, take in the Van Gogh Museum in the morning. Relax over coffee at the Café Américain, with its stunning art nouveau interior. Look into some street markets, either the Albert Cuyp market, the floating Flower Market, or the Waterlooplein flea market. In the evening, take a walk in the Red Light District. (If this isn't your idea of an edifying experience, consider the alternative dining option from Day 1.)

THREE MUST-SEE ATTRACTIONS

✪ **Anne Frankhuis.** Prinsengracht 263 (beside Westermarkt). ☎ **020/556-7100.** Admission 10Dfl ($4.80) adults, 5Dfl ($2.40) children 10–17; children under 10 free. Apr–Aug daily 9am–9pm; Sept–Mar daily 9am–5pm. Tram: 13, 14, 17, or 20 to Westermarkt.

Anne Frank's famous diary was written in a secret annex of this house, where eight Jewish refugees from three separate families lived together in nearly total silence for more than 2 years during World War II. The hiding place Otto Frank found for his family and some friends kept them safe until they were betrayed and their refuge was raided by pro-Nazi police, tragically close to the war's end. Anne and six of the other *onderduikers* (divers or hiders) died in concentration camps. The rooms are still as bare as they were when Anne's father, the only survivor, returned—nothing has been changed. A new wing for temporary exhibits opened in 1999. Note that the lines here can be very long, especially in summer—try going on a weekday morning.

Nearby on Westermarkt is the **Homomonument,** dedicated to the gays and lesbians who were killed during World War II and also a place of remembrance for those who've died of AIDS.

✪ **Rijksmuseum.** Stadhouderskade 42 (behind Museumplein). ☎ **020/674-7000** or 020/674-7047 for taped information in English. Admission 15Dfl ($7) adults, 7.50Dfl ($3.60) children 6–18; children under 6 free. Daily 10am–5pm. Tram: 2, 5, or 20 to Hobbemastraat; 6, 7, or 10 to Spiegelgracht.

The architectural legacy of Holland's 17th-century golden age is all around you in Amsterdam. For the artistic lowdown, head to the neo-Gothic Rijksmuseum, opened in 1885. It holds the world's largest collection of paintings by the Dutch masters, including the most famous: Rembrandt's 1642 *The Night Watch.* Rembrandt, Jacob van Ruysdael, Maerten van Heemskerck, Frans Hals, Paulus Potter, Jan Steen, Jan Vermeer, Pieter de Hooch, Gerard Terborch, and Gerard Dou are all represented, as are Fra Angelico, Tiepolo, Goya, Rubens, Van Dyck, and later artists of the Hague School and the Amsterdam Impressionist movement. You'll also find prints and sculpture, furniture, Asian and Islamic art, china and porcelain, trinkets and glassware, armaments and ship models, 17th-century dollhouses, costumes, screens, badges, and laces.

The long-closed South Wing (now called the New Wing) was reopened in 1996 to exhibit a variety of art objects from Asia, like jewelry, Buddha sculptures, and weapons. And in 1998, the Rijksmuseum introduced ARIA, an interactive multimedia system, so you can learn more about the museum's collections. By touching a screen, you can access information about more than 1,200 artworks, including text, illustrations, video, and animation.

✪ **Van Gogh Museum.** Paulus Potterstraat 7 (at Museumplein). ☎ **020/570-5200.** Admission 15.50Dfl ($7) adults, 5Dfl ($2.40) children 13–17, free for children under 13. Daily 10am–6pm. Tram: 2, 5, or 20 to Paulus Potterstraat; 3, 12, or 16 to Museumplein.

This three-story museum houses the world's largest van Gogh collection—more than 200 paintings displayed chronologically according to the seven distinct periods that defined his short career. They include a progression of 18 paintings produced during the 2 years the artist spent in the south of France, generally considered his artistic high

The World's Smallest Art Museum

Amsterdam boasts the world's smallest art museum, **Reflex,** Weteringchans 79A, opposite the Rijksmuseum (☎ **020/627-2832**). It's only 13.2 square meters large and displays 1,500 miniature paintings, graphics, sculptures, and pictures, including works by Picasso, Lichtenstein, Oldenburg, and Christo. Admission is free, and it's open Tuesday to Saturday 10am to 6pm.

point. The ground floor displays paintings by van Gogh's contemporaries—Toulouse-Lautrec, Gauguin, Monet, Sisley, and others. One flight up is one of the most famous paintings of modern times, *Still Life Vase with Fourteen Sunflowers,* best known simply as *Sunflowers,* and van Gogh's last painting, *Cornfield with Crows,* whose mood seems to presage his suicide in 1890 at the age of 37. Upper floors contain van Gogh drawings, a library, and temporary exhibits. The museum was totally refurbished in 1998–99, with the addition of a new wing designed by Japanese architect Kisho Kurokawa. Note that the lines here can be very long, especially in summer—try going on a weekday morning.

CANALS & CANAL-SIDE HOUSES

A canal-boat cruise is the best way to see old Amsterdam and its large and busy harbor. A typical itinerary includes Centraal Station; the Harlemmersluis floodgates; the Cat Boat (a houseboat—one of around 2,400 in the city—with a permanent population of as many as 150 wayward felines); and both the narrowest building in the city and one of its largest houses still in use as a single-family residence. You may also see the burgomaster's (mayor's) official residence; the "Golden Bend" on Herengracht, traditionally the best address in town; picturesque bridges, including the famous Magere Brug (Skinny Bridge) over the Amstel; and Amsterdam Drydocks.

Trips depart at regular intervals from *rondvaart* (canal circuit) piers in key locations around town and last approximately 1 hour. The majority of launches are docked along Damrak and Prins Hendrikkade near Centraal Station, on Rokin near Muntplein, and near Leidseplein. They leave every 15 to 30 minutes during summer (9am to 9:30pm) and every 45 minutes in winter (10am to 4pm). Average fare is 12 to 18Dfl ($6 to $9) for adults, 10 to 12Dfl ($4.80 to $6) for children 4 to 13. Numerous canal-boat cruise operators offer comparable prices and trips.

HISTORIC BUILDINGS & MONUMENTS

Begijnhof. Gedempte Begijnensloot (at Spui). No telephone. Free admission. Daily until sunset. Tram: 1, 2, or 5 to Spui.

Formerly an almshouse for *begijns,* pious laywomen involved in religious and charitable work, this beautiful cloister of small homes around a 14th-century garden courtyard makes for a perfect escape from the city's bustle. In the southwest corner is one of two surviving wooden houses in Amsterdam, dating from the 15th century. (Construction of wooden houses was prohibited in 1452 after a series of disastrous fires.) Most of the tiny 17th- and 18th-century buildings still house the city's elderly poor, and you should respect their privacy, especially after sunset.

Koninklijk Paleis (Royal Palace). Dam Square. ☎ **020/620-4060.** Admission 7Dfl ($3.35) adults, 5Dfl ($2.40) seniors and children 13–18, 2.50Dfl ($1.20) children 5–12, free for children under 5. Easter and June–July daily 10am–5:30pm, Aug–Oct daily 12:30–5pm; otherwise, generally Tues–Thurs 12:30–5pm, closed mid-Dec to mid Feb. (Opening days and hours are highly variable, and it's best to check before going.) Tram: 1, 2, 4, 5, 9, 13, 14, 16, 17, 20, 24, or 25 to Dam Square.

The 17th-century neoclassical Royal Palace was Amsterdam's town hall for 153 years. It was first used as a palace during the 5-year rule of Louis Bonaparte (Napoleon's brother) in the early 19th century. You can visit its high-ceilinged Citizens' Hall, Burgomasters' Chambers, and Council Room, as well as the Vierschaar—a marble tribunal where death sentences were pronounced during the 17th century. Although this is the monarch's official palace, Queen Beatrix rarely uses it for more than occasional receptions or official ceremonies.

MUSEUMS & GALLERIES

✪ **Amsterdams Historisch Museum.** Kalverstraat 92 and Nieuwezijds Voorburgwal 359. ☎ **020/523-1822.** Admission 12Dfl ($6) adults, 6Dfl ($2.90) children 6–15, free for children under 6. Mon–Fri 10am–5pm; Sat–Sun 11am–5pm. Tram: 1, 2, 4, 5, 9, 16, 20, 24, or 25 to Spui.

In a huge 17th-century former city orphanage that has been beautifully redesigned, this fascinating museum gives you a better understanding of everything you see as you explore the city. Gallery by gallery, century by century, you learn how a small fishing village became a major world trading center. You can also view many famous paintings by Dutch masters in the context of their time and place. Next to the museum is the Schuttersgalerij (Civic Guard Gallery), a narrow, two-story skylit chamber bedecked with a dozen large 17th-century group portraits of militiamen. The hours are the same as for the museum, and admission is free.

Holland Experience. Waterlooplein 17. ☎ **020/422-2233.** Admission 17.50Dfl ($8) adults, 15Dfl ($7) seniors and children under 13. Daily 10am–6pm. Tram: 9, 14, or 20 to Waterlooplein.

A multidimensional film and theater show takes you through Holland's landscapes and culture at different historical periods up to the present. Exhibitions include farming and fishing scenes, and there's a simulated dike collapse.

Joods Historisch Museum (Jewish Historical Museum). Jonas Daniël Meijerplein 2–4 (facing Waterlooplein). ☎ **020/626-9945.** Admission 10Dfl ($4.80) adults, 4.50Dfl ($2.15) children 13–18, 2.50Dfl ($1.20) children 6–12, free for children under 6. Daily 11am–5pm. Tram: 9, 14, or 20 to Waterlooplein.

This museum, in the restored Ashkenazi Synagogue complex, tells the intertwining stories of Jewish identity, religion, culture, and history in the Netherlands through objects, photographs, artworks, and interactive displays. Take time to appreciate the beauty of the buildings, which include Europe's oldest public synagogue.

Museum Het Rembrandthuis. Jodenbreestraat 4–6 (at Waterlooplein). ☎ **020/520-0400.** Admission 12.50Dfl ($6) adults, 7.50Dfl ($3.60) children 6–15, free for children under 6. Mon–Sat 10am–5pm; Sun and holidays 1–5pm. Tram: 9, 14, or 20 to Waterlooplein.

Rembrandt had to leave his home of 19 years in 1658 because of bankruptcy. A recently completed restoration has returned it to the way it looked when Rembrandt lived and worked here. About 120 of the museum's 250 Rembrandt etchings, including self-portraits and landscapes, hang on the walls at any one time and you can see the artist's printing press. Temporary exhibitions are mounted in an adjacent house that belonged to Rembrandt's wife, Saskia. To avoid the crowds, try going early on a weekday morning.

Nederlands Scheepvaartmuseum (Netherlands Maritime Museum). Kattenburgerplein 1 (in the Eastern Dock). ☎ **020/523-2222.** Admission 12.50Dfl ($6) adults, 8Dfl ($3.85) children 17 and under. Tues–Sat 10am–5pm (also Mon mid-June to mid-Sept); Sun noon–5pm. Bus: 22 or 32 to Kattenburgerplein.

A former Amsterdam Admiralty arsenal overlooking Amsterdam harbor provides the backdrop for rooms of ships, ship models, and seascapes. Old maps include a

15th-century Ptolemaic atlas and a sumptuously bound edition of the *Great Atlas* by Jan Blaeu, master cartographer of Holland's golden age. Among the historic papers on display are several pertaining to Nieuwe Amsterdam (New York City) and Nieuwe Nederland (New York State). A full-size replica of the Dutch East India Company sailing ship *Amsterdam*, which foundered off Hastings in 1749, is moored at the wharf, and a replica of an 1854 iron clipper is under construction.

Stedelijk Museum of Modern Art. Paulus Potterstraat 13 (at Museumplein). ☎ **020/573-2911.** Admission 9Dfl ($4.35) adults, 4.50Dfl ($2.15) children 7–16, free for children under 7. Daily 11am–5pm. Tram: 2, 5, or 20 to Paulus Potterstraat; 3, 12, or 16 to Museumplein.

The Stedelijk centers its collection around De Stijl, CoBrA (an expressive, abstract style from the 1950s) and post-CoBrA painting, nouveau réalisme, pop art, color-field painting, zero and minimalist art, and conceptual art. On display are works by such Dutch painters as Karel Appel, Willem de Kooning, and Piet Mondrian; French artists Chagall, Cézanne, Picasso, Renoir, Monet, and Manet; and Americans Calder, Oldenburg, Rosenquist, and Warhol. The museum houses the largest collection outside Russia of abstract painter Kasimir Malevich.

Tropenmuseum (Tropical Museum). Linnaeusstraat 2 (at Mauritskade). ☎ **020/568-8215.** Admission 12.50Dfl ($6) adults, 7.50Dfl ($3.60) children 6–17, free for children under 6. Mon–Fri 10am–5pm; Sat–Sun and holidays noon–5pm. Tram: 7, 9, 10, or 14 to Mauritskade.

Built by the Royal Tropical Institute in the 19th century, this museum is devoted to contemporary culture and problems in tropical areas. Its most interesting exhibits are walk-through model villages that capture daily life in such places as India and Indonesia (minus the inhabitants); tools and techniques used to produce batik, the distinctively dyed Indonesian fabric; and instruments and ornaments one would find in a tropical residence. A new permanent exhibition covers West Asia and North Africa. A section of the museum, Kindermuseum TM Junior (☎ **020/568-8300**), is open only to children 6 to 12 (one adult per child is allowed).

CHURCHES & A SYNAGOGUE

The most important places of worship in Amsterdam are the 14th-century **Nieuwe Kerk,** Holland's coronation church, on Dam Square; 17th-century **Westerkerk,** on Prinsengracht at Westermarkt, which has the tallest, most beautiful tower in Amsterdam (take the elevator to the top for a great view) and is the burial place of Rembrandt; 14th-century **Oude Kerk,** at Oudekerksplein on Oudezijds Voorburgwal in the Red Light District, surrounded by almshouses turned into prostitutes' rooms; and the 17th-century **Portuguese Synagogue,** on Mr. Visserplein, facing the Jewish Historical Museum.

A GREAT ZOO

✪ **Artis Zoo.** Plantage Kerklaan 38–40. ☎ **020/523-3400.** Admission 25Dfl ($12) adults, 17.50Dfl ($8) children 4–11, free for children under 4. Daily 9am–5pm. Tram: 9, 14, or 20 to Plantage Middenlaan.

Established in 1838, this is the oldest zoo in the Netherlands, housing more than 6,000 animals. Also on the property are a planetarium, aquarium, geological and zoological museum, and a children's farm. The aquarium, constructed in 1882 and recently renovated, is well presented, particularly the exhibits on the Amazon River, coral reefs, and Amsterdam's canals, with their fish and garbage.

Diamond-Cutting Demonstrations

Although a diamond-cutting demonstration will probably just consist of a lone polisher working at a small wheel in the back of a jewelry store or in the lobby of a factory building, it will still give you an idea of how a diamond is cut and polished.

The main diamond factories and showrooms are **Amsterdam Diamond Center,** Rokin 1, off Dam Square (☎ **020/624-5787;** tram: 4, 9, 14, 16, 20, 24, or 25); **Coster Diamonds,** Paulus Potterstraat 2–6, near the Rijksmuseum (☎ **020/676-2222;** tram: 2, 5, or 20); **Gassan Diamonds,** Nieuwe Uilenburgerstraat 173–175 (☎ **020/622-5333;** tram: 9, 14, or 20); **Stoeltie Diamonds,** Wagenstraat 13–17 (☎ **020/623-7601;** tram: 4, 9, 14, or 20); and **Van Moppes Diamonds,** Albert Cuypstraat 2–6, at the street market (☎ **020/676-1242;** tram: 16, 24, or 25).

THE RED LIGHT DISTRICT (DE WALLEN/ROSSE BUURT)

The warren of streets around Oudezijds Achterburgwal and Oudezijds Voorburgwal by the Oude Kerk is one of Amsterdam's most famous destinations. It's extraordinary to see women of all nationalities dressed in exotic underwear and perched in windows, knitting, brushing their hair, or just slinking, enticingly, in their seats, waiting for customers. The district has become a major tourist attraction, not only for customers of storefront sex but for sightseers. If you choose to go there, you need to exercise caution. Stick to the busy streets, particularly at night, and be wary of pickpockets at all times. *Warning:* In a neighborhood where anything seems permissible, the one no-no is taking pictures. Violate this rule and your camera could be removed from you and broken. To get there, take tram 4, 9, 16, 20, 24, or 25 to Dam Square, and then pass behind the Grand Hotel Krasnapolsky.

ORGANIZED TOURS

A 3-hour bus tour costs 35 to 40Dfl ($16.85 to $19.25) and includes tickets for a canal cruise. Children 4 to 13 are usually charged half-price. Companies offering tours include **The Best of Holland,** Damrak 34 (☎ **020/623-1539**); **Holland International Excursions,** Dam 6 (☎ **020/551-2800**); **Holland Keytours,** Dam Square 19 (☎ **020/624-7304**); and **Lindbergh Excursions,** Damrak 26 (☎ **020/622-2766**).

A clever way of putting all that water to use, and a great time-saver for anyone in a hurry, the **Museum Boat,** Stationsplein 8 (☎ **020/622-2181**), motors between major museums close to the canals and harbor and offers as good a view as a regular canal-boat cruise. Stops are made every 30 minutes at seven key spots, providing access to 16 museums. The fare for the whole day, including a discount on museum admissions, is 25Dfl ($12) for adults, 20Dfl ($10) for children 13 and under. Half-day tours after 1pm cost 15Dfl ($7), no reduction for children; single round-trip tours cost 20Dfl ($10) for adults, 15Dfl ($7) for children 13 and under.

THE SHOPPING SCENE

Regular shopping hours are Monday 11am to 6pm, Tuesday, Wednesday, and Friday 9am to 6pm, Thursday 9am to 9pm, and Saturday 9am to 5pm. Shops in the Magna Plaza mall, some large department stores, and some other stores are open on Sunday noon to 5pm and shops in the Museum quarter are open every first Sunday of the month.

Best buys include special items the Dutch produce to perfection, or produced to perfection in the past and now retail as antiques—Delftware, pewter, crystal, and old-fashioned clocks—or commodities in which they have significantly cornered a market, like diamonds. If cost is an important consideration, remember the Dutch also have inexpensive specialties, such as cheese, flower bulbs, and chocolate.

For jewelry, trendy clothing, or athletic gear, try the department stores around Dam Square and shops on Kalverstraat and Leidsestraat. For fashion, antiques, and art, shop on Van Baerlestraat, P. C. Hooftstraat, and Nieuwe Spiegelstraat. For fashion boutiques and funky little specialty shops, or a good browse through a flea market or secondhand store, Reestraat, Hartenstraat, Wolvenstraat, and Runstraat are particularly good choices. Amsterdam's top department store, with the best selection and a great cafe, is **De Bijenkorf,** Dam 1 (☎ **020/621-8080; tram: 4, 9, 14, 16, 20, 24, or 25).

MARKETS

You'll find all types of foods, clothing, flowers, plants, and textiles at the **Albert Cuyp Markt,** Albert Cuypstraat (tram: 4, 16, 24, or 25), open 6 days a week. Every Friday there's a secondhand book market on the Spui, with about 25 booths.

The ✪ **Floating Flower Market,** a row of barges permanently moored on the Singel at Muntplein (tram: 4, 9, 14, 16, 20, 24, or 25), sells fresh-cut flowers, plants, ready-to-travel packets of tulip bulbs, and home gardening accessories. Buying flowers here is an Amsterdam ritual. The **Sunday Art Market,** at Thorbeckeplein (tram: 4, 9, 14, or 20), runs March to December, with sculptures, paintings, jewelry, and mixed-media pieces by local artists.

You'll find everything and anything at the **Waterlooplein Flea Market,** at Waterlooplein (metro: Waterlooplein; tram: 9, 14, or 20). On Sunday during summer (late May to September), the junk is replaced for a day by antiques and books. ✪ **Kunst & Antiekcentrum de Looier,** Elandsgracht 109 (☎ 020/624-9038; tram: 7, 10, or 20), is a big indoor antiques market that spreads through several old warehouses along the Jordaan canals. Individual dealers rent booths and corners to show their best wares: antique jewelry, prints, and engravings.

SHOPS

✪ **Focke & Meltzer,** P. C. Hooftstraat 65–67 (☎ 020/664-2311; tram: 2, 5, or 20), is the best one-stop shop for authentic Delft Blue and Makkumware porcelain, as well as Hummel figurines, Leerdam crystal, and a world of other fine china, porcelain, silver, glass, and crystal. Unless you simply must have brand-name articles, you can save considerably on hand-painted pottery at **Heinen,** Prinsengracht 440, off Leidsestraat (☎ 020/627-8299; tram: 1, 2, or 5), and even watch the product being made.

The crafts and curios on sale at **Blue Gold Fish,** Rozengracht 17 (☎ 020/623-3134; tram: 13, 14, 17, or 20), cover a wide range of ceramics, jewelry, household items (including colorful lamps), and textiles, running the gamut from chic to kitsch. Call before you head out to the cooperative **ABK Gallery for Sculpture,** Zeilmakersstraat 15 (☎ 020/625-6332; tram: 3), since it's open only by appointment, Thursday to Sunday noon to 6pm. Opened in 1743, **Jacob Hooy & Co.,** Kloveniersburgwal 10–12 (☎ 020/624-3041; metro: Nieuwmarkt), is a wonderland of fragrant smells offering more than 500 different herbs and spices, along with 30 different teas, sold loose by weight. Everything is stored in wooden drawers and barrels with the name hand-scripted in gold. Lining the counter are fishbowl jars with 30 different types of *dropjes* (drops or lozenges).

H. P. de Vreng en Zonen, Nieuwendijk 75 (☎ 020/624-4581; tram: 1, 2, 5, 13, 17, or 20), creates Dutch liqueurs and gins using old-fashioned methods. Try Old

Amsterdam *jenever* or some of the more flamboyantly colored brews, like the brilliant green *Pruimpje prik in.* **P. G. C. Hajenius,** Rokin 92–96 (☎ **020/623-7494;** tram: 4, 9, 16, 20, 24, or 25), has been the city's leading purveyor of cigars and smoking articles since 1826. Cigars are the house specialty, and there's a room full of Havanas. They also sell long, handmade clay pipes of the kind you see in Old Dutch paintings, as well as ceramic pipes.

A big array of best-sellers, paperbacks, hardcover editions, and magazines is available at **American Book Center,** Kalverstraat 185 (☎ **020/625-5537;** tram: 4, 9, 16, 20, 24, or 25). A landmark amid P. C. Hooftstraat's fashionable stores, **A van der Meer,** P. C. Hooftstraat 112 (☎ **020/662-1936;** tram: 2, 5, or 20), is a quiet place to enjoy antique maps, prints, and engravings, including 17th- and 18th-century Dutch world maps.

AMSTERDAM AFTER DARK

Amsterdam has highly regarded orchestras, ballet, and opera companies, a strong jazz tradition, and a thriving club and dance-bar scene. Its brown cafes—typical Amsterdam bars (see "Brown Cafes," below)—are a highlight of any visit. Cabarets and theaters can be counted on for English-language shows on a regular basis.

Your best source of information on nightlife and culture is the VVV tourist office's monthly *What's On in Amsterdam.* Many hotels have copies for guests, or you can pick up one at VVV offices for 4Dfl (1.90). *De Uitkrant,* a free monthly paper in Dutch, has an even more thorough listing of events and is available in performance venues, clubs, and VVV offices.

For tickets to theatrical and musical events (including rock concerts), contact **Amsterdam Uit Buro (AUB) Ticketshop,** Leidseplein 26 (☎ **020/621-1211**), which can book tickets for almost every venue in town. VVV Amsterdam also books tickets, for a 5Dfl ($2.40) fee.

The Performing Arts

MUSIC & BALLET   Classical music in Amsterdam centers on the world-famous **Royal Concertgebouw Orchestra,** based in the superb Concertgebouw, Concertgebouwplein 2–6 (☎ **020/671-8345;** tram: 3, 5, 12, 16, or 20). Throughout the musical season (September to May) and annual Holland Festival (June to July), the world's greatest orchestras, ensembles, conductors, and soloists travel to Amsterdam to perform here. There are free concerts on Wednesdays at 12:30pm. The box office is open daily 10am to 7pm, with tickets at 25Dfl to 200Dfl ($12 to $96). The **Netherlands Philharmonic Orchestra** and **Netherlands Chamber Orchestra** perform at the Beurs van Berlage, Damrak 243 (☎ **020/627-0466;** tram: 4, 9, 14, 16, 20, 24, or 25). The box office is open Tuesday to Friday 12:30 to 6pm and Saturday noon to 5pm, with tickets at 15Dfl to 55Dfl ($7 to $26).

September to March, the **Netherlands Opera** produces classics at the Muziektheater, Waterlooplein 22 (☎ **020/625-5455;** metro: Waterlooplein; tram: 9, 14, or 20). Also performing at the Muziektheater are two dance companies: **The Dutch National Ballet** and The Hague–based **Netherlands Dance Theater,** whose artistic director/choreographer, Jirí Kylián, has enjoyed great success. The box office is open Monday to Saturday 10am to 8pm and Sunday 11:30am to 6pm, with tickets at 30Dfl to 125Dfl ($14 to $60). Dance performances are occasionally held at the **Felix Meritis Theater,** Keizersgracht 324 (☎ **020/626-2321;** tram: 1, 2, or 5); the box office opens an hour before performances and tickets are 7.50Dfl to 125Dfl ($14 to $60).

THEATER   Amsterdammers speak English so well that Broadway road shows and English-language touring companies often make the city a stop on their European itineraries. Broadway and London musicals also come to Amsterdam.

Look for touring shows at **Koninklijke Theater Carré,** Amstel 115–125 (☎ **020/622-5225;** metro: Wesserplein), but get tickets as far in advance as possible—hot shows sell out fast. The **Stadsschouwburg,** Leidseplein 26 (☎ **020/624-2311;** tram: 1, 2, 5, 6, 7, 10, or 20), is the city's main venue for Dutch theater as well as Dutch and, occasionally, English versions of international plays.

COMEDY THEATER   Compared by *Time* to Chicago's famous Second City troupe, ✪ **Boom Chicago Theater,** Leidsepleintheater, Leidseplein 12 (☎ **020/ 530-7300;** tram: 1, 2, 5, 6, 7, 10, or 20), puts on great improvisational comedy, and Dutch audiences have no problem with the English sketches. You can have dinner and a drink while enjoying the show at a candlelit table. It's open daily in summer, closed Sunday in winter. Tickets are 32.50Dfl ($16); the restaurant opens at 7pm, and meals cost 20Dfl to 25Dfl ($10 to $12).

LIVE-MUSIC CLUBS

Most big-name touring rock and pop acts perform at Ajax soccer club's **Amsterdam Arena,** Arena Boulevard, Amsterdam Zuid-Oost (☎ **020/311-1313;** metro: Amsterdam Arena). **De Ijsbreker,** Weesperzijde 23 (☎ **020/693-9093;** tram: 3), offers the latest in electronic music and anything else that goes out on a musical limb. It has a good cafe with a terrace beside the River Amstel, and music usually begins around 8pm. Cover is 15Dfl to 25Dfl ($7 to $12).

Bimhuis, Oudeschans 73–77 (☎ **020/623-1361;** metro: Nieuwmarkt), is relaxed, but serious about jazz. Top musicians, including European and American stars, often perform here. Closed Tuesdays for jazz workshops. Cover Thursday to Sunday is 15Dfl to 25Dfl ($7 to $12). At the small, comfortable **Alto Jazz Café,** Korte Leidsedwarsstraat 115 (☎ **020/626-3249;** tram: 1, 2, 5, 6, 7, 10, or 20), there's a regular crowd and regular and guest combos in this cafe.

GAY & LESBIAN CLUBS

Amsterdam is the gay capital of Europe, proud of its open and tolerant attitude toward homosexuality. There are lots of bars and dance clubs for gay men all over the city, but fewer lesbian nightspots. Generally the trendier spots are on Reguliersdwarsstraat. You'll find a more casual atmosphere on Kerkstraat near Leidseplein and leather bars on Warmoesstraat.

Some of the more popular places for men are **C-Ring,** Warmoesstraat 96 (☎ **020/623-9604;** tram: 4, 9, 14, 16, 20, 24, or 25), a gay music-cafe where the music tends toward raunchy; **Café April,** Reguliersdwarsstraat 37 (☎ **020/ 623-4254;** tram: 1, 2, or 5), and associated **April's Exit,** Reguliersdwarsstraat 42 (☎ **020/625-8788;** tram: 1, 2, or 5), a disco that attracts a young crowd; **iT,** Amstelstraat 24 (☎ **020/625-0111;** tram: 9, 14, or 20), a flashy disco with a mixed gay and straight crowd; and **Argos,** Warmoesstraat 95 (☎ **020/622-6572;** tram: 4, 9, 14, 16, 20, 24, or 25), Europe's oldest leather bar. **Saarein,** Elandstraat 119 (☎ **020/623-4901;** tram: 7, 10, 17, or 20), is a women-only bar, and **Vive la Vie,** Amstelstraat 7 (☎ **020/624-0114;** tram: 4, 9, 14, or 20), is a lively lesbian bar that hosts occasional parties.

DANCE CLUBS

As long as your attire and behavior suit the management's sensibilities, you should have no problem getting past the bouncer in these clubs. Drinks can be expensive—a beer or Coke averages 10Dfl ($4.80), and a whisky or cocktail 15Dfl ($7).

Escape, Rembrandtplein 11 (☎ **020/622-1111;** tram: 4, 9, 14, or 20), is big and popular, with several dance floors and a capacity of 2,000. Cover is 10DFl to 20Dfl ($4.80 to $9.60), free for students on Thursday. **Melkweg,** Lijnbaansgracht 234a (☎ **020/624-1777;** tram: 1, 2, 5, 6, 7, 10, or 20), is a former hippie hangout turned multipurpose venue that includes a dance club. Temporary membership (required) is 5Dfl ($2.40) for a month; cover is 12Dfl to 35Dfl ($6 to $17).

Paradiso, Weteringschans 6–8 (☎ **020/626-4521;** tram: 1, 2, 5, 6, 7, 10, or 20), presents an eclectic variety of music in a former church. Theme nights range from jazz to raves to disco. Cover is 5 to 35Dfl ($2.40 to $17). At ✪ **Odeon,** Singel 460 (☎ **020/624-9711;** tram: 1, 2, or 5), you can dance to jazz, funk, house, techno, R&B, or classic disco amid graceful surroundings in a 17th-century canal house. Cover is 7.50 to 12.50Dfl ($3.60 to $6). Membership policy is strict at **RoXY,** Singel 465–467 (☎ **020/620-0354;** tram: 4, 9, 14, 16, 20, 24, or 25), one of the hippest places in town, and it's usually hard to get in. Some nights, the membership rules are dropped and anyone can enter. Wednesday is gay night for men; Sunday's Pussy Lounge is women-only. Cover is 10 to 20Dfl ($4.80 to $10).

BROWN CAFES

You haven't tasted Dutch beer until you've tasted it in a *bruine kroeg,* or brown cafe (what Americans would call a bar). Even if you're not a beer lover, brown cafes afford you a peek into the city's everyday life. You find them on almost every corner in old neighborhoods. There is no mistaking them: The smoky, mustard brownness inside comes from centuries of thick smoke and heated conversation. Some have been around since Rembrandt's time. The best are on Prinsengracht, below Westermarkt; at Dam Square; Leidseplein; Spui; and, with a bit of looking, on tiny streets between canals.

Said to be where the builders of the Westerkerk were paid, **Café Chris,** Bloemstraat 42 (☎ **020/624-5942;** tram: 13, 14, 17, or 20), opened in 1624 and has some curious old features, including a toilet that flushes from outside the bathroom door. In a medieval alley, wood-paneled **In de Wildeman,** Kolksteeg 3 (☎ **020/638-2348;** tram: 1, 2, 5, 13, 17, or 20), serves more than 200 kinds of beer. The tile floor and rows of bottles and jars behind the counters are remnants from its early days as a distillery's retail shop. **Hoppe,** Spui 18–20 (☎ **020/420-4420;** tram: 1, 2, or 5), dating from 1670, has become a tourist attraction, but locals love it too, often stopping for a drink on their way home. It's usually standing-room only, and the crowds overflow onto the street.

At **De Vergulde Gaper,** Prinsenstraat 30 (☎ **020/624-8975;** tram: 1, 2, 5, 13, 17, or 20), you can retreat into the cozy interior in bad weather, and in good you can sit on a terrace beside the Prinsengracht—in the unlikely event you get a seat. Opened by Pieter Hoppe in 1786 as a liquor distillery/tasting house, ✪ **'t Smalle,** Egelantiersgracht 12 (☎ **020/623-9617;** tram: 13, 14, 17, or 20), is wonderfully cozy, though you probably won't find a seat or even be able to see one. In good weather, a boat moored on the canal alongside serves as a terrace.

OTHER CAFES

The Grand Cafe concept, combining drinks and fine food in elegant surroundings, has won plenty of devotees, tired of cramped and crowded brown cafes. Among the best are **Café Luxembourg,** Spuistraat 24 (☎ **020/620-6264;** tram 1, 2, or 5), a chic rendezvous that takes some of its menu dishes from top eateries around town; and ✪ **Royal Cafe De Kroon,** Rembrandtplein 15 (☎ **020/625-2011;** tram: 4, 9, 14, or 20), a mix of Louis XVI and tropical decor, overlooking the square. Other chic cafes are **Café Dante,** Spuistraat 320 (☎ **020/638-8839;** tram 1, 2, or 5) whose owners' love of modern art shows itself in a different exhibition every month; ✪ **Café Schiller,** Rembrandtplein 26 (☎ **020/624-9846;** tram: 4, 9, 14, or 20), whose bright glassed-in terrace on the square and finely carved art deco interior makes it popular with artists and writers.

Another notable hangout is **Café Schuim,** Spuistraat 189 (☎ **020/638-9357;** tram 1, 2, or 5), attracting an assortment of creative types. On summer evenings trendies head to the terrace of ✪ **Café Vertigo,** Vondelpark 3 (☎ **020/612-3021;** tram: 1, 3, 6, or 12), on the edge of the park, for the liveliest scene in town. Inside, low arched ceilings, subtle lighting, and unobtrusive music set a mood of casual sophistication.

DAY TRIPS FROM AMSTERDAM
HAARLEM

Haarlem is a city of music and art just 20km (12 miles) west of Amsterdam, traditionally considered the capital's little sister city.

GETTING THERE   From Amsterdam, Haarlem is 20 minutes by train from Centraal Station; the trains leave about every half an hour, and the fare is 10.50Dfl ($5) round-trip. It can also be reached by frequent bus from outside Centraal Station, costing 6 strips of a strippenkart (about 4.60Dfl/$2). By car, take N5/A5 west.

VISITOR INFORMATION   VVV **Haarlem** is at Stationsplein 1 (☎ **0900/ 616-1600;** fax 023/534-0537), outside the train station.

EXPLORING HAARLEM   Haarlem is where Frans Hals, Jacob van Ruysdael, and Pieter Saenredam lived and painted portraits, landscapes, and church interiors while Rembrandt was living and working in Amsterdam. Handel and Mozart made special visits to the city to play the magnificent organ of **St. Bavokerk** (St. Bavo's Church), also known as the Grote Kerk (Great Church), Oude Groenmarkt 23 (☎ **023/ 532-4399**). Look for Frans Hals's tombstone, and for a cannonball imbedded in the wall during the 1572–73 Spanish siege. Don't miss the 1738 Christian Müller Organ, which has 5,068 pipes and is nearly 30m (98 feet) tall; you can hear it at free concerts on Tuesdays and Thursdays, April to October. The church is open Monday to Saturday 10am to 4pm. Admission is 2.50Dfl ($1.20) for adults, 1.50Dfl (70¢) for children under 14.

From St. Bavo's, it's a short walk to Holland's oldest and perhaps most unusual museum, the **Teylers Museum,** Spaarne 16 (☎ **023/531-9010**). It houses drawings by Michelangelo, Raphael, and Rembrandt; fossils, minerals, and skeletons; and an odd assortment of inventions, including the world's biggest electrostatic generator, dating from 1784, and a 19th-century radarscope. The museum is open Tuesday to Saturday 10am to 5pm and Sunday 1 to 5pm. Admission is 8Dfl ($3.85) for adults, 4Dfl ($1.90) for students, seniors, and children 5 to 15, free for children under 5.

Be sure to visit the ✪ **Frans Halsmuseum,** Groot Heiligland 62 (☎ **023/ 516-4200**), whose galleries are halls and chambers of a former seniors' home. Famous paintings by Haarlem School masters hang in settings that look like the 17th-century homes they were originally intended to adorn. Open Monday to Saturday 11am to 5pm, Sunday 1 to 5pm. Admission is 8Dfl ($3.85) for adults, 4Dfl ($1.90) for children 10 to 17, free for children under 10.

An ideal way to view the city is by hourly **canal boat cruise,** operated by Woltheus Cruises from their River Spaarne jetty at Gravensteenbrug (☎ **023/535-7723**). Cruises are April to October at 10:30am, noon, 1:30, 3, and 4:30pm.

ZANDVOORT

If you feel like a breath of sea air, do what Amsterdammers do: Head for Zandvoort on the North Sea coast.

GETTING THERE   Trains leave Amsterdam Centraal Station every hour; transfer at Haarlem. During summer, extra trains go direct from Centraal Station. Journey time is 30 minutes, and the fare is 13.50Dfl ($7) round-trip. Buses leave every 30 minutes from outside Centraal Station. You can go by car via Haarlem on the N5 west, but during summer, there are frequent traffic jams.

VISITOR INFORMATION   VVV **Zandvoort** is at Schoolplein 1 (☎ **023/ 571-7947;** fax 023/571-7003), opposite the bus station.

EXPLORING ZANDVOORT   There's not much more than a beach, but what a beach. Seemingly endless sands are lined in summertime with beach cafes and discos, and the conditions are good for sailboarding. Down from the mainstream beaches are gay and nudist beaches.

   Holland Casino Zandvoort, Badhuisplein 7 (☎ **023/571-8044**), is one of 10 legal casinos in Holland, with roulette, blackjack and more. Dress code is "correct" (collar and tie for men), the minimum age is 18, and you'll need your passport. It's open daily 1:30pm to 2am. Admission is 6Dfl ($2.90).

   You can find tranquillity in the **Kennemer Duinen** and **Amsterdamse Waterleiding Duinen,** protected zones of sand dune and vegetation that play an important role in sea defense. Stroll along paths through woods on the eastern side and across dunes leading west toward the sea. There's beachy shopping and plenty of eating and drinking possibilities in town.

DELFT

Delft is the home of the famous blue-and-white porcelain, but don't let Delftware be your only reason to visit. The small, handsome city is quiet and intimate, with flowers in its flower boxes and linden trees bending over gracious canals. The cradle of the Dutch Republic, Delft is still the burial place of the royal family, and the birthplace and inspiration of artist Jan Vermeer, the 17th-century master of light and subtle emotion.

GETTING THERE   There are trains at least hourly from Amsterdam; the 1-hour trip costs 32Dfl ($15) round-trip. By car, Delft is off the A13, the main The Hague–Rotterdam expressway.

VISITOR INFORMATION   VVV **Delft** is at Markt 83–85 (☎ **015/212-6100;** fax 015/215-8695).

EXPLORING DELFT   Vermeer's house is long gone from Delft, as are his paintings. But you can visit the **Oude Kerk,** Roland Holstlaan 753 (☎ **015/212-3015**), where he's buried, open April to October, Monday to Saturday 10am to 5pm. You can also visit the ✪ **Nieuwe Kerk,** Markt (☎ **015/212-3025**), where Prince William of Orange (Willem van Oranje) and the other members of the House of Oranje-Nassau are buried. Open April to October, Monday to Saturday 9am to 6pm, November to March Monday to Saturday 11am to 4pm.

   The **Prinsenhof Museum,** Sint-Agathaplein 1 (☎ **015/260-2358**), on Oude Delft canal, is where William I of Orange (William the Silent) lived and had his headquarters when he helped found the Dutch Republic. He was assassinated here in 1584, and you can see the musket-ball holes in the stairwell. The Prinsenhof is now a museum of paintings, tapestries, silverware, and pottery. It's open Tuesday to Saturday 10am to 5pm and Sunday 1 to 5pm (also Monday 1 to 5pm June to August). Admission is 5Dfl ($2.40).

A fine collection of Delft tiles graces the wood-paneled setting of the 19th-century mansion that's now the **Lambert van Meerten Museum,** Oude Delft 199 (☎ 015/260-2358). It's open Tuesday to Saturday 10am to 5pm, Sunday 1 to 5pm (closed Sunday November to March). Admission is 3.50Dfl ($1.70).

To view brand-new **Delftware,** and see how it's hand painted, visit the factory showroom of ✪ **De Porceleyne Fles,** Rotterdamseweg 196 (☎ 015/256-0234). It's open April to October, Monday to Saturday 9am to 5pm and Sun 9:30am to 4pm; November to March, Monday to Saturday 9am to 5pm. Admission is free.

THE FLOWER CENTERS

Flowers at **Keukenhof Gardens,** Lisse (☎ 025/465-555), have a short but glorious season. You'll never forget a visit to this meandering 28ha (70-acre) wooded park in the heart of the bulb-producing region, planted each fall by major Dutch growers. Each spring the bulbs burst forth and produce almost eight million tulips, narcissi, daffodils, hyacinths, bluebells, crocuses, lilies, amaryllis, and more. A blaze of color is everywhere in the park and greenhouses, beside brooks and shady ponds, along paths and in neighboring fields, in neat little plots and helter-skelter on lawns. By its own report, it's the greatest flower show on earth.

The park is open late March to late May only, daily 8am to 7:30pm. There are special train-bus connections via Haarlem and the nearby town of Leiden. Admission is 17Dfl ($8) for adults and, 8.50Dfl ($4.10) for children 4 to 12.

Flowers are a billion-guilder-per-year business at **Aalsmeer Flower Auction** (☎ 0297/393-939), held in lakeside Aalsmeer near Schiphol Airport. Every year, three billion flowers and 400 million plants from 8,000 nurseries are auctioned off. Get there early to see the biggest array of flowers and to have as much time as possible to watch the computerized auctioning. As flower lots go by on carts, the first bid to stop the auction "clock" as it works down from 100 to 1 wins the posies. The auction is held Monday to Friday 7:30 to 11am. Bus 172 takes you there from Amsterdam's Centraal Station. Admission is 5Dfl ($2.40) for adults, free for children 12 and under.

VOLENDAM & MARKEN

One of these neighboring villages on the IJsselmeer lake is on the mainland, the other on a former island; one is Catholic, the other Protestant; in one, women wear white caps with wings, and in the other, caps with ribbons—but they are often combined on bus-tour itineraries.

GETTING THERE   There are separate, hourly buses to Volendam and Marken from outside Amsterdam's Centraal Station. The fare is 7.85Dfl ($3.75) round-trip; the trip is 35 minutes to Volendam and 45 minutes to Marken.

VISITOR INFORMATION   VVV Volendam is at Zeestraat 37 (☎ 0299/363-747; fax 0299/368-484). Marken has no VVV office.

EXPLORING VOLENDAM & MARKEN   Volendam is geared for tourism, with souvenir shops, boutiques, and restaurants. Its boat-filled harbor, tiny streets, and traditional houses have an undeniable charm. If you want a snapshot of yourself surrounded by fishermen wearing little caps and balloon-legged pants, Volendammers will gladly pose. They understand that the traditional costume is worth preserving, as is the economy of a small town that lost most of its fishing industry when the Zuiderzee enclosure dam cut it off from the North Sea. You can see such attractions as the fish auction, diamond cutter, clog maker, and the house with a room entirely wallpapered in cigar bands.

✪ **Marken** was an island until a causeway connected it with the mainland, and it remains as insular as ever. Quieter than Volendam, with a village of green-painted houses on stilts around a tiny harbor, it is also more rural. Clusters of farmhouses dot the polders (the reclaimed land from the sea that makes up two-thirds of Holland), and a candy-striped lighthouse stands on the IJsselmeer shore. Marken does not gush over tourists, but it will feed and water them, and let them wander around its pretty streets. Villagers wear traditional costume, as much to preserve the custom as to appease the tourists who pour in daily. The **Marken Historisch Museum,** Kerkbuurt 44 (☎ **0299/601-904**), is a typical house open as a museum from Good Friday to the end of October, Monday to Saturday 10am to 5pm and Sunday noon to 4pm. Admission is 4Dfl ($1.90) for adults and 2Dfl (95¢) for children. A clog maker works in the parking lot during the summer.

13 Norway

by Darwin Porter & Danforth Prince

Norway is a land of tradition, as exemplified by its rustic stave churches—look for these mysterious dark structures with steep gables surmounted by dragon heads and pointed steeples—and folk dances stepped to the airs of a fiddler. But Norway is also modern, a technologically advanced nation that's rich in petroleum and hydroelectric energy. One of the world's last great natural frontiers, Norway is a land of astonishing beauty; its steep and jagged fjords, salmon-teeming rivers, glaciers, mountains, and meadows invite exploration. In winter, the shimmering Northern Lights beckon; in summer, the midnight sun shines late and warm.

1 Oslo

Today Oslo is one of the 10 largest capitals in the world in sheer area, if not in urban buildup. After World War II, Oslo grew to 450 square kilometers (175 square miles). The city is one of the most heavily forested on earth, and fewer than half a million Norwegians live and work here.

One of the oldest Scandinavian capital cities, founded in the mid–11th century, Oslo has never been a mainstream tourist site. But the city is culturally rich with many diversions—enough to fill at least 3 or 4 busy days. It's also the center for many easy excursions along the Oslofjord or to towns and villages in its environs, both north and south.

In recent years Oslo has grown from what even the Scandinavians viewed as a Nordic backwater to one of Europe's happening cities. Restaurants, nightclubs, cafes, shopping complexes, and other venues keep on opening. A kind of Nordic joie de vivre permeates the city; the only drawback is that all this fun is going to cost you—Oslo ranks as one of Europe's most expensive cities.

ESSENTIALS

GETTING THERE   By Plane   Most arrivals are at **Oslo Airport** (☎ **64-81-00-00**), 45km (28 miles) from the city center. This airport serves SAS and other inter-European airlines, including British Airways and Icelandair.

SAS operates a **bus service** from both terminals to the Sentralstasjon train station and other points in Oslo every 10 minutes. The fare for the 40-minute trip is 65NOK ($8). An express train, running every 20 minutes, goes to Sentralstasjon and costs 120NOK ($15).

A cab ride into the city from the airport will cost from 120 to 150NOK ($15 to $19) for up to four passengers.

By Train   Trains from the Continent and from Sweden or Copenhagen pull into **Oslo Sentralstasjon (Central Station),** Jernbanetorget 1 at the beginning of Karl Johans Gate (☎ **81-50-08-88** for information), in the city center. It's open daily 7am to 11pm. From there, you can catch trains heading for Bergen and all other rail links in Norway. From the station, you can also take trams to all major parts of Oslo.

By Car   If you're driving from mainland Europe, the fastest way to reach Oslo is to take the car-ferry from Frederikshavn, Denmark (see below). You can also take a car-ferry from Copenhagen (see below) or drive from Copenhagen by crossing over to Helsingborg, Sweden, from Helsingør, Denmark. Once at Helsingborg, take E-6 north all the way to Stockholm. If you're driving from Stockholm to Oslo, follow E-18 west all the way (trip time: 7 hours). Once you near the outskirts of Oslo from any direction, follow the signs into the SENTRUM, or city center.

By Ferry   Ferries from Europe arrive at Oslo port, a 15-minute walk or a short taxi ride from the city center. From Denmark, car-ferries depart for Oslo from Copenhagen (trip time: 12 hours), Hirtshals (trip time: 9 hours), and Frederikshavn (trip time: $8^1/_2$ hours). Trips start at 400NOK ($51.20) per person round trip. From Strømstad, Sweden, there's a daily crossing in summer to Sandefjord, Norway (trip time: $2^1/_2$ hours); from Sandefjord, it's an easy drive or train ride north to Oslo. Call ☎ **22-41-90-90** or 22-33-50-00 for schedules and information. Reservations are required.

VISITOR INFORMATION   Assistance and information for visitors are available at the **Tourist Information Office,** Vestbaneplassen 1, N-0250 Oslo (☎ **22-83-00-50;** bus 27). Free maps, brochures, sightseeing tickets, and guide services are available. The office is open in June, daily 9am to 6pm; July and August, daily 9am to 7pm; May and September, Monday to Saturday 9am to 4pm; January to April and October to December, Monday to Friday 9am to 4pm.

There's also an Oslo-only **information office** at the Oslo Sentralstasjon (Central Station), Jernbanetorget 1, at the beginning of Karl Johans Gate (no phone), open daily 8am to 11pm.

CITY LAYOUT   Oslo is at the mouth of the 95km (60-mile) Oslofjord. Opening onto the harbor is **Rådhusplassen** (City Hall Square), dominated by the modern City Hall, a major attraction. Guided bus tours leave from this square, and the launches that cruise the fjords depart from the pier facing the municipal building. (You can catch ferries to the Bygdøy Peninsula from the quay at Rådhusplassen.)

Out on a promontory to the east is the **Akershus Castle.** At **Bygdøy,** the much larger peninsula that juts out to the west, are four of Oslo's major attractions: the Viking ships, the Polar Ship *Fram* Museum, the *Kon-Tiki* Museum, and the Folk Museum.

Karl Johans Gate, Oslo's main street (especially for shopping and strolling) is north of City Hall Square. This boulevard begins at Oslo **Sentralstasjon** (Central Station) and stretches all the way to the 19th-century **Royal Palace** at the western end. A short walk from the palace is the famed **Student's Grove** (the University of Oslo is nearby), where everybody gathers on a summer day to socialize. Dominating this area is the **National Theater.** South of the theater and near the harbor is **Stortingsgaten,** another shopping street.

Oslo

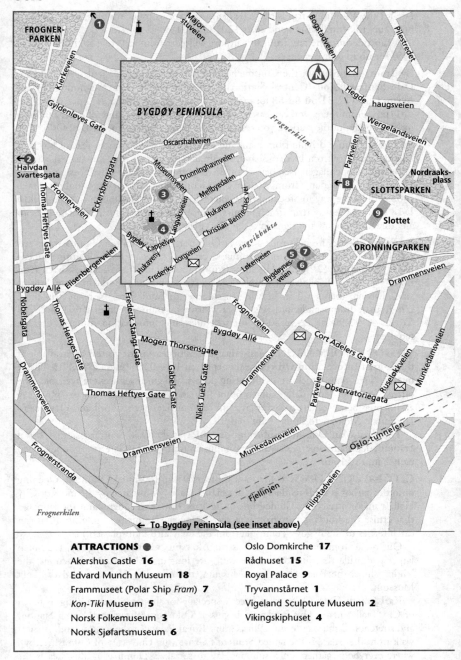

ATTRACTIONS ●

Akershus Castle **16**
Edvard Munch Museum **18**
Frammuseet (Polar Ship *Fram*) **7**
Kon-Tiki Museum **5**
Norsk Folkemuseum **3**
Norsk Sjøfartsmuseum **6**

Oslo Domkirche **17**
Rådhuset **15**
Royal Palace **9**
Tryvannstårnet **1**
Vigeland Sculpture Museum **2**
Vikingskiphuset **4**

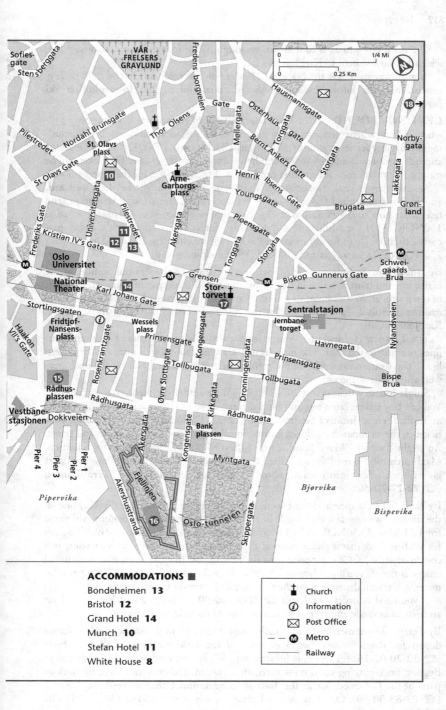

ACCOMMODATIONS ■

Bondeheimen **13**

Bristol **12**

Grand Hotel **14**

Munch **10**

Stefan Hotel **11**

White House **8**

Legend:
- † Church
- (i) Information
- ✉ Post Office
- — Ⓜ Metro
- —— Railway

The main city square is **Stortorvet,** although it's no longer the center of city life, which has now shifted to Karl Johans Gate.

At a subway stop near the National Theater you can catch an electric train to **Tryvannstårnet,** the loftiest lookout in Scandinavia, and to the **Holmenkollen Ski Jump.**

GETTING AROUND   A 24-hour **Tourist Ticket (Turistkort)** lets you travel anywhere in Oslo whenever you wish, by bus, tram, subway, local railway, or boat, including the Bygdøy ferries in summer. The Tourist Ticket costs 20NOK ($2.55) for adults and half price for children 4 to 15; children 3 and under travel free. The ticket will be stamped when it's used for the first time and will then be good for the next 24 hours.

An even better deal, especially for short-term visitors, might be the **OsloCard,** which allows unlimited travel by public transportation, free parking validation, and free admission to all museums and major tourist attractions. A 1-day pass costs 150NOK ($19) for adults and 50NOK ($6) for children up to 15; a 2-day pass costs 220NOK ($28) for adults and 60NOK ($8) for children; and a 3-day pass costs 250NOK ($32) for adults and 70NOK ($9) for children.

By Bus, Tram & Subway   Jernbanetorget, in front of the Central Station, is the major bus and tram terminal in Oslo. Most buses and trams passing through the heart of town stop at Wessels Plass, next to the Parliament (Stortinget), or at Stortorvet, the main marketplace. Many also stop at the National Theater or University Square on Karl Johans Gate.

The **T-banen (subway)** has four main lines running to the east of Oslo and four lines running to the west. The most heavily traveled routes by tourists are the eastern lines. The western lines take in Holmenkollen and residential and recreational areas west and north of the city.

Single-journey tickets cost 20NOK ($2.55) for adults; children travel for half fare. You can buy tickets from bus and tram drivers, or you can purchase them in advance at Trafikanten in front of Sentralstasjon (☎ 22-17-70-30). You must cancel your ticket in the automated machines located in subway stations and on buses and trams. An eight-coupon "Maxi" card costs 115NOK ($15), half price for children. Maxi cards can be used for unlimited transfers within 1 hour of the time the ticket is stamped. For information about timetables and fares, call **Trafikanten** (☎ 22-17-70-30).

By Taxi   The cheapest and most spontaneous way to get a taxi involves hailing one on the street or waiting at a taxi stand. In either case, the initial meter reading will range from 24.50 to 29.50NOK ($3.15 to $3.80), depending on the time of day. If you call for a cab and ask that it pick you up at a specific address, the initial meter reading will cost from 46NOK ($6), depending on the time of day. In either case, after your initial charge is noted, you'll pay between 7.75NOK ($1) and 11.20NOK ($1.45) per kilometer you travel, depending on the time day and however far you travel.

If you need to order a taxi, call ☎ **22-38-80-90,** 24 hours a day. Reserve at least an hour in advance and be prepared to be placed on hold indefinitely.

By Ferry   In warmer months, usually from mid-April until late September, ferries depart for Bygdøy from Pier 3 in front of the Oslo Rådhuset. Call **Båtservice** (☎ 22-20-07-15) for schedule information. We recommend using a ferry or bus to Bygdøy since parking conditions there are crowded. Other ferries leave for various parts of the Oslofjord; ask at the **Tourist Information Office** at Vestbaneplassen 1 (☎ 22-83-00-50). One-way fare to Bygdøy or any destination in Oslo is 25NOK ($3.20).

By Bicycle   Den Rustne Eike, Vestbaneplassen 2 (☎ **22-83-52-08;** T-banen: Stortinget), rents bikes at moderate rates, complete with free maps of interesting routes in Oslo and its environs. The cost is 140 to 190NOK ($18 to $24) for 24 hours, or 600 to 900NOK ($77 to $115) per week, with a 1,500NOK ($192) deposit or valid picture ID required. Helmets are included at no charge and a child's seat is available for 200NOK ($26) per day or 700NOK ($90) per week. It's open May to October, daily from 9am to 6pm; off-season, Monday to Friday 2am to 6pm.

Fast Facts: Oslo

American Express   American Express Reisebyrå, Karl Johans Gate (☎ **22-98-37-00**), is open Monday to Friday 9am to 6pm and Saturday 10am to 3pm.

Business Hours   Most **banks** are open Monday to Friday 8:15am to 3:30pm (Thursday to 5pm). The Fellesbanken's Exchange at the Oslo Central Railway Station (tel. 22-41-26-11) is open Monday to Friday 8am to 11pm, Saturday 8am to 7pm, and Sunday 8am to noon. There's a bank at Fornebu Airport, open daily 7am to 10:30pm, and another at Gardermoen Airport. Most **businesses** are open Monday to Friday 9am to 4pm. **Stores** are generally open Monday to Friday 9am to 5pm (many stay open late on Thursday to 6 or 7pm) and Saturday 9am to 1 or 2pm. Sunday closings are observed.

Currency   You'll pay your way in Norway in Norwegian **kroner** (**KR**). There're 100 øre in 1 krone. Notes are issued in denominations of 5, 10, and 20 kroner. The exchange rate used in this chapter was $1 = 7.79 Norwegian kroner, or 1 Norwegian krone = 15 U.S. cents. The ratio for the British pound to the krone fluctuates constantly. At press time, £1 = approximately 12.88NOK (or 1NOK = 0.07p). The Euro rate was currently fixed at 8.29NOK (or 1 KR = €0.12).

Dentists   In an emergency, contact the **Tøyen Senter,** Kolstadgate 18 (☎ **22-67-78-00;** T-banen: Groønen), open daily 11am to 2pm and 7 to 10pm. For private dentists, look under *Tannleger* ("tooth doctors") in volume 1B of the telephone directory; there's rarely a language barrier.

Doctors   Oslo's most prominent emergency clinic is the 24-hour **Oslo Municipal Casualty Clinic (Legavakten)** at Storgata 40 (☎ **22-11-70-70** or 22-00-81-60; T-banen: Groønland). For more routine medical assistance, contact Oslo's biggest hospital, **Ullavel,** Kirkeveien 166 (☎ **22-11-80-80;** T-banen: Brattikollen). To consult a private doctor (nearly all of whom speak English), check the telephone directory or ask at your hotel for a recommendation.

Drugstores   A 24-hour pharmacy is **Jernbanetorvets Apotek,** Jernbanetorget 4A (☎ **22-41-24-82;** T-banen: Jernbanetorget).

Embassies & Consulates   The Embassy of the **United States** is at Drammensveien 18, N-0255 Oslo 2 (☎ **22-44-85-50;** T-banen: Nationaltheatret); **United Kingdom,** at Thomas Heftyes Gate 8, N-0264 Oslo 2 (☎ **23-13-27-00;** T-banen: Nationaltheatret); **Canada,** at Oscarsgate 20, N-0244 Oslo 3 (☎ **22-99-53-00;** T-banen: Nationaltheatret); and **South Africa**, Drammensveien 88C, N-0255 (☎ **23-27-32-20;** T-banen: Nationaltheatret). Visitors from Ireland and New Zealand should contact the British Embassy. Australians should contact the Canadian Embassy.

Emergencies   Dial the Oslo **police** at ☎ **112;** report a **fire** at ☎ **110;** call an **ambulance** at ☎ **113.**

Internet Access   If you want to check your email, try the **Underworld-Internet Café & Bar,** Akersgata 39, Oslo (☎ **22-33-38-98;** T-banen: Stortinget).

Post Office   The **Oslo General Post Office** is at Dronningensgate 15 (☎ **22-40-78-10;** T-banen: Jernbanetorget), though the entrance is at the corner of Prinsensgate. It's open Monday to Friday 8am to 6pm, Saturday 9am to 3pm; it's closed Sunday and public holidays.

Telephone   The country code for Norway is **47,** and the city code for Oslo is **22.** For operator assistance in English, dial ☎ **115.**

International calls can be made from **Telenor's Telecommunications Office,** Kongensgate 21 (☎ **22-40-55-09;** T-banen: Stortinget), open Monday to Friday 9am to 8pm, Saturday 10am to 5pm, and Sunday noon to 6pm. The entrance is on Prinsensgate. Toll-free international access codes are: **AT&T** (☎ **800/19011), MCI** (☎ **800/19912),** or **Sprint** (☎ **800/19877).**

WHERE TO STAY
EXPENSIVE
Bristol. Kristian IV's Gate 7, N-0164 Oslo 1. ☎ **22-82-60-00.** Fax 22-82-60-01. www.bristol.no. E-mail: booking@bristol.no. 141 units. A/C MINIBAR TV TEL. 1,795NOK ($230) double; 3,500NOK ($448) suite. Children 14 and under stay free in parents' room. Rates include breakfast. AE, DC, MC, V. Parking 130NOK ($17). T-banen: Stortinget.

In the heart of the city, on a side street north of Karl Johans Gate, this 1920s hotel is warm, inviting, and luxurious. The Moorish-inspired lobby, with its Winter Garden and Library Bar, sets the elegant tone. Rooms range from medium to spacious and are especially comfortable, with excellent, firm mattresses. Although the plumbing in some of the bathrooms is a bit antiquated, you'll find hair dryers. Some units are no smoking. The Bristol's meal options range from sandwiches and lighter fare to the more formal intimacy of the Bristol Grill.

✪ **Grand Hotel.** Karl Johans Gate 31, N-0159 Oslo 1. ☎ **800/223-5652** in the U.S., or 22-42-93-90. Fax 47-23-21-00. E-mail: reservation@grand-hotel.no. 287 units. MINIBAR TV TEL. 2,840NOK ($364) double; 4,350NOK ($557) suite. Rates include buffet breakfast. AE, DC, MC, V. Parking 120NOK ($15). T-banen: Stortinget.

Norway's leading hotel, on the wide boulevard that leads to the Royal Palace, is a completely renovated 1874 building. Rooms range from medium to large and have excellent beds with firm mattresses. Bathrooms have a hair dryer and big fluffy towels. Some rooms are air-conditioned. The hotel has several restaurants, serving both international and Scandinavian food. The Palmen and the Grand Café offer live entertainment, as does the nightclub, Bonanza. Facilities include an indoor swimming pool, sauna, and solarium.

MODERATE
Bondeheimen. Rosenkrantzgate 8 (entrance on Kristian IV's Gate), N-0159 Oslo 1. ☎ **800/528-1234** in the U.S., or 22-42-95-30. Fax 22-41-94-37. www.bestwestern.com. 81 units. MINIBAR TV TEL. 1,045–1,060NOK ($134–$136) double Mon–Thurs; 850–875NOK ($109–$112) double Fri–Sun. Rates include breakfast. AE, DC, MC, V. Parking 125NOK ($16). Tram: 7 or 11.

In the city center, Bondeheimen has been associated with the Best Western hotel chain for the past decade. Rooms are medium-size and comfortable, with excellent beds with fine, frequently renewed mattresses. Many bathrooms are small with minimum shelf space. There's an inexpensive cafeteria serving homemade Norwegian dishes. Unfortunately for guests, this makes the place popular with bus tours, so be warned. The hotel does not have a license to serve alcohol.

Stefan Hotel. Rosenkrantzgate 1, N-0159 Oslo 1. ☎ **22-42-92-50.** Fax 23-31-55-55. E-mail: stefan@os.telia.no. 138 units. A/C MINIBAR TV TEL. 1,015NOK ($130) double Mon–Thurs; 775NOK ($99) double Fri–Sun. Rates include breakfast. AE, DC, MC, V. Parking 110NOK ($14). Tram: 11, 17, or 18.

This clean, comfortable hotel boasts an excellent location in the city center. Built in 1952, it has been modernized and much improved. Rooms are well furnished and maintained. Two have facilities for travelers with disabilities, and all but eight are air-conditioned. The Restaurant Stefan is recommended (see "Where to Dine," below). There's also a cozy hotel bar.

INEXPENSIVE

Munch. Munchsgaten 5, N-0130 Oslo 1. ☎ **22-42-42-75.** Fax 22-20-64-69. 212 units. MINIBAR TV TEL. 870NOK ($111) double Mon–Thurs; 690NOK ($88) double Fri–Sun. Rates include breakfast. AE, DC, MC, V. Parking 100NOK ($13). T-banen: Stortinget. Tram: 7 or 11. Bus: 37.

Built in 1983, this solid, nine-floor hotel offers good-value accommodations (by Oslo standards), each floor reached by elevator. Although not overly large, rooms are cozy and well heated, with firm and frequently renewed mattresses and reproductions of Edvard Munch's paintings. Bathrooms tend to be tiny, with showers or shower/tub combinations.

White House. President Harbitz Gate 18, N-0259 Oslo 2. ☎ **22-44-19-60.** Fax 22-55-04-30. 21 units. MINIBAR TV TEL. 995NOK ($127) double Mon–Thurs; 795NOK ($102) double Fri–Sun. Rates include breakfast. AE, DC, MC, V. Free parking. Tram: 1.

The White House lies in the forested residential district of Breskeby, a short walk from the rear of the Royal Palace. Set on a steeply sloping lot, and greatly modernized since its original construction around 1900 as a private home, it attracts a loyal clientele that appreciates the hotel's small scale and sense of intimacy. Rooms have a cozy Norwegian charm, almost like something encountered in the countryside. They range from small to medium, but have good beds and firm mattresses, and snug but adequate bathrooms (mostly with shower units). The in-house restaurant, Den Lelle Sondue, has an outdoor wooden deck looking down over the street in front.

WHERE TO DINE

Norwegians are as fond of smørbrød (smorgasbord) as the Danes, (you'll see it offered everywhere for lunch), except they spell it differently. Basically, this means bread and butter, but it is really an open-faced sandwich that can be stacked with virtually anything, including ham with a slice of peach resting on top or perhaps a mound of dill-flavored shrimp.

EXPENSIVE

D'Artagnan. Øvre Slottsgate 16. ☎ **22-41-50-62.** Reservations required. Main courses 250–300NOK ($32–$38); 5-course fixed-price menu 625NOK ($80). AE, DC, MC, V. Mon–Fri (also Sat Oct–Christmas) 6–11pm. Closed July–Aug 5 and Dec 22–Jan 3. Bus: 27, 29, 30, 41, or 61. FRENCH.

D'Artagnan is one of Oslo's most elegant and upscale restaurants. Amid flickering candles and bouquets of flowers, you'll enjoy menu items that change with the seasons but might include a salad of king crab from Finnmark with avocado and grapefruit segments, yogurt-marinated reindeer with a boysenberry sauce, wild duck served with roasted mixed nuts and a port wine sauce, and one of the most unusual dishes of all: wild lamb from the mountains of central Norway, served with an herb-flavored mustard sauce. Always featured in various salads and main dishes is salmon, smoked on the premises using various types of wood and tea leaves.

✪ Statholdergaarden. Rådhusgate 11. ☎ **22-41-88-00.** Reservations recommended. Main courses 525–695NOK ($67–$89); fixed-price 6-course menu 635NOK ($81). Mon–Sat 6–10pm. Tram 11, 15, 18. NOUVELLE NORWEGIAN/FRENCH.

One of the most richly historic restaurant settings in Oslo is directed by one of the capital's most feted and successful chefs, Bent Stiansen. The setting, beneath stucco-covered and frescoed ceilings, was built in 1640 as the governor's headquarters. Menu items change frequently, according to the season. Examples include grilled crayfish served with a scallop and salmon tartare, and thyme-infused codfish with a crabmeat mousse and two sauces. (One is a simple white wine sauce; the other is based on a rare vanilla bean imported from Thailand.) One of the most appealing and all-time favorite dishes we've enjoyed was a lightly fried Arctic char with sautéed Savoy cabbage, deep-fried black roots, and a lime beurre blanc. Don't confuse this upscale and prestigious site with the less expensive bistro, Statholderstueakroen, that occupies the building's vaulted cellar.

MODERATE

Grand Café. In the Grand Hotel, Karl Johans Gate 31. ☎ **22-42-93-90.** Reservations recommended. Main courses 195–260NOK ($25–$33). AE, DC, MC, V. Mon–Sat 11am–11pm, Sun noon–11pm. T-banen: Stortinget. INTERNATIONAL.

This is the grand old cafe of Oslo, steeped in legend and tradition—in fact, atmosphere and tradition are more compelling than the cuisine. A large mural depicts among many others, Ibsen, who once enjoyed whale steaks here, and Edvard Munch. The menu relies on the best of Norwegian country traditions (after all, how many places still serve elk stew?). Choices range from a napoleon with coffee to a full meal; you'll find fried stingray, standard veal and beef dishes, and reindeer steaks. Sandwiches for 65 to 70NOK ($8 to $9) are also available. This is tasty, unpretentious cooking that will win you over if you like solid, honest, and earthy flavors, but more importantly, this is the place to be seen.

✪ Restaurant Stefan. In the Stefan Hotel, Rosenkrantzgate 1. ☎ **22-42-92-50.** Reservations recommended. Main courses 175–225NOK ($22–$29); lunch smörgåsbord 185NOK ($24). Mon–Fri 11:30am–2:30pm and 4:30–9:45pm, Sat noon–2:30pm and 5–9:45pm. Smörgåsbord daily at lunch and Thurs–Fri at dinner. Tram: 7 or 11. NORWEGIAN.

This bustling, unpretentious restaurant is better known than the hotel that houses it. It's especially popular at lunchtime, when the locals come for the city's best smörgåsbord, a buffet laden with traditional Norwegian foods. Samplings usually include cucumber salad, fish and meat salads, sausages, meatballs, potato salad, smoked fish, assorted Norwegian cheeses, and breads. Selections from the à la carte menu include "Stefan's special platter," an old-fashioned but flavorful dish that incorporates slices of reindeer, moose meat, and ox tongue, with lingonberries and potatoes.

INEXPENSIVE

Brasserie 45. Karl Johans Gate 45. ☎ **22-41-34-00.** Reservations recommended. Main courses 89–179NOK ($11–$23). AE, DC, MC, V. Mon–Thurs noon–midnight; Fri–Sat noon–1am; Sun 2–11pm. T-Bana: Centrum. CONTINENTAL.

Airy, artful, and stylish, this bistro lies one floor above street level and overlooks the biggest fountain along the showplace promenade of downtown Oslo. You'll be attended by uniformed staff bearing steaming platters of dishes that include especially flavorful versions of fried catfish with lemon-garlic sauce; fried chicken in a spicy tomato-based sweet-and-sour sauce; pork schnitzels with béarnaise sauce and shrimp; and a tartare of salmon with dill-enriched boiled potatoes. Dessert might include a chocolate terrine with cloudberry-flavored sorbet. The cuisine is ambitious, but lives up to its promise.

Det Gamla Rådhus (Old Town Hall). Nedre Slottsgate 1. ☎ **22-42-01-07.** Reservations recommended. Main courses 185–240NOK ($24–$31). AE, DC, MC, V. Mon–Sat 4pm– midnight. (Kroen Bar Mon–Sat 4pm–midnight.) Bus: 27, 29, 30, 41, or 61. NORWEGIAN.

The oldest restaurant in Oslo, Gamla Rådhus is located in what in 1641 was Oslo's Town Hall. At noon you can sit in the spacious dining room and choose from an array of open-face sandwiches (smørbrød). À la carte dinner selections include fresh fish, game, and Norwegian specialties. Ingredients are fresh, and the service accommodating.

Engebret Café. Bankplassen 1. ☎ **22-33-66-94.** Reservations recommended. Main courses 198–289NOK ($25–$37); smørbrød 55–65NOK ($7–$8). AE, DC, MC, V. Mon–Fri 11am–11pm, Sat noon–11pm. Bus: 27, 29, or 30. NORWEGIAN.

An enduring Oslovian favorite since 1857, this restaurant is housed in two 400-year-old joined landmark buildings directly north of Akershus Castle. It has an old-fashioned atmosphere and good food. During lunch, a tempting selection of open-face sandwiches is available. The menu grows more elaborate in the evening when you might begin with a terrine of game with blackberry/port-wine sauce or fish soup. You can then order such traditional dishes as trout in sour cream with boiled potatoes and pickled cucumber, red wild boar with whortleberry sauce, or smoked or roast reindeer fillets served in a port wine cream sauce with seasonal vegetables.

SEEING THE SIGHTS
IN THE BYGDØY PENINSULA

✪ **Vikingskiphuset (Viking Ship Museum).** Huk Aveny 35, Bygdøy. ☎ **22-43-83-79.** Admission 30NOK ($3.85) adults, 10NOK ($1.30) children. May–Aug daily 9am–6pm; Sept daily 11am–5pm; Apr daily 11am–4pm; Nov–Mar daily 11am–3pm. Oct daily 11am–4pm. Ferry: Pier 3 facing the Rådhuset (summer only). Bus: 30 from the National Theater to polar ship *Fram* and *Kon-Tiki* Museum (see below).

Displayed here are three Viking burial vessels that were excavated on the shores of the Oslofjord and preserved in clay. The most spectacular find is the 9th-century *Oseberg*, discovered near Norway's oldest town. This 20m (64-foot) dragon ship features a wealth of ornaments and is the burial chamber of a Viking queen and her slave. The *Gokstad* find is an outstanding example of Viking vessels because it's so well preserved. The smaller *Tune* ship was never restored. Look for the *Oseberg* animal-head post, the elegantly carved sleigh used by Viking royalty, and the *Oseberg* four-wheeled cart.

Frammuseet (Polar Ship *Fram*). Bygdøynesveien. ☎ **22-43-83-70.** Admission 25NOK ($3.20) adults, 10NOK ($1.30) students and children. May 1–15 daily 10am–4:45pm; May 16–Aug daily 9am–5:45pm; Sept daily 10am–4:45pm; Mar–Apr Mon–Fri 11am–3:45pm, Sat–Sun 11am–3:45pm; Oct–Nov Mon–Fri 10am–3:45pm, Sat–Sun 11am–3:45pm; Dec–Feb Sat–Sun 11am–4:45pm. Ferry: Pier 3 facing the Rådhuset (summer only). Bus: 30 from the National Theater.

A long walk from the Viking ships, the Frammuseet contains the sturdy polar exploration ship *Fram*, which Fridtjof Nansen sailed across the Arctic (1893–96). The vessel was later used by Norwegian explorer Roald Amundsen, the first man to reach the South Pole (1911).

Kon-Tiki **Museum.** Bygdøynesveien 36. ☎ **23-08-67-67.** Admission 30NOK ($3.85) adults, 10NOK ($1.30) children, 20NOK ($2.55) students, and 70NOK ($9) family tickets (up to 4). Apr–May and Sept daily 10:30am–5pm; June–Aug daily 9:30am–5:45pm; Oct–Mar daily 10:30am–4pm. Ferry: Pier 3 facing the Rådhuset (summer only). Bus: 30 from the National Theater.

Kon-Tiki is the world-famed balsa-log raft that the young Norwegian scientist Thor Heyerdahl and his five comrades sailed in for 7,000km (4,300 miles) in 1947—all the way from Callao, Peru, to Raroia, Polynesia. Besides the raft, there're other exhibits from Heyerdahl's subsequent visit to Easter Island, including an Easter Island family cave, with a collection of sacred lava figurines.

Norsk Sjøfartsmuseum (Norwegian Maritime Museum). Bygdøynesveien 37. ☎ **22-43-82-40.** Admission (museum and boat hall) 30NOK ($3.85) adults, 15NOK ($1.90) children. May–Sept daily 10am–7pm; Oct–Apr Mon, Wed, Fri–Sat, 10:30am–4pm, Tues and Thurs 10:30am–7pm. Ferry: Pier 3 facing the Rådhuset (summer only). Bus: 30 from the National Theater.

This museum, which contains complete a ship's deck with helm and chart house, and a three-deck-high section of the passenger steamer *Sandnaes*, chronicles the maritime history and culture of Norway. The Boat Hall features a fine collection of original small craft. The fully restored polar vessel *Gjoa*, used by Roald Amundsen in his search for America's Northwest Passage, is also on display. The three-masted schooner *Svanen* (Swan) is moored at the museum.

Norsk Folkemuseum (Norwegian Folk Museum). Museumsveien 10. ☎ **22-12-37-00.** Admission 50NOK ($6) adults, 10NOK ($1.30) children 7–16. Jan 1–May 14 and Sept 15–Dec 31, Fri–Sat 11am–3pm, Sun 11am–4pm; May 15–June 14 and Sept 1–Sept 14, daily 10am–5pm; June 15–Aug 31, 10am–6pm. Ferry: Pier 3 facing the Rådhuset (summer only). Bus: 30 from the National Theater.

From all over Norway, 140 original buildings have been transported and reassembled on 14ha (35 acres) on the Bygdøy Peninsula. This open-air folk museum includes a number of medieval buildings, such as the Raulandstua, one of the oldest wooden dwellings still standing in Norway, and a stave church from about 1200. The rural buildings are grouped together by region of origin, while the urban houses have been laid out in the form of an old town.

IN WESTERN OLSO

✪ **Vigeland Sculpture Museum.** Frogner Park, Nobelsgata 32. ☎ **22-54-25-30.** Museum, 30NOK ($3.85) adults, 15NOK ($1.90) students and children. Park, daily 24 hours. Museum, May–Sept, Tues–Sat 10am–6pm, Sun noon–7pm; Oct–Apr, Tues–Sat noon–4pm, Sun noon–6pm. Parking free; Tram: 12 or 15. Bus: 20.

The lifetime work of Gustav Vigeland, Norway's greatest sculptor, is displayed inside the museum as well as throughout the nearby 30ha (75-acre) Frogner Park in western Oslo. Nearly 211 sculptures in granite, bronze, and iron can be admired. See in particular his four granite columns, symbolizing the fight between humanity and evil (a dragon, the embodiment of evil, embraces a woman). The angry boy is the most photographed statue in the park, but the really celebrated work is the 16m (52-foot) monolith, composed of 121 figures of colossal size—all carved into one piece of stone.

IN EASTERN OSLO

✪ **Edvard Munch Museum.** Tøyengate 53. ☎ **23-24-14-00.** Admission 50NOK ($6) adults, 20NOK ($2.55) students and children under 15. June–mid-Sept daily 10am–6pm; mid-Sept–May Tues–Wed and Fri–Sat 10am–4pm, Thurs and Sun 10am–6pm. T-banen: Tøyen. Bus: 20.

Devoted exclusively to the works of Edvard Munch (1863–1944), Scandinavia's leading painter, this exhibit (Munch's gift to the city), traces his work from early realism to his latter-day expressionism. The collection comprises 1,100 paintings, some 4,500 drawings, around 18,000 prints, numerous graphic plates, six sculptures, and important documentary material.

IN THE CITY CENTER

Akershus Castle. Festnings-Plassen. ☎ **22-41-25-21.** Admission 20NOK ($2.55) adults, 10NOK ($1.30) students and children. May–Sept 15, Mon–Sat 10am–4pm, Sun 12:30–4pm; Apr 15–30 and Sept 16–Oct, Sun 12:30–4pm. Closed Nov–Apr 14. Tram: 1, 2, or 10.

One of the oldest historical monuments in Oslo, Akershus Castle was built in 1300 by King Haakon V Magnusson. It was a fortress and a royal residence for several centuries. A fire in 1527 devastated the northern wing, and the castle was rebuilt and transformed into a Renaissance palace under the Danish-Norwegian king Christian IV. Now it's used for state occasions. A few rooms, including the chapel, are open to the public. In the rectangular court, markings show where the massive medieval keep used to stand. You can wander through two large halls (Olav's and Christian IV's), which occupy the top floor of the north and south wings, respectively. For many, the most interesting part is the dungeon, which includes an "escape-proof room" built for a prisoner, Ole Pedersewn Hoyland. After he was placed in the chamber and realized there was no way he could ever escape, he killed himself.

ATTRACTIONS NEARBY

Tryvannstårnet (Lookout Tower). Voksenkollen. ☎ **22-14-67-11.** Admission 35NOK ($4.50) adults, 20NOK ($2.55) children. May and Sept daily 10am–5pm; June daily 9am–7pm; July daily 9am–10pm; Aug daily 9am–8pm; Oct–Apr Mon–Fri 10am–4pm. T-banen: Holmenkollen SST Line 1 from near the National Theater to Voksenkollen, a 30-minute ride; then a 15-minute walk uphill.

This is the loftiest lookout tower in Scandinavia—the gallery is approximately 580m (1,900 feet) above sea level and offers a view of the Oslofjord with Sweden to the east. A walk down the hill takes you to the famous restaurant Frognerseteren. You can take another 20-minute walk down the hill to the Holmenkollen ski jump, the site of the 1952 Olympic competitions as well as the Holmenkollen Ski Festival, when skiers compete in downhill, slalom, giant slalom, cross-country ski races, and jumping.

Henie-Onstad Kunstsenter (Henie-Onstad Art Center). Høvikodden, Baerum. ☎ **67-80-48-80.** Admission 60NOK ($8) adults, 30NOK ($3.85) ages 25 and under. June–Aug Mon 11am–5pm, Tues–Fri 9am–9pm, Sat–Sun 11am–7pm; Sept–May Tues 9am–9pm, Sat–Mon 11am–6pm. Bus: 151, 152, 251, or 261 for Høvikodden.

On a site beside the Oslofjord 11km (7 miles) west of Oslo, ex-movie star and skating champion Sonja Henie and her husband, Niels Onstad, a shipping tycoon, opened a museum to display their art collection. This especially good 20th-century collection includes some 1,800 works by Munch, Picasso, Matisse, Léger, Bonnard, and Miró. Henie's Trophy Room is impressive, with 600 trophies and medals, including three Olympic gold medals—she was the star at the 1936 competition—and 10 world skating championships.

ORGANIZED TOURS

H. M. Kristiansens Automobilbyrå, Hegdehaugsveien 4 (☎ **22-20-82-06;** bus: 27—departure point for tours), known as H.M.K. tours, has been showing visitors around Oslo for more than a century. All year the agency offers a 3- to 4-hour Oslo sightseeing tour, leaving daily at 10am and 1:30pm. It costs 225NOK ($29) for adults

Exploring the Fjords from Oslo

The scenery around Bergen is more spectacular, but if the Oslo area is your only chance to see Norwegian fjord country, then go for it. The eastern side is sunny and preferable for touring. Along the way you'll pass old Viking ruins, once fortified towns, woodlands, and endless blue waters. Quaint cottages pose on rolling hills that suddenly plunge downward to the deeply blue, narrow depths that dramatically snake their way inland.

Oslofjord links the capital with the open sea. It is studded with islets and sheltered waters. Regrettably, industry has blighted some the shoreline, but there's much that is still pristine, beautiful, and unspoiled, a perfect combination of mountain scenery and fjord waters.

Departing from Pier 3 in front of the Oslo Rådhuset (City Hall), **Båtservice Sightseeing,** Rådhusbrygge 3, Rådhusplassen (☎ **22-20-07-15;** bus 27), offers a 50-minute minicruise boat tour, with a view of the harbor and the city, including the ancient fortress of Akershus and the islands in the inner part of the Oslofjord. Cruises depart mid-May to late August, on the hour daily 11am to 8pm (limited sailing at the season's beginning and end). Adults pay 70NOK ($9); children, 35NOK ($4.50).

An evening fjord cruise, including a maritime buffet at the Norwegian restaurant Lanternen, leaves late June through August, daily at 3:30 and 5:45pm. The 3^1/$_2$-hour cruise costs 325NOK ($42) for adults and 120NOK ($15) for children.

If you have more time, take the 2-hour fjord cruise through the maze of islands and narrow sounds in the Oslofjord. Departures are May to September, daily at 10:30am and 1, 3:30, and 5:45pm; the cost is 140NOK ($18) for adults, 70NOK ($9) for children. Refreshments are available on board. There are variants of this cruise, such as the fjord cruise with lunch, also 2 hours, leaving May to mid-September, daily at 10:30am, and costing 240NOK ($31) for adults, 120NOK ($15) for children. After the cruise, the boat anchors so the passengers can go ashore for lunch at Lanternen Restaurant.

and 115NOK ($15) for children—not including lunch. The tour passes through the city center and makes stops at the Vigeland Sculpture Park, the Holmenkollen ski jump, the Viking Ship Museum, the *Kon-Tiki* Museum, and the Vikingland theme park. A shorter two-hour tour departs daily at 10am and 5:30pm, costing 150NOK ($19) for adults and 80NOK ($10) for children. Tours leave from the Norway information center, Vestbaneplassen 1; you should arrive 15 minutes before departure. Authorized guides speak English.

THE SHOPPING SCENE

Near the marketplace and the cathedral (Oslo Domkirche), **Den Norske Husflids-forening,** Møllergata 4 (☎ **22-42-10-75;** T-banen: Stortinget; bus 17)—or Husfliden, as it's called—is the display and retail center for the Norwegian Association of Home Arts and Crafts, founded in 1891. Today it's almost eight times larger than any of its competitors, with two floors displaying the very finest of Norwegian design in ceramics, glassware, furniture, and woodworking. You can also purchase souvenirs, gifts, textiles, rugs, knotted Rya rugs, embroidery, wrought iron, and fabrics by the yard. Goods are shipped all over the world.

Norway's largest department store, **Steen & Strøm,** Kongensgate 23 (☎ **22-00-40-00;** T-banen: Stortinget), is a treasure house with hundreds of Nordic items spread through 58 individual departments. Look for hand-knit sweaters and caps, hand-painted wooden dishes reflecting traditional Norwegian art, and pewter dinner plates made from old molds. **Heimen Husflid,** Rosenkrantzgate 8 (☎ **22-41-40-50;** T-banen: Nationaltheatret), about a block from Karl Johans Gate, carries folk costumes, antiques, and reproductions. Hand-knit sweaters in traditional Norwegian patterns are a special item, as are pewter and brass items.

William Schmidt, Karl Johans Gate 41 (☎ **22-42-02-88;** T-banen: Stortinget), established in 1853, is a leading purveyor of unique souvenirs, including pewter items (everything from Viking ships to beer goblets), Norwegian dolls in national costumes, wood carvings (the troll collection is the most outstanding in Oslo), and sealskin moccasins. The shop specializes in hand-knit cardigans, pullovers, gloves, and caps; sweaters are made from mothproofed 100% Norwegian wool.

OSLO AFTER DARK

To find out what's happening when you're visiting, pick up *What's On in Oslo,* which details concerts and theaters and other useful information.

Theater, ballet, and opera tickets are sold at various box offices and also at **Billettsentralen,** Karl Johans Gate 35 (☎ **22-41-31-80;** T-banen: Stortinget)—although this service costs quite a bit more than your typical box office. Tickets to sports and cultural events can now be purchased easily and more cheaply via computer linkup at any post office in the city, so when you buy a stamp you can also buy a voucher for a ticket to the ballet, theater, or hockey game.

THE PERFORMING ARTS

Home to the National Theater Company, the **National Theater,** Johans Eidvolls Plass 1 (☎ **22-00-14-00;** T-banen: Nationaltheatret), stages dramatic performances 6 nights a week (Monday to Saturday) every month except June to August. Ticket prices range from 135 to 200NOK ($17 to $26).

Two blocks from the National Theater, **Oslo Konserthus,** Munkedamsveien 14 (☎ **23-11-31-00;** T-banen: Nationaltheatret), is the home of the widely acclaimed Oslo Philharmonic. Performances are given on Thursday and Friday evenings except in June and July, and ticket prices range from 240 to 270NOK ($31 to $35). Big-name jazz and pop acts show up regularly; ticket prices depend on the act.

The 1931 building, originally a movie theater, at Storgaten 23, was adapted for better acoustics and dedicated in 1959 to the **Den Norske Opera (Norwegian National Opera)** (☎ **22-42-94-75;** T-banen: Jernbanetorget). It's also the venue for the National Ballet. Productions of both companies are staged between September and mid-June. Between the two companies, there're generally three performances a week, with the only set performance night being Saturday. Tickets range from 240 to 410NOK ($31 to $53).

The **Norwegian Folk Museum,** on Bygdøy (ferry: Pier 3 near the Rådhuset), often presents folk-dance performances by its own ensemble on summer Sunday afternoons at the museum's open-air theater. Admission is free, as the performance is included in the museum's entrance price.

THE CLUB & MUSIC SCENE

Smuget, Rosenkrantzgate 22 (☎ **22-42-52-62;** T-banen: Nationaltheatret), is the most talked-about nightlife joint in the city, and has the long lines (especially on weekends) to prove it. It's in a 19th-century building in back of the City Hall and has a restaurant, an active dance floor, and a stage where live bands from throughout Europe and the world perform. It's open Monday to Saturday 8pm to 3am; the cover is 60NOK ($8) on weekdays and 80NOK ($10) on Saturday.

With a capacity of 1,200 patrons, the **Rockefeller Music Hall,** Torggata 16 (☎ **22-20-32-32;** T-banen: Stortinget), a combination concert hall and nightclub, is one of the largest establishments of its kind in Oslo. There're live concerts every night, everything from reggae to rock to jazz. Cover runs 60 to 300NOK ($8 to $38). It's usually open Sunday to Thursday 8pm to 2:30am and Friday to Saturday 9pm to 3:30am. Show time is about an hour after the doors open.

A labyrinth of hallways, dance areas, and bars, **Dixie,** Universitetsgata 26 (☎ **22-41-36-33;** T-banen: Nationaltheatret), is one of Oslo's busiest clubs. Inside, you'll find the **New Orleans Restaurant** (☎ **22-42-44-20**), and the high-energy **Barock Disco** (☎ **22-42-44-20**). Barock is open as a bar on Wednesday night and as a disco every Thursday to Saturday 9pm to 3:30am. Entrance on disco nights is 60NOK ($8).

Set immediately behind the Bristol Hotel, **Club Castro,** Kristians IV Gate 7 (☎ **22-41-51-08;** T-banen: Stortinget), is the largest, most visible, and most popular gay bar and disco in Norway. It's open Tuesday to Sunday 9pm to 3:30am.

DAY TRIPS FROM OSLO

The best 1-day excursion from Oslo includes visits to Fredrikstad and Tønsberg, which gives you a chance to explore the scenic highlights of the Oslofjord. A trip to Fredrikstad, in Østfold on the east bank of the Oslofjord, can easily be combined in 1 day with a visit to the port of Tønsberg on the west bank, by crossing over on the ferry from Moss to Horten, then heading south.

Getting There   To reach the first stop, Fredrikstad, take E-6 south from Oslo toward Moss. Continue past Moss until you reach the junction of Route 110, which is sign-posted south of Fredrikstad. About six buses per day depart for the town from the Central Station in Oslo. Trains from Oslo's Central Station depart from Fredrikstad about every 2 hours during the day (trip time:30 minutes).

FREDRIKSTAD   In recent years Fredrikstad, 95km (60 miles) south of Oslo, has become a major tourist center, thanks to its Old Town and 17th-century fortress. Across the river on the west is a modern industrial section, and although a bridge links the two sections, the best way to reach Old Town is by ferry, which costs 5NOK (65¢). The departure point is about 4 blocks from the Fredrikstad railroad station—simply follow the crowd out the main door of the station, make an obvious left turn, and continue down to the shore of the river. It's also possible to travel between the two areas by bus 360 or 362, although most pedestrians opt for the ferry.

Visitor Information   The **Fredrikstad Turistkontor** is on Turistsenteret, Østre Brohode in Gamle Fredrikstad (☎ **69-32-03-30**). June to September, it's open Monday to Friday 8am to 7pm and Saturday10am to 7pm; October to May, hours are Monday to Friday 8am to 4pm.

Fredrikstad was founded in 1567 as a marketplace at the mouth of the River Glomma. **Gamlebyen** (Old Town) became a fortress in 1663 and continued in that role until 1903, boasting some 200 guns in its heyday. It still serves as a military camp. The main guardroom and old convict prison are now the **Fredrikstad Museum,** Gamleslaveri (☎ **69-32-09-01**), open May through September, Monday to Friday 11am to 5pm, Saturday and Sunday noon to 5pm. Admission is 30NOK ($3.85) for adults and 10NOK ($1.30) for children.

Outside the gates of Old Town is **Kongsten Fort,** on what was first called Gallows Hill, an execution site. When Fredrikstad Fortress was built, it was provisionally fortified in 1677, becoming known as Svenskeskremme (Swede Scarer). Present-day Kongsten Fort with its 20 cannons, underground chambers, passages, and countermines, eventually replaced it.

Since Fredrikstad's heyday as a trading port and merchant base, Old Town has attracted craftspeople and artisans, many of whom create their products in the Old Town's historic houses and barns. Many of these glassblowers, ceramic artists, and silversmiths choose not to display or sell their products at their studios, preferring instead to leave the sales aspect to local shops.

En Route to Tønsberg   You can drive back north from Fredrikstad to the town of Moss, where you can take a ferry to Horten. Once at Horten, signs will point the way south for the short drive to Tønsberg. Tønsberg is about 1¹/₂ hours from Oslo, with some 20 trains arriving daily.

TØNSBERG   Bordering the western bank of the Oslofjord, Tønsberg, 100km (64 miles) south of Oslo, is Norway's oldest town. It's divided into a historic area, filled with old clapboard-sided houses, and the commercial center, where the marketplace is located.

Visitor Information   In Tønsberg, **Tourist Information** is at Nedre Langgate 36B, N-3100 Tønsberg (tel. **33-31-02-20**). June and August, it's open Monday to Saturday 10am to 5pm; July hours are daily 10am to 8pm; and September to May, it's open Monday to Friday 10am to 3:30pm.

Tønsberg was founded a year before King Harald Fairhair united parts of the country in 872, and this Viking town became a royal coronation site. Svend Foyn, who invented modern whaling and seal hunting, was born here.

Slottsfjellet, a huge hill fortress directly ahead of the train station, is touted as "the Acropolis of Norway." But it has only some meager ruins, and people mostly come here for the view from the lookout tower. Built in 1888, the **Slottsfjelltårnet** (☎ **33-31-18-72**) is open May 18 to June 23, Monday to Friday 10am to 3pm; June 24 to August 18, daily 11am to 6pm; August 19 to September 15, Saturday and Sunday noon to 5pm; and September 16 to 29, Saturday and Sunday noon to 3pm. Admission is 10NOK ($1.30) for adults and 5NOK (65¢) for children.

Nordbyen is the old and scenic part of town, with well-preserved houses. **Haugar** cemetery, at Møllebakken, is right in the town center, with the Viking graves of King Harald's sons, Olav and Sigrød.

Sem Church, Hageveien 32 (☎ **33-36-93-99**), the oldest in Vestfold, was built of stone in the Romanesque style around 1100. It's open Tuesday to Friday 9am to 2pm; ask at the vestry. Admission is free.

You should also see **Fjerdingen,** a street of charming restored houses. Tønsberg was also a Hanseatic town during the Middle Ages, and some houses have been redone in typical Hanseatic style.

In the **Vestfold Folk Museum,** Frammannsveien 30 (☎ **33-31-29-19**), there're many Viking and whaling treasures. One of the biggest (literally) thrills is the skeleton of a blue whale. There's also a real Viking ship displayed, the *Klastad* from Tjolling, built about A.D. 800. Admission is 30NOK ($3.85) for adults, 20NOK ($2.55) for seniors and students, and 10NOK ($1.30) for children. It's open mid-May to mid-September, Monday to Saturday 10am to 5pm, Sunday and holidays noon to 5pm; mid-September to mid-May, Monday to Friday 10am to 2pm.

2 Bergen & the Fjords

In western Norway the landscape takes on an awesome beauty, with iridescent glaciers, deep fjords that slash into rugged, snowcapped mountains, roaring waterfalls, and secluded valleys that lie at the end of corkscrew-twisting roads. From Bergen the most beautiful fjords to visit are the **Hardanger** (best at blossom time, May and early June), to the south; the **Sogne,** Norway's longest fjord, immediately to the north; and the **Nordfjord,** north of that. A popular excursion on the Nordfjord takes visitors from Loen to Olden along rivers and lakes to the Brixdal Glacier.

If you have time, on the Hardangerfjord you can stop over at one of the fjord resorts, such as Ulvik or Lofthus. From many vantage points it's possible to see the Folgefonn Glacier, Norway's second-largest ice field, which spans more than 250 square kilometers (100 square miles).

Bergen, with its many sightseeing attractions, good hotels and restaurants, and its excellent boat, rail, and coach connections, is the best center for touring the fjord district. This ancient city looms large in Viking sagas. Until the 14th century, it was the seat of the medieval kingdom of Norway. The Hanseatic merchants established a major trading post here, holding sway until the 18th century.

BERGEN: GATEWAY TO THE FJORDS
ESSENTIALS
GETTING THERE   By Plane   The **Bergen Airport** at Flesland, 19km (12 miles) south of the city, offers frequent flights to such larger cities as Copenhagen and London, through which most international flights are routed. In addition, dozens of **SAS** (☎ **67-59-60-50**) and **Braathens SAFE** (☎ **55-99-82-50**) direct flights leave here for nearly every medium-sized city in Norway.

Frequent airport bus service circles from the airport to the SAS Royal Hotel, Braathens SAFE's office at the Hotel Norge, and the city bus station. Buses depart every 20 minutes Monday to Friday and every 30 minutes Saturday and Sunday. The one-way fare is 45NOK ($6).

By Train   Day and night trains arrive from Oslo (trip time: 6 to 8¹/₂ hours). For information, call the Bergen train station at ☎ **55-96-69-00.**

By Bus   Express buses travel to Bergen from Oslo in 11 hours. For long-distance bus information, call ☎ **55-32-14-80.**

By Car   A toll is charged on all vehicles driven into the city center Monday to Friday 6am to 10pm. A single ticket costs 5NOK (65¢); a book of 20 tickets, 90NOK ($12).

To cross from Oslo to Bergen is a mountain drive filled with dramatic scenery. Since the country is split by mountains, there's no direct road. You can take the southern route, E76, going through mountain passes until the junction with Route 47; then head north to the ferry crossing at Kinsarvik that goes across the fjords to E16 leading west to Bergen. The northern route is via Highway 7, going through the resort of Geilo, to the junction with Route 47; then head south to Kinsarvik. After crossing on the ferry, you arrive at E16 and head west to reach Bergen.

VISITOR INFORMATION   Tourist Information, Bryggen 7 (☎ **55-32-14-80**), is open June to August, daily 8:30am to 10pm; May and September daily 9am to 8pm; October to April, Monday to Saturday 9am to 4pm. They'll help you find accommodations, exchange foreign currency, and cash traveler's checks when banks are closed. You can also purchase tickets for city sightseeing or for tours of the fjords.

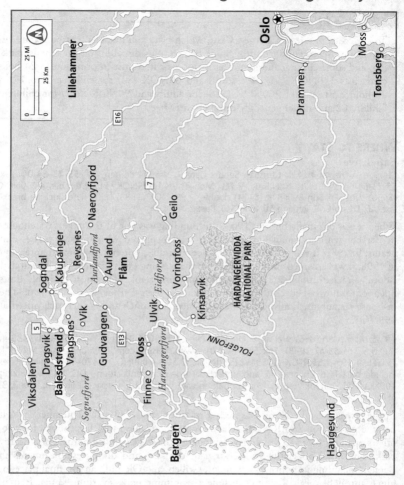

SPECIAL EVENTS The annual **Bergen Festival,** held for 12 days in late May, features performances by regional, national, and international orchestras, dance ensembles, and theater groups. The complete festival schedule is usually available by February of each year. For festival and ticket information, contact the **Bergen Festival office** (☎ **55-21-61-50**).

GETTING AROUND   By Bus   The **Central Bus Station** (Bystasjonen), Strømgaten 8 (☎ **55-55-90-70**), is the terminal for all buses serving the Bergen and the Hardanger area, as well as the airport bus. Gaia Traffic runs a network of yellow-sided **city buses** (☎ **55-59-55-00**) that serve the city center.

By Taxi   Taxis are readily available at the airport, or call ☎ **55-99-70-00.** A ride to the center costs 200 to 240NOK ($26 to $31). Sightseeing by taxi costs about 300 to 360NOK ($38 to $46) per hour.

To cut costs, purchase a **Bergen Card,** which gives you free bus transport and usually free museum entrance throughout Bergen, plus discounts on car rentals, parking, and some cultural and leisure activities. Ask at Tourist Information. A 24-hour card costs 130NOK ($17) for adults and 60NOK ($8) for children 3 to 15. A 48-hour card sells for 200NOK ($26) for adults and 90NOK ($12) for children. Children 2 and under generally travel or enter free.

WHERE TO STAY

Expensive

Clarion Admiral Hotel. Christian Sundts Gate 9, N-5004 Bergen. ☎ **55-23-64-00.** Fax 55-23-64-64. 210 units. MINIBAR TV TEL. Mon–Thurs 1,495NOK ($191) double, 4,200NOK ($538) suite; Fri–Sun 890NOK ($114) double, 2,995NOK ($383) suite. Rates include breakfast. AE, DC, MC, V. Parking 50NOK ($6). Bus: 2, 4, or 11.

When it was originally built in 1906, this building was one of the largest warehouses in Bergen, with six sprawling floors that were peppered with massive trusses and beams. In 1987, it was transformed into a comfortable, tastefully appointed hotel, and in 1998, it was enlarged and renovated into the bustling establishment you'll see today. Rooms and bathrooms are a bit small, but comfortable. The most desirable units open onto flower-bedecked balconies with the best harbor views in town. The in-house restaurant, Emily, offers set-price menus at lunch and dinner each priced at 198NOK ($25).

✪ **Radisson-SAS Hotel Norge.** Ole Bulls Plass 4, N-5001 Bergen. ☎ **800/333-3333** in the U.S., or 55-57-30-00. Fax 55-57-30-01. www.radisson.com. 350 units. A/C MINIBAR TV TEL. 1,195–1,895NOK ($153–$243) double; 2,500–4,000NOK ($320–$512) suite. Rates include breakfast. Children 17 and under stay free in parents' room. DC, MC, V. Parking 100NOK ($13). Book your parking spot along with your room, as space is limited. Bus: 2, 3, or 4.

In the city center, the Norge has been a tradition since 1885. In September 1996 it became part of the SAS Radisson chain. Some rooms have tubs big enough for two, others open onto private balconies overlooking the flower-ringed borders of a nearby park. The hotel offers the widest array of drinking and dining establishments in Bergen, including its gourmet restaurant, Grillen, and Ole Bull, an informal place for lunch and light meals. Facilities include a swimming pool, solarium, sauna, Jacuzzi, gym, and garage.

Moderate

Hotell Hordaheimen. C. Sundtsgate 18, N-5004 Bergen. ☎ **55-23-23-20.** Fax 55-23-49-50. 64 units. TV TEL MINIBAR. Mon–Thurs 1,250NOK ($160) double, Fri–Sun 1,170NOK ($150) double; 1,350NOK ($173) junior suite. Rates include breakfast. AE, DC, MC, V. Free parking (limited spaces). Bus: 1, 5, or 9.

Operated by Bondeungdomslaget i Bergen, sponsors of cultural and folklore programs, the hotel has long been a base for many young people from nearby districts, yet it still considers itself primarily a business hotel. However, school and civic groups traveling together sometimes fill nearly all the rooms. The hotel was built at the turn of the century, but renovated in the 1990s. Rooms are simple and immaculate. The restaurant serves traditional Norwegian dishes.

Rosenkrantz. Rosenkrantzgate 7, N-5003 Bergen. ☎ **55-31-50-00.** Fax 55-31-14-76. 129 units. MINIBAR TV TEL. 1,190NOK ($152) double Sun–Thurs, 750NOK ($96) double Fri–Sat,

2,000NOK ($256) suite daily. Rates include breakfast. AE, DC, MC, V. Parking 70NOK ($9). Bus: 1, 5, or 9.

This simple, unpretentious choice stands near Bryggen in the city center. The lobby, with white marble floors, leads to a comfortable dining room and bar. Rooms are pleasantly furnished. The hotel was recently renovated. Facilities include a TV lounge, a piano bar, and a restaurant serving traditional dishes. Located beside the hotel is a covered parking garage.

Inexpensive
Fagerheim Pensjonat. Kalvedalsveien 49A, N-5018 Bergen. ☎ **90-16-47-80.** Fax 55-90-22-77. 5 units (two with bathroom). 400NOK ($51) double. MC, V. Free parking. Bus: 2, 4, 7, or 11 from the post office.

Small apartments are offered on the grounds of this old-fashioned hillside house. One- and two-bedroom apartments are available for a 3-night minimum stay. Rooms are complete with all modern facilities. Wooden floors, light-colored walls, and marble bathrooms all add to the comfortable atmosphere. Most units have a view of the water and city.

Romantik Hotel Park. Harald Hårfagresgaten 35 and Parkveien 22, N-5000 Bergen. ☎ **55-54-44-60.** Fax 55-54-44-44. 35 units. TV TEL. 850NOK ($109) double. Rates include breakfast. AE, MC, V. Free parking. Bus: 11.

This converted 1890 townhouse is in an attractive university area near Grieghall and Nygård Park. Rooms are traditionally furnished, often with antiques, and vary in size; all have good beds and adequate bathrooms. In summer, a neighboring building accommodates overflow guests. A delicious Norwegian breakfast is served in the dining room; later in the day, sandwiches, small hot dishes, wine, and beer are available there. In the summer, reserve well in advance. The Romantik is a 10-minute walk from the train and bus stations.

WHERE TO DINE
Bryggeloftet/Stuen. Bryggen 11. ☎ **55-31-06-30.** Main courses 140–249NOK ($18–$32); lunch smørbrød 55–199NOK ($7–$25). AE, DC, MC, V. Mon–Sat 11am–11:30pm, Sun 1–11:30pm. Bus: 1, 5, or 9. NORWEGIAN.

This is the best-established restaurant along the harborfront. At street level the Stuen has low ceiling beams, carved banquettes, and 19th-century murals of old Bergen, along with dozens of clipper-ship models. For a more formal meal, head upstairs to the Bryggeloftet, with its high ceilings and wood paneling. A dinner in either section might include fried porbeagle (a form of whitefish) served with shrimp, mussels, and a white-wine sauce; roast reindeer with cream sauce; or pepper steak with a salad. Several different preparations of salmon and herring are featured, along with roast pork with Norwegian sour cabbage. This is a quintessential Norwegian type of place; come here if you're seeking authentic flavors, the type sea captains might have enjoyed a long time ago when they sailed into Bergen harbor.

✪ Finnegaardstuene. Rosenkrantzgate 6. ☎ **55-55-03-00.** Reservations recommended. Main courses 240–320NOK ($31–$41). Set-price 7-course menu 865NOK ($111). AE, DC, MC, V. Mon–Sat 6–11pm. Closed 1 week at Easter and Dec 22–Jan 8. Bus: 5, 21. NORWEGIAN/FRENCH.

At this restaurant, you'll find a richly timbered, partially paneled environment where four small-scale dining rooms create a cozy atmosphere of welcome intimacy. Cuisine revolves around Norwegian ingredients, especially very fresh fish, and classical French methods of preparation. Menus change with the season and the inspiration of the chef, but are likely to include platters of crayfish served with fillets of French foie gras in a cider and foie gras sauce; a gratin of monkfish with sea scallops; fillets of venison with juniper-berry sauce; and breast of duck with lime and fig sauce. We really like the way the chefs have created some culinary magic in sleepy Bergen. The menu is well thought out with carefully prepared dishes.

❂ **To Kokker.** Enhjørninggården. ☎ **55-32-28-16.** Reservations required. Set-price 3-course menu 430–490NOK ($55–$63); 5-course menu 615–630NOK ($79–$81); 7-course menu 695NOK ($89). AE, DC, MC, V. Mon–Sat 5–10pm. FRENCH.

Favored by celebrities, including Britain's Prince Andrew, this restaurant occupies a building reconstructed in 1703 after a fire. Set one floor above street level, it has scarlet-colored walls, a collection of old paintings, and a solidly grounded staff that work competently under pressure. Menu items include such time-tested favorites as lobster soup; whitebait roe with chopped onions, sour cream, and fresh-baked bread; and a fillet of lamb with mustard sauce and pommes Provençal. Savvy local foodies are increasingly gravitating to this restaurant because of the competence of its cuisine and the use of first-rate ingredients.

SEEING THE SIGHTS

In addition to the sights below, take a stroll around **Bryggen (the Quay).** This row of Hanseatic timbered houses, rebuilt along the waterfront after the disastrous fire of 1702, is what remains of medieval Bergen. The northern half burned to the ground as recently as 1955. Bryggen is on UNESCO's World Heritage List as one of the world's most significant cultural and historical re-creations of a medieval settlement. It's a center for arts and crafts, where painters, weavers, and craftspeople have their workshops.

❂ **Det Hanseatiske Museum.** Finnegårdsgaten 1A, Bryggen. ☎ **55-31-41-89.** Admission May–Sept 35NOK ($4.50) adults, Oct–Apr 20NOK ($2.55) adults; free for children. June–Aug daily 9am–5pm; Sept–May daily 11am–2pm. Bus: 1, 5, or 9.

In one of the best-preserved wooden buildings at Bryggen, this museum illustrates Bergen's commercial life on the wharf centuries ago. German merchants, representatives of the Hanseatic League centered in Lübeck, lived in these medieval houses built in long rows up from the harbor. With dried cod, grain, and salt as articles of exchange, fishers from northern Norway met German merchants during the busy summer season. The museum is furnished with authentic articles dating from 1704.

Mariakirke (St. Mary's Church). Dreggen. ☎ **55-31-59-60.** Admission 15NOK ($1.90) adults, free for children. May 18–Sept 10 Mon–Fri 11am–4pm; Sept 11–May 17 Tues–Fri noon–1:30pm. Bus: 1, 5, or 9.

The oldest building in Bergen (its exact date is unknown, but perhaps from the mid–12th century) is this Romanesque church, one of the most beautiful in Norway. Its altar is the oldest ornament in the church, and there's a baroque pulpit, donated by Hanseatic merchants, with carved figures depicting everything from Chastity to Naked Truth. Church-music concerts are given May to August several nights a week.

Fløibanen. Vetrlidsalm 23A. ☎ **55-31-48-00.** Round-trip ticket 40NOK ($5) adults, 20NOK ($2.55) children. May 25–Aug Mon–Fri 7:30am–midnight, Sat 8am–midnight, Sun 9am–midnight; Sept–May 24 Mon–Thurs 7:30am–11pm, Fri 7:30am–11:30pm, Sat 8am–11:30pm, Sun 9am–11pm. Bus: 6.

A short walk from the fish market is the station where the funicular heads up to Fløien, the most famous of Bergen's seven hills. At 320m (1,050 feet), the view of the city, the neighboring hills, and the harbor is worth every øre.

Gamle Bergen. Elsesro, Sandviken. ☎ **55-25-78-50.** Admission 40NOK ($5) adults, 20NOK ($2.55) children and students. Houses, mid-May–Aug, guided tours daily every hour

11am–5pm. Park and restaurant, daily noon–10pm. Bus: 1 or 9 from the city center, leaving every 10 minutes.

At Elsesro and Sandviken is a collection of houses from the 18th and 19th centuries set in a park. Old Town is complete with streets, an open square, and narrow alleyways. Some of the interiors are exceptional, including a merchant's living room in the typical style of the 1870s—padded sofas, heavy curtains, potted plants—a perfect setting for Ibsen's *A Doll's House.*

○ **Troldhaugen (Troll's Hill).** Troldhaugveien 65, Hop. ☎ **55-91-17-91.** Admission 40NOK ($5) adults, free for children under 16. Apr 21–Sept daily 9am–6pm; Oct–Nov Mon–Fri 10am–2pm, Sat–Sun noon–4pm; Jan–Apr 20 Mon–Fri 10am–2pm. Closed Dec. Bus: 20, 21, 30, and 50 leave from the Bergen bus station (platforms 18–20); once the bus lets you off, turn right, walk about 200m (200 yards), turn left at Hopsvegen, and from here follow the signs to Troldhaugen, a 20- to 30-minute walk.

This Victorian house, in beautiful rural surroundings at Hop, near Bergen, was the summer villa of composer Edvard Grieg. The house still contains Grieg's own furniture, paintings, and other mementos. His Steinway grand piano is frequently used at concerts given in the house during the annual Bergen festival, as well as at Troldhaugen's own summer concerts. Grieg and his wife, Nina, are buried in a cliff grotto on the estate.

ORGANIZED TOURS

A 1-hour **tram tour** uses the city tram lines and specially designed red-sided streetcars equipped with multilingual headsets. The tour departs every hour on the hour from Bryggen and costs 70NOK ($9) for adults and 35NOK ($4.50) for children. It operates May through September daily 10am to 7pm.

The most popular and most highly recommended **bus tour** of Bergen is the 3-hour city tour, which departs daily at 10am and covers all major sightseeing attractions. These include Troldhaugen and Old Bergen. It also runs May to September and costs 220NOK ($28) for adults and 140NOK ($18) for children. For information and tickets for either tour, contact the tourist office at Bryggen 7 (☎ **55-32-14-80**).

THE SHOPPING SCENE

Bergen's pedestrian shopping area includes the streets **Gamle Strandgaten, Torgalmenningen,** and **Marken.** Shops are open weekdays from 9am to 4:30pm, except on Thursday, when they close at 7pm. Saturday hours are 9am to 3pm. Shopping centers are open weekdays 9am to 8pm, and close at 4pm on Saturday. When cruise ships are anchored in the harbor, most shops extend their hours to take advantage of the tourist trade. You'll find the widest selection of national handcrafts at **Husfliden I Bergen,** Vågsalmenningen 3 (☎ **55-31-78-70**)—the finest handmade knitwear from the western district, along with woodwork, brass, pewter ware, and national costumes. Especially popular are the selection of hand-turned wooden bowls and ceramics featuring a traditional hand-painted rose motif. The leading outlet for glassware and ceramics, **Prydkunst-Hjertholm,** Olav Kyrres Gate 7 (☎ **55-31-70-27**), purchases much of its merchandise directly from the studios of Norwegian and other Scandinavian artisans who turn out quality goods not only in glass and ceramics, but also in pewter, brass, wood, and textiles.

BERGEN AFTER DARK

Opened in mid-1978, the modern **Grieg Hall (Grieghallen),** Lars Hillesgate 3A (☎ **55-21-61-50**), is Bergen's monumental showcase for music, drama, and a host of other cultural events. The Bergen Symphony Orchestra, founded in 1765, performs here August to May on Thursday and some Fridays.

Norway's oldest theater performs September to June at **Den National Scene,** Engen 1 (☎ **55-54-97-10**). Its repertoire consists of classical Norwegian and international drama and contemporary plays, as well as visiting productions of opera and ballet in conjunction with the annual Bergen Festival. Performances are held Monday to Saturday.

In summer, the **Bergen Folklore dancing troupe** (☎ **55-58-80-10**), arranges a 1-hour folklore program at the Bryggens Museum on Tuesday and Thursday at 9pm. Tickets, which cost 95NOK ($12), are on sale at the tourist information center or at the door. **Ulriken Mountain Concerts** offers free folk and classical concerts weekdays at 7pm between June and August. A round-trip ticket to reach this mountaintop show costs 70NOK ($9) for adults and 35NOK ($4.50) for children, which includes rides on a shuttle bus from the Bergen tourist office (leaving at a quarter past the hour from 9:15am to 8:15pm) and the Ulriken cable car.

The most-frequented pub in the city center, the **Kontoret Pub,** Ole Bulls Plass 8–10 (☎ **55-90-07-60**), is in the Hotel Norge next to the Dickens restaurant/pub. Drinkers can wander freely between the two places, since they're connected. In the Kontoret you can order the same food served at Dickens, though most people seem to come here to drink. It's open Sunday to Thursday 4pm to 1am and Friday and Saturday 4pm to 3am.

Wednesday to Friday, **Engelen,** in the Radisson SAS Royal Hotel (☎ **55-54-30-00**), is one of Bergen's more elegant discos. On these nights an older, sedate crowd gathers to enjoy the music and ambience. On Saturday, however, beware—the atmosphere changes drastically with the arrival of 20-somethings intent on having fun. It's open Wednesday to Saturday 9pm to 3am, with a cover of 50NOK ($6.40); hotel guests enter free.

EXPLORING THE FJORDS

Norway's fjords can be explored from both Oslo and Bergen by ship and car or by a scenic train ride. Here are the details.

BY CAR FROM BERGEN

Bergen is the best departure point for trips to the fjords: To the south lies the famous **Hardangerfjord** and to the north the **Sognefjord,** cutting 180km (111 miles) inland. We've outlined a driving tour of the fjords, starting in Bergen and heading east on Route 7 to Ulvik, a distance of 150km (93 miles).

Ulvik   Ulvik is that rarity: an unspoiled resort. It lies like a fist at the end of an arm of the Hardangerfjord that's surrounded in summer by misty peaks and fruit farms. The village's 1858 church is attractively decorated in the style of the region. It's open June through August, daily 9am to 5pm, and presents concerts.

From Ulvik, you can explore the **Eidfjord** district, which is the northern tip of the Hardangerfjord, home to some 1,000 people and a paradise for hikers. Anglers are attracted to the area because of its mountain trout.

The district contains nearly one-quarter of ✪ **Hardangervidda National Park,** which is on Europe's largest high-mountain plateau. It's home to 20,000 wild reindeer, and well-marked hiking trails connect a series of 15 tourist huts.

Several canyons, including the renowned **Måbø Valley,** lead down from the plateau to the fjords. Here, you'll see the famous 170m (550-foot) **Voringfoss** waterfall; the Valurefoss in Hjømo Valley has a free fall of almost 245m (800 feet).

Part of the 1,000-year-old road across Norway, traversing the Måbø Valley, has been restored for hardy hikers.

En Route to Voss From Ulvik, take Highway 20 to Route 13. Follow Route 13 to Voss, 40km (25 miles) west of Ulvik and 100km (63 miles) east of Bergen.

VOSS Between the Sogne and Hardanger fjords, Voss is a famous year-round resort, also known for its folklore and as the birthplace of football hero Knute Rockne. Maybe the trolls don't strike fear into the hearts of farm children anymore, but they're still called out of hiding to give visitors a little fun.

Voss is a natural base for exploring the two largest fjords in Norway, the Sognefjord to the north and the Hardangerfjord to the south. In and around Voss are glaciers, mountains, fjords, waterfalls, orchards, rivers, and lakes.

A ride on the **Hangursbanen cable car** (☎ 56-51-12-12) offers panoramic views of Voss and the environs. The hardy take the cable car up, then spend the rest of the afternoon strolling down the mountain. A round-trip ride costs 50NOK ($6) for adults, 25NOK ($3.20) for children 8 to 16, and it's free for children 7 and under. The cable-car entrance is on a hillside that's a 10-minute walk north of the town center. It's open in summer and winter, but is closed May and September to November.

Built in 1277, the **Vangskyrkje,** Vangsgata 3 (☎ 56-51-22-78), with a timbered tower, contains a striking Renaissance pulpit, a stone altar and triptych, fine wood carvings, and a painted ceiling. It's a 5-minute walk east of the railroad station. We recommend that you call in advance to reserve an English-speaking guide. Admission is 15NOK ($1.90) for adults, 5NOK (65¢) for children, and free for children 6 and under. The church is open only June through August daily 10am to 4pm. If you arrive when church is closed, it's possible to arrange a private tour of the church by calling the parsonage (☎ 56-51-22-78).

Voss Folkemuseum, Mølster (☎ 56-51-15-11), is a collection of authentically furnished houses that shows what early farm life was like. Lying just north of Voss on a hillside overlooking the town, the museum consists of more than a dozen farmhouses and other buildings, ranging in age from the 1500s to around 1870. Admission is 30NOK ($3.85) for adults, and it's free for children. It's open May and September daily 10am to 5pm; June to August daily 10am to 7pm; and October to April Monday to Friday 10am to 3pm and Sunday noon to 3pm.

A little west of Voss in Finne, **Finnesloftet** (☎ 56-51-11-00) is one of Norway's oldest timbered houses, dating from the mid-13th century. It's a 15-minute walk west of the railway station. Admission is 30NOK ($3.85) for adults and 15NOK ($1.90) for children. It's open June 15 to August 15 daily 10:30am to 4:30pm.

An Excursion to the Sognefjord If you have time, you may want to visit the Sognefjord district, the largest of all Norwegian fjords. From Voss continue north on Route 13 to **Vik.** The scenery is beautiful and the road goes along for miles across a desolate tableland at 900m (3,000 feet) above sea level. The lakes on a summer day appear green, and on the distant slopes is snow.

In Vik, see the stave church, one of the most attractive in Norway; then take the road to **Vangsnes,** where you can make the short car-ferry connection across the Sognefjord to Balestrand or Dragsvik. Once across, take Route 5 north. The highway is steep, bringing you through rolling countryside with waterfalls until you reach **Viksdalen,** about 65km (40 miles) from Dragsvik.

BALESTRAND Long known for its arts and crafts, Balestrand lies on the northern rim of the Sognefjord, at the junction of the Vetlefjord, the Esefjord, and the Fjaerlandsfjord.

Kaiser Wilhelm II, a frequent visitor to Balestrand, presented the district with two statues of old Norse heroes, King Bele and Fridtjof the Bold, which stand in the town center.

What a Ride: Exploring the Fjords by Scenic Train

One of the great train rides of Europe is the ✪ **Bergensbanen** (☎ **55-96-69-00** for information), with five daily departures from Oslo, plus an additional train on Sunday. The most popular routing is Oslo to Bergen, although you can also take the train from Bergen to Oslo, depending on where you land in Norway. We think this is the most scenic and beautiful train ride in the world. Departures are from Oslo Central Station, and the trip takes $7^{1}/_{2}$ to $8^{1}/_{2}$ hours to cut across some of the most panoramic fjord and mountain scenery in Europe. The cost of a one-way ticket is 525NOK ($67) but a 30NOK ($3.85) seat reservation is required.

If your time is more limited, you can take a brief train ride from Bergen that will cover the most panoramic part of the journey.

The most exciting rail journey in Norway is a 12-hour tour from Bergen, encompassing two arms of the Sognefjord. The main feature of this journey—and the reason most passengers take the ride—is the 19km (12-mile) route from Myrdal to Flåm (see above). An electric train "drops" 880m (2,900 feet), past seemingly endless waterfalls. In summer, the tour leaves from the Bergen railroad station daily at 8:05am and 8:30am, and Monday to Friday at 11:48am. Guests may have lunch at Flåm, then board a river steamer for Gudvangen, where they hop on a bus to Voss, then a train back to Bergen. The round-trip fare, excluding meals, is 480NOK ($61) for adults and 240NOK ($31) for children under 12, and 285NOK ($37) for those over 67. Holders of Eurail or Scandinavian Rail Passes get a reduced fare. For more information, contact the Bergen tourist office (☎ **55-32-14-80**).

You can explore by setting out in nearly any direction, on scenic country lanes with little traffic, or a wide choice of marked trails and upland farm tracks. A touring map may be purchased at the **tourist office** in the town center (☎ 57-69-12-55). There's good sea fishing, as well as lake and river trout fishing. Fishing tackle, rowboats, and bicycles can all be rented in the area.

En Route to Flåm   From Balestrand, follow Route 55 east along the Sognefjord, crossing the fjord via ferry at Dragsvik and by bridge at Sogndal. At Sogndal, drive east to Kaupanger, where you'll cross the Ardalsfjord by ferry, south to Revsnes. In Revsnes, pick up Route 11 heading southeast. Drive east until you connect with a secondary road heading southwest through Kvigno and Aurland. When you arrive in Aurland, take Route 601 southwest to the town of Flåm, 95km (60 miles) southeast of Balestrand and 165km (103 miles) east of Bergen.

FLÅM   Flåm (pronounced *Flawm*) lies on the Aurlandsfjord, a tip of the more famous Sognefjord. In the village you can visit the old church dating from 1667, with painted walls done in typical Norwegian country style.

Flåm is an excellent starting point for excursions by car or boat to other well-known centers on the Sognefjord, Europe's longest and deepest fjord. Worth exploring are two of the wildest and most beautiful fingers of the Sognefjord: Nærøyfjord and Aurland-fjord. Ask at the **tourist office,** near the rail station (☎ 57-63-21-06), about a summer-only cruise from Flåm, where you can experience the dramatic scenery of both of these fjords. From Flåm by boat, you can disembark either in Gudvangen or Aurland and continue the tour by coach. Alternatively, you can return to Flåm by train.

There're also a number of easy walks in the Flåm district. The tourist office has a map detailing these walks.

BY SHIP/TOUR FROM BERGEN

There're several ways to visit Sognefjord, Norway's longest fjord, from Bergen. One way is to cross the fjord on an express steamer that travels from Bergen to **Gudvangen.** From Gudvangen, passengers go to Voss (see above), and from Voss a train runs back to Bergen. You can go by boat, bus, and then train for 495NOK ($63) round-trip. Details about this and other tours are available from the **Tourist Information** office in Bergen, Bryggen 7 (☎ **55-32-14-80**).

If you have more than a day to see the fjords in the environs of Bergen, you can take the grandest fjord cruise in the world, a **coastal steamer** going all the way to the North Cape and beyond. The coastal steamers are elegantly appointed ships that travel along the western coast of Norway from Bergen to Kirkenes, carrying passengers and cargo to 34 ports along the Norwegian coast. Eleven ships in all make the journey year-round. The ships sail through Norway's more obscure fjords, providing panoramic scenery and numerous opportunities for adventure. Along the way, sightseeing excursions to the surrounding mountains and glaciers are offered, as well as sails on smaller vessels through some of the more obscure fjords.

The chief operator of these coastal cruises is the **Bergen Line,** 405 Park Ave., New York, NY 10022 (☎ **800/323-7436** or 212/319-1300 in the U.S.). Tours may be booked heading north from Bergen, south from Kirkenes, or round-trip. The 7-day northbound journey costs $912 to $2,797 per person, including meals and taxes. Visitors opting for the southbound trip from Kirkenes pay $772 to $2,367. The round-trip voyage lasts 12 days and costs $1,605 to $4,300 per person.

14 Portugal

by Darwin Porter & Danforth Prince

Lisbon presides over a country that has one of Europe's fastest-growing economies, much of it fueled by investments that have poured in since Portugal joined the European Union. About 260km (160 miles) south of Lisbon, the maritime province of the Algarve, often called the "garden of Portugal," is the southwestern most part of Europe. Its coastline stretches 160km (100 miles) and is dotted with hundreds of beaches—the finest in Portugal.

1 Lisbon & Environs

Lisbon has blossomed into a cosmopolitan city—Europe's smallest capital is no longer a backwater at the far corner of Iberia. Sections along Avenida da Liberdade, the main street, at times evoke Paris in miniature. Sidewalk portrait painters beg to sketch your likeness, artisans offer you jewelry claiming it's gold (you both know it isn't), and vendors peddle handcrafts from embroidery to leather work. Some of the formerly clogged streets of the Baixa have been closed to traffic, and cobblestone pedestrian malls have been created.

Today, after a long slumber, there's excitement again in this city of seven hills. The world dropped in on Lisbon as it celebrated EXPO '98, marking the 500th anniversary of Vasco da Gama's journey to India. Not since the aftermath of the 1755 earthquake was there such a building boom. In spring 1998, a new bridge spanning the Tagus, Ponte Vasco da Gama, opened; this addition to the city's infrastructure has speeded access to other areas of Portugal, including Alentejo province with links to Spain.

In Lisbon, there's postmillennial life after EXPO '98. The site of the last great World's Fair of this century has not become a ghost town. Many of the attractions and facilities remain, including the Oceanarium, the largest aquarium in Europe. The Utopia Pavilion—an indoor stadium with advanced theatrical equipment—becomes Lisbon's first multimedia arena for concerts, sporting events, theatrical shows, and international congresses. The Lisbon Exhibition Center today holds dozens of international affairs every year, and the recreational harbor now has a capacity for between 700 to 900 moorings for leisure craft.

Some 1.6 million people now call Lisbon home, and many Lisboetas (Lisboans), having drifted in from the far corners of the world, don't even speak Portuguese.

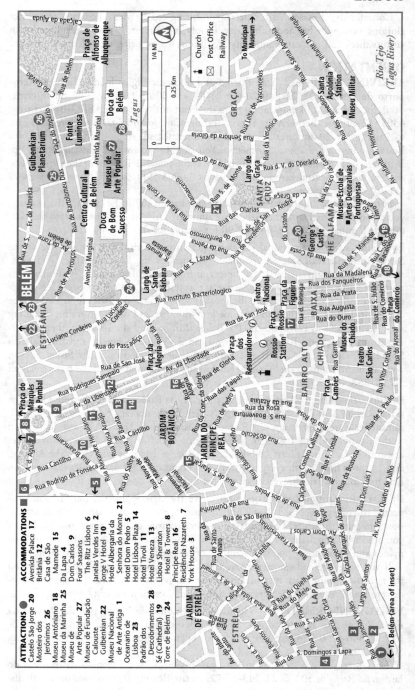

Lisbon

ATTRACTIONS ●
Castelo São Jorge **20**
Mosteiro dos
Jerónimos **26**
Museu Antóniano **18**
Museu da Marinha **25**
Museu de
Arte Popular **27**
Museu de Fundação
Calouste
Gulbenkian **22**
Museu Nacional
de Arte Antiga **1**
Oceanário de
Lisboa **23**
Padrão dos
Descobrimentos **28**
Sé (Cathedral) **19**
Torre de Belém **24**

ACCOMMODATIONS ■
Avenida Palace **17**
Britânia **12**
Casa de São
Mamede **15**
Da Lapa **4**
Dom Carlos **9**
Four Seasons
The Ritz Lisbon **6**
Janelas Verdes Inn **2**
Jorge V Hotel **10**
Hotel Albergaria da
Senhora do Monte **21**
Hotel Dom Pedro **5**
Hotel Lisboa Plaza **14**
Hotel Tivoli **11**
Hotel Veneza **13**
Lisboa Sheraton
Hotel & Towers **8**
Principe Real **16**
Residência Nazareth
York House **3**

Consider an off-season visit, especially in spring or fall, when the city is at its most glorious, before the hot and humid days of July and August. Lisbon isn't infested with visitors then, and you can wander about without fear of being trampled underfoot.

ORIENTATION

ARRIVING   By Plane   Both foreign and domestic flights land at Lisbon's **Aeroporto de Lisboa** (☎ **21-840-20-60;** 21-841-35-00 or 21-840-22-62 for information), located about 6km (4 miles) from the heart of the city. An AERO-BUS costing 430$ ($2.40) goes between the airport and the Cais do Sodré train station from 7am to 9am (every 20 minutes). It makes 10 intermediate stops, including praça dos Restauradores and praça do Comércio. You can also go by taxi. Passengers line up, British style, in a usually well-organized line at the sidewalk in front of the airport. The average fare to central Lisbon is 2,000$ to 3,000$ ($11 to $17). Luggage is 300$ ($1.70) extra per piece.

For ticket sales, flight reservations, and information about the city and the country, you can get in touch with the Lisbon personnel of TAP Air Portugal at praça do Marqués de Pombal 3A (☎ **21-841-69-90** for reservations).

By Train   Most international rail passengers from Madrid and Paris arrive at the **Santa Apolónia Rail Station,** the major terminal, by the Tagus near the Alfama district. Two daily trains make the 10-hour run from Madrid to Lisbon. Rail lines from northern and eastern Portugal also arrive at this station. EXPO '98 brought a new terminal to Lisbon, and it remains the most modern. **Gare de Oriente** at Expo Urbe opened in 1998 and is the hub for some long-distance and suburban trains, including such destinations as Porto, Sintra, the Beiras, Minho, and the Douro. Other rail terminals are **Estaçãodo Rossio,** where you can get trains to Sintra, and the **Cais do Sodré,** with trains to Cascais and Estoril on the Costa do Sol. At **Sul e Sueste,** you can board trains to the Algarve. For **rail information** at any of the terminals, call ☎ **21-888-40-25.**

By Bus   Buses from all over Portugal arrive at the **Rodoviária da Estremadura,** av. Casal Ribeiro 18B (☎ **21-357-77-15**), which lies near praça Saldanha, about a 30-minute walk from the praça dos Restauradores. Buses 1, 21, and 32 will deliver you to the Rossio, and bus 1 goes on to the Cais do Sodré, if you're checked into a hotel at estoril or Cascais. At least 10 buses a day leave for Lagos, a gateway to the Algarve, and 15 buses head north every day to Porto. There are eight daily buses leaving from here for Coimbra, the university city in the north.

By Car   International motorists must arrive through Spain, the only nation connected to Portugal via road. You'll have to cross Spanish border points, which usually poses no great difficulty. The roads are moderately well maintained. From Madrid, if you head west, the main road (N-620) from Tordesillas goes southwest by way of Salamanca and Ciudad Rodrigo to reach the Portuguese frontier at Fuentes de Onoro.

If you have a rented car, make sure that your insurance covers Portugal. Drive on the right side of the road; international signs and symbols are used. There are 15 border crossings, most of which are open daily from 7am to midnight.

VISITOR INFORMATION   The main tourist office in Lisbon is at the **Palácio da Foz,** Praça dos Restauradores, at the Baixa end of avenida da Liberdade (☎ **21-346-63-07;** metro: Restauradores), open Monday to Saturday 9am to 8pm, Sunday 10am to 6pm.

The office above is devoted to Portugal in general, but **Lisboa Turismo,** rua do Jardim do Reqedor 50 (☎ **21-343-36-72;** metro: Rossio), is concerned only with dispensing information about the city itself. It is open from 9am to 6pm. It sells the

Lisbon Card, an open sesame for visitors and an inexpensive and convenient way to see the town. The card provides free city transportation and entrance fees to museums and other attractions, plus discounts to see events. For adults, a 1-day pass cost 1,900$ ($11); 2 days 3,100$ ($17), 3 days, 4,000$ ($22). Children 5 to 11 pay 750$ ($4.20) for 1 day, 1,100$ ($6) for 2 days, and 1,500$ ($8) for 3 days.

CITY LAYOUT   Lisbon is best approached through its gateway, **Praça do Comércio (Commerce Square** or **Black Horse Square),** bordering the Tagus. This is one of Europe's most perfectly planned squares, and it's the site of the Stock Exchange and various government ministries. Directly west stands the late 19th-century City Hall, fronting **Praça do Município.** Heading north from Commerce Square, you enter the bustling Praça Dom Pedro IV, popularly known as the **Rossio.** The "drunken" undulation of the sidewalks, with their arabesques of black and white, have led to the appellation "the dizzy praça."

Opening onto the Rossio is the Teatro Nacional Dona Maria II. If you arrive by train, you'll enter the **Estação do Rossio,** whose exuberant Manueline architecture is worth seeing. Separating the Rossio from Avenida da Liberdade is **Praça dos Restauradores,** named in honor of the Restoration, when the Portuguese chose their own king and freed themselves from 60 years of Spanish rule. The event is marked by an obelisk.

Lisbon's main street is handsomely laid out **Avenida da Liberdade (Avenue of Liberty),** dating from 1880 and once called the "antechamber of Lisbon." Avenida da Liberdade is like a mile-long park, with shade trees, gardens, and center walks for the promenading crowds. Flanking it are fine shops, headquarters for many major airlines, travel agents, coffeehouses with sidewalk tables, and hotels, including the Tivoli. At the top of the avenue is **Praça Marquês de Pombal,** with a statue erected in honor of Pombal, the 18th-century prime minister credited with Lisbon's reconstruction in the aftermath of the 1755 earthquake. Proceeding north, you'll enter **Parque Eduardo VII,** named in honor of Queen Victoria's son, who paid a state visit to Lisbon. In the park is the Estufa Fria, a greenhouse well worth a visit.

GETTING AROUND   CARRIS (☎ 21-363-20-44) operates the network of funiculars, trains, subways, and buses in Lisbon. They sell a *"bihete de assinatura turistico"* good for 4 days of unlimited travel, costing 1,600$ ($9). You can also purchase a 1-day pass for 430$ ($2.40) or a 7-day pass for 2,264$ ($13). Passes are sold in CARRIS booths, open from 8am to 8pm daily, in most Metro stations and network train stations. You must show a passport to purchase one of these passes.

By Metro   Metro stations are designated by large M signs. The subway runs daily 6:30am to 1am. A single ticket costs 80$ (60¢) per ride. You can buy 10 tickets at one time for 550$ ($3.10). For more information, call ☎ 21-355-84-57.

By Bus & Tram   These are among the cheapest in Europe. Electric trams (**eléctricos**) make the steep run up to the Bairro Alto and are usually painted a rich Roman gold. You pay a flat fare of 160$ (90¢) on a bus if you buy the ticket from the driver. The transportation system within the city limits is divided into zones ranging from one to five, and your fare depends on how many zones you traverse. Buses and eléctricos run daily 6am to 1am.

By Electric Train   Lisbon is connected to all the towns and villages along the Portuguese Riviera by a smooth-running modern electric train system. You can board at the waterfront **Cais do Sodré Station** in Lisbon and head up the coast all the way to Cascais. Only one class of seat is offered, and the rides are cheap and generally comfortable. Sintra can't be reached by the electric train. You must go to the **Estação do Rossio,** opening onto Praça Dom Pedro IV, where frequent connections can be made. On the Lisbon-Cascais, Lisbon-Estoril, and Lisbon-Sintra run, the one-way fare is 180$ ($1).

By Taxi Taxis usually are diesel-engine Mercedes, charging a basic fare of 250$ ($1.40) for the first 440m (480 yards). Most fares in the city average 700$ ($3.90), with 20% extra from 10pm to 6am. The driver is allowed by law to tack on another 50% if your luggage weighs more than 30kg (66 pounds). Portuguese tip about 20% of an already modest fare. It is important to verify that the meter has indeed been activated the moment you step into a cab. For a **radio taxi,** call ☎ **21-811-90-00** or 21-793-27-56.

By Car Car-rental kiosks are at the airport as well as in the city center. These include **Avis,** Avenida Praia da Vitoria 12C (☎ **21-356-11-76**); **Hertz,** Qto. Frangelha Baixio, (☎ **21-849-27-22**); and **Budget,** av. Visconte Valmar 36 (☎ **21-994-04-43**). *Warning:* Driving in congested Lisbon is extremely difficult and potentially dangerous; the city has an alarmingly high accident rate and parking is impossible. It's best to wait and rent a car for excursions from the capital.

Fast Facts: Lisbon

American Express This agency is represented by Top Tours, av. Duque de Loulé 108 (☎ **21-315-58-77;** metro: Restauradores), open Monday to Friday 9:30am to 1pm and 2:30 to 6:30pm.

Baby-Sitters Most first-class hotels can provide baby-sitters from lists the concierge keeps. At small places, the sitter is likely to be a relative of the proprietor. Rates are low. You need to request a baby-sitter early in the day.

Business Hours Typically, **shops** are open Monday to Friday 9am to 1pm and 3 to 7pm (though some stay open through lunch) and Saturday 9am to 1pm; some are also open Saturday afternoon. **Banks** are open Monday to Friday 8:30am to 3pm; some offer a foreign-exchange service Monday to Saturday 6 to 11pm.

Currency The Portuguese currency unit is the **escudo,** written **1$00.** Fractions of an escudo (**centavos**) follow the "$"; for example, 100 escudos is written "100$00." Coins are minted in 50 centavos and 1, $2^{1}/_{2}$, 5, 10, 20, 25, 50, 100, and 200 escudos. Notes are printed in 100, 500, 1,000, 2,000, 5,000, and 10,000 escudos. The exchange rate used in this chapter was $1 = 180 escudos, or 1 escudo = 6¢. The ratio of the British pound to the mark fluctuates constantly. At press time, £1 = approximately 344 escudos. The euro rate is currently fixed at 200 escudos (or 1 escudo = €.005).

Dentists/Doctors Contact **Clinica Medical Espanha,** rua Dom Luis de Noroha 32 (☎ **21-796-74-57;** metro: Palhava), where some dentists speak English. Virtually every hotel maintains a list of doctors and dentists who can be called upon in emergencies.

Drugstores A central and well-stocked one is **Farmácia Vall,** Avenida Visconde Valmor 60A (☎ **21-797-30-43;** metro: Saldanha). Pharmacies that are closed post a notice indicating the nearest one that's open.

Embassies/Consulates If you lose your passport or have some other pressing problem, you'll need to get in touch with the **U.S. Embassy,** avenida das Forças Armadas (Sete Rios), 1600 Lisboa (☎ **21-727-33-00;** metro: Entre Campos). Hours are Monday to Friday 8am to 12:30pm and 1:30 to 5pm. If you've lost a passport, the embassy can take photos for you and help you to obtain the proof of citizenship needed to get a replacement. The **Canadian Embassy** is at

Avenida da Liberdade 144, 4th floor, 1250 Lisboa (☎ **21-347-48-92;** metro: Avenida); hours are Monday to Friday 8:30am to 12:30pm and 1:30 to 5pm (in July and August, the embassy closes at 1pm on Fridays). The **British Embassy,** rua São Bernardo 33, 1200 Lisboa (☎ **21-392-40-00;** metro: Avenida), is open Monday to Friday 10am to 12:30pm and 3 to 4:30pm. **Australians and New Zealanders** can refer to the British Embassy. The **Republic of Ireland Embassy,** rua de Imprensa à Estrêla 1, 1200 Lisboa (☎ **21-396-15-69;** metro: Rossio), is open Monday through Friday from 9:30am to noon and 2:30 to 4:30pm.

Emergencies   To call the police or an ambulance in Lisbon, telephone ☎ **112.** In case of fire, call ☎ **21-342-22-22.**

Hospitals   In case of a medical emergency, inquire at your hotel or call your embassy and ask the staff there to recommend an English-speaking physician; or try the **British Hospital,** rua Saraiva de Carvalho 49 (☎ **21-395-50-67;** bus: 7, 40, 49, or 60), where the telephone operator, staff, and doctors all speak English.

Post Office   The general post office is on Praça do Comércio (☎ **21-346-32-31;** metro: Rossio), open Monday to Friday 8:30am to 6:30pm.

Telephone   The **country code** for Portugal is **351.** The **city code** for Lisbon was changed in November 1999 from 01 to 21; use this code when calling from anywhere outside or inside Portugal—you must add it even within Lisbon itself.

You can make a **local call** in Lisbon in one of the many telephone booths. For most **long-distance calls,** particularly transatlantic calls, go to the central post office (see above). Give an assistant here the number you wish, and he or she will make the call, billing you at the end. Some phones are equipped for using calling cards, including American Express and Visa. You can also purchase phone cards from the post office in denominations of 50 units for 555$ ($3.10), 100 units for 1,011$ ($6), or 150 units for 1,624$ ($9). Phone cards can be used at any public phone in Portugal. In hotels, local calls are billed directly to your room. Phone debit cards are used only in public phones in public places. These cards bear one of two different names; T.L.P. or CrediFone. Both are sold at the cashier's desk of most hotels as well as at post offices.

To make an international call using your calling card, and thereby bypassing many of the add-on charges imposed by your hotel, dial the appropriate access number to reach a North American operator or an English-language voice prompt. For **AT&T,** call ☎ **05-017-1288;** for **MCI,** call ☎ **05-017-1234;** for **Sprint,** call ☎ **05-017-1877.**

WHERE TO STAY
IN THE CENTER
Very Expensive

✪ **Da Lapa.** Rua do Pau de Bandeira 4, 1200 Lisboa. ☎ **21-395-00-05.** Fax 21-395-06-65. www.orient-expresshotels.com. E-mail:reservas@hotelapa.com. 102 units. A/C MINIBAR TV TEL. 55,000$–100,000$ ($308–$560) double; from 90,000$ ($504) suite. Rates include breakfast. AE, DC, MC, V. Free parking. Bus: 13 or 27.

We never thought we'd see a hotel replace the Ritz as the premier address, but Da Lapa has done it. Its lushly manicured gardens (huge by urban standards) lie close to the Tagus, south of the city center. All but about 20 of the units are in a six-story modern wing. The public areas have multicolored ceiling frescoes and patterned marble floors in sometimes startling geometric patterns. Embaixada is one of Lisbon's most elegant restaurants (see below). Facilities include an outdoor pool.

Four Seasons Hotel The Ritz Lisbon. Rua Rodrigo Fonseca 88, 1200 Lisboa. ☎ **800/332-3442** in the U.S. or 21-383-20-20. Fax 21-383-17-83. www.fourseasons.com. 284 units. A/C MINIBARS TV TEL. 25,000$–60,000$ ($140–$336) double; from 65,000$ ($364) suite. AE, DC, MC, V. Free parking. Metro: Rotunda; bus: 1, 2, 9, or 32.

One of the most famous and legendary hotels in Lisbon was built by dictator Antonio Salazar in the late 1950s. In 1998, its management contract was taken over by the well-respected Four Seasons group, which immediately embarked on a sweeping upgrade from the English Victorian-themed lobby to the supremely comfortable rooms. Each has its own terrace, about half of them overlooking Edward VII Park. Bathrooms have double basins, hair dryers, and lots of electronic extras. There's a business center and room service, both open 24 hours, an upscale bistro, the Ritz Coffee Shop, and an airy and formal restaurant, Verandah, that's both dignified and pleasant. At press time, there wasn't a health club or swimming pool within the hotel, although guests receive temporary memberships in an up-to-date health and exercise club within the nearby park. Service, especially among the concierge staff, is superb.

○ **Hotel Dom Pedro.** Avenida Engenheiro. Duarte Pacheco, 1070 Lisboa. ☎ **21-389-6600.** Fax 21-389-6601. www.dompedro-hotels.com. E-mail: dp.lisboa@mail. telepac.pt. 262 units. A/C MINIBAR TV TEL 40,000$–60,000$ ($224–$336) double; from 70,000$ ($392) suite. Rates include breakfast. AE, DC, MC, V. Free parking. Metro: Marquês de Pombal.

One Lisbon's newest hotels, rated five stars by the Portuguese government and associated with some of the most glamorous hotels of the Algarve and Madeira, the 21-story Dom Pedro is set within the very central Amoreiras district, across from one of the city's biggest shopping centers. The interior is as conservative and rich-looking as the exterior is futuristic. Rooms are richly furnished. The more upscale of the hotel's two restaurants is the II Gatto Pardo, an Italian restaurant with a leopard-skin theme (see "Where to Dine, " below). Its services are supplemented with an upscale bistro, Le Café.

Expensive

Avenida Palace. Rua ler Dezembro 123, 1200 Lisboa. ☎ **21-346-01-55.** Fax 21-342-28-84. E-mail: hotel.av.palace@mail.telepac.pt. 96 units. A/C MINIBAR TV TEL. 27,000$–36,000$ ($151–$202) double; 55,000$ ($308) junior suite; 75,000$ ($420) suite. Rates include breakfast. AE, DC, MC, V. Free parking. Metro: Restaurador; tram: 35.

Built in 1892 and long closed for a massive overhaul, Avenida Palace is the grandest old-fashioned hotel in Lisbon, a link to the past, a world etched in crystal and antiques. Its location is right at the Rossio is terribly convenient and terribly noisy, but once inside it is another world entirely. Still "The Grand Dame of Lisbon hotels," it retains its belle-epoch aura and elegance, while offering all the modern comforts. Rooms are soundproof against the busy street and supplied with elegant, antique-style furnishings, and deluxe mattresses. The hotel no longer maintains a restaurant.

Hotel Lisboa Plaza. Travessa do Salitre 7, av. da Liberdade, 1269 Lisboa. ☎ **21-346-39-22.** Fax 21-347-16-30. www.heritage.pt. E-mail: plaza.hotels@heritage.pt. 112 units. A/C MINIBAR TV TEL. 23,500$–34,600$ ($132–$194) double; 35,000$–48,000$ ($196–$269) suite. Rates include buffet breakfast. Children 12 and under stay free in parents' room. AE, DC, MC, V. Parking 2,300$ ($13) nearby. Metro: Avenida; bus: 1, 2, 36, or 44.

This family owned and operated hotel in the heart of the city is a charmer, with many appealing art nouveau touches. Rooms—boasting well-stocked bathrooms with hair dryers and in-house videos—are well styled and comfortable. Try for a room in the rear, overlooking the botanical gardens. Quinta d'Avenida restaurant specializes in traditional Portuguese cuisine.

Hotel Tivoli. Av. da Liberdade 185, 1298 Lisboa Codex. ☎ **21-319-89-00.** Fax 21-319-89-50. E-mail: htllisboa@mail.telepac.pt. 357 units. A/C MINIBAR TV TEL.

26,000$–34,000$ ($146–$190) double; from 50,000$ ($280) suite. Rates include continental breakfast. AE, DC, MC, V. Parking 1,600$ ($9). Metro: Avenida; bus: 1, 2, 9, or 32.

The Tivoli has enticing features, including the only hotel pool in central Lisbon. After a much-needed 1998 renovation, it sparkles again, and it boasts extensive facilities. Best of all, its prices aren't extravagant, considering the amenities. The largest and best rooms face the front, though those in the rear are quieter. Some are better appointed and more spacious than others. The wood-paneled O Zodíaco restaurant serves lunch and dinner buffets. The top-floor O Terraço offers a view of Lisbon as well as á la carte meals. Facilities include access to the Tivoli Club, surrounded by a lovely garden, with a pool that can be heated when necessary, a tennis court, and a solarium.

Lisboa Sheraton Hotel & Towers. Rua Latino Coelho 1, 1097 Lisboa. ☎ **800/325-3535** in the U.S., or 21-357-57-57. Fax 21-314-22-92. 388 units. A/C MINIBAR TV TEL. 44,000$ ($246) double; from 90,000$ ($504) suite. AE, DC, MC, V. Parking 1,900$ ($11). Bus: 1, 2, 9, or 32.

This 26-floor skyscraper lies at a traffic-clogged intersection a bit removed from the center, a few blocks north of Praça Marquês de Pombal. Bedrooms don't match the grandeur of the public rooms, but they're generally spacious, and each was renovated in the late '90s. The most desirable are in the tower, opening onto views of the longest bridge in Europe. The hotel's restaurants include the glamour choice, the Alfama Grill. A rooftop bar features live music nightly, and there's an outdoor pool and a health club.

Moderate

Britânia. Rua Rodrigues Sampaio 17, 1150 Lisboa. ☎ 21-315-50-16. Fax 21-315-50-21. www.heritage.pt. E-mail: britania.hotel@heritage.pt. 30 units. A/C MINIBAR TV TEL. 19,500$–30,600$ ($109–$171) double. Rates include buffet breakfast. AE, DC, MC, V. Metro: Avenida; bus: 1, 2, 11, or 21.

In its own way, the Britânia is one of Lisbon's most traditional and refreshingly conservative hotels, designed by well-known Portuguese architect Cassiano Branco in 1944. About a block from Avenida da Liberdade, it boasts a distinguished clientele that returns repeatedly, and an old-fashioned, almost courtly, staff. Rooms contain hair dryers and safes. There's a bar on the premises, and the only meal served is breakfast, but the facilities of the much larger Lisboa Plaza Hotel (with which the Britânia is affiliated) lie just across the busy avenue.

Dom Carlos. Av. Duque de Loulé 121, 1050 Lisboa. ☎ 21-351-25-90. Fax 21-352-07-28. E-mail: hdcarlos@mail.telepac.pt. 76 units. A/C MINIBAR TV TEL. 20,800$ ($117) double; 24,000$ ($134) triple. Rates include buffet breakfast. AE, DC, MC, V. Metro: Marquês de Pombal; bus: 7, 36, 44, or 45.

Just off praça Marquê de Pombal, the Dom Carlos faces its own triangular park dedicated to the partially blind Camilo Castelo Branco, a 19th-century "eternity poet." The curvy facade is all glass, giving guests an outdoorsy feeling reinforced by green trees and beds of orange and red canna. In a neighborhood of similar competitors, this is the best three-star hotel of the lot because its rooms are more spacious and because maintenance is high.

Hotel Veneza. Av. da Liberdade 189, 1200 Lisboa. ☎ 21-352-26-18. Fax 21-352-66-78. E-mail: 3k.hotels@mail.telepack.pt. 36 units. A/C MINIBAR TV TEL. 18,000$ ($101) double. Rates include continental breakfast. AE, DC, MC, V. Parking 1,400$ ($8). Metro: Avenida.

The Veneza, which opened in 1990, occupies one of the few remaining turn-of-the-century palaces that once lined avenida da Liberdade. Inside, a grand staircase leads to the three upper floors. The well-appointed midsize rooms are furnished in a soothing modern style, each with a firm mattress. The staff is pleasant. The Veneza contains a bar but serves no meals other than breakfast. Its position adjacent to the better-equipped Hotel Tivoli (see above) ensures its clients access to all the facilities they might need, including several restaurants, an animated bar, a health club, a pool, and a garden.

✪ **Janelas Verdes Inn.** Rua das Janelas Verdes 47, 1200 Lisboa. ☎ **21-396-81-43.** Fax 21-396-81-44. www.heritage.com. E-mail: jverdes@heritage.pt. 17 units. A/C TV TEL. 29,200$–35,900$ ($164–$201) double. 39,000$–45,300$ ($218–$254) triple. Rates include continental breakfast. AE, DC, MC, V. Bus: 27, 40, 49, or 60.

Owned by the proprietors of the Lisboa Plaza (see above), this aristocratic 18th-century mansion was the home of Portuguese novelist Eça de Queiros. Near the Museum of Ancient Art, its large, luxurious, and marvelously restored rooms have abundant closet space and generous tile bathrooms. The lounges are evocative of a comfortable bourgeois house in turn-of-the-century Lisbon. Breakfast is brought on a tray to your room, to the lounge, or to the rear walled-in terrace.

Príncipe Real. Rua de Alegria 53, 1200 Lisboa. ☎ **21-346-01-16.** Fax 21-342-21-04. E-mail: hbelver@mail.telepac.pt. 24 units. A/C MINIBAR TV TEL. 25,500$–29,000$ ($143–$162) double. Rates include buffet breakfast. AE, DC, MC, V. Metro: Rotunda or Avenida; bus: 2.

This modern five-story hotel, which was built in the 1960s and renovated several times since, is reached after a long, steep climb from Avenida da Liberdade. Selectivity and care are shown in the small but tasteful individualized rooms. Beds, reproductions of fine antiques, have excellent mattresses. The hotel's restaurant opens onto panoramic views of Lisbon and serves excellent Portuguese cuisine. There's also a bar on the premises, but no outlet for health and recreation.

✪ **York House.** Rua das Janelas Verdes 32, 1200 Lisboa. ☎ **21-396-24-35.** Fax 21-397-27-93. E-mail: yorkhouse@mail.telepac.pt. 34 units. TV TEL. 30,000$–41,000$ ($168–$230) double. Rates include buffet breakfast. AE, DC, MC, V. Bus: 27, 40, 49, 54, or 60.

York House mixes the drama of the past with modern convenience. Once a 16th-century convent, it's outside the center of traffic-filled Lisbon, almost opposite the National Art Gallery. York House was tastefully furnished by one of the most distinguished Lisbon designers. The various size rooms have antique beds, good mattresses, and 18th- and 19th-century bric-a-brac. The former monks' dining hall has deep-set windows, large niches for antiques, and, best of all, combined French and Portuguese cuisine. Guests gather in the two-level lounge for before- or after-dinner drinks. On-street parking might be free but is rarely available. The lack of air-conditioning can also be a problem in summer. Book well in advance.

Inexpensive

Casa de São Mamede. Rua da Escola Politécnica 159, 125 Lisboa. ☎ **21-396-31-66.** Fax 21-395-1896. 28 units. TEL. 12,500$ ($70) double, 15,000$ ($84) triple. Rates include continental breakfast. No credit cards. Tram: 24; bus: 22,49, or 58.

Constructed in the 1800s as a villa for the count of Coruche, this building, behind the Botanical Gardens about midpoint between Avenida da Liberdade and the Amoreiras shopping center, was transformed into a hotel in 1945. It's managed by the Marquês family. Breakfast is served in a sunny second-floor dining room decorated with antique yellow-and-blue tiles. Though renovated, rooms retain an aura of their original high-ceilinged, somewhat frayed charm.

Jorge V Hotel. Rua Mouzinho da Silveira 3, 1200 Lisboa. ☎ **21-356-25-25.** Fax 21-315-03-19. 49 units. A/C TV TEL. 14,000$ ($78) double; 18,000$ ($101) suite. Rates include continental breakfast. AE, DC, MC, V. Parking 1,500$ ($8). Metro: Avenida or Marquês de Pombal.

Jorge V, a neat little hotel with a 1960s design, boasts a choice location a block off noisy Avenida da Liberdade. Its facade contains rows of cellular balconies, roomy enough for guests to have breakfast or afternoon "coolers." A tiny elevator takes guests to a variety of aging rooms, which aren't generous in size but are comfortable in a compact way; all have small bathrooms. There's no on-site restaurant, but the in-house bar serves sandwiches and light snacks.

Residência Nazareth. Av. António Augusto de Aguiar 25, 1000 Lisboa. ☎ **21-354-20-16.** Fax 21-356-08-36. 32 units. A/C MINIBAR TV TEL. 8,000$ ($45) double. Rates include continental breakfast. AE, DC, MC, V. Metro: São Sebastião or Park; bus: 31, 41, or 46.

You'll recognize this place by its dusty-pink facade and windows, some of which are surrounded with decorative arches in low relief. Take an elevator to the fourth-floor landing, where, far from the beauticians, hair stylists, and offices below, there's a medieval vaulting you might find in a romanticized Portuguese fortress. The distressed plaster and the wrought-iron lanterns are obvious facsimiles. Even the spacious bar/TV lounge looks like a vaulted cellar. Some rooms, which are very basic, contain platforms, requiring guests to step up or down to the bathroom or to the comfortable bed. A little refurbishing is in order here.

IN THE GRAÇA DISTRICT
Moderate
✪ **Hotel Albergaria da Senhora do Monte.** Calçada do Monte 39, 1100 Lisboa. ☎ **21-886-60-02.** Fax 21-887-77-83. 32 units. A/C TV TEL. 17,500$ ($98) double; 27,500$ ($154) suite. Rates include continental breakfast. AE, DC, MC, V. Metro: Socorro; tram: 28; bus: 12, 17, or 35.

This little hilltop hotel from 1969 has a unique character and was last renovated in 1995. It's perched near a belvedere, the Miradouro Senhora do Monte, with a memorable nighttime view of the city, St. George's Castle, and the Tagus. The intimate living room features tufted sofas and oversize tables and lamps. Multilevel corridors lead to the excellent rooms, all with verandas. There's a panoramic bar on site, but other than breakfast, no meals are served.

WHERE TO DINE
IN THE CENTER
Very Expensive
✪ **Gambrinus.** Rua das Portas de Santo Antão 25. ☎ **21-342-14-66.** Reservations required. Main courses 6,000$–13,000$ ($34–$73). AE, MC, V. Daily noon–1:30am. Metro: Rossio. SEAFOOD.

One of Lisbon's premier restaurants since 1936, Gambrinus is the finest choice for fish and shellfish. It's in the congested heart of the city, off the Rossio near the rail station on a little square behind the National Theater. Have your meal in the severely macho dining room with leather chairs under a cathedral-beamed ceiling or select a little table beside a fireplace on the raised end of the room. The shades and nuances of the cuisine here are definitely to the tastes of the cultivated palate, focused as they are on exciting flavor harmonies. The soups are good, especially the shellfish bisque. The most expensive items, logically, are shrimp and lobster dishes. However, you might try conch with shellfish thermidor or sea bass minhota. If you don't fancy fish but do like your dishes hot, ask for chicken piri-piri. The restaurant also offers elaborate desserts. Coffee with a 30-year-old brandy is the perfect end to a sumptuous meal here.

Expensive

❊ António Clara. Av. da República 38. ☎ **21-799-42-80.** Reservations required. Main courses 2,500$–3,500$ ($14–$20). AE, DC, MC, V. Mon–Sat noon–3pm and 7–10:30pm. Metro: Saldainha. PORTUGUESE/INTERNATIONAL.

This art nouveau villa is famous as the former home of one of Portugal's most revered architects. Although it is no longer as chic and glamorous as it was in the early '90s, it still offers a first-rate cuisine in romantic surroundings. It was built in 1890 by Miguel Ventura Terra (1866–1918), whose photograph hangs amid polished antiques and gilded mirrors. The villa's angled tiled wings seem to embrace visitors as they approach the vaguely Moorish facade. Meals include specialties like smoked swordfish, paella for two, chateaubriand béarnaise, monkfish rice, codfish Margarida da Praça and beef Wellington. These dishes may be familiar, but only the highest-quality ingredients go into them.

Casa da Comida. Travessa de Amoireiras 1. (off rua Alexandre Herculano). ☎ **21-388-53-76.** Reservations required. Main courses 3,200$–5,000$ ($18–$28). AE, DC, MC, V. Mon–Fri 1–3pm; and 8pm–midnight, Sat 8pm–midnight. Metro: Rato. PORTUGUESE/FRENCH.

Casa da Comida, off Rua Alexandre Herculano, is touted by local gourmets as having some of the finest food in Lisbon. You'll find the cuisine good and the atmosphere pleasant. The dining room is handsomely decorated, the bar done in period style, and the walled garden charming. Specialties include roast kid with herbs, a medley of shellfish Casa da Comida, and lobster with vegetables. One speciality is stewed pheasant that has been marinated in port, a recipe dating from the Middle Ages. An excellent selection of wines is available. The food is often more imaginative here than at some of the other top-rated choices.

Clara. Campo dos Mártires da Pátria 49. ☎ **21-885-30-53.** Reservations required. Main courses 2,900$–4,000$ ($16–$22). AE, DC, MC, V. Mon–Sat noon–3:30pm and 7pm–midnight. Closed Aug 1–15. Metro: Avenida. PORTUGUESE/INTERNATIONAL.

In a hillside location amid decaying villas and city squares, this green tile house contains an elegant restaurant. During lunch, you may prefer to sit near the garden terrace's plants and fountain. At night, an indoor seat—perhaps near the large marble fireplace—is more appealing. A piano plays softly at dinner. Specialties include tournedos Clara, stuffed rabbit with red-wine sauce, Valencian paella, filet of sole with orange, and pheasant with grapes. Shellfish dishes are often lethal in price, ranging from 5,600$ ($31) for a shrimp platter to 9,000$ ($50) for a lobster. Prices are based on daily changing market quotations. As in many top Lisbon restaurants, these dishes aren't creative or innovative, but they're often prepared flawlessly. The wine list is very selective, containing mostly Portuguese wines from small scale and prestigious wineries throughout the country's best districts.

❊ Embaixada. In the Da Lapa, rua do Pau de Bandeira 4. ☎ **21-395-00-05.** Reservations recommended. Main courses 2,700$–6,000$ ($15–$34); fixed-price lunch buffet 4,800$ ($27) per person; *menu dégustation* 8,700$ ($49). AE, DC, MC, V. Daily 12:30–3:30pm and 7:30–10:30pm. Bus: 13 or 27; tram: 25 or 28. INTERNATIONAL/PORTUGUESE.

This dignified dining room, with flowered curtains and a view of one of the most lavish gardens in this exclusive neighborhood, is a favorite with diplomats from the foreign embassies and consulates nearby. Especially popular is the fixed-price lunch buffet with an array of international food. The à la carte items are available at lunch and dinner and include, depending on the season, fresh salmon fried with sage, lamb chops with mint sauce, a succulent version of a traditional Portuguese feijoada, and duck breast with pears. While you may not run to phone *Gourmet* magazine, you'll be amply rewarded with deluxe ingredients perfectly handled by the staff.

Escorial. Rua das Portas de Santo Antão 47. ☎ **21-346-44-29.** Reservations recommended. Main courses 3,500$–8,000$ ($20–$45); *menu dégustation* 9,800$ ($55) for 2. AE, DC, MC, V. Daily noon–midnight. Metro: Rossio or Restauradores. INTERNATIONAL.

Near Praça dos Restauradores, this Spanish-owned place combines classic Spanish dishes with an inviting rosewood-paneled dining room. A menu is printed in English (always look for the course of the day). For an appetizer, you may enjoy Portuguese oysters or squid on a skewer. The chef's specialties are barbecued baby goat, beef Stroganoff, or partridge casserole. In spite of its neighborhood, which grows increasingly sleazy at night, Escorial has stood the test of time and remained an enduring though not incredibly innovative favorite.

Il Gatto Pardo. In the Hotel Dom Pedro, av. Engenheiro, Duarte Pacheco. ☎ **21-389-6600.** Reservations recommended. Main courses 2,200$–3,200$ ($12–$18). Set-price menus 6,000$–8,000$ ($34–$45). AE, DC, MC, V. Daily 12:30–3:30pm and 8–11pm. Metro: Marquês de Pombal. ITALIAN.

The most appealing and stylish Italian restaurant in Lisbon is distinctly different from the pasta and pizza joints that until now have passed for Italian within the Portuguese capital. Set on the third floor of the Dom Pedro, it has a smooth and soothing color scheme of beiges and browns, with lots of exposed hardwoods and a leopard-skin theme. Virtually everything was imported from Italy, including many members of the staff, who prepare ultrafresh versions of pasta with clams, risotto with cuttlefish; pappardelle with zucchini and saffron; sea wolf coated in breadcrumbs; grilled swordfish steak in parsley sauce; roasted veal cooked in heady Barolo wine; and duck breast flavored with honey and vinegar sauce. During clement weather, an outdoor terrace that's ringed with potted shrubs and vines provides sweeping views out over the surrounding neighborhood.

Restaurante Tavares. Rua da Misericórdia 37. ☎ **21-342-11-12.** Reservations required. Main courses 6,000$–8,000$ ($34–$45); fixed-price lunch or dinner 10,000$ ($56). AE, DC, MC, V. Mon–Fri 12:30–3pm and 8–10:30pm, Sun 8–10:30pm. Bus: 15. PORTUGUESE/CONTINENTAL.

Lisbon's oldest restaurant, Tavares is a nostalgic favorite, still serving competently prepared food with flawless service. It may be one of the capital's more glittering settings, but it's beginning to show a little wear. Your meal may begin with crepes de marisco prepared with shellfish. A main-course selection may be sole in champagne, stuffed crab Tavares style, or tournedos Grand Duc. Many continental dishes are on the menu, including the classic scallops of veal viennoise. The restaurant nearly always serves such basic Portuguese dishes as sardines and salted codfish.

Sua Excelência. Rua do Conde 34. ☎ **21-390-36-14.** Reservations required. Main courses 2,500$–3,000$ ($14–$17). AE, MC, V. Mon–Tues and Thurs–Fri 1–3pm; Thurs–Tues 8–10:30pm. Closed Sept. Bus: 27 or 49; tram: 25. PORTUGUESE.

Sua Excelência is the creation of Francisco Queiroz, who has created an atmosphere somewhat like that of a fashionable drawing room, with colorful tables in an intimate Portuguese provincial decor. Some dishes are uncommon in Portugal, including Angolan chicken cooked in palm oil with a medley of vegetables. Specialties include prawns piri-piri (not unreasonably hot), lulas a moda da casa (squid stewed in white wine, crème fraîche, and cognac), what Queiroz proclaims the "best smoked swordfish in Portugal," and clams cooked at least five ways. One unusual specialty is "little jacks," a small fish eaten whole, served with a well-flavored "paste" made from

2-day-old bread. The restaurant is just a block up the hill from the entrance to the National Art Gallery.

Moderate

Alemontes. Traversa da Santa Marta 4A. ☎ **21-315-77-93.** Reservations recommended. Main courses 2,500$–4,000$ ($14–$22). AE, MC, V. Daily 12:30–5pm and 7:30pm–midnight. Metro: Marquês de Pombal. PORTUGUESE.

Owners of inexpensive hotels in Lisbon often send their guests to this little bistro, as if it were some special secret to be shared. There is a lot of justification, as the place offers excellent food with good, well-chosen ingredients—all served at a fair price. "We don't get movie stars around here," said one of the waiters, "just people wanting an honest and decent meal." Fadistas entertain nightly, and the place has a real cozy atmosphere, with a simple decor of handcrafted rugs and decorative dishes. Many of the dishes are based on recipes from the Portuguese provinces of Trá-os-Montes. Try such delights as tender loin of veal grilled perfectly and served with fresh potatoes and vegetables. Another excellent prepared regional dishes including hare with white beans or roasted suckling pig on the spit.

Bachus. Largo da Trindade 8–9. ☎ **21-342-28-28.** Reservations recommended. Main courses 1,500$–3,600$ ($8–$20). AE, DC, MC, V. Mon–Fri noon–3pm, Sat 7pm–midnight. Metro: Chiado; bus: 58. INTERNATIONAL.

Amusing murals cover the wood-paneled facade of this restaurant; inside, the decor is elaborate and sophisticated. The ambience is a mix of a salon in a Russian palace, a turn-of-the-century English club, and a stylized Manhattan bistro. Specialties change frequently, depending on market availability. Full meals might include mixed grill Bachus, chateaubriand with béarnaise, mountain goat, beef Stroganoff, shrimp Bachus, or other daily specials. The chef has a conservative approach to his cuisine and reportedly rarely gets any complaints. The wine list is extensive.

Bonjardim. Travessa de Santo Antão 10–12. ☎ **21-342-74-24.** Main courses 1,100$–2,900$ ($6–$16). AE, DC, MC, V. Daily noon–11:30pm. Metro: Restauradores. PORTUGUESE.

Bonjardim caters mostly to families, providing wholesome meals that fit most budgets. The operation has been so successful that it has taken over a building across the street, where the same menu is offered. The restaurant, one of the most popular in Lisbon, is just east of avenida da Liberdade near the grimy praça dos Restauradores. In the main restaurant, the air-conditioned second-floor dining room is designed in rustic Portuguese style. The street-floor dining room, with an adjoining bar, has walls of decorative tiles. During your dinner, the aroma of plump chickens roasting to a golden brown on the charcoal spit is likely to prompt you to try one. An order of this house speciality, called frango no espeto, is adequate for two, with a side dish of french fries. The cook also bakes hake in the Portuguese style; an alternative dish is pork fried with clams.

✪ Conventual. Praça das Flores 45. ☎ **21-390-91-96.** Reservations required. Main courses 2,300$–3,500$ ($13–$20). AE, DC, MC, V. Mon–Fri 12:30–3:30pm and 7:30–11pm, Sat 7:30–11:30pm. Metro: Avenida; bus: 100. PORTUGUESE.

In many ways this is one of our favorite Lisbon restaurants, because of the taste and sensitivity of its gracious owner, Dina Marquês. Many of its admirers (who include the prime minister of Portugal) rank it as the best place to dine in Lisbon today, even though its prices are about a quarter less than at many of its competitors. Once inside, you'll be treated to a display of old panels from baroque churches, religious statues, and bric-a-brac from Mrs. Marquês private collection. The owner invented a few of the delectably flavored recipes, including creamy coriander soup, stewed partridge in port, duck in champagne sauce, grilled monkfish in herb-flavored cream sauce, and stewed clams in a sauce of red peppers, onions, and cream.

Restaurant 33. Rua Alexandre Herculano 33A. ☎ **21-354-60-79.** Reservations recommended. Main courses 2,500$–3,600$ ($14–$20); AE, DC, MC, V. Mon–Fri noon–3:30pm and 8–10:30pm, Sat 8–10pm. Metro: Rotunda; bus: 6 or 9. PORTUGUESE/INTERNATIONAL.

Restaurant 33 is a treasure. Decorated like an English hunting lodge, it lies near many recommended hotels, including the Ritz. Specialties include shellfish rice served in a crab shell, smoked salmon or lobster tour d'Argent, and pepper steak. Large portions, tasty stews, and strong-flavored ingredients characterize the food. You can order a glass of port in the small bar and enjoy the pianist who performs during dinner.

Inexpensive

António Oliveira. Rua Tomá Ribiero 63. ☎ **21-353/87-80.** Main courses 790$–1,500$ ($4.40–$8). MC, V. Mon–Sat 7:30–10:30pm. Metro: Picoas; bus: 44 or 55. PORTUGUESE/INTERNATIONAL.

This place was created for Portuguese businesspeople who want a relaxing ambience and good food. Just a bit away from the din of central traffic, it's a refreshing oasis with blue-and-white glazed earthenware tiles and a free-form blue ceiling. Fish dishes, garnished with vegetables, include fillets with tomato sauce and baked sole. Polvo à lagareira (octopus with broiled potatoes, olive oil, and garlic) is a specialty. From among the fowl and meat dishes, try the *frango na prata* (chicken broiled in foil with potatoes) or pork with clams Alentejana style. The owner/manager recommends his *açorda de marisco,* a stewlike breaded shellfish-and-egg dish that's a treat.

Casa Nostra. Rua de Rosa 84–90. ☎ **21-342-59-31.** Reservations recommended. Regular main courses 1,000$–2,600$ ($6–$15); seafood main courses 1,900$–2,400$ ($11–$13). AE, MC, V. Tues–Fri 12:30–2:30pm and 8–11pm, Sat 8–11pm, Sun 1–2:30pm. Metro: Chiado; tram: 28 or 28B. ITALIAN.

Maria Paola Porru, a movie sound engineer whose travels have exposed her to cinematic circles across Europe, created this postmodern and very hip hideaway in the Bairro Alto. Set behind a century-old, pink-toned deliberately understated facade that you might not immediately recognize as a restaurant, the setting is simple, stylish, and informal. All pastas are homemade on the premises. Accomplished menu items include fettuccine al mascarpone, lasagna, spaghetti with Portuguese clams, and several versions of grilled meat. The preferred dessert of many repeat clients is the Sicilian-style tiramisu, a rich dessert made with ladyfingers, coffee, and mascarpone cream. Despite the fact that this restaurant's official address is on rua de Rosa, its entrance lies around the corner, at travessa de Poco da Cidade 60.

Cervejaria Brilhante. Rua das Portas de Santo Antão 105. ☎ **21-346-14-07.** Main courses 1,600$–3,400$ ($9–$19); tourist menu 1,800$ ($10). AE, DC, MC, V. Daily noon–midnight. Metro: Rossio; bus: 1, 2, 36, 44, or 45. SEAFOOD/PORTUGUESE.

Lisboans from every walk of life stop here for a stein of beer and *mariscos* (seafood). Opposite the Coliseu, the tavern is decorated with stone arches, wood-paneled walls, and pictorial tiles of sea life. You can dine either at the bar or at marble tables. The front window is packed with an appetizing array of king crabs, oysters, lobsters, baby clams, shrimp, and even barnacles. Prices change every day, depending on the market; you pay by the kilo. This is hearty, robust eating. It's a challenge to attract a waiter's attention.

Cervejaria Ribadoura. Av. da Liberdade 155. ☎ **21-354-94-11.** Main courses 1,200$–3,600$ ($7–$20). AE, DC, MC, V. Daily 9am–1:30am. Metro: Avenida; bus: 1, 2, 44, or 45. SEAFOOD.

Cervejaria Ribadoura is one of central Lisbon's typical shellfish-and-beer places, mid-way along the major boulevard at the corner of Rua do Salitre. The decor is simple; the emphasis is on fish. The classic *bacalhau* (codfish) *a Bras* is a good choice; for a lighter bite, try the shrimp omelette. Many diners follow fish with a meat dish. Beware the sautéed pork cutlets with piri-piri, made with red-hot peppers from Angola—only those who've been trained for many years on the most mouth-wilting Indian curries should order this blazing dish.

Cervejaria Trindade. Rua Nova de Trindade 20C. ☎ **21-342-35-06.** Main courses 1,500$–3,000$ ($8–$17). AE, DC, MC, V. Daily 9am–1:30am. Metro: Rossio; bus: 15, 20, 51, or 100. PORTUGUESE.

Cervejaria Trindade is a German beer hall/Portuguese tavern. In operation since 1836, it's the oldest tavern in Lisbon, built on the site of the 13th-century Convento dos Frades Tinos, destroyed in the 1755 earthquake. You can order tasty little steaks and heaps of crisp french-fried potatoes. Many Portuguese prefer *bife na frigideira*—steak with mustard sauce and a fried egg, served in a clay frying pan. The tavern features shellfish, which come from private fish ponds, and the house specialties are *ameijoas* (clams) *à Trindade* and giant prawns.

Pastelaria Sala de Cha Versailles. Av. da República 15A. ☎ **21-354-63-40.** Sandwiches 265$ ($1.50); pastries 130$–160$ (75¢–90¢); plats du jour 1,150$–2,400$ ($6–$13)). AE, MC, V. Daily 7:30am–10pm. Metro: Salvanhe. SANDWICHES/PASTRIES.

Lisbon's most famous teahouse, this place has been declared part of the "national patrimony." In older days, the specialty was Licungo, Mozambique's famed black tea; you can still order it, but nowadays many drinkers enjoy English brands. The Portuguese claim they (not the English) introduced the custom of tea drinking to the English court, after Catherine of Bragança married Charles II in 1662. The decor is rich, with chandeliers, gilt mirrors, stained-glass windows, tall stucco ceilings, and black-and-white-marble floors. You can also order milk shakes, mineral water, and fresh orange juice, along with beer and liquor. Snacks come in many varieties, including codfish balls and toasted ham-and-cheese sandwiches. They now serve a limited array of Portuguese fare that's simple but wholesome.

IN THE CHIADO DISTRICT
Expensive
✪ **Tágide.** Largo da Académia Nacional de Belas Artes 18–20. ☎ **21-342-07-20.** Reservations required. Main courses 2,000$–3,500$ ($11–$20). AE, DC, MC, V. Mon–Fri 12:30–2:30pm and 7:30–10:30pm. Metro: Chiado; tram: 20; bus: 15. PORTUGUESE/INTERNATIONAL.

Tágide has had a prestigious past—once the town house of a diplomat, then a major nightclub, and now one of Lisbon's leading restaurants. It's up from the docks, atop a steep hill overlooking the old part of Lisbon and the Tagus. The Louis XIV dining room's windows look down on the ships moored in the port. Specialties include suprême of halibut with coriander, pork with clams and coriander, and grilled baby goat with herbs. Habitués from the world of Lisbon finance and government, including Portugal's president, are given preferential seating and treatment.

Moderate
A Brasileira. Rua Garrett 120. ☎ **21-346-95-41.** Sandwiches 260$–550$ ($1.45–$3.10); pastries 150$–300$ (85¢–$1.70); meals in restaurant 1,500$–5,000$ ($8–$28). AE, MC, V (restaurant only). Daily 7:30am–2pm. Metro: Rossio. SANDWICHES/PASTRIES.

One of Lisbon's oldest coffeehouses, A Brasileira boasts an art nouveau facade and was once a gathering place of Lisbon literati. Guests sit at small tables on chairs made of tooled leather, amid mirrored walls and marble pilasters. A statue of the great

Portuguese poet Fernando Pessoa sits on a chair side by side with the customers. The restaurant here serves basic fare like omelets, steaks, and fish. Note that you'll pay more for sandwiches and pastries in the restaurant than in the coffee bar.

IN THE ALCÂNTARA
Expensive

Café Alcântara. Rua Maria Luisa Holstein 15. ☎ **21-363-71-76.** Reservations recommended. Main courses 3,500$–7,000$ ($20–$39). AE, DC, MC, V. Daily 8pm–1am. Bar daily 9pm–3am. Bus: 57. FRENCH/PORTUGUESE.

One of Lisbon's most fun and hip dining-and-entertainment complexes, it attracts an international crowd. A 600-year-old warehouse for storing timber, the vast building has forest-green and Bordeaux walls, exposed marble, ceiling fans, burgeoning plants, and simple wooden tables and chairs. Menu items include fillet of salmon with lemon sauce, fresh fish, steak tartare, three different preparations of duck, and a Portuguese platter of the day, which might include fried *bacalhau* (codfish) or a hearty *feijoada* (bean-and-meat stew).

SEEING THE SIGHTS
SIGHTSEEING SUGGESTIONS FOR FIRST-TIME VISITORS

If You Have 1 Day   This is just enough time to take a walking tour of the **Alfama,** Lisbon's most interesting district. Visit the 12th-century **Sé** (cathedral) and take in a view of the city and the river Tagus from the **Santa Luzia Belvedere.** Climb up to the **Castelo São Jorge (St. George's Castle).** Take a taxi or bus to **Belém** to see the **Mosteiro dos Jerónimos (Jerónimos Monastery)** and the **Torre de Belém.** While at Belém. End your day at a **fado café.**

If You Have 2 Days   On Day 2, head for **Sintra,** the single most visited sight in the environs—Byron called it "glorious Eden." You can spend the day here, exploring the castle and other palaces in the panoramic area. Try at least to visit the **Palácio Nacional de Sintra** and the **Palácio Nacional da Pena.** Return to Lisbon for a night at a **fado café.**

If You Have 3 Days   Spend the morning of Day 3 at the **Museu Calouste Gulbenkian,** one of Europe's artistic treasure troves. Have lunch at a *típico* restaurant in the Bairro Alto. In the afternoon see the **Fundção Ricardo Esprito Santo (Museum of Decorative Art)** and the **Museu Nacional de Art Antiga (National Museum of Ancient Art).** At the day's end, wander through **Parque Eduardo VII.**

If You Have 4 or 5 Days   On Day 4, take an excursion from Lisbon (perhaps an organized tour) to visit the fishing village of **Nazaré** and the walled city of **Óbidos.** Those interested in Roman Catholic sights might also want to go to the shrine at **Fátima,** though it would be hectic to see this on the same day. On the final day, slow your pace a bit with a morning at the beach at **Estoril** on Portugal's Costa do Sol. Then continue along the coast to **Cascais** for lunch. After lunch, wander around this old fishing village now turned into a major resort. Go to **Guincho,** 6km (4 miles) along the coast from Cascais, which is near the westernmost point on the European continent and has panoramic views.

Traveler's Tip

If your time is limited, explore the National Coach Museum, the Jerónimos Monastery, and the Alfama with St. George's Castle. At least two art museums merit attention: the Museu Nacional de Art Antiga and the Museu Calouste Gulbenkian.

✪ THE ALFAMA

Old Lisbon lives on in the Alfama district. The wall built by the Visigoths and incorporated into some of the houses is testimony to its ancient past. The Alfama was the Saracen sector centuries before its conquest by the Christians. Some of the buildings were spared from the devastating 1755 earthquake, and the Alfama has retained much of its original charm—narrow cobblestone streets, cages of canaries chirping in the afternoon sun, strings of garlic and pepper inviting you inside *típico* taverns, old street markets, and charming balconies.

One of the best views is from the belvedere of **Largo das Portas do Sol,** near the Museum of Decorative Art. It's a balcony opening onto the sea, overlooking the typical houses as they sweep down to the Tagus. One of the oldest churches is **Santo Estevão (St. Stephen),** at Largo de Santo Estevão. It was first built in the 13th century; the present marble structure dates from the 18th. Also of medieval origin is the **Church of São Miguel (St. Michael),** at Largo de São Miguel, deep in the Alfama on a palm tree—shaded square. **Rua da Judiaria (Street of the Jews)** is another reminder of the past. It was settled largely by Jewish refugees fleeing Spain to escape the Inquisition.

✪ **Castelo São Jorge.** Rua da Costa do Castelo. No phone. Free admission. Apr–Sept, daily 9am–9pm; Oct–Mar, daily 9am–6pm. Bus: 37; tram: 12 or 28.

Believed to have predated the Romans, the hilltop was used as a fortress to guard the Tagus and its settlement below. Beginning in the 5th century A.D., the site was a Visigothic fortification; it fell in the early 8th century to the Saracens. Many of the walls still standing were erected during the centuries of Moorish domination. The Moors were in control until 1147, when Afonso Henríques, the country's first king, chased them out and extended his kingdom south. Even before Lisbon was made the capital of the newly emerging nation, the site was used as a royal palace. For what is the finest view of the Tagus and the Alfama, walk the esplanades and climb the ramparts of the old castle, named in commemoration of an Anglo-Portuguese pact dating from as early as 1371. On the grounds you can stroll through a setting of olive, pine, and cork trees, all graced by swans and rare white peacocks.

Sé (Cathedral). Largo da Sé. ☎ **21-86-67-52.** Admission: Cathedral, free; cloister, 100$ (55¢). Mon–Sat 10am–5pm. Tram: 28 (Graça); bus: 37.

Characterized by twin towers flanking its entrance, the Sé represents an architectural wedding of Romanesque and Gothic. The facade is severe enough to resemble a medieval fortress. When the city was captured early in the 12th century by Christian Crusaders, led by Portugal's first king, Afonso Henríques, the Sé became the first church in Lisbon. It was damaged in the earthquakes of 1344 and 1755.

Inside the rough exterior are many treasures, including the font where St. Anthony of Padua is said to have been christened in 1195. The cloister, built in the 14th century by King Dinis, is of ogival construction, with garlands, a Romanesque wrought-iron grille, and tombs with inscription stones. In the sacristy or Treasury Museum are marbles, relics, valuable images, and pieces of ecclesiastical treasure from the 15th and 16th centuries.

Museu Antóniano. Largo de Santo António de Sé. ☎ **21-886-91-45.** Free admission. Daily 7:30am–7:30pm. Métro: Rossio; bus: 37.

St. Anthony of Padua, an itinerant Franciscan monk who became Portugal's patron saint, was born in 1195 in a house that once stood here. The original church was destroyed by the 1755 earthquake, and the present building was designed by Mateus Vicente in the 18th century. In the crypt, a guide will show you the spot where the

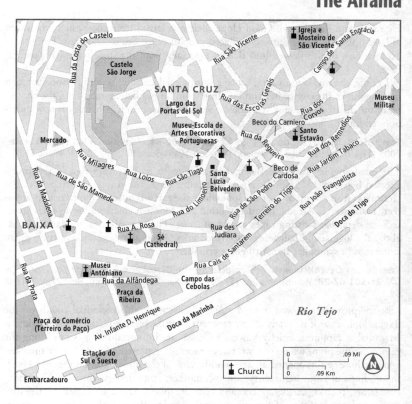

saint was allegedly born (he's buried in Padua, Italy). The devout come to this little church to light candles under his picture. He's known as a protector of young brides and also has a special connection with the children of Lisbon.

THE BAIRRO ALTO

Like the Alfama, the Bairro Alto (Upper City) preserves the characteristics of an older Lisbon. It once was called the heart of the city, probably for both its location and its inhabitants. Many of its buildings survived the 1755 earthquake. Today it's the home of some of the finest fado cafes, making it a center of nightlife. The Bairro Alto is also a fascinating place to visit during the day, when its charming narrow cobblestone streets and alleys, lined with ancient buildings, can be appreciated in the warm light coming off the sea.

From the windows and balconies, streamers of laundry hang out to dry, and there are cages of canaries, parrots, parakeets, and other birds. In the morning, the street scene is made up of housewives emerging from their homes to shop, following the cries of the *varinas* (fishmongers) and other food vendors. At night, the area comes alive with fado clubs, discos, and small bars; Victorian lanterns light the streets; and people stroll along leisurely.

BELÉM

At Belém, the most southwestern district of Lisbon, the Tagus meets the sea. From here the caravels that charted the unknown were launched on their missions: Vasco da Gama to India, Ferdinand Magellan to circumnavigate the globe, and Bartolomeu

Dias to round the Cape of Good Hope. Belém emerged from the Restelo, the point of land from which the ships set sail across the so-called Sea of Darkness. From these explorations, wealth flowed into Belém, especially from the spice trade with the Far East.

In time, the royal family established a summer palace here. Wealthy Lisboans began moving out of the city center and building town houses here, establishing the character of the district. For many years Belém was a separate municipality but is now incorporated into Lisbon as a parish.

Torre de Belém. Praça do Imperio. ☎ **21-362-00-34.** Admission 400$ ($2.25) adults, 200$ ($1.10) children, free for seniors. Tues–Sun 10am–5pm. Bus: 27, 28, 43, 49, or 51.

The quadrangular Tower of Belèm is a monument to Portugal's Age of Discovery. Erected between 1515 and 1520 in Manueline style, the tower is Portugal's classic landmark. It stands on or near the spot where the caravels once set out to sea. Its architect, Francisco de Arruda, blended Gothic and Moorish elements, using such architectural details as twisting ropes carved of stone. The coat-of-arms of Manuel I rests above the loggia, and balconies grace three sides. Along the balustrade of the loggias, stone crosses symbolize the Portuguese crusaders.

Padrão dos Descobrimentos (Memorial to the Discoveries). Praça da Boa Esperança. ☎ **21-301-62-28.** Admission 300$ ($1.70) Tues–Sun 9:30am–6:30pm. Bus: 27, 28, 43 or 49.

Like the prow of a caravel from the Age of Discovery, this memorial stands on the Tagus, looking as if it's ready at any moment to strike out across the Sea of Darkness. Memorable explorers, chiefly Vasco da Gama, are immortalized in stone along the ramps. At the point where the two ramps meet is a representation of Henry the Navigator, whose genius opened up new worlds. One of the stone figures is that of a kneeling Philippa of Lancaster, Henry's English mother; other figures symbolize Crusaders, navigators, monks, cartographers, and cosmographers. Don't be fooled by the dramatic sculptural quality of this monument's exterior: Beneath the heroic representations of figures crucial to the country's history, it contains a permanent exhibition on the role of the Portuguese in exploring the world, as well as temporary exhibition related to the Portuguese experience.

۞ Mosteiro dos Jerónimos (Jerónimos Monastery). Praça do Império. ☎ **21-362-00-34.** Church, free. Cloisters, 500$ ($2.80); children and seniors free. Tues–Sun 10am–5pm. Bus: 27, 28, 29, 43, or 49; tram: 15.

In an expansive mood of celebration, Manuel I, the Fortunate, ordered this monastery built in 1502 to commemorate Vasco da Gama's voyage to India and to give thanks to the Virgin Mary for its success. Manueline, the style of architecture to which the king contributed his name, combines Flamboyant gothic and Moorish influences with elements of the nascent Renaissance in Portugal. The 1755 earthquake damaged the monastery, and extensive restoration, some ill conceived, was carried out. The church interior is divided into a trio of naves, noted for their fragile-looking pillars. Some of the ceilings, like those in the monks' refectory, have a ribbed barrel vault. The "palm tree" in the sacristy is exceptional.

Museu de Marinha (Maritime Museum). Praça do Império. ☎ **21-362-00-19.** Admission 400$ ($2.25) adults, 200$ ($1.10) students; children under 9 and seniors free. Tues–Sun 10am–6pm; (to 5pm off-season). Bus: 27, 28, 29, 43, 49, or 51.

The pageant and the glory that characterized Portugal's domination of the high seas is evoked for posterity in the Maritime Museum, one of the most important in Europe. Appropriately, it's installed in the west wing of the Mosteiro dos Jerónimos. These royal galleys re-create an age of opulence that never feared excess, as exemplified by dragons' heads dripping with gilt and sea monsters coiling with abandon. The museum contains hundreds of models, from 15th-century sailing ships to 20th-century warships. In a special room is a model of the queen's stateroom on the royal yacht of Carlos I, the Bragança king who was assassinated at Praça do Comércio in 1908.

Museu de Arte Popular (Folk Art Museum). Av. de Brasília. ☎ **21-301-16-75.** 300$ ($1.70) adults; free for children 9 and under. Tues–Sun 10am–12:30pm and 2–5pm. Closed holidays. Bus: 27, 28, 29, 43, 49, or 51; tram: 15.

This is the most dramatic exhibition of the folk arts and customs of the Portuguese. The walls of the building are painted by contemporary artists, including Carlos Botelho, Eduardo Anahory, Estréla Faria, Manuel Lapa, Paulo Ferreira, and Tomás de Melo. The 1948 opening of the Folk Art Museum was a result of a campaign for ethnic revival directed by António Ferro. The collections—including ceramics, furniture, wickerwork, clothes, farm implements, and painting—are displayed in five rooms that correspond more or less to the provinces, each of which maintains its own distinct personality.

ELSEWHERE IN LISBON

✪ **Museu Nacional de Arte Antiga (National Museum of Ancient Art).** Rua das Janelas Verdes 9. ☎ **21-396-41-51.** Admission 500$ ($2.80) adults, 250$ ($1.40) students; children 13 and under free. Tues 2–6pm; Wed–Sun 10am–6pm. Bus: 27, 40, 49, or 60; tram: 15 or 18.

This museum occupies two connected buildings: a 17th-century palace and an added edifice built on the site of the old Carmelite Convent of Santo Alberto. The museum has many notable paintings, including the 15th-century famous polyptych from St. Vincent's monastery attributed to Nuno Gonçalves. Outstanding works are Hieronymus Bosch's triptych *The Temptation of St. Anthony;* Hans Memling's *Mother and Child;* Albrecht Dürer's *St. Jerome;* and paintings by Velázquez, Zurbarán, Poussin, and Courbet. Paintings from the 15th through the 19th century trace the development of Portuguese art, and the museum also exhibits a remarkable collection of gold- and silversmiths' work.

✪ **Museu de Fundação Calouste Gulbenkian.** Av. de Berna 45. ☎ **21-795-02-36.** Admission 500$ ($2.80) adults; children 9 and under and seniors free. Free for everyone on Sun. Wed–Sun 10am–6pm, Tues 2–6pm. Metro: Sebastião; bus: 16, 26, 31, 46, or 56.

Opened in 1969, this museum houses the collection of Armenian oil tycoon Calouste Gulbenkian—called by one critic "one of the world's finest private art collections." It covers Egyptian, Greek, and Roman antiquities; remarkable Islamic art; and vases, prints, and lacquerwork from China and Japan. European works include medieval illuminated manuscripts and ivories, 15th- to 19th-century painting and sculpture, 18th-century French decorative works, French impressionist painting, and Lalique jewelry and glassware. Notable are Gulbenkian's two Rembrandts, Rubens's *Portrait of Hélène Fourment,* and Renoir's *Portrait of Madame Claude Monet.*

✪ **Oceanario de Lisboa.** Parque das Nações. ☎ **21-891-7002.** Admission 1,500$ ($8) adults, 800$ ($4.50) students and children 12 and under. Daily 10am–7pm. Metro: Estação do Oriente.

This world-class aquarium remains as the most enduring, and impressive, achievement of EXPO '98, which was meant to propel Portugal into the consciousness of Europe and the world. Defined as the second-biggest aquarium in the world, exceeded in size only by an equivalent facility in Osaka, Japan, it's contained within a stone and glass building whose centerpiece is a 5 million-liter (1.3 million-gallon) holding tank. Its waters are divided into four distinct ecosystems replicating the Atlantic, Pacific, Indian, and Antarctic Oceans. Each is supplemented with land portions on which birds, amphibians, and reptiles flourish. Look for otters in the Pacific, penguins in the Antarctic, Polynesian trees and flowers in the Indian, and puffins, terns, and seagulls in the Atlantic.

ORGANIZED TOURS

Offering seven different year-round tours of Lisbon and its environs, **Star Travel,** travessa Escola Arauio 31 (☎ **21-352-00-00**), is popular with visitors who want to see the sights or get their bearings in and around the city. A daily half-day tour, "Touristic Lisbon" starts with a drive down avenida da Liberdade to Rossio, the heart of the city, and on every day but Monday and holidays the tour concludes at the Coach Museum, which houses the nation's largest collection of coaches. The price of the tour is 5,500$ ($31).

Offered on Tuesday and Thursday, **"Lisbon and the Blue Coast"** is a full-day tour that includes the same sites as "Touristic Lisbon," but which also crosses the Tagus in the afternoon for a drive along the Blue Coast through the "Three Castles" region of Sesimbra, Setubal, and Palmela. Included in the sightseeing is a stop for coffee at the Pousada do Castelo, and a visit to a wine cellar and handcrafts center at Azeitão. The cost is 13,500$ ($76). A similar half-day tour, offered daily, is **"Arrábida/Sesimbra,"** which includes the same stop as the afternoon of the "Blue Coast" tour, with an additional stop in the nature preserve on Arrábida Mountain. The cost is 8,900$ ($50).

For a different view, take the **"Lisbon by Night"** tour, offered on Monday, Wednesday, and Friday evenings throughout the year. The night tour includes the same city stops as the other tours and then delves into the old quarter of Alcântara. The evening concludes with dinner and drinks at a restaurant featuring entertainment by a *fadista*. The price of the tour is 11,000$ ($62) with two drinks at the restaurant, and 13,000$ ($73) for dinner and drinks. A nighttime offering on Tuesday, Thursday, or Saturday, the **"Casino Estoril"** tour has the same itinerary as "Lisbon by Night," but concludes with dinner and an international show at the casino located in the coastal resort of Estoril. The cost is 13,000$ ($73) with two drinks at the casino and 14,500$ ($81) with dinner.

THE SHOPPING SCENE

Baixa, between the Rossio and the Tagus, is a major shopping area. **Rua do Ouro (Street of Gold), Rua da Prata,** and **Rua Augusta** are the principal shopping streets. Another major upscale shopping artery is **Rua Garrett,** in the Chiado; to reach the area, you can take the Santa Justa elevator near the Rossio.

At the **Feira da Ladra,** you can experience the fun of haggling for bargains at an open-air street market. The vendors peddle their wares on Tuesday and Saturday. About a 5-minute walk from the waterfront in the Alfama, the market sits behind the Maritime Museum, adjoining the Pantheon of São Vicente. Start your browsing at Campo de Santa Clara in the Alfama. Portable stalls and individual displays are lined up on this hilly street with its tree-lined center.

AZUELJOS & PORCELEIN   The most unusual buys in Lisbon are *azulejos,* the decorated glazed tiles that are sought by collectors, and pottery from all over Portugal. Pottery with brightly colored roosters from Barcelos is legendary and blue-and-white pottery is made in Coimbra. Our favorites come from Caldas da Rainha, including yellow-and-green dishes in the shape of vegetables, fruit, and animals. Vila Real is known for its black pottery, and polychrome pottery comes from Aceiro. The red-clay pots from the Alentejo region are based on designs that go back to the Etruscans.

Founded in 1741 in the Chiado, ✪ **Sant'Anna,** rua do Alecrim 95–97 (☎ **21-342-25-37;** metro: Estação do Cais do Sodré), is Portugal's leading ceramic center, famous for its azulejos (glazed tiles). The showroom is on Rua do Alecrim, but you can also visit the factory at Calçada da Boa Hora 96; however, you make an appointment by calling ☎ **21-363-31-17).** ✪ **Vista Alegre,** largo do Chiado 18 (☎ **21-347-54-81;** metro: Chiado), turns out some of the finest porcelain dinner services in the country, along with objets d'art and limited editions for collectors and a range of practical day-to-day tableware.

GOLD   One of the very best buys in Portugal is gold. Gold is strictly regulated by the government, which requires jewelers to put a minimum of $19^1/4$ karats in the jewelry they sell. Filigree jewelry, made of fine gold or silver wire, is an art that dates from ancient times. ✪ **W. A. Sarmento,** rua áurea 251 (☎ **21-347-07-83;** metro: Rossio), is the most distinguished silver- and goldsmith in Portugal, specializing in lacy filigree jewelry, including charm bracelets. Well on its way to being a century old, the **Joalharia do Carmo,** rua do Carmo 87B (☎ **21-342-42-00;** metro: Rossio), is one of the best shops in Lisbon for gold filigree work.

ART & ANTIQUES   Along both sides of narrow **rua de S. José** are treasure troves of shops packed with antiques from all over the world. **Rua Dom Pedro V** is another street of antique shops. Near the Ritz Hotel, the **Galleria Sesimbra,** rua Castilho 77 (☎ **21-387-02-91;** metro: Marquês de Pombal), is a top art gallery, mainly displaying Portuguese artists. It was established in the 1970s by an expatriate Scotsman.

OTHER SELECT SHOPS   ✪ **Casa Quintão,** rua Serpa Pinto 12A (☎ **21-346-58-37;** metro: Chiado), is the showcase for Arraiolos carpets. Rugs sold here are priced by the square foot, according to the density of the stitching. Casa Quintão can reproduce intricate Oriental or medieval designs in rugs or tapestries as well as create any customized pattern. The shop, dating from 1880, also sells materials and gives instructions on how to make your own carpets and tapestry-covered pillows.

In the same building as the Hotel Avenida Palace, **Casa Bordados da Madeira,** rua 1 de Dezembro 137 (☎ **21-342-14-47;** metro: Restauradores), offers handmade embroideries from Madeira, and Viana. If you wish to place an order, the staff will mail it to you. ✪ **Casa Regional da Ilha Verde,** rua Paiva de Andrade 4 (☎ **21-342-59-74;** metro: Chiado), is handmade items, especially embroideries from the Azores—that's why it's called the "Regional House of the Green Island." You can get some good buys here. ✪ **Madeira House,** rua Augusta 131–135 (☎ **21-342-68-13;** metro: Chiado), specializes in high-quality regional cottons, linens, and gift items.

For something typically Portuguese, try **Casa das Cortiças,** rua da Escola Politécnica 4–6 (☎ **21-342-58-58;** metro: Rato). "Mr. Cork," the original owner, became somewhat of a legend in Lisbon for offering "everything conceivable" that could be made of cork, of which Portugal controls a hefty part of the world market. He's long gone, but the store carries on.

If you're looking for fado recordings, **Valentim de Carvalho,** Rossio 57 (☎ **21-322-44-00;** metro: Rossio), is the largest outlet in Portugal for records and tapes, with a staggering collection of fado music.

LISBON AFTER DARK

Consult **What's On in Lisbon,** available at most newsstands, for the latest listings. The local newspaper, **Diário de Notícias,** also carries cultural listings, but in Portuguese. No special discount tickets are offered, except that students get 50% off on tickets purchased for the national theater. Also of interest is **Agenda Cultural,** an

The Quintessential Lisbon Experience: Fado

Fado is Portugal's most vivid art form; no visit to Lisbon is complete without at least one night in one of the taverns where this traditional music is heard. Fado is typically sung by women, called *fadistas,* accompanied by guitar and viola. The songs express romantic longing and sadness, *saudade,* the country's sense of nostalgia for the past.

Adega Machado, rua do Norte 91 (☎ **21-347-05-50;** bus: 58 or 100), has passed the test of time and is still one of Portugal's favored fado clubs. Alternating with the fadistas are folk dancers whirling, clapping, and singing their native songs in colorful costumes. Dinner is à la carte, and the cuisine is mostly Portuguese, with a number of regional dishes. Expect to spend 5,000$ to 6,000$ ($28 to $34) for a complete meal. Dining starts at 8:30pm, and the doors don't close until 3am. The first show starts at 9:15pm. Cover (including two drinks) is 2,600$ ($15). It's open Tuesday to Sunday.

Every night at **A Severa,** rua das Gaveas 51 (☎ **21-346-40-06;** bus: 20 or 24), top fadistas sing, both male and female, alternating with folk dancers. In a niche you'll spot a statue honoring the club's namesake, Maria Severa, the legendary 19th-century Gypsy fadista who made fado famous. The kitchen turns out regional dishes based on recipes from the north of Portugal. Expect to spend from 6,000$ ($34) per person for a meal with wine. Cover (including two drinks) is 3,500$ ($20) and the club is open Friday to Wednesday 8pm to 3:30am.

Try to catch the tempestuous Fernanda Maria, the owner of **Lisboa a Noite,** rua das Gaveas 69 (☎ **21-346-85-57;** bus: 58 or 100), when she's about to make her first appearance of the evening. The 17th-century-style setting is rustic yet luxurious (this Bairro Alto club was once a stable). In the rear is an open kitchen and charcoal grill. The price of an average meal is around 8,000$ ($45). Cover (including two drinks) is 3,000$ ($17), and hours are Monday to Saturday 8pm to 3am; shows begin at 9:30pm.

Seemingly every fadista worth her shawl has sung at the old-time **Parreirinha da Alfama,** Beco do Espirito Santo 1 (☎ **21-886-82-09;** bus: 39 or 46), just a minute's walk from the docks of the Alfama. It's fado and fado only here, and it's open daily 8:30pm to 2:30am; music begins at 9:30pm. In the first part of the program, fadistas get all the popular songs out of the way, then settle in to their more classic favorites. You can order a good regional dinner for around 5,000$ ($28) as part of the experience, although many visitors opt to come here just for a drink. Cover (credited toward drinks) is 2,000$ ($11).

English-and Portuguese-language seasonal periodical that's available without charge at cafes, hotels, and at the Lisbon branch of the Portuguese tourist office. Inside, you'll find an abbreviated listing of musical, theatrical, and cultural choices available throughout the city.

THE PERFORMING ARTS

Teatro Nacional de São Carlos, rua Serpa Pinto 9 (☎ **21-346-59-14;** tram: 24, 28, or 28B; bus: 15 or 100), attracts opera and ballet aficionados from all over Europe. Top companies from around the world perform at this 18th-century theater; the season begins in mid-September and extends through July. The box office is open daily from 1 to 7pm. There are no special discounts. Tickets are 2,500$ to 9,600$ ($14 to $54).

Chamber-music and symphony concerts and ballet are presented at the **Teatro Municipal de São Luís,** rua António Maria Cardoso 40 (☎ 21-325-08-00; metro: Estação Cais do Sodré; tram: 10, 28, or 28B). Check locally to see if anything is featured when you are in Lisbon. Tickets range from 1,000$ to 2,500$ ($6 to $14).

Originally built in the 1840s, and restored after a disastrous fire in 1964, the **Teatro Nacional Doña Maria II,** Plaza Dom Piedro IV (Rossio) (☎ 21-342-22-10; metro: Rossio), ranks along with the Teatro San Carlos and the Teatro San Luis as the most important cultural venue in Lisbon. Despite its funding by the Ministry of Culture, it does not limit its repertoire to just Portuguese-language productions, although those are the most common. Thanks to government funding tickets are reasonably priced, costing 1,500$ to 3,000$ ($9 to $17). Students with a valid ID get a 50% discount.

From October to June, concerts, recitals, and occasionally ballet are performed at the **Museu da Fundação Calouste Gulbenkian,** av. de Berna 45 (☎ 21-793-51-31; metro: Sebastião; bus: 16, 18, 26, 31, 42, 46, or 56). Sometimes there are also jazz concerts. You'll have to inquire locally about what is happening at the time of your visit.

BARS

Bachus, largo da Trindade 9 (☎ 21-342-28-28; bus: 58 or 100), is a restaurant and a convivial watering spot. Amid Oriental carpets, fine hardwoods, bronze statues, and intimate lighting, you can hobnob with some of the most glamorous people in Lisbon. Late-night candlelit suppers are served in the bar. The array of drinks is international, costing from 600$ ($3.35). Open daily noon to midnight. There's no cover.

A longtime favorite of journalists, politicians, and foreign actors, the once-innovative **Procópio Bar,** Alto de San Francisco 21A (☎ 21-385-28-51; bus: 9), has become a tried-and-true staple. It might easily become your favorite bar—if you can find it. It lies just off Rua de João Penha, which itself lies off the landmark Praça das Amoreiras. It's open Monday to Saturday from 6pm to 3am. A mixed drink costs from 850$ ($4.75), whereas the price of beer begins at 600$ ($3.35). There's no cover. It's closed August 1 to 15.

Panorama Bar, in the Lisboa Sheraton Hotel, rua Latino Coelho 1 (☎ 21-357-57-57; metro: Picos; bus: 1, 2, 9, or 32), occupies the top floor of one of Portugal's tallest buildings, the 30-story Lisboa Sheraton. The view features the old and new cities, the mighty Tagus, and many towns on the river's far bank. Amid a decor of chiseled stone and stained glass, a polite uniformed staff serves you. You'll pay 1,400$ to 1,800$ ($8 to $10) for a whisky and soda. The bar is open daily 6pm to 2am. There's no cover.

Though the sophisticated restaurant draws many visitors, many people come to **The Bar of the Café Alcântara,** rua Maria Luisa Holstein 15 (☎ 21-363-71-76; bus: 12 or 18), for its bar. The bar is long and curvy, with accessories you might've expected in a railway car pulling into turn-of-the-century Paris. The bar is open nightly 8pm to 3. There's no cover.

You might find the Polynesian theme that permeates **Bora-Bora,** rua da Madalena 201 (☎ 21-887-20-43; metro: Rossio; tram: 12 or 28), to be unexpected and even a bit surreal, but despite that, its concept is all the rage in Lisbon today. Amid an artfully re-created jungle that's filled with images of the South Pacific, you'll hear recorded versions of ukulele music enjoy with a crowd of surfers on a beach. Drinks are fruited, flaming, sunset-colored, and potent. Beers cost 650$ ($3.65); mixed drinks begin at 1,100$ ($6). It's open Sunday to Thursday from 9pm to 2am and Friday and Saturday from 9pm to 3am. There's no cover. Although doors open nightly at 8pm, it's sort of sleepy till around 10pm, when crowds of hipsters tend to wake.

PORT WINE TASTING   A bar devoted exclusively to the drinking and enjoyment of port in all its known types, **Solar do Vinho do Porto,** rua de São Pedro de Alcântara 45 (☎ **21-347-57-07;** bus: 58 or 100), lies near the Bairro Alto and its fado clubs. You enter what appears to be a private living room that offers a relaxing atmosphere enhanced by an open stone fireplace. Owned and sponsored by the Port Wine Institute, Solar displays many artifacts related to the industry. But the real reason for dropping in during the day is for its *lista de vinhos*—there are more than 200 wines from which to choose. Solar is not far from the upper terminus of the Gloria funicular. It's open Monday to Saturday 2pm to midnight. A glass of wine costs 200$ ($1.10) to 4,210$ ($24).

GAY & LESBIAN BARS

Since the collapse of Salazar and the new openness of Lisbon nightlife, at least eight gay bars have sprung up in the district known as **Príncipe Real.** The dark pink **Agua No Bico Bar,** rua de São Marçal 170 (☎ **21-347-28-30;** bus: 15, 58 or 100; tram: 24), is lined with movie posters and filled mainly with young men and the hottest bartenders in Lisbon. You won't see any sign out in front, but there's a discreet brass plaque set on a steeply sloping street lined with dignified 18th-century villas. Recorded music plays in an atmosphere that might remind you of an English pub—but with Iberian art work. Beer costs from 400$ ($2.25); whisky and soda begins at 600$ ($3.35). It's open nightly from 9pm to 2am. There's no cover.

In the narrow streets of the Bairro Alto, **Memorial Bar,** Rua Gustavo de Matos Sequeira 42A (☎ **21-396-88-91;** bus: 58 or 100), is a "household word" for dozens of lesbians, who consider it one of the premier networking sites in Portugal. This small and rather cramped disco with ample bar space welcomes newcomers. There's an occasional round of live entertainment; otherwise, the place is low-key and unpretentious. A beer costs 600$ ($3.35). It's open Tuesday to Saturday from 10pm to 4am, but disco music begins at midnight. On Sunday it's open 4 to 8pm. Cover is 1,000$ ($6).

Queens, rua de Cintura do Porto de Lisboa, Armazém 8, Naves A&B, Doca de Alcantara Norte (☎ **21-395-58-70;** tram: 15), is one of the most frequented gay nightclubs in Lisbon, larger than any of its competitors, and outfitted with an enormous dance floor that's flooded with late-breaking music from a sophisticated sound system. Most of the hip crowd is gay, male, and under 35, although today, in spite of its name, the club also attracts straights. It's open Monday to Saturday 10pm to 6am, or sometimes later, depending on the energy level of the dance floor. Cover is 1,000$ ($6).

DANCE CLUBS

As its name implies, **Docks,** avenida 24 de Julio, at Centro Mare (☎ **21-395-08-56;** tram 15), is adjacent to the Tagus in Alcântara and has windows overlooking the river. Sophisticated and stylish, with a decor that's one of the most beautiful in the neighborhood, it has a 30-ish crowd. It's open Tuesday to Saturday 11:30pm to 6am. Cover is 1,000$ ($6) if full, otherwise free.

Kremlin, Escadinhas da Praia 5 (☎ **21-390-87-60;** bus: 32, or 37), the most energetic and iconoclastic of Lisbon's dance clubs, welcomes a very hip crowd of techno and garage music lovers into an angular and metallic-looking environment that's an artfully surreal takeoff on pomposity of what used to be known as the Soviet dictatorship. Some of that dictatorship lives on in the doorman who evaluates each patron, as they did in the heyday of New York's Studio 54, letting in what he perceives as the young and trendy. It's open Tuesday and Sunday from 11pm to 5am. Cover is 1,000$ ($6).

If you're up for late-night, high-energy partying with student-aged hipsters who like to dance, **Model's,** Travessa Teixeira Junior 6 (☎ **21-363-39-59;** bus: 4, 27, 28, 32;

tram: 15, 18), is the place to go. Within a large and echoing space whose bartops and dance floors are virtually indestructible, you'll find a musical venue that changes every night of the week, and which, according to the preferences of management and the DJs, includes tribal underground, techno, garage, house, and on some nights, a scattering of salsa and merengue. It opens at 11:30pm, staying open till 4am every Tuesday to Sunday. Cover is 1,200$ ($7).

Rock City, rua Cintura do Porto de Lisboa, Armazém (Warehouse) 225 (☎ 21-324-86-36; tram: 15), is one of the few venues in Lisbon devoted to the presentation of live music. In a funky and artfully battered environment that includes guitars hanging from the walls and an airplane suspended from the ceiling, you'll appreciate live rock 'n' rollers performing from a stage near a bar that can get very busy. Regrettably, this place seems to focus on performances by a limited number of bands who appear again and again, usually emulating the hits of such '70s and '80s greats as Bruce Springsteen and Queen. Beer begins at 600$ ($3.35) a bottle. The club opens every night-rather every morning at 2am, remaining open until 7am. Cover (credited toward drinks) is 1,000$ ($6) on Friday and Saturday only.

A DAY TRIP TO THE COSTA DO SOL: THE PORTUGUESE RIVIERA

Lisbon's environs are so intriguing that many fail to see the capital itself, lured by Guincho (near the westernmost point in continental Europe), the Mouth of Hell, and Lord Byron's "glorious Eden" at Sintra. You could spend a day drinking in the wonders of the pretty pink rococo palace at Queluz or enjoying seafood at the Atlantic beach resort of Cascais.

The **Costa do Sol** is the string of beach resorts forming the Portuguese Riviera on the northern bank of the mouth of the Tagus. If you arrive in Lisbon when the sun is shining and the air balmy, consider heading for this cabana-studded shoreline. So near to Lisbon is Estoril that it's easy to dart in and out of the capital to see the sights or visit the fado clubs, while you spend your nights in a hotel by the sea. An inexpensive electric train leaving from the Cais do Sodré in Lisbon makes the trip frequently throughout the day and evening, ending its run in Cascais.

The Riviera is a microcosm of Portugal. Ride out on the train, even if you don't plan to stay there. Along the way you'll pass pastel-washed houses, with red-tile roofs and facades of antique blue and white tiles; miles of modern apartment dwellings; rows of canna, pines, mimosa, and eucalyptus; swimming pools; and in the background, green hills studded with villas, chalets, and new homes. The sun coast is sometimes known as the Costa dos Reis, the "coast of kings," because of all the deposed royalty who have settled there—everybody from exiled kings to pretenders, marquesses from Italy, princesses from Russia, and baronesses from Germany.

ESTORIL   The first stop is 24km (15 miles) west of Lisbon. This chic resort has long basked in its reputation as a playground of monarchs. The **Parque Estoril,** in the town center, is a well-manicured piece of landscaping, a subtropical setting with plants swaying in the breeze. At night, when it's floodlit, you can go for a stroll. The palm trees studding the grounds have prompted many to call it "a corner of Africa." At the top of the park sits the **casino,** offering not only gambling but also international floor shows, dancing, and movies.

Across the railroad tracks is the **beach,** where some of Europe's most fashionable women sun themselves on the peppermint-striped canvas chairs along the Tamariz Esplanade. The atmosphere is cosmopolitan and the beach sandy, unlike the pebbly strand at Nice. If you don't want to swim in the polluted ocean, you can check in at an oceanfront pool for a plunge.

CASCAIS   Just 6km (4 miles) west of Estoril and 30km (19 miles) west of Lisbon, Cascais has more of a Portuguese atmosphere than Estoril, even though it has been increasingly overbuilt. That Cascais is growing is an understatement: It's leapfrogging! Apartment houses, new hotels, and the finest restaurants along the Costa do Sol draw a never-ending stream of visitors every year.

However, the life of the simple fisher folk still goes on. Auctions, called *lotas,* at which the latest catch is sold, still take place on the main square, though a modern hotel has sprouted up in the background. In the small harbor, rainbow-colored fishing boats share space with pleasure craft owned by an international set that flocks to Cascais from early spring until autumn.

The most popular excursion outside Cascais is to the ✪ **Boca de Inferno (Mouth of Hell).** Reached by heading out the highway to Guincho, then turning left toward the sea, the Boca deserves its ferocious reputation. At their peak, thundering waves sweep in with such power and fury they long ago carved a wide hole (*boca*) in the cliffs. However, if you should arrive when the sea is calm, you'll wonder why it's called a cauldron. The Mouth of Hell can be a windswept roar if you don't stumble over too many souvenir hawkers.

The three sandy **beaches** at Cascais are almost as overcrowded as those at Estoril, and the waters here are less polluted but contaminated nonetheless. Hotel pools remain the safer choice. Though there's a dangerous undertow, the best beach—at least from the standpoint of lying on the sand—is Praia do Guincho, around Cabo da Roca, right outside Cascais. The beach has dunes and is mostly uncrowded and relatively pollution free. The continental winds make it a favorite for surfers.

QUELUZ   At the Estação Rossio in Lisbon, take the Sintra line train 15km (9 miles) northwest to Queluz. Trains depart every 15 minutes (trip time: 30 minutes). After leaving the train station in Queluz, take a left turn and follow the signs to the ✪ **Palácio de Queluz,** largo do Palácio (☎ 21-435-00-39), a brilliant example of the rococo in Portugal. Pedro III ordered its construction in 1747, and the work dragged on until 1787. What you see now isn't exactly what it was in the 18th century. Queluz suffered a lot during the French invasions, and almost all its belongings were transported to Brazil with the royal family. A 1934 fire destroyed a great deal of Queluz, but tasteful reconstruction has restored the lighthearted aura of the 18th century. Inside, you can wander through the queen's dressing room, lined with painted panels depicting a children's romp; the Don Quixote Chamber (Dom Pedro was born here and returned from Brazil to die in the same bed); the Music Room, complete with a French grande pianoforte and an 18th-century English harpsichord; and the mirrored throne room adorned with crystal chandeliers. The palace is open Wednesday to Monday (except holidays) from 10am to 1pm and 2 to 5pm. Admission is 500$ ($2.80). It's always free for anyone under 14, and free for general admission every Sunday morning.

SINTRA   Sintra, 29km (18 miles) northwest of Lisbon, is a 45-minute train ride from the Estação Rossio in Lisbon. Lord Byron called it a "glorious Eden," and so it remains. Visitors flock here not only to absorb the town's beauty and scenic setting but also to visit two major sights.

Opening onto the central town square, the ✪ **Palácio Nacional de Sintra,** largo da Rainha D. Amélia (☎ 21-923-00-85), was a royal palace until 1910. Much of it was constructed in the days of the first Manuel, the Fortunate. Two conical chimney towers form the most distinctive landmark on the Sintra skyline. The Swan Room was a favorite of João I, one of the founding kings, father of Henry the Navigator and husband of Philippa of Lancaster. The Room of the Sirens or Mermaids is one of the most elegant in the palace. In the Heraldic or Stag Room, coats-of-arms of aristocratic Portuguese families and hunting scenes are depicted. The palace is rich in paintings and Iberian and Flemish tapestries. But it's at its best when you wander into a tree- and plant-shaded patio and listen to the fountain. Admission is 400$ ($2.25) for adults, half-price for children 6 to 16, and free for anyone 5 and under. The palace is open Thursday to Tuesday 10am to 1 and 2 to 5pm.

Towering over Sintra, the **Palácio Nacional da Pena,** Estrada de Pena (☎ 21-923-02-27), sits on a plateau about 450m (1,500 feet) above sea level. At the top the castle is a soaring agglomeration of towers, cupolas, and battlemented walls. Crossing over a drawbridge, you'll enter the palace proper, whose last royal occupant was Queen Amélia in 1910. Pena has remained much as Amélia left it, which is part of its fascination; it emerges as a rare record of European royal life in the halcyon days preceding World War I. Admission is 475$ ($2.65), free for anyone 14 and under. The palace is open October to May Tuesday to Sunday 10am to 1pm and 2 to 5pm (last admittance at 4:30pm); June to September Tuesday to Sunday 10am to 1pm and 2 to 6:30pm (last admittance 6pm).

2 The Algarve

The maritime province of the Algarve, often called the "garden of Portugal," is the southwesternmost part of Europe. Its coastline stretches 160km (100 miles)—all the way from Henry the Navigator's Cape St. Vincent to the border town of Vila Real de Santo António. The varied coastline contains sluggish estuaries, sheltered lagoons, low-lying areas where the cluck of the marsh hen can be heard, long sandy spits, and promontories jutting out into the white-capped aquamarine foam. Called Al-Gharb by the Moors, the land south of the *serras* (hills) of Monchique and Caldeirão remains a spectacular anomaly that seems more like a transplanted section of the North African coastline. The countryside abounds in vegetation: almonds, lemons, oranges, carobs, pomegranates, and figs.

Many Moorish and even Roman ruins remain. In the character of its fret-cut chimneys, mosquelike cupolas, and cubist houses, a distinct Oriental flavor prevails. Phoenicians, Greeks, Romans, Visigoths, Moors, and Christians all touched this land. However, much of the historic flavor is gone forever, swallowed by a sea of dreary high-rise apartment blocks surrounding most towns. Many former fishing villages, now summer resorts, dot the Algarvian coast: Carvoeiro, Albufeira, Olhão, Portimão. The sea is still the source of life, as it always has been. The marketplaces in the villages sell esparto mats, copperwork, pottery, and almond and fig sweets that are sometimes shaped like birds and fish.

Our tour stretches along the coast, beginning at Lagos, 264km (164 miles) south of Lisbon. From Lagos the road 34km (21 miles) west to Sagres (N-125) generally has minor traffic, unlike in the rest of the Algarve.

LAGOS

Lagos, known to the Lusitanians and Romans as Locobriga and to the Moors as Zawaia, became an experimental shipyard of caravels during the time of Henry the Navigator. Edged by the Costa do Ouro (Golden Coast), the Bay of Sagres at one point in its epic history was big enough to allow 407 warships to maneuver with ease. An ancient port city (one historian traced its origins back to the Carthaginians 3 centuries before the birth of Christ), Lagos was well known by the sailors of Admiral Nelson's fleet.

Actually, not that much has changed since Nelson's day. The reasons to go to Lagos are to enjoy the pleasures of table and beach. In winter, the almond blossoms match the whitecaps on the water and the climate is often warm enough for sunbathing. In town, the flea market sprawls through narrow streets, the vendors selling rattan baskets, earthenware pottery, fruits, vegetables, crude furniture, cutlery, knitted shawls, and leather boots.

Just down the coast, the hustle and bustle of market day is forgotten as the rocky headland of the Ponta da Piedade (Point of Piety) appears. This spot is the most beautiful on the entire coast. Amid the colorful cliffs and secret grottoes carved by the waves are the most flamboyant examples of Manueline architecture.

ESSENTIALS

GETTING THERE   By Ferry & Train   From Lisbon's praça do Comércio, take the ferry across the Tagus to Barreiro. From there, make connections with the Southern Line Railway on its run to Lagos (☎ **21-888-40-25** for information). Three trains per day depart from Lisbon (trip time: 6¹/₂ hours). Tickets cost from 1,900$ ($11) one way.

By Bus   Eight **Rodoviária** buses (☎ **21-357-77-15**) a day make the run between Lisbon and Lagos (trip time: 5 hours) and cost 2,650$ ($15) one way.

By Car   Take N-120 south of Lisbon to Lagos.

VISITOR INFORMATION   The Lagos Tourist Office is at largo Marquês de Pombal (☎ **282-76-30-31**).

WHERE TO STAY

✪   **Casa de São Gonçalo da Lagos.** Rua Cândido dos Reis 73, 8600 Lagos. ☎ **282-76-21-71.** Fax 282-76-39-27. 13 units. TEL. 15,000$–17,000$ ($84–$95) double. Rates include breakfast. AE. Free parking on street if available. Closed Nov–Mar.

This pink villa, with its fancy iron balconies, dates from the 18th century. At the core of Lagos, the antiques-filled home is almost an undiscovered gem. Most of the public lounges and rooms turn, in the Iberian fashion, to the inward peace of a sun-filled patio. All the furnishings are individualized: hand-embroidered linens, period mahogany tables, and ornate beds from Angola. Street-level rooms can be noisy.

Hotel de Lagos. Rua Nova da Aldeia 1, 8600 Lagos. ☎ **282-76-99-67.** Fax 282-76-99-20. E-mail: lagos@mail.telepac.pt. 315 units. A/C TV TEL. 10,960$–27,300$ ($61–$153) double; 15,000$–30,000$ ($84–$168) suite. Rates include breakfast. AE, DC, MC, V. Free parking outside, 1,000$ ($6) garage.

A 20th-century castle of Moorish and Portuguese design, Hotel de Lagos has its own ramparts and moats (a pool and a paddling pool). Standing at the eastern side of the old town, far removed from the beach, this first-class hotel is spread over a hilltop overlooking Lagos; no matter which room you get, you'll have a view, even if it's a courtyard with semitropical greenery. Some rooms have ground-level patios, but most are on the upper six floors; you have a choice of standard or deluxe rooms. The 31-room wing, complete with pool and health club, was added in 1989, and the hotel has its own beach club a mile away.

WHERE TO DINE

Alpendre. Rua António Barbosa Viana 17. ☎ **282-76-27-05.** Reservations recommended. Main courses 1,600$–3,600$ ($9–$20). AE, DC, MC, V. Daily noon–11pm. PORTUGUESE.

Alpendre offers one of the most elaborate and sophisticated menus along the Algarve, but, considering the lackluster competition, that's not saying too much. The food is

The Algarve

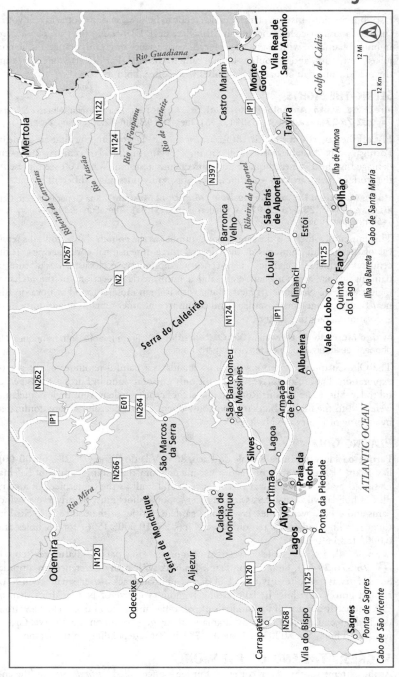

tasty, but the portions aren't large. Service tends to be slow, so don't come here if you're rushed. House specialties include shellfish rice, steak Diane, and fillet of sole sautéed in butter, flambéed with cognac, and served with a sauce of cream, orange and lemon juices, vermouth, and seasonings known only to the chef. For dessert you can opt for the mixed fruits flambé or crepes flambés with coffee, both for two.

SEEING THE SIGHTS

Igreja de Santo António (Church of St. Anthony). Rua General Alberto Silveira. ☎ **282-76-23-01.** Admission 350$ ($1.95). Tues–Sun 9:30am–12:30pm and 2–5pm.

Just off the waterfront sits this 18th-century church. Decorating the altar are some of Portugal's most notable rococo gilt carvings. Begun in the 17th century, they were damaged in the 1755 earthquake but subsequently restored. What you see represents the work of many artisans—at times, each apparently pursuing a different theme.

Museu Municipal Dr. José Formosinho (Municipal Museum). Rua General Alberto Carlos Silveira. ☎ **282-76-23-01.** Admission 350$ ($1.95). Tues–Sun 9:30am–noon and 2–5pm. Closed holidays.

This museum, which has the same phone number as the church above, contains replicas of the fret-cut chimneys of the Algarve, three-dimensional cork carvings, 16th-century vestments, ceramics, 17th-century embroidery, ecclesiastical sculpture, a painting gallery, weapons, minerals, and a numismatic collection. In the archaeological wing are Neolithic artifacts, along with Roman mosaics found at Boca do Rio near Budens, fragments of statuary and columns, and other remains of antiquity from excavations along the Algarve.

Antigo Mercado de Escravos (Old Customs House). Praça Infante Dom Henríques. No phone. Free admission. Open for viewing any time.

The Old Customs House, now in ruins, stands as a painful reminder of the age of exploration. The arcaded slave market, the only one of its kind in Europe, looks peaceful today, but under its four Romanesque arches captives taken from their homelands were sold to the highest bidders. The house opens onto a peaceful square dominated by a statue of Henry the Navigator.

PLAYING GOLF

Parque da Floresta, Budens, Vale do Poco, 8650 Vila do Bispo (☎ **282-69-00-00**), lies 16km (10 miles) west of Lagos, just inland from the fishing hamlet of Salema. Designed by Spanish architect Pepe Gancedo and built as the centerpiece of a complex of holiday villas, it offers sweeping views. Some shots must be driven over vineyards and others over ravines, creeks, and gardens. Critics of the course have cited its rough grading and rocky terrain. Greens fees are 10,000$ ($56) for 18 holes and 6,000$ ($33.60) for 9.

Some 4km (2½ miles) west of Lagos is the par-71 **Palmares** course (☎ **282-76-29-61**), designed by Frank Pennink with many differences in altitude. Some fairways require driving a ball across railroad tracks, over small ravines, or around groves of palms. Its landscaping is more evocative of North Africa than of Europe, partly because of its hundreds of palm, fig, and almond trees. The view from the 17th green is among the most dramatic of any golf course on the Algarve. Greens fees for 18 holes are 6,000$ to 10,000$ ($34 to $56), depending on the season.

SAGRES: "THE END OF THE WORLD"

At the extreme southwestern corner of Europe—once called *o fim do mundo* (the end of the world)—Sagres is a rocky escarpment jutting into the Atlantic Ocean. It was from here that Henry the Navigator, the Infante of Sagres, launched Portugal and the rest of Europe on the seas of exploration. Here he established his school of navigation, where Magellan, Diaz, Cabral, and even Vasco da Gama apprenticed. Henry died in 1460, before the great discoveries of Columbus and Vasco da Gama, but the later explorers owed a debt to him. A virtual ascetic, he brought together the best navigators, cartographers, geographers, scholars, sailors, and builders, infused them with his rigorous devotion, and methodically set Portuguese caravels upon the Sea of Darkness.

ESSENTIALS

GETTING THERE   By Bus   Some 10 **Rodoviária** buses (☎ 282-76-29-44) per day head west from Lagos to Sagres (trip time: 1 hour). A one-way ticket costs 450$ ($2.50).

By Car   From Lagos, drive west on N-125 to Vila do Bispo, where you head south along N-268 to Sagres.

VISITOR INFORMATION   Until Sagres gets a full-time tourist office, these functions will be performed by a privately run travel agency: **Turifo,** praça da República (☎ 282-62-00-03).

WHERE TO STAY

Hotel da Baleeira. Sítio da Baleeira, Sagres, 8650 Vila do Bispo. ☎ **282-624-212.** Fax 282-624-425. E-mail: hotel.baleeira@mail.telepac.pt. 118 units. TV TEL. 18,600$ ($104) double. Rates include breakfast. AE, DC, MC, V. Free parking.

In a ship's-bow position, Hotel da Baleeira is a first-class whaleboat (*baleeira* in Portuguese) spread out above the fishing port with vessels tied up in the harbor. The largest hotel on this land projection, it offers rooms with sea-view balconies. The hotel has nearly doubled the number of its rooms in recent years; the older ones are quite small and some have linoleum floors. Bathrooms are also tiny.

If you're exploring the Algarve and are in Sagres just for the day, you can stop and order lunch or dinner in a dining room cantilevered toward the sea, where every seat has a view. The chef has his own lobster tanks, and the meals are well prepared. Meals begin at 2,500$ ($14). There's also a cocktail lounge, an angular saltwater pool with a snack bar, a flagstone terrace, a tennis court, and a private sandy beach.

Pousada do Infante. Ponta da Atalaia, 8650 Sagres. ☎ **282-642-222.** Fax 282-642-225. www.pousadas.pt. 39 units. MINIBAR TV TEL. 16,300$–25,000$ ($91–$140) double; 20,800$–31,000$ ($117–$174) suite. Rates include breakfast. AE, DC, MC, V. Free parking.

Pousada do Infante, the best address at Sagres, seems like a monastery built by ascetic monks who wanted to commune with nature. You'll be charmed by the rugged beauty of the rocky cliffs, the pounding surf, the sense of the ocean's infinity. Built in 1960, the glistening white-painted government-owned tourist inn is spread along the edge of a cliff projecting rather daringly over the sea. It boasts a long colonnade of arches with an extended stone terrace set with garden furniture. The public rooms are generously proportioned, gleaming with marble and decorated with fine tapestries depicting the exploits of Henry the Navigator. On the second floor are midsize, rather sterile rooms with private balconies. Rooms 1 to 12 are the most desirable. Guests can order the traditional lunch or dinner of the pousadas. Have a before-dinner drink on the terrace. Facilities feature an outdoor saltwater pool, riding stables, and a tennis court; room service is offered. An official annex of the pousada, the Fortaleza do Belixe (see "Where to Dine," below), offers less luxurious rooms.

WHERE TO DINE

Fortaleza do Belixe. Fortaleza do Belixe, Vila do Bispo, 8650 Sagres. ☎ **282-62-41-24.**
Main courses 980$–4,000$ ($6–$22); fixed-price menu 3,500$ ($20). AE, MC, V. Daily 1–3pm
and 7:30–9:30pm. Closed Nov 15–Feb 15. From Sagres, drive west for 5km (3 miles) along
the coastal road, following the signs to Cabo de São Vicente. PORTUGUESE/INTERNATIONAL.

Set on a sandy and rocky stretch of the coastal road stretching between Sagres and the
southwesternmost tip of Portugal, Cabo de São Vicente, this establishment occupies
the much-restored remnants of a medieval fortress built around the heyday of Henry
the Navigator. Although each of its four dining rooms enjoys a partial, or angled, view
of the nearby sea, one in particular offers a wider panorama—ask for it specifically if
you're absolutely enamored of a sea view. The menu offerings are simple, straightforward, and flavorful, and include such items as caldo verde; a tasty fish soup; fried or
grilled squid; grilled swordfish; well-prepared but uncomplicated versions of veal,
pork, and beef; and whatever fresh fish happens to be available from the local market.

In addition to its restaurant, the establishment maintains a quartet of rooms, each
with TV and telephone. With breakfast included, doubles cost 16,000$ ($90).

EXPLORING THE AREA

Both the cape and Sagres (especially from the terrace of the pousada) offer a view of
the sunset. To the ancient world, the cape was the last explored point, although in time
the Phoenicians pushed beyond it. Many mariners thought that when the sun sank
beyond the cape, it plunged over the edge of the world and thus to venture around the
promontory was to face the demons of the unknown.

Today, at the reconstructed site of Henry's windswept fortress on Europe's Land's
End (named after the narrowing westernmost tip of Cornwall, England), you can see
a huge stone compass dial, Venta de Rosa, that Henry is alleged to have used in the
naval studies pursued at Sagres. Housed in the fortress is a small museum of minor
interest that documents some of the area's history. Admission is 300$ ($1.70), and it's
open Tuesday to Sunday from 10am to noon and 2 to 6pm. At a simple chapel,
restored in 1960, sailors are said to have prayed for help before setting out into
unchartered waters. The chapel is closed to the public.

The promontory of Cabo de São Vicente is 5km (3 miles) away. The cape is so
named because, according to legend, the body of St. Vincent arrived mysteriously here
on a boat guided by ravens. Others claim that the body of the patron saint, murdered
at Valencia, Spain, washed up on Lisbon's shore. A lighthouse, the second most powerful in Europe, beams light 100km (60 miles) across the ocean. It's generally open
daily from 8am to noon and 2 to 9pm, but you must get permission from the gate-
keeper to climb it. Here, seagulls glide on the air currents, and on the approach, a few
goats graze on a hill where even the trees are bent from the gusty winds.

No buses connect the cape with Sagres. You must go by car.

OUTDOOR ACTIVITIES

BEACHES Many beaches fringe the peninsula—some attracting nude bathers.
Mareta, at the bottom of the road leading from the center of town toward the water,
is not only the best but the most popular. Rock formations can be seen jutting far out
into the Atlantic. East of town is **Tonel,** also a good sandy beach. The beaches west of
town, **Praia de Baleeira** and **Praia de Martinhal,** are better for windsurfing than for
swimming.

EXPLORING If you'd like to rent a **bike** to explore the cape, go to **Turinfo,** praça
da República in Sagres (☎ **282-62-00-03**). The charge is 1,200$ ($7) per half day. It

also offers **Jeep tours** of the natural preserve of the cape, including lunch, at a cost of 6,900$ ($39).

PRAIA DA ROCHA

En route to Praia da Rocha, off N-125 between Lagos and Portimão, 18km (11 miles) away, you'll find several good beaches and rocky coves, particularly at **Praia dos Três Irmãos** and **Alvor.** But the most popular seaside resort on the Algarve is the creamy yellow beach of Praia da Rocha. At the outbreak of World War II there were only two small hotels on the Red Coast, but nowadays Praia da Rocha is booming, as many have been enchanted by the spell cast by its shoreline and climate.

It's named the Beach of the Rock because of its beautiful sculptural rock formations. At the end of the mussel-encrusted cliff, where the Arcade flows into the sea, are the ruins of the **Fort of St. Catarina,** whose location offers many views of Portimâo's satellite, Ferragudo, and of the bay.

To reach Praia da Rocha from Portimão, you can catch a bus for the 2.5km (1½-mile) trip south. Service is frequent. Algarve buses aren't numbered but are marked by their final destination, such as Praia da Rocha.

WHERE TO STAY

✪ **Bela Vista.** Av. Tómas Cabreira, Praia da Rocha, 8500 Portimão. ☎ **282-450-480.** Fax 282-41-53-69. 14 units. MINIBAR TV TEL. 10,000$–23,000$ ($56–$129) double; 15,000$–34,000$ ($84–$190) suite. Rates include breakfast. AE, DC, MC, V. Free parking.

The Bela Vista, an artfully rustic Moorish-style mansion built during the last century by a wealthy family as a summer home, is set atop its own palisade, with access to a sandy cove where you can swim. In addition to a minaret-type tower at one end of its facade, there's a statue of the Virgin set into the masonry of one of the corners. The villa is ideal for those who respond to the architecture of the past and those who make a reservation way in advance. It's flanked by the owner's home and a simple cliff-edge annex shaded by palm trees. The entry hall has an art nouveau bronze torchère and a winding staircase, with walls almost covered with 19th-century blue and white tiles. Rooms facing the sea, the former master bedrooms, are the most desirable, though all rooms have character. Decorations vary from an inset tile shrine to the Virgin Mary to crystal sconces.

Residencial Sol. Av. Tomás Cabreira 10, Praia da Rocha, 8500 Portimão. ☎ **282-42-40-71.** Fax 282-41-71-99. 22 units. TEL. 8,000$–8,500$ ($45–$48) double; 9,500$ ($53) suite. Rates include breakfast. AE, DC, MC, V. Free parking.

The painted concrete facade of this hotel appears somewhat bleak, in part because of its location near the noisy main street. In this case, however, appearances are deceiving, since the rooms are some of the cleanest, most unpretentious, most attractive in town. Each is designed for two. Those in back are quieter, but the terrace-dotted front units look across the traffic toward a bougainvillea-filled park. The breakfast lounge doubles as a TV room.

WHERE TO DINE

Titanic. Edifício Colúmbia, Rua Engenheiro Francisco Bivar. ☎ **282-42-23-71.** Reservations recommended, especially in summer. Main courses 1,600$–2,800$ ($9–$20). AE, DC, MC, V. Daily 7–11pm. Closed Nov 27–Dec 27. INTERNATIONAL.

Complete with gilt and crystal, the 100-seat air-conditioned Titanic is the most elegant restaurant in town. From its open-view kitchen, it serves the best food, including shellfish and flambé dishes. Even though it's named after the ill-fated luxury liner, it's not on the water but in a modern residential complex. You can dine very well here on such appealing dishes as the fish of the day, pork fillet with mushrooms, prawns à *la plancha* (grilled), Chinese fondue, and sole Algarve. Service is among the best at the resort.

PLAYING GOLF

Vale de Pinta (Pestana Golf), Praia do Carvoeiro (☎ 282-34-09-00), are twin par-72 courses, sharing a clubhouse and staff. They're set amid a landscape of tawny rocks and arid hillocks. Both of them route their players through groves of twisted olive, almond, carob, and fig trees. Views from the fairways, designed in 1992 by Californian Ronald Fream, sweep over the low masses of the Monchique mountains, close to the beach resort of Carvoeiro. Experts cite the layout of these two courses as one of the most varied set of challenges in the competitive world of Portuguese golf. Clusters of bunkers, barrier walls, and abrupt changes in elevation make the course complicated. Greens fees are 8,500$ to 12,000$ ($48 to $67) per person.

PRAIA DOS TRÊS IRMÃOS & ALVOR

You can also visit **Praia dos Três Irmãos (the Beach of the Three Brothers)** for its beach, even if you prefer not to stay here. It's just a 5km (3-mile) drive southwest of Portimão, or you can reach it or the tourist development at Alvor by bus. Service is frequent throughout the day. At Praia dos Três Irmãos, you get 14km (9 miles) of burnished golden sand, broken only by an occasional crag riddled with arched passages. This beach has been discovered by skin divers who explore its undersea grottoes and shoreside cave.

Its neighbor is the whitewashed fishing village of **Alvor,** where Portuguese and Moorish arts and traditions have mingled since the Arabs gave up their 500 years of occupation. Alvor was a favorite coastal haunt of João II. The summer hordes descend on the long strip of sandy beach here. It's not the best in the area, but at least you have space.

WHERE TO STAY

✪ **Carlton Alvor Hotel.** Praia dos Três Irmãos, Alvor, 8500 Portimão. ☎ **282-45-89-00.** Fax 282-45-89-99. E-mail: pestana.hotels@mail.telepac.pt. 216 units. A/C MINIBAR TV TEL. Summer 35,000$–39,300$ ($196–$220) double; from 40,000$ ($224) suite. Rates include buffet breakfast. AE, DC, MC, V. Free parking.

This citadel of hedonism is so self-contained you may never stray from the premises. On a landscaped crest, the luxury hotel has many rooms exposed to the ocean view, gardens, and Olympic-size pool. Rooms are decorated in a classically modern style; most contain oversize beds. Many have private balconies where you can eat breakfast with a view of the Bay of Lagos. Those to avoid are in the rear with so-so views, small balconies, and Murphy beds. Bathrooms are well designed with double basins and lots of towels. The bilevel main dining room boasts three glass walls so every guest has an ocean view. The Grill Maisonette is your best bet. Facilities include a health club.

Le Meridien Penina Golf Hotel. Montes de Alvor, 8502 Portimão. ☎ **800/225-5843** in the U.S., or 282-41-54-15. Fax 282-41-50-00. E-mail: meridienaalg.sm@mail.telepac.pt. 213 units. A/C MINIBAR TV TEL. 42,000$–50,000$ ($235–$280) double; 70,000$–130,000$ ($392–$728) suite. Children 3–11 stay free in parents' room. Rates include breakfast. AE, DC, MC, V. Free parking. Closed Sept 3–Dec 20.

The first deluxe hotel on the Algarve was the Penina Golf, between Portimão and Lagos, a major sporting mecca. Most rooms contain picture windows and honeycomb balconies, with views of the course and pool or vistas of the Monchique hills. Standard rooms are furnished pleasantly, combining traditional pieces with Portuguese provincial spool beds. All are spacious and contain good-sized beds; the so-called attic rooms

Silves: Ghosts of Crusaders & Moors

When you pass through the Moorish-inspired entrance of this hillside town, you'll quickly realize that Silves is unlike other Algarve towns and villages. It lives in the past, recalling its heyday when it was known as Xelb, the seat of Muslim culture in the south before it fell to the crusaders. Christian warriors and earthquakes have been rough on the town.

To reach Silves from Portimão, drive on N-125 east for 8km (5 miles) to Lagoa, a market town that is the junction with N-124 leading 7km (4¹/₂ miles) north to Silves. There is bus service to Silves 8 times a day.

The red-sandstone **Castle of Silves,** crowning the hilltop, may date from the 9th century. From its ramparts you can look down on the saffron-mossed tile roofs of the village houses and the narrow cobbled streets where roosters strut and scrappy dogs sleep peacefully in the doorways. Once the blood of the Muslims, staging their last stand in Silves, "flowed like red wine," as one Portuguese historian wrote, and the cries and screams of women and children resounded over the walls. Inside the walls, the government has planted a flower garden, adorning it with golden chrysanthemums and scarlet poinsettias. In the fortress, water rushes through a huge cistern and a deep well made of sandstone. Below are dungeon chambers and labyrinthine tunnels where the last of the Moors hid out before the crusaders found them and sent them to their deaths.

The 13th-century former **cathedral of Silves** (now a church), down below, was built in the Gothic style. You can wander through its aisles and nave, noting the beauty in their simplicity. Both the chancel and the transept date from a later period, having been built in the Flamboyant Gothic style. The Christian architects who originally constructed it may have torn down an old mosque. Many of the tombs contained here are believed to have been the graves of crusaders who took the town in 1244. The structure is one of the most outstanding religious monuments in the Algarve.

Stop for lunch or dinner at **Ladeira,** Ladeira de São Pedro 1 (☎ **282-44-28-70**). This rustic restaurant is known to virtually everyone in its neighborhood on the western outskirts of Silves. It features grilled fish, home cooking, and regional specialties. Steak Ladeira and mixed-fish *cataplana* (a local stew) are especially good. In season, game like partridge or rabbit is often served. Main courses run 1,200$ to 1,800$ ($7 to $10) and there's a set menu for 1,600$ ($9). It's open Monday to Saturday, noon to 3pm and 6 to 10pm. American Express, MasterCard, and Visa are accepted.

have the most charm, with French doors opening onto terraces. You can dine at any of four restaurants. Facilities include three championship golf courses (one 18 hole and two 9 hole), a private beach with its own snack bar and changing cabins reached by shuttle bus, a pool, and six floodlit hard tennis courts.

WHERE TO DINE

Restaurante O Búzio. Aldeamento da Prainha, Praia dos Três Irmãos. ☎ **282-45-87-72.** Reservations recommended. Main courses 2,500$–4,000$ ($14–$22). AE, DC, MC, V. Daily 7–10:30pm. Closed Nov–Dec. INTERNATIONAL.

This restaurant stands at the end of a road encircling a resort development dotted with exotic shrubbery. Lunch and dinner are served in separate locations, dinner in a room where blue curtains reflect the color of the shimmering ocean you can see at the bottom of the cliffs. Your dinner might include fish soup, gazpacho, carre de borrego Serra da Estrela (grantinée of roast lamb with garlic, butter, and mustard), Italian pasta dishes, or lamb kabobs with saffron-flavored rice. The wine cellar is extensive.

PLAYING GOLF

Penina, Apartado 146 (☎ **282-41-54-15**), lies 5km (3 miles) west of Portimão, farther west than many of the other great golf courses of the Algarve. Completed in 1966, it was one of the first courses here and the universally acknowledged masterpiece of British designer Sir Henry Cotton. It occupies what was once a network of marshy rice paddies, on level terrain that critics said was unsuited for anything except wetlands. The solution involved planting groves of eucalyptus (350,000 trees in all), which grew quickly in the muddy soil, eventually drying it out enough to bulldoze dozens of water traps and a labyrinth of fairways and greens. The course wraps itself around a luxury hotel (the Meridien Penina). Greens fees are 13,500$ ($76) for 18 holes, whereas greens fees for each of the two 9-hole courses are 3,000$ to 4,000$ ($17 to $22) each.

ALBUFEIRA

The cliff-side town of Albufeira, formerly a fishing village, is the St-Tropez of the Algarve. The lazy life, sunshine, and beaches make it a haven for young people and artists, though the old-timers still regard the invasion that began in the late 1960s with some ambivalence. Some residents open the doors of their cottages to those seeking a place to stay. Travelers without the money often sleep in tents on the cliff or under the sky.

The big, bustling resort retains characteristics more closely associated with a North African seaside community. Its streets are steep, and the villas are staggered up and down the hillside. Albufeira rises above a sickle-shaped **beach** that shines in the bright sunlight. A rocky grottoed bluff separates the strip used by the sunbathers from the working beach, where brightly painted fishing boats are drawn up on the sand. Beach access is through a passageway tunneled through the rock.

ESSENTIALS

GETTING THERE   By Train   Trains connect Albufeira with Faro (see below), which has good connections to and from Lisbon. The train station is 6km (4 miles) north of the center, but buses run back and forth to the resort every 30 minutes. The fare is 175$ ($1) one way. Call ☎ **289-80-17-26** for information and schedules.

By Bus   Buses run between Albufeira and Faro every hour; the trip takes 1 hour and costs 570$ ($3.20) one way. Seven buses per day link Portimão with Albufeira, also a 1-hour trip. This trip costs 700$ ($3.90). Call ☎ **289-58-97-55** for information and schedules.

By Car   From Portimão, take N-125 east; from Faro, take N-125 west.

VISITOR INFORMATION   The **Tourist Information Office** is on rua 5 de Outubro (☎ **289-58-52-79**).

WHERE TO STAY

Estalagem do Cerro. Rua Samora Barros, 8200 Albufeira. ☎ and fax **289-58-61-91.** 95 units. A/C TV TEL. 12,000$–16,000$ ($67–$90) double. AE, DC, MC, V. Free parking on street if available.

Estalagem do Cerro captures Algarvian charm yet doesn't neglect modern amenities. This "Inn of the Craggy Hill" is just east of the center at the top of a hill overlooking Albufeira's bay, about a 10-minute walk down to the beach. The older regional-style building has been renovated, but its character has been maintained; it's joined to a modern structure in a similar Moorish style. The tasteful rooms have verandas overlooking the sea, pool, or garden. A panoramic dining room provides good meals. On most nights, guests can dance to disco music, and be provided with some kind of entertainment Monday to Friday. The inn has an outdoor heated pool in a garden setting.

Hotel Montechoro. Rua Alexandre O'Neill, (Apartado 928), 8200 Albufeira. ☎ **289-58-94-23.** Fax 289-58-99-47. E-mail: reservas@grupomontechoro.com. 362 units. A/C TV TEL. 14,600$–29,800$ ($82–$167) double, 21,800$–44,500$ ($122–$249) suite. Rates include buffet breakfast. AE, V. Parking 250$ ($1.40).

This is the largest hotel in and around Albufeira, a four-star resort set in the vacation-oriented suburb of Montechoro, about a mile northeast of Albufeira's center. Rooms are done in a modern and somewhat streamlined style, opening onto views of the sun-baked countryside. The hotel's only drawback is its lack of a beach adjacent to its grounds, though management supplies frequent minivans to both Oura Beach, about a mile away, and the bar-packed center of Albufeira. Dining choices include the Restaurant Montechoro and the more formal Grill das Amendoeiras, on the panoramic fifth floor. Facilities include two pools, eight professional tennis courts, two squash courts, a sauna, and a gym.

WHERE TO DINE

O Cabaz da Praia. Praça Miguel Bombarda 7. ☎ **289-51-21-37.** Reservations recommended. Main courses 2,400$–5,800$ ($13–$33). AE, MC, V. Fri–Wed noon–2:30pm and 7–10:30pm. FRENCH/PORTUGUESE.

The 3-decade-old "Beach Basket" sits on a colorful little square near the Church of São Sebastião, now a museum. In a former fisher's cottage, the restaurant has an inviting ambience and good food. With its large sheltered terrace, it offers diners a view over the main Albufeira beach. Main courses, including favorites like cassoulet of seafood, salade océane, and monkfish with mango sauce, are served with fresh vegetables. The restaurant is renowned for its lemon meringue pie and for its soufflés. If you're visiting in winter call first.

VALE DO LOBO

Almancil, 13km (8 miles) west of Faro and 24km (15 miles) east along N-125 from Albufeira, is a small market town of little interest, yet it's a center for two of the most exclusive tourist developments along the Algarve: **Vale do Lobo,** 6km (4 miles) southeast of Almancil, and **Quinta do Lago,** 10km (6 miles) southeast of town. Both are a golfer's paradise.

WHERE TO STAY

Hotel Dona Filipa. Vale do Lobo, 8136 Almancil ☎ **289-39-41-41.** Fax 289/39-42-88. E-mail: gm1298@fortehotel.com. 162 units. A/C MINIBAR TV TEL. 31,000$–52,000$ ($174–$291) double; 55,000$–68,000$ ($308–$381) junior suite; 74,000$–107,000$ ($414–$599) deluxe suite. Rates include breakfast. AE, DC, MC, V. Free parking.

Dona Filipa is a deluxe golf hotel with impressive grounds embracing 210ha (450 acres) of rugged coastline. The exterior is somewhat uninspired, but a greater dimension was brought to the interior with green-silk banquettes, marble fireplaces, Portuguese ceramic lamps, and old prints over baroque-style love seats. The well-furnished rooms have balconies. The hotel includes a grill restaurant serving an à la carte menu and, by the pool, a coffee shop offering lunch. Facilities include three tennis courts and discounts on greens fees at nearby golf courses.

⊙ Quinta do Lago. Quinta do Lago, 8135 Almancil. ☎ **800/223-6800** in the U.S., or 289-39-66-66. Fax 289-39-63-93. www.quintadologohotel.com. E-mail: info@quintadologohotel.com. 141 units. A/C MINIBAR TV TEL. 35,000$–72,000$ ($196–$403) double; from 85,000$ ($476) suite. Rates include breakfast. AE, DC, MC, V. Free parking.

This hotel is associated with the massive Quinta do Lago resort development, a sprawling, 750ha (1,600-acre) estate that incorporates private villas, golf courses, beachfront, swimming pools, and a host of resort-oriented amenities. The contemporary buildings in Mediterranean style rise three to six floors. Rooms are generally spacious, with balconies that open onto views of the estuary. The Navegadores is an informal grill room overlooking a pool. Facilities include a riding center, one of the best in southern Europe; a 27-hole golf course, designed by American William F. Mitchell, among the top six in Europe; tennis courts; indoor and outdoor pools; a health club and solarium.

WHERE TO DINE

Casa Velha. Quinta do Lago. ☎ 289-39-49-83. Reservations recommended. Main courses 3,800$–4,600$ ($21–$26); fixed-price menu 7,500$ ($42). AE, MC, V. Mon–Sat 7:30–10:30pm. FRENCH.

Casa Velha is an excellent choice. It's not part of the Quinta do Lago resort but overlooks the resort's lake from a century-old farmhouse. The menu is French, with a scattering of Portuguese and international dishes as well. Specialties include a salad of chicken livers and gizzards with leeks and vinaigrette and roasted duck en service (the staff presents different parts of the bird throughout the meal, beginning with the thighs en confit and ending with the breast en magret). Other choices are carefully flavored sea bass, délices of sole, and lobster salad flavored with an infusion of vanilla.

⊙ Restaurant Ermitage. Estrada Almancil-Vale de Lobo. ☎ 289-39-43-29. Reservations recommended. Main courses 3,200$–4,500$ ($18–$25); set menu 9,500$ ($53). AE, MC, V. Tues–Sat 7–10:30pm. Closed 3 weeks in Dec., 2 weeks in Jan, and 1 week in June. From Almancil, drive 3km (2 miles) south, following the signs to Vale de Lobo. ITALIAN/SWISS/INTERNATIONAL.

Our favorite restaurant in the region occupies an 18th-century farmhouse. Surrounded by gardens and flowering vines and built from locally quarried stone, its focal point is a cozy dining room whose fireplaces add warmth in winter and whose outdoor terrace adds beauty in summer. Starters include goose-liver terrine with blackberry sauce and a "symphony of homemade pastas" surrounding a portion of shrimp and spinach-stuffed ravioli with four other pastas and sauces. Main courses, which change with the season and the chef's inspiration, include grilled fish of the day with herb-flavored hollandaise sauce and fillet of monkfish with prawn-and-curry sauce. A favorite dessert is a walnut-flavored parfait with freshly made ice cream and mocha sauce. Your hosts, and the restaurant's manager and chef, are the Dutch-born Willemina Gilhooley and her husband, Vincent.

PLAYING GOLF

Vale do Lobo, Vale do Lobo, 8135 Almancil (☎ 289-39-39-39), has played an important role in establishing Portugal's image as a golfer's mecca. Its name, which means valley of the wolf, suggests some forlorn spot set amid bleak terrain—this course is hardly that. It was designed by British golfer Henry Cotton as three nine-hole courses identified as the Green, the Orange, and the Yellow, but a recent addition of another nine-hole course has caused the management to reconfigure the Green and Orange courses into the 18-hole Oceanfront Course, and the Yellow and (newest of all) the Blue Course into the 18-hole Royal Course. Some of the long shots along both of these courses require driving the ball over ravines, where variable winds make a straight shot difficult. Greens fees, depending on the day of the week, range from 8,000$ to 11,000$ ($45 to $62) for nine holes and 13,500$ to 18,000$ ($76 to $101) for 18 holes.

Since its opening in 1991, **Vila Sol,** Alto do Semino (☎ **289-30-05-05**), has been judged as having the best fairways and the boldest and most inventive contours of any course in the Algarve. Designed by English architect Donald Steel, it's part of a 170ha (362-acre) residential estate. Great care was taken in allowing the terrain's natural contours to determine the layout of the fairways and greens. Vila Sol was selected as host to the Portuguese Open 2 years in a row (1992 and 1993). Golfers especially praise the configuration of holes 6, 8, and 14, which collectively manage to funnel golf balls around and over ponds, creek beds, and pine groves in nerve-racking order. Par is 72, and greens fees for 18 holes are 9,000$ to 15,000$ ($50 to $84).

The most famous and sought-after of this complex's trio of golf courses is the **Vilamoura Old Course,** sometimes called Vilamoura I (☎ **289-31-03-41**), laid out in 1969 by noted English architect Frank Pennink. Its design, texture, and conception are the most English of south Portugal's golf courses, and it's invariably cited for its beauty, its lushness, and the maturity of its trees and shrubberies. Though some of its holes are almost annoyingly difficult (four of them have pars of 5), the course is among the most consistently crowded on the Algarve. Its par is 73, and greens fees are 18,000$ ($101) for 18 holes.

Adjacent to the Old Course are a pair of newer less sought-after courses. They include the **Pinhal Golf Course,** formerly known as Vilamoura II (☎ **289-32-15-62**), noted for the challenging placement of its many copses of pines. Greens fees cost between 5,250$ to 10,500$ ($29 to $59), depending on the season and the time of day. Nearby is the newest of the three, **Laguna Golf Course,** Vilamoura III (☎ **289-31-01-80**), known for its labyrinth of water traps and lakes. Greens fees range from 5,250$ to 8,500$ ($29 to $48), depending on the season and the time of day. Tee-offs in the heat of noon are less expensive than the more sought-after early mornings. Pars for both Pinhal and Laguna are 72.

Quinta do Lago also has superb facilities and is one of the most elegant "tourist estates" on the Algarve. This pine-covered beachfront property has been the retreat of everybody from movie stars to European presidents. The resort's 27 superb holes of golf are also a potent lure.

Of the four golf courses that undulate across the massive Quinta do Lago development, the par-72 ✪ **São Lourenço** (☎ **289-39-65-22**), is the most interesting, challenging, and prestigious. Set amid the grassy wetlands of the Rio Formosa Nature Reserve, home to millions of waterfowl, its contours were crafted by American golf designers William (Rocky) Roquemore and Joe Lee. In 1997, *Golf World* magazine voted it the second most-desirable course in continental Europe as part of its annually revised rating systems. Ironically, although the hotel lies within the confines of Quinto do Logo, it's closely associated with the Meridien Doña Felipa Hotel in Vale do Lobo, 7km (4¹/₂ miles) to the west. The most panoramic hole on this course is the sixth; the most frustrating are the 8th and 18th. Many long drives, especially those aimed at the 17th and 18th holes, soar over the waters of a saltwater lagoon. Greens fees are 12,500$ ($70) for nine holes and 24,000$ ($134) for 18 holes.

Quinta do Lago (☎ **289-39-07-00**), the namesake course of the massive development, is actually composed of two 18-hole golf courses. Quinta do Lago and Rio Formosa. Together they comprise more than 280ha (600 acres) of sandy terrain abutting the Rio Formosa Wildlife Sanctuary. Very few long drives here are over open water; instead, the fairways undulate through cork forests, groves of pine trees, and terrain with sometimes abrupt changes in elevation. Greens fees run 7,500$ ($42) for nine holes and 15,000$ ($84) for 18 holes.

Pinheiros Altos, Quinta do Lago (☎ 289-39-43-40), is one of the most deceptive golf courses on the Algarve, with contours that even professional golfers cite as being far more difficult than they appear at first glance. Abutting the wetland refuge of the Rio Formosa National Park, its 120ha (250 acres) of terrain, designed by U.S. architect Ronald Fream, are dotted with umbrella pines and with dozens of small lakes at nine of the course's 18 holes. Carts navigate their way around the terrain on cobble-covered paths. The par is 73. Greens fees are 7,500$ ($42) for nine holes and 15,000$ ($84) for 18 holes.

FARO

Once loved by the Romans and later by the Moors, Faro is the main city of the Algarve. Since Afonso III drove out the Moors for the last time in 1266, Faro has been Portuguese. On its outskirts an international jet airport brings in thousands of visitors every summer. The airport has done more than anything else to speed tourism not only to Faro but also to the entire Algarve.

ESSENTIALS

GETTING THERE   By Plane   You can fly to Faro from Lisbon in 45 minutes. For **flight information,** call ☎ **289-80-08-01.** You can take bus 14 or 16 to the railway station in Faro. The bus operates daily 7:10am to 9:45pm, leaving every 45 minutes. The one-way fare is 175$ ($1).

By Train   Trains arrive in Faro from Lisbon six times a day (trip time: 4 to 7 hours). One-way fares cost 2,175$ ($12). For rail information in Faro, call the **railway station** at Largo Estação (☎ **289-80-17-26**). For information in Lisbon, dial ☎ **21-888-40-25.**

By Bus   Buses arrive every hour from Lisbon after a 4¹/₂-hour journey. The **bus station** is on avenida da República (☎ **289-89-97-60**), adjacent to the railway station. One-way ticket costs 2,300$ ($13).

By Car   After leaving Vale do Lobo, continue east along N-125 directly into Faro.

VISITOR INFORMATION   The **Tourist Office** is at rua da Misericórdia 8–12 (☎ **289-80-36-04**). At the tourist office, you can pick up a copy of the Algarve Guide to Walks, which will direct you on nature trails in the area.

WHERE TO STAY

Eva. Av. da República, 8000 Faro. ☎ **289-80-33-54.** Fax 289-80-23-04. 148 units. A/C MINIBAR TEL. 16,000$–25,000$ ($90–$140) double; 23,500$–39,400$ ($132–$221) suite. Rates include breakfast. AE, DC, MC, V. Free parking on street if available.

Eva dominates the harbor like a fortress. This modern five-story hotel occupies an entire side of the yacht-clogged harbor. It was beginning to look worn and tired, but a recent rejuvenation has perked it up. There are direct sea views from most rooms, which are furnished in a restrained, even austere, style; some contain minibars. The better rooms open onto the water with large balconies. The Eva's best features are its penthouse restaurant and rooftop pool.

WHERE TO DINE

Dois Irmãos. Largo do Terreiro do Bispo 13–15. ☎ **289-82-33-37.** Reservations recommended. Main courses 950$–3,500$ ($5–$20); set price menu 1,800$ ($10). AE, MC, V. Daily noon–11pm. PORTUGUESE.

This popular Portuguese bistro, founded in 1925, has a no-nonsense atmosphere, yet it has its devotees. The menu is as modest as the place and its prices, but you get a good choice of fresh fish and shellfish. Ignore the paper napkins and concentrate on the fine kettle of fish placed before you. Clams in savory sauce is a favorite, and sole is regularly featured—of course, everything depends on the catch of the day. Service is slow but amiable.

Restaurante Cidade Velha. Rua Domingos Guieiro 19. ☎ **289-82-71-45.** Reservations recommended. Main courses 1,500$–2,500$ ($8–$14). AE, DC, V. Mon–Fri 12:30–2pm and 7:30–10:30pm, Sat 7:30–10:30pm. PORTUGUESE/INTERNATIONAL.

The leading restaurant in town is the Cidade Velha, which used to be one of the best private homes in Faro. You'll find it behind the cathedral, with thick stone walls that were built at least 250 years ago. Your meal will be served in one of a pair of rooms, each with a vaulted brick ceiling. The cookery is first rate, as you'll agree as you feast on smoked swordfish with horseradish, roast rack of lamb with rosemary, roast duck with apricot sauce, or fillet of pork stuffed with dates and walnuts and flavored with port wine.

SEEING THE SIGHTS

The most bizarre attraction in Faro is the **Capela d'Ossos (Chapel of Bones),** entered via a courtyard from the rear of the **Igreja (Church) de Nossa Senhora do Monte do Carmo do Faro,** on largo do Carmo. Erected in the 19th century, this chapel is completely lined with the skulls and bones of human skeletons, an extraordinarily ossicular rococo. In all, it's estimated that there are 1,245 skulls. The chapel is open Monday to Friday 10am to 1pm and 2:30 to 5pm, Saturday 10am to 1pm. Entrance is free to the church but 250$ ($1.40) to the chapel.

Other religious monuments include the old **Sé (cathedral),** largo da Sé, built in the Gothic and Renaissance styles (originally a Muslim mosque stood on this site); and the **Igreja de São Francisco,** largo de São Francisco, with panels of glazed earthenware tiles in milk white and Dutch blue depicting the life of the patron saint. The church is open Monday to Friday 10am to 5pm, Saturday 10am to 1:30pm. Entrance to the church is 250$ ($1.40). Yes, they charge admission to enter the church, somewhat of a rarity in Portugal. Sunday masses are conducted Sunday at 10am and 11am (no charge then, of course).

But most visitors don't come to Faro to look at churches. Rather, they take the harbor ferry to the wide white-sand beaches called the **Praia de Faro,** on an islet. The ride is available only in summer. The beach is also connected to the mainland by bridge, a distance of 6km (4 miles) from the town center. Once here, you can water-ski and fish or just rent a deck chair and umbrella and lounge in the sun.

DAY TRIPS FROM FARO

OLHÃO   Olhão, described as the living re-creation of a Georges Braque collage, is the famous cubist town of the Algarve, so long beloved by painters. In its heart, white blocks stacked one on the other, with flat red-tile roofs and exterior stairs on the stark walls, evoke the aura of the Casbahs of North African cities. But let us not paint too romantic a portrait. Many readers have found it disappointing—dirty, dusty, and too commercial.

If you do go here, try to attend the **fish market** near the waterfront when a *lota* (auction) is underway. Olhão is also known for its bullfights of the sea, in which fishermen wrestle with struggling tuna trapped in nets and headed for the smelly warehouses along the harbor.

For the best view, climb **Cabeça Hill,** its grottos punctured with stalagmites and stalactites, or **St. Michael's Mount,** offering a panorama of the Casbah-like Barreta. Finally, for what is one of the most idyllic beaches on the Algarve, take a 10-minute motorboat ride to the **Ilha de Armona,** a nautical mile away. Olhão is 10km (6^1/$_2$ miles) west of Faro and is reached by going east on N-125.

SÃO BRAS DE ALPORTEL   Traveling north from Faro for 20km (12^1/$_2$ miles), you'll pass through groves of figs, almonds, and oranges, through pine woods where resin collects in wooden cups on the tree trunks. At the end of the run, you'll come on isolated São Bras de Alportel, one of the Algarve's most charming and least-known spots.

Far from the crowded beaches, it attracts those wanting pure air, peace, and quiet— a bucolic setting filled with flowers pushing through nutmeg-colored soil. Northeast of Loulé, this whitewashed, tile-roofed town rarely gets lively except on **market days.** Like its neighbor, Faro, it's noted for its perforated plaster chimneys. Lying at the foot of the Serra do Caldeirão, the whole area has been called one vast garden.

A change of pace from the seaside accommodations is offered at **Pousada de Sao Bras,** Estrada de Lisboa, N2, 8150 Saõ Brás de Alportel (☎ **289-84-23-05**). The government-owned inn built in 1942 is a hilltop villa, with fret-cut limestone chimneys and a crow's-view of the surrounding serras. Many visitors arrive just for lunch or dinner (daily 12:30 to 3pm and 7:30 to 10pm). The 3,650$ ($20) table d'hôte menu offers soup, a fish course, a meat dish, vegetables, and dessert. The cuisine is plain but good. The pousada, the third one built in Portugal, also offers 22 well-furnished rooms, each with air-conditioning, minibar, TV, telephone. The cost is 24,600$ ($138) a day with breakfast included. American Express, MasterCard, and Visa are accepted.

VILA REAL DE SANT ANTÓNIO/MONTE GORDO

Twenty years after the marquês de Pombal rebuilt Lisbon, which had been destroyed in the 1755 earthquake, he sent architects and builders to Vila Real de Santo António, where they reestablished the frontier town on the bank opposite Spain. It took only 5 months. Pombal's motivation was jealousy of Spain. Much has changed, of course, though Praça de Pombal remains. An obelisk stands in the center of the square, which is paved with inlays of black and white tiles radiating like rays of the sun. Separated from its Iberian neighbor by the Guadiana River, Vila Real de Santo António offers a car-ferry between Portugal and Ayamonte, Spain.

Today, Vila Real is a mostly residential and industrial community that prides itself on its royal and antique associations as a border town. It's supplemented today by Monte Gordo, a town whose buildings mostly date from the 1920s and later. Set 3km (2 miles) to the east, it's the site of most of the region's tourist facilities and hotels, with easier access to the sandy beaches that attract tourists every summer from as far away as northern Europe.

ESSENTIALS

GETTING THERE   By Train   The railway facilities in Vila Real are bigger, better accessorized, and more convenient than those in Monte Gordo, which is the site of a railway stopping point but not a bona-fide station. In Vila Real, however, 11 trains per day arrive from Faro (trip time: 2^1/$_2$ hours). Tickets are 500$ ($2.80) each way. Four direct trains arrive from Lagos (even more if you count the ones that require transfers en route), each taking 4^1/$_2$ hours and costing 890$ ($5) each way. For railway information and schedules, call ☎ **21-888-40-25.**

By Bus   It's faster to take the bus from Faro to Vila Real. Five *espressos* per day arrive from Faro (trip time: 1 hour). The cost is 710$ ($4). Eight buses arrive from Lagos (trip time: 4 hours). Call ☎ **289-89-96-61** for information. Buses pull into Vila Real at the bus station on the avenida Da República.

By Car   From Faro, take N-125 85km (53 miles) east to reach our final destination, at the Spanish frontier.

VISITOR INFORMATION   The **tourist office** is on Avenida Infante Henrique in Monte Gordo (☎ **281-54-44-95**).

WHERE TO STAY

In Vila Real

Hotel Apolo. Av. dos Bombeiros Portugueses, 8900 Vila Real de Santo António. ☎ **281-51-24-48.** Fax 281-51-24-50. 42 units. A/C TV TEL. 10,500$–20,000$ ($59–$112) double. Rates include breakfast. AE, DC, MC, V. Free parking.

Hotel Apolo, built in the mid-1980s, lies on the western edge of town as you enter from Monte Gordo or Faro. Near the beach and the river, it attracts vacationers as well as travelers who don't want to cross the Spanish border at night. The hotel is a marginal choice, with a spacious marble-floored lobby leading into a large bar scattered with comfortable sofas and flooded with sunlight. Each of the simply furnished rooms has a balcony.

✪ Hotel Guadiana. Av. da República 94, 8900 Vila Real de Santo António. ☎ **281-51-14-82.** Fax 281-51-14-78. 39 units. A/C TV TEL. 15,000$ ($84) double; from 17,000$ ($95) suite. Rates include breakfast. AE, DC, MC, V. Free parking.

This is the best hotel in town (which isn't saying a lot), housed in a mansion classified as a historic national monument. Close to the river and the Spanish border, it's ideally located for exploring the town, not far from Santo António beach and near the beach attractions of Monte Gordo. Azulejos (decorated tiles) line some of the walls. Rooms are traditional and old-fashioned but have modern amenities. There's a cozy bar, and breakfast is the only meal served.

In Monte Gordo

Hotel Alcázar. Rua de Ceuta, Monte Gordo, 8900 Vila Real de Santo António. ☎ **281-51-01-84.** Fax 281-51-01-49. 97 units. A/C MINIBAR TV TEL. 22,000$ ($123) double; 24,000$–29,000$ ($134–$162) suite. Rates include breakfast. AE, DC, MC, V.

Hotel Alcázar is the best at the resort and was last renovated in 1994. A free-form pool is built on terraces into the retaining walls that shelter it from the wind and extend the hot-weather season late into autumn. The interior is a vaguely Arab-style series of repetitive arches and vaults of distressed concrete. Each rather austere unit contains its own sun terrace and a radio. The basement disco is open in summer. An alluring spot is under the soaring ceiling of the in-house restaurant, where formal meals (rather standard fare) are served.

Hotel dos Navegadores. Monte Gordo, 8900 Vila Real de Santo António. ☎ **281-51-08-60.** Fax 281-51-08-79. 431 units. A/C TEL. 13,000$–26,000$ ($73–$146) double; 32,250$–50,000$ ($181–$280) suite. Rates include breakfast. AE, DC, MC, V. Free parking.

This hotel is popular with vacationing Portuguese and British families, who congregate under the dome covering the atrium's pool. The public rooms are clean and functional, and about three-fourths of the standardized rooms have balconies. The beach is only a 5-minute walk away. There are dull boutiques in a corridor near the pool, along with a hairdresser and a coffee shop. The hotel restaurant serves Portuguese and international dishes (dinner only).

Hotel Vasco da Gama. Av. Infante Dom Henrique, Monte Gordo, 8900 Vila Real de Santo António. ☎and fax **281-51-09-01.** E-mail: vagama@mail.telepac.pt. 172 units. A/C TV TEL. 11,500$–13,000$ ($64–$73) double; 13,500$–26,000$ ($76–$146) suite. Rates include breakfast. AE, DC, MC, V. Free parking.

The entrepreneurs here know what their guests seek—lots of sunbathing and swimming. Though this hotel enjoys a position on a long, sandy beach, it also offers an Olympic pool with a high-dive board and nearly an acre of flagstoned sun terrace. All the Spartan rooms are furnished conservatively, and glass doors open onto balconies. There's an oceanfront dining room.

WHERE TO DINE

Edmundo. Av. da República 55. ☎ **281-54-46-89.** Reservations recommended. Main courses 1,500$–2,800$ ($8–$16). AE, DC, MC, V. Mon–Sat noon–3pm and 7–10pm, Sun 7–10pm. PORTUGUESE.

Edmundo has long been known in the Algarve, attracting Spaniards who often visit just for the day. It overlooks the river and Spain across the water—try to get a sidewalk table. The people who run this place are friendly and proud of their repertoire of local cuisine, especially fresh fish. You might begin with shrimp cocktail, then follow with fried sole, crayfish, or sautéed red mullet. You can also order such meat dishes as lamb cutlets and veal fillet.

EXPLORING VILA REAL

A long esplanade, **Avenida da República,** lines the river, and from its northern extremity you can view the Spanish town across the way. Gaily painted **horse-drawn carriages** take you sightseeing past the shipyards and the lighthouse.

A short drive north on the road to Mertola will take you to the gull-gray castle-fortress of **Castro Marim.** This formidable structure is a legacy of the old border wars between Spain and Portugal. The ramparts and walls watch Spain across the river. Afonso III, who expelled the Moors from this region, founded the original fortress, which was razed by the 1755 earthquake. Inside the walls are the ruins of the **Church of São Tiago,** dedicated to St. James.

Directly southwest of Vila Real is the emerging resort of **Monte Gordo,** which has the greatest concentration of hotels in the eastern Algarve after Faro. Monte Gordo is the last in a long line of Algarvian resorts; it's 3km (2 miles) southwest of the frontier town of Vila Real de Santo António at the mouth of the Guadiana River. Its wide beach, one of the finest along the southern coast of Portugal, is backed by pine-studded lowlands.

Sadly, this was once a sleepy little fishing village. Now young men tend to work in the hotels instead of on the sea, fishing for tips instead of tunny. Monte Gordo has succumbed to high-rises; it often attracts Spaniards from across the border. It has many good hotels, and a number of Europeans use it as their place in the Algarvian sun.

Scotland 15

by Darwin Porter & Danforth Prince

Whether you go to Scotland to seek out your ancestral roots, explore ancient castles, drive the Malt Whisky Trail, or partake in the internationally acclaimed Edinburgh Festival, you'll find a country rich in history, legend, and romance. If it's the outdoors you love, Scotland offers great salmon fishing, peaceful walks in heather-covered Highland hills, and some of the best (and oldest) golf courses.

1 Edinburgh & Environs

Called one of Europe's fairest cities, the "Athens of the North," Edinburgh is the second most visited city in Britain after London. It's a "white-collar" city in contrast to industrialized bastions like Aberdeen and Glasgow. Home of the Royal Mile, Princes Street, and the ever-growing Edinburgh Festival with its action-packed list of cultural events, Edinburgh is both hip and historic. John Knox, Mary, Queen of Scots, Robert Louis Stevenson, Sir Arthur Conan Doyle, Alexander Graham Bell, Sir Walter Scott, Bonnie Prince Charlie, and Deacon Brodie are all part of the city's past; you can walk in their footsteps and explore sights associated with them.

ORIENTATION

GETTING THERE   By Plane   Edinburgh is 632km (393 miles) north of London, about an hour's flying time. **Edinburgh Airport** (☎ **0131/333-1000** for flight info) lies 10km (6 miles) west of the city's center. Flights from within the British Isles and Europe land here; most transatlantic flights go to Glasgow's airport. A double-decker Airlink bus makes the trip between the airport and the city center every 10 minutes, letting you off near Waverley Bridge, between Old Town and New Town; the one-way fare is £3.30 ($6). A taxi suitable for up to 4 passengers into the city costs £14 ($24) or more, depending on traffic.

By Train   Fast air-conditioned InterCity trains with restaurant and bar service link London with Edinburgh. Trains from London's King's Cross or Euston stations arrive in Edinburgh at **Waverley Station,** at the east end of Princes Street (☎ **0345/484-950** in London for information). Trains depart London every hour or so, taking $4^1/2$ to 5 hours. An overnight sleeper requires reservations. Taxis and buses are found right outside the station in Edinburgh.

Edinburgh

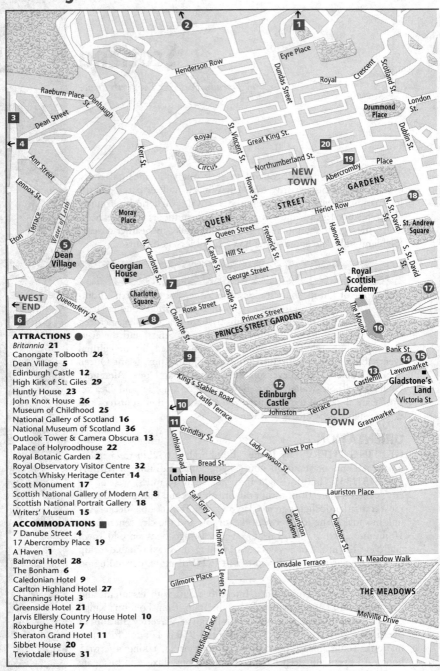

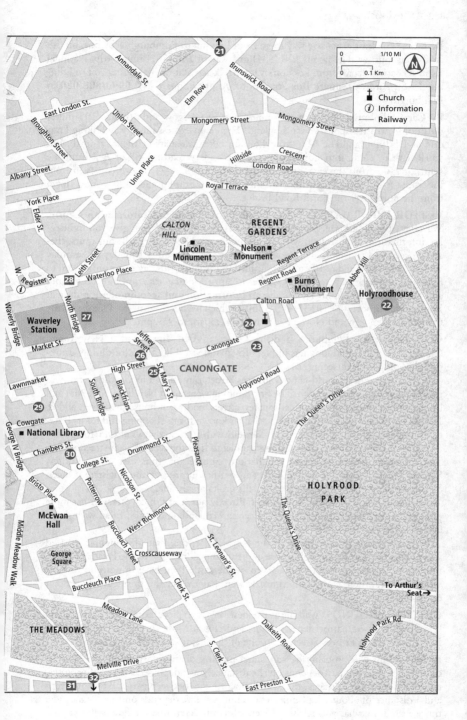

By Bus   The least expensive way to go from London to Edinburgh is by bus, but it's an 8-hour journey. The fare is £20 ($34) one way or £30 ($51) round-trip. National Express coaches depart from London's Victoria Coach Station, delivering you to Edinburgh's **St. Andrew Square Bus Station,** St. Andrew Square (☎ **0990/808-080** in Edinburgh).

By Car   Edinburgh lies 74km (46 miles) east of Glasgow and 169km (105 miles) north of Newcastle upon Tyne in England. There's no express motorway linking London and Edinburgh. The M-1 from London takes you part of the way north, but you'll have to come into Edinburgh along secondary roads: A-68 or A-7 from the southeast, A-1 from the east, or A-702 from the north. A-71 or A-8 comes in from the west, A-8 connecting with M-8 just west of Edinburgh; A-90 comes down from the north over the Forth Road Bridge.

VISITOR INFORMATION   The **Edinburgh & Scotland Information Centre,** Waverley Shopping Plaza, 3 Princes St. (☎ **0131/437-3800**), can give you sightseeing information and can help with accommodations. The center sells bus tours, theater tickets, and souvenirs. It's open May, June, and September Monday to Saturday 9am to 7pm and Sunday 10am to 7pm; July and August Monday to Saturday 9am to 8pm and Sunday 10am to 8pm; October to April Monday to Saturday 9am to 6pm and Sunday 10am to 6pm. There's also an **information and accommodation desk** at Edinburgh Airport (☎ **0131/473-3800**), which is open April to October daily 6:30am to 10:30pm and November to March 7:30am to 9:30pm.

CITY LAYOUT   Edinburgh is divided into an **Old Town** and a **New Town.** Chances are, you'll find lodgings in New Town and visit Old Town for dining, drinking, shopping, or sightseeing.

New Town, with its world-famous **Princes Street,** came about in the 18th century in the "Golden Age" of Edinburgh. The first building went up in New Town in 1767, and by the end of the century, classical squares, streets, and town houses had been added. Princes Street runs straight for about a mile; it's known for its shopping and for its beauty, as it opens onto the **Princes Street Gardens** with stunning views of Old Town.

North of Princes Street, and running parallel to it, is the second great street of New Town, **George Street.** It begins at Charlotte Square and runs east to St. Andrew Square. Directly north of George Street is another impressive thoroughfare, **Queen Street,** opening onto Queen Street Gardens on its north side.

You'll also hear a lot about **Rose Street,** directly north of Princes Street. It has more pubs per square block than any other place in Scotland, and is also filled with shops and restaurants.

Everyone seems to have heard of the **Royal Mile,** the main thoroughfare of Old Town, beginning at Edinburgh Castle and running all the way to the Palace of Holyroodhouse. A famous street to the south of the castle (you have to descend to it) is **Grassmarket,** where convicted criminals were hanged on the dreaded gallows that once stood here.

GETTING AROUND   Walking is the best way to explore Edinburgh, particularly Old Town with its narrow lanes, wynds, and closes. Most attractions are along the Royal Mile, along Princes Street, or in one of the major streets of New Town.

By Bus   This will probably be your chief method of transport within the Scottish capital. The fare you pay depends on the distance you ride, based on a confusing system that derives from "stages" that usually incorporate between two and five bus stops and a distance of about a half-mile. The minimum fare depends on the distance you travel, based on what you tell the driver, who will determine the fare, sell you your ticket, and even make change. Minimum fare is 50p (85¢) for three stages or less, going up to a maximum of £1.60 ($2.70) for travel between 44 or more stages. Children 5 to 15 pay a flat rate of 50p (85¢), regardless of how many stages they traverse, and children 4 and under ride free, and must be accompanied by an adult. There's a family ticket for 2 adults and 4 children for £6 ($10) a day and another for £1.60 ($2.70) which operates 6:30pm onward.

The **Edinburgh Freedom Ticket** allows 1 day of unlimited travel on city buses at a cost of £2.40 ($4.10) for adults and £1.60 ($2.70) for children aged 5 to 15. For daily commuters or for die-hard Scottish enthusiasts, a **RideCard** season ticket allows unlimited travel on all buses at £10.50 ($18) for adults for 1 week and £30.50 ($52) for 4 weeks. Travel must begin on Sunday. Prices for children are £6.50 ($11) for 1 week, £18 ($31) for 4 weeks.

These tickets and further information may be obtained in the city center at the **Waverley Bridge Transport Office,** Waverley Bridge (☎ **0131/554-4494;** bus: 3, 31), open daily 6:30am to 10:30pm or at the Hanover Street office which operates from 9am to 7pm daily. For information on timetables call ☎ **0131/555-6363.**

By Taxi   Cabs can be hailed on the street, or met at any of several taxi stands, each of which lie at prominent intersections throughout the city. Some of the more important of these are at Hanover Street, North St. Andrew Street, Waverley Station, Princes Street (at the Caledonian Hotel), Haymarket Station, Frederick Street, Castle Street, and Lauriston Place. Fares are prominently displayed in the front of each taxi. The meter begins ticking at £1.80 ($3.05). Regardless of the time of day, you'll be charged 20p (35¢) per 300 yards of distance your cab covers. If you phone for a cab to come to a point you specify to them, you'll pay a surcharge of 60p ($1) at any time of the day or night. To call a taxi, dial **City Cabs** (☎ **0131/228-1211**) or **Central Radio Taxi** (☎ **0131/229-2468**).

By Car   Car rentals are relatively expensive, and driving in Edinburgh is a tricky business. It's a warren of one-way streets, with parking spots at a premium. However, a car is convenient, and sometimes a must, for touring the countryside. Most companies will accept your U.S. or Canadian driver's license, provided you have held it for more than a year and are over 21. At the Edinburgh airport, try **Avis** (☎ **0131/333-1866**), **Hertz** (☎ **0131/344-3260**), or **Europcar** (☎ **0131/333-2588**).

By Bicycle   You can rent bikes by the day or by the week from a number of outfits. Nevertheless, bicycling is not a good idea for most visitors because the city is constructed on a series of high ridges and terraces.

You may, however, want to rent a bike for exploring the flatter countryside. Try **Central Cycle Hire,** 13 Lochrin Place (☎ **0131/228-6333;** bus: 10), off Home Street in Tollcross, near the Cameo Cinema. Depending on the type of bike, rates range from £10 to £18 ($17 to $31) per day. A deposit of £50 to £100 ($85 to $170) is imposed. The shop is open Monday through Saturday from 10am to 5:30pm; June through September it also opens Sunday noon to 7pm.

Fast Facts: Edinburgh

American Express   The office is at 139 Princes St. (☎ **0131/225-7881;** bus: 3, 39, 69), 5 blocks from Waverley Station. Open Monday to Wednesday and Friday 9am to 5:30pm and Thursday 9:30am to 5:30pm.

Baby-Sitters   The most reliable services are provided by **Guardians Baby Sitting Service,** 13 Eton Terrace (☎ **0131/343-3870**); or **Care Connections,** 45 Barclay Place (☎ **01506/856-106**).

Business Hours In Edinburgh, **banks** are usually open Monday through Wednesday from 9:30am to 3:45pm, and Thursday and Friday from 9:30am to 5 or 5:30pm. **Shops** are generally open Monday through Saturday from 10am to 5:30 or 6pm; on Thursday stores are open until 8pm. **Offices,** in the main, are open Monday through Friday from 9am to 5pm.

Currency The basic unit of currency is the **pound sterling** (£), which is divided into 100 **pence** (p). There're 1p, 2p, 10p, 20p, 50p, £1, and £2 coins; banknotes are issued in £1, £5, £10, £20, and £50, and £100 denominations. The exchange rate at the time we wrote this chapter was £1 = $1.70.

Currency Exchange There's a **Bureau de Change** of the Clydesdale Bank at 5 Waverley Bridge and at Waverley Market.

Dentists For a dental emergency, go to the **Edinburgh Dental Institute,** 39 Lauriston Place (☎ **0131/536-4900;** bus: 23, 41), open Monday to Friday 9am to 3pm.

Doctors In a medical emergency, you can seek help from the **Edinburgh Royal Infirmary,** 1 Lauriston Place (☎ **0131/536-1000;** bus: 23, 41). Medical attention is available 24 hours.

Drugstores There're no 24-hour drugstores ("chemists" or "pharmacies") in Edinburgh. The major drugstore is **Boots,** 48 Shandwick Place (☎ **0131/ 225-6757;** bus: 3, 31), open Monday to Wednesday and Friday 8am to 6pm, Thursday 8am to 7:30pm, Saturday 8am to 7pm, and Sunday 10am to 5pm.

Embassies/Consulates The Consulate of the **United States** is at 3 Regent Terrace (☎ **0131/556-8315;** bus: 26, 85, or 86), which is an extension of Princes Street beyond Nelson's Monument. All the other embassies are in London.

Emergencies Call ☎ **999** in an emergency to summon the police, an ambulance, or firefighters.

Hospital The best and most convenient is the **Edinburgh Royal Infirmary,** 1 Lauriston Place (☎ **0131/536-1000;** bus: 23, 41).

Internet Access For checking on your mail or sending messages, head to the **Cyberia Edinburgh,** 88 Hanover St. (☎ **0131/220-4405;** e-mail: edinburgh@ cybersurf.co.uk; bus: 23, 41).

Post Office The Edinburgh Branch **Post Office,** St. James's Centre (☎ **0131/ 5508232;** bus: 23 or 41), is open Monday to Friday 9am to 5:30pm and Saturday 9am to noon.

Taxes A 17.5% **value-added tax** (known as **VAT**) is added to all goods and services in Edinburgh, as elsewhere in Britain. There're no special city taxes.

Telephones The United Kingdom's **country code** is **44.** The city code for **Edinburgh** is **0131.** If you're calling from inside the United Kingdom but outside the city code area, dial the complete area code; if you're calling from outside the United Kingdom, drop the zero. As in the United States, if you're calling from inside the code area, dial just the seven-digit number.

Public phones cost 10p (15¢) for the first 3 minutes and accept coins of various denominations. You can also buy a phone card for use in special phones at post offices and newsstands. You can receive U.S. rates for collect or credit card calls by dialing toll free **AT&T** (☎ **0800/890011**), **MCI** (☎ **0800/890222**), or **Sprint** (☎ **0800/890877** or 0500/890877).

WHERE TO STAY
IN THE CENTER
Very Expensive
✪ **Balmoral Hotel.** Princes St., Edinburgh, Lothian EH2 2EQ. ☎ **800/225-5843** in the U.S., or 0131/556-2414. Fax 0131/557-3747. 186 units. A/C MINIBAR TV TEL. Apr–Oct £230–£280 ($391–$476) double; from £375 ($638) suite. Off-season £185–£215 ($315–$366) double; from £298 ($507) suite. AE, DC, MC, V. Parking £15 ($26). Bus: 50.

This legendary establishment was originally opened in 1902 as the largest, grandest, and most impressive hotel in the north of Britain. Its soaring clock tower is a city landmark. Furnished with reproduction pieces, the rooms are distinguished, conservative, and rather large, a graceful reminder of Edwardian sprawl with a contemporary twist. Many benefit from rounded or oversize windows and the many Victorian/Edwardian quirks that were originally designed as part of its charm. The hotel's most elegant eatery is 1 Princes Street (see "Where to Dine," below). Facilities include a large and well-equipped health club with Jacuzzi, sauna, exercise equipment, and a pool.

Caledonian Hotel. Princes St., Edinburgh EH1 2AB. ☎ **0131/459-9988.** Fax 0131/225-6632. 249 units. MINIBAR TV TEL. £225–£315 ($383–$536) double; from £350 ($595) suite. Children 15 and under stay free in parents' room. AE, DC, MC, V. Bus: 33. Parking £7 ($12).

"The Caley" is Edinburgh's most visible hotel, with commanding views over Edinburgh Castle and the Princes Street Gardens. It's built of Dumfriesshire stone, a form of deep red sandstone used in only three other buildings in town. The pastel-colored public areas are reminiscent of Edwardian splendor. Rooms are conservatively but individually styled with reproduction furniture, and are often exceptionally spacious. Fifth-floor rooms are the smallest. Although the accommodations are comparable to other first-class hotels in Edinburgh, the Caledonian lacks the leisure facilities of its major competitor, the Balmoral. Among the hotel eateries, the best food is served in the formal La Pompadour Restaurant.

Expensive
✪ **The Bonham.** 35 Drumsheugh Gardens, Edinburgh EH3 7RN. ☎ **0131/226-6050.** Fax 0131/226-6080. www.thebonham.com. E-mail: reserve@thebonham.com. 48 units. A/C MINIBAR TV TEL. £165–£185 ($272–$305) double; £220 ($363) suite. AE, DC, MC, V. Bus: 23, 27.

One of Edinburgh's newest and most stylish hotels occupies a trio of 19th-century town houses. Rooms are outfitted in an urban and very hip blend of old and new. Each has a high ceiling, a unique decorative theme, and a TV with Internet access. The in-house restaurant, the Restaurant at the Bonham, is one of Edinburgh's finest hotel dining rooms. Amenities include 24-hour room service, concierge, laundry, and baby-sitting.

Carlton Highland Hotel. 19 North Bridge, Edinburgh, Lothian EH1 1SD. ☎ **0131/556-7277.** Fax 0131/556-2691. 197 units. TV TEL. £193 ($328) double; from £250 ($425) suite. Rates include breakfast. Children 14 and under stay free in parents' room. AE, DC, MC, V. Parking £6 ($10). Bus: 55.

The Victorian turrets, Flemish gables, and severe gray stonework rise imposingly from a street corner on the Royal Mile, a few steps from Waverley Station. The former department store has been converted into a bright and airy milieu full of modern conveniences. Rooms have a kind of Scandinavian simplicity, with coffeemakers, hair dryers, and trouser presses. Bathrooms tend to be quite small. The hotel's restaurant, Quills, is designed like a private 19th-century library, and offers an international and Scottish regional menu. The hotel also has a coffee bar, Central Perk, named for the fictional cafe in the sitcom *Friends*. This cafe is open daily from 7am to 8pm. Facilities include an exercise room with a swimming pool, solarium, whirlpool, sauna, two squash courts, and an aerobics studio.

Channings Hotel. South Learmonth Gardens 15, Edinburgh EH4 1EZ. ☎ **0131/315-2226.** Fax 0131/332-9631. www.channings.co.uk. E-mail: reserve@channings.co.uk. 48 units. TV TEL. £125–£170 ($213–$289) double. Rates include breakfast. Children 14 and under stay free in parents' room. AE, DC, MC, V. Bus: 18, 19, 41, or 81.

Five Edwardian terrace houses were combined to create this hotel 7 blocks north of Dean Village in a tranquil residential area. It maintains the atmosphere of a Scottish country house, with oak paneling, ornate fireplaces, molded ceilings, and antiques. Rooms are outfitted in a modern style, with trouser presses and hair dryers. Front units have views of a cobblestoned street. Back units are quieter, and standard rooms are a bit cheaper, but are much smaller. The most desirable units are labeled "Executive," and often have bay windows and wingback chairs. In the downstairs bar and brasserie, a Scottish/French cuisine is served.

Roxburghe Hotel. 38 Charlotte Square, Edinburgh EH2 4HG. ☎ **0131/225-3921.** Fax 0131/220-2518. www.macdonaldhotels.co.uk. E-mail: info@roxburghe.macdonaldhotels. co.uk. 201 units. MINIBAR TV TEL. £180 ($306) double; from £230 ($391) suite. Children 13 and under stay free in parents' room. AE, DC, MC, V. Parking £8 ($14). Bus: 100.

Originally a stately Robert Adam town house, the hotel stands on a tree-filled square a short walk from Princes Street. In 1999, it opened a new wing, more than doubling the original size of the hotel. The old wing maintains a traditional atmosphere with ornate ceilings and woodwork, antique furnishings, and tall arched windows. The new wing offers four-star hotel comfort, completely contemporary styling, and up-to-date furnishings. All rooms have trouser presses, tea/coffeemakers, sewing kits, and deluxe toiletries. There're two restaurants, the Consult, offering a fine à la carte Scottish cuisine, and the more informal Melrose, a bistro with light fare. There's also a trio of bars.

✪ **Sheraton Grand Hotel.** 1 Festival Sq., Edinburgh, Lothian EH3 9SR. ☎ **800/325-3535** in the U.S. and Canada, or 0131/229-9131. Fax 0131/228-4510. 264 units. A/C MINIBAR TV TEL. June–Sept £230–£245 ($391–$417) double; from £340 ($578) suite. Off-season, £145 ($247) double, £215 ($366) suite. Children 16 and under stay free in parents' room. AE, DC, MC, V. Bus: 4, 15, or 44.

This elegant hotel, in a postmodern complex on a former railway siding, a short walk from Princes Street, is the most appealing modern hotel in the capital. There's a team of helpful concierges. The spacious rooms offer double-glazed windows and hair dryers. Rooms on the top three floors have castle views. There are two restaurants: The Terrace, with castle views, a brasserie-style restaurant with a conservatory atmosphere; and the Grill Room, small and intimate with traditional warm wood paneling. A leisure center offers a pool (too small for lap swimming), whirlpool, sauna, and fully equipped gym.

Moderate

17 Abercromby Place. 17 Abercromby Place, Edinburgh EH3 6LB. ☎ **0131/557-8036.** Fax 0131/558-3453. E-mail: eirlyslloyd@virgin.net. 10 units. TV TEL. £100 ($170) double. Rates include breakfast. MC, V. Free parking. Bus: 15 or 100.

Eirlys Lloyd runs this fine B&B, a 5-minute walk north of Princes Street. The five-story gray stone terrace house was home in the 1820s to William Playfair, who designed many of Edinburgh's most visible landmarks, including the Royal Scottish Academy and Surgeon Hall of the Royal College of Surgeons. Rooms vary in size, but all are acceptable with king- to queen-size beds, tea/coffeemakers, and hair dryers. Two rooms are in what was originally conceived as a mews house (living quarters adapted from stables). Evening meals can be arranged with prior notice.

✪ **Sibbet House.** 26 Northumberland St., Edinburgh EH3 6LS. ☎ **0131/556-1078.** Fax 0131/557-9445. www.sibbet-house.co.uk. E-mail: sibbethouse@2etnet.co.uk. 7 units. TV TEL. £90–£110 ($153–$187) double; £130 ($221) suite. Rates include breakfast. MC, V. Free parking. Bus: 13, 23, or 27.

Set on a residential terrace a 5-minute walk from Princes Street, this Georgian house is the cheerful domain of Anita and Jens Steffert, who do everything they can to distinguish their family home from "just another hotel." Rooms are small to medium-size, furnished with antiques (one has a four-poster bed), all with hair dryers. There's a drawing room/salon where glasses will be provided for those who bring their own liquor. The neighborhood offers several restaurants serving evening meals.

Inexpensive

A Haven. 180 Ferry Rd., Edinburgh EH6 4NS. ☎ **0131/554-6559.** Fax 0131/554-5252. www.a-haven.co.uk. E-mail: reservations@a-haven.co.uk. 12 units. TV TEL. £60–£98 ($102–$167) double. Rates include breakfast. AE, MC, V. Free parking. Bus: 1, 6, 7, 25, C3, 17, 14A, 25A.

This semidetached 1862 Victorian house is a 15-minute walk or 5-minute bus ride north of the rail station. Rooms are of various sizes (the biggest on the second floor). Some in back overlook the Firth of Forth, and those in the front open onto views of Arthur's Seat. All come with hospitality trays, computer ports, and hair dryers. Moira and Ronnie Murdock extend a Scottish welcome in this family-type place, and often advise guests about sightseeing. They have a licensed bar, but the only meal served is breakfast.

Greenside Hotel. 9 Royal Terrace, Edinburgh EH7 5AB. ☎ and fax **0131/557-0022.** 15 units. TV TEL. £45–£90 ($77–$153) double. Rates include breakfast. AE, DC, MC, V. Bus: 4, 15, or 44.

This 1786 Georgian house is furnished with antiques to give it the right spirit. There are singles, doubles, twins, and three family rooms, all centrally heated and all with private bathrooms. Rooms, refurbished in 1998, open onto views of a private garden or the Firth of Forth and are so large that 10 of them contain a double bed and two singles. There's a color TV in the lounge, where coffee and tea are available all day, and four-course Scottish dinners can be arranged.

✪ **7 Danube Street.** 7 Danube St., Edinburgh EH4 1NN. ☎ **0131/332-2755.** Fax 0131/343-3648. www.aboutedinburgh.com/danube. E-mail: 7.danubestreet@virgin.net. 5 units. £90 ($149) double. Rates include breakfast. MC, V. Free parking nearby. Bus: 28.

This B&B is in Stockbridge, a quiet, stylish residential neighborhood a 10-minute walk north of the center. It's the 1825 home of Fiona Mitchell-Rose and her husband, Colin. The establishment is proud of its charmingly decorated rooms that reflect Fiona's experience as a decorator in London. Rooms look out onto the sloping garden. The most desirable has a four-poster bed and direct garden access. All have perfumed soaps and shampoos, adapters, and nail files. You're likely to meet your hosts and other guests in the formal dining room in the morning, where the lavish breakfast is inspired by Scotland's old-fashioned agrarian tradition.

WEST OF THE CENTER

Jarvis Ellersly Country House Hotel. 4 Ellersly Rd., Edinburgh EH12 6HZ. ☎ **0131/337-6888.** Fax 0131/313-2543. 57 units. TV TEL. £139 ($236) double; £154 ($262) suite. AE, DC, MC, V. Free parking. Take A-8 4km (2 1/2 miles) west of the city center. Bus: 2, 2A, 21, 26, 31, 36, 36A.

Standing in walled gardens, this three-story Edwardian country house offers the privacy of a home. It's in a dignified west-end residential section near the Murrayfield rugby grounds, about a 5-minute ride from the center, and is one of Edinburgh's best moderately priced hotels. The well-equipped rooms (with hair dryers) vary in size and are in either the main house or in a less desirable annex. After recent refurbishments, the hotel is better than ever, and service is first class. The hotel possesses a well-stocked wine cellar and offers good-tasting Scottish and French meals. Room service and laundry/valet are offered.

SOUTH OF THE CENTER

✪ **Teviotdale House.** Grange Loan, Edinburgh EH9 2ER. ☎ and fax **0131/667-4376.** E-mail: teviotdale.house@btinternet.com. 7 units. TV TEL. £50–£90 ($85–$153). AE, MC, V. Bus: 42.

Some visitors rate this three-story 1848 house, 10 minutes by bus from Princes Street, Waverley Station, and Edinburgh Castle, as the finest B&B in Edinburgh. Jane E. Coville's attention to detail has earned her an enviable reputation. The house is completely no smoking, and is furnished with antiques. Individually decorated rooms have hair dryers and specialist mattresses; the three largest can accommodate up to four beds. The home-cooked breakfast may be the highlight of your day's dining, and can include smoked salmon, kippers, and home-baked bread and scones.

WHERE TO DINE

IN THE CENTER—NEW TOWN

Expensive

✪ **The Atrium.** 10 Cambridge St. (beneath Saltire Court). ☎ **0131/228-8882.** Reservations recommended. Fixed-price meal £14–£18 ($24–$31) at lunch, main courses £13.50–£18.50 ($23–$31) at dinner. AE, DC, MC, V. Mon–Fri noon–2:30pm and 6–10:30pm, Sat 6–10:30pm. Closed for 1 week at Christmas. MODERN SCOTTISH/INTERNATIONAL.

Since its opening in 1993, the Atrium has been one of the most emulated restaurants in Edinburgh. No more than 60 diners can be accommodated in the "deliberately moody" atmosphere that's a fusion of Argentinean hacienda and stylish Beverly Hills bistro. Flickering oil lamps create shadows on the dark-colored walls while patrons enjoy dishes prepared by chef Alan Metheison. Although offerings vary according to the inspiration of the chef and his manager, our favorites include grilled salmon or roasted sea bass. The latter comes with Dauphinois potatoes, baby spinach, charcoal-grilled eggplant, and baby fennel. Whether it's game or lamb from the Scottish Highlands, dishes have taste, style, and flair. The desserts are equally superb, especially the lemon tart with berry soulis and crème fraîche.

Bonars. 56 St. Mary's St. ☎ **0131/556-5888.** Reservations required. Table d'hôte menu at lunch £10.85–£12.95 ($18–$22); main courses £14.85–£17.35 ($25–$30). MC, V. Daily noon–2pm and 5–10pm. Bus: 1, 6, 34, or 35. MODERN SCOTTISH/FRENCH.

Just off the Royal Mile, between Cowgate and Canongate, this restaurant is ranked among the top 60 in Scotland, and the service is the most polished in town, with crystal and fine bone china. It uses the finest of Scottish ingredients in its classic French cuisine, which is backed up by a carefully chosen wine list. Game and fish are specialties, and each dish, whether from the moors, lochs, or sea, is individually prepared. Some main dishes taste as if you've been transported to the Périgord region of France. The menu changes frequently but has included confit of duck in a Cassis sauce, Scottish salmon, and saddle of hare. The lunch menu is changed monthly, and the dinner menu is adjusted daily, depending upon what is fresh at the market.

No. 1 Princes Street. In the Balmoral Hotel, 1 Princes St. ☎ **0131/556-2414.** Reservations recommended. Main courses £14–£30 ($24–$51); fixed-price lunch £17.50 ($30) for two courses; £19.25 ($33) for 3 courses; fixed-price 5-course dinner £35 ($60). AE, DC, MC, V. Mon–Fri noon–2pm and daily 7–10pm and 10:30 on Fri. SCOTTISH/CONTINENTAL.

This intimate, crimson-colored enclave is the premier restaurant in the Balmoral Hotel. The walls are studded with Scottish memorabilia in formal, yet sporting patterns. This is very much the grand-style hotel dining room, and it offers good food if you don't mind paying high prices. You can sample the likes of pan-seared Isle of Skye monkfish with saffron mussel broth, roulade of Dover sole with langoustine, oyster, and scallop garnish or grilled fillet of Scottish beef served with bourguignonne sauce. For dessert you can have a variety of sorbets, British cheeses, or something more exotic such as mulled wine parfait with a cinnamon sauce. There's a separate vegetarian menu and a wide-ranging wine list with celestial tariffs.

36. 36 Great King St. ☎ **0131/556-3636.** Reservations recommended. Set-price lunch £16.50–£19.50 ($27–$32); dinner main courses £11.50–£18.50 ($19–$31). AE, DC, MC, V. Bus: 23, 27. SCOTTISH/INTERNATIONAL.

The food here is among the most creative and appealing in Edinburgh, thanks to a dependence on fresh produce and the sophisticated applications of chef Malcolm Warham. The setting is a starkly decorated basement, with minimalist white walls and lights that throw off rainbows of color. Menu items might remind you of some of the unusual combinations of ingredients you'd expect in Paris. Truly inspired dishes include a terrine of confit of rabbit with a cucumber and red onion picallili; chilled tomato mousse with warm asparagus-flavored hollandaise and a salad of baby fennel; fillet of Scotch beef with shallot-thyme glaze, dauphinoise potatoes, and Arran island mustard sauce. Also noteworthy are baked fillet of cod wrapped in lard and served with soft onion and a red wine-flavored butter sauce, and roasted beef of guinea fowl with black pudding.

Moderate

Café Saint-Honoré. 34 NW Thistle St. Lane. ☎ **0131/226-2211.** Reservations recommended. Main coures £7.50–£12.50 ($13–$21) at lunch, pretheater fixed-price meal £13.50–£18 ($23–$31), £13.75–£17.25 ($23–$29) at dinner. AE, DC, MC, V. Mon–Fri noon–2:15pm; Mon–Fri (pretheater meal) 5:30–6:30pm; Mon–Sat 7–10pm and sometimes 11pm. Bus: 3, 16, 17, 23, 27, or 31. FRENCH/SCOTTISH.

Between Frederick and Hanover Streets, this is a French-inspired bistro with a dinner format that's much more formal and expensive than its deliberately rapid lunchtime venue. The menu is completely revised each day, based on what's fresh in the market, and whatever the chefs feel inspired to cook. An upbeat and usually enthusiastic staff serves a combination of Scottish and French cuisine that includes venison with juniper berries and wild mushrooms; local pheasant in wine and garlic sauce; or lamb kidneys with broad beans inspired by the cuisine of the region around Toulouse. Fish is very fresh.

Duck's at Le Marché Noir. 2/4 Eyre Place. ☎ **0131/558-1608.** Reservations recommended. Lunch main courses £10–£15 ($17–$25); dinner main courses £12–£17 ($20–$28). AE, DC, MC, V. Mon–Sat noon–2pm and 7–9:30pm. Bus: 23, 27. SCOTTISH/FRENCH.

The cuisine here is more stylish, and more tuned to the culinary sophistication of London, than many other restaurants in Edinburgh. Set within a wood house whose outside and inside are both decorated in shades of dark green, its handful of dishes honor the traditions of Scotland. (An example is their baked haggis in phyllo pastry on a bed of turnip puree and red wine sauce.) More modern dishes include a boudin of chicken and foie gras served with wilted spinach and applesauce; seared salmon with leeks, asparagus, zucchini, and a picked ginger and sesame salad; roasted rack of lamb with thyme juice and roasted vegetables; and grilled red snapper with wild rice and lime-marinated sweet potato pickles.

Haldanes Restaurant. 39A Albany St. ☎ **0131/556-8407.** Reservations recommended. Set-price lunch £10.50–£15 ($17–$25); set-price dinner £22.50–£27.50 ($37–$45). AE, DC, MC, V. Daily noon–2pm and 6–10pm. Bus: 15. SCOTTISH.

Set in the cellar of the Albany Hotel building, within a pair of royal blue and gold-tinted dining rooms, Haldanes features the cuisine of George Kelso. During clement weather, the venue moves into the building's verdant garden. Dinners are conducted like meals at a private country house manor, with polite and deferential service. George applies a light touch to dishes he cooks with innovation and style. Menu items include a traditional haggis in phyllo pastry with tatties (roasted turnips) and whisky sauce; panfried crab cakes with a tomato and spring onion salsa; a panaché of West Coast scallops, monkfish, and salmon with saffron-flavored risotto and roasted asparagus; and a pavé of lamb with mint-flavored herb crust, wild mushrooms, and zucchini. For dessert, try the caramelized lemon tarte with crème fraîche.

Inexpensive
Far Pavilions. 10 Craighleith Rd., Comely Bank. ☎ **0131/332-3362.** Reservations recommended. Lunch main courses £7–£13 ($12–$22), lunch buffet £7.95 ($14) per person, dinner main courses £7–£13 ($12–$22). AE, DC, MC, V. Mon–Fri noon–2pm and Mon–Sat 5:30–11:30pm. Bus: 19, 39, 55, 81, or X91. INDIAN/CONTINENTAL.

Established in 1987, this Indian restaurant offers finely tuned service. You might appreciate a drink in the bar before confronting the long menu with dishes from the former Portuguese colony of Goa and the north Indian province of Punjab. Highly recommended is the house specialty, Murgi Massala, concocted with tandoori chicken that falls off the bone thanks to slow cooking in a garlic-based butter sauce. Menu items include curry dishes influenced by British tastes, as well as authentic platters whose composition is faithful to their original Indian tradition. Most items are suitably pungent, and concocted from lamb, seafood, vegetables, and beef, and the staff is always able to combine the garnishes and side dishes that form a worthy Indian meal.

✪ Henderson's Salad Table. 94 Hanover St. ☎ **0131/225-2131.** Main courses £3.50–£4.75 ($6–$8); fixed-price meal at lunch £4.95 ($8); fixed-price meal at dinner £10.90 ($19). AE, MC, V. Mon–Sat 7:30am–10:45pm. Bus: 23 or 27. VEGETARIAN.

This is a Shangri-la for health-food lovers. At this self-service place, you can pick and choose eggs, carrots, grapes, nuts, yogurt, cheese, potatoes, cabbage, watercress—you name it. Hot dishes such as peppers stuffed with rice and pimiento are served on request, and a vegetarian twist on the national dish of Scotland haggis is usually available. Other well-prepared dishes filled with flavor include cheese and onion potato croquet, vegetable lasagna, and a broccoli and cheese crumble. The homemade desserts include a fresh fruit salad or a cake with double-whipped cream and chocolate sauce. The wine cellar offers 30 wines. Live music, ranging from classical to jazz to folk, is played every evening.

Valvona & Crolla. 19 Elm Row. ☎ **0131/556-6066.** Breakfast £4.95 ($8); pizzas, pastas, or platters £3–£10 ($4.95–$17). AE, DC, MC, V. Cafe with limited food service Mon–Sat 8:30am–5pm; full lunch service Mon–Sat noon–3pm. Bus: 7, 10, 11, 12, or 14. INTERNATIONAL.

In 1872, a recent arrival from Italy opened this restaurant, and it's still going strong. It shares space with a delicatessen and food emporium where exotic coffees, Parma ham, Italian cheeses, and breads, as well as takeaway sandwiches and casseroles, are sold. A satellite room, a few steps down from the main shopping area, contains a cafe and luncheon restaurant where food is very fresh and prices refreshingly low. Here, you can order three kinds of breakfasts (continental, Scottish, or vegetarian) for a fixed price of £3.95 ($7); or platters of pasta, mixed sausages, and cold cuts; crostini, risottos, and omelettes. Don't expect leisurely dining, as the place caters to office workers and shoppers who dash in for midday sustenance, appreciating the informality, low prices, and the freshness of the food.

IN THE CENTER—OLD TOWN

Moderate

Dubh Prais. 123B High St., Royal Mile. ☎ **0131/557-5263.** Reservations recommended. Lunch main courses £6.50 ($11); dinner main courses £10.90–£15.50 ($18–$26). AE, MC, V. Tues–Fri noon–2pm and Tues–Sat 6–10:30pm. Bus: 11. SCOTTISH.

Dub Prais (Gaelic for "The Black Pot") conjures up an image of old-fashioned Scottish recipes bubbling away in a stewpot above a fireplace. Within dining rooms adorned with stenciled versions of thistles, you'll appreciate the meals prepared by members of the McWilliams family, which composes its menu entirely from Scottish produce and raw ingredients. Menu items are time-tested and not at all experimental, but flavorful nonetheless. Examples include smoked salmon; a ragout of wild mushrooms and Ayrshire bacon served with garlic sauce; saddle of venison with juniper sauce; and a supreme of salmon with grapefruit-flavored butter sauce.

Inexpensive

Baked Potato Shop. 56 Cockburn St. ☎ **0131/225-7572.** Reservations not accepted. Food items 50p–£2.80 (85¢–$4.75). No credit cards. Daily 9am–9pm (to 10pm in summer). Bus: 5. VEGETARIAN/WHOLE FOOD.

This is the least expensive restaurant in a very glamorous neighborhood, and it attracts mobs of office workers every day. Many carry their food away. Place your order at the countertop and it will be served in ecology-conscious recycled cardboard containers. Only free-range eggs, whole foods, and vegetarian cheeses are used. Vegetarian cakes are a specialty.

Pierre Victoire. 10–14 Victoria St. ☎ **0131/225-1721.** Reservations recommended. Main courses £6.40–£10 ($11–$17); fixed-price lunch £5.90 ($10) and £6.90 ($12) Sun. MC, V. Daily noon–3pm and 6–11pm. Bus: 1, 34, or 35. FRENCH.

This was the original model for a series of franchises that have sprouted up in recent years in six other areas of Edinburgh. Many residents still prefer the original to the newer versions. It's an ideal, if chaotic, stopover if you're antique shopping and climbing Victoria Street. It's also one of the most popular evening gathering places as it keeps long hours. Wine specials are posted on the chalkboard. In a bistro setting with crowded tables, you can order grilled mussels in garlic with Pernod butter, salmon with ginger, or roast pheasant with Cassis. Vegetarians will also find selections to suit their taste.

SOUTH OF THE CENTER

○ Kelly's. 46 W. Richmond St. ☎ **0131/668-3847.** Reservations recommended. Fixed-price 3-course dinner £27 ($46); 3-course lunch £11 ($19). DC, MC, V. Mon–Sat noon–2pm and 6–10pm. Bus: 11, 12, or 14. MODERN SCOTTISH/MODERN FRENCH.

Catering to a crowd of barristers, artists, financiers, and employees of the nearby university, this stylish restaurant is a 20-minute walk south of the center in a residential neighborhood. The place offers an intimate setting decorated with flowers, watercolors, and unusual ceramics. Focusing on fresh ingredients and vaguely inspired by the culinary techniques of the late British cuisine authority Robert Carrier, the menu includes such dishes as asado of lamb in olive and herb crust with spicy couscous, roast breast of Barbary duck with black pepper and blueberries or ravioli of lobster with asparagus. Dessert might include a caramelized lemon tart.

LEITH

In the northern regions of Edinburgh, Leith is the old port town, opening onto the Firth of Forth. Once it was a city in its own right until it (and its harbor facilities) was slowly absorbed into Edinburgh.

Moderate

Vintner's Room. The Vaults, 87 Giles St., Leith. ☎ **0131/554-6767.** Reservations recommended. Table d'hôte meal £11–£14.50 ($19–$25) at lunch, £15–£19.50 ($26–$33) at dinner. AE, MC, V. Mon–Sat noon–2pm and 7–10:30pm. Closed 2 weeks at Christmas. Bus: 7 or 10. FRENCH/SCOTTISH.

This stone-fronted building was originally constructed around 1650 as a warehouse for barrels of Bordeaux (claret) and port that came in from Europe's mainland. Near the entrance, beneath a venerable ceiling of oaken beams, a wine bar serves platters and drinks beside a large stone fireplace. Most diners, however, head for the small but elegant dining room, illuminated by flickering candles. Here, elaborate Italianate plasterwork decorates a room that functioned 300 years ago as the site of wine auctions. A robust cuisine includes seafood salad with mango mayonnaise, a terrine of pigeon and duck, loin of pork with mustard sauce, and venison in a bitter chocolate sauce.

SEEING THE SIGHTS
SIGHTSEEING SUGGESTIONS FOR FIRST TIME VISITORS

If You Have 1 Day   Visit Edinburgh Castle as soon as it opens in the morning, then walk the Royal Mile to the Palace of Holyroodhouse, former abode of Mary, Queen of Scots. Look out over the city from the vantage point of Arthur's Seat, and stroll through Princes Street Gardens, capping your day with a walk along the major shopping thoroughfare, Princes Street.

If You Have 2 Days   In the morning of your second day, head for Old Town again, but this time explore its narrow streets, wynds, and closes, and visit the John Knox House, the High Kirk of St. Giles, and the small museums. After lunch, climb the Scott Monument for a good view of Old Town and the Princes Street Gardens. Spend the rest of the afternoon exploring the National Gallery of Scotland.

If You Have 3 Days   Spend Day 3 getting acquainted with the major attractions of New Town, including the National Museum of Scotland, National Portrait Gallery, Georgian House, and Royal Botanic Garden.

If You Have 4 or 5 Days   On the fourth day, take a trip west to Stirling Castle and see some of the dramatic scenery of the Trossachs. On the fifth day you'll feel like a native, so seek out some of the city's minor but interesting attractions, such as the Camera Obscura, the Scotch Whisky Heritage Centre, and Dean Village.

THE ROYAL MILE

The Royal Mile stretches from Edinburgh Castle all the way to the Palace of Holyroodhouse. Walking along, you'll see some of the most interesting old structures in Edinburgh, with their turrets, gables, and towering chimneys. Take bus 1, 6, 23, 27, 30, 34, or 36 to reach the various spots along the Royal Mile.

High Kirk of St. Giles. High St. ☎ **0131/225-9442.** Free admission, but £1 ($1.65) donation suggested. Easter–Sept Mon–Fri 9am–7pm, Sat 9am–5pm, Sun 1–5pm; Oct–Easter Mon–Sat 9am–5pm, Sun 1–5pm. Sun services at 8, 10 and 11:30am and 6 and 8pm.

Built in 1120, a short walk downhill from Edinburgh Castle, this church is one of the most important architectural landmarks along the Royal Mile. It combines a dark and brooding stone exterior with surprisingly graceful and delicate flying buttresses. One of its outstanding features is its **Thistle Chapel,** housing beautiful stalls and notable heraldic stained-glass windows. A group of cathedral guides is available at all times to conduct tours.

Writers' Museum. In Lady Stair's House, off Lawnmarket. ☎ **0131/529-4901.** Free admission. Mon–Sat 10am–5pm.

This 1622 house takes its name from a former owner, Elizabeth, the dowager countess of Stair. Today it's a treasure trove of portraits, relics, and manuscripts relating to three of Scotland's greatest men of letters. The Robert Burns collection includes his writing desk, rare manuscripts, portraits, and many other items. Also on display are some of Sir Walter Scott's possessions, including his pipe, chess set, and original manuscripts. The museum holds one of the most significant Robert Louis Stevenson collections anywhere, including personal belongings, paintings, photographs, and early editions.

Museum of Childhood. 42 High St. ☎ **0131/529-4142.** Free admission. Mon–Sat 10am–5pm; during the Edinburgh Festival, also Sun 2–5pm.

The world's first museum devoted solely to the history of childhood stands just opposite John Knox' House. Contents of its four floors range from antique toys to games to exhibits on health, education, and costumes, plus video presentations and an activity area. Because of the youthful crowd it naturally attracts, it ranks as the noisiest museum in town.

John Knox' House. 43–45 High St. ☎ **0131/556-9579.** Admission £1.95 ($3.20) adults, £1.50 ($2.45) seniors/students, 75p ($1.25) children. Mon–Sat 9:45am–4:30pm.

Even if you're not interested in the reformer who founded the Scottish Presbyterian Church, you may want to visit his house, as it's characteristic of the "lands" that used to flank the Royal Mile. All of them are gone now, except Knox's house, with its timbered gallery. Inside, you'll see the tempera ceiling in the Oak Room, along with exhibitions of Knox memorabilia.

The People's Story. 163 Canongate. ☎ **0131/529-4057.** Free admission. Mon–Sat 10am–5pm (Aug also Sun 2–5pm). Bus 1.

If you continue walking downhill along Canongate toward Holyroodhouse, you'll see one of the handsomest buildings on the Royal Mile. Built in 1591, the **Canongate Tolbooth** was once the courthouse, prison, and center of municipal affairs for the burgh of Canongate. Now it contains a museum celebrating the social history of the inhabitants of Edinburgh from the late 18th century to the present, with lots of emphasis on the cultural displacements of the Industrial Revolution.

Huntly House. 142 Canongate. ☎ **0131/529-4143.** Free admission. Mon–Sat 10am–5pm; during the Edinburgh Festival, also Sun 2–5pm. Bus: 1.

Across from the Canongate Tolbooth is this fine example of a restored 16th-century mansion. Today it functions as Edinburgh's principal museum of local history. The interior contains faithfully crafted reproductions of rooms inspired by the city's traditional industries, including exhibits devoted to glassmaking, pottery, wool processing, and cabinetry, always with a focus on the stamina and struggles of the workers who labored within.

Scotch Whisky Heritage Centre. 354 Castlehill. ☎ **0131/220-0441.** Admission £4.95 ($8) adults, £3.50 ($6) seniors, £2.50 ($4.15) students with ID, £2.50 ($4.15) ages 5 to 17; children 4 and under free. Daily 10am–5pm.

This center is privately funded by a conglomeration of Scotland's biggest distillers. It highlights the economic effect of whisky on both Scotland and the world and illuminates the centuries-old traditions associated with whisky making, showing the science and art of distilling. There's a 7-minute audiovisual show and an electric car ride past 13 sets showing historic moments in the whisky industry. For £10 ($17) extra, you can sample two whiskies during the tour. A tour entitling you to sample five whiskies and take away a miniature bottle is £18 ($30) per person.

HISTORIC SITES

✪ **Edinburgh Castle.** Castlehill. ☎ **0131/225-9846.** Admission £6.50 ($11) adults, £2 ($3.40) children 15 and under. Apr–Sept daily 9:30am–5:15pm; Oct–Mar daily 9:30am–4:15pm. Bus: 1 or 6.

Although its early history is vague, it's believed that Edinburgh was built on the dead volcano, Castle Rock. It's known that in the 11th century Malcolm III (Canmore) and his Saxon queen, later venerated as St. Margaret, founded a castle on this same spot. The only fragment left of their original castle—in fact the oldest structure in Edinburgh—is **St. Margaret's Chapel.** Built in the Norman style, the oblong structure dates principally from the 12th century.

Inside the castle you can visit the **State Apartments,** particularly Queen Mary's bedroom, where Mary, Queen of Scots gave birth to James VI of Scotland (later James I of England). The highlight is the Crown Chamber, which houses the Honours of Scotland (Scottish Crown Jewels), used at the coronation of James VI, along with the scepter and the sword of state of Scotland.

You can also view the Stone of Scone or "Stone of Destiny," on which Scottish kings had been crowned since time immemorial. Edward I of England carried the stone off to Westminster Abbey in 1296, where it rested under the British coronation chair. It was finally returned to its rightful home in Scotland in November 1996, where it was welcomed with much pomp and circumstance.

✪ **Palace of Holyroodhouse.** Canongate, at the eastern end of the Royal Mile. ☎ **0131/556-7371.** Admission £5.50 ($9) adults, £4 ($7) seniors, £2.70 ($4.60) children 15 and under; £13 ($22) family pass for 2 adults and 2 children. Mon–Sat 9:30am–4:45pm, Sun 10:30–4:40pm. Closed 2 weeks in May and 3 weeks in late June and early July (dates vary). Bus: 1 or 6.

This palace was built adjacent to an Augustinian abbey established by David I in the 12th century. The nave, now in ruins, remains today. James IV founded the palace nearby in the early part of the 16th century, but only the north tower is left. Much of what you see today was ordered built by Charles II.

The most dramatic incident in the history of Holyroodhouse occurred in the old wing when Mary, Queen of Scots was in residence. Her Italian secretary, David Rizzio, was murdered (with 56 stab wounds) in the audience chamber by Mary's husband, Lord Darnley, and his accomplices. The palace suffered long periods of neglect, although it basked in glory at the ball thrown by Bonnie Prince Charlie in the mid–18th century. The present queen and Prince Philip live at Holyroodhouse whenever they visit Edinburgh. When they're not in residence, the palace is open to visitors.

For Mr. Hyde Fans

Near Gladstone's Land is **Brodie's Close,** a stone-floored alleyway. You can wander into the alley for a view of old stone houses that'll make you think you've stepped into a scene from a BBC production of a Dickens novel. It was named in honor of the notorious Deacon Brodie, a respectable councilor by day and a thief by night (he was the inspiration for Robert Louis Stevenson's *The Strange Case of Dr. Jekyll and Mr. Hyde,* though Stevenson set his story in foggy London town, not in Edinburgh). Brodie was hanged in 1788, and the mechanism used for the hangman's scaffolding had previously been improved by Brodie himself—for use on others, of course. Across the street is the most famous pub along the Royal Mile: **Deacon Brodie's Tavern** (see below).

MORE ATTRACTIONS

Scott Monument. In the East Princes St. Gardens. ☎ **0131/529-4068.** Admission £2.50 ($4.25). Mar–May and Oct, Mon–Sat 9am–6pm, Sun 10am–6pm; June–Sept, Mon–Sat 9am–8pm, Sun 10am–6pm; Nov–Feb, Mon–Sat 9am–4pm, Sun 10am–4pm. Bus: 1 or 6.

Completed in the mid-19th century, the Gothic-inspired Scott Monument is the most famous landmark of Edinburgh. Sir Walter Scott's heroes are carved as small figures in the monument, and you can climb to the top. You can also see the first-ever **floral clock,** which was constructed in 1904, in the West Princes Street Gardens. The monument reopened in the spring of 1999 following a major restoration.

✪ **National Gallery of Scotland.** 2 The Mound. ☎ **0131/624-6200.** Free admission. Mon–Sat 10am–5pm, Sun 2–5pm (during the festival, Mon–Sat 10am–6pm, Sun 11am–6pm). Bus: 3, 21, or 26.

This museum is located in the center of Princes Street Gardens. The gallery is rather small, but the collection was chosen with great care and has been expanded considerably by bequests, gifts, and loans. The duke of Sutherland has lent the museum some paintings, including two Raphaels, Titian's two Diana canvases and his Venus rising from the sea, and the *Seven Sacraments,* a work of the great 17th-century Frenchman Nicolas Poussin. The Spanish masters are represented as well. You can also see excellent examples of English painting: Gainsborough's *The Hon. Mrs. Graham* and Constable's *Dedham Vale,* along with works by Turner, Reynolds, and Hogarth. Naturally, the work of Scottish painters is prominent, including Alexander Naysmith and Henry Raeburn, whose most famous work, *The Reverend Walker,* can be seen.

Outlook Tower & Camera Obscura. Castlehill. ☎ **0131/22-3709.** Admission £3.95 ($7) adults, £2.50 ($4.25) seniors and children. Open Apr–Oct Mon–Fri 9:30am–6pm, Sat–Sun 10am–6pm, until 7:30pm in July and 7pm in Aug; Nov–Mar daily 10am–5pm. Bus: 1 or 6.

The 1853 periscope is at the top of the Outlook Tower from which you can view a panorama of the surrounding city. Trained guides point out the landmarks and talk about Edinburgh's fascinating history. In addition, there're several entertaining exhibits, all with an optical theme, and a well-stocked shop selling books, crafts, and compact discs.

Royal Observatory Visitor Centre. Blackford Hill. ☎ **0131/668-8405.** Admission £3 ($5) adults; £2 ($3.40) students and seniors and children 5–16; free for children 4 and under. Mon–Fri 10am–5pm, Sat–Sun noon–5pm. Bus: 40 or 41.

On display here are the works of the Scottish National Observatory at home and abroad, featuring the finest images of astronomical objects, Scotland's largest telescope, and antique instruments. There's also a panoramic view of the city from the balcony. An exhibit, *The Universe,* uses photographs, videos, computers, and models to take you on a cosmic whirlwind tour from the beginning of time to the farthest depths of space in a couple of hours.

National Museum of Scotland (NMS). Chambers St. ☎ **0131/227-4422.** Admission £3 ($5) adults, £1.50 ($2.55) seniors and students, and free for children under 18; supplement for some temporary exhibitions. Mon and Wed–Sat 10am–5pm, Tues 10am–8pm, Sun noon–5pm. Walk south from Waverley Station for 10 min. to reach Chambers St. or take bus no. 3, 7, 21, 30, 31, 53, 69, or 80.

In 1998 two long-established museums, the Royal Museum of Scotland and the National Museum of Antiquities, were united into this single institution 2 blocks south of the Royal Mile. The museum showcases exhibits in the decorative arts, ethnography, natural history, geology, archaeology, technology, and science. Six modern galleries distill billions of years of Scottish history, a total of 12,000 items ranging from rocks found on the island of South Uist dating back 2.9 billion years to a Hillman Imp, one of the last 500 cars manufactured at the Linwood plant near Glasgow before it closed in 1981. One gallery is devoted to Scotland's role as an independent nation before it merged with the United Kingdom in 1707. One gallery, devoted to industry and empire from 1707 to 1914, includes exhibits on shipbuilding, whisky distilling, the railways, and such textiles as the tartan and paisley.

✪ **Scottish National Gallery of Modern Art.** Belford Rd. ☎ **0131/556-8921.** Free admission, except for some temporary exhibits. Mon–Sat 10am–5pm, Sun 2–5pm. Bus: 13, or take 18, 20, or 41; ask the driver for the stop closest to the museum and then take the 5-minute walk up Queensferry Terrace and Belford Rd. to the gallery.

In 1984 Scotland's national collection of 20th-century art moved into a gallery converted from a former 1828 school building. It's set on 5.5ha (12 acres) of grounds, just a 15-minute walk from the west end of Princes Street. The collection is international in scope and high in quality despite its modest size. Major sculptures outside the building include pieces by Henry Moore and Barbara Hepworth. Inside, the collection ranges from a fauve Derain and cubist Braque and Picasso to recent works by Paolozzi. There's a strong representation of English and Scottish artists—William Turner, John Constable, Henry Raeburn, and David Wilkie to name a few. Works by Matisse, Miró, Kirchner, Kokoschka, Ernst, Ben Nicholson, Nevelson, Balthus, Lichtenstein, Kitaj, and Hockney are also on view.

Scottish National Portrait Gallery. 1 Queen St. ☎ **0131/624-6200.** Free admission, except for some temporary exhibits. Mon–Sat 10am–5pm, Sun 2–5pm. Bus: 18, 20, or 41.

Housed in a red stone Victorian Gothic building by Rowand Anderson, this portrait gallery gives you a chance to see what the famous people of Scottish history looked like. The portraits, several by Ramsay and Raeburn, include everybody from Mary, Queen of Scots to Sean Connery, from Flora Macdonald to Irvine Welsh.

A STEP BACK IN TIME AT HISTORIC DEAN VILLAGE

The village is one of the most photographed sights in the city. Set in a valley about 30m (100 feet) below the level of the rest of Edinburgh, it's full of nostalgic charm. The settlement dates from the 12th century, and for many centuries it was a grain-milling center. The current residents worked hard to restore the old buildings—many of which were converted into flats and houses—and managed to maintain all of the original Brigadoon-like charm. A few minutes from the West End, it's located at the end of Bell's Brae, off Queensferry Street, on the Water of Leith. You can enjoy a celebrated view by looking downstream under the high arches of Dean Bridge, designed

Britannia: The People's Yacht

In case the queen never invited you to sail aboard her 125m (412-foot) yacht, there's still a chance to go aboard this world famous vessel. Launched on April 16, 1953, the luxury yacht was decommissioned December 11, 1997. Today, the yacht—technically a Royal Navy ship—which has sailed more than a million miles, rests at anchor in the port of Leith, 3km (2 miles) from the center of Edinburgh. The gangplank is now lowered for the public, whereas it once was lowered for such world leaders as Mahatma Gandhi, Tony Blair, and Nelson Mandela.

British taxpayers spent £160 million maintaining the yacht throughout most of the '90s. Even a major refit would have prolonged the vessel's life for only a few more years. Because of budgetary constraints, a decision was made to put it in dry dock. The public reaches the vessel by going through a visitor center designed by Sir Terence Conran. At its centerpiece is the yacht's 12m (41-foot) tender floating in a pool.

Once on board, you're guided around all five decks by an audio tour. You can also visit the drawing room and the Royal Apartments, once occupied by the likes of not only the queen, but Prince Philip and princes William, Harry, Edward, and Andrew, as well as princesses Anne and Margaret. Even the engine room, the galleys, and the captain's cabin can be visited.

All tickets should be booked as far in advance as possible by calling ☎ **0131/ 555-5566.** The yacht is open daily except Christmas, with the first tour beginning at 10:30am, the last tour at 3:50pm. Lasting 90 to 120 minutes, each tour is self-guided with the use of a headset lent to participants. Adults pay £6.50 ($11), seniors £5 ($9), and ages 5 to 15 £3.75 ($6); those 4 and under visit for free. A family ticket, good for two adults and up to two children, is £18 ($31). From Waverley Bridge, take either city bus (Lothian Transport) X50, or else the Guide Friday tour bus which is marked all over its sides with the words BRITANNIA.

by Telford in 1833. The most scenic walk is along the water in the direction of St. Bernard's Well.

A GARDEN

Gardeners and nature lovers will be attracted to the **Royal Botanic Garden,** Inverleith Row (☎ **0131/552-7171**). Main areas of interest are Exhibition Hall, Alpine House, the Demonstration Garden, annual and herbaceous borders (summer only), the copse, the Woodland Garden, Wild Garden, Arboretum, Peat Garden, Rock Garden, Heath Garden, and the Pond. Admission is by voluntary donation, and it's open April to August 9:30am to 7pm, March and September 9:30am to 6pm, February and October 9:30am to 5pm, and November to January 9:30am to 4pm.

ORGANIZED TOURS

If you want a quick introduction to the principal attractions in and around Edinburgh, consider one or more of the tours offered by **Lothian Region Transport,** 14 Queen St. (☎ **0131/555-6363**). You won't find a cheaper way to hit the highlights. The buses leave from Waverley Bridge, near the Scott Monument. The tours are given April to late October; a curtailed winter program is also offered.

You can see most of the major sights of Edinburgh, including the Royal Mile, the Palace of Holyroodhouse, Princes Street, and Edinburgh Castle, by double-deck motor coach for £7.50 ($13) for adults, £6 ($10) for seniors and students, and £1.50 ($2.55) for children. This ticket is valid all day on any LRT Edinburgh Classic Tour bus, which allows passengers to get on and off at any of the 15 stops along its routes. Buses start from Waverley Bridge every day beginning at 9:15am, departing every 15 minutes in summer and about every 30 minutes in winter, then embark on a circuit of Edinburgh, which if you remain on the bus without ever getting off will take about 2 hours. Commentary is offered along the way.

Tickets for any of these tours can be bought at LRT offices at Waverley Bridge, or at 14 Queen St., or at the tourist information center in Waverley Market. Advance reservations are a good idea. For more information, call ☎ **0131/555-6363,** 24 hours a day.

THE SHOPPING SCENE

The best buys are in tartans and woolens, along with bone china and Scottish crystal. Princes Street, George Street, and the Royal Mile are the major shopping arteries. Here are a few suggestions.

Looking for a knitted memento? Moira-Anne Leask, owner of the **Shetland Connection,** 491 Lawnmarket (☎ **0131/225-3525;** bus: 1), promotes the skills of the Shetland knitter, and her shop is packed with sweaters, hats, and gloves in colorful Fair Isle designs. She also offers hand-knitted mohair, Arran, and Icelandic sweaters. Her oldest knitter is 90 years old! Items range from fine-ply cobweb shawls to chunky ski sweaters handcrafted by skilled knitters in top-quality wool.

If you've ever suspected that you might be Scottish, **Tartan Gift Shops,** 54 High St. (☎ **0131/558-3187;** bus 1), has a chart indicating the place of origin, in Scotland, of your family name. You'll then be faced with a bewildering array of hunt-and-dress tartans. The high-quality wool is sold by the yard as well as in the form of kilts for both men and women.

Clan Tartan Centre, 70–74 Bangor Rd., Leith (☎ **0131/553-5100;** bus: 7, 10), is one of the leading specialists in Edinburgh, regardless of which clan you claim as your own. If you want help in identifying a particular tartan, the staff at this shop will assist you. There's also the **James Pringle Woollen Mill,** 70–74 Bangor Rd., Leith (☎ **0131/553-5161;** bus: 7, 10), which produces a large variety of top-quality wool items, including a range of Scottish knitwear—cashmere sweaters, tartan and tweed ties, travel rugs, tweed hats, and tam o'shanters. In addition, the mill has the only Clan Tartan Centre in Scotland, where more than 2,500 sets and trade designs are accessible through their research facilities.

Edinburgh Crystal factory, Eastfield, Penicuik (☎ **01968/675128;** bus: 62, 64, 65, 81, or 87), lies about 16km (10 miles) south of Edinburgh, just off A-701 to Peebles. It's devoted entirely to handmade crystal glassware, and you can take tours to watch glassmakers at work Monday to Friday 9am to 3:30pm. There's a free minibus link from Waverley Station, which leaves on the hour and runs Monday to Friday 10am to 4pm and on the weekend 11am to 2pm. April to September, weekend tours are also given between 11am and 2:30pm. At the Visitor Centre is a factory shop where the world's largest collection of Edinburgh crystal is on view and for sale. You can find inexpensively priced factory seconds.

For beautiful wall hangings, you can make your own brass rubbings or buy them ready-made from the **Scottish Stone and Brass Rubbing Centre,** Trinity Apse, Chalmers Close, near the Royal Mile (☎ **0131/556-4364;** bus: 1). You can visit the center's collection of replicas molded from ancient Pictish stones, rare Scottish brasses, and medieval church brasses.

The two best department stores in Edinburgh are **Debenham's,** 109–112 Princes St. (☎ **0131/2251320;** bus: 3, 31, 69), and **Jenners,** 48 Princes St. (☎ **0131/ 2252442;** bus: 3, 31, 69). Both stock Scottish and international merchandise.

Other Scottish shopping venues worth checking out include **Old Town Weaving Company,** 555 Castlehill (☎ **0131/226-1555;** bus: 1), where you can converse with various craftspeople and purchase some of their work. If you're interested in old-fashioned Scottish crafts, this is the place. Established in 1866, **Hamilton & Inches,** 87 George St. (☎ **0131/225-4898;** bus: 41, 42), is a gold and silversmith with both modern and antique designs. It has a stunning late Georgian interior as well.

EDINBURGH AFTER DARK

For a thorough list of entertainment options during your stay, pick up a copy of *The List,* a biweekly entertainment paper available at the Tourist Information Office for £1.90 ($3.25).

FESTIVALS

The highlight of Edinburgh's year—some would say the only time when the real Edinburgh emerges—comes in the last weeks of August during the ✪ **Edinburgh International Festival.** Since 1947, the festival has attracted artists and companies of the highest international standard in all fields of the arts, including music, opera, dance, theater, exhibition, poetry, and prose, and "Auld Reekie" takes on a cosmopolitan air.

During the festival, one of the most exciting spectacles is the Military Tattoo on the floodlit esplanade in front of Edinburgh Castle, high on its rock above the city. Vast audiences watch the precision marching of Scottish regiments and military units from all parts of the world, and of course the stirring skirl of the bagpipes and the swirl of the kilt.

Less predictable in quality but greater in quantity is the **Edinburgh Festival Fringe,** an opportunity for anybody—professional or nonprofessional, an individual, a group of friends, or a whole company of performers—to put on a show wherever they can find an empty stage or street corner. Late-night reviews, outrageous and irreverent contemporary drama, university theater presentations, maybe even a full-length opera—Edinburgh gives them all free rein. A **Film Festival,** a **Jazz Festival,** a **Television Festival,** and a **Book Festival** (every second year) all overlap at varying times during August.

Ticket prices vary from £5 ($9) up to about £50 ($85) a seat. Information can be obtained at **Edinburgh International Festival,** The Hub, Castle Hill, Edinburgh EH1 7ND (☎ **0131/473-2000;** fax 0131/473-2003; www.go-edinburgh.co.uk). The office is open Monday to Friday 9:30am to 5:30pm.

Other sources of event information include **Edinburgh Festival Fringe,** 180 High St., Edinburgh EH1 1BW (☎ **0131/226-5257**); **Edinburgh Book Festival,** 137 Dundee St., Edinburgh EH11 1BG (☎ **0131/228-5444**); **Edinburgh Film Festival,** 88 Lothian Rd., Edinburgh EH3 9BZ (☎ **0131/228-4051**); and **Edinburgh Military Tattoo,** 32 Market St., Edinburgh EH1 1QB (☎ **0131/225-1188**).

THEATER

Edinburgh has a lively theater scene. In 1994, the ✪ **Festival Theatre,** 13–29 Nicolson St. (☎ **0131/662-1112** for administration, 0131/529-6000 for tickets during non-festival times, or 0131/225-5756 for tickets during the festival; bus: 3, 31, 33), opened in time for some aspects of the Edinburgh Festival. Set on the eastern edge of Edinburgh, near the old campus of the University of Edinburgh, it has since been called "Britain's de facto Dance House" because of its sprung floor, its enormous stage (the largest in Britain), and its suitability for opera presentations of all kinds. Tickets are £5.50 to £45.50 ($9 to $77).

Another major theater is the **King's Theatre,** 2 Leven St. (☎ **0131/529-6000;** bus: 10, 11), a 1,600-seat Victorian venue offering a wide repertoire of classical entertainment, including ballet, opera, and West End productions. The **Netherbow Arts Centre,** 43 High St. (☎ **0131/556-9579;** bus: 1), has been called "informal," and productions here are often experimental and delightful—new Scottish theater at its best. Ask about lunchtime performances.

The resident company of **Royal Lyceum Theatre,** Grindlay Street (☎ **0131/248-4848;** bus: 11, 15), also has an enviable reputation; its presentations range from the works of Shakespeare to new Scottish playwrights. The **Traverse Theatre,** Cambridge Street (☎ **0131/228-1404;** bus: 11, 15), is one of the few theaters in Britain funded solely to present new plays by British writers and first translations into English of international works. In a modern location, it now offers two theaters under one roof: Traverse 1 seats 250 and Traverse 2 seats 100.

BALLET, OPERA & CLASSICAL MUSIC

The **Scottish Ballet** and the **Scottish Opera** perform at the **Playhouse Theatre,** 18–22 Greenside Place (☎ **0131/557-2590;** bus: 7, 14), which, with 3,100 seats, is the town's largest theater. The **Scottish Chamber Orchestra** makes its home at the **Queen's Hall,** Clerk Street (☎ **0131/668-2019;** bus: 3, 33, 31), also a major venue for the Edinburgh International Festival.

FOLK MUSIC & CEILIDHS

Folk music is presented in many clubs and pubs in Edinburgh, but these strolling players tend to be somewhat erratic or irregular in their appearances. It's best to read notices in pubs and talk to the tourist office to see where the ceilidh will be on the night of your visit.

Some hotels regularly feature traditional Scottish music in the evenings. You might check with the **Carlton Highland Hotel** on North Bridge (☎ **0131/556-7277;** bus: 3, 31, 33) or the **George Hotel** 19–21 George St. (☎ **0131/225-1251;** bus: 3, 31, 33). **Jamie's Scottish Evening** is presented at the King James Hotel on Leith Street (☎ **0131/556-0111;** bus: 7, 14) Tuesday through Sunday at 7pm, costing £38 ($65) for dinner, wine, and show.

DANCE & ROCK CLUBS

The **Cavendish,** 3 West Tollcross (☎ **0131/228-3252;** bus: 11, 15, or 23), isn't necessarily where you go to hear the next Oasis or Blur, but who knows? A rock-and-roll

---

A Wee Dram for Fans of Malt Whisky

It requires a bit of an effort to reach it (take bus 10A, 16, or 17 from Princes Street to Leith), but for fans of malt whisky, the **Scotch Malt Whisky Society** has been called "The Top of the Whisky Pyramid" by distillery-industry magazines in Britain. It's on the second floor of a 16th-century warehouse at 87 Giles St., Leith (☎ **0131/554-3451**), and was originally designed to store Bordeaux and port wines from France and Portugal. All you can order are single-malt whiskies, served neat, usually in a dram (unless you want yours watered down with branch water) and selected from a staggering choice of whiskies from more than 100 distilleries throughout Scotland. Hours are Monday to Friday 10am to 11pm, Saturday 10am to 2:30pm and from 5 to 11pm.

legend might be born here every Friday or Saturday night when the doors open at 10pm and close at 2am. There's a dress code—that is, no tennis shoes or jeans. The bar is open Thursday to Saturday 10pm to 3am, with a £6 ($10) cover Friday and Saturday.

The glamorous **Club Mercado,** 36–39 Market St. (☎ **0131/226-4224;** bus: 1), attracts an 18- to 35-year-old crowd. Once the headquarters of the British Rail's Scottish branch, it hangs suspended over the tracks behind the city's main station. On Friday, the action kicks off with free-admission TFIS, which stands for a somewhat saltier version of "Thank God It's Friday"; it runs 5 to 10pm and caters to youngish workers who indulge in the cut-price drinks while tapping to the kitsch music. Other special nights are alternate–Saturday Viva (a night of eclectic music attracting all sorts from toughs to drag queens) and The Colours of Love (basically a rave featuring the latest house music); both charge £8 to £10 ($13 to $17). Sunday's Bubbalicious is student night, charging £3 to £4 ($4.95 to $7), and the first Sunday of the month is gay night, charging £5 ($8). Generally, cover runs £3 to £10 ($4.95 to $17), and it's open daily 10pm to 3am.

Po Na Na, 43B Frederick St. (☎ **0131/226-2224;** bus: 80), is a branch of Britain's most successful nightclub chain. The theme is a Moroccan Casbah, thanks to wall mosaics, brass lanterns, and artifacts shipped in from Marrakech. You'll dance in the cellar of a transformed 19th-century building, beneath a tented ceiling illuminated with strobes. Expect 25- to 40-year-olds and a highly danceable mix of house and funk. Po Na Na isn't specifically gay but does draw a strong gay following. It's open daily 8pm to 3am, with a cover running £2 to £3 ($3.30 to $4.95). **Revolution,** 31 Lothian Rd. (☎ **0131/229-7670;** bus: 11, 15), is Edinburgh's largest nightclub, popular with an under-25 crowd and with a capacity for 1,500. Mainstream contemporary dance music (plus five bars) attracts the crowds, and there are theme and student nights. Cover is £3 to £7 ($4.95 to $12), and it's open Wednesday to Sunday 10pm to 2am.

In the basement of the Dome Bar & Grill, **Whynot,** 14 George St. (☎ **0131/ 624-8633;** bus: 41, 42), is a hot new entertainment complex that opened in the former Bank of Scotland building across from the George Inter-Continental Hotel. It has low ceilings with veil-like curtains above the dance floor and lots of seating coves tucked away for privacy. The club swings Thursday to Sunday 10pm to 3am. On Thursday, there's a £3 to £7.50 ($4.95 to $12) cover for dancing to the music of the 1960s, 1970s, and 1980s. Friday features mainstream pop, with a £5 ($8) cover, and Saturday features contemporary dance music, with a £7.50 ($12) cover. Behind the main Post Office and Waverley Station is ○ **The Venue,** 15 Calton Rd. (☎ **0131/ 557-3073;** bus: 26), the principal stage for live music. Some of the biggest bands in the United Kingdom perform here, and other entertainment is by Scottish wannabes. Posters and flyers around town will let you know what's on at any given time. This large hall isn't open unless there's a concert, and admission fees and times are on a per-show basis, so call for details.

PUBS & BARS

Edinburgh's most famous pub, **Café Royal Circle Bar,** 17 W. Register St. (☎ **0131/ 556-1884;** bus: 3, 31, 33), is a long-enduring favorite. One part is now occupied by the Oyster Bar of the Café Royal, but life in the Circle Bar continues at its old pace. The opulent trappings of the Victorian era are still to be seen. Go up to the serving counter, which stands like an island in a sea of drinkers, and place your order.

The Abbotsford, 3 Rose St. (☎ **0131/225-5276;** bus: 3, 31, 33), is near the eastern end of Rose Street, a short walk from Princes Street. This pub has served stiff drinks and oceans of beer since it was founded in 1887. Inside, the gaslight era is alive and thriving, thanks to a careful preservation of the original dark paneling, long, battered tables, and an ornate plaster ceiling. The inventories of beer on tap changes about once a week, supplementing a roster of single-malt scotches. Platters of food, priced at from £2.50 to £6.60 ($4.25 to $11), are dispensed from the bar. Established in 1806, **Deacon Brodie's Tavern,** 435 Lawnmarket (☎ **0131/225-6531;** bus: 1), is the neighborhood pub along the Royal Mile. It perpetuates the memory of Deacon Brodie, good citizen by day, robber by night (see above). The tavern and wine cellars contain a restaurant and lounge bar.

GAY BARS & CLUBS

C. C. Bloom's, 23–24 Greenside Place (☎ **0131/556-9331;** bus: 7, 14), is one of the most popular gay bars in Edinburgh. The upstairs bar offers drinks and same-sex camaraderie. The downstairs club features dancing to a wide range of music, and one night a week is set aside for karaoke. Attracting a larger female clientele than most other gay bars in Edinburgh is **Planet Out,** 6 Baxters Place (☎ **0131/524-0061;** bus: 8, 9, or 19). It's mainly a place to sit and enjoy a drink, but once a month there's a theme night with drink specials and activities. Another gay venue is **Cafe Habana,** 22 Greenside Place (☎ **0131/556-4349;** bus: 7, 14). This pub answers the eternal question of what's under the kilt. Gays enjoy the cafe downstairs or the disco upstairs on Friday and Saturday nights.

DAY TRIPS FROM EDINBURGH

LINLITHGOW In this royal burgh, a county town in West Lothian, 29km (18 miles) west of Edinburgh, Mary, Queen of Scots was born. From Edinburgh direct trains (☎ **0345/484950**) run every 15 minutes during the day to Linlithgow (trip time: 20 minutes). Round-trip fare is £4.60 ($8) for adults, £2.30 ($3.90) for children. Buses also leave from St. Andrew's Square in Edinburgh (☎ **01324/613-777** for schedules), every 20 minutes (trip time: 1 hour). Round-trip fare is £4.15 ($7) for adults, £2.10 ($3.55) for children. Motorists can take A902 to Corstorphine, then A8 to M9, getting off at the signposted junction (no. 3) to Linlithgow.

The roofless ✪ **Linlithgow Palace** (☎ **01506/842-896**), birthplace of Mary, Queen of Scots in 1542, can still be explored today, even if it's but a shell of its former self. The queen's suite was in the north quarter, but was rebuilt for the homecoming of James VI (James I of England) in 1620. The palace burned to the ground in 1746. The Great Hall is on the first floor, and a small display shows some of the more interesting architectural relics. The ruined palace is 1km (half a mile) from Linlithgow Station. Admission is £2.50 ($4.25) for adults, £1.90 ($3.25) for seniors, £1 ($1.70) for children. Hours are daily 9:30am to 6:30pm (last admission 6pm).

South of the palace stands the medieval kirk of **St. Michael's Parish Church** (☎ **01506/842188**), open only May to September 10am to 4:30pm. It's been where many a Scottish monarch has worshipped since its consecration in 1242. Despite being ravaged by the disciples of John Knox and transformed into a stable by Cromwell, it's one of Scotland's best examples of a parish church.

In the midst of beautifully landscaped grounds, laid out along the lines of Versailles, sits ✪ **Hopetoun House** (☎ **0131/331-2451**), 16km (10 miles) from Edinburgh. This is Scotland's greatest Adam mansion, and a fine example of 18th-century architecture. The splendid reception rooms are filled with 18th-century furniture, paintings, statuary, and other artworks. From a rooftop platform you see a panoramic view of the Firth of Forth. You can take the nature trail, explore the deer parks, investigate the Stables Museum, or stroll through the formal gardens, all on the grounds. The house is 3km (2 miles) from the Forth Road Bridge near South Queensferry, off A-904. If you don't have a car, take a cab from the rail station in Linlithgow for about £7 to £9 ($12 to $15). Admission is £5 ($9) for adults, £4.50 ($8) for seniors, £2.70 ($4.60) for children; family ticket (for up to six) £15 ($26). Open Easter weekend, May to September and weekends in October, daily from 10am to 5:30pm (last admission 4:30pm).

NORTH BERWICK   This royal burgh, created in the 14th century, was once an important Scottish port. In East Lothian, 39km (24 miles) east from Edinburgh, it's today a holiday resort popular with the Scots. Visitors are drawn to its golf courses, beaches, and harbor life on the Firth of Forth. You can climb the rocky shoreline or enjoy the heated outdoor swimming pool in July and August.

Trains (☎ 0345/484950) leave from Edinburgh about every half hour for the 30-minute trip, roundtrip costing £4 ($6.80) for adults or £2 ($3.40) for children. Buses (☎ 0131/366-39233) also leave from Charlotte Square in Edinburgh at 33 minutes past the hour daily from 8:03am to 5:33pm, taking 1¼ hours and costing £2.75 ($4.70) round-trip for adults or £1.40 ($2.40) for children. Motorists follow A198 from Edinburgh to North Berwick (it's signposted all the way).

At the **information center,** Quality Street (☎ 01620/892-197), you can pick up information on boat trips to the offshore islands, including **Bass Rock,** a volcanic island that is a breeding ground for about 10,000 gannets (a type of seabird). Hours are Monday to Saturday 9am to 1:30pm and 2:30 to 5pm.

Some 3km (2 miles) east of North Berwick, and 40km (25 miles) east of Edinburgh on A-198, stand the ruins of the 14th-century diked and rose-colored **Tantallon Castle** (☎ 01620/892-727). This was the ancient stronghold of the Douglases until their defeat by Cromwell's forces in 1650. Overlooking the Firth of Forth, the castle ruins are still formidable, with a square, five-story central tower and a dovecote, plus the shell of its east tower, a D-shaped structure with a wall from the central tower. The best way to get to the castle is by car; there're buses that run every 2 hours from North Berwick. The castle can be visited April to September, daily 9:30am to 6:30pm; the rest of the year it's open Monday to Wednesday and Saturday 9:30am to 4pm, Thursday 9:30am to 4:30pm, and Sunday 2 to 4:30pm. Admission is £2.50 ($4.25) for adults, £1.90 ($3.25) for seniors, and £1 ($1.70) for children.

DIRLETON   This little town, a preservation village, vies for the title of "prettiest village in Scotland." The town plan, drafted in the early 16th century, is essentially unchanged today. Dirleton has two greens shaped like triangles, with a pub opposite Dirleton Castle, placed at right angles to a group of cottages. It's on the Edinburgh–North Berwick road (A-198), 8km (5 miles) west of North Berwick and 31km (19 miles) east of Edinburgh. Buses (☎ 0131/663-9233) leave from St. Andrew's Square station in Edinburgh at 10 past and 20 to the hour (trip time: 1 hour). The last bus departs at 5:10pm. One-way fare is £1.60 ($2.70) for adults or 85p ($1.45) for children.

A rose-tinted 13th-century castle with surrounding gardens, once the seat of the wealthy Anglo-Norman de Vaux family, **Dirleton Castle** (☎ 01620/850330) looks like a fairy-tale fortification, with its towers, arched entries, and oak ramp. Ruins of the Great Hall and kitchen can be seen, as well as what's left of the lord's chamber where the de Vaux family lived. The 16th-century main gate has a hole through which boiling tar or water could be poured to discourage unwanted visitors. The castle's country garden and bowling green are still in use. Admission is £2.50 ($4.25) for adults, £1.90 ($3.25) for seniors, £1 ($1.70) for children. You can tour the castle April to September, Monday to Saturday 9:30am to 6pm, Sunday 10am to 6pm; October to March, Monday to Saturday 9:30am to 4pm, Sunday 2 to 4pm.

2 Tayside & Grampian

Tayside and Grampian, two history-rich sections in northeast Scotland, offer a vast array of sightseeing, even though they're relatively small areas. Tayside, for example, is about 137km (85 miles) east to west, and some 97km (60 miles) south to north. The two regions share the North Sea coast between the Firth of Tay in the south and the Firth of Moray farther north. The so-called Highland Line separating the Lowlands in the south from the Highlands in the north crosses both regions. The Grampians, the highest mountain range in Scotland, are to the west of this line.

Carved out of the old counties of Perth and Angus, **Tayside** is named for its major river, the 190km (119-mile) Tay. The region is easy to explore, and its tributaries and dozens of lochs and Highland streams are among the best salmon and trout waters in Europe. One of the loveliest regions of Scotland, Tayside is filled with heather-clad Highland hills, long blue lochs under tree-lined banks, and miles and miles of walking trails. Perth and Dundee are among the six leading cities of Scotland. Tayside provided the backdrop for many novels by Sir Walter Scott, including *The Fair Maid of Perth, Waverley,* and *The Abbot.* Its golf courses are world famous, ranging from the trio of 18-hole courses at Gleneagles to the open championship links at Carnoustie.

The **Grampian region** has Aberdeen, Scotland's third-largest city, and Braemar, site of the most famous of the Highland gatherings. The queen herself comes here to holiday at Balmoral Castle, her private residence, a tradition dating back to the days of Queen Victoria and her consort, Prince Albert. As you journey on the scenic roads of Scotland's northeast, you'll pass heather-covered moorland and peaty lochs, wood glens and salmon-filled rivers, granite-stone villages and ancient castles, and fishing harbors as well as North Sea beach resorts.

After exploring Edinburgh, you can tour Tayside and Grampian. Perth, 70km (44 miles) north of Edinburgh, makes the best "gateway" to the region.

PERTH

From its majestic position on the Tay, the ancient city of Perth was the capital of Scotland until the middle of the 15th century. It's here that the Highlands meet the Lowlands. Perth itself has few historic buildings. The main attraction, Scone Place, lies on the outskirts.

ESSENTIALS

GETTING THERE   By Train   ScotRail provides service between Edinburgh and Perth (trip time: 90 minutes), with continuing service to Dundee. The trip to Perth costs £9 ($15) from Edinburgh; phone ☎ **0345/484950** for 24-hour information.

By Bus   Edinburgh and Perth are connected by frequent bus service (trip time: 1¹/₂ hours). The fare is £4.70 ($8). For more information and schedules, check with CityLink (☎ **0990/505050**).

By Car   To reach Perth from Edinburgh, take A-90 northwest and go across the Forth Road Bridge, continuing north along M-90 (trip time: 1¹/₂ hours).

VISITOR INFORMATION   The **tourist information center** is at Lower City Mills, West Mill St. (☎ **01738/638353**), and is open April to June daily 9am to 6pm,

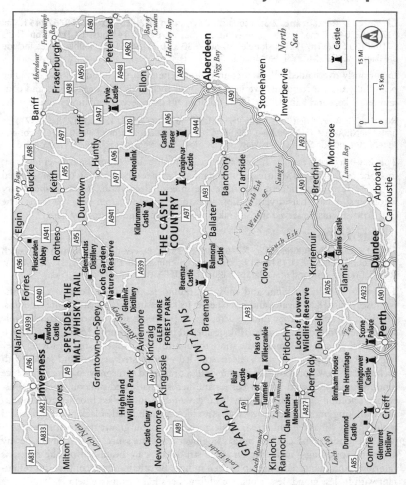

July to September daily 9am to 8pm, October daily 9am to 6pm, and November to March, Monday to Saturday 9am to 5pm.

WHERE TO STAY

Dupplin Castle. Near Aberdalgie, Perth PH2 0PY. ☎ **01738/623224.** Fax 01738/444140. www.dupplin.co.uk. E-mail: dupplin@netcomuk.co.uk. 7 units. TEL. £110 ($187) double. Rates include breakfast. MC, V. From Perth, follow the main highway to Glasgow, turning left onto B-9112 toward Aberdalgie and Forteviot.

Only a 1-hour drive from Edinburgh, this modern, severely dignified mansion was built in 1968 by well-known architect Schomber Scott to replace the last of the three castles that had once risen proudly from the site. Surrounded by 14ha (30 acres) of forest and spectacular gardens (some of its specimens are 250 years old), the site is one of the most beautiful near Perth. Rooms are rented in a spirit of elegance and good manners. Views from many overlook the valley of the River Earn. Meals, which must be booked 24 hours in advance, cost £28 ($48).

✪ **Hotel & Restaurant.** 2 St. Leonard's Bank, Perth PH2 8EB. ☎ **01738/622451.** Fax 01738/622046. E-mail: centuryhousehotel@compuserve.com. 14 units. TV TEL. Mon–Thurs £110–£125.50 ($187–$213) double, Fri–Sun £80–£90 ($136–$153) double. Rates include breakfast. AE, DC, MC, V. Free parking.

Luxuriously overhauled, this is a country-house hotel in the middle of the city. The beautifully decorated rooms overlook the South Inch Park. All are spacious and contain teamakers and hair dryers. Light traditional fare is served in country-house style.

Hunting Tower. Crieff Rd., Perth PH1 3JT. ☎ **01738/583771.** Fax 01738/583777. 34 units. MINIBAR TV TEL. £99.50–£129.50 ($169–$220) double, from £99.50 ($169) cottage suite. Rates include Scottish breakfast. AE, DC, MC, V. Drive 6km (3^1/$_2$ miles) west on A-85.

This late-Victorian country house, about a 10-minute drive from the city center, is set in 1.5ha (3^1/$_2$ acres) of well-manicured gardens, with a modern wing of rooms added in 1998. Taste and concern went into the interior decoration. Rooms, which vary wildly in size, have hair dryers, radios, and trouser presses. Seven have spa baths. The fine Scottish cuisine served in the Oak Room is reason enough to stay here.

WHERE TO DINE

✪ **Let's Eat.** 77–79 Kinnoul St. ☎ **01738/643377.** Reservations recommended. Lunch main courses £6.50–£11 ($11–$19); dinner main courses £8–£15 ($14–$26). AE, MC, V. Tues–Sat noon–2pm and 6:30–9:45pm. BRITISH/INTERNATIONAL.

The most visually striking, and most appealing, restaurant in Perth occupies the premises of an 1822 theater and intersperses its tables amid its soaring white columns. There's a particularly cozy lounge, site of a log-burning iron stove and comfortable sofas, where you might want a drink or aperitif before your meal. Menu items, which change frequently, are among the most thoughtful and sophisticated in town. They might include a gratin of goat's cheese studded with roasted peppers and served with rocket salad, new potatoes, and chutney; fillet of roasted venison with port wine sauce (and in some cases with juniper berries and herbs); marinated tuna on a bed of couscous; a selection of terrins that vary from day to day; and grilled brochettes of monkfish with king prawns, rice, and salad. Also look for handmade black puddings served with "smash" (mashed potatoes), applesauce, and onion gravy; risotto studded with wild mushrooms; and chicken breasts in ginger-and-lime sauce. Dessert might be any of several "puddings" including an apple strudel that are headlined on the menu as "glorious" and that usually live up to their billing. Be careful not to confuse this restaurant with its less grand, less expensive sibling, Let's Eat Again (see below).

Let's Eat Again. 33 George St. ☎ **1738/633771.** Reservations recommended. Main courses £5–£9 ($9–$15). AE, MC, V. Tues–Sat noon–2pm and 6:30–9:30pm. BRITISH/INTERNATIONAL.

Set behind the bright-yellow-with-lime-green trim of what was originally a 19th-century private home, this upbeat bistro caters to the young-at-heart with well-prepared but relatively inexpensive versions of Mediterranean and international cuisine like what you might have expected in a trendy eatery in London. Your meal might begin with charcoal-grilled Mediterranean vegetables with mozzarella; smoked haddock and chive-laced risotto; smoked local venison with spicy pears; salmon and codfish cakes with lemon-flavored butter sauce; roasted salmon with sun-dried tomatoes and pesto; and Thai-style chicken curry with noodles. Be careful not to confuse this restaurant with the more upscale Let's Eat, under the same management (see above).

Littlejohn's. 24 St. John's St. ☎ **01738/639888.** Main courses £3.95–£12.85 ($7–$22). AE, DC, MC, V. Daily 10am–11pm. INTERNATIONAL.

Set on one of Perth's busiest commercial streets, behind a century-old facade, this restaurant has one large dining room with old-fashioned wood paneling, antique signs, and lots of Scottish charm. Despite the conservative nature of the setting, the food offerings are eclectic and include pizzas, pastas, Mexican tortillas, burgers, steaks, and an occasional lobster dish.

SEEING THE SIGHTS

Kirk of St. John the Baptist. 31 St. John Place. ☎ **01738/622241.** Free admission. Mon–Fri 10am–noon and 2–4pm.

This is the main sightseeing attraction of "the fair city." It's believed that the original foundation is from Pictish times. The present choir dates from 1440 and the nave from 1490. In 1559 John Knox preached his famous sermon here attacking idolatry, which caused a turbulent wave of iconoclasm to sweep across the land. In its wake, religious artifacts, stained glass, and organs were destroyed all over Scotland. The church was restored as a World War I memorial in the mid-1920s.

Branklyn Garden. 116 Dundee Rd. (A-85), in Branklyn. ☎ **01738/625535.** Admission £2.50 ($4.25) adults, £1.70 ($2.90) children, students, and seniors; family ticket £6.40 ($11). Mar–Oct daily 9:30am–sunset; closed in winter.

Once the finest 1ha (2 acres) of private garden in Scotland, the garden now belongs to the National Trust for Scotland. It has a superb collection of rhododendrons, alpines, and herbaceous and peat-garden plants from all over the world.

A DAY TRIP TO SCONE

Old Scone, 3km (2 miles) from Perth on the River Tay, was the ancient capital of the Picts. On a lump of sandstone called the "Stone of Destiny," the early Scottish monarchs were enthroned. In 1296 Edward I, the "Hammer of the Scots," moved the stone to Westminster Abbey, and for hundreds of years it rested under the chair on which British monarchs were crowned. The Scots have always bitterly resented this theft, and at last, it has been returned to Scotland, to find a permanent home in Edinburgh Castle, where it can be viewed by the public.

The seat of the earls of Mansfield and birthplace of David Douglas of fir-tree fame, **Scone Palace,** along A-93 (☎ **01738/552300**), was largely rebuilt in 1802, incorporating the old palace of 1580. Inside is an impressive collection of French furniture, china, ivories, and 16th-century needlework, including bed hangings executed by Mary, Queen of Scots. A fine collection of rare conifers is found on the grounds in the Pinetum. Rhododendrons and azaleas grow profusely in the gardens and woodlands around the palace. To reach the palace, head northeast of Perth on A-93. The site is open Good Friday to mid-October only, daily 9:30am to 5pm. Admission is £5.40 ($9) for adults, £4.60 ($8) seniors, £3.20 ($5) for children 16 years old and under, including entrance to both house and grounds. Admission to the grounds only is £2.70 ($4.60) for adults and £1.60 ($2.70) for children.

Where to Stay & Dine

✪ **The Murrayshall.** New Scone, Perthshire PH2 7PH. ☎ **01738/551171.** Fax 01738/552595. 27 units. TV TEL. £120–£130 ($204–$221) double; from £150–£160 ($255–$272) suite; lodge £150 ($255). Rates include Scottish breakfast. AE, DC, MC, V. Take A-94 2.5km (1½ miles) east of New Scone.

Murrayshall, an elegant country-house hotel and restaurant set in 300 acres of parkland, was completely refurbished in 1987 and reopened as one of the showpieces of Perthshire. The Victorian mansion offers its own 18-hole, par-73 golf course, interspersed with trees, water hazards, and white-sand bunkers. The hotel is traditionally styled and offers the finest dining in the area in its Old Masters restaurant.

GLENEAGLES

This famous golfing center and sports complex is on a moor between Strathearn and Strath Allan. Gleneagles has four **18-hole golf courses:** King's Course, the longest one; Queen's Course, next in length; Prince's Course, shortest of all; and Glendevon, the newest of the quartet, built in 1980. They're among the best in Scotland, and the sports complex is one of the best-equipped in Europe.

ESSENTIALS

GETTING THERE   By Train   The 15-minute ride from Perth costs £3 ($4.95). The trip takes 1 hour and 40 minutes from Edinburgh and costs £8 ($14). For information call ☎ **0345/484950.**

By Bus   The only service departs from Glasgow. The trip takes slightly more than an hour and costs £6 ($10). For information and schedules, call ☎ **01738/26847.**

By Car   Gleneagles is on A-9, about halfway between Perth and Stirling, a short distance from the village of Auchterarder. It lies 88km (55 miles) from Edinburgh and 72km (45 miles) from Glasgow.

VISITOR INFORMATION   The year-round tourist center is at 90 High St., Auchterarder (☎ **01764/663450**). Open November to March Monday to Friday 9:30am to 5pm, Saturday 11am to 3pm; April to June Monday to Saturday 9:30am to 5:30pm, Sunday 11am to 4pm; July and August Monday to Saturday 9am to 7pm, Sunday 11am to 6pm, and September and October Monday to Saturday 9:30am to 5:30pm, Sunday 11am to 4pm.

WHERE TO STAY & DINE

✪ **Auchterarder House.** Auchterarder PH3 1DZ. ☎ **01764/663646.** Fax 01764/ 662939. www.wrensgroup.com. 15 units. TV TEL. £160–£300 ($272–$510) double. Rates include Scottish breakfast. AE, DC, MC, V. Free parking.

Auchterarder House, 1.5km (1 mile) from Gleneagles, sits on its own grounds off B-8062 between Auchterarder and Crieff. A fine example of 1830s architecture and construction in the Scots Jacobean style, the mansion house has been completely restored and the interior refurbished to a high standard of luxury by its present owners in a mix of Victorian and modern. The house has elegant public areas and comfortable rooms, all with amenities that aim to please a discerning clientele. At lunch or dinner in the Victorian dining room or in the library, you can choose from a French or British menu.

Gleneagles Hotel. Auchterarder PH3 1NF. ☎ **01764/662231.** Fax 01764/662134. www.gleneagles.com. E-mail: resort.sales@gleneagles.com. 229 units. MINIBAR TV TEL. £315–£380 ($536–$646) double; from £535 ($910) suite. Rates include Scottish breakfast. AE, DC, MC, V. Free parking. Take A-9 1 1/2 miles southwest of Auchterarder.

Gleneagles Hotel stands on its own 390ha (830-acre) estate. Built in isolated grandeur in 1924, it was then the only five-star hotel in Scotland. The service and elegant decor here are among the finest in the country. The luxurious rooms offer views of hills and glens, as well as hair dryers, ironing boards, and trouser presses. You can dine in the Strathearn, paying £42.50 ($72) for a table d'hôte dinner (daily 7 to 9:30pm). The chef uses fresh Scottish and French produce, cooked in a light style while still incorporating traditional flair and imagination. Service is impeccable. The hotel's country club, enclosed in a glass dome to provide a year-round tropical climate, offers members and guests use of a swimming pool, whirlpool, Turkish bath, saunas, plunge pool, and children's pool. The legendary golf courses are the main attraction, however.

Gleneagles guests pay £80 ($132) per person in summer and nonresidents pay £100 ($170).

CRIEFF

From Perth, head west on A-85 for 29km (18 miles) to Crieff. At the edge of the Perthshire Highlands, with good fishing and golf, Crieff makes a pleasant stopover. This small burgh was the seat of the court of the earls of Strathearn until 1747, and the gallows in its marketplace was once used to execute Highland cattle rustlers.

You can take a "day trail" into **Strathearn,** the valley of the River Earn, the very center of Scotland. Here highland mountains meet gentle Lowland slopes, and moorland mingles with rich green pastures. North of Crieff, the road to Aberfeldy passes through the narrow pass of the **Sma' Glen,** a famous spot of beauty, with hills rising on either side to 600m (2,000 feet).

ESSENTIALS

GETTING THERE   By Train   There's no direct service. The nearest rail stations are at Gleneagles, 14km (9 miles) away, and at Perth, 29km (18 miles) away. Call ☎ **0345/484950** for information and schedules.

By Bus   Once you arrive in Perth, you'll find regular connecting bus service hourly during the day. For information and schedules, call **Stagecoach** at ☎ **01738/629339.** The bus service from Gleneagles is too poor to recommend.

By Taxi   From Gleneagles a taxi will cost from £20 to £30 ($34 to $51).

VISITOR INFORMATION   The year-round **tourist information office** is in the Town Hall on High Street (☎ **01764/652578**). Open November to March, Monday to Friday 9:30am to 5pm, Saturday 11am to 3pm; April to June, Monday to Saturday 9:30am to 5:30pm, Sunday 11am to 4pm; July and August, Monday to Saturday 9am to 7pm, Sunday 11am to 6pm, and September and October, Monday to Saturday 9:30am to 5:30pm, Sunday 11am to 4pm.

WHERE TO STAY & DINE

Murraypark Hotel. Connaught Terrace, Crieff PH7 3DJ. ☎ **01764/653731.** Fax 01764/655311. 19 units. TV TEL. £75 ($128) double or suite. Rates include Scottish breakfast. AE, DC, MC, V. Free parking.

This stone-fronted house lies in a residential neighborhood about a 10-minute walk from Crieff's center. In 1993, a new wing was opened, enlarging the public areas and the number of simply furnished rooms. The restaurant's cuisine is based on Scottish, French, and international inspirations.

SEEING THE SIGHTS

Glenturret Distillery Ltd. Hwy. A-85, Glenturret. ☎ **01764/656565.** Guided tours £3.50 ($6) adults, £3 ($5) seniors, £2.30 ($3.90) persons 12–17, free for children 11 and under. Mar–Dec Mon–Sat 9:30am–6pm, Sun noon–6pm, Feb Mon–Fri 11:30am–4pm, Sun noon–4pm. Closed Jan and Dec 25–26. Take A-85 toward Comrie; 1.5km (³/₄ mile) from Crieff, turn right at the crossroads; the distillery is a .5km (¹/₄ mile) up the road.

Scotland's oldest distillery, Glenturret was established in 1775 on the banks of the River Turret. Visitors can see the milling of malt, mashing, fermentation, distillation, and cask filling, followed by a free "wee dram" dispensed at the end of the tour. Guided tours take about 25 minutes and leave at frequent intervals—sometimes as often as every 10 minutes when there's a demand for it. This can be followed or preceded by a 20-minute video, *The Water of Life,* that's presented adjacent to a small museum devoted to the implements of the whisky trade.

Drummond Castle Gardens. Grimsthorpe, Crieff. ☎ **01764/681257.** Admission £3 ($5) adults, £2 ($3.40) seniors, £1.50 ($2.55) children. May–Oct daily 2–6pm; Easter weekend 2–6pm. Closed Nov–Apr. Take A-822 for 5km (3 miles) south of Crieff.

The gardens of Drummond Castle, first laid out in the early 17th century by John Drummond, second earl of Perth, are among the finest formal gardens in Europe. There's a panoramic view from the upper terrace, overlooking an example of an early Victorian parterre in the form of St. Andrew's Cross. The multifaceted sundial by John Mylne, master mason to Charles I, has been the centerpiece since 1630.

PLAYING GOLF

Crieff Golf Club (☎ **01764/652909**) has two courses—both with panoramic views and excellent facilities. The most challenging is the 18-hole Fern Tower, a par-71 course with three par-5 holes. The Dornock is a 64-par, 9-hole course with three par-3 holes. It's not quite as difficult as the Fern Tower, but a test nonetheless. Greens fees for the Fern Tower are £25 ($43) per round Monday to Friday, and £33 ($56) on weekends. Greens fees for the Dornock are £10 ($17) for 9 holes and £14 ($24) for 18 holes. Carts cost £15 ($26) per round. From April to October, the golf club is open 8am to 11pm; November to March to Friday 11am to 6pm and Saturday and Sunday 11am to 11pm.

ABERFELDY

The "Birks o' Aberfeldy" are among the beauty spots made famous by the poet Robert Burns. Once a Pictish center, this small town makes a fine base for touring Perthshire's glens and lochs. Loch Tay lies 10km (6 miles) to the west; Glen Lyon, 24km (15 miles) west; and Kinloch Rannoch, 29km (18 miles) northwest. The town's shops offer good buys in tweeds and tartans, plus other items of Highland dress.

ESSENTIALS

GETTING THERE   By Train   There's no direct service into Aberfeldy. You can take a train to either Perth or Pitlochry, then continue the rest of the way by bus. Call ☎ **0345/484950** for schedules.

By Bus   Connecting buses at either Perth or Pitlochry make the final journey to Aberfeldy. The private bus line **Stagecoach** (☎ **01738/629339**) handles much of the bus travel to the smaller towns and villages in the area.

By Car   From Crieff, take A-822 on a winding road north to Aberfeldy. The 48km (30-mile) drive from Perth takes 30 to 45 minutes.

VISITOR INFORMATION   The **tourist office** is at The Square (☎ **01887/ 820276**). Hours are July and August daily 9:30am to 5pm; April to June, and September and October daily 9am to 5:30pm, and October to March Monday to Saturday 9am to 5:30pm.

WHERE TO STAY & DINE

Farleyer House Hotel. Hwy. B-846, Aberfeldy PH15 2JE. ☎ **01887/820332.** Fax 01887/829430. www.farleyer.com. E-mail: reservations@farleyer.com. 19 units. TV TEL. £100–£200 ($170–$340) double; £110–£190 ($187–$323) family suite. AE, DC, MC, V. Take B-846 for 2 miles west of Aberfeldy.

A tranquil oasis, this hotel of character stands on 33ha (70 acres) of grounds in the Tay Valley. Although restored and altered over the years, the building dates back to the 1500s. The staff entertains guests as if they were in a private home. The public areas are immaculate and beautifully furnished, and the rooms are well maintained and comfortable. The internationally renowned Menzies Restaurant offers a fixed-price menu of five courses that changes daily.

PLAYING GOLF

Aberfeldy Golf Club, at Aberfeldy (☎ **01887/820535**), is a flatland course located on the banks of the River Tay. It's an 18-hole par 68 that is viewed as a "challenge" by the local pro. The River Tay comes into play on several holes, and if you're not careful, you'll be making trips back to the Pro Shop for more balls. Greens fees are £14 ($24) for 18 holes (or £16 ($27) on weekends), and cart fees are £2 ($3.40) per round (pull carts). April to October the club is open daily 8am to 11pm. During other months, call first to see if they're open: it depends on the weather.

DUNKELD

A cathedral town, Dunkeld lies in a thickly wooded valley of the Tay River at the edge of the Perthshire Highlands. Once a major ecclesiastical center, it's one of the seats of ancient Scottish history and an important center of the Celtic church.

ESSENTIALS

GETTING THERE   By Train   Trains from Perth arrive every 2 hours and cost £5 ($9). Travel time by train is 1¹/₂ hours. Call ☎ **0345/484950** for information and schedules.

By Bus   Pitlochry-bound buses leaving from Perth make a stopover in Dunkeld, letting you off at the Dunkeld Car Park, which is at the train station (trip time: 50 minutes). The cost is £3.10 ($5). Contact **Stagecoach** at ☎ **01738/629339.**

By Car   From Aberfeldy, take A-827 east until you reach the junction of A-9 heading south to Dunkeld.

VISITOR INFORMATION   A **tourist information office** is at The Cross (☎ **01350/727688**). It's open April to June, Monday to Saturday 9:30am to 5:30pm and Sunday 11am to 4pm; July 1 to September 8, Monday to Saturday 9am to 7:30pm and Sunday 11am to 7pm; September 9 to October 27, Monday to Saturday 9:30am to 5:30pm and Sunday 11am to 4pm; October 28 to December, Monday to Saturday 9:30am to 1:30pm (closed January to March).

WHERE TO STAY & DINE

✪ **Kinnaird.** Kinnaird, Kinnaird Estate, Dunkeld PH8 0LB. ☎ **01796/482440.** Fax 01796/482289. www.kinnairdestate.com. E-mail: enquiry@kinnairdestate.com. 9 units and 8 estate cottages. TV TEL. £345 ($587) double; £440 ($748) suite; £290–£900 ($493–$1,530) estate cottages. Rates include dinner and Scottish breakfast. MC, V. Free parking. No children under 12 accepted in the hotel.

On a 4,200ha (9,000-acre) private estate, this is a small hotel of great warmth, charm, and comfort. Built in 1770 as a hunting lodge, the house has been restored to its previous grandeur. All the beautifully furnished rooms have king-size beds, private bathrooms, and views. Some rooms overlook the valley of the River Tay; others open onto gardens and woodlands. Kinnaird House Restaurant brings a high-caliber cuisine to the area. The chef cooks in the modern, postnouvelle British and continental style, depending on fresh ingredients, with changing menus based on the season. Sporting facilities on the estate include salmon and trout fishing, roe stalking, and shooting for pheasant, grouse, and duck.

Stakis Dunkeld House Resort Hotel. Dunkeld PH8 0HX. ☎ **01350/727771.** Fax 01350/728924. E-mail: reservations@dunkeld.stakis.co.uk. 97 units. MINIBAR TV TEL. £130 ($221) double; from £180–£200 ($306–$340) suite. Rates include Scottish breakfast. AE, DC, MC, V.

The hotel, offering the quiet dignity of life in a Scottish country house, is ranked as one of the leading leisure and sports hotels in the area. On the banks of the Tay, the surrounding grounds—132ha (280 acres) in all—make for a park-like setting. The house is beautifully kept, and rooms come in a wide range of styles, space, and furnishings. In 1999, an outhouse was converted into an extra wing offering another nine rooms. Its restaurant is one of the finest in the area, paying homage to its "Taste of Scotland" dishes, but also serving international selections. Salmon and trout fishing are possible right on the grounds, and facilities include an indoor swimming pool and all-weather tennis courts.

SEEING THE SIGHTS

Founded in A.D. 815, the **Cathedral of Dunkeld** was converted from a church to a cathedral in 1127 by David I. It stands on Cathedral Street in a scenic setting along the River Tay. The cathedral was first restored in 1815, and traces of the 12th-century structure remain today. Admission is free, and the cathedral is open May to September Monday to Saturday 9:30am to 6:30pm, Sunday 2 to 6:30pm; October to April, Monday to Saturday 9:30am to 4pm.

The National Trust for Scotland has restored many of the old houses and shops around the marketplace and cathedral. The trust owns 20 houses on High Street and Cathedral Street as well. Many of these houses were constructed in the closing years of the 17th century after the rebuilding of the town following the Battle of Dunkeld. The Trust runs the **Ell Shop,** The Cross (☎ **01350/727460**), which specializes in Scottish handcrafts. Easter weekend to December 24, it's open Monday to Saturday 10am to 5:30pm.

The **Scottish Horse Museum,** The Cross (no phone), has exhibits tracing the history of the Scottish Horse Yeomanry, a cavalry force first raised in 1900. The museum is open Easter to October only, Saturday to Wednesday 10am to noon and 1:50 to 5pm. Admission is free.

Shakespeare fans may want to seek out the oak and sycamore in front of the destroyed Birnam House, a mile to the south. This was believed to be a remnant of the **Birnam Wood** in *Macbeth;* you may recall, "Macbeth shall never vanquished be until great Birnam Wood to high Dunsinane Hill shall come against him."

The Hermitage, lying off A-9 about 3km (2 miles) west of Dunkeld, was called a "folly" when it was constructed in 1758 above the wooded gorge of the River Braan. Today it makes for one of the most scenic woodland walks in the area.

PLAYING GOLF

Dunkeld & Birnam, at Dunkeld (☎ **01350/727524**), is touted as the best in the area. The 18-hole course is not too long, but can be quite difficult. It's edged in many areas with bracken, and many a golfer has had to take a drop instead of searching for the errant ball. There're sweeping views of the surrounding environs. Greens fees: Monday through Friday £11 ($19) for 18 holes; Saturday and Sunday £16 ($27) for 18 holes. There are no electric carts; pull carts are available for £2 ($3.40) per round. Hours are daily 7am to 11pm April to September. October to March greens fees are reduced to £5 ($9) and hours are daily 8am to 4pm. There's no official dress code, although if the starter feels you are not dressed "appropriately" you will be asked to "smarten up" the next time you play the course.

DUNDEE & GLAMIS CASTLE

This royal burgh and old seaport is an industrial city on the north shore of the Firth of Tay. When steamers took over the whaling industry from sailing vessels, Dundee became the leading home port for the ships from the 1860s until World War I. Long known for its jute and flax operations, we think today of the Dundee fruitcakes, marmalades, and jams. This was also the home of the man who invented stick-on postage stamps, James Chalmers. Dundee has a raffish charm and serves well as a base for a trip to Glamis Castle.

Spanning the Firth of Tay is the **Tay Railway Bridge,** opened in 1888. Constructed over the tidal estuary, the bridge is some 3km (2 miles) long, one of the longest in Europe. There's also a road bridge 2km (1¼ miles) long, with four traffic lanes and a walkway in the center.

ESSENTIALS

GETTING THERE   By Train   ScotRail offers frequent service between Perth, Dundee, and Aberdeen. One-way fare from Perth to Dundee is £4.40 ($8); from Aberdeen, £16.80 ($29). Phone ☎ **0345/484950** for schedules and departure times.

By Bus   CityLink buses offer frequent bus service from Edinburgh and Glasgow. Call ☎ **0990/505050** for information.

By Car   The fastest way to reach Dundee is to cut south back to Perth along A-9 and link up with A-972 going east.

VISITOR INFORMATION   The **tourist information office** is at 21 Castle St. (☎ **01382/434664**). Hours are April to September, Monday to Saturday 9am to 6pm, Sunday 10am to 4pm; October to March, Monday to Saturday 9am to 5pm.

WHERE TO STAY

Invercarse Hotel. 371 Perth Rd., Dundee DD2 1PG. ☎ **01382/669231.** Fax 01382/644112. 44 units. TV TEL. £90 ($153) double; £100 ($170) suite. Rates include Scottish breakfast. AE, DC, MC, V. Free parking.

In landscaped gardens overlooking the River Tay, this privately owned hotel lies 5km (3 miles) west of the heart of Dundee. Many prefer it for its fresh air, tranquil location, and Victorian country-house aura. Well-maintained rooms come in a variety of sizes and open onto views across the Tay to the hills of the Kingdom of Fife. Guests can enjoy drinks in the bar, and later order a continental or Scottish cuisine.

Stakis Earl Grey Hotel. Earl Grey Place, Dundee DD1 4DE. ☎ **01382/229271.** Fax 01382/200072. E-mail: reservations@dundee.stakis.co.uk. 129 units. TV TEL. £105–£125 ($179–$213) double; from £175 ($298) suite. AE, DC, MC, V. Free parking. Bus: 1A, 1B, or 20.

This chain hotel helped rejuvenate the once-seedy waterfront of Dundee. Built in a severe modern style, it takes its name from a famous English tea, which most often accompanies marmalade and Dundee fruitcakes, the city's two most famous products. Some of the well-furnished rooms overlook the Firth, the river, or the Tay Bridge. Guests can dine at Juliana's Table, featuring buffet-style meals along with table d'hôte lunches and dinners. Facilities include a heated indoor swimming pool, exercise equipment, sauna, and whirlpool.

WHERE TO DINE

Jahangir Tandoori. 1 Sessions St. (at the corner of Hawk Hill). ☎ **01382/202022.** Reservations recommended. Main courses £6.50–£15 ($11–$26). AE, MC, V. Daily 5pm–midnight. INDIAN.

Built around an indoor fishpond in a dining room draped with the soft folds of an embroidered tent, this is one of the most exotic restaurants in the region. Meals are prepared with fresh ingredients and cover the gamut of recipes from both north and south India. Some preparations are slow-cooked in clay pots (tandoori) and seasoned to the degree of spiciness you prefer. Both meat and meatless dishes are available.

SEEING THE SIGHTS

For a panoramic view of Dundee, the Tay bridges across to Fife, and mountains to the north, go to **Dundee Law,** a 175m (572-foot) hill just north of the city. The hill is an ancient volcanic plug.

HMS *Unicorn*. Victoria Dock. ☎ **01382/200900.** Admission £4 ($7) adults, £3 ($5) seniors and children; £10 ($17) family ticket. Easter–Oct daily 10am–5pm, Jan–Easter Mon–Fri 10am–4pm. Bus: 6, 23, or 78.

This 46-gun wooden ship of war commissioned in 1824 by the Royal Navy, now the oldest British-built ship afloat, has been restored and visitors can explore all four decks: the quarterdeck with 32-pound cannonades, the gun deck with its battery of 18-pound cannons and the captain's quarters, the berth deck with officers' cabins and crews' hammocks, and the orlop deck and hold. Various displays portraying life in the sailing navy and the history of the *Unicorn* make this a rewarding visit.

Broughty Castle. Castle Green, Broughty Ferry. ☎ **01382/436916.** Free admission. July–Sept Mon 11am–5pm, Tues–Thurs 10am–1pm and 2–5pm, Sun 2–5pm; Oct–June Mon 11am–5pm, Tues–Thurs 10am–1pm and 2–5pm. Bus: 75 or 76.

This 15th-century estuary fort lies about 6km (4 miles) east of the city center on the seafront, at Broughty Ferry, a little fishing hamlet and once the terminus for ferries crossing the Firth of Tay before the bridges were built. Besieged by the English in the 16th century, and attacked by Cromwell's army under General Monk in the 17th century, it was eventually restored as part of Britain's coastal defenses in 1861. Its gun battery was dismantled in 1956, and it's now a museum with displays on local history, arms and armor, and Dundee's whaling story. The observation area at the top of the castle provides fine views of the Tay estuary and northeast Fife.

PLAYING GOLF

Caird Park, at Dundee (☎ 01382/453606), is an 18-hole, par-72 course that presents most golfers with an average challenge. The course is quite flat, but there're more than a few bunkers to navigate. There's also a restaurant and bar on the premises. Greens fees are £15 ($26) for 18 holes, or £25 ($43) for a day ticket. No carts of any sort are allowed on the course, and there's no particular dress code. The park is open April to October daily 7am to 8pm.

A DAY TRIP TO GLAMIS

The little village of Glamis (pronounced without the "i") grew up around **Glamis Castle,** Castle Office, Glamis (☎ 01307/840393). Next to Balmoral Castle, visitors to Scotland most want to see Glamis Castle for its link with the crown. For 6 centuries it has been connected to members of the British royal family. The Queen Mother was brought up here; and Princess Margaret was born here, becoming the first royal princess born in Scotland in 3 centuries. The present owner is the queen's great-nephew. The castle contains Duncan's Hall—the Victorians claimed this was where Macbeth murdered King Duncan, but in the play, the murder takes place at Macbeth's castle (Cawdor?) near Inverness. In fact, Shakespeare was erroneous, as well—he had Macbeth named Thane of Glamis, but Glamis wasn't made a thaneship (a sphere of influence in medieval Scotland) until years after the play takes place.

The present Glamis Castle dates from the early 15th century, but there're records of a castle having been in existence in the 11th century. Glamis Castle has been in the possession of the Lyon family since 1372, and it contains some fine plaster ceilings, furniture, and paintings.

The castle is open to the public, with access to the Royal Apartments and many other rooms, as well as the fine gardens, the end of March to the end of October only, daily 10:30am to 5:30pm. Admission to the castle and gardens is £5.40 ($9.20) adults, £2.80 ($4.75) children. If you wish to visit the grounds only, the charge is £2.50 ($4.25) adults, £1.40 ($2.40) children. Buses run between Dundee and Glamis. The 35-minute ride costs £3.70 ($6) one way. *Note:* Buses don't run on Sunday, and they don't stop in front of the castle, which lies 1.5km (1 mile) from the bus stop.

Where to Stay

Castleton House. Eassie by Glamis, Forfar, Tayside DD8 1SJ. ☎ **01307/840340.** Fax 01307/840506. www.dundeechamber.co.uk/castleton. E-mail: castleton@fastnet.co.uk. 6 units. TV TEL. £100 ($170) double. Children 10 and under stay free in parents' room. Rates include Scottish breakfast. MC, V. Drive 5km (3 miles) west of Glamis on A-94.

This Victorian hotel has been restored with love and care by its owners, Anthony and Sheila Lilly. In cool weather you're greeted by welcoming coal fires in both the bar and public lounge; the youthful staff is the most considerate we've encountered in the area. Rooms of various sizes are furnished with reproductions of antiques. The chef features a set luncheon and a fixed-price dinner, and the menu changes daily but is based on the freshest produce in any given season.

Where to Dine

Strathomore Arms. The Square Glamis. ☎ **01307/840248.** Reservations recommended. Main courses £5.50–£15 ($9–$26). MC, V. Daily noon–2pm and 6:30–9pm. CONTINENTAL/ SCOTTISH.

Try this place near the castle for one of the best lunches in the area. You might begin with freshly made soup of the day or the fresh prawns. Some of the dishes regularly featured might include steak pie or venison. For something a little more exotic there's the Indian chicken breast, marinated in yogurt and spices; and for vegetarians phyllo parcels stuffed with asparagus and cauliflower.

BRAEMAR

In the heart of some of Grampian's most beautiful scenery, Braemar is not only known for its own castle, but it also makes a good center from which to explore Balmoral Castle (see "Ballater & Balmoral Castle," below). In this Highland village, set against a massive backdrop of hills covered with heather in summer, Clunie Water joins the River Dee. The massive **Cairn Toul** towers over Braemar, reaching a height of 1,293m (4,241 feet).

ESSENTIALS

GETTING THERE   By Train   Take the train to Aberdeen, then continue the rest of the way by bus. For information and schedules, call ☎**0345/484950.**

By Bus   Buses run daily from Aberdeen to Braemar at the rate of 6 per day (trip time: 2 hours). One-way fare is £6.50 ($11). The bus and train stations in Aberdeen are next to each other on Guild Street (☎ **01224/212266** for information about schedules).

By Car   To reach Braemar from Dundee, return west toward Perth, then head north along A-93, following the signs into Braemar. The 113km (70-mile) drive will take 70 to 90 minutes.

VISITOR INFORMATION   The year-round **Braemar Tourist Office** is in The Mews, Mar Road (☎ **013397/42208**). In June, hours are daily 10am to 6pm; July and August daily 9am to 7pm, and in September daily 10am to 1pm and 2 to 6pm.

Playing the World's Oldest Course

At **St. Andrew's,** 23km (14 miles) southeast of Dundee and 82km (51 miles) northeast of Edinburgh, the rules of golf in Britain and the world were codified and arbitrated. Golf was played for the first time in the 1400s, probably on the site of St. Andrew's Old Course, and enjoyed by Mary, Queen of Scots here in 1567. All six of St. Andrew's golf courses are open to the public on a more-or-less democratic basis—ballots are polled one day in advance. To participate in the balloting, you first must be staying in St. Andrews for a minimum of 2 days and you must be able to present a current handicap certificate issued by the governing golf body of your home country. If you meet those requirements, you can enter the ballot in person at the golf course, or by phone at ☎ **01334/466666,** before 1:45pm on the day before the one on which you wish to play. At 2pm each day, the balloting is drawn, and the following day's players are announced at 4pm. Bear in mind that your wait to play will most likely be from 4 to 6 days; however, some lucky players get on the course the next day. Players who call the golf course several weeks in advance to make reservations can often circumvent the balloting system, depending on demand.

The **Old Course,** St. Andrews, Golf Place, St. Andrew's, Fife (☎ **01334/466666**), is a 6,000m (6,566-yard) 18-hole course billed as "the Home of Golf." Greens fees are £75 ($128) per round April to September or £34 ($58) otherwise. A caddy will cost £27 ($46) plus tip. Golf clubs rent for £15 ($26) per round. Electric carts are not allowed, and you can rent a cart only on afternoons May to September for £3 ($5). The course is a par 72.

To reach St. Andrews from Edinburgh, travel along the A90 north to Dunfermline. From there, continue northeast along A910, which becomes A915 at Leven. From Leven, drive northeast on A915 directly to St. Andrews (trip time: 1 hour).

In off-season hours are Monday to Saturday 10am to 1pm and 2 to 5pm, Sunday noon to 5pm.

SPECIAL EVENTS   The spectacular ✪ **Royal Highland Gathering** takes place annually in late August or early September in the Princess Royal and Duke of Fife Memorial Park. The queen herself often attends the gathering. These ancient games are thought to have been originated by King Malcolm Canmore, a chieftain who ruled much of Scotland at the time of the Norman conquest of England. He selected his hardiest warriors from all the clans for a "keen and fair contest."

Call the tourist office (see "Visitor Information," above) for more information. Braemar is overrun with visitors during the gathering—anyone thinking of attending would be wise to reserve accommodations anywhere within a 32km (20-mile) radius of Braemar no later than early April.

WHERE TO STAY & DINE

Braemar Lodge Hotel. 6 Glenshee Rd., Braemar AB35 5YQ. ☎ and fax **013397/41627.** 7 units. TV. £50–£72 ($85–$122) double; £200–£400 ($340–$680) log cabin. Rates include Scottish breakfast. MC, V. Free parking. Closed Nov.

This hotel, popular with skiers who frequent the nearby Glenshee slopes, is set on 1ha (2 acres) of grounds at the head of Glen Clunie. Rooms have a strikingly modern decor. Dinner, served in the restaurant from 5:30pm, includes Scottish regional dishes on the à la carte menu. The food is excellent. The chef's specialties include venison with red wine, bacon, mushroom, and onion sauce, steaks served in a creamy pepper sauce, and sautéed fillet of trout with hollandaise sauce. The hotel is on the road to the Glenshee ski slopes near the cottage where Robert Louis Stevenson wrote *Treasure Island*. On the grounds three log cabins have been recently built. Fully equipped with all modern conveniences, they can sleep up to six persons.

Invercauld Arms Thistle Hotel. Braemar AB35 5YR. ☎ **013397/41605.** Fax 013397/41428. 68 units. £139 ($236) double. Rates include Scottish breakfast. AE, DC, MC, V. Free parking. Bus: 201.

The oldest part of this old granite building dates from the 18th century. In cool weather there's a roaring log fire on the hearth. You can go hill walking and see deer, golden eagles, and other wildlife. Fishing and, in winter, skiing are other pursuits in the nearby area. Rooms are comfortably furnished, but rather uninspired. In the pub close by, you'll meet the "ghilles" and "stalkers" (hunting and fishing guides) and then return to the Scottish and international fare served at the hotel.

SEEING THE SIGHTS

If you're a royal family watcher, you might be able to spot members of the family, even the queen, at **Crathie Church,** 14km (9 miles) east of Braemar on A-93 (☎ **013397/ 42208**), where they attend Sunday services when in residence. Services are at 11:30am; otherwise the church is open to view April to October, Monday to Saturday 9:30am to 5:30pm and on Sunday 2 to 5:30pm.

Nature lovers may want to drive to the **Linn of Dee,** 10km (6 miles) west of Braemar, a narrow chasm on the River Dee, which is a local beauty spot. Other beauty spots include Glen Muick, Loch Muick, and Lochnagar. A **Scottish Wildlife Trust Visitor Centre,** reached by a minor road, is located in this Highland glen, off the South Deeside road. An access road joins B-976 at a point 26km (16 miles) east of Braemar. The tourist office (see above) will give you a map pinpointing these beauty spots.

Braemar Castle. On the Aberdeen-Ballater-Perth Rd. (A-93). ☎ **013397/41219.** Admission £2.50 ($4.25) adults, £2 ($3.40) seniors and students, £1 ($1.70) ages 5–15; free for age 4 and under. Mon after Easter to Oct, Sat–Thurs 10am–6pm. Closed Nov–Easter. Take A93 .8km (¹/₂ mile) northeast of Braemar.

This romantic 17th-century castle is a fully furnished private residence with architectural grace, scenic charm, and historical interest. The castle has barrel-vaulted ceilings and an underground prison and is known for its remarkable star-shaped defensive curtain wall.

PLAYING GOLF

Braemar Golf Course, at Braemar (☎ **013397/41618**), is the highest golf course in the country. The green of the second hole is 380m (1,250 feet) above sea level—this is the trickiest hole on the course. Pro golf commentator Peter Alliss has deemed it "the hardest par 4 in all of Scotland." Set on a plateau, the hole is bordered on the right by the River Clunie and lined on the left by rough. Greens fees are as follows: Monday to Friday £13 ($22) for 18 holes and £18 ($31) for a day ticket; Saturday and Sunday £16 ($27) for 18 holes and £21 ($36) for a day ticket. Pull carts can be rented for £2 ($3.40) per day and sets of clubs can be borrowed for £5 ($9) per day. The only dress code is "be reasonable." The course is open only April to October daily (call in advance as hours can vary).

BALLATER & BALMORAL CASTLE

Ballater is a vacation resort center on the Dee River, with the Grampian Mountains in the background. The town still centers around its Station Square, where the royal family used to be photographed as they arrived to spend vacations. The railway is now closed.

ESSENTIALS

GETTING THERE   By Train   Go to Aberdeen and continue the rest of the way by connecting bus. For rail schedules and information, call ☎ **0345/484950.**

By Bus   Buses run hourly from Aberdeen to Ballater. The bus and train stations in Aberdeen are next to each other on Guild Street (☎ **01224/212266** for information). Bus 201 from Braemar runs to Ballater (trip time: 1¹/₄ hours). The fare is £3 ($5).

By Car   From Braemar, go east along A-93.

VISITOR INFORMATION   The **tourist information office** is at Station Square (☎ **013397/55306**). Hours are July and August, daily 10am to 1pm and 2 to 6pm; September and October and May and June, Monday to Saturday 10am to 1pm and 2 to 5pm, Sunday 1 to 5pm. Closed November through April.

WHERE TO STAY

Craigendarroch Hotel and Country Club. Braemar Rd., Ballater AB35 5XA. ☎ **013397/ 55858.** Fax 013397/55447. www.hilton.com. E-mail: holidays@stakis.co.uk. 45 units. TV TEL. £141 ($240) double; £216 ($367) suite. Rates include Scottish breakfast. Half board £10 ($17) extra per person. AE, DC, MC, V.

This hotel, built in the Scottish baronial style, is set amid old trees on a 13ha (28-acre) estate. Modern comforts have been added, but the owners have tried to maintain a 19th-century aura. The public rooms include a regal oaken staircase and a large sitting room. The fair-size rooms open onto views of the village of Ballater and the River Dee. Each is furnished in individual style; all have hair dryers, trouser presses, private bathrooms (with showers), and small refrigerators (not minibars). Public facilities are luxurious, especially the study with oak paneling, a log fire, and book-lined shelves. Facilities include the Leisure Club with a spa pool, two swimming pools, a sauna, and a solarium.

Monaltrie Hotel. 5 Bridge Sq., Ballater AB35 5QJ. ☎ **013397/55417.** Fax 013397/55180. 24 units. TV TEL. £60–£70 ($102–$119) double. Rates include Scottish breakfast. AE, DC, MC, V. Free parking.

This hotel, the first in the region, was built in 1835 of Aberdeen granite to accommodate the clients of a now-defunct spa. Today it bustles with a clientele who come for the live music in its pub and for the savory food served in its two restaurants. The more unusual of the two is a Thai restaurant, which serves dinner only, Thursday through Tuesday from 7 to 10pm. Rooms contain comfortable beds.

WHERE TO DINE

Green Inn. 9 Victoria Rd., Ballater AB35 5QQ. ☎ and fax **013397/55701.** Reservations required. Fixed-price menu £24 ($41) for 2 courses, £28.50 ($48) for 3 courses. AE, DC, MC, V. Mar–Oct daily 7–9pm, and Nov–Feb Tues–Sat 7–9pm. SCOTTISH.

In the heart of town, this establishment was once a temperance hotel. Now it's one of the finest dining rooms in town, especially for traditional Scottish dishes. The chef places emphasis on local produce, including homegrown vegetables when available. In season, loin of venison is served with a bramble sauce, and you can always count on fresh salmon and the best of Angus beef. Three very simply furnished double rooms are rented here, all with private bathrooms (with shower) and TV. Half board costs £55 ($94) per person.

Oaks Restaurant. In the Craigendarroch Hotel and Country Club, Braemar Rd. ☎ **013397/55858.** Reservations strongly recommended. Fixed-price 4-course dinner £27.50 ($47). AE, DC, MC, V. Daily 7–10:30pm. BRITISH.

The most glamorous restaurant in the region, the Oaks is in the century-old mansion that was originally built by the "marmalade kings" of Britain, the Keiller family. (The company's marmalade is still a household word throughout the United Kingdom.) This is the most upscale of the three restaurants in a resort complex that includes hotel rooms, time-share villas, and access to a nearby golf course. To start, try the venison and duck terrine flavored with orange and brandy and served with a warm black conch vinaigrette. Other main courses include roast rack of lamb, breast of Grampian chicken, loin of venison, or fillet of Aberdeen Angus beef.

THE CASTLE

Balmoral Castle. Balmoral, Ballater. ☎ **013397/42334.** Admission £4 ($7) adults, £3 ($5) seniors, £1 ($1.70) for children 5–16, free 4 and under. Apr 10–May 3 Mon–Sat 10am–5pm; June 1–Aug 2, daily 10am–5pm. Closed Aug 3–Apr 9. Crathie bus from Aberdeen to the Crathie station; Balmoral Castle is signposted from there (a short walk).

"This dear paradise" is how Queen Victoria described Balmoral Castle, rebuilt in the Scottish baronial style by her "beloved" Albert and completed in 1855. Today Balmoral, 13km (8 miles) west of Ballater, is still a private residence of the British sovereign, and its principal feature is a 30m (100-foot) tower. On the grounds are many memorials to the royal family. In addition to the gardens there're country walks, pony trekking, souvenir shops, and a refreshment room. Of the actual castle, only the ballroom is open to the public; it houses an exhibition of pictures, porcelain, and works of art.

PLAYING GOLF

Ballater Golf Club, at Ballater (☎ **013397/55567**), is one of the more scenic courses in the area. Set in a bowl of mountains and situated on the banks of the River Dee, this is a 5,155m (5,638-yard), par-67 course. Greens fees are as follows: Monday through Friday, £18 ($31) for 18 holes or £27 ($46) for a day ticket; Saturday and Sunday, £21 ($36) for 18 holes or £31 ($53) for a day ticket. There're no electric carts for hire; pull-carts rent for £2 ($3.40) per day. Dress should be smart but casual. The course is open daily April to September 7:30am to sunset. From October to March hours are daily 9am to sunset but only if the weather permits.

THE CASTLE COUNTRY

The city of **Aberdeen,** Scotland's "third city," is bordered by fine sandy beaches (if you're a polar bear) and is one of the largest fishing ports in the country. However, far more interesting to visitors with limited time is the array of 40 inhabited castles on the city's periphery, which has earned the area the title of "castle country." Since time is limited for most motorists, we've spotlighted only the most intriguing.

ESSENTIALS

GETTING THERE   By Train   Scotrail runs trains from Edinburgh to Aberdeen at the rate of nine per day Monday to Saturday and 10 per day on Sunday, costing £31 ($51) for a one-way ticket. For information, call ☎0345/484950.

By Bus   Scottish Citylink (☎ 08705/505050) arrives in Aberdeen from Edinburgh at the rate of at least one bus per hour during the day, costing £13.50 ($23) one way.

WHERE TO STAY

Mannofield Hotel. 447 Great Western Rd., Aberdeen AB10 6NL. Tel. **01224/315-888.** Fax 01224/208-971. 9 units. TV TEL. £69 ($114) double. Rates include Scottish breakfast. AE, DC, MC, V. Free parking. Bus: 18, 24.

Built of silver granite around 1880, this hotel is a Victorian fantasy, with step gables, turrets, spires, bay windows, and a sweeping mahogany-and-teakwood staircase. Owners Bruce and Dorothy Cryle offer a warm Scottish welcome. The nicely sized guest rooms, refurbished in 1998 with paisley curtains and quilts, include tea/coffeemakers and hair dryers. The hotel, a favorite of visiting businesspeople from other parts of Britain, contains a good restaurant.

✪ Marcliffe at Pitfodels. N. Deeside Rd., Aberdeen AB1 9YA. Tel. **01224/861-000.** Fax 01224/868-860. www.nettrak.co.uk/marcliffe. E-mail: reservations@marcliffe.com. 42 units. MINIBAR TV TEL. £115–£165 ($190–$272) double. AE, DC, MC, V. Free parking. Drive about a mile off A90 at the Aberdeen ring road, A93.

On Aberdeen's western edge, this traditional manor house was built around a courtyard and stands on 6 acres of landscaped grounds. The Oriental rugs, placed on stone floors, and the tartan sofas set the mood in the public rooms; a scattering of antiques add a grace note. The spacious guest rooms are furnished in Chippendale and reproduction pieces, with armchairs and desks, plus extras like hair dryers and even fresh milk in the minibar. The conservatory restaurant offers regional dishes, and the more expensive Invery Room is favored by businesspeople entertaining out-of-town guests.

WHERE TO DINE

Elrond's Cafe Bar. In the Caledonian Thistle Hotel, 10–14 Union Terrace. ☎ **01224/640-233.** Main courses £7–£9 ($12–$15); pot of tea with pastry £2 ($3.30). AE, DC, MC, V. Mon–Sat 10am–midnight, Sun 10am–11pm. Bus: 16 or 17. INTERNATIONAL.

White marble floors, a long oak-capped bar, evening candlelight, and a garden-inspired decor create the ambience. No one will mind if you show up just for a drink, a pot of tea, a midday salad or snack, or a full-blown feast. Specialties are burgers, steaks, pastas, fresh fish, lemon chicken supreme, chicken Kiev, and vegetarian dishes. This isn't the world's greatest food, but it's popular nevertheless. Though it's in one of Aberdeen's well-known hotels, the restaurant has a separate entrance onto Union Terrace.

Ferryhill House. Bon Accord St., Aberdeen AB11 6UA. Tel. **01224/590-867.** Fax 01224/586-947. Reservations recommended Sat–Sun. Main courses £6–£12 ($10–$20). AE, DC, MC, V. Free parking. Bus: 16. INTERNATIONAL.

In its own park and garden on Aberdeen's southern outskirts, Ferryhill House was built 250 years ago by the region's most successful brick maker/quarry master. It has Georgian detailing, but recent refurbishment has removed many of the original panels and all the ceiling beams. The restaurant boasts one of the region's largest collections of single-malt whiskies—more than 140 brands. There's a fireplace for chilly afternoons and a beer garden for midsummer, as well as a conservatory. Food items include steak or vegetable tempura, chicken dishes like chicken fajita, fried haddock fillet, pastas, and chili. Ferryhill House also rents nine standard guest rooms, with TVs, phones, and hair dryers. Breakfast included, the double rate is £79 ($130) Sunday to Thursday and £50 ($83) Friday and Saturday.

SEEING THE CASTLES

Castle Fraser. Sauchen, Inverurie. ☎ **01330/833463.** Admission £4.40 ($8) adults, £2.90 ($4.95) seniors, £1.30 ($2.20) children, free for age 4 and under. Easter weekend and Oct, Sat–Sun 2–4:45pm; May–June, daily 1:30–5pm; July–Aug, daily 11am–4:45pm; Sept, daily

1:30–5:30pm. Closed Nov–Mar. Head 5km (3 miles) south of Kemnay, 26km (16 miles) west of Aberdeen, off A944.

One of the most impressive of the fortresslike castles of Mar, Castle Fraser stands in a 12ha (25-acre) parkland setting. The sixth laird, Michael Fraser, began the structure in 1575, and his son finished it in 1636. Its Great Hall is spectacular, and you can wander around the grounds, which include an 18th-century walled garden.

Kildrummy Castle. Hwy. A-97, Kildrummy. ☎ **019755/71331.** Admission £1.80 ($3.05) adults, £1.30 ($2.20) seniors, 75p ($1.30) children. Easter–Sept daily 9:30am–6:30pm; Oct–Nov daily 9:30am–4pm. Closed Dec–Easter. Take A-97 for 56km (35 miles) west of Aberdeen; it's signposted off A-97, 16km (10 miles) west of Alford.

This is the most extensive example of a 13th-century castle in Scotland. Once the ancient seat of the earls of Mar, you can still see the four round towers, the hall, and the chapel from the original structure. The great gatehouse and other remains date from the 16th century. The castle played a major role in Scottish history up to 1715, when it was dismantled.

Fyvie Castle. Turriff, on the Aberdeen-Banff road. ☎ **01651/891266.** Admission £4.40 ($8) adults, £2.90 ($4.95) seniors and children. Easter–June and Sept daily 1:30–4:45pm; July–Aug daily 11am–4:45pm; Oct Sat–Sun 1:30–4:45pm. Closed Nov–Mar. Take A947 for 37km (23 miles) northwest of Aberdeen.

The National Trust for Scotland opened this castle to the public in 1986. The oldest part, dating from the 13th century, is the grandest existing example of Scottish baronial architecture. There're five towers, named after Fyvie's five families—the Prestons, Melddrums, Setons, Gordons, and Leiths—who lived here over 5 centuries. Originally built in a royal hunting forest, Fyvie means "deer hill" in Gaelic. The interior, created by the first Lord Leith of Fyvie, a steel magnate, reflects the opulence of the Edwardian era. His collections contain arms and armor, 16th-century tapestries, and important artworks by Raeburn, Gainsborough, and Romney. The castle is rich in ghosts, curses, and legends.

✪ **Craigievar Castle.** Hwy. A980, 10km (6 miles) south of Alford. ☎ **013398/83635.** Admission £6 ($10) adults, £4 ($7) seniors/children. Castle May–Sept daily 1:30–4:45pm. Grounds year-round daily 9:30am–sunset. Head west on A96 to alford, then south on A980.

Structurally unchanged since its completion in 1626, Craigievar Castle is an exceptional tower house where Scottish baronial architecture reached its pinnacle of achievement. It has contemporary plaster ceilings in nearly all its rooms. The castle had been continuously lived in by the descendants of the builder, William Forbes, until it came under the care of the National Trust for Scotland in 1963. The family collection of furnishings is complete. Some 6km (4 miles) south of the castle, clearly signposted on a small road leading off A980, near Lumphanan, is **Macbeth's Cairn,** where the historical Macbeth is supposed to have fought his last battle. Built of timber in a rounded format known by historians as "motte and bailey," it's now nothing more than a steep-sided rounded hillock marked with a sign and a flag.

SPEYSIDE & THE MALT WHISKY TRAIL

Much of the Speyside region covered in this section is in the Moray district, on the southern shore of the Moray Firth, a great inlet cutting into the northeastern coast of Scotland. The district stretches in a triangular shape south from the coast to the wild heart of the Cairngorm Mountains near Aviemore. It's a land steeped in history, as its many castles, battle sites, and ancient monuments testify. It's also a good place to fish and, of course, play golf. Golfers can purchase a 5-day ticket from tourist information centers that will allow them to play at more than 11 courses in the area.

One of the best of these courses is **Boat of Garten,** Speyside (☎ **01479/831282**). Relatively difficult, the almost 5,500m (6,000-yard) course is dotted with many bunkers and wooded areas. April to October greens fees are £21 ($36) Monday to Friday and hours are 7:30am to 11pm. Saturday greens fees are £31 ($53), and hours are 10am to 4pm. In winter, call to see if the course is open. Greens fees are then reduced to £10 ($17). Pull-carts can be rented for £2 ($3.40) and electric carts are available for £5 ($9). Dress reasonably; blue jeans are not acceptable.

The valley of the second-largest river in Scotland, the Spey, lies north and south of Aviemore. It's a land of great natural beauty. The Spey is born in the Highlands above Loch Laggan, which lies 64km (40 miles) south of Inverness. Little more than a creek at its inception, it gains in force, fed by the many "burns" that drain water from the surrounding hills. It's one of Scotland's great rivers for salmon fishing, and it runs between the towering Cairngorms on the east and the Monadhliath Mountains on the west. Its major center is Grantown-on-Spey.

The major tourist attraction in the area is the **Malt Whisky Trail,** 113km (70 miles) long, running through the glens of Speyside. Here distilleries, many of which can be visited, are known for their production of *uisge beatha* or "water of life." "Whisky" is its more familiar name.

Half the malt distilleries in the country lie along the River Spey and its tributaries. Here peat smoke and Highland water are used to turn out single-malt (unblended) whisky. There're five malt distilleries in the area: **Glenlivet, Glenfiddich, Glenfarclas, Strathisla,** and **Tamdhu.** Allow about an hour each to visit them.

The best way to reach Speyside from Aberdeen is to take A-96 northwest, sign-posted Elgin. If you're traveling north on the A-9 road from Perth and Pitlochry, your first stop might be at Dalwhinnie, which has the highest whisky distillery in the world at 575m (1,888 feet). It's not in the Spey Valley but is at the northeastern end of Loch Ericht, with views of lochs and forests.

KEITH

Keith, 18km (11 miles) northwest of Huntly, grew up because of its strategic location, where the main road and rail routes between Inverness and Aberdeen cross the River Isla. It has an ancient history, but owes its present look to the "town planning" of the late 18th and early 19th centuries. Today it's a major stopover along the Malt Whisky Trail.

The oldest operating distillery in the Scottish Highlands, the **Strathisla Distillery,** on Seafield Avenue (☎ **01542/783044**), was established in 1786. Hours are February to mid-March, Monday to Friday 9:30am to 4pm; mid-March to November 30, Monday to Saturday 9:30am to 4pm, Sunday 12:30 to 4pm; closed December and January. Admission is £4 ($7) for adults, free for ages 8 to 18, children 7 and under not admitted. The admission fee includes a £2 ($3.40) voucher redeemable in the distillery shop against a 70cl bottle of whisky. Be warned that tours of this distillery are self-guided.

Where to Stay

Grange House. Grange, near Keith AB55 6RY. ☎ and fax **01542/870206.** www.aboutscotland.com/banff/grangehouse.html. 2 units. £50 ($85) double. Rate includes breakfast. No credit cards. From Keith, drive 5km (3 miles) east of town, following the signs to Banff, into the hamlet of Grange.

This dignified-looking stone house was constructed in 1815 as the manse (home of a minister) for the nearby Church of Scotland, which is still the most prominent building in this tiny hamlet. Doreen Blanche, assisted by her husband Bill, rents two well-decorated and comfortable rooms within her private home. The venue is upscale, charming, and comfortable, with a calm and quiet that's enhanced by the 4ha (8 acres) of park and garden that surrounds this isolated place. Ask the owners to point out the late Victorian addition here, completed in 1898, that greatly enlarged the size of the original house. Smoking is not permitted inside.

DUFFTOWN

James Duff, the fourth earl of Fife, founded this town in 1817. The four main streets of town converge at the battlemented **clock tower,** which is also the tourist information center. A center of the whisky-distilling industry, Dufftown is surrounded by seven malt distilleries. The family-owned **Glenfiddich Distillery** is on A-941, just north of Dufftown (☎ **01340/820373**). It's open Monday to Friday 9:30am to 4:30pm; Easter to mid-October it's also open on Saturday 9:30am to 4:30pm and on Sunday noon to 4:30pm. Guides in kilts show visitors around the plant and explain the process of distilling. A film of the history of distilling is also shown. At the finish of the tour, you're given a dram of malt whisky to sample. The tour is free, but there's a souvenir shop where the owners hope you'll spend a few pounds.

Other sights include **Balvenie Castle,** along A-941 (☎ **01340/820121**), the ruins of a moated stronghold from the 14th century on the south side of the Glenfiddich Distillery. During her northern campaign against the earl of Huntly, Mary, Queen of Scots spent 2 nights here. It's open April to September, daily 9:30am to 6pm. Admission is £1.20 ($2.05) for adults, 90p ($1.55) seniors, and 50p (85¢) for children 15 and under.

Mortlach Parish Church in Dufftown is one of the oldest places of Christian worship in the country. It's reputed to have been founded in 566 by St. Moluag. A Pictish cross stands in the graveyard. The present church was reconstructed in 1931 and incorporates portions of an older building.

Where to Dine

Taste of Speyside. 10 Balvenie St. ☎ **01340/820860.** Reservations recommended in the evening. Main courses £9.50–£12.50 ($16–$21); Speyside platter £8.80 ($15) at lunch, £10.40 ($18) at dinner. MC, V. Daily 11am–5pm and 6–9pm. Closed Nov–Feb. SCOTTISH.

True to its name, this restaurant in the town center, just off the main square, avidly promotes a Speyside cuisine as well as malt whiskies, and in the bar you can buy the product of each of Speyside's 46 distilleries. A platter including a slice of smoked salmon, smoked venison, smoked trout, pâté flavored with malt whisky, locally made cheese (cow or goat), salads, and homemade oat cakes is offered at noon and at night. Nourishing soup is made fresh daily and is served with homemade bread. There's also a choice of meat pies, including venison with red wine and herbs or rabbit. For dessert, try Scotch Mist, which contains fresh cream, malt whisky, and crumbled meringue.

ROTHES

A Speyside town with five distilleries, Rothes is just to the south of the Glen of Rothes, 100km (62 miles) northwest of Aberdeen. Founded in 1766, the town lies between Ben Aigan and Conerock Hill. The original settlement grew up around **Rothes Castle,** ancient stronghold of the Leslie family, who lived here until 1622. Only a single massive wall of the castle remains.

Among the several distilleries launched by the Grant family is the **Glen Grant Distillery** (☎ **01542/783318**), opened in the mid-19th century. It's located right outside town (signposted from the center). Admission is £2.50 ($4.25) adults, free for children ages 8 to 18, children 7 and under not allowed. The visit includes a tour of both the gardens and distillery, a taste of whisky, plus a £2 ($3.40) voucher applied against one of the large bottles of whisky on sale here. June to September hours are Monday to Saturday 10am to 5pm, Sunday 11:30am to 5pm. March to May and in October hours are Monday to Saturday 10am to 4pm, and Sunday from 11:30am to 4pm.

Where to Stay & Dine

Rothes Glen Hotel. Rothes AB38 7AQ. ☎ **01340/831254.** Fax 01340/831566. E-mail: rothesglen@compuserve.com. 15 units. TV TEL. £100–£150 ($170–$255) double. Rates include Scottish breakfast. MC, V. Take A-941 5km (3 miles) north of Rothes.

The old turreted house was designed by the architect who built Balmoral. It's surrounded by about 18ha (40 acres) of fields with grazing Highland cattle. This historic building retains many of its original pieces of furniture. The dining room serves good, wholesome meals in true Scottish tradition. A fixed-price four-course dinner is offered for £32.50 ($55).

GRANTOWN-ON-SPEY

This vacation resort, with its gray granite buildings, is 55km (34 miles) southeast of Inverness, in a wooded valley from which it commands views of the Cairngorm Mountains. It's a key center of winter sports in Scotland. Fishers are also attracted to this setting, because the Spey is renowned for its salmon. One of Scotland's many 18th-century planned towns, it was founded on a heather-covered moor in 1765 by Sir James Grant of Grant and became the seat of that ancient family. The town was famous in the 19th century as a Highland tourist center.

From a base here, you can explore the valleys of the Don and Dee, the Cairngorms, and Culloden Moor, scene of the historic battle in 1746, when Bonnie Prince Charlie and his army were defeated.

A year-round **tourist information office** is on High Street (☎ **01479/872773**). Hours April to October are daily 9am to 7pm, Sunday 10am to 5pm; November to March, Monday to Friday 9am to 5pm, Saturday 10am to 5pm.

Where to Stay

Garth Hotel. The Square, Castle Rd., Grantown-on-Spey, Morayshire PH26 3HN. ☎ **01479/872836.** Fax 01479/872116. 17 units. TV TEL. £59–£69 ($100–$117) double. Rates include Scottish breakfast. MC, V. Free parking.

The elegant, comfortable Garth stands on 2ha (4 acres) of ground beside the town square. Guests enjoy the use of a spacious upstairs lounge, whose high ceilings, wood-burning stove, and vine-covered veranda make it an attractive place for morning coffee or afternoon tea. The comfortable and handsomely furnished rooms have all the necessary amenities. Extensive and selective meals with a French slant favor "Taste of Scotland" dishes, with emphasis on fresh local produce, including seafood, salmon, venison, game, and beef.

Tulchan Lodge. Advie, Grantown-on-Spey PH26 3PW. ☎ **01807/510200.** Fax 01807/510234. www.tulchanestateoffice.co.uk. 13 units. TEL. £350–£500 ($595–$850) double. Rates include full board. No credit cards. Closed Feb–Mar. Drive 14km (9 miles) northeast of Grantown on B-9102.

Tulchan Lodge, built in 1906 to serve as the 10,800ha (23,000-acre) Tulchan Estate's fishing and shooting lodge, is a place for both sports-oriented visitors and travelers who want to experience a place designed with the elegance required by Edward VII, who came here for sports. The lodge has panoramic views of the Spey Valley, and each room is different in size and furnishings. In the two elegant dining rooms, Scottish and international dishes are served, with particular attention to Scottish beef, lamb, game, and fresh local seafood. The vegetables are grown in the lodge's garden. Only full-board residents are accepted. Facilities include a tennis court, nature trails, and a golf course nearby.

Where to Dine

Craggan Mill. Hwy. A-95 1km (³/₄ mile) south of Grantown-on-Spey. ☎ **01479/872288.** Reservations recommended. Main courses £3.95–£12.50 ($7–$21). MC, V. May–Sept daily noon–2pm and 6–10pm; Oct–Apr Tues–Sun 7–10pm. Closed the first 2 weeks in Nov. BRITISH/ITALIAN.

This licensed restaurant and lounge bar, a 10-minute walk south of the town center, is housed in a restored ruined granite mill whose waterwheel is still visible. The owners offer British or Italian cuisine at attractive prices. Your appetizer might be smoked trout in deference to Scotland, or ravioli, inspired by sunny Italy. Main courses might be breast of chicken with cream or chicken cacciatore, followed by a dessert of rum-raisin ice cream or peach Melba. You've probably had better versions of all the dishes offered here, but what you get isn't bad. A good selection of Italian wines is also offered.

GLENLIVET

As you leave Grantown-on-Spey and head east along A-95, drive to the junction with B-9008; go south and you won't miss the **Glenlivet Distillery.** The location of the **Glenlivet Reception Centre** (☎ **01542/783220**) is 16km (10 miles) north of the nearest town, Tomintoul. Near the River Livet, a Spey tributary, this distillery is one of the most famous in Scotland. It's open mid-March to October Monday to Saturday 10am to 4pm, and Sunday 12:30 to 4pm. July and August, Monday to Saturday 10am to 6pm and Sunday 12:30pm to 6pm. The £2.50 ($4.25) admission fee for visitors over 18 includes a £2 ($3.40) voucher off the purchase of a bottle of whisky.

Back on A-95, you can visit the **Glenfarclas Distillery** at Ballindalloch (☎ **01807/500245**), one of the few malt whisky distilleries that's still independent of the giants. Founded in 1836, Glenfarclas is managed by the fifth generation of the Grant family. It's open all year, Monday to Friday 9am to 5pm; June to September, it's also open Saturday 10am to 4pm and Sunday 12:30 to 4:30pm. There's a small craft shop, and each visitor is offered a dram of Glenfarclas Malt Whisky. The admission of £3.50 ($6) is for visitors over 18 and there's a discount of £7 ($12) on any purchase of £10 ($17) or more.

Where to Stay

Minmore House Hotel. Glenlivet, Ballindalloch AB37 9DB. ☎ **01807/590378.** Fax 01807/590472. www.smoothhound.co.uk/hotels/minmore.html. 10 units. TEL. £110–£150 ($187–$255) double. Rates include breakfast, afternoon tea, and 5-course dinner. MC, V. Closed mid-Oct to mid-Apr.

Standing on 2ha (5 acres) of private grounds adjacent to the Glenlivet Distillery, this impressive country house was the home of the distillery owners before becoming a hotel. The hotel operators have elegantly furnished their drawing room, which opens onto views of the Ladder Hills and an outdoor swimming pool. Well-furnished rooms have tea/coffeemakers, and drinks can be enjoyed in the oak-paneled lounge bar, which has an open log fire on chilly nights. The Scottish food is excellent, served in a Regency-style dining room with mahogany tables and matching chairs.

KINCRAIG

Kincraig enjoys a scenic spot at the northern end of Loch Insh, overlooking the Spey Valley to the west and the Cairngorm Mountains to the east. Near Kincraig, the most notable sight is the **Highland Wildlife Park** (☎ **01540/651270**), a natural area of

Spotting Nessie

Sir Peter Scott's *Nessitera rhombopteryx* continues to elude her pursuers. "Nessie," as she's more familiarly known, has captured the imagination of the world, drawing thousands of visitors yearly to Loch Ness. The Loch Ness monster has been described as one of the world's greatest mysteries. Half a century ago A82 was built alongside the banks of the loch's western shores. Since that time many more sightings have been recorded.

All types of high-tech underwater contraptions have searched for the Loch Ness monster, but no one can find her. Dr. Robert Rines and his associates at the Academy of Applied Science in Massachusetts maintain an all-year watch with sonar-triggered cameras and strobe lights suspended from a raft in Urquhart Bay.

The loch is 39km (24 miles) long, 1.5km (1 mile) wide, and some 230m (755 feet) deep. Even if the monster doesn't put in an appearance, you can enjoy the loch seascape. In summer, you can take boat cruises across Loch Ness from both Fort Augustus and Inverness.

Buses from either Fort Augustus or Inverness traverse A82, taking you to Drumnadrochit. Call ☎ **0990/808080** for schedules and more information. The bucolic hamlet of Drumnadrochit lies a mile from Loch Ness at the entrance to Glen Urquhart. It's the nearest village to the part of the loch from which sightings of the monster have been reported most frequently.

From Grantown-on-Spey, take A938 west until you merge with northwest-bound E15/A9, which leads to Inverness, on the north tip of Loch Ness. From Inverness, travel on the A82 south, which runs the length of the western shoreline. The eastern shoreline can be traveled by following signposted rural roads from Inverness.

parkland with a collection of wildlife, some of which is extinct elsewhere in Scotland. Herds of European bison, red deer, shaggy Highland cattle, wild horses, St. Kilda Soay sheep, and roe deer range the park. In enclosures are wolves, polecats, wildcats, beavers, badgers, and pine martens. Protected birds to see are golden eagles and sev-eral species of grouse—of special interest is the capercaillie ("horse of the woods"), a large Eurasian grouse native to Scotland's pine forests. There's a visitor center with a gift shop, cafe, and exhibition areas. Ample parking and a picnic site are also available.

You need a car to go through the park; walkers are discouraged and are picked up by park rangers. The park is open every day at 10am. April and October, the last entrance is at 4pm, except during July and August, when the last entrance is at 5pm. November to March, the last entrance is at 2pm. All people and vehicles are expected to vacate the park within 2 hours of the day's last admission. Admission to the park is £6.30 ($11) for adults, £5.25 ($9) for seniors, and £4.20 ($7) for children. A family ticket costs £21 ($36).

KINGUSSIE

Your next stop along the Spey might be at the little summer vacation resort and winter ski center of Kingussie (it's pronounced King-*you*-see), just off A-9, the capital of Badenoch, a district known as "the drowned land" because the Spey can flood the valley when the snows of a severe winter melt in the spring.

Kingussie, 188km (117 miles) northwest of Edinburgh, 66km (41 miles) south of Inverness, and 18km (11 miles) southwest of Aviemore, practically adjoins Newtonmore (see below), directly northeast along A-86.

Highland Folk Museum, Duke St. (☎ **01540/661307**), is the first folk museum established in Scotland (1934), and its collections are based on the life of the Highlanders. You'll see domestic, agricultural, and industrial items. Open-air exhibits are a turf kailyard (kitchen garden), a Lewis "black house," and old vehicles and carts. Traditional events such as spinning, music making, and handcraft fairs are held throughout the summer. Admission is £3 ($5) for adults, £2 ($3.40) for children and seniors, £10 ($17) for a family ticket. Hours are April to October Monday to Friday 10:30am to 4pm, Saturday and Sunday 1 to 4pm.

A summer-only **tourist center** is on King Street (☎ **01540/661297**). It's open only May 22 to September 22, Monday to Saturday 10am to 1pm and 2 to 6pm, and on Sunday 10am to 1pm and 2 to 5pm.

Where to Stay

Homewood Lodge. Newtonmore Rd., Kingussie PH21 1HD. ☎ **01540/661507.** www.bigfoot.com/tildahomeward-lodge. E-mail: homeward-lodge@bigfoot.com. 4 units. £40 ($68) double. Rates include Scottish breakfast. No credit cards. Free parking.

One of the best B&Bs in the area, this small Highland house offers large, simply furnished rooms for either two travelers or families. In a garden and woodland setting, the house has a sitting room with an open fire. Good traditional local fare is served in the evening (reservations recommended). Summer barbecues are also offered, and children are welcome.

Osprey Hotel. Ruthven Rd. (at High St.), Kingussie PH21 1EN. ☎ and fax **01540/661510.** www.ospreyhotel.freeserve.co.uk. E-mail: aiteeen@ospreyhotel.freeserve.co.uk. 8 units. £85–£98 ($145–$167) double. Rates include half board. AE, DC, MC, V. Free parking.

This 1895 Victorian structure, 275m (300 yards) from the rail station, is a convenient place to stay, with comfortable although very plain rooms, all with hot and cold running water, central heating, electric blankets, and electric fires. The hotel has a licensed bar, residents' lounge, and TV lounge. Baby-sitting and baby-listening service is provided; laundry and ironing facilities are available. The place is known for its pure, fresh, 100% homemade food. Prime Scottish meats are served; in summer, salmon and trout from local rivers are offered either fresh or peat-smoked.

Where to Dine

The Cross. Tweed Mill Brae, off the Ardbroilach road, Kingussie PH21 1TC. ☎ **01540/661166.** Fax 01540/661080. Reservations recommended. Fixed-price 5-course dinner £35 ($60). MC, V. Wed–Mon 7–9pm. Closed Dec–Feb. SCOTTISH.

This chic restaurant comes as a surprise: In an out-of-the-way setting in a remote Highland village, it serves superlative meals that involve theater as much as fine food. The restaurant stands on 2ha (4 acres), with the Gynack Burn running through the grounds. The main building is an old tweed mill. The restaurant has an open-beam ceiling and French doors leading out onto a terrace over the water's edge where al fresco dinners are served. Specialties depend on the availability of produce in the local markets and might include venison Francatelli, wild pigeon with grapes, or Highland lamb with sorrel.

Nine rooms are rented in a new building. Each room is different in size and style—for example, two rooms have canopied beds, and another has a balcony overlooking the mill pond. Doubles, including half board, cost £190 ($323). Personal service and attention to detail go into the running of this place, operated by Ruth and Tony Hadley, and Ruth's cooking has put it on the gastronomic map of Scotland.

NEWTONMORE

This Highland resort in Speyside is a good center for the Grampian and Monadhliath mountains, and it offers excellent fishing, golf, pony trekking, and hill walking. A track from the village climbs past the Calder River to Loch Dubh and the massive 940m (3,087-foot) **Carn Ban,** where eagles fly. **Castle Cluny,** ancient seat of the MacPherson chiefs, is 10km (6 miles) west of Newtonmore.

You may want to stop and have a look at **Clan Macpherson House & Museum,** Main Street (☎ **01540/673332**). Displayed are clan relics and memorials, including the Black Chanter and Green Banner as well as a "charmed sword," and the broken fiddle of the freebooter, James MacPherson—a Scottish Robin Hood. Relics associated with Bonnie Prince Charlie are also here. An annual clan rally is held in August. Admission is free, but donations are accepted. It's open Monday to Saturday 10am to 5pm, Sunday 2:30 to 5pm, but only April to October.

Where to Stay

Pines Hotel. Station Rd., Newtonmore PH20 1AR. ☎ **01540/673271.** 5 units. TV. £50–£75 ($85–$128) double. Rates include Scottish breakfast. No credit cards. Free parking. Closed Dec 28–Jan 15.

Built in 1903, this somber-looking house sits on a hill overlooking the Spey Valley, and lies just west of the hamlet's center. Your hosts are Colin and Pamela Walker, migrants from Brighton, who charge the bargain price of £25 ($43) for a double if it's taken by one person. Rooms contain beverage-making facilities and hair dryers are available on request. All have pleasant views of the Highland countryside. The food is wholesome, straightforward Scottish cuisine, made from fresh ingredients such as salmon, lamb, venison, and Aberdeen Angus beef. His wife, Pamela, is an expert on desserts and has a particular interest in creating treats for diabetics.

Spain 16

by Darwin Porter & Danforth Prince

The fascinating history of Spain is perceptible in towns small and large, but this country of 40 million is no relic mired in the past. Spain today is a vital and exciting place. This land of sun-drenched beaches, terraced vineyards, sleepy villages, and jeweled Moorish palaces is undergoing a remarkable cultural renaissance. Spain's rebirth is tied to both the death of Franco and the nation's 1986 entry into the European Union. Contemporary art, literature, cinema, and fashion are the tools of new and original expression, and cafes and bars hum with animated discussion about politics, society, and Spain's newfound prosperity.

1 Madrid & Environs

Landlocked Madrid lies on a windswept and often arid plain, beneath a sky that has been described as Velázquez blue. Certain poets have even labeled Madrid the "gateway to the skies": *de Madrid al cielo.* The city is populated by adopted sons and daughters from virtually every region of Spain, adding to its cosmopolitan gloss. Despite its influence as the cultural beacon of the Spanish-speaking world and its quintessentially Spanish nature, Madrid lacks features that for many bespeak Spain: a beach, an ancient castle or cathedral, an archbishop. Madrileños long ago learned how to compensate: They substituted long strolls through the city's verdant parks and along its *paseos,* and they built an elegant palace and erected countless churches, many with baroque ornamentation and gilt.

Artists and writers gravitate to the newly revitalized Madrid and its fertile artistic climate. This is the city, after all, that is itself a central character in Pedro Almodóvar's films, such as *All About My Mother.* Spaniards—and particularly Madrileños—pursue nightlife with passion; they stay awake till the wee hours and top off the night by congregating, as late as 6am, over hot chocolate and *churros* (fried fingerlike doughnuts). But despite the city's many pleasures, Madrileños recognize that their city is also a place for work, evidenced by the spate of emerging local industries, services, and products.

ORIENTATION

GETTING THERE   By Plane   Barajas (☎ **91-305-83-43** for airport information), 14km (9 miles) east of the city center, Madrid's international airport, has two terminals—one international, the other domestic. A conveyor belt connects the two.

Maddid

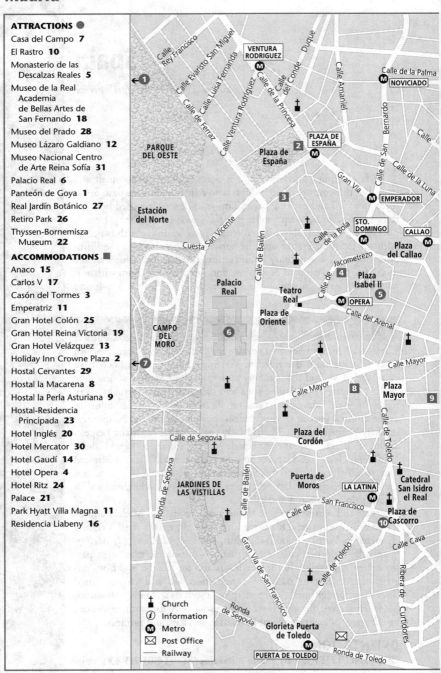

Calle Rey Francisco
Calle Evaristo San Miguel
Calle Luisa Fernanda
Calle de la Palma
NOVICIADO
Calle de Ferraz
Calle Ventura Rodríguez
Calle de la Princesa
Calle del Conde
Duque
VENTURA
RODRIGUEZ
PARQUE
DEL OESTE
Plaza de
España
PLAZA DE
ESPAÑA
Calle Amaniel
Calle de San Bernardo
Calle de la Luna
Calle
Gran Vía
EMPERADOR
Estación
del Norte
Calle de San Vicente
Cuesta San Vicente
Calle de Bailén
Calle de la Bola
Calle de Jacometrezo
STO.
DOMINGO
CALLAO
Plaza
del Callao
Palacio
Real
CAMPO
DEL
MORO
Teatro
Real
Plaza de
Oriente
Plaza
Isabel II
OPERA
Calle del Arenal
Calle de Segovia
Calle Mayor
Calle Mayor
Plaza del
Cordón
Plaza
Mayor
Calle de Toledo
Ronda de Segovia
JARDINES DE
LAS VISTILLAS
Calle de Bailén
Puerta de
Moros
LA LATINA
San Francisco
Calle de
Catedral
San Isidro
el Real
Plaza de
Cascorro
Calle Cava
Ribera de Curtidores
Gran Vía de San Francisco
Ronda
de Segovia
Glorieta Puerta
de Toledo
PUERTA DE TOLEDO
Ronda de Toledo

† Church
ⓘ Information
Ⓜ Metro
✉ Post Office
— Railway

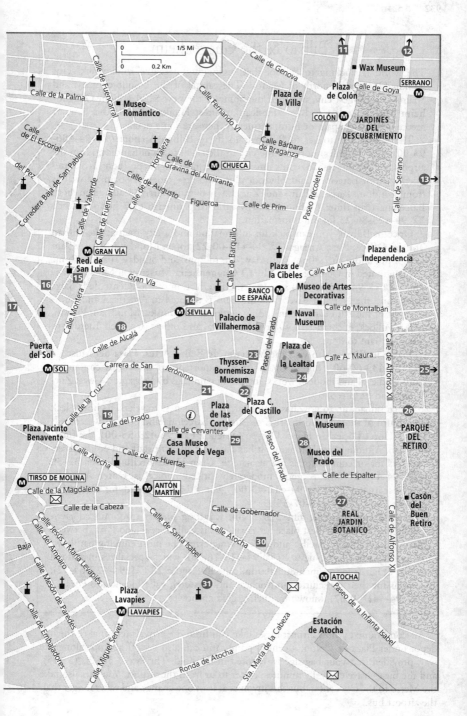

Bilbao & the Guggenheim

The world is flocking to Bilbao, that "ugly, gray, decaying smokestack" city, 395km (246 miles) north of Madrid. The capital of the Basque country, and Spain's sixth largest city, Bilbao is the home of the new $100 million **Guggenheim Museum,** designed by American architect Frank Gehry. If this new art mecca is on your Spain or Europe itinerary, here are some details:

The easiest way to get to Bilbao is to fly to **Bilbao Airport** (☎ **94-486-93-00**), 8km (5 miles) north of the city in the small town of Sandica. From the airport, yellow bus A-3247 runs into the city center. Flights on Iberia arrive frequently from Barcelona and Madrid, plus other key cities in Spain, as well as from London, Paris, Milan, and Zurich. Two trains arrive daily from both Barcelona (trip time: 11 hours) and Madrid (trip time: 6 or 7 hours); phone ☎ **94-423-86-23** for rail information.

Once in Bilbao, you can pick up information and a city map at the **Bilbao Tourist Office,** Plaza Arriaga (☎ **94-416-00-22**), open Monday to Friday 9am to 1:30pm and 4 to 7:30pm, Saturday 9am to 2pm, and Sunday 10am to 2pm.

Inaugurated in October 1997, the ✪ **Guggenheim Museum** at Muella Abandoiba 2 (☎ **94-423-27-99**) stands at the intersection of the Puente de la Salve bridge and the Nervión River. The museum is devoted to American and European art of the 20th century, including works by Kandinsky, Mondrian, Picasso, Ernst, Pollock, Lichtenstein, Oldenburg, Serra, and others. It's open Tuesday to Sunday 10am to 8pm.

While in Bilbao, also visit the **Museum de Bellas Artes,** Plaza del Museo 2 (☎ **94-439-60-60**), one of Spain's most important art museums, containing both medieval and modern works, including paintings by Velásquez, Goya, Zurbarán, and El Greco.

Since Bilbao, up to now has mainly attracted business travelers, its hotels lack the charm of those found in art cities such as Barcelona and Seville. We consider the **Hotel López de Haro,** Obispo Orueta 2 (☎ **94-423-55-00**), the finest in town. Although sterile looking, it has the most efficient staff and polished service. Its major competitor is the also-sterile **Gran Hotel Ercilla,** Ercilla 37–39 (☎ **94-410-20-00**). A good moderately priced choice is **Hotel Avenida,** Zumalacárregui 40 (☎ **94-412-43-00**). For a bargain, head for **Roquefer,** Lotería 2–4 (☎ **94-415-07-55**).

Basque cuisine is the finest in Spain, featuring *pintxos* (pronounced *peen-chohz*), or tapas. The best place for tapas bars is Calle Licenciado Poza, between Alameda del Doctor Areilza and calle Iparraguirre. The most enticing bar, however, is **Victor,** Plaza Nueva 2 (☎ **94-415-16-78**), which specializes in seafood tapas. Other favorites include **Atlanta,** calle Rodríguez 28 (☎ **94-427-64-72**), famous for their prosciutto sandwiches, and **Busterri,** calle Licenciado Poza 42 (☎ **94-441-50-67**), known for their grilled anchovies.

Air-conditioned yellow airport buses take you from the arrivals terminal to the bus depot under Plaza de Colón, a central point. You can also get off at stops along the way, provided that your baggage isn't stored in the hold. The fare is 385Pts ($2.45), and the buses leave every 15 minutes, either to or from the airport. You can also take the Metro to the city center, but this involves at least one change and takes longer than the airport bus.

If you go into town by taxi, expect to pay 4,000Pts ($25) and up, plus surcharges for the trip to/from the airport and for baggage handling. If you take an unmetered limousine, negotiate the price in advance.

By Train   Madrid has three major railway stations: **Atocha,** Avenida Ciudad de Barcelona (Metro: Atocha RENFE), for trains to Lisbon, Toledo, Andalusia, and Extremadura; **Chamartín,** in the northern suburbs at Augustín de Foxá (Metro: Chamartín), for trains to Barcelona, Asturias, Cantabria, Castilla y León, the Basque country, Aragón, Catalonia, Levante (Valencia), Murcia, and the French border; and **Estación Príncipe Pío** or Norte, Po. del Rey 30 (Metro: Norte), for trains to northwest Spain (Salamanca and Galicia). For information about connections from any of these stations, call **RENFE,** Spanish State Railways (☎ **91-328-90-20** daily 7am to 11pm). For tickets, go to the principal office of RENFE, Alcalá 44 (Metro: Banco de España), open Monday to Friday 9am to 8pm.

By Bus   Madrid has at least eight major bus terminals, including the large **Estación Sur de Autobuses,** calle Méndez Alvaro (☎ **91-468-42-00;** Metro: Alvaro). Most buses pass through this station.

By Car   The following are the major highways into Madrid, with information on driving distances to the city: Rte. NI from Irún, 507km (315 miles); NII from Barcelona, 626km (389 miles); NIII from Valencia, 349km (217 miles); NIV from Cádiz, 624km (388 miles); NV from Badajoz, 409km (254 miles); and NVI from Galicia, 602km (374 miles).

VISITOR INFORMATION   The most convenient **tourist office** is on the ground floor of the 40-story Torre de Madrid, Plaza de España (☎ **91-429-31-77;** Metro: Banco de España); it's open Monday to Friday 9am to 7pm and Saturday 9:30am to 1pm. Ask for a street map of the next town on your itinerary, especially if you're driving.

CITY LAYOUT   In modern Spain, all roads and rail and phone lines lead to Madrid. The capital has outgrown all previous boundaries and is branching out in all directions.

Every new arrival ought to find the **Gran Vía,** which cuts a winding path across the city beginning at **Plaza de España,** where you'll find one of Europe's tallest skyscrapers, Edificio España. On this principal avenue is the largest concentration of shops, hotels, restaurants, and movie houses. **Calle de Serrano,** in the Salamanca neighborhood, is a runner-up in terms of importance.

South of the avenue lies the **Puerta del Sol.** All road distances in Spain are measured from this square. However, its significance has declined, and today it's prime hunting ground for pickpockets and purse-snatchers. Here **calle de Alcalá** begins and runs for 4km (2¹/₂ miles).

Plaza Mayor is the heart of Old Madrid, an attraction in itself with its mix of French and Georgian architecture. (Again, be wary, especially late at night.) Pedestrians pass under the arches of the huge square onto the narrow streets of the old town, where you can find some of the capital's most intriguing restaurants and tascas.

The area south of Plaza Mayor—known as **barrios bajos**—merits exploration. The narrow cobblestone streets are lined with 16th- and 17th-century architecture. Directly south of the plaza is the **Arco de Cuchilleros,** a street packed with markets, restaurants, flamenco clubs, and taverns.

Gran Vía ends at calle de Alcalá, and at this juncture lies **Plaza de la Cibeles,** with its fountain to Cybele, "the mother of the gods," and what has become known as "the cathedral of post offices." From Cibeles, the wide **Paseo de Recoletos** begins a short run to **Plaza de Colón.** From this latter square rolls the serpentine **Paseo de la**

Castellana, flanked by expensive shops, apartment buildings, luxury hotels, and foreign embassies.

Back at Cibeles again: Heading south is **Paseo del Prado,** where you'll find Spain's
major attraction, the **Museo del Prado,** as well as the **Jardín Botánica** (Botanical
Garden). The paseo also leads to the Atocha Station. To the west of the garden lies the
Parque del Retiro, once reserved for royalty, with restaurants, nightclubs, a rose garden, and two lakes.

GETTING AROUND

Getting around Madrid isn't easy, because everything is spread out. Even many
Madrileño taxi drivers, often new arrivals from outside the city or a foreign country,
are unfamiliar with their own city once they're off the main boulevards.

ON FOOT   This is the perfect way to see Madrid, especially the narrow streets of
the old town. If you're going to another district (and chances are that your hotel will
be outside the old town), you can take the bus or Metro. For such a large city, Madrid
can be covered amazingly well on foot, because so much of what will interest a visitor
lies in various clusters.

BY SUBWAY (METRO)   The Metro system is easy to learn and convenient. The
central converging point is the Puerta del Sol, and the fare is 120Pts (75¢) for a one-
way trip. The Metro operates daily 6am to 1:30am; avoid rush hours if possible. For
information, call ☎ **91-429-31-77.** You can save money on public transportation by
purchasing a 10-trip ticket known as a *bonos*—for the Metro it costs 660Pts ($4.15).

BY BUS   A bus network also services the city and suburbs, with routes clearly shown
at each stop on a schematic diagram. Buses are fast and efficient because they travel
along special lanes. Both red and yellow buses charge 135Pts (85¢) per ride.

For 600Pts ($3.80) you can purchase a 10-trip ticket (but without transfers) for
Madrid's bus system. It's sold at **Empresa Municipal de Transportes,** Plaza de Cibeles
(☎ **91-406-88-00**), where you can also purchase a guide to the bus routes. The office
is open daily 8am to 2pm.

The hop-off, hop-on **Madrid Vision Bus** lets you set your own pace and itinerary. A
scheduled panoramic tour lasts a half hour, provided that you don't get off the bus. Otherwise, you can opt for an unlimited number of stops, exploring at your leisure. The
Madrid Vision makes four complete tours daily, two in the morning and two in the afternoon; on Sunday and Monday buses depart only in the morning. Check with **Trapsa
Tours** (☎ **91-767-17-43**) for departure times, which are variable. The full-day tour with
unlimited stops, costs 2,200Pts ($14). You can board the bus at the Madrid tourist office.

BY TAXI   Even though cab fares have risen recently, they're still reasonable. When
you flag down a taxi, the meter should register 115Pts (70¢); for every kilometer thereafter, the fare increases by 85Pts (55¢). A supplement is charged for trips to the rail
station or the bullring, as well as on Sundays and holidays. The ride to Barajas Airport
carries a 400Pts ($2.50) surcharge, and there's a 180Pts ($1.15) supplement for trips
from the rail stations. In addition, there's a 140Pts (90¢) supplement on Sundays and
holidays, plus a 150Pts (95¢) supplement at night. It's customary to tip about 10% of
the fare. To call a taxi, dial ☎ **91-447-51-80.**

BY CAR   Driving is nightmarish and potentially dangerous in very congested
Madrid—it always feels like rush hour. It's not a good idea to maintain a rental car
while staying in the city. It's nearly impossible to park, and rental cars are the frequent
targets of thieves. Should you want to rent a car to tour the environs, however, you'll
have several choices. In addition to its office at Barajas Airport (☎ **91-393-72-22**),
Avis has a main office downtown at Gran Vía 60 (☎ **91-205-42-73**). **Hertz,** too, has

an office at Barajas Airport (☎ **91-393-72-28**) and another in the heart of Madrid in the Edificio España, Gran Vía 88 (☎ **91-541-99-24**). **Budget Rent-a-Car** maintains an office at Barajas Airport (☎ **91-393-72-16**).

BY BICYCLE   Ever wonder why you see so few people riding bicycles in Madrid? Those who tried were overcome by the traffic pollution. Plus, the traffic would be very difficult to contend with. It's better to walk.

Fast Facts: Madrid

American Express   For your mail or banking needs, you can go to the American Express office at the corner of Marqués de Cubas and Plaza de las Cortes 2, across the street from the Palace Hotel (☎ **91-322-55-00;** Metro: Gran Vía). Open Monday to Friday 9am to 5:30pm and Saturday 9am to noon.

Baby-Sitters   Most major hotels can arrange for baby-sitters, called *canguros* (kangaroos!) in Spanish. Usually the concierge keeps a list of reliable nursemaids and will contact them for you, provided that you give adequate notice. Rates vary considerably but are fairly reasonable. Although some baby-sitters in Madrid speak English, don't count on it. You may also want to contact La Casa de la Abuela, calle Condes Torreanas 4 (☎ **91-574-30-94**), in the prestigious Barrio Madrid, where "grandmother's house" offers childcare combined with creative exercises and workshops in a child-friendly environment. It's open year-round; prices vary.

Currency   The unit of currency is the Spanish **peseta (Pts),** with coins of 1, 5, 10, 25, 50, 100, 200, and 500 pesetas. Be aware that the 500-peseta coin is easily confused with the 100-peseta coin. Learn to distinguish them by size. Notes are issued in 1,000, 2,000, 5,000, and 10,000-peseta denominations. The rate of exchange used in this chapter was $1 = 156Pts, or 1Pts = .0063¢. The ratio of the British pound to the peseta fluctuates constantly. At press time, £1 = approximately 258Pts (or 1Pts = £0.003). The Euro rate was currently fixed at 166.38Pts (or 100Pts = €0.006).

Dentist/Doctor   For an English-speaking dentist or doctor, contact the U.S. Embassy, calle Serrano 75 (☎ **91-587-22-00**); it maintains a list of dentists and doctors who have offered their services to Americans abroad. For dental services, consult also Unidad Médica Anglo-Americana, Conde de Arandá 1 (☎ **91-435-18-23;** Metro: Retiro), near Plaza de Independencia; office hours are Monday to Friday 9am to 8pm, though there's a 24-hour answering service.

Drugstores   For a late-night pharmacy, dial ☎ **098** or look in the daily newspaper under "Farmacias de Guardia" to learn what drugstores are open after 8pm. Another way to find out is to go to any pharmacy, even if it's closed—it will have posted a list of nearby pharmacies that are open late on that date.

Embassies/Consulates   The Embassy of the **United States,** Calle Serrano 75 (☎ **91-587-22-00;** Metro: Núñez de Balboa), is open Monday to Friday 9:30am to noon and 3 to 5pm. The Embassy of **Canada,** Núñez de Balboa 35 (☎ **91-423-32-50;** Metro: Velázquez), is open Monday to Friday 9am to 5:15pm. The **United Kingdom** Embassy, calle Fernando el Santo, 16 (☎ **91-319-02-00;** Metro: Colón), is open Monday to Friday from 9am to 1:30pm and 3 to 6pm. The Republic of **Ireland** embassy, Paseo de La Castellana, 46 (☎ **91-576-35-00;** Metro: Serrano), is open Monday to Friday from 10am

Madrid Metro

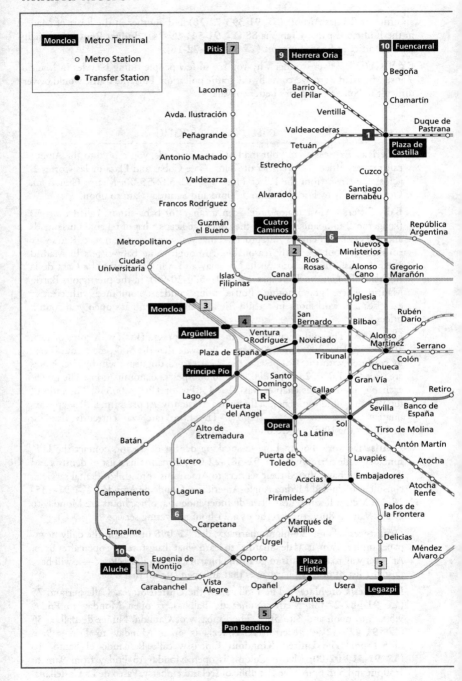

Moncloa — Metro Terminal
o — Metro Station
● — Transfer Station

Pitis 7

9 Herrera Oria

10 Fuencarral

Lacoma

Barrio del Pilar

Begoña

Avda. Ilustración

Ventilla

Chamartín

Peñagrande

Valdeacederas

Duque de Pastrana

Antonio Machado

Tetuán

1

Estrecho

Plaza de Castilla

Valdezarza

Alvarado

Cuzco

Francos Rodríguez

Santiago Bernabéu

Guzmán el Bueno

Cuatro Caminos

República Argentina

Metropolitano

6

Nuevos Ministerios

Ciudad Universitaria

2

Ríos Rosas

Canal

Alonso Cano

Gregorio Marañón

Islas Filipinas

Quevedo

Iglesia

Moncloa 3

San Bernardo

Bilbao

Rubén Darío

Argüelles 4

Ventura Rodríguez

Noviciado

Alonso Martínez

Serrano

Plaza de España

Tribunal

Colón

Príncipe Pío

Santo Domingo

Chueca

Retiro

R

Callao

Gran Vía

Lago

Puerta del Angel

Sevilla

Banco de España

Batán

Alto de Extremadura

Opera

Sol

Tirso de Molina

Lucero

La Latina

Antón Martín

Puerta de Toledo

Lavapiés

Atocha

Campamento

Laguna

Acacias

Embajadores

Atocha Renfe

6

Pirámides

Palos de la Frontera

Empalme

Carpetana

Marqués de Vadillo

Delicias

10

Urgel

Méndez Alvaro

Aluche 5

Eugenia de Montijo

Oporto

Plaza Elíptica

3

Carabanchel

Vista Alegre

Opañel

Usera

Legazpi

Abrantes

5 Pan Bendito

936

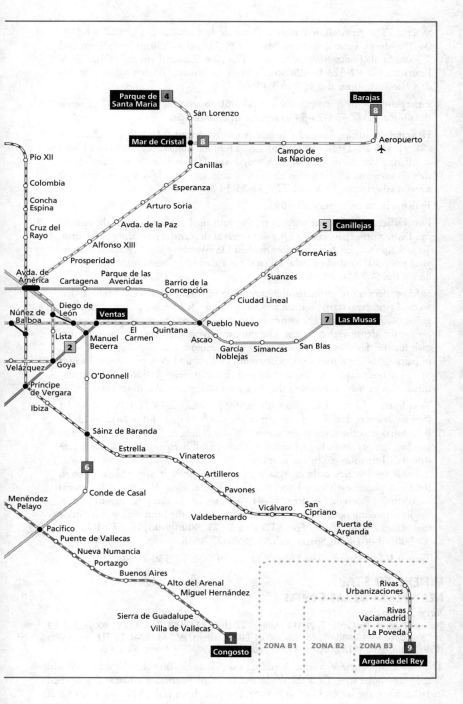

to 2pm. The **Australian** Embassy, Paseo de la Castellana, 143 (☎ **91-579-04-28;** Metro: Cuzco), is open Monday to Thursday 8:30am to 1:30pm and 2:30 to 5pm, Friday 8:30am to 2pm. The **New Zealand** embassy, Plaza de la Lealtad, 2 (☎ **91-523-02-26;** Metro: Banco de España), is open Monday to Friday 9am to 1:30pm and 2:30 to 5:30pm.

Emergencies   In an emergency, call ☎ **080** to report a **fire,** ☎ **091** to reach the **police,** or ☎ **734-25-54** to request an **ambulance.**

Hospitals/Clinics   Unidad Médica Anglo-Americana, Conde de Arandá 1 (☎ **91-435-18-23;** Metro: Retiro), isn't a hospital but a private outpatient clinic offering the services of various specialists. This isn't an emergency clinic, though someone on the staff is always available. It's open daily 9am to 8pm. For a real medical emergency, call ☎ **734-25-54** for an ambulance.

Police   In an emergency, dial **091.**

Post Office   If you don't want to receive your mail at your hotel or the American Express office, direct it to *Lista de Correos* at the central post office in Madrid. To pick up mail, go to the window marked LISTA, where you'll be asked to show your passport. Madrid's central office is the Palacio de Comunicaciones at Plaza de Cibeles (☎ **396-20-00**).

Safety   Because of an increasing crime rate in Madrid, the U.S. Embassy has warned visitors to leave their valuables in a hotel safe or other secure place when going out. Your passport may be needed, however, as the police may stop foreigners for identification checks. The embassy advises that you carry only enough cash for the day's needs. Purse snatching is common, and criminals often work in pairs, grabbing purses from pedestrians, cyclists, and even cars. Several scams to divert one's attention are well known. Even a friendly, "Do you know the time?" can be used to establish that you are a foreigner and distract you.

Telephone   To call Spain from the United States, dial 011 followed by **34** (Spain's country code) and the city code (for example, 1 for Madrid, 3 for Barcelona) plus the seven-digit number. When calling in Spain from one city to another, the city prefix begins with a 9. Thus, to call Barcelona from Madrid, one would dial 93 followed by the number.

For **long-distance calls,** especially transatlantic ones, it may be best to go to the main phone exchange, Locutorio Gran Vía, at Gran Vía 30, or Locutorio Recoletos, at Paseo de Recoletos 37–41. You may not be lucky enough to find an English-speaking operator, but you can fill out a simple form that will facilitate the placement of a call. For **AT&T,** call ☎ **900/99-0011;** for **MCI,** call ☎ **900/99-0014;** for **Sprint,** call ☎ **800/877-4646.**

Transit Information   For Metro information, call ☎ **530-19-80.**

WHERE TO STAY
NEAR PLAZA DE LAS CORTES
Very Expensive

Palace. Plaza de las Cortes 7, 28014 Madrid. ☎ **800/325-3535** in the U.S., 800/325-3589 in Canada, or 91-360-80-00. Fax 91-360-81-00. 465 units. A/C MINIBAR TV TEL. 63,000Pts ($397) double; from 185,000Pts ($1,166) suite. AE, DC, MC, V. Metro: Banco de España.

The Palace, an ornate Victorian "wedding cake" that captures the elegant pre-World War I grand hotel style, faces the Prado and Neptune Fountain. When it first opened in 1912, it was the largest hotel in Europe. Everyone from Dalí to Picasso, from Sarah Bernhardt to Sophia Loren, has spent the night. Nevertheless, it doesn't achieve the snob appeal of its sibling, the Ritz (under the same management). Rooms are conservative and traditional, boasting plenty of space and large bathrooms with lots of amenities. The elegant dining choice is La Cupola, serving Italian specialties along with some of the more famous dishes of the Spanish cuisine. Less expensive is La Rotonda, a site reserved for an ongoing roster of buffets. Club Neptuno, a new fitness center, is the most advanced in Madrid, commanding a panoramic rooftop location.

Inexpensive
Hostal Cervantes. Cervantes 34, 28014 Madrid. ☎ and fax **91-429-27-45.** 12 units. 6,000Pts ($38) double. No credit cards. Metro: Banco de España.

One of Madrid's most pleasant family run-hotels, the much-restored, circa 1940s Cervantes has been widely appreciated by our readers for years. You'll take a tiny birdcage-style elevator to the immaculately maintained second floor of this stone-and-brick building. Rooms contains a bed and spartan furniture. No breakfast is served, but the owners, the Alfonsos, will direct you to one of several nearby cafes. The hotel is convenient to the Prado, Retiro Park, and the older sections of Madrid.

NEAR PLAZA DE ESPAÑA
Expensive
Holiday Inn Crowne Plaza. Plaza de España, 8, 28013 Madrid. ☎ **800/465-4329** in the U.S., or 91-547-12-00. Fax 91-548-23-89. E-mail: reservas@crowneplaza.es. 306 units. A/C MINIBAR TV TEL. 29,500Pts ($186) double; from 32,000Pts ($202) suite. AE, DC, MC, V. Free parking. Metro: Plaza de España.

The Plaza, built in 1953, might be called the Waldorf-Astoria of Spain. A massive rose-and-white structure, it soars to a central 26-story tower. One of the tallest skyscrapers in Europe, it's a landmark visible for miles around. Once one of the best hotels in Spain, the Plaza no longer enjoys such a lofty position, having fallen way down the list in the wake of all the new deluxe hotels built in Madrid. Accommodations include both conventional doubles and luxurious suites; the latter have sitting rooms and abundant amenities. The quieter rooms are on the upper floors.

Moderate
✪ **Hotel Opera.** Cuesta de Santo Domingo 2, 28013 Madrid. ☎ **91-541-2800.** Fax 91-541-6923. E-mail: hotelopera@phoenix.net. 79 units. A/C TV TEL. 14,200Pts ($89) double. AE, DC, MC, V. Metro: Opera.

Don't judge this little discovery by its dreary gray facade and its narrow little windows. The place livens up considerably once you go inside. Set close to the royal palace and the opera house, the hotel isn't regal, but offers first-rate comfort and a warm welcome from the English-speaking staff. Rooms range from medium to surprisingly spacious, each fitted with first-rate twin or double beds with quality mattresses. Bathrooms are also excellent, with dual basins. El Café de la Opera is a popular rendezvous point, and you might also want to patronize the lovely little bar even if you're not a guest. It's adorned with fabric-covered walls and horsy art. The Opera remains one of Madrid's relatively undiscovered boutique hotels.

Inexpensive
Casón del Tormes. Calle del Río 7, 28013 Madrid. ☎ **91-541-97-46.** Fax 91-541-18-52. 63 units. A/C TV TEL. 10,200Pts ($64) double, 12,900Pts ($81) triple. MC, V. Parking 1,600Pts ($10). Metro: Plaza de España.

The attractive three-star Casón del Tormes, set behind a 4-story red-brick facade with stone-trimmed windows, is around the corner from the Royal Palace and Plaza de España. The long, narrow lobby contains wood paneling, a marble floor, and a bar opening onto a separate room. The individually styled rooms aren't not spectacular, but they are generally roomy and comfortable.

ON OR NEAR THE GRAN VÍA

Expensive

Hotel Gaudí. Gran Vía 9, 28013 Madrid. ☎ **91-531-22-22.** Fax 91-531-54-69. www. hoteles-catalonia.es. E-mail: catalon@hoteles-catalonia.es. 88 units. A/C MINIBAR TV TEL. 26,900Pts ($169) double; 40,000Pts ($252) suite. AE, DC, MC, V. Metro: Gran Vía.

In a turn-of-the-century building in the heart of Madrid, this hotel is located in a beautifully restored landmark Modernist building. It was constructed in 1898 by Emilio Salas y Cortes, one of the teachers of the great Barcelona architect, Gaudí. It was completely overhauled and expanded in 1998. Some of the most important attractions of Madrid are within an easy walk, including the Prado, the Thyssen Museum, and the Plaza Mayor with its rustic taverns. Rooms come in a number of sizes, but each is comfortably furnished and beautifully maintained with hair dryers and safes. Facilities include a fitness center, Jacuzzi, and sauna.

Moderate

Carlos V. Maestro Vitoria 5, 28013 Madrid. ☎ **91-531-41-00.** Fax 91-531-37-61. www.h.carlosv.es. E-mail: recepcion@hotelcarlosV.com. 67 units. A/C MINIBAR TV TEL. 14,565Pts ($92). AE. Parking 1,175Pts ($7). Metro: Puerta del Sol.

Once the featured hotel in the pioneering *Spain on $5 a Day,* this establishment is still going strong and still offering good value, even though its prices are no longer $2.50 a night. Renovations have much improved this centrally located hotel, directly north of Puerta del Sol. The medium-sized rooms are sparkling dryers. Try for one of the top-floor rooms with little balconies overlooking the central city.

Residencia Liabeny. Salud 3, 28013 Madrid. ☎ **91-531-90-00.** Fax 91-532-74-21. 222 units. A/C MINIBAR TV TEL. 11,200Pts ($71) double, 15,400Pts ($97) triple. AE, MC, V. Parking 1,605Pts ($10). Metro: Puerta del Sol, Callao, or Gran Vía.

This hotel, named after the original owner, is in a prime location midway between the tourist highlights of the Gran Vía and the Puerta del Sol. The comfortable, contemporary rooms, though newly redecorated, are a bit too pristine for our tastes. The masculine cocktail bar is more warming, and the functional-looking dining room is strictly for convenience. A coffee shop is also on the premises, and good laundry service and personalized attention from the staff add to the allure.

Inexpensive

Anaco. Tres Cruces 3, 28013 Madrid. ☎ **91-522-46-04.** Fax 91-531-64-84. 40 units. A/C TV TEL. 7,850–12,500Pts ($49–$79) double; 11,100–16,175Pts ($70–$102) triple. AE, DC, MC, V. Parking 1,500Pts ($9). Metro: Gran Vía, Callao, or Puerta del Sol.

Modest yet modern, with a simple boxy design from 1963, Anaco is just off the main shopping thoroughfare, the Gran Vía. Opening onto a tree-shaded plaza, it attracts those seeking a resting place that features contemporary appurtenances and cleanliness. Rooms are compact, with built-in headboards, reading lamps, and lounge chairs. Ask for one of the five terraced rooms on the top floor, which rent at no extra charge. The hotel has a bar/cafeteria/restaurant open daily.

NEAR THE PUERTA DEL SOL

Expensive

Gran Hotel Reina Victoria. Plaza de Santa Ana 14, 28012 Madrid. ☎ **91-531-45-00.** Fax 91-522-03-07. 201 units. A/C MINIBAR TV TEL. 21,000Pts ($132) double; from 26,250Pts ($165) suite (includes breakfast). AE, DC, MC, V. Parking 1,800Pts ($11). Metro: Tirso de Molina or Puerta del Sol.

Since a renovation and upgrading by Spain's Tryp Hotel Group, this hotel is less staid and more impressive than ever. Though it's in a congested and noisy neighborhood in the center of town, Reina Victoria opens onto its own sloping plaza, rich in tradition as a meeting place of intellectuals during the 17th century. Rooms contain sound-resistant insulation, safes, and bathrooms with many amenities. The lobby bar, Manuel Rodriguez Manolete, displays bullfighting memorabilia, and there's a good in-house restaurant, El Ruedo.

Inexpensive

Hostal la Macarena. Cava de San Miguel 8, 28005 Madrid. ☎ **91-365-92-21.** Fax 91-364-27-57. 25 units. TV TEL. 5,500Pts ($35) double; 7,500Pts ($47) triple; 8,500Pts ($54) quad. MC, V. Metro: Puerta del Sol, Opera, or La Latina.

Known for its reasonable prices and praised by readers for the warmth of its reception, this unpretentious, clean hostel is run by the Ricardo González family. Its 19th-century facade, accented with belle-époque patterns and individual balconies, offers an ornate contrast to the chiseled simplicity of the ancient buildings facing it. One of the hostel's assets is its location on a street (an admittedly noisy one) immediately behind Plaza Mayor, near one of the best clusters of tascas in Madrid. Windows facing the street have double panes. No breakfast is served on site, but there's an array of neighborhood cafes.

Hostal la Perla Asturiana. Plaza de Santa Cruz 3, 28012 Madrid. ☎ **91-366-46-00.** Fax 91-366-46-08. E-mail: perlaasturiana@mundivia.es. 30 units. TV TEL. 4,066Pts ($26) double, 5,564Pts ($35) triple. AE, MC, V. Parking: 2,400Pts ($15). Metro: Puerta del Sol.

Ideal for those who want to stay in the heart of Old Madrid (1 block off Plaza Mayor and 2 blocks from the Puerta del Sol), this small family run establishment has a courteous staff member at the desk 24 hours a day for security and convenience. You can socialize in the small, comfortable lobby. Rooms are clean but simple and often cramped. Many inexpensive restaurants and tapas bars are nearby. No breakfast is served.

Hostal-Residencia Principado. Zorrilla 7, 28014 Madrid. ☎ and fax **91-429-81-87.** 15 units. TV. 6,000Pts ($38) double. AE, MC, V. Metro: Sevilla or Banco de España. Bus: 5, 9, or 53.

The two-star Principado is a real find. Located one floor above street level in a well-kept turn-of-the-century town house, it's run by a gracious owner who keeps everything clean and inviting. New tiles, attractive bedspreads, and curtains give the rooms a fresh look. Safety boxes are provided. No meals are served, but most guests retreat to a nearby cafe for breakfast.

✪ Hotel Inglés. Calle Echegaray 8, 28014 Madrid. ☎ **91-429-65-51.** Fax 91-420-24-23. 58 units. TV TEL. 8,500Pts ($54) double; 12,305Pts ($78) suite. AE, DC, MC, V. Parking 1,391Pts ($9). Metro: Puerta del Sol or Sevilla.

On a central street lined with lively tascas, this hotel has welcomed overnight guests since it opened in 1853. It's more modern and impersonal than it was when Virginia Woolf made it her address in Madrid. The lobby is air-conditioned, though the rooms aren't. Rooms are unpretentious and contemporary, all well maintained. Guests who open their windows at night are likely to hear noise from the enclosed courtyard, so light sleepers beware. The comfortable armchairs in the TV lounge are likely to be filled with avid soccer fans. There's a simple cafeteria on the premises, serving drinks and uncomplicated platters daily from 7:30am to 11pm.

NEAR ATOCHA STATION

Moderate

Hotel Mercátor. Calle Atocha 123, 28012 Madrid. ☎ **91-429-05-00.** Fax 91-369-12-52. 87 units. MINIBAR TV TEL. 8,700Pts ($55) double; 12,200Pts ($77) suite. AE, DC, MC, V. Parking 1,740Pts ($11). Metro: Atocha or Antón Martín.

Only a 3-minute walk from the Prado, Reina Sofía, and Thyssen-Bornemisza museums, the circa 1953 Mercátor draws a clientele seeking a good hotel—orderly, well run, and clean, with enough comforts and conveniences to please the weary traveler. The public areas are simple and minimalistic, in a vaguely modern way. Some rooms are more inviting than others, especially those with desks and armchairs. Twenty-one units are air-conditioned. It has a bar and cafeteria serving light meals: *platos combinados* (combination plates) and the like.

NEAR RETIRO & SALAMANCA

Very Expensive

✪ **Hotel Ritz.** Plaza de la Lealtad 5, 28014 Madrid. ☎ **800/225-5843** in the U.S. and Canada, or 91-521-28-57. Fax 91-532-87-76. www.ritz.es. 156 units. A/C MINIBAR TV TEL. 48,000–58,000Pts ($302–$365) double; 60,000–71,000Pts ($378–$447) suite. AE, DC, MC, V. Parking 4,000Pts ($25). Metro: Banco de España.

Spain's most famous hotel, encased in an early 20th-century shell of soaring ceilings and graceful columns, is Madrid's most prestigious address. Billions of pesetas have been spent on renovations since the British-based Forte chain acquired it. The result is a bastion of glamour. The Ritz was built at the command of Alfonso XIII, with the aid of César Ritz, in 1908. Rooms contain fresh flowers, well-accessorized bathrooms, and TVs with video movies and satellite reception. In the hotel's formal restaurant, Goya, the chefs present an international menu featuring a paella that's Madrid's most elaborate.

Park Hyatt Villa Magna. Paseo de la Castellana 22, 28046 Madrid. ☎ **800/223-1234** in the U.S. and Canada, or 91-587-12-34. Fax 91-431-22-86. www.travelweb.com/hyatt.html. 182 units. A/C MINIBAR TV TEL. 55,000Pts ($347) double; from 60,000Pts ($378) suite. AE, DC, MC, V. Parking 3,000Pts ($19). Metro: Rubén Darío.

One of Europe's finest hotels, the nine-story Park Hyatt is set behind a bank of pines and laurels on the city's most fashionable boulevard. Today it's an even finer choice than the Palace and is matched in luxury, ambience, and tranquillity only by the Ritz. This luxury palace offers plush but dignified rooms decorated in Louis XVI, English Regency, or Italian provincial style. The Berceo serves international food in a glamorous setting, Berceo Le Divellec, a branch of the most famous fish restaurant of Paris, serves international seafood in a glamorous setting, and there's also Tse-Yang, an upscale Chinese restaurant and a lavish English-style bar. The hotel is known for its summer terraces, set in gardens.

Expensive

Emperatriz. López de Hoyos 4, 28006 Madrid. ☎ **91-563-80-88.** Fax 91-563-98-04. 158 units. A/C MINIBAR TV TEL. 22,500Pts ($142) double; 27,000Pts ($170) suite. AE, DC, MC, V. Metro: Rubén Darío.

This eight-story hotel is just off the wide Paseo de Castellana, only a short walk from some of Madrid's most deluxe hotels, but it charges relatively reasonable rates. Rooms (classically styled and comfortable, with both traditional and modern furniture) remain much finer than the somewhat unimaginative public areas. Ask for a seventh-floor room, where you'll get a private terrace at no extra charge. There's a bar and restaurant on site, serving both Spanish and international food, plus 24-hour room service.

Our Favorite Tascas

Don't starve waiting around for Madrid's fashionable 9:30 or 10pm dinner hour. Throughout the city you'll find *tascas,* bars that serve wine and platters of tempting hot and cold hors d'oeuvres known as tapas: mushrooms, salads, baby eels, shrimp, lobster, mussels, sausage, ham, and, in one establishment at least, bull testicles. Below we've listed our favorite tapas bars. Keep in mind you can often save pesetas by ordering at the bar rather than occupying a table.

Casa Mingo, Paseo de la Florida 2 (☎ 91-547-79-18; Metro: Norte), has been known for decades for its cider, both still and bubbly. The perfect accompanying tidbit is a piece of Asturian cabrales (goat cheese), but the roast chicken is the specialty of the house. There's no formality here, since customers share big tables under the vaulted ceiling in the dining room; in summer, the staff sets up tables and wooden chairs out on the sidewalk. This isn't so much a restaurant as it is a bodega/taverna that serves food daily 11am to midnight. Hemingway and celebrated bullfighter Luís Miguel Domínguín used to frequent the casual **Cervecería Alemania,** Plaza de Santa Ana 6 (☎ 91-429-70-33; Metro: Alonso Martín or Tirso de Molina)—ask the waiter to point out Hemingway's table. However, it earned its name because of its long-ago German clients. Opening onto one of the liveliest little plazas in Madrid, it clings to its early-1900s traditions, and you can sit at one of the tables, leisurely sipping beer or wine, since the waiters make no attempt to hurry you along. To accompany your beverage, try the fried sardines or a Spanish omelette. It's open Sunday to Thursday 11am to 12:30am and Friday and Saturday 11am to 2am.

Unique in Madrid, the **Cervecería Santa Bárbara,** Plaza de Santa Bárbara 8 (☎ 91-319-04-049; Metro: Alonzo Martínez; bus: 3, 7, or 21), is an outlet for a beer factory, and the management has spent a lot to make it modern and inviting. Hanging globe lights and spinning ceiling fans create an attractive ambience, as does the black-and-white marble floor. You go here for beer, of course: *cerveza negra* (black beer) or *cerveza dorada* (golden beer). The local brew is best accompanied by homemade potato chips or by fresh shrimp, lobster, crabmeat, or barnacles. You can either stand at the counter or go to one of the wooden tables for waiter service. It's open daily 11:30am to midnight. Many Madrileños begin their nightly tasca crawl at the **Taberna Toscana,** Manuel Fernandez y Gonzales 10 (☎ 91-429-60-31; Metro: Puerta del Sol or Sevilla). The ambience is that of a village inn far removed from 21st-century Madrid. You sit on crude country stools, under sausages, peppers, and sheaves of golden wheat that hang from the age-darkened beams. The long tiled bar is loaded with tasty tidbits, including the house specialties: *lacón y cecina* (boiled ham), *habas* (broad beans) with Spanish ham, and *chorizo* (a sausage of red peppers and pork)—almost meals in themselves. Especially delectable are the kidneys in sherry sauce and the snails in hot sauce. It's open Tuesday to Saturday noon to 4pm and 8pm to midnight (closed August).

Grand Hotel Velázquez. Calle de Velázquez 62, 28001 Madrid. ☎ **91-575-28-00.** Fax 91-575-28-09. 146 units. A/C MINIBAR TV TEL. 16,000Pts ($101) double; from 18,000Pts ($113) suite. AE, DC, MC, V. Parking 2,200Pts ($14). Metro: Retiro.

On an affluent residential street near the center of town, this hotel has an art deco facade and a 1940s interior filled with well-upholstered furniture and richly grained paneling. Be advised that this is a very Spanish hotel with less international exposure than some of its more cosmopolitan competitors. Several public rooms lead off a central oval area; one of them includes a bar area. As in many hotels of its era, the rooms vary; some are large enough for entertaining, with a small but separate sitting area for reading or watching TV. This is one of the most attractive medium-size hotels in Madrid, with plenty of comfort and convenience.

Moderate

Gran Hotel Colón. Pez Volador 11, 28007 Madrid. ☎**91-573-59-00.** Fax 91-573-08-09. 380 units. A/C MINIBAR TV TEL. 12,000–15,000Pts ($76–$95) double. AE, DC, MC, V. Parking 1,800Pts ($11). Metro: Sainz de Baranda.

East of Retiro Park, Gran Hotel Colón is a few minutes from the city center by Metro. It offers comfortable yet moderately priced rooms. More than half have private balconies, and all contain comfortably traditional furniture, much of it built-in. Other assets include two dining rooms and a bar.

WHERE TO DINE
NEAR PLAZA DE LAS CORTÉS
Expensive

El Espejo. Paseo de Recoletos 31. ☎ **91-308-23-47.** Reservations required. Menú del día 3,000Pts ($18). AE, DC, MC, V. Sun–Fri 1–4pm and 9pm–midnight, Sat 9pm–1am. Metro: Banco de España or Colón. Bus: 27. INTERNATIONAL.

Here you'll find good-tasting food and one of the most perfectly crafted art nouveau decors in Madrid. If the weather is good, you can choose one of the outdoor tables, served by uniformed waiters who carry food across the busy street to a green area flanked with trees and strolling pedestrians. There's also a charming cafe/bar. Menu items include grouper ragout with clams, steak tartare, guinea fowl with Armagnac, and lean duck meat with pineapple.

Inexpensive

La Trucha. Manuel Fernández González 3. ☎ **91-429-58-33.** Reservations recommended. Main courses 1,800–2,800Pts ($11–$18). AE, V. Mon–Sat 12:30–4pm and 7:30pm–midnight. Metro: Sevilla. SPANISH/SEAFOOD.

With its Andalusian tavern ambience, La Trucha boasts a street-level bar and a small dining room. The arched ceiling and whitewashed walls are festive with hanging braids of garlic, dried peppers, and onions; on the lower level there's a second bustling area. The specialty is fish, and there's a complete à la carte menu including *trucha* (trout), *verbenas de ahumados* (smoked delicacies), a stew called *fabada* (made with beans, Galician ham, black sausage, and smoked bacon), and *comida casera rabo de toro* (home-style oxtail). No one should miss nibbling on the *tapas variadas* in the bar.

ON OR NEAR THE GRAN VÍA
Expensive

La Barraca. Reina 29–31. ☎ **91-532-71-54.** Reservations recommended. Main courses 4,000–5,000Pts ($25–$32); fixed-price menu 3,500–4,000Pts ($22–$25). AE, DC, MC, V. Daily 1–4pm and 8:30pm–midnight. Metro: Gran Vía or Bancode España. Bus: 1, 2, or 74. VALENCIAN.

This longtime local favorite right off the Gran Vía is like a country inn. There're four different dining rooms, colorfully cluttered with ceramics, paintings, photographs, Spanish lanterns, flowers, and local artifacts. The Valencian-style restaurant is recommended for its tasty Levante cooking. The house specialty, paella à la Barraca, is made with pork and chicken. Specialties in the appetizer category include *desgarrat* (a salad of codfish and red peppers), mussels in a white-wine sauce, and shrimp sautéed with garlic. In addition to the recommended paella, you can select at least 16 rice dishes, including black rice and queen paella. Main-dish specialties include brochette of anglerfish and prawns and rabbit with fines herbs.

Moderate

El Mentidero de la Villa. Santo Tomé 6. ☎ **91-308-12-85.** Reservations required. Main courses 2,000–5,000Pts ($13–$32); menú del día 1,450Pts ($9). AE, DC, MC, V. Mon–Fri 1:30–4pm and 9pm–midnight, Sat 9pm–midnight. Closed last 2 weeks of Aug. Metro: Alonso Martínez, Colón, or Gran Vía. Bus: 37. SPANISH/FRENCH.

This "Gossip Shop" is certainly a multicultural experience. The owner describes the cuisine as "modern Spanish with Japanese influence; the cooking technique is French." The result is usually a graceful achievement, as each ingredient in every dish manages to retain its natural flavor. The kitchen prepares such adventuresome dishes as black spaghetti, flavored with squid ink, served with lobster sauce, mussels, and medallions of crayfish; an avocado/crabmeat/watercress and bacon salad; rack of lamb stuffed with minced leg of lamb that's been enhanced with a pepper/white wine/and potato sauce. Despite many newer desserts, the most popular remains a sherry trifle that British visitors usually applaud.

✪ **Mad Cafe Club.** Calle Virgin de los Peligros 4. ☎ **91-532-62-28.** Reservations recommended. Main courses 1,700–2,200Pts ($11–$14); fixed-price menu (at lunch only) 1,700Pts ($11). AE, DC, MC, V. Mon–Wed 1–4pm and 9:30pm–3am; Thurs–Sat 1–4pm and 9:30pm–4am. Dinner served until 12:30am. Metro: Sevilla, Gran Vía. INTERNATIONAL.

This restaurant/bar in the very center of Madrid is a fine representative of the new Spain and is a popular night-time haunt for the fashionable. Decorated in a stark minimalist style, it recalls the early Soviet Constructivist artists. There's also a garden where diners and drinkers can languish on the hot summer nights. Staples include starters such as goat cheese on caramelized onions and corral salad, which is comprised of wild chicken marinated in vinegar and cream in four types of lettuce. Other dishes to savor are marinated salmon with dill and golden caviar, which is black, from an inland sea in the dry southern province of Murcia. This is appropriately served with Japanese seaweed and the fresh seasonal vegetables are presented al dente. Desserts include an apple tart, not too sweet and topped with egg yolk.

NEAR THE PUERTA DEL SOL

Expensive

Casa Paco. Plaza de la Puerta Cerrada 11. ☎ **91-366-31-66.** Reservations required. Main courses 1,800–5,000Pts ($11–$32); fixed-price menu 3,600Pts ($23). DC. Mon–Sat 1:30–3:45pm and 8:30–11:45pm. Closed Aug. Metro: Puerta del Sol, Opera, or La Latina. Bus: 3, 21, or 65. STEAK.

Madrileños defiantly name Casa Paco, beside Plaza Mayor in the old town, when someone has the nerve to put down Spanish steaks. They know that here you can get the thickest, juiciest steaks in Spain, priced according to weight. Señor Paco was the first in Madrid to sear steaks in boiling oil before serving them on plates so hot that the almost-raw meat continues to cook, preserving the natural juices. The two-story restaurant offers three dining rooms. Reservations are imperative—otherwise, you face a long wait. Casa Paco isn't just a steak house. You can start with fish soup and proceed to a dish such as grilled sole, lamb, or Casa Paco cocido, the famous chickpea/meat soup of Madrid.

Lhardy. Carrera de San Jerónimo 8. ☎ **91-521-33-85.** Reservations recommended in the upstairs dining room. Main courses 7,500–10,000Pts ($47–$63). AE, DC, MC, V. Mon–Sat 1–3:30pm and 8:30–11:30pm. Closed Aug. Metro: Puerta del Sol. SPANISH/INTERNATIONAL.

Lhardy has been a Madrileño legend since it opened in 1839 as a gathering place for the city's literati and political leaders. Its street level contains what might be the most elegant snack bar in Spain. In a dignified setting of marble and varnished hardwoods, cups of steaming consommé are dispensed from silver samovars into delicate porcelain cups. The real culinary skill of the place, however, is visible on Lhardy's second floor, where you'll find a formal restaurant decorated in the ornate style of Isabel Segunda. Specialties include many preparations of fresh fish; tripe in a garlicky tomato-and-onion/wine sauce; and cocido, the chickpea stew of Madrid, made with sausage, pork, and vegetables. Soufflé sorpresa (baked Alaska) is the dessert specialty.

Platerías Comedor. Plaza de Santa Ana 11. ☎ **91-429-70-48.** Reservations recommended. Main courses 5,500–7,500Pts ($35–$47). AE, DC, MC, V. Mon–Fri 1:30–4pm and 9pm–midnight, Sat 9pm–midnight. Metro: Puerta del Sol. SPANISH.

One of the most charming dining rooms in Madrid, Platerías Comedor has richly brocaded walls and a graceful setting originally built in 1862. Despite the busy socializing on the plaza outside, this serene oasis makes few concessions to the new generation in its food, decor, or formally attired waiters. Specialties are beans with clams, stuffed partridge with cabbage and sausage, hake prepared in several variations, magret of duckling with orange sauce or pomegranates, duck liver with white grapes, veal stew with snails and mushrooms, and guinea hen with figs and plums. You might finish with passion fruit sorbet.

Moderate

Café de Oriente. Plaza de Oriente 2. ☎ **91-541-39-74.** Reservations recommended (in formal restaurant only). In cafe, tapas 850Pts ($5), coffee 550Pts ($3.45). In restaurant, main courses 7,000–7,500Pts ($44–$47). AE, DC, MC, V. Café daily 8:30am–12:30am (till 2:30am Fri–Sat). Restaurant daily 1–4pm and 9pm–midnight. Metro: Opera. FRENCH/SPANISH.

With the allure of a setting on one of Madrid's most historic and regal-looking squares, the Oriente manages both bistro-style informality and some very grand dining. In the more formal richly accessorized cellar, intricate, stylish Basque cuisine is served at 10 tables suitable for Spanish royalty. Expect lots of high-powered corporate groups that dine in the private dining rooms nestled off to the side of the central room. On the street level, you'll find a less intense, more workaday crowd of cafe patrons who appreciate the rich array of tapas, the dozens of small tables, coffee, wine, and foaming mugs of beer, and a set-price menu that's one of the bargains of this gilt-edged neighborhood.

Inexpensive

Casa Alberto. Huertas 18. ☎ **91-429-93-56.** Reservations recommended. Main courses 2,006–4,000Pts ($13–$25). AE, DC, MC, V. Tues–Sun 8:30am–1:30pm. Metro: Antón Martín. CASTILIAN.

One of the oldest tascas in the neighborhood, Casa Alberto is on the street level of the house where Miguel de Cervantes lived briefly in 1614 and contains an appealing mixture of bullfighting memorabilia, engravings, and reproductions of old master paintings. Tapas are continually replenished from platters on the bar top, but there's also a sit-down dining area in the back for more substantial meals. Specialties include fried squid, shellfish in green sauce, *chorizo* (sausage) in cider sauce, and several versions of baked or roasted lamb. If you don't come for a meal, it's also a great place to sit down and have a cold beer or glass of *vino tinto* and a wedge of tortilla española.

Hylogui. Ventura de la Vega 3. ☎ **91-429-73-57.** Reservations recommended. Main courses 1,500–4,500Pts ($9–$28); fixed-price menu 1,200–1,800Pts ($8–$11). AE, MC, V. Mon–Sat 1:30–4:30pm and 9pm–midnight, Sun 1–4:30pm. Metro: Sevilla. SPANISH.

Hylogui, a local legend since the 1930s, is one of the largest dining rooms along Ventura de la Vega, but there're many arches and nooks for privacy. One globe-trotting American wrote enthusiastically that he took all his Madrid meals here, finding the soup pleasant and rich, the flan soothing, the regional wine dry, and the prices affordable. The food is old-fashioned Spanish home-style cooking.

Near Retiro & Salamanca
Very Expensive

Alkalde. Jorge Juan 10. ☎ **91-576-33-59.** Reservations required. Main courses 5,000–5,600Pts ($32–$35); fixed-price menu from 4,500Pts ($28). AE, DC, MC, V. Daily 1:15–4:30pm and 8:30pm–midnight. Closed Sat–Sun July–Aug. Metro: Retiro or Serrano. Bus: 8, 21, 29, or 53. BASQUE/INTERNATIONAL.

Alkalde serves top-quality Spanish food in an old tavern setting decorated like a Basque inn, with beamed ceilings and hams hanging from the rafters. Upstairs is a large *típico* tavern; downstairs is a maze of stone-sided cellars that are pleasantly cool in summer. Basque cookery is the best in Spain, and Alkalde honors that tradition nobly. You might begin with the cream-of-crabmeat soup, followed by *gambas a la plancha* (grilled shrimp), chicken cutlets, or *cigalas* (crayfish). Other well-recommended dishes are *mero en salsa verde* (brill in a green sauce), trout Alkalde, stuffed peppers, and chicken steak.

Horcher. Alfonso XII 6. ☎ **91-532-35-96.** Reservations required. Jackets and ties required for men. Main courses 5,500–7,500Pts ($35–$47). AE, DC, MC, V. Mon–Fri 1:30–4pm and 8:30pm–midnight, Sat 8:30pm–midnight. Metro: Retiro. GERMAN/INTERNATIONAL.

Horcher originated in Berlin in 1904. Prompted by a tip from a high-ranking German officer that Germany was losing the war, Herr Horcher moved his restaurant to Madrid in 1943. The restaurant has continued its grand European traditions, including excellent service, ever since. You might try the skate or shrimp tartare or the distinctive warm hake salad. The venison stew in green pepper with orange peel and the crayfish with parsley and cucumber are the type of elegant fare served with impeccable style; you can sample game dishes like wild boar or roast wild duck in autumn. Other main courses include veal scaloppini in tarragon and sea bass with saffron.

Viridiana. Juan de Mena 14. ☎ **91-523-44-78.** Reservations recommended. Main courses 6,000–10,000Pts ($38–$63). AE, MC, V. Mon–Sat 1:30–4pm and 9pm–midnight. Closed Aug and 1 week at Easter. Metro: Banco. INTERNATIONAL.

Praised as one of Madrid's top restaurants, Viridiana is known for the creative imagination of chef and part-owner Abraham García, a cinema historian and self-taught chef who named his restaurant after the Luís Buñuel 1961 classic. Menu specialties are usually contemporary adaptations of traditional recipes and change frequently according to the availability of the ingredients. Examples are tartare of tuna, a salad of exotic lettuces with smoked salmon, fillet steak with truffles, guinea fowl stuffed with herbs and wild mushrooms, baby squid with curry served on a bed of lentils, and roast lamb in puff pastry with fresh basil. A delectable dish is vineyard snails cooked in vine leaves, rosemary, tomato sauce, and pimientos.

Expensive

El Amparo. Callejón de Puígcerdá 8 (at the corner of Jorge Juan). ☎ **91-431-64-56.** Reservations required. Main courses 13,000–14,000Pts ($82–$88); fixed-price menu 10,000Pts ($63). AE, MC, V. Mon–Fri 1:30–3:30pm and 9am–11:30pm, Sat 9:30–11:30pm. Closed the week before Easter and 1 week in Aug. Metro: Goya; bus: 21 or 53. BASQUE.

Behind the cascading vines on its facade, this is one of Madrid's most elegant gastro-nomic enclaves, a pioneer of a new type of cuisine. It introduced (some 16 years ago) cod cheeks in a smooth puree of red peppers. You are served innovative food in a for-mer carriage house, including, for example, ravioli with crayfish dressed in balsamic vinegar and a vanilla-scented oil. A sloping skylight floods the interior with sun by day; at night, pinpoints of light from the high-tech hanging lanterns create intimate shadows. A battalion of polite uniformed waiters serves well-prepared nouvelle-cuisine versions of cold marinated salmon with tomato sorbet, delectable fish salads, bisque of shellfish with Armagnac, ravioli stuffed with seafood, a platter of steamed fish of the day, and steamed hake with pepper sauce.

La Gamella. Alfonso XII 4. ☎ **91-532-45-09.** Reservations required. Main courses 5,500–6,000Pts ($35–$38). AE, DC, MC, V. Mon–Fri 1:30–4pm and 9pm–midnight, Sat 9pm–midnight. Closed 2 weeks around Easter and 2 weeks in Aug. Metro: Retiro; bus: 19. CALIFORNIAN/CASTILIAN.

In 1988, La Gamella's Illinois-born owner, former choreographer Dick Stephens, moved his restaurant into this 19th-century building. Low-key, glamorous, and sooth-ing, the restaurant serves a roster of ongoing staples, plus some newfangled cuisine that in North America might be referred to as fusion. Examples of the latter include what has been called "the only edible hamburger in Madrid" and steak tartare spiked with Jack Daniels, as well as more upscale food such as sliced duck liver in truffle sauce, duck breast with sweet-and-sour sauce, spicy Thai chicken, and a perennial favorite of quiche made with Spanish sausage and red peppers. Also look for creative dishes such as their fish of the day with a poblano sauce, served on a bed of corn pud-ding. Fried goose liver, served as a supremely upscale main course, is the most expen-sive item on the menu.

Inexpensive
Gran Café de Gijón. Paseo de Recoletos 21. ☎ **91-521-54-25.** Reservations required for restaurant. Main courses 4,500–7,000Pts ($28–$44); fixed-price menu 1,500Pts ($9). MC, V. Daily 8am–2am. Metro: Banco de España, Colón, or Recoletos. SPANISH.

Each European capital has a coffeehouse that traditionally attracts the literati. In Madrid it's the Gijón, which opened in 1888. Artists and writers still patronize this venerated cafe; many spend hours over one cup of coffee. Hemingway made the place famous for Americans. Gijón has open windows looking out onto the wide paseo, as well as a large terrace for sun worshipers and bird-watchers. Along one side is a stand-up bar and on the lower level is a restaurant. The cookery is the "way it used to be" in Madrid.

CHAMBERÍ
Very Expensive
Jockey. Amador de los Ríos 6. ☎ **91-319-24-35.** Reservations required. Main courses 10,000–12,500Pts ($63–$79). AE, DC, MC, V. Mon–Sat 1–4pm and 9pm–midnight. Closed Aug. Metro: Colón. INTERNATIONAL.

Beginning in 1945, this was Spain's premier restaurant, though competition is severe today. At any rate, it's still a favorite of international celebrities, and some of the more faithful patrons look on it as their private club. Against the wood-paneled walls are a dozen prints of horses mounted by jockeys—hence the name of the place. The chef prides himself on coming up with new and creative dishes. Try his fatted duck with ginger and citrus sauce, or slices of Jabugo ham. His cold melon soup with shrimp is soothing on a hot day, especially when followed by grill-roasted young pigeon from Talavera cooked in its own juice or monkfish en papillote with Mantua sauce. Stuffed small chicken Jockey style is a specialty.

Las Cuatro Estaciones. General Ibañez Ibero 5. ☎ **91-553-63-05.** Reservations required. Main courses 7,000Pts ($44); fixed-price dinner 5,500Pts ($35). AE, DC, MC, V. Mon–Fri 1:30–5:30pm and 9pm–midnight, Sat 9–11:30pm. Closed Aug. Metro: Guzmán el Bueno. MEDITERRANEAN.

Praised by gastronomes and horticulturists, Las Cuatro Estaciones has become a neck-and-neck rival with the prestigious Jockey. Each person involved in food preparation spends a prolonged apprenticeship at one of the great restaurants of France. In addition to superb food, the establishment prides itself on the masses of flowers that change with the season, plus a modern and softly inviting decor. Representative specialties are petite marmite of fish and shellfish, imaginative preparations of salmon, a salad of eels, black rice with squid ink and squid, hake with a tomato and garlic butter sauce, and a three-fish platter with fines herbes.

Inexpensive

La Bola. Calle de la Bola, 5. ☎ **91-547-69-30.** Reservations required. Main courses 1,500–3,150Pts ($9–$20); fixed-price menu 1,250Pts ($8). No credit cards. Mon–Sat 1–4pm, daily 8:30pm–midnight. Metro: Plaza de España or ópera; bus: 1 or 2. MADRILEÑA.

This is just the taberna in which to savor the 19th century. Just north of the Teatro Real, La Bola hangs on to tradition like a tenacious bull. Time has passed, but not inside this restaurant: The soft, traditional atmosphere; the gentle and polite waiters; the Venetian crystal; the Carmen-red draperies; and the aging velvet preserve the 1870 ambience. Ava Gardner, with her entourage of bullfighters, used to patronize this establishment, but that was long before La Bola became so well known to tourists. Grilled sole, fillet of veal, and roast veal are regularly featured. Basque-style hake and grilled salmon also are well recommended. A host of refreshing dishes to begin your meal includes grilled shrimp, red-pepper salad, and lobster cocktail.

OFF PLAZA MAYOR

Moderate

✪ **Sobrino de Botín.** Calle de Cuchilleros 17. ☎ **91-366-42-17.** Reservations required. Main courses 3,500–5,000Pts ($22–$32); fixed-price menu 3,700Pts ($23). AE, DC, MC, V. Daily 1–4pm and 8pm–midnight. Metro: La Latina, Puerto del Sol, or Opera. SPANISH.

Ernest Hemingway made Sobrino de Botín famous. In the final pages of *The Sun Also Rises,* Jake invites Lady Brett there for the Segovian specialty, roast suckling pig, washed down with Rioja Alta. By merely entering its portals you step back to 1725, the year the restaurant was founded. You'll see an open kitchen with a charcoal hearth, hanging copper pots, an 18th-century tile oven for roasting the suckling pig, and a big pot of regional soup whose aroma wafts across the room. The other house specialty is roast Segovian lamb. But if you're not in the mood for those, you can order an excellent and robust fillet steak. You can accompany your meal with Valdepeñas or Aragón wine, or even sangría.

CHAMARTIN

Expensive

✪ **Zalacaín.** Alvarez de Baena, 4. ☎ **91-561-48-40.** Reservations required. Main courses 10,000–15,000Pts ($63–$95). AE, DC, MC, V. Mon–Fri 1:15–4pm, Mon–Sat 9pm–midnight. Closed week before Easter and Aug. Metro: Rubén Darío. INTERNATIONAL.

Outstanding in both food and decor, Zalacaín opened in 1973 and introduced nouvelle cuisine to Spain. Zalacaín is small, exclusive, and expensive. It has the atmosphere of an elegant old mansion: The walls are covered with textiles, and some are decorated with Audubon-type paintings. Men should wear jackets and ties. The menu features many Basque and French specialties, often with nouvelle cuisine touches. It might offer a superb sole in a green sauce, but it also knows the glory of grilled pig's feet. Among the most recommendable main dishes are oysters with caviar and sherry jelly; crêpes stuffed with smoked fish; ravioli stuffed with mushrooms, foie gras, and truffles; and Spanish bouillabaisse. For dessert, we'd suggest one of the custards, perhaps raspberry or chocolate.

Moderate
El Olivo Restaurant. General Gallegos 1. ☎ **91/359-15-35.** Reservations recommended. Main courses 2,500–4,000Pts ($16–$25); fixed-price meals 1,500–2,000Pts ($9–$13). AE, V. Tues–Sat 1–4pm and 9pm–midnight. Closed Aug 15–31 and 4 days around Easter. Metro: Plaza de Castilla. MEDITERRANEAN.

Locals praise the success of French-born Jean Pierre Vandelle in recognizing the international appeal of two of Spain's most valuable culinary resources, olive oil and sherry. Designed in tones of green and amber, it's the only restaurant in Spain that wheels a cart stocked with 40 regional olive oils from table to table. From the cart, diners select a variety to soak up with chunks of rough-textured bread that is, according to your taste, seasoned with a dash of salt. Menu specialties include grilled fillet of monkfish marinated in herbs and olive oil, then served with black-olive sauce over a compote of fresh tomatoes, and four preparations of codfish arranged on a single platter and served with a pil-pil sauce. Desserts might be one of several different chocolate pastries. A wide array of reasonably priced Bordeaux and Spanish wines can accompany your meal.

SEEING THE SIGHTS
Madrid has changed drastically in recent years. It is no longer fair to say that this lively European capital has only the Prado, and after you see that, you should head for Toledo or El Escorial. As you'll discover, Madrid has something to amuse and delight everyone.

SIGHTSEEING SUGGESTIONS FOR FIRST-TIME VISITORS
If You Have 1 Day   If you have just arrived in Spain after a long flight, don't tackle too much on your first day. Spend the morning seeing a few of the masterpieces at the Prado, one of the world's great art museums. It's best to arrive when it opens at 9am (remember, it's closed Monday). Have lunch and then visit the Palacio Real (Royal Palace). Have an early dinner near Plaza Mayor.

If You Have 2 Days   On Day 2 visit the Thyssen-Bornemisza Museum in the morning, strolled around Madrid's medieval area, and visited the Museo Nacional Centro de Arte Reina Sofía in the late afternoon or early evening (it closes at 9pm most nights). Here you can see Picasso's *Guernica* plus other great art of the 20th century. Have dinner once again at one of the many restaurants off Plaza Mayor.

If You Have 3 Days   On your third day take a trip to Toledo, where you can visit the Cathedral, the Santa Cruz Museum, and the Alcázar. Return to Madrid in the evening.

If You Have 4 or 5 Days   On Day 4 take a 1-hour train ride to the Monastery of San Lorenzo de El Escorial, in the foothills of the Sierra de Guadarrama. Return to Madrid in the evening. On Day 5 you could take a trip to Segovia or ávila.

THE TOP MUSEUMS
✪ **Museo del Prado.** Paseo del Prado. ☎ **91-330-28-00.** Admission 500Pts ($3.15), 250Pts ($1.60) students, free children 11 and under and seniors. Tues–Sat 9am–7pm, Sun and holidays 9am–2pm. Closed Jan 1, Good Friday, May 1, and Dec 25. Metro: Banco de España or Atocha; bus: 10, 14, 27, 34, 37, 45, or M6.

With more than 7,000 paintings, the Prado is one of the most important repositories of art in the world. It began as a royal collection and was enhanced by the Hapsburgs. In paintings of the Spanish school the Prado has no equal, so on your first visit, concentrate on the Spanish masters. You'll find a treasure trove of works by El Greco, the Crete-born artist who lived much of his life in Toledo. Look for *Las Meninas,* the museum's most famous painting, and other works by the incomparable Diego Velázquez. The incomparable Francisco de Goya collection includes his unflattering portraits of his patron, Charles IV, and his family, as well as the *Clothed Maja* and the *Naked Maja* and pictures from his black period. Look also for paintings by Zurbarán and Murillo, and be sure to search out Flemish genius Hieronymus Bosch's best-known work, *The Garden of Earthly Delights.* **Paseo del Arte,** priced at 1,275 Pts. ($8) grants admission to the Museo del Prado, Museo Thyssen-Bornemisza, and the Cento de Arte Reina Sofía, and the pass is sold at all three museums.

○ **Thyssen-Bornemisza Museum.** Palacio de Villahermosa, Paseo del Prado 8. ☎ **91-369-01-51.** Admission 700Pts ($4.40) adults, 450Pts ($2.85) seniors and students, free children 11 and under. Tues–Sun 10am–7pm. Metro: Banco de España; bus: 1, 2, 5, 9, 10, 14, 15, 20, 27, 34, 45, 51, 52, 53, 74, 146, or 150.

The Thyssen-Bornemisza family's unrivaled private collection was amassed over a period of about 60 years. Baron von Thyssen is married to a Spaniard, who desperately wanted to see the collection permanently reside in her native Spain. When it went on the market, Spain acquired it for $350 million. To house the collection, an 18th-century Villahermosa Palace, adjacent to the Prado, was retrofitted so that by following the order of the various rooms a logical sequence of European and American painting can be traced from the 13th through the 20th century. The nucleus of the collection consists of 700 world-class paintings. They include works by El Greco, Velázquez, Dürer, Rembrandt, Watteau, Canaletto, Caravaggio, Frans Hals, Hans Memling, and Goya, among many others.

Museo Nacional Centro de Arte Reina Sofía. Santa Isabel 52. ☎ **91-467-50-62.** Admission 500Pts ($3.15) adults, 250Pts ($1.60) students and children 11 and under. Mon and Wed–Sat 10am–9pm, Sun 10am–2:30pm. Metro: Atocha; bus: 6, 14, 26, 27, 32, 45, 57, or C.

Madrid's greatest repository of 20th-century art is here, in a high-ceilinged showplace named after the Greek-born wife of Spain's present king. One of Europe's largest museums, it was designated "the ugliest building in Spain" by the Catalán architect Oriol Bohigas, though many are thrilled with the huge glass-enclosed elevators on the outside. Special emphasis inside is paid to the great 20th-century artists of Spain: Juan Gris, Dalí, and Miró. Picasso's masterpiece, *Guernica,* now rests here after a long and troubling nomadic history. (During Franco's reign, it was in New York's Museum of Modern Art, per Picasso's request.) This antiwar piece immortalizes the blanket bombing by the German Luftwaffe for Franco during the Spanish Civil War of the village of Guernica, cradle of the Basque nation.

○ **Palacio Real (Royal Palace).** Plaza de Oriente, calle de Bailén 2. ☎ **91-542-00-59.** Admission 950Pts ($6) adults, 350Pts ($2.20) seniors, students, and children 11 and under; self-guided tour 850Pts ($5). Mon–Sat 9am–5pm, Sun 9am–2pm. Metro: Opera or Plaza de España.

This huge palace was begun in 1738 on the site of the Madrid Alcázar, which burned in 1734. Some of its 2,000 rooms are open to the public, though others are still used for state business. The guided tour includes the Reception Room, the State Apartments, the Armory, and the Royal Pharmacy. The rooms are literally stuffed with art treasures and antiques—salon after salon of monumental grandeur, with no apologies for the damask, mosaics, stucco, Tiepolo ceilings, gilt and bronze, chandeliers, and paintings. In the Armory you'll see a fine collection of weaponry.

MORE ATTRACTIONS

Museo de la Real Academia de Bellas Artes de San Fernando (Fine Arts Museum). Alcalá 13. ☎ **91-522-14-91.** Tues–Fri 300Pts ($1.90) adults, 150Pts (95¢) students, free for children and seniors 60 and over; Sat–Sun free for everyone. Tues–Fri 9am–7pm, Sat–Mon 9am–2:30pm. Metro: Puerta del Sol or Sevilla; bus: 15, 20, 51, 52, or M12.

An easy stroll from the Puerta del Sol, the Fine Arts Museum is located in the restored and remodeled 17th-century baroque palace of Juan de Goyeneche. The collection—more than 1,500 paintings and 570 sculptures, ranging from the 16th century to the present—was started in 1752 during the reign of Fernando VI (1746–59). It emphasizes works by Spanish, Flemish, and Italian artists. Masterpieces by El Greco, Rubens, Velázquez, Zurbarán, Ribera, Cano, Coello, Murillo, and Sorolla are here. The Goya collection in itself is worth a visit. Goya was a member of the academy since 1780, and the museum houses two of his self-portraits, along with a full-size portrait of the actress, La Tirana, and the royal "favorite" Manuel Godoy, plus the carnival scene, *Burial of the Sardine,* and eight more oils.

Panteón de Goya (Goya's Tomb). Glorieta de San António de la Florida. ☎ **91-542-07-22.** Admission 300Pts ($1.90) adults, 150Pts (95¢) seniors and children 17 and under. Tues–Fri 10am–2pm and 4–8pm, Sat–Sun 10am–2pm. Metro: Principe Pio; bus: 41, 46, 75, or C.

Several blocks beyond the North Station lies Goya's tomb, containing one of his masterpieces: an elaborately beautiful fresco depicting the miracles of St. Anthony on the dome and cupola of the little hermitage of San António de la Florida. This has been called Goya's Sistine Chapel. Already deaf when he began the painting, Goya labored from dawn to dusk for 16 weeks, painting with sponges rather than brushes. By depicting common street life—stone masons, prostitutes, and beggars—Goya raised the ire of the nobility. However, when Carlos IV viewed it and approved, the formerly "outrageous" painting was deemed acceptable.

✪ Museo Lázaro Galdiano. Serrano 122. ☎ **91-561-60-84.** Admission 500Pts ($3.15) adults, 150Pts (95¢) students, free for seniors and children 11 and under. Tues–Sun 10am–2pm. Closed holidays and Aug. Metro: Gregorio Marámon; bus: 9, 16, 19, 51, or 89.

This well-preserved 19th-century mansion bulges with artworks of all kinds. Take the elevator to the top floor and work your way down; there are 15th-century hand-woven vestments, swords and daggers, royal seals, 16th-century crystal from Limoges, Byzantine jewelry, Italian bronzes from ancient times to the Renaissance, and medieval armor. There are also works by the Old Masters El Greco, Velázquez, Zurbarán, Ribera, Murillo, and Valdés-Leal, and Tiepolo and Guardi, and a section is devoted to works by the English artists Reynolds, Gainsborough, and Constable.

✪ Monasterio de las Descalzas Reales. Plaza de las Descalzas Reales. ☎ **91-454-87-00.** Admission 650Pts ($4.10) adults, 350Pts ($2.20) seniors and children 11 and under. Tues–Thurs and Sat 10:30am–12:30pm and 4–5pm, Fri 10:30am–12:30pm, Sun 11am–1:15pm. Bus: 1, 2, 5, 20, 46, 52, 53, 74, M1, M2, M3, or M5. From Plaza del Callao, off Gran Vía, walk down Postigo de San Martín to Plaza de las Descalzas Reales; the convent is on the left.

In the mid–16th century, aristocratic women came to this convent to take the veil. Each of them brought a dowry, making this one of the richest convents in the land. But by the mid–20th century the convent sheltered mostly poor women. Although it contained a priceless collection of art treasures, the sisters were forbidden to auction anything. The state intervened, and the pope granted special dispensation to open the convent as a museum. In the Reliquary are the noblewomen's dowries, one of which is said to include bits of wood from the True Cross; another, some bones of St. Sebastian. The most valuable painting is Titian's *Caesar's Money*. The Flemish Hall shelters other fine works, including paintings by Hans de Beken and Breugel the Elder, and tapestries based on Rubens's cartoons.

PARKS & GARDENS

Casa de Campo (Metro: Lago or Batán), the former royal hunting grounds, is composed of miles of parkland lying south of the Royal Palace across the Manzanares River. You can see the gate through which the kings rode out of the palace grounds—either on horseback or in carriages—on their way to the park. Casa de Campo has a variety of trees and a lake, usually filled with rowers. You can have drinks and light refreshments around the water or go swimming in a municipally operated pool. The park can be visited daily 8am to 9pm.

Retiro Park (Metro: Retiro), originally a playground for the Spanish monarchs and their guests, extends over 165ha (350 acres). The huge palaces that once stood here were destroyed in the early 19th century and only the former dance hall, Casón del Buen Retiro (housing the Prado's modern works), and the building containing the Army Museum remain. The park boasts numerous fountains and statues, plus a large lake. There're also two exposition centers, the Velásquez and Crystal Palaces (built to honor the Philippines in 1887) and a lakeside monument, erected in 1922 in honor of Alfonso XII. In summer, the rose gardens are worth a visit, and you'll find several places where you can have inexpensive snacks and drinks. The park is open daily 24 hours, but it's safest, like most public parks, during the day (7am to 8:30pm).

Across calle de Alfonso XII, at the southwest corner of Retiro Park, is the **Real Jardín Botánico (Royal Botanical Garden),** Plaza de Murillo 2 (☎ **91-420-30-17;** Metro: Atocha; bus: 10, 14, 19, 32, or 45). Founded in the 18th century, the garden contains more than 100 species of trees and 3,000 types of plants. Also on the premises are an exhibition hall and a library specializing in botany. The park is open daily 10am to 9pm; admission is 200Pts ($1.25) for adults and 100Pts (65¢) for children.

ORGANIZED TOURS

One of Spain's largest tour operators is **Pullmantours,** Plaza de Oriente 8 (☎ **91-541-18-07;** Metro: Opera). Regardless of its destination or duration, virtually every tour departs from the Pullmantour terminal at that address. Half-day tours of Madrid include an artistic tour at 4,000Pts ($25) per person, which provides entrance to a selection of the city's museums, and a panoramic half-day tour for 3,000Pts ($19).

Southward treks to **Toledo** are the most popular full-day excursions. They cost 7,000Pts ($44). These tours, including lunch, depart daily at 9:30am from the above-mentioned departure point, last all day, and include ample opportunities for wandering at will through the city's narrow streets. You can take an abbreviated morning tour of Toledo, without stopping for lunch, for 5,300Pts ($33). May to September, these half-day visits to Toledo are conducted in both the morning and afternoon; the rest of the year, they depart only in the afternoon.

Another popular tour stops briefly in Toledo and continues on to visit both the monastery at **El Escorial** and **Valle de los Caídos** (the Valley of the Fallen) before returning the same day to Madrid. With lunch included, this all-day excursion costs 11,300Pts ($71).

A final touring option involves Pullmantour's full-day excursions from Madrid that incorporate both **Segovia** and **Ávila**—both focal points of Spanish culture and history—on the same day. Departing every day at 8:45am, and returning the same day at 6:30pm, they cost 7,500Pts ($47) for participants who don't want lunch included in their experience, and from 8,900Pts ($56) for those who opt for lunch.

THE SHOPPING SCENE

Tirso de Molina, the 17th-century playwright, called Madrid "a shop stocked with every kind of merchandise." Its estimated 50,000 stores sell everything from high-fashion clothing to flamenco guitars to art and ceramics.

THE MAIN SHOPPING AREAS

The sheer diversity of shops in Madrid's **center** is staggering. Their densest concentration lies immediately north of Puerta del Sol, radiating out from calle del Carmen, calle Montera, and calle Preciados.

Conceived, designed, and built in the 1910s and 1920s as a showcase for the city's best shops, hotels, and restaurants, the **Gran Vía** has since been eclipsed by other shopping districts, although its art nouveau and art deco glamour still survives. The bookshops here are among the best in the city, as are outlets for fashion, shoes, jewelry, and handcrafts from all regions of Spain. Under the arcades of the **Plaza Mayor** are exhibitions of lithographs and oil paintings, and within 3 or 4 blocks in every direction you'll find tons of souvenir shops.

The **Salamanca** district is known throughout Spain as the quintessential upper-bourgeois neighborhood. Here you'll find exclusive furniture, fur, and jewelry shops as well as several department stores. The main streets are calle de Serrano and calle de Veláquez. The district lies northeast of the center of Madrid, a few blocks north of Retiro Park. Its most central Metro stops are Serrano and Veláquez.

SOME NOTEWORTHY SHOPS

Established in 1904 as the "first house of Spanish ceramics," **Antigua Casa Talavera,** Isabel la Católica 2 (☎ **91-547-34-17;** Metro: Santo Domingo; bus: 1, 2, 46, 70, 75, or 148), has wares that include a sampling of regional styles from every major area of Spain. Sangría pitchers, dinnerware, tea sets, plates, and vases are all handmade. Inside one of the showrooms is an interesting selection of tiles painted with scenes from bullfights, dances, and folklore. One series of tiles depicts famous paintings at the Prado.

El Arco de los Cuchilleros Artesanía de Hoy, Plaza Mayor 9 (basement level) (☎ **91-365-26-80;** Metro: Puerta del Sol or Opera), is devoted to unusual craft items from throughout Spain. The merchandise is one-of-a-kind, Spanish, and in most cases contemporary, and includes a changing array of pottery, leather, textiles, wood carvings, glassware, wickerwork, papier-mâché, and silver jewelry.

El Corte Inglés, Preciados 3 (☎ **91-379-80-00;** Metro: Puerta del Sol), is the mother of all Spanish department stores, and this is the flagship store in Madrid. It sells Spanish handcrafts and also glamorous fashion articles, such as Pierre Balmain designs, for about a third less than in most European capitals. **Lasarte,** Gran Vía 44 (☎ **91-521-49-22;** Metro: Callao), is Madrid's, and Spain's, largest outlet for Lladró porcelain—the most characteristic and memorable form of fine porcelain made in Spain. You'll find at least 1,500 styles of figurines here, priced from 3,000Pts ($19) for a small plate. Since Lladró introduces and recalls about 50 new models every year, the establishment's inventory is constantly rotating. Anything you buy here can be shipped.

Since 1846, **Loewe,** Gran Vía 8 (☎ **91-522-68-15;** Metro: Gran Vía), has been Spain's most elegant leather store. Its designers have always kept abreast of changing tastes and styles, but the inventory still retains a timeless chic. The store sells luggage,

Spain's Biggest Flea Market

Foremost among Madrid flea markets is **El Rastro,** Plaza Cascorro and Ribera de Curtidores (Metro: La Latina; bus: 3 or 17), which occupies a roughly triangular district of streets and plazas a few minutes' walk south of Plaza Mayor. This market will delight anyone attracted to a mishmash of fascinating junk interspersed with bric-a-brac and paintings. But thieves are rampant here (hustling more than just antiques), so secure your wallet carefully, be alert, and proceed with caution. Open Saturday and Sunday only 9:30am to 1:30pm and to a lesser extent from 5 to 8pm.

handbags, and jackets for men and women (in leather or suede). At **Casa de Diego,** Puerto del Sol 12 (☎ **91-522-66-43;** Metro: Puerto del Sol), you'll find a wide inventory of fans, ranging from plain to fancy, from plastic to exotic hardwood, from cost-conscious to lavish.

MADRID AFTER DARK

In summer, Madrid sponsors a series of plays, concerts, and films, and the city takes on the air of a virtual free festival. Pick up a copy of *Guía del Ocio* (available at most newsstands) for listings of these events. This guide also provides information about occasional discounts for commercial events, such as the concerts given in Madrid's parks. Also check the program of the Fundación Juan March, calle Castello 77 (☎ **91-435-42-40;** Metro: Núñez de Balboa), which frequently stages free classical and chamber music concerts.

Flamenco in Madrid is geared mainly to tourists with fat wallets, and nightclubs are expensive. But since Madrid is preeminently a city of song and dance, you can often be entertained at very little cost—in fact, for the price of a glass of wine or beer, if you sit at a bar with live entertainment.

Tickets to dramatic and musical events usually range from 700 to 19,000Pts ($4.40 to $120), with discounts of up to 50% granted on certain days (usually Wednesday and early performances on Sunday). In the event your choice is sold out, you may be able to get tickets (with a reasonable markup) at **Localidades Galicia,** Plaza del Carmen 1 (☎ **91-531-27-32;** Metro: Puerta del Sol). This agency, however, mainly markets tickets to bullfights and sports events. It's open Tuesday to Sunday 9:30am to 1pm and 4:30 to 7:30pm.

THE PERFORMING ARTS

For those who speak Spanish, **Compañía Nacional de Nuevas Tendencias Escénicas** is an avant-garde troupe that performs new—and often controversial—works by undiscovered writers. **Compañía Nacional de Teatro Clásico,** as its name suggests, is devoted to the Spanish classics, including works by the ever-popular Lope de Vega or Tirso de Molina.

Among dance companies, **Ballet Nacional de España** is devoted exclusively to Spanish dance; its performances are always well attended. The national ballet company of the country is the **Ballet Lírico Nacional.** Also look for performances by choreographer Nacho Duato's **Compañía Nacional de Danza.**

World-renowned flamenco sensation António Canales and his troupe, **Ballet Flamenco António Canales,** offer high-energy, spirited performances. Productions are centered around Canales's impassioned *Torero*—his interpretation of a bullfighter and the physical and emotional struggles within the man. For tickets and information, call ☎ 91-531-27-32.

CLASSICAL MUSIC

Madrid's opera company is the **Teatro de la Opera,** and its symphony orchestra is the outstanding **Orquesta Sinfónica de Madrid** (at Teatro Real, see recommendation).

Reopened in 1997 after a massive $157 million renovation, the **Teatro Real,** Plaza Isabel II (☎ **91-516-06-60;** Metro: Opera), is one of the world's finest stage and acoustic settings for opera. Its extensive state-of-the-art equipment affords elaborate stage designs and special effects. Luís Antonio García Navarro, the internationally heralded maestro from Valencia, is the musical and artistic director of the Royal Opera House, at least until 2002. He'll be working with leading Spanish lyric talents, including Plácido Domingo. Today, the building is the home of the Compañía del Teatro Real and is major venue for classical music and opera. On November 19, 1850, under the reign of Queen Isabel II, the Royal Opera house opened its doors with Donizetti's *La Favorita.* Tickets are 2,000 to 16,500Pts ($13 to $104).

Auditorio Nacional de Música, Príncipe de Vergara 146 (☎ **91-337-01-00;** Metro: Cruz del Rayo), is the ultramodern home of both the **National Orchestra of Spain,** which pays particular attention to the music of Spanish composers, and the **National Chorus of Spain.** Just north of Madrid's Salamanca district, it ranks as a major addition to the competitive circles of classical music in Europe. Tickets are 1,000 to 6,000Pts ($6 to $38).

FLAMENCO

One of the best flamenco clubs in town, **Café de Chinitas,** Torija 7 (☎ **91-559-51-35;** Metro: Santo Domingo; bus: 1 or 2), is one floor above street level in a 19th-century building midway between the Opera and the Gran Vía. It features an array of (usually) Gypsy-born flamenco artists from Madrid, Barcelona, and Andalusia, whose acts and performers change about once a month. You can arrange for dinner before the show. Open Monday to Saturday, with dinner served 9 to 11pm and the show lasting 10:30pm to 3am. Reservations are recommended. Dinner and show cost from 9,800Pts ($62); show and 1 drink 4,450Pts ($28).

Following an upswing in interest in flamenco after a period of declining interest in the 1980s, **Casa Patas,** calle Cañizares 10 (☎ **91-369-04-96;** Metro: Tirso de Molina), is now one of the best places to see "true" flamenco as opposed to the more tourist-oriented version. It's also a bar/restaurant, with space reserved in the rear for flamenco. Shows are presented at 10pm Thursday through Saturday and during Madrid's major fiesta month of May. The club itself is open daily from 9pm to 5am. Admission is 3,000Pts ($19).

CABARET

Since the mid-1990s, **Café de Foro,** calle San Andres 38 (☎ **91-445-37-52;** Metro: Bilbao; bus: 40, 147, 149, or N19), in the Malasaña district has been one of the most fashionable places in Madrid to hang out after dark. Patronizing the club are members of the literati along with a large student clientele. You never know exactly what the program for the evening will be, though live music such as pop, rock, merengue, salsa, or flamenco generally starts at 11pm. Cabaret is often featured, along with live merengue and salsa. It's open daily 7pm to 3am. Admission is free, but cover might be imposed for a specially booked act.

Scala Melía Castilla, calle Capitán Haya 43 (entrance at Rosario Pino 7) (☎ **91-571-44-11;** Metro: Cuzco), Madrid's most famous dinner show, is a major

Las Vegas–style spectacle. The program is varied—you might see international or Spanish ballet, magic acts, ice skaters, whatever. Most definitely, you'll be entertained by a live orchestra. It's open Tuesday to Saturday 8:30pm to 3am. Dinner is served beginning at 9pm; the show is presented at 10:30pm. Reservations are needed for the 90-minute show, which is changed annually. It's been running successfully since 1981. Dinner and show are 10,200Pts ($64). Show and 1 drink are 5,300Pts ($33).

JAZZ

Off Plaza de Santa Ana, **Café Central,** Plaza del Angel 10 (☎ **91-369-41-43;** Metro: Antón Martín), has a vaguely art deco interior, with an unusual series of stained-glass windows. Many of the patrons read newspapers and talk at the marble-top tables during the day, but the ambience is far more animated during the nightly jazz sessions. It's open Sunday to Thursday 1:30pm to 2:30am and Friday and Saturday 1:30pm to 3:30am; live jazz is offered daily 10pm to 2am. Cover is 1,500Pts ($9).

With dozens of small tables and a huge bar in its dark and smoky interior, **Clamores,** Albuquerque 14 (☎ **91-445-79-38;** Metro: Bilbao), is the largest and one of the most popular jazz clubs in Madrid. It has thrived because of the American and Spanish jazz bands that appear here. The place is open daily 6pm to 3am or so, but jazz is presented only Tuesday to Saturday. Tuesday to Thursday, performances are at 11pm and 1am; Saturday at 11:30pm and 1:30am. There're no live performances Sunday or Monday. Cover Tuesday to Saturday is 500 to 1,100Pts ($3.15 to $7), depending on the act.

DANCE CLUBS

A copycat of the hot clubs of London and New York, the bileveled **Bocaccio,** calle Marqués de la Ensenada 16 (☎ **91-308-49-81;** Metro: Colón), caters to the most beautiful and trendiest people of Madrid. Low key during the week, it lets its hair down on the weekends. The first level is known as *Infierno* (Hell), and is the most intense level of the two, awash in sex, drugs, alcohol, and the techno beats of British pop, complete with scarlet velour couches for a color match of the motif. The upstairs is trés chic, as you have your drinks on antique chairs and couches, admiring the collection of art and tapestries that adorn the walls. Open Monday to Thursday from 7 to 11pm, Friday and Saturday 7pm to 6am, and Sunday 7pm to 3am. Cover is 500 to 1,200Pts ($3.15 to $8).

Kapital, Atocha 125 (☎ **91-420-29-06;** Metro: Antón Martín), is the most sprawling, labyrinthine, and multicultural dance club in Madrid. In what was formerly a theater, it contains seven levels, each with at least one bar, and a sometimes radically different ambience and musical theme in each. If you grow tired of the sometimes frenetic dancing on the lower levels, keep climbing: Things get calmer and more laid-back as you rise. In warm weather, the seventh floor opens onto an outdoor terrace. It's open Thursday to Sunday from 11:30pm to 5:30am. Cover, with first drink included, is 2,000Pts ($13).

Kathmandu, Señores de Luzón 3 (☎ **91-541-52-53;** Metro: Sol), is Madrid's club of the moment. Cutting-edge music echoes through the nightclub—reggae, jungle, hip-hop, jazzy funk. At this alternative disco, be prepared for a dizzy psychedelic experience. The club would feel right at home set among some Soho dives in New York. Decidedly androgynous, it's an Asian-inspired, ultramodern scoff at normalcy. The bar on the top floor is a curious retreat with Tibetan textiles draped from the ceiling. Nepalese art decorates part of the downstairs. At times the floor becomes so overcrowded you think the club will sink, but it carries on with wild abandon. Open Thursday from 10am to 5am, Friday and Saturday from 10am until 6am. Cover is 1,000Pts ($6), including first drink.

Pubs & Bars

Bar Cock, De la Reina 16 (☎ 91-532-28-26; Metro: Gran Vía), attracts some of the most visible artists, actors, models, and filmmakers in Madrid, among them the award-winning Spanish director Pedro Almódovar. The name comes from the word *cocktail,* or so they say. The decoration is elaborately unique, in contrast to the hip clientele. It's open daily 7pm to 3am; closed December 24 to 31.

Beloved by Hemingway, who had quite a few drinks here, ✪ **Chicote,** Gran Vía 12 (☎ 91-532-67-37; Metro: Gran Vía), is Madrid's most famous cocktail bar. It's a classic, with the same 1930s decor it had when the foreign press sat out the Civil War here. Even the seats are original. Long a favorite of artists and writers, the bar became a haven for prostitutes in the late Franco era. No more. It's back in the limelight again, a sophisticated and much frequented rendezvous. It's open daily 7:30pm to 3am.

One of the best located bars in town, the fashionable **El Aljibe,** 4 Plaza de Oriente (☎ 91-548-46-20; Metro: Opera), at the majestic Plaza de Oriente, lies in a historic section in the very heart of the city. Velázquez lived at No. 4 on the square where he painted *Las Meninas.* Fancy coffees and elegant drinks are served here in a setting that reveals the remains of Madrid's medieval stone wall. Arabic tapestries form a part of the decor. Open daily 7pm to 3am.

The 1847 construction of the **Palacio Gaviria,** calle del Arenal 9 (☎ 91-526-60-69; Metro: Puerta del Sol or Opera), was heralded as the architectural triumph of one of the era's most flamboyant aristocrats, the marqués de Gaviria. Famous as one of the paramours of Isabel II, he outfitted his palace with the ornate jumble of neoclassical and baroque styles that later became known as Isabelino. In 1993, after extensive renovations, the building was opened to the public as a concert hall for the occasional presentation of classical music and as a late-night cocktail bar. Ten high-ceilinged rooms now function as richly decorated multipurpose areas for guests to wander and dance in what is the most kitschy and rococo disco in Madrid. Open Monday to Friday 10pm to 3am, Saturday and Sunday 11pm to 5am. Cover is 1,500Pts ($9), including your first drink.

Gay & Lesbian Clubs & Cafes

Plaza de Chueca (Metro: Chueca) has no fewer than four gay cafes lining the square's edges and something approaching a gay living room (with a healthy number of lesbians as well) is created every evening from 8pm to early the next morning. Open daily 1:30pm to 4am, both **Café Figueroa,** calle Augusto Figueroa 17 (☎ 91-521-16-73), and **Café Aquarella,** calle Gravina 10 (☎ 91-522-21-43), have elevated gay table-hopping to a fine art. A diverse clientele includes both gay men and lesbians.

Leading the way as one of the various lesbian bars now established in Plaza de Chueca, the **Sutileza,** Plaza de Chueca (no phone), is the perfect starting point for the discerning lesbian on the prowl. The crowd is predominately women with a few gay men thrown in for good measure. May to September there's an outside terrazza that competes with the other lesbian bars in the square, namely Escape and **Truco,** a *bar de copas* at Gravina 10 (☎ 91-532-89-21). The atmosphere at all the bars is friendly and frequently quite cruisey, and they're all open Tuesday to Thursday and Sunday 8pm to 3am, and Friday and Saturday 9pm to 4am.

One of the predominant gay bars of Madrid, a center for gay consciousness-raising and gay cruising (though they say the name refers to automobile driving), **Cruising,** Perez Galdos, 5 (☎ 91-521-51-43; Metro: Chueca), has probably been visited at least once by virtually every gay male in Castile. There're virtually no women inside, but always a hustler looking for a tourist john. It doesn't get crowded or lively until late at night. Open daily from 7pm to 3:30am. Beer costs from 400 to 500Pts ($2.50 to $3.15).

CAVE CRAWLING

To capture a glimpse of the unique Madrid joie de vivre, visit some *mesones* and *cuevas,* many found in the *barrios bajos.* From Plaza Mayor, walk down Arco de Cuchilleros until you find a Gypsy-like cave that fits your fancy.

The bartenders at the **Mesón del Champiñón,** Cava de San Miguel 17 (no phone; Metro: Puerta del Sol or Opera), keep a brimming bucket of sangría behind the long stand-up bar as a thirst quencher for the crowd. The name of the establishment means mushroom, and that's exactly what you'll see depicted in various sizes along sections of the vaulted ceilings. A more appetizing way to experience a champiñón is to order a *ración* (serving) of grilled, stuffed, and salted mushrooms, served with toothpicks. Open daily 7pm to 1:30am. Our favorite cueva in the area, the **Mesón de la Guitarra,** Cava de San Miguel 13 (☎ **91-559-95-31;** Metro: Puerta del Sol or Opera), is loud and exciting any night of the week, and it's as warmly earthy as anything you'll find in Madrid. The decor combines terra-cotta floors, antique brick walls, hundreds of sangría pitchers clustered above the bar, murals of gluttons, old rifles, and faded bullfighting posters. Like most things in Madrid, the place doesn't get rolling until around 10:30pm. Open daily 7pm to 2am.

DAY TRIPS FROM MADRID

TOLEDO   If you have only 1 day for an excursion outside Madrid, go to Toledo, 66km (42 miles) to the southwest, a place made special by its blending of Arab, Jewish, Christian, and even Roman and Visigothic elements. Declared a national landmark, the city that inspired El Greco in the 16th century has remained relatively unchanged in parts of its central core. You can still stroll through streets barely wide enough for a man and his donkey.

Getting There   Daily **RENFE** trains run here frequently. Those departing Madrid's Atocha Station run daily 7:05am to 8:40pm; those leaving Toledo for Madrid run daily 6:30am to 8:55pm. Travel time is approximately 1 hour 15 minutes, and a one-way fare costs 745Pts ($4.70). For train information in Madrid call ☎ **91-328-90-20;** in Toledo call ☎ **925-22-30-99.**

Bus transit between Madrid and Toledo is faster and more convenient than travel by train. Buses, operated by several companies, the largest of which include Continental and Galiano, depart from Madrid's South Bus Station (Estacíon Sur de Autobuses), calle Méndez Alvaro (☎ **91-527-29-61** for tickets and information). Buses depart at 30-minute intervals every day 6:30am to 10pm, and a one-way ticket costs 585Pts ($3.70).

Motorists exit Madrid via Cibeles (Paseo del Prado) and take N-401 south.

The **tourist office** is at Puerta de Bisagra (☎ **925-22-08-43**), open Monday to Friday 9am to 6pm, Saturday 9am to 7pm, and Sunday 9am to 3pm.

Exploring Toledo   Ranked among the greatest of Gothic structures, the ✪ **Cathedral,** Arcos de Palacio (☎ **925-22-22-41;** bus: 5 or 6), actually reflects a variety of styles because of the more than 2¹/₂ centuries that went into its construction, from 1226 to 1493. The portals have witnessed many historic events, including the proclamation of Joanna the Mad and her husband, Philip the Handsome, as heirs to the throne of Spain. Among its art treasures, the *transparente* stands out—a wall of marble and florid baroque alabaster sculpture overlooked for years because of the cathedral's poor lighting. The sculptor Narciso Tomé cut a hole in the ceiling, much to the consternation of Toledans, and now light touches the high-rising angels, a *Last Supper* in alabaster, and a Virgin in ascension. The 16th-century Capilla Mozárabe, containing works by Juan de Borgona, is another curiosity of the cathedral. The Treasure

Room has a 500-pound 15th-century gilded monstrance—allegedly made with gold brought back from the New World by Columbus—that's still carried through the streets of Toledo during the feast of Corpus Christi. Admission to the cathedral is free; admission to the Treasure Room is 500Pts ($3.15). Open Monday to Saturday 10:30am to 1pm and 3:30 to 7pm, Sunday 10:30am to 1:30pm and 4 to 7pm.

Alcázar, calle General Moscardó 4, near Plaza de Zocodover (☎ **925-22-30-38;** bus: 5 or 6), at the eastern edge of the old city, dominates the Toledo skyline. It became famous at the beginning of the Spanish Civil War when it underwent a 72-day siege that almost destroyed it. Today it has been rebuilt and turned into an army museum, housing such exhibits as a plastic model of what the fortress looked like after the Civil War, electronic equipment used during the siege, and photographs taken during the height of the battle. A walking tour gives a realistic simulation of the siege. Admission is 200Pts ($1.25). Entrance is free on Wednesday and always free for children 9 and under. It's open Tuesday to Sunday 9:30am to 2pm (6:30pm July to September).

Today a museum of art and sculpture, the ✪ **Museo de Santa Cruz,** Miguel de Cervantes 3 (☎ **925-22-10-36;** bus: 5 or 6), was originally a 16th-century Spanish Renaissance hospice, founded by Cardinal Mendoza—"the third king of Spain"—who helped Ferdinand and Isabella gain the throne. The facade is almost more spectacular than any of the exhibits inside. It's a stunning architectural achievement in the classical plateresque style. The major artistic treasure inside is El Greco's *The Assumption of the Virgin,* his last known work. Paintings by Goya and Ribera are also on display. Admission is free. Open Tuesday to Saturday 10am to 6:30pm, Sunday 10am to 2pm, Monday 10am to 2pm and 4 to 6:30pm. To get here, pass beneath the granite archway on the eastern edge of Plaza de Zocodover and walk about 1 block.

SAN LORENZO DE EL ESCORIAL   The second most important excursion from Madrid is the austere Royal Monastery of San Lorenzo de El Escorial, 30 miles to the west. Philip II ordered the construction of this rectangular granite-and-slate monster in 1563, two years after he moved his capital to Madrid. Once the haunt of aristocratic Spaniards, El Escorial is now a resort where hotels and restaurants flourish in summer, as hundreds flock here to escape the heat of the capital.

Getting There   More than two dozen trains depart daily from Madrid's Atocha, Nuevos Ministerios, and Chamartín stations (trip time: $1^{1}/_{4}$ hours). During summer extra coaches are added. For schedules and information, call ☎91-328-90-20.

The Office of Empresa Herranz, calle del Rey 27 in El Escorial (☎ **91-890-41-22**), runs some 40 buses per day back and forth between Madrid's Moncloa Station and El Escorial; on Sunday service is curtailed to 10 buses. Trip time is 1 hour, and a round-trip fare is 790Pts ($5).

Motorists can follow NVI (marked on some maps as A-6) from the northwest perimeter of Madrid toward Lugo, La Coruña, and El Escorial. After about half an hour, fork left onto C-505 toward San Lorenzo. Driving time from Madrid is about an hour.

The **tourist information office** is at Floridablanca 10 (☎ **91-890-59-03**), open Monday to Friday 10am to 2pm and 3 to 5pm and Saturday 10am to 2pm.

Exploring the Monastery   The huge granite fortress of the ✪ **Real Monasterio de San Lorenzo de El Escorial,** calle San Lorenzo de El Escorial 1 (☎ **91-890-59-03**), houses a wealth of paintings and tapestries and serves as a burial place for Spanish kings. Foreboding both inside and out because of its sheer size and institutional look, El Escorial took 21 years to complete. Philip II, who collected many of the paintings exhibited here in the New Museums, didn't appreciate El Greco and favored Titian.

But you'll still find El Greco's *The Martyrdom of St. Maurice,* rescued from storage, and his *St. Peter.* Other superb works are Titian's *Last Supper* and Velázquez's *The Tunic of Joseph.* The Royal Library houses a priceless collection of 60,000 volumes—one of the most significant in the world. The displays range from the handwriting of St. Teresa of Avila to medieval instructions on playing chess.

You can also visit the Philip II Apartments; these are strictly monastic, and Philip called them the "cell for my humble self" in this "palace for God." The Apartments of the Bourbon Kings are lavishly decorated, in contrast to Philip's preference for the ascetic.

A comprehensive ticket costs 1,100Pts ($7) for adults and 350Pts ($2.20) for children. The monastery is open Tuesday to Sunday: April to September 10am to 7pm and October to March 10pm to 6pm.

SEGOVIA Less commercial than Toledo, Segovia, 87km (54 miles) northwest of Madrid, typifies the glory of Old Castile. Wherever you look, you'll see reminders of a golden era—whether it's the most spectacular Alcázar on the Iberian Peninsula or the well-preserved and still-functioning Roman aqueduct. Segovia lies on the slope of the Guadarrama Mountains, where the Eresma and Clamores Rivers converge. This ancient city stands in the center of the most castle-rich part of Castile. Isabella was proclaimed queen of Castile here in 1474.

Getting There Fifteen trains leave Madrid's Chamartín and Atocha stations every day (trip time: 2 hours). A one-way rail fare from Madrid costs 775Pts ($4.90). Segovia's station, **Paseo Obispo Quesada** (☎ 921-42-07-74), is a 20-minute walk from the town center. Bus 3 departs every quarter hour for Plaza Mayor.

Buses arrive and depart from the **Estacionamiento Municipal de Autobuses,** Paseo de Ezequile González 10 (☎ 921-42-77-25), near the corner of Avenida Fernández Ladreda and the steeply sloping Paseo Conde de Sepúlveda. There are 10 to 15 buses a day to and from Madrid (which depart from Paseo de la Florida 11; Metro: Norte). A one-way bus fare from Madrid to Segovia sells for 765Pts ($4.80).

Motorists can take NVI (on some maps it's known as A-6) or the Autopista del Nordeste northwest from Madrid, toward León and Lugo. At the junction with Rte. 110 (signposted Segovia), turn northeast.

The **tourist office** is at Plaza Mayor 10 (☎ 921-46-03-34), open daily 10am to 2pm and 5 to 8pm.

Exploring Segovia You'll view the castle ✪ **El Alcázar,** Plaza de la Reina Victoria Eugenia (☎ 921-46-07-59; bus: 3), first from below, at the junction of the Clamores and Eresma Rivers. It's on the west side of Segovia, and you may not spot it when you first enter the city. But that's part of the surprise. The castle dates back to the 12th century, and royal romance is inextricably associated with it. Isabella first met Ferdinand here, and today you can see a facsimile of her dank bedroom. Walk the battlements of this once-impregnable castle, from which its occupants hurled down boiling oil onto the enemy below. Brave the hazardous stairs of the tower, built by Isabella's father as a prison, for a panoramic view of Segovia. Admission is 325Pts ($2.05) for adults, 400Pts ($2.50) for children 8 to 14, and free for children 7 and under. The castle is open daily, April to September 10am to 7pm and October to March 10am to 6pm. Take either calle Vallejo, calle de Velarde, calle de Daoiz, or Paseo de Ronda.

The ✪ **Roman aqueduct,** Plaza del Azoguejo, is an architectural marvel built by the Romans more than 2,000 years ago. Until recent times, it is still used to carry water. Constructed of mortarless granite, it consists of 118 arches, and in one two-tiered section it soars 30m (95 feet) to its highest point. The Spanish call it simply El Puente. It spans Plaza del Azoguejo, the old market square, stretching nearly 730m

(800 yards). When the Moors took Segovia in 1072, they destroyed 36 arches, which were rebuilt under Ferdinand and Isabella in 1484.

Constructed between 1515 and 1558, the ✪ **Cabildo Catedral de Segovia,** Plaza de la Catedral, Marqués del Arco (☎ **921-46-22-05**), is the last Gothic cathedral built in Spain. Fronting historic Plaza Mayor, it stands on the spot where Isabella I was proclaimed queen of Castile. Affectionately called La Dama de las Catedrales ("the Lady of Cathedrals"), it contains numerous treasures, such as the Blessed Sacrament Chapel (created by the flamboyant Churriguera); stained-glass windows; elaborately carved choir stalls; and 16th- and 17th-century paintings, including a reredos portraying the deposition of Christ from the cross by Juan de Juni. Admission to the cathedral is free; admission to the cloisters, museum, and chapel room is 50Pts (30¢) for adults and 250Pts ($1.60) for children. Open daily spring and summer 9am to 7pm and off-season 9am to 6pm.

2 Barcelona & Environs

Hardworking Barcelona enjoys the most diversified and prosperous economy of any region in Spain. And culturally, it is as rich as any. Its roster of natives and longtime residents—the *modernista* architect Antoni Gaudí, artists Pablo Picasso, Salvador Dalí, and Joan Miró, as well as the opera star Montserrat Caballé—have been instrumental in defining Catalan culture.

As one local newspaper critic put it, "If there were an award for the city that has done the most in the last few years to rebuild, reclaim, and expand while maintaining its elegance and charm, Barcelona would win hands down." The years that led up to and immediately following the 1992 Olympics made a huge difference to the city. Residual benefits from the games have included a roster of impressive new hotels, top-notch sporting facilities, the refurbishing of an airport capable of funneling 18 million annual visitors into Catalonia, and new ring roads that have alleviated some crucial traffic problems. And Barcelona, despite its dearly protected Catalán cultural and linguistic identity, continues a proud role as Spain's literary and publishing headquarters.

With a reputation as the savviest business center in Spain, Barcelona boasts buildings by I. M. Pei, Arata Isozaki, Richard Meier, Norman Foster, Victorio Gregotti, and native son Ricardo Bofill. Miles of grimy industrial waterfronts have been returned to clean and sandy beaches. In fact, the entire city has been reoriented toward the Mediterranean, whereas it once almost seemed to turn its back on the sea. Flower stalls, bird cages, and decorative pavements along the gorgeous pedestrian boulevard Les Rambles have been rejuvenated, and a state-of-the-art transportation network carries visitors past monuments that look better than when they were first erected. Unlike either of its landlocked competitors, Seville or Madrid, Barcelona welcomes the newest phenomenon in tourism, the cruise-ship industry.

Despite the city's burgeoning population (and the regrettable growth in both drug addiction and street crime), people are flocking to the newly revived Barcelona. Nearly 40% of tourists to Spain go to Catalonia, and many are repeat visitors.

ORIENTATION

GETTING THERE **By Plane** Even post-Olympics, most transatlantic passengers are obliged to change aircraft in Madrid before continuing on to Barcelona. The only exception is **TWA** (☎ **800/892-4141**), which maintains nonstop transatlantic service to Barcelona from New York. Within Spain, by far the most likely carrier is **Iberia** (☎ **800/772-4642**), which offers a string of peak-hour shuttle flights at 15-minute intervals between Madrid and Barcelona. Service from Madrid to Barcelona at less congested times of the day averages around one flight every 30 to 40 minutes. **Air**

Europa (☎ 93-298-33-28) and **Spanair** (☎ 93-298-33-62) also run shuttles between Madrid and Barcelona. These flights are generally cheaper than Iberia; frequency of shuttle flights depends on demand, with more occurring in the early morning and late afternoon.

The **Aeropuerto de Barcelona,** 08820 Prat de Llobregat (☎ 93-298-38-38), lies 12km (7½ miles) southwest of the city. A train runs at 30-minute intervals between the airport and Barcelona's Estació Central de Barcelona-Sants daily 6:14am to 10:44pm (10:14pm is the last city departure, 6:14am the first airport departure). The 21-minute trip costs 305Pts ($1.90) Monday to Friday or 485Pts ($3.05) Saturday and Sunday. If your hotel lies near Plaça de Catalunya, you might opt for an Aerobús that runs daily every 15 minutes from 5:30am to 10pm. The fare is 475Pts ($3). A taxi from the airport into central Barcelona will cost about 3,000Pts ($19).

By Train   The *Barcelona Talgo* train provides rail service between Paris and Barcelona in 11½ hours. For many other connections from the mainland of Europe, it'll be necessary to change trains at Port Bou. Most trains issue seat and sleeper reservations.

Trains departing from the **Estació de Franca,** Avenida Marqués de l'Argentera, cover long distances in Spain as well as international routes. There are express night trains to Paris, Zurich, Milan, and Geneva. All the international routes served by the state-owned RENFE rail company use the Estació de Franca, including some of its most luxurious express trains, such as the *Pau Casals* and *Talgo Catalán.* From this station, you can book tickets to the major cities: Madrid (five *talgos,* 7 hours; three *rápidos,* 10 hours), Seville (two per day, 10½ hours), and Valencia (11 per day, 4 hours). For general **RENFE information,** call ☎ 93-490-02-02.

By Bus   Bus travel to Barcelona is cheaper than the train, faster than all but the *talgos,* and very popular among Spaniards who travel frequently between the two main cities. **Enatcar,** Estació del Nord (☎ 93-245-25-28), operates five buses per day to Madrid (trip time: 8 hours) and 10 buses per day to Valencia (trip time: 4½ hours). A one-way ticket to Madrid costs 2,140Pts ($14); a one-way ticket to Valencia is 2,900Pts ($18).

By Car   From France (the usual road approach to Barcelona), the major access route is at the eastern end of the Pyrenees. You have a choice of the express highway (E-15) or the more scenic coastal road. From France, it's possible to approach Barcelona via Toulouse. Cross the border into Spain at Puigcerdá (frontier stations are there), near the principality of Andorra. From here, take N-152 to Barcelona. From Madrid, take N-2 to Zaragoza, then A-2 to El Vendrell, followed by A-7 to Barcelona.

VISITOR INFORMATION   A conveniently located tourist office is the **Oficina de Informacio de Turisme de Barcelona**, Plaça de Catalunya, 17-S (☎ 93-304-31-35; Metro: Plaça de Catalunya). It's open daily from 9am to 9pm.

CITY LAYOUT   **Plaça de Catalunya** (Plaza de Cataluña in Spanish) is the city's heart; the world-famous Rambles (Ramblas) and the grand boulevard Paseo de Gracia, its arteries. Les Rambles begin at Plaça Portal de la Pau, with its 50m (164-foot) monument to Columbus and a panoramic view of the port, and stretch north to Plaça de Catalunya, with its fountains and trees.

At the end of Les Rambles is the **Barri Xinés** (Barrio Chino, the "Chinese Quarter"), which in the past was notorious as a haven of prostitution and drugs. It is being cleaned up, but is still not a terribly safe district; it's best viewed during the day. Off Les Rambles is **Plaça Reial** (Plaza Real in Spanish), Barcelona's most harmoniously proportioned square.

The major wide boulevards are **Avinguda Diagonal** and **Passeig de Colom** and the elegant shopping street **Passeig de Gràcia** (Paseo de Gracia). A short walk from Les

Barcelona

ATTRACTIONS ●

Catedral de Barcelona **29**
Fundació Antoni Tàpies **17**
Fundació Joan Miró **6**
La Pedrera **14**
La Sagrada Família **12**
Monument á Colón **31**
Montjuïc **7**
Museu Barbier-Mueller Art Precolombi **34**
Museu d'Art Contemporáreo de Barcelona **23**
Museu d'Art Modern **35**
Museu de la Ciència **9**
Museu Frederic Marès/ Museu Sentimental **27**
Museu Marítim **30**
Museu Nacional d'Art de Catalunya **5**
Museu Picasso **33**
Parc Güell **11**
Poble Espanyol **4**
Tibidabo Mountain **10**

ACCOMMODATIONS ■

Astoria **13**
Barcelona Hilton **2**
Claris **16**
Colón **28**
Condes de Barcelona **15**
Derby/Gran Derby **8**
Duques de Bergara **21**
Granvía **19**
Hespería **3**
Hostal Levante **32**
Hostal Neutral **18**
Hotel Arts **36**
Le Meridien Barcelona **24**
Mesón Castilla **22**
Montecarlo **25**
Regencia Colón **26**
Rey Juan Carlos I **1**
Ritz **20**

1
TIBIDABO
2
3
Avinguda de Madrid
Carrer del Vallespir
Carrer de Berlin
Carrer de Numancia
Carrer de la Infanta Carlota Joaquima
Carrer de Còrsega
Carrer de Rossello
Carrer de Sant Antoni
Carrer de Provença
Carrer de Sants de la Creu Coberta
Avinguda de Roma
Carrer de Tarragona
Pià de la Pau
Carrer d'Entrença
Carrer de Rocafort
Carrer de Calabria
Carrer de Viladomat
Carretera de la Bordeta
Plaça de Espanya
Carrer de Sant Fructuós
Gran Vía de les Corts Catalanes
Carrer de Sepulveda
Av. de Marques de Comillas
Av. de la Riena Maria Cristina
Avinguda de Paral-lel
Carrer de Floridablanca
Carrer de Tamarit
Carrer de Manso
Carrer del Parlament
4
5
6
Avinguda de l'Estadi
Estadi Olímpic
Avinguda de Miramar
PARC DE MONTJUÏC
PARC D'ATRACCIONS DE MONTJUÏC
7
Passeig de Josep Carner

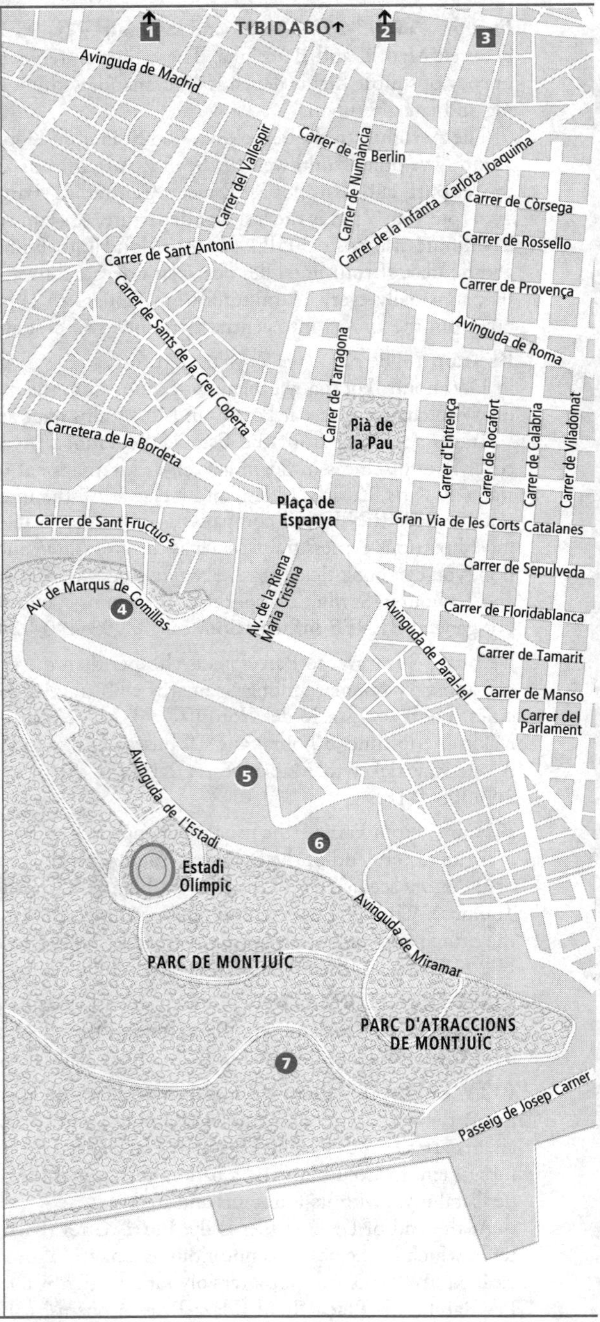

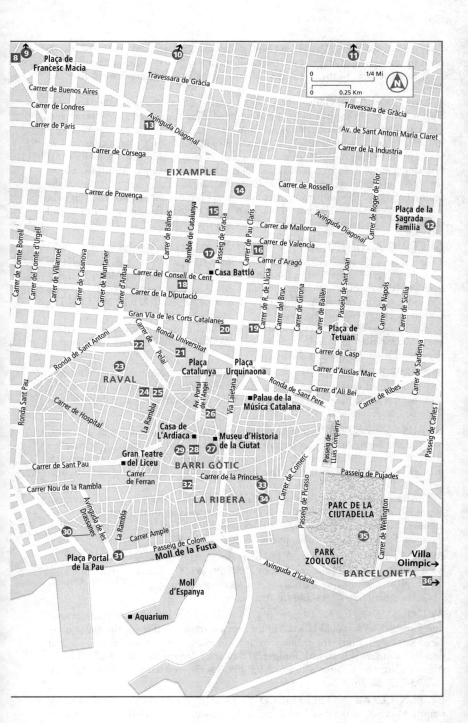

Rambles will take you to **Passeig del Moll de la Fusta,** a waterfront promenade developed for the Olympic renewal with some of the finest (but not the cheapest) restaurants in Barcelona. To the east is the old port of the city, **La Barceloneta,** from the 18th century.

Barri Gòtic (Barrio Gótico, the Gothic Quarter) lies to the east of Les Rambles. This is the site of the city's oldest buildings, including the cathedral and many gorgeous palaces with central courtyards. North of Plaça de Catalunya, the **Eixample** unfolds. An area of wide boulevards, in contrast to the Gothic Quarter, it contains two major roads leading out of Barcelona, Avinguda Diagonal and Gran Vía de les Corts Catalánes. Another major area, **Gràcia,** lies north of the Eixample. **Montjuïc,** one of the mountains of Barcelona, begins at Plaça d'Espanya, a traffic rotary. This was the setting for the 1992 Summer Olympic Games and is today the site of Vila Olimpica. The other mountain is **Tibidabo,** in the northwest, offering fine views of the city and the Mediterranean and boasting an amusement park.

GETTING AROUND

To save money on public transport, buy one of the transportation cards, each valid for 10 trips: **Tarjeta T-1,** for 780Pts ($4.90), is good for the Metro, bus, Montjuïc funicular, and Tramvía Blau, which runs from Passeig de Sant Gervasi/Avinguda del Tibidabo to the bottom part of the funicular to Tibidabo; **Tarjeta T-2,** for 720Pts ($4.55), is valid on everything but the bus.

Passes (*abonos temporales*) are available at any Metro station or at the office of **Transports Metropolita de Barcelona,** calle Go 2123 (☎ **93-298-70-00** for information), open Monday to Friday 8am to 5pm.

BY SUBWAY (METRO)   Barcelona's underground railway system, the Metro, consists of five main lines. Two commuter trains also service the city, fanning out to the suburbs. A one-way fare is 145Pts (90¢), and the major station for all subway lines is Plaça de Catalunya.

BY BUS   Some 50 bus lines traverse the city, and the driver issues a ticket as you board at the front. Most buses operate daily 6:30am to 10pm; some night buses go along the principal arteries 10pm to 4am. Buses are color-coded—red ones cut through the city center during the day, and blue ones do the job at night. A one-way fare is 145Pts (90¢).

The **Barcelona "Moon Express"** is a tourist train that runs through the city from 10pm to 2am and costs 700Pts ($4.40) for a ride. It takes in the city's most scenic highlights at night, including floodlit Gothic buildings. Tickets can be purchased on the train. For more information, phone ☎ **906-30-12-82.**

BY TAXI   Each yellow-and-black taxi bears the letters *sp* (*servicio público*) on both its front and its rear. The basic rate begins at 300Pts ($1.90). For each additional kilometer in the slow-moving traffic, you're assessed a charge of 110 to 118Pts (70¢ to 75¢). For a taxi, call ☎ **93-330-08-04.**

BY CAR   Driving is a headache in congested Barcelona, and it's potentially dangerous. However, a car would be ideal to tour the environs. All three of the major U.S.-based car-rental firms are represented in Barcelona, both at the airport and at downtown offices. Check with **Budget,** at Barcelona Airport 71 (☎ **93-298-35-00**); **Avis,** at Carrer de Casanova 209 (☎ **93-209-95-33**); or **Hertz,** at Carrer Tuset 10 (☎ **93-217-80-76**).

BY FUNICULAR & TELEFÉRICO   Two of Barcelona's high-altitude vantage points, Montjuïc and Tibidabo, accessible by funicular, are visited for a panoramic overview of the city. The departure point for Tibidabo lies on the northern outskirts

Barcelona Metro

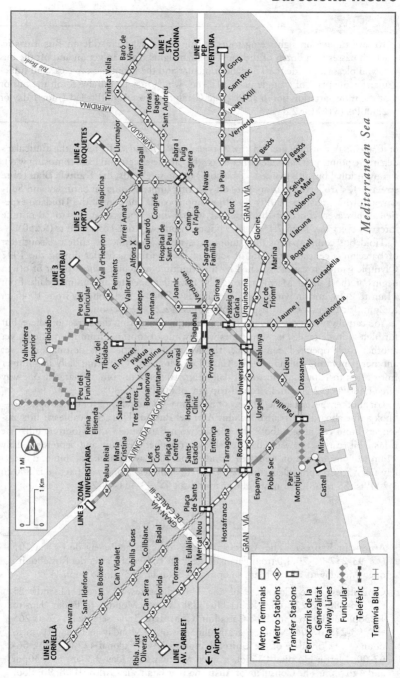

To save money on sightseeing tours during summer, take a ride on **Bus Turistic,** which passes by a dozen of the most popular sights. You can get on and off the bus as you please and ride the Tibidabo funicular and the Montjuïc cable car and funicular for the price of a single ticket. Tickets, which may be purchased on the bus or at the transportation booth at Plaça de Catalunya, cost 1,900Pts ($12) for 1 day or 2,500Pts ($16) for 2 days.

of Barcelona's central core, on the *Avinguda del Tibidabo*. To reach the funicular's departure point, you can take either a taxi (by far the easiest and least confusing way), a conventional bus (it's marked "Tibidabo") or, on weekends, the **Tramvía Blau (blue streetcar),** a trolleycar that operates only during limited hours on Saturday and Sunday, and which charges 300Pts ($1.90) to hop aboard. The core of the Tibidabo experience, however, concerns the funicular itself, which operates at 20- to 30-minute intervals every day from 7:15am to 9:45pm. A one-way ride costs 400Pts ($2.50).

Tibidabo's counterpart is the panoramic eyrie of Montjuïc, a gentle rise southeast of Barcelona's central core. Site of some of the sporting activities during the 1992 Olympic games, it can be reached by the Montjuïc funicular, whose point of origin begins at the Parallel Metro station. The funicular operates in summer daily from 11am to 8pm, and in winter only on Saturday, Sunday, and holidays from 10:45am to 2pm. It charges a round-trip fare of 350Pts ($2.20) per person.

You can always get off the funicular at Montjuïc, exploring the attractions here, but for high-altitude freaks, it's sometimes worthwhile to continue from Montjuïc on yet another cable-operated conveyance, the Montjuïc teleférico. Its destination is yet another panoramic hilltop and the Castell de Montjuïc. Operating daily in summer from 11am to 10pm, and in winter daily from 10:45am to 8pm, it charges a one-way fare of 400Pts ($2.50); and a round-trip fare of 600Pts ($3.80).

For another spectacular aerial view of Barcelona—definitely not for the acrophobic—book a ride aboard the **Transbordador Aeri del Puerto.** This aerial cable car lifts passengers hundreds of feet above the port between Barceloneta and Montjuïc hill. The ride's a bit scary, so be warned. The cable car runs between July and September daily 11am to 9pm; off-season hours are Sunday and Tuesday noon to 5:45pm and Saturday noon to 6:15pm. Departures are every 15 minutes; a one-way passage is 800 to 1,200Pts ($5 to $8). For more information, call ☎ **93-441-48-20.**

Fast Facts: Barcelona

American Express The American Express office is at Passeig de Gràcia 101 (☎ **93-217-00-70;** Metro: Diagonal), near the corner of Carrer del Rosselló. It's open Monday to Friday 10am to 6pm and Saturday 9:30am to noon.

Consulates The Consulate of the **United States,** at Reina Elisenda 23 (☎ **93-280-22-27;** train: Reina Elisenda), is open Monday to Friday 9am to 12:30pm and 3 to 5pm. The **Canadian Consulate,** Travessera de les Corts 265 (☎ **93-215-07-04;** Metro: Plaça Molina), is open Monday to Friday 10am to noon. The Consulate of the **United Kingdom,** Av. Diagonal 477 (☎ **93-366-62-00;** Metro: Hospital Clínic), is open Monday to Friday 9:30am to 1:30pm and 4 to 5pm. The Consulate of **Australia** is at Gran Vía Carlos III 98, 9th floor (☎ **93-330-94-96;** Metro: María Cristina), open Monday to Friday 10am to noon.

Currency See "Fast Facts: Madrid."

Currency Exchange Most banks will exchange currency Monday to Friday 8:30am to 2pm and Saturday 8:30am to 1pm. A major *oficina de cambio* (exchange office) is operated at the Estació Central de Barcelona-Sants, the principal rail station; it's open Monday to Saturday 8:30am to 10pm and Sunday 8:30am to 2pm and 4:30 to 10pm. There are three major banks at Plaça de Catalunya, including La Caixa, with currency exchange windows frequented by tourists.

Dentists Call **Clinica Dental Beonadex**, Paseo Bona Nova 69, 3rd floor (☎ **93-418-44-33;** bus: 22), for an appointment. It is open Monday from 3 to 9pm and Tuesday through Friday from 8am to 3pm.

Drugstores The most central one is Farmacia Manuel Nadal i Casas, Rambla de Canaletes 121 (☎ **93-317-49-42;** Metro: Plaça de Catalunya), open daily 9am to 1:30pm and 4:30 to 10pm. After hours, various pharmacies take turns staying open at night. All pharmacies that are not open do post the names and addresses of after-hours pharmacies in the area.

Emergencies In an emergency, phone ☎ **080** to report a **fire,** ☎ **092** to call the **police,** and ☎ **061** to request an **ambulance.**

Hospitals Barcelona has many hospitals and clinics, including **Hospital Clínic,** Casanova 143 (☎ **93-227-54-00**), and **Hospital de la Santa Creu i Sant Pau,** at the intersection of Carrer Cartagena and Carrer Sant Antoni Maria Claret (☎ **93-291-90-00;** Metro: Hospital de Sant Pau).

Post Office The main post office is at Plaça d'Antoni López (☎ **93-219-71-97;** Metro: Jaume I). It's open Monday to Friday 8am to 9pm and Saturday 9am to 1pm.

Safety Be particularly careful with cameras, purses, and wallets, all favorite targets of thieves and pickpockets in Barcelona—particularly on the world-famous Rambles. The southern part of Les Rambles, near the waterfront, is the most dangerous section, especially at night. Proceed with caution.

Telephone The **country code** for Spain is **34.** The **city code** for Barcelona is **3;** use this code when calling from outside Spain. If you're within Spain, use **93.**

To make an **international call,** dial **07,** wait for the tone, and dial the country code, the area code, and the number. Note that an international call from a public phone booth requires stacks and stacks of 100 peseta coins. As an alternative, purchase a **phone card** from a tobacco shop (*estanco*), the post office, or other authorized dealer.

Transit Information For general **RENFE** (train) information, dial ☎ **93-490-02-02.** For **airport** information, call ☎ **93-478-50-00.**

WHERE TO STAY
CIUTAT VELLA (OLD CITY)
Expensive
Hotel Colón. Av. de la Catedral 7, 08002 Barcelona. ☎ **800/845-0636** in the U.S., or 93-301-14-04. Fax 93-317-29-15. E-mail: colon@nexus.es. 147 units. A/C MINIBAR TV TEL. 20,000–35,000Pts ($126–$221) double; from 40,000Pts ($252) suite. AE, DC, MC, V. Bus: 16, 17, 19, or 45.

This postwar hotel is blessed with one of the most dramatic locations in Barcelona, opposite the cathedral's main entrance. Inside you'll find conservative and slightly old-fashioned public areas and a helpful staff. Rooms are filled with comfortable furniture and (despite recent renovations) an appealingly dowdy kind of charm. Though lacking views, those in back are quieter. Sixth-floor rooms with balconies overlooking the square are the most desirable. Some lower rooms are dark. The hotel maintains two well-recommended restaurants, the Grill (continental specialties) and the Carabela (Catalan specialties).

✪ **Le Meridien Barcelona.** Rambles 111, 08002 Barcelona. ☎ **800/543-4300** in the U.S., or 93-318-62-00. Fax 93-301-77-76. 206 units. A/C MINIBAR TV TEL. 25,000–35,000Pts ($158–$221) double; from 40,000Pts ($252) suite. AE, DC, MC, V. Parking 2,000Pts ($13). Metro: Liceu or Plaça de Catalunya.

This nine-story tower is the finest hotel in the old town, thanks in large part to a major refurbishment in 1997. It's superior in both amenities and comfort to its closest rival, the Colón. Rooms are spacious and comfortable, with double-glazed windows, extralarge beds, 18 TV channels, three in-house videos, two phones, bathrooms with heated floors, and hair dryers. The hotel contains a comfortable bar and an excellent restaurant, Le Patio.

Moderate

✪ **Duques de Bergara.** Bergara 11. ☎ **93-301-51-51.** Fax 93-317-34-42. 150 units. A/C MINIBAR TV TEL. 28,900Pts ($182) double, 32,900Pts ($207) triple. AE, DC, MC, V. Metro: Catalunya.

Barcelona's newest upscale hotel occupies what was originally the private 1899 townhouse of the Duke of Bergara (look for his coat of arms in the stained glass panels of the reception area). Public areas artfully contain paneling, stained glass, and decorative accessories originally installed by modernist architect Emilio Salas I Cortes. In 1998, a new, seven-story tower was added. Rooms are outfitted with conservatively traditional comforts. On the premises are a restaurant (El Duc), a bar and cafe one floor above the lobby, and an outdoor swimming pool.

Granvía. Gran Vía de les Cortes Catalanes, 642, 08007 Barcelona. ☎ **93-318-19-00.** Fax 93-318-99-97. 50 units. A/C MINIBAR TV TEL. 12,500Pts ($79) double. AE, DC, MC, V. Metro: Plaça de Catalunya.

A grand hotel on one of the most fashionable boulevards in Barcelona, the Granvía has public areas that reflect the opulence of the 1860s. It's your best choice if you want to feel like royalty. The traditional rooms are comfortable rather than luxurious. Expect fancifully shaped headboards and pastel-colored chenille bedspreads along with upholstery that needs refreshing. Rooms come in a variety of shapes and sizes. The courtyard, graced with a fountain and palm trees, is set with tables for alfresco drinks; in the garden room off the courtyard, continental breakfast is served. Centrally heated in the winter, the hotel has one drawback: street noise, which might disturb the light sleeper.

Hotel Regencia Colón. Carrer Sagristans 13–17, 08002 Barcelona. ☎ **93-318-98-58.** Fax 93-317-28-22. 55 units. A/C MINIBAR TV TEL. 9,500Pts ($60) double; 16,000Pts ($101) triple. AE, DC, MC, V. Metro: Jaume 1 or Urquinaona.

This stately stone hotel stands behind the more prestigious, superior, and expensive Hotel Colón in the shadow of the cathedral. The formal lobby seems a bit dour, but the well-maintained rooms are comfortable and often roomy, albeit worn. Rooms are insulated against sound, and 40 of them have full-tub bathrooms, the remainder have showers only. The hotel is a good value for Barcelona.

✪ **Mesón Castilla.** Carrer Valldoncella 5, 08002 Barcelona. ☎ **93-318-21-82.** Fax 93-412-40-20. 56 units. A/C MINIBAR TV TEL. 9,500Pts ($60) double. V. Parking 2,200Pts ($14). Metro: Plaça de la Universitat.

This two-star hotel, originally established in 1952, occupies a former apartment building with an interior that contains occasional touches of art nouveau detailing. Owned and operated by the Spanish hotel chain HUSA, the Castilla is clean, charming, and well maintained. Its nearest rival is the Regencia Colón, to which it is comparable in atmosphere. Rooms, which benefited from a renovation in 1997, are comfortable—beds have ornate headboards—and some open onto large terraces.

Montecarlo. Ramble dels Estudis 124, 08002 Barcelona. ☎ **93-412-04-04.** Fax 93-318-73-23. E-mail: montecarlobcn@abaforum.es. 60 units. A/C MINIBAR TV TEL. 9,500Pts ($60) double; 16,400Pts ($103) triple. AE, DC, MC, V. Parking 2,000Pts ($13). Metro: Plaça de Catalunya.

This hotel, beside the wide and sloping promenade of Les Rambles, was built around 200 years ago as an opulent private home. In the 1930s it was transformed into the comfortably unpretentious hotel you'll find today. Rooms are efficiently decorated. Double-glazed windows help keep out some of the noise. The public areas include some of the building's original accessories, with carved doors, a baronial fireplace, and crystal chandeliers.

Inexpensive

Hostal Levante. Baïxada de Sant Miguel 2, 08002 Barcelona. ☎ **93-317-95-65.** Fax 93-317-05-26. E-mail: hostallevante@mx3.redestb.es. 27 units (7 with bathroom). 2,800Pts ($18) double without bathroom; 4,400Pts ($28) double with bathroom. AE, V. Metro: Liceu or Jaume 1.

The small and very simple rooms here are scattered over two floors of a 200-year-old building connected by a cramped and creaking elevator. Drawbacks are that you're likely to be confronted with lots of screaming children, relatives of the family that owns the place. Benefits include a position in the heart of the historic Barri Gótic, near the Plaça de Sant Jaume, and clean, utterly unpretentious rooms. No meals are served, and the place is strictly laissez-faire, but a worthy choice for its location and rock-bottom prices.

Hostal Neutral. Rambla de Catalunya 42, 08007 Barcelona. ☎ **93-487-63-90.** 35 units (28 with full bathroom, 7 with shower only [no toilet]). TEL. 3,370Pts ($21) double with shower only (no toilet); 5,955Pts ($38) double with bathroom. MC, V. Metro: Paseo de Gracia.

In 1917, the original innkeeper of this establishment acquired two floors of a six-floor, 1890s building and transformed it into a simple pension. The name he chose, Hostal Neutral, may seem odd to many present-day guests, but it reflected his neutrality during the armed conflicts of World War I that had by then engulfed all of Europe. Today, it functions as an older but highly recommendable pension; the affordable rooms are "neutral" in their decor, but clean and comfortable nonetheless. Breakfast, the only meal available, is served in a salon with a coffered ceiling, and there's a TV lounge on the premises.

SUR DIAGONAL

Very Expensive

Barcelona Hilton. Av. Diagonal 589–591, 08014 Barcelona. ☎ **800/445-8667** in the U.S. and Canada, or 93-495-77-77. Fax 93-495-77-00. www.hilton.com. 286 units. A/C MINIBAR TV TEL. 32,000Pts ($202) double; from 36,000Pts ($227) suite. AE, DC, MC, V. Parking 3,000Pts ($19). Metro: María Cristina.

This five-star property, opposite the gates to the fairgrounds (beyond that, to the Olympic Stadium), is a huge 11-floor corner structure. The lobby is sleek with lots of marble, and the public lounges are furnished with black leather and velvet chairs. Most rooms are rather large and finely equipped. Furnishings are Hilton-standardized, but with amenities such as private safes. The Restaurant Cristal Garden serves well-prepared international and Spanish menus in a relaxed but polished setting. Less expensive meals are served informally at Le Bistro. There's a small and somewhat cramped exercise room on the hotel's sixth floor, but serious exercise buffs will head for a health club a half mile away, with which the Hilton maintains a cooperative relationship.

Claris. Carrer de Pau Claris, 150, 08009 Barcelona. ☎ **800/888-4747** in the U.S., or 93-487-62-62. Fax 93-215-79-70. www.derbyhotels.es. E-mail: info@derbyhotels.es. 120 units. A/C MINIBAR TV TEL. Mon–Thurs 32,700Pts ($206) double; from 40,900Pts ($258) suite. Fri–Sun 35,000Pts ($221) double; from 45,000Pts ($284) suite. Fri–Sun rates include breakfast. AE, DC, MC, V. Parking 2,250Pts ($14). Metro: Passeig de Gràcia.

One of the most unusual hotels in Barcelona, the postmodern Claris is one of only two five-star grand luxe hotels in the city center. It opened in 1992, in time for the Olympics, and includes a pool and garden on its roof, a minimuseum of Egyptian antiquities on its second floor, and two restaurants, one of which, Beluga, specializes in different brands of caviar. Rooms are painted an iconoclastic blue-violet and incorporate copies of ancient Egyptian art with state-of-the-art electronic accessories.

✪ Hotel Ritz. Gran Vía de les Corts Catalanes, 668, 08010 Barcelona. ☎ **93-318-52-00.** Fax 93-318-01-48. 122 units. A/C MINIBAR TV TEL. 30,000–45,000Pts ($189–$284) double; 60,000Pts ($378) suite. AE, DC, MC, V. Parking 3,500Pts ($22). Metro: Passeig de Gràcia.

Acknowledged as the finest, most prestigious, and most architecturally distinguished hotel in Barcelona, the Ritz was built in art deco style in 1919. It has welcomed more millionaires, celebrities, and aristocrats than any other hotel in northeastern Spain. One of the finest features is its cream-and-gilt neoclassical lobby, featuring marble floors and potted palms. Rooms are formal and richly furnished, sometimes with Regency furniture; bathrooms are accented with mosaics and tubs inspired by those in ancient Rome. The elegant Restaurant Diana serves French and Catalán cuisine amid soaring ceilings and crystal chandeliers.

Rey Juan Carlos I/Conrad International Barcelona. Av. Diagonal 661, 08028 Barcelona. ☎ **800/445-8355** in the U.S., or 93-448-08-08. Fax 93-364-42-64. www.lhw.com. 432 units. A/C MINIBAR TV TEL. Mon–Thurs 40,000Pts ($252) double, 60,000Pts ($378) suite; Fri–Sun 23,000Pts ($145) double, 52,500Pts ($331) suite. AE, DC, MC, V. Free parking for guests. Metro: Zona Universitaria.

Named for the Spanish king, who attended its opening and who has visited it several times since, this is the only five-star choice that competes effectively against the Ritz and Claris. Opened in 1992, in time for the Olympics, it rises 17 stories from a position at the northern end of the Diagonal. At one end of the soaring inner atrium, a bank of glass-sided elevators glide silently up and down. Rooms contain many electronic extras, conservatively comfortable furnishings, and in many cases, views out over Barcelona to the sea. The hotel's most elegant restaurant is Chez Vous, a glamorous and panoramic locale with impeccable service and French/Catalan meals. Amenities include a swimming pool, health club, and business center.

Expensive

Hotel Condes de Barcelona. Passeig de Gràcia, 73–75, 08008 Barcelona. ☎ **93-488-22-00.** Fax 93-488-06-14. www.condesdebarcelona.com. E-mail: cbhotel@ condesdebarcelona.com. 183 units. A/C MINIBAR TV TEL. 31,000Pts ($195) double; 35,000–55,000Pts ($221–$347) suite. AE, DC, MC, V. Parking 2,000Pts ($13). Metro: Passeig de Gràcia.

No longer looking as fresh as it did for the 1992 Olympics, this hotel has fallen a bit but still has quite a bit of charm, and its public areas contain more references to medieval Barcelona than any other hotel in town. Business was so good that it opened a 74-room extension, which regrettably lacks the élan of the original. The curved lobby-level bar and its adjacent restaurant add a touch of art deco. Some of the comfortable rooms are beginning to show wear and tear, but all have soundproof windows. The hotel has a Jacuzzi on the fifth floor.

Moderate

Hotel Derby/Hotel Gran Derby. Loreto, 21–25, and Loreto, 28, 08029 Barcelona. ☎ **93-322-32-15.** Fax 93-419-68-20. www.derbyhotels.es. E-mail: info@derbyhotels.es. 141 units. A/C MINIBAR TV TEL. 21,000–28,000Pts ($132–$176) double; 22,000–26,000Pts ($139–$164) suite. AE, DC, MC, V. Parking 2,200Pts ($14). Metro: Hospital Clínic.

In two separate buildings, these twin hotels are in a tranquil neighborhood about 2 blocks south of the busy intersection of Avinguda Diagonal and Avinguda Sarría. The Derby offers conventional rooms and the Gran Derby (across the street) contains suites, many of which have small balconies overlooking a flowered courtyard. (All drinking, dining, and entertainment facilities are in the Derby.) Rooms and suites are outfitted with simple furniture in a variety of styles, each comfortable and quiet. A coffee shop and bistro in the Hotel Derby serves sandwiches and light platters throughout the day.

Inexpensive

Hotel Astoria. París, 203, 08036 Barcelona. ☎ **93-209-83-11.** Fax 93-202-30-08. www.derbyhotels.es. E-mail: info@derbyhotels.es. 117 units. A/C MINIBAR TV TEL. 9,000–15,000Pts ($57–$95) double. AE, DC, MC, V. Metro: Diagonal.

One of our favorites, the 1954 Astoria has an art deco facade that makes it appear older than it is. The high ceilings, geometric designs, and brass-studded detailings in the public areas could be Moorish or Andalusian. The comfortable rooms are soundproofed. The more old-fashioned ones have warm textures of exposed cedar and elegant modern accessories. There's a bar on the premises but the only meal served is breakfast.

NORTE DIAGONAL
Moderate

Hotel Hesperia. Los Vergós, 20, 08017 Barcelona. ☎ **93-204-55-51.** Fax 93-204-43-92. www.hoteles-hesperia.es. 134 units. A/C MINIBAR TV TEL. Mon–Thurs 16,500Pts ($104) double. Fri–Sun 10,000Pts ($63) double. AE, DC, MC, V. Parking 1,750Pts ($11). Metro: Tres Torres.

Built in the late 1980s, this six-story hotel, on the northern edge of the city, a 12-minute taxi ride from the center, sits in one of Barcelona's most pleasant residential neighborhoods. You'll pass a Japanese rock garden to reach the stone-floored reception area, with its adjacent bar. Sunlight floods the monochromatic interiors of the rooms. The uniformed staff offers fine service. A restaurant on the premises serves a regional cuisine.

VILA OLÍMPICA
Expensive

Hotel Arts. Carrer de la Marina, 19-21, 08005 Barcelona. ☎ **800/241-3333** in the U.S., or 93-221-10-00. Fax 93-221-10-70. www.ritzcarlton.com. 453 units. A/C MINIBAR TV TEL. Mon–Thurs 50,000Pts ($315) double; from 55,000Pts ($347) suite. Fri–Sun 30,000Pts ($189) double; 40,000Pts ($252) suite. AE, DC, MC, V. Parking 3,200Pts ($20). Metro: Ciudadela–Vila Olímpica.

This hotel, managed by the luxury-conscious Ritz-Carlton chain, occupies 33 floors of one of Spain's tallest buildings, a 44-floor postmodern tower. The location is about 2.5km (1½ miles) southwest of Barcelona's historic core, adjacent to the sea and the Olympic Village. Its decor is contemporary and elegant, including a lobby sheathed in slabs of soft gray and yellow marble and rooms outfitted in pastel yellow or blue. Views from the rooms sweep out over the skyline and the Mediterranean. The food and drink facilities are the best of any hotel in Barcelona, including a summer-only bar set beside the pool. Other facilities include a fitness center.

WHERE TO DINE
Ciutat Vella (Old City)
Expensive

Agut d'Avignon. Carrer Trinitat 3. ☎ **93-302-60-34.** Reservations required. Main courses 5,500–7,500Pts ($35–$47). AE, MC, V. Daily 1–3:30pm and 9pm–11:30am. Metro: Jaume I or Liceu. CATALAN.

One of our favorite restaurants in Barcelona is near Plaça Reial, in a tiny alleyway (the cross street is calle d'Avinyó 8). The restaurant explosion here has toppled Agut d' Avignon from its once stellar position, but partly because of its nostalgic charm, it's still going strong. A small 19th-century vestibule leads to the multilevel dining area that has two balconies and a main hall and is evocative of a hunting lodge. Specialties range from the strictly traditional to the culinary avant-garde and are likely to include local shrimp with aioli (garlicky mayonnaise), acorn-squash soup served in its shell, fisher's soup with garlic toast, duck with figs, and haddock stuffed with shellfish, the latter a dish that's forever associated with Catalonia.

Casa Leopoldo. Carrer Sant Rafael 24. ☎ **93-441-30-14.** Reservations required. Main courses 5,500–10,000Pts ($35–$63); fixed-price menu 4,000Pts ($25). AE, DC, MC, V. Tues–Sun 1–4pm and Tues–Sat 9–11pm. Closed 1 week in Aug and at Easter. Metro: Liceu. SEAFOOD.

An excursion through the streets of the Barri Xinés contributes to the sense of adventure of coming to this warm and surprisingly sophisticated restaurant. It has thrived here since 1929, within a building erected in 1780. It offers some of the freshest seafood in town, and caters to a loyal clientele. There's a popular stand-up tapas bar in front, then two dining rooms, one slightly more formal than the other. Specialties include oxtail stew; fried sea bass with chives, lemon, olive oil, and garlic; shellfish soup, and deep-fried eels. An enduring specialty, prepared only for two, is an enormous platter of fish and shellfish that's configured entirely as a meal unto itself.

Moderate

Brasserie Flo. Jonqueras 10. ☎ **93-319-31-02.** Reservations recommended. Main courses 4,500–6,000Pts ($28–$38); fixed-price menu 2,280Pts ($14). AE, DC, MC, V. Mon–Thurs 1–4pm and 8:30pm–midnight, Fri–Sun 1–4pm and 8:30pm–1am. Metro: Urquinaona. FRENCH/INTERNATIONAL.

The art deco dining room here is spacious, palm-filled, comfortable, and air-conditioned. Installed in a handsomely restored warehouse, it's as close as Barcelona gets to offering a brasserie you might find in Alsace. Menu items are equally divided between specialties from the bistro traditions of France and Catalonia. French-derived items include fresh foie gras and large platters of *choucroute* (sauerkraut) served with sausages, pork chops, and a steamed ham hock. Catalan specialties include *mariscado* (shellfish stew), *parillada de mariscos* (mixed grilled shellfish), *caldereta* of lobster, and fresh seasonal oysters.

Can Culleretes. Quintana, 5. ☎ **93-317-64-85.** Reservations recommended. Main courses 2,500–3,500Pts ($16–$22). DC, V. Tues–Sun 1:30–4pm, Tues–Sat 9–11:30pm. Closed 3 weeks in July. Metro: Liceu. Bus: 14 or 59. CATALÁN.

Founded in 1786 as a *pastelería* (pastry shop) in the Barri Gòtic, this oldest of Barcelona restaurants still retains many architectural features. All three dining rooms are decorated in Catalan style, with tile dadoes and wrought-iron chandeliers. The well-prepared food, mostly seafood, features authentic dishes of northeastern Spain, including sole Roman style, *zarzuela à la marinara* (shellfish medley), *canalones* (cannelloni), fillet of sole with clams, and paella. October to January special game dishes are available, including *perdiz* (partridge).

Egipte. La Rambla 79. ☎ **93-317-74-80.** Reservations recommended. Main courses 1,500–3,000Pts ($9–$19); fixed-price menu (Mon–Sat) 1,125–2,500Pts ($7–$16). AE, DC, MC, V. Mon–Sat 1–4pm and 8pm–midnight. Metro: Liceu. CATALAN/SPANISH.

A favorite among locals, this tiny place, set amid narrow medieval streets, behind the central marketplace, is lively day and night. The excellent menu includes spinach vol-au-vent (traditionally served with an egg on top), *lengua de ternera* (tongue), and *berengeras* (stuffed eggplant), a chef's specialty. The local favorite is codfish prepared several ways, including one savory version in cream sauce. A savory beginning to your meal is baked bread layered with ham and a salty Catalan cheese. Expect hearty market-fresh food and a total lack of pretension.

Els Quatre Gats. Montsió 3. ☎ **93-302-41-40.** Reservations required Sat–Sun. Main courses 2,000–3,500Pts ($13–$22); fixed-price lunch 1,500Pts ($9). AE, MC, V. Restaurant, Mon–Sat 1–4pm and 9pm–midnight; cafe, daily 8am–2am. Metro: Plaça de Catalunya. CATALAN.

A Barcelona legend since 1897, the "Four Cats" was the favorite of Picasso and other artists. In their heyday, their works decorated the walls of this cafe on a narrow cobblestone street near the cathedral. Today a *tertulia* (clublike) bar in the heart of the Barri Gòtic, it was restored but retains its fine old look. The good food is prepared in an unpretentious style of Catalan cooking called *cuina de mercat* (based on whatever looked fresh at the market that day).

✪ Los Caracoles. Escudellers 14. ☎ **93-302-31-85.** Reservations required. Main courses 5,000–9,000Pts ($32–$57). AE, DC, MC, V. Daily 1pm–midnight. Metro: Drassanes. CATALAN/SPANISH.

Set in a labyrinth of narrow cobblestone streets, Los Caracoles has been the port's most colorful restaurant since 1835. It has won acclaim for its spit-roasted chicken, roast suckling pig, roast suckling lamb, and its namesake, snails. In summer tables are placed outside. The excellent food features all sorts of Spanish and Catalan specialties, especially a mixed grill of seafood or a medley of fried fish in sauce. Although a number-one tourist stop, it's not a tourist trap but delivers the same aromatic and robust food it always did.

✪ Restaurant Hoffman. Argentería 74–78. ☎ **93-319-58-89.** Reservations required. Main courses 1,300–3,300Pts ($8–$21); set lunch (wine and coffee included) 4,600Pts ($29). AE, DC, MC, V. Mon–Fri 1:30–4pm and 9pm–midnight. Metro: Jaume I. CATALAN/FRENCH/INTERNATIONAL.

This restaurant's creative cuisine close association with a well-respected training school for future employees of Catalonia's hotel and restaurant industry have made it one of the most famous in Barcelona. The decor is eclectic—masses of verdant plants and fresh flowers, old photographs, and dramatic oil paintings. During clement weather, tables are also set up outside. Menu items change every 2 months and are often concocted from ingredients acquired in nearby France. Examples include a superb version of *fine tarte* with deboned sardines; foie gras wrapped in puff pastry; a ragout of crayfish with green risotto; and a succulent version of pig's feet with eggplant. Especially flavorful is a fillet steak cooked in Rioja wine and served with a confit of shallots and a gratin of potatoes. Fondant of chocolate makes a worthy dessert.

Inexpensive

Biocenter. Pintor Fortuny 25. ☎ **93-301-45-83.** Fixed-price menu 1,125Pts ($8). Main courses 700–1,200Pts ($4.40–$8). No credit cards. Mon–Sat 9am–5pm. (Bar, Mon–Sat 9am–11pm.) Metro: Plaça de Catalunya. VEGETARIAN.

This is Barcelona's largest and best-known vegetarian restaurant, a funky, counterculture sort of place. Meals are served in two ground-floor dining rooms, whose walls are decorated with the paintings and artworks of the owner and his colleagues. There's a salad bar, an array of vegetarian casseroles, such soups as gazpacho and lentil, and a changing selection of seasonal vegetables.

Garduña. Mercado La Boquería. Morera 17-19. ☎ **93-302-43-23.** Reservations recommended. Main courses 1,500–4,500Pts ($9–$28); fixed-price menu 1,000Pts ($6). AE, MC, V. Daily 1–4pm and 8pm–midnight. Metro: Liceu. CATALÁN.

Battered and somewhat ramshackle, this famous restaurant in La Boquería, the covered food market, enjoys a fashionable reputation among actors, sculptors, writers, and painters who appreciate a blue-collar atmosphere. Because of its position near the back of the market, you'll pass endless rows of fresh produce, cheese, and meats that whet your appetite before you reach it. You can dine downstairs, near a crowded bar, or a bit more formally upstairs. The food is ultra-fresh and might include "hors d'oeuvres of the sea," *canalones* (cannelloni) Rossini, grilled hake with herbs, seafood rice, fillet steak with green peppercorns, or zarzuela of fresh fish.

Pitarra. Avinyó 56. ☎ **93-301-16-47.** Reservations required. Main courses 3,500Pts ($22); fixed-price lunch 1,200Pts ($8). AE, DC, MC, V. Mon–Sat 1–4pm and 8:30–11pm. Metro: Liceu. CATALAN.

This restaurant in the Barri Gòtic was named after the 19th-century Catalán playwright who lived and wrote his plays and poetry in the back room. Menu items read like a roster of traditional Catalan specialties, and most of them are flavorful. Examples include mushroom crêpes layered with strips of duck meat; pork chops smothered with morel mushrooms; an ultratraditional version of sea bass baked with tomatoes, peppers, onions, and garlic. There're also two forms of paella served here: the Valencian version with fish, shellfish, and assorted meats, and an all-seafood version beloved by Catalonians.

SUR DIAGONAL
Very Expensive

Beltxenea. Mallorca 275. ☎ **93-215-30-24.** Reservations recommended. Main courses 3,000–6,900Pts ($19–$43); menú degustación 8,000Pts ($50). AE, DC, MC, V. Mon–Fri 1:30–3:30pm and Mon–Sat 8:30–11:30pm. Closed 2 weeks in Aug. Metro: Passeig de Gràcia. BASQUE/INTERNATIONAL.

In a late 19th-century modernist apartment building, this restaurant celebrates the nuances and subtleties of Basque cuisine. Since the Basques are noted as the finest chefs in Spain, the cuisine is grand indeed, and the restaurant is one of the most elegantly and comfortably furnished in Barcelona. Save a visit for that special night—it's worth the money. The cuisine reflects the inspiration of the chef and the availability of ingredients. Examples are hake either fried with garlic or garnished with clams and served with fish broth. Roast lamb, grilled rabbit, and pheasant are well prepared and succulent, as are the desserts. Summer dining is possible out in the formal garden.

✪ **La Dama.** Av. Diagonal 423. ☎ **93-202-06-86.** Reservations required. Main courses 7,000–9,150Pts ($44–$58); fixed-price menu 2,000–8,500Pts ($13–$54). AE, DC, MC, V. Daily 1–4pm and 8:30–11:30pm. Metro: Provença. CATALÁN/INTERNATIONAL.

Located one floor above street level, this stylish and well-managed place is one of the few Barcelona restaurants that deserves and gets a Michelin star. La Dama serves a clientele of local residents and civic dignitaries with impeccable taste. You'll climb a short flight of sinuous stairs to reach the dining room. Specialties may include warm scampi salad with orange zest; house-style pig's trotters with mushrooms and truffles; tenderloin of beef layered with foie gras; salmon steak served with vinegar derived from cava and onions; an abundant seasonal platter of autumn mushrooms; and succulent preparations of lamb, fish and shellfish, beef, and veal.

Inexpensive

Ca La María. Tallers 76 bis. ☎ **93-318-89-93.** Reservations recommended. Main courses 1,100–4,000Pts ($7–$25). AE, DC, MC, V. Daily 1:30–3:45pm; Tues–Sat 8:30–10:45pm. Metro: Plaça de la Universida. CATALAN.

This small, family-operated, good-natured, and charming restaurant accommodates only 36 guests, who dine in cozy intimacy on a quiet square opposite a Byzantine-style church near Plaça de la Universitat. With some recent exceptions, menu items are endearingly homelike—provided you grew up in a family of Catalan cooks. Examples include anglerfish with brown garlic sauce, fillet of sole with mushrooms and prawns, tournedos with cèpe mushrooms, and a veal fillet "Café de Paris."

NORTE DIAGONAL

Very Expensive

✪ **Botafumiero.** Gran de Gràcia 81. ☎ **93-218-42-30.** Reservations recommended for dining rooms, not necessary for meals at the bar. Main courses 2,500–6,000Pts ($16–$38); fixed-price menus 8,000–13,000Pts ($50–$82). AE, DC, MC, V. Mon–Sat 1pm–1am, Sun 1–5pm. Metro: Fontana. SEAFOOD.

Although the competition is severe, this well-managed *restaurante marisquería* (seafood restaurant) consistently serves Barcelona's finest seafood. Much of the allure comes from the attention to detail paid by the white-jacketed staff. You can dine at the bar or in one of the attractive dining rooms with light-grained panels, polished brass, and paintings by Galician artists. Menu items include grilled sea bass with a paprika, garlic, olive oil, and lemon sauce; braised grouper with cider and cava sauce; and baked hake with a tomato-herb sauce. The establishment prides itself on its fresh- and saltwater fish, clams, mussels, lobster, crayfish, scallops, and several varieties of crustaceans that you may never have seen before.

Neichel. Pedralbes 16. ☎ **93-334-06-99.** Reservations required. Main courses 3,000–4,500Pts ($19–$28). AE, DC, MC, V. Mon–Sat 1:30–3:45pm and 8:30–11pm. Closed Aug and holidays. Metro: María Christina. MEDITERRANEAN.

Alsatian-born Jean Louis Neichel has been called "the most brilliant ambassador French cuisine has ever had in Spain." Focusing on a light-textured culinary display that uses olive oil instead of butter and cream, Neichel prepares dishes that include fresh foie gras with a confit of figs; crayfish salad with a truffle-studded vinaigrette; a salad of wild mushrooms with a carpaccio of wild duck; John Dory with pulverized shellfish suspended in an emulsion of olive oil; baby monkfish with Mediterranean herbs and a confit of sweet peppers; and fillet of beef stuffed with foie gras and served with a sauce made from a heady Spanish red wine known as *merlap*. In 1996, the dessert cart at this glamorous restaurant won an award as the most appealing roster of desserts in Spain.

MOLL DE LA FUSTA & BARCELONETA

Expensive

Can Costa. Passeig Don Juan de Borbò 70. ☎ **93-221-59-03.** Reservations recommended. Main courses 2,000–4,200Pts ($13–$26). AE, MC, V. Daily 1:30–4pm; Mon–Sat 8–11:30pm. Metro: Barceloneta. SEAFOOD.

One of the most long-lived seafood restaurants in this seafaring town is Can Costa, whose big windows overlook the water. Established in the late 1930s, it contains two busy dining rooms, a uniformed, well-seasoned staff, and an outdoor terrace where clients can take advantage of the streaming sunlight and harbor-front breezes. Fresh seafood rules the menu here, prepared according to traditional recipes. They include the best baby squid in town—it's sautéed in a flash so that it has an almost grilled flavor, and is almost never overcooked or too rubbery. A chef's specialty that has endured through many a season is *fideuá de piex,* which is equivalent to a classic Valencian shellfish paella, except in this case, noodles are used in lieu of rice. All the desserts are homemade by the kitchen staff daily.

Can Solé. 4 Carrer Sant Carles. ☎ **93-221-50-12.** Reservations required. Main courses 5,000–6,000Pts ($32–$38). AE, DC, MC, V. Tues–Sun 1–4pm; Tues–Sat 8:30–11:30pm. Metro: Barceloneta. CATALÁN.

In Barceloneta at the harbor, Can Solé still honors the traditions of this former fishing village. Many of the seafood joints here are too touristy for our tastes, but this one is authentic and delivers good value. The decor is rustic and a bit raffish, with wine barrels, lots of noise, and excellent food. Begin with the sweet tiny clams or the codfish cakes, perhaps some bouillabaisse. Little langoustines are an eternal but expensive favorite, and everything is aromatically perfumed with fresh garlic. You might also sample one of the seafood rice dishes. Desserts are so good they're worth saving room for, especially the orange pudding or the praline ice cream.

Moderate

Siete Puertas (also known as 7 Portes). Passeig d'Isabel II, 14. ☎ **93-319-30-33.** Reservations required. Main courses 3,000–4,500Pts ($19–$28). AE, DC, MC, V. Daily 1pm–1am. Metro: Barceloneta. SEAFOOD.

This is a lunchtime favorite for businesspeople (the Stock Exchange is across the way) and an evening favorite for in-the-know clients who have made it their preferred restaurant in Catalonia. It's been going since 1836. Regional dishes—the portions are enormous—include fresh herring with onions and potatoes, a different paella daily (sometimes with shellfish, for example, or with rabbit), and a wide array of fresh fish, succulent oysters, and an herb-laden stew of black beans with pork or white beans with sausage.

Inexpensive

Cal Pep. 8 Plaça des les Olles. ☎ **93-310-79-61.** Reservations needed. Main courses 1,200–1,800Pts ($8–$11). AE, V. Mon 8:30–11:30pm, Tues–Sat 1–4:30pm and 8:30–11:30pm. Closed Aug. Metro: Barceloneta. CATALAN.

One of the dining secrets of Barcelona, Cal Pep lies close to the Picasso Museum and is a slice of local life. On a tiny postage stamp square, it's generally packed, and the food is some of the tastiest in the old town. There's actually a Pep himself, and he's a great host, going around to see that everybody is one happy family. In the rear is a small dining room but most patrons like to occupy one of the counter seats up front. From the pans in the rear emerge a selection of perfectly cooked dishes that might launch you into your meal. Try the fried artichokes or the mixed medley of seafood that includes small sardines. Tiny clams come swimming in a well-seasoned broth given extra spice by a sprinkling of hot peppers. A delectable tuna dish comes with a sesame sauce and fresh salmon is flavored with such herbs as basil—sublime.

SEEING THE SIGHTS

Spain's second-largest city is also its most cosmopolitan and avant-garde. Barcelona is filled with landmark buildings and world-class museums offering many sightseeing opportunities. These include Antoni Gaudí's Sagrada Familia, Museu Picasso, Barcelona's Gothic cathedral, and Les Rambles, the famous tree-lined promenade cutting through the heart of the old quarter.

SIGHTSEEING SUGGESTIONS FOR FIRST-TIME VISITORS

If You Have 1 Day Spend the morning exploring the Barri Gótic. In the afternoon visit Antoni Gaudí's unfinished masterpiece, La Sagrada Família, before returning to the heart of the city for a walk down Les Rambles. To cap your day, take the funicular to the fountains at Montjuïc or go to the top of Tibidabo for a panoramic view of Barcelona and its harbor.

If You Have 2 Days   On Day 2, visit the Museu Picasso in the Gothic Quarter. Then stroll through the surrounding district, the Barri de la Ribera, which is filled with Renaissance mansions and is the site of the gorgeous church Santa María del Mar. Follow this with a ride to the top of the Columbus Monument for a panoramic view of the harbor front. Have a seafood lunch at La Barceloneta and in the afternoon, stroll up Les Rambles again. Explore Montjuïc and visit the Museu d'Art de Catalunya if time remains. End the day with a meal at Los Caracoles, a famous restaurant in the old city, just off Les Rambles.

If You Have 3 Days   On Day 3, make a pilgrimage to the monastery of Montserrat, about 45 minutes outside of Barcelona, to see the venerated Black Virgin and a host of artistic and scenic attractions. Try to time your visit to hear the 50-member boys' choir.

If You Have 4 or 5 Days   On Day 4, take a morning walk along the harborfront, or in the modernist Eixample section of Barcelona, the planned urban expansion area from 1860. Have lunch on the pier. In the afternoon visit Montjuïc again to tour the Fundació Joan Miró and walk through the Poble Espanyol, a miniature village with reproductions of representative regional architecture, created for the 1929 World's Fair. On Day 5, take another excursion from the city. If you're interested in history, visit the former Roman city of Tarragona to the south. If you want to unwind on a beach, head south to Sitges.

THE TOP ATTRACTIONS

✪ Catedral de Barcelona. Plaça de la Seu. ☎ **93-315-15-54.** Cathedral, free; museum, 100Pts (65¢); cloisters, 50Pts (30¢). Cathedral, daily 8am–1:30pm and 4–7:30pm; museum and cloisters, daily 10am–1pm. Metro: Jaume I.

Barcelona's cathedral is a celebrated example of Catalonian Gothic. Except for the 19th-century west facade, the basilica was begun at the end of the 13th century and completed in the mid–15th century. The three naves, cleaned and illuminated, have splendid Gothic details. With its large bell towers, blending of medieval and Renaissance styles, beautiful cloister, high altar, side chapels, sculptured choir, and Gothic arches, it ranks as one of Spain's most impressive cathedrals. The cloister, illuminated on Saturday and fiesta days, contains a museum of medieval art.

Fundació Joan Miró. Plaça de Neptú, Parc de Montjuïc. ☎ **93-329-19-08.** Admission 800Pts ($5) adults, 450Pts ($2.85) students, free for children 14 and under. Tues–Wed and Fri–Sat 10am–8pm (July–Sept) or 10am–7pm (Oct–June); Thurs 10am–9:30pm, Sun 10am–2:30pm. Bus: 61 from Plaza d'España.

Born in 1893, Joan Miró went on to become one of Spain's greatest painters, known for his whimsical abstract forms and brilliant colors. Some 10,000 works by this Catalán surrealist, including paintings, graphics, and sculptures, have been collected here. The building has been greatly expanded in recent years, following the design of the Catalán architect Josep Lluís Sert, a close friend of Miró's. An exhibition in a modern wing charts (in a variety of media) Miró's complete artistic evolution, from his first drawings at the age of 8 to his last works. Touring international shows of considerable interest are also held at the Fundació Miró.

✪ La Sagrada Família. Mallorca 401. ☎ **93-207-30-31.** Church, 800Pts ($5), including a 12-minute video about Gaudí's religious and secular works; elevator to the tower (about 200 ft.), 200Pts ($1.25). Apr–Aug, daily 9am–8pm; Mar and Sept, daily 9am–7pm; Oct–Feb, daily 9am–6pm. Metro: Sagrada Família.

An Ancient Neighborhood to Explore

The ✪ **Barri Gótic** is Barcelona's old aristocratic quarter, parts of which have survived from the Middle Ages. Spend at least 2 or 3 hours exploring the Gothic Quarter's narrow streets and squares. Start by walking up Carrer del Carme, east of Les Rambles. A nighttime stroll takes on added drama, but exercise extreme caution. The buildings, for the most part, are austere and sober, the cathedral being the crowning achievement. Roman ruins and the vestiges of 3rd-century walls add further interest. This area is intricately detailed and filled with many attractions that are easy to miss.

Gaudí's incomplete masterpiece is one of the most idiosyncratic works of architecture in the world. If you have time to see only one Catalan landmark, make it this one. Begun in 1882 and still incomplete at Gaudí's death in 1926, this incredible church—the Temple of the Holy Family—is a bizarre wonder. The languid, amorphous structure embodies the essence of Gaudí's style, which some have described as art nouveau run rampant. The spires—Gaudí planned to construct a total of 12 to reflect the 12 disciples—look a bit like dripping candles. Work continues on the structure but without any sure idea of what Gaudí intended, so disagreements are constant. The newest sculptures have provoked outrage among many art critics. Still, some predict that the church will be completed in the mid–21st century.

✪ **Museu Picasso.** Montcada 15–19. ☎ **93-319-63-10.** Admission 700Pts ($4.40) adults, 300Pts ($1.90) students, free for children 17 and under. Tues–Sat 10am–8pm, Sun 10am–3pm. Metro: Jaume I.

Two converted palaces on a medieval street have been turned into a museum housing works by Pablo Picasso, who donated some 2,500 of his paintings, engravings, and drawings to the museum in 1970. Picasso was particularly fond of Barcelona, where he spent much of his formative youth. In fact, some of the paintings were done when Picasso was 9. One portrait, from 1896, depicts his stern aunt, Tía Pepa. Another, completed at the turn of the century when Picasso was 16, depicts *Science and Charity* (his father was the model for the doctor). Many of the works, especially the early paintings, show the artist's debt to van Gogh, El Greco, and Rembrandt; a famous series, *Las Meninas* (1957), is said to "impersonate" the work of Velázquez. From his Blue Period, the *La Vie* drawings are perhaps the most interesting.

Parc Güell. ☎ **93-424-38-09.** Free admission. May–Sept, daily 10am–9pm; Oct–Apr, daily 10am to 6pm. Bus: 27, 60, 85, or 73.

This fanciful park on the northern tier of Barcelona's inner core is much more than green space. It was begun by Antoni Gaudí as a real-estate venture for a wealthy friend, Count Eusebi Güell, a well-known Catalan industrialist, but never completed. Only two houses were constructed, but Gaudí's whimsical creativity, seen in soaring columns that impersonate trees and splendid winding benches of broken mosaics, is on abundant display. The city took over the property in 1926 and turned it into a public park. The panoramic views are excellent.

MORE ATTRACTIONS

Monument à Colom (Columbus Monument). Portal de la Pau. ☎ **93-302-52-24.** Admission 250Pts ($1.60) adults, 150Pts (95¢) children 4–12, free for children 3 and under. Sept 25–May 31, Mon–Fri 10am–2pm and 3:30–6:30pm, Sat–Sun and holidays

10am–6:30pm; June 1–Sept 24, daily 9am–8:30pm. Closed Jan 1, Jan 6, and Dec 25–26. Metro: Drassanes. Bus: 14, 18, 36, 57, 59. 64.

This monument to Christopher Columbus was erected at Barcelona's harborfront on the occasion of the Universal Exhibition of 1888. It's divided into four parts: a plinth with bronze bas-reliefs depicting the principal feats of Columbus; the base of the column, consisting of an eight-sided polygon; the column itself, rising 50m (167 feet); and finally a 8m (25-foot) bronze statue of Columbus himself by Rafael Ataché. Inside the iron column, an elevator ascends to the mirador, where a panoramic view of Barcelona and its harbor unfolds.

Museu d'Art Contemporáreo de Barcelona (MACBA). Plaça de los Angels. ☎ **93-412-08-10.** Admission 750Pts ($4.70); 550Pts ($3.45) seniors and students, free ages 12 and under. Tues–Fri noon–8:30pm, Sat 10am–8pm, Sun 10am–3pm. Metro: Plaça de Catalunya.

A soaring, glistening edifice in Barcelona's Raval district, the Museum of Contemporary Art is to Barcelona what the Pompidou Center is to Paris. Designed by American architect Richard Meier, the building itself is a work of art, manipulating sunlight to offer brilliant natural interior lighting. On display in the 6,875 square meters (74,000 square feet) of exhibit space is the work of such modern luminaries as Tápies, Klee, Miró, and many others. The museum contains a library, bookshop, and cafeteria.

Poble Espanyol. Marqués de Comilias, Parc de Montjuïc. ☎ **93-325-78-66.** Village, 750Pts ($4.70) adults, 550Pts ($3.45) seniors, students, and children 7–11, free for children 6 and under; audiovisual hall, free. Mon 9am–8pm, Tues–Thurs 9am–2am, Fri–Sat 9am–4am, Sun 9am–midnight. Bus: 13 or 50.

In this re-created Spanish village, built for the 1929 World's Fair, various regional architectural styles are reproduced. The infrastructure is crumbling a bit and the format has grown stale and a bit corny, but it remains an enduring attraction nonetheless. There're 115 life-size reproductions of buildings and monuments, ranging from the 10th to the 20th century. The center of the village has an outdoor cafe. Shops sell crafts from all the provinces, and in some of them you can see artists at work, printing fabric or blowing glass. The village has 14 restaurants of varying styles, a dance club, and eight musical bars. The whole attraction is a lot more appealing at night.

ADDITIONAL MUSEUMS

Fundació Antoni Tàpies. Aragó 255. ☎ **93-487-03-15.** Admission 750Pts ($4.70) adults, 350Pts ($2.20) students and children 10–18, free for children 9 and under. Tues–Sun 11am–8pm. Metro: Passeig de Gràcia.

When it opened in 1990, this became Barcelona's third museum devoted to the work of a single artist. Antoni Tàpies probably has the greatest international renown of any living artist in Spain. In 1984 Tàpies set up the foundation bearing his name, and the city of Barcelona donated an ideal site near the Passeig de Gràcia in Eixample. One of Barcelona's landmark buildings, the splendid brick-and-iron structure was built between 1881 and 1884 by the Gaudí contemporary exponent of Catalán modernism, Lluís Domènech i Montaner. The core of the museum is a collection of works by Tàpies (most contributed by the artist), covering the stages of his career as it evolved into abstract expressionism.

Museu Barbier-Mueller Art Precolombí. Carrer de Montcada 14. ☎ **93-319-76-03.** Admission 500Pts ($3.15) adults, 250Pts ($1.60) students, free children under 12. Free admission on the first Sat of every month. Tues–Sat 10am–8pm, Sun and holidays 10am–3pm. Metro: Jaume. Bus: 14, 17, 19, 39, 40, 45, or 51.

Opened by Queen Sofia in the spring of 1997, this is one of the most prominent collections of pre-Columbian art in the world. Encased in the Palacio Nadal, built during the Middle Ages and restored, the collection contains almost 6,000 pieces of tribal or ancient art. Pre-Columbian cultures created religious, funerary, and ornamental objects of great stylistic variety with relatively simple means. They were especially outstanding in stone sculpture and ceramic objects. For example, the Olmecs, who settled on the coast of the Gulf of Mexico at the beginning of the first millennium B.C., executed notable monumental sculpture in stone and magnificent figures in jade. Rich in exhibits is the Mayan culture, the most homogenous and widespread of its time, its origins going back to 1000 B.C.

Museu de la Ciència (Science Museum). Teodoro Roviralta, 55. ☎ **93-212-60-50.** Admission to museum and planetarium, 550Pts ($3.45) adults, 350Pts ($2.20) children 16 and under. Museum only 400Pts ($2.50) adults, 250Pts ($1.60) children. Planetarium only 200Pts ($1.25). Tues–Sun 10am–8pm. Bus: 17, 22, 58, or 73.

The science museum's modern design and hands-on activities have made it a major cultural attraction. You can touch, listen, watch, and participate in a variety of hands-on exhibits designed to convey a sense of wonder about science and technology. From the beauty of life in the sea to the magic of holograms, the museum offers a world of science to discover. Watch the world turn beneath the Foucault pendulum, ride on a human gyroscope, hear a friend whisper from 18m (20 yards) away, feel an earthquake, or use the tools of a scientist to examine intricate life forms with microscopes and video cameras.

Museu Frederic Marés/Museu Sentimental. Plaça de Santa Iú 5–6. ☎ **93-310-58-00.** Admission (to both museums) 300Pts ($1.90), free for children 15 and under. Tues–Sat 10am–5pm, Sun 10am–2pm. Metro: Jaume I. Bus: 17, 19, or 45.

One of the biggest repositories of medieval sculpture in the region is the Frederic Marès Museum, just behind the cathedral. It's housed in an ancient palace whose interior courtyards, chiseled stone, and soaring ceilings are impressive in their own right, an ideal setting for the hundreds of polychrome sculptures. The sculpture section dates from pre-Roman times to the 20th century. Also housed here is the Museu Sentimental, a collection of everyday items that help to illustrate life in Barcelona during the past 2 centuries.

Museu Marítim. Av. de las Drassanes. ☎ **93-318-32-45.** Admission 800Pts ($5), 400Pts ($2.50) seniors and young adults 15–18, and children 14 and under are free. Apr–Oct Tues–Sun 10am–7pm, winter Tues–Sat 10am–6pm, Sun 10am–2pm. Closed holidays. Metro: Drassanes. Bus: 14, 18, 36, 38, or 57.

In the formal Royal Shipyards of the Drassanes Reials, this 13th-century civil Gothic complex was used for the construction of ships for the Catalan-Aragonese rulers. The most outstanding exhibition here is a reconstruction of *La Galería Real* of Don Juan of Austria, a lavish royal galley. Another special exhibit features a map by Gabriel de Vallseca that was owned by explorer Amerigo Vespucci.

Museu Nacional d'Art de Catalunya. Palau Nacional, Parc de Montjuïc. ☎ **93-622-03-06.** Admission 900Pts ($6) adults, 400Pts ($2.50) children 7–20, free children under 7. Tues–Wed and Fri–Sat 10am–7pm, Thurs 10am–9pm, Sun 10am–2:30pm. Metro: Espanya.

This recently reopened and redesigned museum is the world's major depository of Gothic and Romanesque Catalan art, a treasure trove of this important region of the world. More than 100 pieces, including sculptures, icons, and frescoes, are on display.

The highlight of the museum is the collection of murals from various Romanesque churches throughout Catalonia.

Museu d'Art Modern. Plaça do Armaj, Parque de la Ciudadela. ☎ **93-319-57-28.** Admission 500Pts ($3.15) adults, 250Pts ($1.60) students and seniors 65 and over, free for children 6 and under. Tues–Sat 10am–7pm, Sun 10am–2:30pm. Closed Jan 1 and Dec 25. Metro: Arc de Triomf. Bus: 14, 16, 17, 39, or 40.

This museum shares a wing of the Palau de la Ciutadela with the Catalonian Parliament. Constructed in the 1700s, it once formed part of Barcelona's defenses as an arsenal. Its collection of art focuses on the early 20th century and features the work of Catalan artists, including Martí Alsina, Vayreda, Casas, Fortuny, and Rusiñol. The collection also encompasses modernist furniture, including designs by architect Puig i Cadafalch.

PARKS & GARDENS

While Barcelona is not a city of abundant green space, most people head to the hills for a respite from the density and activity of the city below. The mountain park of **Montjuïc** has splashing fountains, gardens, outdoor restaurants, and museums. This is where the principal Olympic stadiums are located. The re-created village, the Poble Espanyol, and the Joan Miró Foundation are also in the park. There are many walks and vantage points for viewing the Barcelona skyline.

Another attraction, **Tibidabo Mountain,** offers the finest panoramic view of Barcelona. A funicular takes you up 490m (1,600 feet) to the summit. The funicular runs daily 7:15am to 9:45pm and costs 400Pts ($2.50) each way. The ideal time to visit this summit north of the port (the culmination of the Sierra de Collcerola) is at sunset, as the city lights begin to flicker. A slightly kitschy amusement park—with Ferris wheels that spin over Barcelona—has been here for years. There's also a church in this carnival-like setting called Santa Creu ("Sacred Heart"), plus restaurants and mountaintop hotels. From Plaça John Kennedy take the funicular uphill, or catch any of the buses from central Barcelona labeled TIBIDABO.

ORGANIZED TOURS

Pullmantur, Gran Vía de les Corts Catalánes 635 (☎ **93-317-12-97**), offers a morning tour departing from the terminal at the above address at 9:30am, taking in the cathedral, the Gothic Quarter, the Rambles, the monument to Columbus, and the Spanish Village and the Olympic Stadium. It costs 4,750Pts ($30). An afternoon tour leaves at 3:30pm, with visits to some of the most outstanding buildings in the Eixample, including Gaudí's Sagrada Família, Parc Güell, and a stop at the Picasso Museum. This tour costs 4,750Pts ($30). Pullmantur also offers several excursions into the environs. The daily tour of the monastery of Montserrat departs at 9:30am and returns to the city at 2:30pm. Tours include a visit to the Royal Basilica to view the famous sculpture of the Black Virgin. The tour returns to Barcelona to the harbor, where passengers have the option to remain for the afternoon. Tours cost 5,800Pts ($37).

Another company that offers tours of Barcelona and the surrounding countryside is **Juliatours,** Ronda Universitat 5 (☎ **93-317-64-54;** Metro: Universitat). Itineraries are similar to those above, with similar prices. One, the Visita Ciudad Artistica, offers a tour of Barcelona focusing on the city's artistic significance. Tours pass many of Gaudí's brilliant buildings, including La Sagrada Família. Also included are visits to the Museu Picasso or Museu d'Art Modern, depending on the day of your tour. Tours cost 4,700Pts ($30) and leave at 3:30pm and again at 7pm.

THE SHOPPING SCENE
THE BEST SHOPPING STREETS

The main shopping street in Barcelona is **Passeig de Gràcia.** Stroll this street from the Avinguda Diagonal to the Plaça de Catalunya, and you'll pass some of Barcelona's most elegant boutiques.

In the **old quarter,** the principal shopping streets are the Ramblas, Carrer del Pi, Carrer de la Palla, and Avenguda Portal de l'Angel. Moving north in the Eixample are Passeig de Catalunya, Passeig de Gràcia, and Rambla de Catalunya. Going even farther north, Avinguda Diagonal is a major shopping boulevard. Via Augusta is another prominent street.

Another shopping expedition is to the **Mercat de la Boquería,** Rambla, 101, near Carrer del Carme. Here you'll see a wide array of straw bags and regional products, along with handsome displays of fruits, vegetables, cheeses, meats, and fish.

THE BEST BUYS

Barcelona, a city of design and fashion, offers a wealth of shopping opportunities. In addition to modern, attractively designed, and stylish clothing, shoes, and decorative objects are often good buys. Designs for both women and men are sold at **Groc,** Ramble de Catalunya 100 (☎ **93-215-74-74;** Metro: Plaça de Catalunya). One of the most stylish shops in Barcelona, the Catalan designer Antonio Miró's shop is expensive but filled with high-quality apparel made from the finest of natural fibers. The men's store is downstairs, the women's store one flight up. Miró has a newer, fancier, and bigger store a few blocks down the Ramble, Consejo de Ciento 349 (☎ **93-487-06-70**).

Adolfo Dominguez, 32 Passeig de Gracia (☎ **93-487-41-70**), has been called "the Spanish Armani." Suits in earth tones for both men and women have a rather austere but very stylish look. One of the best showcases for Catalan fashion designers for women is **On Land,** 273 Carrer Valencia (☎ **93-215-56-25**). For designer housewares and the best in Spanish contemporary furnishings, your best bet is **Vincón,** Passeig de Gràcia, 96 (☎ **93-215-60-50**), housed in the former home of artist Ramón Casas.

In the city of Miró, Tàpies, and Picasso, **art** is a major business. You'll find dozens of galleries, especially in the Barri Gótic and around the Picasso Museum. In business since 1840, **Sala Parés,** Petritxol 5 (☎ **93-318-70-20;** Metro: Plaça de Catalunya), is one of the city's finest art galleries. Paintings are displayed in a two-story amphitheater; exhibitions change about once a month. Petritxol is one of the nicest shopping and strolling streets in the Gothic Quarter. At **Art Picasso,** Tapineria 10 (☎ **93-310-49-57;** Metro: Jaume I), you can get good lithographs of works by Picasso, Miró, and Dalí, as well as T-shirts with the designs of these masters and books. Tiles sold here often carry their provocatively painted scenes.

Unless you're seeking some specialty item, one of your best bets for **antiques** is **El Bulevard des Antiquarius,** Passeig de Gràcia, 55 (no central phone). This 70-unit complex, just off one of the city's most aristocratic avenues, has a huge collection of art and antiques assembled in a series of boutiques, and there's also a cafe-bar on the upper level. Most shoppers from abroad settle happily for **handcrafts,** and the city is rich in offerings, ranging from simple pottery to handmade furniture. Named after the Victorian English illustrator, **Beardsley,** Petritxol 12 (☎ **93-301-05-76;** Metro: Plaça de Catalunya), is on the same street where the works of Picasso and Dalí were exhibited before they became world famous. The wide array of gifts includes a little bit of everything from everywhere—dried flowers, writing supplies, silver dishes, unusual bags and purchases, and lots more.

At **Itaca,** Carrer Ferran 26 (☎ **93-301-30-44;** Metro: Liceu), you'll find a wide array of handmade pottery, not only from Catalonia but also from Spain, Portugal, Mexico, and Morocco. The merchandise has been selected for its basic purity, integrity, and simplicity. If your time and budget are limited, you may want to patronize Barcelona's major department store, **El Corte Inglés,** Plaça de Catalunya (☎ **93-302-12-12;** Metro: Plaça de Catalunya). The store sells everything from Spanish handcrafts to high-fashion items to Catalan records and food. The store also has restaurants and cafés and offers a number of consumer-related services, such as a travel agent. It will arrange for the mailing of purchases back home.

BARCELONA AFTER DARK

Your best source of information about the cornucopia known as Barcelona nightlife appears within either of two magazines, *Guia del Ocio,* and its less comprehensive counterpart, *La Semana de Barcelona.* The price of both publications is 125Pts (80¢). Both are in Spanish, but the listings seem to be worded in ways that even non-native speakers can benefit a lot from referring to them. Both publications are available at virtually every news kiosk along Les Rambles.

Culture and the arts are deeply ingrained in the Catalan soul. The performing arts are strong here—this is the city, after all, that produced the opera legends Plácido Domingo, José Carreras, and Montserrat Caballé. Other, more popular arts take place on the street, especially along Les Rambles, where crowds often gather around a singer or mime.

THE PERFORMING ARTS

Founded in 1847, **Gran Teatre del Liceu,** Rambla de Caputxins 61 (☎ **93-485-99-13**), was once one of the world's leading opera stages until destroyed by fire on January 31, 1997. When it burned, distraught crowds gathered outside on the Ramblas, and the singer Montserrat Caballé wept. Following a complete restoration, the theater reopened in 1999. The auditorium's appearance and its capacity of 2,320 seats is much the same as before. But many technical improvements have been made, including a modernized stage. It focuses on Opera, dance performances, concerts, and recitals. Box office hours open 1 hour before the presentation. Tickets cost from 2,000Pts to 28,000Pts ($12 to $168).

Mercat de Les Flors, Lleida 59 (☎ **93-426-18-75;** Metro: Plaça de Espanya), the other major Catalan theater, is housed in a building constructed for the 1929 International Exhibition at Montjuïc. Peter Brook used it for a 1983 presentation of *Carmen.* Innovators in drama, dance, and music are showcased here, as are modern dance companies from Europe, including troupes from Italy and France. The 999-seat house also contains a restaurant overlooking the rooftops of the city. Tickets are 2,000 to 3,000Pts ($13 to $19).

In a city of architectural highlights, ✪ **Palau de la Música Catalán,** Sant Francesc de Paula 2 (☎ **93-268-10-00;** Metro: Urquinaona), recently named to the roster of UNESCO World Heritage sites, stands out. In 1908, Lluís Doménech i Montaner, a Catalan architect, designed this fantastical modernist structure, including stained glass, ceramics, statuary, and ornate lamps. It stands today, restored, as a classic example of modernism. Classical concerts, leading recitals, and the occasional jazz and pop performance are presented here. The box office is open Monday to Friday 10am to 9pm and Saturday 3 to 9pm. Ticket prices depend on the presentation, usually 1,000 to 3,500Pts ($6 to $22).

FLAMENCO

El Tablao de Carmen, Poble Espanyol de Montjuïc (☎ 93-325-68-95; Metro: Plaça de Espanya, then a 10-minute walk), is the most durable of Barcelona's flamenco shows, with a reputation for authenticity and dancers who derive from Andalusia. It's set on the panoramic highlands of Montjuïc, within the Poble Espanyol compound. You can either eat dinner—traditional Catalan specialties—at tables set up in front of the stage, or dine elsewhere and opt just for a drink or two as the dancers clap and stamp. The club is open Tuesday to Sunday 8pm to midnight or later. During the week, they sometimes close around 1am, often staying open until 2 or 3am on week-ends (everything depends on business). The first show is always at 9:30pm, and sec-ond show Tuesday through Thursday and Sunday is at 11:30pm and on Friday and Saturday at midnight. Reservations are encouraged. Dinner and show are 7,800Pts ($49); show and one drink, 4,200Pts ($26).

At the southern end of Les Rambles, you'll hear the strum of the guitar, the sound of rhythmic hand clapping punctuated by staccato heels, and the haunting sound of the flamenco, a tradition since 1968 at **Tablao Flamenco Cordobés,** Les Rambles 35 (☎ 93-317-66-53; Metro: Drassanes or Liceu). Head upstairs to an Andalusian-style room where performances take place with the traditional *cuadro flamenco*—singers, dancers, and guitarist. Cordobés is said to be the best showcase for flamenco in Barcelona. November 1 to March 15 (except for 1 week in December), the show begins at 10pm. March 15 to October shows are offered nightly at 9:30 and 11:15, with meals beginning about an hour before show time. Reservations are required. Din-ner and show is 7,800Pts ($49); show and one drink, 4,200Pts ($26).

A CABARET

The ✪ **Bodega Bohemia,** Lancaster 2 (☎ 93-302-50-61; Metro: Liceu), off Les Rambles, is a Barcelona institution. This cabaret extraordinaire rates as high camp—a talent showcase for theatrical personalities whose joints aren't so flexible but who per-form with bracing dignity. Curiously, most audiences fill up with young people, who cheer, boo, catcall, and scream with laughter—and the old-timers on stage love it. In all, it's an incredible entertainment bargain if your tastes lean slightly to the bizarre. The street outside is none too safe; take a taxi right to the door. Open daily 11pm to 4am.

DANCE CLUBS

In the basement of a commercial-looking shopping center, **Bikini,** Deu I Mata 105 (☎ 093-322-00-05; Metro: Les Corts), is one of the most comprehensive and wide-ranging nightlife compounds in the city, with at least two venues for dancing in every conceivable genre (including funky, rock-and-roll, and golden-oldie music). There's a separate room for Puerto Rican salsa (the owners refer to it as a "salsoteca") and a very large area where fans of emerging musical groups applauds wildly to the music of their favorite band of the minute. The venue changes every night of the week, and has even been known to include sophisticated adaptations of conventional tango music. Open Monday to Thursday 7pm to 4:30am, Friday and Saturday 7pm to 6am. Cover is 1,000 to 2,500Pts ($6 to $16).

The chic atmosphere of **Up and Down,** Numancia Diagonal, 179 (☎ 93-205-51-94; Metro: María Cristina), attracts the elite of Barcelona, spanning a generation gap. The more mature patrons, specifically the black-tie, post-opera crowd, head for the upstairs section, leaving the downstairs to the loud music and "flaming youth." Up and Down is the most cosmopolitan disco in Barcelona, with a carefully planned ambience, impeccable service, and a welcoming atmosphere. Technically, this is a private club and you can be turned away at the door. The disco is open Tuesday to

Saturday from 12:30am to anytime between 5am and 6:30am, depending on business. Cover is 1,800 to 3,000Pts ($11 to $19), including first drink.

JAZZ & BLUES

Long beloved by jazz aficionados, **Barcelona Pipa Club,** Plaça Reial 3 (☎ 93-302-47-32; Metro: Liceu), is for pure devotees. Ring the buzzer and you'll be admitted (at least we hope you will) to a club reached after a climb of two flights up a seedy run-down building. A series of five rooms are decorated with displays or photographs of pipes—naturally Sherlock Holmes gets in on the act. Depending on the performer, music ranges from New Orleans jazz to Brazilian rhythms. Jazz is featured Thursday to Sunday 10pm to 5am, although the club with its comfortable bar is open daily during the same hours. Cover is 1,030Pts ($7).

In the heart of the Barric Gotic, **Jamboree,** Plaça Reial 17 (☎ 93-301-75-64; Metro: Liceu), has long been one of the city's premier venues for good blues and jazz. However, it varies its musical performances and doesn't feature jazz every night, perhaps a Latin dance band. Sometimes a world-class performer will appear here, but most likely it'll be a younger group. Shows are at midnight, and the club is open daily 9pm to 5am. Cover is 1,500Pts ($9).

CHAMPAGNE BARS

The Catalans call their own version of champagne *cava.* In Spanish, champagne bars are called *champanerías,* and in Catalán the name is *xampanyerías.* These Spanish wines are often excellent, said by some to be better than their French counterparts.

Located in an old part of Barcelona, **La Cava del Palau,** Verdaguer I Callis, 10 (☎ 93-310-07-22; Metro: Urquinaona), is a favorite of the after-concert crowd. Live music is sometimes presented, accompanied by a wide assortment of cheeses, cold cuts, pâtés, and fresh anchovies. It's open Monday to Friday 1:30 to 4pm and 8pm to 2am, Saturday 8pm to 2am.

Someone had to fashion a champagne bar after the Bogart-Bergman film, and **Xampanyería Casablanca,** Bonavista, 6 (☎ 93-237-63-99; Metro: Passeig de Gràcia), is it. Four kinds of house *cava* are served by the glass. The staff also serves a good selection of tapas, especially pâtés. The Casablanca is close to the Passeig de Gràcia. It's open Sunday to Thursday 6:45pm to 2:30am and Friday and Saturday 6:45pm to 3am.

GAY & LESBIAN CLUBS

Gay residents of Barcelona refer to **Chaps,** Av. Diagonal 365 (☎ 93-215-53-65; Metro: Diagonal), a saloon-style watering hole, as Catalonia's premier leather bar. However, the dress code usually steers more toward boots and jeans than leather and chains. Set behind a pair of swinging doors evocative of the old American West, Chaps contains two bar areas and is open daily 9pm to 3am.

Behind a pair of unmarked doors, in a neighborhood of art nouveau buildings, **Martin's Disco,** Passeig de Gràcia 130 (☎ 93-218-71-67; Metro: Passeig de Gràcia), is one of the more popular gay dance clubs in Barcelona. In a series of all-black rooms, you'll wander through a landscape of men's erotic art, upended oil drums (used as cocktail tables), and the disembodied front-end chassis of yellow cars set amid the angular surfaces of the drinking and dancing areas. Another bar supplies drinks to a large room where films are shown. Open daily midnight to 5am. Cover, including the first drink, is 1,000Pts ($6).

Santanassa, Carrer Aribau 27 (no phone: Metro: Universidad), is a regular staple on Barcelona's gay circuit, with a bar and dance floor along with provocative art, plus a clientele whose percentage of gay women has greatly increased in the past several years. However, gay males are still the dominant sex. Open nightly 11pm to 3am. Cover is 1,000Pts ($6), including your first drink, only on Friday and Saturday.

DAY TRIPS FROM BARCELONA

PENEDÉS WINERIES   From the Penedés wineries comes the famous *cava* (Catalan champagne), which you can sample in Barcelona's champagne bars. You can see where this wine originates by driving 40km (25 miles) from Barcelona via highway A-2, Exit 27. There're also daily trains from Barcelona-Sants to Sant Sadurní d'Anoia, home to 66 cava firms.

The winery best equipped to receive visitors is **Codorníu** (☎ **93-818-32-32**), the largest producer of cava—some 40 million bottles a year. Your best bet is to visit Codorníu by car because public transportation is unreliable. Tours, conducted Monday to Friday 9am to 5pm, are presented in English and take 1½ hours; they visit some of the 16km (10 miles) of underground cellars by electric cart. Take a sweater, even on a hot day. The tour ends with a cava tasting.

SITGES   One of the most frequented resorts of southern Europe, Sitges, 40km (25 miles) south of Barcelona, is the brightest spot on the Costa Dorada. It's crowded in summer, mostly with affluent young northern Europeans, many of them gay. For years the resort was patronized largely by prosperous middle-class industrialists from Barcelona, but those rather staid days have gone; Sitges is as lively today as Benidorm and Torremolinos down the coast, but it's nowhere near as tacky. It has earned a reputation as a gay resort, but the attitude is hardly in-your-face.

Sitges has long been known as a city of culture thanks in part to resident artist/playwright/Bohemian mystic Santiago Rusiñol. The 19th-century modernist movement largely began at Sitges, and the town remained the scene of artistic encounters and demonstrations long after modernism waned. Sitges continued as a resort of artists, attracting such giants as Salvador Dalí and the poet Federico García Lorca. Then the Spanish Civil War (1936–39) erased what has come to be called the "golden age" of Sitges.

Getting There   RENFE runs trains from Barcelona-Sants or Passeig de Gràcia to Sitges. Between 5:45am and 10pm daily, there's a train at the rate of one every 10 to 15 minutes (trip time: 40 minutes). Call ☎ **93-490-02-02** in Barcelona for information about schedules. A one-way ticket costs 305Pts ($1.90).

Sitges is a 45-minute drive from Barcelona along C-246, a coastal road. An express highway, A-7, opened in 1991. The coastal road is more scenic, but it can be extremely slow on weekends because of the heavy traffic, as all of Barcelona seemingly heads for the beaches.

The **tourist information office** is at Carrer Sínis Morera 1 (☎ **93-894-42-51**). Open June to September 15 daily 9am to 9pm; September 16 to May, Monday to Friday 9am to 2pm and 4 to 6:30pm, Saturday 10am to 1pm.

Exploring Sitges   It's the **beaches** that attract most visitors. They have showers, bathing cabins, and stalls. Kiosks rent such items as motorboats and air cushions for fun on the water. Beaches on the eastern end and those inside the town center are the most peaceful, including **Aiguadoiç** and **Els Balomins. Playa San Sebastián, Fragata Beach,** and **"Beach of the Boats"** (under the church and next to the yacht club) are the area's family beaches. Most young people go to the **Playa de la Ribera,** in the west.

Beaches aside, Sitges has a handful of interesting museums. The Catalán artist Santiago Rusiñol combined two 16th-century cottages to make the house that contains the **Museu Cau Ferrat,** Carrer del Fonollar (☎ **93-894-03-64**). He lived and worked here and upon his death in 1931 he willed it to Sitges along with his art collection. The museum collection includes two paintings by El Greco and several small Picassos, including *The Bullfight.* A number of Rusiñol's works are displayed. Admission is 500Pts ($3.15) for adults, 200Pts ($1.25) for students, and free for children 15 and under. A combination ticket to this museum and the two below is 700Pts ($4.40) for adults or 350Pts ($2.20) for students and children. All three museums keep the same hours: June 22 to September 10 Tuesday to Saturday 9:30am to 3pm and 4 to 9pm, Sunday 9:30am to 3pm. The rest of the year, hours are Tuesday to Friday 9:30am to 2pm and 4 to 6pm, Saturday 9:30am to 2pm and 4 to 8pm, and Sunday 9:30am to 3pm.

Opened by the king and queen of Spain, the **Museu Maricel,** Carrer del Fonallar (☎ 93-894-03-64), contains art donated by Dr. Jesús Pérez Rosales. The palace, owned by American Charles Deering when it was built right after World War I, is in two parts connected by a small bridge. The museum has a good collection of Gothic and Romantic paintings and sculptures, as well as many fine Catalán ceramics. There are also three noteworthy works by Rebull and an allegorical painting of World War I by Sert. Admission is 500Pts ($3.15) for adults, 250Pts ($1.60) for students, and free for children 15 and under. See Museu Cau Ferrat above for combination ticket and hours.

Museu Romàntic ("Can Llopis"), Sant Gaudenci 1 (☎ 93-894-29-69), re-creates the daily life of a Sitges landowning family in the 18th and 19th centuries. The family rooms, furniture, and household objects are most interesting. You'll also find wine cellars and an important collection of antique dolls (upstairs). Admission is 300Pts ($1.90) for adults, 150Pts (95¢) for students, and free for children 15 and under. See Museu Cau Ferrat above for combination ticket and hours.

MONTSERRAT   Lying 56km (35 miles) northwest of Barcelona, Montserrat ("the serrated mountain") is the most popular day excursion, though it's too crowded for Sunday visits. The winds blow cold at Montserrat, even in summer, so take along warm sweaters, jackets, or coats; in winter, thermal underwear might not be a bad idea.

Getting There   The best and most exciting way to go is via the Catalán railway— Ferrocarrils de la Generalitat de Catalunya (Manresa line), with five trains a day leaving from Plaça de Espanya in Barcelona. The central office is at Plaça de Catalunya 1 (☎ 93-205-15-15). The train connects with an aerial cableway (Aeri de Montserrat), included in the rail passage. Expect to spend 1,855Pts ($12), including the funicular.

Motorists can take N-2 southwest of Barcelona toward Tarragona, turning west at the junction with N-11. The signposts and exit to Montserrat will be on your right. From the main road, it's 14km (9 miles) to the monastery through dramatic scenery, with eerie rock formations.

The **tourist office** is at Plaça de la Creu (☎ 93-877-77-77), open daily 10am to 5:30pm.

Exploring Montserrat   Sitting atop a 1,210m (4,000-foot) mountain 11km (7 miles) long and 6km (3¹/₂ miles) wide, Montserrat is one of the most important pilgrimage spots in Spain. Thousands travel here every year to see and touch the 12th-century statue of **La Moreneta (The Black Virgin),** the patron saint of Catalonia. The 50-member ✪ **Escolanía** (boys' choir) is one of Europe's oldest and most renowned, dating from the 13th century. At 1pm daily, you can hear them singing "Salve Regina" and the "Virolai" (hymn of Montserrat) in the Nostra Senyora de Montserrat. The basilica is open daily 8 to 10:30am and noon to 6:30pm. Admission is free. To view the Black Virgin (12th- or 13th-century) statue, enter the church through a side door to the right. At Plaça de Santa María you can also visit the **Museu de Montserrat** (☎ 93-877-77-77), known for its collection of ecclesiastical paintings, including works by Caravaggio and El Greco. The museum is open Monday to Friday 9:30am to 6pm, Saturday and Sunday 9:30am to 6:30pm, charging 500Pts ($3.15) for adults or 250Pts ($1.60) for children and students.

Trains from Barcelona stop at the base of the mountain, where a 9-minute funicular ride takes you the final leg of the journey to the 1,255m (4,119-foot) peak, Sant Jeroni. The funicular operates every 20 minutes April to October, daily 10am to 6:40pm. The cost is included in the price of the train ride to Montserrat. From the top, you'll see not only all Catalonia but also the Pyrenees and the islands of Majorca and Ibiza.

3 Andalusia & the Costa del Sol

This once-great stronghold of Muslim Spain is incredibly rich in history and tradition, containing some of the country's most celebrated sightseeing treasures: the Mezquita (mosque) in Córdoba, the Alhambra in Granada, and the great Gothic cathedral in Seville. This is also the land of the famed *pueblos blancos* ("white villages") and interminable, undulating olive groves. Give Andalusia a week and you'll still have only skimmed the surface of its many offerings.

This dry, mountainous region also embraces the Costa del Sol (Málaga, Marbella, and Torremolinos are covered here), a popular beach strip of Spain. Go to the Costa del Sol for resorts, after-dark fun, and relaxation; visit Andalusia for its architectural wonders, beauty, and relaxed way of life.

The mild winter climate and almost-guaranteed sunshine in summer have made the razzle-dazzle Costa del Sol shoreline a year-round attraction. It begins at the western frontier harbor city of Algeciras and stretches east to the port city of Almería. Sandwiched between these points is a steep, rugged coastline, with poor-to-fair beaches, set against the Sierra Nevada. You'll find sandy coves, whitewashed houses, olive trees, lots of new apartment houses, fishing boats, golf courses, souvenir stands, fast-food outlets, and widely varied flora—both human and vegetable. From June to October the coast is mobbed, so make sure that you've nailed down a reservation.

A driving tour of Andalusia and the Costa del Sol can begin at the "gateway" city of Córdoba, 418km (260 miles) southwest of Madrid. The city lies astride NIV (E-5) connecting Madrid with Seville.

CÓRDOBA

Ten centuries ago Córdoba was one of the world's greatest cities. The capital of Muslim Spain, it was Europe's largest city (with a population of 900,000) and a cultural and intellectual center. This seat of the Western Caliphate flourished, constructing public baths, mosques, a great library, and palaces. But greedy hordes descended on the city, sacking ancient buildings and carting off art treasures. Despite these assaults, Córdoba retains traces of its former glory—enough to rival Seville and Granada as the most fascinating city in Andalusia.

Today this provincial capital is known chiefly for its mosque, but it abounds in other artistic and architectural riches, especially its domestic dwellings. The old Arab and Jewish quarters are famous for their narrow streets lined with whitewashed homes and flower-filled patios and balconies; it's perfectly acceptable to walk along gazing into the courtyards.

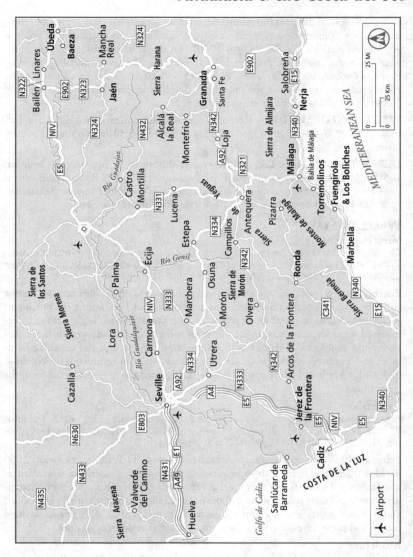

Andalusia & the Costa del Sol

MEDITERRANEAN SEA

25 Mi

25 Km

Úbeda
Baeza
Mancha Real
N324
Linares
Bailén
N322
E902
N323
Sierra Harana
Jaén
Salobreña
E902
E15
Nerja
Granada
Santa Fe
NIV
N324
N432
Alcalá la Real
Montefrío
N342
Loja
A92
Sierra de Almijara
Málaga
Bahía de Málaga
N340
E5
Castro
Río Guadajoz
Montilla
N331
Lucena
Yeguas
Antequera
N321
Torremolinos
Fuengirola
& Los Boliches
Estepa
N334
Campillos
Pizarra
Marbella
N340
Écija
Río Genil
Osuna
N342
Sierra de Morón
Ronda
Morón
N340
Palma
Marchena
Sierra de los Santos
Sierra Morena
Lora
Río Guadalquivir
Carmona
NIV
N333
Olvera
Arcos de la Frontera
C341
Sierra Bermeja
E15
Cazalla
N630
N334
Utrera
N333
N342
Seville
A92
A4
E5
Jerez de la Frontera
N340
E803
Sanlúcar de Barrameda
Costa de la Luz
Cádiz
NIV
E5
N435
Sierra Aracena
N433
Valverde del Camino
N431
A49
E1
Huelva
Golfo de Cádiz

✈ Airport

ESSENTIALS

GETTING THERE   Córdoba is a railway junction for routes to the rest of Andalusia and the rest of Spain. There're about 22 *talgo* and AVE trains daily between Córdoba and Madrid (trip time: 1¹/₂ to 2 hours). Other trains (*tranvías*) take 5 to 8 hours
for the same trip. There're also 25 trains from Seville every day (1¹/₂ hours). The main
rail station is on the town's northern periphery, at Av. de América 130, near the corner of Avenida de Cervantes. For information about **RENFE** services in Córdoba, call
☎ 957/40-02-02.

There're several different bus companies, each of which maintains a separate terminal. The town's most important bus terminal is at calle Torrito 10, one block south of Av. Medina Azahara, 29 (☎ 957-40-40-40), on the western outskirts of town (just west of the gardens beside Paseo de la Victoria). From the bus terminal operated by Empresa Bacoma, Av. de Cervantes, 22 (☎ 957-40-40-40), a short walk south of the railway station, there're three buses per day to Seville (trip time: 2 hours) and five daily buses to Jaén (3 hours). Buses arrive here from Madrid (5¹/₂ hours).

VISITOR INFORMATION   Córdoba's **tourist information office** is at Calle Torrijos 10 (☎ 957-47-12-35). Open Monday to Saturday 9:30am to 8pm and Sunday 10am to 2pm.

DEPARTING BY CAR   Take NIV toward Seville but try to stop over in Carmona, 105km (65 miles) to the southwest. Partially surrounded by its Roman walls, this is one of the most scenic towns in all of Andalusia. You can lunch here at the parador. After lunch, continue on NIV for another 39km (24 miles) into Seville.

WHERE TO STAY
Very Expensive
✪ **El Conquistador Hotel.** Magistral González Francés 15, 14003 Córdoba. ☎ **957-48-11-02.** Fax 957-47-46-77. 102 units. A/C TV TEL. 15,000Pts ($95) double; from 25,000Pts ($158) suite. AE, DC, MC, V. Parking 1,500Pts ($9). Bus: 12.

Benefiting from one of the most evocative locations in Córdoba, just across a narrow street from one side of the Mezquita, this hotel opened in 1986 within the much renovated premises of an interconnected pair of 19th-century villas. Triple rows of stone-trimmed windows and ornate iron balustrades shelter a marble-and-granite lobby that opens into an interior courtyard filled with seasonal flowers, a pair of splashing fountains, and a symmetrical stone arcade. The quality, size, and comfort of the rooms—each with a black-and-white marble floor—have earned the hotel four stars from the government.

Expensive
Parador Nacional de la Arruzafa. Av. de la Arruzafa 33, 14012 Córdoba. ☎ **957-27-59-00.** Fax 957-28-04-09. 96 units. A/C MINIBAR TV TEL. 17,500Pts ($110) double; 21,500Pts ($135) suite. AE, DC, MC, V. Free parking.

Lying 4km (2¹/₂ miles) outside town in the suburb of El Brillante, this circa 1960 parador (named after an Arab word meaning "palm grove") offers the conveniences and facilities of a luxurious resort hotel at reasonable rates. Built atop the foundations of a former caliphate palace, it's one of the finest paradors in Spain, with a view, a pool, and a tennis court. The spacious rooms have been furnished with fine dark-wood pieces, and some have balconies. The restaurant serves regional specialties.

Moderate
Hotel González. Manríquez 3, 14003 Córdoba. ☎ **957-47-98-19.** Fax 957-48-61-87. 17 units. A/C TV TEL. 7,500–9,500Pts ($47–$60) double; 11,000Pts ($69) triple; 19,000Pts ($120) quad. Rates include breakfast. AE, DC, MC, V. Parking 1,400Pts ($9).

Within walking distance of Córdoba's major monuments, the González is clean and decent but not a lot more. The hotel's the result of a radical reconstruction of a crumbling antique house that was so comprehensive that very little of the original core is still visible. Rooms are functionally furnished and comfortable. In the hotel restaurant, you can sample both regional and national specialties. Readers have praised the staff's attitude.

Sol Inn Gallos. Medina Azahara 7, 14005 Córdoba. ☎ **800/336-3542** in the U.S., or 957-23-55-00. Fax 957-23-16-36. 114 units. A/C TV TEL. 7,250Pts ($46) double; 9,250Pts ($58) triple. AE, DC, MC, V.

Half a block from a wide, tree-shaded boulevard on the western edge of town, this aging 1977 hotel stands eight floors high, crowned by an informal roof garden. The blandly international hotel is a favorite of groups and commercial travelers. The comfortable but small rooms have many extra comforts, such as balconies, and the outdoor pool is a pleasure during summer. The hotel also offers a restaurant, a drinking lounge, and a spacious lobby.

Inexpensive

Hostal el Triunfo. Corregidor Luís de la Cerda 79, 14003 Córdoba. ☎ **957-47-55-00.** Fax 957-48-68-50. 50 units. A/C TV TEL. 5,000Pts ($32) double; 6,500Pts ($41) triple. AE, DC, MC, V. Parking 1,500Pts ($9). Bus: 12.

Opposite the mosque and a block from the northern bank of the Guadalquivir River is a real find—a simple hotel with a formal entrance; a pleasant, white-walled lounge; and comfortable, well-furnished rooms. El Triunfo offers polite and efficient service. The three-floor hotel has no elevator; its only other drawback is that the bells of the Mezquita cathedral may make it difficult for one to sleep.

Hotel Riviera. Plaza de Aladreros 5, 14001 Córdoba. ☎ **957-47-30-00.** Fax 957-47-60-18. 30 units. A/C TV TEL. 3,700–4,500Pts ($23–$28) double; 5,500–6,500Pts ($35–$41) triple. AE, DC, V.

The genial owner of this 1978 hotel is likely to be behind the reception desk when you arrive. His establishment—on a triangular plaza in a commercial section of town a short walk south of the train station—offers very clean "no-frills" accommodations. No meals are served, but many cafes are within walking distance.

WHERE TO DINE
Moderate

✪ El Caballo Rojo. Cardinal Herrero 28, Plaza de la Hoguera. ☎ **957-47-53-75.** Reservations required. Main courses 1,200–2,500Pts ($8–$16). AE, DC, MC, V. Daily 1–4:30pm and 8pm–midnight. Bus: 12. SPANISH.

This restaurant is the most popular in Andalusia, and except for La Almudaina, it's Córdoba's best, though often overrun by tourists. The place has a noise level matched by no other restaurant in town, but the skilled waiters seem to cope with all demands. Within walking distance of the Mezquita in the old town, it's down a long open-air passage flanked with potted geraniums and vines. Try a variation on the usual gazpacho—almond-flavored broth with apple pieces. In addition to Andalusian dishes, the chef offers Sephardic and Mozarabic specialties, an example of the latter being monkfish with pine nuts, currants, carrots, and cream. Real aficionados come for the *rabo de toro* (stew made with the tail of an ox or a bull).

La Almudaina. Plaza de los Santos Mártires 1. ☎ **957-47-43-42.** Reservations required. Main courses 2,000–6,000Pts ($13–$38); fixed-price menu 1,500Pts ($9). AE, DC, MC, V. Mon–Sat noon–5pm and 8:30pm–midnight, Sun noon–5pm. Closed Sun July–Aug. Bus: 12. SPANISH/FRENCH.

Fronting the river in what used to be the Jewish Quarter, La Almudaina is one of the most attractive restaurants in Andalusia, where you can dine in one of the lace-curtained salons or on a glass-roofed central courtyard. Specialties include salmon crêpes; a wide array of fish, such as hake with shrimp sauce; and meats, such as pork loin in wine sauce. For dessert, try the not-too-sweet chocolate crepe. The cuisine's success is in its use of very fresh ingredients that are deftly handled by the kitchen.

Inexpensive

Restaurante Da Vinci. Plaza de los Chirinos 6. ☎ **957-47-75-17.** Reservations required. Main courses 1,200–2,200Pts ($8–$14); menú del día 1,100Pts ($7). V. Daily 1:30–4:30pm and 8pm–midnight. ITALIAN/INTERNATIONAL.

This ranks as one of the leading restaurants in town. Although it's not as highly rated as those above, for value it has both of them beat. Both the cuisine and the decor are a blend of Andalusian, international, and Italian influences. Menu items include a choice of roast meats (veal, pork, beefsteak, and lamb), a selection of pastas and salads, and many kinds of fish and seafood, especially hake, monkfish, squid, and salmon. This is standard Andalusian fare, with no innovation and little flair, but it's still good.

EXPLORING CÓRDOBA

✪ **Alcázar de los Reyes Cristianos.** Amador de los Ríos. ☎ **957-42-01-51.** Admission 425Pts ($2.70) adults, 150Pts (95¢) children. May–Sept, Tues–Sat 10am–2pm and 6–8pm, Sun 10am–3pm; Oct–Apr, Tues–Sat 9:30am–3pm and 4:30–6:30pm, Sun 9:30am–3pm. Bus: 3 or 12.

Commissioned in 1328 by Alfonso XI (the "Just"), the Alcázar de los Reyes Cristianos (Alcázar of the Christian Kings), is a fine example of military architecture. Ferdinand and Isabella governed Castile from this fortress on the river as they prepared to reconquer Granada, the last Moorish stronghold in Spain. Columbus journeyed here to fill Isabella's ears with his plans for discovery. Two blocks southwest of the mosque, the quadrangular building is notable for powerful walls and a trio of towers: the Tower of the Lions, the Tower of Allegiance, and the Tower of the River. The Tower of the Lions contains intricately decorated ogival ceilings that are the most notable example of gothic architecture in Andalusia. The beautiful gardens (illuminated May to September, Tuesday to Saturday 10pm to 1am) and the Moorish bathrooms are celebrated attractions. The Patio Morisco is a lovely spot, its pavement decorated with the arms of León and Castile.

✪ **Mezquita-Catedral de Córdoba.** Calle Cardenal Herrero. ☎ **957-47-05-12.** Admission 750Pts ($4.70) adults, 375Pts ($2.35) children 12 and under. Daily May–Sept 10am–7pm, Oct–Apr 10am–6pm. Bus: 3 or 12.

Dating from the 8th century, the mosque here was the crowning Muslim architectural achievement in the West, rivaled only by the one at Mecca. Córdoba's is a fantastic labyrinth of red-and-white-striped pillars. To the astonishment of visitors, a cathedral sits awkwardly in the middle of the mosque, disturbing the purity of the lines. The 16th-century cathedral, a blend of many styles, is impressive in its own right, with an intricately carved ceiling and baroque choir stalls. Additional ill-conceived annexes later turned the mezquita into an architectural oddity. Its most interesting feature is the mihrab, a domed shrine of Byzantine mosaics that once housed the Koran. After exploring the interior, stroll through the Courtyard of the Orange Trees, which has a beautiful fountain.

Museo de Bellas Artes de Córdoba. Plazuela del Potro 1. ☎ **957-47-33-45.** Admission 250Pts ($1.60), free for children 11 and under. June 15–Sept 15, Tues–Sat 10am–2pm and 5–7pm, Sun 10am–1:30pm; Sept 16–June 14, Tues–Sat 10am–2pm and 5–7pm, Sun 10am–1:30pm. Bus: 3 or 4.

Housed in an old hospital, the Fine Arts Museum contains medieval Andalusian paintings, examples of Spanish baroque art, and works by many of Spain's important 19th- and 20th-century painters, including Goya. The museum is east of the Mezquita, about a block south of the Church of St. Francis (San Francisco).

Museo Municipal de Arte Taurino. Plaza de las Bulas (also called Plaza Maimónides. ☎ **957-20-10-56.** Admission 425Pts ($2.70), free for children 17 and under 1. May–Sept, Tues–Sat 10:30am–2pm and 6–8pm, Sun 9:30am–3pm; Oct–Apr, Mon–Sat 10am–2pm and 5–7pm, Sun 9:30am–3pm. Bus: 3 or 12.

Memorabilia of great bullfights are housed in this museum, a 16th-century building in the Jewish Quarter, inaugurated in 1983. Its ample galleries recall Córdoba's great bullfighters with "suits of light," pictures, trophies, posters, even stuffed bulls' heads. You'll see Manolete in repose and the blood-smeared uniform of El Cordobés—both of these famous matadors came from Córdoba.

THE SHOPPING SCENE

The largest and most comprehensive association of craftspeople in Córdoba is **Arte Zoco,** on calle de los Júdios (no phone). Opened in the Jewish quarter as a business cooperative in the mid-1980s, it assembles the creative output of about a half dozen artisans, whose media include leather, wood, silver, crystal, terra-cotta, and iron. Some of the artisans maintain on-premises studios, which you can visit to check out the techniques and tools they use to pursue their crafts. The center is open Monday to Friday 9:30am to 8pm and Saturday and Sunday 9:30am to 2pm. The workshops and studios of the various artisans open and close according to the whims of their occupants but are usually open Monday to Friday 10am to 2pm and 5:30 to 8pm.

At **Meryan,** Calleja de las Flores 2 (☎ **957-47-59-02**), you can see artisans plying their ancient craft of leather-making in a 250-year-old building. Most items must be custom ordered, but there're some ready-made pieces for sale, including cigarette boxes, jewel cases, attaché cases, book and folio covers, and ottoman covers. Meryan is open Monday to Friday 9am to 8pm and Saturday 9am to 2pm.

SEVILLE

Seville, the capital of Andalusia, is justly famous for its beauty and romance. It lies 550km (341 miles) southwest of Madrid and 217km (135 miles) northwest of Málaga. In spite of the sultry (some would say oppressive) heat in summer and its many problems, such as rising unemployment and street crime, it remains one of the most charming Spanish cities. Don Juan, Carmen, and that wily barber, Figaro—aided by Mozart, Bizet, and Rossini—have given Seville a romantic reputation it seems unable to live down. If a visitor can see only two Spanish cities in a lifetime, they ought to be Seville and Toledo.

Unlike most Spanish cities, Seville has fared well under most of its conquerors—the Romans, Arabs, and Christians. When Spain entered its 16th-century golden age, Seville funneled gold from the New World into the rest of the country. Columbus docked here after his journey to America.

ESSENTIALS

GETTING THERE   From Seville's **San Pablo Airport,** calle Almirante Lobo (☎ **95-467-29-81**), 10km (6 miles) north of the center of Seville, beside the highway leading to and signposted to Carmona, Iberia flies several times a day to and from Madrid and Barcelona, with routes from here fanning out across the world. A bus, identified by the sign AE (*Aeropuerto*), runs at frequent intervals between the airport, the bus station, and strategic points within the city center. Train service into Sevilla is now centralized into the Estación Santa Justa, Avenida Kansas City (☎ **95-454-02-02** for information and reservations). Buses C1 and C2 travel between the railway station and the town's bus station at Prado de San Sebastian.

The high-speed AVE train between Madrid and Seville charges between 7,000 and 9,500Pts ($44 and $60) each way, depending on when you travel (trip time: 2¹/₂ hours). It makes 14 cross-country runs a day, with a stop in Córdoba. Between Seville and Córdoba, the AVE train takes 50 minutes, the *talgo* train 1¹/₂ hours, and conventional trains, which charge 980Pts ($6) each way between the two Andalusian cities, about 2 hours each way, with many stops en route.

Most buses arrive and depart from the city's largest **bus terminal,** on the southeast edge of the old city, at Prado de San Sebastián, calle José María Osborne 11 (☎ **95-441-71-11**). Many lines also converge on Plaza de la Encarnación, on Plaza Nueva, in front of the cathedral on Avenida Constitución, and at Plaza de Armas (across the street from the old train station, Estación de Córdoba). From here, buses from several companies make frequent runs to and from Córdoba (trip time: 2¹/₂ hours). For information and prices, call **Alsina Graells** at ☎ **95/441-88-11.**

VISITOR INFORMATION   The tourist office, **Oficina de Información del Turismo,** at Av. de la Constitución 21B (☎ **95-422-14-04**), is open Monday to Saturday 9am to 7pm and Sunday and holidays 10am to 2pm.

DEPARTING BY CAR   After Seville, the next major city of interest in Andalusia is Granada. To get there, you can drive along one of Europe's most fabled beach strips, the Costa del Sol, beginning at Marbella, the chicest enclave. Take A-4 (E-5) south toward Cádiz, bypassing the city by going along NIV, where you connect with N340 heading southeast. This coastal road will take you past Algeciras and Gibraltar and through the resort of Estepona until you reach Marbella.

WHERE TO STAY
Very Expensive
✪ **Hotel Alfonso XIII.** San Fernando 2, 41004 Sevilla. ☎ **800/221-2340** in the U.S. and Canada, or 95-422-28-50. Fax 95-421-60-33. www.ittsheraton.com. 146 units. A/C MINIBAR TV TEL. 35,000–45,000Pts ($221–$284) double; from 60,000–95,000Pts ($378–$599) suite. AE, DC, MC, V. Parking 2,750Pts ($17).

At the southwestern corner of the gardens fronting Seville's famous Alcázar, this turn-of-the-century rococo monument is a legendary hotel and Seville's premier address. Now under the management of the luxury division of Sheraton, the ITT group, it reigns supreme in Seville as a bastion of glamour. Built in the Mudéjar/Andalusian Revival style, it contains halls that glitter with hand-painted tiles, acres of marble and mahogany, antique furniture embellished with intricately embossed leather, and a spacious floor plan that are nothing short of majestic. The San Fernando restaurant offers Italian/continental cuisine.

Expensive
Hoel Inglaterra. Plaza Nueva 7, 41001 Sevilla. ☎ **95-422-49-70.** Fax 95-456-13-36. 116 units. A/C TV TEL. May–Mar, 15,000-20,000Pts ($95–$126) double. Apr, 25,000–29,000Pts ($158–$183) double. AE, DC, MC, V. Parking 1,500Pts ($9).

Opened in 1857 and since modernized into a glossy seven-story contemporary design, this eminently respectable and rather staid hotel lies a 5-minute walk southwest of the cathedral. Much of its interior is sheathed with white and gray marble, and the furnishings include ample use of Spanish leather and floral-patterned fabrics. Rooms still have old-fashioned touches of Iberian gentility; the best are on the fifth floor. The sunny restaurant serves well-prepared fixed-price meals from a frequently changing international menu.

Moderate
Bécquer. Calle de los Reyes Católicos 4, 41001 Sevilla. ☎ **95-422-89-00.** Fax 95-421-44-00. 118 units. A/C TV TEL. 15,000Pts ($95) double. AE, DC, MC, V. Parking 1,500Pts ($9). Bus: 21, 31, 32, or 33.

Seville

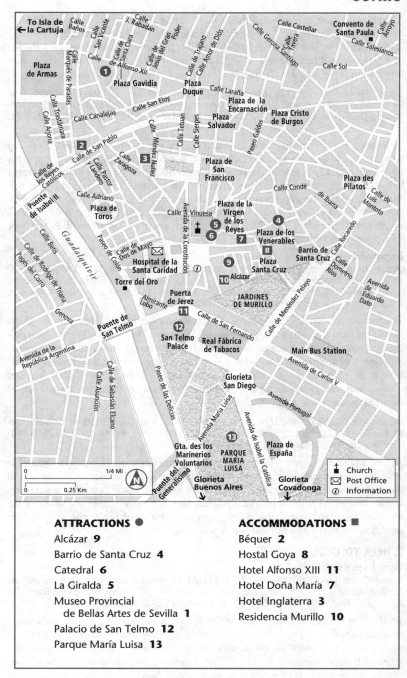

ATTRACTIONS ●

Alcázar **9**

Barrio de Santa Cruz **4**

Catedral **6**

La Giralda **5**

Museo Provincial
de Bellas Artes de Sevilla **1**

Palacio de San Telmo **12**

Parque María Luisa **13**

ACCOMMODATIONS ■

Béquer **2**

Hostal Goya **8**

Hotel Alfonso XIII **11**

Hotel Doña María **7**

Hotel Inglaterra **3**

Residencia Murillo **10**

A short walk from the action of the Seville bullring (Maestranza) and only 2 blocks from the river, the Bécquer lies on a street of cafes where you can order tapas and drink Andalusian wine. The Museo de Bellas Artes also is nearby. The hotel occupies the site of a mansion and retains many objets d'art rescued before that building was demolished. Rooms are functionally furnished, well kept, and reasonably comfortable.

Hotel Doña María. Don Remondo 19, 41004 Sevilla. ☎ **95-422-49-90.** Fax 95-421-95-46. 69 units. A/C TV TEL. Mar–June and Sept–Dec 15,000–25,000Pts ($95–$158) double; Jan–Feb and July–Aug 11,000Pts ($69) double. AE, DC, MC, V. Parking 2,000Pts ($13).

Its location a few steps from the cathedral creates a dramatic view from the rooftop terrace. Originally built in 1969, this well-conceived four-star four-story hotel has since been radically upgraded. Tasteful Iberian antiques fill the stone lobby and upper halls. The ornate neoclassical entry is offset with a pure-white facade and iron balconies. Amid the flowering plants on the upper floor, you'll find a pool ringed with garden-style lattices and antique wrought-iron railings. Each of the one-of-a-kind rooms is well furnished and comfortable, though some are rather small. A few have four-poster beds; others, a handful of antique reproductions.

Inexpensive

Hostal Goya. Mateus Gago 31, 41004 Sevilla. ☎ **95-421-11-70.** Fax 95-456-02-88. 20 units (10 with bathrooms). Jan–Mar and May–Dec 5,990Pts ($38) double without bathroom, 6,400Pts ($40) double with bathroom. Apr 7,000Pts ($44) double without bathroom, 8,000Pts ($50) double with bathroom. No credit cards.

The location of this 1960s-era hotel, within a narrow-fronted building in the oldest part of the barrio, is one of the Goya's strongest virtues. The building's ornate iron railings and old-fashioned Andalusian-style facade conceal rooms that, although extremely simple and spartan, and without TV or phone, can be cozy nonetheless. Guests congregate in the marble-floored salon, where a skylight floods the slightly battered couches and chairs with sunlight. There's no restaurant on the premises, but lots of cafes nearby serve morning coffee.

Residencia Murillo. Calle Lope de Rueda 7–9, 41004 Sevilla. ☎ **95-421-60-95.** Fax 95-421-96-16. 57 units. TEL. 5,000–7,000Pts ($32–$44) double; 8,000–10,000Pts ($50–$63) triple. AE, DC, MC, V. Parking 2,000Pts ($13) nearby.

Tucked away on a narrow street in the heart of Santa Cruz, the old quarter, the 1950s style Murillo (named after the artist who used to live in this district) is almost next to the Alcázar's gardens. Inside, the lounges have some fine architectural characteristics and antique reproductions; behind a grilled screen is a retreat for drinks. Many of the rooms we inspected were cheerless and gloomy, so have a look before checking in. Like all of Seville's hotels, the Murillo is in a noisy area.

WHERE TO DINE
Very Expensive

Egaña Oriza. San Fernando 41. ☎ **95-422-72-11.** Reservations required. Main courses 3,000–6,000Pts ($19–$38). AE, DC, MC, V. Mon–Fri 1:30–4pm and 9–midnight, Sat 9–11:30pm. (Bar, daily 9am–midnight.) Closed Aug. BASQUE/INTERNATIONAL.

Seville's best restaurant lies in a mansion built as a showplace for the city's 1929 international exposition. The restaurant is one of the few that specializes in game in Andalusia—a province that's otherwise devoted to seafood. The restaurant was established by Basque-born owner/chef José Mari Egaña, who managed to combine his passion for hunting with his flair for cooking his catch. Many of the raw ingredients that go into the dishes were trapped or shot in Andalusia. Try the salad of wild partridge, casserole of wild boar with cherries and raisins, quenelles of duck in a potato nest with apple puree, rice with stewed thrush, hake cooked in a salt crust, or even woodcock flamed in Spanish brandy.

Expensive

Casa Robles. Calle Alvarez Quintero 58. ☎ **95-421-31-50.** Reservations recommended. Main courses 1,000–3,000Pts ($6–$19); fixed-price menus 3,500–5,000Pts ($22–$32). AE, DC, MC, V. Daily 1–4:30pm and 8pm–1am. ANDALUSIAN.

This restaurant began its life as an unpretentious bar/bodega in 1954 and developed into a courteous but bustling dining hall on two floors of a building a short walk from the cathedral. Amid an all-Andalusian decor, you can enjoy some surprisingly complicated dishes, most of them flavorful and well prepared, in a setting that retains touches of old-fashioned formality. Menu items include fish soup in the Andalusian style, *lubina con naranjas* (sea bass with Sevillana oranges); a suprême of hake garnished with clams, shrimp, and strips of Serrano ham; and fillet of beef layered with foie gras.

Moderate

✪ **Enrique Becerra.** Gamazo 2. ☎ **95-421-30-49.** Reservations recommended. Main courses 2,000–3,500Pts ($13–$22). AE, DC, MC, V. Mon–Sat 1–5pm and 8pm–midnight. ANDALUSIAN.

Off Plaza Nueva and near the cathedral, this restaurant has flourished since 1979 and might provide one of your best meals in Seville. The restaurant takes its name from its owner, a smart and helpful host. A popular tapas bar and Andalusian dining spot, it offers an intimate setting and a hearty welcome. The gazpacho here is among the city's best, and the sangría is served ice cold. Specialties include hake real, sea bream Bilbaon style, rockfish cooked in Amontillada sherry, and oxtail braised in red wine. Many vegetarian dishes are also featured.

Inexpensive

Hostería del Laurel. Plaza de los Venerables 5, 41001 Sevilla. ☎ **95-422-02-95.** Reservations recommended. Main courses 850–2,500Pts ($5–$16). AE, DC, MC, V. Daily noon–4pm and 7:30pm–midnight. ANDALUSIAN.

In one of the most charming buildings on tiny, difficult-to-find Plaza de los Venerables in the labyrinthine Barrio de Santa Cruz, this hideaway restaurant has iron-barred windows stuffed with plants. Some kind of inn has been functioning within this antique building since the 1600s, and as such, it's one of the oldest restaurants in the city. Many diners delay their entrance into the plant-filled dining room until after a round of drinks—preferably sherry—at the beamed and smoke-stained tapas bar. Fish and grilled meats are typical of the region, and served in generous portions.

EXPLORING SEVILLE

✪ **Alcázar.** Plaza del Triunfo. ☎ **95-450-23-23.** Entrance is north of the cathedral. Admission 700Pts ($4.40). Apr–Sept, Tues–Sat 9:30am–8pm, Sun 9:30am–6pm. Oct–Mar, Tues–Sat 9:30am–6pm, Sun 9:30am–2:30pm.

A magnificent 14th-century Mudéjar palace, the Alcázar, the oldest royal residence in Europe still in use, was built by Pedro the Cruel. From the Dolls' Court to the Maidens' Court through the domed Ambassadors' Room, it contains some of the finest work of Sevillian artisans. In many ways it evokes the Alhambra at Granada. Ferdinand and Isabella, who at one time lived in the Alcázar, welcomed Columbus here on his return from America. On the top floor, the Oratory of the Catholic Monarchs has a fine altar in polychrome tiles made by Pisano in 1504.

✪ **Catedral.** Plaza del Triunfo, Av. de la Constitución. ☎ **95-421-49-71.** Admission, including Giralda Tower, 700Pts ($4.40), 200Pts ($1.25) children and students (free 12 and under). Mon–Sat 11–5pm, Sun 2–6pm.

The largest Gothic building in the world, Seville's cathedral was designed by builders with a stated goal—that "those who come after us will take us for madmen." Construction began in the late 1400s and took centuries to complete. Built on the site of an ancient mosque, the cathedral claims to contain the remains of Columbus, with his tomb mounted on four statues.

Works of art abound, many of them architectural, such as the 15th-century stained-glass windows, the iron screens (*rejas*) closing off the chapels, the elaborate 15th-century choir stalls, and the Gothic reredos above the main altar. Emerge into the sunlight in the Patio of Orange Trees, with its fresh citrus scents and chirping birds.

✪ **La Giralda.** Plaza del Triunfo. Entrance through the cathedral (admission is included with cathedral).

Just as Big Ben symbolizes London, La Giralda conjures up Seville. This Moorish tower, next to the cathedral, is the city's most famous monument. Erected as a minaret in the 12th century, it has seen later additions, such as 16th-century bells. To climb it is to take the walk of a lifetime. There're no steps—you ascend an endless ramp. If you make it to the top, you'll have a dazzling view of Seville.

Museo Provincial de Bellas Artes de Sevilla. Plaza del Museo 9. ☎ **95-422-18-29.** Admission 250Pts ($1.60), free for students. Tues 3–8pm, Wed–Sat 9am–8pm, Sun 9am–3pm. Bus: 21, 24, 30, or 31.

A lovely old convent off calle de Alfonso XII, this museum houses an important Spanish art collection. Some art experts claim that after the two leading art museums of Madrid, this is the most valuable and significant repository of art in Spain. A whole gallery is devoted to two paintings by El Greco, and works by Zurbarán are exhibited; however, the devoutly religious paintings of the Seville-born Murillo are the highlights. An entire wing is given over to macabre paintings by the 17th-century artist Valdés-Leál. The top floor, which displays modern paintings, is less interesting.

SHOPPING

Artesanía Textil, calle Sierpes 70 (☎ **95-456-28-40**), specializes in the nubbly and roughly textured textiles, including linens and embroidery, that reflect the earthiness of contemporary Spanish art. Weavings (some of which use linen, others the rough fibers of Spanish sheep) are the specialty here.

Close to Seville's town hall, **Ceramics Martian,** calle Sierpes 74 (☎ **95-421-34-13**), sells a wide array of painted tiles and ceramics, all made in or near Seville. Many of the pieces exhibit ancient geometric patterns of Andalusia. Near the cathedral, **El Postigo,** calle Arfe (☎ **95-456-00-13**), contains one of the biggest selections in town of the ceramics for which Andalusia is famous. Some of the pieces are much, much too big to fit into your suitcase; others—especially the hand-painted tiles—make charming souvenirs that can be packed with your luggage.

Carmen fluttered her fan and broke hearts in ways that Andalusian maidens have done for centuries. **Casa Rubio,** calle Sierpes 56 (☎ **95-422-68-72**), stocks a large collection of fans and castanets that range from the austere or dramatic to some of the most florid and fanciful aids to coquetry available in Spain.

SEVILLE AFTER DARK

In the 1990s Seville finally got its own opera house, **Teatro de la Maestranza,** Núñez de Balboa (☎ **95-422-65-73**), which quickly became a premier venue for world-class

Don't-Miss Strolls: The Barrio de Santa Cruz & Parque María Luisa

What was once a ghetto for Spanish Jews, who were forced out of Spain in the 15th century in the wake of the Inquisition, the ✪ **Barrio de Santa Cruz** today is Seville's most colorful district. Near the old walls of the Alcázar, winding medieval streets with names like Vida (Life) and Muerte (Death) open onto pocket-size plazas. Balconies with draping bougainvillea and potted geraniums jut out over this labyrinth, and through numerous wrought-iron gates you can glimpse patios filled with fountains and plants. To enter the Barrio Santa Cruz, turn right after leaving the Patio de Banderas exit of the Alcázar. Turn right again at Plaza de la Alianza and go down calle Rodrigo Caro to Plaza de Doña Elvira. Use caution when strolling through the area, particularly at night; many robberies have occurred here.

About a 7-minute walk northeast of the cathedral on the northern edge of the Barrio de Santa Cruz is the **Casa de Pilatos,** Plaza Pilatos, 1 (☎ **95/422-50-55**). This 16th-century palace of the dukes of Medinaceli recaptures the splendors of the past, combining Gothic, Mudéjar, and plateresque styles in its courtyards, fountains, and salons. Don't miss the two old carriages or the rooms filled with Greek and Roman statues. Admission to the museum is 1,000Pts ($7), the patios and gardens 500Pts ($3.50). The museum is open daily 10am to 2pm and 4pm to 6pm; patio and gardens, daily 9am to 7pm.

Parque María Luisa, dedicated to María Luisa, sister of Isabella II, was once the grounds of the Palacio de San Telmo, Avenida de Roma. Its baroque facade visible behind the deluxe Alfonso XIII Hotel, the palace today houses a seminary. The former private royal park is now open to the public. Running south along the Guadalquivir River, the park attracts those who want to take boat rides, walk along paths bordered by flowers, jog, or go bicycling. The most romantic way to traverse it is by rented horse and carriage, but this can be expensive, depending on your negotiation with the driver. Exercise caution while walking through this park as many muggings have been reported.

---

operatic performances. Jazz, classical music, and even the quintessentially Spanish zarzuelas (operettas) are also performed here. The opera house can't be visited except during performances. The box office is open daily 11am to 2pm and 5 to 8pm. Tickets vary in cost depending on the attraction.

In central Seville on the riverbank between two historic bridges, ✪ **El Patio Sevillano,** Paseo de Cristóbal Colón 11 (☎ **95-421-41-20**), is a showcase for Spanish folk song and dance, performed by exotically costumed dancers. The presentation includes a wide variety of Andalusian flamenco and songs, as well as classical pieces by composers like Falla, Albéniz, Granados, and Chueca. Three shows are presented nightly at 7:30, 10, and 11:45pm. From November to February there're only two shows nightly at 7:30 and 10pm. Admission, including one drink, is 3,800Pts ($24).

MARBELLA

Though it's packed with tourists, ranking just behind Torremolinos in popularity, Marbella is still the most exclusive resort along the Costa del Sol—with such bastions of posh as the Marbella Club. Despite the hordes, Marbella remains a pleasant

Andalusian town at the foot of the Sierra Blanca, 80km (50 miles) east of Gibraltar and 76km (47 miles) east of Algeciras, or 600km (373 miles) south of Madrid.

Traces of the past are found in its palatial town hall, its medieval ruins, and its ancient Moorish walls. Marbella's most charming area is the **old quarter,** with narrow cobblestone streets and Arab houses, centering around Plaza de los Naranjos.

The biggest attractions in Marbella, however, are **El Fuerte** and **La Fontanilla,** the two main beaches. There are other, more secluded beaches, but you need your own transportation to get to them.

ESSENTIALS

GETTING THERE   Twenty buses run between Málaga and Marbella daily, plus three buses that come in from Madrid and another three from Barcelona.

VISITOR INFORMATION   The **tourist office** is on Glorieta de la Fontanilla (☎ **95-277-14-42**), open April to October, Monday to Friday 9:30am to 9pm and Saturday 10am to 2pm. Another **tourist office** is on Plaza Naranjos (☎ **95-282-35-50**), keeping the same hours.

DEPARTING BY CAR   From Marbella, it's just a short drive east along E-15 to Fuengirola, though traffic tends to be heavy.

WHERE TO STAY

Hostal El Castillo. Plaza San Bernabé 2, 29600 Marbella. ☎ **95-277-17-39.** 26 units. 3,500–5,000Pts ($22–$32) double. MC, V.

This small 1960s hotel is at the foot of the castle in the narrow streets of the old town. The spartan rooms are scrubbed clean and look out onto a small, covered courtyard. No meals are served, but many cafes, suitable for breakfast, lie nearby.

Hotel El Fuerte. Av. del Fuerte, 29600 Marbella. ☎ **800/448-8355** in the U.S., or 95-286-15-00. Fax 95-282-44-11. 263 units. A/C MINIBAR TV TEL. 11,000–21,000Pts ($69–$132) double; from 25,000Pts ($158) suite. AE, DC, MC, V. Parking 650Pts ($4.10).

El Fuerte is the largest and most recommendable hotel in the center of Marbella. An underground tunnel leads beneath an all-pedestrian traffic-free promenade to the sands of the beach. Built in 1957, it was last renovated in 1994. It caters to a sedate clientele of conservative northern Europeans. There's a palm-fringed pool across the street from a sheltered lagoon and a wide-open beach. The hotel offers a handful of terraces, some shaded by flowering arbors.

Los Monteros. Carretera de Cádiz, km 187, 29600 Marbella. ☎ **95-277-17-00.** Fax 95-282-37-21. 180 units. A/C MINIBAR TV TEL. 20,000–28,000Pts ($126–$176) double; from 35,000Pts ($221) suite. Rates include breakfast. AE, DC, MC, V. Free parking.

Los Monteros, 365m (400 yards) from a beach and 4km (2¹/₂ miles) east of Marbella, is one of the most tasteful resort complexes along the Costa del Sol, attracting those seeking intimacy and luxury. It reopened in 1998 after a radical upgrade. The hotel offers various salons, Andalusian/Japanese in concept, with open fireplaces, a library, and terraces. Rooms are brightly decorated and have terraces. The hotel has a bar and four restaurants on different levels that open onto flower-filled patios, gardens, and fountains. Grill El Corzo is one of the finest grill rooms along the coast. Other facilities include several pools, a beach club with a heated indoor pool, 10 tennis courts, and a riding club. The tennis courts and riding club are operated independently of the hotel.

✪   **Marbella Club.** Bulevar Príncipe Alfonso von Hohenlohe, 29600 Marbella. ☎ **800/448-8355** in the U.S., or 95-282-22-11. Fax 95-282-98-84. 136 units. A/C MINIBAR TV TEL. 30,000–60,000Pts ($189–$378) double; 45,000–60,000Pts ($284–$378) suite; 110,000–220,000Pts ($693–$1,386) bungalow. AE, DC, MC, V. Free parking.

This exclusive enclave was established in 1954, sprawling over a landscaped property that slopes from its roadside reception area down to the beach. It's composed of small, ecologically conscious clusters of garden pavilions, bungalows, and small-scale annexes (none taller than two stories). Rooms have private balconies or terraces. The Marbella Club Restaurant moves from indoor shelter to an outdoor terrace according to the season. There're two pools and a beach with a lunch restaurant. Golf can be arranged nearby, and tennis courts are within a 2-minute walk.

WHERE TO DINE

Balcón de la Virgen. Remedios 2. ☎ **95-277-60-92.** Reservations recommended. Main courses 1,200–2,800Pts ($8–$18). AE, MC, V. Daily 7pm–midnight. Closed Tues Nov–May. SPANISH.

Set in the historic core of old Marbella, this restaurant is named after a 200-year-old statue of the Virgin that adorns a wall niche surrounded by flowers and vines—the focal point of the antique house that contains it. You'll find it within a short walk of the Plaza de los Naranjos, and regardless of when you arrive, it's likely to be well patronized because of its floral charm, good food, attentive service, and reasonable prices. The menu—derived mostly from Andalusia and, to a lesser degree, the rest of Spain—features Málaga-style meat stew, baked hake with olive oil and herbs, marinated swordfish, roasted pork, and grilled fillets of beef.

✪ **La Hacienda.** Urbanización Hacienda Las Chapas, Carretera de Cádiz, km 193. ☎ **95-283-12-67.** Reservations recommended. Main courses 2,000–4,000Pts ($13–$25); fixed-price menu 5,500Pts ($35). AE, DC, MC, V. Summer, daily 8:30–11:30pm; winter, Wed–Sun 1–3:30pm and 8:30–11:30pm. Closed Nov 15–Dec 20. INTERNATIONAL.

La Hacienda, a tranquil choice 13km (8 miles) east of Marbella, enjoys a reputation for serving some of the best food along the Costa del Sol. In cooler months, you can dine in the rustic tavern before an open fireplace; in fair weather, meals are served on a patio partially encircled by open Romanesque arches. The chef is likely to offer foie gras with lentils, lobster croquettes (as an appetizer), and roast guinea hen with cream, minced raisins, and port. The food has a great deal of flavor, is presented with style, and is prepared with the freshest ingredients available. Although the food is admirable, the service is sometimes lacking.

MARBELLA AFTER DARK

Near Puerto Banús, **Casino Nueva Andalucía Marbella,** Urbanización Nueva Andalucía (☎ **95-281-40-00**), is on the lobby level of the Andalucía Plaza Hotel. It lies in an upscale development surrounded by foreign-owned condos and verdant golf courses, 7km (4¹/₂ miles) from Marbella's center beside the road leading to Cádiz. Gambling includes individual games such as French and American roulette, blackjack, punto y banco, craps, and chemin de fer. Entrance to the casino is 600Pts ($3.80), and you'll have to present a valid passport. You can dine before or after gambling in the Casino Restaurant. The casino is open daily 8pm to 4 or 5am. La Caseta Bar offers flamenco shows at 11pm Friday to Saturday. Entrance is free but drinks cost 1,800Pts ($11) and up.

FUENGIROLA & LOS BOLICHES

The twin fishing towns of Fuengirola and Los Boliches lie halfway between the more famous resorts of Marbella and Torremolinos. The promenade along the water stretches some 4km (2¹/₂ miles) with the less developed Los Boliches a short distance from Fuengirola.

The towns don't have the facilities or drama of Torremolinos and Marbella. Except for two major luxury hotels, Fuengirola and Los Boliches are cheaper, though, and that has attracted a horde of budget-conscious European tourists. Most visitors prefer Fuengirola, which is a bit more upscale and "human looking" than Los Boliches, which is to an increasing degree viewed as a satellite of the larger and more interesting Fuengirola. Both resorts lie within a 20-minute walk of each other.

On a promontory overlooking the sea, the ruins of 10th-century **San Isidro Castle** can be seen. Access to them is forbidden most of the year, so they usually have to be admired from outside. Sometimes in July and August, but only at rare intervals, they are used for presentations of classical music. The **Santa Amalja, Carvajal,** and **Las Gaviotas beaches** are broad, clean, and sandy. Everybody goes to the big **flea market** at Recinto Ferial at Fuengirola on Tuesday.

ESSENTIALS

GETTING THERE From Torremolinos, take the Metro (a local train line that's only partly underground) from Torremolinos's railway station, in the La Nogalera district (look for the RENFE sign). The 20-minute ride will carry you to any of four stops in Fuengirola and Los Boliches. Trains depart at 30-minute intervals throughout the day and evening. Fuengirola is also on the main Costa del Sol bus route from both Algeciras in the west and Málaga in the east. Call ☎ **95-747-12-35** for more information.

VISITOR INFORMATION The **tourist information office** is at Av. Jesús Santos Reino 6 (☎ **95-747-12-35**). Open Monday to Friday 9:30am to 2pm and 5 to 8pm and Saturday 10am to 1pm.

DEPARTING BY CAR From Fuengirola, it's a short drive northeast along E-15 to Torremolinos.

WHERE TO STAY

✪ **Byblos Andaluz.** Urbanización Mijas Golf, 29640 Fuengirola. ☎ **95-246-02-50.** Fax 95-247-67-83. 144 units. A/C MINIBAR TV TEL. 30,000–45,000Pts ($189–$284) double; 35,000–50,000Pts ($221–$315) suite. AE, DC, MC, V. Free parking.

This luxurious resort is in a golf club setting 6km (4 miles) from Fuengirola and 8km (5 miles) from the beach. The grounds contain a white minaret, Moorish arches, tile-adorned walls, and an orange-tree patio inspired by the Alhambra grounds. Two 18-hole golf courses designed by Robert Trent Jones, tennis courts, spa facilities, a gym, and pools bask in the Andalusian sunshine. The health spa is in a handsome classic structure. Rooms and suites are elegantly and individually designed and furnished in Roman, Arabic, Andalusian, and rustic styles. Private sun terraces and lavish bathrooms add to the comfort. The dining choices include Le Nailhac, with French cuisine.

Las Pirámides. Paseo Marítimo, 29640 Fuengirola. ☎ **95-247-06-00.** Fax 95-258-32-97. 316 units. A/C MINIBAR TV TEL. 12,000–18,000Pts ($76–$113) double; 15,000–25,000Pts ($95–$158) suite. Rates include breakfast. AE, MC, V. Parking 1,000Pts ($6).

This resort is much favored by travel groups from northern Europe. Built in 1970 and renovated in 1996, it's a citylike compound, about 45m (50 yards) from the beach, with seemingly every kind of diversion: flamenco shows every Saturday on the large patio; a cozy bar and lounge; traditionally furnished sitting rooms; a coffee shop; a poolside bar; and a gallery of boutiques and tourist facilities, such as car-rental agencies. Rooms have slick modern styling, as well as terraces. It lies within a 2-minute walk from the center of Fuengirola.

WHERE TO DINE

La Langosta. Calle Francisco Cano, 1, Los Boliches. ☎ **95-247-50-49.** Main courses 1,400–3,000Pts ($9–$19); fixed-price menus 1,500–3,500Pts ($9–$22). AE, DC, MC, V. Mon–Sat 7pm–midnight. SPANISH/SEAFOOD.

Just a stone's throw from Fuengirola in Los Boliches, this is one of the best-recommended restaurants in the area. The stylish two-story art deco dining room comes as welcome relief from the ever-present Iberian "rustic style" that adorns so many restaurants in the region. A variety of seafood is featured on the menu (the place is just two blocks from the beach), as well as Spanish dishes that include chicken and prawns with a medley of sauces, mussels, and salmon. Lobster is prepared thermidor style, or virtually any way you want; among the beef offerings is an especially succulent version of chateaubriand. The staff here seems particularly well trained and helpful.

TORREMOLINOS

This is the most famous Mediterranean beach resort in Spain. It's a gathering place for international visitors, a melting pot of Europeans and Americans. Many relax here after a whirlwind tour of Europe—the living's easy, the people are fun, and there're no historic monuments to visit. Thus the sleepy fishing village of Torremolinos has been engulfed in a cluster of concrete-walled resort hotels. Prices are on the rise, but it nevertheless remains one of Europe's vacation bargains. The sands along the beachfront tend to be gritlike and grayish. The best beaches are **El Bajondillo** and **La Carihuela,** the latter bordering an old fishing village. All beaches here are public, but don't expect changing facilities. Although it's technically not allowed, many women go topless on the beaches.

ESSENTIALS

GETTING THERE   Torremolinos is served by the nearby Málaga airport, 14km (9 miles) west. There're also frequent rail departures from the terminal at Málaga; for information, call ☎ **95-237-29-56.** Buses run frequently between Málaga and Torremolinos; for information, call ☎ **95-235-00-61.**

VISITOR INFORMATION   The **tourist information office** at Plaza de las Comunidades Autonomas (☎ **95-822-10-22**). Open daily 8am to 3pm.

DEPARTING BY CAR   From Torremolinos, continue east along E-15 for 11km (7 miles) into Málaga.

WHERE TO STAY

Hotel Las Palomas. Carmen Montes 1, 29620 Torremolinos. ☎ **95-238-50-00.** Fax 95-238-64-66. 303 units. TEL. 6,200–10,000Pts ($39–$63) double. AE, DC, MC, V.

Built during Torremolinos's construction boom (1968), this well-managed low-rise hotel is one of the town's most attractive, surrounded by gardens. A 1-minute walk from the beach and a 10-minute walk south of the town center, it has an Andalusian decor that extends into the rooms, a formal entrance, and a clientele of repeat visitors. Rooms have private balconies. None are air-conditioned, though guests can open windows and balcony doors to catch the sea breezes. Three pools are on-site.

Sol Don Pablo. Paseo Marítimo, s/n, 29620 Torremolinos. ☎ **95-238-38-88.** Fax 95-238-37-83. 443 units. A/C MINIBAR TV TEL. 10,500–20,000Pts ($66–$126) double. Rates include buffet breakfast. AE, DC, MC, V.

One of the most desirable hotels in Torremolinos is housed in a modern building that's located a minute from the beach and surrounded by its own garden and playground. The surprise is the glamorous interior, which borrows heavily from Moorish palaces and medieval castles. Splashing fountains are found in the arched-tile arcades, and niches with life-size stone statues of nude figures line the grand staircase. The comfortably furnished rooms have sea-view terraces and private bathrooms. There're several places where you can order a drink, but the restaurant serves only buffets for lunch and dinner. The full day and night entertainment program includes fitness classes, dancing to a live band, and a disco.

Sol Élite Aloha Puerto. Calle Salvador Allende, 45, 29620 Torremolinos. ☎ **800/336-3542** in the U.S., or 95-238-70-66. Fax 95-238-57-01. 430 units. A/C MINIBAR TV TEL. 12,000–19,000Pts ($76–$120) double. Rates include buffet breakfast. AE, DC, MC, V.

Heralded as one of the most modern hotels along the Costa del Sol when it was built in 1972, this now-aging hotel stands on the seashore in the residential suburb of El Saltillo, on the southwestern edge of Torremolinos. Away from the noise of the town center, it offers spacious rooms, all defined by the hotel as minisuites. Each faces the sea, the Benalmádena marina, or the beach, and each contains a separate sitting area. Guests are given a choice of two restaurants and four bars. The most popular lunchtime option is a poolside buffet that includes an all-you-can-eat medley. The two swimming pools are heated.

WHERE TO DINE

Casa Juan. Calle Mar 14, La Carihuela. ☎ **95-238-4106.** Reservations recommended. Main courses 1,200–2,500Pts ($8–$16). AE, DC, MC, V. Tues–Sun 12:30–4:30pm and 7:30pm–midnight. Closed Dec. SEAFOOD.

This seafood restaurant west of Torremolinos center is set within a modern-looking building in the old-timey satellite hamlet of La Carihuela. Menu items include selections from a lavish display of fish and shellfish prominently positioned near the entrance. Dishes include a fried platter of mixed fish; several different versions of codfish; meat or fish kabobs; and paella. Of special note is *lubina a la sal*—sea bass that's packed in layers of roughly textured salt, which is then broken open at your table and deboned in front of you. Whenever it gets busy (which is frequently), the staff is likely to rush around hysterically and at times, even brusquely, although many of the restaurant's local fans think this only adds to its charm.

El Gato Viudo. La Nogalera 8. ☎ **95-238-51-29.** Main courses 800–1,900Pts ($5–$12). AE, DC, MC, V. Nov–Apr Thurs–Tues 1–4pm and 6–11:30pm. May–Oct daily 1–4pm and 6–11:30pm. SPANISH.

Simple and amiable, this old-fashioned tavern with sidewalk seating occupies the street level and cellar of a building off calle San Miguel. The menu includes tasty dishes such as platters of grilled fish; marinated hake; roasted pork, steak, and veal; calamari with spicy tomato sauce; grilled shrimp; and shellfish or fish soup.

TORREMOLINOS AFTER DARK

One of the major casinos along the Costa del Sol, **Casino Torrequebrada,** Carretera de Cádiz 220, Benalmádena Costa (☎ **95-244-25-45**), is on the lobby level of the Hotel Torrequebrada. The Torrequebrada combines a nightclub/cabaret, a restaurant, and an array of tables devoted to blackjack, chemin de fer, punto y banco, and two kinds of roulette. The nightclub presents a flamenco show every Tuesday to Saturday at 10:30pm. Many visitors prefer to attend just the show, paying 4,500Pts ($28) for entrance (includes the first drink). Dinner is served Wednesday to Saturday at 9pm and costs 8,800Pts ($55), which includes admission to the show. The casino is especially lively in midsummer. The casino, its facilities, and its gaming tables are open daily 9pm to 4am. The entrance fee to the gaming rooms is 600Pts ($3.80). You need a passport to enter.

MÁLAGA

Málaga is a bustling commercial and residential center whose economy doesn't depend exclusively on tourism. Its chief attraction is the mild off-season climate—summer can be sticky. Málaga's most famous native son is Pablo Picasso, born in 1881 at Plaza de la Merced, in the center of the city.

ESSENTIALS

GETTING THERE **Iberia** has flights every 2 hours into Málaga from Madrid. To make reservations, call ☎ **800/772-4642** in the United States. There're at least five trains a day from Madrid (trip time: $4^1/2$ hours). For rail information in Málaga, call **RENFE** at ☎ **95-221-31-22.** Buses from all over Spain arrive at the terminal on Paseo de los Tilos, behind the RENFE office. Málaga is linked by bus to all the major cities of Spain, including eight buses per day from Madrid (trip time: 7 hours) and 7 per day from Seville (13 hours). Call ☎ **95-235-00-61** in Málaga for **bus information.**

VISITOR INFORMATION The **tourist information office** at Pasaje de Chinitas 4 (☎ **95-221-34-45**) is open Monday to Friday 9am to 7pm and Saturday and Sunday 9am to 2pm. Keeping longer hours is **Municipal,** Av. Cervantes 1 (☎ **95-260-44-10**), open Monday to Friday 8:15am to 2:45pm and 4:30 to 7pm, Saturday 9:30am to 1:30pm.

DEPARTING BY CAR From Málaga, N-340, a curving, winding road, heads east to Nerja.

WHERE TO STAY

Parador de Málaga-Gibralfaro. Monte Gibralfaro, 29016 Málaga. ☎ **95-222-19-02.** Fax 95-222-19-04. 38 units. A/C MINIBAR TV TEL. 17,500Pts ($110) double. AE, DC, MC, V. Free parking.

Originally established in 1948, and renovated in the 1990s, this parador is located immediately adjacent to the foundations of a medieval castle. Although the feeling inside is modern-day and streamlined, it enjoys a scenic position overlooking the city and the Mediterranean, with views of the bullring, mountains, and beaches. Rooms, with private entrances, have living-room areas and wide glass doors opening onto sun terraces with garden furniture. They're tastefully decorated with modern furnishings and reproductions of Spanish antiques. On the premises are two dining rooms with a reputation for good food served in generous portions.

Parador Nacional del Golf. Carretera de Málaga, Torremolinos, 29080 Apartado 324, Málaga. ☎ **95-238-12-55.** Fax 95/238-89-63. 60 units. A/C MINIBAR TV TEL. 14,000Pts ($88) double. AE, DC, MC, V. Free parking.

A resort hotel created by the Spanish government, this hacienda-style parador is flanked by a golf course on one side and the Mediterranean on another. It's 3km (2 miles) from the airport, 10km ($6^1/2$ miles) from Málaga, and 4km ($2^1/2$ miles) from Torremolinos. Rooms have balconies with a view of the golfing greens, the circular pool, or the water; some are equipped with Jacuzzis. Long tile corridors lead to the air-conditioned public areas, graciously furnished lounges, and a restaurant.

WHERE TO DINE

Café de Paris. Vélez Málaga 8. ☎ **95-222-50-43.** Reservations required. Main courses 2,500–3,500Pts ($16–$22); menú del día 1,500Pts ($9). AE, DC, MC, V. Mon–Sat 1–4pm and 8:30pm–midnight. Closed July 1–15. Bus: 13. FRENCH/SPANISH.

Málaga's best restaurant is in La Malagueta, the district surrounding the Plaza de Toros (bullring). Proprietor/chef de cuisine José García Cortés worked at many important dining rooms before carving out his own niche here. Much of the Cortés's cuisine has been adapted from classic French dishes to please the Andalusian palate. Menus are changed frequently, reflecting both the chef's imagination and the availability of produce. You might be served crepes gratinées (filled with baby eels) or local white fish baked in salt (it doesn't sound good but is excellent). Meat Stroganoff is made here not with the usual cuts of beef but with ox meat. Other specialties include artichokes Café de Paris stuffed with foie gras and a succulent version of hake that's stuffed with pulverized shellfish and served with a fish-based tomato sauce.

EXPLORING MÁLAGA

The remains of the ancient Moorish **Alcazaba,** Plaza de la Aduana, Alcazabilla (☎ 95-221-60-05; bus: 4, 18, 19, or 24), are within easy walking distance of the city center, off Paseo del Parque (plenty of signs point the way up the hill). The fortress was erected in the 9th or 10th century, though there have been later additions and reconstructions. Ferdinand and Isabella stayed here when they reconquered the city. The Alcazaba now houses an archaeological museum, with exhibits of cultures ranging from Greek to Phoenician to Carthaginian. Admission to the museum is 30Pts (20¢).

The 16th-century Renaissance **cathedral,** Plaza Obispo (☎ 95-221-59-17; bus: 14, 18, 19, or 24), in Málaga's center, was built on the site of a great mosque and suffered damage during the Civil War. But it remains vast and impressive, reflecting changing styles of interior architecture. Its most notable attributes are the richly ornamented choir stalls by Ortiz, Mena, and Michael. Admission is 200Pts ($1.25). It's open daily 10am to 12:45pm and 4 to 6:30pm; closed holidays.

NERJA

Nerja, 51km (32 miles) east of Málaga, is known for its good beaches and small coves, its seclusion, its narrow streets and courtyards, and its whitewashed, flat-roofed houses. Nearby is one of Spain's greatest attractions, the Cave of Nerja (see below).

At the mouth of the Chillar River, Nerja gets its name from an Arabic word, *narixa,* meaning "bountiful spring." Its most dramatic spot is the **Balcón de Europa,** a palm-shaded promenade that juts out into the Mediterranean. The sea-bordering walkway was built in 1885 in honor of a visit from king Alfonso XIII in the wake of an earthquake that had shattered part of nearby Málaga. The phrase "Balcón de Europa" is said to have been coined by the king during one of the speeches he made in Nerja praising the beauty of the panoramas around him. To reach the best beaches, head west from the Balcón and follow the shoreline.

ESSENTIALS

GETTING THERE   There's no railway station in Nerja, so railway passengers get off in Málaga and then go by bus. Nerja is well serviced by buses from Málaga—at least 10 per day make the 90-minute run. Buses depart from a point immediately adjacent to the railway station. For bus information in both Málaga and Nerja, call ☎ 95-235-00-61.

VISITOR INFORMATION   The **tourist information office** is at Puerta del Mar 2 (☎ 95-252-15-31). Open Monday to Friday 10am to 2pm and 5:30 to 8:30pm and Saturday 10am to 1pm.

DEPARTING BY CAR   From Nerja, N-340 continues east to Salobreña, where you can connect with E-902 heading north to Granada.

WHERE TO STAY

✪ Parador Nacional de Nerja. Calle Almuñecar 8, Playa de Burriana-Tablazo, 29780 Nerja. **☎ 95-252-00-50.** Fax 95-252-19-97. 80 units. A/C MINIBAR TV TEL. 12,500–20,000Pts ($79–$126) double. AE, DC, MC, V. Free parking.

A 5-minute walk from the center of town, this government-owned hotel takes the best of modern motel designs and blends them with a classic Spanish ambience of beamed ceilings, tile floors, and hand-loomed draperies. It was built in the 1960s on the edge of a cliff, around a flower-filled courtyard with a splashing fountain, and its social life centers around the large pool and tennis courts. There's a sandy beach below, reached by an elevator, plus lawns and gardens. Rooms are spacious and furnished in an understated but tasteful style. International and Spanish meals are served in the hotel restaurant.

WHERE TO DINE

Restaurante Rey Alfonso. Paseo Balcón de Europa. **☎ 95-252-09-58.** Reservations recommended. Main courses 900–2,100Pts ($6–$13). AE, DC, MC, V. Thurs–Tues 11am–4pm and 7–11pm. Closed Nov. SPANISH/INTERNATIONAL.

Few visitors to the Balcón de Europa realize they're standing directly above one of the most unusual restaurants in town. You enter from the bottom of a flight of stairs that skirts the rocky base of what was designed in the late 19th century as a *miradore* (viewing station), which juts seaward as an extension of the town's main square. The restaurant's menu and interior decor don't hold many surprises, but the close-up view of the crashing waves makes dining here worthwhile. Specialties include a well-prepared paella valenciana, tournedos Nerja (flambéed with mushrooms) and entrecôte Rey Alfonso with a red wine and cream sauce, five preparations of sole (from grilled to meunière), and crayfish in whisky sauce.

EXPLORING A CAVE

The most popular outing from either Málaga or Nerja is to the **✪ Cueva de Nerja** (Cave of Nerja), Carretera de Maro (**☎ 95-252-96-35**), which scientists believe was inhabited from 25,000 to 2,000 B.C. This prehistoric stalactite and stalagmite cave lay undiscovered until 1959, when it was found by chance by a handful of boys. When fully opened, it revealed a wealth of treasures left from the days of the cave dwellers, including Paleolithic paintings. These depict horses and deer, but as of this writing they're not open to public viewing. The archaeological museum in the cave contains a number of prehistoric artifacts. You can walk through its stupendous galleries, where the ceiling soars to a height of 60m (200 feet).

The cave is open daily 10am to 2pm and 4 to 6:30pm (to 8pm July and August). Admission is 650Pts ($4.10) for adults, 300Pts ($1.90) for children 6 to 12, and free for children 5 and under. If you want to visit the Nerja caves directly from Málaga, buses depart from Málaga's railway station, then stop en route at Málaga's Muelle de Heredia, at intervals of between 60 and 90 minutes every day between 7am and 8:15pm. The trip takes about an hour.

GRANADA

Granada, 122km (76 miles) northeast of Málaga, is 670m (2,200 feet) above sea level. It sprawls over two main hills, the Alhambra and the Albaicín, and it's crossed by two rivers, the Genil and the Darro. The **Cuesta de Gomérez** is one of the most important streets in Granada, climbing uphill from Plaza Nueva, the center of the modern city, to the Alhambra, Spain's major tourist attraction. This former stronghold of Moorish Spain, in the foothills of the snowcapped Sierra Nevada range, is replete with romance and folklore. In his *Tales of the Alhambra,* Washington Irving used the symbol of the city, the pomegranate (*granada*), to conjure up a spirit of romance.

ESSENTIALS

GETTING THERE   Iberia flies to Granada once or twice daily from both Barcelona and Madrid. Granada's airport (☎ **958-24-52-00**) is 16km (10 miles) west of the city center, in the hamlet of Chauchina. Airline ticketing problems and airline information is more easily handled at the **Iberia** ticketing office in the city center, at Plaza Isabel la Católica 2 (☎ **958-22-75-92**). A shuttle bus makes runs several times a day between the airport and the city center, at hours that are timed to coincide with the arrival and departures of flights. The buses meander through the city center before heading out to the airport, but the most convenient and central place to catch one is on the Gran Vía de Colón, immediately in front of the city's cathedral. Passage costs 425Pts ($2.70) each way.

Two **trains** daily connect Granada with Madrid's Atocha Station (trip time: 6 to 8 hours). Granada's railway station is on calle Dr. Jaime García Royo (☎ **958-27-12-72**), at the end of Avenida Andaluces.

Most buses pull into the station on the fringe of Granada at Carretera de Madrid. **Alsina Graells** (☎ **958-18-50-10**) is the most useful company here, offering 6 buses per day to Córdoba (3 hours), 12 per day from Jaen (1¹/₂ hours), 9 per day from Madrid (5 hours), 15 from Málaga (2 hours), and 6 from Sevilla (3 hours).

VISITOR INFORMATION   The **tourist information office** is at Plaza de Mariana Pineda 10 (☎ **958-22-66-88**), open Monday to Friday 9am to 7pm and Saturday 10am to 2pm.

WHERE TO STAY

Hotel América. Real de la Alhambra 53, 18009 Granada. ☎ **958-22-74-71.** Fax 958-22-74-70. 14 units. A/C TEL. 15,000Pts ($95) double; 18,000Pts ($113) suite. AE, DC, MC, V. Closed Dec–Feb. Bus: 2.

Located within the ancient Alhambra walls, this is one of Granada's small hotels built during the 19th-century administration of Napoléon's brother. Walk through the covered entry of this former villa into the shady patio that's lively yet intimate, with large trees, potted plants, and ferns. Other plants cascade down the white plaster walls and entwine with the ornate grillwork. Garden chairs and tables are set out for home-cooked Spanish meals. The living room of this homey retreat is graced with a collection of regional decorative objects; some of the rooms have Andalusian reproductions.

Hotel Granada Center. Av. Fuentenueva, s/n, 18002 Granada. ☎ **958-20-50-00.** Fax 958-28-96-96. 172 units. A/C MINIBAR TV TEL. 20,500Pts ($129) double; 60,000Pts ($378) suite. AE, DC, MC, V. Parking 1,300–1,800Pts ($8–$11).

One of the most recommendable modern hotels in Granada opened in 1992 adjacent to the university. Its seven-story design allowed its architects to create a marble-floored, glass-covered atrium at its center, where elevators rise like glass cages against one wall, and potted plants and armchairs are bathed in natural light from above. Rooms are comfortable, with ample use of postmodern furniture and slabs of polished stone, especially in the bathrooms. Al Zagal, the hotel's restaurant, serves adequate Andalusian and international fare, though the service could be greatly improved. Amenities include room service, laundry and dry cleaning service, conference rooms, in-house garage, baby-sitting, and currency exchange.

Hotel Rallye. Camino de Ronda 107, 18003 Granada. ☎ **958-27-28-00.** Fax 958-27-28-62. 79 units. A/C MINIBAR TV TEL. 13,200Pts ($83) double. AE, DC, MC, V. Parking 1,400Pts ($9). Bus: 1 or 5.

Some locals consider this one of the best hotels in town, and it's a relatively good value for the price. Built as a three-star hotel in 1964, it was thoroughly upgraded into a four-star format in 1990. It's a 15-minute walk from the cathedral, on the northern perimeter of Granada's urban center. Rooms are comfortable and well maintained, and the in-house restaurant, the Rallye, serves very good meals.

Hotel Residencia Cóndor. Constitución 6, 18012 Granada. ☎ **958-28-37-11.** Fax 958-28-38-50. 104 units. A/C TV TEL. 10,300–13,000Pts ($65–$82) double. AE, DC, MC, V. Parking 1,300Pts ($8). Bus: 6, 8, 9, or 10.

The attractive 1987 design of this hotel helps make it one of Granada's best in its price range. In 1997, following renovations, it was upgraded to four-star status. It's in the center of town, a 5-minute walk from the cathedral. Many of the pleasant rooms have terraces, and all have light-grained contemporary furniture. The hotel's restaurant serves both Spanish and international cuisine, and there's also a cafeteria for snacks, although room service is available 24 hours a day.

✪ Parador Nacional de San Francisco. Alhambra, 18009 Granada. ☎ **800/343-0020** in the U.S., or 958-22-14-40. Fax 958-22-22-64. 36 units. A/C MINIBAR TV TEL. 33,000Pts ($208) double. AE, DC, MC, V. Free parking. Bus: 13.

Spain's most famous parador—and the hardest to get a room at—is housed in an old brick building with a new annex, set on the grounds of the Alhambra. The decor is tasteful, and the place evokes a lot of history and a rich Andalusian ambience. The parador itself is a former convent founded by the Catholic monarchs immediately after they conquered the city in 1492. One side opens onto its own lovely gardens and the other fronts the Alhambra. From its terrace, you'll have views of the Generalife gardens and the Sacromonte caves. Rooms are generally spacious and comfortable.

The best lunch option after visiting the Alhambra is this parador, where you can dine alfresco overlooking the gardens. The menu is one of the finest of the hotel dining rooms of Granada, and the chefs base it on what was freshest at the market that day. The cuisine features regional dishes of Andalusia and Spanish national specialties. When in doubt, order the gazpacho and grilled fish.

Amenities include concierge, currency exchange, room service, and laundry.

WHERE TO DINE

Cunini. Plaza de la Pescadería 14. ☎ **958-25-07-77.** Reservations recommended. Main courses 2,200–5,500Pts ($14–$35); fixed-price menu 5,000Pts ($32). AE, DC, MC, V. Tues–Sun noon–4pm and 8pm–midnight. SEAFOOD.

The array of seafood specialties offered here, perhaps a hundred selections, extends even to the tapas served at the long, stand-up bar. After a drink or two, patrons move on to the paneled ground-floor restaurant, where the cuisine reflects the whole of Spain. Meals often begin with soup, such as *sopa sevillana* (with ham, shrimp, and whitefish). Also popular is a deep fry of small fish called a *fritura Cunini;* other specialties are rice with seafood, *zarzuela* (fish stew), smoked salmon, and grilled shrimp. Plaza de la Pescadería is adjacent to the Gran Vía de Colón, just below the cathedral.

Restaurante Sevilla. Calle Oficios 12. ☎ **958-22-12-23.** Reservations recommended. Main courses 1,200–3,500Pts ($8–$22); fixed-price menu 2,000Pts ($13). AE, DC, MC, V. Mon–Sat 1–4pm and 8–11pm, Sun 1–4pm. SPANISH/ANDALUSIAN.

Attracting a mixed crowd of all ages, the Sevilla was the favorite restaurant of such hometown boys as García Lorca and Manuel de Falla. Our most recent meal included gazpacho, Andalusian veal, and dessert (selections included caramel custard and fresh fruit). To break the gazpacho monotony, try *sopa virule*, made with pine nuts and chicken breasts. For a main course, we recommend the *cordero à la pastoril* (lamb with herbs and paprika). The best dessert is bananas flambé. You can dine inside, where it's pleasantly decorated, or on the terrace.

⊙ **Ruta del Valleta.** Carretera de la Sierra Nevada, km 5.5, Cenés de la Vega. ☎ **958-48-61-34.** Reservations recommended. Main courses 2,200–3,000Pts ($14–$19); fixed-price menus 4,000–7,000Pts ($25–$44). AE, DC, MC, V. Mon–Sat 1–4:30pm and 8pm–midnight, Sun 1–4:30pm. ANDALUSIAN/INTERNATIONAL.

Despite its origins in 1976 as an unpretentious roadhouse restaurant, this place rapidly evolved into what's usually acclaimed as the best restaurant in or around Granada. It's in the hamlet of Cenés de la Vega, about 6km (3^1/$_2$ miles) northwest of Granada's center, and contains six dining rooms of various sizes, all decorated with a well-planned mix of English and Andalusian furniture and accessories. Menu items change with the seasons but are likely to include roast suckling pig, breast of duck in a sweet-and-sour sauce, roasted game birds such as pheasant and partridge (often served with Rioja wine sauce), and preparations of fish and shellfish.

Exploring Granada

⊙ **Alhambra.** Palacio de Carlos V. ☎ **958-22-09-12.** Comprehensive ticket, including Alhambra and Generalife (below), 725Pts ($4.55); Museo Bellas Artes, 250Pts ($1.60); Museo de la Alhambra, 250Pts ($1.60); illuminated visits, 725Pts ($4.55). Mar–Oct, daily 9am–7:45pm, floodlit visits daily 10pm–midnight; Nov–Feb, daily 9am–5:45pm, floodlit visits daily 8–10pm. Bus: 2. Note: Crowds can be overwhelming at the Alhambra. Some visitors arriving after 10am might not be admitted until 1:30pm or later, and if you arrive after 4pm, there's a chance you won't get in at all.

The last remaining fortress-palace in Spain, built for the conquering caliphs of old, the Alhambra is a once-royal city surrounded by walls—it's actually a series of three palaces leading from one to the other as if part of a whole. You'll enter a world of *The Arabian Nights,* where sultans of old conducted state business, raised their families, and were entertained by their harems.

You may be surprised by its somewhat somber exterior. You have to walk across the threshold to discover the true delights of this Moorish palace. The most-photographed part is the Court of Lions, named after its highly stylized fountain. This was the heart of the palace, the most private section. Opening onto the court are the Hall of the Two Sisters, where the "favorite" of the moment was kept, and the Gossip Room, a factory of intrigue. In the dancing room in the Hall of Kings, entertainment was provided nightly to amuse the sultan's party. You can see the room where Washington Irving lived (in the chambers of Charles V) while he was compiling his *Tales of the Alhambra.*

Charles V may have been horrified when he saw the cathedral placed in the middle of the great mosque at Córdoba, but he's responsible for his own architectural meddling here, building a Renaissance palace at the Alhambra—though it's quite beautiful, it's terribly out of place. Today, it houses the **Museo de la Bellas Artes en la Alhambra** (☎ 958-22-48-43), a site devoted to painting and sculpture from the 16th to the 19th centuries, and the **Museo de la Alhambra** (☎ 958-22-62-79), which focuses more intensely on the region's breathtaking traditions of Hispanic-Muslim art and architecture. Both museums are open Monday to Saturday 9am to 2pm.

⊙ **Generalife.** Alhambra, Cerro de Sol. ☎ **958-22-09-12.** Comprehensive ticket, including Alhambra and Generalife, 725Pts ($4.55). For hours, see the Alhambra above.

The sultans used to spend their summers in this palace (pronounced hay-nay-rahl-*ee*-fay), safely locked away with their harems. Built in the 13th century to overlook the

Alhambra, the Generalife depends for its glory on its gardens and courtyards. Don't expect an Alhambra in miniature: The Generalife was always meant to be a retreat, even from the splendors of the Alhambra.

Catedral and Capilla Real. Plaza de la Lonja, Gran Vía de Colón 5. ☎ **958-22-29-59.** Admission to cathedral, 300Pts ($1.90); chapel, 150Pts (95¢). Cathedral and chapel, daily 10:30am–1:30pm and 4–7pm (closes at 6:30pm in winter).

The richly ornate Spanish Renaissance cathedral, with its spectacular altar, is one of the country's great architectural highlights, acclaimed for its beautiful facade and gold-and-white decor. It was begun in 1521 and completed in 1714. Behind the cathedral (entered separately) is the flamboyant Gothic **Royal Chapel** where lie the remains of Isabella and Ferdinand. It was their wish to be buried in recaptured Granada, not Castile or Aragón. The coffins are remarkably tiny—a reminder of how short they must have been. Accenting the tombs is a wrought-iron grill, a masterpiece. Occupying much larger tombs are the remains of their daughter, Joanna the Mad, and her husband, Philip the Handsome. The Capilla Real abuts the cathedral's eastern edge.

ALBAICÍN

This old Arab quarter, on one of the two main hills of Granada, doesn't belong to the city of 19th-century buildings and wide boulevards. It, and the surrounding Gypsy caves of Sacromonte, are holdovers from the past. The Albaicín once flourished as the residential section of the Moors, even after the city's reconquest, but it fell into decline when the Christians drove them out. This narrow labyrinth of crooked streets escaped the fate of much of Granada, which was torn down in the name of progress. Fortunately, it has been preserved, as have its plazas, whitewashed houses, villas, and the decaying remnants of the old city gate. Here and there, you can catch a glimpse of a private patio filled with fountains and plants, a traditional and graceful-appearing way of life that flourishes today. To reach the Albaicín from the medieval and 19th-century center of Granada, take bus 7 to calle de Pagés. Alternatively, you can hop aboard any of the small red-and-white buses marked "ALBAICÍN" that make runs at 15-minute intervals from the Plaza Isabel la Católica. The buses operate daily from 7am to 11pm; the fare is 120Pts (70¢).

THE GYPSY CAVES OF SACROMONTE

The Gypsy Caves of Sacromonte are a tourist trap, one of the most obviously commercial and shadowy rackets in Spain. Yet visitors seem to flock to them in spite of the warnings. It's safer to go on an organized tour. A visit to the caves is almost always included as part of the morning and (more frequently) afternoon city tours offered every day by such companies as **Grana Vision** (☎ **958-13-58-04**). A tour of Granada, including not only the caves but the cathedral, the monastery, the royal chapel, and the Albaicín, costs 5,000Pts ($32) per person. Tours depart daily at 4:30pm, ending at 7pm. Night tours of the caves (when they're at their most eerie, evocative, and, unfortunately, larcenous) are usually offered only to those who can assemble 10 or more people into a group. Before agreeing to a tour, negotiate the price carefully.

THE SHOPPING SCENE

The **Alcaicería,** once the Moorish silk market, is next to the cathedral in the lower city. The narrow streets of this rebuilt village of shops are filled with vendors selling the arts and crafts of the province. The Alcaicería offers you one of Spain's most splendid assortments of tiles, castanets, and wire figures of Don Quixote chasing windmills. The jewelry found here compares favorably with the finest Toledan work. For the window shopper, in particular, it makes a pleasant stroll.

Artesanía Albaicín (Tienda Eduardo Ferrer Lucena), calle del Agua 19 (☎ 958-27-90-56), is one of the Arab Quarter's most enduring outlets for the intricately tooled leather for which Andalusia is famous. Also in the Arab quarter, **Cerámica Aliatar,** Plaza de Aliatar 18 (☎ 958-27-80-89), is the place to head for a wide assortment of charming ceramic water and wine pitchers, serving platters, dinner plates, and garden pots.

GRANADA AFTER DARK

The best **flamenco** show in Granada is staged at the **Jardines Neptuno,** calle Arabial (☎ 958-25-11-12), nightly at 10:15pm. The acts are a bit racy, though they've been toned down. In addition to flamenco, performers attired in regional garb perform folk dances and present guitar concerts. The show takes place in a garden setting. There's a high cover charge of 3,800Pts ($24), including your first drink. It's best to take a taxi here to the location about a mile south of the center.

Sweden 17

by Darwin Porter & Danforth Prince

Although it was founded 7 centuries ago, Stockholm didn't become Sweden's capital until the mid–17th century. Today it's the capital of a modern welfare state with a strong focus on leisure activities and access to nature only a few minutes away.

Stockholm & Environs

Stockholm (pop. 1.4 million) is built on 14 islands in Lake Mälaren, marking the beginning of an archipelago of 24,000 islands, skerries, and islets that stretches all the way to the Baltic Sea. It's a city of bridges and islands, towers and steeples, cobblestone squares and broad boulevards, Renaissance splendor and steel-and-glass skyscrapers. The medieval walls of Gamla Stan (the Old Town) no longer stand, but the winding streets have been preserved. You can even go fishing in downtown waterways, thanks to a long-ago decree from Queen Christina.

Once an ethnically homogeneous society, Stockholm has experienced a vast wave of immigration in the past several years. More than 10% of Sweden's residents are immigrants or children of immigrant parents, with most coming from other Scandinavian countries. Because of Sweden's strong stance on human rights, the country has also become a major destination for political and social refugees from Africa and the Middle East and the former Yugoslavia as well.

An important aspect of Stockholm today is a growing interest in cultural activities. Over the past quarter of a century, attendance at live concerts has grown, book sales are up, and more and more people are visiting museums.

ORIENTATION

GETTING THERE   By Plane   You'll arrive at **Stockholm Arlanda Airport,** about 45km (28 miles) north of Stockholm on the E-4 highway. A long, covered walkway connects the international and domestic terminals. For information on flights, call ☎ **08/797-61-00. SAS** (☎ **800/221-2350**) is the most common carrier, but **TWA** (☎ **800/221-2000**) and **Delta** (☎ **800/241-4141**) also fly daily from New York, and **American Airlines** (☎ **800/443-7300**) offers daily flights from Chicago.

A **bus** outside the terminal building goes to the City Terminal, Klarabergsviadukten, in the city center every 10 to 15 minutes (trip

Stockholm

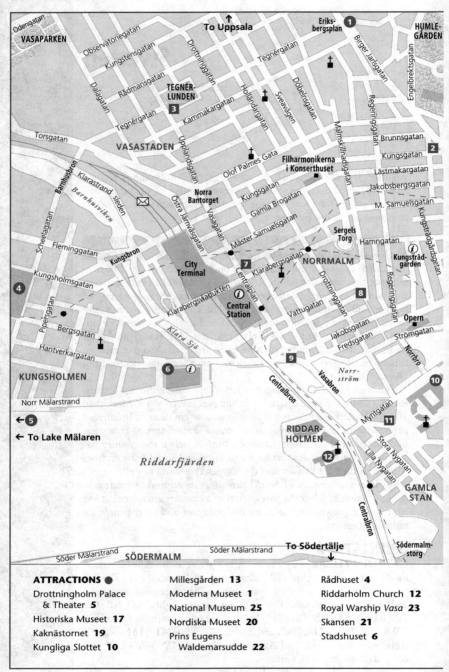

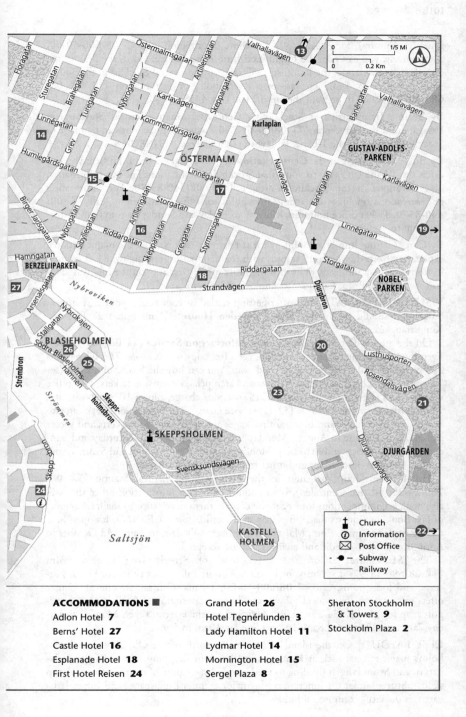

time: 35 minutes), for 70SEK ($9). For more information, call ☎ **08/600-10-00.** Alternatively, you can take the **Flight Taxi limousine service.** Go to the desk in the arrivals hall at Arlanda; the limousine will take you to central Stockholm for 300 to 350SEK ($37 to $43). For advance reservations or information call ☎ **08/ 686-10-10.** A taxi to or from the airport will cost 435SEK ($53).

By Train   Trains arrive at Stockholm's **Centralstationen (Central Station)** on Vasagatan, in the city center (☎ **08/69-67-540**), where connections can be made to Stockholm's subway, the T-bana. Follow the sign marked TUNNELBANA.

By Bus   Buses arrive at the **Centralstationen** on Vasagatan, and from here you can catch the T-bana (subway) to your final Stockholm destination. For bus information or reservations in the Stockholm area, call ☎ **08/440-85-70.** For information or reservations on buses departing Stockholm for other destinations, call ☎ **08/ 440-8570.** Ticket office hours are Monday to Friday and Sunday 9am to 6pm; Saturday 9am to 4pm.

By Car   Getting into Stockholm by car is relatively easy because the major national expressway from the south, E-4, joins with the national express highway E-3 coming in from the west and leads right into the heart of the city. Stay on the highway until you see the turnoff for Central Stockholm or Centrum.

VISITOR INFORMATION   After getting settled in your room, your first stop in Stockholm should be **Sverige Huset (Sweden House),** Hamnagatan 27 (T-bana: Kungsträdgården).

On the ground floor is the **Stockholm Information Service** (☎ **08/789-24-90**). Even if you desire no other information, get a free copy of *Stockholm This Week* for its lists of special and free events and good map. You can buy the Stockholm Card (see "Traveler's Tip") here, as well as city tour and archipelago-excursion tickets. This office will reserve a hotel room for a 60SEK ($7) service charge, plus a 10% deposit, or a youth hostel room for a 20SEK ($2.45) service charge. The reservations desk can also book summer cottages and overnight packages and sell tickets to concerts and soccer games. It's open June to August, Monday to Friday 8am to 7pm, Saturday and Sunday 9am to 5pm; September to May, Monday to Friday 9am to 6pm and Saturday and Sunday 10am to 3pm. Maps and other free material are available.

Hotell Centralen, Vasagatan in the main hall of Central Station (☎ **08/ 789-24-25**; T-bana: Centralen), is an authorized tourist information office that will also book accommodations for free if you contact them in advance by mail, telephone, or fax. Booking requests made in person at the office cost 50SEK ($6). It's open June to August daily 7am to 9pm; May and September daily 8am to 7pm; and October to April 9am to 6pm. Credit and charge cards are accepted.

The **SL Center** is on the lower level of Sergels Torg in Norrmalm (☎ **08/686-11-97**; if it's busy, or if you need only info about times for buses, subways, and local trains, call ☎ **08/600-10-00**; T-bana: Centralen). The SL Center offers information about local subway and bus transportation and sells a good transport map for 35SEK ($4.25), as well as tickets for the system. Open Monday to Friday 7am to 6:30pm, and Saturday and Sunday 10am to 5pm.

CITY LAYOUT   On the island of Norrmalm north of the Old Town are Stockholm's major streets, such as **Kungsgatan** (the main shopping street), **Birger Jarlsgatan,** and **Strandvägen** (leading to the Djurgården—home of many of the city's top sights). **Stureplan,** at the junction of the major avenues Kungsgatan and Birger Jarlsgatan, is the city's commercial hub.

About 4 blocks west of the Stureplan rises **Hötorget City,** a landmark of modern urban planning that includes five 18-story skyscrapers. Its main traffic-free artery is the **Sergelgatan,** a 3-block shopper's promenade that eventually leads to the modern sculptures in the center of the **Sergels Torg.** About 9 blocks south of the Stureplan, at **Gustav Adolfs Torg,** are the Royal Dramatic Theater and the Royal Opera House. A block east of the flaming torches of the Royal Opera House is the verdant north-south stretch of **Kungsträdgården,** part avenue, part public park, which serves as a popular gathering place for students and as a resting perch for shoppers. Three blocks southeast, on a famous promontory, lie the landmark Grand Hotel and the National Museum.

Kungsholmen, King's Island, is across a narrow canal from the rest of the city, a short walk west of the Central Station. It's visited chiefly by those wanting to tour Stockholm's elegant Stadshuset (City Hall). South of the island where **Gamla Stan** (Old Town) is located and separated from it by a narrow but much-navigated stretch of water is **Södermalm,** the southern district of Stockholm. Quieter than its northern counterpart, it's an important residential area with a distinctive flavor of its own.

To the east of Gamla Stan, on a large and forested island completely surrounded by the complicated waterways of Stockholm, is **Djurgården** (Deer Park). The rustically unpopulated summer pleasure ground of Stockholm, it's the site of many of the city's most popular attractions: the open-air museums of Skansen, the *Vasa* man-of-war, Gröna Lund's Tivoli, the Waldemarsudde estate of the "painting prince" Eugen, and the Nordic Museum.

GETTING AROUND

Walking is the best way to get to know the city. In any case, you have to explore Gamla Stan on foot, as cars are banned from most of the streets. Djurgården and Skeppsholmen are other popular haunts for strolling.

BY SUBWAY (TUNNELBANA OR T-BANA)   Subways (called Tunnelbana or T-bana) and buses are operated by **SL,** the city transportation network, and charge according to a zone system—the price increases the farther you go. Most places you'll visit in central Stockholm will cost 14SEK ($1.70), payable at the Tunnelbana and bus entrance. The subway system is fast, efficient, and far-reaching. Color-coded maps are on station walls and printed in most tourist publications. Timetables for each train are also posted. Subway entrances are marked with a blue T on a white background. For information about schedules, routes, and fares, call ☎ **08/600-10-00.**

One ticket costs 14SEK ($1.70) and is good for 1 hour (use it as often as you want), or you can get a strip of 20 coupons for 95SEK ($12). Your best transportation bet is to purchase a **tourist season ticket.** A 1-day card costs 60SEK ($7) and is valid for

---

Traveler's Tip

Costing just 199SEK ($24) for 1 day, 398SEK ($49) for 2 days, or 498SEK ($61) for 3 days, the **Stockholmskortet (Stockholm Card)** is a personal discount card that includes unlimited travel on Stockholm's public transport network (except airport buses), admission to most museums, and a guidebook to the city. You can also take a free sightseeing tour with City Sightseeing, which allows you to get on and off as often as you choose, looking at the sights according to your own schedule. You also get boat sightseeing at half price, plus a one-way ticket to Drottningholm Palace. Cards are sold at the tourist information counter at Sweden House and at Hotell Centralen at Central Station, and each is valid for one adult and two children 17 and under.

24 hours of unlimited travel by T-bana, bus, and commuter train in Stockholm. It also includes passage on the ferry to Djurgården. Most visitors will probably want the 3-day card for 120SEK ($15), valid for 72 hours in both Stockholm and the adjacent county. The 3-day card is also valid for admission to Skansen, Kaknästornet, and Gröna Lund. Children under 18 pay 36SEK ($4.40) for a 1-day card or 72SEK ($9) for a 3-day card, but children up to age 7 can travel free with an adult. Tickets are sold at tourist-information offices, in subway stations, and at most news vendors. You can buy day passes at the SL center (see "Visitor Information," above).

If you're paying with cash or using a strip ticket, pass through the gate and tell the person in the ticket booth where you're going. He or she will either ask for your fare or stamp your ticket. If you have a Stockholm Card, just flash it. Sometimes the ticket collector is absent; in these instances, few commuters wait for the collector to return—they just walk through.

BY BUS   A bus will fill the need when the T-bana isn't convenient. The two systems have been coordinated to complement each other. Many visitors use a bus to reach Djurgården (though you can walk there), since the T-bana doesn't go there. Enter through the front door and pay the driver, show your Stockholm Card, or have your strip ticket stamped. For a list of bus routes, purchase the *SL Stockholmskartan,* available for 45SEK ($6) at the Stockholm Information Service in the Sweden House or the SL Center (see "Visitor Information," above). Many buses depart from Normalmstorg, catercorner to Kungsträdgården and 2 blocks from Sweden House.

BY FERRY   Ferries run between Gamla Stan (near the bridge to Södermalm) and Djurgården year-round, providing the best link between these two. In summer, boats depart every 15 minutes 9am to midnight (to 10:40pm Sunday); in winter, daily every 20 minutes 9am to 6pm. The ride costs 20SEK ($2.45) adults, half price for seniors and children 7 to 18. Passage is free for ages 6 and under. Ferries also run between Nybroplan and Djurgården (summer only) and between Slussen and Djurgården (year-round). Contact **Vaxholmsbolaget** (☎ 08/679-58-30) for more information.

An offbeat experience that you might want to try if you're fond of ocean voyages involves overnight ferryboats between Stockholm and Helsinki, across the Gulf of Bothnia. **Silja Line** (☎ 08/22-21-40), whose itineraries and prices are closely matched by **Viking Line** (☎ 08/452-40-00), operates ships that depart from both Stockholm and Helsinki every evening at 6pm, and which pull into Helsinki or Stockholm after a 13^{1}/$_{2}$-hour transit. If you opt to visit Helsinki from Stockholm for the day, you'll enjoy about 9 hours of touring the city before the departure of your ship back to Stockholm. Depending on the season, your cabin, and the day of the week, round-trip fares for two persons sharing a cabin range from 1,284 to 4,800SEK ($157 to $586). Meals and drinks on board cost extra.

BY TAXI   Taxis are expensive in Stockholm—in fact, they're among the most expensive in the world, with a double-tiered charge that applies both for the distance you travel, and for the time your ride takes. The meter begins at 28SEK ($3.40), after which the per-kilometer charge ranges from 6.60 to 9.80SEK (80¢ to $1.20), and the per-minute charge ranges from 4.60 to 4.95SEK (55¢ to 60¢). Both of those variables depend on the time of day or night, and the day of the week you travel, but the outcome is that taxi rides within Stockholm can easily cost as much as 100SEK ($12). If you're heading from anywhere in downtown Stockholm to Arlanda airport, there's a set-price charge of 435SEK ($53) that's valid for up to four passengers and their luggage. Taxis whose dome lights display the word LEDIG aren't otherwise engaged, and can be hailed on the street. If you want to call for a taxi, the most reputable taxi companies include **Taxi Stockholm** (☎ 08/15-00-00 or 08/15-04-00), **Taxi Kurir**

(☎ **08/30-00-00**), and **Taxicard** (☎ **08/97-00-00**). Note that there're some occasional independent, unmetered taxis within Stockholm, which tend to be frowned upon by local authorities. If you opt to travel within one of these, negotiate a reasonable fare with the driver before leaving the curb.

BY CAR   Each of the major car-rental firms are represented in Stockholm, including Avis and Hertz, both of which maintain offices at Arlanda Airport (**Hertz:** ☎ **08/797-9900; Avis:** ☎ **08/797-9970**) and in locations a few steps from Stockholm's main railway station. Hertz's downtown office is at Vasagatan 26 (☎ **08/240-720**); Avis's downtown office is at Vasagatan 10B (☎ **08/20-20-60**). Rentals at both organizations are usually cheaper if you reserve them by phone before leaving North America. For reservations and information within the United States and Canada, call Avis at ☎ **800/331-2112** or Hertz at ☎ **800/654-3001.**

BY BICYCLE   The best place to go cycling is on Djurgården. You can rent bicycles from **Skepp o Hoj,** Djurgårdsbron (☎ **08/660-57-57**), for about 150SEK ($18) per day or 500SEK ($61) per week. A valid credit-card number is held on deposit on any bicycle rental. The shop is open May through August, daily 9am to 9pm.

Fast Facts: Stockholm

American Express   American Express is at Norrlandsgatan 21 (☎ **08/679-78-80;** T-Bana: Mariatorget), open Monday to Friday from 9am to 6pm (until 5pm in winter) and Saturday from 10am to 3pm (until 1pm in winter).

Currency   You'll pay your way in Stockholm in SwedishKr (**KR**) or crowns (singular, **krona**), internationally abbreviated SEK, which are divided into 100 **öre.** Bills come in denominations of 10, 20, 50, 100, and 1,000KR. Coins are issued in 50 öre, as well as 1, 5, and 10KR. The exchange rate used in this chapter was $1 = 8.14SEK, or 1KR = 10¢. The ratio of the British pound to the crown fluctuates constantly. At press time, £1 = approximately 13.46SEK (or 1SEK = 7p). The euro rate was currently fixed at 8.67SEK (or 1SEK = €0.12).

Dentists   Emergency dental treatment is offered at **St. Eriks Hospital,** Fleminggatan 22 (☎ **08/654-11-17;** T-bana: Fridhemsplan), open daily 8am to 8:30pm.

Doctors   If you need emergency medical care, check with **Medical Care Information** (☎ **08/463-91-00**). There's also a private clinic, **City Akuten,** at Holländargartan 3 (☎ **08/412-29-61;** T-bana: Skanstull).

Drugstores   One 24-hour pharmacy is **C. W. Scheele,** Klarabergsgatan 64 (☎ **08/454-81-00;** T-bana: Centralen).

Embassies/Consulates   The **U.S. Embassy** is at Strandvägen 101, S-115 89 Stockholm (☎ **08/783-53-00;** T-bana: Östermalmstorg); the **British Embassy** (☎ **08/671-90-00**) is at Skarpögatan 6–8 (mailing address: P.O. Box 27819, S-115 93 Stockholm); the **Canadian Embassy** is at Tegelbacken 4, S-103 23 Stockholm (☎ **08/453-30-00;** T-bana: Centralen); the **Irish Embassy** (☎ **08/661-80-05;** T-bana: Östermalmstorg) is at Östermalmsgatan 97 (mailing address: P.O. Box 10326, S-100 55 Stockholm); the **Australian Embassy** (☎ **08/613-29-00;** T-bana: Hötorget) is at Sergels Torg 12 (mailing address: P.O. Box 7003, S-103 86 Stockholm), and the **South Africa Embassy** is at Linnég 76, S-115 00 Stockholm (☎ **08/24-39-50;** T-bana: Östermalmstorg). **New Zealand** doesn't maintain an embassy in Sweden.

Emergencies   Call ☎ **90-000** anywhere in Sweden if you need an ambulance, the police, or fire department.

Hospitals   Call **Medical Care Information** at ☎ **08/463-91-00** and an English-speaking operator will inform you of the hospital closest to you.

Internet Access   Stockholm's first Internet cafe is **Café Access,** Kulturhuset (☎ **08/508-31-400;** e-mail: staff@cafeaccess.se; T-bana: Kungsträdgården), in the Stockholm Culture House in the heart of the city. It is open Monday 11am to 6pm, Tuesday to Thursday 10am to 7pm, Friday 10am to 6pm, Saturday 10 to 5pm and Sunday noon to 4pm.

Post Office   The main post office is at Vasagatan 28–34 (☎ **08/781-20-00**), open Monday to Friday from 8am to 7am and Saturday 10am to 2pm. Mail can be sent c/o general delivery as follows: Post Restante, c/o Postens Huyudkontor (Main Post Office), Vasagatan 28–34, S-10 430 Stockholm, Sweden.

Telephone   The **country code** for Sweden is **46.** The **city code** for Stockholm is **8;** use this code when you're calling from outside Sweden. If you're within Sweden but not in Stockholm, use **08.** If you're calling within Stockholm, simply leave off the code and dial the regular phone number.

Instructions in English are posted in **public phone boxes,** which can be found on street corners. Very few phones in Sweden are coin operated; most require the purchase of a phone card (called a **Telekort**). You can obtain phone cards at most newspaper stands and tobacco shops.

You can make international calls from the **TeleCenter Office** on the Central Station's ground floor (☎ **08/456-74-94**), open daily 8am to 9pm, except major holidays. Long-distance rates are posted. To make a collect or calling card call, dial one of the following access numbers to reach an American operator or an English-language voice prompt: **AT&T** ☎ **020/795-611; MCI** ☎ **020/795-9222;** and **Sprint** ☎ **020/799-011.**

For **directory assistance,** dial ☎ **0018.** For directory listings or other information for Stockholm or other parts of Sweden only, dial ☎ **07975;** for other parts of Europe, dial ☎ **07977.**

Transit Information   For information on all services, including buses and subways (Tunnelbana), even suburban trains (*pendeltåg*), call ☎ **08/600-10-00.** Or else visit the SL Center (see "Visitor Information," above) on the lower level of Sergels Torg. It provides information about transportation and also sells a map of the city's system, as well as tickets and special discount passes.

WHERE TO STAY

If you want to stay in an hotel convenient to your flight, there's nothing closer than the **Radisson SAS SkyCity Hotel,** Stockholm/Arlanda Airport, 190 45 Stockholm/Arlanda (☎ **08/59077300;** fax 08/59378100). With 230 modernized and tastefully styled rooms, it is right in the airport complex. As you check out of your hotel, you're virtually at the check-in for your flight, as this hotel lies midway between two of the busiest terminals (numbers 4 and 5) at the airport. Doubles cost 1,195SEK ($146) every Friday to Sunday; during July and otherwise, 1,895SEK ($231) each. There's also a bar, fitness center, and international restaurant.

Nearby, accessible from the main airport terminals via yellow-sided airport bus 14, but not accessible via covered walkway, is the SkyCity Hotel's twin, the nearly identical, 300-room **SAS Arlandia Hotel,** Bernstocksvägen 1, 190 45 Stockholm/Arlanda (☎ **08/59361-800;** fax 08/59361-970), charging comparable rates. *Note:* The hotel has a slightly different spelling from the name of the airport.

Traveler's Tip

Most European capitals experience high season in summer, when hordes of tourists arrive. But the situation is different in Stockholm. Although most tourists arrive in summer, the city's hotels are more dependent on business travelers than tourists. Consequently, hotels sometimes *lower* their prices in summer. Even during the busier winter season, hotels will often lower prices on Friday, Saturday, and possibly Sunday nights. It always pays to ask if any discounts are available.

A shuttle bus between the hotels and Stockholm's main railway station, and charges 60SEK ($7) per person each way. It's marked **Flygbus** and it's silver.

IN THE CITY CENTER

Very Expensive

✪ **Grand Hotel.** Södra Blaisieholmshamnen 8, S-103 27 Stockholm. ☎ **08/679-35-00.** Fax 08/611-86-86. E-mail: guest@grandhotel.se. 307 units. MINIBAR TV TEL. 2,395–3,060SEK ($292–$373) double, from 7,000SEK ($854) suite. Rates include breakfast. AE, DC, MC, V. Parking 290SEK ($35). T-bana: Kungsträdgården; bus: 46, 55, 62, or 76.

Opposite the Royal Palace, this hotel is grand indeed, the only five-star hotel in Sweden. Built in 1874, it has been continuously renovated, but its old-world style has been maintained. Rooms come in all shapes and sizes, but each is elegant, and some have air-conditioning. The mattresses and level of comfort are the finest in town. The spacious bathrooms have heated floors, fluffy towels, and hair dryers. The Grand Veranda specializes in traditional food served from a buffet, and the Franska Matsalen is the hotel's gourmet restaurant.

Expensive

Berns' Hotel. Näckströmsgatan 8, S-111 47 Stockholm. ☎ **08/614-07-00.** Fax 08/566-32-201. 65 units. A/C MINIBAR TV TEL. 2,340–2,740SEK ($286–$334) double, from 3,240SEK ($395) suite. Rates include breakfast. AE, DC, MC, V. Parking 295SEK ($36). T-bana: Östermalmstorg.

During its 19th-century heyday, this was Sweden's most elegant hotel, with a lush gilded-age interior. Rooms range from medium to spacious; each is soundproof, has a satellite TV, CD player, and a good-size bathroom containing such amenities as fluffy towels, hair dryers, a phone, and a makeup mirror. Some units are no smoking. The open-air terrace on the hotel's rooftop offers views over the city's historic core. The Salonger is the hotel's major restaurant (see "Where to Dine," below).

Lydmar Hotel. Sturegatan 10, S-114 36 Stockholm. ☎ **08/566-11-300.** Fax 08/566-11-301. E-mail: info@lydmar.se. 56 units. MINIBAR TV TEL. 1,700–1,950SEK ($207–$238) double; 2,600SEK ($317) junior suite. Rates include buffet breakfast. AE, DC, MC, V. Parking 250SEK ($31). T-bana: Östermalmstorg; bus: 41, 46, 56, or 91.

Opposite the garden of the King's Library, in what looks like an office building, the Lydmar opened in 1930. The exceptionally well-maintained rooms are traditionally furnished and range from small singles to medium-size doubles. Mattresses are firm and frequently renewed, and bathrooms are state of the art, with a generous supply of good towels and adequate space. Both Swedish and international cuisines are served in the hotel's restaurant; there's a rooftop terrace where you can enjoy drinks in summer, and a popular lobby bar.

Sergel Plaza. Brunkebergstorg 9, S-103 27 Stockholm. ☎ **08/22-66-00.** Fax 08/21-50-70. E-mail: sergel.plaza.hotel@provobis.se. 418 units. A/C TV TEL. 1,950–2,800SEK ($238–$342) double; 6,500SEK ($793) suite. Rates include breakfast. AE, DC, MC, V. Parking 210SEK ($26). T-bana: Centralen; bus: 47, 52, or 69.

This hotel at the entrance to Drottninggatan, the main shopping street, is one of the city's best. The elegant decor includes 18th-century artwork and antiques. It's a bastion of comfort and good taste, as reflected by the beautifully decorated, generally spacious rooms. All contain firm mattresses, have good double-glazed windows, and average-size, immaculately maintained bathrooms with plenty of soft towels and a hair dryer. Some units are no smoking and wheelchair accessible. The Anna Rella gourmet restaurant offers both Swedish and international specialties. Facilities include saunas, solariums, and Jacuzzis.

Sheraton Stockholm Hotel & Towers. Tegelbacken 6, S-101 23 Stockholm. ☎ **800/325-3535** in the U.S. and Canada, or 08/412-34-00. Fax 08/412-34-09. E-mail: sheraton-stockholm@ittsheraton.com. 470 units. A/C MINIBAR TV TEL. 1,200–2,650SEK ($146–$323) double; from 3,500SEK ($427) suite. Rates include breakfast. AE, DC, MC, V. Parking 160SEK ($20). T-bana: Centralen.

Sheathed with Swedish granite, this hotel rises eight stories across the street from Stockholm's City Hall. Short on charm, it is, however, excellent by chain hotel standards. Rooms, the largest in the city, feature mirrored closets, one king or two double beds, good firm mattresses, and bedside controls. Most have sweeping views. The medium-size bathrooms have hair dryers and heated racks with fluffy towels. Some have bidets. A pair of ethnic brasseries, Die Ecke and Le Bistro, serve German and French specialties, respectively.

Moderate

Castle Hotel. Riddargatan 14, S-114 35 Stockholm. ☎ **08/679-57-00.** Fax 08/611-20-22. www.castle/hotel.se. E-mail: receptionen@castle/hotel.se. 49 units. TV TEL. 825–1,550SEK ($101–$189) double; 1,450–2,400SEK ($177–$293) suite. Rates include breakfast. AE, DC, MC, V. T-bana: Östermalmstorg.

In an expensive neighborhood a short walk east of the center, this 1920 house was originally an apartment building. The good-size rooms are adorned with art deco accessories and twin beds with excellent mattresses. The tidy, medium-size bathrooms have lots of towels and ample shelf space. Discounts are offered on various weekends throughout the year.

Esplanade Hotel. Strandvägen 7A, S-114 56 Stockholm. ☎ **08/663-07-40.** Fax 08/662-59-92. E-mail: hotel@esplanadesto.se. 34 units. TV TEL. 1,300–1,825SEK ($159–$223) double. Rates include breakfast. AE, DC, MC, V. T-bana: Östermalmstorg. Bus: 47 or 69.

This informal hotel was constructed in 1910 as a simple boarding house. Single rooms are minuscule, but doubles, for the most part, are more spacious, with double-glazed windows, trouser presses, extra-long beds with comfortable mattresses, and medium-size bathrooms with fluffy towels. Many rooms have minibars, and four have a water view. The English lounge has a balcony with a view of the Djurgården. Breakfast is the only meal served.

Mornington Hotel. Nybrogatan 53, S-102 44 Stockholm. ☎ **800/528-1234** in the U.S., or 08/663-12-40. Fax 08/662-21-79. E-mail: mornington.hotel-sth@wmhotels.se. 141 units. TV TEL. June 26–Aug 9, 1,250SEK ($153) double; Aug 10–June 25, 1,695–2,100SEK ($207–$256) double; year-round 2,400SEK ($293) suite. Rates include breakfast. AE, DC, MC, V. Parking 200SEK ($24). Closed Dec 23–26. T-bana: Östermalmstorg; bus: 49, 54, or 62.

This efficiently modern establishment has a concrete exterior brightened with rows of flower boxes. The lobby is enhanced with a small rock garden and modern versions of Chesterfield armchairs. Rooms, many quite small, are kept in tiptop shape, with excellent mattresses on comfortable beds. No-smoking rooms and units for guests with disabilities are available. Bathrooms are medium size; many have showers but no tubs. The sauna and Turkish bath are free. The Restaurant Eleonora serves international and Swedish cuisine.

Stockholm Plaza. Birger Jarlsgatan 29, S-103 95 Stockholm. ☎ **08/566-22-00.** Fax 08/566-22-020. E-mail: stockholm.plaza@elite.se. 151 units. TV TEL. 1,090–1,795SEK ($133–$219) double; 2,180–3,100SEK ($266–$378) suite. Rates include breakfast. AE, DC, MC, V. Parking 220SEK ($27). T-bana: Hötorget or Östermalmstorg.

This is an inviting choice in the city center. The small to medium-size rooms have light, fresh interiors with firm beds. The medium-size bathrooms are kept immaculately and provided with hair dryers and fluffy towels. On the premises is an elegant upscale French-style brasserie serving Gallic and Swedish specialties.

Inexpensive

Adlon Hotel. Vasagatan 42, S-111 20 Stockholm. ☎ **08/402-65-00.** Fax 08/20-86-10. www.adlon.se. E-mail: hotel@adlon.se. 72 units. TV TEL. 1,330–1,580SEK ($162–$193) double. Rates include breakfast. AE, DC, MC, V. Parking 230SEK ($28). T-bana: Centralen.

The Adlon was originally built in the 1890s, but a 1990 renovation created a more comfortable look, and improvements have been frequent ever since. The rather small but beautifully maintained rooms are comfortably furnished and have new mattresses. Bathrooms, though small, contain hair dryers. Some 70% are designated no-smoking. The Adlon is near the Central Station and is convenient to buses heading for Arlanda Airport.

Hotel Tegnérlunden. Tegnérlunden 8, S-113 59 Stockholm. ☎ **08/34-97-80.** Fax 08/32-78-18. E-mail: info.tegener@swedenhotels.se. 103 units. TV TEL. 800–1,395SEK ($98–$170) double. Rates include breakfast. AE, DC, MC, V. Parking 135SEK ($16). Bus: 47, 53, or 69 from the Central Station.

In a 19th-century building at the edge of a park, this hotel's best feature is its tasteful rooms, each blissfully quiet, opening onto the rear. They come in a variety of sizes and shapes, with most on the small to medium side. Each is well maintained but furnished in a somewhat functional Scandinavian style evocative of a good motel. Nonetheless, you'll be comfortable here, (especially on the excellent Swedish mattresses). Bathrooms, although tidy, are small with only adequate towels. There's a sauna.

IN GAMLA STAN (OLD TOWN)

First Hotel Reisen. Skeppsbron 12, S-111 30 Stockholm. ☎ **08/22-32-60.** Fax 08/20-15-59. 114 units. MINIBAR TV TEL. 2,148–2,348SEK ($262–$286) double; 3,500–4,500SEK ($427–$549) suite. Rates include breakfast. AE, DC, MC, V. Bus: 43, 46, 55, 59, or 76.

This Old Town hotel facing the water benefited from a 1997 renovation. Dating from the 17th century, the three-building structure attractively combines the old and the new. The medium-size rooms are comfortably furnished and stylishly modern, mattresses are frequently renewed. Top-floor units open onto small balconies. The generous bathrooms are equipped with massaging showerheads, scales, heated towels racks, fluffy towels, and a phone. Some no-smoking units are available. The main restaurant is the warm and nautical Quarter Deck; the Clipper Club piano bar specializes in simple snacks.

✪ **Lady Hamilton Hotel.** Storkyrkobrinken 5, S-111 28 Stockholm. ☎ **08/23-46-80.** Fax 08/411-11-48. E-mail: info@lady-hamilton.se. 34 units. MINIBAR TV TEL. 1,450–2,090SEK ($177–$255) double. Rates include breakfast buffet. AE, DC, MC, V. Parking 255SEK ($31). T-bana: Gamla Stan; bus: 48.

This historic hotel on a quiet street scatters dozens of antiques in its medium-size rooms. Top-floor units have skylights and memorable views. Beds have firm, frequently renewed mattresses. Bathrooms come in a variety of sizes, from spacious to cramped. All have heated racks with plenty of fluffy towels, heated floors, and a hair dryer, although only some have tubs (the rest offer showers only). Some no-smoking rooms are available. Simple food, such as sandwiches, along with beer and wine, are served in the breakfast room throughout the day. There's also a sauna.

WHERE TO DINE
IN THE CITY CENTER
Very Expensive

Operakällaren. Operahuset, Kungsträdgården ☎ **08/676-58-00.** Reservations required. Main courses 300SEK ($37); fixed-price menu 600SEK ($73) for 3 courses, 700SEK ($85) for 4 courses; 7-course *menu dégustation* 1,000SEK ($122). AE, DC, MC, V. Daily 5–10pm. Closed July. T-bana: Kungsträdgarden. FRENCH/SWEDISH.

Opposite the Royal Palace is Sweden's most famous and luxurious restaurant. Its elegant classic decor and style are reminiscent of a royal court banquet at the turn of the last century. Dress formally (the dress code isn't strictly enforced, but men are encouraged to wear jackets and ties) to enjoy its impeccable service and house specialties, including the platter of northern delicacies, with everything from smoked eel to smoked reindeer along with Swedish red caviar. You may wish to sip a drink in the Café Opera, with its magnificent crystal chandeliers and a ceiling painted by Vicke Andrén, or smoke an after-dinner cigar in the new cigar bar. A glass-enclosed outer room has a lofty ceiling and is brightly sunlit during the day. After midnight, the cafe turns into a popular disco (see "Stockholm After Dark," below).

✪ **Paul & Norbert.** Strandvägen 9. ☎ **08/663-81-83.** Reservations required. Main courses 285–685SEK ($35–$84); 8-course *grand menu de frivolité* 1,050SEK ($128). AE, DC, MC, V. Mon–Fri noon–2pm and 6:30–10:30pm. Closed July and Dec 23–Jan 6. T-bana: Östermalmstorg. CONTINENTAL.

In a patrician residence dating from 1873, this is Stockholm's most innovative restaurant. Seating only 30 people at nine tables, it has a vaguely art deco decor, with beamed ceilings, and dark paneling. Owners Paul Beck and Norbert Lang worked in many of the top restaurants of Europe before opening this establishment. Lang's foie gras is the finest in town. Main courses, which change seasonally, tend to favor game and game birds; examples include juniper-marinated noisettes of reindeer with cheese, and escargot-filled breast of guinea fowl in rosemary sauce with garlic and onion. The seafood menu offers sole and salmon dishes along with a daily catch.

Wedholms Fisk. Nybrokajen 17. ☎ **08/611-78-74.** Reservations required. Main courses 235–280SEK ($29–$34); fixed-price lunch 90–190SEK ($11–$23). AE, DC, MC, V. Mon–Fri 11:30am–11pm, Sat 7–11pm. Closed July. T-bana: Östermalmstorg. SWEDISH/FRENCH.

This classic restaurant is one of the best in Stockholm. Housed in an old building whose decor has been stripped down to its basics, it has no curtains in the windows and no carpets, but the display of modern paintings by Swedish artists is riveting. You might begin with marinated herring with garlic and bleak roe, or tartare of salmon with salmon roe. The chef has reason to be proud of such dishes as perch poached with clams and saffron sauce; prawns marinated in herbs and served with Dijon hollandaise; and grilled fillet of sole with a Beaujolais sauce. For dessert, try the home-made vanilla ice cream with cloudberries. The cuisine is both innovative and traditional. How many places today would prepare a chèvre mousse to accompany a simple tomato salad? (On the other hand, they dare serve Grandmother's favorite: cream stewed potatoes.)

Expensive

Teatergrillen. Nybrogatan 3. ☎ **08/611-70-44.** Reservations recommended. Main courses 150–300SEK ($18–$37). AE, DC, MC, V. Mon–Fri 11:30am–3pm; Mon–Fri 6pm–midnight. Closed July. T-bana: Östermalmstorg. Bus: 46. SWEDISH/FRENCH.

Located near the Royal Dramatic Theater, this restaurant is appropriately decorated with theatrical memorabilia. It's divided into a small, windowless grill room and a spacious main room that's filled with fresh flowers and has views of the surrounding neighborhood. Many traditional, home-style Swedish dishes are offered at lunch. Each noon features a different specialty—perhaps sautéed fish in a tarragon sauce with rice or pork schnitzel with thyme-flavored fried potatoes. At dinner the cuisine is considerably upgraded with the likes of halibut with chanterelles in a curry sauce or pikeperch appearing with mussels in a citrus-flavored tomato broth. Increasingly, the chefs have become more innovative, offering such appetizers as deep-fried chicken in a peanut sauce accompanied by a coriander and mint salad.

Moderate

Akvarium. Kungsträdgården. ☎ **08/100-626.** Reservations recommended. Main courses 100–198SEK ($12–$24); set-price lunches 60SEK ($7). AE, DC, MC, V. Mon–Thurs 11am–midnight; Fri 5pm–3am, Sat–Sun 11:30am–3am. T-bana: Kungsträdgården. CONTINENTAL.

Don't expect bubbling fish tanks. This hip and stylish restaurant's name derives from its former incarnation as a seafood restaurant. You'll find a bustling kitchen that's open to view, a bar dotted with colored lamps, and a big veranda that accommodates diners who appreciate the light of midsummer. Menu items include "duck espresso" (breast of duck with port wine sauce and plums), veal saltimbocca (with ham), tagliatelle with mussels, clams, and squid ink; grilled butterfish with pesto sauce; and an all-vegetarian version of ravioli stuffed with porcini mushrooms.

✪ Eriks Bakfica. Fredrikshovsgatan 4. ☎ **08/660-15-99.** Reservations recommended. Main courses 80–245SEK ($10–$30); 3-course entrecôte dinner 350SEK ($43); 5 courses 445SEK ($54). AE, DC, MC, V. Mon–Fri 11:30am–midnight, Sat 5–midnight, Sun 5–10pm. Bus: 47. SWEDISH.

Though there are other restaurants here bearing the name Eriks, this one is relatively moderate and offers particularly good value. It features a small, bustling bistro with a bar and background music, and a quieter main dining room with muted yellow walls and antique furnishings. The menu features a handful of Swedish dishes from the tradition of *husmanskost* (wholesome home cooking). There's a daily choice of herring appetizers. Main courses include grilled char with lobster sauce, and grilled veal schnitzel with mushrooms and a red wine sauce. We suggest you try the archipelago stew, a ragout of fish flavored with tomatoes and served with garlic mayonnaise. If none of these strike your fancy, stick to the cheeseburger with a special secret sauce.

KB Restaurant. Smålandsgatan 7. ☎ **08/679-60-32.** Reservations recommended. Main courses 200SEK ($24); fixed-price lunch 145SEK ($18); fixed-price dinner 217SEK ($26). AE, DC, MC, V. Mon–Fri 11:30am–2pm and 5–11pm, Sat 5–11pm; Bar, Mon–Sat 11:30am–midnight. Closed June 23–Aug 7. T-bana: Östermalmstorg. SWEDISH/CONTINENTAL.

This has been a traditional artists' rendezvous since opening on New Year's Eve 1931. It still features the original dark wood furniture; the dark red and green color scheme and wall-to-wall carpeting were added more recently. Located in the center of town, KB offers good Swedish cookery as well as continental dishes. The fish dishes are especially recommended. You might begin with any of a number of herring starters followed by baked North Sea cod with broad beans and lobster in lemon sauce, or perhaps fried pigeon with onion marmalade, potato terrine, and currant pepper sauce.

Inexpensive

✪ **Bakfickan.** Jakobs Torg 12. ☎ **08/676-58-09.** Reservations not accepted. Main courses 85–159SEK ($10–$19). AE, DC, MC, V. July Mon–Sat 5pm–midnight. Aug–June, Mon–Sat 11:30am–midnight. T-bana: Kungsträdgården. SWEDISH.

Tucked away in the back of the swanky Operakällaren restaurant (see above), the "Hip Pocket" is a chic place to get a moderately priced meal. It's a small art nouveau room, meticulously maintained since 1904. There's seating for 30 diners at tables surrounding a horseshoe-shaped bar. Although it's within the Operakällaren, it has its own kitchen and a separate menu. Main courses might include grilled marinated fillet of cod with mustard sabayon, or perhaps sautéed roulades of pork stuffed with Swedish cheese in cider sauce and served with mashed vegetables and lingonberries. You'll always find salmon butterfly with béarnaise sauce and fried parsley, or thinly sliced beef tenderloin with horseradish, egg yolk, and mashed potatoes.

Lisa Elmquist. Östermalms Saluhall, Nybrogatan 31. ☎ **08/660-92-32.** Reservations recommended. Main courses 150–200SEK ($18–$24). AE, DC, MC, V. Mon–Thurs 10am–6pm, Fri 9am–7pm, Sat 9am–3:30pm. T-bana: Östermalmstorg. SEAFOOD.

Under the soaring roof and amid the food stalls of Stockholm's produce market (the Östermalms Saluhall), sits this likable cafe/oyster bar. The menu varies daily according to the catch, but might include fried monkfish with scampi and mixed vegetables, and boiled lemon sole with tarragon sauce and trout roe. Some people just order a portion of shrimp with bread and butter for 85 to 115SEK ($10 to $14). On Saturday, when only the bar is open, only cold and raw seafood items are available.

Prinsens. Mäster Samuelsgatan 4. ☎ **08/611-13-31.** Reservations required Sun. Main courses 150–225SEK ($18–$27); fixed-price lunch 85SEK ($10). AE, DC, MC, V. Mon–Sat 11:30am–2:30pm and 4:30–10:30pm, Sun 5–9:30pm. T-bana: Östermalmstorg. SWEDISH.

A 2-minute walk from the Stureplan, this is a favorite haunt of artists and has been feeding people since 1897. Diners are seated on one of two levels, and in summer some tables are placed outside. The cuisine is fresh and flavorful and includes daily dishes and traditional Swedish menu items such as veal patty with homemade lingonberry preserves, sautéed fjord salmon, and roulades of beef. The most popular item on the menu is a fillet of beef, served with fried potatoes and onions, marinated cucumbers, and egg yolk and mayonnaise on the side. For dessert, try the homemade vanilla ice cream.

IN GAMLA STAN (OLD TOWN)

Very Expensive

Eriks. Österlånggatan 17. ☎ **08/23-85-00.** Reservations required 2 days in advance. Main courses 285–485SEK ($35–$59); luncheon plates 90–200SEK ($11–$24); 10-course *menu dégustation* 800–1,195SEK ($98–$146). AE, DC, MC, V. Mon–Fri 11am–3pm and 6–11pm, Sat noon–3:30am and 5:30–11pm. Closed July and Dec 25–Jan 1. T-bana: Gamla Stan. FRENCH.

This restaurant, which occupies two floors of a building dating from the 1600s in the Old Town, has a warmly autumnal color scheme and English country-house decor. It is the domain of Erik Lallerstedt, one of the great master chefs of Stockholm. You can select from such appetizers as a warm lobster salad with leeks, tomatillos, and a lobster dressing; or perhaps goose-liver terrine with truffle soufflé. The chef's top specialty is fried duckling served in two courses—the breast in cider sauce is followed by the leg in green-pepper sauce. Fish selections include the catch of the day, or perfectly prepared lobster, turbot, and halibut with a chervil-and-champagne sauce, accompanied by wild rice.

Expensive

Den Gyldene Freden. Österlånggatan 51. ☎ **08/24-97-60.** Reservations recommended. Main courses 175–340SEK ($21–$42). AE, DC, MC, V. Mon–Fri 5pm–midnight; Sat 1pm–midnight. Closed July 2–Aug 2, bank holidays. T-bana: Gamla Stan. SWEDISH.

The "Golden Peace" is Stockholm's oldest tavern, opened in 1722. Its building is owned by the Swedish Academy, and members frequent the place on Thursday night. The cozy dining rooms, named for Swedish historic figures, are divided between the traditional 18th-century pub and the medieval cellar vaults. You get good traditional Swedish cooking here, and the chefs are especially fond of fresh Baltic fish and game from the forests of Sweden. Specials include roast reindeer in juniper-berry sauce with a timbale of black grouse; fried sole served with lemon, horseradish, and butter; and breast of pigeon and leg of guinea hen stuffed with duck liver and asparagus in sherry sauce.

Fem Små Hus. Nygrånd 10. ☎ **08/10-87-75.** Reservations required. Main courses 200SEK ($24). AE, DC, MC, V. Tues–Sat 5pm–midnight. Sun–Mon 5–10pm. T-bana: Gamla Stan. SWEDISH/FRENCH.

This historic restaurant, whose cellars date from the 17th century, is furnished like the interior of a private castle, with European antiques and oil paintings. It's actually five houses with nine dining rooms. After being shown to a candlelit table, you can order seasonal classic Swedish cuisine—fried fillet of reindeer served with a juniper-berry sauce, half an artichoke filled with vegetable ragout, and a French potato gratinée. The most popular dish on the menu, named after a woman who at one time ran a speakeasy in the cellars of these buildings, is veal Anna Lynberg, in a morel cream sauce flavored with Gorgonzola. Fish dishes include fresh salmon slightly oven baked, then served in a Chablis sauce with fresh asparagus, trout caviar, and boiled potatoes, or grilled turbot with ratatouille and basil butter.

Moderate

Cattelin Restaurant. Storkyrkobrinken 9. ☎ **08/20-18-18.** Reservations recommended. Main courses 89–185SEK ($11–$23); fixed-price lunch (Mon–Fri 11am–2pm only) 55SEK ($7). AE, DC, MC, V. Mon–Fri 11am–10pm, Sat noon–11pm; Sun 1–9pm. T-bana: Gamla Stan. SWEDISH.

Don't expect genteel service at this boisterous restaurant where the clattering of china can be almost deafening at times. Furniture, paintings, everything but the paint is part of the original 1927 decor. Economical menu items include fried brill with mushrooms and pressed potatoes, sliced beef with mushrooms and fried potatoes, and Swedish meatballs. The swordfish with lobster sauce, filet mignon black and white, and trout with white wine sauce and spinach are other options.

EXPLORING STOCKHOLM

Everything from the *Vasa* Ship Museum to the changing of the guard at the Royal Palace to the Gröna Tivoli amusement park will keep you intrigued. Even just window shopping for well-designed Swedish crafts can be a great way to spend an afternoon.

SIGHTSEEING SUGGESTIONS FOR FIRST-TIME VISITORS

If You Have 1 Day   Take a ferry to Djurgården to visit the **Royal Warship *Vasa*,** Stockholm's most famous attraction, and to explore the open-air **Skansen** folk museum. In the afternoon, walk through **Gamla Stan** (Old Town) and have dinner at one of its restaurants.

If You Have 2 Days   On Day 2, get up early and visit the **Kaknästornet** TV tower for a panoramic view of Stockholm, its many islands, and the archipelago. Go to the

Nordic Museum for insight into 5 centuries of life in Sweden. After lunch, visit the **Millesgården** of Lidingö, the sculpture garden and former home of Carl Milles.

If You Have 3 Days   Spend your third morning walking through the center of Stockholm and doing some shopping. At noon (1pm on Sunday), return to Gamla Stan to see the **changing of the guard at the Royal Palace.** View this French-inspired building that has been the residence of Swedish kings for more than 700 years. In the afternoon, see the attractions at the **National Museum.**

If You Have 4 or 5 Days   On Day 4, take one of the many tours of the **Stockholm archipelago.** Return to Stockholm and spend the evening at the **Gröna Tivoli** amusement park on Djurgården. On your last day, visit **Drottningholm Palace** and its 18th-century theater. In the afternoon, explore the university town of **Uppsala,** north of Stockholm, easily reached by public transportation.

THE TOP ATTRACTIONS
At Djurgården

✪ **Royal Warship** *Vasa.* Galärvarvet, Djurgården. ☎ **08/519-54-800.** Admission 60SEK ($7) adults, 35SEK ($4.25) students, 10SEK ($1.20) children 7–15; children under 7 free. June 10–Aug 20 daily 9:30am–7pm; Aug 21–June 9 daily 10am–5pm. Closed Jan 1, May 1, and Dec 24–25 and 31. Bus: 44 or 47; ferry from Slussen all year, from Nybroplan summer only.

This 17th-century man-of-war is the number-one attraction in Scandinavia—and for good reason. Housed in a museum specially constructed for it at Djurgården near Skansen, the *Vasa* is the world's oldest identified and complete ship.

In 1628, on its maiden voyage and in front of thousands of horrified onlookers, the Royal Warship *Vasa* capsized and sank almost instantly to the bottom of Stockholm harbor. When it was salvaged in 1961, more than 4,000 coins, carpenters' tools, and other items of archaeological interest were found on board. Best of all, 97% of the 700 original sculptures were retrieved. Carefully restored and preserved, they're back aboard the ship, which looks stunning now that it once again carries grotesque faces, lion masks, fish-shaped bodies, and other carvings, some with their original paint and gilt.

✪ **Skansen.** Djurgården 49–51. ☎ **08/442-80-00.** Admission 30–50SEK ($3.65–$6) adults, 10SEK ($1.20) ages 7–14, free 6 and under. Historic buildings, May–Aug daily 11am–6pm; Sept–Apr daily 11am–4pm. Bus: 44 or 47 from central Stockholm; ferry from Slussen to Djurgården.

Often called "Old Sweden in a Nutshell," this 35ha (75-acre) open-air museum, near Gröna Lund's Tivoli, contains more than 150 dwellings, most from the 18th and 19th centuries. Exhibits range from a windmill to a manor house to a complete town quarter. Browsers can explore the old workshops and see where the early book publishers, silversmiths, and pharmacists plied their trade. Handcrafts (glassblowing, for example) are demonstrated here, along with peasant crafts like weaving and churning. Folk dancing and open-air symphonic concerts are also featured (see "Stockholm After Dark").

Nordiska Museet (Nordic Museum). Djurgårdsvägen 6–16, Djurgården. ☎ **08/519-56-000.** Admission 60SEK ($7) adults, 50SEK ($6) seniors, 20SEK ($2.45) children 7–15, free for children under 7. Tues–Sun 10am–9pm. Bus: 44, 47, or 69.

This museum houses an impressive collection of implements, costumes, and furnishings of Swedish life from the 1500s to the present. Highlights are period costumes ranging from matching garters and ties for men to purple flowerpot hats from the 1890s. In the basement is an extensive exhibit of the tools of the Swedish fishing trade, plus relics from nomadic Lapps.

The Changing of the Royal Guard

Even the most hurried traveler will want to see the **changing of the Royal Guard.** You can watch the parade of the military guard daily in summer and on Wednesday and Sunday in winter (on all other days you can see only the changing of the guard). The parade route on weekdays begins at Sergels Torg and proceeds along Hamngatan, Kungsträdgårdsgatan, Strömgatan, Gustav Adolfs Torg, Norrbro, Skeppsbron, and Slottsbacken. On Sunday the guard departs from the Army Museum, going along Riddargatan, Artillerigatan, Strandvägen, Hamngatan, Kungsträdgårdsgatan, Strömgatan, Gustav Adolfs Torg, Norrbro, Skeppsbron, and Slottsbacken. For information on the time of the march, ask at the Information Service in the Sweden House (see "Visitor Information," above). The actual changing of the guard takes place at noon Monday to Saturday (at 1pm on Sunday) in front of the Royal Palace in Gamla Stan.

Prins Eugens Waldemarsudde. Prins Eugens Väg 6, Djurgården. ☎ **08/662-18-33.** Admission 60SEK ($7) adults, 40SEK ($4.90) students and seniors, free for children 16 and under. June–Aug Tues–Sun 11am–5pm; Sept–May Tues–Sun 11am–4pm. Bus: 47 to the end of the line.

This once-royal residence is today an art gallery and a memorial to one of the most famous royal artists in recent history, Prince Eugen (1865–1947). The youngest of King Oscar II's four children, he was credited with making innovative contributions to the techniques of Swedish landscape paintings, specializing in depictions of his favorite regions in central Sweden. Among his most visible works are the murals on the inner walls of the Stadshuset.

On Gamla Stan & Neighboring Islands

☼ Kungliga Slottet (Royal Palace). Kungliga Husgeradskammaren (☎ **08/402-61-32** for Royal Apartments and Treasury; ☎ **08/402-61-30** for Royal Armoury; ☎ **08/402-61-30** for Museum of Antiquities. Royal Apartments, 50SEK ($6) adults, 40SEK ($4.90) students, 15SEK ($1.85) children 7–18. Royal Armoury, 60SEK ($7) adults, 40SEK ($4.90) students, 20SEK ($2.45) children. Museum of Antiquities, 50SEK ($6) adults, 40SEK ($4.90) students. Treasury 50SEK ($6) adults, 40SEK ($4.90) seniors and students. Children under 7 are admitted free to all. Apartments and Treasury, May–Aug daily 10am–4pm, Sept–Apr Tues–Sun noon–3pm. Royal Armoury, year-round Tues–Sun 11am–4pm, May 1–Aug 30 Mon 11am–4pm. Royal Apartments off-limits during official government receptions. Museum of Antiquities, June–Aug daily 10am–4pm, Sept–May daily noon–3pm. T-bana: Gamla Stan; bus: 43, 46, 59, or 76.

Severely dignified, even cold looking on the outside, this palace has a lavish interior designed in the Italian baroque style. Kungliga Slotta is one of the few official residences of a European monarch that's open to the public. Although the Swedish king and queen prefer to live at Drottningholm, this massive 608-room showcase, built between 1691 and 1754, remains their official address.

The most popular rooms include the **State Apartments;** look for at least three magnificent baroque ceiling frescoes and fine tapestries. In the building's cellar is the **Stattkammaren (Treasury),** the repository for Sweden's crown jewels. Most intriguing to any student of war and warfare is the **Royal Armoury,** whose entrance is on the castle's rear side, at Slottsbacken 3. Gustavas III's collection of sculpture from the days of the Roman Empire can be viewed in the **Antikmuseum** (Museum of Antiquities).

Riddarholm Church. Riddarholmen. ☎ **08/402-61-30.** Admission 20SEK ($2.45) adults, 10SEK ($1.20) students and children. May and Sept Wed and Sat–Sun noon–3pm; June–Aug daily noon–4pm. Closed Oct–Apr. T-bana: Gamla Stan.

The second-oldest church in Stockholm is on the tiny island of Riddarholmen, next to Gamla Stan. It was founded in the 13th century as a Franciscan monastery. Almost all the royal heads of state are entombed here, except for Christina, who is buried in Rome. There're three principal royal chapels, including one, the Bernadotte wing, that belongs to the present ruling family.

In the City Center

Historiska Museet (Museum of National Antiquities). Narvavägen 13–17. ☎ **08/51-95-56-00.** Admission 60SEK ($7) adults, 50SEK ($6) seniors and students, 35SEK ($4.25) children 7–15, free for children under 7. Apr–Sept Tues–Sun 11am–5pm; Oct–Mar Tues–Sun 11am–5pm (until 8pm on Thurs). T-bana: Karlaplan or Östermalmstorg; bus: 44, 47, 54, 56, 69, or 76.

If you're interested in Swedish history, especially the Viking era, here you'll find the nation's finest repository of relics left by those legendary conquerors who once terrorized Europe. Many relics have been unearthed from ancient burial sites. The collection of artifacts ranges from prehistoric to medieval times, including Viking stone inscriptions and coins minted in the 10th century. The Gold Room features authentic Viking silver and gold jewelry, large ornate charms, elaborate bracelet designs found nowhere else in the world, and a unique neck collar from Färjestaden.

National Museum (National Museum of Fine Arts). Blasieholmskajen. ☎ **08/519-54-300.** Admission 60SEK ($7) adults, 40SEK ($4.90) seniors and students, free for children under 16. Tues and Thurs 11am–8pm, Wed and Fri–Sun 11am–5pm. T-bana: Kungsträdgården; bus: 46, 62, 65, or 76.

At the tip of a peninsula, a short walk from the Royal Opera House and the Grand Hotel, is Sweden's state treasure house of paintings and sculpture, one of the oldest museums in the world. The first floor is devoted to applied arts (silverware, handcrafts, porcelain, furnishings), but first-time visitors may want to head directly to the second floor to the painting collection with works by Rembrandt and Rubens, Lucas Cranach's most amusing *Venus and Cupid,* and a rare collection of Russian icons from the Moscow School of the mid–16th century. The most important room in the gallery has one whole wall devoted to Rembrandt—*Portrait of an Old Man* and *Portrait of an Old Woman,* along with his *Kitchen Maid.*

Moderna Museet (Museum of Modern Art). Skeppsholmen. ☎ **08/519-55-200.** Admission 60SEK ($7) adults, 40SEK ($4.90) seniors and students, free for children 15 and under. Tues–Thurs 11am–10pm, Fri–Sun 11am–6pm. T-bana: Rådmansgatan; bus: 65 to Skeppsholmen.

This museum focuses on contemporary works by Swedish and international artists, including kinetic sculptures. Highlights are a small but good collection of cubist art by Picasso, Braque, and Léger; Matisse's *Apollo* découpage; the famous *Enigma of William Tell* by Salvador Dalí; and works by Brancusi, Max Ernst, Giacometti, and Arp, among others.

Stadshuset (Stockholm City Hall). Hantverkargatan 1. ☎ **08/508-29-059.** Admission 50SEK ($6) adults, seniors, students; free for children under 12. Tower, May–Sept daily 10am–4pm. City Hall tours (subject to change), June–Sept daily at 10am, 11am, noon, and 2pm; Oct–May daily at 10am and noon. T-bana to Central Station or Rådhuset; bus: 48 or 62.

Built in what is called the "National Romantic Style," the Stockholm City Hall, on the island of Kungsholmen, is one of Europe's finest examples of modern architecture.

Designed by Ragnar Ostberg, the redbrick structure is dominated by a lofty square tower 106m (348 feet) high, topped by three gilt crowns and the national coat-of-arms. The Nobel Prize banquet takes place here in the Blue Hall. About 18 million pieces of gold and colored mosaics made of special glass cover the walls, and the southern gallery contains murals by Prince Eugen, the painter prince.

Just Outside Stockholm

❂ Drottningholm Palace and Theater. Ekerö, Drottningholm. ☎ **08/402-62-80.** Palace, 50SEK ($6) adults, 30SEK ($3.65) students and persons under 26. Theater, 50SEK ($6) adults, 30SEK ($3.65) students and persons under 26. Chinese Pavilion, 50SEK ($6) adults, 30SEK ($3.65) students and persons under 26. All 3 are free for children 15 and under. Palace, May daily 11am–4:30pm, June–Aug 10am–4:30pm, Sept noon–3:30pm; closed weekdays Oct–Apr. Theater, guided tours in English, May–Aug 12:30, 1:30, 2:30, 3:30, and 4:30pm, and Sept 1:30, 2:30, and 3:30pm; closed Oct–Apr. Chinese Pavilion, May–Aug 11am–4:30pm, Sept noon–3:30pm, Oct 1–3:30pm; closed Oct–Mar. All hours are daily. There're two ways of reaching Drottningholm. The first is by steamboat, which takes 50 min. and costs 75SEK ($9) round-trip adults or 50SEK ($6) children 6–11. Boats leave from Stadshusbron, beside Stockholm's City Hall, daily, early June–mid-Aug on the hour 10am–4pm and at 6pm and May–early June and mid-August to early September 10am–2pm (to 4pm on weekends). Contact **Strömma Kanalbolaget** at ☎ **08/23-33-75** (fax 08/20-50-31) for more information. **Stockholm City Sightseeing** (☎ **08/587-140-30**) offers round-trips to Drottningholm in turn-of-the-century boats. You can also take the T-Bana to Brommaplan, then connect to any Mälarö bus for Drottningholm.

Originally conceived as the centerpiece of Sweden's royal court, this regal complex of stately buildings sits on an island in Lake Mälaren. Dubbed the Versailles of Sweden, Drottningholm, or Queen's Island, is about 11km (7 miles) west from Stockholm. The palace—loaded with courtly art and furnishings—is surrounded by fountains and parks, and still functions as one of the official residences of the country's royal family. On the grounds is one of the most perfectly preserved 18th-century theaters in the world, **Drottningholm Court Theater** (☎ **08/759-04-06**), with 30 annual performances (mostly 18th-century operas) between May and September. The theater only seats 450, and performances often sell out long in advance. (For ticket information, see "Stockholm After Dark," below.)

❂ Millesgården. Carl Milles Väg 2, Lidingö. ☎ **08/446-75-90.** Admission 80SEK ($10) adults, 50SEK ($6) seniors and students, 30SEK ($3.65) children 7–16, free for children under 7. May–Sept, daily 10am–5pm; Oct–Apr, Tues–Sun noon–4pm. T-bana: Ropsten, then bus to Torsviks torg or train to Torsvik.

On the island of Lidingö, northeast of Stockholm, is Carl Milles's former villa and sculpture garden beside the sea, now a museum. Many of his best-known works are displayed here (some are copies), as are works of other artists. Milles (1875–1955), who relied heavily on mythological themes, was Sweden's most famous sculptor.

A VIEW ON HIGH

Kaknästornet (Kaknäs Television Tower). Ladugårdsvägen 60. ☎ **08/789-24-35.** Admission 25SEK ($3.05) adults, 15SEK ($1.85) children 7–15, free for children under 7. May–Aug daily 9am–10pm; Sept–Apr daily 10am–9pm. Closed Dec 24–25. Bus: 69 from Central Station.

The tallest man-made structure in Scandinavia, this radio/television tower stands 155m (508 feet) high. Two elevators take visitors to an observation platform, where you can see everything from the cobblestone streets of the Old Town to the city's modern concrete-and-glass structures and the archipelago beyond.

An Amusement Park

Gröna Lunds Tivoli. Djurgården. ☎ **08/587-50-100.** Admission 40SEK ($4.90) adults, free for children 12 and under. Apr–Sept daily noon–11pm or midnight (hours are subject to change; call for exact hours). Bus: 44 or 47; Djurgården ferry from Nybroplan.

Unlike its Copenhagen namesake, this is an amusement park, not a fantasyland. For those who like Coney Island–type thrills, it's a good nighttime adventure.

Organized Tours

Stockholm City Sightseeing (☎ 08/587-140-30) operates the best tours. From early June to early August, 1¹/₂-hour tours leave from the Opera House at 10 and 1pm; the cost is 130SEK ($16) for adults and half price for children 6 to 11. Ask about the combination excursions that include walking, touring by bus, and/or taking a boat.

Also offered are boat tours of the city, departing from Strömkajen, in front of the Grand Hotel. (Locals insist that the best way to explore their city is by boat.) Get tickets at the kiosk topped with yellow flags with a red *S* on them. The company's "Under the Bridges of Stockholm" tour takes 2 hours and costs 140SEK ($17) for adults and half price for children 6 to 15; it's offered mid-April to mid-December. The hour-long "Royal Canal Tour" runs mid-May to early September for 90SEK ($11).

THE SHOPPING SCENE

A whopping 25% goods tax makes shopping in Sweden expensive, and you can get most items at home for less money. On the positive side, Swedish stores usually stock items of the highest quality. Favorite buys include crystal, clothing, and Scandinavian-design furniture.

For the best shopping and window-shopping, stroll along the streets of **Gamla Stan** (especially **Västerlånggatan**), filled with boutiques, art galleries, and jewelry stores. Attractive shops and galleries can also be found along the **Hornsgats-Puckeln** (the Hornsgatan-Hunchback, a reference to the shape of the street), on **Södermalm.** Other good browsing streets are **Hamngatan, Birger Jarlsgatan, Biblioteksgatan,** and **Kungsgatan,** all in **Norrmalm.**

Blås & Knåda, Hornsgatan 26 (☎ 08/642-77-67; T-bana: Slussen), sells the products of a cooperative of 50 Swedish ceramic artists and glassmakers. Prices begin at 160SEK ($20) for small functional pieces, and go way up for museum-quality works of art. Bone china, stoneware dinner services, and other fine table and decorative ware are made at **Keramiskt Centrum Gustavsberg** (Gustavsberg Ceramics Center) (☎ 08/570-356-58; bus: 422 or 24400), on Värmdö Island, about 21km (13 miles) east of Stockholm.

Traveler's Tip

Many stores offer tax rebates to visitors spending over 200SEK ($24). When you make your purchase, ask the retailer for a Tax Free Check (valid for 1 month) and leave your purchase sealed until you leave the country. At any border crossing on your way out of Sweden (or at repayment centers in Denmark, Finland, or Norway), show both the check (to which you've added your name, address, and passport number) and the purchase to an official at the tax-free desk. You'll get a cash refund of about 16% to 18% in U.S. dollars (or seven other currencies) after the service charge has been deducted (remember not to check the purchase in your luggage until after you receive the refund). For more information, call ☎ 0410/613-01.

In the center of Stockholm, the largest department store in Sweden is **Åhlesns City,** Klarabergsgatan 50 (☎ **08/676-60-00;** T-bana: T-Centralen), with a gift shop, a restaurant, and a famous food department. Also seek out the fine collection of home textiles and Orrefors and Kosta crystal ware. **Nordiska Kompanient,** Hamngatan 18–20 (☎ **08/762-80-00;** T-bana: Kungsträdgården), NK for short, is another high-quality department store. Most of the big names in Swedish glass are displayed at NK, including Orrefors (see the Nordic Light collection) and Kosta. Swedish handcrafted items are in the basement. Stainless steel is also a good buy in Sweden. Greta Garbo got her start in the millinery department at **PUB,** Hötorget 13 (☎ **08/239-915;** T-bana: Hötorget), a popular department store that sells middle-bracket clothing and good-quality housewares.

At **Loppmarknaden I Skärholmen (Skärholmen Shopping Center),** Skärholmen (☎ **08/710-00-60;** T-bana: 13 or 23 to Skärholmen, a 20-minute ride), the biggest flea market in northern Europe, you might find *anything.* Try to go on Saturday or Sunday (the earlier the better) when the market is at its peak. Weekend admission is 10SEK ($1.20), but weekdays are free. **Geocity,** Tysta Marigången 5, Tegélbacken (☎ **08/411-11-40;** T-bana: T-Centralen), offers exotic mineral crystals, jewelry, Scandinavian gems, Baltic amber, and lapidary equipment. Its staff includes two certified gemologists who'll cut and set any gem you select, as well as appraise jewelry you already own. Its inventory includes stones from Scandinavia and around the world, including Greenland, Madagascar, Siberia, and South America.

An unusual outlet, **Slottsbodarna (Royal Gift Shop),** in the south wing of the Royal Palace, Slottsbacken (☎ **08/402-60-48;** T-bana: Gamla Stan), sells items related to or copied from the collections in the Royal Palace, re-created in silver, gold, brass, pewter, textiles, and glass. Every item is made in **Sweden. Svensk Hemslojd (Society for Swedish Handcrafts),** Sveavägen 44 (☎ **08/23-21-15;** T-bana: Hötorget), has a wide selection of glass, pottery, gifts, and wooden and metal handcrafts, the work of some of Sweden's best artisans. You'll also see a display of hand-woven carpets, upholstery fabrics, tapestries, lace, and embroidered items; and you can even find beautiful yarns for your own weaving and embroidery.

STOCKHOLM AFTER DARK

Pick up a copy of *Stockholm This Week,* distributed at the Stockholm Information Service in the Sweden House (see "Visitor Information," above), to see what's on.

THE PERFORMING ARTS

All the major opera, theater, and concert performances begin in autumn, except for special summer festival performances. Fortunately, most of the major opera and theatrical performances are funded by the state, which keeps the ticket price reasonable.

Founded by King Gustavus III in 1766, the ✪ **Drottningsholm Slottsteater,** Drottningholm (☎ **08/660-82-25;** T-bana: Brommaplan), stands on an island in Lake Mälaren, 11km (7 miles) from Stockholm. It stages operas and ballets with full 18th-century regalia, complete with period costumes and wigs. The theater, a short walk from the royal residence, seats only 450 patrons, which makes tickets hard to come by. Eighteenth-century music performed on antique instruments is a perennial favorite. The season is May to September and most performances begin at 7:30pm, lasting $2^{1}/_{2}$ to 4 hours. Ticket are 100 to 500SEK ($12 to $61) and should be ordered at least 2 months in advance by phoning the number above and giving your American Express card number (only American Express is accepted).

Filharmonikerna I Konserthuset (Concert Hall). Hötorget 8 (☎ **08/8-786-02-00;** T-bana: Hötorget), home of the **Stockholm Philharmonic Orchestra,** is the

---

Special Events with a Local Flavor at Skansen

The open-air museum **Skansen** (see "The Top Attractions," above) arranges traditional seasonal festivities like autumn market days and a Christmas Fair as well as summer concerts, sing-alongs, and guest performances. Folk dancing is staged June to August, Monday to Saturday at 7pm and Sunday at 2:30 and 4pm. Live music accompanies outdoor dancing June to August, Monday to Friday 8:30 to 11:30pm. Admission is 30SEK ($3.65) adults and 10SEK ($1.20) children 7 to 14; children under 7 are free.

---

principal place to hear classical music in Sweden. (The Nobel Prizes are also awarded here.) Constructed in 1920, the building houses two concert halls—one, seating 1,600, is better suited for major orchestras; the other, seating 450, is suitable for chamber music groups. Box office hours are Monday through Friday noon to 6pm, Saturday 11am to 3pm. Tickets are 50 to 500SEK ($6 to $61).

Founded in 1773 by King Gustavus III, who was assassinated here at a masked ball, the **Operan (Royal Opera House),** Gustav Adolfs Torg (☎ 08/24-82-40; T-bana: Kungsträdgården), is the home of the **Royal Swedish Opera** and the **Royal Swedish Ballet.** The present building dates from 1898. Performances are usually Monday to Saturday at 7:30pm (closed mid-June to August). The box office is open Monday to Friday noon to 7:30pm (to 6pm if no performance is scheduled) and Saturday noon to 3pm. Tickets are 100 to 500SEK ($12 to $61); many are discounted 10% to 20% for seniors and students.

NIGHTCLUBS

Café Opera, Operahuset, Kungsträdgården (☎ 08/676-58-07; T-bana: Kungsträdgården)—Swedish beaux arts at its best—functions as a bistro, brasserie, and tearoom during the day and as one of the most popular nightclubs in Stockholm at night. (Don't confuse this spot with the opera's main dining room, the Operakällaren, whose entrance is through a different door). Near the entrance of the cafe is a stairway leading to one of the Opera House's most beautiful corners, the clublike Operabaren (Opera Bar). It's open Monday to Saturday 11:30am to 3am and Sunday 1pm to 3am. There's no cover before 10pm, 80SEK ($10) after.

Göta Källare, in the Medborgplatsen subway station, Södermalm (☎ 08/642-08-28; T-bana: Medborgplatsen), is the largest and most successful supper-club–style dance hall in Stockholm, with a long list of clients who have met here, and subsequently fallen in love and gotten married. Large, echoing, and paneled with lots of wood in a *faux-español* style, it has a large terrace that surrounds an enormous tree, and a restaurant. Expect a crowd aged 45 and older, and music from a live orchestra (performing "Strangers in the Night" a bit too frequently). The place is open every night from 8:30pm. Cover is 60SEK ($7) before 9:30pm; 95SEK ($12) after.

ROCK & JAZZ CLUBS

Some of Sweden's and the world's best known jazz musicians regularly play **Fasching,** Kungsgatan 63 (☎ 08/21-62-67; T-bana: T-Centralen). It's so small, you almost feel like you're in the band. Weekend late nights are for dancing, and after midnight on Friday there's salsa; Saturday late is dedicated to soul. Hours can be irregular, so it's best to call in advance, but it's usually open nightly from 7pm to at least 2am. Cover is 60 to 225SEK ($7 to $27).

The Swedish branch of **Hard Rock Cafe,** Sveavägen 75 (☎ **08/16-03-50;** T-bana: Hötorget), is fun and gregarious. Sometimes an American, British, or Scandinavian band gives a live concert; otherwise it's the sound system. Club sandwiches, hamburgers, T-bone steaks, and barbecued spareribs are available. Open in summer, Sunday to Thursday 11am to 1am and Friday and Saturday 11am to 3am; in winter, Sunday to Thursday 11am to midnight and Friday and Saturday 11am to 1am. There's no cover.

Pub Engelen/Nightclub Kolingen, Kornhamnstorg 59B (☎ **08/20-10-92;** T-bana: Gamla Stan), is a three-in-one combination consisting of the Engelen Pub, the Restaurant Engelen, and the Nightclub Kolingen in the cellar. The restaurant, which serves some of the best steaks in town, is open Sunday to Thursday 5 to 11:30pm and Friday to Saturday 5pm to 1:30am. Swedish groups (mostly) perform live in the pub daily from 8:30pm to midnight—usually soul, funk, and rock. The pub is open Tuesday to Thursday from 4pm to 1am, Friday and Saturday from 4pm to 2am, and Sunday from 5pm to 1am. In the cellar (which dates from the 15th century), the Nightclub Kolingen is a disco nightly from 10pm to about 3am. Pub and nightclub cover is 40 to 60SEK ($4.90 to $7) Monday to Friday after 9pm. You must be 23 or over to enter.

BARS

One of the hippest and most talked-about bars in Stockholm, **Tiger Bar/Havana Bar,** 18 Kungsgatan (☎ **08-244-700;** T-bana: Östermalmstorg), attracts a bevy of supermodels and TV actors. It's divided into a street-level site (the Tiger Bar) that's outfitted in black leather upholstery and a postmodern kind of cool, and a basement-level recreation of pre-Castro Cuba (the Havana Bar) that's outfitted with plastic palms and the deliberately garish colors associated with Old Havana's most raunchy 1950s-era excesses. You're likely to hear anything from recorded disco (every Friday and Saturday beginning at midnight), and live salsa and merengue (every Wednesday from 9pm to 5am). The place is open Wednesday and Thursday from 7pm to 3am, and Friday and Saturday from 7pm to 4am.

Named after the builder of the deluxe Grand Hotel, the **Cadier Bar,** Södra Blasieholmshamnen 8 (☎ **08/679-35-00;** T-bana: Kungsträdgården), enjoys a view of the harbor and Royal Palace. It's one of the most sophisticated places for a rendezvous in Stockholm. You can also enjoy light meals at any time of day in the extension overlooking the waterfront. Open Monday to Saturday noon to 2am and Sunday noon to 12:30am; a piano player performs Monday to Saturday 9:30pm to 1:30am.

A GAY BAR

If you're gay, consider slugging back a round or two at **Sidetrack,** Wollmar Yxkullsgatan 7 (☎ **08/641-1688;** T-bana: Mariatorget). Small, and committed to shunning any semblance of trendiness, it was named after its founder's favorite gay bar in Chicago. It's open every night 6pm to 1am. Tuesdays here seem to be something of an institution in gay Stockholm. Other nights, however, it's fine too—something like a Swedish version of a bar and lounge at your local bowling alley where everyone happens to be into same-sex encounters.

DAY TRIPS FROM STOCKHOLM

SKOKLOSTER CASTLE **Skokloster,** S-746 96 Skokloster (☎ **018/38-60-77**), is a splendid 17th-century castle and one of the most interesting baroque museums in Europe. It's next to Lake Mälaren, 64km (40 miles) west of Stockholm and 40km (31 miles) south of Uppsala. Original interiors aside, the castle is noted for its rich collections of paintings, furniture, applied art, tapestries, arms, and books. Admission is 60SEK ($7) for adults, 50SEK ($6) for seniors, 30SEK ($3.65) for students and children. Guided tours are conducted May to August daily every hour at 11am to 4pm; in September daily at noon; and in April and October on Saturday and Sunday only at 1, 2, and 3pm. The site is closed November to March.

Skokloster Motor Museum (☎ **018/38-61-00**), on the palace grounds, contains the largest collection of vintage automobiles and motorcycles in the country. One of the most notable cars is a 1905 8-horsepower De Dion Bouton. Unlike the castle, the museum is open all year. It costs 40SEK ($4.90) for adults, 10SEK ($1.20) for children 7 to 14, and it's free for children 6 and under. It's open only May to September daily 11am to 5pm and October to April, every Saturday and Sunday from 11am to 5pm.

Getting There   From Stockholm take a train to the hamlet of Bålsta, which lies 19km (12 miles) from the castle. At the village train station, you can either take bus 894 directly to Skokloster, or call for a taxi from a direct telephone line that's prominently positioned just outside the railway station.

UPPSALA   The major university city of Sweden, Uppsala, 68km (42 miles) northwest of Stockholm, is the most popular destination for day-trippers from Stockholm, and for good reason. Uppsala not only has a great university, but also a celebrated 15th-century cathedral. Even in the time of the Vikings, this was a religious center, the scene of animal and human sacrifices in honor of the old Norse gods, and was once the center of royalty as well. Queen Christina occasionally held court here. The church is still the seat of the archbishop, and the first Swedish university was founded here in 1477.

Getting There   The town is easily reached by train from Stockholm's Central Station. Trains leave about every hour during peak daylight hours (trip time: 45 minutes). Boats from Stockholm to Uppsala (or vice versa) also stop at Skokloster and Sigtuna. Check with the tourist office in Stockholm or Uppsala for details.

Visitor Information   The **tourist office** is at Fyris Torg 8 (☎ **018/27-48-00**), open Monday to Friday 10am to 6pm and Saturday 10am to 3pm.

Exploring Uppsala   At the end of Drottninggatan is the **Carolina Rediviva (University Library)** (☎ **018/471-00-00;** bus: 6, 7, or 22), with its more than five million volumes and 40,000 manuscripts, among them many rare works from the Middle Ages. But the manuscript that really draws visitors is the *Codex Argenteus* (Silver Bible), translated into the old Gothic language in the middle of the 3rd century and copied in about A.D. 525. It's the only book extant in the old Gothic script. Also worth seeing is *Carta Marina,* the earliest map (1539), a fairly accurate map of Sweden and its neighboring countries. Admission is free. The Library's exhibition room is open Monday to Friday 9am to noon.

Linnaeus Garden and Museum, Svartbäcksgatan 27 (☎ **018/13-65-40** for the museum, or 018/10-94-90 for the garden; walk straight from the rail station to Kungsgatan, and go for about 10 minutes to Svartbäcksgatan), is the former home of Swedish botanist Carl von Linné, known as Carolus Linnaeus, who developed a classification system for the world's plants and flowers. This museum is on the spot where he restored Uppsala University's botanical garden, which resembles a miniature baroque garden. His detailed sketches and descriptions of the garden have been faithfully followed. Admission to the museum is 20SEK ($2.45) for adults and free for children. Admission to the gardens is 20SEK ($2.45) for adults and free for children under 12. The gardens are open May to August daily 9am to 9pm and September daily 9am to 7pm. The museum is open June to mid-September, Tuesday to Sunday noon to 4pm.

The largest cathedral in Scandinavia at nearly 120m (400 feet) tall, the twin-spired Gothic ✪ **Uppsala Domkyrka,** Domkyrkoplan 5 (☎ **018/18-72-01;** bus: 1 and 2), was founded in the 13th century. It was severely damaged in 1702 in a disastrous fire that swept over Uppsala, then was restored near the turn of the last century. Among the regal figures buried in the crypt is Gustavus Vasa. The remains of St. Erik, patron saint of Sweden, are entombed in a silver shrine. Botanist Linnaeus and philosopher-theologian Emanuel Swedenborg are also buried here. A small museum displays ecclesiastical relics of Uppsala. Admission to the cathedral is free; museum admission is 30SEK ($3.65) for adults and 20SEK ($2.45) for children 7 to 15 (free for children under 7). The cathedral is open daily from 8am to 6pm.

✪ **GRIPSHOLM CASTLE** On an island in Lake Mälaren, Gripsholm Castle (Gripsholm Slottsfervaltning), P.O. Box 14, 64721 Mariefred (☎ **0159/101-94)**— the fortress built by Gustavus Vasa in the late 1530s—is one of the best-preserved castles in Sweden. It lies near Mariefred, an idyllic small town known for its vintage narrow-gauge railroad.

Even though Gripsholm was last occupied by royalty (Charles XV) in 1864, it's still a royal castle. Its outstanding features include a large collection of portrait paintings depicting obscure branches of the Swedish monarchy, its brooding architecture, and its 18th-century theater built for the amusement of the 18th-century actor-king Gustavus III. It's open May to August daily 10am to 4pm; in September, Tuesday to Friday 10am to 3pm; October to March, Saturday and Sunday only, noon to 3pm. Admission is 50SEK ($6) for adults and 25SEK ($3.05) for children under 12.

Getting There The castle is 68km (42 miles) southwest of Stockholm, easily reached either by the E-20 south or by taking the fast X-2000 train from Stockholm's main railway station (trip time: 35-minutes). In summertime, you might also opt to take a ferryboat from Stockholm's Klara Malarstrand Pier, near Stadshuset. Your best bet is to take one of the ferries that departs every Monday to Friday at 10am for an arrival at Mariefred at 1:30pm. It's a 5-minute stroll from the Mariefred pier to the castle.

18 Switzerland

by Darwin Porter & Danforth Prince

Switzerland evokes images of towering peaks, mountain lakes, lofty pastures, and alpine villages, but it also offers a rich cultural life in cities such as sophisticated Geneva and perfectly preserved medieval Bern.

1 Geneva

Geneva is in the Rhône Valley at the southwestern corner of Lake Geneva (Lac Léman in French), between the Jura Mountains and the Alps. It's the capital of the canton of Geneva, the second-smallest canton in the Swiss confederation.

Switzerland's second-largest city is truly cosmopolitan. The setting is idyllic, on one of the biggest alpine lakes and within view of the glorious pinnacle of Mont Blanc. Filled with parks and promenades, the city becomes a virtual garden in summer. It's also one of the world's healthiest cities because the prevailing north wind blows away any pollution.

The yachts bobbing in the harbor and the Rolls-Royces cruising the promenades testify that Geneva is home to some of the richest people in the world. Its state religion is said to be banking—half of Switzerland's banks are located here.

Geneva has long held a position as a center of enlightenment and humane tolerance. Over the years it has offered a refuge to such controversial figures as Voltaire, Lenin, and native son Jean-Jacques Rousseau. Geneva also hosted Knox and Calvin, the religious reformers, and provided a safe haven for many artists. Today the headquarters of the International Red Cross and the World Health Organization are here, and it attracts many other international organizations.

ORIENTATION

GETTING THERE **By Plane** The **Geneva-Cointrin Airport** (☎ 022/717-71-11), though busy, is compact and easily negotiated. **Swissair** (☎ 800/221-4750 in the U.S.) has the most frequent flights from North America to Geneva. **American Airlines** (☎ 800/433-7300) makes daily nonstop flights from Chicago to Zurich where planes fly frequently into Geneva. Connections can also be made on **United Airlines** (☎ 800/241-6522) with a daily nonstop flight from Washington to Zurich with a connection to Geneva.

Finally **Air Canada** (☎ **800/776-3000**) flies nonstop daily from Toronto to Zurich where passengers then wing their way to Geneva on one of several frequent flights.

To get into the center of Geneva, there's a train station linked to the air terminal with trains leaving about every 8 to 20 minutes from 5:39am to 11:36pm (trip time: 7 minutes); the one-way fare is 8.40SF ($6) first class and 5SF ($3.35) second class. A taxi into town costs 30SF ($20) and up, or you can take bus 10 for 2.20SF ($1.45).

By Train   Geneva's busiest, most central, and most visible CFF (Chemins de fer fédéraux) rail station is **Gare Cornavin** (sometimes referred to as Genève-Cornavin), place Cornavin (☎ **022/157-22-22** or 022/05-12-25-14-92). Don't confuse it with **Gare Genève-Cointrin,** near the airport, which handles some of the spillover from its larger sibling. Conveniently, some trains heading off to other regions of Switzerland and the rest of Europe from Genève-Cointrin don't require transfers in Genève-Cornavin, a fact that's appreciated by many airline passengers flying to other parts of the country.

By Car   From Lausanne, head southwest on N1 to the very "end of southwestern Switzerland."

By Lake Steamer   Llate May to late September there are frequent daily arrivals by Swiss lake steamer from Montreaux, Vevey, and Lausanne (you can use your Eurailpass). If you're staying in the Left Bank (Old Town), get off at the Jardin Anglais stop in Geneva; Mont Blanc and Pâquis are the Right Bank stops. For more information, call ☎ **022/312-52-23.**

VISITOR INFORMATION   The **Office du Tourisme de Genève,** 3 rue du Mont-Blanc (☎ **022/909-70-00**), is at Gare Cornavin. The staff provides information and can arrange hotel reservations (in Geneva and throughout Switzerland) and excursion bookings, and can refer you to car-rental agencies. The office is open June 15 to September 15, Monday to Friday 8am to 6pm and Saturday to Sunday 8am to 5pm; the rest of the year, it's open Monday to Saturday 9am to 6pm.

CITY LAYOUT   Geneva is divided by **Lake Geneva (Lac Léman)** and the **Rhône River** into two sections: the Right Bank and Left Bank. You may rent an audio-guided tour in English from the tourist office (see above) for 10SF ($7). This tour covers more than two dozen highlights in Old Town and comes with a cassette player, and map. A 50SF ($37) deposit is required.

Rive Gauche (Left Bank)   This compact and colorful area is the oldest section. Here you'll find Old Town, some major shopping streets, the famous Flower Clock, the university, and several important museums. **Grand' Rue** is Old Town's well-preserved main street, flanked by many houses from the 15th and 18th centuries. The street winds uphill from the ponts de l'Ile; at place Bel-Air it becomes rue de la Cité, then Grand' Rue, and finally rue Hôtel-de-Ville. Eventually it reaches **place du Bourg-de-Four**—one of Geneva's most historic squares (Rousseau was born in no. 40).

South of this street is **promenade des Bastions,** a greenbelt area with a monument to the Reformation; it overlooks the Arve River. Directly to the west, in the northern corner of promenade des Bastions, is **place Neuve,** Geneva's finest square. From place Neuve, you can take **rue de la Corraterie,** once surrounded by the city wall, to the Rhône and the **ponts de l'Ile.** On this bridge is the Tour de l'Ile, what's left of the 13th-century bishop's castle.

On the shore of Lake Geneva is the **Jardin Anglais** (English Garden) with its Flower Clock, and farther out are the **Parc La Grange** and **Parc des Eaux-Vives.**

Rive Droite (Right Bank)   You can cross to the other side of the Rhône on any of several bridges, including **pont du Mont-Blanc, pont de la Machine, pont des**

Geneva

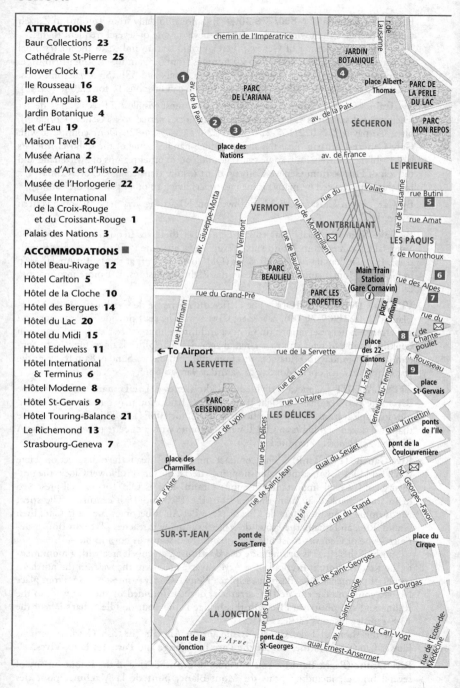

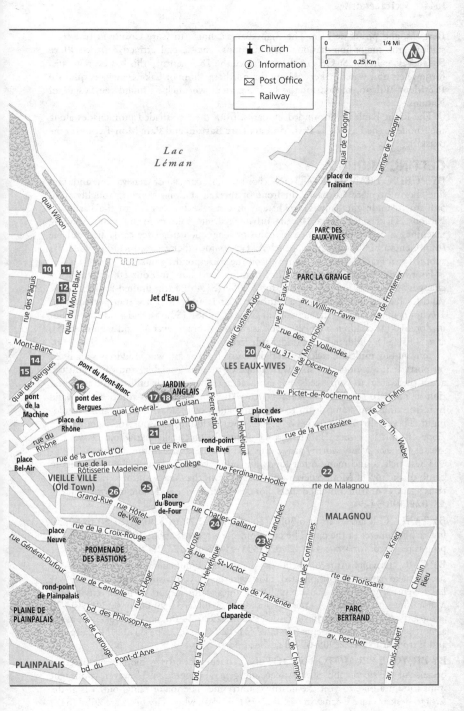

Bergues, and **ponts de l'Ile.** The Right Bank is home to **Gare Cornavin** (the train station), the major international organizations, and several attractive parks. **Place St-Gervais** is in the St-Gervais district; since the 18th century this has been an area for jewelers and watchmakers. Along the northern shore of Lake Geneva is **quai du Président-Wilson,** named for the U.S. president who helped found the League of Nations.

The Right Bank is surrounded by parks, from the tree-shaded promenades along the Rhône to the **Parc de la Perle du Lac, Parc Barton,** and **Parc Mon-Repos** on the outskirts.

GETTING AROUND

BY PUBLIC TRANSPORTATION   For the most part, all of Geneva's bus and tram lines begin at place Cornavin, in front of the rail station—running roughly from 5:30am to midnight daily. From here, you can take bus F or 8 to the Palais des Nations. Tickets for **Zone 10,** the urban area, are sold from automatic vending machines at each stop, operated by coins or magnetic cards (free cards are available from Geneva public transport agencies). Tickets for other zones, including Geneva's suburbs and France, are sold by drivers on the corresponding buses.

Four **basic tickets** are provided: free transfers for 1 hour in Zone 10, with as many changes as you wish on any vehicle, for 2.20SF ($1.45); a trip limited to three stops, valid for half an hour, allowing a return trip, at 1.50SF ($1); free transportation for $1^{1}/_{2}$ hours in all zones of the network of Geneva, at 4SF ($2.65); and a ride for 1 hour in Zone 10 for children 6 to 12 as well as seniors (women over 62 and men over 65), at 1.50SF ($1); children 5 and under ride free.

You can buy **multiuse tickets** and **daily cards** from agents whose addresses are listed on posts at the various stops. A wide range of these is available, and often you can adapt the system to your needs. For example, a daily ticket for unlimited transportation in Zone 10 is 5SF ($3.35) for as many trips and changes as you need; it's valid from the time you stamp it up to the termination of the day's service, around midnight. There's also a daily ticket at 8.50SF ($6) including transportation not only in Zone 10, but in Zones 21, 31, and 41, taking in practically the whole network of greater Geneva. Many worthy attractions and restaurants are in the suburbs.

These tickets and many other kinds, including combined bus/cable-car tickets to climb to the top of Mont Salève, are available from the Geneva public transport systems agencies or from official dealers. For customer service and more information, call ☎ **022/308-34-34.**

BY TAXI   Cab fares start at 6.30SF ($4.20), plus 2.70 to 3.30SF ($1.80 to $2.20) for each kilometer in the city. The fare from the airport is about 30SF ($20). No tipping is required; for a taxi, call ☎ **022/331-41-33** or 022/320-20-20.

BY CAR   Driving isn't recommended—parking is too difficult and the many one-way streets make navigation complicated. However, should you wish to rent a car and tour Lake Geneva, you'll find many rental companies at the airport or in the city center. Major offices include **Avis,** 44 rue de Lausanne (☎ **022/731-90-00,** or 022/929-03-30 at the airport); **Budget,** 36 rue de Zurich (☎ **022/900-24-00,** or 022/798-22-52 at the airport); **Hertz,** 60 rue de Berne (☎ **022/731-12-00,** or 022/798-11-02 at the airport); and **Europcar** (☎ **022/909-69-90** at the airport).

BY BICYCLE OR MOTOR SCOOTER   Touring the city by bicycle isn't practical because of the steep cobblestone streets and general congestion. However, you might want to rent a bike to visit the nearby countryside. The major rental outlet is at the *bagages* desk at **Gare Cornavin** (☎ **022/791-02-50**), where city bikes are 26SF ($17) per day and mountain bikes 35SF ($23) per day.

If you're interested in renting a motor scooter, try **Horizon Motos,** 51 rue de Lausanne (☎ **022/732-29-90**), where rentals begin at 35SF ($23) per day.

Fast Facts: Geneva

American Express   The American Express office at 7 rue du Mont-Blanc (☎ **022/731-76-00;** bus: 1) is open Monday to Friday 8:30am to 5:30pm and Saturday 9am to noon.

Baby-Sitters   A list of agencies is available at the tourist office. Hotels will also secure an English-speaking sitter for you, or you can call **Service de Placement de l'Université,** 4 rue de Candolle (☎ **022/329-39-70;** tram: 12). Call this office before noon if you want a sitter at night.

Business Hours   Most **banks** are open Monday to Friday 8:30am to 4:30pm (to 5:30pm on Wednesday). Most **offices** are open Monday to Friday 8am to noon and 2 to 6pm, though this can vary. It's always best to call first.

Consulates   If you lose your passport or have other business with your home government, go to your nation's consulate: **United States,** Route de Près Bois 29 (☎ **022/798-16-15;** tram to Gare Genè-Cointrin [airport]); **Australia,** 56–58 rue Moillebeau (☎ **022/918-29-00**); **Canada,** 1 chemin du Pré-de-la-Bichette (☎ **022/919-92-00;** bus: 5, 8, or 18); **New Zealand,** 28A chemin du Petit-Saconnex (☎ **022/734-95-30;** bus: 3); the **United Kingdom,** 37–39 rue de Vermont (☎ **022/918-24-00;** bus: 3), or **South Africa**, rue de Rhône 65 (☎ **022/849-54-54;** bus: 2, 9, or 22).

Currency   The basic unit of currency is the **Swiss franc (SF),** made up of 100 centimes. Notes are in denominations of 10, 20, 50, 100, 500, and 1,000 francs, and coin denominations are 5, 10, 20, and 50 centimes and 1, 2, and 5 francs. At press time, the rate of exchange used in this chapter was $1 = 1.50SF, or 1SF = 65¢; £1 = approximately 2.48SF. The Euro rate is 1.59SF = €1.

Currency Exchange   The money exchange at **Gare Cornavin,** 10 place Cornavin (☎ **022/375-33-60;** tram to Gare Cornavin), is open daily 8:30am to 8:30pm. For other financial transactions, the **Société de Banque Suisse** (Swiss Bank Corporation) is at 2 rue de la Confédération (☎ **022/375-75-75;** bus: 12).

Dentists   English-speaking dentists are available at one of the *cliniques dentaires* at 5 rue Malombré (☎ **022/346-64-44;** tram: 12), Monday to Friday 7:30am to 8pm and Saturday to Sunday 8am to 6pm.

Doctors   In a medical emergency, call ☎ **022/320-25-11;** or arrange an appointment with an English-speaking doctor at the **Hôpital Cantonal,** 24 rue Micheli-du-Crest (☎ **022/372-3311;** tram: 12).

Drugstores   One of the world's biggest drugstores, **Pharmacie Principale,** Confédération-Centre, rue de la Confédération (☎ **022/318-66-60;** bus: 12), offers everything from medicine to clothing, perfumes, optical equipment, cameras, and photo supplies. It's open Monday to Friday 9am to 7pm and Saturday 9am to 5pm.

Emergencies   In an emergency, dial ☎ **117** for the police, ☎ **144** for an ambulance, and ☎ **118** to report a fire.

Hospitals   You can go to the **Hôpital Cantonal,** 24 rue Micheli-du-Crest
(☎ **022/372-3311**).

Internet Access   Global Café, 71 rue des Rois (☎ **022/328-2619**; bus: 1, 4,
or 44), is open Monday 2 to 11pm, Tuesday to Saturday 10am to 11pm; e-mail:
info@globalcafe.ch.

Post Office   The city's main post office, **Bureau de Poste Montbrillant,** rue de
Gares (☎ **022/739-21-11**; tram to Gare Cornavin), offers a full range of telephone, telegraph, and mail-related services Monday to Friday 8am to 10:45pm,
Saturday 8am to 10pm, and Sunday noon to 8pm. There's a branch, which offers
less extensive services, at **Gare Cornavin,** 16 rue de Gares (☎ **022/739-24-15**),
open Monday to Friday 6am to 10:45pm, Saturday 6am to 8pm, and Sunday
noon to 8pm.

Taxes   Geneva has no special city tax. All goods and services throughout
Switzerland have a 6.5% value-added tax (VAT) attached, however.

Telephones/Telex/Fax   The **country code** for Switzerland is **41.** The **city code**
for Geneva is **22;** use this code when you're calling from outside Switzerland. If
you're within Switzerland but not in Geneva, use **022.** If you're calling within
Geneva, simply leave off the code and dial the regular phone number.

A big **long-distance phone center** is at the main train station, Gare Cornavin,
place Cornavin; it's open 24 hours. It's much cheaper to make your long-distance
calls here than at your hotel—some Geneva hotels add a 40% surcharge to long-
distance calls. Telegrams and faxes can be sent at the post office at 16 rue des
Gares (☎ **022/739-24-61**), 2 blocks from the train station. For **AT&T,** call
☎ **888/288-4685;** for **Sprint,** call ☎ **800/877-4646;** for **MCI,** call ☎ **800/
444-4141.**

WHERE TO STAY
ON THE RIGHT BANK
Very Expensive

Hôtel Beau-Rivage. 13 quai du Mont-Blanc, CH-1201 Genève. ☎ **022/716-66-66.** Fax
022/716-60-60. E-mail: info@beau-rivage.ch. 97 units. MINIBAR TV TEL. 520–740SF
($347–$494) double; from 1,980SF ($1,321) suite. AE, DC, MC, V. Parking 30SF ($20). Bus: 1.

This landmark 1865 hotel receives our highest recommendation for its traditional
Victorian charm and impeccable service. However, you pay dearly for them. The
"romantic" rooms are bigger than the "classical." Double-glazing cuts down on street
noise, and each unit has a roomy bathroom, with robes and a hair dryer. Some rooms
are air-conditioned, and those in front open onto views of the Right Bank. The more
elegant of the hotel's two restaurants is Le Chat-Botté (see "Where to Dine," below).

Hôtel des Bergues. 33 quai des Bergues, CH-1211 Genève. ☎ **022/908-70-00.** Fax
022/908-70-90. www.hoteldesbergues.com. E-mail: info@hoteldesbergues.com. 120 units.
A/C MINIBAR TV TEL. 465–795SF ($310–$530) double; from 2,200SF ($1,467) suite. AE, DC,
MC, V. Parking 35SF ($23) per night. Bus: 7.

This elegant hotel once catered to the monarchs of Europe. It has long been ranked
by *Institutional Investor* as one of the world's top hotels, grandly memorable from its
central position at the edge of the Rhône. The staff is the most hospitable in Geneva.
Rooms have Directoire and Louis-Philippe furnishings. Those ranked superior on the
Bel Etage floor are the finest choices, although lake view rooms are more expensive.
Bathrooms have tub/shower combinations, phones, hair dryers, full-length mirrors,
and thick towels. The two restaurants and bar are highly recommended.

☉ Le Richemond. Jardin Brunswick, CH-1211 Genève. ☎ **022/715-70-00.** Fax 022/715-70-01. www.richemond.ch. E-mail: reservations@richemond.ch. 91 units. A/C MINI-BAR TV TEL. 640–740SF ($427–$494) double; from 990SF ($660) suite. AE, DC, MC, V. Parking 45SF ($30). Bus: 1.

Le Richemond is Geneva's greatest hotel and counts some of the world's most prominent people among its guests. Erected in 1875, the neoclassical building is near the lake, across from a small park. Nearly half of the units are suites. A large number are renovated every year but even those between rehabs look as good as new. This is true Grand Hotel living, with luxurious beds and spacious bathrooms with hair dryers, robes, and a basket of expensive toiletries. Some rooms are reserved for nonsmokers. Gentilhomme is among the finest dining rooms in Geneva, and Le Jardin is the city's most fashionable cafe.

Moderate

Hôtel Carlton. 22 rue Amat, CH-1202 Genève. ☎ **022/908-68-50.** Fax 022/908-68-68. E-mail: carlton@swissonline.ch. 123 units. TV TEL. 150–240SF ($100–$160) double. Rates include buffet breakfast. AE, DC, MC, V. Parking 10SF ($7). Bus: 4.

This hotel is about 7 city blocks east of the rail station and near the waterfront views of quai du Président-Wilson. Rooms have minimal sitting areas but good beds and fine linen. Bathrooms feature both shower and tubs. Lunch and dinner are served in the restaurant/grill, Le Canard Laqué, with a menu that includes an extensive salad buffet and fresh fish.

Hôtel du Midi. 4 place Chevelu, CH-1211 Genève. ☎ **022/731-78-00.** Fax 022/731-00-20. E-mail: midihotel@irpolink.ch. 90 units. A/C MINIBAR TV TEL. 210–245SF ($140–$163) double; 450SF ($300) suite. Rates include continental breakfast. AE, DC, MC, V. Bus: 7.

On a tree-lined square near the center of Geneva, this salmon-colored eight-story hotel resembles an apartment building. Rooms, though not spectacular, are well maintained and comfortable, with double-glazed windows to keep out traffic noise, warming racks for towels, and safes. Bathrooms are a bit cramped but have adequate shelf space. The hotel maintains a small restaurant at street level open only Monday to Friday.

Hôtel Edelweiss. 2 place de la Navigation, CH-1201 Genève. ☎ **022/731-36-58.** Fax 022/738-85-33. 39 units. MINIBAR TV TEL. 225SF ($150) double. Rates include continental breakfast. AE, DC, MC, V. Parking 15SF ($10). Bus: 1.

This brown-and-white hotel, built in the early 1960s, towers above its neighbors near quai du Président-Wilson. Its rustic interior decor contrasts with its modern exterior. Rooms, cozy with pinewood furniture crafted in country-Swiss style, have sitting areas and desk space, but bathrooms are small and devoid of many amenities. Its little restaurant is patronized by locals and is inexpensively priced.

Hôtel Moderne. 1 rue de Berne, CH-1211 Genève. ☎ **022/732-81-00.** Fax 022/738-26-58. www.hotelmoderne.ch. E-mail: info@hotelmoderne.ch. 54 units. TV TEL. 180–190SF ($120–$127) double. Rates include buffet breakfast. AE, DC, MC, V. Bus: 10.

This seven-story white rectangle is near the rail station and the lake. Public areas are modern, with Nordic furniture and abstract angles and curves. Rooms, with sound-proof windows, are modern, clean and sunny, though predictably furnished and a bit sterile. Some are reserved for nonsmokers. You'll probably wish the bathrooms had more room to spread out your stuff. Baby-sitting, room service, and laundry facilities are available. The hotel's restaurant serves only breakfast, but there's an Italian restaurant in the building. The nearest parking is at the Cornavin rail station's underground garage nearby.

Strasbourg-Geneva. 10 rue J.-J.-Pradier, CH-1201 Genève. ☎ **800/528-1234** in the U.S., or 022/906-58-00. Fax 022/738-42-08. www.hotel-strasbourg-geneva.ch. E-mail: info@hotel-strasbourg-geneva.ch. 53 units. MINIBAR TV TEL. 200–240SF ($133–$160) double; 300–500SF ($200–$334) suite. Rates include continental breakfast. AE, DC, MC, V. Bus: 1, 2, 3, 4, 8, 12, 13, or 44.

Close to the rail station, this building was constructed around 1900, though many renovations—the most recent in 1999—have kept it looking fresh. The most spacious rooms tend to be those on the lower floors. The compact, tiled bathrooms are minimally equipped. Run by a local family, this hotel is affiliated with Best Western.

Inexpensive

✪ **Hôtel de la Cloche.** 6 rue de la Cloche, CH-1211 Genève. ☎ **022/732-94-81.** Fax 022/738-16-12. 8 units, 3 with bathroom. TV. 85SF ($57) double without bathroom, 120SF ($80) double with bathroom; 95SF ($63) triple without bathroom; 140SF ($93) quad without bathroom. AE, MC, V. Bus: 1.

This small hotel, one of Geneva's best deals, occupies the second floor of a 19th-century apartment building on a narrow street behind the Noga Hilton. Unpretentious despite a glamorous location, it's run by an elderly widow, Mme Chabbey. Rooms are spacious, well cared for, and designed with an eye to old-fashioned comfort. Some have views over a quiet inner courtyard and others open onto views over the lake. Private bathrooms have rather cramped shower stalls; corridor bathrooms are well maintained, and there's rarely a wait. Breakfast is the only meal served.

Hôtel International & Terminus. 20 rue des Alpes, CH-1201 Genève. ☎ **022/732-80-95.** Fax 022/732-18-43. 53 units. MINIBAR TV TEL. 200SF ($133) double. Rates include continental breakfast. AE, DC, MC, V. Bus: 6, 10, or 33.

This hotel lies across from the main entrance of Geneva's railway station and has been run by three generations of the Cottier family. Built around 1900, it was radically upgraded in 1999, with pairs of smaller rooms reconfigured into larger units. Don't expect grand style, the allure of this place is its exceedingly good value. Bathrooms seem to have been added as an afterthought in areas not designed for them, and are a bit cramped. The restaurant, La Veranda, serves some of the most reasonable meals in Geneva, and also keeps the pizza ovens' piping hot.

Hôtel St-Gervais. 20 rue des Corps-Saints, CH1201 Genève. ☎ and fax **022/732-45-72.** 26 units, 2 with bathroom. 78SF ($52) double without bathroom, 98SF ($65) double with bathroom. AE, MC, V. Tram: 1, 3, 4, 5, or 6.

This good-value hotel lies in an old-fashioned, vaguely nondescript building within Geneva's medieval core, a 3-minute walk from Gare Cornavin. Though it has the kind of quirky idiosyncrasies that appeal to architects and historic renovators, its minimalist furnishings and conservative decor are a bit lackluster. Most rooms have a sink, but the hall bathrooms are frequently tidied for the next guest's use. There's a convivial pub on the ground floor.

ON THE LEFT BANK

Moderate

Hôtel Touring-Balance. 13 place Longemalle, CH-1204 Genève. ☎ **022/818-62-62.** Fax 022/818-62-61. 58 units. MINIBAR TV TEL. 250SF ($167) double; 350–500SF ($233–$334) suite. Rates include buffet breakfast. AE, DC, MC, V. Parking 28SF ($19). Bus 6, 8, or 9.

Previously two hotels across the street from each other, the Touring-Balance is in the heart of the Left Bank's shopping district. A radical renovation in 1999 transformed the lobby with a theme like that of an Italian garden, complete with *jardinières* and potted plants. Rooms in both sections are comparable in style and amenities. Upper floors are more modern than the traditional lower floors. Some units are air-conditioned. Bathrooms are compact, neat, and well kept. There's a coffee shop adjacent to the lobby in the Touring.

Inexpensive

Hôtel du Lac. 15 rue des Eaux-Vives, CH-1207 Genève. ☎ **022/735-45-80.** Fax 022/735-45-82. 26 units, none with bathroom. 80SF ($53) double; 110SF ($73) triple. Rates include continental breakfast. No credit cards. Bus: 9 from the train station to place des Eaux-Vives.

This small budget hotel in the old city occupies the sixth and seventh floors of an apartment building. The Swiss-Italian managers don't pretend to offer first-class service, but they make up for it with their hospitality. Although rooms are small and the mattresses somewhat thin and used, this minimalist place is one of the best values in a very expensive city. Most have a phone and a balcony. There are no private bathrooms, but the public bathrooms are quite decent.

WHERE TO DINE
ON THE RIGHT BANK
Very Expensive

✪ **Le Chat-Botté.** In the Hôtel Beau-Rivage, 13 quai du Mont-Blanc. ☎ **022/716-66-66.** Reservations required. Main courses 40–51SF ($27–$34); set-price menu 60–145SF ($40–$97) at lunch, 115–145SF ($77–$97) at dinner. AE, DC, MC, V. Daily noon–2pm and 7–10pm. Bus: 6 or 33. FRENCH.

"Puss in Boots" is in one of Geneva's grandest hotels. Decorated with tapestries, sculpture, and rich upholstery, and graced by a polite staff, it serves delectable food. In nice weather you can dine on the flower-decked terrace, overlooking the Jet d'Eau. The cuisine, though inspired by French classics, is definitely contemporary. The large selection includes fillets of red mullet vinaigrette, lobster salad with eggplant "caviar," and breast of chicken stuffed with vegetables. Highly recommended is delicate perch fillet from Lake Geneva, sautéed until it's golden and sometimes served with fava beans. In the autumn gourmets flock here for the roast saddle of roebuck, prepared only for two or more diners.

Le Cygne. In the Noga Hilton International, 19 quai du Mont-Blanc. ☎ **022/908-90-85.** Reservations required. Main courses 38–64SF ($25–$43); fixed-price meal 58–78SF ($39–$52) at lunch, 75–155SF ($50–$103) at dinner. AE, DC, MC, V. Daily noon–2pm and 7–10pm. Closed 1 week in Jan, 11 days at Easter, and 3 weeks in July. Bus: 1. FRENCH.

Le Cygne overlooks the harbor with the famous Jet d'Eau and, in the distance, the Alps. A refined cuisine is offered, with impeccable service. The menu changes seasonally and may present such choices as terrine of blackened chicken in crayfish- and anise-flavored aspic. Also good are the smoked fillet of sea bass with truffle-flavored vinaigrette and the roasted lamb with coriander and tomatoes stuffed with moussaka. Five elaborate carts, each laden with a different selection, make one of the most spectacular arrays of desserts in Switzerland.

Le Neptune. In the Hôtel du Rhône, 1 quai Turrettini. ☎ **022/731-98-31.** Reservations required. Main courses 45–62SF ($30–$41); fixed-price meal 65SF ($43) at lunch; 65–125SF ($43–$83) at dinner. AE, DC, MC, V. Mon–Fri noon–2pm and 7:30–10pm. Bus: 6, 8, 10, or 15. SEAFOOD.

At one of Geneva's finest seafood restaurants, the decor is intimate, intensely floral, and graced with an enormous fresco displaying an inside view of Neptune's kingdom. Though the menu changes based on market conditions, you're likely to be offered such dishes as herbed vichyssoise with hazelnut oil and a dollop of foie gras; cassolette of oysters seasoned with algae-flavored butter sauce; or Atlantic sea bass roasted in a salt crust with thyme. If you're not in the mood for fish, try rack of Scottish lamb in puff pastry with spices or partridge roasted en casserole with autumn herbs.

Expensive

La Mère Royaume. 9 rue des Corps-Saints. ☎ **022/732-70-08.** Reservations required. Brasserie, main courses 15–26SF ($10–$17); fixed-price menu 36–48SF ($24–$32). Restaurant, main courses 28–48SF ($19–$32); fixed-price menus 50–98SF ($33–$65). AE, DC, MC, V. Mon–Fri noon–2pm and 7–10:30pm, Sat 7–10:30pm. Bus: 4, 6, or 7. FRENCH.

Opened around the turn of the century, this is one of the oldest restaurants in town. It's named after a heroine who in 1602 poured boiling stew over a Savoyard soldier's head and cracked his skull with the kettle. With an antecedent like that, you'd expect some of the heartiest fare in Geneva, but instead the kitchen offers perfectly cooked French specialties such as *omble chevalier,* a delicate Lake Geneva whitefish known as "the world's most divine trout." Less expensive meals are served in the brasserie.

Moderate

✪ **Chez Jacky.** 9–11 rue Necker. ☎ **022/732-86-80.** Reservations recommended. Main courses 38–42SF ($25–$28); business lunch 40SF ($27); fixed-price dinner 55–85SF ($37–$57). AE, DC, MC, V. Mon–Fri 11am–2pm and 6:30–11pm. Closed first week of Jan and 3 weeks in Aug. Bus: 5, 10, or 44. SWISS.

This French provincial bistro should be better known, though it already attracts everyone from grandmothers to young skiers en route to Verbier. It's the domain of Jacky Gruber, an exceptional chef from Valais. There's a subtlety in M. Gruber's cooking that suggests the influence of his mentor, Frédy Giradet, once hailed as the world's greatest chef. You might begin with Chinese cabbage and mussels and continue with fillet of turbot roasted with thyme or beautifully prepared pink duck on spinach with onion confit. Be prepared to wait for each course.

Le Boeuf Rouge. 17 rue Alfred-Vincent (at the corner of rue Paquis). ☎ **022/732-75-37.** Reservations recommended. Main courses 29–49SF ($19–$33); set-price lunches 17–35SF ($11–$23); set-price dinners 43–47SF ($29–$31). AE, DC, MC, V. Mon–Fri noon–2pm and 7–10:30pm. Bus: 1. LYONNAIS.

Few other restaurants in Geneva's center work so hard to bring you an authentic version of the brasserie-style cuisine of Lyon. As such, you'll find authentic versions of such dishes as Lyonnais sausage with scalloped potatoes; chateaubriand in red wine sauce; blood sausage; and quenelles of pike-perch, any of which might be preceded by a delectable version of onion soup or green salad with croutons and bacon. The decor is appealingly kitschy, complete with lots of art nouveau posters and late 19th-century ceramics. The staff here is brusque but kindly.

ON THE LEFT BANK

Expensive

Le Béarn. 4 quai de la Poste. ☎ **022/321-00-28.** Reservations required. Main courses 30–64SF ($20–$43); fixed-price meal 55–160SF ($37–$107) at lunch, 90–160SF ($60–$107) at dinner. AE, DC, MC, V. Mon–Fri noon–2pm; Mon–Sat 7:15–10pm. Closed mid-July to mid-Aug and Sat June–Sept. Bus: 2, 10, or 22. FRENCH.

Jean-Paul Goddard and his excellent staff have created the best restaurant in Geneva's business center. With only 10 tables, everything is on a small scale, and the service is personal. There are two dining areas in the Empire style. The chefs prepare dishes like morels stuffed with fresh asparagus tips, roasted Scottish thrush (one of the world's most expensive birds), and a platter called "three terrines of autumn" (rabbit, partridge, and thrush).

Moderate

Au Pied de Cochon. 4 place du Bourg-de-Four. ☎ **022/310-47-97.** Reservations recommended. Main courses 25–38SF ($17–$25). AE, DC, MC, V. Daily noon–2:30pm and 6:30–11pm (closed Sun June–Aug). Bus: 2 or 22; tram: 12. LYONNAISE/SWISS.

Come here for hearty Lyonnaise fare if you don't mind smoke and noise. A lot of young people are attracted to this place, as well as lawyers from the Palais de Justice across the way, artists, and local workers. The cooking is like grandma's—provided she came from Lyon. Naturally, the namesake *pieds de cochon* (pigs' feet) is included on the menu, along with *petit salé* (lamb), tripe and some of the best grilled andouillettes (sausages made of chitterlings) in Geneva.

Brasserie de l'Hôtel de Ville. 19 Grand Rue. ☎ **022/311-70-30.** Reservations recommended. Main courses 30–45SF ($20–$30); set-price menus 49–90SF ($33–$60). AE, DC, MC, V. Daily 11am–11:30pm. Bus: 17. SWISS.

This is one of the most deliberately archaic-looking restaurants in Geneva, with a reputation that goes back to 1764 and a clientele that prefers its old-fashioned decor and its choice of menu items absolutely not change. Within a dining room loaded with antique or semiantique kitsch, you can enjoy dialogues with antique dealers and their clients. The menu is stylish and fashionable, offering such time-tested Swiss dishes as fondue, *tafelspits* (boiled beef), Wiener schnitzel, glazed ham served with béarnaise sauce; fillets of perch and fera from the nearby lake.

Brasserie Lipp. Confédération-Centre, 8 rue de la Confédération. ☎ **022/311-10-11.** Reservations recommended. Main courses 23–45SF ($15–$30); fixed-price menus 55–75SF ($37–$50); plats du jour 175SF ($117) lunch only. AE, DC, MC, V. Daily 7am–12:45am. Bus: 12. SWISS.

This bustling place is named after the famous Parisian brasserie, and when you enter (especially at lunch) and see the waiters in black jackets with long white aprons rushing about, you'll think you've been transported to France. The impossibly long menu contains a sampling of the repertoire of bistro dishes, but like its namesake, the Geneva Lipp specializes in several versions of charcuterie. You can also order three kinds of pot-au-feu and such classics as Toulousain cassoulet with confit de canard (duckling), available in autumn and winter. The fresh oysters are among the best in the city, and tables are placed outside in summer.

La Coupole. 116 rue du Rhône. ☎ **022/787-50-10.** Main courses 34–44SF ($23–$29); fixed-price menus 49–70SF ($33–$47). AE, DC, MC, V. Fri–Sat and Mon 11:30am–2:30pm and 7–11:30pm, Tues–Thurs 11:30am–2:30pm and 7–10:30pm. Bus: 2, 9, or 22; tram: 12. SWISS.

This is a true brasserie, and far more elegant than its Parisian namesake. The place is most popular at noon, especially with shoppers and office workers. Fanciful and fun, it's dotted with grandfather clocks, a bronze *Venus,* Edwardian palms, and comfortable banquettes. The menu is limited but well selected; the *cuisine du marché* (cooking based on market-fresh ingredients) is some of the finest in this part of town. Chefs search the market in the early morning for the freshest and best of ingredients, then quickly compose a day's menu based on their purchases.

L'Aïoli. 6 rue Adrien-Lachenal. ☎ **022/736-79-71.** Reservations not necessary. Main courses 20–29SF ($13–$19); *menu dégustation* 69SF ($46). AE, DC, MC, V. Tues–Sat 11am–2:30pm and 7–10:30pm. Closed Aug. Bus: 1 or 6; tram: 12. PROVENÇAL.

This popular neighborhood restaurant stands opposite Le Corbusier's Maison de Verre. Something of a local secret, it offers personalized service and the finest Provençal cooking in town. An evening meal includes an appetizer, a first plate, a main dish, cheese, a dessert, coffee, and wine (you can spend more by ordering à la carte). Frogs' legs Provençal are simmered in a savory tomato, onion and garlic sauce, and also recommended is the lamb gigot, in which the meat is infused with fresh herbs and garlic and baked to a tender perfection. The chefs also prepare a delectable Provence-derived lamb stew called gardiane camarguaise.

✪ La Favola. 15 rue Jean-Calvin. ☎ **022/311-74-37.** Reservations required. Main courses 39.50–47.50SF ($26–$32). AE, MC, V. Mon–Fri noon–2pm and 7:15–10pm. Closed 1 week at Christmas, 2 weeks between July–Aug. Tram: 12. TUSCAN/ITALIAN.

This is the best Italian dining spot in Geneva, and its most devoted habitués go even further, hailing it as the best restaurant in Geneva. Within a few steps of the Cathédrale St-Pierre, it contains two cramped dining rooms and boasts a family-managed staff. The menu is small and short but choice, varying with the availability of ingredients and the season. Look for such dishes as carpaccio of beef; *vitello tonnato* (paper-thin veal with a tuna sauce); lobster salad; potato salad with cèpe mushrooms; and ravioli made on-site with either eggplant or mushrooms.

Le Lyrique. 12 bd. du Théâtre. ☎ **022/328-00-95.** Reservations recommended. Restaurant, main courses 25–40SF ($17–$27); fixed-price menu 47–60SF ($31–$40). Brasserie, main courses 20–30SF ($13–$20); fixed-price menu (lunch or dinner) 36–45SF ($24–$30). AE, MC, V. Mon–Fri noon–2pm and 6:30–10pm. Bus: 2 or 22. SWISS.

Le Lyrique contains both a formal restaurant and a brasserie. The restaurant opened in 1981, but was cleverly patterned on late 19th-century models. It bustles with urban vitality and is very tuned to the arts and business lives of Geneva. When there's a special presentation at the nearby Grand Théâtre de Genève on Saturday or Sunday, the restaurant is open. The brasserie, which has a terrace, is open all day but serves hot meals only during the hours mentioned above. In the restaurant, you can try such carefully prepared dishes as fillet of sea wolf with grapefruit segments, a roulade of rabbit with pasta maison, and tagliatelle with scampi. In the brasserie, menu items include chicken suprême with ravioli and leeks and an assiette Lyrique, a meal in itself that combines four vegetarian and fish dishes—tartare of salmon, tartare of vegetables, terrine of vegetables, and eggplant "caviar."

Pizzeria da Paolo. 3 rue du Lac. ☎ **022/736-3049.** Reservations recommended. Pizza 13.50–20SF ($9–$13). Main platters 21–40SF ($14–$27). AE, DC, MC, V. Daily 11:45am–2pm and 6:45–11pm. Tram 12. ITALIAN/PIZZA.

Bustling, convivial, and completely unpretentious, this simple pizzeria offers a cozy, wood-sheathed setting from a position very close to the water jet that's the very symbol of Geneva. Inside, a staff member will accept your order for pizza. There are more than 20 kinds offered—the house specialty is a Pizza Paolo, made from fresh spinach and cheese. But if pizzas aren't your thing, there's also a full complement of chicken parmigiana; stuffed and roasted turkey, fresh salads, ham dishes, and fresh fish. Don't expect glamour or too much cosseting from the overworked staff—instead, you'll get a dose of reality, everyday grittiness, good value, and some filling and very tasty Italian food.

Restaurant du Palais de Justice. 8, place du Bourg-de-Four. ☎ **022/318-37-37.** Main courses 20–41SF ($13–$27); fondues 21–39SF ($14–$26). AE, DC, MC, V. Mon–Sat noon–2:15pm and 6:45–10:30pm. Bus: 2 or 22. SWISS/ITALIAN/FRENCH.

An inviting place with lots of atmosphere, this restaurant is in the old town on a colorful square, across from the Palais de Justice. It was established in the late 1950s in a medieval building complete with a cellar with a vaulted ceiling, and has thrived ever since. The building contains three dining rooms. Small pizzas, fondues, and *plats du jour*, including an array of beef dishes, draw the crowds, as do such dishes as fillet of lamb with baby vegetables. The food is in the usual brasserie style, nothing special but nothing really bad either.

Inexpensive

Taverne de la Madeleine. 20 rue Toutes-Ames. ☎ **022/310-60-70.** Reservations recommended. Main courses 13–24SF ($9–$16); *plat du jour* 14SF ($9). MC, V. Sept–June Mon–Fri 7:30am–6pm (last food order at 4pm), Sat 9am–4:30pm (last food order at 2:30pm); July–Aug Tues–Sat 7:30am–9pm. Tram: 12; bus: 2. SWISS.

This very good restaurant is set against the old city wall beside the Eglise de la Madeleine. The restaurant was opened about 80 years ago in a century-old building. The brusquely efficient staff caters to a lunchtime business crowd, and the place is operated by a philanthropic organization that forbids the consumption of alcohol (alcohol-free beer is available). You can order a variety of well-prepared dishes or specials like four types of pasta, vegetarian sandwiches, and a big plate of osso buco (braised veal shank) with *pommes frites.* The kitchen prides itself on its fillet of lake perch meunière style (in butter sauce) or Vevey style with exotic mushrooms.

SEEING THE SIGHTS

You can see most of Geneva on foot, which is the best way to familiarize yourself with the city.

SIGHTSEEING SUGGESTIONS FOR FIRST-TIME VISITORS

If You Have 1 Day   Begin the day by viewing the spectacular water fountain, **Jet d'Eau,** and the **Flower Clock** in the Jardin Anglais. Then take a **steamer cruise** of Lake Geneva. Return in the early afternoon and explore the Left Bank's **Old Town.** Have dinner at a restaurant on or around place du Bourg-de-Four.

If You Have 2 Days   Spend Day 1 as above. On Day 2, visit some of the most important museums, each completely different. It'll take a full day of sightseeing to absorb the **Musée d'Art et d'Histoire,** the **Musée International de la Croix-Rouge et du Croissant-Rouge (Red Cross Museum),** and the **Palais des Nations.**

If You Have 3 Days   Spend Days 1 and 2 as above. On Day 3, take a stroll along the quays of Geneva in the morning, and in the afternoon go on an organized excursion to the Alps, including Mont Blanc, for a panoramic view.

If You Have 4 or 5 Days   Spend Days 1 to 3 as above. On Day 4, take a lake steamer to Lausanne. You'll have time to explore its old town and walk its lakeside quays at Ouchy before returning to Geneva in the evening. On Day 5, take another lake steamer, this time to Montreux; after visiting this lakeside resort, take a trip outside the town to see the Château de Chillon, immortalized by Lord Byron.

THE TOP ATTRACTIONS

In addition to the sights below, Geneva's top attractions are the ✪ **Jet d'Eau,** the famous fountain that has virtually become the city's symbol; the **Flower Clock,** in the Jardin Anglais; and the **Old Town,** the oldest part of the city.

Baur Collections. 8 rue Munier-Romilly. ☎ **022/346-17-29.** Admission 5SF ($3.35) adults, free for children. Tues–Sun 2–6pm. Bus: 1 or 8.

The collections, housed in a 19th-century mansion with a garden, constitute a private exhibit of artworks from China (10th to 19th century) and Japan (17th to 20th century). On display are jade, ceramics, lacquer, ivories, and delicate sword fittings.

Maison Tavel. 6 rue du Puits-St-Pierre. ☎ **022/310-29-00.** Free admission. Tues–Sun 10am–5pm. Bus: 3, 5 or 17.

Built in 1303 and partially reconstructed after a fire in 1334, this is the city's oldest house and one of its newest museums. The museum exhibits historical collections from Geneva dating from the Middle Ages to the mid–19th century. The Magnin relief in the attic is outstanding, as is the copper-and-zinc model of 1850s Geneva. Objects of daily use are displayed in the old living quarters.

Musée Ariana. 10 av. de la Paix. ☎ **022/48-54-50.** Free admission, but 5SF ($3.35) for special exhibits. Wed–Mon 10am–5pm. Bus: 8 or F.

To the west of the Palais des Nations, this Italian Renaissance building was constructed by Gustave Revilliod, the 19th-century Genevese patron who began the collection. Today it's one of the top porcelain, glass, and pottery museums in Europe. Here you'll see Sèvres, Delft faïence, and Meissen porcelain, as well as pieces from Japan and China. It's also the headquarters of the International Academy of Ceramics.

✪ **Musée d'Art et d'Histoire (Museum of Art and History).** 2 rue Charles-Galland. ☎ **022/418-26-00.** Free admission. Tues–Sun 10am–5pm. Bus: 2, 3, 5, 7, 12, or 16.

Geneva's most important museum is between boulevard Jacques-Dalcroze and boulevard Helvétique. Displays include prehistoric relics, Greek vases, medieval stained glass, 12th-century armor, Swiss timepieces, and Flemish and Italian paintings. The Etruscan pottery and medieval furniture are quite impressive. A 1444 altarpiece by Konrad Witz depicts the "miraculous" draught of fishes. Many galleries also contain works by such artists as Rodin, Renoir, Le Corbusier, Picasso, Chagall, Corot, Monet, and Pissarro.

Musée de l'Horlogerie (Watch Museum). 15 route de Malagnou. ☎ **022/418-64-70.** Free admission. Wed–Mon 10am–5pm. Bus: 6 or C tram: 12.

This town house chronicles the history of watches and clocks from the 16th century. It displays everything from sand timers to sundials, though most of the exhibits are concerned with Geneva's watches, usually from the 17th and 18th centuries. The enameled watches of the 19th century are particularly intriguing (many play chimes when you open them).

✪ **Musée International de la Croix-Rouge et du Croissant-Rouge (International Red Cross and Red Crescent Museum).** 17 av. de la Paix. ☎ **022/748-95-11.** Admission 10SF ($7) adults, 5SF ($3.35) seniors, students, and children. Wed–Mon 10am–5pm. Bus: 18, F, V or Z.

Here you can experience the legendary past of the Red Cross in the city where it started; it's across from the visitors' entrance to the European headquarters of the United Nations. The dramatic story from 1863 to the present is revealed through displays of rare documents and photographs, films, multiscreen slide shows, and cycloramas. You're taken from the battlefields of Europe to the plains of Africa to see the Red Cross in action. When Henry Dunant founded the Red Cross in Geneva in 1863, he needed a recognizable symbol to suggest neutrality. The Swiss flag (a white cross on a red field), with the colors reversed, ended up providing the perfect symbol for one of the world's greatest humanitarian movements.

✪ **Palais des Nations.** Parc de l'Ariana, 14 av. de la Paix. ☎ **022/907-48-96.** Admission 8.50SF ($6) adults, 6.50SF ($4.35) students, 4SF ($2.65) children under 6. July–Aug daily 9am–6pm; Sept–June daily 10am–noon and 2–4pm. Bus: 5, 8, 18, F, V, or 2.

Surrounded by ancient trees and modern monuments, these buildings comprise the second-largest complex in Europe after Versailles. Until 1936, the League of Nations met at the Palais Wilson, when the League's headquarters were transferred to the Palais des Nations. The international organization continued minor activities through the war years until it was dissolved in 1946, just as the newly created United Nations met in San Francisco. Today the Palais des Nations is the headquarters of the United Nations in Europe, with a modern wing added in 1973.

Inside are a **philatelic museum** and the **League of Nations Museum,** though the building itself is the most interesting attraction. Daily tours leave from the visitors' entrance at 14 av. de la Paix, opposite the Red Cross building. For information, contact the **Visitors' Service,** United Nations Office, 14 av. de la Paix (☎ **022/ 907-45-60**).

RELIGIOUS MONUMENTS

The old town, **Vieille Ville,** on the Left Bank, is dominated by the ✪ **Cathédrale St-Pierre,** Cour St-Pierre (☎ **022/311-75-75**), built in the 12th and 13th centuries and partially reconstructed in the 15th century. Recent excavations have disclosed that a Christian sanctuary was here as early as A.D. 400. In 1536, the people of Geneva gathered in the cloister of St-Pierre's and voted to make the cathedral Protestant. The church has a modern organ with 6,000 pipes. The northern tower was reconstructed at the end of the 19th century, with a metal steeple erected between the two stone towers. If you don't mind the 145 steps, you can climb to the top of the north tower for a panoramic view.

To enter the St-Pierre archaeological site, called **Site Archéologique de St-Pierre,** go through the entrance in the Cour St-Pierre, at the right corner of the cathedral steps. The underground passage extends under the present cathedral and the High Gothic (early 15th-century) **Chapelle des Macchabées,** which adjoins the church's southwestern corner. The chapel was restored during World War II, after having been used as a storage room following the Reformation. Excavations have revealed baptisteries, a crypt, the foundations of several cathedrals, the bishop's palace, 4th-century mosaics, and sculptures and geological strata.

The cathedral, tower, and excavations are open June to September daily 9am to 7pm; October to May Monday to Saturday 10am to noon and 2 to 5pm, Sunday 11am to 12:30pm and 1:30 to 5pm. Admission is 3SF ($2).

ORGANIZED TOURS

A 2-hour city tour is operated daily by **Key Tours S.A.,** 7 rue des Alpes, square du Mont-Blanc (☎ **022/731-41-40**). The tour starts from the Gare Routière, the bus station at place Dorcière, near the Key Tours office. From November through March, a tour is offered only once a day at 2pm; the rest of the year, two tours leave daily, at 10am and 2pm. A bus will drive you through the city to see the monuments, landmarks, and lake promenades. In the Old Town, you can take a walk down to the Bastions Park to the Reformation Wall. After an English-language tour through the International Center—where you'll be shown the headquarters of the International Red Cross—the bus returns to its starting place. Adults pay 35SF ($23), children 4 to 12 accompanied by an adult are 18SF ($12), and children 3 and under go free.

THE SHOPPING SCENE

As one might suspect, watches, knives, cheese, and chocolate are among Geneva's best buys. Check prices carefully; many Swiss watches are currently cheaper in the United States than in Switzerland. Swiss army knives are still a good deal, and as for chocolate, well, it's incomparable and just not the same when you buy it in another country.

Geneva's Left Bank shopping area is along the exclusive **rue du Rhône** and adjacent streets. Here you'll find shop after shop of designer fashions and expensive watches. Along the winding streets of the **Old City** you can explore antiques stores

Exploring Geneva's Parks & Gardens

If you walk along the quays, heading north as if to Lausanne, you'll come to some of the lushest parks in Geneva. **Parc Mon–Repos** is off avenue de France and **La Perle du Lac** lies off rue de Lausanne. Directly to the right is the **Jardin Botanique (Botanical Garden),** opened in 1902. It has an alpine garden, a little zoo, greenhouses, and exhibitions; you can visit it free daily October through April 9:30am to 5pm and May through September 8am to 7:30pm.

Back at lakeside, you can take a boat to the other bank, getting off at quai Gustave-Ador. From here you can explore two more lakeside parks—**Parc la Grange,** which has the most extravagant rose garden in Switzerland (especially in June), and, next to it, **Parc des Eaux-Vives.**

When you leave the Botanical Garden on the Left Bank, you can head west, along avenue de la Paix, about a mile north from pont du Mont-Blanc, to the Palais des Nations in **Parc de l'Ariana.**

and galleries. For Swiss army knives and watches, stroll along the pedestrians-only **rue du Mont-Blanc** on the Right Bank. You'll find an endless assortment of watches, knives, and other souvenirs, all priced similarly.

Colorful **outdoor markets,** overflowing with flowers and fruit, take place several times a week at places Rive, Coutance, Carouge, and others. A **flea market** is held every Wednesday and Saturday on the Plaine de Plainpalais; markets for books take place on place de la Madeleine on most days during summer.

SELECT SHOPS   Virtually all the inventory at **Antiquorum,** 2 rue du Mont-Blanc (☎ **022/738-02-22;** bus: 1), consists of antique jewelry and antique watches—a sure attraction for a city that derives so much of its income from selling timepieces. The array includes some of the world's most historically important watches.

The aroma of chocolate from the **Confiserie Rohr,** 3 place du Molard (☎ **022/ 311-63-03;** bus: 9, 10, or 12), practically pulls you in off the street. You'll find chocolate-covered truffles, "gold" bars with hazelnuts, and poubelles au chocolat (chocolate "garbage pails"). There's another branch at 42 rue du Rhône (☎ **022/ 311-68-76;** bus: 2, 9, or 22).

On place du Molard, **Bon Genie,** 34 rue du Marché (☎ **022/818-11-11;** tram 12), is a department store selling high-fashion women's clothing and a limited selection of men's. Its windows display art objects from local museums alongside designer clothes. Geneva's largest department store, **Globus & Grand Passage,** 48 rue du Rhône (☎ **022/319-50-50;** bus: 2, 9, or 22), has just about everything: a travel bureau, an agency selling theater tickets, a hairdresser, a newsstand, a handful of boutiques, a restaurant, and a sandwich shop. **Bruno Magli,** 47 rue du Rhône (☎ **022/ 311-53-77;** bus: 2, 9, or 22), is one of Geneva's best-stocked shoe stores, with an elegant variety of Italian shoes, purses, and accessories. This outlet of the Bologna-based chain stocks mainly women's shoes.

Opposite pont du Mont-Blanc, the chrome-and-crystal **Bucherer,** 45 rue du Rhône (☎ **022/319-62-66;** bus: 2, 9, or 22), sells expensive watches and diamonds. The store offers such name brands as Rolex, Piaget, Baume & Mercier, Tissot, Rado, and Swatch. The third floor is filled with relatively inexpensive watches. Once you're on that floor, you'll also find a large selection of cuckoo clocks, music boxes, embroideries, and souvenirs, as well as porcelain pillboxes and other gift items.

Established over a century ago, **Leinen Langenthal,** 13 rue du Rhône (☎ **022/ 310-65-10;** bus: 2, 9, or 22), boasts an enviable reputation for good-quality merchandise and a showroom on the city's most prestigious shopping street, across from the Union des Banques Suisses. The merchandise includes napery, towels, bed linens, and "table suites," some of it embroidered by hand in the Swiss lace center of St-Gallen.

At the corner of rue de la Fontaine, **Jouets Weber,** 12 rue de la Croix-d'Or (☎ **022/310-42-55;** bus: 2 or 12), is the best toy store in the city. It has all kinds of children's toys, from slide shows to cartoon characters, as well as dolls and sports equipment.

GENEVA AFTER DARK

For a preview of events at the time of your visit, pick up a copy of the monthly **"List of Events"** issued by the tourist office.

THE PERFORMING ARTS

Modeled on Paris's Opéra Garnier, the **Grand Théâtre de Genève,** Place Neuve (☎ **022/418-31-30;** bus: 12), was opened in 1879, and is often included in lists of the world's ten best opera houses. It burned down in 1951 and was subsequently rebuilt in the same style, except for the modern auditorium, which has seating for 1,488. From September to July, it presents about eight operas and two ballets, as well as recitals and chamber music concerts. Tickets are 24 to 145SF ($16 to $97) for opera, 18 to 124SF ($12 to $83) for ballet.

The 1,866-seat **Victoria Hall,** 14 rue du Général-Dufour, is home to the celebrated **Orchestre de la Suisse Romande** (☎ **022/32881-21;** bus: 12). The orchestra is Geneva's most famous musical institution. For 50 years, its conductor was Ernst Ansermet and, through this maestro, it was closely associated with Igor Stravinsky. Tickets are 16 to 62SF ($11 to $41).

THE CLUB & MUSIC SCENE

In the suburb of Carouges, **Au Chat Noir,** 13 rue Vautier, Carouges (☎ **022/ 343-49-93;** tram: 12 from Place Bel-Air), is the current hot spot in town, a venue for funk, rock, salsa, jazz, and some good old New Orleans blues. It's crowded on weekends but the club will take reservations. A changing repertoire of concerts is presented nightly at either 9 or 10pm. The club itself is open Monday to Thursday 6pm to 4am, Friday 6pm to 5am, Saturday 9pm to 5am, and Sunday 9am to 4am. After a few drinks, you begin to fear that the car suspended from the ceiling might fall in on you. Cover is 10 to 15SF ($7 to $10).

The fun, unpretentious **Arthur's Club,** Centre I.C.C., Rte. des Près-Bois 20 (☎ **022/791-77-00;** tram to Gare Genève-Cointrin), near the Geneva airport, is committed to preserving a healthy balance of clients between the ages of 18 and 45. Inside, each of the ten different bars manages to attract a minisubculture all its own, so regardless of your age or preferences, you'll eventually find something or someone that appeals to you. On busy nights, expect as many as 2,500 clients, many of whom dance, dance, dance, crammed inside. It's open Friday and Saturday 10am to 5am. The location is. Cover is 25SF ($17) and includes the first drink.

Griffin's Club, 36 bd. Helvétique (☎ **022/735-12-18;** bus 26), is the choicest club in Geneva. Technically, it's private—you may or may not get in, depending on the mood of the management at the time of your visit. On Friday and Saturday, precedence is usually given to members. Jackets are required for men. The decor of the place, much of which is in a basement, is gilt and gray, with lots of live plants and large paintings in the restaurant. The restaurant serves main courses priced at 38 to 50SF ($25 to $33) nightly from 8pm till 3:30am. The disco opens at 11pm and closes between 5 and 6am, depending on the night of the week. There's no cover.

The private **Club 58,** 15 Glacis de Rive (☎ 022/735-15-15; bus: 26), allows non-members to enter, although men are required to wear jackets. It's mainly a disco, but there's an attached restaurant. Occasionally the club presents some top names in show business. It opens daily at 10pm; the restaurant opens at 8pm. Drinks in the club cost 25SF ($17). Cover is 15 to 20SF ($10 to $13). **L'Interdit,** Quai du Seujet 18 (☎ 022/738-90-91; bus: 12), isn't as difficult to get into as other clubs in Geneva. It's hip, heterosexual, and worthy of a visit if you want to meet attractive strangers of the opposite sex. There's also a restaurant here, but the main appeal is the dancing, which starts every night at 10pm and lasts until around 5am. Cover is 20SF ($13), including first drink.

Within its genre, **Velvet,** 7 rue de Jeu-de-l'Arc (☎ 022/735-00-00; bus: 26), is a safe and well-recommended nightclub, but it isn't for the timid, and unless you're an unusually brazen woman, or firmly attached to an attentive male escort, it's more appropriate as a nighttime venue for (temporarily) unattached men. It's very heterosexual, very permissive, and loaded with working women waiting for a male visitor to buy them a drink of, perhaps, champagne. In most instances, its tawdrier aspects are rather artfully concealed, although that's a tall order for a venue where, beginning around 11pm, as many as 32 international beauties, many of them topless, begin strutting their stuff in a nonstop, informally choreographed *spectacle* that continues, on and off, till around 5am. There's a restaurant and a disco on the premises. It's open nightly from 10pm till 5am. On Sunday, the restaurant is closed, but not the cabaret and bar. Drinks begin at 19SF ($13), but usually average around 24SF ($16) each. There's no cover Sunday to Thursday; cover is 10SF ($7) Friday and Saturday.

BARS

Sheathed in mahogany, brass, and dark-green upholstery, the fashionable **Bar des Bergues,** in the Hôtel des Bergues, 33 quai des Bergues (☎ 022/908-70-00; bus: 7), is decorated with a series of late 19th-century menus from the Cercle des Arts et des Lettres. Though most people come just for a drink or two, the place also serves lunches and platters from the hotel's top-notch kitchen. Ask the barman for the list of daily specials. Beginning in the early evening, there's an international array of pianists.

Though this is technically the aperitif bar for the elegant Restaurant Le Gentilhomme, many visitors consider **Le Jardin,** in the Hôtel Richemond, Jardin Brunswick (☎ 022/715-77-20; bus: 1 or 9), an attractive and stylish option in its own right. It attracts a chic crowd, ranging from U.S.-based beneficiaries of corporate mergers to Zurich bankers to glamorous women in $50,000 furs.

GAY GENEVA

Many lesbian groups meet at the **Centre Femmes Nathalie Barney (Le Maison),** 30 av. Peshier. (☎ 022/789-26-00; tram: 12), in the Champel district. It's the best-organized outlet for gay women in French-speaking Switzerland and is named for Nathalie Barney, a well-known lesbian liberationist (from Dayton, Ohio) who ran a salon in Paris at the turn of the last century. Different social and political gatherings take place several nights a week. The center maintains a restaurant open for group dinners only on designated nights of the week and a women's bar open only Friday and Saturday nights.

In the district of Servette, **Dialogai,** 57 av. de Wendt (☎ 022/906-40-40; bus: 12), provides multilingual information and advice. On the basement-level premises are a library, a cafe and bar, and meeting rooms for Wednesday-night dinners and Saturday-night dancing parties. The organization publishes a list—free to anyone who asks—of the gay bars of Geneva and French-speaking Switzerland, and is the best conduit to Geneva's male homosexual network.

Le Loft and Le Night Fever, 20 quai du Seujet (☎ 022/738-28-28; bus: 12), are set within the same building and managed by the same team. These two gay bars offer a convivial venue for drinking and dancing. Shows begin every night at 11pm. The place functions as a cafe throughout the day, serving croissants and café au lait to office workers as early as 6am, but its most amusing times are nightly beginning around 10pm and lasting till around 3am.

DAY TRIPS FROM GENEVA

MONT SALÈVE   The limestone ridge of Mont Salève (House Mountain) is 6km (4 miles) south of Geneva in France, so you'll need your passport. Its peak is at 1,200m (4,000 feet). If you have a car, you can take a road that goes up the mountain; it's also popular with rock climbers. Bus 8 will take you to Veyrier, on the French border, where there's a passport and Customs control. A 6-minute cable-car ride will carry you to a height of 1,140m (3,750 feet) on Mont Salève. From the top you'll have a panoramic sweep of the Valley of the Arve, with Geneva and Mont Blanc in the background.

✪ MONT BLANC & CHAMONIX   We highly recommend a Mont Blanc excursion, an all-day trip to Chamonix, France, by bus and a cable-car ride to the 3,850m (12,610-foot) summit of the Aiguille du Midi. The tour leaves Geneva at 8am and returns at 6pm daily. Buses leave from Gare Routière, and you must take your passport.

Other climbs on this tour are Vallée Blanche by télécabin, an extension of the Aiguille du Midi climb, April through October; to Mer de Glâce via electric rack railway to the edge of the glacier, from which you may descend to the ice grotto (the climb isn't available in winter); and to Le Brevent, an ascent by cable car to a rocky belvedere at 2,400m (7,900 feet), facing the Mont Blanc range.

An English-speaking guide will accompany your bus tour. Key Tours S.A., 7 rue des Alpes (place du Mont-Blanc), Case Postale 1745, CH-1211 Genève (☎ 022/731-41-40), require a minimum of eight people per trip. Tours begin at 208SF ($139) for adults and 104SF ($69) for children.

LAKE GENEVA CRUISES   Two companies offer cruises on Lac Léman. The smaller one, Mouettes Genevoises Navigation, 8 quai du Mont-Blanc (☎ 022/732-29-44), specializes in small-scale boats carrying only about 100 passengers. Each features some kind of guided (pre-recorded) commentary, in French and English. An easy promenade that surveys the landscapes and bird life along the uppermost regions of the Rhône draining the lake is the company's "Tour du Rhône" (Rhône River Tour). The trip originates at a point adjacent to Geneva's pont de l'Ile and travels downstream for about 15km (9 miles) to the Barrage de Verbois (Verbois Dam) and back. From April through October, departures are daily at 2:15pm and also Wednesday, Thursday, Saturday, and Sunday at 10am. It costs 22SF ($15) for adults and 15SF ($10) for children 4 to 12; free for children under 4. The same company also offers 1¼-hour tours (four times a day) and 2-hour tours (twice a day) out onto the lake. The longer tour includes a pre-recorded commentary on the celebrity residences and ecology of the lake. It's 12SF ($8) for the shorter tour and 20SF ($13) for the longer tour; no stops are made en route.

Bateaux de la Mouette's largest competitor, **CGN (Compagnie General de Navigation),** quai du Mont-Blanc (☎ **022/312-52-23**), offers roughly equivalent tours, May through September, that last an hour and depart 4 to 6 times a day from the company's piers along the quai du Mont-Blanc. Known as "Les Belles Rives Genevoises," they charge 11SF ($7) for adults and 6SF ($4) for children 6 to 16 (children under 6 free). Tours include pre-recorded commentaries and are about as long in duration as many short-term visitors to the city really want.

2 Bern & the Berner Oberland

Dating from the 12th century, Bern is one of the loveliest and oldest cities in Europe. Since much of its medieval architecture has remained untouched, the United Nations declared it a world landmark in 1983. As the capital of Switzerland, it's also a city of diplomats and the site of many international organizations and meetings.

Bern is a convenient center for exploring the lakes and peaks of the Berner Oberland—a vast recreation area only minutes from the capital, sprawling between the Reuss River and Lake Geneva. It's an important center for winter sports, one of the best-equipped areas for downhill skiers, and a challenging place for hikers and mountain climbers. The 4,158m (13,642-foot) Jungfrau and the 4,274m (14,022-foot) Finsteraarhorn are the highest alpine peaks. The canton of Bern, encompassing most of the area, is Switzerland's second largest, and contains 260 square kilometers (100 square miles) of glaciers.

The best center for exploring the Berner Oberland is Interlaken, a popular summer resort. Summer and winter playgrounds are at Gstaad, Grindelwald, Kandersteg, and Mürren. You can ski in the mountains in winter and surf, sail, and water-ski on Lake Thun in summer.

BERN

The modern mingles harmoniously with the old in this charming city. Contemporary buildings are discreetly designed to blend in with the historic environment. The city stands on a thumb of land that's bordered on three sides by the Aare River, and several bridges connect the old part of the city with the newer sections.

Market days in Bern are Tuesday and Saturday, when people from the outlying areas come to town to sell their produce and wares. If you're fortunate enough to arrive on the fourth Monday of November, you'll witness the centuries-old Zwiebelmarkt (Onion Market). This is the city's last big event before the onset of winter, as residents traditionally stock up on onions in anticipation of the first snows.

ORIENTATION

GETTING THERE   By Plane   The **Bern-Belp Airport** (☎ **031/960-21-11**) is 10km (6 miles) south of the city in Belpmoos. International flights arrive from London, Paris, and Nice, but transatlantic jets are not able to land here. Fortunately, it's a short hop to Bern from the international airports in Zurich and Geneva.

Taxis are about 45SF ($30) to the city center, so it's better to take the shuttle bus that runs between the airport and the Bahnhof (train station), costing 14SF ($9) one way.

By Train   Bern has direct connections to the continental rail network that includes France, Italy, Germany, and the Benelux countries, even Scandinavia and Spain. The superfast TGV train connects Paris with Bern (trip time: 4¹/₂ hours). Bern also lies on major Swiss rail links, particularly those connecting Geneva and Zurich (trip time: 90 minutes).

Bern

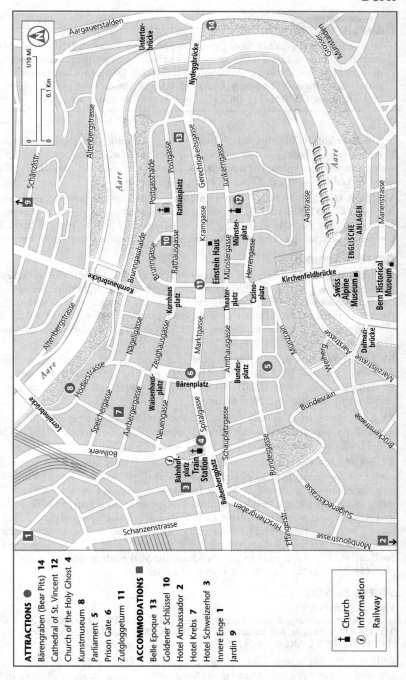

ATTRACTIONS ●
Bärengraben (Bear Pits) **14**
Cathedral of St. Vincent **12**
Church of the Holy Ghost **4**
Kunstmuseum **8**
Parliament **5**
Prison Gate **6**
Zutglogeturm **11**

ACCOMMODATIONS ■
Belle Epoque **13**
Goldener Schlüssel **10**
Hotel Ambassador **2**
Hotel Krebs **7**
Hotel Schweizerhof **3**
Innere Enge **1**
Jardin **9**

✝ Church
ⓘ Information
—— Railway

1061

Traveler's Tip

To save time, and possibly money, you can purchase a **1-day ticket** for 6SF ($4), entitling you to unlimited travel on the SVB network. Just get the ticket stamped at the automatic machine before you begin your first trip. One-day tickets are available at the ticket offices at Bubenbergplatz 5 (☎ **031/321-06-31**) and in the underpass of the Bahnhof (☎ **031/321-06-41**), as well as at other outlets in the city.

The **Bahnhof**, on Bahnhofplatz, is in the center of town near all the major hotels. If your luggage is light, you can walk to your hotel; otherwise, take one of the taxis waiting outside the station. For **information** about tickets and train schedules for the Swiss Federal Railways, call ☎ **157-22-22** (no area code).

VISITOR INFORMATION The **Bern Tourist Office,** in the Bahnhof, on Bahnhofplatz (☎ **031/328-12-12**), is open June to September, daily 9am to 8:30pm; October to May, Monday to Saturday 9am to 6:30pm and Sunday 10am to 5pm. If you need help finding a hotel room, the tourist office can make a reservation for you.

GETTING AROUND

BY BUS & TRAM The public transportation system, the **Stadtische Verkehrsbetriebe (SVB),** is a reliable 77km (48-mile) network of buses and trams. Before you board, purchase a ticket from the self-service automatic machines at each stop (conductors don't sell tickets). If you're caught traveling without one, you'll be fined 50SF ($33). A short-range ticket (six stations) costs 1.50SF ($1); a regular ticket, valid for 45 minutes one-way only, is 2.40SF ($1.60).

BY TAXI You can catch a taxi at the public cab stands, or you can call a dispatcher. Try Nova Taxi at ☎ **031/301-11-11.** The meter registers as 6SF ($4) when you get in, then goes up to 3.10SF ($2.05) per kilometer. After 8pm and until 6am daily, the per kilometer rate rises to 3.50SF ($2.35).

BY CAR Don't try to drive in the city; use your car for exploring the environs. Car-rental companies in Bern include **Hertz,** Casinoplatz at Kochergasse 1 (☎ **031/318-21-60**), and **Avis,** Wabernstrasse 41 (☎ **031/372-13-13**).

BY BICYCLE The Altstadt is compressed into such a small area that it's better to cover it on foot rather than on a bike. Bicycles aren't allowed on the many pedestrians-only streets anyway. However, in Greater Bern and its environs there are 400km (248 miles) of cycling paths. These are marked on a special cycling map available at the tourist office (see above). Bicycle lanes are indicated by yellow on parts of the road network. The point of departure for most official cycling routes is Bundesplatz (Parliament Square). Special red signs will guide you through a wide variety of landscapes. For 22SF ($15) per day, you can rent bicycles at the **SBB Railway Station,** Bahnhofplatz (☎ **157-22-22**). Call the day before for a reservation.

WHERE TO STAY

Very Expensive

Hotel Schweizerhof. Bahnhofplatz 11, CH-3001 Bern. ☎ **031/326-80-80.** Fax 031/326-80-90. 84 units. A/C MINIBAR TV TEL. 380–450SF ($253–$300) double; from 600SF ($400) suite. AE, DC, MC, V. Parking 26SF ($17). Tram: 3, 9, or 12.

Built in 1859, this central hotel managed by the Gauer family is popular with diplomats and remains the grandest hotel in the Swiss capital. It contains many antiques and some of the best decorative art in Bern. Some rooms are quite contemporary, others more antique; some are air-conditioned. The luxurious bathrooms contain cosmetics bars, hair dryers, tubs with shower, and robes. There are several formal restaurants, including the Schultheissenstube, our favorite, which offers attentive service.

Expensive

○ Belle Epoque. Gerechtigkeitsgasse 18, CH-3001 Bern. ☎ **031/311-43-36.** Fax 031/311-39-36. www.belle-epoque.ch. E-mail: info@belle-epoque.ch. 17 units. MINIBAR TV TEL. 250–315SF ($167–$210) double; 280–380SF ($187–$253) suite. AE, DC, MC, V. Bus: 12.

One of the highlights of this renovated medieval home in Bern's historic core is a bar outfitted like an art and antiques gallery, lined with late 19th- and early 20th-century oil paintings and filled with Jugendstil (German art nouveau) furnishings and comfortable settees. Room boasts reproduction turn-of-the-century furniture, 1920s light fixtures, and engravings. Many bathrooms have both tubs and showers. A tiny restaurant is used mainly for breakfast, although it's often possible to order light meals at other times.

Innere Enge. Engestrasse 54, CH-3012 Bern. ☎ **031/309-61-11.** Fax 301/309-61-12. 26 units. MINIBAR TV TEL. 260–390SF ($173–$260) double. Rates include continental breakfast. AE, DC, MC, V. Free parking. Bus: 21 from the rail station.

When you tire of impersonal bandboxes, head for this small, choice hotel. The light, spacious, and airy rooms have style and character, with traditional (if not antique) beds and roomy bathrooms, sometimes with a tub/shower combination. Many have a view of the Bernese Alps. Swiss regional and international dishes are served in the restaurant, and jazz acts are booked in the Louis Armstrong Bar.

Moderate

Hotel Ambassador. Seftigenstrasse 99, CH-3007 Bern. ☎ **031/371-41-11.** Fax 031/371-41-17. 97 units. MINIBAR TV TEL. 176–196SF ($117–$131) double. AE, DC, MC, V. Free parking. Tram: 9.

This nine-story hotel in a neighborhood of older houses with red-tile roofs is not far from the train station and easily reached by tram. Rooms come with refrigerators, and many have a view of the Bundeshaus. They tend to be smallish and furnished somewhat impersonally, but they're well maintained. Dining choices include the Restaurant Pavilion Café and the Japanese Teppan Restaurant, and there's a sauna, a solarium, and a 24-hour indoor pool.

Hotel Krebs. Genfergasse 8, CH-3011 Bern. ☎ **031/311-49-42.** Fax 031/311-10-35. 46 units (41 with bathroom). TV TEL. 130SF ($87) double without bathroom, 160-175SF ($106.70–$117) double with bathroom. Rates include buffet breakfast. AE, DC, MC, V. Tram: 3 or 9.

This three-star hotel near the train station shares its ground floor with a store. Rooms are rather Spartan but occasionally sunny, and wood paneling adds more warmth. Some rooms can be converted for families. The singles, without bathroom, are among the more reasonably priced in the area. Private bathrooms are small, and a little short of shelf space; those in the hall are tidily kept.

Inexpensive

○ Goldener Schlüssel. Rathausgasse 72, CH-3011 Bern. ☎ **031/311-02-16.** Fax 031/311-56-88. 29 units (21 with bathroom). TV TEL. 110SF ($73) double without bathroom, 142SF ($95) double with bathroom; 149SF ($99) triple without bathroom, 185SF ($123) triple with bathroom. Rates include continental breakfast. AE, MC, V. Free parking. Bus: 12; tram: 9.

In the heart of Altstadt, opening onto Rathausgasse, the building housing this little inn dates from the 13th century, when it was used as a stable. Rooms are beautifully maintained. As it's fairly busy on the street outside, ask for a rear room if you want less noise. If you're a bargain hunter, ask for a room without bathroom—the hallway plumbing is adequate. The hotel's sidewalk cafe does a thriving business throughout summer, and the restaurant offers reasonably priced meals (see "Where to Dine," below).

Jardin. Militarstrasse 38, CH-3014 Bern. ☎ **031/333-01-17.** Fax 031/333-09-43. 17 units. TV TEL. 133SF ($89) double; 195SF ($130) triple. Rates include breakfast. AE, DC, MC, V. Free parking. Tram: 9 to Breitenrainplatz.

In 1985, this building just north of the city center was converted from a restaurant and apartment building into a modern and warmly appealing hotel. Rooms are larger than virtually any others in their price range. The hotel is run by identical twins Andy and Daniel Balz, whose similarities may confuse you; one or the other is almost always available to help guests. Joggers and nature lovers appreciate the verdant areas across the street; they're part of the land surrounding Bern's largest military academy. The still-flourishing Jardin restaurant is recommended (see "Where to Dine," below).

WHERE TO DINE
Expensive

Della Casa. Schauplatzgasse 16. ☎ **031/311-21-42.** Reservations recommended. Main courses 21-36.50SF ($14–$24);fixed-price menu 23SF ($15). AE, DC, MC, V (downstairs only). Mon–Fri 11am–2pm and 6–9:30pm, Sat 9:30am–3pm. Upstairs level closed in July (downstairs dining room remains open). Tram: 3, 5, or 9. CONTINENTAL.

From under an arcade, you enter a low-ceilinged paneled room that's often crowded with chattering diners. For those eager to follow the latest political trends and opinions, an inner room has all the day's newspapers—indeed, the place has been called Switzerland's "unofficial Parliament headquarters." Upstairs is a quieter, somewhat more formal dining room. The menu features continental and Italian dishes. Two of our favorites are the ravioli maison and the fried zucchini; a popular meat specialty is filet mignon à la bordelaise with Créole rice. More typical, however, is the calf's heart with onions, tomatoes and potatoes with an herbed vinaigrette.

Jack's Brasserie (Stadt Restaurant). In the Hotel Schweizerhof, Bahnhofplatz 11. ☎ **031/311-45-01.** Reservations recommended. Main courses 25–60SF ($17–$40); set-price menu 70SF ($47). AE, DC, MC, V. Daily 11:45am–1:45pm and 6:15–10:45pm. Limited menu daily 1:45–6:15pm. Tram: 3, 9, or 12. FRENCH/CONTINENTAL.

Although this restaurant is configured as one of the less formal eateries within the also-recommended Schweizerhof, it's perfectly acceptable as the site for an important meal or even a celebratory dinner, with or without business clients. Nostalgically outfitted in a style that might remind you of a Lyonnais bistro, replete with paneling, banquettes, and etched glass, it bustles in a way that's chic, convivial, and matter-of-fact, all at the same time. Menu items include fish soup, the kind of Weinerschitzels that hang over the sides of the plate, a succulent version of sole meunière and sea bass, veal head vinaigrette for real regional flavor, tender pepper steaks, and smaller platters piled high with salads, risottos, and succulent pastas.

Räblus. Zeughausgasse 3. ☎ **031/311-59-08.** Reservations required. Main courses 16–35SF ($11–$23); 3 course fixed-price menus 28–55SF ($19–$37). AE, DC, MC, V. Mon–Wed 6pm–1:30am, Thurs 6pm–2:30am and Fri–Sat 6pm–3:30am. Tram: 3 or 9. FRENCH/SWISS REGIONAL.

Centrally located near the Clock Tower, this 200-year-old restaurant has a ground-floor bar where you can stop for an aperitif before proceeding up to the richly paneled, sculpture-filled dining room. The kitchen prepares a French cuisine with a definite Swiss/German influence. Try such dishes as saffron-flavored sole, potpourri of seafood flavored with Pernod, or citrus-flavored veal.

Moderate

Restaurant Harmonie. Hotelgasse 3. ☎ **031/313-11-41.** Reservations recommended. Main courses 18–40SF ($12–$27). MC, V. Mon and Sat 3–11:30pm, Tues–Fri 8am–11:30pm. Closed mid-July to mid-Aug. Tram 9. SWISS/BERNESE.

Located at the corner of Münstergasse a few blocks from the Houses of Parliament, this art nouveau local favorite evokes 1890s Paris with its grimy overlay. It has been in the hands of the Gyger family since 1915. Service is efficient, and tables are spaced far enough apart to allow a feeling of privacy. There are two separate dining rooms and a handful of sidewalk tables set beneath ivy-clad trellises. You get the same regional specialties that Grandmother Gyger might have served between the wars: pork sausage with rösti, tripe with tomatoes, and cheese fondues. In the unlikely event that you're not ravenously hungry, the simple platter of cooked ham might be consumed with pickles, pickled onions, and sliced bread.

Goldener Schlüssel. Rathausgasse 72. ☎ **031/311-02-16.** Reservations recommended. Main courses 25–35SF ($17–$23); fixed-price lunch 16.80–21.80SF ($11–$15). AE, MC, V. Sun–Thurs 7am–11:30pm, Fri–Sat 7am–12:30am. Tram: 9; bus: 12. SWISS.

You'll relish both the food and the bustling atmosphere at this very Swiss restaurant, where the old planking and stonework of a 13th-century building can be seen overhead. Serving wholesome food in ample portions, the restaurant is on the street level of a budget-priced hotel of the same name. Specialties include a well-flavored *mignon d'agneau au poivre vert* (tenderloin of lamb with green-pepper sauce and corn croquettes), *schweinbratwurst mit zwiebelsauce* (butter-fried sausage with onion sauce), and rösti.

Ratskeller. Gerechtigkeitsgasse 81. ☎ **031/311-17-71.** Reservations recommended. Main courses 12–50SF ($8–$33); fixed-price lunch 17SF ($11). AE, DC, MC, V. Daily 11:30am–2pm and 6–10pm. Tram: 9. SWISS.

This historic establishment has old masonry, modern paneling, and a battalion of busy waitresses serving ample portions of good, rib-sticking food. Specialties include rack of lamb à la diable for two, an omelette soufflé aux fruits, veal kidneys Robert, and côte de beau in butter sauce. Your best bet is the *egli* (tiny fillet of perch) with white sauce on a bed of spinach. Prized by gourmets, this tiny fish is native to the lakes around Bern.

Inexpensive

Jardin. Militärstrasse 38. ☎ **031/333-01-17.** Reservations recommended. Main courses 12–38SF ($8–$25); set price menu 15SF ($10). AE, DC, MC, V. Mon–Sat 11am–2pm and 5–10pm. Tram: 9 to Breitenrainplatz. INTERNATIONAL.

Set in the previously recommended hotel of the same name, this stately looking restaurant flourished long before the hotel was established in 1985. Part of its appeal derives from its ability to be as formal or informal as you want; consequently, it serves snacks such as cheese croquettes to accompany your foaming mugfuls of beer, as well as more substantial grilled steaks, minced Zürich-style veal with rösti potatoes, and schnitzels of pork with braised cabbage.

SEEING THE SIGHTS

The **Zutgloggeturm (Clock Tower),** on Kramgasse, was built in the 12th century and restored in the 16th. Four minutes before every hour, crowds gather for the world's oldest (since 1530) and biggest horological puppet show: Mechanical bears, jesters,

---

Taking a Cable-Train to Mont Gurten

The most panoramic attraction in the immediate vicinity is the ✪ **belvedere atop Mont Gurten,** where there's also a children's fairyland and a walking area. The belvedere is connected to Bern by the Gurtenbahn cable-train, one of the fastest in all Europe. The train departs from a station beside the Monbijoustrasse, about 2.5km (1¹/₂ miles) from Bern's center. Round-trip passage on the cable-train is 7SF ($4.65). The train operates year-round, daily 7:30am to sunset. For details, contact **Gurtenbahn Bern,** Eigerplatz 3 (☎ **031/961-23-23**). To reach the departure platform, take tram 9 to the Gurtenbahn station for 2.40SF ($1.60) each way. If you're driving, follow the road signs to Thun. There's a parking lot in the hamlet of Wabern, a short walk from the cable-train station.

---

and emperors put on an animated performance. The tower marked the west gate of Bern until 1250.

The ✪ **Bärengraben (Bear Pits),** on the opposite side of the river, is a deep moon-shaped den where bears, Bern's mascots, have been kept since 1480. According to legend, when the duke of Zähringen established the town in 1191, he sent his hunters into the encircling woods, which were full of wild game. The duke promised to name the city after the first animal slain, which was a Bär (bear). Since then the town has been known as Bärn or Bern. Today, the bears are beloved, pampered, and fed by residents and visitors (carrots are most appreciated). The **Nydegg Bridge (Nydegg-brücke)** was built over one of the gorges of the Aare River; its central stone arch has a span of 55m (180 feet) and affords a sweeping view of the city from its center. Below the Bear Pits, you can visit the **Rosengarten** (Rose Gardens), from which there's a much-photographed view of the medieval sector and the river.

✪ **Cathedral of St. Vincent.** Münsterplatz. ☎ **031/312-04-62.** Cathedral, free; viewing platform, 3SF ($2) adults, 1SF (65¢) children. Easter Sun–Oct, Tues–Sat 10am–5pm, Sun 11am–5pm; off-season, Tues–Fri 10am–noon and 2–4pm, Sat 10am–noon and 2–5pm, Sun 11:30am–2pm. Viewing platform closes half an hour before cathedral. Bus: 12.

The Münster is one of Switzerland's newer Gothic churches; although dating from 1421, the belfry was completed only in 1893. The most exceptional feature of this three-aisle pillared basilica is the tympanum over the main portal, depicting the Last Judgment with more than 200 figures, some painted. Mammoth 15th-century stained-glass windows line the chancel. The 1523 choir stalls brought the Renaissance to Bern. In the Matter Chapel is a remarkable stained-glass window, the *Dance of Death,* created in the last year of World War I, but based on a much older design. The 90m (300-foot) belfry offers a panoramic sweep, though you must climb 270 steps to get to the viewing platform. Outside the basilica on Münsterplatz is the 1545 Moses Fountain.

✪ **Kunstmuseum (Fine Arts Museum).** Hodlerstrasse 12. ☎ **031/311-09-44.** Permanent collection, 6SF ($4) adults, 4SF ($2.65) seniors; special exhibit, 10–15SF ($7–$10) extra. Tues 10am–9pm, Wed–Sun 10am–5pm. Bus: 20.

The world's largest collection of Swiss-born Paul Klee's works is the star attraction here. The Klee collection includes 40 oils and 2,000 drawings, gouaches, and watercolors. Other works emphasize the 19th and 20th centuries. The important 20th-century collection has works by Kandinsky, Modigliani, Matisse, Soutine, and Picasso, and by the

Surrealist and Constructivist schools as well as contemporary Swiss artists. There's also a collection of Italian 14th-century primitives, notably Fra Angelico's *Virgin and Child*, and Swiss primitives, including the *Masters of the Carnation*.

Organized Tours

Highly recommended is the **2-hour bus tour** leaving from the tourist office at the Bahnhof, at Bahnhofplatz. An English-speaking guide will take you through the city's residential quarters, past museums, and down to the Aare River, which flows below the houses of Parliament. You'll see the Rose Gardens and the Late Gothic cathedral and stroll under the arcades to the Clock Tower. After visiting the Bear Pits, you'll be led through medieval streets and back to the railroad station. Tours are offered June through September daily at 2pm; November through March, only Saturday at 2pm; and April, May and October, Monday to Saturday at 2pm. The cost is 23SF ($15) for adults, and 11.50SF ($8) for children 6 to 16; children 5 and under are free.

The tourist office also conducts 2-hour **walking tours** of Bern from May to October. Tours leave daily at 11am from the tourist office and at 11:15am from Zytglogge. The cost is 12SF ($8) for adults and 6SF ($4) for children 6 to 16; children 5 and under are free.

BERN AFTER DARK

This Week in Bern, distributed free by the tourist office, has a list of cultural events.

PERFORMING ARTS   The **Bern Symphony Orchestra,** one of Switzerland's finest, is directed by the widely acclaimed Russian-born Dmitrij Kitajenko; famous guest conductors also frequently appear. Performances are usually at the concert facilities in the **Bern Casino,** Herrengasse 25 (☎ 031/311-42-42).

Major opera and ballet performances are usually staged in the century-old **Stadttheater,** Kornhausplatz 20 (☎ 031/312-17-77). Plays and dance programs are presented in the **Theater am Käfigturm,** Spitalgasse 4 (☎ 031/311-61-00). Plays are usually in German, and to a lesser degree, French. Contemporary German-language theater is featured in the **Kleintheater,** Kramgasse 6 (☎ 031/320-26-26).

WINE CELLARS & TRADITIONAL MUSIC   ✪ **Klötzlikeller,** 62 Gerechtigkeitsgasse (☎ 031/311-74-56), the oldest wine tavern in Bern, is near the Gerechtigkeitsbrunnen (Fountain of Justice), the first fountain you see on your walk from the Bear Pits to the Clock Tower. Watch for the lantern outside an angled cellar door. The tavern, dating from 1635, is owned by the city and leased to an independent operator (by tradition, an unmarried woman). Some 20 wines are sold by the glass, with prices ranging from 7.40SF ($4.95). The traditional kitchen serves various dinner plates from 22 to 42SF ($15 to $28) that change every 6 weeks, but reflect regional specialties and prices. The bar is open Tuesday to Saturday 4pm to 12:30am.

Kornhaus Keller, Kornhausplatz 18 (☎ 031/311-11-33), a former grain warehouse in the Altstadt, is the city's best-known wine cellar. The symmetrical stone building, with an arcade on the ground floor, seats 462 diners in a baronial atmosphere; musical acts are often performed in the evening. Main courses—go for the classic, a plate of smoked meats and sauerkraut—range from 18 to 44SF ($12 to $29); the tagesteller (a meal itself and the daily), costs 18.50SF ($12), but is served only at lunch. Food service is daily 11:30am to 1:45pm and 6 to 9:45pm, but guests usually linger over their drinks till around midnight.

A JAZZ CLUB   The Louis Armstrong Bar, site of **Marians' Jazzroom** in the Innere Enge Hotel, Engerstrasse 54 (☎ 031/309-61-11), has its own separate entrance from the hotel. Unique in Bern, it's a setting for not only food and drink, but the finest traditional jazz performed live by top artists from around the world. It's open Tuesday to Thursday 7:30pm to 1am, Friday and Saturday 7:30pm to 2am. On Saturday, there is a Concert Apéro from 4 to 6:30pm and on some Sundays there is a Jazz Brunch from 10am to 1:30pm. Cover is 15 to 45SF ($10 to $30), depending on the act. Closed June 6 to September 6.

A GAY BAR   Samurai Club, Aarbergergasse 35 (☎ **031/311-88-03**), draws many people who work in the local embassies, Bern locals, and young men from the Bernese Oberland in for a night on the town. Women are also welcome. The club is open Sunday to Thursday 5pm to 2:30am; Friday and Saturday 5pm to 3:30am. On weekdays 5 to 8pm, beer is 3.50SF ($2.35); at other times, 4.80SF ($3.20).

A CASINO   Across the river from the oldest section of Bern, the **Kursaal, Schanzlistrasse** 71–77 (☎ **031/333-10-10** or 031/333-18-55), is the only place in town to gamble. Indeed, it's a great spot for novices to learn gambling, because serious money rarely changes hands here. Betting is limited to 1 to 5SF (65¢ to $3.35), as required by Swiss law. It's open daily noon to 3:30am, and admission is free. Drinks cost 10 to 12SF ($7 to $8). There's also a restaurant, serving nightly from 5:30 to 10pm. In addition, a dance hall, called Insight, charges an admission of 15SF ($10). It's open on Thursday from 9pm to 2am, on Friday and Saturday from 9pm to 3:30am, and on Sunday from 3 to 7pm. Kursaal passport needed for this casino.

THE BERNER OBERLAND

The Berner Oberland is Valhalla for walkers, hikers, and skiers. Here nature's scenery satisfies both the most ambitious adventurer and the slowest stroller. It's one of the world's best-equipped regions for winter sports, and walking trails branch out from almost every junction. Most of these are paved and signposted, with distances posted and estimated walking times given. Most tourist offices, including those at Interlaken (see below), will provide guidance and suggested itineraries.

EXPLORING THE AREA BY TRAIN & BICYCLE   If you're not driving, you'll find that public transport is quite adequate for exploring the area. You can buy a **transportation pass** for the Bernese Oberland from the Swiss Rail System. The train ticket is valid for 7 days, and costs 165SF ($110) in second class and 202SF ($135) in first class. Another pass, valid for 15 days, costs 205SF ($137) in second class and 251SF ($167) in first class. With the 7-day pass, you'll travel free for 3 days and pay a reduced fare for the final 4. With a 15-day pass, you'll travel free for 5 days and pay reduced fares for the rest of the time. Children travel at half price. The pass is valid on most railroads; all mountain trains, cable cars, chair lifts, steamers on Lakes Thun and Brienz; and most postal-bus lines in the area. The ticket also qualifies you for a 25% reduction on the Kleine Scheidegg-Eigergletscher-Jungfraujoch railway, the Mürren-Schilthorn aerial cable line, and the bus to Grosse Scheidegg and Bussalp.

Cycling tours through the Berner Oberland often begin at Interlaken. Hundreds of miles of cycling paths cover the area. Separate from the network of hiking paths, the bicycle routes are signposted and marked on rental maps distributed at bike rental

Traveler's Tip

You must purchase the pass at least 1 week before you arrive. For information about the pass, call ☎ **212/757-5944** in New York City, ☎ **310/640-8900** in Los Angeles, ☎ **312/332-9900** in Chicago, or ☎ **416/695-2090** in Toronto.

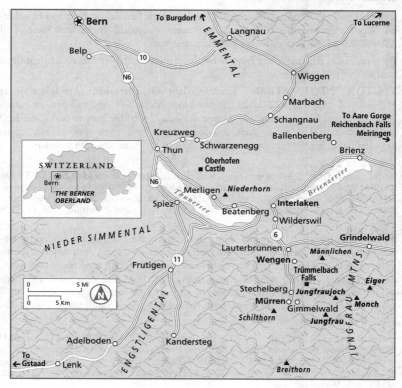

agencies. Some 13 rail stations in the Berner Oberland offer bike rental services, and rates are reasonable. For example, families can rent four bikes (two for adults, two for children 15 and under) for an all-inclusive price of 35SF ($23) per day or 198SF ($132) per week. Individual rentals cost 26SF ($17) per day or 80SF ($53) per week. You must make reservations at least the evening before the tour at any of the rail stations providing the service. Call ☎ **033/828-73-19** or 033/826-47-50 for reservations.

INTERLAKEN

Interlaken is the Berner Oberland's tourist capital. Cableways and cog railways designed for steeply inclined hills and mountains connect it with most of the region's villages. A dazzling sight is the snowy heights of the Jungfrau, which rises a short distance to the south.

The "town between the lakes" (Thun and Brienz) has been a holiday resort for more than 300 years. Though it was once a summer resort, it has developed into a year-round playground. Interlaken charges low-season prices in January and February, when smaller resorts at higher altitudes charge their highest rates. The most expensive time to visit is midsummer, when high-altitude ski resorts often charge their lowest rates.

Essentials

GETTING THERE   By Train   There are several trains daily between Zurich and Interlaken (trip time: 2 hours) and between Bern and Interlaken (40 minutes). Frequent train service also connects Geneva and Interlaken (2¹/₂ hours). Though the town has two rail stations, about 3km (2 miles) apart, **Interlaken East** and **Interlaken West,** most of the city center lies near or around Interlaken West. Call ☎ 157-22-22 (no area code) for schedules and fares.

By Car   To reach Interlaken from Bern, drive south on N6 to Spiez, then continue west on N8 to Interlaken.

VISITOR INFORMATION   The **Tourism Organization Interlaken** is at Höheweg 37 (☎ **033/822-21-21**), in the Hotel Metropole, and will provide itineraries for hikers. It's open July and August, Monday to Friday 8am to noon and 1:30 to 6:30pm, Saturday 8am to 5pm, and Sunday 5 to 7pm; the rest of the year, hours are Monday to Friday 8am to noon and 2 to 6pm and Saturday 8am to noon.

Where to Stay

Hotel Beau-Site. Seestrasee 16, CH-3800 Interlaken. ☎ **033/826-75-75.** Fax 033/826-75-85. www.beausite.ch. E-mail: info@beausite.ch. 50 units (43 with bathroom). TEL. 110SF ($73) double without bathroom, 200–260SF ($133–$173) double with bathroom. Rates include continental breakfast. AE, DC, MC, V. Free parking outside, 20SF ($13) in garage.

A short walk from the Interlaken West train station, this hotel is surrounded by spacious gardens with parasol-shaded card tables and chaise lounges in summer, and provides a pleasant, relaxing oasis. Rooms are modern; some open onto mountain views, and most have TVs and minibars. Rooms on upper floors are a bit small and often rented as singles. The spotless bathrooms, though a bit small, have adequate shelf space. The hotel has two fine restaurants, the budget-priced Stübli and the more elegant and expensive Veranda.

Hotel Bellevue. Marktgasse 59, CH-3800 Interlaken. ☎ **033/822-44-31.** Fax 033/822-92-50. www.interlakentourism.ch./alplodge. E-mail: alplodge@interlakentourism.ch. 38 units. MINIBAR TV TEL. 168–280SF ($112–$187) double. Half-price reduction for children up to 12 sharing parents' room. Half board 32SF ($21) per person. Rates include buffet breakfast. AE, DC, MC, V. Free parking.

The Bellevue, in a central spot opening directly on the Aare, retains something of its original 1789 design as a mock fortified castle and is surrounded by an English-style garden. The modernized rooms, in a variety of shapes and sizes, often have balconies with a view of the river and the distant mountains. All contain a mixture of modern and traditional furniture. Bathrooms are compact, often with a tub and shower. Breakfast and dinner are served in the formal dining room, and guests relax in a nicely furnished salon facing the garden and a view of the Alps.

Hotel de la Paix. Bernastrasse 24, CH-3800 Interlaken. ☎ **033/822-70-44.** Fax 033/822-87-28. E-mail: delapaix@quicknet.ch. 22 units. TV. 110–150SF ($73–$100) double. Rates include buffet breakfast. AE, DC, MC, V. Free parking. Closed mid-Oct to mid-Mar.

This family-run hotel is a block from the Westbahnhof (Interlaken West). You'll recognize it by its ornate roofline, which is gabled and tiled like a house in a Brothers Grimm fairy tale. Gillian and Georges Etterli offer a pleasant, relaxed atmosphere. Rooms are simply but comfortably furnished. Those downstairs are quite spacious. Bathrooms are small. A four-course dinner is available every night for 30SF ($20).

Park-Hotel Mattenhof. Hauptstrasse, Matten, CH-3800 Interlaken. ☎ **033/821-61-21.** Fax 033/822-28-88. 76 units. TV TEL. June–Sept and Dec 26–Jan 1, 260SF ($173) double; off-season, 180SF ($120) double. Rates include buffet breakfast. AE, DC, MC, V. Free parking. Bus: 5.

This old-fashioned hotel is in a secluded area at the edge of a forest 1.5km (1 mile) south of the center; you can reach it by heading away from the center toward

Wilderswil. Originally a simple 19th-century pension, it adopted a mock-medieval look complete with high pointed roof, tower, loggias, and balconies after a massive 1908 enlargement. The Bühler family offers a calm retreat, with terraces, manicured lawns, and panoramic views of the Alps. Rooms come in a variety of sizes and bathrooms are compact. Facilities include a pool, a tennis court, play areas, terraces, bars, and restaurants.

Swiss Inn. Général-Guisan-Strasse 23, CH-3800 Interlaken. ☎ **033/822-36-26.** Fax 033/823-23-03. www.swiss-inn.com. E-mail: info@swiss-inn.ch. 10 units. TV TEL. 100–140SF ($67–$93) double; 120–180SF ($80–$120) apt for two, 150–200SF ($100–$133) apt for four. Rates in double include buffet breakfast. AE, MC, V. Free parking.

This is a small-scale Edwardian-era inn with balconies, gables, and a sense of economy. Mrs. Vreny Müller Lohner offers conventional doubles that are simply decorated and a bit spare. Bathrooms are very small and have shower stalls. There are also some self-contained apartments with kitchens that receive clean-up service only once a week. Guests have access to a lounge, a sitting area with a fireplace, a laundry, and within the garden, a barbecue grill.

✪ **Victoria-Jungfrau Grand Hotel & Spa.** Höheweg 41, CH-3800 Interlaken. ☎ **800/ 223-6800** in the U.S., or 033/828-28-28. Fax 033/828-28-80. www.victoria-jungfrauch E-mail: interlaken@victoria-jungfrau.ch. 216 units. MINIBAR TV TEL. Summer 560–640SF ($374–$427) double. Winter 420–480SF ($280–$320) double. Year-round from 600SF ($400) junior suite; from 1,150SF ($767) suite. Half board 90SF ($60) per person extra. AE, DC, MC, V. Parking free outside, 18SF ($12) in garage.

Since 1865, this has been one of Switzerland's most important resort properties. In richly ornate Victorian styling, it sits in the town center at the foot of rigidly symmetrical gardens. The hotel boasts one of the best-trained staffs in the country. Deluxe rooms open onto views of the Jungfrau. Nearly all are spacious, and feature amenities such as bedside controls, irons and ironing boards. Bathrooms have tub/shower combinations and hair dryers. Dining choices include La Terrasse, a gourmet restaurant with a pianist and a winter garden, and Jungfraustube, a rustic restaurant with traditional Swiss dishes and charcoal-grilled specialties. Facilities include a pool, indoor and outdoor tennis courts, a sauna, a solarium, whirlpools, steam baths, and one of Switzerland's best spas.

Where to Dine

Gasthof Hirschen. Hauptstrasse 11, Matten. ☎ **033/822-15-45.** Reservations recommended. Main courses 18–99SF ($12–$66). AE, DC, MC, V. Thurs–Mon 11:30am–2pm and 6–10pm. SWISS.

This hotel restaurant offers some of the best and most reasonably priced meals in town, and the menu is varied. The potato soup with mountain cheese is the finest we've ever tasted. Other appetizers include salmon-filled ravioli. For a main dish, try sautéed calves' liver, fillet of beef bordelaise, broiled trout, or chateaubriand. The Hirschen operates its own farm, and many of the items it features are home-grown, including Bio-Angus beef, veal, cheese, and fresh vegetables and herbs.

Il Bellini. In the Hotel Metropole, Höheweg 37. ☎ **033/828-66-66.** Reservations recommended Fri–Sun. Main courses 27–36SF ($18–$24); pastas 14–20SF ($9–$13). AE, DC, MC, V. Daily 11:30am–2pm and 6:30–10pm. ITALIAN.

This is the finest Italian restaurant in the area, with food that evokes some of the best trattorie south of the border. One floor above the lobby of the tallest hotel in Interlaken, it's done in a graceful 19th-century rendition of pale pinks and greens. An assortment of antipasti from the buffet or a homemade minestrone is followed by such main courses as beefsteak Florentine, saltimbocca (veal with ham), or chicken breast grilled with tomatoes and mozzarella. The fish selections are limited but well chosen, and can be grilled on request.

Schuh. Höheweg 56. ☎ **033/822-94-41.** Main courses 20–52SF ($13–$35); set price menu 37–41SF ($25–$27). AE, DC, MC, V. Tues–Sun 8am–11pm. Closed Oct 25–Dec 9. SWISS/CONTINENTAL.

This attractive restaurant and tearoom in the center of town has a sunny terrace with a view of the Jungfrau. The calf's liver is excellent, perfectly grilled and seasoned, and their daily soups are pure homemade goodness. Salads rely on market fresh ingredients, and the desserts often incorporate locally-grown berries and fruits. Their pastries are justifiably acclaimed as the finest in the area. A pianist provides music.

Exploring Interlaken
What you do in Interlaken is walk. You can walk at random, as there are panoramic views in virtually all directions, or, if you'd like some guidance, go to the tourist office for a copy of *What to Do in Interlaken;* it maps out walks of all levels of difficulty.

The **Höheweg** covers 16ha (35 acres) in the middle of town, between the west and east train stations. Once the property of Augustinian monks, it was acquired in the mid–19th century by Interlaken's hotel keepers, who turned it into a park. As you stroll along **Höhenpromenade,** admire the famous view of the Jungfrau. Another beautiful sight is the **flower clock** at the Kursaal (casino), and you'll also see **fiacres** (horse-drawn cabs). The promenade is lined with hotels, cafes, and gardens.

Cross over the Aare River to **Unterseen,** built in 1280 by Berthold von Eschenbach. Here you can visit the **parish church,** with its Late Gothic tower from 1471. This is one of the most photographed sights in the Berner Oberland. The Mönch mountain appears on the left of the tower, the Jungfrau on the right.

Back in Interlaken, visit the **Touristik-Museum der Jungfrau-Region,** am Stadthausplatz, Obere Gasse 26 (☎ **033/822-98-39**), the country's first regional museum of tourism, showing development over the past 2 centuries. It's open May to mid-October, Tuesday to Sunday 2 to 5pm. Admission is 5SF ($3.35), or 3SF ($2) with a Visitor's Card. Children 12 and under pay 2SF ($1.35).

For a sightseeing fiacre ride, go to the Westbahnhof. The half-hour round-trip is 35SF ($23) for one or two, plus 10SF ($7) for each extra person; children 7 to 16 are charged half fare, and those 6 and under ride free.

Other attractions include animal parks, afternoon concerts, and the luscious pastries sold in cafes. During summer, you can sit in covered grandstands and watch Schiller's version of the William Tell story. Steamers carry passengers across Lakes Brienz and Thun.

MÜRREN
At 1,650m (5,414 feet) above the Lauterbrunnen Valley, Mürren is the highest permanently inhabited village in the Berner Oberland. It's an exciting excursion from Interlaken in summer and a major ski resort in winter. Downhill skiing was developed and the slalom invented here in the 1920s, and Mürren is also the birthplace of modern alpine racing.

Essential
GETTING THERE **By Train** Trains from Interlaken to Mürren's train station require a change of equipment in both Lauterbrunen and Grutschalp. The combined trip takes an hour from Interlaken, and a roundtrip fare costs 16.80SF ($11).

By Bus & Car A regular postal-bus service departs once an hour from Lauterbrunnen to the hamlet of Stechelberg, the last town along the Lauterbrunnen Valley road,

Glaciers in the Sky: A Trip to Jungfraujoch

A trip to ✪ **Jungfraujoch,** at 3,454m (11,333 feet), can be the highlight of your visit. Since the 1860s it's been the highest rail station in Europe. It's also one of the most expensive: A round-trip tour is 169.40SF ($113) first class or 159SF ($106) second. However, families can fill out a Family Card form, available at the rail station; it allows children 16 and under to ride free. There are departures from Interlaken's East Railway Station (**Bahnhof Interlaken Ost**) every hour in winter, and every half hour in summer, but for true aficionados of the experience, the area is at its panoramic best if you depart at 8:05am and return to Bahnhof Interlaken Ost at 4pm. You'll get to see the mountain when it is most dazzlingly lit, and will have enough time for a leisurely lunch. To check times, contact the sales office of **Jungfrau Bahnen** (Jungfrau Railways), Höheweg 37 (☎ **033/ 828-71-11**).

Once at the Jungfraujoch terminus, you may feel a little giddy until you get used to the air. You'll find much to do in this eerie world high up, Jungfrau. But take it slowly—your metabolism will be affected and you may tire quickly.

Within a 5-minute, well-marked walk from the Jungfraujoch railway terminus is an elevator that leads to the famed ✪ **Eispalast (Ice Palace).** Here you'll be walking within what's called "eternal ice"—caverns hewn out of the slowest-moving section of the glacier. Cut 20m (65 feet) below the glacier's surface, they were begun in 1934 by a Swiss guide and subsequently enlarged and embellished with additional sculptures. The cost of entrance to the Ice Palace is included in the price of a railway ticket to the Jungfraujoch. Hours of the Ice Palace coincide with the arrival of the first train in the morning and the departure of the last train in the evening.

After returning to the station, you can take the **Sphinx Tunnel** to another elevator. This one takes you up 108m (356 feet) to an observation deck called the **Sphinx Terraces,** overlooking the saddle between the Mönch and Jungfrau peaks. You can also see the **Aletsch Glacier,** a 23km (14-mile) river of ice—the longest in Europe. The snow melts into Lake Geneva and eventually flows into the Mediterranean.

the end of the line for cars and buses, and the departure point for a cable car which runs uphill to Mürren. The cable car that continues from Stechelberg on to Mürren departs at 30-minute intervals, costs 28.80SF ($19) round-trip, and takes about 10 minutes each way.

VISITOR INFORMATION   The **Mürren Tourist Information Bureau** is at the Sportzentrum (☎ **033/856-86-86**), and is open Monday to Friday 9am to noon and 2 to 5pm.

Where to Stay

Hotel Alpenruh. CH-3825 Mürren. ☎ **033/856-88-00.** Fax 033/856-88-88. 26 units. www.schilthorn.ch. E-mail: alpuh@tcnet.ch. A/C MINIBAR TV TEL. 180–250SF ($120–$167) double. 50% discount for children 12 and under sharing parents' room. Half board 30SF ($20) per person. Rates include breakfast. AE, DC, MC, V.

In the most congested, yet still charming, section of the village, the Alpenruh has a plusher interior than its chalet-style facade implies. The old building was upgraded to three-star status without sacrificing any of its small-scale charm. Rooms have pine paneling and a mix of antique and contemporary furniture; most have a view of the Jungfrau. The tidy bathrooms are small, compact, and efficiently organized.

Hotel Blumental. CH-3825 Mürren. ☎ **033/855-18-26.** Fax 033/855-36-86. 16 units. MINIBAR TV. 130–190SF ($87–$127) double. Half board 25SF ($17) per person. Rates include buffet breakfast. AE, DC, V.

Centrally located and redecorated and remodeled, this is a small chalet-type hotel, with stone masonry and wood-paneled public areas. Run by the von Allmen family, it offers a cozy atmosphere inspired by the nearby mountains. Several rooms have private balconies. The small bathrooms have shower stalls. The hotel also operates a French restaurant La Grotte.

Hotel Eiger. CH-3825 Mürren. ☎ **033/856-54-54.** Fax 033/856-54-56. www.muerren. ch/eiger. E-mail: eiger@muerren.ch. 44 units. TV TEL. Summer 220–280SF ($147–$187) d ouble; 460–480SF ($307–$320) suite. Winter 260–340SF ($173–$227) double; 520–680SF ($347–$454) suite. Rates include breakfast. AE, DC, MC, V. Closed Easter to mid-June and mid-Sept to Dec 19.

Founded in the 1920s and last renovated in 1994, this chalet is the longest-established hotel in Mürren. The public areas are warmly decorated, and many of the windows have panoramic views. Rooms are small, cozy, comfortable, and decorated in a typical alpine style. The hotel, managed by Annelis Stähli-von Allmen and family, lies across the street from the terminus of the cable car from Lauterbrunne. There's a fine restaurant (see "Where to Dine," below) and a popular après-ski bar.

Where to Dine
✪ Eigerstübli. In the Hotel Eiger. ☎ **033/856-54-64.** Reservations recommended. Main courses 21–49SF ($14–$33). AE, DC, MC, V. Daily 11:30am–2pm and 6–9pm. Closed Easter to mid-June and mid-Sept to mid-Dec. SWISS.

Here you'll find Mürren's best food, served in a festive ambience. The cuisine includes fondue as well as an international range of hearty specialties well suited to the alpine heights and chill. Try, for example, roast lamb shoulder with lentils, roast breast of duck with orange sauce, or poached fillet of trout with a sauce flavored with alpine herbs. All main dishes may be ordered with rösti.

Hitting the Slopes & Other Active Endeavors
There are 48km (30 miles) of prepared ski runs, including 16 downhills; the longest run measures 12km (7¹/₂ miles). For cross-country skiers there's a 12km (7¹/₂-mile) track in the Lauterbrunnen Valley, 10 minutes by railway from Mürren.

The alpine **Sportzentrum (Sports Center)** (☎ 033/856-86-86), in the middle of Mürren, is one of the finest in the Berner Oberland. The modern building has an indoor pool, a lounge, a snack bar, an outdoor skating rink, a tourist information office, and a children's playroom and library. There are facilities for playing squash, outdoor tennis, and curling. Hotel owners subsidize the operation, tacking the charges onto your hotel bill. Supplemental charges include 16 to 22SF ($11 to $15) per hour for tennis or per 45-minute session for squash and 13 to 16SF ($9 to $11) per hour for use of the sauna. The facility is usually open Monday to Friday 9am to noon and 2 to 6pm, and from Christmas through April and July to mid-September, also on Saturday from 1 to 6:30pm and Sunday from 1 to 5:30pm; but check locally as these times can vary.

Nearby Excursions
The famous **Mürren-Allmendhubel Cableway** leaves from the northwestern edge of Mürren. From the high destination, there's a panoramic view of the Lauterbrunnen Valley as far as Wengen and Kleine Scheidegg, and between mid-June and late August,

the alpine meadows are covered with wildflowers. A hill walk in this region might be a highlight of your trip. The cable car operates daily 8am to 5pm. However, there are annual closings for maintenance in May and in November. It costs 12SF ($8) per person round-trip.

The most popular excursion from Mürren is a cable-car ride to the ✪ **Schilthorn,** famous for its 360° view. The panorama extends from the Jura to the Black Forest and includes the Eiger, Mönch, and Jungfrau. The Schilthorn is also called "Piz Gloria" after the James Bond film *On Her Majesty's Secret Service,* partly filmed at this dramatic location. Today Piz Gloria is the name of the revolving restaurant here, and the summit is the start of the world's longest downhill ski race. The cable car to Schilthorn leaves every 30 minutes. A round-trip ticket is 87SF ($58.05), and the journey to the top takes 20 minutes. For details, call ☎ **033/823-14-44.**

WENGEN

The Mönch, Jungfrau, and Eiger loom above this sunny resort, built on a sheltered terrace high above the Lauterbrunnen Valley, at about 1,270m (4,160 feet). Wengen (pronounced *Ven*-ghen) is one of the more chic and better-equipped ski and mountain resorts in the Berner Oberland. It has 30 hotels in all price categories, as well as 500 apartments and chalets for rent.

In the 1830s, the International Lauberhorn Ski Race was established here. At that time, Wengen was a farm community, but the Brits popularized the resort after World War I. Parts of the area retain their rural charm, but the main street is filled with cafes, shops, and restaurants. No cars are allowed in Wengen, but the streets still bustle with service vehicles and electric luggage carts.

Essentials

GETTING THERE   By Train   Take the train (frequent service) from Interlaken East to Lauterbrunnen. For information, call ☎ **157-22-22** (no area code). From here, the journey to Wengen is by cog railway, a 15-minute trip. A one-way fare is 5.40SF ($3.60).

By Car   Unlike Mürren, Wengen, 26km (16 miles) south of Interlaken, can be reached by car—at least for part of the trip. From Interlaken, head south in the direction of Wilderswil, following the minor signposted road to Lauterbrunnen, where there are garages or open-air spaces for parking. After that, it's cog railway the rest of the way to Wengen.

VISITOR INFORMATION   The **Wengen Tourist Information Office** (☎ **033/ 855-14-14**) is in the center of the resort and is signposted. It's open Monday to Friday 8am to noon and 2 to 6pm, Saturday 8:30 to 11:30am only.

Where to Stay

Hotel Eden. CH-3823 Wengen. ☎ **033/855-16-34.** Fax 033/855-39-50. 30 units (6 with bathroom). Summer 144SF ($96) double without bathroom, 158SF ($105) double with bathroom. Winter 164SF ($109) double without bathroom, 184SF ($123) double with bathroom. Half board 30SF ($20) per person. Rates include breakfast. AE, DC, MC, V.

You'll feel comfortable and at home in this economy oasis that stands among guest houses and private chalets above the commercial center of town. Kerstin Bucher directs a cooperative staff. Meals are served in a simple modern room with a few frivolous touches. There's a small TV lounge and a tiny Jägerstübli, where guests mix with locals over Swiss wine and specialties. Although the rooms are a bit Spartan, the beds are comfortable. Only a few units have private bathrooms, and these are quite small without much room for your stuff.

Hotel Eiger. CH-3823 Wengen. ☎ **800/528-1234** in the U.S. and Canada, or 033/855-11-31. Fax 033/855-10-30. www.wengen.com./hotel/eiger. E-mail: eiger@wengen. com. 33 units. TV TEL. Summer 184–206SF ($123–$137) double. Winter 204–228SF ($136–$152) double. Suite for two, 240–342SF ($160–$228). Half board 25SF ($17) per person. Rates include breakfast. AE, DC, MC, V. Closed mid-Apr to June 1 and Nov.

Rustic timbers cover the walls and ceilings of this attractive hotel behind the cog-railway station. Karl Fuchs and his family offer spacious attractive rooms with balconies. A modern dining room has views of the Jungfrau massif and the Lauterbrunnen Valley. Rooms have cozy, alpine styling, but bathrooms are small and cramped. In the lobby is an inviting sitting area with a fireplace, and there's a bar reserved for hotel guests.

Where to Dine

Hotel Hirschen Restaurant. In the Hotel Hirschen. ☎ **033/855-15-44.** Reservations recommended. Main courses 14.50–44.50SF ($10–$30); set price menu 39.50–69.50SF ($26–$46). DC, MC, V. Mon–Fri 5–11pm; Sat–Sun 11:30am–2:30pm and 5–11pm (closed Wed over the summer and Tues over the winter). Closed mid-Apr to May and Sept–Dec 15. SWISS.

This quiet retreat at the foot of the slopes has true alpine flavor. The rear dining room is decorated with hunting trophies, pewter, and wine racks. Johannes Abplanalp and his family offer a dinner special called Galgenspiess—fillet of beef, veal, and pork flambéed at your table. Other dishes include fillet of breaded pork, rump steak Café de Paris, and fondue Bacchus (in white-wine sauce), bourguignonne (hot oil), or chinoise (hot bouillon). A hearty lunch is winzerrösti, consisting of country ham, cheese, and a fried egg with homemade rösti.

Exploring the Area

The ski area around Wengen is highly developed, with both straight and serpentine trails carved into the sides of such sloping geological formations as Männlichen, Kleine Scheidegg, Lauberhorn, and Eigergletscher. A triumph of alpine engineering, the town and its region contain three mountain railways, two aerial cableways, one gondola, five chairlifts, nine ski lifts, and three practice lifts. You'll also find a branch of the Swiss ski school, more than 12km (7 miles) of trails for cross-country skiing, an indoor and outdoor skating rink, a curling hall, an indoor pool, and a day nursery.

In summer, the district attracts hill climbers from all over Europe. Hiking trails are well maintained and carefully marked, with dozens of unusual detours to hidden lakes and panoramas.

Nearby Attractions

In winter, skiers take the cableway to **Männlichen,** at 2,236m (7,335 feet), which opens onto a panoramic vista of the treacherous Eiger. From here, there's no direct run back to Wengen; however, skiers can enjoy an uninterrupted ski trail stretching 7km (4¹/₂ miles) to Grindelwald.

There are many sights you can visit up and down the Lauterbrunnen Valley from either Wengen or Grindelwald. **Trümmelbach Falls** plunges in five powerful cascades through a gorge. An elevator built through the rock leads to a series of galleries; the last stop is at a wall where the upper fall descends (bring a raincoat). You can visit the falls daily May to June and September to October 9am to 5pm and July to August 8:30am to 6pm. Admission is 10SF ($7) adults and 4SF ($2.65) children 6 to 16 and free for children 5 and under. It takes about 45 minutes to reach the falls on foot. For information, call ☎ **033/855-32-32.** The postal bus from Lauterbrunnen departs once an hour and stops at Trümmelbach Falls; fares are 1.20SF (80¢) adults and a .60SF (40¢) children.

You might also want to visit the base of the **Staubbach Waterfall,** which plunges nearly 300m (1,000 feet) in a sheer drop over a rock wall in the valley above Lauterbrunnen. Lord Byron compared this waterfall to the "tail of the pale horse ridden by Death in the Apocalypse."

GRINDELWALD

The "glacier village" of Grindelwald, both a summer and a winter resort, is set against a backdrop of the Wetterhorn and the towering north face of the Eiger. Grindelwald is surrounded with folkloric hamlets, swift streams, and as much alpine beauty as you're likely to find anywhere in Switzerland. It's also easier to reach from Interlaken than either Wengen or Mürren. Though at first, the hiking options and cable car networks might seem baffling, the tourist office can provide helpful maps.

Essentials
GETTING THERE   By Train   The Berner Oberland Railway (BOB) leaves from the Interlaken East station (trip time: 35 minutes). Call ☎ **157-22-22** (no area code) for information.

VISITOR INFORMATION   Grindelwald's **tourist office** is at Sportszentrum, Hauptstrasse, CH-3818 Grindelwald (☎ **033/854-12-12**), open mid-June to late September Monday to Friday 8am to 7pm, Saturday 8am to 5pm, Sunday 9 to 11am and 3 to 5pm. Otherwise, hours are Monday to Friday 8am to 6pm, Saturday 8am to noon, and Sunday 10am to noon and 3 to 5pm.

Where to Stay
✪ **Grand Hotel Regina.** CH-3818 Grindelwald. ☎ **800/223-6800** in the U.S. or 033/854-54-55. Fax 033/853-47-17. 98 units. MINIBAR TV TEL. 420SF ($280) double; from 1,000SF ($667) suite. AE, DC, MC, V. Parking free outside, 158SF ($105) in garage. Closed mid-Oct to Dec 18.

Across from the Grindelwald train station, this turn-of-the-century hotel is part rustic, part urban slick. The facade of the hotel's oldest part has an imposing set of turrets with red-tile roofs. Antiques blend with modern furnishings into a harmonious whole, and the beds are exceedingly comfortable. Bathrooms are well maintained, with robes and a hair dryer. A steel-and-glass extension houses sports facilities, and live music is performed at the disco. Both set price and à la carte menus are served in the restaurant. There are indoor and outdoor pools, a sauna, a solarium, and two tennis courts.

Hotel Eiger. CH-3818 Grindelwald. ☎ **033/853-31-31.** Fax 033/853-31-30. www.eiger-grindelwald.ch. E-mail: hotel@grindelwald.ch. 50 units. MINIBAR TV TEL. Summer 196–276SF ($131–$184) double. Winter 266–296SF ($177–$197) double. Half board 35SF ($23) per person. Rates include buffet breakfast. AE, DC, MC, V. Free parking outdoors; 6–12SF ($4–$8) in garage.

This hotel appears to be a collection of interconnected balconies, each on a different plane, angled toward the alpine sunshine and built of contrasting shades of white stucco and natural wood. The interior is attractive and unpretentious, with lots of warmly tinted wood, hanging lamps, and contrasting lights. Rooms range from small to medium; each has a soft, snug bed, and a compact bathroom with adequate shelf space. The Gepsi-Bar offers live music, recently released songs, and "evergreen" (mountain) tunes. The Heller family offers a bar and restaurant, including a steakhouse, and the facilities include a sauna, a steam bathroom, and a children's playroom.

Hotel Hirschen. CH-3818 Grindelwald. ☎ **033/854-84-84.** Fax 033/854-84-80. www.grindelwald.ch. E-mail: hirschen.grindelwald@bluewin.ch. 28 units. TV TEL. 120–192SF ($80–$128) double. Half board 28SF ($19) per person. Rates include continental breakfast. AE, DC, MC, V. Free parking outside; 8SF ($5) garage. Closed Nov–Dec 19.

In the three-star Hirschen, the Bleuer family offers one of the resort's best values. Rooms are a bit small but each is cozy, warm, and a great place to retreat to on a cold winter's night. Bathrooms are tiny but tidy. It has a respectable dining room as well as a popular bowling alley in the cellar.

Where to Dine

Il Mercato. In the Hotel Spinne. ☎ **033/854-88-88.** Reservations recommended. Main courses 13–21SF ($9–$14). AE, DC, MC, V. Daily 11am–2pm and 6:30–10:30pm. Closed Oct to mid-Dec. ITALIAN/SWISS.

The decor is elegant and alpine, with Italian touches. The dining room's centerpiece is a large window with a sweeping view over the mountains; during warm weather, tables are set on the terrace. Menu items include virtually everything Italian, with an emphasis on cold-weather dishes from the Val d'Aosta (northern Italy's milk and cheese district). A tempting array of dishes based on market-fresh ingredients changes daily. Especially good are the risottos, simmered rice dishes that come in infinite varieties. The chefs also specialize in grilled meats and homemade salads, which even in the dead of winter use fresh, crisp ingredients. Their pizzas are the best in town. Daily pastas are featured, each with a succulent sauce.

✪ **Restaurant Français.** In the Hotel Belvedere. ☎ **033/854-54-54.** Reservations recommended. Main courses 30–45SF ($20–$30); set price menu 52–65SF ($35–$43). AE, DC, MC, V. Daily noon–1pm and 6:45–9pm. INTERNATIONAL.

Special buffets feature at Grindelwald's best restaurant. After you study the ever-changing menu to the soothing sounds of a live pianist, you may decide on an appetizer of game terrine, Grindewald air-dried meat, or thinly sliced lamb carpaccio. On recent visits, dishes have included poached turbot fillet on zucchini, peppercorn-coated lamb entrecôte and breast of guinea fowl with red wine and prunes.

Seeing the Glaciers

Adjacent to the base of the **Lower Grindelwald Glacier (Untere Gletscher)** is a sheltered observation gallery offering a look at the rock-strewn ravine formed by the glacier and its annual snowmelt. The half-mile gallery stretches past deeply striated rocks, which include formations of colored marble worn smooth by the glacier's erosion. Don't expect a view of the glacier from this point, as you'll have go to a higher altitude, at least in summer, to see the actual ice. The gallery is easy to reach on foot or by car from the center of Grindelwald. Yellow-sided buses labeled GLETSCHER-SCHLUCHT depart from a point in front of Grindelwald's rail station at least four times a day, year-round, for the lower glacier and points beyond. Passage to the lower glacier costs 11.20SF ($7) each way, but since the distance from the center of Grindelwald is about 4km (2¹/₂ miles), in nice weather, many hardy souls opt to trek across well-marked hiking trails instead.

A more exotic destination farther afield is the **Blue Ice Grotto,** whose frozen mass is part of the Upper Grindelwald Glacier (Obere Gletscher). Popular with hill climbers, it's a 3-hour hike (which includes navigating up an 890-step alpine staircase) or a 15-minute bus ride from the Lower Grindelwald Glacier. The upper and lower glaciers are separated by rocky cliffs and flow in different valleys. At midday, the 45m (150-foot) -thick ice walls of the grotto take on an eerie blue tinge. Local guides assure you that though the grotto—and the glacier containing it—are moving slowly downhill, you're perfectly safe. The grotto is open daily mid-June to October 9am to 6pm. If you don't want to make the uphill trek on foot from Grindelwald, a yellow-sided bus marked GROSSE SCHEIDEGG departs at approximately 1-hour intervals, year-round, during daylight hours. Round-trip fares from Grindelwald to the Obere

Gletscher and its grotto cost 11.20SF ($7). *Note:* Once you get off the bus, you'll still have to climb 900 steps to reach the grotto.

Hiking & Mountain Climbing

Grindelwald and environs offer dozens of challenging paths and mountain trails that are well marked and maintained. Outdoor adventures range from an exhilarating ramble across the gentle incline of an alpine valley to a dangerous trek with ropes and pitons along the north face of Mount Eiger. The choice depends on your inclination, degree of experience, and mountaineering skills. Maps showing the paths, trails, and their various elevations are available at the town's tourist office.

From Grindelwald, you can reach the high-altitude plateau known as **First Mountain** at 2,168m (7,113 feet) after a 30-minute ride on a six-passenger gondola ("bubble car"). The round-trip transport is 45SF ($30). You can stop at such intermediate stations as Bort and Grindel (a site that some locals refer to as Scheckfeld) on your way to **First Mountain terminal and sun terrace.** From First, where there are dining facilities, you'll have many hiking possibilities into the neighboring Bussalp or Grosse Scheidegg area. Also, from First, an hour's brisk hike will take you to the still high-altitude waters of **Bachalpsee** (Lake Bachalp). Buses depart from Grindelwald from both Bussalp and Grosse Scheidegg if you opt not to walk all the way back.

Faulhorn, at 2,681m (8,796 feet), is a historic vantage point with a panorama of untouched alpine beauty. Near the summit is the Faulhorn Hotel (☎ **033/ 853-27-13**), which has been here for more than 150 years. Faulhorn is a 7-hour hike from Grindelwald. For a shorter climb, take either the bus to Bussalp, the cable car to First, or the train to Schynige Platte. From any of these intermediate points, climbers can continue their treks on to Faulhorn. Hikes from Bussalp take 2³/₄ hours; from First, 2¹/₂ hours; and from Schynige Platte, 4 hours.

Grosse Scheidegg, at 1,961m (6,434 feet), is a famous pass between the Grindelwald and Rosenlaui valleys. You can hike here in 3 hours from Grindelwald or can take a 40-minute bus ride from Grindelwald to Grosse Scheidegg and begin hill walking at a point that's far from the village traffic and crowds. Round-trip bus passage from Grindelwald to Grosse Scheidegg is 32SF ($21).

KANDERSTEG

Between Grindelwald and Gstaad, Kandersteg is a popular resort at one of the southern points of the Berner Oberland. It's a tranquil and lovely mountain village with rust- and orange-colored rooftops and green Swiss meadows. The summer and winter resort is spread over 4km (2¹/₂ miles), so nothing is crowded. The village itself is at the foot of the 3,660m (12,000-foot) Blumlisalp chain and provides access to six remote alpine hamlets.

Kandersteg developed as a resting point on the road to the Gemmi Pass, which long ago linked the Valais with the Berner Oberland. The village still has many old farmhouses and a tiny church from the 16th century.

Essentials

GETTING THERE   By Train   Kandersteg is at the northern terminus of the 14km (9-mile) Lotschberg Tunnel, which, ever since the beginning of World War I, has linked Bern with the Rhône Valley. The railroad that runs through the tunnel can transport cars. Trains leave every 30 minutes; no reservations are necessary. The resort is also served by the Bern-Lotschberg-Simplon railway. Call ☎ **157-22-22** (no area code) for information. The station is in the center of town.

By Car   Kandersteg is 43km (27 miles) southwest of Interlaken. Take N8 east to where the Kandersteg road then heads south into the mountains. The journey from Spiez to Kandersteg along a well-built road takes only 20 minutes.

VISITOR INFORMATION The **Kandersteg Tourist Office,** Hauptstrasse CH-3718 Kandersteg (☎ **033/675-80-80**), is open Monday to Friday 8am to noon and 2 to 6pm.

Where to Stay & Dine

Hotel Adler. CH-3718 Kandersteg. ☎ **033/675-80-10.** Fax 033/675-80-11. www.kandessteg. ch./adler. 24 units. MINIBAR TV TEL. Feb–Mar and July–Sept 170–210SF ($113–$140) double. Off-season, 160SF ($107) double. Rates include breakfast. Half-board 25SF ($17). AE, DC, MC, V. Closed Nov 22–Dec 26. Free parking.

An open fire crackling in the foyer sets the tone at this cozy inn, a wood-sided chalet on the main street near the town center. The fourth-generation owner, Andreas Fetzer, and his Finnish-born wife, Eija, offer comfortable pinewood-paneled rooms, some with Jacuzzis. Almost all open onto a private balcony. The small, neat bathrooms are inviting and have adequate shelf space. The Adler-Bar is one of the most popular après-ski hangouts, and there's also a brasserie (the Adlerstube) as well as a relatively formal restaurant.

Outdoor Activities

Around Kandersteg is an extensive network of level footpaths and strategically located benches; these paths are open year-round. In summer, qualified riders in proper clothes can rent horses at the local riding school. In winter, the resort attracts cross-country skiers and downhill novices (top-speed skiers go elsewhere). It has a cable car, two chairlifts, and four ski tows; the National Nordic Ski Center offers a ski-jumping station. The 2.5km (1¹/₂-mile) cross-country ski trail is floodlit in the evening, and other facilities include an indoor and outdoor ice rink.

Excursions Nearby

The most popular excursion from Kandersteg is to **Oeschinensee (Lake Oeschinen),** high above the village. The lake is surrounded by the snow-covered peaks of the Blumlisalp, towering 1,830m (6,000 feet) above the extremely clear water. You can walk to it from the Victoria Hotel or take a chairlift, costing 16.20SF ($11), to the Oeschinen station and walk down from that point. If you opt to walk, allow about 1¹/₂ hours, or 2 hours if you'd like to stroll. Many visitors who take the chairlift decide to hike back to Kandersteg. Be aware, however, of the steep downhill grade.

Another popular excursion is to **Klus Gorge.** Park your car at the cable station's lower platform at Stock and walk 3km (2 miles) to the gorge, which was formed by the abrasive action of the Kander River. The rushing water creates a romantic, even primeval, setting. However, you must watch your step, as the path gets very slippery in places because the spray coats the stones and pebbles and has fostered a layer of moss. There's a tunnel over the gorge, but in winter, the access route is dangerous and icebound.

GSTAAD

Against a backdrop of glaciers and mountain lakes, Gstaad is a haven for the rich and famous. Built at the junction of four quiet valleys near the southern tip of the Berner Oberland, Gstaad was once only a place to change horses on the grueling trip by carriage through the Berner Oberland. As the rail lines developed, it grew into a resort for the wealthy who flocked to the Palace Hotel, which promised the ultimate in luxury.

The town retains much of its late 19th-century charm. Some first-time visitors, however, say that the resort is a bore if you can't afford to stay at the Gstaad Palace or mingle with the stars in their private chalets. Yet the town has many moderately priced hotels, taverns, and guest houses, with an allure of their own.

Essentials

GETTING THERE   By Train   Gstaad is on the local train line connecting Interlaken with Montreux and several smaller towns in central-southwest Switzerland. About a dozen trains come into Gstaad every day from both cities, each of which is a rail junction with good connections to the rest of Switzerland. Travel time from Montreux can be as little as $1^1/_3$ hours; from Interlaken, about 30 minutes, sometimes with a change of train at the hamlet of Zweisimmen. Call ☎ 157-22-22 (no area code) for information.

By Car   From Spiez, follow Route 11 southwest to Gstaad.

VISITOR INFORMATION   The **Gstaad-Saanenland Tourist Association,** CH-3780 Gstaad (☎ **033/748-81-81**), can help you find hotels, restaurants, and attractions if the signposts don't point you in the right direction. It's open Monday to Friday 8am to noon and 1:30 to 6pm and Saturday 9am to noon only.

Where to Stay

✪ Hostellerie Alpenrose. Hauptstrasse, CH-3778 Schönried Gstaad. ☎ **033/744-67-67.** Fax 033/744-67-12. 19 units. MINIBAR TV TEL. Summer 300–450SF ($200–$300) double. Winter 300–720SF ($200–$480) double. Half board 35SF ($23) per person extra. AE, DC, MC, V. Free parking. Closed Nov.

For those who like the charm of a small inn, this is the preferred choice, the only Relais & Châteaux listing within 50km (30 miles). Its owner, Michel von Siebenthal, is a memorable host, setting the fashionable tone of the chalet, which is famous for its restaurants. The pine-paneled public areas are exquisitely decorated with rustic furnishings. Rooms are tastefully appointed and have mountain views and private safes. Bathrooms have hairdryers and showers, but no tubs. Although the original house has more character, accommodations in the contemporary annex are more spacious and luxurious—some are fireplace suites, quite romantic on a wintry night. Facilities include a sauna, whirlpool, and solarium.

✪ Hotel Olden. Hauptstrasse, CH-3780 Gstaad. ☎ **033/744-34-44.** Fax 033/744-61-64. 15 units. MINIBAR TV TEL. 318SF ($212) double. Rates include continental breakfast. AE, DC, MC, V. Free parking. Closed late Apr to late May.

This is a low-key and gracefully unpretentious hotel, a sort of Victorian country inn set amid a sometimes chillingly glamorous landscape. The facade is painted with regional floral designs and pithy bits of folk wisdom, with embellishments carved or painted into the stone lintels around many of the doors. The folkloric alpine-style rooms are very cozy. The small bathrooms don't have a lot of extras, but maintenance is spotless. Rooms in the chalet wing are generally roomier and more up to date.

Palace Hotel Gstaad. CH-3780 Gstaad. ☎ **800/223-6800** in the U.S., or 033/748-50-50. 124 units. MINIBAR TV TEL. Summer 510–790SF ($340–$527) double; from 1,700SF ($1,134) suite. Winter 890–1,160SF ($594–$774) double; from 2,190SF ($1,461) suite. Rates include breakfast. Half board 75–80SF ($50–$53) per person extra. AE, DC, MC, V. Parking free outside, 18SF ($12) in garage. Closed end of Mar to mid-June and late Sept to shortly before Christmas (dates vary).

This landmark hotel is on a wooded hill overlooking the center of Gstaad. It's one of the most sought-after luxury hideaways in the world, attracting corporation heads, film stars, jet-setters, and the titled. The nerve center of this chic citadel is an elegantly paneled main salon, with an eternal flame burning in the baronial stone fireplace. Radiating halls lead to superb restaurants, bars, discos, and sports facilities. Rooms (some large enough for Elizabeth Taylor and all her husbands) are country deluxe with regional artifacts, cheerful print wallpaper and rustic pine furnishings. Bathrooms are exceedingly luxurious with fluffy robes, dual basins, and hair dryers. Facilities include an indoor pool with an underwater sound system, a fitness center, a sauna, a solarium, and tennis courts.

Where to Dine

Olden Restaurant. In the Hotel Olden, Hauptstrasse. ☎ **033/744-34-44.** Reservations recommended. Main courses 28–75SF ($19–$50). AE, DC, MC, V. Daily noon–2:30pm and 6:30–10:30pm. Closed mid-Apr to mid-May and 2 weeks in Nov. MEDITERRANEAN/SWISS.

This most elegant of the several dining areas in the above-recommended hotel attracts visiting celebrities. The service is formal and refined, the food as good as, or better than anything in the area. The always tempting menu might include smoked salmon, fresh goose-liver terrine, shrimp bisque with green peppercorns, house-style tagliatelle, raclette, veal cutlet milanese, Scottish lamb, and sea bass with olives, potatoes, tomatoes, and onions. Although there are grander restaurants in Gstaad, and dining rooms serving a more haute cuisine, the Olden remains our most satisfying choice year after year after countless visits.

⚫ **Restaurant Chesery.** Lauenenstrasse. ☎ **033/744-24-51.** Reservations required. Main courses 45–65SF ($30–$43); set price lunch 49–64SF ($33–$43); set-price dinner 128–148SF ($85–$99). AE, DC, MC, V. Tues–Sun 11:30am–2:30pm and 7pm–midnight. Closed mid-Oct to mid-Dec and in winter (Tues–Fri) for lunch. Closed after Easter–June 10. FRENCH/SWISS.

One of Switzerland's 10 best restaurants perches at an elevation of 1,100m (3,600 feet). Natural stone floors and polished pine walls pair naturally with a menu that changes daily, but is always based on the freshest of ingredients—grouse from Scotland, Charolais beef from France, truffles from Umbria. Try the salt-crusted sea bass with wild rice or chicken Houban (a special breed from France). In the basement bar, Casino, a piano player entertains nightly; the bar is open 6pm to around 3am.

Skiing & Hiking

The resort is rich in **sports facilities.** Many skiers stay in Gstaad and go to one of the nearby ski resorts in the daytime. Cable cars take passengers to altitudes of 1,500m and 3,000m (5,000 and 10,000 feet)—at the higher altitude there's skiing even in summer. Other facilities include tennis courts, heated indoor and outdoor pools, and some 320km (200 miles) of hiking trails. Many of these scenic trails are possible to walk or hike year-round (the tourist office will advise). The Gstaad International Tennis Tournament, held the second week in July, is the most important tennis event in Switzerland.

Skiers setting off from Gstaad have access to 70 lifts, mountain railroads, and gondolas. The altitude of Gstaad's highest skiable mountain is 2,000m (6,550 feet), with a vertical drop of 1,084m (3,555 feet). Most beginner and intermediate runs are east of the village in **Eggli,** a sunny, south-facing ski area that's reached by cable car.

Wispellan-Sanetch is good for afternoon skiing, and has lots of runs down to the village. At the summit is the Glacier des Diablerets, at 3,000m (9,900 feet). **Wasserngrat,** prized by skilled skiers for its powder skiing on steep slopes, is reached from the south side of the resort.

Appendix

A Average Travel Times by Rail

AMSTERDAM TO
Berlin 8¹/₂ hr.
Cologne 3 hr.
Copenhagen 11¹/₂ hr.
Frankfurt 6 hr.
Munich 8¹/₂ hr.
Paris 4¹/₄ hr.
Zurich 10 hr.

ATHENS TO
Munich 42¹/₂ hr.
Vienna 43 hr.

AVIGNON TO
Barcelona 6¹/₂ hr.
Paris 3¹/₂ hr.

BARCELONA TO
Madrid 7 hr.
Paris 11¹/₂ hr.

BATH TO
London 1¹/₄ hr.

BERLIN TO
Frankfurt 6 hr.
Munich 7 hr.
Paris 11 hr.
Prague 6¹/₂ hr.

BERN TO
Interlaken 1 hr.
Milan 4¹/₂ hr.
Paris 4¹/₂ hr.
Zurich 1¹/₂ hr.

BORDEAUX TO
Paris 3 hr.

BRUSSELS TO
Frankfurt 5¹/₂ hr.
London 2³/₄ hr.
Paris 1¹/₂ hr.

BUDAPEST TO
Frankfurt 15¹/₂ hr.
Prague 9¹/₂ hr.
Vienna 4 hr.

CANNES TO
Paris 6 hr.

COPENHAGEN TO
Oslo 10¹/₂ hr.
Paris 15 hr.
Stockholm 8 hr.

EDINBURGH TO
London 4 hr.

FLORENCE TO
Geneva 8 hr.
Milan 3 hr.
Paris 12¹/₂ hr.
Rome 1¹/₂ hr.
Venice 3 hr.
Zurich 8 hr.

FRANKFURT TO
Munich 3¹/₂ hr.
Paris 6¹/₄ hr.
Prague 8 hr.
Salzburg 5 hr.
Vienna 8 hr.
Zurich 5 hr.

GENEVA TO
Milan   4¹/₄ hr.
Paris   3¹/₂ hr.
Venice   8 hr.

GLASGOW TO
London   5 hr.

GRANADA TO
Madrid   6¹/₂ hr.

HELSINKI TO
Stockholm   10 hr.

INNSBRUCK TO
Munich   3 hr.
Vienna   8 hr.
Zurich   5 hr.

LAUSANNE TO
Milan   4¹/₂ hr.
Paris   3³/₄ hr.

LILLEHAMMER TO
Oslo   2¹/₂ hr.

LISBON TO
Madrid   10 hr.

LONDON TO
Paris   3 hr.

LUXEMBOURG TO
Paris   4 hr.

LUZERNE TO
Paris   7¹/₂ hr.
Venice   8 hr.

LYON TO
Nice   5 hr.
Paris   2 hr.

MADRID TO
Malaga   7 hr.

MARSEILLE TO
Paris   4¹/₄ hr.

MILAN TO
Nice   5 hr.
Paris (day)   6³/₄ hr.
Rome   5 hr.
Venice   3 hr.
Zurich   4¹/₂ hr.

MUNICH TO
Paris   8¹/₂ hr.
Prague   7¹/₂ hr.
Rome   11 hr.
Salzburg   2 hr.
Venice   9 hr.
Vienna   4³/₄ hr.
Zurich   5 hr.

NANTES TO
Paris   2 hr.

NAPLES TO
Rome   2 hr.

NICE TO
Paris   6¹/₂ hr.
Rome   10 hr.
Venice   10 hr.

OSLO TO
Stockholm   6¹/₂ hr.

PARIS TO
Rome   15 hr.
Salzburg   10 hr.
Strasbourg   4 hr.
Toulouse   5 hr.
Tours   1 hr.
Venice   12¹/₄ hr.
Vienna   13¹/₂ hr.
Zurich   6 hr.

PISA TO
Rome   4 hr.

PRAGUE TO
Vienna   5 hr.

ROME TO
Siena   3 hr.
Venice   4¹/₂ hr.
Zurich   8¹/₂ hr.

SALZBURG TO
Vienna   4 hr.

VENICE TO
Vienna   8 hr.

VIENNA TO
Zurich   12 hr.

B Metric Conversions

LIQUID VOLUME

To convert	multiply by
U.S. gallons to liters	3.8
Liters to U.S. gallons	.26
U.S. gallons to imperial gallons	.83
Imperial gallons to U.S. gallons	1.2
Imperial gallons to liters	4.55

1 liter = .26 gal   1 gal = 3.8 liters

DISTANCE

To convert	multiply by
Inches to centimeters	2.54
Centimeters to inches	.39
Feet to meters	.30
Meters to feet	3.28
Yards to meters	.91
Meters to yards	1.09
Miles to kilometers	1.61
Kilometers to miles	.62

1 mi = 1.6km   1km = .62 mi   1 ft = .30m   1m = 3.3 ft

WEIGHT

To convert	multiply by
Ounces to grams	28.35
Grams to ounces	.35
Pounds to kilograms	.45
Kilograms to pounds	2.20

1 oz = 28g   1 g = .04 oz   1 lb = 4555kg   1 kg = 2.2 lb

TEMPERATURE

C°	−18°	−10	0	10	20	30	40

F°	0°	10	20	30	40	50	60	70	80	90	100

To **convert °F to °C,** subtract 32 and multiply by $5/9$ (.555).
To **convert °C to °F,** multiply by 1.8 and add 32.
32°F = 0°C

C Clothing Size Conversions

WOMEN'S CLOTHING

American	6	8	10	12	14	16
Continental	36	38	40	42	44	46
British	8	10	12	14	16	18

WOMEN'S SHOES

American	5	6	7	8	9	10
Continental	36	37	38	39	40	41
British	4	5	6	7	8	9

CHILDREN'S CLOTHING

American	3	4	5	6	6X
Continental	98	104	110	116	122
British	18	20	22	24	26

CHILDREN'S SHOES

American	8	9	10	11	12	13	1	2	3
Continental	24	25	27	28	29	30	32	33	34
British	7	8	9	10	11	12	13	1	2

MEN'S SUITS

American	34	36	38	40	42	44	46	48
Continental	44	46	48	50	52	54	56	58
British	34	36	38	40	42	44	46	48

MEN'S SHIRTS

American	$14\frac{1}{2}$	15	$15\frac{1}{2}$	16	$16\frac{1}{2}$	17	$17\frac{1}{2}$	18
Continental	37	38	39	41	42	43	44	45
British	$14\frac{1}{2}$	15	$15\frac{1}{2}$	16	$16\frac{1}{2}$	17	$17\frac{1}{2}$	18

MEN'S SHOES

American	7	8	9	10	11	12	13
Continental	$39\frac{1}{2}$	41	42	43	$44\frac{1}{2}$	46	47
British	6	7	8	9	10	11	12

Index

Index

Index

Notes

Notes

Frommer's® National Park Guides

Family Vacations in the
  National Parks
Grand Canyon

National Parks of the
  American West
Rocky Mountain

Yellowstone & Grand Teton
Yosemite & Sequoia/
  Kings Canyon
Zion & Bryce Canyon

Frommer's® Memorable Walks

Chicago
London

New York
Paris

San Francisco
Washington, D.C.

Frommer's® Great Outdoor Guides

New England
Northern California

Southern California & Baja
Southern New England

Washington & Oregon

Frommer's® Born to Shop Guides

Born to Shop: China
Born to Shop: France

Born to Shop: Italy
Born to Shop: London

Born to Shop: New York
Born to Shop: Paris

Frommer's® Irreverent Guides

Amsterdam
Boston
Chicago
Las Vegas

London
Los Angeles
Manhattan
New Orleans

Paris
San Francisco
Seattle & Portland
Vancouver

Walt Disney World
Washington, D.C.

Frommer's® Best-Loved Driving Tours

America
Britain
California

Florida
France
Germany

Ireland
Italy
New England

Scotland
Spain
Western Europe

The Unofficial Guides®

Bed & Breakfasts in
  California
Bed & Breakfasts in
  New England
Bed & Breakfasts in
  the Northwest
Beyond Disney
Branson, Missouri
California with Kids
Chicago

Cruises
Disneyland
Florida with Kids
Golf Vacations in the
  Eastern U.S.
The Great Smoky &
  Blue Ridge
  Mountains
Inside Disney

Hawaii
Las Vegas
London
Miami & the Keys
Mini Las Vegas
Mini-Mickey
New Orleans
New York City
Paris

Safaris
San Francisco
Skiing in the West
Walt Disney World
Walt Disney World
  for Grown-ups
Walt Disney World
  for Kids
Washington, D.C.

Special-Interest Titles

Frommer's Britain's Best Bed & Breakfasts and
  Country Inns
Frommer's Britain's Best Bike Rides
The Civil War Trust's Official Guide
  to the Civil War Discovery Trail
Frommer's Caribbean Hideaways
Frommer's Food Lover's Companion to France
Frommer's Food Lover's Companion to Italy
Frommer's Gay & Lesbian Europe
Frommer's Exploring America by RV
Hanging Out in Europe
Israel Past & Present

Mad Monks' Guide to California
Mad Monks' Guide to New York City
Frommer's The Moon
Frommer's New York City with Kids
The New York Times' Unforgettable
  Weekends
Places Rated Almanac
Retirement Places Rated
Frommer's Road Atlas Britain
Frommer's Road Atlas Europe
Frommer's Washington, D.C., with Kids
Frommer's What the Airlines Never Tell You